© Éditions D & G MOTTE
281, route de Lavaux
Case Postale 288 - CH 1095 Lutry

PEUGEOT
Golf Guide

1000

golf courses

The Millennium Guide

Europe

Austria
Belgium
Czech Rep.
Denmark
England
Finland
France
Germany
Ireland
Luxemburg
Netherlands
Norway
Portugal
Russia
Scotland
Spain
Sweden
Switzerland
Turkey
Wales

PEUGEOT

Automobiles Peugeot have been an active and prominent part of the extraordinary expansion of communications in the 20th century, courtesy of which golf has become a sport and a leisure activity right around the world. Because golfers are constantly in search of new horizons, this latest edition of the Peugeot Golf Guide will be their indispensable companion in the 21st century. It gives a detailed run-down of the 1,000 top courses throughout Europe designed as a work of authority to satisfy their curiosity and their passion for the game.

Automobiles Peugeot a participé de manière active et prestigieuse à l'extraordinaire développement des communications au XXe siècle, grâce auxquelles le golf est devenu un sport et un loisir dans l'ensemble de la planète.

Parce que les joueurs recherchent sans cesse de nouveaux espaces, la présente édition du Peugeot Golf Guide va les accompagner dans le XXIe siècle en leur présentant de manière approfondie les 1.000 meilleurs parcours dans l'Europe entière, pour assouvir en pleine connaissance de cause leur curiosité et leur passion.

Peugeot Automobiles hat unsere Welt mobiler gemacht, die Kommunikation gesteigert und so dazu beigetragen, dass Golf auf der ganzen Welt als Sport und Freizeitaktivität ständig wächst. Golfer suchen immer neue Herausforderungen, neue Plätze. Die aktuelle Ausgabe des Peugeot Golf Guide wird für Golfer der unverzichtbare Begleiter ins neue Jahrtausend, weil er unbestechlich und mit Autorität die besten 1000 Plätze Europas beschreibt. Peugeot har haft en aktiv

4

❿ och framträdande roll i den fantastiska utveckling som vi har sett under 1900-talet vad gäller kommunikation.

Under samma tid har golf blivit en sport och fritidssysselsättning som utövas över hela världen. Eftersom golfare ständigt är på jakt efter nya utmaningar kommer Peugeot Golf Guide att bli en oumbärlig följeslagare i 2000-talet. I Guiden får du en detaljerad redovisning över Europas 1000 bästa golfbanor – ett utmärkt stöd för den passionerade golfaren som vill stilla sin nyfikenhet för spelet...

---

❿ Automóviles Peugeot ha aportado activamente su prestigio para colaborar en el extraordinario desarollo de las comunicaciones del siglo XX, gracias a las cuales el deporte del golf se puede disfrutar con placer en todo el planeta. Para que los aficionados puedan seguir buscando nuevos espacios, la presente edición de la Guía de Golf Peugeot les acompaña en el tránsito al siglo XXI, presentándoles de manera seria y muy documentada los mil mejores campos de golf de Europa,

con el fin de que puedan satisfacer con pleno conocimiento de causa su curiosidad y pasión.

---

❿ La Peugeot Automobili ha avuto un ruolo attivo e saliente nella straordinaria espansione della comunicazione nel 20° secolo, grazie alla quale il golf è diventato uno sport e un'attività per il tempo libero in ogni parte del mondo. Siccome i golfisti sono sempre alla ricerca di nuovi orizzonti, quest'ultima edizione della Peugeot Golf Guide sarà la loro indispensabile compagna nel 21° secolo. Offre una panoramica dettagliata dei 1000 migliori campi d'Europa ed è stata progettata per essere un'opera competente, in grado di soddisfare la loro curiosità e la loro passione per il gioco.

Éric Peugeot

"UN SWING,
C'EST COMME UNE SIGNATURE."

Fred Couples.

Fred Couples, depuis qu'il a rejoint le circuit professionnel, a démontré un grand talent naturel. Avec son style personnel fait de puissance, d'aisance, de décontraction, et son swing merveilleusement rythmé, il fait rêver le monde du golf. Il n'est pas surprenant qu'il ait choisi une montre qui allie la performance et le style avec autant de succès. Une Rolex Day-Date.

ROLEX
GENÈVE

NOTICE TO ALL GOLF RETAILERS & STAFF

SELLING THE NEW HAWK EYE IRONS DOES NOT ENTITLE YOU TO WEAR AN ADVANCED COACHING BADGE.

Unless you are made of titanium and tungsten and possess a particularly low centre of gravity, please don't claim that you can suddenly make golfers hit the ball with more control and accuracy.

Leading to results.

"Private Banking. Made by Deutsche Bank." is providing you with the full range of financial products and consulting services to obtain superior financial results. The service combines the expertise of a leading international bank with the exclusive customer attention offered by a private bank. Utilizing our renowned first class research facilities and global network, your personal relationship-manager customizes the investment strategy that is best suited for your individual needs.

Private Banking worldwide: More than 100 locations in 34 countries.
Argentina · Australia · Austria · Bahrain · Belgium · Brazil · Cayman Islands
Channel Islands · Chile · Egypt · France · Germany · Hong Kong · India · Indonesia
Italy · Japan · Luxembourg · Malaysia · Monaco · Netherlands · Pakistan
Philippines · Portugal · Singapore · Spain · Sri Lanka · Switzerland · Taiwan
Thailand · United Kingdom · Uruguay · USA · Venezuela

Private Banking.
Made by Deutsche Bank.

Deutsche Bank

Vos nouvelles collaboratrices sont petites, plates, pleines de puces, mais gèrent intelligemment votre budget carburants.

TOTAL invente la première carte pétrolière de paiement à puce : la carte GR Actys. Il s'agit d'une nouvelle génération de carte qui va révolutionner le marché en permettant pour la première fois, aux entreprises disposant d'un parc automobile, d'associer les conducteurs à la maîtrise du budget carburants. Grâce à la puce de la carte GR Actys, le conducteur peut notamment consulter, après chaque plein, sa consommation au 100 km. Il est alerté en cas de saisie incohérente du kilométrage. En créant la carte GR Actys, TOTAL a eu le souci d'optimiser la gestion de votre budget carburants et d'établir une relation de confiance avec vos conducteurs. Consultez le site Internet : www.gr.total.fr **VOUS NE VIENDREZ PLUS CHEZ NOUS PAR HASARD.**

CONTENTS	Page	SOMMAIRE	Page

R I V I E R A
Côte d'Azur

Winter thrills

autumn traditions

spring excitement

summer celebrations

365 new reasons to love golf.

Here, under the splendid sunshine of the Côte d'Azur, each new day brings a new emotional experience. From grand museums to colourful market places, from age-old villages to sparkling palaces. From the clear sky of Winter to the bright lights of Summer, from the blossoming of Spring to the serenity of Autumn, an intense world packed with emotion awaits you. 365 days to taste the flavour of festivities or discovery, each second rich in pleasure and marvellous moments. 1999: the Côte d'Azur offers you an entire year as its season.

Brochure on request :
Comité Régional du Tourisme Riviera Côte d'Azur
55, Promenade des Anglais - BP 1602 - 06011 Nice Cedex 1 - France
http://www.crt-riviera.fr · e-mail : crt06@crt-riviera.fr

Côte d'Azur
Four seasons, a thousand emotions

PEUGEOT GOLF GUIDE 2000/2001

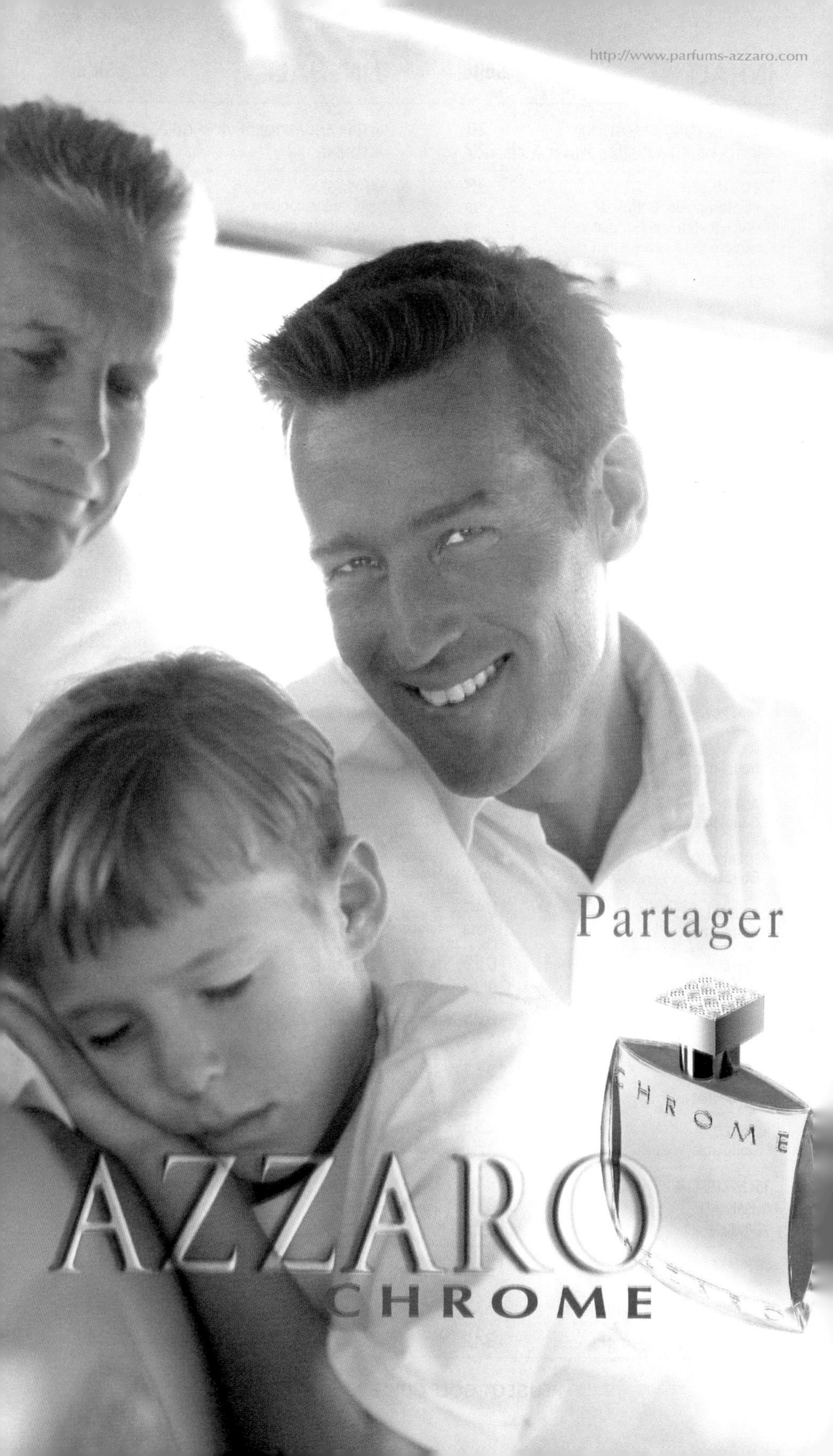
http://www.parfums-azzaro.com
Partager
CHROME
AZZARO
CHROME

HOW TO USE YOUR PEUGEOT GOLF GUIDE
COMMENT UTILISER LE PEUGEOT GOLF GUIDE
WIE DER PEUGEOT GOLF GUIDE BENUTZT WIRD

POSITION ON THE MAP

Situation sur la carte	Läge på kartan
Lage auf der Karte	Placering på kortet
Situación en el mapa	Kartta-sivu
Situatie op de kaart	Avmerket sted
Localização no mapa	på kartet
Posizione sulla carta	

When calling from abroad, remember to omit the first digit (nearly always a 0) immediately after the international dialling code. E.g.: for (49) 09178 - 98 960, dial (49) 9178 98 960

PHONE NUMBER FOR BOOKING OFFICE

Numéro de téléphone pour réserver
Telefonnummer für Reservierung
Numero de teléfono para reservar
Tel No voor reserveringen
Numero de telefone para reservar
Numero telefonico per prenotare
Telefonnummer för reservation
Telefonnummer til reservation af starttid
Lähtöajan varaus
Telefonnummer forå bestille tee-time

FEES MAIN SEASON

Tarifs en haute saison
Preisliste hochsaison
Precios temporada alta
Hoogseizoen tarieve
Tarifas da época alta
Tariffe alta stagione
Tariff hög säsong
Priser i højsæson
Green-fees
Tariffer i høysesongen

POSITION ON THE MAP

Situation sur la carte
Lage auf der Karte
Situación en el mapa
Situatie op de kaart
Localização no mapa
Posizione sulla carta
Läge på kartan
Placering på kortet
Kartta-sivu
Avmerket sted på kartet

LITTLE	MUCH
Peu	Beaucoup
Wenig	Viel
Poco	Mucho
Weinig	Veel
Pouco	Muito
Poco	Molto
Få	Många
Lille	Meget
Vähän	Paljon
Lite	Mye

0   12   24   36
0 ➝ 24
ADVISED GOLFING ABILITY (HCP)

Niveau de jeu recommandé
Empfohlene Spielstärke
Nivel de juego aconselado
Aanbevolen golfvaardigheid
Nivel de jogo recomendado
Livello di gioco consigliato
Rekommenderad spelnivå
Anbefalet golfkunnen
Tasoitusvaatimus
Anbefalt golfnivå

FAIR	EXCELLENT
Passable	Excellent
Mittelmässig	Hervorragend
Mediana	Excelente
Aanvaardboar	Uitstekend
Suficiente	Excelente
Passabile	Eccellente
Godkänd	Förträfflig
Rimelig	Fantastik
Hyvä	Erinomainen
Godbra	Utmerket

20

RECOMMENDED HOLIDAYS

Vacances recommandées — Località di vacanze raccomandata
Empfohlener Ferienort — Rekommenderad semesterort
Sitio de vacaciones recomendado — Anbefalet som feriested
Aanbevolen vacantie-oord — Suositellaan lomanviettopaikkana
Local de férias recomendado — Anbefalt feriested

RECOMMENDED GOLFING STAY

Séjour de golf recommandé
Empfohlener Golf Aufenthalt
Estancia de golf recomendada
Aanbevolen golf vacantie
Estadia de golf recomendada
Soggiorno golfistico raccomandato
Rekommenderad golfvistelse
Anbefalet til golfophold
Suositellaan golfin pelaamisen
Anbefalt golfopphold

ROYAL WEST NORFOLK (Brancaster) ⟩ 17 7 6

If you are one of those golfers who go for nature, wildlife and vegetation, this course is for you, set in a landscape of dunes and salt-marshes that flood at every high tide and which are home to a host of wild animals. Brancaster is famous for its railway sleeper bunkers and its devilish greens, which are tough to put on and tough to reach because they are small and often hit with long irons. If it's windy, you can forget it. Get out on the course, by all means, and enjoy what is an uplifting experience for any golfer, but go around in matchplay and play to see who pays for the drink at the bar. You won't want to leave the clubhouse, which has never been anything else but old and smells of wood, woods and balatas. Time has stood still at Brancaster, which is why you feel so privileged to be here. A little on the short side, did you say? What the hell.

Si vous êtes de ces golfeurs qui sont aussi amoureux de la nature, de la flore et de la faune, ce parcours est pour vous, dans un paysage de dunes et de marais salés inondés lors des grandes marées, qui abritent une vie sauvage très riche. Brancaster est célèbre pour ses bunkers renforcés par des traverses de chemin de fer, mais aussi pour des greens diaboliques, difficiles à toucher car ils sont petits et souvent attaqués avec des longs fers, et difficiles à putter. Les jours de vent, n'insistez pas : jouez car l'expérience est exaltante, mais en match-play, avec un enjeu à consommer au Clubhouse. Il est vieux depuis toujours, il y règne une odeur de bois en bois et de balatas, il fait bon y rester. Ici, le temps s'est arrêté, c'est pourquoi on s'y sent autant privilégié. Le parcours est un peu court ? Et alors...

SCORE FOR THE COURSE (1 TO 20)

17

Note du parcours (1 à 20)
Benotung des Golfplatzes (1 bis 20)
Nota del campo (1 a 20)
Waardering van de baan (1 tot 20)
Nota do percurso (1 a 20)
Giudizio sul percorso (1 a 20)
Banans betyg (1 till 20)
Klassificering af banen (1 til 20)
Kentän laatuluokitus (1 to 20)
Rangering av golfbanen (1-20)

Royal West Norfolk Golf Club	1892		
ENG - BRANCASTER, Norfolk PE31 8 AY			

Office	Secrétariat	(44) 01485 - 210 223
Pro shop	Pro-shop	(44) 01485 - 210 616
Fax	Fax	(44) 01485 - 210 087
Situation	Situation	

12 km from Hunstanton (pop. 4 736)
30 km from King's Lynn (pop. 41 281)

Annual closure	Fermeture annnuelle	no
Weekly closure	Fermeture hebdomadaire	

Fees main season
Tarifs haute saison 18 holes

	Week days Semaine	We/Bank holidays We/Férié
Individual Individuel	£ 39	£ 49
Couple Couple	£ 78	£ 98

In August, no visitor unless playing with a member

Caddy	Caddy	on request
Electric Trolley	Chariot électrique	no
Buggy	Voiturette	no
Clubs	Clubs	no

Credit cards Cartes de crédit
Visa - Mastercard (Pro shop goods & green fees)

Access Accès : London M11. Cambridge A10 to King's Lynn. A149 North through Hunstanton to Brancaster. Turn left into Beach Road, continue across marsh.
Map 4 on page 495 Carte 4 Page 495

GOLF COURSE PARCOURS

17/20

Site	Site	
Maintenance	Entretien	
Architect	Architecte	Holcombe Ingleby
Type	Type	seaside course, links
Relief	Relief	
Water in play	Eau en jeu	
Exp. to wind	Exposé au vent	
Trees in play	Arbres en jeu	

Scorecard	Chp.	Mens	Ladies
Carte de score	Chp.	Mess.	Da.
Length Long.	5785	5785	5334
Par	71	71	75

Advised golfing ability	0 12 24 36
Niveau de jeu recommandé	
Hcp required	Handicap exigé	certificate

CLUB HOUSE & AMENITIES
CLUB HOUSE ET ANNEXES

7/10

Pro shop	Pro-shop	
Driving range	Practice	
Sheltered	couvert	no
On grass	sur herbe	yes
Putting-green	putting-green	yes
Pitching-green	pitching green	no

HOTEL FACILITIES
ENVIRONNEMENT HOTELIER

6/10

HOTELS HÔTELS

Le Strange Arms — Hunstanton 12 km
36 rooms, D £ 70
Tel (44) 01485 - 534 411
Fax (44) 01485 - 534 724

Cingham Hall — Grimston 25 km
12 rooms, D £ 100
Tel (44) 01485 - 600 250
Fax (44) 01485 - 601 191

RESTAURANTS RESTAURANT

Gurney's — Burnham Market 7 km
Tel (44) 01328 - 738937

The Hoste Arms — Burnham Market 7 km
Tel (44) 01328 - 738777

639

SCORE FOR THE CLUB HOUSE AND ANNEXES (1 TO 10)

7

Note du Club House et annexes (1 à 10)
Benotung des Klubhauses (1 bis 10)
Nota del Club House (1 a 10)
Waardering van het Club House (1 tot 10)
Nota do Club House (1 a 10)
Giudizio sul Club House (1 a 10)
Klubhus betyg (1 till 10)
Klassificering af Klubhuset (1 til 10)
Klubitalon laatuluokitus (1 to 10)
Rangering av Klubhus (1-10)

SCORE FOR HOTEL FACILITIES (1 TO 10)

6

Note de l'environnement hôtelier (1 à 10)
Benotung des Hotelangebots (1 bis 10)
Nota del complejo hotelero (1 a 10)
Waardering van het Hotel and ongeving (1 tot 10)
Nota das infraestructuras hoteleiras (1 a 10)
Giudizio su offerta alberghiera (1 a 10)
Hotellomgivningens betyg (1 till 10)
Klassificering af hotelfaciliteterne (1 til 10)
Hotellin laatuluokitus (1 to 10)
Rangering av Hotel (1-10)

21

D 1000 F: BEST ROOM PRICE FOR 2 PEOPLE (MAIN SEASON)

Premier prix chambre 2 personnes (haute saison)
Preis Hotelzimmer für 2 personen (Hauptsaison)
Primer precio habitación 2 personas (temporada alta)
1e Klas prijs 2 persoons kamer (hoog seizoen)
Primeiro preço quarto duplo (época alta)
Primo prezzo camera doppia (2 persone), alta stagione
Lägsta rumspris för 2 pers. under högsäsong
Lavere pris for dobbeltværelse (højsæson)
Alennus 2-hengen huoneesta
Lavere pris for et tommans rom (høysesong)

Bell Hotel
RECOMMENDED BY THE PEUGEOT GOLF GUIDE

Recommandé par le Peugeot Golf Guide
Empfohlen durch Peugeot Golf Guide
Recomendado por el Peugeot Golf Guide
Aanbevolen door de Peugeot Golf Guide
Recomendado pelo Peugeot Golf Guide
Raccomandato da Peugeot Golf Guide
Rekommanderat av Peugeot Golf Guide
Anbefalet af Peugeot Golf Guide
Opaan suositettelema (Peugeot Golf Guide)
Anbefalt av Peugeot Golf Guide

Certains parcours révèlent l'excellence.

Qu'importent fairways en dévers, bunkers sournois et greens pentus. Concentration, précision, sang-froid, sens de l'anticipation ont toujours construit les plus belles cartes. Et c'est dans la régularité, tout au long d'un parcours, que vous appréciez la parfaite maîtrise d'un partenaire.

La gestion de votre patrimoine exige plus encore. A la Banque Piguet, nous cultivons aussi solidité et discrétion. Jour après jour, avec constance, nous employons notre savoir-faire à élaborer des stratégies gagnantes, taillées à l'exacte mesure de vos besoins. Car, comme en compétition, chaque coup est déterminant pour le score.

BANQUE PIGUET & CIE S.A.

DEPUIS 1856

GENÈVE
Place de l'Université 5 – CH-1205 Genève
Téléphone (+41 22) 322 88 00

LAUSANNE
Rue du Grand-Chêne 8 – CH-1003 Lausanne
Téléphone (+41 21) 310 10 10

YVERDON-LES-BAINS
Rue de la Plaine 14 – CH-1400 Yverdon
Téléphone (+41 24) 423 43 00

Foreword

Standard of facilities

As opposed to hotel or restaurant guides, there was no such thing as a qualitative guide to golf courses. Yet as all golf-lovers know, every course is different and standards of excellence vary. Besides the unquestionable class of championship courses that everyone wants to play, there are all the others. «Remoter» courses, little gems in the depths of Europe, public courses with simple layouts, pretentiously labelled «international» courses where layouts often have no regard for common sense, and the small budget courses where the architect has worked wonders...

Six years ago, we began to take a long, hard look at golf courses in Europe, putting ourselves verry firmly in the shoes of the golfer who pays to play and who expects standards of service to match his or her expectations. This "millenium" edition is the initial successful outcome of this approach, since all European countries are included whenever, of course, their courses hit the mark.

1,000 selected courses

Over the past six years, we have visited and played 1,500 18-hole golf courses. We did so anonymously so we could see them like an ordinary golfer. Of all the courses we played, we selected 1000 which are open to the public, at least during weekdays. But we have also included many private courses where you can always try your luck.

Three scores for each course

In our scoring system, the score for the course is explicitely given out of 20, while the score for the club-house and facilities and local hotel accommodation are clearly marked out of 10. So to our mind, the actual course score has a greater significance, while the other marks allows us to tone down the considerable differences seen in golfing and hotel accommodation from one country to the next.

On each page you will find the three scores in the top right-hand corner. The first concerns the actual course, the second is for the Club-House and facilities, and the third is for surrounding hotel accomodation. A little golfer indicates a few days golfing is recommended, a sun recommends a full holiday stay, including non-golfers.

Standard of facilities

We gave a general score to the course, but in the same way we also assessed the quality of the Club-House and related services: styling and comfort of buildings, practice and additional facilities.

Hotel accommodation

Lastly, we assessed the regions's hotel facilities. Some highly reputed restaurants were thus selected, as were hotels from different categories so that there would be something for every budget. Our assessment of hotel standards indicates most importantly the numbers and diversity of hotel facilities within the immediate vicinity of the golf.

Philosophy of the Guide

One last word to stress the fact that inaccuracies or errors are bound to creep in when working with such a mass of information. Our goal is to help golfers and also golf courses to raise standards in order to provide ever better service and the best possible course to play on. Their prosperity dependa on how demanding players are in this respect. As demanding as if every green-fee golfer were sent by our Guide.

LANVIN
L'HOMME

EAU DE TOILETTE POUR HOMME

Avant-propos

Un véritable « Guide »

Contrairement aux guides des hôtels ou des restaurants, il n'existait aucun guide qualitatif des parcours à l'échelle européenne. Mais, tous les amateurs de golf le savent, la qualité des parcours est variable. A côté des parcours de championnat, que les meilleurs veulent affronter, il est des parcours ignorés qui sont de petits joyaux, des golfs publics au dessin très simple et aux ambitions réduites, des parcours prétentieux et décevants, des parcours à petit budget où l'architecte a fait des prodiges... Il y a six ans, nous avons entrepris un travail de fond sur les golfs d'Europe, en se situant résolument du côté de ceux qui paient pour jouer et attendent un service à hauteur de leurs attentes. Cette édition «Millenium» est un premier aboutissement de cette démarche, car tous les pays d'Europe y sont compris, lorsque leurs parcours sont à la hauteur des attentes, bien sûr.

1000 parcours retenus

Nous avons visité et joué 1.500 parcours de 18 trous au cours des six dernières années. Et chaque fois de manière anonyme, comme n'importe quel golfeur. Parmi tous ces parcours , nous en avons retenu 1000 ouverts au public, au moins en semaine, mais aussi la grande majorité des parcours privés où vous pourrez essayer d'avoir accès.

Une « triple note »

La note du parcours est explicitement exprimée sur 20, les notes relatives au Club-house et à ses équipements, et à l'environnement hôtelier sont clairement indiquées sur 10. Pour nous, la note du parcours est ainsi prépondérante, les autres permettent d'atténuer les fortes différences des installations et de l'hôtellerie d'un pays à l'autre. Sur chaque page, vous trouverez en haut et à droite les trois notes. La première concerne le parcours, la seconde le Club-House et ses équipements, la troisième l'environnement hôtelier. Un petit golfeur indique un séjour de golf recommandé, un soleil un séjour de vacances recommandé.

Qualité des installations

Nous avons attribué une note globale aux parcours, et une autre pour la qualité du Club-House et de ses équipements : esthétique et confort des bâtiments, qualité des installations d'entraînement, etc...

Environnement hôtelier

Enfin, nous avons étudié l'environnement hôtelier dans la région. Certains restaurants de bonne réputation sont sélectionnés, de même que des hôtels de différentes catégories. La note attribuée n'exprime pas seulement un jugement sur les hôtels, mais elle signale surtout la quantité et la diversité des équipements hôteliers à proximité du parcours.

La philosophie du Peugeot Golf Guide

Un dernier mot pour souligner qu'il est impossible d'échapper à certaines imprécisions ou erreurs, avec une telle masse d'informations. Notre but est d'aider les golfeurs, et aussi les Clubs à progresser pour proposer toujours de meilleurs servies et un parcoutrs aussi bon que possible. Leur prospérité dépend de leur réputation et de leur exigence. Comme si chaque visiteur était envoyé par le Guide...

Figoni & Falaschi. Talbot Lago T150 SS, 1938.

Léman Collection, 1998.

*Available as fountain pen, roller/fibre-tip pen, ballpoint pen and mechanical pencil,
in ruby red, sapphire blue, racing green and ebony black.*

Make your mark

CARAN d'ACHE
OF SWITZERLAND

CARAN d'ACHE SA • P.O. Box 332 • CH-1226 Thônex-Geneva • TEL. +41 22 348 0204 • FAX +41 22 348 7521
For more information, please visit our website: www.carandache.ch

Vorwort

Ein echter Golffuhrer

Im Gegensatz zu den zahlreichen Hotel- und Restaurantführern gab es bisher noch keinen Golfplatzführer, der die Plätze kritisch und objektiv bewertet. Neben den begehrten und allseits bekannten Plätzen und grossen Meisterschaftsplätzen, gibt es auch einige unentdeckte Juwele, unbekannte Plätze, öffentliche Plätze mit einfachem, aber reizvollem Design, Plätze, die mit einem kleinen Budget entstanden sind, wo aber der Architekt Wunder vollbrachte. Vor sechs Jahren haben wir begonnen, uns die Golfplätze in Europa genau und kritisch anzusehen. Wir haben uns in die Lage von Golfer versetzt, die Greenfee zahlen und einen Platz und einen Service erwarten, der ihren Ansprüchen entspricht. Diese Millenium-Ausgabe" ist die erste, die unser ursprünglich gesetztes Ziel erreicht, nämlich Golfplätze in ganz Europa zu beschreiben und zu bewerten - allerdings nur sofern die Plätze den hohen Ansprüchen dieses Golfführers genügen.

1000 Golfplätze ausgewählt

Wir haben in den vergangenen fünf Jahren 1500 18-Loch-Plätze besucht und darauf gespielt. Und zwar immer anonym, so dass wir einen Platz in seinem üblichen Zustand beurteilen konnten, wie ihn jeder Spieler antreffen kann. Von den 1100 bespielten Plätzen haben wir öffentlich zugängliche ausgewählt, darunter sind jedoch auch viele private Golfplätze, die nur beschränkt zugänglich sind.

Eine dreifache Note

In unserem Bewertungssystem ist die höchste Bewertungszahl für den Platz 20 Punkten, während für das Clubhaus, die sonstigen Einrichtungen und die regionale Hotelleriet bereits 10 Punkte die Höchstnoteist. Die Bewertung des Parcours ist für uns ausschlaggebend; die anderen Noten ermöglichen eine differenzierte Beurteilung der von Land zu Land recht unterschlieden Anlagen

und Unterkunftsmöglichkeiten. Auf jeder Seite finden Sie oben rechts drei Noten. Die erste für den Platz, die zweite für das Clubhaus und seine Einrichtungen, die dritte für das Hotelangebot der Umgebung. Ein kleiner Golfspieler zeigt an, dass Golfferien empfohlen werden können, eine Sonne, dass auch allgemein ein Ferienaufenthalt empfehlenswert ist.

Qualität der Einrichtungen

Eine Gesamtnote haben wir dem Golfplatz erteilt, eine zweite der Qualität des Clubhauses und seinen Einrichtungen: Ästhetik und Komfort der Gebäude, Trainingsanlagen usw. Auch die Professionalität des Empfangs wurde bei der Bewertung berücksichtigt.

Hotelangebot der Umgebung

Schliesslich haben wir das Hotelangebot der Umgebung untersucht. Es wurden einige gute Restaurants sowie Hotels und Gästezimmer verschiedener Kategorien ausgewählt. Die erteilte Note ist nicht nur Ausdruck eines Urteils über die Hotels, sondern steht vor allem für die Grösse und Vielseitigkeit des Hotelangebots in der Umgebung des Golfplatzes.

Die Philosophie des Guide

Es ist uns sehr wohl bewusst, dass bei einer solchen Fülle von Informationen gewisse Ungenauigkeiten oder Fehler möglich sind. Unser Ziel ist es Golfer bei der Auswahl lohnenswerte Plätze zu helfen, aber auch die Golfanlagen dazu anzuspornen Greenfee-Spielern den Platz in bestmöglichem Zustand anzubieten und den Standard ihres Service zu verbessern. Der finanzielle Erfolg vieler Golfanlagen hängt auch davon ab, wie zufrieden Greenfeespieler nach ihrer Runde sind. Golfspieler sind anspruchsvoll - und jede Golfanlage sollte Gastspieler so behandeln, als seien Tester für unseren Golfführer.

The Finest Golf Resorts® COLLECTION

Adare Manor Hotel: One of the finest golf resorts

THE FINEST GOLF RESORT COLLECTION

ILLUSTRATES THE MOST PRESTIGIOUS GOLF RESORTS

FROM ACROSS THE GLOBE

TO ORDER YOUR COPY

Visit: www.finestgolfresorts.com

OR COMPLETE THE SUBSCRIPTION CARD WITHIN
INSIDE THE TOUR '99

Inledning

Inom hotell- och restaurangbranschen har det länge funnits guideböcker, däremot har det saknats en kvalitetsguide över golfbanor. Ändå vet alla passionerade golfspelare att alla banor skiljer sig från varandra. Naturligtvis vill alla spela på mästerskapbanor, men det finns också en uppsjö av andra banor. En del ligger långt från allfarsvägarna, andra är gömda pärlor mitt i Europa, och så finns det naturligtvis "public courses" – banor med enklare layouter men som å andra sidan är öppna för alla. Det finns banor i vilka massor med pengar har plöjts ned där layouten är huvudlös. Det finns banor med minimala budgetar men där arkitekten har gjort underverk.

För sex år sedan började vi titta närmare på golfbanorna i Europa. Vi utgick från den vanlige golfspelaren och vilka förväntningar och krav som finns när vi kommer till en bana. Denna millenium-utgåva är resultatet av detta arbete. Alla europeiska länder är representerade. En del länder har fler banor med, andra färre. Vi har utgått från banornas kvalitet, och inget annat.

1 000 utvalda banor

Över de senaste sex åren har vi besökt och spelat 1 500 golfbanor. Vi besökte dem anonymt och utan att avslöja vår t syfte. Av alla banor vi har spelat har vi valt ut 1 000 stycken, de allra flesta är öppna för allmänheten – åtminstone under vardagar. En del är privata, men ringer du dem finns det oftast alltid en möjlighet att komma ut.

Tre rankingar för varje bana

Vårt poängberäkningssystem för banorna går från 1-20 poäng. Poängberäkningssystemet för hotellen och klubbhusen går från 1-10. Naturligtvis ligger tonvikten i vår ranking på själva banorna, dessa är också enklare att poängsätta än hotellen. Hotellens kvalitet varierar mycket från land till land och detta gör det svårare att gradera dem.

På varje sida kommer du uppe i högra hörnet se våra tre poäng som vi utfärdar per respektive bana. Den första poängen rör banan, den andra poängen gäller klubbhuset och den tredje poängen hotellen i närheten av banan.

Anläggningens standard

När vi har satt poäng på banan har vi även tagit hänsyn till anläggningens standard: klubbhusets kvalitet †och design, övningsfält och andra faciliteter.

Hotell

Vi har även †bedömt hotellen i respektive region, och dessutom har vi valt ut några högklassiga restauranger. När vi har valt hotell har vi även tagit med hotell som passar alla slags plånböcker. Hotellens geografiska närhet till golfbanan har varit av största betydelse.

Sist men inte minst

Ett sista ord på vägen: I en sådan här omfattande produktion kan felaktigheter och inaktuell information krypa in. Vårt mål är att hjälpa golfare men också uppmuntra golfbanor till att höja standarden. Vi vill tipsa om de bästa banorna du kan spela och den service du kan få där. Hur klubbarna lyckas på detta område beror på vilka krav som ställs på dem.

29

Introduccion

Una auténtica guía

En Europa hay muchas guía de hoteles y restaurantes pero faltaba una guía cualitativa de campos de golf. Además de la incuestionable categoría de los recorridos de campeonato que todo il mundo desea jugar, tenemos campos escondidos en el interior de Europa que son verdaderas joyas, golfs públicos elementales, recorridos "internacionales" pretenciosos cuyo diseño tiene muy poco sentido común, y otros que se han hecho con pocos recursos y donde el arquitecto ha hecho maravillas. Hace sei años empezamos a visitar los campos de golf de Europa con espiritu crítico, intentando ponernos en la piel del jugador que paga por jugar y, por lo tanto, tiene derecho a esperar que el servicio que recibe colme sus expéctativas. Con esta edición del milenio ofrecemos por primera vez la obra que satisaface nuestro objetivo, puesto que incluye todos los países europeos donde hay campos de golf que, por supuesto, alcanzan el nivel de calidad requerido.

Una selección de 1.000 campos

Durante los últimos seis años hemos visitado y jugado en 1.500 campos de 18 hoyos. Lo hemos hecho siempre de manera anónima, como cualquier jugador de paso. Para esta edición hemos hecho una selección de 1.000 campos abiertos al público, que admiten green-fees al menos entre semana, aunque también hemos incorporado clubs privados en los que, con suerte, también se puede encontrar la manera de jugar.

Triple nota

En el sistema de puntuación que hemos empleado, la nota del campo se valora sobre 20, mientras las notas de la casa-club y sus instalaciones, y la de los recursos hoteleros próximos, se puntúan sobre 10. Por lo tanto, nuestro criterio da preponderancia e la nota del campo, mientras con las otras dos salvamos las evidentes diferencias en cuanto a instalaciones, servicios y hostelería que existen de un país a otro. Encontrará usted tres notas en la parte superior derecha de cada página. La primera se refiere al recorrido, la segunda a la casa-club y sus instalaciones y la tercera, a la estructura hotelera de la zona. La silueta de un golfista indica que se recomienda para pasar más de un día; cuando aparece un sol quiere decir qe se recomienda, incluso a los no golfistas, para unas vacaciones.

Calidad de las instalaciones

Concedemos una nota general al campo pero también queremos dejar constancia de la calidad y servicios de la casa-club: para ello se tienen en consideración la estética y la comodidad del conjunto, el estado de campo de prácticas y las instalaciones complementarias.

Infraestructura hotelera

Finalmente, consideramos la infraestructura hotelera de la zona. Se han seleccionado buenos restaurantes y hoteles de varias categorías para diferentes presupuestos. La calificación hotelera se fija, sobre todo, en la cantidad de servicios que se ofrecen y en su proximidad al campo de golf.

Filosofia de la Guía de Golf Peugeot

Por último, somos muy conscientes de que cuando se maneja tal cantidad de datos siempre pueden escarpase ciertas imprecisiones a algun error. Pretendemos ser una referencia para los jugadores y un incentivo para que los campos mejoren sus servicios y tengan el recorrido de juego en les mejores condiciones posibles. Su prosperidad depende de que los jugadores aprecien sus cualidades. Esta guía prepara al golfista a comprender el nivel de calidad que puede exigirse en cada uno de los campos que visite pagando un green-fee.

GOLF
& TURISMO

LA RIVISTA CHE TI PARLA DI...

- grandi **tornei**
- i **protagonisti**
- **viaggi** e **vacanze**
- **resort** e alberghi
- la **tecnica**
- i nostri **test**
- ...e **altro** ancora

Go. Tu. srl - Via Winckelmann, 2 - 20146 MILANO
tel. +39.02.424191 - e-mail: golfeturismo@touritel.com

Introduzione

Una guida attendibile

Contrariamente alle guide degli alberghi o dei ristoranti, non esisteva alcuna guida qualitativa dei campi da golf su scala europea. Ma, come tutti i giocatori sanno, la qualit‡ dei percorsi è molto varia. A fianco di percorsi da campionato, che i migliori giocatori vogliono sfidare, troviamo dei campi poco conosciuti che sono dei piccoli gioielli, dei golf pubblici di disegno semplice e di modeste ambizioni, dei percorsi pretenziosi e deludenti, dei percorsi realizzati con piccoli budget dove l'architetto ha fatto miracoli... Da sei anni abbiamo intrapreso un lavoro meticoloso su tutti i golf in Europa, cercando di metterci dalla parte di coloro che pagano per giocare e si aspettano un servizio all'altezza delle loro aspettative. Questa edizione «Millenium» è il primo esito del grande lavoro, perchè ci sono davvero tutti i paesi d'Europa, sempre che, ovviamente, i loro percorsi siano all'altezza.

1000 percorsi selezionati

Abbiamo visitato e giocato in 1500 percorsi di 18 buche nel corso degli ultimi sei anni e ogni volta in maniera anonima, come un golfista qualsiasi. Tra tutti questi campi ne abbiamo scelti 1000 aperti al pubblico, almeno in settimana, ma anche la maggioranza dei percorsi privati dove potrete provare ad accedere.

Un « voto triplo »

Il voto del percorso è esplicitamente espresso in ventesimi, i voti relativi al club-house ed alle sue attrezzature così come quello degli alberghi nei dintorni è indicato in decimi. Per noi il voto attribuito ai percorsi è assolutamente preponderante, gli altri voti permettono di attenuare le grandi differenze che si incontrano nei servizi e nel settore alberghiero da un paese all'altro.

In ogni pagina, troverete in alto a destra i tre voti: il primo riguarda il percorso, il secondo il club-house e le sue attrezzature, il terzo i servizi alberghieri. Il simbolo di un golfista indica che è consigliata una sosta per giocare a golf , un sole indica che è consigliata una sosta per una vacanza.

Qualita' degli impianti

Abbiamo attribuito un voto globale ai percorsi ed un altro alla qualità dei club-house e delle attrezzature: per estetica, comodità, qualità delle strutture, ecc.

Offerta alberghiera nei dintorni

Infine, abbiamo approfondito l'offerta alberghiera nei dintorni. Sono stati selezionati alcuni ristoranti che godono già di una buona reputazione ma anche alberghi di differenti categorie. Il voto attribuito non esprime soltanto un giudizio sugli alberghi e sui ristoranti ma segnala soprattutto la quantità e la varietà delle attrezzature di questo tipo vicino al campo da golf.

La filosofia della Peugeot Golf Guide

Un'ultima parola per ricordare che è impossibile sfuggire a qualche imprecisione o a qualche errore quando si tratta una tale massa d'informazioni. Il nostro scopo rimane quello di agevolare i golfisti ma anche quello di aiutare i circoli a progredire per proporre servizi sempre più gradevoli e un percorso sempre migliore. La loro fortuna dipende dalla loro reputazione e dalle loro esigenze. Come se ogni visitatore fosse stato mandato dalla Guida ...

30 ANS DE TROPHÉE

LANCÔME

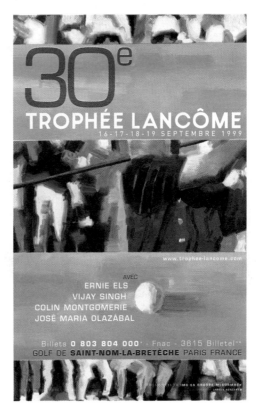

Follow the course of events via the World's

Daily Newspaper.

EBEL

LES ARCHITECTES DU TEMPS

"Chronographe 1911" en acier et or avec fond saphir. Chronographe automatique avec certificat de chronomètre. Garantie internationale de 5 ans.

COLIN MONTGOMERIE ET SON CHRONOGRAPHE

portrait par Hans Gissinger

CLASSIFICATION OF COURSES
CLASSEMENT DES PARCOURS
EINTEILUNG DER GOLFPLÄTZE
VI RANKAR BANORNA
CLASIFICACION DE LOS RECORRIDOS
CLASSIFICA DEI PERCORSI

This classification gives priority consideration to the score awarded to the actual course.
Ce classement donne priorité à la note attribuée au parcours.
Diese Einteilung berücksichtigt in erster Linie die dem Golfplatz erteilte Note.
Rankingen syftar endast på golfbanan.
Esta clasificación da prioridad a la nota atribuida al recorrido.
Questa classifica è ordinata secondo il punteggio assegnato al percorso.

A: Austria   B: Belgium   Ch: Switzerland   Cz: Czech Republic   Da: Denmark   E: Spain
Eng: England   F: France   Fi: Finland   G: Germany   I: Republic of Ireland
L: Luxembourg   N: Nederland   Nw: Norway   P: Portugal   R: Russia   S: Sweden   Sc: Scotland
T: Turkey   U: Northern Ireland (Ulster)   W: Wales

Course score	Club-house and facilities	Hotel facility score
Note du parcours	Note du Club-house et annexes	Note de l'environnement hôtelier
Note für den Golfplatz	Note für das Clubhaus und die Einrichtungen	Note für das Hotelangebot der Umgebung
Banans betyg	Klubhus och omngivninges betyg	Hotellomgivninges betyg
Nota del recorrido	Nota del club-house y anejos	Nota de la infraestructura hotelera
Giudizio sul percorso	Giudizio sul Club house	Giudizio su offerta alberghiera

19/20

| 19 | 7 | 7 | Ballybunion *Old Course* | I | 839 | Page |

19	7	7	Ballybunion *Old Course*	I	839
19	8	6	Bordes (Les)	F	239
19	5	6	Carnoustie *Championship*	Sc	715
19	8	5	Ganton	Eng	573
19	7	6	Muirfield	Sc	759
19	7	8	Nairn	Sc	762
19	7	8	Portmarnock	I	894
19	9	7	Royal Birkdale (The)	Eng	629
19	6	7	Royal County Down	UL	934
19	7	7	Royal Dornoch Championship	Sc	776
19	7	8	Royal Lytham & St Anne's	Eng	635
19	7	6	Royal Porthcawl	W	819
19	7	7	Royal Portrush *Dunluce Links*	UL	935
19	7	5	Royal St George's	Eng	638
19	7	7	Royal Troon *Old Course*	Sc	778
19	9	8	Turnberry *Ailsa Course*	Sc	792
19	8	6	Valderrama	E	1213

39

AUGUSTE THOUARD

INTERNATIONAL PROPERTY CONSULTANTS

An international group with specialiesed professionals working together to meet your property requirements

Agency, Consulting, Valuation, Property management, Interior design.

Tous les services d'un Groupe International réunis au service de votre immobilier :

Transactions, Conseil, Expertise, Gestion, Aménagement intérieur.

Score	Course	Country	Page
	18/20		
18 7 7	Alwoodley (The)	Eng	523
18 7 6	Barsebäck	S	1231
18 7 7	Biella - Le Betulle	I	959
18 8 6	Blairgowrie *Rosemount*	Sc	706
18 7 6	Burnham & Berrow	Eng	542
18 8 7	Castelconturbia		
	Giallo + Azzurro	I	963
18 6 8	Castletown	Eng	549
18 9 7	Celtic Manor *Roman Road*	W	804
18 7 6	Chantilly *Vineuil*	F	255
18 8 6	Chart Hills	Eng	550
18 6 5	Club zur Vahr (Garlstedt)	D	398
18 5 6	County Louth	I	855
18 7 6	Cruden Bay	Sc	718
18 8 6	Domaine Impérial	Ch	1294
18 8 6	Eindhoven	N	1019
18 7 6	El Saler	E	1144
18 5 6	European (The)	I	867
18 6 7	Falkenstein	D	404
18 7 5	Falsterbo	S	1242
18 6 5	Fontanals	E	1148
18 7 7	Formby	Eng	568
18 9 7	Gleneagles *King's*	Sc	735
18 8 7	Gut Altentann	A	98
18 7 8	Haagsche	N	1025
18 8 7	Halmstad	S	1252
18 7 7	Hillside	Eng	585
18 7 6	Ilkley	Eng	590
18 8 6	Kempferhof (Le)	F	293
18 8 8	Kennemer	N	1030
18 6 6	Lahinch	I	883
18 7 7	Las Brisas	E	1171
18 6 4	Machrihanish	Sc	755
18 7 5	Médoc *Les Châteaux*	F	302
18 7 7	Moortown	Eng	609
18 9 8	Mount Juliet	I	889
18 5 6	National *L'Albatros*	F	307
18 7 8	Noordwijk	N	1032
18 7 8	North Berwick	Sc	765
18 6 6	Notts (Hollinwell)	Eng	614
18 7 5	Örebro	S	1266
18 6 6	Pennard	W	816
18 7 7	PGA de Catalunya	E	1196
18 6 7	Prestwick	Sc	771
18 8 9	Puerta de Hierro		
	Puerta de Hierro 2	E	1200

Score	Course	Country	Page
18 7 6	Real Sociedad		
	Club de Campo	E	1202
18 7 8	Royal Aberdeen		
	Balgownie Links	Sc	774
18 8 7	Royal Liverpool (Hoylake)	Eng	634
18 6 6	Royal North Devon		
	(Westward Ho!)	Eng	637
18 6 5	Royal St David's	W	820
18 7 7	Royal Zoute	B	121
18 6 8	S. Lourenço	P	1085
18 7 6	Saunton *East Course*	Eng	645
18 8 7	Scharmützelsee *Nick Faldo*	D	457
18 5 4	Seascale	Eng	647
18 9 7	Seddiner See *Südplatz*	D	467
18 7 4	Silloth-on-Solway	Eng	653
18 7 6	Sotogrande	E	1209
18 6 5	Southerness	Sc	781
18 7 7	Southport & Ainsdale	Eng	655
18 8 8	St Andrews *Old Course*	Sc	785
18 7 4	St Enodoc *Church Course*	Eng	656
18 8 8	Sunningdale *New Course*	Eng	661
18 8 8	Sunningdale *Old Course*	Eng	662
18 7 6	Tenby	W	822
18 7 6	Tralee	I	908
18 7 7	Walton Heath *Old Course*	Eng	675
18 8 7	Wentworth *West Course*	Eng	678
18 7 6	West Sussex	Eng	685
18 7 7	Woburn *Dukes Course*	Eng	690
18 7 8	Woodhall Spa	Eng	694
	17/20		
17 7 7	Aberdovey	W	799
17 7 7	Aloha	E	1127
17 6 5	Ashburnham	W	800
17 9 9	Bad Griesbach *Brunnwies*	D	386
17 6 5	Ballyliffin *Glashedy Links*	I	841
17 7 6	Barbaroux	F	229
17 8 7	Berkshire (The) *Blue Course*	Eng	529
17 8 7	Berkshire (The) *Red Course*	Eng	530
17 7 6	Beuerberg	D	393
17 6 5	Blackmoor	Eng	532
17 8 7	Bogogno	I	960
17 6 6	Bowood G&CC	Eng	535
17 7 6	Brampton	Eng	536
17 7 6	Bro-Bålsta	S	1235
17 7 7	Broadstone	Eng	538
17 8 7	Buckinghamshire (The)	Eng	540

41

Sentir bon. Se sentir bien.

EAU DYNAMISANTE CLARINS.

Le plaisir du parfum, l'efficacité des plantes.

Première Eau de Toilette de Beauté, l'Eau Dynamisant parfume, hydrate,* raffermit, vitalise. D'un seul geste, elle offre réunis, le parfum et l'action traitante des plantes.

* Les couches supérieures de l'épiderme.

Pour elle comme pour lui.

Eau Dynamisante, un regain de fraîcheur et de dynamisme, à tout moment de la journée, même sous le soleil.

Le plaisir décliné.

Lait Hydratant Parfumé, pour une peau souple, lisse et satinée. Gel Moussant Parfumé, d'une douceur extrême, pour la douche et le bain.

Lait Hydratant Parfumé
"Eau Dynamisante"

Moisturizing Body Lotion

CLARINS

Gel Moussant Parfumé
"Eau Dynamisante"

Shower Gel

CLARINS
PARIS

Eau Dynamisante

fraîcheur fermeté vitalité

Eau de Soins
CLARINS
PARIS

CLARINS
PARIS

L'expérience et l'efficacité du soin.

Une question-beauté? Demandez cons à votre parfumeur ou écrivez à Clarins vous répondra personnellement.

Clarins Conseil. 4, rue Berteaux-Dumas 92203 Neuilly-sur-Seine Cedex.

Score	Course	Country	Page	Score	Course	Country	Page
17 7 7	Caldy	Eng	543	17 6 5	Moliets	F	304
17 8 8	Carden Park			17 7 7	Monifieth	Sc	756
	Nicklaus Course	Eng	547	17 8 7	Montecastillo	E	1185
17 7 7	Carlisle	Eng	548	17 5 6	Montrose	Sc	757
17 7 7	Castillo de Gorraiz	E	1136	17 8 7	Moor Park High Course	Eng	608
17 7 7	Clitheroe	Eng	552	17 5 5	Moray	Sc	758
17 8 7	Colony Club Gutenhof	A	92	17 7 6	Moscow	Ru	1316
17 7 8	Conwy	W	805	17 8 6	Motzener See	D	441
17 4 3	County Sligo	I	856	17 7 7	Neguri	E	1187
17 7 7	Cumberwell Park	Eng	555	17 8 6	Nobilis	T	1319
17 8 8	Dalmahoy East Course	Sc	719	17 7 6	North Hants	Eng	613
17 6 7	Downfield	Sc	720	17 6 8	North Wales (Llandudno)	W	814
17 8 7	East Sussex National			17 6 5	Oberfranken	D	449
	East Course	Eng	560	17 7 7	Orchardleigh	Eng	615
17 7 6	El Prat Verde	E	1143	17 6 5	Panmure	Sc	766
17 7 6	Emporda	E	1145	17 6 8	Penha Longa	P	1076
17 7 8	Fairhaven	Eng	561	17 7 5	Pléneuf-Val-André	F	316
17 7 7	Ferndown Old Course	Eng	564	17 7 8	Portmarnock Links	I	895
17 7 7	Fontainebleau	F	274	17 6 5	Praia d'El Rey	P	1079
17 6 7	Forest Pines Forest + Pines	Eng	567	17 8 7	Prestbury	Eng	624
17 7 8	Frankfurter GC	D	406	17 7 5	Pyle & Kenfig	W	817
17 7 8	Fulford	Eng	571	17 8 7	Ravenstein	B	117
17 7 8	Fürstlicher GC Bad Waldsee	D	408	17 6 5	Royal Cinque Ports	Eng	630
17 7 8	Genève	Ch	1297	17 7 8	Royal Mougins	F	327
17 9 7	Gleneagles Monarch's	Sc	736	17 7 6	Royal West Norfolk		
17 7 6	Grenoble Bresson	F	285		(Brancaster)	Eng	639
17 8 7	Gullane No 1	Sc	740	17 7 7	Rungsted	Da	143
17 9 7	Gut Lärchenhof	D	412	17 7 7	Saint-Germain	F	332
17 7 7	Gütersloh (Westfälischer GC)	D	416	17 8 6	San Roque	E	1203
17 8 6	Hubbelrath	D	425	17 5 7	Sandiway	Eng	644
17 7 6	Hunstanton	Eng	588	17 8 7	Scharmützelsee		
17 7 8	I Roveri	I	974		Arnold Palmer	D	456
17 8 8	K Club	I	877	17 8 6	Schloss Nippenburg	D	465
17 6 8	Kilmarnock (Barassie)	Sc	744	17 7 5	Schloss Wilkendorf	D	466
17 6 7	Köln	D	430	17 6 4	Seacroft	Eng	646
17 7 7	Krefelder	D	432	17 7 5	Seaton Carew	Eng	648
17 7 7	Kristianstad	S	1258	17 8 7	Seefeld-Wildmoos	A	99
17 8 6	La Cala Norte	E	1158	17 7 7	Seignosse	F	341
17 7 8	La Moye	Eng	594	17 7 8	Sevilla	E	1207
17 7 5	Ladybank	Sc	746	17 7 6	Sherwood Forest	Eng	652
17 7 5	Larvik	Nw	1052	17 5 5	Shiskine (Blackwaterfoot)	Sc	780
17 8 7	Le Querce	I	980	17 5 7	Skövde	S	1270
17 7 4	Lerma	E	1174	17 8 7	Slaley Hall	Eng	654
17 6 5	Limère	F	298	17 7 7	Spa (Les Fagnes)	B	123
17 8 6	Linden Hall	Eng	595	17 7 5	Spérone	F	344
17 6 6	Lindrick	Eng	596	17 8 8	St Andrews New Course	Sc	784
17 6 7	Ljunghusen	S	1261	17 7 7	St George's Hill	Eng	657
17 7 7	Machrie	Sc	754	17 9 7	St Mellion Nicklaus Course	Eng	658
17 7 7	Mittelrheinischer	D	440	17 7 6	St. Dionys	D	470

43

Tradition. Heritage. Integrity.

Admirable traits in golf. And in a golf car.

The best golf car in the world.™

Club Car (UK) Plc • Dunmore Court • Wootton Road • Abingdon • Oxfordshire, OX13 6BH, England • 0044-1235-537-575 • Fax: 0044-1235-537-5
Club Car, France • 8 Rue D'Anjou • 92517 Boulogne CEDEX, France • 0033-141-41-5939 • Fax: 0033-141-41-5985
Club Car Divaco Benelux B.V. • Mariniersweg 2 • NL 3941 • XK Dourn, Netherlands • 0031-343-416484 • Fax: 0031-343-412245
Club Car, Inc./Ingersoll-Rand • P.O. Box 204658 • Augusta, GA USA 30917 • 706-863-3000 Ext. 2601 • Fax: 706-863-5808 • www.clubcar.

Score	Course	Country	Page
17 7 8	Stenungsund	S	1272
17 8 8	Stoke Poges	Eng	659
17 5 5	Stuttgarter Solitude	D	474
17 6 6	Tain	Sc	789
17 6 7	Touquet (Le) *La Mer*	F	349
17 7 7	Trevose *Championship*	Eng	672
17 8 6	Ullna	S	1278
17 6 4	Villette d'Anthon		
	Les Sangliers	F	354
17 7 7	Wallasey	Eng	673
17 6 7	Waterville	I	914
17 7 7	West Lancashire	Eng	683
17 5 7	Western Gailes	Sc	795
17 6 7	Whittington Heath	Eng	688

16/20

Score	Course	Country	Page
16 5 4	Aisses (Les) *Rouge/Blanc*	F	215
16 7 7	Antwerp	B	107
16 7 6	Ashridge	Eng	524
16 6 5	Åtvidaberg	S	1230
16 5 7	Ayr (Belleisle)	Sc	701
16 7 7	Ballybunion		
	Cashen (*New Course*)	I	838
16 7 7	Båstad *Old Course*	S	1232
16 6 9	Bath	Eng	526
16 7 7	Beau Desert	Eng	527
16 6 5	Belle-Dune	F	232
16 7 7	Bergisch Land Wuppertal	D	391
16 7 6	Berkhamsted	Eng	528
16 8 9	Berlin-Wannsee	D	392
16 7 7	Bodensee-Weissensberg	D	395
16 6 7	Bokskogen	S	1233
16 7 6	Bondues *Blanc*	F	237
16 7 6	Bonmont	E	1132
16 6 5	Borre	Nw	1049
16 7 6	Bowood (Cornwall)	Eng	534
16 7 7	Bråviken	S	1234
16 7 6	Buxtehude	D	397
16 6 6	Camberley Heath	Eng	544
16 6 6	Carlow	I	847
16 5 3	Carn	I	848
16 6 6	Castlerock	UL	925
16 6 6	Charmeil	F	256
16 6 8	Chiberta	F	259
16 8 8	Club de Campo	E	1138
16 7 3	Courson *Vert/Noir*	F	262

Score	Course	Country	Page
16 8 5	Cromstrijen	N	1016
16 9 6	Dartmouth	Eng	556
16 8 7	De Pan	N	1017
16 6 4	Dingle (Ceann Sibeal)	I	859
16 7 8	Disneyland Paris		
	Never Land + Wonderland	F	265
16 5 6	Donegal (Murvagh)	I	860
16 6 5	Donnerskirchen-Neusiedlersee	A	94
16 9 7	Druids Glen	I	863
16 7 8	Duke's Course St Andrews	Sc	723
16 5 6	Dunbar	Sc	725
16 6 7	East Devon	Eng	559
16 8 5	Efteling	N	1018
16 7 4	El Bosque	E	1141
16 7 6	Enniscrone	I	866
16 7 6	Espoo	Fi	153
16 6 7	Estérel Latitudes	F	269
16 7 6	Europasportregion-Zell am See		
	Schmittenhöhe	A	95
16 7 6	Feldafing	D	405
16 7 7	Flommen	S	1244
16 8 5	Fontana	A	96
16 7 4	Forsbacka	S	1245
16 6 5	Fortrose & Rosemarkie	Sc	733
16 7 5	Frösåker	S	1247
16 7 7	Glasson	I	872
16 7 8	Golf del Sur	E	1151
16 7 5	Golfresort Haugschlag-		
	Waldviertel	A	97
16 7 6	Gouverneur (Le) *Le Breuil*	F	279
16 6 6	Grande Bastide (La)	F	281
16 6 4	Grande-Motte (La)		
	Les Flamants Roses	F	282
16 5 8	Grange	I	874
16 7 5	Gut Thailing	D	414
16 7 7	Hadley Wood	Eng	575
16 8 7	Hamburg-Ahrensburg	D	417
16 6 6	Hanau-Wilhelmsbad	D	419
16 8 6	Haninge	S	1253
16 6 6	Hankley Common	Eng	577
16 7 7	Hannover	D	420
16 6 6	Hardelot *Les Pins*	F	287
16 7 7	Hayling	Eng	580
16 7 8	Helsinki	Fi	154
16 7 6	Herkenbosch	N	1026
16 7 7	Hilversum	N	1027
16 8 6	Himmerland *New Course*	Da	137
16 7 6	Hindhead	Eng	586
16 6 5	Holstebro	Da	138

45

Europe

Score	Course	Country	Page	Score	Course	Country	Page
16 7 5	Holyhead	W	807	16 7 8	Parkstone	Eng	618
16 6 6	Hossegor	F	289	16 6 5	Peralada	E	1195
16 8 8	Houtrak	N	1029	16 6 6	Perranporth	Eng	620
16 6 7	Huddersfield (Fixby)	Eng	587	16 8 8	Pevero	I	994
16 7 6	Iffeldorf	D	426	16 8 6	Pleasington	Eng	621
16 7 8	Inverness	Sc	743	16 7 7	Poggio dei Medici	I	995
16 7 7	Ipswich (Purdis Heath)	Eng	591	16 6 5	Pont Royal	F	318
16 7 8	Is Molas	I	975	16 5 5	Portsalon	I	896
16 8 8	Islantilla	E	1156	16 7 7	Portstewart Strand Course	UL	932
16 7 4	Isle Adam (L')	F	290	16 6 4	Powfoot	Sc	770
16 7 6	Isle of Purbeck	Eng	592	16 6 7	Prestwick St Nicholas	Sc	772
16 7 6	John O'Gaunt	Eng	593	16 8 9	Puerta de Hierro		
16 7 7	Jönköping	S	1254		Puerta de Hierro 1	E	1199
16 8 7	Joyenval *Marly*	F	291	16 7 7	Purmerend	N	1035
16 7 7	Kikuoka	LU	128	16 6 4	Rebetz	F	322
16 7 8	Killarney *Killeen Course*	I	880	16 7 7	Reichswald-Nürnberg	D	454
16 8 6	La Cala *Sur*	E	1159	16 8 9	Roma - Acquasanta	I	999
16 7 8	La Moraleja *La Moraleja 2*	E	1166	16 7 6	Rosapenna	I	899
16 7 7	La Zagaleta	E	1169	16 7 9	Royal Burgess	Sc	775
16 6 5	Lanark	Sc	747	16 8 7	Royal Dublin	I	901
16 7 8	Las Americas	E	1170	16 7 7	Royal Guernsey	Eng	632
16 7 7	Lausanne	Ch	1300	16 7 8	Royal Jersey	Eng	633
16 9 7	Le Robinie	I	981	16 8 7	Royal Musselburgh	Sc	777
16 6 6	Leven	Sc	749	16 7 8	Royal Wimbledon	Eng	640
16 7 4	Limburg	B	112	16 7 4	Sablé-Solesmes		
16 7 6	Liphook	Eng	597		La Forêt/La Rivière	F	328
16 7 7	Los Naranjos	E	1176	16 6 5	Saint-Jean-de-Monts	F	333
16 5 6	Luffness New	Sc	752	16 8 8	Saint-Nom-la-Bretèche *Rouge*	F	336
16 6 7	Lundin	Sc	753	16 8 7	Sarfvik *New Course*	Fi	158
16 7 5	Lunds Akademiska	S	1262	16 7 7	Sart-Tilman	B	122
16 7 5	Lüneburger Heide	D	436	16 7 7	Schloss Braunfels	D	458
16 7 7	Manchester	Eng	601	16 8 7	Schloss Langenstein	D	461
16 8 8	Marco Simone	I	983	16 8 7	Schloss Liebenstein		
16 8 7	Marriott St Pierre *Old Course*	W	811		Gelb + Blau	D	462
16 7 8	Maspalomas	E	1180	16 7 7	Schloss Myllendonk	D	464
16 7 6	Mediterraneo	E	1181	16 6 6	Scotscraig	Sc	779
16 6 7	Mijas *Los Lagos*	E	1182	16 8 7	Semlin am See	D	468
16 8 9	Milano	I	985	16 7 4	Soufflenheim	F	343
16 7 5	Montpellier-Massane	F	306	16 7 7	Southerndown	W	821
16 7 7	München-Riedhof	D	443	16 8 8	St Andrews Jubilee Course	Sc	783
16 6 7	Neckartal	D	446	16 7 7	St Margaret's	I	906
16 7 5	Nefyn & District	W	812	16 7 6	St. Eurach	D	471
16 7 6	Nîmes-Campagne	F	309	16 6 7	Stavanger	Nw	1056
16 9 6	Northop Country Park	W	815	16 7 6	Steiermärkischer Murhof	A	100
16 7 7	Novo Sancti Petri	E	1188	16 8 9	Stockholm	S	1273
16 7 6	Olgiata	I	990	16 7 5	Stolper Heide	D	473
16 6 6	Österåker	S	1267	16 6 8	Swinley Forest	Eng	663
16 7 6	Pals	E	1192	16 7 7	Täby	S	1275
16 7 5	Paris International	F	313	16 6 4	Thurlestone	Eng	671

46

Score	Course	Country	Page
16 8 8	Torino - La Mandria		
	Percorso Blu	I	1001
16 9 8	Turnberry Arran Course	Sc	793
16 6 6	Ulzama	E	1212
16 8 7	Vale of Glamorgan	W	823
16 7 7	Vasatorp	S	1281
16 7 9	Venezia	I	1003
16 7 7	Vilamoura I (Old Course)	P	1091
16 8 9	Villa D'Este	I	1005
16 7 6	Villamartin	E	1214
16 6 5	Visby	S	1283
16 7 6	Walddörfer	D	479
16 7 6	Walton Heath New Course	Eng	674
16 6 6	Wantzenau (La)	F	356
16 8 7	Waterloo La Marache	B	125
16 7 6	Wendlohe A-Kurs + B-Kurs	D	481
16 8 7	Wentworth East Course	Eng	677
16 7 6	West Cornwall	Eng	681
16 7 5	West Kilbride	Sc	794
16 6 7	Weston-Super-Mare	Eng	686
16 7 6	Wilmslow	Eng	689
16 7 6	Wittelsbacher	D	483
16 6 6	Woking	Eng	691
16 7 6	Woodenbridge	I	918
16 7 6	Worplesdon	Eng	695
16 7 6	Zaudin	E	1215

15/20

Score	Course	Country	Page
15 6 4	Ableiges Les Etangs	F	213
15 6 7	Adare	I	836
15 6 5	Ailette (L')	F	214
15 6 6	Albi	F	217
15 7 6	Alloa	Sc	699
15 7 7	Amarilla	E	1128
15 7 7	Amsterdam	N	1012
15 8 6	Apremont	F	222
15 7 5	Arendal	Nw	1048
15 6 6	Aroeira	P	1068
15 7 6	Asserbo	Da	133
15 7 7	Augsburg	D	383
15 7 7	Bad Abbach-Deutenhof	D	384
15 5 7	Bad Bevensen	D	385
15 9 9	Bad Griesbach-Sagmühle		
	Sagmühle	D	387
15 6 5	Baden	F	227

Score	Course	Country	Page
15 7 7	Bâle-Hagenthal	F	228
15 6 7	Ballater	Sc	703
15 6 5	Ballyliffin Old Course	I	842
15 7 7	Bamberg	D	390
15 8 8	Barlassina	I	957
15 7 3	Batouwe	N	1014
15 7 8	Baule (La) Rouge	F	230
15 5 6	Belvoir Park	UL	922
15 7 8	Bergamo - L'Albenza		
	Blu + Giallo	I	958
15 6 5	Berwick-upon-Tweed	Eng	531
15 7 8	Bitburger Land	D	394
15 8 6	Blairgowrie Lansdowne	Sc	705
15 7 6	Blumisberg	Ch	1291
15 5 7	Bolton Old Links	Eng	533
15 7 6	Bondues Jaune	F	238
15 7 8	Boulie (La) La Vallée	F	240
15 6 4	Bresse (La)	F	241
15 7 7	Bretesche (La)	F	243
15 7 6	Broekpolder	N	1015
15 6 6	Brokenhurst Manor	Eng	539
15 7 7	Brora	Sc	708
15 8 9	Bruntsfield	Sc	709
15 6 5	Bude & North Cornwall	Eng	541
15 5 6	Came Down	Eng	545
15 7 8	Cannes-Mougins	F	246
15 6 6	Canyamel	E	1134
15 6 5	Cap d'Agde	F	247
15 7 6	Capdepera	E	1135
15 6 5	Cardigan	W	802
15 7 4	Carmarthen	W	803
15 7 7	Castelgandolfo	I	964
15 8 8	Castello di Tolcinasco	I	965
15 7 6	Cély	F	249
15 6 7	Chamonix	F	252
15 6 6	Clandeboye Dufferin Course	UL	926
15 3 5	Cork GC	I	854
15 7 5	County Tipperary	I	857
15 7 3	Courson Lilas/Orange	F	261
15 6 6	Coxmoor	Eng	554
15 6 6	Crail	Sc	716
15 7 7	Crieff Ferntower Course	Sc	717
15 7 5	Dachstein Tauern /		
	Schladming	A	93
15 6 7	Delamere Forest	Eng	557
15 7 7	Denham	Eng	558
15 5 5	Dooks	I	861
15 7 9	Duddingston	Sc	721
15 6 6	Duff House Royal	Sc	722

47

Score	Course	Country	Page
15 7 5	Dumfries & County	Sc	724
15 6 6	Dundalk	I	864
15 7 7	Dunfermline	Sc	726
15 7 7	Düsseldorfer	D	400
15 6 8	East Renfrewshire	Sc	727
15 7 6	El Prat *Amarillo*	E	1142
15 7 6	Elgin	Sc	729
15 6 6	Elie	Sc	730
15 6 6	Engadin	Ch	1295
15 6 5	Esbjerg	Da	134
15 7 5	Esery	F	268
15 8 7	Essener Oefte	D	403
15 6 5	Etiolles *Les Cerfs*	F	270
15 7 6	European Tour Club		
	(Kungsängen)	S	1239
15 7 9	Evian	F	272
15 9 5	Fågelbro	S	1240
15 4 7	Fanø	Da	135
15 6 6	Felixstowe Ferry		
	Martello Course	Eng	563
15 7 5	Feucherolles	F	273
15 6 3	Fjällbacka	S	1243
15 7 6	Fota Island	I	869
15 7 8	Franciacorta	I	971
15 7 7	Frégate	F	278
15 7 7	Fureso	Da	136
15 7 7	Gendersteyn	N	1021
15 9 7	Gleneagles *Queen's*	Sc	737
15 7 6	Goes	N	1022
15 7 8	Gog Magog *Old Course*	Eng	574
15 4 4	Golden Eagle	P	1071
15 7 7	Golf d'Aro	E	1150
15 6 7	Göteborg	S	1249
15 7 6	Graafschap	N	1023
15 7 5	Gränna	S	1250
15 7 6	Gujan-Mestras	F	286
15 7 6	Gut Kaden		
	Platz B + Platz C	D	411
15 6 6	Gut Ludwigsberg	D	413
15 7 5	Gut Waldhof	D	415
15 7 9	Haggs Castle	Sc	741
15 7 5	Hainaut		
	Bruyere-Quesnoy-Etangs	B	110
15 6 8	Hallamshire	Eng	576
15 6 6	Hamburg-Holm	D	418
15 7 7	Harrogate	Eng	578
15 8 7	Hawkstone Park		
	Hawkstone	Eng	579
15 6 7	Hermitage	I	876

Score	Course	Country	Page
15 6 6	Herreria	E	1155
15 7 7	Hertfordshire (The)	Eng	582
15 6 7	High Post	Eng	584
15 7 5	Hof Trages	D	423
15 6 7	Hoge Kleij	N	1028
15 7 6	Hohenpähl	D	424
15 7 6	Im Chiemgau	D	427
15 7 6	Isernhagen	D	428
15 7 6	Jakobsberg	D	429
15 8 7	Joyenval *Retz*	F	292
15 5 8	Kalmar	S	1255
15 7 6	Karlovy Vary	Cz	1313
15 6 6	Karlstad	S	1257
15 7 8	Killarney *Mahony's Point*	I	881
15 4 5	Kingussie	Sc	745
15 6 5	Kirkistown Castle	UL	927
15 7 6	Knock	UL	928
15 6 6	Kungsbacka	S	1259
15 7 7	La Manga *Norte*	E	1162
15 7 8	La Moraleja *La Moraleja 1*	E	1165
15 8 7	La Quinta	E	1167
15 6 5	La Sella	E	1168
15 7 7	Langland Bay	W	808
15 7 4	Largue (La)	F	295
15 7 5	Læsø *Seaside*	Da	140
15 6 6	Les Bois	Ch	1301
15 7 5	Letham Grange *Old Course*	Sc	748
15 7 6	Lichtenau-Weickershof	D	433
15 7 6	Limerick County	I	885
15 7 8	Lindau-Bad Schachen	D	434
15 7 6	Lisburn	UL	929
15 5 8	Llandudno (Maesdu)	W	809
15 9 7	London Golf Club		
	International	Eng	599
15 8 8	Lübeck-Travemünder	D	435
15 7 8	Lugano	Ch	1302
15 7 7	Luttrellstown	I	886
15 7 8	Lytham Green Drive	Eng	600
15 8 7	Manor House		
	(Castle Combe)	Eng	603
15 7 8	Marbella	E	1178
15 7 6	Masia Bach	E	1179
15 7 7	Master Master	Fi	155
15 7 5	Médoc *Les Vignes*	F	303
15 5 7	Mendip	Eng	604
15 8 7	Meon Valley *Meon Course*	Eng	605
15 7 7	Mere	Eng	606
15 7 5	Mölle	S	1264
15 7 7	Møn	Da	141

48

Score	Course	Country	Page	Score	Course	Country	Page
15 6 7	Monkstown	I	888	15 7 8	Saint Donat	F	329
15 7 7	Montenmedio	E	1186	15 7 4	Saint-Endréol	F	331
15 5 5	Mullion	Eng	610	15 8 8	Saint-Nom-la-Bretèche *Bleu*	F	335
15 6 7	Münchner-Strasslach	D	444	15 4 7	Samsø	Da	144
15 6 6	Murcar	Sc	760	15 7 7	Schloss Egmating	D	459
15 6 7	Nairn Dunbar	Sc	763	15 6 6	Schloss Klingenburg	D	460
15 7 7	National GC	T	1318	15 7 6	Schloss Lüdersburg *Old/New*	D	463
15 7 7	Neuhof	D	447	15 6 6	Seapoint	I	902
15 7 8	New Golf Deauville			15 8 7	Sempachersee	Ch	1309
	Rouge/Blanc	F	308	15 7 6	Shanklin & Sandown	Eng	649
15 6 7	Newbury & Crookham	Eng	611	15 6 7	Sherborne	Eng	650
15 6 7	Newport	W	813	15 7 6	Sheringham	Eng	651
15 7 5	Nordcenter *Benz Course*	Fi	156	15 7 5	Sint Nicolaasga	N	1038
15 5 3	Nunspeet *North/East*	N	1033	15 8 6	Slieve Russell	I	904
15 6 6	Oberschwaben Bad Waldsee	D	450	15 7 5	Söderåsen	S	1271
15 7 7	Old Head	I	893	15 7 7	Sonnenalp	D	469
15 7 7	Oostende	B	114	15 8 6	St. Leon-Rot	D	472
15 7 7	Oosterhout	N	1034	15 7 8	Stoneham	Eng	660
15 7 7	Öschberghof	D	451	15 7 6	Strathaven	Sc	788
15 7 9	Oslo	Nw	1054	15 6 6	Sybrook	N	1039
15 8 8	Palazzo Arzaga	I	992	15 6 8	Sylt	D	475
15 6 7	Pannal	Eng	617	15 7 4	Taulane	F	346
15 7 7	Patriziale Ascona	Ch	1307	15 9 8	The Belfry *Brabazon*	Eng	666
15 5 4	Peterhead	Sc	767	15 9 8	The Belfry *PGA National*	Eng	667
15 8 5	Pickala *Seaside Course*	Fi	157	15 7 7	The Island	I	907
15 7 9	Pineda	E	1197	15 6 5	Thornhill	Sc	791
15 7 6	Ploemeur Océan	F	317	15 7 4	Toulouse Palmola	F	347
15 6 6	Pornic	F	320	15 7 6	Toulouse-Seilh *Rouge*	F	348
15 8 7	Portal *Championship*	Eng	622	15 6 5	Troia	P	1087
15 7 7	Porters Park	Eng	623	15 6 5	Tullamore	I	911
15 6 7	Portpatrick (Dunskey)	Sc	769	15 7 6	Tutzing	D	478
15 7 7	Powerscourt	I	897	15 7 6	Twente	N	1041
15 6 7	Praha Karlstejn	Cz	1315	15 6 5	Val Queven	F	352
15 7 8	Quinta do Lago *B/C*	P	1082	15 6 7	Vale do Lobo		
15 7 8	Quinta do Lago *Ria Formosa*	P	1083		*Royal Golf Course*	P	1089
15 6 5	Quinta do Peru	P	1084	15 7 5	Värnamo	S	1280
15 7 6	Rathsallagh	I	898	15 7 4	Vaucouleurs (La) *Les Vallons*	F	353
15 6 6	Rolls of Monmouth (The)	W	818	15 6 7	Växjö	S	1282
15 7 7	Roncemay	F	326	15 7 7	Vejle *Blue + Red Slings*	Da	147
15 7 7	Rosendael	N	1037	15 7 8	Warwickshire (The)	Eng	676
15 5 6	Ross-on-Wye	Eng	627	15 7 7	Wasserburg Anholt	D	480
15 7 7	Roxburghe (The)	Sc	773	15 7 6	Wentorf-Reinbeker	D	482
15 7 7	Royal Belfast	UL	933	15 7 7	West Berkshire	Eng	679
15 7 6	Royal Cromer	Eng	631	15 6 6	West Hill	Eng	682
15 8 6	Royal Latem	B	120	15 7 7	West Surrey	Eng	684
15 7 5	Royal Oak	Da	142	15 7 7	Westport	I	916
15 6 8	Royal Winchester	Eng	641	15 7 7	Whitekirk	Sc	797
15 8 8	Rudding Park	Eng	642	15 7 6	Woodbrook	I	917
15 7 8	Rya	S	1268	15 9 6	Woodbury Park *The Oaks*	Eng	693

49

Score	Course	Country	Page	Score	Course	Country	Page
15 7 6	Wouwse Plantage	N	1042	14 6 5	Casteljaloux	F	248
15 7 6	Zumikon	Ch	1311	14 6 6	Castletroy	I	850
				14 7 7	Cerdaña	E	1137
				14 8 6	Chailly (Château de)	F	250
				14 5 7	Chambon-sur-Lignon (Le)	F	251
				14 6 3	Champ de Bataille	F	253
				14 7 7	Chantaco	F	254
14 7 6	A 6	S	1229	14 6 4	Chaumont-en-Vexin	F	257
14 7 6	Abenberg	D	382	14 7 6	Cheverny	F	258
14 6 6	Aboyne	Sc	698	14 8 7	Collingtree Park	Eng	553
14 8 7	Albarella	I	954	14 6 6	Connemara	I	853
14 6 5	Alcaidesa	E	1123	14 6 7	Cosmopolitan	I	968
14 7 5	Alhaurin	E	1124	14 5 5	Courtown	I	858
14 6 6	Almerimar	E	1126	14 7 8	Crans-sur-Sierre	Ch	1293
14 6 6	Alyth	Sc	700	14 6 5	Dieppe-Pourville	F	263
14 7 7	Ambrosiano	I	955	14 6 7	Divonne	F	266
14 7 8	Amirauté (L')	F	218	14 7 7	Domtal-Mommenheim	D	399
14 7 6	Anderstein	N	1013	14 7 7	Dromoland Castle	I	862
14 7 8	Arcangues	F	224	14 9 6	Drottningholm	S	1236
14 6 4	Ardglass	UL	920	14 6 3	Edzell	Sc	728
14 6 6	Arras	F	225	14 7 7	Ekerum	S	1237
14 6 8	Baberton	Sc	702	14 7 7	Elfrather Mühle	D	401
14 7 7	Bad Liebenzell	D	388	14 7 7	Eschenried	D	402
14 6 6	Bad Wörishofen	D	389	14 7 5	Eslöv	S	1238
14 7 7	Badgemore Park	Eng	525	14 7 6	Estepona	E	1147
14 7 6	Ballykisteen	I	840	14 6 5	Etretat	F	271
14 7 7	Banchory	Sc	704	14 7 7	Falkenberg	S	1241
14 6 6	Bangor	UL	921	14 6 7	Falmouth	Eng	562
14 6 7	Beaufort	I	843	14 7 4	Falnuee	B	109
14 7 7	Bélesbat	F	231	14 8 9	Firenze - Ugolino	I	969
14 7 5	Béthemont	F	234	14 6 6	Fontcaude	F	275
14 7 7	Bhearna	I	844	14 7 6	Fontenailles *Blanc*	F	276
14 6 8	Biarritz-le-Phare	F	235	14 7 4	Fontenelles (Les)	F	277
14 6 5	Bitche	F	236	14 8 8	Forest of Arden		
14 6 7	Boat of Garten	Sc	707		Arden Course	Eng	566
14 6 6	Bonalba	E	1131	14 6 6	Forfar	Sc	732
14 6 5	Brancepeth Castle	Eng	537	14 8 6	Formby Hall	Eng	569
14 6 7	Braunschweig	D	396	14 6 7	Forsgården	S	1246
14 7 6	Brest Iroise	F	242	14 7 6	Fränkische Schweiz	D	407
14 7 6	Brigode	F	244	14 7 7	Frilford Heath *Red Course*	Eng	570
14 6 6	Buchanan Castle	Sc	710	14 7 6	Fürstliches Hofgut		
14 6 6	Burntisland	Sc	711		Kolnhausen	D	409
14 6 6	Campoamor	E	1133	14 8 6	Gainsborough-Karsten Lakes	Eng	572
14 7 8	Cannes Mandelieu			14 7 6	Galway Bay	I	870
	Old Course	F	245	14 7 8	Gardagolf	I	972
14 8 8	Carden Park *Cheshire Course*	Eng	546	14 7 8	Garlenda	I	973
14 6 8	Cardiff	W	801	14 6 7	Garmisch-Partenkirchen	D	410
14 6 5	Cardross	Sc	713	14 6 6	Gävle	S	1248
14 5 6	Carnoustie *Burnside*	Sc	714	14 4 5	Gelpenberg	N	1020

50

Score	Course	Country	Page	Score	Course	Country	Page
14 7 8	Glamorganshire	W	806	14 7 6	Märkischer Potsdam	D	438
14 7 7	Glen	Sc	734	14 5 6	Massereene	UL	931
14 5 4	Golspie	Sc	738	14 6 6	Memmingen Gut Westerhart	D	439
14 7 6	Gouverneur (Le) *Montaplan*	F	280	14 7 8	Modena	I	986
14 6 5	Granada	E	1152	14 6 7	Monte Carlo (Mont Agel)	F	305
14 6 7	Grantown on Spey	Sc	739	14 8 7	Monticello	I	989
14 4 4	Granville *Les Dunes*	F	283	14 6 7	Moor Allerton	Eng	607
14 6 5	Greenore	I	875	14 5 5	Mullingar	I	891
14 6 6	Grenland	Nw	1050	14 7 8	Murrayshall	Sc	761
14 7 4	Grevelingenhout	N	1024	14 8 6	Nahetal	D	445
14 7 6	Gruyère (La)	Ch	1298	14 6 4	Nes	Nw	1053
14 7 6	Guadalhorce	E	1153	14 6 7	Neuchâtel	Ch	1305
14 7 7	Guadalmina *Sur*	E	1154	14 5 5	Newtonmore	Sc	764
14 6 4	Haut-Poitou	F	288	14 7 7	Obere Alp	D	448
14 6 6	Hechingen-Hohenzollern	D	421	14 6 7	Oliva Nova	E	1189
14 6 7	Henley	Eng	581	14 7 5	Omaha Beach		
14 7 6	Hetzenhof	D	422		La Mer/Le Bocage	F	310
14 8 8	Hever	Eng	583	14 6 4	Ormskirk	Eng	616
14 6 7	Huntercombe	Eng	589	14 7 4	Osona Montanya	E	1191
14 6 6	Huntly	Sc	742	14 6 6	Oudenaarde	B	115
14 6 6	Interlaken	Ch	1299	14 7 7	Padova	I	991
14 6 6	Karlshamn	S	1256	14 6 4	Panoramica	E	1193
14 7 6	Keerbergen	B	111	14 6 5	Pedreña	E	1194
14 6 6	Kilkea Castle	I	878	14 7 7	Penina	P	1077
14 6 5	Killorglin	I	882	14 7 7	Pinheiros Altos	P	1078
14 4 6	Korsør	Da	139	14 6 6	Pinnau	D	452
14 7 4	La Dehesa	E	1160	14 6 7	Pitlochry	Sc	768
14 7 7	La Manga *Oeste*	E	1163	14 6 4	Porcelaine (La)	F	319
14 7 7	La Manga *Sur*	E	1164	14 7 8	Punta Ala	I	996
14 6 7	Lacanau	F	294	14 8 7	Quinta da Beloura	P	1080
14 8 8	Las Palmas	E	1172	14 6 4	Raray (Château de)		
14 6 7	Lauswolt	N	1031		La Licorne	F	321
14 7 5	Laval-Changé *La Chabossière*	F	296	14 6 7	Reichsstadt Bad Windsheim	D	453
14 8 8	Le Pavoniere	I	979	14 8 7	Rheinhessen	D	455
14 7 5	Le Prieuré *Ouest*	F	297	14 7 6	Rigenée	B	118
14 7 7	Lignano	I	982	14 6 5	Rijk van Nijmegen		
14 8 6	Lindö Park	S	1260		Nijmeegse Baan	N	1036
14 6 5	Littlestone	Eng	598	14 6 5	Rinkven *Red - White*	B	119
14 6 4	Llanymynech	W	810	14 6 4	Rochefort-Chisan	F	325
14 7 6	Longniddry	Sc	750	14 6 6	Rochester & Cobham	Eng	626
14 6 7	Los Arqueros	E	1175	14 7 6	Royal Ashdown Forest	Eng	628
14 6 8	Lothianburn	Sc	751	14 7 8	Royal Mid-Surrey *Outer*	Eng	636
14 6 5	Madeira	P	1072	14 7 7	Saint-Cloud *Vert*	F	330
14 7 6	Main-Taunus	D	437	14 7 5	Saint-Laurent	F	334
14 7 5	Maison Blanche	F	299	14 7 5	Saint-Thomas	F	337
14 6 8	Makila Golf Club	F	300	14 7 6	Salgados	P	1086
14 8 6	Mannings Heath			14 6 6	San Sebastián	E	1204
	Waterfall Course	Eng	602	14 7 7	Sand Moor	Eng	643
14 7 6	Mariánské Lázne	Cz	1314	14 5 4	Savenay	F	340

51

Europe

Score			Course	Country	Page	Score			Course	Country	Page
14	7	6	Schönenberg	Ch	1308	13	6	5	Annonay-Gourdan	F	221
14	5	6	Sct. Knuds	Da	145	13	6	6	Arcachon	F	223
14	7	7	Simon's	Da	146	13	7	7	Asolo	I	956
14	6	5	Skellefteå	S	1269	13	6	7	Atalaya *Old Course*	E	1129
14	6	7	Son Vida	E	1208	13	6	6	Athlone	I	837
14	7	8	Spiegelven	B	124	13	5	4	Augerville	F	226
14	8	8	St Andrews *Eden Course*	Sc	782	13	5	5	Aura	Fi	152
14	6	6	St Helen's Bay	I	905	13	7	6	Bad Ragaz	Ch	1290
14	5	4	St Laurence	Fi	159	13	7	6	Belas	P	1069
14	8	6	Talma	Fi	160	13	6	7	Bendinat	E	1130
14	7	6	Tandridge	Eng	664	13	7	7	Bercuit	B	108
14	7	7	TAT Golf Belek	T	1320	13	7	5	Besançon	F	233
14	7	5	Tawast	Fi	161	13	6	6	Blainroe	I	845
14	7	8	Tegernseer Bad Wiessee	D	476	13	7	7	Bologna	I	961
14	7	5	Thetford	Eng	668	13	7	6	Breitenloo	Ch	1292
14	7	6	Thorndon Park	Eng	669	13	6	7	Bundoran	I	846
14	7	7	Thorpeness	Eng	670	13	6	8	Ca' della Nave	I	962
14	7	7	Torekov	S	1276	13	6	5	Cairndhu	UL	923
14	7	7	Torrequebrada	E	1211	13	6	7	Callander	Sc	712
14	7	6	Toxandria	N	1040	13	6	8	Castle	I	849
14	6	7	Tranås	S	1277	13	7	6	Castle Hume	UL	924
14	7	6	Tulfarris	I	910	13	6	9	Cervia	I	966
14	6	6	Tyrifjord	Nw	1057	13	4	6	Charleville	I	851
14	7	5	Val de Sorne	F	351	13	7	7	Cherasco	I	967
14	6	6	Vale da Pinta	P	1088	13	6	7	Chesterfield	Eng	551
14	8	7	Varese	I	1002	13	6	7	Citywest	I	852
14	7	7	Vila Sol	P	1090	13	7	5	Cognac	F	260
14	7	7	Vilamoura			13	7	7	Costa Brava	E	1139
			Vilamoura III (Laguna)	P	1093	13	6	6	Costa Dorada	E	1140
14	6	5	Volcans (Les)	F	355	13	6	7	Dinard	F	264
14	6	6	Waterford	I	912	13	7	4	Domont-Montmorency	F	267
14	5	6	Waterford Castle	I	913	13	7	8	Elm Park	I	865
14	6	8	West Byfleet	Eng	680	13	7	6	Ennetsee-Holzhäusern	Ch	1296
14	8	6	Westerwood	Sc	796	13	8	4	Escorpion	E	1146
14	6	6	Wheatley	Eng	687	13	7	7	Estoril	P	1070
14	4	5	Wimereux	F	357	13	7	6	Faithlegg	I	868
14	7	7	Woodbridge	Eng	692	13	6	6	Falkirk Tryst	Sc	731
14	7	7	Zuid Limburgse	N	1043	13	5	5	Filey	Eng	565
						13	6	6	Galway GC	I	871
						13	7	5	Girona	E	1149
						13	4	7	Glen of the Downs	I	873
						13	7	7	Gloria Golf Resort	T	1317
						13	6	7	Grand Ducal de Luxembourg	LU	127
						13	7	6	Grasse	F	284

13/20

Score			Course	Country	Page	Score			Course	Country	Page
13	5	7	Aix-les-Bains	F	216	13	7	6	Gullbringa	S	1251
13	6	7	Aldeburgh	Eng	522	13	7	6	Hauger	Nw	1051
13	8	8	Almenara	E	1125	13	7	6	Jarama R.A.C.E.	E	1157
13	6	5	Amnéville	F	219	13	7	6	Kilkenny	I	879
13	6	6	Anjou-Champigné	F	220	13	6	6	Königsfeld	D	431

52

Europe

Score	Course	Country	Page	Score	Course	Country	Page
13 7 6	La Duquesa	E	1161	13 6 4	Prince's *Himalayas-Shore*	Eng	625
13 7 7	La Margherita	I	976	13 6 5	Pula	E	1201
13 7 7	La Pinetina	I	977	13 7 7	Quinta da Marinha	P	1081
13 6 8	La Rocca	I	978	13 7 8	Rapallo	I	997
13 7 5	Lauro	E	1173	13 7 6	Reims-Champagne	F	323
13 7 6	Lee Valley	I	884	13 7 6	Riva dei Tessali	I	998
13 6 7	Luzern	Ch	1303	13 7 8	Riviéra Golf Club	F	324
13 7 6	Lyckorna	S	1263	13 5 6	Rosslare	I	900
13 4 6	Málaga	E	1177	13 7 7	Royal Portrush *Valley*	UL	936
13 7 8	Malahide			13 7 6	Sainte-Baume (La)	F	338
	Red + Blue + Yellow	I	887	13 7 7	Sainte-Maxime	F	339
13 6 6	Malone	UL	930	13 6 5	Sant Cugat	E	1205
13 7 7	Margara	I	984	13 6 7	Santa Ponsa	E	1206
13 5 4	Mazamet-La Barouge	F	301	13 7 7	Servanes	F	342
13 6 7	Mijas *Los Olivos*	E	1183	13 6 6	Shannon	I	903
13 9 8	Molinetto	I	987	13 6 4	Sorknes	Nw	1055
13 7 6	Mont-Garni	B	113	13 6 7	Stirling	Sc	786
13 7 6	Montado	P	1073	13 5 5	Stonehaven	Sc	787
13 5 5	Monte Mayor	E	1184	13 7 6	Strasbourg Illkirch		
13 8 7	Montecchia	I	988		*Jaune + Rouge*	F	345
13 6 5	Montreux	Ch	1304	13 6 6	Sundsvall	S	1274
13 6 5	Mount Wolsley	I	890	13 4 6	Taymouth Castle	Sc	790
13 6 7	Mülheim	D	442	13 7 6	Tehidy Park	Eng	665
13 7 5	Newcastle West	I	892	13 7 7	Torremirona	E	1210
13 7 7	Niederbüren	Ch	1306	13 7 6	Touraine	F	350
13 7 7	North Foreland	Eng	612	13 7 6	Tramore	I	909
13 7 5	Öijared *Gamla banan*	S	1265	13 8 7	Treudelberg	D	477
13 7 8	Olivar de la Hinojosa	E	1190	13 6 6	Upsala	S	1279
13 6 7	Opio Valbonne	F	311	13 7 8	Verona	I	1004
13 7 5	Ozoir-la-Ferrière			13 7 7	Vilamoura		
	Château/Monthéty	F	312		*Vilamoura II (Pinhal)*	P	1092
13 6 7	Palheiro	P	1074	13 6 5	Warrenpoint	UL	937
13 6 6	Palingbeek	B	116	13 7 9	Wien-Freudenau	A	101
13 7 5	Palmares	P	1075	13 6 6	Wylihof	Ch	1310
13 7 9	Parco de' Medici	I	993				
13 8 8	Patshull Park Hotel	Eng	619	12 7 6	West Waterford	I	915
13 6 8	Pau	F	314				
13 7 7	Pessac	F	315				
13 6 4	Playa Serena	E	1198				

53

Europe

ARCHITECTS AND COURSES
ARCHITECTES ET PARCOURS
ARCHITEKTEN UND GOLFPLÄTZE
ARKITEKTER OCH GOLFBANOR
ARQUITECTOS Y RECORRIDOS
ARCHITETTI E PERCORSI

Architect Golf course	Country	Score			Page
John Abercromby					
Worplesdon	Eng	16	7	6	695
Marc Adam/Patrick Fromanger					
Cély	F	15	7	6	249
Bitche	F	14	6	5	236
Peter Alliss					
Alcaidesa	E	14	6	5	1123
Cannes-Mougins	F	15	7	8	246
Manor House (Castle Combe)	Eng	15	8	7	603
The Belfry *Brabazon*	Eng	15	9	8	666
Peter Alliss & Dave Thomas					
Baule (La) *Rouge*	F	15	7	8	230
Anders Amilon					
Bokskogen	S	16	6	7	1233
Lyckoma	S	13	7	6	1263
Lars Andreasson					
Læsø *Seaside*	Da	15	7	5	140
Javier Arana					
Neguri	E	17	7	7	1187
Club de Campo	E	16	8	8	1138
Ulzama	E	16	6	6	1212
Jarama R.A.C.E.	E	13	7	6	1157
El Saler	E	18	7	6	1144
Aloha	E	17	7	7	1127
El Prat *Verde*	E	17	7	6	1143
Cerdaña	E	14	7	7	1137
Guadalmina *Sur*	E	14	7	7	1154
Lauri Arkkola					
Helsinki	Fi	16	7	8	154
Aura	Fi	13	5	5	152
Austrogolf					
Golfresort Haugschlag-Waldviertel	A	16	7	5	97
Bill Baker					
Bretesche (La)	F	15	7	7	243
Amirauté (L')	F	14	7	8	218
Brigode	F	14	7	6	244
Haut-Poitou	F	14	6	4	288

Architect Golf course	Country	Score			Page
Harold Baker					
Oudenaarde	B	14	6	6	115
Palingbeek	B	13	6	6	116
Seve Ballesteros					
Novo Sancti Petri	E	16	7	7	1188
Pont Royal	F	16	6	5	318
Alhaurin	E	14	7	5	1124
Los Arqueros	E	14	6	7	1175
Oliva Nova	E	14	6	7	1189
Westerwood	Sc	14	8	6	796
Gunnar Bauer					
Falsterbo	S	18	7	5	1242
R.& F. M. Benjumea					
Pineda	E	15	7	9	1197
Bradford Benz					
La Zagaleta	E	16	7	7	1169
Nordcenter *Benz Course*	Fi	15	7	5	156
Stig Bergendorff					
Flommen	S	16	7	7	1244
Robert Berthet					
Sainte-Baume (La)	F	13	7	6	338
Nicholas Bielenberg					
Luttrellstown	I	15	7	7	886
R.J. Browne					
Bhearna	I	14	7	7	844
Biratti, Cavalsani					
Monticello	I	14	8	7	989
Cecil R. Blandford					
Varese	I	14	8	7	1002
Arcachon	F	13	6	6	223
Cecil R. Blandford & Peter Gannon					
Milano	I	16	8	9	985
Firenze - Ugolino	I	14	8	9	969
James Braid					
Gleneagles *King's*	Sc	18	9	7	735
Pennard	W	18	6	6	816
Southport & Ainsdale	Eng	18	7	7	655

54

Architect Golf course	Country	Score			Page
James Braid					
St Enodoc *Church Course*	Eng	18	7	4	656
Tenby	W	18	7	6	822
Brampton	Eng	17	7	6	536
Clitheroe	Eng	17	7	7	552
Dalmahoy *East Course*	Sc	17	8	8	719
Fairhaven	Eng	17	7	8	561
Hunstanton	Eng	17	7	6	588
(James Braid)					
La Moye	Eng	17	7	8	594
North Hants	Eng	17	7	6	613
Ayr (Belleisle)	Sc	16	5	7	701
Fortrose & Rosemarkie	Sc	16	6	5	733
Grange	I	16	5	8	874
Holyhead	W	16	7	5	807
Ipswich (Purdis Heath)	Eng	16	7	7	591
Lundin	Sc	16	6	7	753
Nefyn & District	W	16	7	5	812
Perranporth	Eng	16	6	6	620
Powfoot	Sc	16	6	4	770
Royal Musselburgh	Sc	16	8	7	777
Alloa	Sc	15	7	6	699
Ballater	Sc	15	6	7	703
Berwick-upon-Tweed	Eng	15	6	5	531
Brora	Sc	15	7	7	708
East Renfrewshire	Sc	15	6	8	727
Gleneagles *Queen's*	Sc	15	9	7	737
Hawkstone Park *Hawkstone*	Eng	15	8	7	579
Kirkistown Castle	UL	15	6	5	927
Langland Bay	W	15	7	7	808
Mere	Eng	15	7	7	606
Shanklin & Sandown	Eng	15	7	6	649
Tullamore	I	15	6	5	911
Bangor	UL	14	6	6	921
Boat of Garten	Sc	14	6	7	707
Buchanan Castle	Sc	14	6	6	710
Henley	Eng	14	6	7	581
Lothianburn	Sc	14	6	8	751
Mullingar	I	14	5	5	891
Newtonmore	Sc	14	5	5	764
Thorpeness	Eng	14	7	7	670
Stirling	Sc	13	6	7	786
Taymouth Castle	Sc	13	4	6	790
Scotscraig	Sc	16	6	6	779
Golspie	Sc	14	5	4	738
Sherborne	Eng	15	6	7	650
James Braid, Herbert Fowler, Harry S. Colt					
Aberdovey	W	17	7	7	799
G. Bruns					
Isernhagen	D	15	7	6	428

Architect Golf course	Country	Score			Page
Douglas Brasier					
Kristianstad	S	17	7	7	1258
Ljunghusen	S	17	6	7	1261
Åtvidaberg	S	16	6	5	1230
Växjö	S	15	6	7	1282
Karlshamn	S	14	6	6	1256
Gullbringa	S	13	7	6	1251
Öijared *Gamla banan*	S	13	7	5	1265
Olivier Brizon					
Aïsses (Les) *Rouge/Blanc*	F	16	5	4	215
Pessac	F	13	7	7	315
A.C. Brown/Willie Park					
Grantown on Spey	Sc	14	6	7	739
Ture Bruce					
Barsebäck	S	18	7	6	1231
Vasatorp	S	16	7	7	1282
Mölle	S	15	7	5	1264
Söderåsen	S	15	7	5	1271
Eslöv	S	14	7	5	1238
Lindö Park	S	14	8	6	1260
Mr Buchanan					
West Byfleet	Eng	14	6	8	680
Yves Bureau					
Saint-Jean-de-Monts	F	16	6	5	333
Baden	F	15	6	5	227
Val Queven	F	15	6	5	352
Fontenelles (Les)	F	14	7	4	277
Omaha Beach					
La Mer/Le Bocage	F	14	7	5	310
Burrows					
Hilversum	N	16	7	7	1027
CS Butchark					
Porters Park	Eng	15	7	7	623
Sir Guy Campbell					
West Sussex	Eng	18	7	6	685
Ashridge	Eng	16	7	6	524
Killarney *Mahony's Point*	I	15	7	8	881
Prince's *Himalayas-Shore*	En	13	6	4	625
Sir Guy Campbell & Hutchinson					
Wimereux	F	14	4	5	357
Willie Campbell					
Seascale	Eng	18	5	4	647
Machrie	Sc	17	7	7	754
Enrique Canales					
Islantilla	E	16	8	8	1156

Architect Golf course	Country	Score			Page
S. Carrera					
Molinetto	I	13	9	8	987
Doug Carrick					
Fontana	A	16	8	5	96
Tony Carroll					
Castle Hume	UL	13	7	6	924
Giulio Cavalsani					
Punta Ala	I	14	7	8	996
M. Chantepie					
Etretat	F	14	6	5	271
Hubert Chesneau, Robert von Hagge					
National L'Albatros	F	18	5	6	307
Neil Coles					
PGA de Catalunya	E	18	7	7	1196
Gainsborough-Karsten Lakes	Eng	14	8	6	572
Harry S. Colt					
Royal Portrush Dunluce Links	UL	19	7	7	935
Alwoodley (The)	Eng	18	7	7	523
Eindhoven	N	18	8	6	1019
Falkenstein	D	18	6	7	404
Haagsche	N	18	7	8	1025
Ilkley	Eng	18	7	6	590
Kennemer	N	18	8	8	1030
Royal Zoute	B	18	7	7	121
Sunningdale New Course	Eng	18	8	8	661
Wentworth West Course	Eng	18	8	7	678
Blackmoor	Eng	17	6	5	532
County Sligo	I	17	4	3	856
Frankfurter GC	D	17	7	8	406
Moor Park High Course	Eng	17	8	7	608
Prestbury	Eng	17	8	7	624
Pyle & Kenfig	W	17	7	5	817
Saint-Germain	F	17	7	7	332
Sherwood Forest	Eng	17	7	6	652
St George's Hill	Eng	17	7	7	657
Stoke Poges	Eng	17	8	8	659
Trevose Championship	Eng	17	7	7	672
Whittington Heath	Eng	17	6	7	688
Royal Dublin	I	16	8	7	901
De Pan	N	16	8	7	1017
Isle of Purbeck	Eng	16	7	6	592
Manchester	Eng	16	7	7	601
Royal Wimbledon	Eng	16	7	8	640
Bath	Eng	16	6	9	526
Swinley Forest	Eng	16	6	8	663
Camberley Heath	Eng	16	6	6	544
Thurlestone	Eng	16	6	4	671
Wentworth East Course	Eng	16	8	7	677

Architect Golf course	Country	Score			Page
Harry S. Colt					
Belvoir Park	UL	15	5	6	922
Brokenhurst Manor	Eng	15	6	6	539
Denham	Eng	15	7	7	558
Royal Belfast	UL	15	7	7	933
Brancepeth Castle	Eng	14	6	5	537
Cannes Mandelieu Old Course	F	14	7	8	245
Chantaco	F	14	7	7	254
Longniddry	Sc	14	7	6	750
Pedreña	E	14	6	5	1194
Saint-Cloud Vert	F	14	7	7	330
Tandridge	Eng	14	7	6	664
Thorndon Park	Eng	14	7	6	669
Castle	I	13	6	8	849
Chesterfield	Eng	13	6	7	551
Málaga	E	13	4	6	1177
Harry S. Colt, Alison					
Granville Les Dunes	F	14	4	4	283
Harry S. Colt, MacKenzie					
Knock	UL	15	7	6	928
E. Connaughton					
Charleville	I	13	4	6	851
Bill Coore					
Médoc Les Châteaux	F	18	7	5	302
J.-Cl. Cornillot					
Arras	F	14	6	6	225
Cornish & Silva					
Ambrosiano	I	14	7	7	955
C.K. Cotton					
Downfield	Sc	17	6	7	720
Marriott St Pierre Old Course	W	16	8	7	811
Patriziale Ascona	Ch	15	7	7	1307
Ross-on-Wye	Eng	15	5	6	627
C.W. Hunter					
Portpatrick (Dunskey)	Sc	15	6	7	769
C.K. Cotton & John Harris					
Bologna	I	13	7	7	961
C.K. Cotton & Sutton					
Bergamo - L'Albenza					
Blu + Giallo	I	15	7	8	958
C.K. Cotton, Penninck, Mancinelli					
Keerbergen	B	14	7	6	111
Is Molas	I	16	7	8	975
Gardagolf	I	14	7	8	972

56

Architect Golf course	Country	Score	Page
C.K. Cotton, Dreyer			
Sct. Knuds	Da	14 5 6	145
C.K. Cotton, Cruikshank			
Venezia	I	16 7 9	1003
Henry Cotton			
Olgiata	I	16 7 6	990
Vale do Lobo			
Royal Golf Course	P	15 6 7	1089
Penina	P	14 7 7	1077
Arthur Croome			
Liphook	Eng	16 7 6	597
Marco Croze			
Lignano	I	14 7 7	982
Cervia	I	13 6 9	966
Cherasco	I	13 7 7	967
La Margherita	I	13 7 7	976
(Marco Croze)			
La Rocca	I	13 6 8	978
Riva dei Tessali	I	13 7 6	998
Juan de la Cuadra			
La Sella	E	15 6 5	1168
Robert E. Cupp			
East Sussex National			
East Course	Eng	17 8 7	560
Baldovino Dassù			
Poggio dei Medici	I	16 7 7	995
Deutsche Golf Consult			
Öschberghof	D	15 7 7	451
Mülheim	D	13 6 7	442
Olivier Dongradi			
Augerville	F	13 5 4	226
Frederik Dreyer			
Esbjerg	Da	15 6 5	134
Jönköping	S	16 7 7	1254
B. Ducwing			
Pau	F	13 6 8	314
Joan Dudok van Heel			
Wittelsbacher	D	16 7 6	483
Im Chiemgau	D	15 7 6	427
Herkenbosch	N	16 7 6	1026
Oosterhout	N	15 7 7	1034
Anderstein	N	14 7 6	1013
George Duncan			
Stonehaven	Sc	13 5 5	787

Architect Golf course	Country	Score	Page
Tom Dunn			
Broadstone	Eng	17 7 7	538
Royal Cinque Ports	Eng	17 6 5	630
Seacroft	Eng	17 6 4	646
Weston-Super-Mare	Eng	16 6 7	686
Woking	Eng	16 6 6	691
Bude & North Cornwall	Eng	15 6 5	541
Came Down	Eng	15 5 6	545
Felixstowe Ferry			
Martello Course	Eng	15 6 6	563
Sheringham	Eng	15 7 6	651
Tom Dunn, Harry Vardon			
Ganton	Eng	19 8 5	573
Tom Dunn, Willie Park			
Lindrick	Eng	17 6 6	596
Willie Dunn			
Biarritz-le-Phare	F	14 6 8	235
Dinard	F	13 6 7	264
Pete & P.B. Dye			
Barbaroux	F	17 7 6	229
Pete Dye			
Domaine Impérial	CH	18 8 6	1294
Franciacorta	I	15 7 8	971
Björn Eriksson			
Fågelbro	S	15 9 5	1240
Ramón Espinosa			
Fontanals	E	18 6 5	1148
Mediterraneo	E	16 7 6	1181
Golf d'Aro	E	15 7 7	1150
Bonalba	E	14 6 6	1131
Eschauzier & Thate			
Graafschap	N	15 7 6	1023
European Golf Design			
Asolo	I	13 7 7	956
Nick Faldo			
Chart Hills	Eng	18 8 6	550
Scharmützelsee *Nick Faldo*	D	18 8 7	457
Jim Fazio			
Le Querce	I	17 8 7	980
Marco Simone	I	16 8 8	983
David Feherty			
National GC	T	15 7 7	1318
Heinz Fehring			
München-Riedhof	D	16 7 7	443

57

Architect Golf course	Country	Score			Page
Heinz Fehring					
Fürstliches Hofgut Kolnhausen	D	14	7	6	409
Henrik Jacobsen					
Samsø	Da	15	4	7	144
Michael Fenn					
Toulouse Palmola	F	15	7	4	347
Brest Iroise	F	14	7	6	242
Saint-Laurent	F	14	7	5	334
Besançon	F	13	7	5	233
Reims-Champagne	F	13	7	6	323
Touraine	F	13	7	6	350
Willie Fernie					
Royal Troon *Old Course*	Sc	19	7	7	778
Shiskine (Blackwaterfoot)	Sc	17	5	5	780
Southerndown	W	16	7	7	821
Dumfries & County	Sc	15	7	5	724
Strathaven	Sc	15	7	6	788
Thornhill	Sc	15	6	5	791
Cardross	Sc	14	6	5	713
Pitlochry	Sc	14	6	7	768
Flera					
Örebro	S	18	7	5	1266
Anders Forsbrand					
European Tour Club					
(Kungsängen)	S	15	7	6	1239
Jean-Pascal Fourès					
Rebetz	F	16	6	4	322
Laval-Changé *La Chabossière*	F	14	7	5	296
Grasse	F	13	7	6	284
Herbert Fowler					
Saunton *East Course*	Eng	18	7	6	645
Walton Heath *Old Course*	Eng	18	7	7	675
Berkshire (The) *Blue Course*	Eng	17	8	7	529
Berkshire (The) *Red Course*	Eng	17	8	7	530
Beau Desert	Eng	16	7	7	527
Delamere Forest	Eng	15	6	7	557
West Surrey	Eng	15	7	7	684
Herbert Fowler, Harry S. Colt					
Royal Lytham & St Anne's	Eng	19	7	8	635
Herbert Fowler, Tom Simpson					
North Foreland	Eng	13	7	7	612
Ronald Fream					
Disneyland Paris *Never Land*					
+ *Wonderland*	F	16	7	8	265
Isle Adam (L')	F	16	7	4	290
Montpellier-Massane	F	16	7	5	306

Architect Golf course	Country	Score			Page
Ronald Fream					
Cap d'Agde	F	15	6	5	247
Frégate	F	15	7	7	278
Arcangues	F	14	7	8	224
Pinheiros Altos	P	14	7	7	1078
Vale da Pinta	P	14	6	6	1088
Patrick Fromanger					
Bélesbat	F	14	7	7	231
Didier Fruchet					
Gouverneur (Le) *Le Breuil*	F	16	7	6	279
Gouverneur (Le) *Montaplan*	F	14	7	6	280
Les Furber					
Praha Karlstejn	Cz	15	6	7	1315
Angel Gallardo, Peter Alliss					
Playa Serena	E	13	6	4	1198
José Gancedo					
Lerma	E	17	7	4	1174
Golf del Sur	E	16	7	8	1151
Canyamel	E	15	6	6	1134
Torrequebrada	E	14	7	7	1211
Costa Dorada	E	13	6	6	1140
Monte Mayor	E	13	5	5	1184
Peter Gannon					
Villa D'Este	I	16	8	9	1005
Jean Garaïalde					
Porcelaine (La)	F	14	6	4	319
Cognac	F	13	7	5	260
Jonathan Gaunt					
Linden Hall	Eng	17	8	6	595
Michel Gayon					
Sablé-Solesmes					
La Forêt/La Rivière	F	16	7	4	328
Ailette (L')	F	15	6	5	214
Esery	F	15	7	5	268
Etiolles *Les Cerfs*	F	15	6	5	270
Pornic	F	15	6	6	320
Saint-Endréol	F	15	7	4	331
Vaucouleurs (La) *Les Vallons*	F	15	7	4	353
Casteljaloux	F	14	6	5	248
Chambon-sur-Lignon (Le)	F	14	5	7	251
Fontenailles *Blanc*	F	14	7	6	276
Savenay	F	14	5	4	340
Gloria Golf Resort	T	13	7	7	1317
Charles Gibson					
Royal Porthcawl	W	19	7	6	819

58

Europe

Architect Golf course	Country	Score			Page
Andrew Gilbert					
Kilkea Castle	I	14	6	6	878
Golden Bear Design					
La Moraleja *La Moraleja 2*	E	16	7	8	1166
Antonio Lucena Gomez					
Herreria	E	15	6	6	1155
G.H. Gowring					
Berkhamsted	Eng	16	7	6	528
I.E. Grant					
Cardigan	W	15	6	5	802
Gratenau					
St. Dionys	D	17	7	6	470
Karl F. Grohs					
Bitburger Land	D	15	7	8	394
Eddie Hackett					
Waterville	I	17	6	7	914
Carn	I	16	5	3	848
Dingle (Ceann Sibeal)	I	16	6	4	859
Donegal (Murvagh)	I	16	5	6	860
Enniscrone	I	16	7	6	866
Killarney *Killeen Course*	I	16	7	8	880
Dooks	I	15	5	5	861
Castletroy	I	14	6	6	850
Connemara	I	14	6	6	853
Greenore	I	14	6	5	875
Killorglin	I	14	6	5	882
Malahide *Red + Blue + Yellow*	I	13	7	8	887
West Waterford	I	12	7	6	915
Donald Harradine					
Europasportregion-Zell am See					
Schmittenhöhe	A	16	7	6	95
Beuerberg	D	17	7	6	393
Seefeld-Wildmoos	A	17	8	7	99
(Donald Harradine)					
Schloss Myllendonk	D	16	7	7	464
Düsseldorfer	D	15	7	7	400
Hamburg-Holm	D	15	6	6	418
Lugano	CH	15	7	8	1302
Schloss Klingenburg	D	15	6	6	460
Sonnenalp	D	15	7	7	469
Sylt	D	15	6	8	475
Zumikon	CH	15	7	6	1311
Bad Wörishofen	D	14	6	6	389
Chaumont-en-Vexin	F	14	6	4	257
Grevelingenhout	N	14	7	4	1024
Neuchâtel	CH	14	6	7	1305

Architect Golf course	Country	Score			Page
(Donald Harradine)					
Schönenberg	CH	14	7	6	1308
Tegernseer Bad Wiessee	D	14	7	8	476
Bad Ragaz	CH	13	7	6	1290
Breitenloo	CH	13	7	6	1292
Niederbüren	CH	13	7	7	1306
Opio Valbonne	F	13	6	7	311
Sainte-Maxime	F	13	7	7	339
Strasbourg Illkirch					
Jaune + Rouge	F	13	7	6	345
Peter Harradine					
Maison Blanche	F	14	7	5	299
FA Harris					
Berlin-Wannsee	D	16	8	9	392
John D. Harris					
Shannon	I	13	6	6	903
Albarella	I	14	8	7	954
Garlenda	I	14	7	8	973
Lacanau	F	14	6	7	294
Padova	I	14	7	7	991
La Pinetina	I	13	7	7	977
Verona	I	13	7	8	1004
Harris & Associates					
Courtown	I	14	5	5	858
Hauser					
Neuhof	D	15	7	7	447
Hawtree & Son					
Blainroe	I	13	6	6	845
Girona	E	13	7	5	1149
Båstad *Old Course*	S	16	7	7	1232
Hawtree & Taylor					
High Post	Eng	15	6	7	584
F. Hawtree					
Royal Birkdale (The)	Eng	19	9	7	629
Hillside	Eng	18	7	7	585
Waterloo *La Marache*	B	16	8	7	125
Pals	E	16	7	6	1192
Bondues *Jaune*	F	15	7	6	238
Gog Magog *Old Course*	Eng	15	7	8	574
John O'Gaunt	Eng	16	7	6	593
Limburg	B	16	7	4	112
Saint-Nom-la-Bretèche *Rouge*	F	16	8	8	336
Lisburn	UL	15	7	6	929
Royal Latem	B	15	8	6	120
Saint-Nom-la-Bretèche *Bleu*	F	15	8	8	335
The Island	I	15	7	7	907
Westport	I	15	7	7	916

59

Architect Golf course	Country	Score			Page
F. Hawtree					
Woodbridge	Eng	14	7	7	692
Zuid Limburgse	N	14	7	7	1043
Le Prieuré *Ouest*	F	14	7	5	297
Son Vida	E	14	6	7	1208
Massereene	UL	14	5	6	931
Rochefort-Chisan	F	14	6	4	325
Bendinat	E	13	6	7	1130
Domont-Montmorency	F	13	7	4	267
Malone	UL	13	6	6	930
Anjou-Champigné	F	13	6	6	220
Martin Hawtree					
Rudding Park	Eng	15	8	8	642
Simon's	Da	14	7	7	146
TAT Golf Belek	T	14	7	7	1320
Siegfried Heinz					
Domtal-Mommenheim	D	14	7	7	399
Rolf Henning-Jensen					
Møn	Da	15	7	7	141
Rubens Henriquez					
Las Americas	E	16	7	8	1170
Sandy Herd					
Harrogate	Eng	15	7	7	578
Lytham Green Drive	Eng	15	7	8	600
Pannal	Eng	15	6	7	617
Sandy Herd, James Braid					
Wilmslow	Eng	16	7	6	689
E.D. Hess					
Wendlohe *A-Kurs + B-Kurs*	D	16	7	6	481
Wentorf-Reinbeker	D	15	7	6	482
L. Hewson					
Ballybunion *Old Course*	I	19	7	7	839
Alan Higgins					
Carden Park *Cheshire Course*	Eng	14	8	8	546
Reijo Hillberg					
Pickala Seaside Course	Fi	15	8	5	157
Tawast	Fi	14	7	5	161
Harold Hilton					
Ferndown *Old Course*	Eng	17	7	7	564
Ormskirk	Eng	14	6	4	616
Thomas Himmel					
Fürstlicher GC Bad Waldsee	D	17	7	8	408
Pierre Hirigoyen					
San Sebastián	E	14	6	6	1204

Architect Golf course	Country	Score			Page
Karl-Heinz Hoffmann					
Mittelrheinischer	D	17	7	7	440
Col. S.V. Hotchkin					
Woodhall Spa	Eng	18	7	8	694
Brian Huggett					
Orchardleigh	Eng	17	7	7	615
Bowood (Cornwall)	Eng	16	7	6	534
Charles Hunter					
Prestwick St Nicholas	Sc	16	6	7	772
Ibergolf					
Granada	E	14	6	5	1152
Holcombe Ingleby					
Royal West Norfolk (Brancaster)	En	17	7	6	639
John Jacobs					
Buckinghamshire (The)	Eng	17	8	7	540
Northop Country Park	W	16	9	6	815
Apremont	F	15	8	6	222
Patshull Park Hotel	Eng	13	8	8	619
Wolfgang Jersombek					
Jakobsberg	D	15	7	6	429
Peter Johnson					
Vale of Glamorgan	W	16	8	7	823
Gerard Jol					
Houtrak	N	16	8	8	1029
Tom Jones					
Llandudno (Maesdu)	W	15	5	8	809
E. Jonson-Sedibe					
Gut Waldhof	D	15	7	5	415
Jean Jottrand					
Falnuee	B	14	7	4	109
Armin Keller					
Nahetal	D	14	8	6	445
Rheinhessen	D	14	8	7	455
Ron Kirby					
Elfrather Mühle	D	14	7	7	401
Spiegelven	B	14	7	8	124
Escorpion	E	13	8	4	1146
Ron Kirby, Joe Carr					
Old Head	I	15	7	7	893
Ron Kirby/Golden Bear					
London Golf Club *International*	Eng	15	9	7	599

60

Architect Golf course	Country	Score			Page
Kothe					
Hanau-Wilhelmsbad	D	16	6	6	419
C. Kramer					
Tutzing	D	15	7	6	478
D.C. van Krimpen					
Rosendael	N	15	7	7	1037
Kosti Kuronen					
Master *Master*	Fi	15	7	7	155
Guadalhorce	E	14	7	6	1153
St Laurence	Fi	14	5	4	159
Dr W. Laidlaw Purves					
Royal St George's	Eng	19	7	5	638
Littlestone	Eng	14	6	5	598
Hugues Lambert					
Villette d'Anthon *Les Sangliers*	F	17	6	4	354
Val de Sorne	F	14	7	5	351
Patrice Lambert					
Saint-Thomas	F	14	7	5	337
Bernhard Langer					
Bad Griesbach *Brunnwies*	D	17	9	9	386
Portmarnock Links	I	17	7	8	895
Schloss Nippenburg	D	17	8	6	465
Soufflenheim	F	16	7	4	343
Stolper Heide	D	16	7	5	473
Dachstein Tauern /					
Schladming	A	15	7	5	93
Béthemont	F	14	7	5	234
Modena	I	14	7	8	986
Panoramica	E	14	6	4	1193
Charles Lawrie					
Woburn *Dukes Course*	Eng	18	7	7	690
Hankley Common	Eng	16	6	6	577
Joseph Lee					
S. Lourenço	P	18	6	8	1085
Vilamoura					
Vilamoura III (Laguna)	P	14	7	7	1093
Patrice Léglise					
Raray (Château de) *La Licorne*	F	14	6	4	321
Bernhard von Limburger					
Club zur Vahr (Garlstedt)	D	18	6	5	398
Gütersloh (Westfälischer GC)	D	17	7	7	416
Hubbelrath	D	17	8	6	425
Köln	D	17	6	7	430
Krefelder	D	17	7	7	432
Oberfranken	D	17	6	5	449

Architect Golf course	Country	Score			Page
Bernhard von Limburger					
Stuttgarter Solitude	D	17	5	5	474
Feldafing	D	16	7	6	405
Hamburg-Ahrensburg	D	16	8	7	417
Hannover	D	16	7	7	420
Neckartal	D	16	6	7	446
Schloss Braunfels	D	16	7	7	458
(Bernhard von Limburger)					
Steiermärkischer Murhof	A	16	7	6	100
Walddörfer	D	16	7	6	479
Augsburg	D	15	7	7	383
Bâle-Hagenthal	F	15	7	7	228
Blumisberg	CH	15	7	6	1291
Essener Oefte	D	15	8	7	403
Wasserburg Anholt	D	15	7	7	480
Main-Taunus	D	14	7	6	437
Atalaya *Old Course*	E	13	6	7	1129
Sune Linde					
Frösåker	S	16	7	5	1247
Forsgården	S	14	6	7	1246
Karl Litten					
Warwickshire (The)	Eng	15	7	8	676
José Luis Lopez					
Estepona	E	14	7	6	1147
George Low, Sandy Herd					
Pleasington	Eng	16	8	6	621
Sandy Lyle					
Schloss Wilkendorf	D	17	7	5	466
Tom MacAuley					
Cromstrijen	N	16	8	5	1016
Purmerend	N	16	7	7	1035
Twente	N	15	7	6	1041
Mont-Garni	B	13	7	6	113
Montecchia	I	13	8	7	988
Alister Mackenzie					
Blairgowrie *Rosemount*	Sc	18	8	6	706
Moortown	Eng	18	7	7	609
Rungsted	Da	17	7	7	143
Hadley Wood	Eng	16	7	7	575
Bolton *Old Links*	Eng	15	5	7	533
Duff House Royal	Sc	15	6	6	722
Cork GC	I	15	3	5	854
Sand Moor	Eng	14	7	7	643
Galway GC	I	13	6	6	871
Charles MacKenzie					
Fulford	Eng	17	7	8	571

61

Architect Golf course	Country	Score		Page
John MacPherson				
Elgin	Sc	15 7 6		729
Brian Magnusson				
Bråviken	S	16 7 7		1234
Alejandro Maldonado				
Montenmedio	E	15 7 7		1186
Malling Petersen				
Vejle *Blue + Red Slings*	Da	15 7 7		147
Malling/Gundtoft				
Royal Oak	Da	15 7 5		142
Dan Maples				
Capdepera	E	15 7 6		1135
C.H. Mayo				
Thetford	Eng	14 7 5		668
J. McAllister				
Athlone	I	13 6 6		837
Dr McCuaig				
Seaton Carew	Eng	17 7 5		648
Peter McEvoy				
Powerscourt	I	15 7 7		897
Rathsallagh	I	15 7 6		898
Glen of the Downs	I	13 4 7		873
Woodbrook (remod.)	I	15 7 6		917
M. McKenna				
Hermitage	I	15 6 7		876
Paddy Merrigan				
Slieve Russell	I	15 8 6		904
Tulfarris	I	14 7 6		910
Woodenbridge	I	16 7 6		918
Faithlegg	I	13 7 6		868
David Mezzacane				
Cosmopolitan	I	14 6 7		968
Parco de' Medici	I	13 7 9		993
Johnny Miller				
Collingtree Park	Eng	14 8 7		553
William Mitchell				
Quinta do Lago B/C	P	15 7 8		1082
Quinta do Lago *Ria Formosa*	P	15 7 8		1083
Theodore Moon				
Kilmarnock (Barassie)	Sc	17 6 8		744
Léonard Morandi				
Nîmes-Campagne	F	16 7 6		309

Architect Golf course	Country	Score		Page
John Morgan				
Forest Pines *Forest + Pines*	Eng	17 6 7		567
Tim Morisson				
Cairndhu	UL	13 6 5		923
Hossegor	F	16 6 6		289
J. Morris				
Royal Liverpool (Hoylake)	Eng	18 8 7		634
Caldy	Eng	17 7 7		543
Tom Morris				
Royal County Down	UL	19 6 7		934
Carnoustie *Championship*	Sc	19 5 6		715
Muirfield	Sc	19 7 6		759
Nairn	Sc	19 7 8		762
Royal Dornoch *Championship*	Sc	19 7 7		776
Lahinch	I	18 6 6		883
Royal North Devon				
(Westward Ho!)	Eng	18 6 6		637
Machrihanish	Sc	18 6 4		755
Ladybank	Sc	17 7 5		746
Moray	Sc	17 5 5		758
Tain	Sc	17 6 6		789
Rosapenna	I	16 7 6		899
Dunbar	Sc	16 5 6		725
Lanark	Sc	16 6 5		747
Luffness New	Sc	16 5 6		752
Royal Burgess	Sc	16 7 9		775
West Kilbride	Sc	16 7 5		794
Crail	Sc	15 6 6		716
Alyth	Sc	14 6 6		700
Forfar	Sc	14 6 6		732
Callander	Sc	13 6 7		712
Tom Morris/James Braid				
Wallasey	Eng	17 7 7		673
John Morrison				
Biella - Le Betulle	I	18 7 7		959
Stockholm	S	16 8 9		1273
Torino - La Mandria *Blu*	I	16 8 8		1001
Lunds Akademiska	S	16 7 5		1262
Lüneburger Heide	D	16 7 5		436
Barlassina	I	15 8 8		957
John Morrison				
Toxandria	N	14 7 6		1040
M. Nakowsky				
Divonne	F	14 6 7		266
M. Narbel				
Lausanne	CH	16 7 7		1300

62

Architect Golf course	Country	Score	Page
Falco Nardi			
Lauro	E	13 7 5	1173
Santa Ponsa	E	13 6 7	1206
Robin Nelson			
Champ de Bataille	F	14 6 3	253
Peter Nicholson			
Hever	Eng	14 8 8	583
M. Nicholson			
Crans-sur-Sierre	CH	14 7 8	1293
Jack Nicklaus			
Gut Altentann	A	18 8 7	98
Mount Juliet	I	18 9 8	889
Carden Park *Nicklaus Course*	Eng	17 8 8	547
Gleneagles *Monarch's*	Sc	17 9 7	736
Gut Lärchenhof	D	17 9 7	412
Montecastillo	E	17 8 7	1185
St Mellion *Nicklaus Course*	Eng	17 9 7	658
Le Robinie	I	16 9 7	981
Paris International	F	16 7 5	313
La Moraleja *La Moraleja 1*	E	15 7 8	1165
Palazzo Arzaga	I	15 8 8	992
Nicklaus Design			
Hertfordshire (The)	Eng	15 7 7	582
Tommy Nordström			
Borre	Nw	16 6 5	1049
Peter Nordwall			
Bro-Bålsta	S	17 7 6	1235
Skövde	S	17 5 7	1270
Stenungsund	S	17 7 8	1272
Gränna	S	15 7 5	1250
A 6	S	14 7 6	1229
Ekerum	S	14 7 7	1237
C. Noskowski			
Karlovy Vary	Cz	15 7 6	1313
Christy O'Connor Jr			
Glasson	I	16 7 7	872
Fota Island	I	15 7 6	869
Galway Bay	I	14 7 6	870
Citywest	I	13 6 7	852
Lee Valley	I	13 7 6	884
Mount Wolsley	I	13 6 5	890
Peter O'Hare			
Monkstown	I	15 6 7	888
José Maria Olazábal			
Sevilla	E	17 7 8	1207

Architect Golf course	Country	Score	Page
José Maria Olazábal			
Masia Bach	E	15 7 6	1179
Arnold Palmer			
Tralee	I	18 7 6	908
K Club	I	17 8 8	877
Scharmützelsee			
Arnold Palmer	D	17 8 7	456
Castello di Tolcinasco	I	15 8 8	965
Le Pavoniere	I	14 8 8	979
Ca' della Nave	I	13 6 8	962
Willie Park			
Silloth-on-Solway	Eng	18 7 4	653
Sunningdale *Old Course*	Eng	18 8 8	662
Parkstone	Eng	16 7 8	618
Bruntsfield	Sc	15 8 9	709
Duddingston	Sc	15 7 9	721
Peterhead	Sc	15 5 4	767
Stoneham	Eng	15 7 8	660
West Hill	Eng	15 6 6	682
Baberton	Sc	14 6 8	702
Burntisland	Sc	14 6 6	711
Huntercombe		14 6 7589	Eng
Willie Park, Harry S. Colt			
Formby	Eng	18 7 7	568
Willie Park Jr			
Notts (Hollinwell)	Eng	18 6 6	614
(Willie Park Jr)			
Montrose	Sc	17 5 6	757
Antwerp	B	16 7 7	107
Portstewart *Strand Course*	UL	16 7 7	932
Dieppe-Pourville	F	14 6 5	263
Waterford	I	14 6 6	912
Greger Paulsson			
Upsala	S	13 6 6	1279
Frank Pennink			
Noordwijk	N	18 7 8	1032
Vilamoura			
Vilamoura I (Old Course)	P	16 7 7	1091
Aroeira	P	15 6 6	1068
Broekpolder	N	15 7 6	1015
Kungsbacka	S	15 6 6	1259
Gelpenberg	N	14 4 5	1020
Gut Kaden *Platz B + Platz C*	D	15 7 6	411
Lauswolt	N	14 6 7	1031
Palmares	P	13 7 5	1075
Vilamoura *Vilmaoura II (Pinhal)*	P	13 7 7	1092

63

Europe

Architect Golf course	Country	Score			Page
Jeremy Pern					
Charmeil	F	16	6	6	256
Dartmouth	Eng	16	9	6	556
Wantzenau (La)	F	16	6	6	356
Ableiges *Les Etangs*	F	15	6	4	213
Albi	F	15	6	6	217
Bresse (La)	F	15	6	4	241
Largue (La)	F	15	7	4	295
Les Bois	Ch	15	6	6	1301
Roncemay	F	15	7	7	326
Toulouse-Seilh *Rouge*	F	15	7	6	348
Gruyère (La)	Ch	14	7	6	1298
Anders Person					
Göteborg	S	15	6	7	1249
WG Pikeman					
Portmarnock	I	19	7	8	894
Manuel Piñero					
La Quinta	E	15	8	7	1167
La Dehesa	E	14	7	4	1160
Chris Pittman					
Fontcaude	F	14	6	6	275
Gary Player					
Zaudin	E	16	7	6	1215
Taulane	F	15	7	4	346
Almerimar	E	14	6	6	1126
Jean-Marie Poellot					
Feucherolles	F	15	7	5	273
P. Postel					
Iffeldorf	D	16	7	6	426
Alain Prat					
Pléneuf-Val-André	F	17	7	5	316
Gujan-Mestras	F	15	7	6	286
Rainer Preismann					
Bad Abbach-Deutenhof	D	15	7	7	384
PSA Projects					
Formby Hall	Eng	14	8	6	569
P. Puttman					
Villamartin	E	16	7	6	1214
Quenouille					
Ploemeur Océan	F	15	7	6	317
Ted Ray					
Sandiway	Eng	17	5	7	644
R. Reuss					
Luzern	CH	13	6	7	1303

Architect Golf course	Country	Score			Page
R. Reuss					
Wylihof	CH	13	6	6	1310
Alan Rijks					
Batouwe	N	15	7	3	1014
Gendersteyn	N	15	7	7	1021
Sybrook	N	15	6	6	1039
José Rivero					
Olivar de la Hinojosa	E	13	7	8	1190
Cabell Robinson					
Castillo de Gorraiz	E	17	7	7	1136
La Cala *Norte*	E	17	8	6	1158
Limère	F	17	6	5	298
Praia d'El Rey	P	17	6	5	1079
Grande Bastide (La)	F	16	6	6	281
La Cala *Sur*	E	16	8	6	1159
Evian	F	15	7	9	272
Palheiro	P	13	6	7	1074
W.R. Robinson					
Clandeboye *Dufferin Course*	UL	15	6	6	926
Paul Rolin					
Amsterdam	N	15	7	7	1012
Nunspeet *North/East*	N	15	5	3	1033
Sint Nicolaasga	N	15	7	5	1038
Rigenée	B	14	7	6	118
Rijk van Nijmegen					
Rijk van Nijmegen	N	14	6	5	1036
Rinkven *Red - White*	B	14	6	5	119
Erik Röös					
Fjällbacka	S	15	6	3	1243
Rocky Roquemore					
Golden Eagle	P	15	4	4	1071
Quinta do Peru	P	15	6	5	1084
Makila Golf Club	F	14	6	8	300
Belas	P	13	7	6	1069
James Ross					
Asserbo	Da	15	7	6	133
Mackenzie Ross					
Castletown	Eng	18	6	8	549
Southerness	Sc	18	6	5	781
Maspalomas	E	16	7	8	1180
Glen	Sc	14	7	7	734
Las Palmas	E	14	8	8	1172
Estoril	P	13	7	7	1070
Mazamet-La Barouge	F	13	5	4	301
Turnberry *Ailsa Course*	Sc	19	9	8	792
Turnberry *Arran Course*	Sc	16	9	8	793

64

Architect Golf course	Country	Score			Page

Jean-Manuel Rossi
| Belle-Dune | F | 16 | 6 | 5 | 232 |
| Amnéville | F | 13 | 6 | 5 | 219 |

Kurt Rossknecht
Colony Club Gutenhof	A	17	8	7	92
Motzener See	D	17	8	6	441
Donnerskirchen-Neusiedlersee	A	16	6	5	94
Gut Thailing	D	16	7	5	414
Bad Griesbach-Sagmühle					
Sagmühle	D	15	9	9	387
Gut Ludwigsberg	D	15	6	6	413
Hof Trages	D	15	7	5	423
Hohenpähl	D	15	7	6	424
Schloss Egmating	D	15	7	7	459
Sempachersee	CH	15	8	7	1309

Lucien Roux
| Volcans (Les) | F | 14 | 6 | 5 | 355 |

Pat Ruddy
European (The)	I	18	5	6	867
Ballyliffin					
Glashedy Links	I	17	6	5	841
Druids Glen	I	16	9	7	863
St Margaret's	I	16	7	7	906

Bob Sandow
| Badgemore Park | Eng | 14 | 7 | 7 | 525 |

Gregorio Sanz
| Campoamor | E | 14 | 6 | 6 | 1133 |

Ben Sayers
| Castlerock | UL | 16 | 6 | 6 | 925 |

Ulrich Schmidt
| Bad Bevensen | D | 15 | 5 | 7 | 385 |

Erik Schnack
| Holstebro | Da | 16 | 6 | 5 | 138 |

Hannes Schreiner
| St. Leon-Rot | D | 15 | 8 | 6 | 472 |

Archdeacon Scott
| Royal Ashdown Forest | Eng | 14 | 7 | 6 | 628 |

Jan Sederholm
Larvik	Nw	17	7	5	1052
Espoo	Fi	16	7	6	153
Haninge	S	16	8	6	1253
Himmerland *New Course*	Da	16	8	6	137
Sarfvik *New Course*	Fi	16	8	7	158
Fureso	Da	15	7	7	136
Grenland	Nw	14	6	6	1050

Jan Sederholm
| Tyrifjord | Nw | 14 | 6 | 6 | 1057 |

F.L. Segales
| Pula | E | 13 | 6 | 5 | 1201 |

T. Shannon
| Dundalk | I | 15 | 6 | 6 | 864 |

William Side
| Mullion | Eng | 15 | 5 | 5 | 610 |

W. Siegmann
| Buxtehude | D | 16 | 7 | 6 | 397 |
| Schloss Lüdersburg *Old/New* | D | 15 | 7 | 6 | 463 |

Archie Simpson
| Murcar | Sc | 15 | 6 | 6 | 760 |
| Aboyne | Sc | 14 | 6 | 6 | 698 |

Bob Simpson
Royal Aberdeen					
Balgownie Links	Sc	18	7	8	774
Crieff *Ferntower Course*	Sc	15	7	7	717
Edzell	Sc	14	6	3	728

Tom Simpson
Chantilly *Vineuil*	F	18	7	6	255
Cruden Bay	Sc	18	7	6	718
Carlisle	Eng	17	7	7	548
Fontainebleau	F	17	7	7	274
Ravenstein	B	17	8	7	117
Spa (Les Fagnes)	B	17	7	7	123
Carlow	I	16	6	6	847
Chiberta	F	16	6	8	259
Hardelot *Les Pins*	F	16	6	6	287
Puerta de Hierro					
Puerta de Hierro 1	E	16	8	9	1199
Sart-Tilman	B	16	7	7	122
Hainaut					
Bruyere-Quesnoy-Etangs	B	15	7	5	110
New Golf Deauville					
Rouge/Blanc	F	15	7	8	308
Oostende	B	15	7	7	114
County Louth	I	18	5	6	855

Cameron Sinclair
| Whitekirk | Sc | 15 | 7 | 7 | 797 |

Nils Sköld
| Forsbacka | S | 16 | 7 | 4 | 1245 |

(Nils Sköld)
Täby	S	16	7	7	1275
Visby	S	16	6	5	1283
Karlstad	S	15	6	6	1257

65

Architect Golf course	Country	Score			Page
(Nils Sköld)					
Värnamo	S	15	7	5	1280
Torekov	S	14	7	7	1276
Nils Sköld, Karlsson					
Skellefteå	S	14	6	5	1269
Nils Sköld, Jan Sederholm					
Gävle	S	14	6	6	1248
Fred Smith					
Stavanger	Nw	16	6	7	1056
Des Smyth					
Limerick County	I	15	7	6	885
Seapoint	I	15	6	6	902
Ballykisteen	I	14	7	6	840
Waterford Castle	I	14	5	6	913
Junl Søgaard					
Sorknes	Nw	13	6	4	1055
Jorge Soler					
Peralada	E	16	6	5	1195
Duarte Sotto Mayor					
Quinta da Beloura	P	14	8	7	1080
Montado	P	13	7	6	1073
Thierry Sprecher					
Chailly (Château de)	F	14	8	6	250
Annonay-Gourdan	F	13	6	5	221
Servanes	F	13	7	7	342
Arthur Spring					
Beaufort	I	14	6	7	843
Newcastle West	I	13	7	5	892
Christoph Staedler					
Semlin am See	D	16	8	7	468
Märkischer Potsdam	D	14	7	6	438
John Stagg					
West Berkshire	Eng	15	7	7	679
Donald Steel					
Efteling	N	16	8	5	1018
Amarilla	E	15	7	7	1128
Goes	N	15	7	6	1022
Hoge Kleij	N	15	6	7	1028
Portal Championship	Eng	15	8	7	622
Wouwse Plantage	N	15	7	6	1042
Forest of Arden					
Arden Course	Eng	14	8	8	566
Rochester & Cobham	Eng	14	6	6	626
Vila Sol	P	14	7	7	1090
Treudelberg	D	13	8	7	477

Architect Golf course	Country	Score			Page
Donald Steel/GK. Smith					
Letham Grange Old Course	Sc	15	7	5	748
Adrian Stiff					
Cumberwell Park	Eng	17	7	7	555
J. Hamilton Stutt					
Costa Brava	E	13	7	7	1139
Meon Valley Meon Course	Eng	15	8	7	605
Murrayshall	Sc	14	7	8	761
Woodbury Park The Oaks	Eng	15	9	6	693
Dunfermline	Sc	15	7	7	726
Rafael Sundblom					
Halmstad	S	18	8	7	1252
Rya	S	15	7	8	1268
Drottningholm	S	14	9	6	1236
Sundsvall	S	13	6	6	1274
Rafael Sundblom/Gierdsjö					
Kalmar	S	15	5	8	1255
Tranås	S	14	6	7	1277
Dieter Sziedat					
Hetzenhof	D	14	7	6	422
J.H. Taylor					
Touquet (Le) La Mer	F	17	6	7	349
Hayling	Eng	16	7	7	580
Hindhead	Eng	16	7	6	586
Carmarthen	W	15	7	4	803
Royal Cromer	Eng	15	7	6	631
Royal Winchester	Eng	15	6	8	641
Frilford Heath Red Course	Eng	14	7	7	570
Royal Mid-Surrey Outer	Eng	14	7	8	636
Tecnoa					
Torremirona	E	13	7	7	1210
David Thomas					
Bowood G&CC	Eng	17	6	6	535
El Prat Amarillo	E	15	7	6	1142
Nobilis	T	17	8	6	1319
San Roque	E	17	8	6	1203
Blairgowrie Lansdowne	Sc	15	8	6	705
Roxburghe (The)	Sc	15	7	7	773
The Belfry PGA National	Eng	15	9	8	667
La Manga Oeste	E	14	7	7	1163
Almenara	E	13	8	8	1125
Slaley Hall	Eng	17	8	7	654
Osona Montanya	E	14	7	4	1191
Thomas/Puttman					
La Manga Norte	E	15	7	7	1162
La Manga Sur	E	14	7	7	1164

66

Architect Golf course	Country	Score			Page
John Thompson					
Aldeburgh	Eng	13	6	7	522
Peter Thomson					
Duke's Course St Andrews	Sc	16	7	8	723
Mr Thompson					
Portsalon	I	16	5	5	896
Capt. Tippett					
Tramore	I	13	7	6	909
R. Trent Jones Jr					
Puerta de Hierro					
Puerta de Hierro 2	E	18	8	9	1200
Seddiner See Südplatz	D	18	9	7	467
Grenoble Bresson	F	17	7	6	285
Moscow	Ru	17	7	6	1316
Penha Longa	P	17	6	8	1076
Bonmont	E	16	7	6	1132
Saint Donat	F	15	7	8	329
Robert Trent Jones					
Valderrama	E	19	8	6	1213
Castelconturbia					
Giallo + Azzurro	I	18	8	7	963
Celtic Manor Roman Road	W	18	9	7	804
Las Brisas	E	18	7	7	1171
Sotogrande	E	18	7	6	1209
Genève	CH	17	7	8	1297
I Roveri	I	17	7	8	974
Spérone	F	17	7	5	344
Moliets	F	17	6	5	304
Pevero	I	16	8	8	994
Joyenval Marly	F	16	8	7	291
Ballybunion Cashen					
(New Course)	I	16	7	7	838
Bodensee-Weissensberg	D	16	7	7	395
Los Naranjos	E	16	7	7	1176
Bondues Blanc	F	16	7	6	237
El Bosque	E	16	7	4	1141
Estérel Latitudes	F	16	6	7	269
Mijas Los Lagos	E	16	6	7	1182
Grande-Motte (La)					
Les Flamants Roses	F	16	6	4	282
Joyenval Retz	F	15	8	7	292
Marbella	E	15	7	8	1178
Castelgandolfo	I	15	7	7	964
Adare	I	15	6	7	836
Chamonix	F	15	6	7	252
Troia	P	15	6	5	1087
Dromoland Castle	I	14	7	7	862
Moor Allerton	Eng	14	6	7	607
Madeira	P	14	6	5	1072

Architect Golf course	Country	Score			Page
Robert Trent Jones					
Riviéra Golf Club	F	13	7	8	324
Bercuit	B	13	7	7	108
La Duquesa	E	13	7	6	1161
Mijas Los Olivos	E	13	6	7	1183
Quinta da Marinha	P	13	7	7	1081
Sven Tumba					
Ullna	S	17	8	6	1278
Österåker	S	16	6	6	1267
Jeremy Turner					
Hauger		13	7	6 1051	N
J. H. Turner					
Newbury & Crookham	Eng	15	6	7	611
Reverend Tyack					
West Cornwall	Eng	16	7	6	681
Iwao Uematsu					
Kikuoka	LU	16	7	7	128
Urbis Planning					
Rolls of Monmouth (The)	W	15	6	6	818
Harry Vardon					
Kingussie	Sc	15	4	5	745
Mendip	Eng	15	5	7	604
Bundoran	I	13	6	7	846
Pedro Vasconcelos					
Salgados	P	14	7	6	1086
M. Verdieri					
Ennetsee-Holzhäusern	CH	13	7	6	1296
Engadin	CH	15	6	6	1295
O. van der Vynckt					
Cheverny	F	14	7	6	258
Robert von Hagge					
Bordes (Les)	F	19	8	6	239
Kempferhof (Le)	F	18	8	6	293
Real Sociedad					
Club de Campo	E	18	7	6	1202
Bogogno	I	17	8	7	960
Emporda	E	17	7	6	1145
Royal Mougins	F	17	7	8	327
Seignosse	F	17	7	7	341
Courson Vert/Noir	F	16	7	3	262
Courson Lilas/Orange	F	15	7	3	261
Robert Walker					
Cardiff	W	14	6	8	801
Philip Walton					
County Tipperary	I	15	7	5	857

67

Architect Golf course	Country	Score			Page	Architect Golf course	Country	Score			Page
Philip Walton						**Unknown architects**					
St Helen's Bay	I	14	6	6	905	Newport	W	15	6	7	813
Henrik Wartiainen						Oberschwaben Bad Waldsee	D	15	6	6	450
Talma	Fi	14	8	6	160	Oslo	Nw	15	7	9	1054
Rod Whitman						Abenberg	D	14	7	6	382
Médoc *Les Vignes*	F	15	7	5	303	Ardglass	UL	14	6	4	920
Unknown architects						Bad Liebenzell	D	14	7	7	388
Burnham & Berrow	Eng	18	7	6	542	Braunschweig	D	14	6	7	396
North Berwick	Sc	18	7	8	765	Carnoustie *Burnside*	Sc	14	5	6	714
Prestwick	Sc	18	6	7	771	Eschenried	D	14	7	7	402
Royal St David's	W	18	6	5	820	Falkenberg	S	14	7	7	1241
St Andrews *Old Course*	Sc	18	8	8	785	Falmouth	Eng	14	6	7	562
Ashburnham	W	17	6	5	800	Fränkische Schweiz	D	14	7	6	407
Conwy	W	17	7	8	805	Garmisch-Partenkirchen	D	14	6	7	410
Gullane *No 1*	Sc	17	8	7	740	Glamorganshire	W	14	7	8	806
Monifieth	Sc	17	7	7	756	Hechingen-Hohenzollern	D	14	6	6	421
West Lancashire	Eng	17	7	7	683	Huntly	Sc	14	6	6	742
North Wales (Llandudno)	W	17	6	8	814	Interlaken	CH	14	6	6	1299
Panmure	Sc	17	6	5	766	Korsør	Da	14	4	6	139
St Andrews *New Course*	Sc	17	8	8	784	Llanymynech	W	14	6	4	810
Western Gailes	Sc	17	5	7	795	Mannings Heath					
Bergisch Land Wuppertal	D	16	7	7	391	Memmingen Gut Westerhart	D	14	6	6	439
East Devon	Eng	16	6	7	559	Obere Alp	D	14	7	7	448
Huddersfield (Fixby)	Eng	16	6	7	587	Pinnau	D	14	6	6	452
Inverness	Sc	16	7	8	743	Reichsstadt Bad Windsheim	D	14	6	7	453
Leven	Sc	16	6	6	749	*Waterfall Course*	Eng	14	8	6	602
Reichswald-Nürnberg	D	16	7	7	454	Mariánské Lázne	Cz	14	7	6	1314
Roma - Acquasanta	I	16	8	9	999	Monte Carlo (Mont Agel)	F	14	6	7	305
Royal Guernsey	Eng	16	7	7	632	Nes	Nw	14	6	4	1053
Royal Jersey	Eng	16	7	8	633	St Andrews *Eden Course*	Sc	14	8	8	782
Schloss Langenstein	D	16	8	7	461	Wheatley	Eng	14	6	6	687
Schloss Liebenstein						Aix-les-Bains	F	13	5	7	216
Gelb + Blau	D	16	8	7	462	Elm Park	I	13	7	8	865
St. Eurach	D	16	7	6	471	Falkirk Tryst	Sc	13	6	6	731
St Andrews *Jubilee Course*	Sc	16	8	8	783	Filey	Eng	13	5	5	565
Walton Heath *New Course*	Eng	16	7	6	674	Grand Ducal de Luxembourg	LU	13	6	7	127
Arendal	Nw	15	7	5	1048	Kilkenny	I	13	7	6	879
Ballyliffin *Old Course*	I	15	6	5	842	Königsfeld	D	13	6	6	431
Bamberg	D	15	7	7	390	Margara	I	13	7	7	984
Boulie (La) *La Vallée*	F	15	7	8	240	Montreux	CH	13	6	5	1304
Coxmoor	Eng	15	6	6	554	Ozoir-la-Ferrière					
Elie	Sc	15	6	6	730	*Château/Monthéty*	F	13	7	5	312
Fanø	Da	15	4	7	135	Rapallo	I	13	7	8	997
Haggs Castle	Sc	15	7	9	741	Rosslare	I	13	5	6	900
Hallamshire	Eng	15	6	8	576	Royal Portrush Valley	UL	13	7	7	936
Lichtenau-Weickershof	D	15	7	6	433	Sant Cugat	E	13	6	5	1205
Lindau-Bad Schachen	D	15	7	8	434	Tehidy Park	Eng	13	7	6	665
Lübeck-Travemünder	D	15	8	8	435	Warrenpoint	UL	13	6	5	937
Münchner-Strasslach	D	15	6	7	444	Wien-Freudenau	A	13	7	9	101
Nairn Dunbar	Sc	15	6	7	763						

68

RECOMMENDED SEASONS
SAISONS RECOMMANDEES
EMPFOHLENE JAHRESZEITEN
REKOMMANDERADE MÅNADER
EPOCA DEL AÑO ACONSEJADA
MESI CONSIGLIATI

Seasons Golf course	Country	Score	Page	Seasons Golf course	Country	Score	Page
1 2 3 4 5 6 7 8 9 10 11 12				1 2 3 4 5 6 7 8 9 10 11 12			
Albi	F	15 6 6	217	La Manga *Sur*	E	14 7 7	1164
Amarilla	E	15 7 7	1128	La Sella	E	15 6 5	1168
Arcachon	F	13 6 6	223	Lacanau	F	14 6 7	294
Aroeira	P	15 6 6	1068	Las Americas	E	16 7 8	1170
Baule (La) *Rouge*	F	15 7 8	230	Las Palmas	E	14 8 8	1172
Belas	P	13 7 6	1069	Madeira	P	14 6 5	1072
Bendinat	E	13 6 7	1130	Maspalomas	E	16 7 8	1180
Biarritz-le-Phare	F	14 6 8	235	Mediterraneo	E	16 7 6	1181
Bonalba	E	14 6 6	1131	Médoc *Les Châteaux*	F	18 7 5	302
Bretesche (La)	F	15 7 7	243	Médoc *Les Vignes*	F	15 7 5	303
Campoamor	E	14 6 6	1133	Moliets	F	17 6 5	304
Cannes Mandelieu				Montado	P	13 7 6	1073
Old Course	F	14 7 8	245	Montenmedio	E	15 7 7	1186
Cannes-Mougins	F	15 7 8	246	Montpellier-Massane	F	16 7 5	306
Canyamel	E	15 6 6	1134	Oliva Nova	E	14 6 7	1189
Cap d'Agde	F	15 6 5	247	Palheiro	P	13 6 7	1074
Capdepera	E	15 7 6	1135	Palmares	P	13 7 5	1075
Chiberta	F	16 6 8	259	Pals	E	16 7 6	1192
Cosmopolitan	I	14 6 7	968	Penha Longa	P	17 6 8	1076
Costa Dorada	E	13 6 6	1140	Penina	P	14 7 7	1077
Dieppe-Pourville	F	14 6 5	263	Peralada	E	16 6 5	1195
El Bosque	E	16 7 4	1141	Pevero	I	16 8 8	994
El Saler	E	18 7 6	1144	PGA de Catalunya	E	18 7 7	1196
Escorpion	E	13 8 4	1146	Pineda	E	15 7 9	1197
Estérel Latitudes	F	16 6 7	269	Pinheiros Altos	P	14 7 7	1078
Estoril	P	13 7 7	1070	Ploemeur Océan	F	15 7 6	317
Etretat	F	14 6 5	271	Praia d'El Rey	P	17 6 5	1079
Garlenda	I	14 7 8	973	Pula	E	13 6 5	1201
Golden Eagle	P	15 4 4	1071	Punta Ala	I	14 7 8	996
Golf d'Aro	E	15 7 7	1150	Quinta da Beloura	P	14 8 7	1080
Golf del *Sur*	E	16 7 8	1151	Quinta da Marinha	P	13 7 7	1081
Grande Bastide (La)	F	16 6 6	281	Quinta do Lago *B/C*	P	15 7 8	1082
Granville *Les Dunes*	F	14 4 4	283	Quinta do Lago			
Hardelot *Les Pins*	F	16 6 6	287	*Ria Formosa*	P	15 7 8	1083
Hossegor	F	16 6 6	289	Quinta do Peru	P	15 6 5	1084
Is Molas	I	16 7 8	975	Rapallo	I	13 7 8	997
La Manga *Norte*	E	15 7 7	1162	Riva dei Tessali	I	13 7 6	998
La Manga *Oeste*	E	14 7 7	1163	Riviéra Golf Club	F	13 7 8	324

69

RECOMMENDED SAISONS

Seasons Golf course	Country	Score	Page
1 2 3 4 5 6 7 8 9 10 11 12			
Roma - Acquasanta	I	16 8 9	999
Royal Mougins	F	17 7 8	327
S. Lourenço	P	18 6 8	1085
Saint Donat	F	15 7 8	329
Saint-Jean-de-Monts	F	16 6 5	333
Saint-Laurent	F	14 7 5	334
Saint-Thomas	F	14 7 5	337
Salgados	P	14 7 6	1086
San Roque	E	17 8 6	1203
Santa Ponsa	E	13 6 7	1206
Savenay	F	14 5 4	340
Seignosse	F	17 7 7	341
Son Vida	E	14 6 7	1208
Sotogrande	E	18 7 6	1209
Torremirona	E	13 7 7	1210
Touquet (Le) *La Mer*	F	17 6 7	349
Troia	P	15 6 5	1087
Val Queven	F	15 6 5	352
Valderrama	E	19 8 6	1213
Vale da Pinta	P	14 6 6	1088
Vale do Lobo			
Royal Golf Course	P	15 6 7	1089
Vila Sol	14	7 71090	P
Vilamoura			
Vilamoura I (Old Course)	P	16 7 7	1091
Vilamoura			
Vilamoura II (Pinhal)	P	13 7 7	1092
Vilamoura			
Vilamoura III (Laguna)	P	14 7 7	1093
Villamartin	E	16 7 6	1214
Wimereux	F	14 4 5	357

Seasons Golf course	Country	Score	Page
1 2 3 4 5 6 7 8 9 10 11 12			
Costa Brava	E	13 7 7	1139
El Prat *Amarillo*	E	15 7 6	1142
El Prat *Verde*	E	17 7 6	1143
Girona	E	13 7 5	1149
Nîmes-Campagne	F	16 7 6	309
Novo Sancti Petri	E	16 7 7	1188
Sant Cugat	E	13 6 5	1205

Seasons Golf course	Country	Score	Page
1 2 3 4 5 6 7 8 9 10 11 12			
Alhaurin	E	14 7 5	1124
Almenara	E	13 8 8	1125
Almerimar	E	14 6 6	1126
Aloha	E	17 7 7	1127
Atalaya *Old Course*	E	13 6 7	1129
Estepona	E	14 7 6	1147

70

Seasons Golf course	Country	Score	Page
1 2 3 4 5 6 7 8 9 10 11 12			
Guadalmina *Sur*	E	14 7 7	1154
La Cala *Norte*	E	17 8 6	1158
La Cala *Sur*	E	16 8 6	1159
Málaga	E	13 4 6	1177
Marbella	E	15 7 8	1178
Mijas *Los Lagos*	E	16 6 7	1182
Mijas *Los Olivos*	E	13 6 7	1183
Olgiata	I	16 7 6	990

Seasons Golf course	Country	Score	Page
1 2 3 4 5 6 7 8 9 10 11 12			
Karlstad	S	15 6 6	1257

Seasons Golf course	Country	Score	Page
1 2 3 4 5 6 7 8 9 10 11 12			
Albarella	I	14 8 7	954
Franciacorta	I	15 7 8	971
Gardagolf	I	14 7 8	972
Le Querce	I	17 8 7	980
Lignano	I	14 7 7	982
Palazzo Arzaga	I	15 8 8	992
Pornic	F	15 6 6	320
Venezia	I	16 7 9	1003

Seasons Golf course	Country	Score	Page
1 2 3 4 5 6 7 8 9 10 11 12			
Aisses (Les) *Rouge/Blanc*	F	16 5 4	215
Barbaroux	F	17 7 6	229
Belle-Dune	F	16 6 5	232
Bonmont	E	16 7 6	1132
Chantaco	F	14 7 7	254
Club de Campo	E	16 8 8	1138
Emporda	E	17 7 6	1145
Gujan-Mestras	F	15 7 6	286
Hayling	Eng	16 7 7	580
Mazamet-La Barouge	F	13 5 4	301
Opio Valbonne	F	13 6 7	311
Royal Zoute	B	18 7 7	121
Saint-Endréol	F	15 7 4	331
Sainte-Maxime	F	13 7 7	339
San Sebastián	E	14 6 6	1204
Spérone	F	17 7 5	344

Seasons Golf course	Country	Score	Page
1 2 3 4 5 6 7 8 9 10 11 12			
Alcaidesa	E	14 6 5	1123
Aldeburgh	Eng	13 6 7	522
Castelgandolfo	I	15 7 7	964
Guadalhorce	E	14 7 6	1153
Islantilla	E	16 8 8	1156
La Duquesa	E	13 7 6	1161
La Quinta	E	15 8 7	1167

Europe

Seasons Golf course	Country	Score		Page
1 2 3 4 5 6 7 8 9 10 11 12				
La Zagaleta	E	16	7 7	1169
Las Brisas	E	18	7 7	1171
Lauro	E	13	7 5	1173
Los Arqueros	E	14	6 7	1175
Los Naranjos	E	16	7 7	1176
Marco Simone	I	16	8 8	983
Monte Mayor	E	13	5 5	1184
Montecastillo	E	17	8 7	1185
Panoramica	E	14	6 4	1193
Parco de' Medici	I	13	7 9	993
Playa Serena	E	13	6 4	1198
Sevilla	E	17	7 8	1207
Torrequebrada	E	14	7 7	1211
Zaudin	E	16	7 6	1215
1 2 3 4 5 6 7 8 9 10 11 12				
Arcangues	F	14	7 8	224
Asolo	I	13	7 7	956
Baden	F	15	6 5	227
Bergamo - L'Albenza				
Blu + Giallo	I	15	7 8	958
Berkshire (The) Blue Course	Eng	17	8 7	529
Berkshire (The) Red Course	Eng	17	8 7	530
Bordes (Les)	F	19	8 6	239
Buckinghamshire (The)	Eng	17	8 7	540
Ca' della Nave	I	13	6 8	962
Casteljaloux	F	14	6 5	248
Castello di Tolcinasco	I	15	8 8	965
1 2 3 4 5 6 7 8 9 10 11 12				
Castillo de Gorraiz	E	17	7 7	1136
Cély	F	15	7 6	249
Cervia	I	13	6 9	966
Champ de Bataille	F	14	6 3	253
Chantilly Vineuil	F	18	7 6	255
Charleville	I	13	4 6	851
Chart Hills	Eng	18	8 6	550
Cork GC	I	15	3 5	854
County Louth	I	18	5 6	855
County Sligo	I	17	4 3	856
Denham	Eng	15	7 7	558
Dinard	F	13	6 7	264
East Sussex National				
East Course	Eng	17	8 7	560
Etiolles Les Cerfs	F	15	6 5	270
European (The)	I	18	5 6	867
Ferndown Old Course	Eng	17	7 7	564
Firenze - Ugolino	I	14	8 9	969

Seasons Golf course	Country	Score		Page
1 2 3 4 5 6 7 8 9 10 11 12				
Fontainebleau	F	17	7 7	274
Frégate	F	15	7 7	278
Gog Magog Old Course	Eng	15	7 8	574
Gouverneur (Le) Le Breuil	F	16	7 6	279
Gouverneur (Le) Montaplan	F	14	7 6	280
Grande-Motte (La)				
Les Flamants Roses	F	16	6 4	282
Henley	Eng	14	6 7	581
Hermitage	I	15	6 7	876
Hubbelrath	D	17	8 6	425
Jarama R.A.C.E.	E	13	7 6	1157
La Dehesa	E	14	7 4	1160
La Margherita	I	13	7 7	976
La Moraleja La Moraleja 1	E	15	7 8	1165
La Moraleja La Moraleja 2	E	16	7 8	1166
La Pinetina	I	13	7 7	977
La Rocca	I	13	6 8	978
Le Pavoniere	I	14	8 8	979
Le Robinie	I	16	9 7	981
Limère	F	17	6 5	298
Littlestone	14	6	5598	Eng
Makila Golf Club	F	14	6 8	300
Milano	I	16	8 9	985
Modena	I	14	7 8	986
Molinetto	I	13	9 8	987
Monte Carlo (Mont Agel)	F	14	6 7	305
Montecchia	I	13	8 7	988
Monticello	I	14	8 7	989
National L'Albatros	F	18	5 6	307
Neguri	E	17	7 7	1187
Newbury & Crookham	Eng	15	6 7	611
North Foreland	Eng	13	7 7	612
Olivar de la Hinojosa	E	13	7 8	1190
Oostende	B	15	7 7	114
Osona Montanya	E	14	7 4	1191
Parkstone	Eng	16	7 8	618
Pau	F	13	6 8	314
Pedreña	E	14	6 5	1194
Perranporth	Eng	16	6 6	620
Poggio dei Medici	I	16	7 7	995
Pont Royal	F	16	6 5	318
Portmarnock	I	19	7 8	894
Portmarnock Links	I	17	7 8	895
Prince's Himalayas-Shore	Eng	13	6 4	625
Puerta de Hierro				
Puerta de Hierro 1	E	16	8 9	1199
Puerta de Hierro				
Puerta de Hierro 2	E	18	8 9	1200

71

RECOMMENDED SEASONS

Seasons Golf course	Country	Score			Page
1 2 3 4 5 6 7 8 9 10 11 12					
Ravenstein	B	17	8	7	117
Rebetz	F	16	6	4	322
Rochefort-Chisan	F	14	6	4	325
Rosslare	I	13	5	6	900
Royal County Down	UL	19	6	7	934
Royal Dublin	I	16	8	7	901
Royal St George's	19	7	5638		Eng
Royal Wimbledon	16	7	8640		Eng
Sainte-Baume (La)	F	13	7	6	338
Servanes	F	13	7	7	342
Stoke Poges	Eng	17	8	8	659
Sunningdale *New Course*	Eng	18	8	8	661
Sunningdale *Old Course*	Eng	18	8	8	662
Swinley Forest	Eng	16	6	8	663
The Island	I	15	7	7	907
Thorndon Park	Eng	14	7	6	669
Thorpeness	Eng	14	7	7	670
Toulouse Palmola	F	15	7	4	347
Varese	I	14	8	7	1002
Verona	I	13	7	8	1004
Villa D'Este	I	16	8	9	1005
Walton Heath *New Course*	Eng	16	7	6	674
Walton Heath *Old Course*	Eng	18	7	7	675
West Berkshire	Eng	15	7	7	679
West Hill	Eng	15	6	6	682
Woking	Eng	16	6	6	691
Woodbridge	Eng	14	7	7	692
Worplesdon	Eng	16	7	6	695
1 2 3 4 5 6 7 8 9 10 11 12					
Gloria Golf Resort	T	13	7	7	1317
National GC	T	15	7	7	1318
Nobilis	T	17	8	6	1319
TAT Golf Belek	T	14	7	7	1320
1 2 3 4 5 6 7 8 9 10 11 12					
Granada	E	14	6	5	1152
1 2 3 4 5 6 7 8 9 10 11 12					
Annonay-Gourdan	F	13	6	5	221
Barlassina	I	15	8	8	957
Brigode	F	14	7	6	244
Bude & North Cornwall	Eng	15	6	5	541
Caldy	Eng	17	7	7	543
Castlerock	UL	16	6	6	925
Cherasco	I	13	7	7	967
Cognac	F	13	7	5	260
Dartmouth	Eng	16	9	6	556

Seasons Golf course	Country	Score			Page
1 2 3 4 5 6 7 8 9 10 11 12					
Dingle (Ceann Sibeal)	I	16	6	4	859
East Devon	Eng	16	6	7	559
Elie	Sc	15	6	6	730
Falmouth	Eng	14	6	7	562
Goes	N	15	7	6	1022
Greenore	I	14	6	5	875
Gullane *No 1*	Sc	17	8	7	740
Haagsche	N	18	7	8	1025
Hainaut					
Bruyere-Quesnoy-Etangs	B	15	7	5	110
Huddersfield (Fixby)	Eng	16	6	7	587
Isle of Purbeck	Eng	16	7	6	592
Lisburn	UL	15	7	6	929
Luttrellstown	I	15	7	7	886
Masia Bach	E	15	7	6	1179
Mullion	Eng	15	5	5	610
New Golf Deauville					
Rouge/Blanc	F	15	7	8	308
Noordwijk	N	18	7	8	1032
Nunspeet *North/East*	N	15	5	3	1033
Orchardleigh	Eng	17	7	7	615
Pessac	F	13	7	7	315
Portstewart Strand Course	UL	16	7	7	932
Royal Guernsey	Eng	16	7	7	632
Royal Portrush *Dunluce Links*	UL	19	7	7	935
Royal Portrush Valley	UL	13	7	7	936
Saunton *East Course*	Eng	18	7	6	645
Shannon	I	13	6	6	903
Thurlestone	Eng	16	6	4	671
Tullamore	I	15	6	5	911
Turnberry *Ailsa Course*	Sc	19	9	8	792
Turnberry *Arran Course*	Sc	16	9	8	793
Waterford Castle	I	14	5	6	913
West Byfleet	Eng	14	6	8	680
Woodbury Park *The Oaks*	Eng	15	9	6	693
1 2 3 4 5 6 7 8 9 10 11 12					
Ambrosiano	I	14	7	7	955
Badgemore Park	Eng	14	7	7	525
Ballybunion Cashen					
(*New Course*)	I	16	7	7	838
Ballybunion *Old Course*	I	19	7	7	839
Ballyliffin *Glashedy Links*	I	17	6	5	841
1 2 3 4 5 6 7 8 9 10 11 12					
Ballyliffin *Old Course*	I	15	6	5	842
Beaufort	I	14	6	7	843
Blainroe	I	13	6	6	845

72

Seasons Golf course	Country	Score			Page
`1 2 3 4 5 6 7 8 9 10 11 12`					
Bogogno	I	17	8	7	960
Bologna	I	13	7	7	961
Burnham & Berrow	Eng	18	7	6	542
Camberley Heath	Eng	16	6	6	544
Delamere Forest	Eng	15	6	7	557
Domtal-Mommenheim	D	14	7	7	399
Dooks	I	15	5	5	861
Dromoland Castle	I	14	7	7	862
Druids Glen	I	16	9	7	863
Elfrather Mühle	D	14	7	7	401
Enniscrone	I	16	7	6	866
Fontanals	E	18	6	5	1148
Frankfurter GC	D	17	7	8	406
Galway Bay	I	14	7	6	870
Galway GC	I	13	6	6	871
Grasse	F	13	7	6	284
Gut Waldhof	D	15	7	5	415
Hamburg-Ahrensburg	D	16	8	7	417
Hanau-Wilhelmsbad	D	16	6	6	419
Hankley Common	Eng	16	6	6	577
Herreria	E	15	6	6	1155
Hertfordshire (The)	Eng	15	7	7	582
Hever	Eng	14	8	8	583
Hindhead	Eng	16	7	6	586
Hof Trages	D	15	7	5	423
Huntercombe	Eng	14	6	7	589
I Roveri	I	17	7	8	974
Ipswich (Purdis Heath)	Eng	16	7	7	591
Isle Adam (L')	F	16	7	4	290
Jakobsberg	D	15	7	6	429
La Moye	Eng	17	7	8	594
Lahinch	I	18	6	6	883
Lausanne	CH	16	7	7	1300
Lerma	E	17	7	4	1174
Lugano	CH	15	7	8	1302
Margara	I	13	7	7	984
Mere	Eng	15	7	7	606
Moor Park *High Course*	Eng	17	8	7	608
Muirfield	Sc	19	7	6	759
Mülheim	D	13	6	7	442
München-Riedhof	D	16	7	7	443
Münchner-Strasslach	D	15	6	7	444
Neuhof	D	15	7	7	447
Newcastle West	I	13	7	5	892
Ormskirk	Eng	14	6	4	616
Padova	I	14	7	7	991
Portsalon	I	16	5	5	896
Rathsallagh	I	15	7	6	898

Seasons Golf course	Country	Score			Page
`1 2 3 4 5 6 7 8 9 10 11 12`					
Roxburghe (The)	Sc	15	7	7	773
Royal Ashdown Forest	Eng	14	7	6	628
Royal Cinque Ports	Eng	17	6	5	630
Royal Latem	B	15	8	6	120
Royal Mid-Surrey *Outer*	Eng	14	7	8	636
Saint-Germain	F	17	7	7	332
Seacroft	Eng	17	6	4	646
Seapoint	I	15	6	6	902
Sherborne	Eng	15	6	7	650
Southerness	Sc	18	6	5	781
St George's Hill	Eng	17	7	7	657
St Helen's Bay	I	14	6	6	905
Stuttgarter Solitude	D	17	5	5	474
Tandridge	Eng	14	7	6	664
Torino - La Mandria					
Percorso Blu	I	16	8	8	1001
Toulouse-Seilh *Rouge*	F	15	7	6	348
Tralee	I	18	7	6	908
Tramore	I	13	7	6	909
Ulzama	E	16	6	6	1212
Villette d'Anthon *Les Sangliers*	F	17	6	4	354
Walddörfer	D	16	7	6	479
Waterloo *La Marache*	B	16	8	7	125
Waterville	I	17	6	7	914
Wentorf-Reinbeker	D	15	7	6	482
West Surrey	Eng	15	7	7	684
West Sussex	Eng	18	7	6	685
Weston-Super-Mare	Eng	16	6	7	686
Woburn *Dukes Course*	Eng	18	7	7	690

`1 2 3 4 5 6 7 8 9 10 11 12`					
Aberdovey	W	17	7	7	799
Ailette (L')	F	15	6	5	214
Aix-les-Bains	F	13	5	7	216
Alloa	Sc	15	7	6	699
Alwoodley (The)	Eng	18	7	7	523
Alyth	Sc	14	6	6	700
Amirauté (L')	F	14	7	8	218
Anderstein	N	14	7	6	1013
Anjou-Champigné	F	13	6	6	220
Antwerp	B	16	7	7	107
Apremont	F	15	8	6	222
Ardglass	UL	14	6	4	920
Ashburnham	W	17	6	5	800
Ashridge	Eng	16	7	6	524
Asserbo	Da	15	7	6	133

73

Seasons Golf course	Country	Score	Page		Seasons Golf course	Country	Score	Page
`1 2 3 4 5 6 7 8 9 10 11 12`					Cardigan	W	15 6 5	802
Athlone I	13	6 6	837		Cardross	Sc	14 6 5	713
Augerville	F	13 5 4	226		Carlow	I	16 6 6	847
Augsburg	D	15 7 7	383		Carmarthen	W	15 7 4	803
Ayr (Belleisle)	Sc	16 5 7	701		Carn	I	16 5 3	848
Bad Abbach-Deutenhof	D	15 7 7	384		Carnoustie *Burnside*	Sc	14 5 6	714
Bad Ragaz	CH	13 7 6	1290		Carnoustie *Championship*	Sc	19 5 6	715
Ballykisteen	I	14 7 6	840		Castelconturbia			
Bamberg	D	15 7 7	390		*Giallo + Azzurro*	I	18 8 7	963
Bangor	UL	14 6 6	921		Castle Hume	UL	13 7 6	924
Bath	Eng	16 6 9	526		Celtic Manor *Roman Road*	W	18 9 7	804
Batouwe	N	15 7 3	1014		Charmeil	F	16 6 6	256
Beau Desert	Eng	16 7 7	527		Clandeboye *Dufferin Course*	UL	15 6 6	926
Bélesbat	F	14 7 7	231		Clitheroe	Eng	17 7 7	552
Bercuit	B	13 7 7	108		Club zur Vahr (Garlstedt)	D	18 6 5	398
Bergisch Land Wuppertal	D	16 7 7	391		Collingtree Park	Eng	14 8 7	553
Berkhamsted	Eng	16 7 6	528		Connemara	I	14 6 6	853
Berlin-Wannsee	D	16 8 9	392		Conwy	W	17 7 8	805
Béthemont	F	14 7 5	234		County Tipperary	I	15 7 5	857
Beuerberg	D	17 7 6	393		Courson *Lilas/Orange*	F	15 7 3	261
Biella - Le Betulle	I	18 7 7	959		Courson *Vert/Noir*	F	16 7 3	262
Bitburger Land	D	15 7 8	394		Crail	Sc	15 6 6	716
Bitche	F	14 6 5	236		Crieff *Ferntower Course*	Sc	15 7 7	717
Blackmoor	Eng	17 6 5	532		Cromstrijen	N	16 8 5	1016
Blairgowrie *Lansdowne*	Sc	15 8 6	705		Cruden Bay	Sc	18 7 6	718
Blairgowrie *Rosemount*	Sc	18 8 6	706		Cumberwell Park	Eng	17 7 7	555
Bodensee-Weissensberg	D	16 7 7	395		Dalmahoy *East Course*	Sc	17 8 8	719
Bolton *Old Links*	Eng	15 5 7	533		De Pan	N	16 8 7	1017
Bondues *Blanc*	F	16 7 6	237		Disneyland Paris *Never Land*			
Bondues *la vallée*	F	15 7 6	238		+ *Wonderland*	F	16 7 8	265
Boulie (La) *La Vallée*	F	15 7 8	240		Domaine Impérial	CH	18 8 6	1294
Bowood (Cornwall)	Eng	16 7 6	534		Domont-Montmorency	F	13 7 4	267
Bowood G&CC	Eng	17 6 6	535		Donegal (Murvagh)	I	16 5 6	860
Brampton	Eng	17 7 6	536		Duff House Royal	Sc	15 6 6	722
Brancepeth Castle	Eng	14 6 5	537		Duke's Course St Andrews	Sc	16 7 8	723
Brest Iroise	F	14 7 6	242		Dumfries & County	Sc	15 7 5	724
Broadstone	Eng	17 7 7	538		Dunbar	Sc	16 5 6	725
Broekpolder	N	15 7 6	1015		Dundalk	I	15 6 6	864
Brokenhurst Manor	Eng	15 6 6	539		Düsseldorfer	D	15 7 7	400
Bruntsfield	Sc	15 8 9	709		Efteling	N	16 8 5	1018
Buchanan Castle	Sc	14 6 6	710		Eindhoven	N	18 8 6	1019
Bundoran	I	13 6 7	846		Elm Park	I	13 7 8	865
Burntisland	Sc	14 6 6	711		Ennetsee-Holzhäusern	CH	13 7 6	1296
Buxtehude	D	16 7 6	397		Eschenried	D	14 7 7	402
Cairndhu	UL	13 6 5	923		Esery	F	15 7 5	268
Came Down	Eng	15 5 6	545		Essener Oefte	D	15 8 7	403
Carden Park *Cheshire Course*	Eng	14 8 8	546		Fairhaven	Eng	17 7 8	561
Carden Park *Nicklaus Course*	Eng	17 8 8	547		Faithlegg	I	13 7 6	868
Cardiff	W	14 6 8	801		Falkenstein	D	18 6 7	404

74

Europe

Seasons Golf course	Country	Score	Page	Seasons Golf course	Country	Score	Page
`1 2 3 4 5 6 7 8 9 10 11 12`				Hillside	Eng	18 7 7	585
Falkirk Tryst	Sc	13 6 6	731	Hilversum	N	16 7 7	1027
Falnuee	B	14 7 4	109	Himmerland *New Course*	Da	16 8 6	137
Falsterbo	S	18 7 5	1242	Hoge Kleij	N	15 6 7	1028
Fanø	Da	15 4 7	135	Holyhead	W	16 7 5	807
Felixstowe Ferry				Hunstanton	Eng	17 7 6	588
Martello Course	Eng	15 6 6	563	Ilkley	Eng	18 7 6	590
Feucherolles	F	15 7 5	273	John O'Gaunt	Eng	16 7 6	593
Filey	Eng	13 5 5	565	K Club	I	17 8 8	877
Fontcaude	F	14 6 6	275	Keerbergen	B	14 7 6	111
Fontenailles *Blanc*	F	14 7 6	276	Kempferhof (Le)	F	18 8 6	293
Fontenelles (Les)	F	14 7 4	277	Kennemer	N	18 8 8	1030
Forest of Arden *Arden Course*	Eng	14 8 8	566	Kikuoka	LU	16 7 7	128
Formby	Eng	18 7 7	568	Kilkea Castle	I	14 6 6	878
Formby Hall	Eng	14 8 6	569	Kilkenny	I	13 7 6	879
Fortrose & Rosemarkie	Sc	16 6 5	733	Killorglin	I	14 6 5	882
Fota Island	I	15 7 6	869	Kilmarnock (Barassie)	Sc	17 6 8	744
Frilford Heath *Red Course*	Eng	14 7 7	570	Kirkistown Castle	UL	15 6 5	927
Fürstlicher GC Bad Waldsee	D	17 7 8	408	Knock	UL	15 7 6	928
Fürstliches Hofgut Kolnhausen	D	14 7 6	409	Köln	D	17 6 7	430
Ganton	Eng	19 8 5	573	Krefelder	D	17 7 7	432
Gelpenberg	N	14 4 5	1020	Ladybank	Sc	17 7 5	746
Gendersteyn	N	15 7 7	1021	Lanark	Sc	16 6 5	747
Genève	CH	17 7 8	1297	Langland Bay	W	15 7 7	808
Glamorganshire	W	14 7 8	806	Lauswolt	N	14 6 7	1031
Glasson	I	16 7 7	872	Le Prieuré *Ouest*	F	14 7 5	297
Glen	Sc	14 7 7	734	Lee Valley	I	13 7 6	884
Glen of the Downs	I	13 4 7	873	Letham Grange			
Gleneagles King's	Sc	18 9 7	735	*Old Course*	Sc	15 7 5	748
Gleneagles *Monarch's*	Sc	17 9 7	736	Leven	Sc	16 6 6	749
Gleneagles Queen's	Sc	15 9 7	737	Lichtenau-Weickershof	D	15 7 6	433
Golspie	Sc	14 5 4	738	Limburg	B	16 7 4	112
Göteborg	S	15 6 7	1249	Limerick County	I	15 7 6	885
Graafschap	N	15 7 6	1023	Lindau-Bad Schachen	D	15 7 8	434
Grenoble Bresson	F	17 7 6	285	Lindrick	Eng	17 6 6	596
Grevelingenhout	N	14 7 4	1024	Liphook	Eng	16 7 6	597
Gut Kaden *Platz B + Platz C*	D	15 7 6	411	Llandudno (Maesdu)	W	15 5 8	809
Gut Lärchenhof	D	17 9 7	412	Llanymynech	W	14 6 4	810
Gut Thailing	D	16 7 5	414	London Golf Club			
Gütersloh (Westfälischer GC)	D	17 7 7	416	*International*	Eng	15 9 7	599
Hadley Wood	Eng	16 7 7	575	Longniddry	Sc	14 7 6	750
Hallamshire	Eng	15 6 8	576	Lübeck-Travemünder	D	15 8 8	435
Hamburg-Holm	D	15 6 6	418	Luffness New	Sc	16 5 6	752
Hannover	D	16 7 7	420	Lundin	Sc	16 6 7	753
Haut-Poitou	F	14 6 4	288	Lyckorna	S	13 7 6	1263
Hawkstone Park *Hawkstone*	Eng	15 8 7	579	Lytham Green Drive	Eng	15 7 8	600
Hechingen-Hohenzollern	D	14 6 6	421	Machrie	Sc	17 7 7	754
Hetzenhof	D	14 7 6	422	Machrihanish	Sc	18 6 4	755
High Post	Eng	15 6 7	584	Main-Taunus	D	14 7 6	437

75

Seasons Golf course	Country	Score	Page
1 2 3 4 5 6 7 8 9 10 11 12			
Malahide			
Red + Blue + Yellow	I	13 7 8	887
Malone	UL	13 6 6	930
Manchester	Eng	16 7 7	601
Mannings Heath			
Waterfall Course	Eng	14 8 6	602
Manor House (Castle Combe)	Eng	15 8 7	603
Marriott St Pierre *Old Course*	W	16 8 7	811
Mendip	Eng	15 5 7	604
Mittelrheinischer	D	17 7 7	440
Monifieth	Sc	17 7 7	756
Monkstown	I	15 6 7	888
Mont-Garni	B	13 7 6	113
Montreux	Ch	13 6 5	1304
Montrose	Sc	17 5 6	757
Moor Allerton	Eng	14 6 7	607
Moray	Sc	17 5 5	758
Motzener See	D	17 8 6	441
Mount Juliet	I	18 9 8	889
Mount Wolsley	I	13 6 5	890
Mullingar	I	14 5 5	891
Murcar	Sc	15 6 6	760
Murrayshall	Sc	14 7 8	761
Nahetal	D	14 8 6	445
Nairn	Sc	19 7 8	762
Nairn Dunbar	Sc	15 6 7	763
Neckartal	D	16 6 7	446
Nefyn & District	W	16 7 5	812
Newport	W	15 6 7	813
North Berwick	Sc	18 7 8	765
North Hants	Eng	17 7 6	613
North Wales (Llandudno)	W	17 6 8	814
Northop Country Park	W	16 9 6	815
Notts (Hollinwell)	Eng	18 6 6	614
Oberschwaben Bad Waldsee	D	15 6 6	450
Omaha Beach			
La Mer/Le Bocage	F	14 7 5	310
Oosterhout	N	15 7 7	1034
Öschberghof	D	15 7 7	451
Oudenaarde	B	14 6 6	115
Ozoir-la-Ferrière			
Château/Monthéty	F	13 7 5	312
Palingbeek	B	13 6 6	116
Paris International	F	16 7 5	313
Patriziale Ascona	CH	15 7 7	1307
Patshull Park Hotel	Eng	13 8 8	619
Pennard	18	6	6816 W
Peterhead	15	5	4767 Sc

Seasons Golf course	Country	Score	Page
1 2 3 4 5 6 7 8 9 10 11 12			
Pinnau	14	6	6452 D
Pitlochry	Sc	14 6 7	768
Pleasington	Eng	16 8 6	621
Pléneuf-Val-André	F	17 7 5	316
Porcelaine (La)	F	14 6 4	319
Portal *Championship*	Eng	15 8 7	622
Porters Park	Eng	15 7 7	623
Portpatrick (Dunskey)	Sc	15 6 7	769
Powfoot	Sc	16 6 4	770
Prestbury	Eng	17 8 7	624
Prestwick	Sc	18 6 7	771
Prestwick St Nicholas	Sc	16 6 7	772
Purmerend	N	16 7 7	1035
Pyle & Kenfig	W	17 7 5	817
Real Sociedad			
Club de Campo	E	18 7 6	1202
Reichswald-Nürmberg	D	16 7 7	454
Reims-Champagne	F	13 7 6	323
Rheinhessen	D	14 8 7	455
Rigenée	B	14 7 6	118
Rijk van Nijmegen			
Rijk van Nijmegen	N	14 6 5	1036
Rinkven *Red - White*	B	14 6 5	119
Rochester & Cobham	Eng	14 6 6	626
Rolls of Monmouth (The)	W	15 6 6	818
Roncemay	F	15 7 7	326
Rosapenna	I	16 7 6	899
Rosendael	N	15 7 7	1037
Royal Belfast	UL	15 7 7	933
Royal Birkdale (The)	Eng	19 9 7	629
Royal Burgess	Sc	16 7 9	775
Royal Cromer	Eng	15 7 6	631
Royal Dornoch *Championship*	Sc	19 7 7	776
Royal Jersey	Eng	16 7 8	633
Royal Liverpool (Hoylake)	Eng	18 8 7	634
Royal Lytham & St Anne's	Eng	19 7 8	635
Royal Musselburgh	Sc	16 8 7	777
Royal North Devon			
(Westward Ho!)	Eng	18 6 6	637
Royal Porthcawl	W	19 7 6	819
Royal St David's	W	18 6 5	820
Royal Troon *Old Course*	Sc	19 7 7	778
Royal West Norfolk			
(Brancaster)	Eng	17 7 6	639
Royal Winchester	Eng	15 6 8	641
Rungsted	Da	17 7 7	143
Rya	S	15 7 8	1268
Sablé-Solesmes			

76

Seasons Golf course	Country	Score	Page
1 2 3 4 5 6 7 8 9 10 11 12			
La Forêt/La Rivière	F	16 7 4	328
Saint-Cloud *Vert*	F	14 7 7	330
Saint-Nom-la-Bretèche *Bleu*	F	15 8 8	335
Saint-Nom-la-Bretèche *Rouge*	F	16 8 8	336
Samsø	Da	15 4 7	144
Sand Moor	Eng	14 7 7	643
Sandiway	Eng	17 5 7	644
Sart-Tilman	B	16 7 7	122
Scharmützelsee			
Arnold Palmer	D	17 8 7	456
Scharmützelsee *Nick Faldo*	D	18 8 7	457
Schloss Braunfels	D	16 7 7	458
Schloss Egmating	D	15 7 7	459
Schloss Klingenburg	D	15 6 6	460
Schloss Liebenstein			
Gelb + Blau	D	16 8 7	462
Schloss Wilkendorf	D	17 7 5	466
Scotscraig	Sc	16 6 6	779
Sct. Knuds	Da	14 5 6	145
Seascale	Eng	18 5 4	647
Seaton Carew	Eng	17 7 5	648
Seddiner See *Südplatz*	D	18 9 7	467
Sheringham	Eng	15 7 6	651
Simon's	Da	14 7 7	146
Slieve Russell	I	15 8 6	904
Soufflenheim	F	16 7 4	343
Southerndown	W	16 7 7	821
Southport & Ainsdale	Eng	18 7 7	655
Spa (Les Fagnes)	B	17 7 7	123
Spiegelven	B	14 7 8	124
St Andrews *Eden Course*	Sc	14 8 8	782
St Andrews *Jubilee Course*	Sc	16 8 8	783
St Andrews *New Course*	Sc	17 8 8	784
St Andrews *Old Course*	Sc	18 8 8	785
St Enodoc *Church Course*	Eng	18 7 4	656
St Margaret's	I	16 7 7	906
St Mellion *Nicklaus Course*	Eng	17 9 7	658
St. Dionys	D	17 7 6	470
St. Leon-Rot	D	15 8 6	472
Stolper Heide	D	16 7 5	473
Stoneham	Eng	15 7 8	660
Strasbourg Illkirch			
Jaune + Rouge	F	13 7 6	345
Sybrook	N	15 6 6	1039
Sylt	D	15 6 8	475
Tain	Sc	17 6 6	789
Tehidy Park	13	7 6665	Eng
Tenby	W	18 7 6	822

Seasons Golf course	Country	Score	Page
1 2 3 4 5 6 7 8 9 10 11 12			
The Belfry *Brabazon*	Eng	15 9 8	666
The Belfry *PGA National*	Eng	15 9 8	667
Thetford	Eng	14 7 5	668
Thornhill	Sc	15 6 5	791
Touraine	F	13 7 6	350
Toxandria	N	14 7 6	1040
Treudelberg	D	13 8 7	477
Trevose Championship	Eng	17 7 7	672
Tulfarris	I	14 7 6	910
Twente	N	15 7 6	1041
Vale of Glamorgan	W	16 8 7	823
Vaucouleurs (La) *Les Vallons*	F	15 7 4	353
Vejle *Blue + Red Slings*	Da	15 7 7	147
Volcans (Les)	F	14 6 5	355
Wallasey	Eng	17 7 7	673
Wantzenau (La)	F	16 6 6	356
Warrenpoint	UL	13 6 5	937
Warwickshire (The)	Eng	15 7 8	676
Wasserburg Anholt	D	15 7 7	480
Waterford	I	14 6 6	912
Wendlohe *A-Kurs + B-Kurs*	D	16 7 6	481
Wentworth *East Course*	Eng	16 8 7	677
Wentworth *West Course*	Eng	18 8 7	678
West Cornwall	Eng	16 7 6	681
West Kilbride	Sc	16 7 5	794
West Lancashire	Eng	17 7 7	683
Western Gailes	Sc	17 5 7	795
Westport	I	15 7 7	916
Wheatley	Eng	14 6 6	687
Whitekirk	Sc	15 7 7	797
Whittington Heath	Eng	17 6 7	688
Wien-Freudenau	A	13 7 9	101
Wilmslow	Eng	16 7 6	689
Wittelsbacher	D	16 7 6	483
Woodbrook	I	15 7 6	917
Woodenbridge	I	16 7 6	918
Woodhall Spa	Eng	18 7 8	694
Wouwse Plantage	N	15 7 6	1042
Zuid Limburgse	N	14 7 7	1043
1 2 3 4 5 6 7 8 9 10 11 12			
Barsebäck	S	18 7 6	1231
Båstad *Old Course*	S	16 7 7	1232
Blumisberg	CH	15 7 6	1291
Breitenloo	CH	13 7 6	1292
Castle	I	13 6 8	849
Chesterfield	Eng	13 6 7	551

77

Seasons Golf course	Country	Score	Page
1 2 **3 4 5 6** 7 **8 9 10** 11 12			
Ekerum	S	14 7 7	1237
Elgin	Sc	15 7 6	729
Eslöv	S	14 7 5	1238
Flommen	S	16 7 7	1244
Forest Pines *Forest + Pines*	Eng	17 6 7	567
Fulford	Eng	17 7 8	571
Gainsborough-Karsten Lakes	Eng	14 8 6	572
Gruyère (La)	Ch	14 7 6	1298
Haggs Castle	Sc	15 7 9	741
Kristianstad	S	17 7 7	1258
Ljunghusen	S	17 6 7	1261
Mölle	S	15 7 5	1264
Moortown	Eng	18 7 7	609
Neuchâtel	Ch	14 6 7	1305
Newtonmore	Sc	14 5 5	764
Pannal	Eng	15 6 7	617
Raray (Château de) *La Licorne*	F	14 6 4	321
Ross-on-Wye	Eng	15 5 6	627
Rudding Park	Eng	15 8 8	642
Sherwood Forest	Eng	17 7 6	652
Söderhåsen	S	15 7 5	1271
Torekov	S	14 7 7	1276
Vasatorp	S	16 7 7	1281
Visby	S	16 6 5	1283
Westerwood	Sc	14 8 6	796
Zumikon	CH	15 7 6	1311

Seasons Golf course	Country	Score	Page
1 2 3 **4 5 6 7 8** 9 **10** 11 12			
Abenberg	D	14 7 6	382
Ableiges *Les Etangs*	F	15 6 4	213
Aboyne	Sc	14 6 6	698
Adare	I	15 6 7	836
Amnéville	F	13 6 5	219
Amsterdam	N	15 7 7	1012
Bad Griesbach *Brunnwies*	D	17 9 9	386
Bad Griesbach-Sagmühle *Sagmühle*	D	15 9 9	387
Bad Liebenzell	D	14 7 7	388
Bad Wörishofen	D	14 6 6	389
Banchory	Sc	14 7 7	704
Belvoir Park	UL	15 5 6	922
Bhearna	I	14 7 7	844
Bresse (La)	F	15 6 4	241
Brora	Sc	15 7 7	708
Castletroy	I	14 6 6	850
Cerdaña	E	14 7 7	1137
Chailly (Château de)	F	14 8 6	250
Chambon-sur-Lignon (Le)	F	14 5 7	251

Seasons Golf course	Country	Score	Page
1 2 3 **4 5** 6 7 **8 9 10** 11 12			
Chaumont-en-Vexin	F	14 6 4	257
Cheverny	F	14 7 6	258
Citywest	I	13 6 7	852
Colony Club Gutenhof	A	17 8 7	92
Courtown	I	14 5 5	858
Dachstein Tauern / Schladming	A	15 7 5	93
Divonne	F	14 6 7	266
Donnerskirchen-Neusiedlersee	A	16 6 5	94
Duddingston	Sc	15 7 9	721
East Renfrewshire	Sc	15 6 8	727
Edzell	Sc	14 6 3	728
Esbjerg	Da	15 6 5	134
Europasportregion-Zell am See Schmittenhöhe	A	16 7 6	95
Evian	F	15 7 9	272
Falkenberg	S	14 7 7	1241
Fontana	A	16 8 5	96
Forfar	Sc	14 6 6	732
Furesø	Da	15 7 7	136
Garmisch-Partenkirchen	D	14 6 7	410
Golfresort Haugschlag-Waldviertel	A	16 7 5	97
Grand Ducal de Luxembourg	LU	13 6 7	127
Grange	I	16 5 8	874
Gut Ludwigsberg	D	15 6 6	413
Herkenbosch	N	16 7 6	1026
Hohenpähl	D	15 7 6	424
Holstebro	Da	16 6 5	138
Houtrak	N	16 8 8	1029
Huntly	Sc	14 6 6	742
Iffeldorf	D	16 7 6	426
Im Chiemgau	D	15 7 6	427
Inverness	Sc	16 7 8	743
Isernhagen	D	15 7 6	428
Joyenval *Marly*	F	16 8 7	291
Joyenval *Retz*	F	15 8 7	292
Killarney *Killeen Course*	I	16 7 8	880
Killarney *Mahony's Point*	I	15 7 8	881
Königsfeld	D	13 6 6	431
Korsør	Da	14 4 6	139
Læsø Seaside	Da	15 7 5	140
Les Bois	CH	15 6 6	1301
Linden Hall	Eng	17 8 6	595
Maison Blanche	F	14 7 5	299
Märkischer Potsdam	D	14 7 6	438
Memmingen Gut Westerhart	D	14 6 6	439
Meon Valley *Meon Course*	Eng	15 8 7	605

Europe

Golf course	Country	Score	Page

`1 2 3 4 [5] 6 7 [8] 9 [10] 11 12`

Golf course	Country	Score	Page
Møn	Da	15 7 7	141
Obere Alp	D	14 7 7	448
Oberfranken	D	17 6 5	449
Öijared *Gamla banan*	S	13 7 5	1265
Powerscourt	I	15 7 7	897
Reichsstadt Bad Windsheim	D	14 6 7	453
Royal Aberdeen			
Balgownie Links	Sc	18 7 8	774
Royal Oak	Da	15 7 5	142
Schloss Langenstein	D	16 8 7	461
Schloss Myllendonk	D	16 7 7	464
Schloss Nippenburg	D	17 8 6	465
Semlin am See	D	16 8 7	468
Sempachersee	CH	15 8 7	1309
Shanklin & Sandown	Eng	15 7 6	649
Sint Nicolaasga	N	15 7 5	1038
Slaley Hall	Eng	17 8 7	654
St. Eurach	D	16 7 6	471
Steiermärkischer Murhof	A	16 7 6	100
Stonehaven	Sc	13 5 5	787
Taulane	F	15 7 4	346
Taymouth Castle	Sc	13 4 6	790
Upsala	S	13 6 6	1279
Val de Some	F	14 7 5	351
West Waterford	I	12 7 6	915
Wylihof	CH	13 6 6	1310

`1 2 3 4 [5] 6 7 [8] 9 [10] 11 12`

Golf course	Country	Score	Page
A 6	S	14 7 6	1229
Arendal	Nw	15 7 5	1048
Arras	F	14 6 6	225
Åtvidaberg	S	16 6 5	1230
Aura	Fi	13 5 5	152
Baberton	Sc	14 6 8	702
Bad Bevensen	D	15 5 7	385
Bâle-Hagenthal	F	15 7 7	228
Berwick-upon-Tweed	Eng	15 6 5	531
Besançon	F	13 7 5	233
Boat of Garten	Sc	14 6 7	707
Bokskogen	S	16 6 7	1233
Borre	Nw	16 6 5	1049
Braunschweig	D	14 6 7	396
Bråviken	S	16 7 7	1234
Bro-Bålsta	S	17 7 6	1235
Callander	Sc	13 6 7	712
Carlisle	Eng	17 7 7	548
Castletown	Eng	18 6 8	549
Coxmoor	Eng	15 6 6	554

`1 2 3 4 [5] 6 7 [8] 9 10 11 12`

Golf course	Country	Score	Page
Downfield	Sc	17 6 7	720
Drottningholm	S	14 9 6	1236
Dunfermline	Sc	15 7 7	726
Espoo	Fi	16 7 6	153
European Tour Club			
(Kungsängen)	S	15 7 6	1239
Fågelbro	S	15 9 5	1240
Feldafing	D	16 7 6	405
Fjällbacka	S	15 6 3	1243
Forsgården	S	14 6 7	1246
Fränkische Schweiz	D	14 7 6	407
Frösåker	S	16 7 5	1247
Gränna	S	15 7 5	1250
Grantown on Spey	Sc	14 6 7	739
Grenland	Nw	14 6 6	1050
Gullbringa	S	13 7 6	1251
Gut Altentann	A	18 8 7	98
Halmstad	S	18 8 7	1252
Haninge	S	16 8 6	1253
Harrogate	Eng	15 7 7	578
Hauger	Nw	13 7 6	1051
Helsinki	Fi	16 7 8	154
Jönköping	S	16 7 7	1254
Karlovy Vary	Cz	15 7 6	1313
Karlshamn	S	14 6 6	1256
Kungsbacka	S	15 6 6	1259
Largue (La)	F	15 7 4	295
Larvik	Nw	17 7 5	1052
Laval-Changé *La Chabossière*	F	14 7 5	296
Lindö Park	S	14 8 6	1260
Lothianburn	Sc	14 6 8	751
Lunds Akademiska	S	16 7 5	1262
Lüneburger Heide	D	16 7 5	436
Luzern	CH	13 6 7	1303
Mariánské Lázne	Cz	14 7 6	1314
Massereene	UL	14 5 6	931
Master *Master*	Fi	15 7 7	155
Nes	Nw	14 6 4	1053
Niederbüren	Ch	13 7 7	1306
Nordcenter *Benz Course*	Fi	15 7 5	156
Old Head	I	15 7 7	893
Örebro	S	18 7 5	1266
Oslo	Nw	15 7 9	1054
Österåker	S	16 6 6	1267
Panmure	Sc	17 6 5	766
Pickala Seaside Course	Fi	15 8 5	157
Praha Karlstejn	Cz	15 6 7	1315
Sarfvik *New Course*	Fi	16 8 7	158

79

RECOMMENDED SEASONS

Seasons Golf course	Country	Score		Page
`1 2 3 4 5 6 7 8 9 10 11 12`				
Schönenberg	Ch	14 7	6	1308
Shiskine (Blackwaterfoot)	Sc	17 5	5	780
Silloth-on-Solway	Eng	18 7	4	653
Sonnenalp	D	15 7	7	469
Sorknes	Nw	13 6	4	1055
St Laurence	Fi	14 5	4	159
Stavanger	Nw	16 6	7	1056
Stenungsund	S	17 7	8	1272
Stirling	Sc	13 6	7	786
Stockholm	S	16 8	9	1273
Strathaven	Sc	15 7	6	788
Talma	Fi	14 8	6	160
Tawast	Fi	14 7	5	161
Tegernseer Bad Wiessee	D	14 7	8	476
Tranås	S	14 6	7	1278
Tutzing	D	15 7	6	478
Tyrifjord	Nw	14 6	6	1057
Ullna	S	17 8	6	1278
Värnamo	S	15 7	5	1280
`1 2 3 4 5 6 7 8 9 10 11 12`				
Interlaken	CH	14 6	6	1299

Seasons Golf course	Country	Score		Page
`1 2 3 4 5 6 7 8 9 10 11 12`				
Chamonix	F	15 6	7	252
Schloss Lüdersburg Old/New	D	15 7	6	463
`1 2 3 4 5 6 7 8 9 10 11 12`				
Forsbacka	S	16 7	4	1245
Kalmar	S	15 5	8	1255
Skövde	S	17 5	7	1270
Täby	S	16 7	7	1275
Växjö	S	15 6	7	1282
`1 2 3 4 5 6 7 8 9 10 11 12`				
Ballater	Sc	15 6	7	703
Crans-sur-Sierre	Ch	14 7	8	1293
Engadin	Ch	15 6	6	1295
Gävle	S	14 6	6	1248
Kingussie	Sc	15 4	5	745
Moscow	Ru	17 7	6	1316
Seefeld-Wildmoos	A	17 8	7	99
Skellefteå	S	14 6	5	1269
Sundsvall	S	13 6	6	1274

RECOMMENDED GOLFING STAY
SEJOUR DE GOLF RECOMMANDÉ
FÜR GOLFFERIEN EMPFOHLEN
REKOMMENDERADE GOLFVISTELSE
ESTANCIA DE GOLF RECOMENDADA
SOGGIORNO GOLFISTICO CONSIGLIATI

Golf course	Country	Score			Page
Almerimar	E	14	6	6	1126
Aloha	E	17	7	7	1127
Antwerp	B	16	7	7	107
Bad Griesbach *Brunnwies*	D	17	9	9	386
Bad Griesbach-Sagmühle Sagmühle	D	15	9	9	387
Ballybunion *Old Course*	I	19	7	7	839
Ballyliffin *Glashedy Links*	I	17	6	5	841
Ballyliffin *Old Course*	I	15	6	5	842
Barbaroux	F	17	7	6	229
Barsebäck	S	18	7	6	1231
Belle-Dune	F	16	6	5	232
Berkshire (The) *Blue Course*	Eng	17	8	7	529
Berkshire (The) *RedCourse*	Eng	17	8	7	530
Blairgowrie *Lansdowne*	Sc	15	8	6	705
Blairgowrie *Rosemount*	Sc	18	8	6	706
Bogogno	I	17	8	7	960
Bondues *Blanc*	F	16	7	6	237
Bondues *Jaune*	F	15	7	6	238
Bordes (Les)	F	19	8	6	239
Brampton	Eng	17	7	6	536
Bretesche (La)	F	15	7	7	243
Buckinghamshire (The)	Eng	17	8	7	540
Burnham & Berrow	Eng	18	7	6	542
Canyamel	E	15	6	6	1134
Carden Park *Nicklaus Course*	Eng	17	8	8	547
Carlisle	Eng	17	7	7	548
Carnoustie *Burnside*	Sc	14	5	6	714
Carnoustie *Championship*	Sc	19	5	6	715
Castelconturbia Giallo + Azzurro	I	18	8	7	963
Castillo de Gorraiz	E	17	7	7	1136
Castletown	Eng	18	6	8	549
Celtic Manor *Roman Road*	W	18	9	7	804
Chart Hills	Eng	18	8	6	550
Chiberta	F	16	6	8	259
Club de Campo	E	16	8	8	1138
Club zur Vahr (Garlstedt)	D	18	6	5	398
County Louth	I	18	5	6	855
County Sligo	I	17	4	3	856
Courson *Lilas/Orange*	F	15	7	3	261
Courson *Vert/Noir*	F	16	7	3	262
Cruden Bay	Sc	18	7	6	718
Dalmahoy *East Course*	Sc	17	8	8	719
Dartmouth	Eng	16	9	6	556
De Pan	N	16	8	7	1017
Domaine Impérial	CH	18	8	6	1294
Druids Glen	I	16	9	7	863
East Sussex National *East Course*	Eng	17	8	7	560
Eindhoven	N	18	8	6	1019
El Prat *Amarillo*	E	15	7	6	1142
El Prat *Verde*	E	17	7	6	1143
El Saler	E	18	7	6	1144
Emporda	E	17	7	6	1145
European (The)	I	18	5	6	867
Evian	F	15	7	9	272
Fairhaven	Eng	17	7	8	561
Falsterbo	S	18	7	5	1242
Felixstowe Ferry *Martello Course*	Eng	15	6	6	563
Ferndown *Old Course*	Eng	17	7	7	564
Fontanals	E	18	6	5	1148
Forest Pines *Forest + Pines*	Eng	17	6	7	567
Formby	Eng	18	7	7	568
Fürstlicher GC Bad Waldsee	D	17	7	8	408
Ganton	Eng	19	8	5	573
Genève	CH	17	7	8	1297
Gleneagles *King's*	Sc	18	9	7	735
Gleneagles *Monarch's*	Sc	17	9	7	736
Gleneagles *Queen's*	Sc	15	9	7	737
Gouverneur (Le) *Le Breuil*	F	16	7	6	279

81

Europe

Golf course	Country	Score		Page	Golf course	Country	Score		Page
Gouverneur (Le) *Montaplan*	F	14 7	6	280	Meon Valley *Meon Course*	Eng	15 8	7	605
Grande Bastide (La)	F	16 6	6	281	Mijas *Los Lagos*	E	16 6	7	1182
Grande-Motte (La)					Mijas *Los Olivos*	E	13 6	7	1183
Les Flamants Roses	F	16 6	4	282	Mittelrheinischer	D	17 7	7	440
Guadalmina *Sur*	E	14 7	7	1154	Moliets	F	17 6	5	304
Gujan-Mestras	F	15 7	6	286	Montecastillo	E	17 8	7	1185
Gullane *No 1*	Sc	17 8	7	740	Montpellier-Massane	F	16 7	5	306
Gut Altentann	A	18 8	7	98	Moor Park *High Course*	Eng	17 8	7	608
Gut Kaden Platz B + Platz C	D	15 7	6	411	Moray	Sc	17 5	5	758
Haagsche	N	18 7	8	1025	Motzener See	D	17 8	6	441
Hainaut					Mount Juliet	I	18 9	8	889
Bruyere-Quesnoy-Etangs	B	15 7	5	110	Nairn	Sc	19 7	8	762
Halmstad	S	18 8	7	1252	National *L'Albatros*	F	18 5	6	307
Hanau-Wilhelmsbad	D	16 6	6	419	Neguri	E	17 7	7	1187
Hardelot *Les Pins*	F	16 6	6	287	Nîmes-Campagne	F	16 7	6	309
Hawkstone Park *Hawkstone*	Eng	15 8	7	579	Noordwijk	N	18 7	8	1032
Hayling	Eng	16 7	7	580	Oberschwaben Bad Waldsee	D	15 6	6	450
Hillside	Eng	18 7	7	585	Oostende	B	15 7	7	114
Hilversum	N	16 7	7	1027	Örebro	S	18 7	5	1266
Himmerland *New Course*	Da	16 8	6	137	Pals	E	16 7	6	1192
Holstebro	Da	16 6	5	138	Penha Longa	P	17 6	8	1076
Hossegor	F	16 6	6	289	Pléneuf-Val-André	F	17 7	5	316
Hunstanton	Eng	17 7	6	588	Pont Royal	F	16 6	5	318
I Roveri	I	17 7	8	974	Portal *Championship*	Eng	15 8	7	622
Islantilla	E	16 8	8	1156	Portmarnock	I	19 7	8	894
Isle of Purbeck	Eng	16 7	6	592	Portmarnock Links	I	17 7	8	895
John O'Gaunt	Eng	16 7	6	593	Portstewart *Strand Course*	UL	16 7	7	932
K Club	I	17 8	8	877	Praia d'El Rey	P	17 6	5	1079
Kalmar	S	15 5	8	1255	Pyle & Kenfig	W	17 7	5	817
Kempferhof (Le)	F	18 8	6	293	Quinta do Lago *B/C*	P	15 7	8	1082
Kennemer	N	18 8	8	1030	Quinta do Lago *Ria Formosa*	P	15 7	8	1083
Killarney *Killeen Course*	I	16 7	8	880	Ravenstein	B	17 8	7	117
Killarney *Mahony's Point*	I	15 7	8	881	Roncemay	F	15 7	7	326
La Cala *Norte*	E	17 8	6	1158	Royal Birkdale (The)	Eng	19 9	7	629
La Cala *Sur*	E	16 8	6	1159	Royal Cinque Ports	Eng	17 6	5	630
La Dehesa	E	14 7	4	1160	Royal County Down	UL	19 6	7	934
La Manga *Norte*	E	15 7	7	1162	Royal Dornoch				
La Manga *Oeste*	E	14 7	7	1163	*Championship*	Sc	19 7	7	776
La Manga *Sur*	E	14 7	7	1164	Royal Dublin	I	16 8	7	901
La Moraleja *La Moraleja 1*	E	15 7	8	1165	Royal Liverpool (Hoylake)	Eng	18 8	7	634
La Moraleja *La Moraleja 2*	E	16 7	8	1166	Royal Lytham & St Anne's	Eng	19 7	8	635
La Quinta	E	15 8	7	1167	Royal North Devon				
Lahinch	I	18 6	6	883	(Westward Ho!)	Eng	18 6	6	637
Las Brisas	E	18 7	7	1171	Royal Porthcawl	W	19 7	6	819
Lausanne	CH	16 7	7	1300	Royal Portrush *Dunluce Links*	UL	19 7	7	935
Limère	F	17 6	5	298	Royal Portrush *Valley*	UL	13 7	7	936
Ljunghusen	S	17 6	7	1261	Royal St David's	W	18 6	5	820
Los Naranjos	E	16 7	7	1176	Royal St George's	Eng	19 7	5	638
Machrihanish	Sc	18 6	4	755	Royal Troon *Old Course*	Sc	19 7	7	778
Madeira	P	14 6	5	1072	Royal West Norfolk				
Marriott St Pierre *Old Course*	W	16 8	7	811	(Brancaster)	Eng	17 7	6	639
Mediterraneo	E	16 7	6	1181	Royal Zoute	B	18 7	7	121
Médoc *Les Châteaux*	F	18 7	5	302	Rungsted	Da	17 7	7	143
Médoc *Les Vignes*	F	15 7	5	303	S. Lourenço	P	18 6	8	1085

82

Golf course	Country	Score		Page
Sablé-Solesmes				
La Forêt/La Rivière	F	16 7	4	328
Saint Donat	F	15 7	8	329
Saint-Jean-de-Monts	F	16 6	5	333
Saint-Nom-la-Bretèche	F	16 8	8	336
San Roque	E	17 8	6	1203
San Sebastián	E	14 6	6	1204
Saunton East Course	Eng	18 7	6	645
Scharmützelsee				
Arnold Palmer	D	17 8	7	456
Scharmützelsee Nick Faldo	D	18 8	7	457
Schloss Liebenstein	D	16 8	7	462
Seddiner See Südplatz	D	18 9	7	467
Seignosse	F	17 7	7	341
Skövde	S	17 5	7	1270
Slaley Hall	Eng	17 8	7	654
Sotogrande	E	18 7	6	1209
Southport & Ainsdale	Eng	18 7	7	655
Spa (Les Fagnes)	B	17 7	7	123
Spérone	F	17 7	5	344
Spiegelven	B	14 7	8	124
St Andrews Eden Course	Sc	14 8	8	782
St Andrews Jubilee Course	Sc	16 8	8	783
St Andrews New Course	Sc	17 8	8	784
St Andrews Old Course	Sc	18 8	8	785
St Enodoc Church Course	Eng	18 7	4	656
St Mellion Nicklaus Course	Eng	17 9	7	658
Stoke Poges	Eng	17 8	8	659
Sunningdale New Course	Eng	18 8	8	661

Golf course	Country	Score		Page
Sunningdale Old Course	Eng	18 8	8	662
Taulane	F	15 7	4	346
The Belfry	Eng	15 9	8	666
Torino - La Mandria				
Percorso Blu	I	16 8	8	1001
Toulouse-Seilh Rouge	F	15 7	6	348
Touquet (Le) La Mer	F	17 6	7	349
Tralee	I	18 7	6	908
Trevose Championship	Eng	17 7	7	672
Troia	P	15 6	5	1087
Turnberry Ailsa Course	Sc	19 9	8	792
Turnberry Arran Course	Sc	16 9	8	793
Valderrama	E	19 8	6	1213
Vilamoura I (Old Course)	P	16 7	7	1091
Vilamoura II (Pinhal)	P	13 7	7	1092
Vilamoura III (Laguna)	P	14 7	7	1093
Villamartin	E	16 7	6	1214
Villette d'Anthon Les Sangliers	F	17 6	4	354
Wallasey	Eng	17 7	7	673
Walton Heath New Course	Eng	16 7	6	674
Walton Heath Old Course	Eng	18 7	7	675
Warwickshire (The)	Eng	15 7	8	676
Waterloo La Marache	B	16 8	7	125
Waterville	I	17 6	7	914
Wentworth East Course	Eng	16 8	7	677
Wentworth West Course	Eng	18 8	7	678
West Lancashire	Eng	17 7	7	683
Woburn Dukes Course	Eng	18 7	7	690
Woodhall Spa	Eng	18 7	8	694

83

RECOMMENDED GOLFING HOLIDAYS
VACANCES RECOMMANDEES
FÜR EINEN FERIENAUFENTHALT EMPFOHLEN
REKOMMENDERAD SEMESTERORT
FÉRIAS RECOMENDADAS
LOCALITÀ DI VACANZE CONSIGLIATI

Golf course	Country	Score	Page	Golf course	Country	Score	Page
Aix-les-Bains	F	13 5 7	216	Falsterbo	S	18 7 5	1242
Albarella	I	14 8 7	954	Fanø	Da	15 4 7	135
Aloha	E	17 7 7	1127	Fjällbacka	S	15 6 3	1243
Amirauté (L')	F	14 7 8	218	Flommen	S	16 7 7	1244
Arcachon	F	13 6 6	223	Forsgården	S	14 6 7	1246
Arcangues	F	14 7 8	224	Frégate	F	15 7 7	278
Båstad	S	16 7 7	1232	Gardagolf	I	14 7 8	972
Baule (La) *Rouge*	F	15 7 8	230	Garlenda	I	14 7 8	973
Belas	P	13 7 6	1069	Garmisch-Partenkirchen	D	14 6 7	410
Biarritz-le-Phare	F	14 6 8	235	Gleneagles *King's*	Sc	18 9 7	735
Bodensee-Weissensberg	D	16 7 7	395	Gleneagles *Monarch's*	Sc	17 9 7	736
Bonmont	E	16 7 6	1132	Gleneagles *Queen's*	Sc	15 9 7	737
Brokenhurst Manor	Eng	15 6 6	539	Golfresort			
Cannes Mandelieu	F	14 7 8	245	Haugschlag-Waldviertel	A	16 7 5	97
Cannes-Mougins	F	15 7 8	246	Grande Bastide (La)	F	16 6 6	281
Cap d'Agde	F	15 6 5	247	Grande-Motte (La)			
Capdepera	E	15 7 6	1135	Les Flamants Roses	F	16 6 4	282
Cervia	I	13 6 9	966	Gujan-Mestras	F	15 7 6	286
Chamonix	F	15 6 7	252	Hardelot *Les Pins*	F	16 6 6	287
Chantaco	F	14 7 7	254	Hossegor	F	16 6 6	289
Charleville	I	13 4 6	851	Im Chiemgau	D	15 7 6	427
Chiberta	F	16 6 8	259	Is Molas	I	16 7 8	975
Cosmopolitan	I	14 6 7	968	Islantilla	E	16 8 8	1156
Costa Dorada	E	13 6 6	1140	Kungsbacka	S	15 6 6	1259
Crans-sur-Sierre	CH	14 7 8	1293	La Cala *Norte*	E	17 8 6	1158
Dachstein Tauern / Schladming	A	15 7 5	93	La Cala *Sur*	E	16 8 6	1159
Dinard	F	13 6 7	264	La Manga *Norte*	E	15 7 7	1162
Disneyland Paris				La Manga *Oeste*	E	14 7 7	1163
Never Land + Wonderland	F	16 7 8	265	La Manga *Sur*	E	14 7 7	1164
Ekerum	S	14 7 7	1237	La Moye	Eng	17 7 8	594
El Bosque	E	16 7 4	1141	La Sella	E	15 6 5	1168
El Saler	E	18 7 6	1144	Lacanau	F	14 6 7	294
Emporda	E	17 7 6	1145	Langland Bay	W	15 7 7	808
Engadin	CH	15 6 6	1295	Læsø Seaside	Da	15 7 5	140
Esbjerg	Da	15 6 5	134	Lignano	I	14 7 7	982
Estérel Latitudes	F	16 6 7	269	Lindau-Bad Schachen	D	15 7 8	434
Estoril	P	13 7 7	1070	Ljunghusen	S	17 6 7	1261
Europasportregion-Zell am See				Llandudno (Maesdu)	W	15 5 8	809
Schmittenhöhe	A	16 7 6	95	Lübeck-Travemünder	D	15 8 8	435
Falmouth	Eng	14 6 7	562	Lugano	Ch	15 7 8	1302

Golf course	Country	Score			Page
Madeira	P	14	6	5	1072
Makila Golf Club	F	14	6	8	300
Marbella	E	15	7	8	1178
Maspalomas	E	16	7	8	1180
Mediterraneo	E	16	7	6	1181
Mijas *Los Lagos*	E	16	6	7	1182
Mijas *Los Olivos*	E	13	6	7	1183
Moliets	F	17	6	5	304
Mölle	S	15	7	5	1264
Monte Carlo (Mont Agel)	F	14	6	7	305
Mullion	Eng	15	5	5	610
New Golf Deauville *Rouge/Blanc*	F	15	7	8	308
North Wales (Llandudno)	W	17	6	8	814
Novo Sancti Petri	E	16	7	7	1188
Obere Alp	D	14	7	7	448
Öschberghof	D	15	7	7	451
Palazzo Arzaga	I	15	8	8	992
Palheiro	P	13	6	7	1074
Palmares	P	13	7	5	1075
Pals	E	16	7	6	1192
Patriziale Ascona	CH	15	7	7	1307
Penha Longa	P	17	6	8	1076
Penina	P	14	7	7	1077
Pennard	W	18	6	6	816
Pevero	I	16	8	8	994
Pinheiros Altos	P	14	7	7	1078
Playa Serena	E	13	6	4	1198
Pornic	F	15	6	6	320
Praia d'El Rey	P	17	6	5	1079
Pula	E	13	6	5	1201
Punta Ala	I	14	7	8	996
Quinta da Marinha	P	13	7	7	1081
Quinta do Lago *B/C*	P	15	7	8	1082

Golf course	Country	Score			Page
Quinta do Lago *Ria Formosa*	P	15	7	8	1083
Quinta do Peru	P	15	6	5	1084
Rapallo	I	13	7	8	997
Riva dei Tessali	I	13	7	6	998
Riviéra Golf Club	F	13	7	8	324
Royal Guernsey	Eng	16	7	7	632
Royal Jersey	Eng	16	7	8	633
Royal Mougins	F	17	7	8	327
Rungsted	Da	17	7	7	143
Rya	S	15	7	8	1268
S. Lourenço	P	18	6	8	1085
Saint Donat	F	15	7	8	329
Saint-Laurent	F	14	7	5	334
Sainte-Maxime	F	13	7	7	339
Salgados	P	14	7	6	1086
Seefeld-Wildmoos	A	17	8	7	99
Spérone	F	17	7	5	344
Steiermärkischer Murhof	A	16	7	6	100
Sylt	D	15	6	8	475
Torekov	S	14	7	7	1276
Torrequebrada	E	14	7	7	1211
Touquet (Le) *La Mer*	F	17	6	7	349
Vale da Pinta	P	14	6	6	1088
Vale do Lobo *Royal Golf Course*	P	15	6	7	1089
Venezia	I	16	7	9	1003
Vila Sol	P	14	7	7	1090
Vilamoura *Vilamoura I* (Old Course)	P	16	7	7	1091
Vilamoura *Vilamoura II* (Pinhal)	P	13	7	7	1092
Vilamoura *Vilamoura III* (Laguna)	P	14	7	7	1093
Villa D'Este	I	16	8	9	1005

Europe

85

Österreich

I n Österreich, dem Land der Berge, sind in den letzten Jahren viele Golfplätze enststanden. So sind viele Wintersportorte auch beliebte Sommerreiseziele. In Österreich findet man derzeit rund 75 Plätze, auf denen 50.000 einheimische Golfer die Schläger schwingen. Golf in Österreich ist ein Sport, auf den meisten Plätzen geht man zu Fuss. Obwohl die Winter in der Alpenrepublik streng sind, setzen die Greenkeeper allen Ehrgeiz daran, einen perfekt gepflegten Platz zu präsentieren. Die meisten Plätze liegen idyllisch, das herrliche Alpenpanorama wird Besucher beeindrucken. Ob Sie in Österreich einen Golfurlaub verbringen oder nur mal eben zwischendurch eine Runde Golf spielen: Es wird ein angenehme Überraschung werden, zumal die österreichische Gastfreundschaft und das einzigartige Land sie faszienieren wird.

A ustria, a land of mountains, has quickly built up a number of golf courses which are the ideal complement to the country's many skiing resorts. There are now more than 75 courses for almost 50,000 golfers. Naturally, golf here is a real sport and walking a tradition; and despite the harsh winters, producing a course in good shape is a question of honour. Often located in idyllic natural settings, the picture postcard appearance of most courses is a joy to behold for foreign visitors. Whether here for a golfing holiday or for a quick round in between other delightful holiday activities, you are in for some great surprises and hospitality typical of a country unlike any other.

87

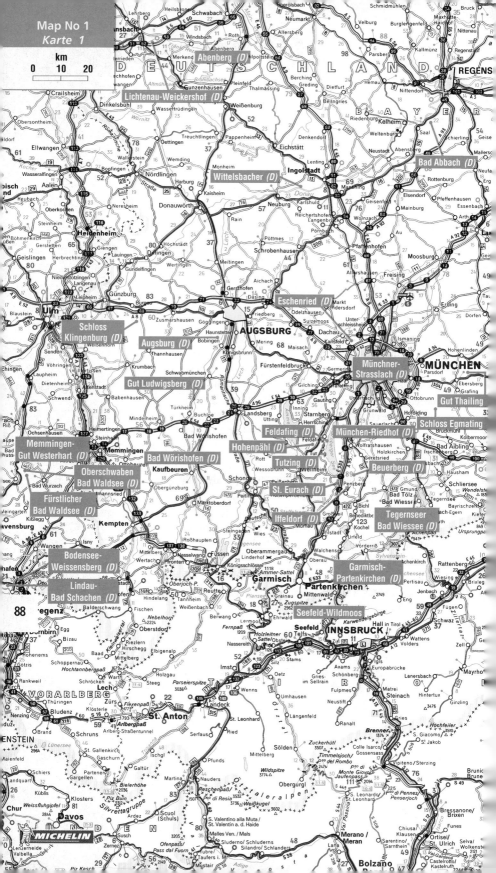

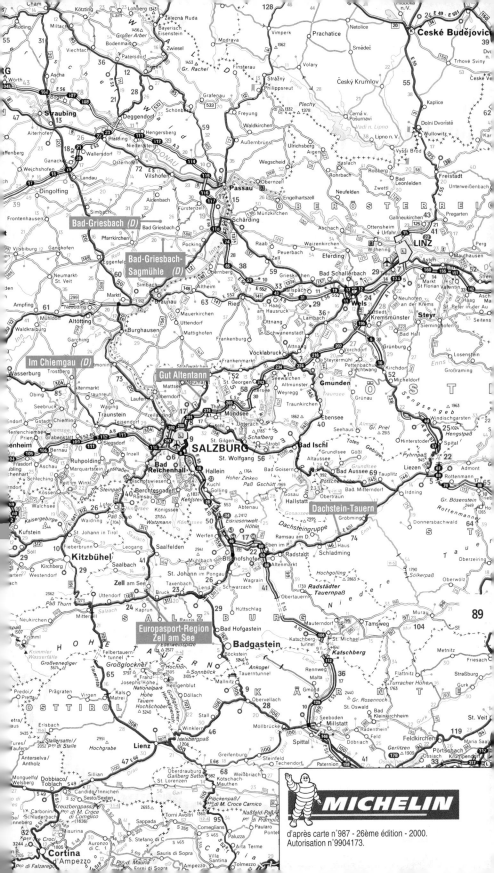

EINTEILUNG DER GOLFPLÄTZE
CLASSIFICATION OF COURSES

Diese Einteilung berücksichtigt in erster Linie die dem Golfplatz erteilte Note
This classification gives priority consideration
to the score awarded to the actual course

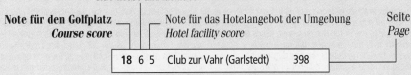

Note für das Clubhaus und die Einrichtungen
Club-house and facilities

Note für den Golfplatz ____ ┌ Note für das Hotelangebot der Umgebung   Seite
    Course score   *Hotel facility score*   *Page*

18 6 5   Club zur Vahr (Garlstedt)   398

Note	Golfplatz	Seite	Note	Golfplatz	Seite
18 8 7	Gut Altentann	98	**16** 7 5	Golfresort Haugschlag-	
17 8 7	Colony Club Gutenhof	92		Waldviertel	97
17 8 7	Seefeld-Wildmoos	99	**16** 7 6	Steiermärkischer Murhof	100
16 6 5	Donnerskirchen-Neusiedlersee	94	**15** 7 5	Dachstein Tauern /	
16 7 6	Europasportregion-Zell			Schladming	93
	am See *Schmittenhöhe*	95	**13** 7 9	Wien-Freudenau	101
16 8 5	Fontana	96			

EINTEILUNG DES HOTELANGEBOTS
DER UMGEBUNG
CLASSIFICATION OF HOTELS FACILITIES

Note	Golfplatz	Seite	Note	Golfplatz	Seite
13 7 **9**	Wien-Freudenau	101	16 7 **6**	Steiermärkischer Murhof	100
17 8 **7**	Colony Club Gutenhof	92	15 7 **5**	Dachstein Tauern / Schladming	93
18 8 **7**	Gut Altentann	98	16 6 **5**	Donnerskirchen-Neusiedlersee	94
17 8 **7**	Seefeld-Wildmoos	99	16 8 **5**	Fontana	96
16 7 **6**	Europasportregion-Zell am See		16 7 **5**	Golfresort Haugschlag-	
	Schmittenhöhe	95		Waldviertel	97

TYP DES GOLFPLATZES TYPE OF COURSE

Golfplatz	Seite	Golfplatz	Seite	Golfplatz	Seite
hilly		**mountain**		**parkland**	
Seefeld-Wildmoos	99	Dachstein Tauern /		Colony Club Gutenhof	92
inland		Schladming	93	Gut Altentann	98
Europasportregion-Zell am See		Seefeld-Wildmoos	99	Steiermärkischer Murhof	100
Schmittenhöhe	95	**open country**		**links style**	
Fontana	96	Gut Altentann	98	Donnerskirchen-Neusiedlersee	94
Golfresort Haugschlag-		Dachstein Tauern Schladming	93	**residential**	
Waldviertel	97	Donnerskirchen-		Fontana	96
Wien-Freudenau	101	Neusiedlersee	94		

Das modernste mit allen Angeboten versehene Golfresort in der Wiener Region, das auf zwei einander im Stil und Qualität sehr ähnliche 18-Loch Golfkurse stolz sein kann. Mit allem Respekt vor Kurt Rossknecht's layouts, wäre es interessant ob ein anderer Architekt seinen eigenen Stil in einen der beiden Kurse gebracht hätte, deren Spielbahnen sich meist entlang alter Baumbestände schlängeln. Beide Kurse passen perfekt in das Landschaftsbild wobei alle Hindernisse klar sichtbar sind und Sorge tragen, dass Sie für alle Spielstärken als gerecht empfunden werden. An die 50 Fairwaybunker verlangen ebensolche Präzision wie eine ähnliche Anzahl von Hindernissen von den gut konturierten und gut proportionierten Greens. Das flache Terrain erlaubt den Enthusiasten alle 36 Löcher an einem Tag zu spielen ohne sich dabei zu sehr zu verausgaben um abendlich die Wiener Staatsoper, die Philharmoniker oder den «Heurigen» - ein kleines gemütliches Gasthaus in dem der heurige Wein serviert wird - besuchen zu können.

This complex is the most modern of all the golf facilities in the region of Vienna, boasting two 18-hole courses of similar style. With all due respect to Kurt Rossknecht's layouts, it would have been interesting if another architect had added his own style to one of the two on terrain which mostly winds its way through age-old trees. At least both courses blend in perfectly with the landscape, but do so without actually vanishing completely, as the difficulties are clearly visible. Another noticeable feature is the way they cater to all levels of play. Fifty or so fairway bunkers call for a certain degree of precision, while a similar number of traps form the last line of defence in front of well-contoured and nicely sized greens. The flat terrain will allow die-hard enthusiasts to play 36 holes in a day without too much trouble, followed by an evening in Staatsoper at the Philharmonia or in the «Heurigen», little open air restaurants which serve young wines.

Colony Club Gutenhof		1990
Gutenhof		
A - 2325 HIMBERG		

Office	Sekretariat	(43) 022358 7055-10
Pro shop	Pro shop	(43) 022358 7055-35
Fax	Fax	(43) 022358 7055-14
Situation	Lage	
Wien (pop. 1 640 000), 10 km		
Annual closure	Jährliche Schliessung	no
Weekly closure	Wöchentliche Schliessung	no

Fees main season
Preisliste hochsaison 18 holes

	Week days Woche	We/Bank holidays We/Feiertag
Individual Individuell	ÖS 500,-	ÖS 800,-
Couple Ehepaar	ÖS 1000,-	ÖS 1600,-

Caddy	Caddy	no
Electric Trolley	Elektrokarren	ja
Buggy	Elektrischer Wagen	ja
Clubs	Leihschläger	ja

Credit cards Kreditkarten
VISA - Eurocard - MasterCard - DC

Access Zufahrt : Wien, A4.
Exit (Ausfahrt) Schwechat-Himberg. → Moosbrunn.
2 km S. of Himberg, → Golfplatz
Map 2 on page 90 Karte 2 Seite 90

GOLF COURSE
PLATZ   **17** /20

Site	Lage	
Maintenance	Instandhaltung	
Architect	Architekt	Kurt Rossknecht H.G. Erhardt
Type	Typ	parkland
Relief	Relief	
Water in play	Platz mit Wasser	
Exp. to wind	Wind ausgesetzt	
Trees in play	Platz mit Bäumen	

Scorecard Scorekarte	Chp. Chp.	Mens Herren	Ladies Damen
Length Länge	6350	6200	5600
Par	73	73	73

Advised golfing ability Empfohlene Spielstärke	0 12 24 36
Hcp required	Min. Handicap	no

CLUB HOUSE & AMENITIES
KLUBHAUS UND NEBENGEBÄUDE   **8** /10

Pro shop	Pro shop	
Driving range	Übungsplatz	
Sheltered	überdacht	10 mats
On grass	auf Rasen	yes
Putting-green	Putting-grün	yes
Pitching-green	Pitching-grün	yes

HOTEL FACILITIES
HOTEL BESCHREIBUNG   **7** /10

HOTELS HOTELS

Hotel Sacher		Wien
108 rooms, D ÖS 3900,-		18 km
Tel (43) 01 51 456, Fax (43) 01 51 456 - 810		
Hotel im Palais Schwarzenberg		Wien
44 rooms, D ÖS 4000,-		16 km
Tel (43) 01 798 45 15, Fax (43) 01 798 47 14		
Holiday Inn Crowne Plaza		Wien
367 rooms, D ÖS 2500,-		10 km
Tel (43) 01 72 777, Fax (43) 01 72 951 06		
Zum Guten Hirten		Himberg
11 rooms, D ÖS 990,-		5 km
Tel (43) 02235 875 82, Fax (43) 02235 87582-27		

RESTAURANTS RESTAURANT

Steirereck - Tel (43) 01713 3168		Wien 15 km
Novelli - Tel(43) 01513 4200-0		Wien 15 km

92

Skisportsfans werden von Schladming (80 km von Salzburg) schon gehört haben, daher ist es Zeit auch den Golffans das Resort näherzubringen, das über einen der besten Bernhard Langer-Design Kurse aus den frühen 90-er Jahren verfügt. Auf einer Seehöhe von 750 m umgeben von Bergen mit Schneespitzen könnte man einen körperlich anstrengenden Kurs erwarten, doch dieser ist leicht begehbar und spult seinen Weg zwischen kleinen Hügeln mit Bäumen ab. Das Terrain ist gut kanalisiert, man braucht sich um die gefürchteten Sommergewitter keine Sorge zu machen. Kleine Seen und Wasserläufe sind am halben Platz im Spiel, da aber keines der 18 Löcher sehr lange ausgefallen sind, kann man immer auf sicher spielen, ohne viel Distanz zu verlieren. Der Kurs macht visuell und technisch grossen Spass und zählt mit seinem gut positionierten chaletähnlichen Clubhaus zu den besten Layouts des Landes. Der 2-fache US Masterssieger Bernhard Langer scorte nur 71, ein Beweis dafür, dass die vorhandene natur nicht so leicht zu bewältigen ist.

Skiers and sports-lovers will have heard of the resort of Schladming, 50 miles from Salzburg, so it is about time that golf enthusiasts got to know this course, one of the best designed by Bernhard Langer in the early 1990s. At an altitude of 750 metres (2,475 feet) laid out in a setting surrounded by mountains and eternal snows, you might expect a physically demanding course. In actual fact, this one is easily walkable as it winds its way between little hills covered with trees. And as the terrain is well drained, there is no need to worry about those summer showers. Small lakes and stretches of water are in play on one half of the course, but as the 18 holes are never very long, you can play safe without ever losing too much distance. Visually attractive and technically great fun to play, this course with a chalet-style club-house is one of the most pleasant layouts in the whole country.

Dachstein Tauern
Golf & Country Club — 1990
Oberhaus 59
A - 8967 HAUS IM ENNSTAL

Office	Sekretariat	(43) 03686 2630
Pro shop	Pro shop	(43) 03686 2630
Fax	Fax	(43) 03686 2630 15
Situation	Lage	

Salzburg (pop. 147 000), 80 km

Annual closure	Jährliche Schliessung	no
Weekly closure	Wöchentliche Schliessung	no

Fees main season
Preisliste hochsaison 18 holes

	Week days Woche	We/Bank holidays We/Feiertag
Individual Individuell	ÖS 650,-	ÖS 750,-
Couple Ehepaar	ÖS 1300,-	ÖS 1500,-

Caddy	Caddy	no
Electric Trolley	Elektrokarren	ÖS 60,-
Buggy	Elektrischer Wagen	ÖS 250,-
Clubs	Leihschläger	ÖS 250,-

Credit cards Kreditkarten
VISA - Eurocard - MasterCard - AMEX - DC

Dachsteingruppe

GOLF

Gröbming
Liezen (A9) →

Ramsau — Weissenbach Aich

146 — Haus

Schladming

Radstadt
Salzburg (A10)

0   2   4 km

Access Zufahrt : Salzburg, A10.
Exit (Ausfahrt) → Radstadt, Schladming, 146/E651.
After Schladming, Golf 2 km.
Map 1 on page 89 Karte 1 Seite 89

GOLF COURSE
PLATZ — 15/20

Site	Lage	▰▰▰▰▱
Maintenance	Instandhaltung	▰▰▰▰▱
Architect	Architekt	Bernhard Langer
Type	Typ	mountain, open space
Relief	Relief	▰▰▰▱▱
Water in play	Platz mit Wasser	▰▰▰▱▱
Exp. to wind	Wind ausgesetzt	▰▰▱▱▱
Trees in play	Platz mit Bäumen	▰▰▰▱▱

Scorecard Scorekarte	Chp. Chp.	Mens Herren	Ladies Damen
Length Länge	5895	5524	5182
Par	71	71	71

Advised golfing ability	0	12	24	36
Empfohlene Spielstärke		▰▰▰▰▰▰▰		
Hcp required Min. Handicap	36			

CLUB HOUSE & AMENITIES
KLUBHAUS UND NEBENGEBÄUDE — 7/10

Pro shop	Pro shop	▰▰▰▰▱
Driving range	Übungsplatz	▰▰▰▱▱
Sheltered	überdacht	7 mats
On grass	auf Rasen	no (60 mats)
Putting-green	Putting-grün	yes
Pitching-green	Pitching-grün	yes

93

HOTEL FACILITIES
HOTEL BESCHREIBUNG — 5/10

HOTELS HOTELS
Alte Post — Schladming
40 rooms, D ÖS 1260,- — 3 km
Tel (43) 03687 22571, Fax (43) 03687 22571-8

Sporthotel Royer — Schladming
127 rooms, D ÖS 1200,- — 3 km
Tel (43) 03687 200, Fax (43) 03687 200-94

RESTAURANTS RESTAURANT
Alte Post — Schladming
Tel (43) 03687 22571 — 3 km

Während man sich in dieser Region befindet sollte man keinesfalls den vor der ungarischen Grenze befindlichen Postkarten-Ort Mörbisch versäumen. Dem steht der Ort Donnerskirchen kaum nach, speziell für seine exzellente Weinproduktion. Am Kurs ist mehr die Frage nach Wasser als Wein und die beschränkt sich auf kleine oder weniger kleine frontal- oder seitliche Seen. Im Gegensatz dazu gibt es auch einige Out-of-bounds-Areale während Bäume selten ins Spiel kommen. Manchmal erinnert der Kurs an eine «Links» insbesondere weil häufig der Wind pfeift. Golfer die eine Runde Lochwettspiel absolvieren wollen, werden diesen Platz lieben, denn er eignet sich in Österreich als einer der besten Kurse für strategisches und taktisches Spiel. Es ist auch ein angenehmer Kurs für alle Spielklassen obwohl sich alle klar sein müssen, dass auch in Österreich die Golfbälle nicht schwimmen.

While you are in this region, don't miss the little town of Mörbisch (to the south), a real colour picture postcard just before the Hungarian border. The village of Donnerskirchen is no less agreeable, particularly for its excellent wine production. On the course it is more a question of water than wine, as there is no shortage of the stuff in the form of small and not so small lateral and frontal lakes. In contrast, and although there are also quite a few out-of-bounds areas, trees seldom come into play and the course sometimes has a links look about it, an interesting proposition when there is wind about. Golfers who like a round of match-play will love this place, one of the best courses in Austria through the strategic and tactical options on offer. It is also a pleasant course for golfers of all abilities, even though they may well have to reflect upon the fact that even in Austria, golf balls don't float. A course with a well-balanced spread of difficulties, which needs playing several times for it to stick in the memory.

Club Danube Golf-Neusiedlersee		1989
A - 7082 DONNERSKIRCHEN		

Office	Sekretariat	(43) 02683 8171
Pro shop	Pro shop	(43) 02683 8171
Fax	Fax	(43) 02683 817 231
Situation	Lage	
Wien (pop. 1 640 000), 60 km		
Annual closure	Jährliche Schliessung	yes
		1/12 → 31/3
Weekly closure	Wöchentliche Schliessung	no

Fees main season
Preisliste hochsaison full day

	Week days Woche	We/Bank holidays We/Feiertag
Individual Individuell	ÖS 550,-	ÖS 550,-
Couple Ehepaar	ÖS 1100,-	ÖS 1100,-

Caddy	Caddy	no
Electric Trolley	Elektrokarren	no
Buggy	Elektrischer Wagen	yes
Clubs	Leihschläger	yes

Credit cards Kreditkarten
VISA - Eurocard - MasterCard - DC

Access Zufahrt : Wien, A4 → Parndorf, Györ. Exit (Ausfahrt) Parndorf, 50/s31 → Einsiedeln. Donnerskirchen → Golfplatz.
Map 2 on page 90 Karte 2 Seite 90

GOLF COURSE
PLATZ
16/20

Site	Lage	
Maintenance	Instandhaltung	
Architect	Architekt	Kurt Rossknecht H.G. Erhardt
Type	Typ	open country, links style
Relief	Relief	
Water in play	Platz mit Wasser	
Exp. to wind	Wind ausgesetzt	
Trees in play	Platz mit Bäumen	

Scorecard Scorekarte	Chp. Chp.	Mens Herren	Ladies Damen
Length Länge	6221	5931	5559
Par	72	72	72

Advised golfing ability	0	12	24	36
Empfohlene Spielstärke				
Hcp required	Min. Handicap	36		

CLUB HOUSE & AMENITIES
KLUBHAUS UND NEBENGEBÄUDE
6/10

Pro shop	Pro shop	
Driving range	Übungsplatz	
Sheltered	überdacht	4 mats
On grass	auf Rasen	yes
Putting-green	Putting-grün	yes
Pitching-green	Pitching-grün	yes

HOTEL FACILITIES
HOTEL BESCHREIBUNG
5/10

HOTELS HOTELS

Hotel Burgenland	Eisenstadt
88 rooms, D ÖS 1590,-	11 km
Tel (43) 02682 6960, Fax (43) 02682 655-31	

Seehotel Rust	Rust
110 rooms, D ÖS 1800,-	15 km
Tel (43) 02685 381-0, Fax (43) 02685 381-419	

Hotel Wende	Neusiedl am See
106 rooms, D ÖS 1460,-	25 km
Tel (43) 02167 8111, Fax (43) 02167 8111-649	

Sporthotel Rust	Rust
47 rooms, D ÖS 1100,-	15 km
Tel (43) 02685 641-80, Fax (43) 02685 641-858	

EUROPASPORTREGION -Zell am See ✹ 16 7 6

Zell am See und Kaprun sind Ausgangspunkte für die innerhalb von 75 km liegenden Naturschauspiele wie Grossglöckner-Hochalpenstrasse als auch Nationalsparks Hohe Tauern. Auf 750 m Seehöhe bietet der Club zwei gleichwertige 18-Loch Kurse die kaum unabhängig der grandiosen Umgebung bewertet werden können. Es ist schwer sich nicht priviligiert und zufrieden zu fühlen wenn man auf den saftigen grünen Fairways am Fuss von Gletschern und schneebedeckten Bergen spaziert, noch dazu wo das Terrain des Platzes als völlig flach bezeichnet werden kann. Der Kurs «Schmittenhöhe» wartet mit mehreren Wasserhindernissen und einigen von Bäumen verteidigten Dog-Legs auf, die aber von allen Spielklassen ohne Probleme bewältigt werden können. Der «Kitzsteinhorn»-Kurs, etwas trickreicher oder etwas weniger leicht, vor allem beim ersten Mal. Eine grossartige Sommerferien-Gegend.

Two superb holiday resorts, Zell-am-See and Kaprun mark the starting point of the sublime Grossglockner-Hochalpenstrasse, an itinerary of 75 km which is both fun and wild in the national park of Hoch Tauern. At an altitude of 750 m (2,475 feet), Europasportregion boasts two equally attractive 18 hole courses which cannot be judged independently of this sublime setting. It is hard indeed not to feel privileged and contented walking the green turf of fairways at the foot of snow-capped mountains and glaciers. More, as the courses are laid out in a valley free of sloping terrain, you know you are in for a great days golfing, particularly on the «Schmittenhöhe», with which we are concerned here. The course is covered by any number of ponds and other stretches of water and a few dog-legs protected by trees call for caution, but players of all abilities can tee it up here without too much to worry about. The other course, the «Kitzsteinhorn», is a little trickier, or at least a little less easy to get to grips with when playing for the first time. A great summer holiday site.

Golfclub Europasportregion- -Zell am See
1984

Golfstrasse 25
A - 5700 ZELL AM SEE

Office	Sekretariat	(43) 06542 561 61
Pro shop	Pro shop	(43) 06542 564 82
Fax	Fax	(43) 06542 561 61-16
Situation	Lage	

Salzburg (pop. 147 000), 85 km

Annual closure	Jährliche Schliessung	yes
		15/11 → 1/4
Weekly closure	Wöchentliche Schliessung	no

Fees main season
Preisliste hochsaison full day

	Week days Woche	We/Bank holidays We/Feiertag
Individual Individuell	ÖS 650,-	ÖS 750,-
Couple Ehepaar	ÖS 1300,-	ÖS 1500,-

Caddy	Caddy	ÖS 300,-
Electric Trolley	Elektrokarren	yes
Buggy	Elektrischer Wagen	yes
Clubs	Leihschläger	yes

Credit cards Kreditkarten
VISA - Eurocard - MasterCard - AMEX - DC

Access Zufahrt : Salzburg, A10/E55. Exit (Ausfahrt)
Bischofshofen, 311 → Zell am See, → Kaprun.
Map 1 on page 89 Karte 1 Seite 89

GOLF COURSE 16/20
PLATZ

Site	Lage	▰▰▰▰▰▰▱
Maintenance	Instandhaltung	▰▰▰▰▰▰▱
Architect	Architekt	Donald Harradine Hermann Schauer
Type	Typ	inland
Relief	Relief	▰▰▰▱▱▱▱
Water in play	Platz mit Wasser	▰▰▰▰▱▱▱
Exp. to wind	Wind ausgesetzt	▰▰▱▱▱▱▱
Trees in play	Platz mit Bäumen	▰▰▰▰▱▱▱

Scorecard	Chp.	Mens	Ladies
Scorekarte	Chp.	Herren	Damen
Length Länge	6219	5790	5051
Par	72	72	72

Advised golfing ability		0 12 24 36
Empfohlene Spielstärke		▰▰▰▰▰▰▱
Hcp required	Min. Handicap	no

CLUB HOUSE & AMENITIES 7/10
KLUBHAUS UND NEBENGEBÄUDE

Pro shop	Pro shop	▰▰▰▰▰▱▱
Driving range	Übungsplatz	▰▰▰▰▱▱▱
Sheltered	überdacht	7 mats
On grass	auf Rasen	yes
Putting-green	Putting-grün	yes
Pitching-green	Pitching-grün	yes

HOTEL FACILITIES 6/10
HOTEL BESCHREIBUNG

HOTELS HOTELS
Hotel Salzburger Hof — Zell am See
50 rooms, D from ÖS 2600,- — 4 km
Tel (43) 06542 765, Fax (43) 06542 765-66

Burgruine Kaprun — Kaprun
37 rooms, D ÖS 1980,- — 9 km
Tel (43) 06547 8306, Fax (43) 06542 8306-60

Schloss Prielau — Zell am See
8 rooms, D ÖS 2500,- — 6 km
Tel (43) 06542 72609, Fax (43) 06542 720609-55

RESTAURANTS RESTAURANT
Schloss Prielau — Zell am See
Tel (43) 06542 72609 — 6 km

95

Ein typischer «technischer» Kurs, der ausschaut als wäre er aus Florida in die Vororte Wiens transportiert worden. Wie auch immer, auf der künstlerischen Seite wurden keine Fehler gemacht, das Gesamtbild ist vortrefflich. Die Architekten Doug Carrick und Hand Erhard haben sich der Versuchung der übermässigen Länge erfolgreich widersetzt, trotzdem macht es den Platz speziell von den rückwärtigen Tees kaum leichter. Eine weise Entscheidung von weiter vorne abzuschlagen macht den Kurs etwas bezwingbarer und man hat bei den vielen Wasserhindernissen und gefährlichen Bunker weniger zu weinen. Die Annäherung auf die stark konturierten Greens ist das Schwierigste und man braucht oft den hohen Eisenschlag der eine, bei einem Kurs der extrem dem Winde ausgesetzt ist, heikle Entscheidung darstellt. Ein spektakuläres Layout für technisch anspruchsvolles Golf, aber Besucher die bodenständiges und Wiener Charme suchen, werden ein wenig überrascht sein.

This is your typical «technical» course, which looks to have been beamed up from Florida down to the suburbs of Vienna. Whatever the excellence and appeal, there is no mistaking the artificial side. At least architects Doug Carrick and Hans Erhard successfully resisted the temptation of excessive yardage; although this hardly makes the layout any easier, especially from the back tees, the course does mellow somewhat if you wisely tee off further forward. This way, you will have less to fear from the many water hazards and the most dangerous bunkers. The approach to highly contoured greens is all the more difficult in that you often need to hit lofted iron shots, a tricky proposition on a course that is exposed to the wind. A spectacular layout which technically speaking makes for excellent golfing, but visitors looking for local colour and Viennese charm will be a touch surprised.

Golf & Sportclub Fontana — 1997

Fontana Allee 1
A - 2522 OBERWALTERSDORF

Office	Sekretariat	(43) 02253 606 401
Pro shop	Pro shop	(43) 02253 606 412
Fax	Fax	(43) 02253 606 403
Situation	Lage	

Wien (pop. 1.640.000), 35 km

Annual closure	Jährliche Schliessung	yes
	1/11 → 28/2	
Weekly closure	Wöchentliche Schliessung	no

Fees main season
Preisliste hochsaison 18 holes

	Week days Woche	We/Bank holidays We/Feiertag
Individual Individuell	ÖS 1000,-	ÖS 1300,-
Couple Ehepaar	ÖS 2000,-	ÖS 2600,-
Caddy Caddy		no
Electric Trolley Elektrokarren		ÖS 300,-
Buggy Elektrischer Wagen		no
Clubs Leihschläger		ÖS 350

Credit cards Kreditkarten
VISA - Eurocard - MasterCard - AMEX - DC

GOLF COURSE / PLATZ — 16/20

Site	Lage	
Maintenance	Instandhaltung	
Architect	Architekt	Doug Carrick Hans Erhard
Type	Typ	inland, residential
Relief	Relief	
Water in play	Platz mit Wasser	
Exp. to wind	Wind ausgesetzt	
Trees in play	Platz mit Bäumen	

Scorecard Scorekarte	Chp. Chp.	Mens Herren	Ladies Damen
Length Länge	6088	5643	5012
Par	72	72	72

Advised golfing ability		0 12 24 36
Empfohlene Spielstärke		
Hcp required	Min. Handicap	36

CLUB HOUSE & AMENITIES / KLUBHAUS UND NEBENGEBÄUDE — 8/10

Pro shop	Pro shop	
Driving range	Übungsplatz	
Sheltered	überdacht	no
On grass	auf Rasen	yes
Putting-green	Putting-grün	yes
Pitching-green	Pitching-grün	yes

HOTEL FACILITIES / HOTEL BESCHREIBUNG — 5/10

HOTELS HOTELS

Imperial	Wien	
128 rooms, D ÖS 7000,-	35 km	
Tel (43) 01501 100, Fax (43) 01501 104-10		
Biedermeier	Wien	
203 rooms, D ÖS 2450,-	35 km	
Tel (43) 01716 710, Fax (43) 01716 715 03		
Das Triest	Wien	
73 rooms, D ÖS 2800,-	35 km	
Tel (43) 01589 180, Fax (43) 01589 1818		

RESTAURANTS RESTAURANT

Academie	Wien	
Tel (43) 01 713 8256	35 km	
Selina - Tel (43) 01 405 6404	Wien 35 km	
Steirer Stub'n - Tel (43) 01 544 4349	Wien 35 km	

96

Access Zufahrt : Wien A2 → Graz. Exit (Ausfahrt) Baden. 210 to Oberwatersdorf.
Map 2 on page 90 Karte 2 Seite 90

Obwohl in Österreich, könnte dieses Layout auch zu den besseren Kursen in der tschechischen Republik zählen, umso mehr es sehr nahe der Grenze des wundervollen Südböhmens liegt. Das Land von Bauernhöfen, Seen und Wäldern läuft in diesen Teil Nordösterreichs über. Der Kurs wurde auf hügeligem Terrain entlang von Sumpfland und vielen Wäldern angelegt, wobei die Bäume nur auf ein Drittel der Spielbahnen das Spiel gefährden. Wasser sollte weniger problematisch werden ausser am 4. Loch, einem Inselgrün. Eine Gruppe von Architekten Austrogolf, die für das Design des Kurses verantwortlich zeichnen, initierte nicht den amerikanischen Layout-Trend - im Gegenteil, sie planten ein Modell der Diskretion als wäre nichts natürlicher als ein Golfplatz auf diesem Platz. Es ist ein hübscher Kurs (nahe des 1. Abschlages wird im Frühling 2000 ein Hotel und eine zweite 18-Loch Anlage eröffnet) mit durchschnittlichen Schwierigkeiten der von allen Spielklassen bewältigt werden kann.

This layout, stands very close to the frontier of the Czech Republic and particularly to the magnificent region of southern Bohemia. This land of farms, lakes and forests runs over into this part of Northern Austria. The course was laid out over very lightly rolling landscape full of woods and marshes, although the trees are dangerous only on about one third of the holes. The water shouldn't bother you too much, except on the 4th hole which has an island green. Austrogolf, the group of architects who designed this course, did not set out to imitate the ongoing trend of American style layouts; to the contrary, they succeeded in building a model of discretion, as if nothing could be more natural than a golf course right here. This is a pretty course with average difficulties, playable by golfers of all abilities. Another 18-hole course is under construction, and an hotel opens in the Spring of 2000, close to the first tee of the present course.

Golfresort Haugschlag-Waldviertel 1990
A - 3874 HAUGSCHLAG

Office	Sekretariat	(43) 02865 8441
Pro shop	Pro shop	(43) 02865 8441
Fax	Fax	(43) 02865 5004
Situation	Lage	
Gmünd, 24 km		
Annual closure	Jährliche Schliessung	no
Weekly closure	Wöchentliche Schliessung	no

Fees main season
Preisliste hochsaison full day

	Week days Woche	We/Bank holidays We/Feiertag
Individual Individuell	ÖS 490,-	ÖS 600,-
Couple Ehepaar	ÖS 980,-	ÖS 1200,-
Caddy	Caddy	ÖS 300,-
Electric Trolley	Elektrokarren	ÖS 120,-
Buggy	Elektrischer Wagen	ÖS 390,-
Clubs	Leihschläger	ÖS 200,-

Credit cards Kreditkarten
VISA - Eurocard - MasterCard

Access Zufahrt : • Wien, A22, E49 → Horn, Schrems, Gmünd • Linz, E14 B38, B41 to Gmünd.• Then, B30, B5 to Einsgarn, → Litschau, Haugschlag.
Map 2 on page 90 Karte 2 Seite 90

GOLF COURSE
PLATZ 16/20

Site	Lage	
Maintenance	Instandhaltung	
Architect	Architekt	Austrogolf
Type	Typ	inland
Relief	Relief	
Water in play	Platz mit Wasser	
Exp. to wind	Wind ausgesetzt	
Trees in play	Platz mit Bäumen	

Scorecard	Chp.	Mens	Ladies
Scorekarte	Chp.	Herren	Damen
Length Länge	6359	6128	5377
Par	72	72	72

Advised golfing ability		0 12 24 36
Empfohlene Spielstärke		
Hcp required	Min. Handicap	36

CLUB HOUSE & AMENITIES
KLUBHAUS UND NEBENGEBÄUDE 7/10

Pro shop	Pro shop	
Driving range	Übungsplatz	
Sheltered	überdacht	8 mats
On grass	auf Rasen	yes
Putting-green	Putting-grün	yes
Pitching-green	Pitching-grün	yes

HOTEL FACILITIES
HOTEL BESCHREIBUNG 5/10

HOTELS HOTELS
Resort Hotel — Haugschlag
37 rooms, D ÖS 1180,- — on site
Tel (43) 02865 8441, Fax (43) 02865 5004

RESTAURANTS RESTAURANT
Perzy — Rottach 6 km

97

Der obligatorische Jack Nicklaus-Kurs jedes Landes und so macht auch Österreich keinen Unterschied zu fast allen europäischen Nationen. Man ist in Salzburg, der Geburtsstadt Mozarts, einer historischen Stadt par excellence. Wie auch immer, der Stil von Jack Nicklaus als Architekt ist näher zu Wagner als zu der leuchtenden Inspiration und dem Humor von Mozart. Die Kennzeichen sind alle da: die Strenge des Layouts, die Stetigkeit an Schwierigkeiten. Golfer, die schon mehrere Jack Nicklaus-Kurse gespielt haben werden seinen Stil in Form der Greens oder Bunker bzw. in der Anlage mancher Spielbahnen, wiedererkennen. Das ist der einzige Makel wenn man die unerwartete oder verschnörkelte Inspiration einer Pete Dyes in Vergleich zieht. In der Nähe des Wallersees, in einer für diese Gegend typischen und offenen Lichtungen und den ins Spiel kommenden zwei Seen, Wasserläufen und Sümpfen, umgeben von Bergen und Wäldern zählt Altentann zum beeindruckendsten Golfkurs des Landes.

Here, we are in Salzburg, the home of Mozart and historical city par excellence bathed in incomparable sunlight. However, the style of Jack Nicklaus the architect is closer to Wagner than to the luminous inspiration and humour of Mozart. The hallmarks are all here: the rigour of the layout, the spectacular continuity in holes and difficulties, and sheer efficiency. Golfers who have played a lot of Jack Nicklaus courses will recognize his style in the form of greens and bunkers, and even through the shape of certain holes. This is the only blot when compared to the more unexpected and probably more baroque inspirations of someone like Pete Dye. Located above lake Wallersee in moderately rolling landscape that is typical of the region, the course alternates between woodland and open space and features two lakes, stretches of water and marshes that often come into play. This is clearly the most impressive golf course in Austria.

Golf & Country Club Gut Altentann 1989
Hof 54
A - HENNDORF AM WALLERSEE

Office	Sekretariat	(43) 06214 6026-0
Pro shop	Pro shop	(43) 06214 6026-12
Fax	Fax	(43) 06214 6026-81
Situation	Lage	

Salzburg (pop. 147 000), 15 km

Annual closure	Jährliche Schliessung	yes
		1/11 → 31/3
Weekly closure	Wöchentliche Schliessung	no

Fees main season
Preisliste hochsaison 18 holes

	Week days Woche	We/Bank holidays We/Feiertag
Individual Individuell	ÖS 850,-	ÖS 850,-
Couple Ehepaar	ÖS 1700,-	ÖS 1700,-
Caddy	Caddy	ÖS 300,-
Electric Trolley	Elektrokarren	ÖS 170,-
Buggy	Elektrischer Wagen	ÖS 650,-
Clubs	Leihschläger	ÖS 200,-

Credit cards Kreditkarten
VISA - Eurocard - MasterCard - AMEX - DC

Access Zufahrt : Salzburg, 1 → Strasswalchen. In Henndorf, turn right → Altentann, → Golfplatz.
Map 1 on page 89 Karte 1 Seite 89

GOLF COURSE
PLATZ
18/20

Site	Lage	
Maintenance	Instandhaltung	
Architect	Architekt	Jack Nicklaus
Type	Typ	parkland, open country
Relief	Relief	
Water in play	Platz mit Wasser	
Exp. to wind	Wind ausgesetzt	
Trees in play	Platz mit Bäumen	

Scorecard Scorekarte	Chp. Chp.	Mens Herren	Ladies Damen
Length Länge	6223	5812	5415
Par	72	72	72

Advised golfing ability	0	12	24	36
Empfohlene Spielstärke				
Hcp required	Min. Handicap	34		

CLUB HOUSE & AMENITIES
KLUBHAUS UND NEBENGEBÄUDE
8/10

Pro shop	Pro shop	
Driving range	Übungsplatz	
Sheltered	überdacht	10 mats
On grass	auf Rasen	yes
Putting-green	Putting-grün	yes
Pitching-green	Pitching-grün	yes

HOTEL FACILITIES
HOTEL BESCHREIBUNG
7/10

HOTELS HOTELS

Sheraton Salzburg — Salzburg
163 rooms, D from ÖS 3500,- — 15 km
Tel (43) 0662 889 990, Fax (43) 0662 881 776

Österreichischer Hof — Salzburg
120 rooms, D from ÖS 4000,- — 15 km
Tel (43) 0662 889 77, Fax (43) 0662 889 7714

Goldener Hirsch — Salzburg
70 rooms, D from ÖS 4000,- — 14 km
Tel (43) 0662 808 40, Fax (43) 0662 843 349

RESTAURANTS RESTAURANT

Goldener Hirsch - Tel (43) 0662 808 40 — Salzburg 14 km

Brandstätter — Salzburg-Liefering
Tel (43) 0662 434 535 — 18 km

Pfefferschiff — Hallwang-Söllheim
Tel (43) 0662 661 242 — 10 km

98

Seefeld-Wildmoos ist bemerkenswert für seine Ruhe und Abgeschiedenheit die nur von Vögel und Golfer zart unterbrochen wird. Der Kurs liegt auf einem Plateau inmitten einer Waldlandschaft dessen Bergszenerie eine derartige Gemütsruhe kreiert, dass sie nicht einmal von einer Golfrunde zerstört werden kann und ist keinesfalls leicht, denn das hügelige Terrain wurde von Don Harradine gewissenhaft in Layout miteinbezogen. Verhältnismässig schwer dagegen die Back-Tee Version. Die Schwierigkeiten sind klar sichtbar aber die manchmal engen Spielbahnen erfordern gute Strategie und sorgfältige Schlagausführung. Trotz der Steilhänge (schwer zu gehen für nicht fite Golfer) hat der intelligente Kurs keine blinden Grüns - ein Zeichen des Architekten der für Besucher und Erstmalsspieler Verständnis zeigt, so auch der Club, der Greenfeespieler herzlich willkommen heisst. Und die können ihre erfolgreiche Bewältigung des «Bermuda Dreiecks» - Löcher 13 bis 15 - bei der hervorragenden heimischen Küche zelebrieren.

Seefeld-Wildmoos is remarkable for the absolute silence that reigns here, broken only very delicately by birds and golfers. The course is set on a plateau surrounded by woodland, where the scenery of mountains and trees create a sort of serenity that not even a round of golf could upset. It is by no means easy, however, as the hilly landscape has been faithfully designed into the layout by Harradine. Comparatively easy for mid-handicappers, it is a trickier proposition from the back tees. Difficulties are clearly visible but the sometimes narrow fairways call for good strategy and accurate shot-making. Despite the slopes (hard going for unfit golfers), this very intelligent course has hardly any blind greens, a sign of an architect who cares for visitors and first-time players. Talking of whom, green-fees are very warmly welcomed and can celebrate their handling of the «Bermuda triangle» - holes 13 to 15 - by tasting some of the excellent local cuisine.

Golfclub Seefeld-Wildmoos — 1970

Postfach 22
A - 6100 SEEFELD

Office	Sekretariat	(43) 05212 3003
Pro shop	Pro shop	(43) 05212 3003-19
Fax	Fax	(43) 05212 3722-22
Situation	Lage	

Innsbruck (pop. 120 000), 20 km

Annual closure	Jährliche Schliessung	1/11 → 30/4
Weekly closure	Wöchentliche Schliessung	no

Fees main season
Preisliste hochsaison full day

	Week days Woche	We/Bank holidays We/Feiertag
Individual Individuell	ÖS 630,-	ÖS 730,-
Couple Ehepaar	ÖS 1260,-	ÖS 1460,-

Seefeld hotels guests: – 25 %

Caddy	Caddy	no
Electric Trolley	Elektrokarren	yes
Buggy	Elektrischer Wagen	no
Clubs	Leihschläger	yes

Credit cards Kreditkarten
VISA - Eurocard - MasterCard

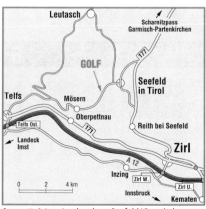

Access Zufahrt : Innsbruck, → Seefeld/Garmisch-Partenkirchen. In Seefeld, → Telfs, → Golfplatz.
Map 1 on page 88 Karte 1 Seite 88

GOLF COURSE / PLATZ — 17 /20

Site	Lage	
Maintenance	Instandhaltung	
Architect	Architekt	Donald Harradine
Type	Typ	mountain, hilly
Relief	Relief	
Water in play	Platz mit Wasser	
Exp. to wind	Wind ausgesetzt	
Trees in play	Platz mit Bäumen	

Scorecard Scorekarte	Chp. Chp.	Mens Herren	Ladies Damen
Length Länge	5960	5393	4676
Par	72	70	70

Advised golfing ability	0	12	24	36
Empfohlene Spielstärke				
Hcp required Min. Handicap	36			

CLUB HOUSE & AMENITIES / KLUBHAUS UND NEBENGEBÄUDE — 8 /10

Pro shop	Pro shop	
Driving range	Übungsplatz	
Sheltered	überdacht	4 mats
On grass	auf Rasen	yes
Putting-green	Putting-grün	yes
Pitching-green	Pitching-grün	yes

99

HOTEL FACILITIES / HOTEL BESCHREIBUNG — 7 /10

HOTELS HOTELS

Hotel Klosterbau		Seefeld
100 rooms, D ÖS 2400,-		4 km
Tel (43) 05212 26210, Fax (43) 05212 3885		
Goldener Adler		Innsbruck
37 rooms, D ÖS 1600,-		20 km
Tel (43) 0512 571 111, Fax (43) 0512 584 409		
Karwendelhof		Seefeld
42 rooms, D ÖS 1200,-		4 km
Tel (43) 05212 265-5, Fax (43) 05212 265-544		

RESTAURANTS RESTAURANT

Sir Richard		Seefeld
Tel (43) 05212 2093		6 km
Klosterbräu		Seefeld 4 km
Tel (43) 05212 262 70		

Neben den berühmten Städten Salzburg oder Wien sollte man die Chance nicht vergeben sich auch Graz anzusehen, das über eine grosse historische Altstadt als auch über ein aussergewöhnliches Zeughaus mit mehr als 30.000 Waffen verfügt... aber keine Golfschläger. Auf mässiger Höhe gelegen, ist der Kurs meist schon ab März bespielbar, am vergnüglichsten und schönsten im Sommer und Herbst. Während man wie meistens in Österreich einen hügeligen Kurs erwartet, ist Murhof eine Art Riesenpark der komplett eben ist. Umgeben von einen kleinen Fluss und herrlichen alten Bäumen, die trotz sehr angenehmer Umgebung seriöse Bedrohungen für unberechenbare Drives darstellen. Gute Spieler können, unter der Voraussetzung sie verstehen auch ihre feine Technik zum richtigen Zeitpunkt einzusetzen, jederzeit attackieren aber trotzdem ist niemand ein guter Score sicher. Das Hotel beim Kurs ist typisch österreichischer Landhausstil.

Next to the famous cities of Salzburg or Vienna, don't miss the chance to see Graz, which has preserved one of the largest old historical districts in the Germanic world and an extraordinary arsenal (Zeughaus) housing more than 30,000 weapons... but no golf clubs. At a moderate altitude, this course is playable from the Spring onwards but is naturally most enjoyable in the Summer and Autumn. While you might expect hilly and almost mountainous courses in Austria, this one is a sort of large park which is virtually flat, encircled by a river and covered with trees that form both a very pleasant environment and a serious threat to wayward drives. Good players can attack the course head on without expecting to understand the finer technicalities, as honest and open are the watchwords here. No-one of course is ever sure of a good score. The hotel on site is pure Austrian country style.

Steiermärkischer Golf-Club Murhof 1963

Frohnleiten
A - 8130 FROHNLEITEN-MURHOF

Office	Sekretariat	(43) 03126 3010
Pro shop	Pro shop	(43) 03126 3010
Fax	Fax	(43) 03126 300 029
Situation	Lage	

Graz, 20 km

Annual closure	Jährliche Schliessung	no
Weekly closure	Wöchentliche Schliessung	no

Fees main season
Preisliste hochsaison 18 holes

	Week days Woche	We/Bank holidays We/Feiertag
Individual Individuell	ÖS 660,-	ÖS 860,-
Couple Ehepaar	ÖS 1320,-	ÖS 1720,-

Golfhotel guests : – 50%

Caddy	Caddy	no
Electric Trolley	Elektrokarren	yes
Buggy	Elektrischer Wagen	no
Clubs	Leihschläger	yes

Credit cards Kreditkarten
VISA - DC

100

Access Zufahrt : Graz A9, S35.
2nd exit (2. Ausfahrt) Peggau. → Murhof, Golfplatz.
Map 2 on page 90 Karte 2 Seite 90

GOLF COURSE
PLATZ   16/20

Site	Lage	
Maintenance	Instandhaltung	
Architect	Architekt	B. von Limburger
Type	Typ	parkland
Relief	Relief	
Water in play	Platz mit Wasser	
Exp. to wind	Wind ausgesetzt	
Trees in play	Platz mit Bäumen	

Scorecard Scorekarte	Chp. Chp.	Mens Herren	Ladies Damen
Length Länge	6381	6198	5414
Par	72	72	72

Advised golfing ability Empfohlene Spielstärke		0 12 24 36
Hcp required	Min. Handicap	36

CLUB HOUSE & AMENITIES
KLUBHAUS UND NEBENGEBÄUDE   7/10

Pro shop	Pro shop	
Driving range	Übungsplatz	
Sheltered	überdacht	no
On grass	auf Rasen	yes
Putting-green	Putting-grün	yes
Pitching-green	Pitching-grün	yes

HOTEL FACILITIES
HOTEL BESCHREIBUNG   6/10

HOTELS HOTELS
Golfhotel Murhof   Golf Club
20 rooms, D ÖS 1880,-   on site
Tel (43) 03126 3000, Fax (43) 03126 30029

Austria Trend Hotel Europa   Graz 24 km
114 rooms, D ÖS 1200,-
Tel (43) 0316 7076-0, Fax (43) 0316 7076-606

RESTAURANTS RESTAURANT
Der Pichlmaier   Graz 22 km
Tel (43) 0316 471 597

Würde dieser Kurs in einem ländlichen Gebiet und nicht im Herzen des Praters, wenige Minuten vom historischen Zentrum Wiens entfernt, liegen hätte er keinerlei Bedeutung. Nein, mehr - der Kurs liegt inmitten einer Pferderennbahn - eine Tatsache die jeden Enthusiasmus entschlummern lässt. Jene Bäume die glücklicherweise gewachsen sind, leiten die Spielbahnen. Andere Schwierigkeiten sind die Bunker, hohes Rough und zwei Wasserhindernisse, wovon eines am 5. Loch ins Spiel kommt. Wien-Freudenau ist Österreichs ältester Golfclub und war schon Gastgeber grosser Turniere. Er hat die grösste Tradition im Land und ähnelt im Grunde genommen, britischen Clubs. Ein typischer Mitgliederclub mit wenig Schwierigkeiten für jedes Leistungsniveau. Wenn man eine der schönsten Städte Europas besucht wird man einen Stopp auf diesem Kurs um seinen Schwung in Schwung zu halten, nicht bereuen.

If it were laid out in the countryside rather than at the heart of Prater, a few minutes from the historical centre of Vienna, this course would probably not merit any significant detour. What is more, it is sited virtually in the middle of a hippodrome, a fact that evidently stunted any enthusiasm to move much earth. Fortunately, the trees have grown and now pleasantly line the holes. Other difficulties come from bunkers, tall rough and two water hazards, one of which is very much in play on the 5th hole. The Wien-Freudenau golf club is Austria's oldest and has hosted very many top tournaments. It is still one of the country's great traditional and virtually British clubs, a typical members' club with a course designed for them without too many difficulties, whatever the playing ability. With that said, when visiting one of the finest cities in Europe, a little stop-off here is an opportunity you won't regret to polish up your swing.

Golf-Club Wien — 1901

Freudenau 65 A
A - 1020 WIEN

Office	Sekretariat	(43) 01728 9564
Pro shop	Pro shop	(43) 01728 3790
Fax	Fax	(43) 01789 56420
Situation	Lage	

in Wien (pop. 1 640 000)

Annual closure	Jährliche Schliessung	no

Weekly closure Wöchentliche Schliessung
Monday, restaurant

Fees main season
Preisliste hochsaison full day

	Week days Woche	We/Bank holidays We/Feiertag
Individual Individuell	ÖS 800,-	*
Couple Ehepaar	ÖS 1600,-	*

* Week ends: only with a member

Caddy	Caddy	no
Electric Trolley	Elektrokarren	no
Buggy	Elektrischer Wagen	no
Clubs	Leihschläger	no

Credit cards Kreditkarten no

Access Zufahrt : Wien → Prater, Lusthaus
Map 2 on page 90 Karte 2 Seite 90

GOLF COURSE / PLATZ — 13/20

Site	Lage	
Maintenance	Instandhaltung	
Architect	Architekt	unknown
Type	Typ	inland
Relief	Relief	
Water in play	Platz mit Wasser	
Exp. to wind	Wind ausgesetzt	
Trees in play	Platz mit Bäumen	

Scorecard Scorekarte	Chp. Chp.	Mens Herren	Ladies Damen
Length Länge	5861	5697	5050
Par	70	70	70

Advised golfing ability Empfohlene Spielstärke	0	12	24	36

Hcp required Min. Handicap 28

CLUB HOUSE & AMENITIES / KLUBHAUS UND NEBENGEBÄUDE — 7/10

Pro shop	Pro shop	
Driving range	Übungsplatz	
Sheltered	überdacht	8 mats
On grass	auf Rasen	yes
Putting-green	Putting-grün	yes
Pitching-green	Pitching-grün	yes

101

HOTEL FACILITIES / HOTEL BESCHREIBUNG — 9/10

HOTELS HOTELS

Holiday Inn Crowne Plaza — Wien
367 rooms, D ÖS 2500,- — 4 km
Tel (43) 01 72 777, Fax (43) 01 72 951 06

Renaissance Penta Vienna Hotel — Wien
342 rooms, D ÖS 3600,- — 5 km
Tel (43) 01711 750, Fax (43) 01711 7590

Erzherzog Rainer — Wien
84 rooms, D ÖS 2220,- — 7 km
Tel (43) 01501 110, Fax (43) 01501 11350

RESTAURANTS RESTAURANT

Walter Bauer — Wien
Tel (43) 01512 9871 — 6 km

Fadinger — Wien
Tel (43) 01533 4341 — 7 km

Zum Kukuck — Wien
Tel (43) 01512 8470 — 6 km

"Al bij al is het hier op aarde nog zo slecht niet."

406 Coupé

PEUGEOT

Belgique
België
Luxembourg

L a Belgique compte plus de 33.000 joueurs de golf pour 45 parcours de 18 trous environ. Les golfs présentés ici sont ouverts au public. Certes, une partie d'entre eux peut être difficile d'accès en week-end, en raison de leur grand nombre de membres, mais les voyageurs ont souvent la possibilité d'y jouer en semaine. Pour les joueurs belges comme pour les étrangers, le fait d'être muni d'une lettre d'introduction de leur propre club peut cependant faciliter les choses.

B elgië heeft meer dan 33.000 spelers op ongeveer 45 banen 18-holesbanen. De meeste golfclubs in Peugeot Golf Guide zijn vrij toegankelijk voor het publiek. In sommige raakt men wel moeilijker binnen tijdens het week-end, wegens hun groot aantal leden, maar 'reizigers' bevinden zich meestal gemakkelijker in de mogelijkheid om tijdens de week te spelen. Voor Belgische en buitenlandse spelers is een introductiebrief van de eigen club vaak een goed idee, om de zaken eenvoudiger te maken.

B elgium has more than 33,000 golfers playing on around 50 eighteen-hole courses. All golf courses presented in this Guide are open to the public. Some may be difficult to play on week-ends owing to the number of members, but travelling green-feers should often be able to play during the week. Carrying a letter of introduction from your club may be a help, both for Belgian and foreign players.

CLASSEMENT DES PARCOURS
RANGSCHIKKING VAN DE TERREINEN
CLASSIFICATION OF COURSES

Note du Club-house et annexes
Cijfer van het Club-House & dependances
Club-house and facilities

Note du parcours
Cijfer van het terrein
(Course score)

Note de l'environnement hôtelier
Cijfer van hotelaccomodatie in de omgeving
Hotel facility score

18 7 7	Royal Zoute		B	121	Page Bladzijde

Note	Parcours	Pays	Page	Note	Parcours	Pays	Page
18 7 7	Royal Zoute	B	121	**14** 7 4	Falnuee	B	109
17 8 7	Ravenstein	B	117	**14** 7 6	Keerbergen	B	111
17 7 7	Spa (Les Fagnes)	B	123	**14** 6 6	Oudenaarde	B	115
16 7 7	Antwerp	B	107	**14** 7 6	Rigenée	B	118
16 7 7	Kikuoka	L	128	**14** 6 5	Rinkven *Red - White*	B	119
16 7 4	Limburg	B	112	**14** 7 8	Spiegelven	B	124
16 7 7	Sart-Tilman	B	122	**13** 7 7	Bercuit	B	108
16 8 7	Waterloo *La Marache*	B	125	**13** 6 7	Grand Ducal		
15 7 5	Hainaut				de Luxembourg	L	127
	Bruyere-Quesnoy-Etangs	B	110	**13** 7 6	Mont-Garni	B	113
15 7 7	Oostende	B	114	**13** 6 6	Palingbeek	B	116
15 8 6	Royal Latem	B	120				

CLASSEMENT DE L'ENVIRONNEMENT HOTELIER
RANGSCHIKKING VAN DE HOTELACCOMODATIE
CLASSIFICATION OF HOTELS FACILITIES

106

Note	Parcours	Pays	Page	Note	Parcours	Pays	Page
14 7 **8**	Spiegelven	B	124	14 7 **6**	Keerbergen	B	111
16 7 **7**	Antwerp	B	107	13 7 **6**	Mont-Garni	B	113
13 7 **7**	Bercuit	B	108	14 6 **6**	Oudenaarde	B	115
13 6 **7**	Grand Ducal			13 6 **6**	Palingbeek	B	116
	de Luxembourg	L	127	14 7 **6**	Rigenée	B	118
16 7 **7**	Kikuoka	L	128	15 8 **6**	Royal Latem	B	120
15 7 **7**	Oostende	B	114	15 7 **5**	Hainaut		
17 8 **7**	Ravenstein	B	117		*Bruyere-Quesnoy-Etangs*	B	110
18 7 **7**	Royal Zoute	B	121	14 6 **5**	Rinkven *Red - White*	B	119
16 7 **7**	Sart-Tilman	B	122	14 7 **4**	Falnuee	B	109
17 7 **7**	Spa (Les Fagnes)	B	123	16 7 **4**	Limburg	B	112
16 8 **7**	Waterloo *La Marache*	B	125				

Créé en 1888, remodelé par Willie Park en 1913 et Tom Simpson en 1930, c'est l'un des plus anciens golfs d'Europe Continentale et le plus ancien golf de Belgique, mais il ne fait vraiment pas son âge. Comme il a conservé son caractère «old-style», il n'est pas utile de driver comme John Daly, ni d'avoir le toucher au putting d'un Corey Pavin. Mais il ne faut surtout pas sous-estimer les difficultés du tracé, ce parcours a une main de fer dans un gant de velours. Tous les architectes de golf pourraient d'ailleurs s'inspirer de l'intelligence du tracé, du placement très stratégique des bunkers, de la mise en jeu des arbres et de la bruyère. Ici, les principales difficultés concernent surtout les meilleurs joueurs, mais le parcours est une inspiration pour tous. Jouer ici est un vrai bonheur, et plus encore avec la pression d'une compétition. Et le charme visuel du lieu ajoute encore au plaisir.

Created in 1888 then redesigned by Willie Park in 1913 and Tom Simpson in 1930, this is Belgium's oldest club, although it looks as young as ever. Having the privilege of being an old-style course, its length doesn't mean having to drive à la John Daly and the subtle greens hardly require the putting touch of a Corey Pavin. But the trouble in store should never be under-estimated, as this is an iron hand in a velvet glove. The remarkably intelligent layout, highly strategic bunkering and the presence and use of trees and heather are an example for all modern designers. Here, the main difficulties have cleverly been reserved for the better players, but the general layout is an inspiration for us all. Playing here is a real pleasure, and playing with the pressure of a tournament even more so. The site adds visual charm to the enjoyment of golfing.

Royal Antwerp Golf Club		1888
G. Capiaulei, 2		
B - 2950 KAPELLEN		
Office	Secrétariat	(32) 03 - 666 84 56
Pro shop	Pro-shop	(32) 03 - 666 46 87
Fax	Fax	(32) 03 - 666 44 37
Situation	Situation	
Antwerpen / Anvers (pop. 403 072), 15 km		
Brussel / Bruxelles, 48 km		
Annual closure	Fermeture annuelle	no
Weekly closure	Fermeture hebdomadaire	
no Monday (lundi), pro shop closed		

Fees main season Tarifs haute saison full day

	Week days Semaine	We/Bank holidays We/Férié
Individual Individuel	3 000 BF	*
Couple Couple	6 000 BF	*

GF: 2 250 BF if member of Belgian Golf Federation - *
W/E: members & guests only

Caddy	Caddy	no
Electric Trolley	Chariot électrique	no
Buggy	Voiturette	1200 BF
Clubs	Clubs	no

Credit cards Cartes de crédit VISA - Eurocard

Access Accès : E19 Anvers → Breda, Exit 5 → N11
Map 1 on page 104 Carte 1 Page 104

GOLF COURSE / PARCOURS — 16/20

Site	Site	
Maintenance	Entretien	
Architect	Architecte	Willie Park Jr Tom Simpson
Type	Type	parkland
Relief	Relief	
Water in play	Eau en jeu	
Exp. to wind	Exposé au vent	
Trees in play	Arbres en jeu	

Scorecard Carte de score	Chp. Chp.	Mens Mess.	Ladies Da.
Length Long.	6187	6155	5252
Par	73	73	73

Advised golfing ability Niveau de jeu recommandé	0	12	24	36
Hcp required Handicap exigé	28			

CLUB HOUSE & AMENITIES / CLUB HOUSE ET ANNEXES — 7/10

Pro shop	Pro-shop	
Driving range	Practice	
Sheltered	couvert	4 mats
On grass	sur herbe	yes
Putting-green	putting-green	yes
Pitching-green	pitching green	yes

HOTEL FACILITIES / ENVIRONNEMENT HOTELIER — 7/10

HOTELS HÔTELS
Hilton — Antwerpen
199 rooms, D 10 900 BF — 15 km
Tel (32) 03 - 204 12 12, Fax (32) 03 - 204 12 13

Alfa Theater — Antwerpen
122 rooms, D 5 700 BF — 15 km
Tel (32) 03 - 231 17 20, Fax (32) 03 - 233 88 58

Rubens — Antwerpen
35 rooms, D 6 500 BF — 15 km
Tel (32) 03 - 222 48 48, Fax (32) 03 - 225 19 40

RESTAURANTS RESTAURANT
De Bellefleur — Kapellen
Tel (32) 03 - 664 67 19 — 1 km

't Fornuis — Antwerpen
Tel (32) 03 - 233 62 70 — 15 km

107

De son propre aveu, Robert Trent Jones n'a pas donné son meilleur, et on ne retrouve notamment pas ici son dessin de bunkers. Certains trous sont assez fatigants et «tricky», mais d'autres valent le déplacement. Le relief très mouvementé interdit de quitter les fairways, et les frappeurs se sentiront souvent privés de leur liberté d'expression, du moins s'ils souhaitent absolument jouer leur driver. L'arrosage des fairways a néanmoins rendu plus facile le choix des zones de réception des balles. Les greens bien défendus, pas toujours très accueillants aux balles et souvent rapides proposent un sérieux challenge au putting. Après avoir joué plusieurs fois ce parcours, on en comprend mieux les pièges, mais il ne perdra pas complètement son caractère hasardeux. Un conseil : jouer au soleil et en voiturette, pour mieux profiter du décor arboré et des superbes panoramas sur le Brabant wallon.

You won't find here the bunkers that have come to typify Robert Trent Jones, and he readily admits that this is not one of his best courses. A number of holes are tiring and tricky but others are probably good enough to make you feel it was all worthwhile. The hilly terrain means you are best advised to keep it in the fairway, so big-hitters, if they insist on using the driver, might easily run into trouble. More optimistically, fairway sprinklers have made the choice of landing area a little easier. The greens, well-guarded, often slick but not always as receptive as they might be, are a stiff challenge to the best putter. After several rounds here you will begin to understand the traps a little better but the course is never completely risk-free. One piece of advice: play in sunny weather and with a buggy to make the most of the tree-covered landscape and wonderful views over the Walloon Brabant.

Golf de Bercuit

1965

Domaine de Bercuit, Les Gottes, 3
B - 1390 GREZ-DOICEAU

Office	Secrétariat	(32) 010 - 84 15 01
Pro shop	Pro-shop	(32) 010 - 84 15 01
Fax	Fax	(32) 010 - 84 55 95
Situation	Situation	

Wavre (pop. 27 162), 5 km
Bruxelles / Brussel, 30 km

Annual closure	Fermeture annuelle	no
Weekly closure	Fermeture hebdomadaire	no

Monday (lundi), Pro-shop & Secretariat closed

Fees main season
Tarifs haute saison 18 holes

	Week days Semaine	We/Bank holidays We/Férié
Individual Individuel	1 450 BF	2 600 BF
Couple Couple	2 900 BF	5 200 BF
Caddy Caddy	no	
Electric Trolley Chariot électrique	500 BF	
Buggy Voiturette	1 200 BF	
Clubs Clubs	500 BF	

Credit cards Cartes de crédit
VISA - Eurocard - MasterCard

Access Accès : E411 Bruxelles → Namur, Exit (Sortie) 8
→ Grez Doiceau, turn right on N243,
2 km on left hand side → Dion
Map 1 on page 105 Carte 1 Page 105

GOLF COURSE
PARCOURS

13/20

Site	Site	
Maintenance	Entretien	
Architect	Architecte	Robert Trent Jones
Type	Type	forest
Relief	Relief	
Water in play	Eau en jeu	
Exp. to wind	Exposé au vent	
Trees in play	Arbres en jeu	

Scorecard	Chp.	Mens	Ladies
Carte de score	Chp.	Mess.	Da.
Length Long.	5931	5931	5208
Par	72	72	72

Advised golfing ability		0 12 24 36
Niveau de jeu recommandé		
Hcp required	Handicap exigé	32 Men, 36 Ladies

CLUB HOUSE & AMENITIES
CLUB HOUSE ET ANNEXES

7/10

Pro shop	Pro-shop	
Driving range	Practice	
Sheltered	couvert	10 mats
On grass	sur herbe	no
Putting-green	putting-green	yes
Pitching-green	pitching green	yes

HOTEL FACILITIES
ENVIRONNEMENT HOTELIER

7/10

HOTELS HÔTELS

Le Domaine des Champs		Wavre
18 rooms, D 2 800 BF		5 km
Tel (32) 010 - 22 75 25, Fax (32) 010 - 24 17 31		

Novotel - 102 rooms, D 3 200 BF		Wavre
Tel (32) 010 - 41 13 63, Fax (32) 010 - 41 19 22		5 km

Château du Lac		Genval
84 rooms, D 9 500 BF		11 km
Tel (32) 02 - 655 71 11, Fax (32) 02 - 655 74 44		

RESTAURANTS RESTAURANT

Château du Lac		Genval
Tel (32) 02 - 655 71 11		11 km

Le Vert Délice - Tel (32) 010 - 22 90 01		Wavre 5 km

Le Jardin Gourmand		Wavre
Tel (32) 010 - 24 15 26		5 km

Un joli Club, avec son Club house dans les anciennes écuries voûtées remontant au Moyen-Age, le charme d'un paysage vallonné, la présence de deux rivières. Les puristes pourront relever une rupture avec la tradition, avec cinq par 3 (dont quatre au retour) et trois par 5, pour un par 70 et une longueur réduite. La grande difficulté consiste à tenir compte des dénivellations pour choisir les clubs, et aussi pour placer les drives : il suffit d'un peu d'inattention pour voir les obstacles très en jeu, et manquer quelques greens surélevés qu'il vaut mieux toucher directement. Jean Jottrand a produit un dessin agréable, bien qu'un peu rustique, mais si l'on regrette son imagination un peu timide, ce parcours reste accessible à tous niveaux. On conseillera plutôt de jouer ici entre amis, pour le plaisir, sans vouloir chercher d'émotions visuelles et golfiques très violentes.

A pretty golf club, with a club-house in former vaulted stables dating from the middle ages, rolling landscape and two rivers. The purists will point to the break from tradition, as this short course is a par 70 with five par 3s (four of which are on the back 9) and three par 5s. The major difficulty is assessing the slopes and hills before choosing your club, and positioning the tee-shot. A momentary lapse of concentration can take you straight into the hazards and result in missing some of the elevated greens, which you are well advised to pitch directly. Jean Jottrand has produced a pleasant layout, perhaps a little on the rustic side, but despite the regrettable lack of imagination, the course is playable by golfers of all levels. Your best bet here is a round with friends, just for fun, without looking for true visual or golfing excitement.

Golf de Falnuée — 1987

55, rue E. Pirson
B - 5032 MAZY

Office	Secrétariat	(32) 081 - 63 30 90
Pro shop	Pro-shop	(32) 081 - 63 30 90
Fax	Fax	(32) 081 - 63 37 64
Situation	Situation	

Namur (pop. 97 845), 15 km

Annual closure	Fermeture annuelle	no
Weekly closure	Fermeture hebdomadaire	monday (lundi)

Fees main season
Tarifs haute saison 18 holes

	Week days Semaine	We/Bank holidays We/Férié
Individual Individuel	900 BF	1 400 BF
Couple Couple	1 800 BF	2 800 BF

Caddy	Caddy	no
Electric Trolley	Chariot électrique	400 BF/18 trous
Buggy	Voiturette	1 000 BF
Clubs	Clubs	400 BF

Credit cards Cartes de crédit
VISA - Eurocard - Mastercard - AMEX - DC

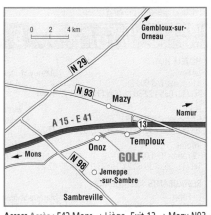

```
        0    2    4 km          Gembloux-sur-
                               Orneau
          N 29
          N 93      Mazy
                              Namur
     A 15 - E 41          13
                      Temploux
  Mons      Onoz
          N 98       GOLF
          Jemeppe
          -sur-Sambre
      Sambreville
```

Access Accès : E42 Mons → Liège, Exit 13 → Mazy N93
Map 1 on page 105 Carte 1 Page 105

GOLF COURSE / PARCOURS — 14/20

Site	Site	
Maintenance	Entretien	
Architect	Architecte	Jean Jottrand
Type	Type	country, forest
Relief	Relief	
Water in play	Eau en jeu	
Exp. to wind	Exposé au vent	
Trees in play	Arbres en jeu	

Scorecard Carte de score	Chp. Chp.	Mens Mess.	Ladies Da.
Length Long.	5590	5590	4750
Par	70	70	70

Advised golfing ability
Niveau de jeu recommandé — 0 12 24 36

Hcp required — Handicap exigé — 36

CLUB HOUSE & AMENITIES / CLUB HOUSE ET ANNEXES — 7/10

Pro shop	Pro-shop	
Driving range	Practice	
Sheltered	couvert	6 mats
On grass	sur herbe	no, 14 mats open air
Putting-green	putting-green	yes
Pitching-green	pitching green	yes

109

HOTEL FACILITIES / ENVIRONNEMENT HOTELIER — 4/10

HOTELS HÔTELS

Beauregard — Namur
51 rooms, D 3250 BF — 15 km
Tel (32) 081 - 23 00 28, Fax (32) 081 - 24 12 09

Grand Hôtel de Flandre — Namur
33 rooms, D 3 000 BF — 15 km
Tel (32) 081 - 23 18 68, Fax (32) 081 - 22 80 60

Les Tanneurs — Namur
16 rooms, D 6 000 BF — 15 km
Tel (32) 081 - 23 19 99, Fax (32) 081 - 22 97 03

RESTAURANTS RESTAURANT

La Bergerie — Lives-sur-Meuse
Tel (32) 081 - 58 06 13 — 20 km

Biétrumé Picar — Namur
Tel (32) 081 - 23 07 39 — 15 km

Pour le 18 trous traditionnel (Bruyères et Quesnoy), une architecture classique de Tom Simpson, sur un terrain sablonneux jouable toute l'année. Les obstacles sont bien visibles, stratégiquement bien placés, notamment les bunkers de fairway, s'ajoutant aux nombreux arbres du parcours (certains bois devraient être aujourd'hui éclaircis), qui donnent un sentiment de calme et de charme tout à fait plaisants. Mais c'est un aspect trompeur, car les greens bien défendus sont accessibles après des drives bien placés et de bons coups de fers. Pour bien scorer, il faut maîtriser les balles levées, avec assez d'effet quand les greens sont rapides. Ce parcours au caractère britannique réserve de grandes satisfactions, avec un petit parfum d'autrefois très agréable. «Les Etangs» (9 trous) complètent cet équipement, avec beaucoup de trous en dog-leg. Très scénique et plus «moderne», il exige un jeu très long et précis, au milieu des pins.

The traditional 18-hole course is a classic design from Tom Simpson on sandy soil that is playable all year. The hazards are clearly visible and strategically well located, especially the fairway bunkers, adding to the many trees on the course which give a pleasing impression of tranquillity and charm (some woods should be thined). But appearances can be deceptive, and here the well-defended greens, always perfectly in line with well-placed drives, call for some pretty sharp ironwork. Good scores need tight pitch and lob shots, and backspin too, when the greens are fast. The course has a pleasant British flavour and can give immense satisfaction with its very pleasant olde worlde charm. The 9-hole course ("Les Etangs") completes the picture and includes a lot of dog-legs. Now mature, very scenic and more "modern" (i.e. lots of water), it demands both length and precision through the pine-trees.

Royal Golf Club du Hainaut — 1933

2, rue de la Verrerie
B - 7050 ERBISOEUL

Office	Secrétariat	(32) 065 - 22 94 74
Pro shop	Pro-shop	(32) 065 - 22 79 29
Fax	Fax	(32) 065 - 22 51 54
Situation	Situation	

Mons (pop. 77 021), 5 km
Bruxelles / Brussel, 60 km

Annual closure	Fermeture annuelle	no
Weekly closure	Fermeture hebdomadaire	no

Fees main season
Tarifs haute saison 18 holes

	Week days Semaine	We/Bank holidays We/Férié
Individual Individuel	1 500 FB	2 000 FB
Couple Couple	3 000 FB	4 000 FB

Caddy	Caddy	no
Electric Trolley	Chariot électrique	no
Buggy	Voiturette	1 000 BF
Clubs	Clubs	no

Credit cards Cartes de crédit
VISA - Eurocard - Mastercard - DC

110

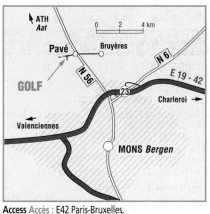

Access Accès : E42 Paris-Bruxelles,
Exit (Sortie) 23, N6 → Mons, N56 → Ath
Map 1 on page 104 Carte 1 Page 104

GOLF COURSE PARCOURS — 15/20

Site	Site	
Maintenance	Entretien	
Architect	Architecte	Tom Simpson
Type	Type	forest, hilly
Relief	Relief	
Water in play	Eau en jeu	
Exp. to wind	Exposé au vent	
Trees in play	Arbres en jeu	

Scorecard Carte de score	Chp. Chp.	Mens Mess.	Ladies Da.
Length Long.	6042	6042	5318
Par	72	72	72

Advised golfing ability		0	12	24	36
Niveau de jeu recommandé					
Hcp required	Handicap exigé	36			

CLUB HOUSE & AMENITIES CLUB HOUSE ET ANNEXES — 7/10

Pro shop	Pro-shop	
Driving range	Practice	
Sheltered	couvert	yes
On grass	sur herbe	no, mats open air
Putting-green	putting-green	yes
Pitching-green	pitching green	yes

HOTEL FACILITIES ENVIRONNEMENT HOTELIER — 5/10

HOTELS HÔTELS

La Forêt — Masnuy St-Jean
51 rooms, D 3 900 BF — 4 km
Tel (32) 065 - 72 36 85, Fax (32) 065 - 72 41 44

Lido — Mons
67 rooms, D 3 900 BF — 6 km
Tel (32) 065 - 32 78 00, Fax (32) 065 - 84 37 22

Infotel — Mons
19 rooms, D 3 000 BF — 6 km
Tel (32) 065 - 35 62 21, Fax (32) 065 - 35 62 24

RESTAURANTS RESTAURANT

La Forêt — Masnuy St-Jean
Tel (32) 065 - 72 36 85 — 4 km

Devos — Mons
Tel (32) 065 - 35 13 35 — 6 km

De namen van de architecten alleen al zijn een aanduiding voor een grondige kennis van de golfsport. Op 38 hectare zijn ze erin geslaagd een par 70 met 6 zeer afwisselende par 3 te herbergen. Dit is een klassiek parcours, zeer kort en vlak (het kan zeer vlug gespeeld worden), maar het is een echte "challenge" qua precisie en intelligent spel. Het is geschikt voor alle handicaps, en speciaal op prijs gesteld door de dames, waarvan de besten tee-offs hebben die quasi gelijk zijn aan die van de heren. Goed onderhouden met netjes opgeruimd onderhout : dit is de perfecte golf om zichzelf een pleziertje te gunnen, maar ook om het spel met de kleinere "irons" wat bij te schaven, dankzij zeer interessante approaches van de greens naargelang de positie van de vlaggen. Talrijke "out of bounds" zetten de slordige spelers wat onder druk, en verschillende strategisch aangelegde vijvers zorgen voor wat subtiliteit, vooral op de 2, 15 en 18, een par 4 langs de rand van een vijver, waarboven het Club-House uittorent.

The names of the architects obviously denote in-depth knowledge of the game of golf. They have successfully squeezed a par 70 into 38 hectares (95 acres), with 6 very different par 3s. This is a classical, very short and flat course (ideal for fast play), but also a challenge of precision and intelligence. Suitable for all levels, it is particularly popular with the ladies, the best of whom tee off very close to the men's tees. Well upkept with the rough and undergrowth also neatly cleared, this is a perfect course for enjoying yourself and honing your short irons; some of the approach shots are a real treat, depending on the pin positions. Wayward golfers will feel the pressure of a lot of out-of-bounds, and several strategic lakes call for subtle strategy, especially holes 2, 15 and 18, a par 4 edged by a lake and overlooked by the club-house.

Keerbergen Golf Club — 1968
Vlieghavenlaan, 50
B - 3140 KEERBERGEN

Office	Secretariaat	(32) 015 - 23 49 61
Pro shop	Pro shop	(32) 015 - 23 49 63
Fax	Fax	(32) 015 - 23 57 37
Situation	Locatie	

Mechelen / Malines (pop. 69 430), 10 km
Brussel / Bruxelles, 25 km

Annual closure	Jaarlijkse sluiting	no
Weekly closure	Wekelijkse sluitingsdag	no

Monday (maandag), restaurant closed

Fees main season
Hoogseizoen tarieven 18 holes

	Week days Weekdagen	We/Bank holidays We/Feestdagen
Individual Individueel	1 300 BF	1 800 BF
Couple Paar	2 600 BF	3 600 BF

Caddy	Caddy	no
Electric Trolley	Electrische trolley	no
Buggy	Buggy	1 000 BF/18 holes
Clubs	Clubs	600 BF/18 holes

Credit cards Creditkaarten VISA - Mastercard - DC

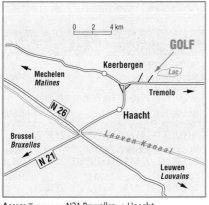

GOLF

Keerbergen *Lac*

Mechelen Malines

Tremolo →

N 26

Haacht

Brussel Bruxelles

N 21

Leuwen Louvains

Leuven Kanaal

0 2 4 km

Access Toegang : N21 Bruxelles → Haacht,
→ Keerbergen, → Tremolo, Golf
Map 1 on page 105 Auto kaart 1 Blz 105

GOLF COURSE / BAAN — 14/20

Site	Terrein	■■■■■□
Maintenance	Onderhoud	■■■■■□
Architect	Architect	Cotton, Penninck Lawree
Type	Type baan	parkland, residential
Relief	Reliëf	■■□□□□
Water in play	Waterhazards	■■■□□□
Exp. to wind	Windgevoelig	■■■□□□
Trees in play	Bomen	■■■■□□

Scorecard Scorekaart	Chp. Back tees	Mens Heren	Ladies Damen
Length Lengte	5600	5530	4867
Par	70	70	70

Advised golfing ability Aanbevolen golfvaardigheid	0 12 24 36	
Hcp required Vereiste hcp	36	

CLUB HOUSE & AMENITIES / CLUB HOUSE EN ANNEXEN — 7/10

Pro shop	Pro shop	■■■■□□
Driving range	Oefenbaan	■■■■□□
Sheltered	overdekt	3 mats
On grass	op gras	no, 10 mats open air
Putting-green	putting-green	yes
Pitching-green	pitching-green	yes

HOTEL FACILITIES / HOTELS IN OMGEVING — 6/10

HOTELS HOTELS
Alfa Alba - 43 rooms, D 6 700 BF — Mechelen 10 km
Tel. (32) 015 - 42 03 03, Fax (32) 015 - 42 37 88

Berkenhof — Keerbergen 1 km
7 rooms, D 8 250 BF
Tel. (32) 015 - 73 01 01, Fax (32) 015 - 73 02 02

Den Grooten Wolsack — Mechelen 10 km
14 rooms, D 3 700 BF
Tel. (32) 015 - 21 86 03, Fax (32) 015 - 21 86 28

RESTAURANTS RESTAURANT
The Paddock - Tel (32) 015 - 51 19 34 Keerbergen 1 km
D'Hoogh - Tel (32) 015 - 21 75 53 Mechelen 10 km
Berkenhof - Tel (32) 015 - 73 01 01 Kerbergen1 km

111

Midden in een natuurreservaat en een landschap van sparren en berken, typerend voor de Kempen, wordt dit licht golvend terrein een ware streling voor het oog als de heide in bloei staat, op het einde van de zomer en in de herfst. Het is het stroke-play parcours bij uitstek, met een harmonisch speelritme, enkele moeilijke pieken die ges- preksstof vormen voor achteraf (sommige par 4 zijn hardnekkig), zeer mooie par 5 en een juweeltje, de 8, een kleine technische par 4 zoals men er geen meer durft ontwerpen. Het design van FW Hawtree is van een op en top Brits classicisme, het ontwerp ziet eruit alsof de natuur zelf het zo gewild heeft, mooi gelegen tussen de heide en het bos, en het heeft een zeer "intelligente" bunkering (recent gerestaureerde bunkers rond vijf greens). Daar het terrein zeer goed uitgebalanceerd is, met werkelijke verschillen tussen de champion tees en de andere, is het er zeer aangenaam spelen op elk niveau, en keert men met plezier nog eens terug. Onderhoud is nu zeer goed.

Set in a nature reserve of pine and birch that are typical of the Campine region, this slightly rolling course is a beauti- ful sight when the heather is in full bloom in late summer and in autumn. This is an excellent course for stroke-play, neatly balanced with a few memorable tough moments on the back nine (some par 4s are really hard going), some fa- bulous par 5s and a gem of a hole, the 8th, which is a short but very technical 4-par, the likes of which are hardly ever found these days. F.W. Hawtree's layout is a pure British classic, winding its way almost naturally between heather and wood with particularly intelligent bunkering (newly restored bunkers around five greens). Because it is so well ba- lanced, with real differences between the tournament and hacker tees, it is pleasant to play, again and again, whate- ver your level. Upkeep is very good now.

Limburg Golf & Country Club   1967

Golfstraat 1
B - 3530 HOUTHALEN

Office	Secretariaat	(32) 089 - 38 35 43
Pro shop	Pro shop	(32) 089 - 84 32 04
Fax	Fax	(32) 089 - 84 12 08
Situation	Locatie	

Hasselt (pop. 64 722), 15 km

Annual closure	Jaarlijkse sluiting	no
Weekly closure	Wekelijkse sluitingsdag	no

Monday (maandag),
Pro-shop & Restaurant closed (bar open)

Fees main season
Hoogseizoen tarieven 18 holes

	Week days Weekdagen	We/Bank holidays We/Feestdagen
Individual Individueel	1 450 BF	1 850 BF
Couple Paar	2 900 BF	3 700 BF
Caddy Caddy	no	
Electric Trolley Electrische trolley	no	
Buggy Buggy	1 200 BF/18 holes	
Clubs Clubs	no	

Credit cards Creditkaarten VISA - Eurocard - Mastercard

Access Toegang : E314 Brussel → Aix-la-Chapelle,
Exit 29, N715 → Eindhoven, Houthalen, → Golf
Map 1 on page 105 Auto kaart 1 Blz 105

GOLF COURSE
BAAN   16/20

Site	Terrein	
Maintenance	Onderhoud	
Architect	Architect	Fred Hawtree
Type	Type baan	forest, heathland
Relief	Reliëf	
Water in play	Waterhazards	
Exp. to wind	Windgevoelig	
Trees in play	Bomen	

Scorecard Scorekaart	Chp. Back tees	Mens Heren	Ladies Damen
Length Lengte	6128	5750	5156
Par	72	72	72

Advised golfing ability Aanbevolen golfvaardigheid	0 12 24 36
Hcp required Vereiste hcp	W/E: 32 Men, 36 Ladies

CLUB HOUSE & AMENITIES
CLUB HOUSE EN ANNEXEN   7/10

Pro shop	Pro shop	
Driving range	Oefenbaan	
Sheltered	overdekt	14 mats
On grass	op gras	no, 9 mats open air
Putting-green	putting-green	yes
Pitching-green	pitching-green	yes

HOTEL FACILITIES
HOTELS IN OMGEVING   4/10

HOTELS HOTELS

Scholteshof   Hasselt
11 rooms, D 12 000 BF   15 km
Tel (32) 011 - 25 02 02, Fax (32) 011 - 25 43 28

Holiday Inn   Hasselt
106 rooms, D 6 900 BF   15 km
Tel (32) 011 - 24 22 00, Fax (32) 011 - 22 39 35

Hassotel - 30 rooms, D 3 820 BF   Hasselt
Tel (32) 011 - 22 64 92, Fax (32) 011 - 22 94 77   15 km

Century - 17 rooms, D 2 500 BF   Hasselt
Tel (32) 011 - 22 47 99, Fax (32) 011 - 23 18 24   15 km

RESTAURANTS RESTAURANT

Scholteshof - Tel (32) 011 - 25 02 02   Hasselt 15 km

De Barrier - Tel (32) 011 - 52 55 25   Houthalen 3 km

112

Avec quelques arbres en moins (2, 13, 14, 17) qui empiètent sur la bonne ligne de jeu, l'élagage de certaines branches et un plus large net1toyage des sous-bois, Mont-Garni donnerait plus encore de plaisir aux golfeurs, rendrait plus évidente la stratégie de jeu et ne punirait vraiment que les coups lâchés. En revanche, le challenge est réel, beaucoup de trous sont intéressants, même si les pars 3 sont plus longs que vraiment subtils (leurs départs sont mal orientés). Il faut constamment se méfier des arbres et des étangs, qui rendent cependant le site assez séduisant : sur ce parcours demandant de la précision, on ne conseillera les départs arrière qu'aux joueurs de très bon niveau, les autres s'y amuseront beaucoup en match-play, en famille ou entre amis de niveau équivalent. On suivra avec intérêt l'évolution de ce parcours, et les non-golfeurs peuvent préférer le centre équestre sur place que porter les sacs...

With fewer trees right in the line of fire (on the 2nd, 13th, 14 th and 17th holes), the trimming of a few branches and more extensive clearing of undergrowth, Mont-Garni would be even more enjoyable to play, would make game strategy more obvious and would punish only the really wayward shot. However, the challenge here hits you in the eye, with a lot of interesting holes, even though the par 3s are longer than they are subtle. You have to be constantly on the outlook to avoid the trees and lakes, which at the same time add to the course's appeal. On a course like this, which demands precision play, we would recommend the back-tees only for the better players ; the others can move forward and have fun with the family or friends with a round of match-play. It will be interesting to see how this course evolves. Rather than lug golf bags around, non-golfers may prefer the riding stables next door.

Golf du Mont-Garni — 1990

Rue du Mont-Garni, 3
B - 7331 BAUDOUR

Office	Secrétariat	(32) 065 - 62 27 19
Pro shop	Pro-shop	(32) 065 - 62 27 19
Fax	Fax	(32) 065 - 62 34 10
Situation	Situation	

Mons / Bergen (pop. 77 021), 7 km

Annual closure	Fermeture annuelle	no
Weekly closure	Fermeture hebdomadaire	no

Fees main season
Tarifs haute saison 18 holes

	Week days Semaine	We/Bank holidays We/Férié
Individual Individuel	1 000 BF	1 500 BF
Couple Couple	2 000 BF	3 000 BF

Caddy	Caddy	no
Electric Trolley	Chariot électrique	no
Buggy	Voiturette	1 000 BF
Clubs	Clubs	50 BF

Credit cards Cartes de crédit
VISA - Eurocard - Mastercard

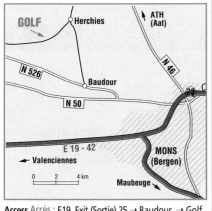

Access Accès : E19, Exit (Sortie) 25 → Baudour, → Golf
Map 1 on page 104 Carte 1 Page 104

GOLF COURSE / PARCOURS — 13/20

Site	Site	
Maintenance	Entretien	
Architect	Architecte	Tom MacAuley
Type	Type	forest, open country
Relief	Relief	
Water in play	Eau en jeu	
Exp. to wind	Exposé au vent	
Trees in play	Arbres en jeu	

Scorecard Carte de score	Chp. Chp.	Mens Mess.	Ladies Da.
Length Long.	6353	6041	5615
Par	74	74	74

Advised golfing ability	0	12	24	36
Niveau de jeu recommandé				
Hcp required Handicap exigé	28			

CLUB HOUSE & AMENITIES / CLUB HOUSE ET ANNEXES — 7/10

Pro shop	Pro-shop	
Driving range	Practice	
Sheltered	couvert	8 mats
On grass	sur herbe	yes
Putting-green	putting-green	yes
Pitching-green	pitching green	yes

113

HOTEL FACILITIES / ENVIRONNEMENT HOTELIER — 6/10

HOTELS HÔTELS

Château de la Cense aux Bois — Nimy
10 rooms, D 4 900 BF — 5 km
Tel (32) 065 - 31 60 00, Fax (32) 065 - 36 11 55

Lido - 67 rooms, D 3 900 BF — Mons
Tel (32) 065 - 32 78 00, Fax (32) 065 - 84 37 22 — 7 km

Auberge Le 19ème — Thulin
20 rooms, D 4 000 BF — 10 km
Tel (32) 065 - 65 01 56

Hôtel de la Forêt — Masnuy St Jean
51 rooms, D 3 900 BF — 10 km
Tel (32) 065 - 72 36 85, Fax (32) 065 - 72 41 44

RESTAURANTS RESTAURANT

Fernez - Tel (32) 065 - 64 44 67 — Baudour 1 km

Devos - Tel (32) 065 - 35 13 35 — Mons 7 km

Het is nu bekend dat de originele design van de hand van Tom Simpson is. Het is een feit dat moderne aanpassingen niet steeds even succesvol zijn; daarom heft Martin Hawtree het effect van de links willen respecteren en waren zijn hervormingen slechts miniem. Toch is de design van hole 3, een par 3 van 200 meter, niet echt overtuigend binnen de stijl van het geheel. The holes langs de zee (van 5 tot 10) blijven indrukwekkend met hun zeer nadrukkelijk links-design. Eigenlijk ontbreken we daar 20 hectaren duinen! Het parcours blijft een serieuze fysieke inspanning vergen, vooral als er wind staat, en het is zeker een goede test voor spelers, die het lage balspel willen oefenen. Maar bij mooi weer is Oostende een parcours voor alle niveaus. De waterhindernissen die op het parcoursplan getekend staan, vormen niet echt een moeilijkheid, want de voornaamste problemen schuilen in de bunkers, het struikgewas en de rough. Eenmaal op de green aanbeland, bent u veilig: ze zijn mooi vlak en gemakkelijk bespeelbaar.

We now know that the original architect was Tom Simpson, and even though modern restyling operations are not always as successful as they are supposed to be, Martin Hawtree set out to respect the feel of this links course and made only slight changes. Having said that, his work on hole N°3, a 200-metre par 3, has raised more than a few disapproving eyebrows as far as unity of style is concerned. The seaside holes (5 to 10) are as remarkable as ever with a very distinct links flavour. In fact, what is missing here is about 50 acres of sand-dunes, although the course that crosses the dunes is a good physical exercise when the wind blows and a stiff test as to a player's ability to hit low shots. In fine weather, Oostende is a course for all golfers: the few water hazards shown on the course map are not really in play and the main problems are the very many bunkers, bushes and the rough.

Koninklijke Golf Club Oostende — 1903

Koninklijke baan 2
B - 8420 DE HAAN

Office	Secretariaat	(32) 059 - 23 32 83
Pro shop	Pro shop	(32) 059 - 23 32 83
Fax	Fax	(32) 059 - 23 37 49
Situation	Locatie	

close to Oostende (pop. 67 257)

Annual closure	Jaarlijkse sluiting	no
Weekly closure	Wekelijkse sluitingsdag	no

Tuesday (diensdag): restaurant closed

Fees main season
Hoogseizoen tarieven 18 holes

	Week days Weekdagen	We/Bank holidays We/Feestdagen
Individual Individueel	1 500 BF	2 200 BF
Couple Paar	3 000 BF	4 400 BF

Caddy	Caddy	no
Electric Trolley	Electrische trolley	no
Buggy	Buggy	1 300 BF
Clubs	Clubs	no

Credit cards Creditkaarten VISA - Eurocard - DC

Access Toegang : N34 De Haan-Oostende
Map 1 on page 104 Auto kaart 1 Blz 104

GOLF COURSE / BAAN — 15/20

Site	Terrein	
Maintenance	Onderhoud	
Architect	Architect	Tom Simpson M. Hawtree,1990
Type	Type baan	seaside course, links
Relief	Reliëf	
Water in play	Waterhazards	
Exp. to wind	Windgevoelig	
Trees in play	Bomen	

Scorecard Scorekaart	Chp. Back tees	Mens Heren	Ladies Damen
Length Lengte	5517	5246	4648
Par	70	70	70

Advised golfing ability Aanbevolen golfvaardigheid	0	12	24	36

Hcp required Vereiste hcp 34

CLUB HOUSE & AMENITIES / CLUB HOUSE EN ANNEXEN — 7/10

Pro shop	Pro shop	
Driving range	Oefenbaan	
Sheltered	overdekt	9 mats
On grass	op gras	no, 5 mats open air
Putting-green	putting-green	yes
Pitching-green	pitching-green	yes

HOTEL FACILITIES / HOTELS IN OMGEVING — 7/10

HOTELS HOTELS

Manoir Carpe Diem — De Haan (Le Coq)
15 rooms, D 4 500 BF — 2 km
Tel (32) 059 - 23 32 83, Fax (32) 059 - 23 33 96

Auberge des Rois-Beach — De Haan
23 rooms, D 4 500 BF — 2 km
Tel (32) 059 - 23 30 18, Fax (32) 059 - 23 60 78

Azur - 16 rooms, D 2 800 BF — De Haan
Tel (32) 059 - 23 83 16, Fax (32) 059 - 23 83 17 — 2 km

Hôtel de la Forêt — Masnuy St Jean
51 rooms, D 3 900 BF — 10 km
Tel (32) 065 - 72 36 85, Fax (32) 065 - 72 41 44

RESTAURANTS RESTAURANT

Villa Maritza - Tel (32) 059 - 50 88 08 — Oostende 1 km

't Vistrapje - Tel (32) 059 - 80 23 82 — Oostende 1 km

Om een mooie wandeling te maken in een uitgestrekt park (prachtige beuken!) met nadien een drankje in een club-house, dat ingericht is in een kasteel van de XIXe eeuw, is men in Oudenaarde aan het juiste adres. Als men echter een golfparcours "van sterke emoties" zoekt, dat een grote sportieve uitdaging vormt, kan men al beter van de back tees vertrekken. Hier heeft men vooral aan het genoegen van de leden gedacht! Het parcours van Oudenaarde heeft onlangs enkele wijzigingen ondergaan, die niet al te gelukkig zijn uitgevallen, omdat er enkele "goeie ouwe holes" werden geïntegreerd in een nieuw circuit van 9 holes. De nieuwe holes, die de oude verdwenen holes op het bestaande parcours vervangen, vergen wel enige athletische vastberadenheid, maar missen de charme van een echt leuke golf. Het oude parcours, als het vanaf de back tees wordt gespeeld, biedt mede dankzij de talrijke hindernissen een niet te onderschatten uitdaging, zowel qua lengte als qua precisie. De greens zijn goed zichtbaar en niet te erg door bunkers omzoomd. Naast de grote "monumenten" in de golfwereld, moeten er ook terreinen zoals dit zijn...

Personal assessment here depends on what you expect from a golf course. If you are looking primarily for a pleasant stroll through a large estate (with some beautiful beech trees) between Escaut and Vieil Escaut, before returning and relaxing in a club house converted from a mid-19th century castle, then Oudenaarde is for you. But if you are looking for exciting golf and a real sporting challenge, then drive on. Emphasis here is on pleasing members, most of whom are only average golfers. The main course (18 holes since 1976) is not very long and offers no great originality. The hazards are of no great danger and the greens are clearly in view with few bunkers. The 9-hole course built in 1991 is even shorter. But alongside the giant courses of this world, we also need courses like this...

Golf & Country-Club Oudenaarde   1976

Kortrukstraat 52
B - 9790 WORTEGEM-PETEGEM

Office	Secretariaat	(32) 055 - 33 41 61
Pro shop	Pro shop	(32) 055 - 33 41 63
Fax	Fax	(32) 055 - 31 98 49
Situation	Locatie	

Oudenaarde (pop. 27 012), 3 km
Gent / Gand (pop. 210 704), 25 km

Annual closure	Jaarlijkse sluiting	no
Weekly closure	Wekelijkse sluitingsdag	no

Wednesday (woensdag): restaurant closed (bar open)

Fees main season
Hoogseizoen tarieven 18 holes

	Week days Weekdagen	We/Bank holidays We/Feestdagen
Individual Individueel	1 200 BF	1 500 BF
Couple Paar	2 400 BF	3 000 BF

Caddy	Caddy	no
Electric Trolley	Electrische trolley	no
Buggy	Buggy	1000 BF
Clubs	Clubs	no

Credit cards Creditkaarten VISA

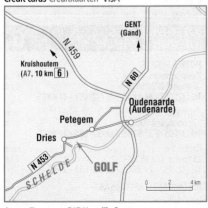

Kruishoutem (A7, 10 km 6)
N 459
GENT (Gand)
N 60
Oudenaarde (Audenarde)
Petegem
Dries
N 453
SCHELDE
GOLF

0   2   4 km

Access Toegang : E17 Kortrijk-Gent,
Exit 8 De Pinte, N60 → Ronse, N453 → Kortrijk
Map 1 on page 104 Auto kaart 1 Blz 104

GOLF COURSE / BAAN   14/20

Site	Terrein	
Maintenance	Onderhoud	
Architect	Architect	Harold Baker
Type	Type baan	parkland
Relief	Reliëf	
Water in play	Waterhazards	
Exp. to wind	Windgevoelig	
Trees in play	Bomen	

Scorecard Scorekaart	Chp. Back tees	Mens Heren	Ladies Damen
Length Lengte	6172	5774	5337
Par	72	72	72

Advised golfing ability Aanbevolen golfvaardigheid	0 12 24 36	
Hcp required Vereiste hcp	36	

CLUB HOUSE & AMENITIES / CLUB HOUSE EN ANNEXEN   6/10

Pro shop	Pro shop	
Driving range	Oefenbaan	
Sheltered	overdekt	12 mats
On grass	op gras	no, 6 mats open air
Putting-green	putting-green	yes
Pitching-green	pitching-green	yes

HOTEL FACILITIES / HOTELS IN OMGEVING   6/10

HOTELS HOTELS

Le Shamrock — Ronse — 12 km
5 rooms, D 3 250 BF
Tel (32) 055 - 21 55 29, Fax (32) 055 - 21 56 83

La Pomme d'Or — Oudenaarde — 3 km
8 rooms, D 1 600 BF
Tel (32) 055 - 31 19 00, Fax (32) 055 - 30 08 44

De Rantere — Oudenaarde — 3 km
20 rooms, D 1 700 BF
Tel (32) 055 - 31 89 88, Fax (32) 055 - 33 01 11

RESTAURANTS RESTAURANT

't Craeneveldt — Oudenaarde — 3 km
Tel (32) 055 - 31 72 91

Le Shamrock — Ronse — 12 km
Tel (32) 055 - 21 55 29

115

Gelegen langs de rand van het natuurdomein Palingbeek, doet dit parcours denken aan de esthetiek van de golf op z'n Amerikaans uit de jaren '70. Het betreft een terrein met weinig reliëf (helemaal niet vermoeiend), met enkele nogal ongevaarlijke waterhindernissen, waar de architect geen risico's heeft genomen om de stempel van zijn persoonlijkheid op het parcours te drukken (behalve op de 18). Zelfs de eerste keer staat de speler nooit voor verrassingen en verliest hij geen ballen. Deze ongedwongenheid kan veel spelers geruststellen, en indien ze al moeite hebben op de lange par 4, spelen ze toch meestal hun handicap. De greens zijn mooi ontworpen, en in goede staat, zoals trouwens het hele terrein. Er ontbreekt enkel wat beweging in het terrein zelf om het technisch gezien wat interessanter, en uit visueel oogpunt wat aangenamer te maken.

On the edge of the Palingbeek nature park, this course has all the look and appeal of american style courses at the beginning of the 1970s, and in particular the cachet of Trent Jones, minus his strategic genius. Over flattish terrain (easy on the legs), dotted with a few not too hostile water hazards, the architect backed away from the risks involved in asserting his personality on the course (except on the 18th). Players will meet with few surprises and lose few or no balls, even the first time out. In contrast, many will find such limpidity reassuring and probably play to their handicap, despite a few problems perhaps on the long par 4s. The greens are well shaped and in good condition, as is the course as a whole. The only thing missing is a little shifting of earth to make the course technically more appealing and visually more attractive.

Golf & Country Club de Palingbeek 1992
Eekhofstraat 14
B - 8902 HOLLEBEKE

Office	Secretariaat	(32) 057 - 20 04 36
Pro shop	Pro shop	(32) 057 - 20 04 36
Fax	Fax	(32) 057 - 21 89 58
Situation	Locatie	

Ieper / Ypres (pop. 34 874), 6 km
Kortrijk / Courtrai (pop. 74 044), 30 km

Annual closure	Jaarlijkse sluiting	27/1→18/2
Weekly closure	Wekelijkse sluitingsdag	no

Fees main season
Hoogseizoen tarieven 18 holes

	Week days Weekdagen	We/Bank holidays We/Feestdagen
Individual Individueel	1 300 BF	1 500 BF
Couple Paar	2 600 BF	3 000 BF

Caddy	Caddy	no
Electric Trolley	Electrische trolley	no
Buggy	Buggy	1 200 BF/18 holes
Clubs	Clubs	yes

Credit cards Creditkaarten VISA - Eurocard

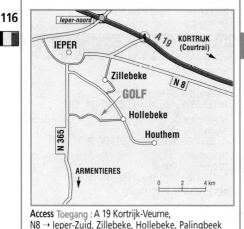

Access Toegang : A 19 Kortrijk-Veurne,
N8 → Ieper-Zuid, Zillebeke, Hollebeke, Palingbeek
Map 1 on page 104 Auto kaart 1 Blz 104

GOLF COURSE
BAAN   13/20

Site	Terrein	
Maintenance	Onderhoud	
Architect	Architect	Harold Baker
Type	Type baan	open country
Relief	Reliëf	
Water in play	Waterhazards	
Exp. to wind	Windgevoelig	
Trees in play	Bomen	

Scorecard Scorekaart	Chp. Back tees	Mens Heren	Ladies Damen
Length Lengte	6165	6165	5221
Par	72	72	72

Advised golfing ability		0 12 24 36
Aanbevolen golfvaardigheid		
Hcp required	Vereiste hcp	36

CLUB HOUSE & AMENITIES
CLUB HOUSE EN ANNEXEN   6/10

Pro shop	Pro shop	
Driving range	Oefenbaan	
Sheltered	overdekt	8 mats
On grass	op gras	yes
Putting-green	putting-green	yes
Pitching-green	pitching-green	yes

HOTEL FACILITIES
HOTELS IN OMGEVING   6/10

HOTELS HOTELS
Kemmelberg   Kemmel
16 rooms, D 3 250 BF   8 km
Tel (32) 057 - 44 41 45, Fax (32) 057 - 44 40 89

Regina   Ieper
17 rooms, D 2 700 BF   6 km
Tel (32) 057 - 21 88 88, Fax (32) 057 - 21 90 20

Rabbit Inn   Ieper
28 rooms, D 2 950 BF   6 km
Tel (32) 057 - 21 70 00, Fax (32) 057 - 21 94 74

RESTAURANTS RESTAURANT

Kemmelberg   Kemmel
Tel (32) 057 - 44 41 45   8 km

Host. St Nicolas   Ieper
Tel (32) 057 - 20 06 22   6 km

116

Le Roi Léopold II a été à l'origine d'Oostende et du Ravenstein. Il fit appel à un architecte «royal», le grand Tom Simpson, dont le dessin a été largement préservé. Chênes, bouleaux, cèdres bleus, ormes et saules offrent un spectacle qui ferait oublier le parcours, si celui-ci n'était d'une si évidente qualité. Il offre des drives sans gros problèmes (sauf aux 2, 4, 11 et 17), mais les attaques de green sont passionnantes car le putting ne sera pas ensuite évident. Les greens ne sont pas très ondulés, mais leurs surfaces sont plus difficiles à lire qu'il n'y paraît. Le Ravenstein peut être joué à tous les niveaux, mais les meilleurs y trouveront quelques défis de premier ordre, alors que sa longueur reste modérée, selon les exigences modernes en tout cas. Un «must». Plusieurs trous ont été «modernisés» par Martin Hawtree, en reculant les greens aux 14 et 18, et aussi (c'est moins convaincant) avec des buttes et des bunkers aux 9 et 18.

King Léopold II was the instigator of the courses at Oostende and Ravenstein. He called in a "royal" architect, the great Tom Simpson, whose design has remained largely unscathed. The impressive oak, birch, blue cedar, elm and willow trees could almost make you forget the course if it wasn't such an excellent layout. The tee shot is never too much of a problem (except on 2nd, 4th, 11th and 17th holes), but the approach shots are all the more exciting in that putting here is an equally challenging proposition. These are hardly what you would call undulating greens, but the putting surface is hard to read . Ravenstein can be played by golfers of all abilities, but the most proficient will find a number of challenges of the highest order, even though by modern standards the course posts only moderate yardage. Essential visiting. Several holes have been «modernized» by Martin Hawtree, holes 14 and 18 have been lengthened (the greens pushed back) but the sandhills on the 8th and the bunkers on the 9th and 18th holes fail to impress.

Royal Golf Club de Belgique — 1905

Château de Ravenstein
B - 3080 TERVUREN

Office	Secrétariat	(32) 02 - 767 58 01
Pro shop	Pro-shop	(32) 02 - 767 55 60
Fax	Fax	(32) 02 - 767 28 41
Situation	Situation	

Bruxelles / Brussel, 6 km

Annual closure	Fermeture annuelle	no
Weekly closure	Fermeture hebdomadaire	no

Fees main season
Tarifs haute saison full day

	Week days Semaine	We/Bank holidays We/Férié
Individual Individuel	2 000 BF	1 500 BF*
Couple Couple	4 000 BF	3 000 BF*

* Members guests only

Caddy	Caddy	on request
Electric Trolley	Chariot électrique	no
Buggy	Voiturette	no
Clubs	Clubs	no

Credit cards Cartes de crédit
VISA - Eurocard - AMEX (Pro shop & restaurant only)

Access Accès : In Bruxelles, Avenue de Tervuren →
Tervuren, go through Les Quatre Bras, → Golf
Map 1 on page 104 Carte 1 Page 104

GOLF COURSE / PARCOURS — 17/20

Site	Site	
Maintenance	Entretien	
Architect	Architecte	Tom Simpson
Type	Type	parkland, forest
Relief	Relief	
Water in play	Eau en jeu	
Exp. to wind	Exposé au vent	
Trees in play	Arbres en jeu	

Scorecard Carte de score	Chp. Chp.	Mens Mess.	Ladies Da.
Length Long.	6033	5775	5088
Par	72	72	72

Advised golfing ability		0 12 24 36
Niveau de jeu recommandé		
Hcp required	Handicap exigé	20 Men, 24 Ladies

CLUB HOUSE & AMENITIES / CLUB HOUSE ET ANNEXES — 8/10

Pro shop	Pro-shop	
Driving range	Practice	
Sheltered	couvert	10 mats
On grass	sur herbe	no, 12 mats open air
Putting-green	putting-green	yes
Pitching-green	pitching green	yes

117

HOTEL FACILITIES / ENVIRONNEMENT HOTELIER — 7/10

HOTELS HÔTELS
Montgomery — Woluwé-Saint-Pierre
61 rooms, D 10 000 BF — 5 km
Tel (32) 02 - 741 85 11, Fax (32) 02 - 741 85 00

Château du Lac — Genval
84 rooms, D 9 500 BF — 10 km
Tel (32) 02 - 655 71 11, Fax (32) 02 - 655 74 44

Lambeau — Woluwé-Saint-Lambert
24 rooms, D 3 000 BF — 6 km
Tel (32) 02 - 732 51 70, Fax (32) 02 - 732 54 90

RESTAURANTS RESTAURANT
Des Trois Couleurs — Woluwé-Saint-Pierre
Tel (32) 02 - 770 33 21 — 5 km

Le Vignoble de Margot — Woluwé-Saint-Pierre
Tel (32) 02 - 779 23 23 — 5 km

Très ouvert et peu arboré, c'est un parcours délicat quand le vent souffle. Les défauts originels du dessin ont été peu à peu gommés par Christophe Descampe, frère de la grande joueuse belge. De nouveaux plans d'eau et des plantations devraient faire progresser cette réalisation dont l'entretien est de très bonne qualité. Les trous sont assez bien équilibrés et imposent un rythme de jeu agréable, mais on notera surtout la qualité technique des par 5. Les roughs sont bien en jeu, les greens assez vastes et moyennement modelés sont bien défendus, ce qui impose un jeu précis. Assez naturel au départ, et sans prétendre au titre de chef-d'oeuvre, Rigenée progresse toujours dans le bon sens. L'ambiance y reste très familiale et sportive, on a plaisir à le souligner.

This very open and almost treeless course is a tricky proposition when the wind gets up. The original flaws have been gradually designed out by Christophe Descampe, the brother of the great Belgian player. New stretches of water and plantation programmes should keep the course moving in the right direction, helped by excellent upkeep. The holes are well balanced for a pleasant playing rhythm, but most notable is the technical excellence of the par 5s. The rough is very much in play, and the rather large and averagely contoured greens are well defended, thus calling for some precision play. A natural layout at the outset and with no pretence to the masterpiece label, Rigenée is improving all the time. The atmosphere is one of family entertainment and sport, an important point that deserves a special mention.

Golf de Rigenée — 1981

Rue du Châtelet, 62
B - 1495 VILLERS-LA-VILLE

Office	Secrétariat	(32) 071 - 87 77 65
Pro shop	Pro-shop	(32) 071 - 87 77 65
Fax	Fax	(32) 071 - 87 77 83
Situation	Situation	

Bruxelles / Brussel, 35 km
Nivelles (pop. 21 883), 15 km

Annual closure	Fermeture annuelle	no

Weekly closure	Fermeture hebdomadaire	no

Monday (lundi) : restaurant closed

Fees main season
Tarifs haute saison le parcours

	Week days Semaine	We/Bank holidays We/Férié
Individual Individuel	1 100 BF	2 200 BF
Couple Couple	2 200 BF	4 400 BF

1 800 BF before 10.00 (We)

Caddy	Caddy	no
Electric Trolley	Chariot électrique	no
Buggy	Voiturette	800 BF
Clubs	Clubs	300 BF

Credit cards Cartes de crédit VISA - DC

Access Accès : N93 Nivelles → Namur,
Marbais → Villers-la-Ville, Golf 2 km
Map 1 on page 105 Carte 1 Page 105

GOLF COURSE / PARCOURS — 14/20

Site	Site	
Maintenance	Entretien	
Architect	Architecte	Paul Rolin C. Descampe
Type	Type	open country
Relief	Relief	
Water in play	Eau en jeu	
Exp. to wind	Exposé au vent	
Trees in play	Arbres en jeu	

Scorecard Carte de score	Chp. Chp.	Mens Mess.	Ladies Da.
Length Long.	6354	6036	5111
Par	73	73	73

Advised golfing ability	0 12 24 36
Niveau de jeu recommandé	
Hcp required Handicap exigé	30 Men, 36 Ladies

CLUB HOUSE & AMENITIES / CLUB HOUSE ET ANNEXES — 7/10

Pro shop	Pro-shop	
Driving range	Practice	
Sheltered	couvert	12 mats
On grass	sur herbe	yes (summer)
Putting-green	putting-green	yes
Pitching-green	pitching green	yes

HOTEL FACILITIES / ENVIRONNEMENT HOTELIER — 6/10

HOTELS HÔTELS

Hostellerie La Falise — Baisy-Thy
6 rooms, D 3 000 BF
Tel (32) 067 - 77 35 11, Fax (32) 067 - 79 04 94

Nivelles-Sud — Nivelles
115 rooms, D 1 950 BF — 15 km
Tel (32) 067 - 21 87 21, Fax (32) 067 - 22 10 88

Grand Hôtel de Waterloo — Waterloo
71 rooms, D 7 500 BF — 15 km
Tel (32) 02 - 352 18 15, Fax (32) 02 - 352 18 88

RESTAURANTS RESTAURANT

Hostellerie La Falise — Baisy-Thy
Tel (32) 067 - 77 35 11

Le Vert d'Eau — Lasne
Tel (32) 02 - 633 54 52 — 15 km

118

Na een mooie toegangsweg door de bossen, valt direct het professionalisme van de club op, door de kwaliteit van de installaties en het onderhoud van het terrein. Dit laatste bestaat uit 3 combineerbare 9-holes, van gelijke moeilijkheidsgraad (vooral de bomen en water) en met greens zonder enige variatie qua esthetiek, vaak verhoogd en smal. Men mist persoonlijkheid en stijl in de architectuur van dit parcours, en krijgt veeleer een indruk van eentonigheid, dermate dat men om het even welke combinatie van 18 holes kan spelen en toch een tamelijk duidelijk beeld van het geheel krijgt. Een voordeel is dat de moeilijkheidsgraad voor elk spelniveau min of meer gelijk is, maar de betere handicaps zullen zich wel ietwat gefrustreerd voelen wegens het gebrek aan grotere uitdagingen. Ze kunnen echter wel genieten van een mooie wandeling in een aangename omgeving van berken en sparren, met een rijke fauna.

After a pleasant drive through the woods, you can tell the club's professionalism by the standard of facilities and the upkeep of the course. There are three combinable 9-hole courses offering the same level of difficulty (basically trees and water) and similar-looking greens that are often narrow and elevated. It is a pity about the lack of personality and style, which creates a slight feeling of monotony, to the point where you can play any 18-hole combination and get exactly the same impression of the site. On the upside, we noticed the average difficulty for all players, although very low handicappers might feel frustrated at the lack of real challenge. At least they will enjoy a pretty stroll over a pleasant estate of birch and pine trees, and the extensive wildlife to keep them company.

Rinkven Golf Club — 1981

Sint-Jobsteenweg, 120
B - 2970 SCHILDE

Office	Secretariaat	(32) 03 - 380 12 80
Pro shop	Pro shop	(32) 03 - 385 82 13
Fax	Fax	(32) 03 - 384 29 33
Situation	Locatie	

Antwerpen / Anvers (pop. 403 072), 15 km

Annual closure	Jaarlijkse sluiting	no
Weekly closure	Wekelijkse sluitingsdag	no

Fees main season
Hoogseizoen tarieven 18 holes

	Week days Weekdagen	We/Bank holidays We/Feestdagen
Individual Individueel	1 600 BF	2 500 BF
Couple Paar	3 200 BF	5 000 BF

Caddy	Caddy	no
Electric Trolley	Electrische trolley	400 BF
Buggy	Buggy	900 BF
Clubs	Clubs	no

Credit cards Creditkaarten — no

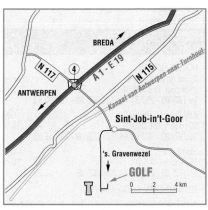

Access Toegang : E19 Anvers → Breda, Exit (Sortie)
St-Job-in-'t Goor → 's Gravenwesel → Golf
Map 1 on page 105 Auto kaart 1 Blz 105

GOLF COURSE / BAAN — 14/20

Site	Terrein	
Maintenance	Onderhoud	
Architect	Architect	Paul Rolin
Type	Type baan	forest
Relief	Reliëf	
Water in play	Waterhazards	
Exp. to wind	Windgevoelig	
Trees in play	Bomen	

Scorecard Scorekaart	Chp. Back tees	Mens Heren	Ladies Damen
Length Lengte	6140	6046	5388
Par	72	72	72

Advised golfing ability
Aanbevolen golfvaardigheid — 0 12 24 36

Hcp required Vereiste hcp — 28

CLUB HOUSE & AMENITIES / CLUB HOUSE EN ANNEXEN — 6/10

Pro shop	Pro shop	
Driving range	Oefenbaan	
Sheltered	overdekt	6 mats
On grass	op gras	no, 9 mats open air
Putting-green	putting-green	yes
Pitching-green	pitching-green	yes

119

HOTEL FACILITIES / HOTELS IN OMGEVING — 5/10

HOTELS HOTELS

Alfa De Keyser — Antwerpen
115 rooms, D 8 000 BF — 15 km
Tel (32) 03 - 234 01 35, Fax (32) 03 - 232 39 70

Hilton — Antwerpen
199 rooms, D 10 900 BF — 15 km
Tel (32) 03 - 204 12 12, Fax (32) 03 - 204 12 13

Rubens — Antwerpen
35 rooms, D 6 500 BF — 15 km
Tel (32) 03 - 222 48 48, Fax (32) 03 - 225 19 40

RESTAURANTS RESTAURANT

Apicius — Schilde
Tel (32) 03 - 383 45 65 — 5 km

't Fornuis — Antwerpen
Tel (32) 03 - 233 62 70 — 15 km

Deze golfclub werd in 1909 geopend en was bekend onder de naam «les Buttes Blanches». Greens en bunkers werden in de jaren '50 hertekend door Hawtree. Het gebrek aan ruimte brengt ook een beperking in afstand met zich mee, en "out of bounds" op de helft van de holes. Het grote park is aangeplant met prachtige bomen, eiken, dennen, en beuken van meer dan 200 jaar oud, wat voor een zeer aantrekkelijke omgeving zorgt. De hindernissen zijn hoofdzakelijk bunkers, maar ook enkele vijvers en grachten, niet echt moeilijk. Het design is tamelijk eenvoudig, en de strategie voor de hand liggend, behalve op 6 en de 18, met blinde drives. De strategie om de greens te bereiken, is niet ingewikkeld te noemen; zelfs niet de keuze van de club, behalve voor de approach van vijf ervan, die verhoogd zijn. Dankzij een afwisselend design, een matig reliëf en een opvallende charme en volkomenheid, kan Latem een parcours bieden, dat voor elk spelersniveau een plezier betekent. De zanderige bodem en de volledige irrigatie maken het mogelijk in alle seizoenen te spelen.

Opened back in 1909, this Golf Club was known under the name of «Les Buttes Blanches». The greens and bunkers were redesigned by Hawtree in the 1950s. Lack of space has resulted in a shortish course and out-of-bounds on at least half of the holes. The estate is covered with some beautiful trees - oak, pine and beech - often more than 200 years old, and makes for a very attractive setting. The main hazards are the bunkers, but there are a number of ponds and ditches awaiting the mis-hit shot. The layout is clear and strategy obvious, except on the 6 and 18th holes, where the drive is blind. Approach shots are not too complex, either, and choice of club is more or less straightforward, except for the five elevated greens. A varied layout and averagely hilly, the course is not made for the very best players, but the rest will have fun. Sandy soil and comprehensive irrigation facilities make this a course that is playable virtually all year.

Royal Latem Golf Club — 1909
B - 9380 ST-MARTENS-LATEM

Office	Secretariaat	(32) 09 - 282 54 11
Pro shop	Pro shop	(32) 09 - 282 57 65
Fax	Fax	(32) 09 - 282 90 19
Situation	Locatie	

Gent / Gand (pop. 210 704), 10 km

Annual closure	Jaarlijkse sluiting	no
Weekly closure	Wekelijkse sluitingsdag	no

Monday (maandag) : restaurant closed

Fees main season
Hoogseizoen tarieven full day

	Week days Weekdagen	We/Bank holidays We/Feestdagen
Individual Individueel	1 750 BF	2 250 BF
Couple Paar	3 500 BF	4 500 BF

Caddy	Caddy	no
Electric Trolley	Electrische trolley	no
Buggy	Buggy	1200 BF/18 holes
Clubs	Clubs	no

Credit cards Creditkaarten VISA - Eurocard

GOLF COURSE / BAAN — 15/20

Site	Terrein	
Maintenance	Onderhoud	
Architect	Architect	Fred Hawtree
Type	Type baan	forest, residential
Relief	Reliëf	
Water in play	Waterhazards	
Exp. to wind	Windgevoelig	
Trees in play	Bomen	

Scorecard Scorekaart	Chp. Back tees	Mens Heren	Ladies Damen
Length Lengte	5767	5767	5143
Par	72	72	72

Advised golfing ability Aanbevolen golfvaardigheid	0	12	24	36

Hcp required	Vereiste hcp	36 weekdays, 28 W/E

CLUB HOUSE & AMENITIES / CLUB HOUSE EN ANNEXEN — 8/10

Pro shop	Pro shop	
Driving range	Oefenbaan	
Sheltered	overdekt	3 mats
On grass	op gras	no, 13 mats open air
Putting-green	putting-green	yes
Pitching-green	pitching-green	yes

HOTEL FACILITIES / HOTELS IN OMGEVING — 6/10

HOTELS HOTELS

Auberge du Pêcheur — Sint-Martens
26 rooms, D 3 200 BF — 1,5 km
Tel (32) 09 - 282 31 44, Fax (32) 09 - 282 90 58

Alfa Flanders Hotel — Gent
50 rooms, D 6 000 BF — 10 km
Tel (32) 09 - 222 60 65, Fax (32) 09 - 220 16 05

Holyday Inn Expo — Gent
137 rooms, D 5 700 BF — 10 km
Tel (32) 09 - 220 24 24, Fax (32) 09 - 222 66 22

RESTAURANTS RESTAURANT

Auberge du Pêcheur — Sint-Martens
Tel (32) 09 - 282 31 44 — 1,5 km

De Klokkeput — Sint Martens
Tel (32) 09 - 282 97 75 — 1.5 km

120

Access Toegang : E40 Brussel-Oostende,
Exit (Sortie) 14, N43 → Kortrijk, → Golf
Map 1 on page 105 Auto kaart 1 Blz 105

Un parcours centenaire qui ne paraît pas trop difficile, en tout cas lorsque le haut rough n'est pas trop proche, mais c'est un formidable défi quand le vent se met à souffler. Pour juger de sa qualité, on peut faire confiance au témoignage de joueurs aussi connaisseurs d'architecture de golf que Nick Faldo, et à la signature de Harry Colt, l'un des plus grands créateurs de parcours de l'histoire du golf. Malgré tout, Le Zoute ne dissimule jamais ses difficultés, ce qui permet de savoir où placer son départ pour mieux préparer le coup suivant vers des greens rapides et bien modelés, défendus avec intelligence et subtilité. Le chemin le plus direct est clairement défini entre les dunes et les arbres, mais ne prenez pas trop vite confiance en vous, les fairways roulants peuvent réserver quelques positions de balle inconfortables et inattendues. Un classique que tous les golfeurs doivent jouer un jour ou l'autre, et un des meilleurs links du continent.

A hundred-year old course which does not look too tough, or at least not when you stay well away from the tall grass in the rough. When the winds blows, though, it is a terrific challenge for anyone. Its reputation has long been established, tributes from players such as Nick Faldo are a reference indeed, as is the label of H.S. Colt, one of greatest golf course designers in the history of golf. Anyway, Le Zoute never tries to hide any of its difficulties, notably placing the tee-shot for an easier approach shot to fast and well-contoured greens, that are cleverly and subtly defended. The "straight and narrow" is clearly laid out betwen dunes and trees, but don't feel too confident too soon. Some of the rolling fairways can provide unusual and unexpected positions. A very classic course and one that all golfers should know sooner or later. One of the best links courses in continental Europe.

Royal Zoute Golf Club   1945
Caddiespad 14
B - 8300 KNOKKE-HEIST

Office	Secrétariat	(32) 050 - 60 12 27
Pro shop	Pro-shop	(32) 050 - 60 19 60
Fax	Fax	(32) 050 - 62 30 29
Situation	Situation	

close to Knokke-Heist (pop. 31 237)

Annual closure	Fermeture annuelle	no
Weekly closure	Fermeture hebdomadaire	no

Fees main season
Tarifs haute saison 18 holes

	Week days Semaine	We/Bank holidays We/Férié
Individual Individuel	2 500 BF	3 500 BF
Couple Couple	5 000 BF	7 000 BF

Caddy	Caddy	1 000 BF
Electric Trolley	Chariot électrique	yes
Buggy	Voiturette	yes
Clubs	Clubs	yes

Credit cards Cartes de crédit   no

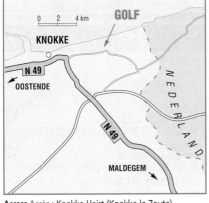

GOLF

KNOKKE

N 49

OOSTENDE

N 49

NEDERLAND

MALDEGEM

0   2   4 km

Access Accès : Knokke-Heist (Knokke-le-Zoute)
Map 1 on page 105 Carte 1 Page 105

GOLF COURSE
BAAN   18/20

Site	Site	
Maintenance	Entretien	
Architect	Architecte	Harry S. Colt
Type	Type	links
Relief	Relief	
Water in play	Eau en jeu	
Exp. to wind	Exposé au vent	
Trees in play	Arbres en jeu	

Scorecard Carte de score	Chp. Chp.	Mens Mess.	Ladies Da.
Length Long.	6172	6172	5416
Par	72	72	72

Advised golfing ability	0 12 24 36
Niveau de jeu recommandé	
Hcp required Handicap exigé	20 Men, 24 Ladies

CLUB HOUSE & AMENITIES
CLUB HOUSE EN ANNEXEN   7/10

Pro shop	Pro-shop	
Driving range	Practice	
Sheltered	couvert	20 mats
On grass	sur herbe	no, 6 mats open air
Putting-green	putting-green	yes
Pitching-green	pitching green	yes

HOTEL FACILITIES
HOTELS IN OMGEVING   7/10

HOTELS HÔTELS
Royal Zoute Golf Club   Golf
7 rooms, D 6 000 BF   on site
Tel (32) 050 - 60 16 17, Fax (32) 050 - 62 24 26

Manoir du Dragon   Het Zoute
8 rooms, D 8 500 BF   1 km
Tel (32) 050 - 62 35 36, Fax (32) 050 - 61 57 96

Villa Verdi   Het Zoute
8 rooms, D 4 950 BF   1 km
Tel (32) 050 - 62 35 72, Fax (32) 050 - 62 11 46

RESTAURANTS RESTAURANT
Chez Jean   Knokke
Tel (32) 050 - 61 49 57   2 km

Le Rembrandt   Knokke
Tel (32) 050 - 61 06 61   1 km

121

C'est l'un des meilleurs parcours de match-play de Belgique. La longueur de certains trous (dont quelques terribles par 4), leur relief raisonnable et naturel, la présence insistante des arbres, et des greens diaboliques le rendent difficile à scorer, notamment pour les joueurs de moins de 12 de handicap, qui pourront vraiment y tester leur jeu. Il faut établir sa stratégie dès le départ en fonction des positions de drapeau. Son relief mesuré, son excellent rythme, son honnêteté et la beauté du site traduisent bien le génie de son architecte Tom Simpson. Le lac du 14, qui cassait l'harmonie du dessin a été heureusement supprimé. La qualité de l'entretien ajoute encore au plaisir : Le Royal Sart-Tilman mérite un large détour pour sa franchise, son intérêt, son absence de «vices cachés», son confort général et son ambiance chaleureuse.

This is one of Belgium's finest match-play courses. The length of some holes(some pretty hard par 4s), the measured, natural relief, the looming presence of trees and devilishly tricky greens make scoring a tough business, especially for players with a handicap under 12, who will find this a real test. Game strategy must be set before starting out, and be geared to the pin positions. The measured relief and excellent balance, plus the course's honesty and the beauty of the site are a good reflection on the genius of architect Tom Simpson. The lake on the 14th, which broke the harmony of the layout has been filled in. The standard of upkeep only enhances the enjoyment of playing here. Royal Sart Tilman is well worth the time and journey for its openness, appeal, absence of hidden vices, general pleasantness and warm atmosphere.

Royal Golf Club du Sart-Tilman — 1939

Route de Condroz, 541
B - 4031 ANGLEUR

Office	Secrétariat	(32) 04 - 336 20 21
Pro shop	Pro-shop	(32) 04 - 336 20 21
Fax	Fax	(32) 04 - 337 20 26
Situation	Situation	

Liège / Luik (pop. 155 999), 5 km

Annual closure	Fermeture annuelle	no
Weekly closure	Fermeture hebdomadaire	no

Monday (lundi) : Pro-shop closed

Fees main season
Tarifs haute saison 18 holes

	Week days Semaine	We/Bank holidays We/Férié
Individual Individuel	1 600 BF	2 100 BF
Couple Couple	3 200 BF	4 200 BF

Caddy	Caddy	no
Electric Trolley	Chariot électrique	no
Buggy	Voiturette	1 500 BF/18 holes
Clubs	Clubs	no

Credit cards Cartes de crédit
VISA - Eurocard - Mastercard - AMEX - DC

LIEGE
MEUSE
Ougrée
N 63
Sart Tilman
N 30
GOLF
TILFF
MARCHE
(en Famenne)
N 63
0   1   2 km

Access Accès : N63 Liège - Marche
Map 1 on page 105 Carte 1 Page 105

GOLF COURSE
PARCOURS — 16/20

Site	Site	▰▰▰▰▱
Maintenance	Entretien	▰▰▰▱▱
Architect	Architecte	Tom Simpson
Type	Type	forest, hilly
Relief	Relief	▰▰▰▰▱
Water in play	Eau en jeu	▰▱▱▱▱
Exp. to wind	Exposé au vent	▰▰▱▱▱
Trees in play	Arbres en jeu	▰▰▰▰▱

Scorecard Carte de score	Chp. Chp.	Mens Mess.	Ladies Da.
Length Long.	6000	5624	5367
Par	72	72	72

Advised golfing ability
Niveau de jeu recommandé

0	12	24	36

Hcp required Handicap exigé   36

CLUB HOUSE & AMENITIES
CLUB HOUSE ET ANNEXES — 7/10

Pro shop	Pro-shop	▰▰▰▱▱
Driving range	Practice	▰▰▱▱▱
Sheltered	couvert	10 mats
On grass	sur herbe	no, 7 mats open air
Putting-green	putting-green	yes
Pitching-green	pitching green	yes

HOTEL FACILITIES
ENVIRONNEMENT HOTELIER — 7/10

HOTELS HÔTELS

Ramada		Liège
105 rooms, D 6 600 BF		5 km
Tel (32) 041 - 21 77 11, Fax (32) 041 - 21 77 01		
Bedford		Liège
149 rooms, D 6 950 BF		5 km
Tel (32) 041 - 28 81 11, Fax (32) 041 - 27 45 75		
Holiday Inn		Liège
214 rooms, D 6 600 BF		5 km
Tel (32) 041 - 42 60 20, Fax (32) 041 - 43 48 10		

RESTAURANTS RESTAURANT

Max		Liège
Tel (32) 04 - 222 08 59		5 km
La Ciboulette		Flemalle
Tel (32) 04 - 275 19 65		6 km

122

La signature de Tom Simpson est une garantie de parcours technique et stratégique. De relief modéré, c'est un des bons exemples d'architecture classique «inland», où il faut maîtriser l'ensemble de son jeu pour éviter les bois, les roughs et autres bunkers, admirablement disposés. Le placement du drive est essentiel, notamment sur quatre longs par 4, mais le travail ne s'arrête pas là, car les greens sont bien défendus, leurs surfaces assez subtiles à lire. Dans un site d'une parfaite tranquillité, on a l'impression de prendre une retraite pour méditer non seulement sur le golf, mais aussi sur l'intelligente sobriété de l'architecture, révélant une connaissance parfaite des joueurs de tous niveaux, mais sans jamais dissimuler les pièges. Exigeant, ce parcours donne un plaisir que l'on souhaite retrouver très souvent. Les 12 (par 5), 7 et 15 (par 4) sont de pures merveilles. Et l'arrosage automatique a encore amélioré l'ensemble.

The Tom Simpson label is the guarantee of a technical and strategic course. This moderately hilly layout is one of the classic examples of inland architecture, where every part of your game has to be in shape to avoid the woods, rough and admirably located bunkers. Placing the tee-shot is essential, especially on the four long par 4s, but the job doesn't stop there, because the greens are well defended and the putting surfaces tricky to read. On a site of perfect tranquillity, you get the impression of being in a sanctuary from where to meditate not only about the course, but also about the smart discretion of a layout, which reveals good insight into every golfing ability but never conceals the traps. It is a demanding course but an enjoyable one, too. The type you like to come back and play again and again. 7th, 12th and 15th are architectural masterpieces. And the automatic watering system has made the course still better.

Royal Golf Club des Fagnes — 1929

Avenue de l'Hippodrome, 1
B - 4900 SPA

Office	Secrétariat	(32) 087 - 79 30 30
Pro shop	Pro-shop	(32) 087 - 79 30 32
Fax	Fax	(32) 087 - 79 30 39
Situation	Situation	

Spa (pop. 9 953), 2 km

Annual closure	Fermeture annuelle	no
Weekly closure	Fermeture hebdomadaire	no

Fees main season
Tarifs haute saison 18 holes

	Week days Semaine	We/Bank holidays We/Férié
Individual Individuel	1 800 BF	2 000 BF
Couple Couple	3 600 BF	4 000 BF

Caddy	Caddy	no
Electric Trolley	Chariot électrique	no
Buggy	Voiturette	1 200 BF each people
Clubs	Clubs	no

Credit cards Cartes de crédit VISA - Eurocard - AMEX

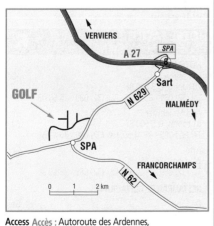

VERVIERS
A 27 SPA
Sart
GOLF N 629
MALMÉDY
SPA
FRANCORCHAMPS
N 62

0   1   2 km

Access Accès : Autoroute des Ardennes,
Exit (Sortie) Spa → Golf
Map 2 on page 105 Carte 2 Page 105

GOLF COURSE / BAAN — 17/20

Site	Site	
Maintenance	Entretien	
Architect	Architecte	Tom Simpson
Type	Type	forest, hilly
Relief	Relief	
Water in play	Eau en jeu	
Exp. to wind	Exposé au vent	
Trees in play	Arbres en jeu	

Scorecard Carte de score	Chp. Chp.	Mens Mess.	Ladies Da.
Length Long.	6040	5671	5276
Par	72	72	72

Advised golfing ability
Niveau de jeu recommandé — 0   12   24   36
Hcp required Handicap exigé 36

CLUB HOUSE & AMENITIES / CLUB HOUSE EN ANNEXEN — 7/10

Pro shop	Pro-shop	
Driving range	Practice	
Sheltered	couvert	2 mats
On grass	sur herbe	no, 9 mats open air
Putting-green	putting-green	yes
Pitching-green	pitching green	yes

HOTEL FACILITIES / HOTELS IN OMGEVING — 7/10

HOTELS HÔTELS
Dorint — Spa
97 rooms, D 5 000 BF — 2 km
Tel (32) 087 - 77 25 81, Fax (32) 087 - 77 41 74

Alfa Balmoral — Spa
34 rooms, D 5 950 BF — 2 km
Tel (32) 087 - 79 21 41, Fax (32) 087 - 79 21 51

La Heid des Pairs — Spa
11 rooms, D 5 600 BF — 4 km
Tel (32) 087 - 77 43 46, Fax (32) 087 - 77 06 44

RESTAURANTS RESTAURANT
Brasserie du Grand Maur — Spa
Tel (32) 087 - 77 36 16 — 2 km

Manoir de Lebiolles — Creppe
Tel (32) 087 - 77 04 20 — 6 km

123

Een terrein dat een juist uitgebalanceerd spel vraagt. De eerste 9 holes, in de bossen, eisen veel nauwkeurigheid en aandacht bij het plaatsen van de drives. De laatste 9 liggen temidden van de heide, en zijn ook langer, meer bepaald drie van de par 4. De moeilijkheden, fairway bunkers en waterhindernissen, zijn goed zichtbaar en op een slimme manier gesitueerd; de architect, Ron Kirby, had een goed inzicht in de mogelijkheden van de spelers, en dit op verschillende niveaus. Hij heeft tegelijk echter ook zoveel mogelijk het natuurlijke uitzicht van het terrein proberen te bewaren, en het prachtig geïntegreerd. De perfecte uitdunning van het onderhout is opmerkelijk. De greens zijn mooi ontworpen, niet te golvend, maar de speler moet, bij het bepalen van zijn strategie, rekening houden met de plaatsing van de vlaggen. Het terrein is tamelijk heuvelachtig, maar kan gemakkelijk te voet worden gespeeld. Geplaatst op een voormalige stortplaats, heeft dit terrein zeer vlug een plaats verworven onder de goede, recente realisaties, die waar men herinneringen aan overhoudt, behalve van de 7 de hole.

A course that demands a solid all-round game. The front nine, in the woods, call for precision in the extreme and a lot of care when placing the tee-shot. The back nine are in the heather and are longer, notably three of the par 4s. The difficulties, fairway bunkers and water hazards are clear to see and astutely located, revealing designer Ron Kirby's insight when it comes to understanding golfers of differing abilities. At the same time, he has preserved the course's natural look as far as possible, and the way it fits into the surroundings is exemplary. The undergrowth has been conveniently cleared to avoid penalising players too heavily, the greens are well designed and slope quite a bit, but the pin positions must be watched carefully if you want to establish an effective game strategy. The site is hilly but easily walkable.

Spiegelven Golf Club Genk   1988

Wiemesmeerstraat 109
B - 3600 GENK

Office	Secretariaat	(32) 089 - 35 96 16
Pro shop	Pro shop	(32) 089 - 36 20 60
Fax	Fax	(32) 089 - 36 41 84
Situation	Locatie	

Genk (pop. 45 906), 10 km
Hasselt (pop. 64 722), 20 km

| Annual closure | Jaarlijkse sluiting | no |
| Weekly closure | Wekelijkse sluitingsdag | no |

Fees main season
Hoogseizoen tarieven 18 holes

	Week days Weekdagen	We/Bank holidays We/Feestdagen
Individual Individueel	1 300 BF	1 800 BF
Couple Paar	2 600 BF	3 600 BF

Caddy	Caddy	no
Electric Trolley	Electrische trolley	no
Buggy	Buggy	1 200 BF
Clubs	Clubs	1 000 BF
Credit cards Creditkaarten		no

124

Access Toegang : E314, Exit 32, N744 → Zutendal, Golf
Map 2 on page 105 Auto kaart 2 Blz 105

GOLF COURSE
BAAN   14/20

Site	Terrein	
Maintenance	Onderhoud	
Architect	Architect	Ron Kirby

Type	Type baan	forest
Relief	Reliëf	
Water in play	Waterhazards	
Exp. to wind	Windgevoelig	
Trees in play	Bomen	

Scorecard Scorekaart	Chp. Back tees	Mens Heren	Ladies Damen
Length Lengte	6198	6198	5436
Par	72	72	73

Advised golfing ability		0	12	24	36
Aanbevolen golfvaardigheid					
Hcp required	Vereiste hcp	36			

CLUB HOUSE & AMENITIES
CLUB HOUSE EN ANNEXEN   7/10

Pro shop	Pro shop	
Driving range	Oefenbaan	
Sheltered	overdekt	9 mats
On grass	op gras	yes
Putting-green	putting-green	yes
Pitching-green	pitching-green	yes

HOTEL FACILITIES
HOTELS IN OMGEVING   8/10

HOTELS HOTELS

La Réserve — Golf
70 rooms, D 3 900 BF
Tel (32) 089 - 35 58 28, Fax (32) 089 - 35 58 03

Alfa Molenvijer — Genk — 3 km
81 rooms, D 5 500 BF
Tel (32) 089 - 36 41 50, Fax (32) 089 - 36 41 51

Arte — Genk — 5 km
24 rooms, D 2 650 BF
Tel (32) 089 - 35 20 06, Fax (32) 089 - 36 10 36

RESTAURANTS RESTAURANT

Da Vinci — Genk — 5 km
Tel (32) 089 - 35 17 61

't Konijtje — Genk — 5 km
Tel (32) 089 - 35 26 45

Les Français ne trouveront guère que Waterloo soit une «morne plaine» (le retour est assez vallonné), et le parcours de «La Marache», plus ancien parcours du «Lion» voisin, doit être abordé avec prudence et sagesse. Très bon exemple de l'architecture de Hawtree, il se déroule dans un environnement boisé plaisant, et souvent dangereux. Les seconds coups sont ici très intéressants, même si beaucoup des très grands greens sont assez ouverts pour y parvenir en roulant. Il est important d'être droit, même si la longueur de ce parcours est appréciable, mais chacun, selon son niveau, pourra y prendre plaisir. Les bons et longs drivers pourront cependant s'exprimer, sans trop de souci des tragédies bien plus graves dont Waterloo a été le cadre autrefois ! Ce complexe s'étend au total sur 150 hectares, et ses équipements sont dignes de ces dimensions.

Even the French could hardly describe Waterloo as the "cheerless plain" it was once said to be (the back 9 are over rolling terrain), and "La Marache", older than the neighbouring "Lion" course, should be approached with caution and good sense. An excellent example of Hawtree architecture, the course unwinds in a pleasant but often hazardous woodland environment. The second shots are interesting propositions here, even though many of the very large greens have no frontal hazard and so can be reached with chipped or low approach shots. It is important to play straight at Waterloo, the course is pretty long but every one can enjoy playing here. However, wild-hitters will be at ease, and in the past Waterloo has seen worst disasters than wayward tee-shots! The full complex stretches over 150 hectares (370 acres) and facilities are of an equally high standard.

Royal Waterloo Golf Club — 1960

Vieux chemin de Wavre 50
B - 1380 LASNE

Office	Secrétariat	(32) 02 - 633 18 50
Pro shop	Pro-shop	(32) 02 - 633 43 16
Fax	Fax	(32) 02 - 633 28 66
Situation	Situation	

Bruxelles / Brussel, 20 km

Annual closure	Fermeture annuelle	no
Weekly closure	Fermeture hebdomadaire	no

Monday (lundi): restaurant & Pro shop closed

Fees main season
Tarifs haute saison full day

	Week days Semaine	We/Bank holidays We/Férié
Individual Individuel	1 750 BF	2 950 BF
Couple Couple	3 500 BF	5 900 BF

Caddy	Caddy	1 000 BF
Electric Trolley	Chariot électrique	400 BF
Buggy	Voiturette	1 200 BF
Clubs	Clubs	no

Credit cards Cartes de crédit VISA - Eurocard

BRUSSEL

WATERLOO
Waterloo - Lasne
GOLF
Ohain
La Marache
R 0
BRUSSEL
CHARLEROI (A 7)

0   2   4 km

Access Accès : Bruxelles E, → Wavre, → Waterloo
Map 1 on page 105 Carte 1 Page 105

GOLF COURSE / PARCOURS — 16/20

Site	Site	
Maintenance	Entretien	
Architect	Architecte	F. Hawtree
Type	Type	country, parkland
Relief	Relief	
Water in play	Eau en jeu	
Exp. to wind	Exposé au vent	
Trees in play	Arbres en jeu	

Scorecard Carte de score	Chp. Chp.	Mens Mess.	Ladies Da.
Length Long.	6235	5887	5541
Par	72	72	72

Advised golfing ability	0	12	24	36
Niveau de jeu recommandé				
Hcp required Handicap exigé	28			

CLUB HOUSE & AMENITIES / CLUB HOUSE ET ANNEXES — 8/10

Pro shop	Pro-shop	
Driving range	Practice	
Sheltered	couvert	20 mats
On grass	sur herbe	yes
Putting-green	putting-green	yes
Pitching-green	pitching green	yes

125

HOTEL FACILITIES / ENVIRONNEMENT HOTELIER — 7/10

HOTELS HÔTELS

Grand Hôtel — Waterloo
71 rooms, D 7 500 BF — 6 km
Tel (32) 02 - 352 18 15, Fax (32) 02 - 352 18 88

Château du Lac — Genval
84 rooms, D 9 500 BF — 5 km
Tel (32) 02 - 655 71 11, Fax (32) 02 - 655 74 44

Auberge de Waterloo — Rhode-Saint-Genèse
84 rooms, D 5 300 BF — 12 km
Tel (32) 02 - 358 35 80, Fax (32) 02 - 358 38 06

RESTAURANTS RESTAURANT

Auberge d'Ohain — Ohain
Tel (32) 02 - 653 64 97 — 3 km

La Maison du Seigneur — Waterloo
Tel (32) 02 - 354 07 50 — 6 km

La faible longueur du "Grand Ducal" plaira à la grande majorité des joueurs de tous niveaux. Mais que les bons frappeurs se méfient, les arbres sont très beaux, mais les éviter constitue la difficulté essentielle d'un parcours dont l'esthétique très britannique (quelques "cross-bunkers") coïncide bien avec les traditions golfiques cultivées ici. Les bunkers sont assez nombreux, mais défendent les greens sans méchanceté aucune. Ceux-ci sont de dimensions très raisonnables, mais leurs pentes exigent de l'attention. Le vallonnement du terrain reste modéré, sauf au 6, un long par 4 en montée, et seul trou vraiment difficile. En revanche, le 18, un par 5, laissera une bonne impression, car il présente une bonne occasion de birdie. En résumé, un parcours où le driver n'est pas indispensable, généralement en bon état, et très agréable quand on visite le pays. Cependant, les avions de l'aéroport tout proche manquent parfois de respect au golf...

The short yardage of the "Grand Ducal" will appeal to the vast majority of golfers of all levels. Yet the big-hitters should beware, the trees might look a pretty picture, but avoiding them is one of the main difficulties on a course, whose very attractive and very British style (with a few cross-bunkers to boot) perfectly reflects the golfing traditions nurtured in this part of the world. There are a lot of bunkers, which defends the greens but are never unduly spiteful. The greens themselves are very reasonably sized, but their slopes call for careful reading. This is a moderately hilly course, but is especially steep on the 6th, a long uphill 4-par and the only really tough hole. In contrast, the 18th, a par 5, should leave you liking the course because the birdie here is a definite possibility. In a word or two, this is a course where the driver can easily stay in the bag. It is in good condition and very pleasant to play when you visit the "Grand Duché". Unfortunately, the planes from the neighbouring airport don't always respect the game of golf...

Golf Club Grand Ducal   1936

Route de Trèves, 1
L - 2633 SENNINGERBERG

Office	Secrétariat	(352) 34 00 90
Pro shop	Pro-shop	(352) 34 83 94
Fax	Fax	(352) 34 83 91
Situation	Situation	

Luxembourg (pop. 75 377), 6 km

Annual closure	Fermeture annuelle	no
Weekly closure	Fermeture hebdomadaire	no

Fees main season
Tarifs haute saison 18 holes

	Week days Semaine	We/Bank holidays We/Férié
Individual Individuel	1 500 FLUX	2 000 FLUX
Couple Couple	3 000 FLUX	4 000 FLUX

Caddy	Caddy	no
Electric Trolley	Chariot électrique	no
Buggy	Voiturette	no
Clubs	Clubs	150 FLUX
Credit cards Cartes de crédit		VISA - Eurocard

Access Accès : N1 Luxembourg → Airport (Aéroport)
Map 1 on page 73 Carte 1 Page 73

GOLF COURSE
PARCOURS   13/20

Site	Site	
Maintenance	Entretien	
Architect	Architecte	Unknown
Type	Type	parkland
Relief	Relief	
Water in play	Eau en jeu	
Exp. to wind	Exposé au vent	
Trees in play	Arbres en jeu	

Scorecard Carte de score	Chp. Chp.	Mens Mess.	Ladies Da.
Length Long.	5782	5782	5179
Par	71	71	71

Advised golfing ability		0 12 24 36
Niveau de jeu recommandé		
Hcp required	Handicap exigé	36 weekdays, 28 W/E

CLUB HOUSE & AMENITIES
CLUB HOUSE ET ANNEXES   6/10

Pro shop	Pro-shop	
Driving range	Practice	
Sheltered	couvert	9 mats
On grass	sur herbe	yes
Putting-green	putting-green	yes
Pitching-green	pitching green	yes

HOTEL FACILITIES
ENVIRONNEMENT HOTELIER   7/10

HOTELS HÔTELS

Sheraton Aérogolf — Aéroport
145 rooms, D 9 000 FLUX — 1 km
Tel (352) 34 05 71, Fax (352) 34 02 17

Le Royal — Luxembourg
165 rooms, D 10 500 FLUX — 6 km
Tel (352) 416 16, Fax (352) 22 59 48

Cravat — Luxembourg
59 rooms, D 7 200 FLUX — 6 km
Tel (352) 22 19 75, Fax (352) 22 67 11

RESTAURANTS RESTAURANT

Clairefontaine — Luxembourg
Tel (352) 46 22 11 — 6 km

Le Grimpereau — Senningerberg
Tel (352) 43 67 87 — 1 km

126

Sans atteindre des sommets, ce parcours créé en 1991 ne déçoit jamais. Sur chaque départ, on sait exactement où jouer, et les différences visuelles d'un trou à l'autre renouvellent constamment l'intérêt du jeu. Sans être sublime, le site est agréablement boisé et vallonné (facile à jouer à pied), souvent à flanc de côteau, et l'architecte en a utilisé habilement les contours. En l'absence d'arbres, quelques mouvements de terrain ont été créés, mais sans le côté spectaculaire qu'un von Hagge aurait pu donner à cet espace très ouvert. Les principaux obstacles sont les bunkers, qui sont près d'une centaine, certains de grande taille, et placés autant pour capter les balles égarées que pour définir les trous. De fait, le crayon d'Iwao Uematsu a subi des influences américaines, en particulier pour la forte défense des greens et les formes de ceux-ci. L'ouverture prochaine d'un hôtel sur place ne peut que faire mieux connaître ce parcours.

Although not what you would call a top-flight course, this 1991 layout is great golfing every time. From each tee-box you know exactly where to play and the visual differences from one hole to the next keep it constantly interesting. The site is pleasantly wooded over lightly rolling terrain (easily walkable) often on the side of a hill, and the architect very cleverly used the natural topology. Where there are no trees, he shifted a little earth, but without going to the lengths you might have found if someone like von Hagge had been let loose here. The main hazards are bunkers, almost a hundred in all, some of which are huge and placed to both snap up mis-hit shots and define the holes. As a result, the design of Iwao Uematsu has undergone a definite American influence, particularly concerning the well-guarded greens and the shape of the putting surfaces. The future opening of a hotel should help to make this a better known course.

Kikuoka Country Club — 1991

Scheierhaff
L - 5412 CANACH

Office	Secrétariat	(352) 35 61 35
Pro shop	Pro-shop	(352) 35 61 35
Fax	Fax	(352) 35 74 50
Situation	Situation	

Luxembourg (pop. 75 377), 17 km

Annual closure	Fermeture annuelle	no
Weekly closure	Fermeture hebdomadaire	no

Fees main season
Tarifs haute saison full day

	Week days Semaine	We/Bank holidays We/Férié
Individual Individuel	2 060 FLUX	2 575 FLUX
Couple Couple	4 120 FLUX	5 150 FLUX
Monday & Tuesday (Lundi/Mardi): 1 400 FLUX		

Caddy	Caddy	on request
Electric Trolley	Chariot électrique	485 FLUX
Buggy	Voiturette	1 500 FLUX
Clubs	Clubs	1 150 FLUX

Credit cards Cartes de crédit
VISA - Eurocard - MasterCard - AMEX - DC

Access Accès : Luxembourg → Airport (Aréoport).
E29 → Saarbrücken. At Sandweiler, N28 and
CR 144 → Wormeldange, Golf on right hand side
Map 0 on page 0 Carte 0 Page 0

GOLF COURSE PARCOURS — 16/20

Site	Site	
Maintenance	Entretien	
Architect	Architecte	Iwao Uematsu
Type	Type	open country
Relief	Relief	
Water in play	Eau en jeu	
Exp. to wind	Exposé au vent	
Trees in play	Arbres en jeu	

Scorecard Carte de score	Chp. Chp.	Mens Mess.	Ladies Da.
Length Long.	6404	5943	5202
Par	72	72	72

Advised golfing ability Niveau de jeu recommandé	0	12	24	36
Hcp required Handicap exigé	36			

CLUB HOUSE & AMENITIES CLUB HOUSE ET ANNEXES — 7/10

Pro shop	Pro-shop	
Driving range	Practice	
Sheltered	couvert	yes
On grass	sur herbe	tyes
Putting-green	putting-green	yes
Pitching-green	pitching green	yes

127

HOTEL FACILITIES ENVIRONNEMENT HOTELIER — 7/10

HOTELS HÔTELS
Mercure Hotel — on site
70 rooms, ask in June 2000
Tel (352) 35 61 35, Fax (352) 35 79 50

Hôtel des Vignes — Remich
24 rooms, D 3 500 FLUX — 12 km
Tel (352) 69 91 48, Fax (352) 69 84 63

La Bergerie — Geyershaff (Echternach)
15 rooms, D 4 000 FLUX — 18 km
Tel (352) 72 85 041, Fax (352) 72 85 08

RESTAURANTS RESTAURANT
Restaurant de la Forêt — Remich
Tel (352) 694 73 — 12 km

Saint Michel - Tel (352) 22 32 15 — Luxembourg 17 km

La Bergerie — Geyershaff (Echternach)
Tel (352) 794 64 — 18 km

Danmark

Danmark er det sydligste af de Skandisnaviske lande og kilmaet er det mildeste. Man skal imidlertid ikke ignorere at Vesterhavet og Østersøen aldrig er langt væk og vejret kan i denne del af verden tit være meget fugtig. Her falder nok regn til at landskabeter grønt og græsset er tæt og frodigt. Det er naturligtvis ideelt for golf, en sport som har 85,000 danske udøvere og her er ca. 100 18 huls golfbaner. Danmark har både inland og kyst golfbaner, links, og til tider er banen kreeret på en af de mange øer eller tæt på et af badestæderne. I Danmark er man aldrig mere end 30km fra havet. Det kan være svært at få en sydeuropæer til at bade på disse kanter, men danskerne er robuste og flere top spillere i verdensklasse kommer herfra. Den bedst kendte er naturligtvis Thomas Bjørn.

Denmark is the southernmost Scandinavian country and climate-wise is also the mildest. Having said that, the North and Baltic Seas are never far away and it can sometimes be very wet in this part of the world, with enough rain to ensure lush landscapes and thick grass. This is, if course, ideal for golf, a sport played by 85,000 Danes on almost one hundred 18-hole courses. Denmark boasts both inland and coastal courses, sometimes nestling on the country's many islands, or again close to seaside resorts. Anyone from southern Europe would need a lot of prompting to bathe in these cold waters, but the Danes are a hardy bunch and have produced some top world golfers, the best known of whom is, of course, Thomas Bjorn.

129

d'après carte n°985 - 8ème édition - 2000.
Autorisation n°9904173.

KLASSIFIKATION AF GOLFBANER
CLASSIFICATION OF COURSES

Denne klassifikation giver prioritet til bedømmelsen af banens standard.

This classification gives priority consideration
to the score awarded to the actual course.

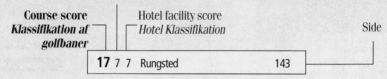

Club-house and facilities
Klassifikation af Klubhuset

Course score
Klassifikation af
golfbaner

Hotel facility score
Hotel Klassifikation

Side

17 7 7   Rungsted   143

Klass.	Golfbaner		Side	Klass.	Golfbaner	Side
17 7 7	Rungsted	✳	143	**15** 7 5	Læsø Seaside ✳	140
16 8 6	Himmerland *New Course*	🏌	137	**15** 7 7	Møn	141
16 6 5	Holstebro	🏌	138	**15** 7 5	Royal Oak	142
15 7 6	Asserbo		133	**15** 4 7	Samsø	144
15 6 5	Esbjerg	✳	134	**15** 7 7	Vejle *Blue + Red Slings*	147
15 4 7	Fanø	✳	135	**14** 4 6	Korsør	139
15 7 7	Furesø		136	**14** 5 6	Sct. Knuds	145

HOTEL KLASSIFIKATION
CLASSIFICATION OF HOTELS FACILITIES

Denne Klassifikation giver prioritet til bedømmelsen af hotellets faciliteter.

This classification gives priority consideration
to the score awarded to the hotel facilities.

Club-house and facilities
Klassifikation af Klubhuset

Course score
Klassifikation af golfbaner

Hotel facility score
Hotel Klassifikation

Side

132

16 6 **9**   Bath   Fng   526

Klass.	Golfbaner		Side	Klass.	Golfbaner		Side
17 7 **7**	Rungsted	Da	143	15 7 **6**	Asserbo	Da	133
15 7 **7**	Furesø	Da	136	14 5 **6**	Sct. Knuds	Da	145
15 7 **7**	Møn	Da	141	14 4 **6**	Korsør	Da	139
15 7 **7**	Vejle *Blue + Red Slings*	Da	147	15 7 **5**	Læsø Seaside	Da	140
15 4 **7**	Samsø	Da	144	15 7 **5**	Royal Oak	Da	142
14 7 **7**	Simon's	Da	146	16 6 **5**	Holstebro	Da	138
14 4 **7**	Fanø	Da	135	15 6 **5**	Esbjerg	Da	134
16 8 **6**	Himmerland *New Course*	Da	137				

Nordsjælland er behagelig langt fra den københavnske golf-alfarvej. Herligger Asserbo, ikke så langt fra Hillerød og fra Frederiksborg Slot, der står på tresmå øer, og hvis park for nylig er blevet beriget med landets smukkeste haveanlæg i romantisk stil. Banen er temmelig kuperet (el-vogn tilrådes), og skråninger er på to trediedele af hullerne udnyttet, så ens approach-slag skal spilles enten op eller ned for at komme på green. Derfor er det vigtigt, at man er omhyggelig med sit valg af jern. Det er nu ikke nødvendigt at spille her 20 gange for at vide, hvad du skal, for trods højdeforskellene byder banen ikke på særlig mange blinde slag. Den er tværtimod åben og ærlig. Greens er fornuftigt designede og ligger godt beskyttet. Flere steder er såvel enkeltstående som klynger af træer i allerhøjeste grad i spil, og der er vandhazarder med i billedet især på de sidste ni huller. En meget smukt og dejlig afsides beliggende bane, der ikke er sværere, end at alle kan være med. Ikke Sjællands bedste, men altid en fornøjelse at vende tilbage til.

A little removed from the destinations most frequented by the Danish capital's city folk, this course is located close to the royal castle of Frederiksborg in Hillerød, curiously built on three islands and now the Museum of Danish History. The terrain is hilly (buggy recommended) and the slopes have been cleverly used by the architects, who deliberately placed the greens of at least twelve holes with either an uphill or downhill approach. However, you don't have to play here a hundred times to draw up a game strategy, as he course has nothing to hide. The greens are well guarded and rather well designed, there are a few dangerous trees to negotiate (particularly on holes 1 and 4) and water hazards are also a part of the scene, especially on the back 9, although they are seldom really dangerous. A pretty course in a calm, isolated setting, playable by all. This is hardly the course of the century but it is always a pleasure coming back here.

Asserbo Golf Club — 1946

Bødkergaardsvej
DK - 3300 FREDERIKSVÆRK

Office	Sekretariat	(45) 47 72 14 90
Pro shop	Pro-shop	(45) 47 72 12 84
Fax	Fax	(45) 47 72 14 26
Situation	Sted	

Hillerød, 20 km

Annual closure	Årlig lukkeperiod	no
Weekly closure	Ugentlig lukketid	no

Fees main season
Priser i hojsæson 18 holes

	Week days Hverdage	We/Bank holidays Helligdag
Individual Individuelt	220 DKr	280 DKr
Couple Paar	440 DKr	560 DKr

Junior : – 50%

Caddy	Caddie	no
Electric Trolley	Bagvogn	no
Buggy	Golf car	150 DKr
Clubs	Koller	150 DKr

Credit cards Creditkord VISA - Eurocard - DC

Access Adgang : København E4 → Helsingør. 50 km,
19 → Hillerød, 16 → Frederiksværk. → Liseleje.
1 km → Golf
Map 1 on page 131 Kort 1 på side 131

GOLF COURSE / BAN — 15/20

Site	Sted	
Maintenance	Vedligeholdese	
Architect	Arkitekt	James Ross Peter Samuelsen
Type	Type	parkland, hilly
Relief	Lettelse	
Water in play	Vand i spil	
Exp. to wind	Udsat vind	
Trees in play	Træer i spil	

Scorecard Scorekort	Chp. Back tee	Mens Herre tee	Ladies Dame tee
Length Længde	5861	5861	4915
Par	72	72	72

Advised golfing ability	0	12	24	36

Hcp required	Max. handicap	30

CLUB HOUSE & AMENITIES / KLUBHUSET OG FACILITETER — 7/10

Pro shop	Pro-shop	
Driving range	Driving range	
Sheltered	Ly	no
On grass	på græs	no, 8 mats open air
Putting-green	Putting-green	yes
Pitching-green	Indspilsgreen	yes

133

HOTEL FACILITIES / HOTEL FACILITETERNE — 6/10

HOTELS HOTEL

Sankt Helene Centret — Tisvildeleje
12 rooms, D 660 DKr — 5 km
Tel (45) 48 70 98 50, Fax (45) 48 70 98 97

Hotel Hillerød — Hillerød
32 rooms, D 480 DKr — 20 km
Tel (45) 48 24 08 00, Fax (45) 48 24 08 74

RESTAURANTS RESTAURANT

Le Provençal — Hornbæk
Tel (45) 49 76 11 77 — 40 km

Søstjernen — Raageleje
Tel (45) 48 71 53 27 — 20 km

Vestjyllands marsk, sandklitter og strande langs Vesterhavet er ikke Danmarks golf-mekka. Synd, for de baner, området byder på, er temmelig gode. Som nu for eksempel Esbjergs fine gamle mesterskabsbane, der - som den altid er det, især når det blæser - ved DM i 1999 var en skrap test for de bedste spillere. Her bliver ikke lavet stribevis af 5 under par-runder! Banen er uden egentlige vand-hazarder, og der er heller ikke mange træer. Dens hovedforhindringer er en række meget velplacerede bunkers, især på de sidste ni huller, og så den altid tilstedeværende. Læg dertil, at hullerne er meget flade, og man kunne få det indtryk, at de er meget ens. Javist, men mere naturlig bane i så barske omgivelser skal man lede længe efter, i hvert fald i Danmark. Den er indbegrebet af underspillet charme, og man føler sig virkelig i pagt med naturen på runden. Ni relativt nye huller er med til at gøre et besøg mere varieret.

The west coast of Jutland is not the most popular area of Denmark for tourists, but it certainly has its share of romance with infinite stretches of moor-land which seem to merge with the sand dunes alongside the North Sea. The first good reason for coming here is the pretty medieval town of Ribe, a major trading centre and port from the Viking era. Another reason is this golf course, the only real seaside course in a country where you are never far from the sea. Strangely enough, there are no water hazards on this pretty layout. There are not many trees, either, and the main difficulties lie with some excellent bunkering, particularly in the fairways on the back 9, and the ever present wind. Should we add that the holes are very flat, you might get the impression that they are all much the same. In actual fact, what is a very natural course in a rather rough setting is a picture of subtlety and charm, helped by the impression of isolation you get when playing here. An extra 9 holes enhance these qualities still further.

Esbjerg Golfklub — 1964

Sønderhedevej 11
DK - 6710 ESBJERG V

Office	Sekretariat	(45) 75 26 92 19
Pro shop	Pro-shop	(45) 75 26 92 72
Fax	Fax	(45) 75 26 94 19
Situation	Sted	

Esbjerg, 15 km

Annual closure	Årlig lukkeperiod	no
Weekly closure	Ugentlig lukketid	no

Fees main season
Priser i hojsæson full day

	Week days Hverdage	We/Bank holidays Helligdag
Individual Individuelt	200 DKr	200 DKr
Couple Paar	400 DKr	400 DKr

Juniors : – 50%

Caddy	Caddie	no
Electric Trolley	Bagvogn	15 DKr
Buggy	Golf car	200 DKr
Clubs	Koller	150 DKr

Credit cards Creditkord VISA - Eurocard - DC

Access Adgang : E20, Exit → 463 → Blåvand.
→ Marbæk/Golf
Map 1 on page 130 Kort 1 på side 130

GOLF COURSE / BAN — 15/20

Site	Sted	
Maintenance	Vedligeholdese	
Architect	Arkitekt	Frederik Dreyer
Type	Type	seaside course
Relief	Lettelse	
Water in play	Vand i spil	
Exp. to wind	Udsat vind	
Trees in play	Træer i spil	

Scorecard Scorekort	Chp. Back tee	Mens Herre tee	Ladies Dame tee
Length Længde	5728	5728	4977
Par	71	71	71

Advised golfing ability	0	12	24	36

Hcp required	Max. handicap	36

CLUB HOUSE & AMENITIES / KLUBHUSET OG FACILITETER — 6/10

Pro shop	Pro-shop	
Driving range	Driving range	
Sheltered	Ly	5 mats
On grass	på græs	yes (04 →10)
Putting-green	Putting-green	yes
Pitching-green	Indspilsgreen	yes

HOTEL FACILITIES / KLUBHUSET OG FACILITETER — 5/10

HOTELS HOTEL

Britannia — Esbjerg 15 km
85 rooms, D 700 DKr
Tel (45) 75 13 01 11, Fax (45) 75 45 20 85

Hjerting — Esbjerg 15 km
55 rooms, D 750 DKr
Tel (45) 75 11 52 44

RESTAURANTS RESTAURANT

Pakhuset — Esbjerg 15 km
Tel (45) 75 12 74 55

Henne Kirkeby Kro — Henne 30 km
Tel (45) 75 25 54 00

Schackenborg Slotskro — Møgeltonder 70 km
Tel (45) 74 83 83 83

134

Ti minutter med færgen fra Esbjerg - og man er i helt andre omgivelser på Fanø. Et kig inden for i banens "kontor" med efterfølgende spil på banen, og man kunne tilføje: I en helt anden tidsalder. Fanø er Danmarks ældste bane, fra før verden gik af lave. Den åbnede i 1901, og tre af hullerne samt én green, den 7., fra det originale hulforløb eksisterer den dag i dag. Hullerne løber ikke helt ud til vandet, men der er ikke desto mindre tale om Danmarks eneste linksbane udlagt blandt de for links-baner karakteristiske sandklitter. Disse er banens fornemste forhindringer. Dels fordi de ikke er rare at stifte bekendtskab med for éns bold, dels fordi de resulterer i mange mere eller mindre blinde slag, både fra tee og ind til green. Det kræver adskillige runder at finde ud af, hvordan banens spidsfindigheder skal tackles. Med syv par 3-huller og ingen par 5-huller er banen dog så kort, at man godt kan spille to af disse runder på samme dag og alligevel have tid tid til en tur på den kilometerlange og meget brede strand lige ved siden af.

This course, located on the island of Fanø, is just opposite the town of Esbjerg, which is also well worth a visit via a 10-minute boat-trip. Only a few houses here and there are able to counter the sensation of travelling through time on a course opened in 1901 and doubtless designed by a Brit, judging by the style (the green on hole N° 7 is most original). Although not exactly by the sea, this is a real links course using the dunes, and of course the wind, are the main obstacles. The tall rough is omnipresent but the dunes carefully conceal a number of greens and fairways, resulting in a number of blind shots and blind greens. You will need several rounds to size up the layout and understand its subtle features. Moreover, it is not because this course is short that it should be underestimated, but you can easily play it twice in a day, with no trouble. With seven par 3s and no par 5, here is a course offering a lot of excitement and a few surprises.

Fanø Golf Links — 1901

Sdr. Banksti 2
DK - 6720 NORDBY

Office	Sekretariat	(45) 75 16 14 00
Pro shop	Pro-shop	(45) 75 16 14 00
Fax	Fax	(45) 75 16 14 00
Situation	Sted	
Esbjerg, 12 mn (Ferry)		
Annual closure	Årlig lukkeperiod	no
Weekly closure	Ugentlig lukketid	no

Fees main season
Priser i højsæson full day

	Week days Hverdage	We/Bank holidays Helligdag
Individual Individuelt	190 DKr	190 DKr
Couple Paar	380 DKr	380 DKr
Junior : – 50 %		

Caddy	Caddie	no
Electric Trolley	Bagvogn	no
Buggy	Golf car	no
Clubs	Koller	40 DKr

Credit cards Creditkord VISA - DC

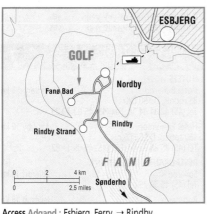

ESBJERG

GOLF

Fanø Bad
Nordby
Rindby
Rindby Strand
F A N Ø
Sønderho

0	2	4 km
0		2,5 miles

Access Adgang : Esbjerg, Ferry. → Rindby.

Map 1 on page 130 Kort 1 på side 130

GOLF COURSE / BAN — 15/20

Site	Sted	▰▰▰▰▱
Maintenance	Vedligeholdese	▰▰▰▱▱
Architect	Arkitekt	unknown
Type	Type	links
Relief	Lettelse	▰▰▱▱▱
Water in play	Vand i spil	▰▱▱▱▱
Exp. to wind	Udsat vind	▰▰▰▱▱
Trees in play	Træer i spil	▰▱▱▱▱

Scorecard Scorekort	Chp. Back tee	Mens Herre tee	Ladies Dame tee
Length Længde	4423	4423	3772
Par	65	65	65

Advised golfing ability	0	12	24	36

Hcp required   Max. handicap   no

CLUB HOUSE & AMENITIES / KLUBHUSET OG FACILITETER — 4/10

Pro shop	Pro-shop	▰▰▱▱▱
Driving range	Driving range	▰▰▱▱▱
Sheltered	Ly	no
On grass	på græs	no
Putting-green	Putting-green	yes
Pitching-green	Indspilsgreen	no

HOTEL FACILITIES / HOTEL FACILITETERNE — 7/10

HOTELS HOTEL
Fanø Badeland — Rindby 1
126 rooms, D 695 DKr
Tel (45) 75 16 60 00, Fax (45) 75 16 60 11

Sønderhø Kro — Sønderho 5 km
18 rooms, D 680 DKr
Tel (45) 75 16 40 09, Fax (45) 75 16 43 85

RESTAURANTS RESTAURANT
Sønderho Kro — Sønderho 5 km
Tel (45) 75 16 40 09

Nørdby Kro — Nordby 2 km
Tel(45) 75 16 35 89

135

Det er næsten ikke til at tro, at man her befinder sig inden for det, der kaldes Storkøbenhavn. Så idyllerisk og fjernt fra storbyens larm fremtræder Furesø - selv om der kun er 20 km til Rådhuspladsen. Banen har tre forskellige nihullers sløjfer, der kan kombineres efter ønske. Spil dem alle tre - og du får virkelig noget for pengene. Tre af de originale 18 huller blev for nogle år tilbage erstattet med nye og betydelig bedre huller, og i 1996 kom så ni helt nye huller til. De byder på forholdsvis åben golf med skrap rough, mens de oprindelige 18 huller har karakter af parkbane, hvor bevoksning, træer og adskillige store og små vand-hazarder står for underholdningen. Brug gerne en baneguide, første gang du spiller banen. Den er måske lidt kort for de længst-slående, men det råder dens spidsfindigheder mere end bod på. Mht. kupering er den lidt over gennemsnittet.

Although on the outskirts of the city of Copenhagen, the Furesø golf course is set in very calm surroundings. In this sanctuary lying next door to a bustling city, where as it happens there are a thousand things to do other than just seeing the mermaid, this course offers 27 holes of golf. The whole course is definitely on the hilly side but the going is never too steep. Three of the first 18 holes have been recently altered for the better, and an extra 9 holes have been laid out over more open land than that used for the original 18 hole course, where the vegetation creates a number of hazards. At least the trees are more visible than certain water hazards; there is no shortage of water, but some watery graves are hidden and can create some unpleasant surprises. If you can't play here several times, then you should at least tee off with locals who know the course first time out. Although a little on the short side for the longer hitters, this is an imaginative and well-landscaped course that generally speaking has been very carefully laid out.

Furesø Golf Club — 1974

Hestkøb Vænge 4
DK - 3460 BIRKERØD

Office	Sekretariat	(45) 42 81 74 44
Pro shop	Pro-shop	(45) 42 81 77 17
Fax	Fax	(45) 42 81 02 24
Situation	Sted	

København, 15 km

Annual closure	Årlig lukkeperiod	no
Weekly closure	Ugentlig lukketid	no

Fees main season
Priser i hojsæson full day

	Week days Hverdage	We/Bank holidays Helligdag
Individual Individuelt	200 DKr	280 DKr
Couple Paar	400 DKr	560 DKr

Juniors : – 50%

Caddy	Caddie	no
Electric Trolley	Bagvogn	30 DKr
Buggy	Golf car	no
Clubs	Koller	150 DKr

Credit cards Creditkord VISA - Eurocard - DC

136

Access Adgang : E16, Exit 10 → Birkerød, Birkerød Parkvej, Duemosevej, → Golf.
Map 1 on page 131 Kort 1 på side 131

GOLF COURSE
BAN 15/20

Site	Sted	
Maintenance	Vedligeholdese	
Architect	Arkitekt	Jan Sederholm
Type	Type	parkland
Relief	Lettelse	
Water in play	Vand i spil	
Exp. to wind	Udsat vind	
Trees in play	Træer i spil	

Scorecard	Chp.	Mens	Ladies
Scorekort	Back tee	Herre tee	Dame tee
Length Længde	5596	5596	4776
Par	72	72	71

Advised golfing ability   0 12 24 36

Hcp required   Max. handicap   31

CLUB HOUSE & AMENITIES
KLUBHUSET OG FACILITETER 7/10

Pro shop	Pro-shop	
Driving range	Driving range	
Sheltered	Ly	no
On grass	på græs	yes (04 → 10)
Putting-green	Putting-green	yes
Pitching-green	Indspilsgreen	yes

HOTEL FACILITIES
HOTEL FACILITETERNE 7/10

HOTELS HOTEL

Hotel Birkerød   Birkerød 3 km
35 rooms, D 550 DKr
Tel (45) 42 81 44 30, Fax (45) 45 82 30 29

Hotel Eremitage   Lyngby 10 km
130 rooms, D 850 DKr
Tel (45) 45 88 77 00, Fax (45) 45 88 17 82

RESTAURANTS RESTAURANT

Søllerød Kro   Søllerød 10 km
Tel (45) 45 80 25 05

Rotunden   Hellerup 15 km
Tel (45) 39 61 26 96

Den Røde Cottage   Klampenborg10 km
Tel (45) 39 90 46 14

Den gamle vikinge-begravelsesplads Lindholm samt Rold Skov, Danmarks største, er blandt seværdighederne i nærheden af Himmerland. Selv PÅ dette 36-hullers anlæg er der andet at tage sig til end at spille golf, stå på vandski på Gatten sø f.eks. Banerne kaldes Old Course og New Course. Den sidste er tegnet Jan Sederholm, og det bærer greens som altid præg af: De er udlagt, så greenkeeperen har mulighed for meget forskellige flagplaceringer. Området er relativt fladt og åbent. Vand-hazarder her og der giver nærmest indtryk af amerikansk parkbane, og det samme gør de i visse tilfælde meget store fairwaybunkers. 18. hul er en glimrende afslutning - lige op til klubhuset, hvor man kan sidde og følge dristige spilleres forsøg på at skære hjørnet af den sø, der æder sig ind i fairway på det kun godt 300 m lange hul. New Course er en krævende bane, også fordi den er temmelig lang, og det skyldes blandt andet et af golfverdenens meget sjældne par 6-huller - i dette tilfæde det 10., som er hele 610 m.

The eastern region of Jutland is more protected from oceanic influences than the west coast and the landscapes are more lush with alternating meadows and forests. After a visit to Ålborg, Europe's cleanest city, don't miss Lindholm Høje, an age-old Viking cemetery kept in perfect condition. The same goes for Rold Skov, the country's largest forest, before reaching Himmerland. This 36-hole resort comprises the New Course, designed by Jan Sederholm, whose greens most connoisseurs would recognize, always laid out in the true spirit of the game. In relatively flat and clear open space, the scattering of a few hazards gives a slightly American flavour, and the same goes for the large fairway bunkers. Well designed and demanding, this layout is probably difficult for inexperienced players, but they will find a welcome on the other course here (very pleasant golfing). A curiosity is the par-6 10th hole... reachable in 3 by the longer hitters.

Himmerland Golf Klub — 1993

Centervej 1 - Gatten
DK - 9640 FARSØ

Office	Sekretariat	(45) 96 49 61 00
Pro shop	Pro-shop	(45) 96 49 61 09
Fax	Fax	(45) 98 66 14 56
Situation	Sted	

Aalborg, 50 km

Annual closure	Årlig lukkeperiod	no
Weekly closure	Ugentlig lukketid	no

Fees main season
Priser i hojsæson full day

	Week days Hverdage	We/Bank holidays Helligdag
Individual Individuelt	230 DKr	320 DKr
Couple Paar	460 DKr	640 DKr

Junior : – 50 %

Caddy	Caddie	no
Electric Trolley	Bagvogn	no
Buggy	Golf car	320 DKr
Clubs	Koller	100 DKr

Credit cards Creditkord VISA - Eurocard - DC

Access Adgang : E 45 Århus - Ålborg.
Exit (Frakørsel) 33, 535 → Aars. 29 → Løgstør.
Map 1 on page 130 Kort 1 på side 130

GOLF COURSE / BAN — 16/20

Site	Sted	
Maintenance	Vedligeholdese	
Architect	Arkitekt	Jan Sederholm
Type	Type	country, open country
Relief	Lettelse	
Water in play	Vand i spil	
Exp. to wind	Udsat vind	
Trees in play	Træer i spil	

Scorecard Scorekort	Chp. Back tee	Mens Herre tee	Ladies Dame tee
Length Længde	6102	6102	5347
Par	73	73	73

Advised golfing ability 0 12 24 36

Hcp required Max. handicap 36

CLUB HOUSE & AMENITIES / KLUBHUSET OG FACILITETER — 8/10

Pro shop	Pro-shop	
Driving range	Driving range	
Sheltered	Ly	no
On grass	på græs	yes
Putting-green	Putting-green	yes
Pitching-green	Indspilsgreen	yes

HOTEL FACILITIES / HOTEL FACILITETERNE — 6/10

HOTELS HOTEL

Golfagergård Motel 24 rooms, D 250 DKr Tel (45) 98 66 30 98	Gatten 1 km
Himmerland Golf Hotel 48 rooms, D 610 DKr Tel (45) 96 49 61 00, Fax (45) 98 66 14 66	Farsø 2 km

RESTAURANTS RESTAURANT

Himmerland Golf Hotel Tel (45) 96 49 61 00	Farsø 2 km

137

Denne bane er næsten altid at finde på danske golferes top 3. Den ligger i et tidligere plantageområde og må om nogen betegnes som en skovbane. Fairways er forholdsvis brede, men kommer du først uden for fairway, kan der være problemer med overhovedet at finde den igen. Det er ingen overdrivelse, men forholdet mellem brede fairways og straffende skov er helt rigtigt, og det forklarer, hvorfor banen kun har ganske få bunkers. Træerne - mellem hvilke man går i storladen isolation - er sammen med en række vand-hazarder alt rigeligt til at holde selv den bedste spiller i ørerne. Men Holstebro er også en åben og ærlig bane. Spilleplanen for hvert hul er klar. Kun på dogleg-huller kan man ikke se green fra tee-stedet. Greens er vel-designede uden de store ondulationer. Banen ER svær - men så byder Holstebros anlæg også på en ni-hullers bane for de lidt mindre skrappe.

This course is regularly ranked amongst the country's top three, even by those people who have never played here. That's what reputation can do for you. It is located in a former plantation, which explains the very many trees. The fairways are wide, but if you spray the ball left or right you might end up not actually knowing how to get back onto the «short stuff». That's no exaggeration. It all gives a marvellous sensation of isolation and explains why there are few green-side bunkers and just a single fairway bunker; the trees and water hazards are enough to keep most players on their toes. With this said, Holstebro is a very forthright course: game strategy is immediately clear, there are no blind greens (except on the dog-legs) and greens are well designed without any excessively steep slopes. Spectacular for its forest setting, very pleasant for its peace and quiet but a little tough for high-handicappers, Holstebro is worth a visit. What's more, there is another shortish 9 hole course, which is perfect for all the family.

Holstebro Golfklub — 1970

Brandsbjergvet 4
DK - 7570 VEMB

Office	Sekretariat	(45) 97 48 51 55
Pro shop	Pro-shop	(45) 97 48 52 93
Fax	Fax	(45) 97 48 52 93
Situation	Sted	

Århus, 100 km - Holstebro, 15 km

Annual closure	Årlig lukkeperiod	no
Weekly closure	Ugentlig lukketid	no

Fees main season
Priser i højsæson full day

	Week days Hverdage	We/Bank holidays Helligdag
Individual Individuelt	200 DKr	220 DKr
Couple Paar	400 DKr	440 DKr

Juniors : – 50%

Caddy	Caddie	no
Electric Trolley	Bagvogn	no
Buggy	Golf car	180 DKr
Clubs	Koller	100 DKr

Credit cards Creditkord VISA - Eurocard - DC

138

Access Adgang : Århus: 16 → Herning,
18 → Holstebro. 16, 12 km → Ulfborg, → Golf.
Map 1 on page 130 Kort 1 på side 130

GOLF COURSE
BAN — **16**/20

Site	Sted	
Maintenance	Vedligeholdese	
Architect	Arkitekt	Erik Schnack
Type	Type	forest, parkland
Relief	Lettelse	
Water in play	Vand i spil	
Exp. to wind	Udsat vind	
Trees in play	Træer i spil	

Scorecard Scorekort	Chp. Back tee	Mens Herre tee	Ladies Dame tee
Length Længde	5853	5853	4705
Par	72	72	72

Advised golfing ability — 0 12 24 36

Hcp required — Max. handicap — no

CLUB HOUSE & AMENITIES
KLUBHUSET OG FACILITETER — **6**/10

Pro shop	Pro-shop	
Driving range	Driving range	
Sheltered	Ly	no
On grass	på græs	yes (04 → 10)
Putting-green	Putting-green	yes
Pitching-green	Indspilsgreen	yes

HOTEL FACILITIES
HOTEL FACILITETERNE — **5**/10

HOTELS HOTEL
Schaumburg — Holstebro 15 km
80 rooms, D 650 DKr
Tel (45) 97 42 31 11, Fax (45) 97 42 72 82

Royal Holstebro — Holstebro 15 km
65 rooms, D 1040 DKr
Tel (45) 97 40 23 33, Fax (45) 97 40 30 87

RESTAURANTS RESTAURANT
NR. Wosborg — Vemb 8 km
Tel (45) 97 48 17 40

Teaterrestauranten — Herning 40 km
Tel (45) 97 12 20 77

Sevel Kro — Sevel 20 km
Tel (45) 97 44 80 11

Denne glimrende bane har hidtil ligget langt fra såvel København som Vestdanmark, men med Storebæltsbroen er den pludselig kommet tidsmæssigt meget tættere på Fyn og Jylland. Banen er designet af medlemmerne, og det forklarer måske lidt af dens af og til særprægede layout. Som fx 7. hul, der er et zigzaggende par 5, hvor man virkelig skal tænke sig om, før man slår. Det skal man faktisk på de fleste huller, og man gør klogt i at lade driver'en blive i bag'en det meste af tiden. Selv om banen er relativt flad, er approach-slagene til et par greens blinde. Især 5. green kan være svær at ramme. Ellers er hullernes layout gennemgående præget af opfindsomhed, og efterhånden som runden skrider frem, bygges der op til belønning: 15. og 16. hul byder på fænomenal udsigt over vandet, som de begge løber langs med. Det er værd at lægge mærke til, at 9. hul ikke fører ind til klubhuset.

The new bridge over the Storebælt, linking the islands of Sjælland and Fyn, has made it easier to drive to this latter province, described by Andersen as the garden of Denmark, and he should know. From Korsør, it is now quick and convenient to go and visit the provincial capital of Odense, the old district of which looks like a collection of theatrical props. The Korsør course was designed by club members, which explains some of the layout's more original features such as hole N° 7, a zigzagging par 5 where you really do need to think before you shoot. In fact the same can be said for nearly all the holes. One of the best ideas here is to leave the driver in the bag and stick to long irons. A few greens are blind, despite the flattish terrain, and none more so than the contentious hole N° 5. Otherwise you'll find holes that are full of imagination, some splendid views over the arm of the sea splitting the two islands, and a number of holes at the end of the course which bring the Storebælt river into play.

Korsør Golf Klub   1964

Ørnumvej 8
DK - 4220 KORSØR

Office	Sekretariat	(45) 53 57 18 36
Pro shop	Pro-shop	(45) 53 57 40 18
Fax	Fax	(45) 53 57 18 39
Situation	Sted	

Korsør, 2 km

Annual closure	Årlig lukkeperiod	no
Weekly closure	Ugentlig lukketid	no

Fees main season
Priser i hojsæson full day

	Week days Hverdage	We/Bank holidays Helligdag
Individual Individuelt	160 DKr	200 DKr
Couple Paar	320 DKr	400 DKr

Junior : – 50%

Caddy	Caddie	no
Electric Trolley	Bagvogn	25 DKr
Buggy	Golf car	150 DKr
Clubs	Koller	100 DKr

Credit cards Creditkord   VISA - Eurocard - MasterCard

Access Adgang : E20 Exit 42. Tårnkorgvej, Ørnumvej → Golf.
Map 1 on page 131 Kort 1 på side 131

GOLF COURSE
BAN   14/20

Site	Sted	
Maintenance	Vedligeholdese	
Architect	Arkitekt	Unknown
Type	Type	seaside course, country
Relief	Lettelse	
Water in play	Vand i spil	
Exp. to wind	Udsat vind	
Trees in play	Træer i spil	

Scorecard Scorekort	Chp. Back tee	Mens Herre tee	Ladies Dame tee
Length Længde	5773	5773	4969
Par	73	73	73

Advised golfing ability	0	12	24	36

Hcp required	Max. handicap	36

CLUB HOUSE & AMENITIES
KLUBHUSET OG FACILITETER   4/10

Pro shop	Pro-shop	
Driving range	Driving range	
Sheltered	Ly	no
On grass	på græs	yes (04 → 10)
Putting-green	Putting-green	yes
Pitching-green	Indspilsgreen	yes

139

HOTEL FACILITIES
HOTEL FACILITETERNE   6/10

HOTELS HOTEL

Tårnborg Park Hotel   Korsør 1 km
110 rooms, D 650 DKr
Tel (45) 58 35 01 10, Fax (45) 58 35 01 20

Hotel Frederik II   Slagelse 15 km
50 rooms, D 520 DKr
Tel (45) 58 53 03 22, Fax (45) 58 53 16 22

Hesselet   Nyborg 10 km
85 rooms, D 850 DKr
Tel (45) 65 31 30 29, Fax (45) 65 31 29 58

RESTAURANTS RESTAURANT

Babette   Vordingborg 45 km
Tel (45) 55 34 30 30

Hesselet   Nyborg 10 km
Tel (45) 65 31 29 58

LÆSØ SEASIDE

★ 15 7 5

Med 90 minutters sejltur fra Frederikshavn eller en lille times taxi-flyvning fra Roskilde er saltsydningens, krebsenes og biernes ø Læsø ikke et sted, man sådan lige lægger vejen forbi. Men er du allerede i Nordjylland for at spille golf, bør du gøre turen ud til øens naturskønne, varierede og svære bane. Svær, fordi man på kun ét af dens 15 lange huller hiver driver'en op af bag'en uden at betænke sig. På de resterende 14 er landingsområderne enten meget smalle, eller også er hullet dogleg, så der kræves den helt rigtige længde på slaget for at bolden kommer til at ligge rigtigt. Slår man skævt, straffes man hårdt af træer med dertil hørende tyk underskov. Eller af høj rough som den, der på det prægtige par 5 afslutningshul klemmer fairway til maks. 25 meter. Vand-hazarder, der ikke alle er lige tydelige, gør ikke banen nemmere. Læsø er banen for folk, der har mange slag i bag'en, og har du ikke det, første gang du besøger banen, så glem din score og nyd i stedet, hvor naturligt det kan lade sig gøre at udlægge en golbane.

Here, you can hit your wayward shots without too many people watching in a tranquil setting made to feel even more isolated by the thick trees and rough. By contrast, you won't have much opportunity to use the driver, either because the fairways are narrow or because the turn of the dog-legs are too close, or because the water hazards lurk dangerously close to the most adventurous way forward. Fortunately, there are few bunkers, which would only have compounded the issue. In fact, this is a course designed for seasoned golfers who can quickly adjust their game. The first time out, you might be put off by the demands of the course; in this case, forget your handicap and focus on discovering the course. You will understand and appreciate the course better the next time out. Over an area naturally suited to golf, the architect didn't have to move much earth, and this is noticeable in the already «mature» feel to the complex.

Læsø Seaside Golfklub 1995

Prof. Johansensvej 2
DK - 9940 Læsø

Office	Sekretariat	(45) 98 49 84 00
Pro shop	Pro-shop	(45) 98 49 84 00
Fax	Fax	–
Situation	Sted	

Frederikshavn, 90 mn (Ferry)

Annual closure	Årlig lukkeperiod	no
Weekly closure	Ugentlig lukketid	no

Fees main season
Priser i hojsæson full day

	Week days Hverdage	We/Bank holidays Helligdag
Individual Individuelt	180 DKr	180 DKr
Couple Paar	360 DKr	360 DKr

Junior : – 50%

Caddy	Caddie	no
Electric Trolley	Bagvogn	no
Buggy	Golf car	no
Clubs	Koller	40 DKr

Credit cards Creditkord VISA - Eurocard - DC

140

GOLF

Østerby Havn

Frederikshavn

Østerby

Vesterø Havn

Vesterø Mejeriby

Skoven

Hvent

L Æ S Ø

0 2 4 km
0 2,5 miles

Access Adgang : Frederikshavn, 90 mn Ferry.
Vesterø → Østerby
Map 1 on page 130 Kort 1 på side 130

GOLF COURSE
BAN
15/20

Site	Sted	
Maintenance	Vedligeholdese	
Architect	Arkitekt	Lars Andreasson
Type	Type	seaside course, forest
Relief	Lettelse	
Water in play	Vand i spil	
Exp. to wind	Udsat vind	
Trees in play	Træer i spil	

Scorecard Scorekort	Chp. Back tee	Mens Herre tee	Ladies Dame tee
Length Længde	6068	6068	5250
Par	74	74	74

Advised golfing ability 0 12 24 36

Hcp required Max. handicap 36

CLUB HOUSE & AMENITIES
KLUBHUSET OG FACILITETER
7/10

Pro shop	Pro-shop	
Driving range	Driving range	
Sheltered	Ly	–
On grass	på græs	no, 8 mats open air
Putting-green	Putting-green	yes
Pitching-green	Indspilsgreen	no

HOTEL FACILITIES
HOTEL FACILITETERNE
5/10

HOTELS HOTEL

Læsø Seaside Hotel	Læsø
16 rooms, D 700 DKr	
Tel (45) 48 99 88 00, Fax (45) 98 49 84 00	
Hotel Nygaard	Østerby
18 rooms, D 510 DKr	5 km
Tel (45) 98 49 16 66, Fax (45) 98 49 84 00	

RESTAURANTS RESTAURANT

Hotel Nygaard	Østerby
Tel (45) 98 49 16 66	5 km
Delikaten	Vesterø
Tel (45) 98 49 99 01	10 km

Begynd gerne en udflugt til golfbanen på Møn med at køre for langt. Fortsætter du forbi banen, der ligger umiddelbart øst for Stege, ender du nemlig helt ude på øens østkyst, og her er det et helt fantastisk syn, at opleve morgensolens stråler ramme de majestætiske hvide klinter. En anden af øens attraktioner er de fine middelalderlige kalkmalerier, der kan ses i flere kirker ikke langt fra banen. Den forholdsvis nye bane, der i hesteskoform strækker sig rundt om inderste del af Stege Nor, er i glimrende stand, og man lægger straks mærke til de fine fairways. Det begynder blødt med forholdsvis åbne huller, men strammer til på de sidste ni, hvor vand-hazarder og især rough straffer den, der slår skævt. 14. hul, et langt par 4, er strålende i al sin enkelhed: Lidt op ad bakke zigzagger fairway'en sig mellem den bølgende rough op til green'en, hvor en enkel bunker står vagt. Alt i alt en ærlig og ikke alt for kuperet bane, hvor golfere på alle niveauer kan være med.

Møn is hardly the best known of the many islands in Denmark, and as a result has retained unspoiled many of its natural treasures, including the huge white beaches, dunes, forests and amazing white chalk cliffs. Art-loving golfers will not want to miss visiting the three churches in the village of Stege, decorated with Middle Age frescos. On the course, these same golfers will want to know how to sometimes bend the ball when they stray off the excellent fairways on holes lined with trees, although there are enough more open holes to make up for poor accuracy. Caution is required however, as the tall rough is a very dangerous proposition on about half a dozen holes (particularly the 14th) and often more so than water, which only really comes into play on 3 holes. After reconnoitring, you'll find this an honest course, relatively playable by golfers of all abilities and sufficiently steep in places to recommend a buggy for unfit golfers.

Møn Golfklub — 1995

Klintevej 118
DK - 4780 STEGE

Office	Sekretariat	(45) 55 81 32 60
Pro shop	Pro-shop	(45) 55 81 39 69
Fax	Fax	(45) 55 81 32 60
Situation	Sted	

Vordingborg, 20 km

Annual closure	Årlig lukkeperiod	no
Weekly closure	Ugentlig lukketid	no

Fees main season
Priser i højsæson 18 holes

	Week days Hverdage	We/Bank holidays Helligdag
Individual Individuelt	210 DKr	260 DKr
Couple Paar	420 DKr	520 DKr

Junior : – 50%

Caddy	Caddie	no
Electric Trolley	Bagvogn	no
Buggy	Golf car	250 DKr
Clubs	Koller	80 DKr

Credit cards Creditkord VISA - Eurocard - DC

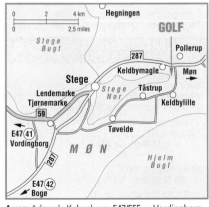

GOLF

Access Adgang : København, E47/E55 → Vordingborg. → Stege.
Map 1 on page 131 Kort 1 på side 131

GOLF COURSE / BAN — 15/20

Site	Sted	
Maintenance	Vedligeholdese	
Architect	Arkitekt	Rolf Henning-Jensen
Type	Type	country, hilly
Relief	Lettelse	
Water in play	Vand i spil	
Exp. to wind	Udsat vind	
Trees in play	Træer i spil	

Scorecard Scorekort	Chp. Back tee	Mens Herre tee	Ladies Dame tee
Length Længde	5917	5917	4974
Par	72	72	72

Advised golfing ability   0   12   24   36

Hcp required   Max. handicap   no

CLUB HOUSE & AMENITIES / KLUBHUSET OG FACILITETER — 7/10

Pro shop	Pro-shop	
Driving range	Driving range	
Sheltered	Ly	no
On grass	på græs	yes
Putting-green	Putting-green	yes
Pitching-green	Indspilsgreen	yes

HOTEL FACILITIES / HOTEL FACILITETERNE — 7/10

HOTELS HOTEL

Præstekilde Hotel — Stege
30 rooms, D 740 DKr — next to Golf
Tel (45) 55 86 87 88, Fax (45) 55 81 36 34

Hotel Stege Bugt — Stege 2 km
35 rooms, D 620 DKr
Tel (45) 55 81 54 54, Fax (45) 55 81 58 90

Hotel Store Klint - 14 rooms, D 780 DKr — Borre 10 km
Tel (45) 55 81 90 08

RESTAURANTS RESTAURANT

Præstekilde Hotel — Stege
Tel (45) 55 86 87 88 — next to Golf

Babette - Tel(45) 55 34 30 30 — Vordingborg 20 km

Skipperkrøn - Tel (45) 55 99 22 00 — Præstø 30 km

141

Ved bredden af Jels Sø ligger Royal Oak, opkaldt efter det egetræ, hvor kongen engang gjorde holdt, og som stadig står. Træer af mere moderat størrelse er i spil flere steder på denne fine, der åbnede i 1992, og med bunkers og vand-hazarder spredt tilsvarende ud er problemerne ligeligt fordelt og samtidig tydelige for enhver. Den mest imponerende vand-hazard er dog selve Jels Sø, der gør flere af hullerne på de første ni ualmindelig smukke. Trods sin ærlige karakter kan banen være svær at score på, især hvis størrelsen på de vel-designede, hurtige greens udnyttes til at stille flagene svært. Banen har sammen med Simon's ry for at være den mest velplejede i Danmark, og det gør den altid til en fornøjelse at spille.

On the shores of lake Jels, the Royal Oak takes its name from the oak tree under which the king and his son rested when on the road to Vejen. It is not, however, the only tree on this course, first opened in 1992 on an estate located in the middle of Jutland. Many others are clearly in play, giving this course the look of a fabulous park, especially beautiful for the holes along the lake. With bunkers and water hazards, difficulties are evenly spread around the course and are clearly visible to allow the golfer to immediately feel at ease. Despite the visual simplicity, you need several rounds here to collect any sort of score, which will also particularly depend on the pin positions on rather large, well designed and often very fast greens. Generally speaking, green-keeping and maintenance here are first rate, resulting as always in more enjoyable golf. Rather spectacular while retaining its naturalness, this is a quality course, which is obviously much appreciated for its peaceful location and impressive landscape.

Royal Oak Golf Club 1992

Golfvej, Jels
DK - 6630 RØDDING

Office	Sekretariat	(45) 74 55 32 94
Pro shop	Pro-shop	(45) 74 55 32 95
Fax	Fax	(45) 74 55 32 94
Situation	Sted	

Vejen, 15 km

Annual closure	Årlig lukkeperiod	no

Weekly closure	Ugentlig lukketid	no

Fees main season
Priser i højsæson full day

	Week days Hverdage	We/Bank holidays Helligdag
Individual Individuelt	280 DKr	280 DKr
Couple Paar	560 DKr	560 DKr

Junior : – 50%

Caddy	Caddie	no
Electric Trolley	Bagvogn	30 DKr
Buggy	Golf car	250 DKr
Clubs	Koller	140 DKr

Credit cards Creditkord VISA - Eurocard - DC

142

Access Adgang : E45. Exit → Kolding Syd.
403. → Jels, → Golf.
Map 1 on page 130 Kort 1 på side 130

GOLF COURSE
BAN   15/20

Site	Sted	
Maintenance	Vedligeholdese	
Architect	Arkitekt	Malling/Gundtoft

Type	Type	parkland
Relief	Lettelse	
Water in play	Vand i spil	
Exp. to wind	Udsat vind	
Trees in play	Træer i spil	

Scorecard	Chp.	Mens	Ladies
Scorekort	Back tee	Herre tee	Dame tee
Length Længde	6087	6087	5243
Par	72	72	72

Advised golfing ability	0	12	24	36

Hcp required	Max. handicap	30

CLUB HOUSE & AMENITIES
KLUBHUSET OG FACILITETER   7/10

Pro shop	Pro-shop	
Driving range	Driving range	
Sheltered	Ly	no
On grass	på græs	yes (04 → 10)
Putting-green	Putting-green	yes
Pitching-green	Indspilsgreen	yes

HOTEL FACILITIES
HOTEL FACILITETERNE   5/10

HOTELS HOTEL

Skibelund Krat	Vejen
45 rooms, D 670 DKr	15 km
Tel (45) 75 36 07 21, Fax (45) 75 36 62 70	

Koldingford	Kolding
140 rooms, D 850 DKr	45 km
Tel (45) 75 51 00 00, Fax (45) 75 51 00 51	

Danhotel	Rødding
80 rooms, D 700 DKr	10 km
Tel (45) 74 55 28 69, Fax (45) 74 55 31 07	

RESTAURANTS RESTAURANT

Schackenborg Slotskro	Møgeltonder
Tel (45) 74 83 83 83	60 km

Holdbi Kro	Kruså
Tel (45) 74 67 30 00	60 km

En meget berømt bane - ikke kun fordi den er fra 1936 og således en af landets ældste, men fordi dens originale layout skyldes C.A. MacKenzie, bror til ingen ringere end Augusta-skaberen Alister MacKenzie. I det nordsjællandske Strandvejsområde, der domineres af marinaer og millionvillaer - og ikke langt fra Karen Blixens fødested Rungstedlund, der i dag fungerer Blixen-museum - ligger en af Danmarks bedste baner. Den er udlagt blandt masser af store træer, der taler deres tydelige sprog om banens alder. Få men velplacerede bunkers og ikke mindst et vandløb, der krydser ikke færre end syv huller, sørger for, at den ikke specielt lange bane alligevel er svær at score på. Banen er ikke særlig kuperet. Der står en aura af diskret afmålthed omkring banen. Alting er i balance. Og så har banen flere karakteristisk smukke og egenartede huller: Det ubrudte skovparti langs højre side af det lange 4. hul. Den grydeagtige green nede mellem træerne på det korte 6. hul. De store rhododendron-buske bag 15. green. Rungsted er en bane man husker.

This is one of Denmark's more famous courses... because it dates back to 1936 and was one of the country's first layouts, and because it is situated in a magnificent region. Starting out from the capital Copenhagen and heading north towards Sjælland, the coast road reveals some superb villas, a number of small harbours with marinas, and a view of Sweden on the other side of the Øresund straits. The golf course was laid out in a huge park, only slightly scarred by a railway line, where huge trees and very well designed bunkers testify to the art of a designer in a class of his own. Water hazards are cleverly used and well in play without ever looking artificial, and greens are well-guarded without the need for massive protection. There is a sense of measure to everything about this discreet and well-balanced course, rather a tough proposition for beginners but one which fairly rewards good and well shaped shots.

Rungsted Golf Klub — 1936

Vester Stationsvej 16
DK - 2960 RUNGSTED KYST

Office	Sekretariat	(45) 45 86 34 44
Pro shop	Pro-shop	(45) 45 86 34 14
Fax	Fax	(45) 45 86 57 70
Situation	Sted	

København, 25 km

Annual closure	Årlig lukkeperiod	no
Weekly closure	Ugentlig lukketid	no

Fees main season
Priser i højsæson 18 holes

	Week days Hverdage	We/Bank holidays Helligdag
Individual Individuelt	325 DKr	375 DKr
Couple Paar	650 DKr	750 DKr
Junior : – 50 %		

Caddy	Caddie	no
Electric Trolley	Bagvogn	no
Buggy	Golf car	no
Clubs	Koller	250 DKr

Credit cards Creditkord
VISA - Eurocard - MasterCard - DC

Access Adgang : E47, Exit Hørsholm C. → Rungsted, → Golf.
Map 1 on page 131 Kort 1 på side 131

GOLF COURSE / BAN — 17/20

Site	Sted	
Maintenance	Vedligeholdese	
Architect	Arkitekt	C.A. MacKenzie
Type	Type	forest, parkland
Relief	Lettelse	
Water in play	Vand i spil	
Exp. to wind	Udsat vind	
Trees in play	Træer i spil	

Scorecard Scorekort	Chp. Back tee	Mens Herre tee	Ladies Dame tee
Length Længde	5761	5760	5164
Par	71	71	71

Advised golfing ability — 0 12 24 36

Hcp required — Max. handicap — 36

CLUB HOUSE & AMENITIES / KLUBHUSET OG FACILITETER — 7/10

Pro shop	Pro-shop	
Driving range	Driving range	
Sheltered	Ly	no
On grass	på græs	yes (04 → 10)
Putting-green	Putting-green	yes
Pitching-green	Indspilsgreen	yes

HOTEL FACILITIES / HOTEL FACILITETERNE — 7/10

HOTELS HOTEL

Store Kro — Fredensborg 10 km
40 rooms, D 650 DKr
Tel (45) 48 48 00 47, Fax (45) 48 48 45 61

Nybogaard — Kvistgaard 5 km
15 rooms, D 800 DKr
Tel (45) 49 16 16 60, Fax (45) 49 16 16 80

Scanticon Borupgaard — Snekkersten
45 rooms, D 780 DKr
Tel (45) 49 22 03 33, Fax (45) 49 22 03 99

RESTAURANTS RESTAURANT

Nokken - Tel (45) 45 57 13 14 — Rungsted 5 km
Søllerød Kro - Tel (45) 45 80 25 05 — Søllerød 10 km
Taarbæk Kro - Tel (45) 39 63 00 96 — Taarbæk 15 km

143

Nogle af Danmarks bedste baner synes at spille kostbare i den forstand, at de ikke er sådan lige at komme til. Det gælder Læsø Seaside og det gælder banen på Samsø, Strisserens ø midt i Danmark. Det tager mindst en time at sejle med færge fra Jylland eller Sjælland, men tiden er godt givet ud, for Samsø-banen er måske den smukkest beliggende i Danmark. På to trediedele af de 18 huller går man med udsigt over Kattegat. Som helhed er banen nænsomt og stort set uden planering af jord udlagt i terræn, der for det meste skråner ned mod havet. Lidt bunkers, lidt vand-hazarder, lidt træer - alt er i balance. Og som altid, når Henrik Jakobsen har designet en bane, ligger forhindringerne, hvor de skal. Helt ned til vandet kommer man på 8. hul, et par 3, der har Kattegat som uendeligt bagtæppe, og på 16. hul, der løber langs med og kun en lille meter oven for selve stranden. Eneste anke ved banen er, at den er relativt kort, samt at klubhuset ikke har nogen egentlig restaurant.

Samsø can be reached by ferry from Kalundborg (Sjælland) or Hov (Jutland) but it really is worth the trouble and the wait. The terrain made available to Henryk Jacobsen was ideal. Laudable concern for blending the course into the landscape, a few cleverly placed bunkers and a number of water hazards have produced a great layout. The successful outcome also required a lot of good taste and insight into the game, and there are often several solutions for reaching the medium-sized but well designed greens. From the many holes that stick in the mind, the signature hole is the most memorable, the par-3 8th hole whose green is backed by the ocean. A very pleasant course for all golfing abilities, where the only criticism might be lack of yardage (except when the wind blows) and hilly contours for senior players, but the latter is simply an excuse to stop, catch your breath and admire the scenery. Bring a packed lunch as there is no restaurant.

Samsø Golf Club — 1992

Besser Kirkevej 24
DK - 8305 Samsø

Office	Sekretariat	(45) 86 59 22 18
Pro shop	Pro-shop	(45) 86 59 22 18
Fax	Fax	(45) 86 59 22 21
Situation	Sted	
on Samsø Island		
Annual closure	Årlig lukkeperiod	no
Weekly closure	Ugentlig lukketid	no

Fees main season
Priser i hojsæson full day

	Week days Hverdage	We/Bank holidays Helligdag
Individual Individuelt	185 DKr	220 DKr
Couple Paar	370 DKr	440 DKr
Junior : – 50 %		

Caddy	Caddie	no
Electric Trolley	Bagvogn	no
Buggy	Golf car	150 DKr
Clubs	Koller	125 DKr

Credit cards Creditkord VISA - Eurocard - DC

144

Access Adgand : Kalundborg, Ferry → Samsø - Hov
(Jutland), Ferry → Sælvig
Map 1 on page 131 Kort 1 på side 131

GOLF COURSE BAN — 15/20

Site	Sted	
Maintenance	Vedligeholdese	
Architect	Arkitekt	Henrik Jacobsen
Type	Type	seaside course, country
Relief	Lettelse	
Water in play	Vand i spil	
Exp. to wind	Udsat vind	
Trees in play	Træer i spil	

Scorecard Scorekort	Chp. Back tee	Mens Herre tee	Ladies Dame tee
Length Længde	5600	5600	4865
Par	72	72	72

Advised golfing ability	0	12	24	36

Hcp required   Max. handicap   36

CLUB HOUSE & AMENITIES KLUBHUSET OG FACILITETER — 4/10

Pro shop	Pro-shop	
Driving range	Driving range	
Sheltered	Ly	no
On grass	på græs	yes (04 → 10)
Putting-green	Putting-green	yes
Pitching-green	Indspilsgreen	yes

HOTEL FACILITIES HOTEL FACILITETERNE — 7/10

HOTELS HOTEL
Flinch's Hotel — Tranebjerg 5 km
25 rooms, D 475 DKr
Tel (45) 86 59 17 22, Fax (45) 86 59 35 50

Ballen Badehotel — Ballen 5 km
30 rooms, D 600 DKr
Tel (45) 86 59 17 99, Fax (45) 86 59 06 59

Motel Sølyst — Vesterløkken 5 km
20 rooms, D 520 DKr
Tel (45) 86 59 16 59, Fax (45) 86 59 16 99

RESTAURANTS RESTAURANT
Ved Kæret - Tel (45) 86 59 61 22 — Nordby 20 km
Skipperly - Tel (45) 86 59 10 18 — Ballen 5 km
Ballen Badehotel - Tel (45) 86 59 17 99 — Ballen 5 km

Måske den nemmeste bane at finde i hele Danmark, fordi man ser ned på den fra motorvejen mellem Nyborg og Storebæltsbroen. Alligevel virker støjen kun generende på et par huller. Resten af runden går man dybt inde blandt træerne eller nede ved vandet. Egentlige vand-hazarder er der kun ganske få af. Dén på det 450 meter lange 16. hul er til gengæld imponerende: Det er selve Storebælt, man kan forsøge at skære så meget af i sit drive, som man tør. Ellers sørger især de tydeligvis gamle træer og også bunkers for problemerne på den næsten helt flade bane. Sct. Knuds mangler de tekniske raffinementer, der skal til for at udfordre den dygtige spiller, men kan så til gengæld spilles uden problemer af folk med højt handicap.

Here is an easy-to-find course: the motorway that crosses the three major regions of Denmark (Sjælland, Fyn and Jutland) runs along about 6 or 7 holes but is only really a nuisance on holes 10 and 11. If you can forget it is there, this well-wooded and very pleasant site is most pleasant. On the clearer sections of the course, the trees give way to the Storebælt, particularly on the 16th, a magnificent short par 5. This belt of sea is moreover the only water hazard on the course, the other hazards being more classical and typically British in the form of trees (sometimes very much in play) and the standard bunkers. All this gives a very open course, which hides none of its difficulties. For the more demanding player, though, it probably lacks a little technical subtlety to be played too often. With that said, you will have fun golfing here with all the family or with friends, even with widely differing abilities.

Sct. Knuds Golfklub		1954
Sliphavnsvej 16		
DK - 5800 Nyborg		
Office	Sekretariat	(45) 65 37 12 12
Pro shop	Pro-shop	(45) 65 30 02 04
Fax	Fax	(45) 65 30 28 04
Situation	Sted	
Nyborg, 2 km		
Annual closure	Årlig lukkeperiod	no
Weekly closure	Ugentlig lukketid	no
Fees main season		
Priser i højsæson full day		

	Week days Hverdage	We/Bank holidays Helligdag
Individual Individuelt	200 DKr	250 DKr
Couple Paar	400 DKr	500 DKr
Junior : – 50 %		

Caddy	Caddie	no
Electric Trolley	Bagvogn	30 DKr
Buggy	Golf car	200 DKr
Clubs	Koller	150 DKr

Credit cards Creditkord VISA - Eurocard - DC

Kerteminde
Odense
Hjulby
Regstrup
Skabohuse
46
E20
NYBORG
Vindinge
45 Svendborg
163
Svendborg
Nyborg Fjord
GOLF
0 2 4 km
0 2,5 miles

Access Adgang : København E20 → Odense.
Nyborg, → Golf.
Map 1 on page 131 Kort 1 på side 131

GOLF COURSE BAN			**14**/20
Site	Sted		
Maintenance	Vedligeholdese		
Architect	Arkitekt		Cotton/Dreyer
Type	Type		forest, open country
Relief	Lettelse		
Water in play	Vand i spil		
Exp. to wind	Udsat vind		
Trees in play	Træer i spil		

Scorecard Scorekort	Chp. Back tee	Mens Herre tee	Ladies Dame tee
Length Længde	5810	5810	4880
Par	72	72	72

Advised golfing ability	0	12	24	36

Hcp required   Max. handicap   32

CLUB HOUSE & AMENITIES KLUBHUSET OG FACILITETER		**5**/10
Pro shop	Pro-shop	
Driving range	Driving range	
Sheltered	Ly	no
On grass	på græs	yes (03 → 11)
Putting-green	Putting-green	yes
Pitching-green	Indspilsgreen	yes

HOTEL FACILITIES HOTEL FACILITETERNE		**6**/10
HOTELS HOTEL		
Hesselet		Nyborg
85 rooms, D 850 DKr		2 km
Tel (45) 65 31 30 29, Fax (45) 65 31 29 58		
Nyborg Strand		Nyborg
120 rooms, D 900 DKr		3 km
Tel (45) 65 31 31 31, Fax (45) 65 31 37 01		
RESTAURANTS RESTAURANT		
Hos Svend		Svendborg
Tel (45) 62 22 07 95		30 km
Hesselet		Nyborg
Tel (45) 65 31 29 58		2 km
Sognegården		Millinge
Tel (45) 62 68 11 11		40 km

145

Med sin placering kun få kilometer ned ad motorvejen fra Helsingør er Simon's en bane, svenskere gerne betaler de temmelig mange penge, det koster at spille den. For de ved, at de - lige som alle andre - får noget for pengene. Fremragende stand, først og fremmest - banen regnes sammen med Royal Oak for Danmarks bedst holdte. Og en bane, der er sværere, end den ser ud til - ikke mindst på grund af dens meget store, ondulerede og efter danske forhold lynhurtige greens samt de små græstuer, der flankerer mange af dem på tre sider. Banen har været vært for adskillige turneringer på Challenge-touren, og det ses på fairways, de er ikke specielt brede. En stor sø dominerer det korte 10. hul, hvor man skal slå over for at komme på green, og det 18., hvis 460 meter lange venstre side ER søen. Banen er ikke specielt kuperet, men byder alligevel på en del blinde slag og skjulte forhindringer. Især approach-slaget til den højtliggende 3. green er svært.

A few miles from here, don't miss Helsingør and make sure you visit the castle of Kronborg on a foggy night; this is the castle of Elsenor, the setting for Shakespeare's Hamlet. The old houses in town are worth visiting as much as the castle, which in fact is more Renaissance than medieval in style. The course was opened only very recently on a pleasant site, despite the closeness of the motorway. A large lake is in play on the 10th and the 18th, a now classic par 5 edged by water up the whole of the left side. The course is not hilly but five of the greens and several hazards are almost blind, which does not help things first time out on the course. Likewise, you will need to concentrate over the whole round, not necessarily a good thing for pace of play and relaxation. Simon's is well worth a visit, even though we might have imagined a more «dramatic» course in this part of the world...

Simon's Golf Klub — 1993

Nybovej 5
DK - 3490 KVISTGAARD

Office	Sekretariat	(45) 49 19 13 28
Pro shop	Pro-shop	(45) 49 19 48 76
Fax	Fax	(45) 49 19 14 70
Situation	Sted	

København, 30 km

Annual closure	Årlig lukkeperiod	no
Weekly closure	Ugentlig lukketid	no

Fees main season
Priser i højsæson 18 holes

	Week days Hverdage	We/Bank holidays Helligdag
Individual Individuelt	275 DKr	375 DKr
Couple Paar	550 DKr	750 DKr

Junior : – 50 %

Caddy	Caddie	no
Electric Trolley	Bagvogn	no
Buggy	Golf car	75 DKr
Clubs	Koller	200 Dkr

Credit cards Creditkord VISA - Eurocard - DC

146

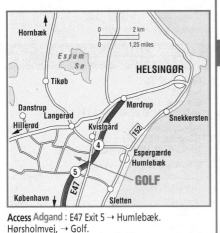

Access Adgang : E47 Exit 5 → Humlebæk.
Hørsholmvej, → Golf.
Map 1 on page 131 Kort 1 på side 131

GOLF COURSE 14/20
BAN

Site	Sted	
Maintenance	Vedligeholdese	
Architect	Arkitekt	Martin Hawtree
Type	Type	inland, country
Relief	Lettelse	
Water in play	Vand i spil	
Exp. to wind	Udsat vind	
Trees in play	Træer i spil	

Scorecard Scorekort	Chp. Back tee	Mens Herre tee	Ladies Dame tee
Length Længde	5787	5787	5064
Par	72	72	72

Advised golfing ability   0   12   24   36

Hcp required   Max. handicap   30

CLUB HOUSE & AMENITIES 7/10
KLUBHUSET OG FACILITETER

Pro shop	Pro-shop	
Driving range	Driving range	
Sheltered	Ly	no
On grass	på græs	no, 10 mats open air
Putting-green	Putting-green	yes
Pitching-green	Indspilsgreen	yes

HOTEL FACILITIES 7/10
HOTEL FACILITETERNE

HOTELS HOTEL
Nybogaard — Kvistgaard
15 rooms, D 800 DKr — on site
Tel (45) 49 16 16 60, Fax (45) 49 16 16 80

Store Kro — Fredensborg
40 rooms, D 650 DKr — 10 km
Tel (45) 48 48 00 47, Fax (45) 48 48 45 61

Scantilon Borupgaard — Snekkersten
45 rooms, D 780 DKr — 6 km
Tel (45) 49 22 03 33, Fax (45) 49 22 03 99

RESTAURANTS RESTAURANT

Nokken - Tel (45) 45 57 13 14	Rungsted 10 km
Jan Hurtigkarl - Tel(45) 49 70 90 03	Ålsgårde 5 km
Taarbæk Kro - Tel(45) 39 63 00 96	Taarbæk 20 km

Legoland ligger lige i nærheden, i Billund, dér er alt i miniatureformat. På Vejle-banen er der ikke miniature over hverken banens niveau eller dens træer. Tværtimod. Storladen er det ord, der bedst beskriver træerne, højdeforskellene og isolationen på den såkaldte blå banes ni huller. Det 4. hul er helt fantastisk. Når man står på tee-stedet og ser de store træer og de høje klippesider, skulle man ikke tro at man befinder sig i en dansk skov. Vejles anlæg består også af en rød og en gul bane, i alt 27 huller der byder på meget stor variation. Anlægget har flere gange lagt huller til Danish Open på damernes Europa-tour. Kombinationen blå/rød bane hører med en course slope på 139 til blandt de allersværeste 18 huller i Danmark. Ikke specielt lang, men smal og med svære dogleg-huller. De ni gule huller kom til i 1994. De er længere og af mere åben karakter. Kombinationen rød/gulbane er banen for den mindre øvede spiller.

When you are in this region, you simply have to drive a few miles west towards Billund... a little town of no special interest except Legoland, an incredible miniature world built with the famous plastic cubes that are a favourite toy for children all over the world. And since there is a child in every golfer, find a little inspiration to get to grips with the 27 holes at Vejle, of which the «Blue» 9-hole course is without a doubt the hardest test of golf in Denmark. What it lacks in yardage it makes up for with some devilish dog-legs, the tremendous challenge of the forest and some disconcerting, sometimes even excessive, differences in level and altitude. The «Red» course, a 9-holer which originally completed the Blue course, is hardly any easier for wayward hitters, whereas the Yellow course, opened in 1994, is both more open and forthright, despite the number of small water hazards. For mid-handicappers and inexperienced players, we would recommend a «Red/Yellow» mix.

Vejle Golf Club — 1972

Ibækvej 46
DK - 7100 VEJLE

Office	Sekretariat	(45) 75 85 81 85
Pro shop	Pro-shop	(45) 75 85 81 43
Fax	Fax	(45) 75 85 83 01
Situation	Sted	

Vejle, 5 km

Annual closure	Årlig lukkeperiod	no
Weekly closure	Ugentlig lukketid	no

Fees main season
Priser i hojsæson full day

	Week days Hverdage	We/Bank holidays Helligdag
Individual Individuelt	250 DKr	250 DKr
Couple Paar	500 DKr	500 DKr

Junior : – 50 %

Caddy	Caddie	no
Electric Trolley	Bagvogn	no
Buggy	Golf car	200 DKr
Clubs	Koller	100 DKr

Credit cards Creditkord VISA - Eurocard - DC

Access Adgang : E45 Exit 61. Vejle, Andkjærvej, → Golf.
Map 1 on page 130 Kort 1 på side 130

GOLF COURSE
BAN — 15/20

Site	Sted	
Maintenance	Vedligeholdese	
Architect	Arkitekt	Malling Petersen
Type	Type	forest, hilly
Relief	Lettelse	
Water in play	Vand i spil	
Exp. to wind	Udsat vind	
Trees in play	Træer i spil	

Scorecard Scorekort	Chp. Back tee	Mens Herre tee	Ladies Dame tee
Length Længde	5532	5532	4646
Par	72	72	72

Advised golfing ability: 0 12 24 36

Hcp required   Max. handicap   36

CLUB HOUSE & AMENITIES
KLUBHUSET OG FACILITETER — 7/10

Pro shop	Pro-shop	
Driving range	Driving range	
Sheltered	Ly	no
On grass	på græs	yes (04 → 10)
Putting-green	Putting-green	yes
Pitching-green	Indspilsgreen	yes

HOTEL FACILITIES
HOTEL FACILITETERNE — 7/10

HOTELS HOTEL

Munkebjerg	Vejle 3 km
150 rooms, D 850 DKr	
Tel (45) 76 42 85 00, Fax (45) 75 72 08 86	
Vejle Center	Vejle 5 km
65 rooms, D 600 DKr	
Tel (45) 75 72 45 00, Fax (45) 75 72 46 60	

RESTAURANTS RESTAURANT

Munkjeberg Hotel Restaurant	Vejle 3 km
Tel (45) 76 42 85 00	
Merlot	Vejle 5 km
Tel (45) 75 83 88 44	
Da Franco	Vejle 5 km
Tel (45) 75 82 57 67	

147

Suomi

The Millennium Guide

Suomi on kahden vuodenajan maa. Kuusi, jopa kahdeksankin kuukautta pitkä talvi, pohjoisesta etelään asti, ja kesä, yhtä intensiivinen ja loistelias. Niiden väliin jäävät kesä ja syksy ovat yhtä ihmeelliset kuin lyhyetkin. Golfia Suomessa pelataan toukokuusta syyskuun loppupuolelle, mutta täällä voi silti pelata kaksin verroin kauemmin kuin missään muualla, sillä Suomen kesäyö on vain lyhyt hämärän hetki. Parantumattomina luonnonystävinä suomalaiset ovat tietenkin ryhtyneet harrastamaan golfia, jota he pelaavat lumenlähdöstä ensi lumeen saakka. Suomessa on nykyisin avoinna 91 golfkenttää (joista yli 50 on 18-reikäisiä), jotka huolehtivat 60 000:sta golfinpelaajasta. Ja koska golfia pidetään Suomessa oikeana urheilulajina, on täällä jo riittävästi hyviä pelaajia, jotka ovat antaneet monta hyvää näytöstä joukkueiden maailmanmestaruuskisoissa.

This is a land of two seasons. Winter, which lasts from six to eight months, from north to south, and summer, equally intense and spectacular. Between the two, Spring and Autumn are as wonderful as they are short. Golf in Finland is played from May to late September, but you can play for twice as long as anywhere else. In the summer, nighttime is just a brief period of dusk. As inveterate nature-lovers, the Finns have naturally taken to golf, which is played as soon as the ice has thawed until the first winter snowfall. Today, there are 91 courses open (more than 50 eighteen-holers) catering to 60,000 golfers. And as here golf is a real sport, there are already enough good players for Finland to have produced many a good performance in the world team championships.

GOLFIKENTTIEN LUOKITUS
CLASSIFICATION OF COURSES

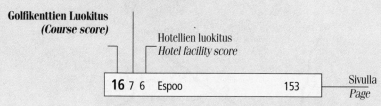

Klubitalon luokitus
Club-house and facilities

Golfikenttien Luokitus
(Course score)

Hotellien luokitus
Hotel facility score

16 7 6	Espoo	153	Sivulla *Page*

Luokitus	Golfkenttä	Sivulla	Luokitus	Golfkenttä	Sivulla
16 7 6	Espoo	153	**15** 8 5	Pickala *Seaside Course*	157
16 7 8	Helsinki	154	**14** 5 4	St Laurence	159
16 8 7	Sarfvik *New Course*	158	**14** 8 6	Talma	160
15 7 7	Master *Master*	155	**14** 7 5	Tawast	161
15 7 5	Nordcenter *Benz Course*	156	**13** 5 5	Aura	152

HOTELLIEN LUOKITUS
CLASSIFICATION OF HOTELS FACILITIES

Note	Parcours	Pays	Page	Note	Parcours	Pays	Page
16 7 8	Helsinki		154	13 5 5	Aura		152
15 7 7	Master *Master*		155	15 7 5	Nordcenter *Benz Course*		156
16 8 7	Sarfvik *New Course*		158	15 8 5	Pickala *Seaside Course*		157
16 7 6	Espoo		153	14 7 5	Tawast		161
14 8 6	Talma		160	14 5 4	St Laurence		159

KENTÄN OMINAISUUS TYPE DE PARCOURS

149

Note	Parcours	Pays	Page	Note	Parcours	Pays	Page
forest				**Master***Master*		15 7 7	155
Nordcenter *Benz Course*		15 7 5	156	St Laurence		14 5 4	159
Sarfvik *New Course*		16 8 7	158	Talma		14 8 6	160
St Laurence		14 5 4	159	**seaside course**			
Talma		14 8 6	160	Pickala *Seaside Course*		15 8 5	157
Tawast		14 7 5	161	**inland**			
open country				Tawast		14 7 5	161
Espoo		16 7 6	153	**links**			
parkland				Pickala *Seaside Course*		15 8 5	157
Aura		13 5 5	152	**skogsdungar**			
Helsinki		16 7 8	154	Helsinki		16 7 8	154

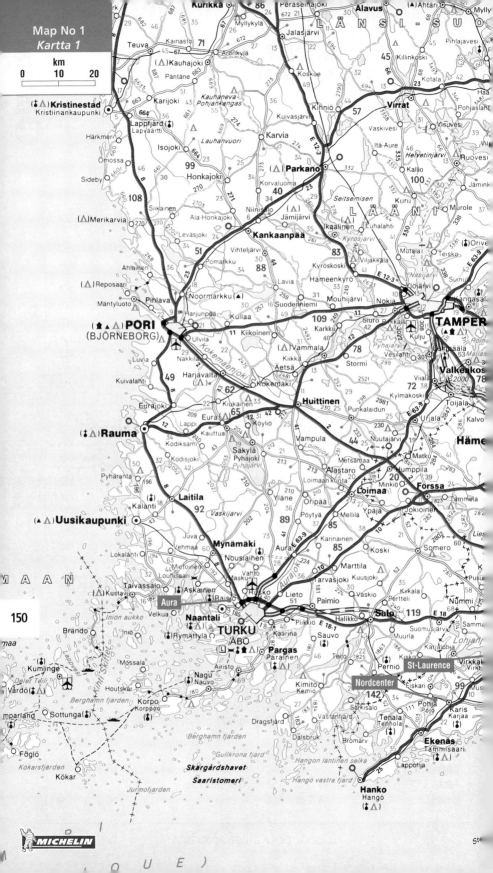

151

Turku (ruotsiksi Åbo) oli kauan Suomen pääkaupunki, ja se on edelleenkin hyvin vilkas kaupunki niin kulttuurillisesti kuin taloudellisestikin. Turun palo v. 1827 jätti jälkensä, ja tämän päivän Turku onkin hyvin nykyaikainen kaupunki, jossa matkailija viihtyy erinomaisesti, samoin kuin tuhansista saarista muodostuvassa Turun saaristossakin. Aura Golfin kenttä on rakennettu yhdelle näistä saarista, Ruissaloon, ja kuten useimmilla Suomen kentillä on täälläkin kesä- ja heinäkuussa käytännössä mahdollista pelata golfia ympäri vuorokauden. Tämä vanhaan linnanpuistoon rakennettu puistokenttä on ihastuttava suurine metsineen, joissa kasvaa jopa yli 400 vuotta vanhoja tammia. Kenttä avattiin v. 1958. Kokonaisuus on hyvä ja pitkät ja lyhyet reiät vuorottelevat hienosti. Kaksi par 4 -reikää on pituudeltaan yli 400 metriä, mutta jos pelaaja lyö kauas, on hänellä mahdollisuus siirtyä par 5 -rei'ille kahdella lyönnillä. Lisäksi kentällä on kaksi todella lyhyttä par 4 -reikää.

Turku (or Åbo in Swedish, the country's second most widely-spoken language), was the capital of Finland for many a year and is still a busy city, particularly through the frequent sea-links with Sweden and the Baltic ports. After the great fire of 1827, this is now a very modern city and still as attractive as ever with the thousands of islands making up the Turku archipelago. The Aura golf course is laid out on one such isle, the island of Ruissalo, and like most other courses in Finland is playable almost 24 hours a day in June and July. It is a superb park thick with woods, in a former castle estate where some of the oak trees are over 400 years old. The course was opened in 1958 and is a great layout with holes of reasonable length; two of the par 4s are over 400 metres long and big-hitters can expect to reach the par 5s in two and make light work of some short par 4s. A wonderful site and very enjoyable course.

Aura Golf   1958

Ruissalo 85
FIN - 20100 TURKU

Office	Toimisto	(358) 2 - 258 9201
Pro shop	Pro shop	(358) 2 - 258 9201
Fax	Fax	(358) 2 - 258 9121
Situation	Sijainti	

Turku, 5 km

Annual closure	Kenttä suljetaan	no
Weekly closure	Suljetan viikolla	no

Fees main season
Green fee 18 holes

	Week days Arkipäivisin	We/Bank holidays Pyhäpäivisin
Individual Henkilö	FIM 200	FIM 250
Couple Pari	FIM 400	FIM 500

Caddy	Caddy	no
Electric Trolley	Sähkörattaat	no
Buggy	Golfauto	FIM 150
Clubs	Mailat	FIM 100

Credit cards Luottokortit
VISA - Eurocard - MasterCard - AMEX - DC

GOLF COURSE
GOLFBANEN   13/20

Site	Sijainti	
Maintenance	Hoito	
Architect	Arkkitehti	Lauri Arkkola Pekka Sivula
Type	Kentän luonne	parkland
Relief	Vapautuminen	
Water in play	Vesiesteitä	
Exp. to wind	Tuulta	
Trees in play	Puita	

Scorecard Tuloskortti	Chp. Champ. tii	Mens Miest. tii	Ladies Naist. tii
Length Pituus	5843	5614	4841
Par	71	71	71

Advised golfing ability   0   12   24   36
Tasoitusvaatimus
Hcp required   Hcp-vaatimus   36

CLUB HOUSE & AMENITIES
KLUBHUS OG OMGIVELSER   5/10

Pro shop	Pro shop	
Driving range	Driving range	
Sheltered	suoja	yes
On grass	ruoholla	yes (Summer)
Putting-green	putting-green	yes
Pitching-green	pitching-green	yes

HOTEL FACILITIES
HOTELFASILITETER   5/10

HOTELS
Scandic Marina Palace   Turku
183 rooms, D FIM 530 (We)/830   8 km
Tel (358) 02 - 336 300

RESTAURANTS RAVINTOLA

Marina Palace   Turku
Tel (358) 02 - 336 300   8 km

Hermanni   Turku
Tel (358) 02 - 220 3333   8 km

Harald   Turku
Tel (358) 02 - 276 5050   8 km

152

Access Pääsy : On Ruissalo island, W. of Turku.
Map 1 on page 150 Kartta 1 sivulla : 150

Espoon (ruotsiksi Esbo) ympäristössä on joitakin Suomen tunnetuimmista rakennuksista. Espoon kirkossa voi katsella keskiaikaisia seinämaalauksia.vähän kauempana, Tapiolassa, voi käydä kävelyllä puistoissa ja puutarhoissa (kaupunki rakennettiin 1950-luvulla). Arkkitehti Saarisen kotina olleessa Hvitträskin huvilassa, joka on nykyisin museona, on yöpynyt monia kuuluisuuksia,kuten esimerkiksi Gorki, Sibelius ja Edvard Munch. Espoon golfkenttä puolestaan edustaa ruotsalaista arkkitehtuuria. Sen on piirtänyt kenttäarkkitehtinä tunnettu Jan Sederholm. Pituudeltaan ja vaikeusasteeltaan Espoon kenttää voidaan pitää oikeana mestaruuskilpailukenttänä. Kenttä sijaitsee melko avoimessa maastossa, joten vaarana voi olla, että kentällä tuulee. Kokonaisuus on nerokkaasti rakennettu, ja tasoerojen vuoksi voi mailan valinta osoittautua pulmalliseksi. Niin alemmissa kuin ylemmissäkin tasoitusryhmissä pelaavilla voi olla vaikeuksia päästä kunnon pistemääriin. Griinit ovat pieniä ja niiden sijainti on suojainen.

From the church of Espoo (Esbo), housing medieval mural frescoes, to the garden city of Tapiola, a model in mid-20th century town-planning, to Hvitträsk, a romantic style castle where the most illustrious guests have included Gorki, Sibelius, and Edvard Munch, you have some of the finest examples of the Finnish art of building all within a few miles of each other. The Espoo golf course, for its part, is an example of well-known Swedish art by course architect Jan Sederholm. It has the length and the hazards to rightfully claim the title of championship course in wide open space that is so exposed that the wind is almost always a constant threat to your ball. Both natural and cleverly laid out, this is a difficult course to score well on, whatever your golfing ability, particularly on account of subtle and sometimes steep terrain, which makes the choice of club a little more complicated. The greens are on the small side and very well guarded.

Espoo Golf Club — 1977

P.O. Box 26
FIN - 02781 ESPOO

Office	Toimisto	(358) 9 - 2190 3444
Pro shop	Pro shop	(358) 9 - 2190 3444
Fax	Fax	(358) 9 - 2190 3434
Situation	Sijainti	

Helsinki (pop. 492 000), 15 km

Annual closure	Kenttä suljetaan	no
Weekly closure	Suljetan viikolla	no

Fees main season
Green fee 18 holes

	Week days Arkipäivisin	We/Bank holidays Pyhäpäivisin
Individual Henkilö	FIM 180	*
Couple Pari	FIM 360	*

* Members only

Caddy	Caddy	no
Electric Trolley	Sähkörattaat	no
Buggy	Golfauto	FIM 200
Clubs	Mailat	FIM 100

Credit cards Luottokortit
VISA - Eurocard - MasterCard - AMEX - DC

Access Pääsy : Helsinki, road 101/110 →
Kauniainen/Grankulla, E18/50 → Kauklahti/Masala.
Exit Masala, go left of the motorway.
Map 1 on page 151 Kartta 1 sivulla : 151

GOLF COURSE / GOLFBANEN — 16/20

Site	Sijainti	
Maintenance	Hoito	
Architect	Arkkitehti	Jan Sederholm
Type	Kentän luonne	open country
Relief	Vapautuminen	
Water in play	Vesiesteitä	
Exp. to wind	Tuulta	
Trees in play	Puita	

Scorecard Tuloskortti	Chp. Champ. tii	Mens Miest. tii	Ladies Naist. tii
Length Pituus	6155	5940	5245
Par	72	72	72

Advised golfing ability Tasoitusvaatimus	0	12	24	36
Hcp required Hcp-vaatimus	36			

CLUB HOUSE & AMENITIES / KLUBHUS OG OMGIVELSER — 7/10

Pro shop	Pro shop	
Driving range	Driving range	
Sheltered	suoja	yes
On grass	ruoholla	yes (Summer)
Putting-green	putting-green	yes
Pitching-green	pitching-green	yes

HOTEL FACILITIES / HOTELFASILITETER — 6/10

HOTELS
Majvik — Espoo
100 rooms, D FIM 760 — 10 km
Tel (358) 09 - 295 511

RESTAURANTS RAVINTOLA
Majvik — Espoo
Tel (358) 09 - 295 511 — 10 km

153

Helsingissä (ruotsiksi Helsingfors) tuntuu voimakkaasti 1900 luvun suurien arkkitehtien Eliel Saarisen ja Alvar Aallon vaikutus. Jos haluaa nähdä vanhoja, perinteisiä rakennuksia, on Seurasaaren ulkomuseo, joka sijaitsee vain lyhyen bussimatkan päässä kaupungista, käymisen arvoinen. Kaupunkia on kutsuttu Itämeren tyttäreksi, ja Seurasaari (Fölisön) on vain yksi sitä ympäröivistä saarista. Vaikka Suomen ilmasto asettaakin rajoituksensa on golf saanut nopeasti jalansijaa urheilulajina. Helsingin Golfklubin kenttä on Suomen vanhin ja se sijaitsee lähellä keskustaa. Kerho on järjestänyt monia suuria amatöörikilpailuja. Lauri Arkkolan kauniiseen lehtomaisemaan suunnittelemalla kentällä on ilmiselviä brittiläisiä esikuvia. Kenttää kehystävät jättimäiset puut, maasto on tasaista ja väylät erinomaiset. Vesiesteitä on vain muutama, kolmen reiän kohdalla on kuitenkin otettava huomioon joki. Kenttä on houkuttelevan avoin ja liikkuminen on helppoa, mutta täällä on kuitenkin vaikea päästä hyviin pistelukemiin. Reikien pituus vaihtelee, joten on viisasta pitää mukanaan kaikki 14 mailaa.

Helsinki has been marked by successive trends in architecture and by the great designers of the 20th century like Saarinen or Alvar Aalto. To find old traditional buildings, the open-air Seurasaari Ulkomuseo museum is a short bus ride on one of the many isles and peninsulas spread around Helsinki, known as «the daughter of the Baltic». In a country where nature commands so much respect, the game of golf has quickly gained a foothold despite the sometimes harsh climate, and the Helsinki golf club, virtually within the city limits, is the oldest. Designed by Lauri Arkkola with a very definite British influence, this is a magnificent park with some wonderful trees, virtually flat terrain and great fairways. There are not many water hazards, just a stream that only really comes into play on three holes, on a course which is very forthright, easy to play on foot but hard to score well. Holes come in all lengths so pack the full 14 clubs.

Helsinki Golf Club — 1932
Talin Kartano
FIN - 00350 HELSINKI

Office	Toimisto	(358) 09 - 550 235
Pro shop	Pro shop	(358) 09 - 550 235
Fax	Fax	(358) 09 - 550 235
Situation	Sijainti	

within Helsinki (pop. 492 000)

Annual closure	Kenttä suljetaan	no
Weekly closure	Suljetan viikolla	no

Fees main season
Green fee 18 holes

	Week days Arkipäivisin	We/Bank holidays Pyhäpäivisin
Individual Henkilö	FIM 200	FIM 220
Couple Pari	FIM 400	FIM 440

Caddy	Caddy	no
Electric Trolley	Sähkörattaat	no
Buggy	Golfauto	no
Clubs	Mailat	FIM 100

Credit cards Luottokortit — no

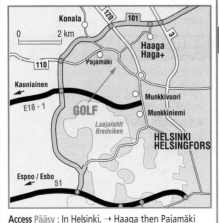

154

Access Pääsy : In Helsinki, → Haaga then Pajamäki
Map 1 on page 151 Kartta 1 sivulla : 151

GOLF COURSE
GOLFBANEN — 16/20

Site	Sijainti	
Maintenance	Hoito	
Architect	Arkkitehti	Lauri Arkkola
Type	Kentän luonne	parkland,
Relief	Vapautuminen	
Water in play	Vesiesteitä	
Exp. to wind	Tuulta	
Trees in play	Puita	

Scorecard Tuloskortti	Chp. Champ. tii	Mens Miest. tii	Ladies Naist. tii
Length Pituus	5715	5465	4783
Par	71	71	71

Advised golfing ability — 0 12 24 36
Tasoitusvaatimus
Hcp required — Hcp-vaatimus — 36

CLUB HOUSE & AMENITIES
KLUBHUS OG OMGIVELSER — 7/10

Pro shop	Pro shop	
Driving range	Driving range	
Sheltered	suoja	yes
On grass	ruoholla	yes (Summer)
Putting-green	putting-green	yes
Pitching-green	pitching-green	yes

HOTEL FACILITIES
HOTELFASILITETER — 8/10

HOTELS

Scandic Hotel Kalastajatorrpa — Helsinki
235 rooms, D FIM 560/1250 — 3 km
Tel (358) 09 - 45 811

Rivoli Jardin — Helsinki
53 rooms, D FIM 930 — 5 km
Tel (358) 09 - 177 880

RESTAURANTS RAVINTOLA

Kalastajorrpa — Helsinki
Tel (358) 09 - 45 811 — 3 km

Havis Amanda — Helsinki
Tel (358) 09 - 666 882 — 5 km

Savoy — Helsinki
Tel (358) 09 - 4684 40020 — 5 km

Espoo (ruotsiksi Esbo) on Helsingin rajanaapuri ja yksi Suomen suurimmista kaupungeista. Lähes 90 prosenttia rakennuksista on rakennettu vuoden 1960 jälkeen, mutta alue oli aikaisemmin tunnettu monista kartanoistaan, jotka sijaitsivat vanhan rantatien tuntumassa. Master Golf klubin kaksi 18-reikäistä kenttää on rakennettu tähän näyttävään ympäristöön. Forest-kenttä kaikkine puineen on saanut varsin osuvan nimen. Laajassa puistomaisemassa sijaitseva Master-kenttä on vielä parempi. Ensimmäiset seitsemän reikää ovat avoimia, mutta kierroksen loppuosassa on paljon vettä, mukaan luettuna lampi, joka on otettava huomioon etenkin viimeisten yhdeksän reiän kohdalla. Kenttä on erittäin tasapainoinen ja soveltuu kaikenlaisille pelaajille. Master-kenttä onkin suomalaisten golfinpelaajien suosiossa ammattitaitoisen palvelun ja kenttien erinomaisen kunnon ansiosta.

Espoo/Esbo is one of the largest cities in Finland and today virtually adjoins Helsinki. While almost 90% of the housing dates from the 1960s and thereafter, this used to be a region of a extensive properties not far from the old coast road. This grand golf club, with two 18-hole courses, is laid out on one such former estate. The first course, «the Forest», has the name it deserves and boasts any number of age-old trees. The second, «the Master», is even better and sprawls over a huge park. While the first seven holes are laid out over wide open space, the rest of the course features a lot of water, including a lake which spectacularly comes into play on half the holes, especially on the back nine. Well-balanced overall, open and adapting to players of all abilities, the «Master» is a very popular course with Finnish golfers, a fact equally explained to some extent by very professional administration and excellent maintenance.

Master Golf Club   1988
Bodomintie 4
FIN - 02940 ESPOO

Office	Toimisto	(358) 09 - 253 7002
Pro shop	Pro shop	(358) 09 - 253 7002
Fax	Fax	(358) 09 - 253 7027
Situation	Sijainti	

Helsinki (pop. 492 000), 15 km

| Annual closure | Kenttä suljetaan | no |
| Weekly closure | Suljetan viikolla | no |

Fees main season
Green fee 18 holes

	Week days Arkipäivisin	We/Bank holidays Pyhäpäivisin
Individual Henkilö	FIM 200	FIM 240
Couple Pari	FIM 400	FIM 480

Caddy	Caddy	no
Electric Trolley	Sähkörattaat	no
Buggy	Golfauto	FIM 150
Clubs	Mailat	FIM 100

Credit cards Luottokortit
VISA - Eurocard - MasterCard - AMEX - DC

GOLF
Myllyjärvi Kvarnträsk
Pakankylä Backby
Pünametsä Brunskogen
Kalajärvi
Bodominjärvi
Bodom
Vantaa Vanda
KEHA III RING III
50
Veikkola
Helsinki
110
E18 - 1
Kauniainen Grankulla
Espoo Esbo
0   2   4 km

Access Pääsy : Helsinki, take 50/E18, Exit Bodominjärvi/Bodom, go left towards the lake.
Map 1 on page 151 Kartta 1 sivulla : 151

GOLF COURSE
GOLFBANEN   15 /20

Site	Sijainti	▰▰▰▰▱
Maintenance	Hoito	▰▰▰▰▱
Architect	Arkkitehti	Kosti Kuronen
Type	Kentän luonne	parkland
Relief	Vapautuminen	▰▰▱▱▱
Water in play	Vesiesteitä	▰▰▰▰▱
Exp. to wind	Tuulta	▰▰▱▱▱
Trees in play	Puita	▰▰▰▱▱

Scorecard Tuloskortti	Chp. Champ. tii	Mens Miest. tii	Ladies Naist. tii
Length Pituus	6042	5696	4847
Par	72	72	72

Advised golfing ability Tasoitusvaatimus	0 12 24 36
	▰▰▰▱
Hcp required	Hcp-vaatimus	no

CLUB HOUSE & AMENITIES
KLUBHUS OG OMGIVELSER   7 /10

Pro shop	Pro shop	▰▰▰▰▱
Driving range	Driving range	▰▰▰▰▱
Sheltered	suoja	yes
On grass	ruoholla	yes (Summer)
Putting-green	putting-green	yes
Pitching-green	pitching-green	yes

155

HOTEL FACILITIES
HOTELFASILITETER   7 /10

HOTELS
Kaisankoti	Espoo
80 rooms, D FIM 560	3 km
Tel (358) 09 - 887 191	

RESTAURANTS RAVINTOLA
| Kaisankoti | Espoo |
| Tel (358) 09 - 887 191 | 3 km |

Vain 75 kilometrin päässä Helsingistä sijaitsee Nordcenter, joka on 36-reikäinen kenttä kuten lähellä olevat Pickalan ja Sarfvikin kentätkin. Lohjanjärven rannalle rakennettu Nordcenter on kahden amerikkalaisen suunnittelema, varsin eksklusiivinen kenttä, joka ei varmaankaan oudoksuta niitä, jotka ovat pelanneet golfia USA:ssa. Ronald Freamin suunnittelema kenttä on avoin ja maaston korkeuserot ovat suuret (suosittelemme golfauton käyttöä). Neljä reikää pelataan vedenrajassa. Nordcenterissä suosittelemme korkeuseroiltaan helpompaa Benz kenttää, jolla liikkuminen ei ole yhtä rasittavaa kuin Fream kentällä. Tämän kentän on piirtänyt Bradford Benz, ja metsineen ja vesistöineen se tuntuu paljon "suomalaisemmalta". Vesi ja puut tulevat mukaan peliin kymmenen reiän kohdalla. Väylät ovat leveitä ja pieleen menneistä lyönneistä voi täällä pelastautua: varomattomuudesta ei sakoteta. Takatiiltä ei kuitenkaan kannata pelata, vaikka kenttä onkin avoin eikä sisällä salattuja vaikeuksia. Riittää kun lyö klubitiiltä. Nordcenter on täydellinen "resort"-kenttä.

Here is another 36-hole resort just 75 km from Helsinki in a setting that overlooks the lake of Lohjanjarvi. This happens to be a very exclusive club, which called on the services of two American architects to design the courses on which any American would feel very much at home. The course designed by Ronald Fream is very open and very hilly (buggy recommended) where four holes run along the shores of the lake. We would recommend the less hilly and so more easily walkable course designed by Bradford Benz, which is more specifically Finnish in its landscape of wood and water, both of which are very much in play on about ten holes. The fairways are wide, so the less accurate or less cautious golfers should get by without too much damage to their card. Don't think twice about opting for the front tees, at least to get to know the layout, even though the course is very open and hides nothing. A great golfing resort.

Nordcenter Golf & Country Club — 1993
FIN - 10410 ÅMINNEFORS

Office	Toimisto	(358) 19 - 238 850
Pro shop	Pro shop	(358) 19 - 238 850
Fax	Fax	(358) 19 - 238 871
Situation	Sijainti	

Helsinki (pop. 492 000), 75 km

Annual closure	Kenttä suljetaan	no
Weekly closure	Suljetan viikolla	no

Fees main season
Green fee 18 holes

	Week days Arkipäivisin	We/Bank holidays Pyhäpäivisin
Individual Henkilö	FIM 260	*
Couple Pari	FIM 520	*

* Members' guests only

Caddy	Caddy	no
Electric Trolley	Sähkörattaat	yes
Buggy	Golfauto	FIM 160
Clubs	Mailat	FIM 100

Credit cards Luottokortit
VISA - Eurocard - MasterCard - AMEX - DC

156

Tenala Tenhola
Pohja Pojo
Pinjainen Billnäs
Åminnafors
GOLF
Karis Karjaa
Domargård
Pohjanlahti Pojoviken
Tenala Tenhola
Helsinki / Lohja Helsingfors / Lojo
Ekenäs Tammisaari

Access Pääsy : Helsinki, E18, them road 25
→ Lohja/Karis, → Pohja, turn left → Åminnefors
Map 1 on page 151 Kartta 1 sivulla : 151

GOLF COURSE / GOLFBANEN — 15/20

Site	Sijainti	
Maintenance	Hoito	
Architect	Arkkitehti	Bradford Benz
Type	Kentän luonne	forest
Relief	Vapautuminen	
Water in play	Vesiesteitä	
Exp. to wind	Tuulta	
Trees in play	Puita	

Scorecard Tuloskortti	Chp. Champ. tii	Mens Miest. tii	Ladies Naist. tii
Length Pituus	6023	5740	4853
Par	72	72	72

Advised golfing ability Tasoitusvaatimus	0	12	24	36
Hcp required Hcp-vaatimus	36			

CLUB HOUSE & AMENITIES / KLUBHUS OG OMGIVELSER — 7/10

Pro shop	Pro shop	
Driving range	Driving range	
Sheltered	suoja	yes
On grass	ruoholla	no
Putting-green	putting-green	yes
Pitching-green	pitching-green	yes

HOTEL FACILITIES / HOTELFASILITETER — 5/10

HOTELS
Fiskars Värdhus — Åminnefors
6 rooms, D FIM 520 — 6 km
Tel (358) 019 - 237 355

RESTAURANTS RAVINTOLA
Fiskars Värdhus — Åminnefors
Tel (358) 019 - 237 355 — 6 km

Pickalan Golfclubiin kuuluu suuri urheilulaitos tenniskenttineen ja hevostalleineen, ja täällä voi purjehtia sekä pelata golfia kahdella kentällä. Sijainti Itämeren rannalla on upea, ja toinen, kentistä kapeampi, on-kin saanut nimekseen Seaside. Leveämpi kenttä on nimeltään Park. Seaside-kenttään kuuluu vähemmän puita, mutta sitäkin enemmän vesiesteitä, patoja ja lammikoita, joita yhdistää pieni joki. Vesi on mukana pe-lissä kahdentoista reiän kohdalla, mikä asettaa suuria vaatimuksia aloituslyönnille ja rankaisee epäonnistuneista jat-kolyönneistä. Griinien ympärillä on bunkkerointeja, harvemmin vettä. Jos kyseessä on vain harjoituskierros, sopii kenttä hyvin kaikenlaisille pelaajille: ensiksi vaaratekijöiden arviointi, seuraavaksi aloituslyönti, ja sitten voikin vain toivoa parasta. Hyvänä uutisena mainittakoon, että Seaside ei sisällä todella pitkiä reikiä.. Tuuli sen sijaan on aina otettava huomioon. Park-kenttä on myös erittäin hyvä ja kerhotalo, ravintola ja alueen vuokramökit ovat erinomaiset.

This golf club is a sporting complex which features tennis courts, horse-riding, sailing and two golf courses. The loca-tion is quite magnificent, on the Baltic coastline, which, as the name suggests, serves as a backdrop for the «Seaside» course. Tighter than the «Park Course», «Seaside» has very few trees but a lot of water in the shape of ponds and small lakes, linked by a small river. Water actually comes into play on about a dozen holes as frontal or lateral hazards and is more dangerous for the drive or wayward second shot than when really attacking the greens, where the bunkers take over. In practice, players of all abilities can play here, calculate the risks they are willing to take and hope for the best. There are no excessively long holes here, good news for big-hitters, who will nonetheless have to reckon with the wind. The second course has much to be said for it, as do the club-house, restaurant and chalets for rent on site.

Pickala Golf Club — 1986

Golfkuja 5
FIN - 02580 SIUNTIO

Office	Toimisto	(358) 09 - 221 90844
Pro shop	Pro shop	(358) 09 - 221 90844
Fax	Fax	(358) 09 - 221 90899

Situation Sijainti
Helsinki (pop. 492 000), 45 km

Annual closure	Kenttä suljetaan	no
Weekly closure	Suljetan viikolla	no

Fees main season
Green fee 18 holes

	Week days Arkipäivisin	We/Bank holidays Pyhäpäivisin
Individual Henkilö	FIM 180	FIM 220
Couple Pari	FIM 360	FIM 440

Caddy	Caddy	no
Electric Trolley	Sähkörattaat	no
Buggy	Golfauto	FIM 200
Clubs	Mailat	FIM 150

Credit cards Luottokortit
VISA - Eurocard - MasterCard - AMEX - DC

Access Pääsy : Helsinki, road 51 →
Kirkkonummi/Kyrkslatt, in Pickala/Pickala → Golf
Map 1 on page 151 Kartta 1 sivulla : 151

GOLF COURSE / GOLFBANEN — 15/20

Site	Sijainti	
Maintenance	Hoito	
Architect	Arkkitehti	Reijo Hillberg
Type	Kentän luonne	seaside course, links
Relief	Vapautuminen	
Water in play	Vesiesteitä	
Exp. to wind	Tuulta	
Trees in play	Puita	

Scorecard Tuloskortti	Chp. Champ. tii	Mens Miest. tii	Ladies Naist. tii
Length Pituus	6118	5758	4880
Par	71	71	71

Advised golfing ability Tasoitusvaatimus	0	12	24	36
Hcp required Hcp-vaatimus	36			

CLUB HOUSE & AMENITIES / KLUBHUS OG OMGIVELSER — 8/10

Pro shop	Pro shop	
Driving range	Driving range	
Sheltered	suoja	yes
On grass	ruoholla	yes (Summer)
Putting-green	putting-green	yes
Pitching-green	pitching-green	yes

157

HOTEL FACILITIES / HOTELFASILITETER — 5/10

HOTELS

Majvik	Espoo
100 rooms, D FIM 760	25 km

Tel (358) 09 - 295 511

RESTAURANTS RAVINTOLA

Majvik	Espoo
Tel (358) 09 - 295 511	25 km

SARFVIK NEW COURSE

16 8 7

Sarfvik Golfklubista on kehittynyt kaikkien tavoittelema, Suomen eksklusiivisin ja kallein kerho. Vaikka kenttiä on kaksi, voi täällä pelata greenfee-vieraana ainoastaan viikonloppuisin ja silloinkin vain jonkun kerhonjäsenen seurassa. Molempien kenttien suunnittelusta vastaa Jan Sederholm, joka on yksi Ruotsin tuotteliaimpia arkkitehtejä. Pelaaminen on nautinnollista molemmilla kentillä, vaikkakin eri syistä: Old Course on tasainen, avoin puistokenttä kun taas New Course on mäkinen ja kiemurtelee metsän läpi. Jälkimmäinen on kentistä haastavampi, koska tasoerot vaikeuttavat oikean mailan valintaa. Tämän lisäksi on palloa välillä taivutettava, ellei halua päätyä puiden sekaan. Samanaikaisesti metsä luo miellyttävän erillisyyden ja rauhan tunteen. Muutama vesieste luo elävyyttä kaiken vihreyden keskellä, ja griinibunkkerit, joita ei ole kovin monta, on erittäin hyvin sijoitettu. New Course on erittäin hyvä kenttä, joka vaatii pelaajaltaan keskittäytymistä, jos haluaa pelata taitoaan vastaavasti. Täällä pelaamiseen voi varata pitkän kesäpäivän ja pelata molemmat kentät.

The «Sarfvik Golfklubi» has become Finland's most highly coveted, most exclusive and most expensive golf club. And even though there are two courses, you can only play here on week-ends if accompanied by a member. Both courses were laid out by Jan Sederholm and both are very enjoyable in their very different ways. The «Old Course» is flat like a park with wide open space, while the «New Course» is hilly and runs through a forest. The latter is the most challenging of the two, as the steep topography adds to the difficulty of club selection and players need to be able to bend the ball to keep out of the trees. At the same time, the forest landscape gives a great feeling of isolation and tranquillity, while a few water hazards give visual variety to all the shades of green around you, not forgetting the few but well located sand traps by the greens. A very fine complex where you need to concentrate long and hard to play to your handicap.

Sarfvik Golf Club — 1984
Finnbyntie 30
FIN - 02430 MASALA

Office	Toimisto	(358) 09 - 221 9000
Pro shop	Pro shop	(358) 09 - 221 9000
Fax	Fax	(358) 09 - 297 7134
Situation	Sijainti	

Helsinki (pop. 492 000), 15 km

Annual closure	Kenttä suljetaan	no
Weekly closure	Suljetan viikolla	no

Fees main season
Green fee 18 holes

	Week days Arkipäivisin	We/Bank holidays Pyhäpäivisin
Individual Henkilö	FIM 320	*
Couple Pari	FIM 640	*

* Members'guests only

Caddy	Caddy	no
Electric Trolley	Sähkörattaat	no
Buggy	Golfauto	FIM 150
Clubs	Mailat	FIM 150

Credit cards Luottokortit
VISA - Eurocard - MasterCard - AMEX - DC

158

Access Pääsy : Helsinki, 51 → Kirkkonummi/Kyrkslatt.
After Espoonlahti and bridge, turn left → Sarfvik
Map 1 on page 151 Kartta 1 sivulla : 151

GOLF COURSE / GOLFBANEN — 16/20

Site	Sijainti	
Maintenance	Hoito	
Architect	Arkkitehti	Jan Sederholm
Type	Kentän luonne	forest
Relief	Vapautuminen	
Water in play	Vesiesteitä	
Exp. to wind	Tuulta	
Trees in play	Puita	

Scorecard Tuloskortti	Chp. Champ. tii	Mens Miest. tii	Ladies Naist. tii
Length Pituus	5854	5547	4696
Par	72	72	72

Advised golfing ability
Tasoitusvaatimus — 0 12 24 36
Hcp required — Hcp-vaatimus — no

CLUB HOUSE & AMENITIES / KLUBHUS OG OMGIVELSER — 8/10

Pro shop	Pro shop	
Driving range	Driving range	
Sheltered	suoja	yes
On grass	ruoholla	yes (Summer)
Putting-green	putting-green	yes
Pitching-green	pitching-green	yes

HOTEL FACILITIES / HOTELFASILITETER — 7/10

HOTELS
Majvik — Espoo
100 rooms, D FIM 760 — 9 km
Tel (358) 09 - 295 511

RESTAURANTS RAVINTOLA
Majvik — Espoo
Tel (358) 09 - 295 511 — 9 km

PEUGEOT GOLF GUIDE 2000/2001

ST LAURENCE

14	5	4

Kenttä sijaitsee aivan Lohjan kaupungin ja Lohjanjärven tuntumassa. Kymmenen prosenttia Etelä-Suomen pinta-alasta on vettä ja Lohjanjärvi on alueen toiseksi suurin järvi. Arkkitehti Kosti Kuronen, joka on yksi Suomen parhaista amatöörigolfareista, on epäilemättä tuntenut houkutusta vesiesteiden käyttöön. Vesi on tietenkin mukana kuvassa, mutta Kurosen perus- ratkaisu on varovaisempi ja kenttä sulautuu hyvin metsä- ja peltomaisemaansa. Vaikka Suomen golfkausi on lyhyt on St. Laurence aina erinomaisessa kunnossa. Väylät ja griinibunkkeristo on suunniteltu hyvin, samoin kuin suuret viheriöt, joilla kannattaa pysytellä lipun tuntumassa, muuten seuraa "three put". Griinit ovat melko kumpuilevia, suhteellisen kovia, nopeudeltaan sopivia ja hyvin suojattuja. St. Laurence on erittäin miellyttävä kenttä, pelaajan valmiuksista riippumatta.

The course is located within the immediate vicinity of the town of Lohja and lake Lohjanjärvi, the largest in southern Finland, where ten percent of surface area is made up of lakes. Kosti Kuronen, one of the top Finnish golfers, was obviously tempted to pepper the course with water hazards, but while paying an obvious tribute to the very strategic style of American architecture, he resisted the easy option of excess water and preserved a more typical setting of forest and fields. Although the golfing season is short in Finland, this very neatly landscaped course is always in very satisfactory condition, a compliment that is valid for the well-located fairway and green-side bunkers, the fairways and very large greens, where you need to keep it near the pin if you want avoid three putts. The putting surfaces are slightly undulating, rather firm, not too slick and well guarded. A very pleasant course, regardless of playing ability.

St Laurence Golf — 1989

Kaivurinkatu 133
FIN - 08 200 LOHJA

Office	Toimisto	(358) 019 - 386 603
Pro shop	Pro shop	(358) 019 - 386 603
Fax	Fax	(358) 019 - 386 666
Situation	Sijainti	

Lohja, 5 km

Annual closure	Kenttä suljetaan	no
Weekly closure	Suljetan viikolla	no

Fees main season
Green fee 18 holes

	Week days Arkipäivisin	We/Bank holidays Pyhäpäivisin
Individual Henkilö	FIM 200	FIM 220
Couple Pari	FIM 400	FIM 440

Caddy	Caddy	no
Electric Trolley	Sähkörattaat	no
Buggy	Golfauto	no
Clubs	Mailat	FIM 50

Credit cards Luottokortit
VISA - Eurocard - MasterCard - AMEX - DC

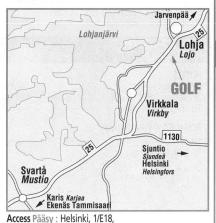

Access Pääsy : Helsinki, 1/E18,
then road 25 → Lohja/Lojo
Map 1 on page 151 Kartta 1 sivulla : 151

GOLF COURSE / GOLFBANEN — 14/20

Site	Sijainti	
Maintenance	Hoito	
Architect	Arkkitehti	Kosti Kuronen

Type	Kentän luonne	forest, parkland
Relief	Vapautuminen	
Water in play	Vesiesteitä	
Exp. to wind	Tuulta	
Trees in play	Puita	

Scorecard Tuloskortti	Chp. Champ. tii	Mens Miest. tii	Ladies Naist. tii
Length Pituus	5769	5769	5018
Par	72	72	72

Advised golfing ability Tasoitusvaatimus	0	12	24	36
Hcp required Hcp-vaatimus	36			

CLUB HOUSE & AMENITIES / KLUBHUS OG OMGIVELSER — 5/10

Pro shop	Pro shop	
Driving range	Driving range	
Sheltered	suoja	yes
On grass	ruoholla	yes (Summer)
Putting-green	putting-green	yes
Pitching-green	pitching-green	yes

HOTEL FACILITIES / HOTELFASILITETER — 4/10

HOTELS
Mustio Castle — Lohja
30 rooms, D FIM 880 (w. GF) — 30 km
Tel (358) 019 - 362 31

RESTAURANTS RAVINTOLA
Mustio Castle — Lohja
Tel (358) 019 - 362 31 — 30 km

159

Musiikista kiinnostunut pelaaja jatkaa kentältä Tuusulanjärven rannalla sijaitsevaan Ainolaan, missä säveltäjä Jean Sibelius asui suurimman osan elämästään. Lähistöllä on myös Gauguinin oppilaana olleen taidemaalari Pekka Halosen talo. Niin Halosen kuin Sibeliuksenkin inspiraation lähteitä olivat Suomen kansa, luonto ja legendat. Golf Talman klubitalo on rakennettu suomalaisten taide- ja suunnitteluperinteiden hengessä. 27-reikäisen kentänkin luulisi silloin olevan erikoisemman, mutta kokonaisuus on varsin hillitty, ja maisema sisältää niin metsäosuuksia kuin puistomaisempiakin alueita. Jos pelaa vain 18 reikää, ovat A- ja B-väylä golfteknisesti vaikein osuus. Muutoin erot eivät ole suuria. Erityistä kiitosta ansaitsevat erinomaiset harjoitusmahdollisudet, jotka kohottavat kokonaisvaikutelmaa.

Music-lovers will want to push a little further north-west from this course as far as Ainola on the shores of lake Tuusula. This is where the composer Jean Sibelius spent most of his life. A little further still and you can visit the house and studio of the painter Pekka Halonen, a student with Gauguin. The two men were inspired by the Finnish people, their legends and nature. The club-house here follows the country's tradition of art and design, and as such might leave you expecting a more exceptional and stylish course than is actually the case. As it happens, the 27 holes here are rather more sedate in a calm setting between parkland and forest. If you play only 18 holes, the combination of the two nine-hole A and B courses is perhaps the most difficult golf-wise, but there is little difference between the three. The whole complex is enhanced by the excellence of the practice facilities.

Golf Talma — 1989

Nygårdintie
FIN - 04240 TALMA

Office	Toimisto	(358) 9 - 239 6166
Pro shop	Pro shop	(358) 9 - 239 6166
Fax	Fax	(358) 9 - 239 6131
Situation	Sijainti	

Helsinki (pop. 492 000), 30 km

Annual closure	Kenttä suljetaan	no
Weekly closure	Suljetan viikolla	no

Fees main season
Green fee 18 holes

	Week days Arkipäivisin	We/Bank holidays Pyhäpäivisin
Individual Henkilö	FIM 170	FIM 220
Couple Pari	FIM 340	FIM 440

Caddy	Caddy	no
Electric Trolley	Sähkörattaat	no
Buggy	Golfauto	FIM 150
Clubs	Mailat	FIM 100

Credit cards Luottokortit
VISA - Eurocard - MasterCard - AMEX - DC

160

Access Pääsy : Helsinki, road 4/E75 → Järvenpää.
Exit Kerava, turn right on road 148 → Sibbo,
then left on 140, then right → Talma/Tallmo → Golf
Map 1 on page 151 Kartta 1 sivulla : 151

GOLF COURSE GOLFBANEN — 14/20

Site	Sijainti	
Maintenance	Hoito	
Architect	Arkkitehti	Henrik Wartiainen
Type	Kentän luonne	forest, parkland
Relief	Vapautuminen	
Water in play	Vesiesteitä	
Exp. to wind	Tuulta	
Trees in play	Puita	

Scorecard Tuloskortti	Chp. Champ. tii	Mens Miest. tii	Ladies Naist. tii
Length Pituus	5855	5855	4995
Par	72	72	72

Advised golfing ability Tasoitusvaatimus	0 12 24 36	
Hcp required Hcp-vaatimus	36	

CLUB HOUSE & AMENITIES KLUBHUS OG OMGIVELSER — 8/10

Pro shop	Pro shop	
Driving range	Driving range	
Sheltered	suoja	yes
On grass	ruoholla	yes (Summer)
Putting-green	putting-green	yes
Pitching-green	pitching-green	yes

HOTEL FACILITIES HOTELFASILITETER — 6/10

HOTELS

Sokos Hotel Vantaa	Vantaa
162 rooms, D FIM 460 (We)/780	20 km
Tel (358) 09 - 857 851	

RESTAURANTS RAVINTOLA

Sokos Hotel Vantaa	Vantaa
Tel (358) 09 - 857 851	20 km
Chique	Vantaa
Tel (358) 09 - 8234 832	

TAWAST

Hämeenlinnan (ruotsiksi Tavastehus) Tawast-kenttä sijaitsee upeassa rantamaisemassa. Metsät rikkovat vain harvakseltaan alueen rikkaita vesistöjä, joilla voi tehdä laivamatkoja järveltä toiselle. Alue on yksi Suomen suurimmista turistikeskuksista, ja suurimmat kaupungit ovat nimeltään Tampere (Tammerfors) ja Savonlinna (Nyslott). Tawastin kenttä sijaitsee Katumajärven rannalla, puistomaisemassa, ja arkkitehdillä on ollut siinä määrin mieltymys dog leg -välien käyttöön, että pelaaja yllättyy, kun par 3 -reiät ovatkin suoria. Tawastin kokonaisuus on kuitenkin erittäin †mielenkiintoinen, joskin kenttä on lyhyenlainen monien Suomen kenttien tapaan. Arkkitehdit hemmottelevat kuntoilijagolfareita! Tawast vaatii keskittymistä monien esteiden selvittämiseksi. Pelaajalta vaaditaan erilaisten lyöntien hallintaa tasoerojen aiheuttamien tilanteiden hallitsemiseksi. Vanhan kartanon talliin rakennettu kerhotalo on erittäin viihtyisä ja tyylikäs.

Hämeenlinna (Tavastehus) is one of the gateways to the wonderful region of lakes, interrupted only occasionally by forests, where you can set out on almost endless water cruises across lakes that are often inter-linked by stretches of water. This is one of the country's major tourist areas, around the two centres of Tempere and Savonlinna. The Tawast course lies along one of these superb lakes in a wood-covered parkland landscape where the architect seems to have been hell-bent on producing nothing but dog-legs. It's a wonder he did not curve the par 3s as well. Having said that, this is an interesting layout, albeit not very long, where the designers had a lot of thought for mid-handicappers. Every golfer here will have to negotiate all types of hazard, try every shot in the book and cope with a number of different situations. Facilities are good, including a very pleasant and stylish club-house in the old stables of a former lordly estate.

Tawast Golf & Country Club — 1987

Tawastintie 48
FIN - 13270 HÄMEENLINNA

Office	Toimisto	(358) 03 - 619 7502
Pro shop	Pro shop	(358) 03 - 619 7502
Fax	Fax	(358) 03 - 619 7503
Situation	Sijainti	

Annual closure	Kenttä suljetaan	no
Weekly closure	Suljetan viikolla	no

Fees main season
Green fee 18 holes

	Week days Arkipäivisin	We/Bank holidays Pyhäpäivisin
Individual Henkilö	FIM 180	FIM 180
Couple Pari	FIM 360	FIM 360

Caddy	Caddy	no
Electric Trolley	Sähkörattaat	no
Buggy	Golfauto	FIM 200
Clubs	Mailat	FIM 100

Credit cards Luottokortit
VISA - Eurocard - MasterCard - AMEX - DC

Access Pääsy : Helsinki, E12 → Tampere.
Exit Hämeenlinna.
Map 1 on page 151 Kartta 1 sivulla : 151

GOLF COURSE / GOLFBANEN — 14/20

Site	Sijainti	
Maintenance	Hoito	
Architect	Arkkitehti	Reijo Hillberg
Type	Kentän luonne	forest, inland
Relief	Vapautuminen	
Water in play	Vesiesteitä	
Exp. to wind	Tuulta	
Trees in play	Puita	

Scorecard Tuloskortti	Chp. Champ. tii	Mens Miest. tii	Ladies Naist. tii
Length Pituus	6063	5741	5019
Par	72	72	72

Advised golfing ability — 0 12 24 36
Tasoitusvaatimus
Hcp required — Hcp-vaatimus — 36

CLUB HOUSE & AMENITIES / KLUBHUS OG OMGIVELSER — 7/10

Pro shop	Pro shop	
Driving range	Driving range	
Sheltered	suoja	yes
On grass	ruoholla	yes (Summer)
Putting-green	putting-green	yes
Pitching-green	pitching-green	yes

161

HOTEL FACILITIES / HOTELFASILITETER — 5/10

HOTELS
Vanajanlinna Castle Hotel — Hämeenlinna
50 rooms, D FIM 700 (w. GF) — 3 km
Tel (358) 03 - 619 6565

RESTAURANTS RAVINTOLA
Vanajanlinna — Hämeenlinna
Tel (358) 03 - 619 6565 — 3 km

Sur terre
comme dans un rêve.

www.peugeot.fr

Les roues sur terre, la tête dans les nuages, c'est sur cette idée que Peugeot s'est basé pour créer un véritable rêve automobile : le Coupé

Disponible en 2 motorisations, le 2.0 L/135 ch pour le dynamisme et le 3.0 L V6/194 ch pour la force et la puissance, cette voiture est égalem

synonyme de technologie et de sécurité avec l'ABS, l'antidémarrage, la condamnation centralisée des portes et ses coussins gonfla

conducteur et passager. L'air conditionné (régulé sur V6), le pommeau du levier de

vitesse habillé de cuir et aluminium ainsi que l'autoradio, huit haut-parleurs, avec

commande au volant en font une illustration parfaite du plaisir de conduire et de se

laisser conduire. Au volant du Coupé 406 vous pourrez enfin découvrir le plaisir de

voyager sur terre comme dans un rêve.

POUR QUE L'AUTOMOBILE SOIT TOUJOURS UN PLAISIR.

406 PEUGEO

Ⓕrance

France

Le golf en France ne s'est développé qu'à partir des années 80, et compte aujourd'hui plus de 280.000 golfeurs pour plus de 500 parcours, dont plus de 350 de 18 trous. Il reste de la place pour les visiteurs! Premier du monde pour le tourisme, le pays commence seulement à être considéré comme une destination golfique, et ses arguments ne manquent pas. Vous trouverez ici les meilleurs parcours ouverts au public. Les grands golfs privés traditionnels acceptent parfois les visiteurs, en semaine notamment, et en été, mais sans en faire vraiment la promotion. Avec une lettre d'introduction de votre club, vous pouvez tenter votre chance auprès des plus réputés: par exemple Chantilly, Saint-Germain, Fontainebleau, Saint-Nom-la-Bretèche, le Paris International, Joyenval, La Boulie. Tous figurent dans ce Guide... sauf Morfontaine, complètement fermé.

Golf in France only really took off from the 1980s onward, and today there are more than 280,000 golfers for more than 500 courses, of which more than 350 are eighteen-hole layouts. So there is room enough for visitors. A world leader for tourisme, France is now only starting to be considered as a golfing destination, and it has a lot going for it. We have included here the best courses open to the public. The great traditional private courses sometimes admit visitors, especially during the week and summer, but they never really promote the idea. With a letter of introduction from your club, you can try your luck at some of the more highly-reputed courses such as Chantilly, Saint-Germain, Fontainebleau, Saint-Nom-la-Bretèche, Paris International, Joyenval and La Boulie in the greater Paris area. All are featured in this edition, except Morfontaine, closed for all visitors.

163

The Millennium Guide

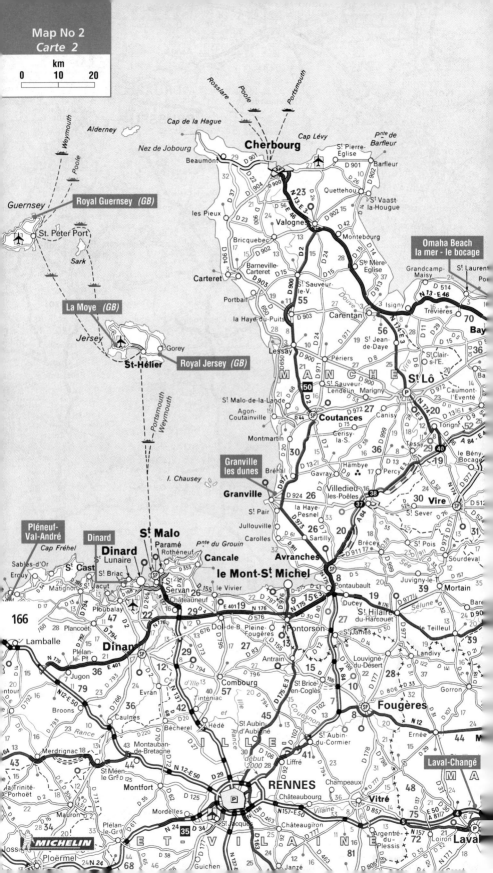

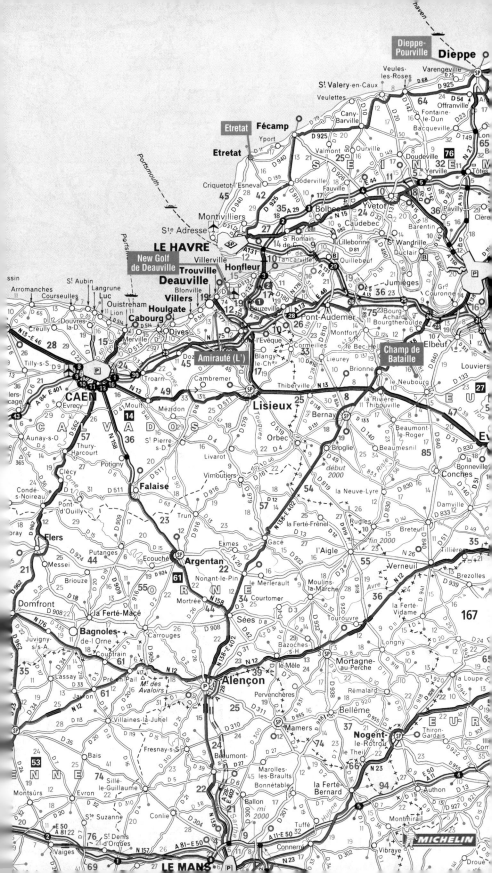

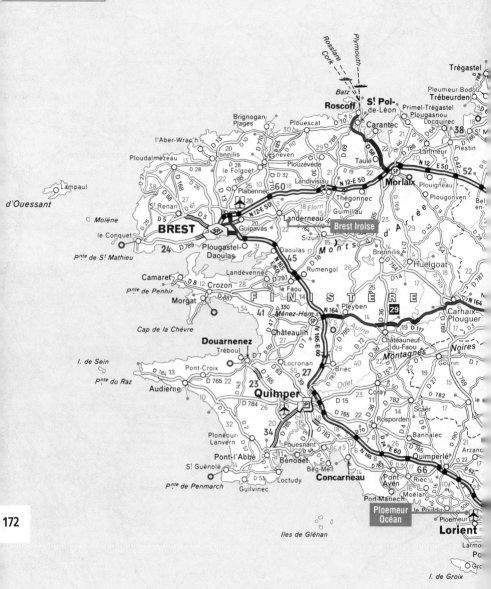

km
0   10   20

Rosslare
Cork

Plymouth

Batz

Trégastel

Pleumeur-Bodou
Trébeurden
Roscoff   St Pol-
de-Léon   Primel-Trégastel
Plougasnou
Locquirec   38

Brignogan
Plages   Plouescat   Carantec

l'Aber-Wrac'h   Plouzévédé   30   St   Lanmeur   Plestin

Ploudalmézeau   Lannilis   Lesneven   29 D 788   69   D 786   Plouigneau

Lampaul   le Folgoët   Plouzévédé   Landivisiau   N 12-E 50   Morlaix   Plouigneau   52

d'Ouessant   St Renan   Plabennec   60   18   Thégonnec   Plougonven

Molène   Guimiliau

le Conquet   BREST   Landerneau   Brest Iroise   Huelgoat

Pnte de St Mathieu   24   Plougastel-
Daoulas   Daoulas   Sizun   15   Brennilis

Camaret   Crozon   Landévennec   Rumengol   le Faou   Pleyben   Carhaix
Plouguer

Pnte de Penhir   Morgat   Ménez-Hom   330   N 164   29

Cap de la Chèvre   Châteaulin   Châteauneuf-
du-Faou   Noires

I. de Sein   Douarnenez   Tréboul   Locronan   Briec   Montagnes   Gourin

Pnte du Raz   Pont-Croix   55   27   Odet   Coray   Scaër

Audierne   23   Quimper   Rosporden   Bannalec   Quimperlé

Ploneour-
Lanvern   34   Fouesnant   66   Riec

Pont-l'Abbé   Bénodet   Beg-Meil   Pont-
Aven   Moëlan   le Pouldu

St Guénolé   Loctudy   Concarneau   Port-Manech   Ploemeur
Océan   Lorient

Pnte de Penmarch   Guilvinec   Iles de Glénan   I. de Groix

172

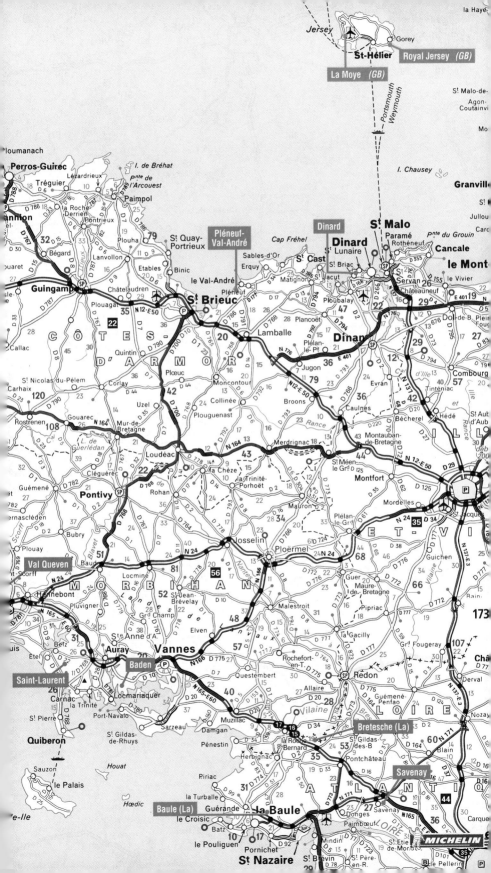

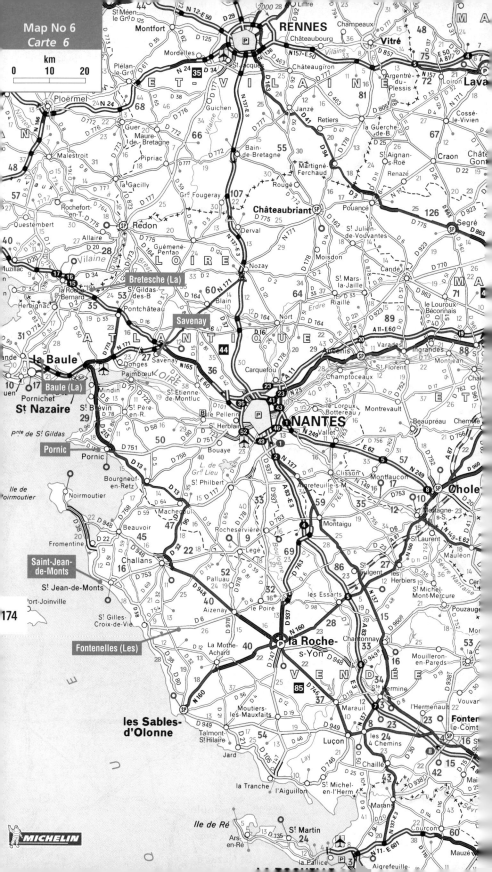

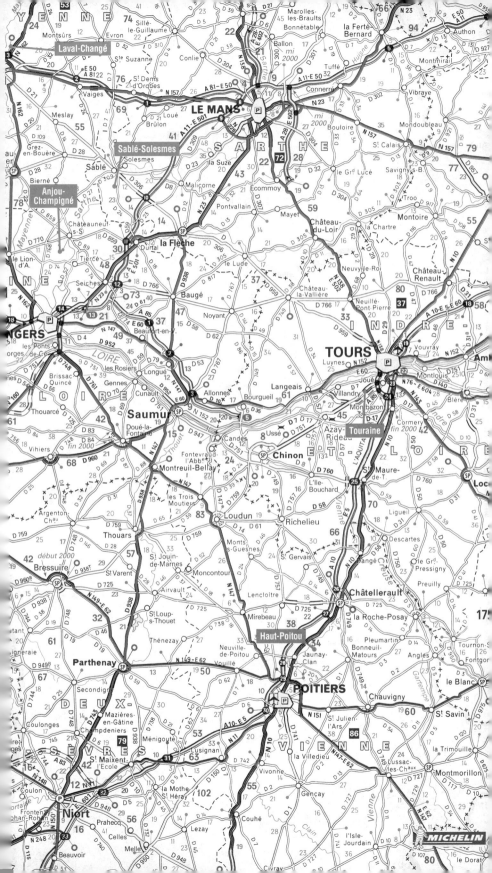

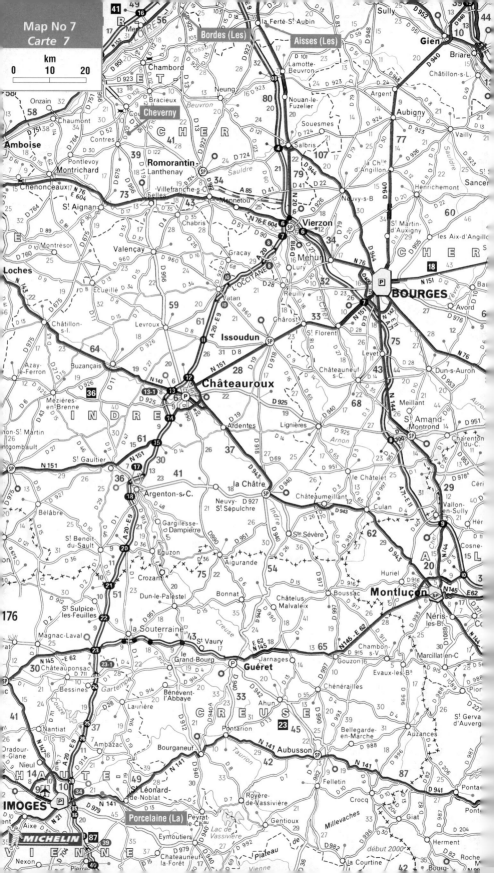

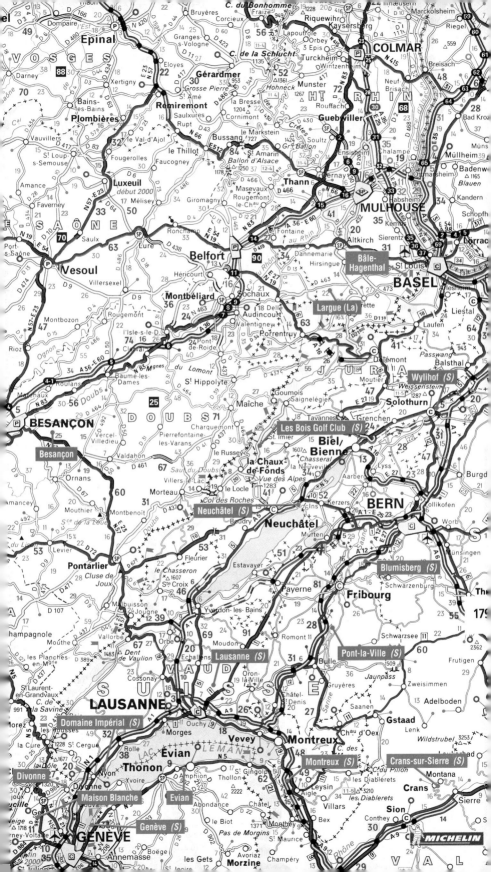

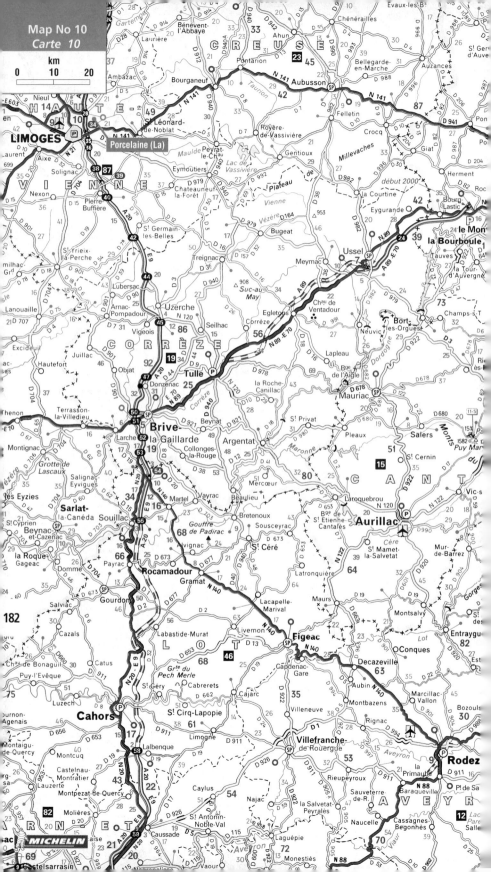

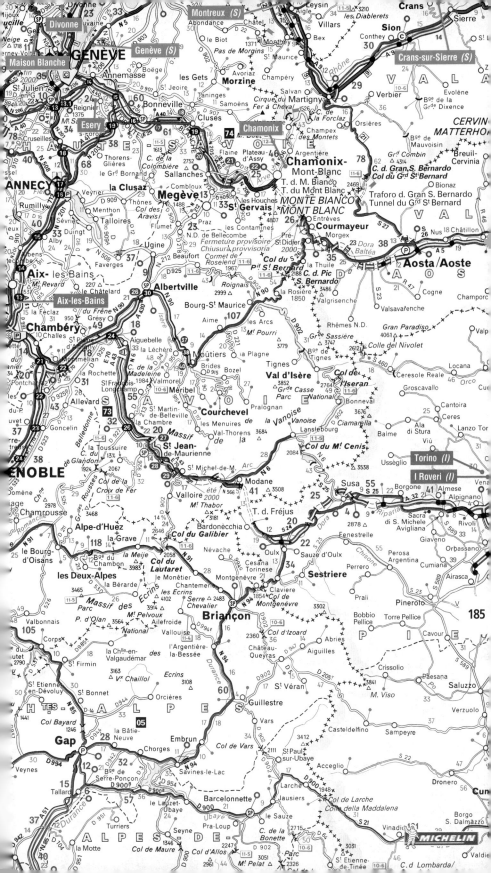

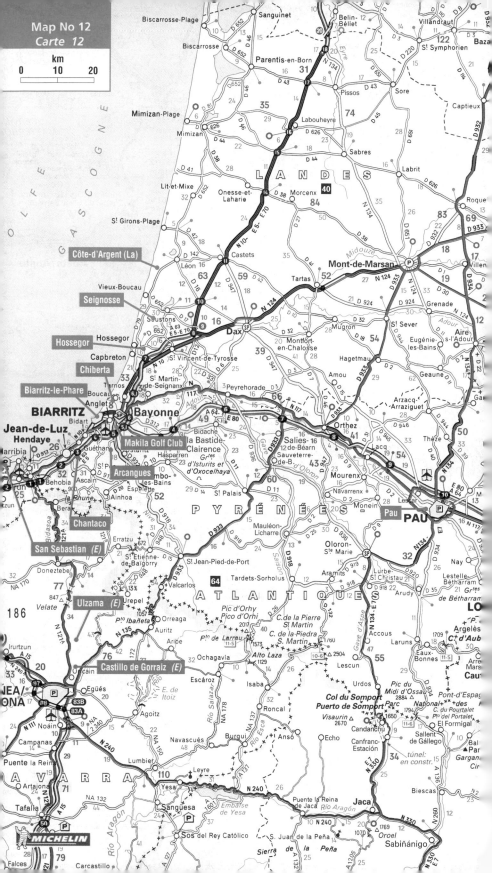

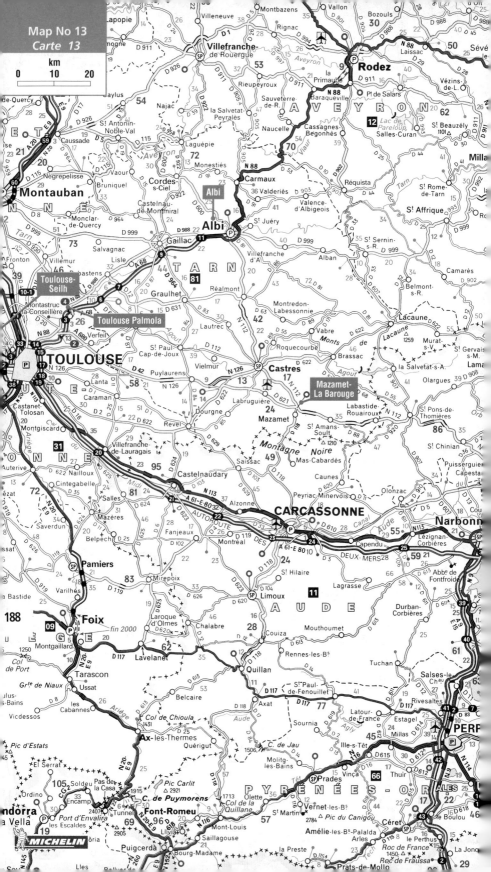

189

MICHELIN

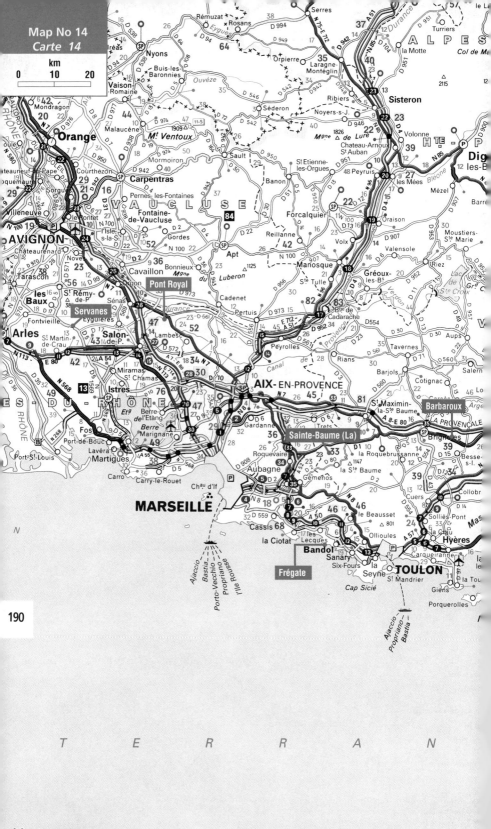

km
0   10   20

Serres
Rémuzat
Rosans
D 994
Eyguians
D 949
ALPES
Col de Ma
la Motte
2115

Nyons
Buis-les-
Baronnies
Orpierre
Laragne-
Montéglin
64
Ribiers
Noyers-s-J.
Sisteron
23

Vaison-
Romaine
Ouvèze
Séderon
Mgne de Lure
Chateau-Arnoux
St Auban
Volonne
HTE-P
Dig
les-B

Mondragon
20
RHÔNE
42
Malaucène
44
Mt Ventoux
Sault
St Etienne-
les-Orgues
Banon
Peyruis
les Mées
Mézel

Orange
Courthézon
Mormoiron
Forcalquier
Mgne
Volx
Manosque
Oraison
Moustiers-
Ste Marie
Riez

Carpentras
VAUCLUSE
Pernes-les-Fontaines
Fontaine-
de-Vaucluse
84
Apt
Reillanne
42
Ste Tulle
Gréoux-
les-B.
Valensole
Lac
de
Ste Croix

AVIGNON
Le Pontet
L'Isle-
s-la-S.
Gordes
N 100
Bonnieux
Luberon
Cadenet
Manosque
82
83
Bce de
Cadarache
Aups

Tarascon
Châteaurenard
Cavaillon
Pont Royal
Servanes
Eyguières
Salon
Pertuis
Rians
Tavernes

les
Baux
St Rémy-
de-P.
Sénas
Lambesc
St Chamas
Peyrolles
Barjols
Cotignac
Salern

Arles
St Martin-
de-Crau
43
Miramas
Istres
76
AIX-EN-PROVENCE
81
St Maximin-
la-Ste Baume
Barbaroux
A PROVENCALE

DU
RHÔNE
Fos
Berre-
l'Etang
Berre
Marignane
47
Gardanne
45
Trets
Sainte-Baume (La)
la Roquebrussanne
Brignoles
39

Port-de-Bouc
Lavéra
Martigues
Carro
Carry-le-Rouet
Roquevaire
33
la Ste Baume
Cuers
39

MARSEILLE
Chau d'If
Aubagne
Gémenos
le Beausset
Solliès-Pont
Collobr

Cassis
68
la Ciotat
les
Lecques
Ollioules
la Crau
Hyères

Frégate
Bandol
Sanary
Six-Fours
la
Seyne
St Mandrier
TOULON
Giens
Porquerolles

190

Cap Sicié
Ajaccio
Propriano-
Bastia

T E R R A N

MICHELIN

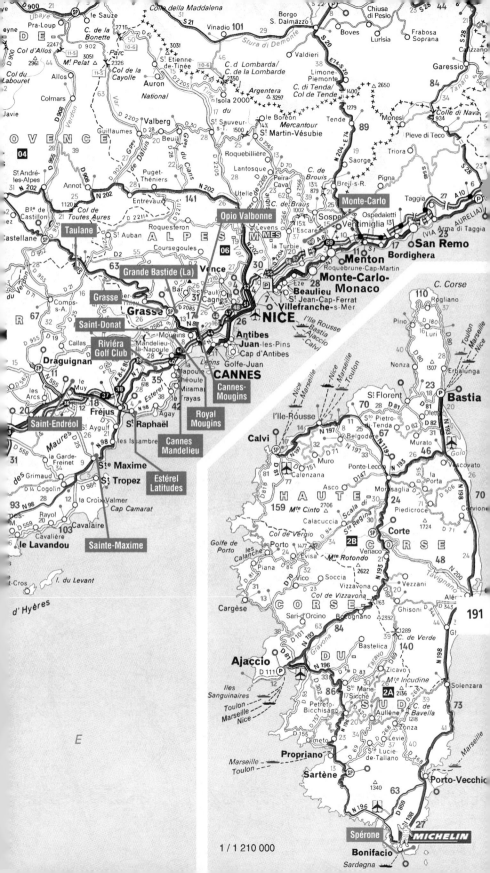

Bayer

Bayer
l'approche
parfaite

Knox out 240 Jardin : 240 g/l diazinon micro-encapsulé - A.M.M n° 8500591 - Emploi autorisé dans les jardins. - Engrais gazon longue durée : Engrais NK (20.20) sous forme de sels d'aminés - N 15% - P2O5 5% - K2O 8% - MgO 3% - A.M.M. n° 8600575 - Emploi autorisé dans les jardins. - Hédonal MP-D Jardin : 300 g/l équivalent acide du mécoprop - 130 g/l d'équivalent acide du 2.4-D - A.M.M n° 9500556 - Classé Xn - Emploi autorisé dans les jardins. 8% - sulfate de fer 50% - 2.4-D 0.7% - dicamba 0.1% - A.M.M n°9420113. - NPK 20-10-10 - Engrais gazon + désherbant : 2.1170 Engrais NPK 20-5-8 + 2% MgO + 32% SO3 + 1% Fe - Azote (N) 20% dont 9% ammoniacal - 7% uréique - 4% organique de synthèse. - Engrais gazon triple action :

Engrais - Traitement - Désherbant

BAYER S.A.
Département Jardin
Division Agro
49-51, Quai De Dion Bouton
92815 PUTEAUX CEDEX

CLASSEMENT DES PARCOURS FRANÇAIS
CLASSIFICATION OF FRENCH COURSES

Ce classement donne priorité à la note attribuée au parcours .
This classification gives priority consideration
to the score awarded to the actual course.

Club-house and facilities
Note du Club-house et annexes

Course score
Note du parcours

Hotel facility score
Note de l'environnement hôtelier

Page

19	8	6	Bordes (Les)	239

Note			Parcours	Page	Note			Parcours	Page
19	8	6	Bordes (Les)	239	**16**	7	5	Montpellier-Massane	306
18	7	6	Chantilly *Vineuil*	255	**16**	7	6	Nîmes-Campagne	309
18	8	6	Kempferhof (Le)	293	**16**	7	5	Paris International	313
18	7	5	Médoc *Les Châteaux*	302	**16**	6	5	Pont Royal	318
18	5	6	National *L'Albatros*	307	**16**	6	4	Rebetz	322
17	7	6	Barbaroux	229	**16**	7	4	Sablé-Solesmes	
17	7	7	Fontainebleau	274				*La Forêt/La Rivière*	328
17	7	6	Grenoble Bresson	285	**16**	6	5	Saint-Jean-de-Monts	333
17	6	5	Limère	298	**16**	8	8	Saint-Nom-la-Bretèche *Rouge*	336
17	6	5	Moliets	304	**16**	7	4	Soufflenheim	343
17	7	5	Pléneuf-Val-André	316	**16**	6	6	Wantzenau (La)	356
17	7	8	Royal Mougins	327	**15**	6	4	Ableiges *Les Etangs*	213
17	7	7	Saint-Germain	332	**15**	6	5	Ailette (L')	214
17	7	7	Seignosse	341	**15**	6	6	Albi	217
17	7	5	Spérone	344	**15**	8	6	Apremont	222
17	6	7	Touquet (Le) *La Mer*	349	**15**	6	5	Baden	227
17	6	4	Villette d'Anthon		**15**	7	7	Bâle-Hagenthal	228
			Les Sangliers	354	**15**	7	8	Baule (La) *Rouge*	230
16	5	4	Aisses (Les) *Rouge/Blanc*	215	**15**	7	6	Bondues *Jaune*	238
16	6	5	Belle-Dune	232	**15**	7	8	Boulie (La) *La Vallée*	240
16	7	6	Bondues *Blanc*	237	**15**	6	4	Bresse (La)	241
16	6	6	Charmeil	256	**15**	7	7	Bretesche (La)	243
16	6	8	Chiberta	259	**15**	7	8	Cannes-Mougins	246
16	7	3	Courson *Vert/Noir*	262	**15**	6	5	Cap d'Agde	247
16	7	8	Disneyland Paris		**15**	7	6	Cély	249
			Never Land + Wonderland	265	**15**	6	7	Chamonix	252
16	6	7	Estérel Latitudes	269	**15**	7	3	Courson *Lilas/Orange*	261
16	7	6	Gouverneur (Le) *Le Breuil*	279	**15**	7	5	Esery	268
16	6	6	Grande Bastide (La)	281	**15**	6	5	Etiolles *Les Cerfs*	270
16	6	4	Grande-Motte (La)		**15**	7	9	Evian	272
			La Forêt/La Rivière	282	**15**	7	5	Feucherolles	273
16	6	6	Hardelot *Les Pins*	287	**15**	7	7	Frégate	278
16	6	6	Hossegor	289	**15**	7	6	Gujan-Mestras	286
16	7	4	Isle Adam (L')	290	**15**	8	7	Joyenval *Retz*	292
16	8	7	Joyenval *Marly*	291	**15**	7	4	Largue (La)	295

195

Et un, et deux, et trois...

la fête continue !

Après avoir remporté le premier appel d'offres de mobilier urbain pour une grande ville de France avec Rennes, Adshel transforme l'essai en obtenant coup sur coup les contrats pour les abris voyageurs de Montpellier et de Lyon, pour le plus grand bénéfice des annonceurs et des collectivités locales.

ADSHEL
Mobilier Urbain

197

CLASSEMENT DE L'ENVIRONNEMENT HOTELIER
CLASSIFICATION OF HOTELS FACILITIES

This classification gives priority consideration
to the score awarded to the hotel facilities.

Ce classement donne priorité à la note attribuée à l'environnement hôtelier

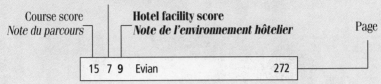

Club-house and facilities
Note du Club-house et annexes

Course score
Note du parcours

Hotel facility score
Note de l'environnement hôtelier

Page

| 15 | 7 | 9 | Evian | 272 |

Note			Parcours	Page	Note			Parcours	Page
15	7	**9**	Evian	272	15	8	**7**	Joyenval *Retz*	292
14	7	**8**	Amirauté (L')	218	14	6	**7**	Lacanau	294
14	7	**8**	Arcangues	224	14	6	**7**	Monte Carlo (Mont Agel)	305
15	7	**8**	Baule (La) *Rouge*	230	13	6	**7**	Opio Valbonne	311
14	6	**8**	Biarritz-le-Phare	235	13	7	**7**	Pessac	315
15	7	**8**	Boulie (La) *La Vallée*	240	15	7	**7**	Roncemay	326
14	7	**8**	Cannes Mandelieu *Old Course*	245	14	7	**7**	Saint-Cloud *Vert*	330
15	7	**8**	Cannes-Mougins	246	17	7	**7**	Saint-Germain	332
16	6	**8**	Chiberta	259	13	7	**7**	Sainte-Maxime	339
16	7	**8**	Disneyland Paris		17	7	**7**	Seignosse	341
			Never Land + Wonderland	265	13	7	**7**	Servanes	342
14	6	**8**	Makila Golf Club	300	17	6	**7**	Touquet (Le) *La Mer*	349
15	7	**8**	New Golf Deauville		15	6	**6**	Albi	217
			Rouge/Blanc	308	13	6	**6**	Anjou-Champigné	220
13	6	**8**	Pau	314	15	8	**6**	Apremont	222
13	7	**8**	Riviéra Golf Club	324	13	6	**6**	Arcachon	223
17	7	**8**	Royal Mougins	327	14	6	**6**	Arras	225
15	7	**8**	Saint Donat	329	17	7	**6**	Barbaroux	229
15	8	**8**	Saint-Nom-la-Bretèche *Bleu*	335	16	7	**6**	Bondues *Blanc*	237
16	8	**8**	Saint-Nom-la-Bretèche *Rouge*	336	15	7	**6**	Bondues *Jaune*	238
13	5	**7**	Aix-les-Bains	216	19	8	**6**	Bordes (Les)	239
15	7	**7**	Bâle-Hagenthal	228	14	7	**6**	Brest Iroise	242
14	7	**7**	Bélesbat	231	14	7	**6**	Brigode	244
15	7	**7**	Breteche (La)	243	15	7	**6**	Cély	249
14	5	**7**	Chambon-sur-Lignon (Le)	251	14	8	**6**	Chailly (Château de)	250
15	6	**7**	Chamonix	252	18	7	**6**	Chantilly *Vineuil*	255
14	7	**7**	Chantaco	254	16	6	**6**	Charmeil	256
13	6	**7**	Dinard	264	14	7	**6**	Cheverny	258
14	6	**7**	Divonne	266	14	6	**6**	Fontcaude	275
16	6	**7**	Estérel Latitudes	269	14	7	**6**	Fontenailles *Blanc*	276
17	7	**7**	Fontainebleau	274	16	7	**6**	Gouverneur (Le) *Le Breuil*	279
15	7	**7**	Frégate	278	14	7	**6**	Gouverneur (Le) *Montaplan*	280
16	8	**7**	Joyenval *Marly*	291	16	6	**6**	Grande Bastide (La)	281

199

Air France vous emmène partout et plus loin au cœur du monde.

Réseau Air France :
267 escales dans 81 pays,
34 millions de passagers par an.

Renseignez-vous dans votre agence Air France ou votre agence de voyages.

AIR FRANCE

GAGNER LE COEUR DU MONDE

201

CANNES
LA VIE EST UN FESTIVAL

FORFAITS "SPECIAL GOLF"
6 NUITS + 5 GREEN-FEES

INFORMATIONS - RESERVATIONS
0 810 06 12 12
+ 33 810 06 12 12

CANNES
CÔTE D'AZUR

Direction Générale du Tourisme et des Congrès (S.EM.E.C.)
Palais des Festivals - La Croisette - BP 272 - 06403 Cannes Cedex - France
Tél. +33 (0)4 93 39 01 01 - Fax. +33 (0)4 93 99 37 06
www.cannes-on-line.com - E.mail : semloisi@palais-festivals-cannes.fr

CAP CREATION - CANNES

SEJOUR DE GOLF RECOMMANDÉ
RECOMMENDED GOLFING STAY

France

Parours	Note	Page	Parours	Note	Page
Barbaroux	17 7 6	229	Médoc *Les Vignes*	15 7 5	303
Belle-Dune	16 6 5	232	Moliets	17 6 5	304
Bondues *Blanc*	16 7 6	237	Montpellier-Massane	16 7 5	306
Bondues *Jaune*	15 7 6	238	National *L'Albatros*	18 5 6	307
Bordes (Les)	19 8 6	239	Nîmes-Campagne	16 7 6	309
Bretesche (La)	15 7 7	243	Pléneuf-Val-André	17 7 5	316
Chiberta	16 6 8	259	Pont Royal	16 6 5	318
Courson *Lilas/Orange*	15 7 3	261	Roncemay	15 7 7	326
Courson *Vert/Noir*	16 7 3	262	Sablé-Solesmes		
Evian	15 7 9	272	*Forêt/La Rivière*	16 7 4	328
Gouverneur (Le) *Le Breuil*	16 7 6	279	Saint Donat	15 7 8	329
Gouverneur (Le) *Montaplan*	14 7 6	280	Saint-Jean-de-Monts	16 6 5	333
Grande Bastide (La)	16 6 6	281	Saint-Nom-la-Bretèche *Bleu*	15 8 8	335
Grande-Motte (La)			Saint-Nom-la-Bretèche *Rouge*	16 8 8	336
Les Flamants Roses	16 6 4	282	Seignosse	17 7 7	341
Gujan-Mestras	15 7 6	286	Spérone	17 7 5	344
Hardelot *Les Pins*	16 6 6	287	Taulane	15 7 4	346
Hossegor	16 6 6	289	Toulouse-Seilh *Rouge*	15 7 6	348
Kempferhof (Le)	18 8 6	293	Touquet (Le) *La Mer*	17 6 7	349
Limère	17 6 5	298	Villette d'Anthon *Les Sangliers*	17 6 4	354
Médoc *Les Châteaux*	18 7 5	302			

VACANCES RECOMMANDEES
RECOMMENDED GOLFING HOLIDAYS

Parours	Note	Page	Parours	Note	Page
Aix-les-Bains	13 5 7	216	Grande Bastide (La)	16 6 6	281
Amirauté (L')	14 7 8	218	Grande-Motte (La)	16 6 4	282
Arcachon	13 6 6	223	Gujan-Mestras	15 7 6	286
Arcangues	14 7 8	224	Hardelot Les Pins	16 6 6	287
Baule (La) *Rouge*	15 7 8	230	Hossegor	16 6 6	289
Biarritz-le-Phare	14 6 8	235	Lacanau	14 6 7	294
Cannes Mandelieu			Makila Golf Club	14 6 8	300
Old Course	14 7 8	245	Moliets	17 6 5	304
Cannes-Mougins	15 7 8	246	Monte Carlo (Mont Agel)	14 6 7	305
Cap d'Agde	15 6 5	247	New Golf Deauville *Rouge/Blanc*	15 7 8	308
Chamonix	15 6 7	252	Pornic	15 6 6	320
Chantaco	14 7 7	254	Riviéra Golf Club	13 7 8	324
Chiberta	16 6 8	259	Royal Mougins	17 7 8	327
Dinard	13 6 7	264	Saint Donat	15 7 8	329
Disneyland Paris	16 7 8	265	Saint-Laurent	14 7 5	334
Estérel Latitudes	16 6 7	269	Sainte-Maxime	13 7 7	339
Frégate	15 7 7	278	Spérone	17 7 5	344

203

Quel Caddy préférez-vous ?

Le geste naturel est d'acheter son matériel chez un vrai spécialiste. Seul GOLF PLUS vous fait rencontrer des professionnels, des conseillers pour qui le golf est une seconde nature. Pas de têtes de gondole chez GOLF PLUS, uniquement des têtes de club.

Choix des marques, dernières nouveautés, essai avant l'achat, contrat prix, échange de la série sous 21 jours, un bon parcours commence toujours chez GOLF PLUS.

G O L F
P L U S

Le Club des Clubs

Catalogue gratuit sur simple demande

Type	Note			Page	Type	Note			Page
copse					Cannes-Mougins	15	7	8	246
Amirauté (L')	14	7	8	218	Chambon-sur-Lignon (Le)	14	5	7	251
Cognac	13	7	5	260	Champ de Bataille	14	6	3	253
Fontenelles (Les)	14	7	4	277	Chantaco	14	7	7	254
New Golf Deauville					Chantilly *Vineuil*	18	7	6	255
Rouge/Blanc	15	7	8	308	Charmeil	16	6	6	256
Omaha Beach					Cheverny	14	7	6	258
La Mer/Le Bocage	14	7	5	310	Chiberta	16	6	8	259
					Domont-Montmorency	13	7	4	267
country					Estérel Latitudes	16	6	7	269
Anjou-Champigné	13	6	6	220	Fontainebleau	17	7	7	274
Baden	15	6	5	227	Grasse	13	7	6	284
Bâle-Hagenthal	15	7	7	228	Gujan-Mestras	15	7	6	286
Besançon	13	7	5	233	Hardelot *Les Pins*	16	6	6	287
Cognac	13	7	5	260	Haut-Poitou	14	6	4	288
Kempferhof (Le)	18	8	6	293	Hossegor	16	6	6	289
Laval-Changé					Isle Adam (L')	16	7	4	290
La Chabossière	14	7	5	296	Joyenval *Marly*	16	8	7	291
Maison Blanche	14	7	5	299	Joyenval *Retz*	15	8	7	292
Nîmes-Campagne	16	7	6	309	Lacanau	14	6	7	294
Pont Royal	16	6	5	318	Largue (La)	15	7	4	295
Porcelaine (La)	14	6	4	319	Limère	17	6	5	298
Saint-Thomas	14	7	5	337	Mazamet-La Barouge	13	5	4	301
Sainte-Baume (La)	13	7	6	338	Médoc *Les Vignes*	15	7	5	303
Servanes	13	7	7	342	Moliets	17	6	5	304
Strasbourg Illkirch					Opio Valbonne	13	6	7	311
Jaune + Rouge	13	7	6	345	Pessac	13	7	7	315
Val Queven	15	6	5	352	Pornic	15	6	6	320
Vaucouleurs (La) *Les Vallons*	15	7	4	353	Raray (Château de) *La Licorne*	14	6	4	321
Villette d'Anthon *Les Sangliers*	17	6	4	354	Reims-Champagne	13	7	6	323
Volcans (Les)	14	6	5	355	Rochefort-Chisan	14	6	4	325
					Roncemay	15	7	7	326
forest					Royal Mougins	17	7	8	327
Ailette (L')	15	6	5	214	Saint-Endréol	15	7	4	331
Aisses (Les) *Rouge/Blanc*	16	5	4	215	Saint-Germain	17	7	7	332
Amnéville	13	6	5	219	Saint-Jean-de-Monts	16	6	5	333
Apremont	15	8	6	222	Saint-Laurent	14	7	5	334
Augerville	13	5	4	226	Seignosse	17	7	7	341
Bâle-Hagenthal	15	7	7	228	Soufflenheim	16	7	4	343
Baule (La) *Rouge*	15	7	8	230	Taulane	15	7	4	346
Besançon	13	7	5	233	Toulouse Palmola	15	7	4	347
Béthemont	14	7	5	234	Touraine	13	7	6	350
Bitche	14	6	5	236	Val Queven	15	6	5	352
Bordes (Les)	19	8	6	239	Villette d'Anthon *Les Sangliers*	17	6	4	354
Boulie (La) *La Vallée*	15	7	8	240					
Bresse (La)	15	6	4	241	**hilly**				
Bretesche (La)	15	7	7	243	Ableiges *Les Etangs*	15	6	4	213
Cannes Mandelieu *Old Course*	14	7	8	245	Arcachon	13	6	6	223

205

Type	Note			Page		Type	Note			Page
Arcangues	14	7	8	224		Esery	15	7	5	268
Augerville	13	5	4	226		Volcans (Les)	14	6	5	355
Barbaroux	17	7	6	229						
Béthemont	14	7	5	234		**open country**				
Bitche	14	6	5	236		Ableiges *Les Etangs*	15	6	4	213
Chambon-sur-Lignon (Le)	14	5	7	251		Bresse (La)	15	6	4	241
Chaumont-en-Vexin	14	6	4	257		Brest Iroise	14	7	6	242
Divonne	14	6	7	266		Casteljaloux	14	6	5	248
Domont-Montmorency	13	7	4	267		Chailly (Château de)	14	8	6	250
Esery	15	7	5	268		Charmeil	16	6	6	256
Evian	15	7	9	272		Courson *Lilas/Orange*	15	7	3	261
Fontcaude	14	6	6	275		Courson *Vert/Noir*	16	7	3	262
Frégate	15	7	7	278		Disneyland Paris Never Land				
Grasse	13	7	6	284		+ Wonderland	16	7	8	265
Lacanau	14	6	7	294		Etiolles *Les Cerfs*	15	6	5	270
Laval-Changé *La Chabossière*	14	7	5	296		Gouverneur (Le) *Le Breuil*	16	7	6	279
Maison Blanche	14	7	5	299		Gouverneur (Le) *Montaplan*	14	7	6	280
Makila Golf Club	14	6	8	300		Grande Bastide (La)	16	6	6	281
Monte Carlo (Mont Agel)	14	6	7	305		Haut-Poitou	14	6	4	288
Paris International	16	7	5	313		Médoc *Les Châteaux*	18	7	5	302
Pont Royal	16	6	5	318		Montpellier-Massane	16	7	5	306
Royal Mougins	17	7	8	327		Sablé-Solesmes				
Saint Donat	15	7	8	329		*La Forêt/La Rivière*	16	7	4	328
Saint-Endréol	15	7	4	331		Savenay	14	5	4	340
Sainte-Maxime	13	7	7	339		Toulouse-Seilh *Rouge*	15	7	6	348
Seignosse	17	7	7	341		Wantzenau (La)	16	6	6	356
Spérone	17	7	5	344		Aix-les-Bains	13	5	7	216
inland						**parkland**				
Chantilly *Vineuil*	18	7	6	255		Ailette (L')	15	6	5	214
						Aisses (Les) *Rouge/Blanc*	16	5	4	215
links						Albi	15	6	6	217
Albi	15	6	6	217		Annonay-Gourdan	13	6	5	221
Barbaroux	17	7	6	229		Apremont	15	8	6	222
Chiberta	16	6	8	259		Arras	14	6	6	225
Dieppe-Pourville	14	6	5	263		Bélesbat	14	7	7	231
Dinard	13	6	7	264		Bondues *Blanc*	16	7	6	237
Granville *Les Dunes*	14	4	4	283		Bondues *Jaune*	15	7	6	238
National *L'Albatros*	18	5	6	307		Bretesche (La)	15	7	7	243
Médoc *Les Châteaux*	18	7	5	302		Brigode	14	7	6	244
Moliets	17	6	5	304		Cannes-Mougins	15	7	8	246
Pornic	15	6	6	320		Cély	15	7	6	249
Saint-Jean-de-Monts	16	6	5	333		Chamonix	15	6	7	252
Touquet (Le) *La Mer*	17	6	7	349		Chantaco	14	7	7	254
Vaucouleurs (La) Les Vallons	15	7	4	353		Chaumont-en-Vexin	14	6	4	257
Wimereux	14	4	5	357		Divonne	14	6	7	266
						Evian	15	7	9	272
mountain						Feucherolles	15	7	5	273
Chamonix	15	6	7	252		Fontenailles *Blanc*	14	7	6	276
Grenoble Bresson	17	7	6	285		Hardelot *Les Pins*	16	6	6	287

207

Mon Combi radio-réveil,
il fait tout sauf le café.

TV VIDEO
► **COMBI**

Le Philips TV Combi radio-réveil sait tout faire. La télé est non
seulement un magnétoscope mais aussi un radio réveil. Avec lui les matins
ne se ressemblent pas, c'est sans doute pour ça qu'il est unique. Petit, il a
su malgré tout prendre une grande place dans ma vie. www.philips.com

PHILIPS

Faisons toujours mieux.

SHOWVIEW   Le combi Philips radio réveil est équipé du système ShowView®
la façon la plus simple de programmer votre magnétoscope.
www.showview.com

Type	Note			Page	Type	Note			Page
Joyenval *Retz*	15	8	7	292	Etretat	14	6	5	271
Joyenval *Marly*	16	8	7	291	Frégate	15	7	7	278
Kempferhof (Le)	18	8	6	293	Grande-Motte (La)				
Largue (La)	15	7	4	295	*Les Flamants Roses*	16	6	4	282
Le Prieuré *Ouest*	14	7	5	297	Omaha Beach				
Limère	17	6	5	298	*La Mer/Le Bocage*	14	7	5	310
Makila Golf Club	14	6	8	300	Pléneuf-Val-André	17	7	5	316
Mazamet-La Barouge	13	5	4	301	Ploemeur Océan	15	7	6	317
Monte Carlo (Mont Agel)	14	6	7	305	Spérone	17	7	5	344
New Golf Deauville									
Rouge/Blanc	15	7	8	308	**open country**				
Nîmes-Campagne	16	7	6	309	Baule (La) *Rouge*	15	7	8	230
Opio Valbonne	13	6	7	311	Bordes (Les)	19	8	6	239
Ozoir-la-Ferrière					Cap d'Agde	15	6	5	247
Château/Monthéty	13	7	5	312	Cheverny	14	7	6	258
Paris International	16	7	5	313	Etretat	14	6	5	271
Pau	13	6	8	314	Feucherolles	15	7	5	273
Rebetz	16	6	4	322	Isle Adam (L')	16	7	4	290
Reims-Champagne	13	7	6	323	Médoc *Les Vignes*	15	7	5	303
Riviéra Golf Club	13	7	8	324	Raray (Château de)				
Saint-Cloud *Vert*	14	7	7	330	La Licorne	14	6	4	321
Saint Donat	15	7	8	329	Rebetz	16	6	4	322
Saint-Nom-la-Bretèche *Bleu*	15	8	8	335	Roncemay	15	7	7	326
Saint-Nom-la-Bretèche *Rouge*	16	8	8	336	Soufflenheim	16	7	4	343
Savenay	14	5	4	340					
Touraine	13	7	6	350	**residential**				
Val de Sorne	14	7	5	351	Bondues *Blanc*	16	7	6	237
					Bondues *Jaune*	15	7	6	238
residential					Estérel Latitudes	16	6	7	269
Biarritz-le-Phare	14	6	8	235	Grande-Motte (La)				
Fontcaude	14	6	6	275	*Les Flamants Roses*	16	6	4	282
					Montpellier-Massane	16	7	5	306
seaside course					Pessac	13	7	7	315
Arcachon	13	6	6	223	Riviéra Golf Club	13	7	8	324
Baden	15	6	5	227	Saint-Nom-la-Bretèche *Bleu*	15	8	8	335
Belle-Dune	16	6	5	232	Saint-Nom-la-Bretèche *Rouge*	16	8	8	336
Cannes Mandelieu *Old Course*	14	7	8	245	Sainte-Maxime	13	7	7	339
Cap d'Agde	15	6	5	247	Toulouse Palmola	15	7	4	347
Dieppe-Pourville	14	6	5	263	Toulouse-Seilh *Rouge*	15	7	6	348
Dinard	13	6	7	264	Wantzenau (La)	16	6	6	356

209

Comme lui, lisez GOLF SENIOR

Abonnez-vous !

1 an = 140 FF ou 21,34 euros

2 ans = 200 FF ou 30,50 euros

et il vous sera adressé
un cadeau de bienvenue par retour.

BULLETIN D'ABONNEMENT (à photocopier)

à compléter et à envoyer avec votre règlement à :
E.G.O - BP 5 - 78124 MAREIL-SUR-MAULDRE (FRANCE)

Nom :..Prénom :...

Adresse :...

Code postal :.................Ville:.............................Pays:...................

RELIEF DES PARCOURS
GEOGRAPHICAL RELIEF

211

Votre handicap baisse
quand votre tranquillité augmente.

**Gestion et distribution des matériels publi-promotionnels
et des documents techniques et administratifs. Gestion d'économat.**

- Un engagement de tous les instants
- Une grande implication dans l'action
- Une disponibilité et une réactivité immédiate
- Le respect de la culture client

Depuis de nombreuses années, EURODISPACH assure la logistique
des produits de communication d'AUTOMOBILE PEUGEOT

Siège social : 8, avenue Albert-Einstein
ZI du Coudray BP8 93152 Le Blanc-Mesnil Cedex
Tél : 01 48 14 73 73 - Fax : 01 48 14 73 13
http//www.eurodispatch.fr

Service commercial :
Tél : 01 48 14 73 15 - Fax : 01 48 14 72 02

EURODISPATCH
Le sens du plus

ABLEIGES LES ETANGS

En plaine et dans les vallons du Vexin, l'architecture du 18 trous des «Etangs» présente des styles différents, sans rupture trop marquée. Le haut du domaine s'apparente aux links, avec de jolis mouvements de terrain, alors que la partie basse est plus «américaine». La plupart des drives, tout comme les approches, exigent une bonne technique et un placement attentif, en raison des nombreux obstacles très en jeu, qu'il s'agisse des bunkers, du rough ou de l'eau. L'architecte Jeremy Pern a généreusement modelé et défendu les greens (deux ont été refaits), où les positions de drapeau peuvent changer radicalement le jeu. Les reliefs du terrain rendent assez physique ce parcours (mais il y a 45 voiturettes), à jouer des départs normaux au dessus de 10 de handicap. C'est un très bon test, mais l'entretien reste à surveiller, certains trous pouvant être très humides.

On the plain and through the vales of Vexin, the architecture of the 18 hole «Etangs» course features a number of different styles stitched together in almost seamless fashion. The upper section is links territory, with attractive sandhills and dips, while the lower section is more American in its layout. Most tee-shots and approach-shots demand good technique and careful placing of the ball owing to the numerous hazards in play, ranging from unforgiving rough to water. Architect Jeremy Pern has generously contoured and defended the greens (two of them have been remodeled), where the pin-positions can radically change the course. Ableiges can be a tiring course on foot (45 golf cars are available), and the back-tees should be for single-figure handicappers only. All in all, a great test of golf, but as some of the holes tend to be very wet, the course requires extra careful upkeep.

Golf Club d'Ableiges — 1989

Chaussée Jules César
F - 95450 ABLEIGES

Office	Secrétariat	(33) 01 30 27 97 00
Pro shop	Pro-shop	(33) 01 34 27 97 00
Fax	Fax	(33) 01 30 27 97 10
Situation	Situation	

Pontoise (pop. 27 150), 9 km SE
Paris (pop. 2 175 200), 40 km SE

Annual closure	Fermeture annuelle	no
Weekly closure	Fermeture hebdomadaire	no

Fees main season
Tarifs haute saison 18 holes

	Week days Semaine	We/Bank holidays We/Férié
Individual Individuel	150 F	290 F
Couple Couple	300 F	580 F

Tuesday (Mardi): GF + lunch, 150 F

Caddy	Caddy	no
Electric Trolley	Chariot électrique	70 F/full day
Buggy	Voiturette	90 F
Clubs	Clubs	50 F/full day

Credit cards Cartes de crédit CB

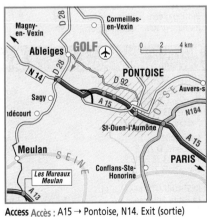

Access Accès : A15 → Pontoise, N14. Exit (sortie)
Ableiges, → Golf
Map 3 on page 168 Carte 3 Page 168

GOLF COURSE PARCOURS — 15/20

Site	Site	
Maintenance	Entretien	
Architect	Architecte	Jeremy Pern Jean Garaïalde
Type	Type	open country, hilly
Relief	Relief	
Water in play	Eau en jeu	
Exp. to wind	Exposé au vent	
Trees in play	Arbres en jeu	

Scorecard Carte de score	Chp. Chp.	Mens Mess.	Ladies Da.
Length Long.	6261	5634	5274
Par	72	72	72

Advised golfing ability	0 12 24 36
Niveau de jeu recommandé	
Hcp required Handicap exigé	35, 30 We

CLUB HOUSE & AMENITIES CLUB HOUSE ET ANNEXES — 6/10

Pro shop	Pro-shop	
Driving range	Practice	
Sheltered	couvert	15 mats
On grass	sur herbe	no, 10 mats open air
Putting-green	putting-green	yes
Pitching-green	pitching green	yes

HOTEL FACILITIES ENVIRONNEMENT HOTELIER — 4/10

HOTELS HÔTELS
Astrée — Pontoise
55 rooms, D 540 F — 10 km
Tel (33) 01 34 24 94 94,
Fax (33) 01 34 24 95 15

Campanile — Pontoise
80 rooms, D 295 F — 10 km
Tel (33) 01 30 38 55 44,
Fax (33) 01 30 30 48 87

RESTAURANTS RESTAURANT
Gérard Cagna — Cormeilles-en-Vexin
Tel (33) 01 34 66 61 56 — 4 km

Le Chiquito — La Bonneville
Tel (33) 01 30 36 40 23 — 5 km

213

AILETTE (L')

15 6 5

L'Ailette maintient son statut de très bon golf public. Bien que vallonné, il n'est pas difficile à jouer à pied, mais quelques greens très surélevés peuvent déconcerter au premier abord, accentuant le côté technique et tactique du parcours. Ses difficultés augmentent à mesure que l'on joue les départs reculés, mais il reste à la portée des joueurs moyens, toujours nombreux ici. On remarquera l'alternance de trous assez reposants et de trous plus difficiles, ce qui donne un bon rythme au jeu, et des possibilités de reprendre des forces quand il le faut. Les greens sont vastes et francs, et bien défendus par des bunkers dessinés avec soin. Le parcours propose des trous dans des bois généralement assez éloignés, et les obstacles d'eau sont dangereux sans être trop préoccupants. Le site du Chemin des Dames, témoin de la première Guerre Mondiale, n'est plus le théâtre que de pacifiques batailles...

Ailette has retained its status as an excellent public course. Although far from flat, the course is not too tiring to walk around. A number of elevated greens are a little disconcerting at first and emphasise the course's technical and tactical sides. The difficulties of playing here increase as you tee-off further back, but Ailette is playable by mid-to-high handicappers, of whom there are many here. This is a nicely balanced course, with pleasant alternation between tough and easier holes allowing players breathing space and the chance to recuperate. The greens are huge, forthright and well-defended by well-designed bunkers. Some holes run through woodland, although the trees are usually not too close, and the water hazards are dangerous but never over-bearing. The site of Chemin des Dames, a testimony to World War I, is now simply the theatre of more peaceful conflict with a little white ball.

Golf de l'Ailette
F - 02860 CERNY-EN-LAONNOIS
1988

Office	Secrétariat	(33) 03 23 24 83 99
Pro shop	Pro-shop	(33) 03 23 24 81 24
Fax	Fax	(33) 03 23 24 84 66
Situation	Situation	

Laon (pop. 26 490), 17 km

Annual closure	Fermeture annuelle	no
Weekly closure	Fermeture hebdomadaire	

Club-house: tuesday / mardi (01/09 → 31/03)

Fees main season
Tarifs haute saison full day

	Week days Semaine	We/Bank holidays We/Férié
Individual Individuel	185 F	240 F
Couple Couple	370 F	480 F

Caddy	Caddy	no
Electric Trolley	Chariot électrique	no
Buggy	Voiturette	200 F/18 holes
Clubs	Clubs	30 F/full day

Credit cards Cartes de crédit
VISA - CB - Eurocard - MasterCard

Access Accès : A 26, Exit (Sortie) Laon-Chambry.
D 967 → Fismes
Map 1 on page 165 Carte 1 Page 165

GOLF COURSE
PARCOURS
15/20

Site	Site	
Maintenance	Entretien	
Architect	Architecte	Michel Gayon
Type	Type	forest, parkland
Relief	Relief	
Water in play	Eau en jeu	
Exp. to wind	Exposé au vent	
Trees in play	Arbres en jeu	

Scorecard Carte de score	Chp. Chp.	Mens Mess.	Ladies Da.
Length Long.	6127	5759	5180
Par	72	72	72

Advised golfing ability
Niveau de jeu recommandé   0 12 24 36

Hcp required Handicap exigé   35

CLUB HOUSE & AMENITIES
CLUB HOUSE ET ANNEXES
6/10

Pro shop	Pro-shop	
Driving range	Practice	
Sheltered	couvert	5 mats
On grass	sur herbe	yes
Putting-green	putting-green	yes
Pitching-green	pitching green	yes

HOTEL FACILITIES
ENVIRONNEMENT HOTELIER
5/10

HOTELS HÔTELS
Mercure Holigolf	Golf
58 rooms, D 570 FF	
Tel (33) 03 23 24 84 85	
Fax (33) 03 23 24 81 20	
Campanile	Laon
47 rooms, D 295 F	17 km
Tel (33) 03 23 23 15 05	
Fax (33) 03 23 23 04 25	

RESTAURANTS RESTAURANT
La Petite Auberge	Laon
Tel (33) 03 23 23 02 38	17 km
Bannière de France	Laon
Tel (33) 03 23 23 21 44	17 km

214

AISSES (LES) ROUGE/BLANC

16 5 4

Cet ensemble est composé de trois neuf trous combinables, le Rouge, le Blanc et le Bleu, dans un domaine de 250 hectares. Sur les deux premiers parcours, d'immenses bunkers sont à la fois des obstacles (mais ils ne sont pas trop profonds) et des éléments d'architecture pour mieux préciser les trous dans l'espace. Le paysage de Sologne est calme et séduisant, mais le relief est absent, et les architectes n'ont pas voulu modeler beaucoup le terrain. Sur le dernier 9 trous, les obstacles d'eau prennent le relais des bunkers. La végétation est assez naturelle, avec les bouleaux, hêtres, sapins et chênes de la région. Un ensemble plaisant, mais inachevé (le Club-House est toujours insuffisant), qui ne mérite pas à lui seul un long détour, mais constitue un élément intéressant dans le remarquable équipement golfique de la région (avec Les Bordes et Limère).

This is a complex of three combinable 9-hole courses - Red, White and Blue - over an estate of some 250 hectares. The first two are marked by huge bunkers (although not too deep) which are at once the main hazards and the principal features of this lay-out. The Sologne landscape is calm and appealing, but the area is flat and the architects visibly avoided shaping the course. On the Blue course, bunkers are largely replaced by water. Vegetation is mostly natural, with birch, beech, pine and oak trees, typical of this area. A pleasant but incomplete venue (the club-house is still inadequate) which is hardly worth a long journey on its own, but which nicely completes some remarkable golfing facilities in this region (with Les Bordes and Limère).

Golf des Aisses   1992

Domaine des Aisses
F - 45240 LA FERTÉ-SAINT-AUBIN

Office	- Secrétariat	(33) 02 38 64 80 87
Pro shop	Pro-shop	(33) 02 38 64 80 87
Fax	Fax	(33) 02 38 64 80 85
Situation	Situation	

Orléans (pop. 105 110), 24 km

Annual closure	Fermeture annuelle	
		yes 1/1 → 10/1
Weekly closure	Fermeture hebdomadaire	
	wednesday (mercredi) / 1/11→28/2	

Fees main season
Tarifs haute saison full day

	Week days Semaine	We/Bank holidays We/Férié
Individual Individuel	200 F	280 F
Couple Couple	400 F	510 F
Caddy Caddy		no
Electric Trolley Chariot électrique		no
Buggy Voiturette		180 F/18 holes
Clubs Clubs		50 F/full day

Credit cards Cartes de crédit
VISA - CB - Eurocard - MasterCard - AMEX

Access Accès : A71 Orléans → Bourges, Exit (Sortie) Orléans La Source. N20 → La Ferté-St-Aubin, 1 km. D17 → Golf, on the left.
Map 3 on page 168 Carte 3 Page 168

GOLF COURSE
PARCOURS   **16**/20

Site	Site	
Maintenance	Entretien	
Architect	Architecte	Olivier Brizon Groupe Taiyo
Type	Type	forest, parkland
Relief	Relief	
Water in play	Eau en jeu	
Exp. to wind	Exposé au vent	
Trees in play	Arbres en jeu	

Scorecard	Chp.	Mens	Ladies
Carte de score	Chp.	Mess.	Da.
Length Long.	6438	6125	5202
Par	72	72	72

Advised golfing ability		0	12	24	36
Niveau de jeu recommandé					
Hcp required	Handicap exigé	no			

CLUB HOUSE & AMENITIES
CLUB HOUSE ET ANNEXES   **5**/10

Pro shop	Pro-shop	
Driving range	Practice	
Sheltered	couvert	no
On grass	sur herbe	yes
Putting-green	putting-green	yes
Pitching-green	pitching green	yes

215

HOTEL FACILITIES
ENVIRONNEMENT HOTELIER   **4**/10

HOTELS HÔTELS
Château des Muids   La Ferté-Saint-Aubin
23 rooms, D 630 F   3 km
Tel (33) 02 38 64 65 14
Fax (33) 02 38 76 50 08

L'Orée des Chênes   La Ferté-Saint-Aubin
23 rooms, D 600 F   3 km
Tel (33) 02 38 64 84 00
Fax (33) 02 38 64 84 20

RESTAURANTS RESTAURANT
Ferme de la Lande   La Ferté-Saint-Aubin
Tel (33) 02 38 76 64 37   3 km

Les Brémailles   La Ferté-Saint-Aubin
Tel (33) 02 38 76 56 60   3 km

Ce parcours a été créé en 1936 pour répondre aux demandes de la clientèle étrangère de cette jolie ville d'eaux. Le terrain ne manque pas de charme, mais le rythme des trous est saccadé, donnant une sensation d'assemblage désordonné : du 6 au 12, on trouve cinq par 3 ! Avec des par 4 en général très courts et trois des cinq par 5 prenables en deux, un bon score est à la portée de tous les joueurs, par rapport à leur niveau bien sûr. S'ils évitent quelques hors-limites dangereux, les joueurs du meilleur niveau seront vite frustrés par le manque de difficultés et de longueur de ce parcours, mais ils prendront du plaisir à jouer en famille ou avec des amis de plus faible niveau. Bien boisé, mais assez humide, surtout au retour, Aix-les-Bains est l'occasion d'une agréable promenade. On souhaiterait un remodelage de ce tracé un peu désuet, notamment aux alentours des petits greens...

This course was opened in 1936 to cater to the numerous foreign visitors heading to this pretty spa town. It is a charming site, sure enough, but the general layout lacks any sort of pattern, rather as if the holes were just thrown together. For example, there are five par 3s between the 6th and 12th holes. With the par 4s generally pretty short and three of the five par 5s reachable in two, a good score is within the capability of most players, depending of course on their level of proficiency. If they avoid the few dangerous out-of-bounds, the better players will quickly feel a little frustrated at the lack of difficulty and yardage, but should have fun playing with the family or with friends of lesser ability. There are a lot of trees and the course is damp, especially on the back nine, but Aix-les-Bains is the opportunity to enjoy a pleasant round of golf, even though the slightly outdated layout could do with a little restyling, especially around the small greens.

Golf Club d'Aix-les-Bains 1937

Avenue du Golf
F - 73100 AIX-LES-BAINS

Office	Secrétariat	(33) 04 79 61 23 35
Pro shop	Pro-shop	(33) 04 79 61 31 56
Fax	Fax	(33) 04 79 34 06 01
Situation	Situation	

Aix-les-Bains (pop. 24 680), 1 km

Annual closure	Fermeture annuelle	no
Weekly closure	Fermeture hebdomadaire	no

Fees main season
Tarifs haute saison full day

	Week days Semaine	We/Bank holidays We/Férié
Individual Individuel	280 F	280 F
Couple Couple	560 F	560 F
Caddy	Caddy	no
Electric Trolley	Chariot électrique	70 F/18 holes
Buggy	Voiturette	200 F/18 holes
Clubs	Clubs	50 F/full day

Credit cards Cartes de crédit
VISA - CB - Eurocard - MasterCard - AMEX - DC

AIX-LES-BAINS

Lac du Bourget
Rumilly/Annecy
Yenne
GOLF
N 201
Drumettaz
A 43-E 70
Aix-les-Bains
N 504
Le-Bourget ✈
du-Lac
Chambéry N.
D 991
N 201
Chambéry
0 2 4 km

Access Accès : Grenoble, A43, Exit (Sortie) Aix Sud,
→ Aix-les-Bains, → Golf
Map 11 on page 185 Carte 11 Page 185

GOLF COURSE
PARCOURS 13/20

Site	Site	▬▬▬
Maintenance	Entretien	▬▬▬
Architect	Architecte	
Type	Type	parkland
Relief	Relief	▬▬
Water in play	Eau en jeu	▬
Exp. to wind	Exposé au vent	▬
Trees in play	Arbres en jeu	▬▬

Scorecard	Chp.	Mens	Ladies
Carte de score	Chp.	Mess.	Da.
Length Long.	5627	5404	4966
Par	71	71	71

Advised golfing ability	0	12	24	36
Niveau de jeu recommandé		▬▬▬		
Hcp required	Handicap exigé	35		

CLUB HOUSE & AMENITIES
CLUB HOUSE ET ANNEXES 5/10

Pro shop	Pro-shop	▬▬▬
Driving range	Practice	▬▬
Sheltered	couvert	5 mats
On grass	sur herbe	no, 17 mats open air
Putting-green	putting-green	yes
Pitching-green	pitching green	yes

HOTEL FACILITIES
ENVIRONNEMENT HOTELIER 7/10

HOTELS HÔTELS
Campanile — on site
60 rooms, D 270 F
Tel (33) 04 79 61 30 66, Fax (33) 04 79 61 30 66

Ariana — Aix-les-Bains
60 rooms, D 720 F — 1 km
Tel (33) 04 79 61 79 79, Fax (33) 04 79 61 79 00

Le Manoir — Aix-les-Bains
73 rooms, D 695 F — 1 km
Tel (33) 04 79 61 44 00, Fax (33) 04 79 35 67 67

RESTAURANTS RESTAURANT
Le Manoir — Aix-les-Bains
Tel (33) 04 79 61 44 00

Park Hôtel — Aix-les-Bains
Tél(33) 04 79 34 19 19

216

Dans un très joli environnement à proximité du Tarn, ce parcours a été modelé dans un paysage de campagne par Jeremy Pern, auteur de nombreux parcours en France. On y retrouve sa mise en jeu traditionnelle de nombreux bunkers et d'obstacles d'eau, ici en jeu sur une demi-douzaine de trous, mais sans trop pénaliser les joueurs peu expérimentés, et de nombreuses références au style de links que l'architecte a souvent mis en évidence. Grâce à un bon équilibre entre les trous techniques et les trous plus faciles, les joueurs peuvent évoluer dans un bon rythme de jeu, sans pression excessive. Lors de notre dernière visite, l'entretien restait toujours honnête, meilleur sur les trous en bordure du Tarn parfois assez humides, et les roughs laissés au naturel, avec le risque d'y perdre des balles. Cette difficulté risque de rebuter inutilement certains joueurs bien que les fairways soient assez larges et le tracé très agréable.

Architect Jeremy Pern has designed many courses in France, including this one located in beautiful surroundings near the River Tarn. His traditional use of countless bunkers and water hazards is very much to the fore, coming into play on half a dozen holes but without penalising the less experienced players. The more difficult holes alternate agreeably with the easier ones to give a good playing pattern without too much pressure. During our visit, the greenkeeping and general upkeep were much better alongside the river. The rough, too, was sufficiently overgrown for a number of balls to end up lost. The fairways are larger than before, but this is still a point that needs watching, as it mars for some players what is obviously a very pleasant golf course.

Golf Club d'Albi — 1989

Château de Lasbordes
F - 81000 ALBI

Office	Secrétariat	(33) 05 63 54 98 07
Pro shop	Pro-shop	(33) 05 63 54 98 07
Fax	Fax	(33) 05 63 47 21 55
Situation	Situation	

Albi (pop. 46 580), 4 km

Annual closure	Fermeture annuelle	no
Weekly closure	Fermeture hebdomadaire	no

Fees main season
Tarifs haute saison full day

	Week days Semaine	We/Bank holidays We/Férié
Individual Individuel	170 F	230 F
Couple Couple	340 F	460 F

Seniors: wednesday (mardi) 100 F.

Caddy	Caddy	no
Electric Trolley	Chariot électrique	no
Buggy	Voiturette	170 F/18 holes
Clubs	Clubs	50 F/full day

Credit cards Cartes de crédit
VISA - CB - Eurocard - MasterCard

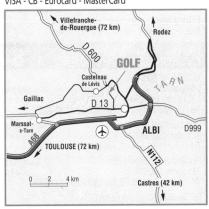

Access Accès : Toulouse, A 68 et N 88 →Albi.
Albi → Villefranche-de-Rouergue, → Golf
Map 13 on page 188 Carte 13 Page 188

GOLF COURSE / PARCOURS — 15/20

Site	Site	
Maintenance	Entretien	
Architect	Architecte	Jeremy Pern Jean Garaïalde
Type	Type	parkland, links
Relief	Relief	
Water in play	Eau en jeu	
Exp. to wind	Exposé au vent	
Trees in play	Arbres en jeu	

Scorecard Carte de score	Chp. Chp.	Mens Mess.	Ladies Da.
Length Long.	6199	5759	5226
Par	72	72	72

Advised golfing ability Niveau de jeu recommandé	0	12	24	36
Hcp required Handicap exigé	35			

CLUB HOUSE & AMENITIES / CLUB HOUSE ET ANNEXES — 6/10

Pro shop	Pro-shop	
Driving range	Practice	
Sheltered	couvert	8 mats
On grass	sur herbe	no, 18 mats open air
Putting-green	putting-green	yes
Pitching-green	pitching green	no

217

HOTEL FACILITIES / ENVIRONNEMENT HOTELIER — 6/10

HOTELS HÔTELS

La Réserve — Fonvialane
24 rooms, D 1 300 F — 3 km
Tel (33) 05 63 60 80 80, Fax (33) 05 63 47 63 60

Host. Saint-Antoine — Albi
44 rooms, D 850 F — 4 km
Tel (33) 05 63 54 04 04, Fax (33) 05 63 47 10 47

Host. du Vigan — Albi
40 rooms, D 350 F — 4 km
Tel (33) 05 63 54 01 23, Fax (33) 05 63 47 05 42

RESTAURANTS RESTAURANT

Le Grand Ecuyer — Cordes
Tel (33) 05 63 53 79 50 — 20 km

Moulin de la Mothe — Albi
Tel (33) 05 63 60 38 15 — 4 km

Dominant un paysage normand de bocage et de marais, le Club house luxueux paraît annoncer un parcours exceptionnel. Ce n'est pas vraiment le cas. Avec ses larges boulevards, des obstacles de fairway peu dangereux, des greens sans grande personnalité et très peu défendus, la stratégie de jeu est évidente, et la motivation s'estompe si on joue souvent ici. Les obstacles d'eau constituent les seules véritables difficultés, les bunkers étant peu profonds et éloignés des limites des greens. Si les joueurs expérimentés regretteront le manque de «souffle» du parcours, au demeurant bien entretenu, les joueurs de tous niveaux pourront y évoluer facilement, ce qui est bien la fonction de ce club «de vacances» et de week-end. Les installations d'entraînement sont de bonne qualité, et sept trous peuvent être éclairés (trois du 18 trous et quatre du parcours d'initiation).

Overlooking a Norman landscape of farmsteads and marshland, the luxurious club-house seems to suggest an exceptional course. This is not really so. With wide open fairways, a few benign fairway hazards, and greens with little character and even fewer bunkers to defend them, the course has no hidden dangers and can border on the monotonous if played often. The only real difficulties are the water hazards, as the bunkers are shallow and generally well away from the greens. While the more experienced player may regret the course's lack of gusto, (despite excellent upkeep, it should be said), players of all levels will find this an easy way to improve their game, which is exactly what this «holiday» and week-end course sets out to do. Practice facilities are good and seven holes can be lit up (three from the 18 hole course and four from the pitch 'n putt).

Golf Club de l'Amirauté — 1993
Tourgéville
F - 14800 DEAUVILLE

Office	Secrétariat	(33) 02 31 88 38 00
Pro shop	Pro-shop	(33) 02 31 88 38 00
Fax	Fax	(33) 02 31 88 32 00
Situation	Situation	

Deauville (pop. 4 260), 7 km

Annual closure	Fermeture annuelle	no
Weekly closure	Fermeture hebdomadaire	no

Fees main season
Tarifs haute saison full day

	Week days Semaine	We/Bank holidays We/Férié
Individual Individuel	250 F	350 F
Couple Couple	500 F	700 F
Caddy Caddy		on request
Electric Trolley Chariot électrique		150 F/18 holes
Buggy Voiturette		220 F/18 holes
Clubs Clubs		100 F/full day

Credit cards Cartes de crédit
VISA - CB - Eurocard - MasterCard

218

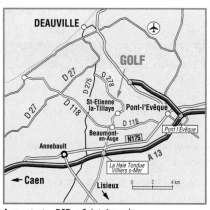

Access Accès : D27 → Saint-Arnoult,
D 275 → Beaumont-en-Auge, → Golf
Map 2 on page 167 Carte 2 Page 167

GOLF COURSE / PARCOURS — 14/20

Site	Site	▰▰▰▱▱
Maintenance	Entretien	▰▰▰▱▱
Architect	Architecte	Bill Baker
Type	Type	copse, country
Relief	Relief	▰▱▱▱▱
Water in play	Eau en jeu	▰▰▰▱▱
Exp. to wind	Exposé au vent	▰▱▱▱▱
Trees in play	Arbres en jeu	▰▱▱▱▱

Scorecard Carte de score	Chp. Chp.	Mens Mess.	Ladies Da.
Length Long.	6017	5806	5195
Par	73	73	73

Advised golfing ability — 0 12 24 36
Niveau de jeu recommandé
Hcp required Handicap exigé — no

CLUB HOUSE & AMENITIES / CLUB HOUSE ET ANNEXES — 7/10

Pro shop	Pro-shop	▰▰▰▱▱
Driving range	Practice	▰▰▰▱▱
Sheltered	couvert	42 mats
On grass	sur herbe	no, 10 mats open air
Putting-green	putting-green	yes
Pitching-green	pitching green	yes

HOTEL FACILITIES / ENVIRONNEMENT HOTELIER — 8/10

HOTELS HÔTELS
L'Amirauté — Touques
232 rooms, D 1 290 F — 6 km
Tel (33) 02 31 81 82 83, Fax (33) 02 31 81 82 93

Hôtel du Golf — Saint-Arnoult
180 rooms, D 1800 F — 6 km
Tel (33) 02 31 14 24 00, Fax (33) 02 31 14 24 01

Hostellerie de Tourgéville — Tourgéville
25 rooms, D 850 F — 4 km
Tel (33) 02 31 14 48 68, Fax (33) 02 31 14 48 69

RESTAURANTS RESTAURANT
Le Ciro's — Deauville
Tel (33) 02 31 14 31 31 — 7 km

Le Central — Trouville
Tel (33) 01 31 88 80 84 — 7 km

AMNÉVILLE

13	6	5

Situé au coeur du centre touristique thermal d'Amnéville, ce parcours est accidenté et physique, mais bénéficie d'un environnement boisé très tranquille (chênes, hêtres, bouleaux) qui constitue l'essentiel des difficultés. Dans son dessin, l'architecte Jean-Manuel Rossi a conservé et suivi le caractère naturel du terrain. En revanche, il a beaucoup travaillé les greens, généralement de bonne taille. Les obstacles sont bien visibles, mais certains trous comme le 2, le 5, le 11 et le 17 sont délicats à négocier, et obligent à savoir jouer tous les coups. Amusant à jouer en famille, notamment en match-play, Amnéville est difficile à scorer pour tous les niveaux de jeu, mais plus encore pour les néophytes. En revanche, les situations de jeu sont assez variées pour que l'on revienne volontiers jouer ici. Dans une région pauvre en parcours de qualité, celui-ci s'impose comme le plus intéressant.

Located at the heart of the spa and tourist town of Amnéville, this is a hilly and physically testing course, laid out in a peaceful, woodland setting. Indeed, the oak, beech and birch trees are the main hazards on the course. In this lay-out, architect Jean-Manuel Rossi has preserved and espoused the natural features of the terrain. By contrast, he has done a lot of switchback work on the greens, which are generally quite large. The hazards are visible, but a number of holes, like the 2nd, 5th, 11th and 17th, are tricky little numbers and require the full range of shots. Fun to play with the family, particulary in match-play, Amnéville is a tough course for anyone to card low scores, especially beginners. Yet there so many different playing situations that can arise here that you always want to come back for more. In a region where golf courses are few and far between, this has to be the best.

Amnéville Cité Thermale — 1993
Boulevard de l'Europe
F - 57360 AMNEVILLE

Office	Secrétariat	(33) 03 87 71 30 13
Pro shop	Pro-shop	(33) 03 87 71 30 13
Fax	Fax	(33) 03 87 70 26 96
Situation	Situation	

Metz pop. 119 590, 15 km, Thionville pop. 39 712, 15 km

Annual closure	Fermeture annuelle	no
Weekly closure	Fermeture hebdomadaire	no

Fees main season
Tarifs haute saison full day

	Week days Semaine	We/Bank holidays We/Férié
Individual Individuel	160 F	220 F
Couple Couple	320 F	440 F

Wednesday & Friday (Merc. et Vend.),
GF + lunch, 180 F

Caddy	Caddy	no
Electric Trolley	Chariot électrique	60 F/18 holes
Buggy	Voiturette	150 F/18 holes
Clubs	Clubs	40 F/full day

Credit cards Cartes de crédit
VISA - CB - Eurocard - MasterCard

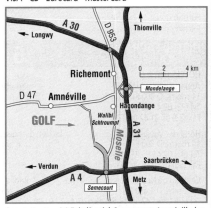

Access Accès : A4 Exit (Sortie) Semecourt, Amnéville les Thermes → «Centre touristique et thermal», → Golf
Map 4 on page 171 Carte 4 Page 171

GOLF COURSE / PARCOURS — 13/20

Site	Site	
Maintenance	Entretien	
Architect	Architecte	Jean-Manuel Rossi
Type	Type	forest
Relief	Relief	
Water in play	Eau en jeu	
Exp. to wind	Exposé au vent	
Trees in play	Arbres en jeu	

Scorecard Carte de score	Chp. Chp.	Mens Mess.	Ladies Da.
Length Long.	5985	5985	5618
Par	71	71	71

Advised golfing ability Niveau de jeu recommandé	0	12	24	36
Hcp required Handicap exigé	35			

CLUB HOUSE & AMENITIES / CLUB HOUSE ET ANNEXES — 6/10

Pro shop	Pro-shop	
Driving range	Practice	
Sheltered	couvert	10 mats
On grass	sur herbe	no, 20 mats open air
Putting-green	putting-green	yes
Pitching-green	pitching green	yes

HOTEL FACILITIES / ENVIRONNEMENT HOTELIER — 5/10

HOTELS HÔTELS
Diane — Amnéville
46 rooms, D 340 F — 1 km
Tel (33) 03 87 70 16 33, Fax (33) 03 87 72 36 72

Orion — Amnéville
44 rooms, D 280 F — 1 km
Tel (33) 03 87 70 20 20, Fax (33) 03 87 72 36 21

Saint-Eloi — Amnéville
47 rooms, D 330 F — 1 km
Tel (33) 03 87 70 32 62, Fax (33) 03 87 71 71 59

RESTAURANTS RESTAURANT
La Forêt (Hôtel Diane) — Amnéville
Tel (33) 03 87 70 34 34 — 1 km

Orion — Amnéville
Tel (33) 03 87 70 20 20 — 1 km

219

Dessiné en 1988 par Frédéric Hawtree dans un domaine de 200 hectares, ce parcours est orné et défendu par de nombreux plans d'eau (pas trop en jeu) habités par une faune sauvage, ce qui amplifie l'aspect naturel voulu par l'architecte. Quelques grands arbres et des haies de bocage rythment le terrain et viennent parfois assez en jeu pour poser des problèmes aux joueurs peu précis. Les bunkers de fairway et de green ne sont pas très profonds, et disposés de manière classique : on aurait aimé un peu plus de variété de ce côté. Sans prétendre être exceptionnel, cet ensemble d'honorable facture convient à tous les niveaux, les meilleurs jouant résolument des départs arrière, où les trous proposent une belle montée en puissance jusqu'à la fin.

Designed in 1988 by Fred Hawtree in an estate of some 200 hectares, this course is enhanced and defended by countless stretches of water (which do not over-affect play) and is populated by wildlife which amplifies the natural aspect the architect was looking for. The course is dotted with a few large trees and hedges, which can cause problems for wayward hitters. The fairway bunkers are not particularly deep and are laid out in classic fashion. Indeed, a little variety would have been welcome here. Without claiming to be outstanding, this is a very decent golf course for players of all standards, the best of whom will move straight to the back-tees and enjoy the way the course gradually becomes more difficult from one hole to the next.

Anjou Golf & Country Club 1990
Route de Cheffes
F - 49330 CHAMPIGNE

Office	Secrétariat	(33) 02 41 42 01 01
Pro shop	Pro-shop	(33) 02 41 42 01 01
Fax	Fax	(33) 02 41 42 04 37
Situation	Situation	

Angers (pop. 141 400), 25 km

Annual closure	Fermeture annuelle	no
Weekly closure	Fermeture hebdomadaire	no

Fees main season
Tarifs haute saison full day

	Week days Semaine	We/Bank holidays We/Férié
Individual Individuel	180 F	220 F
Couple Couple	360 F	440 F
Caddy	Caddy	no
Electric Trolley	Chariot électrique	no
Buggy	Voiturette	150 F/18 holes
Clubs	Clubs 1/2 série	80 F/full day

Credit cards Cartes de crédit
VISA - CB - Eurocard - MasterCard - AMEX

220

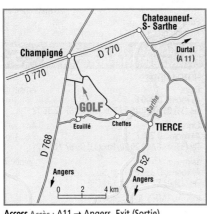

Access Accès : A11 → Angers, Exit (Sortie)
11 → Durtal. D859 → Châteauneuf.
D770 → Champigné, → Golf
Map 6 on page 175 Carte 6 Page 175

GOLF COURSE
PARCOURS
13/20

Site	Site	
Maintenance	Entretien	
Architect	Architecte	Frederic Hawtree
Type	Type	country
Relief	Relief	
Water in play	Eau en jeu	
Exp. to wind	Exposé au vent	
Trees in play	Arbres en jeu	

Scorecard Carte de score	Chp. Chp.	Mens Mess.	Ladies Da.
Length Long.	6227	5979	5241
Par	72	72	72

Advised golfing ability		0 12 24 36
Niveau de jeu recommandé		
Hcp required	Handicap exigé	35

CLUB HOUSE & AMENITIES
CLUB HOUSE ET ANNEXES
6/10

Pro shop	Pro-shop	
Driving range	Practice	
Sheltered	couvert	6 mats
On grass	sur herbe	no, 17 mats open air
Putting-green	putting-green	yes
Pitching-green	pitching green	no

HOTEL FACILITIES
ENVIRONNEMENT HOTELIER
6/10

HOTELS HÔTELS
Appartements du Golf — on site
11 rooms, D 300 F
Tel (33) 02 41 42 01 01,
Fax (33) 02 41 42 04 37

Hôtel des Voyageurs — Le Lion d'Angers
14 rooms, D 300 F — 6 km
Tel (33) 02 41 95 81 81,
Fax (33) 02 41 95 84 80

Château de Noirieux — Briollay
19 rooms, D 1 650 F — 16 km
Tel (33) 02 41 42 50 05, Fax (33) 02 41 37 91 00

RESTAURANTS RESTAURANT
Château de Noirieux — Briollay
Tel (33) 02 41 42 50 05 — 16 km

A l'exception des trois premiers trous, ce parcours ouvert en 1988 est situé dans le parc d'un petit château, clos de hauts murs, ce qui garantit une atmosphère très calme. Sa longueur reste raisonnable et son relief modéré, ce qui permet de le jouer sans grande fatigue, du moins si l'on a de bonnes jambes. L'eau vient en jeu sur une demi-douzaine de trous (étangs, ruisseau, fossés), mais essentiellement sur le 11 et le 15. Les greens ne sont pas très grands, ce qui exige un jeu de fers assez exact, mais permet de ne pas craindre les 3-putts toujours vexants, une fois que l'on y est en sécurité. Quelques beaux arbres (notamment des cyprès bleus) et un bon placement des bunkers amènent à recommander de faire attention pour préserver un bon score : les longs frappeurs se feront souvent dominer par les bons joueurs de fers. Mais tous les niveaux de jeu peuvent cohabiter ici.

With the exception of the first three holes, this 1988 course is laid out in the grounds of a small castle surrounded by high walls, so you couldn't hope for a more tranquil atmosphere. Length is reasonable and the course none too hilly, so you can walk it easily, if you are fit. Water comes into play on half a dozen holes (lakes, a stream and ditches), but is basically dangerous on the 11th and 15th. The greens are not large, so accurate ironwork is a must. But once home on the green, you have less chance of recording those irksome 3-putts. A few beautiful trees (notably some fine blue cypress) and astutely-placed bunkers keep golfers on their toes if they want to hold their score down. Long-hitters will probably be outplayed here by good iron players, but all in all, this is a course for all types of player.

Golf Annonay-Gourdan — 1988

Saint-Clair
F - 07430 SAINT-CLAIR-ANNONAY

Office	Secrétariat	(33) 04 75 67 03 84
Pro shop	Pro-shop	(33) 04 75 67 03 84
Fax	Fax	(33) 04 75 67 79 50
Situation	Situation	

Lyon, pop. 413 090, 81 km
Saint-Etienne pop. 201 570, 40 km

| Annual closure | Fermeture annuelle | no |
| Weekly closure | Fermeture hebdomadaire | no |

Fees main season
Tarifs haute saison 18 holes

	Week days Semaine	We/Bank holidays We/Férié
Individual Individuel	180 F	230 F
Couple Couple	310 F	410 F

2 GF + 2 lunches + golfcar = 650 F

Caddy	Caddy	no
Electric Trolley	Chariot électrique	70 F/18 holes
Buggy	Voiturette	180 F/18 holes
Clubs	Clubs	70 F/18 holes

Credit cards Cartes de crédit
VISA - CB - Eurocard - MasterCard

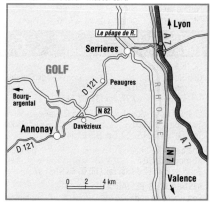

GOLF D 121 Peaugres
Bourg-argental
N 82
Annonay Davézieux
D 121

Le péage de R.
Serrieres
Lyon
A7
RHONE
A7
N7
Valence

0   2   4 km

Access Accès : A7 Lyon - Valence,
Exit (Sortie) Chanas, → Annonay, N82 → Saint-Etienne
Map 11 on page 184 Carte 11 Page 184

GOLF COURSE PARCOURS — 13/20

Site	Site	
Maintenance	Entretien	
Architect	Architecte	Thierry Sprecher Géry Watine
Type	Type	parkland
Relief	Relief	
Water in play	Eau en jeu	
Exp. to wind	Exposé au vent	
Trees in play	Arbres en jeu	

Scorecard Carte de score	Chp. Chp.	Mens Mess.	Ladies Da.
Length Long.	5900	5557	5252
Par	72	72	72

| Advised golfing ability Niveau de jeu recommandé | 0 | 12 | 24 | 36 |
| Hcp required | Handicap exigé | no | | |

CLUB HOUSE & AMENITIES CLUB HOUSE ET ANNEXES — 6/10

Pro shop	Pro-shop	
Driving range	Practice	
Sheltered	couvert	6 mats
On grass	sur herbe	yes
Putting-green	putting-green	yes
Pitching-green	pitching green	yes

HOTEL FACILITIES ENVIRONNEMENT HOTELIER — 5/10

HOTELS HÔTELS
Hôtel d'Ay — on site
35 rooms, D 400 F
Tel (33) 04 75 67 01 00,
Fax (33) 04 75 67 07 38

Hôtel du Midi — Annonay 4 km
40 rooms, D 270 F
Tel (33) 04 75 33 23 77,
Fax (33) 04 75 33 02 43

RESTAURANTS RESTAURANT
Marc et Christine — Annonay 4 km
Tel (33) 04 75 33 46 97

La Halle — Annonay 4 km
Tel (33) 04 75 32 04 62

221

Même si l'on pense toujours que le parcours aurait pu faire l'objet d'un investissement aussi important que le luxueux Club house, son entretien remarquable est un point fort. Conçu par John Jacobs, il reste très agréable à parcourir, avec 14 trous en forêt d'Halatte et les autres organisés autour de pièces d'eau. L'ensemble est plat, facile à marcher avec les départs très proches des greens. Certes, le dessin de John Jacobs ne propose pas de grands chocs visuels, la stratégie de jeu est assez évidente, mais faute d'affrontements épiques avec le parcours, on appréciera le silence des lieux et la majesté du cadre. Apremont n'a sans doute pas droit à l'appellation de chef-d'oeuvre, dans la mesure où les meilleurs golfeurs trouveront ses défis techniques un peu modestes, mais la majorité des joueurs y passeront une bonne journée, et pourront espérer «tourner» dans leur handicap.

Even though we still feel the course could have benefited from the same investment that was obviously given to the luxurious club-house, remarkable upkeep and green-keeping are definitely the club's forte. Designed by John Jacobs, this is a very pleasant course to play, with 14 holes in the forest of Halatte and the others laid out around lakes. The whole course is flat, with very little distance between green and next tee. There is nothing strikingly visual about this layout, and game strategy is pretty obvious, but in the absence of epic confrontation with the course, players will enjoy the silence and the majestic setting. Apremont could never really claim the label of golfing masterpiece in that the better player will find the technical challenge within easy reach, but most players spend a good day's golfing here and can hold out hopes of playing to their handicap.

Apremont Golf-Club
1992
F - 60300 APREMONT

Office	Secrétariat	(33) 03 44 25 61 11
Pro shop	Pro-shop	(33) 03 44 25 61 11
Fax	Fax	(33) 03 44 25 11 72
Situation	Situation	

Chantilly (pop. 11 340), 6 km - Senlis (pop. 14 430), 7 km

Annual closure	Fermeture annuelle	no
Weekly closure	Fermeture hebdomadaire	monday
		1/10→31/3

Fees main season
Tarifs haute saison full day

	Week days Semaine	We/Bank holidays We/Férié
Individual Individuel	250 F	480 F
Couple Couple	480 F	720 F
Caddy Caddy		no
Electric Trolley Chariot électrique		70 F/full day
Buggy Voiturette		180 F/18 holes
Clubs Clubs série		120 F/full day

Credit cards Cartes de crédit
VISA - CB - Eurocard - MasterCard - AMEX - JCB

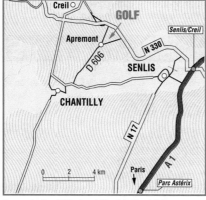

Access Accès : A1 Paris → Lille, Exit (Sortie) 8
Senlis/Creil. N 330 → Creil.
7 km. after Senlis, → Apremont on the left
Map 1 on page 164 Carte 1 Page 164

GOLF COURSE
PARCOURS
15/20

Site	Site	
Maintenance	Entretien	
Architect	Architecte	John Jacobs
Type	Type	forest, parkland
Relief	Relief	
Water in play	Eau en jeu	
Exp. to wind	Exposé au vent	
Trees in play	Arbres en jeu	

Scorecard Carte de score	Chp. Chp.	Mens Mess.	Ladies Da.
Length Long.	6436	5843	5395
Par	72	72	72

Advised golfing ability		0	12	24	36
Niveau de jeu recommandé					
Hcp required	Handicap exigé	no			

CLUB HOUSE & AMENITIES
CLUB HOUSE ET ANNEXES
8/10

Pro shop	Pro-shop	
Driving range	Practice	
Sheltered	couvert	no
On grass	sur herbe	no,
		30 mats open air
Putting-green	putting-green	yes
Pitching-green	pitching green	no

HOTEL FACILITIES
ENVIRONNEMENT HOTELIER
6/10

HOTELS HÔTELS
Golf Hôtel — Domaine de Chantilly
111 rooms, D 2 000 F — 4 km
Tél (33) 03 44 58 47 77, Fax (33) 03 44 58 50 11

Château Hôtel Mont-Royal — La Chapelle-en-Serval
100 rooms, D 1 600 FF — 15 km
Tél (33) 03 44 54 50 50, Fax (33) 03 44 54 50 20

Château de la Tour — Gouvieux
41 rooms, D 930 F — 8 km
Tél (33) 03 44 62 38 38, Fax (33) 03 44 57 31 97

RESTAURANTS RESTAURANTS
Restaurant du golf — Apremont
Tél (33) 03 44 25 61 11 — on site

Verbois — Saint-Maximin
Tél (33) 03 44 24 06 22 — 4 km

222

Depuis longtemps, c'est le golf des Bordelais en week-end, et des vacanciers du Pyla. Que l'on n'attende donc pas un parcours très moderne ni audacieux. En pays de vieille tradition britannique, les architectes Blandford et Pierre Hirigoyen ont dessiné un parcours sans grands éclats, épousant sans trop le bousculer un terrain accidenté à l'aller, et plus plat au retour. Avec le relief, l'approche de certains greens surélevés n'est pas toujours simple ; les fairways souvent étroits, bien défendus par les arbres, imposent de placer les coups de départ, quitte à laisser le driver dans le sac. Mais le parcours est assez court, et la précision plus souvent récompensée que la longueur. Avec les travaux de drainage sur la partie basse du parcours, il est jouable toute l'année. Les non-golfeurs de la famille trouveront de nombreuses activités dans la station balnéaire d'Arcachon, en haute saison. Le Club-House est placé au sommet de cet ensemble, l'ambiance est familiale et amicale.

This has long been the traditional week-end course for the good folk of Bordeaux and holiday-makers at Pylat, so don't expect a modern or bold layout here. In a region of British tradition, architects Blandford and Pierre Hirigoyen laid out a subdued course which embraces but never disrupts the hilly terrain on the front nine and the flatter holes around the back. The broken relief means that the second shot to a number of elevated greens is not always easy. And a few tight fairways, well-defended by trees, require a well-placed tee-shot, even if that means leaving the driver in the bag. But the course is short, and precision is more often better rewarded than length off the tee. With the lower section of the course now fitted with a drainage system, Arcachon is playable all year. Non-golfers in the family will find lots to do in the seaside resort of Arcachon in summer, while the club-house overlooking the course offers a friendly family atmosphere.

Golf d'Arcachon — 1952

35, boulevard d'Arcachon
F - 33260 LA TESTE

Office	Secrétariat	(33) 05 56 54 44 00
Pro shop	Pro-shop	(33) 05 57 52 62 83
Fax	Fax	(33) 05 56 66 86 32
Situation	Situation	

Arcachon (pop. 11 770), 3 km

Annual closure	Fermeture annuelle	no
Weekly closure	Fermeture hebdomadaire	no

Fees main season
Tarifs haute saison full day

	Week days Semaine	We/Bank holidays We/Férié
Individual Individuel	270 F	270 F
Couple Couple	460 F	460 F

Caddy	Caddy	no
Electric Trolley	Chariot électrique	no
Buggy	Voiturette	150 F/18 holes
Clubs	Clubs	70 F/full day

Credit cards Cartes de crédit
VISA - CB- Eurocard - MasterCard - AMEX

Access Accès : N250 → La Teste → Pyla-sur-Mer
Map 9 on page 181 Carte 9 Page 181

GOLF COURSE / PARCOURS — 13/20

Site	Site	▰▰▰▱▱
Maintenance	Entretien	▰▰▰▱▱
Architect	Architecte	Cecil R. Blandford Pierre Hirrigoyen
Type	Type	seaside course, hilly
Relief	Relief	▰▰▰▱▱
Water in play	Eau en jeu	▰▱▱▱▱
Exp. to wind	Exposé au vent	▰▰▱▱▱
Trees in play	Arbres en jeu	▰▰▰▱▱

Scorecard Carte de score	Chp. Chp.	Mens Mess.	Ladies Da.
Length Long.	5953	5746	5065
Par	72	72	72

Advised golfing ability		0 12 24 36
Niveau de jeu recommandé		▰▰▰▰▱
Hcp required	Handicap exigé	35 (summer)

CLUB HOUSE & AMENITIES / CLUB HOUSE ET ANNEXES — 6/10

Pro shop	Pro-shop	▰▰▰▱▱
Driving range	Practice	▰▰▰▱▱
Sheltered	couvert	6 mats
On grass	sur herbe	no, 36 mats open air
Putting-green	putting-green	yes
Pitching-green	pitching green	yes

HOTEL FACILITIES / ENVIRONNEMENT HOTELIER — 6/10

HOTELS HÔTELS

Séminaris — Arcachon
19 rooms, D 740 F — 3 km
Tél (33) 05 56 83 25 87, Fax (33) 05 57 52 22 41

Deganne — Arcachon
57 rooms, D 800 F — 3 km
Tél (33) 05 56 83 99 91, Fax (33) 05 56 83 87 92

Grand Hôtel Richelieu — Arcachon
43 rooms, D 780 F — 3 km
Tél (33) 05 56 83 16 50, Fax (33) 05 56 83 47 78

Le Parc — Arcachon
30 rooms, D 570 F — 3 km
Tél (33) 05 56 83 10 58, Fax (33) 05 56 54 05 30

RESTAURANTS RESTAURANTS

L'Ombrière — Arcachon
Tél (33) 05 56 83 86 20 — 3 km

223

Le site offre de jolies vues sur la campagne basque et les Pyrénées, avec un bon rythme entre les trous dégagés et les trous boisés. Il a fallu beaucoup modifier le terrain accidenté pour le rendre jouable, mais de nombreux dévers et pentes étaient inévitables, et peuvent entraîner des coups délicats : il faut savoir jouer des balles à effets. Pour cela, on ne le conseillera pas aux débutants, ni aux seniors, à moins de jouer en voiturette. Comme souvent avec l'architecte Ronald Fream, les bunkers et les greens sont très travaillés et bien en jeu, mais c'est logique pour un parcours aassez court : vive la précision... Et aussi un peu la chance, car la franchise n'est pas le point fort de ce dessin. Ce golf très technique doit être reconnu avant d'espérer un bon score, il offre des caractéristiques bien différentes des autres parcours de la région. Quelques travaux ont été entrepris pour améliorer le tracé.

The setting provides beautiful views over the Basque countryside and the Pyrenees, and there is a nice balance between woodland holes and holes through open country. A lot of earth was moved to make this once rugged landscape into a playable course, but inevitably slopes and hills still remain and can lead to some tricky shots. Being able to flight the ball is more of an advantage than usual. For this reason we would not recommend Arcangues to beginners or to seniors, unless on wheels. As is often the case with Ronald Fream, the bunkers and greens have been given a lot of careful thought, which is only logical for a course as short as this. The watchword here is precision play... with perhaps a bit of luck thrown in, as the layout is not as forthright as it might be. Arcangues is a very technical course that needs a little reconnaissance work before hoping to card a good score. And its features are very different from the other courses in the region.

Golf d'Arcangues — 1991
Club House
F - 64200 ARCANGUES

Office	Secrétariat	(33) 05 59 43 10 56
Pro shop	Pro-shop	(33) 05 59 43 10 56
Fax	Fax	(33) 05 59 43 12 60
Situation	Situation	

Biarritz (pop. 28 740), 6 km
Bayonne (pop. 40 050), 10 km

Annual closure	Fermeture annuelle	no
Weekly closure	Fermeture hebdomadaire	monday
	(lundi)	30/10→1/3

Fees main season
Tarifs haute saison 18 holes

	Week days Semaine	We/Bank holidays We/Férié
Individual Individuel	300 F	300 F
Couple Couple	550 F	550 F

Caddy	Caddy	no
Electric Trolley	Chariot électrique	no
Buggy	Voiturette	150 F/18 holes
Clubs	Clubs	60 F

Credit cards Cartes de crédit
VISA - CB - Eurocard - MasterCard

224

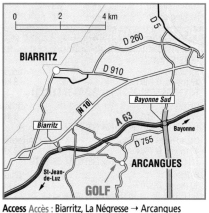

Access Accès : Biarritz, La Négresse → Arcangues
Map 12 on page 186 Carte 12 Page 186

GOLF COURSE / PARCOURS — 14/20

Site	Site	▰▰▰▰▱
Maintenance	Entretien	▰▰▰▱▱
Architect	Architecte	Ronald Fream
Type	Type	hilly
Relief	Relief	▰▰▰▱▱
Water in play	Eau en jeu	▰▰▱▱▱
Exp. to wind	Exposé au vent	▰▰▱▱▱
Trees in play	Arbres en jeu	▰▰▰▰▱

Scorecard Carte de score	Chp. Chp.	Mens Mess.	Ladies Da.
Length Long.	6092	5687	5243
Par	72	72	72

Advised golfing ability Niveau de jeu recommandé	0 12 24 36	
Hcp required	Handicap exigé	35

CLUB HOUSE & AMENITIES / CLUB HOUSE ET ANNEXES — 7/10

Pro shop	Pro-shop	▰▰▰▰▱
Driving range	Practice	▰▰▰▱▱
Sheltered	couvert	5 mats
On grass	sur herbe	yes
Putting-green	putting-green	yes
Pitching-green	pitching green	yes

HOTEL FACILITIES / ENVIRONNEMENT HOTELIER — 8/10

HOTELS HÔTELS

Le Palais — Biarritz
134 rooms, D 2 000 F — 6 km
Tel (33) 05 59 41 64 00, Fax (33) 05 59 41 67 99

Château de Brindos — Anglet
12 rooms, D 1300 F — 8 km
Tel (33) 05 59 23 17 68, Fax (33) 05 59 23 48 47

Hôtel Laminak — Arbonne
10 rooms, D 560 F — 4 km
Tel (33) 05 59 41 95 40, Fax (33) 05 59 41 87 65

RESTAURANTS RESTAURANTS

Auberge d'Achtal — Arcangues
Tel (33) 05 59 43 05 56

Les Platanes — Biarritz
Tel (33) 05 59 23 13 68 — 6 km

ARRAS

En dehors des routes touristiques, mais profitant d'une grosse promotion grâce à son Président Gervais Martel, patron de l'équipe de football de Lens, ce parcours mérite le détour, surtout quand il est préparé pour les compétitions. Amusant et très varié quand il est joué des départs avancés, il devient beaucoup plus technique des départs arrière (hommes ou dames). Il faut alors pas mal d'intelligence stratégique et de lucidité, un bon sens du placement de la balle. Assez vallonné, il cache parfois ses dangers, avec quelques trous aveugles, péché mignon de l'architecte. Il faut donc bien le repérer avant d'espérer faire un score : il y a tout de même 12 trous avec de l'eau. Le site est agréable, avec une esthétique de parc à l'anglaise, quelques dénivellées mais pas insurmontables. Le seul gros défaut est que le parcours absorbe assez lentement les pluies. Un hôtel doit ouvrir sur le site au cours de l'année 2000, ce qui devrait encore améliorer la notoriété de ce golf sympathique.

Off the tourist track, this course is worth going out of your way for, especially when set up for tournaments. A bag of fun and variety when played from the front tees, the layout is much more technical when played from the tips (men's and ladies), calling for strategic intelligence, clear-thinking and good sense for placing the ball. This rather hilly course sometimes hides its hazards with a few blind holes that the architect couldn't resist. So you will need to check these out before hoping to card any sort of score, talking of which we might also add that there are 12 holes with water. The site is pleasant, a sort of English-style park with a few climbs and slopes, but nothing too insurmountable. The only real flaw here is that the terrain takes a while to soak up the rain. A hotel is due to open in the year 2000, an addition which should further improve the reputation of this very pleasant course.

Golf Club d'Arras		1990
F - 62223 ANZIN- SAINT-AUBIN		

Office	Secrétariat	(33) 03 21 50 24 24
Pro shop	Pro-shop	(33) 03 21 50 24 24
Fax	Fax	(33) 03 21 50 27 22
Situation	Situation	
Arras (pop. 39 000), 4 km		
Annual closure	Fermeture annuelle	no
Weekly closure	Fermeture hebdomadaire	no

Fees main season
Tarifs haute saison 18 holes

	Week days Semaine	We/Bank holidays We/Férié
Individual Individuel	190 F	280 F
Couple Couple	380 F	560 F

Caddy	Caddy	no
Electric Trolley	Chariot électrique	no
Buggy	Voiturette	yes
Clubs	Clubs	yes

Credit cards Cartes de crédit
VISA - CB - Eurocard - MasterCard - AMEX

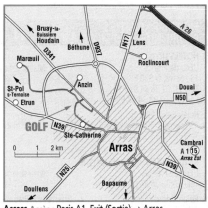

Access Accès : Paris A1. Exit (Sortie) → Arras.
N39→ Le Touquet, D64 → Golf.
Map 1 on page 164 Carte 1 Page 164

GOLF COURSE
PARCOURS
14/20

Site	Site	
Maintenance	Entretien	
Architect	Architecte	J.-Cl. Cornillot
Type	Type	parkland
Relief	Relief	
Water in play	Eau en jeu	
Exp. to wind	Exposé au vent	
Trees in play	Arbres en jeu	

Scorecard	Chp.	Mens	Ladies
Carte de score	Chp.	Mess.	Da.
Length Long.	5846	5846	4830
Par	72	72	72

Advised golfing ability	0 12 24 36
Niveau de jeu recommandé	
Hcp required Handicap exigé	35

CLUB HOUSE & AMENITIES
CLUB HOUSE ET ANNEXES
6/10

Pro shop	Pro-shop	
Driving range	Practice	
Sheltered	couvert	20 mats
On grass	sur herbe	yes (05 → 10)
Putting-green	putting-green	yes (2)
Pitching-green	pitching green	yes

HOTEL FACILITIES
ENVIRONNEMENT HOTELIER
6/10

HOTELS HÔTELS
L'Univers	Arras
37 rooms, D 490 F	4 km
Tel (44) 03 21 71 34 01, Fax (44) 03 21 71 41 42	

Mercure	Arras
80 rooms, D 520 F	4 km
Tel (44) 03 21 23 88 88, Fax (44) 03 21 23 88 89	

Ibis	Arras
63 rooms, D 300 F	4 km
Tel (44) 03 21 23 61 61, Fax (44) 03 21 71 31 31	

RESTAURANTS RESTAURANT
La Faisanderie	Arras
Tel (44) 03 21 48 20 76	4 km
Le Régent - Tel (44) 03 21 71 51 09	Arras 4 km
La Coupole d'Arras - Tel (44) 03 21 71 88 44	Arras 4 km

225

Pas très long, et bien accidenté, ce récent parcours bénéficie d'un bel environnement forestier, et de la présence d'un château du XVIIᵉ siècle, qui devrait être aménagé un jour en véritable Club house. Pour l'instant, les installations restent très sommaires. A côté de très jolis trous, certains autres sont fort contestables, notamment un par 5 et quelques par 3 où des arbres empiètent fortement sur la ligne de jeu. On doit aussi signaler la présence de quelques greens aveugles, qui ne sont pas très «golfiques», obligent non seulement à bien connaître le parcours mais aussi la position des drapeaux. Un dernier regret : la difficulté excessive du 18, qui laisse sur une impression mitigée. La beauté du cadre et les promesses du lieu incitent à conseiller une visite, mais le manque de franchise du parcours et son entretien encore moyen nous incitent toujours à reporter un jugement définitif.

Not very long and rather hilly, this course lies in a beautiful setting of forest enhanced by a 17th century castle, shortly due to be refurbished to form the club-house. For the time being, facilities are pretty basic. Alongside some very pretty holes, others are very questionable, notably one par 5 and a few par 3s, where trees come right into the firing line. There are also a few blind greens, which do not make for good golf and which require prior knowledge of the course and the pin-position. Our last little regret is the excessively difficult 18th hole, which leaves the golfer with a mixed impression of the course as a whole. The beauty and promise of the setting and site make this a visit we would recommend, but with the course's lack of fairness and still only very average upkeep, we feel we should reserve final judgment.

Golf du Château d'Augerville — 1995

Place du Château
F - 45330 AUGERVILLE-LA-RIVIERE

Office	Secrétariat	(33) 02 38 32 12 07
Pro shop	Pro-shop	(33) 02 38 32 12 07
Fax	Fax	(33) 02 38 32 12 15
Situation	Situation	

Nemours (pop. 12 075), 25 km
Pithiviers (pop. 9 327), 20 km

Annual closure	Fermeture annuelle	no
Weekly closure	Fermeture hebdomadaire	no

Fees main season
Tarifs haute saison full day

	Week days Semaine	We/Bank holidays We/Férié
Individual Individuel	180 F	280 F
Couple Couple	360 F	560 F

Caddy	Caddy	no
Electric Trolley	Chariot électrique	no
Buggy	Voiturette	100 F/18 holes
Clubs	Clubs	70 F/18 holes

Credit cards Cartes de crédit
VISA - CB - Eurocard - MasterCard

226

Access Accès : A6 Exit (Sortie) Ury, N152 →
Malesherbes, D958 → Puiseaux, → Golf
Map 3 on page 168 Carte 3 Page 168

GOLF COURSE / PARCOURS — 13/20

Site	Site	
Maintenance	Entretien	
Architect	Architecte	Olivier Dongradi
Type	Type	forest, hilly
Relief	Relief	
Water in play	Eau en jeu	
Exp. to wind	Exposé au vent	
Trees in play	Arbres en jeu	

Scorecard Carte de score	Chp. Chp.	Mens Mess.	Ladies Da.
Length Long.	6268	5466	4699
Par	72	72	72

Advised golfing ability	0	12	24	36
Niveau de jeu recommandé				

Hcp required	Handicap exigé	35 (We)

CLUB HOUSE & AMENITIES / CLUB HOUSE ET ANNEXES — 5/10

Pro shop	Pro-shop	
Driving range	Practice	
Sheltered	couvert	no
On grass	sur herbe	yes
Putting-green	putting-green	yes
Pitching-green	pitching green	no

HOTEL FACILITIES / ENVIRONNEMENT HOTELIER — 4/10

HOTELS HÔTELS
L'Ecu de France — Malesherbes
13 rooms, D 350 F — 7 km
Tel (33) 02 38 34 87 25
Fax (33) 02 38 34 68 99

Relais Saint Georges — Pithiviers
43 rooms, D 370 F — 20 km
Tel (33) 02 38 30 40 25
Fax (33) 02 38 30 09 05

RESTAURANTS RESTAURANTS
L'Ecu de France — Malesherbes
Tel (33) 02 38 34 87 25 — 7 km

Relais Briardis — Briarres-sur-Essonne
Tel (33) 02 38 32 11 22 — 3 km

BADEN

15	6	5

Sans être un véritable links, Baden est un excellent parcours de bord de mer, dominant l'estuaire de la rivière d'Auray. Seuls quelques trous sont vraiment tracés dans les pins, mais on n'a jamais l'impression de monotonie, étant donnée la variété du tracé. Les reliefs du terrain, les arbustes, une végétation assez sauvage, quelques arbres isolés, et le dessin d'Yves Bureau en font un lieu de charme pour les yeux, et pour le jeu. Sans être d'une difficulté extrême, il offre aux meilleurs joueurs un défi constant, parfois rehaussé par le vent, tout en permettant aux joueurs moyens et même aux novices de passer une journée agréable. Un morceau de choix dans une région bien équipée en golfs. L'entretien y est variable, mais généralement correct, et le Club house n'est pas vraiment à la hauteur du lieu.

While not a real links, Baden is an excellent seaside course overlooking the estuary of the river Auray. Only a few holes are laid out really amongst the pine-trees, but given the variety, the course is never boring. The sloping terrain, bushes, wild-growing vegetation, a few isolated trees and the layout of Yves Bureau make this a charming course both to look at and play. Although not over-difficult, the challenge to the better player never eases and is sometimes made tougher when the wind gets up. At the same time, high-handicappers and even beginners can enjoy a good day out. A choice venue in a region well-endowed with golf courses. Upkeep is good but the club-house not quite up to scratch.

Golf de Baden — 1989

Kernic
F - 56870 BADEN

Office	Secrétariat	(33) 02 97 57 18 96
Pro shop	Pro-shop	(33) 02 97 57 18 96
Fax	Fax	(33) 02 97 57 22 05
Situation	Situation	

Auray (pop. 10 320), 8 km
Vannes (pop. 45 640), 13 km

Annual closure	Fermeture annuelle	no
Weekly closure	Fermeture hebdomadaire	no

Fees main season
Tarifs haute saison full day

	Week days Semaine	We/Bank holidays We/Férié
Individual Individuel	260 F	260 F
Couple Couple	520 F	520 F

Caddy	Caddy	on request
Electric Trolley	Chariot électrique	60 F/18 holes
Buggy	Voiturette	150 F/18 holes
Clubs	Clubs	50 F/18 holes

Credit cards Cartes de crédit
VISA - CB - Eurocard - MasterCard

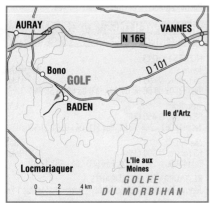

Access Accès : N165 → Le Bono, → Baden, Golf
Map 5 on page 173 Carte 5 Page 173

GOLF COURSE / PARCOURS — 15/20

Site	Site	
Maintenance	Entretien	
Architect	Architecte	Yves Bureau
Type	Type	seaside course, country
Relief	Relief	
Water in play	Eau en jeu	
Exp. to wind	Exposé au vent	
Trees in play	Arbres en jeu	

Scorecard Carte de score	Chp. Chp.	Mens Mess.	Ladies Da.
Length Long.	6110	5761	5235
Par	72	72	72

Advised golfing ability Niveau de jeu recommandé	0	12	24	36
Hcp required Handicap exigé	35			

CLUB HOUSE & AMENITIES / CLUB HOUSE ET ANNEXES — 6/10

Pro shop	Pro-shop	
Driving range	Practice	
Sheltered	couvert	no
On grass	sur herbe	yes
Putting-green	putting-green	yes
Pitching-green	pitching green	yes

HOTEL FACILITIES / ENVIRONNEMENT HOTELIER — 5/10

HOTELS HÔTELS

Hostellerie Abbatiale — Le Bono
71 rooms, D 450 F — 3 km
Tel (33) 02 97 57 84 00, Fax (33) 02 97 57 83 00

Le Gavrinis — Toulbroch
19 rooms, D 460 F — 2 km
Tel (33) 02 97 57 00 82, Fax (33) 02 97 57 09 47

Auberge du Forban — Le Bono
21 rooms, D 320 F — 3 km
Tel (33) 02 97 57 88 65, Fax (33) 02 97 57 92 76

RESTAURANTS RESTAURANTS

Régis Mahé — Vannes
Tel (33) 02 97 42 61 41 — 13 km

Le Pressoir — Vannes
Tel (33) 02 97 60 87 63 — 13 km

227

15 7 7

Dans un très beau site de campagne et de bois, ce parcours est une sorte d'enclave suisse en France. Dessiné par l'architecte allemand von Limburger, auteur de très nombreux parcours classiques dans son pays natal, il est assez long, et quelques reliefs accentués obligent à réfléchir sur les choix de club. Sans présenter de caractère très original sur le plan visuel, c'est un parcours stratégique intelligent, avec des obstacles bien visibles, mais pas excessivement dangereux (sauf les arbres). Ces difficultés raisonnables amènent à le conseiller à tous les niveaux de joueurs classés, dans la mesure où ils pourront attaquer les greens, largement ouverts, en faisant rouler la balle. Mais pour jouer son handicap, il vaut mieux savoir faire des balles à effet. La deuxième partie du parcours, la plus boisée, est techniquement la plus intéressante. A connaître.

In a beautiful setting of countryside and woodland, this course is a sort of a Swiss enclave in France. Laid out by German architect Bernhard von Limburger, it is longish and a few hilly mounds call for care when choosing the club to play. Although visually speaking the course is nothing to write home about, it is a strategically intelligent layout, with clearly visible but not excessively dangerous hazards (except the trees). We would therefore recommend it to high-handicappers and better, especially since the greens are wide open and reachable with easier chip shots. Being able to move the ball both ways (deliberately) will definitely be helpful for players looking to play to their handicap. The second part of the course, where the woods are thicker, is technically speaking the most interesting. Worth getting to know.

Golf & Country Club de Bâle   1968
Route de Wentzwiller
F - 68220 HAGENTHAL-LE-BAS

Office	Secrétariat	(33) 03 89 68 50 91
Pro shop	Pro-shop	(33) 03 89 68 51 61
Fax	Fax	(33) 03 89 68 55 66
Situation	Situation	

Bâle/Basel (pop. 171 000), 9 km

Annual closure	Fermeture annuelle	no
Weekly closure	Fermeture hebdomadaire	no

Fees main season
Tarifs haute saison full day

	Week days Semaine	We/Bank holidays We/Férié
Individual Individuel	320 F	*
Couple Couple	640 F	*

* We: no green fees

Caddy	Caddy	no
Electric Trolley	Chariot électrique	60 F/18 holes
Buggy	Voiturette	no
Clubs	Clubs	80 F/full day

Credit cards Cartes de crédit
VISA - CB - Eurocard - MasterCard

Mulhouse
Lörrach/St-Louis
Saint-Louis
D 12 bis
D 419
D 105
A 35
Hesingue
D 419
Altkirch
Belfort
Buschwiller
Hegenheim
D 473
BALE
Folgensbourg
GOLF
D 12 b
Suisse
D 16
Hagenthal
0   2   4 km

Access Accès : • Mulhouse A35 Exit (Sortie) Saint-Louis, → Aéroport, D473 → Hesingue, → Folgensbourg, D16 → Hagenthal. • Bâle → Hegenheim. • Belfort D419 → Bâle **Map 8 on page 179** Carte 8 Page 179

GOLF COURSE PARCOURS   15/20

Site	Site	
Maintenance	Entretien	
Architect	Architecte	B. von Limburger
Type	Type	forest, country
Relief	Relief	
Water in play	Eau en jeu	
Exp. to wind	Exposé au vent	
Trees in play	Arbres en jeu	

Scorecard Carte de score	Chp. Chp.	Mens Mess.	Ladies Da.
Length Long.	6255	5938	5497
Par	72	72	72

Advised golfing ability   0   12   24   36
Niveau de jeu recommandé
Hcp required   Handicap exigé   32

CLUB HOUSE & AMENITIES CLUB HOUSE ET ANNEXES   7/10

Pro shop	Pro-shop	
Driving range	Practice	
Sheltered	couvert	5 mats
On grass	sur herbe	no, 40 mats open air
Putting-green	putting-green	yes
Pitching-green	pitching green	yes

HOTEL FACILITIES ENVIRONNEMENT HOTELIER   7/10

HOTELS HÔTELS
Jenny   Hagenthal
26 rooms, D 495 F   1 km
Tel (33) 03 89 68 50 09, Fax (33) 03 89 68 58 64

Trois Rois   Bâle
98 rooms, D 450 CHF   9 km
Tel (41) 061 - 261 52 52, Fax (41) 061 - 261 21 53

Merian   Bâle
65 rooms, D 300 CHF   9 km
Tel (41) 061 - 681 00 00, Fax (41) 061 - 681 11 01

RESTAURANTS RESTAURANTS
Jenny - Tel (33) 03 89 68 50 09   Hagenthal-le-Bas 1 km
Ancienne Forge   Hagenthal-le-Haut
Tel (33) 03 89 68 56 10   1 km
Stucki - Tél(41) 061 - 361 82 22   Bâle 9 km

BARBAROUX

| | 17 | 7 | 6 |

Un parcours controversé, notamment par son style composite, comme s'il s'agissait d'un catalogue : on a l'impression de se trouver successivement en Irlande, en Ecosse, aux Etats-Unis. Mais le paysage sauvage de Provence modère ce manque d'unité. Barbaroux est une succession de tests dont il serait vain de vouloir décrire tous les détails. Les mouvements de terrain créés par Pete et P.B. Dye, le dessin des bunkers et des greens constituent non seulement un spectacle permanent, mais aussi une série de difficultés que bien peu sauront maîtriser. Ici, la première qualité est de savoir accepter que l'on ne fait pas toujours un bon score avec du bon jeu, bref, savoir accepter d'être battu par un grand parcours, pas trop fréquenté. L'inversion pratique de l'aller et du retour a un peu diminué l'impact du finale originel mais facilité le jeu à pied. Quand l'entretien est à la hauteur, ce parcours est vraiment une expérience à vivre.

A controversial course, primarily because of its contrasting styles, the impression here is one of a mail-order catalogue for world golf-courses; one minute you feel you could be in Ireland, the next in Scotland and the next in the United States. Yet the wild Provence landscape tempers any lack of unity, making Barbaroux a succession of ordeals, all the details of which can hardly be described here. The contoured fairways, created by Pete and P.B. Dye, and the design of the greens and bunkers make not only for a never-ending spectacle but also for a series of difficulties that few golfers will find easy to master. Here, lesson number one is admitting that good play does not always end up as a good score, in other words accepting defeat at the hands of a great course that is never too crowded. The convenient reversal of the front and back nine has diminished somewhat the impact of the course's original «grand finale». When green-keeping is up to standard, this is an essential golfing experience.

Golf Club de Barbaroux — 1989

Route de Cabasse
F - 83170 BRIGNOLES

Office	Secrétariat	(33) 04 94 69 63 63
Pro shop	Pro-shop	(33) 04 94 69 63 63
Fax	Fax	(33) 04 94 59 00 93
Situation	Situation	

Brignoles (pop. 11 240), 9 km

Annual closure	Fermeture annuelle	no
Weekly closure	Fermeture hebdomadaire	no

Fees main season
Tarifs haute saison 18 holes

	Week days Semaine	We/Bank holidays We/Férié
Individual Individuel	280 F	280 F
Couple Couple	560 F	560 F

Seniors: wednesdays (merc.), 2 GF + golf car: 570 F

Caddy	Caddy	no
Electric Trolley	Chariot électrique	no
Buggy	Voiturette	200 F/18 holes
Clubs	Clubs	60 F/full day

Credit cards Cartes de crédit
VISA - CB - Eurocard - MasterCard - AMEX

Access Accès : A8 Toulon-Cannes, Exit (Sortie) Brignoles, N7 → Flassans, Le Luc, 1,5 km, turn left on D79 → La Cabane **Map 14 on page 190** Carte 14 Page 190

GOLF COURSE / PARCOURS — 17/20

Site	Site	
Maintenance	Entretien	
Architect	Architecte	Pete & P.B. Dye
Type	Type	hilly, links
Relief	Relief	
Water in play	Eau en jeu	
Exp. to wind	Exposé au vent	
Trees in play	Arbres en jeu	

Scorecard Carte de score	Chp. Chp.	Mens Mess.	Ladies Da.
Length Long.	6124	5653	5168
Par	72	72	72

Advised golfing ability Niveau de jeu recommandé	0 12 24 36
Hcp required	Handicap exigé	no

CLUB HOUSE & AMENITIES / CLUB HOUSE ET ANNEXES — 7/10

Pro shop	Pro-shop	
Driving range	Practice	
Sheltered	couvert	no
On grass	sur herbe	yes
Putting-green	putting-green	yes
Pitching-green	pitching green	yes

229

HOTEL FACILITIES / ENVIRONNEMENT HOTELIER — 6/10

HOTELS HÔTELS

Golf de Barbaroux — on site
24 rooms, D 480 F
Tel (33) 04 94 69 63 63,
Fax (33) 04 94 59 00 93

La Grillade au feu de bois — Flassans-sur-Issole
16 rooms, D 900 F — 8 km
Tel (33) 04 94 69 71 20,
Fax (33) 04 94 59 66 11

RESTAURANTS RESTAURANTS

Le Lingousto — Cuers
Tel (33) 04 94 28 69 10 — 25 km

Neuf des 18 trous originaux de Alliss et Thomas en 1978 ont été conservés, les neuf autres ont été séparés pour constituer un parcours de par 35. Pour compléter le «grand» parcours, Michel Gayon a tracé neuf trous supplémentaires. Ils sont intercalés entre le 4 et le 14, ce qui rompt la monotonie des allers et retours d'autrefois (les anciens 10 à 16). Bien sûr, le manque d'unité de style est flagrant, mais le plaisir d'évoluer dans la campagne de La Baule reste intact. Tout aussi stratégiques que les autres, les «greens et bunkers Gayon» sont dessinés avec plus d'attention et de relief (à remarquer le double green des 5 et 12), et l'on pourrait souhaiter que l'architecte retravaille les neuf trous originaux afin de donner plus d'harmonie à cet ensemble bien organisé pour passer des vacances. Pendant l'année 2000, deux nouveaux 9 trous de Gayon et Lebreton vont modifier et encore élargir le paysage du golf de la Baule.

Nine of the original 18 holes designed by Alliss and Thomas in 1978 have been retained, while the other nine now form a separate par 35 course. To complete the main course, Michel Gayon designed nine additional holes, which have been inserted between the 4th and the 14th, and so break up the monotony of the earlier up and down holes (formerly holes 10 to 16). Obviously, there is a clear lack of unity in style, but the pleasure of walking La Baule countryside is as great as ever. As strategic as on the other holes, the «Gayon» greens and bunkers have been more carefully designed, with sharper relief (note the double green shared by the 5th and 12th holes), Hopefully the architect will redesign the nine original holes to create a more harmonious feel to this course, which is nicely organised for holiday-makers. But in the year 2000, two new 9 hole courses (designed by Gayon and Lebreton) will change and expand still further the golfing landscape of La Baule.

Golf de La Baule
1994

Domaine de Saint-Denac
F - 44117 SAINT-ANDRE-DES-EAUX

Office	Secrétariat	(33) 02 40 60 46 18
Pro shop	Pro-shop	(33) 02 40 60 46 18
Fax	Fax	(33) 02 40 60 41 41
Situation	Situation	

St-Nazaire (pop. 64 810), 12 km
La Baule (pop. 14 850), 7 km

Annual closure	Fermeture annuelle	no
Weekly closure	Fermeture hebdomadaire	tuesday
	(mardi) 1/11 → 31/3	

Fees main season
Tarifs haute saison full day

	Week days Semaine	We/Bank holidays We/Férié
Individual Individuel	330 F	330 F
Couple Couple	660 F	660 F
Caddy	Caddy	no
Electric Trolley	Chariot électrique	no
Buggy	Voiturette	200 F/18 holes
Clubs	Clubs	100 F/full day

Credit cards Cartes de crédit
VISA - CB - Eurocard - MasterCard - AMEX

230

Access Accès : La Baule → La Baule-Escoublac,
cross the road N171. → Golf
Map 5 on page 173 Carte 5 Page 173

GOLF COURSE
PARCOURS
15/20

Site	Site	▬▬▬▬▭▭
Maintenance	Entretien	▬▬▬▬▬▭
Architect	Architecte	Alliss & Thomas Michel Gayon
Type	Type	forest, open country
Relief	Relief	▬▬▭▭▭▭
Water in play	Eau en jeu	▬▬▬▭▭▭
Exp. to wind	Exposé au vent	▬▬▭▭▭▭
Trees in play	Arbres en jeu	▬▬▬▭▭▭

Scorecard	Chp.	Mens	Ladies
Carte de score	Chp.	Mess.	Da.
Length Long.	6127	5769	5176
Par	72	72	72

Advised golfing ability		0　12　24　36
Niveau de jeu recommandé		▬▬▬▬▭▭
Hcp required	Handicap exigé	30 (main season)

CLUB HOUSE & AMENITIES
CLUB HOUSE ET ANNEXES
7/10

Pro shop	Pro-shop	▬▬▬▬▭▭
Driving range	Practice	▬▬▬▭▭▭
Sheltered	couvert	10 mats
On grass	sur herbe	yes
Putting-green	putting-green	yes
Pitching-green	pitching green	yes

HOTEL FACILITIES
ENVIRONNEMENT HOTELIER
8/10

HOTELS HÔTELS
Castel Marie-Louise · La Baule
31 rooms, D 2 000 F · 7 km
Tel (33) 02 40 11 48 38, Fax (33) 02 40 11 48 35

Hermitage · La Baule
217 rooms, D 2 000 F · 7 km
Tel (33) 02 40 11 46 46, Fax (33) 02 40 11 46 45

Le Manoir du Parc · La Baule
18 rooms, D 550 F · 7 km
Tel (33) 02 40 60 24 52, Fax (33) 02 40 60 55 96

RESTAURANTS RESTAURANTS
La Marcandrerie · La Baule
Tel (33) 02 40 24 03 12 · 7 km

L'Hermitage · La Baule
Tel (33) 02 40 11 46 46 · 7 km

Avec dix hectares de plus et davantage de génie architectural, on aurait pu avoir un grand parcours. Mais c'est tout de même un parcours très correct et visuellement plaisant qu'une refonte du bunkering pourrait rapidement améliorer. La plupart des 60 et quelque bunkers sont trop étendus et surtout sans grand relief. De même, on peut trouver les greens beaucoup trop vastes, souvent disproportionnés avec le coup à jouer. On peut également penser que les obstacles d'eau sont trop regroupés sur la fin, et pas toujours bien placés (les joueurs peu expérimentés auront du mal à finir), mais les architectes avaient il est vrai un cahier des charges très contraignant sur ce secteur. Reste que malgré ces observations, l'ensemble ne manque ni de beauté, ni de qualités ni de grandeur, que l'hôtellerie sur place est de bonne qualité, et que les plus charmantes des femmes ont parfois des défauts, à bien regarder. Longtemps fermé, Bélesbat paraît repartir du bon pied.

With another 25 acres and little more imagination, this could have been a masterpiece. As it stands, this is a good and visually attractive course that could be easily improved with some changes made to the bunkering. Most of the 60 or something bunkers are too expansive and especially devoid of any topology. Likewise, you might find the greens much too large and disproportionate to the shot you need to play. You might also find that there is too much poorly positioned water hogging the back nine (inexperienced players will find the last few holes something of an ordeal) but it is true to say that the architects were given highly restrictive specifications in this respect. Despite everything, the whole course has much to be said for it in terms of beauty and quality and the on-site hotel is excellent. Let's face it, even the most beautiful face can have flaws when taking a really close look.

Golf de Bélesbat — 1990
F - 91820 BOUTIGNY-SUR-ESSONNE

Office	Secrétariat	(33) 01 69 23 19 10
Pro shop	Pro-shop	(33) 01 69 23 19 10
Fax	Fax	(33) 01 69 23 19 10
Situation	Situation	

Fontainebleau (pop. 15 714), 25 km

Annual closure	Fermeture annuelle	no
Weekly closure	Fermeture hebdomadaire	no

Fees main season
Tarifs haute saison 18 holes

	Week days Semaine	We/Bank holidays We/Férié
Individual Individuel	200 F	400 F
Couple Couple	400 F	800 F

Tuesday: 2 players for 1 green fee
(mardi, 1 GF pour 2 joueurs)

Caddy	Caddy	no
Electric Trolley	Chariot électrique	no
Buggy	Voiturette	170 F/18 holes
Clubs	Clubs	120 F

Credit cards Cartes de crédit
VISA - CB - Eurocard - MasterCard - AMEX - DC - JCB

Access Accès : Paris A6 Exit (sortie) 11 → Le Coudray.
D948 → Milly-la-Forêt. 9 km turn right on D83 → La Ferté-Alais. 4 km turn left on D153 to Boutigny. → Golf. Map 3 on page 168 Carte 3 Page 168

GOLF COURSE / PARCOURS — 14/20

Site	Site	
Maintenance	Entretien	
Architect	Architecte	Patrick Fromanger
Type	Type	parkland
Relief	Relief	
Water in play	Eau en jeu	
Exp. to wind	Exposé au vent	
Trees in play	Arbres en jeu	

Scorecard Carte de score	Chp. Chp.	Mens Mess.	Ladies Da.
Length Long.	6030	5698	5111
Par	72	72	72

Advised golfing ability 0 12 24 36
Niveau de jeu recommandé
Hcp required Handicap exigé 35

CLUB HOUSE & AMENITIES / CLUB HOUSE ET ANNEXES — 7/10

Pro shop	Pro-shop	
Driving range	Practice	
Sheltered	couvert	4 mats (with net)
On grass	sur herbe	no
Putting-green	putting-green	yes
Pitching-green	pitching green	yes

231

HOTEL FACILITIES / ENVIRONNEMENT HOTELIER — 7/10

HOTELS HÔTELS
Domaine de Belesbat — on site
61 rooms, D 985 F
Tel (33) 01 69 23 19 00, Fax (33) 01 69 23 19 01

Mercure — Le Coudray-Montceaux
125 rooms, D 650 F — 22 km
Tel (33) 01 64 99 00 00, Fax (33) 01 64 93 95 55

Bas Bréau — Barbizon
12 rooms, D 1200 F — 25 km
Tel (33) 01 60 66 40 05, Fax (33) 01 60 69 22 89

RESTAURANTS RESTAURANTS
Le Pavillon — Golf, on site
Tel (33) 01 69 23 19 00

Auberge d'Auvers Galant — Auvers
Tel (33) 01 64 24 51 20 — 10 km

BELLE-DUNE

Constituant l'une des bonnes réalisations récentes, ce golf public conserve ses qualités, bien que la plupart des bunkers n'aient toujours pas été «ensablés», alors qu'ils auraient apporté des contrastes visuels dans une symphonie de verts, et accentué le caractère de links, même si l'environnement est boisé sur un grand nombre de trous. Plusieurs greens sont presque aveugles, et leurs contours peuvent paraître parfois excessifs, mais on retrouve ces caractéristiques sur de nombreux links britanniques. Epousant les contours de dunes tourmentées (parfois de façon exagérée), ce golf est assez physique pour les golfeurs rouillés mais reste jouable à pied. Alors que les arbres protègent certains trous, d'autres plus dénudés deviennent très difficiles quand le vent est violent : il faudra alors davantage «limiter les dégâts» que rechercher les exploits. Un Club-House dans le style local complète cet équipement de bonne qualité, où l'accueil peut être cependant très «fonctionnaire»...

One of several excellent achievements of late, this public course retains a lot of its quality, although unfortunately most of the bunkers are still awaiting their sand. This is important to add a little visual contrast to a sea of green and to emphasise the links side to the course, even though a number of holes are more reminiscent of a woodland course. Several greens are almost blind and some of the slopes are a little excessive, but that is often the way it is on many British links. The course hugs the sometimes excessively twisting dunes, and although hilly, even the rustier golfers can play it without a buggy. While trees protect some of the holes, others are exposed and become a very tricky proposition once the wind gets up. The result is often an exercise in damage limitation rather than a quest for a good card. A Club-house in pure local style completes the high quality facilities at a course where the reception might sometimes seem off-hand.

Golf de Belle-Dune — 1993

Promenade du Marquenterre
F - 80790 FORT-MAHON-PLAGE

Office	Secrétariat	(33) 03 22 23 45 50
Pro shop	Pro-shop	(33) 03 22 23 45 50
Fax	Fax	(33) 03 22 23 93 41
Situation	Situation	

Le Touquet (pop. 5 590), 25 km
Berck-Plage (pop. 14 160), 20 km

Annual closure	Fermeture annuelle	no
Weekly closure	Fermeture hebdomadaire	no

only Fridays in winter (vendredi en hiver seulement)

Fees main season
Tarifs haute saison 18 holes

	Week days Semaine	We/Bank holidays We/Férié
Individual Individuel	210 F	260 F
Couple Couple	370 F	440 F
Caddy	Caddy	no
Electric Trolley	Chariot électrique	75 F/18 holes
Buggy	Voiturette	225 F/18 holes
Clubs	Clubs	60 F/full day

Credit cards Cartes de crédit VISA - CB - Eurocard

Access Accès : N1 Abbeville-Boulogne, → Rue,
→ Quend-Plage, D32 → Fort-Mahon-Plage, → Golf
Map 1 on page 164 Carte 1 Page 164

GOLF COURSE / PARCOURS — 16/20

Site	Site	
Maintenance	Entretien	
Architect	Architecte	Jean-Manuel Rossi
Type	Type	seaside course, forest
Relief	Relief	
Water in play	Eau en jeu	
Exp. to wind	Exposé au vent	
Trees in play	Arbres en jeu	

Scorecard Carte de score	Chp. Chp.	Mens Mess.	Ladies Da.
Length Long.	5952	5562	5008
Par	72	72	72

Advised golfing ability		0 12 24 36
Niveau de jeu recommandé		
Hcp required	Handicap exigé	35

CLUB HOUSE & AMENITIES / CLUB HOUSE ET ANNEXES — 6/10

Pro shop	Pro-shop	
Driving range	Practice	
Sheltered	couvert	10 mats
On grass	sur herbe	no, 150 mats open air
Putting-green	putting-green	yes
Pitching-green	pitching green	yes

HOTEL FACILITIES / ENVIRONNEMENT HOTELIER — 5/10

HOTELS HÔTELS
La Terrasse — Fort-Mahon-Plage
56 rooms, D 395 F — 1 km
Tel (33) 03 22 23 37 77, Fax (33) 03 22 23 36 74

Le Lion d'Or - 16 rooms, D 340 F — Rue 12 km
Tel (33) 03 22 25 74 18, Fax (33) 03 22 25 66 63

La Chipodière — Fort-Mahon-Plage
18 rooms, D 300 F — 1 km
Tel (33) 03 22 27 70 36, Fax (33) 03 22 23 38 16

RESTAURANTS RESTAURANTS
La Grenouillère — La Madelaine sous Montreuil
Tel (33) 03 21 06 07 22 — 12 km

La Terrasse — Fort-Mahon-Plage
Tel (33) 03 22 23 37 77 — 1 km

Auberge Le Fiacre — Routhiauville
Tél(33) 03 22 23 47 30 — 2 km

232

BESANÇON

Un golf très équilibré : le parcours se déroule dans un site agréable, entre plaine et forêt, il n'est pas trop plat, ni trop mouvementé, pas trop facile, ni trop difficile, avec très peu d'eau. Il offre ainsi un bon dosage des obstacles, une bonne alternance de trous faciles et plus délicats : de quoi satisfaire les débutants et les joueurs moyens, sans les effrayer par des difficultés hors de leurs compétences. Certes, les joueurs de haut niveau n'y trouveront alors pas leur compte, mais ce n'est pas la vocation de ce golf de les satisfaire exclusivement, il est essentiellement fréquenté par les joueurs de la région. Dessiné par Michael Fenn, il représente un style de parcours bien adapté à un usage «local», mais sans mériter vraiment le détour. Mais, d'avril à octobre, si vous êtes dans la région, vous avez l'assurance d'y passer une journée détendue.

A nicely balanced course, pleasantly located between plain and forest, not too flat and not too hilly, not too easy yet none too difficult, with little in the way of water. Hazards are astutely dispensed here and there, with easier holes alternating pleasantly with harder numbers, giving enough to satisfy beginners and twenty-plus handicappers without scaring them off with hazards that might be beyond them. Better players will certainly feel a touch of frustration, but there again the course was not designed with only them in mind. It is basically played by local players. Designed by Michael Fenn, the course's style is well suited to local golfing but not really worth any long trip out of your way. But if you are in the region between April and October, drop by and enjoy a good day out.

Golf Club de Besançon — 1972

La Chevillotte
F - 25620 MAMIROLLE

Office	Secrétariat	(33) 03 81 55 73 54
Pro shop	Pro-shop	(33) 03 81 55 86 13
Fax	Fax	(33) 03 81 55 88 64
Situation	Situation	

Besançon (pop. 113 820), 12 km

Annual closure	Fermeture annuelle	no
Weekly closure	Fermeture hebdomadaire	no

Fees main season
Tarifs haute saison full day

	Week days Semaine	We/Bank holidays We/Férié
Individual Individuel	200 F	250 F
Couple Couple	400 F	500 F

Caddy	Caddy	no
Electric Trolley	Chariot électrique	100 F/18 holes
Buggy	Voiturette	150 F/18 holes
Clubs	Clubs	50 F/full day

Credit cards Cartes de crédit
VISA - CB - Eurocard - MasterCard

Access Accès : Besançon N57 → Pontarlier / Lausanne, → Saône, → Golf
Map 8 on page 179 Carte 8 Page 179

GOLF COURSE / PARCOURS — 13/20

Site	Site	
Maintenance	Entretien	
Architect	Architecte	Michael Fenn
Type	Type	forest, country
Relief	Relief	
Water in play	Eau en jeu	
Exp. to wind	Exposé au vent	
Trees in play	Arbres en jeu	

Scorecard Carte de score	Chp. Chp.	Mens Mess.	Ladies Da.
Length Long.	6070	5705	5117
Par	72	72	72

Advised golfing ability		0 12 24 36
Niveau de jeu recommandé		
Hcp required	Handicap exigé	35

CLUB HOUSE & AMENITIES / CLUB HOUSE ET ANNEXES — 7/10

Pro shop	Pro-shop	
Driving range	Practice	
Sheltered	couvert	7 mats
On grass	sur herbe	no, 20 mats open air
Putting-green	putting-green	yes
Pitching-green	pitching green	yes

HOTEL FACILITIES / ENVIRONNEMENT HOTELIER — 5/10

HOTELS HÔTELS
Mercure-Parc Micaud — Besançon 12 km
95 rooms, D 600 F
Tel (33) 03 81 80 14 44, Fax (33) 03 81 53 29 83

Nord — Besançon 12 km
44 rooms, D 3020 F
Tel (33) 03 81 81 34 56, Fax (33) 03 81 81 85 96

Ibis Centre — Besançon 12 km
49 rooms, D 365 F
Tel (33) 03 81 81 02 02, Fax (33) 03 81 81 89 65

RESTAURANTS RESTAURANTS
Mungo Park — Besançon 12 km
Tel (33) 03 81 81 28 01

Le Chaland — Besançon 12 km
Tel (33) 03 81 80 61 61

233

BÉTHEMONT

Les premiers et derniers trous donnent l'impression d'un parcours physique, mais la plupart des trous sont situés sur un plateau. Il est assez court, mais bordé d'arbres souvent bien en jeu, avec un grand nombre de bunkers, de beaux obstacles d'eau, et quelques doglegs assez diaboliques. La signature de Bernhard Langer est évidente en ce qu'elle réclame beaucoup de précision avec les fers, pas mal de réflexion avant de jouer, plus que de la longueur. Dans ces conditions, une seule visite ne suffit pas pour prétendre le maîtriser, et les joueurs moyens risquent de le trouver trop exigeant pour eux au premier abord, d'autant que les greens sont souvent très modelés. On ne saurait placer Béthemont parmi les grands parcours de la région parisienne, mais on peut y passer une bonne journée. Assez humide, il ne saurait être conseillé en dehors de la période de mai à octobre, où son entretien devient très correct.

The 1st and 18th at Béthemont give the impression of a physically demanding course, but in reality the majority of holes are laid out on a plateau. Rather short by today's standards, the course is edged by what sometimes seem to be unmissable trees and is generously dotted with bunkers, attractive water hazards and a few devilish dog-legs. This is a Bernhard Langer design, and it shows, calling for precision ironwork and a lot of thought before each stroke. Length off the tee is secondary. Under these conditions, a single round is hardly enough to get to grips with the course and the less experienced player may well find it too demanding first time out, especially with the undulating greens. Perhaps not one of the greatest courses around Paris, Béthemont does however make for an excellent day's golfing. Owing to the wet, we would not recommend the course outside the May to October period, when upkeep and green-keeping are very good.

Béthemont Chisan Club — 1989
12, rue du Parc de Béthemont
F - 78300 POISSY

Office	Secrétariat	(33) 01 39 75 51 13
Pro shop	Pro-shop	(33) 01 39 75 51 13
Fax	Fax	(33) 01 39 75 49 90
Situation	Situation	

Paris (pop. 2 175 200), 25 km

Annual closure	Fermeture annuelle	no
Weekly closure	Fermeture hebdomadaire	tuesday
		mardi

Fees main season
Tarifs haute saison full day

	Week days Semaine	We/Bank holidays We/Férié
Individual Individuel	250 F	500 F
Couple Couple	500 F	1 000 F

Caddy	Caddy	on request
Electric Trolley	Chariot électrique	no
Buggy	Voiturette	no
Clubs	Clubs	100 F/full day

Credit cards Cartes de crédit
VISA - CB - Eurocard - MasterCard - AMEX - JCB

234

Access Accès : A13 Paris-Rouen, Exit (Sortie) Poissy → Chambourcy, roundabout → Saint-Germain, 1st road on the right.
Map 15 on page 192 Carte 15 Page 192

GOLF COURSE / PARCOURS — 14/20

Site	Site	
Maintenance	Entretien	
Architect	Architecte	Bernhard Langer
Type	Type	forest, hilly
Relief	Relief	
Water in play	Eau en jeu	
Exp. to wind	Exposé au vent	
Trees in play	Arbres en jeu	

Scorecard Carte de score	Chp. Chp.	Mens Mess.	Ladies Da.
Length Long.	6035	5550	5128
Par	72	72	72

Advised golfing ability Niveau de jeu recommandé		0 12 24 36
Hcp required Handicap exigé	35	

CLUB HOUSE & AMENITIES / CLUB HOUSE ET ANNEXES — 7/10

Pro shop	Pro-shop	
Driving range	Practice	
Sheltered	couvert	5 mats
On grass	sur herbe	no, 9 mats open air
Putting-green	putting-green	yes
Pitching-green	pitching green	no

HOTEL FACILITIES / ENVIRONNEMENT HOTELIER — 5/10

HOTELS HÔTELS

Moulin d'Orgeval — Orgeval
14 rooms, D 800 F — 5 km
Tel (33) 01 39 75 85 74,
Fax (33) 01 39 75 48 52

Novotel — Orgeval
119 rooms, D 580 F — 5 km
Tel (33) 01 39 22 35 11,
Fax (33) 01 39 75 48 93

RESTAURANTS RESTAURANTS

L'Esturgeon — Poissy
Tel (33) 01 39 65 00 04 — 4 km

Dessiné il y a plus de 100 ans par Willie Dunn, ce parcours a été tellement modifié qu'il n'a plus rien du quasi «links» des origines. Ayant perdu ses trous de bord de mer, c'est devenu un joli golf de parc, très court, ce qui ne veut pas dire facile à scorer. Les greens peuvent être rendus démoniaques, et même une attaque avec un petit fer peut alors s'avérer redoutable. Les fairways sont séparés par de minces rideaux d'arbres et arbustes, et si l'on n'est pas précis, il vaut mieux s'en écarter franchement que de rester entre deux fairways. Mais, sauf aux 1, 15 et 16, il est inutile de jouer le driver au départ, un bois 3 ou un long fer suffit largement. On peut considérer «Le Phare» comme un peu désuet, mais il porte la tradition irremplaçable du golf des origines en Pays Basque, et peut être joué à tous les niveaux. Le prix du green-fee est peut-être anormalement élevé pour ce type de parcours.

Laid out more than 100 years ago by Willie Dunn, this course has seen so much change that there is virtually nothing left of the original links. Having lost its sea-side holes, it has become a pretty parkland course, very short but by no means easy. The greens can be devilishly tricky, and even short iron approach shots can prove to be a formidable ordeal. The fairways are separated by thin rows of trees and bushes, so if you are going to stray left or right, go the whole way to avoid being stuck in the middle ground. The 3-wood or a long iron will suffice here, except on the 1st, 15th and 16th holes where you can go for your driver. «Le Phare» could be considered a little antiquated, but it bears the irreplaceable tradition of the origins of golf in the Basque country and can be played by golfers of all levels. The green fee has become probably abnormally high for this type of course.

Golf de Biarritz-Le-Phare 1888
2, avenue Edith-Cavell
F - 64200 BIARRITZ

Office	Secrétariat	(33) 05 59 03 71 80
Pro shop	Pro-shop	(33) 05 59 03 71 80
Fax	Fax	(33) 05 59 03 26 74
Situation	Situation	

Biarritz (pop. 28 740), 1 km

Annual closure	Fermeture annuelle	no
Weekly closure	Fermeture hebdomadaire	no

only tuesday out of main season (mardi basse saison)

Fees main season
Tarifs haute saison 18 holes

	Week days Semaine	We/Bank holidays We/Férié
Individual Individuel	330 F	330 F
Couple Couple	595 F	595 F

Caddy	Caddy	on request
Electric Trolley	Chariot électrique	70 F/18 holes
Buggy	Voiturette	200 F/18 holes
Clubs	Clubs	50 F/full day

Credit cards Cartes de crédit
VISA - CB - Eurocard - MasterCard - AMEX

Access Accès : A63 Exit (Sortie) Biarritz la Négresse, →
Biarritz, → Anglet
Map 12 on page 186 Carte 12 Page 186

GOLF COURSE
PARCOURS 14/20

Site	Site	
Maintenance	Entretien	
Architect	Architecte	Willie Dunn
Type	Type	residential
Relief	Relief	
Water in play	Eau en jeu	
Exp. to wind	Exposé au vent	
Trees in play	Arbres en jeu	

Scorecard Carte de score	Chp. Chp.	Mens Mess.	Ladies Da.
Length Long.	5376	5059	4633
Par	69	69	69

Advised golfing ability		0 12 24 36
Niveau de jeu recommandé		
Hcp required	Handicap exigé	35

CLUB HOUSE & AMENITIES
CLUB HOUSE ET ANNEXES 6/10

Pro shop	Pro-shop	
Driving range	Practice	
Sheltered	couvert	8 mats
On grass	sur herbe	no, 7 mats open air
Putting-green	putting-green	yes
Pitching-green	pitching green	no

HOTEL FACILITIES
ENVIRONNEMENT HOTELIER 8/10

HOTELS HÔTELS
Le Palais
134 rooms, D 2 000 F
Tel (33) 05 59 41 64 00, Fax (33) 05 59 41 67 99
Biarritz
1 km

Regina et Golf
61 rooms, D 1350 F
Tel (33) 05 59 41 33 00, Fax (33) 05 59 41 33 99
Biarritz
1 km

Miramar
110 rooms, D 2 000 F
Tel (33) 05 59 41 30 00, Fax (33) 05 59 24 77 20
Biarritz
1 km

RESTAURANTS RESTAURANTS
Café de Paris
Tel (33) 05 59 24 19 53
Biarritz
1 km

Les Platanes
Tel (33) 05 59 23 13 68
Biarritz
2 km

235

14	6	5

Son excellent entretien distingue ce parcours, ainsi que son site pittoresque, entouré de forêt. Assez accidenté pour offrir de beaux points de vue sur la région, mais aussi demander une bonne forme physique, ses difficultés sont assez visibles pour être abordé sans complexes dès la première fois. L'architecture de Fromanger et Adam a conservé le caractère naturel du lieu, elle manque un peu de grandeur, mais la franchise de leur dessin est à souligner. Il n'a pas été possible d'éviter un green aveugle (le 14), mais s'il reste le seul, les autres sont assez bien défendus pour exiger souvent de porter la balle. Quelques obstacles d'eau ponctuent le paysage, mais ils sont assez peu en jeu. Assez facile des départs avancés, le parcours progresse en difficultés à mesure que l'on recule, et sa longueur est plus effective qu'au vu de la carte, en raison des importantes dénivellations.

A course that stands out for its excellent upkeep, plus a picturesque setting surrounded by a forest. Hilly enough to provide some fine views over the region and to require a good pair of legs, the course's difficulties are visible enough for players to cope first time out. The architecture, by Fromanger and Adam, has preserved the site's natural character, and although not a great layout, the course is open and fair, a point we would like to emphasise. They were unable to avoid one blind green (the 14th), while the others are defended enough to require lofted shots almost every time. The landscape is dotted with water hazards which don't really come into play. Easy enough from the front tees, it logically gets harder as you move back, and the overall yardage plays longer than you might guess from the card, owing to some steep slopes.

Golf de Bitche　　　　1988
Rue des Prés
F - 57230 BITCHE

Office	Secrétariat	(33) 03 87 96 15 30
Pro shop	Pro-shop	(33) 03 87 96 10 00
Fax	Fax	(33) 03 87 96 08 04
Situation	Situation	

Sarreguemines (pop. 23 117), 33 km - Haguenau, 43 km

Annual closure	Fermeture annuelle	yes
		25/12 → 1/1
Weekly closure	Fermeture hebdomadaire	no

Fees main season
Tarifs haute saison 18 holes

	Week days Semaine	We/Bank holidays We/Férié
Individual Individuel	190 F	290 F
Couple Couple	380 F	580 F

Caddy	Caddy	no
Electric Trolley	Chariot électrique	no
Buggy	Voiturette	200 F/18 holes
Clubs	Clubs	70 F/full day

Credit cards Cartes de crédit
VISA - CB - Eurocard - MasterCard

236

Access Accès : A32 → Metz, Exit (Sortie)
Sarreguemines, N62 → Bitche
Map 4 on page 171 Carte 4 Page 171

GOLF COURSE
PARCOURS　　　　**14**/20

Site	Site	
Maintenance	Entretien	
Architect	Architecte	Marc Adam
		Patrick Fromanger
Type	Type	forest, hilly
Relief	Relief	
Water in play	Eau en jeu	
Exp. to wind	Exposé au vent	
Trees in play	Arbres en jeu	

Scorecard Carte de score	Chp. Chp.	Mens Mess.	Ladies Da.
Length Long.	6074	5759	5127
Par	72	72	72

Advised golfing ability Niveau de jeu recommandé	0	12	24	36

Hcp required　Handicap exigé　35 (We)

CLUB HOUSE & AMENITIES
CLUB HOUSE ET ANNEXES　　**6**/10

Pro shop	Pro-shop	
Driving range	Practice	
Sheltered	couvert	6 mats
On grass	sur herbe	yes
Putting-green	putting-green	yes
Pitching-green	pitching green	yes

HOTEL FACILITIES
ENVIRONNEMENT HOTELIER　　**5**/10

HOTELS HÔTELS
Relais des Châteaux-Forts　　　　　　　Bitche
30 rooms, D 365 F　　　　　　　　　　　800 m
Tél (33) 03 87 96 14 14, Fax (33) 03 87 96 07 36

Auberge de Strasbourg　　　　　　　　Bitche
11 rooms, D 290 F　　　　　　　　　　　1 km
Tél (33) 03 87 96 00 44, Fax (33) 03 87 06 10 60

RESTAURANTS RESTAURANTS
Relais des Châteaux-Forts　　　　　　　Bitche
Tél (33) 03 87 96 14 14　　　　　　　　800 m

Auberge de la Tour　　　　　　　　　　Bitche
Tél(33) 03 87 96 29 25　　　　　　　　1 km

Auberge de Strasbourg　　　　　　　　Bitche
Tél (33) 03 87 96 00 44　　　　　　　　1 km

BONDUES BLANC ♪ 16 7 6

Le «Blanc» offre la particularité d'offrir neuf trous de Robert Trent Jones père et neuf trous du fils. L'architecture est évidemment très américaine, avec de multiples obstacles d'eau, en jeu sur près d'une douzaine de trous. Qaund ils le peuvent, les membres se réfugient sur le "Jaune", moins pénalisant de ce point de vue. Comme les arbres sont peu menaçants, marquant simplement les limites des trous, a panoplie des obstacles est complétée par de nombreux bunkers, protégeant à la fois les arrivées de drive et les greens. Cependant, le parcours n'est pas très long, et, une fois familiarisé avec l'eau, il n'est pas impossible de jouer son handicap. Certes, les joueurs de niveau moyen auront du mal à scorer, mais ce 18 trous amène une rupture des habitudes tout à fait bienvenue. Les greens sont de bonne dimension, assez profonds pour poser des problèmes de choix de club.

The «Blanc» course has the peculiarity of featuring nine holes designed by Robert Trent Jones Sr et nine by his son Robert Trent Jones Jr. This is evidently a very American style course with countless water hazards in play on almost a dozen holes. Whenever they can, members seek solace on the «Jaune» course, a little easier a far as water is concerned. Since the trees offer very little threat and are there simply to demarcate the holes, the panoply of hazards is completed by numerous bunkers, protecting both the tee-shot landing site and the greens. With this said, the course is not too long, and once you have become acquainted with the water, playing to your handicap is not impossible. High handicappers might be hard put to card a good score, but this 18-hole layout makes a welcome break from your everyday course. The greens are nicely sized and deep enough to pose a few problems for club selection.

Golf de Bondues — 1967
Château de la Vigne
F - 59910 BONDUES

Office	Secrétariat	(33) 03 20 23 20 62
Pro shop	Pro-shop	no Pro shop
Fax	Fax	(33) 03 20 23 24 11
Situation	Situation	

Lille (pop. 178 300), 6 km
Tourcoing (pop. 93 760), 4 km

Annual closure	Fermeture annuelle	no
Weekly closure	Fermeture hebdomadaire	tuesday mardi

Fees main season
Tarifs haute saison full day

	Week days Semaine	We/Bank holidays We/Férié
Individual Individuel	200 F	300 F
Couple Couple	300 F	450 F

Caddy	Caddy	no
Electric Trolley	Chariot électrique	no
Buggy	Voiturette	200 F/18 holes
Clubs	Clubs	no

Credit cards Cartes de crédit VISA - CB

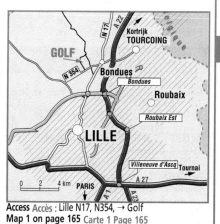

Access Accès : Lille N17, N354, → Golf
Map 1 on page 165 Carte 1 Page 165

GOLF COURSE / PARCOURS — 16/20

Site	Site	
Maintenance	Entretien	
Architect	Architecte	R. Trent Jones Sr R. Trent Jones Jr residential
Type	Type	
Relief	Relief	
Water in play	Eau en jeu	
Exp. to wind	Exposé au vent	
Trees in play	Arbres en jeu	

Scorecard Carte de score	Chp. Chp.	Mens Mess.	Ladies Da.
Length Long.	6012	5576	5072
Par	72	72	72

Advised golfing ability
Niveau de jeu recommandé   0   12   24   36

Hcp required Handicap exigé   34

CLUB HOUSE & AMENITIES / CLUB HOUSE ET ANNEXES — 7/10

Pro shop	Pro-shop	
Driving range	Practice	
Sheltered	couvert	8 mats
On grass	sur herbe	no, 20 mats open air
Putting-green	putting-green	yes
Pitching-green	pitching green	yes

HOTEL FACILITIES / ENVIRONNEMENT HOTELIER — 6/10

HOTELS HÔTELS
Sofitel — Marcq-en-Barœul
125 rooms, D 900 F — 5 km
Tél (33) 03 20 72 17 30, Fax (33) 03 20 89 92 34

Alliance — Lille
80 rooms, D 1 000 F — 6 km
Tél (33) 03 20 30 62 62, Fax (33) 03 20 42 94 25

Mercure — Roubaix
92 rooms, D 560 F — 5 km
Tél (33) 03 20 73 40 00, Fax (33) 03 20 73 22 42

RESTAURANTS RESTAURANTS
L'Huitrière - Tél (33) 03 20 55 43 41 — Lille 6 km
Auberge de la Garenne — Bondues 2 km
Tél (33) 03 20 46 20 20
Château Blanc Tél (33) 03 20 21 81 41 — Verlinghem 6 km

237

Bondues est l'un des grands clubs traditionnels de la région lilloise, et d'un accès parfois difficile en week-end. Le parcours «Jaune» est signé Fred Hawtree, dans la pure tradition britannique, avec assez peu d'obstacles d'eau, mais des arbres bien en jeu et des bunkers de dessin sans originalité particulière de forme, mais toujours bien placés. En revanche, il n'est pas très facile de mémoriser le parcours, sans grande personnalité ni recherche esthétique très affirmée. Il n'en est pas plus facile pour autant d'y scorer. Bondues «Jaune» fait partie de ces parcours classiques parfaitement adaptés à leur destination : il a été essentiellement conçu pour ses membres (qui trouvent facilement leurs marques et leurs habitudes) et non pour des voyageurs de passage. Certes, la région n'est pas vraiment une destination de vacances, mais la réouverture du parcours «Blanc» en a fait une halte très intéressante, avec deux parcours complémentaires.

Bondues is one of the great traditional clubs from the Lille region and is sometimes difficult to play on week-ends. The «Jaune» course was designed by Fred Hawtree in the pure British tradition, i.e. few water hazards but trees very much in play and bunkers that, although hardly original in shape and design, are always well placed. This is not a course that sticks in the memory ; it has no clear-cut personality or research into style, although that doesn't mean it is any easier to score on. Bondues «Jaune» is one of those classic courses that is perfectly suited to the people it was designed for, i.e. basically club members (who can easily find their landmarks and habits) and not for green-feers passing through. Sure, the region is not really a holiday destination, but the re-opening of the «Blanc» course has made it a very interesting stop-off, with two complementary layouts.

Golf de Bondues		1967
Château de la Vigne		
F - 59910 BONDUES		
Office	Secrétariat	(33) 03 20 23 20 62
Pro shop	Pro-shop	no Pro shop
Fax	Fax	(33) 03 20 23 24 11
Situation	Situation	
Lille (pop. 178 300), 6 km		
Tourcoing (pop. 93 760), 4 km		
Annual closure	Fermeture annuelle	no
Weekly closure	Fermeture hebdomadaire	tuesday mardi

Fees main season
Tarifs haute saison full day

	Week days Semaine	We/Bank holidays We/Férié
Individual Individuel	200 F	300 F
Couple Couple	300 F	450 F

Caddy	Caddy	no
Electric Trolley	Chariot électrique	no
Buggy	Voiturette	200 F/18 holes
Clubs	Clubs	no

Credit cards Cartes de crédit VISA - CB

238

Access Accès : Lille N17, N354, → Golf
Map 1 on page 165 Carte 1 Page 165

GOLF COURSE
PARCOURS   15/20

Site	Site	
Maintenance	Entretien	
Architect	Architecte	Frederic Hawtree
Type	Type	parkland, residential
Relief	Relief	
Water in play	Eau en jeu	
Exp. to wind	Exposé au vent	
Trees in play	Arbres en jeu	

Scorecard	Chp.	Mens	Ladies
Carte de score	Chp.	Mess.	Da.
Length Long.	6260	5878	5150
Par	73	73	73

Advised golfing ability	0	12	24	36
Niveau de jeu recommandé				
Hcp required	Handicap exigé	34		

CLUB HOUSE & AMENITIES
CLUB HOUSE ET ANNEXES   7/10

Pro shop	Pro-shop	
Driving range	Practice	
Sheltered	couvert	8 mats
On grass	sur herbe	no, 20 mats open air
Putting-green	putting-green	yes
Pitching-green	pitching green	yes

HOTEL FACILITIES
ENVIRONNEMENT HOTELIER   6/10

HOTELS HÔTELS
Sofitel — Marcq-en-Barœul
125 rooms, D 900 F — 5 km
Tel (33) 03 20 72 17 30, Fax (33) 03 20 89 92 34

Alliance - 80 rooms, D 1 000 F — Lille
Tel (33) 03 20 30 62 62, Fax (33) 03 20 42 94 25 — 6 km

Mercure - 92 rooms, D 560 F — Roubaix
Tel (33) 03 20 73 40 00, Fax (33) 03 20 73 22 42 — 5 km

RESTAURANTS RESTAURANTS
L'Huitrière - Tel (33) 03 20 55 43 41 — Lille 6 km
Auberge de la Garenne — Bondues
Tel (33) 03 20 46 20 20 — 2 km
Château Blanc — Verlinghem
Tel (33) 03 20 21 81 41 — 6 km

BORDES (LES)

Si ce parcours reste incontestablement au premier rang français, son entretien est devenu moins rigoureux depuis la disparition de son fondateur Marcel Bich, mais il reste très bon. Il fait partie de ces parcours impossibles à ignorer, pour son tracé d'une grande variété de jeu et de stratégie, et pour son environnement : Les Bordes est une initiation à la Sologne, le parcours un lieu de méditation sur la vérité de son propre jeu, où il est impossible de maquiller ses faiblesses. Notre jugement précédent reste entier : si vous l'abordez avec simplicité, intelligence et humilité, il pourra se montrer généreux. Le practice, le Club-House, les chambres rustiques sont exemplaires. Ici, l'argent investi ne s'étale pas, comme si cet ensemble récent avait des siècles d'existence. Désormais largement ouvert aux membres extérieurs, c'est un «incontournable» du golf, comme une grande adresse gastronomique où le prix du plaisir n'a pas d'importance.

While still undoubtedly one of France's top-rate courses, upkeep has fallen away somewhat since the death of its founder, Marcel Bich, but remains very good. Les Bordes is one of those courses you simply have to play for its variety in layout, its ever-changing game strategy and its setting. Les Bordes is an introduction to the Sologne and the course an arena of meditation for the truth about your golfing ability. Any chinks in your game are ruthlessly exposed. Our previous judgment is still valid. If you approach the course with simplicity, intelligence and humility, it can be rewarding in terms of score. The driving range, club-house and country-style rooms are excellent, with no ostentatious signs of new investment, rather as if this recently-designed course had been around for centuries. Now wide-open to green-feers, Les Bordes is an absolute must and a great address for excellent food. Here, the price of sheer pleasure matters little.

Golf International des Bordes   1987
F - 41220 SAINT-LAURENT-NOUAN

Office	Secrétariat	(33) 02 54 87 72 13
Pro shop	Pro-shop	(33) 02 54 87 72 13
Fax	Fax	(33) 02 54 87 78 61
Situation	Situation	

Beaugency pop. 6 910, 11 km Orléans pop. 105 110, 30 km

Annual closure	Fermeture annuelle	no
Weekly closure	Fermeture hebdomadaire	no

Fees main season
Tarifs haute saison 18 holes

	Week days Semaine	We/Bank holidays We/Férié
Individual Individuel	375 F	575 F
Couple Couple	650 F	1 000 F

Seniors 250 F (weekdays/semaine)

Caddy	Caddy	no
Electric Trolley	Chariot électrique	no
Buggy	Voiturette	250 F/18 holes
Clubs	Clubs	150 F/full day

Credit cards Cartes de crédit
VISA - CB - Eurocard - MasterCard - AMEX

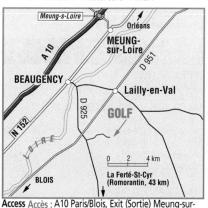

Access Accès : A10 Paris/Blois, Exit (Sortie) Meung-sur-Loire, N152 → Beaugency. In Beaugency → Lailly-en-Val. Cross over the Loire, → La Ferté Saint- Cyr (D925) **Map 3 on page 168** Carte 3 Page 168

GOLF COURSE
PARCOURS   19/20

Site	Site	
Maintenance	Entretien	
Architect	Architecte	Robert von Hagge
Type	Type	forest, open country
Relief	Relief	
Water in play	Eau en jeu	
Exp. to wind	Exposé au vent	
Trees in play	Arbres en jeu	

Scorecard Carte de score	Chp. Chp.	Mens Mess.	Ladies Da.
Length Long.	6412	6023	5317
Par	72	72	72

Advised golfing ability Niveau de jeu recommandé	0	12	24	36
Hcp required Handicap exigé	no			

CLUB HOUSE & AMENITIES
CLUB HOUSE ET ANNEXES   8/10

Pro shop	Pro-shop	
Driving range	Practice	
Sheltered	couvert	no
On grass	sur herbe	yes
Putting-green	putting-green	yes
Pitching-green	pitching green	yes

HOTEL FACILITIES
ENVIRONNEMENT HOTELIER   6/10

HOTELS HÔTELS
Dormy House   on site
20 rooms, D 950 F
Tel (33) 02 54 87 72 13, Fax (33) 02 54 87 78 61

La Tonnellerie 15 rooms, D 600 F   Tavers
Tel (33) 02 38 44 68 15, Fax (33) 02 38 44 10 01   10 km

Les Chênes Rouges   Villeny
10 rooms, D 800 F   20 km
Tel (33) 02 54 98 23 94, Fax (33) 02 54 98 23 99

Relais des Templiers 14 rooms, D 240 F   Beaugency
Tel (33) 02 38 44 53 78   7 km

RESTAURANTS RESTAURANTS
Ferme de la Lande   La Ferté-Saint-Aubin
Tel (33) 02 38 76 64 37

Auberge Gourmande   Baule
Tel (33) 02 38 45 01 02   20 km

239

Le seul véritable reproche que l'on puisse faire à ce parcours, c'est que les arbres ont pris une telle densité depuis les origines que s'ils constituent un bon écran contre l'autoroute voisine, on peut éprouver sinon une sensation de claustrophobie, du moins se trouver à l'étroit. Ce n'est pas fait pour ceux qui aiment les grands espaces. Parcours original du Golf de Paris, devenu Golf du Racing-Club de France (le plus grand club omnisports français), «La Vallée» réclame un jeu très complet, des drives puissants et droits, des fers très précis pour des greens souvent assez animés, et une grande maîtrise des coups de rattrapage (balles basses sous les arbres !). Sans oublier les sorties de bunker car ils protègent solidement les greens. Quelques coups aveugles sont ici inévitables en raison du relief général assez prononcé mais sans fatigue excessive (sauf au 9). A connaître.

The only real reproach you can level at this course is that the trees have grown so thick since its inception that, while now they form an effective sound barrier from the neighbouring motorway, they also create a feeling if not of claustrophobia then at least of having very little space to play in. This is not a course for golfers who love wide open expanses. The original Golf de Paris course and now one of the two courses of the Racing-Club de France (France's biggest all sports club), «La Vallée» requires a good all-round game, powerful and straight driving, accurate ironwork for greens that are often lively affairs, and mastery in the art of recovery (particularly hitting very low shots from under the trees). And that's not forgetting escaping from bunkers that offer a solid line of defence around the greens. A few blind shots were unavoidable here owing to the general relief of the terrain, which is hilly but not too tiring (except the 9th). Well worth knowing.

Golf de La Boulie - Racing Club de France
1901
F - 78000 VERSAILLES

Office	Secrétariat	(33) 01 39 50 59 41
Pro shop	Pro-shop	(33) 01 39 49 92 77
Fax	Fax	(33) 01 39 49 04 16
Situation	Situation	

Paris (pop. 2 175 200), 22 km

Annual closure	Fermeture annuelle	no
Weekly closure	Fermeture hebdomadaire	tuesday mardi

Fees main season
Tarifs haute saison 18 holes

	Week days Semaine	We/Bank holidays We/Férié
Individual Individuel	400 F	500 F*
Couple Couple	800 F	1 000 F*

* members' guests (sur invitation d'un membre)

Caddy	Caddy	on request
Electric Trolley	Chariot électrique	80 F/18 holes
Buggy	Voiturette	no
Clubs	Clubs	150 F/18 holes
Credit cards Cartes de crédit		no

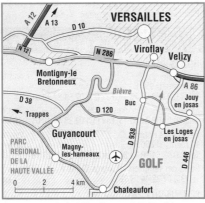

Access Accès : Paris A13 → Rouen, Exit (Sortie)
Versailles-Vaucresson. D182 → Versailles, D185 →
Château, → Versailles-Chantiers. N186 → Golf.
Map 15 on page 192 Carte 15 Page 192

GOLF COURSE PARCOURS   15/20

Site	Site	
Maintenance	Entretien	
Architect	Architecte	
Type	Type	forest
Relief	Relief	
Water in play	Eau en jeu	
Exp. to wind	Exposé au vent	
Trees in play	Arbres en jeu	

Scorecard Carte de score	Chp. Chp.	Mens Mess.	Ladies Da.
Length Long.	5995	5698	5062
Par	72	72	72

Advised golfing ability	0 12 24 36
Niveau de jeu recommandé	
Hcp required Handicap exigé	24 Men, 28 Ladies

CLUB HOUSE & AMENITIES CLUB HOUSE ET ANNEXES   7/10

Pro shop	Pro-shop	
Driving range	Practice	
Sheltered	couvert	15 mats
On grass	sur herbe	no, 5 mats open air
Putting-green	putting-green	yes
Pitching-green	pitching green	yes

HOTEL FACILITIES ENVIRONNEMENT HOTELIER   8/10

HOTELS HÔTELS

Trianon Palace   Versailles
94 rooms, D 1 800 F   3 km
Tel (33) 01 30 84 38 00, Fax (33) 01 39 49 00 77

Pavillon Trianon   Versailles
98 rooms, D 1 000 F   3 km
Tel (33) 01 30 84 38 00, Fax (33) 01 39 51 57 79

Résidence du Berry   Versailles
38 rooms, D 600 F   3 km
Tel (33) 01 39 49 07 07, Fax (33) 01 39 50 59 40

RESTAURANTS RESTAURANTS

Les Trois Marches Tel (33) 01 39 50 13 21 Versailles 3 km

Valmont - Tel (33) 01 39 51 39 00   Versailles 3 km

Le Potager du Roy   Versailles
Tél (33) 01 39 50 35 34   3 km

240

BRESSE (LA)

15 6 4

Dans une région très calme, sur un terrain peu fatigant, Jeremy Pern a dessiné un parcours faisant appel à toutes les qualités : puissance, précision du grand jeu, subtilité du petit jeu, finesse du putting. Certes, il est difficile à jouer quand il est mouillé, mais il prend toute sa dimension aux beaux jours. Le rythme de jeu est excellent, avec une bonne alternance de trous de plaine et de trous tracés dans les bois, permettant à tous les goûts de trouver leur plaisir. Les golfeurs expérimentés auront l'occasion d'affronter des défis intéressants, notamment pour choisir leurs clubs, mais les joueurs de tous niveaux ne sont jamais vraiment découragés. Les greens, assez modelés, sont délicats à interpréter, et peuvent «charger la carte» quand on ne parvient pas à les lire. Le Club-House est sympathique, la restauration de bonne qualité est typique d'une région où l'on sait bien manger. L'entretien est actuellement revu dans le bon sens.

In a calm region on flattish terrain, Jeremy Pern has designed a course which requires just about every golfing skill: power and precision off the tee, a sharp and clever short game and fine putting. It might be hard to play in damp conditions, but when the sun shines the course comes into its own. The tempo of play is good here, with a pleasant mixture of alternating open-field and woodland holes. In fact, there's something for all tastes. The more experienced golfer will enjoy the opportunity to get to grips with a number of interesting challenges, especially for club selection, but the lesser player will never really feel too despondent, either. The undulating greens are not always easy to read and can, as always, add a few unwelcome strokes to the card when mis-read. The club-house is very pleasant and the food is good... typical, you might suppose, of a region where they know what good food is all about. Green-keeping is only average on what is a naturally wet course, but efforts are being made to put this right.

Golf-Club de la Bresse — 1990
Domaine de Mary
F - 01400 CONDEISSIAT

Office	Secrétariat	(33) 04 74 51 42 09
Pro shop	Pro-shop	(33) 04 74 51 42 09
Fax	Fax	(33) 04 74 51 40 09
Situation	Situation	

Bourg-en-Bresse (pop. 40 970), 15 km

Annual closure	Fermeture annuelle	no
Weekly closure	Fermeture hebdomadaire	no

Fees main season
Tarifs haute saison full day

	Week days Semaine	We/Bank holidays We/Férié
Individual Individuel	200 F	250 F
Couple Couple	350 F	450 F

Caddy	Caddy	no
Electric Trolley	Chariot électrique	70 F/18 holes
Buggy	Voiturette	200 F/18 holes
Clubs	Clubs 1/2 série	50 F/full day

Credit cards Cartes de crédit
VISA - CB - Eurocard - MasterCard - AMEX

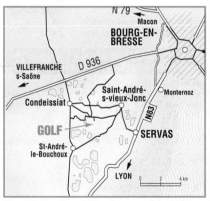

Access Accès : • Lyon, N83 → Bourg-en-Bresse. Servas, → Condeissiat • Mâcon A40, Exit (Sortie) Bourg-en-Bresse Nord, D936 → Châtillon-sur-Chalaronne, on the left, Condeissiat → Servas
Map 11 on page 184 Carte 11 Page 184

GOLF COURSE
PARCOURS
15/20

Site	Site	
Maintenance	Entretien	
Architect	Architecte	Jeremy Pern
Type	Type	open country, forest
Relief	Relief	
Water in play	Eau en jeu	
Exp. to wind	Exposé au vent	
Trees in play	Arbres en jeu	

Scorecard Carte de score	Chp. Chp.	Mens Mess.	Ladies Da.
Length Long.	6217	5748	5190
Par	72	72	72

Advised golfing ability Niveau de jeu recommandé		0 12 24 36
Hcp required	Handicap exigé	no

CLUB HOUSE & AMENITIES
CLUB HOUSE ET ANNEXES
6/10

Pro shop	Pro-shop	
Driving range	Practice	
Sheltered	couvert	7 mats
On grass	sur herbe	yes
Putting-green	putting-green	yes
Pitching-green	pitching green	no

241

HOTEL FACILITIES
ENVIRONNEMENT HOTELIER
4/10

HOTELS HÔTELS

Georges Blanc	Vonnas
32 rooms, D 1000 F	7 km
Tel (33) 04 74 50 00 10, Fax (33) 04 74 50 08 80	
La Résidence des Saules	Vonnas
10 rooms, D 600 F	7 km
Tel (33) 04 74 50 90 51, Fax (33) 04 74 50 08 80	
Hôtel de France	Bourg-en-Bresse
46 rooms, D 400 F	12 km
Tel (33) 04 74 23 30 24, Fax (33) 04 74 23 69 90	

RESTAURANTS RESTAURANTS

Jacques Guy	Bourg-en-Bresse
Tel (33) 04 74 45 29 11	15 km
Georges Blanc	Vonnas
Tel (33) 04 74 50 90 90	7 km

BREST IROISE

Tracé en paysage de landes, ce golf est le plus occidental de France. Michael Fenn y a dessiné un parcours épousant un terrain qui se prêtait bien à la construction d'un golf, avec un certain nombre de dénivellations pour rompre la monotonie. Elles permettent d'offrir de beaux points de vue sur la campagne et les Monts d'Arée. Le paysage - sinon le jeu - est agrémenté d'une végétation rustique et dense, de genêts et de gros rochers. De longueur raisonnable, il est accessible à tous les niveaux, avec des greens généralement très fermes, et bien défendus par des bunkers au dessin cependant sans grande subtilité. L'entretien a beaucoup progressé, grâce à d'importants travaux de drainage. Le Club-House venant d'être transféré au Golf hôtel tout proche, totalement modernisé, Brest Iroise devient une véritable destination de week-end.

Laid out amidst heath and moorland, this is France's western-most course. Michael Fenn has designed a course that hugs terrain that was almost made for golf, with a number of slopes to break the monotony. This gives some fine views over the country and the Monts d'Arée. The landscape, and the round, is enhanced with some thick country bush, gorse-bushes and rocks. Reasonable in length, golfers of all standards can play here and enjoy greens that are generally hard and well defended by some pretty ordinary bunkers. Upkeep has improved considerably thanks to some extensive drainage work, and now that the club-house has been transferred to the nearby and totally refurbished Golf hotel, Brest Iroise is now a real week-end destination.

Golf de Brest Iroise — 1976
Parc de Lann-Rohou, Saint-Urbain
F - 29800 LANDERNEAU

Office	Secrétariat	(33) 02 98 85 16 17
Pro shop	Pro-shop	(33) 02 98 85 16 17
Fax	Fax	(33) 02 98 85 19 39
Situation	Situation	

Landerneau (pop. 14 720), 4 km
Brest (pop. 147 950), 24 km

Annual closure	Fermeture annuelle	no
Weekly closure	Fermeture hebdomadaire	no

Fees main season
Tarifs haute saison full day

	Week days Semaine	We/Bank holidays We/Férié
Individual Individuel	230 F	260 F
Couple Couple	460 F	520 F

Caddy	Caddy	no
Electric Trolley	Chariot électrique	no
Buggy	Voiturette	120 F/18 holes
Clubs	Clubs	50 F/full day

Credit cards Cartes de crédit
VISA - CB - Eurocard - MasterCard - AMEX - DC

242

Access Accès : • N12, D170 → Landerneau, → Golf
• N165, Daoulas → Landerneau, → Golf
Map 5 on page 172 Carte 5 Page 172

GOLF COURSE / PARCOURS — 14/20

Site	Site	
Maintenance	Entretien	
Architect	Architecte	Michael Fenn
Type	Type	open country
Relief	Relief	
Water in play	Eau en jeu	
Exp. to wind	Exposé au vent	
Trees in play	Arbres en jeu	

Scorecard Carte de score	Chp. Chp.	Mens Mess.	Ladies Da.
Length Long.	5672	5464	4873
Par	71	71	71

Advised golfing ability	0	12	24	36
Niveau de jeu recommandé				
Hcp required	Handicap exigé	no		

CLUB HOUSE & AMENITIES / CLUB HOUSE ET ANNEXES — 7/10

Pro shop	Pro-shop	
Driving range	Practice	
Sheltered	couvert	11 mats
On grass	sur herbe	no, 9 mats open air
Putting-green	putting-green	yes
Pitching-green	pitching green	yes

HOTEL FACILITIES / ENVIRONNEMENT HOTELIER — 6/10

HOTELS HÔTELS
Golf Hôtel de l'Iroise — Golf, on site
44 rooms, D 350 F
Tel (33) 02 98 85 16 17,
Fax (33) 02 98 85 19 39

Le Clos du Pontic — Landerneau 3 km
32 rooms, D 350 F
Tel (33) 02 98 21 50 91,
Fax (33) 02 98 21 34 33

RESTAURANTS RESTAURANTS
Le Clos du Pontic — Landerneau 3 km
Tel (33) 02 98 21 50 91

La Mairie — Landerneau 3 km
Tel (33) 02 98 85 01 83

BRETESCHE (LA)

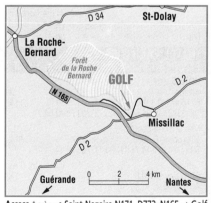 **15 7 7**

D'un parcours sans grande longueur, on attendrait des greens très travaillés et bien défendus, dont l'approche soit d'autant plus compliquée qu'on les attaque avec des petits fers. Ce n'est pas la difficulté technique qui inspirera pour sublimer son jeu. Heureusement, l'environnement de parc est très joli, le château séduisant pour les étrangers : ce lieu typique d'une certaine idée de la France plaît beaucoup. S'il est difficile de souligner un quelconque aspect surprenant du parcours, sinon l'habituel trou en boomerang (le 16 ici) de l'architecte Bill Baker, le plaisir d'évoluer sur ce parcours bien entretenu est évident. Le dessin des trous est honorable, les greens et bunkers sans grosses difficultés, leurs défenses raisonnables. Cela fait donc un parcours très plaisant pour y évoluer en famille, et pour la majorité des joueurs, dans un ensemble très soigné. Les meilleurs attendent sans doute des défis de plus grande ampleur.

Over a shortish course, you might expect carefully designed and well-defended greens, made even more complicated by the fact that the approach shot is more often than not a short iron. However here, it is certainly not the technical difficulty that will inspire golfers to better things. Fortunately, the park's surroundings are very pretty and the castle appealing to foreigners, who like the spot for the way it represents a typical picture thay have of France. While it is difficult to underline any one surprising aspect of the course, excepting the usual boomerang hole by designer Bill Baker (the 16th), the pleasure of playing here on a well-manicured course is obvious. The holes are pleasantly laid out, and the greens and bunkers are none too difficult and reasonably well-defended. All in all, this gives a course without too much danger which is agreeable to play with all the family and players of almost every ability, especially since the whole complex has been carefully designed. Perhaps the very best players could expect tougher challenges.

Golf de la Breteche — 1967

Domaine de la Breteche
F - 44780 MISSILLAC

Office	Secrétariat	(33) 02 51 76 86 86
Pro shop	Pro-shop	(33) 02 51 76 86 86
Fax	Fax	(33) 02 40 88 36 28
Situation	Situation	

Redon (pop. 9 260), 24 km
La Baule (pop. 14 850), 30 km

Annual closure	Fermeture annuelle	no
Weekly closure	Fermeture hebdomadaire	no

Fees main season
Tarifs haute saison full day

	Week days Semaine	We/Bank holidays We/Férié
Individual Individuel	320 F	320 F
Couple Couple	640 F	640 F
Caddy Caddy		on request
Electric Trolley Chariot électrique		no
Buggy Voiturette		250 F/18 holes
Clubs Clubs		100 F/full day

Credit cards Cartes de crédit
VISA - CB - Eurocard - MasterCard - AMEX

Access Accès : • Saint-Nazaire N171, D773, N165 → Golf
• La Baule D774, N165 → Golf
Map 6 on page 174 Carte 6 Page 174

GOLF COURSE PARCOURS — 15/20

Site	Site	
Maintenance	Entretien	
Architect	Architecte	Bill Baker
Type	Type	forest, parkland
Relief	Relief	
Water in play	Eau en jeu	
Exp. to wind	Exposé au vent	
Trees in play	Arbres en jeu	

Scorecard Carte de score	Chp. Chp.	Mens Mess.	Ladies Da.
Length Long.	6080	5809	5136
Par	72	72	72

Advised golfing ability		0 12 24 36
Niveau de jeu recommandé		
Hcp required	Handicap exigé	35

CLUB HOUSE & AMENITIES CLUB HOUSE ET ANNEXES — 7/10

Pro shop	Pro-shop	
Driving range	Practice	
Sheltered	couvert	10 mats
On grass	sur herbe	yes
Putting-green	putting-green	yes
Pitching-green	pitching green	yes

HOTEL FACILITIES ENVIRONNEMENT HOTELIER — 7/10

HOTELS HÔTELS
Golf de la Breteche — on site
27 rooms, D 1000 F
Tel (33) 02 51 76 86 96, Fax (33) 02 40 66 99 47

Cottage de la Breteche — on site
30 rooms, 3890 F/week
Tel (33) 02 40 88 31 18

Domaine de Bodeuc — Nivillac
8 rooms, D 590 F — 12 km
Tel (33) 02 99 90 89 63, Fax (33) 02 99 90 90 32

Auberge de Kerhinet — Saint-Lyphard
7 rooms, D 300 F — 14 km
Tel (33) 02 40 61 91 46, Fax (33) 02 40 61 97 57

RESTAURANTS RESTAURANTS
Auberge Bretonne — La Roche-Bernard
Tel (33) 02 99 90 60 28 — 11 km

243

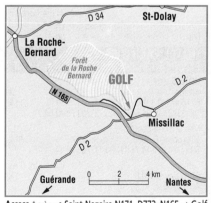

Ce parcours signé Harold Baker est l'un des grands clubs traditionnels des Lillois, dont beaucoup y ont élu résidence, mais l'impression d'un golf immobilier n'est pas trop pesante car les maisons sont de bonne qualité. Assez plat, quelques obstacles d'eau, un bon nombre de bunkers, et les arbres lui donnent des allures de grand parc à la britannique, d'allure assez harmonieuse et séduisante. A côté de cet environnement, c'est un parcours aussi agréable pour les joueurs de bon niveau que pour les joueurs moyens. Certes, ce n'est pas un test d'une énorme difficulté, l'architecture est restée sobre, peut-être même un peu timide, mais on a visiblement recherché à favoriser le plaisir du jeu en famille. Un vrai «golf de membres» où les golfeurs de passage seront mieux accueillis en semaine, les week-ends étant souvent chargés.

This Harold Baker course is one of the great traditional clubs of Lille and many people have bought homes here. The quality standard of houses fortunately rules out any great impression of this being a property development course. Being rather flat, with a few water hazards and a good number of bunkers, Brigode looks like a British park, at once harmonious and attractive. Alongside this setting, the course is pleasant for skilled and less skilful golfers alike. It is certainly not too tough a test for the better golfer, as the architecture is unobtrusive and even a little on the shy side, but the designers visibly were looking to promote the pleasure of family golfing. This is a real «members' club» where green-fees get a warmer welcome during the week. Week-ends are often heavily booked.

Golf de Brigode   1967

36, avenue du Golf
F - 59650 VILLENEUVE-D'ASCQ

Office	Secrétariat	(33) 03 20 91 17 86
Pro shop	Pro-shop	no Pro shop
Fax	Fax	(33) 03 20 05 96 36
Situation	Situation	

Lille (pop. 178 300), 11 km

Annual closure	Fermeture annuelle	no
Weekly closure	Fermeture hebdomadaire	tuesday (mardi)

Fees main season
Tarifs haute saison 18 holes

	Week days Semaine	We/Bank holidays We/Férié
Individual Individuel	200 F	300 F
Couple Couple	400 F	600 F

Caddy	Caddy	no
Electric Trolley	Chariot électrique	no
Buggy	Voiturette	200 F/18 holes
Clubs	Clubs	50 F/18 holes

Credit cards Cartes de crédit
VISA - CB - Eurocard - MasterCard

244

Access Accès : «Rocade» Paris-Gand • Paris/Lille, Exit (Sortie) Pont de Bois → Annappes-cousinerie • Gand-Tourcoing, Exit (Sortie) Roubaix-Est, 1 km on the right → Annappes. 2 km, in front of Stadium → Golf
Map 1 on page 165 Carte 1 Page 165

GOLF COURSE
PARCOURS   14/20

Site	Site	
Maintenance	Entretien	
Architect	Architecte	Bill Baker
Type	Type	parkland
Relief	Relief	
Water in play	Eau en jeu	
Exp. to wind	Exposé au vent	
Trees in play	Arbres en jeu	

Scorecard Carte de score	Chp. Chp.	Mens Mess.	Ladies Da.
Length Long.	6106	6106	5152
Par	72	72	72

Advised golfing ability   0   12   24   36
Niveau de jeu recommandé
Hcp required Handicap exigé   30

CLUB HOUSE & AMENITIES
CLUB HOUSE ET ANNEXES   7/10

Pro shop	Pro-shop	
Driving range	Practice	
Sheltered	couvert	6 mats
On grass	sur herbe	no, 34 mats open air
Putting-green	putting-green	yes
Pitching-green	pitching green	no

HOTEL FACILITIES
ENVIRONNEMENT HOTELIER   6/10

HOTELS HÔTELS

Alliance   Lille
80 rooms, D 1 000 F   11 km
Tel (33) 03 20 30 62 62, Fax (33) 03 20 42 94 25

Mercure Lille-Centre   Lille
102 rooms, D 580 F   11 km
Tel (33) 03 20 14 71 47, Fax (33) 03 20 14 71 48

Campanile   Villeneuve-d'Ascq
47 rooms, D 350 F   1 km
Tel (33) 03 20 91 83 10, Fax (33) 03 20 67 21 18

RESTAURANTS RESTAURANTS

L'Huitrière   Lille
Tel (33) 03 20 55 43 41   11 km

La Porte de Gand   Lille
Tel (33) 03 20 74 28 66   11 km

Si personne ne sait qui a dessiné le 18 trous original de Mandelieu, on sait que le grand architecte Harry Colt a participé à son remaniement, comme en témoigne la forme des bunkers, parfois assez profonds pour poser problème aux joueurs moyens. Pourtant, ce sont les pins parasols qui constituent les principaux obstacles, leur envergure impressionnante rendant bien étroits les fairways. Les techniciens adorent ce parcours, car la plupart des coups de départ demandent des effets de fade ou de draw, un contrôle précis des trajectoires, un choix de club très subtil pour se retrouver en bonne position et signer les birdies que l'on peut espérer. Si sa longueur ne répond plus tout à fait aux exigences du jeu moderne, Cannes-Mandelieu reste un parcours de charme, dont le rajeunissement paraît porter ses fruits. Les par 3 (il y en a cinq) y sont d'une remarquable diversité.

While no-one knows exactly who laid out the original 18 holes at Mandelieu, we do know that the great Harry Colt had a hand in re-designing the course, as seen in the shape of the bunkers that are sometimes deep enough to cause high-handicappers a few headaches. Yet the main hazards here are the huge parasol pines, which stretch majestically upward and outward and make a number of fairways a little on the tight side. The more technically-minded golfers love this course, because the majority of tee-shots require draws or fades, precise flight control and very careful club selection to get into the right position to line up the birdies we all hope and pray for. While not as long as the modern game might require, Cannes-Mandelieu remains a charming course, where restyling work seems to be having the right effect. The five par 3s are remarkable for their variety.

Golf de Cannes Mandelieu Old Course
1891

Route du Golf
F - 06210 MANDELIEU

Office	Secrétariat	(33) 04 92 97 32 00
Pro shop	Pro-shop	(33) 04 92 97 32 00
Fax	Fax	(33) 04 93 49 92 90
Situation	Situation	

Cannes (pop. 68 670), 5 km

Annual closure	Fermeture annuelle	no
Weekly closure	Fermeture hebdomadaire	no

Fees main season
Tarifs haute saison full day

	Week days Semaine	We/Bank holidays We/Férié
Individual Individuel	330 F	330 F
Couple Couple	660 F	660 F

Caddy	Caddy	no
Electric Trolley	Chariot électrique	60 F/18 holes
Buggy	Voiturette	180 F/18 holes
Clubs	Clubs	100 F/full day

Credit cards Cartes de crédit
VISA - CB - Eurocard - MasterCard - AMEX

Access Accès : A8 Exit (Sortie) Mandelieu-La Napoule,
→ Mandelieu, → « Old Course »
Map 14 on page 191 Carte 14 Page 191

GOLF COURSE
PARCOURS
14/20

Site	Site	
Maintenance	Entretien	
Architect	Architecte	Harry Colt
Type	Type	seaside course, forest
Relief	Relief	
Water in play	Eau en jeu	
Exp. to wind	Exposé au vent	
Trees in play	Arbres en jeu	

Scorecard Carte de score	Chp. Chp.	Mens Mess.	Ladies Da.
Length Long.	5676	5676	4973
Par	71	71	71

Advised golfing ability		0 12 24 36
Niveau de jeu recommandé		
Hcp required	Handicap exigé	28

CLUB HOUSE & AMENITIES
CLUB HOUSE ET ANNEXES
7/10

Pro shop	Pro-shop	
Driving range	Practice	
Sheltered	couvert	10 mats
On grass	sur herbe	yes
Putting-green	putting-green	yes
Pitching-green	pitching green	yes

245

HOTEL FACILITIES
ENVIRONNEMENT HOTELIER
8/10

HOTELS HÔTELS
Hostellerie du Golf — Mandelieu — 1 km
39 rooms, D 660 F
Tel (33) 04 93 49 11 66, Fax (33) 04 92 97 04 01

Majestic — Cannes — 5 km
263 rooms, D 2 200 F
Tel (33) 04 92 98 77 00, Fax (33) 04 93 38 97 90

Paris — Cannes — 5 km
50 rooms, D 700 F
Tel (33) 04 93 38 30 89, Fax (33) 04 93 39 04 61

RESTAURANTS RESTAURANTS
La Palme d'Or — Cannes — 5 km
Tel (33) 04 92 98 74 14

Arcimboldo - Tél(33) 04 93 94 14 15 — Cannes

Villa des Lys (Majestic) - Tel (33) 04 92 98 77 00 — Cannes

Longtemps le club le plus prestigieux et le mieux entretenu de la région, il s'est un peu endormi face à la concurrence, mais paraît vouloir retrouver son prestige. Sa séduction apparente dissimule ses réelles difficultés. Les obstacles d'eau ne sont pas nombreux, mais ils sont placés de manière très stratégique. Si on peut avoir l'impression de pouvoir signer un bon score, le parcours résiste bien, notamment parce qu'il est difficile de récupérer le par quand on a manqué un green. Très divers dans son tracé, très bien paysagé, il ne récompense que les meilleurs, et surtout les techniciens du golf, les manieurs de balles. Pendant plus de dix ans, Cannes-Mougins a servi de cadre à un Open européen, ce qui a contribué à améliorer la qualité du terrain et à imposer des transformations. La grandeur passée de Cannes-Mougins revit parfois ici mais l'accueil est rarement chaleureux.

For many a year the region's most prestigious and best-kept golf course, Cannes-Mougins has of late been caught napping by competitors. It only now seems to be striving to recover some of its prestige. The course's outer appeal tends to hide the real difficulties. There are not many water hazards, but what water there is is strategically placed. And while signing for a good score might look a possibility, the course always fights back, more notably because saving par can be so hard when you miss a green. Full of variety and nicely landscaped, this course rewards only the best, and especially the technicians who can flight the ball. Cannes-Mougins has hosted a top European Open event for more than 10 years, which has helped to improve the quality of the course and led to necessary changes. You sometimes get glimpses of the past greatness of Cannes-Mougins, but there is rarely a warm welcome to be had here.

Golf Country Club de Cannes Mougins
1978

175, Avenue du Golf
F - 06250 MOUGINS

Office	Secrétariat	(33) 04 93 75 79 13
Pro shop	Pro-shop	(33) 04 93 75 53 32
Fax	Fax	(33) 04 93 75 27 60
Situation	Situation	

Cannes (pop. 68 670), 9 km

Annual closure	Fermeture annuelle	no
Weekly closure	Fermeture hebdomadaire	no

Fees main season
Tarifs haute saison full day

	Week days Semaine	We/Bank holidays We/Férié
Individual Individuel	400 F	450 F
Couple Couple	680 F	760 F

Caddy	Caddy	on request
Electric Trolley	Chariot électrique	no
Buggy	Voiturette	280 F/18 holes
Clubs	Clubs	yes

Credit cards Cartes de crédit
VISA - CB - Eurocard - MasterCard - AMEX

246

Access Accès : A8. Exit (Sortie) Mougins, → Grasse,
Exit (Sortie) Antibes, → Golf
Map 14 on page 191 Carte 14 Page 191

GOLF COURSE
PARCOURS
15/20

Site	Site	▰▰▰▰▱
Maintenance	Entretien	▰▰▰▰▱
Architect	Architecte	Peter Alliss Dave Thomas
Type	Type	forest, parkland
Relief	Relief	▰▰▱▱▱
Water in play	Eau en jeu	▰▰▱▱▱
Exp. to wind	Exposé au vent	▰▰▱▱▱
Trees in play	Arbres en jeu	▰▰▰▱▱

Scorecard Carte de score	Chp. Chp.	Mens Mess.	Ladies Da.
Length Long.	6263	5889	5314
Par	72	72	72

Advised golfing ability		0 12 24 36
Niveau de jeu recommandé		▰▰▰▱
Hcp required	Handicap exigé	24 Men, 28 Ladies

CLUB HOUSE & AMENITIES
CLUB HOUSE ET ANNEXES
7/10

Pro shop	Pro-shop	▰▰▰▰▱
Driving range	Practice	▰▰▰▱▱
Sheltered	couvert	5 mats
On grass	sur herbe	yes
Putting-green	putting-green	yes
Pitching-green	pitching green	yes

HOTEL FACILITIES
ENVIRONNEMENT HOTELIER
8/10

HOTELS HÔTELS

Hôtel de Mougins 50 rooms, D 1 070 F Tel (33) 04 92 92 17 07, Fax (33) 04 92 92 17 08		Mougins
Les Muscadins 8 rooms, D 900 F Tel (33) 04 93 92 28 28, Fax (33) 04 92 92 88 23		Mougins 5 km
Le Manoir de l'Etang 15 rooms, D 1 000 F Tel (33) 04 93 90 01 07, Fax (33) 04 92 92 20 70		Mougins 5 km

RESTAURANTS RESTAURANTS

Les Muscadins Tel (33) 04 92 28 28 28		Mougins 5 km
Le Moulin de Mougins - Tel (33) 04 93 75 78 24		Mougins 5 km
L'Amandier de Mougins Tel (33) 04 93 90 00 91		Mougins 5 km

CAP D'AGDE

Le dessin de Ronald Fream est de grande qualité, et même si l'entretien a progressé, les abords immédiats des fairways restent trop rocailleux, ce qui pose toujours des problèmes quand on y envoie sa balle. Tous les trous demandent une bonne dose de réflexion avant de prendre de risques nécessaires pour espérer un bon score. Même si les obstacles sont bien visibles, leur nombre et leur placement stratégique poseront des problèmes aux débutants. Les joueurs moyens s'en sortiront mieux, et les frappeurs devront être d'une grande précision, surtout quand le vent souffle, ce qui arrive assez souvent ici. Une belle réussite architecturale, mais qui exigerait un entretien parfait. La station balnéaire de Cap d'Agde est très proche et pas bien belle, mais sa présence n'est pas trop envahissante, grâce aux modelages du parcours, et à une certaine végétation.

This layout, designed by Ronald Fream, is excellent, but the areas immediately skirting the fairways are still too rocky and so pose a few problems for wayward shots. All the holes here require careful thought before taking the risks required if you hope to card a good score. Even though most hazards are there to be seen, their number and strategic placement might be a little too much for beginners. Mid-handicappers should get by a little easier, although big-hitters should aim for precision, espcially when the wind gets up, as it does fairly often. In architectural terms this is an impressive site, but one which requires perfect upkeep. The seaside resort of Cap d'Agde is close by and hardly the most beautiful sight on earth, but the way the course is contoured and the vegetation keep most of it out of view.

Golf du Cap d'Agde — 1989

4, avenue des Alizés
F - 34300 CAP D'AGDE

Office	Secrétariat	(33) 04 67 26 54 40
Pro shop	Pro-shop	(33) 04 67 26 54 40
Fax	Fax	(33) 04 67 26 97 00
Situation	Situation	

Béziers (pop. 71 000), 22 km

Annual closure	Fermeture annuelle	no
Weekly closure	Fermeture hebdomadaire	no

Fees main season
Tarifs haute saison full day

	Week days Semaine	We/Bank holidays We/Férié
Individual Individuel	260 F	260 F
Couple Couple	520 F	520 F

Caddy	Caddy	no
Electric Trolley	Chariot électrique	no
Buggy	Voiturette	140 F/18 holes
Clubs	Clubs	60 F/full day

Credit cards Cartes de crédit
VISA - CB - Eurocard - MasterCard

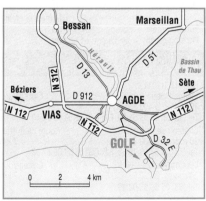

Access Accès : A9 Exit (Sortie) 34 → Agde, → « Ile des Loisirs », golf in front of «Aqualand»
Map 13 on page 189 Carte 13 Page 189

GOLF COURSE / PARCOURS — 15/20

Site	Site	▰▰▰▱
Maintenance	Entretien	▰▰▰▱
Architect	Architecte	Ronald Fream
Type	Type	seaside course, open country
Relief	Relief	▰▱▱▱
Water in play	Eau en jeu	▰▰▱▱
Exp. to wind	Exposé au vent	▰▰▰▰
Trees in play	Arbres en jeu	▰▰▱▱

Scorecard Carte de score	Chp. Chp.	Mens Mess.	Ladies Da.
Length Long.	6301	6160	5204
Par	72	72	72

Advised golfing ability
Niveau de jeu recommandé   0   12   24   36

Hcp required   Handicap exigé   no

CLUB HOUSE & AMENITIES / CLUB HOUSE ET ANNEXES — 6/10

Pro shop	Pro-shop	▰▰▰▱
Driving range	Practice	▰▰▰▱
Sheltered	couvert	no
On grass	sur herbe	yes
Putting-green	putting-green	yes
Pitching-green	pitching green	yes

247

HOTEL FACILITIES / ENVIRONNEMENT HOTELIER — 5/10

HOTELS HÔTELS

Hôtel du Golf   Cap d'Agde
50 rooms, D 660 F   1,5 km
Tel (33) 04 67 26 87 03, Fax (33) 04 67 26 26 89

Capaô   Cap d'Agde
45 rooms, D 700 F   2 km
Tel (33) 04 67 26 99 44, Fax (33) 04 67 26 55 41

Azur   200 m du golf
33 rooms, D 500 F
Tel (33) 04 67 26 98 22, Fax (33) 04 67 26 48 14

RESTAURANTS RESTAURANTS

La Tamarissière   Agde
Tel (33) 04 67 94 20 87   2 km

La Table d'Emilie   Marseillan
Tel (33) 04 67 77 63 59   6 km

CASTELJALOUX

14	6	5

L'une des belles réussites de l'architecte Michel Gayon dans une région assez à l'écart des grands circuits golfiques, mais très agréable pour de grands week-ends ou des vacances. Les cinq premiers trous du parcours se situent au milieu des pins et des chênes, avant qu'il s'élargisse dans un vaste espace autour d'un lac. Ses reliefs ne sont pas trop accentués, mais suffisants pour éviter l'écueil de la monotonie visuelle, permettant une grande variété de trous en montée ou en descente, avec cependant quelques coups aveugles. Très bien équilibré au plan du rythme de jeu, ce parcours n'offre pas de trous très longs, ce qui permet aux joueurs de tous niveaux d'y évoluer sans problèmes de cohabitation. Le golf fait partie d'un complexe sportif permettant aux non-golfeurs de décliner l'honneur de tirer le chariot : ils ont mieux à faire ! Seul problème, un entretien parfois bien défaillant. A surveiller...

One of Michel Gayon's finest achievements in a region rather off the beaten track when it comes to golf courses, yet a pleasant spot for long week-ends or holidays. The first five holes run through pine-trees and oaks, before broadening out into a vast area around a lake. The course is not too hilly, but slopes enough to avoid visual monotony and to provide a good variety of uphill and downhill holes, plus, unfortunately, a few blind shots. Nicely balanced for a brisk round of golf, the course has no really long holes, so is suitable for golfers of all handicaps to get along together. The golf course is part of a sports complex to tempt non-players away from pulling trolleys, and they certainly will have better things to do here.The only problem is maintenance, which is sometimes pretty poor. Watch out!

Casteljaloux Golf Club — 1989
Avenue du Lac
F - 47700 CASTELJALOUX

Office	Secrétariat	(33) 05 53 93 51 60
Pro shop	Pro-shop	(33) 05 53 93 51 60
Fax	Fax	(33) 05 53 20 90 98
Situation	Situation	

Agen (pop. 30 550), 60 km
Bordeaux (pop. 211 200), 90 km

Annual closure	Fermeture annuelle	no
Weekly closure	Fermeture hebdomadaire	no

Fees main season
Tarifs haute saison full day

	Week days Semaine	We/Bank holidays We/Férié
Individual Individuel	130 F	170 F
Couple Couple	260 F	340 F

Caddy	Caddy	no
Electric Trolley	Chariot électrique	no
Buggy	Voiturette	160 F/18 holes
Clubs	Clubs	60 F/full day

Credit cards Cartes de crédit
VISA - CB - Eurocard - MasterCard

Access Accès : A62 Bordeaux-Agen, Exit (Sortie) Marmande, D933 → Casteljaloux, → Mont-de-Marsan, Golf 3 km. **Map 12 on page 187** Carte 12 Page 187

GOLF COURSE PARCOURS — 14/20

Site	Site	
Maintenance	Entretien	
Architect	Architecte	Michel Gayon
Type	Type	open country
Relief	Relief	
Water in play	Eau en jeu	
Exp. to wind	Exposé au vent	
Trees in play	Arbres en jeu	

Scorecard Carte de score	Chp. Chp.	Mens Mess.	Ladies Da.
Length Long.	5916	5484	4983
Par	72	72	72

Advised golfing ability Niveau de jeu recommandé	0	12	24	36

Hcp required — Handicap exigé — no

CLUB HOUSE & AMENITIES CLUB HOUSE ET ANNEXES — 6/10

Pro shop	Pro-shop	
Driving range	Practice	
Sheltered	couvert	6 mats
On grass	sur herbe	no, 14 mats open air
Putting-green	putting-green	yes
Pitching-green	pitching green	yes

HOTEL FACILITIES ENVIRONNEMENT HOTELIER — 5/10

HOTELS HÔTELS
Village Hôtel — Casteljaloux 250 m
10 rooms, D 400 F
Tel (33) 05 53 93 51 60, Fax (33) 05 53 93 04 10

Château de Ruffiac — Route de Ruffiac 7 km
20 rooms, D 480 F
Tel (33) 05 53 93 18 63, Fax (33) 05 53 89 67 93

Les Cordeliers — Casteljaloux 2 km
24 rooms, D 290 F
Tel (33) 05 53 93 02 19

RESTAURANTS RESTAURANT
Le Trianon — Marmande 23 km
Tel (33) 05 53 20 80 94

Vieille Auberge — Casteljaloux 2 km
Tel (33) 05 53 93 01 36

248

CÉLY

15	7	6

Dessiné par Fromanger et Adam, ce parcours a été remodelé à la suite de son achat par un groupe japonais, il est alors devenu un véritable jardin, très paysagé, où le moindre détail était soigné. Longtemps célèbre par un Club house luxueux et un entretien éblouissant, digne de véritables manucures, il a subi quelques revers financiers et ces avantages se sont aujourd'hui estompés, révélant les insuffisances du tracé. C'est un très agréable parcours, mais il manque de longueur et de difficultés stratégiques pour passionner les joueurs de bon niveau. Son tracé est agréable, les attaques de green sont très intéressantes, les trous sont de profils variés, mais il manque sans doute un zeste de génie et de «souffle» pour en faire un «grand» parcours. Jouer Cély est à recommander, le jouer souvent est une autre question. Un regret, le bruit de l'autoroute toute proche.

Originally designed by Fromanger and Adam, Cély has been restyled further to a buy-out by a Japanese group. It is now very much a landscaped garden in style, where no detail, no matter how small, has been overlooked. Famous for its luxurious club-house and manicured fairways and greens, the club has met with a few financial difficulties and these features have lost some of their shine, revealing in the process some of the layout's shortcomings. This is a very pleasant course, but it lacks the length and strategic complexity to excite the best players. The layout is pleasing with some interesting approach shots to the greens, and the holes offer variety enough, but it is almost certainly lacks that touch of genius and the staying power to be a truly great course. A round of golf at Cély is to be recommended, but playing it often is another matter. The one drawback is the noise from the adjacent A6 motorway.

Cély Golf Club — 1990

Château de Cély, route de Saint-Germain
F - 77930 CELY-EN-BIERE

Office	Secrétariat	(33) 01 64 38 03 07
Pro shop	Pro-shop	(33) 01 64 38 03 07
Fax	Fax	(33) 01 64 38 08 78
Situation	Situation	

Fontainebleau (pop. 15 710), 14 km
Melun (pop. 35 320), 12 km

Annual closure	Fermeture annuelle	no
Weekly closure	Fermeture hebdomadaire	no

Fees main season
Tarifs haute saison full day

	Week days Semaine	We/Bank holidays We/Férié
Individual Individuel	300 F	400 F
Couple Couple	600 F	800 F

Ladies' day on thursday (jeudi) : GF + tea time: 250 F

Caddy	Caddy	no
Electric Trolley	Chariot électrique	100 F/18 holes
Buggy	Voiturette	no
Clubs	Clubs	100 F/full day

Credit cards Cartes de crédit
VISA - CB - Eurocard - MasterCard - AMEX - DC - JCB

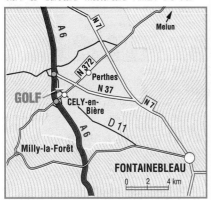

Access Accès : • A6 Paris → Lyon, Exit (Sortie)
Fontainebleau, Milly-la-Forêt • A 6 Lyon → Paris, Exit
(Sortie) Cély **Map 3 on page 168** Carte 3 Page 168

GOLF COURSE / PARCOURS — 15/20

Site	Site	
Maintenance	Entretien	
Architect	Architecte	Marc Adam Patrick Fromanger
Type	Type	parkland
Relief	Relief	
Water in play	Eau en jeu	
Exp. to wind	Exposé au vent	
Trees in play	Arbres en jeu	

Scorecard Carte de score	Chp. Chp.	Mens Mess.	Ladies Da.
Length Long.	6026	5739	5118
Par	72	72	72

Advised golfing ability	0	12	24	36
Niveau de jeu recommandé				

Hcp required	Handicap exigé	30

CLUB HOUSE & AMENITIES / CLUB HOUSE ET ANNEXES — 7/10

Pro shop	Pro-shop	
Driving range	Practice	
Sheltered	couvert	no
On grass	sur herbe	yes
Putting-green	putting-green	yes
Pitching-green	pitching green	yes

249

HOTEL FACILITIES / ENVIRONNEMENT HOTELIER — 6/10

HOTELS HÔTELS

Bas Bréau — Barbizon
12 rooms, D 1200 F — 7 km
Tel (33) 01 60 66 40 05, Fax (33) 01 60 69 22 89

Les Pléïades — Barbizon
23 rooms, D 560 F — 7 km
Tel (33) 01 60 66 40 25, Fax (33) 01 60 69 41 68

Aigle Noir — Fontainebleau
49 rooms, D 1050 F — 14 km
Tel (33) 01 60 74 60 00, Fax (33) 01 60 74 60 01

RESTAURANTS RESTAURANTS

Le Bas Bréau — Barbizon
Tel (33) 01 60 66 40 05 — 7 km

Le Grand Veneur — Barbizon
Tel (33) 01 60 66 40 44 — 7 km

Avec ce golf à proximité de Dijon et de l'autoroute A6 (sans bruits), le propriétaire souhaitait faire un «links» à l'intérieur des terres. Il n'a pas souhaité faire de plantations dans cet espace d'origine agricole parcouru par un ruisseau, et parsemé de quelques grandes pièces d'eau. L'architecture de Thierry Sprecher et Géry Watine est de bonne qualité et de bon goût, mais reste un peu timide et sans originalité frappante. Alors que les intentions originelles auraient demandé quelques modelages et davantage de violence visuelle, ils sont peu importants. Ce qui peut laisser une impression de platitude, avec pour avantage de permettre aux joueurs de tous niveaux de ne pas connaître trop de problèmes. Le château du domaine a été aménagé avec des chambres d'hôtel et un restaurant gastronomique, qui ont beaucoup contribué à la réputation du parcours.

The owner of this course, located near Dijon and the A6 motorway (no noise), set out to create an inland links. He also had no intention of planting trees or bushes on a site which was originally farming land crossed by a stream and dotted with a few stretches of water. The design by Thierry Sprecher and Géry Watine is high class and in good taste, but lacks boldness and originality. While original designs would have required a little shaping of ground and greater visual impact, neither one nor the other is very much in evidence. This gives an impression of flatness and a round of golf where players of all levels should stay out of trouble. The estate's castle has been refurbished with hotel rooms and a gourmet restaurant, which have done much to enhance the course's reputation.

Golf Club du Château de Chailly — 1990
F - 21320 CHAILLY-SUR-ARMENCON

Office	Secrétariat	(33) 03 80 90 30 40
Pro shop	Pro-shop	(33) 03 80 90 30 40
Fax	Fax	(33) 03 80 90 30 05

Situation Situation
Dijon pop. 146 700, 55 km Pouilly-en-Auxois pop. 1 370, 5 km

Annual closure Fermeture annuelle — yes
1/1 → 31/1

Weekly closure Fermeture hebdomadaire — no

Fees main season
Tarifs haute saison full day

	Week days Semaine	We/Bank holidays We/Férié
Individual Individuel	200 F	300 F
Couple Couple	400 F	600 F

Caddy	Caddy	no
Electric Trolley	Chariot électrique	60 F/18 holes
Buggy	Voiturette	250 F/18 holes
Clubs	Clubs	100 F/full day

Credit cards Cartes de crédit
VISA - CB - Eurocard - MasterCard

250

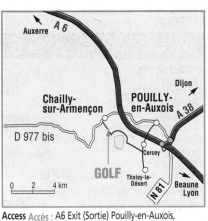

Access Accès : A6 Exit (Sortie) Pouilly-en-Auxois,
D977 bis → Saulieu
Map 7 on page 177 Carte 7 Page 177

GOLF COURSE
PARCOURS — 14/20

Site	Site	■■■■□□
Maintenance	Entretien	■■■■□□
Architect	Architecte	Thierry Sprecher Géry Watine
Type	Type	open country
Relief	Relief	■■□□□□
Water in play	Eau en jeu	■■■□□□
Exp. to wind	Exposé au vent	■■■■□□
Trees in play	Arbres en jeu	■■□□□□

Scorecard	Chp.	Mens	Ladies
Carte de score	Chp.	Mess.	Da.
Length Long.	6146	5844	5224
Par	72	72	72

Advised golfing ability — 0 12 24 36
Niveau de jeu recommandé
Hcp required Handicap exigé — no

CLUB HOUSE & AMENITIES
CLUB HOUSE ET ANNEXES — 8/10

Pro shop	Pro-shop	■■■■□□
Driving range	Practice	
Sheltered	couvert	12 mats
On grass	sur herbe	no, 8 mats open air
Putting-green	putting-green	yes
Pitching-green	pitching green	yes

HOTEL FACILITIES
ENVIRONNEMENT HOTELIER — 6/10

HOTELS HÔTELS
Château de Chailly — Chailly, on site
42 rooms, D 1 900 F
Tel (33) 03 80 90 30 30, Fax (33) 03 80 90 30 00

Château de Sainte-Sabine — Sainte-Sabine 14 km
16 rooms, D 750 F
Tel (33) 03 80 49 22 01, Fax (33) 03 80 49 20 01

Hostellerie du Château — Châteauneuf 15 km
18 rooms, D 430 F
Tel (33) 03 80 49 22 00, Fax (33) 03 80 49 21 27

RESTAURANTS RESTAURANT
La Côte d'Or — Saulieu 20 km
Tel (33) 03 80 90 53 53

L'Armançon — on site
Tel (33) 03 80 90 30 30

CHAMBON-SUR-LIGNON (LE)

14	5	7

Dans les montagnes au sud de Saint-Etienne, tout près de la vieille cité épiscopale du Puy-en-Velay, la petite ville de Chambon sur Lignon est au départ de randonnées superbes du printemps à l'automne car à mille mètres d'altitude, les hivers sont parfois rigoureux. Il fallait pas mal de foi pour y construire un golf. Sans prétention aucune, il vaut largement le déplacement. Visuellement, et par le caractère de son architecture insinuée dans un relief assez conséquent, il rappelle parfois les parcours des Highlands écossais, avec en prime quelques panoramas somptueux, depuis les départs du 6 et du 13 en particulier. Nul ici ne peut prétendre au luxe d'une maintenance à l'américaine, mais l'atmosphère est très sympathique, l'entretien reste correct, avec généralement de bons greens, bien dessinés. Quelques coups aveugles réservent des émotions (au 14), inévitables avec les dénivelées : voiturette conseillée.

In the mountains to the south of Saint Etienne, close to the old Episcopal city of Puy-en-Velay, the small town of Chambon sur Lignon is the starting point for some wonderful hikes. From spring to autumn that is, because at an altitude of 1,000 metres, the winters in this part of the world are sometimes harsh. It took a lot of faith to build a golf course here, but this unpretentious layout is well worth a visit. Visually, and through architecture which winds it way through some marked topology, it is sometimes reminiscent of the Scottish highland courses with a few splendid vistas to boot, particularly from the 6th and 13th tees. Nobody should expect US-style standards of maintenance here, but the atmosphere is jovial and maintenance pretty fair, with good and well-designed greens by and large. A few blind shots will set the pulse racing (on the 14th hole), but this was hardly to be avoided on a rather hilly course where a buggy is recommended if you want to play 18 holes without stopping off for lunch.

Golf du Chambon-sur-Lignon — 1994

Riondet, La Pierre de la Lune, BP 12
F - 43400 LE CHAMBON-SUR-LIGNON

Office	Secrétariat	(33) 04 71 59 28 10
Pro shop	Pro-shop	(33) 04 71 59 28 10
Fax	Fax	(33) 04 71 65 87 14
Situation	Situation	

Saint-Etienne (pop. 199 396), 68 km
Valence (pop. 63 437), 70 km

Annual closure	Fermeture annuelle	yes
		15/11 → 29/3
Weekly closure	Fermeture hebdomadaire	no

Fees main season
Tarifs haute saison 18 holes

	Week days Semaine	We/Bank holidays We/Férié
Individual Individuel	220 F	220 F
Couple Couple	440 F	440 F

Caddy	Caddy	no
Electric Trolley	Chariot électrique	no
Buggy	Voiturette	150 F/18 holes
Clubs	Clubs	50 F/full day

Credit cards Cartes de crédit VISA - Eurocard - MasterCard

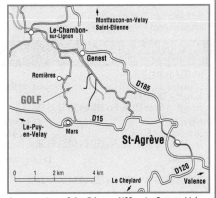

Access Accès : • Saint-Etienne, N88 → Le-Puy-en-Velay. Yssingeaux, D103 → Tence, D151 → Le Chambon-sur-Lignon. SE, D103, D155 → Golf. • Valence, D533 → Lamastre, St Agrève. D185, D151 → Chambon-sur-Lignon. **Map 10 on page 183** Carte 10 Page 183

GOLF COURSE / PARCOURS — 14/20

Site	Site	
Maintenance	Entretien	
Architect	Architecte	Michel Gayon
Type	Type	hilly, forest
Relief	Relief	
Water in play	Eau en jeu	
Exp. to wind	Exposé au vent	
Trees in play	Arbres en jeu	

Scorecard Carte de score	Chp. Chp.	Mens Mess.	Ladies Da.
Length Long.	5950	5476	4639
Par	72	72	72

Advised golfing ability		0	12	24	36
Niveau de jeu recommandé					
Hcp required	Handicap exigé	35			

CLUB HOUSE & AMENITIES / CLUB HOUSE ET ANNEXES — 5/10

Pro shop	Pro-shop	
Driving range	Practice	
Sheltered	couvert	4 mats
On grass air	sur herbe	no, 11 mats open
Putting-green	putting-green	yes
Pitching-green	pitching green	yes

HOTEL FACILITIES / ENVIRONNEMENT HOTELIER — 7/10

HOTELS HÔTELS
Bel Horizon — Le Chambon-sur-Lignon
20 rooms, D 350 F — 5 km
Tel (33) 04 71 59 74 39, Fax (33) 04 71 59 79 81

Bois Vialotte — Le Chambon-sur-Lignon
17 rooms, D 345 F — 3 km
Tel (33) 04 71 59 74 03, Fax (33) 04 71 65 86 32

Domaine de Rilhac — Saint-Agrève
7 rooms, D 460 F — 8 km
Tel (33) 04 75 30 20 20, Fax (33) 04 75 30 20 00

Château d'Urbilhac 12 rooms, D 700 F — Lamastre 3 km
Tel (33) 04 75 06 42 11, Fax (33) 04 75 06 52 75

RESTAURANTS RESTAURANT
Domaine de Rilhac — Saint-Agrève
Tel (33) 04 75 30 20 20 — 8 km
Vidal, Tél(33) 04 71 08 70 50 St-Julien-Chapteuil 25 km

251

Dessiné par Robert Trent Jones, ce parcours souffrait d'un entretien très en deçà de son architecture, mais les travaux récents de drainage ont été assez efficaces. Les greens demandent aussi une attention permanente à cette altitude. Dans un site exceptionnel dans la vallée de Chamonix, orné de sapins et de bouleaux, il n'a de golf de montagne que son paysage, car son relief est très modéré. Parcouru par de petits ruisseaux et par l'Arve, ses difficultés ne sont pas insurmontables pour un joueur de bon niveau capable de réfléchir sur la stratégie mais il peut être délicat pour un débutant, en raison de l'étroitesse de ses fairways. Conçu comme un golf de vacances, il peut être joué plusieurs fois sans ennui, mais ses difficultés assez subtiles apparaissent vite quand on chasse un bon score... C'est néanmoins l'un des tout meilleurs parcours de montagne.

Designed by Robert Trent Jones, this course has suffered from a standard of upkeep well below that of its layout, but the recent drainage work has had effective results. At this altitude, the greens require constant maintenance. Laid out in an exceptional site in the valley of Chamonix, lined with fir and birch trees, the only thing mountaineous about this course is the landscape, because the actual terrain is flat. Crossed by a number of streams and the gushing Arve river, the difficulties here are not impossible for a player with good ability and a strategic brain, but it can pose a problem or two for beginners owing to a number of tight fairways. Designed as a holiday course, you can play it several times with the same fun and enthusiasm, although the subtle difficulties tend to emerge pretty quickly when you are after a good score. In the final reckoning, this is one of Europe's best Alpine golf courses.

Golf Club de Chamonix — 1934

35, route du Golf
F - 74400 CHAMONIX

Office	Secrétariat	(33) 04 50 53 06 28
Pro shop	Pro-shop	(33) 04 50 53 45 23
Fax	Fax	(33) 04 50 53 38 69
Situation	Situation	

Chamonix (pop. 9 700), 3 km
Genève (pop. 167 200), 85 km

Annual closure	Fermeture annuelle	yes
		1/12 → 30/4
Weekly closure	Fermeture hebdomadaire	no

Fees main season
Tarifs haute saison full day

	Week days Semaine	We/Bank holidays We/Férié
Individual Individuel	350 F	350 F
Couple Couple	700 F	700 F
Caddy Caddy		no
Electric Trolley Chariot électrique		no
Buggy Voiturette		200 F/18 holes
Clubs Clubs		100 F/full day

Credit cards Cartes de crédit
VISA - CB - Eurocard - MasterCard

Map 11 on page 185 Carte 11 Page 185

252

0   2   4 km

Argentière
GOLF
N 506
Genève, Annecy
A 40
CHAMONIX
N 205
Aiguille du Midi
SAINT-GERVAIS
MEGEVE
Mont Blanc

Access Accès : • Genève, A40 → Chamonix
• Megève, N212, D909, N205

GOLF COURSE PARCOURS — 15/20

Site	Site	
Maintenance	Entretien	
Architect	Architecte	Robert Trent Jones
Type	Type	parkland, mountain
Relief	Relief	
Water in play	Eau en jeu	
Exp. to wind	Exposé au vent	
Trees in play	Arbres en jeu	

Scorecard	Chp.	Mens	Ladies
Carte de score	Chp.	Mess.	Da.
Length Long.	6075	5735	5347
Par	72	72	72

Advised golfing ability		0 12 24 36
Niveau de jeu recommandé		
Hcp required	Handicap exigé	35

CLUB HOUSE & AMENITIES CLUB HOUSE ET ANNEXES — 6/10

Pro shop	Pro-shop	
Driving range	Practice	
Sheltered	couvert	6 mats
On grass	sur herbe	no, 18 mats open air
Putting-green	putting-green	yes
Pitching-green	pitching green	yes

HOTEL FACILITIES ENVIRONNEMENT HOTELIER — 7/10

HOTELS HÔTELS
Le Labrador — Chamonix, on site
32 rooms, D 780 F
Tel (33) 04 50 55 90 09, Fax (33) 04 50 53 15 85

Albert 1er — Chamonix
30 rooms, D 1 500 F — 2 km
Tel (33) 04 50 53 05 09, Fax (33) 04 50 53 95 48

Beausoleil — Le Lavancher
15 rooms, D 570 F — 2 km
Tel (33) 04 50 54 00 78, Fax (33) 04 50 54 17 34

RESTAURANTS RESTAURANTS
Albert 1er — Chamonix
Tel (33) 04 50 53 05 09 — 2 km

Le Crochon — Chamonix
Tel (33) 04 50 53 41 78 — 2 km

CHAMP DE BATAILLE

En dehors du premier et du dernier trou, directement inspirés de l'architecture à la française, et assez insipides, ce parcours accidenté, dessiné par Nelson et Huau, est une jolie promenade dans les bois, avec quelques spécimens d'arbres magnifiques, mais des fairways généralement de bonne taille. De nombreux sapins font parfois imaginer être en montagne, alors que nous sommes au coeur de la Normandie. Chez les architectes, on sent les paysagistes sans doute plus que les golfeurs, mais si l'on peut regretter un certain manque de souffle, il n'y a pas de fautes graves, ce qui incite à le recommander davantage aux amoureux de belles balades en famille (ou avec des amis) qu'aux joueurs de haut niveau à la recherche de grands défis. Les écuries du château ont été aménagées pour recevoir le Club House.

Excepting the first and last holes, directly inspired by French style architecture but otherwise totally uninspired, this hilly course, designed by Nelson and Huau, is a beautiful stroll through the woods, where some magnificent trees leave enough room for some decently sized fairways. With some of the pine-trees, you'd think you were in the Alps, rather than in the heart of Normandy. Architecturally speaking, the course is the work of landscapers rather than golfers, but if we overlook a little lack of punch, there is nothing at all wrong with this course, which is to be recommended more for family outings (or rounds with friends) rather than for skilful players looking for a tough challenge. The castle's stables have been refurbished and converted into a club-house.

Golf du Champ de Bataille — 1988

Château du Champ-de-Bataille
F - 27110 LE NEUBOURG

Office	Secrétariat	(33) 02 32 35 03 72
Pro shop	Pro-shop	(33) 02 32 35 03 72
Fax	Fax	(33) 02 32 35 83 10
Situation	Situation	

Evreux (pop. 49 100), 27 km

Annual closure	Fermeture annuelle	no
Weekly closure	Fermeture hebdomadaire	no

Fees main season
Tarifs haute saison 18 holes

	Week days Semaine	We/Bank holidays We/Férié
Individual Individuel	220 F	350 F
Couple Couple	400 F	630 F

Caddy	Caddy	on request
Electric Trolley	Chariot électrique	no
Buggy	Voiturette	220 F/18 holes
Clubs	Clubs	no

Credit cards Cartes de crédit
VISA - CB - Eurocard - MasterCard - AMEX

Access Accès : • Evreux, N13 → Lisieux → Le Neubourg
• Caen or Lisieux, N13 → Evreux → Le Neubourg
Map 2 on page 167 Carte 2 Page 167

GOLF COURSE / PARCOURS — 14/20

Site	Site	
Maintenance	Entretien	
Architect	Architecte	Robin Nelson Thierry Huau
Type	Type	forest
Relief	Relief	
Water in play	Eau en jeu	
Exp. to wind	Exposé au vent	
Trees in play	Arbres en jeu	

Scorecard Carte de score	Chp. Chp.	Mens Mess.	Ladies Da.
Length Long.	5983	5600	5130
Par	72	72	72

Advised golfing ability
Niveau de jeu recommandé   0 12 24 36

Hcp required   Handicap exigé   no

CLUB HOUSE & AMENITIES / CLUB HOUSE ET ANNEXES — 6/10

Pro shop	Pro-shop	
Driving range	Practice	
Sheltered	couvert	no
On grass	sur herbe	yes (Summer)
Putting-green	putting-green	yes
Pitching-green	pitching green	yes

HOTEL FACILITIES / ENVIRONNEMENT HOTELIER — 3/10

HOTELS HÔTELS
Le Logis de Brionne   Brionne
12 rooms, D 390 F   5 km
Tel (33) 02 32 44 81 73
Fax (33) 02 32 45 10 92

Pré Saint-Germain   Louviers
30 rooms, D 550 F   20 km
Tel (33) 02 32 40 48 48
Fax (33) 02 32 50 75 60

RESTAURANTS RESTAURANTS
Hôtel de France   Evreux
Tel (33) 02 32 39 09 25   27 km

253

CHANTACO

Ce parcours, l'un des plus célèbres de la Côte Basque, reste incontournable par son charme, son ambiance et sa tradition sportive, cultivée par la famille Lacoste. Mais son manque de longueur ou l'espace commun au practice et au trou n°16 ne peuvent lui accorder le titre de grand golf. Relativement accidenté, il est cependant plus fatigant d'en déjouer les pièges que d'y marcher. Il donne l'impression de promettre une journée tranquille, mais résiste bien aux ambitieux : souvent étroit, avec quelques dévers redoutables et de petits greens, il demande plus de précision que de longueur. Si l'on ne cherche pas à défier un monstre pendant ses vacances, Chantaco reste par beau temps (il peut être humide) un parcours plaisant. L'architecte originel était Harry Colt, mais la diversité des styles rencontrés laisse à penser que son travail a été modifié...

Chantaco, one of the Basque Coast's most celebrated golf courses, is a must for its charm, atmosphere and sporting tradition, nurtured by the Lacoste family. But for the lack of space and the common area shared by the driving range and the 16th hole, it could be ranked as one of the greats in the area. Although rather a hilly lay-out, the most tiring thing about Chantaco is not so much the walking but trying to avoid the traps. It gives the impression of a quiet day's golfing, but even the most ambitious golfer will find it more than a handful. Often tight, with a few formidably sloping fairways and small greens, the course demands precision more than length off the tee. Avoid trying to defy this monster during your holidays and you will find Chantaco a very pleasant course when the weather is fine (it can get very wet). The original architect was Harry Colt, but with the variety of styles around the course, we suspect his design might have been altered here and there.

Golf de Chantaco — 1928

Route d'Ascain
F - 64500 SAINT-JEAN-DE-LUZ

Office	Secrétariat	(33) 05 59 26 14 22
Pro shop	Pro-shop	(33) 05 59 26 21 45
Fax	Fax	(33) 05 59 26 48 37
Situation	Situation	

Saint-Jean-de-Luz (pop. 13 030), 2 km
Biarritz (pop. 28 740), 15 km

Annual closure	Fermeture annuelle	no
Weekly closure	Fermeture hebdomadaire	tuesday

except during holidays (mardi sauf vacances)

Fees main season
Tarifs haute saison 18 holes

	Week days Semaine	We/Bank holidays We/Férié
Individual Individuel	340 F	340 F
Couple Couple	680 F	680 F
Caddy Caddy		on request
Electric Trolley Chariot électrique		80 F/18 holes
Buggy Voiturette		200 F/18 holes
Clubs Clubs		80 F/full day

Credit cards Cartes de crédit
VISA - CB - Eurocard - MasterCard

254

Access Accès : A63 Biarritz → Saint-Jean-de-Luz, Exit (Sortie) Saint-Jean-de-Luz Nord, D918 → Chantaco, Ascain
Map 12 on page 186 Carte 12 Page 186

GOLF COURSE
PARCOURS — 14/20

Site	Site	
Maintenance	Entretien	
Architect	Architecte	Harry Colt
Type	Type	forest, parkland
Relief	Relief	
Water in play	Eau en jeu	
Exp. to wind	Exposé au vent	
Trees in play	Arbres en jeu	

Scorecard Carte de score	Chp. Chp.	Mens Mess.	Ladies Da.
Length Long.	5722	5385	5224
Par	70	70	70

Advised golfing ability		0	12	24	36
Niveau de jeu recommandé					
Hcp required	Handicap exigé	no			

CLUB HOUSE & AMENITIES
CLUB HOUSE ET ANNEXES — 7/10

Pro shop	Pro-shop	
Driving range	Practice	
Sheltered	couvert	4 mats
On grass	sur herbe	no, 25 mats open air
Putting-green	putting-green	yes
Pitching-green	pitching green	yes

HOTEL FACILITIES
ENVIRONNEMENT HOTELIER — 7/10

HOTELS HÔTELS
Chantaco — on site
22 rooms, D 1 600 F
Tel (33) 05 59 26 14 76, Fax (33) 05 59 26 35 97

La Devinière — Saint-Jean-de-Luz
8 rooms, D 750 F — 2 km
Tel (33) 05 59 26 05 51, Fax (33) 05 59 51 26 38

Parc Victoria — Saint-Jean-de-Luz
10 rooms, D 1250 F — 2 km
Tel (33) 05 59 26 78 78, Fax (33) 05 59 26 78 08

RESTAURANTS RESTAURANTS
Taverne Basque — Saint-Jean-de-Luz
Tel (33) 05 59 26 01 26 — 2 km

Chez Dominique — Ciboure
Tel (33) 05 59 47 29 16 — 3 km

«Vineuil» reste l'incontournable grand classique en France, et si le passage du golf à 36 trous en a modifié le déroulement, notamment le finale de ce 18 trous, aucune blessure n'a été infligée aux trous «Simpson», une marque de respect dont bien des golfs auraient dû s'inspirer. Et bien des architectes aussi, qui devraient faire des stages prolongés ici, tant s'y exprime la grandeur dans la sobriété et la franchise, la subtilité technique dans la beauté esthétique. Hautement stratégique, diaboliquement intelligent, Vineuil exige une stratégie exactement adaptée à ses limites du moment, et se révèle un sérieux examen de passage des capacités à jouer au golf. Très difficile des départs les plus reculés, plus aimable des départs normaux, parfois un peu injuste pour les dames de très bon niveau (de leurs départs), c'est simplement un très grand parcours (mais l'entretien est toujours moyen...).

The «Vineuil» course is still France's great classic contribution to golf, and while the upgrading to 36 holes has changed the way the course unwinds, particularly the finish of the former 18 holes, no harm has been done to Simpson's original layout, a mark of respect that many golf clubs might have done well to ponder. And many designers, as well, who should come here for extended training to see just how well greatness can spring from discretion and honesty, and technical subtlety from sheer beauty. Highly strategic and devilishly intelligent, Vineuil requires strategy tailored to your limitations on the day, and can prove to be a very serious examination of your golfing ability. Very tough indeed from the back tees and sometimes a little unfair for the best ladies players (from their own tees), this is simply a really great course (although green-keeping is still fair only).

Golf de Chantilly — 1909
F - 60500 CHANTILLY

Office	Secrétariat	(33) 03 44 57 04 43
Pro shop	Pro-shop	(33) 03 44 58 26 72
Fax	Fax	(33) 03 44 57 26 54
Situation	Situation	

Paris (pop. 2 175 200), 41 km - Chantilly (pop. 11 341), 2 km

Annual closure	Fermeture annuelle	no
Weekly closure	Fermeture hebdomadaire	thursday (jeudi)

Fees main season
Tarifs haute saison 18 holes

	Week days Semaine	We/Bank holidays We/Férié
Individual Individuel	400 F	—
Couple Couple	800 F	—

We : members and guests only (membres et leurs invités)

Caddy	Caddy	on request/250 F
Electric Trolley	Chariot électrique	100 F/18 holes
Buggy	Voiturette	no
Clubs	Clubs	150 F/full day

Credit cards Cartes de crédit
VISA - CB - Eurocard - MasterCard

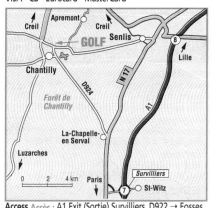

Access Accès : A1 Exit (Sortie) Surviliers, D922 → Fosses. N17 → La Chapelle en Serval. In La Chapelle, go left D924 → Chantilly. Après le Château, à droite → Vineuil, Golf. **Map 3 on page 168** Carte 3 Page 168

GOLF COURSE
PARCOURS — 18/20

Site	Site	
Maintenance	Entretien	
Architect	Architecte	Tom Simpson
Type	Type	forest, inland
Relief	Relief	
Water in play	Eau en jeu	
Exp. to wind	Exposé au vent	
Trees in play	Arbres en jeu	

Scorecard Carte de score	Chp. Chp.	Mens Mess.	Ladies Da.
Length Long.	6396	5664	4809
Par	71	71	74

Advised golfing ability		0 12 24 36
Niveau de jeu recommandé		
Hcp required	Handicap exigé	35

CLUB HOUSE & AMENITIES
CLUB HOUSE ET ANNEXES — 7/10

Pro shop	Pro-shop	
Driving range	Practice	
Sheltered	couvert	4 mats
On grass	sur herbe	yes
Putting-green	putting-green	yes
Pitching-green	pitching green	yes

255

HOTEL FACILITIES
ENVIRONNEMENT HOTELIER — 6/10

HOTELS HÔTELS

Le Parc — Chantilly
58 rooms, D 540 F — 3 km
Tel (33) 03 44 58 20 00, Fax (33) 03 44 57 31 10

Château de la Tour — Gouvieux
41 rooms, D 930 F — 6 km
Tel (33) 03 44 62 38 38, Fax (33) 03 44 57 31 97

Relais d'Aumale — Montgrésin
24 rooms, D 740 F — 8 km
Tel (33) 03 44 54 61 31, Fax (33) 03 44 54 69 15

RESTAURANTS RESTAURANTS

Relais Condé — Chantilly
Tel (33) 03 44 57 05 75 — 3 km

Le Verbois — St-Maximin
Tel (33) 03 44 24 06 22 — 5 km

CHARMEIL

Avec une moitié de trous en forêt et l'autre en plaine, ce parcours est assez plat, mais jamais monotone. Jeremy Pern aime l'architecture de links, et le montre par son modelage de buttes et une grande utilisation de bunkers de toutes tailles, y compris des «pot-bunkers». Les obstacles d'eau sont pratiquement tous naturels, y compris un étang de trois hectares, ce qui apporte de jolis éléments paysagers. Un joueur réfléchi peut toujours jouer la sécurité, ce qui rend le parcours amusant pour tous les niveaux, les difficultés étant visibles. Franc et plaisant, il peut cependant être un peu long pour les joueurs de plus de 24 de handicap. Les greens sont assez faciles à lire, mais certaines attaques sont délicates à apprécier. Ce beau tracé bénéficie d'un entretien correct, mais il vaut mieux jouer pendant les périodes sèches, car il supporte mal l'humidité.

With half the holes in the woods and the other half in open country, this is a fairly flat but never boring course. Architect Jeremy Pern is fond of links layouts and shows it here, with carefully shaped mounds and the widespread use of bunkers in all shapes and sizes, and a number of pot-bunkers. Nearly all the water is natural, including a lake of some 7 acres or more, which adds to the pretty landscape. A thoughtful player, as always, can play safe, thus making this an amusing course for all players of all abilities, as the difficulties are there to be seen. Honest and pleasant to play, it can however be a little long for high-handicappers. The greens are easy to read but some approach shots tend to be a little tricky to assess. The standard of green-keeping for this fine layout is average. And as it doesn't like rain, this is a course for the drier days.

Golf du Charmeil — 1987

Saint-Quentin-sur-Isère
F - 38210 SAINT-QUENTIN-SUR-ISERE

Office	Secrétariat	(33) 04 76 93 67 28
Pro shop	Pro-shop	(33) 04 76 93 67 28
Fax	Fax	(33) 04 76 93 62 04
Situation	Situation	

Grenoble (pop. 150 750), 24 km

Annual closure	Fermeture annuelle	no
Weekly closure	Fermeture hebdomadaire	no

Fees main season
Tarifs haute saison full day

	Week days Semaine	We/Bank holidays We/Férié
Individual Individuel	195 F	260 F
Couple Couple	390 F	520 F

Tuesday/mardi (1.05 → 30.11) : GF+lunch+competition, 195 F.

Caddy	Caddy	no
Electric Trolley	Chariot électrique	no
Buggy	Voiturette	120 F/18 holes
Clubs	Clubs	50 F/full day

Credit cards Cartes de crédit
VISA - CB - Eurocard - MasterCard - AMEX - DC

256

Access Accès : • Grenoble A49 → Valence
• Lyon A48 → Grenoble → A49 Valence, Exit (Sortie)
Tullins → Saint-Quentin-sur-Isère
Map 11 on page 184 Carte 11 Page 184

GOLF COURSE
PARCOURS — 16 /20

Site	Site	
Maintenance	Entretien	
Architect	Architecte	Jeremy Pern Jean Garaïalde
Type	Type	open country, forest
Relief	Relief	
Water in play	Eau en jeu	
Exp. to wind	Exposé au vent	
Trees in play	Arbres en jeu	

Scorecard Carte de score	Chp. Chp.	Mens Mess.	Ladies Da.
Length Long.	6251	5852	5277
Par	73	73	73

Advised golfing ability Niveau de jeu recommandé	0 12 24 36
Hcp required Handicap exigé	no

CLUB HOUSE & AMENITIES
CLUB HOUSE ET ANNEXES — 6 /10

Pro shop	Pro-shop	
Driving range	Practice	
Sheltered	couvert	8 mats
On grass	sur herbe	no, 20 mats open air
Putting-green	putting-green	yes
Pitching-green	pitching green	no

HOTEL FACILITIES
ENVIRONNEMENT HOTELIER — 6 /10

HOTELS HÔTELS
Golf Hôtel du Charmeil — on site
50 rooms, D 520 F
Tel (33) 04 76 93 67 28, Fax (33) 04 76 93 62 04

Auberge de Malatras — Tullins
19 rooms, D 290 F — 6 km
Tel (33) 04 76 07 02 30, Fax (33) 04 76 07 76 48

Campanile — Saint-Egrène
39 rooms, D 305 F — 10 km
Tel (33) 04 76 75 57 88, Fax (33) 04 76 75 06 49

RESTAURANTS RESTAURANTS
Philippe Serratrice — Voiron
Tel (33) 04 76 05 29 88 — 16 km

La Table d'Ernest — Grenoble
Tel (33) 04 76 43 19 56 — 24 km

CHAUMONT-EN-VEXIN

| 14 | 6 | 4 |

C'est à la fois l'aîné et le voisin de Rebetz, dans un site constitué de deux plateaux de niveaux très différents (un peu physique pour les seniors). L'allée de l'entrée comme le château font un lieu assez prestigieux, mais pas aussi luxueux qu'on pourrait le croire. En fait, tout cela fait penser à une belle «campagne». Dessiné par Donald Harradine, le parcours est plutôt franc, même si certaines dénivelées, quelques greens élevés, ou à plateaux peuvent obliger à réfléchir. Très divers de décor comme de tracé, les 18 trous constituent pourtant un ensemble assez cohérent. Si les difficultés dépendent pour beaucoup de la vitesse des greens, il faut être constamment attentif, car quelques ruisseaux et de puissants arbres sont une menace constante. Pour la beauté du cadre comme pour l'intérêt d'un parcours amusant à tous les niveaux, Chaumont-en-Vexin (ou Bertichère comme on le nomme souvent) mérite une visite, même si ce n'est pas tout à fait un «grand» parcours.

This is the older neighbour of Rebetz on a site of two plateaus of very different heights (tough on the legs, especially for seniors). The driveway and the castle make this a very prestigious location but it is not as luxurious as you might imagine. In fact there is a beautiful «country» style to the whole site. The course, designed by D. Harradine, is candid enough, although a few slopes, elevated greens and plateaus call for some serious thought before putting club to ball. Although different in setting and layout, the 18 holes form a rather consistent whole, and while the difficulty here depends for a large part on the speed of the greens, you have to be constantly on your toes owing to the threat of streams and some sturdy trees. Chaumont-en-Vexin (or Bertichère as it is often called) is fun for golfers of all abilities owing to the beauty of the setting and appeal of the course. Nobody would call this a «great» course, but it is well worth a visit.

Golf de Chaumont-en-Vexin		1968
Château de Bertichère		
F - 60240 CHAUMONT-EN-VEXIN		
Office	Secrétariat	(33) 03 44 49 00 81
Pro shop	Pro-shop	(33) 03 44 49 00 81
Fax	Fax	(33) 03 44 49 32 71
Situation	Situation	
Cergy-Pontoise (pop. 90 000), 25 km		
Annual closure	Fermeture annuelle	no
Weekly closure	Fermeture hebdomadaire	no

Fees main season			
Tarifs haute saison 18 holes			
		Week days Semaine	We/Bank holidays We/Férié
Individual Individuel		150 F	300 F
Couple Couple		300 F	600 F

Caddy	Caddy	no
Electric Trolley	Chariot électrique	no
Buggy	Voiturette	yes
Clubs	Clubs	yes

Credit cards Cartes de crédit
VISA - CB - Eurocard - MasterCard

Access Accès : Paris A15 → Pontoise, N14 → Magny-en-Vexin, D153 → Chaumont-en-Vexin.
Chaumont → Golf Bertichère.
Map 1 on page 164 Carte 1 Page 164

GOLF COURSE
PARCOURS
14/20

Site	Site	
Maintenance	Entretien	
Architect	Architecte	Donald Harradine
Type	Type	parkland, hilly
Relief	Relief	
Water in play	Eau en jeu	
Exp. to wind	Exposé au vent	
Trees in play	Arbres en jeu	

Scorecard Carte de score	Chp. Chp.	Mens Mess.	Ladies Da.
Length Long.	6197	6197	5266
Par	72	72	72

Advised golfing ability		0	12	24	36
Niveau de jeu recommandé					
Hcp required	Handicap exigé	no			

CLUB HOUSE & AMENITIES
CLUB HOUSE ET ANNEXES
6/10

Pro shop	Pro-shop	
Driving range	Practice	
Sheltered	couvert	8 mats
On grass	sur herbe	yes
Putting-green	putting-green	yes
Pitching-green	pitching green	yes

257

HOTEL FACILITIES
ENVIRONNEMENT HOTELIER
4/10

HOTELS HÔTELS
Appartements sur place — Golf, on site
10 rooms, D. 100 → 1.500 F
Tel (33) 03 44 49 00 81, Fax (33) 03 44 49 32 71

Château de la Rapée — Bazincourt-sur-Epte
12 rooms, D 790 F — 13 km
Tel (33) 02 32 55 11 61, Fax (33) 02 32 55 95 65

Moderne — Gisors
30 rooms, D 395 F — 10 km
Tel (33) 02 32 55 23 51, Fax (33) 02 32 55 08 75

RESTAURANTS RESTAURANTS
Le Cappeville — Gisors
Tel (33) 03 32 55 11 08 — 10 km

Le Cygne — Gisors
Tel (33) 02 33 55 23 76 — 10 km

CHEVERNY

A proximité immédiate du château historique de Cheverny, ce parcours contribue au «parcours golfique» des Châteaux de la Loire. Il se déroule largement en forêt, mais aussi autour de l'étang de la Rousselière. De nombreux petits obstacles d'eau apportent des éléments de jeu bienvenus dans cet espace très plat, mais toujours humide en saison pluvieuse. L'architecte Olivier van der Vynckt a très peu bougé le terrain, recherché la subtilité des formes, notamment au niveau des alentours de green, mais on aurait souhaité que le terrain soit davantage modelé, ne serait-ce que pour mieux définir les trous dans cet espace, et donner de meilleurs points de repère. Le rythme de jeu est plaisant, les différents départs permettent de l'adapter à tous les niveaux. Une réalisation de bonne facture, avec un Club-House sympathique.

In the immediate vicinity of the historic Château de Cheverny, the course of the same name is one of a trail of golfing venues amidst the castles of the Loire valley. It is laid out mostly through a forest but also around a lake. Numerous minor water hazards add welcome spice to a very flat setting, which is always wet in autumn and winter. Architect Olivier van der Vinckt moved very little earth and preferred a more subtle touch, particularly around the greens. However, a little more shaping of terrain would have been welcome, if only to create greater definition for individual holes and clearer points of reference. Overall, the balance is pleasing and the difference in tee-off areas makes this a course for all abilities. A good quality course with a friendly club-house.

Golf de Cheverny — 1988

La Rousselière
F - 41700 CHEVERNY

Office	Secrétariat	(33) 02 54 79 24 70
Pro shop	Pro-shop	(33) 02 54 79 24 70
Fax	Fax	(33) 02 54 79 25 52
Situation	Situation	

Blois (pop. 49 310), 15 km

Annual closure	Fermeture annuelle	no
Weekly closure	Fermeture hebdomadaire	tuesday

during winter (mardi en hiver)

Fees main season
Tarifs haute saison full day

	Week days Semaine	We/Bank holidays We/Férié
Individual Individuel	200 F	280 F
Couple Couple	320 F	500 F

GF + lunch : weekdays (semaine) 270 F, We 330 F

Caddy	Caddy	no
Electric Trolley	Chariot électrique	no
Buggy	Voiturette	150 F/18 holes
Clubs	Clubs	80 F/full day

Credit cards Cartes de crédit
VISA - CB - Eurocard - MasterCard - AMEX

GOLF COURSE
PARCOURS
14/20

Site	Site	
Maintenance	Entretien	
Architect	Architecte	O. van der Vynckt
Type	Type	forest, open country
Relief	Relief	
Water in play	Eau en jeu	
Exp. to wind	Exposé au vent	
Trees in play	Arbres en jeu	

Scorecard Carte de score	Chp. Chp.	Mens Mess.	Ladies Da.
Length Long.	6276	5830	4933
Par	71	71	71

Advised golfing ability		0	12	24	36
Niveau de jeu recommandé					
Hcp required	Handicap exigé	no			

CLUB HOUSE & AMENITIES
CLUB HOUSE ET ANNEXES
7/10

Pro shop	Pro-shop	
Driving range	Practice	
Sheltered	couvert	5 mats
On grass	sur herbe	no, 15 mats open air
Putting-green	putting-green	yes
Pitching-green	pitching green	yes

HOTEL FACILITIES
ENVIRONNEMENT HOTELIER
6/10

HOTELS HÔTELS

Château du Breuil — Cour-Cheverny
18 rooms, D 900 F — 2 km
Tel (33) 02 54 44 20 20, Fax (33) 02 54 44 30 40

Les Trois Marchands — Cour-Cheverny
36 rooms, D 350 F — 2 km
Tel (33) 02 54 79 96 44, Fax (33) 02 54 79 25 60

Saint Hubert — Cour-Cheverny
18 rooms, D 320 F — 2 km
Tel (33) 02 54 79 96 60, Fax (33) 02 54 79 21 17

RESTAURANTS RESTAURANTS

Les Trois Marchands — Cour-Cheverny
Tel (33) 02 54 79 96 44 — 2 km

Restaurant du Golf — Golf on place
Tel (33) 02 54 79 23 02

258

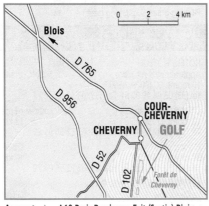

Access Accès : A10 Paris-Bordeaux, Exit (Sortie) Blois →
D765 → Romorantin → Cour-Cheverny, → Golf
Map 3 on page 168 Carte 3 Page 168

Un des grands exemples français de links, signé par le légendaire Tom Simpson. L'essentiel de son dessin a été préservé, même si les aspects les plus sauvages ont été gommés par l'arrosage automatique et certaines «améliorations». La disparition de quelques difficultés a rendu le parcours plus accessible à tous les niveaux, surtout par beau temps comme sur tous ces types de golfs en bord de mer. Les greens sont de bonne qualité, les obstacles bien visibles, la stratégie assez évidente, l'absence de relief et le confort d'un sol sablonneux rendent la marche plaisante. Mais, quand le vent souffle, Chiberta devient un test où la maîtrise des trajectoires de balles est essentielle et les spécialistes du petit jeu s'en donneront à cœur joie. Les équipements du Club house restent spartiates, mais l'entretien a été très amélioré. A jouer sans réserve, y compris par mauvais temps !

One of the great French examples of a links course, designed by the legendary Tom Simpson. The original basic design has been preserved, although the wilder features have been smoothed away by automatic sprinklers and a number of «improvements». With fewer difficulties, the course is more accessible to all golfers, especially in fine weather (as always). The greens are good, the hazards clearly visible, strategy is pretty obvious, and the absence of any real relief with the comfort of sandy soil make for a pleasant walk. But once the wind gets up, Chiberta becomes a test where ball-control is essential and where players with a tight short game will come into their own. Club-house facilities are as Spartan as ever but upkeep has been much improved. A must, even in bad weather!

Golf de Chiberta — 1927

104, bd des Plages
F - 64600 ANGLET

Office	Secrétariat	(33) 05 59 52 51 10
Pro shop	Pro-shop	(33) 05 59 63 17 87
Fax	Fax	(33) 05 59 52 51 11
Situation	Situation	

3 km Biarritz (pop. 28 740), 3 km

Annual closure	Fermeture annuelle	no
Weekly closure	Fermeture hebdomadaire	thursday
		16/9 → 30/4

Fees main season
Tarifs haute saison full day

	Week days Semaine	We/Bank holidays We/Férié
Individual Individuel	330 F	330 F
Couple Couple	540 F	540 F

Summer : – 40 % after 18.00

Caddy	Caddy	200 F/18 holes
Electric Trolley	Chariot électrique	70 F/18 holes
Buggy	Voiturette	no
Clubs	Clubs	70 F/full day

Credit cards Cartes de crédit
VISA - CB - Eurocard - MasterCard - AMEX

Access Accès : A63, Exit (Sortie) Biarritz.
Biarritz → Anglet
Map 12 on page 186 Carte 12 Page 186

GOLF COURSE PARCOURS — 16/20

Site	Site	▰▰▰▱▱
Maintenance	Entretien	▰▰▰▰▱
Architect	Architecte	Tom Simpson
Type	Type	links, forest
Relief	Relief	▰▰▱▱▱
Water in play	Eau en jeu	▰▱▱▱▱
Exp. to wind	Exposé au vent	▰▰▰▱▱
Trees in play	Arbres en jeu	▰▰▱▱▱

Scorecard Carte de score	Chp. Chp.	Mens Mess.	Ladies Da.
Length Long.	5650	5313	4882
Par	71	71	71

Advised golfing ability Niveau de jeu recommandé	0	12	24	36

Hcp required Handicap exigé 35

CLUB HOUSE & AMENITIES CLUB HOUSE ET ANNEXES — 6/10

Pro shop	Pro-shop	▰▰▰▱▱
Driving range	Practice	▰▰▱▱▱
Sheltered	couvert	8 mats
On grass	sur herbe	no, 8 mats open air
Putting-green	putting-green	yes
Pitching-green	pitching green	no

259

HOTEL FACILITIES ENVIRONNEMENT HOTELIER — 8/10

HOTELS HÔTELS

Hôtel Chiberta et du Golf — on site
98 rooms, D 1 000 F
Tel (33) 05 59 58 48 48, Fax (33) 05 59 63 57 84

La Résidence — on site
50 rooms, D 600 F
Tel (33) 05 59 52 87 65, Fax (33) 05 59 63 59 19

Hôtel Palais — Biarritz 3 km
156 rooms, D 1800 F
Tel (33) 05 59 41 64 00, Fax (33) 05 59 41 67 99

Château de Brindos — Anglet 2 km
12 rooms, D 1300 F
Tel (33) 05 59 23 17 68, Fax (33) 05 59 23 48 47

RESTAURANTS RESTAURANTS

Château de Brindos — Anglet
Tel (33) 05 59 23 17 68

Dans une région très touristique en raison de ses vignobles (... et fameux alcools), la création de ce golf public était bienvenue, et on remarquera d'abord son Club-House sympathique, construit dans une ancienne ferme. Le paysage est un mélange plaisant de campagne et de bocages et le relief assez modéré. L'architecture du parcours est agréable visuellement et très honnête sur le plan du jeu, sans recherche excessive d'originalité. Les coups imprécis ne sont rarement pénalisés sévèrement car les fairways sont assez larges, les greens peu complexes et les bunkers rarement très dangereux. Seuls deux trous comportent des obstacles d'eau. Visiblement, ce parcours a été conçu pour les joueurs moyens, ce qui en fait un «produit» utile et de qualité estimable pour la majorité des golfeurs, de la région ou de passage. Les meilleurs joueurs ne s'y ennuieront pas.

The opening of a public course was most welcome in a region where vineyards (and the famous spirits they produce) attract tourists in their droves. Just as welcoming is the club-house built in an old farmhouse. The landscape is a pleasing «blend» (this is cognac country, after all) of open country and green pastures, and the course can be rather hilly in places. The design is visually attractive and very forthright in golfing terms, albeit not excessively original. Wayward shots are only rarely heavily penalised, as the fairways are rather wide, the greens comparatively straightforward and the bunkers seldom too dangerous. There are water hazards on two holes only. The course was visibly designed for the average golfer, thus making it a «useful» product of considerable class for the majority of golfers, whether local or passing through. But even the best players will enjoy their golf here.

Golf du Cognac — 1988

Saint-Brice
F - 16100 COGNAC

Office	Secrétariat	(33) 05 45 32 18 17
Pro shop	Pro-shop	(33) 05 45 32 37 60
Fax	Fax	(33) 05 45 35 10 76
Situation	Situation	

Cognac (pop. 19 520), 5 km
Angoulême (pop. 42 880), 32 km

Annual closure	Fermeture annuelle	no
Weekly closure	Fermeture hebdomadaire	tuesday
	(mardi) 30/9 → 30/4	

Fees main season
Tarifs haute saison full day

	Week days Semaine	We/Bank holidays We/Férié
Individual Individuel	240 F	240 F
Couple Couple	420 F	420 F
Caddy Caddy	no	
Electric Trolley Chariot électrique	80 F/18 holes	
Buggy Voiturette	150 F/18 holes	
Clubs Clubs	50 F/full day	

Credit cards Cartes de crédit
VISA - CB - Eurocard - MasterCard

260

Access Accès : Cognac N141 → Angoulême,
D15 → Saint-Brice, → Golf
Map 9 on page 181 Carte 9 Page 181

GOLF COURSE / PARCOURS — 13/20

Site	Site	
Maintenance	Entretien	
Architect	Architecte	Jean Garaïalde
Type	Type	copse, country
Relief	Relief	
Water in play	Eau en jeu	
Exp. to wind	Exposé au vent	
Trees in play	Arbres en jeu	

Scorecard Carte de score	Chp. Chp.	Mens Mess.	Ladies Da.
Length Long.	6142	5665	5266
Par	72	72	72

Advised golfing ability Niveau de jeu recommandé	0 12 24 36
Hcp required	Handicap exigé	35

CLUB HOUSE & AMENITIES / CLUB HOUSE ET ANNEXES — 7/10

Pro shop	Pro-shop	
Driving range	Practice	
Sheltered	couvert	12 mats
On grass	sur herbe	oui
Putting-green	putting-green	oui
Pitching-green	pitching green	oui

HOTEL FACILITIES / ENVIRONNEMENT HOTELIER — 5/10

HOTELS HÔTELS
L'Echassier
21 rooms, D 510 F
Tel (33) 05 45 35 01 09, Fax (33) 05 45 32 22 43
Châteaubernard
5 km

Les Pigeons Blancs
7 rooms, D 500 F
Tel (33) 05 45 82 16 36, Fax (33) 05 45 82 29 29
Cognac
5 km

Domaine du Breuil
24 rooms, D 350 F
Tel (33) 05 45 35 32 06, Fax (33) 05 45 35 48 06
Cognac
5 km

RESTAURANTS RESTAURANTS
Les Pigeons Blancs
Tel (33) 05 45 82 16 36
Cognac
5 km

L'Echassier
Tel (33) 05 45 35 01 09
Cognac
5 km

Grand club omnisports, le Stade Français a créé un complexe golfique composé de quatre neuf trous combinables, dont la configuration idéale. est Vert-Noir et Lilas-Orange . Ce dernier 18 trous est un peu moins long, mais aussi exigeant techniquement. Dans un immense espace, Bob von Hagge a beaucoup modelé le terrain pour isoler les fairways, lui donnant un aspect un peu lunaire. L'esthétique est assez américaine, sans refuser pour autant certaines références aux links. Le «Orange» est assez accidenté, sans être vraiment fatigant : après quatre trous assez tranquilles, il en offre cinq de toute beauté, où les scores peuvent s'alourdir. Plus classique, le «Lilas» met en jeu quelques redoutables obstacles d'eau, généralement plus intimidants visuellement que dangereux. Ici, l'important est d'être précis, et de bien maîtriser le petit jeu quand on manque les greens.

Le Stade Français, one of the country's leading multi-sports clubs, has created a golf complex formed from four combinable 9-hole courses. The ideal combinations are Green and Black (see after) and Lilac and Orange (see here). The latter is a little less long but technically just as demanding. Over a huge area of land, Bob van Hagge has shifted a lot of earth to isolate the fairways and form a sort of lunar landscape. Although rather American in style, there is something of the links about all four courses. The «Orange» course is hilly but not too tiring. After four quietish holes, the next five are simply beautiful... and can ruin your card. The «Lilac» course, a little more classical if you will, involves some formidable water hazards, which are generally more intimidating to the eye than dangerous to the score. What matters here is straight-hitting and a sharp short game when you miss the greens.

Golf Courson-Monteloup

1991

Stade Français
F - 91680 COURSON-MONTELOUP

Office	Secrétariat	(33) 01 64 58 80 80
Pro shop	Pro-shop	(33) 01 64 58 89 69
Fax	Fax	(33) 01 64 58 83 06
Situation	Situation	

Les Ulis (pop. 27 160), 15 km
Paris (pop. 2 175 200), 34 km

Annual closure	Fermeture annuelle	no
Weekly closure	Fermeture hebdomadaire	
	wednesday (mercredi)	

Fees main season
Tarifs haute saison full day

	Week days	We/Bank holidays
	Semaine	We/Férié
Individual Individuel	250 F	500 F
Couple Couple	500 F	1 000 F

150 F after 16.00 - Seniors : 150 F (weekdays/semaine)

Caddy	Caddy	on request
Electric Trolley	Chariot électrique	80 F/18 holes
Buggy	Voiturette	200 F/18 holes
Clubs	Clubs	100 F/full day

Credit cards Cartes de crédit
VISA - CB - Eurocard - MasterCard

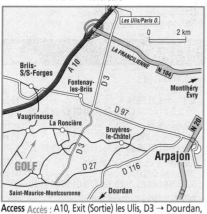

Access Accès : A10, Exit (Sortie) les Ulis, D3 → Dourdan,
Château de Courson, La Roncière, → Golf
Map 15 on page 192 Carte 15 Page 192

GOLF COURSE
PARCOURS

15/20

Site	Site	
Maintenance	Entretien	
Architect	Architecte	Robert von Hagge
Type	Type	open country
Relief	Relief	
Water in play	Eau en jeu	
Exp. to wind	Exposé au vent	
Trees in play	Arbres en jeu	

Scorecard	Chp.	Mens	Ladies
Carte de score	Chp.	Mess.	Da.
Length Long.	6171	5746	4987
Par	72	72	72

Advised golfing ability		0 12 24 36
Niveau de jeu recommandé		
Hcp required	Handicap exigé	35 / 24-28 We

CLUB HOUSE & AMENITIES
CLUB HOUSE ET ANNEXES

7/10

Pro shop	Pro-shop	
Driving range	Practice	
Sheltered	couvert	15 mats
On grass	sur herbe	no,
		25 mats open air
Putting-green	putting-green	yes
Pitching-green	pitching green	yes

261

HOTEL FACILITIES
ENVIRONNEMENT HOTELIER

3/10

HOTELS HÔTELS
Mercure — Les Ulis
108 rooms, D 630 F — 13 km
Tel (33) 01 69 07 63 96, Fax (33) 01 69 07 92 00

Campanile — Les Ulis
49 rooms, D 295 F — 13 km
Tel (33) 01 69 28 60 60, Fax (33) 01 69 28 06 35

Abbaye les Vaux de Cernay — Cernay-la-Ville
58 rooms, D 800 F — 11 km
Tel (33) 01 34 85 23 00, Fax (33) 01 34 85 11 60

RESTAURANTS RESTAURANTS
Le Saint-Clément — Arpajon
Tel (33) 01 64 90 21 01 — 9 km

COURSON VERT/NOIR 🏌 | 16 | 7 | 3 |

Les quatre 9 trous de Courson constituent une véritable création en trois dimensions à partir d'un terrain sans grand relief naturel. Sur le «Vert», il vaut mieux partir des départs avancés, car sa longueur peut décourager les joueurs moyens (les pars 4 sont redoutables). Le «Noir» est moins brutal, parfois accidenté, mais les derniers trous mettent beaucoup d'eau en jeu. Le paysage ne manque pas de majesté, et les trous ont été bien isolés par la création de buttes spectaculaires, dont l'aspect visuel ne plaît pas à tous ! Très protégés par de beaux bunkers, les greens sont très vastes et souvent à multiples plateaux : il faut choisir celui où est le drapeau pour ne pas craindre les «trois-putts». Comme les par 5 sont difficilement prenables en deux coups, il est difficile d'y scorer très bien. Un parcours où il faut utiliser la tête autant que les clubs. L'entretien n'est pas toujours au niveau du green-fee...

The four 9-hole courses at Courson form a genuine 3-dimensional creation built out of terrain with no great natural relief. On the «Green» course, swallow your pride and play from the forward tees; it is long enough to discourage any mid-handicapper (the par 4s are quite formidable). The «Black» course is a little kinder and sometimes hilly, and the last few holes involve a lot of water. There is something very majestic about the landscape here, and the holes are clearly separated by spectacular sand-hills and hillocks, which from a visual point of view are not to everyone's liking. The greens are huge, often multi-tiered and defended by magnificent bunkers, so wayward approach shots are often greeted with 3 putts. And as the par 5s are tough to reach in two, a good score is not always easy. A typical course where brains are almost as important as your clubs. Maintenance is not always on a par with the size of the green-fee.

Golf Courson-Monteloup 1991

Stade Français
F - 91680 COURSON-MONTELOUP

Office	Secrétariat	(33) 01 64 58 80 80
Pro shop	Pro-shop	(33) 01 64 58 89 69
Fax	Fax	(33) 01 64 58 83 06
Situation	Situation	

Les Ulis (pop. 27 160), 15 km - Paris (pop. 2 175 200), 34 km

Annual closure	Fermeture annuelle	yes
		25/12 → 1/1

Weekly closure Fermeture hebdomadaire
wednesday mercredi

Fees main season
Tarifs haute saison full day

	Week days Semaine	We/Bank holidays We/Férié
Individual Individuel	250 F	500 F
Couple Couple	500 F	1 000 F

150 F after 16.00 - Seniors : 150 F (weekdays/semaine)

Caddy	Caddy	on request
Electric Trolley	Chariot électrique	80 F/18 holes
Buggy	Voiturette	200 F/18 holes
Clubs	Clubs	100 F/full day

Credit cards Cartes de crédit
VISA - CB - Eurocard - MasterCard

262

Access Accès : A10, Exit (Sortie) les Ulis, D3 → Dourdan, Château de Courson, La Roncière, → Golf
Map 15 on page 192 Carte 15 Page 192

GOLF COURSE PARCOURS · 16/20

Site	Site	
Maintenance	Entretien	
Architect	Architecte	Robert von Hagge
Type	Type	open country
Relief	Relief	
Water in play	Eau en jeu	
Exp. to wind	Exposé au vent	
Trees in play	Arbres en jeu	

Scorecard Carte de score	Chp. Chp.	Mens Mess.	Ladies Da.
Length Long.	6570	6043	5348
Par	72	72	72

Advised golfing ability		0 12 24 36
Niveau de jeu recommandé		
Hcp required	Handicap exigé	35

CLUB HOUSE & AMENITIES CLUB HOUSE ET ANNEXES · 7/10

Pro shop	Pro-shop	
Driving range	Practice	
Sheltered	couvert	15 mats
On grass	sur herbe	no, 25 mats open air
Putting-green	putting-green	yes
Pitching-green	pitching green	yes

HOTEL FACILITIES ENVIRONNEMENT HOTELIER · 3/10

HOTELS HÔTELS
Mercure *** — Les Ulis
108 rooms, D 630 F — 13 km
Tel (33) 01 69 07 63 96, Fax (33) 01 69 07 92 00

Campanile ** — Les Ulis
49 rooms, D 295 F — 13 km
Tel (33) 01 69 28 60 60, Fax (33) 01 69 28 06 35

Abbaye les Vaux de Cernay *** — Cernay-la-Ville
58 rooms, D 800 F — 11 km
Tel (33) 01 34 85 23 00, Fax (33) 01 34 85 11 60

RESTAURANTS RESTAURANT
Le Saint-Clément — Arpajon
Tel (33) 01 64 90 21 01 — 9 km

Un golf familial, dont le parcours tracé par le grand Willie Park en 1897, a été notablement modifié depuis, notamment après la dernière guerre et l'occupation. 9 des 27 trous d'avant-guerre n'ont alors pas été réouverts. Situé en bord de mer, ce n'est pas exactement un links, étant donné la nature du terrain mais les conditions de jeu en sont souvent proches (attention au vent !). Le style du parcours est très britannique, avec des greens bien protégés., mais souvent accessibles avec des «pitch and run». Sa longueur reste raisonnable, mais les scores ne sont pas toujours tels qu'on pourrait les espérer au vu de la carte. Le relief est modéré, ce qui convient bien aux joueurs de tous âges comme de tous niveaux. L'ambiance est sans prétention mais très plaisante, comme la simplicité des équipements. On ne perd certes pas sa journée à jouer ici, entre amis et en famille.

A family course designed by the great Willie Park in 1897 but considerably restyled, particularly since the end of last war and the occupation. Nine of the 27 pre-war holes have not been re-opened. Laid out along the sea-shore, this is not exactly a links course, given the nature of the terrain, but conditions of play are often very similar (watch out for the wind). Dieppe is a very British style course with well protected greens that can often be reached with bump and run shots. It is a reasonable length, but scores are not always as low as you might have hoped for when looking at the card. It is rather hilly but suitable for players of all ages and abilities. The atmosphere is unpretentious and pleasant, as is the simplicity of facilities. You certainly will not waste your time spending a day's golfing here, with friends or the family.

Dieppe-Pourville Golf Club		1897
Route de Pourville		
F - 76200 DIEPPE		

Office	Secrétariat	(33) 02 35 84 25 05
Pro shop	Pro-shop	(33) 02 32 84 25 05
Fax	Fax	(33) 02 35 84 97 11
Situation	Situation	

Dieppe (pop. 5 890), 2 km

Annual closure	Fermeture annuelle	no
Weekly closure	Fermeture hebdomadaire	no

Fees main season
Tarifs haute saison full day

	Week days Semaine	We/Bank holidays We/Férié
Individual Individuel	190 F	240 F
Couple Couple	380 F	480 F

Caddy	Caddy	on request
Electric Trolley	Chariot électrique	no
Buggy	Voiturette	150 F/18 holes
Clubs	Clubs	100 F/full day

Credit cards Cartes de crédit
VISA - CB - Eurocard - MasterCard

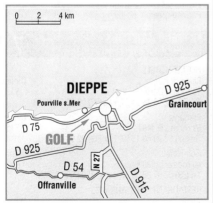

DIEPPE
Pourville s.Mer
D 925
Graincourt
D 75
GOLF
D 925
D 54
N 27
D 915
Offranville

Access Accès : Dieppe → Pourville
Map 1 on page 164 Carte 1 Page 164

GOLF COURSE
PARCOURS
14/20

Site	Site	▬▬▬▬
Maintenance	Entretien	▬▬▬
Architect	Architecte	Willie Park Jr
Type	Type	seaside course, links
Relief	Relief	▬
Water in play	Eau en jeu	▭
Exp. to wind	Exposé au vent	▬▬▬
Trees in play	Arbres en jeu	▬

Scorecard Carte de score	Chp. Chp.	Mens Mess.	Ladies Da.
Length Long.	5763	5489	4866
Par	70	70	70

Advised golfing ability	0	12	24	36
Niveau de jeu recommandé				
Hcp required	Handicap exigé	no		

CLUB HOUSE & AMENITIES
CLUB HOUSE ET ANNEXES
6/10

Pro shop	Pro-shop	▬▬▬
Driving range	Practice	▬▬
Sheltered	couvert	10 mats
On grass	sur herbe	yes
Putting-green	putting-green	yes
Pitching-green	pitching green	yes

263

HOTEL FACILITIES
ENVIRONNEMENT HOTELIER
5/10

HOTELS HÔTELS
La Présidence · Dieppe
89 rooms, D 490 F
Tel (33) 02 35 84 31 31, Fax (33) 02 35 84 86 70

Aguado · Dieppe
56 rooms, D 455 F
Tel (33) 02 35 84 27 00, Fax (33) 02 35 06 17 61

Auberge du Clos Normand · Martin-Eglise
8 rooms, D 460 F · 7 km
Tel (33) 02 35 04 40 34, Fax (33) 02 35 04 48 49

RESTAURANTS RESTAURANTS
La Mélie · Dieppe
Tel (33) 02 35 84 21 19

Auberge du Trou Normand · Pourville
Tel (33) 02 35 84 59 84

Fondé en 1883, ce parcours a été, comme Biarritz, originellement dessiné par Willie Dunn, mais remanié à tel point, au cours des années, qu'il ne reste qu'une dizaine de trous d'une esthétique spécifiquement écossaise. Ils suffisent à faire de Dinard un golf à connaître. Sa longueur peut paraître dérisoire, même avec un par 68, mais elle devient démesurée quand le vent souffle. Alors, il faut une tête de spécialiste en balistique pour calculer les dérives ! Et un seul par 5 offre une franche occasion de birdie. Ailleurs, la difficulté vient du choix de club, et l'on se retrouve sans cesse «entre deux clubs» pour chercher les drapeaux. Les greens bien défendus et souvent de petite taille obligent à une grande précision. Un golf surtout amusant, dont l'ambiance est très sportive, à jouer avec les golfeurs de tous niveaux. L'arrosage des fairways a un peu amélioré l'entretien en été, la vue sur la mer reste splendide par tous les temps.

Opened in 1883, this course was originally designed, like Biarritz, by Willie Dunn, but it has been restyled so many times over the years that only about ten holes have preserved their special Scottish flavour. And they alone are enough to make Dinard a course worth knowing. The length may appear derisory by today's standards, even as a par 68, but when the wind howls, it feels and plays much longer. A specialist in ballistics can come in handy to calculate flight and deviation! Only one par 5 provides a real birdie chance. Elsewhere, difficulties arise from club selection, and players are often stuck «between two clubs» for their approach shots. The greens are often small and well defended, thus calling for extreme precision. An entertaining course with a great sporting atmosphere, to be played with golfers of all levels. The watering of fairways has slightly improved upkeeping during summer months. The view over the sea is splendid whatever the weather.

Golf de Dinard
1887
Boulevard de la Houle
F - 35 800 SAINT-BRIAC-SUR-MER

Office	Secrétariat	(33) 02 99 88 32 07
Pro shop	Pro-shop	(33) 02 99 88 30 55
Fax	Fax	(33) 02 99 88 04 53
Situation	Situation	

Dinard (pop. 9 920), 5 km

Annual closure	Fermeture annuelle	no
Weekly closure	Fermeture hebdomadaire	no

Fees main season
Tarifs haute saison full day

	Week days Semaine	We/Bank holidays We/Férié
Individual Individuel	300 F	300 F
Couple Couple	600 F	600 F

Caddy	Caddy	no
Electric Trolley	Chariot électrique	no
Buggy	Voiturette	150 F/18 holes
Clubs	Clubs	yes

Credit cards Cartes de crédit
VISA - CB - Eurocard - MasterCard

264

GOLF St-Lunaire **Dinard** **St-Malo**
St-Briac-S-Mer
D 603
D 168   D 168
Châteauneuf-
d'Ille-et-Vilaine
Ploubalay
D 266
D 2

Access Accès : Dinard → Saint-Lunaire, → Golf
Map 5 on page 173 Carte 5 Page 173

GOLF COURSE
PARCOURS
13/20

Site	Site	
Maintenance	Entretien	
Architect	Architecte	Willie Dunn
Type	Type	seaside course, links
Relief	Relief	
Water in play	Eau en jeu	
Exp. to wind	Exposé au vent	
Trees in play	Arbres en jeu	

Scorecard Carte de score	Chp. Chp.	Mens Mess.	Ladies Da.
Length Long.	5137	4992	4651
Par	68	68	68

Advised golfing ability	0 12 24 36
Niveau de jeu recommandé	
Hcp required Handicap exigé	35

CLUB HOUSE & AMENITIES
CLUB HOUSE ET ANNEXES
6/10

Pro shop	Pro-shop	
Driving range	Practice	
Sheltered	couvert	4 mats
On grass	sur herbe	yes
Putting-green	putting-green	yes
Pitching-green	pitching green	yes

HOTEL FACILITIES
ENVIRONNEMENT HOTELIER
7/10

HOTELS HÔTELS
Reine Hortense   Dinard
13 rooms, D 980 F   5 km
Tel (33) 02 99 46 54 31, Fax (33) 02 99 88 15 88

Printania   Dinard
59 rooms, D 440 F   5 km
Tel (33) 02 99 46 13 07, Fax (33) 02 99 46 26 32

Golf Hôtel   St-Briac
40 rooms, D 520 F   on place
Tel (33) 02 99 88 30 30, Fax (33) 02 99 88 07 87

RESTAURANTS RESTAURANTS
Altaïr   Dinard
Tel (33) 02 99 46 13 58   5 km

Restaurant du Decolle   St Lunaire
Tel (33) 02 99 46 01 70   2 km

Ce n'est pas encore un énorme complexe golfique comme Disneyworld à Orlando, mais Disneyland Paris offre un 18 trous et un 9 trous, construits par Ronald Fream sur un terrain plat, mais fortement modelé. Cet ensemble n'est pas d'une trop grande complexité technique, les pièges sont immédiatement visibles et les grands espaces favorisent les longs frappeurs. Cependant, les contours assez tourmentés des greens et quelques difficultés stratégiques permettent aux techniciens d'y exprimer leur virtuosité. L'ensemble présente un visage très américain, il ne faudra pas s'en étonner, avec bon nombre d'obstacles d'eau. Si les trois parcours affirment peu à peu leur personnalité, le Club House et les équipements sont fonctionnels, mais ils manquent de chaleur. C'est un complexe évidemment commercial, sans véritable vie de Club... On aime ou pas.

This is not yet your actual outsized golfing complex as in Disneyworld Orlando, but Disneyland Paris presently provides an 18-hole and a 9-hole course built by Ronald Fream over flat terrain bulldozed into shape. Technically speaking, the course is not too complex, as traps are immediately visible and wide open space is a gift for long-hitters. However, the twisting greens and a number of strategic difficulties also give the technicians a chance to practice their skills. Not surprisingly, the whole layout has a very American look to it with a good number of water hazards. While the three courses gradually forge a personality, the Club House and facilities are functional, but lack warmth or soul. This is obviously a business venture without any real club life, so not to everyone's liking.

Golf Disneyland Paris — 1992

Allée de la Mare-Houleuse
F - 77450 MAGNY-LE-HONGRE

Office	Secrétariat	(33) 01 60 45 68 90
Pro shop	Pro-shop	(33) 01 60 45 68 90
Fax	Fax	(33) 01 60 45 68 33
Situation	Situation	

Paris (pop. 2 175 200), 38 km

Annual closure	Fermeture annuelle	no
Weekly closure	Fermeture hebdomadaire	no

Fees main season
Tarifs haute saison 18 holes

	Week days Semaine	We/Bank holidays We/Férié
Individual Individuel	160 F	290 F
Couple Couple	320 F	580 F

Caddy	Caddy	no
Electric Trolley	Chariot électrique	no
Buggy	Voiturette	150 F/18 holes
Clubs	Clubs	150 F/full day

Credit cards Cartes de crédit
VISA - CB - Eurocard - MasterCard - AMEX - DC - JCB

Access Accès : A4 Paris-Metz/Nancy, → «Parc Disneyland Paris»
Map 15 on page 193 Carte 15 Page 193

GOLF COURSE / PARCOURS — 16/20

Site	Site	▬▬
Maintenance	Entretien	▬▬▬
Architect	Architecte	Ronald Fream
Type	Type	open country
Relief	Relief	▬
Water in play	Eau en jeu	▬▬
Exp. to wind	Exposé au vent	▬▬
Trees in play	Arbres en jeu	▬▬

Scorecard / Carte de score	Chp. / Chp.	Mens / Mess.	Ladies / Da.
Length Long.	6032	5593	5172
Par	72	72	72

Advised golfing ability Niveau de jeu recommandé	0	12	24	36
Hcp required Handicap exigé	35			

CLUB HOUSE & AMENITIES / CLUB HOUSE ET ANNEXES — 7/10

Pro shop	Pro-shop	▬▬
Driving range	Practice	▬▬
Sheltered	couvert	10 mats
On grass	sur herbe	yes
Putting-green	putting-green	yes
Pitching-green	pitching green	yes

HOTEL FACILITIES / ENVIRONNEMENT HOTELIER — 8/10

HOTELS HÔTELS

Centrale de réservation	on site

Tel (33) 01 60 30 60 30

Disneyland	1 km

500 rooms, D 2 500 F
Tel (33) 01 60 45 65 00, Fax (33) 01 60 45 65 33

Séquoia Lodge	1 km

1001 rooms, D 1 000 F
Tel (33) 01 60 45 51 00, Fax (33) 01 60 45 51 33

Cheyenne	1 km

1000 rooms, D 695
Tel (33) 01 60 45 62 00, Fax (33) 01 60 45 62 33

RESTAURANTS RESTAURANT

Invention - Tel (33) 01 60 45 65 00	Hôtel Disneyland
Cape Cod et Yacht Club	Hôtel New-Port

Tel (33) 01 60 45 55 00

265

14	6	7

Avec six par 4, six par 5 et six par 3, le parcours de Divonne est original, mais le fait de commencer et de terminer par des par 3 n'est pas son point fort. Dominant le Lac Léman, ce parcours de moyenne montagne est assez bien rythmé pour ne pas être épuisant, quand il n'est pas trop humide. L'environnement boisé est très plaisant (en automne notamment), et permet au minimum de transformer une mauvaise partie en jolie promenade. Peut-être un peu difficile pour les joueurs non classés, Divonne permet cependant aux golfeurs de tous niveaux de jouer ensemble, et constitue un challenge appréciable pour les meilleurs frappeurs : ils auront de multiples occasions de prendre des risques, même si l'absence de subtilités stratégiques empêche de renouveler constamment le plaisir. C'est en tout cas une halte de qualité pendant un séjour à la belle saison.

With six par 4s, six par 5s and six par 3s, Divonne is an original course, but starting and finishing with par 3s is hardly its strong point. Overlooking lake Geneva, Divonne is a mid-mountain course which is not too tiring, when the weather is not too damp. The woody surroundings are very pleasant (especially in autumn) and at the very least can help change a rotten round into a pleasant walk. Divonne might be a little too tough for very high handicappers but it does allow golfers of all abilities to play together. It is certainly quite some challenge for the longerhitters, who have countless opportunities to take risks, even though the course lacks strategic subtlety. At all events, this is a great stop-off over the summer months.

Golf de Divonne — 1931
F - 01220 DIVONNE-LES-BAINS

Office	Secrétariat	(33) 04 50 40 34 11
Pro shop	Pro-shop	(33) 04 50 40 34 11
Fax	Fax	(33) 04 50 40 34 25
Situation	Situation	

Genève (pop. 172 486), 17 km

Annual closure	Fermeture annuelle	no

Weekly closure Fermeture hebdomadaire
no tuesday (mardi): restaurant 15/12 → 15/03

Fees main season
Tarifs haute saison full day

	Week days Semaine	We/Bank holidays We/Férié
Individual Individuel	300 F	500 F
Couple Couple	600 F	1 000 F
Caddy Caddy		on request
Electric Trolley Chariot électrique		150 F/18 holes
Buggy Voiturette		220 F/18 holes
Clubs Clubs		160 F/full day

Credit cards Cartes de crédit
VISA - CB - Eurocard - MasterCard - AMEX - DC - JCB

266

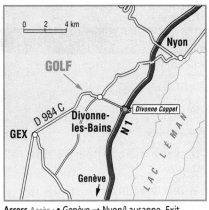

GOLF

Nyon

D 984 C

Divonne-les-Bains

Divonne Coppet

GEX

N1

LAC LÉMAN

Genève

Access Accès : • Genève → Nyon/Lausanne, Exit (Sortie) Divonne, → Golf
• Gex (France) D 984 → Divonne
Map 8 on page 179 Carte 8 Page 179

GOLF COURSE / PARCOURS — 14/20

Site	Site	
Maintenance	Entretien	
Architect	Architecte	M. Nakowsky Donald Harradine
Type	Type	parkland, hilly
Relief	Relief	
Water in play	Eau en jeu	
Exp. to wind	Exposé au vent	
Trees in play	Arbres en jeu	

Scorecard Carte de score	Chp. Chp.	Mens Mess.	Ladies Da.
Length Long.	6035	5607	5087
Par	72	72	72

Advised golfing ability   0   12   24   36
Niveau de jeu recommandé
Hcp required Handicap exigé   35

CLUB HOUSE & AMENITIES / CLUB HOUSE ET ANNEXES — 6/10

Pro shop	Pro-shop	
Driving range	Practice	
Sheltered	couvert	10 mats
On grass	sur herbe	no, 12 mats open air
Putting-green	putting-green	yes
Pitching-green	pitching green	yes

HOTEL FACILITIES / ENVIRONNEMENT HOTELIER — 7/10

HOTELS HÔTELS
Le Grand Hôtel   500 m
115 rooms, D 1 200 F
Tel (33) 04 50 40 34 34, Fax (33) 04 50 40 34 24

Château de Divonne   Divonne
22 rooms, D 950 F   2 km
Tel (33) 04 50 20 00 32, Fax (33) 04 50 20 03 73

Auberge des Chasseurs   Echenevex
15 rooms, D 800 F   9 km
Tel (33) 04 50 41 54 07, Fax (33) 04 50 41 90 61

RESTAURANTS RESTAURANTS
Château de Divonne   Divonne
Tel (33) 04 50 20 00 32

La Terrasse   Divonne
Tel (33) 04 50 40 35 39

DOMONT-MONTMORENCY

13	7	4

Depuis 1966, Domont a conquis une réputation de club très familial, où l'accueil est toujours agréable. L'architecture manque un peu de style, mais l'architecte n'a visiblement pas souhaité bouleverser le terrain. Comme l'eau n'est en jeu que sur un seul trou, que les nombreux bunkers sont bien placés (ils ont tous été regarnis), mais rarement très profonds, les difficultés tiennent essentiellement à la présence imposante de beaux arbres souvent serrés les uns contre les autres. Ils donnent une impression trompeuse de parcours étroit : en fait, les arrivées de drive sont assez larges. Les accidents du terrain compliquent le choix de club, mais aussi l'exécution des coups quand on se trouve dans un dévers. Cependant, le parcours étant assez court, rien n'oblige à prendre des risques avec le driver, et les joueurs précis réussissent mieux ici que les frappeurs. Un parcours très plaisant.

Since 1966, Domont has built up the reputation of a very family club where visitors are always warmly welcomed. The layout lacks a wee bit of style, but the architect was clearly keen not to disrupt the natural terrain. With water in play on one hole only, and with numerous bunkers that, although cleverly placed, are never too deep, the main problems here come essentially from the beautiful trees that closely line nearly every fairway. They give the false impression of narrow fairways, but in fact the drive landing areas are wide enough. The undulating terrain makes club selection a little more difficult than usual, and stroke-making is never easy on some of the sloping fairways. On the upside, the course is comparatively short, so there's no need to risk the driver. All in all, a very pleasant golf course where the straight player will almost certainly card a better score than the long-hitters.

Golf de Domont-Montmorency — 1966

Route de Montmorency
F - 95330 DOMONT

Office	Secrétariat	(33) 01 39 91 07 50
Pro shop	Pro-shop	(33) 01 39 91 07 50
Fax	Fax	(33) 01 39 91 25 70
Situation	Situation	

Enghien (pop. 10 080), 10 km - Paris (pop. 2 175 200), 20 km

Annual closure	Fermeture annuelle	no
Weekly closure	Fermeture hebdomadaire	tuesday (mardi)

Fees main season
Tarifs haute saison full day

	Week days Semaine	We/Bank holidays We/Férié
Individual Individuel	250 F	480 F
Couple Couple	500 F	960 F
Caddy Caddy		no
Electric Trolley Chariot électrique		100 F/18 holes
Buggy Voiturette		180 F/18 holes
Clubs Clubs		yes

Credit cards Cartes de crédit
VISA - CB - Eurocard - Mastercard - AMEX - DC - JCB

Access Accès : Paris, A1 then N1 → Beauvais,
Exit (Sortie) Domont-Ezanville → Montmorency
Map 15 on page 192 Carte 15 Page 192

GOLF COURSE
PARCOURS
13/20

Site	Site	▮▮▮▮▮▯
Maintenance	Entretien	▮▮▮▮▮▯
Architect	Architecte	Fred Hawtree
Type	Type	forest, hilly
Relief	Relief	▮▮▮▮▯▯
Water in play	Eau en jeu	▮▯▯▯▯▯
Exp. to wind	Exposé au vent	▮▮▯▯▯▯
Trees in play	Arbres en jeu	▮▮▮▮▯▯

Scorecard Carte de score	Chp. Chp.	Mens Mess.	Ladies Da.
Length Long.	5874	5569	5008
Par	71	71	71

Advised golfing ability		0 12 24 36
Niveau de jeu recommandé		▮▮▯▯
Hcp required	Handicap exigé	30

CLUB HOUSE & AMENITIES
CLUB HOUSE ET ANNEXES
7/10

Pro shop	Pro-shop	▮▮▮▮▮▯
Driving range	Practice	▮▮▮▮▯▯
Sheltered	couvert	15 mats
On grass	sur herbe	no
Putting-green	putting-green	yes
Pitching-green	pitching green	no

HOTEL FACILITIES
ENVIRONNEMENT HOTELIER
4/10

HOTELS HÔTELS
Grand Hôtel — Enghien
47 rooms, D 1 000 F — 10 km
Tel (33) 01 34 12 80 00, Fax (33) 01 34 12 73 81

Novotel Château de Maffliers — Maffliers
80 rooms, D 660 F — 7 km
Tel (33) 01 34 08 35 35, Fax (33) 01 34 69 97 49

RESTAURANTS RESTAURANTS
Au Cœur de la Forêt — Montmorency
Tel (33) 01 39 64 99 19 — 5 km

Auberge Landaise — Enghien
Tel (33) 02 34 12 78 36 — 10 km

267

Très fréquenté par les Suisses, ce parcours a été dessiné par Michel Gayon sur un terrain accidenté, avec très peu d'arbres. Ses difficultés viennent essentiellement des dévers, du relief, des rivières traversant les fairways et de quelques mares. Il serait sans doute plus délicat à négocier avec des roughs plus épais. Les greens sont dessinés avec beaucoup de soin, protégés par le relief naturel du terrain et par un grand nombre de bunkers, tout comme les arrivées de drive. Pour les joueurs à partir de 15 de handicap, il peut être très long, mais de nombreux départs différents permettent de se faire un parcours «à sa main», si l'on ne veut pas trop forcer son talent. Le rythme général est assez saccadé, avec des trous difficiles en succession, puis des moments de relâchement, mais la fin de parcours est technique, montant en puissance à partir du 13.

Very popular with Swiss golfers, Esery was designed by Michel Gayon over a hilly terrain with very few trees. The major difficulty comes from the sloping fairways, the relief, the rivers crossing the fairways and a few ponds. It would certainly be a tougher test with thicker rough. The greens have been very carefully designed and are very well defended, not only by the naturally hilly terrain but also by well-placed bunkers. The same goes for the fairways at driving distance. For players with handicaps in the upper teens, this could prove to be a very long course, but the large number of tees let you tailor the course to your own ability if you don't feel up to the test. The overall rhythm is a little disjointed with a series of difficult holes followed by a number of easier ones. The run-in is more technical, getting harder from the 13th hole onwards.

Golf Club d'Esery 1990
Esery
F - 74930 REIGNIER

Office	Secrétariat	(33) 04 50 36 58 70
Pro shop	Pro-shop	(33) 04 50 31 20 15
Fax	Fax	(33) 04 50 36 57 62
Situation	Situation	

Genève (pop. 172 486), 12 km

Annual closure	Fermeture annuelle	no
Weekly closure	Fermeture hebdomadaire	no

Monday (lundi): Club-house closed

Fees main season
Tarifs haute saison 18 holes

	Week days Semaine	We/Bank holidays We/Férié
Individual Individuel	280 F	400 F
Couple Couple	560 F	800 F
Caddy Caddy		on request
Electric Trolley Chariot électrique		100 F/18 holes
Buggy Voiturette		200 F/18 holes
Clubs Clubs		100 F/full day

Credit cards Cartes de crédit
VISA - CB - Eurocard - MasterCard

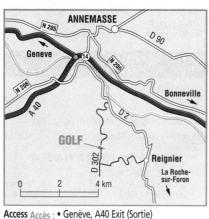

Access Accès : • Genève, A40 Exit (Sortie)
Annemasse → Reignier
• Annecy, A41 Exit (Sortie) 14, → Reignier
Map 11 on page 185 Carte 11 Page 185

GOLF COURSE
PARCOURS 15/20

Site	Site	
Maintenance	Entretien	
Architect	Architecte	Michel Gayon
Type	Type	mountain, hilly
Relief	Relief	
Water in play	Eau en jeu	
Exp. to wind	Exposé au vent	
Trees in play	Arbres en jeu	

Scorecard	Chp.	Mens	Ladies
Carte de score	Chp.	Mess.	Da.
Length Long.	6350	6044	5100
Par	72	72	72

Advised golfing ability		0 12 24 36
Niveau de jeu recommandé		
Hcp required	Handicap exigé	30

CLUB HOUSE & AMENITIES
CLUB HOUSE ET ANNEXES 7/10

Pro shop	Pro-shop	
Driving range	Practice	
Sheltered	couvert	10 mats
On grass	sur herbe	no, 10 mats open air
Putting-green	putting-green	yes
Pitching-green	pitching green	no

HOTEL FACILITIES
ENVIRONNEMENT HOTELIER 5/10

HOTELS HÔTELS
Mercure — Annemasse
78 rooms, D 570 F — 7 km
Tél (33) 04 50 92 05 25, Fax (33) 04 50 87 14 57

Ibis — Archamps
84 rooms, D 320 F — 12 km
Tél (33) 04 50 95 38 18, Fax (33) 04 50 95 38 95

Hôtel des Bergues — Genève
123 rooms, D 320 CHF — 12 km
Tél (41) 022 - 731 50 50, Fax (41) 022 - 732 19 8

RESTAURANTS RESTAURANTS
Le Béarn — Genève
Tél (41) 022 - 321 00 28 — 12 km

Le Chat Botté — Genève
Tél (41) 022 - 731 02 21 — 12 km

268

ESTÉREL LATITUDES

Dans un environnement de pins, et sur un terrain modérément accidenté, Robert Trent Jones a tracé un parcours techniquement très intéressant, d'une grande diversité de difficultés et souvent spectaculaire : notamment le 15, petit par 3 où il faut franchir un véritable gouffre. Il faut savoir bien travailler la balle pour y scorer convenablement, et choisir soigneusement son club à chaque coup, le driver n'étant certes pas obligatoire sur chaque départ. Des dizaines de bunkers et quelques obstacles d'eau très en jeu imposent de définir soigneusement sa stratégie. Les greens sont le point faible de ce parcours tactique, non par leur entretien, mais par leurs ondulations excessives (sur une demi-douzaine) qui laissent trop de place à la chance... Un parcours à connaître, malgré la présence des maisons qui enserrent ce golf de style «resort».

In a setting of pine forest and pretty hilly countryside, Robert Trent Jones has laid out what is technically a very interesting course with a number of varied and often spectacular hazards. This is particularly so on the 15th, a short 3-par, where a sort of chasm separates tee from green. Careful club selection and ball-control are the key to a goodish score at Esterel, and the driver can certainly be banished on several holes. Dozens of bunkers and a few water hazards call for deliberate strategy. The weak point on this tactical course comes from the greens, not through their upkeep, but because of excessive slope and undulation (on half a dozen holes), which leave too much to chance. A course worth knowing, despite the presence of villas now all around this resort style complex.

Golf Estérel Latitudes — 1989

Avenue du Golf
F - 83700 SAINT-RAPHAEL

Office	Secrétariat	(33) 04 94 52 68 30
Pro shop	Pro-shop	(33) 04 94 52 68 30
Fax	Fax	(33) 04 94 52 68 31
Situation	Situation	

Saint-Raphaël (pop. 26 610), 3 km

Annual closure	Fermeture annuelle	no
Weekly closure	Fermeture hebdomadaire	no

Fees main season
Tarifs haute saison full day

	Week days Semaine	We/Bank holidays We/Férié
Individual Individuel	285 F	285 F
Couple Couple	570 F	570 F

Caddy	Caddy	on request
Electric Trolley	Chariot électrique	70 F/18 holes
Buggy	Voiturette	200 F/18 holes
Clubs	Clubs	150 F/full day

Credit cards Cartes de crédit
VISA - CB - Eurocard - MasterCard - AMEX - DC

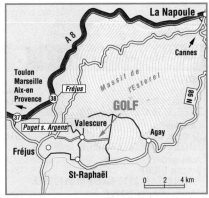

Access Accès : A 8, Exit (Sortie) Fréjus Saint-Raphaël,
→ Saint-Raphaël, then Agay and Valescure
Map 14 on page 191 Carte 14 Page 191

GOLF COURSE PARCOURS — 16/20

Site	Site	
Maintenance	Entretien	
Architect	Architecte	R. Trent Jones Sr
Type	Type	forest, residential
Relief	Relief	
Water in play	Eau en jeu	
Exp. to wind	Exposé au vent	
Trees in play	Arbres en jeu	

Scorecard Carte de score	Chp. Chp.	Mens Mess.	Ladies Da.
Length Long.	5921	5533	5108
Par	71	71	71

Advised golfing ability		0 12 24 36
Niveau de jeu recommandé		
Hcp required	Handicap exigé	35

CLUB HOUSE & AMENITIES CLUB HOUSE ET ANNEXES — 6/10

Pro shop	Pro-shop	
Driving range	Practice	
Sheltered	couvert	15 mats
On grass	sur herbe	yes
Putting-green	putting-green	yes
Pitching-green	pitching green	no

HOTEL FACILITIES ENVIRONNEMENT HOTELIER — 7/10

HOTELS HÔTELS
Latitudes Valescure — on site
95 rooms, D 1 100 F
Tél (33) 04 94 52 68 00, Fax (33) 04 94 44 61 37

San Pedro — Saint-Raphaël
28 rooms, D 850 F — 8 km
Tél (33) 04 94 19 90 20, Fax (33) 04 94 40 57 20

RESTAURANTS RESTAURANT
L'Arbousier — Saint-Raphaël
Tél (33) 04 94 95 25 00 — 4 km

San Pedro — Saint-Raphaël
Tél(33) 04 94 19 90 20 — 8 km

269

Construit dans une très vaste clairière (on souhaiterait plus d'arbres), avec quelques maisons assez séduisantes, Etiolles est un exemple de bon parcours commercial, indulgent aux coups décentrés, et donc accessible à tous. Dessiné par Michel Gayon, il permet à chacun de trouver son bonheur. Les fairways (de bonne dimension) sont bien isolés par des buttes importantes, qui non seulement ajoutent du relief à un terrain assez plat, mais ramènent volontiers les balles en jeu. Les greens sont vastes, mais pas trop difficiles à lire. Ils ne sont pas trop défendus quand l'approche se fait avec un long fer ou un bois. Parmi les trous remarquables, on distinguera le 18, de physionomie très américaine dans son dessin, ramenant vers le Club House de style colonial. L'entretien est très correct, et le neuf trous adjacent de bonne qualité.

Laid out over a huge clearing (a few more trees would be welcome), with some very attractive houses, Etiolles is a good example of a successful business golfing venture. Designed by Michel Gayon, there is something for everyone here. The wide fairways are neatly isolated by mounds, which not only add a little relief to a flat terrain but also obligingly bring the ball back into play. The greens are large but not too difficult to read, and are open to long approaches with a long iron or fairway wood. One of the most remarkable holes is the very American style 18th, leading the player back to the colonial style club-house. Upkeep is very good, and the same goes for the adjacent 9-hole course.

Golf d'Etiolles — 1990

Vieux Chemin de Paris
F - 91450 ETIOLLES

Office	Secrétariat	(33) 01 60 75 49 49
Pro shop	Pro-shop	(33) 01 60 75 49 49
Fax	Fax	(33) 01 60 75 64 20
Situation	Situation	

Paris (pop. 2 175 200), 37 km - Evry (pop. 455 530), 3 km

Annual closure	Fermeture annuelle	no
Weekly closure	Fermeture hebdomadaire	no

Fees main season
Tarifs haute saison full day

	Week days Semaine	We/Bank holidays We/Férié
Individual Individuel	260 F	390 F
Couple Couple	400 F	600 F

After 16.00, GF 150 F/weekdays, 200 F/We

Caddy	Caddy	no
Electric Trolley	Chariot électrique	65 F/18 holes
Buggy	Voiturette	200 F/18 holes
Clubs	Clubs	50 F/full day

Credit cards Cartes de crédit
VISA - CB - Eurocard - MasterCard - Amex

270

Access Accès : A6, Exit (Sortie) Melun Sénart/Marne-la-Vallée, Francilienne (N104) 3 km, Exit (Sortie) Etiolles
Map 15 on page 193 Carte 15 Page 193

GOLF COURSE / PARCOURS — 15/20

Site	Site	
Maintenance	Entretien	
Architect	Architecte	Michel Gayon
Type	Type	open country
Relief	Relief	
Water in play	Eau en jeu	
Exp. to wind	Exposé au vent	
Trees in play	Arbres en jeu	

Scorecard Carte de score	Chp. Chp.	Mens Mess.	Ladies Da.
Length Long.	6239	5710	5272
Par	73	73	73

Advised golfing ability 0 12 24 36
Niveau de jeu recommandé
Hcp required Handicap exigé no

CLUB HOUSE & AMENITIES / CLUB HOUSE ET ANNEXES — 6/10

Pro shop	Pro-shop	
Driving range	Practice	
Sheltered	couvert	9 mats
On grass	sur herbe	no, 12 mats open air
Putting-green	putting-green	yes
Pitching-green	pitching green	yes

HOTEL FACILITIES / ENVIRONNEMENT HOTELIER — 5/10

HOTELS HÔTELS

Mercure — Evry
114 rooms, D 600 F — 3 km
Tél (33) 01 69 47 30 00, Fax (33) 01 69 47 30 10

Campanile — Saint-Germain-lès-Corbeil
47 rooms, D 295 F — 5 km
Tél (33) 01 69 89 12 13, Fax (33) 01 69 89 11 89

Auberge de l'Ile de Saussay — Ile de Saussay
7 rooms, D 450 F — 17 km
Tél (33) 01 64 93 20 12, Fax (33) 01 69 93 39 88

Climat - 44 rooms, D 275 F — Tigery
Tél (33) 01 69 89 19 00, Fax (33) 01 69 89 19 12 — 3 km

RESTAURANTS RESTAURANT

La Mare au Diable — Moissy-Cramayel
Tél (33) 01 64 10 20 90 — 13 km

La vue sur la mer, les falaises et la ville est splendide. On ne se lassera pas du 10, plongeant au drive en bord de mer, pour remonter ensuite vers le green sur un plateau. Ouvert à tous les vents, ce parcours a fait l'objet de modifications depuis sa création en 1908. Pour le classer parmi les grands links, il faudrait reprendre pas mal de bunkers, quelques greens aux surfaces souvent sans intérêt, et déplacer plusieurs départs, mais ce golf familial ne dispose pas des moyens des clubs prestigieux et les améliorations ne peuvent être que progressives. Cela dit, on peut jouer ici plusieurs jours avec beaucoup de plaisir, par beau temps au moins. Quand le vent souffle, c'est une bataille contre le parcours, et il vaut mieux jouer en match-play ! L'atmosphère du club est sympathique, le profil général du parcours en fait un « challenge » attachant, ne serait ce que pour travailler les balles basses.

The view over the sea, cliffs and the town is magnificent, and the 10th hole, with a drive plunging seaward from the cliffs before sweeping back up to an elevated green, is a moment to cherish. Exposed to all winds, the course has been altered several times since its creation in 1908, but to be ranked among the truly great links, some tees need moving and a number of bunkers require attention, as do the putting surfaces on several greens. But this is a family club that lacks the resources of the more prestigious courses, and improvements can only come gradually. With this said, you can play here time and time again and enjoy every minute, at least if the weather holds. When the wind blows, it is a tough battle with the course and match-play is the obvious resort. The club has a friendly atmosphere and the general layout of the course makes it a pleasing challenge, if only for the opportunity to practice those low-trajectory shots.

Golf d'Etretat — 1908

Route du Havre
F - 76790 ETRETAT

Office	Secrétariat	(33) 02 35 27 04 89
Pro shop	Pro-shop	(33) 02 35 28 56 67
Fax	Fax	(33) 02 35 29 49 02
Situation	Situation	

Fécamp (pop. 20 800), 16 km
Le Havre (pop. 197 210), 30 km

Annual closure	Fermeture annuelle	no
Weekly closure	Fermeture hebdomadaire	no

tuesday (mardi): restaurant closed

Fees main season
Tarifs haute saison full day

	Week days Semaine	We/Bank holidays We/Férié
Individual Individuel	200 F	330 F
Couple Couple	360 F	590 F

Caddy	Caddy	no
Electric Trolley	Chariot électrique	no
Buggy	Voiturette	180 F/18 holes
Clubs	Clubs	no

Credit cards Cartes de crédit
VISA - CB - Eurocard - MasterCard

Access Accès : D940 Etretat-Le Havre
Map 2 on page 167 Carte 2 Page 167

GOLF COURSE / PARCOURS — 14/20

Site	Site	
Maintenance	Entretien	
Architect	Architecte	M. Chantepie D. Fruchet (4 trous)
Type	Type	seaside course, open country
Relief	Relief	
Water in play	Eau en jeu	
Exp. to wind	Exposé au vent	
Trees in play	Arbres en jeu	

Scorecard Carte de score	Chp. Chp.	Mens Mess.	Ladies Da.
Length Long.	6072	5681	5137
Par	72	72	72

Advised golfing ability   0   12   24   36
Niveau de jeu recommandé
Hcp required   Handicap exigé   35 - 28 We

CLUB HOUSE & AMENITIES / CLUB HOUSE ET ANNEXES — 6/10

Pro shop	Pro-shop	
Driving range	Practice	
Sheltered	couvert	3 mats
On grass	sur herbe	no, 5 mats open air
Putting-green	putting-green	yes
Pitching-green	pitching green	no

271

HOTEL FACILITIES / ENVIRONNEMENT HOTELIER — 5/10

HOTELS HÔTELS
Dormy House Golf Hôtel — 500 m
49 rooms, D 650 F
Tél (33) 02 35 27 07 88, Fax (33) 02 35 29 86 19

Le Donjon — Etretat — 2 km
10 rooms, D 700 F
Tél (33) 02 35 27 08 23, Fax (33) 02 35 29 92 24

Les Falaises - 24 rooms, D 400 F — Etretat — 2 km
Tél (33) 02 35 27 02 77

RESTAURANTS RESTAURANTS
Le Belvédère — Etretat — 2 km
Tél (33) 02 35 20 13 76

Le Galion — Etretat — 2 km
Tél (33) 02 35 29 48 74

Le remodelage effectué par Cabell Robinson en 1990 a «réveillé» et beaucoup amélioré ce parcours et le remplacement récent du 3 (par 3) a fait disparaître son trou le plus contestable. Les greens sont maintenant très protégés, avec des jeux de buttes et de nombreux bunkers très en jeu, mettant beaucoup plus l'accent sur les aspects techniques du jeu. Si les joueurs très moyens ont parfois regretté ces nouvelles difficultés, le parcours a repris son rang parmi les meilleurs de la région lémanique. Assez accidenté (voiturette conseillée pour les seniors), quasiment comme un golf de montagne, Evian n'est pas très long, mais les dénivellations peuvent être trompeuses, notamment au 15, petit par 3 très spectaculaire dominant le lac Léman. Le plus joli point de vue du parcours, couronnant l'impression très agréable d'évoluer dans un beau parc.

The restyling carried out by Cabell Robinson in 1990 has revived and much improved this course, and the recent replacement of hole N° 3 (a par 3) has seen the end of one of the course's more controversial holes. The greens are now particularly well defended, with a series of sand-hills and easy-to-hit bunkers, thus placing much more emphasis on the technical side of the game. While high-handicappers may often come to regret these new difficulties, the course has recovered its status as one of the best courses in the region. Hilly enough to be virtually a mountain course (buggy recommended for seniors), Evian is not very long, but the steep slopes can be deceiving, especially on the 15th, a highly spectacular short par 3 overlooking Lake Geneva. This is the prettiest spot on the course and crowns the very pleasant impression of playing golf in a beautiful park.

Royal Golf Club Evian 1904
B.P. No 8
F - 74502 EVIAN

Office	Secrétariat	(33) 04 50 75 46 66
Pro shop	Pro-shop	(33) 04 50 75 51 96
Fax	Fax	(33) 04 50 75 65 54
Situation	Situation	

Evian (pop. 8 900), 2.5 km
Genève (pop. 172 486), 46 km

Annual closure	Fermeture annuelle	yes
		15/12 → 31/1
Weekly closure	Fermeture hebdomadaire	no

Fees main season
Tarifs haute saison 18 holes

	Week days Semaine	We/Bank holidays We/Férié
Individual Individuel	310 F	380 F
Couple Couple	620 F	760 F

After 18.00 : – 50%

Caddy	Caddy	160 F/18 holes
Electric Trolley	Chariot électrique	130 F/18 holes
Buggy	Voiturette	280 F/18 holes
Clubs	Clubs	100 F/18 holes

Credit cards Cartes de crédit
VISA - CB - Eurocard - MasterCard - AMEX - DC - JCB

272

Access Accès : Genève → Evian, take right → Golf
Map 8 on page 179 Carte 8 Page 179

GOLF COURSE
PARCOURS
15/20

Site	Site	▰▰▰▰▱
Maintenance	Entretien	▰▰▰▰▱
Architect	Architecte	Cabell Robinson
Type	Type	parkland, hilly
Relief	Relief	▰▰▰▰▱
Water in play	Eau en jeu	▰▰▱▱▱
Exp. to wind	Exposé au vent	▰▰▱▱▱
Trees in play	Arbres en jeu	▰▰▰▱▱

Scorecard Carte de score	Chp. Chp.	Mens Mess.	Ladies Da.
Length Long.	6006	5651	5094
Par	72	72	72

Advised golfing ability		0 12 24 36
Niveau de jeu recommandé		▰▰▰▰▱
Hcp required	Handicap exigé	35

CLUB HOUSE & AMENITIES
CLUB HOUSE ET ANNEXES
7/10

Pro shop	Pro-shop	▰▰▰▰▱
Driving range	Practice	▰▰▰▰▱
Sheltered	couvert	10 mats
On grass	sur herbe	yes
Putting-green	putting-green	yes
Pitching-green	pitching green	yes

HOTEL FACILITIES
ENVIRONNEMENT HOTELIER
9/10

HOTELS HÔTELS
Le Royal — Evian 3 km
125 rooms, D 1900 F
Tél (33) 04 50 26 85 00, Fax (33) 04 50 75 61 00

L'Ermitage — Evian 2 km
90 rooms, D 1600 F
Tél (33) 04 50 26 85 00, Fax (33) 04 50 75 61 00

La Verniaz « Relais & Châteaux » — Evian 2 km
35 rooms, D 1 000 F
Tél (33) 04 50 75 04 90, Fax (33) 04 50 70 78 92

Bourgogne et Ducs de Savoie — Evian 2 km
30 rooms, D 520 F
Tél (33) 04 50 75 01 05, Fax (33) 04 50 75 04 05

RESTAURANTS RESTAURANT
La Toque Royale — Evian 2,5 km
Tél (33) 04 50 26 87 10

FEUCHEROLLES

Un parcours assez vallonné, mais où la mise en oeuvre des reliefs a été faite avec intelligence, et le souci d'éviter les coups aveugles. Cette franchise a beaucoup contribué à sa réputation. Très varié, le dessin de l'américain Jean-Marie Poellot met en jeu tous les types d'obstacles et exige tous les coups de golf; il propose fréquemment des choix stratégiques intéressants, et des situations de petit jeu excitantes. La maturité du parcours et l'abondance des plantations contribuent au charme du jeu. Les trous sont de bonne longueur, à l'exception du 13, un par 3 démesuré, mais on ne recommandera les départs arrière qu'aux handicaps à un chiffre. Très travaillés, les greens demandent beaucoup de finesse et d'attention pour ne pas perdre trop de points au putting. Le fonctionnement du club est complètement commercial, mais l'ensemble reste accueillant. Le Club-House est à la hauteur.

A comparatively hilly course where relief has been employed intelligently to carefully avoid blind shots. This straight and honest side to the layout has done much to help the course's reputation. The very varied design of American architect Jean-Marie Poellot brings all types of hazard into play and demands every shot in the book. Interestingly, the layout often gives a choice of strategy and some exciting situations for short-play around the greens. The maturity of the course and the numerous plantations do much to add to the charm of playing here. All the holes are of a good length, except the outsized 13th hole, a par-3 of over 200 metres, but generally the back-tees are to be recommended for single-figure handicappers. A lot of work has gone into the greens, which require more than a touch of finesse if you want to avoid too many 3-putts (and who doesn't?). The club is a totally commercial affair, but the whole complex extends a warm welcome with a club-house worthy of the rest.

Golf de Feucherolles — 1993

Sainte-Gemme
F -78810 FEUCHEROLLES

Office	Secrétariat	(33) 01 30 54 94 94
Pro shop	Pro-shop	(33) 01 30 54 94 94
Fax	Fax	(33) 01 30 54 92 37
Situation	Situation	

St-Germain-en-Laye (pop. 39 920), 12 km
Paris (pop. 2 175 200), 39 km

Annual closure	Fermeture annuelle	no
Weekly closure	Fermeture hebdomadaire	tuesday
	(mardi) 1/11 → 28/2	

Fees main season
Tarifs haute saison 18 holes

	Week days Semaine	We/Bank holidays We/Férié
Individual Individuel	350 F	490 F
Couple Couple	700 F	980 F
Caddy	Caddy	on request
Electric Trolley	Chariot électrique	no
Buggy	Voiturette	120 F/18 holes
Clubs	Clubs	150 F/full day

Credit cards Cartes de crédit
VISA - CB - Eurocard - MasterCard - AMEX - DC - JCB

Access Accès : Paris A13 → Versailles, Exit (Sortie)
Saint-Germain-en-Laye → Saint-Nom-la- Bretèche,
→ Feucherolles
Map 15 on page 193 Carte 15 Page 193

GOLF COURSE / PARCOURS — 15/20

Site	Site	
Maintenance	Entretien	
Architect	Architecte	Jean-Marie Poellot
Type	Type	parkland, open country
Relief	Relief	
Water in play	Eau en jeu	
Exp. to wind	Exposé au vent	
Trees in play	Arbres en jeu	

Scorecard	Chp.	Mens	Ladies
Carte de score	Chp.	Mess.	Da.
Length Long.	6358	5887	5486
Par	72	72	72

Advised golfing ability	0	12	24	36
Niveau de jeu recommandé				
Hcp required	Handicap exigé	no		

CLUB HOUSE & AMENITIES / CLUB HOUSE ET ANNEXES — 7/10

Pro shop	Pro-shop	
Driving range	Practice	
Sheltered	couvert	no
On grass	sur herbe	no, 12 mats open air
Putting-green	putting-green	yes
Pitching-green	pitching green	no

273

HOTEL FACILITIES / ENVIRONNEMENT HOTELIER — 5/10

HOTELS HÔTELS

La Forestière — Saint-Germain
25 rooms, D 950 F — 12 km
Tél (33) 01 39 10 38 38, Fax (33) 01 39 73 73 88

Le Pavillon Henri IV — Saint-Germain
42 rooms, D 1 290 F — 12 km
Tél (33) 01 39 10 15 15, Fax (33) 01 39 93 73 93

Ermitage des Loges — Saint-Germain
57 rooms, D 660 F — 12 km
Tél (33) 01 39 21 50 90, Fax (33) 01 39 21 50 91

RESTAURANTS RESTAURANTS

Les Trois Marches — Versailles
Tél (33) 01 39 50 13 21 — 10 km

Le Potager du Roy — Versailles
Tél (33) 01 39 50 35 34 — 10 km

Situé à l'orée de la superbe forêt de Fontainebleau, ce parcours est l'un des plus tranquilles de la région parisienne. Il fait partie de ces grands refuges d'une certaine tradition britannique, bien que l'on puisse regretter que certaines retouches aient été apportées au dessin de Simpson au cours des années, notamment sur quelques greens. Un regret mineur en regard des satisfactions visuelles et golfiques que l'on peut éprouver ici, au milieu des chênes, des pins et des hêtres, où l'on devine parfois les ombres des biches, où l'on dérange souvent lièvres et lapins. Grâce au terrain très sablonneux et au gazon très souple, on peut découvrir ici toute l'année un parcours plus que plaisant, pas trop difficile, bien que les greens soient souvent petits et parfois très torturés, mais où un bon score n'est jamais le fait du hasard. Un parcours complet.

This course, lying on the edge of the magnificent forest of Fontainebleau, is one of the quietest around Paris. It is one of those great bastions of British tradition, although some might regret the way Simpson's layout has been retouched here and there over the years, particularly on some of the greens. This is only a minor gripe given the visual and golfing pleasure to be had here amidst the oak, pine and beech trees, where you can sometimes make out the shape of deer or disturb hares and rabbits. With very sandy terrain and plush grass, you can play this more than pleasant and not too difficult course all year, although the greens are often small and very torturous. A complete course where a good score is never down to chance.

Golf de Fontainebleau — 1909
Route d'Orléans
F - 77300 FONTAINEBLEAU

Office	Secrétariat	(33) 01 64 22 22 95
Pro shop	Pro-shop	(33) 01 64 22 74 19
Fax	Fax	(33) 01 64 22 63 76
Situation	Situation	

Fontainebleau (pop. 15 714), 1 km

Annual closure	Fermeture annuelle	no
Weekly closure	Fermeture hebdomadaire	tuesday (mardi)

Fees main season
Tarifs haute saison full day

	Week days Semaine	We/Bank holidays We/Férié
Individual Individuel	350 F	—
Couple Couple	700 F	—

We : only members (membres seuls) - 07/08: We 500 F

Caddy	Caddy	190 F/18 holes
Electric Trolley	Chariot électrique	no
Buggy	Voiturette	no
Clubs	Clubs	100 F/full day

Credit cards Cartes de crédit
VISA - CB - MasterCard - Eurocard

274

Access Accès : A6 Exit (Sortie) Fontainebleau. N7 → Fontainebleau. «Carrefour de l'Obélisque», N152 → Malesherbes. Golf 500 m on right hand side.
Map 3 on page 168 Carte 3 Page 168

GOLF COURSE / PARCOURS — 17/20

Site	Site	
Maintenance	Entretien	
Architect	Architecte	Tom Simpson
Type	Type	forest
Relief	Relief	
Water in play	Eau en jeu	
Exp. to wind	Exposé au vent	
Trees in play	Arbres en jeu	

Scorecard Carte de score	Chp. Chp.	Mens Mess.	Ladies Da.
Length Long.	6074	5711	5168
Par	72	72	72

Advised golfing ability		0 12 24 36
Niveau de jeu recommandé		
Hcp required	Handicap exigé	24 Men, 28 Ladies

CLUB HOUSE & AMENITIES / CLUB HOUSE ET ANNEXES — 7/10

Pro shop	Pro-shop	
Driving range	Practice	
Sheltered	couvert	6 mats
On grass	sur herbe	yes
Putting-green	putting-green	yes
Pitching-green	pitching green	yes

HOTEL FACILITIES / ENVIRONNEMENT HOTELIER — 7/10

HOTELS HÔTELS
Aigle Noir — Fontainebleau 1 km
49 rooms, D 1050 F
Tél (33) 01 60 74 60 00, Fax (33) 01 60 74 60 01

Mercure — Fontainebleau 1 km
97 rooms, D 800 F
Tél (33) 01 64 69 34 34, Fax (33) 01 64 69 34 39

Ibis — Fontainebleau 1 km
80 rooms, D 460 F
Tél (33) 01 64 23 45 25, Fax (33) 01 64 23 42 22

RESTAURANTS RESTAURANTS
Bas- Bréau — Barbizon 10 km
Tél (33) 01 60 66 40 05

Le Vieux Logis — Thomery 10 km
Tél (33) 01 60 96 44 77

Grand Veneur - Tél (33) 01 60 66 40 44 Barbizon 9 km

Dans un environnement immobilier manquant singulièrement de beauté, ce parcours a été dessiné par Chris Pittman sur un terrain relativement accidenté. Quelques accidents de terrain (ravin au 11), de petits arbustes, la garrigue et quelques grands arbres interviennent pour compliquer le jeu, ainsi que des dénivellations et dévers parfois préoccupants. Si l'on ajoute quelques trous en bordure de rivière, des greens bien modelés et des bunkers assez profonds pour inciter à s'entraîner avant de les affronter, les joueurs trouveront là un parcours varié et amusant, mais les meilleurs estimeront sans doute qu'il manque «un petit quelque chose» pour en faire un grand parcours. Néammoins, c'est un bon complément dans une région de bonne qualité golfique, notamment avec La Grande Motte, Massane, Cap d'Agde et Nîmes-Campagne.

Laid out in an environment of property development singularly lacking in appeal, this course was designed by Chris Pittman over comparatively hilly terrain. A few drastic features (a ravine on the 11th), small bushes, the «garrigue» and a few big trees actively complicate the course, as do some of the steep slopes and inclines, which can cause considerable concern. Add to this a few holes alongside a river, well-contoured greens and bunkers that are deep enough to prompt some sand practice before the round, and you have here a varied and amusing course, but one where the best players will doubtless feel that there is something missing for it to become a great course. Nevertheless, this is a good additional course in a great region for golf, with in particular La Grande Motte, Massane, Cap d'Agde and Nîmes-Campagne in the neighbourhood.

Golf de Fontcaude — 1991

Domaine de Fontcaude
F - 34990 JUVIGNAC

Office	Secrétariat	(33) 04 67 03 34 30
Pro shop	Pro-shop	(33) 04 67 03 34 30
Fax	Fax	(33) 04 67 03 34 51
Situation	Situation	

Montpellier (pop. 210 860), 2 km

Annual closure	Fermeture annuelle	no
Weekly closure	Fermeture hebdomadaire	no

Fees main season
Tarifs haute saison full day

	Week days Semaine	We/Bank holidays We/Férié
Individual Individuel	260 F	260 F
Couple Couple	520 F	520 F

Caddy	Caddy	no
Electric Trolley	Chariot électrique	60 F/18 holes
Buggy	Voiturette	125 F/18 holes
Clubs	Clubs 1/2 série	60 F/full day

Credit cards Cartes de crédit
VISA - CB - Eurocard - MasterCard - AMEX - DC - JCB

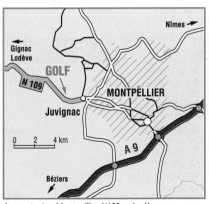

Access Accès : Montpellier, N109 → Lodève
Map 13 on page 189 Carte 13 Page 189

GOLF COURSE PARCOURS — 14/20

Site	Site	
Maintenance	Entretien	
Architect	Architecte	Chris Pittman
Type	Type	residential, hilly
Relief	Relief	
Water in play	Eau en jeu	
Exp. to wind	Exposé au vent	
Trees in play	Arbres en jeu	

Scorecard	Chp.	Mens	Ladies
Carte de score	Chp.	Mess.	Da.
Length Long.	6292	5917	5056
Par	72	72	72

Advised golfing ability	0	12	24	36
Niveau de jeu recommandé				
Hcp required Handicap exigé	35			

CLUB HOUSE & AMENITIES CLUB HOUSE ET ANNEXES — 6/10

Pro shop	Pro-shop	
Driving range	Practice	
Sheltered	couvert	5 mats
On grass	sur herbe	yes
Putting-green	putting-green	yes
Pitching-green	pitching green	yes

275

HOTEL FACILITIES ENVIRONNEMENT HOTELIER — 6/10

HOTELS HÔTELS
Golf de Fontcaude — on site
46 rooms, D 510 F
Tél (33) 04 67 03 34 10, Fax (33) 04 67 03 34 51

New Hôtel du Midi — Montpellier
47 rooms, D 380 F — 2 km
Tél (33) 04 67 92 69 61, Fax (33) 04 67 92 73 63

Demeure des Brousses — Montpellier
17 rooms, D 580 F — 2 km
Tél (33) 04 67 65 77 66, Fax (33) 04 67 22 22 17

RESTAURANTS RESTAURANT
Jardin des Sens — Montpellier
Tél (33) 04 67 79 63 38 — 2 km

Le Chandelier — Montpellier
Tél (33) 04 67 15 34 38 — 2 km

FONTENAILLES BLANC

| 14 | 7 | 6 |

Dans cet ensemble de 27 trous, le 18 trous «Blanc» est considéré comme le pacours principal, même si le «Rouge» propose aussi quelques bons trous. L'architecte Michel Gayon a travaillé avec dextérité et imagination ce vaste espace plat et joliment boisé. Il faut profiter de quelques trous assez courts pour ne pas trop gâter une carte de score forcément mise à mal sur d'autres trous, exigeant beaucoup de puissance au drive. C'est en général un parcours mieux adapté aux frappeurs qu'aux techniciens. En tout cas, certains obstacles cachés impliquent de le jouer plusieurs fois pour bien le connaître avant d'espérer bien y scorer. L'entretien du parcours est généralement de bonne qualité, mais il est un peu humide en hiver, notamment dans les zones les plus boisées. Le complexe Club house-Hôtel est assez confortable et plaisant pour que l'on s'y attarde.

In this 27-hole complex, the 18-hole «White» course is considered to be the main layout, although the 9-hole «Red» alternative also features a few interesting holes. Architect Michel Gayon has employed a lot of skill and imagination in developing this enormous flat space, which has more than its fair share of woodland. Here, you take advantage of a few short holes in order to protect a card that will definitely be hard pushed to survive some of the others, which require power-play and length off the tee. Generally speaking, this is a course for long-hitters rather than for technicians. In any case, a number of hidden hazards call for several outings before hoping to card a good score. Upkeep is generally good, but the course is bit damp in winter, especially in the woodier areas. The club-house/hotel complex is comfortable and pleasant enough to warrant spending some time here.

Golf de Fontenailles — 1991
Domaine de Bois-Boudran
F - 77370 FONTENAILLES

Office	Secrétariat	(33) 01 64 60 51 52
Pro shop	Pro-shop	(33) 01 64 60 51 00
Fax	Fax	(33) 01 60 67 52 12
Situation	Situation	

Melun (pop. 35 320), 25 km

Annual closure	Fermeture annuelle	yes
		24/12 → 2/1
Weekly closure	Fermeture hebdomadaire	no

Fees main season
Tarifs haute saison full day

	Week days Semaine	We/Bank holidays We/Férié
Individual Individuel	200 F	350 F
Couple Couple	350 F	600 F

after 16.00 : 125 (weekdays) et 200 F (We)

Caddy	Caddy	no
Electric Trolley	Chariot électrique	no
Buggy	Voiturette	200 F/18 holes
Clubs	Clubs	60 F/full day

Credit cards Cartes de crédit
VISA - CB - Eurocard - MasterCard - AMEX - DC - JCB

276

Access Accès : • A4 Paris-Nancy, N104 → Troyes,
N19 → Provins • A5 → Melun, Exit (Sortie) 16
Châtillon-la-Borde, D408 → Nangis
Map 3 on page 169 Carte 3 Page 169

GOLF COURSE
PARCOURS

14/20

Site	Site	
Maintenance	Entretien	
Architect	Architecte	Michel Gayon
Type	Type	parkland
Relief	Relief	
Water in play	Eau en jeu	
Exp. to wind	Exposé au vent	
Trees in play	Arbres en jeu	

Scorecard Carte de score	Chp. Chp.	Mens Mess.	Ladies Da.
Length Long.	6256	5900	5299
Par	72	72	72

Advised golfing ability		0 12 24 36
Niveau de jeu recommandé		
Hcp required	Handicap exigé	35 (We)

CLUB HOUSE & AMENITIES
CLUB HOUSE ET ANNEXES

7/10

Pro shop	Pro-shop	
Driving range	Practice	
Sheltered	couvert	5 mats
On grass	sur herbe	yes (Summer)
Putting-green	putting-green	yes
Pitching-green	pitching green	yes

HOTEL FACILITIES
ENVIRONNEMENT HOTELIER

6/10

HOTELS HÔTELS
Domaine de Bois-Boudran — on site
48 rooms, D 1 000 F
Tel (33) 01 64 60 51 00
Fax (33) 01 60 67 52 12

Le Dauphin — Nangis
13 rooms, D 300 F — 6 km
Tel (33) 01 64 08 00 27
Fax (33) 01 64 08 12 97

RESTAURANTS RESTAURANTS
Le Dauphin — Nangis
Tel (33) 01 64 08 00 27 — 6 km

La Forge — Fontenailles
Tel (33) 01 64 08 44 11 — 1 km

A proximité de Saint-Jean-de-Monts, ce golf complète un bel itinéraire dans la province historique de Vendée. A proximité de la station balnéaire de Saint-Gilles-Croix-de-Vie, l'architecte Yves Bureau a conçu un parcours très propre (comme à son habitude) et pour tous niveaux, dans un site de campagne aux reliefs très doux, dans un paysage de chênes verts et de pins maritimes. Des plans d'eau pas trop en jeu agrémentent un dessin sans pièges, adapté à tous les types de joueurs, en harmonie visuelle avec les marais de la région. Ce parcours est de bonne longueur des départs arrière, ce qui permettra aux meilleurs de s'exprimer avec plaisir mais sans trop de soucis. Un joli golf de vacances, où le vent peut apporter un piment, et quelques surprises supplémentaires.

Close to Saint-Jean-de-Monts, this course is a fine addition to a great golfing itinerary through the historical province of La Vendée. Not far from the seaside resort of Saint-Gilles-Croix-de-Vie, architect Yves Bureau has, as usual, designed a very neat golf course for all golfers in gently undulating countryside, lined with oak trees and maritime pines. Stretches of water enhance a layout that is free of hidden traps and tailored to all types of golfer. Visually, the course also blends in well with the region's marshlands. This is a good length course from the back tees, thus giving the better players the chance to show their mettle without too much to worry about. All in all, a pretty holiday course where the wind can add a little spice and a few extra surprises.

Golf des Fontenelles — 1990
F - 85220 L'AIGUILLON-SUR-VIE

Office	Secrétariat	(33) 02 51 54 13 94
Pro shop	Pro-shop	(33) 02 51 54 13 94
Fax	Fax	(33) 02 51 55 45 77
Situation	Situation	

St-Gilles-Croix-de-Vie (pop. 6 290), 10 km
Nantes (pop. 252 030), 65 km

Annual closure	Fermeture annuelle	no
Weekly closure	Fermeture hebdomadaire	monday
	(lundi) 01/11 → 31/03	

Fees main season
Tarifs haute saison full day

	Week days Semaine	We/Bank holidays We/Férié
Individual Individuel	255 F	255 F
Couple Couple	510 F	510 F
Caddy Caddy	no	
Electric Trolley Chariot électrique	no	
Buggy Voiturette	150 F/18 holes	
Clubs Clubs	50 F/full day	

Credit cards Cartes de crédit
VISA - CB - Eurocard - MasterCard

Access Accès : • Sables d'Olonne D32 → Challans
• La Roche-sur-Yon → Aizenay/Saint-Gilles-Croix-de-Vie D6. Go through Coëx, Golf 2 km.
Map 6 on page 174 Carte 6 Page 174

GOLF COURSE / PARCOURS — 14/20

Site	Site	
Maintenance	Entretien	
Architect	Architecte	Yves Bureau
Type	Type	copse
Relief	Relief	
Water in play	Eau en jeu	
Exp. to wind	Exposé au vent	
Trees in play	Arbres en jeu	

Scorecard Carte de score	Chp. Chp.	Mens Mess.	Ladies Da.
Length Long.	6205	5824	5311
Par	72	72	72

Advised golfing ability Niveau de jeu recommandé	0	12	24	36

Hcp required   Handicap exigé   no

CLUB HOUSE & AMENITIES / CLUB HOUSE ET ANNEXES — 7/10

Pro shop	Pro-shop	
Driving range	Practice	
Sheltered	couvert	10 mats
On grass	sur herbe	yes
Putting-green	putting-green	yes
Pitching-green	pitching green	yes

277

HOTEL FACILITIES / ENVIRONNEMENT HOTELIER — 4/10

HOTELS HÔTELS
Le Château de la Vérie — Challans
19 rooms, D 880 F — 22 km
Tel (33) 02 51 35 33 44, Fax (33) 02 51 35 14 84

Le Lion d'Or — Saint-Gilles-Croix-de-Vie
55 rooms, D 380 F — 10 km
Tel (33) 02 51 55 50 39, Fax (33) 02 51 55 22 84

Embruns — Saint-Gilles-Croix-de-Vie
14 rooms, D 4580 F — 10 km
Tel (33) 02 51 55 11 40, Fax (33) 02 51 55 11 20

RESTAURANTS RESTAURANTS
Les Embruns — Saint-Gilles-Croix-de-Vie
Tel (33) 02 51 55 11 40 — 10 km

La Grand Roche — Bretignolles-sur-Mer
Tel (33) 02 51 90 15 21 — 10 km

L'architecte Ronald Fream a tiré le meilleur parti d'un site très accidenté (en voie d'urbanisation), mais qui propose de belles vues sur la mer et des trous spectaculaires. Il faut payer le prix de ce décor tourmenté, dans une région où les reliefs sont très accentués : de nombreux dévers peuvent compliquer les trajectoires de balle, quelques coups sont aveugles (moins qu'on pourrait le croire), le rough est souvent très pénalisant, les fairways parfois étroits, et quelques rochers viennent dangereusement en jeu. Très bien paysagé, très technique, c'est un parcours que l'on prendra du plaisir à jouer en voiturette, ou au minimum avec un chariot électrique, pour conserver des forces physiques et mentales, non seulement pour choisir les bons clubs, mais aussi pour les utiliser. Si l'on connaît mal le parcours, il ne faut pas trop penser au score, mais commencer en match-play.

Architect Ronald Fream has made good use of a very hilly site (now being built upon more and more) which features fine views of the sea and some spectacular holes. But this twisted and winding scenery comes at a cost in a region of rolling hills and dales. A lot of slanting fairways make life a little difficult at times, a few shots are blind (but less so than you might imagine), the rough gives no quarter, the fairways are sometimes very tight indeed and a few rocks loom dangerously at strategic areas. Beautifully landscaped and a technically demanding course, Frégate is good fun to play in a buggy in order to preserve mental and physical strength, not only for choosing the right club but also for using them in the right way. If you don't know the course, don't worry too much about the score and go around in match-play.

Golf de Frégate — 1992

Route de Bandol RD 559
F - 83270 SAINT-CYR-SUR-MER

Office	Secrétariat	(33) 04 94 29 38 00
Pro shop	Pro-shop	(33) 04 94 29 38 00
Fax	Fax	(33) 04 94 29 96 94
Situation	Situation	

Bandol (pop. 7 430), 3 km
Toulon (pop. 167 620), 25 km

Annual closure	Fermeture annuelle	no
Weekly closure	Fermeture hebdomadaire	no

Fees main season
Tarifs haute saison full day

	Week days Semaine	We/Bank holidays We/Férié
Individual Individuel	320 F	320 F
Couple Couple	640 F	640 F
Caddy Caddy		on request
Electric Trolley Chariot électrique		100 F/18 holes
Buggy Voiturette		200 F/18 holes
Clubs Clubs		100 F/18 holes

Credit cards Cartes de crédit
VISA - CB - Eurocard - MasterCard - AMEX

Access Accès : • A50 Marseille → Toulon, Exit (Sortie) Saint-Cyr-sur-Mer • A50 Toulon → Marseille, Exit Bandol, D559
Map 14 on page 190 Carte 14 Page 190

GOLF COURSE PARCOURS — 15/20

Site	Site	▣▣▣▣▣▣
Maintenance	Entretien	▣▣▣▣▣▣
Architect	Architecte	Ronald Fream
Type	Type	seaside course, hilly
Relief	Relief	▣▣▣▣▢
Water in play	Eau en jeu	▣▢▢▢▢
Exp. to wind	Exposé au vent	▣▣▢▢▢
Trees in play	Arbres en jeu	▣▣▣▢▢

Scorecard Carte de score	Chp. Chp.	Mens Mess.	Ladies Da.
Length Long.	6209	5847	4950
Par	72	72	72

Advised golfing ability Niveau de jeu recommandé	0	12	24	36

Hcp required Handicap exigé 35

CLUB HOUSE & AMENITIES CLUB HOUSE ET ANNEXES — 7/10

Pro shop	Pro-shop	▣▣▣▢▢
Driving range	Practice	▣▣▣▢▢
Sheltered	couvert	4 mats
On grass	sur herbe	no, 46 mats open air
Putting-green	putting-green	yes
Pitching-green	pitching green	no

HOTEL FACILITIES ENVIRONNEMENT HOTELIER — 7/10

HOTELS HÔTELS

Frégate — on site
138 rooms, D 1 500 F
Tel (33) 04 94 29 39 39, Fax (33) 04 94 29 39 40

L'Ile Rousse — Bandol
53 rooms, D 1 400 F — 3 km
Tel (33) 04 94 29 33 00, Fax (33) 04 94 29 49 49

Bérard — La Cadière-d'Azur
40 rooms, D 700 F — 7 km
Tel (33) 04 94 90 11 43, Fax (33) 04 94 90 01 94

RESTAURANTS RESTAURANTS

L'Ile Rousse — Bandol
Tel (33) 04 94 29 33 00 — 3 km

Le Mas des Vignes — on site
Tel (33) 04 94 29 39 39

278

Des deux 18 trous de ce complexe ambitieux, Le Breuil est le plus «héroïque» dans son déroulement, notamment avec neuf trous insinués entre les superbes étangs de la Dombe, dont l'aspect sauvage a été préservé. D'énormes travaux de drainage lui permettent d'être jouable en toutes saisons. Plat et long, c'est l'un des parcours les plus techniques et exigeants de la région lyonnaise, mais il affiche clairement ses difficultés stratégiques, notamment avec des roughs imposants. On pourra lui reprocher le peu de variété de ses par 3, un manque de modelage des alentours de green et des bunkers. Délicat pour les joueurs peu expérimentés, il doit absolument être joué des départs normaux par les golfeurs moyens. Les greens sont peu complexes à lire, mais les difficultés étaient suffisantes pour ne pas en rajouter à ce niveau. Le Club-House établi dans de magnifiques bâtiments anciens est complété d'un hôtel sur le site.

"Le Breuil" is the boldest of the two 18-hole courses in this ambitious golfing resort, with nine holes winding their way through the superb lakes of La Dombe, which have lost nothing of their wild natural character. Very extensive draining work has made this a course for all seasons. Flat and long, it is one of the most technical and demanding courses in the Lyons region, but the strategic difficulties are clearly visible. The few criticisms that might be levelled are the lack of diversity of par 3s and the lack of relief around the greens and bunkers. A tricky proposition for inexperienced players, this is a course that should be played from the normal tees for mid-handicappers. The greens are straightforward to read, but the course is already difficult enough without adding any more around the pin. In addition to the club-house, laid out in magnificent old buildings, there is an on-site hotel.

Golf du Gouverneur — 1992
Château du Breuil
F - 01390 MONTHIEUX

Office	Secrétariat	(33) 04 72 26 40 34
Pro shop	Pro-shop	(33) 04 72 26 40 34
Fax	Fax	(33) 04 72 26 41 61
Situation	Situation	

Lyon (pop. 413 090), 28 km
Bourg-en-Bresse (pop. 40 970), 38 km

Annual closure	Fermeture annuelle	no
Weekly closure	Fermeture hebdomadaire	no

Fees main season
Tarifs haute saison 18 holes

	Week days Semaine	We/Bank holidays We/Férié
Individual Individuel	200 F	280 F
Couple Couple	350 F	480 F

Tuesday (Mardi), 150 F

Caddy	Caddy	no
Electric Trolley	Chariot électrique	50 F/18 holes
Buggy	Voiturette	180 F/18 holes
Clubs	Clubs	90 F/full day

Credit cards Cartes de crédit
VISA - CB - Eurocard - MasterCard - AMEX

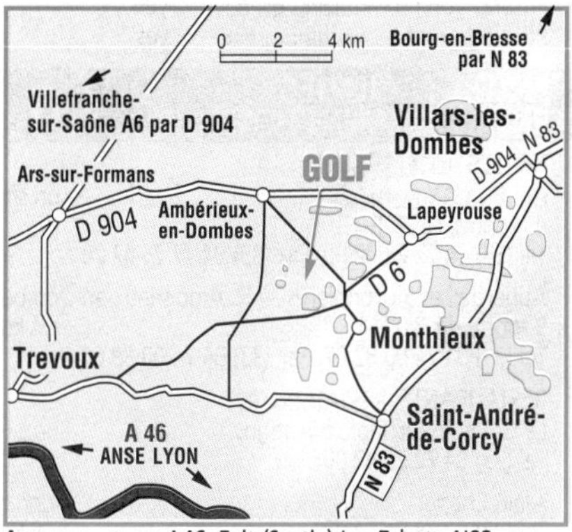

[Map]

0   2   4 km   Bourg-en-Bresse par N 83

Villefranche-sur-Saône A6 par D 904
Ars-sur-Formans
D 904
Ambérieux-en-Dombes
GOLF
Villars-les-Dombes
N 83
D 904
Lapeyrouse
D 6
Trevoux
Monthieux
A 46
ANSE LYON
N 83
Saint-André-de-Corcy

Access Accès : • A46, Exit (Sortie) Les Echets, N83 → Bourg-en- Bresse. St-André de Corcy → Monthieux • A6, Exit Villefranche, → Bourg, Ars, Ambérieux-en-Dombes → Monthieux
Map 11 on page 184 Carte 11 Page 184

GOLF COURSE / PARCOURS — 16/20

Site	Site	▬▬▬▬▬▬□
Maintenance	Entretien	
Architect	Architecte	Didier Fruchet George Will
Type	Type	open country
Relief	Relief	
Water in play	Eau en jeu	▬▬□□□
Exp. to wind	Exposé au vent	▬▬▬□□
Trees in play	Arbres en jeu	▬▬▬□□

Scorecard	Chp.	Mens	Ladies
Carte de score	Chp.	Mess.	Da.
Length Long.	6535	6165	4940
Par	72	72	72

Advised golfing ability	0	12	24	36
Niveau de jeu recommandé				
Hcp required	Handicap exigé	35		

CLUB HOUSE & AMENITIES / CLUB HOUSE ET ANNEXES — 7/10

Pro shop	Pro-shop	▬▬▬▬□
Driving range	Practice	▬▬▬▬□
Sheltered	couvert	10 mats
On grass	sur herbe	yes
Putting-green	putting-green	yes
Pitching-green	pitching green	yes

HOTEL FACILITIES / ENVIRONNEMENT HOTELIER — 6/10

HOTELS HÔTELS
Hôtel Le Gouverneur   on site
45 rooms, D 590F
Tel (33) 04 72 26 42 00, Fax (33) 04 72 26 42 20

Auberge Les Bichonnières   Ambérieux-en-Dombes
9 rooms, D 320 F   4 km
Tel (33) 04 74 00 82 07, Fax (33) 04 74 00 89 61

RESTAURANTS RESTAURANT
Le Gouverneur/Table d'Antigny   on site
Tel (33) 04 72 26 42 00

Alain Chapel   Mionnay 8 km
Tel (33) 04 78 91 82 02

Auberge des Chasseurs   Bouligneux 8 km
Tel (33) 04 74 98 10 02

Auberge de Rancé   Rancé 5 km
Tel (33) 04 74 00 87 08

279

Ce parcours plus «humain» que Le Breuil est accessible à tous les niveaux, même si quelques trous sont abondamment protégés par des obstacles d'eau. A peine plus accidenté, il n'est jamais fatigant, sa technicité comme sa franchise le rendent très plaisant, et si les bons joueurs auront plus d'émotions sur le parcours voisin, ils ne doivent pas se laisser abuser par l'apparente amabilité de Montaplan. Quelques trous boisés (surtout à l'aller) apportent une certaine variété à ce paysage typique de la Dombes, et un programme de plantations sur d'autres trous va mieux encore le «dessiner» visuellement. On remarquera la qualité et les reliefs subtils des greens, et les progrès de son entretien après l'achèvement des drainages. Les joueurs non classés auront ici l'occasion d'aborder un parcours de golf présentant pratiquement toutes les difficultés possibles sans se faire trop peur.

Slightly more "human" than "Breuil", the Montaplan course is within the reach of golfers of all levels, even though some holes are heavily protected by water hazards. Although slightly more hilly, the course's technical challenge and openness make it a very pleasant golfing experience. And while the better player will proably find its neighbour more exciting, no-one should be fooled by the apparent friendliness of Montaplan. A few holes amidst the trees (especially on the front nine) add a little variety to this typical landscape of La Dombes, and a plantation programme on other holes will eventually enhance the whole layout from a visual angle. We noted the excellence and subtle contours of the greens, and the progress achieved in upkeep further to drainage work. Here, beginners and high-handicappers have the opportunity to tackle a course which features just about every difficulty you can find on a golf course, without ever being too fearsome.

Golf du Gouverneur — 1992

Château du Breuil
F - 01390 MONTHIEUX

Office	Secrétariat	(33) 04 72 26 40 34
Pro shop	Pro-shop	(33) 04 72 26 40 34
Fax	Fax	(33) 04 72 26 41 61
Situation	Situation	

Lyon (pop. 413 090), 28 km
Bourg-en-Bresse (pop. 40 970), 38 km

Annual closure	Fermeture annuelle	no
Weekly closure	Fermeture hebdomadaire	no

Fees main season
Tarifs haute saison 18 holes

	Week days Semaine	We/Bank holidays We/Férié
Individual Individuel	180 F	250 F
Couple Couple	300 F	430 F

Tuesday (mardi), 150 F

Caddy	Caddy	no
Electric Trolley	Chariot électrique	50 F/18 holes
Buggy	Voiturette	180 F/18 holes
Clubs	Clubs	90 F/full day

Credit cards Cartes de crédit
VISA - CB - Eurocard - MasterCard - AMEX

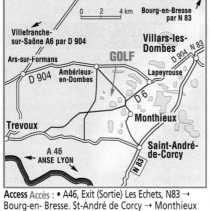

Access Accès : • A46, Exit (Sortie) Les Echets, N83 → Bourg-en- Bresse. St-André de Corcy → Monthieux
• A6, Exit Villefranche, → Bourg, Ars, Ambérieux-en-Dombes → Monthieux
Map 11 on page 184 Carte 11 Page 184

GOLF COURSE PARCOURS — 14/20

Site	Site	
Maintenance	Entretien	
Architect	Architecte	Didier Fruchet George Will
Type	Type	open country
Relief	Relief	
Water in play	Eau en jeu	
Exp. to wind	Exposé au vent	
Trees in play	Arbres en jeu	

Scorecard Carte de score	Chp. Chp.	Mens Mess.	Ladies Da.
Length Long.	5959	5678	5069
Par	72	72	72

Advised golfing ability	0	12	24	36
Niveau de jeu recommandé				
Hcp required Handicap exigé	35			

CLUB HOUSE & AMENITIES CLUB HOUSE ET ANNEXES — 7/10

Pro shop	Pro-shop	
Driving range	Practice	
Sheltered	couvert	10 mats
On grass	sur herbe	yes
Putting-green	putting-green	yes
Pitching-green	pitching green	yes

HOTEL FACILITIES ENVIRONNEMENT HOTELIER — 6/10

HOTELS HÔTELS

Hôtel Le Gouverneur — on site
45 rooms, D 590F
Tel (33) 04 72 26 42 00, Fax (33) 04 72 26 42 20

Auberge Les Bichonnières — Ambérieux-en-Dombes
9 rooms, D 320 F — 4 km
Tel (33) 04 74 00 82 07, Fax (33) 04 74 00 89 61

RESTAURANTS RESTAURANTS

Le Gouverneur/Table d'Antigny — on site
Tel (33) 04 72 26 42 00

Alain Chapel — Mionnay
Tel (33) 04 78 91 82 02 — 8 km

Auberge des Chasseurs — Bouligneux
Tel (33) 04 74 98 10 02 — 8 km

Auberge de Rancé — Rancé
Tel (33) 04 74 00 87 08 — 5 km

280

Ce 18 trous créé par le Club Med a pris une place de choix parmi les bons parcours de la région. L'architecte Cabell Robinson a voulu faire un parcours « tous usages », jouable par tous, même si quelques obstacles d'eau peuvent effrayer les débutants. Les arrivées de drive sont assez larges, mais la densité des roughs incite à taper droit. Les obstacles tiennent essentiellement des mouvements de terrain et des vastes bunkers, souvent très en jeu, qui délimitent bien les fairways. Le programme de plantations commence à atténuer atténuer une certaine imprécision des trous, dans un si vaste espace. Les greens sont assez modelés pour imposer une grande maîtrise du petit jeu et du putting. Amusant à jouer et très divers, ce parcours est facile à jouer à pied, ce n'est pas si fréquent sur la Côte d'Azur. Seul inconvénient : les joueurs sont nombreux ici, et pas toujours très rapides... Jouez tôt le matin !

This 18-hole course, commissioned by the Club Med, now ranks among the best in the region. Architect Cabell Robinson set out to build an "all-purpose" course for all golfers, even though a number of water hazards might well scare the true beginner. At driving distance, the fairways are wide enough, but the thick rough is a good reason for hitting in the fairway. The basic hazards here are the graded fairways and huge bunkers, which are often fully in play and clearly demarcate the playing area. The new plantation programme begins to give greater definition to some holes laid out over such a wide area. The greens are well-contoured and require a sharp short game and good putting. Fun to play with variety all round, this is an easily walkable course, which is seldom the case on courses on the French Riviera. The only drawback is the number of players and frequent slow play... Play early in the morning!

Golf de la Grande Bastide — 1990

Chemin des Picholines
F - 06740 CHATEAUNEUF-DE-GRASSE

Office	Secrétariat	(33) 04 93 77 70 08
Pro shop	Pro-shop	(33) 04 93 77 70 08
Fax	Fax	(33) 04 93 77 72 36
Situation	Situation	

Nice (pop. 345 670), 27 km
Cannes (pop. 68 670), 17 km

Annual closure	Fermeture annuelle	no
Weekly closure	Fermeture hebdomadaire	no

Fees main season
Tarifs haute saison full day

	Week days Semaine	We/Bank holidays We/Férié
Individual Individuel	280 F	310 F
Couple Couple	560 F	620 F

GF evening (soir) 200 F/weekdays, 230 F/We

Caddy	Caddy	no
Electric Trolley	Chariot électrique	no
Buggy	Voiturette	190 F/18 holes
Clubs	Clubs	100 F/full day

Credit cards Cartes de crédit
VISA - CB - Eurocard - MasterCard - AMEX

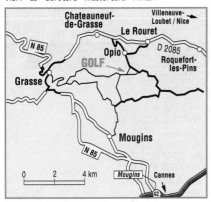

Access Accès : • Cannes, N85 → Valbonne
• Nice, A8 Exit (Sortie) Villeneuve-Loubet → Grasse, Roquefort-les-Pins, → Opio
Map 14 on page 191 Carte 14 Page 191

GOLF COURSE PARCOURS — 16/20

Site	Site	
Maintenance	Entretien	
Architect	Architecte	Cabell Robinson
Type	Type	open country
Relief	Relief	
Water in play	Eau en jeu	
Exp. to wind	Exposé au vent	
Trees in play	Arbres en jeu	

Scorecard Carte de score	Chp. Chp.	Mens Mess.	Ladies Da.
Length Long.	6105	5610	5175
Par	72	72	72

Advised golfing ability		0	12	24	36
Niveau de jeu recommandé					
Hcp required	Handicap exigé	35			

CLUB HOUSE & AMENITIES CLUB HOUSE ET ANNEXES — 6/10

Pro shop	Pro-shop	
Driving range	Practice	
Sheltered	couvert	no
On grass	sur herbe	no, 4 mats with nets
Putting-green	putting-green	yes
Pitching-green	pitching green	yes

HOTEL FACILITIES ENVIRONNEMENT HOTELIER — 6/10

HOTELS HÔTELS
Club Méditerranée — Opio
400 rooms, D 1 200F — 2 km
Tel (33) 04 93 09 71 00 - Fax (33) 04 93 77 33 57

Hôtel des Parfums — Grasse
60 rooms, D 750 F — 4 km
Tel (33) 04 92 42 35 35 - Fax (33) 04 93 36 35 48

Hôtel du Patti — Grasse
50 rooms D 420 F — 4 km
Tel (33) 04 93 36 01 00 - Fax (33) 04 93 36 36 40

RESTAURANTS RESTAURANTS
Bastide Saint Antoine — Grasse
Tel (33) 04 93 70 94 94 — 5 km

L'Auberge Fleurie — Valbonne
Tel (33) 04 93 12 02 80 — 5 km

281

GRANDE-MOTTE (LA) LES FLAMANTS ROSES

| 16 | 6 | 4 |

En paysage d'étangs, à partir d'un terrain sans relief naturel, et très peu boisé Robert Trent Jones a signé un parcours de grande qualité, modelé avec une grande intelligence, sans jamais donner l'impression de monotonie. Certes, les longs frappeurs peuvent s'y déchaîner, mais les seconds coups, le petit jeu et le putting demandent beaucoup d'inspiration., et les joueurs précis pourront y réussir. L'eau joue un rôle important, mais sans sévérité excessive. Avec une bonne connaissance de ce parcours bien défini dans l'espace (notamment par la tonte du fairway et du petit rough) et un peu de réflexion, tous les joueurs peuvent y prendre plaisir, à l'exception des débutants, qui trouveront avec un joli parcours de 6 trous et un 18 trous de par 58 de quoi largement s'occuper et s'aguerrir. La Grande Motte est un golf commercial, mais le Club house manque de chaleur... et de distinction.

Set in a landscape of lakes with no natural relief and very few trees, Robert Trent Jones has cleverly shaped a high class course which never seems monotonous. Long-hitters can definitely open their shoulders, but approach shots, short play and putting call for a lot of inspiration which should suit the more accurate players. Water is a significant part of the course but is never too severe a test. When you know this neatly laid-out course well (especially the tidily-mown fairways and short rough) and with a little careful thought, every golfer will enjoy playing here, except beginners, who can learn the ropes and get to grips with the compact 6-holer and the par-58 18 hole course. La Grande Motte is a business venture course but the club-house lacks both warmth... and distinction.

Golf de La Grande-Motte — 1987

BP 16
F - 34280 LA GRANDE-MOTTE

Office	Secrétariat	(33) 04 67 56 05 00
Pro shop	Pro-shop	(33) 04 67 29 93 02
Fax	Fax	(33) 04 67 29 18 84
Situation	Situation	

Montpellier (pop. 210 860), 22 km
La Grande-Motte (pop. 5 010), 1 km

Annual closure	Fermeture annuelle	no
Weekly closure	Fermeture hebdomadaire	no

Fees main season
Tarifs haute saison full day

	Week days Semaine	We/Bank holidays We/Férié
Individual Individuel	260 F	260 F
Couple Couple	520 F	520 F

Caddy	Caddy	no
Electric Trolley	Chariot électrique	no
Buggy	Voiturette	160 F/18 holes
Clubs	Clubs	80 F/18 holes

Credit cards Cartes de crédit
VISA - CB - Eurocard - MasterCard

Access Accès : • Nîmes, A9, Exit (Sortie) 26 Gallargues, N113 → Lunel, D61 → La Grande-Motte • Montpellier A9 Exit Fréjorgues, D21 et D62 → La Grande-Motte
Map 13 on page 189 Carte 13 Page 189

GOLF COURSE PARCOURS — 16/20

Site	Site	
Maintenance	Entretien	
Architect	Architecte	R. Trent Jones Sr
Type	Type	seaside course, residential
Relief	Relief	
Water in play	Eau en jeu	
Exp. to wind	Exposé au vent	
Trees in play	Arbres en jeu	

Scorecard Carte de score	Chp. Chp.	Mens Mess.	Ladies Da.
Length Long.	6161	5768	5220
Par	72	72	72

Advised golfing ability		0	12	24	36
Niveau de jeu recommandé					
Hcp required	Handicap exigé	35

CLUB HOUSE & AMENITIES CLUB HOUSE ET ANNEXES — 6/10

Pro shop	Pro-shop	
Driving range	Practice	
Sheltered	couvert	no
On grass	sur herbe	yes
Putting-green	putting-green	yes
Pitching-green	pitching green	yes

HOTEL FACILITIES ENVIRONNEMENT HOTELIER — 4/10

HOTELS HÔTELS
Frantour — on site
80 rooms, D 500 F
Tel (33) 04 67 29 88 88
Fax (33) 04 67 29 17 01

Golf Hôtel — 300 m
43 rooms, D 450 F
Tel (33) 04 67 29 72 00
Fax (33) 04 67 29 12 44

RESTAURANTS RESTAURANTS
Jardin des Sens — Montpellier
Tel (33) 04 67 79 63 38 — 22 km

Le Chandelier — Montpellier
Tel (33) 04 67 15 34 38 — 22 km

282

GRANVILLE LES DUNES

14	4	4

Originellement dessiné par Colt et Allison, Granville était un chef-d'oeuvre à l'écart des sentiers battus. Ce grand links était malheureusement traversé par une petite route, qui a obligé à modifier beaucoup de trous, alors qu'elle aurait sans doute pu être déviée. Hélas, ces trous n'ont pas été les seuls altérés, et une bonne partie du caractère a été perdue (les nouveaux bunkers n'ont rien à voir avec l'esthétique originelle). Il s'agissait là d'un véritable trésor caché, au niveau du Touquet et de Chiberta, mais il a suffi de quelques décisions hâtives pour détruire cinquante ans de tradition. S'il reste néammoins une bonne douzaine de bons trous, qui justifient à eux seuls une visite, on est bien obligé de passer par les autres. Granville est une bonne leçon de prudence et de respect pour les golfs qui veulent s'engager dans un remodelage.

Originally designed by Colt and Allison, Granville used to be a masterpiece off the beaten track. Unfortunately, this great links course has been crossed by a small road, which could have been re-routed, and a number of holes have had to be altered. Worse, other features of the course have also been tampered with, and a lot of its character has disappeared (the new bunkers have nothing common with the original style). This used to be a real gem of a course, pleasantly remote and on a par with Le Touquet or Chiberta, but a few hasty decisions were enough to destroy fifty years of tradition. While there are still a dozen excellent holes, which are worth the visit in themselves, there is no avoiding the others. Granville is a stern lesson in caution and respect for any golf course that might be considering a change in style and design.

Golf de Granville — 1928

Pavillon du Golf
F - 50290 BREVILLE

Office	Secrétariat	(33) 02 33 50 23 06
Pro shop	Pro-shop	(33) 02 33 50 23 06
Fax	Fax	(33) 02 33 61 91 87
Situation	Situation	

Granville (pop. 12 410), 6 km

Annual closure	Fermeture annuelle	no
Weekly closure	Fermeture hebdomadaire	no

Fees main season
Tarifs haute saison full day

	Week days Semaine	We/Bank holidays We/Férié
Individual Individuel	240 F	240 F
Couple Couple	400 F	400 F
Caddy Caddy		no
Electric Trolley Chariot électrique		no
Buggy Voiturette		100 F/18 holes
Clubs Clubs		60 F/full day

Credit cards Cartes de crédit
VISA - CB - Eurocard - MasterCard

Access Accès : Avranches D973 → Granville, Bréville s/Mer
Map 2 on page 166 Carte 2 Page 166

GOLF COURSE PARCOURS — 14/20

Site	Site	■■■■■□
Maintenance	Entretien	■■■■□
Architect	Architecte	Colt, Alison M. Hawtree (1992)
Type	Type	links
Relief	Relief	■■□□□
Water in play	Eau en jeu	■□□□□
Exp. to wind	Exposé au vent	■■■■□
Trees in play	Arbres en jeu	■■□□□

Scorecard Carte de score	Chp. Chp.	Mens Mess.	Ladies Da.
Length Long.	5835	5835	4835
Par	71	71	71

Advised golfing ability Niveau de jeu recommandé	0	12	24	36

Hcp required Handicap exigé 35

CLUB HOUSE & AMENITIES
CLUB HOUSE ET ANNEXES — 4/10

Pro shop	Pro-shop	■■■■□
Driving range	Practice	■■■□□
Sheltered	couvert	10 mats
On grass	sur herbe	yes
Putting-green	putting-green	yes
Pitching-green	pitching green	yes

283

HOTEL FACILITIES
ENVIRONNEMENT HOTELIER — 4/10

HOTELS HÔTELS
La Beaumonderie — Bréville-sur-Mer
12 rooms, D 870 F — 1 km
Tel (33) 02 33 50 36 36
Fax (33) 02 33 50 36 45

Hôtel des Bains — Granville
45 rooms, D 850 F — 6 km
Tel (33) 02 33 50 17 31
Fax (33) 02 33 50 89 22

RESTAURANTS RESTAURANTS
Hôtel de la Mer — Granville
Tel (33) 02 33 50 01 86 — 6 km

Le Relais des Iles — Coudeville
Tel (33) 02 33 61 66 66 — 1 km

GRASSE

13	7	6

On a toujours le sentiment que ce parcours dessiné par Jean-Pascal Fourès n'a pas été achevé, ou pas par le même architecte, tant le style est inégal. A côté de très jolis trous (le 2 ou le 7), d'autres paraissent d'une étonnante banalité, certains greens dépourvus de défenses. La forêt de chênes est belle, mais réserve peu d'espace au parcours. Les fairways étroits sont bordés de roughs très cailloux, obligeant à une grande prudence, ou une extrême précision. Mais, à 600 mètres d'altitude, les points de vue sur la région de Cannes et la mer sont magnifiques, et le climat contraste en été avec les chaleurs du littoral. Les joueurs assez droits prendront cependant du plaisir à faire une belle balade en moyenne montagne, plutôt que de vouloir batailler contre le parcours. Comme il est plutôt accidenté, on leur conseille la voiturette...

This layout, designed by Jean-Pascal Fourès, is so inconsistent in style as to leave the lasting impression of a course that has never really been completed, or at least not by the same architect. Next to some very pretty holes (the 2nd or 7th, for example), others seem amazingly ordinary and some greens are totally undefended. The oak-forest is a real beauty but leaves little space for the course. The tight fairways are edged with very stoney rough calling for great care or extreme precision (or both). But at 600 m above-sea level, the views over the Mediterranean and the region of Cannes are magnificent and the climate in summer is a pleasant contrast with the heat on the Riviera. Straight-hitters will have more fun roaming through this upland terrain than they will trying to take on the course. Being rather hilly, we recommend a buggy every time.

Grasse Country-Club — 1992

Lieu-dit «Claux Amic»
F - 06130 GRASSE

Office	Secrétariat	(33) 04 93 60 55 44
Pro shop	Pro-shop	(33) 04 93 60 55 44
Fax	Fax	(33) 04 93 60 55 19
Situation	Situation	

Grasse (pop. 41 380), 5 km

Annual closure	Fermeture annuelle	no
Weekly closure	Fermeture hebdomadaire	no

Fees main season
Tarifs haute saison full day

	Week days Semaine	We/Bank holidays We/Férié
Individual Individuel	280 F	300 F
Couple Couple	560 F	600 F

Tuesday (Mardi): GF 180 F (except holidays and 07/08)

Caddy	Caddy	no
Electric Trolley	Chariot électrique	no
Buggy	Voiturette	180 F/18 holes
Clubs	Clubs	50 F/full day

Credit cards Cartes de crédit
VISA - CB - Eurocard - MasterCard - AMEX - JCB

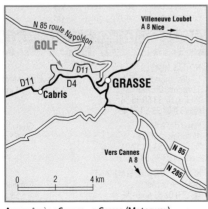

Access Accès : Cannes, → Grasse (Motorway).
In Grasse → Grasse Country Club
Map 14 on page 191 Carte 14 Page 191

GOLF COURSE / PARCOURS — 13/20

Site	Site	▮▮▮▮▮▯
Maintenance	Entretien	▮▮▮▮▯▯
Architect	Architecte	Jean-Pascal Fourès
Type	Type	forest, hilly
Relief	Relief	▮▮▮▮▮▯
Water in play	Eau en jeu	▮▯▯▯▯▯
Exp. to wind	Exposé au vent	▮▮▯▯▯▯
Trees in play	Arbres en jeu	▮▮▮▮▯▯

Scorecard Carte de score	Chp. Chp.	Mens Mess.	Ladies Da.
Length Long.	6021	5413	4662
Par	72	72	72

Advised golfing ability Niveau de jeu recommandé		0 12 24 36
Hcp required	Handicap exigé	no

CLUB HOUSE & AMENITIES / CLUB HOUSE ET ANNEXES — 7/10

Pro shop	Pro-shop	▮▮▮▮▮▯
Driving range	Practice	▮▮▮▯▯▯
Sheltered	couvert	no
On grass	sur herbe	yes
Putting-green	putting-green	yes
Pitching-green	pitching green	no

HOTEL FACILITIES / ENVIRONNEMENT HOTELIER — 6/10

HOTELS HÔTELS

Grasse Country-Club — on site
15 rooms, D 1200 F
Tel (33) 04 93 60 55 44, Fax (33) 04 93 60 55 19

Hôtel des Parfums — Grasse
60 rooms, D 750 F — 5 km
Tel (33) 04 92 42 35 35, Fax (33) 04 93 36 35 48

Bastide Saint Antoine — Grasse
11 rooms, D 1 200 F — 5 km
Tel (33) 04 93 70 94 94, Fax (33) 04 93 70 94 95

RESTAURANTS RESTAURANTS

Bastide Saint Antoine — Grasse
Tel (33) 04 93 70 94 94 — 5 km

Pierre Baltus — Grasse
Tel (33) 04 93 36 32 90 — 5 km

284

GRENOBLE BRESSON

17 7 6

Ce terrain reste très accidenté, parfois même épuisant (voiturette conseillée), mais Robert Trent Jones Jr a réussi l'exploit de ne pas imposer de coups aveugles. Cependant, il n'a pu éviter de faire trois ou quatre trous assez indifférents dans un ensemble autrement de belle qualité, et même excitant à parcourir. Souvent spectaculaire, ce parcours ne livre pas facilement ses secrets, et mérite d'être joué plusieurs fois, ne serait-ce que pour négocier les greens. Dans un paysage quasiment montagnard, des hêtres, des chênes et des genêts apportent des touches de végétation au modelage des fairways, à la sculpture des nombreux bunkers. Quelle que soit la beauté de la balade, la maîtrise du jeu que réclame Bresson incite à ne pas le recommander aux joueurs à haut handicap. Ce parcours exige un dessin précis des fairways et un entretien très attentif, ce n'est pas toujours le cas actuellement.

This is a very hilly and sometimes exhausting course (buggy recommended) but Robert Trent Jones Jr has achieved the virtually impossible by avoiding blind shots. In contrast, there was no other way around three or four rather ordinary holes in an otherwise excellent setting, which makes for exciting golf. This sometimes spectacular course does not give up its secrets easily and deserves a number of rounds, if only to get to grips with the greens. In virtually mountainous landscape, oak-trees, beech and gorse add a touch of vegetation to the contoured fairways and numerous bunkers. But however beautiful the scenery, the skill required to play Bresson is perhaps beyond the abilities of high-handicappers. The course requires tightly-mown fairways and very careful upkeep, which is not always the case at the present time.

Golf International de Grenoble — 1990

Route de Montavie
F - 38320 BRESSON

Office	Secrétariat	(33) 04 76 73 65 00
Pro shop	Pro-shop	(33) 04 76 73 65 00
Fax	Fax	(33) 04 76 73 65 51
Situation	Situation	

Grenoble (pop. 150 750), 5 km - Vizille (pop. 7 100), 8 km

Annual closure	Fermeture annuelle	no
Weekly closure	Fermeture hebdomadaire	no

Fees main season
Tarifs haute saison full day

	Week days Semaine	We/Bank holidays We/Férié
Individual Individuel	240 F	280 F
Couple Couple	480 F	560 F

Caddy	Caddy	no
Electric Trolley	Chariot électrique	no
Buggy	Voiturette	170 F/18 holes
Clubs	Clubs	70 F/full day

Credit cards Cartes de crédit
VISA - CB - Eurocard - MasterCard

Access Accès : Lyon A48 → Chambéry. At toll (Péage) go to the «Rocade», Exit 5, Eybens, Bresson → Tavernolles, → Golf
Map 11 on page 184 Carte 11 Page 184

GOLF COURSE / PARCOURS — 17/20

Site	Site	
Maintenance	Entretien	
Architect	Architecte	R. Trent Jones Jr
Type	Type	mountain
Relief	Relief	
Water in play	Eau en jeu	
Exp. to wind	Exposé au vent	
Trees in play	Arbres en jeu	

Scorecard Carte de score	Chp. Chp.	Mens Mess.	Ladies Da.
Length Long.	6345	5836	5356
Par	73	73	73

Advised golfing ability Niveau de jeu recommandé	0 12 24 36
Hcp required Handicap exigé	no

CLUB HOUSE & AMENITIES / CLUB HOUSE ET ANNEXES — 7/10

Pro shop	Pro-shop	
Driving range	Practice	
Sheltered	couvert	20 mats
On grass	sur herbe	yes
Putting-green	putting-green	yes
Pitching-green	pitching green	yes

285

HOTEL FACILITIES / ENVIRONNEMENT HOTELIER — 6/10

HOTELS HÔTELS
Chavant — Bresson
9 rooms, D 780 F — 2 km
Tel (33) 04 76 25 25 38, Fax (33) 04 76 62 06 55

Château de la Commanderie — Eybens
25 rooms, D 720 F — 2 km
Tel (33) 04 76 25 34 58, Fax (33) 04 76 24 07 31

Park Hôtel — Grenoble
40 rooms, D 1 500 F — 5 km
Tel (33) 04 76 85 81 23, Fax (33) 04 76 46 49 88

Grand Hôtel - 44 rooms, D 605 F — Uriage
Tel (33) 04 76 89 10 80, Fax (33) 04 76 89 04 62 — 7 km

RESTAURANTS RESTAURANTS
Chavant — Bresson
Tel (33) 04 76 25 25 38 — 2 km

Auberge Napoléon — Grenoble
Tel (33) 04 76 87 53 64 — 5 km

Entre Arcachon et Bordeaux, ce 18 trous (complété par un petit 9 trous) a été dessiné par Alain Prat avec beaucoup de bon sens : il n'a pas voulu exagérer les difficultés et son tracé ne pénalise que ceux qui prennent des risques excessifs. Le terrain plat a été légèrement modelé pour les besoins de la cause, et le sol sablonneux est idéal pour le golf. Le déroulement dans les pins et la bruyère est agréable, avec des difficultés mesurées pour ne rebuter personne, les principaux dangers (en dehors de quelques obstacles d'eau) étant constitués par les bunkers et les arbres, qui laissent souvent libres les accès aux vastes greens. Mais les débutants auront sans doute du mal quand ils sont très défendus. On peut jouer facilement ici toute l'année : les hivers sont plutôt doux, le parcours supporte bien les intempéries et son entretien reste de bonne qualité.

Located between Arcachon and Bordeaux, this 18-hole course was designed by Alain Prat (with an adjoining 9 hole course). Using a lot of good sense, he has avoided any excessive difficulties and the layout only penalises the players who take one risk too many. The flat terrain has been slightly graded for greater relief and the sandy subsoil is ideal for a golf course. It winds its way pleasantly through pinetrees and heather, with playing difficulties carefully gauged to avoid scaring the lesser player. Aside from the few water hazards, the main problems are the bunkers and trees, which generally speaking afford easy access to the greens. Beginners will probably find the going a little harder when dealing with some of the better-defended holes. You can easily play here all year, as the winters are mild, the ground withstands all weathers and upkeep is generally good.

Golf de Gujan-Mestras   1990
Route de Sanguinet
F - 33470 GUJAN-MESTRAS

Office	Secrétariat	(33) 05 57 52 73 73
Pro shop	Pro-shop	(33) 05 57 52 73 73
Fax	Fax	(33) 05 56 66 10 93
Situation	Situation	

Gujan-Mestras (pop. 11 430), 6 km
Arcachon (pop. 11 770), 12 km

Annual closure	Fermeture annuelle	no
Weekly closure	Fermeture hebdomadaire	no

Fees main season
Tarifs haute saison full day

	Week days Semaine	We/Bank holidays We/Férié
Individual Individuel	270 F	270 F
Couple Couple	450 F	450 F

Caddy	Caddy	no
Electric Trolley	Chariot électrique	no
Buggy	Voiturette	130 F/18 holes
Clubs	Clubs	60 F/full day

Credit cards Cartes de crédit
VISA - CB - Eurocard - MasterCard - AMEX - DC

B A S S I N
D ' A R C A C H O N

ARCACHON

Gujan-Mestras

N 250

A 63 Bordeaux

GOLF

D 652

Sanguinet

Parc régional
des Landes de Gascogne

0   2   4 km

Access Accès : Bordeaux, A63, Exit (Sortie) Arcachon, at Aqua City, → Golf
Map 9 on page 181 Carte 9 Page 181

GOLF COURSE PARCOURS   15/20

Site	Site	▉▉▉▉▉▉□
Maintenance	Entretien	▉▉▉▉▉▉□
Architect	Architecte	Alain Prat
Type	Type	forest
Relief	Relief	▉▉□□□
Water in play	Eau en jeu	▉▉▉□□
Exp. to wind	Exposé au vent	▉▉▉□□
Trees in play	Arbres en jeu	▉▉▉▉□

Scorecard Carte de score	Chp. Chp.	Mens Mess.	Ladies Da.
Length Long.	6225	6005	5185
Par	72	72	72

Advised golfing ability   0   12   24   36
Niveau de jeu recommandé
Hcp required   Handicap exigé   35

CLUB HOUSE & AMENITIES CLUB HOUSE ET ANNEXES   7/10

Pro shop	Pro-shop	▉▉▉▉▉□
Driving range	Practice	▉▉▉▉□
Sheltered	couvert	8 mats
On grass	sur herbe	yes
Putting-green	putting-green	yes
Pitching-green	pitching green	yes

HOTEL FACILITIES ENVIRONNEMENT HOTELIER   6/10

HOTELS HÔTELS
La Guérinière   Gujan-Mestras
27 rooms, D 550 F   6 km
Tel (33) 05 56 66 08 78
Fax (33) 05 56 66 13 39

Séminaris   Arcachon
19 rooms, D 740 F   12 km
Tel (33) 05 56 83 25 87
Fax (33) 05 57 52 22 41

Deganne   Arcachon
57 rooms, D 800 F   12 km
Tel (33) 05 56 83 99 91
Fax (33) 05 56 83 87 92

RESTAURANTS RESTAURANTS
L'Ombrière   Arcachon
Tel (33) 05 56 83 86 20   12 km

286

Depuis sa création en 1931, «Les Pins» est un des excellents exemples du style de Tom Simpson et reste un parcours plus passionnant et plus franc que le récent parcours des «Dunes», bien qu'il soit beaucoup plus sec en été. Quelques coups sont aveugles, mais faussement trompeurs et sans véritable gêne pour le jeu. Avec des greens subtils, des bunkers diaboliquement placés, le parcours exige une grande précision, et de savoir profiter des occasions d'attaquer. On a ici l'impression de devoir simplement suivre les pas de l'architecte pour le négocier correctement, tant son dessin paraît empreint de bon sens. «Les Pins» est de ces parcours polis par le temps que l'on doit d'autant plus connaître si l'on joue surtout des golfs «modernes». Les Anglais ne s'y trompent pas, ils y viennent nombreux. Mais les visites en été ont montré que ce parcours pouvait aussi être en très mauvais état quand il n'est pas arrosé... Attention !

Designed in 1931 by Tom Simpson, «Les Pins» is still a more exciting and forthright course than the more recent «Les Dunes», although the latter is drier in summer. Some shots are blind but never really deceive the player or affect play. With subtle greens and devilishly well-placed bunkers, this course cries out for precision stroke-making and the ability to utilise opportunities for attacking play. The impression is one of simply following in the footsteps of the architect in order to play the course correctly. That is how sensible the layout is. «Les Pins» is one of those courses that becomes more polished with time and is a must for anyone raised exclusively on «modern» courses. The British know a good golf course when they see one, and a lot of Brits come and play here. But our visits during the summer months have shown that this course, without an automatic watering system, can also be in very poor condition. So watch out.

Golf d'Hardelot-les-Pins 1931
3, avenue du Golf
F - 62152 HARDELOT

Office	Secrétariat	(33) 03 21 83 73 10
Pro shop	Pro-shop	(33) 03 21 83 73 10
Fax	Fax	(33) 03 21 83 24 33
Situation	Situation	

Boulogne s/Mer (pop. 43 670), 15 km

Annual closure	Fermeture annuelle	no
Weekly closure	Fermeture hebdomadaire	no

Fees main season
Tarifs haute saison 18 holes

	Week days Semaine	We/Bank holidays We/Férié
Individual Individuel	300 F	350 F
Couple Couple	600 F	700 F

Caddy	Caddy	no
Electric Trolley	Chariot électrique	no
Buggy	Voiturette	200 F/18 holes
Clubs	Clubs	100 F/full day

Credit cards Cartes de crédit
VISA - CB - Eurocard - MasterCard - AMEX

Access Accès : • Boulogne, A16 → Calais, N1 → Montreuil, through Pont-de-Briques, turn right on D940 → Hardelot • Montreuil, N1 → Boulogne-sur-Mer, or D940 coming from Le Touquet
Map 1 on page 164 Carte 1 Page 164

GOLF COURSE / PARCOURS 16/20

Site	Site	
Maintenance	Entretien	
Architect	Architecte	Tom Simpson
Type	Type	forest, parkland
Relief	Relief	
Water in play	Eau en jeu	
Exp. to wind	Exposé au vent	
Trees in play	Arbres en jeu	

Scorecard Carte de score	Chp. Chp.	Mens Mess.	Ladies Da.
Length Long.	5870	5870	5137
Par	72	72	72

Advised golfing ability		0	12	24	36
Niveau de jeu recommandé					
Hcp required	Handicap exigé	35			

CLUB HOUSE & AMENITIES / CLUB HOUSE ET ANNEXES 6/10

Pro shop	Pro-shop	
Driving range	Practice	
Sheltered	couvert	6 mats
On grass	sur herbe	no, 6 mats open air
Putting-green	putting-green	yes
Pitching-green	pitching green	yes

HOTEL FACILITIES / ENVIRONNEMENT HOTELIER 6/10

HOTELS HÔTELS
Hôtel du Parc — Hardelot
80 rooms, D 1 400 F — 1 km
Tel (33) 03 21 33 22 11, Fax (33) 03 21 83 29 71

Cléry — Hesdin-l'Abbé
19 rooms, D 795 F — 7 km
Tel (33) 03 21 83 19 83, Fax (33) 03 21 87 52 59

Régina — Hardelot
40 rooms, D 345 F — 1 km
Tel (33) 03 21 83 81 88, Fax (33) 03 21 87 44 01

RESTAURANTS RESTAURANTS
La Matelote — Boulogne-sur-Mer
Tel (33) 03 21 30 17 97 — 15 km

Host. de la Rivière — Pont-de-Briques
Tel (33) 03 21 32 22 81 — 7 km

287

Un parcours paradoxalement difficile pour une région où les néophytes sont nombreux, avec un relief qui rend assez fatigants les neuf derniers trous, tracés dans une zone agréable de pins et de bouleaux. A cause de sa longueur (même avec un par 73), on conseillera à tous de ne pas partir des départs les plus reculés, s'ils espèrent jouer leur handicap. Les neuf premiers trous sont plus plats, avec des obstacles d'eau pas trop pénalisants. L'architecture du parcours manque certes de charme et d'originalité (le 13 est joli), mais les greens sont en majorité bien dessinés. En résumé, un golf à jouer si l'on se trouve dans la région, notamment pour compléter un séjour en famille, un petit parcours de 9 trous permettant de loger les débutants. Une base de loisirs est toute proche, ainsi que le Futuroscope de Poitiers.

A paradoxically tough course in region where beginners abound. The sloping terrain makes the back 9 a tiring but pleasant walk through pines and birch trees. Haut Poitou is a long course, and even at a par 73 we would not recommend the back tees to anyone wishing to play to his handicap. The front 9 are flatter with water hazards that could be rated as avoidable and so not too heavy on the score. The overall architecture probably lacks originality and charm (although the 13th is a pretty hole), but the majority of greens are well-designed. In short, a course worth playing if you are in the region, especially if you are with the family, as a neighbouring 9 hole pitch 'n putt is ideal for beginners. The course is also close to a leisure centre and to the Futuroscope.

Golf Club du Haut-Poitou   1987
F - 86130 SAINT-CYR

Office	Secrétariat	(33) 05 49 62 53 62
Pro shop	Pro-shop	(33) 05 49 62 53 62
Fax	Fax	(33) 05 49 88 77 14
Situation	Situation	

Châtellerault (pop. 34 670), 15 km
Poitiers (pop. 78 890), 20 km

Annual closure	Fermeture annuelle	no
Weekly closure	Fermeture hebdomadaire	no

Fees main season
Tarifs haute saison full day

	Week days Semaine	We/Bank holidays We/Férié
Individual Individuel	170 F	200 F
Couple Couple	290 F	350 F

Caddy	Caddy	no
Electric Trolley	Chariot électrique	no
Buggy	Voiturette	130 F/18 holes
Clubs	Clubs	50 F/full day

Credit cards Cartes de crédit
VISA - CB - Eurocard - MasterCard - AMEX

GOLF COURSE
PARCOURS   14/20

Site	Site	
Maintenance	Entretien	
Architect	Architecte	Bill Baker
Type	Type	open country, forest
Relief	Relief	
Water in play	Eau en jeu	
Exp. to wind	Exposé au vent	
Trees in play	Arbres en jeu	

Scorecard	Chp.	Mens	Ladies
Carte de score	Chp.	Mess.	Da.
Length Long.	6590	6124	5569
Par	73	73	73

Advised golfing ability	0	12	24	36
Niveau de jeu recommandé				
Hcp required	Handicap exigé	no		

CLUB HOUSE & AMENITIES
CLUB HOUSE ET ANNEXES   6/10

Pro shop	Pro-shop	
Driving range	Practice	
Sheltered	couvert	18 mats
On grass	sur herbe	yes
Putting-green	putting-green	yes
Pitching-green	pitching green	yes

HOTEL FACILITIES
ENVIRONNEMENT HOTELIER   4/10

HOTELS HÔTELS
Château de la Ribaudière   Chasseneuil
41 rooms, D 840 F   12 km
Tel (33) 05 49 52 86 66, Fax (33) 05 49 52 86 32

Mercure Poitiers Nord   Chasseneuil
89 rooms, D 590 F   12 km
Tel (33) 05 49 52 90 41, Fax (33) 05 49 52 51 72

Agora   Dissay
43 rooms, D 350 F   2 km
Tel (33) 05 49 52 62 42, Fax (33) 05 49 52 62 62

RESTAURANTS RESTAURANTS
Maxime   Poitiers
Tel (33) 05 49 41 09 55   20 km

Benjamin   Dissay
Tel (33) 05 49 52 42 37   2 km

288

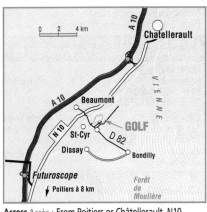

Access Accès : From Poitiers or Châtellerault, N10,
Exit (Sortie) Beaumont, → Golf
Map 6 on page 175 Carte 6 Page 175

Un des grands classiques de la «Côte Basque», dont l'architecture rappelle les parcours intérieurs traditionnels de Grande-Bretagne, où les obstacles sont essentiellement les arbres et les bunkers. Dans un espace aussi évidemment fait pour le golf, il n'était guère utile de beaucoup modeler le terrain (pas de bulldozers à l'époque). Depuis les années 30, le dessin n'a pas pris une ride, sauf qu'il devrait être adapté au jeu actuel, en déplaçant (sans modifier leur forme) les bunkers de fairway des par 4, qui pénalisent surtout les joueurs moyens. Le parcours est plat, et de bonne qualité toute l'année, grâce au sol sablonneux. Les obstacles bien visibles, la variété des trous et le profil des greens en font un test de stratégie et de jeu, qui masque ses réelles difficultés sous un visage souriant. Un excellent parcours, qu'il s'agisse de jouer en compétition, ou en famille.

One of the great classics on the Basque coast with a layout reminiscent of traditional British inland courses, where the hazards are primarily trees and bunkers. On a site so obviously made for golf, there was hardly any need to shape the terrain (anyway there were no bulldozers around at the time). Since the 1930s, the course looks and feels as young as ever. But it might be better adjusted to the needs of modern play by shifting (without any change in shape) the fairway bunkers on the par 4s, which tend nowadays to penalise mid-handicappers more than anyone else. The course is flat and plays beautifully all year thanks to the sandy sub-soil. Clearly visible hazards, variety and the neat greens make this a fine test of golfing ability and strategy, and one that conceals its real difficulties beneath a cheerful exterior. An excellent course for tournaments or for all the family.

Golf Club d'Hossegor — 1930

Avenue du Golf
F - 40150 HOSSEGOR

Office	Secrétariat	(33) 05 58 43 56 99
Pro shop	Pro-shop	(33) 05 58 43 56 99
Fax	Fax	(33) 05 58 43 98 52
Situation	Situation	

Dax (pop. 19 310), 32 km
Bayonne (pop. 40 050), 20 km

Annual closure	Fermeture annuelle	no
Weekly closure	Fermeture hebdomadaire	tuesday

mardi (except holidays)

Fees main season
Tarifs haute saison full day

	Week days Semaine	We/Bank holidays We/Férié
Individual Individuel	350 F	350 F
Couple Couple	700 F	700 F
Caddy Caddy		on request
Electric Trolley Chariot électrique		100 F/18 holes
Buggy Voiturette		no
Clubs Clubs		no

Credit cards Cartes de crédit
VISA - CB - Eurocard - MasterCard

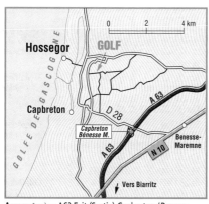

Hossegor GOLF

Capbreton

Capbreton Bénesse M.

Benesse-Maremne

Vers Biarritz

0 2 4 km

Access Accès : A63 Exit (Sortie) Capbreton / Benesse-Marenne → «Hossegor Centre Ville»
Map 12 on page 186 Carte 12 Page 186

GOLF COURSE PARCOURS — 16/20

Site	Site	▰▰▰▱▱
Maintenance	Entretien	▰▰▰▰▱
Architect	Architecte	Tim Morisson
Type	Type	forest
Relief	Relief	▰▱▱▱▱
Water in play	Eau en jeu	▰▱▱▱▱
Exp. to wind	Exposé au vent	▰▰▱▱▱
Trees in play	Arbres en jeu	▰▰▰▰▱

Scorecard Carte de score	Chp. Chp.	Mens Mess.	Ladies Da.
Length Long.	6001	5867	5037
Par	71	71	71

Advised golfing ability	0 12 24 36
Niveau de jeu recommandé	▰▰▰▱
Hcp required Handicap exigé	24 Men, 28 Ladies (main season)

CLUB HOUSE & AMENITIES CLUB HOUSE ET ANNEXES — 6/10

Pro shop	Pro-shop	▰▰▰▱▱
Driving range	Practice	▰▰▱▱▱
Sheltered	couvert	20 mats
On grass	sur herbe	no
Putting-green	putting-green	yes
Pitching-green	pitching green	no

289

HOTEL FACILITIES ENVIRONNEMENT HOTELIER — 6/10

HOTELS HÔTELS

Beauséjour — Hossegor
45 rooms, D 650 F — 2 km
Tel (33) 05 58 43 51 07, Fax (33) 05 58 43 70 13

Hôtel du Golf — on site
9 rooms, D 400 F
Tel (33) 05 58 43 50 59, Fax (33) 05 58 43 98 52

Les Hortensias du Lac — Hossegor
21 rooms, D 450 F — 2 km
Tel (33) 05 58 43 99 00, Fax (33) 05 58 43 42 81

RESTAURANTS RESTAURANTS

Les Huîtrières du Lac — Hossegor
Tel (33) 05 58 43 51 48 — 2 km

Regalty — Capbreton
Tel (33) 05 58 72 22 80 — 3 km

Ce parcours a vite conquis une belle réputation. Par sa franchise, par la très grande variété de dessin et d'environnement des trous, tracés en partie dans une forêt, en partie sur un beau plateau. Le seul inconvénient, c'est de passer de l'une à l'autre : il serait astucieux de prévoir des navettes, tant les montées sont épuisantes. La stratégie de jeu est évidente dès la première visite, les fairways sont larges, mais le placement de la balle est crucial pour pouvoir ensuite approcher les greens en bonne position, car leurs modelages et leurs dimensions exigent beaucoup d'attention. L'architecte Ronald Fream a beaucoup modelé le terrain, dans une synthèse heureuse des tendances britannique et américaine, permettant à tous les niveaux et tous les styles de jeu de s'exprimer. Les arbres et bunkers sont bien en jeu, et l'eau présente sur trois trous seulement. Une bonne réussite.

This course has rapidly gained a fine reputation for its fairness and for the great variety in the design and setting of holes, some of which are laid out through a forest, others on a pretty plateau. The only drawback is walking from one part of the course to the other. The climb is so exhausting that a shuttle service might be in order. Game strategy is clear from the very first visit; the fairways are wide, but it is essential to position the tee-shot accurately in order to get a good look at greens whose slopes and size require great care. Architect Ronald Fream has shaped the terrain a great deal and created a happy combination of British and American trends. The course is fun for golfers of all abilities and styles. The trees and bunkers are clearly in play and water threatens on just three holes. A good success.

Golf de l'Isle-Adam — 1995

1, chemin des Vanneaux
F - 95290 L'ISLE-ADAM

Office	Secrétariat	(33) 01 34 08 11 11
Pro shop	Pro-shop	(33) 01 34 08 11 11
Fax	Fax	(33) 01 34 08 11 19
Situation	Situation	

Paris (pop. 2 175 200), 35 km - Chantilly (pop. 11 340), 21 km

Annual closure	Fermeture annuelle	yes
	24/12 → 1/1	
Weekly closure	Fermeture hebdomadaire	tuesday (mardi)

Fees main season
Tarifs haute saison full day

	Week days Semaine	We/Bank holidays We/Férié
Individual Individuel	250 F	375 F
Couple Couple	500 F	750 F
Caddy Caddy		no
Electric Trolley Chariot électrique		70 F/18 holes
Buggy Voiturette		no
Clubs Clubs		150 F/full day

Credit cards Cartes de crédit
VISA - CB - Eurocard - MasterCard - AMEX - DC

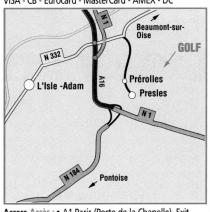

Access Accès : • A1 Paris (Porte de la Chapelle), Exit (Sortie) Beauvais, N1, Exit Beaumont-sur-Oise • A15 Paris (Porte de Clignancourt), → Pontoise, → N184, Exit Beaumont-sur-Oise **Map 1 on page 165** Carte 1 Page 165

GOLF COURSE / PARCOURS — 16/20

Site	Site	▆▆▆▆▆▁
Maintenance	Entretien	▆▆▆▆▁▁
Architect	Architecte	Ronald Fream
Type	Type	forest, open country
Relief	Relief	▆▆▁▁▁▁
Water in play	Eau en jeu	▆▆▆▁▁▁
Exp. to wind	Exposé au vent	▆▆▁▁▁▁
Trees in play	Arbres en jeu	▆▆▆▆▁▁

Scorecard / Carte de score	Chp. / Chp.	Mens / Mess.	Ladies / Da.
Length Long.	6230	5711	5152
Par	72	72	72

Advised golfing ability	0	12	24	36
Niveau de jeu recommandé		▆▆▆▆		
Hcp required Handicap exigé	35			

CLUB HOUSE & AMENITIES / CLUB HOUSE ET ANNEXES — 7/10

Pro shop	Pro-shop	▆▆▆▆▁
Driving range	Practice	▆▆▆▁▁
Sheltered	couvert	12 mats
On grass	sur herbe	yes (summer)
Putting-green	putting-green	yes
Pitching-green	pitching green	yes

HOTEL FACILITIES / ENVIRONNEMENT HOTELIER — 4/10

HOTELS HÔTELS
Novotel Château de Maffliers — Maffliers
80 rooms, D 660 F — 7 km
Tel (33) 01 34 08 35 35
Fax (33) 01 34 69 97 49

Etap Hôtel — L'Isle-Adam
68 rooms, D 185 F — 1 km
Tel (33) 01 34 69 09 85
Fax (33) 01 34 69 11 85

RESTAURANTS RESTAURANTS
Relais Fleuri — L'Isle-Adam
Tel (33) 01 34 69 01 85 — 2 km

Gai Rivage — L'Isle Adam
Tel (33) 01 34 69 01 09 — 2 km

290

JOYENVAL MARLY

16	8	7

Après bien des péripéties, le Golf de Joyenval semble avoir trouvé sa vitesse de croisière, et sait parfois entr'ouvrir ses portes, bien qu'il soit très privé. L'avantage d'une fréquentation réduite, c'est que son entretien, notamment au niveau des greens, est généralement excellent. Des deux parcours, Marly est celui qui a le moins souffert des contraintes administratives, souvent abusives, liées à la proximité du Désert de Retz (monument historique), mais on aimerait voir les trous souvent mieux définis par des plantations. Dans ces conditions, on ne voit souvent plus que les bunkers, aussi impressionnants à voir qu'à visiter. Très varié de paysage et de style, ce parcours est d'autant plus technique que les greens sont très difficiles à lire. Les équipements annexes, Club house et practice sont de premier ordre.

After a lot of starting and stopping, the Joyenval club now looks to be up and running and sometimes even opens its gate to outsiders, despite being a very private club. The upside of being under-played is that their greenkeeping and the greens in particular are generally good. Of the two courses, Marly is the one that suffered the least from often excessive administrative requirements related to the closeness of the Désert de Retz (an historical landmark), although we would like to see the holes better defined with a tree planting program. Under these conditions you often see only the bunkers, which are as impressive to see as they are to be in. Very varied in style and landscape, the course is made all the more technical by greens that are very difficult to read. Club house and practice facilities are first class.

Golf de Joyenval — 1992

Chemin de la Tuilerie
F - 78240 CHAMBOURCY

Office	Secrétariat	(33) 01 39 22 27 61
Pro shop	Pro-shop	(33) 01 39 22 27 50
Fax	Fax	(33) 01 30 65 94 26
Situation	Situation	
Paris (pop. 2 175 200), 28 km		
Annual closure	Fermeture annuelle	no
Weekly closure	Fermeture hebdomadaire	monday (lundi)

Fees main season
Tarifs haute saison 18 trous

	Week days Semaine	We/Bank holidays We/Férié
Individual Individuel	*	*
Couple Couple	*	*

* upon application (sur demande): limitations of access

Caddy	Caddy	on request/250 F
Electric Trolley	Chariot électrique	100 F/18 holes
Buggy	Voiturette	250 F/18 holes
Clubs	Clubs	100 F/18 holes

Credit cards Cartes de crédit
VISA - CB - Eurocard - MasterCard

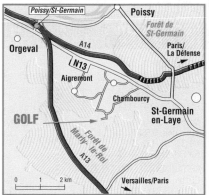

Access Accès : A13 Exit (Sortie) → Saint-Germain.
N13 → Poissy, → Orgeval. After Chambourcy,
take left → Désert de Retz, Golf de Joyenval.
Map 15 on page 192 Carte 15 Page 192

GOLF COURSE PARCOURS — 16/20

Site	Site	
Maintenance	Entretien	
Architect	Architecte	R. Trent Jones Sr
Type	Type	parkland, forest
Relief	Relief	
Water in play	Eau en jeu	
Exp. to wind	Exposé au vent	
Trees in play	Arbres en jeu	

Scorecard Carte de score	Chp. Chp.	Mens Mess.	Ladies Da.
Length Long.	6249	5776	5272
Par	72	72	72

Advised golfing ability		0 12 24 36
Niveau de jeu recommandé		
Hcp required	Handicap exigé	no

CLUB HOUSE & AMENITIES
CLUB HOUSE ET ANNEXES — 8/10

Pro shop	Pro-shop	
Driving range	Practice	
Sheltered	couvert	5 mats
On grass	sur herbe	yes
Putting-green	putting-green	yes
Pitching-green	pitching green	yes

291

HOTEL FACILITIES
ENVIRONNEMENT HOTELIER — 7/10

HOTELS HÔTELS
Pavillon Henri IV — Saint-Germain
42 rooms, D 1 290 F — 4 km
Tel (33) 01 39 10 15 15
Fax (33) 01 39 93 73 93

Novotel — Orgeval
119 rooms, D 580 F — 4 km
Tel (33) 01 39 22 35 11
Fax (33) 01 39 75 48 93

RESTAURANTS RESTAURANTS
L'Esturgeon — Poissy
Tel (33) 01 39 65 00 04 — 5 km

Cazaudehore — Saint-Germain
Tel (33) 01 30 61 64 64 — 5 km

Le site est exceptionnel, entre la forêt de Marly et une vallée que les poètes n'aurait pas reniée, à proximité immédiate du Désert de Retz, folie architecturale dûe à l'imagination d'un gentilhomme du XVIII ème siècle. On aurait d'ailleurs aimé que le parcours soit vraiment une réponse moderne à cet esprit baroque, mais le crayon parfois austère de Trent Jones a permis de limiter au minimum les contraintes. Il reste quelques trous de haute volée, entre forêt et plaine, entre parc et jardin, avec des aspects évidemment américains dans leur franchise et leur brutalité, mais aussi britanniques quand les contours deviennent plus flous, plus subtils. Très scénique, moins stratégique que «Marly», ce parcours est aussi moins exigeant pour les joueurs moyens.

The site is outstanding, between the forest of Marly and a valley to make any poet wax lyrical, within the immediate vicinity of the Désert de Retz, a piece of architecture folly born from the imagination of an 18th century gentleman. We would have liked this course really to be a modern response to this baroque spirit, but the often austere design of Trent Jones helped keep restrictions to a minimum. There are a few top-notch holes between forest and plain, park-land and garden, obviously looking very American in their honesty and toughness, but also British when contours grow a little less sharp and more subtle. Very scenic and less strategic than Marly, Retz is also less demanding for the average golfer.

Golf de Joyenval — 1992

Chemin de la Tuilerie
F - 78240 CHAMBOURCY

Office	Secrétariat	(33) 01 39 22 27 61
Pro shop	Pro-shop	(33) 01 39 22 27 50
Fax	Fax	(33) 01 30 65 94 26
Situation	Situation	

Paris (pop. 2 175 200), 28 km

Annual closure	Fermeture annuelle	no
Weekly closure	Fermeture hebdomadaire	monday (lundi)

Fees main season
Tarifs haute saison 18 holes

	Week days Semaine	We/Bank holidays We/Férié
Individual Individuel	*	*
Couple Couple	*	*

* upon application (sur demande): limitations of access

Caddy	Caddy	on request/250 F
Electric Trolley	Chariot électrique	100 F/18 holes
Buggy	Voiturette	250 F/18 holes
Clubs	Clubs	100 F/18 holes

Credit cards Cartes de crédit
VISA - CB - Eurocard - MasterCard

Access Accès : A13 Exit (Sortie) → Saint-Germain.
N13 → Poissy, → Orgeval. After Chambourcy,
take left → Désert de Retz, Golf de Joyenval.
Map 15 on page 192 Carte 15 Page 192

GOLF COURSE PARCOURS — 15/20

Site	Site	
Maintenance	Entretien	
Architect	Architecte	R. Trent Jones Sr
Type	Type	forest, parkland
Relief	Relief	
Water in play	Eau en jeu	
Exp. to wind	Exposé au vent	
Trees in play	Arbres en jeu	

Scorecard Carte de score	Chp. Chp.	Mens Mess.	Ladies Da.
Length Long.	6211	5728	5248
Par	72	72	72

Advised golfing ability		0 12 24 36
Niveau de jeu recommandé		
Hcp required	Handicap exigé	no

CLUB HOUSE & AMENITIES
CLUB HOUSE ET ANNEXES — 8/10

Pro shop	Pro-shop	
Driving range	Practice	
Sheltered	couvert	5 mats
On grass	sur herbe	yes
Putting-green	putting-green	yes
Pitching-green	pitching green	yes

HOTEL FACILITIES
ENVIRONNEMENT HOTELIER — 7/10

HOTELS HÔTELS
Pavillon Henri IV — Saint-Germain
42 rooms, D 1 290 F — 4 km
Tel (33) 01 39 10 15 15
Fax (33) 01 39 93 73 93

Novotel — Orgeval
119 rooms, D 580 F — 4 km
Tel (33) 01 39 22 35 11
Fax (33) 01 39 75 48 93

RESTAURANTS RESTAURANTS
L'Esturgeon — Poissy
Tel (33) 01 39 65 00 04 — 5 km

Cazaudehore — Saint-Germain
Tel (33) 01 30 61 64 64 — 5 km

292

KEMPFERHOF (LE)

18 8 6

Ce parcours signé Von Hagge donne d'abord une impression de finition et de soin du détail : le plaisir des yeux commence en arrivant sur le site. Dans un environnement de campagne, avec des sapins, des hêtres et des bouleaux, il est difficile d'oublier le plaisir des yeux et de jouer son handicap mais ce parcours sans reliefs prononcés est jouable à tous les niveaux (les néophytes seront cependant intimidés par quelques obstacles d'eau dangereux). Très sélectif, le tracé demande souvent de travailler la balle et de démontrer sa maîtrise de tous les clubs, avec un accent aigu sur la précision, notamment pour approcher les vastes greens, très travaillés. Tous les obstacles étant visibles, ce parcours ne cache rien de ses exigences. Le terrain a été beaucoup modelé, mais la nature a repris ses droits, donnant au lieu une belle impression de calme. Une incontestable réussite, dans une région magnifique.

This Von Hagge course gives the initial impression of careful grooming and attention to detail. The beauty of the site is apparent the moment you arrive. In a country setting of pine-trees, beech and birch, playing to your handicap might be too much to ask, but this flattish course can be played by all (although beginners may be unsettled by a few dangerous water hazards). We found this a very selective course, calling for skill in ball-control and stroke-making, and great emphasis on precision-play, especially for approaching the huge and carefully designed greens. As all the hazards are there to be seen, the course hides nothing of what it demands from golfers. The terrain has been contoured to a considerable extent, but mother nature has regained the upper hand to give an overall impression of tranquillity. A great course in a fabulous region.

Kempferhof Golf Club — 1990

351, rue du Moulin
F - 67115 PLOBSHEIM

Office	Secrétariat	(33) 03 88 98 72 72
Pro shop	Pro-shop	(33) 03 88 98 72 72
Fax	Fax	(33) 03 88 98 74 76
Situation	Situation	

Strasbourg (pop. 252 260), 15 km

Annual closure	Fermeture annuelle	yes
		21/12 → 12/1
Weekly closure	Fermeture hebdomadaire	tuesday
	(mardi) 01/11 → 01/04	

Fees main season
Tarifs haute saison 18 holes

	Week days Semaine	We/Bank holidays We/Férié
Individual Individuel	350 F	500 F
Couple Couple	700 F	1 000 F

Caddy	Caddy	no
Electric Trolley	Chariot électrique	no
Buggy	Voiturette	200 F/18 holes
Clubs	Clubs	no

Credit cards Cartes de crédit
VISA - CB - Eurocard - MasterCard - AMEX

Access Accès : Strasbourg A35, Exit (Sortie) N°5
Baggersee → Eschau, → Plobsheim, → Golf
Map 4 on page 171 Carte 4 Page 171

GOLF COURSE / PARCOURS — 18/20

Site	Site	
Maintenance	Entretien	
Architect	Architecte	Robert von Hagge
Type	Type	parkland, country
Relief	Relief	
Water in play	Eau en jeu	
Exp. to wind	Exposé au vent	
Trees in play	Arbres en jeu	

Scorecard Carte de score	Chp. Chp.	Mens Mess.	Ladies Da.
Length Long.	5980	5583	4816
Par	72	72	72

Advised golfing ability Niveau de jeu recommandé	0 12 24 36
Hcp required Handicap exigé	35, We

CLUB HOUSE & AMENITIES / CLUB HOUSE ET ANNEXES — 8/10

Pro shop	Pro-shop	
Driving range	Practice	
Sheltered	couvert	10 mats
On grass	sur herbe	yes
Putting-green	putting-green	yes
Pitching-green	pitching green	yes

293

HOTEL FACILITIES / ENVIRONNEMENT HOTELIER — 6/10

HOTELS HÔTELS
Kempferhof Hotel — Golf
13 rooms, D 600 / 1 500 F — on site
Tel (33) 03 88 98 72 72, Fax (33) 03 88 98 74 76

Holiday Inn Garden Court — Illkirch 5 km
68 rooms, D 680 F
Tel (33) 03 88 40 84 84, Fax (33) 03 88 66 22 83

Alizés — Lipsheim 3 km
49 rooms, D 360 F
Tel (33) 03 88 59 02 00, Fax (33) 03 88 64 21 61

RESTAURANTS RESTAURANTS
Buerehiesel — Strasbourg 13 km
Tel (33) 03 88 45 56 65

Le Crocodile — Strasbourg 13 km
Tel (33) 03 88 32 13 02

Dans ce site magnifique et tranquille, modérément vallonné, et au milieu d'une forêt de pins, ce parcours aurait pu être un chef d'œuvre. Mais le dessin de John Harris est simplement de bonne qualité, mais une demi-douzaine de trous sortent cependant de l'ordinaire. Des obstacles d'eau apportent un élément paysager intéressant, et posent quelques interrogations avant de jouer, mais ils ne sont pas effrayants. Certes, il faut jouer plusieurs fois pour bien comprendre la stratégie idéale en fonction des différents départs, mais seuls les mauvais coups sont vraiment punis. Même si les débutants auront des difficultés sur certains trous étroits, les golfeurs de tous niveaux peuvent passer un séjour vivifiant au grand air et à proximité de l'Atlantique, pratiquement toute l'année car le sol sablonneux du parcours absorbe bien la pluie. Le nouveau green-keeper a fait des merveilles pour amener l'entretien à très bon niveau.

Gently rolling through a pine forest in a balmy and magnificent setting, this course could have been a masterpiece. As it is, the layout designed by John Harris is simply a good course, although half a dozen holes clearly emerge as out of the ordinary. Water hazards are an attractive addition to the general landscape and call for a little thought before shaping the shot, but they are less than awesome. Naturally, you need to play the course several times to grasp the ideal strategy depending on the tees you choose, but here, only the really bad shots are penalised. Although beginners (and even proficient players) will find a number of holes a little on the tight side, golfers of all abilities can spend an invigorating holiday in the sea-air close to the Atlantic Ocean. And they can play virtually all year round, as the sandy soil quickly soaks up the rain. The new green-keeper has made an excellent job of keeping the course in prime condition.

Golf de Lacanau — 1980

Domaine de l'Ardilouse
F - 33680 LACANAU

Office	Secrétariat	(33) 05 56 03 92 98
Pro shop	Pro-shop	(33) 05 56 03 92 98
Fax	Fax	(33) 05 56 26 30 57
Situation	Situation	

Bordeaux (pop. 211 200), 50 km

Annual closure	Fermeture annuelle	no
Weekly closure	Fermeture hebdomadaire	no

Fees main season
Tarifs haute saison full day

	Week days Semaine	We/Bank holidays We/Férié
Individual Individuel	240 F	240 F
Couple Couple	420 F	420 F

Caddy	Caddy	no
Electric Trolley	Chariot électrique	no
Buggy	Voiturette	150 F/18 holes
Clubs	Clubs	45 F/full day

Credit cards Cartes de crédit
VISA - CB - Eurocard - MasterCard - AMEX - DC

294

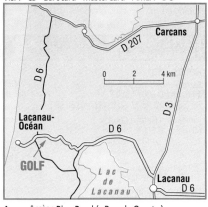

Access Accès : Ring Road (« Rocade Ouest »)
of Bordeaux, Exit (Sortie) No 7, N 215,
D6 → Lacanau Océan
Map 9 on page 180 Carte 9 Page 180

GOLF COURSE / PARCOURS — 14/20

Site	Site	
Maintenance	Entretien	
Architect	Architecte	John Harris
Type	Type	forest, hilly
Relief	Relief	
Water in play	Eau en jeu	
Exp. to wind	Exposé au vent	
Trees in play	Arbres en jeu	

Scorecard Carte de score	Chp. Chp.	Mens Mess.	Ladies Da.
Length Long.	5932	5512	5065
Par	72	72	72

Advised golfing ability 0 12 24 36
Niveau de jeu recommandé
Hcp required Handicap exigé 35 (summer/été)

CLUB HOUSE & AMENITIES / CLUB HOUSE ET ANNEXES — 6/10

Pro shop	Pro-shop	
Driving range	Practice	
Sheltered	couvert	10 mats
On grass	sur herbe	yes
Putting-green	putting-green	yes
Pitching-green	pitching green	yes

HOTEL FACILITIES / ENVIRONNEMENT HOTELIER — 7/10

HOTELS HÔTELS
Hôtel du Golf — Domaine de l'Ardilouse
50 rooms, D 600 F — on site
Tel (33) 05 56 03 92 92, Fax (33) 05 56 26 30 57

Les Maisons de l'Ardilouse — on site
30 rooms, 3 395 F/week
Tel (33) 05 56 03 92 92

Relais de Margaux — Margaux
61 rooms, D 900 F — 25 km
Tel (33) 05 57 88 38 30, Fax (33) 05 57 88 31 73

RESTAURANTS RESTAURANTS
Savoie — Margaux
Tel (33) 05 57 88 31 76 — 25 km

La Vieille Auberge — Lacanau
Tel (33) 05 56 26 50 40 — 3 km

Dans une jolie propriété, traversée par la ligne Maginot, offrant alternativement un environnement de forêt et des trous de style links, ce parcours est accidenté mais plaisant, avec quelques pièces d'eau. Plus impressionnant visuellement que réellement, ses obstacles principaux sont les nombreux bunkers et les arbres. Les bunkers de green sont bien travaillés, mais parfois peu visibles. Ils constituent les principales difficultés, avec les arbres, mais La Largue est surtout délicat à négocier par le choix de clubs, étant donné sa topographie très vallonnée (voiturette recommandée pour les seniors). Les départs et fairways sont bien entretenus, les greens sont de bonne qualité et bien conçus : certains surélevés demandent de porter la balle. Un parcours d'entraînement de 9 trous permet de faire tranquillement progresser les enfants ou amis peu expérimentés encore.

This is a hilly and pleasant course with a few stretches of water, located on a pretty estate crossed by the Maginot line. Part woodland and part links, this is a visually impressive layout where the main hazards are the trees and numerous bunkers. The green-side bunkers in particular are well-designed, but sometimes hard to spot. The course is perhaps less impressive once you are on it, with the main difficulty coming from the trees, bunkers and club selection, owing to the hilly terrain (a buggy is recommended for senior players). The tees and fairways are in good condition and the greens are well laid-out and upkept. A number of elevated greens call for long high approaches. A 9-hole practice course is good news for children and friends still learning the game.

Golf de La Largue — 1989

Chemin du Largweg
F - 68580 MOOSLARGUE

Office	Secrétariat	(33) 03 89 07 67 67
Pro shop	Pro-shop	(33) 03 89 07 67 67
Fax	Fax	(33) 03 89 25 62 83
Situation	Situation	

Bâle (pop. 171 000), 30 km
Altkirch (pop. 5 090), 24 km

Annual closure	Fermeture annuelle	yes
		15/12 → 10/2
Weekly closure	Fermeture hebdomadaire	no

Fees main season
Tarifs haute saison 18 holes

	Week days Semaine	We/Bank holidays We/Férié
Individual Individuel	250 F	350 F
Couple Couple	500 F	700 F
GF 140 F le soir		
Caddy	Caddy	no
Electric Trolley	Chariot électrique	no
Buggy	Voiturette	220 F/18 holes
Clubs	Clubs	70 F/full day

Credit cards Cartes de crédit
VISA - CB - Eurocard - MasterCard

Access Accès : • Mulhouse → Altkirch → Hirsingue →
Seppois • Bâle, Motorway → Delémont, Exit Reinach
sud → Therwil → Leymen → Linsdorf → Ferrette →
Moos **Map 8 on page 179** Carte 8 Page 179

GOLF COURSE / PARCOURS — 15/20

Site	Site	
Maintenance	Entretien	
Architect	Architecte	Jeremy Pern
		Jean Garaïalde
Type	Type	forest, parkland
Relief	Relief	
Water in play	Eau en jeu	
Exp. to wind	Exposé au vent	
Trees in play	Arbres en jeu	

Scorecard Carte de score	Chp. Chp.	Mens Mess.	Ladies Da.
Length Long.	6200	5724	5415
Par	72	72	72

Advised golfing ability	0	12	24	36
Niveau de jeu recommandé				
Hcp required Handicap exigé	35			

CLUB HOUSE & AMENITIES / CLUB HOUSE ET ANNEXES — 7/10

Pro shop	Pro-shop	
Driving range	Practice	
Sheltered	couvert	22 mats
On grass	sur herbe	no, 34 mats open air
Putting-green	putting-green	yes
Pitching-green	pitching green	yes

295

HOTEL FACILITIES / ENVIRONNEMENT HOTELIER — 4/10

HOTELS HÔTELS

Le Petit Kohlberg		Lucelle
35 rooms, D 300 F		12 km
Tel (33) 03 89 40 85 30		
Fax (33) 03 89 40 89 40		
Aux Deux Clefs		Ferrette
7 rooms, D 270 F		9 km
Tel (33) 03 89 40 80 56		
Fax (33) 03 89 08 10 47		

RESTAURANTS RESTAURANTS

Ottié		Hirtzbach
Tel (33) 03 89 40 93 22		15 km
Au Raisin		Moernach
Tel (33) 03 89 40 80 73		5 km

| 14 | 7 | 5 |

Malheureusement à proximité immédiate de l'autoroute, ce parcours a été dessiné par Jean-Pascal Fourès dans un site dégagé et de relief assez prononcé. On souhaiterait une délimitation plus franche des fairways et des roughs (surtout entre le 1, le 9 et le 18) afin de mieux orienter le jeu du visiteur, d'autant que le manque d'arbres ne permet pas facilement de se repérer. Le tracé général, de longueur raisonnable, est de bonne qualité, avec quelques coups aveugles, mais inévitables en raison du terrain. Les greens sont raisonnablement modelés, et de très bonne qualité. Ce golf n'est pas vraiment un lieu traditionnel de vacances, mais il a visiblement été pensé pour des membres permanents, et pour tous les niveaux de jeu. Ses jolis points de vue sur la Mayenne et son ambiance plairont aux visiteurs de passage dans la région...

Unhappily located within the immediate vicinity of a motorway, this course was designed by Jean-Pascal Fourès in an open and rather hilly site. We would have preferred clearer demarcation between fairway and rough (especially between the 1st, 9th and 18th holes) for the visitor to get a clearer picture of the course. Bearings are already hard to find because there are no trees to speak of. The general layout is of reasonable length and good standard, although there are the few unavoidable blind holes on such sloping terrain. The greens are reasonably well contoured and excellent to play. This course is not really in traditional holiday country, but it has visibly been designed for permanent members and golfers of all playing skills. Pretty panoramas over the Mayenne river and the club's atmosphere will appeal to visitors passing through.

Golf de Laval-Changé 1992
«La Chabossière»
F - 53810 CHANGE

Office	Secrétariat	(33) 02 43 53 16 03
Pro shop	Pro-shop	(33) 02 43 53 16 03
Fax	Fax	(33) 02 43 49 35 15
Situation	Situation	

Laval (pop. 50 470), 5 km

Annual closure	Fermeture annuelle	no
Weekly closure	Fermeture hebdomadaire	no

Fees main season
Tarifs haute saison full day

	Week days Semaine	We/Bank holidays We/Férié
Individual Individuel	180 F	220 F
Couple Couple	290 F	350 F

Caddy	Caddy	no
Electric Trolley	Chariot électrique	60 F/18 holes
Buggy	Voiturette	150 F/18 holes
Clubs	Clubs	50 F/full day

Credit cards Cartes de crédit
VISA - CB - Eurocard - MasterCard

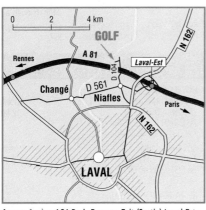

0   2   4 km

GOLF

Rennes
A 81
Laval-Est
D 104
Changé
D 561
Niafles
Paris
N 162
N 162
LAVAL

Access Accès : A81 Paris-Rennes, Exit (Sortie) Laval-Est
Map 2 on page 166 Carte 2 Page 166

GOLF COURSE / PARCOURS
14/20

Site	Site	
Maintenance	Entretien	
Architect	Architecte	Jean-Pascal Fourès
Type	Type	country, hilly
Relief	Relief	
Water in play	Eau en jeu	
Exp. to wind	Exposé au vent	
Trees in play	Arbres en jeu	

Scorecard Carte de score	Chp. Chp.	Mens Mess.	Ladies Da.
Length Long.	6068	5669	5132
Par	72	72	72

Advised golfing ability Niveau de jeu recommandé		0 12 24 36
Hcp required	Handicap exigé	35

CLUB HOUSE & AMENITIES / CLUB HOUSE ET ANNEXES
7/10

Pro shop	Pro-shop	
Driving range	Practice	
Sheltered	couvert	10 mats
On grass	sur herbe	yes
Putting-green	putting-green	yes
Pitching-green	pitching green	yes

HOTEL FACILITIES / ENVIRONNEMENT HOTELIER
5/10

HOTELS HÔTELS

Les Blés d'Or 8 rooms, D 520 F Tel (33) 02 43 53 14 10, Fax (33) 02 43 49 02 84		Laval 5 km
Impérial Hôtel 34 rooms, D 420 F Tel (33) 02 43 53 55 02, Fax (33) 02 43 49 16 74		Laval 5 km

RESTAURANTS RESTAURANTS

Bistro de Paris Tel (33) 02 43 56 98 29		Laval 5 km
Table Ronde Tel (33) 02 43 53 43 33		Changé 2 km
Le Capucin Gourmand Tel (33) 02 43 66 02 02		Laval 5 km

296

Ceux qui connaissent le style Hawtree ne seront guère étonnés d'un tracé plus qu'honnête mais sans grandes surprises. Le parcours «Est» est sans doute plus varié et amusant, mais moins bien équilibré : le parcours «Ouest» constitue à l'évidence la référence de ce golf, même s'il débute curieusement par un par 3. Dans un site à la fois de grand parc orné de quelques très beaux specimens d'arbres, le parcours se déroule de manière assez conventionnelle avec des défenses de green le plus souvent latérales, quelques mouvements sur les surfaces de putting, un bon équilibre des difficultés, une longueur très respectable, mais peu de chocs visuels ou de très grands défis techniques. Peu d'autres options que de taper loin et droit, de bien frapper ses fers et de putter correctement ! Autrement dit, on est heureux d'avoir joué ce classique, à tous les sens du terme, mais pas forcément ému. L'arrosage automatique a bien arrangé cet ensemble souvent sec en été, mais il reste très humide en hiver.

Golfers acquainted with the Hawtree style will not be surprised by this more than fair layout where there is little to raise any golfer's eyebrows. The «East» course is certainly most varied and fun to play, although it lacks balance. The «West» course is evidently the club's «flagship», even though strangely it starts off with a par 3. On a site of wide parkland and a few fine trees, the course unwinds in a very classical style with greens often guarded by lateral bunkers, a few contours on the greens, well-balanced difficulties, very respectable yardage but few visual thrills or tough technical challenges. There is nothing else for it but to hit the ball long and straight, strike some clean iron shots and putt properly. In other words, you are glad to have played this classic layout, in every sense of the term, but not necessarily too excited. The automatic sprinklers have done much to help a course that often gets very dry in summer, but stays wet in winter.

Golf du Prieuré — 1965

F - 78440 SAILLY

Office	Secrétariat	(44) 01 34 76 65 65
Pro shop	Pro-shop	(44) 01 34 76 78 29
Fax	Fax	(44) 01 34 76 65 50
Situation	Situation	

Arras (pop. 90 000), 22 km

Annual closure	Fermeture annuelle	no
Weekly closure	Fermeture hebdomadaire	no

Fees main season
Tarifs haute saison 18 holes

	Week days Semaine	We/Bank holidays We/Férié
Individual Individuel	260 F	340 F
Couple Couple	520 F	680 F

W.E. : members' guests only (invitation d'un membre)

Caddy	Caddy	250 F
Electric Trolley	Chariot électrique	yes
Buggy	Voiturette	260 F/18 holes
Clubs	Clubs	no

Credit cards Cartes de crédit
VISA - CB - Eurocard - MasterCard

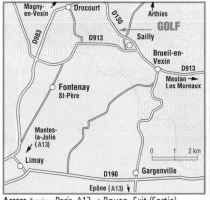

Access Accès : Paris, A13 → Rouen. Exit (Sortie) Meulan/Les Mureaux. After bridge over river Seine, take D913 to Oinville, Brueil-en-Vexin. 1 km after, turn right into Sailly, Golf 2 km
Map 3 on page 168 Carte 3 Page 168

GOLF COURSE PARCOURS — 14/20

Site	Site	▬▬▬▬▬□
Maintenance	Entretien	▬▬▬▬▬□
Architect	Architecte	Fred Hawtree
Type	Type	parkland
Relief	Relief	
Water in play	Eau en jeu	▬□□□□
Exp. to wind	Exposé au vent	▬▬□□□
Trees in play	Arbres en jeu	▬▬▬□□

Scorecard Carte de score	Chp. Chp.	Mens Mess.	Ladies Da.
Length Long.	6301	5716	5346
Par	72	72	72

Advised golfing ability
Niveau de jeu recommandé   0   12   24   36

Hcp required   Handicap exigé   35

CLUB HOUSE & AMENITIES CLUB HOUSE ET ANNEXES — 7/10

Pro shop	Pro-shop	▬▬▬▬□
Driving range	Practice	▬▬▬▬□
Sheltered	couvert	7 mats
On grass	sur herbe	no, 43 mats open air
Putting-green	putting-green	yes
Pitching-green	pitching green	yes

HOTEL FACILITIES ENVIRONNEMENT HOTELIER — 5/10

HOTELS HÔTELS

Mercure — Meulan
56 rooms, D 700 F — 12 km
Tel (33) 01 34 74 63 63, Fax (33) 01 34 74 00 98

Moulin d'Orgeval — Orgeval
14 rooms, D 800 F — 27 km
Tel (33) 01 39 75 85 74, Fax (33) 01 39 75 48 52

RESTAURANTS RESTAURANTS

Galiote — Mantes-la-Jolie
Tel (44) 01 34 77 03 02 — 12 km

Auberge de la Truite — Rosay
Tel (33) 01 34 76 30 52 — 22 km

Le Bon Vivant — Poissy
Tel (44) 01 39 65 02 14

297

L'un des meilleurs parcours français récents, et un quasi sans fautes sur le plan de l'architecture. Cabell Robinson a réussi à faire un parcours réellement accessible à tous les niveaux, et passionnant pour tous les joueurs. Plat et peu fatigant, il est modérément modelé, mais toujours dans l'intérêt du jeu. Beaucoup d'arbres, de bunkers et quelques obstacles d'eau viennent menacer ceux qui manquent les fairways pourtant assez larges, les approches de green peuvent être délicates, et les placements de drapeau rendent plus intéressants encore les greens subtils et intelligemment construits. Sans excès esthétiques inutiles, le parcours se déroule avec un excellent rythme de difficultés. Dans un environnement agréable et absorbant bien l'eau, Limère mérite le détour, et un séjour, même si le Club house n'est pas vraiment digne de l'ensemble.

One of the finest recent courses built in France and virtually faultless in terms of architecture. Cabell Robinson has succeeded in producing a course that can be played by, and will excite, golfers of all levels. Flat and relaxing, the terrain has been given quite a bit of shape, but always in the right way. A lot of trees, bunkers and a few water hazards threaten balls that miss the fairways (although these are pleasantly wide), approach-shots to the greens can be tricky and pin-positions make the subtle and cleverly built greens even more enticing. Without any needless visual effects, the course unwinds with a nice balance of hazards and difficulties. In a pleasant setting which soaks up the rain as fast as it falls, Limère is well worth the trip and a few days stay, even though the club-house does not quite meet the standard of the actual course.

Golf de Limère — 1992

Allée de la Pomme-de-Pin
F - 45160 ARDON

Office	Secrétariat	(33) 02 38 63 89 40
Pro shop	Pro-shop	(33) 02 38 63 89 40
Fax	Fax	(33) 02 38 63 05 20
Situation	Situation	

Orléans (pop. 105 110), 13 km

Annual closure	Fermeture annuelle	no
Weekly closure	Fermeture hebdomadaire	no

Fees main season
Tarifs haute saison 18 holes

	Week days Semaine	We/Bank holidays We/Férié
Individual Individuel	220 F	320 F
Couple Couple	440 F	640 F

Caddy	Caddy	no
Electric Trolley	Chariot électrique	no
Buggy	Voiturette	120 F/18 holes
Clubs	Clubs	60 F/full day

Credit cards Cartes de crédit
VISA - CB - Eurocard - MasterCard - AMEX - DC

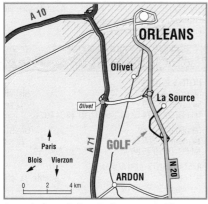

Access Accès : → Orléans La Source, sortie Olivet,
RN20 → La Source, → Golf
Map 3 on page 168 Carte 3 Page 168

GOLF COURSE / PARCOURS — 17/20

Site	Site	
Maintenance	Entretien	
Architect	Architecte	Cabell Robinson
Type	Type	forest, parkland
Relief	Relief	
Water in play	Eau en jeu	
Exp. to wind	Exposé au vent	
Trees in play	Arbres en jeu	

Scorecard Carte de score	Chp. Chp.	Mens Mess.	Ladies Da.
Length Long.	6232	5769	5264
Par	72	72	72

Advised golfing ability		0	12	24	36
Niveau de jeu recommandé					
Hcp required	Handicap exigé	no			

CLUB HOUSE & AMENITIES / CLUB HOUSE ET ANNEXES — 6/10

Pro shop	Pro-shop	
Driving range	Practice	
Sheltered	couvert	9 mats
On grass	sur herbe	yes
Putting-green	putting-green	yes
Pitching-green	pitching green	yes

HOTEL FACILITIES / ENVIRONNEMENT HOTELIER — 5/10

HOTELS HÔTELS
Domaine des Portes de Sologne — on site
120 rooms, D 700 F
Tel (33) 02 38 49 99 99, Fax (33) 02 38 49 99 00

Rivage — Olivet
17 rooms, D 490 F — 6 km
Tel (33) 02 38 66 02 93, Fax (33) 02 38 56 31 11

Novotel Orléans — La Source
107 rooms, D 530 F — 3 km
Tel (33) 02 38 63 04 28, Fax (33) 02 38 69 24 04

RESTAURANTS RESTAURANTS
Rivage — Olivet
Tel (33) 02 38 66 02 93 — 6 km

Les Antiquaires — Orléans
Tel (33) 02 38 53 52 35 — 13 km

La Poutrière — Orléans
Tel (33) 02 38 66 02 30 — 13 km

MAISON BLANCHE

14	7	5

Avec des vues magnifiques sur les Alpes et un Club house luxueux, on attendait un parcours mieux entretenu en dehors des mois d'été : il faut être impeccable face à la concurrence des autres golfs de la région lémanique, devenue une destination de golf du printemps à l'automne. Et d'autant plus que le terrain supporte mal l'humidité. Dessiné par Peter Harradine et Olivier Dongradi, le parcours comprend de nombreux obstacles d'eau, des arbres très en jeu et des reliefs assez prononcés (surtout au retour). Ils peuvent poser des problèmes aux débutants, mais les autres joueurs prendront plaisir à un tracé intéressant, sinon inoubliable, et garderont au minimum l'impression d'une belle balade en montagne. On regrettera que les bunkers n'aient pas été davantage travaillés, ils ne gênent que les joueurs peu expérimentés, souvent terrorisés dans le sable.

With magnificent views over the Alps and a luxurious club-house, we were expecting a course in better condition than this outside the summer months. Upkeep has to be immaculate in the face of competition from other courses in the region of Geneva, which is nowadays a spring and autumn golf destination. What's more, the terrain here does not take too kindly to wet weather. Designed by Peter Harradine and Olivier Dongradi, the course features a number of water hazards and trees, both very much in play, plus some undulating fairways (especially on the back 9). These may pose a few problems for beginners, but other players will have fun on this interesting if not unforgettable layout, and at the very least will feel like having enjoyed a beautiful mountain stroll. The bunker locations might have been given a little more thought, as at present the sand bothers only the inexperienced player.

Golf de Maison Blanche — 1992

Naz-Dessous
F - 01170 ECHENEVEX

Office	Secrétariat	(33) 04 50 42 44 42
Pro shop	Pro-shop	(33) 04 50 42 47 27
Fax	Fax	(33) 04 50 42 44 43
Situation	Situation	

Genève (pop. 172 486), 15 km
Gex (pop. 6 620), 2 km

Annual closure	Fermeture annuelle	yes
		20/12 → 1/3
Weekly closure	Fermeture hebdomadaire	no

Fees main season
Tarifs haute saison 18 holes

	Week days Semaine	We/Bank holidays We/Férié
Individual Individuel	320 F	—
Couple Couple	640 F	—

We: members only (membres seulement)

Caddy	Caddy	on request
Electric Trolley	Chariot électrique	no
Buggy	Voiturette	200 F/18 holes
Clubs	Clubs	100 F/full day

Credit cards Cartes de crédit
VISA - CB - Eurocard - MasterCard

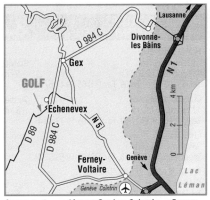

Access Accès : → Airport Genève-Cointrin → Ferney-Voltaire, → Gex, → Golf, on left hand side
Map 8 on page 179 Carte 8 Page 179

GOLF COURSE / PARCOURS — 14/20

Site	Site	
Maintenance	Entretien	
Architect	Architecte	Peter Harradine Olivier Dongradi
Type	Type	country, hilly
Relief	Relief	
Water in play	Eau en jeu	
Exp. to wind	Exposé au vent	
Trees in play	Arbres en jeu	

Scorecard Carte de score	Chp. Chp.	Mens Mess.	Ladies Da.
Length Long.	6142	5775	5180
Par	72	72	72

Advised golfing ability Niveau de jeu recommandé	0 12 24 36
Hcp required Handicap exigé	30

CLUB HOUSE & AMENITIES / CLUB HOUSE ET ANNEXES — 7/10

Pro shop	Pro-shop	
Driving range	Practice	
Sheltered	couvert	10 mats
On grass	sur herbe	no, 20 mats open air
Putting-green	putting-green	yes
Pitching-green	pitching green	yes

299

HOTEL FACILITIES / ENVIRONNEMENT HOTELIER — 5/10

HOTELS HÔTELS
Auberge des Chasseurs — Echenevex 2 km
15 rooms, D 800 F
Tel (33) 04 50 41 54 07, Fax (33) 04 50 41 90 61

La Mainaz — Mijoux 8 km
25 rooms, D 500 F
Tel (33) 04 50 41 31 10, Fax (33) 04 50 41 31 77

Le Parc — Gex 2 km
17 rooms, D 350 F
Tel (33) 04 50 41 50 18, Fax (33) 04 50 42 37 29

RESTAURANTS RESTAURANTS
La Champagne - Tel (33) 04 50 20 13 13 — Divonne 8 km
La Marée - Tel (33) 04 50 20 01 87 — Divonne 8 km
La Cravache - Tel (33) 04 50 41 69 61 — Gex 2 km

Peuplé de très beaux chênes, cet espace très vaste a permis de créer de larges fairways et de préserver l'isolement d'un trou à l'autre. Rocky Roquemore a dessiné un parcours de style américain sur fond de Pyrénées, avec des trous très variés, où l'on passe de la montagne aux plaines bordées d'obstacles d'eau. Les reliefs sont assez prononcés (sur trois trous), mais il était difficile de faire autrement dans cette superbe région et seuls les golfeurs en bonne condition physique pourront y évoluer sans voiturette. Avec près de 6200 mètres du fond, c'est un parcours solide pour les bons joueurs, mais les départs normaux permettent aux golfeurs de niveau moyen d'être à l'aise : les obstacles sont bien visibles, la stratégie assez évidente, les difficultés bien réparties. L'entretien est bon, mais le terrain est fragile par temps humide.

Lined with beautiful age-old oaks, this huge site gave the designer the possibility to lay out wide fairways and keep holes well apart. Rocky Roquemore has produced an American style layout set beneath the Pyrenees. Variety is the key word, ranging from mountain-side holes to lower-level holes edged with water hazards. It is pretty hilly (3 holes in particular) but it would have been difficult to do otherwise in this superb region. If you are not in top shape, take a buggy. This course plays 6,200 metres from the back tees, so is a good test for the better player, but the middle tees are perfect for the mid-handicapper. The hazards are visible, the strategy pretty obvious and difficulties are evenly spread around the course. Overall, the course is well looked after, but the terrain tends to suffer in wet conditions.

Makila Golf Club   1992

Route de Cambo-Biarritz
F - 64200 BASSUSSARRY

Office	Secrétariat	(33) 05 59 58 42 42
Pro shop	Pro-shop	(33) 05 59 58 42 42
Fax	Fax	(33) 05 59 58 42 48
Situation	Situation	

Biarritz (pop. 28 740), 5 km
Bayonne (pop. 40 050), 6 km

Annual closure	Fermeture annuelle	no
Weekly closure	Fermeture hebdomadaire	no

Fees main season
Tarifs haute saison 18 holes

	Week days Semaine	We/Bank holidays We/Férié
Individual Individuel	300 F	300 F
Couple Couple	550 F	550 F

Caddy	Caddy	no
Electric Trolley	Chariot électrique	no
Buggy	Voiturette	160 F/18 holes
Clubs	Clubs	100 F/18 holes

Credit cards Cartes de crédit
VISA - CB - Eurocard - MasterCard

300

Access Accès : A63, Exit (Sortie) N° 5 Bayonne Sud →
Cambo D932. Golf 800 m. after roundabout
Map 12 on page 186 Carte 12 Page 186

GOLF COURSE PARCOURS   14/20

Site	Site	▬▬▬▬
Maintenance	Entretien	▬▬▬▬
Architect	Architecte	Rocky Roquemore
Type	Type	parkland, hilly
Relief	Relief	▬▬▬
Water in play	Eau en jeu	▬▬
Exp. to wind	Exposé au vent	▬▬
Trees in play	Arbres en jeu	▬▬▬

Scorecard Carte de score	Chp. Chp.	Mens Mess.	Ladies Da.
Length Long.	6176	5790	5067
Par	72	72	72

Advised golfing ability	0	12	24	36
Niveau de jeu recommandé		▬▬▬▬		
Hcp required Handicap exigé	no			

CLUB HOUSE & AMENITIES CLUB HOUSE ET ANNEXES   6/10

Pro shop	Pro-shop	▬▬▬▬
Driving range	Practice	▬▬▬
Sheltered	couvert	10 mats
On grass	sur herbe	yes
Putting-green	putting-green	yes
Pitching-green	pitching green	no

HOTEL FACILITIES ENVIRONNEMENT HOTELIER   8/10

HOTELS HÔTELS

Le Palais   Biarritz
134 rooms, D 2 000 F   5 km
Tel (33) 05 59 41 64 00, Fax (33) 05 59 41 67 99

Château de Brindos   Anglet
12 rooms, D 1300 F   8 km
Tel (33) 05 59 23 17 68, Fax (33) 05 59 23 48 47

Chiberta   Anglet
98 rooms, D 1 000 F   8 km
Tel (33) 05 59 58 48 48, Fax (33) 05 59 63 57 84

RESTAURANTS RESTAURANTS

Café de Paris   Biarritz
Tel (33) 05 59 24 19 53   5 km

Auberge d'Achtal   Arcangues
Tel (33) 05 59 43 05 56   2 km

Les neuf premiers trous ont été conçus par Mackenzie Ross, puis remodelés et complétés par le cabinet Hawtree. Avec 5600 mètres, il peut paraître court, mais c'est un par 70. Les longs frappeurs pourront s'y déchaîner, sans trop craindre les arbres de ce grand parc (beaucoup de pins). Les joueurs moyens s'amuseront aussi, car les obstacles sont bien visibles, certains trous très courts, les roughs sont propres et les sous-bois bien nettoyés. Le terrain est assez plat pour être facilement marché, ce qui accentue la sensation générale de tranquillité et de golf reposant (à conseiller aux seniors). Les difficultés existent pourtant, mais elles sont aisément négociables si l'on possède un bon jeu de petits fers : les greens ne sont pas bien grands. L'environnement, l'ambiance amicale et l'utilisation rationnelle d'une surface réduite en font une halte agréable.

The first nine holes were designed by Mackenzie Ross, then completed and redesigned by Hawtree. It might appear short at just 5600 metres, but it is a par 70 where long hitters will be able to open their shoulders without worrying too much about the trees (there are a lot of pines). The average golfer can also have fun, because the hazards are clearly visible, a number of holes are short, the rough is trimmed and the undergrowth kept clear. The terrain is flat enough to make this an easily walkable course and add to the overall impression of a peaceful, relaxing golf course (recommended for seniors). But it is no push-over, and the difficulties are there to be negotiated - an easier proposition if your short irons are in good shape. Accuracy is at a premium because the greens are not enormous. The general setting, friendly atmosphere and rational utilisation of limited space make this a very pleasant stop-off.

Golf Club de Mazamet-La Barouge 1956
F - 81660 PONT-DE-LARN

Office	Secrétariat	(33) 05 63 61 06 72
Pro shop	Pro-shop	(33) 05 63 61 06 72
Fax	Fax	(33) 05 63 61 13 03
Situation	Situation	

Castres (pop. 44 810), 16 km
Toulouse (pop. 358 690), 84 km

Annual closure	Fermeture annuelle	no
Weekly closure	Fermeture hebdomadaire	no

Fees main season
Tarifs haute saison full day

	Week days Semaine	We/Bank holidays We/Férié
Individual Individuel	175 F	235 F
Couple Couple	350 F	470 F

Caddy	Caddy	no
Electric Trolley	Chariot électrique	no
Buggy	Voiturette	200 F/18 holes
Clubs	Clubs	no

Credit cards Cartes de crédit
VISA - CB - Eurocard - MasterCard

CASTRES
0   2   4 km

N 112
N 112
D 621
GOLF
D 65
MAZAMET
↓ Carcassone

Access Accès : Mazamet, N 112 → Castres, → Golf
Map 13 on page 188 Carte 13 Page 188

GOLF COURSE PARCOURS   13/20

Site	Site	
Maintenance	Entretien	
Architect	Architecte	Mackenzie Ross Fred Hawtree
Type	Type	parkland, forest
Relief	Relief	
Water in play	Eau en jeu	
Exp. to wind	Exposé au vent	
Trees in play	Arbres en jeu	

Scorecard Carte de score	Chp. Chp.	Mens Mess.	Ladies Da.
Length Long.	5635	5427	4898
Par	70	70	70

Advised golfing ability		0 12 24 36
Niveau de jeu recommandé		
Hcp required	Handicap exigé	no

CLUB HOUSE & AMENITIES CLUB HOUSE ET ANNEXES   5/10

Pro shop	Pro-shop	
Driving range	Practice	
Sheltered	couvert	6 mats
On grass	sur herbe	no
Putting-green	putting-green	yes
Pitching-green	pitching green	no

301

HOTEL FACILITIES ENVIRONNEMENT HOTELIER   4/10

HOTELS HÔTELS
La Métairie Neuve   Bout-du-Pont-de-Larn
14 rooms, D 480 F   1 km
Tel (33) 05 63 97 73 50, Fax (33) 05 63 61 94 75

H. Jourdan   Mazamet
11 rooms, D 360 F   1 km
Tel (33) 05 63 61 56 93, Fax (33) 05 63 61 83 38

Demeure de Flore   Lacabarède
12 rooms, D 490 F   16 km
Tel (33) 05 63 98 32 32, Fax (33) 05 63 98 47 56

Occitan   Castres
42 rooms, D 420 F   14 km
Tel (33) 05 63 35 34 20, Fax (33) 05 63 35 70 32

RESTAURANTS RESTAURANT
H. Jourdan   Mazamet
Tel (33) 05 63 61 56 93   1 km

Si le parcours des «Vignes» est une agréable promenade en plaine et dans une pinède, le parcours des «Châteaux» est de meilleur cru encore (nous sommes en plein Bordelais), et sa réputation est largement méritée. Dû au crayon habile de l'Américain Bill Coore, il se déroule dans un paysage de plaine dénudé, modelé comme un links, mais sans les dunes. Des obstacles d'eau et des «ditchs» viennent parfois perturber la quiétude du golfeur, mais les ondulations du fairway, le dessin des bunkers, la bonne densité des roughs et le profil des vastes greens en font l'un des parcours les plus remarquables de la région. Les amateurs de paysages boisés peuvent sans doute lui reprocher une légère monotonie visuelle, mais il s'avère de plus en plus intéressant, à mesure qu'on le joue. C'est le parcours le plus technique de la région, et très facile à jouer à pied. Plus il prend de la maturité, plus il s'impose parmi les grands parcours français.

While "Les Vignes" course (The Vines) is a pleasant stroll through open country and a pine forest, the «Châteaux» course is an even better vintage (we are to the west of Bordeaux) and well worth its reputation. Designed by the American Bill Coore, the course unfolds over flat open country and is designed to play like a links course, but without the dunes. Some water hazards and ditches can be a little trying, but the rolling fairways, the well-designed bunkers, the thick rough and the profile of the huge greens make this one of the region's finest courses. People who prefer woodland courses will probably knock "Les Châteaux" as being visually boring, but this course gets better and better the more you play it. The most technical course in the region and easily walkable. The more it matures, the more Le Médoc has to be ranked amongst the best courses in France.

Golf du Médoc — 1989

Chemin de Courmateau
F - 33290 LE PIAN-MEDOC

Office	Secrétariat	(33) 05 56 70 11 90
Pro shop	Pro-shop	(33) 05 56 70 11 90
Fax	Fax	(33) 05 56 70 11 99
Situation	Situation	

Bordeaux (pop. 211 200), 15 km

| Annual closure | Fermeture annuelle | no |
| Weekly closure | Fermeture hebdomadaire | no |

Fees main season
Tarifs haute saison full day

	Week days Semaine	We/Bank holidays We/Férié
Individual Individuel	250 F	300 F
Couple Couple	500 F	600 F

Caddy	Caddy	on request
Electric Trolley	Chariot électrique	80 F/18 holes
Buggy	Voiturette	200 F/18 holes
Clubs	Clubs	80 F/18 holes

Credit cards Cartes de crédit
VISA - CB - Eurocard - MasterCard - AMEX

Access Accès : Bordeaux, Ring road (Rocade), Exit (Sortie) N° 7 → Lacanau, go right on D1 → Le Verdon
Map 9 on page 180 Carte 9 Page 180

GOLF COURSE PARCOURS — 18/20

Site	Site	
Maintenance	Entretien	
Architect	Architecte	Bill Coore
Type	Type	open country, links
Relief	Relief	
Water in play	Eau en jeu	
Exp. to wind	Exposé au vent	
Trees in play	Arbres en jeu	

Scorecard Carte de score	Chp. Chp.	Mens Mess.	Ladies Da.
Length Long.	6316	5765	5120
Par	71	71	71

| Advised golfing ability Niveau de jeu recommandé | 0 12 24 36 |
| Hcp required Handicap exigé | no |

CLUB HOUSE & AMENITIES CLUB HOUSE ET ANNEXES — 7/10

Pro shop	Pro-shop	
Driving range	Practice	
Sheltered	couvert	15 mats
On grass	sur herbe	yes
Putting-green	putting-green	yes
Pitching-green	pitching green	yes

HOTEL FACILITIES ENVIRONNEMENT HOTELIER — 5/10

HOTELS HÔTELS
Relais de Margaux — Margaux
61 rooms, D 900 F — 13 km
Tel (33) 05 57 88 38 30, Fax (33) 05 57 88 31 73

Bayonne — Bordeaux
36 rooms, D 800 F — 15 km
Tel (33) 05 56 48 00 88, Fax (33) 05 56 48 41 60

RESTAURANTS RESTAURANTS
Le Chapon Fin — Bordeaux
Tel (33) 05 56 79 10 10 — 15 km

Le Vieux Bordeaux — Bordeaux
Tel (33) 05 56 52 94 36 — 15 km

Jean Ramet — Bordeaux
Tel (33) 05 56 44 12 51 — 15 km

302

Sur un terrain généralement plat, l'ensemble des 36 trous du golf du Médoc peut être facilement joué dans la journée. Après le paysage très peu arboré du parcours des «Châteaux», le parcours des «Vignes» offre un contraste heureux, et des difficultés moins affirmées. Les amoureux des parcours dans les arbres seront comblés car un certain nombre de trous se situent dans une petite pinède, aux ombrages plaisants. Les autres trous offrent une végétation plus légère, mais néammoins souvent en jeu. Tout comme sur l'autre parcours, les greens sont de bonne qualité, et sans reliefs excessifs. Certes, «Les Châteaux» représente un défi plus constant, mais cet ensemble s'est incontestablement imposé comme l'un des tout meilleurs dans une région très touristique, et comme l'ensemble le plus intéressant à proximité immédiate de Bordeaux.

Laid out over what is generally flat terrain, the 36 holes at Le Pian Médoc can easily be played in one day. After the tree-less landscape of "Les Châteaux", "Les Vignes" provides a welcome contrast and plays a little more easily. Golfers who love playing woodland courses will be spoilt here, as a number of holes wind their way through a pretty and shady pine forest. The others provide a little lighter vegetation which nonetheless is very much in play. As with "Les Châteaux", the greens are excellent and not too undulating. Although a little less challenging, "Les Vignes" is still one of the best courses in a very busy tourist region, and the two courses together are the most attractive golfing proposition within the immediate vicinity of Bordeaux.

Golf du Médoc — 1991

Chemin de Courmateau
F - 33290 LE PIAN-MEDOC

Office	Secrétariat	(33) 05 56 70 11 90
Pro shop	Pro-shop	(33) 05 56 70 11 90
Fax	Fax	(33) 05 56 70 11 99
Situation	Situation	

Bordeaux (pop. 211 200), 15 km

Annual closure	Fermeture annuelle	no
Weekly closure	Fermeture hebdomadaire	no

Fees main season
Tarifs haute saison full day

	Week days Semaine	We/Bank holidays We/Férié
Individual Individuel	250 F	300 F
Couple Couple	500 F	600 F

Caddy	Caddy	on request
Electric Trolley	Chariot électrique	80 F/18 holes
Buggy	Voiturette	200 F/18 holes
Clubs	Clubs	80 F/18 holes

Credit cards Cartes de crédit
VISA - CB - Eurocard - MasterCard - AMEX

Access Accès : Bordeaux, Ring road (Rocade), Exit (Sortie) N° 7 → Lacanau, go right on D1 → Le Verdon
Map 9 on page 180 Carte 9 Page 180

GOLF COURSE PARCOURS — 15/20

Site	Site	
Maintenance	Entretien	
Architect	Architecte	Rod Whitman
Type	Type	forest, open country
Relief	Relief	
Water in play	Eau en jeu	
Exp. to wind	Exposé au vent	
Trees in play	Arbres en jeu	

Scorecard Carte de score	Chp. Chp.	Mens Mess.	Ladies Da.
Length Long.	6220	5694	5136
Par	71	71	71

Advised golfing ability Niveau de jeu recommandé	0	12	24	36
Hcp required Handicap exigé	no			

CLUB HOUSE & AMENITIES CLUB HOUSE ET ANNEXES — 7/10

Pro shop	Pro-shop	
Driving range	Practice	
Sheltered	couvert	15 mats
On grass	sur herbe	yes
Putting-green	putting-green	yes
Pitching-green	pitching green	yes

303

HOTEL FACILITIES ENVIRONNEMENT HOTELIER — 5/10

HOTELS HÔTELS
Relais de Margaux — Margaux
61 rooms, D 900 F — 13 km
Tel (33) 05 57 88 38 30, Fax (33) 05 57 88 31 73

Bayonne — Bordeaux
36 rooms, D 800 F — 15 km
Tel (33) 05 56 48 00 88, Fax (33) 05 56 48 41 60

RESTAURANTS RESTAURANTS
Le Chapon Fin — Bordeaux
Tel (33) 05 56 79 10 10 — 15 km

Le Vieux Bordeaux — Bordeaux
Tel (33) 05 56 52 94 36 — 15 km

Jean Ramet — Bordeaux
Tel (33) 05 56 44 12 51 — 15 km

Ce parcours remarquable a été réalisé dans la forêt de pins des Landes (treize trous), et en bord de mer (cinq trous). L'architecte Robert Trent Jones l'a incontestablement signé, avec des enjeux techniques et stratégiques dénotant une connaissance profonde du golf : si les joueurs de haut niveau y trouveront un «challenge» difficile, partir des départs avancés permet davantage d'erreurs. Visuellement, ses fameux bunkers dentelés défendent remarquablement les greens, dont trois sont pratiquement aveugles ; leurs surfaces sont modelées sans excès. Les fairways largement tondus favorisent le rythme de jeu, et la nature sablonneuse du sol permet de jouer facilement toute l'année. Il n'est pas trop fatigant, mais les distances entre greens et départs sont parfois importantes. Un bon 9 trous annexe permet d'occuper les débutants de la famille.

This remarkable course was laid out in the pine forests of Les Landes (for 13 holes) and along the coast (five holes). Welcome to a typical Robert Trent Jones design, where the technical and strategic challenges reflect an in-depth knowledge of golf. While the more proficient golfer will find this a tough challenge, playing from the forward tees is, funnily enough, often more conducive to error. The famous jagged bunkers are a remarkable form of defence for the greens, three of which are virtually blind, and the putting surfaces are neatly but never excessively contoured. The closely-cropped fairways help speed up the game and the sandy sub-soil keeps the course easily playable all year. This is not a tiring course, but distances between holes are sometimes a little on the long side. A good adjoining 9 hole course is ideal for beginners in the family.

Golf de Moliets 1989
Rue Mathieu Desbieys
F - 40660 MOLIETS

Office	Secrétariat	(33) 05 58 48 54 65
Pro shop	Pro-shop	(33) 05 58 48 54 65
Fax	Fax	(33) 05 58 48 54 88
Situation	Situation	

Dax (pop. 19 310), 35 km - Bayonne (pop. 40 050), 40 km

Annual closure	Fermeture annuelle	no
Weekly closure	Fermeture hebdomadaire	no

Fees main season
Tarifs haute saison 18 holes

	Week days Semaine	We/Bank holidays We/Férié
Individual Individuel	330 F	330 F
Couple Couple	590 F	590 F

Caddy	Caddy	on request
Electric Trolley	Chariot électrique	no
Buggy	Voiturette	150 F/18 holes
Clubs	Clubs	60 F/full day

Credit cards Cartes de crédit
VISA - CB - Eurocard - MasterCard

304

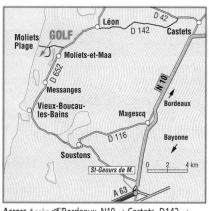

Access Accès : • Bordeaux, N10 → Castets. D142 → Léon, Moliets • Bayonne, N10 → Magescq, D116 → Soustons, D652 → Vieux-Boucau-les-Bains, Moliets
Map 12 on page 186 Carte 12 Page 186

GOLF COURSE
PARCOURS 17/20

Site	Site	▰▰▰▰▱
Maintenance	Entretien	▰▰▰▱▱
Architect	Architecte	Robert Trent Jones
Type	Type	forest, links
Relief	Relief	▰▰▱▱▱
Water in play	Eau en jeu	▰▱▱▱▱
Exp. to wind	Exposé au vent	▰▰▰▱▱
Trees in play	Arbres en jeu	▰▰▰▱▱

Scorecard	Chp.	Mens	Ladies
Carte de score	Chp.	Mess.	Da.
Length Long.	6172	5823	5329
Par	72	72	72

Advised golfing ability		0	12	24	36
Niveau de jeu recommandé			▰▰▰▱		
Hcp required	Handicap exigé	30			

CLUB HOUSE & AMENITIES
CLUB HOUSE ET ANNEXES 6/10

Pro shop	Pro-shop	▰▰▰▱▱
Driving range	Practice	▰▰▰▱▱
Sheltered	couvert	10 mats
On grass	sur herbe	yes
Putting-green	putting-green	yes
Pitching-green	pitching green	yes

HOTEL FACILITIES
ENVIRONNEMENT HOTELIER 5/10

HOTELS HÔTELS
Royal Green Parc | Moliets
Villas 5 500 F/week | on site
Tel (33) 05 58 48 57 57, Fax (33) 05 58 48 57 58

Hôtel du Golf | Moliets
4 rooms, D 800 F | on site
Tel (33) 05 58 49 16 00, Fax (33) 05 58 49 16 29

Côte d'Argent | Vieux-Boucau
34 rooms, D 330 F | 10 km
Tel (33) 05 58 48 13 17, Fax (33) 05 58 48 01 15

RESTAURANTS RESTAURANTS
Restaurant du Golf | Moliets
Tel (33) 05 58 48 44 55 | on site

Relais de la Poste | Magescq 20 km
Tel (33) 05 58 47 70 25

MONTE CARLO (MONT AGEL) ✳ 14 6 7

Quand on évoque le golf de Monte Carlo, on pourrait s'attendre à une sorte de produit à l'américaine, flashy. Bref, très Principauté. En fait, le plus somptueux ici, c'est le panorama. A plus de 800 mètres, Monaco apparaît en contrebas comme un village de poupée, et la vue s'étend à l'infini sur la Méditerranée, les Riviera française et italienne, parfois même la Corse. Quand au golf, il est d'une surprenante sobriété, ce qui est bien la marque du vrai luxe. On vient ici pour jouer dans une atmosphère presque familiale, pas pour se faire voir. Le parcours a fait l'objet, depuis plusieurs années, d'impressionnants travaux pour lui donner un peu de longueur et de largeur. Très britannique de style, il n'est certes pas d'une grande difficulté, à priori, mais les greens sont assez petits, les pieds pas toujours à plat. La précision et la finesse l'emporteront toujours sur la force. Ici, on vous demande de l'élégance... princière bien sûr.

When you talk about golf in Monte Carlo, you might expect a sort of sumptuous, American style and even flashy course... worthy of a principality, maybe. In actual fact, the most sumptuous part about this layout is the view. Monaco lies 800 metres below you like a doll's village and the vista stretches over the Mediterranean right across the French and Italian Rivieras. Sometimes you can even see Corsica. The actual course is a picture of sobriety, but isn't that the sign of real luxury? You come and play here in an almost family atmosphere, not just to be seen. In recent years the course has been given some impressive refurbishing work to make it longer and wider. Very British in style, it is certainly not the hardest course around, on the face of it, but the greens are smallish, flat lies are rare to come by. Accuracy and finesse are more valuable assets than brute strength on a course where you are asked for a little golfing elegance, in princely style, of course.

Monte Carlo Golf Club		1911
Route du Mont Agel		
06320 LA TURBIE		
Office	Secrétariat	(33) 04 92 41 50 70
Pro shop	Pro-shop	(33) 04 92 41 04 46
Fax	Fax	(33) 04 93 41 09 55
Situation	Situation	
Monaco (pop. 29 972), 15 km - Nice (pop. 342 439), 16 km		
Annual closure	Fermeture annuelle	no
Weekly closure	Fermeture hebdomadaire	no

Fees main season		
Tarifs haute saison 18 holes		
	Week days Semaine	We/Bank holidays We/Férié
Individual Individuel	400 F	500 F
Couple Couple	800 F	1000 F

Caddy	Caddy	250 F
Electric Trolley	Chariot électrique	120 F/18 holes
Buggy	Voiturette	no
Clubs	Clubs	80 F/full day

Credit cards Cartes de crédit
VISA - Eurocard - MasterCard

Access Accès : 10 km N. of Monaco. → La Turbie, → Mont Agel, Monte Carlo Golf Club.
Map 14 on page 191 Carte 14 Page 191

GOLF COURSE / PARCOURS — 14/20

Site	Site	
Maintenance	Entretien	
Architect	Architecte	unknown
Type	Type	hilly, parkland
Relief	Relief	
Water in play	Eau en jeu	
Exp. to wind	Exposé au vent	
Trees in play	Arbres en jeu	

Scorecard Carte de score	Chp. Chp.	Mens Mess.	Ladies Da.
Length Long.	5683	5683	4938
Par	71	71	71

Advised golfing ability	0	12	24	36
Niveau de jeu recommandé				
Hcp required Handicap exigé	32			

CLUB HOUSE & AMENITIES / CLUB HOUSE ET ANNEXES — 6/10

Pro shop	Pro-shop	
Driving range	Practice	
Sheltered	couvert	4 mats
On grass	sur herbe	no
Putting-green	putting-green	yes
Pitching-green	pitching green	yes

HOTEL FACILITIES / ENVIRONNEMENT HOTELIER — 7/10

HOTELS HÔTELS
Hotel de Paris — Monaco — 15 km
160 rooms, D 3400 F
Tel (377) 92 16 30 00, Fax (377) 92 16 38 50

Hotel Hermitage — Monaco — 15 km
215 rooms, D 2950 F
Tel (377) 92 16 40 00, Fax (377) 92 16 38 52

Balmoral — Monaco — 15 km
64 rooms, D 1050 F
Tel (377) 93 50 62 37, Fax (377) 93 15 08 69

RESTAURANTS RESTAURANTS
Café de Paris — Monaco — 15 km
Tel (377) 92 16 20 20

Louis XV — Monaco — 15 km
Tel (377) 92 16 30 01

Chez Gianni - Tel (377) 93 30 46 33 — Monaco 15 km

305

MONTPELLIER-MASSANE ♪ 16 7 5

Dessiné par Ronald Fream, le golf de Massane n'est certes pas à conseiller aux débutants, car ils risquent de sentir certaines difficultés au dessus de leurs moyens. Et, pour vraiment s'amuser, les joueurs simplement moyens devront absolument choisir les départs avancés. En revanche, les golfeurs confirmés y trouveront de quoi tester l'ensemble de leur jeu. De nombreux obstacles d'eau, des bunkers frontaux, différentes alternatives d'attaque des trous obligent à savoir précisément quand décider de rester court ou de passer les obstacles, quelle tactique choisir : il faut parfois se résigner à la prudence pour ramener un bon score. Ce parcours se joue avec ses clubs, et vraiment avec sa tête. Les bunkers et les greens sont remarquablement dessinés, ce qui accentue encore la nécessité d'un petit jeu complet et bien aiguisé. Un parcours parfois controversé, mais vraiment à connaître.

Designed by Ronald Fream, the Massane course is definitely not for beginners, but if the average hacker wants to enjoy a good round of golf, he should make straight for the front tees. By contrast, skilled golfers will find this an excellent test for every aspect of their game. Numerous water hazards, front bunkers and different lines of approach to the green force players into tactical decisions and into choosing exactly when to lay up short or when to carry the hazard. A good score sometimes comes more from caution than from daring. This is another course where you really do play with your clubs and your brains. The bunkers and greens are remarkably well designed and only emphasise the need for an all-round and well-honed short game. A sometimes controversial course but one worth knowing.

Golf de Montpellier-Massane   1988
Mas de Massane
F - 34670 BAILLARGUES

Office	Secrétariat	(33) 04 67 87 87 89
Pro shop	Pro-shop	(33) 04 67 87 87 89
Fax	Fax	(33) 04 67 87 87 90

Situation Situation
Montpellier (pop. 210 860), 13 km
Nîmes (pop. 128 470), 34 km

Annual closure	Fermeture annuelle	no
Weekly closure	Fermeture hebdomadaire	no

Fees main season
Tarifs haute saison full day

	Week days Semaine	We/Bank holidays We/Férié
Individual Individuel	270 F	270 F
Couple Couple	540 F	540 F

Caddy	Caddy	no
Electric Trolley	Chariot électrique	70 F/18 holes
Buggy	Voiturette	180 F/18 holes
Clubs	Clubs	60 F/full day

Credit cards Cartes de crédit
VISA - CB - Eurocard - MasterCard - AMEX - DC

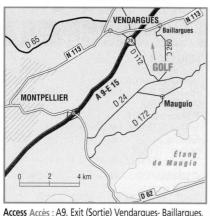

Access Accès : A9, Exit (Sortie) Vendargues- Baillargues,
N113 → Baillargues
Map 13 on page 189 Carte 13 Page 189

GOLF COURSE
PARCOURS   16/20

Site	Site	■■■□□
Maintenance	Entretien	■■■■□
Architect	Architecte	Ronald Fream
Type	Type	open country, residential
Relief	Relief	■□□□□
Water in play	Eau en jeu	■■■□□
Exp. to wind	Exposé au vent	■■■□□
Trees in play	Arbres en jeu	■■□□□

Scorecard	Chp.	Mens	Ladies
Carte de score	Chp.	Mess.	Da.
Length Long.	6550	6044	5098
Par	72	72	72

Advised golfing ability		0 12 24 36
Niveau de jeu recommandé		■■■■□
Hcp required	Handicap exigé	no

CLUB HOUSE & AMENITIES
CLUB HOUSE ET ANNEXES   7/10

Pro shop	Pro-shop	■■■■□
Driving range	Practice	■■■□□
Sheltered	couvert	12 mats
On grass	sur herbe	yes (120 places)
Putting-green	putting-green	yes
Pitching-green	pitching green	yes

HOTEL FACILITIES
ENVIRONNEMENT HOTELIER   5/10

HOTELS HÔTELS
Golf-Hôtel   on site
32 rooms, D 540 F
Tel (33) 04 67 87 87 87, Fax (33) 04 67 87 87 90

New Hôtel du Midi   Montpellier
47 rooms, D 380 F   13 km
Tel (33) 04 67 92 69 61, Fax (33) 04 67 92 73 63

Demeure des Brousses   Montpellier
17 rooms, D 580 F   13 km
Tel (33) 04 67 65 77 66, Fax (33) 04 67 22 22 17

RESTAURANTS RESTAURANTS
Jardin des Sens   Montpellier
Tel (33) 04 67 79 63 38   13 km
Le Chandelier   Montpellier
Tel (33) 04 67 15 34 38   13 km

306

L'Albatros (site de plusieurs Peugeot Opens de France) est un parcours de championnat, réservé aux moins de 24 de handicap. Dessiné par H. Chesneau et R. von Hagge, il alterne des trous à l'américaine et des trous typiques de bord de mer, insinués entre d'énormes dunes artificielles prévues pour accueillir les spectateurs. En contrebas sur le parcours, le dépaysement est total. La moindre erreur stratégique ou technique peut s'avérer catastrophique sur chacun des 18 trous, défendus par toutes sortes d'obstacles, mais aux difficultés bien réparties, où les quatre derniers trous sont toujours décisifs. Il vaut mieux jouer en match-play si l'on n'est pas dans sa meilleure forme. Pour atténuer cette exigence, le parcours est d'une parfaite franchise, et le résultat est à hauteur de la performance du joueur. A connaître absolument... même si le site est laid (l'hôtel !) et l'entretien pas toujours à la hauteur.

The «Albatros» (the venue for several Peugeot French Opens) is a championship course reserved for players with a minimum handicap of 24. Designed by Hubert Chesneau and Von Hagge, this is a combination course where US style target golf alternates with typical links holes set amidst huge artificial dunes, designed with the spectators in mind. Down in the playing arena it's whole a different story. The slightest strategic or technical slip can lead to disaster on any one of the 18 holes, all of which are defended by every sort of hazard. And although difficulties are finely balanced over the whole course, the last 4 holes are decisive. If you are not on top of your game, try match-play. Although demanding, the course is forthright and the score on your card the reflection of just how well you played! An absolute must... even though surroundings and maintenance does not always measure up.

Le Golf National — 1990

2, avenue du Golf
F - 78280 GUYANCOURT

Office	Secrétariat	(33) 01 30 43 36 00
Pro shop	Pro-shop	(33) 01 30 43 36 00
Fax	Fax	(33) 01 30 43 85 58
Situation	Situation	

Paris (pop. 2 175 200), 30 km Versailles (pop. 87 790), 14 km

Annual closure	Fermeture annuelle	no
Weekly closure	Fermeture hebdomadaire	

wednesday mercredi (01/11 → 30/06)

Fees main season
Tarifs haute saison 18 holes

	Week days Semaine	We/Bank holidays We/Férié
Individual Individuel	260 F	390 F
Couple Couple	520 F	780 F

Seniors (tuesday/mardi) / Ladies (thursday/jeudi) :
GF + lunch 220 F

Caddy	Caddy	no
Electric Trolley	Chariot électrique	70 F/18 holes
Buggy	Voiturette	no
Clubs	Clubs	50 F/full day

Credit cards Cartes de crédit
VISA - CB - Eurocard - MasterCard

Access Accès : • Paris A13, A12 → St-Quentin en Y., Exit (Sortie) Montigny-le-Bretonneux • Paris N118 → Chartres (A10), Exit Saclay, D36 → Châteaufort, Trappes **Map 15 on page 192** Carte 15 Page 192

GOLF COURSE / PARCOURS — 18/20

Site	Site	▬▬▬□□□□
Maintenance	Entretien	▬▬▬▬□□□
Architect	Architecte	Hubert Chesneau
		Robert von Hagge consultant
Type	Type	links
Relief	Relief	▬▬□□□□□
Water in play	Eau en jeu	▬▬▬▬□□□
Exp. to wind	Exposé au vent	▬▬▬▬▬□□
Trees in play	Arbres en jeu	▬▬□□□□□

Scorecard Carte de score	Chp. Chp.	Mens Mess.	Ladies Da.
Length Long.	6515	6155	5200
Par	72	72	72

Advised golfing ability
Niveau de jeu recommandé
0 12 24 36
▬▬▬▬▬▬□

Hcp required Handicap exigé 24 Men. 28 Ladies (We)

CLUB HOUSE & AMENITIES / CLUB HOUSE ET ANNEXES — 5/10

Pro shop	Pro-shop	▬▬▬▬□□□
Driving range	Practice	▬▬▬▬□□□
Sheltered	couvert	30 mats
On grass	sur herbe	yes
Putting-green	putting-green	yes
Pitching-green	pitching green	yes

HOTEL FACILITIES / ENVIRONNEMENT HOTELIER — 6/10

HOTELS HÔTELS

Novotel — Guyancourt
130 rooms, D 690 F — on site
Tel (33) 01 30 57 65 65, Fax (33) 01 30 57 65 00

Abbaye les Vaux de Cernay — Cernay-la-Ville
58 rooms, D 800 F — 17 km
Tel (33) 01 34 85 23 00, Fax (33) 01 34 85 11 60

Le Relais de Voisins — Voisin-le-Bretonneux
54 rooms, D 295 F — 2 km
Tel (33) 01 30 44 11 55, Fax (33) 01 30 44 02 04

RESTAURANTS RESTAURANTS

Les Trois Marches — Versailles
Tel (33) 01 39 50 13 21 — 14 km

La Belle Epoque — Châteaufort
Tel (33) 01 39 56 95 48 — 4 km

307

NEW GOLF DEAUVILLE ROUGE BLANC ✳ 15 7 8

Un ensemble de 27 trous avec un bon 9 trous et un 18 trous de bon niveau, de style très britannique, assez vallonné sans être trop fatigant. Dessiné en 1929 par Tom Simpson, il a été agrandi et beaucoup remanié par Henry Cotton en 1964. Dans un agréable paysage normand, ce parcours avait tendance à se banaliser mais un dessin plus précis des limites de fairways et des roughs, la modification de certains bunkers, la décoration même lui ont donné une nouvelle jeunesse, et imposent maintenant de réfléchir sur la stratégie : les joueurs de bon niveau devraient y revenir. Il s'agit certes d'un golf commercial, pour les golfeurs en week-end et en vacances, et il convient d'assurer leur plaisir, mais les progrès réalisés incitent à le remonter notablement dans la hiérarchie. C'est de nouveau le meilleur parcours de la région, on souhaite que l'accueil y soit toujours agréable.

A 27-hole complex with a good 9-hole course and an excellent British style 18-hole layout over rolling countryside. Designed in 1929 by Tom Simpson, it was enlarged and very much restyled by Henry Cotton in 1964. Set in pleasant Norman countryside, the course was beginning to look a bit ordinary, but clearer demarcation of the fairways and rough, plus changes to certain bunkers and to the general decor have given Deauville a new lease of life. Good players should and almost certainly do return for more of the same. This is a business venture, of course, for weekenders and holiday-makers, and their enjoyment is naturally important, but with what has been achieved here, we can only review the course's ranking upwards. This is once again the best course in the region, and we would like to see the hospitality always friendly.

New Golf de Deauville — 1929

Saint-Arnoult
F - 14800 DEAUVILLE

Office	Secrétariat	(33) 02 31 14 24 24
Pro shop	Pro-shop	(33) 02 31 14 24 24
Fax	Fax	(33) 02 31 14 24 25
Situation	Situation	

Deauville (pop. 4 260), 3 km

Annual closure Fermeture annuelle — no

Weekly closure Fermeture hebdomadaire — tuesday
mardi (except holidays)

Fees main season
Tarifs haute saison full day

	Week days Semaine	We/Bank holidays We/Férié
Individual Individuel	300 F	400 F
Couple Couple	600 F	800 F

After 16.00: GF 200 F (weekdays), 250 F (weekends)

Caddy	Caddy	180 F/18 holes
Electric Trolley	Chariot électrique	no
Buggy	Voiturette	200 F/18 holes
Clubs	Clubs	50 F/full day

Credit cards Cartes de crédit
VISA - CB - Eurocard - MasterCard - AMEX - DC

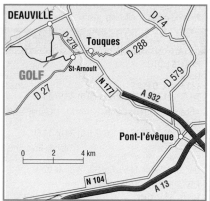

Access Accès : Paris A13, Exit (Sortie) Deauville,
N177 → Deauville. Touques, D27 → New Golf
Map 2 on page 167 Carte 2 Page 167

GOLF COURSE PARCOURS — 15/20

Site	Site	
Maintenance	Entretien	
Architect	Architecte	Tom Simpson
		Henry Cotton
Type	Type	parkland, copse
Relief	Relief	
Water in play	Eau en jeu	
Exp. to wind	Exposé au vent	
Trees in play	Arbres en jeu	

Scorecard Carte de score	Chp. Chp.	Mens Mess.	Ladies Da.
Length Long.	5951	5705	5035
Par	71	71	71

Advised golfing ability — 0 12 24 36
Niveau de jeu recommandé
Hcp required Handicap exigé — 24 Men, 28 Ladies

CLUB HOUSE & AMENITIES CLUB HOUSE ET ANNEXES — 7/10

Pro shop	Pro-shop	
Driving range	Practice	
Sheltered	couvert	22 mats
On grass	sur herbe	yes (summer)
Putting-green	putting-green	yes
Pitching-green	pitching green	yes

HOTEL FACILITIES ENVIRONNEMENT HOTELIER — 8/10

HOTELS HÔTELS

Hôtel du Golf — Deauville
180 rooms, D 1 800 F — on site
Tel (33) 02 31 14 24 00, Fax (33) 02 31 14 24 01

Normandy — Deauville
252 rooms, D 1 600 F — 3 km
Tel (33) 02 31 98 66 22, Fax (33) 02 31 98 66 23

Ferme St-Siméon — Honfleur
31 rooms, D 2 000 F — 15 km
Tel (33) 02 31 81 78 00, Fax (33) 02 31 89 48 48

RESTAURANTS RESTAURANTS

Le Central — Trouville
Tel (33) 01 31 88 80 84 — 5 km

Le Ciro's — Deauville
Tel (33) 02 31 14 31 31 — 3 km

Ferme St-Siméon — Honfleur
Tel (33) 02 31 81 78 00 — 15 km

308

D'une année sur l'autre, on a plaisir à retrouver ce « classique » de la région, et de tradition sportive bien établie. Comme un ami d'enfance, il ne change pas. Dessiné par Morandi et Donald Harradine, il s'impose toujours comme un vrai parcours de championnat, surtout quand souffle le vent. Alors, les chênes et cyprès bleus deviennent redoutables, et les balles basses obligatoires, d'autant que quelques obstacles d'eau stratégiques viennent perturber le jugement comme la confiance. Les greens sont généralement bien dessinés, pas toujours très vastes. Pour les bons joueurs, la précision devra s'allier alors à la puissance, car les trous sont rarement courts des départs arrière : les joueurs lucides ne devront pas hésiter à choisir les départs normaux. Ce golf toujours bien entretenu est très fréquenté par ses nombreux membres, il est conseillé de réserver en toute saison.

Year in year out, it's always a pleasure to play this "classic" course which enjoys a well established sporting tradition. Like a life-long friend, Nîmes Campagne never changes. Designed by Morandi and Donald Harradine, this is a real championship course, especially when the wind blows. Then the oaks and the blue cypress trees are formidable foes, which make low-flighted balls a must, especially since a few strategic water hazards can affect both judgment and confidence. The greens are generally well-designed and not always that large. For the better player, the course demands both power and precision, as holes are seldom short from the back tees. Clear-headed average golfers should use the normal tees. The course is very well upkept and played by a large number of members, so whatever the season, always book a tee-off time.

Golf de Nîmes-Campagne		1968
Route de Saint-Gilles		
F - 30900 NIMES		

Office	Secrétariat	(33) 04 66 70 17 37
Pro shop	Pro-shop	(33) 04 66 70 17 37
Fax	Fax	(33) 04 66 70 03 14
Situation	Situation	
Nîmes (pop. 128 470), 10 km		
Annual closure	Fermeture annuelle	no
Weekly closure	Fermeture hebdomadaire	no

Fees main season
Tarifs haute saison full day

	Week days Semaine	We/Bank holidays We/Férié
Individual Individuel	270 F	270 F
Couple Couple	5400 F	500 F

After 17.00 : – 50 %

Caddy	Caddy	no
Electric Trolley	Chariot électrique	no
Buggy	Voiturette	150 F/18 holes
Clubs	Clubs	80 F/full day

Credit cards Cartes de crédit
VISA - CB - Eurocard - MasterCard

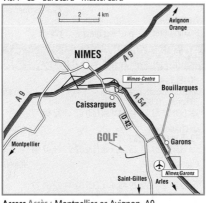

Access Accès : Montpellier or Avignon, A9,
Exit (Sortie) Nîmes Centre, D42 → Saint-Gilles,
go right of the airport, → Golf
Map 13 on page 189 Carte 13 Page 189

GOLF COURSE
PARCOURS 16/20

Site	Site	
Maintenance	Entretien	
Architect	Architecte	Léonard Morandi Donald Harradine
Type	Type	country, parkland
Relief	Relief	
Water in play	Eau en jeu	
Exp. to wind	Exposé au vent	
Trees in play	Arbres en jeu	

Scorecard Carte de score	Chp. Chp.	Mens Mess.	Ladies Da.
Length Long.	6135	5599	5045
Par	72	72	72

Advised golfing ability		0	12	24	36
Niveau de jeu recommandé					
Hcp required	Handicap exigé	35			

CLUB HOUSE & AMENITIES
CLUB HOUSE ET ANNEXES 7/10

Pro shop	Pro-shop	
Driving range	Practice	
Sheltered	couvert	2 mats
On grass	sur herbe	no, 20 mats open air
Putting-green	putting-green	yes
Pitching-green	pitching green	yes

HOTEL FACILITIES
ENVIRONNEMENT HOTELIER 6/10

HOTELS HÔTELS
Imperator Concorde   Nîmes
61 rooms, D 1 000 F   10 km
Tel (33) 04 66 21 90 30, Fax (33) 04 66 67 70 25

Les Aubuns   Caissargues
30 rooms, D 495 F   6 km
Tel (33) 04 66 70 10 44, Fax (33) 04 66 70 14 97

New Hôtel La Baume   Nîmes
34 rooms, D 420 F   10 km
Tel (33) 04 66 76 28 42, Fax (33) 04 66 76 28 45

RESTAURANTS RESTAURANTS
Alexandre   Garons
Tel (33) 04 66 70 08 99   4 km

Les Alizés   Nîmes
Tel (33) 04 66 67 08 17   10 km

309

Les trois 9 trous sont combinables, mais « L'Etang », assez dénudé et accidenté, n'est pas aussi caractéristique que « Le Bocage » (dans un paysage typiquement normand) et « La Mer ». Ces deux derniers parcours forment la combinaison la plus cohérente au plan du jeu et de l'unité esthétique, où l'architecte Yves Bureau a utilisé les reliefs naturels sans trop bouleverser le terrain, ponctuant la route des greens de quelques grands bunkers. «La Mer», assez vallonné, propose quelques trous sur un plateau dominant l'une des plages du Débarquement, avec de magnifiques points de vue sur la côte et la mer. Ces trous sur la mer n'ont pas vraiment le caractère de links, étant donné la nature du sol et l'absence de dunes (ils se rapprochent du style d'Etretat), mais le vent peut les rendre redoutables pour le jeu et surtout pour les scores. Une réalisation sympathique et de qualité.

The three nine hole courses can be played in any combination, but «L'Etang», a barren and hilly layout, does not have the character of «Le Bocage» (in typically Norman countryside) or «La Mer». The latter two form the most consistent combination in terms of golfing and visual unity, where architect Yves Bureau has employed the natural relief without too much excavation work, dotting the fairways with a few large bunkers. «La Mer», which unwinds over rolling landscape, includes a few holes on a plateau overlooking one of the D-Day beaches and providing magnificent views over the coastline and English channel. The seaboard holes are hardly your typical links holes, given the nature of the soil and the absence of dunes (they are more in the Etretat style), but the wind can play havoc with your game and your card. A very pleasant golf course of excellent standard.

Omaha Beach Golf Club — 1987

La Ferme Saint-Sauveur
F - 14520 PORT-EN-BESSIN

Office	Secrétariat	(33) 02 31 21 72 94
Pro shop	Pro-shop	(33) 02 31 22 76 45
Fax	Fax	(33) 02 31 51 79 61
Situation	Situation	

Bayeux (pop. 14 700), 10 km

Annual closure	Fermeture annuelle	no
Weekly closure	Fermeture hebdomadaire	tuesday
	(mardi): 15/11 → 15/03	

Fees main season
Tarifs haute saison full day

	Week days Semaine	We/Bank holidays We/Férié
Individual Individuel	260 F	260 F
Couple Couple	520 F	520 F

Caddy	Caddy	on request
Electric Trolley	Chariot électrique	70 F/18 holes
Buggy	Voiturette	170 F/18 holes
Clubs	Clubs	60 F/full day

Credit cards Cartes de crédit
VISA - CB - Eurocard - MasterCard

310

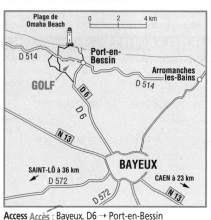

Access Accès : Bayeux, D6 → Port-en-Bessin
Map 2 on page 166 Carte 2 Page 166

GOLF COURSE PARCOURS — 14/20

Site	Site	
Maintenance	Entretien	
Architect	Architecte	Yves Bureau
Type	Type	seaside course, copse
Relief	Relief	
Water in play	Eau en jeu	
Exp. to wind	Exposé au vent	
Trees in play	Arbres en jeu	

Scorecard Carte de score	Chp. Chp.	Mens Mess.	Ladies Da.
Length Long.	6229	5867	5384
Par	72	72	72

Advised golfing ability	0	12	24	36
Niveau de jeu recommandé				
Hcp required Handicap exigé	no			

CLUB HOUSE & AMENITIES CLUB HOUSE ET ANNEXES — 7/10

Pro shop	Pro-shop	
Driving range	Practice	
Sheltered	couvert	15 mats
On grass	sur herbe	no, 35 mats open air
Putting-green	putting-green	yes
Pitching-green	pitching green	yes

HOTEL FACILITIES ENVIRONNEMENT HOTELIER — 5/10

HOTELS HÔTELS

Mercure Omaha Beach		on site
39 rooms, D 500 F		
Tel (33) 02 31 22 44 44, Fax (33) 02 31 22 66 77		
La Chenevière		Commes
19 rooms, D 1 220 F		2 km
Tel (33) 02 31 51 25 25, Fax (33) 02 31 21 47 98		
Château de Sully		Bayeux
24 rooms, D 650 F		8 km
Tel (33) 02 31 22 29 48, Fax (33) 02 31 22 64 77		

RESTAURANTS RESTAURANTS

Marine		Port-en-Bessin
Tel (33) 02 31 21 70 08		2 km
Château de Sully		Bayeux
Tel (33) 02 31 22 29 48		6 km

OPIO VALBONNE

13 | **6** | **7**

Parcours traditionnel de la région de Cannes, Opio Valbonne vit toujours sur sa réputation, mais les nouveaux parcours ont amené de nouvelles exigences, notamment par rapport à l'entretien, qui n'est pas ici le point fort. Dans un espace modérément accidenté agréablement vallonné, l'architecte Donald Harradine s'est appuyé sur la richesse de la végétation locale, sans bouleverser le paysage. On apprécie son aspect naturel , mais le dessin manque certainement de grandeur. Une petite rivière vient en jeu sur de nombreux trous, mais les obstacles principaux autour des petits greens sont des bunkers au dessin banal, dont le remodelage est toujours en projet. Pas très long (surtout à l'aller), il se joue facilement, et la succession de deux par 5 pour terminer permet de sauver sa carte si besoin est. Un bel ensemble, mais le green-fee n'est pas des plus avantageux...

The traditional course in the region of Cannes, Opio Valbonne is still living on its reputation, but new courses in the neighbourhood have brought new requirements. This is particularly true for upkeep, which is hardly Valbonne's forte. Set over rather hilly terrain, architect Donald Harradine focused on the wealth of the local vegetation without upsetting the landscape. You will enjoy the natural look to the course, but the layout definitely lacks ambition. A little river comes into play on many holes, but the main hazards around the small greens are the very ordinary bunkers, which are still due to be redesigned shortly. This is not a very long course (especially the front nine) and it plays quite easily. The last two holes are easyish par 5s which can sometimes rescue your card if you are in trouble. A fine course, but green-fees are hardly the cheapest you can find.

Golf Opio Valbonne		1963
Château de la Bégude - Route de Roquefort-les-Pins		
F - 06650 OPIO		
Office	Secrétariat	(33) 04 93 12 00 08
Pro shop	Pro-shop	(33) 04 93 12 05 29
Fax	Fax	(33) 04 93 12 26 00
Situation	Situation	
Grasse (pop. 41 390), 10 km		
Annual closure	Fermeture annuelle	no
Weekly closure	Fermeture hebdomadaire	no

Fees main season
Tarifs haute saison 18 holes

	Week days Semaine	We/Bank holidays We/Férié
Individual Individuel	330 F	360 F
Couple Couple	660 F	720 F

Caddy	Caddy	no
Electric Trolley	Chariot électrique	no
Buggy	Voiturette	200 F/18 holes
Clubs	Clubs	100 F/18 holes

Credit cards Cartes de crédit
VISA - CB - Eurocard - MasterCard - AMEX - JCB

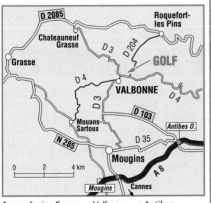

Access Accès : Cannes → Valbonne, → Antibes,
turn left → Roquefort-les-Pins
Map 14 on page 191 Carte 14 Page 191

GOLF COURSE / PARCOURS

13/20

Site	Site	
Maintenance	Entretien	
Architect	Architecte	Donald Harradine
Type	Type	forest, parkland
Relief	Relief	
Water in play	Eau en jeu	
Exp. to wind	Exposé au vent	
Trees in play	Arbres en jeu	

Scorecard Carte de score	Chp. Chp.	Mens Mess.	Ladies Da.
Length Long.	5931	5931	4963
Par	72	72	72

Advised golfing ability		0	12	24	36
Niveau de jeu recommandé					
Hcp required	Handicap exigé	35			

CLUB HOUSE & AMENITIES / CLUB HOUSE ET ANNEXES

6/10

Pro shop	Pro-shop	
Driving range	Practice	
Sheltered	couvert	3 mats
On grass	sur herbe	no, 50 mats open air
Putting-green	putting-green	yes
Pitching-green	pitching green	yes

HOTEL FACILITIES / ENVIRONNEMENT HOTELIER

7/10

HOTELS HÔTELS

Hôtel du Golf *** — sur place
32 chambres, D 490 F

Pullman **** — Sophia-Antipolis
104 chambres, D 690 F — 4 km S.E.
Tel (33) 04 92 96 68 78, Fax (33) 04 92 96 68 96

RESTAURANTS RESTAURANTS

Auberge du Colombier — Roquefort-les-Pins
Tel (33) 04 92 60 33 00 — 3 km

L'Auberge Fleurie — Valbonne
Tel (33) 04 93 12 02 80 — 2 km

Bistro de Valbonne — Valbonne
Tel (33) 04 93 12 05 59 — 2 km

311

Dans un superbe parc plat, mais avec un sol parfois humide, de larges avenues bordées de grands arbres offrent le sentiment d'espace que l'on attend traditionnellement d'un golf. Même si certains trous restent assez étroits et réclament un jeu précis, les longs frappeurs trouveront aussi de quoi s'exprimer. On peut regretter que les fairways ne soient guère modelés, ce qui facilite le jeu, il est vrai, mais les meilleurs joueurs n'y trouveront pas tout à fait un test complet de leur jeu. Les bunkers sont avec les arbres les principaux obstacles, l'eau ne venant en jeu que sur deux trous. Golf de membres, c'est le parcours le plus « parisien » à l'est de Paris, comme en témoigne le très bourgeois Club-House, une vénérable maison de maître. Un très décent parcours de 9 trous, avec beaucoup d'obstacles d'eau, complète cet équipement de bon niveau, sinon exceptionnel.

In a beautiful, flat park which is sometimes a little damp underfoot, wide fairways lined by tall trees give the feeling of space you expect from a golf course. Although some holes are rather tight and demand precision play, long-hitters can let fly at Ozoir. We thought it a shame that no contouring has been done to the fairways. True, they are easier to play as they are, but they could be made more challenging for the better players. Bunkers and trees are the main hazards, as water enters the fray on only two holes. Very much a "members' club", Ozoir is the most "Parisian" course to the east of Paris, as seen with the classy clubhouse, a fine mansion. A very decent 9-holer with a lot of water hazards completes this excellent, if not to say exceptional, golfing complex.

Ozoir-la-Ferrière — 1928
Château des Agneaux
F - 77330 OZOIR-LA-FERRIERE

Office	Secrétariat	(33) 01 60 02 60 79
Pro shop	Pro-shop	(33) 01 64 40 18 51
Fax	Fax	(33) 01 64 40 28 20
Situation	Situation	

Paris (pop. 2 175 200), 36 km
Pontault-Combault (pop. 26 800), 5 km

Annual closure	Fermeture annuelle	no
Weekly closure	Fermeture hebdomadaire	no

Fees main season
Tarifs haute saison full day

	Week days Semaine	We/Bank holidays We/Férié
Individual Individuel	210 F	400 F
Couple Couple	420 F	800 F

Caddy	Caddy	no
Electric Trolley	Chariot électrique	yes
Buggy	Voiturette	150 F/18 holes
Clubs	Clubs	80 F/full day

Credit cards Cartes de crédit
VISA - CB - Eurocard - MasterCard

312

GOLF COURSE / PARCOURS — **13**/20

Site	Site	
Maintenance	Entretien	
Architect	Architecte	unknown
Type	Type	parkland
Relief	Relief	
Water in play	Eau en jeu	
Exp. to wind	Exposé au vent	
Trees in play	Arbres en jeu	

Scorecard Carte de score	Chp. Chp.	Mens Mess.	Ladies Da.
Length Long.	6085	5720	5220
Par	71	71	71

Advised golfing ability
Niveau de jeu recommandé   0   12   24   36
Hcp required   Handicap exigé   24 Men, 28 Ladies

CLUB HOUSE & AMENITIES / CLUB HOUSE ET ANNEXES — **7**/10

Pro shop	Pro-shop	
Driving range	Practice	
Sheltered	couvert	2 mats
On grass	sur herbe	no, 15 mats open air
Putting-green	putting-green	yes
Pitching-green	pitching green	yes

HOTEL FACILITIES / ENVIRONNEMENT HOTELIER — **5**/10

HOTELS HÔTELS
Le Manoir — Fontenay-Trésigny
20 rooms, D 800 F — 18 km
Tel (33) 01 64 25 91 17, Fax (33) 01 64 25 95 49

Château de la Grande Romaine — Lesigny
88 rooms, D 800 F — 2 km
Tel (33) 01 64 43 16 00, Fax (33) 01 64 43 16 10

Le Pavillon Bleu — Ozoir-la-Ferrière
38 rooms, D 285 F — 2 km
Tel (33) 01 64 40 05 56, Fax (33) 01 64 40 29 74

RESTAURANTS RESTAURANTS
Le Canadel — Pontault-Combault
Tel (33) 01 64 43 45 47 — 5 km

La Gueulardière — Ozoir-la-Ferrière
Tel (33) 01 60 02 94 56 — 2 km

Access Accès : A4 Paris → Nancy, Exit (Sortie)
Emerainville. N104 («la Francilienne») → Pontault-Combault, N4 → Ozoir-la-Ferrière
Map 15 on page 193 Carte 15 Page 193

PARIS INTERNATIONAL

Avec sa situation très favorable au nord de Paris et à proximité de l'aéroport Charles-de-Gaulle, ce parcours était d'autant plus espéré au moment de sa création que son dessin avait été confié à Jack Nicklaus. Mais autant on peut reconnaître sa patte sur une douzaine de trous, où un espace très ouvert lui permettait de donner sa pleine mesure, autant on a l'impression qu'il s'est trouvé moins à l'aise et à l'étroit dans les trous en forêt, où l'on a du mal à variment identifier sa signature, et où les très bons joueurs auront plus de mal à s'exprimer. Ces réserves viennent surtout du fait que l'on attendait beaucoup de Nicklaus. Pour garder le meilleur souvenir du parcours, on conseillera de commencer par le retour et de faire ensuite l'aller. A connaître néanmoins, mais on évitera les journées humides, que le terrain supporte cependant un peu mieux grâce à de gros travaux.

Neatly located to the north of Paris close to Charles-de-Gaulle airport, this course was long awaited in that the designer was a one Jack Nicklaus. But as easily as you will recognize his style on a dozen or so holes, where wide open space gave him full scope od expression, as easily you will feel that the great man was not quite comfortable and a little cramped on the holes through the forest. Here, his style is not nearly as evident and even good players will have problems coming to terms with the course. These reservations are of course voiced because much was expected of Nicklaus. To get the best impression of this course, we would advise you to start from the 10th. Worth playing nonetheless, but avoid the wet days as the terrain does not take too well to water (a new drainage has improved it).

Paris International Golf Club — 1990

18, route du Golf
F - 95560 BAILLET-en-FRANCE

Office	Secrétariat	(33) 01 34 69 90 00
Pro shop	Pro-shop	(33) 01 34 69 90 00
Fax	Fax	(33) 01 34 69 97 15
Situation	Situation	

Paris (pop. 2 175 200), 30 km

Annual closure	Fermeture annuelle	no
Weekly closure	Fermeture hebdomadaire	monday (lundi)

Fees main season
Tarifs haute saison 18 holes

	Week days Semaine	We/Bank holidays We/Férié
Individual Individuel	350 F	500 F
Couple Couple	700 F	1 000 F

Caddy	Caddy	on request
Electric Trolley	Chariot électrique	80 F/18 holes
Buggy	Voiturette	200 F/18 holes
Clubs	Clubs	140 F/full day

Credit cards Cartes de crédit
VISA - CB - Eurocard - MasterCard - AMEX - DC - JCB

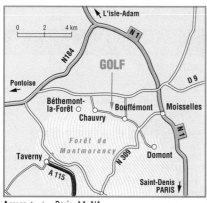

Access Accès : Paris, A1, N1.
Turn left on D3 → Baillet-en-France
Map 15 on page 192 Carte 15 Page 192

GOLF COURSE / PARCOURS — 16/20

Site	Site	
Maintenance	Entretien	
Architect	Architecte	Jack Nicklaus
Type	Type	parkland, hilly
Relief	Relief	
Water in play	Eau en jeu	
Exp. to wind	Exposé au vent	
Trees in play	Arbres en jeu	

Scorecard Carte de score	Chp. Chp.	Mens Mess.	Ladies Da.
Length Long.	6319	5905	4910
Par	72	72	72

Advised golfing ability		0 12 24 36
Niveau de jeu recommandé		
Hcp required	Handicap exigé	no

CLUB HOUSE & AMENITIES / CLUB HOUSE ET ANNEXES — 7/10

Pro shop	Pro-shop	
Driving range	Practice	
Sheltered	couvert	no
On grass	sur herbe	yes
Putting-green	putting-green	yes
Pitching-green	pitching green	yes

HOTEL FACILITIES / ENVIRONNEMENT HOTELIER — 5/10

HOTELS HÔTELS
Le Grand Hôtel — Enghien
45 rooms, D 1 000 F — 14 km
Tel (33) 01 39 34 10 00, Fax (33) 01 39 34 10 01

Campanile — Taverny
76 rooms, D 295 F — 10 km
Tel (33) 01 30 40 10 85, Fax (33) 01 30 40 10 87

Median — Goussainville
49 rooms, D 495 F — 10 km
Tel (33) 01 39 88 93 93, Fax (33) 01 39 88 75 65

RESTAURANTS RESTAURANTS
Gai Rivage — L'Isle Adam
Tel (33) 01 34 69 01 09 — 9 km

Au Cœur de la Forêt — Montmorency
Tel (33) 01 39 64 99 19 — 11 km

313

PAU

13	6	8

C'est le plus ancien golf d'Europe continentale, ce pourrait être uniquement un lieu de pélerinage. Mais si le parcours n'est pas un chef-d'oeuvre, il est fort amusant et relaxant à jouer même s'il n'a plus grand chose des origines. Il a au moins gardé le goût de la décoration florale et les arbres ont fort grandi, tout en laissant des vues séduisantes sur les Pyrénées. La présence du Gave de Pau apporte un intérêt au jeu, dont les seules difficultés consistent à apprécier les distances : le parcours est plat et étroit (avec beaucoup de hors-limites). Sa longueur réduite peut décevoir les vedettes du driver, mais c'est parfait pour affûter ses petits fers. Le putting et le petit jeu jouent évidemment un rôle essentiel, et les progrès de l'entretien ont augmenté encore le plaisir des amateurs. On aimera la chaleur de l'accueil dans le Sud-Ouest, le charme des lieux, la situation pratiquement en ville et le culte de l'esprit des origines.

This is the oldest course on the continent of Europe and could get by simply as a place of pilgrimage. But while the course is hardly a masterpiece, it is great fun and relaxing to play even though there is little left of its original features. At least it has retained the tasteful floral decoration and the trees have grown, leaving some attractive sights over the Pyrenees. The «Gave de Pau» (a mountain stream) adds a little spice to your round, the only real difficulty of which is appreciating the distances: the course is flat and tight (with a lot of out-of-bounds to cope with). The short yardage might disappoint long-drivers, but it is perfect for honing your short irons. Putting and a good short game obviously play a key role and improved maintenance has done much to enhance the pleasure of playing here. The warm welcome of the South-West of France, the charming site, a virtually town-centre course and the course's long-standing origins make this a lovely walk, perhaps accompanied by the old golfing spirits of the 19th century.

Pau Golf-Club		1856
Rue du Golf		
F - 64140 BILLERE		
Office	Secrétariat	(33) 05 59 32 02 33
Pro shop	Pro-shop	(33) 05 59 92 15 46
Fax	Fax	(33) 05 59 62 42 57
Situation	Situation	
Pau (pop. 82 150), 2 km		
Annual closure	Fermeture annuelle	no
Weekly closure	Fermeture hebdomadaire	no
monday (lundi): restaurant closed		
Fees main season		
Tarifs haute saison full day		

	Week days Semaine	We/Bank holidays We/Férié
Individual Individuel	250 F	250 F
Couple Couple	430 F	430 F

Winter months (Basse saison) : 200 F (weekdays)/340 F (weekends)

Caddy	Caddy	no
Electric Trolley	Chariot électrique	no
Buggy	Voiturette	no
Clubs	Clubs	60 F/full day

Credit cards Cartes de crédit
VISA - CB - Eurocard - MasterCard

314

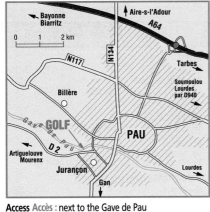

Access Accès : next to the Gave de Pau and «Parc National»
Map 12 on page 186 Carte 12 Page 186

GOLF COURSE
PARCOURS

13/20

Site	Site	
Maintenance	Entretien	
Architect	Architecte	B. Ducwing
Type	Type	parkland
Relief	Relief	
Water in play	Eau en jeu	
Exp. to wind	Exposé au vent	
Trees in play	Arbres en jeu	

Scorecard Carte de score	Chp. Chp.	Mens Mess.	Ladies Da.
Length Long.	5312	5067	4418
Par	69	69	69

Advised golfing ability	0	12	24	36
Niveau de jeu recommandé				
Hcp required Handicap exigé	35			

CLUB HOUSE & AMENITIES
CLUB HOUSE ET ANNEXES

6/10

Pro shop	Pro-shop	
Driving range	Practice	
Sheltered	couvert	5 mats
On grass	sur herbe	no, 15 mats open air
Putting-green	putting-green	yes
Pitching-green	pitching green	yes

HOTEL FACILITIES
ENVIRONNEMENT HOTELIER

8/10

HOTELS HÔTELS
Clarine — Pau
41 rooms, D 390 — 2 km
Tel (33) 05 59 82 58 00, Fax (33) 05 59 27 30 20

Commerce — Pau
51 rooms, D 320 F — 2 km
Tel (33) 05 59 27 24 40, Fax (33) 05 59 83 81 74

Novotel — Lescar
89 rooms, D 540 F — 6 km
Tel (33) 05 59 32 17 32, Fax (33) 05 59 32 34 98

RESTAURANTS RESTAURANTS
Chez Pierre — Pau
Tel (33) 05 59 27 76 86 — 2 km
Le Viking - Tel (33) 05 59 84 02 91 — Pau 2 km
Chez Ruffet - Tel (33) 05 59 06 25 13 — Jurançon 2 km

PESSAC

13 **7** **7**

Avec un 18 trous et un 9 trous, cet ensemble est principalement situé dans une pinède entourée de villas pas trop perturbantes. Le site était intéressant, mais l'architecte n'a malheureusement pas tiré la quintessence de ses possibilités. Beaucoup de trous se ressemblent, et donnent une impression de monotonie, même si l'environnement est agréable. Certaines difficultés sont peu gênantes pour les bons joueurs mais pénalisent inutilement les joueurs moyens, qui devront composer également avec la proximité de la forêt sur plusieurs trous. Les obstacles d'eau artificiels ont été joliment dessinés, et l'absence de relief permet de jouer sans fatigue plus de 18 trous dans la journée. Accessible aux joueurs de tous niveaux, ce parcours mérite une visite si l'on passe dans la région, d'autant que les travaux entrepris ont amélioré l'entretien du terrain de nature sablonneuse, en particulier les greens.

An 18-hole and 9-hole golf resort is sited primarily in a pine forest, surrounded by a number of unobtrusive villas. The site was an interesting one but the architect unfortunately failed to make the most of its potential. A lot of holes are similar and create an impression of monotony, even though the surroundings are very pleasant. Some hazards don't really bother the better players but do needlessly penalise the mid-handicappers, who also have to cope with an encroaching forest on several holes. The artificial water hazards have been prettily designed and the course's flatness makes 18 holes an easy proposition in one day. Accessible to players of all abilities, Pessac is well worth a visit if you are in the region, especially since maintenance work has considerably improved the state of the sandy terrain, particularly the greens.

Golf de Pessac — 1989

Rue de la Princesse
F - 33600 PESSAC

Office	Secrétariat	(33) 05 57 26 03 33
Pro shop	Pro-shop	(33) 05 57 26 03 33
Fax	Fax	(33) 05 56 36 52 89
Situation	Situation	

Bordeaux (pop. 211 200), 10 km

Annual closure	Fermeture annuelle	no
Weekly closure	Fermeture hebdomadaire	no

Fees main season
Tarifs haute saison full day

	Week days Semaine	We/Bank holidays We/Férié
Individual Individuel	160 F	220 F
Couple Couple	320 F	440 F

Tuesday (mardi): Ladies & Seniors130 F

Caddy	Caddy	no
Electric Trolley	Chariot électrique	no
Buggy	Voiturette	100 F/18 holes
Clubs	Clubs	60 F/full day

Credit cards Cartes de crédit
VISA - CB - Eurocard - MasterCard - AMEX - DC

Access Accès : Bordeaux Ring road West («Rocade Ouest»), Exit (Sortie) No 12 → «Zoo de Pessac»
Map 9 on page 180 Carte 9 Page 180

GOLF COURSE
PARCOURS

13/20

Site	Site	▬▬▬
Maintenance	Entretien	▬▬▬
Architect	Architecte	Olivier Brizon
Type	Type	forest, residential
Relief	Relief	▬
Water in play	Eau en jeu	▬▬
Exp. to wind	Exposé au vent	▬
Trees in play	Arbres en jeu	▬▬

Scorecard	Chp.	Mens	Ladies
Carte de score	Chp.	Mess.	Da.
Length Long.	6242	5848	5465
Par	72	72	72

Advised golfing ability	0	12	24	36
Niveau de jeu recommandé		▬▬▬		

Hcp required	Handicap exigé	no

CLUB HOUSE & AMENITIES
CLUB HOUSE ET ANNEXES

7/10

Pro shop	Pro-shop	▬▬▬
Driving range	Practice	▬▬
Sheltered	couvert	10 mats
On grass	sur herbe	yes
Putting-green	putting-green	yes
Pitching-green	pitching green	yes

315

HOTEL FACILITIES
ENVIRONNEMENT HOTELIER

7/10

HOTELS HÔTELS

La Réserve		Pessac
22 rooms, D 650 F		5 km
Tel (33) 05 57 26 58 28, Fax (33) 05 56 36 31 02		
Relais de Margaux		Margaux
61 rooms, D 900 F		35 km
Tel (33) 05 57 88 38 30, Fax (33) 05 57 88 31 73		
Mercure Château-Chartrons		Bordeaux
144 rooms, D 760 F		10 km
Tel (33) 05 56 43 15 00, Fax (33) 05 56 69 15 21		

RESTAURANTS RESTAURANTS

Le Chapon Fin		Bordeaux
Tel (33) 05 56 79 10 10		10 km
Jean Ramet		Bordeaux
Tel (33) 05 56 44 12 51		10 km
Rose des Vents		Bordeaux
Tel (33) 05 56 48 55 85		10 km

PLÉNEUF-VAL-ANDRÉ

	17	7	5

Une jolie réussite signée par Alain Prat, en bordure de mer, sans pour autant se rattacher au style de links traditionnels. On remarquera une bonne montée en puissance des difficultés du parcours. De même que sur chacun des trous : les fairways sont généralement assez larges, ce qui facilite la plupart des tee-shots, mais les greens sont particulièrement défendus par de nombreux bunkers de sable et d'herbe, stratégiquement placés. Le trou le plus spectaculaire est le 11, un par 5 au départ arrière situé sur un éperon rocheux, dans la partie la plus accidentée du parcours. Mais ce n'est pas un golf trop fatiguant. On notera aussi la qualité particulière des installations d'entraînement, et de jolis points de vue, mais le Club house ne mérite sans doute pas les mêmes compliments. L'entretien est seulement correct, greens et départs étaient très moyens au moment de nos visites.

A pretty layout by Alain Prat along the sea-shore, but without the traditional links style. Difficulties gradually increase as the day wears on, a good thing, and each hole has generally rather wide fairways for easier tee-shots. However, the greens are well defended by numerous bunkers and dips, all strategically located. The most spectacular hole is the 11th, a par 5 whose back-tee is placed on a rocky spur on the hilliest part of the course. But there is nothing too tiring about Pleneuf. Practice facilities are very good. There are also some pretty viewpoints, but unfortunately there is not too much that can be said in favour of the club-house. Maintenance is fair only; when we visited, the greens and tee-boxes were in no more than average condition.

Golf de Pléneuf-Val-André — 1992
Rue de la Plage des Vallées
F - 22370 PLENEUF-VAL-ANDRE

Office	Secrétariat	(33) 02 96 63 01 12
Pro shop	Pro-shop	(33) 02 96 63 01 12
Fax	Fax	(33) 02 96 63 01 06
Situation	Situation	

Saint-Brieuc (pop. 44 750), 25 km

Annual closure	Fermeture annuelle	no
Weekly closure	Fermeture hebdomadaire	no

Fees main season
Tarifs haute saison 18 holes

	Week days Semaine	We/Bank holidays We/Férié
Individual Individuel	270 F	270 F
Couple Couple	540 F	540 F

Caddy	Caddy	no
Electric Trolley	Chariot électrique	no
Buggy	Voiturette	120 F/18 holes
Clubs	Clubs	50 F/full day

Credit cards Cartes de crédit
VISA - CB - Eurocard - MasterCard - AMEX - DC

316

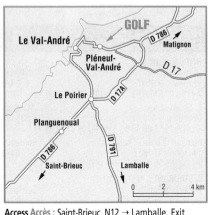

Access Accès : Saint-Brieuc, N12 → Lamballe, Exit (Sortie) Saint-René. D786 → Pléneuf- Val-André
Map 5 on page 173 Carte 5 Page 173

GOLF COURSE / PARCOURS — 17/20

Site	Site	
Maintenance	Entretien	
Architect	Architecte	Alain Prat
Type	Type	seaside course
Relief	Relief	
Water in play	Eau en jeu	
Exp. to wind	Exposé au vent	
Trees in play	Arbres en jeu	

Scorecard Carte de score	Chp. Chp.	Mens Mess.	Ladies Da.
Length Long.	6052	5752	5125
Par	72	72	72

Advised golfing ability Niveau de jeu recommandé	0 12 24 36
Hcp required Handicap exigé	no

CLUB HOUSE & AMENITIES / CLUB HOUSE ET ANNEXES — 7/10

Pro shop	Pro-shop	
Driving range	Practice	
Sheltered	couvert	10 mats
On grass	sur herbe	yes
Putting-green	putting-green	yes
Pitching-green	pitching green	yes

HOTEL FACILITIES / ENVIRONNEMENT HOTELIER — 5/10

HOTELS HÔTELS
Grand Hôtel — Val-André
39 rooms, D 440 F — 1 km
Tel (33) 02 96 72 20 56, Fax (33) 02 96 63 00 24

Le Fanal — Fréhel
9 rooms, D 340 F — 17 km
Tel (33) 02 96 41 43 19

Manoir de Vaumadeuc — Pleven
14 rooms, D 1 000 F — 22 km
Tel (33) 02 96 84 46 17, Fax (33) 02 96 84 40 16

RESTAURANTS RESTAURANTS
La Cotriade — Pléneuf-Val-André
Tel (33) 02 96 63 06 90 — 1 km

Le Haut Guen — Pléneuf-Val-André
Tel (33) 02 96 72 25 07

La Mer — Val-André
Tel (33) 02 96 72 20 44 — 1 km

A proximité de Lorient, c'est un vaste espace de bord de mer et de campagne, sans guère plus de végétation que de bas buissons de lichens, mais dans le voisinage peu gracieux d'une grande carrière de sable et de gravier. Dommage, car ce parcours ouvert en 1990 et signé Quenouille est agréable, avec quelques jolis trous, des fairways bien fournis, des greens très corrects et de bons bunkers. Certains coups et approches sont assez techniques, mais les difficultés ne sont pas très accentuées, ce qui permet à tous les niveaux d'y évoluer simultanément. Quelques trous longent la mer, mais sans rendre vraiment un hommage évident aux parcours britanniques de situation analogue. Un plaisant parcours dans une région aujourd'hui bien fournie en golfs, mais il faut cependant en surveiller l'entretien.

Close to Lorient, a wide open space along the seaboard with hardly any more vegetation than a few low-cut lichen bushes, but set in a rather unsightly neighbourhood of a large sand and gravel quarry. This is a pity, because Ploemeur, designed by Quenouille and opened in 1990, is a pleasant course with a few pretty holes, well-grassed fairways, very decent greens and some good bunkers to boot. Some shots require a lot of technique but the difficulties are never excessive, so that players of all aspirations can enjoy a round together. A few holes run along the sea-shore, but there is nothing to obviously compare with British courses in a similar setting. A pleasant course in a region that today has more than its fair share of golfing facilities, but a tight rein needs to be kept on upkeep.

Golf de Ploemeur Océan — 1990

Saint-Jude - Kerham
F - 56270 PLOEMEUR

Office	Secrétariat	(33) 02 97 32 81 82
Pro shop	Pro-shop	(33) 02 97 32 81 82
Fax	Fax	(33) 02 97 32 80 90
Situation	Situation	

Lorient (pop. 59 270), 10 km

Annual closure	Fermeture annuelle	no
Weekly closure	Fermeture hebdomadaire	no

Fees main season
Tarifs haute saison 18 holes

	Week days Semaine	We/Bank holidays We/Férié
Individual Individuel	260 F	260 F
Couple Couple	520 F	520 F

Caddy	Caddy	no
Electric Trolley	Chariot électrique	no
Buggy	Voiturette	150 F/18 holes
Clubs	Clubs	50 F/full day

Credit cards Cartes de crédit
VISA - CB - Eurocard - MasterCard

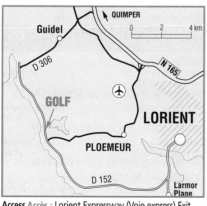

Access Accès : Lorient Expressway (Voie express) Exit Ploemeur → Airport Lann-Bihoué → Fort Bloqué
Map 5 on page 172 Carte 5 Page 172

GOLF COURSE / PARCOURS — 15/20

Site	Site	
Maintenance	Entretien	
Architect	Architecte	Quenouille & MacAuley
Type	Type	seaside course
Relief	Relief	
Water in play	Eau en jeu	
Exp. to wind	Exposé au vent	
Trees in play	Arbres en jeu	

Scorecard Carte de score	Chp. Chp.	Mens Mess.	Ladies Da.
Length Long.	5957	5495	4959
Par	72	72	72

Advised golfing ability
Niveau de jeu recommandé   0   12   24   36
Hcp required   Handicap exigé   no

CLUB HOUSE & AMENITIES / CLUB HOUSE ET ANNEXES — 7/10

Pro shop	Pro-shop	
Driving range	Practice	
Sheltered	couvert	16 mats
On grass	sur herbe	yes
Putting-green	putting-green	yes
Pitching-green	pitching green	no

HOTEL FACILITIES / ENVIRONNEMENT HOTELIER — 6/10

HOTELS HÔTELS

Les Astéries — Ploemeur
36 rooms, D 360 F — 4 km
Tel (33) 02 97 86 21 97, Fax (33) 02 97 86 34 33

Le Vivier — Lomener
14 rooms, D 480 F — 6 km
Tel (33) 02 97 82 99 60, Fax (33) 02 97 82 88 89

Château de Locguénolé — Hennebont
22 rooms, D 1 200 F — 20 km
Tel (33) 02 97 76 76 76, Fax (33) 02 97 76 82 35

RESTAURANTS RESTAURANTS

L'Amphitryon - Tel (33) 02 97 83 34 04 — Lorient 10 km

Le Poisson d'Or — Lorient
Tel (33) 02 97 21 57 06 — 10 km

Château de Locguénolé — Hennebont
Tel (33) 02 97 76 76 76 — 20 km

317

Premier parcours français signé par Severiano Ballesteros, Pont Royal bénéficie d'un excellent entretien. La dimension généreuse des bunkers peut obliger à de longues sorties du sable, une spécialité du champion espagnol, et un cauchemar des amateurs comme de la plupart des professionnels. Avec de grands arbres, divers obstacles d'eau (rivière, étangs), quelques dangereux ravins, un relief assez accidenté (voiturette conseillée), Pont Royal réclame pas mal de technique, de sens tactique et une grande habileté dans le choix de clubs, ce qui le rendra difficile aux joueurs peu expérimentés. Les frappeurs auront de belles occasions de prendre des risques, avec émotions garanties. Plusieurs trous au dessin quelque peu torturé exigent d'être préalablement reconnus avant d'être négociés correctement, surtout quand souffle le mistral, assez fréquent ici !

The first French course designed by Seve Ballesteros, Pont Royal is kept in excellent condition. The very large bunkers can lead to some very long escape shots from sand, one of the Spanish champion's specialities but often a nightmare for amateurs and pros alike. With large trees, various water hazards (a river and ponds), a few dangerous ravines and a hilly landscape (buggy recommended), Pont Royal requires a lot of technique, a good tactical mind and skill in choosing the right club. This makes it a difficult proposition for inexperienced players. Long-hitters have exciting opportunities to take risks, but several holes with a twisted layout need a little reconnaissance before hoping to make par, especially when the Mistral is blowing.

Pont Royal Golf Club
F - 13370 MALLEMORT   1992

Office	Secrétariat	(33) 04 90 57 40 79
Pro shop	Pro-shop	(33) 04 90 57 40 79
Fax	Fax	(33) 04 90 49 46 05
Situation	Situation	

Salon-de-Provence (pop. 34 050), 20 km

Annual closure	Fermeture annuelle	no
Weekly closure	Fermeture hebdomadaire	no

Fees main season
Tarifs haute saison 18 holes

	Week days Semaine	We/Bank holidays We/Férié
Individual Individuel	300 F	300 F
Couple Couple	600 F	600 F

Caddy	Caddy	no
Electric Trolley	Chariot électrique	no
Buggy	Voiturette	200 F/18 holes
Clubs	Clubs	100 F/full day

Credit cards Cartes de crédit
VISA - CB - Eurocard - MasterCard

318

Access Accès : A7, Exit (Sortie) Sénas,
N7 → Aix-en-Provence, Golf 10 km
Map 14 on page 190 Carte 14 Page 190

GOLF COURSE
PARCOURS   **16**/20

Site	Site	
Maintenance	Entretien	
Architect	Architecte	Seve Ballesteros
Type	Type	country, hilly
Relief	Relief	
Water in play	Eau en jeu	
Exp. to wind	Exposé au vent	
Trees in play	Arbres en jeu	

Scorecard Carte de score	**Chp.** Chp.	**Mens** Mess.	**Ladies** Da.
Length Long.	6307	6036	5356
Par	72	72	72

Advised golfing ability		0 12 24 36
Niveau de jeu recommandé		
Hcp required	Handicap exigé	35

CLUB HOUSE & AMENITIES
CLUB HOUSE ET ANNEXES   **6**/10

Pro shop	Pro-shop	
Driving range	Practice	
Sheltered	couvert	no
On grass	sur herbe	yes
Putting-green	putting-green	yes
Pitching-green	pitching green	no

HOTEL FACILITIES
ENVIRONNEMENT HOTELIER   **5**/10

HOTELS HÔTELS
Moulin de Vernègues   Vernègues
34 rooms, D 1 000 F   1 km
Tel (33) 04 90 59 12 00, Fax (33) 04 90 59 15 90

Abbaye de Sainte-Croix   Salon-de-Provence
24 rooms, D 900 F   12 km
Tel (33) 04 90 56 24 55, Fax (33) 04 90 56 31 12

Bastide de Capelongue   Bonnieux
17 rooms, D 1 800 F   20 km
Tel (33) 04 90 75 89 78, Fax (33) 04 90 75 93 03

RESTAURANTS RESTAURANTS
Abbaye de Sainte-Croix   Salon-de-Provence
Tel (33) 04 90 56 24 55   12 km

Le Mas du Soleil   Salon-de-Provence
Tel (33) 04 90 56 06 53   12 km

Bastide de Capelongue   Bonnieux
Tel (33) 04 90 75 89 78   20 km

PORCELAINE (LA)

14 6 4

Avec son relief accidenté et son sol, La Porcelaine est plus agréable à jouer aux beaux jours, du printemps à l'automne, quand la végétation prend des couleurs fort séduisantes. Ce parcours signé Jean Garaialde a été conçu comme une alternative privée au golf de Limoges, le premier golf public en France. Des obstacles d'eau entrent en jeu sur la moitié des trous, et constituent, avec quelques arbres stratégiquement utilisés, les principales entraves à de bons scores. Ce parcours très «campagnard» a été destiné essentiellement à satisfaire l'ensemble des membres, résidents dans la région de Limoges, et reste jouable effectivement à tous niveaux. Cependant, les grands voyageurs de golf se livrent fatalement au jeu des comparaisons, et trouveront certainement son architecture sans éclat, et sans grandes surprises, mais son ambiance très agréable.

With its steep slopes and soil, La Porcelaine is most pleasant to play when the weather is at its best, from spring to autumn, and when the vegetation blooms into colour. This course, designed by French champion Jean Garaialde, was designed as a private alternative to Limoges, France's first public course. Water hazards are in play on one half of the course and, along with some strategically located trees, are the main stumbling blocks to a good score. This is a very "country" style course, designed first and foremost to satisfy local members, and is effectively playable by golfers of all levels. However, hardened golf-trotters will make their usual and unavoidable comparisons and will certainly find that this design lacks sparkle and surprise. But this is a golf club with a very pleasant atmosphere.

Golf de la Porcelaine — 1988
Célicroux
F - 87350 PANAZOL

Office	Secrétariat	(33) 05 55 31 10 69
Pro shop	Pro-shop	(33) 05 55 31 10 69
Fax	Fax	(33) 05 55 31 10 69
Situation	Situation	

Limoges (pop. 133 460), 6 km

Annual closure	Fermeture annuelle	no
Weekly closure	Fermeture hebdomadaire	tuesday
	(mardi): 01/10 → 31/03	

Fees main season
Tarifs haute saison full day

	Week days Semaine	We/Bank holidays We/Férié
Individual Individuel	200 F	200 F
Couple Couple	400 F	400 F

Caddy	Caddy	no
Electric Trolley	Chariot électrique	no
Buggy	Voiturette	150 F/18 holes
Clubs	Clubs	50 F/full day

Credit cards Cartes de crédit
VISA - CB - Eurocard - MasterCard

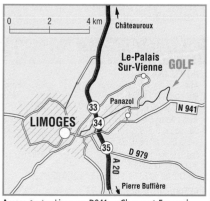

Access Accès : Limoges, D941 → Clermont-Ferrand, → Golf
Map 7 on page 176 Carte 7 Page 176

GOLF COURSE / PARCOURS — **14**/20

Site	Site	
Maintenance	Entretien	
Architect	Architecte	Jean Garaïalde
Type	Type	country
Relief	Relief	
Water in play	Eau en jeu	
Exp. to wind	Exposé au vent	
Trees in play	Arbres en jeu	

Scorecard Carte de score	Chp. Chp.	Mens Mess.	Ladies Da.
Length Long.	6035	5562	5218
Par	72	72	72

Advised golfing ability		0 12 24 36
Niveau de jeu recommandé		
Hcp required	Handicap exigé	35

CLUB HOUSE & AMENITIES / CLUB HOUSE ET ANNEXES — **6**/10

Pro shop	Pro-shop	
Driving range	Practice	
Sheltered	couvert	4 mats
On grass	sur herbe	yes
Putting-green	putting-green	yes
Pitching-green	pitching green	no

319

HOTEL FACILITIES / ENVIRONNEMENT HOTELIER — **4**/10

HOTELS HÔTELS
Chapelle Saint-Martin — Saint-Martin-du-Fault
10 rooms, D 800 F — 18 km
Tel (33) 05 55 75 80 17, Fax (33) 05 55 75 89 50

Royal Limousin — Limoges
77 rooms, D 680 F — 6 km
Tel (33) 05 55 34 65 30, Fax (33) 05 55 34 55 21

Gd-Saint-Léonard — Saint-Léonard-de-Noblat
14 rooms, D 300 F — 13 km
Tel (33) 05 55 56 18 18, Fax (33) 05 55 56 98 32

RESTAURANTS RESTAURANTS
Philippe Redon — Limoges
Tel (33) 05 55 34 66 22 — 6 km

Amphytrion — Limoges
Tel (33) 05 55 33 36 39 — 6 km

A partir du neuf trous existant depuis 1929, Michel Gayon a reconstruit un 18 trous très intéressant en 1991, dans un espace assez accidenté. C'est une région traditionnelle de vacances, au sud de Nantes, mais il n'est jamais vraiment difficile d'y trouver un départ. De plus, le sol sablonneux permet de le recommander toute l'année. Cinq trous sont agrémentés de pins, les treize autres se trouvent dans une zone de bord de mer, où les fairways sont séparés par des buttes, créant ainsi un peu d'intimité. On regrettera qu'ils soient à peu près tous parallèles, mais cela permet aux frappeurs sauvages de s'écarter du droit chemin sans être trop pénalisés, ni menacer les joueurs de tous niveaux pouvant évoluer ici. Ce parcours est assez long des départs arrière, mais la disposition des différents départs permet cependant de se faire un parcours « à sa main ».

Starting out with a 9-holer opened in 1929, Michel Gayon rebuilt a very interesting 18-hole course in 1991 over very hilly terrain. This is traditional holiday territory, to the south of Nantes, but getting a tee-off time poses no real problem. In addition, the sandy sub-soil is playable all year. Five holes are enhanced with pine-trees, the thirteen others run along the sea-shore, where the fairways are separated by sandhills and are sometimes a little too close together. It is a shame they all run more or less parallel, up and down, although this allows wild-hitters to wander off the straight and narrow without too much penalty and encourages players of all abilities to play here together. Rather long from the back, the number of different tees allows golfers to choose a course to suit their game.

Golf de Pornic — 1929

Avenue Sacalby-Newby
F - 44210 SAINTE-MARIE-SUR-MER

Office	Secrétariat	(33) 02 40 82 06 69
Pro shop	Pro-shop	(33) 02 40 82 06 69
Fax	Fax	(33) 02 40 82 80 65
Situation	Situation	Pornic (pop. 9 810),

Nantes (pop. 252 030), 52 km

Annual closure	Fermeture annuelle	no
Weekly closure	Fermeture hebdomadaire	

Wednesday (mercredi) (winter/hiver)

Fees main season
Tarifs haute saison full day

	Week days Semaine	We/Bank holidays We/Férié
Individual Individuel	240 F	240 F
Couple Couple	480 F	480 F

Caddy	Caddy	no
Electric Trolley	Chariot électrique	no
Buggy	Voiturette	150 F/18 holes
Clubs	Clubs	50 F/full day

Credit cards Cartes de crédit
VISA - CB - Eurocard - MasterCard

320

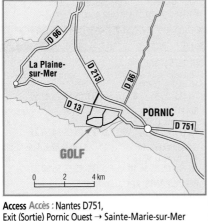

La Plaine-sur-Mer
D 96
D 273
D 86
D 13
PORNIC
D 751
GOLF

0 2 4 km

Access Accès : Nantes D751,
Exit (Sortie) Pornic Ouest → Sainte-Marie-sur-Mer
Map 6 on page 174 Carte 6 Page 174

GOLF COURSE PARCOURS — 15/20

Site	Site	
Maintenance	Entretien	
Architect	Architecte	Michel Gayon
		Jacques Lebreton
Type	Type	links, forest
Relief	Relief	
Water in play	Eau en jeu	
Exp. to wind	Exposé au vent	
Trees in play	Arbres en jeu	

Scorecard Carte de score	Chp. Chp.	Mens Mess.	Ladies Da.
Length Long.	6112	5545	5017
Par	72	72	72

Advised golfing ability		0 12 24 36
Niveau de jeu recommandé		
Hcp required	Handicap exigé	no

CLUB HOUSE & AMENITIES CLUB HOUSE ET ANNEXES — 6/10

Pro shop	Pro-shop	
Driving range	Practice	
Sheltered	couvert	6 mats
On grass	sur herbe	yes
Putting-green	putting-green	yes
Pitching-green	pitching green	no

HOTEL FACILITIES ENVIRONNEMENT HOTELIER — 6/10

HOTELS HÔTELS

Alliance — Pornic
90 rooms, D 1 020 F — 2 km
Tel (33) 02 40 82 21 21, Fax (33) 02 40 82 80 89

Relais Saint-Giles — Pornic
28 rooms, D 370 F — 2 km
Tel (33) 02 40 82 02 25

Les Sablons — Sainte-Marie
30 rooms, D 420 F — 1 km
Tel (33) 02 40 82 09 14, Fax (33) 02 40 82 04 26

RESTAURANTS RESTAURANTS

Le Beau Rivage — Pornic
Tel (33) 02 40 82 03 08 — 2 km

Anne de Bretagne — La Plaine-sur-Mer
Tel (33) 02 40 21 54 72 — 10 km

RARAY (CHÂTEAU DE) LA LICORNE

14	6	4

Un entretien moyen ne rend pas pleine justice à ce parcours d'inspiration très britannique, tracé par le professionnel français Patrice Léglise. Plusieurs trous inspirés de l'architecture de links ont été tracés en plaine, et les autres dans la même esthétique dans une belle forêt, au terrain assez humide. Le dessin des bunkers est particulièrement réussi, de même que leur placement très stratégique. L'ensemble est d'une grande franchise, les difficultés techniques sont réelles mais raisonnables, avec quelques fossés d'apparence naturelle. Le 18, dans une allée bordée de grands arbres, est d'une esthétique « à la française » très adéquate pour le retour vers le château, autrefois utilisé comme décor du film « La Belle et la Bête » de Jean Cocteau, et que l'on aimerait voir parfaitement restauré. Le parcours étant plat, il permet aux joueurs de tous âges d'y évoluer. A jouer en « saison sèche ».

Only average maintenance does not do full justice to this very British style course, laid out by the French professional Patrice Léglise. There are several holes in open countryside that are reminiscent of the best links courses, while the others, equally attractive, run through a beautiful forest over rather damp terrain. The bunkers are particularly well-designed, as is their strategic positioning. The whole course is an honest test of golf with real but reasonable technical difficulties and a few natural-looking ditches. The 18th hole, laid out along a wide alley edged by large trees is very French in style and a suitable way to return to the castle which, may it be said, was used for filming «The Beauty and the Beast» by Jean Cocteau. A little restoration work here would be welcome. A flat course for golfers of all ages, but preferably in dry weather.

Château de Raray — 1988
4, rue Nicolas Lancy
F - 60810 RARAY

Office	Secrétariat	(33) 03 44 54 70 61
Pro shop	Pro-shop	(33) 03 44 54 70 61
Fax	Fax	(33) 03 44 54 74 97
Situation	Situation	

Senlis (pop. 14 430), 6 km Paris (pop. 2 175 200), 54 km

Annual closure	Fermeture annuelle	no
Weekly closure	Fermeture hebdomadaire	tuesday (mardi)

Fees main season
Tarifs haute saison full day

	Week days Semaine	We/Bank holidays We/Férié
Individual Individuel	220 F	400 F
Couple Couple	440 F	700 F

Week ends : GF 250 F after 15.30

Caddy	Caddy	no
Electric Trolley	Chariot électrique	no
Buggy	Voiturette	150 F/18 holes
Clubs	Clubs	100 F/full day

Credit cards Cartes de crédit
VISA - CB - Eurocard - MasterCard

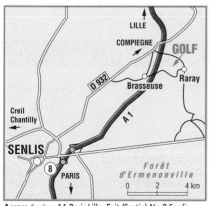

Access Accès : A1 Paris Lille, Exit (Sortie) No 8 Senlis
→ Creil/Chantilly, D932 → Compiègne,
→ Château de Raray
Map 1 on page 164 Carte 1 Page 164

GOLF COURSE
PARCOURS
14/20

Site	Site	
Maintenance	Entretien	
Architect	Architecte	Patrice Léglise
Type	Type	forest, open country
Relief	Relief	
Water in play	Eau en jeu	
Exp. to wind	Exposé au vent	
Trees in play	Arbres en jeu	

Scorecard	Chp.	Mens	Ladies
Carte de score	Chp.	Mess.	Da.
Length Long.	6455	5915	5460
Par	72	72	72

Advised golfing ability	0	12	24	36
Niveau de jeu recommandé				
Hcp required	Handicap exigé	35 (We)		

CLUB HOUSE & AMENITIES
CLUB HOUSE ET ANNEXES
6/10

Pro shop	Pro-shop	
Driving range	Practice	
Sheltered	couvert	8 mats
On grass	sur herbe	yes
Putting-green	putting-green	yes
Pitching-green	pitching green	yes

HOTEL FACILITIES
ENVIRONNEMENT HOTELIER
4/10

HOTELS HÔTELS
Château de Raray — on site
10 rooms, D 1 200 F
Tel (33) 03 44 54 70 61, Fax (33) 03 44 54 74 97

Auberge de Fontaine — Fontaine-Chaalis
7 rooms, D 295 F — 11 km
Tel (33) 03 44 54 20 22, Fax (33) 03 44 60 25 38

RESTAURANTS RESTAURANT
Le Vieux Logis — Fleurines
Tel (33) 03 44 54 10 13 — 10 km

La Maison du Gourmet — Le Meux
Tel (33) 03 44 91 10 10 — 12 km

321

Toujours avec ses excellents greens (notamment en hiver), ce parcours reconnu pour la qualité et la variété de son architecture (Jean-Pascal Fourès), profite toujours de la pousse des nombreuses plantations. Les zones de plaine constituant la majorité du terrain sont ainsi bien mieux paysagées, et les différents trous mieux délimités. Relativement aisé par beau temps, il devient plus complexe avec le vent, souvent fréquent ici, comme sur un links, auxquels certains trous font référence. L'eau vient en jeu sur huit trous, complétant bien la diversité des obstacles rencontrés. Les greens sont souvent très modelés, et les placements de drapeau peuvent en modifier considérablement l'attaque. Sans être absolument exceptionnel, ce parcours a magnifiquement utilisé un budget limité. Le Club-House est une véritable maison de campagne où l'accueil est chaleureux.

With the greens as good as ever (especially in winter) and on a par with the quality and variety of architecture (designed by Jean-Pascal Fourès) which has helped to build the course's excellent reputation, Rebetz is all the better now the extensive plantation programme has started to take root. The areas of open countryside which form the largest part of the course are much better landscaped and the holes have gained in individuality. Relatively easy in fine weather, the frequent wind makes playing golf a trickier business, rather as if playing a links course. Indeed, a few holes could be taken as seaside holes. Water is in play on eight holes and completes the diversity of the course's hazards. The greens are often well-contoured and pin-positions can considerably change the configuration of approach shots. Without being really exceptional, the course has put restricted resources to magnificent use. The club-house is a genuine country-style manor and extends a warm welcome to all.

Golf Club de Rebetz — 1988

Route de Noailles
F - 60240 CHAUMONT-EN-VEXIN

Office	Secrétariat	(33) 03 44 49 15 54
Pro shop	Pro-shop	(33) 03 44 49 15 54
Fax	Fax	(33) 03 44 49 14 26
Situation	Situation	

Paris (pop. 2 175 200), 67 km Gisors (pop. 9 480), 10 km

Annual closure	Fermeture annuelle	no
Weekly closure	Fermeture hebdomadaire	no

Fees main season
Tarifs haute saison full day

	Week days Semaine	We/Bank holidays We/Férié
Individual Individuel	150 F	350 F
Couple Couple	300 F	700 F

Friday (vendredi) : GF 100 F

Caddy	Caddy	no
Electric Trolley	Chariot électrique	60 F/18 holes
Buggy	Voiturette	200 F/18 holes
Clubs	Clubs	60 F/full day

Credit cards Cartes de crédit
VISA - CB - Eurocard - MasterCard

322

Access Accès : A15 Pontoise, N14 → Magny-en-Vexin, turn right on D153 → Chaumont-en-Vexin, turn right in Chaumont-en-Vexin → Golf
Map 1 on page 164 Carte 1 Page 164

GOLF COURSE PARCOURS — 16/20

Site	Site	
Maintenance	Entretien	
Architect	Architecte	Jean-Pascal Fourès
Type	Type	parkland, open country
Relief	Relief	
Water in play	Eau en jeu	
Exp. to wind	Exposé au vent	
Trees in play	Arbres en jeu	

Scorecard Carte de score	Chp. Chp.	Mens Mess.	Ladies Da.
Length Long.	6409	5885	5317
Par	73	73	73

Advised golfing ability
Niveau de jeu recommandé — 0   12   24   36
Hcp required   Handicap exigé   35 (We)

CLUB HOUSE & AMENITIES CLUB HOUSE ET ANNEXES — 6/10

Pro shop	Pro-shop	
Driving range	Practice	
Sheltered	couvert	14 mats
On grass	sur herbe	yes
Putting-green	putting-green	yes
Pitching-green	pitching green	no

HOTEL FACILITIES ENVIRONNEMENT HOTELIER — 4/10

HOTELS HÔTELS
Château de la Rapée   Bazincourt-sur-Epte
12 rooms, D 790 F   13 km
Tel (33) 02 32 55 11 61, Fax (33) 02 32 55 95 65

Moderne   Gisors
30 rooms, D 395 F   10 km
Tel (33) 02 32 55 23 51, Fax (33) 02 32 55 08 75

RESTAURANTS RESTAURANTS
Cappeville   Gisors
Tel (33) 02 35 55 11 08   10 km

Le Cygne   Gisors
Tel (33) 02 33 55 23 76   10 km

REIMS-CHAMPAGNE

Relativement plat et dans un espace très agréablement boisé, c'est une sorte de grand domaine avec un joli château où tous les grands noms du Champagne ont laissé leur marque. Les 9 trous construits en 1927 ont été remodelés et portés à 18 trous par Michael Fenn en 1977. Leur dessin suit les contours du terrain sans imagination particulière et seuls les par 5 sortent un peu de l'ordinaire. Les arbres constituent les principaux obstacles, mais ils font plus de peur que de mal. En dépit d'un assez bon rythme de jeu, on ne fera certainement pas de long détour pour venir jouer ici, mais si l'on passe dans la région, la visite sera sympathique et amusante. Nous sommes peut-être difficiles, mais on imagine qu'il serait possible de remodeler et rajeunir le parcours sans lui retirer son caractère familial.

Relatively flat but in a pleasant woodland setting, this is a sort of large estate around a pretty castle where all the great names in champagne have left their mark. Originally a nine-hole course opened in 1927, it was upgraded to 18 holes by Michael Fenn in 1977. The layout follows the contours of the terrain without too much imagination, and only the par 5s really stand out. The main hazards here are the trees, but their bark (no pun intended) is worse than their bite. Despite a good playing tempo, it is hard to envisage making any long detour to come and play here, but if you are in the region, Reims-Champagne is a pleasant and amusing visit. Perhaps we are being a little too hard, but we believe this course could be redesigned for the better without detracting from its family-style character.

Reims-Champagne — 1977

Château des Dames de France
F - 51390 GUEUX

Office	Secrétariat	(33) 03 26 05 46 10
Pro shop	Pro-shop	(33) 03 26 05 46 10
Fax	Fax	(33) 03 26 05 46 19
Situation	Situation	

Reims (pop. 180 620), 5 km

Annual closure	Fermeture annuelle	no
Weekly closure	Fermeture hebdomadaire	monday

lundi: restaurant (11 → 03)

Fees main season
Tarifs haute saison full day

	Week days Semaine	We/Bank holidays We/Férié
Individual Individuel	200 F	280 F
Couple Couple	400 F	560 F

After 16.00 : GF 120/180

Caddy	Caddy	no
Electric Trolley	Chariot électrique	no
Buggy	Voiturette	150 F/18 holes
Clubs	Clubs	90 F/full day

Credit cards Cartes de crédit VISA - CB

← Soissons
Muizon
N 31
A 26
REIMS
Reims-Tinqueux
GOLF Gueux
A 4
Vrigny
RD 380
Château-Thierry
PARIS
N 51
Pargny-les-Reims
Epernay

0   2   4 km

Access Accès : A4 Exit (Sortie) Reims Tinqueux →
Soissons, → Gueux
Map 3 on page 169 Carte 3 Page 169

GOLF COURSE / PARCOURS — 13/20

Site	Site	▓▓▓▓▓░
Maintenance	Entretien	▓▓▓▓░░
Architect	Architecte	Michael Fenn
Type	Type	parkland, forest
Relief	Relief	▓▓░░░░
Water in play	Eau en jeu	▓▓▓░░░
Exp. to wind	Exposé au vent	▓▓░░░░
Trees in play	Arbres en jeu	▓▓▓▓▓░

Scorecard Carte de score	Chp. Chp.	Mens Mess.	Ladies Da.
Length Long.	6042	5902	5097
Par	72	72	72

Advised golfing ability	0	12	24	36
Niveau de jeu recommandé		▓▓▓▓░░		
Hcp required Handicap exigé	35			

CLUB HOUSE & AMENITIES / CLUB HOUSE ET ANNEXES — 7/10

Pro shop	Pro-shop	▓▓▓▓░░
Driving range	Practice	▓▓▓▓░░
Sheltered	couvert	4 mats
On grass	sur herbe	no, 20 mats open air
Putting-green	putting-green	yes
Pitching-green	pitching green	yes

323

HOTEL FACILITIES / ENVIRONNEMENT HOTELIER — 6/10

HOTELS HÔTELS

Les Crayères — Reims, 5 km
16 rooms, D 1 500 F
Tel (33) 03 26 82 80 80, Fax (33) 03 26 82 65 52

Grand Hôtel des Templiers — Reims, 5 km
19 rooms, D 1 400 F
Tel (33) 03 26 88 55 08, Fax (33) 03 26 47 80 60

La Paix — Reims, 5 km
104 rooms, D 670 F
Tel (33) 03 26 40 04 08, Fax (33) 03 26 47 75 04

RESTAURANTS RESTAURANTS

Les Crayères — Reims, 5 km
Tel (33) 03 26 82 80 80

Vigneraie — Reims, 5 km
Tel (33) 03 26 88 67 27

Chardonnay - Tel (33) 03 26 06 08 60 — Reims 5 km

Non loin du parcours centenaire de Mandelieu, le Riviera s'inscrit dans un paysage totalement différent, démontrant la diversité des paysages français dans un espace pourtant réduit. Quelques trous assez plats et larges contrastent avec des trous «de montagne» souvent étroits par leur dessin. Les arbres, de nombreux bunkers et quelques obstacles d'eau créent de nombreuses difficultés, accentuées par des greens surélevés et les dénivellations, qui amènent à conseiller de jouer en voiturette. Certains trous manquent un peu de franchise, et les visiteurs connaissant mal le parcours seront bien inspirés de jouer sans se soucier du score. Un golf parfois surprenant, au rythme heurté, où il faut garder la tête froide. Mais quelques modifications récentes du tracé en ont singulièrement amélioré la franchise. Un ensemble en gros progrès.

Not far from the centenary course of Cannes-Mandelieu, the Riviera course is located in a totally different setting, as if to demonstrate the variety of French landscapes over a relatively limited surface area. A few flat and wide holes are in stark contrast with the mountain-style holes, which are often tight in layout. The trees, countless bunkers and a few water hazards create a lot of problems, emphasised by elevated greens and by steep slopes (buggy recommended). Some holes are lacking in openness and visitors who are not familiar with the course would be well advised to forget any idea of keeping score. A sometimes surprising course and a little unevenly balanced. A cool head can see you home safely. However, a few recent changes to the layout have most definitely made this a more open course. Remarkable progress is now being achieved.

Riviéra Golf Club — 1991

Avenue des Amazones
F - 06210 MANDELIEU-LA NAPOULE

Office	Secrétariat	(33) 04 92 97 49 49
Pro shop	Pro-shop	(33) 04 90 97 49 49
Fax	Fax	(33) 04 92 97 49 42
Situation	Situation	

Cannes (pop. 68 670), 8 km

Annual closure	Fermeture annuelle	no
Weekly closure	Fermeture hebdomadaire	no

Fees main season
Tarifs haute saison 18 holes

	Week days Semaine	We/Bank holidays We/Férié
Individual Individuel	280 F	300 F
Couple Couple	560 F	600 F

Caddy	Caddy	no
Electric Trolley	Chariot électrique	no
Buggy	Voiturette	180 F/18 holes
Clubs	Clubs	100 F/full day

Credit cards Cartes de crédit
VISA - CB - MasterCard - AMEX

324

Access Accès : A8 Exit (Sortie Mandelieu-La Napoule),
In Mandelieu, turn right on RN7 → Fréjus
Map 14 on page 191 Carte 14 Page 191

GOLF COURSE PARCOURS — 13/20

Site	Site	
Maintenance	Entretien	
Architect	Architecte	R. Trent Jones Sr
Type	Type	parkland, residential
Relief	Relief	
Water in play	Eau en jeu	
Exp. to wind	Exposé au vent	
Trees in play	Arbres en jeu	

Scorecard Carte de score	Chp. Chp.	Mens Mess.	Ladies Da.
Length Long.	5736	5195	4830
Par	72	72	72

Advised golfing ability Niveau de jeu recommandé	0 12 24 36
Hcp required Handicap exigé	35

CLUB HOUSE & AMENITIES CLUB HOUSE ET ANNEXES — 7/10

Pro shop	Pro-shop	
Driving range	Practice	
Sheltered	couvert	no
On grass	sur herbe	yes
Putting-green	putting-green	yes
Pitching-green	pitching green	yes

HOTEL FACILITIES ENVIRONNEMENT HOTELIER — 8/10

HOTELS HÔTELS

Hôtellerie du Golf — Mandelieu
55 rooms, D 640 F — 2 km
Tel (33) 04 93 49 11 66, Fax (33) 04 92 97 04 01

Majestic — Cannes
263 rooms, D 2 200 F — 8 km
Tel (33) 04 92 98 77 00, Fax (33) 04 93 38 97 90

Paris — Cannes
50 rooms, D 700 F — 8 km
Tel (33) 04 93 38 30 89, Fax (33) 04 93 39 04 61

RESTAURANTS RESTAURANTS

L'Oasis — La Napoule
Tel (33) 04 93 49 95 52 — 4 km

L'Armorial — La Napoule
Té l(33) 04 93 49 91 80 — 4 km

Le Riou - Tel(33) 04 93 49 95 56 — La Napoule 3 km

C'est un plaisir dont on ne se lasse pas de retrouver ce type de parcours en forêt, tel que l'on ne peut plus guère en construire aujourd'hui. Ce parcours classique, dessiné par Fred Hawtree, et ouvert en 1964, a été ensuite acquis par le groupe japonais Chisan. Ce parcours offre de magnifiques lumières au printemps et en automne, ajoutant à l'agrément du jeu sur un sol de sable et de terre de bruyère. On peut ainsi l'apparenter à des parcours « inland » « tel que The Berkshire. Ce n'est sans doute pas un chef-d'oeuvre absolu, mais il reste très plaisant à jouer, offrant une grande variété de coups, et nécessitant un bon travail des trajectoires de balle. Les obstacles sont essentiellement les arbres, souvent très dangereux car le parcours est assez étroit, mais aussi les bunkers de fairway et de green, et le relief, parfois assez accidenté pour troubler dans le choix de clubs.

It is always a pleasure to play this type of woodland course, which nowadays is virtually impossible to build. This classic layout, designed by Fred Hawtree, was opened in 1964 and subsequently purchased by the Japanese group Chisan. The light and reflections in spring and autumn are a joy to behold, adding to the pleasure of playing on sandy sub-soil and moor-land. This gives it much in common with inland courses such as The Berkshire. Rochefort is probably not an absolute masterpiece, but it is a very pleasant course to play, requiring a whole variety of shots and ball-control. The hazards are basically the trees, often dangerous as they lean over some pretty tight fairways. But don't forget the fairway and green-side bunkers, either, or the sharp relief which makes club selection harder than usual.

Rochefort-Chisan Country Club — 1964

Route de la Bâte
F - 78730 ROCHEFORT-EN-YVELINES

Office	Secrétariat	(33) 01 30 41 31 81
Pro shop	Pro-shop	(33) 01 30 41 31 81
Fax	Fax	(33) 01 30 41 94 01
Situation	Situation	

Rambouillet (pop. 24 340), 15 km - Paris, 45 km

Annual closure	Fermeture annuelle	no
Weekly closure	Fermeture hebdomadaire	thursday (jeudi)

Fees main season
Tarifs haute saison full day

	Week days Semaine	We/Bank holidays We/Férié
Individual Individuel	250 F	450 F
Couple Couple	500 F	900 F

Wednesdays (merc.), 200 F
Ladies : GF 150 F on Fridays (vend.)

Caddy	Caddy	no
Electric Trolley	Chariot électrique	100 F/18 holes
Buggy	Voiturette	250 F/18 holes
Clubs	Clubs	100 F/full day

Credit cards Cartes de crédit
VISA - CB - Eurocard - MasterCard - AMEX - DC - JCB

Access Accès : A10 Paris Chartres/Orléans, Exit (Sortie) Dourdan
Map 3 on page 168 Carte 3 Page 168

GOLF COURSE PARCOURS — **14**/20

Site	Site	
Maintenance	Entretien	
Architect	Architecte	Fred Hawtree
Type	Type	forest
Relief	Relief	
Water in play	Eau en jeu	
Exp. to wind	Exposé au vent	
Trees in play	Arbres en jeu	

Scorecard Carte de score	Chp. Chp.	Mens Mess.	Ladies Da.
Length Long.	5735	5165	5165
Par	71	71	71

Advised golfing ability Niveau de jeu recommandé		0 12 24 36
Hcp required Handicap exigé		24 Men, 28 Ladies (We)

CLUB HOUSE & AMENITIES CLUB HOUSE ET ANNEXES — **6**/10

Pro shop	Pro-shop	
Driving range	Practice	
Sheltered	couvert	8 mats
On grass	sur herbe	no, 10 mats open air
Putting-green	putting-green	yes
Pitching-green	pitching green	yes

HOTEL FACILITIES ENVIRONNEMENT HOTELIER — **4**/10

HOTELS HÔTELS

Abbaye les Vaux de Cernay — Cernay-la-Ville
58 rooms, D 800 F — 11 km
Tel (33) 01 34 85 23 00, Fax (33) 01 34 85 11 60

Auberge du Gros Marronnier — Senlisse
16 rooms, D 425 F — 13 km
Tel (33) 01 30 52 51 69, Fax (33) 01 30 52 55 91

Blanche de Castille - 41 rooms, D 750 F — Dourdan
Tel (33) 01 64 59 90 90, Fax (33) 01 64 59 48 90 — 9 km

RESTAURANTS RESTAURANT

La Brazoucade — Rochefort-en-Yvelines
Tel (33) 01 30 41 49 09 — 2 km

L'Escu de Rohan — Rochefort-en-Yvelines
Tel (33) 01 30 41 31 33 — 2 km

325

Tracé principalement en forêt de chênes, hêtres et bouleaux (avec une demi-douzaine de trous de style links), et sur un terrain peu accidenté, ce parcours porte sans aucun doute la signature de Jeremy Pern, pour le nombre et le dessin des bunkers, de fairways comme de défense des greens. Le dessin est assez varié pour exiger tous les types de coups, ou même offrir un choix entre les approches roulées à la britannique et le «jeu de cible» à l'américaine. Les obstacles d'eau sont peu nombreux et pas trop dangereux, tous les niveaux de jeu peuvent donc cohabiter sur ce golf plaisant, dans un décor très agréable. Les greens sont de bonne dimension, et généralement très modelés : attention aux trois putts... L'ouverture d'un très joli hôtel sur place, avec une bonne table, fait de ce golf un ensemble plein de charme et une bonne destination de week-end.

This course is basically laid out through a forest of oak, beech and birch trees (plus half a dozen links holes) over flattish terrain. Looking at the number and design of bunkers, the fairways and greens, there is no doubt that this is a Jeremy Pern creation. The layout is varied enough to demand every shot in the book or even offer a choice between British "bump and run" shots and American-style target golf. Water hazards are few and far between and not too dangerous, so players of all abilities can play this pleasant course in a very attractive setting. The greens are large and slope a lot, so watch out for the 3 putts. The opening of a very pretty hotel in situ with excellent food makes this a very charming course indeed.

Domaine de Roncemay 1991
F - 89110 CHASSY

Office	Secrétariat	(33) 03 86 73 50 50
Pro shop	Pro-shop	(33) 03 86 73 50 62
Fax	Fax	(33) 03 86 73 69 46
Situation	Situation	

Joigny (pop. 9 690), 19 km - Auxerre (pop. 38 810), 20 km

Annual closure	Fermeture annuelle	no
Weekly closure	Fermeture hebdomadaire	no

Fees main season
Tarifs haute saison full day

	Week days Semaine	We/Bank holidays We/Férié
Individual Individuel	200 F	280 F
Couple Couple	400 F	600 F

Summer (été) after 17.00 : GF 120 F

Caddy	Caddy	no
Electric Trolley	Chariot électrique	85 F/18 holes
Buggy	Voiturette	200 F/18 holes
Clubs	Clubs	50 F/18 holes

Credit cards Cartes de crédit
VISA - CB - Eurocard - MasterCard - AMEX - DC - JCB

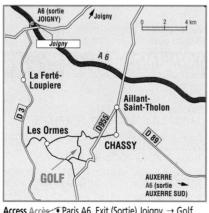

Access Accès : • Paris A6, Exit (Sortie) Joigny, → Golf
• Lyon A6, Exit (Sortie) Auxerre Nord → Aillant-sur-Tholon par D 89, → Golf
Map 3 on page 169 Carte 3 Page 169

326

GOLF COURSE
PARCOURS   15/20

Site	Site	
Maintenance	Entretien	
Architect	Architecte	Jeremy Pern
Type	Type	forest, open country
Relief	Relief	
Water in play	Eau en jeu	
Exp. to wind	Exposé au vent	
Trees in play	Arbres en jeu	

Scorecard Carte de score	Chp. Chp.	Mens Mess.	Ladies Da.
Length Long.	6401	5808	5257
Par	72	72	72

Advised golfing ability		0	12	24	36
Niveau de jeu recommandé					
Hcp required	Handicap exigé	35			

CLUB HOUSE & AMENITIES
CLUB HOUSE ET ANNEXES   7/10

Pro shop	Pro-shop	
Driving range	Practice	
Sheltered	couvert	12 mats
On grass	sur herbe	yes
Putting-green	putting-green	yes
Pitching-green	pitching green	yes

HOTEL FACILITIES
ENVIRONNEMENT HOTELIER   7/10

HOTELS HÔTELS

Domaine de Roncemay 16 rooms, D 750 F Tel (33) 03 86 73 50 50, Fax (33) 03 86 73 69 46	Chassy on site
A la Côte Saint-Jacques 29 rooms, D 1 000 F Tel (33) 03 86 62 09 70, Fax (33) 03 86 91 49 70	Joigny 19 km
Modern'Hôtel 21 rooms, D 500 F Tel (33) 03 86 62 16 28, Fax (33) 03 86 62 44 33	Joigny 19 km

RESTAURANTS RESTAURANTS

La Côte Saint-Jacques Tel (33) 03 86 62 09 70	Joigny 19 km
Jean-Luc Barnabet Tel (33) 03 86 51 68 88	Auxerre 20 km

Bob von Hagge a intelligemment tiré profit d'un espace réduit, et créé un parcours excitant et spectaculaire, qui ne laisse pas indifférent. Au moins pour pouvoir en juger, Royal Mougins mérite une visite attentive. Certains joueurs discutent le « modernisme » du parcours comme son étroitesse, mais celle-ci est plus visuelle que réelle : certes, de nombreux mouvements de terrain animent de manière spectaculaire les limites de fairway, mais ils ramènent volontiers la balle en jeu. Ici, il faut jouer avec sa tête, et rester précis, ne serait-ce que pour éviter les obstacles d'eau menaçants qui ponctuent le parcours. Mais comme sa longueur est raisonnable, les frappeurs peuvent facilement jouer leurs coups de départ avec un bois 3 ou un long fer. La plupart du temps, les seconds coups seront joués avec des petits et moyens fers, ce qui ne devrait pas poser de problèmes aux joueurs expérimentés... Le prix de la journée n'est pas vraiment à la portée d'une famille avec enfants !

Bob von Hagge has made very intelligent use of limited space and created an exciting and spectacular course, with no room for indifference. Royal Mougins is well worth a close visit if only to judge for yourself. Some players question the course's modernism and tightness, but the latter is visual rather than real. We agree that the slanting terrain sometimes adds rather spectacular goings-on at the edges of the fairway, but it also helps bring the ball back into play. This is a course you play with your brains, where precision play is at a premium, if only to avoid the water hazards dotted around the 18 holes. But being of reasonable length, big-hitters can easily tee off with a 3-wood or long iron. Approach shots are played mostly with short or mid-irons, so experienced players should not find the going too tough... The price you pay for a full day's golfing is on the highest side for a family of four.

Royal Mougins Golf Club — 1993

424, avenue du Roi
F - 06250 MOUGINS

Office	Secrétariat	(33) 04 92 92 49 69
Pro shop	Pro-shop	(33) 04 92 92 49 79
Fax	Fax	(33) 04 92 92 49 70
Situation	Situation	

Cannes (pop. 68 670), 10 km - Grasse (pop. 41 390), 20 km

Annual closure	Fermeture annuelle	no
Weekly closure	Fermeture hebdomadaire	no

Fees main season
Tarifs haute saison full day

	Week days Semaine	We/Bank holidays We/Férié
Individual Individuel	1 000 F*	1 000 F*
Couple Couple	2 000 F*	2 000 F*

* GF all-day + practice + lunch

Caddy	Caddy	on request
Electric Trolley	Chariot électrique	70 F/18 holes
Buggy	Voiturette	100 F/18 holes
Clubs	Clubs	100 F/full day

Credit cards Cartes de crédit
VISA - CB - Eurocard - MasterCard - AMEX

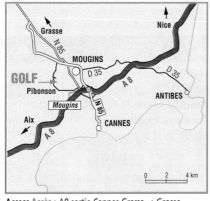

Access Accès : A8 sortie Cannes-Grasse → Grasse,
3e sortie Mougins Pibonson, Saint-Martin
Map 14 on page 191 Carte 14 Page 191

GOLF COURSE / PARCOURS — 17/20

Site	Site	
Maintenance	Entretien	
Architect	Architecte	Robert von Hagge
Type	Type	forest, hilly
Relief	Relief	
Water in play	Eau en jeu	
Exp. to wind	Exposé au vent	
Trees in play	Arbres en jeu	

Scorecard Carte de score	Chp. Chp.	Mens Mess.	Ladies Da.
Length Long.	6004	5697	4926
Par	71	71	71

Advised golfing ability		0 12 24 36
Niveau de jeu recommandé		
Hcp required	Handicap exigé	30

CLUB HOUSE & AMENITIES / CLUB HOUSE ET ANNEXES — 7/10

Pro shop	Pro-shop	
Driving range	Practice	
Sheltered	couvert	no
On grass	sur herbe	yes
Putting-green	putting-green	yes
Pitching-green	pitching green	yes

327

HOTEL FACILITIES / ENVIRONNEMENT HOTELIER — 8/10

HOTELS HÔTELS

Mas Candille — Mougins
23 rooms, D 900 F — 3 km
Tel (33) 04 93 90 00 85, Fax (33) 04 92 92 85 56

Hôtel de Mougins — Mougins
50 rooms, D 1 070 F — 3 km
Tel (33) 04 92 92 17 07, Fax (33) 04 92 92 17 08

Le Manoir de l'Etang — Mougins
15 rooms, D 1 000 F — 3 km
Tel (33) 04 93 90 01 07, Fax (33) 04 92 92 20 70

RESTAURANTS RESTAURANTS

Les Muscadins — Mougins
Tel (33) 04 92 28 28 28 — 3 km

Le Feu Follet — Mougins
Tel (33) 04 93 90 15 78 — 3 km

La Ferme de Mougins — Mougins
Tel (33) 04 93 90 03 74 — 3 km

Entre les villes d'Angers et du Mans, cet ensemble de 27 trous s'est s'imposé dans le groupe de tête des parcours français, alors que l'on ne s'attendait pas à trouver des tracés d'une telle qualité en pleine campagne. Entre la Sarthe et la Forêt de Pincé, Michel Gayon a dessiné trois 9 trous combinables de longueur raisonnable et le terrain moyennement accidenté permet de les jouer tous en une seule journée. Sur la combinaison «La Forêt-La Rivière», l'eau intervient sur une dizaine de trous, sans être trop effrayante pour autant. «La Cascade» revendique un caractère plus écossais, avec beaucoup de bosses, de bunkers d'herbe et de sable, mais aussi un peu d'eau, comme au 8. On éprouve ici une très bonne impression d'espace et de calme, propice à la concentration que réclame ce golf à connaître, hors des circuits golfiques traditionnels.

Between Angers and Le Mans, this 27-hole complex has edged its way into the group of leading French courses at a time when no-one was expecting such a great layout right out in the country. Michel Gayon has designed three inter-combinable 9-hole courses of reasonable length, stretching between the river Sarthe and a large forest. On flattish terrain, all three can be played in one day. On the "Forêt-Rivière" combination, water is present on ten holes but is never too intimidating. "La Cascade" is more Scottish in nature, with lots of sandhills, grass- and sand-bunkers, and also a little water, like on the 8th. Here you get a great feeling of space and of tranquillity, suitable for the concentration required when playing a course like this. A club that is well worth discovering outside the traditional golfing circuits.

Golf de Sablé-Solesmes — 1991
Domaine de l'Outinière, route de Pincé
F - 72300 SABLE-SUR-SARTHE

Office	Secrétariat	(33) 02 43 95 28 78
Pro shop	Pro-shop	(33) 02 43 95 28 78
Fax	Fax	(33) 02 43 92 39 05
Situation	Situation	

La Flèche (pop. 14 950), 26 km
Le Mans (pop. 145 500), 59 km

Annual closure	Fermeture annuelle	no
Weekly closure	Fermeture hebdomadaire	no

Fees main season
Tarifs haute saison full day

	Week days Semaine	We/Bank holidays We/Férié
Individual Individuel	230 F	290 F
Couple Couple	420 F	520 F

Caddy	Caddy	no
Electric Trolley	Chariot électrique	60 F/18 holes
Buggy	Voiturette	200 F/18 holes
Clubs	Clubs	60 F/full day

Credit cards Cartes de crédit
VISA - CB - Eurocard - MasterCard

GOLF
Sablé-sur-Solesmes

Pincé
Forêt de Pincé
Précigné
D 306
LE MANS
ANGERS
A 11
Sablé/La Flèche
D 24
La Flèche

0   2   4 km

Access Accès : Le Mans-Angers, A11 Exit (Sortie) La Flèche, turn right on D306 → Sablé-sur-Sarthe
Map 6 on page 175 Carte 6 Page 175

GOLF COURSE / PARCOURS — 16/20

Site	Site	■■■■□□
Maintenance	Entretien	■■■■■□
Architect	Architecte	Michel Gayon
Type	Type	open country
Relief	Relief	■□□□□□
Water in play	Eau en jeu	■■■□□□
Exp. to wind	Exposé au vent	■■□□□□
Trees in play	Arbres en jeu	■□□□□□

Scorecard Carte de score	Chp. Chp.	Mens Mess.	Ladies Da.
Length Long.	6207	5753	5250
Par	72	72	72

Advised golfing ability		0 12 24 36
Niveau de jeu recommandé		■■■■■
Hcp required	Handicap exigé	35

CLUB HOUSE & AMENITIES / CLUB HOUSE ET ANNEXES — 7/10

Pro shop	Pro-shop	■■■■□□
Driving range	Practice	■■■■■□
Sheltered	couvert	7 mats
On grass	sur herbe	yes
Putting-green	putting-green	yes
Pitching-green	pitching green	yes

HOTEL FACILITIES / ENVIRONNEMENT HOTELIER — 4/10

HOTELS HÔTELS
Grand Hôtel — Solesmes
34 rooms, D 600 F — 4 km
Tel (33) 02 43 95 45 10, Fax (33) 02 43 95 22 26

Haras de la Potardière — Crosnières
17 rooms, D 650 F — 20 km
Tel (33) 02 43 45 83 47, Fax (33) 02 43 45 81 06

RESTAURANTS RESTAURANTS
Escu du Roy — Sablé
Tel (33) 02 43 95 90 31 — 6 km

Hostellerie Saint-Martin — Sablé
Tel (33) 02 43 95 00 03 — 6 km

Martin Pêcheur — Golf
Tel (33) 02 43 95 97 55 — on site

328

SAINT-CLOUD VERT

14 7 7

Etre le Club le plus proche de Paris a beaucoup contribué à sa réputation, mais aussi à la difficulté d'y venir jouer. A côté du petit parcours «Jaune,» dont une bonne moitié des trous ne manquent pas d'intérêt, le «Vert» a reçu de nombreuses compétitions internationales, même si sa longueur peut paraître aujourd'hui insuffisante. Il a été dessiné par Harry S. Colt, mais a fait l'objet de divers aménagements qui peuvent parfois donner l'impression de styles différents, en particulier pour ceux des bunkers. Très agréable dans son déroulement, avec des vues superbes sur Paris, pas trop accidenté, ornementé d'une végétation somptueuse (à voir en automne !), c'est l'une des plus jolies oasis de la région, à déguster pendant les soirées d'été quand les membres sont en vacances ailleurs. L'entretien n'est pas toujours au niveau de ce grand club.

Being the closest club to Paris has done much for its reputation and for the difficulty encountered in being able to play here. Alongside the little «Jaune» course, where a good half of the holes offer much appeal, the «Vert» course has hosted many international tournaments even though its length, by today's standards, may appear a little on the short side. It was designed by Harry Colt but has been restyled in a variety of ways which can sometimes give the impression of different styles joined together, especially as far as the bunkers are concerned. The course unwinds very pleasantly with some superb views over Paris, is not too hilly and is cloaked with some lush vegetation (gorgeous in Autumn). This is one of the region's prettiest oases, a great «watering hole» to enjoy on Summer evenings when the members are on holiday elsewhere. Up keep is not more than average.

Golf de Saint-Cloud		1912
60, rue du 19 Janvier		
F - 92380 GARCHES		
Office	Secrétariat	(33) 01 47 01 01 85
Pro shop	Pro-shop	(33) 01 47 41 01 45
Fax	Fax	(33) 01 47 01 19 57
Situation	Situation	Paris , 15 km
Annual closure	Fermeture annuelle	no
Weekly closure	Fermeture hebdomadaire	monday (lundi)

Fees main season
Tarifs haute saison 18 holes

	Week days Semaine	We/Bank holidays We/Férié
Individual Individuel	450 F*	600 F**
Couple Couple	900 F	1 200 F

* members' guests (invitation)
** with a member (avec un membre)

Caddy	Caddy	on request
Electric Trolley	Chariot électrique	80 F/18 holes
Buggy	Voiturette	no
Clubs	Clubs	yes

Credit cards Cartes de crédit
VISA - CB - Eurocard - MasterCard

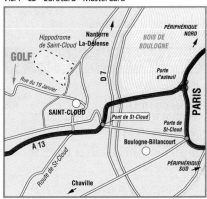

Access Accès : Paris Porte Maillot,
Bois de Boulogne → Suresnes. Pont de Suresnes,
Bld H. Sellier, → Hippodrome St Cloud.
Turn right into Rue du 19 janvier. → Golf St Cucufa.
Map 15 on page 192 Carte 15 Page 192

GOLF COURSE / PARCOURS — **14**/20

Site	Site	
Maintenance	Entretien	
Architect	Architecte	Harry S. Colt
Type	Type	parkland
Relief	Relief	
Water in play	Eau en jeu	
Exp. to wind	Exposé au vent	
Trees in play	Arbres en jeu	

Scorecard Carte de score	Chp. Chp.	Mens Mess.	Ladies Da.
Length Long.	5975	5975	4985
Par	72	72	72

Advised golfing ability		0 12 24 36
Niveau de jeu recommandé		
Hcp required	Handicap exigé	24 Men, 28 Ladies

CLUB HOUSE & AMENITIES / CLUB HOUSE ET ANNEXES — **7**/10

Pro shop	Pro-shop	
Driving range	Practice	
Sheltered	couvert	46 mats
On grass	sur herbe	no
Putting-green	putting-green	yes (2)
Pitching-green	pitching green	yes

HOTEL FACILITIES / ENVIRONNEMENT HOTELIER — **7**/10

HOTELS HÔTELS

Villa Henri IV		Saint-Cloud
36 rooms, D 550 F		4 km
Tel (33) 01 46 02 59 30, Fax (33) 01 49 11 11 02		
Quorum		Saint-Cloud
58 rooms, D 565 F		4 km
Tel (33) 01 47 71 22 33, Fax (33) 01 46 02 75 64		
Concorde La Fayette		Paris Pte Maillot
950 rooms, D 1 500 F		10 km
Tel (33) 01 40 68 50 68, Fax (33) 01 40 68 50 43		

RESTAURANTS RESTAURANTS

Guy Savoy		Paris 17e
Tel (33) 01 43 80 40 61		12 km
Le Petit Colombier		Paris 17e
Tel (33) 01 43 80 28 54		11 km
Michel Rostang		Paris 17e
Tel (33) 01 47 63 40 77		12 km

329

Saint Donat a été un des premiers parcours de la région à présenter une architecture «moderne». Robert Trent Jones Jr lui a donné des contours très variés, utilisant avec intelligence la végétation existante, les reliefs (surtout au retour) et modelant sans excès les espaces plus plats. Ce qui donne un dessin très précis, où les méandres d'une petite rivière viennent en jeu sur une bonne demi-douzaine de trous. De nombreux bunkers et des bouquets d'arbres (notamment de très beaux vieux chênes) constituent des obstacles parfois préoccupants. Ici, il faut s'appuyer sur la technique, la sagesse dans le choix de club et pas sur la longueur, mais les joueurs de tous niveaux peuvent y évoluer, après une petite période d'adaptation. Alors que les dix premiers trous sont assez plats, le retour est accidenté et beaucoup plus torturé, mais assez facile à marcher en condition physique normale.

Saint Donat was one of the first courses in this region with so-called «modern» architecture. Robert Trent Jones Jr moulded the course into a variety of shapes, making intelligent use of existing vegetation and relief (especially on the back nine) and contouring the flatter areas without ever going over the top. The result is a very precise layout, where the meanders of a small river come into play on half a dozen or so holes. A good number of bunkers and groups of trees (including some beautiful oaks) form some pretty worrying hazards. Emphasis should be on technique and prudence in the choice of club, not on length. But after a period of adjustment, all players can enjoy a round of golf here. While the first ten holes are rather flat, the last eight are hilly and more tricky encounters but easily walkable for the average able-bodied golfer.

Golf de Saint Donat — 1993
270, route de Cannes
F - 06130 PLAN-DE-GRASSE

Office	Secrétariat	(33) 04 93 09 76 60
Pro shop	Pro-shop	(33) 04 93 09 76 60
Fax	Fax	(33) 04 93 09 76 63
Situation	Situation	

Grasse (pop. 41 390), 2 km - Cannes (pop. 68 670), 18 km

Annual closure	Fermeture annuelle	no
Weekly closure	Fermeture hebdomadaire	no

Fees main season
Tarifs haute saison 18 holes

	Week days Semaine	We/Bank holidays We/Férié
Individual Individuel	320 F	320 F
Couple Couple	640 F	640 F

End of afternoon (en soirée): GF 220 F

Caddy	Caddy	no
Electric Trolley	Chariot électrique	100 F/18 holes
Buggy	Voiturette	200 F/18 holes
Clubs	Clubs	80 F/18 holes

Credit cards Cartes de crédit
VISA - CB - Eurocard - MasterCard - AMEX - DC

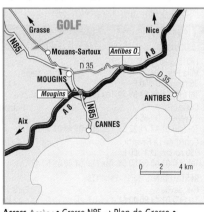

Access Accès : • Grasse N85 → Plan-de-Grasse • Cannes, Motorway → N85 Grasse, Mouans-Sartoux, → Golf de Saint Donat
Map 14 on page 191 Carte 14 Page 191

GOLF COURSE / PARCOURS — 15/20

Site	Site	▰▰▰▱▱
Maintenance	Entretien	▰▰▰▰▱
Architect	Architecte	R. Trent Jones Jr
Type	Type	hilly, parkland
Relief	Relief	▰▰▰▱▱
Water in play	Eau en jeu	▰▰▱▱▱
Exp. to wind	Exposé au vent	▰▰▰▱▱
Trees in play	Arbres en jeu	▰▰▰▱▱

Scorecard Carte de score	Chp. Chp.	Mens Mess.	Ladies Da.
Length Long.	6031	5558	5082
Par	71	71	71

Advised golfing ability		0	12	24	36
Niveau de jeu recommandé				▰▰	
Hcp required Handicap exigé	30				

CLUB HOUSE & AMENITIES / CLUB HOUSE ET ANNEXES — 7/10

Pro shop	Pro-shop	▰▰▰▰▱
Driving range	Practice	▰▰▰▱▱
Sheltered	couvert	6 mats
On grass	sur herbe	no, 30 mats open air
Putting-green	putting-green	yes
Pitching-green	pitching green	yes

HOTEL FACILITIES / ENVIRONNEMENT HOTELIER — 8/10

HOTELS HÔTELS

Hôtel de Mougins — Mougins
50 rooms, D 1 070 F — 6 km
Tel (33) 04 92 92 17 07, Fax (33) 04 92 92 17 08

Le Manoir de l'Etang — Mougins
15 rooms, D 1 000 F — 6 km
Tel (33) 04 93 90 01 07, Fax (33) 04 92 92 20 70

Domaine de l'Albatros — Mouans-Sartoux
44 rooms, D 310 F — 500 m
Tel (33) 04 79 68 26 26, Fax (33) 04 79 68 26 29

RESTAURANTS RESTAURANTS

Bastide Saint Antoine — Grasse
Tel (33) 04 93 70 94 94 — 2 km

Les Muscadins — Mougins
Tel (33) 04 92 28 28 28 — 6 km

330

Dans un paysage typique de Provence, ce parcours de Michel Gayon en épouse les reliefs, d'où quelques greens aveugles, dont certains d'ailleurs auraient pu être évités. Certains coups forcément hasardeux atténuent le plaisir que l'on peut éprouver sur ce golf en pleine nature, dont le relief accentué invite à jouer en voiturette. Parce que la tactique de jeu n'est pas évidente à assimiler, parce qu'il faut connaître le parcours pour bien évaluer les distances, parce que que la chance joue ici un rôle important, on s'amusera beaucoup plus en match-play (où tout peut arriver) qu'en stroke play. Avec plusieurs trous spectaculaires et pour la beauté de son environnement, Saint-Endreol vaut incontestablement le détour. Le 17 a été conçu comme un par 5, mais reste toujours inscrit en par 4. Ne tenez pas compte de la carte, jouez le en par 5, vous serez moins déçu par votre score.

Laid out in typical Provence style countryside, Michel Gayon's course hugs the contours of the landscape and in the process provides a number of blind greens, some of which could have been avoided. Certain hazardous shots tend to dampen the enjoyment of this course right out in the country, and whose hilly terrain make a buggy a wise decision. This is a match-play course (where anything can happen) rather than a course for stroke-play, simply because the tactics needed here are not always obvious, because you need to know the course to evaluate distances, and because luck plays perhaps a bigger role than usual. With several spectacular holes and a beautiful setting, Saint Endréol is most certainly well worth the visit. The 17th was designed like a par 5 but stays a par 4. Forget what's written on the card and play it in 5 to avoid disappointment.

Golf de Saint-Endréol — 1992

Route de Bagnols-en-Forêt
F - 83920 LA MOTTE-EN-PROVENCE

Office	Secrétariat	(33) 04 94 51 89 89
Pro shop	Pro-shop	(33) 04 94 51 89 89
Fax	Fax	(33) 04 94 51 89 90
Situation	Situation	

Draguignan (pop. 30 180), 10 km
Saint-Raphaël (pop. 26 620), 18 km

Annual closure	Fermeture annuelle	no
Weekly closure	Fermeture hebdomadaire	no

Fees main season
Tarifs haute saison 18 holes

	Week days Semaine	We/Bank holidays We/Férié
Individual Individuel	330 F	330 F
Couple Couple	660 F	660 F

Caddy	Caddy	on request
Electric Trolley	Chariot électrique	no
Buggy	Voiturette	150 F/18 holes
Clubs	Clubs	80 F/full day

Credit cards Cartes de crédit
VISA - CB - Eurocard - MasterCard - AMEX

Access Accès : Saint-Raphaël, N7, Exit (Sortie) Le Muy, D54 → La Motte-en- Provence, → Golf
Map 14 on page 191 Carte 14 Page 191

GOLF COURSE — PARCOURS — 15/20

Site	Site	
Maintenance	Entretien	
Architect	Architecte	Michel Gayon
Type	Type	hilly, forest
Relief	Relief	
Water in play	Eau en jeu	
Exp. to wind	Exposé au vent	
Trees in play	Arbres en jeu	

Scorecard Carte de score	Chp. Chp.	Mens Mess.	Ladies Da.
Length Long.	6219	5940	5011
Par	72	72	72

Advised golfing ability		0	12	24	36
Niveau de jeu recommandé					
Hcp required	Handicap exigé	35			

CLUB HOUSE & AMENITIES — CLUB HOUSE ET ANNEXES — 7/10

Pro shop	Pro-shop	
Driving range	Practice	
Sheltered	couvert	7 mats
On grass	sur herbe	no, 15 mats open air
Putting-green	putting-green	yes
Pitching-green	pitching green	yes

HOTEL FACILITIES — ENVIRONNEMENT HOTELIER — 4/10

HOTELS HÔTELS

Résidence du Golf — Golf
15 Suites, D 600/900 F — on site
Tel (33) 04 64 51 89 89, Fax (33) 04 64 51 89 90

Le Logis du Guetteur — Les Arcs
10 rooms, D 630 F — 6 km
Tel (33) 04 94 99 51 10, Fax (33) 04 94 99 51 29

Les Gorges de Pennafort — Callas
16 rooms, D 7950 F — 11 km
Tel (33) 04 94 76 66 51, Fax (33) 04 94 76 67 23

RESTAURANTS RESTAURANTS

Les Pignatelles — La Motte
Tel (33) 04 94 70 25 70 — 5 km

Le Logis du Guetteur — Les Arcs
Tel (33) 04 94 99 51 10 — 6 km

Les Gorges de Pennafort — Callas11 km
Tel (33) 04 94 76 66 51

331

On le considère parfois comme trop court, c'est peut-être vrai pour les meilleurs professionnels, mais bien suffisant pour 99,99 % des golfeurs, qui ont souvent du mal à y jouer leur handicap ! On y verra plutôt la quintessence de l'architecture britannique sur un terrain très plat et très ramassé, avec un très bon rythme d'enchaînement des trous et des difficultés, quelques reliefs subtils, notamment en approche des greens et sur les greens, généralement très vastes. Un seul regret, le nouveau green du 2, sans rapport avec le style « d'époque ». Les obstacles essentiels sont les arbres, majestueux mais pas oppressants, et surtout les bunkers, typiques des idées stratégiques de Colt, et souvent de formes très belles. Scorer ici demande un jeu très complet, et d'abord de ne pas se laisser endormir par la tranquille séduction du lieu.

Saint-Germain may well sometimes be considered too short for the top pros but it certainly is long enough for 99,99% of golfers who often find playing to their handicap here something of an exploit. We see it rather as the quintessence of British-style design over very flat and very squat landscape. There is a remarkable flow of continuity between holes and difficulties and some subtly-shaped terrain, particularly when approaching or actually on the generally very large greens. Our one regret is the new green on the 2nd hole, which has nothing in common with the course's «period» style. The basic hazards are trees, majestic enough but not too interfering, and especially bunkers, typical of designer Colt's ideas of strategy and often wonderfully shaped. You need an all-round game to score well here and don't let the balmy appeal of the site distract you from the task at hand.

Golf de Saint-Germain — 1922

Route de Poissy
F - 78100 SAINT-GERMAIN-EN-LAYE

Office	Secrétariat	(33) 01 39 10 30 30
Pro shop	Pro-shop	(33) 01 39 73 87 48
Fax	Fax	(33) 01 39 10 30 31
Situation	Situation	

Paris , 26 km - Saint-Germain (pop. 39 320), 4 km

Annual closure	Fermeture annuelle	no
Weekly closure	Fermeture hebdomadaire	monday (lundi)

Fees main season
Tarifs haute saison 18 holes

	Week days Semaine	We/Bank holidays We/Férié
Individual Individuel	400 F	—
Couple Couple	800 F	—

We : only member and guests (membres et leurs invités)

Caddy	Caddy	on request/200 F
Electric Trolley	Chariot électrique	no
Buggy	Voiturette	no
Clubs	Clubs	150 F/full day

Credit cards Cartes de crédit
VISA - CB - Eurocard - MasterCard - AMEX

332

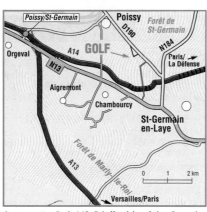

Access Accès : Paris A13, Exit (Sortie) → Saint-Germain.
N13 → Poissy, N184 then D190 → Poissy. Golf on left
hand side. **Map 15 on page 192** Carte 15 Page 192

GOLF COURSE / PARCOURS — 17/20

Site	Site	▬▬▬▬
Maintenance	Entretien	▬▬▬▬
Architect	Architecte	Harry S. Colt
Type	Type	forest
Relief	Relief	▬
Water in play	Eau en jeu	
Exp. to wind	Exposé au vent	▬
Trees in play	Arbres en jeu	▬▬

Scorecard Carte de score	Chp. Chp.	Mens Mess.	Ladies Da.
Length Long.	6117	5805	5224
Par	72	72	72

Advised golfing ability
Niveau de jeu recommandé — 0 12 24 36

Hcp required Handicap exigé — 24 Men, 28 Ladies

CLUB HOUSE & AMENITIES / CLUB HOUSE ET ANNEXES — 7/10

Pro shop	Pro-shop	▬▬▬
Driving range	Practice	▬▬▬
Sheltered	couvert	17 mats
On grass	sur herbe	yes
Putting-green	putting-green	yes
Pitching-green	pitching green	yes

HOTEL FACILITIES / ENVIRONNEMENT HOTELIER — 7/10

HOTELS HÔTELS

La Forestière (Cazaudehore) — Saint-Germain
25 rooms, D 950 F — 5 km
Tel (33) 01 39 73 36 60, Fax (33) 01 39 73 93 88

Pavillon Henri IV — Saint-Germain
42 rooms, D 1 290 F — 4 km
Tel (33) 01 39 10 15 15, Fax (33) 01 39 93 73 93

Ermitage des Loges — Saint-Germain
57 rooms, D 660 F — 5 km
Tel (33) 01 39 21 50 90, Fax (33) 01 39 21 50 91

RESTAURANTS RESTAURANTS

Cazaudehore — Saint-Germain
Tel (33) 01 30 61 64 64 — 5 km

La Feuillantine — Saint-Germain
Tel (33) 01 34 51 04 24 — 4 km

Ce parcours s'est vite imposé parmi les meilleurs parcours de ces dernières années, et il maintient son standing. Il prouve que l'on peut faire de bons parcours même avec de petits budgets... Situé en bord de mer, son dessin est un hommage à l'architecture de links, même dans la dizaine de trous (parfois très étroits) situés dans une forêt de pins maritimes et de chênes verts. Les fairways très modelés, les greens souvent à double ou même triple plateau suivent les reliefs des dunes, dans un souci évident de préserver la nature. L'architecte Yves Bureau a joué davantage sur la nécessité de précision que sur la longueur, mais le vent peut rendre ce parcours démoniaque. Les Britanniques n'y seront certes pas dépaysés ! Le parcours est jouable sans problème toute l'année, et ses tarifs très raisonnables en font l'un des meilleurs rapports qualité/prix de France.

This course quickly became established as one of the best new layouts in recent years and has preserved its status. It also proves that good courses are possible even on low budgets. Laid out along the sea, this is a hommage to links golf, even though ten or so holes (sometimes very tight indeed) wind their way through a forest of maritime pines and oak trees. The highly contoured fairways and two- or even three-tiered greens hug the relief of the dunes with obvious emphasis on preserving the natural landscape. Architect Yves Bureau has played more on the need for precision rather than length, but the wind can make this a devilishly hard course. The British will certainly feel at home here. Saint Jean de Monts is easily playable all year and green fees are very reasonable, thus making this one of the best values for money in France.

Golf de Saint-Jean-de-Monts — 1988

Avenue des Pays-de-la-Loire
F - 85160 SAINT-JEAN-DE-MONTS

Office	Secrétariat	(33) 02 51 58 82 73
Pro shop	Pro-shop	(33) 02 51 58 82 73
Fax	Fax	(33) 02 51 59 18 32
Situation	Situation	

Challans (pop. 14 200), 17 km - Nantes (pop. 252 030), 70 km

Annual closure	Fermeture annuelle	no
Weekly closure	Fermeture hebdomadaire	no

tuesday (mardi), club-house closed from 01/11 to 31/03

Fees main season
Tarifs haute saison full day

	Week days Semaine	We/Bank holidays We/Férié
Individual Individuel	280 F	280 F
Couple Couple	560 F	560 F

GF + lunch 320 F

Caddy	Caddy	no
Electric Trolley	Chariot électrique	80 F/18 holes
Buggy	Voiturette	150 F/18 holes
Clubs	Clubs	70 F/full day

Credit cards Cartes de crédit
VISA - CB - Eurocard - MasterCard - AMEX

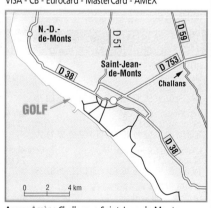

Access Accès : Challans → Saint-Jean-de-Monts, → Golf
Map 6 on page 174 Carte 6 Page 174

GOLF COURSE
PARCOURS   16/20

Site	Site	
Maintenance	Entretien	
Architect	Architecte	Yves Bureau
Type	Type	forest, links
Relief	Relief	
Water in play	Eau en jeu	
Exp. to wind	Exposé au vent	
Trees in play	Arbres en jeu	

Scorecard Carte de score	Chp. Chp.	Mens Mess.	Ladies Da.
Length Long.	5962	5620	5026
Par	72	72	72

Advised golfing ability Niveau de jeu recommandé		0 12 24 36
Hcp required Handicap exigé	35	

CLUB HOUSE & AMENITIES
CLUB HOUSE ET ANNEXES   6/10

Pro shop	Pro-shop	
Driving range	Practice	
Sheltered	couvert	10 mats
On grass	sur herbe	no, 20 mats open air
Putting-green	putting-green	yes
Pitching-green	pitching green	yes

HOTEL FACILITIES
ENVIRONNEMENT HOTELIER   5/10

HOTELS HÔTELS

Mercure		100 m
44 rooms, D 720 F		
Tel (33) 02 51 59 15 15, Fax (33) 02 51 59 91 03		
Hôtel de la Plage	N.-D.-de-Monts	5 km
49 rooms, D 485 F		
Tel (33) 02 51 58 83 09, Fax (33) 02 51 58 97 12		
Château de la Vérie	Challans	15 km
23 rooms, D 880 F		
Tel (33) 02 51 35 33 44, Fax (33) 02 51 35 14 84		

RESTAURANTS RESTAURANTS

Hôtel de la Plage	N.-D.-de-Monts	5 km
Tel (33) 02 51 58 83 09		
Petit St-Jean	St-Jean-de-Monts	1 km
Tel (33) 02 51 59 78 50		

333

Beaucoup de golfs prétendent convenir à tout le monde, mais ce n'est pas toujours vrai. Ici, oui : Saint-Laurent est un parcours réellement praticable par les joueurs de tous niveaux, même les joueurs de haut handicap, qui y perdront moins de balles que de points. Situé dans un bel espace vallonné et planté de pins ou de chênes, le 18 trous signé par Michael Fenn se déroule sans imagination particulière, mais il a été conçu et réalisé très sérieusement. Son entretien de bonne qualité incite à en recommander la visite, d'autant que cette belle région est une destination traditionnelle de vacances. Avec la mer et les activités balnéaires à proximité, un golfeur pourra sans trop mauvaise conscience abandonner sa famille quelques heures. Le 9 trous signé Yves Bureau est un lieu idéal pour initier les aspirants golfeurs.

A lot of courses claim to be suitable for all golfers, but are not. Saint Laurent is one of the exceptions, with a course that really is playable by golfers of all abilities, even high-handicappers, who will probably lose fewer balls than they drop strokes. Located in rolling landscape planted with pines and oak-trees, the 18-hole course, designed by Michael Fenn, unfolds with no great imagination, but it was designed and built with the most serious intentions. Excellent upkeep makes it well worth a visit, especially in this beautiful holiday region. With the sea and holiday resorts nearby, golfers can abandon the family for a few hourse without remorse. The 9-hole course designed by Yves Bureau is the ideal venue for beginners and new-comers to the game.

Golf de Saint-Laurent — 1976

Ploemel
F - 56400 AURAY

Office	Secrétariat	(33) 02 97 56 85 18
Pro shop	Pro-shop	(33) 02 97 56 85 18
Fax	Fax	(33) 02 97 56 89 99
Situation	Situation	
Auray (pop. 10 320), 11 km - Vannes (pop. 45 640), 44 km		
Annual closure	Fermeture annuelle	no
Weekly closure	Fermeture hebdomadaire	no

Fees main season
Tarifs haute saison full day

	Week days Semaine	We/Bank holidays We/Férié
Individual Individuel	260 F	260 F
Couple Couple	520 F	520 F

Caddy	Caddy	no
Electric Trolley	Chariot électrique	no
Buggy	Voiturette	150 F/18 holes
Clubs	Clubs	50 F/full day

Credit cards Cartes de crédit
VISA - CB - Eurocard - MasterCard

334

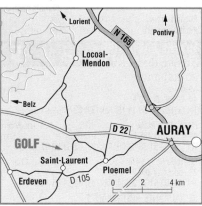

Access Accès : N165 (« Voie Express »), Exit (Sortie)
Carnac-Quiberon, D22 → Belz-Etel. 6 km → Golf
Map 5 on page 172 Carte 5 Page 172

GOLF COURSE / PARCOURS — 14/20

Site	Site	
Maintenance	Entretien	
Architect	Architecte	Michael Fenn
Type	Type	forest
Relief	Relief	
Water in play	Eau en jeu	
Exp. to wind	Exposé au vent	
Trees in play	Arbres en jeu	

Scorecard Carte de score	Chp. Chp.	Mens Mess.	Ladies Da.
Length Long.	6112	6112	5247
Par	72	72	72

Advised golfing ability
Niveau de jeu recommandé   0 12 24 36
Hcp required   Handicap exigé   35

CLUB HOUSE & AMENITIES / CLUB HOUSE ET ANNEXES — 7/10

Pro shop	Pro-shop	
Driving range	Practice	
Sheltered	couvert	10 mats
On grass	sur herbe	yes
Putting-green	putting-green	yes
Pitching-green	pitching green	yes

HOTEL FACILITIES / ENVIRONNEMENT HOTELIER — 5/10

HOTELS HÔTELS
Bleu Marine — 200 m
42 rooms, D 655 F
Tel (33) 02 97 56 88 88, Fax (33) 02 97 56 88 28

Best Western Celtique — Carnac
49 rooms, D 700 F — 7 km
Tel (33) 02 97 52 11 49, Fax (33) 02 97 52 71 10

Château de Locguénolé — Hennebont
22 rooms, D 1 200 F — 23 km
Tel (33) 02 97 76 76 76, Fax (33) 02 97 76 82 35

RESTAURANTS RESTAURANTS
La Closerie du Kerdrain — Auray
Tel (33) 02 97 56 61 27 — 10 km

Chebaudière — Auray
Tel (33) 02 97 24 09 84 — 10 km

Saint-Nom fut à son ouverture un événement, un exemple aussi de golf résidentiel prestigieux, qui, après des efforts patients, a acquis aujourd'hui beaucoup de maturité, en même temps que les arbres en prenaient. Comme le «Rouge», celui-ci a été dessiné par Fred Hawtree, mais beaucoup de changements ont été apportés depuis, souvent avec bonheur, et de nombreux arbres plantés, ce qui constitue un bienfait visuel et technique. Un léger vallonnement le rend agréable à jouer, et ajoute de l'intérêt au choix de clubs. Mieux qu'un parent pauvre d'un parent prestigieux, ce parcours offre quelques pars 4 très musclés, et peu de vraies occasions de birdies. L'entretien est de très bon niveau, le Club-house superbe.

When first opened, Saint Nom was an event and a fine example of a prestigious residential golf club which after much patient work has today grown to maturity in pace with the trees. Like the « Rouge » course, the « Bleu » layout was designed by Fred Hawtree, although a lot of changes have been made to it since, often to the better, with many new trees planted to add visual and technical appeal. The slightly rolling landscape makes it a pleasant course to play and adds to the importance of choosing the right club. Better than a poor relation to a prestigious neighbour, this layout contains a number of very demanding par 4s and few real birdie chances. Greenkeeping is of very high standard and the Club-house simply superb.

Golf de Saint-Nom-la-Bretèche — 1959

Hameau de la Tuilerie Bignon
F - 78860 SAINT-NOM-LA-BRETECHE

Office	Secrétariat	(33) 01 30 80 04 40
Pro shop	Pro-shop	(33) 01 30 80 04 40
Fax	Fax	(33) 01 34 62 87 04
Situation	Situation	

Paris (pop. 2 175 200), 22 km - Versailles (pop. 87 789), 9 km

Annual closure	Fermeture annuelle	no
Weekly closure	Fermeture hebdomadaire	tuesday (mardi)

Fees main season
Tarifs haute saison 18 holes

	Week days Semaine	We/Bank holidays We/Férié
Individual Individuel	500 F	600 F*
Couple Couple	1 000 F	1 200 F*

* with a member (accompagné d'un membre)

Caddy	Caddy	250 F
Electric Trolley	Chariot électrique	100 F/18 holes
Buggy	Voiturette	medical reasons
Clubs	Clubs	yes

Credit cards Cartes de crédit VISA - CB - Eurocard

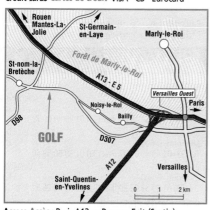

Access Accès : Paris A13 → Rouen. Exit (Sortie) Versailles-Ouest. → Versailles. 500 m turn right on D307 → Noisy-le-Roy, Saint-Nom-la-Bretèche
Map 15 on page 192 Carte 15 Page 192

GOLF COURSE / PARCOURS — 15/20

Site	Site	
Maintenance	Entretien	
Architect	Architecte	Fred Hawtree
Type	Type	parkland, residential
Relief	Relief	
Water in play	Eau en jeu	
Exp. to wind	Exposé au vent	
Trees in play	Arbres en jeu	

Scorecard Carte de score	Chp. Chp.	Mens Mess.	Ladies Da.
Length Long.	6167	5674	4971
Par	72	72	72

Advised golfing ability		0 12 24 36
Niveau de jeu recommandé		
Hcp required	Handicap exigé	24 Men, 28 Ladies

CLUB HOUSE & AMENITIES / CLUB HOUSE ET ANNEXES — 8/10

Pro shop	Pro-shop	
Driving range	Practice	
Sheltered	couvert	5 mats
On grass	sur herbe	no, 19 mats open air
Putting-green	putting-green	yes
Pitching-green	pitching green	yes

335

HOTEL FACILITIES / ENVIRONNEMENT HOTELIER — 8/10

HOTELS HÔTELS

Trianon Palace — Versailles
94 rooms, D 1 800 F — 9 km
Tel (33) 01 30 84 38 00, Fax (33) 01 39 49 00 77

Résidence du Berry — Versailles
38 rooms, D 600 F — 9 km
Tel (33) 01 39 49 07 07, Fax (33) 01 39 50 59 40

Ibis — Versailles
85 rooms, D 400 F — 9 km
Tel (33) 01 39 53 03 30, Fax (33) 01 39 50 06 31

RESTAURANTS RESTAURANTS

La Marée de Versailles — Versailles
Tel (33) 01 30 21 73 73 — 9 km

Les Trois Marches — Versailles
Tel (33) 01 39 50 13 21 — 9 km

SAINT-NOM-LA-BRETÈCHE ROUGE ♪ | 16 | 8 | 8

Ce parcours a été rendu célèbre par le Trophée Lancôme, qui se dispute maintenant sur un composite des deux parcours. On ne joue plus sept des derniers trous, venir ici est donc l'occasion de les redécouvrir. Le «Rouge» nécessite un driving très précis si l'on veut espérer scorer, et attaquer les greens en bonne posture. La stratégie de jeu est assez claire, la seule chose que l'on ne maîtrise pas immédiatement, c'est le putting, car les contours des greens sont peu visibles, mais souvent déconcertants. Assez vallonné, mais sans être trop fatiguant à marcher, ce parcours réclame de savoir faire (et bien faire) tous les coups de golf. La variété du dessin, la progression des difficultés permet de renouveler l'intérêt : jouer ici pour le plaisir ou en compétition n'est pas du tout la même chose !

This course owes its fame to the Trophée Lancôme, which these days is played on a combination of the two courses. Seven of the last «Rouge» holes are not used, so playing here yourself is the opportunity to get to know them. The «Rouge» course requires very straight driving if you want to card a good score and attack the greens from the ideal position. Game strategy is clear enough and the only thing you will immediately find anything but easy is your putting. The contours of these greens are not particularly visible and often disconcerting. rather hilly but not too tiring on the legs, this course demands every shot in the book (played accordingly to the book). The variety of the layout and the way difficulties slowly pile up make this an interesting course every time. But here, playing for fun and playing in a tournament are two very different propositions.

Golf de Saint-Nom-la-Bretèche — 1959

Hameau de la Tuilerie Bignon
F - 78860 SAINT-NOM-LA-BRETECHE

Office	Secrétariat	(33) 01 30 80 04 40
Pro shop	Pro-shop	(33) 01 30 80 04 40
Fax	Fax	(33) 01 34 62 87 04
Situation	Situation	

Paris (pop. 2 175 200), 22 km - Versailles (pop. 87 789), 9 km

Annual closure	Fermeture annuelle	no
Weekly closure	Fermeture hebdomadaire	tuesday (mardi)

Fees main season
Tarifs haute saison 18 holes

	Week days Semaine	We/Bank holidays We/Férié
Individual Individuel	500 F	600 F*
Couple Couple	1 000 F	1 200 F*

* with a member (accompagné d'un membre)

Caddy	Caddy	250 F
Electric Trolley	Chariot électrique	100 F/18 holes
Buggy	Voiturette	medical reasons
Clubs	Clubs	yes

Credit cards Cartes de crédit VISA - CB - Eurocard

GOLF COURSE / PARCOURS — 16/20

Site	Site	
Maintenance	Entretien	
Architect	Architecte	Fred Hawtree
Type	Type	parkland, residential
Relief	Relief	
Water in play	Eau en jeu	
Exp. to wind	Exposé au vent	
Trees in play	Arbres en jeu	

Scorecard Carte de score	Chp. Chp.	Mens Mess.	Ladies Da.
Length Long.	6252	5726	4920
Par	72	72	72

Advised golfing ability	0	12	24	36
Niveau de jeu recommandé				

Hcp required Handicap exigé 24 Men, 28 Ladies

CLUB HOUSE & AMENITIES / CLUB HOUSE ET ANNEXES — 8/10

Pro shop	Pro-shop	
Driving range	Practice	
Sheltered	couvert	5 mats
On grass	sur herbe	no, 19 mats open air
Putting-green	putting-green	yes
Pitching-green	pitching green	yes

HOTEL FACILITIES / ENVIRONNEMENT HOTELIER — 8/10

HOTELS HÔTELS

Trianon Palace — Versailles 9 km
94 rooms, D 1 800 F
Tel (33) 01 30 84 38 00, Fax (33) 01 39 49 00 77

Résidence du Berry — Versailles 9 km
38 rooms, D 600 F
Tel (33) 01 39 49 07 07, Fax (33) 01 39 50 59 40

Ibis — Versailles 9 km
85 rooms, D 400 F
Tel (33) 01 39 53 03 30, Fax (33) 01 39 50 06 31

RESTAURANTS RESTAURANTS

La Marée de Versailles — Versailles 9 km
Tel (33) 01 30 21 73 73

Les Trois Marches — Versailles 9 km
Tel (33) 01 39 50 13 21

336

Access Accès : Paris A13 → Rouen. Exit (Sortie) Versailles-Ouest. → Versailles. 500 m turn right on D307 → Noisy-le-Roy, Saint-Nom-la-Bretèche
Map 15 on page 192 Carte 15 Page 192

Près de Béziers, ce parcours offre un préjugé favorable, par son arrivée dans la garrigue, par l'environnement et les couleurs de la nature. Le tracé du parcours signé Patrice Lambert ne dément pas cette première impression. Sans apporter d'idées vraiment originales ni d'émotions de jeu exceptionnelles, les 18 trous sont généralement de bonne facture, peu fatigants à jouer, et le climat local comme la nature du sol permettent d'y jouer toute l'année, seul le vent pouvant augmenter les difficultés. L'architecte y a inclus quelques trous délicats (comme le 7 ou le 16 par exemple), mais aussi plusieurs trous assez reposants pour ne pas trop surcharger la carte, et permettre de le conseiller à tous les niveaux. Les équipements de ce club sympathique sont propres et de bonne qualité, sans prétention aucune, on se sent un peu en famille ici.

This course, close to Béziers, immediately gives a pleasing first impression as you drive along a track through the colourful garrigue (Mediterranean shrub). The actual layout, designed by P. Lambert, lives up to this impression. Without any really original ideas or excitement, the 18 holes make for good golfing over flattish terrain, and the local climate and the soil keep the course playable all year. Only the wind can come along and pose a few problems. There are a few very tricky holes (the 7th and 16th, for example), and also some more relaxing numbers to keep the score down and make this a course for everyone. The facilities in this very friendly club are good and stylish, and the visitor will very quickly feel one of the family.

Golf de Saint-Thomas — 1992

Route de Pézenas
F - 34500 BEZIERS

Office	Secrétariat	(33) 04 67 39 03 09
Pro shop	Pro-shop	(33) 04 67 39 00 61
Fax	Fax	(33) 04 67 39 10 65
Situation	Situation	

Béziers (pop. 71 000), 10 km

Annual closure	Fermeture annuelle	no
Weekly closure	Fermeture hebdomadaire	no

Fees main season
Tarifs haute saison 18 holes

	Week days Semaine	We/Bank holidays We/Férié
Individual Individuel	280 F	280 F
Couple Couple	560 F	560 F

Caddy	Caddy	no
Electric Trolley	Chariot électrique	no
Buggy	Voiturette	180 F/18 holes
Clubs	Clubs	50 F/full day

Credit cards Cartes de crédit
VISA - CB - Eurocard - MasterCard - AMEX

Access Accès : A9, Exit (Sortie) Béziers Est,
Expressway (« voie rapide »), → Bassan,
go through «le Rouge gorge», over bridge, → Golf
Map 13 on page 189 Carte 13 Page 189

GOLF COURSE / PARCOURS — 14/20

Site	Site	
Maintenance	Entretien	
Architect	Architecte	Patrice Lambert
Type	Type	country
Relief	Relief	
Water in play	Eau en jeu	
Exp. to wind	Exposé au vent	
Trees in play	Arbres en jeu	

Scorecard Carte de score	Chp. Chp.	Mens Mess.	Ladies Da.
Length Long.	6130	5762	4996
Par	72	72	72

Advised golfing ability Niveau de jeu recommandé	0	12	24	36

Hcp required Handicap exigé no

CLUB HOUSE & AMENITIES / CLUB HOUSE ET ANNEXES — 7/10

Pro shop	Pro-shop	
Driving range	Practice	
Sheltered	couvert	4 mats
On grass	sur herbe	no, 12 mats open air
Putting-green	putting-green	yes
Pitching-green	pitching green	yes

HOTEL FACILITIES / ENVIRONNEMENT HOTELIER — 5/10

HOTELS HÔTELS

Impérator 45 rooms, D 440 F Tel (33) 04 67 49 02 25, Fax (33) 04 67 28 92 30		Béziers 10 km
Du Nord 40 rooms, D 450 F Tel (33) 04 67 28 34 09, Fax (33) 04 67 49 00 37		Béziers 10 km
Château de Lignan 49 rooms, D 700 F Tel (33) 04 67 37 91 47, Fax (33) 04 67 37 99 25		Lignan-sur-Orb 15 km

RESTAURANTS RESTAURANTS

Le Framboisier Tel (33) 04 67 49 90 00		Béziers 10 km
Potinière Tel(33) 04 67 76 35 30		Béziers 10 km
Château de Lignan Tel (33) 04 67 37 91 47		Lignan-sur-Orb 15 km

337

Ce 18 trous aurait pu être une complète réussite si l'on ne trouvait çà et là quelques «idées d'architecte» plus paysagères que golfiques. Alors qu'un parcours commercial doit pouvoir être joué dès la première fois sans cacher ses obstacles, on peut penser que certains trous manquent de franchise, parallèlement à d'autres presque trop faciles. La stratégie n'est alors pas évidente. De fait, on a l'impression d'un ensemble de bonnes idées graphiques, mais pas toujours bien disposées sur le plan du jeu, d'où une impression de manque d'unité. Les joueurs moyens ou débutants seront sans doute moins exigeants que les joueurs qui attachent une grande importance à la logique des obstacles, au rythme d'un parcours. En dépit de ces appréciations, pour la beauté de l'environnement et la bonne qualité de son entretien, ce parcours mérite néanmoins une visite.

This 18-hole course could have been a total success if it weren't for a few architectural ideas here and there, that have more to do with landscaping than with golf. And since a commercial course should be playable first time out without concealing its hazards, there is reason to believe that some holes are a little on the sneaky side, as opposed to others that are almost too easy. The overall impression is that of a whole series of good graphic ideas that are not always well translated into golfing language, hence the feeling of a disjointed layout. Mid-handicappers and beginners will probably be less demanding in this respect than players who attach considerable importance to the logic of hazards and the overall balance of a course. Despite these views, the course is well worth a visit for the beauty of the setting and the standard of upkeep.

Golf de la Sainte-Baume — 1988
F - 83860 NANS-LES-PINS

Office	Secrétariat	(33) 04 94 78 60 12
Pro shop	Pro-shop	(33) 04 94 78 92 74
Fax	Fax	(33) 04 94 78 63 52
Situation	Situation	

Marseille (pop. 800 550), 44 km

Annual closure	Fermeture annuelle	no
Weekly closure	Fermeture hebdomadaire	no

Fees main season
Tarifs haute saison 18 holes

	Week days Semaine	We/Bank holidays We/Férié
Individual Individuel	260 F	260 F
Couple Couple	520 F	520 F

Seniors : GF 180 F on thursdays (jeudis)

Caddy	Caddy	no
Electric Trolley	Chariot électrique	80 F/18 holes
Buggy	Voiturette	200 F/18 holes
Clubs	Clubs	80 F/full day

Credit cards Cartes de crédit
VISA - CB - Eurocard - MasterCard - AMEX

338

GOLF COURSE / PARCOURS — 13/20

Site	Site	
Maintenance	Entretien	
Architect	Architecte	Robert Berthet
Type	Type	country
Relief	Relief	
Water in play	Eau en jeu	
Exp. to wind	Exposé au vent	
Trees in play	Arbres en jeu	

Scorecard Carte de score	Chp. Chp.	Mens Mess.	Ladies Da.
Length Long.	6167	5984	5205
Par	72	72	72

Advised golfing ability Niveau de jeu recommandé	0	12	24	36

Hcp required Handicap exigé 35

CLUB HOUSE & AMENITIES / CLUB HOUSE ET ANNEXES — 7/10

Pro shop	Pro-shop	
Driving range	Practice	
Sheltered	couvert	10 mats
On grass	sur herbe	yes
Putting-green	putting-green	yes
Pitching-green	pitching green	yes

HOTEL FACILITIES / ENVIRONNEMENT HOTELIER — 6/10

HOTELS HÔTELS
Domaine de Châteauneuf — 400 m
30 rooms, D 1 000 F
Tel (33) 04 94 78 90 06, Fax (33) 04 94 78 63 30

Plaisance — Saint-Maximin
13 rooms, D 350 F — 7 km
Tel (33) 04 94 78 16 74, Fax (33) 04 94 78 18 39

Hôtel de France — Saint-Maximin
26 rooms, D 380 F — 7 km
Tel (33) 04 94 78 00 14, Fax (33) 04 94 59 83 80

RESTAURANTS RESTAURANTS
Domaine de Châteauneuf — 400 m
Tel (33) 04 94 78 90 06

Château de Nans — Nans-les-Pins
Tel (33) 04 94 78 92 06 — 2 km

Access Accès : A8 Aix-en-Provence → Nice, Exit (Sortie)
Saint-Maximin → La Sainte-Baume, Nans-les-Pins
Map 14 on page 190 Carte 14 Page 190

Il faut parfois grimper haut (il y a un téléphérique entre le 10 et le 11), et ce parcours est épuisant à pied, mais les vues sur la baie de Saint-Tropez et le massif des Maures récompensent les efforts. Taillé pour une bonne part dans la colline, il n'est pas d'une grande franchise, même si les travaux ont atténué les rebonds indésirables. On comprend que l'architecte Donald Harradine ait adapté son dessin au terrain, mais certains greens aveugles auraient pu être évités. Les fairways sont rarement larges, de nombreux pins empiètent sur les trajectoires de balle mais la longueur assez réduite du parcours permet de laisser souvent le driver de côté. Il faut soigneusement éviter de jouer en stroke-play, mais on peut s'amuser en match-play. Pour les joueurs peu expérimentés, ce parcours peut être décourageant par le nombre de situations délicates qu'il peut réserver. Qu'ils profitent alors du spectacle splendide.

You sometimes have to scale considerable heights (a cable-car links the 10th and 11th holes) and the course is generally speaking exhausting to walk, but the views over the bay of Saint Tropez and the Maures uplands are more than worth the effort. Mostly cut out of a hill, this can be a deceitful course, even though recent work has reduced the unexpected and unwarranted kick. Architect Donald Harradine understandably adapted his layout to the terrain, but certain blind greens could have been avoided. The fairways are seldom wide and numerous pine-trees encroach upon the ball's flight-path, but on this short course, you can always leave the driver in the bag. Make a point of not playing stroke-play, have fun with match-play. A sometimes dispiriting course for inexperienced golfers, but they'll love the view.

Golf de Sainte-Maxime — 1991

Route du Débarquement
F - 83120 SAINTE-MAXIME

Office	Secrétariat	(33) 04 94 55 02 02
Pro shop	Pro-shop	(33) 04 94 55 02 02
Fax	Fax	(33) 04 93 55 02 03
Situation	Situation	

Ste-Maxime (pop. 10 010), 2 km
Draguignan (pop. 30 180), 24 km

Annual closure	Fermeture annuelle	no
Weekly closure	Fermeture hebdomadaire	no

Fees main season
Tarifs haute saison 18 holes

	Week days Semaine	We/Bank holidays We/Férié
Individual Individuel	320 F	320 F
Couple Couple	640 F	640 F

Caddy	Caddy	no
Electric Trolley	Chariot électrique	no
Buggy	Voiturette	150 F/18 holes
Clubs	Clubs	80 F/full day

Credit cards Cartes de crédit
VISA - CB - Eurocard - MasterCard - AMEX - DC

GOLF
D 25
N 98
La Nartelle
Cap des Sardinaux
SAINTE-MAXIME
N 98
Beauvallon
D 98 A
SAINT-TROPEZ
D 559
0   2   4 km

Access Accès : A8 Exit (Sortie) 36,
D25 → Sainte-Maxime, → Golf
Map 14 on page 191 Carte 14 Page 191

GOLF COURSE / PARCOURS — 13 /20

Site	Site	▰▰▰▰▱
Maintenance	Entretien	▰▰▰▱▱
Architect	Architecte	Donald Harradine
		Peter Harradine
Type	Type	hilly, residential
Relief	Relief	▰▰▰▰▱
Water in play	Eau en jeu	▰▱▱▱▱
Exp. to wind	Exposé au vent	▰▰▱▱▱
Trees in play	Arbres en jeu	▰▰▰▰▱

Scorecard Carte de score	Chp. Chp.	Mens Mess.	Ladies Da.
Length Long.	6155	5705	5143
Par	71	71	71

Advised golfing ability		0 12 24 36
Niveau de jeu recommandé		▰▰▰▱
Hcp required	Handicap exigé	35

CLUB HOUSE & AMENITIES / CLUB HOUSE ET ANNEXES — 7 /10

Pro shop	Pro-shop	▰▰▰▰▱
Driving range	Practice	▰▰▰▱▱
Sheltered	couvert	4 mats
On grass	sur herbe	yes
Putting-green	putting-green	yes
Pitching-green	pitching green	yes

HOTEL FACILITIES / ENVIRONNEMENT HOTELIER — 7 /10

HOTELS HÔTELS

Golf Plaza — on site
111 rooms, D 1 350 F
Tel (33) 04 94 56 66 66, Fax (33) 04 94 56 66 00

Hostellerie de la Belle Aurore — Sainte-Maxime
17 rooms, D 2 000 F — 2 km
Tel (33) 04 94 96 02 45, Fax (33) 04 94 96 63 87

Mas des Brugassières — Plan de la Tour
14 rooms, D 550 F — 11 km
Tel (33) 04 94 43 72 42, Fax (33) 04 94 43 00 20

RESTAURANTS RESTAURANTS

Hostellerie de la Belle Aurore — Sainte-Maxime
Tel (33) 04 94 96 02 45 — 2 km

L'Amiral — Sainte-Maxime
Tel (33) 04 94 43 99 36 — 2 km

Le Daniéli — Sainte-Maxime
Tel (33) 04 94 43 96 45 — 2 km

339

Entre Nantes et Saint-Nazaire, et dominant la Loire, Savenay est situé au coeur d'une région aujourd'hui très fournie en golfs de qualité. Un voyage de golf est ainsi agréable pour tous les niveaux, de la Vendée à la côte sud de Bretagne, dans des paysages très caractéristiques de ces régions. Ce parcours plutôt long (complété par un 9 trous d'entraînement) a été dessiné par Michel Gayon dans un site alternant les trous larges volontiers inspirés des «links» (par leur dessin et l'abondance des bunkers stratégiques), et des trous plus intimes, notamment les 7 et 8, le long d'une pièce d'eau. Les arbres (beaucoup de châtaigniers) sont assez nombreux, mais sans que l'on éprouve une impression d'étouffement. Un petit regret : le grand nombre de trous parallèles. Et toujours un entretien correct.

Between Nantes and Saint Nazaire, overlooking the Loire river, Savenay stands at the heart of a region which today boasts a number of excellent courses. This makes a golfing holiday to Brittany a pleasant proposition for all, from the Vendée to the southern Breton coastline, in typical settings. This is a rather long course (there is also a 9 hole pitch 'n putt) designed by Michel Gayon, on a site where deliberately wide holes, designed and strategically bunkered in true links style, alternate with more intimate holes, notably the 7th and 8th along a stretch of water. Trees abound (a lot of chestnut trees) but are never too imposing a presence. The one little regret is the number of holes running parallel. And still a good upkeep.

Golf de Savenay — 1990

Le Chambeau
F - 44260 SAVENAY

Office	Secrétariat	(33) 02 40 56 88 05
Pro shop	Pro-shop	(33) 02 40 56 88 05
Fax	Fax	(33) 02 40 56 89 04
Situation	Situation	

Saint-Nazaire (pop. 64 810), 26 km

Annual closure	Fermeture annuelle	no
Weekly closure	Fermeture hebdomadaire	tuesday
	(mardi) : 1/11→1/3	

Fees main season
Tarifs haute saison 18 holes

	Week days Semaine	We/Bank holidays We/Férié
Individual Individuel	225 F	225 F
Couple Couple	450 F	450 F

Caddy	Caddy	no
Electric Trolley	Chariot électrique	no
Buggy	Voiturette	150 F/18 holes
Clubs	Clubs	50 F/full day

Credit cards Cartes de crédit
VISA - CB - Eurocard - MasterCard

340

Access Accès : • Saint-Nazaire N171, Exit (Sortie)
Châteaubriand • Nantes N165, Exit Blain-Bouvron
Map 6 on page 174 Carte 6 Page 174

GOLF COURSE / PARCOURS — 14/20

Site	Site	
Maintenance	Entretien	
Architect	Architecte	Michel Gayon
Type	Type	open country, parkland
Relief	Relief	
Water in play	Eau en jeu	
Exp. to wind	Exposé au vent	
Trees in play	Arbres en jeu	

Scorecard Carte de score	Chp. Chp.	Mens Mess.	Ladies Da.
Length Long.	6339	5778	5370
Par	73	73	73

Advised golfing ability Niveau de jeu recommandé	0	12	24	36
Hcp required Handicap exigé	35			

CLUB HOUSE & AMENITIES / CLUB HOUSE ET ANNEXES — 5/10

Pro shop	Pro-shop	
Driving range	Practice	
Sheltered	couvert	9 mats
On grass	sur herbe	no, 60 mats open air
Putting-green	putting-green	yes
Pitching-green	pitching green	yes

HOTEL FACILITIES / ENVIRONNEMENT HOTELIER — 4/10

HOTELS HÔTELS
Auberge du Chêne Vert — Savenay
20 rooms, D 240 F — 1 km
Tel (33) 02 40 56 90 16, Fax (33) 02 40 56 99 60

Manoir du Rodoir — La Roche-Bernard
26 rooms, D 490 F — 30 km
Tel (33) 02 99 90 82 68, Fax (33) 02 99 90 76 22

Berry — Saint-Nazaire
27 rooms, D 550 F — 23 km
Tel (33) 02 40 22 42 61, Fax (33) 02 40 22 45 34

RESTAURANTS RESTAURANTS
L'An II — Saint-Nazaire
Tel (33) 02 40 00 95 33 — 23 km

Au Bon Accueil — Saint-Nazaire
Tel (33) 02 40 22 07 05 — 23 km

Un parcours qui ne laisse personne indifférent. A proximité du parcours très plat d'Hossegor, il se déroule dans un paysage très accidenté, planté de pins et de chênes-liège. Les différences de dénivellation et l'étroitesse des fairways incitent à le conseiller aux joueurs en forme et golfiquement aguerris, qui devront bien étudier leur stratégie. En revanche, il n'est pas très long (notamment les par 3, sauf le 16), et demande un jeu de fers précis, en particulier pour attaquer les drapeaux, car les greens sont très modelés et de dimensions très variées. Les contours de fairway très travaillés et les abords des greens sont typiquement de von Hagge, de même que l'alternance de bunkers de sable et d'herbe et le dessin des pièces d'eau (sur cinq trous). Souvent spectaculaire et intimidant, il ne se maîtrise pas au premier abord. C'est un parcours follement amusant en match-play.

A course that leaves no-one indifferent. Close to the flat course of Hossegor, Seignosse unwinds over very hilly terrain planted with pine-trees and cork oaks. The steep slopes and narrow fairways mean this is a golf for seasoned players on top of their game, who will need to study their strategy. By contrast, the course is short (especially the par 3s, except the 16th) and requires precision ironwork, especially when attacking the contoured greens of all sizes. The rolling fairways and edges of the greens are typical of von Hagge, as are the alternating grass-bunkers and sand-traps and the design of the water hazards (on five holes). Often spectacular and intimidating, most golfers will have trouble first time out. A good course and great fun in match-play.

Golf de Seignosse

1989

Avenue du Belvédère
F - 40510 SEIGNOSSE

Office	Secrétariat	(33) 05 58 41 68 30
Pro shop	Pro-shop	(33) 05 58 41 68 30
Fax	Fax	(33) 05 58 41 68 31
Situation	Situation	

Bayonne (pop. 40 050), 28 km - Dax (pop. 19 310), 37 km

Annual closure	Fermeture annuelle	no
Weekly closure	Fermeture hebdomadaire	no

Fees main season
Tarifs haute saison 18 holes

	Week days Semaine	We/Bank holidays We/Férié
Individual Individuel	350 F	350 F
Couple Couple	700 F	700 F

Caddy	Caddy	no
Electric Trolley	Chariot électrique	no
Buggy	Voiturette	140 F/18 holes
Clubs	Clubs	40 F/full day

Credit cards   Cartes de crédit
VISA - CB - Eurocard - MasterCard - AMEX - DC

Access Accès : • Bayonne A63 → Bordeaux,
Exit (Sortie) Capbreton → Capbreton/Hossegor
• Bordeaux A63 → Bayonne,
Exit Saint-Geours-de-Marenne → Seignosse
Map 12 on page 186 Carte 12 Page 186

GOLF COURSE
PARCOURS

17/20

Site	Site	▮▮▮▮▮▯
Maintenance	Entretien	▮▮▮▮▮▯
Architect	Architecte	Robert von Hagge
Type	Type	forest, hilly
Relief	Relief	▮▮▮▮▯▯
Water in play	Eau en jeu	▮▮▮▯▯▯
Exp. to wind	Exposé au vent	▮▮▯▯▯▯
Trees in play	Arbres en jeu	▮▮▮▮▯▯

Scorecard	Chp.	Mens	Ladies
Carte de score	Chp.	Mess.	Da.
Length Long.	6124	5774	5069
Par	72	72	72

Advised golfing ability	0	12	24	36
Niveau de jeu recommandé			▮▮▮▮	

Hcp required   Handicap exigé   no

CLUB HOUSE & AMENITIES
CLUB HOUSE ET ANNEXES

7/10

Pro shop	Pro-shop	▮▮▮▮▮▯
Driving range	Practice	▮▮▮▮▮▯
Sheltered	couvert	10 mats
On grass	sur herbe	yes
Putting-green	putting-green	yes
Pitching-green	pitching green	yes

HOTEL FACILITIES
ENVIRONNEMENT HOTELIER

7/10

HOTELS HÔTELS
Golf Hôtel Blue Green   on site
45 rooms, D 710 F
Tel (33) 05 58 41 68 40, Fax (33) 05 58 41 68 41

Beauséjour   Hossegor
45 rooms, D 650 F   5 km
Tel (33) 05 58 43 51 07, Fax (33) 05 58 43 70 13

Les Hortensias du Lac   Hossegor
21 rooms, D 450 F   5 km
Tel (33) 05 58 43 99 00, Fax (33) 05 58 43 42 81

RESTAURANTS RESTAURANTS
Les Huîtrières du Lac   Hossegor
Tel (33) 05 58 43 51 48   5 km

Auberge du Cheval Blanc   Bayonne
Tel (33) 05 59 59 01 33   28 km

341

Servanes ne peut renier sa Provence, avec les reliefs blancs et rocailleux des Alpilles, les oliviers, cyprès et platanes, et parfois un méchant coup de mistral, qui devrait empoisonner les golfeurs, mais ils en sont relativement protégés ici. Dans un site de campagne à peu près préservé d'immobilier, Sprecher et Watine ont dessiné un parcours bien paysagé, techniquement honnête, mais sans imagination excessive. Les contours de fairway auraient sans doute pu être mieux travaillés : en Provence, on préfère les sentiers aux boulevards. Autrement, il n'y a pas de grands commentaires à faire, sinon que, tout comme les joueurs de niveau moyen, les joueurs peu expérimentés trouveront ici le calme et de quoi assouvir leur passion naissante dans un cadre magnifique, à proximité du splendide village des Baux de Provence.

Servanes is Provence through and through, with the white rocky terrain of the Alpilles, cypress and plane trees, and sometimes a gust of mistral which can play havoc, although golfers are relatively sheltered on this course. On a country site more or less protected from property development, Sprecher and Watine have designed a nicely landscaped course which is technically fair but none too rich in imagination. The fairways could certainly have been better contoured, and in Provence they prefer pathways to boulevards. Otherwise, there is little else to say, except that high-handicappers and beginners alike will find the calm and the course they are looking for to satisfy their nascent enthusiasm for the game. All this in a magnificent setting close to the splendid village of Baux de Provence.

Golf Country-Club de Servanes   1989

Domaine de Servanes
F - 13890 MOURIES

Office	Secrétariat	(33) 04 90 47 59 95
Pro shop	Pro-shop	(33) 04 90 47 65 70
Fax	Fax	(33) 04 90 47 52 58
Situation	Situation	

Arles (pop. 52 050), 25 km

Annual closure	Fermeture annuelle	no
Weekly closure	Fermeture hebdomadaire	no

Fees main season
Tarifs haute saison full day

	Week days Semaine	We/Bank holidays We/Férié
Individual Individuel	250 F	250 F
Couple Couple	500 F	500 F

2 GF + 2 lunches + golf car: 750 F

Caddy	Caddy	no
Electric Trolley	Chariot électrique	no
Buggy	Voiturette	200 F/18 holes
Clubs	Clubs	100 F/full day

Credit cards Cartes de crédit
VISA - CB - Eurocard - MasterCard - AMEX - DC

342

Access Accès : A54 / N113 Nîmes-Arles, → Marseille,
Exit (Sortie) Saint-Martin-de-Crau → Mouriès
Map 14 on page 190 Carte 14 Page 190

GOLF COURSE PARCOURS   13/20

Site	Site	
Maintenance	Entretien	
Architect	Architecte	Thierry Sprecher Géry Watine
Type	Type	country
Relief	Relief	
Water in play	Eau en jeu	
Exp. to wind	Exposé au vent	
Trees in play	Arbres en jeu	

Scorecard Carte de score	Chp. Chp.	Mens Mess.	Ladies Da.
Length Long.	6101	5675	5150
Par	72	72	72

Advised golfing ability   0   12   24   36
Niveau de jeu recommandé
Hcp required   Handicap exigé   35

CLUB HOUSE & AMENITIES CLUB HOUSE ET ANNEXES   7/10

Pro shop	Pro-shop	
Driving range	Practice	
Sheltered	couvert	4 mats
On grass	sur herbe	yes
Putting-green	putting-green	yes
Pitching-green	pitching green	yes

HOTEL FACILITIES ENVIRONNEMENT HOTELIER   7/10

HOTELS HÔTELS
Oustau de Baumanière   Les Baux-de-Provence
11 rooms, D 1 500 F   8 km
Tel (33) 04 90 54 33 07, Fax (33) 04 90 54 40 46

Cabro d'Or   Les Baux-de-Provence
31 rooms, D 820 F   8 km
Tel (33) 04 90 54 33 21, Fax (33) 04 90 54 45 98

Val Baussenc - 21 rooms, D 680 F   Maussane
Tel (33) 04 90 54 38 90, Fax (33) 04 90 54 33 36   7 km

RESTAURANTS RESTAURANTS
Oustau de Baumanière   Les Baux-de-Provence
Tel (33) 04 90 54 33 07   8 km

Lou Pantaï   Maussane
Tel (33) 04 90 54 39 27   7 km

La Riboto de Taven   Les Baux-de-Provence
Tel (33) 04 90 54 34 23   8 km

SOUFFLENHEIM

16	7	4

Avec ce nouveau parcours, l'Alsace confirme son statut de région golfique de qualité. Bernhard Langer offre un dessin très technique, où les obstacles sont visuellement et réellement menaçants. La présence de nombreux bunkers de greens et de fairways (un peu trop de sable pour l'instant) comme des obstacles d'eau (sur 14 trous) exige une attention constante et impose un rythme soutenu, mais les joueurs peu expérimentés pourront trouver des solutions et s'y amuser, en jouant des départs avancés. De nombreuses buttes séparent les fairways et entourent la plupart des greens, ajoutant du relief à cet espace naturellement plat, et entouré de forêts. Les greens sont de bonne dimension, souvent bien modelés, ajoutant à l'intérêt du jeu. Quelques modifications récentes du tracé ont encore amélioré le plaisir d'y jouer, mais le parcours a toujours du mal à absorber les pluies.

With this new course, Alsace has confirmed its status as a great region for golf. Bernhard Langer has created a very technical layout where hazards are visually and truly threatening. The numerous green-side and fairway bunkers (containing a little too much sand at the moment) and the water hazards (on 14 holes) demand constant care and establish a nice balance, but inexperienced golfers will find the answer and have fun by playing from the front tees. The fairways are separated by numerous sandhills, which also surround most of the greens, thus adding relief to a naturally flat terrain encircled by a forest. The greens are large and often well contoured, thus adding extra spice to the course. A few recent changes to the course have improved still further the pleasure of playing here, but the terrain still has problems soaking up the rain.

Soufflenheim Baden Baden — 1995

Allée du Golf
F - 67620 SOUFFLENHEIM

Office	Secrétariat	(33) 03 88 05 77 00
Pro shop	Pro-shop	(33) 03 88 05 77 00
Fax	Fax	(33) 03 88 05 77 01
Situation	Situation	

Strasbourg (pop. 252 260), 40 km
Haguenau (pop. 27 670), 15 km

Annual closure	Fermeture annuelle	no
Weekly closure	Fermeture hebdomadaire	no

Restaurant closed on monday (lundi), from 01/01 to 01/03

Fees main season
Tarifs haute saison 18 holes

	Week days / Semaine	We/Bank holidays / We/Férié
Individual Individuel	300 F	400 F
Couple Couple	600 F	800 F

Caddy	Caddy	on request
Electric Trolley	Chariot électrique	no
Buggy	Voiturette	170 F/18 holes
Clubs	Clubs	100 F/18 holes

Credit cards Cartes de crédit
VISA - CB - Eurocard - MasterCard - DC

Access Accès : Strasbourg, A4, Exit (Sortie) Karlsruhe-Lauterburg to D300. 15 km, Exit Soufflenheim → Golf
Map 4 on page 171 Carte 4 Page 171

GOLF COURSE / PARCOURS — 16/20

Site	Site	▰▰▰▰▱
Maintenance	Entretien	▰▰▰▱▱
Architect	Architecte	Bernhard Langer
Type	Type	forest, open country
Relief	Relief	▰▰▱▱▱
Water in play	Eau en jeu	▰▰▰▰▱
Exp. to wind	Exposé au vent	▰▰▱▱▱
Trees in play	Arbres en jeu	▰▰▰▱▱

Scorecard	Chp.	Mens	Ladies
Carte de score	Chp.	Mess.	Da.
Length Long.	6208	5872	5459
Par	72	72	72

Advised golfing ability		0 12 24 36
Niveau de jeu recommandé		▰▰▰▰▱
Hcp required	Handicap exigé	35

CLUB HOUSE & AMENITIES / CLUB HOUSE ET ANNEXES — 7/10

Pro shop	Pro-shop	▰▰▰▰▱
Driving range	Practice	▰▰▰▱▱
Sheltered	couvert	35 mats
On grass	sur herbe	no, 70 mats open air
Putting-green	putting-green	yes
Pitching-green	pitching green	yes

HOTEL FACILITIES / ENVIRONNEMENT HOTELIER — 4/10

HOTELS HÔTELS

Europe — Haguenau
81 rooms, D 350 F — 14 km
Tel (33) 03 88 93 58 11, Fax (33) 03 88 06 05 43

Kaiserhof — Haguenau
15 rooms, D 330 F — 14 km
Tel (33) 03 88 73 43 43, Fax (33) 03 88 73 28 91

RESTAURANTS RESTAURANTS

Auberge du Cheval Blanc — Schweighouse-sur-Moder
Tel (33) 03 88 72 76 96 — 18 km

A l'Agneau — Sessenheim
Tel(33) 03 88 86 95 55 — 5 km

Au Bœuf — Sessenheim
Tel (33) 03 88 86 97 14 — 5 km

Barberousse — Haguenau
Tel (33) 03 88 73 31 09 — 14 km

343

Dans un des sites les plus magnifiques d'Europe, Robert Trent Jones a tracé le parcours en plein maquis, à l'exception de six trous absolument splendides en bord de falaise, d'où l'on découvre la Méditerranée et la Sardaigne en arrière-plan. Pas très long, mais très technique et assez accidenté (voiturette conseillée), ce parcours spectaculaire ne peut laisser indifférent. Si on peut l'estimer difficile pour les joueurs peu expérimentés, on peut en revanche adorer son tracé parfois déconcertant, ses provocations, ses greens très modelés. Avec ses couleurs, ses lumières, les odeurs de la flore, c'est un parcours assez magique, mais parfois injuste quand le vent vient lui donner un air d'Ecosse en plein soleil. Alors, ceux qui maîtrisent mal les balles basses peuvent souffrir ! Une cinquantaine de maisons de belle architecture sont dissimulées dans ce vaste domaine.

On one of Europe's most fabulous sites, Robert Trent Jones designed this course amid gorse and heathland, with the exception of six absolutely splendid holes atop the cliffs, from where Sardinia can be viewed in the distance over the shimmering Mediterranean. Not particularly long but very much a course for the technician and hilly to boot (buggy recommended), this spectacular course leaves no-one indifferent. While it may be considered tough for inexperienced golfers, you have to love the sometimes disconcerting layout, the provocative nature of the course and the switchback greens. With its colours, light and fragrances, this is a magic course, but one which is sometimes unjust when the wind gets up and brings along a breath of Scottish air in the Corsican sun. In this case, low shots are a must to keep a decent score. Fifty or so villas are nicely hidden on this vast estate.

Golf de Spérone — 1990
Domaine de Spérone
F - 20169 SPERONE

Office	Secrétariat	(33) 04 95 73 17 13
Pro shop	Pro-shop	(33) 04 95 73 17 13
Fax	Fax	(33) 04 95 73 17 85
Situation	Situation	

Bonifacio (pop. 2 680), 6 km

Annual closure	Fermeture annuelle	yes
		6/1→3/2

Weekly closure Fermeture hebdomadaire
thursday afternoon (jeudi ap-m) from 01/05 to 30/09

Fees main season
Tarifs haute saison full day

	Week days Semaine	We/Bank holidays We/Férié
Individual Individuel	390 F	390 F
Couple Couple	780 F	780 F

16/09 to 15/06: GF 330 F

Caddy	Caddy	no
Electric Trolley	Chariot électrique	no
Buggy	Voiturette	220 F/18 holes
Clubs	Clubs	60 F/full day

Credit cards Cartes de crédit
VISA - CB - Eurocard - MasterCard - AMEX - DC

Access Accès : Bonifacio → Phare de Pertusato, → Golf
Map 14 on page 191 Carte 14 Page 191

GOLF COURSE / PARCOURS — 17/20

Site	Site	
Maintenance	Entretien	
Architect	Architecte	R. Trent Jones Sr
Type	Type	seaside course, hilly
Relief	Relief	
Water in play	Eau en jeu	
Exp. to wind	Exposé au vent	
Trees in play	Arbres en jeu	

Scorecard Carte de score	Chp. Chp.	Mens Mess.	Ladies Da.
Length Long.	6130	5603	5197
Par	72	72	72

Advised golfing ability Niveau de jeu recommandé	0	12	24	36

Hcp required Handicap exigé 28

CLUB HOUSE & AMENITIES / CLUB HOUSE ET ANNEXES — 7/10

Pro shop	Pro-shop	
Driving range	Practice	
Sheltered	couvert	no
On grass	sur herbe	yes
Putting-green	putting-green	yes
Pitching-green	pitching green	yes

HOTEL FACILITIES / ENVIRONNEMENT HOTELIER — 5/10

HOTELS HÔTELS
A Trama — Bonifacio
25 rooms, D 800 F — 4 km
Tel (33) 04 95 73 17 17, Fax (33) 04 95 73 17 79

Genovese — Bonifacio
14 rooms, D 1 700 F — 6 km
Tel (33) 04 95 73 12 34, Fax (33) 04 95 73 09 03

Roy d'Aragon — Bonifacio
31 rooms, D 700 F — 6 km
Tel (33) 04 95 73 03 99, Fax (33) 04 95 73 07 94

RESTAURANTS RESTAURANTS
Stella d'Oro — Bonifacio
Tel (33) 04 95 73 03 63 — 6 km

Quatre Vents — Bonifacio
Tel (33) 04 95 73 07 50 — 6 km

Le golf des Strasbourgeois, avant la création de la Wantzenau et du Kempferhof. L'architecture semble plus traditionnelle, avec quelques obstacles d'eau seulement, surtout sur le Rouge, où les arbres ajoutent d'autres difficultés. Les trous les plus durs sont groupés au début du Jaune, mais cet ensemble reste rassurant, et ne suscite pas de grandes émotions visuelles ou techniques chez les meilleurs joueurs. En revanche, les nombreux membres y évoluent avec plaisir en famille, d'autant que les fairways sont excellents en toutes saisons. Les greens sont bien défendus, mais il est toujours possible d'y accéder en faisant rouler la balle. Il s'agit là avant tout d'un club pour les locaux, cependant ouvert aux joueurs extérieurs (accès limité en week-end). De passage à Strasbourg, ils y passeront une journée plaisante. Après la rénovation du Club house, des travaux bienvenus sur le parcours en ont rehaussé le niveau, au niveau des bunkers notamment.

This was the traditional golf club of Strasbourg before Wantzenau and Kempferhof came along. By comparison, the architecture looks morez traditional with only a few water hazards, notably on the Red course, where trees add further difficulties. The hardest holes are grouped at the start of the Yellow course, but the full layout is somewhat reassuring and will hardly cause much visual or technical stirrings among the best players. By contrast, the many members enjoy playing here with the family, especially since the fairways are in excellent condition all year round. The greens are well defended but not from the front, thus allowing the easier chipped (or topped!) shot onto the putting surface. This is first and foremost a club for the locals, although the course is open to green-feers (not so easy on week-ends). When passing through Strasbourg, they can spend a pleasant day. After rehabilitation of the Club house, welcome work on the course has improved standards, particularly when it comes to bunkering.

Golf de Strasbourg-Ilkirch 1934
Route du Rhin
F - 67400 ILLKIRCH

Office	Secrétariat	(33) 03 88 66 17 22
Pro shop	Pro-shop	(33) 03 88 67 22 85
Fax	Fax	(33) 03 88 65 05 67
Situation	Situation	Strasbourg, 12 km
Annual closure	Fermeture annuelle	yes
		22/12 → 3/1
Weekly closure	Fermeture hebdomadaire	no

Restaurant closed on wednesday (mercredi)

Fees main season
Tarifs haute saison 18 holes

	Week days Semaine	We/Bank holidays We/Férié
Individual Individuel	250 F	300 F*
Couple Couple	500 F	600 F*

* We main season, members only
(membres seulement haute saison)

Caddy	Caddy	no
Electric Trolley	Chariot électrique	no
Buggy	Voiturette	200 F/18 holes
Clubs	Clubs	no

Credit cards Cartes de crédit
VISA - CB - Eurocard - MasterCard

Access Accès : • Strasbourg A35, Exit (Sortie) Baggersee, 1st roundabout → Markolsheim, 2nd roundabout, Expressway, → Golf • Colmar N83, go through Fegersheim → Illkirch
Map 4 on page 171 Carte 4 Page 171

GOLF COURSE PARCOURS 13/20

Site	Site	
Maintenance	Entretien	
Architect	Architecte	Donald Harradine
Type	Type	country
Relief	Relief	
Water in play	Eau en jeu	
Exp. to wind	Exposé au vent	
Trees in play	Arbres en jeu	

Scorecard Carte de score	Chp. Chp.	Mens Mess.	Ladies Da.
Length Long.	6105	5782	5194
Par	73	73	73

Advised golfing ability Niveau de jeu recommandé	0 12 24 36
Hcp required Handicap exigé	35

CLUB HOUSE & AMENITIES CLUB HOUSE ET ANNEXES 7/10

Pro shop	Pro-shop	
Driving range	Practice	
Sheltered	couvert	15 mats
On grass	sur herbe	yes (not in winter)
Putting-green	putting-green	yes
Pitching-green	pitching green	yes

HOTEL FACILITIES ENVIRONNEMENT HOTELIER 6/10

HOTELS HÔTELS
Holiday Inn Garden Court — Illkirch
68 rooms, D 680 F — 3 km
Tel (33) 03 88 40 84 84, Fax (33) 03 88 66 22 83

Alsace — Illkirch
40 rooms, D 300 F — 3 km
Tel (33) 03 88 66 41 60, Fax (33) 03 88 67 04 64

Alizés — Lipsheim
49 rooms, D 360 F — 6 km
Tel (33) 03 88 59 02 00, Fax (33) 03 88 64 21 61

RESTAURANTS RESTAURANTS
Buerehiesel — Strasbourg
Tel (33) 03 88 45 56 65 — 12 km

Au Crocodile — Strasbourg
Tel (33) 03 88 32 13 02 — 12 km

Maison Kammerzell et Baumann — Strasbourg
Tel (33) 03 88 32 42 14 — 12 km

345

A moyenne altitude, ce parcours n'est ouvert que huit mois par an, dans un site isolé et très naturel donnant une sensation de calme extrême. Gary Player a complètement remodelé un ancien tracé, avec beaucoup de goût et d'intelligence du jeu. On peut regretter un certain manque de souci de spectacle golfique, mais il a visiblement voulu préserver la beauté du lieu (l'automne y est splendide). Son tracé est très intéressant, sa difficulté globale raisonnable, il demande cependant une bonne technique pour être négocié avec succès. Les joueurs de tous niveaux peuvent y évoluer, de préférence en voiturette car les reliefs sont assez prononcés. Le plaisir ne sera certes pas éternellement renouvelé, car la stratégie sur chaque trou est pratiquement toujours la même, mais il sera toujours de grande qualité. Les amoureux de la nature vont adorer Taulane, d'autant que l'hôtel sur place est très agréable.

At mid-altitude, Taulane is open just eight months a year in an isolated and very natural setting of extreme tranquillity. Gary Player completely restyled an old layout with considerable taste and golfing nous. Perhaps sadly there was a little lack of concern for the visual side of things, but he clearly set out to preserve the beauty of the site (magnificent in autumn). The layout is very interesting and overall difficulty quite reasonable, but a good round here requires a sound technique. Players of all levels will enjoy Taulane, preferably on 4-wheels since some of the slopes are on the steep side. But it is hard to imagine golfers enjoying playing here again and again, as game strategy is virtually the same for each hole. Yet this is good golfing. Nature-enthusiasts will love the site, which also boasts a very pleasant hotel.

Golf de Taulane — 1992

RN 85
F - 83840 LA MARTRE

Office	Secrétariat	(33) 04 93 60 31 30
Pro shop	Pro-shop	(33) 04 93 60 31 30
Fax	Fax	(33) 04 93 60 33 23
Situation	Situation	

Grasse (pop. 41 380), 50 km

Annual closure	Fermeture annuelle	yes
	1/11 → 1/4	
Weekly closure	Fermeture hebdomadaire	no

Fees main season
Tarifs haute saison 18 holes

	Week days Semaine	We/Bank holidays We/Férié
Individual Individuel	400 F	400 F
Couple Couple	800 F	800 F

Caddy	Caddy	on request
Electric Trolley	Chariot électrique	75 F/18 holes
Buggy	Voiturette	220 F/18 holes
Clubs	Clubs	150 F/full day

Credit cards Cartes de crédit
VISA - CB - Eurocard - MasterCard - AMEX - DC

346

Vers Castellane (17 km du golf)
GOLF
Le Logis-du-Pin
Séranon
La Martre
Le Castellas 1068 m
Vers Grasse (44 km)
Vers Comps-s-Artuby Draguignan
La Bastide

0   2   4 km

Access Accès : From Nice or Cannes → Grasse/Digne → Le Logis du Pin, « Route Napoléon »
Map 14 on page 191 Carte 14 Page 191

GOLF COURSE / PARCOURS — 15/20

Site	Site	
Maintenance	Entretien	
Architect	Architecte	Gary Player
Type	Type	forest
Relief	Relief	
Water in play	Eau en jeu	
Exp. to wind	Exposé au vent	
Trees in play	Arbres en jeu	

Scorecard Carte de score	Chp. Chp.	Mens Mess.	Ladies Da.
Length Long.	6269	5822	5341
Par	72	72	72

Advised golfing ability Niveau de jeu recommandé	0 12 24 36
Hcp required Handicap exigé	24 Men, 28 Ladies

CLUB HOUSE & AMENITIES / CLUB HOUSE ET ANNEXES — 7/10

Pro shop	Pro-shop	
Driving range	Practice	
Sheltered	couvert	10 mats
On grass	sur herbe	yes
Putting-green	putting-green	yes
Pitching-green	pitching green	yes

HOTEL FACILITIES / ENVIRONNEMENT HOTELIER — 4/10

HOTELS HÔTELS
Château de Taulane — on site
44 rooms, D 1 200 F
Tel (33) 04 93 40 60 80, Fax (33) 04 93 60 37 48

Château de Trigance — Trigance
10 rooms, D 900 F — 20 km
Tel (33) 04 94 76 91 18, Fax (33) 04 94 85 68 99

RESTAURANTS RESTAURANTS
Nouvel Hôtel du Commerce — Castellane
Tel (33) 04 92 83 61 00 — 15 km

L'Ancienne Station — La Martre
Tel (33) 04 93 60 38 48 — 1 km

15	7	4

Un club très vivant et professionnel, où il fait bon s'arrêter. Bien à l'abri du vent, avec de beaux chênes, quelques trouées offrant de jolies vues sur la vallée du Tarn, ce parcours a bien respecté l'environnement. Cette réussite générale rend certainement exigeant. Pour en faire un grand parcours, on souhaiterait par exemple que les bunkers soient un peu plus profonds, ce qui impliquerait une révision des avant-greens. Mais, en l'état, il faut déjà savoir jouer tous les coups, et utiliser tous les clubs du sac : les joueurs de bon handicap apprécieront particulièrement sa technicité. Assez varié pour ne jamais être ennuyeux, le tracé de Michael Fenn a évité les trous parallèles, et offre un rythme de jeu bien équilibré, alternant les trous difficiles et les trous plus reposants. Un golf très familial, avec une bonne politique sportive, qui mérite largement la visite.

A very lively, professional club where it is always a pleasure to stop-off. Nicely sheltered from the wind, this is a course that has espoused its environment and is laid out amidst some beautiful oaks. A few holes provide splendid views over the Tarn river. This initial very positive impression makes the visitor a little more demanding when it comes to the rest. For example, a great course would require slightly deeper bunkers and consequently a little re-design work around the greens. But as it is, it demands every shot in the book and probably every club in your bag. Low handicappers in particular will enjoy the course's technical aspect. With enough variety never to be boring, Michael Fenn's layout has avoided parallel holes and provides a nicely balanced course, alternating difficult holes with the not so difficult. A very family-style course, very well organised sports-wise and well worth the visit.

Golf de Toulouse Palmola	1974
F - 31660 BUZET-SUR-TARN	

Office	Secrétariat	(33) 05 61 84 20 50
Pro shop	Pro-shop	(33) 05 61 84 20 50
Fax	Fax	(33) 05 61 84 48 92
Situation	Situation	
Toulouse (pop. 358 680), 20 km		
Annual closure	Fermeture annuelle	no
Weekly closure	Fermeture hebdomadaire	tuesday (mardi)

Fees main season		
Tarifs haute saison full day		
	Week days Semaine	We/Bank holidays We/Férié
Individual Individuel	210 F	350 F
Couple Couple	420 F	600 F

Caddy	Caddy	no
Electric Trolley	Chariot électrique	no
Buggy	Voiturette	200 F/18 holes
Clubs	Clubs	80 F/full day

Credit cards Cartes de crédit
VISA - CB - Eurocard - MasterCard

SAINT-SULPICE
GOLF
N 2088
D 630
A 68
Albi
Buzet
D 2
Montastruc-La-Conseillère
N 88
Toulouse
0   2   4 km

Access Accès : • A 68 Toulouse → Albi, Exit (Sortie) No 4 Gémil-Buzet sur Tarn • Albi → Toulouse, Exit Montastruc la Conseillère, → Albi (N88), → Golf
Map 13 on page 188 Carte 13 Page 188

GOLF COURSE
PARCOURS

15/20

Site	Site	
Maintenance	Entretien	
Architect	Architecte	Michael Fenn
Type	Type	forest, residential
Relief	Relief	
Water in play	Eau en jeu	
Exp. to wind	Exposé au vent	
Trees in play	Arbres en jeu	

Scorecard	Chp.	Mens	Ladies
Carte de score	Chp.	Mess.	Da.
Length Long.	6156	5949	5292
Par	72	72	72

Advised golfing ability		0 12 24 36
Niveau de jeu recommandé		
Hcp required	Handicap exigé	24-28 (We)

CLUB HOUSE & AMENITIES
CLUB HOUSE ET ANNEXES

7/10

Pro shop	Pro-shop	
Driving range	Practice	
Sheltered	couvert	4 mats
On grass	sur herbe	yes
Putting-green	putting-green	yes
Pitching-green	pitching green	yes

HOTEL FACILITIES
ENVIRONNEMENT HOTELIER

4/10

HOTELS HÔTELS
Château de Saint-Lieux — Saint-Lieux
12 rooms, D 300 F — 13 km
Tel (33) 05 63 41 60 87

A l'Hôtel - 47 rooms, D 250 F — L'Union
Tel (33) 05 61 09 06 06, Fax (33) 05 61 74 21 32 — 13 km

Campanile — L'Union
72 rooms, D 295 F — 13 km
Tel (33) 05 61 74 00 40, Fax (33) 05 61 09 53 38

RESTAURANTS RESTAURANT
Les Jardins de l'Opéra — Toulouse
Tel (33) 05 61 23 07 76 — 20 km

Michel Sarran — Toulouse
Tel (33) 05 61 12 32 32 — 20 km

7 Place Saint-Sernin — Toulouse
Tel (33) 05 62 30 05 30 — 20 km

347

Un Jeremy Pern typique. A partir d'un terrain plat, il a bien travaillé ses mouvements de terrain comme ses bunkers, de toutes formes et de toutes dimensions. Les greens sont vastes, avec des reliefs subtils, permettant de multiples positions de drapeaux. Les obstacles d'eau jouent aussi un grand rôle dans la stratégie, mais ils peuvent être dangereux s'il y a du vent. Autrement, les joueurs prudents peuvent jouer à l'écart. Peu boisé, il a fait l'objet de programmes immobiliers, mais pas trop agressifs visuellement. Ce parcours de style américain réclame un jeu très complet, et notamment un petit jeu bien affûté, il joue donc bien son rôle de «formation de golfeurs». Ici, la chance ne peut jouer aucun rôle dans un bon score. Les installations sont fonctionnelles, mais pas très chaleureuses : ce n'est pourtant pas hors de portée d'un golf commercial...

This is a typical Jeremy Pern layout, starting out with flat terrain and carefully designing-in sloping terrain and bunkers of all shapes and sizes. The greens are huge with subtle breaks, allowing numerous different pin positions. Water hazards play a major role in game strategy here and can be very dangerous if there is wind around. Otherwise, the cautious player will lay up or play around them. There are few trees but a number of property developments, which fortunately are not too hard on the eye. Toulouse-Seilh is an American style course requiring an all-round game and some slick short irons, thereby fulfilling its role as a course for "schooling golfers". A good score here owes little or nothing to luck. The facilities are functional but not over-welcoming, surely a feature that a business venture course like this should be able to afford.

Golf de Toulouse-Seilh Latitudes　　1988

Route de Grenade
F - 31860 SEILH

Office	Secrétariat	(33) 05 62 13 14 14
Pro shop	Pro-shop	(33) 05 62 13 14 14
Fax	Fax	(33) 05 61 42 34 17
Situation	Situation	

Toulouse (pop. 358 680), 10 km

Annual closure	Fermeture annuelle	no
Weekly closure	Fermeture hebdomadaire	no

Fees main season
Tarifs haute saison full day

	Week days Semaine	We/Bank holidays We/Férié
Individual Individuel	170 F	250 F
Couple Couple	340 F	500 F

Special fees in July and August (07/08)

Caddy	Caddy	no
Electric Trolley	Chariot électrique	no
Buggy	Voiturette	120 F/18 holes
Clubs	Clubs	50 F/full day

Credit cards Cartes de crédit
VISA - CB - Eurocard - MasterCard - AMEX - DC

348

Access Accès : A62 or A61 → Toulouse, Exit (Sortie) Saint-Jory → Lespinasse → Blagnac, → Golf
Map 12 on page 187 Carte 12 Page 187

GOLF COURSE / PARCOURS　　15/20

Site	Site	
Maintenance	Entretien	
Architect	Architecte	Jeremy Pern Jean Garaïalde
Type	Type	open country, residential
Relief	Relief	
Water in play	Eau en jeu	
Exp. to wind	Exposé au vent	
Trees in play	Arbres en jeu	

Scorecard Carte de score	Chp. Chp.	Mens Mess.	Ladies Da.
Length Long.	6330	5862	5018
Par	72	72	72

			0　12　24　36
Advised golfing ability Niveau de jeu recommandé			
Hcp required Handicap exigé			28 (We)

CLUB HOUSE & AMENITIES / CLUB HOUSE ET ANNEXES　　7/10

Pro shop	Pro-shop	
Driving range	Practice	
Sheltered	couvert	30 mats
On grass	sur herbe	yes
Putting-green	putting-green	yes
Pitching-green	pitching green	yes

HOTEL FACILITIES / ENVIRONNEMENT HOTELIER　　6/10

HOTELS HÔTELS

Maeva Latitudes　　　　　　　　　　on site
115 rooms, D 500 F
Tel (33) 05 62 13 14 15, Fax (33) 05 61 59 77 97

Diane　　　　　　　　　　　　　　　Toulouse
35 rooms, D 450 F　　　　　　　　　　10 km
Tel (33) 05 61 07 59 52, Fax (33) 05 61 86 38 94

Grand Hôtel de l'Opéra　　　　　　　Toulouse
49 rooms, D 700 F　　　　　　　　　　10 km
Tel (33) 05 61 21 82 66, Fax (33) 05 61 23 41 04

RESTAURANTS RESTAURANTS

Frégate　　　　　　　　　　　　　　Toulouse
Tel (33) 05 61 21 62 45　　　　　　　　10 km

Le Pastel　　　　　　　　　　　Toulouse-Mirail
Tel (33) 05 62 87 84 30　　　　　　　　18 km

Cantaloupe - Tel (33) 05 61 55 34 01　　Toulouse 10 km

Ce 18 trous est le chef-d'œuvre du Touquet, mais son rétablissement dans un tracé proche de celui d'avant-guerre, n'a pas toujours été faite avec la rigueur architecturale nécessaire à toute restauration d'un «monument historique» : on distingue nettement les différences de style. Il offre des reliefs modérés, des fairways très travaillés, quelques bunkers redoutables, et des greens parfois déconcertants, dans une végétation clairsemée, mais souvent en jeu. Une bonne partie des trous se déroulent dans des dunes spectaculaires : ici, il faut être humble avec son golf, car les punitions pour les coups manqués sont immédiates. Et quand le vent s'en mêle, la patience s'impose. Alors, les «manieurs de balles» et les tacticiens prennent le dessus sur les purs frappeurs. Difficile pour les débutants, c'est un parcours passionnant pour les joueurs aguerris. L'autre 18 trous (La Forêt), n'est pas dans la même catégorie, mais reste intéressant.

This 18-hole course is the masterpiece of Le Touquet. The course has been remodelled back to a layout very close to the original pre-war design, but not with the architectural thoroughness required by the restoration of an historical monument. The differences in style clearly stand out. «La Mer» is moderately hilly, boasts carefully designed fairways, a few formidable bunkers and sometimes disconcerting greens amidst sparse vegetation that nonetheless is often in play. A good number of holes are laid out among some spectacular dunes, where golfers need to be humble with their golf: mis-hit shots are punished immediately. And when the wind blows, patience, too, is a virtue. Flighters of the ball and the shrewd tactician will find the going easier than the long-hitter. A tough course for beginners, a great course for the seasoned golfer. The other 18-hole layout (La Forêt), is not in the same class but is still an enjoyable course to play.

Golf du Touquet — 1904

Avenue du Golf
F - 62520 LE TOUQUET

Office	Secrétariat	(33) 03 21 06 28 00
Pro shop	Pro-shop	(33) 03 21 06 28 00
Fax	Fax	(33) 03 21 06 28 01
Situation	Situation	

Le Touquet (pop. 5 590), 2.5 km
Montreuil (pop. 2 450), 18 km

Annual closure	Fermeture annuelle	no
Weekly closure	Fermeture hebdomadaire	no

Fees main season
Tarifs haute saison full day

	Week days Semaine	We/Bank holidays We/Férié
Individual Individuel	270 F	350 F
Couple Couple	540 F	700 F

01/11 → 31/03: GF Weekdays 140 F, We 180 F

Caddy	Caddy	on request
Electric Trolley	Chariot électrique	no
Buggy	Voiturette	240 F/18 holes
Clubs	Clubs	80 F/full day

Credit cards Cartes de crédit
VISA - CB - Eurocard - MasterCard - AMEX

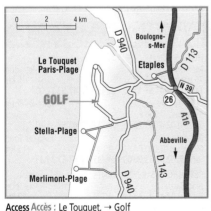

Access Accès : Le Touquet, → Golf
Map 1 on page 164 Carte 1 Page 164

GOLF COURSE PARCOURS — 17/20

Site	Site	
Maintenance	Entretien	
Architect	Architecte	J.H. Taylor Harry S. Colt
Type	Type	links
Relief	Relief	
Water in play	Eau en jeu	
Exp. to wind	Exposé au vent	
Trees in play	Arbres en jeu	

Scorecard Carte de score	Chp. Chp.	Mens Mess.	Ladies Da.
Length Long.	6330	6330	5346
Par	72	72	72

Advised golfing ability   0   12   24   36
Niveau de jeu recommandé

Hcp required Handicap exigé   24 Men, 28 Ladies

CLUB HOUSE & AMENITIES CLUB HOUSE ET ANNEXES — 6/10

Pro shop	Pro-shop	
Driving range	Practice	
Sheltered	couvert	25 mats
On grass	sur herbe	yes
Putting-green	putting-green	yes
Pitching-green	pitching green	yes

349

HOTEL FACILITIES ENVIRONNEMENT HOTELIER — 7/10

HOTELS HÔTELS
Manoir   on site
41 rooms, D 800 F
Tel (33) 03 21 06 28 28, Fax (33) 03 21 06 28 29

Westminster   Le Touquet
115 rooms, D 1 200 F   2,5 km
Tel (33) 03 21 05 48 48, Fax (33) 03 21 05 45 45

Novotel   Le Touquet
149 rooms, D 800 F   2,5 km
Tel (33) 03 21 09 85 00, Fax (33) 03 21 09 85 10

RESTAURANTS RESTAURANT
Flavio-Club de la Forêt   Le Touquet
Tel (33) 03 21 05 10 22   2,5 km

Le Café des Arts   Le Touquet
Tel(33) 03 21 05 21 55   2,5 km

L'Escale - Tel (33) 03 21 05 23 22   Le Touquet 5 km

Un vrai parc de Touraine, avec beaucoup de beaux arbres et une ambiance très familiale, où l'on se sent vite à l'aise. Michael Fenn y a tracé un parcours très varié, mais un peu conformiste, avec quelques trous délicats en raison de fairways étroits, compensés par de grandes «avenues» où les longs frappeurs pourront se déchaîner. L'ensemble n'est pas très long, le relief modérément accidenté, ce qui convient bien à une clientèle de joueurs moyens assez droits, mais les joueurs peu précis peuvent avoir quelques problèmes, car les greens ne sont pas non plus immenses. Pour agrémenter l'incertitude du jeu, quelques pièces d'eau et ruisseaux sont stratégiquement bien utilisés. Dans cette région très touristique des châteaux de la Loire, les visiteurs passeront une journée très agréable et éventuellement encourageante quant à leurs scores sur ce parcours (un peu humide en hiver).

A real Touraine park with many beautiful trees and a very family atmosphere where you soon feel at home. Michael Fenn has designed a course of great variety but a little conformist in nature. The few troublesome holes with tight fairways are offset somewhat by some wide «avenues» where big hitters can let fly. On the whole this is not a very long course, hilly in parts, and is particularly suitable for the average golfer who plays straight. Wayward hitters will have a few more problems, because the greens are also rather small. To add a little spice to uncertainty, a few stretches of water and streams are used to good strategic effect. In this holiday region of the Loire and castles, visitors will spend a very pleasant day's golfing on a course that can be a little wet in winter but which can be encouraging score-wise.

Golf de Touraine — 1972

Château de la Touche
F - 37510 BALLAN-MIRE

Office	Secrétariat	(33) 02 47 53 20 28
Pro shop	Pro-shop	(33) 02 47 53 20 28
Fax	Fax	(33) 02 47 53 31 54
Situation	Situation	

Tours (pop. 129 500), 12 km

Annual closure	Fermeture annuelle	no
Weekly closure	Fermeture hebdomadaire	no

Restaurant closed on tuesday (mardi)

Fees main season
Tarifs haute saison full day

	Week days Semaine	We/Bank holidays We/Férié
Individual Individuel	230 F	300 F
Couple Couple	460 F	600 F

Caddy	Caddy	on request
Electric Trolley	Chariot électrique	no
Buggy	Voiturette	200 F/18 holes
Clubs	Clubs	100 F/full day

Credit cards Cartes de crédit
VISA - CB - Eurocard - MasterCard

350

TOURS

Loire
Cher 4 km

Joué-les-Tours

GOLF D 751

BALLAN-MIRÉ

Ouverture 2000

BLOIS POITIERS

A 10

Azay-le-Rideau
Chinon

Access Accès : A10 Exit (Sortie) Chambray-les-Tours →
Tours → Joué-les-Tours, Chinon → Ballan-Miré
Map 6 on page 175 Carte 6 Page 175

GOLF COURSE / PARCOURS — 13/20

Site	Site	▬▬▬
Maintenance	Entretien	▬▬▬
Architect	Architecte	Michael Fenn
Type	Type	parkland, forest
Relief	Relief	▬▬
Water in play	Eau en jeu	▬
Exp. to wind	Exposé au vent	▬
Trees in play	Arbres en jeu	▬▬▬

Scorecard Carte de score	Chp. Chp.	Mens Mess.	Ladies Da.
Length Long.	5671	5424	4778
Par	71	71	71

Advised golfing ability Niveau de jeu recommandé	0	12	24	36

Hcp required	Handicap exigé	35 (We)

CLUB HOUSE & AMENITIES / CLUB HOUSE ET ANNEXES — 7/10

Pro shop	Pro-shop	▬▬▬
Driving range	Practice	
Sheltered	couvert	8 mats
On grass	sur herbe	no, 10 mats open air
Putting-green	putting-green	yes
Pitching-green	pitching green	yes

HOTEL FACILITIES / ENVIRONNEMENT HOTELIER — 6/10

HOTELS HÔTELS

Mercure — Joué-les-Tours
75 rooms, D 550 F — 5 km
Tel (33) 02 47 53 16 16, Fax (33) 02 47 53 14 00

Château de Beaulieu — Joué-les-Tours
19 rooms, D 750 F — 5 km
Tel (33) 02 47 53 20 26, Fax (33) 02 47 53 84 20

Escurial — Joué-les-Tours
60 rooms, D 280 F — 5 km
Tel (33) 02 47 53 60 00, Fax (33) 02 47 67 75 33

RESTAURANTS RESTAURANTS

Jean Bardet — Tours
Tel (33) 02 47 41 41 11 — 12 km

Charles Barrier — Tours
Tel (33) 02 47 54 20 39 — 12 km

Kiosque - Tel (33) 02 47 53 35 02 — Ballan-Miré 2 km

VAL DE SORNE

| 14 | 7 | 5 |

Dans une région pas très riche en golfs, la création de ce golf était bienvenue. Dessiné sur un terrain modérément accidenté par Hugues Lambert dans un style plus américain que britannique, il comporte des obstacles d'eau sur une demi-douzaine de trous. En jouant des départs avancés et même si certains dévers obligent à jouer dans la pente, il est accessible à tous les niveaux, à l'exception du 16, un par 4 difficile dont le green est entouré d'eau. Le déroulement du parcours est assez agréable, sans être d'un tracé vraiment exceptionnel, les arbres sont souvent bien en jeu (comme au 13), mais il vaut mieux le visiter entre mai et octobre, même si des drainages ont été effectués. Les greens sont de dimensions et de difficultés moyenne : leur modelage un peu timide conviendra à tous les handicaps, et leurs défenses ne sont pas trop hermétiques.

This course was most welcome in a region where golf playing facilities are few and far between. Laid out over a moderately hilly terrain by Hugues Lambert in a rather more American style than British, it features water hazards on half a dozen or so holes. From the front-tees, and despite the sloping fairways, the course can be played by golfers of all abilities, with the possible exception of the 16th, a difficult par 4 where the green is surrounded by water. The course unfolds in a pleasant manner without ever being outstanding, and the trees are often very much in play (on the 13th, for example). And even though drainage work is now complete, the best time to play here is between May and October. The greens are of average size and difficulty, and are sufficiently flat and bunkerless to appeal to all handicaps.

Golf du Val de Sorne — 1993

Vernantois
F - 39570 LONS-LE-SAUNIER

Office	Secrétariat	(33) 03 84 43 04 80
Pro shop	Pro-shop	(33) 03 84 43 04 80
Fax	Fax	(33) 03 84 47 31 21
Situation	Situation	

Lons-le-Saunier (pop. 19 140), 6 km

Annual closure	Fermeture annuelle	no
Weekly closure	Fermeture hebdomadaire	no

Fees main season
Tarifs haute saison 18 holes

	Week days Semaine	We/Bank holidays We/Férié
Individual Individuel	230 F	280 F
Couple Couple	460 F	560 F

Caddy	Caddy	no
Electric Trolley	Chariot électrique	60 F/18 holes
Buggy	Voiturette	200 F/18 holes
Clubs	Clubs	50 F/full day

Credit cards Cartes de crédit
VISA - CB - Eurocard - MasterCard - AMEX - DC

Access Accès : Lons-le-Saunier → Macornay,
then → Vernantois, → Golf
Map 8 on page 178 Carte 8 Page 178

GOLF COURSE PARCOURS — 14/20

Site	Site	
Maintenance	Entretien	
Architect	Architecte	Hugues Lambert
Type	Type	parkland
Relief	Relief	
Water in play	Eau en jeu	
Exp. to wind	Exposé au vent	
Trees in play	Arbres en jeu	

Scorecard Carte de score	Chp. Chp.	Mens Mess.	Ladies Da.
Length Long.	6270	6000	5056
Par	72	72	72

Advised golfing ability Niveau de jeu recommandé		0 12 24 36
Hcp required	Handicap exigé	no

CLUB HOUSE & AMENITIES CLUB HOUSE ET ANNEXES — 7/10

Pro shop	Pro-shop	
Driving range	Practice	
Sheltered	couvert	5 mats
On grass	sur herbe	no, 30 mats open air
Putting-green	putting-green	yes
Pitching-green	pitching green	no

HOTEL FACILITIES ENVIRONNEMENT HOTELIER — 5/10

HOTELS HÔTELS
Hôtel du Golf — Vernantois
36 rooms, D 625 F — on site
Tel (33) 03 84 43 04 80, Fax (33) 03 84 47 31 21

Hostellerie des Monts-de-Vaux — Poligny
10 rooms, D 950 F — 29 km
Tel (33) 03 84 37 12 50, Fax (33) 03 84 37 09 07

Moulin de Bourgchâteau — Louhans
18 rooms, D 550 F — 26 km
Tel (33) 03 85 75 37 12, Fax (33) 03 85 75 45 11

RESTAURANTS RESTAURANTS
La Comédie — Lons-le-Saunier
Tel (33) 03 84 24 20 66 — 6 km

Auberge de Chavannes — Courlans
Tel (33) 03 84 47 05 52 — 8 km

Relais d'Alsace — Lons-le-Saunier
Tel (33) 03 84 47 24 70 — 6 km

351

Un site vallonné dans la vallée du Scorff, et en pleine campagne bretonne, ponctuée de beaux arbres, notamment des chênes et châtaigniers, qui protègent bien du vent assez fréquent dans la région. Comme à son habitude, l'architecte Yves Bureau a dessiné un parcours très plaisant et diversifié, bien paysagé et assez large pour être rassurant, assez technique pour renouveler l'intérêt. Les bons scores ne sont pourtant pas si faciles car il faut tenir compte des dénivellations et de la présence de nombreux bunkers bien découpés. Les greens sont de bonne dimension, et bien construits, les obstacles d'eau peu nombreux. Tous les niveaux de jeu peuvent cohabiter ici, les joueurs moyens comme les meilleurs handicaps. Comme souvent en Bretagne, on peut y croiser de nombreux Britanniques. Une curiosité, la présence d'un tumulus antique.

This is a site of rolling landscape in the Scorff valley, at the heart of Breton countryside. It is dotted with some fine trees, particularly oak and horse-chestnut, which afford good protection from the frequent wind. As usual, architect Yves Bureau has laid out a very pleasant course, full of variety, well-landscaped and wide enough to reassure most of us, and technically difficult enough to keep it interesting. Yet good scores here are not always easy to come by, courtesy of some steep slopes and numerous nicely outlined bunkers. The greens are of a good size and well designed, and water hazards are rare. All golfers can play together here. And as is often the case in Brittany, the course is a favourite with British golfers. One little curiosity is the presence of a «tumulus», or sepulchral mound, on the course.

Golf de Val Queven — 1990

Kerruisseau
F - 56530 QUEVEN

Office	Secrétariat	(33) 02 97 05 17 96
Pro shop	Pro-shop	(33) 02 97 05 17 96
Fax	Fax	(33) 02 97 05 19 18
Situation	Situation	

Lorient (pop. 59 270), 8 km

Annual closure	Fermeture annuelle	no
Weekly closure	Fermeture hebdomadaire	no

Fees main season
Tarifs haute saison 18 holes

	Week days Semaine	We/Bank holidays We/Férié
Individual Individuel	260 F	260 F
Couple Couple	520 F	520 F

Caddy	Caddy	no
Electric Trolley	Chariot électrique	no
Buggy	Voiturette	150 F/18 holes
Clubs	Clubs	50 F/full day

Credit cards Cartes de crédit
VISA - CB - Eurocard - MasterCard

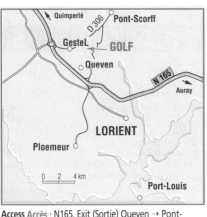

Access Accès : N165, Exit (Sortie) Queven → Pont-Scorff. Queven, 1 km → Golf
Map 5 on page 173 Carte 5 Page 173

GOLF COURSE / PARCOURS — 15/20

Site	Site	■■■■□□
Maintenance	Entretien	■■■■□□
Architect	Architecte	Yves Bureau
Type	Type	country, forest
Relief	Relief	■■■■□□
Water in play	Eau en jeu	■□□□□□
Exp. to wind	Exposé au vent	■■□□□□
Trees in play	Arbres en jeu	■■■□□□

Scorecard Carte de score	Chp. Chp.	Mens Mess.	Ladies Da.
Length Long.	6140	5750	5200
Par	72	72	72

Advised golfing ability		0 12 24 36
Niveau de jeu recommandé		
Hcp required	Handicap exigé	35

CLUB HOUSE & AMENITIES / CLUB HOUSE ET ANNEXES — 6/10

Pro shop	Pro-shop	■■■■□□
Driving range	Practice	■■■■□□
Sheltered	couvert	10 mats
On grass	sur herbe	yes
Putting-green	putting-green	yes
Pitching-green	pitching green	yes

HOTEL FACILITIES / ENVIRONNEMENT HOTELIER — 5/10

HOTELS HÔTELS

Château de Locguénolé — Hennebont
22 rooms, D 1 200 F — 11 km
Tel (33) 02 97 76 76 76, Fax (33) 02 97 76 82 35

Les Moulins du Duc — Moëlan-sur-Mer
27 rooms, D 800 F — 16 km
Tel (33) 02 98 39 60 73, Fax (33) 02 98 39 75 56

RESTAURANTS RESTAURANTS

L'Amphitryon — Lorient
Tel (33) 02 97 83 34 04 — 5 km

Le Jardin Gourmand — Lorient
Tel (33) 02 97 64 17 24 — 8 km

Poisson d'Or — Lorient
Tel (33) 02 97 21 57 06 — 8 km

352

Beaucoup moins boisé que l'autre parcours du lieu, «La Rivière», «Les Vallons» est d'un style radicalement différent, où l'architecte Michel Gayon a rendu hommage aux links britanniques. Il s'agit d'une sorte de parcours de bord de mer, sans la mer bien sûr, avec de nombreuses buttes et roughs délimitant bien les fairways, et donnant du relief à un terrain originellement assez plat. Il n'est pas très long, et les longs frappeurs pourront se livrer, mais c'est un parcours plus dangereux et difficile à scorer qu'il n'y paraît, d'autant que le vent y est rarement absent, et que les greens peuvent être parfois complexes à lire. Alors, il faudra exprimer toutes les ressources de son petit jeu pour sauver le score. Bien entretenu, le complexe de La Vaucouleurs est un ensemble à connaître pour sa variété, à jouer plutôt quand les journées sont belles.

With little or no woodland, «Les Vallons» is radically different from «La Rivière» (the other course on the site) and is something of a tribute by architect Michel Gayon to British style links golfing. It is certainly a sort of seaside course, without the sea, of course, with a number of sandhills and rough clearly defining the fairways and giving considerable relief to terrain that was originally flat. It is not very long and big-hitters can let fly, but the course is more dangerous and harder to master than it looks, especially since the wind is never very far away and some of the greens are tricky to read. In this case, only a sharp short game will save your card. Well looked after with good green-keeping, the estate of La Vaucouleurs is a complex worth getting to know for its variety, but better played in dry weather.

Golf-Club de la Vaucouleurs — 1989
F - 78910 CIVRY-LA-FORET

Office	Secrétariat	(33) 01 34 87 62 29
Pro shop	Pro-shop	(33) 01 34 87 76 27
Fax	Fax	(33) 01 34 87 70 09
Situation	Situation	

Mantes-la-Jolie (pop. 45 080), 20 km - Paris, 61 km
Annual closure Fermeture annuelle yes
22/12 → 1/1
Weekly closure Fermeture hebdomadaire
wednesday/mercredi, from 01/10 to 31/03

Fees main season
Tarifs haute saison full day

	Week days Semaine	We/Bank holidays We/Férié
Individual Individuel	200 F	350 F
Couple Couple	350 F	650 F

Tuesday (mardi): GF 150 F. Friday (vendr.) : GF + lunch 250 F

Caddy	Caddy	on request
Electric Trolley	Chariot électrique	no
Buggy	Voiturette	150 F/18 holes
Clubs	Clubs	50 F/full day

Credit cards Cartes de crédit
VISA - CB - Eurocard - MasterCard - AMEX

Access Accès : A13 Paris/Rouen, Exit (Sortie) Mantes-la-Jolie, D983 → Houdan. In Orvilliers, turn right → Golf
Map 3 on page 168 Carte 3 Page 168

GOLF COURSE / PARCOURS — 15/20

Site	Site	
Maintenance	Entretien	
Architect	Architecte	Michel Gayon
Type	Type	links, country
Relief	Relief	
Water in play	Eau en jeu	
Exp. to wind	Exposé au vent	
Trees in play	Arbres en jeu	

Scorecard Carte de score	Chp. Chp.	Mens Mess.	Ladies Da.
Length Long.	5638	5082	4833
Par	70	70	70

Advised golfing ability 0 12 24 36
Niveau de jeu recommandé
Hcp required Handicap exigé no

CLUB HOUSE & AMENITIES / CLUB HOUSE ET ANNEXES — 7/10

Pro shop	Pro-shop	
Driving range	Practice	
Sheltered	couvert	6 mats
On grass	sur herbe	yes (summer)
Putting-green	putting-green	yes
Pitching-green	pitching green	yes

353

HOTEL FACILITIES / ENVIRONNEMENT HOTELIER — 4/10

HOTELS HÔTELS
Dousseine — Anet
20 rooms, D 280 F — 16 km
Tel (33) 01 37 41 49 93, Fax (33) 01 37 41 90 54

Le Plat d'Etain — Houdan
8 rooms, D 330 F — 11 km
Tel (33) 01 30 59 60 28, Fax (33) 01 34 89 21 11

RESTAURANTS RESTAURANTS
La Poularde — Houdan
Tel (33) 01 30 59 60 50 — 11 km

Le Donjon — Houdan
Tel (33) 01 30 59 79 14 — 11 km

Le très honnête 18 trous des «Brocards» signé par Michael Fenn n'est pas exaltant, mais il permet à tous les niveaux d'évoluer agréablement. Le nouveau 18 trous (Les Sangliers) signé par Hugues Lambert mérite largement le détour, mais ce sont les joueurs de moins de 24 de handicap qui l'apprécieront davantage. Très long (parfois à l'excès), avec de l'eau en jeu sur la moitié des trous, quelques buttes et pas mal de bunkers, il exige un jeu très complet, et beaucoup de puissance si l'on veut tenir son handicap, même des départs avancés. Ses nombreux obstacles impliquent de le jouer plusieurs fois avant d'en comprendre les aspects stratégiques. Si l'on manque les greens, bien travaillés, on peut parfois y rentrer en roulant, mais il vaut mieux soigner la balle. C'est incontestablement l'un des tout meilleurs parcours de la région. Ce golf privé est difficile d'accès en week-end (sauf l'été).

«Les Brocards», is a fair and unpretentious 18-hole course, designed by Michael Fenn, and a pleasant round of golf for golfers of all levels. The new 18-hole course («Les Sangliers»), laid out by Hugues Lambert, is a much more enticing proposition, although a 24 handicap would seem to be the minimum requirement for enjoying the course. Very long (sometimes excessively so) with water on half the holes, a few sandhills and a lot of bunkers, the course demands an all-round game and power, even from the front tees. The countless hazards imply several exploratory rounds before fully understanding the strategic side to the course. Missed greens can sometimes be reached with chip shots, but controlled lob and pitch shots are important here. This is unquestionably one of the region's very best courses, and being private is difficult to play on week-ends (except in summer).

Golf Club de Lyon — 1992
F - 38280 VILLETTE-D'ANTHON

Office	Secrétariat	(33) 04 78 31 11 33
Pro shop	Pro-shop	(33) 04 72 02 28 76
Fax	Fax	(33) 04 72 02 48 27
Situation	Situation	

Lyon (pop. 413 090), 20 km

Annual closure	Fermeture annuelle	no
Weekly closure	Fermeture hebdomadaire	no

Fees main season
Tarifs haute saison 18 holes

	Week days Semaine	We/Bank holidays We/Férié
Individual Individuel	220 F	280 F
Couple Couple	440 F	560 F

Caddy	Caddy	on request
Electric Trolley	Chariot électrique	70 F/18 holes
Buggy	Voiturette	200 F/18 holes
Clubs	Clubs	100 F/full day

Credit cards Cartes de crédit
VISA - CB - Eurocard - MasterCard

Access Accès : • Lyon, «Rocade Est», Exit (Sortie) Meyzieu le Carreau → Villette d'Anthon • A42 Bourg-en-Bresse Lyon, Exit (Sortie) Balan, → Jons, Villette d'Anthon
Map 11 on page 184 Carte 11 Page 184

GOLF COURSE / PARCOURS — 17 /20

Site	Site	
Maintenance	Entretien	
Architect	Architecte	Hugues Lambert
Type	Type	forest, country
Relief	Relief	
Water in play	Eau en jeu	
Exp. to wind	Exposé au vent	
Trees in play	Arbres en jeu	

Scorecard Carte de score	Chp. Chp.	Mens Mess.	Ladies Da.
Length Long.	6727	6228	5395
Par	72	72	72

Advised golfing ability			0 12 24 36
Niveau de jeu recommandé			
Hcp required	Handicap exigé	35	

CLUB HOUSE & AMENITIES / CLUB HOUSE ET ANNEXES — 6 /10

Pro shop	Pro-shop	
Driving range	Practice	
Sheltered	couvert	12 mats
On grass	sur herbe	yes
Putting-green	putting-green	yes
Pitching-green	pitching green	yes

HOTEL FACILITIES / ENVIRONNEMENT HOTELIER — 4 /10

HOTELS HÔTELS

Mont-Joyeux — Meyzieu
20 rooms, D 590 F — 12 km
Tel (33) 04 78 04 21 32, Fax (33) 04 72 02 85 72

Auberge de Jons — Jons
26 rooms, D 440 F — 3 km
Tel (33) 04 78 31 29 85, Fax (33) 04 72 02 48 24

Villa Florentine — Lyon (Vieux-Lyon)
16 rooms, D 2 100 F — 20 km
Tel (33) 04 72 56 56 56, Fax (33) 04 72 40 90 56

RESTAURANTS RESTAURANTS

Paul Bocuse — Collonges-au-Mont-d'Or
Tel (33) 04 72 42 90 90 — 25 km

Léon de Lyon — Lyon
Tel (33) 04 72 10 11 12 — 20 km

Le Jura (Bouchon) — Lyon
Tel (33) 04 78 42 20 57 — 20 km

354

Situé à près de 900 mètres d'altitude au pied du Puy de Dôme, ce parcours peut parfois être gelé le matin, sauf en été. Environné de bouleaux, de pins, de buissons sauvages et de bruyère, il présente une forte montée du 9 au 10, mais pas assez épuisante pour obliger à prendre une voiturette. Le dessin du professionnel local, Lucien Roux, ne prétend certes pas aux plus hautes distinctions, mais il reste plus que correct, avec une bonne utilisation des arbres et des bunkers, quelques greens délicats à double plateau, et un bon rythme de distribution des difficultés. Le parcours peut paraître un peu long du fond, mais les balles portent plus loin en altitude, et les départs avancés (notamment sur les longs par 3) permettent de prendre beaucoup de plaisir dans ce golf sympathique et très familial, situé dans un environnement magnifique et calme.

Lying 900 metres above sea level at the foot of the Puy de Dôme, this course is often frost-bound in the morning outside the summer months. Surrounded by birch trees, pines, wild bushes and heather, there is steep climb between the 9th and 10th, although not tiring enough to warrant a buggy. Designed by local pro Lucien Roux, the layout cannot and would not claim any of the higher accolades, but it is more than a decent course, with excellent use of trees and bunkers, a few tricky, two-tiered greens and nicely balanced hazards and headaches. The course looks a little long from the back-tees, but the thin air at altitude adds length to the drive. Playing from the front tees (especially the long par 3s) is great fun in this very friendly and family-style club, located in a magnificently calm setting.

Golf des Volcans — 1985

La Bruyère des Moines
F - 63870 ORCINES

Office	Secrétariat	(33) 04 73 62 15 51
Pro shop	Pro-shop	(33) 04 73 62 19 19
Fax	Fax	(33) 04 73 62 26 52
Situation	Situation	

Clermont-Ferrand (pop. 136 180), 8 km

Annual closure	Fermeture annuelle	no
Weekly closure	Fermeture hebdomadaire	tuesday
		mardi (01/12 → 01/04)

Fees main season
Tarifs haute saison full day

	Week days Semaine	We/Bank holidays We/Férié
Individual Individuel	250 F	260 F
Couple Couple	500 F	520 F

Caddy	Caddy	no
Electric Trolley	Chariot électrique	no
Buggy	Voiturette	180 F/18 holes
Clubs	Clubs	100 F/full day

Credit cards Cartes de crédit
VISA - CB - Eurocard - MasterCard

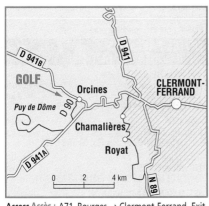

Access Accès : A71, Bourges → Clermont-Ferrand, Exit (Sortie) Clermont-Ferrand Centre → Le Puy-de-Dôme → Orcines
Map 7 on page 177 Carte 7 Page 177

GOLF COURSE / PARCOURS — 14/20

Site	Site	
Maintenance	Entretien	
Architect	Architecte	Lucien Roux
Type	Type	country, mountain
Relief	Relief	
Water in play	Eau en jeu	
Exp. to wind	Exposé au vent	
Trees in play	Arbres en jeu	

Scorecard Carte de score	Chp. Chp.	Mens Mess.	Ladies Da.
Length Long.	6286	6106	5312
Par	72	72	72

Advised golfing ability Niveau de jeu recommandé	0	12	24	36
Hcp required Handicap exigé	35			

CLUB HOUSE & AMENITIES / CLUB HOUSE ET ANNEXES — 6/10

Pro shop	Pro-shop	
Driving range	Practice	
Sheltered	couvert	20 mats
On grass	sur herbe	no, 20 mats open air
Putting-green	putting-green	yes
Pitching-green	pitching green	yes

355

HOTEL FACILITIES / ENVIRONNEMENT HOTELIER — 5/10

HOTELS HÔTELS
Hôtel Radio — Chamalières
25 rooms, D 750 F — 3 km
Tel (33) 04 73 30 87 83, Fax (33) 04 73 36 42 44

Galliéni — Clermont-Ferrand
80 rooms, D 275 F — 8 km
Tel (33) 04 73 93 59 69, Fax (33) 04 73 34 89 29

Europe Hôtel — Chamalières
34 rooms, D 360 F — 3 km
Tel (33) 04 73 37 61 35, Fax (33) 04 73 31 16 59

RESTAURANTS RESTAURANTS
Hôtel Radio — Chamalières 3 km
Tel (33) 04 73 30 87 33

Bernard Andrieux — Durtol
Tel (33) 04 73 19 25 00 — 5 km

Clavé - Tel (33) 04 73 36 46 30 — Clermont-Ferrand

WANTZENAU (LA)

16 6 6

C'est un peu la Floride à l'alsacienne, avec un Club House de style résolument local et plutôt réussi. Le paysage est parsemé d'étangs venant en jeu sur neuf des 18 trous, essentiellement au retour, ce qui crée une forte pression sur les joueurs peu expérimentés. On signalera la grande qualité de dessin des par 5, très risqués à attaquer au deuxième coup, et l'habileté de Jeremy Pern à tirer parti d'un espace très plat. Les mouvements de terrain sont subtils, les greens assez vastes, mais leur entrée est généralement ouverte, ce qui permet de jouer la sécurité dans la plupart des cas, quitte à faire confiance à son petit jeu pour sauver le par. Même si l'on est bien loin de tout océan, le vent peut intervenir de manière importante, et surprenante, sur ce parcours de très bonne facture, aux obstacles bien visibles, et très technique quel que soit le départ choisi.

Welcome to Florida in Alsace, where US style golf combines with a rather attractive local-style club-house. The landscape is dotted with lakes in play on 9 of the 18 holes, basically on the back nine, and puts a lot of pressure on inexperienced players. The par 5s are particularly well-laid out, and going for the green in 2 is risky business. Architect Jeremy Pern has cleverly made the best of very flat terrain. There has been some clever grading work and the greens are huge and generally undefended up-front, thus allowing players to play safe, even if it means counting on their short game to save par. Although the course is far from any sea, the wind can get up and make a big difference on this excellent and skilful course, whatever tees you play from. All the hazards are clearly visible.

Golf de la Wantzenau — 1991

CD 302
F - 67610 LA WANTZENAU

Office	Secrétariat	(33) 03 88 96 37 73
Pro shop	Pro-shop	(33) 03 88 96 37 73
Fax	Fax	(33) 03 88 96 34 71
Situation	Situation	

Strasbourg (pop. 252 260), 12 km

Annual closure	Fermeture annuelle	no
Weekly closure	Fermeture hebdomadaire	no

monday (mardi): restaurant closed during winter (hiver)

Fees main season
Tarifs haute saison 18 holes

	Week days Semaine	We/Bank holidays We/Férié
Individual Individuel	280 F	400 F
Couple Couple	560 F	800 F
Caddy	Caddy	no
Electric Trolley	Chariot électrique	no
Buggy	Voiturette	200 F/18 holes
Clubs	Clubs	50 F/full day

Credit cards Cartes de crédit
VISA - CB - Eurocard - MasterCard

Access Accès : Strasbourg, D468 → La Wantzenau,
→ Golf
Map 4 on page 171 Carte 4 Page 171

GOLF COURSE
PARCOURS — 16/20

Site	Site	
Maintenance	Entretien	
Architect	Architecte	Jeremy Pern
		Jean Garaïalde
Type	Type	open country, residential
Relief	Relief	
Water in play	Eau en jeu	
Exp. to wind	Exposé au vent	
Trees in play	Arbres en jeu	

Scorecard Carte de score	Chp. Chp.	Mens Mess.	Ladies Da.
Length Long.	6325	6142	5167
Par	72	72	72

Advised golfing ability Niveau de jeu recommandé	0 12 24 36
Hcp required Handicap exigé	35

CLUB HOUSE & AMENITIES
CLUB HOUSE ET ANNEXES — 6/10

Pro shop	Pro-shop	
Driving range	Practice	
Sheltered	couvert	8 mats
On grass	sur herbe	yes
Putting-green	putting-green	yes
Pitching-green	pitching green	yes

HOTEL FACILITIES
ENVIRONNEMENT HOTELIER — 6/10

HOTELS HÔTELS

Relais de la Poste — La Wantzenau
19 rooms, D 650 F — 3 km
Tel (33) 03 88 59 24 80, Fax (33) 03 88 59 24 89

Aigle d'Or — Reichstett
17 rooms, D 450 F — 2 km
Tel (33) 03 88 20 07 87, Fax (33) 03 88 81 83 75

Holiday Inn — Strasbourg
170 rooms, D 1 250 F — 10 km
Tel (33) 03 88 37 80 00, Fax (33) 03 88 37 07 04

RESTAURANTS RESTAURANTS

A la Barrière — La Wantzenau
Tel (33) 03 88 96 20 23 — 3 km

Cour des Chasseurs — La Wantzenau
Tel (33) 03 88 96 24 83 — 3 km

356

Si l'on recherche seulement le confort et luxe, il faut passer son chemin, les installations étant spartiates. En revanche, cette simplicité contribue à en faire probablement le parcours français le plus proche des premiers links d'Ecosse, jusqu'aux trous de lapins dans le sol sablonneux. Généralement plat, avec une multitude de profonds bunkers, Wimereux peut présenter un visage aussi souriant et indulgent par beau temps (quand les balles roulent bien) qu'il peut se montrer brutal dès que souffle le vent. Créé en 1907, il a été remanié en 1958 sans trop perdre de son caractère ni de son charme un peu désuet. Ce refus de tout aspect sophistiqué, l'absence d'obstacles d'eau (la mer est à 200 mètres) et d'arbres en jeu peuvent rassurer les amateurs de tous niveaux, qui devront néanmoins éviter les écarts, le grand rough étant redoutable.

If you are looking for comfort and luxury and nothing else, drive on, as the facilities here are Spartan. In contrast, simplicity probably helps make this the closest French course to the original Scottish links, even as far as the rabbit-holes in the sandy soil. Generally flat with a number of deep bunkers, Wimereux can be as leisurely and forgiving in fine weather (when the ball rolls a long way) as it can be mean and unloving when the wind blows. Created in 1907, it was restyled in 1958 without sacrificing too much of the original character or olde worlde charm. This refusal of anything over-sophisticated, the absence of water hazards (the sea is 200 metres away) and trees in play is enough to reassure golfers of all playing abilities, as long as they keep on the straight and narrow. Be warned, the rough is wicked.

Golf de Wimereux — 1907

Route d'Ambleteuse
F - 62930 WIMEREUX

Office	Secrétariat	(33) 03 21 32 43 20
Pro shop	Pro-shop	(33) 03 21 32 43 20
Fax	Fax	(33) 03 21 33 62 21
Situation	Situation	

Boulogne-sur-Mer (pop. 43 670), 6 km

Annual closure	Fermeture annuelle	no
Weekly closure	Fermeture hebdomadaire	no

monday (lundi): restaurant closed from 01/10 to 30/06

Fees main season
Tarifs haute saison full day

	Week days Semaine	We/Bank holidays We/Férié
Individual Individuel	230 F	290 F
Couple Couple	460 F	580 F

Caddy	Caddy	no
Electric Trolley	Chariot électrique	no
Buggy	Voiturette	200 F/18 holes
Clubs	Clubs	yes

Credit cards Cartes de crédit
VISA - CB - Eurocard - MasterCard

Access Accès : Boulogne s/Mer, D940 → Wimereux
Map 1 on page 164 Carte 1 Page 164

GOLF COURSE / PARCOURS — 14/20

Site	Site	
Maintenance	Entretien	
Architect	Architecte	Campbell & Hutchinson links
Type	Type	
Relief	Relief	
Water in play	Eau en jeu	
Exp. to wind	Exposé au vent	
Trees in play	Arbres en jeu	

Scorecard Carte de score	Chp. Chp.	Mens Mess.	Ladies Da.
Length Long.	6150	5887	5184
Par	72	72	72

Advised golfing ability Niveau de jeu recommandé	0	12	24	36

Hcp required	Handicap exigé	35 (We)

CLUB HOUSE & AMENITIES / CLUB HOUSE ET ANNEXES — 4/10

Pro shop	Pro-shop	
Driving range	Practice	
Sheltered	couvert	20 mats
On grass	sur herbe	yes
Putting-green	putting-green	yes
Pitching-green	pitching green	yes

HOTEL FACILITIES / ENVIRONNEMENT HOTELIER — 5/10

HOTELS HÔTELS

Centre — Wimereux
25 rooms, D 350 F — 2 km
Tel (33) 03 21 32 41 08, Fax (33) 03 21 33 82 48

Paul et Virginie — Wimereux
15 rooms, D 450 F — 2 km
Tel (33) 03 21 32 42 12, Fax (33) 03 21 87 65 85

Atlantic — Wimereux
10 rooms, D 480 F — 2 km
Tel (33) 03 21 32 41 01, Fax (33) 03 21 87 46 17

RESTAURANTS RESTAURANTS

Le Relais de la Brocante — Wimille
Tel (33) 03 21 83 19 31 — 3 km

La Matelote — Boulogne-sur-Mer
Tel (33) 03 21 30 17 97 — 6 km

357

Die Form. Die Sinne.
Das PEUGEOT 406 Coupé.

Mehr Infos unter: www.peugeot.de oder 0 18 05/300 206 (DM 0,24/Min

In der Natur erkennt man Schönheit und Perfektion auf den ersten Blick. So verbindet das PEUGEOT 406 Coupé zeitlose Eleganz mit modernster Technik und verkörpert die pure Faszination von Kraft und Ästhetik. Steigen Sie ein und erleben Sie den Beginn einer neuen Leidenschaft – für alle Sinne des Lebens.

PEUGEOT. Mit Sicherheit mehr Vergnügen.

406

PEUGEO

Deutschland

The Millennium Guide

Deutschland erlebt immer noch einen Golf-boom. In den letzten zehn Jahren hat sich die Anzahl der Spieler auf 320.000 verdreifacht. Jedes Jahr entstehen zwischen 30 und 40 neue Anlagen. Derzeit gibt es in Deutschland knapp 600 Plätze. All diese Plätze stehen Gastspielern offen, allerdings mit der Einschränkung, dass am Woche-nende auf vielen Plätzen Gäste nur in Begleitung eines Mitglieds spielen dürfen. Doch fast alle Clubs sind auf Greenfee-Einnahmen angewiesen, so dass Gastgspieler überall willkommen sind. Fast alle deutschen Clubs verlangen einen Handicap-Nach-weise und den Mitgliedsausweis eines anerkannten Golfclubs.

Germany is still in the grips of a golf boom. Within the last decade the number of golfers who are members of a club has tripled to 320,000 and each year 30 to 40 new courses are being built. Right now the number of golf courses in Germany is approaching the 600 mark, all of which are open to visitors, with the restriction that many clubs on weekends only allow green-feers if accompanied by a member. But as most German clubs rely on green-fees to boost their income, guests are welcome everywhere but will require a handicap certificate and proof of membership of a bona fide golf club.

Germany

359

d'après carte n°987 - 26ème édition - 2000.
Autorisation n°9904173.

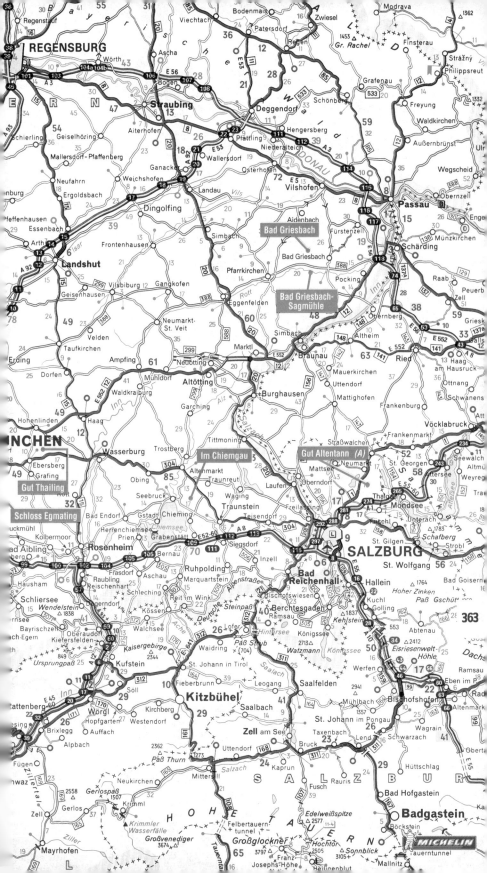

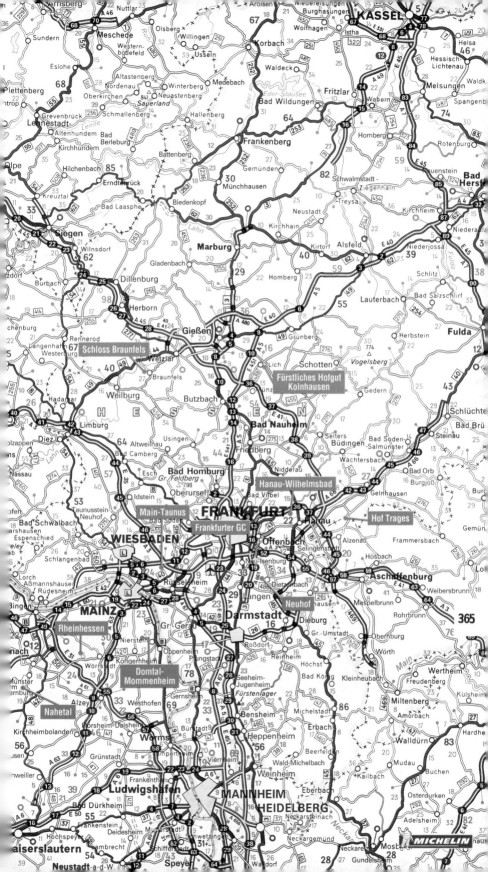

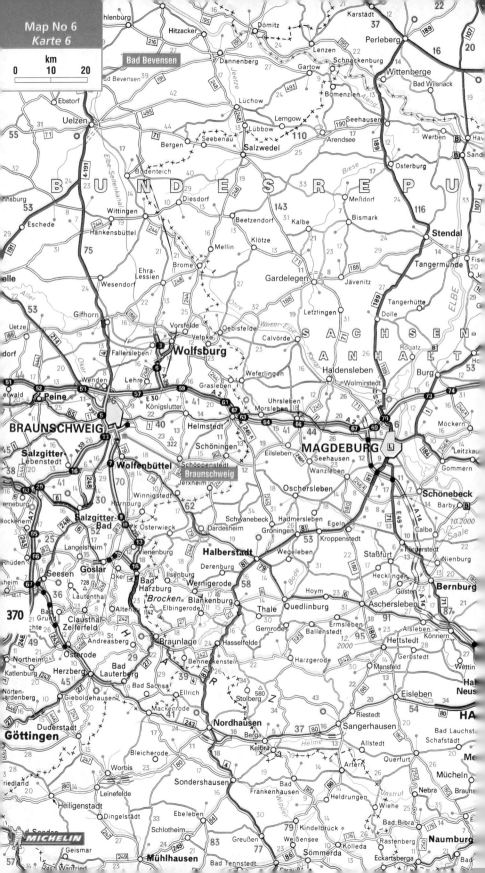

Car Audio and Navigation Systems

Watch Superman,

listen to Mozart, play Supermario

and keep an eye on the

road. All at the same time.

Alpine Electronics GmbH
Kreuzerkamp 7-11 40878 Ratingen
Tel. +49 21 02 45 50 Fax. +49 21 02 44 53 21

Alpine Electronics of U.K Ltd.
13 Tanner Drive Blakelands Milton Keynes MK14 5BU
Tel. +44 19 08 61 15 56 Fax. +44 19 08 61 84 20

Alpine Italia S.p.A.
V.le C.Colombo, 8 20090 Trezzano s/N MI
Tel. +39 02 48 47 81 Fax. +39 02 48 40 35 55

Alpine Electronics de Espana S.A.
Portal de Gamarra 36, Pabellón, 32 01013 Vitoria (Alava) APDO 133
Tel. +34 945 28 35 88 Fax. +34 945 28 34 61

Alpine Electronics France S.A.R.L.
98, Rue de la Belle Etoile Z.I.Paris Nord II 95945 Roissy Charles de Gaulle Cedex
Tel. +33 1 48 63 89 89 Fax. +33 1 48 63 25 81

www.alpine-europe.com

EINTEILUNG DER GOLFPLÄTZE
CLASSIFICATION OF COURSES

Diese Einteilung berücksichtigt in erster Linie die
dem Golfplatz erteilte Note

This classification gives priority consideration
to the score awarded to the actual course

Note für das Clubhaus und die
Einrichtungen

Note für den Golfplatz
Course score

Note für das Hotelangebot der Umgebung
Hotel facility score

Seite
Page

18	6	5	Club zur Vahr (Garlstedt)	398

Note			Golfplatz	Seite	Note			Golfplatz	Seite
18	6	5	Club zur Vahr (Garlstedt)	398	**16**	7	7	Reichswald-Nürnberg	454
18	6	7	Falkenstein	404	**16**	7	7	Schloss Braunfels	458
18	8	7	Scharmützelsee *Nick Faldo*	457	**16**	8	7	Schloss Langenstein	461
18	9	7	Seddiner See *Südplatz*	467	**16**	8	7	Schloss Liebenstein	
17	9	9	Bad Griesbach *Brunnwies*	386				*Gelb + Blau*	462
17	7	6	Beuerberg	393	**16**	7	7	Schloss Myllendonk	464
17	7	8	Frankfurter GC	406	**16**	8	7	Semlin am See	468
17	7	8	Fürstlicher GC Bad Waldsee	408	**16**	7	6	St. Eurach	471
17	9	7	Gut Lärchenhof	412	**16**	7	5	Stolper Heide	473
17	7	7	Gütersloh (Westfälischer GC)	416	**16**	7	6	Walddörfer	479
17	8	6	Hubbelrath	425	**16**	7	6	Wendlohe *A-Kurs + B-Kurs*	481
17	6	7	Köln	430	**16**	7	6	Wittelsbacher	483
17	7	7	Krefelder	432	**15**	7	7	Augsburg	383
17	7	7	Mittelrheinischer	440	**15**	7	7	Bad Abbach-Deutenhof	384
17	8	6	Motzener See	441	**15**	5	7	Bad Bevensen	385
17	6	5	Oberfranken	449	**15**	9	9	Bad Griesbach-Sagmühle	
17	8	7	Scharmützelsee *Arnold Palmer*	456				*Sagmühle*	387
17	8	6	Schloss Nippenburg	465	**15**	7	7	Bamberg	390
17	7	5	Schloss Wilkendorf	466	**15**	7	8	Bitburger Land	394
17	7	6	St. Dionys	470	**15**	7	7	Düsseldorfer	400
17	5	5	Stuttgarter Solitude	474	**15**	8	7	Essener Oefte	403
16	7	7	Bergisch Land Wuppertal	391	**15**	7	6	Gut Kaden *Platz B + Platz C*	411
16	8	9	Berlin-Wannsee	392	**15**	6	6	Gut Ludwigsberg	413
16	7	7	Bodensee-Weissensberg	395	**15**	7	5	Gut Waldhof	415
16	7	6	Buxtehude	397	**15**	6	6	Hamburg-Holm	418
16	7	6	Feldafing	405	**15**	7	5	Hof Trages	423
16	7	5	Gut Thailing	414	**15**	7	6	Hohenpähl	424
16	8	7	Hamburg-Ahrensburg	417	**15**	7	6	Im Chiemgau	427
16	6	6	Hanau-Wilhelmsbad	419	**15**	7	6	Isernhagen	428
16	7	7	Hannover	420	**15**	7	6	Jakobsberg	429
16	7	6	Iffeldorf	426	**15**	7	6	Lichtenau-Weickershof	433
16	7	5	Lüneburger Heide	436	**15**	7	8	Lindau-Bad Schachen	434
16	7	7	München-Riedhof	443	**15**	8	8	Lübeck-Travemünder	435
16	6	7	Neckartal	446	**15**	6	7	Münchner-Strasslach	444

375

EINTEILUNG DES HOTELANGEBOTS DER UMGEBUNG
CLASSIFICATION OF HOTELS FACILITIES

Note für das Clubhaus und die Einrichtungen
Club-house and facilities

Note für
den Golfplatz
Course score

Note für das Hotelangebot der Umgebung
Hotel facility score

17 9 **9** Bad Griesbach *Brunnwies* 314

Seite
Page

EINTEILUNG DES HOTELANGEBOTS DER UMGEBUNG

FÜR EINEN FERIENAUFENTHALT EMPFOHLEN
RECOMMENDED GOLFING HOLIDAYS

FÜR GOLFFERIEN EMPFOHLEN
RECOMMENDED GOLFING STAY

Golfplatz	Note			Seite	Golfplatz	Note			Seite
Bad Griesbach *Brunnwies*	17	9	9	386	Motzener See	17	8	6	441
Bad Griesbach-Sagmühle	15	9	9	387	Oberschwaben Bad Waldsee	15	6	6	450
Club zur Vahr (Garlstedt)	18	6	5	398	Scharmützelsee *Arnold Palmer*	17	8	7	456
Fürstlicher GC Bad Waldsee	17	7	8	408	Scharmützelsee *Nick Faldo*	18	8	7	457
Gut Kaden *Platz B + Platz C*	15	7	6	411	Schloss Liebenstein *Gelb + Blau*	16	8	7	462
Hanau-Wilhelmsbad	16	6	6	419	Seddiner See *Südplatz*	18	9	7	467
Mittelrheinischer	17	7	7	440					

TYP DES GOLFPLATZES
TYPE OF COURSE

Golfplatz	Note			Seite	Golfplatz	Note			Seite
country					Fürstlicher GC Bad Waldsee	17	7	8	408
Bad Bevensen	15	5	7	385	Gut Waldhof	15	7	5	415
Braunschweig	14	6	7	396	Hannover	16	7	7	420
Fränkische Schweiz	14	7	6	407	Hohenpähl	15	7	6	424
Hamburg-Holm	15	6	6	418	Hubbelrath	17	8	6	425
Hannover	16	7	7	420	Iffeldorf	16	7	6	426
Lichtenau-Weickershof	15	7	6	433	Isernhagen	15	7	6	428
Pinnau	14	6	6	452	Köln	17	6	7	430
Schloss Liebenstein *Gelb + Blau*	16	8	7	462	Krefelder	17	7	7	432
Schloss Nippenburg	17	8	6	465	Lüneburger Heide	16	7	5	436
Seddiner See *Südplatz*	18	9	7	467	Mülheim	13	6	7	442
Wendlohe *A-Kurs + B-Kurs*	16	7	6	481	Nahetal	14	8	6	445
					Neckartal	16	6	7	446
forest					Oberfranken	17	6	5	449
Abenberg	14	7	6	382	Oberschwaben Bad Waldsee	15	6	6	450
Augsburg	15	7	7	383	Reichswald-Nürnberg	16	7	7	454
Bad Liebenzell	14	7	7	388	Schloss Myllendonk	16	7	7	464
Bergisch Land Wuppertal	16	7	7	391	Scharmützelsee *Arnold Palmer*	17	8	7	456
Berlin-Wannsee	16	8	9	392	Semlin am See	16	8	7	468
Bodensee-Weissensberg	16	7	7	395	Sonnenalp	15	7	7	469
Braunschweig	14	6	7	396	Stuttgarter Solitude	17	5	5	474
Buxtehude	16	7	6	397	St. Eurach	16	7	6	471
Club zur Vahr (Garlstedt)	18	6	5	398	Walddörfer	16	7	6	479
Düsseldorfer	15	7	7	400	Wasserburg Anholt	15	7	7	480
Eschenried	14	7	7	402	Wentorf-Reinbeker	15	7	6	482
Essener Oefte	15	8	7	403	Wittelsbacher	16	7	6	483
Falkenstein	18	6	7	404					
Frankfurter GC	17	7	8	406	**inland**				
Fränkische Schweiz	14	7	6	407	Schloss Wilkendorf	17	7	5	466

379

Golfplatz	Note			Seite
links				
Scharmützelsee *Nick Faldo*	18	8	7	457
Sylt	15	6	8	475
moorland				
Hamburg-Holm	15	6	6	418
St. Dionys	17	7	6	470
mountain				
Feldafing	16	7	6	405
Iffeldorf	16	7	6	426
Sonnenalp	15	7	7	469
Tegernseer Bad Wiessee	14	7	8	476
Tutzing	15	7	6	478
open country				
Abenberg	14	7	6	382
Bad Abbach-Deutenhof	15	7	7	384
Bad Liebenzell	14	7	7	388
Bad Griesbach *Brunnwies*	17	9	9	386
Bamberg	15	7	7	390
Bitburger Land	15	7	8	394
Buxtehude	16	7	6	397
Domtal-Mommenheim	14	7	7	399
Elfrather Mühle	14	7	7	401
Eschenried	14	7	7	402
Fürstlicher GC Bad Waldsee	17	7	8	408
Fürstliches Hofgut Kolnhausen	14	7	6	409
Gut Kaden *Platz B + Platz C*	15	7	6	411
Gut Lärchenhof	17	9	7	412
Gut Ludwigsberg	15	6	6	413
Gut Thailing	16	7	5	414
Hechingen-Hohenzollern	14	6	6	421
Hetzenhof	14	7	6	422
Hof Trages	15	7	5	423
Im Chiemgau	15	7	6	427
Isernhagen	15	7	6	428
Jakobsberg	15	7	6	429
Königsfeld	13	6	6	431
Main-Taunus	14	7	6	437
Memmingen Gut Westerhart	14	6	6	439
Motzener See	17	8	6	441
Mülheim	13	6	7	442
München-Riedhof	16	7	7	443
Münchner-Strasslach	15	6	7	444
Neckartal	16	6	7	446
Obere Alp	14	7	7	448
Öschberghof	15	7	7	451
Pinnau	14	6	6	452
Reichsstadt Bad Windsheim	14	6	7	453

Golfplatz	Note			Seite
Rheinhessen	14	8	7	455
Schloss Egmating	15	7	7	459
Schloss Langenstein	16	8	7	461
Schloss Nippenburg	17	8	6	465
St. Leon-Rot	15	8	6	472
Sylt	15	6	8	475
Stuttgarter Solitude	17	5	5	474
Treudelberg	13	8	7	477
Wendlohe *A-Kurs + B-Kurs*	16	7	6	481
parkland				
Bad Griesbach-Sagmühle				
Sagmühle	15	9	9	387
Club zur Vahr (Garlstedt)	18	6	5	398
Bad Wörishofen	14	6	6	389
Bodensee-Weissensberg	16	7	7	395
Beuerberg	17	7	6	393
Falkenstein	18	6	7	404
Garmisch-Partenkirchen	14	6	7	410
Gut Ludwigsberg	15	6	6	413
Gut Waldhof	15	7	5	415
Gütersloh (Westfälischer GC)	17	7	7	416
Hamburg-Ahrensburg	16	8	7	417
Hanau-Wilhelmsbad	16	6	6	419
Hohenpähl	15	7	6	424
Hof Trages	15	7	5	423
Lichtenau-Weickershof	15	7	6	433
Lindau-Bad Schachen	15	7	8	434
Lübeck-Travemünder	15	8	8	435
Märkischer Potsdam	14	7	6	438
Memmingen Gut Westerhart	14	6	6	439
Mittelrheinischer	17	7	7	440
Neuhof	15	7	7	447
Oberfranken	17	6	5	449
Oberschwaben Bad Waldsee	15	6	6	450
Öschberghof	15	7	7	451
Scharmützelsee *Arnold Palmer*	17	8	7	456
Schloss Braunfels	16	7	7	458
Schloss Klingenburg	15	6	6	460
Schloss Lüdersburg *Old/New*	15	7	6	463
Schloss Myllendonk	16	7	7	464
Semlin am See	16	8	7	468
St. Leon-Rot	15	8	6	472
Stolper Heide	16	7	5	473
Tegernseer Bad Wiessee	14	7	8	476
Walddörfer	16	7	6	479
Wasserburg Anholt	15	7	7	480
Wentorf-Reinbeker	15	7	6	482

Golfplatz	Note	Seite	Golfplatz	Note	Seite
seaside course			Hechingen-Hohenzollern	14 6 6	421
Lübeck-Travemünder	15 8 8	435	Hetzenhof	14 7 6	422
			Hubbelrath	17 8 6	425
			Jakobsberg	15 7 6	429
hilly			Königsfeld	13 6 6	431
Augsburg	15 7 7	383	München-Riedhof	16 7 7	443
Bad Griesbach *Brunnwies*	17 9 9	386	Obere Alp	14 7 7	448
Bamberg	15 7 7	390	Rheinhessen	14 8 7	455
Bergisch Land Wuppertal	16 7 7	391	Schloss Langenstein	16 8 7	461
Bitburger Land	15 7 8	394			

HÖHE DES GOLFPLATZES
COURSES ALTITUDE > 500 M

Hôhe	Golfplatz		Seite	Hôhe	Golfplatz		Seite
500	Fürstlicher GC Bad Waldsee	17 7 8	408	600	Oberschwaben Bad Waldsee	15 6 6	450
500	Im Chiemgau	15 7 6	427	600	Schloss Egmating	15 7 7	459
530	Augsburg	15 7 7	383	600	Garmisch-Partenkirchen	14 6 7	410
530	Eschenried	14 7 7	402	605	St. Eurach	16 7 6	471
550	Gut Thailing	16 7 5	414	618	Beuerberg	17 7 6	393
550	Schloss Klingenburg	15 6 6	460	650	Bad Wörishofen	14 6 6	389
550	Bad Liebenzell	14 7 7	388	700	Feldafing	16 7 6	405
550	Hechingen-Hohenzollern	14 6 6	421	700	Hohenpähl	15 7 6	424
560	Bodensee-Weissensberg	16 7 7	395	700	Öschberghof	15 7 7	451
580	Münchner-Strasslach	15 6 7	444	700	Tutzing	15 7 6	478
600	Iffeldorf	16 7 6	426	700	Memmingen Gut Westerhart	14 6 6	439
600	München-Riedhof	16 7 7	443	800	Sonnenalp	15 7 7	469
600	Gut Ludwigsberg	15 6 6	413	800	Obere Alp	14 7 7	448

PEUGEOT

Der Golfplatz liegt so nahe bei Nürnberg, dass man sich in dieser deutschen Hochburg des Mittelalters, in der Albrecht Dürer wohnte, gut einquartieren kann. Die Altstadt und das Germanische Nationalmuseum lohnen einen erholsamen Tag zwischen zwei Partien Golf. Die Spielbahnen liegt in einem flachen Gelände mit vielen Bäumen. Die riesigen Bäume stellen einen wichtigen Teil der Schwierigkeiten dar, unter anderem verlangen auch die Fairways und die Länge von gewissen Par 4 bei bestimmten Abschlägen eine sehr sorgfältige Auswahl des Schlägers: wenn man den Ball nicht lange und gerade schlagen kann, muss man einige Bogeys in Kauf nehmen. Die Bunker sind recht zahlreich, aber meist nur um die mittelgrossen, wenig welligen Greens angeordnet. Zwei Greens sind erhöht und zwei auf doppelten Stufen angelegt. Eine ehrliche, offene Anlage, auch wenn die Gestaltung und die Ausprägung der Erhebungen zu wünschen übrig lässt.

The Abenberg course is close enough to Nürnberg for you to establish base-camp in this high spot of Middle-Age Germany, where Albrecht Dürer once lived. The old town and the Germanisches Nationalmuseum are well worth a day's rest between two rounds of golf. This course is laid out on basically flat terrain in very woody countryside, so big trees are not surprisingly a major factor in the difficulties awaiting you on either side of the fairways. On top of that, the length of some par 4s calls for very careful club selection from a number of tees. If you are not too sure of hitting it long and straight, there'll be a few bogeys in store. Bunkers abound but are basically placed around averagely-sized greens with few contours. Two greens are elevated, two are two-tiered. A very decent course, but perhaps lacking a little contouring work to give the layout greater shape.

Golf Club Abenberg e.V. 1988
Am Golfplatz 19
D - 91183 ABENBERG

Office	Sekretariat	(49) 09178 - 98 960
Pro shop	Pro shop	(49) 09178 - 98 960
Fax	Fax	(49) 09178 - 989 698
Situation	Lage	

Nürnberg (pop. 498 000), 25 km

Annual closure Jährliche Schliessung 1/12 → 28/2

Weekly closure Wöchentliche Schliessung no
Monday (Montag) : Restaurant closed

Fees main season
Preisliste hochsaison full day

	Week days Woche	We/Bank holidays We/Feiertag
Individual Individuell	DM 70,-	DM 90,-
Couple Ehepaar	DM 140,-	DM 180,-

under 22 years, Students: – 50% on weekdays (Montag-Freitag)

Caddy	Caddy	no
Electric Trolley	Elektrokarren	no
Buggy	Elektrischer Wagen	no
Clubs	Leihschläger	yes

Credit cards Kreditkarten
VISA - Eurocard - MasterCard - AMEX

382

Access Zufahrt : A6 Nürnberg → Heilbronn. Exit (Ausf.)
Schwabach West/ Abenberg. B466 → Abenberg
Map 4 on page 366 Karte 4 Seite 366

GOLF COURSE
PLATZ **14**/20

Site	Lage	▬▬▬▬▭
Maintenance	Instandhaltung	▬▬▬▬▭
Architect	Architekt	unknown
Type	Typ	forest, open country
Relief	Begehbarkeit	▬▬▭▭▭
Water in play	Platz mit Wasser	▬▬▭▭▭
Exp. to wind	Wind ausgesetzt	▬▬▭▭▭
Trees in play	Platz mit Bäumen	▬▬▬▬▭

Scorecard Scorekarte	Chp. Chp.	Mens Herren	Ladies Damen
Length Länge	6127	6127	5454
Par	72	72	72

Advised golfing ability		0 12 24 36
Empfohlene Spielstärke		▬▬▬▬▭
Hcp required	Min. Handicap	36

CLUB HOUSE & AMENITIES
KLUBHAUS UND NEBENGEBÄUDE **7**/10

Pro shop	Pro shop	▬▬▬▬▭
Driving range	Übungsplatz	▬▬▬▬▭
Sheltered	überdacht	6 mats
On grass	auf Rasen	yes
Putting-green	Putting-grün	yes
Pitching-green	Pitching-grün	yes

HOTEL FACILITIES
HOTEL BESCHREIBUNG **6**/10

HOTELS HOTELS
Burghotel Abenberg Abenberg
17 rooms, D DM 120,- 500 m
Tel (49) 09178 - 982 990, Fax (49) 09178-98 29910

Hotel-Gasthof Meyerle Haag
24 rooms, D DM 120,- 9 km
Tel (49) 09122 - 5158, Fax (49) 09122 - 158 58

Zum Heidenberg Büchenbach-Kühendorf
32 rooms, D DM 140,- 4 km
Tel (49) 09171 - 84 40, Fax (49) 09171 - 84 480

RESTAURANTS RESTAURANT
Goldener Stern Schwabach
Tel (49) 09122 - 2335 10 km

Zirbelstube Nürnberg-Worzeldorf
Tel (49) 0911 - 998 820 25 km

AUGSBURG

15 | **7** | **7**

Auf dem Heimatplatz von Bernhard Langer lauert überall Gefahr. Die erste Runde wird man wohl damit beschäftigt sein, die Strategie für die zweite Runde zu analysieren, da die Hindernisse kaum sichtbar sind. Die Bäume dominieren und im Unterholz gehen die Bälle leicht verloren. Auf diesem Platz benötigt man alle Schlagvarianten. Zudem darf die Konzentration nie erlahmen, denn es gibt keine einfachen Löcher. Es ist ein anspruchsvoller, interessanter Platz, die Schwierigkeiten sind gut verteilt und überfordern einen geübteren Spieler nicht. Zögern Sie jedoch nicht, die vorderen Abschläge zu wählen, wenn sie nicht in golferischer oder körperlicher Hochform sind, denn der Platz ist recht anstrengend zu begehen.. Ob man den Golfplatz nun mag oder nicht, zumindest wird man die Ruhe und der Charme dieses Ortes, ganz in der Nähe der schönen Stadt Augsburg, geniessen.

On Bernhard Langer's home course danger lurks everywhere. First time out, you spend your time studying game strategy and how you might apply it for your next visit, as not all the hazards are visible. As the trees are very present and the undergrowth swallows up many a ball, you soon realize that for a good score here, you need flighted shots and constant concentration. Be warned : there is no one easy hole. This is a demanding, competent and exciting course but the difficulties are well spread out and shouldn't be too much for even inexperienced players. Don't think twice about playing from the front tees if your game - and physical fitness - are not in tip-top condition, as Augsburg can be tough on the legs. Whether you like the course or not, you are bound to appreciate the tranquillity and charm of the spot, close to the pretty town of Augsburg.

Golf-Club Augsburg e.V. **1953**

Engelshofer Strasse 2
D - 86399 BOBINGEN-BURGWALDEN

Office	Sekretariat	(49) 08234 - 5621
Pro shop	Pro shop	(49) 08234 - 7311
Fax	Fax	(49) 08234 - 7855
Situation	Lage	

Augsburg (pop. 265 000), 10 km - München, 78 km

Annual closure	Jährliche Schliessung	no
Weekly closure	Wöchentliche Schliessung	no

Monday (Montag) : Restaurant closed

Fees main season
Preisliste hochsaison full day

	Week days Woche	We/Bank holidays We/Feiertag
Individual Individuell	DM 60,-	DM 90,-
Couple Ehepaar	DM 120,-	DM 180,-

under 21 years/Students : – 50 %

Caddy	Caddy	no
Electric Trolley	Elektrokarren	DM 25,-
Buggy	Elektrischer Wagen	no
Clubs	Leihschläger	DM 15,-
Credit cards Kreditkarten		no

Access Zufahrt : A8 München-Augsburg. Exit (Ausf.) Augsburg-West. Exit Gersthofen Süd, B17 → Exit Königsbrunn. Right → Bobingen, Strassberg. Golf → Burgwalden **Map 2 on page 362** Karte 2 Seite 362

GOLF COURSE **15**/20
PLATZ

Site	Lage	▰▰▰▰▰▱
Maintenance	Instandhaltung	▰▰▰▰▱▱
Architect	Architekt	B. von Limburger
		Donald Harradine
Type	Typ	forest, hilly
Relief	Begehbarkeit	▰▰▰▰▱▱
Water in play	Platz mit Wasser	▰▱▱▱▱▱
Exp. to wind	Wind ausgesetzt	▰▰▱▱▱▱
Trees in play	Platz mit Bäumen	▰▰▰▰▰▱

Scorecard Scorekarte	Chp. Chp.	Mens Herren	Ladies Damen
Length Länge	6018	6018	5347
Par	72	72	72

Advised golfing ability	0	12	24	36
Empfohlene Spielstärke	▰▰▰▰▰▰▰▱			
Hcp required Min. Handicap	36			

CLUB HOUSE & AMENITIES **7**/10
KLUBHAUS UND NEBENGEBÄUDE

Pro shop	Pro shop	▰▰▰▰▱▱
Driving range	Übungsplatz	▰▰▰▰▱▱
Sheltered	überdacht	3 mats
On grass	auf Rasen	yes
Putting-green	Putting-grün	yes
Pitching-green	Pitching-grün	yes

HOTEL FACILITIES **7**/10
HOTEL BESCHREIBUNG

HOTELS HOTELS

Steigenberger Drei Mohren 107 rooms, D DM 300,- Tel (49) 0821 - 50 360, Fax (49) 0821 - 157 864	Augsburg 10 km
Schempp 46 rooms, D DM 130,- Tel (49) 08234 - 3046, Fax (49) 08234 - 4098	Bobingen 3 km
Romantik Augsburger Hof 36 rooms, D DM 200,- Tel (49) 0821 - 314 083, Fax (49) 0821 - 38 322	Augsburg 15 km
Dom Hotel 43 rooms, D DM 190,- Tel (49) 0821 - 153 031, Fax (49) 0821 - 510 126	Augsburg 12 km

RESTAURANTS RESTAURANT

Oblinger - Tel (49) 0821 - 345 8392	Augsburg 12 km
Fuggerei-Stube - Tel (49) 0821 - 30 870	Augsburg 12 km

383

Dieser Platz liegt südlich der Stadt Regensburg, die in ihrem Stadtbild die Geschichte des Deutschen Kaiserreichs widerspiegelt. Viele Gebäude stammen noch aus dem Mittelalter und der Renaissance. Diese Verbundenheit mit der deutschen Geschichte wird in der Walhalla symbolisiert, einem Denkmal hoch über der Donau, das Ludwig I. von Bayern errrichten liess. Der neue Platz in der Kurstadt Bad Abbach, der auf weit offenem Gelände erbaut wurde, gilt schon heute als einer der besten neuen Plätze in Bayern. Der Platz weist keine Heimtücken auf, hier kann man auf Birdies hoffen, statt ständig Bogeys oder Schlimmeres zu befürchten. Bad Abbach hat sich damit in der Kürze der Zeit einen vorzüglichen Ruf erworben, obwohl es ein wenig abseits der grossen Touristenrouten liegt. Die Schwierigkeiten sind gut über den Platz verteilt. Der Platz ist für Golfer aller Spielstärken gut zubewältigen. Sein einziger Nachteil ist das bergige Gelände, sodass Golfer, die körperlich nicht fit sind, schnell ermüden.

This course is located to the south of the city of Regensburg, one of the high-spots of the history of the German Empire where much of the architecture recalls the Middle Ages and the Renaissance. Such union with German history is equally symbolized by the Walhalla, a sort of memorial overlooking the Danube erected by Louis I of Bavaria. This recent course, laid out in a spa city over rather wide open space, has become established as one of the better new courses in Bavaria. Rather forthright and indulgent to golfers who tend to stumble across birdies rather than actively go looking for them, this Rainer Preismann design tends to bare its teeth more to the reckless golfer. Nicely balanced and with a rather likeable personality, Bad Abbach is making a name for itself on account of its excellent attributes, despite being a little off the busier tourist routes. With difficulties fairly spread around the course and playable by golfers of all levels, its only failing is perhaps the hilly terrain which make this a tiring round of golf for physically unfit players.

Golfclub Bad Abbach-Deutenhof — 1996

Gut Deutenhof
D - 93077 BAD ABBACH

Office	Sekretariat	(49) 09405 - 953 20
Pro shop	Pro shop	(49) 09405 - 953 20
Fax	Fax	(49) 09405 - 953 219
Situation	Lage	

Regensburg (pop. 137 000), 10 km

Annual closure	Jährliche Schliessung	no
Weekly closure	Wöchentliche Schliessung	no

Fees main season
Preisliste hochsaison 18 holes

	Week days Woche	We/Bank holidays We/Feiertag
Individual Individuell	DM 60,-	DM 80,-
Couple Ehepaar	DM 120,-	DM 160,-

under 21 years/Students : – 50%

Caddy	Caddy	no
Electric Trolley	Elektrokarren	DM 15,-
Buggy	Elektrischer Wagen	DM 45,-
Clubs	Leihschläger	DM 20,-

Credit cards Kreditkarten VISA- Eurocard - MasterCard

Access Zufahrt : München A93 → Regensburg.
Exit (Ausfahrt) Hausen, → Teugn, → Lengfeld.
Golf on right hand side.
Map 2 on page 362 Karte 2 Seite 362

GOLF COURSE / PLATZ — 15/20

Site	Lage	
Maintenance	Instandhaltung	
Architect	Architekt	Rainer Preismann DeutscheGolf-Consult
Type	Typ	open country
Relief	Begehbarkeit	
Water in play	Platz mit Wasser	
Exp. to wind	Wind ausgesetzt	
Trees in play	Platz mit Bäumen	

Scorecard Scorekarte	Chp. Chp.	Mens Herren	Ladies Damen
Length Länge	6179	5817	5159
Par	72	72	72

Advised golfing ability Empfohlene Spielstärke	0	12	24	36

Hcp required Min. Handicap 35

CLUB HOUSE & AMENITIES / KLUBHAUS UND NEBENGEBÄUDE — 7/10

Pro shop	Pro shop	
Driving range	Übungsplatz	
Sheltered	überdacht	6 mats
On grass	auf Rasen	yes
Putting-green	Putting-grün	yes
Pitching-green	Pitching-grün	yes

HOTEL FACILITIES / HOTEL BESCHREIBUNG — 7/10

HOTELS HOTELS

Parkhotel Maximilian — Regensburg
52 rooms, D DM 300,- — 10 km
Tel (49) 0941 - 568 50, Fax (49) 0941 - 529 42

Clubhaus — Golf
12 rooms, D DM 150,- — on site
Tel (49) 09405 - 953 230, Fax (49) 09405 - 953 239

Altstadthotel Arch — Regensburg
68 rooms, D DM 300,- — 10 km
Tel (49) 0941 - 502 060, Fax (49) 0941 -502 06168

RESTAURANTS RESTAURANT

Historisches Eck — Regensburg
Tel (49) 0941 - 58 920 — 10 km

Alte Münz — Regensburg
Tel (49) 0941 - 54 886 — 10 km

384

BAD BEVENSEN

Dieser Platz im ländlichen Norddeutschland wirkt auf den ersten Blick wie ein grosser Bauernhof, eine Atmosphäre wie man sie selten auf modernen Plätzen findet. Hier ist man weit weg von der Hektik der Grossstadt. Die freundliche Umgebung führt leicht dazu, dass man den Platz unterschätzt - ein Fehler. Das Gelände ist ziemlich hügelig, aber gut begehbar. Einige blinde Löchern wollen mit Überlegung attackiert werden. Die Schwierigkeiten sind gut über den Platz verteilt und meist vom Abschlag deutlich zu erkennen. Einziger Schwachpunkt ist das erste Loch, bei dem gute Spieler und Longhitter über eine Pferdekoppel abschlagen müssen. Der Platz ist originell, gut in die Landschaft eingepasst, allerdings werden hohe Handicaps auf diesem Platz Mühe haben, vor allem, wenn sie mit einstelligen Golfern unterwegs sind. Obwohl der Platz nicht sonderlich lang, ist es keineswegs einfach mit einem guten Ergebnis ins Clubhaus zurückzukehren.

Here were are in the middle of the North German countryside on a course that looks like a huge farm in a rural setting. Bad Bevensen gives new meaning to the expression "getting away from it all". This sort of scenery from another age is something of a rarity on modern golf courses. In such a friendly setting, you might be tempted to underestimate the course, but watch out. The terrain is relatively hilly but definitely walkable, and some virtually blind holes call for extreme caution. Elsewhere, difficulties of all sorts are mostly visible from the tees and cleverly spread around. We did have our reservations about the first hole, where long-hitters have to drive over a horse corral. Original and finely-landscaped, the course as a whole can prove to be awkward when playing amongst players of different abilities, as higher-handicappers will have problems overcoming all the difficulties and keeping up with the others. Despite being on the short side, this is a difficult course to score on.

Golf Club Bad Bevensen e.V. — 1991

Dorfstrasse 22
D - 29575 ALTENMEDINGEN, ORSTEIL SECKLENDORF

Office	Sekretariat	(49) 05821 - 98 250
Pro shop	Pro shop	(49) 05821 - 98 250
Fax	Fax	(49) 05821 - 42 595
Situation	Lage	

Lüneburg (pop. 65 000), 24 km

Annual closure	Jährliche Schliessung	no
Weekly closure	Wöchentliche Schliessung	no

Fees main season
Preisliste hochsaison 18 holes

	Week days Woche	We/Bank holidays We/Feiertag
Individual Individuell	DM 55,-	DM 75,-
Couple Ehepaar	DM 110,-	DM 150,-

under 21 Jahre/Studenten: – 50 %

Caddy	Caddy	no
Electric Trolley	Elektrokarren	no
Buggy	Elektrischer Wagen	DM 50,-
Clubs	Leihschläger	DM 20,-

Credit cards Kreditkarten no

Access Zufahrt : Hamburg, A250 → Lüneburg.
B4 → Uelzen. Exit (Ausf.) Bad Bevensen
→ Secklendorf Altenmedingen. Secklendorf → Golf.
Map 6 on page 370 Karte 6 Seite 370

GOLF COURSE PLATZ — 15/20

Site	Lage	
Maintenance	Instandhaltung	
Architect	Architekt	Ulrich Schmidt
Type	Typ	country
Relief	Begehbarkeit	
Water in play	Platz mit Wasser	
Exp. to wind	Wind ausgesetzt	
Trees in play	Platz mit Bäumen	

Scorecard Scorekarte	Chp. Chp.	Mens Herren	Ladies Damen
Length Länge	5808	5808	5163
Par	71	71	71

Advised golfing ability		0	12	24	36
Empfohlene Spielstärke					
Hcp required	Min. Handicap	no			

CLUB HOUSE & AMENITIES KLUBHAUS UND NEBENGEBÄUDE — 5/10

Pro shop	Pro shop	
Driving range	Übungsplatz	
Sheltered	überdacht	2 mats
On grass	auf Rasen	yes
Putting-green	Putting-grün	yes
Pitching-green	Pitching-grün	yes

HOTEL FACILITIES HOTEL BESCHREIBUNG — 7/10

HOTELS HOTELS
Zur Amtsheide — Bad Bevensen
90 rooms, D DM 190,- — 3 km
Tel (49) 05821 - 851, Fax (49) 05821 - 853 38

Grünings Landhaus — Bad Bevensen
40 rooms, D DM 200,- — 5 km
Tel (49) 05821 - 984 00, Fax (49) 05821 - 984 041

Hotel Ascona — Bad Bevensen
100 rooms, D DM 200,- — 3 km
Tel (49) 05821 - 550, Fax (49) 05821 - 427 18

RESTAURANTS RESTAURANT
Zur Linde — Secklendorf
Tel (49) 05821 - 7589 — 100 m

Zur Amtsheide — Bad Bevensen
Tel (49) 05821 - 1249 — 3 km

Grünings Restaurant — Bad Bevensen
Tel (49) 05821 - 984 00 — 5 km

385

Das Golf Resort Bad Griesbach umfasst vier 18-Loch Anlagen. Brunnwies sowie Sagmühle sind die beiden Top-Plätze des Resorts; Uttlau und Lederbach haben ebenfalls ihre Qualitäten, sind aber sehr hügelig. Brunnwies ist zwar auch auf unebenem Terrain angelegt, dieser Eindruck wird aber durch die hervorragende Platzgestaltung des Architekten Bernhard Langer weitgehend entschärft. Auffallend ist die sorgfältige Gestaltung des Geländes vom Abschlag zum Grün, wodurch die einzelnen Löchern eine deutliche Form und Definition erhalten. Grosse Beachtung wurde auch der Anlage breiter Fairways, sowie der Fairway- und Grünbunker geschenkt, die noch stärker ins Spiel kommen als die Bäume und das Wasser. Von den hinteren Abschlägen sind einige Löcher sehr lang, aber auch diese Bahnen sind von weiter vorne gespielt durchaus zu bewältigen. Gute Spieler tun sich auf Brunnwies schwerer als Durchschnittsgolfer, genau so soll es sein. Eine faszinierende Anlage mit einem sehr schönen Clubhaus im Stil der lokalen Bauernhöfe.

This enormous resort comprises four 18-hole courses. The present course and Sagmühle are the two gems, while Uttlau and Lederbach, despite their qualities, are very hilly (buggy recommended). Brunnwies is steep, too, but the excellence of architect Bernhard Langer tends to keep your mind off geographical considerations. The first thing you notice is the care taken over contouring the terrain, from tee to green, giving clear shape, form and physical definition to holes. There was also concern for wide fairways and fairway and green-side bunkers that are even more in play than the trees or water. From the back tees, some of the holes are long ; moving further forward, though, they are much more reasonable. It's tough for the good player but an easier proposition for the average golfer, so who could ask for more ? A spectacular layout with a very pretty club-house in the style of the region's farmhouses.

Golf Resort Bad Griesbach — 1996
Holzhäuser 8
D - 94 086 BAD GRIESBACH

Office	Sekretariat	(49) 08535 - 96 010
Pro shop	Pro shop	(49) 08535 - 96 010
Fax	Fax	(49) 08535 - 960 115
Situation	Lage	

Passau (pop. 50 000), 40 km
Griesbach (pop. 8 200), 3 km

Annual closure	Jährliche Schliessung	15/11 → 15/3
Weekly closure	Wöchentliche Schliessung	no

Fees main season
Preisliste hochsaison 18 holes

	Week days Woche	We/Bank holidays We/Feiertag
Individual Individuell	DM 70,-	DM 80,-
Couple Ehepaar	DM 140,-	DM 160,-

Caddy	Caddy	on request
Electric Trolley	Elektrokarren	DM 15,-
Buggy	Elektrischer Wagen	DM 40,-
Clubs	Leihschläger	yes

Credit cards Kreditkarten Eurocard - MasterCard

Access Zufahrt : A3 Nürnberg-Regensburg-Passau.
Exit (Ausf.) Pocking.
B12 and B388 → Bad Griesbach. → Golf
Map 2 on page 363 Karte 2 Seite 363

GOLF COURSE / PLATZ — 17 /20

Site	Lage	▰▰▰▰▱
Maintenance	Instandhaltung	▰▰▰▰▱
Architect	Architekt	Bernhard Langer
Type	Typ	open country, hilly
Relief	Begehbarkeit	▰▰▰▱▱
Water in play	Platz mit Wasser	▰▰▱▱▱
Exp. to wind	Wind ausgesetzt	▰▰▱▱▱
Trees in play	Platz mit Bäumen	▰▰▰▱▱

Scorecard Scorekarte	Chp. Chp.	Mens Herren	Ladies Damen
Length Länge	6029	5701	5005
Par	70	70	71

Advised golfing ability Empfohlene Spielstärke	0 12 24 36
Hcp required Min. Handicap	no

CLUB HOUSE & AMENITIES / KLUBHAUS UND NEBENGEBÄUDE — 9 /10

Pro shop	Pro shop	▰▰▰▰▱
Driving range	Übungsplatz	▰▰▰▱▱
Sheltered	überdacht	12 mats
On grass	auf Rasen	no, 20 mats open air
Putting-green	Putting-grün	yes
Pitching-green	Pitching-grün	yes

HOTEL FACILITIES / HOTEL BESCHREIBUNG — 9 /10

HOTELS HOTELS
Golfhotel Maximilian — Golf Resort
232 rooms, D DM 300,-
Tel (49) 08532 - 79 50, Fax (49) 08532 - 795 150

Fürstenhof — Golf Resort
148 rooms, D DM 250,-
Tel (49) 08532 - 98 10, Fax (49) 08532 - 981 135

Parkhotel — Golf Resort
162 rooms, D DM 434,-
Tel (49) 08532 - 2 80, Fax (49) 08532 - 28 204

König Ludwig - 186 rooms, D DM 338,- Golf Resort
Tel (49) 08532 - 79 90, Fax (49) 08532 - 799 799

RESTAURANTS RESTAURANT
Fürstenstube — Golf Resort
Tel (49) 08532 - 98 10
Gutshof Uttlau - Tel (49) 08535 - 1890 — Golf Resort

386

Dies ist der älteste der vier Plätze in Deutschlands grösstem Golf-Resort. in etwas Enfernung zu den drei anderen Plätzen gelegen, verläuft Sagmühle auf wesentlich flacherem Gelände im Flusstal der Rott, deren Nebenarm immer wieder die Spielbahnen kreuzt. Wasser, ob als seitliches oder frontales Hindernis, ist die Hauptschwierigkeit auf diesem intelligent konzipierten Golfplatz, der leider häufig recht feucht ist. Um nicht allzuviele Bälle zu verlieren, sollte man daher seine eigenen Schlaglängen gut einschätzen können. Der Platz spielt sich insgesamt nicht allzu lang, sofern man nicht die hinteren Abschläge wählt. Bäume und Bunker sind so in das Platzdesign integriert, dass der Spieler auf der Runde mit allen möglichen Situationen und Hindernissen konfrontiert wird. Die gesamte Anlage, an der Grenze zwischen Bayern und Oberösterreich gelegen, umfasst ausserdem eine riesige Driving Range, eine Golfschule, zwei Kurz-Plätze und bietet zahlreiche weitere Aktivitäten für jeden Geschmack - egal ob Anfänger oder Könner.

This is the "oldest" of the four courses which grace Germany's largest golfing resort. A little out of the way from the three others, it is also much flatter and lies in the valley of the river Rott, a branch of which continually flows in and out of the course. As a frontal or lateral hazard, water is the main difficulty on this intelligently-designed (but often damp) layout, so it helps to know exactly what distance you can cover with each club to avoid losing too many balls. The overall yardage, though, is not excessive providing you steer clear of the back tees. With trees and bunkers, the course appears to be designed to put players in every imaginable situation with every possible hazard. The whole resort, located on the frontier between Bavaria and upper Austria, also features a huge driving range, a golfing school, two small courses and many other activities to keep everyone happy - the good, the not so good and beginners...

Golf-Club Sagmühle — 1984

Schwaim 52
D - 94 086 BAD GRIESBACH

Office	Sekretariat	(49) 08532 - 2038
Pro shop	Pro shop	(49) 08532 - 7173
Fax	Fax	(49) 08532 - 3165
Situation	Lage	

Passau (pop. 50 000), 40 km - Griesbach (pop. 8 200), 3 km

Annual closure Jährliche Schliessung 15/11 → 15/3

Weekly closure Wöchentliche Schliessung no

Fees main season
Preisliste hochsaison 18 holes

	Week days Woche	We/Bank holidays We/Feiertag
Individual Individuell	DM 70,-	DM 80,-
Couple Ehepaar	DM 140,-	DM 160,-

Caddy	Caddy	on request
Electric Trolley	Elektrokarren	DM 15,-
Buggy	Elektrischer Wagen	DM 40,-
Clubs	Leihschläger	yes

Credit cards Kreditkarten Eurocard - MasterCard

Access Zufahrt : A3 Nürnberg-Regensburg-Passau.
Exit (Ausf.) Pocking.
B12 and B388 → Bad Griesbach. → Golf
Map 2 on page 363 Karte 2 Seite 363

GOLF COURSE / PLATZ — 15/20

Site	Lage	
Maintenance	Instandhaltung	
Architect	Architekt	K. Rossknecht
Type	Typ	parkland
Relief	Begehbarkeit	
Water in play	Platz mit Wasser	
Exp. to wind	Wind ausgesetzt	
Trees in play	Platz mit Bäumen	

Scorecard Scorekarte	Chp. Chp.	Mens Herren	Ladies Damen
Length Länge	6168	5916	5220
Par	72	72	72

Advised golfing ability Empfohlene Spielstärke	0 12 24 36
Hcp required Min. Handicap	no

CLUB HOUSE & AMENITIES / KLUBHAUS UND NEBENGEBÄUDE — 9/10

Pro shop	Pro shop	
Driving range	Übungsplatz	
Sheltered	überdacht	12 mats
On grass	auf Rasen	no, 20 mats open air
Putting-green	Putting-grün	yes
Pitching-green	Pitching-grün	yes

387

HOTEL FACILITIES / HOTEL BESCHREIBUNG — 9/10

HOTELS HOTELS
Golfhotel Maximilian — Golf Resort
232 rooms, D DM 300,-
Tel (49) 08532 - 79 50, Fax (49) 08532 - 795 150
Fürstenhof — Golf Resort
148 rooms, D DM 250,-
Tel (49) 08532 - 98 10, Fax (49) 08532 - 981 135
Parkhotel — Golf Resort
162 rooms, D DM 434,-
Tel (49) 08532 - 2 80, Fax (49) 08532 - 28 204
König Ludwig - 186 rooms, D DM 338,- — Golf Resort
Tel (49) 08532 - 79 90, Fax (49) 08532 - 799 799

RESTAURANTS RESTAURANT
Fürstenstube — Golf Resort
Tel (49) 08532 - 98 10
Gutshof Uttlau — Golf Resort
Tel (49) 08535 - 1890

BAD LIEBENZELL

14 | **7** | **7**

Der Kurort Bad Liebenzell gilt als eines der nördlichen Tore zum Schwarzwald, der sich zwischen Karlsruhe und Basel erstreckt. Diese Landschaft ist geprägt von Weinbergen, Koniferen, Bauernhöfen, Kirchen und natürlich den berühmten Kuckucksuhren, die einem helfen die Startzeit nicht zu verschlafen. Auf gut 500 m Höhe, inmitten eines wunderschönen Waldgebietes gelegen, macht einem der hügelige Charakter des Platzes sofort klar, dass man sich hier im Mittelgebirge befindet. Der Platz kann trotzdem gut zu Fuss bewältigt werden. Obwohl erst vor kurzem gebaut, strahlt die Anlage bereits eine gewisse Reife aus, wobei spürbar wird, dass von Anfang an eine natürliche Einbettung der Anlage in die Umgebung Wert gelegt wurde. Man findet hier alle Arten von Hindernissen vor, von denen sicherlich der Wald und das Rough am gefährlichsten einzuschätzen sind, da es schwierig ist, Bälle von dort wieder herauszuspielen. Besonders wohl fühlen werden sich hier Spieler, die den Ball gerade schlagen, aber auch für alle anderen sollte ein guter Score möglich sein. Ein Platz für alle Spielklassen, der allerdings an gute Spieler zu geringe Anforderungen stellt.

The spa town of Bad Liebenzell marks one of the northern gateways to the Black Forest (from Karlsruhe to Basel), in a land of vineyards and conifers, farms and churches, and not forgetting the famous cuckoo clocks to help you make your tee-off time. Located some 500 metres up, this course nestles amid a beautiful part of the forest and is hilly enough to remind players that, although walkable, this is a mid-mountain course. Although recent, the course has already matured, although blending it into the surrounding landscape was obviously a clear priority from the outset. You will find all types of hazard here, the most dangerous unquestionably being the rough and woods, where escape shots are rarely easy. Having said that, although straight hitters will feel relaxed here, you don't have to be a ball-playing wizard to card a good score. A course for all levels, but perhaps just lacking that little something for the better players.

Golfclub Bad Liebenzell e.V.　1990
Golfplatz
D - 75378 BAD LIEBENZELL-MONAKAM

Office	Sekretariat	(49) 07052 - 93 250
Pro shop	Pro shop	(49) 07052 - 93 250
Fax	Fax	(49) 07052 - 9325 25
Situation	Lage	

Pforzheim (pop. 115 000), 15 km

Annual closure	Jährliche Schliessung	1/11 → 28/2
Weekly closure	Wöchentliche Schliessung	no

Fees main season
Preisliste hochsaison full day

	Week days Woche	We/Bank holidays We/Feiertag
Individual Individuell	DM 60,-	DM 80,-
Couple Ehepaar	DM 120,-	DM 160,-

Caddy	Caddy	on request
Electric Trolley	Elektrokarren	DM 7,-
Buggy	Elektrischer Wagen	DM 60,-
Clubs	Leihschläger	DM 10,-
Credit cards Kreditkarten		no

GOLF COURSE
PLATZ　**14**/20

Site	Lage	▰▰▰▰▱
Maintenance	Instandhaltung	▰▰▰▱▱
Architect	Architekt	
Type	**Typ**	forest, open country
Relief	Begehbarkeit	▰▰▰▱▱
Water in play	Platz mit Wasser	▰▱▱▱▱
Exp. to wind	Wind ausgesetzt	▰▰▱▱▱
Trees in play	Platz mit Bäumen	▰▰▰▰▱

Scorecard Scorekarte	Chp. Chp.	Mens Herren	Ladies Damen
Length Länge	6121	6121	5429
Par	72	72	72

Advised golfing ability	0	12	24	36
Empfohlene Spielstärke	▰▰▰▰▰▰▱▱			
Hcp required Min. Handicap	We: 33			

CLUB HOUSE & AMENITIES
KLUBHAUS UND NEBENGEBÄUDE　**7**/10

Pro shop	Pro shop	▰▰▰▰▱
Driving range	Übungsplatz	
Sheltered	überdacht	6 mats
On grass	auf Rasen	yes (April-Nov.)
Putting-green	Putting-grün	yes
Pitching-green	Pitching-grün	yes

HOTEL FACILITIES
HOTEL BESCHREIBUNG　**7**/10

HOTELS HOTELS
Kronen Hotel　Bad Liebenzell
43 rooms, D DM 250,-　3 km
Tel (49) 07052 - 4090
Fax (49) 07052 - 409 420

Waldhotel Post　Bad Liebenzell
52 rooms, D DM 150,-　3 km
Tel (49) 07052 - 932 00
Fax (49) 07052 - 932 099

RESTAURANTS RESTAURANT
Adler　Calw-Stammheim
Tel (49) 07051 - 4287　10 km

Häckermühle　Tiefenbronn-Würmtal
Tel (49) 07234 - 6111　6 km

388

Access Zufahrt : A8 Stuttgart-Karlsruhe.
Exit (Ausf.) Heimsheim. → Bad Liebenzell.
Left → Unterhaugstett. → Golf
Map 1 on page 361 Karte 1 Seite 361

BAD WÖRISHOFEN

14 **6** **6**

Dieser Platz hat einserseits weder schlechte Löcher, andererseits fehlt ihm aber auch ein wirklich herausragendes Loch, das einem im Gedächtnis bleibt. Dennoch ermöglichen das flache Terrain, dass man hier ohne zu ermüden 36 Löcher am Tag spielen und sich dabei ganz auf das eigene Spiel konzentrieren kann. Die Spielstrategie ist offensichtlich. Der Golfplatz ist gut in die Natur integriert und bietet schöne Ausblicke auf den nahen Stausee und die bayerischen Alpen. Zahlreiche Bäume und Büsche grenzen die Löcher gut voneinander ab. Zwar sind einige der Par 4 Löcher recht lang, dafür sind deren Grüns relativ ungeschützt, so dass man trotzdem noch das Par retten kann. Geduldige, methodisch vorgehende Spieler werden hier belohnt. Breite Fairways und nur wenige Wasserhindernisse lassen diesen Golfplatz für alle Spielklassen geeignet erscheinen, jedoch sollte man vorzugsweise unter der Woche spielen, da es am Wochenende ziemlich voll wird.

There is no bad hole here, but there is no signature hole, either, to linger in your memory. The flat terrain can mean squeezing 36 holes into one day without flagging and with no other worry than the state of your game. Game strategy is pretty obvious. Nicely hidden in its natural surroundings and offering pretty views over Staussee and the Bavarian Alps, this course is enhanced with the lush vegetation of trees and bushes which clearly separate holes. Granted, a number of par 4s are long, but the greens are relatively unguarded to help you save par. Patient and methodical players will feel at home here. Accessible to golfers of all abilities with widish fairways and little water to speak of, this is a course to be recommended during the week. Week-ends are crowded.

Golf Club Bad Wörishofen

1977

Schlingener Strasse 27
D - 87668 RIEDEN

Office	Sekretariat	(49) 08346 - 777
Pro shop	Pro shop	(49) 08346 - 777-146
Fax	Fax	(49) 08346 - 1616
Situation	Lage	

Augsburg (pop. 265 000), 58 km
München (pop. 1 300 000), 88 km

Annual closure	Jährliche Schliessung	15/11 → 15/4
Weekly closure	Wöchentliche Schliessung	no

Monday (Montag): Restaurant closed

Fees main season
Preisliste hochsaison full day

	Week days Woche	We/Bank holidays We/Feiertag
Individual Individuell	DM 70,-	DM 90,-
Couple Ehepaar	DM 140,-	DM 180,-

under 21 years/Students : – 50 %

Caddy	Caddy	no
Electric Trolley	Elektrokarren	no
Buggy	Elektrischer Wagen	yes
Clubs	Leihschläger	DM 10,-

Credit cards Kreditkarten no

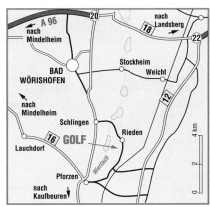

Access Zufahrt : A96 München-Memmingen. Exit (Ausf.)
Bad Wörishofen. → Kaufbeuren. In Schlingen, →
Rieden → Golf **Map 2 on page 362** Karte 2 Seite 362

GOLF COURSE
PLATZ

14/20

Site	Lage	
Maintenance	Instandhaltung	
Architect	Architekt	Donald Harradine
Type	Typ	parkland
Relief	Begehbarkeit	
Water in play	Platz mit Wasser	
Exp. to wind	Wind ausgesetzt	
Trees in play	Platz mit Bäumen	

Scorecard Scorekarte	Chp. Chp.	Mens Herren	Ladies Damen
Length Länge	6177	5798	4937
Par	72	72	70

Advised golfing ability		0 12 24 36
Empfohlene Spielstärke		
Hcp required	Min. Handicap	36

CLUB HOUSE & AMENITIES
KLUBHAUS UND NEBENGEBÄUDE

6/10

Pro shop	Pro shop	
Driving range	Übungsplatz	
Sheltered	überdacht	yes
On grass	auf Rasen	yes
Putting-green	Putting-grün	yes
Pitching-green	Pitching-grün	yes

HOTEL FACILITIES
HOTEL BESCHREIBUNG

6/10

HOTELS HOTELS
Kneipp Kurhotel Fontenay — Bad Wörishofen
60 rooms, D DM 250,- — 6 km
Tel (49) 08247 - 3060, Fax (49) 08247 - 306 185

Kurhotel Kreutzer — Bad Wörishofen
97 rooms, D DM 300:-/520,- — 5 km
Tel (49) 08247 - 35 30, Fax (49) 08247 - 353 138

Kurhotel Residenz — Bad Wörishofen
112 rooms, D DM 382,- — 6 km
Tel (49) 08247 - 35 20, Fax (49) 08247 - 352 214

RESTAURANTS RESTAURANT
Mühlbach — Bad Wörishofen
Tel (49) 08247 - 6039 — 6 km

Jagdhof — Schlingen
Tel (49) 08247 - 4879 — 4 km

389

Der Platz bietet schöne Aussichten auf ein Schloss und das Dorf Altenhof, aber die erhöhte Lage hat auch Nachteile. Das Gelände ist extrem hügelig, so dass wir Senioren und konditionsschwachen Spielern diesen Platz nicht empfehlen können, es sei denn sie lassen sich von jemandem die Golftasche tragen. Darüberhinaus müssen vielfach Bälle aus ganz unterschiedlichen Schräglagen gespielt werden, was hohe Anforderungen an die Beherrschung solcher Schläge stellt. Am besten spielt man hier mitten in der Saison, wenn der Schwung gut funktioniert und man konditionell auf der Höhe ist, da einem der Platz wirklich alles abverlangt. Bamberg hat einen hohen technischen Standard, mit vielen Bäumen und einigen gefährlichen Wasserhindernissen. Hier sein Handicap zu spielen ist eine gute Leistung. Ein Abstecher lohnt sich, wenn man gerade in der Gegend ist.

You are greeted here by some pretty vistas over a castle and the village of Altenhof, but the elevated location does have its drawbacks. The terrain is very hilly so we would definitely not advise seniors and players short on physical fitness to come and play here, unless accompanied by someone to carry their bag. Besides, this configuration results in a good number of shots being played from all sorts of slopes, a good test of skill in this department of your game. The best time to play here is in mid-season, when there is less chance of your swing and legs throwing in the towel. You will need all the strength you can muster. With this said, Bamberg is a course of excellent technical standard with lots of trees and a few dangerous water hazards. Playing to your handicap is already a good performance. Well worth getting to know if you are in the region.

Golfclub Bamberg e.V. auf Gut Leimershof
1973

Gut Leimershof
D - 96149 BREITENGÜSSBACH

Office	Sekretariat	(49) 09547 - 7109
Pro shop	Pro shop	(49) 09547 - 5202
Fax	Fax	(49) 09547 - 7817
Situation	Lage	

Bamberg (pop. 70 000), 15 km

Annual closure	Jährliche Schliessung	1/12 → 28/2
Weekly closure	Wöchentliche Schliessung	no

Monday (Montag): Restaurant closed

Fees main season
Preisliste hochsaison 18 holes

	Week days Woche	We/Bank holidays We/Feiertag
Individual Individuell	DM 60,-	DM 80,-
Couple Ehepaar	DM 120,-	DM 160,-

under 21 years, Students : DM 35,- / DM 45,- (We)

Caddy	Caddy	on request
Electric Trolley	Elektrokarren	no
Buggy	Elektrischer Wagen	no
Clubs	Leihschläger	yes

Credit cards Kreditkarten
VISA - Eurocard - MasterCard - AMEX

Access Zufahrt : BAB Nürnberg-Bamberg. B173 →
Breitengüssbach. → Zückshut → Hohengüssbach
Map 4 on page 366 Karte 4 Seite 366

GOLF COURSE
PLATZ
15/20

Site	Lage	■■■■■□
Maintenance	Instandhaltung	■■■■■□
Architect	Architekt	unknown
Type	Typ	open country, hilly
Relief	Begehbarkeit	■■■■□□
Water in play	Platz mit Wasser	■■■□□□
Exp. to wind	Wind ausgesetzt	■■□□□□
Trees in play	Platz mit Bäumen	■■■■■□

Scorecard Scorekarte	Chp. Chp.	Mens Herren	Ladies Damen
Length Länge	6175	6175	5470
Par	72	72	72

Advised golfing ability		0	12	24	36
Empfohlene Spielstärke					■
Hcp required	Min. Handicap	35			

CLUB HOUSE & AMENITIES
KLUBHAUS UND NEBENGEBÄUDE
7/10

Pro shop	Pro shop	■■■■■□
Driving range	Übungsplatz	■■■■□□
Sheltered	überdacht	5 mats
On grass	auf Rasen	yes
Putting-green	Putting-grün	yes
Pitching-green	Pitching-grün	yes

HOTEL FACILITIES
HOTEL BESCHREIBUNG
7/10

HOTELS HOTELS

Residenzschloss Bamberg — Bamberg
184 rooms, D DM 250,- — 15 km
Tel (49) 0951 - 60 910, Fax (49) 0951 - 609 1701

Hotel Sankt Nepomuk — Bamberg
47 rooms, D DM 200,- — 15 km
Tel (49) 0951 - 9842 0, Fax (49) 0951 - 9842 100

Bamberger Hof-Bellevue — Bamberg
50 rooms, D DM 245,- — 15 km
Tel (49) 0951 - 9855 0, Fax (49) 0951 - 9855 62

RESTAURANTS RESTAURANT

Schlencherla — Bamberg
Tel (49) 0951 - 56 060 — 15 km

Bassanese — Bamberg
Tel (49) 0951 - 57 551 — 15 km

BERGISCH LAND WUPPERTAL

16 7 7

Im Grossraum Düsseldorf findet man in Wuppertal einen der besten klassischen Golfplätze des Landes. Der Platz hat sich seit seiner Eröffnung im Jahre 1928 kaum verändert, aber die Länge des Platzes ist auch für den heutigen Standard ausreichend, auch wenn es keine Meisterschaftsabschläge (Tiger Tees) gibt. Der Platz wirkt auf den ersten Blick nicht allzu einschüchternd. Golfer werden nicht mit übergroflen Schwierigkeiten konfrontiert, es werden keine "Carries" über für Durchschnittsgolfer kaum überwindbare Distanzen verlangt. Trotz des hügeligen Geländes sind die meisten Hindernisse, darunter herrliche alte Bäume, immer gut auszumachen. Die Fairways sind relativ breit und werden nur gelegentlich von Wasser gesäumt. Trotzdem erfordert der Platz alle Konzentration, da die Bunker gut platziert und die Grüns nicht einfachz zu lesen sind. Obwohl hier Golfer aller Spielstärken spielen können, ist ein gutes Bruttoergebnis nicht einfach zu erzielen. Dies ist ein klassischer Club-Platz, den man Dutzende Male spielen kann, ohne ihn als langweilig zu empfinden.

In the sprawling greater Düsseldorf area Wuppertal boasts one of the country's great classic golf courses. The course has changed little since it was opened back in 1928, but yardage still meets today's standards and there are no "tiger" tees to talk of. This apparent friendly face is, what's more, an excellent argument, as golfers can come and enjoy playing here without encountering any impossible difficulties or superhuman angles and distances. Despite the hilly terrain, most of the hazards, including some superb trees, are clearly visible at first glance and the fairways are wide with only a few stretches of water to clutter the wide open spaces. But be careful though, as the bunkering is first rate and the greens tricky to read. While golfers of all abilities can play here, carding a good gross score is certainly no foregone conclusion. A real club course that you can play dozens of times and never grow tired of.

Golf Club Bergisch Land Wuppertal   1928

Siebeneickerstrasse 386
D - 42111 WUPPERTAL

Office	Sekretariat	(49) 02053 - 71 77
Pro shop	Pro shop	(49) 02053 - 48 168
Fax	Fax	(49) 02053 - 73 03
Situation	Lage	

Wuppertal (pop. 390 000), 5 km

Annual closure	Jährliche Schliessung	no
Weekly closure	Wöchentliche Schliessung	no

Fees main season
Preisliste hochsaison 18 holes

	Week days Woche	We/Bank holidays We/Feiertag
Individual Individuell	DM 80,-	*
Couple Ehepaar	DM 160,-	*

We: only with members (nur in Mitgliederbegleitung)

Caddy	Caddy
Electric Trolley	Elektrokarren
Buggy	Elektrischer Wagen
Clubs	Leihschläger

Credit cards Kreditkarten
VISA - Eurocard - MasterCard - AMEX - DC - JCB

Access Zufahrt : A46. Exit (Ausf.) Wuppertal-Katernberg.
→ Neviges/Velbert. 2.5 km turn right → Golf.
Map 3 on page 364 Karte 3 Seite 364

GOLF COURSE
PLATZ   **16**/20

Site	Lage	
Maintenance	Instandhaltung	
Architect	Architekt	unknown
Type	Typ	forest, hilly
Relief	Begehbarkeit	
Water in play	Platz mit Wasser	
Exp. to wind	Wind ausgesetzt	
Trees in play	Platz mit Bäumen	

Scorecard Scorekarte	**Chp.** Chp.	**Mens** Herren	**Ladies** Damen
Length Länge	6037	6037	5334
Par	72	72	72

Advised golfing ability Empfohlene Spielstärke	0	12	24	36

Hcp required Min. Handicap   36

CLUB HOUSE & AMENITIES
KLUBHAUS UND NEBENGEBÄUDE   **7**/10

Pro shop	Pro shop	
Driving range	Übungsplatz	
Sheltered	überdacht	
On grass	auf Rasen	yes
Putting-green	Putting-grün	yes
Pitching-green	Pitching-grün	yes

391

HOTEL FACILITIES
HOTEL BESCHREIBUNG   **7**/10

HOTELS HOTELS

Lindner Golfhotel Juliana	Wuppertal-Barmen
132 rooms, D DM 390,-	7 km
Tel (49) 0202 - 647 50, Fax (49) 0202 - 647 5777	
Intercityhotel Kaiserhof	Wuppertal-Elberfeld
160 rooms, D DM 390,-	5 km
Tel (49) 0202 - 43 060, Fax (49) 0202 - 859 1405	
Villa Christina	Wuppertal-Barmen
7 rooms, D DM 200,-	6 km
Tel (49) 0202 - 621 736, Fax (49) 0202 - 620 499	

RESTAURANTS RESTAURANT

Schmitz Jägerhaus	Wuppertal-Barmen
Tel (49) 0202 - 464 602	12 km
Jagdhaus Mollenkotten	Wuppertal-Barmen
Tel (49) 0202 - 522 643	6 km

| 16 | 8 | 9 |

Der Mauerfall und die Wiedervereinigung Deutschlands haben dem Golfsport in der neuen Hauptstadt Auftrieb verliehen, wobei dieser Golfplatz der älteste Berlins ist 1895 angelegt, wurde der Platz in den 20er Jahren von Grund auf umgestaltet und weist für moderne Ansprüche eine ansenhliche Länge auf. Nach der Wiedervereinigung wurden 1994 die neun Löcher des deutschen Clubs und die 18 Löcher des amerikanischen Clubs wieder zusammengelegt, so dass der Club heute über 18 Löcher des Meisterschaftsplatzes und noch einmal 9 Löcher des Schäferbergplatzes verfügt. Die grösste Schwierigkeit ist es, auf den Spielbahnen zu bleiben und die Bäume entlang den Fairways zu vermeiden, allerdings sind die Fairways bis auf wenige Ausnahmen relativ breit. Die Grüns sind teilweise einfach zu lesen und nicht übermässig geschützt. Wasser kommt nur am 17. Loch, einem Par 3, ins Spiel und auch nur für schwächere Spieler. Diese schöne und für alle Spielstärke gut zu spielende Anlage ist eine reizvolle Abwechslung zu den modernen, neuen Anlagen, die um Berlin herum entstanden sind.

It is the oldest course of Berlin, and the ideal base-camp for people looking to combine sport and culture. Designed back in 1895, the course was radically overhauled in the mid-1920s and now features a very decent length to today's standards. In 1994 the 9 holes of the German club and the 18 holes of the American club were reunited, so the club now boasts an 18 hole championship course and the 9-hole Schäferberg Platz (the old back nine of the American club). The basic problem is that of staying on the fairway and avoiding the trees on both sides, but with few exceptions most fairways are of generous width. There is only one water harzard, on hole 17 (Par 3), but it should only come into play for lesser players. The greens are none too difficult to read, well-contoured but not excessively guarded. A very pleasant course to see and play and an excellent companion for the other modern and more demanding courses in the region.

Golf-Club Berlin-Wannsee e.V. 1895

Golfweg 22
D - 14109 BERLIN

Office	Sekretariat	(49) 030 - 806 7060
Pro shop	Pro shop	(49) 030 - 806 70619
Fax	Fax	(49) 030 - 806 70610
Situation	Lage	

Berlin (pop. 3 500 000), 12 km

Annual closure	Jährliche Schliessung	1/1 → 31/1
Weekly closure	Wöchentliche Schliessung	no

Monday (Montag) : Restaurant closed

Fees main season
Preisliste hochsaison 18 holes

	Week days Woche	We/Bank holidays We/Feiertag
Individual Individuell	DM 110,-	DM 130,-
Couple Ehepaar	DM 220,-	DM 260,-

We & holidays: with members (nur in Mitgliederbegleitung)

Caddy	Caddy	no
Electric Trolley	Elektrokarren	DM 25,-
Buggy	Elektrischer Wagen	no
Clubs	Leihschläger	DM 20,-

Credit cards Kreditkarten VISA - Eurocard - Mastercard

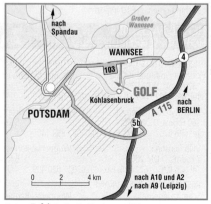

Access Zufahrt : Berlin-Zentrum → Wannsee.
Königstrasse, Chausseestrasse, → Kohlhasenbruck
(Kohlhasenbrücker Strasse), turn right in
Stölpchenweg. **Map 6 on page 371 Karte 6 Seite 371**

GOLF COURSE
PLATZ 16/20

Site	Lage	
Maintenance	Instandhaltung	
Architect	Architekt	FA Harris
Type	Typ	forest
Relief	Begehbarkeit	
Water in play	Platz mit Wasser	
Exp. to wind	Wind ausgesetzt	
Trees in play	Platz mit Bäumen	

Scorecard Scorekarte	Chp. Chp.	Mens Herren	Ladies Damen
Length Länge	6097	6097	5330
Par	72	72	72

Advised golfing ability		0 12 24 36
Empfohlene Spielstärke		
Hcp required	Min. Handicap	34

CLUB HOUSE & AMENITIES
KLUBHAUS UND NEBENGEBÄUDE 8/10

Pro shop	Pro shop	
Driving range	Übungsplatz	
Sheltered	überdacht	11 mats
On grass	auf Rasen	no
Putting-green	Putting-grün	yes
Pitching-green	Pitching-grün	yes

HOTEL FACILITIES
HOTEL BESCHREIBUNG 9/10

HOTELS HOTELS

Hotel Petit Berlin-Wannsee
11 rooms, D DM 148,- 2 km
Tel (49) 030 - 80691 80, Fax (49) 030 - 80691 840

Forsthaus ander Hubertusbrücke Berlin- Wannsee
22 rooms, D DM 300,- 1 km
Tel (49) 030 - 805 3054, Fax (49) 030 - 805 3524

Hotel Griebnitzsee Potsdam-Badelsberg
39 rooms, D DM 190,- 6 km
Tel (49) 033 - 709 10, Fax (49) 033 - 709 111

RESTAURANTS RESTAURANT

Alter Krug Berlin-Dahlem
Tel (49) 030 - 832 5089 9 km

Halali Berlin-Wannsee
Tel (49) 030 - 805 3125 3 km

392

BEUERBERG

Der nationale und internationale Ruf dieses Golfplatzes ist hauptsächlich auf sein aussergewöhnliches Panorama der bayerischen Alpen zurückzuführen. Ihr Anblick tröstet über einen schlechten Score hinweg. Wem es gelingt, seine Aufmerksamkeit nicht nur der Lage und den herrlichen Ausblicken zu widmen, der wird auch vom Platz selbst - einem der besten Entwürfe Donald Harradines - nicht enttäuscht sein. Obwohl recht hoch gelegen, gibt es keine extremen Geländeerhebungen und trotz der vielen Bäume hat man nie den Eindruck, dass diese das Spiel einengen würden. Während die Wasserhindernisse ziemlich bedrohlich wirken, sind die Grüns nur mittelmässig durch Bunker verteidigt. Nach modernen Designkriterien wäre sicherlich eine grössere Anzahl vonw Bunkern angelegt worden, um die besseren Spieler stärker zu fordern. in seinem jetzigen Zustand begünstigt der Platz Spieler mit mittleren und hohen Handicaps. Ein Besuch in Beuerberg lohnt sich in jedem Fall, vor allem auch wegen der hervorragenden Küche. Nach heftigen Regenfällen sollte man den Platz meiden, da er auf Moorboden liegt.

This course's national and international reputation stems widely from the exceptional view here over the Bavarian Alps. The sights can easily make up for a poor score. If you can put the sight and setting to the back of your mind, you won't be disappointed by the course, either, one of the best ever designed by Donald Harradine. Although high up, relief is never excessive, and while trees abound, they never give the impression of narrowness. Rather strangely, there are only three par 3s and five par 5s, but enough short par 4s to hope to bag a few birdies. The water hazards are rather threatening but the greens are only averagely guarded by bunkers: if modern-day criteria were followed, if they had wanted to upset the better players, they might have designed a few more. As it is, the game is made easier for mid- to high-handicappers. Beuerberg is well worth the journey, even more so because the cuisine in the clubhouse is excellent.

Golfclub Beuerberg e.V. — 1983

Gut Sterz
D - 82547 BEUERBERG

Office	Sekretariat	(49) 08179 - 617 728
Pro shop	Pro shop	(49) 08179 - 1229
Fax	Fax	(49) 08179 - 5234
Situation	Lage	

München (pop. 1 300 000), 45 km
Wolfratshausen (pop. 16 000), 15 km

Annual closure	Jährliche Schliessung	15/11 → 15/3
Weekly closure	Wöchentliche Schliessung	no

Fees main season
Preisliste hochsaison 18 holes

	Week days Woche	We/Bank holidays We/Feiertag
Individual Individuell	DM 100,-	DM 120,-
Couple Ehepaar	DM 200,-	DM 240,-

Caddy	Caddy	on request
Electric Trolley	Elektrokarren	yes
Buggy	Elektrischer Wagen	no
Clubs	Leihschläger	yes

Credit cards Kreditkarten — no

Access Zufahrt : A95 München → Garmisch-Partenkirchen. Exit (Ausf.) Seeshaupt, → Beuerberg
Map 2 on page 362 Karte 2 Seite 362

GOLF COURSE PLATZ — 17/20

Site	Lage	
Maintenance	Instandhaltung	
Architect	Architekt	Donald Harradine
Type	Typ	parkland
Relief	Begehbarkeit	
Water in play	Platz mit Wasser	
Exp. to wind	Wind ausgesetzt	
Trees in play	Platz mit Bäumen	

Scorecard	Chp.	Mens	Ladies
Scorekarte	Chp.	Herren	Damen
Length Länge	6264	5820	5204
Par	74	73	73

Advised golfing ability — 0 12 24 36
Empfohlene Spielstärke
Hcp required Min. Handicap — 36

CLUB HOUSE & AMENITIES KLUBHAUS UND NEBENGEBÄUDE — 7/10

Pro shop	Pro shop	
Driving range	Übungsplatz	
Sheltered	überdacht	6 mats
On grass	auf Rasen	yes
Putting-green	Putting-grün	yes
Pitching-green	Pitching-grün	yes

HOTEL FACILITIES HOTEL BESCHREIBUNG — 6/10

HOTELS HOTELS
Gut Faistenberg — Eurasburg-Faistenberg
60 rooms, D DM 275,- — 7 km
Tel (49) 08179 - 1616, Fax (49) 08179 - 433

Posthotel Hofherr — Königsdorf
60 rooms, D DM 175,- — 5 km
Tel (49) 08179 - 5090, Fax (49) 08179 - 659

Jodquellenhof — Bad Tölz
81 rooms, D DM 245,- — 15 km
Tel (49) 08041 - 50 90, Fax (49) 08041 - 509 441

Sprengenöderalm — Eurasburg
8 rooms, D DM 130,- — 6 km
Tel (49) 08179 - 931 00, Fax (49) 08179 - 931 093

RESTAURANTS RESTAURANT
Altes Fährhaus — Bad Tölz
Tel (49) 08041 - 60 30 — 15 km

Weinstube Schwaighofer — Bad Tölz
Tel (49) 08041 - 27 62 — 15 km

393

BITBURGER LAND

| 15 | 7 | 8 |

Die Mittelgebirgslandschaft der südlichen Eifel mit den malerischen Tälern ist ein sehr populäres Feriengebiet unweit von Luxemburg. Der Platz ist wie zu erwarten hügelig, ein Golfwagen ist zumindest an heiss-schwülen Tagen empfehlenswert, da das Gelände sehr offen ist und kaum Sonnenschutz bietet. Durch die grossen Höhenunterschiede sind drei blinde Löcher entstanden, die die Schlägerwahl sehr schwierig machen, insbesondere am 2. Loch, einem Par-3-Loch, mit wesentlich tiefer liegenden Grün. Abgesehen davon ist die Spielstrategie immer vorgeben, die Wasserhindernisse sind klar zu erkennen, dennoch wird man sich auf der zweiten Runde leichter tun. Die Grüns sind ziemlich gross und nicht mir allzu viel Konturen, dafür aber gut verteidigt und dennoch oftmals mit flachen Chips anzuspielen. Karl Grohs entwarf diesen natürlich wirkenden Platz, ohne der Versuchung zu erliegen, mit extremer Länge schwächere Spiele einzuschüchtern. Golfer aller Spielstärken werden diesen Platz geniessen.

This is a very popular region with tourists and lovers of mountain landscapes and nature, with the typical scenery of the small picturesque valleys in the south of Eifel, not far from Luxembourg. The course is hilly, no surprise there, and a buggy is recommended in hot weather as the terrain is very open and exposed. A few sharp changes in altitude have produced three blind greens, which make club selection a tricky business (particularly on the 2nd hole). Apart from that, game strategy is not what you could call complex (the water hazards are clearly in view) but it will be easier second time around, when the half-obscured bunkers will have lost their element of surprise. The greens are rather large, not too sharply contoured and well guarded, but you can often hit them with low running shots. Karl Grohs designed this course with a good deal of imagination, retaining its natural look and refusing to design in the length that puts so many players off. So golfers of all abilities can have fun, whatever the formula and whatever the stakes.

Golf Resort Bitburger Land — 1994
Zur Weilersheck
D - 54636 WISSMANNSDORF

Office	Sekretariat	(49) 06527 - 927 20
Pro shop	Pro shop	(49) 06527 - 927 216
Fax	Fax	(49) 06527 - 927 230
Situation	Lage	

Trier (pop. 99.000), 30 km

Annual closure	Jährliche Schliessung	no
Weekly closure	Wöchentliche Schliessung	no

Fees main season
Preisliste hochsaison 18 holes

	Week days Woche	We/Bank holidays We/Feiertag
Individual Individuell	DM 70,-	DM 90,-
Couple Ehepaar	DM 140,-	DM 180,-

Caddy	Caddy	on request, DM 30,-
Electric Trolley	Elektrokarren	DM 25,-
Buggy	Elektrischer Wagen	DM 50,-
Clubs	Leihschläger	DM 30,-/50,-

Credit cards Kreditkarten
VISA - Eurocard - MasterCard - AMEX

Access Zufahrt : • Köln, A1 → Trier. B51 → Bitburg/Prüm.
• Koblenz, A48 → Trier → Dreieck Vulkaneifel-Daun,
B257 → Bitburg. • Bitburg → Vlanden → «Golf Resort»
Map 3 on page 364 Karte 3 Seite 364

GOLF COURSE
PLATZ — 15/20

Site	Lage	
Maintenance	Instandhaltung	
Architect	Architekt	Karl F. Grohs
Type	Typ	open country, hilly
Relief	Begehbarkeit	
Water in play	Platz mit Wasser	
Exp. to wind	Wind ausgesetzt	
Trees in play	Platz mit Bäumen	

Scorecard Scorekarte	Chp. Chp.	Mens Herren	Ladies Damen
Length Länge	6168	5950	5225
Par	72	72	72

Advised golfing ability 0 12 24 36
Empfohlene Spielstärke
Hcp required Min. Handicap 36

CLUB HOUSE & AMENITIES
KLUBHAUS UND NEBENGEBÄUDE — 7/10

Pro shop	Pro shop	
Driving range	Übungsplatz	
Sheltered	überdacht	12 mats
On grass	auf Rasen	yes
Putting-green	Putting-grün	yes
Pitching-green	Pitching-grün	yes

HOTEL FACILITIES
HOTEL BESCHREIBUNG — 8/10

HOTELS HOTELS
Dorint Hotel & Resort — Biersdorf
100 rooms, D DM 225,- — 3.5 km
Tel (49) 06569 - 990, Fax (49) 06569 - 7909

Waldhaus Seeblick — Biersdorf
21 rooms, D DM 124,- — 3.5 km
Tel (49) 06569 - 9699-0, Fax (49) 06569 - 9699-50

Am Wisselbach — Rittersdorf
23 rooms, D DM 172,- — 3 km
Tel (49) 06561 - 7057, Fax (49) 06561 - 122 93

Blick Instal - 13 rooms, D DM 90,- — Wissmannsdorf
Tel (49) 06527 - 376, Fax (49) 06527 - 247 — 2 km

RESTAURANTS RESTAURANT
Burg Rittersdorf — Rittersdorf
Tel (49) 06561 - 965 70 — 3 km

Simonbräu - Tel (49) 06561 - 3333 — Bitburg 6 km

394

Die Handschrift von Trent Jones ist allein bereits ein Garant für Qualität. Dazu kommt in diesem Fall ein Gelände mit altem Mischwald-Bestand und natürlichen Wasserflächen. Angesichts dieser Vorzüge versteht man die Quelle seiner Inspiriration und das er keinerlei Zugeständnisse an die spielerischen Anforderungen des Platzes machen wollte. Spieler mit hohem Handicap sollten sich daher klaglos darauf einstellen, einige Bälle zu verlieren. Der Platz ist sowohl visuell als auch technisch aussergewöhnlich gut gelungen und hat kaum ein Loch, an dem man sich entspannen könnte. Zu den natürlichen Hindernissen gesellen sich Fairway- und Grünbunker, von denen der Architekt grosszügig Gebrauch gemacht hat. Dennoch ist der Platz fair, da an jedem Loch die Spielstrategie deutlich vorgegeben ist. Spieler, die sich trotzdem an Schlägen versuchen, die ihre Tagesform übersteigen, müssen sich deshalb an der eigenen Nase fassen. Dieser Platz ist ein guter Test und scheint uns aufgrund der umfassenden Anforderungen, die er an die Spieler stellt, besonders geeignet für Wettspiele im Match-Play Format.

The Trent Jones label is already a token of quality. Add to that a site with naturally alternating forest and stretches of water and you will understand his source of inspiration here and his uncompromising refusal of facility. High-handicappers should be ready to lose a lot of balls without complaining. The course is visually and technically just magnificent, with hardly a hole to relax on. Needless to say, the natural hazards have been supplemented by fairway and green-side bunkers generously sprinkled around the course. But this is not a treacherous course, as from each tee game strategy is clear to see and players have only themselves to blame if they attempt to play beyond their current form. This comprehensive course is a tough examination to the most suitable format for amateurs, namely match-play.

Golfclub Bodensee Weissensberg 1986

Lampertsweiler 51
D - 88138 WEISSENSBERG

Office	Sekretariat	(49) 08389 - 89190
Pro shop	Pro shop	(49) 08389 - 89192
Fax	Fax	(49) 08389 - 89 191
Situation	Lage	

Lindau (pop. 25 000), 7 km - Bregenz (Österreich), 15 km

Annual closure	Jährliche Schliessung	no
Weekly closure	Wöchentliche Schliessung	no

01/11 → 01/04 : Restaurant closed

Fees main season
Preisliste hochsaison 18 holes

	Week days Woche	We/Bank holidays We/Feiertag
Individual Individuell	DM 75,-	DM 90,-
Couple Ehepaar	DM 150,-	DM 180,-

under 21 years, Students: DM 45,-/60,-

Caddy	Caddy	on request
Electric Trolley	Elektrokarren	no
Buggy	Elektrischer Wagen	no
Clubs	Leihschläger	yes

Credit cards Kreditkarten
MasterCard

Access Zufahrt : Lindau, → Golf
Map 1 on page 360 Karte 1 Seite 360

GOLF COURSE
PLATZ 16/20

Site	Lage	▬▬▬▬▭
Maintenance	Instandhaltung	▬▬▬▬▭
Architect	Architekt	R. Trent Jones Sr
Type	Typ	forest, parkland
Relief	Begehbarkeit	▬▭▭▭▭
Water in play	Platz mit Wasser	▬▬▬▭▭
Exp. to wind	Wind ausgesetzt	▬▬▭▭▭
Trees in play	Platz mit Bäumen	▬▬▬▬▭

Scorecard	Chp.	Mens	Ladies
Scorekarte	Chp.	Herren	Damen
Length Länge	6112	5856	5189
Par	71	71	71

Advised golfing ability		0 12 24 36
Empfohlene Spielstärke		▬▬▬▬▭
Hcp required	Min. Handicap	no

CLUB HOUSE & AMENITIES
KLUBHAUS UND NEBENGEBÄUDE 7/10

Pro shop	Pro shop	▬▬▬▬▭
Driving range	Übungsplatz	▬▬▬▭▭
Sheltered	überdacht	yes
On grass	auf Rasen	yes
Putting-green	Putting-grün	yes
Pitching-green	Pitching-grün	yes

HOTEL FACILITIES
HOTEL BESCHREIBUNG 7/10

HOTELS HOTELS
Golfhotel Bodensee — Golf
21 rooms, D DM 300,- — on site
Tel (49) 08389 - 8910, Fax (49) 08389 - 89 191

Bayerischer Hof — Lindau-Insel
104 rooms, D DM 400,- — 7 km
Tel (49) 08382 - 91 50, Fax (49) 08382 - 915 591

Hotel Zum Mohren — Wangen-Neuravensburg
29 rooms, D DM 135,- — 5 km
Tel (49) 07528 - 950 0, Fax (49) 07528 - 950 95

Helvetia - 36 rooms, D DM 300,- — Lindau-Insel
Tel (49) 08382 - 40 02, Fax (49) 08382 - 40 04 — 7 km

RESTAURANTS RESTAURANT
Hoyerberg Schlössle — Lindau
Tel (49) 08382 - 25 295 — 7 km

Weinstube Frey — Lindau-Insel
Tel (49) 08382 - 52 78 — 7 km

395

Der Platz ist im typisch britischen Stil konzipiert und vermittelt das Flair eines alten Parks; zudem ist das Gelände für die Gegend recht hügelig. Auffallend sind die geschickt angelegten Fairway- und Grünbunker, welche nicht nur die Löcher optisch voneinander abgrenzen, sondern auch eine sehr wirksame Verteidigung darstellen. Am schwierigsten ist es jedoch seinen Drive gut zu plazieren, was durch eine Reihe sehr enger Fairways erschwert wird. Die dabei geforderte Präzision macht wett, was dem Platz an Länge fehlt. Eine Anzahl blinder Schläge, einige erhöht angelegte Grüns, Höhenunterschiede zwischen Abschlägen und Grüns, sowie relativ kleine Puttflächen erschweren die Schlägerwahl. Braunschweig ist ein spektakulär gestalteter Golfplatz, auf dessen strategisch angelegten Löchern das Spielen grossen Spass macht, wenngleich es Spielern mit mittleren und hohen Handicaps schwer fallen dürfte, hier einen guten Score zu erzielen. Letztere sind gut beraten sich einfach am Spiel zu erfreuen.

A rather hilly course for the region, Braunschweig gives the impression of an old park with a very obvious British style very much to the fore. We noted the clever placing of bunkers (fairway and green) which are as useful for demarcating the layout as they are for protecting it. But the prime difficulty here lies with placing the tee-shot, owing to a number of tight fairways which make up for the course's lack of length. A few blind shots, a number of elevated greens and differences in altitude between tee and green complicate the choice of club, especially since the putting surfaces are generally rather small. A spectacular and prettily landscaped course which is great fun to play and very strategic, although mid- and high-handicappers should not bank too much on carding a good score. They are better off just playing for the fun of it.

Golf-Klub Braunschweig e.V.   1926
Scharzkopffstrasse 10
D - 38126 BRAUNSCHWEIG

Office	Sekretariat	(49) 0531 - 264 240
Pro shop	Pro shop	(49) 0531 - 695 797
Fax	Fax	(49) 0531 - 642 413

Situation Lage
Braunschweig (pop. 260 000), 3 km
Hannover (pop. 510 000), 75 km

Annual closure	Jährliche Schliessung	no

Weekly closure	Wöchentliche Schliessung	no
Monday (Montag): Restaurant closed

Fees main season
Preisliste hochsaison full day

	Week days Woche	We/Bank holidays We/Feiertag
Individual Individuell	DM 60,-	DM 70,-
Couple Ehepaar	DM 120,-	DM 140,-

under 21 years/Students : – 50 %

Caddy	Caddy	no
Electric Trolley	Elektrokarren	no
Buggy	Elektrischer Wagen	no
Clubs	Leihschläger	no

Credit cards Kreditkarten	no

396

Access Zufahrt : Railway station (Hauptbahnhof),
Salzdahlumer Strasse → Krankenhaus
Map 6 on page 370 Karte 6 Seite 370

GOLF COURSE
PLATZ   **14**/20

Site	Lage	▬▬▬▬▬▬▭▭
Maintenance	Instandhaltung	▬▬▬▬▬▬▬▭
Architect	Architekt	Unknown

Type	Typ	country, forest
Relief	Begehbarkeit	▬▬▬▬▬▬▭▭
Water in play	Platz mit Wasser	▬▬▭▭▭▭▭▭
Exp. to wind	Wind ausgesetzt	▬▬▬▭▭▭▭▭
Trees in play	Platz mit Bäumen	▬▬▬▬▬▬▭▭

Scorecard	Chp.	Mens	Ladies
Scorekarte	Chp.	Herren	Damen
Length Länge	6030	6030	5313
Par	72	72	72

Advised golfing ability	0	12	24	36
Empfohlene Spielstärke		▬▬▬▬▬▬▬▬		
Hcp required	Min. Handicap	36		

CLUB HOUSE & AMENITIES
KLUBHAUS UND NEBENGEBÄUDE   **6**/10

Pro shop	Pro shop	▬▬▬▬▬▬▭▭
Driving range	Übungsplatz	▬▬▬▬▭▭▭▭
Sheltered	überdacht	3 mats
On grass	auf Rasen	yes (summer)
Putting-green	Putting-grün	yes
Pitching-green	Pitching-grün	yes

HOTEL FACILITIES
HOTEL BESCHREIBUNG   **7**/10

HOTELS HOTELS
Stadtpalais   Braunschweig
45 rooms, D DM 250,-   3 km
Tel (49) 0531 - 241 024, Fax (49) 0531 - 241 025

Play Off   Braunschweig
174 rooms, D DM 150,-   2 km
Tel (49) 0531 - 263 10, Fax (49) 0531 - 671 19

Fürstenhof   Braunschweig
52 rooms, D DM 160,-   2 km
Tel (49) 0531 - 791 061, Fax (49) 0531 - 791 064

RESTAURANTS RESTAURANT
Gewandhaus   Braunschweig
Tel (49) 0531 - 242 077   3 km

Brabanter Hof   Braunschweig
Tel (49) 0531 - 43 090   3 km

Ein originelles Beispiel der sehr strengen Architektur Siegmanns, bei dem drei verschiedene Stile vorzufinden sind: Wald, offene Fläche und beinahe alpine Landschaft, wobei letztere körperlich die anstrengendste ist (bei drei Löchern). Der Architekt hat sich dem Gelände gefügt, ohne es stark umzugestalten, daher auch der etwas uneinheitliche Stil. Doch der Platz ist dadurch sehr abwechslungsreich und interessant und die Hindernisse sind von den Abschlägen aus gut sichtbar. Man muss jedoch sein Spiel schnell an die Gegebenheiten anpassen können. Buxtehude ist sehr lang, daher ergeben seine sechs Par 5 Löcher ein ansprechendes Par 74. Die Greens sind teils erhöht, teils auf Doppelstufen und recht klein, was äusserste Genauigkeit erfordert. Dafür sind ihre Verteidigungen durchaus zu durchbrechen. Geeignet für die ganze Familie, ohne sich allzusehr um den Score zu kümmern.

An original example of Siegmann's very serious style of architecture, where you find three different styles: one in the woods, another in more open countryside and the last virtually up in the hills and physically the most trying (over three holes). The designer has bowed to the landscape more than he has modelled it, hence the impression of a rather unassertive style. In contrast, the course is great fun to play with a lot of variety and clearly visible hazards from the tees. You have to adjust your game quickly. Buxtehude is very long, but the six par 5s make this a more reasonable par 74. The greens are sometimes elevated and two-tiered, and they are rather small, so tight accuracy is essential. In contrast, their defences are not unbreachable. Play with all the family and don't worry too much about the score.

Golf-Club Buxtehude — 1986
Zum Lehmfeld 1
D - 21614 BUXTEHUDE

Office	Sekretariat	(49) 04161 - 81 333
Pro shop	Pro shop	(49) 04161 - 81 222
Fax	Fax	(49) 04161 - 87 268
Situation	Lage	

Buxtehude (pop. 34 000), 5 km
Hamburg (pop. 1 650 000), 50 km

Annual closure	Jährliche Schliessung	no
Weekly closure	Wöchentliche Schliessung	no

Monday (Montag) : Restaurant closed

Fees main season
Preisliste hochsaison 18 holes

	Week days Woche	We/Bank holidays We/Feiertag
Individual Individuell	DM 60,-	DM 80,-
Couple Ehepaar	DM 120,-	DM 160,-

under 21 years/Students : – 50 %

Caddy	Caddy	on request
Electric Trolley	Elektrokarren	no
Buggy	Elektrischer Wagen	DM 50,-
Clubs	Leihschläger	no

Credit cards Kreditkarten — no

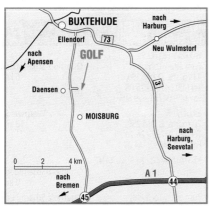

Access Zufahrt : A1 Hamburg-Bremen. Exit (Ausf.)
Hollenstedt → Moisburg, Buxtehude. Daensen → Golf
Map 7 on page 372 Karte 7 Seite 372

GOLF COURSE / PLATZ — 16/20

Site	Lage	■■■■□
Maintenance	Instandhaltung	■■■■□
Architect	Architekt	W. Siegmann
Type	Typ	forest, open country
Relief	Begehbarkeit	■■■■□
Water in play	Platz mit Wasser	■□□□□
Exp. to wind	Wind ausgesetzt	■■□□□
Trees in play	Platz mit Bäumen	■■■■□

Scorecard Scorekarte	Chp. Chp.	Mens Herren	Ladies Damen
Length Länge	6480	6480	5710
Par	74	74	74

Advised golfing ability		0	12	24	36
Empfohlene Spielstärke					
Hcp required	Min. Handicap	36			

CLUB HOUSE & AMENITIES / KLUBHAUS UND NEBENGEBÄUDE — 7/10

Pro shop	Pro shop	■■■■□
Driving range	Übungsplatz	■■■■□
Sheltered	überdacht	5 mats
On grass	auf Rasen	yes
Putting-green	Putting-grün	yes
Pitching-green	Pitching-grün	no

397

HOTEL FACILITIES / HOTEL BESCHREIBUNG — 6/10

HOTELS HOTELS
Seeburg — Buxtehude-Neukloster
14 rooms, D DM 170,- — 5 km
Tel (49) 04161 - 74 100, Fax (49) 04161 - 741 074

Herzog Widukind — Buxtehude
45 rooms, D DM 195,- — 7 km
Tel (49) 04161 - 6460, Fax (49) 04161 - 646 146

Zur Mühle — Buxtehude
36 rooms, D DM 250,- — 7 km
Tel (49) 04161 - 50 650, Fax (49) 04161 - 506 530

Am Stadtpark - 20 rooms, D DM 155,- — Buxtehude
Tel (49) 04161 - 506 810, Fax (49) 04161 - 506 815

RESTAURANTS RESTAURANT
Seeburg — Buxtehude-Neukloster
Tel (49) 04161 - 82 071 — 5 km

Herbstprinz - Tel (49) 04162- 7403 — Jork 8 km

CLUB ZUR VAHR (GARLSTEDT) ⅃ | 18 | 6 | 5 |

1905 erbaut, wurde der Platz Anfang der 60er Jahre neu gestaltet. An vier Löchern kommt Wasser ins Spiel; grosse Pinien dominieren den Platzcharakter. Es gibt insgesamt nur zwei Fairway-Bunker, da das Profil der Doglegs die Spielbahnen bereits sehr anspruchvoll macht. Die Grüns sind bemerkenswert gut verteidigt, obschon die sie umgebenden Bunker weder besonders zahlreich noch allzu bedrohlich sind. Angesichts der Tatsache, dass die meisten Schwierigkeiten gut auszumachen sind und das Gelände nur wenige Unebenheiten aufweist, erkennt man, dass die Probleme, die einem dieser Platz bereitet, sehr subtiler Art sein müssen. Dazu gehören Länge, die Beherrschung einer Vielzahl von Schlagvarianten, die Fähigkeit den Ball vom Abschlag aus so zu plazieren, dass man das Grün mit dem zweiten Schlag gut anspielen kann, sowie die Allgegenwärtigkeit von Bäumen und Heidekraut, die alle verunglückten Schläge bestrafen. Nur die sehr guten Spieler werden sich für die hinteren Abschläge entscheiden, wenngleich die sechs Par 5 Löcher gute Gelegenheiten zu einem Birdie bieten. Es ist ein absolutes Vergnügen hier zu spielen.

This is one of Germany's oldest and most celebrated golf courses. Designed in 1905, it was re-modelled in the early 1960s with water on four holes, tall pine-trees virtually everywhere but only two fairway bunkers. They must have thought that the tight dog-legs were already penalizing enough. The greens are remarkably well guarded, even though the protective bunkers are neither too numerous nor too dangerous. If we add to this the fact that most difficulties are clearly visible and relief never more than a gentle roll, you will understand how subtle the problems are here. Length has a lot to do with this, as does the variety of shots to be played, the positioning of each shot to approach the greens from the best angle and the presence of trees and heather, which punish all wayward shots. Only the very good players will choose the back tees, even though the six par 5s are good opportunities for a birdie 4. A real treat to play.

Club zur Vahr e.V., Bremen, Platz Garlstedter Heide		**1905**
Am Golfplatz 10		
D - 27711 GARLSTEDT/OHZ		
Office	Sekretariat	(49) 0421 - 204 480
Pro shop	Pro shop	(49) 0421 - 231 467
Fax	Fax	(49) 0421 - 244 9248
Situation	Lage	
Bremen (pop. 552 000), 26 km - Bremerhaven , 39 km		
Annual closure	Jährliche Schliessung	1/1 → 1/3
Weekly closure	Wöchentliche Schliessung	no
Monday (Montag): Restaurant closed		
Fees main season		
Preisliste hochsaison 18 holes		

	Week days Woche	We/Bank holidays We/Feiertag
Individual Individuell	DM 70,-	DM 70,-
Couple Ehepaar	DM 140,-	DM 140,-
We: with members (nur in Mitgliederbegleitung)		

Caddy	Caddy	no
Electric Trolley	Elektrokarren	no
Buggy	Elektrischer Wagen	no
Clubs	Leihschläger	no
Credit cards Kreditkarten		no

398

Access Zufahrt : Bremen, A27 → Bremerhaven. Exit (Ausf.) Ihlpol, B6 → Bremerhaven. 10 km until Garlstedt. → Golf on the left.
Map 5 on page 369 Karte 5 Seite 369

GOLF COURSE
PLATZ   18/20

Site	Lage	
Maintenance	Instandhaltung	
Architect	Architekt	B. von Limburger
Type	Typ	forest, parkland
Relief	Begehbarkeit	
Water in play	Platz mit Wasser	
Exp. to wind	Wind ausgesetzt	
Trees in play	Platz mit Bäumen	

Scorecard Scorekarte	Chp. Chp.	Mens Herren	Ladies Damen
Length Länge	6535	6340	5638
Par	74	74	74

Advised golfing ability		0	12	24	36
Empfohlene Spielstärke					
Hcp required	Min. Handicap	36			

CLUB HOUSE & AMENITIES
KLUBHAUS UND NEBENGEBÄUDE   6/10

Pro shop	Pro shop	
Driving range	Übungsplatz	
Sheltered	überdacht	no
On grass	auf Rasen	yes
Putting-green	Putting-grün	yes
Pitching-green	Pitching-grün	yes

HOTEL FACILITIES
HOTEL BESCHREIBUNG   5/10

HOTELS HOTELS
Zum alten Torfkahn   Osterholz-Scharmbeck
11 rooms, D DM 150,-   6 km
Tel (49) 04791 - 76 08
Fax (49) 04791 - 59 606

Eichenhof   Worpswede
20 rooms, D DM 250,-   18 km
Tel (49) 04792 - 26 76
Fax (49) 04792 - 44 27

RESTAURANTS RESTAURANT
Tietjen's Hütte   Osterholz-Scharmbeck
Tel (49) 04791 - 24 15   9 km

Zum alten Torfkahn   Osterholz-Scharmbeck
Tel (49) 04791 - 76 08   6 km

L'Orchidée   Bremen
Tel (49) 0421 - 305 9888   25 km

DOMTAL-MOMMENHEIM

Domtal-Mommenheim ist ein gutes Beispiel für einen Platz, der mit begrenzten Mitteln erbaut wurde. Für das Design zeichnet Siegfried Ernst verantwortlich, der sein Handwerk bei Altmeister Bernhard von Limburger erlernte. Er hatte beim Entwurf vor allem die Mehrzahl der Golfer, also mittlere bis hohe Handicaps, im Auge. Der Platz hat sein Ziel erreicht, Mitglieder und Gastspieler kommen nicht nur aus dem nahegelegenen Mainz. Der Platz wird scheinbar leicht, und dennoch finden auch gute Spieler hier genügend Herausforderung. Dies ist ein Platz, auf dem Longhitter richtig draufhauen können, obwohl es genügend Hindernisse gibt, die aber für gute Spieler selten bedrohlich sind, mit Ausnahme des kurzen 16. Loch (einem Par 3) und dem 18. Loch, bei dem man über Wasser so weit abkürzen kann wie man es sich zutraut. Dennoch muss man den Ball gut treffen, um ein gutes Ergebnis zu erzielen. Alles in allem ist dies ein Platz, auf dem das Spielen in der schönen Umgebung der Weinberge von Rheinhessen richtig Spass macht.

Domtal-Mommenheim is a fine example of a course which was built with a restricted budget, which was designed by owner Siegfried Ernst (who learned his trade as shaper for Bernhard von Limburger) essentially for the vast majority of golfers, i.e. mid-and high-handicappers, and which has successfully reached its target. And by target we don't mean only the inhabitants of Mainz. Yet the apparent facility of this course can be deceiving and good players also have fun playing here. Firstly, long-hitters can open their shoulders because although there is no shortage of hazards they are seldom dangerous, except on the short 16th and on the 18th, where you can cut off as much as you dare over the water hazard. Next, you have to strike the ball well to score well, as shots off-target rarely find any sort of reward. All in all, this is great fun amidst the very pleasant landscape of the Rheinhessen vineyards.

Golf Club Domtal-Mommenheim		1997
Am Golfplatz 1		
D - 55278 MOMMENHEIM		
Office	Sekretariat	(49) 06138 - 920 20
Pro shop	Pro shop	(49) 06138 - 940 170
Fax	Fax	(49) 06138 - 920 222
Situation	Lage	
Mainz (pop. 186 000), 10 km		
Annual closure	Jährliche Schliessung	no
Weekly closure	Wöchentliche Schliessung	no

Fees main season		
Preisliste hochsaison 18 holes		
	Week days Woche	We/Bank holidays We/Feiertag
Individual Individuell	DM 50,-	DM 70,-
Couple Ehepaar	DM 100,-	DM 140,-
under 21 years/Students : – 50 %		

Caddy	Caddy	no
Electric Trolley	Elektrokarren	yes
Buggy	Elektrischer Wagen	DM 40,-
Clubs	Leihschläger	DM 25,-

Credit cards Kreditkarten Eurocard - MasterCard

Access Zufahrt : Mainz A63. Exit (Ausf.)
Nieder-Olm. → Zornheim, → Mommenheim.
1 km → Schwasburg-Nierstein. → Golf.
Map 3 on page 365 Karte 3 Seite 365

GOLF COURSE / PLATZ — 14/20

Site	Lage	
Maintenance	Instandhaltung	
Architect	Architekt	Siegfried Heinz
Type	Typ	open country
Relief	Begehbarkeit	
Water in play	Platz mit Wasser	
Exp. to wind	Wind ausgesetzt	
Trees in play	Platz mit Bäumen	

Scorecard Scorekarte	Chp. Chp.	Mens Herren	Ladies Damen
Length Länge	6155	6092	5283
Par	72	72	72

Advised golfing ability	0	12	24	36
Empfohlene Spielstärke				
Hcp required Min. Handicap	54			

CLUB HOUSE & AMENITIES / KLUBHAUS UND NEBENGEBÄUDE — 7/10

Pro shop	Pro shop	
Driving range	Übungsplatz	
Sheltered	überdacht	8 mats
On grass	auf Rasen	yes
Putting-green	Putting-grün	yes
Pitching-green	Pitching-grün	yes

HOTEL FACILITIES / HOTEL BESCHREIBUNG — 7/10

HOTELS HOTELS
Park Hotel — Nierstein
55 rooms, D DM 260,- — 5 km
Tel (49) 06133 - 5080, Fax (49) 06133 - 508 333

Zum Storchennest — Mommenheim
22 rooms, D DM 110,- — 1 km
Tel (49) 06138 - 1233, Fax (49) 06138 - 1240

Hilton International — Mainz
433 rooms, D DM 230,- — 15 km
Tel (49) 06131 - 245 591, Fax (49) 06131 - 245 589

RESTAURANTS RESTAURANT
Weingut Nack — Gau-Bischofsheim
Tel (49) 06135 - 30 43 — 4 km

Drei Lilien — Mainz
Tel (49) 06131 - 225 068 — 10 km

Rats-und Zunftst. Heilig Geist — Mainz
Tel (49) 06131 - 225 757 — 10 km

399

DÜSSELDORFER

15	7	7

Der Düsseldorfer Golf Club liegt in Ratingen, wenige Kilometer von der Stadtgrenze der Nordrhein-Westfälischen Landes-hauptstadt. Aber trotz der guten Verkehrsanbindung ist der Platz weit von der Hektik der Grossstadt entfernt. Auf einem dicht bewaldeten, hügeligen Gelände entwarf der englische Architekt Donald Harradine 1961 einen Platz, der nicht nur idyllisch gelegen ist, sondern auch mit seinem abwechslungsreichen Design begeistert. Die Hauptschwierigkeit sind die teilweise engen Spielbahnen, der Wald am Rand der Fairways und die drei Teiche sowie einige seitliche Wasserhindernisse. Alle Schwierigkeiten auf diesem Parkland platz sind vom Abschlag aus zu erkennen, etwas, was vor allem bessere Spieler schätzen. Lediglich beim 15. Loch, einem Par 3 von 148 Länge und 80 Metern Höhenunterschied wird man sich beim erstenmal schwertun. Im Juli 1999 wurden nagelneue Grüns eingeweiht, die wesentlich mehr Ondulationen als die alten aufweisen. Jetzt ist auch das Putten auf diesem Platz interessant und abwechslungsreich. Diesen Platz sollte man sich nicht entgehen lassen.

The Düsseldorfer Golf Club is located in Ratingen, a few kilometers from the city limits of the capital of Northrine-Westfalia. The course is easily reached from Düsseldorf but miles away from the hustle and bustle of the big city. English architect Donald Harradine designed a course in a densely wooded area which is not only idyllic but also a pleasure to play, provided your ball stays out of the forest bordering the sometimes narrow fairways. All difficulties on the parkland style course are visible from the tee boxes, a fact better players appreciate. The 15th, a par 3 of 149 metres and an elevation drop of 80 metres, is perhaps the only hole where first-timers will have a hard time picking the right club. In July 1999, the club opened 18 new greens which have far more contours than the old ones and make putting more of a challenge. This is one course not to be missed.

Düsseldorfer Golf Club e.V.   1961
Rittergut Rommeljansweg
D - 40882 RATINGEN

Office	Sekretariat	(49) 02102 - 81 092
Pro shop	Pro shop	(49) 02102 - 83 683
Fax	Fax	(49) 02102 - 81 782
Situation	Lage	

Ratingen (pop. 91 000), 1 km - Düsseldorf, 10 km

Annual closure	Jährliche Schliessung	20/12 → 10/2
Weekly closure	Wöchentliche Schliessung	no

Monday (Montag): Restaurant closed

Fees main season
Preisliste hochsaison full day

	Week days Woche	We/Bank holidays We/Feiertag
Individual Individuell	DM 100,-	DM 100,-
Couple Ehepaar	DM 200,-	DM 200,-

We: with members (nur in Mitgliederbegleitung)
under 21 years / students: – 50 %

Caddy	Caddy	on request, DM 30,-
Electric Trolley	Elektrokarren	DM 20,-
Buggy	Elektrischer Wagen	no
Clubs	Leihschläger	DM 10,-

Credit cards Kreditkarten   no

400

Access Zufahrt : A3, Exit (Ausf.) Ratingen-Wülfrath,
→ Ratingen. 400 m turn right → Golf
Map 3 on page 364 Karte 3 Seite 364

GOLF COURSE
PLATZ   **15**/20

Site	Lage	
Maintenance	Instandhaltung	
Architect	Architekt	Donald Harradine
Type	Typ	forest
Relief	Begehbarkeit	
Water in play	Platz mit Wasser	
Exp. to wind	Wind ausgesetzt	
Trees in play	Platz mit Bäumen	

Scorecard	Chp.	Mens	Ladies
Scorekarte	Chp.	Herren	Damen
Length Länge	5905	5905	5220
Par	71	71	71

Advised golfing ability	0	12	24	36
Empfohlene Spielstärke				
Hcp required Min. Handicap	36			

CLUB HOUSE & AMENITIES
KLUBHAUS UND NEBENGEBÄUDE   **7**/10

Pro shop	Pro shop	
Driving range	Übungsplatz	
Sheltered	überdacht	4 mats
On grass	auf Rasen	yes
Putting-green	Putting-grün	yes
Pitching-green	Pitching-grün	yes

HOTEL FACILITIES
HOTEL BESCHREIBUNG   **7**/10

HOTELS HOTELS

Haus Kronenthal   Ratingen
30 rooms, D DM 230,-   1 km
Tel (49) 02102 - 85 080, Fax (49) 02102 - 850 850

Allgäuer Hof   Ratingen
15 rooms, D DM 165,-   3 km
Tel (49) 02102 - 95 410, Fax (49) 02102 - 954 123

Am Düsseldorfer Platz   Ratingen
49 rooms, D DM 200,-   2 km
Tel (49) 02102 - 20 180, Fax (49) 02102 - 201 850

Breidenbacher Hof   Düsseldorf
130 rooms, D DM 600,-   15 km
Tel (49) 0211 - 13 030, Fax (49) 0211 - 130 3830

RESTAURANTS RESTAURANT

Haus zum Haus - Tel (49) 02102 - 22 586   Ratingen 2 km
Auermühle - Tel(49) 02102 - 81 064   Ratingen 2 km

ELFRATHER MÜHLE

14	7	7

Eine alte, sorgfältig restaurierte Windmühle beeindruckt den Besucher gleich auf Anhieb. Der Eindruck von dem noch ziemlich jungen Platz ist dagegen weniger überwältigend. Trotzdem rechtfertigt sein allgemeiner Zustand, ihn mal zu spielen. Der Stil ist eher amerikanisch, mit einigen Wasserhindernissen, aber nur wenigen Bäumen, was den Platz sehr windanfällig macht. Es ist hier von Vorteil, den Ball flach schlagen zu können. Gleichzeitig wird es schwierig, die gut verteidigten Grüns anzuspielen, wenn man dem Ball nicht genügend Spin mitgibt. Durch den sandigen Untergrund ist der Platz auch bei nassem Wetter gut bespielbar. Das gesamte Layout wurde mit viel Sorgfalt angelegt, insbesondere die zum Teil in mehreren Stufen aufgebauten Grüns, die sehr interessant zu Lesen sind. Einige recht spektakuläre Löcher heben diesen Platz über das allgemeine Niveau hinaus, allerdings fehlt ihm zu einem wirklich grossartigen Kurs das gewisse Etwas. Dennoch eine gute Anlage, deren hügelige ersten neun Löcher zweifellos anspruchsvoller als die zweiten Neun sind.

An old but very carefully restored windmill gives an excellent first impression. The actual course is not quite as exceptional, but the overall standard makes it worth a round or two, even though the layout is still young. The style is a little on the American side, with a few water hazards in play but very few trees. This adds to the difficulties when the wind gets up. Hitting low balls is an asset here, and it is difficult to reach and stay on certain well-protected greens without enough spin on the ball. The sandy soil also makes this a playable course in wet weather. The whole layout has been carefully designed, especially the greens, which are sometimes multi-tiered and always interesting to read. A number of rather spectacular holes lift the overall standard a little above average, but that little spark of genius, which makes a good course a great course, is missing. A competent course all the same with a hilly and doubtless more demanding front nine.

Golf Club Elfrather Mühle GmbH — 1992

An der Elfrather Mühle 145
D - 47802 KREFELD-TRAAR

Office	Sekretariat	(49) 02151 - 496 910
Pro shop	Pro shop	(49) 02151 - 496 922
Fax	Fax	(49) 02151 - 477 459
Situation	Lage	

Krefeld (pop. 242 000), 5 km - Düsseldorf, 30 km

Annual closure	Jährliche Schliessung	no
Weekly closure	Wöchentliche Schliessung	no

Monday (Montag): Restaurant closed

Fees main season
Preisliste hochsaison 18 holes

	Week days Woche	We/Bank holidays We/Feiertag
Individual Individuell	DM 70,-	DM 90,-
Couple Ehepaar	DM 140,-	DM 180,-
Caddy Caddy		on request
Electric Trolley Elektrokarren		DM 20,-
Buggy Elektrischer Wagen		DM 60,-
Clubs Leihschläger		no

Credit cards Kreditkarten
VISA - Eurocard - MasterCard - AMEX - DC

Access Zufahrt : A57 Exit (Ausf.) Krefeld/Gartenstadt. →
Krefeld/Gartenstadt. Right in Werner-Voss-Strasse →
Traar/Elfrath. Left in An der Elfrather Mühle.
Map 3 on page 364 Karte 3 Seite 364

GOLF COURSE
PLATZ

14/20

Site	Lage	
Maintenance	Instandhaltung	
Architect	Architekt	Ron Kirby
		Fritz Beindorf
Type	Typ	open country
Relief	Begehbarkeit	
Water in play	Platz mit Wasser	
Exp. to wind	Wind ausgesetzt	
Trees in play	Platz mit Bäumen	

Scorecard Scorekarte	Chp. Chp.	Mens Herren	Ladies Damen
Length Länge	6544	6160	5370
Par	72	72	72

Advised golfing ability Empfohlene Spielstärke	0	12	24	36
Hcp required Min. Handicap	36/We 28			

CLUB HOUSE & AMENITIES
KLUBHAUS UND NEBENGEBÄUDE

7/10

Pro shop	Pro shop	
Driving range	Übungsplatz	
Sheltered	überdacht	8 mats
On grass	auf Rasen	yes
Putting-green	Putting-grün	yes
Pitching-green	Pitching-grün	yes

HOTEL FACILITIES
HOTEL BESCHREIBUNG

7/10

HOTELS HOTELS

Dorint Hotel		Krefeld-Traar
158 rooms, D DM 250,-		5 km
Tel (49) 02151 - 9560, Fax (49) 02151 - 956 100		
Parkhotel Krefelder Hof		Krefeld
150 rooms, D DM 300,-		5 km
Tel (49) 02151 - 5840, Fax (49) 02151 - 58 435		
Garden Hotel		Krefeld
51 rooms, D DM 200,-		5 km
Tel (49) 02151 - 590 296, Fax (49) 02151 - 590 299		
Zentral Hotel Poststuben		Krefeld
31 rooms, D DM 160,-		5 km
Tel (49) 02151 - 24 656, Fax (49) 02151 - 802 888		

RESTAURANTS RESTAURANT

Koperpot - Tel (49) 02151 - 614 814	Krefeld 5 km
Et Bröckske - Tel (49) 02151 - 29 740	Krefeld 5 km

401

ESCHENRIED

Neues und Altes wurde hier vereint. Die "alten" neun baumgesäumten Spielbahnen wurden ergänzt durch weitere neun Löcher in eher offenem Gelände. Letztere bilden die ersten 9 der jetzigen 18-Loch-Anlage. Beim Bau der neuen Löcher wurde weniger Aufmerksamkeit einem einheitlichen Platzcharakter geschenkt, als vielmehr den Grüns, welche aufgrund ihres weitaus aufwendigeren Designs viel interessanter zu spielen sind als die Grüns der alten Bahnen. Die grössten Probleme bereiten den Spielern die Bäume, doch muss man sich ebenso vor den sehr natürlich wirkenden Wasserläufen und Teichen in acht nehmen. Leider ist das Wasser von den kaum erhöhten Abschlägen häufig nicht einsehbar. Insgesamt kommt Wasser aber eher selten ins Spiel und sollte daher auch unerfahrene Spieler nicht allzu sehr abschrecken. Eschenried ist ein gelungener Golfplatz, den zu spielen vor allem unter der Woche empfehlenswert ist, da er an Wochenenden viele Leute aus dem nahen München und Umgebung anzieht.

New and old. The "old" nine-holer through the trees has been supplemented by a second 9-hole course over more open space, which in fact forms the front nine. Nobody really bothered about respecting unity of character, a good job, too, as far as the greens are concerned, which are much better designed, contoured and amusing to play than those on the first nine-hole course. The main problems come from the trees and, just as importantly, the very natural looking streams and ponds. The only regret is that they could have been more visible from the tee, which have no height to speak of. However, water is hardly ever in play and crossing it should not discourage even inexperienced players. A very competent course that is fun to play during the week. Being close to Munich, it is not always easy playing on week-ends.

Golfclub Eschenried		1983
Kurfürstenweg 10		
D - 85232 ESCHENRIED		

Office	Sekretariat	(49) 08131 - 87 238
Pro shop	Pro shop	(49) 08131 - 86 786
Fax	Fax	(49) 08131 - 567 418
Situation	Lage	

München (pop. 1 300 000), 15 km

Annual closure	Jährliche Schliessung	1/12 → 28/2

Weekly closure	Wöchentliche Schliessung	no

Monday (Montag): Restaurant closed

Fees main season
Preisliste hochsaison 18 holes

	Week days Woche	We/Bank holidays We/Feiertag
Individual Individuell	DM 80,-	DM 100,-
Couple Ehepaar	DM 160,-	DM 200,-

under 21 years/Students : – 50 %

Caddy	Caddy	no
Electric Trolley	Elektrokarren	no
Buggy	Elektrischer Wagen	DM 30,-
Clubs	Leihschläger	DM 30,-

Credit cards Kreditkarten		no

402

Access Zufahrt : A8 München-Stuttgart.
Exit (Ausf.) Langwieder See → Eschenried, → Golf
Map 2 on page 362 Karte 2 Seite 362

GOLF COURSE
PLATZ
14/20

Site	Lage	
Maintenance	Instandhaltung	
Architect	Architekt	
Type	Typ	open country, forest
Relief	Begehbarkeit	
Water in play	Platz mit Wasser	
Exp. to wind	Wind ausgesetzt	
Trees in play	Platz mit Bäumen	

Scorecard Scorekarte	Chp. Chp.	Mens Herren	Ladies Damen
Length Länge	6021	6021	5280
Par	72	72	72

Advised golfing ability		0	12	24	36
Empfohlene Spielstärke					
Hcp required	Min. Handicap	no			

CLUB HOUSE & AMENITIES
KLUBHAUS UND NEBENGEBÄUDE
7/10

Pro shop	Pro shop	
Driving range	Übungsplatz	
Sheltered	überdacht	yes
On grass	auf Rasen	yes
Putting-green	Putting-grün	yes
Pitching-green	Pitching-grün	yes

HOTEL FACILITIES
HOTEL BESCHREIBUNG
7/10

HOTELS HOTELS

Golf Landhaus Eschenried	Eschenried
16 rooms, D DM 140,-	on site
Tel (49) 08131 - 872 38, Fax (49) 08131 - 567 418	

Zur Post	München-Pasing
96 rooms, D DM 250,-	9 km
Tel (49) 089 - 896 950, Fax (49) 089 - 537 319	

Kriemhild	München-Nymphenburg
18 rooms, D DM 180,-	10 km
Tel (49) 089 - 170 077, Fax (49) 089 - 177 478	

RESTAURANTS RESTAURANT

Schlosswirtschaft zur Schwaige	München-Nymphenburg
Tel (49) 089 - 174 421	10 km

Zur Goldenen Gans	München-Pasing
Tel (49) 089 - 837 033	8 km

Dieser Platz inmitten des Tals der Ruhr, ist ein Hort der Ruhe, ein Golfpark mit einigen tropischen Bäumen und einem Klubhaus in einem alten Schloss, das mehr als tausend Jahre alt ist. Die ersten neun Löcher sind hügelig undziemlich eng mit einigen blinden Löchern, die zweiten Neun sind flachener und offener und geben Longhittern die Möglichkeit, den Frust der ersten Neun loszuwerden, aber sie sollten dabei Vorsicht walten lassen, den auch die Back Nine haben Tücken. Kenner der Kunst des Architekten Bernhard von Limburger erkennen sein unverkennbaren Stil. Die Schwierigkeiten sind gut über den Platz verteilt. Der Platz wirkt etwas altmodisch, aber selbst wenn dies nicht der beste Platz im Land ist, ist er immer noch einer der besten der Gegend.

Right in the Ruhr valley, this course is a heaven of tranquillity, a golf park where you will be surprised by some of the tropical trees, and even more so by the club-house set in a former castle which dates back more than a thousand years. Intelligently, the front nine are steep and not very wide (with several blind greens), the back nine are much flatter and open. Big-hitters can give vent to their frustration that mounts over the front nine, but they should be careful: the difficulties are not only on the first nine holes. Connoisseurs of the skills of Bernhard von Limburger will recognize his golfing insight in the way hazards are spread around the course. Others might find this a little dated, but while this is not the most impressive course in the whole country, it is still one of the very best in this region.

Essener Golf-Club Haus Oefte e.V. 1959

Laupendahler Landstrasse
D - 45219 ESSEN

Office	Sekretariat	(49) 02054 - 839 11
Pro shop	Pro shop	(49) 02054 - 847 22
Fax	Fax	(49) 02054 - 838 50
Situation	Lage	

Essen (pop. 670 000), 12 km

Annual closure	Jährliche Schliessung	no
Weekly closure	Wöchentliche Schliessung	no

Fees main season
Preisliste hochsaison 18 holes

	Week days Woche	We/Bank holidays We/Feiertag
Individual Individuell	DM 80,-	DM 100,-
Couple Ehepaar	DM 160,-	DM 200,-

under 21 years/Students : – 50 %

Caddy	Caddy	on request, DM 40,-
Electric Trolley	Elektrokarren	DM 20,-
Buggy	Elektrischer Wagen	no
Clubs	Leihschläger	no

Credit cards Kreditkarten VISA - Eurocard - MasterCard

Access Zufahrt : A52 Essen-Düsseldorf. Exit (Ausf.) Essen-Haarzopf → Werden. Go on E-Werden (Ruhrbrücke), Laupendahler Strasse → E-Kettwig.
Map 3 on page 364 Karte 3 Seite 364

GOLF COURSE PLATZ 15/20

Site	Lage	
Maintenance	Instandhaltung	
Architect	Architekt	B. von Limburger
Type	Typ	forest
Relief	Begehbarkeit	
Water in play	Platz mit Wasser	
Exp. to wind	Wind ausgesetzt	
Trees in play	Platz mit Bäumen	

Scorecard	Chp.	Mens	Ladies
Scorekarte	Chp.	Herren	Damen
Length Länge	6081	6081	5324
Par	72	72	72

Advised golfing ability	0	12	24	36
Empfohlene Spielstärke				
Hcp required	Min. Handicap	32/36		

CLUB HOUSE & AMENITIES KLUBHAUS UND NEBENGEBÄUDE 8/10

Pro shop	Pro shop	
Driving range	Übungsplatz	
Sheltered	überdacht	yes
On grass	auf Rasen	yes
Putting-green	Putting-grün	yes
Pitching-green	Pitching-grün	yes

403

HOTEL FACILITIES HOTEL BESCHREIBUNG 7/10

HOTELS HOTELS

Schloss Hugenpoet — Kettwig
25 rooms, D DM 400,- — 5 km
Tel (49) 02054 - 120 40, Fax (49) 02054 - 120 450

Parkhaus Hügel — Essen-Bredeney
13 rooms, D DM 185,- — 10 km
Tel (49) 0201 - 471 091, Fax (49) 0201 - 444 207

Sengelmannshof — Kettwig
26 rooms, D DM 230,- — 5 km
Tel (49) 02054 - 60 68, Fax (49) 02054 - 832 00

RESTAURANTS RESTAURANT

Residence — Kettwig
Tel (49) 02054 - 89 11 — 5 km

Landhaus Rutherbach — Kettwig
Tel (49) 0201 - 495 246 — 5 km

Parkhaus Hügel — Essen-Bredeney
Tel (49) 0201 - 471 091 — 10 km

FALKENSTEIN

Ein Klassiker traditioneller, englischer Landschaftsarchitektur, umgeben von Wald (Pinien und weisse Birken) und Heidekraut. Auf den ersten Blick fallen die gestalterischen Feinheiten nicht auf, doch wird der Golfplatz durch sie zunehmend interessanter. Die variantenreichen Löcher und die nüchterne Weite des Platzes auf diesem leicht hügeligen Terrain stellen eine echte Herausforderung dar. Die Hindernisse sind einfach und zugleich raffiniert angelegt. Jeder Schlag muss wohlüberlegt sein und alle spielerischen Aspekte müssen in die ‹berlegungen miteinbezogen werden. Die Greens, teils auf mehreren Stufen, teils erhöht, sind immer gut verteidigt und können die Scores ebenso zunichte machen wie unpräzise Schläge. Gerade Löcher wechseln mit spektakulären Doglegs ab. Falkenstein ist wohl einer der schönsten Golfplätze Europas und wird auch mit viel Liebe gepflegt ein grossartiges Beispiel guter Golfarchitektur. Unglücklicherweise ist der Platz für heutige Profiturnier zu kurz, aber für normale Golfer ist dieser Platz lang genug...

One of the great classics and a traditional British design, set in a forest of pine and silver birch, with heather thrown in for good measure. It is not easy to appreciate the subtlety of the course at first sight, but this serves to make the course more exciting every time. The variety of holes and the forbidding size of the layout on moderately hilly terrain produce a thoroughly good test of golf. Hazards are spread with an equal measure of simplicity and strategic intelligence, and each shot demands a lot of thought in every compartment of the game. Sometimes multi-tiered, often elevated but always well-protected, the greens can ruin your card as easily as fluffed shots. With alternating straight holes and spectacular dog-legs, all in beautiful condition, Falkenstein remains one of Europe's greatest courses and a perfect showpiece for golf design. Unfortunately the course is too short for modern tournament pros, but still long enough for all other golfers.

Hamburger Golf Club — 1930

In De Bargen 59
D - 22587 HAMBURG

Office	Sekretariat	(49) 040 - 812 177
Pro shop	Pro shop	(49) 040 - 814 404
Fax	Fax	(49) 040 - 817 315

Situation Lage
Hamburg (pop. 1 650 000), 10 km

Annual closure	Jährliche Schliessung	no
Weekly closure	Wöchentliche Schliessung	no

Monday (Montag): Restaurant closed

Fees main season
Preisliste hochsaison 18 holes

	Week days Woche	We/Bank holidays We/Feiertag
Individual Individuell	DM 75,-	DM 85,-
Couple Ehepaar	DM 150,-	DM 170,-

We: only with members (nur in Mitgliederbegleitung)

Caddy	Caddy	on request
Electric Trolley	Elektrokarren	no
Buggy	Elektrischer Wagen	no
Clubs	Leihschläger	no
Credit cards Kreditkarten		no

Access Zufahrt : A7. → Blankenese. Blankeneser Landtrasse. Risener Landtrasse. Turn left in De Bargen.
Map 7 on page 372 Karte 7 Seite 372

GOLF COURSE / PLATZ — 18/20

Site	Lage	
Maintenance	Instandhaltung	
Architect	Architekt	Harry S. Colt Alison, Morrison
Type	Typ	forest, Park
Relief	Begehbarkeit	
Water in play	Platz mit Wasser	
Exp. to wind	Wind ausgesetzt	
Trees in play	Platz mit Bäumen	

Scorecard Scorekarte	Chp. Chp.	Mens Herren	Ladies Damen
Length Länge	5964	5919	5198
Par	72	72	72

Advised golfing ability Empfohlene Spielstärke	0	12	24	36

Hcp required Min. Handicap 36

CLUB HOUSE & AMENITIES / KLUBHAUS UND NEBENGEBÄUDE — 6/10

Pro shop	Pro shop	
Driving range	Übungsplatz	
Sheltered	überdacht	6 mats
On grass	auf Rasen	yes
Putting-green	Putting-grün	yes
Pitching-green	Pitching-grün	yes

HOTEL FACILITIES / HOTEL BESCHREIBUNG — 7/10

HOTELS HOTELS

Stranhotel Blankenese — Hamburg
15 rooms, D DM 220,- — 4 km
Tel (49) 040 - 861 344, Fax (49) 040 - 864 936

Hotel Senator — Wedel
46 rooms, D DM 178,- — 5 km
Tel (49) 04103 - 80 870, Fax (49) 04103 - 8077250

Hotel Diamant — Wedel
39 rooms, D DM 168,- — 5 km
Tel (49) 04103 - 702 600, Fax (49) 04103 - 702 700

RESTAURANTS RESTAURANT

Flic Flac Bistro — Hamburg
Tel (49) 040 - 865 345 — 2 km

König Pilsener Stuben — Hamburg
Tel (49) 040 - 860 931 — 3 km

404

Feldafing wurde nach Umbau- und Verjüngungsmassnahmen von Heinz Fehring im Jahre 1997 wieder eröffnet, aber es immer noch ein kurzer und enger Platz, allerdings sind die Grüns jetzt stark onduliert. Die Anlage liegt etwas erhöht direkt am Starnberger See, auf einem Gelände, das früher Maximilian II gehörte, dessen Schloss unmittelbar an die Anlage angrenzt. Trotz dieser Lage bietet sich nur selten ein freier Blick auf den See, da der Platz von einer Vielzahl grosser alter Bäume umrahmt wird, die gleichzeitig einen Grossteil der Schwierigkeiten auf diesem Platz darstellen. Bernhard von Limburger hat das ziemlich hügelige Gelände hervorragend zu nutzen verstanden, so dass ein für ihn typisches Design entstanden ist, das sich durch einen nüchtern-eleganten und dabei immer seriösen Stil ausgezeichnet. Feldafing ist ein reizvoller Golfplatz, der sich zudem wunderbar in die ihn umgebende Landschaft einfügt und den man allein schon aus diesem Grund unbedingt kennen lernen sollte.

Feldafing underwent a welcome and successful rejuvenation scheme by Heinz Fehring, but it is still a narrow and short course. Located on an estate formerly belonging to Maximilian II - his castle stands on the edge of the course - Feldafing overlooks the Starnberger See, although the view is not completely clear owing to the very many old trees which form the major share of hazards. Bernhard von Limburger made excellent use of rather hilly terrain (rather tiring when walking) and it is always a pleasure to see his elegant, sober and serious style again. An often spectacular course which blends wonderfully with its natural surroundings. Well worth getting to know.

Golf Club Feldafing e.V.   1926

Tutzinger Strasse 15
D - 82340 TUTZING

Office	Sekretariat	(49) 08157 - 93 340
Pro shop	Pro shop	(49) 08157 - 93 340
Fax	Fax	(49) 08157 - 933 499
Situation	Lage	

München (pop. 1 300 000), 40 km

Annual closure	Jährliche Schliessung	no
Weekly closure	Wöchentliche Schliessung	no

Monday (Montag) : Restaurant closed

Fees main season
Preisliste hochsaison 18 holes

	Week days Woche	We/Bank holidays We/Feiertag
Individual Individuell	DM 100,-	DM 120,-
Couple Ehepaar	DM 200,-	DM 240,-

We: with members (nur in Mitgliederbegleitung)

Caddy	Caddy	on request
Electric Trolley	Elektrokarren	no
Buggy	Elektrischer Wagen	no
Clubs	Leihschläger	yes

Credit cards Kreditkarten	no

Access Zufahrt : A95 München-Starnberg. Exit (Ausf.) Starnberg. Durch Starnberg. B2 → Pöcking. → Tutzing/Deldafing, right on Tutzinger Strasse. 1 km left, Golf. **Map 2 on page 362** Karte 2 Seite 362

GOLF COURSE
PLATZ   16/20

Site	Lage	
Maintenance	Instandhaltung	
Architect	Architekt	B. von Limburger Heinz Fehring
Type	Typ	mountain
Relief	Begehbarkeit	
Water in play	Platz mit Wasser	
Exp. to wind	Wind ausgesetzt	
Trees in play	Platz mit Bäumen	

Scorecard Scorekarte	Chp. Chp.	Mens Herren	Ladies Damen
Length Länge	5738	5482	4795
Par	71	70	70

Advised golfing ability Empfohlene Spielstärke	0 12 24 36
Hcp required Min. Handicap	34

CLUB HOUSE & AMENITIES
KLUBHAUS UND NEBENGEBÄUDE   7/10

Pro shop	Pro shop	
Driving range	Übungsplatz	
Sheltered	überdacht	5 mats
On grass	auf Rasen	yes
Putting-green	Putting-grün	yes
Pitching-green	Pitching-grün	yes

HOTEL FACILITIES
HOTEL BESCHREIBUNG   6/10

HOTELS HOTELS

Kaiserin Elisabeth	Feldafing
70 rooms, D DM 180,-	300 m
Tel (49) 08157 - 930 90	
Fax (49) 08157 -930 9133	

Forsthaus am See	Pöcking-Possenhofen
21 rooms, DM 270,-	2 km
Tel (49) 08157 - 93 010	
Fax (49) 08157 - 4292	

Marina	Bernried
71 rooms, D DM 250,-	7 km
Tel (49) 08158 - 9320	
Fax (49) 08158 - 7117	

RESTAURANTS RESTAURANT

Forsthaus Ilkahöhe	Tutzing
Tel (49) 08158 - 8242	4 km

FRANKFURTER GC

Viele Jahre zählte Frankfurt zu den Plätzen, die bis 1989 gut genug waren, die German Open neunmal auszutragen. Doch fehlt dem Platz die Länge, um heute die Longhitter unter den Tourspielern zu testen... Nichtsdestoweniger ist das Spiel auf diesem wunderschön gelegenen Platz ein reines Vergnügen, auch wenn der nahe Flughafen etwas störend wirkt. Das Layout der leicht hügeligen Anlage ist typisch britisch. Kein Wunder, trägt der Platz doch die Handschrift von Colt und Morrison, die Qualität und hohes technisches Können garantiert, was auch in der im Spielverlauf allmählich spürbaren Steigerung der an den Golfer gestellten Anforderungen zum Ausdruck kommt. Durchschnittliche Spieler werden ihren Spass haben, während die besseren Spieler in guter Form sein müssen, um ein für sie gutes Ergebnis zu erzielen. Der Platz erfordert gerade Schläge ebenso wie die Beherrschung unterschiedlicher Ball-Flugkurven, um die vielen Bäumen vermeiden bzw. um diese herumspielen zu können. Die Grüns sind gut geformt, von mittlerer Grösse und gut verteidigt ohne unzugänglich zu sein.

For many a year this was one of the great courses used for the German Open, but nowadays the course is too short to test the long-hitting tour players. Nevertheless, the Frankfurter is a real joy to play for the beauty of its setting, despite the airport being a shade too close for comfort. The layout is sometimes hilly, but never excessively so. It is plainly very British in style, and the Colt and Morrison label is a guarantee of quality and technical skill, with the course gradually getting harder geared to the golfer's ability. Average players will have fun, but the better players will need to be on their toes to card a good score. Here, of course, you have to play straight and sometimes flight the ball to avoid, or escape from, the many trees. The greens are well-contoured, medium-sized and reasonably well-protected, although never inaccessible. Since the top soil is sand, the course drains very well and can be played even after heavy rainfall.

Frankfurter Golf Club e.V.   1913

Golfstrasse 41
D - 60528 FRANKFURT

Office	Sekretariat	(49) 069 - 666 2318
Pro shop	Pro shop	(49) 069 - 666 2441
Fax	Fax	(49) 069 - 666 7018
Situation	Lage	Frankfurt, 3 km
Annual closure	Jährliche Schliessung	no
Weekly closure	Wöchentliche Schliessung	no

Monday (Montag): Restaurant closed

Fees main season
Preisliste hochsaison 18 holes

	Week days Woche	We/Bank holidays We/Feiertag
Individual Individuell	DM 100,-	DM 115,-
Couple Ehepaar	DM 200,-	DM 230,-

W/E: only with members (nur in Mitgliederbegleitung)
under 21 years/Students: – 50%

Caddy	Caddy	on request
Electric Trolley	Elektrokarren	no
Buggy	Elektrischer Wagen	no
Clubs	Leihschläger	DM 40,-

Credit cards Kreditkarten   no

FRANKFURT

0   2   4 km

Mülheim
GOLF
Hattersheim
OFFENBACH
A 5
43
A 3
A 3
Neu-Isenburg
A 66
MAINZ
44
Sprendlingen
Groß-Gerau
DARMSTADT

Access Zufahrt : A3, Exit (Ausf.) Frankfurt Süd
→ Niederrad, Flughafenstrasse, Golfstrasse.
Map 3 on page 365 Karte 3 Seite 365

GOLF COURSE
PLATZ   17 /20

Site	Lage	
Maintenance	Instandhaltung	
Architect	Architekt	Harry S. Colt
Type	Typ	forest
Relief	Begehbarkeit	
Water in play	Platz mit Wasser	
Exp. to wind	Wind ausgesetzt	
Trees in play	Platz mit Bäumen	

Scorecard Scorekarte	Chp. Chp.	Mens Herren	Ladies Damen
Length Länge	6094	5895	5217
Par	71	71	71

Advised golfing ability	0	12	24	36
Empfohlene Spielstärke				
Hcp required	Min. Handicap		28	

CLUB HOUSE & AMENITIES
KLUBHAUS UND NEBENGEBÄUDE   7 /10

Pro shop	Pro shop	
Driving range	Übungsplatz	
Sheltered	überdacht	yes
On grass	auf Rasen	yes
Putting-green	Putting-grün	yes
Pitching-green	Pitching-grün	yes

HOTEL FACILITIES
HOTEL BESCHREIBUNG   8 /10

HOTELS HOTELS
Arabella Congress Hotel   Frankfurt-Niederrad
393 rooms, D DM 450,-   1 km
Tel (49) 069 - 66 330, Fax (49) 069 - 663 3666

Hugenottenhof   Neu-Isenburg
86 rooms, D DM 180,-   8 km
Tel (49) 06102 - 17 053, Fax (49) 06102 - 25 212

Steigenberger Frankfurter Hof   Frankfurt
332 rooms, D DM 500,-   6 km
Tel (49) 069 - 21 502, Fax (49) 069 - 215 900

RESTAURANTS RESTAURANT
Weinhaus Brückenkeller   Frankfurt
Tel (49) 069 - 284 238   6 km

Weidemann   Frankfurt-Niederrad
Tel (49) 069 - 675 996   2 km

406

FRÄNKISCHE SCHWEIZ

Die beste Zeit diesen Platz zu spielen ist Ende Frühling, wenn die Apfel- und Kirschbäume in voller Blüte stehen. Seit seiner Erweiterung zur 18-Loch-Anlage ist der GC Fränkische Schweiz, zwischen Nürnberg und Bamberg gelegen, zum beliebten Ziel für Golfer geworden. Die eine Hälfte der Löcher liegt im Wald, die andere in offenerem Gelände, wo auch die längsten Löcher zu finden sind und die Spieler mit langem Drive voll zum Zug kommen. Der Platz ist sehr natürlich angelegt. Wenngleich die Bunker besser modelliert sein könnten, bereiten sie doch auch so den meisten Spielern genug Kopfzerbrechen. Dasselbe gilt auch für die Grüns. Während Gestaltung und Formgebung der Grüns bei älteren Anlagen häufig nicht sehr ausgeprägt ist, hat man sich bei neueren Plätzen in dieser Hinsicht an ein aufwendigeres Design gewöhnt. Zusammenfassend können wir sagen, dass dieser Platz einen recht ausgewogenen Eindruck macht, angenehm zu spielen ist und Golfern aller Spielstärken entgegenkommt.

The best season to play here is in late spring, when the apple- and cherry-trees are in blossom. Between Nürnberg and Bamberg, this has been a traditional stop-off for golfers since it was enhanced to 18-hole status in 1989. Half the holes run through the woods, the other half in more open country, where the holes are longer and big-hitters can open their shoulders. The layout is very natural, and while we might have hoped for better contoured bunkers, there is no denying that they do pose a considerable problem for most players. The same observation applies to the greens; while older greens were often a little less elaborate, recent courses have accustomed us to a little more research. Having said that, this is a very pleasant and friendly course for players of all levels, and it is well-balanced throughout. FrÄnkische Schweiz is also a very pretty region...

Golf-Club Fränkische Schweiz e.V.   1974

Kanndorf 8
D - 91320 EBERMANNSTADT

Office	Sekretariat	(49) 09194 - 4827
Pro shop	Pro shop	(49) 09194 - 4827
Fax	Fax	(49) 09194 - 5410
Situation	Lage	

Nürnberg (pop. 498 000), 45 km
Bamberg (pop. 70 000), 35 km

Annual closure	Jährliche Schliessung	no
Weekly closure	Wöchentliche Schliessung	no

Fees main season
Preisliste hochsaison full day

	Week days Woche	We/Bank holidays We/Feiertag
Individual Individuell	DM 60,-	DM 80,-
Couple Ehepaar	DM 120,-	DM 160,-
under 21 years, Students : – 50%		

Caddy	Caddy	no
Electric Trolley	Elektrokarren	no
Buggy	Elektrischer Wagen	no
Clubs	Leihschläger	yes
Credit cards Kreditkarten		no

Access Zufahrt : BAB-A73 Nürnberg-Bamberg. Exit (Ausf.) Forchheim. B470 → Ebermannstadt. → Kanndorf, Golf
Map 4 on page 366 Karte 4 Seite 366

GOLF COURSE
PLATZ   14/20

Site	Lage	■■■■□
Maintenance	Instandhaltung	■■■□□
Architect	Architekt	unknown
Type	Typ	country, forest
Relief	Begehbarkeit	■■■□□
Water in play	Platz mit Wasser	■□□□□
Exp. to wind	Wind ausgesetzt	■■□□□
Trees in play	Platz mit Bäumen	■■■□□

Scorecard Scorekarte	Chp. Chp.	Mens Herren	Ladies Damen
Length Länge	6050	6050	5388
Par	72	72	72

Advised golfing ability	0	12	24	36
Empfohlene Spielstärke	■□			
Hcp required	Min. Handicap	35		

CLUB HOUSE & AMENITIES
KLUBHAUS UND NEBENGEBÄUDE   7/10

Pro shop	Pro shop	■■■□□
Driving range	Übungsplatz	■■■□□
Sheltered	überdacht	3 mats
On grass	auf Rasen	no, 10 mats open air
Putting-green	Putting-grün	yes
Pitching-green	Pitching-grün	yes

HOTEL FACILITIES
HOTEL BESCHREIBUNG   6/10

HOTELS HOTELS
Club Hotel — Golf
15 rooms, D DM 100,- on site
Tel (49) 09194 - 9228, Fax (49) 09194 - 5410

Resengörg — Ebermannstadt
34 rooms, D DM 120,- 2 km
Tel (49) 09194 - 73 930, Fax (49) 09194 - 739 373

Schwanenbrau — Ebermannstadt
13 rooms, D DM 120,- 2 km
Tel (49) 09194 - 209, Fax (49) 09194 - 5836

RESTAURANTS RESTAURANT
Feiler — Muggendorf
Tel (49) 09196 - 322 4 km

Bierbrunnen — Ebermannstadt
Tel (49) 09194 - 5865 5 km

407

Dieser 1998 eröffnete Platz liegt nur 50 m vom wesentlich älteren Golf Club Oberschwaben entfernt, den man mit einem Lobwedge über die Bäume leicht erreichen könnte. Doch der neue Platz ist um vieles reizvoller als der alte Nachbarplatz. Der Platz liegt herrlich eingebettet in einer Waldlandschaft. Die dreimalige deutsche Amateurmeister Thomas Himmel und der Pro Carlo Knauss entwarfen den 18-Loch-Platz. Es ist das erste gemeinsame Werk dieser beiden, und es ist ihnen bestens gelungen. Sie haben dem modernen Trend zu immer mehr Länge widerstanden und betonen statt dessen die Werte von intelligentem und strategischem Golf : easy bogey, tough par. Höhepunkt der Runde sind die Löcher 12 bis 16, die sich um einen riesigen ehemaligen Baggersee schlängeln. Da auch noch ein Hotel direkt am Platz liegt, ist Waldsee ideal für einen Kurzurlaub.

You only need a lobwedge over the trees to reach the neighbouring course of the older GC Oberschwaben, located only 50 metres from this course opened in 1998. But in spite of its youth it is better than the old neighbor. The course is beautifully integrated in a wonderful forest. Three-time German Amateur champion Thomas Himmel and Pro Carlo Knauss collaborated on this course for the first time, and they really got it right the first time. Himmel and Knauss resisted the modern trend to extrem length but stress intelligent and strategic golf: easy bogey, tough par. Highlight of the round are the holes 12 through 16 which meander around a flooded gravel pit. With a wonderful hotel on the site Waldsee is an ideal setting for a short break from daily hum-drum.

Fürstlicher Golfclub Bad Waldsee — 1998

Hopfenweiler 14
D - 88339 BAD WALDSEE

Office	Sekretariat	(49) 07524 -401 7200
Pro shop	Pro shop	(49) 07524 -401 7200
Fax	Fax	(49) 07524 -401 7100
Situation	Lage	

Ravensburg (pop. 46 000), 24 km

Annual closure	Jährliche Schliessung	no
Weekly closure	Wöchentliche Schliessung	no

Fees main season
Preisliste hochsaison 18 holes

	Week days Woche	We/Bank holidays We/Feiertag
Individual Individuell	DM 70,-	DM 90,-
Couple Ehepaar	DM 140,-	DM 180,-

Softspikes mandatory

Caddy	Caddy	no
Electric Trolley	Elektrokarren	DM 25,-
Buggy	Elektrischer Wagen	DM 40,-
Clubs	Leihschläger	DM 20,-

Credit cards Kreditkarten
VISA - Eurocard - MasterCard - AMEX - DC

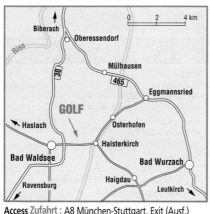

Access Zufahrt : A8 München-Stuttgart. Exit (Ausf.)
Ulm-West. B30 → Bodensee. Bad Waldsee → Golf
Map 1 on page 361 Karte 1 Seite 361

GOLF COURSE / PLATZ — 17/20

Site	Lage	▮▮▮▮▮▮▯
Maintenance	Instandhaltung	▮▮▮▮▮▮▮
Architect	Architekt	Thomas Himmel Carlo Knauss
Type	Typ	forest, open country
Relief	Begehbarkeit	▮▮▮▯▯
Water in play	Platz mit Wasser	▮▮▯▯▯
Exp. to wind	Wind ausgesetzt	▮▮▯▯▯
Trees in play	Platz mit Bäumen	▮▮▮▮▯

Scorecard Scorekarte	Chp. Chp.	Mens Herren	Ladies Damen
Length Länge	6474	6118	5315
Par	72	72	72

Advised golfing ability Empfohlene Spielstärke	0	12	24	36
			▮▮▮▮	

Hcp required Min. Handicap — no

CLUB HOUSE & AMENITIES / KLUBHAUS UND NEBENGEBÄUDE — 7/10

Pro shop	Pro shop	▮▮▮▮▮▮▯
Driving range	Übungsplatz	▮▮▮▮▮▮▯
Sheltered	überdacht	15 mats
On grass	auf Rasen	yes
Putting-green	Putting-grün	yes
Pitching-green	Pitching-grün	yes

HOTEL FACILITIES / HOTEL BESCHREIBUNG — 8/10

HOTELS HOTELS

Hotel im Hofgut — Bad Waldsee
40 rooms, D DM 200,- — on site
Tel (49) 07524 - 4017 0, Fax (49) 07524 -4017 100

Kur-Parkhotel — Bad Waldsee
64 rooms, D DM 200,- — 2 km
Tel (49) 07524 - 97 070, Fax (49) 07524 - 970 775

Altes Tor — Bad Waldsee
28 rooms, D DM 160,- — 2 km
Tel (49) 07524 - 97 190, Fax (49) 07524 - 971 997

RESTAURANTS RESTAURANT

Waldhorn — Ravensburg
Tel (49) 0751 - 36 120 — 20 km

Krone — Schlier
Tel (49) 07529 - 1292 — 25 km

408

Der Architekt Heinz Fehring wurde stark vom amerikanischen Stil beeinflusst, obwohl die vier nahe beim Clubhaus gelegenen Löcher sich deutlich von den restlichen Spielbahnen unterscheiden. Dies war auch nicht anders zu erwarten, angesichts der Tatsache, dass Bäume kaum ins Spiel kommen und Wasserhindernisse, neben dem Wind natürlich, die Hauptschwierigkeiten dieses Platzes bilden. Daher kam ein "natürlicher" Platz von vornherein gar nicht in Frage. Um mit dem Platz gleich beim ersten Mal zurechtzukommen, empfiehlt es sich, sich eine Birdiekarte (Yardage Book) mitzunehmen, da weder die Spielstrategie deutlich vorgegeben, noch ein Grossteil der Hindernisse vom Abschlag aus erkennbar ist - es gibt sogar fünf blinde Löcher. Das schlimmste und einzig vollkommen misslungene Loch ist das 10. Loch, wo man vor lauter Wasser gar nicht weiss, wo man den Abschlag plazieren soll. Glücklicherweise sind die grösstenteils gut gestalteten Grüns wenigstens voll einsehbar. Allen Durchschnittsgolfern empfehlen wir, von den vorderen Abschlägen zu spielen. Einstellige Golfer sollten jedoch auf die Meisterschaftsabschläge gehen...

Designer Heinz Fehring was visibly influenced by the US style of course, even though the four holes close to the clubhouse are rather different from the rest. It could hardly be otherwise, when trees are hardly ever in play and when water hazards provide the main difficulties (with the wind, of course). There was no question of making this a natural course. First time out, you are best advised to take the yardage book with you to get your bearings. Nothing is obvious, not even the hazards are visible and there are, after all, five blind holes. The worst and only really bad hole is the 10th, where water is everywhere and you have no clue where to place your drive. Fortunately, the greens are in view and by and large they are well designed. We would recommend the front tees for all average players, single figure handicapper can use the championship tees.

Golf- und Land-Club
Fürstliches Hofgut Kolnhausen e.V.   1992

D - 35423 LICH

Office	Sekretariat	(49) 06404 - 910 710
Pro shop	Pro shop	(49) 06404 - 910 753
Fax	Fax	(49) 06404 - 910 72
Situation	Lage	

Giessen, 15 km - Frankfurt (pop. 660 000), 55 km

Annual closure	Jährliche Schliessung	no
Weekly closure	Wöchentliche Schliessung	no

Monday (Montag): Restaurant closed

Fees main season
Preisliste hochsaison 18 holes

	Week days Woche	We/Bank holidays We/Feiertag
Individual Individuell	DM 80,-	DM 100,-
Couple Ehepaar	DM 160,-	DM 200,-
under 21 years/Students: – 50%		
Caddy Caddy		DM 50,-
Electric Trolley Elektrokarren		DM 30,-
Buggy Elektrischer Wagen		no
Clubs Leihschläger		DM 30,-

Credit cards Kreditkarten   no

Access Zufahrt : A5 Frankfurt-Kassel. Kambacher Kreuz, A45 → Hanau. Exit (Ausf.) Münzenberg/Lich. → Lich, Golf 5 km. **Map 3 on page 365** Karte 3 Seite 365

GOLF COURSE
PLATZ   14/20

Site	Lage	
Maintenance	Instandhaltung	
Architect	Architekt	Heinz Fehring
Type	Typ	open country
Relief	Begehbarkeit	
Water in play	Platz mit Wasser	
Exp. to wind	Wind ausgesetzt	
Trees in play	Platz mit Bäumen	

Scorecard Scorekarte	Chp. Chp.	Mens Herren	Ladies Damen
Length Länge	6388	6065	5350
Par	73	72	73

		0	12	24	36
Advised golfing ability Empfohlene Spielstärke					
Hcp required Min. Handicap	36				

CLUB HOUSE & AMENITIES
KLUBHAUS UND NEBENGEBÄUDE   7/10

Pro shop	Pro shop	
Driving range	Übungsplatz	
Sheltered	überdacht	6 mats
On grass	auf Rasen	yes
Putting-green	Putting-grün	yes
Pitching-green	Pitching-grün	yes

HOTEL FACILITIES
HOTEL BESCHREIBUNG   6/10

HOTELS HOTELS

Landhaus Klosterwald — Lich
18 rooms, D DM 170,- — 1 km
Tel (49) 06404 - 91 010, Fax (49) 06404 - 910 134

Alte Klostermühle — Lich
26 rooms, D DM 230,- — 1 km
Tel (49) 06404 - 91 900, Fax (49) 06404 - 4867

Tandrias — Giessen
32 rooms, D DM 196,- — 20 km
Tel (49) 0641 - 940 70, Fax (49) 0641 - 940 7499

Steinsgarten — Giessen
129 rooms, D DM 250,- — 15 km
Tel (49) 0641 - 38 990, Fax (49) 0641 - 389 9200

RESTAURANTS RESTAURANT

Zum Stern — Butzbach
Tel (49) 06033 - 7977 — 20 km

409

In unmittelbarer Nähe zu einem der bekanntesten Winter- und Sommersportorte Europas gelegen, verläuft dieser Platz auf so ebenem Terrain, dass man ihn als Flachland-Platz inmitten einer Alpin-Region bezeichnen kann. Der Platz ist daher auch mühelos zu bewältigen. Trotz der schwierigen Witterungsbedingungen - lange kalte Winter, heisse Sommer - macht der Platz einen sehr gepflegten Eindruck. Um auf diesem Platz gut zu spielen, sollte man nicht allzu sehr streuen, da die Fairways, eingegrenzt durch Bäume, Büsche und Felsen, recht schmal sind. Die Tücken dieses Platzes, der deutlich zu erkennende Hindernisse hat, sind eher psychologischer denn realer Natur. Spieler, die den Ball gerade schlagen, werden die Runde geniessen. Dasselbe gilt für Spieler mit mittlerem Handicap sowie jene, denen es an Länge fehlt. Das 'persönliche Par' ist immer möglich. Einen zusätzlichen Anreiz dieses Ortes bietet das ausgezeichnete Restaurant im Clubhaus mit seiner typisch bayerischen Atmosphäre, in dem man einen schönen Golftag ausklingen lassen sollte.

Very close to one of Europe's most celebrated winter and summer resorts, this course is flat enough to be considered a lowland course transposed to the mountains. You can play it tirelessly. Green-keeping is very decent, given the length of the winters and the hot summers, but this is not a course we would recommend to wild hitters: the fairways are tight and guarded by trees, bushes and rocks. The dangers here are perhaps more psychological than real (hazards are clearly visible) and straight players will enjoy their round. The same might apply to mid-handicappers and players lacking length. On most holes you can play your "personal par" (with handicap strokes). To enjoy your day to the full, pop inside the very country-style club-house and enjoy the excellent restaurant and typically Bavarian atmosphere. It is a great bonus for an excellent site..

Golf-Club Garmisch-Partenkirchen e.V. 1928
Gut Buchwies
D - 82496 OBERAU

Office	Sekretariat	(49) 08824 - 8344
Pro shop	Pro shop	(49) 08824 - 1679
Fax	Fax	(49) 08824 - 325
Situation	Lage	München, 81 km

Garmisch-Partenkirchen (pop. 26 500), 8 km

Annual closure	Jährliche Schliessung	1/12 → 31/3
Weekly closure	Wöchentliche Schliessung	no

Monday (Montag): Restaurant closed

Fees main season
Preisliste hochsaison full day

	Week days Woche	We/Bank holidays We/Feiertag
Individual Individuell	DM 70,-	DM 90,-
Couple Ehepaar	DM 140,-	DM 180,-

under 21 years/Students: – 50 %

Caddy	Caddy	on request
Electric Trolley	Elektrokarren	no
Buggy	Elektrischer Wagen	no
Clubs	Leihschläger	DM 20,-

Credit cards Kreditkarten   AMEX

Oberammergau
nach MÜNCHEN
Oberau
GOLF
A 95
Eschenlohe
B 2
nach St Anton
GARMISCH-PARTENKIRCHEN
nach Innsbruck

Access Zufahrt : A95 and B2 München → Garmisch-Partenkirchen. Exit (Ausf.) Oberau. Left over the Loisach → Gut Buchwies, Golf
Map 2 on page 362 Karte 2 Seite 362

GOLF COURSE
PLATZ   **14**/20

Site	Lage	
Maintenance	Instandhaltung	
Architect	Architekt	
Type	Typ	parkland
Relief	Begehbarkeit	
Water in play	Platz mit Wasser	
Exp. to wind	Wind ausgesetzt	
Trees in play	Platz mit Bäumen	

Scorecard Scorekarte	Chp. Chp.	Mens Herren	Ladies Damen
Length Länge	6210	6210	5375
Par	72	72	72

Advised golfing ability		0 12 24 36
Empfohlene Spielstärke		
Hcp required	Min. Handicap	no

CLUB HOUSE & AMENITIES
KLUBHAUS UND NEBENGEBÄUDE   **6**/10

Pro shop	Pro shop	
Driving range	Übungsplatz	
Sheltered	überdacht	8 mats
On grass	auf Rasen	yes
Putting-green	Putting-grün	yes
Pitching-green	Pitching-grün	yes

HOTEL FACILITIES
HOTEL BESCHREIBUNG   **7**/10

HOTELS HOTELS
Grand Hotel Sonnenbichl   Garmisch-Partenkirchen
93 rooms, D DM 250,-   7 km
Tel (49) 08821 - 7020, Fax (49) 08821 - 702 131

Reindl's Partenkirchner Hof   Garmisch-Partenkirchen
65 rooms, D DM 200,-   8 km
Tel (49) 08821 - 58 025, Fax (49) 08821 - 73 401

Tonihof   Eschenlohe
25 rooms, D DM 218,-   5 km
Tel (49) 08824 - 929 30, Fax (49) 08824 - 929 399

RESTAURANTS RESTAURANT
Husar   Garmisch-Partenkirchen
Tel (49) 08821 - 1713   8 km

Alpenhof   Garmisch-Partenkirchen
Tel (49) 08821 - 59 055   8 km

410

Der Turnierplatz (B + C) besteht aus 9 der 18 ursprünglichen Bahnen, sowie weiteren 9 Löchern, die 1993 fertiggestellt wurden. Der schöne A-Platz eignet sich für Spieler mit höherem Handicap. Dank der vorhandenen ‹bung-seinrichtungen (dazu gehören Indoor Driving Range und Putting Grün) zählt Gut Kaden zu den Anlagen gehobener Klasse. Der Fluss Pinnau durchquert das bei Nässe sehr gut abtrocknende Golfgelände, auf dem es sich zudem sehr angenehm läuft. Der Platz liegt ziemlich offen und ist gespickt mit vielen Wasserhindernissen (6 Löcher mit frontalem Wasser) sowie einer beträchtlichen Anzahl geschickt positionierter Bunker. Diese vielfältigen Gefahren sind jedoch gut erkennbar, so dass ein einziger Besuch genügt, den klug angelegten Spielbahnverlauf schätzen zu lernen, was allerdings nicht als Garantie für einen guten Score misszuverstehen ist. Die richtige Schlägerwahl ist hier ausschlaggebend, besonders beim Anspiel der grossflächigen Grüns, die teilweise auf mehreren Stufen angelegt und sehr gut verteidigt sind. Gutes Putten ist gefragt auf diesem Platz, den man spielen sollte, wenn man in der Nähe ist.

The championship course (B + C) is formed from 9 of the original 18 holes and from a further 9 holer completed in 1993. The pretty A course is more suitable for higher-handicappers. Gut Kaden as a whole is a class set-up, thanks in particular to the practice facilities (which include an indoor driving range and putting-green). Crossed by the river Pinnau, this is an estate that drains well and is pleasant to walk. The course is rather open and brings a large number of water hazards into play (6 holes feature frontal water) plus a considerable number of very well-sited bunkers. But these manifold hazards are clearly visible and a single visit is enough for a player to appreciate the intelligent design, if not to guarantee a good score. Here, the choice of club is of key importance, especially when approaching the large greens that are sometimes multi-tiered and very well-guarded. Make sure your putting is in good shape.

Gut Kaden Golf und Land Club — 1986

Kadener Strasse 9
D - 25486 ALVESLOHE

Office	Sekretariat	(49) 04193 - 99 290
Pro shop	Pro shop	(49) 04193 - 99 290
Fax	Fax	(49) 04193 - 992 919
Situation	Lage	

Quickborn (pop. 18 500), 5 km
Norderstedt (pop. 70 500), 10 km

Annual closure	Jährliche Schliessung	no
Weekly closure	Wöchentliche Schliessung	no

Fees main season
Preisliste hochsaison 18 holes

	Week days Woche	We/Bank holidays We/Feiertag
Individual Individuell	DM 70,-	DM 90,-
Couple Ehepaar	DM 140,-	DM 180,-

Monday (Montag): DM 40,- / under 21 years: – 50 %

Caddy	Caddy	no
Electric Trolley	Elektrokarren	no
Buggy	Elektrischer Wagen	no
Clubs	Leihschläger	no
Credit cards Kreditkarten		no

Access Zufahrt : A7 Hamburg-Kiel. Exit (Ausfahrt) Quickborn. Left → Ellerau, Kaltenkirchen. Right → Alveslohe. **Map 7 on page 372** Karte 7 Seite 372

GOLF COURSE
PLATZ **15**/20

Site	Lage	
Maintenance	Instandhaltung	
Architect	Architekt	Frank Pennink (A+B) Karl F. Grohs (C)
Type	Typ	open country
Relief	Begehbarkeit	
Water in play	Platz mit Wasser	
Exp. to wind	Wind ausgesetzt	
Trees in play	Platz mit Bäumen	

Scorecard Scorekarte	Chp. Chp.	Mens Herren	Ladies Damen
Length Länge	6516	6063	5285
Par	72	72	72

Advised golfing ability Empfohlene Spielstärke	0	12	24	36

Hcp required   Min. Handicap   36

CLUB HOUSE & AMENITIES
KLUBHAUS UND NEBENGEBÄUDE **7**/10

Pro shop	Pro shop	
Driving range	Übungsplatz	
Sheltered	überdacht	7 mats
On grass	auf Rasen	yes
Putting-green	Putting-grün	yes
Pitching-green	Pitching-grün	yes

HOTEL FACILITIES
HOTEL BESCHREIBUNG **6**/10

HOTELS HOTELS

Jagdhaus Waldfrieden   Quickborn
14 rooms, D DM 230,-   5 km
Tel (49) 04106 - 3771, Fax (49) 04106 - 69196

Landhaus Quickborn-Heide   Quickborn
18 rooms, D DM 175,-   3 km
Tel (49) 04106 - 76 660, Fax (49) 04106 - 74 969

Parkhotel   Norderstedt
78 rooms, D DM 200,-   20 km
Tel (49) 04052 - 656 0, Fax (49) 04052 -656 6400

RESTAURANTS RESTAURANT

Jagdhaus Waldfrieden   Quickborn
Tel (49) 04106 - 3771   5 km

Restaurant Scheelke   Henstedt-Ulzburg
Tel (49) 04193 - 2207   4 km

411

Man muss amriesigen Tor klingeln, damit man eingelassen werden, man muss sich auf eine saftige Rechnung im Restaurant, das einen Stern im Michelin Guide hat, einstellen (Sparsame können im Bistro speisen) und das teuerste Greenfee in Deutschland bezahlen. Aber das Geld ist gut angelegt: Gut Lärchenhof ist einer der eindrucksvollen neuen Plätze in Deutschland. Der Platz ist ein typisches Beispiel für die Arbeit des Architekten Jack Nicklaus. Wie immer bei Nicklaus findert man ein klares Layout mit sorgfältig angelegten Fairways, strategisch gut platzierten Bunkern, aber auch eine Tendenz alles zu auf kreative Art und Weise zu formen, auch wenn der Platz dann nicht mehr allzu natürlich wirkt oder sich harmonisch in die Landschaft fügt. Nicklaus macht Golf zu einem Spektakel, er entwirft Plätze auf den man den Ball mit unterschiedlichen Flugkurven ins Ziel steuern muss, wo man ein vorzügliches kurzes Spiel und ein guten Touch auf den Grüns haben muss, um einen guten Score zu erzielen. Gut Lärchenhof ist ein moderner Platz im wahrsten Sinne des Wortes, der aber trotzdem selbst für durchschnittliche Golfer gut spielbar ist.

You have to ring a bell to get in here, meet a sizeable bill in the restaurant (boasting a 1 star rating in the Michelin Guide) and pay the most expensive green-fees in Germany. But the money is well spend in one of the most prestigious new courses in recent years. It is a typical example of the work of its architect, Jack Nicklaus. Obviously you will discover the very strategic use of water and sandtraps, a crisp and clear design, very carefully laid-out fairways and a lot of emphasis on shaping everything on the course in an imaginative and also sometimes artificial style. Nothing is really very natural here or subtly blended into the natural surroundings. Nicklaus likes to turn golf into a spectacle, making each course a setting where you have to bend balls, possess an immaculately honed short game and a perfect putting stroke to card a score. Gut Lärchenhof is a modern course in every sense of the word, but is playable even by only very average golfers.

Golf Club Gut Lärchenhof		1997
Hahnenstrasse / Gut Lärchenhof		
D - 50259 PULHEIM		
Office	Sekretariat	(49) 02238 - 923 900
Pro shop	Pro shop	(49) 02238 - 923 170
Fax	Fax	(49)02238 - 923 9010
Situation	Lage	

Köln (pop. 1 005 000), 20 km

Annual closure	Jährliche Schliessung	no
Weekly closure	Wöchentliche Schliessung	no

Fees main season
Preisliste hochsaison 18 holes

	Week days Woche	We/Bank holidays We/Feiertag
Individual Individuell	DM 180,-	DM 180,-
Couple Ehepaar	DM 360,-	DM 360,-

We & holidays: with members (nur in Mitgliederbegleitung)

Caddy	Caddy	no
Electric Trolley	Elektrokarren	no
Buggy	Elektrischer Wagen	DM 50,-
Clubs	Leihschläger	yes

Credit cards Kreditkarten VISA - Eurocard - MasterCard

Access Zufahrt : A57, Exit (Ausf.)26 Köln-Worringen, →
Simmersdorf, → Stommeln, right →
Stommelerbusch. → Gut Lärchenhof
Map 3 on page 364 Karte 3 Seite 364

412

GOLF COURSE
PLATZ
17 /20

Site	Lage	
Maintenance	Instandhaltung	
Architect	Architekt	Jack Nicklaus
Type	Typ	open country
Relief	Begehbarkeit	
Water in play	Platz mit Wasser	
Exp. to wind	Wind ausgesetzt	
Trees in play	Platz mit Bäumen	

Scorecard Scorekarte	Chp. Chp.	Mens Herren	Ladies Damen
Length Länge	6408	6047	5210
Par	72	72	72

Advised golfing ability		0	12	24	36
Empfohlene Spielstärke					
Hcp required	Min. Handicap	24/28			

CLUB HOUSE & AMENITIES
KLUBHAUS UND NEBENGEBÄUDE
9 /10

Pro shop	Pro shop	
Driving range	Übungsplatz	
Sheltered	überdacht	7 mats
On grass	auf Rasen	yes
Putting-green	Putting-grün	yes
Pitching-green	Pitching-grün	yes

HOTEL FACILITIES
HOTEL BESCHREIBUNG
7 /10

HOTELS HOTELS

Ascari — Pulheim
70 rooms, D DM 225,- — 3 km
Tel (49) 02238 - 8040, Fax (49) 02238 - 804 140

Königsdorfer Hof — Frechen
37 rooms, D DM 226- — 6 km
Tel (49) 02234 - 600 70, Fax (49) 02234 - 600 770

Brauhaus Gäffel — Stommeln
18 rooms, D DM 128,- — 3 km
Tel (49) 02238 - 2015, Fax (49) 02238 - 3844

RESTAURANTS RESTAURANT

Restaurant Gut Lärchenhof — Golf
Tel (49) 02238 - 923 100 — on site

Ristorante Ermanno — Frechen
Tel(49) 02234 - 141 63 — 6 km

Früh am Dom — Köln
Tel (49) 0221 - 50 667 — 20 km

Ein Golfplatz für Sportliche, dessen Clubhaus und Einrichtungen bedauerlicherweise nicht den andernorts üblichen höheren Standards entsprechen. Da die Anlage noch relativ jung ist, bleibt zu hoffen, dass sich dies mit der Zeit ändern wird. Die Lage des Platzes ist eindrucksvoll: an klaren Tagen kann man bis zu 150 km weit sehen, insbesondere Richtung Deutsche Alpenstrasse im Süden, an deren Streckenverlauf von Lindau über Garmisch-Partenkirchen nach Salzburg die verrückten Schlösser Ludwigs II von Bayern einen Besuch lohnen. Architekt Rossknecht hat den weitgehend flachen Platz mit einer enormen Vielfalt an Hindernissen versehen, wobei alle Arbeiten mit der für ihn üblichen Sorgfalt ausgeführt wurden. Die Grüns sind ausgezeichnet gestaltet, besonders hervorzuheben ist in diesem Zusammenhang das Inselgrün am 18. Loch. Obschon eine harte Nuss von den hinteren Abschlägen, ist der Platz von weiter vorne durchaus für alle Spielstärken geeignet. Zwischen dem 5. und 17. Loch ändert sich der Charakter des Platzes von Parkland hin zu einem eher amerikanischen Stil, bei dem "target Golf" vom Spieler gefordert wird.

The sporting man's golf course where you might wonder why the clubhouse does not have higher standard facilities. However the course is still young. The location is rather remarkable: on a clear day you can see for 150 km, especially toward the Deutsche Alpenstrasse to the south, the road running from Lindau to Garmisch-Partenkirchen and Salzburg, where the crazy castles of Louis II of Bavaria are well worth a visit. The course has been designed on easily walkable terrain, with the usual care associated with a designer such as Rossknecht, who has included every hazard in the book. The greens are particularly well shaped, especially the island green on the 18th. A tough number from the back tees, the course gets a little more human the further forward you go, making it suitable for all levels. From the 5th to the 17th holes, you leave a park style landscape to encounter a more American style of course, where target golf is the order of the day.

Golfclub zu Gut Ludwigsberg 1988

Augsburgerstrasse 51
D - 86842 TÜRKHEIM

Office	Sekretariat	(49) 08245 - 3322
Pro shop	Pro shop	(49) 08245 - 3934
Fax	Fax	(49) 08245 - 3789
Situation	Lage	

Augsburg (pop. 265 000), 35 km - München, 50 km

Annual closure	Jährliche Schliessung	1/12 → 31/3
Weekly closure	Wöchentliche Schliessung	no

Fees main season
Preisliste hochsaison 18 holes

	Week days Woche	We/Bank holidays We/Feiertag
Individual Individuell	DM 70,-	DM 90,-
Couple Ehepaar	DM 140,-	DM 180,-

Caddy	Caddy	no
Electric Trolley	Elektrokarren	yes
Buggy	Elektrischer Wagen	yes
Clubs	Leihschläger	yes
Credit cards Kreditkarten		no

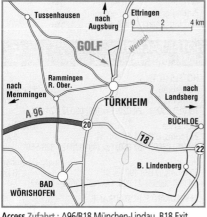

Access Zufahrt : A96/B18 München-Lindau. B18 Exit
(Ausf.) Türkheim-Bad Wörishofen. →
Ettringen/Schwabmünchen. → Golf
Map 2 on page 362 Karte 2 Seite 362

GOLF COURSE
PLATZ   15/20

Site	Lage	
Maintenance	Instandhaltung	
Architect	Architekt	Kurt Rossknecht
Type	Typ	open country, parkland
Relief	Begehbarkeit	
Water in play	Platz mit Wasser	
Exp. to wind	Wind ausgesetzt	
Trees in play	Platz mit Bäumen	

Scorecard	Chp.	Mens	Ladies
Scorekarte	Chp.	Herren	Damen
Length Länge	6159	5867	5395
Par	72	72	72

Advised golfing ability	0	12	24	36
Empfohlene Spielstärke				
Hcp required	Min. Handicap	no		

CLUB HOUSE & AMENITIES
KLUBHAUS UND NEBENGEBÄUDE   6/10

Pro shop	Pro shop	
Driving range	Übungsplatz	
Sheltered	überdacht	5 mats
On grass	auf Rasen	yes
Putting-green	Putting-grün	yes
Pitching-green	Pitching-grün	yes

HOTEL FACILITIES
HOTEL BESCHREIBUNG   6/10

HOTELS HOTELS

Kneipp Kurhotel Fontenay   Bad Wörishofen
60 rooms, D DM 250,-   9 km
Tel (49) 08247 - 3060, Fax (49) 08247 - 306 185

Kurhotel Edelweiss   Bad Wörishofen
52 rooms, D DM 180,-   9 km
Tel (49) 08247 - 35 010, Fax (49) 08247 - 350 175

Allgäuer Hof   Bad Wörishofen
36 rooms, D DM 150,-   9 km
Tel (49) 08247 - 96 990, Fax (49) 08247 - 969 960

Stadthotel - 44 rooms, D DM 160,-   Buchloe
Tel (49) 08241 - 5060, Fax (49) 08241 - 506 135   6 km

RESTAURANTS RESTAURANT

Mühlbach - Tel (49) 08247 - 6039 Bad Wörishofen 9 km

Jagdhof   Bad Wörishofen-Schlingen
Tel (49) 08247 - 4879   13 km

413

Thailing wirkt aufgrund seiner Nähe, demselben Architekten sowie dem Geländecharakter wie der zweieige Zwilling von Schloss Egmating. Nur das hier, insbesondere auf den zweiten 9 Löchern, weitaus öfter Wasser ins Spiel kommt, was diesem Platz einen ganz eigenständigen Charakter verleiht. Die Fairwaybunker sind aus genehmigungs-rechtlichen Gründen noch nicht mit Sand gefüllt, während die hervorragend geformten Grünbunker die sehr sorgfältig gestalteten Grüns (viele davon sind in mehreren Stufen angelegt) sehr wirkungsvoll verteidigen. Dies ist ein weitge-hend offener Golfplatz, dessen umfangreiche Neuanpflanzungen noch einige Jahre brauchen werden, bevor sie eine wirkliche Gefahr darstellen. Man benötigt einige Runden, um mit dem leicht hügeligen Gelände vertraut zu werden. Charakter und Schwierigkeit der Löcher, von denen einige auf Spieler mit hohem Handicap ziemlich einschüchternd wirken können, lassen sich durch mehrere zur Auswahl stehende Abschlag-Boxen verändern. Dies ist eine der viel-versprechendsten neuen Anlagen, die zudem bislang noch nicht überlaufen ist.

This is the false twin to Schloss Egmating through closeness, name of designer and character of terrain. Only here, there is much more water in play, emphatically so on one half of the course, thus giving it its own persona-lity. For administrative reasons, the fairway bunkers are still awaiting their sand, but their green-side counter-parts are well shaped and jealously guard the very carefully crafted putting surfaces (beware the multi-tiered greens). This is by and large an open space course with a lot of newly-planted saplings, which will need a number of years to grow into a real threat. While you need to play here several times to get to grips with a slightly hilly terrain (but never excessively so), the variety of tee-off areas also changes the character of holes, some of which are pretty intimidating for high-handicappers.

Golfclub Gut Thailing e.V. — 1994
Thailing 4
D - 85643 STEINHÖRIG

Office	Sekretariat	(49) 08094 - 9210
Pro shop	Pro shop	(49) 08094 - 9210
Fax	Fax	(49) 08094 - 9220
Situation	Lage	

München (pop. 1 300 000), 35 km
Ebersberg (pop. 10 000), 5 km

Annual closure	Jährliche Schliessung	no
Weekly closure	Wöchentliche Schliessung	no

Fees main season
Preisliste hochsaison 18 holes

	Week days Woche	We/Bank holidays We/Feiertag
Individual Individuell	DM 80,-	DM 100,-
Couple Ehepaar	DM 160,-	DM 200,-

Caddy	Caddy	no
Electric Trolley	Elektrokarren	no
Buggy	Elektrischer Wagen	DM 50,-
Clubs	Leihschläger	yes

Credit cards Kreditkarten Eurocard - Mastercard - AMEX

414

Access Zufahrt : München, A94 → Passau.
Forstinning, B12 → Passau.
Hohenlinden → Ebersberg. 5,5 km, left → Golf
Map 2 on page 363 Karte 2 Seite 363

GOLF COURSE
PLATZ — **16**/20

Site	Lage	▬▬▬▬▬▭
Maintenance	Instandhaltung	▬▬▬▬▬▭
Architect	Architekt	Kurt Rossknecht
Type	Typ	open country
Relief	Begehbarkeit	▬▬▬▭▭
Water in play	Platz mit Wasser	▬▬▬▭▭
Exp. to wind	Wind ausgesetzt	▬▬▭▭▭
Trees in play	Platz mit Bäumen	▬▬▬▭▭

Scorecard Scorekarte	Chp. Chp.	Mens Herren	Ladies Damen
Length Länge	6082	5788	5103
Par	72	72	72

Advised golfing ability		0 12 24 36
Empfohlene Spielstärke		▬▬▬▭
Hcp required	Min. Handicap	36

CLUB HOUSE & AMENITIES
KLUBHAUS UND NEBENGEBÄUDE — **7**/10

Pro shop	Pro shop	▬▬▬▬▭
Driving range	Übungsplatz	▬▬▬▭▭
Sheltered	überdacht	yes
On grass	auf Rasen	yes
Putting-green	Putting-grün	yes
Pitching-green	Pitching-grün	yes

HOTEL FACILITIES
HOTEL BESCHREIBUNG — **5**/10

HOTELS HOTELS
Hölzerbräu — Ebersberg
51 rooms, D DM 140,- — 5 km
Tel (49) 08092 - 24 020, Fax (49) 08092 - 24 031

Klostersee — Ebersberg
23 rooms, D DM 130,- — 5 km
Tel (49) 08092 - 82 850, Fax (49) 08092 - 828 550

Huber — Ebersberg-Oberndorf
50 rooms, D DM 190,- — 8 km
Tel (49) 08092 - 21 026, Fax (49) 08092 - 21 442

RESTAURANTS RESTAURANT
Hölzerbrau — Ebersberg
Tel (49) 08092 - 24 020 — 5 km

Klostersee — Ebersberg
Tel (49) 08092 - 82 850 — 5 km

GUT WALDHOF

In der Umgebung Hamburgs bietet Gut Waldhof eine vom Stil her eher amerikanische Alternative in manchmal hügeligem Gelände zu den bekannten Klassikern. Der Platz verlangt "target golf", insbesondere beim Anspielen der erhöhten und auf mehreren Stufen angelegte Grüns. Spieler, die "bump and run" Schläge bevorzugen, werden es hier schwer haben, doch letztendlich hilt die geforderte Erweiterung des Schlagrepertoires diesen, bessere Golfer zu werden. Die Schwierigkeiten sind gut über den Platz verteilt, wo leichtere Löcher, die zum Entspannen einladen, sich mit solchen abwechseln, an denen hohe Präzision gefordert wird. Manche Hindernisse stellen tatsächliche Gefahren dar, während andere eher psychologischer Natur sind. Dadurch entsteht ein gut ausbalancierter und abwechslungsreicher Gesamteindruck, der sowohl gute als auch weniger gute Spieler zufriedenstellt. Weniger geübten Golfern dürfte es dennoch schwerfallen, allen Anforderungen, die der zum Teil doch sehr anspruchsvollen Platz stellt, gerecht zu werden.

Alongside some of the great classic numbers in the region of Hamburg, Gut Waldhof is a rather American-style alternative where skills in so-called target golf are essential, especially to reach certain elevated and multi-tiered greens (the terrain is sometimes a little on the hilly side). Players who like to bump and run the ball are at a disadvantage here, but a change of habit can only make you a better golfer. Problems are well spread around the course and leave a few lighter breathing spaces between trickier holes, where precision is at a premium. While some hazards are really dangerous, others are more psychological in their intimidation. This leaves an overall impression of variety and balance and will satisfy both the very good and not so good player. The lesser golfers will, nonetheless, be hard pushed to adjust to what is sometimes a challenging layout.

Golfclub Gut Waldhof — 1970

Am Waldhof
D - 24629 KISDORFERWOHLD

Office	Sekretariat	(49) 04194 - 99 740
Pro shop	Pro shop	(49) 04194 - 1005
Fax	Fax	(49) 04194 - 1251
Situation	Lage	

Henstedt-Ulzburg (pop. 21 500), 5 km - Hamburg, 25 km

Annual closure	Jährliche Schliessung	no
Weekly closure	Wöchentliche Schliessung	Monday (Montag)

Fees main season
Preisliste hochsaison 18 holes

	Week days Woche	We/Bank holidays We/Feiertag
Individual Individuell	DM 50,-	DM 70,-
Couple Ehepaar	DM 100,-	DM 140,-

We: only with members (nur in Mitgliederbegleitung)

Caddy	Caddy	no
Electric Trolley	Elektrokarren	no
Buggy	Elektrischer Wagen	DM 50,-/18 holes
Clubs	Leihschläger	no
Credit cards Kreditkarten		no

Access Zufahrt : A7 Hamburg-Kiel. Exit (Ausf.) Kaltenkirchen. B433 → Henstedt Ulzburg. Left → Kisdorferwohld. Right on B432 → Golf
Map 7 on page 372 Karte 7 Seite 372

GOLF COURSE / PLATZ — 15/20

Site	Lage	
Maintenance	Instandhaltung	
Architect	Architekt	E. Jonson-Sedibe
Type	Typ	forest, parkland
Relief	Begehbarkeit	
Water in play	Platz mit Wasser	
Exp. to wind	Wind ausgesetzt	
Trees in play	Platz mit Bäumen	

Scorecard Scorekarte	Chp. Chp.	Mens Herren	Ladies Damen
Length Länge	6044	6044	5318
Par	72	72	72

Advised golfing ability Empfohlene Spielstärke	0	12	24	36
Hcp required Min. Handicap	36			

CLUB HOUSE & AMENITIES / KLUBHAUS UND NEBENGEBÄUDE — 7/10

Pro shop	Pro shop	
Driving range	Übungsplatz	
Sheltered	überdacht	8 mats
On grass	auf Rasen	yes
Putting-green	Putting-grün	yes
Pitching-green	Pitching-grün	yes

HOTEL FACILITIES / HOTEL BESCHREIBUNG — 5/10

HOTELS HOTELS
Hotel Restaurant Scheelke — Henstedt-Ulzburg
5 rooms, D DM 120,- — 5 km
Tel (49) 04193 - 2207, Fax (49) 04193 - 95 590

Schmöker Hof — Norderstedt
80 rooms, D DM 200,- — 10 km
Tel (49) 040 - 526 170, Fax (49) 040 - 526 2231

Tangstedter Mühle — Tangstedt
18 rooms, D DM 150,- — 20 km
Tel (49) 04109 - 279 00, Fax (49) 04109 - 279 013

RESTAURANTS RESTAURANT
Golf Club Restaurant — Gut Waldhof
Tel (49) 04194 - 1010

Hotel Restaurant Scheelke — Henstedt-Ulzburg
Tel (49) 04193 - 2207 — 5 km

415

GÜTERSLOH (WESTFÄLISCHER GC) 17 7 7

Der zwischen Birken und Eichen liegende Platz des Westfälische Golf clubs in Gütersloh geniesst zu recht einen beneidenswerten Ruf. Die Länge des Platzes flösst Respekt ein, ohne die Gesamtlänge eines der modernen Monster aufzuweisen. Doch die von herrlichen alten Bäumen gesäumten Fairways verlangen Präzision, dazu erschweren Wasserhindernisse (Teiche und Gräben) dem ehrgeizigen Golfer das Leben. Wer seine Schläge den vielen Doglegs anpassen kann, wer sicher einen Draw vom Abschlag spielen kann, ist im Vorteil, während der Fade beim Anspielen der grossen und gut verteidigten Gründs zu bevorzugen ist. Dieser Platz ist einer der besten Designs von Bernhard von Limburger, der in Gütersloh ein abwechslungsreiches Layout entwarf, das alle Bereiche des Spiels testet, ohne übermässig spektakulär zu wirken. Der gesamte Platz strahlt eine nüchterne Eleganz und viel Einfallsreichtum des Architekten aus. Dazu kommt noch die wunderschöne Umgebung, die Ruhe und Stille auf den Spielbahnen, die gut von einander getrennt sind.

Laid out amidst birch and oak trees, this course has gained an enviable reputation. The yardage commands respect without ever making this a modern-day monster course but the ever-present trees form a line of defence which calls for great accuracy, a feat that is not always compatible with big-hitting. What's more, water hazards tend to make life more complicated for the more ambitious golfer. There's no doubt that good benders of the ball will be in their element here; the few dog-legs provide the opportunity to show-off that well-honed draw from the tee before changing to fading the ball to pitch the huge and well-guarded greens. This is one of the great designs from Bernhard von Limburger, an excellent connoisseur of golf but no lover of the more decorative style of course. Everything here is very sober in a sort of austere elegance, yet there is no shortage of imagination in the layout. Add to this the beautiful surroundings, peace and quiet and the isolation of each hole and you will understand why this is a great classic course you can't miss.

Westfälischer Golf Club Gütersloh		1969
Gütersloherstrasse 127		
D - 33397 RIETBERG-VARENSELL		

Office	Sekretariat	(49) 05244 - 23 40
Pro shop	Pro shop	(49) 05244 - 18 45
Fax	Fax	(49) 05244 - 13 88
Situation	Lage	
Gütersloh (pop. 90 000), 8 km		
Annual closure	Jährliche Schliessung	no
Weekly closure	Wöchentliche Schliessung	no

Fees main season
Preisliste hochsaison 18 holes

	Week days Woche	We/Bank holidays We/Feiertag
Individual Individuell	DM 60,-	DM 80,-
Couple Ehepaar	DM 120,-	DM 160,-
under 21 years/Students: – 50 %		

Caddy	Caddy	no
Electric Trolley	Elektrokarren	
Buggy	Elektrischer Wagen	DM 50,-
Clubs	Leihschläger	DM 30,-
Credit cards Kreditkarten VISA - Eurocard - MasterCard		

416

Gütersloh
Hannover
Dortmund Essen
24
Veri
A 2
Varensell
GOLF
23
Lintel
Neuenkirchen
Rheda- -Wiedenbrück
Druffel
64
Bokel
Rietberg
0   2   4 km
Paderborn

Access Zufahrt : Hannover A2 → Ruhr. Exit (Ausf.) → Gütersloh. 3rd light, take left on Bruder-Konrad-Strasse, then right → Rietberg. 3.5 km, right → Golf.
Map 5 on page 369 Karte 5 Seite 369

GOLF COURSE / PLATZ 17/20

Site	Lage	
Maintenance	Instandhaltung	
Architect	Architekt	B. von Limburger
Type	Typ	parkland
Relief	Begehbarkeit	
Water in play	Platz mit Wasser	
Exp. to wind	Wind ausgesetzt	
Trees in play	Platz mit Bäumen	

Scorecard Scorekarte	Chp. Chp.	Mens Herren	Ladies Damen
Length Länge	6135	6135	5375
Par	72	72	72

Advised golfing ability
Empfohlene Spielstärke   0   12   24   36

Hcp required   Min. Handicap   35

CLUB HOUSE & AMENITIES / KLUBHAUS UND NEBENGEBÄUDE 7/10

Pro shop	Pro shop	
Driving range	Übungsplatz	
Sheltered	überdacht	6 mats
On grass	auf Rasen	yes
Putting-green	Putting-grün	yes
Pitching-green	Pitching-grün	yes

HOTEL FACILITIES / HOTEL BESCHREIBUNG 7/10

HOTELS HOTELS

Parkhotel Gütersloh — Gütersloh
103 rooms, D DM 260,- — 8 km
Tel (49) 05241 - 8770, Fax (49) 05241 - 877 400

Hotel Stadt Gütersloh — Gütersloh
55 rooms, D DM 245,- — 10 km
Tel (49) 05241 - 1050, Fax (49) 05241 - 105 100

Altdeutsche Gaststätte — Verl
45 rooms, D DM 185,- — 15 km
Tel (49) 05241 - 9660, Fax (49) 05241 - 966 299

RESTAURANTS RESTAURANT

Büdelsrestaurant-Bürmann's Hof — Verl
Tel (49) 05246 - 7970 — 15 km

Stadthalle — Gütersloh
Tel (49) 05241 - 864 269 — 10 km

HAMBURG-AHRENSBURG

16 **8** **7**

Das Original-Platzdesign von Bernhard von Limburger wurde 1977 von Robert Trent Jones leicht verändert. Diese Änderungen haben den Platz für den Durchschnittsgolfer nicht schwerer gemacht, wenngleich jetzt gelegentlich Wasser zu überwinden ist. Kein Par 4 erreicht 400 Meter, einige sind sogar recht kurz, so dass praktisch alle Eisen zum Einsatz kommen. Trotz des eher flachen Geländes gibt es zwei praktisch blinde Grüns, deren Anspiel "target Golf" erfordert. Diese Anforderung gilt im Grunde generell, da die Grüns durchgehend gut verteidigt sind. Dieser im amerikanischen Stil gestaltete Platz, bei dem alle Schwierigkeiten deutlich sichtbar sind, ist eingebettet in eine parkartige Landschaft, in der sich eine Anzahl exotischer Bäume findet. Auffallend ist auch der Abwechslungsreichtum der Löcher, von denen praktisch jedes auf unterschiedliche Art verteidigt wird, sei es in Form von Büschen, Bäumen, Bunkern und/oder Wasserhindernissen. Man braucht einen kühlen Kopf und gute Ballkontrolle, wenn man hier sein Handicap spielen will.

The original design by Bernhard von Limburger was slightly altered in 1977 by Robert Trent Jones. This has not made it any tougher for average players, even though there is now some water to cross. No one par 4 reaches 400 metres, and some are even short, thus allowing a wide choice of irons. Despite rather flat terrain, two greens are virtually blind and call for some target play, but this is a general feature here owing to the well-guarded greens. In a parkland landscape (with a number of exotic varieties of tree), this is a US-style course with difficulties for all to see. Also noteworthy is the variety of holes, with each having practically its own style of defence: bushes, trees, bunkers and/or water hazards. With a cool head and good ball control, you can hope to play to your handicap.

Golf Club Hamburg-Ahrensburg — 1964

Am Haidschlag 39-45
D - 22926 AHRENSBURG

Office	Sekretariat	(49) 04102 - 51 309
Pro shop	Pro shop	(49) 04102 - 57 626
Fax	Fax	(49) 04102 - 81 410
Situation	Lage	

Ahrensburg (pop. 27 000), 500 m - Hamburg, 20 km

Annual closure	Jährliche Schliessung	no
Weekly closure	Wöchentliche Schliessung	no

Monday (Montag): Restaurant closed

Fees main season
Preisliste hochsaison 18 holes

	Week days Woche	We/Bank holidays We/Feiertag
Individual Individuell	DM 70,-	DM 80,-
Couple Ehepaar	DM 140,-	DM 160,-

We: only with members (nur in Mitgliederbegleitung) → 10.00

Caddy	Caddy	on request
Electric Trolley	Elektrokarren	no
Buggy	Elektrischer Wagen	DM 50,-/18 holes
Clubs	Leihschläger	no
Credit cards Kreditkarten		no

Access Zufahrt : A1 Hamburg-Lübeck, Exit (Ausf.) Ahrensburg. B434 → Bargteheide. → Ammersbek. In Bunningstedt, Franz-Kruse-Strasse → "Siedlung Daheim". Am Haidschlag → Golf
Map 7 on page 372 Karte 7 Seite 372

GOLF COURSE
PLATZ

16/20

Site	Lage	▮▮▮▮▮▮▯
Maintenance	Instandhaltung	▮▮▮▮▮▮▯
Architect	Architekt	B. von Limburger
		R. Trent Jones
Type	Typ	parkland
Relief	Begehbarkeit	▮▮▯▯▯
Water in play	Platz mit Wasser	▮▮▮▯▯
Exp. to wind	Wind ausgesetzt	▮▮▯▯▯
Trees in play	Platz mit Bäumen	▮▮▮▮▯

Scorecard Scorekarte	Chp. Chp.	Mens Herren	Ladies Damen
Length Länge	5782	5782	5087
Par	71	71	71

Advised golfing ability	0	12	24	36
Empfohlene Spielstärke		▮▮▮▮▮▮		
Hcp required Min. Handicap	36			

CLUB HOUSE & AMENITIES
KLUBHAUS UND NEBENGEBÄUDE

8/10

Pro shop	Pro shop	▮▮▮▮▯
Driving range	Übungsplatz	▮▮▮▮▮
Sheltered	überdacht	6 mats
On grass	auf Rasen	no,
		10 mats open air
Putting-green	Putting-grün	yes
Pitching-green	Pitching-grün	yes

HOTEL FACILITIES
HOTEL BESCHREIBUNG

7/10

HOTELS HOTELS

Park Hotel Ahrensburg — Ahrensburg
24 rooms, D DM 200,- — 1 km
Tel (49) 04102 - 2300
Fax (49) 04102 - 230 100

Ring Hotel Ahrensburg — Ahrensburg
11 rooms, D DM 160,- — 2 km
Tel (49) 04102 - 51 560
Fax (49) 04102 - 515 656

RESTAURANTS RESTAURANT

Golf Club Restaurant — Golf
Tel (49) 04102 - 57 522 — on site

417

HAMBURG-HOLM

15 6 6

Dieser Golfplatz ist zwar einer der jüngsten Entwürfe von Donald Harradine, doch vermitteln Zustand und die etwas altmodische Platzarchitektur den Eindruck einer bereits viel älteren Anlage. Abgesehen von dem sehr dichten Rough sind die Hindernisse weder übermässig zahlreich noch sonderlich gefährlich. Der Platz wurde offensichtlich mehr mit Augenmerk auf den weniger erfahrenen Durchschnitts-Golfer entworfen, als für die besseren Spieler, denen es hier an Herausforderungen mangelt. Geübte Spieler können hier an ihrem Spiel arbeiten und dabei ohne grosse Anstrengung einen guten Score erzielen. Wir brauchen Plätze wie diesen. Sie bereiten deshalb soviel Vergnügen, weil man auf ihnen eine entspannte Runde Golf spielen kann, ohne das Spiel virtuos beherrschen zu müssen. Ein leicht begehbarer Platz, auf dem man an seinem Spiel feilen kann, bevor man technisch anspruchsvollere Plätze in Angriff nimmt.

This is one of Donald Harradine's latest designs, although the way the course is prepared and the presently rather unfashionable style give the impression of a layout that has been around for some time. So if we forget the thick rough, hazards are neither too numerous nor really dangerous. The course has visibly been designed more for inexperienced mid-handicappers than for the better players, who might find this too easy a challenge. The skilled golfer can check his game here and card a good score without too much effort. We need courses like this; they always provide a great deal of pleasure and make for golf that is all the more relaxing in that you don't need to flight the ball like a virtuoso. It is also a pleasant course to walk. A course for everyone where you can hone your game without too much danger before moving on to more technically demanding layouts.

Golfclub Hamburg-Holm — 1993

Haverkamp 1
D - 25488 HOLM

Office	Sekretariat	(49) 04103 - 91 330
Pro shop	Pro shop	(49) 04103 - 91 330
Fax	Fax	(49) 04103 - 91 330
Situation	Lage	

Hamburg (pop. 1 650 000), 12 km
Wedel (pop. 34 000), 6 km

Annual closure	Jährliche Schliessung	no
Weekly closure	Wöchentliche Schliessung	no

Monday (Montag): Restaurant closed

Fees main season
Preisliste hochsaison 18 holes

	Week days Woche	We/Bank holidays We/Feiertag
Individual Individuell	DM 65,-	DM 80,-
Couple Ehepaar	DM 130,-	DM 160,-

We: only with members (nur in Mitgliederbegleitung)

Caddy	Caddy	no
Electric Trolley	Elektrokarren	no
Buggy	Elektrischer Wagen	no
Clubs	Leihschläger	no

Credit cards Kreditkarten	no

418

Access Zufahrt : A23 Exit (Ausf.) Pinneberg Süd
→ Wedel. Right → Haseldorfer Marsch/Holm
(Lehmweg). 2 km, left (Haverkamp)
Map 7 on page 372 Karte 7 Seite 372

GOLF COURSE
PLATZ **15**/20

Site	Lage	
Maintenance	Instandhaltung	
Architect	Architekt	Donald Harradine
Type	Typ	moorland, country
Relief	Begehbarkeit	
Water in play	Platz mit Wasser	
Exp. to wind	Wind ausgesetzt	
Trees in play	Platz mit Bäumen	

Scorecard Scorekarte	Chp. Chp.	Mens Herren	Ladies Damen
Length Länge	6170	6075	5353
Par	72	72	72

Advised golfing ability		0 12 24 36
Empfohlene Spielstärke		
Hcp required	Min. Handicap	36

CLUB HOUSE & AMENITIES
KLUBHAUS UND NEBENGEBÄUDE **6**/10

Pro shop	Pro shop	
Driving range	Übungsplatz	
Sheltered	überdacht	3 mats
On grass	auf Rasen	yes
Putting-green	Putting-grün	yes
Pitching-green	Pitching-grün	yes

HOTEL FACILITIES
HOTEL BESCHREIBUNG **6**/10

HOTELS HOTELS

Hotel Senator — Wedel
46 rooms, D DM 178,- — 4 km
Tel (49) 04103 - 80 870, Fax (49) 04103 - 8077250

Hotel Diamant — Wedel
39 rooms, D DM 168,- — 5 km
Tel (49) 04103 - 702 600, Fax (49) 04103 - 702 700

Wedel Röhrig — Wedel
27 rooms, D DM 176,- — 5 km
Tel (49) 04103 - 913 60, Fax (49) 04103 - 913 613

RESTAURANTS RESTAURANT

Flic Flac Bistro — Hamburg
Tel (49) 040 - 865 345 — 10 km

Dal Fabbro — Hamburg
Tel (49) 040 - 868 941 — 11 km

HANAU-WILHELMSBAD

⅃ | **16** | **6** | **6**

Der Golfplatz wurde 1939 auf der ehemaligen Fasanenzuchtfarm der Familie Hesse errichtet, ganz in der Nähe von Schloss Wilhelmsbad, einem der zahlreichen Mineral- und Thermalkurorte dieser Gegend. Dieser alte Besitz verfügt über einen grosszügigen alten Baumbestand. Daher rührt auch der Eindruck eines gemütlichen Spaziergangs inmitten eines grossen Parks, den man während der Runde auf dem völlig ebenen Platz gewinnt, dessen 18 Loch ganz mühelos zu gehen sind. Dank ihres anspruchsvollen Layouts war die Anlage in der Vergangenheit mehrmals Austragungsort der Nationalen Offenen Deutschen Golf-Meisterschaften. Die guten Spieler werden versuchen den Amateur-Rekord von 70 Schlägen zu brechen, während die weniger Ehrgeizigen unter uns, von den vorderen Abschlägen aus, einen grossartigen Golftag verbringen können. Da die Runde von Bäumen und einer kleinen Anzahl gefährlicher Wasserhindernisse gewürzt wird, sollten sie nicht zögern, von den vorderen Abschlägen zu spielen. Dies gilt speziell an Loch 7, einem Par 5 von 570 Metern Länge.

This course was designed in 1959 on the former pheasant farm of the Hesse family, close to the castle of Wilhelmsbad, one of the many spas and hydrotherapy centres found in this part of the world. The estate is lavishly lined with old trees, whence the very pleasant impression of a lovely stroll in a huge park without any relief to speak of to stop you from walking the 18 holes. The layout is demanding enough for the National German Championships to have been held here several times, and while skilled players will relish the chance to attack the amateur record of 70, the less ambitious amongst us will play from the forward tees and spend a great day's golfing. The trees and a few dangerous water hazards tend to add a little spice to life, so don't shy away from playing the front tees, especially on the 7th hole, a par 5 of some 570 metres (600 yards plus). The course has no unfair difficulties.

Golf-Club Hanau-Wilhelmsbad e.V. 1959
Wilhelmsbader Allee 32
D - 63454 HANAU-WILHELMSBAD

Office	Sekretariat	(49) 06181 - 82 071
Pro shop	Pro shop	(49) 06181 - 81 775
Fax	Fax	(49) 06181 - 86 967
Situation	Lage	

Frankfurt (pop. 660 000), 20 km - Hanau (pop. 90 000), 3 km

Annual closure	Jährliche Schliessung	no
Weekly closure	Wöchentliche Schliessung	no

Monday (Montag): Restaurant closed

Fees main season
Preisliste hochsaison 18 holes

	Week days Woche	We/Bank holidays We/Feiertag
Individual Individuell	DM 80,-	DM 100,-
Couple Ehepaar	DM 160,-	DM 200,-

We/holidays : with members only (nur in Mitgliederbegleitung)

Caddy	Caddy	no
Electric Trolley	Elektrokarren	no
Buggy	Elektrischer Wagen	no
Clubs	Leihschläger	DM 30,-

Credit cards Kreditkarten — no

Access Zufahrt : Frankfurt, A66. Exit (Ausf.) Hanau Nord. Right on B8/40 until → Wilhelmsbad. 20 m, right (Wilhelmsbader Allee)
Map 3 on page 365 Karte 3 Seite 365

GOLF COURSE
PLATZ   16/20

Site	Lage	
Maintenance	Instandhaltung	
Architect	Architekt	Kothe
Type	Typ	Park
Relief	Begehbarkeit	
Water in play	Platz mit Wasser	
Exp. to wind	Wind ausgesetzt	
Trees in play	Platz mit Bäumen	

Scorecard Scorekarte	Chp. Chp.	Mens Herren	Ladies Damen
Length Länge	6227	6227	5497
Par	73	73	73

Advised golfing ability		0	12	24	36
Empfohlene Spielstärke					

Hcp required Min. Handicap — 32, We: 28

CLUB HOUSE & AMENITIES
KLUBHAUS UND NEBENGEBÄUDE   6/10

Pro shop	Pro shop	
Driving range	Übungsplatz	
Sheltered	überdacht	5 mats
On grass	auf Rasen	yes
Putting-green	Putting-grün	yes
Pitching-green	Pitching-grün	yes

419

HOTEL FACILITIES
HOTEL BESCHREIBUNG   6/10

HOTELS HOTELS
Golfhotel   Golf
7 rooms, D DM 180,-
Tel (49) 06181 - 995 511Brüder-Grimm Hotel   Hanau
95 rooms, D DM 200,-   5 km
Tel (49) 06181 - 30 60, Fax (49) 06181 - 306 512

Villa Stokkum   Hanau-Steinheim
134 rooms, D DM 245,-   5 km
Tel (49) 06181 - 66 40, Fax (49) 06181 - 66 1580

RESTAURANTS RESTAURANT
Brüder-Grimm Hotel   Hanau
Tel (49) 06181 - 33 838   5 km

Der 1923 gebaute Platz wurde später von Bernhard von Limburger umgestaltet, der seine klassische Handschrift hinterliess. Diese zeigt sich in einem klugen Platzdesign, das sich auszeichnet durch die ebenso angemessene wie geschickte Verwendung von Hindernissen, deren Plazierung gute Schläge nicht betraft. Die Lärmbelästigung durch die nahegelegene Autobahn Köln - Hannover wird von den vielen Bäumen etwas gedämpft. Davon abgesehen lohnt sich der Besuch der insgesamt ausgezeichneten Anlage unbedingt. Die bereits erwähnten Bäume erfordern gerade Schläge, um die engen Fairways zu treffen; vielfach ist man sogar gezwungen, einen Fade oder Draw zu spielen, um in die beste Position zu gelangen. Die ziemlich flachen, gut gestalteten Grüns werden von einer Reihe, teilweise sehr tiefer Bunker verteidigt. Die erforderliche Spielstrategie ist offensichtlich, so dass man schon auf der ersten Runde hoffen kann, einen guten Score zu erzielen. Hannover ist einer der besten Plätze der Region und abwechslungsreich genug, um auch bei mehrmaligem Spielen interessant zu bleiben.

Designed in 1923, the course was reshaped by Bernhard von Limburger, who has left his own, very classical stamp with a sensible layout and reasonable use of hazards, always well placed but not too penalizing for good shots. The one regret is the closeness of the Cologne-Hannover motorway, but the general excellence of the course makes it well worth visiting, and the very many trees do tend to dampen the noise somewhat. On the downside, these same trees leave the fairways rather narrow, hence the need to play straight or even flight the ball with fade and draw shots to get into the best position. The greens are well designed and relatively flat, but are protected by a host of bunkers, some of which are often very deep. Game strategy is pretty obvious to try and return a goodish card first time out, and the course is varied enough to keep it interesting. This is one of the region's best courses.

Golf-Club Hannover e.V.   1923
Am Blauen See 120
D - 30823 GARBSEN

Office	Sekretariat	(49) 05137 - 73 068
Pro shop	Pro shop	(49) 05137 - 71 004
Fax	Fax	(49) 05137 - 75 851
Situation	Lage	

Hannover (pop. 510 000), 15 km

Annual closure	Jährliche Schliessung	1/1 → 31/1
Weekly closure	Wöchentliche Schliessung	Monday (Montag)

Fees main season
Preisliste hochsaison full day

	Week days Woche	We/Bank holidays We/Feiertag
Individual Individuell	DM 60,-	DM 80,-
Couple Ehepaar	DM 120,-	DM 1460,-

under 21 years, Students : – 50 %

Caddy	Caddy	no
Electric Trolley	Elektrokarren	no
Buggy	Elektrischer Wagen	yes
Clubs	Leihschläger	yes
Credit cards Kreditkarten		no

420

Access Zufahrt : Hannover, Westschnellweg.
Exit (Ausf.) Herrenhausen.
A2 until Rasthaus «Blauer See». 1,5 km, Golf South of A2
Map 5 on page 369 Karte 5 Seite 369

GOLF COURSE
PLATZ   **16**/20

Site	Lage	
Maintenance	Instandhaltung	
Architect	Architekt	B. von Limburger
Type	Typ	country, forest
Relief	Begehbarkeit	
Water in play	Platz mit Wasser	
Exp. to wind	Wind ausgesetzt	
Trees in play	Platz mit Bäumen	

Scorecard Scorekarte	Chp. Chp.	Mens Herren	Ladies Damen
Length Länge	5846	5681	4994
Par	71	71	71

Advised golfing ability		0 12 24 36
Empfohlene Spielstärke		
Hcp required	Min. Handicap	34

CLUB HOUSE & AMENITIES
KLUBHAUS UND NEBENGEBÄUDE   **7**/10

Pro shop	Pro shop	
Driving range	Übungsplatz	
Sheltered	überdacht	3 mats
On grass	auf Rasen	June → Sept.
Putting-green	Putting-grün	yes
Pitching-green	Pitching-grün	yes

HOTEL FACILITIES
HOTEL BESCHREIBUNG   **7**/10

HOTELS HOTELS
Maritim Grand Hotel Hannover   Hannover
285 rooms, D DM 400,-   15 km
Tel (49) 0511 - 97 370, Fax (49) 0511 - 325195

Landhaus am See   Garbsen-Berenbostel
37 rooms, D DM 200,-   3 km
Tel (49) 05131 - 46 860, Fax (49) 05131 - 468 666

Hotel Wildhage   Garbsen-Hevelse
30 rooms, D DM 200,-   2 km
Tel (49) 05137 - 75 033, Fax (49) 05137 - 75 401

RESTAURANTS RESTAURANT
Landhaus Ammann   Hannover
Tel (49) 0511 - 830 818   15 km

Gattopardo   Hannover
Tel (49) 0511 - 14 375   15 km

HECHINGEN-HOHENZOLLERN 14 6 6

Die Nähe zum Schloss der Hohenzollern - dessen Lage weitaus beeindruckender ist als die nicht so alten Gebäude - haben viel zum Ruf und Bekanntheitsgrad dieses Golfplatzes beigetragen. Seine idyllische Lage ist für viele, in dieser Hinsicht empfängliche Golfer, ein stichhaltiger Grund, hier zu spielen. Wer seine Aufmerksamkeit von der Umgebung dem Platz zuwendet, entdeckt einen hübschen Platz mit engen, häufig baumbestandenen Fairways und einer Anzahl gefährlicher Büsche, welche die Hauptschwierigkeit dieser Anlage darstellen. Zwar gibt es auch Fairway- und Grünbunker, jedoch sind diese nicht wirklich gefährlich genug, um gute Spieler ernsthaft daran hindern zu können, die wohlproportionierten, leicht modellierten Grüns anzuspielen. Geeignet für alle Spielklassen, fehlt es diesem Platz ein wenig an Charakter, um den besseren Spielern auch langfristig Vergnügen zu bereiten. Beim Bau der Anlage stand sicherlich im Vordergrund, dass golfende Familien hier Spass haben sollen.

Being so close to the castle of Hohenzollern (even though the site is more impressive than the not-so-old buildings) has done much for the reputation and recognition of this course. Its idyllic setting is also a sound argument for players who are sensitive to this particular aspect of golf. If you can tear your eyes away from the surroundings, you are left facing a pretty course with narrow fairways often protected by trees and, above all, some dangerous bushes, which form the main hazard. The fairway and green-side bunkers are there all right, but are not really dangerous enough to worry good players unduly and prevent them from homing in on nicely-sized and discreetly contoured greens. Accessible to players of all abilities, this course is a little too short of personality to keep the better players happy for too long. Working for the enjoyment of family golf was certainly a major consideration when designing the course.

Golf Club Hechingen-Hohenzollern 1955
Auf dem Hagelwasen, Postfach 1124
D - 72379 HECHINGEN

Office	Sekretariat	(49) 07471 - 2600
Pro shop	Pro shop	(49) 07471 - 62 272
Fax	Fax	(49) 07471 - 14 776
Situation	Lage	

Hechingen (pop. 16 600), 2 km
Tübingen (pop. 82 000), 25 km

Annual closure	Jährliche Schliessung	1/11 → 31/3
Weekly closure	Wöchentliche Schliessung	no

Monday (Montag): Restaurant closed

Fees main season
Preisliste hochsaison full day

	Week days Woche	We/Bank holidays We/Feiertag
Individual Individuell	DM 60,-	DM 80,-
Couple Ehepaar	DM 120,-	DM 160,-
under 21 years/Students : – 50%		
Caddy	Caddy	no
Electric Trolley	Elektrokarren	yes
Buggy	Elektrischer Wagen	no
Clubs	Leihschläger	DM 10,-
Credit cards Kreditkarten		no

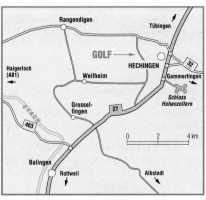

Access Zufahrt : Stuttgart, B27. Tübingen B27
→ Balingen. Hechingen → Burg Hohenzollern,
→ Hechingen-Weilheim, → Golf
Map 1 on page 361 Karte 1 Seite 361

GOLF COURSE / PLATZ 14/20

Site	Lage	
Maintenance	Instandhaltung	
Architect	Architekt	
Type	Typ	open country, hilly
Relief	Begehbarkeit	
Water in play	Platz mit Wasser	
Exp. to wind	Wind ausgesetzt	
Trees in play	Platz mit Bäumen	

Scorecard Scorekarte	Chp. Chp.	Mens Herren	Ladies Damen
Length Länge	6064	6064	5346
Par	72	72	72

Advised golfing ability	0	12	24	36
Empfohlene Spielstärke				
Hcp required Min. Handicap	36			

CLUB HOUSE & AMENITIES / KLUBHAUS UND NEBENGEBÄUDE 6/10

Pro shop	Pro shop	
Driving range	Übungsplatz	
Sheltered	überdacht	6 mats
On grass	auf Rasen	yes (April → Oct.)
Putting-green	Putting-grün	yes
Pitching-green	Pitching-grün	yes

421

HOTEL FACILITIES / HOTEL BESCHREIBUNG 6/10

HOTELS HOTELS
Hotel Brielhof — Hechingen
25 rooms, D DM 200,- — 5 km
Tel (49) 07471 - 4097, Fax (49) 07471 - 16 908

Café Klaiber — Hechingen
28 rooms, D DM 140,- — 3 km
Tel (49) 07471 - 2257, Fax (49) 07471 - 13 918

Stadt Balingen — Balingen
59 rooms, D DM 190,- — 10 km
Tel (49) 07433 - 8021, Fax (49) 07433 - 5119

Domizil — Tübingen
80 rooms, D DM 180,- — 25 km
Tel (49) 07071 - 1390, Fax (49) 07071 - 139 250

RESTAURANTS RESTAURANT
Waldhorn - Tel (49) 07071 - 61 270 — Tübingen 30 km
Rosenau - Tel (49) 07071 - 66 466 — Tübingen 25 km

Dieser erst kürzlich fertiggestellte Golfplatz wird noch ein paar Jahre benötigen, bis er sein volles Potential entfaltet hat, dennoch ist sein jetziger Zustand bereits recht vielversprechend. Angelegt auf leicht hügeligem Gelände, von dem man schöne Blicke auf den Höhenzug der Schwäbischen Alb hat, ist es dem Architekten gelungen, einen Platz zu bauen, dessen Schwierigkeiten gut erkennbar sind, so dass die Spieler sehr schnell die richtige Taktik herausfinden können, um hier einen guten Score zu erzielen. Alles in allem ist der Platz nicht sehr schwierig, so dass es jedem möglich sein sollte, sein Handicap zu spielen. Letzteres dürfte nur dann schwieriger werden, wenn der Wind bläst, da in dem Fall die exponierte Lage des Platzes zum Tragen kommt. Nur dann wird es wirklich nötig, auch die Flugkurve des Balles etwas zu steuern, da selbst die Roughzonen insgesamt eher harmlos sind. Das "Vorzeige-Loch" ist die 17, ein Par 3 von 117 Metern Länge, bei dem ein 70 Meter tiefer gelegenes Grün über ein frontales Wasserhindernis anzuspielen ist. Hetzenhof präsentiert sich als netter, schnörkeloser Platz.

This very recent course will need a few years to mellow before settling into its final physiognomy, but already it promises a great deal. Over a moderately hilly site, with pretty vistas over the "Schwäbische Alb" mountains, the designer has come up with a course where the main difficulties are clearly visible, so that players can quickly grasp the ideal tactics and hope to card some good scores. After all, proportionally speaking this is not a tough course, and anyone can look forward to playing to his or her handicap. This might not be the case if the wind begins to blow, because there's nothing much here to stop it. This is the only time when you need to flight the ball a little, as elsewhere the rough is, on the whole, pretty friendly. The signature hole is the 17th, a 117-metre par 3 with a water hazard in front of the hole, 70 metres downhill. A pleasant and unpretentious course.

Golfclub Hetzenhof e.V.   1995

Hetzenhof 7
D - 73547 LORCH

Office	Sekretariat	(49) 07172 - 9180-13
Pro shop	Pro shop	(49) 07172 - 91800
Fax	Fax	(49) 07172 - 9180-30
Situation	Lage	

Göppingen (pop. 55 000), 10 km
Stuttgart (pop. 559 000), 40 km

Annual closure	Jährliche Schliessung	1/12 → 31/3
Weekly closure	Wöchentliche Schliessung	no

Monday (Montag): Restaurant closed

Fees main season
Preisliste hochsaison 18 holes

	Week days Woche	We/Bank holidays We/Feiertag
Individual Individuell	DM 80,-	DM 80,-
Couple Ehepaar	DM 160,-	DM 160,-

We: with members (nur in Mitgliederbegleitung)

Caddy	Caddy	no
Electric Trolley	Elektrokarren	no
Buggy	Elektrischer Wagen	no
Clubs	Leihschläger	DM 20,-

Credit cards Kreditkarten   no

422

Access Zufahrt : Stuttgart, B29 → Aalen. Exit (Ausf.)
Loch. B927 → Göppingen. → Golf (5 km).
Map 1 on page 361 Karte 1 Seite 361

GOLF COURSE
PLATZ   14/20

Site	Lage	
Maintenance	Instandhaltung	
Architect	Architekt	Dieter Sziedat
Type	Typ	open country, hilly
Relief	Begehbarkeit	
Water in play	Platz mit Wasser	
Exp. to wind	Wind ausgesetzt	
Trees in play	Platz mit Bäumen	

Scorecard Scorekarte	Chp. Chp.	Mens Herren	Ladies Damen
Length Länge	6135	6135	5407
Par	72	72	72

Advised golfing ability		0	12	24	36
Empfohlene Spielstärke					
Hcp required	Min. Handicap	no			

CLUB HOUSE & AMENITIES
KLUBHAUS UND NEBENGEBÄUDE   7/10

Pro shop	Pro shop	
Driving range	Übungsplatz	
Sheltered	überdacht	10 mats
On grass	auf Rasen	yes (April-Sept.)
Putting-green	Putting-grün	yes
Pitching-green	Pitching-grün	yes

HOTEL FACILITIES
HOTEL BESCHREIBUNG   6/10

HOTELS HOTELS
Hohen Linde   Lorch
18 rooms, D DM 100,-   500 m
Tel (49) 07172 - 7443Hotel Sonne   Lorch
25 rooms, D DM 110,-   8 km
Tel (49) 07172 - 7373, Fax (49) 07172 - 8377

Hohenstaufen   Göppingen
50 rooms, D DM 180,-   10 km
Tel (49) 07161 - 6700, Fax (49) 07161 - 70 070

Becher - 65 rooms, D DM 200,-   Donzdorf
Tel (49) 07162 - 20 050, Fax (49) 07162 - 200 555 23 km

RESTAURANTS RESTAURANT
Becher Restaurant de Balzac   Donzdorf
Tel (49) 07162 - 20 050   23 km
Burgrestaurant Staufeneck   Salach 18 km
Tel (49) 07162 - 5028

HOF TRAGES

15 **7** **5**

Kurt Rossknecht hat seinen Ruf als einer der kreativsten Golf-Architekten Europas mit dieser ausgezeichneten Anlage untermauert, die sich als perfekte Ergänzung zu einem der beeindruckendsten Clubhäuser Deutschlands erweist. Der leicht hügelige Platz leugnet nicht die amerikanischen Einflüsse, welche besonders an einer Vielzahl von Wasserhindernissen deutlich werden, die den Spielern, neben einigen durch den Wald verlaufenden Spielbahnen, die grössten Probleme bereiten. Obschon die Schwierigkeiten klar erkennbar sind, muss man doch einige Runden hier spielen, um die vorhandenen strategischen Fallen genau auszumachen. Der Platz ist nicht übermässig lang, so dass Spieler aller Kategorien hier einen schönen Golftag verleben können, sofern sie sich darauf konzentrieren ihr Handicap zu spielen, und keine Schläge unnötig verschenken. Die Grüns sind von guter Qualität, wie auch die gesamte Anlage bereits gut eingewachsen ist. Am 18 Loch, einem schwierigen Par 3, muss man acht geben in Hessen zu bleiben .Wer hier sliced, findet seinen Ball wahrhaft "out of bounds" - nämlich im benachbarten Bayern.

Designer Kurt Rossknecht has asserted his status as one of the most creative course architects in Europe, and this good layout is the perfect complement to one of Germany's most impressive club-houses. Over averagely hilly terrain, the course doesn't try to hide its American influence, and water hazards abound as an obvious danger alongside the stretches through the forest. Even though the difficulties are clearly seen, you need to play the course several times to get a clear picture of the strategic traps. It is not excessively long and players of all levels can spend a good day's golfing if they don't throw strokes away and concentrate on keeping to their handicap. The greens are good and the course has already matured nicely. At the 18th, a tough par 3, be careful to stay in Hesse... if you slice, you will find your ball out of bounds in neighbouring Bavaria!

Golfclub Hof Trages — 1994

Hofgut Trages
D - 65379 FREIGERICHT

Office	Sekretariat	(49) 06055 - 91 380
Pro shop	Pro shop	(49) 06055 - 993 818
Fax	Fax	(49) 06055 - 913 891
Situation	Lage	

Hanau (pop. 90 000), 25 km - Frankfurt (pop. 660 000), 35 km

Annual closure	Jährliche Schliessung	no
Weekly closure	Wöchentliche Schliessung	no

Fees main season
Preisliste hochsaison 18 holes

	Week days Woche	We/Bank holidays We/Feiertag
Individual Individuell	DM 80,-	DM 100,-
Couple Ehepaar	DM 160,-	DM 200,-

under 21 years / Students: DM 35,-

Caddy	Caddy	on request
Electric Trolley	Elektrokarren	no
Buggy	Elektrischer Wagen	DM 50,-
Clubs	Leihschläger	DM 40,-

Credit cards Kreditkarten
VISA - Eurocard - MasterCard - AMEX

Access Zufahrt : A66 Frankfurt → Gelnhausen.
Exit (Ausf.) Erlensee → Rodenbach
→ Niederrodenbach, Oberrodenbach. Golf 3 km
Map 3 on page 365 Karte 3 Seite 365

GOLF COURSE / PLATZ — 15/20

Site	Lage	
Maintenance	Instandhaltung	
Architect	Architekt	Kurt Rossknecht
Type	Typ	parkland, open country
Relief	Begehbarkeit	
Water in play	Platz mit Wasser	
Exp. to wind	Wind ausgesetzt	
Trees in play	Platz mit Bäumen	

Scorecard Scorekarte	Chp. Chp.	Mens Herren	Ladies Damen
Length Länge	5893	5512	4827
Par	71	69	69

Advised golfing ability
Empfohlene Spielstärke — 0 12 24 36

Hcp required Min. Handicap — 36, We: 28

CLUB HOUSE & AMENITIES / KLUBHAUS UND NEBENGEBÄUDE — 7/10

Pro shop	Pro shop	
Driving range	Übungsplatz	
Sheltered	überdacht	8 mats
On grass	auf Rasen	yes
Putting-green	Putting-grün	yes
Pitching-green	Pitching-grün	yes

HOTEL FACILITIES / HOTEL BESCHREIBUNG — 5/10

HOTELS HOTELS

Herrenmühle — Michelbach
28 rooms, D DM 160,- — 7 km
Tel (49) 06023 - 5080
Fax (49) 06023 - 3313

Brüder-Grimm-Hotel — Hanau
95 rooms, D DM 200,- — 25 km
Tel (49) 06181 - 3060
Fax (49) 06181 - 306 512

RESTAURANTS RESTAURANT

Hof Trages Restaurant — Golfplatz
Tel (49) 06055 - 91 380 — on site

Öhlmühle — Mömbris
Tel (49) 06029 - 9500 — 15 km

423

Höhenpähl liegt in einer Parklandschaft zwischen Ammersee und Starnberger See. Trotz der hügeligen Landschaft hat sich Architekt Kurt Rossknekt bemüht, blinde Löcher möglichst zu vermeiden, was ihm aufgrund der Topographie aber nicht immer gelang. Die gesamte Anlage strahlt viel Ruhe aus, ab und an überquert Wild die Fairways. An Löchern, an denen Bäume und Wasser bereits genug Gefahr darstellen, erschweren nicht noch zusätzlich Bunker das Spiele. Ungeübten Spielern werden im Verlauf der Runde, die eine Vielzahl von Problemen für sie bereithält, deutlich ihre Schwächen aufgezeigt. Dieser meist recht enge Platz verlangt vom Spieler sehr kontrolliertes Golf. Erwähnenswert ist auch die "Ehrlichkeit" des Layouts, abgesehen vom 4. Loch, wo ein vom Abschlag aus nicht sichtbarer Graben das Fairway in Höhe der Drive-Landezone kreuzt. Hohenpähl ist zwar anspruchsvoll, jedoch kein "Monsterplatz". Daher ist Loch 8, die schwerste Bahn des Platzes, an der Bogey ein gutes Ergebnis ist, eher die Ausnahme.

Hohenpähl is located in a park land setting between Ammersee and Starnberger See, two of the most beautiful lakes in Bavaria. In spite of the hilly terrain architect Kurt Rossknecht tried everything to avoid blind holes, but the topography decided otherwise. The site is haven of tranquillity, as the rabbits and deer seem to sense as they bound across the fairways. There are no needless traps here: when the trees and water present an obvious danger, this is never compounded by the addition of bunkers. Inexperienced players will certainly encounter a few problems on the way, but they will also get an insight into their weaknesses. This often narrow course demands good control over your game and its honesty deserves a definite mention, except on the 4th hole where a concealed ditch crosses exactly where the drive should land. Although demanding, Hohenpähl is no monster and only the 8th is really tough going. It's a par 4 but the bogey will do nicely. Well worth knowing.

Golf Club Hohenpähl — 1988
D - 82396 PÄHL

Office	Sekretariat	(49) 08808 - 920 20
Pro shop	Pro shop	(49) 08808 - 1308
Fax	Fax	(49) 08808 - 920 222

Situation Lage
München (pop. 1 300 000), 44 km
Weilheim (pop. 18 500), 9 km

Annual closure	Jährliche Schliessung	1/11 → 31/3
Weekly closure	Wöchentliche Schliessung	no

Fees main season
Preisliste hochsaison 18 holes

	Week days Woche	We/Bank holidays We/Feiertag
Individual Individuell	DM 90,-	DM 110,-
Couple Ehepaar	DM 180,-	DM 220,-

We: with members (nur in Mitgliederbegleitung)
under 21 years / Students: - 50%

Caddy	Caddy	on request
Electric Trolley	Elektrokarren	DM 25,-
Buggy	Elektrischer Wagen	no
Clubs	Leihschläger	DM 25,-

Credit cards Kreditkarten — no

424

Access Zufahrt : München, A99 → Garmisch-Partenkirchen. Exit (Ausf.) Starnberg. In Starnberg, B2 → Weilheim. Km 41, turn right → Pähl → Golf
Map 2 on page 362 Karte 2 Seite 362

GOLF COURSE
PLATZ — **15**/20

Site	Lage	
Maintenance	Instandhaltung	
Architect	Architekt	Kurt Rossknecht
Type	Typ	forest, parkland
Relief	Begehbarkeit	
Water in play	Platz mit Wasser	
Exp. to wind	Wind ausgesetzt	
Trees in play	Platz mit Bäumen	

Scorecard Scorekarte	Chp. Chp.	Mens Herren	Ladies Damen
Length Länge	6080	5765	5158
Par	71	71	71

Advised golfing ability	0	12	24	36
Empfohlene Spielstärke				

Hcp required Min. Handicap 36

CLUB HOUSE & AMENITIES
KLUBHAUS UND NEBENGEBÄUDE — **7**/10

Pro shop	Pro shop	
Driving range	Übungsplatz	
Sheltered	überdacht	yes
On grass	auf Rasen	yes
Putting-green	Putting-grün	yes
Pitching-green	Pitching-grün	yes

HOTEL FACILITIES
HOTEL BESCHREIBUNG — **6**/10

HOTELS HOTELS
Kaiserin Elisabeth — Feldafing
70 rooms, D DM 180,- — 15 km
Tel (49) 08157 - 930 90, Fax (49) 08157 -930 9133

Engelhof — Tutzing
12 rooms, D DM 150,- — 4 km
Tel (49) 08158 - 30 61, Fax (49) 08158 - 67 85

Ammersee Hotel — Hersching
40 rooms, D DM 195,- — 20 km
Tel (49) 08152 - 968 70, Fax (49) 08152 - 53 74

RESTAURANTS RESTAURANT
Seehaus — Diessen-Riederau
Tel (49) 08807 - 7300 — 12 km

Forsthaus Ilkahöhe — Tutzing
Tel (49) 08158 - 8242 — 12 km

HUBBELRATH

Hubbelrath gehört zu den Plätzen in Deutschland, die jeder kennen sollte. Er ist gleichzeitig eines der besten Beispiele für das Können Bernhard von Limburgers, dessen Kunst, sich das hier ziemlich hügelige Gelände zunutze zu machen, von wirklich grosser Inspiration zeugt. Aufgrund teilweise nicht immer erkennbarer Schwierigkeiten ist dies ein Platz für erfahrene Spieler. Eine gute Ballkontrolle vorausgesetzt, werden diese mit den Hindernissen besser zurechtkommen als der Rest, auch deswegen, weil sie sich von den vielen blinden Schlägen und Grüns weniger einschüchtern lassen. Die Hindernisse sind ebenso zahlreich wie gefährlich und können den Eindruck eines tückischen Platzes vermitteln. Man braucht schon einige Runden, um den Platz einigermassen in den Griff zu bekommen, was aber angesichts des Vergnügens hier zu spielen, leicht zu verschmerzen ist. Abgeschirmt von der Hektik Düsseldorfs, befindet sich der Platz in erhöhter Lage auf einem bewaldeten Hügel, von wo sich schöne Blicke auf Düsseldorf und Ratingen eröffnen. Hubbelrath offeriert in schöner Umgebung eine sportliche Herausforderung ersten Ranges.

This is one of Germany's courses that everyone should know, and one of the finest testimonies to the skill of Bernhard von Limburger, whose use of a rather hilly terrain can only be described as truly inspired. The sometimes concealed difficulties make this a layout reserved for experienced players; if they know how to control the ball, they will cope with the hazards better than the rest and, importantly, will be somewhat less intimidated by a number of blind shots and greens. The hazards are as numerous as they are truly dangerous and can give you the impression of playing a treacherous course. You certainly need to play several rounds to get to grips with it, but it is always a pleasure to come back here. Sheltered from the rumbling of nearby Düsseldorf, its elevated location on a wood-covered hill provides some fine views over Düsseldorf and Ratingen. Hubbelrath is a lovely walk and an exciting challenge of the highest order.

Golf Club Hubbelrath e.V.　1964

Bergische Landtrasse 700
D - 40629 DÜSSELDORF

Office	Sekretariat	(49) 02104 - 72 178
Pro shop	Pro shop	(49) 02104 - 72 178
Fax	Fax	(49) 02104 - 72 178
Situation	Lage	

Düsseldorf (pop. 570 000), 15 km - Mettmann, 2 km

Annual closure	Jährliche Schliessung	no
Weekly closure	Wöchentliche Schliessung	no

Monday (Montag) : Restaurant closed

Fees main season
Preisliste hochsaison 18 holes

	Week days Woche	We/Bank holidays We/Feiertag
Individual Individuell	DM 100,-	DM 120,-
Couple Ehepaar	DM 200,-	DM 240,-

We: with members (nur in Mitgliederbegleitung)

Caddy	Caddy	DM 40,-
Electric Trolley	Elektrokarren	no
Buggy	Elektrischer Wagen	no
Clubs	Leihschläger	DM 20,-
Credit cards Kreditkarten		no

Access Zufahrt : Düsseldorf, A3 → Oberhausen.
Exit (Ausf.) Düsseldorf-Mettmann. B7 → Mettmann.
800 m, → Golf on the left
Map 3 on page 364 Karte 3 Seite 364

GOLF COURSE
PLATZ　17/20

Site	Lage	▮▮▮▮▮▮▯
Maintenance	Instandhaltung	▮▮▮▮▮▮▯
Architect	Architekt	B. von Limburger
Type	Typ	forest, hilly
Relief	Begehbarkeit	▮▮▮▮▮▮▮
Water in play	Platz mit Wasser	▮▮▯▯▯▯▯
Exp. to wind	Wind ausgesetzt	▮▮▮▯▯▯▯
Trees in play	Platz mit Bäumen	▮▮▮▮▮▮▯

Scorecard Scorekarte	Chp. Chp.	Mens Herren	Ladies Damen
Length Länge	6208	6040	5328
Par	72	72	72

Advised golfing ability		0	12	24	36
Empfohlene Spielstärke		▮▮▮▮▮▮▮▮▮▯			
Hcp required	Min. Handicap	24			

CLUB HOUSE & AMENITIES
KLUBHAUS UND NEBENGEBÄUDE　8/10

Pro shop	Pro shop	▮▮▮▮▮▮▯
Driving range	Übungsplatz	▮▮▮▮▮▮▯
Sheltered	überdacht	11 mats
On grass	auf Rasen	no, 35 mats open air
Putting-green	Putting-grün	yes
Pitching-green	Pitching-grün	yes

425

HOTEL FACILITIES
HOTEL BESCHREIBUNG　6/10

HOTELS HOTELS

Hansa Hotel	Mettmann
178 rooms, D DM 250,-	2 km
Tel (49) 02104 - 98 60, Fax (49) 02104 - 986 150	
Europa Comfort Hotel	Düsseldorf
81 rooms, D DM 169,-	5 km
Tel (49) 0211 - 927 50, Fax (49) 0211 - 927 5666	

RESTAURANTS RESTAURANT

Im Schiffchen	Düsseldorf
Tel (49) 0211 - 401 050	10 km
Am Weinberg	400 m
Tel (49) 0211 - 289 333	
Weinhaus Tante Anna	Düsseldorf
Tel (49) 0211 - 131 163	15 km

IFFELDORF

Der zwischen Garmisch-Partenkirchen und München befindliche Teil Bayerns ist gesegnet mit zahlreichen Golfplätzen, von denen viele in die wunderschöne Voralpenlandschaft zwischen offenem Hügelland und Gebirgsszenerie eingebettet sind. Die meisten dieser Plätze sind naturgemäss ziemlich hügelig und damit ein echter Fitness-Test für die meist stadtverwöhnten Golfer. Iffeldorf ist in dieser Hinsicht ganz anders. Die Anlage ist ein ausgezeichnetes Beispiel für einen Golfplatz mit einem guten, wenn auch nicht herausragendem Design, das einerseits der ganzen Familie ungetrübtes Spielvergnügen bereitet, andererseits aber auch den guten Spielern genügend interessante Herausforderungen stellt. Das Layout ist sehr "ehrlich" und man findet die unterschiedlichsten Hindernisse vor, so dass der Platz auch bei oftmaligem Spielen nicht langweilig wird. Das Sahnestück dieser qualitativ hochwertigen Anlage sind zweifellos die Grüns, die hervorragend gestaltet, von ausreichender Grösse und sorgfältig verteidigt sind.

From Garmisch-Partenkirchen to Munich, Bavaria is full of courses often set in wonderful landscapes between open countryside and mountain scenery, doubtless a little hilly for town folk but a great way to get fit again. The actual course is something else. It is a good example of an excellent golf course, well if not exceptionally designed where all the family can play without any problem and where good players come face to face with interesting challenges. It is a very honest layout where difficulties are evenly spread around the course and varied enough to always enjoy coming back for more. The greens are of the same quality, well designed, reasonably sized and carefully protected.

Golfplatz Iffeldorf e.V.   1990
Gut Rettenberg 3
D - 82393 IFFELDORF

Office	Sekretariat	(49) 08856 - 9255 55
Pro shop	Pro shop	(49) 08856 - 9255 20
Fax	Fax	(49) 08856 - 9255 59
Situation	Lage	

München (pop. 1 300 000), 50 km
Garmisch-Partenkirchen (pop. 26 500, 35 km

Annual closure	Jährliche Schliessung	no
Weekly closure	Wöchentliche Schliessung	no

Fees main season
Preisliste hochsaison 18 holes

	Week days Woche	We/Bank holidays We/Feiertag
Individual Individuell	DM 90,-	DM 110,-
Couple Ehepaar	DM 180,-	DM 220,-

Caddy	Caddy	DM 50,-
Electric Trolley	Elektrokarren	DM 25,-
Buggy	Elektrischer Wagen	DM 50,-
Clubs	Leihschläger	DM 20,-

Credit cards Kreditkarten	VISA - Eurocard - JCB

426

Access Zufahrt : A95 München → Garmisch. Exit (Ausf.) Iffeldorf-Penzberg. → Penzberg, Golf 200 m left towards Gut Rettenberg.
Map 2 on page 362 Karte 2 Seite 362

GOLF COURSE
PLATZ   16/20

Site	Lage	
Maintenance	Instandhaltung	
Architect	Architekt	P. Postel
Type	Typ	forest, mountain
Relief	Begehbarkeit	
Water in play	Platz mit Wasser	
Exp. to wind	Wind ausgesetzt	
Trees in play	Platz mit Bäumen	

Scorecard Scorekarte	Chp. Chp.	Mens Herren	Ladies Damen
Length Länge	5904	5904	5234
Par	72	72	72

Advised golfing ability	0 12 24 36
Empfohlene Spielstärke	
Hcp required	Min. Handicap	no

CLUB HOUSE & AMENITIES
KLUBHAUS UND NEBENGEBÄUDE   7/10

Pro shop	Pro shop	
Driving range	Übungsplatz	
Sheltered	überdacht	3 mats
On grass	auf Rasen	yes
Putting-green	Putting-grün	yes
Pitching-green	Pitching-grün	yes

HOTEL FACILITIES
HOTEL BESCHREIBUNG   6/10

HOTELS HOTELS
Berggeist   Penzberg
46 rooms, D DM 175,-   4 km

Tel (49) 08856 - 8050Sterff   Seeshaupt
18 rooms, D DM 170,-   8 km
Tel (49) 08801 - 1711, Fax (49) 08856 - 2598

Gut Faistenberg   Faistenberg
10 rooms, D DM 200,-   10 km
Tel (49) 08179 - 1200

RESTAURANTS RESTAURANT
La Traviata   Golfplatz
Tel (49) 08856 - 9255 30

Der Golfplatz liegt oberhalb des "bayerischen Meers", wie der Chiemsee als grösster See des bayerischen Voralpenlandes auch häufig genannt wird. Auf einer seiner beiden Inseln findet man das Schloss "Herrenchiemsee", eine der Verrücktheiten König Ludwigs II, der hier eine Kopie von Versailes errichten wollte. Der holländische Architekt Dudok van Heel hat hier einen Platz entworfen, der, ohne grosse technische Schwierigkeiten, ganz auf die Bedürfnisse der Urlauber zugeschnitten ist. Trotzdem ist der Platz anspruchsvoll genug, um nicht uninteressant zu wirken. Nach einigen Runden hat man alle lauernden Gefahren entdeckt, und ist in der Lage, Bunkern und Wasser aus dem Weg zu gehen. Zudem kennt man dann die ideale Spiellinie auf den vielen, von grossen Bäumen gesäumten Fairways. Der Platz hat keine steilen Anstiege und ist somit leicht zu Fuss zu bewältigen. Die Fairways sind von einladender Breite, so dass hier Spieler unterschiedlichen Niveaus problemlos zusammen in einem Flight spielen können. Bessere Spieler sollten sich für die hinteren Abschläge entscheiden.

A course over Chiemsee, or the lake of Bavaria, the region's largest facing the Alps with two pretty islands. One is the site of the "Herrenchiemsee", one of the whimsical notions of King Louis II (and in fact a carbon copy of the Château de Versailles). Dutch architect Dudok van Heel has designed a holiday course with no great technical difficulties, but tough enough to keep it interesting. Play it several times and you will discover the awaiting traps, perhaps be able to keep away from the bunkers and water and negotiate a way through the large trees that line many of the holes. With no steep contours, you can walk the course very easily, and as the fairways are deliciously wide, players of all levels can play together, making sure that the best tee off from the back.

Golfclub Im Chiemgau Chieming — 1984

Kötzing 1
D - 83339 CHIEMING

Office	Sekretariat	(49) 08669 - 873 30
Pro shop	Pro shop	(49) 08669 - 873 30
Fax	Fax	(49) 08669 - 873 333
Situation	Lage	

Chieming (pop. 3 700), 7 km - Traunstein (pop. 17 600), 18 km

Annual closure	Jährliche Schliessung	1/12 → 31/3
Weekly closure	Wöchentliche Schliessung	no

Monday (Montag) : Restaurant closed

Fees main season
Preisliste hochsaison 18 holes

	Week days Woche	We/Bank holidays We/Feiertag
Individual Individuell	DM 70,-	DM 100,-
Couple Ehepaar	DM 140,-	DM 200,-

under 21 years/Students : – 50 %

Caddy	Caddy	no
Electric Trolley	Elektrokarren	no
Buggy	Elektrischer Wagen	no
Clubs	Leihschläger	DM 35,-

Credit cards Kreditkarten	no

Access Zufahrt : A8 München-Salzburg. Exit (Ausf.) Grabenstätt. In Chieming → Laimgrub, Sondermoning. Left → Hart, Golf → Knesing.
Map 2 on page 363 Karte 2 Seite 363

GOLF COURSE
PLATZ — 15/20

Site	Lage	
Maintenance	Instandhaltung	
Architect	Architekt	Dudok van Heel
Type	Typ	open country
Relief	Begehbarkeit	
Water in play	Platz mit Wasser	
Exp. to wind	Wind ausgesetzt	
Trees in play	Platz mit Bäumen	

Scorecard Scorekarte	Chp. Chp.	Mens Herren	Ladies Damen
Length Länge	6221	6069	5416
Par	72	72	72

Advised golfing ability Empfohlene Spielstärke	0	12	24	36

Hcp required	Min. Handicap	36

CLUB HOUSE & AMENITIES
KLUBHAUS UND NEBENGEBÄUDE — 7/10

Pro shop	Pro shop	
Driving range	Übungsplatz	
Sheltered	überdacht	5 mats
On grass	auf Rasen	yes
Putting-green	Putting-grün	yes
Pitching-green	Pitching-grün	yes (2)

HOTEL FACILITIES
HOTEL BESCHREIBUNG — 6/10

HOTELS HOTELS

Unterwirt	Chieming
11 rooms, D DM 100,-	6 km
Tel (49) 08664 - 551, Fax (49) 08664 - 1649	

Gut Ising	Chieming-Ising
105 rooms, D DM 300,-	3 km
Tel (49) 08667 - 790, Fax (49) 08667 - 79 432	

Park-Hotel Traunsteiner Hof	Traunstein
59 rooms, D DM 180,-	20 km
Tel (49) 0861 - 69 041, Fax (49) 0861 - 8512	

Eichenhof	Waging am See
34 rooms, D DM 240,-	30 km
Tel (49) 08681 - 4030, Fax (49) 08681 - 40 325	

RESTAURANTS RESTAURANT

Gut Ising - Tel (49) 08667 - 790	Chieming-Ising
Malerwinkel - Tel (49) 08667 - 488	Seebruck 7 km

427

15 7 6

Ein eher ländlicher Golfplatz, bei dem sich Wald- und Feldflächen abwechseln. Auf den ersten Neun spielt man durch teilweise enge, von alten Bäumen gesäumte Fairways, während die zweiten Neun in offenem Gelände liegen, wo sich hauptsächlich Junganpflanzungen finden. Dadurch gewinnt man den Eindruck, auf zwei unterschiedlichen Platzen zu spielen, auf die man sein Spiel anpassen muss. Während die ersten neun Löcher bei windigen Bedingungen guten Schutz bieten, halten die zweiten Neun für die Spieler einige Überrraschungen bereit. Da die Hindernisse nicht immer deutlich erkennbar sind, bleibt wenig Hoffnung, den Platz auf Anhieb in den Griff zu bekommen. Die Anlage bietet in keiner Hinsicht Aussergewöhnliches, dennoch lohnt ein Besuch, wenn man eh in der Gegend ist. Von den hinteren Abschlägen ist der Platz relativ lang. Wenn man im Familien- oder Freundeskreis unterwegs ist, wo die Spielstärken häufig sehr unterschiedlich sind, empfiehlt es sich deshalb, von etwas weiter vorn zu spielen. Letzteres kommt sicher allen Mitspielern besonders an den wenigen, klug angelegten Wasserhindernissen, entgegen.

This is a country course with alternating woodland and farm landscapes. The course itself chops and changes, from narrow sections through already old trees (the front nine) to wider spaces with smaller saplings (the back nine), giving an impression of two rather different courses to which you need to adapt your game. When the wind blows, you are sheltered up to the 9th hole, but the back nine will have a few surprises in store. And since the hazards are not always clear to see, you can hardly hope to master the course first time around. There is nothing exceptional about the layout, but it is well worth a visit when you are in the region. This is a rather long course from the back tees, so move forward a touch to spend a good day's golfing, especially if you are playing with all the family or among friends of differing abilities. Then you can all cope together with the few very clever water hazards.

Golfclub Isernhagen e.V.   1983
Gut Lohne
D - 30916 ISERNHAGEN

Office	Sekretariat	(49) 05139 - 89 3185
Pro shop	Pro shop	(49) 05139 - 2998
Fax	Fax	(49) 05139 - 27 033
Situation	Lage	

Hannover (pop. 510 000), 14 km

Annual closure	Jährliche Schliessung	no
Weekly closure	Wöchentliche Schliessung	no

Monday (Montag) : Restaurant closed

Fees main season
Preisliste hochsaison full day

	Week days Woche	We/Bank holidays We/Feiertag
Individual Individuell	DM 50,-	DM 70,-
Couple Ehepaar	DM 100,-	DM 140,-

Caddy	Caddy	no
Electric Trolley	Elektrokarren	no
Buggy	Elektrischer Wagen	yes
Clubs	Leihschläger	yes

Credit cards Kreditkarten   no

Access Zufahrt : A7 Exit (Ausf.) Kirchhorst. In Kirchhorst → Neuwarmbüchen. Take left → «Golfplatz Gut Lohne» Map 5 on page 369 Karte 5 Seite 369

GOLF COURSE
PLATZ   **15**/20

Site	Lage	
Maintenance	Instandhaltung	
Architect	Architekt	G. Bruns
Type	Typ	forest, open country
Relief	Begehbarkeit	
Water in play	Platz mit Wasser	
Exp. to wind	Wind ausgesetzt	
Trees in play	Platz mit Bäumen	

Scorecard Scorekarte	Chp. Chp.	Mens Herren	Ladies Damen
Length Länge	6118	6118	5443
Par	72	72	72

Advised golfing ability	0	12	24	36
Empfohlene Spielstärke				
Hcp required Min. Handicap	34			

CLUB HOUSE & AMENITIES
KLUBHAUS UND NEBENGEBÄUDE   **7**/10

Pro shop	Pro shop	
Driving range	Übungsplatz	
Sheltered	überdacht	yes
On grass	auf Rasen	yes
Putting-green	Putting-grün	yes
Pitching-green	Pitching-grün	yes

HOTEL FACILITIES
HOTEL BESCHREIBUNG   **6**/10

HOTELS HOTELS

Queens Hotel   Hannover
176 rooms, D DM 260,-   14 km
Tel (49) 0511 - 51 030, Fax (49) 0511 - 526 924

Sportpark Hotel   Hannover
40 rooms, D DM 160,-   14 km
Tel (49) 0511 - 972 840, Fax (49) 0511 - 972 841

Parkhotel Welfenhof   Isernhagen
110 rooms, D DM 350,-   2 km
Tel (49) 0511 - 65 406, Fax (49) 0511 - 651 050

RESTAURANTS RESTAURANT

Bakkarat im Kasino am Maschsee   Hannover
Tel (49) 0511 - 884 057   14 km

Maritim Seeterrassen   Hannover
Tel (49) 0511 - 884 057   14 km

JAKOBSBERG

15	7	6

Ganz in der Nähe befinden sich auch die Schlösser und der Fels der Lorelei. Der Platz selbst zählt zu den sehr guten Anlagen neueren Datums. Seine grossen Vorzüge liegen in der abwechslungsreichen Gestaltung der Löcher, sowie der klaren Erkennbarkeit der anzuwendenden Spieltaktik. Lediglich der Abschlag an den Löchern 5 und 7 und das Grünanspiel an Loch 17, wo man jeweils sehr auf der Hut sein muss, bilden in dieser Hinsicht eine Ausnahme. Loch 7 ist der einzige Schwachpunkt eines ansonsten sehr ausgewogenen Layouts, bei dem die Hindernisse (Bunker und Wasser) zwar immer im Spiel sind, aber niemals allzu bedrängend wirken. Dies wiederum ermöglicht ein reibungsloses Vorankommen bei Flights, die sich aus Spielern unterschiedlicher Niveaus zusammensetzen, sofern von den, dem Können Aller entsprechenden, Abschlägen gespielt wird. Diesen Golfplatz sollten Sie auf keinen Fall verpassen, zumal die umliegende Region mit ihrer landschaftlichen Schönheit, der Kultur und den Weinbergen ein enormes touristisches Potential bietet.

Located in one of the cradles of German romanticism, overlooking the most boxed-in section of the Rhine valley (the views are superb) and close to the castles and the rock of Loreley, Jakobsberg is one of the very good recent courses. The variety of holes is an asset, as is the clarity of the tactics needed to play here, with the exception of the tee-shot on the 5th and the green on the 17th, which call for particular attention. The 7th is the only weak link on a course that is well-balanced overall, and where difficulties (bunkers and water) are in play but are never too oppressive. This means that players of all levels can get along well together, as long as they are wise enough to choose the right tees. In a region which such fascinating potential for tourists (landscapes, culture and vineyards), this course is a stop-off of considerable merit.

Golf-Club Jakobsberg — 1992
Im Tal der Loreley
D - 56154 BOPPARD-RHENS

Office	Sekretariat	(49) 06742 - 808 491
Pro shop	Pro shop	(49) 06742 - 808 496
Fax	Fax	(49) 06742 - 808 493

Situation Lage
Koblenz (pop. 108 000), 10 km

Annual closure	Jährliche Schliessung	no
Weekly closure	Wöchentliche Schliessung	no

Fees main season
Preisliste hochsaison 18 holes

	Week days Woche	We/Bank holidays We/Feiertag
Individual Individuell	DM 70,-	DM 90,-
Couple Ehepaar	DM 140,-	DM 180,-

under 21 years/Students : – 50 %

Caddy	Caddy	no
Electric Trolley	Elektrokarren	DM 25,-
Buggy	Elektrischer Wagen	DM 50,-
Clubs	Leihschläger	DM 20,-

Credit cards Kreditkarten
VISA - Eurocard - MasterCard - AMEX - DC

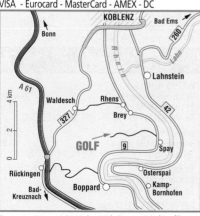

Access Zufahrt : A61 Mainz-Köln/Bonn. Exit (Ausf.)
Koblenz-Waldesch, → Rhens, B9 Brey.
Turn right → Golf
Map 3 on page 364 Karte 3 Seite 364

GOLF COURSE
PLATZ
15/20

Site	Lage	▰▰▰▰▱
Maintenance	Instandhaltung	▰▰▰▰▱
Architect	Architekt	Wolfgang Jersombek
Type	Typ	open country, hilly
Relief	Begehbarkeit	
Water in play	Platz mit Wasser	▰▰▰▱▱
Exp. to wind	Wind ausgesetzt	▰▰▱▱▱
Trees in play	Platz mit Bäumen	▰▰▰▱▱

Scorecard Scorekarte	Chp. Chp.	Mens Herren	Ladies Damen
Length Länge	6351	6114	5363
Par	72	72	72

Advised golfing ability	0	12	24	36
Empfohlene Spielstärke				
Hcp required Min. Handicap	no			

CLUB HOUSE & AMENITIES
KLUBHAUS UND NEBENGEBÄUDE
7/10

Pro shop	Pro shop	▰▰▰▰▱
Driving range	Übungsplatz	▰▰▰▱▱
Sheltered	überdacht	5 mats
On grass	auf Rasen	yes
Putting-green	Putting-grün	yes
Pitching-green	Pitching-grün	yes

429

HOTEL FACILITIES
HOTEL BESCHREIBUNG
6/10

HOTELS HOTELS
Golfhotel Jakobsberg — Golfplatz
108 rooms, D DM 220,-
Tel (49) 06742 - 8080, Fax (49) 06742 - 3069

Bellevue — Boppard 12 km
94 rooms, D DM 300,-
Tel (49) 06742 - 1020, Fax (49) 06742 - 102 602

Rebstock — Boppard 12 km
15 rooms, D DM 180,-
Tel (49) 06742 - 4876, Fax (49) 06742 - 4877

RESTAURANTS RESTAURANT
Königstuhl — Rhens 3 km
Tel (49) 02628 - 2244

Stresemann — Koblenz 15 km
Tel (49) 0261 - 15 464

KÖLN

Abgeschieden von der Aussenwelt, ist "Refrath" ein typischer Vertreter eines im traditionellen Stil erbauten Golfplatzes, bei dem der Waldcharakter dominiert, ohne das dabei der Eindruck von Weitläufigkeit verloren geht. Longhittern, die sich hier etwas beengt fühlen können, mag er ein wenig kurz erscheinen. Für Normalsterbliche hingegen ist er lang genug, nicht zuletzt weil der Weg zum Grün oft blockiert ist, wenn man die zahlreichen Doglegs nicht von der richtigen Seite anspielt. An Hindernissen gibt es neben einem kleinen Bach, der an einigen Löchern ins Spiel kommt, eine grosse Anzahl geschickt plazierter, teilweise tiefer Bunker, die bei ungenauen Schlägen eine Menge Probleme bereiten können. Spieler, die den Ball gerade schlagen, können zahlreiche Grüns auch mit der Variante "bump and run" anspielen, wenngleich grosses Können erforderlich ist, den Ball auf diese Weise nahe der Fahne zu plazieren. Immer makellos gepflegt, zeichnet sich das klare und ehrliche Layout von Köln besonders durch die abwechslungsreiche Gestaltung seiner Löcher - egal ob Par 5, Par 4 oder Par 3 -aus.

Withdrawn from the outside world, "Refrath" stands for the pure tradition of forest golf courses, without forasmuch being too narrow. It may certainly look a little short for the long-hitters (they might feel a little cramped here), but it is long enough for the common mortal, who will see his or her path to the green irritatingly blocked if they take the doglegs on the wrong side. Hazard-wise, there is just one little stream that comes into play on a few holes, but the very many bunkers, well located and sometimes deep, will cause a lot of problems to wayward hitters. The straighter hitters can often bump and run their ball onto the greens, but getting close to the pin needs a lot of skill. Clear, honest and well maintained, KÄln stands out for the diversity of its holes, whether playing the par 5s, the par 4s or the three par 3s, all with remarkable uniformity of style.

Golf- und Land Club Köln   1906

Golfplatz 2, Bensberg-Refrath
D - 51429 BERGISCH-GLADBACH

Office	Sekretariat	(49) 02204 - 927 60
Pro shop	Pro shop	(49) 02204 - 69 192
Fax	Fax	(49) 02204 - 68 192
Situation	Lage	

Köln, 20 km - Bergisch-Gladbach (pop. 104 000), 3 km

Annual closure	Jährliche Schliessung	no
Weekly closure	Wöchentliche Schliessung	no

Monday (Montag) : Restaurant closed

Fees main season
Preisliste hochsaison 18 holes

	Week days Woche	We/Bank holidays We/Feiertag
Individual Individuell	DM 100,-	DM 100,-
Couple Ehepaar	DM 200,-	DM 200,-

We: with members only (nur in Mitgliederbegleitung)

Caddy	Caddy	no
Electric Trolley	Elektrokarren	yes
Buggy	Elektrischer Wagen	no
Clubs	Leihschläger	yes

Credit cards Kreditkarten   no

Access Zufahrt : A3 Frankfurt-Köln. Exit (Ausf.) A4 →
Olpe. Exit Bergisch-Gladbach-Refrath. B55, 1.5 km. →
Bensberg. Dolmanstrasse. Turn right in Altrefratherstr.
Map 3 on page 364 Karte 3 Seite 364

GOLF COURSE
PLATZ   17/20

Site	Lage	
Maintenance	Instandhaltung	
Architect	Architekt	B. von Limburger
Type	Typ	forest
Relief	Begehbarkeit	
Water in play	Platz mit Wasser	
Exp. to wind	Wind ausgesetzt	
Trees in play	Platz mit Bäumen	

Scorecard	Chp.	Mens	Ladies
Scorekarte	Chp.	Herren	Damen
Length Länge	6090	6090	5400
Par	72	72	72

Advised golfing ability	0	12	24	36
Empfohlene Spielstärke				

Hcp required   Min. Handicap   36 (We: 28 Men, 35 Ladies)

CLUB HOUSE & AMENITIES
KLUBHAUS UND NEBENGEBÄUDE   6/10

Pro shop	Pro shop	
Driving range	Übungsplatz	
Sheltered	überdacht	6 mats
On grass	auf Rasen	yes
Putting-green	Putting-grün	yes
Pitching-green	Pitching-grün	yes

HOTEL FACILITIES
HOTEL BESCHREIBUNG   7/10

HOTELS HOTELS

Waldhotel Mangold   Bensberg
21 rooms, D DM 250,-   3 km
Tel (49) 02204 - 95 550, Fax (49) 02204 - 955 560

Gronauer Tannenhof   Gronau
34 rooms, D DM 220,-   3 km
Tel (49) 02204 - 35 088, Fax (49) 02204 - 35 579

Schlosshotel Lerbach   Bergisch-Gladbach
54 rooms, D DM 500,-   3 km
Tel (49) 02202 - 2040, Fax (49) 02202 - 204 940

RESTAURANTS RESTAURANT

Restaurant Dieter Müller   Bergisch-Gladbach
Tel (49) 02202 - 2040   3 km

Eggemans Bürgerhaus   Bergisch-Gladbach
Tel (49) 02202 - 36 134   3 km

430

KÖNIGSFELD

Dieser Teil des Schwarzwaldes zwischen Schwenningen und Freiburg-im-Breisgau ist seit langem ein touristischer Anziehungspunkt und lohnt in der Zeit von Frühling (der hier meist früher kommt als im übrigen Deutschland) bis Herbst einen romantischen Kurzaufenthalt. Golf ist sicher nicht die Hauptattraktion dieser Gegend, deren hügeliges Landschaftsprofil sich für den diesen Sport auch nicht sonderlich eignet, dennoch hat dieser Platz einige Löcher die einen Besuch lohnen, sofern man dafür keinen grossen Umweg in Kauf nehmen muss. Der Platz ist eng und aufgrund einiger blinder oder erhöht angelegter Grüns auch ziemlich "tricky", und bereitet einem damit ständig Kopfzerbrechen bei der Schlägerwahl. Hindernisse gibt es genug, diese sind aber keineswegs unbezwingbar. Spieler, die mit dem Ball einigermassen umgehen können sollten hier gut zurechtkommen. Königsfeld - schön gelegen mit einem weniger schönen Clubhaus - ist etwas für Golfer mit guter Kondition, denen Entspannung wichtiger ist als ein guter Score.

This region of the Black Forest has long been a top spot for tourism and is well worth a short romantic visit between Schwennigen and Freiburg-im-Breisgau, from spring (generally earlier here than in the rest of Germany) to autumn (wunderbar!). Golf was not the prime concern here, as the rather hilly terrain is hardly ideal, but a few holes make a visit worthwhile if it means not going too far out of your way. The course is tight and rather tricky as a whole, with a few blind or elevated greens, and the choice of club is never obvious. There is no shortage of hazards, although these are not insurmountable. A goodish player who can (deliberately) flight the ball a little should come to terms with it. On a site that is much more pleasant than the clubhouse, Königsfeld is fine for players in good physical shape who are looking more for relaxation than a brilliant score.

Golf und Country Club Königsfeld 1990

Angelmoos 20
D - 78126 KÖNIGSFELD-MARTINSWEILER

Office	Sekretariat	(49) 07725 - 93 960
Pro shop	Pro shop	(49) 07725 - 7459
Fax	Fax	(49) 07725 - 939 612
Situation	Lage	

Villingen-Schwenningen (pop. 80 000), 10 km

Annual closure	Jährliche Schliessung	1/11 → 31/3
Weekly closure	Wöchentliche Schliessung	no

Fees main season
Preisliste hochsaison full day

	Week days Woche	We/Bank holidays We/Feiertag
Individual Individuell	DM 70,-	DM 90,-
Couple Ehepaar	DM 140,-	DM 180,-

Caddy	Caddy	no
Electric Trolley	Elektrokarren	no
Buggy	Elektrischer Wagen	no
Clubs	Leihschläger	DM 20,-

Credit cards Kreditkarten — no

Hardt
Weiler
GOLF
Fischbach
Königsfeld
Stuttgart
Konstanz
A 81
0 2 4 km
Triberg
523
35
Villingen
SCHWENNINGEN

Access Zufahrt : A8 Stuttgart-Singen. Exit (Ausf.)
Villingen-Schwenningen → St Georgen. Mönchweiler,
→ Königsfeld, → Golf.
Map 1 on page 361 Karte 1 Seite 361

GOLF COURSE
PLATZ 13/20

Site	Lage	▆▆▆▆▆▁
Maintenance	Instandhaltung	▆▆▆▆▆▁
Architect	Architekt	
Type	Typ	open country, hilly
Relief	Begehbarkeit	▆▆▆▆▁▁
Water in play	Platz mit Wasser	▆▆▁▁▁▁
Exp. to wind	Wind ausgesetzt	▆▆▆▁▁▁
Trees in play	Platz mit Bäumen	▆▆▆▆▁▁

Scorecard Scorekarte	Chp. Chp.	Mens Herren	Ladies Damen
Length Länge	6167	6167	5427
Par	70	70	70

Advised golfing ability Empfohlene Spielstärke	0 12 24 36	▆▆▆▆▆▆▁
Hcp required Min. Handicap	no	

CLUB HOUSE & AMENITIES
KLUBHAUS UND NEBENGEBÄUDE 6/10

Pro shop	Pro shop	▆▆▆▆▁▁
Driving range	Übungsplatz	▆▆▆▆▁▁
Sheltered	überdacht	4 mats
On grass	auf Rasen	yes (summer)
Putting-green	Putting-grün	yes
Pitching-green	Pitching-grün	yes

431

HOTEL FACILITIES
HOTEL BESCHREIBUNG 6/10

HOTELS HOTELS
Fewotel Schwarzwaldtreff — Königsfeld
127 rooms, D DM 220,- — 1 km
Tel (49) 07725 - 8080, Fax (49) 07725 - 808 808

Ochsen — Schönwald
37 rooms, D DM 200,- — 2 km
Tel (49) 07722 - 1045, Fax (49) 07722 - 3018

Bosse — Villingen
36 rooms, D DM 160,- — 8 km
Tel (49) 07721 - 58 011, Fax (49) 07721 - 58 013

Gasthaus Mohren — Fischbach
8 rooms, D DM 100,- — 5 km
Tel (49) 07725 - 37 72, Fax (49) 07725 - 33 46

RESTAURANTS RESTAURANT
Rapp - Tel (49) 07725 - 7621 — Burgberg 3 km
Ochsen - Tel (49) 07722 - 1045 — Schönwald 1 km

17	7	7

Der Platz ist somit typisch für eine Zeit, in der den Architekten weder die technischen noch die finanziellen Mittel zur Verfügung standen, das Gelände grundlegend zu verändern. So folgen die Spielbahnen den kleinen, natürlichen Unebenheiten des Geländes und führen durch teilweise sehr enge, baumgesäumte Fairwayschluchten, was den Spielern präzise Schläge abverlangt. Bei den zehn als Dogleg verlaufenden Bahnen erweist sich eine Draw vom Abschlag als sehr hilfreich. Strategische Überlegungen erfordert in erster Linie das Anspiel der Grüns, die mittelgross, leicht gewellt und halbwegs gut verteidigt sind. "Bump and run" Schläge empfehlen sich nur während der Sommermonate, wenn der Boden hart und trocken ist, ansonsten muss man versuchen die Grüns mit hohen Pitch- und Lobschlägen anzugreifen. Putten ist in den seltensten Fällen eine Formsache, doch wird einem dieser Platz in der Hinsicht wenig Ungemach bereiten. Wasser ist kaum im Spiel, so erkennt man schnell, dass dies die Art von Platz ist, an dem Schläge vorwiegend durch unpräzises Spiel eingebüsst werden.

Built more than 60 years ago, this is a "senior" course that is typical of an age when designers did not have the financial resources to change the lie of the land. The course hugs the lightly rolling natural contours and winds its way (sometimes very tightly) through trees, which call for some straight hitting. A draw off the tee will come in handy as well to cope with the ten dog-legs. The basic strategy lies before you reach the greens, since these are mid-sized, moderately contoured and averagely well-guarded but no more. Bump and run shots are recommended only in summer, when the ground is dry enough, otherwise this is a place for pitchers and lobbers. Actual putting is hardly a formality, but there are few nasty surprises in store. As water is only rarely in play, you will soon realize that this is the kind of course where you insidiously drop strokes through lack of accuracy.

Krefelder Golf Club e.V. 1930

Eltweg 2
D - 47748 KREFELD-LINN

Office	Sekretariat	(49) 02151 - 570 071
Pro shop	Pro shop	(49) 02151 - 520 128
Fax	Fax	(49) 02151 - 572 486

Situation Lage
Krefeld (pop. 242 000), 6 km

Annual closure Jährliche Schliessung no

Weekly closure Wöchentliche Schliessung no
Monday (Montag): Restaurant closed

Fees main season
Preisliste hochsaison full day

	Week days Woche	We/Bank holidays We/Feiertag
Individual Individuell	DM 70,-	DM 90,-
Couple Ehepaar	DM 140,-	DM 180,-

We: with members (nur in Mitgliederbegleitung)
under 21 years/students: – 50 %

Caddy	Caddy	on request, DM 30,-
Electric Trolley	Elektrokarren	no
Buggy	Elektrischer Wagen	no
Clubs	Leihschläger	DM 15,-
Credit cards Kreditkarten		no

432

Access Zufahrt : A57 Köln-Moers. Exit (Ausf.) Krefeld-Oppum. First traffic lights turn right, next ones, right again → Autobahnbrücke. → Golf
Map 3 on page 364 Karte 3 Seite 364

GOLF COURSE
PLATZ **17** /20

Site	Lage	
Maintenance	Instandhaltung	
Architect	Architekt	B. von Limburger
Type	Typ	forest
Relief	Begehbarkeit	
Water in play	Platz mit Wasser	
Exp. to wind	Wind ausgesetzt	
Trees in play	Platz mit Bäumen	

Scorecard Scorekarte	Chp. Chp.	Mens Herren	Ladies Damen
Length Länge	6082	6082	5321
Par	72	72	72

Advised golfing ability 0 12 24 36
Empfohlene Spielstärke

Hcp required Min. Handicap 28

CLUB HOUSE & AMENITIES
KLUBHAUS UND NEBENGEBÄUDE **7** /10

Pro shop	Pro shop	
Driving range	Übungsplatz	
Sheltered	überdacht	6 mats
On grass	auf Rasen	yes
Putting-green	Putting-grün	yes
Pitching-green	Pitching-grün	yes

HOTEL FACILITIES
HOTEL BESCHREIBUNG **7** /10

HOTELS HOTELS

Parkhotel Krefelder Hof Krefeld
150 rooms, D DM 350,- 6 km
Tel (49) 02151 - 5840, Fax (49) 02151 - 58 435

Garden Hotel Krefeld
51 rooms, D DM 200,- 6 km
Tel (49) 02151 - 590 296, Fax (49) 02151 - 590 299

Hansa Hotel Krefeld
107 rooms, D DM 300,- 8 km
Tel (49) 02151 - 8290, Fax (49) 02151 - 829 150

Dorint Sport-und Country-Hotel Krefeld-Traar
158 rooms, D DM 250,- 15 km
Tel (49) 02151 - 9560, Fax (49) 02151 - 956 100

RESTAURANTS RESTAURANT

Koperpot - Tel (49) 02151 - 614 814 Krefeld 8 km

Aquilon - Tel (49) 02151 - 800 207 Krefeld 8 km

LICHTENAU-WEICKERSHOF | 15 | 7 | 6 |

Der Golfplatz befindet sich in unmittelbarer Nachbarschaft der Kleinstadt Ansbach, deren Ortsbild mit seiner Mischung aus mittelalterlichen und barocken Elementen noch heute an die Familie der Hohenzollern erinnert, denen die Stadt einst Ruhm und höfisches Leben verdankte. Der Platz selbst ist eingebettet in eine typisch fränkische Landschaft. Die ersten neun Löcher führen durch hügeliges Gelände, während die zweiten Neun auf flachem, offenem Terrain liegen. Die Bemühungen um die Erhaltung des natürlichen Ökosystems der zum Golfgelände gehörenden Wälder und Wasserläufe haben dem Platz 1994 einen Sonderpreis für Umweltschutz-Massnahmen eingebracht. Eine respektable Länge sowie zahlreiche Hindernisse lassen den Platz eher für gute Golfer geeignet erscheinen, doch selbst denen wird es nicht leicht fallen wird, hier ihr Handicap zu spielen. Dies liegt zum einen an den recht eigenwilligen, aber gut erkennbaren Hindernissen, wie auch an den enorm grossen, hervorragend gestalteten und gut verteidigten Grüns.

Here, we are next door to Ansbach, a small town mingling memories of the Middle Ages and the baroque era, which owed its fame and court life to a Hohenzollern lineage. The course is located in a typical Franconia landscape, with alternating rolling hills (the front 9) and flat open land (on the way in). It cares enough for its appearance and for the balance of an ecosystem of woods and streams to have won a special award in 1994 for environmental protection. Very respectable yardage and the number of hazards make this a course more for the good golfer, who will be hard pushed to play to his or her handicap owing to the course's peculiar difficulties (well visible first time around) and the greens, which are huge, well-contoured and well-guarded. It doesn't have quite the personality to be rated amongst the best, but it does deserve a serious visit.

Golf- und Landclub Lichtenau-Weickershof e.V.   1980

Weickershof 1
D - 91586 LICHTENAU

Office	Sekretariat	(49) 09827 - 920 40
Pro shop	Pro shop	(49) 09827 - 7288
Fax	Fax	(49) 09827 - 920 444
Situation	Lage	

Nürnberg (pop. 498 000), 40 km -Ausbach, 15 km

Annual closure Jährliche Schliessung 30/11 → 28/2

Weekly closure Wöchentliche Schliessung no
Monday (Montag): Restaurant closed

Fees main season
Preisliste hochsaison full day

	Week days Woche	We/Bank holidays We/Feiertag
Individual Individuell	DM 60,-	DM 80,-
Couple Ehepaar	DM 120,-	DM 160,-
Caddy Caddy		on request
Electric Trolley Elektrokarren		yes
Buggy Elektrischer Wagen		yes
Clubs Leihschläger		yes

Credit cards Kreditkarten
VISA - Eurocard - MasterCard - AMEX

Access Zufahrt : BAB A6 Nürnberg-Heilbronn. Exit (Ausf.) Lichtenau. → Golf
Map 4 on page 366 Karte 4 Seite 366

GOLF COURSE PLATZ   15/20

Site	Lage	
Maintenance	Instandhaltung	
Architect	Architekt	Unknown
Type	Typ	parkland, country
Relief	Begehbarkeit	
Water in play	Platz mit Wasser	
Exp. to wind	Wind ausgesetzt	
Trees in play	Platz mit Bäumen	

Scorecard Scorekarte	Chp. Chp.	Mens Herren	Ladies Damen
Length Länge	6132	6132	5400
Par	72	72	72

Advised golfing ability Empfohlene Spielstärke	0 12 24 36
Hcp required Min. Handicap	35

CLUB HOUSE & AMENITIES KLUBHAUS UND NEBENGEBÄUDE   7/10

Pro shop	Pro shop	
Driving range	Übungsplatz	
Sheltered	überdacht	6 mats
On grass	auf Rasen	yes
Putting-green	Putting-grün	yes
Pitching-green	Pitching-grün	yes

433

HOTEL FACILITIES HOTEL BESCHREIBUNG   6/10

HOTELS HOTELS
Golfhotel — Lichtenau
7 rooms, D DM 100,-
Tel (49) 09827 - 920 424, Fax (49) 09827 - 920 424

Am Drechselgarten — Ansbach
85 rooms, D DM 220,- — 15 km
Tel (49) 0981 - 89 020, Fax (49) 0981 - 890 2605

Gasthof Sonne — Neuendettelsau
37 rooms, D DM 150,- — 10 km
Tel (49) 09874 - 5080, Fax (49) 09874 - 50 818

RESTAURANTS RESTAURANT
Weinstube Leidl — Lichtenau
Tel (49) 09827 - 528 — 1 km

Gasthaus um Hochspessart — Lichtenau
Tel (49) 09352 - 1228 — 2 km

Der Golfplatz wurde rund um das Schloss Schönbühl angelegt, und verfügt über ein modernes, sehr komfortables Clubhaus mit einem hervorragenden Restaurant. Die Lage selbst ist beeindruckend, bietet sie doch schöne Ausblicke über den tiefer gelegenen Bodensee (mit der Insel Mainau) und auf die nahen Alpengipfel. In dieser Region grenzen drei Länder aneinander - Deutschland, Österreich und die Schweiz. Daher rührt die Vielfalt der touristischen Attraktionen, über denen man beinahe den Golfsport vergessen könnte. Dies wäre jedoch schade, denn obwohl der Platz weder in spieltechnischer noch ästhetischer Hinsicht Herausragendes bietet, zählt er doch zum besseren Durchschnitt. Mittelklasse-Spielern, deren Streben einem gemütlichen Golftag gilt, bereitet der Platz keine grossen Schwierigkeiten. Aus demselben Grund werden ihn bessere Spieler nicht sonderlich aufregend finden. Letzteren sei empfohlen, sich auf der Runde um die schwächeren Golfer in der Familie zu kümmern, ohne Gefahr zu laufen, sich dadurch den eigenen Score zu ruinieren.

This course is laid out around the castle of SchÄnbühl, with a modern and very comfortable club-house, which includes a very good restaurant. The site itself is quite remarkable, with some superb views over the Bodensee (with the Mainau Island down below) and the peaks of the Alps. This region lies at the crossroads between three countries - Germany, Austria and Switzerland - so there is much for tourists to see and do, perhaps almost enough to coax you off the golf-course. That would be a shame, because although not an exceptional layout in terms of golfing or style, this course rates well above average. It should hardly pose too many problems for average players whose first desire is to spend a relaxing day, but by the same token it will hardly excite the more proficient golfers. They can make up for it by helping the lesser golfers in the family without too much risk of spoiling their own card.

Golf-Club Lindau-Bad Schachen e.V. 1954

Am Schönbühl 5
D - 88131 LINDAU

Office	Sekretariat	(49) 08382 - 78 090
Pro shop	Pro shop	(49) 08382 - 78 090
Fax	Fax	(49) 08382 - 78 998
Situation	Lage	

Lindau (pop. 25 000), 1.5 km

Annual closure Jährliche Schliessung — no

Weekly closure Wöchentliche Schliessung — no
Monday (Montag): Restaurant closed

Fees main season
Preisliste hochsaison 18 holes

	Week days Woche	We/Bank holidays We/Feiertag
Individual Individuell	DM 80,-	DM 100,-
Couple Ehepaar	DM 160,-	DM 200,-

under 21 years / Students : – 50%

Caddy	Caddy	no
Electric Trolley	Elektrokarren	no
Buggy	Elektrischer Wagen	no
Clubs	Leihschläger	no

Credit cards Kreditkarten — no

434

Access Zufahrt : A96 München-Lindau. Exit (Ausf.)
Sigmarszell. 3 km → Golf
Map 1 on page 361 Karte 1 Seite 361

GOLF COURSE
PLATZ   **15**/20

Site	Lage	▰▰▰▰▱
Maintenance	Instandhaltung	▰▰▰▰▱
Architect	Architekt	Unknown
Type	Typ	parkland
Relief	Begehbarkeit	▰▰▱▱▱
Water in play	Platz mit Wasser	▰▰▱▱▱
Exp. to wind	Wind ausgesetzt	▰▰▰▱▱
Trees in play	Platz mit Bäumen	▰▰▰▰▱

Scorecard	Chp.	Mens	Ladies
Scorekarte	Chp.	Herren	Damen
Length Länge	5871	5677	5004
Par	71	71	71

Advised golfing ability   0   12   24   36
Empfohlene Spielstärke   ▰▰▰▱
Hcp required Min. Handicap   36

CLUB HOUSE & AMENITIES
KLUBHAUS UND NEBENGEBÄUDE   **7**/10

Pro shop	Pro shop	▰▰▰▰▱
Driving range	Übungsplatz	▰▰▰▱▱
Sheltered	überdacht	4 mats
On grass	auf Rasen	no
Putting-green	Putting-grün	yes
Pitching-green	Pitching-grün	yes

HOTEL FACILITIES
HOTEL BESCHREIBUNG   **8**/10

HOTELS HOTELS
Bad Schachen   Lindau-Bad Schachen
110 rooms, D DM 300,-   1 km
Tel (49) 08382 - 29 80, Fax (49) 08382 - 25 390

Parkhotel Eden   Lindau-Bad Schachen
26 rooms, D DM 180,-   1 km
Tel (49) 08382 - 58 16, Fax (49) 08382 - 23 730

Bayerischer Hof   Lindau-Insel
104 rooms, D DM 400,-   2 km
Tel (49) 08382 - 91 50, Fax (49) 08382 - 915 591

Villino - 16 rooms, D DM 350,-   Lindau-Hoyren
Tel (49) 08382 - 93 450, Fax (49) 08382 - 64 40   1 km

RESTAURANTS RESTAURANT
Hoyerberg Schlössle   Lindau 1 km
Tel (49) 08382 - 25 295

Schachener Hof   Lindau-Bad Schachen
Tel (49) 08382 - 31 16   1 km

LÜBECK-TRAVEMÜNDER ✳ 15 8 8

Der Strand von Lübeck liegt in Travemünde, einem Seebad mit einem Kasino... und einem Golfplatz. Da viele Löcher nahe an der Ostsee entlang führen, geniesst man während der Runde herrliche Ausblicke. Trotzdem wirkt der Platz mit den vielen alten, prächtigen Bäumen eher wie ein Park. Das vollständig renovierte Clubhaus steht unter Denkmalsschutz. Seit der Eröffnung der ersten neun Löcher im Jahre 1921 sind die 18 Löcher immer wieder überarbeitet und verändert worden. Der Ausbau auf 27 Löcher durch Karl Grohs wird sicherlich den Platz weiter verändern, zumal die Driving Range so verlegt wird, dass man beim Üben immer Meeresblick hat. Aber auch ohne die Erweiterung ist Travemünde ein guter klassischer Platz mit gefährlichen Baumbestand, einigen wohlplatzierten Wasserhindernissen und Bunkern. Da das Gelände mit Ausnahme von zwei Löchern sehr flach ist, ist die Spielstrategie offensichtlich. Dennoch wird man erst nach mehreren Runde die Feinheiten des Platzes kennen. Dieser Platz ist ein lohnenswerter Platz für Golfer aller Spielstärken und mehr als nur ein guter Urlaubsplatz.

The beach of Lübeck is Travemünde, a seaside resort with casino... and golf course. With many of the holes close to the Baltic sea, the course offers some great views, but the magnificent trees make this look more like a park, with a clubhouse listed as an historical monument. Since 1921 the 18 holes have been overhauled again and again, and the new 9-hole layout by Karl Grohs will probably lead to more changes and the driving range being moved so your hitting balls with a sea view. For the time being, this is a good classical course with dangerous trees, a few well-located water hazards and clever bunkering. Since the terrain is virtually flat (except two holes), game strategy is pretty clear, although playing several rounds will help you to discover some of the more subtle touches. The imagination and technical thinking that went into this course make it a very pleasant golf and holidays destination for players of all abilities.

Lübeck-Travemünder Golf-Klub e.V. 1928

Kowitzberg 41
D - 23570 LÜBECK-TRAVEMÜNDE

Office	Sekretariat	(49) 04502 - 74 018
Pro shop	Pro shop	(49) 04502 - 73 975
Fax	Fax	(49) 04502 - 72 184
Situation	Lage	

Lübeck (pop. 215 000), 19 km

Annual closure	Jährliche Schliessung	no
Weekly closure	Wöchentliche Schliessung	no

Fees main season
Preisliste hochsaison 18 holes

	Week days Woche	We/Bank holidays We/Feiertag
Individual Individuell	DM 60,-	DM 80,-
Couple Ehepaar	DM 120,-	DM 160,-

under 21 years / Students : – 50%

Caddy	Caddy	no
Electric Trolley	Elektrokarren	no
Buggy	Elektrischer Wagen	no
Clubs	Leihschläger	DM 30,-

Credit cards Kreditkarten
VISA - Eurocard - MasterCard - AMEX - DC

Access Zufahrt : Hamburg A1 → Travemünde. B75 → Travemünde, → Strand/Brodner Ufte, 100 m Kowizberg Str. **Map 7 on page 373** Karte 7 Seite 373

GOLF COURSE PLATZ 15/20

Site	Lage	
Maintenance	Instandhaltung	
Architect	Architekt	Unknown
Type	Typ	seaside course, parkland
Relief	Begehbarkeit	
Water in play	Platz mit Wasser	
Exp. to wind	Wind ausgesetzt	
Trees in play	Platz mit Bäumen	

Scorecard Scorekarte	Chp. Chp.	Mens Herren	Ladies Damen
Length Länge	6213	6071	5371
Par	72	72	72

Advised golfing ability   0   12   24   36
Empfohlene Spielstärke
Hcp required   Min. Handicap   36

CLUB HOUSE & AMENITIES KLUBHAUS UND NEBENGEBÄUDE 8/10

Pro shop	Pro shop	
Driving range	Übungsplatz	
Sheltered	überdacht	2 bays
On grass	auf Rasen	yes
Putting-green	Putting-grün	yes
Pitching-green	Pitching-grün	yes

435

HOTEL FACILITIES HOTEL BESCHREIBUNG 8/10

HOTELS HOTELS
Strand Hotel   Travemünde
240 rooms, D DM 264,-   1 km
Tel (49) 04502 - 890, Fax (49) 04502 - 744 39

Landhaus Carstens   Timmendorfer Strand
26 rooms, D DM 305   10 km
Tel (49) 04503 - 608 0, Fax (49) 04503 -608 60

Maritim - 104 rooms, D DM 270,-   Travemünde
Tel (49) 04502 - 881 0, Fax (49) 04502 - 744 37   1 km

RESTAURANTS RESTAURANT
Pesel Fischrestaurant   Travemünde
Tel (49) 04502 - 333 0   1.5 km

Restaurante Casabianca   Travemünde
Tel(49) 04502 - 363 1   1.5 km

Hermannshöhe   Travemünde
Tel (49) 04502 - 730 21

Dieser nicht allzu lange, dafür hügelige und körperlich durchaus anstrengende Golfplatz, sollte von den Spielern in keinem Fall unterschätzt werden. Die geschickte Ausnutzung des Geländes spricht für die hervorragenden Golfkenntnisse der Architekten. Die ersten 11 Löcher sind recht eng von Wald begrenzt, so dass Genauigkeit vom Abschlag hier oberstes Gebot ist. Glücklicherweise reicht anstelle des Drivers häufig schon ein Holz 3 oder ein langes Eisen, um in eine Position zu gelangen, von der aus man die Grüns attackieren kann. Letzteres gilt insbesondere für Spieler, die den Ball gut kontrollieren können. Andererseits sind die Grüns in diesem Teil des Platzes nicht sonderlich gut verteidigt. Bei den restlichen Löchern findet man zwar breitere Fairways vor, dafür sind hier die Grüns teilweise erhöht und auch wesentlich besser geschützt. Ein "ehrlicher" Platz auf dem man, trotz leicht zu lesender Grüns, für einen guten Score hart arbeiten muss.

The very reasonable length of this course (pretty hilly and calling for a degree of physical fitness) should not result in golfers underestimating it before their round. The way the land has been used points to an excellent knowledge of the game by its designers. The first eleven holes are narrowish and laid out in a clearly demarcated forest, so accuracy off the tee is the order of the day. Fortunately, the driver can easily be left in the bag, especially since a 3-wood or a long iron is generally enough to find the right spot to attack the greens, particularly for players who can flight the ball. In contrast, the greens on this part of the course are not too heavily guarded. The fairways then grow wider, but, nothing is ever perfect, the greens are better protected and sometimes elevated, although reading them poses no particular problem. An honest course, but you have to work hard for a good score.

Hamburger Land- und Golf Club in der Lüneburger Heide — 1957

Am Golfplatz 24
D - 21218 SEEVETAL

Office	Sekretariat	(49) 04105 - 23 31
Pro shop	Pro shop	(49) 04105 - 23 51
Fax	Fax	(49) 04105 - 52 571
Situation	Lage	

Hittfeld, 2 km - Buchholz (pop. 33 000), 5 km

Annual closure	Jährliche Schliessung	no
Weekly closure	Wöchentliche Schliessung	no

Fees main season
Preisliste hochsaison 18 holes

	Week days Woche	We/Bank holidays We/Feiertag
Individual Individuell	DM 60,-	DM 80,-
Couple Ehepaar	DM 120,-	DM 160,-

under 27 years : – 50 %

Caddy	Caddy	no
Electric Trolley	Elektrokarren	no
Buggy	Elektrischer Wagen	no
Clubs	Leihschläger	no
Credit cards Kreditkarten		no

436

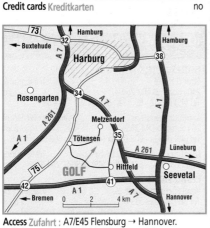

Access Zufahrt : A7/E45 Flensburg → Hannover.
Exit Fleestedt → Hittfeld. 2 km turn right,
Natenbergweg. 1 km, Golf.
Map 7 on page 372 Karte 7 Seite 372

GOLF COURSE
PLATZ — 16/20

Site	Lage	■■■■■■■□□□
Maintenance	Instandhaltung	■■■■■□□□□□
Architect	Architekt	J. Morrison Gärtner
Type	Typ	forest
Relief	Begehbarkeit	■■■■■■■■□□
Water in play	Platz mit Wasser	■■□□□□□□□□
Exp. to wind	Wind ausgesetzt	■■■■□□□□□□
Trees in play	Platz mit Bäumen	■■■■■■□□□□

Scorecard Scorekarte	Chp. Chp.	Mens Herren	Ladies Damen
Length Länge	5903	5903	5202
Par	71	71	71

Advised golfing ability Empfohlene Spielstärke	0	12	24	36
Hcp required Min. Handicap	no			

CLUB HOUSE & AMENITIES
KLUBHAUS UND NEBENGEBÄUDE — 7/10

Pro shop	Pro shop	■■■■■□□□□□
Driving range	Übungsplatz	■■■■■■□□□□
Sheltered	überdacht	6 mats
On grass	auf Rasen	yes
Putting-green	Putting-grün	yes
Pitching-green	Pitching-grün	yes

HOTEL FACILITIES
HOTEL BESCHREIBUNG — 5/10

HOTELS HOTELS
Meyer's — Hittfeld
16 rooms, D DM 170,- — 3 km
Tel (49) 04105 - 612 50, Fax (49) 04105 - 526 55

Hotel Krohwinkel — Hittfeld
7 rooms, D DM 165 — 3 km
Tel (49) 04105 - 24 09, Fax (49) 04105 - 53 799

RESTAURANTS RESTAURANT
Hotel Krohwinkel — Hittfeld
Tel (49) 04105 - 24 09 — 3 km

Hotel Seppenser Mühle — Holm/Seppensen
Tel (49) 04187 - 69 50 — 14 km

MAIN-TAUNUS

Die Lage von Main-Taunus zwischen Wiesbaden und Frankfurt ist ein beachtlicher Vorzug, der zum Teil für die nahe Luftwaffenbasis und den häufigen Blick auf eine Zementfabrik entschädigt. Eine weitere Stärke liegt in der Handschrift Bernhard von Limburgers, auch wenn dieser Platz sicherlich nicht zu dessen besten Arbeiten zählt. Die Junganpflanzungen auf diesem offenen Gelände werden in absehbarer Zeit die intime Atmosphäre dieser Anlage noch verstärken. Als Hindernisse sind die Bäume jedoch keineswegs unüberwindlich. Im Gegensatz dazu kann das Wasser durchaus zum Problem werden. Es kommt bei etwa 10 Löchern ins Spiel und ist der Preis, der für einen Golfplatz mitten in einem Vogelschutzgebiet zu zahlen ist. Die nicht übermässig stark bebunkerten Grüns sind von guter Qualität, allerdings mangelt es ihnen nach heutigem Standard etwas an Form und Gestaltung. Dieser klassische Platz hat ein höchst interessantes und schwieriges Finish, bei dem einem - zumindest auf der ersten Runde - eine Lochbeschreibung sehr gelegen kommt, um die lauernden Hindernisse auszumachen.

The position of Main-Taunus between Wiesbaden and Frankfurt is a considerable advantage, which in part makes up for the closeness of a neighbouring air-base and frequent views of a cement factory. Another strong point is the Bernhard von Limburger label, even though this is not one of his most inspired works. Over this open land, the saplings should eventually add to the intimate atmosphere, but the trees in general are not insurmountable hazards. By contrast, the water can be a problem, coming into play on ten or so holes, a fair price to pay for designing a course in a natural bird reserve. The greens are good but not over-guarded by bunkers, and to modern standards lack a little surface relief. This rather classic design has an intriguing and tough finish, where a map of the course will come in handy to spot the hazards, at least for the first time out.

Golf-Club Main-Taunus e.V.   1980

Lange Seegewann 2
D - 65205 WIESBADEN-DELKENHEIM

Office	Sekretariat	(49) 06122 - 52 550
Pro shop	Pro shop	(49) 06122 - 935 078
Fax	Fax	(49) 06122 - 936 099
Situation	Lage	

Wiesbaden (pop. 271 000), 12 km
Frankfurt (pop. 660 000), 19 km

Annual closure	Jährliche Schliessung	no
Weekly closure	Wöchentliche Schliessung	no

Monday (Montag) : Restaurant closed

Fees main season
Preisliste hochsaison 18 holes

	Week days Woche	We/Bank holidays We/Feiertag
Individual Individuell	DM 80,-	DM 100,-
Couple Ehepaar	DM 160,-	DM 200,-

under 21 years, Students : – 50%

Caddy	Caddy	no
Electric Trolley	Elektrokarren	yes
Buggy	Elektrischer Wagen	yes
Clubs	Leihschläger	no

Credit cards Kreditkarten VISA - Eurocard - MasterCard

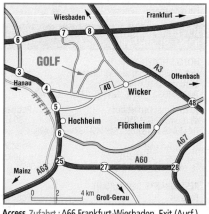

Access Zufahrt : A66 Frankfurt-Wiesbaden. Exit (Ausf.) Wiesbaden Nordenstadt. → Delkenheim, Hochheim.
Map 3 on page 365 Karte 3 Seite 365

GOLF COURSE
PLATZ   14/20

Site	Lage	
Maintenance	Instandhaltung	
Architect	Architekt	B. von Limburger
Type	Typ	open country
Relief	Begehbarkeit	
Water in play	Platz mit Wasser	
Exp. to wind	Wind ausgesetzt	
Trees in play	Platz mit Bäumen	

Scorecard	Chp.	Mens	Ladies
Scorekarte	Chp.	Herren	Damen
Length Länge	6133	5925	5216
Par	72	72	72

Advised golfing ability		0	12	24	36
Empfohlene Spielstärke					

Hcp required   Min. Handicap   36

CLUB HOUSE & AMENITIES
KLUBHAUS UND NEBENGEBÄUDE   7/10

Pro shop	Pro shop	
Driving range	Übungsplatz	
Sheltered	überdacht	6 mats
On grass	auf Rasen	yes
Putting-green	Putting-grün	yes
Pitching-green	Pitching-grün	yes

437

HOTEL FACILITIES
HOTEL BESCHREIBUNG   6/10

HOTELS HOTELS

Nassauer Hof   Wiesbaden
202 rooms, D DM 500,-   10 km
Tel (49) 0611 - 13 30, Fax (49) 0611 - 133 625

Treff Hotel Rhein-Main   Wiesbaden-Nordenstadt
150 rooms, D DM 215,-   5 km
Tel (49) 06122 - 80 10, Fax (49) 06122 - 801 164

Burkartsmühle   Hofheim
28 rooms, D DM 260,-   7 km
Tel (49) 06192 - 25 088, Fax (49) 06192 - 26 869

RESTAURANTS RESTAURANT

Die Ente vom Lehel   Wiesbaden
Tel (49) 0611 - 133 666   10 km

Estragon   Wiesbaden
Tel (49) 0611 - 303 906   10 km

MÄRKISCHER POTSDAM

<table>
<tr><td>14</td><td>7</td><td>6</td></tr>
</table>

Der Westen Berlins ist durchzogen von Kanälen und Seen und Potsdam gilt als historisches Zentrum mit dem wunderschönen Schloss Sanssouci und dem beeindruckenden Neuen Palais, die von Friedrich II von Preussen, einem aufgeklärten und kultivierten Herrscher sowie einem Freund Voltaires, erstellt wurden. Eine Besichtigung der Räumlichkeiten und des 300 Hektaren grossen Parks sollte man nicht verpassen. Etwa eine Viertelstunde von Potsdam ist der Golfplatz Märkischer Potsdam, der 1995 von Christian Städler realisiert wurde. Ein welliges Gelände mit wenig Bäumen, die nie wirklich in die Spielbahn kommen, im Gegensatz zu den Fairway- und Greenbunkern sowie den Wasserhindernissen. Allerdings ist dies kein allzu schwieriger Platz, und die (zahlreichen) Mittelklasse-Spieler werden begeistert sein. Da die Schwierigkeiten gut sichtbar sind, ist es möglich (aber nicht sicher), sein Handicap zu spielen. Ein Platz von durchschnittlich-guter Qualität...

The position of Main-Taunus between Wiesbaden and Frankfurt is a considerable advantage, which in part makes up for the closeness of a neighbouring air-base and frequent views of a cement factory. Another strong point is the Bernhard von Limburger label, even though this is not one of his most inspired works. Over this open land, the saplings should eventually add to the intimate atmosphere, but the trees in general are not insurmountable hazards. By contrast, the water can be a problem, coming into play on ten or so holes, a fair price to pay for designing a course in a natural bird reserve. The greens are good but not over-guarded by bunkers, and to modern standards lack a little surface relief. This rather classic design has an intriguing and tough finish, where a map of the course will come in handy to spot the hazards, at least for the first time out.

Märkischer Golfclub Potsdam e.V. 1995

Schmiedeweg 1
D - 14542 KEMNITZ

Office	Sekretariat	(49) 03327 - 663 70
Pro shop	Pro shop	(49) 03327 - 663 736
Fax	Fax	(49) 03327 - 663 737
Situation	Lage	

Potsdam (pop. 140 000), 20 km
Berlin (pop. 3 500 000), 45 km

Annual closure	Jährliche Schliessung	no
Weekly closure	Wöchentliche Schliessung	no

Fees main season
Preisliste hochsaison 18 holes

	Week days Woche	We/Bank holidays We/Feiertag
Individual Individuell	DM 80,-	DM 100,-
Couple Ehepaar	DM 160,-	DM 200,-

Caddy	Caddy	no
Electric Trolley	Elektrokarren	no
Buggy	Elektrischer Wagen	DM 50,-
Clubs	Leihschläger	DM 25,-

Credit cards Kreditkarten	no

438

Access Zufahrt : Berlin A115 → Magdeburg. Drewitz A10 → Hamburg (Berliner Ring). Exit (Ausf.) Phöben → Golf.
Map 6 on page 371 Karte 6 Seite 371

GOLF COURSE / PLATZ 14/20

Site	Lage	
Maintenance	Instandhaltung	
Architect	Architekt	Christoph Staedler
Type	Typ	parkland
Relief	Begehbarkeit	
Water in play	Platz mit Wasser	
Exp. to wind	Wind ausgesetzt	
Trees in play	Platz mit Bäumen	

Scorecard Scorekarte	Chp. Chp.	Mens Herren	Ladies Damen
Length Länge	6330	6120	5440
Par	72	72	73

Advised golfing ability		0	12	24	36
Empfohlene Spielstärke					
Hcp required	Min. Handicap	32			

CLUB HOUSE & AMENITIES / KLUBHAUS UND NEBENGEBÄUDE 7/10

Pro shop	Pro shop	
Driving range	Übungsplatz	
Sheltered	überdacht	6 mats
On grass	auf Rasen	yes
Putting-green	Putting-grün	yes
Pitching-green	Pitching-grün	yes

HOTEL FACILITIES / HOTEL BESCHREIBUNG 6/10

HOTELS HOTELS
Hotel Landgasthof am Golfplatz — Kemnitz
36 rooms, D DM 140,- — 3 km
Tel (49) 03327 - 4646, Fax (49) 03327 - 464 747

Schlosshotel Cecilienhof — Potsdam
43 rooms, D DM 350,- — 20 km
Tel (49) 0331 - 37 050, Fax (49) 0331 - 292 498

Seidler Art'otel — Potsdam
121 rooms, D DM 380,- — 10 km
Tel (49) 0331 - 9815-510, Fax (49) 0331 - 9815-555

RESTAURANTS RESTAURANT
Pegasus — Potsdam
Tel (49) 0331 - 291 506 — 20 km

Börse — Potsdam
Tel (49) 0331 - 292 505 — 20 km

Dieser Platz wurde in einer Region eröffnet, der es an Golfanlagen nicht mangelt. Man findet ihn unweit von München, Augsburg und Ulm gelegen, in der Umgebung der alten Reichsstadt Memmingen, deren Stadtbild noch gut erhaltene Spuren des Mittelalters und der Renaissance trägt. Trotz seines jungen Alters präsentiert sich der Platz bereits in ausgezeichnetem Zustand, der sich mit der Zeit weiter verbessern sollte. Lediglich der Boden ist noch etwas hart. Die gut gearbeiteten Grüns, die schon dicht mit Gras bewachsen sind, spielen sich etwas weich. Zudem hätte es nicht geschadet, die Grünkörper stärker zu kontourieren, um das Putten, diesen für den Score so ausschlaggebenden Teil des Spiels etwas intersssanter zu machen. Während freistehende Bäume nur vereinzelt eine Rolle spielen, kommt dem Wind als Gefahrenelement eine weitaus grössere Bedeutung zu, insbesondere da man auch noch mit dichtem Rough, Büschen, Fairway- und Grünbunkern, sowie einigen Wasserhindernissen fertigwerden muss. Von mittlerem Schwierigkeitsgrad, ohne nenneswerte Erhebungen, eignet sich der Platz für alle Spielstärken.

This new course was opened in a region where golfing facilities abound, within the immediate vicinity of Munich, Augsburg and Ulm and close to the former imperial city of Memmingen, which has preserved its vestiges of the past (Middle Ages and Renaissance). Despite this being early days, the course is already in excellent condition and should age well (the ground is still a little hard). The well-built greens are already well covered and soft on top, but a little more contouring would not have gone amiss to add a little spice to this department of the game which is so important for scoring. Only a few isolated trees come into play and the wind can be a significant element to be considered, especially with thick rough, bushes, fairway and green-side bunkers and a few water hazards to contend with. Averagely difficult with no significant geographical relief, this is a course for all levels.

Golfclub Memmingen Gut Westerhart e.V. 1994

Westerhart 1b
D - 87740 BUXHEIM

Office	Sekretariat	(49) 08331 - 71 016
Pro shop	Pro shop	(49) 08331 - 71 016
Fax	Fax	(49) 08331 - 71 018
Situation	Lage	

Memmingen (pop. 40 000), 2 km - Ulm (Donau), 55 km

Annual closure	Jährliche Schliessung	1/11 → 1/4
Weekly closure	Wöchentliche Schliessung	no

Monday (Montag): Restaurant closed

Fees main season
Preisliste hochsaison 18 holes

	Week days Woche	We/Bank holidays We/Feiertag
Individual Individuell	DM 60,-	DM 80,-
Couple Ehepaar	DM 120,-	DM 160,-
Students : – 30 %		

Caddy	Caddy	no
Electric Trolley	Elektrokarren	DM 5,-
Buggy	Elektrischer Wagen	DM 50,-
Clubs	Leihschläger	DM 10,-
Credit cards Kreditkarten		no

Access Zufahrt : A96 München-Lindau,
Exit (Ausf.) Aitrach, B12 → Memmingen, → Westerhart
Map 2 on page 362 Karte 2 Seite 362

GOLF COURSE PLATZ 14/20

Site	Lage	▰▰▰▰▱
Maintenance	Instandhaltung	▰▰▰▱▱
Architect	Architekt	Unknown
Type	Typ	parkland, open country
Relief	Begehbarkeit	▰▰▱▱▱
Water in play	Platz mit Wasser	▰▰▱▱▱
Exp. to wind	Wind ausgesetzt	▰▰▰▱▱
Trees in play	Platz mit Bäumen	▰▰▱▱▱

Scorecard Scorekarte	Chp. Chp.	Mens Herren	Ladies Damen
Length Länge	6331	6178	5439
Par	72	72	72

Advised golfing ability		0 12 24 36
Empfohlene Spielstärke		▰▰▰▰▱
Hcp required	Min. Handicap	36

CLUB HOUSE & AMENITIES KLUBHAUS UND NEBENGEBÄUDE 6/10

Pro shop	Pro shop	▰▰▰▱▱
Driving range	Übungsplatz	▰▰▰▱▱
Sheltered	überdacht	10 mats
On grass	auf Rasen	no
Putting-green	Putting-grün	yes
Pitching-green	Pitching-grün	yes

HOTEL FACILITIES HOTEL BESCHREIBUNG 6/10

HOTELS HOTELS

Falken — Memmingen
39 rooms, D DM 180,- — 6 km
Tel (49) 08331 - 47 081, Fax (49) 08331 - 47 086

Park-Hotel an der Stadthalle — Memmingen
90 rooms, D DM 220,- — 6 km
Tel (49) 08331 - 9320, Fax (49) 08331 - 48 439

Allgäuer Tor — Bad Grönenbach
153 rooms, D DM 280,- — 17 km
Tel (49) 08334 - 608 0, Fax (49) 08334 - 608 199

RESTAURANTS RESTAURANT

Weinstube Weber am Bach — Memmingen
Tel (49) 08331 - 2414 — 6 km

Weinhaus Knöringer — Memmingen
Tel (49) 08331 - 2715 — 6 km

439

Der Mittelrheinischer Golfclub liegt gleich neben dem Kurort Bad Ems, wo man sich auf die Behandlung von Hals- und Nasenkrankheiten spezialisiert hat. Der 1928 gebaute Platz ist eingebettet in dichte Vegetation und eröffnet immer wieder schöne Ausblicke auf die Höhenzüge von Eiffel und Taunus. Aufgrund des hügeligen Geländes wird man im Verlauf der Runde mit etwa einem halben Dutzend blinder Schläge konfrontiert. Die Grüns jedoch sind alle gut einsehbar. Leicht gewellt und von mittlerer Grösse bieten sie kaum Anlass für Desaster beim Putten. Golfer, die einen Fade spielen können, haben angesichts der engen Spielbahnen einen kleinen, wenn auch nicht entscheidenden Vorteil. Den Longhittern bieten sich an den fünf Par 5 Löchern gute Birdie-Chancen. Mit ausserdem fünf Par 3 Löchern hat der Platz eine eher ungewöhnliche Konfiguration. Die nicht übermässige Länge des Platzes (nur 9 Löcher verfügen über hintere Abschläge) erleichtert das Miteinander guter und weniger guter Golfer auf einer gemeinsamen Runde. Der Platz lohnt einen Besuch.

The Mittelrheinischer course is located next to the spa of Bad Ems, which specializes in nasal and throat affections. Designed in 1928, the course winds its way through thick vegetation while offering pretty vistas over the Eifel and Taunus uplands. Slightly hilly, the layout entails half a dozen blind shots but all the greens are clearly visible, moderately contoured and of average size (putting disasters are rare). Faders of the ball will enjoy a slight advantage in coping with the narrow fairways, but this is hardly a decisive factor. Long-hitters can look for birdies on the five par 5s; and with five par 3s as well, the course has a rather unusual feel to it. The overall length is very reasonable (there are back tees on 9 holes only) thus making it easier for experienced and inexperienced players to enjoy a round together. Worth knowing.

Mittelrheinischer Golf Club Bad Ems e.V. — 1928

Denzer Heide
D - 56130 BAD EMS

Office	Sekretariat	(49) 02603 - 6541
Pro shop	Pro shop	(49) 02603 - 14 510
Fax	Fax	(49) 02603 - 13 995
Situation	Lage	

Bad Ems (pop. 10 000), 3 km - Koblenz (pop. 108 000), 10 km

Annual closure	Jährliche Schliessung	no
Weekly closure	Wöchentliche Schliessung	no

Monday (Montag): Restaurant closed

Fees main season
Preisliste hochsaison 18 holes

	Week days Woche	We/Bank holidays We/Feiertag
Individual Individuell	DM 70,-	DM 90,-
Couple Ehepaar	DM 140,-	DM 180,-

under 21 years : – 50%

Caddy	Caddy	on request
Electric Trolley	Elektrokarren	yes
Buggy	Elektrischer Wagen	no
Clubs	Leihschläger	yes
Credit cards Kreditkarten		no

GOLF COURSE
PLATZ — 17/20

Site	Lage	
Maintenance	Instandhaltung	
Architect	Architekt	Karl-Heinz Hoffmann
Type	Typ	parkland
Relief	Begehbarkeit	
Water in play	Platz mit Wasser	
Exp. to wind	Wind ausgesetzt	
Trees in play	Platz mit Bäumen	

Scorecard Scorekarte	Chp. Chp.	Mens Herren	Ladies Damen
Length Länge	5925	5925	5243
Par	72	72	72

Advised golfing ability Empfohlene Spielstärke	0	12	24	36
Hcp required Min. Handicap	36			

CLUB HOUSE & AMENITIES
KLUBHAUS UND NEBENGEBÄUDE — 7/10

Pro shop	Pro shop	
Driving range	Übungsplatz	
Sheltered	überdacht	6 mats
On grass	auf Rasen	yes
Putting-green	Putting-grün	yes
Pitching-green	Pitching-grün	yes

HOTEL FACILITIES
HOTEL BESCHREIBUNG — 7/10

HOTELS HOTELS

Golf Hotel Denzerheide — Golfplatz
8 rooms, D DM 100,-
Tel (49) 02603 - 6159, Fax (49) 02603 - 13995

Atlantis Kurhotel — Bad Ems
107 rooms, D DM 250,- — 3 km
Tel (49) 02603 - 7990, Fax (49) 02603 - 799 252

Kleiner Riesen - 28 rooms, D DM 200,- — Koblenz
Tel (49) 0261 - 32 077, Fax (49) 0261 - 160 725 — 10 km

Scandic Crown Hotel - 168 rooms, D DM 320,- — Koblenz
Tel (49) 0261 - 1360, Fax (49) 0261 - 136 1199 — 10 km

RESTAURANTS RESTAURANT

Schweizer Haus — Bad Ems
Tel (49) 02603 - 70 783 — 3 km

Histor. Wirtshaus an der Lahn — Lahnstein
Tel (49) 02621 - 7270 — 15 km

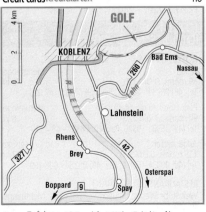

Access Zufahrt : A3 Frankfurt-Köln. Exit (Ausf.)
Montabaur. B49 → Koblenz. → Bad Ems/Denzerheide.
Map 3 on page 364 Karte 3 Seite 364

440

MOTZENER SEE

17 8 6

Dies ist einer der neuen, guten Plätze, die in jüngerer Zeit in Deutschland entstanden sind. Seine hohen technischen Qualitäten werden vor allem den besseren Golfern auffallen. Kurt Rossknecht liess sich beim Bau der Anlage sowohl von amerikanischen wie auch schottischen Stilelementen inspirieren. Entstanden ist dabei ein Platz, der mittels wellenförmiger Fairways und tiefer Bunkerprofile wie die moderne Version eines Linksplatzeses wirkt. Die gut erkennbaren Hindernisse geben die ideale Spiellinie vor. Zudem sind sie so klug positioniert, dass gute Golfschläge nicht bestraft werden. Diese Feststellung gilt im übrigen für das gesamte Layout des Platzes. Allrounder werden diesen Platz ob seines abwechslungsreichen Lochdesigns - an 7 Löchern kommt Wasser ins Spiel - lieben. Je nach Charakter des Loches sind sowohl flache lang ausrollende, als auch hohe Schläge zum Grün gefordert, für deren Ausführung der komplette Schlägersatz herhalten muss. Die grosse Anzahl verschiedener Abschläge erlaubt jedem Golfer eine seiner Spielstärke entsprechende Wahl, aber auch die Möglichkeit je nach Tagesform und Lust zu variieren.

This is one of the best recent courses in Germany, with technical virtues that are more obvious to top level golfers. Kurt Rossknecht was inspired by both American and Scottish styles and has come up with a sort of modernized links (rolling fairways and shaped bunkers). The very clear view of hazards points to the ideal line of play, while their clever positioning and the honest layout never penalizes good golf shots. Good all-round players will love this course, where they can chop and change between low rolled shots and high approaches required by the variety of holes (water is in play on seven holes). Here, you will play every club in the bag. The large number of tees makes this a course that caters to each level of proficiency, and to each player's form and mood... not forgetting that the latter may grow darker with the pin positions on the huge, well-contoured greens.

Berliner Golf- & Country Club am Motzener See e.V.   1991

Am Golfplatz 5
D - 15741 MOTZEN

Office	Sekretariat	(49) 033769 - 50 130
Pro shop	Pro shop	(49) 033769 - 50 128
Fax	Fax	(49) 033769 - 50 134
Situation	Lage	

Berlin (pop. 3 500 000), 40 km - Teupitz (pop. 1 700), 7 km

Annual closure   Jährliche Schliessung   1/1 → 1/2

Weekly closure   Wöchentliche Schliessung   no
Monday (Montag): Restaurant closed

Fees main season
Preisliste hochsaison full day

	Week days Woche	We/Bank holidays We/Feiertag
Individual Individuell	DM 90,-	DM 110,-
Couple Ehepaar	DM 180,-	DM 220,-
under 21 years/Students : - 50 %		
Caddy	Caddy	DM 35,-
Electric Trolley	Elektrokarren	no
Buggy	Elektrischer Wagen	no
Clubs	Leihschläger	DM 35,-
Credit cards Kreditkarten		no

Mittenwalde
Gallun
246
Bestensee
179
Motzener See   Motzen
Pätzer Hintersee
GOLF
nach BERLIN
nach Cottbus Dresden   Töpchin
A 13
Schwerin   **4**   Groß Köris
Teupitzer See
0   2   4 km
Teupitz
5
nach Königs Wusterhausen
3

Access Zufahrt : Berlin, A13 → Dresden. Exit (Ausf.)
Mittenwalde → Gallun-Bestensee → Golf
Map 6 on page 371 Karte 6 Seite 371

GOLF COURSE / PLATZ   **17** /20

Site	Lage	
Maintenance	Instandhaltung	
Architect	Architekt	Kurt Rossknecht
Type	Typ	open country
Relief	Begehbarkeit	
Water in play	Platz mit Wasser	
Exp. to wind	Wind ausgesetzt	
Trees in play	Platz mit Bäumen	

Scorecard Scorekarte	Chp. Chp.	Mens Herren	Ladies Damen
Length Länge	6330	5915	5200
Par	73	72	72

Advised golfing ability   0   12   24   36
Empfohlene Spielstärke
Hcp required   Min. Handicap   36

CLUB HOUSE & AMENITIES / KLUBHAUS UND NEBENGEBÄUDE   **8** /10

Pro shop	Pro shop	
Driving range	Übungsplatz	
Sheltered	überdacht	10 mats
On grass	auf Rasen	yes
Putting-green	Putting-grün	yes
Pitching-green	Pitching-grün	yes

441

HOTEL FACILITIES / HOTEL BESCHREIBUNG   **6** /10

HOTELS HOTELS
Residenz am Motzener See   Motzen
63 rooms, D DM 245,-   1 km
Tel (49) 033769 - 850, Fax (49) 033769 - 85 100

Schlosshotel Teupitz   Teupitz
38 rooms, D DM 200,-   8 km
Tel (49) 033766 - 600, Fax (49) 033766 - 60 455

Lindengarten   Klein Koris
33 rooms, D DM 160,-   5 km
Tel (49) 033766 - 42 063, Fax (49) 033766 - 42 062

RESTAURANTS RESTAURANT
Residenz am Motzener See   Motzen
Tel (49) 033769 - 850   1 km

Schlosshotel Teupitz   Teupitz
Tel (49) 033766 - 600   8 km

Die Anlage macht einen sehr kompletten Eindruck und verfügt über ausgezeichnete Übungseinrichtungen. Der Golfplatz verfügt über weite offene Flächen und deutlich voneinander abgetrennte Spielbahnen und Roughzonen, die ebenso eine Gefahr darstellen wie die traditionellen Hindernisse Wasser, Bäume und Bunker. Mindestens bis Juli lässt man das Rough hier wachsen und verengt somit ganz beträchtlich die Fairway-Landezonen. Das flache Terrain lässt einen, auch wenn man mehr als 18 Loch am Tag spielt, nicht ermüden. Die Grüns sind gut einsehbar, ausgezeichnet geformt und ordentlich verteidigt. Bei der Planung des Platzes wurde offensichtlich auf die Bedürfnisse der Durchschnitts-Golfer Rücksicht genommen, so dass diese sich hier denn auch sehr wohl fühlen werden. Das liegt auch daran, dass es hier wenig gibt, was dem ohnehin geplagten Ego des Golfers zu schaffen macht. Sehr gute Spieler werden allerdings etwas anspruchsvolleren Anlagen vorziehen.

A very comprehensive facility, with good practice installations, but the course is still in its infancy. It will be interesting to keep track of how it matures. There are wide open spaces here, clearly separated fairways and rough that is as much a hazard as the traditional dangers of water, trees and bunkers. Up until July, at least, it is kept long and thick and considerably narrows the fairways. The flattish terrain makes this an easily walkable course, even if you are out to play more than 18 holes in one day. The greens are clearly visible and properly designed with reasonable lines of defence. The designers obviously had the average golfer in mind, and he or she will find this very much to their liking. For once there is not too much here to inflict further suffering on the golfer's much-battered ego. Very good players will doubtless prefer to play on slightly more demanding courses.

Golf Club Mülheim an der Ruhr e.V. 1980

Am Golfplatz 1
D - 45481 MÜLHEIM

Office	Sekretariat	(49) 0208 - 483 607
Pro shop	Pro shop	(49) 0208 - 480 718
Fax	Fax	(49) 0208 - 481 153
Situation	Lage	

Mülheim (pop. 177 000), 10 km -Düsseldorf, 15 km

Annual closure	Jährliche Schliessung	no
Weekly closure	Wöchentliche Schliessung	no

Monday (Montag) : Restaurant closed

Fees main season
Preisliste hochsaison 18 holes

	Week days Woche	We/Bank holidays We/Feiertag
Individual Individuell	DM 90,-	DM 90,-
Couple Ehepaar	DM 180,-	DM 180,-

We: with members (nur in Mitgliederbegleitung) under 21 years/Students : – 50%

Caddy	Caddy	no
Electric Trolley	Elektrokarren	no
Buggy	Elektrischer Wagen	no
Clubs	Leihschläger	no
Credit cards Kreditkarten		no

442

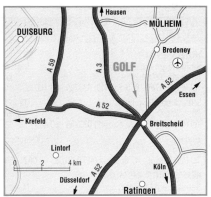

Access Zufahrt : A3 Köln-Duisburg. Exit (Ausf.)
"Autobahnkreuz Breitscheid" → Essen, → Mülheim.
2 km turn left → Golf
Map 3 on page 364 Karte 3 Seite 364

GOLF COURSE
PLATZ   13/20

Site	Lage	
Maintenance	Instandhaltung	
Architect	Architekt	DeutscheGolf Consult
Type	Typ	open country, forest
Relief	Begehbarkeit	
Water in play	Platz mit Wasser	
Exp. to wind	Wind ausgesetzt	
Trees in play	Platz mit Bäumen	

Scorecard	Chp.	Mens	Ladies
Scorekarte	Chp.	Herren	Damen
Length Länge	6159	6159	5466
Par	72	72	72

Advised golfing ability		0	12	24	36
Empfohlene Spielstärke					
Hcp required	Min. Handicap	36			

CLUB HOUSE & AMENITIES
KLUBHAUS UND NEBENGEBÄUDE   6/10

Pro shop	Pro shop	
Driving range	Übungsplatz	
Sheltered	überdacht	8 mats
On grass	auf Rasen	yes
Putting-green	Putting-grün	yes
Pitching-green	Pitching-grün	yes

HOTEL FACILITIES
HOTEL BESCHREIBUNG   7/10

HOTELS HOTELS
Dorint Budget Hotel — Ratingen
118 rooms, D DM 150,- — 3 km
Tel (49) 02102 - 9185, Fax (49) 02102 - 918 900

Novotel Düsseldorf-Ratingen — Ratingen
118 rooms, D DM 280,- — 3 km
Tel (49) 02102 - 1870, Fax (49) 02102 - 18 418

Allgäuer Hof — Ratingen
15 rooms, D DM 165,- — 10 km
Tel (49) 02102 - 95 410, Fax (49) 02102 - 954 123

Steigenberger Parkhotel — Düsseldorf
160 rooms, D DM 450,- — 20 km
Tel (49) 0211 - 13 810, Fax (49) 0211 - 131 679

RESTAURANTS RESTAURANT
Ratinger Stube - Tel (49) 02102 - 24 800 — Ratingen 10 km
Am Kamin - Tel(49) 0208 - 760 036 — Mülheim8 km

MÜNCHEN-RIEDHOF

16	7	7

München-Riedhof liegt in unmittelbarer Nähe zum Starnberger See, einem der grössten bayerischen Seen, auf halbem Weg zwischen München und den bayerischen Alpen. Der von Heinz Fehring entworfene Platz ist vom Layout, dem Pflegezustand und vor allem dem Service her sehr amerikanisch. Greenfeespieler erhalten neben den Pin-Positions auch die Informationen über die "Schnelligkeit" der Grüns (Stimpmeter). Das US-Flair wird durch die vielen Wasserhindernisse (Teiche) verstärkt. Dazu gibt einige Erhebungen im Gelände, die die Schlägerwahl erheblich erschweren. Die Schwierigkeiten sind gut erkennbar. Das gilt auch für die Wasserhindernisse, die für missratene Schläge allerdings weniger Gefahr darstellen, als dies Bäume und Bunker tun. Der grösstenteils spektakuläre, manchmal etwas trügerische Platz bleibt einem gut im Gedächtnis haften, was ein gutes Zeichen ist. Da die Grüns sehr gut verteidigt sind, ist eine gute Ballkontrolle unerlässlich; dennoch werden durchschnittliche Spieler hier ebenso auf ihre Kosten kommmen wie Fortgeschrittene.

The south of Munich is a very privileged region both for sightseeing attractions and the number of courses which offer a wide variety of styles. München-Riedhof is within immediate reach of the Starnberger See, one of Bavaria's largest lakes half-way between Munich and the Bavarian Alps. The course, designed by Heinz Fehring, is not the easiest in the world owing to yardage, water hazards and some steeply contoured terrain, which complicates appreciation of distance. The course is, though, very pleasant to walk around. The difficulties are there to be seen; water is, too, but is not so dangerous for mis-hit shots as the trees and bunkers. Often spectacular and sometimes a wee treacherous, the course sticks in your memory, which is a good sign. As the greens are very well guarded, good ball control is, as always, important, but average players will have as much fun as the experts.

Golfclub München-Riedhof e.V.		**1989**
Riedhof 16		
D - 85244 EGLING-RIEDHOF		

Office	Sekretariat	(49) 08171 - 219 50
Pro shop	Pro shop	(49) 08171 - 219 50
Fax	Fax	(49) 08171 - 219 511
Situation	Lage	
München, 25 km - Wolfratshausen (pop. 16 000), 3 km		

Annual closure	Jährliche Schliessung	no

Weekly closure	Wöchentliche Schliessung	no
Monday (Montag) : Restaurant closed		

Fees main season
Preisliste hochsaison 18 holes

	Week days Woche	We/Bank holidays We/Feiertag
Individual Individuell	DM 160,-	DM 160,-
Couple Ehepaar	DM 320,-	DM 320,-
We: with members (nur in Mitgliederbegleitung)		

Caddy	Caddy	no
Electric Trolley	Elektrokarren	no
Buggy	Elektrischer Wagen	no
Clubs	Leihschläger	no
Credit cards Kreditkarten		no

München
0   2   4 km
Wolfratshausen
Dorfen   **GOLF**
6
Waldram
Starnberger See
A 95
Gartenberg
Loisach
ISAR
Penzberg
Bad Tölz
11

Access Zufahrt : A95 München-Garmisch-Partenkirchen.
Exit (Ausf.) Wolfratshausen, → Autobahn Salzburg-
Wolfratshausen. → Egling
Map 2 on page 362 Karte 2 Seite 362

GOLF COURSE
PLATZ   **16**/20

Site	Lage	
Maintenance	Instandhaltung	
Architect	Architekt	Heinz Fehring
Type	Typ	open country, hilly
Relief	Begehbarkeit	
Water in play	Platz mit Wasser	
Exp. to wind	Wind ausgesetzt	
Trees in play	Platz mit Bäumen	

Scorecard	Chp.	Mens	Ladies
Scorekarte	Chp.	Herren	Damen
Length Länge	6150	6024	5307
Par	72	72	72

Advised golfing ability	0	12	24	36
Empfohlene Spielstärke				
Hcp required Min. Handicap	34			

CLUB HOUSE & AMENITIES
KLUBHAUS UND NEBENGEBÄUDE   **7**/10

Pro shop	Pro shop	
Driving range	Übungsplatz	
Sheltered	überdacht	10 mats
On grass	auf Rasen	yes
Putting-green	Putting-grün	yes
Pitching-green	Pitching-grün	yes

HOTEL FACILITIES
HOTEL BESCHREIBUNG   **7**/10

HOTELS HOTELS

Thalhammer	Wolfratshausen
23 rooms, D DM 170,-	5 km
Tel (49) 08171 - 7149, Fax (49) 08171 - 76 185	
Märchenwald	Wolfratshausen
14 rooms, D DM 130,-	5 km
Tel (49) 08171 - 29 096, Fax (49) 08171 - 22 236	
Ritterhof	Grünwald
20 rooms, D DM 180,-	10 km
Tel (49) 089 - 649 0090, Fax (49) 089 - 649 3012	
Tannenhof	Grünwald
21 rooms, D DM 200,-	10 km
Tel (49) 089 - 641 8960, Fax (49) 089 - 641 5608	

RESTAURANTS RESTAURANT

Patrizierhof	Wolfratshausen
Tel (49) 08171 - 225 33	5 km
Vogelbauer - Tel (49) 08171 - 290 63	Neufahrn 5 km

443

MÜNCHNER-STRASSLACH

15	6	7

In der Umgebung der Metropole München ist dies wohl einer der meist bespielten Golfplätze. Gastspieler sind am Wochenende nur in Begleitung eines Mitglieds erlaubt... Der Platz wurde 1910 inmitten einer typisch bayerischen Landschaft auf leicht hügeligem Terrain angelegt. Auf dem Platz findet sich eine Anzahl wunderschöner grosser Bäume, die an den Doglegs gefährlich ins Spiel kommen. Einige Seen und Wasserläufe sowie knapp 50 sehr sorgfältig plazierte Bunker komplettieren das Repertoire an Hindernissen. Auf den ersten Blick mag der Platz nicht sonderlich schwierig erscheinen, dieser Eindruck wird sich allerdings im Verlauf der Runde revidieren, nicht zuletzt aufgrund einer Reihe schlecht erkennbarer Hindernisse. Auf der zweiten Runde fühlt man sich schon weitaus wohler, da man dann weiss, wie der Platz taktisch zu spielen ist. Der ausgezeichnete Hauptplatz wird ergänzt durch einen nicht minder guten 9-Loch-Kurzplatz, der allerdings noch einwachsen muss.

This is one of the busiest courses around the magnificent greater metropolitan area of Munich, and playing here on week-ends can be very difficult for green-feers. Created in 1910 over averagely-hilly terrain, the course runs over typically Bavarian landscape, with some beautiful big trees (very dangerous on the dog-legs), a few lakes and streams and a little under 50 carefully-located bunkers. At first sight it doesn't look too difficult, but out on the course it can be quite a handful with a number of hazards hidden from view. Second time out, you feel more comfortable and playing tactics are clearer. A class course supplemented by a very good and shortish 9-holer.

Münchner Golf Club e.V., Strasslach 1910

Tölzerstrasse 95
D - 82064 STRASSLACH

Office	Sekretariat	(49) 08170 - 450
Pro shop	Pro shop	(49) 08170 - 7254
Fax	Fax	(49) 08170 - 611
Situation	Lage	

München, 25 km - Strasslach (pop. 2 700), 3 km

Annual closure	Jährliche Schliessung	no
Weekly closure	Wöchentliche Schliessung	no

Monday (Montag): Restaurant closed

Fees main season
Preisliste hochsaison 18 holes

	Week days Woche	We/Bank holidays We/Feiertag
Individual Individuell	DM 120,-	DM 150,-
Couple Ehepaar	DM 240,-	DM 300,-

We: with members (nur in Mitgliederbegleitung): DM 80,-

Caddy	Caddy	no
Electric Trolley	Elektrokarren	yes
Buggy	Elektrischer Wagen	yes
Clubs	Leihschläger	no
Credit cards Kreditkarten		no

GOLF COURSE
PLATZ
15/20

Site	Lage	▮▮▮▮▯
Maintenance	Instandhaltung	▮▮▮▯▯
Architect	Architekt	
Type	Typ	open country
Relief	Begehbarkeit	▮▮▮▯▯
Water in play	Platz mit Wasser	▮▮▯▯▯
Exp. to wind	Wind ausgesetzt	▮▮▮▯▯
Trees in play	Platz mit Bäumen	▮▮▮▯▯

Scorecard Scorekarte	Chp. Chp.	Mens Herren	Ladies Damen
Length Länge	6126	6126	5432
Par	72	72	72

Advised golfing ability		0	12	24	36
Empfohlene Spielstärke		▮▮▮			
Hcp required	Min. Handicap	35			

CLUB HOUSE & AMENITIES
KLUBHAUS UND NEBENGEBÄUDE
6/10

Pro shop	Pro shop	▮▮▮▮▯
Driving range	Übungsplatz	▮▮▮▯▯
Sheltered	überdacht	2 mats
On grass	auf Rasen	yes
Putting-green	Putting-grün	yes
Pitching-green	Pitching-grün	yes

HOTEL FACILITIES
HOTEL BESCHREIBUNG
7/10

HOTELS HOTELS

Ritterhof — Grünwald — 4 km
20 rooms, D DM 180,-
Tel (49) 089 - 649 0090, Fax (49) 089 - 649 3012

Alter Wirt — Grünwald — 4 km
50 rooms, D DM 170,-
Tel (49) 089 - 641 7855, Fax (49) 089 - 641 4266

Schloss Hotel — Grünwald — 4 km
15 rooms, D DM 250,-
Tel (49) 089 - 641 8960, Fax (49) 089 - 641 930 3

RESTAURANTS RESTAURANT

Gasthof zum Wildpark — Strasslach — 1 km
Tel (49) 08170 - 635

Hubertus — Schäfftlern — 5 km
Tel (49) 08178 - 4851

Access Zufahrt : München Süd → Grünwald.
In Grünwald → Bad Tölz. Golf on the left.
Map 2 on page 362 Karte 2 Seite 362

Der Platz wurde 1986 modernisiert, wobei aber die alten Schwierigkeiten erhalten blieben. Erste Notwendigkeit hier ist Präzision, da die Fairways meist nicht sehr breit und zudem von dichtem Wald umgeben sind, was dem Platz den angenehmen Nebeneffekt von Ruhe und Abgeschiedenheit vermittelt. Im vergangenen wurden fast alle Löcher modifiziert und Wasserteiche am 3. Und am 14. Loch gebaut. Der Platz ist sehr ungewöhnlich, da alle zehn Par-4-Löcher und alle vier Par-5-Löcher "blind" sind, d.h. man sieht am Abschlag nur von den Par 3-Löchern die Fahne. Die Spiellinie ist deshalb für bessere Spieler nicht erkennbar. Man benötigt etliche Runden oder die Begleitung eines Platzkenners, um sie herauszufinden. Wer kommt schon auf die Idee am 16. Loch den Ball durch einen Stromleitungsmasten zu schlagen? Schwächere Spieler müssen gerade schlagen und haben dann noch ein langes Eisen oder ein Fairway-Holz zum Grün. Dafür entschädigt der Ausblick auf den spektakulären Rotenfels für diese architektonische Sünde.

Nahetal is situated in the spa town of Bad Münster close to the old Roman town of Bad Kreuznach. The course was modernized in 1986, but the difficulties remain the same. The first is the need to play straight, as the fairways are not always wide and are lined with some pretty dense trees with heavy undergrowth, a feature that adds to a pleasant impression of peace and quiet. Last year most holes have been modified and ponds added on holes 3 and 14. The course design is rather unusual since all par 4s and all par 5s are blind so the flagstick is visible only on the par 3s. The line of play is hardly visible for better players, so you need the advice of a knowledgeable player. Who would think of hitting the drive through an electricity pylon on N° 16? However lesser players have to go the straight route, which means hitting a long iron or a fairway wood into the green. The spectacular view of the Rotenfels makes up for this shortcoming in golf course design.

Golfclub Nahetal e.V. — 1976

Drei Buchen
D - 55583 BAD MÜNSTER AM STEIN-EBERNBURG

Office	Sekretariat	(49) 06708 - 2145
Pro shop	Pro shop	(49) 06708 - 4399
Fax	Fax	(49) 06708 - 1731
Situation	Lage	

Bad Kreuznach (pop. 43 000), 12 km - Mainz, 45 km

Annual closure	Jährliche Schliessung	no
Weekly closure	Wöchentliche Schliessung	no

Monday (Montag) : Restaurant closed

Fees main season
Preisliste hochsaison 18 holes

	Week days Woche	We/Bank holidays We/Feiertag
Individual Individuell	DM 70,-	DM 90,-
Couple Ehepaar	DM 140,-	DM 180,-

under 21 years/Students : – 50 %

Caddy	Caddy	on request, DM 50,-
Electric Trolley	Elektrokarren	DM 18,-
Buggy	Elektrischer Wagen	DM 50,- (medical)
Clubs	Leihschläger	DM 25,-
Credit cards Kreditkarten		only Pro Shop

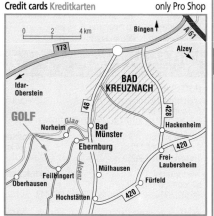

Access Zufahrt : Mainz A60 W, Kreuz Bingen A61 Süd. Exit (Ausf.) Bad Kreuznach. Bad Kreuznach 4s B48 → Bad Münster → Ebernburg. Right in Schlossgartenstr. Right, Wanderweg Dreibuchen.
Map 3 on page 365 Karte 3 Seite 365

GOLF COURSE
PLATZ — **14**/20

Site	Lage	▬▬▬▬▭
Maintenance	Instandhaltung	▬▬▬▬▭
Architect	Architekt	Armin Keller
Type	Typ	forest
Relief	Begehbarkeit	▬▭▭▭▭
Water in play	Platz mit Wasser	▬▬▭▭▭
Exp. to wind	Wind ausgesetzt	▬▭▭▭▭
Trees in play	Platz mit Bäumen	▬▬▬▬▭

Scorecard Scorekarte	Chp. Chp.	Mens Herren	Ladies Damen
Length Länge	6090	6090	5344
Par	72	72	72

Advised golfing ability	0	12	24	36
Empfohlene Spielstärke		▬▬▬▭▭		
Hcp required Min. Handicap	We: 36			

CLUB HOUSE & AMENITIES
KLUBHAUS UND NEBENGEBÄUDE — **8**/10

Pro shop	Pro shop	▬▬▬▬▭
Driving range	Übungsplatz	▬▬▬▬▭
Sheltered	überdacht	10 mats
On grass	auf Rasen	yes
Putting-green	Putting-grün	yes
Pitching-green	Pitching-grün	yes

445

HOTEL FACILITIES
HOTEL BESCHREIBUNG — **6**/10

HOTELS HOTELS
Parkhotel Kurhaus — Bad Kreuznach
100 rooms, D DM 220,- — 12 km
Tel (49) 0671 - 8020, Fax (49) 0671 - 354 77

Landhotel Kauzenberg — Bad Kreuznach
46 rooms, D DM 220,- — 4 km
Tel (49) 0671 - 38 000, Fax (49) 0671 - 380 0124

Hotel am Kurpark — Bad Münster a. Stein
30 rooms, D DM 180,- — 2 km
Tel (49) 06708 - 1292, Fax (49) 06708 - 4648

RESTAURANTS RESTAURANT
Metzlers Gasthof — Bad Kreuznach-Hackenheim
Tel (49) 0671 - 65 312 — 14 km

Die Kauzenburg — Bad Kreuznach
Tel (49) 0671 - 380 0801 — 12 km

NECKARTAL

16 6 7

In unmittelbarer Nähe von Stuttgart gelegen ist der Platz leicht zu erreichen. Nicht-Golfer können sich die Zeit mit einem Besuch von Park, Märchengarten und dem stark von Versailles inspirierten Schloss Ludwigsburg vertreiben. Der nüchtern wirkende Golfplatz spiegelt in keiner Weise den "blühenden Barock" des Schlosses wider. Am Rand eines Waldes auf flachem Gelände angelegt, entwarf Bernhard von Limburger einen in Stil und Taktik eher amerikanisch anmutenden Platz. Länge ist ein entscheidender Faktor um hier erfolgreich zu spielen. Daneben muss man noch mit Bäumen und Rough fertigwerden. Die Grüns sind ausgezeichnet verteidigt, so dass ein gutes Kurzes Spiel vonnöten ist, wenn man sein Handicap hier spielen will. Trotz ansprechender Gestaltung ist der Platz ganz sicher kein Meisterwerk, ein Besuch lohnt sich dennoch allemal.

The course is next door to Stuttgart and so easy to reach. In addition, non-players will have all the time in the world to visit the park, the fairy-tale garden (Märchengarten) and Ludwigsburg castle, disproportionately inspired by Versailles. But there is no trace of the castle's "blossoming baroque style" on this very sober course. Designed by von Limburger along the edge of a forest over flattish terrain, it is rather American in style and in tactics. Length here is a key factor for a successful round and forms the major difficulty with the trees and rough. The greens are protected well enough to demand a very sharp short game if you wish to play to your handicap. Well landscaped, this course is by no means a masterpiece but playing here really is time well spent.

Golfclub Neckartal e.V.   1974

Aldingerstrasse, 975
D - 71638 LUDWIGSBURG-PATTONVILLE

Office	Sekretariat	(49) 07141 - 871 319
Pro shop	Pro shop	(49) 07141 - 84 732
Fax	Fax	(49) 07141 - 81 716
Situation	Lage	

Stuttgart, 15 km - Ludwigsburg (pop. 86 000), 3 km

Annual closure	Jährliche Schliessung	1/11 → 28/2
Weekly closure	Wöchentliche Schliessung	no

Monday (Montag): Restaurant closed

Fees main season
Preisliste hochsaison full day

	Week days Woche	We/Bank holidays We/Feiertag
Individual Individuell	DM 60,-	DM 70,-
Couple Ehepaar	DM 120,-	DM 140,-

Caddy	Caddy	no
Electric Trolley	Elektrokarren	no
Buggy	Elektrischer Wagen	no
Clubs	Leihschläger	DM 10,-

Credit cards Kreditkarten   no

GOLF COURSE
PLATZ   **16**/20

Site	Lage	
Maintenance	Instandhaltung	
Architect	Architekt	B. von Limburger
Type	Typ	forest, open country
Relief	Begehbarkeit	
Water in play	Platz mit Wasser	
Exp. to wind	Wind ausgesetzt	
Trees in play	Platz mit Bäumen	

Scorecard Scorekarte	Chp. Chp.	Mens Herren	Ladies Damen
Length Länge	6278	6278	5493
Par	73	73	73

Advised golfing ability	0 12 24 36
Empfohlene Spielstärke	
Hcp required Min. Handicap	30 Men, 36 Ladies

CLUB HOUSE & AMENITIES
KLUBHAUS UND NEBENGEBÄUDE   **6**/10

Pro shop	Pro shop	
Driving range	Übungsplatz	
Sheltered	überdacht	6 mats
On grass	auf Rasen	yes, April-Nov.
Putting-green	Putting-grün	yes
Pitching-green	Pitching-grün	yes

HOTEL FACILITIES
HOTEL BESCHREIBUNG   **7**/10

HOTELS HOTELS

Schlosshotel Monrepos   Ludwigsburg
81 rooms, D DM 280,-   7 km
Tel (49) 07141 - 3020, Fax (49) 07141 - 302 200

Kronen Stuben   Ludwigsburg
8 rooms, D DM 135,-   4 km
Tel (49) 07141 - 96250

Nestor Hotel   Ludwigsburg
60 rooms, D DM 180,-   4 km
Tel (49) 07141 - 9670, Fax (49) 07141 - 967 113

Adler   Asperg
65 rooms, D DM 250,-   8 km
Tel (49) 07141 - 26 600, Fax (49) 07141 - 266 060

RESTAURANTS RESTAURANT
Adler - Tel (49) 07141 - 26 600   Asperg 8 km

446

Access Zufahrt : A8 Stuttgart-Heilbronn. Exit (Ausf.)
Stuttgart-Zuffenhausen. B27 → Kornwestheim. Exit
Kornwestheim-Nord. → Remseck (Aldinger Strasse).
2 km turn left. **Map 1 on page 361** Karte 1 Seite 361

NEUHOF

Eines soll gleich zu Beginn gesagt sein, Spieler mit hohem Handicap können von dem, an den ersten beiden Löchern ins Spiel kommenden Wasser, leicht abgeschreckt werden. Alles in allem sind die vorhandenen Schwierigkeiten durchaus dazu angetan, den durchschnittlichen "Hacker" permanent zu beunruhigen. Einige extrem lange Par 4 Löcher stellen eine anspruchsvolle Aufgabe selbst für bessere Spieler dar, die auch beim Anspiel einiger frontal von Gräben geschützter Grüns, eine harte Nuss zu knacken haben. Die intelligente Plazierung der Hindernisse spricht für den Sachverstand der Architekten. Die sehr amerikanische Platzarchitektur mit dem Merkmal gut erkennbarer Schwierigkeiten verlangt vom Golfer häufig die Entscheidung, entweder auf Angriff oder auf Sicherheit zu spielen. Bevor man daran geht, auf diesem technisch wie auch taktisch anspruchsvollen Layout, ein gutes Zählspiel-Ergebnis zu erreichen, empfiehlt es sich vorher einige Runden Matchplay zu spielen.

Let it be said right away that here, many high-handicappers may well be seriously put off by the water protecting the first holes. By and large there are quite a few difficulties around, enough to prevent the average hacker from ever really feeling confident. Some very long par 4s will also be a handful for the better players, who will need to think long and hard before trying to hit several greens guarded by frontal ditches. The designers knew their golf and have laid out hazards intelligently. Rather American in style, Neuhof calls for serious debate over whether to "go for it" or lay up. In this sense the difficulties are clear to see, but before envisioning any idea of a good card from this technical and tactical examination of your golfing skills, you are better off trying a few rounds of match-play.

Golf Club Neuhof e.V.   1984

Hofgut Neuhof
D - 63303 DREIEICH

Office	Sekretariat	(49) 06102 - 327 010
Pro shop	Pro shop	(49) 06102 - 33 331
Fax	Fax	(49) 06102 - 327 012
Situation	Lage	

Frankfurt (pop. 660 000), 15 km - Neu-Isenburg, 6 km

Annual closure	Jährliche Schliessung	1/1 → 28/2
Weekly closure	Wöchentliche Schliessung	no

Monday (Montag) : Restaurant closed

Fees main season
Preisliste hochsaison 18 holes

	Week days Woche	We/Bank holidays We/Feiertag
Individual Individuell	DM 100,-	DM 100,-
Couple Ehepaar	DM 200,-	DM 200,-

We: with members (nur in Mitgliederbegleitung) / under 21 years/Students : - 50%

Caddy	Caddy	on request
Electric Trolley	Elektrokarren	no
Buggy	Elektrischer Wagen	no
Clubs	Leihschläger	DM 10,-
Credit cards Kreditkarten		no

Access Zufahrt : A3 Frankfurt-Würzburg. Exit (Ausf.) Offenbach-Kreuz. B661 → Langen/Darmstadt. Exit Dreieich-Götzenhaim. 3 km Golf
Map 3 on page 365 Karte 3 Seite 365

GOLF COURSE
PLATZ   15/20

Site	Lage	
Maintenance	Instandhaltung	
Architect	Architekt	Hauser Patrick Merrigan
Type	Typ	parkland
Relief	Begehbarkeit	
Water in play	Platz mit Wasser	
Exp. to wind	Wind ausgesetzt	
Trees in play	Platz mit Bäumen	

Scorecard Scorekarte	Chp. Chp.	Mens Herren	Ladies Damen
Length Länge	6151	5995	5340
Par	72	72	72

Advised golfing ability		0 12 24 36
Empfohlene Spielstärke		
Hcp required	Min. Handicap	28 Men, 32 Ladies

CLUB HOUSE & AMENITIES
KLUBHAUS UND NEBENGEBÄUDE   7/10

Pro shop	Pro shop	
Driving range	Übungsplatz	
Sheltered	überdacht	yes
On grass	auf Rasen	yes
Putting-green	Putting-grün	yes
Pitching-green	Pitching-grün	yes

447

HOTEL FACILITIES
HOTEL BESCHREIBUNG   7/10

HOTELS HOTELS

Kempinski Hotel Gravenbruch   Neu-Isenburg-
289 rooms, D DM 300,-   Gravenbruch
Tel (49) 06102 - 5050, Fax (49) 06102 - 505 445   5 km

Balance Hotel   Neu-Isenbuch
164 rooms, D DM 300,-   5 km
Tel (49) 06102 - 7460, Fax (49) 06102 - 746 746

Arabella Grand Hotel   Frankfurt
378 rooms, D DM 500,-   15 km
Tel (49) 069 - 29 810, Fax (49) 069 - 298 1810

RESTAURANTS RESTAURANT

Neuer Haferkasten   Neu-Isenburg
Tel (49) 06102 - 35 329   5 km

Grüner Baum   Neu-Isenburg
Tel (49) 06102 - 38 318   5 km

Eine schöne Gegend für Ferien der etwas anderen Art. Mit dem Schwarzwald im Westen, der Schweiz im Süden und dem Bodensee im Osten herrscht hier kein Mangel an Golfgelegenheiten. Zumindest den Nicht-Golfern in der Familie bieten sich eine Vielzahl von Alternativen zur Freizeitgestaltung. Obere Alp ist zwar schon recht hoch gelegen und verläuft auch auf ziemlich hügeligem Gelände, kann deswegen aber noch nicht als "Gebirgsplatz" bezeichnet werden. Dafür spricht auch, dass von den erhöht angelegten Grüns keines wirklich "blind" ist. Obgleich die Platzarchitektur traditionell britisch wirkt, verlangen die gut geschützten Grüns eher nach "target Golf" denn nach für die Insel typischen "bump and run" Schlägen. Auf den ersten Blick erscheint der Platz recht lang. Dieser Eindruck wird aber durch die Ausgewogenheit des Layouts und den aufgrund der Höhenlage weiteren Ballflug, etwas gemildert. Die Trainings-einrichtungen sind hervorragend, insbesondere der Par 3 9-Loch-Platz.

A beautiful region for holidays "with a difference". With the Black Forest to the west, Switzerland to the south and Bodensee to the east, there is no shortage of opportunities to play golf. At least the family's non-golfers will have something to do to pass the time. Obere Alp is set pretty high up, and although rather hilly, it doesn't really qualify for the "mountain course" label. While some greens are elevated, none is really blind, so that's already a point in its favour. Yet they are well guarded enough to require a touch of target golf rather than the British style bump and run, even though the general design has a lot of British tradition about it. The course may seem long, but at altitude balls fly further, and the well balanced layout of the holes here tends to dampen this first impression. Practice facilities are excellent, especially the par 3 nine-hole course.

Golfclub Obere Alp e.V.   1989

Am Golfplatz 1-3
D - 79780 STÜHLINGEN

Office	Sekretariat	(49) 07703 - 92 030
Pro shop	Pro shop	(49) 07703 - 920 330
Fax	Fax	(49) 07703 - 920 318
Situation	Lage	

Donaueschingen (pop. 20 000), 25 km
Stühlingen (pop. 5 000), 8 km

Annual closure	Jährliche Schliessung	1/12 → 31/3
Weekly closure	Wöchentliche Schliessung	no

Fees main season
Preisliste hochsaison 18 holes

	Week days Woche	We/Bank holidays We/Feiertag
Individual Individuell	DM 70,-	DM 90,-
Couple Ehepaar	DM 140,-	DM 180,-

Caddy	Caddy	no
Electric Trolley	Elektrokarren	no
Buggy	Elektrischer Wagen	no
Clubs	Leihschläger	DM 20,-

Credit cards Kreditkarten
VISA - Eurocard - MasterCard

448

Access Zufahrt : A8 Stuttgart-Singen →
Donaueschingen, Stühlingen. Stühlingen, →
Bonndorf. **Map 1 on page 371** Karte 1 Seite 371

GOLF COURSE
PLATZ   **14**/20

Site	Lage	▮▮▮▮▯
Maintenance	Instandhaltung	▮▮▮▮▯
Architect	Architekt	unknown
Type	Typ	open country, hilly
Relief	Begehbarkeit	▮▮▮▯▯
Water in play	Platz mit Wasser	▮▯▯▯▯
Exp. to wind	Wind ausgesetzt	▮▮▯▯▯
Trees in play	Platz mit Bäumen	▮▮▮▯▯

Scorecard	Chp.	Mens	Ladies
Scorekarte	Chp.	Herren	Damen
Length Länge	6147	5966	5268
Par	72	72	72

Advised golfing ability	0	12	24	36
Empfohlene Spielstärke		▮▮▮▯		
Hcp required Min. Handicap	36			

CLUB HOUSE & AMENITIES
KLUBHAUS UND NEBENGEBÄUDE   **7**/10

Pro shop	Pro shop	▮▮▮▮▯
Driving range	Übungsplatz	▮▮▮▮▯
Sheltered	überdacht	14 mats
On grass	auf Rasen	yes (April-Oct.)
Putting-green	Putting-grün	yes
Pitching-green	Pitching-grün	yes

HOTEL FACILITIES
HOTEL BESCHREIBUNG   **7**/10

HOTELS HOTELS
Obere Alp   Golf
15 rooms, D DM 120,-   on site
Tel (49) 07703 - 7820, Fax (49) 07703 - 7053

Mittlere Alp   Golf
10 rooms, D DM 100,-   500 m

Vier Jahreszeiten   Schluchsee
214 rooms, D DM 400,-   20 km
Tel (49) 07703 - 7395Tel (49) 07656 - 703 26, Fax (49) 07656 - 703 23

Hegers Parkhotel Flora   Schluchsee
34 rooms, D DM 200,-   20 km
Tel (49) 07656 - 452, Fax (49) 07656 - 1433

RESTAURANTS RESTAURANT
Hetzel - Tel (49) 07656 - 70 323   Schluchsee 20 km

Schwarzwaldstube   Schluchsee
Tel (49) 07656 - 1200   20 km

Diese ruhige Gegend Frankens wird in erster Linie von Liebhabern barocker Architektur, und mehr noch, von den Besuchern der Bayreuther Festspiele frequentiert. Von wagnerischem Pomp ist beim Golfplatz nichts zu spüren. Oberfranken ist eine klassisch konzipierte Anlage, die sich gut in das unebene Gelände einfügt, und daher vor allem Spielern mit guter Kondition zu empfehlen ist. Schöner, alter Baumbestand schmückt die Landschaft und stellt auf den ersten Blick die Hauptschwierigkeit dar, obschon auch Wasser und Bunker manchmal recht gefährlich werden können. Golfer mittlerer Spielstärke werden sich sicher schwer tun, hier ihr Handicap zu schaffen, obwohl das technische Niveau des Platzes eigentlich von allen Spielern zu meistern ist. Der diskret-elegante Platz, der sich in der Zeit zwischen spätem Frühling und Frühherbst von seiner schönsten Seite zeigt, zählt zweifellos zu den besten Anlagen der Region.

This peaceful region of Franconia comes alive with visits from lovers of baroque architecture and, more particularly, from "pilgrims" to the Bayreuth Festival. But there's nothing grandiose or Wagnerian about this course, which is very classical in style and naturally hugs a terrain that is hilly enough to recommend it basically for golfers in good physical shape. Beautiful old trees enhance the landscape and at first sight form the main hazards, although water and sand are also sometimes a dangerous proposition. Mid-handicappers will certainly find it hard here to achieve a good score, even though the course is technically speaking within the grasp of most golfers. A discreet and elegant course, Oberfranken is at its best from late spring to early autumn and is one of the region's best golfing stop-offs.

Golf Club Oberfranken e.V., Thurnau 1965

Petershof
D - 95349 THURNAU

Office	Sekretariat	(49) 09228 - 319
Pro shop	Pro shop	(49) 09228 - 1022
Fax	Fax	(49) 09228 - 7219
Situation	Lage	

Bayreuth (pop. 72 000), 25 km - Nürnberg, 80 km

Annual closure	Jährliche Schliessung	30/11 → 28/2

Weekly closure	Wöchentliche Schliessung	no

Monday (Montag): Restaurant closed

Fees main season
Preisliste hochsaison full day

	Week days Woche	We/Bank holidays We/Feiertag
Individual Individuell	DM 60,-	DM 80,-
Couple Ehepaar	DM 120,-	DM 160,-

under 21 years/Students : - 50 %

Caddy	Caddy	no
Electric Trolley	Elektrokarren	yes
Buggy	Elektrischer Wagen	yes
Clubs	Leihschläger	yes
Credit cards Kreditkarten		no

Access Zufahrt : Nürnberg, A9 → Berlin.
Exit (Ausf.) Kulmbach-Bayreuth. B505 Exit Thurnau.
Map 4 on page 366 Karte 4 Seite 366

GOLF COURSE
PLATZ
17 /20

Site	Lage	
Maintenance	Instandhaltung	
Architect	Architekt	B. von Limburger
		D. Harradine
Type	Typ	forest, parkland
Relief	Begehbarkeit	
Water in play	Platz mit Wasser	
Exp. to wind	Wind ausgesetzt	
Trees in play	Platz mit Bäumen	

Scorecard Scorekarte	Chp. Chp.	Mens Herren	Ladies Damen
Length Länge	6152	6152	5433
Par	72	72	72

Advised golfing ability	0	12	24	36
Empfohlene Spielstärke				

Hcp required	Min. Handicap	36

CLUB HOUSE & AMENITIES
KLUBHAUS UND NEBENGEBÄUDE
6 /10

Pro shop	Pro shop	
Driving range	Übungsplatz	
Sheltered	überdacht	3 mats
On grass	auf Rasen	yes
Putting-green	Putting-grün	yes
Pitching-green	Pitching-grün	yes

449

HOTEL FACILITIES
HOTEL BESCHREIBUNG
5 /10

HOTELS HOTELS
Brauerei-Gasthof Schnupp   Neudrossenfeld
27 rooms, D DM 175,-   11 km
Tel (49) 09203 - 99 20, Fax (49) 09203 - 99 250

Bayerischer Hof   Bayreuth
49 rooms, D DM 250,-   20 km
Tel (49) 0921 - 78 600, Fax (49) 0921 - 22 085

Goldener Hirsch   Bayreuth
40 rooms, D DM 220,-   20 km
Tel (49) 0921 - 23 046, Fax (49) 0921 - 22 483

RESTAURANTS RESTAURANT

Schloss-Restaurant   Neudrossenfeld
Tel (49) 09203 - 68 368   10 km

Schlosshotel Thiergarten   Bayreuth
Tel (49) 09209 - 98 40   28 km

Der Platz liegt in einer traditionell bayerischen Umgebung, die einer dicht-bewaldeten Parkanlage ähnelt. Am Platz werden in Kürze einige Änderungen vorgenommen, von denen wir hoffen, dass sie das Spielvergnügen noch weiter steigern werden. Es gibt hier jeweils fünf Par 3 und Par 5 Löcher, an denen kürzere Spieler genügend gute Chancen aufs Par haben, der Tatsache Rechnung tragend, dass sich der Durchchnitts-Golfer in dieser Hinsicht an Par 4 Löchern häufig am schwersten tut. Aus dem gleichen Grund sollte man die hinteren Abschläge meiden. Der schön gelegene Platz weist eine respektable Länge auf. Senioren empfehlen wir wegen des etwas hügeligen Geländes die Benutzung eines Golfwagens. Die heikelste Passage lauert zwischen Loch 10 und 12. Da der Boden oft feucht ist und ein halbes Dutzend Grüns erhöht liegen, sollte man einen hohen Pitch beherrschen. Insgesamt sind die einen erwarteten Schwierigkeiten keineswegs so bedrohlich, dass Mittelklasse-Spieler sich davon entmutigen lassen. Angenehm zu spielen und abwechslungsreich gestaltet, lohnt die Anlage einen Besuch sowohl der Lage als auch des Layouts wegen.

In a traditional Bavarian setting of densely wooded park-land, we can firstly only hope that the planned alterations will enhance the pleasure of playing here. With five par 5s and five par 3s, the course gives short-hitters the chance to sign for a few pars, knowing full well that the average hacker has the biggest problems with par 4s. In this case, don't opt for the back-tees. Set in a pretty region, the course is a little hilly for senior players (buggy recommended) and respectable in length; the trickiest section awaits you between the 10th and 12th. Since it is often wet and half a dozen greens are elevated, the high pitch shot is a must, but the hardships here are not threatening enough to discourage the average golfer. Pleasant and nicely varied, this course is worth the trip for both the layout and the site.

Golf-Club Oberschwaben Bad Waldsee — 1968

Fürstliches Hofgut Hopfenweiler
D - 88339 BAD WALDSEE

Office	Sekretariat	(49) 07524 - 5900
Pro shop	Pro shop	(49) 07524 - 48 778
Fax	Fax	(49) 07524 - 6106
Situation	Lage	

Ulm (pop. 110 000), 60 km - Ravensburg (pop. 46 000), 20 km

Annual closure   Jährliche Schliessung   1/11 → 31/3

Weekly closure   Wöchentliche Schliessung   no
Monday (Montag) : Restaurant closed

Fees main season
Preisliste hochsaison 18 holes

	Week days Woche	We/Bank holidays We/Feiertag
Individual Individuell	DM 65,-	DM 90,-
Couple Ehepaar	DM 130,-	DM 180,-
under 21 years/Students : – 50 %		

Caddy	Caddy	no
Electric Trolley	Elektrokarren	no
Buggy	Elektrischer Wagen	no
Clubs	Leihschläger	yes
Credit cards Kreditkarten		no

Biberach
Oberessendorf
Riss
Mülhausen
465
Eggmannsried
GOLF
Haslach
Osterhofen
Haisterkirch
Bad Waldsee
Bad Wurzach
Ravensburg
Haigdau
Leutkirch

Access Zufahrt : A8 München-Stuttgart. Exit (Ausf.)
Ulm-West. B30 → Bodensee. Bad Waldsee → Golf
Map 1 on page 361 Karte 1 Seite 361

GOLF COURSE PLATZ   15/20

Site	Lage	▮▮▮▮▯
Maintenance	Instandhaltung	▮▮▮▮▯
Architect	Architekt	
Type	Typ	forest, parkland
Relief	Begehbarkeit	▮▮▮▯▯
Water in play	Platz mit Wasser	▮▮▯▯▯
Exp. to wind	Wind ausgesetzt	▮▮▮▯▯
Trees in play	Platz mit Bäumen	▮▮▮▮▯

Scorecard Scorekarte	Chp. Chp.	Mens Herren	Ladies Damen
Length Länge	6148	6148	5385
Par	72	72	72

Advised golfing ability Empfohlene Spielstärke	0	12	24	36
Hcp required Min. Handicap	34			

CLUB HOUSE & AMENITIES KLUBHAUS UND NEBENGEBÄUDE   6/10

Pro shop	Pro shop	▮▮▮▮▯
Driving range	Übungsplatz	▮▮▮▯▯
Sheltered	überdacht	yes
On grass	auf Rasen	yes
Putting-green	Putting-grün	yes
Pitching-green	Pitching-grün	yes

HOTEL FACILITIES HOTEL BESCHREIBUNG   6/10

HOTELS HOTELS
Kur-Parkhotel   Bad Waldsee
64 rooms, D DM 200,-   2 km
Tel (49) 07524 - 97 070, Fax (49) 07524 - 970 775

Altes Tor   Bad Waldsee
28 rooms, D DM 160,-   2 km
Tel (49) 07524 - 97 190, Fax (49) 07524 - 971 997

Kurpension Schwabenland   Bad Waldsee
17 rooms, D DM 130,-   2 km
Tel (49) 07524 - 5011

RESTAURANTS RESTAURANT
Waldhorn   Ravensburg
Tel (49) 0751 - 36 120   20 km

Krone   Schlier
Tel (49) 07529 - 1292   25 km

450

ÖSCHBERGHOF

Der ideale Ort um ein paar Golftage zu verbringen und die herrlichen Umgebung von Schwarzwald und Donauquelle zu erkunden. Übernachten können Sie im gut ausgestatteten, komfortablen Hotel der Anlage. Der beachtlich lange Platz wird im Verlauf des Jahres um 9 Löcher erweitert. Er verläuft auf relativ ebenem Gelände und kann so leicht zu Fuss bewältigt werden. Obwohl die Hindernisse alle gut erkennbar sind, muss man mehrere Runden spielen um die strategischen Nuancen des Layouts zu begreifen. Ein Wasserlauf kreuzt acht Spielbahnen und bildet eine der Hauptschwierigkeiten, zu denen ebenfalls zahlreiche Bäume und Bunker zählen. Zum Glück sind die Grüns nicht ausgesprochen gut verteidigt, so dass auch der Durchschnitts-Golfer sie einigermassen gut anspielen kann. Der Platz ist in der Tat so angelegt, dass er nervenschonendes Vergnügen bereitet und schmeichlerische Ergebnisse ermöglicht - ein typischer Urlaubsplatz eben.

An ideal site for a few days golfing, staying in a well-appointed, comfortable hotel (with pool, sauna and jacuzzi) or for exploring this superb region of the Black Forest and sources of the Danube. The course is flat enough for easy walking and during the year will be supplemented by a new 9 holer. It is very reasonable in terms of yardage, but although the hazards are generally visible on each hole, you need several rounds to appreciate the course's strategic "nuances". A stream winds it way across eight holes and forms a major, but not the only, difficulty, as trees and bunkers abound. Fortunately, the greens are not over-protected and approach shots are none too complicated for the average golfer. This is indeed a course designed for enjoyment, where you can card sometimes flattering scores without suffering from nervous exhaustion, so it's just the job the holidays.

Land- und Golf-Club Öschberghof — 1980

Golfplatz 1
D - 78166 DONAUESCHINGEN

Office	Sekretariat	(49) 0771 - 84 525
Pro shop	Pro shop	(49) 0771 - 84 530
Fax	Fax	(49) 0771 - 84 540
Situation	Lage	

Donaueschingen (pop. 20 000), 5 km

Annual closure	Jährliche Schliessung	1/11 → 31/3
Weekly closure	Wöchentliche Schliessung	no

Monday (Montag) : Restaurant closed

Fees main season
Preisliste hochsaison 18 holes

	Week days Woche	We/Bank holidays We/Feiertag
Individual Individuell	DM 90,-	DM 120,-
Couple Ehepaar	DM 180,-	DM 240,-
under 25 years : – 50 %		

Caddy	Caddy	no
Electric Trolley	Elektrokarren	DM 30,-
Buggy	Elektrischer Wagen	DM 40,-/18 holes
Clubs	Leihschläger	DM 25,-

Credit cards Kreditkarten
VISA - Eurocard - MasterCard - AMEX - DC

Access Zufahrt : A81 Stuttgart-Singen. Exit (Ausf.) Bad Dürenheimer Kreuz, E70 → Donaueschingen. Exit Donaueschingen-Mitte. → Golf
Map 1 on page 361 Karte 1 Seite 361

GOLF COURSE / PLATZ — 15/20

Site	Lage	
Maintenance	Instandhaltung	
Architect	Architekt	DeutscheGolf Consult
Type	Typ	open country, parkland
Relief	Begehbarkeit	
Water in play	Platz mit Wasser	
Exp. to wind	Wind ausgesetzt	
Trees in play	Platz mit Bäumen	

Scorecard Scorekarte	Chp. Chp.	Mens Herren	Ladies Damen
Length Länge	6448	5970	5223
Par	74	72	74

Advised golfing ability	0	12	24	36
Empfohlene Spielstärke				

Hcp required Min. Handicap 35

CLUB HOUSE & AMENITIES / KLUBHAUS UND NEBENGEBÄUDE — 7/10

Pro shop	Pro shop	
Driving range	Übungsplatz	
Sheltered	überdacht	10 mats
On grass	auf Rasen	May → Oct.
Putting-green	Putting-grün	yes (2)
Pitching-green	Pitching-grün	yes (2)

451

HOTEL FACILITIES / HOTEL BESCHREIBUNG — 7/10

HOTELS HOTELS

Hotel Öschberghof	500 m
93 rooms, D DM 290,-	
Tel (49) 0771 - 840, Fax (49) 0771 - 84 260	
Concord	Donaueschingen
76 rooms, D DM 165,-	3 km
Tel (49) 0771 - 83 630, Fax (49) 0771 - 836 3120	
Parkhotel Waldegg	Bad Dürrheim
73 rooms, D DM 240,-	10 km
Tel (49) 07726 - 663 100, Fax (49) 07726 - 8001	

RESTAURANTS RESTAURANT

Hotel Öschberghof	500 m
Tel (49) 0771 - 84 610	
Babitzle	Donaueschingen
Tel (49) 0771 - 63 062	5 km

Der Platz verdankt seinen Namen dem Fluss Pinnau, der teilweise entlang des Golfgeländes verläuft. Obwohl der Fluss selbst nie ins Spiel kommt, gibt es andere Wasserhindernisse in bedrohlicher Lage vor den Grüns, um unerfahrene Spieler einzuschüchtern, die hier schnell einige Schläge verlieren können. Spielern mit hohen Handicaps machen auch die Grüns zu schaffen, die teilweise stark onduliert sind, aber in gestalterischer Hinsicht zu wünschen übrig lassen. Dieser Platz favorisiert technisch versierte Spieler, die es verstehen, mit den einzeln stehenden Bäumen fertigzuwerden, die vom Architekten geschickt mit ins strategische Kalkül einbezogen wurden. Der flache Platz ist einfach zu Gehen und trocknet gut ab. Golfer aller Spielstärken können sich hier entfalten, wenngleich methodische Spieler gegenüber Longhittern im Vorteil sind. Wenn möglich sollten Sie an der 10 beginnen, da die zweiten Neun etwas weniger interessant sind als der Rest. Wir empfehlen Matchplay, da auf diesem Platz alles Mögliche passieren kann.

Pinnau takes its name from the river that partly skirts the course. And although this running water never really comes into play, other water hazards in front of the greens are threatening enough to intimidate the more inexperienced players, who can quickly suffer here. High-handicappers will also find the putting surfaces a handful, too, are these are sometimes excessively contoured and lacking in inspiration design-wise. With that said, this is a course for the technicians, who will have to cope with strategically located isolated trees, the finest of which have been smartly used by the designer. Flattish and well-drained, the course is a pleasant one to walk, where golfers of all abilities can unfold their game, even though the thoughtful technician will have the upper hand over the longhitter. If you can, tee off at the 10th, as the back nine are a little less exciting than the rest. And prefer match play, as well, because anything can happen here.

Golf Club An der Pinnau — 1982

Pinneberger Strasse 81a
D - 25451 QUICKBORN-RENZEL

Office	Sekretariat	(49) 04106 - 81 800
Pro shop	Pro shop	(49) 04106 - 60 876
Fax	Fax	(49) 04106 - 82 003
Situation	Lage	

Quickborn (pop. 18 500), 1 km - Hamburg, 25 km

Annual closure	Jährliche Schliessung	no
Weekly closure	Wöchentliche Schliessung	no

Fees main season
Preisliste hochsaison 18 holes

	Week days Woche	We/Bank holidays We/Feiertag
Individual Individuell	DM 70,-	DM 90,-
Couple Ehepaar	DM 140,-	DM 180,-

under 21 years : – 50 %

Caddy	Caddy	on request
Electric Trolley	Elektrokarren	no
Buggy	Elektrischer Wagen	no
Clubs	Leihschläger	no
Credit cards Kreditkarten		no

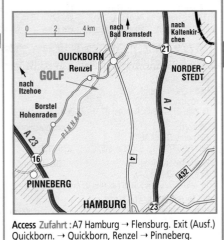

Access Zufahrt : A7 Hamburg → Flensburg. Exit (Ausf.) Quickborn. → Quickborn, Renzel → Pinneberg.
Map 7 on page 372 Karte 7 Seite 372

GOLF COURSE
PLATZ
14/20

Site	Lage	▆▆▆▆▆▆
Maintenance	Instandhaltung	▆▆▆▆▆▆
Architect	Architekt	unknown
Type	Typ	country, open country
Relief	Begehbarkeit	▆▆▆
Water in play	Platz mit Wasser	▆▆▆▆
Exp. to wind	Wind ausgesetzt	▆▆▆
Trees in play	Platz mit Bäumen	▆▆▆▆▆

Scorecard Scorekarte	Chp. Chp.	Mens Herren	Ladies Damen
Length Länge	6188	6023	5231
Par	72	72	72

Advised golfing ability	0	12	24	36
Empfohlene Spielstärke			▆▆▆▆	
Hcp required	Min. Handicap	36		

CLUB HOUSE & AMENITIES
KLUBHAUS UND NEBENGEBÄUDE
6/10

Pro shop	Pro shop	▆▆▆▆
Driving range	Übungsplatz	▆▆▆
Sheltered	überdacht	4 mats
On grass	auf Rasen	yes
Putting-green	Putting-grün	yes
Pitching-green	Pitching-grün	yes

HOTEL FACILITIES
HOTEL BESCHREIBUNG
6/10

HOTELS HOTELS

Jagdhaus Waldfrieden — Quickborn
14 rooms, D DM 230,- — 3 km
Tel (49) 04106 - 3771
Fax (49) 04106 - 69196

Landhaus Quickborn-Heide — Quickborn-Heide
18 rooms, D DM 175,-
Tel (49) 04106 - 77 660
Fax (49) 04106 - 74 969

Wiking Hotel — Henstedt-Ulzburg
36 rooms, D DM 140,- — 10 km
Tel (49) 04193 - 9080, Fax (49) 04193 - 92 323

RESTAURANTS RESTAURANT

Jagdhaus Waldfrieden — Quickborn
Tel (49) 04106 - 3771 — 3 km

Nahe Würzburg und Nürnberg liegt der Golfplatz an der "Romantischen Strasse", die von Würzburg über Augsburg, durch die Schweiz nach Italien führt, und an deren Weg sich immer wieder Städte und Schlösser aus den Epochen des Mittelalters, der Renaissance und des Barock finden. Gleichermassen erwähnenswert sind die Weinberge (Frankenwein) des Maintals. Falls Sie sich von den kulturellen Attraktionen losreissen können, verpassen Sie auf keinen Fall die Golfplätze dieser Gegend, insbesondere nicht diesen, der ebenso handfest und bodenständig ist wie die regionale Küche. Ebene Flächen wechseln sich ab mit hügeligerem Terrain auf einem Platz, der insgesamt einen sehr ausgewogenen Eindruck macht. Die Grüns sind enorm gross und sehr gut verteidigt. Es gibt praktisch keine Bäume, was den Platz sehr windanfällig macht. Einige Wasserhindernisse, gefährliche Bunker, Dickicht und Rough tragen dazu bei, dass der Score voraussichtlich ein paar Schläge über dem Handicap liegen wird. Daher sollten unerfahrene Golfer einfach die Runde geniessen ohne allzu sehr auf ihr Ergebnis zu achten.

Very close to Würzburg and Nürnberg, this course is on the route taken by the "Romantic Road", which started out from Würzburg and ran down to Augsburg then on to Switzerland and Italy, crossing towns and castles testifying to the Middle Ages, the Renaissance and the Baroque period. Equally important are the vineyards in the Main valley (Franconia wine). If you can tear yourself away from the cultural attractions, don't miss the golf courses in this province, especially this one, as serious a layout as the regional cooking. With flat spaces alternating with more hilly terrain and well-balanced overall, the course has huge, well-guarded greens, is virtually tree-less and can get very tough when the wind blows. A few water hazards and dangerous bunkers, the thickets and rough are all there to nudge your score a few strokes above your handicap. Inexperienced golfers will enjoy their round even more if they prefer not to count their score.

Golf Club Reichsstadt Bad Windsheim 1991
Am Weinturm 2
D - 91438 BAD WINDSHEIM

Office	Sekretariat	(49) 09841 - 5027
Pro shop	Pro shop	(49) 09841 - 2497
Fax	Fax	(49) 09841 - 3448
Situation	Lage	

Würzburg (pop. 129 000), 40 km - Nürnberg, 50 km

Annual closure	Jährliche Schliessung	no
Weekly closure	Wöchentliche Schliessung	no

Monday (Montag): Restaurant closed

Fees main season
Preisliste hochsaison full day

	Week days Woche	We/Bank holidays We/Feiertag
Individual Individuell	DM 60,-	DM 80,-
Couple Ehepaar	DM 120,-	DM 160,-

under 21 years/Students : – 50 %

Caddy	Caddy	on request
Electric Trolley	Elektrokarren	no
Buggy	Elektrischer Wagen	no
Clubs	Leihschläger	yes
Credit cards Kreditkarten		no

Access Zufahrt : • A7 Ulm-Würzburg. Exit (Ausf.) Bad Windsheim. B470 → Neustadt/Bad Windsheim. In Bad Windsheim → Oberntief. • Nürnberg → Fürth. B8 to Neustadt. B470 → Bad Windsheim
Map 4 on page 366 Karte 4 Seite 366

GOLF COURSE
PLATZ   14/20

Site	Lage	▰▰▰▱▱
Maintenance	Instandhaltung	▰▰▰▱▱
Architect	Architekt	unknown
Type	Typ	open country
Relief	Begehbarkeit	▰▰▰▱▱
Water in play	Platz mit Wasser	▰▰▱▱▱
Exp. to wind	Wind ausgesetzt	▰▰▰▱▱
Trees in play	Platz mit Bäumen	▰▱▱▱▱

Scorecard Scorekarte	Chp. Chp.	Mens Herren	Ladies Damen
Length Länge	6202	6202	5497
Par	73	73	73

Advised golfing ability		0	12	24	36
Empfohlene Spielstärke					
Hcp required	Min. Handicap	36			

CLUB HOUSE & AMENITIES
KLUBHAUS UND NEBENGEBÄUDE   6/10

Pro shop	Pro shop	▰▰▰▰▱
Driving range	Übungsplatz	▰▰▰▱▱
Sheltered	überdacht	4 mats
On grass	auf Rasen	yes
Putting-green	Putting-grün	yes
Pitching-green	Pitching-grün	yes

HOTEL FACILITIES
HOTEL BESCHREIBUNG   7/10

HOTELS HOTELS
Kurhotel Residenz   Bad Windsheim
128 rooms, D DM 200,-   5 km
Tel (49) 09841 - 910, Fax (49) 09841 - 912 663

Am Kurpark   Bad Windsheim
50 rooms, D DM 160,-   5 km
Tel (49) 09841 - 9020, Fax (49) 09841 - 90 243

Goldener Schwan   Bad Windsheim
22 rooms, D DM 120,-   5 km
Tel (49) 09841 - 5061, Fax (49) 09841 - 79 440

RESTAURANTS RESTAURANT
Neustadt Stuben   Neustadt an der Aisch
Tel (49) 09161 - 5622   20 km

Kurhotel Residenz   Bad Windsheim
Tel (49) 09841 - 910   5 km

453

Der Wald spiegelt wohl am besten den Geist der deutschen Romantik wider. Seine Erhaltung und sein Schutz sind zu einem wichtigen gesellschaftlichen Anliegen, insbesondere der Umweltschützer, geworden. Eine ganze Runde in einem solch mächtigen Wald zu spielen, vermittelt einem das Gefühl von Ruhe und Zufriedenheit - es ist, als wäre man ganz alleine auf der Welt. Hier muss man in Topform sein und den Ball kontrolliert schlagen, um den allgegenwärtigen Pinienbäumen aus dem Weg zu gehen und mit dem Drive in eine Position zu gelangen, die einem das Anspiel der gut durch Bunker verteidigten Grüns ermöglicht. Wenn man gut spielt, werden einen die Wasserläufe und Hindernisse, die ein - wenn auch nicht übermässiges - Gefahrenelement darstellen, weniger einschüchtern. Spieler, denen es an Übung und Genauigkeit fehlt, werden vermutlich einen Einbruch erleben, aber schliesslich zwingt sie ja niemand dazu, all ihre Schläge auch zu zählen. Reichswald ist ohne Zweifel einer der besten Plätze der Region, der auch nach oftmaligem Spielen immer wieder Spass macht.

Forests are one of the key constituents of the German romantic soul; their conservation and protection are now one of society's major concerns, especially with the ecologists. Playing a whole course in a forest such as this procures a feeling of incomparable tranquillity and contentment; on the course, you feel as if you are the only soul in the world. Here, you will need to be on top of your game to keep out of the pine-trees and flight your ball to land the drive in the best position to approach the greens (which are well guarded by bunkers). If you're playing well, you won't be too scared of the streams and hazards that add an element of difficulty but never excessively so. Players with little experience and problems of direction will probably suffer, but they don't have to count every stroke, do they ? One of the region's top layouts, this is a spectacular course which is fun to play again and again.

Golf Club Am Reichswald e.V., Nürnberg   1960

Schiestlstrasse 100
D - 90427 NÜRNBERG

Office	Sekretariat	(49) 0911 - 305 730
Pro shop	Pro shop	(49) 0911 - 305 959
Fax	Fax	(49) 0911 - 301 200
Situation	Lage	

Nürnberg (pop. 498 000), 5 km

Annual closure	Jährliche Schliessung	no
Weekly closure	Wöchentliche Schliessung	no

Monday (Montag): Restaurant closed

Fees main season
Preisliste hochsaison full day

	Week days Woche	We/Bank holidays We/Feiertag
Individual Individuell	DM 70,-	DM 100,-
Couple Ehepaar	DM 140,-	DM 200,-

under 21 years : – 50%

Caddy	Caddy	on request
Electric Trolley	Elektrokarren	no
Buggy	Elektrischer Wagen	no
Clubs	Leihschläger	yes

Credit cards Kreditkarten		no

Access Zufahrt : BAB A3 Nürnberg → Würzburg. Exit (Ausf.) Tennenlohe. B4 → Nürnberg. Kraftshof, turn right → Golf **Map 4 on page 366** Karte 4 Seite 366

GOLF COURSE
PLATZ   16/20

Site	Lage	
Maintenance	Instandhaltung	
Architect	Architekt	unknown
Type	Typ	forest
Relief	Begehbarkeit	
Water in play	Platz mit Wasser	
Exp. to wind	Wind ausgesetzt	
Trees in play	Platz mit Bäumen	

Scorecard Scorekarte	Chp. Chp.	Mens Herren	Ladies Damen
Length Länge	6016	6016	5325
Par	72	72	72

Advised golfing ability		0 12 24 36
Empfohlene Spielstärke		
Hcp required	Min. Handicap	36

CLUB HOUSE & AMENITIES
KLUBHAUS UND NEBENGEBÄUDE   7/10

Pro shop	Pro shop	
Driving range	Übungsplatz	
Sheltered	überdacht	3 mats
On grass	auf Rasen	no, 12 mats open air
Putting-green	Putting-grün	yes
Pitching-green	Pitching-grün	yes

HOTEL FACILITIES
HOTEL BESCHREIBUNG   7/10

HOTELS HOTELS

Maritim	Nürnberg
316 rooms, D DM 350,-	7 km
Tel (49) 0911 - 23 630, Fax (49) 0911 - 236 3836	

Intercity Hotel	Nürnberg
158 rooms, D DM 280,-	7 km
Tel (49) 0911 - 24 780, Fax (49) 0911 - 247 8999	

Dürer-Hotel	Nürnberg
105 rooms, D DM 250,-	7 km
Tel (49) 0911 - 208 091, Fax (49) 0911 - 223 458	

Tassilo	Nürnberg
79 rooms, D DM 250,-	5 km
Tel (49) 0911 - 32 666, Fax (49) 0911 - 326 6799	

RESTAURANTS RESTAURANT

Schwarzer Adler - Tel (49) 0911 - 305 858	Kraftshof 2 km
Alte Post Tel(49) 0911 - 396 215	Kraftshof 2 km

454

RHEINHESSEN

Mit den Nachbarplätzen von Domtal-Mommenhein und Nahetal in der näheren Umgebung, sind die Weinberge zwischen der Mosel und dem Rhein sind ein lohnenswertes Ausflugsziel. Für Golfer bietet sich ein Aufenthalt im exzellenten Hotel im Klubhaus von Rheinhessen an. Hier, ein wenig abseits der ausgetretenen Pfade, kann man sich entspannen, von der Klubhaus-Terasse das phantastische Panorama der Weinberge geniessen. Der Platz ist keineswegs perfekt, weil zu viele Löcher "blind" sind, ein Fehler, der wie schon in Nahetal leicht hätte vermieden werden können. Ein anderer Negativpunkt ist der Graben und der Teich am 14. Loch, einem Par 5, nach 245 m, genau dort, wo der Drive von guten Spielern landet. Dies zwingt dazu, entweder den Ball kurz abzulegen oder ein unkalkulierbares Risiko einzugehen. Wer hier zum erstenmal spielt, wird die Spielstrategie nicht immer erkennen und viele Überraschungen erleben. Dennoch ist das Layout reizvoll, obwohl die vielen Schräglagen viele Golfer überfordern können.

With Domtal-Mommenheim and Nahetal not far away, plus the vineyards of Nahe between the Moselle and the Rhine this is an attractive region to visit. For golfers, a stay at the excellent hotel in the Rheinhessen clubhouse is most relaxing, a little off the beaten track. The club house overlooks the vineyards and provides a superb panorama for everyone to enjoy, not only wine-lovers. The course itself is by no means perfect, as too many holes are blind, a mistake that could have been avoided both here and at Nahetal. Another rather negative feature is the ditch and pond 245 metres from the 14th tee, just where a good drive should be landing. This forces the golfer to take unreasonable risks or to lay up ridiculously short. People playing here for the first time may well encounter problems of strategy and a number of surprises. Otherwise the layout is pleasant enough, the difficulties are often clearly visible and only the contoured relief might handicap players who are technically not on top of their swing.

Golf Club Rheinhessen		1993
Hofgut Wissberg-St. Johann e.V.		

Hofgut Wissberg
D - 55578 ST. JOHANN

Office	Sekretariat	(49) 06701 - 8111
Pro shop	Pro shop	(49) 06701 - 8326
Fax	Fax	(49) 06701 - 8114
Situation	Lage	

Mainz (pop. 186 000), 25 km

Annual closure	Jährliche Schliessung	no
Weekly closure	Wöchentliche Schliessung	no

Fees main season
Preisliste hochsaison 18 holes

	Week days Woche	We/Bank holidays We/Feiertag
Individual Individuell	DM 60,-	DM 90,-
Couple Ehepaar	DM 120,-	DM 180,-

Caddy	Caddy	no
Electric Trolley	Elektrokarren	no
Buggy	Elektrischer Wagen	no
Clubs	Leihschläger	DM 20,-

Credit cards Kreditkarten   no

Access Zufahrt : Mainz, A60, A60 until AK Nahetal
Map 3 on page 365 Karte 3 Seite 365

GOLF COURSE
PLATZ   14/20

Site	Lage	
Maintenance	Instandhaltung	
Architect	Architekt	Armin Keller
Type	Typ	open country, hilly
Relief	Begehbarkeit	
Water in play	Platz mit Wasser	
Exp. to wind	Wind ausgesetzt	
Trees in play	Platz mit Bäumen	

Scorecard Scorekarte	Chp. Chp.	Mens Herren	Ladies Damen
Length Länge	6225	6046	5320
Par	72	72	72

Advised golfing ability		0	12	24	36
Empfohlene Spielstärke					
Hcp required	Min. Handicap	We: 28/36			

CLUB HOUSE & AMENITIES
KLUBHAUS UND NEBENGEBÄUDE   8/10

Pro shop	Pro shop	
Driving range	Übungsplatz	
Sheltered	überdacht	5 mats
On grass	auf Rasen	yes
Putting-green	Putting-grün	yes
Pitching-green	Pitching-grün	yes

HOTEL FACILITIES
HOTEL BESCHREIBUNG   7/10

HOTELS HOTELS

Golf Gasthaus   Rheinhessen
23 rooms, D DM 295,-   on site
Tel (49) 06701 - 916 450, Fax (49) 06701 - 916 455

Landhotel Kauzenberg   Bad Kreuznach
46 rooms, D DM 220,-   15 km
Tel (49) 0671 - 38 000, Fax (49) 0671 - 380 0124

Insel-Stuben   Bad Kreuznach
22 rooms, D DM 180,-   15 km
Tel (49) 0671 - 837 990, Fax (49) 0671 - 837 9955

RESTAURANTS RESTAURANT

Metzlers Gasthof   Hackenheim
Tel (49) 0671 - 653 12   17 km

Krause   Alzey
Tel (49) 06731 - 61 81   10 km

455

SCHARMÜTZELSEE ARNOLD PALMER 17 8 7

Der erst kürzlich erstellte Golfplatz ist Teil eines 36-Loch Resorts, zu dem auch ein von Nick Faldo entworfener 18-Loch Platz gehört. Die Investoren zögerten nicht, für ihr Projekt die Mitarbeit der Besten in Anspruch zu nehmen und beauftragten Arnold Palmer mit dem Bau seines in Deutschland bislang einzigen Platzes. Der amerikanische Stil des in angelegten Platz ist nur auf den ersten 9 Löchern offensichtlich, die zweiten neun Löcher wirken dagegen wie ein alter klassischer Waldplatz und sind der schönste Teil des Platzes. Das Layout ist gut durchdacht und so machen es die vorhandenen Schwierigkeiten nötig, mehrere Runden hier zu spielen, bis man sich mit der Anlage vertraut fühlt. Natürlich ist der Platz, besonders von den hinteren Abschlägen, auch sehr anspruchsvoll. Mehrere Abschlag-Boxen pro Loch ermöglichen es aber jedem Spieler, eine seinem Niveau entsprechende Wahl zu treffen. Besondere Aufmerksamkeit wurde der Gestaltung der Grüns gewidmet, aber auch der Pflegezustand der gesamten Anlage hebt diesen Platz aus der Masse der deutschen Plätze heraus.

The reunification of Germany has opened up new development in this region between Berlin and Frankfurt an der Oder, particularly close to the huge Scharmützelsee. The present very recent course is part of a 36-hole resort which also includes a Nick Faldo offering. The investors didn't hesitate to call on the best, and this is Germany's only course designed by Arnold Palmer. The American style is only obvious on the front nine, the back nine being more like a traditional German forest course. The layout is very intelligent, but the difficulties call for several rounds before getting fully acclimatized. Obviously, it is also very demanding, especially from the back tees, but there are enough tee-boxes for everyone to play the course that suits them best. The greens are especially well-designed and the standard of maintenance of the whole resort makes for two excellent courses.

Sporting Club Berlin Scharmützelsee e.V.		1995
Parkallee 3		
D - 15526 BAD SAAROW		
Office	Sekretariat	(49) 033631 - 5628
Pro shop	Pro shop	(49) 033631 - 5628
Fax	Fax	(49) 033631 - 5270
Situation	Lage	

Frankfurt/Oder (pop. 86 000), 35 km - Berlin, 75 km

Annual closure	Jährliche Schliessung	30/11→1/3
Weekly closure	Wöchentliche Schliessung	no

Fees main season
Preisliste hochsaison 18 holes

	Week days Woche	We/Bank holidays We/Feiertag
Individual Individuell	DM 80,-	DM 100,-
Couple Ehepaar	DM 160,-	DM 200,-
Caddy Caddy		DM 30,-
Electric Trolley Elektrokarren		DM 10,-
Buggy Elektrischer Wagen		DM 60,-
Clubs Leihschläger		DM 20,-

Credit cards Kreditkarten
VISA - Eurocard - MasterCard - AMEX - DC - JCB

456

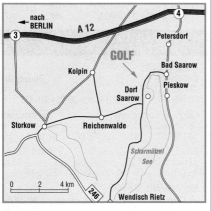

Access Zufahrt : Berlin A12 → Frankfurt/Oder. Exit (Ausf.) Fürstenwalde, → Bad Saarow → Golf.
Map 6 on page 371 Karte 6 Seite 371

GOLF COURSE PLATZ 17 /20

Site	Lage	
Maintenance	Instandhaltung	
Architect	Architekt	Arnold Palmer
Type	Typ	forest, parkland
Relief	Begehbarkeit	
Water in play	Platz mit Wasser	
Exp. to wind	Wind ausgesetzt	
Trees in play	Platz mit Bäumen	

Scorecard Scorekarte	Chp. Chp.	Mens Herren	Ladies Damen
Length Länge	6582	6177	5466
Par	72	72	72

Advised golfing ability Empfohlene Spielstärke	0 12 24 36
Hcp required Min. Handicap	no

CLUB HOUSE & AMENITIES KLUBHAUS UND NEBENGEBÄUDE 8 /10

Pro shop	Pro shop	
Driving range	Übungsplatz	
Sheltered	überdacht	14 mats
On grass	auf Rasen	yes
Putting-green	Putting-grün	yes
Pitching-green	Pitching-grün	yes

HOTEL FACILITIES HOTEL BESCHREIBUNG 7 /10

HOTELS HOTELS
Hotel Kempinski — Golf
201 rooms, D DM 330,- — on site
Tel (49) 033631 - 60, Fax (49) 033631 - 62 000

Landhaus Alte Eichen — Bad Saarow
39 rooms, D DM 156,-/280,- — 3 km
Tel (49) 033631 - 4115, Fax (49) 033631 - 2058

Schloss Hubertushöhe — Storkow
22 rooms, D DM 280,-/650,- — 12 km
Tel (49) 033678 - 43 0, Fax (49) 033678 - 43 100

RESTAURANTS RESTAURANT
Windspiel-Schl. Hubertus Höhe — Storkow
Tel (49) 033678 - 430 — 12 km

Landhaus Alte Eichen — Bad Saarow
Tel (49) 033678 - 4115 — 3 km

SCHARMÜTZELSEE NICK FALDO

| 18 | 8 | 7 |

Grosse Champions müssen sich oft den Vorwurf gefallen lassen, Plätze zu gestalten, ohne die dafür erforderliche Zeit und Mühe aufzuwenden. Auf Nick Faldo trifft dies nicht zu, da bei den leider nur wenigen von ihm bislang entworfenen Platzen seine ganz persönliche Handschrift deutlich erkennbar ist. Angesichts des herausragenden Designs dieses auf flachem, offenen Gelände erbauten Golfplatzes wünscht er sich, dass man bald eimal Gelegenheit bekommt, sein Können an einem Streifen "echten" Links-Terrains auszuprobieren. Die natürlichen und künstlichen Unebenheiten des häufig spektakulär und respekteinflössend anmutenden Geländes nutzt er geschickt für sein Spiel mit Links-typischen Elementen. Ungeachtet dessen eignet sich der Platz für Golfer aller Spielstärken (die hinteren Abschläge sind für die Pros reserviert). Obwohl alle Schwierigkeiten gut erkennbar sind, benötigt man sicherlich einige Runden der Gewöhnung, bevor man hoffen darf, diesen Platz mit einem guten Ergebnis zu absolvieren. Viele Pros lobten den Platz nach den German Open 1998 und 1999 als den besten der gesamten europäischen Tour sowohl vom Design als auch vom Pflegezustand.

Great champions are often accused of signing courses without designing them too much. Not so for Nick Faldo, who visibly leaves his mark on the few (too few even) courses he designs. When you see the excellence of this course over a flat, open site, you can hardly wait to see him get to grips with a grand links site. He has toyed with the links idea here, using the natural and artificial undulations of often very spectacular and intimidating terrain. But golfers of all levels can play here easily enough (the back-tees are for the pros). Although the difficulties are clearly there to be seen, you will need to play this course several times (and in match-play) before even thinking about returning a good card at the end of the day. After the German Open of 1998 and 1999, many European Tour players praised the course as the best of the whole PGA European Tour in design and maintenance.

Sporting Club Berlin Scharmützelsee e.V.

1997

Parkallee 3
D - 15526 BAD SAAROW

Office	Sekretariat	(49) 033631 - 5628
Pro shop	Pro shop	(49) 033631 - 5628
Fax	Fax	(49) 033631 - 5270
Situation	Lage	

Frankfurt/Oder (pop. 86 000), 35 km
Berlin (pop. 3 500 000), 75 km

Annual closure	Jährliche Schliessung	30/11→1/3
Weekly closure	Wöchentliche Schliessung	no

Fees main season
Preisliste hochsaison 18 holes

	Week days Woche	We/Bank holidays We/Feiertag
Individual Individuell	DM 80,-	DM 100,-
Couple Ehepaar	DM 160,-	DM 200,-
Caddy Caddy		DM 30,-
Electric Trolley Elektrokarren		DM 10,-
Buggy Elektrischer Wagen		DM 60,-
Clubs Leihschläger		DM 20,-

Credit cards Kreditkarten
VISA - Eurocard - MasterCard - AMEX - DC - JCB

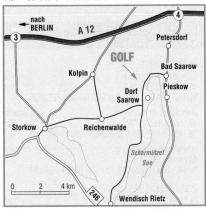

Access Zufahrt : Berlin A12 → Frankfurt/Oder. Exit (Ausf.) Fürstenwalde, → Bad Saarow → Golf.
Map 6 on page 371 Karte 6 Seite 371

GOLF COURSE
PLATZ
18/20

Site	Lage	▬▬▬▬▬▬▬□
Maintenance	Instandhaltung	▬▬▬▬▬▬▬□
Architect	Architekt	Nick Faldo
Type	Typ	links
Relief	Begehbarkeit	▬▬▬□□□□
Water in play	Platz mit Wasser	▬▬□□□□□
Exp. to wind	Wind ausgesetzt	▬▬▬▬□□□
Trees in play	Platz mit Bäumen	▬▬□□□□□

Scorecard Scorekarte	Chp. Chp.	Mens Herren	Ladies Damen
Length Länge	6445	6054	5341
Par	72	72	72

Advised golfing ability		0 12 24 36
Empfohlene Spielstärke		▬▬▬▬▬▬□
Hcp required	Min. Handicap	28

CLUB HOUSE & AMENITIES
KLUBHAUS UND NEBENGEBÄUDE
8/10

Pro shop	Pro shop	▬▬▬▬▬▬□
Driving range	Übungsplatz	▬▬▬▬▬▬□
Sheltered	überdacht	14 mats
On grass	auf Rasen	yes
Putting-green	Putting-grün	yes
Pitching-green	Pitching-grün	yes

457

HOTEL FACILITIES
HOTEL BESCHREIBUNG
7/10

HOTELS HOTELS
Hotel Kempinski — Golf — on site
201 rooms, D DM 330,-
Tel (49) 033631 - 60, Fax (49) 033631 - 62 000

Landhaus Alte Eichen — Bad Saarow — 3 km
39 rooms, D DM 156,-/280,-
Tel (49) 033631 - 4115, Fax (49) 033631 - 2058

Schloss Hubertushöhe — Storkow — 12 km
22 rooms, D DM 280,-/650,-
Tel (49) 033678 - 43 0, Fax (49) 033678 - 43 100

RESTAURANTS RESTAURANT
Windspiel-Schl. Hubertus Höhe — Storkow — 12 km
Tel (49) 033678 - 43 0

Landhaus Alte Eichen — Bad Saarow — 3 km
Tel (49) 033678 - 41 15

SCHLOSS BRAUNFELS

16 7 7

Die alten Bauernhäuser, die einen willkommen heissen, sind gleichermassen beeindruckend wie die Aussicht auf Schloss Braunfels. Der Architekt hat das für einen Golfplatz gut geeignete Gelände absichtlich nur wenig verändert. Die Höhenunterschiede, die einen nicht davon abhalten sollten zu Fuss zu Gehen, spielen eine erhebliche Rolle bei der Schlägerwahl, der wiederum eine Schlüsselrolle zukommt beim Anspiel einiger der zahlreichen, erhöht angelegten Grüns. Priorität hat auch die Vermeidung der Bäume und der Wasserhindernisse, letztere kommen an vier Löchern ins Spiel. Schloss Braunfels verlangt von den Spielern sicherlich kein überdurchschnittliches Können, dennoch kann die Fähigkeit den Ball sowohl mit Draw als auch Fade spielen zu können, bei der Endabrechnung von entscheidendem Vorteil sein. Sein Lage, die Umgebung, Vielseitigkeit und dazu ein komfortables Clubhaus - alles Faktoren, die für diesen Platz sprechen. Zudem liegt Wetzlar ganz in der Nähe, die Heimatstadt von Charlotte, der Heldin in Goethes "Werther".

The old farm buildings that welcome you are impressive, as are the views of Braunfels castle. The designer visibly did not want to upset terrain that is easily adaptable to golf. Although easy enough to play on foot, the slopes need to be reckoned with, at least when it comes to choosing the right club, a key factor here for attacking some of the many elevated greens. The first job is to avoid the trees and the water hazards in play on four holes. Schloss Braunfels certainly does not require above-average virtuosity, but being able to flight the ball both ways can be important in the final count. The location, the comfortable club-house, the setting and variety are major assets, as is the closeness to Wetzlar, the town of Charlotte, Goethe's heroine in "Werther".

Golf Club Schloss Braunfels — 1970

Homburger Hof
D - 35619 BRAUNFELS-LAHN

Office	Sekretariat	(49) 06442 - 4530
Pro shop	Pro shop	(49) 06442 - 5752
Fax	Fax	(49) 06442 - 6683
Situation	Lage	

Wetzlar (pop. 53 000), 15 km - Frankfurt, 80 km

Annual closure	Jährliche Schliessung	no
Weekly closure	Wöchentliche Schliessung	no

Monday (Montag) : Restaurant closed

Fees main season
Preisliste hochsaison 18 holes

	Week days Woche	We/Bank holidays We/Feiertag
Individual Individuell	DM 70,-	DM 90,-
Couple Ehepaar	DM 140,-	DM 180,-

under 21 years/Students : – 50 %

Caddy	Caddy	on request
Electric Trolley	Elektrokarren	no
Buggy	Elektrischer Wagen	no
Clubs	Leihschläger	yes
Credit cards Kreditkarten		no

458

Access Zufahrt : Frankfurt A5 Nord, A45 → Wetzlar.
Exit (Ausf.) Wetzlar Ost, B49 → Limburg. Leun,
→ Braunfels. Restaurant Obermühle, → Golf
Map 3 on page 365 Karte 3 Seite 365

GOLF COURSE
PLATZ — **16**/20

Site	Lage	
Maintenance	Instandhaltung	
Architect	Architekt	B. von Limburger
Type	Typ	parkland
Relief	Begehbarkeit	
Water in play	Platz mit Wasser	
Exp. to wind	Wind ausgesetzt	
Trees in play	Platz mit Bäumen	

Scorecard Scorekarte	Chp. Chp.	Mens Herren	Ladies Damen
Length Länge	6085	6085	5208
Par	73	73	73

Advised golfing ability	0	12	24	36
Empfohlene Spielstärke				

Hcp required Min. Handicap 36

CLUB HOUSE & AMENITIES
KLUBHAUS UND NEBENGEBÄUDE — **7**/10

Pro shop	Pro shop	
Driving range	Übungsplatz	
Sheltered	überdacht	6 mats
On grass	auf Rasen	yes
Putting-green	Putting-grün	yes
Pitching-green	Pitching-grün	yes

HOTEL FACILITIES
HOTEL BESCHREIBUNG — **7**/10

HOTELS HOTELS

Schloss-Hotel Braunfels	Braunfels
36 rooms, D DM 160,-	4 km
Tel (49) 06442 - 3050, Fax (49) 06442 - 305 222	

Zum Alten Amtsgericht	Braunfels
22 rooms, D DM 160,-	3 km
Tel (49) 06442 - 93 480, Fax (49) 06442 - 934 811	

Schloss-Hotel Weilburg	Weilburg
43 rooms, D DM 250,-	8 km
Tel (49) 06471 - 39 096, Fax (49) 06471 - 39 199	

RESTAURANTS RESTAURANT

La Lucia	Weilburg
Tel (49) 06471 - 2130	8 km

Zum Alten Amtsgericht	Braunfels
Tel (49) 06442 - 93 480	3 km

SCHLOSS EGMATING

Der Architekt Kurt Rossknecht versteht es, den von Ihm entworfenen Anlagen seinen ganz persönlichen Stempel aufzudrücken, was in erster Linie in der sorgfältigen Gestaltung und Positionierung von Bunkern und Grüns zum Ausdruck kommt. Da auf Schloss Egmating Wasser nur an einem Loch (4. Loch, Par 3) und so gut wie keine Bäume ins Spiel kommen und auch noch Fairway-Bunker aus Umweltgründen von den Genehmigungsbehörden verboten wurden, ist dies ein Platz, den man leicht unterschätzt. Um einen guten Score zu erzielen, muss man schon bei einigen langen Par-4-Löchern über eine gute Länge verfügen. Auch die langen Par-3-Löcher bevorteilen Longhittern. Wenn der Wind weht, ist es recht den Ball je nach Windrichtung mit Draw oder Fade zu spielen. Die grosse Anzahl von Abschlägen an jedem Loch macht den Platz für alle Spielstärken zugänglich. Die besten Amateure des Deutschen Golf Verband lebten und trainierten von 1992 bis 1996 auf dieser Anlage.

Designer Kurt Rossknecht likes to give courses his own personal stamp, if only through the careful attention he pays to the design of bunkers, to their positioning and to putting surfaces. At Schloss Egmating, water comes into play only on a short par 3, trees hardly feature at all, and on top of that German bureaucracy did not allow fairway bunkers for some environmental reasons. What you will find are greenside bunkers, but the course is still pretty easy. However to reach the greens in regulation you need to able to hit it long, especially on the long par 4s. The long par 3s are no push-over either. If the wind blows, a sound knowledge of the science of trajectories will come in handy as well as the ability to fade or draw the ball. The large number of tee-areas makes this a course for all skills. The best German amateurs lived and practiced here for some time.

Schloss Egmating			1990
Schlosstrasse 15			
D - 85658 EGMATING			

Office	Sekretariat	(49) 08095 - 90 860
Pro shop	Pro shop	(49) 08095 - 908 610
Fax	Fax	(49) 08095 - 9086-66
Situation	Lage	

München (pop. 1 300 000), 25 km
Aying (pop. 3 000), 3 km

Annual closure	Jährliche Schliessung	1/12→31/3
Weekly closure	Wöchentliche Schliessung	no

Fees main season
Preisliste hochsaison 18 holes

	Week days Woche	We/Bank holidays We/Feiertag
Individual Individuell	DM 85,-	DM 110,-
Couple Ehepaar	DM 170,-	DM 220,-

Caddy	Caddy	on request
Electric Trolley	Elektrokarren	yes
Buggy	Elektrischer Wagen	yes
Clubs	Leihschläger	yes
Credit cards Kreditkarten		no

Access Zufahrt : München, A99 Ost. Exit (Ausf.)
Putzbrunn → Oberpframmen → Golf
Map 2 on page 363 Karte 2 Seite 363

GOLF COURSE
PLATZ
15/20

Site	Lage	▬▬▬▬
Maintenance	Instandhaltung	▬▬▬
Architect	Architekt	Kurt Rossknecht
Type	Typ	open country
Relief	Begehbarkeit	▬
Water in play	Platz mit Wasser	▬▬
Exp. to wind	Wind ausgesetzt	▬▬
Trees in play	Platz mit Bäumen	▬

Scorecard	Chp.	Mens	Ladies
Scorekarte	Chp.	Herren	Damen
Length Länge	6381	6116	5324
Par	72	72	72

Advised golfing ability	0	12	24	36
Empfohlene Spielstärke	▬▬▬▬			
Hcp required Min. Handicap	36			

CLUB HOUSE & AMENITIES
KLUBHAUS UND NEBENGEBÄUDE
7/10

Pro shop	Pro shop	▬▬▬
Driving range	Übungsplatz	▬▬▬
Sheltered	überdacht	yes
On grass	auf Rasen	yes
Putting-green	Putting-grün	yes
Pitching-green	Pitching-grün	yes

HOTEL FACILITIES
HOTEL BESCHREIBUNG
7/10

HOTELS HOTELS

Brauereigasthof Aying — Aying
27 rooms, D DM 300,- — 3 km
Tel (49) 08095 - 705, Fax (49) 08095 - 2053

Aigner — Ottobrunn
73 rooms, D DM 250,- — 13 km
Tel (49) 089 - 608 170, Fax (49) 089 -608 3213

Sauerlach Post — Sauerlach
51 rooms, D DM 250,- — 10 km
Tel (49) 08104 - 830, Fax (49) 08104 - 8383

Arabella — München-Bogenhausen
467 rooms, D DM 400,- — 25 km
Tel (49) 089 - 92 320, Fax (49) 089 - 923 24449

RESTAURANTS RESTAURANT

Tantris — München-Schwabing
Tel (49) 089 - 362 061 — 25 km

Haflhof - Tel (49) 08093 - 5336 — Egmating 1 km

459

SCHLOSS KLINGENBURG

| 15 | 6 | 6 |

In einem alten Schlosspark gelegen ist der Platz mit einer Vielzahl herrlicher Bäume unterschiedlicher Art bestanden. Der Ort strahlt, verstärkt durch den umliegenden Wald, eine Aura von Ruhe und Abgeschiedenheit aus. Obwohl der Platz angenehm zu spielen ist, bleibt er angesichts der idealen Voraussetzungen, die den Architekten zu einem Meisterwerk hätten beflügeln sollen, etwas hinter den Erwartungen zurück. Dieser schien jedoch mehr darum besorgt einen spielbaren Platz zu entwerfen als den Platz zu einer echten Herausforderung zu machen. Die wenigen Fairwaybunker haben ein sehr flaches Profil. Bäume, Grünbunker und Wasserhindernisse dagegen stellen eine angemessene Gefahr dar. Abgesehen von den Eröffnungs- und Schlusslöchern verläuft der Platz über relativ ebenes Terrain, auf dem alle Hindernisse gut erkennbar sind. Klingenburgs gut verteidigte Grüns (fünf davon sind blind) verlangen nach "target Golf", so dass Spieler die den Ball faden können einen gewissen Vorteil haben. Theoretisch für Jeden zu bezwingen, bedingt es doch einer guten Form, will man hier einen dem Handicap entsprechenden Score erzielen.

Laid out in old castle grounds, this course has retained some superb varieties of trees, and the impression of peace and tranquillity that exudes from the overall setting is enhanced by the surrounding forest. But while the course is very pleasant to play, it doesn't quite come up to expectations. A site as fine as this should have galvanized the architect into creating greater things. He was probably more concerned with designing a pleasant course rather than looking for stiff challenges, so the rare fairway bunkers are virtually flat, and trees, green-side bunkers and water hazards were most likely thought to be too penalizing. A flattish course (except at the beginning and end) without any hidden traps, Schloss Klingenburg is more of a target golf course with well-protected greens (five of which are blind) and will give greater help to people who fade the ball.

Golf-Club Schloss Klingenburg — 1980

Schloss Klingenburg
D - 89343 JETTINGEN-SCHEPPACH

Office	Sekretariat	(49) 08225 - 30 30
Pro shop	Pro shop	(49) 08225 - 30 320
Fax	Fax	(49) 08225 - 30 350
Situation	Lage	

Augsburg (pop. 265 000), 50 km
Ulm (pop. 110 000), 45 km

Annual closure	Jährliche Schliessung	no
Weekly closure	Wöchentliche Schliessung	no

Monday (Montag): Restaurant closed

Fees main season
Preisliste hochsaison full day

	Week days Woche	We/Bank holidays We/Feiertag
Individual Individuell	DM 70,-	DM 100,-
Couple Ehepaar	DM 140,-	DM 200,-

under 21 years and Students under 27 years: – 50 %

Caddy	Caddy	no
Electric Trolley	Elektrokarren	no
Buggy	Elektrischer Wagen	yes
Clubs	Leihschläger	DM 10,-
Credit cards Kreditkarten		no

460

[map: Günzburg, Burgau, A8, Röfingen, Scheppach, Wettenhausen, Mindel, Jettingen, Ettenbeuren, Schönenberg, Ichenhausen, GOLF, Ried, Burtenbach, Kemnat, Günz, Krumbach, Thannhausen]

Access Zufahrt : A8 Stuttgart-München. Exit (Ausf.)
Burgau. → Jettingen. Schöneberg. 8 km → Golf
Map 2 on page 362 Karte 2 Seite 362

GOLF COURSE
PLATZ   15/20

Site	Lage	▮▮▮▮▮▮▯
Maintenance	Instandhaltung	▮▮▮▮▮▯▯
Architect	Architekt	Donald Harradine
Type	Typ	parkland
Relief	Begehbarkeit	▮▮▮▯▯▯▯
Water in play	Platz mit Wasser	▮▮▯▯▯▯▯
Exp. to wind	Wind ausgesetzt	▮▮▯▯▯▯▯
Trees in play	Platz mit Bäumen	▮▮▮▮▮▯▯

Scorecard Scorekarte	Chp. Chp.	Mens Herren	Ladies Damen
Length Länge	6237	6071	5378
Par	72	72	72

Advised golfing ability		0 12 24 36
Empfohlene Spielstärke		▮▮▮▮▮▯▯
Hcp required Min. Handicap		We: 36

CLUB HOUSE & AMENITIES
KLUBHAUS UND NEBENGEBÄUDE   6/10

Pro shop	Pro shop	▮▮▮▮▯▯▯
Driving range	Übungsplatz	▮▮▮▯▯▯▯
Sheltered	überdacht	yes
On grass	auf Rasen	yes
Putting-green	Putting-grün	yes
Pitching-green	Pitching-grün	yes

HOTEL FACILITIES
HOTEL BESCHREIBUNG   6/10

HOTELS HOTELS
Traubenbräu — Krumbach
10 rooms, D DM 100,- — 15 km
Tel (49) 08282 - 2093, Fax (49) 08282 - 5873

Zettler — Günzburg
49 rooms, D DM 190,- — 19 km
Tel (49) 08221 - 30 008, Fax (49) 08221 - 6714

Ramada — Günzburg
100 rooms, D DM 200,- — 19 km
Tel (49) 08221 - 351 0, Fax (49) 08221 - 351 333

RESTAURANTS RESTAURANT
Gasthof Traubenbräu — Krumbach
Tel (49) 08282 - 32093 — 15 km

Sonnenhof — Thannhausen
Tel (49) 08281 - 2014 — 9 km

Die Nähe zur Schweiz und der schönen Stadt Konstanz, sowie prächtige Ausblicke auf den Bodensee verleihen diesem noch recht neuen Golfplatz eine unbestreitbare Anziehungskraft. Der Föhn kann die Ankunft des Frühlings hier etwas beschleunigen, während der Rest von Deutschland noch vor Kälte bibbert. Das ziemlich hügelige Terrain verlangt vom Spieler eine gute Kondition. Trotz der Geländeunebenheiten sind die Hindernisse gut erkennbar und gibt es keine blinden Grüns. Das Schlüsselwort gilt Kontrolle gilt sowohl für den Ball als auch das eigene Spiel, da die "wilderen" Golfer hier häufig ernsthaft in Schwierigkeiten geraten können. Ehrlich gesagt sollten Anfänger und "Hacker" ihre Schläger hier besser im Auto lassen und stattdessen den guten Spielern zuschauen, es sei denn, sie sind bereit die Runde als Teil des Lernprozesses zu betrachten. Gut ausgewogen und kompetent konzipiert ist Schloss Langenstein ein Muss für den der diese schöne Gegend erkundet.

Being very close to Switzerland and to the pretty town of Konstanz, and offering some fabulous views of the Bodensee, this recent course has unquestionable appeal. The foehn wind can bring spring a little early here, while the rest of Germany is still shivering, but you need to be in good shape, even early in the year, because the terrain is rather hilly. Despite the relief, difficulties are rarely hidden from view and no greens are blind. The key word here is control - of your ball and your game - as the wilder players can often end up in serious trouble. To be honest, even though the course makes for a superb walk, beginners and hackers are better off leaving their clubs in the car and watching the good players ply their trade... unless they consider a round here to be part of the learning process. Well-balanced and tastefully designed, Schloss Langenstein is a must if you are exploring this pretty region.

Country Club Schloss Langenstein 1991

Schloss Langenstein
D - 78359 ORSINGEN-NENZINGEN

Office	Sekretariat	(49) 07774 - 50 651
Pro shop	Pro shop	(49) 07774 - 50 672
Fax	Fax	(49) 07774 - 50 699
Situation	Lage	

Singen (pop. 44 000), 8 km - Stockach (pop. 15 200), 6 km

Annual closure	Jährliche Schliessung	1/12→28/2
Weekly closure	Wöchentliche Schliessung	no

Monday (Montag): Restaurant closed

Fees main season
Preisliste hochsaison 18 holes

	Week days Woche	We/Bank holidays We/Feiertag
Individual Individuell	DM 80,-	DM 100,-
Couple Ehepaar	DM 160,-	DM 200,-

under 21 years / Students : – 50%

Caddy	Caddy	no
Electric Trolley	Elektrokarren	DM 25,-
Buggy	Elektrischer Wagen	yes
Clubs	Leihschläger	DM 10,-
Credit cards Kreditkarten		no

Schwenningen
Eigeltingen
Stockach →
31
Orsingen
GOLF →
A 81
Volkertshausen
A 98
34
Steisslingen
A 98
Singen
33
Schaffhausen
35
Radolfzell →

0　2　4 km

Access Zufahrt : A81 Stuttgart-Singen. Exit (Ausf.) Engen. B31 → Stockach. In Eigeltingen, turn right → Schloss Langenstein. **Map 1 on page 361** Karte 1 Seite 361

GOLF COURSE
PLATZ　16/20

Site	Lage	▰▰▰▰▱
Maintenance	Instandhaltung	▰▰▰▰▱
Architect	Architekt	unknown
Type	Typ	open country, hilly
Relief	Begehbarkeit	▰▰▰▰▱
Water in play	Platz mit Wasser	▰▰▱▱▱
Exp. to wind	Wind ausgesetzt	▰▰▰▱▱
Trees in play	Platz mit Bäumen	▰▰▰▱▱

Scorecard	Chp.	Mens	Ladies
Scorekarte	Chp.	Herren	Damen
Length Länge	6220	6065	5339
Par	73	72	72

Advised golfing ability	0　12　24　36
Empfohlene Spielstärke	▰▰▰▰▰▱▱
Hcp required	Min. Handicap	We: 32/35 (Ladies)

CLUB HOUSE & AMENITIES
KLUBHAUS UND NEBENGEBÄUDE　8/10

Pro shop	Pro shop	▰▰▰▰▱
Driving range	Übungsplatz	▰▰▰▱▱
Sheltered	überdacht	10 mats
On grass	auf Rasen	yes (April → Oct)
Putting-green	Putting-grün	yes
Pitching-green	Pitching-grün	yes

461

HOTEL FACILITIES
HOTEL BESCHREIBUNG　7/10

HOTELS HOTELS

Haus Sättele　Steisslingen
16 rooms, D DM 150,-　5 km
Tel (49) 07738 - 92 200, Fax (49) 07738 - 929 059

Flohr's　Überlingen
8 rooms, D DM 195,-　10 km
Tel (49) 07731 - 93 230, Fax (49) 07731 - 932 323

Art Villa Am See　Radolfzell
9 rooms, D DM 250,-　3 km
Tel (49) 07732 - 944 40, Fax (49) 07732 - 944 410

RESTAURANTS RESTAURANT

Flohr's　Überlingen
Tel (49) 07731 - 93 230　10 km

Salzburger Stub'n　Rielasingen-Worblingen
Tel (49) 07731 - 27 349　12 km

SCHLOSS LIEBENSTEIN GELB + BLAU ⟩ 16 8 7

Der "noble" Golfsport scheint eine Vorliebe dafür zu haben, sich neben Schlössern anzusiedeln. Die äussere Erscheinung kann jedoch täuschen, und so entspricht die Qualität solcher Plätze nicht immer dem gediegenen Stil ihrer Umgebung. Das Schlosshotel ist ein denkmalgeschütztes Monument. Für diese Art von Ehre ist die 27-Loch Anlage sicher noch zu jung, dennoch zeugt die Gestaltung der drei vom Charakter her recht unterschiedlichen 9-Loch-Platze von hinreichend Kompetenz. Longhitter werden sich auf dem "blauen" Platzes mit seinen drohenden Hindernissen und engen Fairways etwas beengt fühlen. Dagegen verzeihen der "gelbe" und der "rote" Platz ungenaue Schläge schon eher. Gute Techniker und Golfer, die wissen wie man sein Handicap spielt, werden hier problemlos zurechtkommen. Trotz des ziemlich hügeligen Terrains (Golf- wagen sind nicht unbedingt notwendig) kann man nur zwei der 27 Grüns als blind bezeichnen. Die richtige Strategie zu wählen ist relativ einfach, da alle Schwierigkeiten gut erkennbar sind. Fazit: ein sehr ansehnlicher Golfplatz.

As a noble sport, golf naturally likes to set up shop next to a castle. But as appearances can be deceptive, not all the courses that opt for the regal style can quite match the setting. Here, the castle hotel is a listed monument, and while its 27 holes are still too young for any form of listing, they have nonetheless been designed with a lot of skill and provide three different 9-holers. Big-hitters will feel the Blue course a little tight, where hazards are threatening and fairways narrow. The "Yellow" and "Red" courses on the other hand are little more lenient on wayward shots. For the technicians and golfers who know how to play to their handicap, the problem is not quite so bad. This is rather a hilly layout (buggies are not really necessary) but only two of the twenty-seven greens could be called blind. Finding the right strategy is easy, especially since all the difficulties are there to be seen. A very respectable course.

Golf- und Landclub Schloss Liebenstein
1982

Schloss Liebenstein
D - 74382 NECKARWESTHEIM

Office	Sekretariat	(49) 07133 - 98 780
Pro shop	Pro shop	(49) 07133 - 12 445
Fax	Fax	(49) 07133 - 987 818
Situation	Lage	

Heilbronn (pop. 126 000), 15 km

Annual closure	Jährliche Schliessung	no

Weekly closure Wöchentliche Schliessung
no Monday (Montag): Restaurant closed

Fees main season
Preisliste hochsaison 18 holes

	Week days Woche	We/Bank holidays We/Feiertag
Individual Individuell	DM 60,-	DM 80,-
Couple Ehepaar	DM 120,-	DM 160,-

Caddy	Caddy	no
Electric Trolley	Elektrokarren	no
Buggy	Elektrischer Wagen	no
Clubs	Leihschläger	yes

Credit cards Kreditkarten	no

Access Zufahrt : A81 Stuttgart-Heilbronn. Exit (Ausf.)
Mundelsheim → Kirchheim. Neckarwestheim → Golf
Map 1 on page 361 Karte 1 Seite 361

462

GOLF COURSE
PLATZ
16/20

Site	Lage	▮▮▮▮▮▮▯
Maintenance	Instandhaltung	▮▮▮▮▮▮▮
Architect	Architekt	unknown
Type	Typ	country
Relief	Begehbarkeit	▮▮▮▮▮▯▯
Water in play	Platz mit Wasser	▮▮▯▯▯▯▯
Exp. to wind	Wind ausgesetzt	▮▮▮▯▯▯▯
Trees in play	Platz mit Bäumen	▮▮▮▮▯▯▯

Scorecard Scorekarte	Chp. Chp.	Mens Herren	Ladies Damen
Length Länge	6220	6220	5496
Par	73	73	73

Advised golfing ability	0 12 24 36
Empfohlene Spielstärke	▮▮▮▮▮▮▯
Hcp required Min. Handicap	We 28

CLUB HOUSE & AMENITIES
KLUBHAUS UND NEBENGEBÄUDE
8/10

Pro shop	Pro shop	▮▮▮▮▮▮▯
Driving range	Übungsplatz	▮▮▮▮▮▮▮
Sheltered	überdacht	6 mats
On grass	auf Rasen	April → Sept.
Putting-green	Putting-grün	yes
Pitching-green	Pitching-grün	yes

HOTEL FACILITIES
HOTEL BESCHREIBUNG
7/10

HOTELS HOTELS
Schloss Liebenstein — 500 m
24 rooms, D DM 220,-
Tel (49) 07133 - 98 990
Fax (49) 07133 - 6045

Hofmann — Neckarwestheim
12 rooms, D DM 100,- — 3 km
Tel (49) 07133 - 7876
Fax (49) 07133 - 4030

RESTAURANTS RESTAURANT
Hofstüble — Neckarwestheim
Tel (49) 07133 - 16 444 — 4 km

Schloss Liebenstein — 500 m
Tel (49) 07133 - 6041

Die 18 von W. Siegmann entworfenen Löcher wurden vor kurzem um eine von Jack Nicklaus geplante 9-Loch-Anlage erweitert. Sämtliche Löcher können als technisch anspruchsvoll und optisch gelungen bezeichnet werden. Wer jedoch nicht alle 27 Löcher spielen kann, dem empfehlen wir - ohne damit den "Goldenen Bären" beleidigen zu wollen - dem einheitlichen Stil des ursprünglichen Platzes den Vorzug zu geben. Dieser Platz mit seinen engen, von grossen Bäume gesäumten Spielbahnen wird von einem Wasserlauf durchschnitten, der an sechs Fairways als nur eines von vielen Wasserhindernissen ins Spiel kommt. Von diesen kleinen Boshaftigkeiten sollten sich auch durchschnittliche Spieler nicht abschrecken lassen. Zwar werden diese hier womöglich keinen guten Score erzielen, aber schliesslich hängt der Spass am Golf nicht allein vom Ergebnis ab. Wer die 27 Löcher erfolgreich bewältigen will, darf in seiner Aufmerksamkeit und Konzentration nie nachlassen. Dieser Platz passt gut in eine Region, der es an anspruchsvollen Golfplätzen nicht mangelt. Er wird einem selbst nach häufigem Spielen nie langweilig.

The 18 holes designed by Siegmann have recently been supplemented by a 9 holer laid out by Jack Nicklaus. They are all as technical as they are agreeable to the eye, but if you cannot play all 27, and without wishing to offend the Golden Bear, you are best advised going for the unity of style offered by the original layout. It is rather narrow, lined with large trees and cut by a stream that crosses the fairways six times as one of the many water hazards. However, Schloss Lüdersburg is not spiteful enough to put off the average player. They may not return a fabulous card, but the fun of golf does not depend solely on performance. The 27 holes call for some hard work if they are to be successfully negotiated, enough to keep the player constantly on his toes. In a region where there is no shortage of challenging golf courses, this one is well placed. What's more, you can play it again and again without a minute's boredom.

Golf- und Landclub Schloss Lüderburg
1986

Lüdersburger Strasse 21
D - 21379 LÜDERSBURG/LÜNEBURG

Office	Sekretariat	(49) 04139 - 69 700
Pro shop	Pro shop	(49) 04139 - 69 700
Fax	Fax	(49) 04139 - 697 070
Situation	Lage	

Lüneburg (pop. 65 000), 15 km - Hamburg, 50 km

Annual closure	Jährliche Schliessung	no
Weekly closure	Wöchentliche Schliessung	no

Fees main season
Preisliste hochsaison 18 holes

	Week days Woche	We/Bank holidays We/Feiertag
Individual Individuell	DM 60,-	DM 90,-
Couple Ehepaar	DM 120,-	DM 180,-

Monday & Tuesday (Montag-Dienstag): DM 30,-

Caddy	Caddy	no
Electric Trolley	Elektrokarren	no
Buggy	Elektrischer Wagen	yes
Clubs	Leihschläger	yes

Credit cards Kreditkarten Eurocard - MasterCard

Brietlingen
nach Hamburg
Lüdersburg
Bardowick **Scharnebeck**
Adendorf
GOLF
Erbstrof
LÜNEBURG
nach Uelzen
nach Dahlenburg
0   2   4 km

Access Zufahrt : A250 Hamburg-Lüneburg. Exit (Ausf.) Lüneburg/Ebersberg. Scranebeck, Lüdersburg.
Map 7 on page 372 Karte 7 Seite 372

GOLF COURSE
PLATZ
15/20

Site	Lage	▰▰▰▱
Maintenance	Instandhaltung	▰▰▰▰
Architect	Architekt	W. Siegmann Jack Nicklaus
Type	Typ	parkland
Relief	Begehbarkeit	▰▱▱▱
Water in play	Platz mit Wasser	▰▰▱▱
Exp. to wind	Wind ausgesetzt	▰▱▱▱
Trees in play	Platz mit Bäumen	▰▰▰▰

Scorecard Scorekarte	Chp. Chp.	Mens Herren	Ladies Damen
Length Länge	6711	6091	5344
Par	73	73	73

Advised golfing ability Empfohlene Spielstärke	0	12	24	36
		▰▰▰▱		

Hcp required Min. Handicap 36

CLUB HOUSE & AMENITIES
KLUBHAUS UND NEBENGEBÄUDE
7/10

Pro shop	Pro shop	▰▰▰▰
Driving range	Übungsplatz	▰▰▰▱
Sheltered	überdacht	yes
On grass	auf Rasen	yes
Putting-green	Putting-grün	yes
Pitching-green	Pitching-grün	yes

463

HOTEL FACILITIES
HOTEL BESCHREIBUNG
6/10

HOTELS HOTELS

Seminaris
Lüneburg
185 rooms, D DM 200,-
16 km
Tel (49) 04131 - 7130, Fax (49) 04131 - 713 128

Hof Reinstorf
Reinstorf
81 rooms, D DM 200,-
15 km
Tel (49) 04137 - 8090, Fax (49) 04137 - 809 100

Heiderose
Lüneburg
21 rooms, D DM 140,-
16 km
Tel (49) 04131 - 44 410, Fax (49) 04131 - 48 357

Lauenburger Mühle
Lauenburg
34 rooms, D DM 170,-
9 km
Tel (49) 04153 - 5890, Fax (49) 04153 - 55 555

RESTAURANTS RESTAURANT

Hof Reinstorf -Tel (49) 04137 - 8090   Reinstorf 15 km
Zum Heidkrug - Tel (49) 04131 -31249 Lüneburg 16 km

Das im Mittelalter erbaute Schloss Myllendonk dient nicht nur als Clubhaus, sondern gibt dem Golfplatz, der im ürigen einen ausgezeichneten Ruf hat, auch seinen Namen. Die schöne Lage täuscht in vielen Fällen über schwerwiegende Schwächen beim Platzdesign hinweg. So enttäuscht uns eine Anzahl sehr nahe beieinander liegender Spielbahnen, trotz der sie begrenzenden schönen Bäume, die das Spiel erschweren. Genaue Drives und kontrolliert geschlagene Bälle sind Voraussetzung, um die Grüns von der besten Position aus angreifen zu können. Aufgrund des sehr ebenen Geländes sind die meisten Hindernisse gut erkennbar. Dies verleiht denen, die hier zum ersten mal spielen, eine gewisse Zuversicht, wenngleich einen das berechtigte Gefühl beschleicht, dass die Wasserläufe und Seen nur darauf lauern, einem das Leben schwer zu machen. Ungeübte Golfer, denen der Platz möglicherweise etwas schwierig erscheint, seien daran erinnert, dass der Score nicht alles ist worum es beim Golf geht.

The castle of Myllendonk, which dates from the Middle Ages, gives this course of excellent repute both its name and its clubhouse. The beauty of the setting can often conceal some glaring errors in design, and while we might regret a number of fairways which are too close to each other, the trees between them are magnificent and really add to the playing difficulty. Accurate driving and flighted shots are vital if you want to have any hope of hitting the greens from the easiest position. As the terrain is very flat, most hazards are clearly visible. This gives the new-comer a certain degree of confidence first time out, even though you can feel that streams and lakes are lying in wait to make life more difficult (a feeling that proves to be true!). Inexperienced golfers might find the layout a little tough, but just tell them that the score is not the only thing in golf...

Golf Club Schloss Myllendonk e.V. Korschenbroich

1965

Myllendonker Strasse 113
D - 41352 KORSCHENBROICH

Office	Sekretariat	(49) 02161 - 641 049
Pro shop	Pro shop	(49) 02161 - 644 955
Fax	Fax	(49) 02161 - 648 806
Situation	Lage	

Mönchengladbach (pop. 260 000), 5 km - Düsseldorf, 25 km

Annual closure	Jährliche Schliessung	no
Weekly closure	Wöchentliche Schliessung	no

Monday (Montag): Restaurant closed

Fees main season
Preisliste hochsaison 18 holes

	Week days Woche	We/Bank holidays We/Feiertag
Individual Individuell	DM 90,-	DM 100,-
Couple Ehepaar	DM 180,-	DM 200,-
Caddy Caddy	no	
Electric Trolley Elektrokarren	no	
Buggy Elektrischer Wagen	no	
Clubs Leihschläger	yes	

Credit cards Kreditkarten no

Access Zufahrt : A44 Exit (Ausf.) Mönchengladbach-Ost
→ "Gewerbegebiet Üdding".
1 km left in Jakobshöhe Strasse. 600 m, left in Myllendonker Strasse. → Schlosshof-Parkplatz.
Map 3 on page 364 Karte 3 Seite 364

GOLF COURSE
PLATZ
16/20

Site	Lage	▬▬▬▬▬▭
Maintenance	Instandhaltung	▬▬▬▬▬▭
Architect	Architekt	Donald Harradine
Type	Typ	parkland, forest
Relief	Begehbarkeit	▬▭▭▭▭
Water in play	Platz mit Wasser	▬▬▬▭▭
Exp. to wind	Wind ausgesetzt	▬▭▭▭▭
Trees in play	Platz mit Bäumen	▬▬▬▬▭

Scorecard Scorekarte	Chp. Chp.	Mens Herren	Ladies Damen
Length Länge	6140	5856	5176
Par	72	72	72

Advised golfing ability		0	12	24	36
Empfohlene Spielstärke				▬▬▬▬	
Hcp required Min. Handicap	36				

CLUB HOUSE & AMENITIES
KLUBHAUS UND NEBENGEBÄUDE
7/10

Pro shop	Pro shop	▬▬▬▬▭
Driving range	Übungsplatz	▬▬▬▭▭
Sheltered	überdacht	no
On grass	auf Rasen	yes (Summer)
Putting-green	Putting-grün	yes
Pitching-green	Pitching-grün	yes

HOTEL FACILITIES
HOTEL BESCHREIBUNG
7/10

HOTELS HOTELS

Queens Hotel — Mönchengladbach-Rheydt
127 rooms, D DM 280,- — 5 km
Tel (49) 02161 - 93 80, Fax (49) 02161 - 938 807

Dorint Hotel — Mönchengladbach
162 rooms, D DM 350,- — 5 km
Tel (49) 02161 - 89 30, Fax (49) 02161 - 87 231

Palazzo — Mönchengladbach
50 rooms, D DM 170,- — 5 km
Tel (49) 02161 - 244 600, Fax (49) 02161 - 244 888

RESTAURANTS RESTAURANT

Tho Penninghof — Mönchengladbach
Tel (49) 02161 - 818 900 — 5 km

Alt Herrenshoff — Korschenbroich
Tel (49) 02161 - 641 080 — 1 km

464

SCHLOSS NIPPENBURG

Die Bäume am Rande der Spielbahnen sind schon etwas seit der Eröffnung im Jahre 1993 gewachsen, aber es wird noch Jahre dauern ehe sie wirklich zur Gefahr werden. Im Augenblick sind die Bunker, Wasser und das Auf und Ab der Spielbahnen mit vielen Schräglagen die Hauptschwierigkeiten. Es gibt drei erhöhte Grüns und ein halbes Dutzend, die tiefer liegen als die Spielbahn. Wenn der Wind hier bläst, ist der Platz um vieles schwieriger. Bernhard Langer hatte beim Entwurf schottische Küstenplätze im Sinn, aber er hat nicht vergessen, dass Golf kein Spiel nur für Professionals und gute Amateure ist. Wenn der Wind nicht bläst, ist der Platz für die Mehrzahl der Golfer gut spielbar, vorausgesetzt sie kommen mit hängenden Balllagen zurecht. Der einzige Nachtal sind die extrem langen Wege vom Grün zum nächsten Abschlag und der ermüdende, bergauf führende Weg vom Parkplatz zum ultramodernen Clubhaus.

The trees alongside this rather open course have grown since it was first opened in 1993, but it will take a few more years before they really become dangerous. For the moment, the main difficulties are the bunkers, water and contoured landscape which leads to sloping lies, three elevated greens and half a dozen downhill greens. If the wind decides to blow, the course assumes a whole new dimension and requires good ball control if you want to card any sort of score, even though the yardage is reasonable. When designing Schloss Nippenburg, Bernhard Langer obviously had the Scottish links style in mind, but according to the proper tradition he never forgot that golf is not a game reserved only for professionals and good amateur players. If the wind is not blowing the course is not too difficult for the majority of players if they can play sloping lies. The only drawback of the course are the long walks from green to the next tee and the long tiring uphill walk from the parking lot to the ultramodern clubhouse.

Schloss Nippenburg Golfclub — 1993
Nippenburg 21
D - 71701 SCHWIEBERDINGEN

Office	Sekretariat	(49) 07150 - 395 30
Pro shop	Pro shop	(49) 07150 - 395 320
Fax	Fax	(49) 07150 - 395 518
Situation	Lage	

Stuttgart (pop. 560 000), 10 km

Annual closure	Jährliche Schliessung	no
Weekly closure	Wöchentliche Schliessung	no

Fees main season
Preisliste hochsaison 18 holes

	Week days Woche	We/Bank holidays We/Feiertag
Individual Individuell	DM 70,-	DM 100,-
Couple Ehepaar	DM 140,-	DM 200,-

Caddy	Caddy	no
Electric Trolley	Elektrokarren	DM 15,-
Buggy	Elektrischer Wagen	DM 50,-/18 holes
Clubs	Leihschläger	DM 15,-

Credit cards Kreditkarten
VISA - Eurocard - Mastercard - AMEX

Access Zufahrt : A81 Stuttgart-Heilbronn. Exit (Ausf.) Stuttgart-Zuffenhausen. B10 → Vaihingen.
Münchingen → Hemmingen. → Golf
Map 1 on page 361 Karte 1 Seite 361

GOLF COURSE / PLATZ — 17/20

Site	Lage	
Maintenance	Instandhaltung	
Architect	Architekt	Bernhard Langer
Type	Typ	country, open country
Relief	Begehbarkeit	
Water in play	Platz mit Wasser	
Exp. to wind	Wind ausgesetzt	
Trees in play	Platz mit Bäumen	

Scorecard Scorekarte	Chp. Chp.	Mens Herren	Ladies Damen
Length Länge	6154	5862	5160
Par	71	70	70

Advised golfing ability — 0 12 24 36
Empfohlene Spielstärke
Hcp required Min. Handicap — no

CLUB HOUSE & AMENITIES / KLUBHAUS UND NEBENGEBÄUDE — 8/10

Pro shop	Pro shop	
Driving range	Übungsplatz	
Sheltered	überdacht	6 mats
On grass	auf Rasen	yes
Putting-green	Putting-grün	yes
Pitching-green	Pitching-grün	yes

465

HOTEL FACILITIES / HOTEL BESCHREIBUNG — 6/10

HOTELS HOTELS
Hotel Mercure — Korntal-Münchingen
208 rooms, D DM 227,- — 3 km
Tel (49) 07150 - 130, Fax (49) 07150 - 132 66

Stohgäu Hotel — Münchingen
47 rooms, D DM 200,- — 3 km
Tel (49) 07150 - 929 30, Fax (49) 07150 - 929 399

Neuwirtshaus Hotel — Stuttgart
31 rooms, D DM 195,- — 10 km
Tel (49) 0711 - 980 630, Fax (49) 0711 -9803 6319

RESTAURANTS RESTAURANT
Muckenstüble — Stuttgart-Weil im Dorf
Tel (49) 0711 - 865 122 — 8 km
Litfass - Tel (49) 0711 - 243 031 — Stuttgart 12 km
Clubhaus Restaurant — Schloss Nippenburg
Tel (49) 07150 - 324 72

Mit Sandy Lyle wurde hier ein weiterer Top-Designer für den Entwurf eines Golfplatzes im Berliner Raum engagiert. Dies ist Lyles erstes Projekt in Kontinental-Europa. Wie in Scharmützelsee handelt es sich dabei um ein Resort mit öffentlichem 18-Loch-Golfplatz. Der aufwendig gebaute Platz erfüllt trotz seines jungen Alters die in ihn gesetzten Erwartungen. Der schottische Champion kennt sich offenbar mit den Feinheiten der Platzarchitektur aus und folgt der Tradition seiner heimatlichen Vorbilder, bei der die Schwierigkeiten meist sehr subtiler Natur sind. Auf ziemlich hügeligem Terrain erbaut, finden sich auf diesem Platz - typisch für die Region - Wasserhindernisse, deren Charakter jedoch nicht so aggressiv ist wie etwa bei amerikanischen Plätzen üblich. Neben vielen Bäumen kommen selbstverständlich auch zahlreiche Bunker ins Spiel, welche die mittel-grossen, gut wenn auch relativ flach gestalteten Grüns verteidigen. Mehrere Runden sind notwendig um sich hier die passende Strategie zu erarbeiten, für deren Umsetzung man alle Schläger benötigen wird.

Another top designer name for a Berlin course is Sandy Lyle, who here designed his first course on the continent of Europe. As at Scharmützelsee, this is a whole resort with an 18-hole public course. It was, of course, given every consideration and despite its early age has come up to expectations. The Scottish champion is a fine connoisseur of architecture and remains very attached to his national tradition, where difficulties are often more on the subtle side. Over rather hilly, but easily walkable, terrain, there are naturally the water hazards inherent in this region, but they are less aggressive than on more American courses. A lot of trees come into play, and many bunkers too, naturally, protecting averagely-sized and well-designed greens without excessive slopes. You need to play here several times to establish a strategy. And you'll want every club in your bag.

Golfclub Schloss Wilkendorf e.V. 1995

Am Weiher 1
D - 15345 WILKENDORF

Office	Sekretariat	(49) 03341 - 330 960
Pro shop	Pro shop	(49) 03341 -330 6920
Fax	Fax	(49) 03341 - 330 961
Situation	Lage	

Berlin (pop. 3 500 000), 70 km - Strausberg, 7 km

Annual closure	Jährliche Schliessung	15/11→15/3
Weekly closure	Wöchentliche Schliessung	no

Monday (Montag): Restaurant closed

Fees main season
Preisliste hochsaison 18 holes

	Week days Woche	We/Bank holidays We/Feiertag
Individual Individuell	DM 70,-	DM 90,-
Couple Ehepaar	DM 140,-	DM 180,-

Caddy	Caddy	no
Electric Trolley	Elektrokarren	DM 25,-
Buggy	Elektrischer Wagen	no
Clubs	Leihschläger	DM 25,-

Credit cards Kreditkarten no

466

Access Zufahrt : B1-5 Berlin → Frankfurt/Oder to Berliner Ring (A10). 1 km left → Strausberg. → Golf.
Map 6 on page 371 Karte 6 Seite 371

GOLF COURSE
PLATZ   17/20

Site	Lage	
Maintenance	Instandhaltung	
Architect	Architekt	Sandy Lyle
Type	Typ	inland
Relief	Begehbarkeit	
Water in play	Platz mit Wasser	
Exp. to wind	Wind ausgesetzt	
Trees in play	Platz mit Bäumen	

Scorecard Scorekarte	Chp. Chp.	Mens Herren	Ladies Damen
Length Länge	6563	6117	5373
Par	74	72	72

Advised golfing ability		0	12	24	36
Empfohlene Spielstärke					
Hcp required	Min. Handicap	36			

CLUB HOUSE & AMENITIES
KLUBHAUS UND NEBENGEBÄUDE   7/10

Pro shop	Pro shop	
Driving range	Übungsplatz	
Sheltered	überdacht	16 mats
On grass	auf Rasen	yes
Putting-green	Putting-grün	yes
Pitching-green	Pitching-grün	yes

HOTEL FACILITIES
HOTEL BESCHREIBUNG   5/10

HOTELS HOTELS
Lakeside Hotel   Strausberg
53 rooms, D DM 166,-   2 km
Tel (49) 03341 - 3469 0, Fax (49) 03341 - 3469 15

Schloss Reichenow   Reichenow
20 rooms, D DM 200,-   15 km
Tel (49) 033437 - 3080, Fax (49) 033437 - 3088 8

Golfakademie   Schloss Wilkendorf
5 rooms, D DM 140,-   on site
Tel (49) 03341 - 330 910, Fax (49) 03341 - 330 961

RESTAURANTS RESTAURANT
Stobber Mühle   Bucklow
Tel (49) 033433 - 668 33   15 km

Goldene Kartoffel   Prötzel
Tel (49) 0334 - 364 92   7 km

Dies ist der erste, und im Moment auch der einzige Platz in Deutschland, den Robert Trent Jones Jr. entworfen hat. Zusammen mit dem Faldo-Platz am Scharmützelsee ist dies wahrscheinlich der beste neue Platz in Deutschland. Er besticht vor allem mit seinem Abwechslungsreichtum und vor allem den geschickt platzierten Bunkern, die optisch attraktiv sind und vor allem jedem Loch eine klare Kontur verleihen. Hinzu kommten einige attraktive Wasserhindernisse (vor allem am 9. und 18. Loch). Insgesamt ist dies ein Platz, der jeden Golfer begeistern wird. Durch geschickte Erdbewegungen wirken manchen Hindernisse und Grüns näher oder weiter entfernt als sie tatsächlich sind, deshalb gilt es der Birdie-Karte (Yardage Book) zu vetrauen. Diese ein Platz der intelligentes Spiel erfordert, aber für alle Spielstärke schwer ist. Wählen Sie deshalb die richtigen Abschläge, die hinter "Tiger-Tees" sind ausschliesslich für Profis und Longhitter. Unglücklicherweise kann man diesen Südplatz nur in Begleistung eines Mitglieds spielen. Der andere Platz des Clubs, der von Rainer Siegmann entworfene Nordplatz ist dagegen ohne Einschränkung für Gastspieler offen.

This is the first, and for the moment the only, course in Germany designed by Robert Trent Jones Jr. With the "Faldo" course at Scharmützelsee, this is probably the best of all the recently built layouts for its variety and remarkable bunkering which, although sometimes deceiving to the eye, perfectly outlines the shape of holes over often very open space. If we add the presence of a few attractive water hazards, you get a course of sheer pleasure. Some clever earthwork here and there might give the illusion of hazards and greens being closer or father away than they actually are, so trust the yardage book. This is a very intelligent course that is tough for everyone, so choose your tees wisely: the "tiger" tees are reserved for very long-hitters. Unfortunately, this "South" course can only be played with a member, the other "North" course has no such restrictions but is much more ordinary.

Golf Club Seddiner See — 1997

Zum Weiher 44
D - 1455 WILDENBRUCH

Office	Sekretariat	(49) 033205 - 7320
Pro shop	Pro shop	(49) 033205 - 73 251
Fax	Fax	(49) 033205 - 73 229
Situation	Lage	

Berlin (pop. 3 500 000), 30 km

Annual closure	Jährliche Schliessung	no
Weekly closure	Wöchentliche Schliessung	no

Monday (Montag): Restaurant closed

Fees main season
Preisliste hochsaison 18 holes

	Week days Woche	We/Bank holidays We/Feiertag
Individual Individuell	* DM 100,-	* DM 120,-
Couple Ehepaar	* DM 200,-	* DM 240,-

* only with members (nur in Mitgliederbegleitung)

Caddy	Caddy	no
Electric Trolley	Elektrokarren	no
Buggy	Elektrischer Wagen	no
Clubs	Leihschläger	DM 54,-

Credit cards Kreditkarten VISA - Eurocard - AMEX

Access Zufahrt : Berlin, A115 Süd, A10 West.
Exit (Ausf.) 12 → Beelitz
Map 6 on page 371 Karte 6 Seite 371

GOLF COURSE / PLATZ — 18/20

Site	Lage	▰▰▰▱▱
Maintenance	Instandhaltung	▰▰▰▱▱
Architect	Architekt	R. Trent Jones Jr
Type	Typ	country
Relief	Begehbarkeit	▰▱▱▱▱
Water in play	Platz mit Wasser	▰▰▱▱▱
Exp. to wind	Wind ausgesetzt	▰▰▱▱▱
Trees in play	Platz mit Bäumen	▰▰▱▱▱

Scorecard Scorekarte	Chp. Chp.	Mens Herren	Ladies Damen
Length Länge	6486	6046	5514
Par	72	72	72

Advised golfing ability		0 12 24 36
Empfohlene Spielstärke		▰▰▰▰
Hcp required	Min. Handicap	34/36

CLUB HOUSE & AMENITIES / KLUBHAUS UND NEBENGEBÄUDE — 9/10

Pro shop	Pro shop	▰▰▰▰▱
Driving range	Übungsplatz	▰▰▰▰▱
Sheltered	überdacht	20 mats
On grass	auf Rasen	yes
Putting-green	Putting-grün	yes
Pitching-green	Pitching-grün	yes

467

HOTEL FACILITIES / HOTEL BESCHREIBUNG — 7/10

HOTELS HOTELS

Seidler Art'otel — Potsdam
121 rooms, D DM 380,- — 15 km
Tel (49) 0331 - 9815-510, Fax (49) 0331 - 9815-555

Sol Inn Hotel — Michendorf
125 rooms, D DM 153,- — 15 km
Tel (49) 033205 - 78-0, Fax (49) 033205 - 78-444

Haus am See — Ferch
21 rooms, D DM 180,- — 12 km
Tel (49) 033209 - 709 55, Fax (49) 033209 - 704 96

Brandenburger Hof — Berlin
87 rooms, D DM 400,- — 30 km
Tel (49) 030 - 214 050, Fax (49) 030 - 214 05 10

RESTAURANTS RESTAURANT

Borchardt - Tel (49) 030 - 229 3144 — Berlin 30 km

Opernpalais Königin Luise — Berlin 30 km
Tel (49) 030 - 20 26 83

Semlin wurde wie auch der Märkische Golfclub Potsdam von Christian Staedler entworfen. Mit ihrem dazugehörigen Hotel entspricht die Anlage einem Resort, und eignet sich somit ausgezeichnet als Wochenend-Ziel für Golfgruppen - auch solche deren Handicaps weit auseinanderklaffen, wenngleich "Hacker" den Platz als etwas zu schwer empfinden mögen. Die Schwierigkeiten sind recht gut erkennbar, so dass man durchaus gleich die erste Runde in Zählspiel absolvieren kann, obschon Matchplay sicherlich genauso viel Spass macht. Das Fehlen gefahrbringender Bäume, die Gestaltung der Grüns und Bunker, sowie das fast völlig ebene Gelände erinnern stark an Florida, damit ist aber nicht eine simple Kopie der dortigen Plätze gemeint. Die Schwierigkeiten sind gut verteilt, so wechseln sich im Verlauf der Runde schwierige und leichtere Löcher miteinander ab. Als sehr hilfreich erweist sich die Fähigkeit den Ball sowohl mit Draw als auch Fade spielen zu können. Die Grüns sind ausgezeichnet und der sandige Boden gewährleistet eine gute Entwässerung.

Like Märkischer Potsdam, Semlin am See chose Christian Staedler as course architect. This is a sort of resort, with a hotel on site, and can be a very decent week-end destination for a group of golfers, even playing to very different handicaps, although the hackers might find it a little too tough for their liking. The difficulties are visible enough to consider stroke-play first time out, although match-play will be at least just as much fun. The absence of dangerous trees, the design of the greens and bunkers and the very slight physical relief are reminiscent of Florida, but this is no carbon copy. The difficulties are well spread around, with tough holes alternating nicely with easier numbers. Moving the ball (deliberately) both ways will be a great help. The greens are excellent and the sandy soil gives good drainage.

Golf- und Landclub Semlin am See   1993

Ferchesarerstrasse
D - 14715 SEMLIN

Office	Sekretariat	(49) 03385 - 5540
Pro shop	Pro shop	(49) 03385 - 554 410
Fax	Fax	(49) 03385 - 554 400
Situation	Lage	

Rathenow (pop. 28 000), 5 km - Berlin, 70 km

Annual closure	Jährliche Schliessung	no
Weekly closure	Wöchentliche Schliessung	no

Fees main season
Preisliste hochsaison 18 holes

	Week days Woche	We/Bank holidays We/Feiertag
Individual Individuell	DM 70,-	DM 90,-
Couple Ehepaar	DM 140,-	DM 180,-

under 21 years/Students : – 50%

Caddy	Caddy	on request, DM 35,-
Electric Trolley	Elektrokarren	no
Buggy	Elektrischer Wagen	DM 50,-
Clubs	Leihschläger	DM 25,-

Credit cards Kreditkarten
VISA - Eurocard - MasterCard - AMEX - DC

nach Rhinow
Hohennauen
Semlin
Ferchesar
nach Briesen
Stechow
GOLF
RATHENOW 188
102
HAVEL
nach Brandenburg
0   2   4 km

Access Zufahrt : Berlin, B5. Brisen, B188 → Rathenow.
Stechow → Ferchesar. → Golf
Map 6 on page 371 Karte 6 Seite 371

GOLF COURSE
PLATZ   16/20

Site	Lage	▰▰▰▰▰▰▱
Maintenance	Instandhaltung	▰▰▰▰▰▰▱
Architect	Architekt	Christoph Staedler
Type	Typ	forest, parkland
Relief	Begehbarkeit	▰▰▱▱▱▱▱
Water in play	Platz mit Wasser	▰▰▱▱▱▱▱
Exp. to wind	Wind ausgesetzt	▰▰▰▰▱▱▱
Trees in play	Platz mit Bäumen	▰▰▰▱▱▱▱

Scorecard Scorekarte	**Chp.** Chp.	**Mens** Herren	**Ladies** Damen
Length Länge	6410	6089	5391
Par	72	72	72

Advised golfing ability Empfohlene Spielstärke	0	12	24	36
			▰▰▰	

Hcp required   Min. Handicap   36

CLUB HOUSE & AMENITIES
KLUBHAUS UND NEBENGEBÄUDE   8/10

Pro shop	Pro shop	▰▰▰▰▰▱▱
Driving range	Übungsplatz	▰▰▰▰▰▰▱
Sheltered	überdacht	5 mats
On grass	auf Rasen	yes
Putting-green	Putting-grün	yes
Pitching-green	Pitching-grün	yes

HOTEL FACILITIES
HOTEL BESCHREIBUNG   7/10

HOTELS HOTELS
Golf- und Landhotel   Golf
72 rooms, D DM 185,-   on site
Tel (49) 03385 - 5540
Fax (49) 03385 - 554 400

Antik Hotel   Semlin
15 rooms, D DM 150,-   500 m
Tel (49) 03385 - 530 053
Fax (49) 03385 - 530 030

Sorat   Brandenburg
88 rooms, D DM 240,-   37 km
Tel (49) 03381 - 5970, Fax (49) 03381 - 597 444

RESTAURANTS RESTAURANT
Golf- und Landhotel   Golf
Tel (49) 03385 - 554 412   on site

468

SONNENALP

15	7	7

Grundsätzlich empfehlen wir nur ungern die Benutzung eines Golfwagens, da das Begehen eines Golfplatzes - insbesondere auf der ersten Runde - unseres Erachtens einen wesentlichen Teil des Spielvergnügens ausmacht. Es erfordert allerdings schon die Fitness und das Können eines Bergsteigers, die Anstiege von Sonnenalp zu bewältigen und dabei noch zwischendurch einen kleinen weissen Ball zu schlagen. Dies ist allerdings der einzige Schwachpunkt eines ansonsten angenehmen Platzes, dessen herrliche Lage einen so manchen Fehler vergessen lässt. Natürlich kann man nicht erwarten, mit den Problemen die das Gelände, die vielen Bäume sowie Hindernisse aller Art und Grösse bereiten, auf Anhieb fertig zu werden. Bevor man diesen Platz zähmen kann, muss man ihn erstmal gründlich kennenlernen. Mit etwas ‹berlegung vor dem Schlag können hier aber durchaus Golfer aller Spielstärken zurechtkommen. Auch wer kein grosser Champion ist kann hier Spass haben, da die Schläge zum Grün nicht allzu anspruchsvoll sind. Ein Wort noch zu der aussergewöhnlichen Zusammenstellung des Platz, es gibt sechs Par 5, sechs Par 4 und sechs Par 3 Löcher.

We never like to recommend a buggy, because walking a course is an integral part of the enjoyment of golf, especially on your first time out. But to scale the heights of Sonnenalp while intermittently hitting a little white ball, you need the fitness and skills of a mountaineer. This is the only weak point of an otherwise pleasant course, where contemplation of a superb site will help you to forget many a mistake. Quite clearly, you cannot hope to master immediately the problems caused by the slopes and hills and the very many trees and hazards that come in all shapes and sizes. To tame this course, you need to get to know it. But players of all abilities can play here, with a little thought before each stroke. And you don't have to be a top champion to have fun, as even approach shots to greens are none too demanding. One last word on the very special configuration here at Sonnenalp: there are six par 5s, six par 3s and six par 4s.

Golfclub Sonnenalp		1975
Sonnenalp		
D - 87527 OFTERSCHWANG		

Office	Sekretariat	(49) 08321 - 27 276
Pro shop	Pro shop	(49) 08321 - 27 297
Fax	Fax	(49) 08321 - 272 238
Situation	Lage	

Oberstdorf (pop. 11 000), 8 km - Sonthofen, 5 km

Annual closure	Jährliche Schliessung	1/12→31/3
Weekly closure	Wöchentliche Schliessung	no

Fees main season
Preisliste hochsaison 18 holes

	Week days Woche	We/Bank holidays We/Feiertag
Individual Individuell	DM 100,-	DM 100,-
Couple Ehepaar	DM 200,-	DM 200,-

Caddy	Caddy	on request, DM 50,-
Electric Trolley	Elektrokarren	DM 30,-
Buggy	Elektrischer Wagen	no
Clubs	Leihschläger	DM 30,-
Credit cards Kreditkarten		no

Sonthofen
Aubach
Ofterschwang
308
Altstädten
Tiefenberg
19
GOLF
Fischen
Schölang
Obermaiselstein
0   2   4 km
Iller
Tiefenbach
Oberstdorf

Access Zufahrt : München A96/B18 → Memmingen. A7 → Kempten. Exit (Ausf). Oberstdorf. B19. Sonthofen. 2 km → Sonnenalp
Map 2 on page 362 Karte 2 Seite 362

GOLF COURSE
PLATZ   15/20

Site	Lage	■■■■■■
Maintenance	Instandhaltung	■■■■■
Architect	Architekt	Donald Harradine
Type	Typ	forest, mountain
Relief	Begehbarkeit	■■■■
Water in play	Platz mit Wasser	■
Exp. to wind	Wind ausgesetzt	■■
Trees in play	Platz mit Bäumen	■■■■■

Scorecard Scorekarte	Chp. Chp.	Mens Herren	Ladies Damen
Length Länge	5719	5227	4444
Par	71	70	70

Advised golfing ability		0	12	24	36
Empfohlene Spielstärke					
Hcp required	Min. Handicap	34			

CLUB HOUSE & AMENITIES
KLUBHAUS UND NEBENGEBÄUDE   7/10

Pro shop	Pro shop	■■■■
Driving range	Übungsplatz	■■■■
Sheltered	überdacht	15 mats
On grass	auf Rasen	no, 25 mats open air
Putting-green	Putting-grün	yes
Pitching-green	Pitching-grün	yes

HOTEL FACILITIES
HOTEL BESCHREIBUNG   7/10

HOTELS HOTELS
Sonnenalp Hotel & Resort — Golf
225 rooms, D DM 500,- (1/2 P) — 400 m
Tel (49) 08321 - 2720, Fax (49) 08321 - 272 242

Dora — Ofterschwang
18 rooms, D DM 160,- — 1.5 km
Tel (49) 08321 - 3509, Fax (49) 08321 - 84 244

Parkhotel Frank — Obertsdorf
68 rooms, D DM 350,- — 10 km
Tel (49) 08322 - 7060, Fax (49) 08322 - 706 286

Kurhotel Filser - 91 rooms, D DM 200,- — Obertsdorf
Tel (49) 08322 - 7080, Fax (49) 08322 - 708 530 10 km

RESTAURANTS RESTAURANT
Alte Post - Tel (49) 08321 - 2508 — Sonthofen 3 km
Grüns Restaurant — Obertsdorf 10 km

469

St. Dionys, in einiger Entfernung zu Hamburg gelegen, bietet einen guten Vorwand zur Erkundung der Lüneburger Heide, einer Moorlandschaft, deren Bild geprägt wird von Pinien, Birken und Heidekraut. Gerade Letzteres taucht diese ansonsten karge Gegend im August und September in üppige Farben. Der Platz selbst weist nur leichte Unebenheiten auf und kann so jedermann empfohlen werden. Die Vegetation ist teilweise sehr dominant, dennoch gibt es auch für Longhitter genügend offene Flächen. Obwohl die gut gestalteten Grüns meist ausgezeichnet verteidigt sind, ist es doch in vielen Fällen möglich, sie flach anzuspielen. Ärgerlich ist die Position einiger Fairwaybunker, durch die gute Schläge bestraft werden können. Es ist nichts Neues, dass für ein gutes Ergebnis lange und gerade Schläge von Bedeutung sind. Diese Feststellung ist hier jedoch - vor allem von den hinteren Abschlägen - ganz besonders zutreffend. Das Vergnügen St. Dionys zu spielen geht weit über den landschaftlichen Reiz der Umgebung hinaus.

St Dionys is some distance from Hamburg, but is a good excuse for discovering the "Lüneburger Heide", moorland dotted with pine-trees and birch and covered with heather. Both add sumptuous colour to rather austere landscape in August and September. The course itself is only moderately hilly and so can be recommended for everyone. The vegetation is sometimes very much to the fore but there is no lack of open space to attract the big-hitters, and while the greens are generally well-designed and frequently well-guarded, you can often run the ball in. One regret is the layout of some fairway bunkers, which can penalize good shots. Saying you have to play long and straight for a good round is stating the obvious, but here it really is very true, especially from the back tees. The fun of playing St Dionys is more than simply admiring the surroundings.

Golf Club St. Dionys — 1972

Widukindweg
D - 21357 ST. DYONIS

Office	Sekretariat	(49) 04133 - 213 311
Pro shop	Pro shop	(49) 04133 - 213 315
Fax	Fax	(49) 04133 - 213 313
Situation	Lage	

Winsen (pop. 27 000), 8 km - Lüneburg, 10 km

Annual closure	Jährliche Schliessung	no
Weekly closure	Wöchentliche Schliessung	no

Fees main season
Preisliste hochsaison 18 holes

	Week days Woche	We/Bank holidays We/Feiertag
Individual Individuell	DM 70,-	DM 90,-
Couple Ehepaar	DM 140,-	DM 180,-

Juniors & Students: – 50%
We: only before 10.00 (Gäste nur bis 10 Uhr)

Caddy	Caddy	no
Electric Trolley	Elektrokarren	no
Buggy	Elektrischer Wagen	no
Clubs	Leihschläger	no

Credit cards Kreditkarten — no

Access Zufahrt : A7 Hamburg → Hannover. Exit (Ausf.) Maschen. A250 → Lüneburg. Exit Winsen Ost. B4 → Lüneburg. Wittorf, left to Barum. → St. Dionys.
Map 7 on page 372 Karte 7 Seite 372

GOLF COURSE / PLATZ — 17/20

Site	Lage	
Maintenance	Instandhaltung	
Architect	Architekt	Gratenau
Type	Typ	moorland
Relief	Begehbarkeit	
Water in play	Platz mit Wasser	
Exp. to wind	Wind ausgesetzt	
Trees in play	Platz mit Bäumen	

Scorecard Scorekarte	Chp. Chp.	Mens Herren	Ladies Damen
Length Länge	6255	6058	5083
Par	72	72	72

Advised golfing ability
Empfohlene Spielstärke — 0   12   24   36

Hcp required   Min. Handicap   36

CLUB HOUSE & AMENITIES / KLUBHAUS UND NEBENGEBÄUDE — 7/10

Pro shop	Pro shop	
Driving range	Übungsplatz	
Sheltered	überdacht	4 mats
On grass	auf Rasen	yes
Putting-green	Putting-grün	yes
Pitching-green	Pitching-grün	yes

HOTEL FACILITIES / HOTEL BESCHREIBUNG — 6/10

HOTELS HOTELS

Hotel Bergström — Lüneburg
52 rooms, D DM 250,- — 11 km
Tel (49) 04131 - 3080
Fax (49) 04131 - 308 499

Landhotel Frank — Lüneburg
32 rooms, D DM 145,- — 2 km
Tel (49) 04133 - 400 90
Fax (49) 04133 - 400 933

RESTAURANTS RESTAURANT

Restaurant Hotel Zum Heidkrug — Lüneburg
Tel (49) 04131 - 31 249 — 11 km

Jagdschänke — Lüdersburg
Tel (49) 04153 - 68 422 — 10 km

Kronen-Bauhaus — Lüneburg
Tel (49) 04133 - 713 200 — 11 km

470

ST. EURACH

Mit seinem dominierenden Clubhaus, dem Platz, dessen Spielbahnen sich durch Bäume und Wälder winden, und dem Blick auf die Alpen im Hintergrund vermittelt St. Eurach den Eindruck von Exklusivität, der durch das Greenfee bestätigt wird. Der Reiz der umgebenden Natur hinterlässt einen ebenso starken Eindruck wie die sehr traditionelle Platz. Der lange und enge Platz wurde durch die von Bernhard Langer vorgenommenen Veränderungen an den Bunkern zusätzlich erschwert. Dennoch ist der Platz kein Monster und im grossen und ganz fair, d.h. gute Schläge werden belohnt, schlechte bestraft. Die BMW International Open, ein Turnier der europäischen PGA Tour wurde hier von 1994 bis 1996 ausgetragen und der Platz dadurch zu seinem Vorteil verändert.

With the estate dominated by the clubhouse, a course winding its way through trees and the Alps visible in the background on a clear day, St Eurach gives the impression of an exclusive site... an impression confirmed by the green fee (so avoid week-ends). When thinking about it, the natural environment leaves a greater impression than the actual course, and it certainly has the glamour to offset a rather bland personality. When it comes to playing, and we hate to put visitors off, high-handicappers will be hard pushed to enjoy their golf here. The layout is long and narrow, and the alterations made to bunkers by Bernhard Langer have added a little spice, but all this implies complete control of your game if you want to excel. You have to feel easy with all your clubs, including those you need for recovery shots. A demanding course to play when on top of your game. Keep to match-play, there are a lot of surprises in store.

St. Eurach Land- und Golf Club e.V. 1973

Eurach 8
D - 82393 IFFELDORF

Office	Sekretariat	(49) 08801 - 1332
Pro shop	Pro shop	(49) 08801 - 1532
Fax	Fax	(49) 08801 - 2523
Situation	Lage	

München (pop. 1 300 000), 35 km - Penzberg, 5 km

Annual closure	Jährliche Schliessung	15/11 →15/4
Weekly closure	Wöchentliche Schliessung	no

Fees main season
Preisliste hochsaison 18 holes

	Week days Woche	We/Bank holidays We/Feiertag
Individual Individuell	DM 100,-	DM 150,-
Couple Ehepaar	DM 200,-	DM 300,-

W/E & holidays: with members (nur in Mitgliederbegleitung)

Caddy	Caddy	on request
Electric Trolley	Elektrokarren	no
Buggy	Elektrischer Wagen	yes
Clubs	Leihschläger	yes
Credit cards Kreditkarten		no

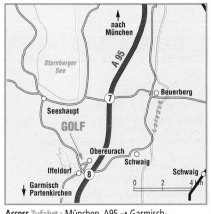

Access Zufahrt : München, A95 → Garmisch-Partenkirchen. Exit (Ausf.) Penzberg → Iffeldorf-Seeshaupt. 1,5 km → Golf on the right.
Map 2 on page 362 Karte 2 Seite 362

GOLF COURSE / PLATZ 16/20

Site	Lage	
Maintenance	Instandhaltung	
Architect	Architekt	unknown
Type	Typ	forest
Relief	Begehbarkeit	
Water in play	Platz mit Wasser	
Exp. to wind	Wind ausgesetzt	
Trees in play	Platz mit Bäumen	

Scorecard Scorekarte	Chp. Chp.	Mens Herren	Ladies Damen
Length Länge	6430	5907	5267
Par	71	71	74

Advised golfing ability	0	12	24	36
Empfohlene Spielstärke				
Hcp required Min. Handicap	28			

CLUB HOUSE & AMENITIES / KLUBHAUS UND NEBENGEBÄUDE 7/10

Pro shop	Pro shop	
Driving range	Übungsplatz	
Sheltered	überdacht	no
On grass	auf Rasen	yes
Putting-green	Putting-grün	yes
Pitching-green	Pitching-grün	yes

471

HOTEL FACILITIES / HOTEL BESCHREIBUNG 6/10

HOTELS HOTELS

Landgasthof Osterseen — Iffeldorf
24 rooms, D DM 200,- — 2 km
Tel (49) 08856 - 10 11, Fax (49) 08856 - 96 06

Stadthotel Berggeist — Penzberg
45 rooms, D DM 150,- — 6 km
Tel (49) 08856 - 80 10, Fax (49) 08856 - 81 913

Gut Faistenberg — Eurasburg-Faistenberg
60 rooms, D DM 275,- — 10 km
Tel (49) 08179 - 1616, Fax (49) 08179 - 433

RESTAURANTS RESTAURANT

Landgasthof Osterseen — Iffeldorf
Tel (49) 08856 - 1011 — 2 km

Stadthotel Berggeist — Penzberg
Tel (49) 08856 - 78 99 — 6 km

ST. LEON-ROT

15	**8**	**6**

Der Platz gehört Dietmar Hopp, der Gründer und ehemalige Vorstandsvorsitzender von SAP. Seltsamer weise wurde dieses luxuriöse und ultra-moderne Projekt nicht von einem der bekannten Golfplatz-Architekten, sondern von einem Landschaftsarchitekten entworfen, der nie zuvor in Leben für das Design eines Golfplatzes verantwortlich gezeichnet hatte. Deshalb musste der Platz für die TPC of Europe gründlich überarbeitet werden, Löcher mussten verlegt werden, so dass der Platz vorüber gehend 19 Löcher aufwies. Das 19. Loch wird künftig das 18. Loch des zweiten Platzes sein, den der englische Golfplatz-Architekt Dave Thomas entwirft und der bis zum Jahre 2001 fertiggestellt werden soll. Trotzdem ist nach den vielen Umbauten ein Platz entstanden, den es sich lohnt zu spielen. Die Hauptschwierigkeit des Platzes sind Wasserhindernisse an neun Löchern (das 7. Loch hat ein Inselgrün) und die viele Biotope, die als seitliches Wasserhinterniss gepflockt sind. Deshalb sind eigentlich nur das erste und das letzte Loch einfach. Diesen Platz wird man nicht so leicht vergessen, auch wenn man für das hohe Greenfee mehr erwartet hätte.

This luxurious and ultra-modern project was laid out not by a high-tech golf course architect but by a skilled landscape gardener, who had never designed a golf course in his life before. As a result, a good part of the course had to be re-shaped in order to host the TPC of Europe in 1999. A second 18-hole course is being built, under the supervision of Dave Thomas, which will be used when the tournament returns to the club in 2001. This is a very decent course all the same. An important feature here is not only the presence of water hazards on nine holes (the 7th has an island green), but also the huge areas protected owing to environmental considerations, which are considered as lateral water hazards. If only because the first and last holes are easy, you will not forget this course in a hurry, but we expected a lot more for the money we paid.

Golf Club St. Leon-Rot — 1997

Opelstrasse 30
D - 68789 ST. LEON-ROT

Office	Sekretariat	(49) 06227 - 860 80
Pro shop	Pro shop	(49) 06227 - 860 899
Fax	Fax	(49) 06227 - 860 888
Situation	Lage	

Heidelberg (pop. 132 000), 15 km

Annual closure	Jährliche Schliessung	no
Weekly closure	Wöchentliche Schliessung	no

Fees main season
Preisliste hochsaison full day

	Week days Woche	We/Bank holidays We/Feiertag
Individual Individuell	DM 120,-	DM 150,-
Couple Ehepaar	DM 240,-	DM 300,-

Caddy	Caddy	on request
Electric Trolley	Elektrokarren	no
Buggy	Elektrischer Wagen	DM 50,-
Clubs	Leihschläger	DM 30,-
Credit cards Kreditkarten		VISA - Eurocard

Access Zufahrt : A6 → Heilbronn. Exit (Ausf.)
Wiesloch/Rauenberg. → Walldorf. 2nd traffic lights
→ St. Leon-Rot. 3rd street, turn left in Opelstrasse.
Map 1 on page 361 Karte 1 Seite 361

472

GOLF COURSE
PLATZ — 15/20

Site	Lage	
Maintenance	Instandhaltung	
Architect	Architekt	Hannes Schreiner
Type	Typ	parkland, open country
Relief	Begehbarkeit	
Water in play	Platz mit Wasser	
Exp. to wind	Wind ausgesetzt	
Trees in play	Platz mit Bäumen	

Scorecard Scorekarte	Chp. Chp.	Mens Herren	Ladies Damen
Length Länge	6587	6047	5329
Par	72	72	72

Advised golfing ability	0	12	24	36
Empfohlene Spielstärke				
Hcp required Min. Handicap	36			

CLUB HOUSE & AMENITIES
KLUBHAUS UND NEBENGEBÄUDE — 8/10

Pro shop	Pro shop	
Driving range	Übungsplatz	
Sheltered	überdacht	15 mats
On grass	auf Rasen	yes
Putting-green	Putting-grün	yes
Pitching-green	Pitching-grün	yes

HOTEL FACILITIES
HOTEL BESCHREIBUNG — 6/10

HOTELS HOTELS
Hotel Walkershof — Reilingen
118 rooms, D DM 350,- — 5 km
Tel (49) 06205 - 9590, Fax (49) 06205 - 959 44

Holiday Inn Walldorf Astoria — Walldorf
158 rooms, D DM 490,- — 6 km
Tel (49) 06227 - 360, Fax (49) 06227 - 36 504

Mondial — Wiesloch
43 rooms, D DM 250,- — 6 km
Tel (49) 06222 - 5760, Fax (49) 06222 - 576 333

RESTAURANTS RESTAURANT
La Chandelle — Wiesloch
Tel (49) 06222 - 5760 — 6 km

Freihof - Tel (49) 06227 - 25 17 — Wiesloch 6 km

Haus Landgraf - Tel (49) 06227 - 40 36 — Walldorf 6 km

STOLPER HEIDE

16	7	5

Stolper Heide ist Bestandteil einer schnell-wachsenden Wohnanlage und ist zweifellos einer der vielversprechendsten Golfplätze in ganz Deutschland. Die Namen Bernhard Langer und Kurt Rossknecht bürgen für ehrlichen Charakter und den Abwechslungsreichtum des Designs, das sich hervorragend an die unterschiedlichen Spielstärken der Golfer anpasst, wenngleich insbesondere die besseren Spieler ihren Spass daran haben werden, die strategischen Herausforderungen des Platzes zu meistern. Auf dem ausgezeichnet und intelligent gestalteten Gelände brauchen die Baüme sicherlich noch Zeit ihr Wachstum zu entfalten, aber bereits jetzt weisen die sorgfältig gearbeiteten Abgrenzungen zwischen Fairway und Rough den Golfer deutlich für den nächsten Schlag. Die Schlusslöcher stellen die Spieler vor allem im Match-Play vor eine interessante Aufgabe. Die Pflegezustand des Platzes, besonders im Bereich der sorgfältig gestalteten Grüns, ist bereits ausgezeichnet.

In a fast-growing residential area, Stolper Heide is one of Germany's most promising courses. The names of Bernhard Langer and Rossknecht were sure-fire guarantees for the honesty and variety of this layout and for the way it adapts to different levels of proficiency, although the better players will have the most fun here solving questions of strategy. Well-landscaped and intelligent, the course needs the trees to grow but the careful way in which the fairways and rough are demarcated means you are never in any doubt as to where the next shot should go. The finishing holes are particularly interesting here if competing in match-play. The green-keeping is already very good, particularly the carefully designed greens.

Stolper Heide Golf Club — 1997

Frihnauer Weg 3
D - 16540 STOLPE

Office	Sekretariat	(49) 03303 - 5490
Pro shop	Pro shop	(49) 03303 - 549 214
Fax	Fax	(49) 03303 - 549 222
Situation	Lage	

Berlin (pop. 3 500 000), 20 km

Annual closure	Jährliche Schliessung	1/1 → 31/1
Weekly closure	Wöchentliche Schliessung	no

Fees main season
Preisliste hochsaison 18 holes

	Week days Woche	We/Bank holidays We/Feiertag
Individual Individuell	DM 80,-	DM 100,-
Couple Ehepaar	DM 160,-	DM 200,-

Caddy	Caddy	no
Electric Trolley	Elektrokarren	no
Buggy	Elektrischer Wagen	no
Clubs	Leihschläger	DM 20,-

Credit cards Kreditkarten
VISA - Eurocard - Mastercard - AMEX

Access Zufahrt : Berlin A111 → Hamburg. Exit (Ausf.) Henningsdorf-Stolpe. Left → Stolpe.
Map 6 on page 371 Karte 6 Seite 371

GOLF COURSE / PLATZ — 16/20

Site	Lage	▰▰▰▰▱
Maintenance	Instandhaltung	▰▰▰▰▱
Architect	Architekt	Bernhard Langer Kurt Rossknecht
Type	Typ	parkland
Relief	Begehbarkeit	▰▱▱▱▱
Water in play	Platz mit Wasser	▰▰▰▱▱
Exp. to wind	Wind ausgesetzt	▰▰▱▱▱
Trees in play	Platz mit Bäumen	▰▰▰▱▱

Scorecard Scorekarte	Chp. Chp.	Mens Herren	Ladies Damen
Length Länge	6255	5974	5222
Par	72	72	72

Advised golfing ability Empfohlene Spielstärke	0	12	24	36

Hcp required   Min. Handicap   36 (weekends)

CLUB HOUSE & AMENITIES / KLUBHAUS UND NEBENGEBÄUDE — 7/10

Pro shop	Pro shop	▰▰▰▱▱
Driving range	Übungsplatz	▰▰▰▱▱
Sheltered	überdacht	15 mats
On grass	auf Rasen	yes
Putting-green	Putting-grün	yes
Pitching-green	Pitching-grün	yes

HOTEL FACILITIES / HOTEL BESCHREIBUNG — 5/10

HOTELS HOTELS

Hotel Palace 282 rooms, D DM 345,- Tel (49) 030 - 250 20 Fax (49) 030 - 262 65 77	Berlin	15 km
Sorat Hotel 120 rooms, D DM 182,- Tel (49) 030 - 439 040 Fax (49) 030 -439 044 44	Berlin-Tegel	8 km
Landgasthof zur Krummen Linde 14 rooms, D DM 160,- Tel (49) 03303 - 502 217 Fax (49) 03303 - 533 630	Stolpe	1 km

RESTAURANTS RESTAURANT

Landgasthof zur Krummen Linde Tel (49) 03303 - 502 217	Stolpe	1 km

473

Ein exemplarisches Beispiel für die Arbeit Bernhard von Limburgers, das sehr gut sein Bemühen, den Anforderungen guter Platzarchitektur gerecht zu werden, veranschaulicht. Solitude erweist sich als echter Gütetest für das Können eines Golfers, insbesondere dessen Fähigkeit gerade Drives zu schlagen. Kraftvollen Spielern werden die Fairways - Genauigkeit vorausgesetzt - vergleichsweise breit erscheinen, aber auch das Anspiel der mittelgrossen, erst kürzlich umgebauten Grüns erfordert in vielen Fällen nochmals höchste Präzision. Kürzere Spieler müssen sich vor allem auf gute lange Eisen und ihr kurzes Spiel verlassen können. Dies gilt im besonderen an den langen Par 4 Löchern, die regulär nur schwer zu erreichen sind, sowie den ausgezeichneten Par 3 Löchern. Wasser kommt nur selten ins Spiel, so ist es primär der Wald, der nicht nur den optischen sondern auch den spieltechnischen Charakter dieses Platzes prägt. Dank eines sehr durchdachten Layouts macht der leicht begehbare Platz einen ausgewogenen Eindruck. Solitude ist eine Anlage, die man kaum ignorieren kann, eignet sich aber eher für die etwas besseren Golfer.

A good example of a von Limburger design and of his concern for the demands of golf. While golf is the examination of a player's abilities, Solitude is a test of value with emphasis on straight driving. If they play straight, powerful hitters will find the fairways comparatively wide, but they will need extreme accuracy to reach a number of mid-sized elevated greens that have been recently reshaped. The shorter-hitters will have to sharpen up their long irons and even their short game on some of the long par 4s, that are tough to hit in regulation, and the very good par 3s. As there is little water to speak of, the course's visual appeal is primarily the forest. The forest is, in fact, the whole point of the course, which is well-balanced, easy on the legs, and a thoroughly well designed affair. It is difficult to overlook Solitude, but it is a course reserved for golfers who can play a bit.

Stuttgarter Golf-Club Solitude — 1968

Am Golfplatz
D - 71297 MÖNSHEIM

Office	Sekretariat	(49) 07044 -911 0410
Pro shop	Pro shop	(49) 07044 -911 0413
Fax	Fax	(49) 07044 -911 0420
Situation	Lage	

Stuttgart (pop. 560 000), 20 km

Annual closure	Jährliche Schliessung	1/12 → 31/3
Weekly closure	Wöchentliche Schliessung	no

Fees main season
Preisliste hochsaison full day

	Week days Woche	We/Bank holidays We/Feiertag
Individual Individuell	DM 80,-	DM 100,-
Couple Ehepaar	DM 160,-	DM 200,-

Week-ends & holidays: only with members
(nur in Mitgliederbegleitung)

Caddy	Caddy	on request
Electric Trolley	Elektrokarren	no
Buggy	Elektrischer Wagen	no
Clubs	Leihschläger	no

Credit cards Kreditkarten — no

474

PFORZHEIM

GOLF
Wurmberg
Mönsheim
Wimsheim
Niefern--Öschelbronn
Mülhacker
Friolzheim
Tiefenbronn nach Stuttgart

0 2 4 km

Access Zufahrt : A8 Stuttgart-Karlsruhe. Exit (Ausf.)
Heimsheim-Mönsheim. Golf → Mönsheim
Map 1 on page 361 Karte 1 Seite 361

GOLF COURSE / PLATZ — 17/20

Site	Lage	
Maintenance	Instandhaltung	
Architect	Architekt	B. von Limburger
Type	Typ	open country, forest
Relief	Begehbarkeit	
Water in play	Platz mit Wasser	
Exp. to wind	Wind ausgesetzt	
Trees in play	Platz mit Bäumen	

Scorecard Scorekarte	Chp. Chp.	Mens Herren	Ladies Damen
Length Länge	6045	6045	5365
Par	72	72	72

Advised golfing ability Empfohlene Spielstärke	0	12	24	36

Hcp required Min. Handicap — 36

CLUB HOUSE & AMENITIES / KLUBHAUS UND NEBENGEBÄUDE — 5/10

Pro shop	Pro shop	
Driving range	Übungsplatz	
Sheltered	überdacht	6 mats
On grass	auf Rasen	yes
Putting-green	Putting-grün	yes
Pitching-green	Pitching-grün	yes

HOTEL FACILITIES / HOTEL BESCHREIBUNG — 5/10

HOTELS HOTELS
Parkhotel — Pforzheim
144 rooms, D 200,- — 12 km
Tel (49 7231) 1610
Fax (49 7044) 1616 90

Hotel Eiss — Leonburg
32 rooms, D DM 170,- — 15 km
Tel (49) 07152 - 9440
Fax (49) 07152 - 42 134

RESTAURANTS RESTAURANT
Häckermühle — Tiefenbronn
Tel (49) 07234 - 6111 — 10 km

Ochsenpost — Tiefenbronn
Tel (49) 07234 - 920 578 — 10 km

Die nördlichste der friesischen Inseln ist einer der elegantesten Urlaubs,-gebiete in Deutschland. Westerland ist das grösste Seebad Deutschlands, Kampen das exklusivste. Auf dieser seltsam geformten Insel von 40km Länge, die von Klippen, Stränden und Dünen gesäumt ist, erwartet man natürlich einen Links Course. Donald Harradine hat hier eine seiner besten Designs abgeliefert, obwohl der Platz nicht mit den Meisterwerken der Links Courses der Britischen Inseln mithalten kann. Auch auf diesem Küstenplatz ist der Wind einbestimmender Faktor. Der sandige Boden sorgt für hervorragende Drainage, aber diese trockene Bodenbeschaffenheit erschwert die Schläge zum Grün. Um die Bälle auf den Grüns zum Halten zubringen, muss man einkalkulieren wie weit der Ball rollt, wobei bei starkem Wind das Beherrschen von "knock-down-shots" hilfreich ist. Es gibt keine blinden Löcher und Fallen, man sieht immer, wohin man den Ball zu spielen hat. Wer ein hohes Ergebnis mit ins Klubhaus bringt, hat schlecht gespielt ganz so wie es sein sollte. Dieser Platz ist auch ein Naturerlebnis in klarer Seeuft, die prickelnd wie Champagner schmeckt.

This is the northernmost of the North Friesian Islands, next to Denmark, where the largest town, Westerland, is Germany's biggest seaside resort. Over this strangely shaped isle (40 km in length) with alternating cliffs, beaches and dunes, a virtual links course was only to be expected. Donald Harradine has produced here a fine design, even though it doesn't really measure up to the British masterpieces. The wind is a key factor, naturally, as is the joy of breathing air as sharp as chilled champagne. The sand gives ideal turf and perfect draining, but the dryness of the soil and the wind make for difficult approach shots to the green. For the ball to stay on the green, you need to know how to roll it on, taking a chance on the likely trajectory. There are no blind shots here and no traps in what is very varied and well-utilised landscape; you can clearly see what needs to be done and you alone are responsible for any high-scoring.

Golf Club Sylt e.V.		1982
D - 25996 WENNINGSTEDT		

Office	Sekretariat	(49) 04651 -453 11
Pro shop	Pro shop	(49) 04651 -455 22
Fax	Fax	(49) 04651 -456 92
Situation	Lage	
Sylt Island, close to Denmark		
Annual closure	Jährliche Schliessung	no
Weekly closure	Wöchentliche Schliessung	no

Fees main season
Preisliste hochsaison 18 holes

	Week days Woche	We/Bank holidays We/Feiertag
Individual Individuell	DM 100,-	DM 100,-
Couple Ehepaar	DM 200,-	DM 200,-

Caddy	Caddy	no
Electric Trolley	Elektrokarren	DM 25,-
Buggy	Elektrischer Wagen	no
Clubs	Leihschläger	DM 35,-

Credit cards Kreditkarten no

Access Zufahrt : Hamburg E45 to Flensburg, then 199 to Niebüll → Westerland/Sylt, Wennigstedt → List
Map 1 on page 130 Karte 1 Seite 130

GOLF COURSE
PLATZ 15/20

Site	Lage	
Maintenance	Instandhaltung	
Architect	Architekt	Donald Harradine
Type	Typ	links, open country
Relief	Begehbarkeit	
Water in play	Platz mit Wasser	
Exp. to wind	Wind ausgesetzt	
Trees in play	Platz mit Bäumen	

Scorecard Scorekarte	Chp. Chp.	Mens Herren	Ladies Damen
Length Länge	6200	5707	5461
Par	72	72	72

Advised golfing ability	0	12	24	36
Empfohlene Spielstärke				
Hcp required Min. Handicap	32			

CLUB HOUSE & AMENITIES
KLUBHAUS UND NEBENGEBÄUDE 6/10

Pro shop	Pro shop	
Driving range	Übungsplatz	
Sheltered	überdacht	20 mats
On grass	auf Rasen	yes
Putting-green	Putting-grün	yes
Pitching-green	Pitching-grün	yes

475

HOTEL FACILITIES
HOTEL BESCHREIBUNG 8/10

HOTELS HOTELS
Rungholt — Kampen
60 rooms, D DM 370,- — 3 km
Tel (49) 04651 - 4480, Fax (49) 04651 - 44 840

Benen-Diken-Hof — Keitum
42 rooms, D DM 300,- — 6 km
Tel (49) 04651 - 938 30, Fax (49) 04651 - 938 383

Stadt Hamburg — Westerland
72 rooms, D DM 400,- — 3 km
Tel (49) 04651 - 8580, Fax (49) 04651 - 858 220

RESTAURANTS RESTAURANT
Landhaus Nösse — Morsum
Tel (49) 04651 - 819 555 — 10 km

Landhaus Stricker — Tinnum
Tel (49) 04651 - 316 72 — 4 km

Manne Pahl - Tel (49) 04651 - 425 10 — Kempen 3 km

Der Platz liegt in einer der schönsten Gegenden Deutschland. Der Platz liegt wunderschön oberhalb des Tegernsees. Leider ist der Platz nicht so schön wie die Gegend, der Platz ist eher wegen seiner illustren Mitgliedschaft als wegen seines Designs berühmt. Neun Löcher sind ordentlich, die anderen neun eher schrecklich. Die Platz ist kurz, aber das Anspielen der relativ kleinen Grüns ist extrem schwierig. Das Clubhaus strahlt viel Gemütlichkeit aus. Mit etwas Glück trifft man hier die Reichen und Schönen Deutschlands, von Boris Becker über Gunter Sachs bis hin zu Willy Bogner. Ein Gang durch die Umkleide mit den Namen auf den Spinden erinnert an das deutsche "Who is Who". Der vielbeschäftigte Donald Harradine entwarf den Platz 1960, aber komplett fertiggestellt wurde er erst im Jahr 1984. Der Platz ist recht hügelig, dennoch benötigen nur ältere oder untrainierte Spieler einen Golfwagen.

It is hardly more than an hour's drive to the Austrian border and not much more to visit Innsbrück once you have discovered all the charms of the lake lying at the foot of the course here. While this layout is hardly a world-beater, it does, like its neighbours, have the advantage of an exceptional natural setting. In this sense, Bavaria is a real golfing destination. Designed in 1960 by Donald Harradine, a decidedly prolific architect, it was only really completed in 1984. It shows all the typical features of its designer, who was undoubtedly less concerned with marking his period than many of his colleagues, but it is very British in style as far as understanding the game at all levels is concerned. We sometimes felt he might have contoured the fairways and bunkers a little more, but this sobriety has the advantage of preserving the terrain's natural aspect. The course is rather hilly but only the more elderly or very unfit golfers will need a buggy.

Tegernseer Golf-Club Bad Wiessee 1960
Robognerhof
D - 83707 BAD WIESSEE

Office	Sekretariat	(49) 08022 - 8769
Pro shop	Pro shop	(49) 08022 - 83 350
Fax	Fax	(49) 08022 - 82 747
Situation	Lage	

Bad Wiessee (pop. 5 000), 1 km - Bad Tölz, 18 km

Annual closure	Jährliche Schliessung	1/12 → 31/3
Weekly closure	Wöchentliche Schliessung	no

Monday (Montag) : Restaurant closed

Fees main season
Preisliste hochsaison 18 holes

	Week days Woche	We/Bank holidays We/Feiertag
Individual Individuell	DM 90,-	DM 120,-
Couple Ehepaar	DM 180,-	DM 240,-

We: ask before coming (begrenzte Spielmöglichkeit)

Caddy	Caddy	on request, DM 50,-
Electric Trolley	Elektrokarren	DM 30,-
Buggy	Elektrischer Wagen	no
Clubs	Leihschläger	DM 35,-

Credit cards Kreditkarten   no

GOLF COURSE
PLATZ `14`/20

Site	Lage	
Maintenance	Instandhaltung	
Architect	Architekt	Donald Harradine
Type	Typ	mountain, parkland
Relief	Begehbarkeit	
Water in play	Platz mit Wasser	
Exp. to wind	Wind ausgesetzt	
Trees in play	Platz mit Bäumen	

Scorecard Scorekarte	Chp. Chp.	Mens Herren	Ladies Damen
Length Länge	5402	5402	4818
Par	70	70	70

Advised golfing ability	0 12 24 36
Empfohlene Spielstärke	
Hcp required	Min. Handicap 36

CLUB HOUSE & AMENITIES
KLUBHAUS UND NEBENGEBÄUDE `7`/10

Pro shop	Pro shop	
Driving range	Übungsplatz	
Sheltered	überdacht	no
On grass	auf Rasen	yes
Putting-green	Putting-grün	yes
Pitching-green	Pitching-grün	yes

HOTEL FACILITIES
HOTEL BESCHREIBUNG `8`/10

HOTELS HOTELS
St. Georg Golf Hotel   Bad Wiessee
28 rooms, D DM 198,-   500 m
Tel (49) 08022 - 819 700, Fax (49) 08022 - 819 611

Wilhelmy   Bad Wiessee
22 rooms, D DM 240,-   1 km
Tel (49) 08022 - 98 680, Fax (49) 08022 - 84 074

Park-Hotel Egerner-Hof   Rottach-Egern
86 rooms, D DM 395,-   6 km
Tel (49) 08022 - 6660, Fax (49) 08022 - 666 200

RESTAURANTS RESTAURANT
Freihaus Brenner   Bad Wiessee
Tel (49) 08022 - 82 004   1 km

Altes Fährhaus   Bad Tölz
Tel (49) 08041 - 60 30   18 km

476

nach München
nach Bad Tölz
Finsterwald
Gmund
nach Miesbach (nach A8)
GOLF
Bad Wiessee
Tegernsee
Österreich
Rottach-Egern
0 2 4 km

Access Zufahrt : A8 München → Salzburg. Exit (Ausf.) Holzkirchen. 318 → Gmund. In Gmund 318 → Bad Wiessee. **Map 2 on page 362** Karte 2 Seite 362

TREUDELBERG

Beim Bau dieses Golfplatzes inmitten eines Naturs3chutzgebietes standen die ökologischen Gesichtspunkte eindeutig im Vordergrund, was zeigt, dass sich Golf und Umwelt durchaus gut vertragen. Treudelberg ist seiner Konzeption nach ein echter Sportclub im Stil amerikanischer Resorts, der aufgrund der angebotenen Palette an Möglichkeiten sicherlich der grösste seiner Art in dieser Region ist. Etwas mehr Charakter würde dem sehr zurückhaltend gestalteten Platz gut zu Gesicht stehen. Da die Anlage sehr stark dem Wind ausgesetzt ist, wären grössere Erdbewegungen wie man sie auch auf flachen Linksplätzen vorfindet, wünschenswert gewesen. Es gibt nur wenig Bäume, dieser Mangel wird aber durch Bunker, zahlreiche Wasserhindernisse sowie, je nach Saison, auch Rough wettgemacht. Ein ganz brauchbarer Platz, auf dem Spieler mit mittleren und hohen Handicaps lernen können, wie man mit Wasserhindernissen zurechtkommt.

This course was laid out in a nature reserve where ecological considerations were top priority. This just goes to show that golf and ecology can get along together. Treudelberg is a real sports club (in the style of US resorts) which is doubtless the largest of its kind in the region, judging by facilities. The course is very discreetly designed, and a little more personality would have been welcome. As exposure to the wind is a dominant factor, we would have liked to see more earth moving and grading, like on links courses, even when flat. Trees are not in great supply, but the bunkers and many water hazards largely make up for that, as does the rough at certain times of year. A useful course where mid- and high-handicappers will learn how to handle water hazards.

Golf & Country Club Treudelberg — 1991

Lehmsaler Landstrasse 45
D - 22397 HAMBURG

Office	Sekretariat	(49) 040 - 60822 500
Pro shop	Pro shop	(49) 040 - 60822 535
Fax	Fax	(49) 040 - 60822 444
Situation	Lage	

Hamburg Zentrum (pop. 1 650 000), 15 km
Hamburg-Poppenbüttel, 3 km

Annual closure	Jährliche Schliessung	no
Weekly closure	Wöchentliche Schliessung	no

Fees main season
Preisliste hochsaison 18 holes

	Week days Woche	We/Bank holidays We/Feiertag
Individual Individuell	DM 75,-	DM 90,-
Couple Ehepaar	DM 150,-	DM 180,-
Caddy Caddy		no
Electric Trolley Elektrokarren		no
Buggy Elektrischer Wagen		DM 50,-
Clubs Leihschläger		DM 30,-

Credit cards Kreditkarten
VISA - Eurocard - MasterCard - AMEX - DC

Access Zufahrt : A7 Hamburg-Flesburg. Exit (Ausf.)
Schnelsen Nord. Right → Airport (Flughafen). →
Poppenbüttel. Left → Lemsahl-Duvenstedt
(Ulzburger Strasse), Lemsahler Landstrasse.
Map 7 on page 372 Karte 7 Seite 372

GOLF COURSE
PLATZ — 13/20

Site	Lage		
Maintenance	Instandhaltung		
Architect	Architekt	Donald Steel	
Type	Typ	open country	
Relief	Begehbarkeit		
Water in play	Platz mit Wasser		
Exp. to wind	Wind ausgesetzt		
Trees in play	Platz mit Bäumen		

Scorecard Scorekarte	Chp. Chp.	Mens Herren	Ladies Damen
Length Länge	6149	6149	5333
Par	72	72	72

Advised golfing ability				
Empfohlene Spielstärke	0	12	24	36
Hcp required Min. Handicap	no			

CLUB HOUSE & AMENITIES
KLUBHAUS UND NEBENGEBÄUDE — 8/10

Pro shop	Pro shop	
Driving range	Übungsplatz	
Sheltered	überdacht	16 mats
On grass	auf Rasen	yes
Putting-green	Putting-grün	yes
Pitching-green	Pitching-grün	yes

HOTEL FACILITIES
HOTEL BESCHREIBUNG — 7/10

HOTELS HOTELS
Treudelberg Marriott — Golf
135 rooms, D DM 300,- — on site
Tel (49) 040 - 608 220, Fax (49) 040 - 608 22 44

Poppenbütteler Hof — Hamburg-Poppenbüttel
32 rooms, D DM 300,- — 3 km
Tel (49) 040 - 602 1072, Fax (49) 040 - 602 3130

Hafen Hamburg — Hamburg
250 rooms, D DM 210,- — 15 km
Tel (49) 040 - 311 130, Fax (49) 040 - 319 2736

Baseler Hof - 149 rooms, D DM 180,- — Hamburg
Tel (49) 040 - 359 060, Fax (49) 040 - 359 06 91 — 15 km

RESTAURANTS RESTAURANT
Ristorante Dante — Hamburg-Lemsahl
Tel (49) 040 - 602 0043 — 5 km

Treudelberg Marriott — Golf
Tel (49) 040 - 608 220 — on site

477

Der auf 700 Meter Höhe gelegene Golfplatz ist wie viele andere Plätzee dieser Region besonders bei Touristen sehr beliebt. Am schönsten spielt sich Tutzing entweder im Herbst oder aber im Frühling, wenn die Vegetation nach dem Winter wieder voll erblüht ist. Die bayerischen Alpen bilden einen malerischen Hintergrund und verstärken so das Spielvergnügen auf dieser ausgezeichneten Anlage mit zahlreichen Bäumen und einigen hübschen Wasserläufen, welche die Spielbahnen - nicht selten zum Verdruss der Golfer - kreuzen. Der Plätze verfügt über keinerlei aussergewöhnliche aufregende Designelemente, sondern spiegelt vielmehr die Absicht des Architekten wider, in erster Linie einen Platz zu bauen, bei dem das Golfvergnügen im Vordergrund steht. Wenn Sie sich in dieser herrlichen Gegend aufhalten, sollten Sie diesen schön gelegenen Golfplatz und das dazugehörige Clubhaus im Stil eines Chalets keinesfalls links liegen lassen.

At an altitude of 700 metres and like most courses in this region very popular with tourists, Tutzing is particularly pleasant to play from the middle of Spring - when the vegetation is filling out after Winter - to the middle of Autumn. The backdrop of the Bavarian Alps adds to the pleasure of this excellent course with its numerous trees and pretty streams which cross the course, sometimes to the distress of the golfer. Don't look for anything outstandingly exciting design-wise here; this is the work of a serious artist who was thinking first and foremost of golfing pleasure. When you are in this superb region, Tutzing is a course not to be missed and a charming site enhanced by the chalet-style clubhouse.

Golf-Club Tutzing e.V.   1983
Deixlfurt
D - 82327 TUTZING

Office	Sekretariat	(49) 08158 - 3600
Pro shop	Pro shop	(49) 08158 - 1761
Fax	Fax	(49) 08158 - 7234
Situation	Lage	

München (pop. 1 300 000), 40 km

Annual closure	Jährliche Schliessung	15/11 →15/2
Weekly closure	Wöchentliche Schliessung	no

Fees main season
Preisliste hochsaison 18 holes

	Week days Woche	We/Bank holidays We/Feiertag
Individual Individuell	DM 80,-	DM 100,-
Couple Ehepaar	DM 160,-	DM 200,-

Caddy	Caddy	no
Electric Trolley	Elektrokarren	DM 50,-
Buggy	Elektrischer Wagen	DM 70,-
Clubs	Leihschläger	DM 50,-

Credit cards Kreditkarten   no

Access Zufahrt : A95 München → Starnberg. Von Starnberg, B2 (Olympiastr.) → Weilheim. After Traubing, 1km left → Deixlfurt.
Map 2 on page 362 Karte 2 Seite 362

GOLF COURSE
PLATZ   **15**/20

Site	Lage	■■■■■□
Maintenance	Instandhaltung	■■■■■□
Architect	Architekt	C. Kramer
Type	Typ	mountain
Relief	Begehbarkeit	■■■■□□
Water in play	Platz mit Wasser	■■■□□□
Exp. to wind	Wind ausgesetzt	■■■□□□
Trees in play	Platz mit Bäumen	■■■■□□

Scorecard Scorekarte	Chp. Chp.	Mens Herren	Ladies Damen
Length Länge	6159	6159	5438
Par	72	72	72

Advised golfing ability		0	12	24	36
Empfohlene Spielstärke					
Hcp required	Min. Handicap	35			

CLUB HOUSE & AMENITIES
KLUBHAUS UND NEBENGEBÄUDE   **7**/10

Pro shop	Pro shop	■■■■□□
Driving range	Übungsplatz	■■■■□□
Sheltered	überdacht	3 mats
On grass	auf Rasen	yes
Putting-green	Putting-grün	yes
Pitching-green	Pitching-grün	yes

HOTEL FACILITIES
HOTEL BESCHREIBUNG   **6**/10

HOTELS HOTELS
Kaiserin Elisabeth   Feldafing
70 rooms, D DM 180,-   3 km
Tel (49) 08157 - 930 90
Fax (49) 08157 -930 9133

Forsthaus am See   Pöcking-Possenhofen
21 rooms, DM 270,-   10 km
Tel (49) 08157 - 93 010
Fax (49) 08157 - 4292

Marina   Bernried
71 rooms, D DM 250,-   12 km
Tel (49) 08158 - 9320, Fax (49) 08158 - 7117

RESTAURANTS RESTAURANT
Forsthaus Ilkahöhe   Tutzing
Tel (49) 08158 - 8242   4 km

478

WALDDÖRFER

| 16 | 7 | 6 |

Wie Ahrensburg ist auch Walddörfer am Ufer des Bredenbeker Sees gelegen, inmitten einer Parklandschaft mit für diese Region typischen Hecken und Bäumen. Dutzende unterschiedlicher Baumarten verleihen vielen Spielbahnen ihren ganz eigenen Charakter. Die hügeligen ersten neun Löcher mit ihren durchgehend engen Fairways zwingen speziell beim Abschlag zur Vorsicht. Die Spielbahnen sind zudem noch recht lang; es gibt vier Par 5, drei Par 3 und zwei Par 4 Löcher. Auf den zweiten Neun wird das Gelände flacher und offener. Besonders bei aufkommendem Wind werden sich selbst Longhitter schwer tun ihr Ergebnis zu reparieren, wenn sie auf den ersten Neun zu sehr gestreut haben. Bemerkenswert am Layout von Walddörfer ist, dass es nur sieben Par 4 Löcher gibt. Die gut erkennbaren Schwierigkeiten kommen stark ins Spiel. Das letzte Wort gebührt der ausgezeichneten 18. Bahn, die den würdigen Abschluss einer grossartigen Golfrunde bildet.

Like Ahrensburg, Walddörfer is located on the banks of Lake Bredenbeker, in a setting of parkland, hedgerows and trees that are typical of the region. The trees are magnificent, with dozens of varieties giving a distinctive flavour to different holes. The front nine is hilly, with generally narrow fairways calling for care, especially off the tee. The holes are pretty long, too, and there are four par 5s, two par 3s and two par 4s. The landscape then becomes flatter and wider, although big-hitters will still be hard-pushed to repair their card if they were too wayward over the front 9, especially if the unstoppable wind gets up. In all, there are only seven par 4s here, a feature that adds to the originality of Walddörfer. Difficulties are very much in play and generally very visible. One last word should go to the 18th, an excellent hole with which to complete a great round of golf.

Golfclub Hamburg-Walddörfer — 1960

Schevenbarg
D - 22949 AMMERSBEK

Office	Sekretariat	(49) 040 - 605 1337
Pro shop	Pro shop	(49) 040 - 605 2725
Fax	Fax	(49) 040 - 605 4879
Situation	Lage	

Ahrensburg (pop. 27 000), 2 km - Hamburg, 20 km

Annual closure	Jährliche Schliessung	no
Weekly closure	Wöchentliche Schliessung	no

Monday (Montag): Restaurant closed

Fees main season
Preisliste hochsaison 18 holes

	Week days Woche	We/Bank holidays We/Feiertag
Individual Individuell	DM 70,-	DM 85,-
Couple Ehepaar	DM 140,-	DM 170,-

We: only with members (nur in Mitgliederbegleitung)

Caddy	Caddy	no
Electric Trolley	Elektrokarren	no
Buggy	Elektrischer Wagen	no
Clubs	Leihschläger	no

Credit cards Kreditkarten — no

BARGTEHEIDE

Timmerhorn

GOLF

Hoisbüttel — Ammersbek — nach LÜBECK

434

AHRENSBURG

nach Hamburg

A 1

0   2   4 km

29
75
28

Access Zufahrt : A1 Hamburg-Lübeck. Exit (Ausf.) Ahrensburg. B434 → Ammersbek. In Ortsteil Hoisbüttel, turn right: Wulfsdorfer Weg → Golf
Map 7 on page 372 Karte 7 Seite 372

GOLF COURSE / PLATZ — 16/20

Site	Lage	▬▬▬▬▬▭
Maintenance	Instandhaltung	▬▬▬▬▬▭
Architect	Architekt	B. von Limburger
Type	Typ	forest, parkland
Relief	Begehbarkeit	▬▬▬▬▭▭
Water in play	Platz mit Wasser	▬▭▭▭▭▭
Exp. to wind	Wind ausgesetzt	▬▬▬▭▭▭
Trees in play	Platz mit Bäumen	▬▬▬▬▭▭

Scorecard Scorekarte	Chp. Chp.	Mens Herren	Ladies Damen
Length Länge	6154	6154	5416
Par	73	73	73

Advised golfing ability Empfohlene Spielstärke	0	12	24	36
Hcp required Min. Handicap	36			

CLUB HOUSE & AMENITIES / KLUBHAUS UND NEBENGEBÄUDE — 7/10

Pro shop	Pro shop	▬▬▬▬▭▭
Driving range	Übungsplatz	▬▬▬▬▭▭
Sheltered	überdacht	8 mats
On grass	auf Rasen	yes
Putting-green	Putting-grün	yes
Pitching-green	Pitching-grün	no

479

HOTEL FACILITIES / HOTEL BESCHREIBUNG — 6/10

HOTELS HOTELS

Park Hotel Ahrensburg 24 rooms, D DM 200,- Tel (49) 04102 - 2300 Fax (49) 04102 - 230 100	Ahrensburg 6 km
Ring Hotel Ahrensburg 11 rooms, D DM 160,- Tel (49) 04102 - 51 560 Fax (49) 04102 - 515 656	Ahrensburg 6 km

RESTAURANTS RESTAURANT

Golfclub Restaurant Tel (49) 040 - 605 4211	Golf on site

WASSERBURG ANHOLT

Ein sehr gepflegter, klassischer Parkland Course mit altem Baumbestand in einem Teil des Schlossparks der Anholter Wasserburg. Der Meisterschaftsplatz wurde von Bernhard von Limburger gekonnt in das Landschaftsschutzgebiet Anholter Schweiz mit seinen beiden Flussläufen Issel und Wasserstrang gelegt. Das Platz ist abwechslungsreich und einprägsam, weil jedes der 18 Löcher seinen eigenenen Charakter hat und spezifische Herausforderung bietet. Besonders reizvoll sind die vier Par-3-Löcher, obwohl sie nach modernen Gesichtspunkten nicht sonderlich lang sind (zwischen 119 und 170 m). Dafür sind sie durch Wasser- und Sandhindernisse sehr gut verteidigt. Die anderen LÖchern erfordern eine Kombination aus präzisem, langen Spiel und strategischem Geschick.

A very well groomed classical parkland course lined by mature trees located in a part of the old park of the water castle (Wasserschloss) Anholt. This championship course was designed by Bernhard von Limburger who laid out the course masterfully in the environmentally protected area of the Anholter Schweiz with the two streams of Issel and Wolfstrang. The course stays in your mind because each and every hole has its own character and challenge. The four par 3 holes on this course really stand out, even though they are not long by modern standards (between 119 and 170 m), but they are well defended by water hazards and sand traps. All other holes require a combination of long, precise shots and strategic skill.

Golf Club Wasserburg-Anholt e.V. — 1974

Am Schloss 3
D - 46419 ISSELBURG-ANHOLT

Office	Sekretariat	(49) 02874 - 915 120
Pro shop	Pro shop	(49) 02874 - 915 130
Fax	Fax	(49) 02874 - 915 128
Situation	Lage	

Bocholt (pop. 70 000), 16 km

Annual closure	Jährliche Schliessung	no
Weekly closure	Wöchentliche Schliessung	no

Monday (Montag): Restaurant closed

Fees main season
Preisliste hochsaison 18 holes

	Week days Woche	We/Bank holidays We/Feiertag
Individual Individuell	DM 50,-	DM 80,-
Couple Ehepaar	DM 100,-	DM 160,-
under 21 years/Students : – 50%		
Caddy	Caddy	on request
Electric Trolley	Elektrokarren	DM 25,-
Buggy	Elektrischer Wagen	DM 60,-
Clubs	Leihschläger	DM 25,-

Credit cards Kreditkarten
Visa - Eurocard - Mastercard - AMEX - DC

Access Zufahrt : A3 Oberhausen → Arnhem, Exit (Ausf.) Rees. B67 → Rees. Right on 458 → Millingen. Right → Anholt. 3 km right on 459 → Wasserburg-Anholt. **Map 5 on page 368** Karte 5 Seite 368

GOLF COURSE
PLATZ — 15/20

Site	Lage	
Maintenance	Instandhaltung	
Architect	Architekt	B. von Limburger
Type	Typ	forest, parkland
Relief	Begehbarkeit	
Water in play	Platz mit Wasser	
Exp. to wind	Wind ausgesetzt	
Trees in play	Platz mit Bäumen	

Scorecard Scorekarte	Chp. Chp.	Mens Herren	Ladies Damen
Length Länge	6115	6115	5371
Par	72	72	72

Advised golfing ability Empfohlene Spielstärke	0	12	24	36

Hcp required	Min. Handicap	36 (week-ends)

CLUB HOUSE & AMENITIES
KLUBHAUS UND NEBENGEBÄUDE — 7/10

Pro shop	Pro shop	
Driving range	Übungsplatz	
Sheltered	überdacht	9 mats
On grass	auf Rasen	yes
Putting-green	Putting-grün	yes
Pitching-green	Pitching-grün	yes

HOTEL FACILITIES
HOTEL BESCHREIBUNG — 7/10

HOTELS HOTELS

Wasserschloss Anholt — Golf / on site
30 rooms, D DM 180/350,-
Tel (49) 02874 - 4590, Fax (49) 02874 - 4035

Nienhaus — Isselburg / 4 km
12 rooms, D DM 140,-
Tel (49) 02874 - 770, Fax (49) 02874 - 45 673

Legeland — Anholt / 1 km
7 rooms, D from DM 110,-
Tel (49) 02874 - 837, Fax (49) 02874 - 45 417

RESTAURANTS RESTAURANT

Wasserschloss Anholt — Golf / on site
Tel (49) 02874 - 4590

Legeland — Anholt / 1 km
Tel (49) 02874 - 837

480

WENDLOHE A-KURS + B-KURS

Die grosszügige Weite Schleswig-Holsteins bildet die ruhige und beschauliche Umgebung für Wendlohe, wo die zahlreichen Bäume kaum beunruhigen, da man seinen Ball auch unter den Bäumen immer in einer guten Lage vorfindet. Wenig Wasser und nur vereinzelte Fairway-Bunker weisen darauf hin, dass die Hauptschwierigkeit im Anspiel der Gröns liegt. Unterschiedlich gross, mit starken Konturen versehen und teilweise auf mehreren Stufen angelegt, sind diese ohne Frage die interessantesten Grüns weit und breit. Sie sind durchgängig gut verteidigt, sehr schnell aber nie unspielbar. Um sie von der richtigen Position aus anzuspielen, bedarf es sehr präziser Eisenschläge. Deswegen wird es einem auch zumindest auf der ersten Runde schwerfallen, ein seinem Handicap entsprechendes Ergebnis zu spielen. Im Winter ist der Platz etwas feucht. Das Clubhaus erfreut sich einer schönen Terrasse, von der aus man das 18. Loch einsehen kann.

The wide open spaces of Schleswig-Holstein provide a calm and pastoral setting at "Auf der Wendlohe", where trees are hardly a worry. There are enough of them, but you always find your ball well-placed when you meet them. With only a little water and few fairway bunkers, you will guess that the main problem is the approach to the greens. These are unquestionably some of the most interesting putting surfaces to contend with in this part of the world, with different sizes, serious contours and multi-tiering. They are generally slick, well-protected but never unplayable. To approach them from the right position, you need a sharp and accurate iron game. This is why returning a card to reflect your handicap is hardly likely, at least not the first time out. A wee damp in winter, the course boasts a pretty terrace overlooking the 18th hole.

Golf Club auf der Wendlohe — 1964

Oldesloher Strasse 251
D - 22457 HAMBURG

Office	Sekretariat	(49) 040 - 550 5014
Pro shop	Pro shop	(49) 040 - 550 6151
Fax	Fax	(49) 040 - 550 3668
Situation	Lage	

Norderstedt (pop. 70 500), 3 km
Hamburg (pop. 1 650 000), 15 km

Annual closure	Jährliche Schliessung	no
Weekly closure	Wöchentliche Schliessung	no

Fees main season
Preisliste hochsaison 18 holes

	Week days Woche	We/Bank holidays We/Feiertag
Individual Individuell	DM 70,-	DM 90,-
Couple Ehepaar	DM 140,-	DM 160,-

We: only with members (nur in Mitgliederbegleitung)

Caddy	Caddy	on request
Electric Trolley	Elektrokarren	no
Buggy	Elektrischer Wagen	no
Clubs	Leihschläger	no
Credit cards Kreditkarten		no

Access Zufahrt : A7 Hamburg-Kiel. Exit (Ausf.) Hamburg-Schnelsen-Nord. 432 → Norderstedt (Oldesloher-Strasse). Left on Wendloher Weg → Golf
Map 7 on page 372 Karte 7 Seite 372

GOLF COURSE / PLATZ — 16/20

Site	Lage	
Maintenance	Instandhaltung	
Architect	Architekt	E.D. Hess
Type	Typ	country, open country
Relief	Begehbarkeit	
Water in play	Platz mit Wasser	
Exp. to wind	Wind ausgesetzt	
Trees in play	Platz mit Bäumen	

Scorecard Scorekarte	Chp. Chp.	Mens Herren	Ladies Damen
Length Länge	6065	6065	5340
Par	72	72	72

Advised golfing ability		0	12	24	36
Empfohlene Spielstärke					
Hcp required	Min. Handicap	36			

CLUB HOUSE & AMENITIES / KLUBHAUS UND NEBENGEBÄUDE — 7/10

Pro shop	Pro shop	
Driving range	Übungsplatz	
Sheltered	überdacht	4 mats
On grass	auf Rasen	yes
Putting-green	Putting-grün	yes
Pitching-green	Pitching-grün	yes

HOTEL FACILITIES / HOTEL BESCHREIBUNG — 6/10

HOTELS HOTELS

Hotel Heuberg — Norderstedt
15 rooms, D DM 150,- — 3 km
Tel (49) 040 - 523 1197
Fax (49) 040 - 523 8067

Hotel Ausspann — Schnelsen
12 rooms, D DM 165,- — 6 km
Tel (49) 040 - 559 8700
Fax (49) 040 - 559 87060

RESTAURANTS RESTAURANT

Golf Club Restaurant — GC Wendlohe
Tel (49) 040 - 550 8583

Champs — Schnelsen
Tel (49) 040 - 559 791-0 — 6 km

481

Dies ist der älteste Golfplatz der Region. Fehlende Länge könnte ihm unter Beurteilung moderner Gesichtspunkte negativ ausgelegt werden, aber dennoch ist er nicht leicht zu spielen. Der Platz entpuppt sich als wahrer Widersacher des Golfers und entspricht so der Philosophie derer, die Golf in erster Linie als Spiel verstehen. Enge Fairways, Doglegs, kleine, oftmals auf mehreren Stufen angelegte Grüns, der ständig ins Spiel kommende Wald, ein Par 3 über eine Schlucht, mehrere Gräben sowie sehr gefährliche Bunker zwingen den Golfer dazu, den Ball permanent kontrolliert zu spielen. Die Schläge zum Grün sind hier häufig dem Angriff auf eine Festung vergleichbar, daher muss man versuchen die Grüns eher hoch denn flach anzuspielen. Leicht zu Gehen, eignet sich der Platz für eine Runde mit der Familie, unabhängig vom Können der Einzelnen, da er auch für Spieler mit hohem Handicap eine interessante Erfahrung darstellt. Der Platz wird etwas einfacher, sobald man einmal alle nicht immer deutlich erkennbaren Hindernisse identifiziert hat.

This is the oldest course in the region. Its lack of length might count against it when judged to modern-day criteria, but it is still not that easy to master. If golf is just a game, then Wentorf-Reinbeker well reflects that image: it is a real adversary for players. Narrow fairways, dog-legs, small greens that are often multi-tiered, a forest that is always in the picture, a par 3 across a gorge, a few ditches and very relevant bunkers constantly oblige players to flight their ball. And to pitch the greens rather than roll their shots, since attacking the greens here is often comparable to taking a fortress! Easily walkable, this is a course for a family outing, whatever the ability of players (it is a good experience for high-handicappers), but it gets easier to play once you have firmly identified the hazards, which are not always clear to see from the tee.

Wentorf-Reinbeker Golf-Club — 1901

Golfstrasse 2
D - 21465 WENTORF/HAMBURG

Office	Sekretariat	(49) 040 - 729 78066
Pro shop	Pro shop	(49) 040 - 720 2141
Fax	Fax	(49) 040 - 720 2141
Situation	Lage	

Reinbek (pop. 24 600), 2 km

Annual closure	Jährliche Schliessung	
Weekly closure	Wöchentliche Schliessung	no

Monday (Montag): Restaurant closed

Fees main season
Preisliste hochsaison 18 Löcher

	Week days Woche	We/Bank holidays We/Feiertag
Individual Individuell	DM 70,-	DM 80,-
Couple Ehepaar	DM 1240,-	DM 160,-

We: only with members (nur in Mitgliederbegleitung)

Caddy	Caddy	no
Electric Trolley	Elektrokarren	no
Buggy	Elektrischer Wagen	no
Clubs	Leihschläger	no

Credit cards Kreditkarten — no

482

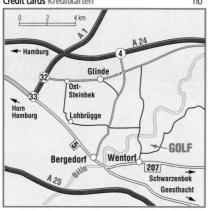

Access Zufahrt : A24 Hamburg → Berlin. Exit (Ausf.) Reinbek. In Reinbek, → Wentorf (Hamburger Strasse). In Mühlenteich, Golfstrasse.
Map 7 on page 372 Karte 7 Seite 372

GOLF COURSE / PLATZ — 15/20

Site	Lage	
Maintenance	Instandhaltung	
Architect	Architekt	E.D. Hess (1991)
Type	Typ	Wald, Park
Relief	Begehbarkeit	
Water in play	Platz mit Wasser	
Exp. to wind	Wind ausgesetzt	
Trees in play	Platz mit Bäumen	

Scorecard Scorekarte	Chp. Chp.	Mens Herren	Ladies Damen
Length Länge	5698	5698	5029
Par	70	70	70

Advised golfing ability Empfohlene Spielstärke		0 12 24 36
Hcp required	Min. Handicap	36

CLUB HOUSE & AMENITIES / KLUBHAUS UND NEBENGEBÄUDE — 7/10

Pro shop	Pro shop	
Driving range	Übungsplatz	
Sheltered	überdacht	4 mats
On grass	auf Rasen	yes
Putting-green	Putting-grün	yes
Pitching-green	Pitching-grün	yes

HOTEL FACILITIES / HOTEL BESCHREIBUNG — 6/10

HOTELS HOTELS

Waldhaus Reinbek — Reinbek — 2 km
12 rooms, D DM 265,-
Tel (49) 040 - 727 520,
Fax (49) 040 - 727 52 10

Sachsenwald Congress Hotel — Reinbek — 2 km
60 rooms, D DM 250,-
Tel (49) 040 - 727 610,
Fax (49) 040 -727 612 15

RESTAURANTS RESTAURANT

Waldhaus Reinbek — Reinbek — 2 km
Tel (49) 040 - 727 520

Unweit der Donau liegt dieser flache Platz in einer parkähnlichen Landschaft mit wunderschönen alten Bäumen, meist Eichen. Die Hauptschwierigkeit dieses Platzes liegt darin, diesen herrlichen Bäumen und dem extrem dicken Rough aus dem Weg zu gehen. Zudem erschweren drei Wasserhindernisse und 17 strategisch geschickt platzierte Fairway-Bunker das Spiel. Die gut gesicherten Grüns sind von herausragender Qualität Sie sind von teilweise immenser Grösse, so dass man den einen oder anderen 3-Putt einkalkulieren muss. Der Clubpräsident seine Königliche Hoheit Herzog Max in Bayern, als Mitglied des von Pine Valley, des R&A, Muirfield und Royal St. Georges ist, besteht in bester schottischer Tradition darauf, dass die Fairways nicht künstlich bewässert werden und keine Entfernungsmarkierungen aufweisen. Imposant ist das moderne Clubhaus mit Wohnmöglichkeit und einem nahegelegene Dormi-Haus. Ein Platz, den man unbedingt spielen muss, wenn man im Grossraum München-Ingolstadt-Augsburg unterwegs ist.

In countryside along the Danube, this is a flat course surrounded by some really beautiful trees, mainly oak, which give the impression of a large English-style park. The main difficulty here is to stay away from these impressive trees and the heavy, thick rough. Three water hazards and 17 strategically placed fairway bunkers add to the difficulty. The greens are well defended and of excellent quality, but some are simply huge, so getting away without at least one 3-putt is a major feat. The club president and de-facto owner, His Royal Highness Duke Max of Bavaria, who is a member of Pine Valley, the R & A, Muirfield and Royal St. George, insists in the best Scottish traditions that there is no irrigation system for the fairways and no distance markers either. Guests can stay either at the ultra modern clubhouse or in the charming dormy-house located two minutes from the course. This is a course not to be missed, if you are in the greater Munich-Ingolstadt-Augsburg area.

Wittelsbacher Golfclub Rohrenfeld-Neuburg — 1988

Gut Rohrenfeld
D - 86633 NEUBURG/DONAU

Office	Sekretariat	(49) 08431 - 44 118
Pro shop	Pro shop	(49) 08431 - 44 118
Fax	Fax	(49) 08431 - 41 301
Situation	Lage	

Ingolstadt (pop. 108 000), 20 km - Augsburg, 45 km

Annual closure	Jährliche Schliessung	no
Weekly closure	Wöchentliche Schliessung	no

Fees main season
Preisliste hochsaison 18 holes

	Week days Woche	We/Bank holidays We/Feiertag
Individual Individuell	DM 70,-	DM 90,-
Couple Ehepaar	DM 140,-	DM 180,-

under 21 years & Students: Special fees

Caddy	Caddy	no
Electric Trolley	Elektrokarren	yes
Buggy	Elektrischer Wagen	yes
Clubs	Leihschläger	yes

Credit cards Kreditkarten MasterCard

Access Zufahrt : München, A9 → Nürnberg. Exit (Ausf.)
Manching B16 → Neuburg. Exit Rohrenfeld → Golf
Map 2 on page 362 Karte 2 Seite 362

GOLF COURSE PLATZ — 16/20

Site	Lage	
Maintenance	Instandhaltung	
Architect	Architekt	Dudok van Heel
Type	Typ	forest
Relief	Begehbarkeit	
Water in play	Platz mit Wasser	
Exp. to wind	Wind ausgesetzt	
Trees in play	Platz mit Bäumen	

Scorecard Scorekarte	Chp. Chp.	Mens Herren	Ladies Damen
Length Länge	6350	6119	5352
Par	72	72	72

Advised golfing ability Empfohlene Spielstärke		0 12 24 36
Hcp required	Min. Handicap	36

CLUB HOUSE & AMENITIES KLUBHAUS UND NEBENGEBÄUDE — 7/10

Pro shop	Pro shop	
Driving range	Übungsplatz	
Sheltered	überdacht	yes
On grass	auf Rasen	yes
Putting-green	Putting-grün	yes
Pitching-green	Pitching-grün	yes

HOTEL FACILITIES HOTEL BESCHREIBUNG — 6/10

HOTELS HOTELS

Wittelsbacher Gästehaus — Golf
26 rooms, D DM 150,- — on site
Tel (49) 08431 - 49 616, Fax (49) 08431 - 41 301

Bergbauer — Neuburg
22 rooms, D DM 155,- — 6 km
Tel (49) 08431 - 47 095, Fax (49) 08431 - 47 090

Blumenhotel — Rain am Lech
63 rooms, D DM 170,- — 20 km
Tel (49) 09090 - 760, Fax (49) 09090 - 764 00

RESTAURANTS RESTAURANT

Arco Schlösschen — Neuburg
Tel (49) 08431 - 22 85 — 6 km

Im Stadttheater — Ingolstadt
Tel (49) 0841 - 93 5150 — 20 km

483

THE NEW PEUGEOT 406 COUPÉ. THE DRIVE OF YOUR LIFE.

Grande-Bretagne Irlande

As far as travel is concerned there are no frontiers. From a golfing point of view, the term « Great Britain and Ireland » covers three criteria, namely geography, language and sport. The best players from both islands were selected for the Ryder Cup team in years gone by, and still are for the Walker Cup and Curtis Cup against the United States. A fourth criterion might be unity of style in terms of golf courses, imposed, despite the variety of landscapes, by the pounding seas around each and every coastline. Seas which, miraculously, have left ample space for the great links courses of England, Scotland, Wales, Northern Ireland and the Republic of Ireland.

When you make choices you necessarily leave yourself open to criticism, and amongst the some 2,500 eighteen-hole courses to be found in this home of golf, we will certainly be accused of having forgotten a number of excellent layouts in Britain and Ireland. Some of them asked not to be included here because they are totally private. But we won't deny the fact that we have also given preference to the more specifically British style course, even though they may appear a little outdated in terms of yardage. In the same way, the scores given to clubhouses were awarded in relation to the general standard of clubhouse found in the British Isles. Some may be considered very low compared to their counterparts in the United States, Japan and even continental Europe. We have considered warmth of atmosphere, respect for tradition and the "golfing" excellence of the site to be of greater importance than marble hallways, thick-pile carpets and gym rooms.

As a general rule, visitors need to be aware of certain local customs. First of all, driving ranges are few and far between. Here people learnt to play out on the course. If you want a few practice swings, bring a bag of balls with you in the boot of your car. Hit them and pick them up yourself on the area provided for practice.

Next, we have done all we can to point out the restrictions on admission to each club, but these may change, as may the minimum handicap required to play the course. We advise you to call in advance every time.

Out on the course, players from Europe will often be surprised at the speed of the game in the UK. Never hesitating to let people play through is one thing, but more importantly they should learn to speed up their own game.

Last but by no means least, always pack a shirt, tie and jacket

//////ALPINE®

Car Audio and Navigation Systems

CAR NAVI®

Now you know
exactly where you're going.
Even when you don't
know where you are.

in your car. Most clubs impose the tie and jacket rule in the bar or restaurant or both, often in the evening but also during the day. So don't get caught out on that one.

En matière de voyage, il n'y a plus de frontières. L'appellation "Grande-Bretagne et Irlande" a trois justifications. D'abord géographique, ensuite linguistique, et enfin sportive : en golf, on unit les meilleurs joueurs des deux îles, autrefois pour disputer la Ryder Cup, aujourd'hui encore pour jouer la Walker Cup et la Curtis Cup contre les Etats-Unis. On pourrait ajouter en dernier lieu une unité de style de parcours, imposée en dépit des diversités des paysages par les assauts de l'océan, de tous côtés, qui ont par miracle laissé de grands espaces vierges pour y tracer les grands links d'Angleterre, d'Ecosse, du Pays de Galles, d'Irlande et d'Irlande du Nord.

Quand on fait des choix, on est forcément vulnérable aux critiques, et on nous reprochera probablement d'avoir "oublié" certains parcours de grande valeur, en Grande-Bretagne et Irlande, parmi les quelques 2.500 parcours de 18 trous que comptent ces berceaux du golf. Certains ont demandé à ne pas figurer ici, car ils sont totalement privés. Mais nous ne cacherons pas avoir aussi privilégié les parcours les plus spécifiquement britanniques de style, même s'ils peuvent parfois paraître désuets par leur manque de longueur. De la même façon, les notes attribuées aux Clubhouses ont été attribuées en relation avec leur niveau général dans les îles britanniques : certains d'entre eux seraient jugés très modestes en comparaison avec leurs équivalents les plus luxueux aux Etats-Unis, au Japon, ou même sur le continent. Pour nous, la chaleur de l'ambiance, le respect de la tradition, la qualité "golfique" du lieu a plus d'importance que le marbre, les moquettes et les salles de mise en forme.

En règle générale, les visiteurs doivent être informés de certaines coutumes locales. D'abord, les practices ou driving ranges sont rares. Ici, on apprenait à jouer sur le parcours. Si vous souhaitez vous entraîner, ayez un sac de balles dans votre coffre, que vous ramasserez vous-même sur les zones prévues à cet effet.

Ensuite, nous avons signalé au maximum les restrictions d'accès dans chaque club, mais elles peuvent changer, tout comme les limites de handicap, nous vous conseillons donc de toujours téléphoner à l'avance.

Sur le parcours, les joueurs du continent seront souvent surpris par la rapidité de jeu sur les parcours. Qu'ils n'hésitent jamais à laisser passer est une chose, mais qu'ils apprennent surtout à accélérer leur propre rythme.

Enfin, ayez toujours dans votre voiture un petit sac avec une chemise de ville, une cravate et une veste. La plupart des clubs imposent "tie and jacket," au bar, au restaurant, ou les deux, souvent le soir, mais aussi dans la journée. Vous ne serez pas pris au dépourvu.

The Millennium Guide

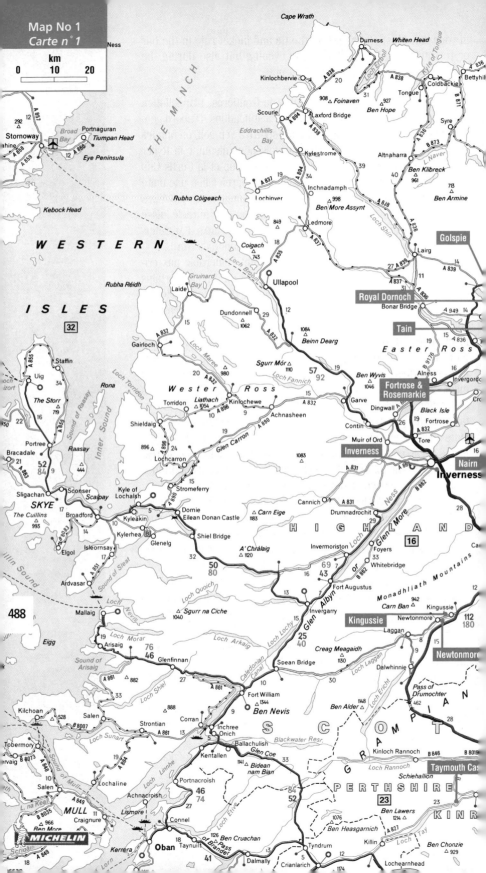

Pentland Firth

Burwick

Dunnet Head

Scrabster 20 Dunnet A 836 John o' Groats
athy Point A 836 Duncansby Head
rich 16 Thurso Castletown B 876
Roadside B 876 Reiss Noss Head
290 21 A 882 Wick

114 24 17 107
183 172

Kinbrace 706 Morven
20

A 897 Helmsdale

Brora
Brora
oie

och Firth
Tarbat Ness

Moray Firth

Moray (Old)
Lossiemouth

Nairn Dunbar
Elgin Buckie Cullen
10 Forres 13 Fochabers A 98 Banff Macduff Kinnairds Head
39 A 940 23 B 9031 Fraserburgh
63 A 941 13 Keith A 95 26 A 98 A 952 Rattray Head
Elgin Rothes 12 A 97 B 9025 13 18 **Peterhead**
22 Craigellachie Dufftown 11 Turriff New Deer B 9029 Mintlaw Peterhead
24 Dava A 95 12 Huntly 22 B 9170 A 948 14 18 Buchan Ness
Grantown- 840 **Huntly** 66 23 A 920 Ellon Cruden Bay
on-Spey 25 15 A 97 109 Oldmeldrum A 920 51 **Cruden Bay**
Dulnain 2 Inverurie 83 Newburgh Stromless
Bridge A 9391 Tomintoul Mossat A 944 Kintore 18 A 947 Lenwick
viemore **Boat of Garten** M O R A Y Craigievar 15 **Murcar** Torshavn
Gorm 1245 Colnabaichin 871 27 Alford Castle 1 **Royal Aberdeen**
Mountains Ben Macdui A 944 A 97 34 A 944 **ABERDEEN**
1309 17 A 980 Crathes 12 A 93
Aboyne Castle 18
Braemar A 93 Aboyne 25 A 93 Banchory Dee
Dee Ballater Balmoral Castle **Ballater** Banchory **Stonehaven**
1155 14 A 957 Stonehaven
O U N T A I N S N. Esk 18
Devil's Elbow 1068 89 A 92
Ghlò 665 Glas Maol 55 22 Inverbervie
1120 A N D Laurencekirk A 92
Pitlochry 3 A N G U S Marikirk **Montrose**
Pitlochry 35 **Edzell** Brechin
14 A 924 **Alyth** Kirriemuir 15 A 935 10 M
A N D Alyth A 926 Glamis 18 B 9128
A 923 Rattray Castle **Forfar** A 932 13
Blairgowrie Glamis Forfar **Letham Grange**
Blairgowrie Dunkeld A 984 Coupar Meigle 455 **Arbroath**
Angus Hills Monifieth A 92
Perth 31 **Dundee** 9 A 930 Carnoustie

489

MICHELIN

d' après cartes n°401 - 19ème édition, n°402 - 17ème édition,
n°403 - 21ème édition, n°404 - 21ème édition - 2000
et n°986 - 19ème édition - 2000. Autorisation n°9904173.

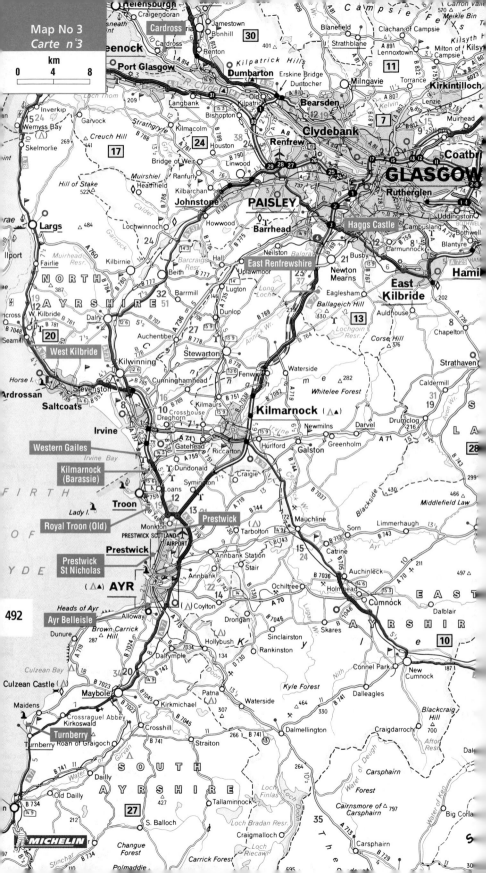

outh
th Shields

NDERLAND

m
g
en
e

Hartlepool

Seaton Carew

ngham Redcar Marske-by-the-Sea
A1085 Saltburn-by-the-Sea
10 Brotton
Guisborough Loftus
liddlesbrough 19 A174 Whitby
A173 27
454 Cleveland Hills
△ 21
North York Moors A169 21
25 National Park 38

B1257 Scalby
Helmsley 13 Pickering **Scarborough**
17
S Filey
H A1039 7 Filey
I Easingwold R B1257 8 A169 22 A1249 11
E Malton Norton Ganton Flamborough Head
B1363 Derwent 18 A1248 Wetwang 13 **Bridlington**
65 E. RIDING
rk 40 O F Gt. Driffield
14 YORKSHIRE A164 Beeford
28 Leven B1244 Hornsea
Fulford Market 17
Weighton 6 **KINGSTON-**
elby Barlby A183 26 38 Beverley **UPON-HULL**
26 Howden M62 61 10 9 13
8 18 B1230 Hedon A1242
Snaith R. Ouse 31 50 10 Humber Bridge Withernsea
39 7 1 Goole River Humber A1033 Patrington
Don Thorne 16 1077 Barton-upon-Humber A1077 Kilnsea
tle 12 Crowle A18 N · L I N C S Immingham Dock Spurn Head
Doncaster 15 4 M180 **Great** Immingham N.E. Rotterdam
Wheatley Brigg A1084 Humberside **Grimsby** Zeebrugge
Epworth A18 Caistor 20 **Cleethorpes**
Bawtry Forest Pines L I N C S
A1 161 Gainsborough 4
A620 Karsten Lakes B631 A1031
Gainsborough Market Rasen Louth Mablethorpe
B638 East A631 A157
Retford A1500 19 Wragby 50 A153 31 A157 Sutton-on-Sea
Tuxford 31 50 A1104 A1104
24 A607 20 Alford A52
Ollerton 39 **Lincoln** Horncastle Partney
sfield 15 B1188 Woodhall Spa B1183 Spilsby 11 **Skegness** Seacroft
26 Sherwood Forest B1191 192 B A155 18
Newark- Leadenham B1178 39 Royal West Norfolk
TTINGHAM on-Trent L I N C O L N 22 24 (Brancaster)
13 21 A153 Woodhall Spa Hunstanton
Bingham 56 A607 60 **Hunstanton** A149
gd 8 35 A153 37 Wells-next-the-Sea Blakeney
24 **Grantham** Sleaford **Boston** 21
39 19 39 B1454 9
Donington A149 22
orough 19 A151 A17 Sandringham Guist
Holbeach House B1145
12 Long Sutton B1454 B1100

The Wash

MICHELIN

Boston
Hunstanton
Wells-next-the-Sea
Sheringham
Cromer
Royal Cromer
Royal West Norfolk
(Brancaster)
Sheringham
Hunstanton
Blakeney
Holt
Mundesley
North Walsham
King's Lynn
N O R F O L K
East Dereham
Swaffham
Watton
Acle
Great
Yarmouth
Gorleston-on-Sea
NORWICH
Wymondham
Attleborough
Lowestoft
Beccles
Thetford
Thetford
Diss
Southwold
Bury St. Edmunds
Newmarket
Stowmarket
Cambridge
Gog Magog
S U F F O L K
Lavenham
Thorpeness
Aldeburgh
Aldeburgh
IPSWICH
Woodbridge
Woodbridge
Haverhill
Ipswich
Ipswich
Felixstowe Ferry
Felixstowe
Harwich
The Naze
Walton-on-the-Naze
Frinton-on-Sea
Colchester
Clacton-on-Sea
E S S E X
Harlow
Chelmsford
Hertfordshire (The)
Maldon
Billericay
Brentwood
Burnham-on-Crouch
Southend-on-Sea
Basildon
Thorndon Park
Canvey Island
Sheerness
North Foreland
Margate
North Foreland
Broadstairs
Rochester
Herne Bay
Ramsgate
Chatham
Whitstable
London Club
Canterbury
Prince's
Rochester & Cobham
Sandwich
Royal St George's
Maidstone
Deal
Royal Cinque Ports
Hever
Chart Hills
Ashford
Dover
Royal
Tunbridge Wells
Tunnel
sous la Manche
Royal Ashdown Forest
Hythe
Folkestone
East Sussex
National
Calais
Littlestone
Hastings
Wimereux (F)
Eastbourne
Wimereux
Beachy Head
Boulogne

MICHELIN

501

41

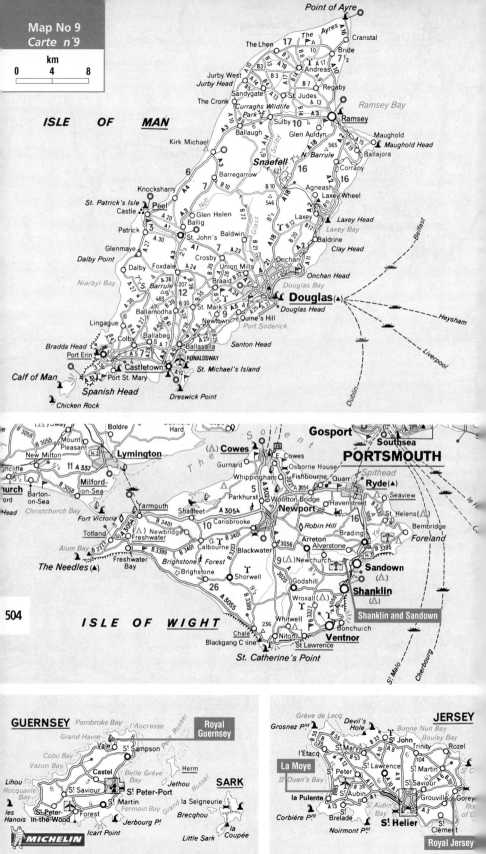

ISLE OF MAN

Point of Ayre
The Ayres
Cranstal
The Lhen
17
A 16
Bride
7½
Jurby West
Jurby Head
Andreas
Regaby
Sandygate
St Judes
The Cronk
Curraghs Wildlife Park
Sulby
10
Ramsey
Ramsey Bay
Ballaugh
Glen Auldyn
Maughold
Kirk Michael
Maughold Head
N. Barrule
Ballajora
Snaefell
565
16
Barregarrow
Corrany
6
16
7
Agneash
Laxey Wheel
546
Knocksharry
Glen Helen
B 22
Laxey
Laxey Head
St Patrick's Isle
Peel
Ballig
Laxey Bay
Castle
Patrick
St John's
Baldwin
Baldrine
Clay Head
Glenmaye
7
Dalby Point
Crosby
Onchan
Dalby
Foxdale
Union Mills
Onchan Head
Niarbyl Bay
S. Barrule
207
Braaid
Douglas Bay
12
Douglas
Ballamodha
St Mark's
Lingague
Newtown
Quine's Hill
Douglas Head
Colby
9
Port Soderick
Ballabeg
Bradda Head
Ballasalla
Santon Head
Port Erin
Castletown
RONALDSWAY
Calf of Man
Port St. Mary
St Michael's Island
Spanish Head
Dreswick Point
Chicken Rock

Heysham
Liverpool
Belfast
Dublin

ISLE OF WIGHT

504

Gosport
Southsea
Cowes
PORTSMOUTH
New Milton
Mount Pleasant
E. Cowes
Lymington
Gurnard
Osborne House
Spithead
Whippingham
Fishbourne
Quarr
Ryde
Milford-on-Sea
Parkhurst
Wootton Bridge
Seaview
Barton-on-Sea
Christchurch Bay
Yarmouth
Shalfleet
Newport
Havenstreet
St Helens
Fort Victoria
Carisbrooke
16
Totland
Newbridge
Freshwater
Robin Hill
Brading
Bembridge
Alum Bay
Blackwater
Arreton
Foreland
The Needles
Freshwater Bay
Brighstone Forest
Alverstone
Newchurch
Brighstone
Shorwell
9
Sandown
Godshill
Shanklin
26
Wroxall
Shanklin and Sandown
Whitwell
Bonchurch
Chale
Niton
Ventnor
Blackgang Chine
St Lawrence
St. Catherine's Point

GUERNSEY

Pembroke Bay
l'Ancresse
Royal Guernsey
Grand Havre
Vale
St Sampson
Cobo Bay
Herm
Vazon Bay
Castel
Belle Grève Bay
Lihou
St Saviour
Jethou
SARK
Rocquaine Bay
St Peter-Port
les Hanois
St Peter-in-the-Wood
Martin
Fermain Bay
la Seigneurie
Forest
Jerbourg Pt
Brecqhou
Icart Point
la Coupée
Little Sark

JERSEY

Grève de Lecq
Devil's Hole
Grosnez Pt
Bonne Nuit Bay
Bouley Bay
St John
Trinity
Rozel
St Mary
St Lawrence
St Martin
La Moye
l'Etacq
St Peter
St Ouen's Bay
St Saviour
la Pulente
St Aubin
Grouville
Gorey
Corbière Pnt
St Brelade
St Helier
Noirmont Pnt
St Clément
Royal Jersey

MICHELIN

CLASSIFICATION OF COURSES
CLASSEMENT DES PARCOURS

This classification gives priority consideration
to the score awarded to the actual course.

Ce classement donne priorité à la note attribuée au parcours.

Club-house and facilities
Note du Club-house et annexes

Course score
Note du parcours

Hotel facility score
Note de l'environnement hôtelier

Page

19 5 6   Carnoustie *Championship*   Sc   715

Score	Course	Country	Page	Score	Course	Country	Page
19 5 6	Carnoustie			**18** 6 6	Royal North Devon		
	Championship	Sc	715		(Westward Ho!)	Eng	637
19 8 5	Ganton	Eng	573	**18** 6 5	Royal St David's	W	820
19 7 6	Muirfield	Sc	759	**18** 7 6	Saunton *East Course*	Eng	645
19 7 8	Nairn	Sc	762	**18** 5 4	Seascale	Eng	647
19 9 7	Royal Birkdale (The)	Eng	629	**18** 7 4	Silloth-on-Solway	Eng	653
19 7 7	Royal Dornoch			**18** 6 5	Southerness	Sc	781
	Championship	Sc	776	**18** 7 7	Southport & Ainsdale	Eng	655
19 7 8	Royal Lytham			**18** 8 8	St Andrews *Old Course*	Sc	785
	& St Anne's	Eng	635	**18** 7 4	St Enodoc *Church Course*	Eng	656
19 7 6	Royal Porthcawl	W	819	**18** 8 8	Sunningdale *New Course*	Eng	661
19 7 5	Royal St George's	Eng	638	**18** 8 8	Sunningdale *Old Course*	Eng	662
19 7 7	Royal Troon *Old Course*	Sc	778	**18** 7 6	Tenby	W	822
19 9 8	Turnberry *Ailsa Course*	Sc	792	**18** 7 7	Walton Heath *Old Course*	Eng	675
18 7 7	Alwoodley (The)	Eng	523	**18** 8 7	Wentworth *West Course*	Eng	678
18 8 6	Blairgowrie *Rosemount*	Sc	706	**18** 7 6	West Sussex	Eng	685
18 7 6	Burnham & Berrow	Eng	542	**18** 7 7	Woburn *Dukes Course*	Eng	690
18 6 8	Castletown	Eng	549	**18** 7 8	Woodhall Spa	Eng	694
18 9 7	Celtic Manor			**17** 7 7	Aberdovey	W	799
	Roman Road	W	804	**17** 6 5	Ashburnham	W	800
18 8 6	Chart Hills	Eng	550	**17** 8 7	Berkshire (The)		
18 7 6	Cruden Bay	Sc	718		*Blue Course*	Eng	529
18 7 7	Formby	Eng	568	**17** 8 7	Berkshire (The)		
18 9 7	Gleneagles *King's*	Sc	735		*Red Course*	Eng	530
18 7 7	Hillside	Eng	585	**17** 6 5	Blackmoor	Eng	532
18 7 6	Ilkley	Eng	590	**17** 6 6	Bowood G&CC	Eng	535
18 6 4	Machrihanish	Sc	755	**17** 7 6	Brampton	Eng	536
18 7 7	Moortown	Eng	609	**17** 7 7	Broadstone	Eng	538
18 7 8	North Berwick	Sc	765	**17** 8 7	Buckinghamshire (The)	Eng	540
18 6 6	Notts (Hollinwell)	Eng	614	**17** 7 7	Caldy	Eng	543
18 6 6	Pennard	W	816	**17** 8 8	Carden Park		
18 6 7	Prestwick	Sc	771		*Nicklaus Course*	Eng	547
18 7 8	Royal Aberdeen			**17** 7 7	Carlisle	Eng	548
	Balgownie Links	Sc	774	**17** 7 7	Clitheroe	Eng	552
18 8 7	Royal Liverpool (Hoylake)	Eng	634	**17** 7 8	Conwy	W	805

PEUGEOT GOLF GUIDE 2000/2001

505

England Wales Scotland

Inside the
TOUR

The Discerning Golfer's Guide to 1999

"The ultimate golfing experience."

Robbie Bishop, Director of Marketing OLD COURSE HOTEL, ST. ANDREW

"Inside The Tour is the very
finest Golf has to offer."

Colin A. Burns, General Manager WINGED FOOT GOLF CLUB

"As publishers of this superb book, you hav
certainly achieved your goal to present th
highest quality articles and other matters
of interest to the keen and dedicated
golfers of the world."

R W Armstrong, Executive Manager BRISBANE GOLF CLUB

"After reading the magazine we would like
to complement you on the content
and presentation."

Keith Lawson, Director of Golf MISSION HILLS GOLF CLUB

"The exceptional quality and
content of the magazine
fits in perfectly with a club
of Westchester's distinction."

James M. Cirillo, General Manager WESTCHESTER COUNTRY CLUB

Visit: www.insidethetour.com

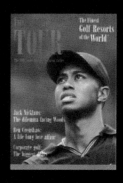

Score	Course	Country	Page
17 7 7	Cumberwell Park	Eng	555
17 8 8	Dalmahoy *East Course*	Sc	719
17 6 7	Downfield	Sc	720
17 8 7	East Sussex National		
	East Course	Eng	560
17 7 8	Fairhaven	Eng	561
17 7 7	Ferndown *Old Course*	Eng	564
17 6 7	Forest Pines		
	Forest + Pines	Eng	567
17 7 8	Fulford	Eng	571
17 9 7	Gleneagles *Monarch's*	Sc	736
17 8 7	Gullane *No 1*	Sc	740
17 7 6	Hunstanton	Eng	588
17 6 8	Kilmarnock (Barassie)	Sc	744
17 7 8	La Moye	Eng	594
17 7 5	Ladybank	Sc	746
17 8 6	Linden Hall	Eng	595
17 6 6	Lindrick	Eng	596
17 7 7	Machrie	Sc	754
17 7 7	Monifieth	Sc	756
17 5 6	Montrose	Sc	757
17 8 7	Moor Park *High Course*	Eng	608
17 5 5	Moray	Sc	758
17 7 6	North Hants	Eng	613
17 6 8	North Wales (Llandudno)	W	814
17 7 7	Orchardleigh	Eng	615
17 6 5	Panmure	Sc	766
17 8 7	Prestbury	Eng	624
17 7 5	Pyle & Kenfig	W	817
17 6 5	Royal Cinque Ports	Eng	630
17 7 6	Royal West Norfolk		
	(Brancaster)	Eng	639
17 5 7	Sandiway	Eng	644
17 6 4	Seacroft	Eng	646
17 7 5	Seaton Carew	Eng	648
17 7 6	Sherwood Forest	Eng	652
17 5 5	Shiskine (Blackwaterfoot)	Sc	780
17 8 7	Slaley Hall	Eng	654
17 8 8	St Andrews *New Course*	Sc	784
17 7 7	St George's Hill	Eng	657
17 9 7	St Mellion		
	Nicklaus Course	Eng	658
17 8 8	Stoke Poges	Eng	659
17 6 6	Tain	Sc	789
17 7 7	Trevose *Championship*	Eng	672
17 7 7	Wallasey	Eng	673
17 7 7	West Lancashire	Eng	683
17 5 7	Western Gailes	Sc	795
17 6 7	Whittington Heath	Eng	688
16 7 6	Ashridge	Eng	524
16 5 7	Ayr (Belleisle)	Sc	701
16 6 9	Bath	Eng	526
16 7 7	Beau Desert	Eng	527
16 7 6	Berkhamsted	Eng	528
16 7 6	Bowood (Cornwall)	Eng	534
16 6 6	Camberley Heath	Eng	544
16 9 6	Dartmouth	Eng	556
16 7 8	Duke's Course		
	St Andrews	Sc	723
16 5 6	Dunbar	Sc	725
16 6 7	East Devon	Eng	559
16 6 5	Fortrose & Rosemarkie	Sc	733
16 7 7	Hadley Wood	Eng	575
16 6 6	Hankley Common	Eng	577
16 7 7	Hayling	Eng	580
16 7 6	Hindhead	Eng	586
16 7 5	Holyhead	W	807
16 6 7	Huddersfield (Fixby)	Eng	587
16 7 8	Inverness	Sc	743
16 7 7	Ipswich (Purdis Heath)	Eng	591
16 7 6	Isle of Purbeck	Eng	592
16 7 6	John O'Gaunt	Eng	593
16 6 5	Lanark	Sc	747
16 6 6	Leven	Sc	749
16 7 6	Liphook	Eng	597
16 5 6	Luffness New	Sc	752
16 6 7	Lundin	Sc	753
16 7 7	Manchester	Eng	601
16 8 7	Marriott St Pierre		
	Old Course	W	811
16 7 5	Nefyn & District	W	812
16 9 6	Northop Country Park	W	815
16 7 8	Parkstone	Eng	618
16 6 6	Perranporth	Eng	620
16 8 6	Pleasington	Eng	621
16 6 4	Powfoot	Sc	770
16 6 7	Prestwick St Nicholas	Sc	772
16 7 9	Royal Burgess	Sc	775
16 7 7	Royal Guernsey	Eng	632
16 7 8	Royal Jersey	Eng	633
16 8 7	Royal Musselburgh	Sc	777
16 7 8	Royal Wimbledon	Eng	640
16 6 6	Scotscraig	Sc	779
16 7 7	Southerndown	W	821
16 8 8	St Andrews		
	Jubilee Course	Sc	783
16 6 8	Swinley Forest	Eng	663
16 6 4	Thurlestone	Eng	671
16 9 8	Turnberry		
	Arran Course	Sc	793

England Wales Scotland

507

England Wales Scotland

Score	Course	Country	Page
16 8 7	Vale of Glamorgan	W	823
16 7 6	Walton Heath		
	New Course	Eng	674
16 8 7	Wentworth East Course	Eng	677
16 7 6	West Cornwall	Eng	681
16 7 5	West Kilbride	Sc	794
16 6 7	Weston-Super-Mare	Eng	686
16 7 6	Wilmslow	Eng	689
16 6 6	Woking	Eng	691
16 7 6	Worplesdon	Eng	695
15 7 6	Alloa	Sc	699
15 6 7	Ballater	Sc	703
15 6 5	Berwick-upon-Tweed	Eng	531
15 8 6	Blairgowrie Lansdowne	Sc	705
15 5 7	Bolton Old Links	Eng	533
15 6 6	Brokenhurst Manor	Eng	539
15 7 7	Brora	Sc	708
15 8 9	Bruntsfield	Sc	709
15 6 5	Bude & North Cornwall	Eng	541
15 5 6	Came Down	Eng	545
15 6 5	Cardigan	W	802
15 7 4	Carmarthen	W	803
15 6 6	Coxmoor	Eng	554
15 6 6	Crail	Sc	716
15 7 7	Crieff Ferntower Course	Sc	717
15 6 7	Delamere Forest	Eng	557
15 7 7	Denham	Eng	558
15 7 9	Duddingston	Sc	721
15 6 6	Duff House Royal	Sc	722
15 7 5	Dumfries & County	Sc	724
15 7 7	Dunfermline	Sc	726
15 6 8	East Renfrewshire	Sc	727
15 7 6	Elgin	Sc	729
15 6 6	Elie	Sc	730
15 6 6	Felixstowe Ferry		
	Martello Course	Eng	563
15 9 7	Gleneagles Queen's	Sc	737
15 7 8	Gog Magog Old Course	Eng	574
15 7 9	Haggs Castle	Sc	741
15 6 8	Hallamshire	Eng	576
15 7 7	Harrogate	Eng	578
15 8 7	Hawkstone Park		
	Hawkstone	Eng	579
15 7 7	Hertfordshire (The)	Eng	582
15 6 7	High Post	Eng	584
15 4 5	Kingussie	Sc	745
15 7 7	Langland Bay	W	808
15 7 5	Letham Grange		
	Old Course	Sc	748
15 5 8	Llandudno (Maesdu)	W	809

Score	Course	Country	Page
15 9 7	London Golf Club		
	International	Eng	599
15 7 8	Lytham Green Drive	Eng	600
15 8 7	Manor House		
	(Castle Combe)	Eng	603
15 5 7	Mendip	Eng	604
15 8 7	Meon Valley		
	Meon Course	Eng	605
15 7 7	Mere	Eng	606
15 5 5	Mullion	Eng	610
15 6 6	Murcar	Sc	760
15 6 7	Nairn Dunbar	Sc	763
15 6 7	Newbury & Crookham	Eng	611
15 6 7	Newport	W	813
15 6 7	Pannal	Eng	617
15 5 4	Peterhead	Sc	767
15 8 7	Portal Championship	Eng	622
15 7 7	Porters Park	Eng	623
15 6 7	Portpatrick (Dunskey)	Sc	769
15 6 6	Rolls of Monmouth (The)	W	818
15 5 6	Ross-on-Wye	Eng	627
15 7 7	Roxburghe (The)	Sc	773
15 7 6	Royal Cromer	Eng	631
15 6 8	Royal Winchester	Eng	641
15 8 8	Rudding Park	Eng	642
15 7 6	Shanklin & Sandown	Eng	649
15 6 7	Sherborne	Eng	650
15 7 6	Sheringham	Eng	651
15 7 8	Stoneham	Eng	660
15 7 6	Strathaven	Sc	788
15 9 8	The Belfry Brabazon	Eng	666
15 9 8	The Belfry PGA National	Eng	667
15 6 5	Thornhill	Sc	791
15 7 8	Warwickshire (The)	Eng	676
15 7 7	West Berkshire	Eng	679
15 6 6	West Hill	Eng	682
15 7 7	West Surrey	Eng	684
15 7 7	Whitekirk	Sc	797
15 9 6	Woodbury Park The Oaks	Eng	693
14 6 6	Aboyne	Sc	698
14 6 6	Alyth	Sc	700
14 6 8	Baberton	Sc	702
14 7 7	Badgemore Park	Eng	525
14 7 7	Banchory	Sc	704
14 6 7	Boat of Garten	Sc	707
14 6 5	Brancepeth Castle	Eng	537
14 6 6	Buchanan Castle	Sc	710
14 6 6	Burntisland	Sc	711
14 8 8	Carden Park		
	Cheshire Course	Eng	546

508

England Wales Scotland

Score	Course	Country	Page	Score	Course	Country	Page
14 6 8	Cardiff	W	801	14 6 4	Ormskirk	Eng	616
14 6 5	Cardross	Sc	713	14 6 7	Pitlochry	Sc	768
14 5 6	Carnoustie *Burnside*	Sc	714	14 6 6	Rochester & Cobham	Eng	626
14 8 7	Collingtree Park	Eng	553	14 7 6	Royal Ashdown Forest	Eng	628
14 6 3	Edzell	Sc	728	14 7 8	Royal Mid-Surrey		
14 6 7	Falmouth	Eng	562		*Outer*	Eng	636
14 8 8	Forest of Arden			14 7 7	Sand Moor	Eng	643
	Arden Course	Eng	566	14 8 8	St Andrews		
14 6 6	Forfar	Sc	732		*Eden Course*	Sc	782
14 8 6	Formby Hall	Eng	569	14 7 6	Tandridge	Eng	664
14 7 7	Frilford Heath			14 7 5	Thetford	Eng	668
	Red Course	Eng	570	14 7 6	Thorndon Park	Eng	669
14 8 6	Gainsborough-Karsten			14 7 7	Thorpeness	Eng	670
	Lakes	Eng	572	14 6 8	West Byfleet	Eng	680
14 7 8	Glamorganshire	W	806	14 8 6	Westerwood	Sc	796
14 7 7	Glen	Sc	734	14 6 6	Wheatley	Eng	687
14 5 4	Golspie	Sc	738	14 7 7	Woodbridge	Eng	692
14 6 7	Grantown on Spey	Sc	739	13 6 7	Aldeburgh	Eng	522
14 6 7	Henley	Eng	581	13 6 7	Callander	Sc	712
14 8 8	Hever	Eng	583	13 6 7	Chesterfield	Eng	551
14 6 7	Huntercombe	Eng	589	13 6 6	Falkirk Tryst	Sc	731
14 6 6	Huntly	Sc	742	13 5 5	Filey	Eng	565
14 6 5	Littlestone	Eng	598	13 7 7	North Foreland	Eng	612
14 6 4	Llanymynech	W	810	13 8 8	Patshull Park Hotel	Eng	619
14 7 6	Longniddry	Sc	750	13 6 4	Prince's *Himalayas-Shore*	Eng	625
14 6 8	Lothianburn	Sc	751	13 6 7	Stirling	Sc	786
14 8 6	Mannings Heath			13 5 5	Stonehaven	Sc	787
	Waterfall Course	Eng	602	13 4 6	Taymouth Castle	Sc	790
14 6 7	Moor Allerton	Eng	607	13 7 6	Tehidy Park	Eng	665
14 7 8	Murrayshall	Sc	761				
14 5 5	Newtonmore	Sc	764				

509

CLASSIFICATION OF HOTELS FACILITIES
CLASSEMENT DE L'ENVIRONNEMENT HOTELIER

This classification gives priority consideration
to the score awarded to the hotel facilities.

Ce classement donne priorité à la note attribuée à l'environnement hôtelier

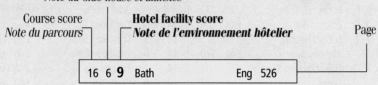

Club-house and facilities
Note du Club-house et annexes

Course score
Note du parcours

Hotel facility score
Note de l'environnement hôtelier

Page

16 6 **9**   Bath   Eng 526

Score			Course	Country	Page	Score			Course	Country	Page
16	6	**9**	Bath	Eng	526	19	7	**8**	Nairn	Sc	762
15	8	**9**	Bruntsfield	Sc	709	18	7	**8**	North Berwick	Sc	765
15	7	**9**	Duddingston	Sc	721	17	6	**8**	North Wales (Llandudno)	W	814
15	7	**9**	Haggs Castle	Sc	741	16	7	**8**	Parkstone	Eng	618
16	7	**9**	Royal Burgess	Sc	775	13	8	**8**	Patshull Park Hotel	Eng	619
14	6	**8**	Baberton	Sc	702	18	7	**8**	Royal Aberdeen		
14	8	**8**	Carden Park						*Balgownie Links*	Sc	774
			Cheshire Course	Eng	546	16	7	**8**	Royal Jersey	Eng	633
17	8	**8**	Carden Park			19	7	**8**	Royal Lytham		
			Nicklaus Course	Eng	547				& St Anne's	Eng	635
14	6	**8**	Cardiff	W	801	14	7	**8**	Royal Mid-Surrey *Outer*	Eng	636
18	6	**8**	Castletown	Eng	549	16	7	**8**	Royal Wimbledon	Eng	640
17	7	**8**	Conwy	W	805	15	6	**8**	Royal Winchester	Eng	641
17	8	**8**	Dalmahoy *East Course*	Sc	719	15	8	**8**	Rudding Park	Eng	642
16	7	**8**	Duke's Course			14	8	**8**	St Andrews *Eden Course*	Sc	782
			St Andrews	Sc	723	16	8	**8**	St Andrews *Jubilee Course*	Sc	783
15	6	**8**	East Renfrewshire	Sc	727	17	8	**8**	St Andrews *New Course*	Sc	784
17	7	**8**	Fairhaven	Eng	561	18	8	**8**	St Andrews *Old Course*	Sc	785
14	8	**8**	Forest of Arden			17	8	**8**	Stoke Poges	Eng	659
			Arden Course	Eng	566	15	7	**8**	Stoneham	Eng	660
17	7	**8**	Fulford	Eng	571	18	8	**8**	Sunningdale *New Course*	Eng	661
14	7	**8**	Glamorganshire	W	806	18	8	**8**	Sunningdale *Old Course*	Eng	662
15	7	**8**	Gog Magog *Old Course*	Eng	574	16	6	**8**	Swinley Forest	Eng	663
15	6	**8**	Hallamshire	Eng	576	15	9	**8**	The Belfry *Brabazon*	Eng	666
14	8	**8**	Hever	Eng	583	15	9	**8**	The Belfry *PGA National*	Eng	667
16	7	**8**	Inverness	Sc	743	19	9	**8**	Turnberry *Ailsa Course*	Sc	792
17	6	**8**	Kilmarnock (Barassie)	Sc	744	16	9	**8**	Turnberry *Arran Course*	Sc	793
17	7	**8**	La Moye	Eng	594	15	7	**8**	Warwickshire (The)	Eng	676
15	5	**8**	Llandudno (Maesdu)	W	809	14	6	**8**	West Byfleet	Eng	680
14	6	**8**	Lothianburn	Sc	751	18	7	**8**	Woodhall Spa	Eng	694
15	7	**8**	Lytham Green Drive	Eng	600	17	7	**7**	Aberdovey	W	799
14	7	**8**	Murrayshall	Sc	761	13	6	**7**	Aldeburgh	Eng	522

510

England Wales Scotland

Score			Course	Country	Page
18	7	7	Alwoodley (The)	Eng	523
16	5	7	Ayr (Belleisle)	Sc	701
14	7	7	Badgemore Park	Eng	525
15	6	7	Ballater	Sc	703
14	7	7	Banchory	Sc	704
16	7	7	Beau Desert	Eng	527
17	8	7	Berkshire (The)		
			Blue Course	Eng	529
17	8	7	Berkshire (The)		
			Red Course	Eng	530
14	6	7	Boat of Garten	Sc	707
15	5	7	Bolton Old Links	Eng	533
17	7	7	Broadstone	Eng	538
15	7	7	Brora	Sc	708
17	8	7	Buckinghamshire (The)	Eng	540
17	7	7	Caldy	Eng	543
13	6	7	Callander	Sc	712
17	7	7	Carlisle	Eng	548
18	9	7	Celtic Manor		
			Roman Road	W	804
13	6	7	Chesterfield	Eng	551
17	7	7	Clitheroe	Eng	552
14	8	7	Collingtree Park	Eng	553
15	7	7	Crieff *Ferntower Course*	Sc	717
17	7	7	Cumberwell Park	Eng	555
15	6	7	Delamere Forest	Eng	557
15	7	7	Denham	Eng	558
17	6	7	Downfield	Sc	720
15	7	7	Dunfermline	Sc	726
16	6	7	East Devon	Eng	559
17	8	7	East Sussex National		
			East Course	Eng	560
14	6	7	Falmouth	Eng	562
17	7	7	Ferndown *Old Course*	Eng	564
17	6	7	Forest Pines		
			Forest + Pines	Eng	567
18	7	7	Formby	Eng	568
14	7	7	Frilford Heath		
			Red Course	Eng	570
14	7	7	Glen	Sc	734
18	9	7	Gleneagles *King's*	Sc	735
17	9	7	Gleneagles *Monarch's*	Sc	736
15	9	7	Gleneagles *Queen's*	Sc	737
14	6	7	Grantown on Spey	Sc	739
17	8	7	Gullane *No 1*	Sc	740
16	7	7	Hadley Wood	Eng	575
15	7	7	Harrogate	Eng	578
15	8	7	Hawkstone Park		
			Hawkstone	Eng	579

Score			Course	Country	Page
16	7	7	Hayling	Eng	580
14	6	7	Henley	Eng	581
15	7	7	Hertfordshire (The)	Eng	582
15	6	7	High Post	Eng	584
18	7	7	Hillside	Eng	585
16	6	7	Huddersfield (Fixby)	Eng	587
14	6	7	Huntercombe	Eng	589
16	7	7	Ipswich (Purdis Heath)	Eng	591
15	7	7	Langland Bay	W	808
15	9	7	London Golf Club		
			International	Eng	599
16	6	7	Lundin	Sc	753
17	7	7	Machrie	Sc	754
16	7	7	Manchester	Eng	601
15	8	7	Manor House		
			(Castle Combe)	Eng	603
16	8	7	Marriott St Pierre		
			Old Course	W	811
15	5	7	Mendip	Eng	604
15	8	7	Meon Valley		
			Meon Course	Eng	605
15	7	7	Mere	Eng	606
17	7	7	Monifieth	Sc	756
14	6	7	Moor Allerton	Eng	607
17	8	7	Moor Park *High Course*	Eng	608
18	7	7	Moortown	Eng	609
15	6	7	Nairn Dunbar	Sc	763
15	6	7	Newbury & Crookham	Eng	611
15	6	7	Newport	W	813
13	7	7	North Foreland	Eng	612
17	7	7	Orchardleigh	Eng	615
15	6	7	Pannal	Eng	617
14	6	7	Pitlochry	Sc	768
15	8	7	Portal *Championship*	Eng	622
15	7	7	Porters Park	Eng	623
15	6	7	Portpatrick (Dunskey)	Sc	769
17	8	7	Prestbury	Eng	624
18	6	7	Prestwick	Sc	771
16	6	7	Prestwick St Nicholas	Sc	772
15	7	7	Roxburghe (The)	Sc	773
19	9	7	Royal Birkdale (The)	Eng	629
19	7	7	Royal Dornoch		
			Championship	Sc	776
16	7	7	Royal Guernsey	Eng	632
18	8	7	Royal Liverpool (Hoylake)	Eng	634
16	8	7	Royal Musselburgh	Sc	777
19	7	7	Royal Troon *Old Course*	Sc	778
14	7	7	Sand Moor	Eng	643
17	5	7	Sandiway	Eng	644

511

England Wales Scotland

Score	Course	Country	Page
15 6 **7**	Sherborne	Eng	650
17 8 **7**	Slaley Hall	Eng	654
16 7 **7**	Southerndown	W	821
18 7 **7**	Southport & Ainsdale	Eng	655
17 7 **7**	St George's Hill	Eng	657
17 9 **7**	St Mellion		
	Nicklaus Course	Eng	658
13 6 **7**	Stirling	Sc	786
14 7 **7**	Thorpeness	Eng	670
17 7 **7**	Trevose *Championship*	Eng	672
16 8 **7**	Vale of Glamorgan	W	823
17 7 **7**	Wallasey	Eng	673
18 7 **7**	Walton Heath		
	Old Course	Eng	675
16 8 **7**	Wentworth *East Course*	Eng	677
18 8 **7**	Wentworth *West Course*	Eng	678
15 7 **7**	West Berkshire	Eng	679
17 7 **7**	West Lancashire	Eng	683
15 7 **7**	West Surrey	Eng	684
17 5 **7**	Western Gailes	Sc	795
16 6 **7**	Weston-Super-Mare	Eng	686
15 7 **7**	Whitekirk	Sc	797
17 6 **7**	Whittington Heath	Eng	688
18 7 **7**	Woburn *Dukes Course*	Eng	690
14 7 **7**	Woodbridge	Eng	692
14 6 **6**	Aboyne	Sc	698
15 7 **6**	Alloa	Sc	699
14 6 **6**	Alyth	Sc	700
16 7 **6**	Ashridge	Eng	524
16 7 **6**	Berkhamsted	Eng	528
15 8 **6**	Blairgowrie *Lansdowne*	Sc	705
18 8 **6**	Blairgowrie *Rosemount*	Sc	706
16 7 **6**	Bowood (Cornwall)	Eng	534
17 6 **6**	Bowood G&CC	Eng	535
17 7 **6**	Brampton	Eng	536
15 6 **6**	Brokenhurst Manor	Eng	539
14 6 **6**	Buchanan Castle	Sc	710
18 7 **6**	Burnham & Berrow	Eng	542
14 6 **6**	Burntisland	Sc	711
16 6 **6**	Camberley Heath	Eng	544
15 5 **6**	Came Down	Eng	545
14 5 **6**	Carnoustie *Burnside*	Sc	714
19 5 **6**	Carnoustie *Championship*	Sc	715
18 8 **6**	Chart Hills	Eng	550
15 6 **6**	Coxmoor	Eng	554
15 6 **6**	Crail	Sc	716
18 7 **6**	Cruden Bay	Sc	718
16 9 **6**	Dartmouth	Eng	556
15 6 **6**	Duff House Royal	Sc	722

Score	Course	Country	Page
16 5 **6**	Dunbar	Sc	725
15 7 **6**	Elgin	Sc	729
15 6 **6**	Elie	Sc	730
13 6 **6**	Falkirk Tryst	Sc	731
15 6 **6**	Felixstowe Ferry		
	Martello Course	Eng	563
14 6 **6**	Forfar	Sc	732
14 8 **6**	Formby Hall	Eng	569
14 8 **6**	Gainsborough-Karsten		
	Lakes	Eng	572
16 6 **6**	Hankley Common	Eng	577
16 7 **6**	Hindhead	Eng	586
17 7 **6**	Hunstanton	Eng	588
14 6 **6**	Huntly	Sc	742
18 7 **6**	Ilkley	Eng	590
16 7 **6**	Isle of Purbeck	Eng	592
16 7 **6**	John O'Gaunt	Eng	593
16 6 **6**	Leven	Sc	749
17 8 **6**	Linden Hall	Eng	595
17 6 **6**	Lindrick	Eng	596
16 7 **6**	Liphook	Eng	597
14 7 **6**	Longniddry	Sc	750
16 5 **6**	Luffness New	Sc	752
14 8 **6**	Mannings Heath		
	Waterfall Course	Eng	602
17 5 **6**	Montrose	Sc	757
19 7 **6**	Muirfield	Sc	759
15 6 **6**	Murcar	Sc	760
17 7 **6**	North Hants	Eng	613
16 9 **6**	Northop Country Park	W	815
18 6 **6**	Notts (Hollinwell)	Eng	614
18 6 **6**	Pennard	W	816
16 6 **6**	Perranporth	Eng	620
16 8 **6**	Pleasington	Eng	621
14 6 **6**	Rochester & Cobham	Eng	626
15 6 **6**	Rolls of Monmouth (The)	W	818
15 5 **6**	Ross-on-Wye	Eng	627
14 7 **6**	Royal Ashdown Forest	Eng	628
15 7 **6**	Royal Cromer	Eng	631
18 6 **6**	Royal North Devon		
	(Westward Ho!)	Eng	637
19 7 **6**	Royal Porthcawl	W	819
17 7 **6**	Royal West Norfolk		
	(Brancaster)	Eng	639
18 7 **6**	Saunton *East Course*	Eng	645
16 6 **6**	Scotscraig	Sc	779
15 7 **6**	Shanklin & Sandown	Eng	649
15 7 **6**	Sheringham	Eng	651
17 7 **6**	Sherwood Forest	Eng	652

512

Score			Course	Country	Page
15	7	6	Strathaven	Sc	788
17	6	6	Tain	Sc	789
14	7	6	Tandridge	Eng	664
13	4	6	Taymouth Castle	Sc	790
13	7	6	Tehidy Park	Eng	665
18	7	6	Tenby	W	822
14	7	6	Thorndon Park	Eng	669
16	7	6	Walton Heath		
			New Course	Eng	674
16	7	6	West Cornwall	Eng	681
15	6	6	West Hill	Eng	682
18	7	6	West Sussex	Eng	685
14	8	6	Westerwood	Sc	796
14	6	6	Wheatley	Eng	687
16	7	6	Wilmslow	Eng	689
16	6	6	Woking	Eng	691
15	9	6	Woodbury Park		
			The Oaks	Eng	693
16	7	6	Worplesdon	Eng	695
17	6	5	Ashburnham	W	800
15	6	5	Berwick-upon-Tweed	Eng	531
17	6	5	Blackmoor	Eng	532
14	6	5	Brancepeth Castle	Eng	537
15	6	5	Bude & North Cornwall	Eng	541
15	6	5	Cardigan	W	802
14	6	5	Cardross	Sc	713
15	7	5	Dumfries & County	Sc	724
13	5	5	Filey	Eng	565
16	6	5	Fortrose & Rosemarkie	Sc	733
19	8	5	Ganton	Eng	573
16	7	5	Holyhead	W	807
15	4	5	Kingussie	Sc	745
17	7	5	Ladybank	Sc	746
16	6	5	Lanark	Sc	747

Score			Course	Country	Page
15	7	5	Letham Grange		
			Old Course	Sc	748
14	6	5	Littlestone	Eng	598
17	5	5	Moray	Sc	758
15	5	5	Mullion	Eng	610
16	7	5	Nefyn & District	W	812
14	5	5	Newtonmore	Sc	764
17	6	5	Panmure	Sc	766
17	7	5	Pyle & Kenfig	W	817
17	6	5	Royal Cinque Ports	Eng	630
18	6	5	Royal St David's	W	820
19	7	5	Royal St George's	Eng	638
17	7	5	Seaton Carew	Eng	648
17	5	5	Shiskine (Blackwaterfoot)	Sc	780
18	6	5	Southerness	Sc	781
13	5	5	Stonehaven	Sc	787
14	7	5	Thetford	Eng	668
15	6	5	Thornhill	Sc	791
16	7	5	West Kilbride	Sc	794
15	7	4	Carmarthen	W	803
14	5	4	Golspie	Sc	738
14	6	4	Llanymynech	W	810
18	6	4	Machrihanish	Sc	755
14	6	4	Ormskirk	Eng	616
15	5	4	Peterhead	Sc	767
16	6	4	Powfoot	Sc	770
13	6	4	Prince's Himalayas-Shore	Eng	625
17	6	4	Seacroft	Eng	646
18	5	4	Seascale	Eng	647
18	7	4	Silloth-on-Solway	Eng	653
18	7	4	St Enodoc Church Course	Eng	656
16	6	4	Thurlestone	Eng	671
14	6	3	Edzell	Sc	728

513

RECOMMENDED GOLFING STAY
SEJOUR DE GOLF RECOMMANDÉ

Course	Country	Score			Page	Course	Country	Score			Page
Berkshire (The)						Machrihanish	Sc	18	6	4	755
Blue Course	Eng	17	8	7	529	Marriott St Pierre					
Berkshire (The)						*Old Course*	W	16	8	7	811
Red Course	Eng	17	8	7	530	Meon Valley *Meon Course*	Eng	15	8	7	605
Blairgowrie *Lansdowne*	Sc	15	8	6	705	Moor Park *High Course*	Eng	17	8	7	608
Blairgowrie *Rosemount*	Sc	18	8	6	706	Moray	Sc	17	5	5	758
Brampton	Eng	17	7	6	536	Nairn	Sc	19	7	8	762
Buckinghamshire (The)	Eng	17	8	7	540	Portal *Championship*	Eng	15	8	7	622
Burnham & Berrow	Eng	18	7	6	542	Pyle & Kenfig	W	17	7	5	817
Carden Park						Royal Birkdale (The)	Eng	19	9	7	629
Nicklaus Course	Eng	17	8	8	547	Royal Cinque Ports	Eng	17	6	5	630
Carlisle	Eng	17	7	7	548	Royal Dornoch					
Carnoustie *Burnside*	Sc	14	5	6	714	*Championship*	Sc	19	7	7	776
Carnoustie						Royal Liverpool (Hoylake)	Eng	18	8	7	634
Championship	Sc	19	5	6	715	Royal Lytham & St Anne's	Eng	19	7	8	635
Castletown	Eng	18	6	8	549	Royal North Devon					
Celtic Manor *Roman Road*	W	18	9	7	804	(Westward Ho!)	Eng	18	6	6	637
Chart Hills	Eng	18	8	6	550	Royal Porthcawl	W	19	7	6	819
Cruden Bay	Sc	18	7	6	718	Royal St David's	W	18	6	5	820
Dalmahoy *East Course*	Sc	17	8	8	719	Royal St George's	Eng	19	7	5	638
Dartmouth	Eng	16	9	6	556	Royal Troon *Old Course*	Sc	19	7	7	778
East Sussex National						Royal West Norfolk					
East Course	Eng	17	8	7	560	(Brancaster)	Eng	17	7	6	639
Fairhaven	Eng	17	7	8	561	Saunton *East Course*	Eng	18	7	6	645
Felixstowe Ferry						Slaley Hall	Eng	17	8	7	654
Martello Course	Eng	15	6	6	563	Southport & Ainsdale	Eng	18	7	7	655
Ferndown *Old Course*	Eng	17	7	7	564	St Andrews *Eden Course*	Sc	14	8	8	782
Forest Pines *Forest + Pines*	Eng	17	6	7	567	St Andrews *Jubilee Course*	Sc	16	8	8	783
Formby	Eng	18	7	7	568	St Andrews *New Course*	Sc	17	8	8	784
Ganton	Eng	19	8	5	573	St Andrews *Old Course*	Sc	18	8	8	785
Gleneagles *King's*	Sc	18	9	7	735	St Enodoc *Church Course*	Eng	18	7	4	656
Gleneagles *Monarch's*	Sc	17	9	7	736	St Mellion *Nicklaus Course*	Eng	17	9	7	658
Gleneagles *Queen's*	Sc	15	9	7	737	Stoke Poges	Eng	17	8	8	659
Gullane *No 1*	Sc	17	8	7	740	Sunningdale *New Course*	Eng	18	8	8	661
Hawkstone Park						Sunningdale *Old Course*	Eng	18	8	8	662
Hawkstone	Eng	15	8	7	579	The Belfry *Brabazon*	Eng	15	9	8	666
Hayling	Eng	16	7	7	580	The Belfry *PGA National*	Eng	15	9	8	667
Hillside	Eng	18	7	7	585	Trevose *Championship*	Eng	17	7	7	672
Hunstanton	Eng	17	7	6	588	Turnberry *Ailsa Course*	Sc	19	9	8	792
Isle of Purbeck	Eng	16	7	6	592	Turnberry *Arran Course*	Sc	16	9	8	793
John O'Gaunt	Eng	16	7	6	593	Wallasey	Eng	17	7	7	673

Course	Country	Score			Page	Course	Country	Score			Page
Walton Heath *New Course*	Eng	16	7	6	674	Wentworth *West Course*	Eng	18	8	7	678
Walton Heath *Old Course*	Eng	18	7	7	675	West Lancashire	Eng	17	7	7	683
Warwickshire (The)	Eng	15	7	8	676	Woburn *Dukes Course*	Eng	18	7	7	690
Wentworth *East Course*	Eng	16	8	7	677	Woodhall Spa	Eng	18	7	8	694

RECOMMENDED HOLIDAYS
VACANCES RECOMMANDEES

Course	Country	Score			Page	Course	Country	Score			Page
Brokenhurst Manor	Eng	15	6	6	539	Llandudno (Maesdu)	W	15	5	8	809
Falmouth	Eng	14	6	7	562	Mullion	Eng	15	5	5	610
Gleneagles *King's*	Sc	18	9	7	735	North Wales (Llandudno)	W	17	6	8	814
Gleneagles *Monarch's*	Sc	17	9	7	736	Pennard	W	18	6	6	816
Gleneagles *Queen's*	Sc	15	9	7	737	Royal Guernsey	Eng	16	7	7	632
La Moye	Eng	17	7	8	594	Royal Jersey	Eng	16	7	8	633
Langland Bay	W	15	7	7	808						

TYPE OF COURSE
TYPE DE PARCOURS

Type / Course		Score			Page	Type / Course		Score			Page
copse						Parkstone	Eng	16	7	8	618
Bath	Eng	16	6	9	526	Rochester & Cobham	Eng	14	6	6	626
Bowood (Cornwall)	Eng	16	7	6	534	Sherwood Forest	Eng	17	7	6	652
Gog Magog *Old Course*	Eng	15	7	8	574	Sunningdale *New Course*	Eng	18	8	8	661
High Post	Eng	15	6	7	584	Sunningdale *Old Course*	Eng	18	8	8	662
Manor House						Swinley Forest	Eng	16	6	8	663
(Castle Combe)	Eng	15	8	7	603	Thetford	Eng	14	7	5	668
						Wentworth *East Course*	Eng	16	8	7	677
downland						Wentworth *West Course*	Eng	18	8	7	678
Southerndown	W	16	7	7	821	Woburn *Dukes Course*	Eng	18	7	7	690
forest						**Heathland**					
Beau Desert	Eng	16	7	7	527	Frilford Heath					
Berkshire (The) *Blue Course*	Eng	17	8	7	529	*Red Course*	Eng	14	7	7	570
Berkshire (The) *Red Course*	Eng	17	8	7	530	Alwoodley (The)	Eng	18	7	7	523
Forest Pines *Forest + Pines*	Eng	17	6	7	567	Alyth	Sc	14	6	6	700

515

England Wales Scotland

Type / Course		Score	Page
Blairgowrie *Lansdowne*	Sc	15 8 6	705
Blairgowrie *Rosemount*	Sc	18 8 6	706
Boat of Garten	Sc	14 6 7	707
Broadstone	Eng	17 7 7	538
Camberley Heath	Eng	16 6 6	544
Edzell	Sc	14 6 3	728
Forfar	Sc	14 6 6	732
Holyhead	W	16 7 5	807
Huntercombe	Eng	14 6 7	589
Ladybank	Sc	17 7 5	746
Thornhill	Sc	15 6 5	791

hilly

Type / Course		Score	Page
Broadstone	Eng	17 7 7	538
Came Down	Eng	15 5 6	545
Dartmouth	Eng	16 9 6	556
Hallamshire	Eng	15 6 8	576
Huddersfield (Fixby)	Eng	16 6 7	587
London Golf Club			
International	Eng	15 9 7	599
Lothianburn	Sc	14 6 8	751
Rolls of Monmouth (The)	W	15 6 6	818

inland

Type / Course		Score	Page
Berkhamsted	Eng	16 7 6	528
Berkshire (The) *Blue Course*	Eng	17 8 7	529
Berkshire (The) *Red Course*	Eng	17 8 7	530
Blackmoor	Eng	17 6 5	532
Blairgowrie *Lansdowne*	Sc	15 8 6	705
Blairgowrie *Rosemount*	Sc	18 8 6	706
Bolton Old Links	Eng	15 5 7	533
Brokenhurst Manor	Eng	15 6 6	539
Caldy	Eng	17 7 7	543
Carden Park *Nicklaus Course*	Eng	17 8 8	547
East Renfrewshire	Sc	15 6 8	727
Falkirk Tryst	Sc	13 6 6	731
Ferndown *Old Course*	Eng	17 7 7	564
Gainsborough-Karsten			
Lakes	Eng	14 8 6	572
Gog Magog *Old Course*	Eng	15 7 8	574
Hankley Common	Eng	16 6 6	577
Hindhead	Eng	16 7 6	586
Ipswich (Purdis Heath)	Eng	16 7 7	591
Lindrick	Eng	17 6 6	596
Liphook	Eng	16 7 6	597
Mannings Heath			
Waterfall Course	Eng	14 8 6	602
Moortown	Eng	18 7 7	609
Newtonmore	Sc	14 5 5	764

Type / Course		Score	Page
North Hants	Eng	17 7 6	613
Notts (Hollinwell)	Eng	18 6 6	614
Orchardleigh	Eng	17 7 7	615
Prestbury	Eng	17 8 7	624
Royal Ashdown Forest	Eng	14 7 6	628
Royal Wimbledon	Eng	16 7 8	640
Royal Winchester	Eng	15 6 8	641
St George's Hill	Eng	17 7 7	657
Stoneham	Eng	15 7 8	660
Swinley Forest	Eng	16 6 8	663
Tehidy Park	Eng	13 7 6	665
Thetford	Eng	14 7 5	668
Thorndon Park	Eng	14 7 6	669
Walton Heath *New Course*	Eng	16 7 6	674
Walton Heath *Old Course*	Eng	18 7 7	675
Wentworth *East Course*	Eng	16 8 7	677
Wentworth *West Course*	Eng	18 8 7	678
West Byfleet	Eng	14 6 8	680
West Hill	Eng	15 6 6	682
West Sussex	Eng	18 7 6	685
Whittington Heath	Eng	17 6 7	688
Wilmslow	Eng	16 7 6	689
Woburn *Dukes Course*	Eng	18 7 7	690
Woking	Eng	16 6 6	691
Woodbridge	Eng	14 7 7	692
Woodbury Park *The Oaks*	Eng	15 9 6	693
Woodhall Spa	Eng	18 7 8	694
Worplesdon	Eng	16 7 6	695

links

Type / Course		Score	Page
Aberdovey	W	17 7 7	799
Ashburnham	W	17 6 5	800
Berwick-upon-Tweed	Eng	15 6 5	531
Brora	Sc	15 7 7	708
Bude & North Cornwall	Eng	15 6 5	541
Burnham & Berrow	Eng	18 7 6	542
Cardigan	W	15 6 5	802
Carnoustie *Burnside*	Sc	14 5 6	714
Carnoustie *Championship*	Sc	19 5 6	715
Castletown	Eng	18 6 8	549
Conwy	W	17 7 8	805
Crail	Sc	15 6 6	716
Cruden Bay	Sc	18 7 6	718
Elie	Sc	15 6 6	730
Falkirk Tryst	Sc	13 6 6	731
Fairhaven	Eng	17 7 8	561
Felixstowe Ferry			
Martello Course	Eng	15 6 6	563
Formby	Eng	18 7 7	568

516

England Wales Scotland

Type / Course		Score			Page	Type / Course		Score			Page
Fortrose & Rosemarkie	Sc	16	6	5	733	Royal West Norfolk					
Golspie	Sc	14	5	4	738	(Brancaster)	Eng	17	7	6	639
Gullane *No 1*	Sc	17	8	7	740	Saunton *East Course*	Eng	18	7	6	645
Hayling	Eng	16	7	7	580	Scotscraig	Sc	16	6	6	779
Hillside	Eng	18	7	7	585	Seascale	Eng	18	5	4	647
Hunstanton	Eng	17	7	6	588	Seacroft	Eng	17	6	4	646
Kilmarnock (Barassie)	Sc	17	6	8	744	Seaton Carew	Eng	17	7	5	648
La Moye	Eng	17	7	8	594	Shanklin & Sandown	Eng	15	7	6	649
Leven	Sc	16	6	6	749	Shiskine (Blackwaterfoot)	Sc	17	5	5	780
Littlestone	Eng	14	6	5	598	Silloth-on-Solway	Eng	18	7	4	653
Luffness New	Sc	16	5	6	752	Southerness	Sc	18	6	5	781
Lundin	Sc	16	6	7	753	Southport & Ainsdale	Eng	18	7	7	655
Machrie	Sc	17	7	7	754	St Andrews *Eden Course*	Sc	14	8	8	782
Machrihanish	Sc	18	6	4	755	St Andrews *Jubilee Course*	Sc	16	8	8	783
Monifieth	Sc	17	7	7	756	St Andrews *New Course*	Sc	17	8	8	784
Montrose	Sc	17	5	6	757	St Andrews *Old Course*	Sc	18	8	8	785
Moray	Sc	17	5	5	758	St Enodoc *Church Course*	Eng	18	7	4	656
Muirfield	Sc	19	7	6	759	Tain	Sc	17	6	6	789
Murcar	Sc	15	6	6	760	Tenby	W	18	7	6	822
Nairn	Sc	19	7	8	762	Trevose *Championship*	Eng	17	7	7	672
Nairn Dunbar	Sc	15	6	7	763	Turnberry *Ailsa Course*	Sc	19	9	8	792
Nefyn & District	W	16	7	5	812	Turnberry *Arran Course*	Sc	16	9	8	793
North Berwick	Sc	18	7	8	765	Wallasey	Eng	17	7	7	673
North Wales (Llandudno)	W	17	6	8	814	West Cornwall	Eng	16	7	6	681
Panmure	Sc	17	6	5	766	West Kilbride	Sc	16	7	5	794
Pennard	W	18	6	6	816	West Lancashire	Eng	17	7	7	683
Perranporth	Eng	16	6	6	620	Western Gailes	Sc	17	5	7	795
Peterhead	Sc	15	5	4	767	Weston-Super-Mare	Eng	16	6	7	686
Powfoot	Sc	16	6	4	770						
Prestwick	Sc	18	6	7	771	**moorland**					
Prestwick St Nicholas	Sc	16	6	7	772	Gleneagles *King's*	Sc	18	9	7	735
Prince's *Himalayas-Shore*	Eng	13	6	4	625	Gleneagles *Monarch's*	Sc	17	9	7	736
Pyle & Kenfig	W	17	7	5	817	Gleneagles *Queen's*	Sc	15	9	7	737
Royal Aberdeen						Lanark	Sc	16	6	5	747
Balgownie Links	Sc	18	7	8	774						
Royal Birkdale (The)	Eng	19	9	7	629	**mountain**					
Royal Cinque Ports	Eng	17	6	5	630	Kingussie	Sc	15	4	5	745
Royal Dornoch						Pitlochry	Sc	14	6	7	768
Championship	Sc	19	7	7	776						
Royal Guernsey	Eng	16	7	7	632	**open country**					
Royal Jersey	Eng	16	7	8	633	Aldeburgh	Eng	13	6	7	522
Royal Liverpool (Hoylake)	Eng	18	8	7	634	Bath	Eng	16	6	9	526
Royal Lytham & St Anne's	Eng	19	7	8	635	Bolton Old Links	Eng	15	5	7	533
Royal North Devon						Came Down	Eng	15	5	6	545
(Westward Ho!)	Eng	18	6	6	637	Chart Hills	Eng	18	8	6	550
Royal Porthcawl	W	19	7	6	819	East Sussex National					
Royal St George's	Eng	19	7	5	638	*East Course*	Eng	17	8	7	560
Royal St David's	W	18	6	5	820	Falmouth	Eng	14	6	7	562
Royal Troon *Old Course*	Sc	19	7	7	778	Ganton	Eng	19	8	5	573

517

TYPE OF COURSE

Type / Course		Score			Page
High Post	Eng	15	6	7	584
Llanymynech	W	14	6	4	810
London Golf Club					
International	Eng	15	9	7	599
Mendip	Eng	15	5	7	604
Mullion	Eng	15	5	5	610
Pannal	Eng	15	6	7	617
Prestbury	Eng	17	8	7	624
Pyle & Kenfig	W	17	7	5	817
Royal Cromer	Eng	15	7	6	631
Sheringham	Eng	15	7	6	651
St Mellion *Nicklaus Course*	Eng	17	9	7	658
The Belfry *Brabazon*	Eng	15	9	8	666
The Belfry *PGA National*	Eng	15	9	8	667
Thorpeness	Eng	14	7	7	670
Thurlstone	Eng	16	6	4	671
West Berkshire	Eng	15	7	7	679
Whitekirk	Sc	15	7	7	797
Wilmslow	Eng	16	7	6	689

parkland

Type / Course		Score			Page
Aboyne	Sc	14	6	6	698
Alloa	Sc	15	7	6	699
Ashridge	Eng	16	7	6	524
Ayr (Belleisle)	Sc	16	5	7	701
Baberton	Sc	14	6	8	702
Badgemore Park	Eng	14	7	7	525
Ballater	Sc	15	6	7	703
Banchory	Sc	14	7	7	704
Bowood G&CC	Eng	17	6	6	535
Bowood (Cornwall)	Eng	16	7	6	534
Brampton	Eng	17	7	6	536
Brancepeth Castle	Eng	14	6	5	537
Bruntsfield	Sc	15	8	9	709
Buchanan Castle	Sc	14	6	6	710
Buckinghamshire (The)	Eng	17	8	7	540
Burntisland	Sc	14	6	6	711
Callander	Sc	13	6	7	712
Camberley Heath	Eng	16	6	6	544
Carden Park					
Cheshire Course	Eng	14	8	8	546
Carden Park					
Nicklaus Course	Eng	17	8	8	547
Cardiff	W	14	6	8	801
Cardross	Sc	14	6	5	713
Carlisle	Eng	17	7	7	548
Carmarthen	W	15	7	4	803
Celtic Manor *Roman Road*	W	18	9	7	804
Chart Hills	Eng	18	8	6	550

Type / Course		Score			Page
Chesterfield	Eng	13	6	7	551
Clitheroe	Eng	17	7	7	552
Collingtree Park	Eng	14	8	7	553
Coxmoor	Eng	15	6	6	554
Crieff *Ferntower Course*	Sc	15	7	7	717
Cumberwell Park	Eng	17	7	7	555
Dalmahoy *East Course*	Sc	17	8	8	719
Dartmouth	Eng	16	9	6	556
Delamere Forest	Eng	15	6	7	557
Denham	Eng	15	7	7	558
Downfield	Sc	17	6	7	720
Duddingston	Sc	15	7	9	721
Duff House Royal	Sc	15	6	6	722
Duke's Course St Andrews	Sc	16	7	8	723
Dumfries & County	Sc	15	7	5	724
Dunfermline	Sc	15	7	7	726
Edzell	Sc	14	6	3	728
Elgin	Sc	15	7	6	729
Forest of Arden					
Arden Course	Eng	14	8	8	566
Formby Hall	Eng	14	8	6	569
Fulford	Eng	17	7	8	571
Gainsborough-Karsten					
Lakes	Eng	14	8	6	572
Golspie	Sc	14	5	4	738
Glamorganshire	W	14	7	8	806
Grantown on Spey	Sc	14	6	7	739
Hadley Wood	Eng	16	7	7	575
Haggs Castle	Sc	15	7	9	741
Hallamshire	Eng	15	6	8	576
Harrogate	Eng	15	7	7	578
Hawkstone Park					
Hawkstone	Eng	15	8	7	579
Henley	Eng	14	6	7	581
Hertfordshire (The)	Eng	15	7	7	582
Hever	Eng	14	8	8	583
Huddersfield (Fixby)	Eng	16	6	7	587
Huntly	Sc	14	6	6	742
Ilkley	Eng	18	7	6	590
Inverness	Sc	16	7	8	743
John O'Gaunt	Eng	16	7	6	593
Langland Bay	W	15	7	7	808
Letham Grange *Old Course*	Sc	15	7	5	748
Linden Hall	Eng	17	8	6	595
Llandudno (Maesdu)	W	15	5	8	809
Longniddry	Sc	14	7	6	750
Lytham Green Drive	Eng	15	7	8	600
Manchester	Eng	16	7	7	601
Manor House					

England Wales Scotland

Type / Course		Score			Page
(Castle Combe)	Eng	15	8	7	603
Marriott St Pierre					
Old Course	W	16	8	7	811
Meon Valley Meon Course	Eng	15	8	7	605
Mere	Eng	15	7	7	606
Moor Allerton	Eng	14	6	7	607
Moor Park High Course	Eng	17	8	7	608
Murrayshall	Sc	14	7	8	761
Newbury & Crookham	Eng	15	6	7	611
Newport	W	15	6	7	813
Northop Country Park	W	16	9	6	815
Orchardleigh	Eng	17	7	7	615
Ormskirk	Eng	14	6	4	616
Patshull Park Hotel	Eng	13	8	8	619
Pleasington	Eng	16	8	6	621
Portal Championship	Eng	15	8	7	622
Porters Park	Eng	15	7	7	623
Portpatrick (Dunskey)	Sc	15	6	7	769
Rochester & Cobham	Eng	14	6	6	626
Rolls of Monmouth (The)	W	15	6	6	818
Ross-on-Wye	Eng	15	5	6	627
Roxburghe (The)	Sc	15	7	7	773
Royal Burgess	Sc	16	7	9	775
Royal Mid-Surrey Outer	Eng	14	7	8	636
Royal Musselburgh	Sc	16	8	7	777
Royal Wimbledon	Eng	16	7	8	640
Rudding Park	Eng	15	8	8	642
Sand Moor	Eng	14	7	7	643
Sandiway	Eng	17	5	7	644
Shanklin & Sandown	Eng	15	7	6	649
Sherborne	Eng	15	6	7	650
Slaley Hall	Eng	17	8	7	654
St George's Hill	Eng	17	7	7	657
St Mellion Nicklaus Course	Eng	17	9	7	658
Stirling	Sc	13	6	7	786
Stoke Poges	Eng	17	8	8	659
Strathaven	Sc	15	7	6	788
Tandridge	Eng	14	7	6	664
Taymouth Castle	Sc	13	4	6	790
Tehidy Park	Eng	13	7	6	665
The Belfry Brabazon	Eng	15	9	8	666
The Belfry PGA National	Eng	15	9	8	667
Thorndon Park	Eng	14	7	6	669
Thornhill	Sc	15	6	5	791
Vale of Glamorgan	W	16	8	7	823
Warwickshire (The)	Eng	15	7	8	676
West Byfleet	Eng	14	6	8	680
West Surrey	Eng	15	7	7	684
Westerwood	Sc	14	8	6	796

Type / Course		Score			Page
Wheatley	Eng	14	6	6	687
Woodbury Park The Oaks	Eng	15	9	6	693
seaside course					
Aberdovey	W	17	7	7	799
Bude & North Cornwall	Eng	15	6	5	541
Burnham & Berrow	Eng	18	7	6	542
Carnoustie Championship	Sc	19	5	6	715
Castletown	Eng	18	6	8	549
Dunbar	Sc	16	5	6	725
East Devon	Eng	16	6	7	559
Falmouth	Eng	14	6	7	562
Felixstowe Ferry					
Martello Course	Eng	15	6	6	563
Filey	Eng	13	5	5	565
Glen	Sc	14	7	7	734
Gullane No 1	Sc	17	8	7	740
Hayling	Eng	16	7	7	580
Hunstanton	Eng	17	7	6	588
Isle of Purbeck	Eng	16	7	6	592
La Moye	Eng	17	7	8	594
Langland Bay	W	15	7	7	808
Leven	Sc	16	6	6	749
Littlestone	Eng	14	6	5	598
Mullion	Eng	15	5	5	610
Nefyn & District	W	16	7	5	812
North Foreland	Eng	13	7	7	612
Ormskirk	Eng	14	6	4	616
Perranporth	Eng	16	6	6	620
Peterhead	Sc	15	5	4	767
Portpatrick (Dunskey)	Sc	15	6	7	769
Prince's Himalayas-Shore	Eng	13	6	4	625
Royal Cinque Ports	Eng	17	6	5	630
Royal Cromer	Eng	15	7	6	631
Royal Guernsey	Eng	16	7	7	632
Royal Jersey	Eng	16	7	8	633
Royal St George's	Eng	19	7	5	638
Royal West Norfolk					
(Brancaster)	Eng	17	7	6	639
Saunton East Course	Eng	18	7	6	645
Seacroft	Eng	17	6	4	646
Seaton Carew	Eng	17	7	5	648
Sheringham	Eng	15	7	6	651
St Enodoc Church Course	Eng	18	7	4	656
Stonehaven	Sc	13	5	5	787
Thorpeness	Eng	14	7	7	670
Thurlestone	Eng	16	6	4	671
Trevose Championship	Eng	17	7	7	672
Wallasey	Eng	17	7	7	673

519

England **W**ales **S**cotland

Type / Course		Score			Page
West Cornwall	Eng	16	7	6	681
Weston-Super-Mare	Eng	16	6	7	686
downland					
Caldy	Eng	17	7	7	543
heathland					
Aldeburgh	Eng	13	6	7	522
Beau Desert	Eng	16	7	7	527
Berkhamsted	Eng	16	7	6	528
Blackmoor	Eng	17	6	5	532
Coxmoor	Eng	15	6	6	554
Delamere Forest	Eng	15	6	7	557
East Devon	Eng	16	6	7	559
Ferndown *Old Course*	Eng	17	7	7	564
Ganton	Eng	19	8	5	573
Hankley Common	Eng	16	6	6	577
Hindhead	Eng	16	7	6	586
Ipswich (Purdis Heath)	Eng	16	7	7	591
Isle of Purbeck	Eng	16	7	6	592
Lindrick	Eng	17	6	6	596
Liphook	Eng	16	7	6	597
Mannings Heath					
Waterfall Course	Eng	14	8	6	602
North Hants	Eng	17	7	6	613
Parkstone	Eng	16	7	8	618
Pleasington	Eng	16	8	6	621
Royal Ashdown Forest	Eng	14	7	6	628
Scotscraig	Sc	16	6	6	779

Type / Course		Score			Page
Sherwood Forest	Eng	17	7	6	652
Stoneham	Eng	15	7	8	660
Sunningdale *New Course*	Eng	18	8	8	661
Sunningdale *Old Course*	Eng	18	8	8	662
Tain	Sc	17	6	6	789
Walton Heath *New Course*	Eng	16	7	6	674
Walton Heath *Old Course*	Eng	18	7	7	675
West Hill	Eng	15	6	6	682
West Sussex	Eng	18	7	6	685
Whittington Heath	Eng	17	6	7	688
Woking	Eng	16	6	6	691
Woodbridge	Eng	14	7	7	692
Woodhall Spa	Eng	18	7	8	694
Worplesdon	Eng	16	7	6	695
meadowland					
Cardigan	W	15	6	5	802
moorland					
East Renfrewshire	Sc	15	6	8	727
Manchester	Eng	16	7	7	601
Moortown	Eng	18	7	7	609
Pannal	Eng	15	6	7	617
upland					
Llanymynech	W	14	6	4	810

520

Angleterre

The Millennium Guide

No, we didn't forget to visit Rye, we simply did not want to get you too excited about a course you will never be able to play, unless accompanied by a member. We haven't included a number of very private clubs, who didn't want to have to reply to inquiries from Peugeot Guide readers. Other clubs do not figure in this year's edition because their course or clubhouse is closed for extensive improvement work. Rest assured, they will be reviewed for next edition. Lastly, other courses were visited but did not deign to reply to requests for practical information: we can only suppose that they have the same attitude to precious income from green-fees. With this said, our choice is neither final nor categorical. Other courses will be added to the guide in the next edition, but all the courses included this year are, to coin a wine phrase, good vintages. You will find the greatest links, the top parkland courses, courses which are ranked amongst the best and also those little "gems" which we hope you will be proud to talk about to your friends.

Non, nous n'avons pas oublié de visiter Rye. Mais nous ne voulions pas vous faire saliver alors que vous ne pourrez jamais y jouer à moins d'être accompagné par un membre. Nous n'avons pas non plus inclus quelques autres clubs très privés, qui ne souhaitaient pas devoir répondre non aux demandes des lecteurs du Guide. Certains clubs ne figurent pas non plus dans cette édition, parce qu'ils ont entrepris des travaux importants sur le parcours ou au Club house. Ils seront revus pour la prochaine édition. D'autres enfin ont été visités, mais n'ont pas daigné répondre aux demandes d'informations pratiques : ils considéreront sans doute de la même manière la manne des green-fees... Cela dit, notre choix n'est ni définitif, ni catégorique. D'autres parcours entreront dans ce Guide dans la prochaine édition. Mais tous les parcours présentés sont, comme on dit en gastronomie, de « bonnes tables. » On y trouve les plus grands links, les meilleurs *parkland,* les parcours qui figurent dans les grands classements, mais aussi quelques petits joyaux dont nous espérons que vous serez fier de parler ensuite à vos amis.

Music lovers might like to know that the English composer Benjamin Britten lived alongside this course for many years. They can also take advantage of their visit here to attend the music festival (in June) in Aldeburgh's superb Snape Maltings. This course is not a grand tournament layout but it is a pleasant holiday course to be included in any golfing tour around this area. Just avoid coming here after any prolonged dry period because the fairways are not watered and get very hard. With gorse and heather in the wings, the holes don't look all that wide and the wind will probably prompt you to play this as you would a links course. But don't let the benevolence of the site make you lower your concentration, either, as there is no shortage of difficulties waiting to make life really complicated. Luckily, inexperienced players can try the 9-hole «River» course to test their progress without getting lost in the heather.

Les amateurs de musique auront une pensée pour le compositeur Benjamin Britten, qui vécut longtemps à côté du golf. Ils en profiteront pour venir au festival de musique (en juin) dans les superbes Snape Maltings d'Aldeburgh. Le présent parcours n'est pas un très grand tracé de championnat, mais il reste un parcours de vacances agréable à intégrer dans un festival de golf dans la région, en évitant toutefois les longues périodes de sécheresse car les fairways ne sont pas arrosés. Avec la présence de bruyère et d'ajoncs, les trous ne paraissent pas bien larges, et le vent incite à jouer comme sur des links. Et l'amabilité apparente du site ne doit pas inciter à baisser sa garde, car les difficultés ne manquent pas de compliquer la quiétude du golfeur. Heureusement pour les joueurs peu expérimentés, le 9 trous supplémentaire («River Course») permet de s'aguerrir sans craindre de se perdre dans la bruyère.

Aldeburgh Golf Club — 1884

Saxmundham Road
ENG - ALDEBURGH, Suffolk IP15 5PE

Office	Secrétariat	(44) 01728 - 452 890
Pro shop	Pro-shop	(44) 01728 - 453 309
Fax	Fax	
Situation	Situation	

38 km from Ipswich (pop. 130 157)
2 km from Aldeburgh (pop. 2 654)

Annual closure	Fermeture annuelle	no
Weekly closure	Fermeture hebdomadaire	no

Fees main season
Tarifs haute saison 18 holes

	Week days Semaine	We/Bank holidays We/Férié
Individual Individuel	£ 35	£ 42
Couple Couple	£ 70	£ 84

£ 24 after 12.00 pm (weekdays)

Caddy	Caddy	on request/£ 15
Electric Trolley	Chariot électrique	£ 5/18 holes
Buggy	Voiturette	no
Clubs	Clubs	£ 7.50/18 holes

Credit cards Cartes de crédit
Visa - Mastercard (Pro shop goods only)

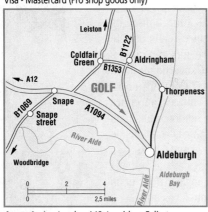

Access Accès : London A12. Ipswich → Felixstowe.
Right unto A1094. Course on left of the road before entering Aldeburgh
Map 7 on page 501 Carte 7 Page 501

GOLF COURSE / PARCOURS — 13/20

Site	Site	
Maintenance	Entretien	
Architect	Architecte	John Thompson Willie Fernie
Type	Type	open country, heathland
Relief	Relief	
Water in play	Eau en jeu	
Exp. to wind	Exposé au vent	
Trees in play	Arbres en jeu	

Scorecard Carte de score	Chp. Chp.	Mens Mess.	Ladies Da.
Length Long.	5698	5238	5238
Par	72	72	74

Advised golfing ability		0 12 24 36
Niveau de jeu recommandé		
Hcp required	Handicap exigé	24

CLUB HOUSE & AMENITIES / CLUB HOUSE ET ANNEXES — 6/10

Pro shop	Pro-shop	
Driving range	Practice	
Sheltered	couvert	no
On grass	sur herbe	yes
Putting-green	putting-green	yes
Pitching-green	pitching green	yes

HOTEL FACILITIES / ENVIRONNEMENT HOTELIER — 7/10

HOTELS HÔTELS

Wentworth Hotel — Aldeburgh
38 rooms, D £ 70 — 2 km
Tel (44) 01728 - 452 312, Fax (44) 01728 - 454 343

Uplands Hotel — Aldeburgh
20 rooms, D £ 65 — 2 km
Tel (44) 01728 - 452 420, Fax (44) 01728 - 454 872

White Lion — Aldeburgh
38 rooms, D £ 60 — 2 km
Tel (44) 01728 - 452 720, Fax (44) 01728 - 452 986

RESTAURANTS RESTAURANTS

New Regatta — Aldeburgh
Tel (44) 01728 - 452011 — 2 km

Lighthouse — Aldeburgh
Tel (44) 01728 - 453377 — 2 km

522

A recently-built clubhouse has only added to the comfort of this remarkable course, which is a revelation for anyone who has never played here before. You have to admit that the partnership between Harry Colt and Alistair Mackenzie will always appeal to connoisseurs. The greens were relaid along the lines of the original layouts, but to modern American specifications. Likewise, several new tee-boxes have helped to restyle the course without changing any of the strategy involved in coping with hazards. Besides the trees, which come into play only for the really bad shot, heather (always impossible to get out of) and especially the bunkers create most of the trouble. On the fairways, finding sand can cost you half a shot. Around the greens, where access is tight, it can cost even more. A demanding course but the fairest adversary you could hope for. You won't forget it in a long, long while.

Un récent Clubhouse n'a fait qu'ajouter du confort à un parcours remarquable qui sera une révélation pour ceux qui ne le connaissent pas encore. Il faut dire que l'association de Harry Colt et Alister MacKenzie ne peut laisser indifférent les connaisseurs. Les greens ont été refaits suivant les dessins originaux, mais avec les spécifications américaines modernes. De même, quelques nouveaux départs ont permis d'adapter le parcours, sans rien changer à la stratégie par rapport aux obstacles. A côté des bois qui ne sont vraiment en jeu que pour les mauvais coups, la bruyère (il est toujours impossible de s'en extraire) et surtout les bunkers constituent l'essentiel des obstacles. Sur les fairways, ils coûtent un demi-coup. Près des greens, dont les ouvertures sont rendues assez étroites, ils peuvent en coûter plus encore. Ce parcours est exigeant, mais il constitue l'adversaire le plus loyal qui soit. On s'en souviendra longtemps.

The Alwoodley Golf Club   1907

Wigton Lane
ENG - LEEDS, Yorkshire LS17 8SA

Office	Secrétariat	(44) 0113 - 268 1680
Pro shop	Pro-shop	(44) 0113 - 268 9603
Fax	Fax	(44) 0113 - 293 9458
Situation	Situation	

8 km N of Leeds (pop. 680 725)

Annual closure	Fermeture annuelle	no
Weekly closure	Fermeture hebdomadaire	no

Fees main season
Tarifs haute saison full day

	Week days Semaine	We/Bank holidays We/Férié
Individual Individuel	£ 50	£ 60
Couple Couple	£ 100	£ 120

Caddy	Caddy	on request/£ 20+tip
Electric Trolley	Chariot électrique	£ 5/18 holes
Buggy	Voiturette	no
Clubs	Clubs	£ 10/18 holes

Credit cards Cartes de crédit
VISA - Eurocard - MasterCard - AMEX - DC
(not for green fees)

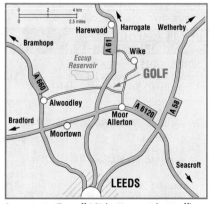

Access Accès : Turn off A61 (→ Harrogate) at traffic lights at Wigton Lane X-roads 8 km N of Leeds.
Map 4 on page 494 Carte 4 Page 494

GOLF COURSE
PARCOURS   18/20

Site	Site	
Maintenance	Entretien	
Architect	Architecte	Harry S. Colt Alister MacKenzie
Type	Type	heathland
Relief	Relief	
Water in play	Eau en jeu	
Exp. to wind	Exposé au vent	
Trees in play	Arbres en jeu	

Scorecard Carte de score	Chp. Chp.	Mens Mess.	Ladies Da.
Length Long.	6017	5671	5097
Par	72	70	73

Advised golfing ability		0 12 24 36
Niveau de jeu recommandé		
Hcp required	Handicap exigé	no

CLUB HOUSE & AMENITIES
CLUB HOUSE ET ANNEXES   7/10

Pro shop	Pro-shop	
Driving range	Practice	
Sheltered	couvert	practice area
On grass	sur herbe	yes
Putting-green	putting-green	yes
Pitching-green	pitching green	yes

523

HOTEL FACILITIES
ENVIRONNEMENT HOTELIER   7/10

HOTELS HÔTELS

Forte Posthouse — Bramhope
123 rooms, D £ 70 — 6 km
Tel (44) 0113 - 284 2911, Fax (44) 0113 - 284 3451

Jarvis Parkway — Bramhope
105 rooms, D £ 98 — 5 km
Tel (44) 0113 - 267 2551, Fax (44) 0113 - 267 4410

Stakis Leeds - 100 rooms, D £ 85 — Leeds, 8 km
Tel (44) 0113 - 273 2323, Fax (44) 0113 - 232 3018

The Calls 41 rooms, D £ 120 — Leeds, 8 km
Tel (44) 0113 - 244 0099, Fax (44) 0113 - 234 4100

RESTAURANTS RESTAURANTS

Pool Court at 42 - Tel (44) 0113 - 244 4242 — Leeds 8 km

Hereford Beefstouw — Leeds 8 km
Tel (44) 0113 - 245 3870

Rascasse - Tel (44) 0113 - 244 6611 — Leeds 8 km

Not far from the Thames valley, the Chiltern Hills and Whipsnade zoo, the largest wildlife reserve in Europe, Ashridge sits right in the middle of this peaceful, wonderful countryside where the aristocrats of yesteryear built superb castles. The course was opened in 1932 and has undergone only minor changes since, even though Henry Cotton was the club professional for many a year. In a superb parkland setting, the course is pleasantly classical in style with each hole having a distinctly individual character. The designers obviously had the pleasure of week-end golfers in mind, and only the sometimes high rough represents any sort of difficulty. Yardage is very reasonable but some of the par 4s are designed to set a very serious challenge. A very good course for all players, male and female.

Non loin de la vallée de la Tamise, des Chiltern Hills, ou de la réserve d'animaux sauvages de Whipsnade, la plus vaste d'Europe, Ashridge est situé au calme dans cette adorable campagne où les familles aristocrates ont bâti de superbes châteaux. Ce parcours date de 1932, et n'a fait l'objet que de minimes modifications, pas même d'Henry Cotton, qui fut longtemps le professionnel du club. Dans un superbe environnement de parc, le dessin est d'un classicisme satisfaisant, chaque trou ayant pourtant un cacatère individuel bien marqué. Les architectes ont visiblement pensé surtout au plaisir des amateurs en week-end, seul le rough, souvent haut et épais, représentant une difficulté importante. La longueur reste très raisonnable, quelques par 4 pouvant présenter de sérieux challenges par leur dessin. Un très bon parcours adapté à tous les joueurs... et joueuses !

Ashridge Golf Club — 1932

Little Gaddesden
ENG - BERKHAMSTED, Herts HP4 1LY

Office	Secrétariat	(44) 01442 - 842 244
Pro shop	Pro-shop	(44) 01442 - 842 307
Fax	Fax	(44) 01442 - 843 770
Situation	Situation	

10 km from Hemel Hemstead (pop. 79 235)
11 km from Aylesbury (pop. 145 935)

Annual closure	Fermeture annuelle	no
Weekly closure	Fermeture hebdomadaire	no

Fees main season
Tarifs haute saison 18 holes

	Week days Semaine	We/Bank holidays We/Férié
Individual Individuel	£ 36	—
Couple Couple	£ 72	—

Weekends: no visitors - No Ladies in spike bar before 2 pm...

Caddy	Caddy	no
Electric Trolley	Chariot électrique	£ 5/18 holes
Buggy	Voiturette	no
Clubs	Clubs	£ 10/18 holes

Credit cards Cartes de crédit
Visa - Eurocard - Mastercard - AMEX - DC (Pro shop only)

GOLF COURSE PARCOURS — 16/20

Site	Site	
Maintenance	Entretien	
Architect	Architecte	Sir Guy Campbell Hutchinson, Hotchkin
Type	Type	parkland
Relief	Relief	
Water in play	Eau en jeu	
Exp. to wind	Exposé au vent	
Trees in play	Arbres en jeu	

Scorecard Carte de score	Chp. Chp.	Mens Mess.	Ladies Da.
Length Long.	5892	5595	5100
Par	72	72	73

Advised golfing ability		0 12 24 36
Niveau de jeu recommandé		
Hcp required	Handicap exigé	certificate

CLUB HOUSE & AMENITIES CLUB HOUSE ET ANNEXES — 7/10

Pro shop	Pro-shop	
Driving range	Practice	
Sheltered	couvert	no
On grass	sur herbe	yes
Putting-green	putting-green	yes
Pitching-green	pitching green	yes

HOTEL FACILITIES ENVIRONNEMENT HOTELIER — 6/10

HOTELS HÔTELS
Pendley Manor - 69 rooms, D £ 90 — Tring, 5 km
Tel (44) 01442 - 891 891, Fax (44) 01442 - 890 687

Hartwell House — Aylesbury
34 rooms, D £ 150 — 12 km
Tel (44) 01296 - 747 444, Fax (44) 01296 - 747 450

Forte Posthouse — Hemel Hempstead
146 rooms, D £ 69 — 10 km
Tel (44) 01442 - 251 122, Fax (44) 01442 - 211 812

Bell Inn — Aston Clinton
15 rooms, D £ 65 — 8 km
Tel (44) 01296 - 630 252, Fax (44) 01296 - 631 250

RESTAURANTS RESTAURANTS
Hartwell House — Aylesbury
Tel (44) 01296 - 747 444 — 12 km

524

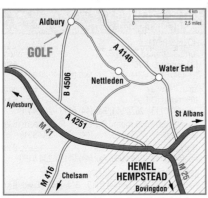

Access Accès : A41 to Berkhamsted. At Northchurch, turn right onto B4506.
Map 8 on page 502 Carte 8 Page 502

BADGEMORE PARK

14 | 7 | 7

Come here in July and dress up for the royal regattas on the Thames. They are held just after Royal Ascot and just before the international polo tournament at Windsor. All three events could be combined and easily be called the «Hat Festival». Here we are in the magnificent Thames valley that would be fun to discover by boat, but only after a good round of golf here for example, where this recent layout designed by Bob Sandow has quickly forged a fine reputation for itself. The one regret is that there is no driving range, but maybe this reflects a desire not to break with a tradition that has also shaped the style of the course: squat, rather tight and with trees looming skyward. Well-balanced, imaginative and very natural in style, Badgemore Park has been improved with new tee-boxes.

Il faut venir en juillet pour les régates royales sur la Tamise, où l'on sort les mêmes toilettes qu'au Royal Ascot, quelques jours plus tôt. Pour faire bon poids, on ajoutera l'International Polo à Windsor. L'ensemble pourrait être dénommé «Festival des Chapeaux.» Nous sommes ici dans l'adorable vallée de la Tamise, que l'on aimera parcourir en bateau. Après une bonne partie de golf, ici par exemple, où ce récent parcours de Bob Sandow s'est vite fait une bonne réputation. On regrette seulement l'absence de practice, mais c'est peut-être un souci de rester dans la tradition, comme en témoigne le style du parcours, bien ramassé, assez étroit, avec des arbres prenant pas mal de place dans le ciel ! Bien équilibré, imaginatif et très naturel, il a été amélioré par la construction de nouveaux départs.

Badgemore Park Golf Club — 1972

Badgemore Park
ENG - HENLEY-ON-THAMES, Oxon RG9 4NR

Office	Secrétariat	(44) 01491 - 572 206
Pro shop	Pro-shop	(44) 01491 - 574 175
Fax	Fax	
Situation	Situation	

1.2 km from Henley (pop. 10 058)
11 km from Maidenhead (pop. 59 605)

Annual closure	Fermeture annuelle	no
Weekly closure	Fermeture hebdomadaire	no

Christmas Day only

Fees main season
Tarifs haute saison 18 holes

	Week days Semaine	We/Bank holidays We/Férié
Individual Individuel	£ 15	£ 25
Couple Couple	£ 30	£ 50
Caddy Caddy	no	
Electric Trolley Chariot électrique	no	
Buggy Voiturette	£ 15/18 holes	
Clubs Clubs	no	

Credit cards Cartes de crédit
Visa - Eurocard - Mastercard - AMEX

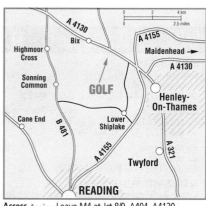

Access Accès : Leave M4 at Jct 8/9, A404, A4130 through Henley-on-Thames. Club house 1.2 km (3/4 m.) after Henley. Map 8 on page 502 Carte 8 Page 502

GOLF COURSE / PARCOURS — 14/20

Site	Site	
Maintenance	Entretien	
Architect	Architecte	Bob Sandow
Type	Type	parkland
Relief	Relief	
Water in play	Eau en jeu	
Exp. to wind	Exposé au vent	
Trees in play	Arbres en jeu	

Scorecard Carte de score	Chp. Chp.	Mens Mess.	Ladies Da.
Length Long.	5500	5082	5036
Par	69	69	72

Advised golfing ability Niveau de jeu recommandé	0	12	24	36
Hcp required Handicap exigé	no			

CLUB HOUSE & AMENITIES / CLUB HOUSE ET ANNEXES — 7/10

Pro shop	Pro-shop	
Driving range	Practice	
Sheltered	couvert	no
On grass	sur herbe	no
Putting-green	putting-green	yes
Pitching-green	pitching green	yes

HOTEL FACILITIES / ENVIRONNEMENT HOTELIER — 7/10

HOTELS HÔTELS
Shepherds - 4 rooms, D £ 48 — Henley, 4 km
Tel (44) 01491 - 628 413

Stonor Arms - 9 rooms, D £ 85 — Stonor, 4 km
Tel (44) 01491 - 638 345, Fax (44) 01491 - 638 863

Holiday Inn — Maidenhead
187 rooms, D £ 120 — 11 km
Tel (44) 01628 - 23 444, Fax (44) 01628 - 770 035

Walton Cottage — Maidenhead
64 rooms, D £ 100 — 11 km
Tel (44) 01628 - 24 394, Fax (44) 01628 - 773 851

RESTAURANTS RESTAURANTS
Stonor Arms - Tel (44) 01491 - 638 345 — Stonor, 4 km
Villa Marina - Tel (44) 01491 - 575 262 — Henley, 4 km
Fredrick's - Tel (44) 01628 - 35 934 Maidenhead, 11 km

525

A highly reputed spa city for more than two centuries, Bath is essential visiting particularly during the music festival held here in May-June, one of the best times to visit England anyway. Very busy on weekends, Bath has several good courses including this one, located on high ground (and providing some splendid views) and laid out over a former stone quarry. Tips from the locals will help you negotiate a number of blind shots and some sloping fairways, avoid some disconcerting kicks and make allowance for wind that can blow your game away. Their help will only increase your enjoyment on what is a rather forgiving course for hackers and beginners, but where better players will need to keep their wits about them if they want to score as well as they hope to. Hardly a major championship course but one with real personality that is well worth getting to know. After your round, go visit the impressive Roman baths in the city centre.

Ville d'eau de grande réputation depuis deux siècles, Bath est aussi à visiter, au moment du festival de musique en mai-juin, l'une des plus belles périodes pour venir en Angleterre. Très fréquenté en week-end, Bath a plusieurs bons golfs, dont celui-ci, situé sur les hauteurs (avec de très belles vues), et dessiné sur le site d'anciennes carrières de pierre. L'aide des joueurs locaux vous aidera à bien négocier quelques coups aveugles et certains fairways en pente, éviter certains rebonds déconcertants, et tenir compte d'un vent qui peut être assez prononcé. Vous n'en apprécierez que mieux ce tracé assez indulgent pour les joueurs moyens ou peu expérimentés, mais où les bons joueurs devront maintenir leur attention en éveil pour faire des scores à hauteur de leurs espérances. Sans être un parcours de championnat, il présente une personnalité à connaître. Ensuite, allez piquer une tête dans les Bains Romains de la ville.

Bath Golf Club — 1883

Sham Castle, North Road
ENG - BATH, Somerset BA2 6JG

Office	Secrétariat	(44) 01225 - 463 834
Pro shop	Pro-shop	(44) 01225 - 466 953
Fax	Fax	(44) 01225 - 331 027
Situation	Situation	

2 km from Bath (pop. 78 689) - 20 km from Bristol

Annual closure	Fermeture annuelle	no
Weekly closure	Fermeture hebdomadaire	no

Christmas Day only

Fees main season
Tarifs haute saison 18 holes

	Week days Semaine	We/Bank holidays We/Férié
Individual Individuel	£ 25	£ 30
Couple Couple	£ 50	£ 60

Full day: £ 30 - £ 40 (weekends)

Caddy	Caddy	no
Electric Trolley	Chariot électrique	£ 10/day
Buggy	Voiturette	no
Clubs	Clubs	£ 12/day

Credit cards Cartes de crédit
Visa - Eurocard - Mastercard (Pro shop goods only)

526

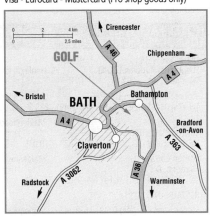

Access Accès : M4 or A36 to Bath. Warminster Road, up North Road, 0,7 km (800 yds) on left up hill. 2 km S of Bath. **Map 6 on page 499** Carte 6 Page 499

GOLF COURSE / PARCOURS — 16/20

Site	Site	
Maintenance	Entretien	
Architect	Architecte	Harry S. Colt (1937)
Type	Type	copse, open country
Relief	Relief	
Water in play	Eau en jeu	
Exp. to wind	Exposé au vent	
Trees in play	Arbres en jeu	

Scorecard Carte de score	Chp. Chp.	Mens Mess.	Ladies Da.
Length Long.	5795	5422	5243
Par	71	71	74

Advised golfing ability Niveau de jeu recommandé	0	12	24	36
Hcp required	Handicap exigé	28 Men, 36 Ladies		

CLUB HOUSE & AMENITIES / CLUB HOUSE ET ANNEXES — 6/10

Pro shop	Pro-shop	
Driving range	Practice	
Sheltered	couvert	no
On grass	sur herbe	yes
Putting-green	putting-green	yes
Pitching-green	pitching green	yes

HOTEL FACILITIES / ENVIRONNEMENT HOTELIER — 9/10

HOTELS HÔTELS

Bath Spa — Bath
91 rooms, D £ 150 — 2 km
Tel (44) 01225 - 444 424, Fax (44) 01225 - 444 006

Homewood Park — Hinton Charterhouse
15 rooms, D £ 130 — 8 km
Tel (44) 01225 - 723 731, Fax (44) 01225 - 723 820

Hunstrete House — Hunstrete
22 rooms, D £ 150 — 8 km
Tel (44) 01761 - 490 490, Fax (44) 01225 - 490 732

RESTAURANTS RESTAURANT

Vellore (Bath Spa Hotel) — Bath
Tel (44) 01225 - 444 424 — 2 km

Garlands — Bath
Tel (44) 01225 - 442 283 — 2 km

Opened in 1921, Beau Desert is aptly named, not because of any similarity with the Sahara but because this is an idyllic golfing retreat. For French readers, the word «Beau» could very easily be replaced by «Elégant». This Fowler layout has of course easily embraced a magnificent setting, using the many trees and often digging bunkers (a little in the Harry Colt style) rather than flanking them with sand-hills. This is not a long course but it is narrow, so the choice of club off the tee is important. Most of the time a 3-wood or a long iron will do to get your ball into the right spot for approaching the greens. The rough is generously lined with heather and gorse, as is often the case on a classic style of course such as this which easily soaks up the rain (rainfalls have been known to occur in this part of the world, even in a Desert). An amusing and little known course.

Ouvert en 1921, Beau Desert porte bien son nom. Sauf qu'il ne s'agit pas d'un quelconque Sahara mais plutôt d'un lieu de retraite idyllique. Et si l'on veut traduire «Beau» en français, ce sera aussi le terme d'élégant que l'on utilisera. Le dessin de Fowler s'est bien sûr adapté à un environnement magnifique, utilisant les nombreux arbres, et creusant souvent les bunkers (un peu dans le style de Colt) au lieu de les flanquer de buttes au-dessus du sol. Ce parcours n'est pas long, mais il est étroit, ce qui oblige à bien réfléchir sur le club à jouer au départ. La plupart du temps, un bois 3 ou un long fer suffisent pour se placer en bonne position par rapport aux greens. La bruyère et les ajoncs garnissent généreusement les roughs, comme sur ces types de parcours classiques supportant bien la pluie, ce qui semble se produire de temps à autre dans ce pays, même dans un Desert. Un parcours amusant et méconnu.

Beau Desert Golf Club — 1921

Hazel Slade
ENG - CANNOCK, Staffs. WS12 5PJ

Office	Secrétariat	(44) 01543 - 422 626
Pro shop	Pro-shop	(44) 01543 - 422 492
Fax	Fax	(44) 01543 - 451 137
Situation	Situation	

5 km from Cannock (pop. 88 833)
25 km from Birmingham (pop. 961 041)

Annual closure	Fermeture annuelle	no
Weekly closure	Fermeture hebdomadaire	no

Fees main season
Tarifs haute saison full day

	Week days Semaine	We/Bank holidays We/Férié
Individual Individuel	£ 35	—
Couple Couple	£ 70	—

No visitors at w/ends

Caddy	Caddy	no
Electric Trolley	Chariot électrique	£ 14/18 holes
Buggy	Voiturette	no
Clubs	Clubs	no

Credit cards Cartes de crédit
VISA - Mastercard - AMEX (Pro shop only)

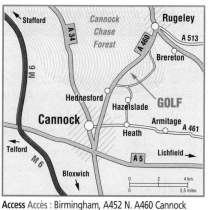

Access Accès : Birmingham, A452 N. A460 Cannock through Hednesford, right at signpost to Hazel Slade, and next left. **Map 7 on page 500** Carte 7 Page 500

GOLF COURSE / PARCOURS — 16/20

Site	Site	
Maintenance	Entretien	
Architect	Architecte	Herbert Fowler
Type	Type	forest, heathland
Relief	Relief	
Water in play	Eau en jeu	
Exp. to wind	Exposé au vent	
Trees in play	Arbres en jeu	

Scorecard Carte de score	Chp. Chp.	Mens Mess.	Ladies Da.
Length Long.	5679	5365	4850
Par	71	70	71

Advised golfing ability	0	12	24	36
Niveau de jeu recommandé				

Hcp required Handicap exigé certificate

CLUB HOUSE & AMENITIES / CLUB HOUSE ET ANNEXES — 7/10

Pro shop	Pro-shop	
Driving range	Practice	
Sheltered	couvert	10 bays
On grass	sur herbe	no
Putting-green	putting-green	yes
Pitching-green	pitching green	yes

527

HOTEL FACILITIES / ENVIRONNEMENT HOTELIER — 7/10

HOTELS HÔTELS
Roman Way - 56 rooms, D £ 65 — Cannock, 5 km
Tel (44) 01543 - 572 121, Fax (44) 01543 - 502 742

Uxbridge Arms - 21 rooms, D £ 32 — Hednesford, 3 km
Tel (44) 01543 - 426 211

Asquith House - 10 rooms, D £ 67 — Birmingham 25 km
Tel (44) 0121 - 454 5282, Fax (44) 0121 - 456 4668

Jonathan's - 30 rooms, D £ 100 — Birmingham 25 km
Tel (44) 0121 - 429 3757, Fax (44) 0121 - 434 3107

RESTAURANTS RESTAURANT
Thrales - Tel (44) 01543 - 255 091 — Lichfield 10 km

Old Farmhouse — Armitage
Tel (44) 01543 - 490 353 — 5 km

Number 282 (Hyatt Regency) — Birmingham
Tel (44) 0121 - 643 1234 — 25 km

Berkhamsted is one of those courses that is close enough to London to be within easy reach and far enough away so as not to be over-crowded. Even so, you still need to call to book a tee-off time. The new clubhouse is just perfect in terms of comfort but you leave your shoes in the hallway. The landscape here is similar to that at Ashridge, a few miles down the road, and is just as respectable and pleasant. The one big difference is that there are no bunkers. This is logical enough in that bunkers are created by sheep and here there are no sheep, just horses in the woods and lots of people out walking. Fortunately they do not come into play. The absence of sand is largely made good by the bushes and heather and by the dips that you might call grass bunkers. Getting out of them with the desired results is never easy, either. The greens are small and so emphasise the need for accuracy. Worth knowing.

Berkhamsted fait partie de ces clubs assez proches de Londres pour en faciliter l'accès, et assez éloignés pour ne pas être trop surchargés, bien qu'il soit toujours nécessaire de téléphoner à l'avance. Le nouveau Clubhouse est tout à fait confortable, mais on laisse ses clous à la porte. On trouve ici un paysage assez proche de celui d'Ashridge, à quelques kilomètres, et un parcours tout aussi respectable et plaisant. Mais avec une grande différence : ici, aucun bunker ! C'est bien logique, les bunkers ont été créés par des moutons, on ne trouve ici que des chevaux dans les bois, et beaucoup de promeneurs, mais rarement en jeu. Ce manque de sable est largement compensé par les buissons et la bruyère, et par des dépressions que l'on peut appeler «bunkers d'herbe,» dont il n'est guère facile de s'extraire avec des résultats garantis. Les greens sont petits, ce qui accentue la nécessité d'être précis. A connaître.

Berkhamsted Golf Club — 1890

The Common
ENG - BERKHAMSTED, Herts HP4 2QB

Office	Secrétariat	(44) 01442 - 865 832
Pro shop	Pro-shop	(44) 01442 - 865 851
Fax	Fax	
Situation	Situation	

1.5 km from Berkhamsted - 8 km from Hemel Hempstead

Annual closure	Fermeture annuelle	no
Weekly closure	Fermeture hebdomadaire	no

Fees main season
Tarifs haute saison 18 holes

	Week days Semaine	We/Bank holidays We/Férié
Individual Individuel	£ 22.50	£ 35
Couple Couple	£ 45	£ 70

Book in advance - Weekends: visitors after 11.30 am

Caddy	Caddy	no
Electric Trolley	Chariot électrique	no
Buggy	Voiturette	no
Clubs	Clubs	£ 10/18 holes

Credit cards Cartes de crédit
Visa - Mastercard - AMEX - JCB (Pro shop goods only)

528

Access Accès : M1, Jct 8 to Hemel Hempstead. At roundabout, take Leighton Buzzard Road. After 4.5 km (3 m.) take Potten End. Turn on left. Golf 4.5 km on left.
Map 8 on page 502 Carte 8 Page 502

GOLF COURSE / PARCOURS — 16/20

Site	Site	▬▬▬▬▬
Maintenance	Entretien	▬▬▬▬▬
Architect	Architecte	G.H. Gowring
Type	Type	inland, heathland
Relief	Relief	▬▬▬
Water in play	Eau en jeu	▬▬
Exp. to wind	Exposé au vent	▬▬▬
Trees in play	Arbres en jeu	▬▬▬▬

Scorecard Carte de score	Chp. Chp.	Mens Mess.	Ladies Da.
Length Long.	5945	5580	5161
Par	71	71	73

Advised golfing ability
Niveau de jeu recommandé

0	12	24	36

Hcp required Handicap exigé   certificate

CLUB HOUSE & AMENITIES / CLUB HOUSE ET ANNEXES — 7/10

Pro shop	Pro-shop	▬▬▬▬
Driving range	Practice	▬▬▬▬
Sheltered	couvert	practice area
On grass	sur herbe	yes
Putting-green	putting-green	yes
Pitching-green	pitching green	yes

HOTEL FACILITIES / ENVIRONNEMENT HOTELIER — 6/10

HOTELS HÔTELS

Pendley Manor — Tring
69 rooms, D £ 90
Tel (44) 01442 - 891 891, Fax (44) 01442 - 890 687

Hartwell House — Aylesbury
34 rooms, D £ 150
Tel (44) 01296 - 747 444, Fax (44) 01296 - 747 450

Forte Posthouse — Hemel Hempstead
146 rooms, D £ 69
Tel (44) 01442 - 251 122, Fax (44) 01442 - 211 812

Bell Inn — Aston Clinton
15 rooms, D £ 65
Tel (44) 01296 - 630 252, Fax (44) 01296 - 631 250

RESTAURANTS RESTAURANT

Hartwell House — Aylesbury
Tel (44) 01296 - 747 444

As it is not always easy to choose between the Red and the Blue courses, play both on either side of lunch. The clubhouse, although renovated, has lost nothing of its charm worthy of characters from P.G. Wodehouse. The trees, not so old but already venerable, are the main setting for this discreet course designed by Herbert Fowler, an equally discreet designer but a real connoisseur of golf (see also Saunton and Walton Heath). The other hazards are fewer in number but just as daunting, for example the bunkers or the stream which crosses several fairways. Here you need every club in your bag, a sign of excellence if ever there was one. Green-keeping is always of the highest standard although without reaching the virtually fanatical levels of preparation that you see all too often these days. Berkshire may not have the «royal» tag but «princely» will do just nicely.

Comme il n'est pas possible de choisir vraiment entre les deux parcours du Berkshire, il faudra jouer les deux, avec une petite visite pour déjeuner à la mi-temps au Clubhouse dont l'intérieur rénové n'a pas perdu son atmosphère digne des héros de P.G. Wodehouse. Les arbres (pas si anciens, mais déjà très vénérables) constituent le décor entourant ce parcours sobrement dessiné par Herbert Fowler, architecte discret, mais toujours aussi connaisseur du jeu de golf (voir aussi Saunton ou Walton Heath). Les autres obstacles ne sont pas très nombreux, mais sont toujours efficaces, comme les bunkers ou le ruisseau traversant plusieurs fairways. Ici, on utilise tous les clubs du sac, c'est un signe de qualité. L'entretien y est de grande qualité, sans les excès de préparation quasi maniaque que l'on voit trop souvent aujourd'hui. Berkshire n'est peut-être pas (ou plus) «Royal,» mais il vous offre un plaisir princier.

The Berkshire Golf Club — 1928

Swinley Road
ENG - ASCOT, Berks SL5 8AY

Office	Secrétariat	(44) 01344 - 621 495
Pro shop	Pro-shop	(44) 01344 - 622 351
Fax	Fax	(44) 01344 - 623 328
Situation	Situation	

3 km from Ascot (pop. 15 244) - 5 km from Bracknell

Annual closure	Fermeture annuelle	no
Weekly closure	Fermeture hebdomadaire	no

Fees main season
Tarifs haute saison 18 holes

	Week days Semaine	We/Bank holidays We/Férié
Individual Individuel	£ 50	—
Couple Couple	£ 100	—

Booking essential - Full weekday: £ 65
No visitors at weekends

Caddy	Caddy	on request/£ 35
Electric Trolley	Chariot électrique	no
Buggy	Voiturette	£ 25/18 holes
Clubs	Clubs	£ 20/18 holes

Credit cards Cartes de crédit
Visa - Mastercard (Pro shop goods only)

Access Accès : M3 Jct 3. A322 → Bracknell.
A332 on right → Ascot. Club house 750 m on left.
Map 8 on page 502 Carte 8 Page 502

GOLF COURSE PARCOURS — 17/20

Site	Site	
Maintenance	Entretien	
Architect	Architecte	Herbert Fowler
Type	Type	inland, forest
Relief	Relief	
Water in play	Eau en jeu	
Exp. to wind	Exposé au vent	
Trees in play	Arbres en jeu	

Scorecard Carte de score	Chp. Chp.	Mens Mess.	Ladies Da.
Length Long.	5635	5420	5077
Par	71	71	73

Advised golfing ability Niveau de jeu recommandé	0 12 24 36
Hcp required Handicap exigé	introduction from home club

CLUB HOUSE & AMENITIES CLUB HOUSE ET ANNEXES — 8/10

Pro shop	Pro-shop	
Driving range	Practice	
Sheltered	couvert	no
On grass	sur herbe	yes
Putting-green	putting-green	yes
Pitching-green	pitching green	yes

HOTEL FACILITIES ENVIRONNEMENT HOTELIER — 7/10

HOTELS HÔTELS

Royal Berkshire - 60 rooms, D £ 140 — Sunninghill
Tel (44) 01344 - 23 322, Fax (44) 01344 - 27 100 — 3 km

Coppid Beech - 205 rooms, D £ 175 — Bracknell
Tel (44) 01344 - 303 333, Fax (44) 01344 - 301 200 8 km

Hilton - 167 rooms, D £ 120 — Bracknell, 5 km
Tel (44) 01344 - 424 801, Fax (44) 01344 - 487 454

Cricketers - 27 rooms, D £ 40 — Bagshot, 4 km
Tel (44) 01276 - 473 196, Fax (44) 01276 - 451 357

RESTAURANTS RESTAURANTS

Stateroom (Royal Berkshire) — Sunninghill
Tel (44) 01344 - 23 322 — 3 km

Jade Fountain — Sunninghill
Tel (44) 01344 - 27 070 — 3 km

The Cottage — Winkfield Row
Tel (44) 01344 - 882 242 — 6 km

529

If you have only ever played here once, you will probably be hard pushed to remember whether it was the Blue course or the Red. They are not quite twins but the similarities of landscape and in length can be confusing. Here is some valuable help: if you played six par 5s, six par 3s and six par 4s, then you played the Red course. You will need at least all those par 5s (some are trimmed to par 4s for certain top tournaments) to bag some birdies and recover what you will have certainly lost on the par 3s. They are all dangerous and making par can be a real problem should you miss the green. You need a steady game and some straight hitting to do well here, particularly with your longer irons. The pines, chestnut trees and birch trees certainly make for a pretty country setting, but you probably won't find them so appealing when you come to add up your score. And even if you do keep out of the trees, there is still the heather to contend with.

Si vous n'avez joué ici qu'une seule fois, vous avez peu de chances de vous souvenir si c'était le «Blue» ou le «Red.» L'un ou l'autre ne sont sans doute pas aussi semblables que des jumeaux, mais même leurs similitudes de longueur peuvent ajouter à la confusion. Une indication précieuse : si vous avez joué six par 5, six par 3 et six par 4, c'était le «Red.» Il faut au moins tous ces par 5 (certains sont ramenés en par 4 dans les grands tournois) pour attraper quelques birdies et récupérer ce que les par 3 vont vous coûter : ils sont tous dangereux et il est très problématique d'y faire le par si vous manquez le green. Il faut ici un jeu solide et bien droit, savoir bien taper les longs fers, car les pins, les châtaigniers et les bouleaux offrent peut-être un cadre bucolique, mais on ne les aime pas toujours autant quand on totalise les scores. Et les éviter ne signifie pas que l'on évitera la bruyère.

The Berkshire Golf Club — 1928

Swinley Road
ENG - ASCOT, Berks SL5 8AY

Office	Secrétariat	(44) 01344 - 621 495
Pro shop	Pro-shop	(44) 01344 - 622 351
Fax	Fax	(44) 01344 - 623 328
Situation	Situation	

3 km from Ascot (pop. 15 244) - 5 km from Bracknell

Annual closure	Fermeture annuelle	no
Weekly closure	Fermeture hebdomadaire	no

Fees main season
Tarifs haute saison 18 holes

	Week days Semaine	We/Bank holidays We/Férié
Individual Individuel	£ 50	—
Couple Couple	£ 100	—

Booking essential - Full weekdays : £ 65
No visitors at weekends

Caddy	Caddy	on request/£ 35
Electric Trolley	Chariot électrique	no
Buggy	Voiturette	£ 25/18 holes
Clubs	Clubs	£ 20/18 holes

Credit cards Cartes de crédit
Visa - Mastercard (Pro shop goods only)

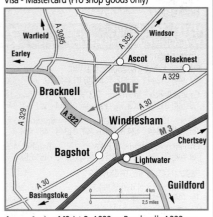

Access Accès : M3 Jct 3. A322 → Bracknell. A332 on right → Ascot. Club house 750 m on left.
Map 8 on page 502 Carte 8 Page 502

GOLF COURSE / PARCOURS — 17/20

Site	Site	
Maintenance	Entretien	
Architect	Architecte	Herbert Fowler
Type	Type	inland, forest
Relief	Relief	
Water in play	Eau en jeu	
Exp. to wind	Exposé au vent	
Trees in play	Arbres en jeu	

Scorecard Carte de score	Chp. Chp.	Mens Mess.	Ladies Da.
Length Long.	5741	5525	5160
Par	72	72	73

Advised golfing ability Niveau de jeu recommandé	0	12	24	36
Hcp required Handicap exigé	introduction from home club			

CLUB HOUSE & AMENITIES / CLUB HOUSE ET ANNEXES — 8/10

Pro shop	Pro-shop	
Driving range	Practice	
Sheltered	couvert	no
On grass	sur herbe	yes
Putting-green	putting-green	yes
Pitching-green	pitching green	yes

HOTEL FACILITIES / ENVIRONNEMENT HOTELIER — 7/10

HOTELS HÔTELS

Royal Berkshire - 60 rooms, D £ 140 — Sunninghill
Tel (44) 01344 - 23 322, Fax (44) 01344 - 27 100 — 3 km

Coppid Beech - 205 rooms, D £ 175 — Bracknell
Tel (44) 01344 - 303 333, Fax (44) 01344 - 301 200 8 km

Hilton - 167 rooms, D £ 120 — Bracknell, 5 km
Tel (44) 01344 - 424 801, Fax (44) 01344 - 487 454

Cricketers - 27 rooms, D £ 40 — Bagshot, 4 km
Tel (44) 01276 - 473 196, Fax (44) 01276 - 451 357

RESTAURANTS RESTAURANTS

Stateroom (Royal Berkshire) — Sunninghill
Tel (44) 01344 - 23 322 — 3 km

Jade Fountain — Sunninghill
Tel (44) 01344 - 27 070 — 3 km

The Cottage — Winkfield Row
Tel (44) 01344 - 882 242 — 6 km

530

BERWICK-UPON-TWEED

15 6 5

A site of endless warring between the English and the Scots, Berwick-upon-Tweed brought peace between both sides and called in designers from both banks of the river Tweed to build a golf course. As you approach, the site looks nothing to write home about, an impression that lasts even as far as the clubhouse, which is simple but functional. The course follows the same style over two wide circles and terrain that is generally on the flat side, with the exception of a few incursions into the sand dunes. This is certainly a less memorable course than others, but its somewhat outdated simplicity, a site between the sea and countryside and the peaceful surroundings combine to create an appealing layout. It would be unthinkable not to play here when in the region, but this slumbering «old lady» is due for some restyling work. In what is an up-and-running project, Dave Thomas has plans to cut out the blind shots and improve the bunkers. Come and play soon, if only to be able to say afterwards how it used to be before.

Eternel théâtre des guerres entre Ecossais et Anglais, Berwick-upon-Tweed a fait la paix pour appeler des architectes des deux bords de la Tweed pour s'occuper du parcours. L'arrivée est sans prétention jusqu'au Clubhouse simple, fonctionnel. Le parcours est dans le même style, en deux boucles sur terrain généralement plat, quelques incursions dans les dunes mises à part. Il n'est sans doute pas aussi mémorable que d'autres, mais sa simplicité un peu surannée, une situation entre campagne et mer, la tranquillité de la région lui donnent un charme certain. Il est impensable de ne pas le jouer quand on passe à proximité, mais on attend un réveil de cette «vieille dame.» Il semble que ce soit toujours un projet, avec les plans de Dave Thomas pour éliminer les coups aveugles et améliorer les bunkers. A jouer vite, rien que pour raconter après comme c'était «avant.»

Berwick-upon-Tweed Golf Club — 1890

Goswick, Beal
ENG - BERWICK-UPON-TWEED,

Office	Secrétariat	(44) 01289 - 387 256
Pro shop	Pro-shop	(44) 01289 - 387 380
Fax	Fax	(44) 01289 - 387 256
Situation	Situation	

7 km S of Berwick-upon-Tweed (pop. 26 731)

Annual closure	Fermeture annuelle	no
Weekly closure	Fermeture hebdomadaire	no

Fees main season
Tarifs haute saison 18 holes

	Week days Semaine	We/Bank holidays We/Férié
Individual Individuel	£ 20	£ 25
Couple Couple	£ 40	£ 50

Full day: £ 25/£ 32

Caddy	Caddy	no
Electric Trolley	Chariot électrique	no
Buggy	Voiturette	no
Clubs	Clubs	£ 14/18 holes

Credit cards Cartes de crédit
Visa - Mastercard (Pro shop goods only)

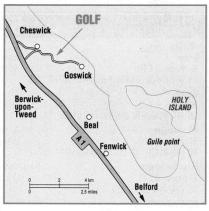

GOLF

Cheswick
Goswick
Berwick-upon-Tweed
Beal
Fenwick
HOLY ISLAND
Guile point
Belford

0 — 2 — 4 km
0 — 2,5 miles

Access Accès : A1 → Berwick-upon-Tweed. Follow signs after Fenwick village.
Map 2 on page 491 Carte 2 Page 491

GOLF COURSE / PARCOURS — 15/20

Site	Site	
Maintenance	Entretien	
Architect	Architecte	James Braid F. Pennink, D. Steel
Type	Type	links
Relief	Relief	
Water in play	Eau en jeu	
Exp. to wind	Exposé au vent	
Trees in play	Arbres en jeu	

Scorecard Carte de score	Chp. Chp.	Mens Mess.	Ladies Da.
Length Long.	5816	5665	5018
Par	72	72	74

Advised golfing ability Niveau de jeu recommandé	0 12 24 36	
Hcp required Handicap exigé	no	

CLUB HOUSE & AMENITIES / CLUB HOUSE ET ANNEXES — 6/10

Pro shop	Pro-shop	
Driving range	Practice	
Sheltered	couvert	no
On grass	sur herbe	yes
Putting-green	putting-green	yes
Pitching-green	pitching green	yes

531

HOTEL FACILITIES / ENVIRONNEMENT HOTELIER — 5/10

HOTELS HÔTELS

Marshall Meadows Country House — Berwick
17 rooms, D £ 75 — 10 km
Tel (44) 01289 - 331 133
Fax (44) 01289 - 331 438

Blue Bell Hotel — Belford
17 rooms, D £ 80 — 10 km
Tel (44) 01668 - 213 543
Fax (44) 01668 - 213 787

Purdy Lodge — Belford
20 rooms, D £ 40 — 10 km
Tel (44) 01668 - 213 000
Fax (44) 01289 - 213 111

Tillmouth Park — Cornhill-on-Tweed
14 rooms, D £ 110 — 25 km
Tel (44) 01890 - 882 255, Fax (44) 01890 - 882 540

Golf is not really about preferring such and such a style of course design, as each has its great side and each its shortcomings. What makes golf such a rich game is the diversity of challenge thrown down to the player. Blackmoor is the perfect example of this, being a very carefully thought out course without the visual gimmickry. Harry Colt placed the hazards, with emphasis as usual on fairness so you see exactly what needs to be done. Given the amount of land available, he preferred a good par 69 to a tricky par 72 and came up with a layout that you will want to play twice in the same day to savour every detail. There are a lot of ditches and especially wonderfully classical bunkers, heather and ubiquitous trees. That sort of description could apply to many other courses, we agree, but Blackmoor has real personality that you meet and feel out on the course.

Il n'est pas question de préférer tel ou tel style d'architecture de golf, chacun a sa grandeur et ses défauts. La richesse du golf vient de cette diversité des défis offerts aux joueurs. Blackmoor est un parfait exemple d'une architecture mûrement pensée, mais sans gadgets visuels. Harry Colt était le maître du placement des obstacles, mais toujours dans un souci de franchise du parcours : on voit ce que l'on doit accomplir. Ici, compte tenu du terrain disponible, il a préféré un bon par 69 à un par 72 «tricky,» et l'on aimera le jouer deux fois dans la journée pour mieux en savourer chaque détail. On trouve ici de nombreux fossés, mais surtout, de manière terriblement classique, les bunkers, la bruyère, les arbres omniprésents : c'est une description que l'on pourrait trouver ailleurs... La personnalité de Blackmoor, vous la trouverez avec votre jeu et votre sensibilité.

Blackmoor Golf Club — 1913
Firgrove Road
ENG - WHITEHILL, Hants GU35 9EH

Office	Secrétariat	(44) 01420 - 472 775
Pro shop	Pro-shop	(44) 01420 - 472 345
Fax	Fax	(44) 01420 - 487 666
Situation	Situation	

10 km from Alton (pop. 16 356) - 10 km from Liphook

Annual closure	Fermeture annuelle	no
Weekly closure	Fermeture hebdomadaire	no

Fees main season
Tarifs haute saison 18 holes

	Week days Semaine	We/Bank holidays We/Férié
Individual Individuel	£ 30	£ 15*
Couple Couple	£ 60	£ 30*

Weekends: * only with member

Caddy	Caddy	no
Electric Trolley	Chariot électrique	£ 5/18 holes
Buggy	Voiturette	no
Clubs	Clubs	no

Credit cards Cartes de crédit
VISA - MasterCard (not for green fees)

GOLF COURSE / PARCOURS — 17/20

Site	Site	
Maintenance	Entretien	
Architect	Architecte	Harry S. Colt
Type	Type	inland, heathland
Relief	Relief	
Water in play	Eau en jeu	
Exp. to wind	Exposé au vent	
Trees in play	Arbres en jeu	

Scorecard Carte de score	Chp. Chp.	Mens Mess.	Ladies Da.
Length Long.	5547	5350	5095
Par	69	69	72

Advised golfing ability Niveau de jeu recommandé	0	12	24	36
Hcp required Handicap exigé	30			

CLUB HOUSE & AMENITIES / CLUB HOUSE ET ANNEXES — 6/10

Pro shop	Pro-shop	
Driving range	Practice	
Sheltered	couvert	practice area
On grass	sur herbe	yes
Putting-green	putting-green	yes
Pitching-green	pitching green	yes

HOTEL FACILITIES / ENVIRONNEMENT HOTELIER — 5/10

HOTELS HÔTELS

Swan — Alton
36 rooms, D £ 70 — 10 km
Tel (44) 01420 - 83 777, Fax (44) 01420 - 87 975

Grange — Alton
30 rooms, D £ 75 — 10 km
Tel (44) 01420 - 86 565, Fax (44) 01420 - 541 346

Alton House — Alton
39 rooms, D £ 60 — 10 km
Tel (44) 01420 - 80 033, Fax (44) 01420 - 89 222

Forte Travelodge — Four Marks
31 rooms, D £ 45 — 11 km
Tel (44) 01420 - 562 659

RESTAURANTS RESTAURANTS

White Hart — Alton (Holybourne)
Tel (44) 01420 - 87 654 — 11 km

Grange - Tel (44) 01420 - 86 565 — Alton 10 km

532

Access Accès : London A3, A31. At signs for Birdworld, A325. Pass Birdworld through Bordon. About 0.75 km out of Bordon, turn right to Blackmoor.
Map 7 on page 500 Carte 7 Page 500

BOLTON OLD LINKS

| 15 | 5 | 7 |

Despite the name, this course has neither the sub-soil nor the physical relief of a real links (it is laid out on the side of a hill). Very close to Manchester, it is still a real change of surroundings for local players, except for the few old factory chimneys you can see in the distance. Bolton Old Links actually lies in some pretty English countryside, full of trees, bushes and a few old flint walls, particularly on the 12th hole where there is also a ravine waiting to ruin your card. Note, too, the small and sloping greens on the short par 4s, and the overall difficulty of the putting surfaces in general (the 17th, for instance). Here lie the origins of some of the greens at Augusta, in which Alister Mackenzie had an active hand. This is one of the region's finest tests of golf where, at least for the first time out and especially if it is windy, you shouldn't bother counting your score. Just have a lot of fun.

Ni par le sol, ni par le relief (il est à flanc de colline), ce n'est un vrai «links,» mais on donna longtemps aux parcours cette dénomination, par extension. Situé à proximité immédiate de Manchester, il n'en est pas moins dépaysant, n'étaient quelques hautes cheminées d'usine au loin. Bolton Old Links est dans une jolie campagne anglaise, avec plein d'arbres et de buissons, quelques vieux murs de pierre, entre autres au 12, qui comprend également un ravin où votre score peut se perdre. A noter encore, la petite taille et les pentes des greens sur les par 4 courts, mais aussi leur difficulté générale (le 17...). On peut retrouver là l'origine de quelques greens d'Augusta, auxquels Alister Mackenzie a si efficacement participé. C'est un des meilleurs tests de golf de la région. La première fois, et surtout s'il y a du vent, on ne compte pas son score, et on s'amuse beaucoup.

Bolton Old Links Golf Club — 1891
Chorley Old Road
ENG - BOLTON, Gtr Manchester BL1 5SU

Office	Secrétariat	(44) 01204 - 842 307
Pro shop	Pro-shop	(44) 01204 - 843 089
Fax	Fax	
Situation	Situation	

5 km NW of Bolton (pop. 258 584)

Annual closure	Fermeture annuelle	no
Weekly closure	Fermeture hebdomadaire	no

Fees main season
Tarifs haute saison full day

	Week days Semaine	We/Bank holidays We/Férié
Individual Individuel	£ 27	£ 40
Couple Couple	£ 54	£ 80

Caddy	Caddy	no
Electric Trolley	Chariot électrique	no
Buggy	Voiturette	no
Clubs	Clubs	no

Credit cards Cartes de crédit — no

to Blackburn
Horwich
B6226
A58
GOLF
BOLTON
A673
6
M61
5
Hindley
to Wigan / Liverpool
Salford
Manchester

0 2 4 km
0 2,5 miles

Access Accès : M61 Jct 5, A58 North, then B6226
Map 4 on page 494 Carte 4 Page 494

GOLF COURSE / PARCOURS — 15/20

Site	Site	
Maintenance	Entretien	
Architect	Architecte	Alister MacKenzie
Type	Type	inland, open country
Relief	Relief	
Water in play	Eau en jeu	
Exp. to wind	Exposé au vent	
Trees in play	Arbres en jeu	

Scorecard / Carte de score	Chp. Chp.	Mens Mess.	Ladies Da.
Length Long.	5830	5490	4995
Par	72	71	73

Advised golfing ability		0 12 24 36
Niveau de jeu recommandé		
Hcp required	Handicap exigé	certificate

CLUB HOUSE & AMENITIES / CLUB HOUSE ET ANNEXES — 5/10

Pro shop	Pro-shop	
Driving range	Practice	
Sheltered	couvert	2 indoor nets
On grass	sur herbe	yes
Putting-green	putting-green	yes
Pitching-green	pitching green	no

533

HOTEL FACILITIES / ENVIRONNEMENT HOTELIER — 7/10

HOTELS HÔTELS
Bolton Moat House — Bolton
126 rooms, D £ 100 — 5 km
Tel (44) 01204 - 383 338, Fax (44) 01204 - 380 777

Last Drop Village — Bromley Cross
80 rooms, D £ 95 — 5 km
Tel (44) 01204 - 591 131, Fax (44) 01204 - 304 122

Broomfield — Bolton
15 rooms, D £ 42 — 6 km
Tel (44) 01204 - 61 570, Fax (44) 01204 - 650 932

RESTAURANTS RESTAURANTS
Bolton Moat House — Bolton
Tel (44) 01204 - 383 338 — 5 km

Last Drop Village — Bromley Cross
Tel (44) 01204 - 591 131 — 5 km

BOWOOD (CORNWALL)

16	7	6

Cornwall is traditionally associated with great links courses, but recent additions such as St Mellion have been designed in rather different landscapes. The same goes for Bowood (not to be confused with the Bowood in Wiltshire), a quite recent course opened in 1992. Laid out in what was once the Black Prince's hunting estate, there are a lot of trees, an unusual feature in Cornwall, many of which the designers have generously brought into play. The style is generally rather British (there is nothing aggressive about this course) although there is a multitude of water hazards in play that most beginners will find rather intimidating. With that said the difficulties are not insurmountable, as long as you can get the ball cleanly up in the air, especially on the 5th hole, a long par 4 with an island green. The clubhouse is huge with pretty views over a country landscape and is to be given 29 rooms to accommodate visitors. Land is also available for housing projects.

On associe la Cornouailles avec les grands links, mais de récentes réalisations comme St Mellion se sont incrites dans des paysages tout différents. C'est le cas de ce Bowood (ne pas confondre avec celui du Wiltshire) ouvert en 1992. Situé dans un ancien domaine de chasse du Prince Noir, on y trouve beaucoup d'arbres (c'est inhabituel dans la région), généreusement mis en jeu par les architectes. Le style est resté assez britannique (le dessin n'est jamais agressif) bien qu'il y ait une multitude d'obstacles d'eau en jeu, que les débutants trouveront intimidants. Cela dit, les difficultés ne sont pas insurmontables... si l'on sait porter la balle, en particulier au 5, un long par 4 avec un green en île. Le Clubhouse est immense, avec de jolies vues sur un paysage rural, et devrait être aménagé avec 29 chambres pour recevoir les visiteurs. Des terrains sont aussi disponibles pour des maisons individuelles.

Bowood Golf Club — 1992

Valley Truckle, Lanteglos
ENG - CAMELFORD, Cornwall PL32 9RF

Office	Secrétariat	(44) 01840 - 213 017
Pro shop	Pro-shop	(44) 01840 - 213 017
Fax	Fax	(44) 01840 - 212 622
Situation	Situation	

65 km NW of Plymouth - 40 km N of Newquay (pop. 17 390)

Annual closure	Fermeture annuelle	no
Weekly closure	Fermeture hebdomadaire	no
Fees main season	Tarifs haute saison	18 holes

	Week days Semaine	We/Bank holidays We/Férié
Individual Individuel	£ 25	£ 25
Couple Couple	£ 50	£ 50
Full day (any): £ 35		

Caddy	Caddy	no
Electric Trolley	Chariot électrique	no
Buggy	Voiturette	£ 25/18 holes
Clubs	Clubs	£ 5/18 holes

Credit cards Cartes de crédit
VISA - Eurocard - MasterCard (Pro-shop goods & restaurant only)

534

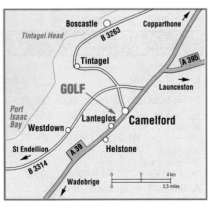

Access Accès : M5, Jct 31 (Exeter), then A30. After Launceston, A395, then A39 South through Camelford. 2 km (1 1/4 m.), turn right on B3266 → Tintagel. First left after garage. **Map 6 on page 498** Carte 6 Page 498

GOLF COURSE / PARCOURS — 16/20

Site	Site	▮▮▮▮▮▯
Maintenance	Entretien	▮▮▮▮▯▯
Architect	Architecte	Brian Huggett Knott/Bridge
Type	Type	copse, parkland
Relief	Relief	▮▮▮▯▯▯
Water in play	Eau en jeu	▮▮▮▮▯▯
Exp. to wind	Exposé au vent	▮▮▯▯▯▯
Trees in play	Arbres en jeu	▮▮▮▮▯▯

Scorecard Carte de score	Chp. Chp.	Mens Mess.	Ladies Da.
Length Long.	6090	5731	5188
Par	72	72	72

Advised golfing ability Niveau de jeu recommandé	0	12	24	36
Hcp required Handicap exigé	certificate			

CLUB HOUSE & AMENITIES / CLUB HOUSE ET ANNEXES — 7/10

Pro shop	Pro-shop	▮▮▮▮▯▯
Driving range	Practice	▮▮▮▮▮▯
Sheltered	couvert	9 bays
On grass	sur herbe	no
Putting-green	putting-green	yes
Pitching-green	pitching green	yes

HOTEL FACILITIES / ENVIRONNEMENT HOTELIER — 6/10

HOTELS HÔTELS

Tintagel Arms Hotel — Tintagel
7 rooms, D £ 50 — 9 km
Tel (44) 01840 - 770 780

Trebrea Lodge — Tintagel
7 rooms, D £ 80 — 9 km
Tel (44) 01840 - 770 410, Fax (44) 01840 - 770 092

Tolcarne House — Boscastle
8 rooms, D £ 60 — 12 km
Tel (44) 01840 - 250 654

Bowood Clubhouse — Camelford
23 rooms, ask for details — on site
Tel (44) 01840 - 213 017

RESTAURANTS RESTAURANT

Port William — Tintagel
Tel (44) 01840 - 770 230 — 8 km

Question: are today's course designers incapable of producing approaches to greens that call for the good old «bump 'n run» shot? Or do they go for the easier option of placing hazards that force players to pitch the greens? We're sorry that Dave Thomas didn't choose to preserve this very British feature here, but his style blends well with the modernity probably required for this sort of course. Bowood is an ambitious resort of a high standard overall where the par 5s are very good, the greens remarkably well defended and where you need to play several rounds before understanding the ins and outs of a very imaginative layout. One word of advice, however: unless you drive straight and long, keep away from the back tees, play further forward and have fun. An impressive resort which is exciting to play, but perhaps not for those continental Europeans who are looking for the traditional English touch of worn tweed and pantaloons.

Les architectes d'aujourd'hui ne sauraient-ils plus dessiner des approches de greens permettant de faire les «bump 'n run» ? C'est plus difficile que de mettre des obstacles obligeant à faire des coups levés. On regrette que Dave Thomas n'ait pu conserver cet art très britannique, même si son style s'adapte bien à la modernité probablement souhaitée dans ce genre de réalisation. Bowood est un domaine ambitieux, de haute qualité générale, où les par 5 sont très réussis, où les greens sont remarquablement défendus, et où il faut jouer plusieurs fois avant de comprendre les subtilités d'un dessin très imaginatif. Un conseil cependant, ne partez pas des départs reculés, à moins de driver fort et droit. Choisissez de vous amuser, avant tout. Un ensemble impressionnant, passionnant à jouer, mais les continentaux aiment aussi le côté old fashioned et tweed râpé.

Bowood Golf & Country Club — 1992

Derry Hill
ENG - CALNE, Wiltshire SN11 9PQ

Office	Secrétariat	(44) 01249 - 822 228
Pro shop	Pro-shop	(44) 01249 - 822 228
Fax	Fax	(44) 01249 - 822 218
Situation	Situation	

8 km from Calne (pop. 13 894)
5 km from Chippenham (pop. 25 794)

Annual closure	Fermeture annuelle	no
Weekly closure	Fermeture hebdomadaire	no

Fees main season
Tarifs haute saison 18 holes

	Week days Semaine	We/Bank holidays We/Férié
Individual Individuel	£ 32	£ 32
Couple Couple	£ 64	£ 64

Full day : £ 42

Caddy	Caddy	no
Electric Trolley	Chariot électrique	no
Buggy	Voiturette	£ 22/18 holes
Clubs	Clubs	£ 15/18 holes

Credit cards Cartes de crédit
VISA - MasterCard (Pro shop goods & restaurant only)

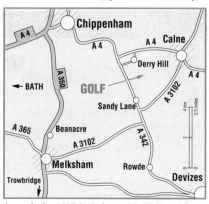

Access Accès : M4 Exit 16, then A420, A3102 to Calne, then A4. At T-junction, turn left → Derry Hill, Golf on left side. Map 6 on page 499 Carte 6 Page 499

GOLF COURSE / PARCOURS — 17/20

Site	Site	
Maintenance	Entretien	
Architect	Architecte	David Thomas
Type	Type	parkland
Relief	Relief	
Water in play	Eau en jeu	
Exp. to wind	Exposé au vent	
Trees in play	Arbres en jeu	

Scorecard Carte de score	Chp. Chp.	Mens Mess.	Ladies Da.
Length Long.	6659	6270	5669
Par	72	72	77

Advised golfing ability		0 12 24 36
Niveau de jeu recommandé		
Hcp required	Handicap exigé	no

CLUB HOUSE & AMENITIES / CLUB HOUSE ET ANNEXES — 6/10

Pro shop	Pro-shop	
Driving range	Practice	
Sheltered	couvert	no
On grass	sur herbe	yes
Putting-green	putting-green	yes
Pitching-green	pitching green	yes

HOTEL FACILITIES / ENVIRONNEMENT HOTELIER — 6/10

HOTELS HÔTELS

Chilvester Hill house — Calne
3 rooms, D £ 75 — 8 km
Tel (44) 01249 - 813 981, Fax (44) 01249 - 814 217

Fenwicks — Lower Goanacre
3 rooms, D £ 45 — 12 km
Tel (44) 01249 - 760 645, Fax (44) 01249 - 821 329

At the Sign of the Angel — Lacock
6 rooms, D £ 50 — 6 km
Tel (44) 01249 - 730 230, Fax (44) 01249 - 730 527

RESTAURANTS RESTAURANTS

George & Dragon — Rowde
Tel (44) 01380 - 723 053 — 9 km

At the Sign of the Angel — Lacock
Tel (44) 01249 - 730 230 — 6 km

535

With Carlisle, this is another little known «gem of a course.» The only thing is finding the opportunity to drive as far as this region and the intuition to stop off here. At 1,000 ft. above sea level, it provides some splendid views over the Lake District peaks which soon soothe your sorely tested golfer's nerves. In fact the whole course gives an impression of peace and tranquillity. This is a typical James Braid layout, where the purity of style - there is nothing superfluous on this course - is plain to see: few fairway bunkers, careful thought required for each shot, punishment in keeping with the errors of your ways and rewards for the good shot. You can pitch high balls into the greens but the wisest decision will always be to roll the ball up to the pin (or thereabouts). Fair (despite a few blind shots), direct and clear, the course is rather hilly and at least looks tiring to play. We say «looks» because the senior members walk it several times a week. So maybe you can too.

Non loin de Carlisle, voici encore un petit joyau méconnu. Mais il faut avoir l'occasion de venir dans cette région, et de l'intuition pour s'y arrêter. A 300 mètres d'altitude, il offre des vues superbes sur les montagnes du Lake District, qui vous calmeront vite si vous êtes arrivé sur les nerfs. Tout comme le parcours vous donnera une sensation de paix. C'est un des plus typiques de James Braid. La pureté de son style, où rien n'est inutile, transparaît ici : peu de bunkers de fairway, une exigence de réflexion avant chaque coup, des punitions à la hauteur des fautes, et des récompenses pour les bons coups. Arrivés à proximité des greens, vous aurez la possibilité de faire des balles levées, mais la bonne décison consiste à la faire rouler. Franc (malgré des coups aveugles), direct et clair, ce parcours est assez accidenté et paraît fatigant, mais les membres seniors le jouent à pied plusieurs fois par semaine. Alors...

Brampton Golf Club — 1920

Tarn Road
ENG - BRAMPTON, Cumbria CA8 1HN

Office	Secrétariat	(44) 016977 - 2255
Pro shop	Pro-shop	(44) 016977 - 2000
Fax	Fax	
Situation	Situation	

15 km from Carlisle (pop. 100 562)

Annual closure	Fermeture annuelle	no
Weekly closure	Fermeture hebdomadaire	no

Fees main season
Tarifs haute saison full day

	Week days Semaine	We/Bank holidays We/Férié
Individual Individuel	£ 20	£ 25
Couple Couple	£ 40	£ 50

Caddy	Caddy	no
Electric Trolley	Chariot électrique	£ 5/18 holes
Buggy	Voiturette	no
Clubs	Clubs	£ 7/18 holes

Credit cards Cartes de crédit
Visa - Mastercard - AMEX (Pro shop goods only)

536

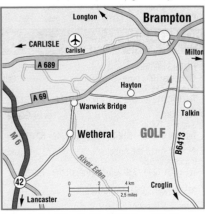

Access Accès : M6 to Carlisle. Jct 43, then A69. At Brampton, B6413 → Castle Carrock. Golf on right side.
Map 2 on page 491 Carte 2 Page 491

GOLF COURSE / PARCOURS — 17/20

Site	Site	
Maintenance	Entretien	
Architect	Architecte	James Braid
Type	Type	parkland
Relief	Relief	
Water in play	Eau en jeu	
Exp. to wind	Exposé au vent	
Trees in play	Arbres en jeu	

Scorecard Carte de score	Chp. Chp.	Mens Mess.	Ladies Da.
Length Long.	5766	5475	4930
Par	72	72	74

Advised golfing ability
Niveau de jeu recommandé — 0   12   24   36

Hcp required Handicap exigé — no

CLUB HOUSE & AMENITIES / CLUB HOUSE ET ANNEXES — 7/10

Pro shop	Pro-shop	
Driving range	Practice	
Sheltered	couvert	no
On grass	sur herbe	yes
Putting-green	putting-green	yes
Pitching-green	pitching green	yes

HOTEL FACILITIES / ENVIRONNEMENT HOTELIER — 6/10

HOTELS HÔTELS

Farlam Hall — Brampton
12 rooms, D £ 140 (Dinner inc) — 3 km
Tel (44) 016977 - 46 234, Fax (44) 016977 - 46 683

Kirby Moor Country House — Brampton
6 rooms, D £ 48 — 5 km
Tel (44) 016977 - 3893, Fax (44) 016977 - 41 847

Crown Hotel — Wetheral
50 rooms, D £ 116 — 13 km
Tel (44) 01228 - 561 888, Fax (44) 01228 - 561 637

Crown + Mitre — Carlisle
97 rooms, D £ 99 — 15 km
Tel (44) 01228 - 25 491, Fax (44) 01228 - 514 553

RESTAURANTS RESTAURANTS

The Weary Sportsman (Pub) — Castle Carrock 5 km
Tel (44) 016977 - 70 230

N° 10 - Tel (44) 01228 - 24 183 — Carlisle, 15 km

BRANCEPETH CASTLE

14	6	5

You come here first and foremost to visit Durham, which has retained many vestiges of the Norman conquest, including a castle and an amazing cathedral which in many ways is quite unique. But this course is not to be outshone, as it is laid out around a castle flanked by a church, which both add to the majesty of what is a fine Harry Colt design. A good number of isolated trees are very much in play and seem to detach themselves from the woods like fairway sentinels. A large ravine is another hazard which has to be crossed three times over a wobbling bridge which can only take six players at a time. A very interesting and sometimes surprising course, where the finishing holes should be handled with the utmost care. The whole site is quite superb, so what more could you ask for?

On vient d'abord ici pour visiter Durham, qui conserve de multiples traces de la conquête normande, dont le château et surtout une cathédrale étonnante, dont certains aspects décoratifs sont uniques. Ce parcours n'est pas en reste, car il a trouvé place auprès d'un château flanqué de son église, ce qui apporte plus encore de majesté au beau dessin de Harry Colt. De nombreux arbres isolés sont bien en jeu, et se détachent comme les gardes des bois environnants. Un grand ravin vient également en jeu, et doit être traversé trois fois sur un pont chancelant qui ne peut supporter plus de six personnes à la fois. Un parcours très intéressant, parfois surprenant, et dont les derniers trous doivent être considérés avec attention. L'endroit est superbe, que demander de plus ?

Brancepeth Castle Golf Club — 1924

Brancepeth Village
ENG - DURHAM, Durham DH7 8EA

Office	Secrétariat	(44) 0191 - 378 0075
Pro shop	Pro-shop	(44) 0191 - 378 0183
Fax	Fax	(44) 0191 - 378 3835
Situation	Situation	

6 km W of Durham (pop. 36 937)

Annual closure	Fermeture annuelle	no
Weekly closure	Fermeture hebdomadaire	no

Fees main season
Tarifs haute saison full day

	Week days Semaine	We/Bank holidays We/Férié
Individual Individuel	£ 29	£ 34
Couple Couple	£ 58	£ 68

Caddy	Caddy	no
Electric Trolley	Chariot électrique	no
Buggy	Voiturette	no
Clubs	Clubs	no

Credit cards Cartes de crédit
VISA - Eurocard - MasterCard

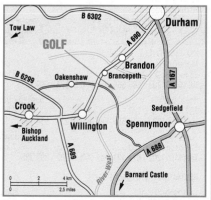

Access Accès : A1 (M) to Durham, then A690 → Crook.
Turn left at crossroads in Brancepeth village. Take slip road left immediately before Castle gates.
Map 2 on page 491 Carte 2 Page 491

GOLF COURSE / PARCOURS — 14/20

Site	Site	
Maintenance	Entretien	
Architect	Architecte	Harry S. Colt
Type	Type	parkland
Relief	Relief	
Water in play	Eau en jeu	
Exp. to wind	Exposé au vent	
Trees in play	Arbres en jeu	

Scorecard Carte de score	Chp. Chp.	Mens Mess.	Ladies Da.
Length Long.	5720	5720	5312
Par	70	70	75

Advised golfing ability Niveau de jeu recommandé	0	12	24	36
Hcp required	Handicap exigé	no		

CLUB HOUSE & AMENITIES / CLUB HOUSE ET ANNEXES — 6/10

Pro shop	Pro-shop	
Driving range	Practice	
Sheltered	couvert	no
On grass	sur herbe	yes
Putting-green	putting-green	yes
Pitching-green	pitching green	yes

537

HOTEL FACILITIES / ENVIRONNEMENT HOTELIER — 5/10

HOTELS HÔTELS
Bridge Toby — Croxdale
46 rooms, D £ 62 — 4 km
Tel (44) 0191 - 378 0524
Fax (44) 0191 - 378 9981

Royal County — Durham
149 rooms, D £ 110 — 6 km
Tel (44) 0191 - 386 6821
Fax (44) 0191 - 386 0704

RESTAURANTS RESTAURANT
County (Royal County) — Durham
Tel (44) 0191 - 386 6821 — 6 km

BROADSTONE

17 | 7 | 7

Some golfers have called Broadstone the Gleneagles of the south. This heather-clad terrain enhanced with pine, birch, oak, chestnut trees and rhododendrons, has kept all the natural appearance of Tom Dunn's original layout, which was later perfected by Harry Colt. Although the holes are often flat, some of the hills are steep and tiring. Never easy to play, the course is a good test for every compartment of your game: length when you need it, accurate ironwork to the rather large but well defended greens, strategy for judging the right distance and flight to avoid the traps, including several dangerous water hazards. If that were not enough, you will also need an excellent short game to make up for mistakes, with lofted or bump 'n roll approach shots, and an acute sense of observation to make the most of the extremely useful experience of local players. Not forgetting your putting and a stop-off at the fountain on the 10th hole, one of the excellent features of a very likeable course.

Certains l'ont appelé le Gleneagles du sud. En terrain de bruyère, orné de pins, bouleaux, chênes, marronniers et rhododendrons, ce terrain a gardé l'aspect naturel du tracé de Tom Dunn, perfectionné et affiné par Harry Colt. Bien que les trous y soient très souvent plats, certaines montées peuvent être assez fatigantes. Peu facile à jouer, c'est un bon test de tous les secteurs de son jeu : la longueur quand il faut porter assez loin la balle, la précision du jeu de fers vers les greens assez grands mais bien protégés, la stratégie quand il faut bien juger des distances et effets pour éviter les obstacles, dont quelques dangereux obstacles d'eau, le petit jeu pour rattraper toutes les fautes, avec des approches levées ou roulées suivant la situation, et l'observation pour tirer profit de l'expérience fort utile des joueurs locaux. Sans oublier le putting ni de s'arrêter à la fontaine du 10, un des attraits d'une très attachante réalisation.

Broadstone Dorset Golf Club   1898
Wentworth Drive, Off Station Approach
ENG - BROADSTONE, Dorset BH18 8DQ

Office	Secrétariat	(44) 01202 - 692 595
Pro shop	Pro-shop	(44) 01202 - 692 835
Fax	Fax	(44) 01202 - 692 595
Situation	Situation	

7 km from Poole (pop. 133 050)
12 km from Bournemouth (pop. 151 300)

Annual closure	Fermeture annuelle	no
Weekly closure	Fermeture hebdomadaire	no

Fees main season	Tarifs haute saison	18 holes
	Week days Semaine	We/Bank holidays We/Férié
Individual Individuel	£ 28	£ 40
Couple Couple	£ 56	£ 80
Full weekday: £ 37 - Book in advance		

Caddy	Caddy	no
Electric Trolley	Chariot électrique	£ 5/18 holes
Buggy	Voiturette	no
Clubs	Clubs	yes (ask Pro)

Credit cards Cartes de crédit
Visa - Mastercard - Amex - DC (Pro shop goods only)

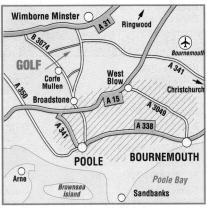

Wimborne Minster — A31 — Ringwood — B3074 — Bournemouth — A341 — GOLF — Corfe Mullen — West Blow — Christchurch — A350 — Broadstone — A15 — A3049 — A341 — A338 — POOLE — BOURNEMOUTH — Arne — Brownsea Island — Poole Bay — Sandbanks

Access Accès : • M3, M27, A31, A349, then Dunyeats Road on the right. • From Poole, B3074, Broadstone Links Road → Blandford, Golf on the right.
Map 6 on page 499 Carte 6 Page 499

GOLF COURSE PARCOURS   17 /20

Site	Site	
Maintenance	Entretien	
Architect	Architecte	Tom Dunn Harry S. Colt (1925)
Type	Type	heathland, hilly
Relief	Relief	
Water in play	Eau en jeu	
Exp. to wind	Exposé au vent	
Trees in play	Arbres en jeu	

Scorecard Carte de score	Chp. Chp.	Mens Mess.	Ladies Da.
Length Long.	5746	5547	4975
Par	70	70	72

Advised golfing ability		0 12 24 36
Niveau de jeu recommandé		
Hcp required	Handicap exigé	certificate

CLUB HOUSE & AMENITIES
CLUB HOUSE ET ANNEXES   7 /10

Pro shop	Pro-shop	
Driving range	Practice	
Sheltered	couvert	no
On grass	sur herbe	yes
Putting-green	putting-green	yes
Pitching-green	pitching green	yes

HOTEL FACILITIES
ENVIRONNEMENT HOTELIER   7 /10

HOTELS HÔTELS

Mansion House — Poole
28 rooms, D £ 90 — 6 km
Tel (44) 01202 - 685 666, Fax (44) 01202 - 665 709

Royal Bath — Bournemouth
124 rooms, D £ 130 — 8 km
Tel (44) 01202 - 555 555, Fax (44) 01202 - 554 158

The Dormy — Ferndown
123 rooms, D £ 100 — 7 km
Tel (44) 01202 - 872 121, Fax (44) 01202 - 895 388

RESTAURANTS RESTAURANTS

La Roche — Poole
Tel (44) 01202 - 707 333 — 6 km

Fisherman's Haunt — Christchurch
Tel (44) 01202 - 484 071 — 10 km

538

Brockenhurst Manor is one of the rare "civilized" spots of the New Forest, one of the finest regions of England over a huge expanse of moorland and oak forest, and a hunting ground for William the Conqueror who helped to create it. The village of Brockenhurst is an excellent starting point for hiking, bicycle rides and horse-trekking, or for playing golf on this Harry Colt course, reached after a very pleasant drive. There is no way you could imagine a course here without trees, and they are a beautiful sight and very much in play, so much so that benders of the ball, in both directions, have a distinct advantage. As is often the case on a Harry Colt layout, the par 3s are wonderful and longer than they look. Another interesting and unusual aspect of this course is that it runs in three loops of 6 holes each, out and back to the club-house. Aside from the trees and bunkers, hazards include a stream which runs along seven holes. Although not really a championship course (it is short), you are guaranteed a great day's golfing.

Brokenhurst Manor est l'un des rares endroits «civilisés» de «New Forest», l'une des plus belles régions d'Angleterre, immense espace de landes et de forêts de chênes, terrain de chasse de Guillaume le Conquérant, qui avait contribué à le créer. Et le village de Brockenhurst est une excellente base de départs pour des randonnées. Ou pour jouer au golf sur ce parcours d'Harry Colt que l'on atteint après une route très plaisante. Ici, on ne pouvait imaginer un parcours sans arbres : ils sont à la fois très beaux visuellement, et très bien mis en jeu. Comme souvent chez Colt, les par 3 sont superbes, et plus longs qu'ils en ont l'air. Autre caractéristique intéressante et inhabituelle, les 18 trous forment trois boucles de six trous revenant au Club house, avec un cours d'eau qui se promène sur sept trous. Bien qu'il ne s'agisse pas vraiment d'un parcours de championnat (il est court), une bonne journée de golf est garantie.

Brokenhurst Manor Golf Club — 1919

Sway Road
ENG - BROKENHURST, Hants. SO42 7SG

Office	Secrétariat	(44) 01590 - 623 332
Pro shop	Pro-shop	(44) 01590 - 623 92
Fax	Fax	(44) 01590 - 624 140
Situation	Situation	

2 km from Brockenhurst (pop. 7 680)
23 km SW of Southampton (pop. 196 864)

Annual closure	Fermeture annuelle	no
Weekly closure	Fermeture hebdomadaire	no
Fees main season	Tarifs haute saison	18 holes

	Week days Semaine	We/Bank holidays We/Férié
Individual Individuel	£ 32	£ 58
Couple Couple	£ 64	£ 116

Full week day: £ 42. Playing with a member £ 17.50/£ 20

Caddy	Caddy	no
Electric Trolley	Chariot électrique	no
Buggy	Voiturette	no
Clubs	Clubs	no

Credit cards Cartes de crédit
VISA - MasterCard (not for green fees)

Access Accès : Southampton M27 → Bournemouth.
Exit 1 onto Lyndhurst. → Brockenhurst.
Golf on B0355 (Sway Road)
Map 7 on page 500 Carte 7 Page 500

GOLF COURSE / PARCOURS — 15/20

Site	Site	
Maintenance	Entretien	
Architect	Architecte	Harry S. Colt
Type	Type	inland
Relief	Relief	
Water in play	Eau en jeu	
Exp. to wind	Exposé au vent	
Trees in play	Arbres en jeu	

Scorecard Carte de score	Chp. Chp.	Mens Mess.	Ladies Da.
Length Long.	5600	5418	5000
Par	70	70	71

Advised golfing ability Niveau de jeu recommandé	0	12	24	36
Hcp required Handicap exigé	24 Men, 36 Women			

CLUB HOUSE & AMENITIES / CLUB HOUSE ET ANNEXES — 6/10

Pro shop	Pro-shop	
Driving range	Practice	
Sheltered	couvert	2 mats + pract. area
On grass	sur herbe	yes
Putting-green	putting-green	yes
Pitching-green	pitching green	no

HOTEL FACILITIES / ENVIRONNEMENT HOTELIER — 6/10

HOTELS HÔTELS

Rhinefield House - 34 rooms, D £ 155   Brockenhurst
Tel (44) 01590 - 622 922, Fax (44) 01590 - 622 800   7 km

Careys Manor - 79 rooms, D £ 160   Brockenhurst 2 km
Tel (44) 01590 - 623 551, Fax (44) 01590 - 622 799

Thatched Cottage   Brockenhurst
5 rooms, D £ 110   2 km
Tel (44) 01590 - 623 090, Fax (44) 01590 - 623 479

Watersplash Hotel   Brockenhurst
23 rooms, D £ 60   2 km
Tel (44) 01590 - 622 344, Fax (44) 01590 - 624 047

RESTAURANTS RESTAURANTS

Le Poussin Tel (44) 01590 - 623 063 Brockenhurst 2 km

Le Blaireau (Careys Manor)   Brockenhurst
Tel (44) 01590 - 623 032   2 km

539

This is one of those resorts that you find either very pretentious or very cosy. All that's missing is the obligatory fitness centre, but that will come. With this said, you would never judge this John Jacobs course to this sort of criteria. The layout was created with much thought given to today's trends in professional and amateur golfing, forcing the player to take decisions as to the line of fire, the type of shot, whether to attack or whether to play safe. Choosing the right tee-boxes for your game is also an important decision. The woods, isolated trees, lakes and bunkers have been used, created or laid out as if geared to all these technical requirements. Dare we say it, here you get the impression of sitting an examination to ascertain your golf playing skills. As a wily craftsman himself, John Jacobs would not necessarily disagree. We will wait until this course mellows a little and acquires the indulgence of some of the more benign «older» courses.

C'est un de ces complexes que l'on trouvera soit très prétentieux, soit très confortable. Il n'y manque que l'inévitable unité de remise en forme, mais cela ne saurait tarder. Cela dit, le parcours dessiné par John Jacobs ne saurait être jugé sur des critères de goût de ce genre ! Le tracé en a été fait avec beaucoup de réflexion sur les tendances des professionnels et des amateurs, il force à prendre des décisions sur la ligne de jeu, le type de coup, l'attaque ou la sécurité, il force même à choisir les départs adaptés à sa force du jour. Les bois, les arbres isolés, les lacs et les bunkers ont été utilisés ou créés, ou disposés en fonction de ces exigences techniques. Dirons-nous que l'on a un peu l'impression de passer un examen d'aptitude à jouer au golf ? Le fin technicien qu'est Jacobs ne dirait pas forcément non. Nous attendrons que ce parcours vieillisse encore pour qu'il adopte l'indulgence des bons vieux golfs.

The Buckinghamshire Golf Club — 1992

Denham Court, Denham Court Drive
ENG - DENHAM, Bucks UB9 5BG

Office	Secrétariat	(44) 01895 - 835 777
Pro shop	Pro-shop	(44) 01895 - 835 777
Fax	Fax	(44) 01895 - 835 210
Situation	Situation	

3 km from Denham - 25 km from Central London

Annual closure	Fermeture annuelle	no
Weekly closure	Fermeture hebdomadaire	no

Fees main season
Tarifs haute saison 18 holes

	Week days Semaine	We/Bank holidays We/Férié
Individual Individuel	£ 60	£ 70
Couple Couple	£ 120	£ 140

Booking 48 hrs in advance

Caddy	Caddy	on request/£ 30
Electric Trolley	Chariot électrique	£ 10/18 holes
Buggy	Voiturette	no
Clubs	Clubs	£ 25/18 holes

Credit cards Cartes de crédit
VISA - Eurocard - MasterCard - AMEX - DC

540

GOLF COURSE / PARCOURS — 17/20

Site	Site	
Maintenance	Entretien	
Architect	Architecte	John Jacobs
Type	Type	parkland
Relief	Relief	
Water in play	Eau en jeu	
Exp. to wind	Exposé au vent	
Trees in play	Arbres en jeu	

Scorecard Carte de score	Chp. Chp.	Mens Mess.	Ladies Da.
Length Long.	6192	5761	5123
Par	72	72	74

Advised golfing ability	0	12	24	36
Niveau de jeu recommandé				
Hcp required Handicap exigé	no			

CLUB HOUSE & AMENITIES / CLUB HOUSE ET ANNEXES — 8/10

Pro shop	Pro-shop	
Driving range	Practice	
Sheltered	couvert	
On grass	sur herbe	yes
Putting-green	putting-green	yes
Pitching-green	pitching green	yes

HOTEL FACILITIES / ENVIRONNEMENT HOTELIER — 7/10

HOTELS HÔTELS

De Vere Bull — Gerrards Cross
93 rooms, D £ 140 — 7 km
Tel (44) 01753 - 885 995, Fax (44) 01753 - 885 504

Copthorne — Slough
217 rooms, D £ 120 — 12 km
Tel (44) 01753 - 516 222, Fax (44) 01753 - 516 237

Courtyard — Slough
148 rooms, D £ 85 — 12 km
Tel (44) 01753 - 551 551, Fax (44) 01753 - 553 333

RESTAURANTS RESTAURANTS

Water Hall — Chalfont St Peter
Tel (44) 01494 - 873 430 — 5 km

Roberto's — Ickenham
Tel (44) 01895 - 632 519 — 4 km

Waterfront Brasserie — Yiewsley
Tel (44) 0181 - 899 1733 — 8 km

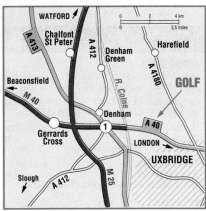

Access Accès : M40 Jct 1. Roundabout on A40, turn into Denham Court Drive, follow signs to the club.
Map 8 on page 502 Carte 8 Page 502

Between Tintagel and the pretty harbour of Clovelly, Bude is a popular seaside resort and starting point for walks and treks, especially for bird-watchers who can take the path that runs along the coast. It is also home to a very pretty links course, almost touching the town, where the wind blows as usual and where you find the standard hazards and unpredictable kicks when the ground is dry. A few blind shots and greens add to the pleasure of discovering this course, particularly when you have given up any idea of keeping score. Good technique, good control for knock-down shots and an excellent short game are essential ingredients at Bude, the latter being helpful for short approaches or escapes from some typical links style bunkers. You won't find this course in the League of Champions, but maintenance is good, the greens are excellent and enjoyment is complete. It is also excellent value for money (good for family).

Entre Tintagel et le joli port de Clovelly, Bude est un lieu de vacances balnéaires, mais il faut avoir le sang d'un Britannique pour aller se baigner. C'est aussi un point de départ de promenades, en particulier pour observer les oiseaux en parcourant le sentier qui longe toute la côte. C'est enfin le site d'un très joli links pratiquement en ville, où le vent joue son rôle, mais aussi les hasards de ce genre de parcours, avec des rebonds imprévisibles quand le sol est sec. Quelques coups et greens aveugles ajoutent au plaisir de la découverte, si l'on évite de compter le score. Une bonne technique, une bonne maîtrise des balles basses, un petit jeu excellent s'imposent, ce dernier aussi bien pour les approches roulées que pour s'extraire de quelques bunkers typiques. Bien sûr, Bude & North Cornwall ne joue pas dans la Ligue des Champions, mais l'entretien est très correct, les greens excellents et le plaisir total. Et un rapport qualité/prix exceptionnel, fort appréciable quand on vient en famille.

Bude & North Cornwall Golf Club		1891
Burn View		
ENG - BUDE, Cornwall EX23 8 DA		

Office	Secrétariat	(44) 01288 - 352 006
Pro shop	Pro-shop	(44) 01288 - 353 635
Fax	Fax	(44) 01288 - 356 855
Situation	Situation	
70 km from Exeter (pop. 98 125)		
Annual closure	Fermeture annuelle	no
Weekly closure	Fermeture hebdomadaire	no

Fees main season			
Tarifs haute saison 18 holes			
		Week days Semaine	We/Bank holidays We/Férié
Individual Individuel		£ 20	£ 20
Couple Couple		£ 40	£ 40
Booking essential (restrictions for visitors)			

Caddy	Caddy	no
Electric Trolley	Chariot électrique	no
Buggy	Voiturette	no
Clubs	Clubs	£ 10

Credit cards Cartes de crédit
VISA - Eurocard - MasterCard (Pro shop goods only)

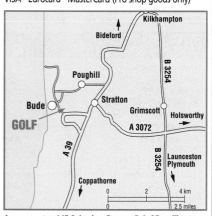

Access Accès : M5 Bristol → Exeter. Exit 27 → Tiverton, Barnstable on A39, then to Bude. Into town, Golf signposted. Map 6 on page 498 Carte 6 Page 498

GOLF COURSE / PARCOURS 15/20

Site	Site	
Maintenance	Entretien	
Architect	Architecte	Tom Dunn
Type	Type	seaside course, links
Relief	Relief	
Water in play	Eau en jeu	
Exp. to wind	Exposé au vent	
Trees in play	Arbres en jeu	

Scorecard Carte de score	Chp. Chp.	Mens Mess.	Ladies Da.
Length Long.	5452	5256	4841
Par	71	71	73

Advised golfing ability		0	12	24	36
Niveau de jeu recommandé					
Hcp required Handicap exigé	certificate				

CLUB HOUSE & AMENITIES / CLUB HOUSE ET ANNEXES 6/10

Pro shop	Pro-shop	
Driving range	Practice	
Sheltered	couvert	practice area
On grass	sur herbe	yes
Putting-green	putting-green	yes
Pitching-green	pitching green	no

HOTEL FACILITIES / ENVIRONNEMENT HOTELIER 5/10

HOTELS HÔTELS

Hartland	Bude
29 rooms, D £ 70	1 km
Tel (44) 01288 - 355 661	
Fax (44) 01288 - 355 664	

Camelot	Bude
21 rooms, D £ 52	1 km
Tel (44) 01288 - 352 361	
Fax (44) 01288 - 355 470	

Bude Haven	Bude
11 rooms, D £ 40	1 km
Tel (44) 01288 - 352 305	

Meva Gwin	Bude
13 rooms, D £ 45	2 km
Tel (44) 01288 - 352 347	
Fax (44) 01288 - 352 347	

541

BURNHAM & BERROW

Played for many a year by J.H. Taylor, this classic course has been profoundly altered throughout the 20th century, in particular to avoid hitting worshippers as they leave the church set in the middle of the course. The changes also cut out many of the blind shots, thereby reducing a little the glorious uncertainty of golf but giving the layout a more forthright feel as it winds its way between majestic sand-dunes. The plant-life here is superb, especially the orchids, and as on many links courses there are very few water hazards (here on the 6th and behind the 13th holes). Dare we say it, these should only bother the higher handicappers. Generally speaking you have to hit the ball straight, as bushes, rough and bunkers await wayward drives, while hilly slopes and pot-bunkers snap up mis-hit approach shots. As the greens are small and steeply contoured, this is a great course for getting your short game together.

Longtemps arpenté par J.H. Taylor, ce classique a été profondément modifié tout au long de ce siècle, en particulier pour éviter d'envoyer aux fidèles de l'église au milieu du parcours. Les modifications ont aussi permis d'éliminer beaucoup de coups aveugles, retirant un peu de la glorieuse incertitude du golf, mais offrant plus de franchise au tracé, à présent mieux insinué entre des dunes majestueuses. On trouve ici une flore sauvage superbe, notamment des orchidées. Comme sur la plupart des links, il y a peu d'obstacles d'eau (au 6 et derrière le 13), mais ils ne concernent que les handicaps élevés. En général, il faut placer la balle, car les buissons, le rough et les bunkers attendent les drives égarés, les mouvements de terrain et les pot bunkers happent les approches imprécises. Comme les greens sont petits et très mouvementés, on travaille son petit jeu sur ce grand parcours...

Burnham & Berrow Golf Club — 1890

St Christophers Way
ENG - BURNHAM-ON-SEA, Somerset TA8 2PE

Office	Secrétariat	(44) 01278 - 785 760
Pro shop	Pro-shop	(44) 01278 - 785 545
Fax	Fax	(44) 01278 - 795 440
Situation	Situation	

50 km SW of Bristol (pop. 376 146)
8 km S of Weston-Super-Mare (pop. 64 935)

Annual closure	Fermeture annuelle	no
Weekly closure	Fermeture hebdomadaire	no
Fees main season	Tarifs haute saison	full day

	Week days Semaine	We/Bank holidays We/Férié
Individual Individuel	£ 36	£ 50
Couple Couple	£ 72	£ 100

Caddy	Caddy	on request
Electric Trolley	Chariot électrique	yes
Buggy	Voiturette	no
Clubs	Clubs	yes

Credit cards Cartes de crédit
Visa - Mastercard (Pro shop goods only)

542

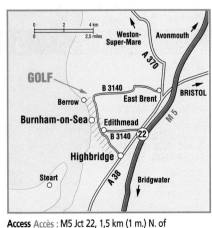

Access Accès : M5 Jct 22, 1,5 km (1 m.) N. of Burnham-on-Sea. Follow signs to Golf.
Map 6 on page 499 Carte 6 Page 499

GOLF COURSE / PARCOURS — 18/20

Site	Site	
Maintenance	Entretien	
Architect	Architecte	Unknown
Type	Type	seaside course, links
Relief	Relief	
Water in play	Eau en jeu	
Exp. to wind	Exposé au vent	
Trees in play	Arbres en jeu	

Scorecard Carte de score	Chp. Chp.	Mens Mess.	Ladies Da.
Length Long.	6151	6012	5227
Par	71	71	74

Advised golfing ability — 0 12 24 36
Niveau de jeu recommandé
Hcp required Handicap exigé — 22 Men, 30 Ladies

CLUB HOUSE & AMENITIES / CLUB HOUSE ET ANNEXES — 7/10

Pro shop	Pro-shop	
Driving range	Practice	
Sheltered	couvert	no
On grass	sur herbe	yes
Putting-green	putting-green	yes
Pitching-green	pitching green	yes

HOTEL FACILITIES / ENVIRONNEMENT HOTELIER — 6/10

HOTELS HÔTELS

Dormy House — Golf on site
4 rooms, D £ 65
Tel (44) 01278 - 785 760
Fax (44) 01278 - 795 440

Grand Atlantic — Weston-Super-Mare 8 km
76 rooms, D £ 75
Tel (44) 01934 - 626 543
Fax (44) 01934 - 415 048

Royal Pier - 36 rooms, D £ 75 — Weston-Super-Mare 8 km
Tel (44) 01934 - 626 644
Fax (44) 01934 - 624 169

RESTAURANTS RESTAURANT

Duets — Weston-Super-Mare 8 km
Tel (44) 01934 - 413 428

CALDY

In a setting formed by the Dee estuary, Flintshire hills and Welsh mountains right in the background, the views from the course provide welcome inspiration, especially towards sun-set. Caldy is a mixture of sloping holes in a parkland setting and links-style seaside holes (3 to 10), and as such offers great variety of style. What's more, being less demanding and less uncompromising than its neighbour, Royal Liverpool, it is not such an intimidating course for the average hacker. Having said that, the number of difficulties (trees, rough, water and sand) makes this a course to be reckoned with, even though the layout is clear and revealing enough for you to know exactly when and where to hit those magic shots. Although slightly hilly in places, no greens are blind but some are elevated, so make allowance for this when choosing your irons. On the down-side, lady golfers here seem to be treated as slightly less than 1st class citizens, there are no spectacular dunes to contend with and no long par 4s... but maybe the wind can change all that.

Le décor réunit l'estuaire de la Dee, les collines du Flintshire et les montagnes du Pays de Galles : de quoi inspirer le joueur, surtout au soleil couchant. Avec son mélange de trous en pente, d'esthétique de parc et de links (du 3 au 10), Caldy offre une superbe variété de styles. De plus, n'étant pas aussi exigeant et brutal que son voisin Royal Liverpool, il intimidera moins le joueur moyen. Pourtant le nombre de difficultés (arbres, rough, eau, bunkers) oblige à réfléchir, mais comme on dispose de toutes les cartes en main - le parcours est d'une grande franchise générale - on peut jouer ses atouts au bon moment. En dépit d'un léger relief, on ne trouve pas de greens aveugles, mais certains étant en élévation, il faut bien choisir ses clubs. Si l'on peut regretter quelque chose, c'est le fait que les femmes ne paraissent pas être ici des citoyens de 1ère classe, l'absence de grandes dunes spectaculaires, le manque de longs par 4 - quoiqu'avec le vent...

Caldy Golf Club — 1908
Links Hey Road
ENG - CALDY, Wirral CH48 1NB

Office	Secrétariat	(44) 0151-625 5660
Pro shop	Pro-shop	(44) 0151-625 1818
Fax	Fax	(44) 0151-625 5660
Situation	Situation	

4 km from Heswall - 18 km from Liverpool (pop. 452 450)

Annual closure	Fermeture annuelle	no
Weekly closure	Fermeture hebdomadaire	no
Fees main season	Tarifs haute saison	full day

	Week days Semaine	We/Bank holidays We/Férié
Individual Individuel	£ 40	*
Couple Couple	£ 80	*

* Members only at week ends

Caddy	Caddy	no
Electric Trolley	Chariot électrique	no
Buggy	Voiturette	£ 15
Clubs	Clubs	no

Credit cards Cartes de crédit
VISA - MasterCard (not for green-fees)

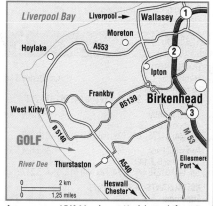

Access Accès : A540 Manchester-Hoylake, → left on D 5140 (Caldy Road), 1st left into Croft Drive East, left into Links Hey Road.
Map 5 on page 497 Carte 5 Page 497

GOLF COURSE / PARCOURS — 17 /20

Site	Site	
Maintenance	Entretien	
Architect	Architecte	John Morris, Donald Steel
Type	Type	inland, downland
Relief	Relief	
Water in play	Eau en jeu	
Exp. to wind	Exposé au vent	
Trees in play	Arbres en jeu	

Scorecard Carte de score	Chp. Chp.	Mens Mess.	Ladies Da.
Length Long.	6001	5710	5208
Par	72	72	74

Advised golfing ability Niveau de jeu recommandé	0	12	24	36
Hcp required Handicap exigé	certificate			

CLUB HOUSE & AMENITIES / CLUB HOUSE ET ANNEXES — 7 /10

Pro shop	Pro-shop	
Driving range	Practice	
Sheltered	couvert	
On grass	sur herbe	yes
Putting-green	putting-green	yes
Pitching-green	pitching green	yes

543

HOTEL FACILITIES / ENVIRONNEMENT HOTELIER — 7 /10

HOTELS HÔTELS
Grove Hotel — Wallasey
14 rooms, D £ 50
Tel (44) 0151 - 630 4558, Fax (44) 0151 - 639 0028

Leasowe Castle Hotel — Moreton
22 rooms, D £ 66
Tel (44) 0151 - 606 9191, Fax (44) 0151 - 678 5551

Bowler Hat — Birkenhead
32 rooms, D £ 85
Tel (44) 0151 - 652 4931, Fax (44) 0151 - 653 8127

Twelfth Man Lodge - 30 rooms, D £ 39 — Greasby
Tel (44) 0151 - 677 5445, Fax (44) 0151 - 678 5085

RESTAURANTS RESTAURANTS
Grove Hotel - Tel (44) 0151 - 630 4558 — Wallasey
Lee Ho - Tel (44) 0151 - 677 6440 — Moreton

CAMBERLEY HEATH

16 6 6

This golf-club, lying almost at the intersection between the counties of Surrey, Hampshire and Berkshire, has an impressive club-house from where you get some equally impressive views over a course that winds its way through trees and heather. Virtually free of water (except the 16th hole), this is a fine example of the exceptional skill of architect Harry Colt and his discreet but totally effective bunkering, the use of trees and natural slopes and the often multi-tiered putting surfaces where down-hill putts should be avoided at all costs. The terrain is hilly enough to get the better of tired legs, an important factor on a course where you will need every ounce of strength to cope with the last three holes, which are often decisive for your card. Depending on the tees you choose, the course can change to such an extent that we would recommend (for "friendly" rounds) changing from one day to the next to vary the fun and test your technique. All in all, a very clever layout.

Ce club, au croisement du Surrey, du Hampshire et du Berkshire, offre depuis son imposant Clubhouse un panorama spectaculaire sur le parcours insinué dans les arbres et la bruyère. Pratiquement sans eau (sauf au 16), c'est un grand exemple de l'art exceptionnel de l'architecte Harry Colt, avec son placement sobre et efficace des bunkers, sa mise en jeu des arbres, son utilisation des pentes naturelles du terrain, et les contours fréquemment à plateaux des greens, où il convient absolument d'éviter les putts en descente. Assez accidenté, il éprouvera les jambes des moins résistants, alors que le jeu réclame ici de garder des forces jusqu'au bout : les trois derniers trous peuvent ainsi retourner le résultat d'une compétition. Suivant le choix des départs, le parcours peut changer à tel point que l'on conseillera (en partie amicale) d'en changer d'un jour à l'autre pour varier les plaisirs et tester sa technique sur ce tracé très intelligent.

Camberley Heath Golf Club — 1913

Golf Drive
ENG - CAMBERLEY, Surrey GU15 1JG

Office	Secrétariat	(44) 01276 - 23 258
Pro shop	Pro-shop	(44) 01276 - 27 905
Fax	Fax	(44) 01276 - 692 505
Situation	Situation	

2 km from Camberley (pop. 46120) - 60 km from London

Annual closure	Fermeture annuelle	no
Weekly closure	Fermeture hebdomadaire	no

Fees main season
Tarifs haute saison full day

	Week days Semaine	We/Bank holidays We/Férié
Individual Individuel	£ 56	*
Couple Couple	£ 112	*
Members only at week ends		
Caddy	Caddy	£ 20
Electric Trolley	Chariot électrique	no
Buggy	Voiturette	£ 35
Clubs	Clubs	£ 30

Credit cards Cartes de crédit — no

Access Accès : London M3 → Basingstoke. Exit 4 → Frimley. Turn left on Portsmouth Road. Golf on the right at Golf Drive.
Map 8 on page 502 Carte 8 Page 502

544

GOLF COURSE / PARCOURS — 16/20

Site	Site	
Maintenance	Entretien	
Architect	Architecte	Harry S. Colt
Type	Type	heathland, parkland
Relief	Relief	
Water in play	Eau en jeu	
Exp. to wind	Exposé au vent	
Trees in play	Arbres en jeu	

Scorecard Carte de score	Chp. Chp.	Mens Mess.	Ladies Da.
Length Long.	5670	5580	4950
Par	72	72	72

Advised golfing ability — 0 12 24 36
Niveau de jeu recommandé
Hcp required — Handicap exigé — certificate

CLUB HOUSE & AMENITIES / CLUB HOUSE ET ANNEXES — 6/10

Pro shop	Pro-shop	
Driving range	Practice	
Sheltered	couvert	
On grass	sur herbe	yes
Putting-green	putting-green	yes
Pitching-green	pitching green	yes

HOTEL FACILITIES / ENVIRONNEMENT HOTELIER — 6/10

HOTELS HÔTELS
Frimley Hall — Camberley 3 km
66 rooms, D £ 105
Tel (44) 01276 - 283 21, Fax (44) 01276 - 691 253

One Oak Toby — Frimley 3 km
40 rooms, D £ 82
Tel (44) 01276 - 691 939, Fax (44) 01276 - 676 088

Pennyhill Park — Bagshot 5 km
70 rooms, D £ 140
Tel (44) 01276 - 471 774, Fax (44) 01276 - 473 217

RESTAURANTS RESTAURANTS
Stateroom — Ascot 12 km
Tel (44) 01344 - 23 322

Ciao Ninety — Ascot 12 km
Tel (44) 01344 - 22 285

CAME DOWN

15	5	6

From Dorchester, it is just a short drive to the coast and Weymouth, a very old seaside resort where you can still see the vestiges of Maiden castle, a stone-age fortress. Even closer is Came Down golf club, a course designed by Tom Dunn, restyled by J.H. Taylor and fine-tuned by Harry Colt. Three top names in golf course design and three great connoisseurs of golf played at every level, indulgent for the less gifted, demanding for the smarter guys. Laid out on a hill, the course has a few climbs to negotiate but nothing too steep, and naturally reserves a few sloping lies. The advantage of this location is the view over the Dorset countryside and some wide open space where big-hitters can open their shoulders despite the risk of landing in some tall rough. You also have the wind to contend with, so keep the ball low and try to run it in. The greens are excellent but often very slick in summer

De Dorchester, il faut quelques minutes pour rejoindre la côte et Weymouth, une très ancienne station balnéaire, ou voir les vestiges de Maiden Castle, une forteresse de l'Age de pierre. Il en faut encore moins pour jouer le parcours de Came Down, dessiné par Tom Dunn, revu par JH Taylor et peaufiné par Harry Colt. Trois grands noms de l'architecture, trois grands connaisseurs du jeu à tous les niveaux, indulgents pour les élèves peu doués, exigeants pour les premiers de la classe. Situé sur une colline, il réserve quelques moments de montées à pied mais sans rien d'excessif, et quelques positions de balle dans différentes pentes. Avantage de la situation, les points de vue sur la campagne du Dorset, et des espaces très ouverts où les frappeurs pourront se déchaîner, avec quelques risques présentés par les hauts roughs. Il faut aussi savoir jouer avec le vent, c'est-à-dire avec sa balle dans le vent, maîtriser les balles basses, et donc les approches roulées : les greens sont de bonne qualité, mais peuvent être très roulants en été.

Came Down Golf Club — 1904
ENG - CAME, DORCHESTER, Dorset DT2 8 NR

Office	Secrétariat	(44) 01305 - 813 494
Pro shop	Pro-shop	(44) 01305 - 812 670
Fax	Fax	(44) 01305 - 813 494
Situation	Situation	

5 km from Dorchester (pop. 15 037)
10 km from Weymouth (pop. 46 065)

Annual closure	Fermeture annuelle	no
Weekly closure	Fermeture hebdomadaire	no
Fees main season	Tarifs haute saison	18 holes

	Week days Semaine	We/Bank holidays We/Férié
Individual Individuel		
Couple Couple		

Prior booking essential

Caddy	Caddy	no
Electric Trolley	Chariot électrique	no
Buggy	Voiturette	no
Clubs	Clubs	yes

Credit cards Cartes de crédit
VISA - Eurocard - MasterCard (Pro shop goods only)

Dorchester
← Bridport
A 35
Whitcombe
Winterborne Herringston
GOLF
A 354
A 352
Warmwell
Broadmayne
Preston
A 353
Weymouth

0   2   4 km
0   2,5 miles

Access Accès : 5 km South of Dorchester. Take A354 head up hill. Keep on same road, Club house on right hand side. **Map 6 on page 499** Carte 6 Page 499

GOLF COURSE / PARCOURS — 15/20

Site	Site	
Maintenance	Entretien	
Architect	Architecte	Tom Dunn J.H. Taylor
Type	Type	open country, hilly
Relief	Relief	
Water in play	Eau en jeu	
Exp. to wind	Exposé au vent	
Trees in play	Arbres en jeu	

Scorecard Carte de score	Chp. Chp.	Mens Mess.	Ladies Da.
Length Long.	5630	5313	5011
Par	70	69	72

Advised golfing ability Niveau de jeu recommandé	0	12	24	36
Hcp required Handicap exigé	certificate			

CLUB HOUSE & AMENITIES / CLUB HOUSE ET ANNEXES — 5/10

Pro shop	Pro-shop	
Driving range	Practice	
Sheltered	couvert	practice area
On grass	sur herbe	yes
Putting-green	putting-green	yes
Pitching-green	pitching green	yes

HOTEL FACILITIES / ENVIRONNEMENT HOTELIER — 6/10

HOTELS HÔTELS
King's Arms — Dorchester 5 km
31 rooms, D £ 100
Tel (44) 01305 - 265 353, Fax (44) 01305 - 260 629

Casterbridge — Dorchester 5 km
14 rooms, D £ 65
Tel (44) 01305 - 264 043, Fax (44) 01305 - 260 884

Junction Hotel — Dorchester 5 km
6 rooms, D £ 45 - Tel (44) 01305 - 268 826

Rex - 31 rooms, D £ 85 — Weymouth 10 km
Tel (44) 01305 - 760 400, Fax (44) 01305 - 760 500

RESTAURANTS RESTAURANTS
Mock Turtle - Tel (44) 01305 - 264 011 Dorchester 5 km
Perry's - Tel (44) 01305 - 785 799 — Weymouth 10 km

545

Another luxury golfing programme with a 125-room hotel. The first course has been open since 1993, the second has opened since summer of 1998, designed by Jack Nicklaus. The present course, laid out by Alan Higgins, represents eventually the second course but is already good enough to warrant a closer examination. It is wide enough to forgive a few errors of direction (except on the 6th and 8th holes) and can prove to be rather an instructive experience because six holes unwind through a forest, six have water and six are very open and so exposed to the wind. This is certainly no tournament course but it is very pleasant to play for all the family, even though you'll need a little patience with beginners (don't you always?) Wet in Winter and very dry in Summer, this is a site to visit in the Spring or Autumn. Practice facilities are excellent.

Encore un programme golfique de luxe, avec hôtel de 125 chambres. Le premier parcours est ouvert depuis 1993, le second est ouvert depuis l'été 1998, avec un excellent dessin de Jack Nicklaus. Le présent tracé de Alan Higgins devient ainsi le complément, mais sa qualité mérite que l'on s'y attarde. Sa largeur permet de pardonner quelques erreurs de direction, sauf aux 6 et 8. En fait, ce parcours s'est assez éducatif car six trous se déroulent dans les arbres, six avec de l'eau et six très ouverts, en particulier au vent. Ce n'est certes pas un parcours de grands championnats, mais un bon parcours très agréable, où toute la famille peut évoluer, même s'il faut un peu de patience avec les plus faibles (n'en faut-il pas toujours ?). Humide en hiver, très sec en été, c'est un site à visiter au printemps et en automne, où les installations d'entraînement sont excellentes.

Carden Park Hotel, Golf Resort & Spa
1993

ENG - CHESTER, Ches. CH3 9DQ

Office	Secrétariat	(44) 01829 - 731 630
Pro shop	Pro-shop	(44) 01829 - 731 500
Fax	Fax	(44) 01829 - 731 625
Situation	Situation	

25 km S of Chester (pop. 115 971) - 15 km W of Nantwich

Annual closure	Fermeture annuelle	no
Weekly closure	Fermeture hebdomadaire	no

Fees main season
Tarifs haute saison 18 holes

	Week days Semaine	We/Bank holidays We/Férié
Individual Individuel	£ 30	£ 30
Couple Couple	£ 60	£ 60

Caddy	Caddy	no
Electric Trolley	Chariot électrique	no
Buggy	Voiturette	£ 15/18 holes
Clubs	Clubs	£ 10/18 holes

Credit cards Cartes de crédit
VISA - Eurocard - MasterCard - AMEX - DC

546

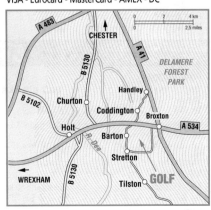

Access Accès : Chester, A41 → Whitchurch. Broxton roundabout, turn right onto A534 → Wrexham. Golf approx. 2.5 km (1.5 m) on left side.
Map 4 on page 494 Carte 4 Page 494

GOLF COURSE
PARCOURS
14/20

Site	Site	
Maintenance	Entretien	
Architect	Architecte	Alan Higgins
Type	Type	parkland
Relief	Relief	
Water in play	Eau en jeu	
Exp. to wind	Exposé au vent	
Trees in play	Arbres en jeu	

Scorecard Carte de score	Chp. Chp.	Mens Mess.	Ladies Da.
Length Long.	5907	5661	5100
Par	72	72	73

Advised golfing ability Niveau de jeu recommandé	0 12 24 36
Hcp required Handicap exigé	no

CLUB HOUSE & AMENITIES
CLUB HOUSE ET ANNEXES
8/10

Pro shop	Pro-shop	
Driving range	Practice	
Sheltered	couvert	13 bays
On grass	sur herbe	oppos. end of range
Putting-green	putting-green	yes
Pitching-green	pitching green	yes

HOTEL FACILITIES
ENVIRONNEMENT HOTELIER
8/10

HOTELS HÔTELS
Carden Park Hotel — on site
125 rooms, D £ 150 (all incl.)
Tel (44) 01829 - 731 000, Fax (44) 01829 - 731 032

Rowton Hall — Chester
42 rooms, D £ 90 — 10 km
Tel (44) 01244 - 335 262, Fax (44) 01244 - 335 464

Broxton Hall — near Chester
12 rooms, D £ 70 — 5 km
Tel (44) 01829 - 782 321, Fax (44) 01829 - 782 330

RESTAURANTS RESTAURANTS
Arkle — Chester
Tel (44) 01244 - 324 024 — 15 km

Crabwall Manor — Chester
Tel (44) 01244 - 851 666 — 15 km

Carden House — Chester
Tel (44) 01244 - 320 004 — 15 km

After Jack Nicklaus Jr., it's now brother Steve who works with dad in his course design business. They have added a second course at the "Cheshire" which, with an on-site hotel, is a great week-end destination. The only problem is the number of golfers here, compounded by the style of a course which is hardly conducive to quick play: water comes into play on more than half the holes. A meandering stream has resulted in double fairways on the 7th and 15th holes, where the risk you are about to take needs even more careful consideration than anywhere else on the course. This is Big Jack's famous "percentage golf". A few large trees complicate things still further, as do the very many bunkers, nearly all large but rather British in style. For once, the architect has not laid out his traditional bunkers with steep walls. Despite this hint of moderation, the course demands target golf, making it a tricky affair for lovers of bump 'n run shot or inveterate toppers of the ball.

Après Jack Nicklaus Jr, c'est le fils Steve qui travaille avec papa. Ils ont ajouté ici un second parcours. Avec l'hôtel sur place, c'est une bonne destination de week-end, mais il risque d'y avoir du monde, et le style du présent parcours ne favorise pas un jeu rapide, avec l'eau en jeu sur une dizaine de trous. Les méandres d'un cours d'eau ont permis de créer des double fairways au 7 et au 15, où l'on devra plus encore qu'ailleurs mesurer les risques avant de jouer : c'est le golf pourcentage cher à Nicklaus. Quelques grands arbres compliquent encore le jeu, ainsi que de nombreux bunkers, souvent grands mais de profils assez britanniques : pour une fois, l'architecte n'a pas trop plaqué ici ses bunkers traditionnels avec des parois abruptes. Malgré cette modération, ce parcours réclame un jeu de cible, ce qui le rend fort délicat pour les habitués du «bump n' run» et les joueurs sans grande expérience.

Carden Park Hotel, Golf Resort & Spa — 1998

ENG - CHESTER, Ches. CH3 9DQ

Office	Secrétariat	(44) 01829 - 731 630
Pro shop	Pro-shop	(44) 01829 - 731 500
Fax	Fax	(44) 01829 - 731 625
Situation	Situation	

25 km S of Chester - 15 km W of Nantwich (pop. 11 695)

Annual closure	Fermeture annuelle	no
Weekly closure	Fermeture hebdomadaire	no

Fees main season
Tarifs haute saison 18 holes

	Week days Semaine	We/Bank holidays We/Férié
Individual Individuel	£ 60*	£ 60*
Couple Couple	£ 120	£ 120

* GF includes buggy

Caddy	Caddy	no
Electric Trolley	Chariot électrique	no
Buggy	Voiturette	£ 15/18 holes
Clubs	Clubs	£ 10/18 holes

Credit cards Cartes de crédit
VISA - Eurocard - MasterCard - AMEX - DC

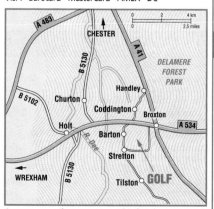

Access Accès : Chester, A41 → Whitchurch. Broxton roundabout, turn right onto A534 → Wrexham. Golf approx. 2.5 km (1.5 m) on left side.
Map 4 on page 494 Carte 4 Page 494

GOLF COURSE / PARCOURS — 17/20

Site	Site	▰▰▱▱
Maintenance	Entretien	▰▰▱▱
Architect	Architecte	Jack Nicklaus Steve Nicklaus
Type	Type	parkland, inland
Relief	Relief	▰▰▱▱
Water in play	Eau en jeu	▰▰▰▱
Exp. to wind	Exposé au vent	▰▰▱▱
Trees in play	Arbres en jeu	▰▰▰▱

Scorecard Carte de score	Chp. Chp.	Mens Mess.	Ladies Da.
Length Long.	6341	5672	4690
Par	72	72	72

Advised golfing ability		0 12 24 36
Niveau de jeu recommandé		
Hcp required	Handicap exigé	no

CLUB HOUSE & AMENITIES / CLUB HOUSE ET ANNEXES — 8/10

Pro shop	Pro-shop	▰▰▰▱
Driving range	Practice	▰▰▰▱
Sheltered	couvert	13 bays
On grass	sur herbe	oppos. end of range
Putting-green	putting-green	yes
Pitching-green	pitching green	yes

547

HOTEL FACILITIES / ENVIRONNEMENT HOTELIER — 8/10

HOTELS HÔTELS

Carden Park Hotel — on site
125 rooms, D £ 150 (all incl.)
Tel (44) 01829 - 731 000, Fax (44) 01829 - 731 032

Rowton Hall — Chester
42 rooms, D £ 90 — 10 km
Tel (44) 01244 - 335 262, Fax (44) 01244 - 335 464

Broxton Hall - 12 rooms, D £ 70 — near Chester
Tel (44) 01829 - 782 321, Fax (44) 01829 - 782 330 5 km

RESTAURANTS RESTAURANTS

Arkle - Tel (44) 01244 - 324 024 — Chester 15 km

Crabwall Manor
Tél(44) 01244 - 851 666 — Chester 15 km

Carden House
Tel (44) 01244 - 320 004 — Chester 15 km

As you drive up past the great links courses from Ayrshire to Carlisle and Scotland, forget the M6 motorway and keep to the A6, which crosses the breath-taking scenery of the Lake District and Hadrian's Wall. If it inspires you the way it inspired Keats, Wordsworth or Beatrix Potter, you could be in for a good day's golfing. Carlisle leaves no-one indifferent, and as this a Tom Simpson design, no-one will be too surprised about that. You will find his trade-mark cross-bunkers (Simpson hated topped shots), greens protected by bunkers on the one side, by bumps and hollows on the other, which offer their own particular brand of difficulty. Plus the never-ending need to think with a clear head on the length and direction of the ideal shot before choosing your club. The par 3s here are outstanding and the par 5s no less memorable. The only shortcoming might be the course's overall length, but hopefully would-be designers will think long and hard before making any alterations.

En remontant des grands links de l'Ayrshire vers Carlisle et l'Ecosse, renoncez à la M6 au profit de l'A6, qui traverse les paysages sublimes du Lake District puis le Mur d'Hadrien. Vous y trouverez peut-être l'inspiration, comme Keats, Wordsworth ou Beatrix Potter. Au moins pour le golf, car Carlisle n'est pas un parcours qui laisse indifférent. La signature de Tom Simpson est une garantie. Vous y trouverez ses cross-bunkers car il haïssait les balles toppées, les greens souvent défendus d'un côté par les bunkers, et de l'autre par des creux et des bosses d'où il n'est guère plus facile de jouer, plus la nécessité de réfléchir sur la longueur et la direction du coup idéal avant de choisir un club. Les par 3 sont ici exceptionnels, les par 5 non moins mémorables. Seul défaut, un certain manque de longueur, mais que l'on réfléchisse bien avant de toucher quoi que ce soit...

Carlisle Golf Club — 1909

Aglionby
ENG - CARLISLE, Cumbria CA4 8AG

Office	Secrétariat	(44) 01228 - 513 029
Pro shop	Pro-shop	(44) 01228 - 513 241
Fax	Fax	(44) 01228 - 513 303
Situation	Situation	

3 km from Carlisle (pop. 100 562)

Annual closure	Fermeture annuelle	no
Weekly closure	Fermeture hebdomadaire	no

Fees main season
Tarifs haute saison 18 holes

	Week days Semaine	We/Bank holidays We/Férié
Individual Individuel	£ 22	£ 30
Couple Couple	£ 44	£ 60

Full days: £ 33/£ 40 - No visitors on Saturdays

Caddy	Caddy	no
Electric Trolley	Chariot électrique	£ 5/18 holes
Buggy	Voiturette	£ 15/18 holes
Clubs	Clubs	no
Credit cards Cartes de crédit		no

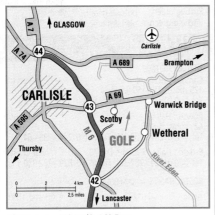

Access Accès : M6 Jct 43, A69 East,
Golf 1 km on the right.
Map 2 on page 491 Carte 2 Page 491

GOLF COURSE / PARCOURS — 17/20

Site	Site	
Maintenance	Entretien	
Architect	Architecte	Tom Simpson Mackenzie Ross
Type	Type	parkland
Relief	Relief	
Water in play	Eau en jeu	
Exp. to wind	Exposé au vent	
Trees in play	Arbres en jeu	

Scorecard Carte de score	Chp. Chp.	Mens Mess.	Ladies Da.
Length Long.	5601	5408	4945
Par	71	71	73

Advised golfing ability Niveau de jeu recommandé	0	12	24	36

Hcp required Handicap exigé — certificate

CLUB HOUSE & AMENITIES / CLUB HOUSE ET ANNEXES — 7/10

Pro shop	Pro-shop	
Driving range	Practice	
Sheltered	couvert	no
On grass	sur herbe	practice area
Putting-green	putting-green	yes
Pitching-green	pitching green	yes

HOTEL FACILITIES / ENVIRONNEMENT HOTELIER — 7/10

HOTELS HÔTELS

Crown Hotel — Wetheral
50 rooms, D £ 116 — 4 km
Tel (44) 01228 - 561 888, Fax (44) 01228 - 561 637

Cumbrian — Carlisle
70 rooms, D £ 95 — 5 km
Tel (44) 01228 - 31 951, Fax (44) 01228 - 47 799

Cumbria Park — Carlisle
49 rooms, D £ 82 — 5 km
Tel (44) 01228 - 22 887, Fax (44) 01228 - 514 796

Crown + Mitre — Carlisle
97 rooms, D £ 99 — 5 km
Tel (44) 01228 - 25 491, Fax (44) 01228 - 514 553

RESTAURANTS RESTAURANTS

No 10 - Tel (44) 01228 - 24 183 — Carlisle 5 km
Crown Hotel - Tel (44) 01228 - 561 888 — Wetheral 4 km

548

In the middle of the Irish Sea, the Isle of Man is reached by ferry or by air from Blackpool. Castletown is located on a sort of triangular-shaped peninsula surrounded by the sea. They say that on the 17th hole, you are driving in Ireland, Scotland, England or Wales. Whatever, this course is exposed to all winds and only the bunkers give any real shelter. Only a few small dunes and rocks give any relief to this flat, superbly-turfed landscape. After the war, Mackenzie Ross brought Castletown back to life with all the talent he showed at Turnberry and even a touch of genius. This is a golfer's paradise on the edge of a rock, but it can be hell if ever a storm sets in and sends players scampering to seek refuge in the hotel on the course. We would recommend a visit here on a fine summer's day.

En plein milieu de la mer d'Irlande, l'Ile de Man est accessible par ferry ou par avion depuis Blackpool. Castletown est situé sur une sorte de presqu'île en forme de triangle cerné par la mer : on dit que du 17, on peut driver en Irlande, en Ecosse, en Angleterre ou au Pays de Galles. En tout cas, ce parcours est ouvert à tous les vents, et seuls les bunkers forment vraiment des abris. Quelques petites dunes et quelques rochers donnent un semblant de relief à ce paysage plat, mais au gazon superbe. Après la guerre, Mackenzie Ross a rendu Castletown à la vie, avec autant de talent qu'à Turnberry, parfois même une forme de génie. C'est un paradis de golfeur sur un bout de rocher, que seule la tempête peut transformer en enfer, mais il ne reste plus alors qu'à se réfugier à l'hôtel sur le site. On conseillera plutôt de venir par une belle journée d'été.

Castletown Golf Club — 1892

Fort Island
ENG - CASTLETOWN, Isle of Man

Office	Secrétariat	(44) 01624 - 822 201
Pro shop	Pro-shop	(44) 01624 - 822 211
Fax	Fax	(44) 01624 - 824 633
Situation	Situation	

4.5 km E of Castletown (pop. 3 152)
15 km SW of Douglas (pop. 22 214)

Annual closure	Fermeture annuelle	no
Weekly closure	Fermeture hebdomadaire	no

Fees main season
Tarifs haute saison 18 holes

	Week days Semaine	We/Bank holidays We/Férié
Individual Individuel	£ 22.50	£ 27.50
Couple Couple	£ 45	£ 55

£ 13 after 4.00 pm

Caddy	Caddy	on request
Electric Trolley	Chariot électrique	£ 9/18 holes
Buggy	Voiturette	£ 20/18 holes
Clubs	Clubs	£ 8/18 holes

Credit cards Cartes de crédit
VISA - Eurocard - MasterCard - AMEX - DC

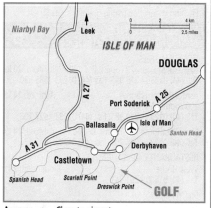

Access Accès : Close to airport
Map 9 on page 504 Carte 9 Page 504

GOLF COURSE PARCOURS — 18/20

Site	Site	■■■■■■□□
Maintenance	Entretien	■■■■■■□□
Architect	Architecte	Mackenzie Ross
Type	Type	seaside course, links
Relief	Relief	□□□□□
Water in play	Eau en jeu	□□□□□
Exp. to wind	Exposé au vent	■■■■□
Trees in play	Arbres en jeu	□□□□□

Scorecard Carte de score	Chp. Chp.	Mens Mess.	Ladies Da.
Length Long.	6040	5880	5072
Par	72	72	73

Advised golfing ability Niveau de jeu recommandé	0	12	24	36
Hcp required Handicap exigé	no			

CLUB HOUSE & AMENITIES CLUB HOUSE ET ANNEXES — 6/10

Pro shop	Pro-shop	■■■■■□
Driving range	Practice	■■■□□
Sheltered	couvert	no
On grass	sur herbe	practice ground only
Putting-green	putting-green	yes
Pitching-green	pitching green	yes

HOTEL FACILITIES ENVIRONNEMENT HOTELIER — 8/10

HOTELS HÔTELS
Links Hotel — Castletown on site
55 rooms, D £ 60
Tel (44) 01624 - 822 201, Fax (44) 01624 - 824 633

Empress — Douglas 15 km
99 rooms, D £ 65
Tel (44) 01624 - 661 155, Fax (44) 01624 - 673 554

Castle Mona — Douglas 15 km
66 rooms, D £ 48
Tel (44) 01624 - 624 540, Fax (44) 01624 - 675 360

RESTAURANTS RESTAURANTS
Chablis Cellar — Castletown 3 km
Tel (44) 01624 - 823 527

Swiss Chalet — Glen Helen 20 km
Tel (44) 01624 - 801 657

Links Hotel - Tel (44) 01624 - 822 201 Castletown, on site

549

They say you shouldn't always expect champions to be great course designers. Well here, Nick Faldo, backed by the top American specialist Steve Smyers, has produced a masterly layout. We admit that our very high score is intended more for experienced players, and many golfers find this course a little over-elaborate with a touch too much sand and water. Those who are afraid that their game might not be up to such a challenge should head shamelessly straight for the front tees. Only there will they learn how to tame a layout which is psychologically rather than really difficult. It was designed with brilliant, bold and uncompromising intelligence. Upholders of the British tradition for discreet courses will be a little surprised here, that's for sure, but you need visual and technical shocks such as this to keep your game moving. The overall excellence of this resort is outstanding.

On ne doit pas toujours espérer des champions qu'ils soient de grands architectes. Epaulé par l'excellent spécialiste américain Steve Smyers, Nick Faldo a réussi un coup de maître. Certes, notre note très favorable est plutôt destinée aux joueurs expérimentés, car beaucoup trouvent ce parcours «trop dessiné,» avec un rien trop de sable et un peu trop d'eau. Ceux qui ont peur que leur jeu ne soit pas à la hauteur des défis présentés choisiront sans honte les départs avancés, ils apprendront à apprivoiser ce tracé plus difficile psychologiquement que réellement, conçu avec une brillante intelligence, avec hardiesse, sans concessions. Certes, les tenants de la tradition britannique d'une architecture discrète seront ici surpris, mais il faut des chocs visuels et techniques de ce genre pour progresser. La qualité générale de ce complexe est exceptionnelle.

Chart Hills Golf Club — 1993
Weeks Lane
ENG - BIDDENDEN, Kent TN27 8JX

Office	Secrétariat	(44) 01580 - 292 222
Pro shop	Pro-shop	(44) 01580 - 292 148
Fax	Fax	(44) 01580 - 292 233
Situation	Situation	

14 km from Ashford (pop. 52 002) - 20 km from Maidstone

Annual closure	Fermeture annuelle	no
Weekly closure	Fermeture hebdomadaire	no
Fees main season	Tarifs haute saison	18 holes

	Week days Semaine	We/Bank holidays We/Férié
Individual Individuel	£ 60	£ 65
Couple Couple	£ 120	£ 130

Mondays & Saturdays: members only

Caddy	Caddy	on request/£ 15
Electric Trolley	Chariot électrique	no
Buggy	Voiturette	£ 20/18 holes
Clubs	Clubs	£ 10/18 holes

Credit cards Cartes de crédit VISA - MasterCard - AMEX

550

Access Accès : • M20, Jct 6 to Maidstone. A274 → Biddenden. After Headcorn, left at Petrol Station, signpost to Smarden • Ashford, A28 to Tenderden, A262 to Biddenden, A274 → Headcorn.
Map 7 on page 501 Carte 7 Page 501

GOLF COURSE PARCOURS — 18/20

Site	Site	
Maintenance	Entretien	
Architect	Architecte	Nick Faldo Steve Smyers
Type	Type	parkland, open country
Relief	Relief	
Water in play	Eau en jeu	
Exp. to wind	Exposé au vent	
Trees in play	Arbres en jeu	

Scorecard Carte de score	Chp. Chp.	Mens Mess.	Ladies Da.
Length Long.	6375	5780	4980
Par	72	72	72

Advised golfing ability — 0 12 24 36
Niveau de jeu recommandé
Hcp required — Handicap exigé — no

CLUB HOUSE & AMENITIES
CLUB HOUSE ET ANNEXES — 8/10

Pro shop	Pro-shop	
Driving range	Practice	
Sheltered	couvert	no
On grass	sur herbe	yes
Putting-green	putting-green	yes
Pitching-green	pitching green	yes (2)

HOTEL FACILITIES
ENVIRONNEMENT HOTELIER — 6/10

HOTELS HÔTELS
Eastwell Manor - 23 rooms, D £ 120   Ashford, 20 km
Tel (44) 01233 - 219 955, Fax (44) 01233 - 635 530

Ashford International   Ashford, 14 km
200 rooms, D £ 100
Tel (44) 01233 - 219 988, Fax (44) 01233 - 627 708

Forte Posthouse - 60 rooms, D £ 60   Ashford, 14 km
Tel (44) 01233 - 625 790, Fax (44) 01233 - 643 176

RESTAURANTS RESTAURANT
West House   Biddenden, 2 km
Tel (44) 01580 - 291 341

Star & Eagle
Tél(44) 01580 - 211 512   Goudhurst, 20 km

Eastwell Manor
Tel (44) 01233 - 219 955   Ashford, 14 km

Derbyshire is richly endowed with golf courses in the National Trust region of the Peak District. Admirers of old English mansions won't want to miss Chatsworth castle and the gardens of Capability Brown and Joseph Paxton. Despite the excellence of the site and the parkland style, this course cannot quite match their sophisticated landscaping, as golf architecture is more a matter of strategy than decoration. Although not one of Harry Colt's masterpieces, Chesterfield is a very pleasant course where strategy (see above!) is not always obvious, and where the sometimes hilly terrain calls for careful club selection. Very natural in its layout with some well-guarded greens that can nonetheless be reached in a variety of ways, this versatile course is well worth a round or two. You wouldn't want to play here for ever but it is a good addition to a golfing holiday in the region.

Le Comté de Derbyshire est bien fourni en parcours de golfs, dans cette région du Parc National de Peak District. Les amateurs de vieilles demeures anglaises ne manqueront pas le Château de Chatsworth, et notamment ses jardins de Capability Brown et Joseph Paxton. En dépit de la qualité de son site et de son aspect de grand parc, ce parcours ne saurait lutter avec leurs créations paysagères sophistiquées, l'architecture de golf étant plus affaire de stratégie que de décoration. Sans être un des grands chefs-d'oeuvre de Harry Colt, Chesterfield est un très agréable parcours, où la stratégie (justement) n'est pas toujours évidente, les quelques reliefs du terrain impliquant des ajustements de choix de club. Très naturel dans son aspect, avec des greens bien défendus, mais accessibles de différentes manières, ce parcours très «versatile» mérite que l'on s'y arrête, même si ce n'est pas pour toujours. C'est en tout cas un bon complément à un voyage golfique dans la région.

Chesterfield Golf Club 1897
ENG - WALTON, CHESTERFIELD, Derbyshire S42 7 LA

Office	Secrétariat	(44) 01246 - 279 256
Pro shop	Pro-shop	(44) 01246 - 276 297
Fax	Fax	(44) 01246 - 276 622
Situation	Situation	

3 km from Chesterfield (pop. 99 403)
20 km from Sheffield, (pop. 501 202)

Annual closure	Fermeture annuelle	no
Weekly closure	Fermeture hebdomadaire	no
Fees main season	Tarifs haute saison	18 holes

	Week days Semaine	We/Bank holidays We/Férié
Individual Individuel	£ 25	*
Couple Couple	£ 34	*

* Members only at week ends

Caddy	Caddy	no
Electric Trolley	Chariot électrique	no
Buggy	Voiturette	no
Clubs	Clubs	no

Credit cards Cartes de crédit
VISA - Eurocard - MasterCard - AMEX
(not for green fees)

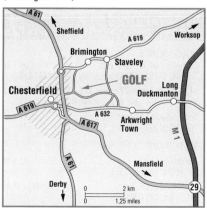

Access Accès : on A 632 (Matlock Road), 3 km from Chesterfield centre town
Map 4 on page 494 Carte 4 Page 494

GOLF COURSE
PARCOURS   13/20

Site	Site	
Maintenance	Entretien	
Architect	Architecte	Harry S. Colt
Type	Type	parkland
Relief	Relief	
Water in play	Eau en jeu	
Exp. to wind	Exposé au vent	
Trees in play	Arbres en jeu	

Scorecard Carte de score	Chp. Chp.	Mens Mess.	Ladies Da.
Length Long.	5635	5468	5029
Par	71	71	73

Advised golfing ability		0 12 24 36
Niveau de jeu recommandé		
Hcp required	Handicap exigé	certificate

CLUB HOUSE & AMENITIES
CLUB HOUSE ET ANNEXES   6/10

Pro shop	Pro-shop	
Driving range	Practice	
Sheltered	couvert	
On grass	sur herbe	yes
Putting-green	putting-green	yes
Pitching-green	pitching green	yes

551

HOTEL FACILITIES
ENVIRONNEMENT HOTELIER   7/10

HOTELS HÔTELS
Riber Hall   Matlock
11 rooms, D £ 145   10 km
Tel (44) 01629 - 582 795, Fax (44) 01629 - 580 475

Portland Hotel   Chesterfield
24 rooms, D £ 66   4 km
Tel (44) 01246 - 234 502, Fax (44) 01246 - 550 915

Sandpiper Hotel   Chesterfield
28 rooms, D £ 75   5 km
Tel (44) 01246 - 450 550, Fax (44) 01246 - 452 805

RESTAURANTS RESTAURANT
Swallow Hotel   South Normanton
Tel (44) 01773 - 812 000   10 km

Sitwell Arms   Renishaw
Tel (44) 01246 - 435 226   10 km

The fairways are carpeted with thick turf which prevents balls from ever rolling too far, trees abound but the fairways are wide and the rough not too severe. A few water hazards threaten and readily swallow up any miscued shots, but they are there to be seen and so won't cause any unpleasant surprises. As on many of James Braid's courses, a sharp short game is of the essence, as is skill in rolling the ball. This is another course that deserves rehabilitation, even if its short yardage may not always be to the liking of golfers who hit the ball a long way. But as long-hitters sometimes tend to hook the ball, the out-of-bounds areas down the left on the front 9 will teach them a little respect. The course's location on the edge of the forest of Bowland in the Ribble Valley makes this an ideal site for a few days off the beaten track exploring rivers, old villages, a Roman camp and an abbey or two.

Ce parcours bénéficie d'un gazon dense, ce qui évite aux balles de trop rouler. Les arbres sont très nombreux, mais les fairways sont larges et les roughs peu pénalisants. Quelques obstacles d'eau menacent ou retiennent quelques mauvais coups, mais ils sont bien visibles et ne sauraient causer de mauvaises surprises. De fait, comme sur de nombreux parcours de James Braid, il est essentiel d'avoir un bon petit jeu, en particulier savoir jouer les balles roulées. Encore un parcours à réhabiliter, même si sa longueur le fait regarder avec indifférence par les frappeurs. Comme ce sont souvent des «hookers,» les hors-limites à gauche à l'aller leur apprendront le respect. Sa situation en bordure de la forêt de Bowland, au coeur de la Ribble Valley, en fait un site idéal pour quelques jours hors des sentiers battus, à la découverte des rivières et vieux villages, d'un camp romain ou d'une abbaye.

Clitheroe Golf Club — 1932

Whalley Road
ENG - PENDLETON, Lancs BB7 1PP

Office	Secrétariat	(44) 01200 - 422 292
Pro shop	Pro-shop	(44) 01200 - 424 242
Fax	Fax	(44) 01200 - 422 292
Situation	Situation	

3 km S of Clitheroe (pop. 13 548)
15 km NE of Blackburn (pop. 136 612)

Annual closure	Fermeture annuelle	no
Weekly closure	Fermeture hebdomadaire	no

Fees main season
Tarifs haute saison full day

	Week days Semaine	We/Bank holidays We/Férié
Individual Individuel	£ 33	£ 39
Couple Couple	£ 66	£ 78
Caddy	Caddy	no
Electric Trolley	Chariot électrique	no
Buggy	Voiturette	no
Clubs	Clubs	no

Credit cards Cartes de crédit
VISA - Eurocard - MasterCard - AMEX - DC - JCB
(Pro shop goods only)

552

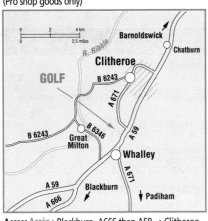

Access Accès : Blackburn, A666 then A59 → Clitheroe.
Golf 3 km on Whalley Road.
Map 4 on page 494 Carte 4 Page 494

GOLF COURSE
PARCOURS — 17/20

Site	Site	
Maintenance	Entretien	
Architect	Architecte	James Braid
Type	Type	parkland
Relief	Relief	
Water in play	Eau en jeu	
Exp. to wind	Exposé au vent	
Trees in play	Arbres en jeu	

Scorecard Carte de score	Chp. Chp.	Mens Mess.	Ladies Da.
Length Long.	5693	5490	4586
Par	71	71	74

Advised golfing ability Niveau de jeu recommandé	0	12	24	36

Hcp required	Handicap exigé	no

CLUB HOUSE & AMENITIES
CLUB HOUSE ET ANNEXES — 7/10

Pro shop	Pro-shop	
Driving range	Practice	
Sheltered	couvert	no
On grass	sur herbe	yes (3 areas)
Putting-green	putting-green	yes
Pitching-green	pitching green	yes

HOTEL FACILITIES
ENVIRONNEMENT HOTELIER — 7/10

HOTELS HÔTELS
Foxfields - 44 rooms, D £ 85 — Whalley 5 km
Tel (44) 01254 - 822 556, Fax (44) 01254 - 824 613

Mytton Old Farm - 27 rooms, D £ 70 — Whalley 5 km
Tel (44) 01254 - 240 662, Fax (44) 01254 - 248 119

Spread Eagle - 10 rooms, D £ 55 — Sawley 6 km
Tel (44) 01200 - 441 202, Fax (44) 01200 - 441 973

RESTAURANTS RESTAURANTS
Northcote Manor — Blackburn 8 km
Tel (44) 01254 - 240 555

Paul Heathcote's — Longridge 18 km
Tel (44) 01772 - 784 969

Auctioner - Tél(44) 01200 - 427 153 — Clitheroe 3 km

Foxfields — Whalley 5 km
Tel (44) 01254 - 822 556

A corner of the United States in England, a nice change of style for the English but continental Europeans might prefer a little more local colour. With water in play on eight of the 18 holes, numerous well-placed bunkers which lack the «feeling» of what a Simpson, a Colt or a Braid might have produced, and well-balanced difficulties geared to the very many different tee-boxes, Collingtree Park is a good, very pleasant and often very interesting American course but without the often acclaimed visual shocks. It doesn't always blend into the surrounding landscape as well as one might have wished. Johnny Miller was a great player but maybe we expected more of him as a course designer. Problems with the greens probably also weighed in our judgment. At all events, there is no disputing the excellence of practice facilities and services on offer.

Un coin d'Etats-Unis en Angleterre, c'est dépaysant pour les Anglais, mais les continentaux attendent plus de couleur locale. Avec de l'eau en jeu sur huit des 18 trous, des bunkers nombreux, et bien placés, mais aux formes moins «sensuelles» que les créations de Simpson, Braid ou Colt, des difficultés bien balancées suivant les différents (et nombreux) départs, Collingtree Park est un bon parcours à l'américaine, très agréable et souvent très intéressant, mais sans les chocs visuels qui emportent totalement l'adhésion. Son intégration à la nature environnante n'est pas toujours aussi complète qu'on le souhaiterait. Johnny Miller a été un très grand joueur de golf, mais on attendait peut-être davantage de lui comme architecte... Et les problèmes des greens influencent sans doute notre jugement. En tout cas, la qualité remarquable des installations d'entraînement et des services offerts est incontestable.

Collingtree Park Golf Club — 1987

Windingbrook Lane
ENG - NORTHAMPTON NN4 0XN

Office	Secrétariat	(44) 01604 - 700 000
Pro shop	Pro-shop	(44) 01604 - 700 000
Fax	Fax	(44) 01604 - 700 000
Situation	Situation	

10 km from Northampton (pop. 180 567)

Annual closure	Fermeture annuelle	no
Weekly closure	Fermeture hebdomadaire	no

Fees main season
Tarifs haute saison 18 holes

	Week days Semaine	We/Bank holidays We/Férié
Individual Individuel	£ 30	£ 40
Couple Couple	£ 60	£ 80

Booking necessary

Caddy	Caddy	no
Electric Trolley	Chariot électrique	no
Buggy	Voiturette	£ 20/18 holes
Clubs	Clubs	£ 15/18 holes

Credit cards Cartes de crédit
VISA - Eurocard - MasterCard - AMEX - DC

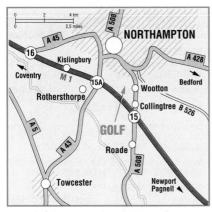

Access Accès : M1 Jct 15, then A508 → Northampton.
10 mins drive, golf on left.
Map 7 on page 500 Carte 7 Page 500

GOLF COURSE / PARCOURS — 14/20

Site	Site	
Maintenance	Entretien	
Architect	Architecte	Johnny Miller
Type	Type	parkland
Relief	Relief	
Water in play	Eau en jeu	
Exp. to wind	Exposé au vent	
Trees in play	Arbres en jeu	

Scorecard Carte de score	Chp. Chp.	Mens Mess.	Ladies Da.
Length Long.	6217	5598	4860
Par	72	72	73

Advised golfing ability Niveau de jeu recommandé	0 12 24 36
Hcp required Handicap exigé	no

CLUB HOUSE & AMENITIES / CLUB HOUSE ET ANNEXES — 8/10

Pro shop	Pro-shop	
Driving range	Practice	
Sheltered	couvert	16 bays (floodlit)
On grass	sur herbe	yes
Putting-green	putting-green	yes
Pitching-green	pitching green	yes

HOTEL FACILITIES / ENVIRONNEMENT HOTELIER — 7/10

553

HOTELS HÔTELS
Stakis Hotel — Northampton
139 rooms, D £ 101 — 1 km
Tel (44) 01604 - 700 666, Fax (44) 01604 - 702 850

Swallow - 120 rooms, D £ 115 — Northampton 10 km
Tel (44) 01604 - 768 700, Fax (44) 01604 - 769 011

Courtyard (Marriott) — Northampton 10 km
104 rooms, D £ 80
Tel (44) 01604 - 22 777, Fax (44) 01604 - 35 454

Lime Trees - 25 rooms, D £ 60 — Northampton 10 km
Tel (44) 01604 - 32 188, Fax (44) 01604 - 233 012

RESTAURANTS RESTAURANTS
La Fontana (Swallow) — Northampton 10 km
Tel (44) 01604 - 768 700

Roadhouse - Tel (44) 01604 - 863 372 — Roade 6 km

French Partridge - Tel (44) 01604 - 870 033 — Horton 7 km

COXMOOR

15 6 6

With Notts, Sherwood Forest and Coxmoor, this region has three no-nonsense courses, of which the latter lies over moorland and is hilly enough to test your fitness as well as your golfing skills. A good score is there for the taking as long as you avoid the traps on some of the dog-leg holes or carry a number of dangerous hazards, but there could be some nasty surprises in store when you come to add up your score. Strategy here is even more important than the standard of your game and the hazards are generally in clear view from the many elevated teeboxes. Very pleasant to play with the family or friends, there is an obvious parallel to be drawn with the many similar courses found in Surrey, the one reservation being the sameness of several holes.

Entre Notts, Sherwood Forest et Coxmoor, cette région dispose de trois parcours peu contestables. Celui-ci est dans un espace de landes, et assez accidenté pour tester la forme physique autant que golfique. Un bon score est à votre portée du moment que vous savez déjouer les pièges de certains doglegs ou survoler quelques obstacles dangereux, mais on peut avoir des surprises au moment de l'addition. La stratégie est ici encore plus importante que la qualité du jeu, et les obstacles sont généralement visibles car beaucoup de départs sont en hauteur. Très agréable à jouer avec des amis ou en famille, que ce soit en stroke play ou en match-play, ce parcours est à mettre en parallèle avec de nombreux parcours similaires du Surrey, avec une petite restriction sur la similarité de plusieurs trous, qui gêne la précision des souvenirs.

Coxmoor Golf Club — 1913

Coxmoor Road
ENG - SUTTON-IN- ASHFIELD, Notts. NG17 5LF

Office	Secrétariat	(44) 01623 - 557 359
Pro shop	Pro-shop	(44) 01623 - 559 906
Fax	Fax	(44) 01623 - 559 854
Situation	Situation	

7 km from Mansfield

Annual closure	Fermeture annuelle	no
Weekly closure	Fermeture hebdomadaire	no

Fees main season	Tarifs haute saison	18 holes
	Week days Semaine	**We/Bank holidays** We/Férié
Individual Individuel	£ 28	—
Couple Couple	£ 56	—

27 holes: £ 36 - Full weekday: £ 40 - No visitors Tuesdays & w/ends

Caddy	Caddy	no
Electric Trolley	Chariot électrique	no
Buggy	Voiturette	no
Clubs	Clubs	no

Credit cards Cartes de crédit
Visa - Eurocard - Mastercard - Amex - Switch
(not for green fees)

554

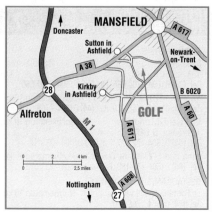

Access Accès : M1 Jct 27. A608 then A611 → Coxmoor
Map 4 on page 494 Carte 4 Page 494

GOLF COURSE PARCOURS — **15**/20

Site	Site	
Maintenance	Entretien	
Architect	Architecte	Unknown
Type	Type	parkland, heathland
Relief	Relief	
Water in play	Eau en jeu	
Exp. to wind	Exposé au vent	
Trees in play	Arbres en jeu	

Scorecard Carte de score	Chp. Chp.	Mens Mess.	Ladies Da.
Length Long.	5914	5626	4936
Par	73	73	74

Advised golfing ability	0	12	24	36
Niveau de jeu recommandé				
Hcp required Handicap exigé	no			

CLUB HOUSE & AMENITIES CLUB HOUSE ET ANNEXES — **6**/10

Pro shop	Pro-shop	
Driving range	Practice	
Sheltered	couvert	practice area
On grass	sur herbe	yes
Putting-green	putting-green	yes
Pitching-green	pitching green	yes

HOTEL FACILITIES ENVIRONNEMENT HOTELIER — **6**/10

HOTELS HÔTELS
Pine Lodge - 20 rooms, D £ 60 — Mansfield 4 km
Tel (44) 01623 - 622 308

Swallow - 157 rooms, D £ 120 — South Normanton
Tel (44) 01773 - 812 000 — 10 km
Fax (44) 01773 - 580 032

Royal Moat House — Nottingham
200 rooms, D £ 100 — 20 km
Tel (44) 0115 - 936 9988, Fax (44) 0115 - 475 667

Stage Hotel - 52 rooms, D £ 53 — Nottingham 20 km
Tel (44) 0115 - 960 3261, Fax (44) 0115 - 969 1040

RESTAURANTS RESTAURANTS
Swallow — South Normanton 10 km
Tel (44) 01773 - 812 000

Sonny's — Nottingham
Tel (44) 0115 - 947 3041 — 20 km

CUMBERWELL PARK

From the back tees, this is a tough course with at least two par 5s that are definitely unreachable in two. The designer made up for this, though, by refusing those huge par 3s and preferring shorter but more technical holes. With four short par 4s, you'll find a good number of opportunities to scent some of those evasive birdies. Adrian Stiff has cleverly combined stress and relaxation. In doing so, he has made Cumberwell Park a very pleasant course to play over gently rolling landscape, dotted with elm and oak trees and crossed by a stream that is very much a part of your game. The terrain has been carefully contoured, without overdoing the visual side but with extra concern for enhancing the course within its environment. For the time being, this promising layout is good value for money and its success has prompted the promoters to begin building a second course. The clubhouse extends a warm welcome and the practice facilities are well above the norm for the UK.

Des départs arrière, c'est un parcours solide, avec au moins deux par 5 pratiquement intouchables en deux, mais l'architecte a compensé en renonçant à ces par 3 interminables, au profit de petits trous plus techniques. Avec quatre par 4 courts, les occasions de birdie ne manqueront pas. Adrian Stiff a bien alterné la tension et la détente, ce qui rend Cumberwell Park très agréable à jouer, dans ce paysage gentiment vallonné et orné de chênes et de pins, où circule un cours d'eau bien mis en jeu. Le modelage du terrain a été fait avec soin, sans excès visuels, mais avec un bon souci de mettre en valeur le parcours dans son environnement. Cette réalisation prometteuse présente pour l'instant un bon rapport qualité/prix, et son succès a incité les promoteurs à entreprendre la construction d'un second parcours. Le Clubhouse est accueillant, les installations de practice très au-dessus des normes britanniques.

Cumberwell Park Golf Club — 1994
ENG - BRADFORD-ON-AVON, Wiltshire, BA15 2PQ

Office	Secrétariat	(44) 01225 - 863 322
Pro shop	Pro-shop	(44) 01225 - 862 332
Fax	Fax	(44) 01225 - 868 160
Situation	Situation	

8 km E of Bath (pop. 78 689)

Annual closure	Fermeture annuelle	no
Weekly closure	Fermeture hebdomadaire	no

Fees main season
Tarifs haute saison 18 holes

	Week days Semaine	We/Bank holidays We/Férié
Individual Individuel	£ 18	£ 25
Couple Couple	£ 36	£ 50

Full day: £ 25 - £ 40 (weekends)

Caddy	Caddy	no
Electric Trolley	Chariot électrique	no
Buggy	Voiturette	£ 15/18 holes
Clubs	Clubs	£ 10/18 holes

Credit cards Cartes de crédit
VISA - MasterCard (Pro shop goods & restaurant only)

Access Accès : On A363 between Bathford and Bradford-on-Avon **Map 6 on page 499** Carte 6 Page 499

GOLF COURSE / PARCOURS — 17/20

Site	Site	
Maintenance	Entretien	
Architect	Architecte	Adrian Stiff
Type	Type	parkland
Relief	Relief	
Water in play	Eau en jeu	
Exp. to wind	Exposé au vent	
Trees in play	Arbres en jeu	

Scorecard Carte de score	Chp. Chp.	Mens Mess.	Ladies Da.
Length Long.	6218	5902	5070
Par	72	72	72

Advised golfing ability Niveau de jeu recommandé	0 12 24 36
Hcp required Handicap exigé	certificate

CLUB HOUSE & AMENITIES / CLUB HOUSE ET ANNEXES — 7/10

Pro shop	Pro-shop	
Driving range	Practice	
Sheltered	couvert	yes
On grass	sur herbe	yes
Putting-green	putting-green	yes
Pitching-green	pitching green	yes

555

HOTEL FACILITIES / ENVIRONNEMENT HOTELIER — 7/10

HOTELS HÔTELS
Widbrook Grange — Bradford-on-Avon
19 rooms, D £ 90 — 3 km
Tel (44) 01225 - 863 173, Fax (44) 01225 - 862 890

The Lodge — Bathford
11 rooms, from D £ 70 — 8 km
Tel (44) 01225 - 858 467, Fax (44) 01225 - 858 172

Old School House — Bathford
4 rooms, D £ 70 — 8 km
Tel (44) 01225 - 859 593, Fax (44) 01225 - 859 590

RESTAURANTS RESTAURANTS
Hole in the Wall — Bath
Tel (44) 01225 - 425 242 — 12 km

Olive Tree — Bath
Tel (44) 01225 - 447 928 — 12 km

DARTMOUTH

Together with Bowood, this is one of the most promising new courses in this very romantic region of moor-land and heathland. It is also as surprising as the gardens of neighbouring Torquay might appear to foreign visitors... they would do the French Riviera proud. This new course is an inland and rather hilly layout (buggy highly recommended, and the club has 30 for hire). Designer Jeremy Pern has created many very good courses on the continent of Europe (particularly in France) but this is probably one of his very best. He has used land very cleverly indeed, forcing players from the back-tees to carry the ball a long way, particularly to clear the many water hazards. First time out, this is your typical match-play course. The clubhouse (with cottages) is remarkably well equipped with a pool, sauna, jacuzzi and gymnasium.

Avec Bowood, c'est l'une des réalisations prometteuses dans cette région très romantique aux paysages de landes, mais souvent aussi surprenante que les jardins de Torquay, dignes de la Riviera française, à quelques kilomètres de Dartmouth, d'où partirent les navires des croisades. Ce nouveau parcours est à l'intérieur des terres, et assez accidenté pour ne pas avoir honte d'emprunter une voiturette (il y en a ici plus de 30). L'architecte Jeremy Pern a fait de nombreux très bons parcours sur le continent (en France notamment), et celui-ci est sans doute l'un de ses tout meilleurs, notamment par l'utilisation très intelligente du terrain, obligeant à porter loin la balle des départs arrière, en particulier au-dessus des nombreux obstacles d'eau. La première fois, c'est le parcours de match-play typique. Le Clubhouse (avec cottages) est remarquablement équipé, avec piscine, sauna, jaccuzi et gymnase.

Dartmouth Golf & Country Club — 1992

Blackawton
ENG - TOTNES, Devon TQ9 7 DE

Office	Secrétariat	(44) 01803 - 712 686
Pro shop	Pro-shop	(44) 01803 - 712 650
Fax	Fax	(44) 01803 - 712 628
Situation	Situation	

12 km S of Totnes (pop. 7 018)
4 km W of Dartmouth (pop. 5 712)

Annual closure	Fermeture annuelle	no
Weekly closure	Fermeture hebdomadaire	no

Fees main season
Tarifs haute saison full day

	Week days Semaine	We/Bank holidays We/Férié
Individual Individuel	£ 25	£ 40
Couple Couple	£ 50	£ 80

Caddy	Caddy	£ 20/18 holes
Electric Trolley	Chariot électrique	no
Buggy	Voiturette	£ 18/18 holes
Clubs	Clubs	£ 10/18 holes

Credit cards Cartes de crédit
VISA - MasterCard (Pro shop goods only)

556

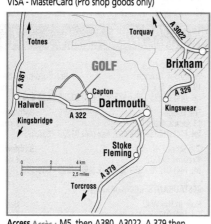

Access Accès : M5, then A380, A3022, A 379 then A3122. Golf on right hand side.
Map 6 on page 499 Carte 6 Page 499

GOLF COURSE
PARCOURS — 16/20

Site	Site	
Maintenance	Entretien	
Architect	Architecte	Jeremy Pern
Type	Type	parkland, hilly
Relief	Relief	
Water in play	Eau en jeu	
Exp. to wind	Exposé au vent	
Trees in play	Arbres en jeu	

Scorecard Carte de score	Chp. Chp.	Mens Mess.	Ladies Da.
Length Long.	6544	6064	5169
Par	72	72	73

Advised golfing ability		0 12 24 36
Niveau de jeu recommandé		
Hcp required	Handicap exigé	certificate

CLUB HOUSE & AMENITIES
CLUB HOUSE ET ANNEXES — 9/10

Pro shop	Pro-shop	
Driving range	Practice	
Sheltered	couvert	4 bays
On grass	sur herbe	no
Putting-green	putting-green	yes
Pitching-green	pitching green	yes

HOTEL FACILITIES
ENVIRONNEMENT HOTELIER — 6/10

HOTELS HÔTELS
Fingals (Old Coombe Farm)   Dittisham
9 rooms, D £ 75   6 km
Tel (44) 01803 - 722 398, Fax (44) 01803 - 722 401

Royal Castle   Dartmouth
25 rooms, D £ 100   8 km
Tel (44) 01803 - 833 033, Fax (44) 01803 - 835 445

Dart Marina   Dartmouth
35 rooms, D £ 75   8 km
Tel (44) 01803 - 832 580, Fax (44) 01803 - 835 040

RESTAURANTS RESTAURANTS
Carved Angel   Dartmouth
Tel (44) 01803 - 832 465   8 km

Billy Budd's   Dartmouth
Tel (44) 01803 - 834 842   8 km

Here we are at the traditional heart of England and this layout seems to be so symbolic of old English golf that even the card still uses the old term «bogey» instead of «par». It is rather as if the course were gently reminding you that you shouldn't expect miracles on the tougher holes. Let's forget that this should be a par 69 and be proud of playing to our handicap. Designed by Herbert Fowler, this is the perfect heathland course with just the right amount of trees, bunkers (sometimes very deep), heather, a splattering of water and the contours to test your legs and pose a few problems of kicks left and right. There is nothing easy about it, but nothing impossible, either. You can pitch your approach or, preferably, roll it onto the green. Golf here is built into nature and the two lie very comfortably together.

C'est ici le coeur traditionnel de l'Angleterre, et ce parcours est comme le symbole des parcours de golf anglais, au point que la carte de score porte le terme «bogey» au lieu de par, comme pour souligner avec indulgence que l'on n'attend pas de miracles sur les trous difficiles. Oublions donc que ce devrait être un par 69, et soyons fier de jouer notre handicap. Dessiné par Herbert Fowler, c'est le parfait parcours de bruyère, avec les arbres qu'il faut, les bunkers qu'il faut (parfois très profonds), la bruyère bien sûr, quelques soupçons d'eau, des reliefs pour tester les jambes et poser quelques problèmes de rebonds. Rien de facile mais rien d'impossible. On peut y jouer des coups levés, mais plutôt des balles roulées. Le golf est ici logé dans la nature, et il s'y trouve bien à l'aise.

Delamere Forest Golf Club — 1910

Station Road, Delamere
ENG - NORTHWICH, Cheshire CW8 2JE

Office	Secrétariat	(44) 01606 - 883 264
Pro shop	Pro-shop	(44) 01606 - 883 307
Fax	Fax	
Situation	Situation	

23 km E of Chester (pop.115 971)

Annual closure	Fermeture annuelle	no
Weekly closure	Fermeture hebdomadaire	no

Fees main season
Tarifs haute saison 18 holes

	Week days Semaine	We/Bank holidays We/Férié
Individual Individuel	£ 30	£ 35
Couple Couple	£ 60	£ 70

Full weekdays: £ 40 - No 3 or 4-balls on w/ends - No visitors on medal day.

Caddy	Caddy	no
Electric Trolley	Chariot électrique	no
Buggy	Voiturette	no
Clubs	Clubs	£ 10/18 holes

Credit cards Cartes de crédit
Visa - Mastercard (Pro shop goods only)

Access Accès : M6 Jct 19, then A556 → Chester. Golf on right side.
Map 4 on page 494 Carte 4 Page 494

GOLF COURSE / PARCOURS — 15/20

Site	Site	
Maintenance	Entretien	
Architect	Architecte	Herbert Fowler
Type	Type	parkland, heathland
Relief	Relief	
Water in play	Eau en jeu	
Exp. to wind	Exposé au vent	
Trees in play	Arbres en jeu	

Scorecard Carte de score	Chp. Chp.	Mens Mess.	Ladies Da.
Length Long.	5463	5463	4972
Par	72	72	72

Advised golfing ability Niveau de jeu recommandé	0	12	24	36

Hcp required Handicap exigé no

CLUB HOUSE & AMENITIES / CLUB HOUSE ET ANNEXES — 6/10

Pro shop	Pro-shop	
Driving range	Practice	
Sheltered	couvert	no
On grass	sur herbe	yes
Putting-green	putting-green	yes
Pitching-green	pitching green	no

557

HOTEL FACILITIES / ENVIRONNEMENT HOTELIER — 7/10

HOTELS HÔTELS
Nunsmere Hall — Sandiway
31 rooms, D £ 120 — 2 km
Tel (44) 01606 - 543 000, Fax (44) 01606 - 889 055

Hartford Hall — Northwich
20 rooms, D £ 65 — 5 km
Tel (44) 01606 - 75 711, Fax (44) 01606 - 782 285

Rookery Hall — Nantwich
45 rooms, D £ 95 — 20 km
Tel (44) 01270 - 610 016, Fax (44) 01270 - 626 027

Oaklands - 11 rooms, D £ 55 — Weaverham 5 km
Tel (44) 01606 - 853 249, Fax (44) 01606 - 852 419

RESTAURANTS RESTAURANTS
Arkle - Tel (44) 01244 - 324 024 — Chester 22 km
Garden House — Chester
Tel (44) 01244 - 320 004 — 22 km

Along with Aberdovey, this is one of the few golf courses to have its own railway station. It also has the type of Clubhouse architecture that reminds you very much of a country residence, and, last but not least, is the type of course that makes you want to take up golf and continue playing for ever. There is nothing particularly spectacular about it, but no Harry Colt course is ever bland. It also has its share of clichés that are typical of other courses he has designed. Here, there are some cleverly placed bunkers but which never bar the entrance to greens (except on the 11th hole), trees but no forest, no hidden terrors, no heather to bury your ball in and no water hazards. It is also a nice length for players who will never hit it as far as Tiger Woods even if they do use high-tech drivers. A course is always an adversary, but this one is fair and most likeable.

C'est un des seuls golfs, avec Aberdovey, qui dispose de sa propre station de chemin de fer. Il a aussi ce genre de Clubhouse dont l'architecture vous donne des idées de maison de campagne. Et c'est enfin le genre de parcours qui donne envie de commencer le golf, et de continuer à l'aimer au point de devenir un jour «oldest member» quelque part. Il n'a rien de très spectaculaire, mais un tracé de Harry Colt n'est jamais banal, même s'il existe des «clichés,» typiques d'autres parcours qu'il a dessiné. Ici, il y a des bunkers bien placés mais pas en travers de la route du green (sauf au 11), des arbres mais pas de forêt, rien d'horrible n'est caché, il n'y a pas de bruyère pour happer les balles, pas d'obstacles d'eau, et la longueur est très favorable aux joueurs qui n'auront jamais la puissance de Tiger Woods, même avec un driver high-tech. Si le parcours est l'adversaire du golfeur, Denham est un «jolly good fellow.»

Denham Golf Club — 1910

Tilehouse Lane
ENG - DENHAM, Bucks UB9 5DE

Office	Secrétariat	(44) 01895 - 832 022
Pro shop	Pro-shop	(44) 01895 - 832 801
Fax	Fax	(44) 01895 - 835 340
Situation	Situation	

8 km from Slough (pop. 101 066)
25 km from Central London (pop. 6 679 700)

Annual closure	Fermeture annuelle	no
Weekly closure	Fermeture hebdomadaire	no

Christmas Day only

Fees main season Tarifs haute saison — 18 holes

	Week days Semaine	We/Bank holidays We/Férié
Individual Individuel	£ 35	-
Couple Couple	£ 70	-

Full weekday: £ 50 each - No visitors at weekends

Caddy	Caddy	on request/£ 25
Electric Trolley	Chariot électrique	£ 6/18 holes
Buggy	Voiturette	no
Clubs	Clubs	£ 5/18 holes

Credit cards Cartes de crédit — no

Access Accès : M40, Jct 1, A40 → Gerrards Cross, then A412 → Watford. 2nd left to Club house.
Map 8 on page 502 Carte 8 Page 502

GOLF COURSE / PARCOURS — 15/20

Site	Site	
Maintenance	Entretien	
Architect	Architecte	Harry S. Colt
Type	Type	parkland
Relief	Relief	
Water in play	Eau en jeu	
Exp. to wind	Exposé au vent	
Trees in play	Arbres en jeu	

Scorecard Carte de score	Chp. Chp.	Mens Mess.	Ladies Da.
Length Long.	5806	5543	5014
Par	70	70	72

Advised golfing ability
Niveau de jeu recommandé — 0 12 24 36

Hcp required Handicap exigé — 28 Men, 36 Ladies

CLUB HOUSE & AMENITIES / CLUB HOUSE ET ANNEXES — 7/10

Pro shop	Pro-shop	
Driving range	Practice	
Sheltered	couvert	practice area
On grass	sur herbe	yes
Putting-green	putting-green	yes
Pitching-green	pitching green	yes

HOTEL FACILITIES / ENVIRONNEMENT HOTELIER — 7/10

HOTELS HÔTELS

De Vere Bull — Gerrards Cross
93 rooms, D £ 140 — 5 km
Tel (44) 01753 - 885 995, Fax (44) 01753 - 885 504

Copthorne — Slough
217 rooms, D £ 120 — 11 km
Tel (44) 01753 - 516 222, Fax (44) 01753 - 516 237

Courtyard — Slough
148 rooms, D £ 85 — 11 km
Tel (44) 01753 - 551 551, Fax (44) 01753 - 553 333

RESTAURANTS RESTAURANT

Water Hall — Chalfont St Peter
Tel (44) 01494 - 873 430 — 3 km

Roberto's - Tel (44) 01895 - 632 519 — Ickenham 6 km

Waterfront Brasserie — Yiewsley
Tel (44) 0181 - 899 1733 — 10 km

EAST DEVON

This is as if a typical Surrey or Berkshire course had been transplanted to the West country. On the cliff tops here, you would think you were playing at Walton Heath or the Berkshire, complete with tall pine-trees, birch trees and gorse. The marine landscape is something of a bonus, rather like the flowers in Spring. Forgetting the unquestionable visual appeal, East Devon is a very good course where, from the back-tees at least, you need a good solid hit, a long carry and some basic skills in flighting the ball through the wind, as the normally harmless hazards (from the front tees) can come dangerously into play. The course is not too hilly but there are still four blind greens and two others that are elevated. Good, accurate players will enjoy themselves (especially between holes 6 and 9) but the higher-handicappers might not enjoy tangling with the gorse and heather on the tougher holes. At least their golfing superiors will have every opportunity to teach them a thing or two about the tactics of golf.

Au sommet de la falaise, on pourrait parfois se croire parfois dans le Surrey ou le Berkshire, quand la bruyère, les grands pins, les bouleaux, les buissons d'ajoncs rappellent Walton Heath ou The Berkshire : les paysages marins sont un cadeau supplémentaire, tout comme les fleurs au printemps. Tout plaisir visuel mis à part, c'est un très bon parcours, où il faut parfois porter solidement la balle depuis les départs arrière du moins, travailler ses balles dans le vent car les obstacles normalement inoffensifs peuvent venir en jeu. Le relief n'est pas trop prononcé, mais il y a quatre greens aveugles et deux autres en élévation. Les joueurs précis prendront pas mal de plaisir ici (entre le 6 et le 9 en particulier), mais les hauts handicaps risquent d'avoir quelques problèmes avec la bruyère et les trous les plus difficiles. Cela dit, leurs aînés en golf se feront un plaisir de les faire profiter de leur expérience tactique du jeu.

The East Devon Golf Club — 1902

North View Road
ENG - BUDLEIGH SALTERTON, Devon EX 9 6DR

Office	Secrétariat	(44) 01395 - 443 370
Pro shop	Pro-shop	(44) 01395 - 445 195
Fax	Fax	(44) 01395 - 445 547
Situation	Situation	

2 km from Exmouth (pop. 30 386)
10 km from Exeter (pop. 98 125)

Annual closure	Fermeture annuelle	no
Weekly closure	Fermeture hebdomadaire	Monday

Fees main season
Tarifs haute saison 18 holes

	Week days Semaine	We/Bank holidays We/Férié
Individual Individuel	£ 27	£ 35
Couple Couple	£ 54	£ 70

Full day : £ 35/£42

Caddy	Caddy	no
Electric Trolley	Chariot électrique	£ 8
Buggy	Voiturette	no
Clubs	Clubs	£ 10

Credit cards Cartes de crédit — no

Access Accès : M5 Jct 30, Exmouth A370 onto B3179 Budleigh Satterton, to T Jct. Turn right onto B373C, then B3173. Club on the right hand side before town, on Links Road. **Map 6 on page 499** Carte 6 Page 499

GOLF COURSE / PARCOURS — 16/20

Site	Site	
Maintenance	Entretien	
Architect	Architecte	Unknown
Type	Type	seaside course, heathland
Relief	Relief	
Water in play	Eau en jeu	
Exp. to wind	Exposé au vent	
Trees in play	Arbres en jeu	

Scorecard Carte de score	Chp. Chp.	Mens Mess.	Ladies Da.
Length Long.	5616	5301	0
Par	70	70	0

Advised golfing ability Niveau de jeu recommandé		0 12 24 36
Hcp required Handicap exigé	certificate	

CLUB HOUSE & AMENITIES / CLUB HOUSE ET ANNEXES — 6/10

Pro shop	Pro-shop	
Driving range	Practice	
Sheltered	couvert	
On grass	sur herbe	yes
Putting-green	putting-green	yes
Pitching-green	pitching green	yes

559

HOTEL FACILITIES / ENVIRONNEMENT HOTELIER — 7/10

HOTELS HÔTELS

Imperial — Exmouth
57 rooms, D £ 85 — 4 km
Tel (44) 01395 - 274 761, Fax (44) 01395 - 265 161

Barn — Exmouth
11 rooms, D £ 64 — 3 km
Tel (44) 01395 - 224 411, Fax (44) 01395 - 224 411

Long Range — Budleigh Salterton
6 rooms, D £ 43 — 1 km
Tel (44) 01395 - 443 321

Belmont — Sidmouth
51 rooms, D £ 232 — 10 km
Tel (44) 01395 - 512 555, Fax (44) 01395 - 579 101

RESTAURANTS RESTAURANT

River House — Lympstone
Tel (44) 01395 - 265 147 — 8 km

This is a 36-hole complex, although the more intimate «West» course is reserved more for members. The «East» course is more like a tournament layout with mounds designed for spectators. Designed by the very talented Robert Cupp, the American style is never too loud and you can even sometimes roll your ball onto the green. The many different tee-boxes add to the variety and allow you to approach the course with the caution it deserves first time out, as some of the hazards are hard to spot and game strategy requires some careful thought. Start with a round of match-play, an excellent idea especially since the finishing holes are very impressive. The appeal of the site is supplemented by the hotel on site, a superb driving range and a huge clubhouse.

Cet ensemble comprend 36 trous, mais le parcours «Ouest,» plus intime, est à priori réservé aux membres. Celui-ci ressemble davantage à un parcours de tournoi, avec des buttes prévues pour accueillir des spectateurs. Dessiné par le très talentueux Robert Cupp, le style américain n'est pourtant pas trop agressif, il est parfois même possible d'arriver en roulant sur les greens. La multiplicité des départs permet de renouveler chaque fois les plaisirs, mais aussi, la première fois, de reconnaître prudemment le parcours, car certains obstacles sont peu visibles, et la stratégie du jeu réclame aussi quelque réflexion. Commencer par jouer en match-play sera d'autant plus agréable que le «finish» est excellent. Pour situer la séduction du lieu, ajoutons l'hôtel sur place, un practice superbe et un vaste Clubhouse.

East Sussex National   1990
Little Horsted
ENG - UCKFIELD, East Sussex TN22 5ES

Office	Secrétariat	(44) 01825 - 880 088
Pro shop	Pro-shop	(44) 01825 - 880 256
Fax	Fax	(44) 01825 - 880 012
Situation	Situation	

3 km S of Uckfield (pop. 12 090)
10 km N of Lewes (pop. 15 376)

| Annual closure | Fermeture annuelle | no |
| Weekly closure | Fermeture hebdomadaire | no |

Fees main season
Tarifs haute saison 18 holes

	Week days Semaine	We/Bank holidays We/Férié
Individual Individuel	£ 55	£ 55*
Couple Couple	£ 110	£ 110

* Sunday only - Weekdays: £ 80 for 36 holes & meal

Caddy	Caddy	on request/£ 10/15
Electric Trolley	Chariot électrique	no
Buggy	Voiturette	£ 20/18 holes
Clubs	Clubs	£ 15/18 holes

Credit cards Cartes de crédit
VISA - Eurocard - MasterCard - AMEX - DC - JCB

560

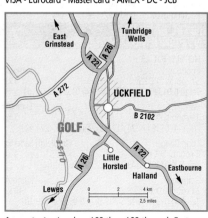

Access Accès : London, A23 then A22 through East Grinstead, Uckfield. Golf 4.5 km South of Uckfield on A22. **Map 7 on page 501** Carte 7 Page 501

GOLF COURSE PARCOURS   17 /20

Site	Site	
Maintenance	Entretien	
Architect	Architecte	Robert E. Cupp
Type	Type	open country
Relief	Relief	
Water in play	Eau en jeu	
Exp. to wind	Exposé au vent	
Trees in play	Arbres en jeu	

Scorecard Carte de score	Chp. Chp.	Mens Mess.	Ladies Da.
Length Long.	6424	6084	4764
Par	72	72	72

Advised golfing ability		0 12 24 36
Niveau de jeu recommandé		
Hcp required	Handicap exigé	certificate

CLUB HOUSE & AMENITIES CLUB HOUSE ET ANNEXES   8 /10

Pro shop	Pro-shop	
Driving range	Practice	
Sheltered	couvert	no
On grass	sur herbe	yes
Putting-green	putting-green	yes
Pitching-green	pitching green	yes

HOTEL FACILITIES ENVIRONNEMENT HOTELIER   7 /10

HOTELS HÔTELS
Horsted Place Hotel   Uckfield
20 rooms, D £ 130   adjacent
Tel (44) 01825 - 750 581
Fax (44) 01825 - 750 459

Hooke Hall   Uckfield
9 rooms, D £ 65   3 km
Tel (44) 01825 - 761 578
Fax (44) 01825 - 768 025

RESTAURANTS RESTAURANTS
Horsted Place Hotel   Uckfield
Tel (44) 01825 - 750 581   adjacent

Pailin   Lewes
Tel (44) 01273 - 473 906   10 km

La Scaletta (Hooke Hall)   Uckfield
Tel (44) 01825 - 761 578   3 km

17 **7** **8**

Golfers who love lush green courses, neatly mown rough, soft greens and trees which shelter from the wind, and who like to get a tan in the process should avoid all the courses on this side of England. On this coast you play golf with all the clubs in your bag, with your head, your technical know-how, all the inspiration you can muster and with locals who will explain where you should hit the ball and where the greens and pins actually are. Fairhaven is simply a great course, not really beautiful from the style point of view, but honest, absorbing, exciting and very well maintained. There are others that have all these attributes but they don't have the pureness of style. To play well here, it's always the same thing: hit it straight, hard and clean. Otherwise don't bother too much counting your strokes, take the gimmies or make full use of the strokes you are given.

Ceux qui aiment les parcours bien verts, les roughs bien tondus, les greens bien mous, les arbres qui abritent du vent, et bronzer en plus, doivent éviter tous les golfs de cette côte d'Angleterre. Ici, on joue au golf avec tous ses clubs et sa tête, avec son bagage technique, avec l'inspiration du moment et avec les joueurs du coin qui vont vous expliquer où sont les points cardinaux, s'il y a des drapeaux au bout des fairways, et où. Fairhaven est simplement un grand parcours pas très très beau (au sens esthétique du terme), mais franc, absorbant, passionnant, très bien entretenu. Il en est d'autres qui ont toutes ces qualités, mais pas la pureté du style. Pour bien le jouer, il faut la même chose, taper droit, fort, nettement. Ou alors ne pas trop s'occuper de compter les coups, ceux que l'on donne et ceux que l'on reçoit.

Fairhaven Golf Club — 1922

Lytham Hall Park, Ansdell
ENG - LYTHAM ST ANNE'S, Lancs FY8 4JU

Office	Secrétariat	(44) 01253 - 736 741
Pro shop	Pro-shop	(44) 01253 - 736 976
Fax	Fax	(44) 01253 - 731 461
Situation	Situation	

close to Lytham St Anne's (pop. 40 866)
9 km from Blackpool (pop. 146 069)

Annual closure	Fermeture annuelle	no
Weekly closure	Fermeture hebdomadaire	no

Fees main season
Tarifs haute saison 18 holes

	Week days Semaine	We/Bank holidays We/Férié
Individual Individuel	£ 35	—
Couple Couple	£ 70	—

Full weekdays : £ 45 / Weekends: limited access (upon request)

Caddy	Caddy	no
Electric Trolley	Chariot électrique	no
Buggy	Voiturette	no
Clubs	Clubs	no

Credit cards Cartes de crédit
VISA - MasterCard (Pro shop goods only)

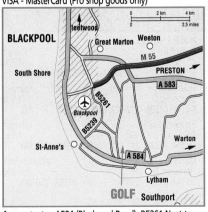

BLACKPOOL Fleetwood, Great Marton, Weeton
M 55 — PRESTON — A 583
South Shore — B5261 — Blackpool — B5259
St-Anne's — A 584 — Warton — Lytham
GOLF Southport

Access Accès : A584 (Blackpool Road). B5261 Next to rugby ground **Map 5 on page 497** Carte 5 Page 497

GOLF COURSE / PARCOURS — 17 /20

Site	Site	■■■■■□
Maintenance	Entretien	
Architect	Architecte	James Braid Jim Steer
Type	Type	links
Relief	Relief	■□□□□
Water in play	Eau en jeu	□□□□□
Exp. to wind	Exposé au vent	■■■■□
Trees in play	Arbres en jeu	■□□□□

Scorecard Carte de score	Chp. Chp.	Mens Mess.	Ladies Da.
Length Long.	6195	5847	5386
Par	74	72	75

Advised golfing ability — 0 12 24 36
Niveau de jeu recommandé
Hcp required Handicap exigé — 28 Men, 36 Ladies

CLUB HOUSE & AMENITIES / CLUB HOUSE ET ANNEXES — 7 /10

Pro shop	Pro-shop	■■■■□
Driving range	Practice	■■□□□
Sheltered	couvert	no
On grass	sur herbe	(pract.ground only)
Putting-green	putting-green	yes
Pitching-green	pitching green	yes

561

HOTEL FACILITIES / ENVIRONNEMENT HOTELIER — 8 /10

HOTELS HÔTELS
Clifton Arms Hotel - 44 rooms, D £ 86 — Lytham
Tel (44) 01253 - 739 898 — 2 km
Fax (44) 01253 - 730 657

Glendover Hotel - 63 rooms, D £ 76 — Lytham St Anne's
Tel (44) 01253 - 723 241 — 3 km

Dalmeny - 130 rooms, D £ 75 — Lytham St Anne's
Tel (44) 01253 - 712 236 — 3 km
Fax (44) 01253 - 724 447

Bedford - 36 rooms, D £ 59 — Lytham St Anne's
Tel (44) 01253 - 724 636 — 3 km
Fax (44) 01253 - 729 244

RESTAURANTS RESTAURANTS
Pleasant Street - Tel (44) 01253 - 788 786 Lytham 2 km
Tiggy's Italian - Tel (44) 01253 - 714 714 — Lytham 2 km
Grand Hotel - Tel (44) 01253 - 721 288 — Lytham 3 km

The development work here over recent years has significantly raised the standard of this course but fortunately has not made it all that much harder. Meaning that most players can enjoy Falmouth without being put off by excessive difficulties. It would have been a pity to deter holiday-makers and deprive them of some superb views over the sea from atop the cliffs. Even though very good players will enjoy this course, it is to be recommended primarily for 12 handicappers and upwards. In windy weather, it is a different picture altogether, but then it always is on courses as exposed as this. This is when you need to hit those low shots and know how to roll the ball down to the greens. There are a few trees in play all the same, but the main hazards are the bunkers, which also define the fairways and alignment of drives and approach shots. An unpretentious course and golf club (with a good driving range, something of a rarity in Britain) to be included in any decent tour of Cornwall.

Les travaux d'aménagement du parcours au cours des dernières années en ont sensiblement relevé le standard, mais il n'a pas été vraiment durci pour autant. La plupart des joueurs pourront ainsi l'apprécier sans être découragés par d'excessives difficultés. Il aurait été dommage de rebuter les vacanciers, et de les priver de vues superbes sur l'océan, du haut des falaises. Même si les très bons joueurs s'y amuseront, on conseillera surtout Falmouth à partir de 12 de handicap. Quand le vent souffle, c'est une tout autre affaire, mais c'est le cas sur tous les parcours aussi ouverts, il faut alors savoir maîtriser les balles basses et en apprécier le roulement. Quelques arbres sont parfois en jeu, mais les bunkers sont à la fois les principaux obstacles et les repères pour définir les fairways et pour s'aligner. Un parcours et un club sans prétention (avec un bon practice, pour une fois dans le pays), à inscrire dans un grand «tour» de la Cornouailles.

Falmouth Golf Club — 1928

Swanpool Road
ENG - FALMOUTH, Cornwall TR11 5 BQ

Office	Secrétariat	(44) 01326 - 311 262
Pro shop	Pro-shop	(44) 01326 - 314 296
Fax	Fax	(44) 01326 - 317 783
Situation	Situation	

1.5 km from Falmouth (pop. 19 217)

Annual closure	Fermeture annuelle	no
Weekly closure	Fermeture hebdomadaire	no

Fees main season	Tarifs haute saison	18 holes
	Week days / Semaine	We/Bank holidays / We/Férié
Individual Individuel	£ 20	£ 20
Couple Couple	£ 40	£ 40
Full day: £ 26		

Caddy	Caddy	no
Electric Trolley	Chariot électrique	no
Buggy	Voiturette	£ 15
Clubs	Clubs	£ 8

Credit cards Cartes de crédit
VISA - Eurocard - MasterCard - AMEX - DC
(Pro shop goods only)

562

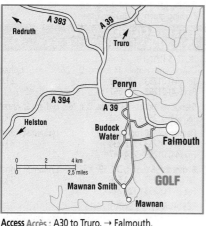

Access Accès : A30 to Truro. → Falmouth.
West of Swanpool Beach. Follow signs.
Map 6 on page 498 Carte 6 Page 498

GOLF COURSE / PARCOURS — 14/20

Site	Site	▰▰▰▱
Maintenance	Entretien	▰▰▰▱
Architect	Architecte	Unknown
Type	Type	seaside course, open country
Relief	Relief	▰▰▱▱▱
Water in play	Eau en jeu	▰▰▱▱▱
Exp. to wind	Exposé au vent	▰▰▰▱▱
Trees in play	Arbres en jeu	▰▰▱▱▱

Scorecard / Carte de score	Chp. / Chp.	Mens / Mess.	Ladies / Da.
Length Long.	5344	5169	4977
Par	71	71	72

Advised golfing ability		0	12	24	36
Niveau de jeu recommandé			▰▰▰▰		
Hcp required	Handicap exigé	certificate			

CLUB HOUSE & AMENITIES / CLUB HOUSE ET ANNEXES — 6/10

Pro shop	Pro-shop	▰▰▰▱
Driving range	Practice	▰▰▰▱
Sheltered	couvert	7 bays
On grass	sur herbe	yes
Putting-green	putting-green	yes
Pitching-green	pitching green	yes

HOTEL FACILITIES / ENVIRONNEMENT HOTELIER — 7/10

HOTELS HÔTELS

Royal Duchy — Falmouth
40 rooms, D £ 175 — 1,5 km
Tel (44) 01326 - 313 042, Fax (44) 01326 - 319 420

St Michael's of Falmouth — Falmouth
65 rooms, D £ 118 — 1,5 km
Tel (44) 01326 - 312 707, Fax (44) 01326 - 211 772

Penmere Manor — Falmouth
38 rooms, D £ 105 — 1,5 km
Tel (44) 01326 - 211 411, Fax (44) 01326 - 317 588

Meudon — Mawnan Smith
28 rooms, D £ 170 — 8 km
Tel (44) 01326 - 250 541, Fax (44) 01326 - 250 543

RESTAURANTS RESTAURANTS

Pennypots — Truro
Tel (44) 01209 - 820 347 — 15 km

This is the fifth oldest club in the history of English golf and a course little known to the majority of golfers on the continent. Yet this is a top notch links course, without the spectacular dunes of the west coast but slightly reminiscent of the courses in Scotland's East Lothian. Re-designed by Henry Cotton after the second world war which left the site in ruins, Tom Dunn's original layout is now a challenge of the highest order despite being rather on the short side. Cut in two by a road, the course's most interesting holes run along the sea-shore. These are the last six holes which make for a highly interesting finish, especially when the wind blows a little (it does happen). A course to bravely go out and pitch into, in the same way as Julie Hall and Jo Hockley, who both learnt their trade here, the hard way.

C'est le cinquième club de l'histoire du golf en Angleterre, et un parcours dont bien peu de continentaux ont entendu parler. C'est pourtant un links de première qualité, sans les dunes spectaculaires de la côte ouest, mais qui n'est pas sans rappeler les parcours de l'East Lothian en Ecosse. Remodelé par Henry Cotton, après la Seconde Guerre Mondiale qui l'avait laissé en ruines, le dessin de Tom Dunn est aujourd'hui redevenu un challenge de premier ordre, même avec sa longueur réduite. Séparé en deux par une route, il offre ses trous les plus intéressants le long de la mer, et ce sont justement les six derniers, ce qui permet un finale des plus intéressants, quand le vent daigne souffler un peu (ce qui arrive). Un parcours à attaquer avec bravoure, comme savent le faire Julie Hall et Jo Hockley, formées ici, à la dure !

Felixstowe Ferry Golf Club — 1880

Ferry Road
ENG - FELIXSTOWE, Suffolk IP11 9RY

Office	Secrétariat	(44) 01394 - 286 834
Pro shop	Pro-shop	(44) 01394 - 283 975
Fax	Fax	
Situation	Situation	

18 km from Ipswich (pop. 130 157)
1 km from Felixstowe (pop. 23 189)

Annual closure	Fermeture annuelle	no
Weekly closure	Fermeture hebdomadaire	no

Fees main season
Tarifs haute saison 18 holes

	Week days Semaine	We/Bank holidays We/Férié
Individual Individuel	£ 22	
Couple Couple	£ 44	

No visitors at weekends.

Caddy	Caddy	no
Electric Trolley	Chariot électrique	£ 5/18 holes
Buggy	Voiturette	no
Clubs	Clubs	no

Credit cards Cartes de crédit
Visa - Mastercard - AMEX (Pro shop goods only)

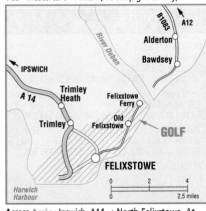

Access Accès : Ipswich, A14 → North Felixstowe. At beach, continue on the left. Course entrance on the right. **Map 7 on page 501** Carte 7 Page 501

GOLF COURSE / PARCOURS — 15/20

Site	Site	
Maintenance	Entretien	
Architect	Architecte	Tom Dunn
		Henry Cotton (1947)
Type	Type	seaside course, links
Relief	Relief	
Water in play	Eau en jeu	
Exp. to wind	Exposé au vent	
Trees in play	Arbres en jeu	

Scorecard Carte de score	Chp. Chp.	Mens Mess.	Ladies Da.
Length Long.	5645	5562	4935
Par	72	72	72

Advised golfing ability		0 12 24 36
Niveau de jeu recommandé		
Hcp required	Handicap exigé	certificate

CLUB HOUSE & AMENITIES / CLUB HOUSE ET ANNEXES — 6/10

Pro shop	Pro-shop	
Driving range	Practice	
Sheltered	couvert	no
On grass	sur herbe	yes
Putting-green	putting-green	yes
Pitching-green	pitching green	yes

HOTEL FACILITIES / ENVIRONNEMENT HOTELIER — 6/10

HOTELS HÔTELS

Orwell Hotel — Felixstowe
58 rooms, D £ 78 — 2 km
Tel (44) 01394 - 309 955, Fax (44) 01394 - 670 687

Waverley — Felixstowe
19 rooms, D £ 75 — 2 km
Tel (44) 01394 - 282 811, Fax (44) 01394 - 670 185

Fludyer Arms Hotel — Felixstowe
8 rooms, D £ 40 — 2 km
Tel (44) 01394 - 283 279, Fax (44) 01394 - 670 754

RESTAURANTS RESTAURANTS

Orwell Hotel - Tel (44) 01394 - 309955 — Felixstowe 2 km

St Peter's - Tel (44) 01473 - 210810 — Ipswich 18 km

Mortimer's on the Quay — Ipswich
Tel (44) 01473 - 230225 — 18 km

563

With sand, heather, pine-trees and conifers, Ferndown is first and foremost a beautiful site with a simple but very functional clubhouse. Once a very dry course during rain-free summers, the course is now watered automatically so that you no longer get those infuriatingly unfair kicks left and right down the fairway, especially on the doglegs. Be careful with Ferndown, because despite the impression of dealing with a fair and open course, some of the trees are more in play than you think and a number of ditches lie hidden in the rough. Good scores depend a lot on your driving, not only to avoid the dangerous fairway bunkers but also to get the ball in the right spot and have a good shot at the green. Although close to Bournemouth, this is not just a simple holiday course but one that has staged some top tournaments: a little short for the big boys, but ideal for the top ladies.

De sable et de bruyère, orné de pins et de sapins, Ferndown est d'abord un bel endroit, avec un Clubhouse sans prétentions architecturales, mais très fonctionnel. Autrefois très sec lors des étés sans pluie, il bénéficie maintenant d'un arrosage qui a retiré certains rebonds imprévus et souvent injustes, en particulier sur les nombreux doglegs. Il faut se méfier de Ferndown, car on a l'impression d'un parcours très franc, alors que certains arbres sont plus en jeu qu'ils ne paraissent, et des fossés se dissimulent dans les roughs. Les bons scores dépendent beaucoup du driving, pour non seulement éviter les dangereux bunkers de fairway, mais aussi placer la balle en bonne position pour attaquer les greens. Bien que proche de Bournemouth, il vaut bien mieux qu'un simple parcours de vacances. Il fut le théâtre de grandes compétitions : un peu court pour les machos, il était idéal pour les proettes.

Ferndown Golf Club — 1914

119, Golf Links Road
ENG - FERNDOWN, Dorset BH22 8BU

Office	Secrétariat	(44) 01202 - 874 602
Pro shop	Pro-shop	(44) 01202 - 873 825
Fax	Fax	(44) 01202 - 873 926
Situation	Situation	

8 km from Bournemouth (pop. 151 300)
5 km from Poole (pop. 133 050)

Annual closure	Fermeture annuelle	no
Weekly closure	Fermeture hebdomadaire	no
Fees main season	Tarifs haute saison	18 holes

	Week days Semaine	We/Bank holidays We/Férié
Individual Individuel	£ 40	£ 45
Couple Couple	£ 80	£ 90

Full day: £ 45 - £ 50 (weekends)

Caddy	Caddy	no
Electric Trolley	Chariot électrique	no
Buggy	Voiturette	£ 20/18 holes
Clubs	Clubs	£ 15/18 holes

Credit cards Cartes de crédit
Visa - Eurocard - Mastercard - Amex
(Pro shop goods only)

564

Access Accès : M3 last exit, then A31 to Trickett's Cross, then A348 to Ferndown, follow signs → Golf.
Map 6 on page 499 Carte 6 Page 499

GOLF COURSE / PARCOURS — 17/20

Site	Site	
Maintenance	Entretien	
Architect	Architecte	Harold Hilton
Type	Type	inland, heathland
Relief	Relief	
Water in play	Eau en jeu	
Exp. to wind	Exposé au vent	
Trees in play	Arbres en jeu	

Scorecard Carte de score	Chp. Chp.	Mens Mess.	Ladies Da.
Length Long.	5895	5651	5176
Par	71	71	72

Advised golfing ability		0 12 24 36
Niveau de jeu recommandé		
Hcp required	Handicap exigé	28 Men, 30 Ladies

CLUB HOUSE & AMENITIES / CLUB HOUSE ET ANNEXES — 7/10

Pro shop	Pro-shop	
Driving range	Practice	
Sheltered	couvert	no
On grass	sur herbe	yes
Putting-green	putting-green	yes
Pitching-green	pitching green	no

HOTEL FACILITIES / ENVIRONNEMENT HOTELIER — 7/10

HOTELS HÔTELS
Mansion House — Poole
28 rooms, D £ 90 — 8 km
Tel (44) 01202 - 685 666, Fax (44) 01202 - 665 709

Royal Bath — Bournemouth
124 rooms, D £ 130 — 5 km
Tel (44) 01202 - 555 555, Fax (44) 01202 - 554 158

The Dormy — Ferndown
123 rooms, D £ 100 — 0,5 km
Tel (44) 01202 - 872 121, Fax (44) 01202 - 895 388

RESTAURANTS RESTAURANTS
La Roche — Poole
Tel (44) 01202 - 707 333 — 5 km

Fisherman's Haunt — Christchurch
Tel (44) 01202 - 484 071 — 10 km

With the exception of Ganton, there are not all that many very good courses in this region, even though Scarborough was one of the very first English seaside resorts which, like others, has been in slow and steady decline since the end of the war. Not far from Filey (to the south), you will want to visit the white cliffs of Flamborough Head and Bempton, a huge sea-bird reserve. Because nature-lovers are often golf-lovers as well, we would recommend a round here, although don't expect to find the course of the century. It might be beside the sea, but Filey is anything but a links course running through dunes. It plays that way though, firstly because of the wind and secondly because of the sandy soil. The layout is more than a hundred years old and has not been radically altered since, even though any course endures some changes over time. Filey is hundreds of other courses you find in Britain, offering nothing particularly spectacular or luxurious but a club where golfers cultivate a certain style of life.

Scarborough était l'une des toutes premières stations balnéaires anglaises, mais sa vogue a décliné après la seconde guerre mondiale. Au sud de Filey, on ne manquera pas les falaises calcaires de Flamborough Head et Bempton, énorme colonie d'oiseaux de mer. Les amateurs de nature étant souvent aussi des amoureux de golf, on leur conseillera une visite ici, bien que ce ne soit pas le parcours du siècle. Nous sommes en bord de mer, mais ce parcours n'a rien d'un links au milieu de dunes, bien que le jeu à y développer soit tout à fait comparable, à cause du vent d'abord, bien entendu, mais aussi de la nature sablonneuse du sol. Depuis plus d'un siècle, le dessin n'a pas été vraiment modifié, même si un parcours de golf se transforme. C'est un golf comme on en trouve des centaines dans le pays, sans rien de spectaculaire ou de luxueux, mais où on continue à cultiver une certaine forme de jeu et de convivialité hors des modes.

Filey Golf Club — 1897

West Avenue
ENG - FILEY, North Yorkshire YO14 9BQ

Office	Secrétariat	(44) 01723 - 513 293
Pro shop	Pro-shop	(44) 01723 - 513 134
Fax	Fax	-
Situation	Situation	

12 km from Scarborough (pop. 38 809)

Annual closure	Fermeture annuelle	no
Weekly closure	Fermeture hebdomadaire	no
Fees main season	Tarifs haute saison	18 holes

	Week days Semaine	We/Bank holidays We/Férié
Individual Individuel	£ 21	£ 21
Couple Couple	£ 42	£ 42

Full day: £ 28

Caddy	Caddy	no
Electric Trolley	Chariot électrique	£ 5
Buggy	Voiturette	no
Clubs	Clubs	no

Credit cards Cartes de crédit
VISA - Eurocard - MasterCard - AMEX - Switch
(not for green fees)

0 — 2 km
0 — 1,25 miles

Scarborough
A 165
Lebberston
Gristhorpe
A 1039
Filey
Muston
GOLF
Kingston-upon-Hull

Access Accès : A64 Leeds-York-Scarborough. After Taxton town, A1039 → Filey. Golf on a private road off end of West Avenue in south end of Filey.
Map 4 on page 494 Carte 4 Page 494

GOLF COURSE / PARCOURS — 13/20

Site	Site	
Maintenance	Entretien	
Architect	Architecte	Unknown
Type	Type	seaside course
Relief	Relief	
Water in play	Eau en jeu	
Exp. to wind	Exposé au vent	
Trees in play	Arbres en jeu	

Scorecard	Chp.	Mens	Ladies
Carte de score	Chp.	Mess.	Da.
Length Long.	5501	5317	5078
Par	70	70	73

Advised golfing ability		0 12 24 36
Niveau de jeu recommandé		
Hcp required	Handicap exigé	no

CLUB HOUSE & AMENITIES / CLUB HOUSE ET ANNEXES — 5/10

Pro shop	Pro-shop	
Driving range	Practice	
Sheltered	couvert	
On grass	sur herbe	yes
Putting-green	putting-green	yes
Pitching-green	pitching green	no

565

HOTEL FACILITIES / ENVIRONNEMENT HOTELIER — 5/10

HOTELS HÔTELS

Sea Brink Hotel — Filey
21 rooms, D £ 45 — 2 km
Tel (44) 01723 - 513 392

White Lodge Hotel — Filey
19 rooms, D £ 60 — 2 km
Tel (44) 01723 - 514 771, Fax (44) 01723 - 516 590

Crown — Scarborough
77 rooms, D £ 70 — 12 km
Tel (44) 01723 - 373 491, Fax (44) 01723 - 362 271

Seafield Hotel — Filey
13 rooms, D £ 35 — 2 km
Tel (44) 01723 - 513 715

RESTAURANTS RESTAURANT

Jade Garden — Scarborough
Tel (44) 01723 - 369 099 — 12 km

The very fine hotel today belongs to the Marriott Group, as does the course. The «Aylesford» hotel is very respectable and perfectly complements this «Arden» course, which is technically a very interesting layout, especially for the better player. All in all, it is a very pleasant spot for a few days golfing with a group or with the family, even if you are playing with golfers of very different abilities. We would simply recommend avoiding the wetter months as the soil takes a long time to soak up surface water. «Arden» was designed by Donald Steel and features many different tee-boxes, of which we would advise the yellow tees, at least for your first round, unless you are a good player of long irons. A tricky course overall with quite a few water hazards, trees which neatly outline the fairways and thick rough, Arden can only get better and better in what is a very professional golfing resort.

Le très bel hôtel appartient aujourd'hui au groupe Marriott, tout comme les parcours. Le «Aylesford» est fort honorable, et complète agréablement le «Arden», plus intéressant techniquement, en particulier pour les meilleurs joueurs. C'est ainsi un lieu très agréable pour passer quelques jours en groupe ou en famille, même si les niveaux de golf sont très différents. On recommandera simplement d'éviter les mois très humides, car le sol a du mal à évacuer les excès d'eau. Le «Arden» a été dessiné par Donald Steel, qui a fait un tracé avec de multiples départs, dont nous conseillerons les «jaunes,» au moins la première fois, à moins d'être un solide joueur de longs fers et de savoir lever la balle. Assez «tricky» en général, avec pas mal d'obstacles d'eau, des arbres sculptant bien les trous, un rough épais, c'est un parcours qui peut nettement progresser, dans un complexe très professionnel.

Marriott Forest of Arden Golf Club — 1970
Maxstoke Lane
ENG - MERIDEN, Warwicks. CV7 7HR

Office	Secrétariat	(44) 01676 - 522 335
Pro shop	Pro-shop	(44) 01676 - 522 335
Fax	Fax	(44) 01676 - 523 711
Situation	Situation	

16 km NW of Coventry (pop. 294 387)
24 km W of Birmingham (pop. 961 041)

Annual closure	Fermeture annuelle	no
Weekly closure	Fermeture hebdomadaire	no

Fees main season
Tarifs haute saison 18 holes

	Week days Semaine	We/Bank holidays We/Férié
Individual Individuel	£ 60	£ 70
Couple Couple	£ 120	£ 140
Caddy Caddy		on request/£ 30
Electric Trolley Chariot électrique		no
Buggy Voiturette		£ 25/18 holes
Clubs Clubs		£ 20/18 holes

Credit cards Cartes de crédit
VISA - Eurocard - MasterCard - AMEX - DC

Access Accès : M42 Jct 6, then A45 → Coventry. After 1.5 km (1 m), left into Shepherds Lane, by «Little Chef». Golf 2 km on the left.
Map 7 on page 500 Carte 7 Page 500

566

GOLF COURSE PARCOURS — 14/20

Site	Site	
Maintenance	Entretien	
Architect	Architecte	Donald Steel
Type	Type	parkland
Relief	Relief	
Water in play	Eau en jeu	
Exp. to wind	Exposé au vent	
Trees in play	Arbres en jeu	

Scorecard Carte de score	Chp. Chp.	Mens Mess.	Ladies Da.
Length Long.	6420	5867	5106
Par	72	72	72

Advised golfing ability — 0 12 24 36
Niveau de jeu recommandé
Hcp required Handicap exigé — no

CLUB HOUSE & AMENITIES
CLUB HOUSE ET ANNEXES — 8/10

Pro shop	Pro-shop	
Driving range	Practice	
Sheltered	couvert	6 bays
On grass	sur herbe	no
Putting-green	putting-green	yes
Pitching-green	pitching green	yes

HOTEL FACILITIES
ENVIRONNEMENT HOTELIER — 8/10

HOTELS HÔTELS

Marriott Forest of Arden Hotel — Meriden
215 rooms, D £ 115 — on site
Tel (44) 01676 - 522 335, Fax (44) 01676 - 523 711

Manor (De Vere) - 74 rooms, D £ 95 — Meriden 3 km
Tel (44) 01676 - 522 735, Fax (44) 01676 - 522 186

Haigs - 13 rooms, D £ 68 — Balsall Common 6 km
Tel (44) 01676 - 533 004, Fax (44) 01676 - 535 132

Arden — Nat. Ex. Centre, Birmingham
146 rooms, D £ 79 — 6 km
Tel (44) 01675 - 443 221

RESTAURANTS RESTAURANTS

Sir Edward Elgar's — Birmingham
Tel (44) 0121 - 452 1144 — 24 km

Number 282 (at Hyatt Regency) — Birmingham
Tel (44) 0121 - 643 1234 — 24 km

It is easier than you might think to get a course all wrong when the terrain is not up to standard. Not so here, where the impression is one of a site blessed by Mother Nature and given the able help of John Morgan. He had to know how to trace the right path through a forest, how to define an intelligent layout, adapt the course to players of different levels, individualise the holes while respecting overall harmony, bring hazards into play without penalising the good shots, and keep a few surprises in store so that it's fun to play again and again. There are courses with which you have an affair and courses which you embrace for life. Forest Pines would be in the latter category, but we will wait a while to see whether it stays as good as it is right now as it comes of age. Opened in 1996 and also featuring a good standard 9 hole course («The Beeches»), this is a resort you cannot afford to miss.

Il est plus facile qu'on ne le croit de rater un parcours alors que le terrain s'y prête. Ici, on peut avoir l'impression que Mère Nature a béni les lieux, mais John Morgan lui a donné un coup de main. Il fallait savoir tracer la route dans la forêt, définir un itinéraire intelligent, adapter son parcours aux différents niveaux de jeu, individualiser les trous tout en conservant une harmonie générale, mettre en jeu les obstacles sans pénaliser les bons coups de golf, et réserver des surprises pour que le plaisir ne soit pas émoussé après la première fois. Il est des parcours avec lesquels on a une liaison et d'autres que l'on épouse. Celui-ci pourrait bien faire partie de la seconde catégorie, même si l'on attend encore un peu pour voir s'il garde sa qualité actuelle en prenant quelques rides. Ouvert en 1996, et proposant également un 9 trous de bonne facture («Beeches»), c'est un ensemble à connaître sans faute.

Forest Pines 1996

Ermine Street, Broughton
ENG - BRIGG, Lincs DN20 04Q

Office	Secrétariat	(44) 01652 - 650 756
Pro shop	Pro-shop	(44) 01652 - 650 756
Fax	Fax	(44) 01652 - 650 495
Situation	Situation	

10 km E of Scunthorpe (pop. 61 550)

Annual closure	Fermeture annuelle	no
Weekly closure	Fermeture hebdomadaire	no

Fees main season
Tarifs haute saison 18 holes

	Week days Semaine	We/Bank holidays We/Férié
Individual Individuel	£ 30	£ 30
Couple Couple	£ 60	£ 60

Full day: £ 35

Caddy	Caddy	on request
Electric Trolley	Chariot électrique	no
Buggy	Voiturette	£ 15/18 holes
Clubs	Clubs	£ 5/18 holes

Credit cards Cartes de crédit
VISA - Eurocard - MasterCard - AMEX - Switch

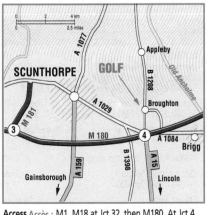

SCUNTHORPE **GOLF** Appleby
Broughton
Brigg
Gainsborough Lincoln

Access Accès : M1, M18 at Jct 32, then M180. At Jct 4, Golf 2 km North
Map 4 on page 495 Carte 4 Page 495

GOLF COURSE
PARCOURS

17/20

Site	Site	
Maintenance	Entretien	
Architect	Architecte	John Morgan
Type	Type	forest
Relief	Relief	
Water in play	Eau en jeu	
Exp. to wind	Exposé au vent	
Trees in play	Arbres en jeu	

Scorecard Carte de score	Chp. Chp.	Mens Mess.	Ladies Da.
Length Long.	6262	5920	5295
Par	73	73	74

Advised golfing ability		0 12 24 36
Niveau de jeu recommandé		
Hcp required	Handicap exigé	certificate

CLUB HOUSE & AMENITIES
CLUB HOUSE ET ANNEXES

6/10

Pro shop	Pro-shop	
Driving range	Practice	
Sheltered	couvert	17 bays
On grass	sur herbe	yes
Putting-green	putting-green	yes
Pitching-green	pitching green	yes

HOTEL FACILITIES
ENVIRONNEMENT HOTELIER

7/10

567

HOTELS HÔTELS

Briggate Lodge 86 rooms, D £ 78 Tel (44) 01652 - 650 770 Fax (44) 01652 - 650 495	Golf on site
Scunthorpe 86 rooms, D £ 60 Tel (44) 01724 - 842 223	Scunthorpe 10 km
Royal Hotel 42 rooms, D £ 65 Tel (44) 01724 - 282 233	Scunthorpe 10 km

RESTAURANTS RESTAURANTS

Brigg Hotel + Restaurant Tel (44) 01652 - 657 633	Brigg 7 km
Briggate Lodge Tel (44) 01652 - 650 770	Golf on site

It is easier to play here as a green-feer (the course is often deserted on weekdays) than to become a member. In this sort of golfing paradise, the latter is perfectly understandable. The layout, soil and dunes bear the hallmark of a links course, but there are trees on a good number of holes, meaning that the wind is not such an important factor as it can be on the region's other links courses. Donald Steel has recently lengthened the course but has taken nothing away from the highly strategic and penalising placing of bunkers, laid out initially by Willie Park then improved upon by Harry Colt. Seen overall, this is a unique and exciting course which offers a permanent challenge. Playing here is a blissful experience, except perhaps for the ladies, who have their own course (a gem) and their own clubhouse. No comment.

Il est plus facile de jouer ici en visiteur (en semaine, c'est souvent désert) que d'y devenir membre. On comprend que ce soit difficile, car Formby est une sorte de paradis. Le dessin, le sol, les dunes sont ceux des links, mais les arbres y sont assez présents sur une bonne partie des trous pour que le vent ne soit pas un facteur aussi terriblement important que sur les autres links de la région. Donald Steel a récemment allongé le parcours, mais sans rien ôter du placement très stratégique et pénalisant des bunkers, établi par Willie Park d'abord, mais surtout par Harry Colt. Au total, le caractère de ce parcours est unique, le jeu passionnant, le challenge permanent. On éprouve ici une impression de bonheur... sauf les Dames, qui ont un parcours à elles (un petit bijou) et leur propre Clubhouse. Sans commentaires.

Formby Golf Club — 1895

Freshfields
ENG - FORMBY, Lancs L37 1LQ

Office	Secrétariat	(44) 01704 - 872 164
Pro shop	Pro-shop	(44) 01704 - 873 090
Fax	Fax	
Situation	Situation	

8 km S of Southport (pop. 90 959)
23 km N of Liverpool (pop. 452 450)

Annual closure	Fermeture annuelle	no
Weekly closure	Fermeture hebdomadaire	no

Fees main season	Tarifs haute saison		full day
		Week days	We/Bank holidays
		Semaine	We/Férié
Individual Individuel		£ 50	£ 50
Couple Couple		£ 100	£ 100
Caddy	Caddy		on request
Electric Trolley	Chariot électrique		no
Buggy	Voiturette		no
Clubs	Clubs		no

Credit cards Cartes de crédit
VISA - Eurocard - MasterCard - AMEX - DC - JCB
(Pro shop goods only)

568

Access Accès : Off A565 Liverpool → Southport.
Formby, green lane to Victoria Road (signposted),
near Freshfields Rail Station.
Map 5 on page 497 Carte 5 Page 497

GOLF COURSE / PARCOURS — 18/20

Site	Site	
Maintenance	Entretien	
Architect	Architecte	W. Park, H.S. Colt F. Pennink, D. Steel
Type	Type	links
Relief	Relief	
Water in play	Eau en jeu	
Exp. to wind	Exposé au vent	
Trees in play	Arbres en jeu	

Scorecard	Chp.	Mens	Ladies
Carte de score	Chp.	Mess.	Da.
Length Long.	6293	6030	0
Par	72	72	0

Advised golfing ability	0	12	24	36
Niveau de jeu recommandé				
Hcp required	Handicap exigé	24 (Males only)!!!		

CLUB HOUSE & AMENITIES / CLUB HOUSE ET ANNEXES — 7/10

Pro shop	Pro-shop	
Driving range	Practice	
Sheltered	couvert	no
On grass	sur herbe	yes
Putting-green	putting-green	yes
Pitching-green	pitching green	yes

HOTEL FACILITIES / ENVIRONNEMENT HOTELIER — 7/10

HOTELS HÔTELS
Dormy House (Males only!!!) — Formby Golf Club
7 rooms, £ 60 (twin & single) — on site
Tel (44) 01704 - 872 164, Fax (44) 01704 - 833 028

Blundellsands - 41 rooms, D £ 70 — Crosby 10 km
Tel (44) 0151 - 924 6515, Fax (44) 0151 - 931 5364

Park - 62 rooms, D £ 34 — Netherton 10 km
Tel (44) 0151 - 525 7555, Fax (44) 0151 - 525 2481

RESTAURANTS RESTAURANTS
Ristorante del Secolo — Liverpool
Tel (44) 0151 - 236 4004 — 18 km

Est, Est, Est! — Liverpool
Tel (44) 0151 - 708 6969 — 18 km

Tree Tops Hotel — Formby
Tel (44) 01704 - 879 651 — 1 km

Very close to Birkdale, Hillside, Formby and Southport & Ainsdale, this new country course is anything but a links. So players who don't like the sometimes lunar and often brutal type of landscape found on your typical links course will find a more «human» alternative waiting for them here. There are not too many trees for the moment but a lot have been planted, so the course can only get better over the years. There are a whole lot of hazards but the only really surprising traps are the ditches that cross about a dozen fairways. On the flat side and exposed to the wind, Formby Hall seems to call for low shots, but your approach work to the well-defended greens will need some high iron shots as well. Fortunately, the greens are big enough for the balls that run rather than pitch. At all events the members seem to like it here, which augurs well for the future of this still young course.

Si près de Birkdale, Hillside, Formby ou Southport & Ainsdale, ce nouveau parcours en campagne n'a rien d'un links, mais certains joueurs n'aiment pas trop l'esthétique parfois lunaire, austère, ou même violente de ce type de parcours, ils trouveront ici une alternative plus «humaine.» Les arbres n'y sont pas encore nombreux, mais beaucoup ont été plantés, et ce parcours ne saurait qu'évoluer dans le bon sens avec les années. Les obstacles sont nombreux, mais les seuls vraiment surprenants sont les fossés traversant une douzaine de fairways. Assez plat, exposé au vent, Formby Hall semble appeler des balles basses, mais les coups vers les greens bien protégés obligent souvent à les lever, à moins de savoir vite les arrêter. Heureusement, ces greens sont assez vastes. En tout cas, les membres semblent apprécier, ce qui rend optimiste quant à la progression de ce parcours encore bien jeune.

Formby Hall Golf Club — 1996
Southport Old Road
ENG - FORMBY, Lancs

Office	Secrétariat	(44) 01704 - 875 699
Pro shop	Pro-shop	(44) 01704 - 875 699
Fax	Fax	(44) 01704 - 832 134
Situation	Situation	

12 km from Southport (pop. 90 959)
21 km from Liverpool (pop. 452 450)

Annual closure	Fermeture annuelle	no
Weekly closure	Fermeture hebdomadaire	no
Fees main season	Tarifs haute saison	18 holes

	Week days Semaine	We/Bank holidays We/Férié
Individual Individuel	£ 25	£ 30
Couple Couple	£ 50	£ 60

Full weekdays: £ 45

Caddy	Caddy	on request
Electric Trolley	Chariot électrique	no
Buggy	Voiturette	£ 20/18 holes
Clubs	Clubs	no

Credit cards Cartes de crédit
VISA - Eurocard - MasterCard - AMEX - DC - JCB

Access Accès : Off A565 (Liverpool → Southport) just beyond Formby turn-off, close to Coast Road traffic lights. Opposite RAF Station at Woodvale.
Map 5 on page 497 Carte 5 Page 497

GOLF COURSE / PARCOURS — 14/20

Site	Site	
Maintenance	Entretien	
Architect	Architecte	PSA Projects
Type	Type	parkland
Relief	Relief	
Water in play	Eau en jeu	
Exp. to wind	Exposé au vent	
Trees in play	Arbres en jeu	

Scorecard Carte de score	Chp. Chp.	Mens Mess.	Ladies Da.
Length Long.	6203	5791	5143
Par	72	72	72

Advised golfing ability Niveau de jeu recommandé	0 12 24 36
Hcp required	Handicap exigé	28 Men, 36 Ladies

CLUB HOUSE & AMENITIES / CLUB HOUSE ET ANNEXES — 8/10

Pro shop	Pro-shop	
Driving range	Practice	
Sheltered	couvert	24 mats
On grass	sur herbe	no
Putting-green	putting-green	yes
Pitching-green	pitching green	yes

569

HOTEL FACILITIES / ENVIRONNEMENT HOTELIER — 6/10

HOTELS HÔTELS
Treetops Hotel — Formby
D £ 78 — 5 km
Tel (44) 01704 - 879 651

Blundellsands — Crosby
41 rooms, D £ 70 — 10 km
Tel (44) 0151 - 924 6515
Fax (44) 0151 - 931 5364

Park — Netherton
62 rooms, D £ 34 — 10 km
Tel (44) 0151 - 525 7555
Fax (44) 0151 - 525 2481

RESTAURANTS RESTAURANTS
Formby Hall Golf Club — Formby
Tel (44) 01704 - 872 164 — on site

Ristorante del Secolo — Liverpool
Tel (44) 0151 - 236 4004

FRILFORD HEATH RED COURSE

14	7	7

Although the club has three 18-hole courses, the "Red Course" is still the one most people refer to. The first four holes, recent enough to adapt to an impressive number of tee-boxes and greens around the club-house, are a little out of keeping with the rest, especially the bunkering, but the course quickly slips back into the typical style of JH Taylor (albeit restyled by JH Turner). This is a frequently hilly layout and tough going for the physically... and technically unfit golfer. As not all the trouble in store is visible at first sight, the tee-shot here is more important than ever for your final score. Strangely enough for a course as British in style and atmosphere as this one, you are better off hitting high balls (sometimes a risky business when the wind swirls between the trees) either to carry some well-placed fairway bunkers or to hit the well-guarded greens. An often under-estimated course but a class layout in a complex where the number of courses provides peaceful golfing in a busy neighbourhood.

Ce club propose trois 18 trous dont le «Red Course» reste le parcours de référence. Certes, les quatre premiers trous sont récents afin d'aménager une grande quantité de départs et de greens près du Club house, et détonnent un peu, notamment pour ce qui est du bunkering, mais on retrouve vite le style de JH Taylor, révisé par JH Turner. Le parcours est assez accidenté, difficile pour les joueurs peu entraînés, physiquement... et techniquement. Toutes les difficultés ne sont pas visibles au premier coup d'oeil, alors que la qualité des drives conditionne généralement la qualité du score. Assez curieusement pour un parcours aussi britannique d'ambiance et de style, il vaut mieux faire des trajectoires hautes (aléatoires quand le vent tourbillonne dans les arbres), soit pour porter la balle au dessus de quelques bunkers de fairway bien placés, soit pour rejoindre des greens bien défendus. Un parcours souvent sous-estimé, mais de bonne classe.

Frilford Heath Golf Club — 1908

Frilford Heath
ENG - ABINGDON, Oxfordshire OX13 5NW

Office	Secrétariat	(44) 01865 - 390 864
Pro shop	Pro-shop	(44) 01865 - 390 887
Fax	Fax	(44) 01865 - 390 823
Situation	Situation	

5 km from Abingdon (pop. 30 771) - 12 km from Oxford

Annual closure	Fermeture annuelle	no
Weekly closure	Fermeture hebdomadaire	no

Fees main season
Tarifs haute saison full day

	Week days Semaine	We/Bank holidays We/Férié
Individual Individuel	£ 45	£ 60
Couple Couple	£ 90	£ 120
£ 28 with a member		
Caddy	Caddy	on request
Electric Trolley	Chariot électrique	£ 5
Buggy	Voiturette	£ 18
Clubs	Clubs	£ 8.50

Credit cards Cartes de crédit
VISA - MasterCard - AMEX - DC
(Green fees & Pro shop only)

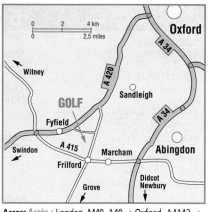

Access Accès : London, M40, A40 → Oxford, A4142 → Abingdon. A415 → Frilford, A338 on right hand side. **Map 7 on page 500** Carte 7 Page 500

570

GOLF COURSE PARCOURS — 14/20

Site	Site	
Maintenance	Entretien	
Architect	Architecte	J.H. Taylor
Type	Type	Heathland
Relief	Relief	
Water in play	Eau en jeu	
Exp. to wind	Exposé au vent	
Trees in play	Arbres en jeu	

Scorecard Carte de score	Chp. Chp.	Mens Mess.	Ladies Da.
Length Long.	6159	5931	5234
Par	73	73	73

Advised golfing ability	0	12	24	36
Niveau de jeu recommandé				

Hcp required   Handicap exigé   certificate

CLUB HOUSE & AMENITIES CLUB HOUSE ET ANNEXES — 7/10

Pro shop	Pro-shop	
Driving range	Practice	
Sheltered	couvert	practice area only
On grass	sur herbe	yes
Putting-green	putting-green	yes
Pitching-green	pitching green	yes

HOTEL FACILITIES ENVIRONNEMENT HOTELIER — 7/10

HOTELS HÔTELS

Upper Riches — Abingdon
25 rooms, D £ 95 — 5 km
Tel (44) 01235 - 522 311, Fax (44) 01235 - 555 182

Abingdon Lodge — Abingdon
63 rooms, D £ 83 — 5 km
Tel (44) 01235 - 553 456, Fax (44) 01235 - 554 117

Old Parsonage — Oxford
30 rooms, D £ 190 — 12 km
Tel (44) 01865 - 310 210, Fax (44) 01865 - 311 262

RESTAURANTS RESTAURANTS

Le Manoir aux Quat'Saisons — Great Milton (A329)
Tel (44) 01844 - 278 881 — 20 km

Fifteen North Parade — Oxford
Tel (44) 01865 - 513 773 — 12 km

Gee's - Tel (44) 01865 - 53 540 — Oxford 12 km

Even before the excellence of the course, Fulford has always been famed for its standard of green-keeping, a reputation enhanced further by the staging here of the English Open and Benson & Hedges International tournaments. Sure, the very low scores carded by the pros have shown that the course might now be a little short for them, but they also holed any number of putts. The greens have always been fast and true, adding to the pleasure of playing here, and the course is definitely long enough for most of us. This is a driver course, not power-wise but in terms of accuracy off the tee, as approach shots must be played from the right spot (bunkers are often on one side of the green only) and will vary according to pin positions. A tactical, technical and fair course for all levels, Fulford has retained its dominant position in York, a superb city to visit with a pedestrians-only centre.

Avant même la qualité de son parcours, Fulford a toujours été renommé pour la qualité de son entretien en général. Et la venue de l'English Open comme celle du Benson & Hedges International ont ensuite accentué cette réputation. Certes, les scores très bas des professionnels ont montré que le parcours était maintenant un peu «court» pour eux, mais ils rentraient aussi beaucoup de putts... Les greens sont toujours rapides et fermes, ce qui n'ajoute qu'un peu plus de plaisir, et le parcours est bien assez «long» pour la majorité d'entre nous. C'est un parcours de driver, pas en termes de puissance, mais de précision, car il faut aborder les greens dans un bon angle (bunkers souvent d'un seul côté), et qui peut varier selon les placements de drapeaux. Tactique et technique, franc et pour tous niveaux, Fulford conserve sa situation dominante à York, qui reste une superbe ville à visiter, avec son centre ville piétonnier.

Fulford Golf Club — 1935

Hessington Lane
ENG - YORK, Yorkshire Y01 5DY

Office	Secrétariat	(44) 01904 - 413 579
Pro shop	Pro-shop	(44) 01904 - 412 882
Fax	Fax	(44) 01904 - 416 918
Situation	Situation	

3 km S. of York (pop. 98 745)

Annual closure	Fermeture annuelle	no
Weekly closure	Fermeture hebdomadaire	no

Fees main season
Tarifs haute saison 18 holes

	Week days Semaine	We/Bank holidays We/Férié
Individual Individuel	£ 30	—
Couple Couple	£ 60	—

Full weekday: £ 40 - Limited access at w/ends

Caddy	Caddy	no
Electric Trolley	Chariot électrique	£ 5/18 holes
Buggy	Voiturette	£ 20/18 holes
Clubs	Clubs	no

Credit cards Cartes de crédit
VISA - MasterCard (not for Green fees)

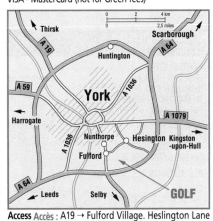

Access Accès : A19 → Fulford Village. Heslington Lane on left. Follow signs for University.
Map 4 on page 495 Carte 4 Page 495

GOLF COURSE / PARCOURS — 17/20

Site	Site	
Maintenance	Entretien	
Architect	Architecte	Charles MacKenzie
Type	Type	parkland
Relief	Relief	
Water in play	Eau en jeu	
Exp. to wind	Exposé au vent	
Trees in play	Arbres en jeu	

Scorecard Carte de score	Chp. Chp.	Mens Mess.	Ladies Da.
Length Long.	6100	5698	4875
Par	72	72	74

Advised golfing ability Niveau de jeu recommandé	0	12	24	36
Hcp required Handicap exigé	28 Men, 36 Ladies			

CLUB HOUSE & AMENITIES / CLUB HOUSE ET ANNEXES — 7/10

Pro shop	Pro-shop	
Driving range	Practice	
Sheltered	couvert	practice area
On grass	sur herbe	yes
Putting-green	putting-green	yes
Pitching-green	pitching green	yes

571

HOTEL FACILITIES / ENVIRONNEMENT HOTELIER — 8/10

HOTELS HÔTELS

Middlethorpe Hall — York, 2 km
30 rooms, D £ 120
Tel (44) 01904 - 641 241, Fax (44) 01904 - 620 176

Forte Posthouse — York, 3 km
139 rooms, D £ 70
Tel (44) 01904 - 707 921, Fax (44) 01904 - 702 804

Novotel — York, 3 km
124 rooms, D £ 76
Tel (44) 01904 - 611 660, Fax (44) 01904 - 610 925

Arndale Hotel - 10 rooms, D £ 65 — York, 3 km
Tel (44) 01904 - 702 424

RESTAURANTS RESTAURANTS

Melton's — York, 3 km
Tel (44) 01904 - 634 341

19 Grape Lane — York, 3 km
Tel (44) 01904 - 636 366

This club was purchased in 1985 by Ping, who run a golf equipment factory nearby, so don't be surprised by the manufacturer's dominant presence, particularly in the Pro Shop. The original course, played at a time when the club was called Thonock, has been restyled by Brian Waites and goes very well with this one, a more ambitious affair with a lot of water in play and few trees as yet. A lot have been planted, though, so visually the course can only get better. For the moment, the contours of the land and the bunkers do not always give you a clear idea of what you have to do. From the back tees this is a tough proposition which is probably too hard to handle for many average golfers. Further forward, the course is a fair and much more accessible test. A very serious course in a comparatively deserted region golf-wise with an impressive clubhouse (there is an excellent coffee-house for snacks).

Ce club a été acheté en 1985 par Ping, dont l'usine de matériel de golf est située à Gainsborough, on ne sera pas étonné de sentir cette présence, en particulier au Pro-shop ! Le parcours de l'époque où le club s'appelait Thonock avait été remodelé par Brian Waites et complète bien celui-ci, plus ambitieux, avec beaucoup d'eau en jeu, peu d'arbres encore mais certaines plantations vont le faire visuellement évoluer. Pour l'instant, les mouvements de terrain et les bunkers ne précisent pas toujours parfaitement ce qu'il faut faire, le «yardage book» (carnet de parcours) sera utile. Des départs arrière, c'est un solide parcours où beaucoup souffriront, mais les départs avancés proposent un test très franc et accessible à beaucoup. Une réalisation très sérieuse dans une région un peu déserte, avec un Clubhouse impressionnant (excellent Coffee shop pour une petite faim).

Gainsborough Golf Club Karsten Lakes — 1997

Thonock
ENG - GAINSBOROUGH, Lincs DN21 1PZ

Office	Secrétariat	(44) 01427 - 613 088
Pro shop	Pro-shop	(44) 01427 - 612 278
Fax	Fax	(44) 01427 - 810 172
Situation	Situation	

1.5 km N of Gainsborough - 30 km W of Lincoln

Annual closure	Fermeture annuelle	no
Weekly closure	Fermeture hebdomadaire	no
Fees main season	Tarifs haute saison	18 holes

	Week days Semaine	We/Bank holidays We/Férié
Individual Individuel	£ 25	£ 25
Couple Couple	£ 50	£ 50
Full day: £ 35		

Caddy	Caddy	no
Electric Trolley	Chariot électrique	no
Buggy	Voiturette	£ 25/18 holes
Clubs	Clubs	£ 12/18 holes

Credit cards Cartes de crédit
VISA - MasterCard - AMEX - Switch

572

Access Accès : M1 Jct 32, then M18,
Jct 1 then A631 to Gainsborough. A 159 golf 1.5 km N.
Map 4 on page 495 Carte 4 Page 495

GOLF COURSE PARCOURS 14/20

Site	Site	
Maintenance	Entretien	
Architect	Architecte	Neil Coles
Type	Type	inland, parkland
Relief	Relief	
Water in play	Eau en jeu	
Exp. to wind	Exposé au vent	
Trees in play	Arbres en jeu	

Scorecard Carte de score	Chp. Chp.	Mens Mess.	Ladies Da.
Length Long.	6279	5901	5310
Par	72	72	72

Advised golfing ability
Niveau de jeu recommandé   0   12   24   36
Hcp required   Handicap exigé   certificate

CLUB HOUSE & AMENITIES CLUB HOUSE ET ANNEXES 8/10

Pro shop	Pro-shop	
Driving range	Practice	
Sheltered	couvert	20 bays
On grass	sur herbe	no
Putting-green	putting-green	yes
Pitching-green	pitching green	yes

HOTEL FACILITIES ENVIRONNEMENT HOTELIER 6/10

HOTELS HÔTELS
Hickmont Hill Hotel   Gainsborough
8 rooms, D £ 50   2 km
Tel (44) 01427 - 613 639
Fax (44) 01427 - 677 591

White Swan Hotel   Gainsborough
12 rooms, D £ 52   20 km
Tel (44) 01724 - 762 342
Fax (44) 01724 - 764 268

RESTAURANTS RESTAURANTS

Cross Keys   Gainsborough
Tel (44) 01427 - 788 314   5 km

White Heather   Gainsborough
Tel (44) 01427 - 878 604

Arizona's   Golf Club
Tel (44) 01427 - 810 173   on site

This is one of the very few inland courses to find favour with links enthusiasts. The sea must have stretched this far in times gone by because you can still find sea-shells in the sand and the soil is of the kind found on every links course. Located between the resort of Scarborough and the superb city of York (a former Viking stronghold), this is a sheer masterpiece of a course where Dunn, Vardon, Harry Colt and C.K. Cotton all had a hand in its design. The links style is all the more obvious in that trees come into play only on a very few holes. Elsewhere, the fairways are bordered by bushes, tall grass and rough, while deep hungry bunkers snap up anything within reach. But all the hazards are there to be seen and the course is not responsible for your shortcomings (or is it?). The slick greens are well-protected but leave the way open for bump 'n roll shots. As we were saying, all that is missing is the sea.

C'est l'un des seuls «inland» à trouver grâce auprès des amoureux des links. La mer devait autrefois venir ici, car on a retrouvé des coquillages dans le sable et le sol est celui des links. Entre la station balnéaire de Scarborough et la ville superbe d'York (ancienne place forte viking), il y a ce chef d'oeuvre absolu où Tom Dunn, Harry Vardon, Harry Colt et C.K. Cotton ont apporté leur contribution. Le style de links est d'autant plus flagrant que les arbres ne sont en jeu que sur quelques trous. Ailleurs, les buissons, les hautes herbes du rough délimitent les fairways, de profonds bunkers pleins d'appétit attrapent tout ce qui passe à portée. Mais tous les obstacles sont bien en vue, et le parcours n'est pas responsable de vos fautes. Les greens subtils et bien défendus laissent néanmoins la porte ouverte aux approches roulées. Il ne manque que la mer, on vous le disait.

Ganton Golf Club — 1891

Ganton
ENG - SCARBOROUGH, Yorkshire YO12 4PA

Office	Secrétariat	(44) 01944 - 710 329
Pro shop	Pro-shop	(44) 01944 - 710 260
Fax	Fax	(44) 01944 - 710 922
Situation	Situation	

15 km SW of Scarborough (pop. 38 809)

Annual closure	Fermeture annuelle	no
Weekly closure	Fermeture hebdomadaire	no

Fees main season
Tarifs haute saison full day

	Week days Semaine	We/Bank holidays We/Férié
Individual Individuel	£ 43	£ 48
Couple Couple	£ 86	£ 96

Caddy	Caddy	on request
Electric Trolley	Chariot électrique	£ 5/18 holes
Buggy	Voiturette	no
Clubs	Clubs	no

Credit cards Cartes de crédit
VISA - MasterCard - Switch (not for green fees)

Scarborough, Whitby, Cayton Bay, Forest Park, East Ayton, West Ayton, Wykeham, Irton, Pickering, Brompton, Cayton, Filey, GOLF, Ganton, Malton/Norton, Staxton, Bridlington

A 170, A 64, A1261, A 165, A1039, B1249

Access Accès : On A64 Leeds-York-Scarborough, 15 km before Scarborough
Map 4 on page 495 Carte 4 Page 495

GOLF COURSE / PARCOURS — 19/20

Site	Site	▬▬▬▬▬▬▬▢
Maintenance	Entretien	▬▬▬▬▬▬▬▢
Architect	Architecte	Tom Dunn, H. Vardon H.S. Colt, CK Cotton
Type	Type	open country, heathland
Relief	Relief	▬▬▬▢▢▢▢▢
Water in play	Eau en jeu	▬▢▢▢▢▢▢▢
Exp. to wind	Exposé au vent	▬▬▬▬▢▢▢▢
Trees in play	Arbres en jeu	▬▬▬▢▢▢▢▢

Scorecard Carte de score	Chp. Chp.	Mens Mess.	Ladies Da.
Length Long.	6061	5827	5447
Par	73	73	75

Advised golfing ability   0   12   24   36
Niveau de jeu recommandé   ▬▬▬▬▬▬▢▢
Hcp required Handicap exigé   24 Men, 36 Ladies

CLUB HOUSE & AMENITIES / CLUB HOUSE ET ANNEXES — 8/10

Pro shop	Pro-shop	▬▬▬▬▬▬▢▢
Driving range	Practice	▬▬▬▬▬▢▢▢
Sheltered	couvert	practice area
On grass	sur herbe	yes
Putting-green	putting-green	yes
Pitching-green	pitching green	yes

573

HOTEL FACILITIES / ENVIRONNEMENT HOTELIER — 5/10

HOTELS HÔTELS

Crescent Hotel — Scarborough
20 rooms, D £ 60 — 15 km
Tel (44) 01723 - 360 929, Fax (44) 01723 - 354 126

Crown (Forte) — Scarborough
77 rooms, D £ 65 — 15 km
Tel (44) 01723 - 373 491, Fax (44) 01723 - 362 271

Ganton Greyhound — Ganton
18 rooms, D £ 50 — 500 m
Tel (44) 01944 - 710 116, Fax (44) 01944 - 710 738

RESTAURANTS RESTAURANTS

Jade Garden (Chinese) — Scarborough
Tel (44) 01723 - 369 099 — 15 km

Lanterna — Scarborough
Tel (44) 01723 - 363 616 — 15 km

GOG MAGOG OLD COURSE

15 7 8

The landscape in this part of the country is generally so flat that it could hardly have inspired early course designers who probably had little more than ploughs and wheelbarrows to move earth. If you don't play much golf here, you will enjoy visiting Cambridge, Ely, Bury St. Edmonds or the Fens with their windmills. Gog Magog, though, is the exception to the rule and is laid out over some small hills which are easy to walk. The club has a long tradition of hospitality (but is closed to green-feers on weekends) and also a second course, Wandlesbury, which has everything perhaps except the charm of this Old Course. There are not too many trees but they are sometimes placed to block your second shot if the drive is not perfect. A fair and shortish course which rewards good shots, Gog Magog is pleasant to play with friends or with the family, whatever their level.

Le paysage de cette région est en général d'une platitude qui ne pouvait guère inspirer les architectes de golf des origines, qui ne disposaient guère que de charrues et de brouettes pour modeler le terrain. Faute de beaucoup jouer, la visite de Cambridge, d'Ely, de Bury St Edmunds ou les marais des Fens avec leurs moulins à vent sont déjà un dépaysement. Gog Magog est l'exception à la règle, et a trouvé place sur de petites collines assez aimables pour les jambes. Ce club a la longue tradition d'accueil (mais fermé aux visiteurs en week-end) offre un second parcours, Wandlesbury, mais le Old Course garde tout son charme. Les arbres n'y sont pas trop nombreux, mais parfois placés pour bloquer les seconds coups si les drives n'ont pas été parfaits. Honnête, récompensant les bons coups de golf, pas très long, c'est un parcours agréable pour jouer en famille ou avec des amis, quel que soit leur niveau.

The Gog Magog Golf Club		**1901**
ENG - SHELFORD BOTTOM, Cambridgeshire CB2 4AB		

Office	Secrétariat	(44) 01223 - 247 626
Pro shop	Pro-shop	(44) 01223 - 246 058
Fax	Fax	(44) 01223 - 414 990
Situation	Situation	
4 km from Cambridge (pop. 91 535)		
Annual closure	Fermeture annuelle	no
Weekly closure	Fermeture hebdomadaire	no

Fees main season
Tarifs haute saison 18 holes

	Week days Semaine	We/Bank holidays We/Férié
Individual Individuel	£ 30	—
Couple Couple	£ 60	—

Full day: £ 37.50 - No visitors at weekends - Booking advisable

Caddy	Caddy	no
Electric Trolley	Chariot électrique	£ 6/18 holes
Buggy	Voiturette	no
Clubs	Clubs	£ 7.50/18 holes

Credit cards Cartes de crédit
Visa - Mastercard - AMEX (Pro shop goods only)

574

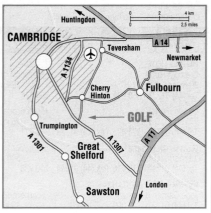

Access Accès : Cambridge A1307 SE. Second roundabout turn left → Fulbourn. Entrance 200 m on the right. **Map 7 on page 501** Carte 7 Page 501

GOLF COURSE PARCOURS

15/20

Site	Site	
Maintenance	Entretien	
Architect	Architecte	F.W. Hawtree
Type	Type	inland, copse
Relief	Relief	
Water in play	Eau en jeu	
Exp. to wind	Exposé au vent	
Trees in play	Arbres en jeu	

Scorecard Carte de score	Chp. Chp.	Mens Mess.	Ladies Da.
Length Long.	5760	5565	5010
Par	70	70	71

Advised golfing ability	0	12	24	36
Niveau de jeu recommandé				
Hcp required Handicap exigé	22			

CLUB HOUSE & AMENITIES
CLUB HOUSE ET ANNEXES

7/10

Pro shop	Pro-shop	
Driving range	Practice	
Sheltered	couvert	no
On grass	sur herbe	yes
Putting-green	putting-green	yes
Pitching-green	pitching green	yes

HOTEL FACILITIES
ENVIRONNEMENT HOTELIER

8/10

HOTELS HÔTELS
University Arms — Cambridge
114 rooms, D £ 80 — 4 km
Tel (44) 01223 - 351 241, Fax (44) 01223 - 315 256

Arundel House — Cambridge
105 rooms, D £ 65 — 4 km
Tel (44) 01223 - 367 701, Fax (44) 01223 - 367 721

Centennial — Cambridge
39 rooms, D £ 65 — 4 km
Tel (44) 01223 - 314 652, Fax (44) 01223 - 315 443

RESTAURANTS RESTAURANTS
Sycamore House — Little Shelford
Tel (44) 01223 - 843396 — 3 km

Midsummer House — Cambridge
Tel (44) 01223 - 69299 — 4 km

Whichever direction you're travelling, London just seems never-ending. The strangest thing is that you start finding golf courses where you would never expect them and, what's more, in calm secluded spots. Less than a mile from Cockfosters tube station, Hadley Wood is one such course, where a very smart clubhouse is surrounded by flowers and bushes whose colours contrast sharply with the grey (or blue) skies. The same elegance and eye for detail are found in what is a very distinguished layout by Alister Mackenzie, landscaped like a garden and whose bunkers, streams and lakes look like items of decoration straight out of a magazine. But deceptive as ever, even the sweetest looking courses can prove deadly and easily end any hope of a good score.

Que l'on aille dans n'importe quelle direction, Londres semble ne jamais finir. Le plus étrange est de parvenir à trouver beaucoup de golfs là où on ne penserait pas en chercher, et à les trouver dans des endroits calmes. Hadley Wood fait partie de ces sites privilégiés, à moins d'un mile du métro Cockfosters. Autour du très beau Clubhouse, fleurs et arbustes témoignent une fois de plus d'un amour des végétaux coloriés qui tranchent avec le ciel gris (et d'ailleurs parfois bleu !). On retrouve cette élégance, ce souci du détail dans le tracé très distingué d'Alister Mackenzie, paysagé comme un jardin, où les bunkers, les petits cours d'eau et les lacs paraissent des éléments d'un décor pour magazine. Mais il faut se méfier des apparences, les dessins les plus évidents peuvent être meurtriers, du moins si l'on tente de faire un bon score.

Hadley Wood Golf Club — 1922

Beech Hill
ENG - BARNET, Herts EN4 0JJ

Office	Secrétariat	(44) 0181 - 449 4328
Pro shop	Pro-shop	(44) 0181 - 449 3285
Fax	Fax	(44) 0181 - 364 8633
Situation	Situation	

16 km N of Central London (pop. 6 679 700)

Annual closure	Fermeture annuelle	no
Weekly closure	Fermeture hebdomadaire	no

Fees main season
Tarifs haute saison 18 holes

	Week days Semaine	We/Bank holidays We/Férié
Individual Individuel	£ 33	—
Couple Couple	£ 66	—

Full weekday: £ 44 - No visitors at weekends

Caddy	Caddy	on request/£ 40
Electric Trolley	Chariot électrique	£ 6/18 holes
Buggy	Voiturette	no
Clubs	Clubs	£ 7.50/18 holes

Credit cards Cartes de crédit
VISA - MasterCard - AMEX (extra charge, no credit cards in Clubhouse)

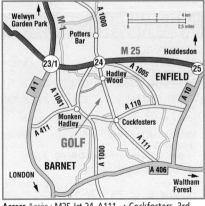

Access Accès : M25 Jct 24. A111 → Cockfosters. 3rd right into Beech Hill. Golf 400 m on left.
Map 8 on page 503 Carte 8 Page 503

GOLF COURSE / PARCOURS — 16/20

Site	Site	
Maintenance	Entretien	
Architect	Architecte	Alister MacKenzie
Type	Type	parkland
Relief	Relief	
Water in play	Eau en jeu	
Exp. to wind	Exposé au vent	
Trees in play	Arbres en jeu	

Scorecard Carte de score	Chp. Chp.	Mens Mess.	Ladies Da.
Length Long.	5811	5612	4710
Par	72	70	73

Advised golfing ability Niveau de jeu recommandé	0 12 24 36
Hcp required Handicap exigé	certificate

CLUB HOUSE & AMENITIES / CLUB HOUSE ET ANNEXES — 7/10

Pro shop	Pro-shop	
Driving range	Practice	
Sheltered	couvert	no
On grass	sur herbe	yes
Putting-green	putting-green	yes
Pitching-green	pitching green	yes

HOTEL FACILITIES / ENVIRONNEMENT HOTELIER — 7/10

HOTELS HÔTELS

West Lodge Park — Hadley Wood
45 rooms, D £ 120 — 1 km
Tel (44) 0181 - 440 8311, Fax (44) 0181 - 449 3698

Royal Chace — Enfield
92 rooms, D £ 85 — 3 km
Tel (44) 0181 - 366 6500, Fax (44) 0181 - 367 7191

Holiday Inn Garden Court — Brent Cross
152 rooms, D £ 85 — 9 km
Tel (44) 0181 - 201 8686, Fax (44) 0181 - 455 4660

Forte Posthouse — South Mimms
120 rooms, D £ 70 — 8 km
Tel (44) 01707 - 643 311, Fax (44) 01707 - 646 728

RESTAURANTS RESTAURANTS

West Lodge Park — Hadley Wood
Tel (44) 0181 - 440 8311 — 1 km

575

As this is probably not the most popular part of Yorkshire with tourists, the courses around Sheffield are played mostly by two types of golfer: the locals and large numbers of travelling businessmen. They will definitely enjoy playing at Hallamshire, which would certainly be better known if located in a more fashionable golfing county like Surrey, for example. This is a course of moorland and woods over rolling but easily walkable terrain, where, surprise, surprise, there is no water. The tall rough is out of play (or should be) and the turf lush and springy, so unless you are here in the middle of a drought you won't have to contend with bad kicks. There are a few blind holes here and there, but if you play with a local golfer from the club, he will guide you around and help you avoid any unpleasant surprises. Hallamshire is a well-balanced course where playing to your handicap is never a foregone conclusion, perhaps owing to a tendency to underestimate the hazards and ignore the dangers behind a friendly exterior. A very respectable course.

Ce n'est certes pas la partie la plus touristique du Yorkshire, et les parcours aux alentours de Sheffield, mis à part les joueurs locaux, sont surtout fréquentés par les «businessmen» en déplacement. Ils apprécierontHallamshire, dont la notoriété aurait été plus grande s'il avait par exemple été situé dans le Surrey. Parcours de landes et de bois, dans un paysage animé mais facile à parcourir à pied, il est dénué d'obstacles d'eau, ce qui est rare de nos jours. Le haut rough n'est pas en jeu, le gazon bien souple, les surprises au rebond ne sont à craindre que par sécheresse. On trouve çà et là quelques coups aveugles, mais avec un bon «pilote» habitué du club, pas de mauvaises surprises non plus. Pourtant, il n'est pas si facile de jouer ici son handicap, peut être parce que l'on a tendance à en sous-estimer les difficultés, à ne pas sentir les dents derrière une amabilité de façade. Bien équilibré, c'est un parcours fort respectable.

Hallamshire Golf Club — 1897

The Club House
ENG - SANDYGATE, SHEFFIELD, S. Yorks. S10 44A

Office	Secrétariat	(44) 01142 - 302 153
Pro shop	Pro-shop	(44) 01723 - 305 222
Fax	Fax	(44) 01723 - 305 656
Situation	Situation	

3 km W of Sheffield (pop. 501 202)

Annual closure	Fermeture annuelle	no
Weekly closure	Fermeture hebdomadaire	no

Fees main season
Tarifs haute saison 18 holes

	Week days Semaine	We/Bank holidays We/Férié
Individual Individuel	£ 30	£ 35
Couple Couple	£ 60	£ 70

Caddy	Caddy	yes
Electric Trolley	Chariot électrique	no
Buggy	Voiturette	no
Clubs	Clubs	no

Credit cards Cartes de crédit
VISA - MasterCard - Switch (not for green fees)

576

Access Accès : A57 from Sheffield city centre, left fork at Crosspool (pub), 1.5 km to the golf.
Map 4 on page 494 Carte 4 Page 494

GOLF COURSE / PARCOURS — 15/20

Site	Site	■■■■□
Maintenance	Entretien	■■■■□
Architect	Architecte	Unknown
Type	Type	parkland, hilly
Relief	Relief	■■■□□
Water in play	Eau en jeu	■□□□□
Exp. to wind	Exposé au vent	■■□□□
Trees in play	Arbres en jeu	■■■□□

Scorecard Carte de score	Chp. Chp.	Mens Mess.	Ladies Da.
Length Long.	0	0	0
Par	0	0	0

Advised golfing ability		0 12 24 36
Niveau de jeu recommandé		■■■■□
Hcp required	Handicap exigé	certificate

CLUB HOUSE & AMENITIES / CLUB HOUSE ET ANNEXES — 6/10

Pro shop	Pro-shop	■■■■□
Driving range	Practice	■■■■□
Sheltered	couvert	
On grass	sur herbe	yes
Putting-green	putting-green	yes
Pitching-green	pitching green	yes

HOTEL FACILITIES / ENVIRONNEMENT HOTELIER — 8/10

HOTELS HÔTELS
Beauchief Hotel — Sheffield
40 rooms, D £ 70 — 4 km
Tel (44) 0114 - 202 0500, Fax (44) 0114 - 350 197

Sheffield Moat House — Sheffield
95 rooms, D £ 82 — 8 km
Tel (44) 01142 - 829 988, Fax (44) 01142 - 378 140

Middle Wood Hull Hotel — Sheffield
20 rooms, D £ 50 — 4 km
Tel (44) 01142 - 863 919, Fax (44) 01142 - 864 188

RESTAURANTS RESTAURANTS
All Bar One — Sheffield 4 km
Tel (44) 01142 - 303 298

Le Neptune - Tél(44) 0114 - 279 6677 — Sheffield 4 km

Bistro Casablanca — Sheffield 5 km
Tel (44) 01142 - 490 720

First of all a word of praise for the slick, very fast greens and the flawless green-keeping. Might this be a tribute to Bobby Locke, one of the greatest putters of all time who for years lived right beside this course? Hankley Common used to be very dry in Summer but now has automatic sprinklers which tend to lengthen the course and stress the need for long-hitting. Keep it straight, too, because the fairway bunkers snap up anything remotely off-line, and even if you miss the sand, there's enough heather to keep you busy for longer than you would like, finding ways of getting your ball back into play. The felling of a number of trees has exposed the course to the wind and sometimes gives a part of the course an unexpected links character, with all the technical challenge that that entails. A final word for the beautiful finishing holes, especially the 18th, where our advice is always to take one club more than you think you need to hit the green.

D'abord un mot pour les greens subtils, très rapides et d'un entretien irréprochable, comme en hommage à l'un des meilleurs putters de tous les temps, Bobby Locke, qui habita longtemps à côté d'ici. Longtemps très sec en été, ce parcours bénéficie maintenant de l'arrosage automatique, qui l'a en quelque sorte «allongé,» renforçant la nécessité d'être long, et droit car les nombreux bunkers de fairway accueillent avec le sourire les balles incertaines. Et quand on réussit à les passer, la bruyère est volontaire pour les retenir un certain temps. L'abattage de nombreux arbres a exposé davantage les joueurs au vent, ce qui donne parfois un caractère de links inattendu à certains trous, avec l'exigence technique que cela représente. A signaler enfin, la beauté du finale, en particulier du 18ème trou : prenez toujours un club de plus pour jouer le green.

Hankley Common Golf Club		**1897**
Tilford Road, Tilford		
ENG - FARNHAM, Surrey GU10 2DD		
Office	Secrétariat	(44) 01252 - 792 493
Pro shop	Pro-shop	(44) 01252 - 793 761
Fax	Fax	(44) 01252 - 792 493
Situation	Situation	
6 km from Farnham (pop. 30 430)		
Annual closure	Fermeture annuelle	no
Weekly closure	Fermeture hebdomadaire	no

Fees main season		
Tarifs haute saison full day		
	Week days Semaine	We/Bank holidays We/Férié
Individual Individuel	£ 50	£ 50*
Couple Couple	£ 100	£ 100*
* For 18 holes and after 2.00 pm		

Caddy	Caddy	no
Electric Trolley	Chariot électrique	no
Buggy	Voiturette	no
Clubs	Clubs	no
Credit cards Cartes de crédit		no

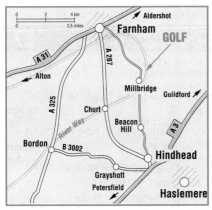

Access Accès : A3 (→ Portsmouth). After Devils Punch Bowl, turn right onto Tilford Road. Golf Club is approx; 6 km (4 m) on the right.
Map 7 on page 500 Carte 7 Page 500

GOLF COURSE / PARCOURS — **16**/20

Site	Site	
Maintenance	Entretien	
Architect	Architecte	Charles Lawrie
Type	Type	inland, heathland
Relief	Relief	
Water in play	Eau en jeu	
Exp. to wind	Exposé au vent	
Trees in play	Arbres en jeu	

Scorecard Carte de score	Chp. Chp.	Mens Mess.	Ladies Da.
Length Long.	5795	5503	5002
Par	71	71	72

Advised golfing ability Niveau de jeu recommandé	0	12	24	36
Hcp required	Handicap exigé	certificate		

CLUB HOUSE & AMENITIES / CLUB HOUSE ET ANNEXES — **6**/10

Pro shop	Pro-shop	
Driving range	Practice	
Sheltered	couvert	no
On grass	sur herbe	yes
Putting-green	putting-green	yes
Pitching-green	pitching green	yes

HOTEL FACILITIES / ENVIRONNEMENT HOTELIER — **6**/10

HOTELS HÔTELS
Bush (Forte Heritage) — Farnham
66 rooms, D £ 85 — 5 km
Tel (44) 01252 - 715 237, Fax (44) 01252 - 733 530

Bishop's Table — Farnham
16 rooms, D £ 85 — 5 km
Tel (44) 01252 - 710 222, Fax (44) 01252 - 733 494

Pride of the Valley — Churt
11 rooms, D £ 70 — 5 km
Tel (44) 01428 - 605 799, Fax (44) 01428 - 605 875

RESTAURANTS RESTAURANTS
Wings Cottage — Farnborough
Tel (44) 01252 - 544 141 — 10 km

Fleur de Sel — Haslemere
Tel (44) 01428 - 651 462 — 10 km

Banaras (Indian) — Farnham
Tel (44) 01252 - 734 081 — 5 km

577

This course is close to Knaresborough, one of the oldest towns in the country. The superb surroundings in this region are further enhanced by the spa city of Harrogate, the Yorkshire Dales and the ruins of Fountains Abbey with its gardens and... fountains. There are several superb courses around here, and this is one of them. With neighbouring Pannal, Harrogate is one of Sandy Herd's best layouts on woody terrain (the trees are never too thick) which is hilly enough to conceal one or two difficulties. In other words, strategy is never simple the first time out and errors of positioning or direction can easily require the use of every club you have available. Although not a terribly spectacular course, it is an excellent examination of talent and technique that connoisseurs of the game will appreciate on its merits.

Le présent parcours est tout proche de Knaresborough, une des plus vieilles villes du pays. La ville d'eau d'Harrogate, le Parc National des Yorkshire Dales, ou encore les ruines de l'Abbaye, les temples à l'antique et les jeux d'eau des jardins de Fountains Abbey ajoutent encore à l'agrément de l'environnement superbe de cette région. Elle est pourvue de plusieurs parcours de qualité et celui-ci ne détonne pas auprès d'eux. Avec son voisin Pannal, c'est un des meilleurs tracés de Sandy Herd. Le terrain est boisé mais sans devoir inquiéter les claustrophobes, assez accidenté, ce qui dissimule quelques difficultés. La stratégie n'est alors pas évidente à la première visite, et les erreurs de placement ou de direction peuvent obliger à sortir tous les coups de son sac. Sans être un parcours très spectaculaire, c'est en fait un excellent examen du talent et de la technique, que les bons connaisseurs apprécieront à sa juste valeur.

Harrogate Golf Club — 1892

Forest Lane Head
ENG - HARROGATE, North Yorkshire HG2 7 TF

Office	Secrétariat	(44) 01423 - 862 999
Pro shop	Pro-shop	(44) 01423 - 862 547
Fax	Fax	(44) 01423 - 860 073
Situation	Situation	

3 km E of Harrogate (pop. 143 526)

Annual closure	Fermeture annuelle	no
Weekly closure	Fermeture hebdomadaire	no

Fees main season
Tarifs haute saison 18 holes

	Week days Semaine	We/Bank holidays We/Férié
Individual Individuel	£ 28	£ 40
Couple Couple	£ 56	£ 80

Full day: £ 32/£ 40

Caddy	Caddy	no
Electric Trolley	Chariot électrique	no
Buggy	Voiturette	no
Clubs	Clubs	no

Credit cards Cartes de crédit
VISA - Eurocard - MasterCard

578

Access Accès : Harrogate, A 59 → Knaresborough.
Golf 3 km on right hand side
Map 4 on page 494 Carte 4 Page 494

GOLF COURSE / PARCOURS — 15/20

Site	Site	
Maintenance	Entretien	
Architect	Architecte	Sandy Herd
Type	Type	parkland
Relief	Relief	
Water in play	Eau en jeu	
Exp. to wind	Exposé au vent	
Trees in play	Arbres en jeu	

Scorecard Carte de score	Chp. Chp.	Mens Mess.	Ladies Da.
Length Long.	5617	5483	5127
Par	69	69	72

Advised golfing ability		0	12	24	36
Niveau de jeu recommandé					

Hcp required	Handicap exigé	certificate

CLUB HOUSE & AMENITIES / CLUB HOUSE ET ANNEXES — 7/10

Pro shop	Pro-shop	
Driving range	Practice	
Sheltered	couvert	
On grass	sur herbe	yes
Putting-green	putting-green	yes
Pitching-green	pitching green	yes

HOTEL FACILITIES / ENVIRONNEMENT HOTELIER — 7/10

HOTELS HÔTELS

Majestic Hotel — Harrogate 5 km
152 rooms, D £ 110
Tel (44) 01423 - 568 972, Fax (44) 01423 - 521 332

Nidd Hall — Harrogate 5 km
56 rooms, D £ 150
Tel (44) 01423 - 771 598, Fax (44) 01423 - 770 931

Green Park — Harrogate 5 km
49 rooms, D £ 83
Tel (44) 01423 - 504 681, Fax (44) 01423 - 536 811

RESTAURANTS RESTAURANTS

The Bistro - Tel (44) 01423 - 530 708 — Harrogate 5 km

La Bergerie — Harrogate 5 km
Tel (44) 01423 - 500 089

Drum and Monkey — Harrogate 5 km
Tel (44) 01423 - 502 650

A strange place where the «Follies» of Hawkstone Park could be a setting for a video game with caves, secret passages or little monuments, all hidden in lush vegetation. They also say that King Arthur is buried somewhere on this estate. What is certain is that Sandy Lyle learnt how to play here. Today, this is a real resort with a hotel and two courses, including «Hawkstone», which was designed by James Braid, with some of the greens in the style of Alister Mackenzie. The course was restored and adapted to the modern game by Brian Huggett, who also laid out the resort's other 18-hole course. Imaginative, sometimes spectacular, very well landscaped and blending perfectly with its environment, this is a course whose subtleties will probably appeal more to the better golfer. Non-golfers can always visit the pretty town of Shrewsbury in the footsteps of Cadfael, the hero of the medieval murder novels by Ellis Peters.

Etrange endroit où les «Follies» de Hawkstone Park pourraient servir de cadre à un jeu vidéo avec grottes, passages secrets ou petits monuments, tous cachés dans une végétation très riche. On murmure que le Roi Arthur aurait été enterré sur ce domaine, mais la seule chose certaine, c'est que Sandy Lyle a appris le golf ici. C'est aujourd'hui un resort, avec hôtel et deux parcours, dont le «Hawkstone» est un James Braid avec certains greens à la Alister Mackenzie, restauré et adapté au jeu moderne par Brian Huggett, qui a également signé l'autre 18 trous du domaine. Imaginatif, parfois spectaculaire, bien paysagé mais en même temps magnifiquement intégré à son environnement, c'est un parcours dont les joueurs d'un bon niveau apprécieront le plus les subtilités. Les autres pourront chercher dans la jolie ville de Shrewsbury les traces de Frère Cadfael, héros des romans policiers médiévaux d'Ellis Peters.

Hawkstone Park Hotel — 1920

Weston-under-Redcastle
ENG - SHREWSBURY, Shropshire SY4 5UY

Office	Secrétariat	(44) 01939 - 200 611
Pro shop	Pro-shop	(44) 01939 - 200 611
Fax	Fax	(44) 01939 - 200 311
Situation	Situation	

19 km N of Shrewsbury (pop. 91 749)

Annual closure	Fermeture annuelle	no
Weekly closure	Fermeture hebdomadaire	no
Fees main season	Tarifs haute saison	18 holes

	Week days Semaine	We/Bank holidays We/Férié
Individual Individuel	£ 27	£ 34.50
Couple Couple	£ 54	£ 69

Full day: £ 40/£ 48

Caddy	Caddy	on request/£ 20
Electric Trolley	Chariot électrique	£ 7.50/18 holes
Buggy	Voiturette	£ 23/18 holes
Clubs	Clubs	£ 12/18 holes

Credit cards Cartes de crédit
VISA - Eurocard - MasterCard - AMEX

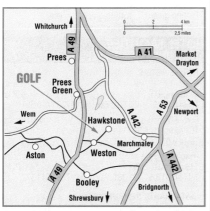

Access Accès : M6 Birmingham → Liverpool. Jct 10A through Telford, A5 → Shrewsbury. A49 North. Follow signs for Hawkstone Historic Park
Map 5 on page 496 Carte 5 Page 496

GOLF COURSE / PARCOURS — 15/20

Site	Site	
Maintenance	Entretien	
Architect	Architecte	James Braid
Type	Type	parkland
Relief	Relief	
Water in play	Eau en jeu	
Exp. to wind	Exposé au vent	
Trees in play	Arbres en jeu	

Scorecard	Chp.	Mens	Ladies
Carte de score	Chp.	Mess.	Da.
Length Long.	5842	5519	5153
Par	72	72	72

Advised golfing ability	0	12	24	36
Niveau de jeu recommandé				
Hcp required	Handicap exigé	certificate		

CLUB HOUSE & AMENITIES / CLUB HOUSE ET ANNEXES — 8/10

Pro shop	Pro-shop	
Driving range	Practice	
Sheltered	couvert	no
On grass	sur herbe	yes
Putting-green	putting-green	yes
Pitching-green	pitching green	yes

579

HOTEL FACILITIES / ENVIRONNEMENT HOTELIER — 7/10

HOTELS HÔTELS

Hawkstone Park Hotel — Weston, on site
65 rooms, D £ 120
Tel (44) 01939 - 200 611
Fax (44) 01939 - 200 311

Albrighton Hall — Albrighton, 12 km
39 rooms, D £ 95
Tel (44) 01939 - 291 000
Fax (44) 01939 - 291 123

Prince Rupert — Shrewsbury, 19 km
62 rooms, D £ 68
Tel (44) 01939 - 499 955
Fax (44) 01939 - 357 306

RESTAURANTS RESTAURANT

Hawkstone Park Hotel — Weston, on site
Tel (44) 01939 - 200 611

The southern coast of England has very few genuine links courses. Rye (totally private) can claim the label, and so can Hayling, whose reputation has never gone beyond England despite being designed by Tom Simpson, a hallmark of quality. As usual, the hazards are remarkably well located with the best route to the green always being the most dangerous (as with Donald Ross). At the same time visibility is 90% perfect so you can get to grips with the course from the first time out. Here you are adapting your game all the time, but that is one of the pleasures of golf. This easy-walking course is ideal for the holidays if you are not too concerned about your card. Close to the beach and a very rich nature reserve, Hayling deserves a good visit.

Cette côte sud de l'Angleterre propose bien peu de sites de vrais links, seul Rye (totalement privé) pouvant prétendre en être un. Ainsi que Hayling, dont la notoriété n'a pas dépassé les frontières, en dépit de la signature de Tom Simpson, une garantie de qualité. Comme d'habitude avec lui, le placement des obstacles est remarquable, la meilleure route étant toujours la plus dangereuse (comme avec Donald Ross), et la visibilité est à 90 % parfaite, de manière à pouvoir entrer dans le vif du sujet dès la première visite. Les problèmes posés diffèrent d'un trou à l'autre, et d'un vent à l'autre, ce qui oblige à s'adapter sans cesse, mais c'est un des plaisirs du golf. Peu fatigant à marcher, c'est un parcours idéal pour les vacances, si l'on n'est pas trop soucieux de son score. Proche de la plage et d'une très riche réserve naturelle, Hayling mérite une visite attentive.

Hayling Golf Club   1883
Links Lane
ENG- HAYLING ISLAND, Hampshire PO11 0BX

Office	Secrétariat	(44) 01705 - 464 446
Pro shop	Pro-shop	(44) 01705 - 464 491
Fax	Fax	(44) 01705 - 464 46
Situation	Situation	

15 km from Portsmouth - 8 km from Havant (pop. 46 510)

Annual closure	Fermeture annuelle	no
Weekly closure	Fermeture hebdomadaire	no

Fees main season
Tarifs haute saison 18 holes

	Week days Semaine	We/Bank holidays We/Férié
Individual Individuel	£ 25	£ 30
Couple Couple	£ 50	£ 60

Full day: £ 30/40 - Weekends: no green-fees before 10.00 am

Caddy	Caddy	no
Electric Trolley	Chariot électrique	£ 7.50/18 holes
Buggy	Voiturette	no
Clubs	Clubs	no

Credit cards Cartes de crédit
VISA - MasterCard (Pro shop goods only)

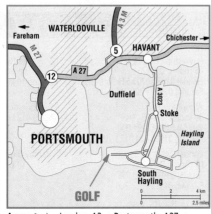

Access Accès : London, A3 → Portsmouth, A27 → Havant. A 3023 to Hayling Island. Seafront, turn right **Map 7 on page 500** Carte 7 Page 500

580

GOLF COURSE
PARCOURS   16/20

Site	Site	
Maintenance	Entretien	
Architect	Architecte	J.H. Taylor
		Tom Simpson
Type	Type	seaside course, links
Relief	Relief	
Water in play	Eau en jeu	
Exp. to wind	Exposé au vent	
Trees in play	Arbres en jeu	

Scorecard Carte de score	Chp. Chp.	Mens Mess.	Ladies Da.
Length Long.	5870	5675	5220
Par	71	71	74

Advised golfing ability		0 12 24 36
Niveau de jeu recommandé		
Hcp required	Handicap exigé	certificate

CLUB HOUSE & AMENITIES
CLUB HOUSE ET ANNEXES   7/10

Pro shop	Pro-shop	
Driving range	Practice	
Sheltered	couvert	2 mats
On grass	sur herbe	no
Putting-green	putting-green	yes
Pitching-green	pitching green	no

HOTEL FACILITIES
ENVIRONNEMENT HOTELIER   7/10

HOTELS HÔTELS
Bear   Havant
42 rooms, D £ 70   8 km
Tel (44) 01705 - 486 501, Fax (44) 01705 - 470 551

Forte Posthouse   Portsmouth
163 rooms, D £ 59   15 km
Tel (44) 01705 - 827 651, Fax (44) 01705 - 756 715

Hospitality Inn   Portsmouth
113 rooms, D £ 75   15 km
Tel (44) 01705 - 731 281, Fax (44) 01705 - 817 572

RESTAURANTS RESTAURANTS
Cockle Warren Cottage   Hayling Island
Tel (44) 01705 - 463226   1 km

MA Bakers   Hayling Island
Tel (44) 01705 - 463226   1 km

We have already talked about this very popular region of Henley (see Badgemore) and the Thames Valley with its pretty villages and timbered houses: the Tudor style is gradually replaced by flint as you move towards the Cotswolds. Another landmark to visit is the Uffington White Horse, carved out of chalk on the hillside. While you are here, play this pretty little Henley course with unpretentious facilities and clubhouse but a well-thought out design by James Braid. There is nothing really distinctive about this course but it makes for a good day's golfing with friends of all different playing levels. You will have a good round relaxing between two more difficult courses in the region, have fun at very little cost and might almost believe you play golf better than you ever thought possible. With that said, proceed with care, as even the most benign course can turn spiteful at times.

Avec Badgemore Park, nous avons évoqué cette région très courue d'Henley et de la vallée de la Tamise, avec les petits villages aux maisons à colombages, qui deviennent peu à peu maisons de pierre à mesure que l'on va vers les Costwolds. Il faudra aussi voir le «Cheval Blanc» d'Uffington, gigantesque figure de craie préhistorique. Et aussi penser à jouer ce joli parcours d'Henley, au Clubhouse et aux installations assez modestes, au dessin bien pensé de James Braid. Certes, il n'offre pas de caractère particulier très notable, mais il permet de passer une bonne journée avec des joueurs de tous niveaux, en guise de détente entre deux parcours plus difficiles, de se faire plaisir à peu de frais, et presque de croire que l'on joue mieux qu'on ne l'imaginait. Il faut cependant faire attention, les parcours les plus souriants ont aussi des dents.

Henley Golf Club — 1908

Harpsden
ENG - HENLEY-ON-THAMES, Oxon RG9 4HG

Office	Secrétariat	(44) 01491 - 575 742
Pro shop	Pro-shop	(44) 01491 - 575 710
Fax	Fax	(44) 01491 - 412 179
Situation	Situation	

3 km from Henley (pop. 10 058)
10 km from Reading (pop. 128 877)

Annual closure	Fermeture annuelle	no
Weekly closure	Fermeture hebdomadaire	no

Christmas Day only

Fees main season	Tarifs haute saison	full day
	Week days Semaine	We/Bank holidays We/Férié
Individual Individuel	£ 30	—
Couple Couple	£ 60	—

No visitors at weekends

Caddy	Caddy	no
Electric Trolley	Chariot électrique	yes (summer)
Buggy	Voiturette	no
Clubs	Clubs	£ 15/18 holes

Credit cards Cartes de crédit
Visa - Mastercard (not for green fees)

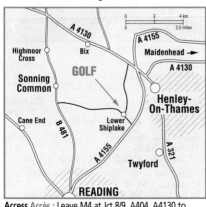

Access Accès : Leave M4 at Jct 8/9, A404, A4130 to Henley-on-Thames, then A4155 → Reading, turn right through Harpsden Village, Golf on the right.
Map 8 on page 502 Carte 8 Page 502

GOLF COURSE / PARCOURS — 14/20

Site	Site	
Maintenance	Entretien	
Architect	Architecte	James Braid
Type	Type	parkland
Relief	Relief	
Water in play	Eau en jeu	
Exp. to wind	Exposé au vent	
Trees in play	Arbres en jeu	

Scorecard Carte de score	Chp. Chp.	Mens Mess.	Ladies Da.
Length Long.	5696	5517	4931
Par	70	70	73

Advised golfing ability
Niveau de jeu recommandé
0   12   24   36

Hcp required   Handicap exigé   certificate

CLUB HOUSE & AMENITIES / CLUB HOUSE ET ANNEXES — 6/10

Pro shop	Pro-shop	
Driving range	Practice	
Sheltered	couvert	no
On grass	sur herbe	yes
Putting-green	putting-green	yes
Pitching-green	pitching green	yes

HOTEL FACILITIES / ENVIRONNEMENT HOTELIER — 7/10

HOTELS HÔTELS

Shepherds - 4 rooms, D £ 48   Henley 3 km
Tel (44) 01491 - 628 413

Holiday Inn - 107 rooms, D £ 105   Reading 10 km
Tel (44) 01734 - 259 988, Fax (44) 01734 - 391 665

Forte Posthouse - 138 rooms, D £ 69   Reading 10 km
Tel (44) 01734 - 875 485, Fax (44) 01734 - 311 958

Great House   Sonning-on-Thames
34 rooms, D £ 85   5 km
Tel (44) 01734 - 692 277, Fax (44) 01734 - 441 296

RESTAURANTS RESTAURANTS

Villa Marina - Tel (44) 01491 - 575 262   Henley 3 km

French Horn   Sonning-on-Thames
Tel (44) 01734 - 692 204   5 km

L'Ortolan   Shinfield
Tel (44) 01734 - 883 783   18 km

581

The Tudor style architecture of this listed clubhouse gives an excellent first impression when you arrive here. You might expect a traditional course, but in fact you are met with excellent practice facilities and a very modern layout by Nicklaus Design, the company that Jack built. Nicklaus did not actually design this course in person, but over a rather limited area you find the same strategic approach with well designed and often large bunkers, water which comes very much into play but which can be avoided, and huge, well-contoured greens. The front nine are very interesting, the back nine a little less so. The whole layout doubtless still needs to mature a little. Being so close to London, this very tranquil course deserves more than one visit.

L'architecture Tudor d'un Clubhouse classé donne d'emblée une impression de majesté. On attendrait un parcours très traditionnel. En fait, il y a ici de remarquables installations d'entraînement, et un parcours de dessin très moderne, créé par Nicklaus Design, la société du grand joueur et architecte américain, qui n'a pas vraiment signé lui-même le parcours. On y trouve cependant, sur un espace assez réduit, la même approche stratégique, avec des bunkers très dessinés et souvent grands, des obstacles d'eau bien en jeu, mais dont il est possible (et conseillé) de ne pas trop s'approcher, des greens vastes et très travaillés. L'aller est très intéressant, le retour un peu moins. L'ensemble a encore besoin de mûrir, sans aucun doute. Si proche de Londres, ce parcours très tranquille mérite plus qu'une visite.

The Hertfordshire Golf & Country Club   1995

Broxbournebury Mansion, White Stubbs Lane
ENG - BROXBOURNE, Herts EN10 7 PY

Office	Secrétariat	(44) 01992 - 466 666
Pro shop	Pro-shop	(44) 01992 - 466 666
Fax	Fax	(44) 01992 - 470 326
Situation	Situation	

8 km S of Hertford (pop. 22 176) - 5 km N of Cheshunt

Annual closure	Fermeture annuelle	no
Weekly closure	Fermeture hebdomadaire	no
Fees main season	Tarifs haute saison	18 holes

	Week days Semaine	We/Bank holidays We/Férié
Individual Individuel	£ 21	£ 25
Couple Couple	£ 42	£ 50
Full day : £ 33/39 each		

Caddy	Caddy	no
Electric Trolley	Chariot électrique	no
Buggy	Voiturette	£ 18 (summer)
Clubs	Clubs	£ 10/18 holes

Credit cards Cartes de crédit
VISA - MasterCard (not for green fees)

582

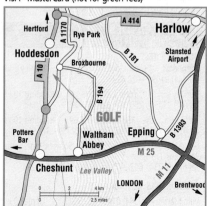

Access Accès : M25. At Jct 25 take A10 → Cambridge.
Exit for Turnford, take A1170 to Bell Lane. Turn left,
Bell Lane becomes White Stubbs Lane. Course
on right. **Map 8 on page 503** Carte 8 Page 503

GOLF COURSE PARCOURS   15/20

Site	Site	
Maintenance	Entretien	
Architect	Architecte	Nicklaus Design
Type	Type	parkland
Relief	Relief	
Water in play	Eau en jeu	
Exp. to wind	Exposé au vent	
Trees in play	Arbres en jeu	

Scorecard Carte de score	Chp. Chp.	Mens Mess.	Ladies Da.
Length Long.	5750	5403	4390
Par	70	70	70

Advised golfing ability Niveau de jeu recommandé	0	12	24	36

Hcp required Handicap exigé   28 Men, 36 Ladies

CLUB HOUSE & AMENITIES CLUB HOUSE ET ANNEXES   7/10

Pro shop	Pro-shop	
Driving range	Practice	
Sheltered	couvert	30 bays
On grass	sur herbe	yes (May → Oct)
Putting-green	putting-green	yes
Pitching-green	pitching green	yes

HOTEL FACILITIES ENVIRONNEMENT HOTELIER   7/10

HOTELS HÔTELS

Cheshunt Marriott	Cheshunt
133 rooms, D £ 110	4 km
Tel (44) 01992 - 451 245, Fax (44) 01992 - 440 120	

Churchgate Manor	Old Harlow
82 rooms, D £ 80	12 km
Tel (44) 01279 - 420 246, Fax (44) 01279 - 437 720	

Harlow Moat House	Harlow
118 rooms, D £ 65	10 km
Tel (44) 01279 - 829 988, Fax (44) 01279 - 635 094	

White Horse	Hertingfordbury
42 rooms, D £ 90	9 km
Tel (44) 01992 - 586 791, Fax (44) 01992 - 550 809	

RESTAURANTS RESTAURANT

Cheshunt Marriott	Cheshunt
Tel (44) 01992 - 451 245	4 km

An impressive site and one of the great new clubs you need to know in the South-West of England which is now so easy to reach courtesy of Eurotunnel. The course, clubhouse and hotel have been laid out in the estate of a castle where Ann Boleyn spent her childhood before briefly becoming Henry VIII's second wife. A stream is in play on almost one half of the course before running into the castle lake, but the hazard is psychologically rather than really dangerous. The trees are much more of a problem and those already on the estate have been supplemented by young plantations which will gradually make their presence felt on the fairways and alter the course as the years go by. As a general rule, Nicholson has made good use of existing features, particularly on the dog-legs, and has created enough variety for the course to be constantly enjoyable. Good work and a pretty place to spend a fine day's golfing.

Un site impressionnant, et l'un des grands nouveaux clubs à connaître dans le sud-ouest de l'Angleterre, si facilement accessible maintenant par Eurotunnel. Le golf, le Clubhouse et l'hôtel ont été créés dans le domaine d'un château où Ann Boleyn passa son enfance, avant d'être la seconde et passagère épouse d'Henry VIII. Le parcours met en jeu sur près de la moitié des trous un cours d'eau se jetant dans le lac du château, mais cet obstacle est plus psychologique que vraiment dangereux. Les arbres le sont bien davantage, et ceux existant dans le parc ont été complétés par de jeunes plantations, qui viendront empiéter sur les fairways et modifier le parcours avec les années. En règle générale, Nicholson a fait bon usage des éléments existant, en particulier sur les doglegs, et donné assez de diversité pour que le plaisir soit constamment renouvelé. Du bon travail et un joli endroit pour passer une bonne journée de golf.

Hever Golf Club — 1993
ENG - HEVER, Kent TN8 7NG

Office	Secrétariat	(44) 01732 - 700 771
Pro shop	Pro-shop	(44) 01732 - 700 785
Fax	Fax	(44) 01732 - 700 775
Situation	Situation	

3 km from Edenbridge (pop. 7 581)
10 km from Tonbridge (pop. 101 765)

Annual closure	Fermeture annuelle	no
Weekly closure	Fermeture hebdomadaire	no

Fees main season
Tarifs haute saison 18 holes

	Week days Semaine	We/Bank holidays We/Férié
Individual Individuel	£ 29	£ 45
Couple Couple	£ 58	£ 90

Visitors after 11.00 pm on weekends

Caddy	Caddy	no
Electric Trolley	Chariot électrique	no
Buggy	Voiturette	£ 20/18 holes
Clubs	Clubs	£ 25/18 holes

Credit cards Cartes de crédit VISA - MasterCard - AMEX

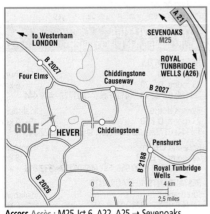

Access Accès : M25 Jct 6, A22, A25 → Sevenoaks.
Limpsfield B269 to Crocham Hill, Four Elms, Bough Beech → Hever Castle
Map 7 on page 501 Carte 7 Page 501

GOLF COURSE
PARCOURS — 14/20

Site	Site	
Maintenance	Entretien	
Architect	Architecte	Peter Nicholson
Type	Type	parkland
Relief	Relief	
Water in play	Eau en jeu	
Exp. to wind	Exposé au vent	
Trees in play	Arbres en jeu	

Scorecard	Chp.	Mens	Ladies
Carte de score	Chp.	Mess.	Da.
Length Long.	6302	6085	5144
Par	72	72	73

Advised golfing ability	0	12	24	36
Niveau de jeu recommandé				

Hcp required   Handicap exigé   certificate

CLUB HOUSE & AMENITIES
CLUB HOUSE ET ANNEXES — 8/10

Pro shop	Pro-shop	
Driving range	Practice	
Sheltered	couvert	no
On grass	sur herbe	yes
Putting-green	putting-green	yes
Pitching-green	pitching green	yes

583

HOTEL FACILITIES
ENVIRONNEMENT HOTELIER — 8/10

HOTELS HÔTELS

Hever Golf Hotel — on site
15 rooms, D £ 79
Tel (44) 01732 - 700 136
Fax (44) 01732 - 700 138

Rose & Crown — Tonbridge 10 km
48 rooms, D £ 80
Tel (44) 01732 - 357 966
Fax (44) 01732 - 357 194

RESTAURANTS RESTAURANTS

Honours Mill — Edenbridge 4 km
Tel (44) 01732 - 866757

The Office — Tonbridge 10 km
Tel (44) 01732 - 353660

Here we are out in the country, with wild peacocks strutting around the clubhouse, jet fighters and trainers flying overhead to disturb your putting stroke, and an obligatory stop at tea-time to taste the delicious cakes. High Post is a hilly course which can be tough on the legs and on your score, but the chalky terrain drains well and doesn't get heavy after rain. The fairways are wide and the rough not too exacting, except when you get too close to the hawthorn bushes. High Post might easily have led a quiet life out of the headlines, except that Peter Alliss drew attention to the course by rating the 9th hole as one of the best 18 holes in England. It is certainly the best without a single grain of sand, and the hollows and grassy sand-hills are often a tougher proposition than bunkers.

Ici, on est à la campagne. Des paons sauvages se promènent autour du Clubhouse, des avions de chasse et d'entraînement vous dérangent quand vous puttez, il faut s'arrêter à l'heure du thé pour déguster quelques fameux Cakes. On monte et on descend, ce qui tire sur les jambes comme sur les scores, mais le terrain crayeux est bien draînant, ce qui évite un sol trop lourd par temps de pluie. Les fairways sont larges, les roughs pas trop pénalisants, sauf auprès des nombreux buissons d'aubépine. On pouvait croire que High Post poursuivra sa vie tranquille à l'écart des grandes histoires, quand Peter Alliss attira l'attention sur ce parcours, en classant son 9 parmi les 18 meilleurs trous d'Angleterre. C'est en tout cas le meilleur où il n'y ait pas un grain de sable, et les dépressions ou buttes d'herbe sont souvent moins faciles à négocier que les bunkers.

High Post Golf Club — 1931

Great Durnford
ENG - SALISBURY, Wiltshire SP4 6AT

Office	Secrétariat	(44) 01722 - 782 356
Pro shop	Pro-shop	(44) 01722 - 782 219
Fax	Fax	(44) 01722 - 782 356
Situation	Situation	

6 km N of Salisbury (pop. 105 318)

Annual closure	Fermeture annuelle	no
Weekly closure	Fermeture hebdomadaire	no

Restaurant: limited service on Mondays

Fees main season
Tarifs haute saison 18 holes

	Week days Semaine	We/Bank holidays We/Férié
Individual Individuel	£ 23	£ 28
Couple Couple	£ 46	£ 56

Full day: £ 30 - £ 35 (weekends)

Caddy	Caddy	no
Electric Trolley	Chariot électrique	£ 5/18 holes
Buggy	Voiturette	no
Clubs	Clubs	no

Credit cards Cartes de crédit
Visa - Mastercard (Pro shop goods only)

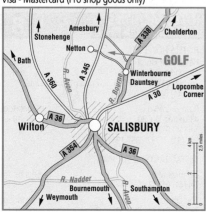

Access Accès : M3 to Southampton, then M27. Jct 2, A36 to Salisbury, then A345 → Amesbury. Golf on right side. **Map 6 on page 499** Carte 6 Page 499

GOLF COURSE / PARCOURS — 15/20

Site	Site	
Maintenance	Entretien	
Architect	Architecte	Hawtree & Taylor
Type	Type	copse, open country
Relief	Relief	
Water in play	Eau en jeu	
Exp. to wind	Exposé au vent	
Trees in play	Arbres en jeu	

Scorecard Carte de score	Chp. Chp.	Mens Mess.	Ladies Da.
Length Long.	5738	5490	5172
Par	70	69	73

Advised golfing ability Niveau de jeu recommandé	0	12	24	36

Hcp required	Handicap exigé	certificate (weekends)

CLUB HOUSE & AMENITIES / CLUB HOUSE ET ANNEXES — 6/10

Pro shop	Pro-shop	
Driving range	Practice	
Sheltered	couvert	no
On grass	sur herbe	yes
Putting-green	putting-green	yes
Pitching-green	pitching green	yes

HOTEL FACILITIES / ENVIRONNEMENT HOTELIER — 7/10

HOTELS HÔTELS

Milford Hall — Salisbury
35 rooms, D £ 70 — 6 km
Tel (44) 01722 - 417 411, Fax (44) 01722 - 419 444

Byways House — Salisbury
23 rooms, D £ 50 — 6 km
Tel (44) 01722 - 328 364, Fax (44) 01722 - 322 146

Rose and Crown — Harnham
28 rooms, D £ 130 — 8 km
Tel (44) 01722 - 399 955, Fax (44) 01722 - 339 816

RESTAURANTS RESTAURANTS

Just Brahms' — Salisbury
Tel (44) 01722 - 328 402 — 6 km

Rose and Crown — Harnham
Tel (44) 01722 - 399 955 — 8 km

584

A quiet course up until 1962, Hillside took on a new dimension with the acquisition of dune-land which Fred Hawtree set to work on. A part of the course is lined by pine-trees, forming an unusual setting rather as if the trees had been plucked and placed on a real links. The first holes run along the railway line and set a «down-the-middle» tone from the very beginning. The dunes and tall rough are more concentrated on the back nine (which won the admiration of Jack Nicklaus) and the fairways run between the dune valleys. In such a motley landscape where the wind can have such a diverse influence on the ball, it is not a bad idea to know how it blows in order to stay on track. Highly manicured but still looking very natural, always pleasant to play and walk on with this links-type soil, Hillside is certainly not the best known links course outside England but it is a must to play.

Parcours tranquille jusqu'en 1962, Hillside a pris une dimension nouvelle avec l'acquisition de terrains travaillés par Fred Hawtree en zone dunaire. De grands pins ornent une partie du parcours, formant un cadre inhabituel, comme un décor posé sur un links authentique. Les premiers trous longent la voie ferrée et annoncent qu'il sera impossible de se relâcher. Les dunes et les haut roughs sont davantage concentrés sur le retour (qui faisait l'admiration de Nicklaus), les fairways glissant dans les vallées. Dans un paysage aussi divers où le vent peut influer de manière différente sur la balle, il n'est pas mauvais de connaître les effets pour rester en piste. Très soigné, tout en conservant un aspect naturel, toujours agréable avec ce genre de sol de links si agréable à marcher et à jouer. Hillside n'est sans doute pas le plus connu des links hors des frontières, mais il est inévitable.

Hillside Golf Club		1923
Hastings Road, Hillside		
ENG - SOUTHPORT, Lancs PR8 2 LU		

Office	Secrétariat	(44) 01704 - 567169
Pro shop	Pro-shop	(44) 01704 - 568360
Fax	Fax	(44) 01704 - 563192
Situation	Situation	
3 km S of Southport (pop. 90 959)		
28 km N of Liverpool (pop. 452 450)		

Annual closure	Fermeture annuelle	no
Weekly closure	Fermeture hebdomadaire	no
Fees main season	Tarifs haute saison	18 holes

	Week days Semaine	We/Bank holidays We/Férié
Individual Individuel	£ 40	£ 50
Couple Couple	£ 80	£ 100
Full weekdays: £ 50		

Caddy	Caddy	on request/£ 25+tip
Electric Trolley	Chariot électrique	no
Buggy	Voiturette	yes
Clubs	Clubs	£ 2 each/18 holes

Credit cards Cartes de crédit
VISA - Eurocard - MasterCard - AMEX - DC - JCB
(not for green-fees)

Access Accès : Off A565 Liverpool → Southport, between Hillside railway station and Royal Birkdale gates. Map 5 on page 497 Carte 5 Page 497

GOLF COURSE
PARCOURS
18/20

Site	Site	
Maintenance	Entretien	
Architect	Architecte	Fred Hawtree (1962)
Type	Type	links
Relief	Relief	
Water in play	Eau en jeu	
Exp. to wind	Exposé au vent	
Trees in play	Arbres en jeu	

Scorecard	Chp.	Mens	Ladies
Carte de score	Chp.	Mess.	Da.
Length Long.	6165	5920	5345
Par	72	72	75

Advised golfing ability	0	12	24	36
Niveau de jeu recommandé				
Hcp required	Handicap exigé	certificate		

CLUB HOUSE & AMENITIES
CLUB HOUSE ET ANNEXES
7/10

Pro shop	Pro-shop	
Driving range	Practice	
Sheltered	couvert	no
On grass	sur herbe	yes
Putting-green	putting-green	yes
Pitching-green	pitching green	yes

585

HOTEL FACILITIES
ENVIRONNEMENT HOTELIER
7/10

HOTELS HÔTELS

Cambridge House Hotel	Southport
18 rooms, D £ 51	5 km
Tel (44) 01704 - 538 372, Fax (44) 01704 - 547 183	

Scarisbrick	Southport
77 rooms, D £ 90	3 km
Tel (44) 01704 - 543 000, Fax (44) 01704 - 533 335	

Stutelea	Southport
24 rooms, D £ 80	3 km
Tel (44) 01704 - 544 220, Fax (44) 01704 - 500 232	

RESTAURANTS RESTAURANTS

The Warehouse	Southport
Tel (44) 01704 - 544 662	3 km

Valentino's	Southport
Tel (44) 01704 - 538 401	3 km

The Jasmin Tree	Southport
Tel (44) 01704 - 530 141	3 km

For a few days golfing in this region of Surrey, on the border with Hampshire and Sussex, Hindhead is one of a threesome which includes Hankley Common and West Surrey. This is very country landscape and a little tiring if you are pulling your own cart. The two parts of the course are very different, with the first 9 holes played in a valley (rather unusual in Surrey) and the back 9 at the top of a hill. From a visual point of view the front 9 are more memorable, especially the 6th, a 3-par looking down steeply onto a well-protected green. Before your round, go and have a drink at the bar, enjoy the magnificent view over the 18th hole and listen to the locals explaining how to play the course. It all comes down to one pint of best bitter and two ideas: keep it straight and keep out of the heather. They could also tell you to avoid the trees and bushes as well, but one look is enough for that to go without saying.

Pour quelques jours de golf dans cette région du Surrey à la limite du Hampshire et du Sussex, Hindhead apporte sa contribution à Hankley Common et West Surrey, dans un paysage très campagnard, mais un peu fatigant s'il faut aussi tirer son chariot. Les deux parties du parcours sont très différentes, les neuf premiers étant joués dans une vallée (c'est peu habituel dans le Surrey) et les neuf derniers au sommet d'une colline. Visuellement, l'aller est plus mémorable, on se souviendra en particulier du 6, un par 3 au green en contrebas et très défendu. Avant de jouer, allez donc faire un tour au bar où les vues sur le 18 sont magnifiques, et où les locaux vous expliqueront la stratégie du parcours. Elle tient en une pinte et deux idées : restez droit et évitez la bruyère. On ne vous dira pas d'éviter aussi les bois et buissons, cela va sans dire en jetant un seul coup d'oeil.

Hindhead Golf Club — 1904
Churt Road
ENG - HINDHEAD, Surrey GU26 6HX

Office	Secrétariat	(44) 01428 - 604 614
Pro shop	Pro-shop	(44) 01428 - 604 458
Fax	Fax	(44) 01428 - 608 508
Situation	Situation	

4 km from Haslemere (pop. 7 326)

Annual closure	Fermeture annuelle	no
Weekly closure	Fermeture hebdomadaire	no

Fees main season	Tarifs haute saison		18 holes
		Week days Semaine	We/Bank holidays We/Férié
Individual Individuel		£ 36	£ 44
Couple Couple		£ 72	£ 88

Caddy	Caddy	no
Electric Trolley	Chariot électrique	no
Buggy	Voiturette	no
Clubs	Clubs	no

Credit cards Cartes de crédit
VISA - MasterCard (not for greenfees)

586

Access Accès : London, A3 (→ Portsmouth). Approx. 9 km (5 m) after Milford, turn right onto A287 → Hindhead, Farnham. After Beacon Hill, golf on right side. **Map 7 on page 500** Carte 7 Page 500

GOLF COURSE / PARCOURS — 16/20

Site	Site	
Maintenance	Entretien	
Architect	Architecte	J.H. Taylor
Type	Type	inland, heathland
Relief	Relief	
Water in play	Eau en jeu	
Exp. to wind	Exposé au vent	
Trees in play	Arbres en jeu	

Scorecard Carte de score	Chp. Chp.	Mens Mess.	Ladies Da.
Length Long.	5735	5520	4992
Par	70	69	72

Advised golfing ability	0	12	24	36
Niveau de jeu recommandé				
Hcp required	Handicap exigé	certificate		

CLUB HOUSE & AMENITIES / CLUB HOUSE ET ANNEXES — 7/10

Pro shop	Pro-shop	
Driving range	Practice	
Sheltered	couvert	2 nets
On grass	sur herbe	yes
Putting-green	putting-green	yes
Pitching-green	pitching green	yes

HOTEL FACILITIES / ENVIRONNEMENT HOTELIER — 6/10

HOTELS HÔTELS
Pride of the Valley — Churt
11 rooms, D £ 70 — 2 km
Tel (44) 01428 - 605 799, Fax (44) 01428 - 605 875

Lythe Hill — Haslemere
28 rooms, D £ 85 — 6 km
Tel (44) 01428 - 651 251, Fax (44) 01428 - 644 131

Georgian — Haslemere
24 rooms, D £ 75 — 4 km
Tel (44) 01428 - 651 555, Fax (44) 01428 - 661 304

RESTAURANTS RESTAURANTS
Undershaw - Tel (44) 01428 - 604 039 — Hindhead 1 km

Fleur de Sel — Haslemere
Tel (44) 01428 - 651 462 — 4 km

Auberge de France — Haslemere
Tel (44) 01428 - 651 251 — 4 km

This was one of the centres of the great industrial revolution in the 19th century. Industries here included coal-mining, today illustrated by the Yorkshire Mining Museum, and textiles, one of the centres of which was Halifax, a few miles down the road. If you are with the family, take the children to visit the Eureka Museum, a sort of living compendium of science. It might take your mind off golf, despite this Huddersfield course, where another youngster, Sandy Herd, learnt how to play well enough to win the British Open in 1902. He must have had pretty sturdy legs too, because this is a very hilly course. Also called Fixby, the layout is lined with trees and strategy is by no means simple because it is so hard to judge the right distances and trajectories you need to place the drive and attack the greens. A classic layout where only good shots get their just desserts. Isn't that how it should be?

C'était une des grandes régions de la révolution industrielle au XIXème siècle. Un bassin minier illustré aujourd'hui par le Musée Minier du Yorkshire, une région d'industrie textile aussi, dont l'une des capitales était Halifax, à quelques kilomètres d'ici. En famille, vous y amènerez aussi vos jeunes enfants au Musée Eureka, une sorte de livre vivant de la science. De quoi vous distraire de votre passion du golf exercée à Huddersfield, où un autre jeune enfant, Sandy Herd, apprit un jeu qui le mena à la victoire au British Open 1902. Il a au moins acquis ici, sur un terrain bien accidenté, les jambes solides nécessaires à de bons appuis du swing. Appelé aussi Fixby, ce parcours est très boisé, la stratégie n'y est pas évidente tant il est difficile d'y juger des distances et des trajectoires nécessaires, pour placer les drives au bon endroit comme pour attaquer les greens. Un parcours au déroulement classique, où seuls les bons coups seront récompensés. C'est l'essentiel.

Fixby Golf Club — 1891

Fixby Hall, Lightridge Road
ENG - FIXBY, HUDDERSFIELD, W. Yorks. HD2 2EP

Office	Secrétariat	(44) 01484 - 420 110
Pro shop	Pro-shop	(44) 01484 - 426 463
Fax	Fax	(44) 01484 - 424 623
Situation	Situation	

3 km S. of Huddersfield (pop. 147 726)

Annual closure	Fermeture annuelle	no
Weekly closure	Fermeture hebdomadaire	no
Fees main season	Tarifs haute saison	18 holes

	Week days Semaine	We/Bank holidays We/Férié
Individual Individuel	£ 30	£ 40
Couple Couple	£ 60	£ 80

Full day: £ 40/£ 50

Caddy	Caddy	no
Electric Trolley	Chariot électrique	£ 5
Buggy	Voiturette	no
Clubs	Clubs	no

Credit cards Cartes de crédit
VISA - Eurocard - MasterCard - Switch
(Pro shop goods only)

Access Accès : M62 Exit 24 to roundabout. 3rd exit →
Brighouse. 1 km to lights, turn right. Turn right
again onto Lightridge Road. Golf 500 m on right.
Map 4 on page 494 Carte 4 Page 494

GOLF COURSE / PARCOURS — 16/20

Site	Site	
Maintenance	Entretien	
Architect	Architecte	Unknown
Type	Type	parkland, hilly
Relief	Relief	
Water in play	Eau en jeu	
Exp. to wind	Exposé au vent	
Trees in play	Arbres en jeu	

Scorecard Carte de score	Chp. Chp.	Mens Mess.	Ladies Da.
Length Long.	5825	5470	5020
Par	71	71	71

Advised golfing ability Niveau de jeu recommandé	0	12	24	36

Hcp required Handicap exigé certificate

CLUB HOUSE & AMENITIES / CLUB HOUSE ET ANNEXES — 6/10

Pro shop	Pro-shop	
Driving range	Practice	
Sheltered	couvert	
On grass	sur herbe	yes
Putting-green	putting-green	yes
Pitching-green	pitching green	yes

587

HOTEL FACILITIES / ENVIRONNEMENT HOTELIER — 7/10

HOTELS HÔTELS
Hilton Nation — Huddersfield
100 rooms, D £ 90 — 5 km
Tel (44) 01422 - 375 431, Fax (44) 01422 - 310 067

The Lodge Hotel — Huddersfield
11 rooms, D £ 70 — 9 km
Tel (44) 01484 - 431 001, Fax (44) 01484 - 421 590

Old Golf House — Outlane - Huddersfield
50 rooms, D £ 70 — 3 km
Tel (44) 01422 - 379 311, Fax (44) 01422 - 372 694

RESTAURANTS RESTAURANTS
Weaver's Shed — Golcar
Tel (44) 01484 - 654 284 — 4 km

Brook's — Brighouse
Tel (44) 01484 - 715 284 — 5 km

Maharadjah — Huddersfield
Tel (44) 01484 - 535 037 — 4 km

If you mentioned East Anglia to the majority of continental golfers who are unfamiliar with England, they'd probably think you were talking about a make of car. In fact it is a region and home to some of the country's finest links including Hunstanton, nestling in a superb landscape of dunes, wild grass and scrubby bushes. From the 4th to the 15th holes, after a comparatively placid start, the course winds in every direction and makes that all-important judgment for each shot even more complicated. And just to prove once and for all that golf is an unfair game, this course boasts a famous par 3 hole with a blind green. In contrast, neither the sea nor the beach is out of bounds. Hunstanton plays host to major amateur tournaments, which is only fair dues for this often unorthodox and uplifting course. You might find it more enjoyable if you lose your scoring pencil.

On peut parier que pour les continentaux (qui ne connaissent guère l'Angleterre), East Anglia est le nom d'une voiture. Dans cette région, on trouve quelques-uns des plus beaux links du pays, dont Hunstanton, blotti dans un superbe paysage de dunes couronnées d'herbes folles et de buissons touffus. Du 4 au 15, après un départ assez calme, les trous ne cessent de tourner dans toutes les directions, ce qui n'est pas fait pour faciliter le jugement, pourtant plus que nécessaire ici. Pour faire définitivement comprendre que le golf n'est pas un jeu juste, on trouve ici un fameux par 3 avec green aveugle. En revanche, ni la mer ni la plage ne sont hors limites. Hunstanton reçoit de grandes compétitions amateur, c'est justice, avec ce tracé souvent peu orthodoxe, exaltant et d'autant plus amusant que l'on a perdu son crayon pour noter le score.

Hunstanton Golf Club — 1891

Golf Course Road
ENG - OLD HUNSTANTON, Norfolk PE36 6JQ

Office	Secrétariat	(44) 01485 - 532 811
Pro shop	Pro-shop	(44) 01485 - 532 751
Fax	Fax	(44) 01485 - 532 319
Situation	Situation	

1 km from Hunstanton (pop. 4 736)
27 km from King's Lynn (pop. 41 281)

Annual closure	Fermeture annuelle	no
Weekly closure	Fermeture hebdomadaire	no

Fees main season
Tarifs haute saison 18 holes

	Week days Semaine	We/Bank holidays We/Férié
Individual Individuel	£ 42	£ 53
Couple Couple	£ 84	£ 106

Caddy	Caddy	no
Electric Trolley	Chariot électrique	no
Buggy	Voiturette	no
Clubs	Clubs	no

Credit cards Cartes de crédit
Visa - Mastercard - AMEX (Pro shop goods only)

588

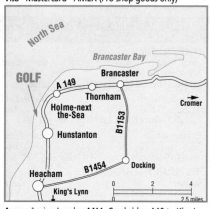

Access Accès : London M11. Cambridge A10 to King's Lynn. A149 North through Hunstanton to Old Hunstanton. Turn left → Golf course.
Map 4 on page 495 Carte 4 Page 495

GOLF COURSE PARCOURS — 17 /20

Site	Site	
Maintenance	Entretien	
Architect	Architecte	James Braid George Fernie
Type	Type	seaside course, links
Relief	Relief	
Water in play	Eau en jeu	
Exp. to wind	Exposé au vent	
Trees in play	Arbres en jeu	

Scorecard Carte de score	Chp. Chp.	Mens Mess.	Ladies Da.
Length Long.	6061	5700	5375
Par	72	72	75

Advised golfing ability Niveau de jeu recommandé	0 12 24 36
Hcp required Handicap exigé	certificate

CLUB HOUSE & AMENITIES CLUB HOUSE ET ANNEXES — 7 /10

Pro shop	Pro-shop	
Driving range	Practice	
Sheltered	couvert	no
On grass	sur herbe	yes
Putting-green	putting-green	yes
Pitching-green	pitching green	no

HOTEL FACILITIES ENVIRONNEMENT HOTELIER — 6 /10

HOTELS HÔTELS
Le Strange Arms — Hunstanton
36 rooms, D £ 70 — 200 m
Tel (44) 01485 - 534 411, Fax (44) 01485 - 534 724

Congham Hall — Grimston
12 rooms, D £ 100 — 28 km
Tel (44) 01485 - 600 250, Fax (44) 01485 - 601 191

Duke's Head — King's Lynn
71 rooms, D £ 70 — 27 km
Tel (44) 01553 - 774 996, Fax (44) 01553 - 763 556

RESTAURANTS RESTAURANTS
The Hoste Arms — Burnham Market
Tel (44) 01328 - 738777 — 15 km

Rococo — King's Lynn
Tel (44) 01553 - 771483 — 27 km

HUNTERCOMBE

14	6	7

At the beginning of the century, Daimlers and then a bus would ferry players to and from Henley railway station. Those were the good old days when service and hospitality meant more than they do today. Huntercombe has become a members' course where green-feers are tolerated on week-days only, although from our experience with no great enthusiasm. This is a pity because here is a layout, designed by Willie Park Jr. over heather and gorse, which is an excellent course, demanding an accurate and serious game. On this very classical and so very British course, keep your head down and don't let yourself be distracted by the pretty view over the plain of Oxford. While in the region, spend a good day out in Oxford and visit Blenheim Palace, the castle of the Dukes of Marlborough whose gardens were designed by Capability Brown.

Au début du siècle, des Daimler puis un autobus du club faisaient l'aller-retour jusqu'à la gare d'Henley pour en ramener les joueurs. C'était l'époque héroïque où le service et l'accueil voulaient dire davantage qu'aujourd'hui. Huntercombe est devenu un golf de membres où l'accès en semaine est toléré, mais pas forcément enthousiaste d'après notre expérience. C'est dommage car le tracé de Willie Park Jr en terrain de bruyère est d'excellente qualité, il exige un jeu précis et sérieux, où on ne lèvera la tête que pour admirer de jolis panoramas sur la plaine d'Oxford. Un parcours très classique et terriblement britannique. Dans la région, il ne faudra pas oublier de passer une bonne journée à Oxford et au Blenheim Palace, château des ducs de Marlborough, où les jardins créés par le grand paysagiste Capability Brown vous donneront des idées.

Huntercombe Golf Club — 1902

Nuffield
ENG - HENLEY-ON-THAMES, Oxon RG9 5SL

Office	Secrétariat	(44) 01491 - 641 207
Pro shop	Pro-shop	(44) 01491 - 641 241
Fax	Fax	(44) 01491 - 642 060
Situation	Situation	

10 km from Henley (pop. 10 058)
5 km from Wallingford (pop. 6 616)

Annual closure	Fermeture annuelle	no
Weekly closure	Fermeture hebdomadaire	no

Fees main season
Tarifs haute saison 18 holes

	Week days Semaine	We/Bank holidays We/Férié
Individual Individuel	—	—
Couple Couple	—	—
Greenfees on request		

Caddy	Caddy	no
Electric Trolley	Chariot électrique	no
Buggy	Voiturette	no
Clubs	Clubs	no

Credit cards Cartes de crédit — no

Access Accès : Leave M4 at Jct 8/9, A404, A4130 through Henley, → Oxford. Clubhouse on the left after 10 km (6 m.)
Map 8 on page 502 Carte 8 Page 502

GOLF COURSE / PARCOURS — 14/20

Site	Site	
Maintenance	Entretien	
Architect	Architecte	Willie Park
Type	Type	heathland
Relief	Relief	
Water in play	Eau en jeu	
Exp. to wind	Exposé au vent	
Trees in play	Arbres en jeu	

Scorecard Carte de score	Chp. Chp.	Mens Mess.	Ladies Da.
Length Long.	5671	5498	5115
Par	70	70	72

Advised golfing ability Niveau de jeu recommandé		0	12	24	36
Hcp required	Handicap exigé	certificate			

CLUB HOUSE & AMENITIES / CLUB HOUSE ET ANNEXES — 6/10

Pro shop	Pro-shop	
Driving range	Practice	
Sheltered	couvert	no
On grass	sur herbe	yes
Putting-green	putting-green	yes
Pitching-green	pitching green	no

HOTEL FACILITIES / ENVIRONNEMENT HOTELIER — 7/10

HOTELS HÔTELS
George — Wallingford
39 rooms, D £ 72 — 5 km
Tel (44) 01491 - 836 665, Fax (44) 01491 - 835 359

Springs — North Stoke
34 rooms, D £ 120 — 5 km
Tel (44) 01491 - 836 687, Fax (44) 01491 - 836 877

Swan Diplomat — Streatley
46 rooms, D £ 120 — 9 km
Tel (44) 01491 - 873 737, Fax (44) 01491 - 872 554

RESTAURANTS RESTAURANTS
Leatherne Bottel — Goring
Tel (44) 01491 - 872 667 — 8 km

Beetle and Wedge — Moulsford
Tel (44) 01491 - 651 381 — 7 km

589

Welcome to the beautiful region of the Yorkshire Dales, where you can visit the Wharfe valley and Ilkley, Fountains Abbey and the town of Haworth, home to the Brontë sisters. While you are here, don't forget to play this superb course designed by Colt and Mackenzie, where the river Wharfe threatens your card on seven holes. Flat and laid out in picturesque landscape, Ilkley is a charming course where nothing is easy but where nothing is impossible, either. Just avoid the trees, the fairway bunkers and the traps beside the greens. Nothing could be simpler. The greenside bunkers also tend to obstruct the obvious approach route to what are generally excellent putting surfaces. A good score is by no means a certainty here, as there are only two par 5s for the chance of a birdie, five par 3s and a few long par 4s where you can easily waste precious strokes. Mark James, Gordon Brand and Colin Montgomerie are members here, and this course is good enough to make you feel almost envious.

De cette très belle région, on retiendra le Parc National des Vallées du Yorkshire, dont celle de la Wharfe qui irrigue Ilkley, le très bel et très curieux ensemble religieux et aristocratique de Fountains Abbey, et la ville d'Haworth, foyer des soeurs Brontë. Et l'on n'oubliera pas de jouer ce superbe parcours, dessiné par Colt et Mackenzie, où la Wharfe vient en jeu sur sept trous. Plat et dans un paysage pittoresque, c'est un parcours de charme, où rien n'est facile, mais rien impossible. Il suffit d'éviter les arbres, les bunkers de fairway, les bunkers de greens qui ferment l'entrée de greens généralement en condition parfaite. Un bon score n'est pas donné d'avance car il n'y a que deux par 5 pour espérer des birdies, cinq par 3 et quelques longs par 4 pour gaspiller toute ses réserves. Mark James, Gordon Brand et Colin Montgomerie sont membres ici, on n'est pas loin de les envier.

Ilkley Golf Club — 1890
Middleton
ENG - ILKLEY, Yorkshire LS29 0BE

Office	Secrétariat	(44) 01943 - 600 214
Pro shop	Pro-shop	(44) 01943 - 607 463
Fax	Fax	(44) 01943 - 607 463
Situation	Situation	

1.5 km from Ilkley (pop. 13 530)
25 km from Leeds (pop. 680 725)

Annual closure	Fermeture annuelle	no
Weekly closure	Fermeture hebdomadaire	no
Fees main season	Tarifs haute saison	full day

	Week days Semaine	We/Bank holidays We/Férié
Individual Individuel	£ 35	£ 40
Couple Couple	£ 70	£ 80
Weekdays: £ 15 after 5.00 pm		

Caddy	Caddy	on request
Electric Trolley	Chariot électrique	£ 5/18 holes
Buggy	Voiturette	no
Clubs	Clubs	£ 7/18 holes

Credit cards Cartes de crédit
VISA - MasterCard - AMEX - Delta - Switch
(£ 1 added charge for green-fees)

590

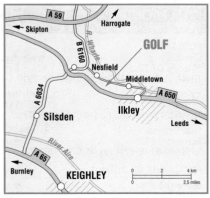

Access Accès : From Leeds, A660, then A65 W → Ilkley, Skipton. In Ilkley, turn right at town centre traffic lights and then second left.
Map 4 on page 494 Carte 4 Page 494

GOLF COURSE PARCOURS — 18/20

Site	Site	
Maintenance	Entretien	
Architect	Architecte	Harry S. Colt Alister MacKenzie
Type	Type	parkland
Relief	Relief	
Water in play	Eau en jeu	
Exp. to wind	Exposé au vent	
Trees in play	Arbres en jeu	

Scorecard Carte de score	Chp. Chp.	Mens Mess.	Ladies Da.
Length Long.	5636	5357	5120
Par	69	69	73

Advised golfing ability Niveau de jeu recommandé	0 12 24 36
Hcp required	Handicap exigé	no

CLUB HOUSE & AMENITIES CLUB HOUSE ET ANNEXES — 7/10

Pro shop	Pro-shop	
Driving range	Practice	
Sheltered	couvert	practice area
On grass	sur herbe	yes
Putting-green	putting-green	yes (3)
Pitching-green	pitching green	yes (2)

HOTEL FACILITIES ENVIRONNEMENT HOTELIER — 6/10

HOTELS HÔTELS
Rombalds — Ilkley
13 rooms, D £ 85 — 1 km
Tel (44) 01943 - 603 201, Fax (44) 01943 - 600 298

Grove — Ilkley
6 rooms, D £ 54 — 1 km
Tel (44) 01943 - 600 298

Randell's — Skipton
76 rooms, D £ 100 — 12 km
Tel (44) 01756 - 700 100, Fax (44) 01756 - 700 107

RESTAURANTS RESTAURANTS
Box Tree - Tel (44) 01943 - 608 484 — Ilkley 1 km
Cow and Calf — Ilkley
Tel (44) 01943 - 607 335 — 1 km
David Woolley's — Burley-in-Wharfedale
Tel (44) 01943 - 864 602 — 5 km

This is exactly the hide-out you dream of when the wind is too strong to attempt the links course on the coast. It is also the opportunity to discover what is much more than an understudy course, an unthinkable notion for a course designed by James Braid. Even though the great man designed more than a hundred courses, he always succeeded in squeezing the very best out of the land or in creating an extraordinary challenge. Like on the 17th, a par 5 which would be quite harmless if he hadn't placed a few pot bunkers to make you wonder about the length of your second shot. If you decide to lay up, you have a tough third shot on your hands. Then there is the 4th hole where the green is hidden in a vale; if your drive is not just perfect, you have a blind second shot to contend with. Just a few examples to prove that nothing is given away here, and that «old» courses and «old» architects can still teach today's over-confident youngsters a thing or two.

C'est exactement le refuge dont on rêve quand le vent souffle trop pour aller sur les links de la côte. Et c'est l'occasion de découvrir ce qui est bien mieux qu'une doublure. Dire qu'il a été dessiné par James Braid devrait être une signature suffisante. Même s'il a fait des centaines de parcours, il a toujours su tirer du terrain la quintessence, ou alors créer des défis inédits. Comme au 17, un par 5 qui serait anodin s'il n'avait placé quelques pot bunkers pour que l'on s'interroge sur la longueur du second coup : si on décide de rester court, le troisième coup ne sera pas facile ! Prenons le 4, un énorme par 4 où le green est caché dans un vallon : si le drive n'est pas exceptionnel, le second coup est aveugle. De rares exemples pour dire que rien n'est ici donné, que les «vieux» architectes et les «vieux» parcours peuvent encore donner des leçons aux jeunes stars trop sûres d'elles.

Ipswich Golf Club — 1895

Purdis Heath, Bucklesham Road
ENG - IPSWICH, Suffolk IP 3 88VQ

Office	Secrétariat	(44) 01473 - 727 474
Pro shop	Pro-shop	(44) 01473 - 724 017
Fax	Fax	(44) 01473 - 715 236
Situation	Situation	

5 km from Ipswich (pop. 130 157)

Annual closure	Fermeture annuelle	no
Weekly closure	Fermeture hebdomadaire	no

Fees main season
Tarifs haute saison 18 holes

	Week days Semaine	We/Bank holidays We/Férié
Individual Individuel	£ 30	—
Couple Couple	£ 60	—

Full day: £ 45 - No visitors at weekends - Booking essential

Caddy	Caddy	no
Electric Trolley	Chariot électrique	no
Buggy	Voiturette	no
Clubs	Clubs	no

Credit cards Cartes de crédit
Visa - Mastercard (Pro shop goods only)

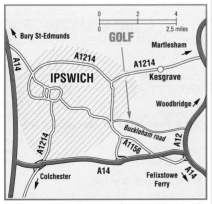

Bury St-Edmunds **GOLF** **Martlesham**
A1214 A1214 Kesgrave
IPSWICH Woodbridge
Bucklesham road A12 A1156
A14 **Colchester** A14 **Felixstowe Ferry**

Access Accès : Ipswich A14 E. Left at roundabout by St Augustine's Church. Golf into Bucklesham Road
Map 7 on page 501 Carte 7 Page 501

GOLF COURSE / PARCOURS — 16/20

Site	Site	
Maintenance	Entretien	
Architect	Architecte	James Braid
Type	Type	inland, heathland
Relief	Relief	
Water in play	Eau en jeu	
Exp. to wind	Exposé au vent	
Trees in play	Arbres en jeu	

Scorecard Carte de score	Chp. Chp.	Mens Mess.	Ladies Da.
Length Long.	5792	5792	5172
Par	71	71	73

Advised golfing ability Niveau de jeu recommandé	0	12	24	36
Hcp required Handicap exigé	certificate			

CLUB HOUSE & AMENITIES / CLUB HOUSE ET ANNEXES — 7/10

Pro shop	Pro-shop	
Driving range	Practice	
Sheltered	couvert	no
On grass	sur herbe	yes
Putting-green	putting-green	yes
Pitching-green	pitching green	no

591

HOTEL FACILITIES / ENVIRONNEMENT HOTELIER — 7/10

HOTELS HÔTELS

Suffolk Grange — Ipswich
60 rooms, D £ 75 — 2 km
Tel (44) 01473 - 272 244
Fax (44) 01473 - 272 484

Novotel - 100 rooms, D £ 55 — Ipswich
Tel (44) 01473 - 232 400 — 5 km
Fax (44) 01473 - 232 414

Marlborough — Ipswich
21 rooms, D £ 70 — 5 km
Tel (44) 01473 - 257 677
Fax (44) 01473 - 226 927

RESTAURANTS RESTAURANTS

St Peter's — Ipswich
Tel (44) 01473 - 210810 — 5 km

Galley — Ipswich
Tel (44) 01473 - 281131 — 5 km

This is the kind of course where the superb views add a point or two to the artistic score. In the distance are the busy south-coast resorts of Poole and Bournemouth, and the Solent. Here you have all the peace and quiet of superb country landscape on the edge of a natural reserve for plant and bird-lovers. The broom and heather add to the decoration and to the problems awaiting players who are wayward or blown off line by the wind. Design-wise this is not exactly a links course but it does require the same skills of flighting and rolling the ball, of trying to outwit and outfox the course. A pretty site for a long weekend with a very pleasant clubhouse, warm welcome, excellent food and a classy additional 9 hole course where you can leave the less gifted members of the family to discover the joys of golf.

C'est le genre de parcours où la qualité des vues donne un petit point de «note artistique» en plus. Au loin, les stations très fréquentées de Poole, Bournemouth, le Solent. Ici, c'est le calme dans un superbe paysage de campagne, en bordure d'une réserve naturelle pour amoureux de plantes et d'oiseaux. Les genêts et la bruyère apportent un élément de décor, mais pas mal aussi d'empoisonnement aux joueurs peu précis, ou emportés par le vent. Ce parcours n'est pas exactement un links dans son style d'architecture, mais il demande les mêmes qualités, savoir travailler la balle, la faire rouler comme il faut, avoir aussi un peu de ruse, être en quelque sorte plus intelligent que le parcours. Un joli lieu de long week-end, avec un Clubhouse très agréable, un accueil chaleureux, une bonne cuisine et un 9 trous supplémentaire de bonne facture pour poser les joueurs les moins compétents de la famille.

Isle of Purbeck Golf Club   1892
ENG - SWANAGE, Dorset BH19 3AB

Office	Secrétariat	(44) 01929 - 450 354
Pro shop	Pro-shop	(44) 01929 - 450 354
Fax	Fax	(44) 01929 - 450 501
Situation	Situation	

12 km S of Poole (pop. 133 050)
5 km from Swanage (pop. 9 037)

Annual closure	Fermeture annuelle	no
Weekly closure	Fermeture hebdomadaire	no

Fees main season
Tarifs haute saison 18 holes

	Week days Semaine	We/Bank holidays We/Férié
Individual Individuel	£ 26	£ 32
Couple Couple	£ 52	£ 64

Full day: £ 35 - £ 40 (weekends) - £ 18 after 4.00 pm

Caddy	Caddy	no
Electric Trolley	Chariot électrique	no
Buggy	Voiturette	£ 40/day
Clubs	Clubs	£ 10/18 holes

Credit cards Cartes de crédit VISA - MasterCard

592

Access Accès : • Ferry from Sandbanks to Studland
• Poole, A351 through Wareham and B3351 →
Studland **Map 6 on page 499** Carte 6 Page 499

GOLF COURSE
PARCOURS   **16**/20

Site	Site	
Maintenance	Entretien	
Architect	Architecte	Harry S. Colt
Type	Type	seaside course, heathland
Relief	Relief	
Water in play	Eau en jeu	
Exp. to wind	Exposé au vent	
Trees in play	Arbres en jeu	

Scorecard	Chp.	Mens	Ladies
Carte de score	Chp.	Mess.	Da.
Length Long.	5730	5450	5080
Par	70	70	73

Advised golfing ability	0	12	24	36
Niveau de jeu recommandé				
Hcp required	Handicap exigé		28 Men, 36 Ladies	

CLUB HOUSE & AMENITIES
CLUB HOUSE ET ANNEXES   **7**/10

Pro shop	Pro-shop	
Driving range	Practice	
Sheltered	couvert	no
On grass	sur herbe	yes
Putting-green	putting-green	yes
Pitching-green	pitching green	yes

HOTEL FACILITIES
ENVIRONNEMENT HOTELIER   **6**/10

HOTELS HÔTELS
Havenhurst   Swanage
17 rooms, D £ 50   5 km
Tel (44) 01929 - 424 224

Mortons House   Corfe Castle
16 rooms, D £ 80   5 km
Tel (44) 01929 - 480 988, Fax (44) 01929 - 480 280

Crowthorne   Swanage
8 rooms, D £ 44   5 km
Tel (44) 01929 - 422 108

RESTAURANTS RESTAURANTS

Cauldron Bistro   Swanage
Tel (44) 01929 - 422 671   5 km

The Galley   Swanage
Tel (44) 01929 - 427 299   5 km

JOHN O'GAUNT

) 16 | 7 | 6

A great club, as British as you could ever imagine, with two 18-hole courses and a huge and very comfortable clubhouse with wonderful old-style architecture. John O'Gaunt is close enough to London to be within easy reach but far enough not to be too busy, at least during the week. The trees are magnificent and give the course a very park-like appearance, adding style to what is a very discreet layout from Hawtree, at least for the main course. A classic layout which calls for no particular comment but which gives an impression of balance and fulfilment when you play it, especially for lovers of traditional courses that seem to have been around for ever. The other course, Carthagena, opened in 1981, is more of a heather-land course.

Un grand club bien britannique comme on l'imagine, avec deux parcours de 18 trous et un vaste Clubhouse à l'architecture ancienne digne d'une bonne série policière télévisée, et parfaitement confortable. John O'Gaunt est assez proche de Londres pour être facilement accessible, mais assez loin pour ne pas être trop encombré, en tout cas en semaine. Les arbres y sont magnifiques, donnant une allure de parc, qui convient bien à l'esthétique assez sobre de Hawtree, pour le parcours principal en tout cas. Très classique, c'est le genre de réalisation qui n'appelle pas de commentaires particuliers, mais donne une impression d'équilibre et de plénitude quand on le joue. Pour amoureux des bons parcours traditionnels, qui donnent l'impression d'être là depuis toujours. L'autre parcours, Carthagena, inauguré en 1981, est plus proche d'un style de terre de bruyère.

John O'Gaunt Golf Club — 1948

Sutton Park
ENG - SANDY, Bedshire SG19 2LY

Office	Secrétariat	(44) 01767 - 260 360
Pro shop	Pro-shop	(44) 01767 - 260 094
Fax	Fax	(44) 01767 - 261 381
Situation	Situation	

18 km from Bedford (pop. 13 066)
35 km from Cambridge (pop. 91 933)

Annual closure	Fermeture annuelle	no
Weekly closure	Fermeture hebdomadaire	no

Fees main season
Tarifs haute saison full day

	Week days Semaine	We/Bank holidays We/Férié
Individual Individuel	£ 45	£ 50
Couple Couple	£ 90	£ 100

Caddy	Caddy	no
Electric Trolley	Chariot électrique	no
Buggy	Voiturette	£ 18/18 holes
Clubs	Clubs	no

Credit cards Cartes de crédit not for greenfees

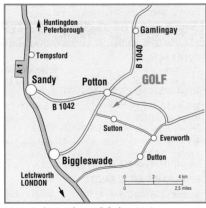

Access Accès : London A1 (M), then A1. At Biggleswade, turn on B1040 → Potton. Golf on right side before Potton.
Map 7 on page 500 Carte 7 Page 500

GOLF COURSE / PARCOURS — 16/20

Site	Site	
Maintenance	Entretien	
Architect	Architecte	Fred Hawtree
Type	Type	parkland
Relief	Relief	
Water in play	Eau en jeu	
Exp. to wind	Exposé au vent	
Trees in play	Arbres en jeu	

Scorecard Carte de score	Chp. Chp.	Mens Mess.	Ladies Da.
Length Long.	5861	5593	5112
Par	71	71	75

Advised golfing ability Niveau de jeu recommandé		0 12 24 36
Hcp required Handicap exigé		28 Men, 36 Ladies

CLUB HOUSE & AMENITIES / CLUB HOUSE ET ANNEXES — 7/10

Pro shop	Pro-shop	
Driving range	Practice	
Sheltered	couvert	no
On grass	sur herbe	yes
Putting-green	putting-green	yes
Pitching-green	pitching green	yes

HOTEL FACILITIES / ENVIRONNEMENT HOTELIER — 6/10

HOTELS HÔTELS
Stratton House - 31 rooms, D £ 38   Biggleswade 3 km
Tel (44) 01767 - 312 442, Fax (44) 01767 - 600 416

Holiday Inn Garden Court   Sandy
56 rooms, D £ 45   3 km
Tel (44) 01767 - 692 220, Fax (44) 01767 - 680 452

Wyboston Lakes   Wyboston
102 rooms, D £ 50   10 km
Tel (44) 01480 - 212 625, Fax (44) 01480 - 223 000

Barns Country Club   Bedford
48 rooms, D £ 67   18 km
Tel (44) 01234 - 270 044, Fax (44) 01234 - 273 102

RESTAURANTS RESTAURANTS
St Helena   Elstow (Bedford)
Tel (44) 01234 - 344 848   20 km

Barns Country Club   Bedford
Tel (44) 01767 - 270 044   16 km

593

Designed by James Braid, La Moye has been considerably lengthened and altered to become the great tournament course of the Channel Islands and long-time home to the Jersey Open. Laid out over the dunes and rolling mounds on the promontory overlooking St Ouen's Bay, it provides an outstanding view and a constantly entertaining challenge. Length and wind together don't make reaching the greens any easier, some of which are blind, all of which are well protected by bunkers or sand-hills. In this setting, only a sharp short game can help save a normal score. If you don't understand how to roll the ball up to the pin ask the pro or some of the local players. During the long evenings of May and early Summer, there are few places on earth where you can get so much pleasure out of playing golf.... no matter how well or badly you are playing.

Originellement dessiné par James Braid, La Moye a été considérablement allongé et modifié, et représente le grand parcours de championnat des iles anglo-normandes, où s'est longtemps disputé le Jersey Open. Tracé sur les dunes et ondulations du promontoire dominant St Ouen's Bay, il offre un panorama exceptionnel et constitue un défi constamment intéressant. Cette longueur combinée au vent ne facilite pas l'accès aux greens, dont certains sont presque aveugles, et tous bien protégés par des bunkers ou les ondulations du terrain. Dans ces conditions, la qualité du petit jeu peut seule garantir un score correct, mais si on n'arrive pas à comprendre comment faire rouler la balle jusqu'au drapeau, il faut demander au pro ou aux joueurs locaux ! Au cours des longues fins de journée du mois de mai au début de l'été, il y a peu d'endroits où l'on puisse éprouver autant de plaisir à jouer au golf. Bien ou mal, peu importe.

La Moye Golf Club — 1902

La Moye
ENG - ST BRELADE, Jersey JE3 8GQ

Office	Secrétariat	(44) 01534 - 43 401
Pro shop	Pro-shop	(44) 01534 - 47 166
Fax	Fax	(44) 01534 - 47 289
Situation	Situation	

10 km W of St Helier (pop. 28 123) - 4 km W of St Aubin

Annual closure	Fermeture annuelle	no
Weekly closure	Fermeture hebdomadaire	no

Fees main season
Tarifs haute saison 18 holes

	Week days Semaine	We/Bank holidays We/Férié
Individual Individuel	£ 40	£ 45*
Couple Couple	£ 80	£ 90*

* only after 2.30 pm at weekends - Full weekday: £55

Caddy	Caddy	no
Electric Trolley	Chariot électrique	£ 5/18 holes
Buggy	Voiturette	£ 18/18 holes
Clubs	Clubs	£ 12/18 holes

Credit cards Cartes de crédit VISA - MasterCard

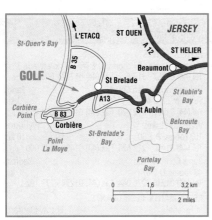

Access Accès : St Helier A1 through St Aubin, then A13 → St Brelade.
Map 9 on page 504 Carte 9 Page 504

GOLF COURSE PARCOURS — 17/20

Site	Site	
Maintenance	Entretien	
Architect	Architecte	James Braid
Type	Type	seaside course, links
Relief	Relief	
Water in play	Eau en jeu	
Exp. to wind	Exposé au vent	
Trees in play	Arbres en jeu	

Scorecard Carte de score	Chp. Chp.	Mens Mess.	Ladies Da.
Length Long.	5998	5775	5320
Par	72	72	74

Advised golfing ability		0 12 24 36
Niveau de jeu recommandé		
Hcp required	Handicap exigé	24 Men, 30 Ladies

CLUB HOUSE & AMENITIES CLUB HOUSE ET ANNEXES — 7/10

Pro shop	Pro-shop	
Driving range	Practice	
Sheltered	couvert	10 mats
On grass	sur herbe	no
Putting-green	putting-green	yes
Pitching-green	pitching green	yes

HOTEL FACILITIES ENVIRONNEMENT HOTELIER — 8/10

HOTELS HÔTELS

L'Horizon — St Brelade's Bay
107 rooms, D £ 150 — 2 km
Tel (44) 01534 - 43 101, Fax (44) 01534 - 46 269

St Brelade's Bay — St Brelade's Bay
80 rooms, D £ 120 — 2 km
Tel (44) 01534 - 46 141, Fax (44) 01534 - 47 278

Sea Crest — Corbière 2 km
7 rooms, D £ 80
Tel (44) 01534 - 46 353, Fax (44) 01534 - 47 316

RESTAURANTS RESTAURANTS

Broome's - Tel (44) 01534 - 42 760 — St Aubin 4 km

Star Grill (L'Horizon) — St Brelade's Bay
Tel (44) 01534 - 43 101 — 2 km

Sea Crest — Corbière
Tel (44) 01534 - 46 353 — 2 km

It was the superb hotel of the same name that added this 18-hole course to its estate, which includes a semi-detached pub transformed, quite logically, into a clubhouse. The owners love the end result, and quite rightly so. They wanted a course that was playable by all, an extremely difficult task but one that Jonathan Gaunt managed to achieve. This is a fair course that you can get to grips with right away, as the thick rough and rather frequent hazards (ditches and lakes) only penalise the truly wayward shot. Only two holes really call for high pitching shots, and even then the distances involved are short. Despite the course's tender age, green-keeping is excellent on a site where everything has been done so very professionally. Pleasant to play, challenging from the back tees and set in a very peaceful part of the country where there is a lot to do and see, Linden Hall is one of the excellent surprises to have emerged in recent years.

C'est le superbe hôtel du même nom qui a ajouté ce récent 18 trous à son domaine, comprenant un pub mitoyen transformé (c'était logique) en Clubhouse. Les propriétaires aiment leur réalisation, ils n'ont pas tort. Ils voulaient un parcours jouable par tous, ce qui reste bien le plus difficile, mais Jonathan Gaunt a bien rempli sa tâche. D'abord, c'est un parcours franc, jouable directement, mais le rough épais, comme les assez nombreux obstacles d'eau (fossés et lacs) ne pénalisent que les coups lâchés. Seuls deux trous obligent vraiment à porter la balle, mais ce sont alors de petits coups. L'entretien est excellent en dépit de la jeunesse du parcours, mais les choses ont été faites très professionnellement. Plaisant à jouer, exigeant des départs arrière, situé dans une région très calme avec beaucoup de choses à faire et à voir, c'est une des très bonnes surprises de ces dernières années.

Linden Hall Hotel & Golf Club — 1997
ENG - LONGHORSLEY, Northumberland

Office	Secrétariat	(44) 01670 - 516 611
Pro shop	Pro-shop	(44) 01670 - 788 050
Fax	Fax	(44) 01670 - 788 544
Situation	Situation	

10 km from Morpeth (pop. 14 394)
40 km from Newcastle (pop. 259 541)

Annual closure	Fermeture annuelle	no
Weekly closure	Fermeture hebdomadaire	no

Fees main season
Tarifs haute saison 18 holes

	Week days Semaine	We/Bank holidays We/Férié
Individual Individuel	£ 22.50	£ 30
Couple Couple	£ 45	£ 60

Caddy	Caddy	no
Electric Trolley	Chariot électrique	no
Buggy	Voiturette	£ 20/18 holes
Clubs	Clubs	£ 10/18 holes

Credit cards Cartes de crédit
VISA - Eurocard - MasterCard - DC - JCB

Access Accès : A1. After Morpeth, A697.
Golf at Longhorsley Village.
Map 2 on page 491 Carte 2 Page 491

GOLF COURSE / PARCOURS — 17/20

Site	Site	
Maintenance	Entretien	
Architect	Architecte	Jonathan Gaunt
Type	Type	parkland
Relief	Relief	
Water in play	Eau en jeu	
Exp. to wind	Exposé au vent	
Trees in play	Arbres en jeu	

Scorecard Carte de score	Chp. Chp.	Mens Mess.	Ladies Da.
Length Long.	6128	5857	4977
Par	72	72	72

Advised golfing ability		0 12 24 36
Niveau de jeu recommandé		
Hcp required	Handicap exigé	24 Men, 36 Ladies

CLUB HOUSE & AMENITIES / CLUB HOUSE ET ANNEXES — 8/10

Pro shop	Pro-shop	
Driving range	Practice	
Sheltered	couvert	no
On grass	sur herbe	yes (not in winter)
Putting-green	putting-green	yes
Pitching-green	pitching green	yes

595

HOTEL FACILITIES / ENVIRONNEMENT HOTELIER — 6/10

HOTELS HÔTELS
Linden Hall Hotel — Longhorsley / on site
50 rooms, D £ 120
Tel (44) 01670 - 516 611
Fax (44) 01670 - 788 544

Bondgate House Hotel — Alnwick / 20 km
8 rooms, D £ 45
Tel (44) 01665 - 602 025
Fax (44) 01665 - 602 554

Orchard — Rothbury / 15 km
6 rooms, D £ 70
Tel (44) 01669 - 620 684

RESTAURANTS RESTAURANT
Linden Hall Hotel — Longhorsley / on site
Tel (44) 01670 - 516 611

Lindrick was for a long while the last course where the American Ryder Cup team actually lost. And while it can be considered to be a very short course for the most powerful pros, it was once the venue for the British Ladies Open and showed itself to be most suitable for that event. For amateurs, men or women, this is a magnificent test of golf in heather-land shorn of any trees to speak of. It demands a style of play similar to when playing on a links course. Driving is very important, if only to avoid the well-placed bunkers and especially the very tough and highly penalising rough with ball-eating bushes. But the fairways are so wonderfully groomed that you won't want to miss them. Original for its landscape, intelligent for its strategic layout, natural-looking, fun to play and never all that busy, Lindrick is a must.

Lindrick fut longtemps le dernier parcours à avoir vu défaite l'équipe américaine de Ryder Cup. Et s'il peut être considéré comme un parcours très court pour les pros les plus puissants, il fut une fois le théâtre d'un British Open féminin qui le montrait bien adapté aux «proettes». Pour les amateurs, hommes ou femmes, ce magnifique test de golf en pleine terre de bruyère, avec assez peu d'arbres, demande un style de jeu assez analogue à celui des links. Le driving est très important, ne serait-ce que pour éviter les bunkers bien placés, mais surtout un rough très sévère, très pénalisant, avec en supplément des buissons mangeurs de balles. Mais les fairways sont d'une telle qualité que l'on serait assez stupide de les manquer ! Original par son paysage, intelligent par ses aspects stratégiques, naturel dans son aspect, amusant à apprivoiser, et assez peu fréquenté, Lindrick est un «Must.

Lindrick Golf Club — 1891

Lindrick
ENG - WORKSOP, Notts S81 8BH

Office	Secrétariat	(44) 01909 - 475 282
Pro shop	Pro-shop	(44) 01909 - 475 820
Fax	Fax	(44) 01909 - 488 685
Situation	Situation	

5 km W of Worksop (pop. 38 222) - 20 km E of Sheffield

Annual closure	Fermeture annuelle	no
Weekly closure	Fermeture hebdomadaire	no

Fees main season	Tarifs haute saison	full day
	Week days Semaine	We/Bank holidays We/Férié
Individual Individuel	£ 45	—
Couple Couple	£ 90	—

No visitors: Tuesdays and Weekends

Caddy	Caddy	no
Electric Trolley	Chariot électrique	no
Buggy	Voiturette	no
Clubs	Clubs	no

Credit cards Cartes de crédit
Visa - Mastercard - AMEX - DC - Switch
(Pro shop goods & restaurant only)

596

Access Accès : M1 Jct 31. A 57 East → Worksop.
Golf on right side after South Anston.
Map 4 on page 494 Carte 4 Page 494

GOLF COURSE
PARCOURS — 17/20

Site	Site	
Maintenance	Entretien	
Architect	Architecte	Tom Dunn, W. Park Herbert Fowler
Type	Type	inland, heathland
Relief	Relief	
Water in play	Eau en jeu	
Exp. to wind	Exposé au vent	
Trees in play	Arbres en jeu	

Scorecard Carte de score	Chp. Chp.	Mens Mess.	Ladies Da.
Length Long.	5945	5643	5195
Par	74	71	74

Advised golfing ability Niveau de jeu recommandé	0	12	24	36

Hcp required   Handicap exigé   certificate

CLUB HOUSE & AMENITIES
CLUB HOUSE ET ANNEXES — 6/10

Pro shop	Pro-shop	
Driving range	Practice	
Sheltered	couvert	practice areas
On grass	sur herbe	yes (2 grounds)
Putting-green	putting-green	yes
Pitching-green	pitching green	yes

HOTEL FACILITIES
ENVIRONNEMENT HOTELIER — 6/10

HOTELS HÔTELS
Red Lion - 30 rooms, D £ 56   Todwick 5 km
Tel (44) 01909 - 771 654, Fax (44) 01909 - 773 704

Aston Hall Hotel - 21 rooms, D £ 96   Aston 6 km
Tel (44) 01142 - 872 309, Fax (44) 01142 - 873 228

Van Dyk - 16 rooms, D £ 55   Clowne 8 km
Tel (44) 01246 - 810 219, Fax (44) 01246 - 819 566

Forte Travelodge - 40 rooms, D £ 35   Worksop 4 km
Tel (44) 01909 - 501 528

Hunter House - 23 rooms, D £ 48   Sheffield 20 km
Tel (44) 0114 - 266 2709, Fax (44) 0114 - 268 6370

RESTAURANTS RESTAURANTS
Old Vicarage - Tel (44) 0114 - 247 5814 Ridgeway 15 km
Le Neptune - Tel (44) 0114 - 279 6677   Sheffield 20 km

Hampshire is one of those counties whose villages, landscape and greenery seem to symbolise the English countryside as seen in films. The drive to Liphook and the hospitality awaiting visitors in the clubhouse are this and more. The designer has bent the course to match the landscape instead of the opposite, maybe because the excavators in service in the 1920s were not up to moving much earth. Liphook is a gem of a course and the hazards penalise absolutely every mis-hit shot. As they are clearly visible, the sanction comes as no surprise. The charming landscape might make you think this to be a kindly course, but nothing could be further from the truth. You need to flight the ball and play with care or else resign yourself to trying to hack your ball out of the heather. Add to this slick subtle greens and you have the full picture: Liphook is an exciting course whose visual discretion cleverly hides the difficulties in store.

Le Hampshire est l'une de ces régions qui symbolisent par leurs villages, leur paysage, leur végétation ce qu'est la campagne anglaise, comme dans les films. L'arrivée au golf de Liphook, comme l'hospitalité du Clubhouse vont dans le même sens. L'architecte a plié le parcours au paysage au lieu du contraire, mais il faut bien dire que, dans les années 20, les engins de terrassement ne permettaient pas de bouger beaucoup de terre. Liphook est un petit joyau, et les obstacles pénalisent absolument tous les coups manqués. Comme ils sont bien visibles, on ne saurait en être surpris. Le charme du paysage peut faire penser à un parcours aimable. Ce n'est pas le cas, il faut savoir travailler la balle, jouer avec prudence, ou alors accepter de devoir sortir ses balles de la bruyère. Si l'on ajoute la subtilité des greens, on aura compris : c'est un parcours passionnant, dont la discrétion visuelle cache bien les difficultés.

Liphook Golf Club 1922

Wheatsheaf Enclosure
ENG - LIPHHOK, Hants GU30 7EH

Office	Secrétariat	(44) 01428 - 723 271
Pro shop	Pro-shop	(44) 01428 - 723 271
Fax	Fax	(44) 01428 - 724 853
Situation	Situation	

2 km from Liphook - 8 km from Petersfield (pop. 12 618)

Annual closure	Fermeture annuelle	no
Weekly closure	Fermeture hebdomadaire	no
Fees main season	Tarifs haute saison	18 holes

	Week days Semaine	We/Bank holidays We/Férié
Individual Individuel	£ 37	£ 37
Couple Couple	£ 74	£ 74

Full day: £ 47 - Sunday: only after 12.00 pm -
Saturday : booking in advance

Caddy	Caddy	no
Electric Trolley	Chariot électrique	no
Buggy	Voiturette	no
Clubs	Clubs	£ 7.50/18 holes

Credit cards Cartes de crédit
Visa - Mastercard (Pro shop goods only)

Access Accès : A3 London to Portsmouth. B2131, then B2070 (old A3). Golf on the right after Railway line
Map 7 on page 500 Carte 7 Page 500

GOLF COURSE
PARCOURS 16/20

Site	Site	▬▬▬
Maintenance	Entretien	▬▬▬
Architect	Architecte	Arthur Croome
Type	Type	inland, heathland
Relief	Relief	▬
Water in play	Eau en jeu	▬
Exp. to wind	Exposé au vent	▬▬
Trees in play	Arbres en jeu	▬▬▬

Scorecard	Chp.	Mens	Ladies
Carte de score	Chp.	Mess.	Da.
Length Long.	5550	5270	4975
Par	70	70	72

Advised golfing ability		0 12 24 36
Niveau de jeu recommandé		
Hcp required	Handicap exigé	certificate

CLUB HOUSE & AMENITIES
CLUB HOUSE ET ANNEXES 7/10

Pro shop	Pro-shop	▬▬▬
Driving range	Practice	▬▬
Sheltered	couvert	2 mats
On grass	sur herbe	no
Putting-green	putting-green	yes
Pitching-green	pitching green	yes

597

HOTEL FACILITIES
ENVIRONNEMENT HOTELIER 6/10

HOTELS HÔTELS
Lythe Hill   Haslemere
28 rooms, D £ 85   10 km
Tel (44) 01428 - 651 251, Fax (44) 01428 - 644 131

Georgian   Haslemere
24 rooms, D £ 75   10 km
Tel (44) 01428 - 651 555, Fax (44) 01428 - 661 304

Langrish House   Langrish
18 rooms, D £ 65   11 km
Tel (44) 01730 - 266 941, Fax (44) 01730 - 260 543

RESTAURANTS RESTAURANTS
Fleur de Sel   Haslemere
Tel (44) 01428 - 651 462   10 km

Lythe Hill   Haslemere
Tel (44) 01428 - 651 251   10 km

Having failed to get on the very private Rye course, make it along to Littlestone. It is not in the same league, but not to be sniffed at, either. Without ever being boring, the first seven holes are pretty ordinary, at least from a visual viewpoint. It is only after the 8th hole that the landscape really comes to life. And while you won't see any really impressive dunes, you are rarely on the flat with your feet level with your ball. Naturally the wind plays a very important role, especially since it is virtually never blowing in the same direction from the 7th to the 15th holes. The same goes for the last three holes, but here you have other things to worry about. This is a devilishly tough finish to the course, starting with a par 4 and a horrendous second shot, followed by a par 3 where you are likely to need more than one tee shot, and finally a par 5 dotted with bunkers. This is an excellent holiday course in summer. For the rest of the year you will need to shape all kinds of different shots.

Faute de pouvoir aller jouer Rye, aux portes fermement closes, Littlestone est loin d'être négligeable, même s'il n'est pas dans la même catégorie. Les sept premiers trous commencent de manière assez banale, du moins visuellement, même si les architectes ont réussi à ne jamais faire ennuyeux, mais le paysage s'anime à partir du 8. Et si l'on ne verra pas de dunes très impressionnantes, on se retrouve rarement les pieds au même niveau que la balle. Le vent joue un rôle très important, d'autant plus qu'il n'est jamais dans le même sens du 7 au 15. Il sera le même dans les trois derniers trous, mais ce finale est assez diabolique avec un par 4 où le second coup est terrible, puis un par 3 où le coup de départ risque d'être suivi de bien d'autres, et enfin un par 5 constellé de bunkers. En été, c'est un excellent parcours de vacances. Le reste de l'année, il faut savoir fabriquer tous les coups de golf.

Littlestone Golf Club   1888

St Andrews Road, Littlestone
ENG - NEW ROMNEY, Kent TN28 8RB

Office	Secrétariat	(44) 01797 - 363 355
Pro shop	Pro-shop	(44) 01797 - 362 231
Fax	Fax	
Situation	Situation	

adjacent to New Romney
30 km from Ashford (pop. 52 000)

Annual closure	Fermeture annuelle	no
Weekly closure	Fermeture hebdomadaire	no

Fees main season
Tarifs haute saison 18 holes

	Week days Semaine	We/Bank holidays We/Férié
Individual Individuel	£ 30	£ 45
Couple Couple	£ 60	£ 90

Full day: £ 42/50 - Some restrictions during weekends

Caddy	Caddy	no
Electric Trolley	Chariot électrique	no
Buggy	Voiturette	no
Clubs	Clubs	no

Credit cards Cartes de crédit VISA - MasterCard

598

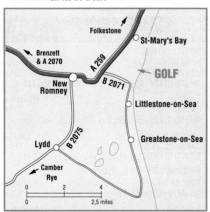

Access Accès : Ashford, A2070 to New Romney. Follow signs to Littlestone. Turn left at seafront
Map 7 on page 501 Carte 7 Page 501

GOLF COURSE
PARCOURS   14/20

Site	Site	▮▮▮▮▮▮▯
Maintenance	Entretien	▮▮▮▮▮▮▮
Architect	Architecte	W. Laidlaw Purves Alistair Mackenzie
Type	Type	seaside course, links
Relief	Relief	
Water in play	Eau en jeu	▮▮▮▯▯
Exp. to wind	Exposé au vent	▮▮▮▮▯
Trees in play	Arbres en jeu	▯▯▯▯▯

Scorecard	Chp.	Mens	Ladies
Carte de score	Chp.	Mess.	Da.
Length Long.	5823	5497	5140
Par	71	71	73

Advised golfing ability	0	12	24	36
Niveau de jeu recommandé				
Hcp required Handicap exigé	24			

CLUB HOUSE & AMENITIES
CLUB HOUSE ET ANNEXES   6/10

Pro shop	Pro-shop	▮▮▮▮▮▯
Driving range	Practice	▮▮▮▮▯
Sheltered	couvert	no
On grass	sur herbe	yes
Putting-green	putting-green	yes (2)
Pitching-green	pitching green	yes (2)

HOTEL FACILITIES
ENVIRONNEMENT HOTELIER   5/10

HOTELS HÔTELS
Hythe Imperial - 98 rooms, D £ 100   Hythe 10 km
Tel (44) 01303 - 267 441, Fax (44) 01303 - 264 610

Romney Bay House   Littlestone
11 rooms, D £ 90   adjacent
Tel (44) 01797 - 364 747, Fax (44) 01797 - 367 156

Stade Court - 42 rooms, D £ 75   Hythe 10 km
Tel (44) 01303 - 268 263, Fax (44) 01303 - 261 803

Broadacre Hotel   New Romney
10 rooms, D £ 50   1 km
Tel (44) 01797 - 362 381

RESTAURANTS RESTAURANTS
Romney Bay House   Littlestone
Tel (44) 01797 - 364747   adjacent

Hythe Imperial   Hythe
Tel (44) 01303 - 267441   10 km

LONDON GOLF CLUB INTERNATIONAL

| 15 | 9 | 7 |

These days, when you want to build a fashionable layout you call in someone like Jack Nicklaus to design it. This is what happened with the "Heritage Course", for members only, but this "International" course, open to all, was left to his Golden Bear company and architect Ron Kirby. The contrary might have been a more preferable option, opening the best of the two courses to players with the ability to play it, but such golfers can seldom afford this kind of membership. At all events, you are best advised to play here when it is dry, as both layouts get very wet in the rain. Having had our gripe, this course is excellent and still wide open, as the trees are young. The wide fairways give welcome breathing space and the huge greens require shots close to the pin to avoid three-putting. The key to a successful round lies with the second shot; the greens are stoutly guarded with sand-traps and water hazards on four holes. The layout is certainly imaginative and brimming with design know-how, but with a green-fee this high you expect something exceptional.

Quand on veut faire un ensemble à la mode, on demande à Jack Nicklaus de le dessiner. Il l'a fait effectivement pour le «Heritage Course», réservé aux membres et a laissé à son collaborateur Ron Kirby le tracé de celui-ci, «International», ouvert au public. Il aurait été préférable de faire le contraire et d'ouvrir le meilleur des deux parcours aux joueurs susceptibles de le maîtriser, mais ils ont rarement les moyens d'être membres. Cela dit, le présent parcours est d'excellente qualité, très ouvert car les arbres sont petits, avec des fairways larges permettant de se déchaîner, et de vastes greens où il faut viser le drapeau pour ne pas risquer trois putts : la clef du succès réside ici dans les seconds coups. Les défenses de greens sont solides, avec des bunkers ou des obstacles d'eau sur quatre trous. Certes, le dessin est imaginatif, mais pour un tel montant de green-fee, on attend l'exceptionnel...

The London Golf Club — 1993

South Ash Manor Estate
ENG - ASH, Near SEVENOAKS, Kent TN15 7EN

Office	Secrétariat	(44) 01474 - 879 899
Pro shop	Pro-shop	(44) 01474 - 879 899
Fax	Fax	(44) 01474 - 879 912
Situation	Situation	

24 km from Sevenoaks (pop. 19 617) - 42 km from London

Annual closure	Fermeture annuelle	no
Weekly closure	Fermeture hebdomadaire	no

Fees main season	Tarifs haute saison	18 holes
	Week days Semaine	**We/Bank holidays** We/Férié
Individual Individuel	£ 70	—
Couple Couple	£ 140	—

Visitors: Monday → Thursday only
Prior booking essential

Caddy	Caddy	£ 30 on request
Electric Trolley	Chariot électrique	£ 7
Buggy	Voiturette	£ 18
Clubs	Clubs	£ 30

Credit cards Cartes de crédit VISA- MasterCard - AMEX

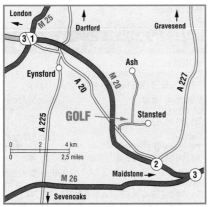

Access Accès : London M20 Exit 2. Turn left → West Kingsdown on A20. 3 km (2 m) on right, sign to Stansted and Golf course. Entrance 100 m on left.
Map 7 on page 501 Carte 7 Page 501

GOLF COURSE / PARCOURS — 15/20

Site	Site	
Maintenance	Entretien	
Architect	Architecte	Ron Kirby Golden Bear
Type	Type	open country, hilly
Relief	Relief	
Water in play	Eau en jeu	
Exp. to wind	Exposé au vent	
Trees in play	Arbres en jeu	

Scorecard Carte de score	**Chp.** Chp.	**Mens** Mess.	**Ladies** Da.
Length Long.	6305	5917	4945
Par	72	72	72

Advised golfing ability Niveau de jeu recommandé	0	12	24	36
Hcp required Handicap exigé	no			

CLUB HOUSE & AMENITIES / CLUB HOUSE ET ANNEXES — 9/10

Pro shop	Pro-shop	
Driving range	Practice	
Sheltered	couvert	no
On grass	sur herbe	yes
Putting-green	putting-green	yes
Pitching-green	pitching green	yes

599

HOTEL FACILITIES / ENVIRONNEMENT HOTELIER — 7/10

HOTELS HÔTELS

Brands Hatch Place - 41 rooms, D £ 100 Fawkham 5 km
Tel (44) 01474 - 872 239, Fax (44) 01474 - 879 652

Brands Hatch Thistle   Brands Hatch
135 rooms, D £ 80   5 km
Tel (44) 01474 - 854 900, Fax (44) 01474 - 853 220

Anchor & Hope   Ash 2 km
6 rooms, D £ 40(w. breakfast)
Tel (44) 01474 - 872 382

RESTAURANTS RESTAURANTS

Brands Hatch Place   Fawkham 5 km
Tel (44) 01474 - 872 239

The Bull Hotel   Wroxham Heath 5 km
Tel (44) 01474 - 885 522

Club's restaurant   Club house
Tel (44) 01474 - 879 899   on site

Being close to the popular seaside resort of Blackpool, all the courses in the region are always busy on week-ends and in the Summer. And Summer is the only season when Lytham Green Drive, although not a links course, can be played like one. The rest of the year it plays much longer than the card would suggest as the fairways are heavily grassed. This was, in fact, one of the most immaculately prepared courses we encountered, hence our enthusiasm for the very advanced plans to extend and enlarge a very pretty and very elegant layout. Enjoy the course while it is still playing short, when it looks just great but probably plays a little more easily than you think. Walking the fairways in this sort of manicured park is recreation indeed after the thrills and spills of the coastal links courses.

La proximité de Blackpool, station balnéaire de grand renom et paradis du jeu, assure une importante fréquentation des golfs de la région en week-end et en été. Cette dernière saison est la seule époque où, sans être un links, Lytham Green Drive peut se jouer comme tel. Le reste de l'année, il paraît plus long que la carte ne l'indique, car le gazon est très fourni. C'était d'ailleurs cette année l'un des parcours les plus impeccablement préparés que nous ayions vus, et l'on ne peut qu'accueillir avec faveur les projets très avancés d'extension et d'agrandissement de ce très joli et très élégant parcours. Profitez des moments où il est encore court, où il est aussi plus séduisant que vraiment difficile : jouer dans un parc aussi manucuré représente une sorte de récréation après avoir connu l'exaltation sur les grands links de la côte.

Lytham Green Drive Golf Club — 1922

Ballam Road
ENG - LYTHAM, Lancs FY8 4 LE

Office	Secrétariat	(44) 01253 - 737 390
Pro shop	Pro-shop	(44) 01253 - 737 379
Fax	Fax	(44) 01253 - 731 350
Situation	Situation	

1 km from Lytham St Anne's (pop. 40 866)
10 km from Blackpool (pop. 146 069)

Annual closure	Fermeture annuelle	no
Weekly closure	Fermeture hebdomadaire	no

Fees main season
Tarifs haute saison 18 holes

	Week days Semaine	We/Bank holidays We/Férié
Individual Individuel	£ 25	£ 30
Couple Couple	£ 50	£ 60

Full weekdays: £ 30 each

Caddy	Caddy	no
Electric Trolley	Chariot électrique	no
Buggy	Voiturette	no
Clubs	Clubs	£ 10/18 holes
Credit cards Cartes de crédit		no

600

Access Accès : M6, Jct 32, M55 → Blackpool.
Peel Corner lights to Ballam Road. Club on the left.
Map 5 on page 497 Carte 5 Page 497

GOLF COURSE / PARCOURS — 15/20

Site	Site	
Maintenance	Entretien	
Architect	Architecte	Sandy Herd Jim Steer
Type	Type	parkland
Relief	Relief	
Water in play	Eau en jeu	
Exp. to wind	Exposé au vent	
Trees in play	Arbres en jeu	

Scorecard Carte de score	Chp. Chp.	Mens Mess.	Ladies Da.
Length Long.	5543	5390	5057
Par	70	70	73

Advised golfing ability Niveau de jeu recommandé		0 12 24 36
Hcp required	Handicap exigé	28 Men, 36 Ladies

CLUB HOUSE & AMENITIES / CLUB HOUSE ET ANNEXES — 7/10

Pro shop	Pro-shop	
Driving range	Practice	
Sheltered	couvert	no
On grass	sur herbe	yes
Putting-green	putting-green	yes
Pitching-green	pitching green	yes

HOTEL FACILITIES / ENVIRONNEMENT HOTELIER — 8/10

HOTELS HÔTELS
Clifton Arms Hotel - 44 rooms, D £ 86   Lytham 2 km
Tel (44) 01253 - 739 898, Fax (44) 01253 - 730 657

Glendover Hotel   Lytham St Anne's
63 rooms, D £ 76   3 km
Tel (44) 01253 - 723 241

Dalmeny   Lytham St Anne's
130 rooms, D £ 75   3 km
Tel (44) 01253 - 712 236, Fax (44) 01253 - 724 447

Bedford   Lytham St Anne's
36 rooms, D £ 59   3 km
Tel (44) 01253 - 724 636, Fax (44) 01253 - 729 244

RESTAURANTS RESTAURANT
Pleasant Street - Tel (44) 01253 - 788 786   Lytham 2 km
Tiggy's Italian - Tel (44) 01253 - 714 714   Lytham 2 km
Grand Hotel - Tel (44) 01253 - 721 288   Lytham 3 km

Very close to the city of Manchester, this fine course is easy to play during the week, particularly for meetings where business and extreme pleasure mix very well indeed. Practice facilities are excellent, which is not always the case in Britain. The layout is not very long but the tee-boxes are well placed to provide each category of player with a good challenge. On an open moorland landscape, the course is very exposed to the wind which can become a major obstacle, particularly on the dog-leg holes, where, as on all Harry Colt courses, you need to think long and hard about where to put your drive to get the right approach to the greens, which are protected by bushes, trees and bunkers. Strategy is to the fore again at the 12th, where hitting the driver will leave you a short approach shot but on a sloping lie, while a 2 iron will leave you on a flat part of the fairway but with a longer approach to the green. A rather hilly course (buggy recommended), Manchester offers some fine views to make up for the difficulty of club selection.

Proche de Manchester, ce beau parcours est très accessible en semaine, notamment pour des réunions d'affaires joignant l'utile au très agréable. Il offre aussi, c'est rare, de bons équipements d'entraînement. Le tracé n'est pas très long, et les départs assez bien placés pour offrir un bon «challenge» à toutes les catégories de joueurs. Dans son paysage de lande, il est très exposé au vent, qui peut devenir l'obstacle essentiel, notamment sur les doglegs où il faut réfléchir sur sa ligne pour avoir les greens ouverts, comme sur beaucoup de dessins d'Harry Colt. Ils sont protégés par des buissons, arbres et bunkers. Stratégie encore au 12, où jouer le drive vous fera jouer un second coup court, mais dans une pente, alors que jouer un fer du départ vous permettra d'avoir les pieds à plat, mais un coup plus long. Assez accidenté, Manchester offre de très belles vues, comme pour compenser la difficulté de sélection de clubs.

Manchester Golf Club — 1882

Hopwood Cottage, Middleton
ENG - MANCHESTER M24 2QP

Office	Secrétariat	(44) 0161 - 643 3202
Pro shop	Pro-shop	(44) 0161 - 643 2638
Fax	Fax	(44) 0161 - 643 9174
Situation	Situation	

10km N of Manchester (pop. 404 861)
6 km S of Rochdale (pop. 202 164)

Annual closure	Fermeture annuelle	no
Weekly closure	Fermeture hebdomadaire	no
Fees main season	Tarifs haute saison	18 holes

	Week days Semaine	We/Bank holidays We/Férié
Individual Individuel	£ 30	—
Couple Couple	£ 60	—

Full weekdays: £ 40 - No visitors at weekends

Caddy	Caddy	no
Electric Trolley	Chariot électrique	£ 5/18 holes
Buggy	Voiturette	no
Clubs	Clubs	no

Credit cards Cartes de crédit
VISA - Eurocard - MasterCard

Access Accès : M62 Jct 20, then A627(M) → Oldham.
First exit, follow A664 signs. Club on the right over humped back bridge.
Map 4 on page 494 Carte 4 Page 494

GOLF COURSE / PARCOURS — 16/20

Site	Site	
Maintenance	Entretien	
Architect	Architecte	Harry S. Colt
Type	Type	parkland, moor-land
Relief	Relief	
Water in play	Eau en jeu	
Exp. to wind	Exposé au vent	
Trees in play	Arbres en jeu	

Scorecard Carte de score	Chp. Chp.	Mens Mess.	Ladies Da.
Length Long.	5873	5660	5198
Par	72	72	74

Advised golfing ability		0 12 24 36
Niveau de jeu recommandé		
Hcp required	Handicap exigé	certificate

CLUB HOUSE & AMENITIES / CLUB HOUSE ET ANNEXES — 7/10

Pro shop	Pro-shop	
Driving range	Practice	
Sheltered	couvert	no
On grass	sur herbe	yes
Putting-green	putting-green	yes
Pitching-green	pitching green	yes

HOTEL FACILITIES / ENVIRONNEMENT HOTELIER — 7/10

HOTELS HÔTELS

Norton Grange — Castleton 5 km
51 rooms, D £ 120
Tel (44) 01706 - 630 788, Fax (44) 01706 - 649 313

Midway Park Hotel — Castleton 5 km
24 rooms, D £ 90
Tel (44) 01706 - 632 881, Fax (44) 01706 - 653 522

Victoria and Albert — Manchester 10 km
128 rooms, D £ 132
Tel (44) 0161 - 832 1188, Fax (44) 0161 - 834 2484

RESTAURANTS RESTAURANTS

French Connection — Norden 6 km
Tel (44) 01706 - 50 167

After Eight — Rochdale7 km
Tél(44) 01706 - 46 432

601

If we were to give golf course clubhouses a score for artistic content, Mannings Heath would be up there with the front-runners. And a good thing too, because after the 18th hole here you have the one idea of relaxing and putting your feet up. This is a steeply sloping course in a charming corner of Sussex, where golf can be a strenuous exercise (but you knew that already). So buggy and caddie are recommended. Between the woods, the sections of heather and the parkland, find time to admire the landscape and many squirrels, they might give you some valuable inspiration. Although not a long course, you need a good golfing brain to score well. Some drives have to be long enough to be able to see the green for the approach shot (2nd, 4th or 8th holes), while tee-shots on the par 3s need careful thought and execution to avoid the meanders of the Horkins. The 10th hole, with its cascade, is a particularly memorable experience, as is the par 4 11th hole. The second «Kingfisher» course is very pleasant but less testing.

Si l'on devait décerner une note artistique aux Clubhouses, Mannings Heath serait dans le peloton de tête. Tant mieux, car on a l'unique idée de se re-poser dans ce manoir après le 18, tant les ondulations de ce charmant coin de campagne du Sussex font du golf un sport (pour ceux qui en doutaient). Chariot électrique ou caddie conseillé. Entre les bois, les parties de bruyère ou de parc, on doit se donner le temps d'admirer le paysage, et le jeu des écureuils : c'est un bon prétexte pour reprendre ses esprits car, en dépit de sa faible longueur, il ne s'agit pas de jouer sans cervelle. Certains drives doivent être assez longs pour pouvoir ensuite apercevoir le green (2, 4 ou 8), et les coups de départ bien calculés sur les par 3 pour éviter la présence fréquente des méandres du Horkins : on retiendra en particulier le 10 avec sa cascade. Ou encore un par 4, le 11. Le second parcours, Kingfisher, est très plaisant, mais moins décisif.

Mannings Heath Golf Club — 1905

Fullers, Hammerspond Road, Manning Heath
ENG - HORSHAM, W. Sussex RH13 6PG

Office	Secrétariat	(44) 01403 - 210 228
Pro shop	Pro-shop	(44) 01403 - 210 228
Fax	Fax	(44) 01403 - 270 974
Situation	Situation	

3.5 km SE of Horsham (pop. 42 552)
12 km SW of Crawley (pop. 87 644)

Annual closure	Fermeture annuelle	no
Weekly closure	Fermeture hebdomadaire	no

Fees main season
Tarifs haute saison full day

	Week days Semaine	We/Bank holidays We/Férié
Individual Individuel	£ 42	£ 55
Couple Couple	£ 84	£ 110
Caddy	Caddy	on request/£ 36
Electric Trolley	Chariot électrique	£ 10/18 holes
Buggy	Voiturette	£ 26/18 holes
Clubs	Clubs	£ 20/18 holes

Credit cards Cartes de crédit
VISA - MasterCard - AMEX - DC

602

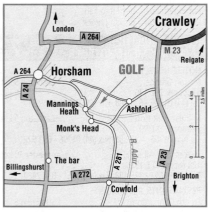

Crawley

London A 264
M 23 Reigate
A 264 Horsham GOLF
A 24
Mannings Heath Ashfold
Monk's Head
Billingshurst The bar A 281 A 23
A 272 Brighton
Cowfold
R. Adur

Access Accès : M23 Jct 11, through Pease Pottage to Grouse Lane (left hand side). 5 km (3.5 m.) to T junction, right and first left to Golf.
Map 7 on page 500 Carte 7 Page 500

GOLF COURSE PARCOURS — 14/20

Site	Site	▮▮▮▮▯
Maintenance	Entretien	▮▮▮▮▯
Architect	Architecte	Unknown
Type	Type	inland, heathland
Relief	Relief	▮▮▮▮▮
Water in play	Eau en jeu	▮▮▮▯▯
Exp. to wind	Exposé au vent	▮▮▮▯▯
Trees in play	Arbres en jeu	▮▮▮▮▯

Scorecard Carte de score	Chp. Chp.	Mens Mess.	Ladies Da.
Length Long.	5805	5460	4920
Par	73	71	73

Advised golfing ability Niveau de jeu recommandé	0	12	24	36
Hcp required	Handicap exigé	certificate		

CLUB HOUSE & AMENITIES CLUB HOUSE ET ANNEXES — 8/10

Pro shop	Pro-shop	▮▮▮▮▯
Driving range	Practice	▮▮▮▯▯
Sheltered	couvert	no
On grass	sur herbe	yes (balls provided)
Putting-green	putting-green	yes
Pitching-green	pitching green	no

HOTEL FACILITIES ENVIRONNEMENT HOTELIER — 6/10

HOTELS HÔTELS
South Lodge — Lower Beeding
37 rooms, D £ 130 — 4 km
Tel (44) 01403 - 891 711
Fax (44) 01403 - 891 766

Ockenden Manor — Cuckfield
20 rooms, D £ 120
Tel (44) 01444 - 416 111
Fax (44) 01444 - 415 549

Cisswood House — Lower Beeding
30 rooms, D £ 85
Tel (44) 01403 - 891 216
Fax (44) 01403 - 891 621

RESTAURANTS RESTAURANT
Jeremy's — Lower Beeding
Tel (44) 01403 - 891 257 — 4 km

MANOR HOUSE (CASTLE COMBE) 15 8 7

It is no coincidence if there are so many buggies here. The superb views from the tee or green come courtesy of some roller-coaster landscape which makes this course something of an ordeal to walk. Designers Alliss and Clark followed the natural lie of the land and evidently had a lot of fun here, alternating pot bunkers or sprawling «sand-traps» and making extensive use of water hazards. All these difficulties are really dangerous because they are so strategic. And the relatively short yardage doesn't mean much when you are constantly shooting uphill or downhill. A spectacular, exciting and, first time out, often a surprising course in a category of its own. You come here for a few days of leisure, staying if you can at Manor House, a pretty piece of architecture with all the most modern amenities. You can also play as a green-feer.

S'il y a autant de voiturettes ici, ce n'est pas par hasard. Les vues superbes du haut des départs ou des greens, c'est au prix de montagnes russes qui rendent le jeu à pied très éprouvant. Les architectes Alliss et Clark ont suivi les contours naturels et se sont bien amusés dans un tel espace, alternant les «pot» bunkers ou de longues étendues de sable, et faisant usage généreux des obstacles d'eau. Toutes ces difficultés sont réellement dangereuses, car très stratégiques, et la longueur relativement faible ne veut pas dire grand chose avec ces changements incessants de niveau. Un parcours spectaculaire, souvent surprenant la première fois, parfois passionnant, et à classer à part. On vient ici passer quelques jours de plaisir, si l'on peut en logeant au Manor House, jolie pièce d'architecture, avec le confort le plus moderne, mais on peut aussi jouer au green-fee.

Manor House (at Castle Combe) 1992
ENG - CASTLE COMBE, Wiltshire SN14 7 PL

Office	Secrétariat	(44) 01249 - 782 982
Pro shop	Pro-shop	(44) 01249 - 783 101
Fax	Fax	(44) 01249 - 782 992
Situation	Situation	

37 km E of Bristol (pop. 376 146)
18 km NE of Bath (pop. 78 689)

Annual closure	Fermeture annuelle	no
Weekly closure	Fermeture hebdomadaire	no
Fees main season	Tarifs haute saison	18 holes

	Week days Semaine	We/Bank holidays We/Férié
Individual Individuel	£ 35	£ 45
Couple Couple	£ 70	£ 90

Full day: £ 55 - £ 70 (weekends)

Caddy	Caddy	no
Electric Trolley	Chariot électrique	no
Buggy	Voiturette	£ 20/18 holes
Clubs	Clubs	£ 10/18 holes

Credit cards Cartes de crédit
VISA - Eurocard - MasterCard (Pro shop goods
& restaurant only)

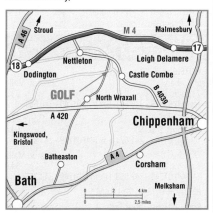

Access Accès : • M4 Jct 17, A350 → Chippenham, A420 on the right, then B4039 N of Castle Combe. • Bath: A46, A420 to Ford, then turn left to Castle Combe.
Map 6 on page 499 Carte 6 Page 499

GOLF COURSE
PARCOURS 15/20

Site	Site	
Maintenance	Entretien	
Architect	Architecte	Peter Alliss Clive Clark
Type	Type	copse, parkland
Relief	Relief	
Water in play	Eau en jeu	
Exp. to wind	Exposé au vent	
Trees in play	Arbres en jeu	

Scorecard Carte de score	Chp. Chp.	Mens Mess.	Ladies Da.
Length Long.	5496	5298	4659
Par	73	71	72

Advised golfing ability		0	12	24	36
Niveau de jeu recommandé					
Hcp required	Handicap exigé	28 Men, 36 Ladies			

CLUB HOUSE & AMENITIES
CLUB HOUSE ET ANNEXES 8/10

Pro shop	Pro-shop	
Driving range	Practice	
Sheltered	couvert	
On grass	sur herbe	yes
Putting-green	putting-green	yes
Pitching-green	pitching green	yes

HOTEL FACILITIES
ENVIRONNEMENT HOTELIER 7/10

HOTELS HÔTELS

Manor House Hotel 44 rooms, D £ 130 Tel (44) 01249 - 782 206 Fax (44) 01249 - 782 159	Golf on site
Castle Inn 7 rooms, D £ 95 Tel (44) 01249 - 783 030 Fax (44) 01249 - 782 315	Castle Combe 1 km
White Hart Inn 11 rooms, D £ 60 Tel (44) 01249 - 782 213 Fax (44) 01249 - 783 075	Ford 3 km

RESTAURANTS RESTAURANT

Manor House Hotel Tel (44) 01249 - 782 206	Golf on site

603

The highest point of this course is more than 1,000 ft. above sea-level from where you can see as far as Glastonbury and the abbey (you need good eyes), Exmoor (you need binoculars) and Wales. If they add America to the list, then you must be at the bar. Despite the altitude, this is not too hilly a course and the turf is wonderfully springy underfoot. This adds comfort to the pleasure of playing a course where you are rarely on the flat, where you need to think, and where you need some good ironwork and razor-sharp putting: the greens come in all shapes, sizes, slopes and contours and rarely forgive poor reading. Although minor details are always being shuffled around, the original 9 hole course by Vardon, later completed by Frank Pennink, remained unchanged until 1988, when the purchase of new land took the par up to 71. The clubhouse is perhaps not the world's prettiest but the atmosphere inside is very friendly, which is better than the other way around.

Le point le plus haut du parcours est à plus de 300 mètres, d'où l'on voit jusqu'à Glastonbury et son abbaye (il faut de bons yeux), Exmoor (il faut des jumelles) et le Pays de Galles. Mais si l'on vous parle de l'Amérique, c'est que vous êtes au bar. Pourtant, le parcours n'est pas trop accidenté, et le gazon est d'une rare souplesse, ce qui ne fait qu'ajouter le confort au plaisir d'un parcours où l'on n'a pas toujours les pieds à plat, où il faut un peu de tête, un très bon jeu de fers et un putting affûté comme un rasoir, car les greens sont de formes, de tailles, et de reliefs variés, ils ne pardonnent pas une lecture négligente. Tout en remaniant en permanence les détails, le dessin de 9 trous par Vardon, complété par Frank Pennink, est resté inchangé jusqu'en 1988, où l'achat de terrains a permis de porter le par à 71. Le Clubhouse n'est peut-être pas le plus joli du monde mais l'atmosphère y est très amicale. C'est mieux que l'inverse

Mendip Golf Club — 1909

Gurney Slade
ENG - BATH, Somerset BA3 4UT

Office	Secrétariat	(44) 01749 - 840 570
Pro shop	Pro-shop	(44) 01749 - 840 793
Fax	Fax	(44) 01749 - 841 439
Situation	Situation	

28 km SW of Bath (pop. 78 689)
38 km S of Bristol (pop. 376 146)

| Annual closure | Fermeture annuelle | no |
| Weekly closure | Fermeture hebdomadaire | no |

Fees main season	Tarifs haute saison	18 holes
	Week days Semaine	We/Bank holidays We/Férié
Individual Individuel	£ 20	£ 30
Couple Couple	£ 40	£ 60

Full weekday: £ 25

Caddy	Caddy	no
Electric Trolley	Chariot électrique	no
Buggy	Voiturette	no
Clubs	Clubs	no

Credit cards Cartes de crédit
Visa - Mastercard (Pro shop goods only)

604

GOLF COURSE / PARCOURS — 15/20

Site	Site	
Maintenance	Entretien	
Architect	Architecte	Harry Vardon
		Frank Pennink (1965)
Type	Type	open country
Relief	Relief	
Water in play	Eau en jeu	
Exp. to wind	Exposé au vent	
Trees in play	Arbres en jeu	

Scorecard	Chp.	Mens	Ladies
Carte de score	Chp.	Mess.	Da.
Length Long.	5833	5653	5452
Par	71	71	75

Advised golfing ability	0	12	24	36
Niveau de jeu recommandé				
Hcp required	Handicap exigé	no		

CLUB HOUSE & AMENITIES / CLUB HOUSE ET ANNEXES — 5/10

Pro shop	Pro-shop	
Driving range	Practice	
Sheltered	couvert	no
On grass	sur herbe	yes
Putting-green	putting-green	yes
Pitching-green	pitching green	yes

HOTEL FACILITIES / ENVIRONNEMENT HOTELIER — 7/10

HOTELS HÔTELS

Shrubbery — Shepton Mallet
7 rooms, D £ 70 — 5 km
Tel (44) 01749 - 346 671, Fax (44) 01749 - 346 581

Ston Easton Park — Ston Easton
19 rooms, D £ 150 — 6 km
Tel (44) 01761 - 241 671, Fax (44) 01749 - 241 377

Thatched Cottage Inn — Shepton Mallet
8 rooms, D £ 70 — 5 km
Tel (44) 01749 - 342 058, Fax (44) 01749 - 343 265

RESTAURANTS RESTAURANTS

Bowlish House (book first) — Shepton Mallet
Tel (44) 01749 - 342 022 — 6 km

Brottens Lodge — Shepton Mallet
Tel (44) 01749 - 880 352 — 8 km

Access Accès : Bristol, A37 → Shepton Mallet, Golf 4.5 km (3 m.) before Shepton Mallet. From Bath, A367.
Map 6 on page 499 Carte 6 Page 499

This southern area of the Downs is a great site for walks and drives (behind the wheel), stretching out in the direction of Winchester, Chichester, Southampton, Beaulieu, Portsmouth and even the Isle of Wight. What's more, the course hotel is convenient and comfortable with an indoor swimming pool, sauna, fitness centre, etc. And as this "resort" also boasts a second 9-hole course (play it twice from two different sets of tee-box), a few days rest here is time well spent. On the Meon course, only real beginners might find the few small lakes a problem, but everyone should take extra care on the 12th and 18th holes. A ditch runs across a large section of the course but is not always that much in play. Elsewhere, a few isolated trees threaten the tee-shot, trees as a whole are generally in play and bunkers, although sparingly used, are very well located. This is an easily walkable course (except perhaps the climb on hole 13) which does not reveal all the trouble in store at first sight. You have better to use the Yardage book.

Cette partie sud des «Downs» est un site de promenades, à pied, ou en voiture pour rayonner vers Winchester, Chichester, Southampton, Beaulieu, Portsmouth ou même l'Ile de Wight. L'hôtel sur le golf est pratique et confortable, avec piscine intérieure, sauna, centre de mise en forme, etc. Et comme ce «resort» comprend un autre 9 trous (jouez-le deux fois de départs très différents !), quelques jours de repos ici seront bien occupés. Sur le «Meon Course», seuls les débutants risquent d'être gênés par quelques petits lacs, mais tous devront s'en méfier au 12 et au 18. Un fossé parcourt une grande partie du terrain, sans être toujours dangereux. A part cela, quelques arbres isolés menacent certains tee-shots, l'ensemble des arbres étant en jeu, et des bunkers bien placés. Assez facile à jouer à pied, ce parcours ne présente pas tous les obstacles au premier abord, il est conseillé de consulter le carnet de parcours.

Marriott Meon Valley Golf & CC — 1976

Sandy Lane
ENG - SHEDFIELD, SOUTHAMPTON SO32 2HQ

Office	Secrétariat	(44) 01329 - 833 455
Pro shop	Pro-shop	(44) 01329 - 836 832
Fax	Fax	(44) 01329 - 834 411
Situation	Situation	

18 km E of Southampton (pop. 196 864)

Annual closure	Fermeture annuelle	no
Weekly closure	Fermeture hebdomadaire	no

Fees main season	Tarifs haute saison	18 holes
	Week days Semaine	**We/Bank holidays** We/Férié
Individual Individuel	£ 34	£ 40
Couple Couple	£ 68	£ 80

Caddy	Caddy	no
Electric Trolley	Chariot électrique	no
Buggy	Voiturette	£ 25
Clubs	Clubs	£ 10

Credit cards Cartes de crédit
VISA - MasterCard - AMEX - DC - Switch - Connect

Access Accès : London M3 onto Southampton, then M27 → Portsmouth. Exit Jct 7, first exit for Botley (A334). → Wickham. On passing Wickham Vineyard, Sandy Lane is the next turning on your left.
Map 7 on page 500 Carte 7 Page 500

GOLF COURSE PARCOURS — 15/20

Site	Site	
Maintenance	Entretien	
Architect	Architecte	Hamilton Stutt
Type	Type	parkland
Relief	Relief	
Water in play	Eau en jeu	
Exp. to wind	Exposé au vent	
Trees in play	Arbres en jeu	

Scorecard Carte de score	Chp. Chp.	Mens Mess.	Ladies Da.
Length Long.	5868	5488	5049
Par	71	71	73

Advised golfing ability — 0 12 24 36
Niveau de jeu recommandé
Hcp required Handicap exigé — certificate

CLUB HOUSE & AMENITIES CLUB HOUSE ET ANNEXES — 8/10

Pro shop	Pro-shop	
Driving range	Practice	
Sheltered	couvert	6 mats
On grass	sur herbe	yes
Putting-green	putting-green	yes
Pitching-green	pitching green	yes

HOTEL FACILITIES ENVIRONNEMENT HOTELIER — 7/10

HOTELS HÔTELS
Meon Valley Hotel — Shedfield
113 rooms, D £ 105 — on site
Tel (44) 01329 - 833 455, Fax (44) 01329 - 834 411

Old House — Wickham
10 rooms, D £ 85 — 3 km
Tel (44) 01329 - 833 049, Fax (44) 01329 - 833 672

Botley Park — Botley
100 rooms, D £ 122 — 8 km
Tel (44) 01489 - 780 888, Fax (44) 01489 - 789 242

RESTAURANTS RESTAURANTS
Treetops (Marriott Hotel) — Shedfield
Tel (44) 01329 - 833 455 — on site

Greens - Tel (44) 01329 - 833 197 — Wickham 3 km

Kings Head — Wickham
Tel (44) 01329 - 832 123 — 3 km

605

Mere was revived in 1985 when the clubhouse was completely overhauled (adding swimming pools, sauna, tennis courts, etc.), an extensive tree-planting program was begun and the course was given new tee-boxes and a new 18th green. The face-lift has «modernised» the original design by Braid and Duncan - you don't have to love the water hazards on the 7th and 8th holes - and generally enhanced the site with a more challenging finish to the course. Some rolling landscape adds a little variety to the layout where there is a pleasant mix of tight and wider holes. Putting and approach shots can be a tricky business on some of the tiered greens. And your best bet here is to pitch the greens rather than roll the ball. This is one of the most accomplished courses in the region of Manchester, a fair test and always a pleasure to play but only on week-days for visitors. Pity about the rather dubious pink scorecard for the ladies.

Mere a été réveillé en 1985 avec une refonte totale du Clubhouse (avec piscines, sauna, tennis, etc), la plantation de nombreux arbres, de nouveaux départs, un nouveau green au 18. Ce rajeunissement a un peu «modernisé» le dessin de Braid et de Duncan - on peut ne pas adorer les obstacles d'eau du 7 et du 8 - mais au profit de l'embellissement général du site, et du renforcement d'un finale très exigeant. Quelques ondulations apportent de la variété au terrain, où le tracé alterne agréablement les trous étroits et les espaces plus larges. Le putting et les approches sont intéressants et délicats à apprécier sur certains greens à plateaux : en général, on devra ici privilégier les coups levés. Dans la région de Manchester, c'est une des réalisations les plus achevées, et le parcours d'une grande franchise reste un plaisir à jouer. En semaine pour les visiteurs. Les dames ont une carte de score rose d'un parfait mauvais goût !

Mere Golf & Country Club — 1934

Chester Road, Mere
ENG - KNUTSFORD, Cheshire WA16 6LJ

Office	Secrétariat	(44) 01565 - 830 155
Pro shop	Pro-shop	(44) 01565 - 830 155
Fax	Fax	(44) 01565 - 830 518
Situation	Situation	

20 km SW of Manchester (pop. 404 861)
3 km NW of Knutsford (pop. 13 352)

Annual closure	Fermeture annuelle	no
Weekly closure	Fermeture hebdomadaire	no

Fees main season
Tarifs haute saison full day

	Week days Semaine	We/Bank holidays We/Férié
Individual Individuel	£ 60	£ 60
Couple Couple	£ 120	£ 120

Visitors: Mondays, Tuesdays and Thursdays only

Caddy	Caddy	on request/£ 25 +tip
Electric Trolley	Chariot électrique	no
Buggy	Voiturette	£ 20/18 holes
Clubs	Clubs	£ 15/18 holes

Credit cards Cartes de crédit
VISA - Eurocard - MasterCard - AMEX - DC

606

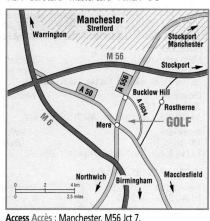

Access Accès : Manchester, M56 Jct 7.
A556 S → Northwich. Golf on left side before A50.
Map 4 on page 494 Carte 4 Page 494

GOLF COURSE / PARCOURS — 15/20

Site	Site	
Maintenance	Entretien	
Architect	Architecte	James Braid George Duncan
Type	Type	parkland
Relief	Relief	
Water in play	Eau en jeu	
Exp. to wind	Exposé au vent	
Trees in play	Arbres en jeu	

Scorecard Carte de score	Chp. Chp.	Mens Mess.	Ladies Da.
Length Long.	6135	5910	5192
Par	71	71	74

Advised golfing ability		0 12 24 36
Niveau de jeu recommandé		
Hcp required	Handicap exigé	certificate

CLUB HOUSE & AMENITIES / CLUB HOUSE ET ANNEXES — 7/10

Pro shop	Pro-shop	
Driving range	Practice	
Sheltered	couvert	no
On grass	sur herbe	no
Putting-green	putting-green	yes
Pitching-green	pitching green	yes

HOTEL FACILITIES / ENVIRONNEMENT HOTELIER — 7/10

HOTELS HÔTELS
Kilton Inn - 28 rooms, D £ 49 — Mere, 1 km
Tel (44) 01565 - 830 420, Fax (44) 01565 - 830 411

The Cottons — Knutsford
73 rooms, D £ 124 — 3 km
Tel (44) 01565 - 650 333, Fax (44) 01565 - 755 351

Victoria and Albert — Manchester
128 rooms, D £ 132 — 20 km
Tel (44) 0161 - 832 1188, Fax (44) 0161 - 834 2484

RESTAURANTS RESTAURANTS
Belle Epoque Brasserie — Knutsford
Tel (44) 01565 - 633 060 — 4 km

Sherlock Holmes — Manchester
Tel (44) 0161 - 832 1188 — 20 km

Magnolia (Cottons) — Knutsford
Tel (44) 01565 - 650 333 — 3 km

It is rare indeed to encounter such a concentration of good golf courses in the northern suburbs of Leeds. With Moortown, Sand Moor and Alwoodley, Moor Allerton is the fourth member of a remarkable crop of courses. Here, though, contrary to the typical Yorkshire moor landscape of the three others, the style is much more that of a parkland course. The changes made to the original layout by Robert Trent Jones have accentuated this trait and even given it a slight American flavour. Hazards come in the form of trees and bunkers (well designed and located) completed by very strategically placed stretches of water. To score well you will have to produce a whole range of shots, meaning that the lesser player could have a hard time of things. A few holes stick in the memory, and although there are other, more spectacular courses in the world, this one deserves a round or two. You will enjoy it.

Il est rare de rencontrer une telle concentration de bons parcours de golf que dans la «banlieue nord» de Leeds. Avec Moortown, Sand Moor et Alwoodley, Moor Allerton constitue le quatrième élément d'un quatuor remarquable. Mais, contrairement aux trois premiers, typiques de la lande du Yorkshire, celui-ci revêt une esthétique beaucoup plus nette de parc. Les modifications apportées par Robert Trent Jones au tracé originel ont d'ailleurs accentué ce caractère, lont même un peu américanisé. Les obstacles sont constitués par les arbres et les bunkers (très bien dessinés et placés), et complétés par la présence de quelques pièces d'eau tout aussi stratégiquement placés. Il faudra développer ici toute une panoplie de coups de golf pour bien scorer, et les joueurs peu expérimentés s'y sentiront sans doute moins à l'aise que les autres. Quelques trous marquent bien la mémoire, et s'il existe à l'évidence des parcours globalement plus mémorables, celui-ci mérite d'être joué et apprécié.

Moor Allerton Golf Club — 1923

Coal Road
ENG - WIKE, LEEDS, West Yorks. LS17 9NH

Office	Secrétariat	(44) 01132 - 661 154
Pro shop	Pro-shop	(44) 01132 - 665 209
Fax	Fax	(44) 01132 - 371 124
Situation	Situation	

5 km N of Leeds (pop. 680 725)

Annual closure	Fermeture annuelle	no
Weekly closure	Fermeture hebdomadaire	no

Fees main season
Tarifs haute saison 18 holes

	Week days Semaine	We/Bank holidays We/Férié
Individual Individuel	£ 41	£ 66
Couple Couple	£ 82	£ 132

Full day: £ 45/£ 77

Caddy	Caddy	on request
Electric Trolley	Chariot électrique	no
Buggy	Voiturette	£ 25
Clubs	Clubs	£ 10

Credit cards Cartes de crédit
VISA - Eurocard - MasterCard - AMEX
(Pro shop goods only)

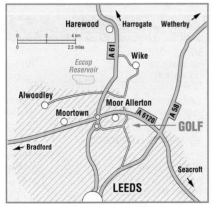

Access Accès : Leeds, A 61 → Harrogate,
then A621 → Moor Allerton
Map 4 on page 494 Carte 4 Page 494

GOLF COURSE / PARCOURS — 14/20

Site	Site	
Maintenance	Entretien	
Architect	Architecte	R. Trent Jones Sr
Type	Type	parkland
Relief	Relief	
Water in play	Eau en jeu	
Exp. to wind	Exposé au vent	
Trees in play	Arbres en jeu	

Scorecard Carte de score	Chp. Chp.	Mens Mess.	Ladies Da.
Length Long.	5823	5526	4878
Par	71	71	73

Advised golfing ability		0 12 24 36
Niveau de jeu recommandé		
Hcp required	Handicap exigé	certificate

CLUB HOUSE & AMENITIES / CLUB HOUSE ET ANNEXES — 6/10

Pro shop	Pro-shop	
Driving range	Practice	
Sheltered	couvert	12 bays
On grass	sur herbe	yes
Putting-green	putting-green	yes
Pitching-green	pitching green	no

HOTEL FACILITIES / ENVIRONNEMENT HOTELIER — 7/10

607

HOTELS HÔTELS
Forte Posthouse — Bramhope
123 rooms, D £ 70 — 7 km
Tel (44) 0113 - 284 2911, Fax (44) 0113 - 284 3451

Jarvis Parkway — Bramhope
105 rooms, D £ 98 — 7 km
Tel (44) 0113 - 267 2551, Fax (44) 0113 - 267 4410

Stakis Leeds — Seacroft - Leeds
100 rooms, D £ 90 — 5 km
Tel (44) 0113 - 273 2323, Fax (44) 0113 - 232 3018

RESTAURANTS RESTAURANTS
Leodis Brasserie — Leeds
Tel (44) 0113 - 242 1010 — 6 km

Brasserie Forty Four — Leeds
Tel (44) 0113 - 234 3232 — 6 km

Sous le nez en ville — Leeds
Tel (44) 0113 - 244 0108 — 6 km

MOOR PARK HIGH COURSE

Originally there were three courses here, two of which have survived beneath the impressive and even intimidating shadows of the clubhouse. The shirt and tie rule is so obvious here that you're surprised to see people actually dressed in casual wear on the course. The «West Course» is on the short side but goes very well with the «High» course, where from the 2nd hole onward you realise you'll need some sort of bearings or benchmarks if you are ever going to card a good score. The yardage book will come in handy for knowing where you should put your drive and for identifying the gardens where your ball should not go (especially on the front 9). A Harry Colt course is never a bland affair and this is no exception to the rule. The last nine holes are particularly memorable with three par 3s more than worthy of the designer's reputation. This is most definitely not the place where you could ever imagine golf becoming a sport for all and sundry, but it is one hell of a good course.

Au départ, il y avait trois parcours, dont deux sont restés sous l'ombre impressionnante, et même intimidante d'un Clubhouse où le port d'une cravate paraît tellement évident qu'on la gardera pour jouer (au cas où). Le «West Course» est assez court, mais constitue un bon complément au «High,» où dès le 2, on comprend qu'il va falloir trouver ses marques pour espérer un score décent. Le «yardage book» ne sera pas inutile pour savoir où poser le drive, et pour identifier (surtout à l'aller) les jardins où il ne faut pas envoyer sa balle. Un parcours dessiné par Harry Colt n'est jamais indifférent, et celui-ci ne fait pas exception à la règle. on gardera un souvenir particulier des neuf derniers trous, avec trois par 3 à la hauteur de la réputation de l'architecte. Certes, ce n'est pas vraiment le lieu où l'on imagine que le golf puisse devenir un sport démocratique, mais c'est un bon parcours !

Moor Park Golf Club — 1923
ENG - RICKMANSWORTH, Herts WD31QN

Office	Secrétariat	(44) 01923 - 773 146
Pro shop	Pro-shop	(44) 01923 - 774 113
Fax	Fax	(44) 01923 - 777 109
Situation	Situation	

35 km from Central London (pop. 6 679 700)
8 km from Watford (pop. 74 566)

Annual closure	Fermeture annuelle	no
Weekly closure	Fermeture hebdomadaire	no

Fees main season
Tarifs haute saison 18 holes

	Week days Semaine	We/Bank holidays We/Férié
Individual Individuel	£ 50	—
Couple Couple	£ 100	—

Full day: £ 75 - Booking essential - No visitors at weekends

Caddy	Caddy	on request/£ 25
Electric Trolley	Chariot électrique	£ 7.50/18 holes
Buggy	Voiturette	£ 25/18 holes
Clubs	Clubs	£ 15/18 holes

Credit cards Cartes de crédit Visa - Mastercard - AMEX

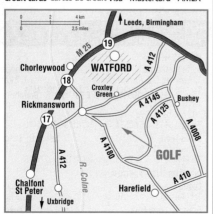

Access Accès : London, M4 Jct 3, A312, A4180,
A404 → Rickmansworth, Golf on the right.
Map 8 on page 502 Carte 8 Page 502

608

GOLF COURSE PARCOURS — 17/20

Site	Site	
Maintenance	Entretien	
Architect	Architecte	Harry S. Colt
Type	Type	parkland
Relief	Relief	
Water in play	Eau en jeu	
Exp. to wind	Exposé au vent	
Trees in play	Arbres en jeu	

Scorecard Carte de score	Chp. Chp.	Mens Mess.	Ladies Da.
Length Long.	6045	5735	5130
Par	72	72	73

Advised golfing ability Niveau de jeu recommandé	0	12	24	36
Hcp required Handicap exigé	certificate			

CLUB HOUSE & AMENITIES CLUB HOUSE ET ANNEXES — 8/10

Pro shop	Pro-shop	
Driving range	Practice	
Sheltered	couvert	no
On grass	sur herbe	yes
Putting-green	putting-green	yes
Pitching-green	pitching green	yes

HOTEL FACILITIES ENVIRONNEMENT HOTELIER — 7/10

HOTELS HÔTELS
Hilton National — Watford
194 rooms, D £ 94 — 8 km
Tel (44) 01923 - 235 881, Fax (44) 01923 - 220 836

Cumberland — Harrow
81 rooms, D £ 80 — 8 km
Tel (44) 0181 - 863 4111, Fax (44) 0181 - 861 5668

RESTAURANTS RESTAURANTS

Percy's — North Harrow
Tel (44) 0181 - 427 2021 — 6 km

Friends — Pinner
Tel (44) 0181 - 866 0286 — 5 km

Trattoria Sorrentina — Harrow
Tel (44) 0181 - 427 9411 — 8 km

With Alwoodley and Sand Moor, here you have a great threesome of courses close to Leeds, certainly not the prettiest city in England one whose region has a lot to be said for it, especially the city of York. The present course, or at least 16 holes of the present course, were designed by Alister Mackenzie while the last two were added in 1989, giving the whole layout more than respectable yardage and leaving the original style untouched. Classic, well-landscaped and with huge greens in excellent condition, the course gives nothing away. By the same token it doesn't steal strokes, either. Here, you score what you deserved to score. The Ryder Cup was held here for the first time in England, as was a particular English Amateur championship where one player had to hit his third shot on the 18th from inside the bar. A good place to go, but only after you have sunk that final putt.

Avec The Alwoodley et Sand Moor, voici un fameux trio de parcours voisins, à proximité de Leeds, qui n'est sans doute pas la plus belle ville d'Angleterre, mais la région ne manque pas de séductions, en particulier avec York. Le présent parcours a été dessiné par Alister Mackenzie. Du moins 16 trous, car deux nouveaux trous ont été ajoutés en 1989, permettant d'afficher maintenant une longueur fort respectable. Le style original n'en a pas été modifié. Classique, bien paysagé, avec de vastes greens généralement excellents, ce parcours ne fait certes pas de cadeaux, mais il ne vole non plus personne : on y fait le score que l'on mérite. La Ryder Cup 1929 s'y est disputée pour la première fois en Grande-Bretagne, tout comme un English Amateur où un joueur dut taper son troisième coup du 18 depuis l'intérieur du bar. On comprend qu'il y soit allé.

Moortown Golf Club — 1909

Harrogate Road
ENG - LEEDS, W. Yorkshire LS17 7DB

Office	Secrétariat	(44) 0113 - 268 6521
Pro shop	Pro-shop	(44) 0113 - 268 3636
Fax	Fax	(44) 0113 - 268 6521
Situation	Situation	

8 km N of Leeds (pop. 680 722)

Annual closure	Fermeture annuelle	no
Weekly closure	Fermeture hebdomadaire	no

Fees main season
Tarifs haute saison 18 holes

	Week days Semaine	We/Bank holidays We/Férié
Individual Individuel	£ 42	£ 47
Couple Couple	£ 84	£ 94

Full day: £ 47 (weekdays) - £ 55 (weekends)

Caddy	Caddy	no
Electric Trolley	Chariot électrique	£ 7/18 holes
Buggy	Voiturette	£ 25/18 holes
Clubs	Clubs	no

Credit cards Cartes de crédit
VISA - Eurocard - MasterCard - DC - Switch
(not for green fees)

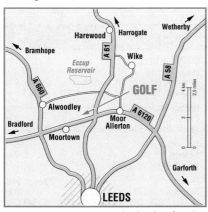

Access Accès : On A61 approx. 8 km (5 m.) N of Leeds
Map 4 on page 494 Carte 4 Page 494

GOLF COURSE / PARCOURS — 18/20

Site	Site	
Maintenance	Entretien	
Architect	Architecte	Alister MacKenzie
Type	Type	inland, moorland
Relief	Relief	
Water in play	Eau en jeu	
Exp. to wind	Exposé au vent	
Trees in play	Arbres en jeu	

Scorecard Carte de score	Chp. Chp.	Mens Mess.	Ladies Da.
Length Long.	6390	5883	5398
Par	72	72	75

Advised golfing ability Niveau de jeu recommandé	0	12	24	36
Hcp required Handicap exigé	certificate			

CLUB HOUSE & AMENITIES / CLUB HOUSE ET ANNEXES — 7/10

Pro shop	Pro-shop	
Driving range	Practice	
Sheltered	couvert	practice area
On grass	sur herbe	yes
Putting-green	putting-green	yes
Pitching-green	pitching green	yes

HOTEL FACILITIES / ENVIRONNEMENT HOTELIER — 7/10

609

HOTELS HÔTELS

Forte Posthouse - 123 rooms, D £ 70 — Bramhope
Tel (44) 0113 - 284 2911, Fax (44) 0113 - 284 3451

Jarvis Parkway - 105 rooms, D £ 98 — Bramhope
Tel (44) 0113 - 267 2551, Fax (44) 0113 - 267 4410

Stakis Leeds - 100 rooms, D £ 85 — Leeds
Tel (44) 0113 - 273 2323, Fax (44) 0113 - 232 3018

The Calls — Leeds
41 rooms, D £ 120
Tel (44) 0113 - 244 0099, Fax (44) 0113 - 234 4100

RESTAURANTS RESTAURANTS

Pool Court at 42 - Tel (44) 0113 - 244 4242 — Leeds

Hereford Beefstouw — Leeds
Tel (44) 0113 - 245 3870

Rascasse — Leeds
Tel (44) 0113 - 244 6611

Before teeing it up on this, the southernmost course in England, you will have already enjoyed a very warm welcome and splendid views. The sea is a sight to behold on windy days, when you are better off playing cards than golf, because on this huge, wide open space, the wind can play havoc. Having said that, the weather is often fine down here, and lovers of the open air and inventive golf, even if they are only average golfers, will have a great time. It might take them a while to reach the greens, but they always get there in the end because no shot is impossible. Despite the bushes and huge reed-beds, which make a part of the course a little spongy underfoot, most of the terrain is sandy and the grass excellent. A few dips and hillocks conceal the foot of the pin on occasions but the course in still very honest and open. The good holes include the 6th, the 7th lined with cross-bunkers and the 10th, a par 4 which can be terrifying to play in a head-wind. This is one of those courses where the golfer really feels very close to nature.

Avant d'aborder le parcours le plus septentrional d'Angleterre, on aura remarqué l'accueil très amical, et un panorama splendide sur les falaises et la mer, grandiose les jours de tempête : dans un espace aussi vaste, le vent s'en donne alors à coeur joie. Mais il y a beaucoup de beaux jours où les amateurs de grand air et d'un golf inventif s'en donneront à coeur joie, même si leur niveau de golf est moyen : s'il faut bien des coups pour arriver au green, aucun d'eux n'est impossible. Une partie du terrain peut être spongieuse avec de vastes roselières, mais la plus grande partie du parcours est sablonneuse, et le gazon excellent. Quelques vallonnements dissimulent certains pieds des drapeaux, mais le parcours est néanmoins d'une grande franchise. On y retiendra parmi bien des bons trous les 6, le 7 avec ses cross-bunkers, la 10 un par 4, qui peut être terrible par vent contraire. Un parcours où le sentiment de communion avec la nature est très fort.

Mullion Golf Club — 1895
ENG - CURY, HELSTON, Cornwall TR12 7BP

Office	Secrétariat	(44) 01326 - 240 685
Pro shop	Pro-shop	(44) 01326 - 241 176
Fax	Fax	(44) 01326 - 240 685
Situation	Situation	

25 km from Falmouth (pop. 19 217)

Annual closure	Fermeture annuelle	no
Weekly closure	Fermeture hebdomadaire	no

Fees main season
Tarifs haute saison full day

	Week days Semaine	We/Bank holidays We/Férié
Individual Individuel	£ 20	£ 25
Couple Couple	£ 40	£ 50

Caddy	Caddy	no
Electric Trolley	Chariot électrique	no
Buggy	Voiturette	£ 15
Clubs	Clubs	no

Credit cards Cartes de crédit — no

GOLF COURSE / PARCOURS — 15/20

Site	Site	▰▰▰▱▱
Maintenance	Entretien	▰▰▰▱▱
Architect	Architecte	William Side
Type	Type	seaside course, open country
Relief	Relief	▰▱▱▱▱
Water in play	Eau en jeu	▰▰▰▱▱
Exp. to wind	Exposé au vent	▰▰▰▰▱
Trees in play	Arbres en jeu	▰▱▱▱▱

Scorecard Carte de score	Chp. Chp.	Mens Mess.	Ladies Da.
Length Long.	5434	5164	4902
Par	70	70	72

Advised golfing ability — 0 12 24 36
Niveau de jeu recommandé
Hcp required — Handicap exigé — certificate

CLUB HOUSE & AMENITIES / CLUB HOUSE ET ANNEXES — 5/10

Pro shop	Pro-shop	▰▰▰▱▱
Driving range	Practice	▰▰▰▱▱
Sheltered	couvert	2 bays
On grass	sur herbe	yes
Putting-green	putting-green	yes
Pitching-green	pitching green	yes

HOTEL FACILITIES / ENVIRONNEMENT HOTELIER — 5/10

HOTELS HÔTELS

Polurrian Hotel — Mullion
38 rooms, D £ 172 (with dinner) — 1 km
Tel (44) 01326 - 240 421, Fax (44) 01326 - 240 083

Nansloe Manor — Helston
7 rooms, D £ 110 — 8 km
Tel (44) 01326 - 574 691, Fax (44) 01326 - 564 680

Tregaddra — Mullion
5 rooms, D £ 38 — 2 km
Tel (44) 01326 - 240 235

Meudon — Mawnan Smith
28 rooms, D £ 170 — 20 km
Tel (44) 01326 - 250 541, Fax (44) 01326 - 250 543

RESTAURANTS RESTAURANT

Helzephron Inn — Gunwallow

610

Access Accès : M4, M5 South, A30 → Penzance,
→ Helston. → Mullion. Follow signs to Golf course.
Map 6 on page 498 Carte 6 Page 498

Horse-racing enthusiasts will already have heard of Newbury, whose racecourse is visible from the 17th hole. But despite being so close, the ground here is far from flat although easy enough to walk. The course was built in 1873, making it one of the oldest in England, and is still popular and busy enough to be closed to non-members on week-ends. Like many of the courses from that period, Newbury & Crookham has a lot of trees and the design has hardly got any younger, but this is not a course to be taken lightly, despite a lack of yardage. It is a very pretty challenge with several holes of the highest order defended by some very well-placed bunkers. There is an obvious need to put your drive in the right place and we would recommend this as a «disciplinary» course for «sprayers». The trees and thick rough will soon get them back on the straight and narrow. The clubhouse is small and not the most cheerful place in the world, but the food is good.

Les amateurs de chevaux connaissent Newbury par son hippodrome, que l'on aperçoit du 17. Malgré ce voisinage, le terrain n'est pas plat, même s'il est facile à jouer à pied. Le parcours a été construit en 1873, ce qui en fait l'un des clubs de golf les plus anciens d'Angleterre, et qui reste très fréquenté car il n'est pas possible d'y jouer en week-end. Comme beaucoup de parcours de cette époque, il est abondamment pourvu d'arbres, et son dessin n'a guère été que rajeuni, mais sa longueur ne doit pas le faire sous-estimer. C'est un très joli challenge, avec plusieurs trous de premier ordre, défendus par des bunkers très bien placés, et la nécessité de placer correctement les drives est évidente : on recommande un petit séjour «disciplinaire» pour les «arroseurs.» Les arbres, mais aussi un rough épais sauront redresser leurs trajectoires. Le Clubhouse est petit et pas très gai, mais la table est très correcte.

Newbury & Crookham Golf Club — 1873

Burysbank Road, Greenham
ENG - NEWBURY, Berks RG19 8BZ

Office	Secrétariat	(44) 01635 - 40 035
Pro shop	Pro-shop	(44) 01635 - 31 201
Fax	Fax	(44) 01635 - 40 045
Situation	Situation	

3 km from Newbury (pop. 136 700) - 25 km from Reading

Annual closure	Fermeture annuelle	no
Weekly closure	Fermeture hebdomadaire	no

Fees main season
Tarifs haute saison 18 holes

	Week days Semaine	We/Bank holidays We/Férié
Individual Individuel	£ 20	—
Couple Couple	£ 40	—

Full day: £ 30 each - No visitors at weekends

Caddy	Caddy	no
Electric Trolley	Chariot électrique	no
Buggy	Voiturette	no
Clubs	Clubs	on request

Credit cards Cartes de crédit
Visa - Mastercard (Pro shop goods only)

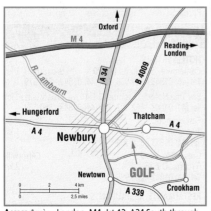

Access Accès : London, M4. Jct 13, A34 South through Newbury. Turn into Newbury Retail Park, 2.5 km SE of Newbury. Golf on left.
Map 7 on page 500 Carte 7 Page 500

GOLF COURSE / PARCOURS — 15/20

Site	Site	
Maintenance	Entretien	
Architect	Architecte	J.H. Turner
Type	Type	parkland
Relief	Relief	
Water in play	Eau en jeu	
Exp. to wind	Exposé au vent	
Trees in play	Arbres en jeu	

Scorecard Carte de score	Chp. Chp.	Mens Mess.	Ladies Da.
Length Long.	5346	5141	4745
Par	69	69	70

Advised golfing ability Niveau de jeu recommandé	0	12	24	36
Hcp required Handicap exigé	no			

CLUB HOUSE & AMENITIES / CLUB HOUSE ET ANNEXES — 6/10

Pro shop	Pro-shop	
Driving range	Practice	
Sheltered	couvert	no
On grass	sur herbe	yes
Putting-green	putting-green	yes
Pitching-green	pitching green	yes

HOTEL FACILITIES / ENVIRONNEMENT HOTELIER — 7/10

HOTELS HÔTELS

Hollington House — Woolton Hill
19 rooms, D £ 160 — 4 km
Tel (44) 01635 - 255 100, Fax (44) 01635 - 255 075

Foley Lodge — Newbury
68 rooms, D £ 115 — 3 km
Tel (44) 01635 - 528 770, Fax (44) 01635 - 528 398

Hilton — Newbury
109 rooms, D £ 105 — 3 km
Tel (44) 01635 - 529 000, Fax (44) 01635 - 529 337

Holiday Inn — Reading
107 rooms, D £ 105 — 25 km
Tel (44) 01734 - 259 988, Fax (44) 01734 - 391 665

RESTAURANTS RESTAURANT

L'Ortolan — Shinfield-Reading
Tel (44) 01734 - 883 783 — 30 km

611

This virtually tree-less course was designed by Fowler and Simpson at the top of some cliffs, which naturally exposes it to all winds and weathers. Winds in the plural, because there are hardly ever two holes running in the same direction, so keep a cool head and control your shots. Beginners will hardly ever be penalised by the rough because it rarely comes into play for their kind of shots. The same applies to the bunker fairways which will more often punish the mistakes made by longer and better players. So you might call this a logical course. At all events it is an excellent venue for playing with all the family because you will also find a real 18-hole course for children (holes measuring between 70 and 140 yards). And this region is the sunniest and driest in all England. Although many of you may know Margate's reputation as a seaside resort, only the really knowledgeable will know that Charles Dickens used to come on holiday here, in Broadstairs, where he wrote David Copperfield.

Pratiquement sans arbres, ce parcours a été dessiné par Fowler et Simpson au sommet de la falaise, ce qui l'expose bien sûr au vent. Aux vents, car on ne trouve pratiquement pas deux trous de suite dans le même sens : il faut garder la tête froide et contrôler ses coups. Les joueurs sans expérience seront peu pénalisés car le rough est rarement en jeu pour eux, tout comme les bunkers de fairway, ce qui pénalise surtout les fautes des meilleurs joueurs : voilà un parcours très logique. Et venir en famille est très agréable car l'on trouve ici un parcours de 18 trous de moins de 130 mètres, à l'échelle des enfants. Et la région est la plus ensoleillée et la moins arrosée d'Angleterre. Si l'on connaît, de réputation, la station balnéaire de Margate, seuls les fanatiques de Charles Dickens savent qu'il prenait ses vacances ici, à Broadstairs, où il écrivit «David Copperfield.»

North Foreland Golf Club   1903

Convent Road
ENG - BROADSTAIRS, Kent CT10 3PU

Office	Secrétariat	(44) 01843 - 862 140
Pro shop	Pro-shop	(44) 01843 - 869 628
Fax	Fax	(44) 01843 - 862 140
Situation	Situation	

1 km from Broadstairs (pop. 23 695) - 3 km from Margate

| Annual closure | Fermeture annuelle | no |
| Weekly closure | Fermeture hebdomadaire | no |

Fees main season
Tarifs haute saison 18 holes

	Week days Semaine	We/Bank holidays We/Férié
Individual Individuel	£ 26	£ 26
Couple Couple	£ 52	£ 52

No visitors Sunday & Monday mornings.
Short course: £ 3 for juniors,

Caddy	Caddy	no
Electric Trolley	Chariot électrique	£ 4/18 holes
Buggy	Voiturette	£ 15/18 holes
Clubs	Clubs	£ 2.50/18 holes

Credit cards Cartes de crédit
Visa - Mastercard - DC (Pro shop goods only)

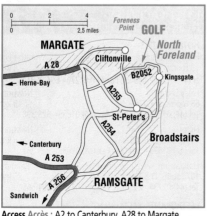

Access Accès : A2 to Canterbury. A28 to Margate,
A299 to Kingsgate (past St Peter's Church), B2052
Map 7 on page 501 Carte 7 Page 501

GOLF COURSE
PARCOURS   13/20

Site	Site	■■■■■■□□□
Maintenance	Entretien	■■■■■■■□□
Architect	Architecte	Fowler & Simpson
Type	Type	seaside course
Relief	Relief	■■■□□□□□□□
Water in play	Eau en jeu	■□□□□□□□□
Exp. to wind	Exposé au vent	■■■■■■■■□
Trees in play	Arbres en jeu	■□□□□□□□□

Scorecard Carte de score	Chp. Chp.	Mens Mess.	Ladies Da.
Length Long.	5790	5564	5185
Par	71	70	75

Advised golfing ability	0	12	24	36
Niveau de jeu recommandé				
Hcp required	Handicap exigé	certificate or letter

CLUB HOUSE & AMENITIES
CLUB HOUSE ET ANNEXES   7/10

Pro shop	Pro-shop	■■■■□□□□□
Driving range	Practice	■■■■■■□□□
Sheltered	couvert	no
On grass	sur herbe	yes
Putting-green	putting-green	yes
Pitching-green	pitching green	no

HOTEL FACILITIES
ENVIRONNEMENT HOTELIER   7/10

HOTELS HÔTELS

Castlemere - 36 rooms, D £ 70   Broadstairs, 1 km
Tel (44) 01843 - 861 566, Fax (44) 01843 - 866 379

Bay Tree Hotel - 11 rooms, D £ 44   Broadstairs, 1 km
Tel (44) 01843 - 862 502, Fax (44) 01843 - 860 589

East Horndon   Broadstairs
10 rooms, D £ 40   1 km
Tel (44) 01843 - 868 306

Greswolde Hotel   Cliftonville
6 rooms, D £ 36   2 km
Tel (44) 01843 - 223 956

RESTAURANTS RESTAURANTS

Marchesi   Broadstairs
Tel (44) 01843 - 862481   1 km

Castlemere   Broadstairs
Tel (44) 01843 - 861566   1 km

612

With Blackmoor and Liphook, North Hants completes an excellent clan of courses in a very beautiful part of Hampshire where Harry Colt, Arthur Croome and here James Braid have left their mark. This is a sort of exercise in style with rather similar spaces hewn out of the heather and woods. With Braid, a very great champion in his time, there is always serious emphasis on making each hole different so that the whole course forms a comprehensive examination of a player's ability. If you want to score well, you will need to flight the ball both ways, and while there are few dog-legs here, there is always a right side and a wrong side of the fairway, depending on pin positions. As the greens are very large and protected in proportion to the theoretical length of the approach shot, you will need to be accurate and self-assured. High-handicappers might not feel all that comfortable here but the majority of amateurs will have a lot of fun. North Hants looks great and plays great.

North Hants forme avec Blackmoor et Liphook une excellente famille de parcours dans cette très belle région du Hampshire, où Harry Colt, Arthur Croome et (ici) James Braid ont apposé leur sceau. C'est une sorte d'exercice de style avec des espaces assez similaires, où la bruyère et les bois constituent la matière à travailler. Avec Braid, qui était un très grand champion, on a toujours un grand souci de différencier chaque trou, afin que l'ensemble constitue un examen complet du joueur. Si l'on veut très bien scorer, il faut travailler la balle dans tous les sens. Et s'il y a très peu de doglegs, il y a toujours un «bon» côté du fairway suivant la position du drapeau. Comme les greens sont très grands et protégés en proportion de la longueur théorique du deuxième coup, il faudra être précis et sûr de soi. Les handicaps élevés ne seront pas très à l'aise, mais la majorité des amateurs prendra beaucoup de plaisir. North Hants est beau et bon.

North Hants Golf Club — 1904

Minley Road
ENG - FLEET, Hants GU13 8BR

Office	Secrétariat	(44) 01252 - 616 443
Pro shop	Pro-shop	(44) 01252 - 616 655
Fax	Fax	(44) 01252 - 811 627
Situation	Situation	

1 km from Fleet - 4 km from Camberley (pop. 46 120)

Annual closure	Fermeture annuelle	no
Weekly closure	Fermeture hebdomadaire	no

Fees main season
Tarifs haute saison 18 holes

	Week days Semaine	We/Bank holidays We/Férié
Individual Individuel	£ 27	—
Couple Couple	£ 54	—

Full day: £ 34 - Weekends: only as a guest of member

Caddy	Caddy	no
Electric Trolley	Chariot électrique	no
Buggy	Voiturette	no
Clubs	Clubs	

Credit cards Cartes de crédit
VISA - Eurocard - MasterCard - DC (Pro shop goods only)

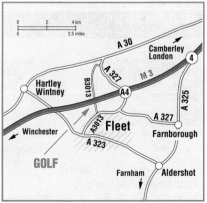

0 2 4 km
0 2,5 miles

A 30 — Camberley London (4)
M 3
Hartley Wintney — A4
B3013 — A 327
A 325
A3013 — **Fleet** — Farnborough
Winchester — A 323
GOLF
Farnham — Aldershot

Access Accès : London M3 Jct 4A → Fleet
Map 8 on page 502 Carte 8 Page 502

GOLF COURSE / PARCOURS — 17/20

Site	Site	
Maintenance	Entretien	
Architect	Architecte	James Braid
Type	Type	inland, heathland
Relief	Relief	
Water in play	Eau en jeu	
Exp. to wind	Exposé au vent	
Trees in play	Arbres en jeu	

Scorecard Carte de score	Chp. Chp.	Mens Mess.	Ladies Da.
Length Long.	5631	5480	4905
Par	69	69	71

Advised golfing ability		0	12	24	36
Niveau de jeu recommandé					
Hcp required	Handicap exigé	24			

CLUB HOUSE & AMENITIES / CLUB HOUSE ET ANNEXES — 7/10

Pro shop	Pro-shop	
Driving range	Practice	
Sheltered	couvert	no
On grass	sur herbe	yes
Putting-green	putting-green	yes
Pitching-green	pitching green	no

HOTEL FACILITIES / ENVIRONNEMENT HOTELIER — 6/10

HOTELS HÔTELS

Frimley Hall — Camberley
66 rooms, D £ 105 — 6 km
Tel (44) 01276 - 283 21, Fax (44) 01276 - 691 253

Forte Crest — Farnborough
110 rooms, D £ 125 — 6 km
Tel (44) 01252 - 545 051, Fax (44) 01252 - 377 210

Falcon — Farnborough
30 rooms, D £ 75 — 6 km
Tel (44) 01252 - 545 378, Fax (44) 01252 - 522 539

RESTAURANTS RESTAURANTS

Wings Cottage — Farnborough
Tel (44) 01252 - 544 141 — 6 km

Chesa — Crondall
Tel (44) 01252 - 850 328 — 4 km

613

NOTTS (HOLLINWELL)

| 18 | 6 | 6 |

In a superb setting with a good old clubhouse the way we all like them, this is one inland course to put up there with the very best. Designed by Willie Park Jr. then given bunkers by J.H. Taylor, this is a nicely modelled course typical of a heathland layout which winds it way amidst silver birch and oak trees. There is little water to speak of, but when there is, watch out. Try the 8th hole from the back tees and you will see what we mean. By and large this is a sort of monster where the back-tees are reserved for very good players who know how to flight a ball. It is a little meeker from the front tees, which for the ladies are even too far forward. Notts is also a great course for the rhythm it strikes up, because it has no time for poor shots (except on hole N° 1, the most forgiving). And because you never play the same two shots twice in a row. The members must love it here.

Dans un environnement superbe, avec un bon vieux Clubhouse tel qu'on les aime, c'est l'un des parcours «inland» à placer parmi les plus grands. Dessiné par Willie Park Jr, le bunkering ayant ensuite été fait par J.H. Taylor, c'est un parcours bien modelé et typique de terre de bruyère, insinué entre les bouleaux blancs et les chênes. L'eau y est peu abondante, mais de quelle manière au 8, des départs arrière ! En règle générale, c'est une sorte de monstre, et jouer du fond est réservé aux joueurs de très bon niveau, et qui savent manoeuvrer la balle. Le parcours est plus doux des départs avancés, qui le sont d'ailleurs un peu trop pour les dames. Notts est aussi un très grand parcours par le rythme qu'il impose, parce qu'il ne supporte pas les coups médiocres (sauf au 1, le trou le plus indulgent), et parce que l'on ne joue jamais deux fois le même coup deux fois de suite. Les membres doivent s'y régaler...

Notts Golf Club Hollinwell — 1887

Hollinwell, Derby Road
ENG - KIRBY-IN-ASHFIELD, Notts NG17 7QR

Office	Secrétariat	(44) 01623 - 753 225
Pro shop	Pro-shop	(44) 01623 - 753 087
Fax	Fax	(44) 01623 - 753 655
Situation	Situation	

20 km N of Nottingham (pop. 270 222)

Annual closure	Fermeture annuelle	no
Weekly closure	Fermeture hebdomadaire	no

Fees main season
Tarifs haute saison 18 holes

	Week days Semaine	We/Bank holidays We/Férié
Individual Individuel	£ 40	—
Couple Couple	£ 80	—

Full weekdays: £ 50 - No visitors at weekends & Bank holidays

Caddy	Caddy	on request/£ 15
Electric Trolley	Chariot électrique	£ 5/18 holes
Buggy	Voiturette	no
Clubs	Clubs	on request

Credit cards Cartes de crédit
Visa - Mastercard (Pro Shop goods only)

614

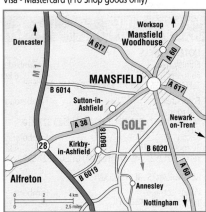

Access Accès : M1 Jct 27. A608 then A611 → Kirby, Mansfield. Golf 3 km on the right.
Map 4 on page 494 Carte 4 Page 494

GOLF COURSE / PARCOURS — 18/20

Site	Site	
Maintenance	Entretien	
Architect	Architecte	Willie Park Jr
Type	Type	inland
Relief	Relief	
Water in play	Eau en jeu	
Exp. to wind	Exposé au vent	
Trees in play	Arbres en jeu	

Scorecard Carte de score	Chp. Chp.	Mens Mess.	Ladies Da.
Length Long.	6398	6250	5187
Par	72	72	74

Advised golfing ability Niveau de jeu recommandé	0	12	24	36	
Hcp required	Handicap exigé	certificate			

CLUB HOUSE & AMENITIES / CLUB HOUSE ET ANNEXES — 6/10

Pro shop	Pro-shop	
Driving range	Practice	
Sheltered	couvert	practice area
On grass	sur herbe	yes
Putting-green	putting-green	yes
Pitching-green	pitching green	yes

HOTEL FACILITIES / ENVIRONNEMENT HOTELIER — 6/10

HOTELS HÔTELS
Pine Lodge - 20 rooms, D £ 60 — Mansfield
Tel (44) 01623 - 622 308 — 8 km

Swallow - 157 rooms, D £ 120 — South Normanton
Tel (44) 01773 - 812 000, Fax (44) 01773 - 580 032 8 km

Royal Moat House — Nottingham
200 rooms, D £ 100 — 20 km
Tel (44) 0115 - 936 9988, Fax (44) 0115 - 475 667

Stage Hotel — Nottingham
52 rooms, D £ 53 — 20 km
Tel (44) 0115 - 960 3261, Fax (44) 0115 - 969 1040

RESTAURANTS RESTAURANTS
Swallow — South Normanton
Tel (44) 01773 - 812 000 — 8 km

Sonny's — Nottingham
Tel (44) 0115 - 947 3041 — 20 km

ORCHARDLEIGH

17	7	7

Designed by Brian Huggett with the help of Peter McEvoy, this is a very ambitious resort with a second course already planned, an hotel, swimming pool and tennis courts. Close to Bath, this is already a course you will want to get to know. A little on the hilly side with a lot of water in play on six holes, Orchardleigh is an American style course calling for some «target golf» to hit the greens. We are a far cry from the traditional «down to earth» game, but the demands of present-day golfers and the nature of available sites mean that is the way golf seems to be moving. So there are few trees in play but a lot of fairway bunkers, as dangerous as water for high-handicappers (which is a bit of shame). On a peaceful site rich in wildlife and neatly landscaped, this is a sound layout which from a technical angle is very interesting to discover and play.

Dessiné par Brian Huggett avec l'aide de Peter McEvoy, c'est un complexe très ambitieux, avec en projet un second parcours, un hôtel, une piscine et des tennis. A proximité de Bath, c'est déjà un parcours à connaître. Assez vallonné, mais sans excès, il présente beaucoup d'obstacles d'eau (en jeu sur un tiers des trous), ce qui donne à l'évidence un style américain que la nécessité de jouer du «jeu de cibles» vers les greens accentue encore. Nous sommes loin du «jeu à terre» de la tradition, mais l'exigence des golfeurs d'aujourd'hui, comme la nature des terrains disponibles imposent cette tendance : on trouve ainsi peu d'arbres en jeu, mais de nombreux bunkers de fairway, aussi dangereux que l'eau pour les hauts handicaps (c'est un peu dommage). Dans un site tranquille, riche en vie sauvage et bien paysagé, c'est une solide réalisation, techniquement très intéressante à découvrir et jouer.

Orchardleigh Golf Club — 1996

Near Frome
ENG - BATH, Somerset BA11 2PH

Office	Secrétariat	(44) 01373 - 454 200
Pro shop	Pro-shop	(44) 01373 - 454 200
Fax	Fax	(44) 01373 - 454 202
Situation	Situation	

18 km S of Bath (pop. 78 689) - 3.5 km NW of Frome

Annual closure	Fermeture annuelle	no
Weekly closure	Fermeture hebdomadaire	no

Fees main season
Tarifs haute saison 18 holes

	Week days Semaine	We/Bank holidays We/Férié
Individual Individuel	£ 30	£ 40
Couple Couple	£ 60	£ 80

Weekends: Visitors only after 11.00 am

Caddy	Caddy	on request/£ 15
Electric Trolley	Chariot électrique	no
Buggy	Voiturette	£ 20/18 holes
Clubs	Clubs	£ 15/18 holes

Credit cards Cartes de crédit VISA - MasterCard

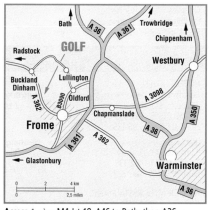

Access Accès : M4 Jct 18, A46 to Bath, then A36 to Frome then A362 → Radstock. 3.5 km NW of Frome, main entrance on right side, before village of Buckland Dinham.
Map 6 on page 499 Carte 6 Page 499

GOLF COURSE / PARCOURS — 17/20

Site	Site	
Maintenance	Entretien	
Architect	Architecte	Brian Huggett
Type	Type	inland, parkland
Relief	Relief	
Water in play	Eau en jeu	
Exp. to wind	Exposé au vent	
Trees in play	Arbres en jeu	

Scorecard Carte de score	Chp. Chp.	Mens Mess.	Ladies Da.
Length Long.	6198	5691	5026
Par	72	72	73

Advised golfing ability Niveau de jeu recommandé		0 12 24 36
Hcp required Handicap exigé		28 Men, 36 Ladies

CLUB HOUSE & AMENITIES / CLUB HOUSE ET ANNEXES — 7/10

Pro shop	Pro-shop	
Driving range	Practice	
Sheltered	couvert	no
On grass	sur herbe	yes
Putting-green	putting-green	yes
Pitching-green	pitching green	yes

HOTEL FACILITIES / ENVIRONNEMENT HOTELIER — 7/10

HOTELS HÔTELS
Woolpack Inn - 10 rooms, D £ 80 — Beckington, 3 km
Tel (44) 01373 - 831 244, Fax (44) 01373 - 831 223

Royal Crescent - 38 rooms, D £ 150 — Bath, 18 km
Tel (44) 01373 - 739 955, Fax (44) 01373 - 339 401

Bloomfield House — Bath
6 rooms, D £ 90 — 18 km
Tel (44) 01225 - 420 105, Fax (44) 01225 - 481 958

RESTAURANTS RESTAURANTS
Woolpack Inn — Beckington
Tel (44) 01373 - 831 244 — 3 km

Brottens Lodge — Doulting
Tel (44) 01749 - 880 352 — 9 km

Bowlish House — Shepton Mallet
Tel (44) 01749 - 342 022 — 12 km

615

Admittedly we are close to the cities of Manchester, Liverpool and Blackburn, but it is still exceptional to see such a concentration of good golf courses in one area. Those on the coast have always attracted the most publicity, but the inland courses have a lot going for them, as well. Take Ormskirk for example, right out in the sticks, far from the hurly-burly of today's modern world. In contrast with links courses, everything here is as green as in those glossy magazines, with birch trees and heather which is a pretty sight indeed... from afar. There is only a single water hazard, on the 3rd hole, but the rough is thick and eats into several fairways. Accurate driving is of the essence, especially on the very many doglegs on which you will have to make a whole range of second shots to reach the greens. The par 3s here are excellent, especially the 14th and 17th holes. Intelligent, natural and very fair, Ormskirk will be a real eye-opener for many golfers.

Certes, nous sommes tout près de Manchester, Liverpool et Blackburn, mais il est exceptionnel de voir une telle concentration de golfs, et de bons golfs. Bien sûr, les parcours de la côte ont bénéficié du maximum de publicité, mais ceux de l'intérieur ne manquent pas d'attraits. Témoin Ormskirk, situé en pleine campagne, très à l'écart des bruits de ce monde. Ici, en contraste avec les links, tout est bien vert comme sur les photos de magazines, avec des bouleaux et la bruyère, si jolie à voir... de loin. Un seul obstacle d'eau, au 3, mais le rough est épais, empiète sur plusieurs fairways, ce qui oblige à la précision des drives, notamment avec les nombreux doglegs qui imposent une très grande variété de seconds coups. On remarquera encore la qualité des par 3, notamment les 14 et 17. Intelligent, naturel et très franc, Ormskirk sera pour beaucoup une découverte.

Ormskirk Golf Club — 1899

Cranes Lane, Lathom
ENG - ORMSKIRK, Lancs L40 5UJ

Office	Secrétariat	(44) 01695 - 572 112
Pro shop	Pro-shop	(44) 01695 - 572 074
Fax	Fax	(44) 01695 - 572 112
Situation	Situation	

22 km N of Liverpool - 2 km E of Ormskirk (pop. 23 425)

Annual closure	Fermeture annuelle	no
Weekly closure	Fermeture hebdomadaire	no

Fees main season
Tarifs haute saison full day

	Week days Semaine	We/Bank holidays We/Férié
Individual Individuel	£ 40	£ 45
Couple Couple	£ 80	£ 90

£ 45 also on Wednesdays

Caddy	Caddy	no
Electric Trolley	Chariot électrique	£ 5/18 holes
Buggy	Voiturette	no
Clubs	Clubs	£ 3/18 holes

Credit cards Cartes de crédit
VISA - Eurocard - MasterCard - AMEX - DC - JCB
(Pro shop goods only)

616

Access Accès : M58 Jct 3. Follow signs to Burscough.
First left at T-junction. Right at Hulton Castle Pub. Right at next T-junction. Golf on right.
Map 5 on page 497 Carte 5 Page 497

GOLF COURSE / PARCOURS — 14/20

Site	Site	
Maintenance	Entretien	
Architect	Architecte	Harold Hilton
Type	Type	parkland, seaside course
Relief	Relief	
Water in play	Eau en jeu	
Exp. to wind	Exposé au vent	
Trees in play	Arbres en jeu	

Scorecard Carte de score	Chp. Chp.	Mens Mess.	Ladies Da.
Length Long.	5898	5786	5107
Par	70	70	73

Advised golfing ability Niveau de jeu recommandé	0	12	24	36

Hcp required Handicap exigé — certificate

CLUB HOUSE & AMENITIES / CLUB HOUSE ET ANNEXES — 6/10

Pro shop	Pro-shop	
Driving range	Practice	
Sheltered	couvert	no
On grass	sur herbe	yes
Putting-green	putting-green	yes
Pitching-green	pitching green	yes

HOTEL FACILITIES / ENVIRONNEMENT HOTELIER — 4/10

HOTELS HÔTELS
Beaufort — Burscough
21 rooms, D £ 70 — 2 km
Tel (44) 01695 - 892 655
Fax (44) 01695 - 895 135

Red Lion — Newburgh
13 rooms, D £ 35 — 3 km
Tel (44) 01257 - 462 336
Fax (44) 01695 - 462 827

RESTAURANTS RESTAURANTS
Pubs in Ormskirk — Ormskirk
— 2 km

Yorkshire has more specialities than just Yorkshire pudding (which for non-English readers is a sort of batter pastry served with roast-beef, especially on a Sunday). There are also excellent golf courses and the hot springs of Harrogate, which were particularly popular before the first world war. But before trying out the city's superb Turkish baths, spend a day on this very fine course, laid out on a plateau which dominates the surrounding region. This is a typical Yorkshire moorland course, very exposed to the wind but with a lot of trees. The difficulties lie with the thickness of the rough, and your score will depend on how well you drive. Despite the slopes, the course is not tiring to walk, only one green and one drive are blind and only a few elevated greens call for high approach shots. Otherwise you can practice your newly acquired art of rolling the ball onto the green. Green-keeping is remarkable, the clubhouse elegant and cosy.

Qu'on le sache, le Yorkshire Pudding n'est pas un dessert, mais une pâte à choux servie avec le rôti du dimanche. Le Yorkshire a d'autre spécialités, dont les bons golfs et les sources thermales à Harrogate, très en activité avant la Grande Guerre. Avant de vous remettre au superbe Sauna Turc de la ville, vous pourrez vous dépenser sur ce très beau parcours, qui vous amène sur un plateau dominant la région. C'est un parcours typique des landes du Comté, très exposé au vent, mais bien arboré. Les difficultés principales tiennent à la densité du rough, et la qualité du drive commande celle du score. En dépit du relief, le parcours n'est pas épuisant, on ne trouve qu'un seul drive et un seul green aveugles, et seules quelques greens surélevés qui appellent des balles levées. Autrement, on peut se livrer à l'amour des balles tendues et des approches roulées. L'entretien est remarquable, le Clubhouse élégant et chaleureux.

Pannal Golf Club

1906

Follifoot Road
ENG - HARROGATE, Yorkshire HG3 1ES

Office	Secrétariat	(44) 01423 - 872 628
Pro shop	Pro-shop	(44) 01423 - 872 620
Fax	Fax	(44) 01423 - 870 043
Situation	Situation	

4 km from Harrogate (pop. 143 530)
21 km from Leeds (pop. 680 725)

Annual closure	Fermeture annuelle	no
Weekly closure	Fermeture hebdomadaire	no

Fees main season
Tarifs haute saison 18 holes

	Week days Semaine	We/Bank holidays We/Férié
Individual Individuel	£ 35	£ 40
Couple Couple	£ 70	£ 80
Full weekdays: £ 40		

Caddy	Caddy	no
Electric Trolley	Chariot électrique	£ 5.50/18 holes
Buggy	Voiturette	no
Clubs	Clubs	no

Credit cards Cartes de crédit
VISA - Eurocard - MasterCard - Axos (not for green fees)

Access Accès : A61 Leeds → Harrogate.
Map 4 on page 494 Carte 4 Page 494

GOLF COURSE
PARCOURS

15/20

Site	Site	
Maintenance	Entretien	
Architect	Architecte	Sandy Herd Charles MacKenzie
Type	Type	open country, moorland
Relief	Relief	
Water in play	Eau en jeu	
Exp. to wind	Exposé au vent	
Trees in play	Arbres en jeu	

Scorecard Carte de score	Chp. Chp.	Mens Mess.	Ladies Da.
Length Long.	5960	5808	5237
Par	72	72	74

Advised golfing ability		0 12 24 36
Niveau de jeu recommandé		
Hcp required	Handicap exigé	24 Men, 28 Ladies

CLUB HOUSE & AMENITIES
CLUB HOUSE ET ANNEXES

6/10

Pro shop	Pro-shop	
Driving range	Practice	
Sheltered	couvert	practice area
On grass	sur herbe	yes
Putting-green	putting-green	yes
Pitching-green	pitching green	yes

HOTEL FACILITIES
ENVIRONNEMENT HOTELIER

7/10

HOTELS HÔTELS
Rudding Park House Hotel   Rudding Park 3 km
50 rooms, D £ 129
Tel (44) 01423 - 871 350, Fax (44) 01423 - 872 286
Sandringham - 6 rooms, D £ 90   Beckwithshaw 5 km
Tel (44) 01423 - 500 722, Fax (44) 01423 - 530 509
Crown - 116 rooms, D £ 80   Harrogate 5 km
Tel (44) 01423 - 567 755, Fax (44) 01423 - 502 284
Ruskin Hotel - 7 rooms, D £ 89   Harrogate 5 km
Tel (44) 01423 - 502 045, Fax (44) 01423 - 506 131

RESTAURANTS RESTAURANTS
Drum & Monkey   Harrogate 5 km
Tel (44) 01423 - 502 650
Clocktower Brasserie   Rudding Park 3 km
Tel (44) 01423 - 872 100
The Bistro - Tel (44) 01423 - 530 708   Harrogate 5 km

617

The best time to come here is in Spring, to see how the rhododendrons add colour to the picturesque landscape of heather and pine, or to listen to the ducks quacking as your ball splashes into its watery grave. Parkstone is virtually in town, between Poole and Bournemouth, one of England's most popular seaside resorts. But everything is peace and quiet in a pretty setting where you feel so privileged to be walking the fairways that it is almost unthinkable not to play well. Yet Willie Park and Harry Colt used their combined talents to set traps and decorate their work of art with heather from where a decent recovery is nigh on impossible. High-handicappers will certainly not consider this to be a holiday course, but after all there is something to be said for being thrown in at the deep end. They'll learn that this is a good course and if they make it to the 18th (a big par 3) they will do the same as everyone else, take one shot more than they expected.

Ici, il faut venir au printemps quand les rhododendrons ajoutent leurs couleurs de fête du printemps au paysage de bruyères et de pins, et les canards leurs cris de joie quand les balles de golf font des ronds dans l'eau. Parkstone est pratiquement en ville, entre Poole et Bournemouth, une des stations balnéaires les plus fréquentées d'Angleterre. Mais on est ici au calme, dans un joli paysage où il est impossible de mal jouer tant on a le sentiment d'être privilégié. Pourtant, Willie Park et Harry Colt se sont ingéniés à tendre des pièges, à décorer leur oeuvre de bruyère dont il est impossible de sortir dignement. Les handicaps un peu élevés ne vont pas trouver qu'il s'agisse d'un parcours de vacances, mais après tout, il faut d'abord apprendre à nager, même au golf. Qu'ils apprennent seulement ce qu'est un bon parcours. Au 18 (un gros par 3), ils feront comme tout le monde, un coup de plus qu'ils n'espèrent.

Parkstone Golf Club — 1910

Links Road, Parkstone
ENG - POOLE, Dorset BH14 9QS

Office	Secrétariat	(44) 01202 - 707 138
Pro shop	Pro-shop	(44) 01202 - 708 092
Fax	Fax	(44) 01202 - 706 027
Situation	Situation	

2 km E of Poole (pop. 133 050)
3 km W of Bournemouth (pop. 151 302)

Annual closure	Fermeture annuelle	no
Weekly closure	Fermeture hebdomadaire	no

Fees main season
Tarifs haute saison 18 holes

	Week days Semaine	We/Bank holidays We/Férié
Individual Individuel	£ 30	£ 40
Couple Couple	£ 60	£ 80

Caddy	Caddy	no
Electric Trolley	Chariot électrique	£ 7/18 holes
Buggy	Voiturette	no
Clubs	Clubs	£ 8/day

Credit cards Cartes de crédit
VISA - MasterCard (Pro shop goods only)

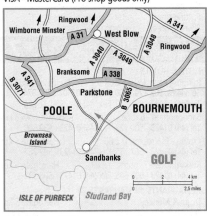

Access Accès : A35 Bournemouth → Poole.
Turn left on St Osmunds Road
Map 6 on page 499 Carte 6 Page 499

GOLF COURSE
PARCOURS — **16**/20

Site	Site	
Maintenance	Entretien	
Architect	Architecte	Willie Park
		James Braid
Type	Type	forest, heathland
Relief	Relief	
Water in play	Eau en jeu	
Exp. to wind	Exposé au vent	
Trees in play	Arbres en jeu	

Scorecard Carte de score	Chp. Chp.	Mens Mess.	Ladies Da.
Length Long.	5690	5405	4952
Par	72	71	71

Advised golfing ability	0 12 24 36
Niveau de jeu recommandé	
Hcp required Handicap exigé	28 Men, 30 Ladies

CLUB HOUSE & AMENITIES
CLUB HOUSE ET ANNEXES — **7**/10

Pro shop	Pro-shop	
Driving range	Practice	
Sheltered	couvert	members & green fees
On grass	sur herbe	yes
Putting-green	putting-green	yes
Pitching-green	pitching green	yes

HOTEL FACILITIES
ENVIRONNEMENT HOTELIER — **8**/10

HOTELS HÔTELS

Haven - 90 rooms, D £ 130 — Sandbanks 2 km
Tel (44) 01202 - 707 333, Fax (44) 01202 - 708 796

Mansion House - 28 rooms, D £ 90 — Poole 2 km
Tel (44) 01202 - 685 666, Fax (44) 01202 - 665 709

East Cliff Court — Bournemouth
70 rooms, D £ 60 — 2 km
Tel (44) 01202 - 554 545, Fax (44) 01202 - 557 456

Wood Lodge — Bournemouth
15 rooms, D £ 60 — 2 km
Tel (44) 01202 - 290 891

RESTAURANTS RESTAURANTS
La Roche — Sandbanks
Tel (44) 01202 - 707 333 — 2 km

Bankes Bistro — Parkstone
Tel (44) 01202 - 736 735 — 0.5 km

618

Nature specialists will often talk to you about Capability Brown, no relation to Calamity Jane, but the father-figure of English landscape gardening in the 18th century in reaction to the more austere French-style gardens. Patshull was laid out in an estate planted by the great man and it gives considerable visual appeal to this very discreet and classical course by John Jacobs. The water hazards certainly add a little extra spice. Some of the trees are dangerously in play because they transform a number of straight holes into dog-legs, so you have to play around them. Not too long, Patshull is a pleasant family course to play on foot, although hiring a buggy is not a bad idea, either, at least for carrying your bags. You don't come here to play top tournaments but to spend a day or two's pleasant golfing. The hotel on site is very well appointed with sauna, pool and jacuzzi, and you can also fish here.

Les spécialistes de la nature vous parleront de Capability Brown, qui n'était pas le cousin de Calamity Jane, mais le père du paysage à l'anglaise au XVIIIème siècle, en réaction contre les austères jardins à la française. C'est dans un domaine qu'il a créé que ce parcours a pris place. Il ajoute un attrait visuel indéniable au tracé très sobre et classique de John Jacobs, où les obstacles d'eau apportent un certain piment. Quelques arbres ont été dangereusement mis en jeu, car ils transforment certains trous droits en doglegs. Il faut savoir tourner autour. Pas trop long, Patshull est très agréable à jouer en famille, à pied éventuellement, mais jouer en voiturette n'est pas mal non plus, au moins pour mettre les sacs de golf. Ici, on ne vient pas jouer de grands championnats, mais passer une ou deux bonnes journées. L'hôtel sur place est très bien équipé, avec sauna, piscine, et jacuzzi. Il est aussi possible de pêcher.

Patshull Park Golf & Country Club   1979
ENG - PATTINGHAM, Shropshire WV6 7HR

Office	Secrétariat	(44) 01902 - 700 100
Pro shop	Pro-shop	(44) 01902 - 700 342
Fax	Fax	(44) 01902 - 700 874
Situation	Situation	

13 km W of Wolverhampton (pop. 242 190)
16 km E of Telford (pop. 119 340)

Annual closure	Fermeture annuelle	no
Weekly closure	Fermeture hebdomadaire	no

Fees main season
Tarifs haute saison 18 holes

	Week days Semaine	We/Bank holidays We/Férié
Individual Individuel	£ 22.50	£ 27.50
Couple Couple	£ 45	£ 55
Caddy Caddy	no	
Electric Trolley Chariot électrique	no	
Buggy Voiturette	£ 19.50/18 holes	
Clubs Clubs	£ 15/18 holes	

Credit cards Cartes de crédit
VISA - Eurocard - MasterCard - AMEX - DC

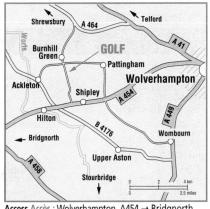

Access Accès : Wolverhampton, A454 → Bridgnorth.
Nearly 4 km (2 1/2 m.) until The Mermaid Inn. Turn right after lights (Tinacre Hill) through Pattingham. Turn right at the Church. Golf 2 km on the right.
Map 7 on page 500 Carte 7 Page 500

GOLF COURSE
PARCOURS   **13**/20

Site	Site	
Maintenance	Entretien	
Architect	Architecte	John Jacobs
Type	Type	parkland
Relief	Relief	
Water in play	Eau en jeu	
Exp. to wind	Exposé au vent	
Trees in play	Arbres en jeu	

Scorecard Carte de score	Chp. Chp.	Mens Mess.	Ladies Da.
Length Long.	5834	5601	5157
Par	72	72	74

Advised golfing ability Niveau de jeu recommandé	0	12	24	36

Hcp required   Handicap exigé   27

CLUB HOUSE & AMENITIES
CLUB HOUSE ET ANNEXES   **8**/10

Pro shop	Pro-shop	
Driving range	Practice	
Sheltered	couvert	
On grass	sur herbe	yes
Putting-green	putting-green	yes
Pitching-green	pitching green	no

HOTEL FACILITIES
ENVIRONNEMENT HOTELIER   **8**/10

HOTELS HÔTELS
Patshull Park Hotel   Golf
49 rooms, D £ 70   on site
Tel (44) 01902 - 700 100, Fax (44) 01902 - 700 874

Hundred House   Norton
10 rooms, D £ 80   7 km
Tel (44) 01952 - 730 353, Fax (44) 01952 - 730 355

Mount (Jarvis)   Tettenhall Wood
55 rooms, D £ 85   10 km
Tel (44) 01902 - 752 055, Fax (44) 01902 - 745 263

RESTAURANTS RESTAURANTS
Old Vicarage   Worfield
Tel (44) 01746 - 716 497   6 km

Lakeside Restaurant   Golf
Tel (44) 01902 - 700 100   on site

619

The cliffs and reefs of the west coast of Cornwall sometimes give way to little bays and fine beaches, such as here and the neighbouring holiday resort of Newquay, a surfer's paradise. It's also pretty good for golfers, too, who should make it along here in the same breath as St Enodoc and Trevose. You are in for a relatively easy round if you don't stray from the fairways, but it's a big «if». The «short stuff» is very tight, hilly (with dips, bumps, mounds and hillocks) and difficult to hit. After climbing up the dunes, you can find yourself in long grass, from where good scoring can pose something of a problem. At first glance you might think this an easy course, as there are very few bunkers. Paradoxically it is easier for mid-handicappers than it is for better players, who often prefer to play their approach shots out of sand rather than in thick grass.

Les falaises et les écueils de la côte ouest de Cornouailles laissent parfois place à de petites criques et même des plages, où ont trouvé place des stations de vacances comme Newquay, un paradis des surfeurs. Mais aussi des golfeurs, qui se doivent de venir ici en même temps qu'à St Enodoc et Trevose. Si l'on ne quitte pas les fairways, le jeu y sera relativement aisé. Mais ils sont très étroits, assez mouvementés (des creux et des bosses, des petites buttes et monticules), et on en sort un peu trop facilement. Après avoir grimpé dans les dunes, on peut alors se retrouver dans des herbes bien hautes, d'où un bon score devient problématique. On peut avoir l'illusion qu'il s'agit d'un parcours facile en jetant un premier coup d'oeil, car les bunkers sont peu nombreux : il est paradoxalement plus facile pour les handicaps moyens que pour les bons, qui préfèrent souvent jouer leurs balles dans le sable que dans l'herbe haute...

Perranporth Golf Club — 1929

The Clubhouse, Budnic Hill
ENG - PERRANPOTH, Cornwall TR6 0AB

Office	Secrétariat	(44) 01872 - 573 701
Pro shop	Pro-shop	(44) 01872 - 572 317
Fax	Fax	(44) 01872 - 573 701
Situation	Situation	

10 km S of Newquay (pop. 17 390)
15 km NW of Truro (pop. 16 522)

Annual closure	Fermeture annuelle	no
Weekly closure	Fermeture hebdomadaire	no

Fees main season
Tarifs haute saison 18 holes

	Week days Semaine	We/Bank holidays We/Férié
Individual Individuel	£ 20	£ 25
Couple Couple	£ 40	£ 50

Caddy	Caddy	no
Electric Trolley	Chariot électrique	no
Buggy	Voiturette	no
Clubs	Clubs	£ 10/day

Credit cards Cartes de crédit
VISA - Eurocard - MasterCard (Pro shop goods only)

GOLF COURSE PARCOURS — 16/20

Site	Site	▰▰▰▰▰▱▱
Maintenance	Entretien	▰▰▰▰▰▱▱
Architect	Architecte	James Braid
Type	Type	seaside course, links
Relief	Relief	▰▰▰▰▱▱▱
Water in play	Eau en jeu	▱▱▱▱▱▱▱
Exp. to wind	Exposé au vent	▰▰▰▱▱▱▱
Trees in play	Arbres en jeu	▱▱▱▱▱▱▱

Scorecard Carte de score	Chp. Chp.	Mens Mess.	Ladies Da.
Length Long.	5722	5460	4880
Par	72	72	72

Advised golfing ability 0 12 24 36
Niveau de jeu recommandé
Hcp required Handicap exigé certificate

CLUB HOUSE & AMENITIES CLUB HOUSE ET ANNEXES — 6/10

Pro shop	Pro-shop	▰▰▰▰▱▱▱
Driving range	Practice	▰▰▰▰▱▱▱
Sheltered	couvert	no
On grass	sur herbe	yes
Putting-green	putting-green	yes
Pitching-green	pitching green	no

HOTEL FACILITIES ENVIRONNEMENT HOTELIER — 6/10

HOTELS HÔTELS

Rose-in-Vale — St Agnes
19 rooms, D £ 70 — 5 km
Tel (44) 01872 - 552 202
Fax (44) 01872 - 552 700

Bristol — Newquay
73 rooms, D £ 75
Tel (44) 01637 - 875 181
Fax (44) 01637 - 879 347

Crantock Bay — Crantock
34 rooms, D £ 80 (w. dinner) — 5 km
Tel (44) 01637 - 830 229
Fax (44) 01637 - 831 111

RESTAURANTS RESTAURANT

Pennypots — Truro
Tel (44) 01209 - 820 347 — 15 km

620

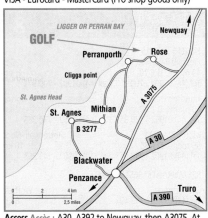

Access Accès : A30, A392 to Newquay, then A3075. At Goonhavern, B3285. Golf on edge of Perranporth, next to beach **Map 6 on page 498** Carte 6 Page 498

This is one the region's great parkland courses and has just treated itself to an impressively sized brand new clubhouse. There are a lot of trees, particularly on the 16th (a par 3) which you have to hit over in order to reach the green, but elsewhere they are rarely in play, except for slicers. The other hazards are the heather and the many large bunkers. Once again, a good score here means you really did play well. You may be lucky once, but rarely twice. Because of the technical challenge here, inexperienced players can expect to sweat a little, so stableford, match-play or a Texas scramble might be a more enjoyable option. This is indeed an excellent course for match-play golf, almost a testimony to the not too distant day and age when match-play was the formula used by all amateur golfers. The general excellence of green-keeping makes a visit here something we would eagerly recommend, despite the proximity of some pretty good links courses.

C'est un des grands parcours «de parc» de cette région, et vient de s'offrir un nouveau Clubhouse de taille impressionnante. On trouve ici beaucoup d'arbres, notamment un au 16 (par 3), qu'il faut survoler pour atteindre le green, mais ils sont rarement très en jeu... sauf pour les sliceurs. Les autres auront plutôt de la bruyère, de grands et nombreux bunkers. Un bon score est forcément la preuve d'un bon jeu. Ici, on peut avoir de la chance une fois, mais rarement deux. En raison de ses exigences techniques, les joueurs peu expérimentés doivent s'attendre à souffrir, on leur conseillera donc le stableford, le match-play ou le scramble ! Car c'est un excellent parcours de match-play, témoin d'un époque pas si lointaine où il s'agissait de la formule de jeu des amateurs. La qualité générale de l'entretien permet de recommander une visite, même si les grands links sont à proximité.

Pleasington Golf Club — 1891

Pleasington
ENG - BLACKBURN, Lancs BB2 5JF

Office	Secrétariat	(44) 01254 - 202 177
Pro shop	Pro-shop	(44) 01254 - 201 630
Fax	Fax	(44) 01254 - 201 028
Situation	Situation	

5 km from Blackburn (pop. 136 612)
10 km from Preston (pop. 126 080)

Annual closure	Fermeture annuelle	no
Weekly closure	Fermeture hebdomadaire	no

Fees main season
Tarifs haute saison full day

	Week days Semaine	We/Bank holidays We/Férié
Individual Individuel	£ 30	£ 35
Couple Couple	£ 60	£ 70

Caddy	Caddy	no
Electric Trolley	Chariot électrique	no
Buggy	Voiturette	no
Clubs	Clubs	£ 7.50/18 holes

Credit cards Cartes de crédit — no

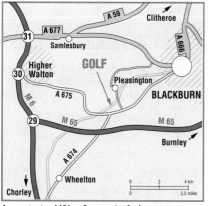

Access Accès : M61 → Preston Jct 9, then M65 → Blackburn. Jct 3, then A674 → Blackburn, to Pleasington Lane. Golf 200 m from Pleasington Station. **Map 5 on page 497** Carte 5 Page 497

GOLF COURSE / PARCOURS — 16/20

Site	Site	
Maintenance	Entretien	
Architect	Architecte	George Low Sandy Herd
Type	Type	parkland, heathland
Relief	Relief	
Water in play	Eau en jeu	
Exp. to wind	Exposé au vent	
Trees in play	Arbres en jeu	

Scorecard Carte de score	Chp. Chp.	Mens Mess.	Ladies Da.
Length Long.	5816	5816	5217
Par	71	71	74

Advised golfing ability Niveau de jeu recommandé	0	12	24	36

Hcp required Handicap exigé — no

CLUB HOUSE & AMENITIES / CLUB HOUSE ET ANNEXES — 8/10

Pro shop	Pro-shop	
Driving range	Practice	
Sheltered	couvert	no
On grass	sur herbe	practice range only
Putting-green	putting-green	yes
Pitching-green	pitching green	yes

HOTEL FACILITIES / ENVIRONNEMENT HOTELIER — 6/10

HOTELS HÔTELS
Swallow Trafalgar Hotel — Samlesbury
78 rooms, D £ 95 — 6 km
Tel (44) 01772 - 877 351, Fax (44) 01772 - 877 424

Forte Posthouse - 121 rooms, D £ 60 — Preston 10 km
Tel (44) 01772 - 259 411, Fax (44) 01772 - 201 923

Millstone - 17 rooms, D £ 85 — Mellor 6 km
Tel (44) 01254 - 813 333, Fax (44) 01254 - 812 628

RESTAURANTS RESTAURANTS
Heathcotes Brasserie — Preston
Tel (44) 01772 - 252 732 — 10 km

Birch House — Preston
Tel (44) 01772 - 251 366 — 10 km

Golf Club — Pleasington
Tel (44) 01254 - 202 177 — on site

621

They needed a big clubhouse here to cater to the number of players on the two 18 hole courses (the second course is the old Oaklands Golf Club). The Championship Course (1989), probably one of Donald Steel's best, is hilly enough for us to recommend a buggy to keep all your strength for playing golf (you will need it). The existing lie of the land was used and enhanced to great effect, completed by some shifting of earth that never clashes with landscape where the impression is more that of a park than open countryside. A little decoration never does any harm, like the little waterfalls on the 15th hole or the plants on the 6th. Owing to the length of this course, you will be hard pushed to play it twice in one day, so you will be pleased to learn that all the hazards are clearly visible, although to avoid them you will have to pitch the ball in high, sometimes flighting it both ways. A fine course.

Il fallait un Clubhouse imposant pour s'accommoder de la fréquentation sur deux 18 trous (le second parcours est l'ancien Oaklands Golf Club). Le Championship Course (1989) est probablement une des meilleures réalisations de Donald Steel, mais on conseillera l'usage d'une voiturette afin de garder assez de forces pour jouer au golf. Le terrain existant a été très bien utilisé et mis en valeur, et complété de mouvements qui ne heurtent jamais un paysage quand même plus proche du parc que de la campagne. Un peu de décoration ne nuit pas, comme les petites cascades du 15 ou les plantations du 6. Comme on jouera difficilement deux fois dans la journée en raison de la longueur du parcours, il faut savoir que tous les obstacles sont bien visibles, mais qu'il vaut mieux savoir bien lever la balle, et parfois la travailler pour réussir. Une belle réalisation.

Portal Golf Club   1989
Cobblers Cross
ENG - TARPORLEY, Cheshire CW6 0DJ

Office	Secrétariat	(44) 01829 - 733 933
Pro shop	Pro-shop	(44) 01829 - 733 933
Fax	Fax	(44) 01829 - 733 928
Situation	Situation	

16 km E of Chester (pop. 115 971)

Annual closure	Fermeture annuelle	no
Weekly closure	Fermeture hebdomadaire	no

Fees main season
Tarifs haute saison 18 holes

	Week days Semaine	We/Bank holidays We/Férié
Individual Individuel	£ 40	£ 40
Couple Couple	£ 80	£ 80

Caddy	Caddy	no
Electric Trolley	Chariot électrique	no
Buggy	Voiturette	£ 20/18 holes
Clubs	Clubs	on request

Credit cards Cartes de crédit
VISA - Eurocard - MasterCard - AMEX - DC

622

Access Accès : Chester A51, then A49. 1 km (0.5 m) north of Tarporley.
Map 4 on page 494 Carte 4 Page 494

GOLF COURSE PARCOURS   15/20

Site	Site	
Maintenance	Entretien	
Architect	Architecte	Donald Steel
Type	Type	parkland
Relief	Relief	
Water in play	Eau en jeu	
Exp. to wind	Exposé au vent	
Trees in play	Arbres en jeu	

Scorecard Carte de score	Chp. Chp.	Mens Mess.	Ladies Da.
Length Long.	6333	5854	5362
Par	73	73	73

Advised golfing ability		0 12 24 36
Niveau de jeu recommandé		
Hcp required	Handicap exigé	no

CLUB HOUSE & AMENITIES CLUB HOUSE ET ANNEXES   8/10

Pro shop	Pro-shop	
Driving range	Practice	
Sheltered	couvert	6 mats
On grass	sur herbe	yes
Putting-green	putting-green	yes
Pitching-green	pitching green	yes

HOTEL FACILITIES ENVIRONNEMENT HOTELIER   7/10

HOTELS HÔTELS
Swan Hotel - 20 rooms, D £ 68.50   Tarporley 5 km
Tel (44) 01829 - 733 838, Fax (44) 01829 - 732 932

Rookery Hall Hotel   Nantwich
45 rooms, D £ 95   10 km
Tel (44) 01270 - 610 016, Fax (44) 01270 - 626 027

Wild Boar   Beeston
37 rooms, D £ 85   6 km
Tel (44) 01829 - 260 309, Fax (44) 01829 - 261 081

Nunsmere Hall   Sandiway
31 rooms, D £ 120   5 km
Tel (44) 01606 - 543 000, Fax (44) 01606 - 889 055

RESTAURANTS RESTAURANTS
Swan Hotel   Tarporley
Tel (44) 01829 - 733 838   5 km

Blue Bell - Tel (44) 01244 - 317 759   Chester 15 km

PORTERS PARK

15 | 7 | 7

This is one of the oldest clubs in Hertfordshire which has recently celebrated its centenary. It was laid out by C.S. Butchart then restyled by J.H. Taylor, especially the bunkering which is remarkable. Bump 'n run shots are frequently a viable option but you often need a good, well-placed drive for the best angle of attack. This is all the more difficult in that high-handicappers seldom have good control over their tee-shots and the contoured fairways here can provide some unpleasant surprises. To make matters worse, a stream comes into play as a frontal hazard on seven holes. Here, either you have the full panoply of shots or you have a sense of improvisation (or both). The second shot also has to be well struck to reach the greens in the best spot. Last but not least, the course finishes with four par 4s of very decent length that can make all the difference whatever formula you are playing. It is great fun playing here (during the week) especially considering the very warm welcome in an impressive and traditional club-house.

Ce club vient de fêter son centenaire. Le parcours dessiné par CS Butchart a été remanié par JH Taylor, en particulier le bunkering, remarquable : les approches roulées sont fréquemment possibles, mais l'angle d'attaque doit souvent avoir été préparé par un drive bien placé. C'est d'autant plus difficile que les amateurs contrôlent rarement leurs coups de départ, que les contours des fairways peuvent réserver des surprises, et qu'un cours d'eau vient en jeu sur sept trous de manière frontale. On doit posséder ici un vaste répertoire de coups de golf, savoir improviser. Et pour parvenir aux greens en bonne position, savoir être précis. On ajoutera que ce parcours se termine par quatre par 4 de longueurs respectables, qui feront la différence aussi bien en match-play qu'en stroke-play. C'est un plaisir de jouer ici (en semaine), d'autant que l'accueil est agréable, le Club house imposant et traditionnel, bien qu'il ne soit pas si ancien.

Porters Park Golf Club		1899
Shenley Hill		
ENG - RADLETT, Herts. WD7 7AZ		

Office	Secrétariat	(44) 01923 - 856 262
Pro shop	Pro-shop	(44) 01923 - 854 366
Fax	Fax	
Situation	Situation	

30 km NW of London - 10 km E of Watford (pop. 74 566)

Annual closure	Fermeture annuelle	no
Weekly closure	Fermeture hebdomadaire	no

Fees main season
Tarifs haute saison 18 holes

	Week days Semaine	We/Bank holidays We/Férié
Individual Individuel	£ 30**	*
Couple Couple	£ 60	*

* With members only at week ends (£ 15)

Caddy	Caddy	no
Electric Trolley	Chariot électrique	£ 5
Buggy	Voiturette	no
Clubs	Clubs	no

Credit cards Cartes de crédit
VISA - Eurocard - MasterCard - AMEX (Pro shop goods only)

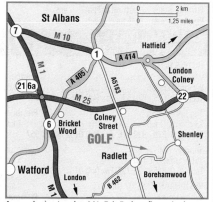

St Albans

GOLF

Radlett

Watford • London • Borehamwood

Hatfield
London Colney
Shenley
Bricket Wood
Colney Street

Access Accès : London M1. Exit 5, then first exit along A41. 300m to a big roundabout, → Radlett on B462. At T-junction mini roundabout, turn right, then first left at next roundabout into Shenley Hill. Golf Club 1,5 km. **Map 8 on page 503** Carte 8 Page 503

GOLF COURSE
PARCOURS
15/20

Site	Site	
Maintenance	Entretien	
Architect	Architecte	CS Butchark J.H. Taylor
Type	Type	parkland
Relief	Relief	
Water in play	Eau en jeu	
Exp. to wind	Exposé au vent	
Trees in play	Arbres en jeu	

Scorecard Carte de score	Chp. Chp.	Mens Mess.	Ladies Da.
Length Long.	5741	5440	5032
Par	70	70	73

Advised golfing ability		0 12 24 36
Niveau de jeu recommandé		
Hcp required	Handicap exigé	certificate

CLUB HOUSE & AMENITIES
CLUB HOUSE ET ANNEXES
7/10

Pro shop	Pro-shop	
Driving range	Practice	
Sheltered	couvert	practice areas
On grass	sur herbe	yes
Putting-green	putting-green	yes
Pitching-green	pitching green	yes

HOTEL FACILITIES
ENVIRONNEMENT HOTELIER
7/10

HOTELS HÔTELS

Hilton National — Watford
194 rooms, D £ 94 — 8 km
Tel (44) 01923 - 235 881, Fax (44) 01923 - 220 836

Edgwarebury — Elstree
47 rooms, D £ 125 — 8 km
Tel (44) 0181 - 953 8227, Fax (44) 0181 - 207 3668

Elstree Moat House — Borehamwood
119 rooms, D £ 135 — 10 km
Tel (44) 0181 - 214 9988, Fax (44) 0181 - 207 3194

Oaklands Toby — Borehamwood
38 rooms, D £ 80 — 10 km
Tel (44) 0181 - 905 1455, Fax (44) 0181 - 905 1370

623

The green-keeper is one of the five «masters» of Britain and his sterling efforts only add to the pleasure of playing one of the very few moorland courses designed by Harry Colt. A huge planting programme has enhanced the course both visually and in terms of giving each hole clearer definition over wide open space. Colt didn't do much to the terrain, he just used it with his usual brilliance, and you might be surprised by some of the sloping fairways. You need an accurate driver here, but the basic work consists in hitting some very-well defended greens which are sometimes tiered, sometimes terraced owing to the lie of the land. You need to play every shot in the book, in every direction. Basically you will want at least one good shot per hole (and some good putts), so you don't have much breathing space. A very sound course that makes an impression on all who play it, although visitors can only tee-off during the week. The ideal time would be a fine Autumn afternoon.

Le greenkeeper est l'un des cinq «Masters» de Grande-Bretagne, son travail ne fait qu'ajouter au plaisir de l'un des seuls dessins de Harry Colt en paysage de lande, auquel un énorme programme de plantations a donné à la fois beauté visuelle et définition des trous dans l'espace. Colt n'a pas beaucoup touché au terrain, il l'a utilisé avec son génie habituel, et certaines inclinaisons des fairways pourront surprendre. Il faut être précis au drive, mais le travail essentiel est dans les approches de greens très protégés, parfois en plateau ou en balcons en raison des mouvements du terrain. Il faut alors savoir jouer tous les coups, et dans tous les sens : il faut au minimum un bon coup de golf par trou (et de bons putts), ce qui ne laisse guère respirer. Un solide parcours qui ne laissera pas indifférent, mais on ne peut le jouer qu'en semaine. A voir par un bel après-midi d'automne

Prestbury Golf Club — 1921

Macclesfield Road
ENG - PRESTBURY, Cheshire SK10 4BJ

Office	Secrétariat	(44) 01625 - 828 241
Pro shop	Pro-shop	(44) 01625 - 828 242
Fax	Fax	
Situation	Situation	

3 km NW of Macclesfield (pop. 49 024)
25 km from Manchester (pop. 404 861)

Annual closure	Fermeture annuelle	no
Weekly closure	Fermeture hebdomadaire	no

Fees main season
Tarifs haute saison full day

	Week days Semaine	We/Bank holidays We/Férié
Individual Individuel	£ 37.50	—
Couple Couple	£ 75	—

No visitors at weekends

Caddy	Caddy	on request/£ 8.50
Electric Trolley	Chariot électrique	£ 5/18 holes
Buggy	Voiturette	no
Clubs	Clubs	£ 5/18 holes

Credit cards Cartes de crédit
VISA - Eurocard - MasterCard - AMEX - DC (Pro shop goods only)

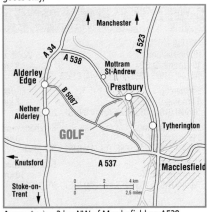

↑ Manchester ↑
A 34 · A 538 · A 523
Mottram St-Andrew
Alderley Edge
B 5067
Prestbury
Nether Alderley
GOLF
Tytherington
Knutsford · A 537 · **Macclesfield**
Stoke-on-Trent ↓
0 — 2 — 4 km
0 — 2.5 miles

Access Accès : 3 km NW of Macclesfield on A538 off A523. **Map 4 on page 494** Carte 4 Page 494

GOLF COURSE / PARCOURS — 17/20

Site	Site	
Maintenance	Entretien	
Architect	Architecte	Harry S. Colt J. Morrison
Type	Type	inland, open country
Relief	Relief	
Water in play	Eau en jeu	
Exp. to wind	Exposé au vent	
Trees in play	Arbres en jeu	

Scorecard Carte de score	Chp. Chp.	Mens Mess.	Ladies Da.
Length Long.	5723	5528	4917
Par	71	71	74

Advised golfing ability
Niveau de jeu recommandé   0   12   24   36

Hcp required Handicap exigé   no

CLUB HOUSE & AMENITIES / CLUB HOUSE ET ANNEXES — 8/10

Pro shop	Pro-shop	
Driving range	Practice	
Sheltered	couvert	no
On grass	sur herbe	yes (own balls)
Putting-green	putting-green	yes
Pitching-green	pitching green	yes

HOTEL FACILITIES / ENVIRONNEMENT HOTELIER — 7/10

HOTELS HÔTELS

White House Manor — Prestbury
9 rooms, D £ 95 — 1 km
Tel (44) 01625 - 829 376, Fax (44) 01625 - 828 627

The Bridge Hotel — Prestbury
23 rooms, D £ 56 — 1 km
Tel (44) 01625 - 829 326, Fax (44) 01625 - 827 557

Shrigley Hall — Adlington
156 rooms, D £ 120 — 5 km
Tel (44) 01625 - 575 757, Fax (44) 01625 - 573 323

RESTAURANTS RESTAURANTS

White House — Prestbury
Tel (44) 01625 - 829 376 — 1 km

The Bridge Hotel — Prestbury
Tel (44) 01625 - 829 326 — 1 km

Mauro's - Tél(44) 01625 - 573 898 — Bollington 2 km

624

13	6	4

Restoration work and alterations since the war, the arranging of the course into 3 nine-hole loops and a commitment to making this a course more for your average golfer have somewhat unseated the original layout by Campbell and Morrison and probably detracted from its overall standard as well. The fairways are wider than they used to be and the bunkers and greens are smaller, thereby reducing the risk of 3-putts. The only really interesting combination is almost certainly «Shore-Himalayas» which, and this is no coincidence, embraces most of the original layout. Of course, alongside Royal St. George and Royal Cinque Ports, a number of less experienced golfers will enjoy their first taste of links golfing with getting too much of a bloody nose. And of course if the wind blows (often a cross-wind here) Prince's can be long and tough. But all the same, the better players will still find the challenge here a little less demanding than it might be. The clubhouse is modern and facilities very respectable.

Les restaurations de l'après-guerre, la disposition en trois boucles de neuf trous, l'adaptation de Prince's aux handicaps moyens ont quelque peu bouleversé le dessin original de Campbell et Morrison. Et l'ont affaibli, il faut bien le dire. Les fairways sont plus larges qu'autrefois, les bunkers souvent plus petits, tout comme les greens : on n'y risque plus trois putts. Et la seule combinaison réellement intéressante est incontestablement «Shore-Himalayas,» où l'on trouve, ce n'est pas un hasard, la majorité du tracé d'origine. Certes, à côté de Royal St George's et de Royal Cinque Ports, certains golfeurs peu aguerris aimeront faire leur expérience des links sans trop se casser les dents. Certes, si le vent souffle (souvent en travers), Prince's peut être être long et difficile. Il n'empêche que les meilleurs joueurs trouveront le défi un peu moins agressif qu'il pourrait l'être. Le Clubhouse est moderne, les équipements convenables.

Prince's Golf Club — 1904
ENG - SANDWICH BAY, Kent CT13 9QB

Office	Secrétariat	(44) 01304 - 611 118
Pro shop	Pro-shop	(44) 01304 - 613 797
Fax	Fax	(44) 01304 - 612 000
Situation	Situation	

4 km from Sandwich (pop. 4 729)
10 km from Deal (pop. 28 504)

Annual closure	Fermeture annuelle	no
Weekly closure	Fermeture hebdomadaire	no

Fees main season
Tarifs haute saison 18 holes

	Week days Semaine	We/Bank holidays We/Férié
Individual Individuel	£ 40	£ 42
Couple Couple	£ 80	£ 84

£ 45/51 for 36 holes (Weekdays/Week-ends)

Caddy	Caddy	no
Electric Trolley	Chariot électrique	no
Buggy	Voiturette	£ 25/18 holes
Clubs	Clubs	£ 20

Credit cards Cartes de crédit VISA - MasterCard - DC

Access Accès : Sandwich, → «The Golf Courses». 3 km Toll gate into Sandwich Bay Estate, left 1 km and left again. Continue 2 km along seafront.
Map 7 on page 501 Carte 7 Page 501

GOLF COURSE PARCOURS — 13/20

Site	Site	■■■■■■□□
Maintenance	Entretien	■■■■■■□□
Architect	Architecte	Sir Guy Campbell John Morrison
Type	Type	seaside course, links
Relief	Relief	■■■□□□□□
Water in play	Eau en jeu	■■■□□□□□
Exp. to wind	Exposé au vent	■■■■■■■□
Trees in play	Arbres en jeu	■□□□□□□□

Scorecard Carte de score	Chp. Chp.	Mens Mess.	Ladies Da.
Length Long.	5860	5614	5260
Par	71	71	73

Advised golfing ability		0 12 24 36
Niveau de jeu recommandé		■■■■■■■
Hcp required	Handicap exigé	no

CLUB HOUSE & AMENITIES CLUB HOUSE ET ANNEXES — 6/10

Pro shop	Pro-shop	■■■■■□□
Driving range	Practice	
Sheltered	couvert	3 mats, members only
On grass	sur herbe	yes
Putting-green	putting-green	yes
Pitching-green	pitching green	yes

HOTEL FACILITIES ENVIRONNEMENT HOTELIER — 4/10

HOTELS HÔTELS
Bell Hotel - 29 rooms, D £ 100 — Sandwich 4 km
Tel (44) 01304 - 613 388, Fax (44) 01304 - 615 308

Jarvis Marina - 59 rooms, D £ 69 — Ramsgate 12 km
Tel (44) 01843 - 588 276, Fax (44) 01843 - 586 866

San Clu - 32 rooms, D £ 80 — Ramsgate 12 km
Tel (44) 01843 - 592 345, Fax (44) 01843 - 580 157

RESTAURANTS RESTAURANTS
Blazing Donkey — Ham, Sandwich
Tel (44) 01304 - 617362 — 7 km

Dunkerleys Restaurant — Deal
Tel (44) 01304 - 375016 — 10 km

Hare & Hounds — Deal
Tel (44) 01304 - 365 429 — 10 km

625

This must be the unluckiest golf club in England. Because of road-works then the Eurostar railway line, it has lost and rebuilt its club-house three times and had a few holes dug up in the process. This latest and hopefully last version was supervised by Donald Steel with new holes and 18 new greens. Once all this upheaval is behind it, the Rochester & Cobham golf club will recover virtually total tranquillity. So despite over 100 years of existence, the course is almost brand new. Some golfers may rue the large number of dog-legs but there was not that much space available. Yardage is, therefore, on the short side and there are three short part 4s that big-hitters will have fun trying to drive without too many risks, as long as there short game is up to it. "Normal" players will also have fun on a course that is within their reach, the main problem being to keep the ball on the small and well-guarded greens.

Le club le plus malchanceux d'Angleterre. A cause de travaux routiers, puis de la voie ferrée d'Eurostar, il a perdu et reconstruit trois fois son Club house, et aussi quelques trous. La dernière (on l'espère) mouture a été dirigée par Donald Steel, avec de nouveaux trous, et 18 nouveaux greens. Une fois ces perturbations achevées, Rochester & Cobham retrouvera un calme quasi absolu. En dépit de son âge plus que centenaire, le parcours est ainsi une nouveauté. Certains regretteront le grand nombre de dog-legs mais l'espace disponible n'était pas immense. Ainsi, la longueur générale n'est pas très grande, mais on trouve trois petits par 4 que certains bons frappeurs auront plaisir à tenter de toucher directement au drive sans trop de risques s'ils ont aussi un bon petit jeu. Les joueurs «normaux» s'amuseront beaucoup ici, sur un tracé à leur portée s'ils savent jouer avec les points de handicap. En fait, le plus difficile pour eux sera de garder la balle sur les greens, car ils ne sont pas immenses et sont bien défendus.

Rochester & Cobham Golf Club	1891
Park Pale	
ENG - ROCHESTER, Kent ME2 3UL	

Office	Secrétariat	(44) 01474 - 823 411
Pro shop	Pro-shop	(44) 01474 - 823 658
Fax	Fax	(44) 01474 - 824 446
Situation	Situation	
8 km from Rochester (pop. 23 971)		
Annual closure	Fermeture annuelle	no
Weekly closure	Fermeture hebdomadaire	no

Fees main season
Tarifs haute saison 18 holes

	Week days Semaine	We/Bank holidays We/Férié
Individual Individuel	£ 30	—
Couple Couple	£ 60	—

Full week day: £ 40 - No visitors at week ends

Caddy	Caddy	no
Electric Trolley	Chariot électrique	no
Buggy	Voiturette	£ 15
Clubs	Clubs	no

Credit cards Cartes de crédit
VISA - MasterCard (not for green fees)

626

Access Accès : London, A2. Cobham exit
(last one before M2). Follow signs to Golf Club.
Map 7 on page 501 Carte 7 Page 501

GOLF COURSE
PARCOURS
14/20

Site	Site	
Maintenance	Entretien	
Architect	Architecte	Donald Steel
Type	Type	forest, parkland
Relief	Relief	
Water in play	Eau en jeu	
Exp. to wind	Exposé au vent	
Trees in play	Arbres en jeu	

Scorecard Carte de score	Chp. Chp.	Mens Mess.	Ladies Da.
Length Long.	5937	5629	5283
Par	71	71	73

Advised golfing ability		0 12 24 36
Niveau de jeu recommandé		
Hcp required	Handicap exigé	certificate

CLUB HOUSE & AMENITIES
CLUB HOUSE ET ANNEXES
6/10

Pro shop	Pro-shop	
Driving range	Practice	
Sheltered	couvert	no
On grass	sur herbe	no
Putting-green	putting-green	yes
Pitching-green	pitching green	yes

HOTEL FACILITIES
ENVIRONNEMENT HOTELIER
6/10

HOTELS HÔTELS
Bridgewood Manor — Rochester
96 rooms, D £ 110 — 6 km
Tel (44) 01634 - 201 333, Fax (44) 01634 - 201 330

Forte Posthouse — Rochester
105 rooms, D £ 70 — 6 km
Tel (44) 01634 - 687 111, Fax (44) 01634 - 864 876

Ye Olde Leather Bottle — Cobham
7 rooms, D £ 40 — 3 km
Tel (44) 01474 - 814 327, Fax (44) 01474 - 812 086

Inn on the Lake — Thong
80 rooms, D £ 65 — 8 km
Tel (44) 01474 - 823 333

RESTAURANTS RESTAURANT
Bridgewood Manor — Rochester
Tel (44) 01634 - 201 333 — 6 km

Driving up from London, you will have stopped off at Stratford-upon-Avon (the birthplace of Shakespeare) and then at Gloucester to visit the cathedral and the docks that have now been transformed into a museum. As you pursue your cultural trek on to Hereford, home of the world's first map (in the cathedral), you drive along the very beautiful Wye valley and stop off in the pretty town that has given its name to this golf course. It was laid out in 1964 in a forest with literally thousands of trees, especially birch, which make this pleasant course such a beautiful site with its small, exciting and very well protected greens. There are a few blind shots but overall this is a very fair course with clearly identifiable hazards. Free of traps, well maintained and very pleasant to play, Ross-on-Wye extends a simple but very friendly welcome to green-feers.

Venant de Londres, vous vous serez arrêté à Stratford-upon-Avon (ville natale de Shakespeare), puis à Gloucester pour visiter la cathédrale et les docks transformés en musée. Avant de poursuivre votre quête culturelle à Hereford où l'on trouve la première carte du monde (à la cathédrale), vous devez passer par la très belle vallée de la Wye et vous arrêter dans la jolie ville qui a donné son nom au parcours. Il date de 1964, a été tracé dans une forêt composée de millions d'arbres, en particulier de bouleaux, qui donnent une grande beauté à ce plaisant parcours, avec de petits greens très animés et bien défendus. On trouve quelques coups aveugles, mais l'ensemble est néanmoins très franc, avec des obstacles clairement identifiables. Sans pièges, bien entretenu, très agréable à jouer, Ross-on-Wye bénéficie également d'un accueil simple, mais très amical.

Ross-on-Wye Golf Club   1964

Two Park, Gorsley
ENG - ROSS-ON-WYE, Hereford HR9 7UT

Office	Secrétariat	(44) 01989 - 720 267
Pro shop	Pro-shop	(44) 01989 - 720 439
Fax	Fax	(44) 01989 - 720 212
Situation	Situation	

20 km W of Gloucester (pop. 101 608)
5 km E of Ross-on-Wye (pop. 9 606)

Annual closure	Fermeture annuelle	no
Weekly closure	Fermeture hebdomadaire	no

Fees main season
Tarifs haute saison 18 holes

	Week days Semaine	We/Bank holidays We/Férié
Individual Individuel	£ 30	£ 30
Couple Couple	£ 60	£ 60
Full day: £ 35		

Caddy	Caddy	no
Electric Trolley	Chariot électrique	£ 6/18 holes
Buggy	Voiturette	no
Clubs	Clubs	£ 5/18 holes

Credit cards Cartes de crédit VISA - MasterCard

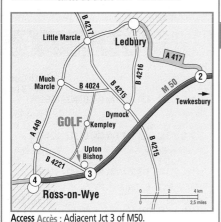

Access Accès : Adjacent Jct 3 of M50.
Map 6 on page 499 Carte 6 Page 499

GOLF COURSE / PARCOURS   15/20

Site	Site	
Maintenance	Entretien	
Architect	Architecte	C.K. Cotton
Type	Type	parkland
Relief	Relief	
Water in play	Eau en jeu	
Exp. to wind	Exposé au vent	
Trees in play	Arbres en jeu	

Scorecard Carte de score	Chp. Chp.	Mens Mess.	Ladies Da.
Length Long.	5897	5443	5130
Par	72	72	73

Advised golfing ability Niveau de jeu recommandé	0	12	24	36

Hcp required   Handicap exigé   certificate

CLUB HOUSE & AMENITIES / CLUB HOUSE ET ANNEXES   5/10

Pro shop	Pro-shop	
Driving range	Practice	
Sheltered	couvert	no
On grass	sur herbe	yes
Putting-green	putting-green	yes
Pitching-green	pitching green	yes

HOTEL FACILITIES / ENVIRONNEMENT HOTELIER   6/10

HOTELS HÔTELS

Chase   Ross-on-Wye
39 rooms, D £ 80   6 km
Tel (44) 01989 - 763 161
Fax (44) 01989 - 768 330

Sunnymount   Ross-on-Wye
6 rooms, D £ 50   6 km
Tel (44) 01989 - 563 880

RESTAURANTS RESTAURANTS

Pheasants   Ross-on-Wye
Tel (44) 01989 - 565 751   6 km

Epicurean   Cheltenham
Tel (44) 01242 - 222 466   30 Km

627

ROYAL ASHDOWN FOREST

14	7	6

Players who can't handle sand breathe an almost audible sigh of relief here, where there is not a single bunker in sight. So it could claim to be the most natural course around, as no-one has ever seen a bunker on wholly natural terrain except perhaps on links courses where grazing sheep keep the place in shape. This was the result of an administrative ban but has now become a sort of coquetry. But don't be too relieved, as there is no shortage of difficulties elsewhere: there are pine and birch trees, a stream on several holes, heather, which is even more dangerous than water that often has to be carried with your drive or even your second shot (on the 12th). As a general rule, and with a couple of exceptions, members will tell you to hit the ball high into the greens, which are rather large, very quick in summer and which slope in all directions. A pretty course and a superb clubhouse.

Alleluia, disent les golfeurs qui restent sur le sable. Il n'y a pas ici un seul bunker, c'est donc le parcours le plus naturel qui soit, car qui a vu des bunkers à l'état naturel, sinon dans les jardins d'enfant et sur les links authentiques où paissent les moutons ? C'était le résultat d'une interdiction administrative, c'est devenu une sorte de coquetterie. Que l'on ne soit pas trop vite soulagé, les difficultés ne manquent pas : les pins et les bouleaux d'abord, un cours d'eau sur plusieurs trous, la bruyère encore, bien plus pénalisante que l'eau, dont il faut souvent franchir des étendues au drive ou même au second coup (au 12). En règle générale, les membres vous souffleront qu'il faut ici lever la balle, sauf pour approcher un ou deux greens. Ceux-ci sont assez grands, avec des pentes dans tous les sens, et très rapides en été. Un joli parcours, avec un superbe Clubhouse.

Royal Ashdown Forest Golf Club — 1989

Chapel Lane, Forest Row
ENG - EAST GRINSTEAD, East Sussex RH18 5LR

Office	Secrétariat	(44) 01342 - 822 018
Pro shop	Pro-shop	(44) 01342 - 822 247
Fax	Fax	(44) 01342 - 825 211
Situation	Situation	

8 km SE of East Grinstead (pop. 24 383)

Annual closure	Fermeture annuelle	no
Weekly closure	Fermeture hebdomadaire	no

Fees main season
Tarifs haute saison full day

	Week days Semaine	We/Bank holidays We/Férié
Individual Individuel	£ 36	£ 40
Couple Couple	£ 72	£ 80
Caddy Caddy		£ 15
Electric Trolley Chariot électrique		no
Buggy Voiturette		no
Clubs Clubs		£ 10/18 holes

Credit cards Cartes de crédit
VISA - Eurocard - MasterCard - AMEX - DC
(not for green fees)

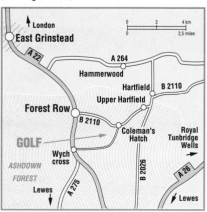

Access Accès : M25 Jct 6 then A22 South through East Grinstead. At Forest Row, turn left into B2110. 0.8 km (1/2 m.) right into Chapel Lane. Top of hill turn left.
Map 7 on page 501 Carte 7 Page 501

628

GOLF COURSE PARCOURS — 14/20

Site	Site	
Maintenance	Entretien	
Architect	Architecte	Archdeacon Scott
Type	Type	inland, heathland
Relief	Relief	
Water in play	Eau en jeu	
Exp. to wind	Exposé au vent	
Trees in play	Arbres en jeu	

Scorecard Carte de score	Chp. Chp.	Mens Mess.	Ladies Da.
Length Long.	5712	5675	5032
Par	72	72	73

Advised golfing ability		0	12	24	36
Niveau de jeu recommandé					
Hcp required	Handicap exigé	certificate			

CLUB HOUSE & AMENITIES CLUB HOUSE ET ANNEXES — 7/10

Pro shop	Pro-shop	
Driving range	Practice	
Sheltered	couvert	no
On grass	sur herbe	yes
Putting-green	putting-green	yes
Pitching-green	pitching green	yes

HOTEL FACILITIES ENVIRONNEMENT HOTELIER — 6/10

HOTELS HÔTELS
Ashdown Park — Wych Cross
89 rooms, D £ 100 — 3 km
Tel (44) 01342 - 824 988, Fax (44) 01342 - 826 206

Brambletye — Forest Row
22 rooms, D £ 60 — 2 km
Tel (44) 01342 - 824 144, Fax (44) 01342 - 824 833

Woodbury House — East Grinstead
14 rooms, D £ 85 — 5 km
Tel (44) 01342 - 313 657, Fax (44) 01342 - 314 801

RESTAURANTS RESTAURANTS
Brambletye — Forest Row
Tel (44) 01342 - 824 144 — 2 km

Chequers Inn — Forest Row
Tel (44) 01342 - 823 333 — 2 km

Royal Birkdale has hosted each and every top tournament: the Open, the Ryder, Walker and Curtis Cups, and the Ladies Open. It has done so more than others probably because this is an open and honest course where you can draw up your strategy according to the wind and not to the imponderables that create the «rough justice» charm of other links. Here, if you stay on the fairway you will avoid any blind shots. If you stray onto the surrounding dunes, you can end up in some very nasty situations indeed. This is a course for the technician and artist, not the big-hitter. Thomson, Watson, Trevino and Miller have all won here, as did Arnold Palmer, a more refined golfer than some might believe. There is no point in describing what could easily fill a whole book. Suffice it to say that Birkdale is unforgettable and that, like a dinner in a top hotel, this immense pleasure comes at a price. So make it a full day's golfing.

Royal Birkdale a reçu toutes les grandes compétitions : l'Open, la Ryder Cup, la Walker Cup, la Curtis Cup, le Ladies Open... Plus que d'autres sans doute, parce que sa franchise permet d'établir la stratégie en fonction du vent, et non des impondérables qui font le charme d'autres links, mais pas toujours dans la justice ! Pas de coups aveugles ici, du moins si l'on reste sur le fairway, car les dunes alentour peuvent vous imposer des situations peu confortables. Ce n'est pas un parcours de frappeur, mais de technicien, d'artiste du travail de la balle : Thomson, Watson, Trevino, Miller ont gagné ici, mais aussi Arnold Palmer, plus fin golfeur qu'on ne le croit. Inutile de décrire ce qui prendrait un livre entier, disons seulement que Birkdale est inoubliable, que cet immense plaisir se paie cher, comme un dîner dans un trois étoiles. Alors, prenez la journée.

The Royal Birkdale Golf Club — 1897

Waterloo Road
ENG - SOUTHPORT, Lancs PR8 2LX

Office	Secrétariat	(44) 01704 - 567 920
Pro shop	Pro-shop	(44) 01704 - 568 857
Fax	Fax	
Situation	Situation	

1.5 km S of Southport (pop. 90 959) - 30 km N of Liverpool

Annual closure	Fermeture annuelle	no
Weekly closure	Fermeture hebdomadaire	no

Fees main season
Tarifs haute saison 18 holes

	Week days Semaine	We/Bank holidays We/Férié
Individual Individuel	£ 75	£ 95*
Couple Couple	£ 150	£ 190*

* Not Saturdays - Full weekdays: £ 95

Caddy	Caddy	on request/£ 23+tip
Electric Trolley	Chariot électrique	£ 6.50/18 holes
Buggy	Voiturette	no
Clubs	Clubs	£ 10/18 holes

Credit cards Cartes de crédit
VISA - Eurocard - MasterCard - AMEX - DC - JCB
(Pro shop goods only)

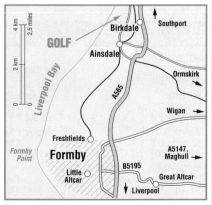

Access Accès : A565 Liverpool → Southport,
1.5 km (1 m.) before Southport.
Map 5 on page 497 Carte 5 Page 497

GOLF COURSE / PARCOURS — 19/20

Site	Site	▰▰▰▰▰▰▱
Maintenance	Entretien	▰▰▰▰▰▰▱
Architect	Architecte	J.H. Taylor F.W. Hawtree
Type	Type	links
Relief	Relief	▰▰▱▱▱▱▱
Water in play	Eau en jeu	▱▱▱▱▱▱▱
Exp. to wind	Exposé au vent	▰▰▰▰▰▱▱
Trees in play	Arbres en jeu	▰▱▱▱▱▱▱

Scorecard Carte de score	Chp. Chp.	Mens Mess.	Ladies Da.
Length Long.	6290	6021	5195
Par	70	72	75

Advised golfing ability
Niveau de jeu recommandé   0   12   24   36

Hcp required   Handicap exigé   28 Men, 36 Ladies

CLUB HOUSE & AMENITIES / CLUB HOUSE ET ANNEXES — 9/10

Pro shop	Pro-shop	▰▰▰▰▰▰▱
Driving range	Practice	▰▰▰▰▱▱▱
Sheltered	couvert	no
On grass	sur herbe	yes
Putting-green	putting-green	yes
Pitching-green	pitching green	yes

629

HOTEL FACILITIES / ENVIRONNEMENT HOTELIER — 7/10

HOTELS HÔTELS

Cambridge House Hotel — Southport 6 km
18 rooms, D £ 51
Tel (44) 01704 - 538 372, Fax (44) 01704 - 547 183

Scarisbrick — Southport 3 km
77 rooms, D £ 90
Tel (44) 01704 - 543 000, Fax (44) 01704 - 533 335

Stutelea - 24 rooms, D £ 80 — Southport 3 km
Tel (44) 01704 - 544 220, Fax (44) 01704 - 500 232

RESTAURANTS RESTAURANTS

The Warehouse — Southport 3 km
Tel (44) 01704 - 544 662

Valentino's - Tel (44) 01704 - 538 401 — Southport 3 km

The Jasmin Tree — Southport 3 km
Tel (44) 01704 - 530 141

Here you are a sliced drive away from the sea but you hardly ever see it. Deal (the course's other name) needs this barrier of dunes to protect the course from the sea-water which is deadly for turf. On a narrow strip of land, dotted with a few dunes and flanked by a little road and houses, you'd think it almost impossible to lay-out such a marvellous course. Less majestic than Royal St. George but more constantly demanding than Prince's, Deal requires the intuition that comes from long years of golfing. For example, knowing that on a particular day a particular shot will need three or even four clubs more. Highly strategic and full of small pot bunkers, this is a lively, clever and smart course which should make you a more intelligent golfer, or else leave you feeling a real fool.

Ici, on est à deux pas de la mer, mais on ne la voit pratiquement jamais. Il faut ce cordon de dunes pour protéger «Deal» (comme on le nomme aussi) des assauts d'eau salée, mortelle pour les gazons. Sur cette étroite langue de terre à peine animée par quelques dunes, longée par une petite route et des maisons, on aurait peine à imaginer pouvoir loger un aussi merveilleux parcours. Moins majestueux que St George's, plus constamment exigeant que Prince's, Deal réclame l'intuition que donne une longue pratique, pour savoir par exemple qu'il faut aujourd'hui trois ou quatre clubs de plus à cause du vent. Hautement stratégique, plein de petits bunkers où seul un mouton peut tenir, c'est un parcours vivant, astucieux et malin, d'où on sort intelligent, ou définitivement stupide.

Royal Cinque Ports Golf Club — 1892
Golf Road
ENG - DEAL, Kent

Office	Secrétariat	(44) 01304 - 374 007
Pro shop	Pro-shop	(44) 01304 - 374 170
Fax	Fax	
Situation	Situation	

adjacent to Deal (pop.28 504)
8 km from Sandwich (pop. 4 729)

Annual closure	Fermeture annuelle	no
Weekly closure	Fermeture hebdomadaire	no

Fees main season
Tarifs haute saison 18 holes

	Week days Semaine	We/Bank holidays We/Férié
Individual Individuel	£ 50	£ 50
Couple Couple	£ 100	£ 100

Visitors strictly by arrangement on weekends - Weekdays after 1.00 pm, £ 40

Caddy	Caddy	on request/£ 20
Electric Trolley	Chariot électrique	£ 5/18 holes
Buggy	Voiturette	£ 20/18 holes
Clubs	Clubs	£ 10/18 holes

Credit cards Cartes de crédit VISA - MasterCard

630

Access Accès : A2, A258 to Deal. Seafront to the end.
Turn left and right into Golf Road
Map 7 on page 501 Carte 7 Page 501

GOLF COURSE PARCOURS — 17/20

Site	Site	▰▰▰▰▱
Maintenance	Entretien	▰▰▰▱▱
Architect	Architecte	Tom Dunn Guy Campbell
Type	Type	seaside course, links
Relief	Relief	
Water in play	Eau en jeu	▰▰▱▱▱
Exp. to wind	Exposé au vent	▰▰▰▰▱
Trees in play	Arbres en jeu	▰▱▱▱▱

Scorecard Carte de score	Chp. Chp.	Mens Mess.	Ladies Da.
Length Long.	6080	5835	5105
Par	72	70	74

Advised golfing ability
Niveau de jeu recommandé — 0 12 24 36

Hcp required Handicap exigé certificate

CLUB HOUSE & AMENITIES CLUB HOUSE ET ANNEXES — 6/10

Pro shop	Pro-shop	▰▰▰▱▱
Driving range	Practice	▰▰▰▱▱
Sheltered	couvert	no
On grass	sur herbe	yes
Putting-green	putting-green	yes
Pitching-green	pitching green	yes

HOTEL FACILITIES ENVIRONNEMENT HOTELIER — 5/10

HOTELS HÔTELS
Royal — Deal 1 km
Tel (44) 01304 - 375 555

Bell Hotel — Sandwich
29 rooms, D £ 100 — 7 km
Tel (44) 01304 - 613 388, Fax (44) 01304 - 615 308

Wallet's Court — St Margaret's Bay
12 rooms, D £ 75 — 8 km
Tel (44) 01304 - 852 424, Fax (44) 01304 - 853 430

RESTAURANTS RESTAURANTS
Dunkerleys Restaurant — Deal
Tel (44) 01304 - 375016 — 1 km

Griffins Head — Chillenden5 km

Chequers Inn — Dealo
Tel (44) 01304 - 636296

Royal Cromer is a select location between Yarmouth and Brancaster. Select firstly for its site atop cliffs which alternate with sandy dunes right down the coastline and afford some superb views. Secondly in historical terms, because this is where they thought up the idea of the Curtis Cup between the top British and American ladies. And last but by no means least for the course, which although not a links has the same sort of difficulties including gorse bushes, wind and beautiful bunkering, for which Harry Colt is largely responsible. Although not quite of the same standard as its illustrious neighbours in this region, and without the typical contours of a links course, this layout is well worth a good visit. While you are here, make the most of your time and see the very pretty old town of Norwich.

Entre Yarmouth et Brancaster, Royal Cromer s'est fait une place de choix. Par sa situation d'abord, au sommet des falaises qui alternent sur toute la côte avec les sites dunaires, et qui offrent des vues superbes. Par l'histoire aussi, car c'est là qu'est née l'idée de la future Curtis Cup, entre les meilleures dames amateur de Grande-Bretagne et des USA. Par le parcours enfin, qui n'est pas un links, mais dont les difficultés en sont bien proches, avec les buissons d'ajoncs, le vent, un «bunkering» de toute beauté, dont Harry Colt est sans doute largement responsable. Sans être tout à fait au niveau de ses illustres voisins de la région, sans avoir ces mouvements de terrain typiques des links, ce parcours mérite une visite approfondie. Et tant que vous êtes là, profitez-en pour visiter la très jolie vieille ville de Norwich.

Royal Cromer Golf Club   1888

Overstrand Road
ENG - CROMER, Norfolk NR27 0JH

Office	Secrétariat	(44) 01263 - 512 884
Pro shop	Pro-shop	(44) 01263 - 512 267
Fax	Fax	(44) 01263 - 512 884
Situation	Situation	

1.5 km from Cromer (pop. 5 025)
32 km from Norwich (pop. 120 895)

Annual closure	Fermeture annuelle	no
Weekly closure	Fermeture hebdomadaire	no

Fees main season
Tarifs haute saison 18 holes

	Week days Semaine	We/Bank holidays We/Férié
Individual Individuel	£ 39	£ 43
Couple Couple	£ 78	£ 86

Caddy	Caddy	no
Electric Trolley	Chariot électrique	no
Buggy	Voiturette	no
Clubs	Clubs	no

Credit cards Cartes de crédit
VISA - MasterCard (Pro shop goods only)

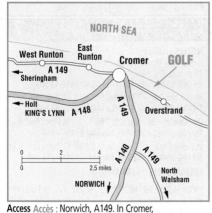

NORTH SEA

West Runton — East Runton — Cromer — GOLF
A 149
Sheringham

← Holt
KING'S LYNN   A 148   A 149   Overstrand

A 140   A 149
2,5 miles   North Walsham

NORWICH ↓

Access Accès : Norwich, A149. In Cromer,
turn right on Coast Road past lighthouse.
Map 7 on page 501 Carte 7 Page 501

GOLF COURSE
PARCOURS   15/20

Site	Site	
Maintenance	Entretien	
Architect	Architecte	J.H. Taylor Harry S. Colt
Type	Type	seaside course, open country
Relief	Relief	
Water in play	Eau en jeu	
Exp. to wind	Exposé au vent	
Trees in play	Arbres en jeu	

Scorecard Carte de score	**Chp.** Chp.	**Mens** Mess.	**Ladies** Da.
Length Long.	5802	5652	5233
Par	72	72	74

Advised golfing ability   0   12   24   36
Niveau de jeu recommandé

Hcp required   Handicap exigé   certificate

CLUB HOUSE & AMENITIES
CLUB HOUSE ET ANNEXES   7/10

Pro shop	Pro-shop	
Driving range	Practice	
Sheltered	couvert	no
On grass	sur herbe	yes
Putting-green	putting-green	yes
Pitching-green	pitching green	no

631

HOTEL FACILITIES
ENVIRONNEMENT HOTELIER   6/10

HOTELS HÔTELS
Cliftonville Hotel   Cromer
30 rooms, D £ 90   1.5 km
Tel (44) 01263 - 512 543

Links Country Park   West Runton
40 rooms, D £ 120   3 km
Tel (44) 01263 - 838 383, Fax (44) 01263 - 838 264

Dormy House   West Runton
14 rooms, D £ 90   3 km
Tel (44) 01263 - 835 537, Fax (44) 01263 - 837 537

RESTAURANTS RESTAURANTS
Westgate Lodge   Cromer
Tel (44) 01263 - 512840   1.5 km

Links Country Park   West Runton
Tel (44) 01263 - 838383   3 km

The Channel Islands are a curious blend of things English and French, with food coming under the latter influence (happily for the French). But golfing here is very British, as seen with this course. Firstly, given the incredible number of players who walks these fairways, Royal Guernsey is very well maintained (but often very dry in Summer). Then it requires good golfing skills and experience of playing in the wind, a capricious element here, often changing directions several times in one round. Under these conditions you don't often damage (pitch) the little greens, at least not as much as one would like. This traditional links course looks as natural as ever despite a number of restyling operations, particularly from Mackenzie Ross and Fred Hawtree. As a bonus, you get splendid views over the sea, the gardens close to the clubhouse... and the cows.

Les îles anglo-normandes (Channel Islands) présentent un curieux mélange d'anglais et de français, cette dernière influence étant aussi sensible (heureusement) sur la cuisine locale. Mais le golf est bien britannique, ce parcours en est l'illustration. D'abord, compte-tenu du nombre incroyable de joueurs qui y passent, il est bien entretenu (mais souvent très sec en été), ensuite, il réclame un jeu très aguerri et une bonne expérience du vent, car celui-ci est capricieux et peut changer plusieurs fois de sens pendant une partie. Dans ces conditions, on n'abîme pas beaucoup les petits greens, du moins aussi vite qu'on le voudrait. Parcours de links traditionnel, il continue à paraître naturel, malgré de nombreuses révisions, surtout de Mackenzie Ross et Fred Hawtree. En prime, les vues sont magnifiques, sur la mer, sur les jardins près du Clubhouse... et sur les vaches.

Royal Guernsey Golf Club 1890
L'Ancresse
ENG - VALE, Guernsey, Channel Islands

Office	Secrétariat	(44) 01481 - 46 523
Pro shop	Pro-shop	(44) 01481 - 45 070
Fax	Fax	(44) 01481 - 43 960
Situation	Situation	

4.5 km N of St Peter Port

Annual closure	Fermeture annuelle	no
Weekly closure	Fermeture hebdomadaire	no

Fees main season
Tarifs haute saison 18 holes

	Week days Semaine	We/Bank holidays We/Férié
Individual Individuel	£ 30	—
Couple Couple	£ 60	—

Thursdays, Saturdays afternoon & Sundays only with a member

Caddy	Caddy	no
Electric Trolley	Chariot électrique	no
Buggy	Voiturette	no
Clubs	Clubs	£ 7.50/18 holes

Credit cards Cartes de crédit
VISA - MasterCard (Pro shop goods only)

632

GOLF MAP
GOLF
L'Ancresse Bay
Grand Havre
L'Ancresse
Vale
St Sampson
GUERNSEY
Belle Grève Bay
Castel
St Peter Port

0	1,6	3,2 km
0		2 miles

Access Accès : Near Pembroke Bay, north of the island
Map 9 on page 504 Carte 9 Page 504

GOLF COURSE / PARCOURS — 16/20

Site	Site	▬▬▬▬▭
Maintenance	Entretien	▬▬▬▭▭
Architect	Architecte	Unknown
Type	Type	seaside course, links
Relief	Relief	
Water in play	Eau en jeu	▬▭▭▭▭
Exp. to wind	Exposé au vent	▬▬▬▬▭
Trees in play	Arbres en jeu	▬▬▭▭▭

Scorecard Carte de score	Chp. Chp.	Mens Mess.	Ladies Da.
Length Long.	5585	5585	5005
Par	70	70	72

Advised golfing ability	0	12	24	36
Niveau de jeu recommandé				
Hcp required Handicap exigé	no			

CLUB HOUSE & AMENITIES / CLUB HOUSE ET ANNEXES — 7/10

Pro shop	Pro-shop	▬▬▬▬▭
Driving range	Practice	▬▬▬▭▭
Sheltered	couvert	no
On grass	sur herbe	no
Putting-green	putting-green	yes
Pitching-green	pitching green	yes

HOTEL FACILITIES / ENVIRONNEMENT HOTELIER — 7/10

HOTELS HÔTELS
Symphony House Hotel — L'Ancresse
15 rooms, D £ 84 — 1 km
Tel (44) 01481 - 45 418, Fax (44) 01481 - 43 581

Pembroke Bay - 12 rooms, D £ 84 — L'Ancresse 100 m
Tel (44) 01481 - 47 573, Fax (44) 01481 - 48 838

De Havelet - 34 rooms, D £ 80 — St Peter Port 5 km
Tel (44) 01481 - 722 199, Fax (44) 01481 - 714 057

St Pierre Park - 132 rooms, D £ 130 — St Peter Port 5 km
Tel (44) 01481 - 782 282, Fax (44) 01481 - 712 041

RESTAURANTS RESTAURANTS

Victor Hugo - Tel (44) 01481 - 782 282 — St Peter Port

The Absolute End — St Peter Port 5 km
Tel (44) 01481 - 723 822

Wellington Boot — St Peter Port 5 km
Tel (44) 01481 - 722 199

Harry Vardon was born next door, just before Ted Ray. Add to that the fact that more recently Tommy Horton learnt how to play here and that makes a lot of champions for one club. The views from the impressive clubhouse are simply magnificent on a course which is a real paradise for golfers, especially players who can produce shots while interpreting every change in land level and get their distances right. In this respect, you are almost better off trusting your eyes than the yardage book. There is no par 4 longer than 400 yards (360 metres), there are five par 3s and only two par 5s at the beginning. Hazards abound and are very well positioned, the deadliest being the sea, at least for slicers. Royal Jersey is very busy in Summer but playable all year because of the warm climate. Spring and Autumn are wonderful times to play here.

Harry Vardon est né à côté, précédant Ted Ray. Si on ajoute que, plus récemment, Tommy Horton a appris le golf ici, cela fait beaucoup de champions pour un seul club. Les vues sont magnifiques depuis l'impressionnant Clubhouse sur ce parcours qui est un véritable paradis pour ceux qui savent fabriquer des coups de golf, en interprétant tous les changements de niveau du terrain, notamment pour les distances. A ce propos, il est presque plus sûr de se fier à ses yeux qu'au carnet de parcours. Aucun par 4 ne dépasse 360 mètres (400 yards), il y a cinq par 3 et seulement deux par 5 placés dès le début, sans doute pour commencer avec le sourire. Les obstacles sont nombreux, très bien placés, le plus redoutable étant la mer, en tout cas pour les sliceurs. Très fréquenté en été, Royal Jersey est jouable toute l'année à cause de la douceur du climat, mais le printemps et l'automne sont sublimes.

Royal Jersey Golf Club — 1878
ENG - GROUVILLE, Jersey JE3 9BD

Office	Secrétariat	(44) 01534 - 854 416
Pro shop	Pro-shop	(44) 01534 - 852 234
Fax	Fax	(44) 01534 - 854 684
Situation	Situation	

7 km E of St Helier (pop. 28 123)
1 km S of Gorey

Annual closure	Fermeture annuelle	no
Weekly closure	Fermeture hebdomadaire	no

Fees main season
Tarifs haute saison 18 holes

	Week days Semaine	We/Bank holidays We/Férié
Individual Individuel	£ 35	£ 40*
Couple Couple	£ 70	£ 80*

* Visitors after 2.30 pm at weekends - Very busy during summer

Caddy	Caddy	no
Electric Trolley	Chariot électrique	£ 10/18 holes
Buggy	Voiturette	no
Clubs	Clubs	£ 10/18 holes

Credit cards Cartes de crédit
VISA - Eurocard - MasterCard - DC (Pro shop goods only)

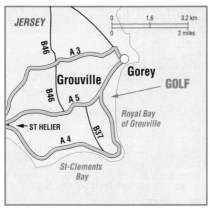

Access Accès : St Helier, A3 → Gorey. Turn right on A4.
Map 9 on page 504 Carte 9 Page 504

GOLF COURSE / PARCOURS — 16/20

Site	Site	
Maintenance	Entretien	
Architect	Architecte	Unknown
Type	Type	seaside course, links
Relief	Relief	
Water in play	Eau en jeu	
Exp. to wind	Exposé au vent	
Trees in play	Arbres en jeu	

Scorecard Carte de score	Chp. Chp.	Mens Mess.	Ladies Da.
Length Long.	5480	5480	4890
Par	70	70	71

Advised golfing ability Niveau de jeu recommandé	0 12 24 36
Hcp required Handicap exigé	28 Men, 36 Ladies

CLUB HOUSE & AMENITIES / CLUB HOUSE ET ANNEXES — 7/10

Pro shop	Pro-shop	
Driving range	Practice	
Sheltered	couvert	no
On grass	sur herbe	no
Putting-green	putting-green	yes
Pitching-green	pitching green	no

HOTEL FACILITIES / ENVIRONNEMENT HOTELIER — 8/10

HOTELS HÔTELS
Longueville Manor — St Saviour/St Helier
30 rooms, D £ 200 — 6 km
Tel (44) 01534 - 25 501, Fax (44) 01534 - 31 613

Old Court House - 58 rooms, D £ 70 — Gorey 1 km
Tel (44) 01534 - 854 444, Fax (44) 01534 - 853 587

De Vere Grand - 110 rooms, D £ 120 — St Helier 7 km
Tel (44) 01534 - 22 301, Fax (44) 01534 - 37 815

Hotel De La Plage — St Helier 7 km
78 rooms, D £ 70
Tel (44) 01534 - 23 474, Fax (44) 01534 - 68 642

RESTAURANTS RESTAURANTS
Longueville Manor — St Saviour/St Helier 6 km
Tel (44) 01534 - 25 501

Jersey Pottery - Tél(44) 01534 - 851 119 — Gorey 1 km

La Petite Pomme — St Helier 7 km
Tel (44) 01534 - 66 608

633

ROYAL LIVERPOOL (HOYLAKE) 》 18 | 8 | 7

Whenever you can, always play a links you don't know with a caddie. With the wind and out-of-bounds (some of which are inside the course), this is particularly true at Hoylake in order to identify certain hazards (the ground is flat) and draw up your game strategy. They say that Hoylake is a match for Carnoustie in terms of difficulty, and they're not wrong, even in fine weather. Here, you need patience, imagination and skill to improvise and invent shots you won't find in golf text-books, particularly on the less spectacular holes where you might be tempted to relax your concentration. There certainly are more spectacular and more baroque-looking courses in the world, but this one is less austere than it looks. Somehow, Hoylake is all a part of English humour; you need wit - a golfing wit - to understand what it's all about.

Quand c'est possible sur les links que vous ne connaissez pas, prenez un caddie. C'est encore plus vrai ici, avec le vent et les hors-limites (certains sont intérieurs), pour identifier certains obstacles car le terrain est plat, et pour établir une stratégie. On dit que Hoylake tient tête à Carnoustie en matière de difficulté. Ce n'est pas faux, même par beau temps : il faut ici de la patience et de l'imagination, savoir improviser, inventer des coups qui ne sont pas dans les livres. Et surtout sur les trous les moins spectaculaires, où l'on aurait tendance à baisser sa garde. Certes, il est des parcours plus impressionnants, visuellement plus baroques, mais celui-ci est moins sévère qu'il n'y paraît. Quelque part, Hoylake participe de l'humour anglais : il faut un certain esprit pour comprendre. Un esprit de joueur.

Royal Liverpool Golf Club — 1869
Meols Drive, Hoylake
ENG - WIRRAL, Cheshire L47 4AL

Office	Secrétariat	(44) 0151 - 632 6757
Pro shop	Pro-shop	(44) 0151 - 632 5868
Fax	Fax	(44) 0151 - 632 3739
Situation	Situation	

5 km from Wallasey
16 km from Liverpool (pop. 452 450)

Annual closure	Fermeture annuelle	no
Weekly closure	Fermeture hebdomadaire	no

Fees main season
Tarifs haute saison 18 holes

	Week days Semaine	We/Bank holidays We/Férié
Individual Individuel	£ 50	£ 75
Couple Couple	£ 100	£ 150

Full weekdays: £ 65

Caddy	Caddy	£ 20 + tip
Electric Trolley	Chariot électrique	£ 5/18 holes
Buggy	Voiturette	no
Clubs	Clubs	£ 15/18 holes

Credit cards Cartes de crédit
VISA - Eurocard - MasterCard - AMEX - DC - JCB

634

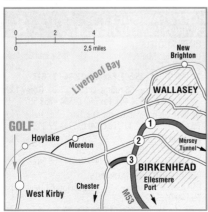

Access Accès : A551/A553 to Hoylake.
Map 5 on page 497 Carte 5 Page 497

GOLF COURSE PARCOURS — 18/20

Site	Site	
Maintenance	Entretien	
Architect	Architecte	Jack Morris
Type	Type	links
Relief	Relief	
Water in play	Eau en jeu	
Exp. to wind	Exposé au vent	
Trees in play	Arbres en jeu	

Scorecard Carte de score	Chp. Chp.	Mens Mess.	Ladies Da.
Length Long.	6345	6139	5180
Par	72	72	74

Advised golfing ability	0	12	24	36
Niveau de jeu recommandé				
Hcp required Handicap exigé	24			

CLUB HOUSE & AMENITIES CLUB HOUSE ET ANNEXES — 8/10

Pro shop	Pro-shop	
Driving range	Practice	
Sheltered	couvert	no
On grass	sur herbe	yes (pract. fairway)
Putting-green	putting-green	yes
Pitching-green	pitching green	yes

HOTEL FACILITIES ENVIRONNEMENT HOTELIER — 7/10

HOTELS HÔTELS
Grove Hotel — Wallasey 6 km
14 rooms, D £ 50
Tel (44) 0151 - 630 4558, Fax (44) 0151 - 639 0028

Leasowe Castle Hotel — Moreton 4 km
22 rooms, D £ 66
Tel (44) 0151 - 606 9191, Fax (44) 0151 - 678 5551

Bowler Hat — Birkenhead 8 km
32 rooms, D £ 85
Tel (44) 0151 - 652 4931, Fax (44) 0151 - 653 8127

Twelfth Man Lodge — Greasby 5 km
30 rooms, D £ 39
Tel (44) 0151 - 677 5445, Fax (44) 0151 - 678 5085

RESTAURANTS RESTAURANTS
Grove Hotel - Tel (44) 0151 - 630 4558 — Wallasey 6 km
Lee Ho - Tél(44) 0151 - 677 6440 — Moreton 4 km

Like Fairhaven, Royal Lytham doesn't look the most spectacular of courses at first sight, nor the most isolated. It is surrounded by houses and a railway line and has no sea-views. In fact you might think it has done everything to avoid any superfluous cosmetic appearance. But this is a golfer's course, and when the wind blows, it is a monster, almost on a par with Carnoustie, the most brutal of all courses in Britain. Fowler, Colt and Simpson joined forces to make this the ultimate test, the obligatory final examination which was later to be fine-tuned by C.K. Cotton. Pure and tough, it reveals all its hazards but you need to play here fifty times or more to take them all in. Green-keeping is excellent and the greens are slick but prone to push balls towards the deep bunkers. At the end of the day, this style of austerity does have its appeal.

Comme Fairhaven, Royal Lytham ne donne pas au premier abord la plus spectaculaire des impressions, ni celle de l'isolement que proposent souvent les golfs. Entouré par les maisons, la voie ferrée et sans aucune vue sur la mer, c'est un parcours dont on pourrait croire qu'il a évité tout aspect décoratif superflu. C'est un parcours pour golfeurs. Avec le vent, c'est un monstre, l'égal presque de Carnoustie, le plus brutal des parcours de Grande-Bretagne. Fowler, Colt et Simpson se sont alliés pour en faire un test absolu, un examen de passage inévitable. C.K. Cotton l'a enfin peaufiné. Pur, dur, il dévoile tous ses obstacles, mais il faut jouer cinquante fois pour bien assimiler. L'entretien est excellent, les greens subtils, mais ils rejettent volontiers la balle vers de profonds bunkers. Finalement, une telle austérité ne manque pas de charme.

Royal Lytham & St Anne's Golf Club 1896

St Patrick's Road South
ENG - LYTHAM, Lancs FY8 3LQ

Office	Secrétariat	(44) 01253 - 724 206
Pro shop	Pro-shop	(44) 01253 - 720 094
Fax	Fax	(44) 01253 - 780 946
Situation	Situation	

Centre of Lytham St Anne's (pop. 40 866)
8 km from Blackpool (pop. 146 069)

Annual closure	Fermeture annuelle	no
Weekly closure	Fermeture hebdomadaire	no

Fees main season
Tarifs haute saison 18 holes

	Week days Semaine	We/Bank holidays We/Férié
Individual Individuel	£ 75	—
Couple Couple	£ 150	—

No visitors at weekends

Caddy	Caddy	on request/£ 25
Electric Trolley	Chariot électrique	no
Buggy	Voiturette	no
Clubs	Clubs	on request

Credit cards Cartes de crédit
VISA - Eurocard - MasterCard - AMEX - DC - JCB

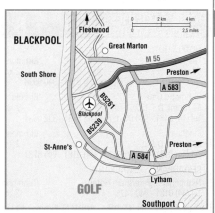

BLACKPOOL
Fleetwood
Great Marton
M 55
South Shore
Preston
A 583
B5261
Blackpool
B5239
St-Anne's
Preston
A 584
Lytham
GOLF
Southport

Access Accès : 1 km from centre of St Anne's
Map 5 on page 497 Carte 5 Page 497

GOLF COURSE / PARCOURS   19/20

Site	Site	
Maintenance	Entretien	
Architect	Architecte	H. Fowler, H.S. Colt T.Simpson/C.K.Cotton
Type	Type	links
Relief	Relief	
Water in play	Eau en jeu	
Exp. to wind	Exposé au vent	
Trees in play	Arbres en jeu	

Scorecard Carte de score	Chp. Chp.	Mens Mess.	Ladies Da.
Length Long.	6202	6011	5232
Par	71	71	75

Advised golfing ability Niveau de jeu recommandé	0 12 24 36	
Hcp required	Handicap exigé	18 maximum

CLUB HOUSE & AMENITIES / CLUB HOUSE ET ANNEXES   7/10

Pro shop	Pro-shop	
Driving range	Practice	
Sheltered	couvert	no
On grass	sur herbe	practice ground only
Putting-green	putting-green	yes
Pitching-green	pitching green	yes

635

HOTEL FACILITIES / ENVIRONNEMENT HOTELIER   8/10

HOTELS HÔTELS
Clifton Arms Hotel - 44 rooms, D £ 86   Lytham 2 km
Tel (44) 01253 - 739 898, Fax (44) 01253 - 730 657

Dalmeny   Lytham St Anne's 2 km
130 rooms, D £ 75
Tel (44) 01253 - 712 236, Fax (44) 01253 - 724 447

Imperial (Forte)   Blackpool 8 km
173 rooms, D £ 120
Tel (44) 01253 - 23 971, Fax (44) 01253 - 751 784

Pembroke - 268 rooms, D £ 120   Blackpool 8 km
Tel (44) 01253 - 23 434, Fax (44) 01253 - 27 864

RESTAURANTS RESTAURANTS
September Brasserie   Blackpool
Tel (44) 01253 - 23 282   8 km

Cromwellian   Kirkham
Tel (44) 01772 - 685 680   13 km

With two courses (including the «Inner» course which is not quite as good), this is one of the great clubs close to London. Unfortunately it lies beneath a flight route in and out of London airport and so, even though located in a residential area, is less tranquil than it might have been. There is a warm welcome for visitors during the week, a none too frequent occurrence in this part of the country. The clubhouse is magnificent with enough golfing mementoes for a small museum. This generally flat course, designed by J.H. Taylor, has no outstanding difficulty, except perhaps some very tough rough that might test a few weak wrists. Except holes 1 (a long par 3) and 17, this is a very decent course for enjoying your golf even when your swing is not quite in tune. The recent automatic watering system has considerably improved the standard of green-keeping after several years of drought.

Avec deux parcours, dont le «Inner» (intérieur) est moins intéressant, c'est un des grands clubs proches de Londres, mais aussi sur le passage des avions de ligne, ce qui perturbe un endroit autrement très calme, bien qu'il soit situé dans une zone résidentielle. L'accueil est agréable en semaine, ce n'est pas forcément si fréquent dans la région. Le Clubhouse est magnifique, avec des souvenirs de golf qui en font un petit musée. Généralement plat, le parcours de JH Taylor n'offre pas de difficultés particulières, bien que quelques zones de rough puissent inquiéter les poignets fragiles. Mis à part le 1 (long par 3) et le 17, c'est un très honorable parcours pour se faire plaisir même quand on n'est pas dans son meilleur swing. Le récent arrosage automatique a permis d'améliorer considérablement son entretien après plusieurs années de sécheresse.

Royal Mid-Surrey Golf Club — 1892
Old Deer Park
ENG - RICHMOND, Surrey TW9 2SB

Office	Secrétariat	(44) 0181 - 940 1894
Pro shop	Pro-shop	(44) 0181 - 940 0459
Fax	Fax	(44) 0181 - 332 2957
Situation	Situation	

1 km from Richmond
15 km from Central London (pop. 6 679 700)

| Annual closure | Fermeture annuelle | no |
| Weekly closure | Fermeture hebdomadaire | no |

Fees main season
Tarifs haute saison full day

	Week days Semaine	We/Bank holidays We/Férié
Individual Individuel	£ 55	—
Couple Couple	£ 110	—

Summer: £ 35 full day after 1.00 pm
Weekends: with member only

Caddy	Caddy	no
Electric Trolley	Chariot électrique	£ 6/18 holes
Buggy	Voiturette	no
Clubs	Clubs	£ 7.50/18 holes
Credit cards Cartes de crédit		not for greenfees

636

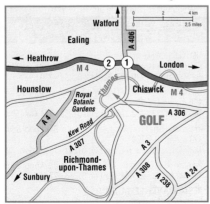

Access Accès : A316, 300 m before Richmond roundabout → London (close to Royal Botanic Gardens).
Map 8 on page 503 Carte 8 Page 503

GOLF COURSE PARCOURS — 14/20

Site	Site	
Maintenance	Entretien	
Architect	Architecte	J.H. Taylor
Type	Type	parkland
Relief	Relief	
Water in play	Eau en jeu	
Exp. to wind	Exposé au vent	
Trees in play	Arbres en jeu	

Scorecard Carte de score	Chp. Chp.	Mens Mess.	Ladies Da.
Length Long.	5747	5450	5231
Par	69	69	73

| Advised golfing ability Niveau de jeu recommandé | 0 | 12 | 24 | 36 |
| **Hcp required** Handicap exigé | certificate | | | |

CLUB HOUSE & AMENITIES CLUB HOUSE ET ANNEXES — 7/10

Pro shop	Pro-shop	
Driving range	Practice	
Sheltered	couvert	4 indoor nets
On grass	sur herbe	yes
Putting-green	putting-green	yes
Pitching-green	pitching green	yes

HOTEL FACILITIES ENVIRONNEMENT HOTELIER — 8/10

HOTELS HÔTELS
Petersham — Richmond
54 rooms, D £ 130 — 2 km
Tel (44) 0181 - 940 7471, Fax (44) 0181 - 940 9998

Richmond Gate — Richmond
64 rooms, D £ 130 — 2 km
Tel (44) 0181 - 940 0061, Fax (44) 0181 - 332 0354

Bingham — Richmond
23 rooms, D £ 85 — 2 km
Tel (44) 0181 - 940 0902, Fax (44) 0181 - 948 8737

RESTAURANTS RESTAURANTS
Nightingales (Petersham Hotel) — Richmond
Tel (44) 0181 - 940 7471 — 2 km

Chez Lindsay - Tel (44) 0181 - 948 7473 Richmond 1 km

McClements — Twickenham
Tel (44) 0181 - 744 9598 — 1 km

This is the oldest links course in England. If you are disappointed when you set eyes on the flat-looking terrain, you certainly won't be once you are out on the course. It might look gentle, but it doesn't play that way. Take the difficulties for example: tight fairways, invisible ditches, small deep bunkers sometimes lined with railway sleepers, very well protected greens where the approach is sometimes blind and rough with sea-gorse where it is nigh on impossible to get the ball back onto the fairway. Sheep crop the grass and bleat at the top of your back-swing, and then there is the wind. If you can keep the ball low, if you know your strengths and weaknesses, if you stay humble in your ambitions and if someone accompanies you around this huge open space, you can spend a great day and get the impression of having walked around a piece of golfing history.

Le plus vieux links d'Angleterre. L'arrivée à «Westward Ho!» peut paraître décevante tant le terrain est sans relief, mais votre partie ne va pas en manquer : c'est beaucoup moins tranquille qu'il n'y paraît. D'abord, les difficultés : fairways étroits, fossés invisibles, bunkers petits et profonds, parfois bordés de traverses, greens très défendus et dont l'entrée est parfois aveugle, dans les roughs et buissons de joncs marins d'où il est impossible de sortir. Des moutons broutent le gazon et bêlent quand vous êtes en haut du backswing. Il y a aussi du vent. Si vous savez jouer des balles basses, si vous connaissez bien vos forces et vos faiblesses, si vous envisagez humblement ce parcours, et si quelqu'un vous oriente dans cet immense espace, vous passerez une merveilleuse journée en ayant l'impression d'avoir mis vos pas dans l'histoire.

Royal North Devon Golf Club   1864
Golf Links Road, Westward Ho!
ENG - BIDEFORD, Devon EX39 7HD

Office	Secrétariat	(44) 01237 - 473 817
Pro shop	Pro-shop	(44) 01237 - 477 598
Fax	Fax	(44) 01237 - 473 456
Situation	Situation	

4 km from Bideford (pop. 13 070)
12 km from Barnstaple (pop. 20 740)

Annual closure	Fermeture annuelle	no
Weekly closure	Fermeture hebdomadaire	no
Book for meals		

Fees main season	Tarifs haute saison	18 holes
	Week days Semaine	We/Bank holidays We/Férié
Individual Individuel	£ 28	£ 34
Couple Couple	£ 56	£ 68
Full day: £ 34 - £ 36 (weekends)		

Caddy	Caddy	no
Electric Trolley	Chariot électrique	no
Buggy	Voiturette	no
Clubs	Clubs	£ 15/day

Credit cards Cartes de crédit
VISA - Eurocard - MasterCard (everywhere except bar)

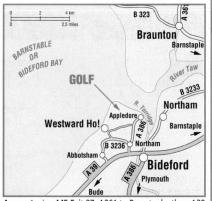

Access Accès : M5 Exit 27, A361 to Barnstaple, then A39 through Northam, take road down Bone Hill past Post Office, keep on left, Clubhouse ahead on hill.
Map 6 on page 498 Carte 6 Page 498

GOLF COURSE
PARCOURS   18/20

Site	Site	
Maintenance	Entretien	
Architect	Architecte	Old Tom Morris
Type	Type	links
Relief	Relief	
Water in play	Eau en jeu	
Exp. to wind	Exposé au vent	
Trees in play	Arbres en jeu	

Scorecard	Chp.	Mens	Ladies
Carte de score	Chp.	Mess.	Da.
Length Long.	5990	5758	5137
Par	71	72	73

Advised golfing ability	0	12	24	36
Niveau de jeu recommandé				
Hcp required	Handicap exigé	certificate		

CLUB HOUSE & AMENITIES
CLUB HOUSE ET ANNEXES   6/10

Pro shop	Pro-shop	
Driving range	Practice	
Sheltered	couvert	no
On grass	sur herbe	yes
Putting-green	putting-green	yes
Pitching-green	pitching green	yes

HOTEL FACILITIES
ENVIRONNEMENT HOTELIER   6/10

HOTELS HÔTELS

Anchorage Hotel   Instow
17 rooms, D £ 50   7 km
Tel (44) 01271 - 860 655
Fax (44) 01271 - 860 767

Newbridge   Northam
10 rooms, D £ 65   1 km
Tel (44) 01237 - 474 989
Fax (44) 01237 - 474 989

Durrant House   Northam
123 rooms, D £ 65   1 km
Tel (44) 01237 - 472 361
Fax (44) 01237 - 421 709

RESTAURANTS RESTAURANT

The Beaver Inn   Appledore
Tel (44) 01237 - 474 822   2 km

637

This is the sort of masterpiece that defies description. If a golf course is to be an adversary offering the toughest resistance to every shot, giving the player the opportunity to shine, sometimes forcing you to take the longer path to get a better shot at your goal, provoking the hardier golfer before breaking him completely but respecting the wise and the knowledgeable, then Royal St. George is one of the very greatest of them all. If we had to find one fault with this regular venue for the British Open, it would be the fact that not all the hazards are clearly visible. You have to play the course a lot to uncover its secrets but this is a privilege reserved for members only. Although the course is open during the week, we would advise visitors to play with a member, or at least with a caddie. You'll enjoy the experience even more.

C'est le genre de chef d'oeuvre qui échappe à toute description. Si un parcours de golf doit être un adversaire qui se défende contre tous les coups, offre des chances de briller à son adversaire, oblige parfois à contourner son objectif pour mieux y revenir ensuite, provoque les téméraires pour mieux les détruire, respecte les sages et les savants, Royal St George's est un des très grands parcours de golf. S'il est un seul défaut à ce links où le British Open revient régulièrement, c'est que tous les obstacles ne sont pas clairement visibles : il faudrait le jouer tous les jours pour en découvrir les secrets, et seuls les membres ont ce privilège. Bien que le parcours soit ouvert en semaine, on conseillera aux visiteurs de jouer avec eux, ou au moins de louer les services d'un caddie. Le plaisir n'en sera que plus grand encore.

Royal St George's Golf Club   1887
ENG - SANDWICH, Kent CT13 9PB

Office	Secrétariat	(44) 01304 - 613 090
Pro shop	Pro-shop	(44) 01304 - 615 236
Fax	Fax	(44) 01304 - 611 245
Situation	Situation	

2 km from Sandwich - 7 km from Deal (pop. 28 504)

Annual closure	Fermeture annuelle	no
Weekly closure	Fermeture hebdomadaire	no

Fees main season
Tarifs haute saison 18 holes

	Week days Semaine	We/Bank holidays We/Férié
Individual Individuel	£ 60	no
Couple Couple	£ 120	no

No visitors during Weekends - Permission required for Ladies to play

Caddy	Caddy	on request/£ 20
Electric Trolley	Chariot électrique	no
Buggy	Voiturette	no
Clubs	Clubs	£ 25/18 holes

Credit cards Cartes de crédit
Visa - Mastercard (Pro shop goods only)

638

Access Accès : Sandwich → «Golf Courses». 1 km along Sandown Road. Club drive on left after last houses **Map 7 on page 501** Carte 7 Page 501

GOLF COURSE
PARCOURS   **19**/20

Site	Site	▮▮▮▮▮▮
Maintenance	Entretien	▮▮▮▮▮▮
Architect	Architecte	Dr W. Laidlaw Purves
Type	Type	seaside course, links
Relief	Relief	▮▮▮▯▯
Water in play	Eau en jeu	▮▮▯▯▯
Exp. to wind	Exposé au vent	▮▮▮▮▯
Trees in play	Arbres en jeu	▮▯▯▯▯

Scorecard Carte de score	Chp. Chp.	Mens Mess.	Ladies Da.
Length Long.	6174	5904	0
Par	70	70	0

Advised golfing ability		0 12 24 36
Niveau de jeu recommandé		▮▮▮▮▯
Hcp required	Handicap exigé	18 Men, 15 Ladies

CLUB HOUSE & AMENITIES
CLUB HOUSE ET ANNEXES   **7**/10

Pro shop	Pro-shop	▮▮▮▮▯
Driving range	Practice	▮▮▮▯▯
Sheltered	couvert	no
On grass	sur herbe	yes
Putting-green	putting-green	yes
Pitching-green	pitching green	yes

HOTEL FACILITIES
ENVIRONNEMENT HOTELIER   **5**/10

HOTELS HÔTELS
Bell Hotel   Sandwich
29 rooms, D £ 100   2 km
Tel (44) 01304 - 613 388
Fax (44) 01304 - 615 308

Jarvis Marina   Ramsgate
59 rooms, D £ 69   12 km
Tel (44) 01843 - 588 276
Fax (44) 01843 - 586 866

Kings Arms   Sandwich
4 rooms, D £ 50   2 km
Tel (44) 1304 - 617 330

RESTAURANTS RESTAURANTS
Dunkerleys Restaurant   Deal
Tel (44) 01304 - 375016   7 km

Griffins Head   Chillenden 10 km

If you are one of those golfers who go for nature, wildlife and vegetation, this course is for you, set in a landscape of dunes and salt-marshes that flood at every high tide and which are home to a host of wild animals. Brancaster is famous for its railway sleeper bunkers and its devilish greens, which are tough to putt on and tough to reach because they are small and often hit with long irons. If it's windy, you can forget it. Get out on the course, by all means, and enjoy what is an uplifting experience for any golfer, but go around in match-play and play to see who pays for the drink at the bar. You won't want to leave the clubhouse, which has never been anything else but old and smells of wood, woods and balatas. Time has stood still at Brancaster, which is why you feel so privileged to be here. A little on the short side, did you say? What the hell.

Si vous êtes de ces golfeurs qui sont aussi amoureux de la nature, de la flore et de la faune, ce parcours est pour vous, dans un paysage de dunes et de marais salés inondés lors des grandes marées, qui abritent une vie sauvage très riche. Brancaster est célèbre pour ses bunkers renforcés par des traverses de chemin de fer, mais aussi pour des greens diaboliques, difficiles à toucher car ils sont petits et souvent attaqués avec des longs fers, et difficiles à putter. Les jours de vent, n'insistez pas : jouez car l'expérience est exaltante, mais en match-play, avec un enjeu à consommer au Clubhouse. Il est vieux depuis toujours, il y règne une odeur de bois en bois et de balatas, il fait bon y rester. Ici, le temps s'est arrêté, c'est pourquoi on s'y sent autant privilégié. Le parcours est un peu court ? Et alors...

Royal West Norfolk Golf Club 1892
ENG - BRANCASTER, Norfolk PE31 8 AY

Office	Secrétariat	(44) 01485 - 210 223
Pro shop	Pro-shop	(44) 01485 - 210 616
Fax	Fax	(44) 01485 - 210 087
Situation	Situation	

12 km from Hunstanton (pop. 4 736)
30 km from King's Lynn (pop. 41 281)

Annual closure	Fermeture annnuelle	no
Weekly closure	Fermeture hebdomadaire	

Fees main season	Tarifs haute saison	18 holes
	Week days	We/Bank holidays
	Semaine	We/Férié
Individual Individuel	£ 39	£ 49
Couple Couple	£ 78	£ 98

In August, no visitor unless playing with a member

Caddy	Caddy	on request
Electric Trolley	Chariot électrique	no
Buggy	Voiturette	no
Clubs	Clubs	no

Credit cards Cartes de crédit
Visa - Mastercard (Pro shop goods & green fees)

GOLF
North Sea
Brancaster Bay
Brancaster
A 149
Thornham
Brancaster Staithe
Cromer →
B1153
Hunstanton
B1454
Docking
Heacham
King's Lynn
0 — 2 — 4
0 — 2,5 miles

Access Accès : London M11. Cambridge A10 to King's Lynn. A149 North through Hunstanton to Brancaster. Turn left into Beach Road, continue across marsh.
Map 4 on page 495 Carte 4 Page 495

GOLF COURSE / PARCOURS — 17/20

Site	Site	
Maintenance	Entretien	
Architect	Architecte	Holcombe Ingleby
Type	Type	seaside course, links
Relief	Relief	
Water in play	Eau en jeu	
Exp. to wind	Exposé au vent	
Trees in play	Arbres en jeu	

Scorecard	Chp.	Mens	Ladies
Carte de score	Chp.	Mess.	Da.
Length Long.	5785	5785	5334
Par	71	71	75

Advised golfing ability	0	12	24	36
Niveau de jeu recommandé				
Hcp required	Handicap exigé	certificate		

CLUB HOUSE & AMENITIES / CLUB HOUSE ET ANNEXES — 7/10

Pro shop	Pro-shop	
Driving range	Practice	
Sheltered	couvert	no
On grass	sur herbe	yes
Putting-green	putting-green	yes
Pitching-green	pitching green	no

639

HOTEL FACILITIES / ENVIRONNEMENT HOTELIER — 6/10

HOTELS HÔTELS
Le Strange Arms — Hunstanton
36 rooms, D £ 70 — 12 km
Tel (44) 01485 - 534 411
Fax (44) 01485 - 534 724

Congham Hall — Grimston
12 rooms, D £ 100 — 25 km
Tel (44) 01485 - 600 250
Fax (44) 01485 - 601 191

RESTAURANTS RESTAURANT
Gurney's — Burnham Market
Tel (44) 01328 - 738937 — 7 km

The Hoste Arms — Burnham Market
Tel (44) 01328 - 738777 — 7 km

Being a very private club (but open to green-fees on week-days) and having been upstaged by other courses a little further out of town, Royal Wimbledon probably doesn't have the reputation it deserves. Yet this is the second oldest course in England, a label that naturally still stands despite serious re-styling by Harry Colt, whose layouts always appeal one way or the other. The course is rather hilly but the club does not provide buggies, for some reason. Luckily, the 18 holes are on the short side, so at least you will be hitting short irons into greens defended by some formidable bunkers, always well placed and often deep. The par 3s, holes 5, 13 and 17, fall into this category. To add to the pleasure of this challenge, the putting surfaces are also remarkably well designed and excellent in quality. And you will have all the time in the world to practice your putting stroke on a famous and equally remarkable practice green, rather like the famous one at Saint Andrews.

Parce qu'il s'agit d'un club très privé (accessible en semaine), parce qu'il a été éclipsé par d'autres golfs plus éloignés, plus campagnards aussi, Royal Wimbledon n'a pas la réputation qu'il mérite. Il s'agit pourtant du second golf créé en Angleterre, mais il a été largement remanié par Harry Colt, dont aucun parcours ne laisse indifférent. Il est assez accidenté mais les voiturettes étant sans doute «shocking», il n'y en a pas. Heureusement, les 18 trous sont assez courts, car il vaut mieux attaquer les greens avec de petits clubs : les bunkers de défense sont redoutables, bien placés et parfois très profonds. Les par 3 n° 5, 13 et 17 sont notamment très défendus. Pour ajouter encore au plaisir, les greens sont remarquablement dessinés et de très bonne qualité de surface. On a tout le loisir de s'y entraîner sur un célèbre et remarquable putting-green, utilisé pour des compétitions spécifiques, à l'instar de celui de St Andrews.

Royal Wimbledon Golf Club   1870

Camp Road
ENG - WIMBLEDON SW19

Office	Secrétariat	(44) 0181 - 946 2125
Pro shop	Pro-shop	(44) 0181 - 946 4606
Fax	Fax	
Situation	Situation	

14 km from Central London (pop. 6 679 699)

Annual closure	Fermeture annuelle	no
Weekly closure	Fermeture hebdomadaire	no

Fees main season
Tarifs haute saison full day

	Week days Semaine	We/Bank holidays We/Férié
Individual Individuel	£ 55	*
Couple Couple	£ 110	*

* Only with a member at week ends

Caddy	Caddy	£ 25
Electric Trolley	Chariot électrique	£ 12
Buggy	Voiturette	no
Clubs	Clubs	£ 8

Credit cards Cartes de crédit
VISA - Eurocard - MasterCard - AMEX - DC
(Pro shop goods only)

640

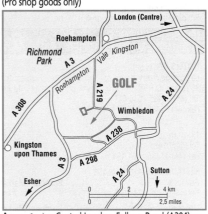

Access Accès : Central London, Fulham Road (A304) →
Putney, then Putney Hill, A219 → Caesar's Camp.
Golf at Wimbledon Common.
Map 8 on page 503 Carte 8 Page 503

GOLF COURSE
PARCOURS   16/20

Site	Site	
Maintenance	Entretien	
Architect	Architecte	Harry S. Colt
Type	Type	inland, parkland
Relief	Relief	
Water in play	Eau en jeu	
Exp. to wind	Exposé au vent	
Trees in play	Arbres en jeu	

Scorecard	Chp.	Mens	Ladies
Carte de score	Chp.	Mess.	Da.
Length Long.	5712	5712	5015
Par	70	70	72

Advised golfing ability		0	12	24	36
Niveau de jeu recommandé					
Hcp required	Handicap exigé	certificate			

CLUB HOUSE & AMENITIES
CLUB HOUSE ET ANNEXES   7/10

Pro shop	Pro-shop	
Driving range	Practice	
Sheltered	couvert	
On grass	sur herbe	yes
Putting-green	putting-green	yes
Pitching-green	pitching green	yes

HOTEL FACILITIES
ENVIRONNEMENT HOTELIER   8/10

HOTELS HÔTELS

Cannizaro House — Wimbledon
44 rooms, D £ 175 — on site
Tel (44) 0181 - 879 1464, Fax (44) 0181 - 879 7338

Forte Travelodge — Morden
32 rooms, D £ 35 — 5 km
Tel (44) 0181 - 640 8227

Kingston Lodge — Kingston-upon-Thames
62 rooms, D £ 130 — 2 km
Tel (44) 0181 - 541 4481, Fax (44) 0181 - 547 1013

RESTAURANTS RESTAURANTS

Gravier's — Kingston-upon-Thames
Tel (44) 0181 - 549 5557 — 4 km

Sonny's - Tel (44) 0181 - 748 0393 — Barnes 5 km

Nightingales — Richmond
Tel (44) 0181 - 940 7471 — 6 km

ROYAL WINCHESTER

The famous Winchester cathedral has the longest nave in Europe and bears vestiges of Norman architecture. It is one of the treasures to be found in this city, others including the legendary Round Table, which was actually built several centuries late! This J.H. Taylor course is also a piece of history, dating from the last century, where you might get the impression you can play a bit until it comes to counting your score. On each tee you will need to think long and hard about the direction of your shot and the club you should play in order to avoid the bunkers. Here the finer technicians of the game are probably better rewarded than thoughtless big-hitters. At least the trees are not too much in play, but there is wind to contend with. A pleasant course to walk (except the 10th), this excellent layout has hardly aged at all, except in yardage, but none of us will lose much sleep about that. Well worth getting to know.

La célèbre cathédrale de Winchester aurait la plus longue nef d'Europe. Elle porte de nombreuses traces de l'architecture normande, mais elle n'est qu'un des trésors d'une très belle ville, dont la Table Ronde de la légende, mais qui fut fabriquée des siècles après ! Le parcours de JH Taylor est aussi une pièce d'histoire plus que centenaire, où l'on aura l'illusion de pouvoir bien jouer jusqu'au moment de compter le score. Sur chaque départ, il faut bien réfléchir à la fois à la trajectoire et au club à utiliser pour ne pas risquer les bunkers. Ici, ce sont les fins techniciens qui seront récompensés, et pas les frappeurs sans cervelle ! Au moins, les arbres ne sont guère en jeu, ce qui laisse d'ailleurs le champ libre aux caprices du vent. Agréable à marcher (sauf le 10), cette excellente réalisation n'a guère pris de l'âge que pour sa longueur, mais cela ne gênera pas grand-monde. A connaître.

Royal Winchester Golf Club — 1888

Sarum Road
ENG - WINCHESTER, Hants SO22 5QE

Office	Secrétariat	(44) 01962 - 852 462
Pro shop	Pro-shop	(44) 01962 - 852 473
Fax	Fax	(44) 01962 - 865 048
Situation	Situation	

2.5 km from Winchester (pop. 96 390)

Annual closure	Fermeture annuelle	no
Weekly closure	Fermeture hebdomadaire	no

Fees main season
Tarifs haute saison full day

	Week days Semaine	We/Bank holidays We/Férié
Individual Individuel	£ 28	—
Couple Couple	£ 56	—

Weekends: only as a guest of member

Caddy	Caddy	no
Electric Trolley	Chariot électrique	no
Buggy	Voiturette	no
Clubs	Clubs	£ 5/18 holes

Credit cards Cartes de crédit VISA - MasterCard

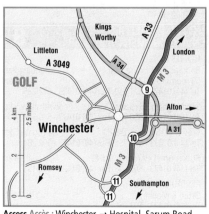

Access Accès : Winchester, → Hospital, Sarum Road, Golf on the right
Map 7 on page 500 Carte 7 Page 500

GOLF COURSE / PARCOURS — 15/20

Site	Site	
Maintenance	Entretien	
Architect	Architecte	J.H. Taylor
Type	Type	inland
Relief	Relief	
Water in play	Eau en jeu	
Exp. to wind	Exposé au vent	
Trees in play	Arbres en jeu	

Scorecard Carte de score	Chp. Chp.	Mens Mess.	Ladies Da.
Length Long.	5585	5416	4950
Par	71	71	72

Advised golfing ability		0 12 24 36
Niveau de jeu recommandé		
Hcp required	Handicap exigé	certificate

CLUB HOUSE & AMENITIES / CLUB HOUSE ET ANNEXES — 6/10

Pro shop	Pro-shop	
Driving range	Practice	
Sheltered	couvert	no
On grass	sur herbe	yes
Putting-green	putting-green	yes
Pitching-green	pitching green	yes

HOTEL FACILITIES / ENVIRONNEMENT HOTELIER — 8/10

HOTELS HÔTELS

Royal Hotel — Winchester
75 rooms, D £ 100 — 2.5 km
Tel (44) 01962 - 840 840, Fax (44) 01962 - 841 582

Lainston House — Winchester
37 rooms, D £ 130 — 3 km
Tel (44) 01962 - 863 588, Fax (44) 01962 - 776 672

Hotel du Vin — Winchester
19 rooms, D £ 80 — 3 km
Tel (44) 01962 - 841 414, Fax (44) 01962 - 842 458

RESTAURANTS RESTAURANTS

Nine the Square — Winchester
Tel (44) 01962 - 864 004 — 3 km

Bistro (Hotel du Vin) — Winchester
Tel (44) 01962 - 841 414 — 3 km

Old Chesil Rectory — Winchester
Tel (44) 01962 - 851 555 — 3 km

641

Faced with administrative restrictions, there was the choice between giving up the ghost or simple ingenuity. Designer Martin Hawtree chose the second option and here has produced one of his best courses. As no bunkers were allowed except in woody areas, there are only 6 greenside bunkers but the edges of the putting surfaces are well contoured with slopes and hollows and the trees are brought into play to be more strategic than decorative. As far as your game is concerned, approach shots are tricky and putting calls for some inspired play. Water has also been cleverly brought into the frame, although on several holes the ladies may have problems carrying it. It will be interesting to see how this interesting project matures, particularly with such a pleasant hotel on site.

Devant les restrictions administratives, on a le choix entre l'abandon et l'ingéniosité. L'architecte Martin Hawtree a choisi la deuxième solution et produit là un de ses meilleurs ouvrages. Comme il était interdit de mettre des bunkers sauf dans les zones boisées, on ne trouve ici que six bunkers de greens, mais les alentours des surfaces de putting sont modelés en reliefs et en creux, et les arbres mis en jeu de manière encore plus stratégique que décorative. Sur le plan du jeu, les approches sont beaucoup plus délicates, et les greens très modelés demandent de l'inspiration. Les obstacles d'eau ont aussi été mis en jeu avec intelligence, mais certaines dames auront peut-être du mal à les franchir sur certains trous en portant la balle. On suivra avec intérêt la maturation de ce projet intéressant, d'autant que l'hôtel sur place est tout à fait agréable

Rudding Park Golf Club — 1995

Rudding Park, Follifoot
ENG - HARROGATE, Yorkshire HG3 1DJ

Office	Secrétariat	(44) 01423 - 872 100
Pro shop	Pro-shop	(44) 01254 - 872 100
Fax	Fax	(44) 01254 - 873 011
Situation	Situation	

5 km from Harrogate (pop. 143 530)
22 km from Leeds (pop. 680 725)

Annual closure	Fermeture annuelle	no
Weekly closure	Fermeture hebdomadaire	no

Fees main season
Tarifs haute saison 18 holes

	Week days Semaine	We/Bank holidays We/Férié
Individual Individuel	£ 18.50	£ 20
Couple Couple	£ 37	£ 40

Full day: £ 30/£ 32.50

Caddy	Caddy	no
Electric Trolley	Chariot électrique	no
Buggy	Voiturette	no
Clubs	Clubs	£ 7.50/18 holes

Credit cards Cartes de crédit
VISA - Eurocard - MasterCard - AMEX - JCB

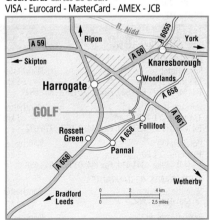

Access Accès : Leeds → Harrogate on A61, then A658 (Harrogate by-pass), follow brown tourist signs for Rudding Park. **Map 4 on page 494** Carte 4 Page 494

GOLF COURSE / PARCOURS — 15/20

Site	Site	
Maintenance	Entretien	
Architect	Architecte	Martin Hawtree
Type	Type	parkland
Relief	Relief	
Water in play	Eau en jeu	
Exp. to wind	Exposé au vent	
Trees in play	Arbres en jeu	

Scorecard Carte de score	Chp. Chp.	Mens Mess.	Ladies Da.
Length Long.	6184	5873	5167
Par	72	72	72

Advised golfing ability Niveau de jeu recommandé	0	12	24	36

Hcp required	Handicap exigé	28 Men, 36 Ladies

CLUB HOUSE & AMENITIES / CLUB HOUSE ET ANNEXES — 8/10

Pro shop	Pro-shop	
Driving range	Practice	
Sheltered	couvert	18 bays
On grass	sur herbe	yes
Putting-green	putting-green	yes
Pitching-green	pitching green	yes

HOTEL FACILITIES / ENVIRONNEMENT HOTELIER — 8/10

HOTELS HÔTELS
Rudding Park House Hotel — Rudding Park
50 rooms, D £ 129 — adjacent
Tel (44) 01423 - 871 350, Fax (44) 01423 - 872 286

Sandringham - 6 rooms, D £ 90 — Beckwithshaw 5 km
Tel (44) 01423 - 500 722, Fax (44) 01423 - 530 509

Crown - 116 rooms, D £ 80 — Harrogate 5 km
Tel (44) 01423 - 567 755, Fax (44) 01423 - 502 284

Ruskin Hotel - 7 rooms, D £ 89 — Harrogate 5 km
Tel (44) 01423 - 502 045, Fax (44) 01423 - 506 131

RESTAURANTS RESTAURANTS
Drum & Monkey — Harrogate
Tel (44) 01423 - 502 650 — 5 km

Clocktower Brasserie — Rudding Parka
Tel (44) 01423 - 872 100

The Bistro - Tel (44) 01423 - 530 708 — Harrogate 5 km

642

SAND MOOR

Modern clubhouses unquestionably lack the charm of their older counterparts but they are more comfortable. Following this same modern trend, many clubs have also laid out practice areas, if only to cater to the ever greater number of players. In 1961, Sand Moor was given a face-lift and at the same time re-styled, adhering most respectfully to the layout of Alister MacKenzie on one side of Alwoodley Lane. The land is rather hilly, but as the use of buggies requires a medical certificate we will simply recommend an electric trolley. Laid out over moorland, the feeling of space here is very pleasant and the rough not too hard on your game, but some of the bunches of trees and carefully placed fairway bunkers do their job very well. We noted the excellence of the par 3s on what is a very good test of golf, albeit a little on the short side for the better players.

Les Clubhouses modernes manquent sans doute un peu du charme des anciens, mais ils ont gagné en confort. De même, bien des clubs ont aménagé des espaces d'entraînement, ne serait-ce que pour répondre à l'élargissement du public. En 1961, Sand Moor s'est ainsi rajeuni et en a profité pour réaménager - avec beaucoup de respect d'ailleurs - le tracé d'Alister Mackenzie d'un seul côté d'Alwoodley Lane. Le terrain est assez accidenté, mais seul un certificat médical permettant de jouer en voiturette, on conseillera le chariot électrique. En terre de lande, la sensation d'espace est ici très agréable, le rough n'est pas trop pénalisant, mais certains bouquets d'arbres et des bunkers de fairway judicieusement placés ne manquent pas de jouer leur rôle. A remarquer enfin, la qualité des pars 3. Un très bon test de golf, un peu court pour les meilleurs joueurs.

Sand Moor Golf Club		1926
Alwoodley Lane		
ENG - LEEDS, W. Yorkshire LS17 7DJ		

Office	Secrétariat	(44) 0113 - 268 5180
Pro shop	Pro-shop	(44) 0113 - 268 3925
Fax	Fax	(44) 0113 - 268 5180
Situation	Situation	
8 km N of Leeds (pop. 680 722)		
Annual closure	Fermeture annuelle	no
Weekly closure	Fermeture hebdomadaire	no

Fees main season
Tarifs haute saison 18 holes

	Week days Semaine	We/Bank holidays We/Férié
Individual Individuel	£ 30	£ 40
Couple Couple	£ 60	£ 80
Full weekdays:£ 38 - No visitors on Saturdays		

Caddy	Caddy	no
Electric Trolley	Chariot électrique	£ 5/18 holes
Buggy	Voiturette	no
Clubs	Clubs	on request

Credit cards Cartes de crédit
VISA - Eurocard - MasterCard - Switch
(+4 % for green fees, not in Club house)

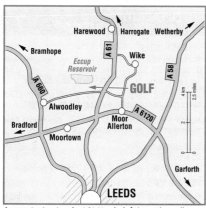

Access Accès : Leeds, A61 North, left into Alwoodley Lane, Golf 0.8 km (1/2 m.) on right hand side.
Map 4 on page 494 Carte 4 Page 494

GOLF COURSE / PARCOURS — 14/20

Site	Site	
Maintenance	Entretien	
Architect	Architecte	Alister MacKenzie
Type	Type	parkland
Relief	Relief	
Water in play	Eau en jeu	
Exp. to wind	Exposé au vent	
Trees in play	Arbres en jeu	

Scorecard Carte de score	Chp. Chp.	Mens Mess.	Ladies Da.
Length Long.	5851	5464	5092
Par	71	71	73

Advised golfing ability Niveau de jeu recommandé		0 12 24 36
Hcp required	Handicap exigé	certificate

CLUB HOUSE & AMENITIES / CLUB HOUSE ET ANNEXES — 7/10

Pro shop	Pro-shop	
Driving range	Practice	
Sheltered	couvert	practice area
On grass	sur herbe	yes
Putting-green	putting-green	yes
Pitching-green	pitching green	yes

HOTEL FACILITIES / ENVIRONNEMENT HOTELIER — 7/10

HOTELS HÔTELS

Forte Posthouse — Bramhope
123 rooms, D £ 70
Tel (44) 0113 - 284 2911, Fax (44) 0113 - 284 3451

Jarvis Parkway — Bramhope
105 rooms, D £ 98
Tel (44) 0113 - 267 2551, Fax (44) 0113 - 267 4410

Stakis Leeds — Leeds
100 rooms, D £ 85
Tel (44) 0113 - 273 2323, Fax (44) 0113 - 232 3018

The Calls - 41 rooms, D £ 120 — Leeds
Tel (44) 0113 - 244 0099, Fax (44) 0113 - 234 4100

RESTAURANTS RESTAURANTS

Pool Court at 42 - Tel (44) 0113 - 244 4242 — Leeds

Hereford Beefstouw - Tél(44) 0113 - 245 3870 — Leeds

Rascasse - Tél(44) 0113 - 244 6611 — Leeds

643

SANDIWAY

17 5 7

Sandiway stands in a little compact group of courses to the east of Chester, the others being Mere and the similarly styled Delamere Forest. If Sandiway was in the western suburbs of London it would surely be better known than it is, but there again for a golfer there is something gratifying about being able to talk about little gems that no-one else has ever set eyes upon. With lots of trees lining sloping fairways, keeping your ball in play is anything but easy, so think twice before taking the driver out of the bag. This very varied course demands good tactics and skill in flighting the ball... at least when it comes to getting out of trouble. A very pretty course and a very intelligent one, too, which demands the same quality from the people who play it.

Sandiway tient bien sa place dans un petit groupe compact à l'est de Chester, qui comprend également Mere et Delamere Forest, le second nommé lui étant le plus comparable par son paysage et son style. Sans nul doute, s'il était dans la banlieue ouest de Londres, ce parcours serait bien plus connu, mais, pour un golfeur, c'est très gratifiant de pouvoir parler des trésors que les autres n'ont jamais vu ! Avec beaucoup d'arbres délimitant les trous, et des fairways souvent en pente, il n'est pas évident d'y garder sa balle en sécurité, il faudra donc réfléchir avant d'empoigner son driver. Très varié, ce parcours exige une tactique solide et souvent de savoir travailler la balle... au moins pour s'extraire des problèmes. Ce très joli parcours est d'une grande intelligence, il en demande aussi aux joueurs.

Sandiway Golf Club — 1921

Chester Road, Sandiway
ENG - NORTHWICH, Cheshire CW8 20 J

Office	Secrétariat	(44) 01606 - 883 247
Pro shop	Pro-shop	(44) 01606 - 883 180
Fax	Fax	(44) 01606 - 883 548
Situation	Situation	

6 km SW of Northwich - 25 km E of Chester (pop. 115 971)

Annual closure	Fermeture annuelle	no
Weekly closure	Fermeture hebdomadaire	no

Fees main season
Tarifs haute saison 18 holes

	Week days Semaine	We/Bank holidays We/Férié
Individual Individuel	£ 30	£ 35
Couple Couple	£ 60	£ 70

Full day: £ 35/£ 40

Caddy	Caddy	no
Electric Trolley	Chariot électrique	£ 5/18 holes
Buggy	Voiturette	no
Clubs	Clubs	no

Credit cards Cartes de crédit
VISA - Eurocard - MasterCard - AMEX (Pro shop goods only)

644

Access Accès : Manchester M56. Jct 7,
A556 → Northwich, Chester.
Golf on left side after Northwich.
Map 5 on page 497 Carte 5 Page 497

GOLF COURSE / PARCOURS — 17/20

Site	Site	
Maintenance	Entretien	
Architect	Architecte	Ted Ray
Type	Type	parkland
Relief	Relief	
Water in play	Eau en jeu	
Exp. to wind	Exposé au vent	
Trees in play	Arbres en jeu	

Scorecard Carte de score	Chp. Chp.	Mens Mess.	Ladies Da.
Length Long.	5791	5438	5071
Par	70	70	73

Advised golfing ability	0	12	24	36
Niveau de jeu recommandé				
Hcp required Handicap exigé	certificate			

CLUB HOUSE & AMENITIES / CLUB HOUSE ET ANNEXES — 5/10

Pro shop	Pro-shop	
Driving range	Practice	
Sheltered	couvert	no
On grass	sur herbe	practice area
Putting-green	putting-green	yes
Pitching-green	pitching green	yes

HOTEL FACILITIES / ENVIRONNEMENT HOTELIER — 7/10

HOTELS HÔTELS
Nunsmere Hall — Sandiway
31 rooms, D £ 120 — 2 km
Tel (44) 01606 - 543 000, Fax (44) 01606 - 889 055

Rookery Hall - 45 rooms, D £ 95 — Nantwich 20 km
Tel (44) 01270 - 610 016, Fax (44) 01270 - 626 027

Hartford Hall - 20 rooms, D £ 65 — Northwich 4 km
Tel (44) 01606 - 75 711, Fax (44) 01606 - 782 285

Tall Trees Lodge — Weaverham
20 rooms, D £ 38 — 3 km
Tel (44) 01606 - 790 824, Fax (44) 01606 - 791 330

RESTAURANTS RESTAURANTS
Nunsmere Hall — Sandiway
Tel (44) 01606 - 889 100 — 2 km

Churche's Mansion — Nantwich
Tel (44) 01270 - 625 933 — 20 km

18	7	6

Saunton does not carry the Royal Seal but if it did it would be well deserved. Harry Vardon dreamed of retiring here, but he was just a professional wasn't he? As such he must have appreciated the amazing balance of the East course, the more fluent of the two. If you play from the back tees, the first four holes will most likely cause irreparable damage to your card. Likewise, if you don't watch out, the last five will finish it off completely. The other holes are not quite so devastating, but the worst danger here is being caught off-guard. Winding between magnificent dunes with sheltered greens, all 18 holes at Saunton make for fantastic golf if you play from the tees that suit your level. The humbler you are, the more fun you will have. Especially since the greens are real beauties.

Si Saunton n'a pas eu droit à l'annoblissement, il ne le mérite pas moins : Harry Vardon rêvait de s'y retirer, mais peut-être n'était-il qu'un professionnel ? Comme tel, il dut apprécier le rythme étonnant de ce parcours Est, le plus éloquent des deux. Quand vous jouez des départs arrière, les quatre premiers trous vont dévorer votre carte, comme les cinq derniers la détruiront définitivement si vous n'y restez pas attentif. Les autres trous sont moins brutaux, mais le pire danger est de baisser la garde. Insinués entre des dunes magnifiques, les greens bien à l'abri, les trous de Saunton apportent un plaisir fou, si l'on joue des départs correspondant à son niveau : plus vous serez humble, plus vous prendrez du plaisir. Et d'autant plus que les greens sont un véritable régal.

Saunton Golf Club 1897

Saunton
ENG - BRAUNTON EX33 1LG

Office	Secrétariat	(44) 01271 - 812 436
Pro shop	Pro-shop	(44) 01271 - 812 013
Fax	Fax	(44) 01271 - 814 241
Situation	Situation	

3 km W of Braunton - 8 km W of Barnstaple (pop. 20 740)

Annual closure	Fermeture annuelle	no
Weekly closure	Fermeture hebdomadaire	no

Fees main season
Tarifs haute saison full day

	Week days Semaine	We/Bank holidays We/Férié
Individual Individuel	£ 37	£ 42
Couple Couple	£ 74	£ 84
Weekends: booking essential		

Caddy	Caddy	on request
Electric Trolley	Chariot électrique	£ 5/18 holes
Buggy	Voiturette	£ 10/18 holes
Clubs	Clubs	£ 15/18 holes

Credit cards Cartes de crédit
VISA - MasterCard (Pro shop goods only)

Access Accès : M5 Jct 27, then A361 to Barnstaple, then A361 to Braunton.
Follow signs to Saunton, golf on the left.
Map 6 on page 498 Carte 6 Page 498

GOLF COURSE
PARCOURS

18/20

Site	Site	
Maintenance	Entretien	
Architect	Architecte	Herbert Fowler
Type	Type	seaside course, links
Relief	Relief	
Water in play	Eau en jeu	
Exp. to wind	Exposé au vent	
Trees in play	Arbres en jeu	

Scorecard	Chp.	Mens	Ladies
Carte de score	Chp.	Mess.	Da.
Length Long.	6123	5800	4555
Par	73	71	74

Advised golfing ability
Niveau de jeu recommandé

0 12 24 36

Hcp required Handicap exigé certificate

CLUB HOUSE & AMENITIES
CLUB HOUSE ET ANNEXES

7/10

Pro shop	Pro-shop	
Driving range	Practice	
Sheltered	couvert	no
On grass	sur herbe	yes (own balls)
Putting-green	putting-green	yes
Pitching-green	pitching green	yes

HOTEL FACILITIES
ENVIRONNEMENT HOTELIER

6/10

HOTELS HÔTELS

Preston House — Saunton
15 rooms, D £ 80 — on site
Tel (44) 01271 - 890 472
Fax (44) 01271 - 890 555

Kittiwell House — Croyde
12 rooms, D £ 108 (dinner inc) — 3 km
Tel (44) 01271 - 890 247
Fax (44) 01271 - 890 469

RESTAURANTS RESTAURANTS

Lynwood House — Barnstaple
Tel (44) 01271 - 43 695 — 8 km

Whiteleaf at Croyde — Croyde
Tel (44) 01271 - 890 266 — 3 km

645

Moving up the coast, this is the only real links course after Hunstanton. The one further on is Seaton Carew which unfortunately lies in such surroundings that only local golfers really enjoy playing there. The landscape at Seacroft will hardly have you gasping with admiration but it is agreeable enough to give this course a pleasant setting. All the holes are neatly laid out in single file, out and in, except the disorderly 6th hole. This makes club selection a little easier when the wind is howling and forces you to hit low shots. In fine weather, you can hit any shot, which makes life easier for those of you who like to hit the ball high. Whatever, the very strategic bunkering here requires a clear-cut tactical approach to every round, but the hazards are visible enough for you to do so. Varied, very authentic and traditional, this is a course you should try.

En remontant la côte, c'est le seul vrai links après Hunstanton, et le suivant sera Seaton Carew, hélas situé dans un tel environnement que seuls les golfeurs locaux y trouveront du plaisir. Les paysages de Seacroft ne vous arracheront pas des cris d'admiration, mais ils sont assez plaisants pour offrir un décor agréable au parcours. Tous les trous sont sagement rangés en file indienne, en aller et retour, mis à part un indiscipliné, le 6. Cet ordre facilite le choix de clubs quand il y a du vent, qui seul vous obligera aux balles basses. Par beau temps, tous les coups sont permis, ce qui peut faciliter le travail de ceux qui savent surtout lever la balle. En tous les cas, le placement très stratégique des bunkers implique de bien définir la tactique de jeu, mais les obstacles sont assez visibles pour ce faire. Varié, très authentique et traditionnel, c'est un parcours à découvrir.

Seacroft Golf Club — 1895

Drummond Road
ENG - SKEGNESS, Lincolnshire PE25 3AU

Office	Secrétariat	(44) 01754 - 763 020
Pro shop	Pro-shop	(44) 01754 - 769 624
Fax	Fax	(44) 01754 - 769 624
Situation	Situation	

1.5 km S of Skegness - 30 km NE of Boston (pop. 53 226)

Annual closure	Fermeture annuelle	no
Weekly closure	Fermeture hebdomadaire	no

Christmas Day

Fees main season	Tarifs haute saison	18 holes
	Week days / Semaine	We/Bank holidays / We/Férié
Individual Individuel	£ 25	£ 30
Couple Couple	£ 50	£ 60

Full day: £ 35/£ 40

Caddy	Caddy	no
Electric Trolley	Chariot électrique	no
Buggy	Voiturette	no
Clubs	Clubs	no

Credit cards Cartes de crédit
VISA - Eurocard - MasterCard - AMEX - DC
(Pro shop goods only)

646

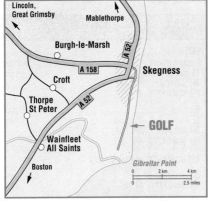

Lincoln, Great Grimsby
Mablethorpe
Burgh-le-Marsh
A 52
A 158 — Skegness
Croft
Thorpe St Peter
A 52
→ GOLF
Wainfleet All Saints
Boston
Gibraltar Point
0   2 km   4 km
0   2.5 miles

Access Accès : A52 to Skegness. 1.5 km S of Skegness alongside Gibraltar Road Bird Sanctuary.
Map 4 on page 495 Carte 4 Page 495

GOLF COURSE / PARCOURS — 17/20

Site	Site	
Maintenance	Entretien	
Architect	Architecte	Tom Dunn
Type	Type	seaside course, links
Relief	Relief	
Water in play	Eau en jeu	
Exp. to wind	Exposé au vent	
Trees in play	Arbres en play	

Scorecard	Chp.	Mens	Ladies
Carte de score	Chp.	Mess.	Da.
Length Long.	5831	5421	5275
Par	71	71	73

Advised golfing ability	0	12	24	36
Niveau de jeu recommandé				
Hcp required	Handicap exigé	certificate		

CLUB HOUSE & AMENITIES / CLUB HOUSE ET ANNEXES — 6/10

Pro shop	Pro-shop	
Driving range	Practice	
Sheltered	couvert	no
On grass	sur herbe	practice ground only
Putting-green	putting-green	yes
Pitching-green	pitching green	yes

HOTEL FACILITIES / ENVIRONNEMENT HOTELIER — 4/10

HOTELS HÔTELS

Crown Hotel		Skegness
28 rooms, D £ 65		400 m
Tel (44) 01754 - 610 760		
Fax (44) 01754 - 610 847		
Vine Hotel		Skegness
21 rooms, D £ 65		1 km
Tel (44) 01754 - 610 611		
Fax (44) 01754 - 769 845		
Links Hotel		Skegness
10 rooms, D £ 50		1 km
Tel (44) 01754 - 761 255		

SEASCALE

A strange place where the Sellafield power station ought to give golfers at least the energy to turn their backs on the cooling towers. When you think of how much flak golf courses get from some environmentalists, it makes you wonder why they don't protect courses from this sort of eyesore. Seascale is a hidden gem, away from the world and off the beaten track. You can talk about this course in glowing terms, no-one will ever argue. An imposing but subtle layout, and odd in that the railway line runs between the course and the sea, Seascale is anything but a fashionable course, just one to severely test any player's capacity for invention and adaptability. As on every links course, you either act positively or suffer the consequences, depending on the state of your game. If you do not know Seascale, then enter it now into your list of best little-known courses.

Etrange endroit où la centrale électrique de Sellafield devrait surtout donner l'énergie aux golfeurs de lui tourner le dos. Quand on sait à quel point on peut ennuyer les golfs avec les problèmes d'environnement, pourquoi ne pas préserver aussi les golfs des pollutions visuelles ? Seascale est un joyau caché, à l'écart du monde et des sentiers battus et, quand vous en parlerez avec émotion, personne ne viendra vous contredire. Puissant et subtil, assez curieux dans la mesure où le chemin de fer passe entre le golf et la mer, Seascale est tout sauf un parcours «fashionable.» Il met en oeuvre la capacité d'invention et d'adaptation des joueurs. Comme sur les links, on agit ou on subit, suivant sa forme du moment. Si vous ne le connaissez pas, c'est un parcours à inscrire à votre tableau de chasse des meilleurs parcours méconnus.

Seascale Golf Club   1893

The Banks
ENG - SEASCALE, Cumbria CA20 1QL

Office	Secrétariat	(44) 01946 - 728 202
Pro shop	Pro-shop	(44) 01946 - 728 202
Fax	Fax	
Situation	Situation	

15 km S of Whitehaven (pop. 9 358)
45 km N of Barrow-in-Furness (pop. 73 125)

Annual closure	Fermeture annuelle	no
Weekly closure	Fermeture hebdomadaire	no

Fees main season	Tarifs haute saison	18 holes
	Week days Semaine	We/Bank holidays We/Férié
Individual Individuel	£ 20	£ 25
Couple Couple	£ 40	£ 50

Full day: £ 25 - £ 30 (Weekends)

Caddy	Caddy	no
Electric Trolley	Chariot électrique	no
Buggy	Voiturette	no
Clubs	Clubs	£ 5/18 holes

Credit cards Cartes de crédit   no

Access Accès : M6 Jct 36, A590 → Barrow-in-Furness.
At Greenodd, A5092, then A595 to Seascale.
Golf N. of village (can't miss it!)
Map 4 on page 494 Carte 4 Page 494

GOLF COURSE
PARCOURS   18/20

Site	Site	
Maintenance	Entretien	
Architect	Architecte	Willie Campbell
Type	Type	links
Relief	Relief	
Water in play	Eau en jeu	
Exp. to wind	Exposé au vent	
Trees in play	Arbres en jeu	

Scorecard	Chp.	Mens	Ladies
Carte de score	Chp.	Mess.	Da.
Length Long.	5840	5554	5226
Par	71	71	74

Advised golfing ability	0	12	24	36
Niveau de jeu recommandé				
Hcp required	Handicap exigé	no		

CLUB HOUSE & AMENITIES
CLUB HOUSE ET ANNEXES   5/10

Pro shop	Pro-shop	
Driving range	Practice	
Sheltered	couvert	no
On grass	sur herbe	yes
Putting-green	putting-green	yes
Pitching-green	pitching green	yes

HOTEL FACILITIES
ENVIRONNEMENT HOTELIER   4/10

HOTELS HÔTELS

Westlakes		Gosforth
9 rooms, D £ 55		4 km
Tel (44) 019467 - 25 221		
Fax (44) 019467 - 25 099		

Howgate		Whitehaven
20 rooms, D £ 60		15 km
Tel (44) 01946 - 66 286		
Fax (44) 01946 - 66 286		

RESTAURANTS RESTAURANT

Westlakes		Gosforth
Tel (44) 019467 - 25 221		4 km

647

The industrial surroundings are certainly not the most pleasant setting for a golf course, but no keen golfer can afford to miss playing this course and getting to grips with the wile and cunning of Alister MacKenzie, the layout's devilishly clever architect. The four holes added by Frank Pennink for spice and variety were laid out in the same spirit. Although rather flat, the course comprises several strings of sand-dunes, just to bother the inaccurate hitter, plus the thickets, bushes and buckthorns that go with them. For all the qualities of this championship course, it is not what you would call intimidating, especially the outward nine. Lesser players might prefer to watch how their betters negotiate the back nine, where certain shots calls for good ball-striking and long carries. This is particularly true on the 17th, probably the trickiest hole of all (and the most deceitful) with a terribly difficult approach shot to an elevated green. And just in case you needed reminding, the wind might also have its say in the final reckoning.

Certes, l'environnement industriel n'est pas des plus réjouissants, mais aucun golfeur acharné ne saurait passer à côté de ce parcours sans affronter les astuces et les ruses d'Alister Mackenzie, son diabolique architecte. Et les quatre trous ajoutés par Frank Pennink, pour varier les plaisirs, ont été créés dans le même esprit. Assez plat, il comprend néanmoins, pour mieux ennuyer le golfeur imprécis, quelques cordons dunaires, avec les arbustes touffus, les buissons et les nerpruns qui vont avec. En dépit de ses qualités de parcours de championnat, il n'est pourtant pas intimidant, en particulier l'aller. Les joueurs peu expérimentés regarderont plutôt leurs «maîtres» négocier le retour, où certains coups demandent des balles solides coups, bien portées. Notamment le 17, sans doute le trou le plus délicat (et le moins franc) de Seaton Carew, par son approche des plus difficiles d'un green surélevé. Et le vent...

Seaton Carew Golf Club — 1925

Tees Road
ENG - HARTLEPOOL, Cleveland TS25 1DE

Office	Secrétariat	(44) 01429 - 890 660
Pro shop	Pro-shop	(44) 01429 - 890 660
Fax	Fax	(44) 01429 - 261 473
Situation	Situation	

5 km S of Hartlepool (pop. 90 409)
10 km N of Middlesbrough (pop. 140 849)

Annual closure	Fermeture annuelle	no
Weekly closure	Fermeture hebdomadaire	no

Fees main season
Tarifs haute saison full day

	Week days Semaine	We/Bank holidays We/Férié
Individual Individuel	£ 29	£ 40
Couple Couple	£ 58	£ 80

Caddy	Caddy	£ 10 (Juniors)
Electric Trolley	Chariot électrique	£ 3
Buggy	Voiturette	£ 16
Clubs	Clubs	£ 10

Credit cards Cartes de crédit
VISA - MasterCard - AMEX - DC (not for green fees)

648

Hartlepool
Seaton Carew ← **GOLF**
Billingham
A 689
A 178
RIVER TEES
0 2 km
0 1,25 miles
Middlesbrough

Access Accès : On Coast Road (A178)
South of Hartlepool
Map 4 on page 495 Carte 4 Page 495

GOLF COURSE / PARCOURS — 17/20

Site	Site	
Maintenance	Entretien	
Architect	Architecte	Dr McCuaig (1874) Alister MacKenzie
Type	Type	links, seaside course
Relief	Relief	
Water in play	Eau en jeu	
Exp. to wind	Exposé au vent	
Trees in play	Arbres en jeu	

Scorecard Carte de score	Chp. Chp.	Mens Mess.	Ladies Da.
Length Long.	6170	5941	4951
Par	73	73	73

Advised golfing ability		0 12 24 36
Niveau de jeu recommandé		
Hcp required	Handicap exigé	certificate

CLUB HOUSE & AMENITIES / CLUB HOUSE ET ANNEXES — 7/10

Pro shop	Pro-shop	
Driving range	Practice	
Sheltered	couvert	
On grass	sur herbe	yes
Putting-green	putting-green	yes
Pitching-green	pitching green	yes

HOTEL FACILITIES / ENVIRONNEMENT HOTELIER — 5/10

HOTELS HÔTELS
Marine Hotel - 25 rooms, D £ 65   Seaton Carew 500 m
Tel (44) 01429 - 266 244, Fax (44) 01429 - 864 144

The Staincliffe   Seaton Carew
20 rooms, D £ 50   500 m
Tel (44) 01429 - 264 301, Fax (44) 01429 - 421 366

Grand Hotel   Hartlepool
50 rooms, D £ 70   5 km
Tel (44) 01429 - 266 345, Fax (44) 01429 - 265 217

RESTAURANTS RESTAURANTS
Krimo's   Seaton Carew
Tel (44) 01429 - 290 022   500 m

Al Syros   Hartlepool
Tel (44) 01429 - 272 525   2 km

Portofinos   Hartlepool
Tel (44) 01429 - 266 166   3 km

Shanklin & Sandown is the best of the seven courses on the Isle of Wight. It is short, naturally, as designers at the turn of the century were wiser than they are today. They weren't unaware of the fact that big-hitters make up only a minority of golfers and that wind can really bother simply anyone, whether blowing with or against the ball. A part of this layout is similar to links golfing, another part is more inland in style with some impressive heather and broom. Despite a distinctly hilly character, there are only three blind drives, otherwise playing strategy is clear. The sole element of chance is the stance and lie, sometimes difficult to negotiate for players who are used to flat courses. With tight fairways and well placed bunkers, we would recommend this course to players who have some control over their ball. Beginners here could easily spend all day looking for theirs.

Shanklin & Sandown se détache parmi les sept parcours de l'Ile de Wight. Il est bien sûr assez court, mais les architectes du début du siècle étaient des sages. Ils n'ignoraient pas que les bons frappeurs ne sont pas les plus nombreux, et que le vent avait tendance à gêner tout le monde, qu'il soit contre ou avec. Ce parcours comporte une partie apparentée aux links et une partie «inland» avec une très belle végétation de bruyère et de genêts. On ne trouve ici, en dépit d'un certain relief, que trois drives aveugles. Autrement, la stratégie à mettre en oeuvre est assez claire, la part de hasard étant préservée par les stances parfois difficiles pour ceux qui jouent habituellement les pieds à plat. Avec ses fairways étroits et ses bunkers bien placés, on le recommendera à ceux qui savent déjà contrôler la balle car les débutants peuvent passer la journée à chercher la leur !

Shanklin & Sandown Golf Club — 1900

The Fairway Lake
ENG - SANDOWN, Isle of Wight PO36 9 PR

Office	Secrétariat	(44) 01983 - 403 217
Pro shop	Pro-shop	(44) 01983 - 404 424
Fax	Fax	(44) 01983 - 403 217
Situation	Situation	

Isle of Wight (pop. 124 580)

Annual closure	Fermeture annuelle	no
Weekly closure	Fermeture hebdomadaire	no

Fees main season
Tarifs haute saison 18 holes

	Week days Semaine	We/Bank holidays We/Férié
Individual Individuel	£ 22	£ 25
Couple Couple	£ 44	£ 50

Saturday: only after 1.00 pm - Sunday: after 9.00 am

Caddy	Caddy	no
Electric Trolley	Chariot électrique	no
Buggy	Voiturette	no
Clubs	Clubs	no

Credit cards Cartes de crédit
VISA - MasterCard (Pro shop goods only)

RYDE

0 — 2 — 4 km
0 — 2.5 miles

ISLE OF WIGHT

← Newport

Bembridge
Brading
Alverston **GOLF**
Sandown
Shanklin

Access Accès : from Cowes A3054 and 3055 to Sandown. Avenue Road on left, then Broadway, Lake Hill on the right, The Fairway on the right.
Map 9 on page 504 Carte 9 Page 504

GOLF COURSE / PARCOURS — 15/20

Site	Site	
Maintenance	Entretien	
Architect	Architecte	James Braid M. Cowper
Type	Type	links, parkland
Relief	Relief	
Water in play	Eau en jeu	
Exp. to wind	Exposé au vent	
Trees in play	Arbres en jeu	

Scorecard Carte de score	Chp. Chp.	Mens Mess.	Ladies Da.
Length Long.	5456	5223	4960
Par	70	70	72

Advised golfing ability
Niveau de jeu recommandé — 0 32
Hcp required Handicap exigé — certificate

CLUB HOUSE & AMENITIES / CLUB HOUSE ET ANNEXES — 7/10

Pro shop	Pro-shop	
Driving range	Practice	
Sheltered	couvert	no
On grass	sur herbe	yes
Putting-green	putting-green	yes
Pitching-green	pitching green	yes

649

HOTEL FACILITIES / ENVIRONNEMENT HOTELIER — 6/10

HOTELS HÔTELS
Brunswick — Shanklin
32 rooms, D £ 60 — 2 km
Tel (44) 01983 - 863 245

Fern Bank — Shanklin
22 rooms, D £ 80 — 2 km
Tel (44) 01983 - 862 790, Fax (44) 01983 - 864 412

Bourne Hall Country — Shanklin
30 rooms, D £ 80 — 2 km
Tel (44) 01983 - 862 820, Fax (44) 01983 - 865 138

RESTAURANTS RESTAURANTS
Bourne Hall Country — Shanklin
Tel (44) 01983 - 862820 — 2 km

Luccombe Chine — Shanklin
Tel (44) 01983 - 862037 — 2 km

This course, about a mile from the city of Sherborne, is testimony to the design skills of James Braid over a country landscape. It was completed in 1936 on a layout dating from 1894. The course is not too hilly but the slopes do pose a few questions, particularly on the sloping fairways of holes 6 and 13. The five par 3s are all excellent holes. The greens are average in size, never blind but do have some stiff slopes at the front on half a dozen holes. This is a fair test and a good family course. For a little culture after your round, drive into town. In the 16th century, the transformation of Sherborne Abbey into a school led to the building being saved at a time when Henry VIII's break with Rome was resulting in the dissolution of monasteries and often the destruction of some of Britain's finest landmarks.

Ce parcours à deux kilomètres de Sherborne reste un bon témoignage de l'architecture de James Braid en paysage de campagne, réalisé en 1936 à partir d'un tracé de 1894. Les reliefs ne sont pas assez importants mais ils permettent d'apporter quelques éléments d'interrogation, en particulier avec les fairways en pente au 6 et au 13. A remarquer aussi, la qualité des cinq par 3. Les greens sont de taille moyenne, jamais aveugles mais avec des pentes sévères en début de surface, sur une demi-douzaine de trous. Aucun green n'est aveugle, ce qui confirme la franchise de ce bon parcours familial. Pour la culture, on ira en ville : au XVIè siècle la transformation de l'abbaye de Sherborne en école a permis de la préserver, après que la rupture d'Henry VIII avec Rome ait eu pour conséquence la dissolution des monastères, leur abandon et souvent la destruction de monuments magnifiques dans toute la Grande-Bretagne.

Sherborne Golf Club — 1894

Higher Clatcombe
ENG - SHERBORNE, Dorset DT9 4RN

Office	Secrétariat	(44) 01935 - 814 431
Pro shop	Pro-shop	(44) 01935 - 812 274
Fax	Fax	(44) 01935 - 814 218
Situation	Situation	

2 km N of Sherborne (pop. 7 606)
10 km E of Yeovil (pop. 28 317)

Annual closure	Fermeture annuelle	no
Weekly closure	Fermeture hebdomadaire	no

Fees main season
Tarifs haute saison full day

	Week days Semaine	We/Bank holidays We/Férié
Individual Individuel	£ 25	£ 30
Couple Couple	£ 50	£ 60

Caddy	Caddy	no
Electric Trolley	Chariot électrique	no
Buggy	Voiturette	no
Clubs	Clubs	ask Pro

Credit cards Cartes de crédit
VISA - MasterCard (Pro shop goods only)

650

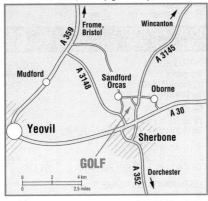

Access Accès : • London M3, Jct 8, A303 to Wincanter, A357 then B3145 → Sherborne. • Bristol A37 to Yeovil, A30 to Sherborne, then B3145 → Wincanton.
Map 6 on page 499 Carte 6 Page 499

GOLF COURSE / PARCOURS — 15/20

Site	Site	
Maintenance	Entretien	
Architect	Architecte	James Braid (1936)
Type	Type	parkland
Relief	Relief	
Water in play	Eau en jeu	
Exp. to wind	Exposé au vent	
Trees in play	Arbres en jeu	

Scorecard Carte de score	Chp. Chp.	Mens Mess.	Ladies Da.
Length Long.	5377	5220	5018
Par	70	70	73

Advised golfing ability Niveau de jeu recommandé	0	12	24	36

Hcp required	Handicap exigé	certificate

CLUB HOUSE & AMENITIES / CLUB HOUSE ET ANNEXES — 6/10

Pro shop	Pro-shop	
Driving range	Practice	
Sheltered	couvert	practice area
On grass	sur herbe	yes
Putting-green	putting-green	yes
Pitching-green	pitching green	no

HOTEL FACILITIES / ENVIRONNEMENT HOTELIER — 7/10

HOTELS HÔTELS

Eastbury — Sherborne
14 rooms, D £ 100 — 2 km
Tel (44) 01935 - 813 131, Fax (44) 01935 - 817 296

Antelope — Sherborne
19 rooms, D £ 65 — 2 km
Tel (44) 01935 - 812 077, Fax (44) 01935 - 816 473

Summer Lodge — Evershot
17 rooms, D £ 100 — 16 km
Tel (44) 01935 - 83 424, Fax (44) 01935 - 83 005

RESTAURANTS RESTAURANTS

Pheasants — Sherborne
Tel (44) 01935 - 815 252 — 2 km

Grange — Oborne
Tel (44) 01935 - 813 463 — 4 km

Less well known than Royal West Norfolk and Hunstanton, Sheringham (together with Royal Cromer) is one of the excellent courses along this magnificent northern coast of East Anglia. Once you have actually found the entrance to the course, some of the views from atop chalk cliffs are quite magnificent. This is not a links course but the wind plays an even more important role in that there are no dunes to offer any shelter. The professionals find Sheringham a little on the short side but the course is looked upon with the greatest respect by the best amateur golfers, for whom the need to improvise and shape shots is an even more essential factor than length. Bunkers play a key role in the definition of each hole and in strategy, but so do the heather and gorse. At least there are no hidden traps on this Tom Dunn layout (created in 1891), and it is perhaps this fairness which deserves our greatest respect.

Moins connu que Royal West Norfolk et Hunstanton, Sheringham est avec Royal Cromer l'un des excellents parcours de cette magnifique côte nord de l'East Anglia, et offre des vues exceptionnelles, du haut de ses falaises de craie... une fois que l'on a trouvé l'entrée du golf. Bien sûr, ce n'est pas un links, mais le vent y joue un rôle encore plus important : il n'y a pas de dunes pour s'en abriter ! Les professionnels le trouvent un peu court, mais c'est un tracé hautement respecté par les meilleurs amateurs, pour qui la nécessité de savoir créer des coups de golf est un facteur plus essentiel que la distance. Les bunkers jouent un rôle important dans la définition des trous et la stratégie, mais peut-être plus encore les buissons d'ajoncs et de fougère. Au moins n'y a-t-il aucun piège caché sur ce dessin de Tom Dunn (en 1891), et cette honnêteté mérite le plus grand respect.

Sheringham Golf Club — 1891

Weybourne Road
ENG - SHERINGHAM, Norfolk NR26 8HG

Office	Secrétariat	(44) 01263 - 822 038
Pro shop	Pro-shop	(44) 01263 - 822 980
Fax	Fax	(44) 01263 - 825 189
Situation	Situation	

8 km from Cromer (pop. 5 025)
35 km from Norwich (pop. 120 895)

Annual closure	Fermeture annuelle	no
Weekly closure	Fermeture hebdomadaire	no

Fees main season
Tarifs haute saison 18 holes

	Week days Semaine	We/Bank holidays We/Férié
Individual Individuel	£ 38	£ 43
Couple Couple	£ 76	£ 86
Booking advised		

Caddy	Caddy	on request/£ 20
Electric Trolley	Chariot électrique	no
Buggy	Voiturette	no
Clubs	Clubs	no

Credit cards Cartes de crédit
Visa - Mastercard - JCB (Pro shop goods only)

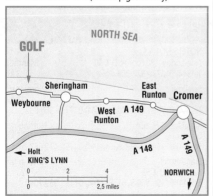

NORTH SEA
GOLF
Sheringham
Weybourne
West Runton
East Runton
Cromer
A 149
Holt
KING'S LYNN
A 148
A 149
NORWICH
0 — 2 — 4
0 — 2,5 miles

Access Accès : Norwich, A140 N to Cromer.
A149 W through Sheringham,
Golf on the right opposite Mobil Garage
Map 7 on page 501 Carte 7 Page 501

GOLF COURSE / PARCOURS — 15/20

Site	Site	
Maintenance	Entretien	
Architect	Architecte	Tom Dunn
Type	Type	seaside course, open country
Relief	Relief	
Water in play	Eau en jeu	
Exp. to wind	Exposé au vent	
Trees in play	Arbres en jeu	

Scorecard Carte de score	Chp. Chp.	Mens Mess.	Ladies Da.
Length Long.	5817	5485	5256
Par	70	70	73

Advised golfing ability		0 12 24 36
Niveau de jeu recommandé		
Hcp required	Handicap exigé	certificate

CLUB HOUSE & AMENITIES / CLUB HOUSE ET ANNEXES — 7/10

Pro shop	Pro-shop	
Driving range	Practice	
Sheltered	couvert	no
On grass	sur herbe	yes
Putting-green	putting-green	yes
Pitching-green	pitching green	yes

HOTEL FACILITIES / ENVIRONNEMENT HOTELIER — 6/10

HOTELS HÔTELS
Beaumaris Hotel — Sheringham
22 rooms, D £ 76 — 500 m
Tel (44) 01263 - 822 370
Fax (44) 01263 - 821 421

Links Country Park — West Runton
40 rooms, D £ 120 — 6 km
Tel (44) 01263 - 838 383
Fax (44) 01263 - 838 264

Sandcliff Private Hotel — Cromer
23 rooms, D £ 50 — 5 km
Tel (44) 01263 - 512 888

RESTAURANTS RESTAURANT
Adlard's — Norwich
Tel (44) 01603 -633522 — 35 km

651

Here we are in Robin Hood country where you can visit the cities of Nottingham and Lincoln and what is left of Sherwood Forest. As you might expect, trees are the main feature on this course and they play a major role throughout. It will be surprising if you don't have to play at least one swirling recovery to get back onto the fairway (the undergrowth is cut back short). Otherwise Harry Colt and James Braid have laid out bunkers as effectively as usual, including around the greens which can be approached in different ways, according to their line of defence. A rather traditional course but with a back 9 that can upset your score. Having spent many years in the shadow of Notts Hollinwell, this hilly course deserves a little limelight of its own.

Nous voici dans le monde de Robin des Bois. Entre une visite à Nottingham et une excursion vers Lincoln, la forêt de Sherwood n'est plus inquiétante que pour les imaginations d'enfants. Comme on pouvait s'y attendre, les arbres constituent l'essentiel du décor de ce parcours, mais un décor qui joue les rôles principaux. Il serait étonnant que vous n'ayiez jamais à jouer de balles à effet pour vous en extraire (les sous-bois sont bien dégagés). Autrement, Harry Colt et James Braid ont développé leur jeu de bunkers toujours aussi efficace, y compris autour des greens. Ceux-ci peuvent cependant être attaqués de différentes manières, selon les lignes de défense. Un parcours assez traditionnel, mais la difficulté du retour peut perturber le score. Longtemps à l'ombre de Notts (Hollinwell), ce parcours très vallonné mérite d'être placé en pleine lumière.

Sherwood Forest Golf Club — 1895

Eakring Road
ENG - MANSFIELD, Notts. NG18 3EW

Office	Secrétariat	(44) 01623 - 626 689
Pro shop	Pro-shop	(44) 01623 - 627 403
Fax	Fax	(44) 01623 - 626 689
Situation	Situation	

25 km N of Nottingham (pop. 270 222) 3 km E of Mansfield

Annual closure	Fermeture annuelle	no
Weekly closure	Fermeture hebdomadaire	no

Fees main season	Tarifs haute saison	18 holes
	Week days Semaine	We/Bank holidays We/Férié
Individual Individuel	£ 35	—
Couple Couple	£ 70	—

Full weekday: £. 45 - No visitors at weekends

Caddy	Caddy	no
Electric Trolley	Chariot électrique	£ 5/18 holes
Buggy	Voiturette	no
Clubs	Clubs	no

Credit cards Cartes de crédit
VISA - Eurocard - MasterCard - Switch - Delta
(not for green fees)

652

Access Accès : M1 Jct 27. Mansfield exit from roundabout. Left at T-junction, left again at next T-junction (8 km or 5 m.). Right at next lights, right again at next T-junction. Left at lights. Right at 3rd mini-roundabout. Golf 1 km on left. **Map 4 on page 495** Carte 4 Page 495

GOLF COURSE
PARCOURS

17 /20

Site	Site	
Maintenance	Entretien	
Architect	Architecte	Harry S. Colt remod. by J. Braid
Type	Type	forest, heathland
Relief	Relief	
Water in play	Eau en jeu	
Exp. to wind	Exposé au vent	
Trees in play	Arbres en jeu	

Scorecard Carte de score	Chp. Chp.	Mens Mess.	Ladies Da.
Length Long.	6028	5654	5082
Par	71	71	73

Advised golfing ability		0	12	24	36
Niveau de jeu recommandé					
Hcp required	Handicap exigé	certificate			

CLUB HOUSE & AMENITIES
CLUB HOUSE ET ANNEXES

7 /10

Pro shop	Pro-shop	
Driving range	Practice	
Sheltered	couvert	practice area
On grass	sur herbe	yes
Putting-green	putting-green	yes
Pitching-green	pitching green	yes

HOTEL FACILITIES
ENVIRONNEMENT HOTELIER

6 /10

HOTELS HÔTELS

Pine Lodge - 20 rooms, D £ 60 — Mansfield
Tel (44) 01623 - 622 308 — 3 km

Swallow — South Normanton
157 rooms, D £ 120 — 18 km
Tel (44) 01773 - 812 000, Fax (44) 01773 - 580 032

Royal Moat House — Nottingham
200 rooms, D £ 100 — 25 km
Tel (44) 0115 - 936 9988, Fax (44) 0115 - 475 667

Stage Hotel — Nottingham
52 rooms, D £ 53 — 25 km
Tel (44) 0115 - 960 3261, Fax (44) 0115 - 969 1040

RESTAURANTS RESTAURANTS

Swallow — South Normanton
Tel (44) 01773 - 812 000 — 18 km

Sonny's - Tel (44) 0115 - 947 3041 — Nottingham 25 km

A course to take in on your way from Liverpool to Scotland, or from Glasgow to England, together with Southerness just opposite on the other side of Solway Firth. Keep looking in this direction, too, because the industrial complex nearby is something of an eyesore. The course's location in the middle of nowhere has kept Silloth from staging any top tournaments, but this does have it advantages: being a quiet course and frequented mostly only by the inhabitants of Carlisle, its overall condition is simply marvellous. It has its enthusiasts, who rate this amongst their top-five links courses, and understandably so. The well-contoured fairways rarely have you standing on flat ground, fairway bunkers have been replaced by heather and gorse, the approaches to greens are tight and putting surfaces are tricky. Bring your best game here and a suitcase because you won't want to leave. Play Silloth before it becomes too fashionable.

Un parcours à inclure dans un voyage de Liverpool vers l'Ecosse, ou de Glasgow vers l'Angleterre, avec celui de Southerness, juste en face, de l'autre côté du Solway Firth. Regardez plutôt de ce côté, car le complexe industriel à proximité n'est pas beau du tout. Sa situation à l'écart de tout a empêché Silloth d'avoir beaucoup de grands championnats, mais il y a un avantage : peu fréquenté, sinon par les habitants de Carlisle, il est dans un état généralement merveilleux. Il a ses amoureux, qui le classent dans leur «Top 5» des links, et on les comprend. Les fairways bien modelés vous mettent rarement à plat, les bunkers de fairway sont remplacés par la bruyère et les ajoncs, les entrées de greens sont étroites, leurs surfaces subtiles. A Silloth-on-Solway, il faut amener son meilleur jeu, et sa valise, car on aura envie de rester... A jouer avant qu'il ne devienne à la mode.

Silloth-on-Solway Golf Club	1892
ENG - SILLOTH-ON-SOLWAY, Cumbria CA5 4AT	

Office	Secrétariat	(44) 016973 - 31 304
Pro shop	Pro-shop	(44) 016973 - 32 404
Fax	Fax	(44) 016973 - 31 782
Situation	Situation	
40 km from Carlisle (pop. 100 562)		

Annual closure	Fermeture annuelle	no
Weekly closure	Fermeture hebdomadaire	no

Fees main season
Tarifs haute saison full day

	Week days	We/Bank holidays
	Semaine	We/Férié
Individual Individuel	£ 25	£ 30
Couple Couple	£ 50	£ 60

Caddy	Caddy	no
Electric Trolley	Chariot électrique	no
Buggy	Voiturette	no
Clubs	Clubs	£ 10/18 holes

Credit cards Cartes de crédit
VISA - Eurocard - MasterCard - AMEX - DC

GOLF
Moricambe Bay · Kirkbride
Skinburness
B5307
Calvo · Newtown Arlosh
Seaville
Silloth
B5300
B5302 · Abbey Town
B5301
Carlisle
Workington
Workington · Wigton
A596
0 2 4 km
0 2,5 miles

Access Accès : M6 to Carlisle, then A595 & A596. At Wigton, B5302 to Silloth Promenade. Go right 200 m.
Map 2 on page 491 Carte 2 Page 491

GOLF COURSE
PARCOURS
18/20

Site	Site	
Maintenance	Entretien	
Architect	Architecte	Willie Park
Type	Type	links
Relief	Relief	
Water in play	Eau en jeu	
Exp. to wind	Exposé au vent	
Trees in play	Arbres en jeu	

Scorecard	Chp.	Mens	Ladies
Carte de score	Chp.	Mess.	Da.
Length Long.	5952	5721	5203
Par	72	72	75

Advised golfing ability	0	12	24	36
Niveau de jeu recommandé				
Hcp required	Handicap exigé	certificate		

CLUB HOUSE & AMENITIES
CLUB HOUSE ET ANNEXES
7/10

Pro shop	Pro-shop	
Driving range	Practice	
Sheltered	couvert	no
On grass	sur herbe	yes
Putting-green	putting-green	yes
Pitching-green	pitching green	yes

HOTEL FACILITIES
ENVIRONNEMENT HOTELIER
4/10

HOTELS HÔTELS
Silloth Golf Hotel	Silloth
21 rooms, D £ 52	200 m
Tél (44) 016973 - 31 438	
Fax (44) 016973 - 32 582	

Crown + Mitre	Carlisle
97 rooms, D £ 99	40 km
Tel (44) 01228 - 25 491	
Fax (44) 01228 - 514 553	

RESTAURANTS RESTAURANT
Silloth Golf Hotel	Silloth
Tel (44) 016973 - 31 438	200 m

653

The Woburn of the north or the Gleneagles of the south, it doesn't matter either way. Slaley Hall is one of those courses that has brought life to a region where good courses were comparatively few and far between. The vegetation is typical of the north, with a good number of pine-trees lining the fairways or adding dark colour to contrast with the lighter greens of the fairways and putting surfaces, the sand in the bunkers and the lakes. Familiar colours to golfers, certainly, but here they just look smarter than anywhere else. The many different playing options add variety to the fun of playing here; you can change the complexion of the course by switching tee-boxes but still keep the same panoply of hazards, including fairway bunkers whose shape (Dave Thomas style) gives this magnificent English style park a little American touch. If you are feeling tired after the very challenging finishing holes, the clubhouse and hotel offer all the facilities of a major golfing resort, enhanced still further with a second course.

Woburn du nord ou Gleneagles du sud, peu importe, Slaley Hall fait partie, des golfs qui ont un peu réveillé une région assez pauvre en grands parcours. La végétation est néanmoins plus typique du nord, avec les nombreux sapins bordant les fairways ou fournissant des couleurs sombres harmonisées à celles des greens et des fairways, au sable des bunkers et aux lacs. Ce sont des couleurs familières aux golfeurs, mais ici plus soignées que partout ailleurs. De multiples options de jeu permettent de varier les plaisirs : d'un jour à l'autre, changez de difficultés en changeant de tees, tout en conservant une panoplie d'obstacles, les formes des bunkers de fairway (à la Dave Thomas !) apportant une touche américaine à ce beau parc à l'anglaise. Si vous êtes un peu fatigué après un finale exigeant, le Clubhouse et l'hôtel offrent tous les services d'un grand «resort», encore amélioré avec un second parcours.

Slaley Hall Hotel & Golf Club		**1988**
Slaley		
ENG - HEXHAM, Northumberland NE47 0BY		

Office	Secrétariat	(44) 01434 - 673 350
Pro shop	Pro-shop	(44) 01434 - 673 154
Fax	Fax	(44) 01434 - 673 152
Situation	Situation	
30 km from Newcastle (pop. 259 541)		
15 km from Hexham (pop. 11 342)		
Annual closure	Fermeture annuelle	no
Weekly closure	Fermeture hebdomadaire	no
Fees main season	Tarifs haute saison	18 holes

	Week days Semaine	We/Bank holidays We/Férié
Individual Individuel	£ 40	—
Couple Couple	£ 80	—

Weekends: members and Hotel guests only

Caddy	Caddy	no
Electric Trolley	Chariot électrique	no
Buggy	Voiturette	£ 20/18 holes
Clubs	Clubs	£ 20/18 holes

Credit cards Cartes de crédit
VISA - Eurocard - MasterCard - AMEX - DC

654

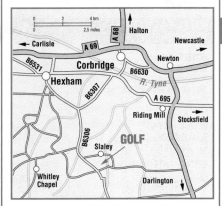

Access Accès : Newcastle, A69 W, turn to Hexham, then B6306 to Slaley.
Map 2 on page 491 Carte 2 Page 491

GOLF COURSE
PARCOURS — **17**/20

Site	Site	
Maintenance	Entretien	
Architect	Architecte	David Thomas
Type	Type	parkland
Relief	Relief	
Water in play	Eau en jeu	
Exp. to wind	Exposé au vent	
Trees in play	Arbres en jeu	

Scorecard	**Chp.**	**Mens**	**Ladies**
Carte de score	Chp.	Mess.	Da.
Length Long.	6320	6085	5255
Par	72	72	75

Advised golfing ability	0	12	24	36
Niveau de jeu recommandé				
Hcp required Handicap exigé		24 Men, 36 Ladies		

CLUB HOUSE & AMENITIES
CLUB HOUSE ET ANNEXES — **8**/10

Pro shop	Pro-shop	
Driving range	Practice	
Sheltered	couvert	8 bays
On grass	sur herbe	yes
Putting-green	putting-green	yes
Pitching-green	pitching green	yes

HOTEL FACILITIES
ENVIRONNEMENT HOTELIER — **7**/10

HOTELS HÔTELS
Slaley Hall Hotel - 139 rooms, D £ 220   Slaley on site
Tel (44) 01434 - 673 350, Fax (44) 01434 - 673 152

Beaumont - 23 rooms, D £ 70   Hexham
Tel (44) 01434 - 602 331   12 km

County - 9 rooms, D £ 58   Hexham
Tel (44) 01434 - 602 030   12 km

Forte Crest   Newcastle
165 rooms, D £ 80   30 km
Tel (44) 0191 - 232 6191, Fax (44) 0191 - 261 8529

RESTAURANTS RESTAURANTS
2 restaurants at Slaley Hall Hotel   Slaley
Tel (44) 01434 - 673 350   on site

Black House - Tel (44) 01434 - 604 744   Hexham10 km

Queen Street - Tél (44) 0191 - 222 0755 Newcastle 30 km

Although it has staged the Ryder Cup and the British Ladies Open, this course has suffered from being overshadowed by its towering neighbours Birkdale and Hillside, although actually there is little to choose between them. It may look short, but only to the better players. For the rest of us it has yardage enough, especially since driving these tight fairways is never easy. The paths to the greens are never very wide, either, and call for bump 'n run shots which can make the job even tougher. In contrast, game strategy will vary with the wind and always be clear: you see exactly what needs to be done. Whether you play here twice or a hundred times, it is always as exciting as that very first day in an elegant, traditional and warm atmosphere.

Bien qu'il ait reçu la Ryder Cup et le British Ladies Open, ce parcours a souffert de l'ombre de ses puissants voisins, Birkdale et Hillside, mais sans vraiment devoir leur envier grand'chose. Il peut paraître court, mais seulement aux meilleurs joueurs : il est bien assez long pour la plupart d'entre nous, en particulier par ce que driver sur ces fairways étroits n'est guère facile. Les entrées de greens ne sont pas toujours très larges, mais on doit les approcher en roulant, ce qui ne facilite pas non plus la tâche. En revanche, la stratégie peut varier en fonction du vent, mais elle apparaît toujours clairement : on voit exactement ce que l'on doit faire. Que l'on joue deux fois ou cent fois, le plaisir est comme au premier jour dans ce club à l'ambiance élégante, traditionnelle et chaleureuse.

Southport & Ainsdale Golf Club — 1922

Bradshaws Lane, Ainsdale
ENG - SOUTHPORT, Lancs PR8 3LG

Office	Secrétariat	(44) 01704 - 578 092
Pro shop	Pro-shop	(44) 01704 - 577 316
Fax	Fax	(44) 01704 - 570 896
Situation	Situation	

5 km S of Southport (pop. 90 959)
26 km N of Liverpool (pop. 452 450)

Annual closure	Fermeture annuelle	no
Weekly closure	Fermeture hebdomadaire	no
Fees main season	Tarifs haute saison	18 holes

	Week days Semaine	We/Bank holidays We/Férié
Individual Individuel	£ 35	£ 45*
Couple Couple	£ 70	£ 90*

* Limited access at weekends - Full weekdays: £ 45

Caddy	Caddy	on request/£ 20+tip
Electric Trolley	Chariot électrique	no
Buggy	Voiturette	no
Clubs	Clubs	£ 7.50/day

Credit cards Cartes de crédit
VISA - Eurocard - MasterCard - AMEX - DC - JCB

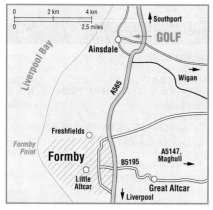

Access Accès : A565 Liverpool → Southport. Ainsdale Village centre, turn left on Bradswhaws Lane
Map 5 on page 497 Carte 5 Page 497

GOLF COURSE / PARCOURS — 18/20

Site	Site	
Maintenance	Entretien	
Architect	Architecte	James Braid
Type	Type	links
Relief	Relief	
Water in play	Eau en jeu	
Exp. to wind	Exposé au vent	
Trees in play	Arbres en jeu	

Scorecard Carte de score	Chp. Chp.	Mens Mess.	Ladies Da.
Length Long.	5950	5924	5052
Par	72	72	74

Advised golfing ability — 0 12 24 36
Niveau de jeu recommandé
Hcp required Handicap exigé — 28 Men, 36 Ladies

CLUB HOUSE & AMENITIES / CLUB HOUSE ET ANNEXES — 7/10

Pro shop	Pro-shop	
Driving range	Practice	
Sheltered	couvert	no
On grass	sur herbe	yes
Putting-green	putting-green	yes
Pitching-green	pitching green	yes

HOTEL FACILITIES / ENVIRONNEMENT HOTELIER — 7/10

HOTELS HÔTELS
Cambridge House Hotel — Southport
18 rooms, D £ 51 — 6 km
Tel (44) 01704 - 538 372, Fax (44) 01704 - 547 183

Scarisbrick — Southport
77 rooms, D £ 90 — 5 km
Tel (44) 01704 - 543 000, Fax (44) 01704 - 533 335

Stutelea — Southport
24 rooms, D £ 80 — 5 km
Tel (44) 01704 - 544 220, Fax (44) 01704 - 500 232

RESTAURANTS RESTAURANTS
The Warehouse — Southport
Tel (44) 01704 - 544 662 — 5 km

Valentino's - Tel (44) 01704 - 538 401 — Southport 5 km

The Jasmin Tree — Southport
Tel (44) 01704 - 530 141 — 5 km

655

You will remember three things about this course: the wonderful views over the Cornish coast and the Camel estuary, the little church on the 10th hole, dug out of the sand 60 years ago, and Himalaya, a giant hill-shaped bunker standing some 80 feet high where you watch golfers walk up and down in a vain attempt to get their ball back in the fairway. But this is not the only hill over steeply undulating terrain, which can be tiring for the fainter-hearted. Some greens are difficult to reach other than with lofted shots, meaning that good scores go to good players. Beginners will spend their time in the dunes and the very thick rough. St. Enodoc is a superb golfing arena, with special mention going to the final holes where you play for the match and an excellent meal in the clubhouse.

Vous vous souviendrez au moins de trois choses : les vues magnifiques sur la côte de Cornouailles et le Camel Estuary, la petite église au 10, tirée du sable il y a 60 ans, et l'Himalaya, gigantesque bunker en forme de colline de 25 mètres de haut, d'où il est distrayant de regarder les joueurs monter et descendre sans parvenir à sortir leur balle. Mais ce n'est pas la seule colline d'un terrain très mouvementé, parfois assez fatigant pour les plus faibles. Certains greens sont difficiles à atteindre autrement qu'avec des balles levées, ce qui réserve les bons scores aux bons joueurs. Les débutants passeront leur vie dans les dunes et dans les roughs très épais. St Enodoc est une superbe arène pour jouer, avec une mention particulière pour les derniers trous quand on y joue le match et un très bon repas au Clubhouse.

St Enodoc Golf Club   1890
Rock
ENG - WADEBRIDGE, Cornwall PL2T 6LD

Office	Secrétariat	(44) 01208 - 863 216
Pro shop	Pro-shop	(44) 01208 - 862 402
Fax	Fax	(44) 01208 - 862 976
Situation	Situation	

10 km from Wadebridge - 32 km from Bodmin

Annual closure	Fermeture annuelle	no
Weekly closure	Fermeture hebdomadaire	no
Fees main season	Tarifs haute saison	18 holes

	Week days Semaine	We/Bank holidays We/Férié
Individual Individuel	£ 35	£ 40
Couple Couple	£ 70	£ 80

Full day: £ 50 - £ 55 (weekends)

Caddy	Caddy	no
Electric Trolley	Chariot électrique	£ 9/day
Buggy	Voiturette	no
Clubs	Clubs	£ 10/18 holes

Credit cards Cartes de crédit
Visa - Mastercard (Pro shop goods only)

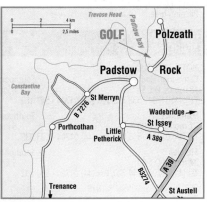

Access Accès : A30 Exeter to Bodmin, then A389 to Wadebridge, follow signs to Rock, drive through Rock, past Boat Club and Matiner's pub, sharp right uphill to Clubhouse (signposted)
Map 6 on page 498 Carte 6 Page 498

GOLF COURSE
PARCOURS   18/20

Site	Site	
Maintenance	Entretien	
Architect	Architecte	James Braid
Type	Type	seaside course, links
Relief	Relief	
Water in play	Eau en jeu	
Exp. to wind	Exposé au vent	
Trees in play	Arbres en jeu	

Scorecard Carte de score	**Chp.** Chp.	**Mens** Mess.	**Ladies** Da.
Length Long.	5619	5450	5115
Par	69	69	73

Advised golfing ability		0 12 24 36
Niveau de jeu recommandé		
Hcp required	Handicap exigé	certificate

CLUB HOUSE & AMENITIES
CLUB HOUSE ET ANNEXES   7/10

Pro shop	Pro-shop	
Driving range	Practice	
Sheltered	couvert	no
On grass	sur herbe	no
Putting-green	putting-green	yes (2)
Pitching-green	pitching green	yes

HOTEL FACILITIES
ENVIRONNEMENT HOTELIER   4/10

HOTELS HÔTELS
Pentire Rocks   New Polzeath
15 rooms, D £ 55   5 km
Tel (44) 01208 - 862 213, Fax (44) 01208 - 862 259

Port Gaverne   Port Isaac
19 rooms, D £ 85   10 km
Tel (44) 01208 - 880 244, Fax (44) 01208 - 880 151

Roskarnon House Hotel   Rock
12 rooms, D £ 40   3 km
Tel (44) 01208 - 862 329, Fax (44) 01208 - 862 785

RESTAURANTS RESTAURANTS
St Kew Inn   St Kew
Tel (44) 01208 - 841 259   12 km

Maltsters Arms   Chapel Amble
Tel (44) 01208 - 812 473   8 km

656

Come and play here in May. If you're game lets you down, you'll probably find some consolation in the rhododendrons in full bloom, whose colours contrast with the purple heather, silver birch and pines to produce a wonderful setting for a superb course designed by Harry Colt. For those of you who are not as fit as you were, this is a very hilly course. If you run out of puff, make it back to the clubhouse and admire the superb views. Actually on the course, the changes of gradient and the slopes call for a little reconnoitring before hoping to card a good score, especially since the greens are very quick, full of breaks and sometimes multi-tiered. A few blind drives or tee-shots to steeply sloping fairways also require extreme accuracy. St George's Hill is not only picturesque, it is also one of the country's very good inland courses.

Venez donc au mois de mai. Si votre jeu vous a déçu, vous vous consolerez à la vue des rhododendrons en pleine floraison, dont les couleurs s'ajoutent aux bruyères pourpres, aux bouleaux blancs, aux pins et aux sapins pour offrir un cadre somptueux au superbe dessin de Harry Colt. Hélas pour ceux qui n'ont pas une excellente forme, ce parcours est très physique. Ils pourront toujours rester au Clubhouse, qui offre des vues superbes. Quant au parcours, ses changements de niveaux et ses pentes exigent une petite reconnaissance préalable avant d'espérer un bon score, d'autant plus que les greens sont rapides, très mouvementés, parfois à plusieurs plateaux. Quelques drives aveugles ou vers des fairways en dévers demandent aussi beaucoup de précision. St George's Hill n'est pas seulement pittoresque, c'est aussi un des très bons parcours «inland» du pays.

St George's Hill Golf Club — 1912

Golf Club Road, St George's Hill
ENG - WEYBRIDGE, Surrey KT13 0NL

Office	Secrétariat	(44) 01932 - 847 758
Pro shop	Pro-shop	(44) 01932 - 847 523
Fax	Fax	(44) 01932 - 821 564
Situation	Situation	

1 km from Weybridge (pop. 7 919)
37 km from Central London (pop. 6 679 700)

Annual closure	Fermeture annuelle	no
Weekly closure	Fermeture hebdomadaire	no
Fees main season	Tarifs haute saison	18 holes

	Week days Semaine	We/Bank holidays We/Férié
Individual Individuel	£ 50	—
Couple Couple	£ 100	—

Full weekday: £ 65 - Weekends: only with a member

Caddy	Caddy	on request/£ 20+tip
Electric Trolley	Chariot électrique	no
Buggy	Voiturette	no
Clubs	Clubs	£ 15/18 holes

Credit cards Cartes de crédit
VISA - Eurocard - MasterCard - AMEX - JCB

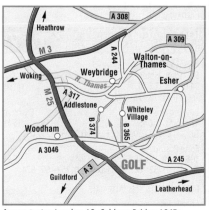

Access Accès : London A3. Cobham Bridge A245 (Byfleet Road). After 2 km (1.2 m.), B374 (Brooklands Road) on right. Golf on right (Golf Club Road).
Map 8 on page 503 Carte 8 Page 503

GOLF COURSE / PARCOURS — 17/20

Site	Site	
Maintenance	Entretien	
Architect	Architecte	Harry S. Colt
Type	Type	inland, parkland
Relief	Relief	
Water in play	Eau en jeu	
Exp. to wind	Exposé au vent	
Trees in play	Arbres en jeu	

Scorecard Carte de score	Chp. Chp.	Mens Mess.	Ladies Da.
Length Long.	5910	5960	5020
Par	70	70	72

Advised golfing ability Niveau de jeu recommandé	0	12	24	36
Hcp required Handicap exigé	certificate			

CLUB HOUSE & AMENITIES / CLUB HOUSE ET ANNEXES — 7/10

Pro shop	Pro-shop	
Driving range	Practice	
Sheltered	couvert	no
On grass	sur herbe	yes
Putting-green	putting-green	yes
Pitching-green	pitching green	no

657

HOTEL FACILITIES / ENVIRONNEMENT HOTELIER — 7/10

HOTELS HÔTELS
Oatlands Park — Weybridge
112 rooms, D £ 145 — 3 km
Tel (44) 01932 - 847 242, Fax (44) 01932 - 842 252

Ship Thistle — Weybridge
39 rooms, D 120 — 1 km
Tel (44) 01932 - 848 364, Fax (44) 01932 - 857 153

Hilton National — Cobham
146 rooms, D £ 120 — 3 km
Tel (44) 01932 - 864 471, Fax (44) 01932 - 868 017

RESTAURANTS RESTAURANTS
Casa Romana — Weybridge 1 km
Tel (44) 01932 - 843 470

Les Alouettes — Esher-Claygate
Tel (44) 01372 - 464 882 — 6 km

Good Earth - Tel (44) 01932 - 462 489 — Esher 4 km

This is a Jack Nicklaus course and golfers who know his style in the United States will recognise the way in which he has bent and twisted the Cornish countryside to fit his requirements. Turning around a hill which is the setting for another 18 hole course, St. Mellion is exposed to all winds and weathers which will make the course even more difficult than usual. Let's be honest here: even from the front tees this course will be beyond most average players. The bunkers, water and lakes are impressive enough to put off any visitor. Equally true though is the fact that it mellows a little more each time you play it. Maybe because you pay less attention to features such as the many tiny, multi-tiered greens. This is a course you cannot pass by, especially given the club's outstanding facilities, but it is not exactly what you would call a holiday course and there is little local colour to talk of. A must to play to form your own opinion. And test the state of your game.

D'accord, St Mellion est signé Jack Nicklaus. Ceux qui connaissent ses parcours aux USA reconnaîtront qu'il a su plier le paysage de Cornouailles à ses volontés. Tournant autour d'une colline où est logé un autre 18 trous, celui-ci est exposé à tous les vents, ce qui renforce encore sa difficulté. Disons-le franchement, même des départs avancés, ce parcours n'est pas à la portée des joueurs moyens. Les bunkers, les cours d'eau, les lacs impressionnent assez pour refroidir le visiteur. Il est vrai que ce parcours s'adoucit à mesure qu'on le joue, on remarque moins que certains greens sont minuscules, beaucoup à plateaux. Il est impossible d'ignorer ce golf, d'autant que les équipements sont remarquables, mais ce n'est pas exactement un parcours de vacances, et l'on cherchera vainement une couleur vraiment locale. A connaître absolument, pour se faire une opinion. Et tester son jeu.

St Mellion International — 1987

St Mellion
ENG - SALTASH, Cornwall PL12 6 SD

Office	Secrétariat	(44) 01579 - 351 351
Pro shop	Pro-shop	(44) 01579 - 350 724
Fax	Fax	(44) 01579 - 350 116
Situation	Situation	

16 km NW of Plymouth (pop. 243 373)

Annual closure	Fermeture annuelle	no
Weekly closure	Fermeture hebdomadaire	no
Fees main season	Tarifs haute saison	18 holes

	Week days Semaine	We/Bank holidays We/Férié
Individual Individuel	£ 35	£ 35
Couple Couple	£ 70	£ 70

Caddy	Caddy	on request
Electric Trolley	Chariot électrique	no
Buggy	Voiturette	£ 18/18 holes
Clubs	Clubs	£ 12.50/18 holes

Credit cards Cartes de crédit
VISA - MasterCard - DC (Pro shop goods & restaurant only)

Access Accès : M5 then A38 to Saltash, then A388 to St Mellion. Golf signposted.
Map 6 on page 498 Carte 6 Page 498

GOLF COURSE / PARCOURS — 17/20

Site	Site	
Maintenance	Entretien	
Architect	Architecte	Jack Nicklaus
Type	Type	parkland, open country
Relief	Relief	
Water in play	Eau en jeu	
Exp. to wind	Exposé au vent	
Trees in play	Arbres en jeu	

Scorecard Carte de score	Chp. Chp.	Mens Mess.	Ladies Da.
Length Long.	6080	5846	5146
Par	72	72	73

Advised golfing ability Niveau de jeu recommandé		0 12 24 36
Hcp required	Handicap exigé	no

CLUB HOUSE & AMENITIES / CLUB HOUSE ET ANNEXES — 9/10

Pro shop	Pro-shop	
Driving range	Practice	
Sheltered	couvert	6 mats
On grass	sur herbe	yes
Putting-green	putting-green	yes
Pitching-green	pitching green	yes

HOTEL FACILITIES / ENVIRONNEMENT HOTELIER — 7/10

HOTELS HÔTELS
St Mellion Hotel — Golf on site
24 rooms, D £ 90
Tel (44) 01579 - 351 351

Bowling Green — Plymouth 16 km
12 rooms, D £ 45
Tel (44) 01752 - 209 090, Fax (44) 01752 - 209 092

Forte Posthouse — Plymouth 16 km
106 rooms, D £ 60
Tel (44) 01752 - 662 828, Fax (44) 01752 - 660 974

RESTAURANTS RESTAURANTS
Chez Nous — Plymouth 16 km
Tel (44) 01752 - 266 793

Danescombe — Calstock 16 km
Tel (44) 01822 - 832 414

658

Agreed, at this price the week-end green-fee is a little high, but we suppose they have to find some sort of deterrent. The most surprising thing here is not the price nor the Clubhouse, re-designed to cater to the addition of a new 9-hole course, hotel rooms and a swimming pool. No, what really surprises the visitor is the absence of heather, found on every other course in the region virtually without exception. We are in the purest «park-land» style, where fairways lined with splendid trees cover space that only Harry Colt could have turned into such a clever course. Everyone talks about the 7th hole, an exemplary par 3, but the rest are no less exciting. With Colt you always have to weigh up the pros and cons of each shot, look twice and watch out for illusions such as hazards that are too visible. If you want to talk about the course, there are some excellent restaurants in the clubhouse.

D'accord, à ce prix en week-end, c'est un peu cher, mais le tarif doit être surtout dissuasif ! Ce qui est le plus surprenant ici, ce n'est pas cela, ni le Clubhouse, bien refait, avec un nouveau 9 trous, des chambres d'hôtel et une piscine. Ce qui est le plus surprenant, c'est qu'il n'y a pas ici de bruyère, comme dans tous les parcours de la région, pratiquement sans exception. Nous sommes dans le style «parkland» le plus pur, avec des fairways décorés d'arbres splendides, dans un espace dont seul un Harry Colt pouvait tirer un parcours d'une telle intelligence. On parle toujours du 7, un par 3 exemplaire, mais les autres ne sont pas moins passionnants à envisager. Avec Colt, il faut toujours regarder à deux fois, se méfier des illusions comme des obstacles trop visibles, il faut toujours peser le pour et le contre de chaque coup. Pour en parler, il y a les excellents restaurants du Clubhouse...

Stoke Poges Golf Club   1908

North Drive, Park Road, Stoke Poges
ENG - SLOUGH, Bucks SL2 4PG

Office	Secrétariat	(44) 01753 - 717 171
Pro shop	Pro-shop	(44) 01753 - 717 172
Fax	Fax	(44) 01753 - 717 181
Situation	Situation	

3 km from Slough (pop. 101 066)
8 km from Windsor (pop. 30 136)

Annual closure	Fermeture annuelle	no
Weekly closure	Fermeture hebdomadaire	no
Fees main season	Tarifs haute saison	18 holes

	Week days Semaine	We/Bank holidays We/Férié
Individual Individuel	£ 50	£ 100
Couple Couple	£ 100	£ 200
Caddy Caddy		on request/£ 25
Electric Trolley Chariot électrique		£ 10/18 holes
Buggy Voiturette		£ 25/18 holes
Clubs Clubs		£ 25/18 holes

Credit cards Cartes de crédit
VISA - Eurocard - MasterCard - AMEX - DC - JCB

Access Accès : M4 Jct 6 at Slough,
A355 → Beaconsfield. At double mini roundabout
in Farnham Royal turn right into Park Road.
Map 8 on page 502 Carte 8 Page 502

GOLF COURSE
PARCOURS   17/20

Site	Site	▰▰▰▰▱
Maintenance	Entretien	▰▰▰▰▱
Architect	Architecte	Harry S. Colt
Type	Type	parkland
Relief	Relief	▰▰▱▱▱
Water in play	Eau en jeu	▰▰▱▱▱
Exp. to wind	Exposé au vent	▰▰▱▱▱
Trees in play	Arbres en jeu	▰▰▰▰▱

Scorecard Carte de score	Chp. Chp.	Mens Mess.	Ladies Da.
Length Long.	6003	5682	5280
Par	71	71	74

Advised golfing ability   0   12   24   36
Niveau de jeu recommandé   ▰▰▰▰▱
Hcp required Handicap exigé   28 Men, 36 Ladies

CLUB HOUSE & AMENITIES
CLUB HOUSE ET ANNEXES   8/10

Pro shop	Pro-shop	▰▰▰▰▱
Driving range	Practice	▰▰▰▰▱
Sheltered	couvert	no
On grass	sur herbe	yes
Putting-green	putting-green	yes
Pitching-green	pitching green	yes

HOTEL FACILITIES
ENVIRONNEMENT HOTELIER   8/10

HOTELS HÔTELS

Stoke Park   Stoke Poges
20 rooms, D £ 275   on site
Tel (44) 01753 - 717171, Fax (44) 01753 - 717181

Copthorne   Slough
217 rooms, D £ 120   5 km
Tel (44) 01753 - 516 222, Fax (44) 01753 - 516 237

Courtyard   Slough
148 rooms, D £ 85   5 km
Tel (44) 01753 - 551 551, Fax (44) 01753 - 553 333

Burnham Beeches   Burnham
73 rooms, D £ 120   4 km
Tel (44) 01628 - 429 955, Fax (44) 01628 - 603 994

RESTAURANTS RESTAURANTS

Club house (3 restaurants)   Stoke Poges on site
Tel (44) 01753 - 717171

Waldo's - Tél(44) 01628 - 668 561   Taplow 6 km

659

A lack of yardage did not prevent Stoneham from staging the first British Masters in 1946 or the Brabazon Trophy in 1993. We'll simply say that this is a good par 70 for golfers who know the course well and pay more attention to their overall score, rather than concentrating on playing to par on each individual hole. At all events, the fairway bunkers should not bother too many players and should ideally be moved to restore their original purpose. The main hazards are now the heather and gorse-bushes, together with the slopes and hills on a site that can be tiring to walk on a number of holes (the 3rd and 18th). This course poses enough problems for us to recommend it first and foremost to experienced players, who will appreciate the uncompromising severity of the challenge. Last but not least, although so close to the port of Southampton, the course is a haven of peace and quiet.

Son manque de longueur n'a pas empêché Stoneham de recevoir le premier British Masters en 1946, ainsi que le Brabazon Trophy en 1993. Nous dirons simplement que c'est un bon par 70 pour ceux qui le connaissent bien et font plus attention au par total qu'au par de chaque trou. En tout cas, les bunkers de fairway ne gêneront pas grand-monde, il faudrait les déplacer pour leur restituer leur fonction originale. Ce sont la bruyère et les buissons d'ajoncs qui sont maintenant les obstacles principaux, avec les changements de niveau ou même les ondulations d'un terrain assez fatigant sur quelques trous (3 et 18). Ce parcours pose assez de problèmes pour qu'on le conseille d'abord aux joueurs expérimentés, qui apprécieront la rigueur sans concession du défi présenté. Enfin, si près du port de Southampton, on est ici parfaitement au calme.

Stoneham Golf Club — 1908

Monks Wood Close
ENG - SOUTHAMPTON, Hampshire SO16 3TT

Office	Secrétariat	(44) 01703 - 769 272
Pro shop	Pro-shop	(44) 01703 - 768 397
Fax	Fax	(44) 01703 - 766 320
Situation	Situation	

Southampton (pop. 196 865)

Annual closure	Fermeture annuelle	no
Weekly closure	Fermeture hebdomadaire	no

Fees main season	Tarifs haute saison	18 holes
	Week days Semaine	**We/Bank holidays** We/Férié
Individual Individuel	£ 36	£ 40
Couple Couple	£ 72	£ 80

18 holes weekdays: £ 29
Under 18 with member, £ 10 any time

Caddy	Caddy	no
Electric Trolley	Chariot électrique	£ 8/18 holes
Buggy	Voiturette	no
Clubs	Clubs	no

Credit cards Cartes de crédit
Visa - Mastercard (Pro shop goods only)

660

Access Accès : M27 Jct 5. Drive towards Southampton. Turn right at first traffic lights on A27 (Bassett Green Road). 1.2 km, turn right into Golf Club.
Map 7 on page 500 Carte 7 Page 500

GOLF COURSE / PARCOURS — 15/20

Site	Site	
Maintenance	Entretien	
Architect	Architecte	Willie Park
Type	Type	inland, heathland
Relief	Relief	
Water in play	Eau en jeu	
Exp. to wind	Exposé au vent	
Trees in play	Arbres en jeu	

Scorecard Carte de score	Chp. Chp.	Mens Mess.	Ladies Da.
Length Long.	5680	5360	4809
Par	72	72	71

Advised golfing ability Niveau de jeu recommandé		0 12 24 36
Hcp required	Handicap exigé	certificate

CLUB HOUSE & AMENITIES / CLUB HOUSE ET ANNEXES — 7/10

Pro shop	Pro-shop	
Driving range	Practice	
Sheltered	couvert	2 mats
On grass	sur herbe	no
Putting-green	putting-green	yes
Pitching-green	pitching green	yes

HOTEL FACILITIES / ENVIRONNEMENT HOTELIER — 8/10

HOTELS HÔTELS

Hilton National 133 rooms, D £ 90 Tel (44) 01703 - 702 700, Fax (44) 01703 - 767 233		Southampton 4 km
De Vere Grand Harbour 169 rooms, D £ 130 Tel (44) 01703 - 633 033, Fax (44) 01703 - 633 066		Southampton 4 km
County 66 rooms, D £ 65 Tel (44) 01703 - 359 955, Fax (44) 01703 - 583 910		Southampton 4 km

RESTAURANTS RESTAURANT

Kuti's Brasserie Tel (44) 01703 - 221585	Southampton 4 km
Old Manor House Tel (44) 01794 - 517353	Romsey 12 km

SUNNINGDALE NEW COURSE

When you find two great courses at the same Club, you always have a slight preference. But don't be disappointed if you cannot play the «Old» course, its «New» counterpart is just as good and some excellent players even prefer it. If you forget the less enchanting and more «manly» landscape, the «New» course has a lot to be said for it. It allows more aggressive driving, although placing the ball is still crucially important. You need to avoid the fairway bunkers (the edges of which are very high), a very dangerous pond on the 15th, and a few wicked ditches. Your ironwork will have to be up to scratch, too, to hit the right spot on greens which readily cast off any mis-hit approach shots. Technical and tactical, lovely to walk but not so easy to score on, this is one of Harry Colt's vintage courses. Make it a whole day here at this very chic Club so you can play both courses.

Quand on trouve deux grands parcours dans le même golf, on a toujours une légère inclination. Que ceux qui ne pourraient jouer le «Old» ne soient pas déçus, le «New» est d'une qualité très comparable, certains excellents joueurs le préférant même. Si l'on fait abstraction d'un paysage moins charmeur, plus «viril,» le New ne manque pas d'arguments. Il autorise des drives plus agressifs, mais le placement de la balle reste crucial : il faut éviter les bunkers de fairway (leurs rebords sont très hauts), une mare très dangereuse au 15, quelques fossés pernicieux, et avoir un excellent jeu de fers pour placer la balle en bonne position sur les greens, qui rejettent sans hésiter les balles un peu approximatives. Technique, tactique, très agréable à marcher, pas facile à scorer, c'est un des bons crus de son architecte Harry Colt. Prenez donc la journée pour jouer les deux parcours de ce club très chic.

Sunningdale Golf Club — 1922

Ridgemount Road
ENG - SUNNINGDALE, Berks SL5 9RW

Office	Secrétariat	(44) 01344 - 612 681
Pro shop	Pro-shop	(44) 01344 - 620 128
Fax	Fax	(44) 01344 - 624 154
Situation	Situation	

10 km from Windsor (pop. 30 136)
5 km from Ascot (pop. 150 244)

Annual closure	Fermeture annuelle	no
Weekly closure	Fermeture hebdomadaire	no
Fees main season	Tarifs haute saison	18 holes

	Week days Semaine	We/Bank holidays We/Férié
Individual Individuel	£ 100	—
Couple Couple	£ 200	—

Visitors from Monday to Thursday - Prior booking essential

Caddy	Caddy	on request/£ 30+tip
Electric Trolley	Chariot électrique	no
Buggy	Voiturette	£ 25/18 holes
Clubs	Clubs	no

Credit cards Cartes de crédit
VISA - MasterCard (Pro shop & green fees only)

Access Accès : London, A30. 1st left after Sunningdale level crossing. Club 300 m on left.
Map 8 on page 502 Carte 8 Page 502

GOLF COURSE / PARCOURS — 18/20

Site	Site	
Maintenance	Entretien	
Architect	Architecte	Harry S. Colt
Type	Type	forest, heathland
Relief	Relief	
Water in play	Eau en jeu	
Exp. to wind	Exposé au vent	
Trees in play	Arbres en jeu	

Scorecard Carte de score	Chp. Chp.	Mens Mess.	Ladies Da.
Length Long.	6022	5798	5256
Par	71	71	74

Advised golfing ability Niveau de jeu recommandé	0 12 24 36
Hcp required Handicap exigé	18 Men, 24 Ladies

CLUB HOUSE & AMENITIES / CLUB HOUSE ET ANNEXES — 8/10

Pro shop	Pro-shop	
Driving range	Practice	
Sheltered	couvert	no
On grass	sur herbe	yes
Putting-green	putting-green	yes
Pitching-green	pitching green	yes

HOTEL FACILITIES / ENVIRONNEMENT HOTELIER — 8/10

661

HOTELS HÔTELS

Berystede — Sunninghill
90 rooms, D £ 120 — 1 km
Tel (44) 01344 - 23 311, Fax (44) 01344 - 872 301

Cricketers — Bagshot
27 rooms, D £ 40 — 3 km
Tel (44) 01276 - 473 196, Fax (44) 01276 - 451 357

Oakley Court — Windsor
91 rooms, D £ 150 — 12 km
Tel (44) 01753 - 609 988, Fax (44) 01628 - 37 011

RESTAURANTS RESTAURANT

Stateroom (Royal Berkshire Hotel) — Sunninghill 1 km
Tel (44) 01344 - 23 322

Ciao Ninety - Tel (44) 01344 - 22 285 — Ascot 3 km

Jade Fountain — Sunninghill
Tel (44) 01344 - 27 070 — 1 km

This is one of those courses where the impression of space unfolding before you is as inviting as it is deceptive. In a magnificent setting, the trees are a sight to behold and are enhanced by heather which has invaded all the rough. When in flower it all looks wonderful, although you might wish you'd never set eyes on it when trying to hack your ball back onto the fairway. Laid out on ideal sandy soil, Sunningdale may lack yardage but is still a model of course design. This is one of Willie Park's masterpieces, such is the need for accuracy and inspiration, for a constant choice of tactics and for control over the full panoply of shots, particularly near the greens. But on a fine day when the ball rolls and rolls and when the greens are at their sublime best, scores can be flattering. This «Old Lady» has boundless charm and appeal.

C'est l'un des parcours où l'impression d'espace devant soi invite au jeu, mais elle peut être aussi trompeuse que la séduction du lieu. Les arbres sont un spectacle, mis en valeur par la bruyère qui envahit tous les roughs, magnifique quand elle prend ses couleurs, impossible quand il faut en déloger sa balle. Construit sur cette terre sablonneuse qui fait de si bons golfs, Sunningdale manque peut-être de longueur, mais reste un modèle d'architecture, et l'un des chefs-d'oeuvre de Willie Park, tant il réclame de précision et d'inspiration, tant il offre constamment des choix tactiques, tant il oblige à disposer de la gamme complète des coups de golf, notamment au petit jeu. Mais en un beau jour d'été où les balles n'en finissent pas de rouler, et où les greens sont à leur sommet, les scores peuvent être flatteurs. Cette «Old Lady» sait toujours se laisser séduire.

Sunningdale Golf Club — 1901

Ridgemount Road
ENG - SUNNINGDALE, Berks SL5 9RW

Office	Secrétariat	(44) 01344 - 612 681
Pro shop	Pro-shop	(44) 01344 - 620 128
Fax	Fax	(44) 01344 - 624 154
Situation	Situation	

10 km from Windsor (pop. 30 136)
5 km from Ascot (pop. 150 244)

Annual closure	Fermeture annuelle	no
Weekly closure	Fermeture hebdomadaire	no

Fees main season	Tarifs haute saison	18 holes	
		Week days Semaine	**We/Bank holidays** We/Férié
Individual Individuel		£ 100	—
Couple Couple		£ 200	—

Visitors: Monday-Thursday only - Prior booking essential

Caddy	Caddy	on request/£ 30+tip
Electric Trolley	Chariot électrique	no
Buggy	Voiturette	£ 25/18 holes
Clubs	Clubs	no

Credit cards Cartes de crédit
VISA - MasterCard (Pro shop & green fees only)

662

Access Accès : London, A30. 1st left after Sunningdale level crossing. Club 300 m on left.
Map 8 on page 502 Carte 8 Page 502

GOLF COURSE PARCOURS — 18/20

Site	Site	
Maintenance	Entretien	
Architect	Architecte	Willie Park
Type	Type	forest, heathland
Relief	Relief	
Water in play	Eau en jeu	
Exp. to wind	Exposé au vent	
Trees in play	Arbres en jeu	

Scorecard Carte de score	Chp. Chp.	Mens Mess.	Ladies Da.
Length Long.	5948	5707	5242
Par	72	70	74

Advised golfing ability Niveau de jeu recommandé		0	12	24	36

Hcp required Handicap exigé — 18 Men, 24 Ladies

CLUB HOUSE & AMENITIES CLUB HOUSE ET ANNEXES — 8/10

Pro shop	Pro-shop	
Driving range	Practice	
Sheltered	couvert	no
On grass	sur herbe	yes
Putting-green	putting-green	yes
Pitching-green	pitching green	yes

HOTEL FACILITIES ENVIRONNEMENT HOTELIER — 8/10

HOTELS HÔTELS
Berystede — Sunninghill
90 rooms, D £ 120 — 1 km
Tel (44) 01344 - 23 311, Fax (44) 01344 - 872 301

Cricketers — Bagshot
27 rooms, D £ 40 — 3 km
Tel (44) 01276 - 473 196, Fax (44) 01276 - 451 357

Oakley Court — Windsor
91 rooms, D £ 150 — 12 km
Tel (44) 01753 - 609 988, Fax (44) 01628 - 37 011

RESTAURANTS RESTAURANT
Stateroom (Royal Berkshire Hotel) — Sunninghill 1 km
Tel (44) 01344 - 23 322

Ciao Ninety - Tel (44) 01344 - 22 285 — Ascot 3 km

Jade Fountain — Sunninghill
Tel (44) 01344 - 27 070 — 1 km

A striking feature is the impression of wide open space despite the impressive mass of trees: the fairways are actually wide and only hugely mis-hit drives can cause real problems for the second shot. Having said that, you will need to be more accurate if you want to hit the greens from the best position and stay on the putting surface, as uncannily they tend to pick out the well-hit shots and reject the rest. As usual with Harry Colt, the tee-boxes, bunkers and greens are at once carefully designed and well-positioned. Here more than ever, try not to count those golfing birdies before they are hatched; granted, the course is not long but it is a par 69 with five par 3s and some long par 4s, the kind of holes which add to your score rather than lower it. Last but not least, we should emphasize that this is a gentleman's club (no Ryder cup here!) where ladies and dogs are nonetheless welcome and where the rules of admission may be relaxed with a prior telephone call to the Secretary.

L'impression d'espace ouvert est frappante, en dépit de la masse imposante des arbres : les fairways sont effective-ment larges, et seuls les drives très égarés peuvent vous préoccuper pour le second coup. Cela dit, il convient d'être plus précis si l'on veut attaquer les greens en bonne position, et y rester, car ils ont assez tendance à trier les bonnes balles et rejeter les moins bonnes. Comme d'habitude avec Harry Colt, les départs comme les bunkers de fairway et de green sont soignés dans leur dessin comme dans leur placement. Il convient aussi de ne pas préjuger de son score avant de l'avoir fait : le parcours n'est pas long, mais c'est un par 69, avec 5 par 3 et quelques longs par 4, le genre de trous qui font les additions plus que les soustractions. Soulignons que c'est un club très «gentlemen « où femmes et chiens sont néanmoins bienvenus, et que les règles d'entrée peuvent s'assouplir avec un coup de téléphone au Secretary.

Swinley Forest Golf Club 1909
Coronation Road
ENG - ASCOT, Berkshire SL9 5LE

Office	Secrétariat	(44) 01344 - 874 979
Pro shop	Pro-shop	(44) 01344 - 874 811
Fax	Fax	(44) 01344 - 874 733
Situation	Situation	

5 km from Ascot (pop. 150 244)

Annual closure	Fermeture annuelle	no
Weekly closure	Fermeture hebdomadaire	no

Fees main season
Tarifs haute saison full day

	Week days Semaine	We/Bank holidays We/Férié
Individual Individuel	£ 65	—
Couple Couple	£ 130	—

No visitors at week ends - Week days: phone before coming

Caddy	Caddy	£ 25 + tip
Electric Trolley	Chariot électrique	no
Buggy	Voiturette	£ 20
Clubs	Clubs	yes

Credit cards Cartes de crédit no

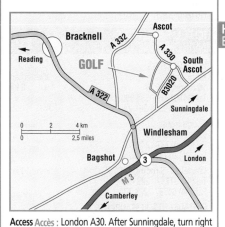

Access Accès : London A30. After Sunningdale, turn right on B3020 and left into Coronation Road. Golf course 1 km on left. **Map 8 on page 502** Carte 8 Page 502

GOLF COURSE
PARCOURS
16/20

Site	Site	
Maintenance	Entretien	
Architect	Architecte	Harry S. Colt
Type	Type	inland, forest
Relief	Relief	
Water in play	Eau en jeu	
Exp. to wind	Exposé au vent	
Trees in play	Arbres en jeu	

Scorecard	Chp.	Mens	Ladies
Carte de score	Chp.	Mess.	Da.
Length Long.	5441	5176	4451
Par	69	68	68

Advised golfing ability		0	12	24	36
Niveau de jeu recommandé					
Hcp required	Handicap exigé	Secretary's discretion			

CLUB HOUSE & AMENITIES
CLUB HOUSE ET ANNEXES
6/10

Pro shop	Pro-shop	
Driving range	Practice	
Sheltered	couvert	no
On grass	sur herbe	no
Putting-green	putting-green	yes
Pitching-green	pitching green	no

663

HOTEL FACILITIES
ENVIRONNEMENT HOTELIER
8/10

HOTELS HÔTELS

Berystede — Sunninghill
90 rooms, D £ 120
Tel (44) 01344 - 23 311, Fax (44) 01344 - 872 301

Cricketers — Bagshot
27 rooms, D £ 40
Tel (44) 01276 - 473 196, Fax (44) 01276 - 451 357

Oakley Court — Windsor
91 rooms, D £ 150
Tel (44) 01753 - 609 988, Fax (44) 01628 - 37 011

RESTAURANTS RESTAURANT

Stateroom (Royal Berkshire Hotel) — Sunninghill
Tel (44) 01344 - 23 322

Ciao Ninety — Ascot
Tel (44) 01344 - 22 285

Jade Fountain — Sunninghill
Tel (44) 01344 - 27 070

A little road leads you one of England's prettiest clubhouses in pure Tudor style. The actual course offers not only some wonderful views over Surrey, Sussex and Kent, but also an exhilarating sensation of open space where most of the tee-boxes are elevated and give a very clear idea of the strategy required. The downside to this hilly landscape is that the course is tiring to walk over the last 9 holes. Tandridge is a rather short course and the wide fairways are an invitation to use your driver, but a few bushes, trees and sometimes very thick rough severely penalise wayward hitting. When approaching the greens, watch out for the bunkers, which are placed well forward. The result is an optical illusion which makes club selection more difficult than usual. The members' favourite hole here is the 14th, where you drive into a valley before hitting your approach shot up the hill towards a very well protected green. Tandridge is a model of simplicity and intelligence, Harry Colt style.

Une petite route vous mène à l'un des plus jolis Clubhouses d'Angleterre, en style Tudor. Le parcours offre non seulement des vues imprenables sur le Surrey, le Sussex et le Kent, mais aussi un sentiment d'espace tout à fait exaltant, car la plupart des départs sont ici en hauteur, donnant une idée très claire de la stratégie. Mais ce relief a l'inconvénient d'être un peu fatigant sur les neuf derniers trous. Tandridge est assez court, et la largeur des fairways permet de sortir souvent le driver, mais quelques buissons, les arbres et un rough parfois dense peuvent punir sévèrement les coups lâchés. A l'approche des greens, il faut remarquer les bunkers placés très en avant, rendant la sélection des clubs difficile en raison des illusions d'optique. Le trou favori des membres est ici le 14, où l'on drive dans une vallée pour remonter ensuite vers un green très défendu : c'est un modèle de simplicité et d'intelligence «à la Colt.»

Tandridge Golf Club
1925
ENG - OXTED, Surrey RH8 9NQ

Office	Secrétariat	(44) 01883 - 712 274
Pro shop	Pro-shop	(44) 01883 - 713 701
Fax	Fax	(44) 01883 - 730 537
Situation	Situation	

10 km E of Reigate - 30 km from Central London

Annual closure	Fermeture annuelle	no
Weekly closure	Fermeture hebdomadaire	no

Fees main season Tarifs haute saison		18 holes
	Week days Semaine	We/Bank holidays We/Férié
Individual Individuel	£ 45*	—
Couple Couple	£ 90*	—

* Restricted to Monday, Wednesday and Thursday (please call in advance)

Caddy	Caddy	no
Electric Trolley	Chariot électrique	no
Buggy	Voiturette	no
Clubs	Clubs	£ 5/18 holes

Credit cards Cartes de crédit
VISA - Eurocard - MasterCard - AMEX - DC (Pro shop goods only)

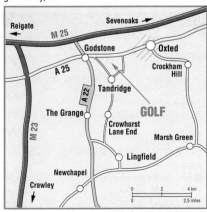

Access Accès : M 25 Jct 7. A22 South → East Grinstead. Left on A25 → Oxted. Golf Club 1.5 km (1 m) on the right. **Map 8 on page 503** Carte 8 Page 503

GOLF COURSE
PARCOURS
14/20

Site	Site	
Maintenance	Entretien	
Architect	Architecte	Harry S. Colt
Type	Type	parkland
Relief	Relief	
Water in play	Eau en jeu	
Exp. to wind	Exposé au vent	
Trees in play	Arbres en jeu	

Scorecard	Chp.	Mens	Ladies
Carte de score	Chp.	Mess.	Da.
Length Long.	5625	5270	4877
Par	70	68	71

Advised golfing ability	0	12	24	36
Niveau de jeu recommandé				
Hcp required	Handicap exigé	certificate		

CLUB HOUSE & AMENITIES
CLUB HOUSE ET ANNEXES
7/10

Pro shop	Pro-shop	
Driving range	Practice	
Sheltered	couvert	2 nets
On grass	sur herbe	yes
Putting-green	putting-green	yes
Pitching-green	pitching green	yes

HOTEL FACILITIES
ENVIRONNEMENT HOTELIER
6/10

HOTELS HÔTELS
Kings Arms — Westerham
16 rooms, D £ 75 — 8 km
Tel (44) 01959 - 562 990
Fax (44) 01959 - 561 240

Bridge House — Reigate
37 rooms, D £ 75 — 10 km
Tel (44) 01737 - 246 801
Fax (44) 01737 - 223 756

Cranleigh - 9 rooms, D £ 75 — Reigate 10 km
Tel (44) 01737 - 223 417
Fax (44) 01737 - 223 734

RESTAURANTS RESTAURANTS
The Dining Room — Reigate 10 km
Tel (44) 01737 - 226 650

The George Inn — Oxted 2 km

664

The very many changes made here were engineered cleverly enough for the course to preserve a sort of seamless feel. Only the recent addition of four lakes for irrigating the tee-boxes and greens probably raised a few eyebrows amongst the locals. This is a parkland course, so since most of the other layouts in the region have more of a links look to them, Tehidy Park adds an extra flavour to an already very comprehensive assortment. The only problem is that the course sometimes takes a while to dry out after rain. Aside from purely golfing considerations, we would recommend a visit here in the Spring, when the primroses, daffodils and violets are in bloom and the rhododendrons compound the already existing difficulties formed by trees, water and bunkers. Over an area that is not as expansive as you might think, you need to hit it straight and work on your recovery shots. More, the 3,000 new oak trees are still only saplings so big-hitters should make the most of it. A country course, close to the sea, and well worth a visit.

Les multiples transformations de ce parcours ont été faites assez habilement, bien que la création récente de quatre lacs pour l'irrigation des départs et des greens ait pu surprendre les anciens habitués du lieu. C'est un parc, et comme la plupart des autres parcours de la région sont plus ou moins apparentés aux links, Tehidy Park fournit une couleur supplémentaire à une palette très complète. En revanche, le parcours a parfois un peu de mal à évacuer l'humidité. En dehors de ses qualités purement golfiques, on recommandera la visite au printemps pour les primevères, les jonquilles et violettes, alors que les rhododendrons ajoutent aux difficultés représentées par les arbres, obstacles d'eau et autres bunkers. Dans cet espace, il convient d'être précis, et de travailler souvent la balle pour se récupérer. Que les frappeurs en profitent : les 3 000 nouveaux chênes n'ont pas encore beaucoup poussé.

Tehidy Park Golf Club — 1922

Tehidy
ENG - CAMBORNE, Cornwall TR14 0HH

Office	Secrétariat	(44) 01209 - 842 208
Pro shop	Pro-shop	(44) 01209 - 842 914
Fax	Fax	(44) 01209 - 843 680
Situation	Situation	

10 km W of Truro (pop 16 522) - 20 km SW of Newquay

Annual closure	Fermeture annuelle	no
Weekly closure	Fermeture hebdomadaire	no
Fees main season	Tarifs haute saison	18 holes

	Week days Semaine	We/Bank holidays We/Férié
Individual Individuel	£ 22.50	£ 27.50
Couple Couple	£ 45	£ 55

Caddy	Caddy	no
Electric Trolley	Chariot électrique	£ 4
Buggy	Voiturette	no
Clubs	Clubs	£ 5
Credit cards Cartes de crédit		no

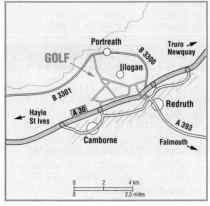

Access Accès : From Exeter, A30 → Penzance.
Exit Camborne/Pool. Right hand fork → Portreath and Tehidy Park GC (signs). At 2nd cross road jct, turn left. 400 m, Tehidy Park GC on left.
Map 4 on page 494 Carte 4 Page 494

GOLF COURSE / PARCOURS — 13/20

Site	Site	
Maintenance	Entretien	
Architect	Architecte	Unknown
Type	Type	inland, parkland
Relief	Relief	
Water in play	Eau en jeu	
Exp. to wind	Exposé au vent	
Trees in play	Arbres en jeu	

Scorecard Carte de score	Chp. Chp.	Mens Mess.	Ladies Da.
Length Long.	5620	5493	5084
Par	72	72	72

Advised golfing ability Niveau de jeu recommandé		0 12 24 36
Hcp required	Handicap exigé	certificate

CLUB HOUSE & AMENITIES / CLUB HOUSE ET ANNEXES — 7/10

Pro shop	Pro-shop	
Driving range	Practice	
Sheltered	couvert	
On grass	sur herbe	yes
Putting-green	putting-green	yes
Pitching-green	pitching green	yes

665

HOTEL FACILITIES / ENVIRONNEMENT HOTELIER — 6/10

HOTELS HÔTELS

Tyack's — Camborne
15 rooms, D £ 90 — on site
Tel (44) 01209 - 612 424, Fax (44) 01209 - 612 435

Alverton Manor — Truro
32 rooms, D £ 99 — 10 km
Tel (44) 01872 - 76 633, Fax (44) 01872 - 222 989

Aviary Court — Illogan
6 rooms, D £ 58 — 5 km
Tel (44) 01209 - 842 256, Fax (44) 01209 - 843 744

RESTAURANTS RESTAURANTS

Pennypots — Truro
Tel (44) 01209 - 820 347 — 10 km

Tricky Dickies — Redruth
Tel (44) 01209 - 219 292 — 3 km

If you don't know how important money and politics are in the choice of Ryder Cup sites, then you won't understand why this course (as others) has hosted the event so many times. This is a resort that is generally quite remarkable with a huge hotel, a whole number of activities on site and three 18-hole golf courses. The Brabazon is a good average parkland course, and as the rough is kept cropped most of the time to speed up play, these flat 18 holes lose something of their character. Actually, two holes here have built the course's reputation; the 10th, a driveable par 4 from the front tees (remember the Ryder Cup) but which most amateurs try to reach from the back. And the 18th, a remarkable high-risk par 4 where the bogey is generally enough to win your match. Having said that, this is a very pleasant and well-balanced course . However, when paying this sort of money to play, the golfer is entitled to expect a higher standard of technical challenge and a little more excitement.

Si l'on ne sait pas à quel point l'argent et la politique sont essentiels dans le choix des sites de la Ryder Cup, on ne comprend pas pourquoi ce parcours (comme d'autres) a reçu tant de fois cette épreuve mythique. Car s'il s'agit d'un «resort» de remarquable qualité générale, avec un immense hôtel et trois 18 trous, le «Brabazon Course» est dans la bonne moyenne des parcours «parkland» du genre. De plus, le rough étant bien coupé la plupart du temps pour accélérer le jeu, ces 18 trous perdent une partie de leur définition. En fait, deux trous ici ont fait la réputation du parcours, le 10, drivable des départs rouges (comme en Ryder Cup), mais que tous les amateurs essaient de driver des départs arrière, et le 18, remarquable par 4 à hauts risques, où un bogey est souvent suffisant pour gagner un match. Cela dit, c'est quand même un parcours très agréable et bien équilibré, mais on est en droit d'attendre un autre niveau technique et émotionnel aussi élevé que le green-fee....

The Belfry — 1977

ENG - WISHAW, North Warwickshire B76 9PR

Office	Secrétariat	(44) 01675 - 470 033
Pro shop	Pro-shop	(44) 01675 - 470 301
Fax	Fax	(44) 01675 - 470 178
Situation	Situation	

10 km from Birmingham (pop. 961 041)
7 km from Sutton Coldfield (pop. 106 001)

Annual closure	Fermeture annuelle	no
Weekly closure	Fermeture hebdomadaire	no

Fees main season	Tarifs haute saison	18 holes
	Week days Semaine	We/Bank holidays We/Férié
Individual Individuel	£ 85	£ 85
Couple Couple	£ 170	£ 170
Caddy Caddy	£ 25	
Electric Trolley Chariot électrique	no	
Buggy Voiturette	£ 30	
Clubs Clubs	£ 15	

Credit cards Cartes de crédit
VISA - Eurocard - MasterCard - AMEX - DC

666

Access Accès : From London: M42 Exit 9. Follow signs to Belfry From Birmingham: A38 to M6, then M42 North at Jct 4A. Exit 9 on M42. Follow signs to Belfry.
Map 7 on page 500 Carte 7 Page 500

GOLF COURSE PARCOURS — 15/20

Site	Site	▮▮▮▮▮▯
Maintenance	Entretien	▮▮▮▮▮▯
Architect	Architecte	Peter Alliss D. Thomas (remod.)
Type	Type	open country, parkland
Relief	Relief	▮▮▮▯▯▯
Water in play	Eau en jeu	▮▮▮▮▯▯
Exp. to wind	Exposé au vent	▮▮▮▯▯▯
Trees in play	Arbres en jeu	▮▮▮▮▯▯

Scorecard Carte de score	Chp. Chp.	Mens Mess.	Ladies Da.
Length Long.	6407	6052	5205
Par	72	72	73

Advised golfing ability		0 12 24 36
Niveau de jeu recommandé		▮▮▮
Hcp required	Handicap exigé	24 Men, 32 Ladies

CLUB HOUSE & AMENITIES CLUB HOUSE ET ANNEXES — 9/10

Pro shop	Pro-shop	▮▮▮▮▯
Driving range	Practice	▮▮▮▮▮
Sheltered	couvert	17 bays
On grass	sur herbe	no
Putting-green	putting-green	yes
Pitching-green	pitching green	no

HOTEL FACILITIES ENVIRONNEMENT HOTELIER — 8/10

HOTELS HÔTELS
The Belfry Hotel - 324 rooms, D £ 175   The Belfry on site
Tel (44) 01675 - 470 033, Fax (44) 01675 - 470 178

New Hall - 62 rooms, D £ 125   Sutton Coldfield 7 km
Tel (44) 0121 - 378 2442, Fax (44) 0121 - 378 4637

Jonathan's - 30 rooms, D £ 100   Birmingham 12 km
Tel (44) 0121 - 429 3757, Fax (44) 0121 - 434 3107

Asquith House - 10 rooms, D £ 67   Birmingham 12 km
Tel (44) 0121 - 454 5282, Fax (44) 0121 - 456 4668

RESTAURANTS RESTAURANTS
La Truffe   Sutton Coldfield 7 km
Tel (44) 0121 - 355 5836

Henry's (Chinese)   Birmingham 10 km
Tel (44) 0121 - 200 1136

French Restaurant   The Belfry
Tel (44) 01675 - 470 033   on site

It is already clear that with the short and tall rough left to grow freely the course would acquire greater definition on terrain that has little natural appeal and where the saplings still have a lot of growing to do. The slight movements of terrain carried out when creating the course would be given more shape and the whole course be more visually attractive. But, as with the Brabazon, the authorities that be have their sights set on a middle-class clientele with money to spend. They also want to enjoy their golf, so scaring them off with tall rough is out of the question. We would recommend that they and others play from the front tees, as a number of water hazards turn very dangerous from the tips (particularly the 4th and 8th). The bunkers have been carefully designed (Dave Thomas style) and decisively brought into play, although some greens can still be reached with bump 'n roll shots. The green-fee is less expensive (well, a little) than at the Brabazon and the layout is almost more likeable than its elder, so much so that perhaps a composite 18 hole setting from the two courses might provide a battlefield with some excitement for the next Ryder Cup.

On devine ici qu'en laissant pousser les roughs et haut roughs, on donnerait un peu plus de mouvement à un terrain sans intérêt naturel, tant que les arbres plantés n'ont pas vraiment grandi. Les légers mouvements de terrain qui ont été créés prendraient qplus d'acuité, et l'oeil serait aussi plus intéressé. Mais, comme pour le «Brabazon», on vise ici une clientèle de niveau moyen, assez argentée, et peut être désireuse de se faire plaisir. On leur conseillera d'ailleurs les départs avancés, car certains obstacles d'eau sont très dangereux depuis le fond (4 et 8 notamment). Les bunkers sont dessinés avec soin (à la Dave Thomas), mis en jeu avec détermination, bien qu'il soit parfois possible de rejoindre les greens en roulant. Le green-fee est (un peu) moins élevé qu'au «Brabazon», et on a presque plus de sympathie pour ce tracé, au point qu'un 18 trous composite des deux ne serait pas si mal pour une Ryder Cup.

The Belfry   1997

ENG - WISHAW, North Warwickshire B76 9PR

Office	Secrétariat	(44) 01675 - 470 033
Pro shop	Pro-shop	(44) 01675 - 470 301
Fax	Fax	(44) 01675 - 470 178
Situation	Situation	

10 km from Birmingham (pop. 961 041)
7 km from Sutton Coldfield (pop. 106 001)

Annual closure	Fermeture annuelle	no
Weekly closure	Fermeture hebdomadaire	no
Fees main season	Tarifs haute saison	18 holes

	Week days Semaine	We/Bank holidays We/Férié
Individual Individuel	£ 70	£ 70
Couple Couple	£ 140	£ 140
Caddy	Caddy	£ 25
Electric Trolley	Chariot électrique	no
Buggy	Voiturette	£ 30
Clubs	Clubs	£ 15

Credit cards Cartes de crédit
VISA - Eurocard - MasterCard - AMEX - DC

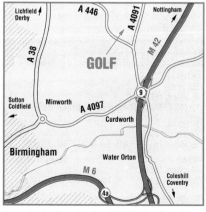

Access Accès : From London: M42 Exit 9. Follow signs to Belfry From Birmingham: A38 to M6, then M42 North at Jct 4A. Exit 9 on M42. Follow signs to Belfry.
Map 7 on page 500 Carte 7 Page 500

GOLF COURSE PARCOURS   15/20

Site	Site	
Maintenance	Entretien	
Architect	Architecte	Dave Thomas
Type	Type	open country, parkland
Relief	Relief	
Water in play	Eau en jeu	
Exp. to wind	Exposé au vent	
Trees in play	Arbres en jeu	

Scorecard Carte de score	Chp. Chp.	Mens Mess.	Ladies Da.
Length Long.	6365	6064	5175
Par	72	72	73

Advised golfing ability Niveau de jeu recommandé	0 12 24 36
Hcp required Handicap exigé	24 Men, 32 Ladies

CLUB HOUSE & AMENITIES CLUB HOUSE ET ANNEXES   9/10

Pro shop	Pro-shop	
Driving range	Practice	
Sheltered	couvert	17 bays
On grass	sur herbe	no
Putting-green	putting-green	yes
Pitching-green	pitching green	no

667

HOTEL FACILITIES ENVIRONNEMENT HOTELIER   8/10

HOTELS HÔTELS
The Belfry Hotel - 324 rooms, D £ 175   The Belfry on site
Tel (44) 01675 - 470 033, Fax (44) 01675 - 470 178

New Hall   Sutton Coldfield
62 rooms, D £ 125   7 km
Tel (44) 0121 - 378 2442, Fax (44) 0121 - 378 4637

Jonathan's - 30 rooms, D £ 100   Birmingham 12 km
Tel (44) 0121 - 429 3757, Fax (44) 0121 - 434 3107

Asquith House - 10 rooms, D £ 67   Birmingham 12 km
Tel (44) 0121 - 454 5282, Fax (44) 0121 - 456 4668

RESTAURANTS RESTAURANTS
La Truffe   Sutton Coldfield
Tel (44) 0121 - 355 5836   7 km

Henry's (Chinese)   Birmingham
Tel (44) 0121 - 200 1136   10 km

French Restaurant   The Belfry
Tel (44) 01675 - 470 033   on site

Between the pretty Georgian town of Swaffham, the national stud-farm of Newmarket, the Neolithic site of Grimes Graves and the beautiful medieval town of Norwich, you might find the time to play this 1912 course which was restyled and lengthened by Donald Steel in 1985. A pity perhaps that the fairways are so wide, but they do prompt the bigger-hitters to open their shoulders and dispatch their ball into the waiting fairway bunkers. There are trees, of course, but not all that close to the fairways. When they do come close, it is to complicate your second shot. Very pretty, calm, well-balanced and with pleasant springy turf over sandy sub-soil, Thetford is not the course of the century but it does enable golfers of all levels to play together very easily. For the less experienced player, however, we would shamelessly recommend the front tees.

Entre les visites de la jolie ville georgienne de Swaffham, du haras national de Newmarket, du site néolithique de Grimes Graves et de la belle ville médiévale de Norwich, il vous restera probablement quelques heures pour jouer ce parcours de 1912, mais remodelé et allongé par Donald Steel en 1985. On regrette que les fairways soient très larges, mais ils incitent les frappeurs à se déchaîner... et à expédier leurs balles dans les bunkers de fairway ! Certes, on trouve aussi des arbres, mais ils ne sont pas très proches des fairways, et quand ils le sont, c'est plutôt pour gêner les seconds coups. Très joli, très calme, bien équilibré, avec un gazon très agréable sur un sol de sable et de tourbe, Thetford n'est pas le parcours du siècle, mais il permet au moins à tous les niveaux d'évoluer en bonne harmonie. On conseillera cependant aux joueurs peu expérimentés de choisir sans honte les départs avancés

Thetford Golf Club — 1912

Brandon Road
ENG - THETFORD, Norfolk IP24 3NE

Office	Secrétariat	(44) 01842 - 752 258
Pro shop	Pro-shop	(44) 01842 - 752 662
Fax	Fax	
Situation	Situation	

2 km from Thetford (pop. 19 900)
50 km from Cambridge (pop. 91 935)

Annual closure	Fermeture annuelle	no
Weekly closure	Fermeture hebdomadaire	no

Fees main season Tarifs haute saison		18 holes
	Week days Semaine	We/Bank holidays We/Férié
Individual Individuel	£ 32	—
Couple Couple	£ 64	—

No visitors during weekends & public holidays
Booking essential

Caddy	Caddy	no
Electric Trolley	Chariot électrique	no
Buggy	Voiturette	no
Clubs	Clubs	no

Credit cards Cartes de crédit
Visa - Mastercard - AMEX (Pro shop goods only)

Access Accès : London M11. Jct 9, A11 → Norwich.
Thetford Bypass B1107 → Brandon, Golf 500 m on the left. **Map 7 on page 501** Carte 7 Page 501

GOLF COURSE PARCOURS — 14/20

Site	Site	
Maintenance	Entretien	
Architect	Architecte	C.H. Mayo Donald Steel (1985)
Type	Type	inland, forest
Relief	Relief	
Water in play	Eau en jeu	
Exp. to wind	Exposé au vent	
Trees in play	Arbres en jeu	

Scorecard Carte de score	Chp. Chp.	Mens Mess.	Ladies Da.
Length Long.	6190	5970	5405
Par	72	72	74

Advised golfing ability		0	12	24	36
Niveau de jeu recommandé					
Hcp required	Handicap exigé	no			

CLUB HOUSE & AMENITIES CLUB HOUSE ET ANNEXES — 7/10

Pro shop	Pro-shop	
Driving range	Practice	
Sheltered	couvert	no
On grass	sur herbe	yes
Putting-green	putting-green	yes
Pitching-green	pitching green	yes

HOTEL FACILITIES ENVIRONNEMENT HOTELIER — 5/10

HOTELS HÔTELS
Bell Hotel — Thetford
46 rooms, D £ 70 — 2 km
Tel (44) 01842 - 754 455, Fax (44) 01842 - 755 552

Strattons — Swaffham
7 rooms, D £ 78 — 25 km
Tel (44) 01760 - 723 845, Fax (44) 01760 - 720 458

Angel — Bury St Edmunds
41 rooms, D £ 90 — 20 km
Tel (44) 01284 - 753 926, Fax (44) 01284 - 750 092

RESTAURANTS RESTAURANTS
Mortimer's — Bury St Edmunds
Tel (44) 01284 - 760623 — 20 km

Strattons - Tel (44) 01760 - 723845 — Swaffham 25 km

Theobalds - Tel (44) 01359 - 231707 — Ixworth 17 km

Essex is not really a golfing county like Surrey, for example, on the other side of London. But some of the courses here do stand out, like this one, laid out in 1920 over a former hunting estate which sports a gigantic neo-classical mansion where everyone seems to speak in whispered tones. The clubhouse is more modern and less imposing, but jacket and tie are required. This is one course of the hundreds designed by Harry Colt, as intelligent in its layout, as imaginative in its use of the land and as fair and open as the others. When you realise how few technical resources they had at the time (1920), it makes you think how much many modern designers could learn from this style of layout. Of course, like many British courses from another age, this one lacks length but the vast majority of players won't complain. A course for everyone, even the best.

L'Essex n'est pas vraiment une région à golf comme peut l'être le Surrey par exemple, de l'autre côté de Londres. Mais quelques parcours se distinguent comme celui-ci, créé en 1920 dans un ancien domaine de chasse orné d'une gigantesque bâtisse néo-classique que l'on dénomme «mansion,» et dans laquelle on doit parler à voix basse. Le Clubhouse est plus moderne, moins imposant, mais on y porte veste et cravate. C'est un parcours parmi les centaines créés par Harry Colt, aussi intelligent dans son déroulement, imaginatif dans son utilisation du terrain, aussi franc et honnête que les autres. Quand on imagine le manque de moyens techniques à l'époque (1920), bien des architectes modernes devraient y prendre des leçons. Bien sûr, comme la plupart des parcours britanniques d'autrefois, il manque de longueur, mais l'immense majorité des joueurs ne s'en plaindra pas. Pour tous, même les meilleurs.

Thorndon Park Golf Club		1920
Ingrave		
ENG - BRENTWOOD, Essex CM13 3RH		
Office	Secrétariat	(44) 01277 - 811 666
Pro shop	Pro-shop	(44) 01277 - 810 736
Fax	Fax	
Situation	Situation	
3 km from Brentwood (pop. 70 600)		
35 km from Central London (pop. 6 679 700)		
Annual closure	Fermeture annuelle	no
Weekly closure	Fermeture hebdomadaire	no
Fees main season	Tarifs haute saison	18 holes

	Week days Semaine	We/Bank holidays We/Férié
Individual Individuel	£ 30	—
Couple Couple	£ 60	—
Booking essential - No visitors at weekends		
Caddy	Caddy	no
Electric Trolley	Chariot électrique	no
Buggy	Voiturette	no
Clubs	Clubs	£ 5/18 holes

Credit cards Cartes de crédit
Visa - Mastercard (Pro shop goods only)

Access Accès : London E, A11 then A12 to Brentwood.
A 128 SE → East Horndon. Golf on the right.
Map 7 on page 501 Carte 7 Page 501

GOLF COURSE
PARCOURS
14/20

Site	Site	
Maintenance	Entretien	
Architect	Architecte	Harry S. Colt
Type	Type	parkland, inland
Relief	Relief	
Water in play	Eau en jeu	
Exp. to wind	Exposé au vent	
Trees in play	Arbres en jeu	

Scorecard	Chp.	Mens	Ladies
Carte de score	Chp.	Mess.	Da.
Length Long.	5845	5620	4580
Par	71	71	72

Advised golfing ability	0	12	24	36
Niveau de jeu recommandé				
Hcp required	Handicap exigé	certificate		

CLUB HOUSE & AMENITIES
CLUB HOUSE ET ANNEXES
7/10

Pro shop	Pro-shop	
Driving range	Practice	
Sheltered	couvert	no
On grass	sur herbe	yes
Putting-green	putting-green	yes
Pitching-green	pitching green	no

HOTEL FACILITIES
ENVIRONNEMENT HOTELIER
6/10

HOTELS HÔTELS
Forte Posthouse   Brentwood
113 rooms, D £ 69   5 km
Tel (44) 01277 - 260 260, Fax (44) 01277 - 264 264

Marygreen Manor   Brentwood
32 rooms, D £ 110   6 km
Tel (44) 01277 - 225 252, Fax (44) 01277 - 262 809

Forte Travelodge   East Horndon
22 rooms, D £ 35   4 km
Tel (44) 01277 - 810 819

Ivy Hill - 34 rooms, D £ 85   Ingatestone 12 km
Tel (44) 01277 - 353 040, Fax (44) 01277 - 355 038

RESTAURANTS RESTAURANTS
Marygreen Manor   Brentwood
Tel (44) 01277 - 225 252   6 km

Forte Posthouse   Brentwood
Tel (44) 01277 - 260 260   5 km

669

Thorpeness is just outside Aldeburgh, not far from Minsmere nature reserve in Dunwich, where you can watch an incredible variety of birds. The hotel-clubhouse is excellent and makes this a fine destination, especially since there is an abundance of good courses round and about (Ipswich, Aldeburgh, Woodbridge, Felixstowe Ferry, etc.). This one was initially designed in 1923 by James Braid and slightly re-shaped in 1965. Here, you keep out of the heather and avoid the lupins, very pretty when in flower but not the ideal place to put your ball. An uncomplicated layout, prepared to make life easier for the average golfer, but one which requires good placing of the ball, so don't think twice about playing an iron off the tee (except perhaps for the half a dozen long par 4s). Other landmarks to cap a very pleasant day's golfing are a wind-mill, a curious «house in the clouds» and an unsightly nuclear power station in the distance.

Thorpeness est juste à l'extérieur d'Aldeburgh, non loin de la réserve naturelle de Minsmere à Dunwich, d'où l'on peut observer une incroyable variété d'oiseaux. L'Hôtel-Clubhouse est de grande qualité, ce qui en fait une destination tout à fait agréable, d'autant que les bons parcours alentour ne manquent pas (Ipswich, Aldeburgh, Woodbridge, Felixstowe Ferry...). Celui-ci a été dessiné par James Braid en 1923, et légèrement retouché vers 1965. On veillera à éviter les bruyères et les buissons de lupin, très jolis en fleur, mais dont il vaut mieux ne pas s'approcher avec une balle de golf. Ce tracé sans histoires, préparé pour faciliter les choses, nécessite avant tout un bon placement : il ne faut pas hésiter à jouer des fers au départ, sauf sur la demi-douzaine de longs par 4. Pour décorer une très agréable journée, un moulin à vent, un curieuse «maison dans les nuages,» et une centrale nucléaire au loin, pas bien belle.

Thorpeness Golf Club — 1923
ENG - THORPENESS, Suffolk IP16 4NH

Office	Secrétariat	(44) 01728 - 452 176
Pro shop	Pro-shop	(44) 01728 - 454 926
Fax	Fax	(44) 01728 - 453 869
Situation	Situation	

3 km from Aldeburgh (pop. 2 654)
39 km from Ipswich (pop. 130 157)

Annual closure	Fermeture annuelle	no
Weekly closure	Fermeture hebdomadaire	no

Fees main season Tarifs haute saison — 18 holes

	Week days Semaine	We/Bank holidays We/Férié
Individual Individuel	£ 25	£ 30
Couple Couple	£ 50	£ 60
Under 18: £ 15 (full day) - After 3.00 pm £ 15 / £ 18		

Caddy	Caddy	no
Electric Trolley	Chariot électrique	£ 5/18 holes
Buggy	Voiturette	£ 30/18 holes
Clubs	Clubs	no

Credit cards Cartes de crédit VISA - MasterCard

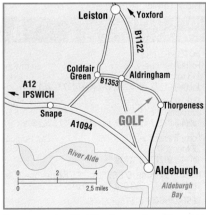

Access Accès : Ipswich A12 → Saxmundham. Turn right on B119 → Leiston. At Leiston, turn right on B1353
Map 7 on page 501 Carte 7 Page 501

GOLF COURSE / PARCOURS — 14/20

Site	Site	
Maintenance	Entretien	
Architect	Architecte	James Braid
Type	Type	seaside course, open country
Relief	Relief	
Water in play	Eau en jeu	
Exp. to wind	Exposé au vent	
Trees in play	Arbres en jeu	

Scorecard Carte de score	Chp. Chp.	Mens Mess.	Ladies Da.
Length Long.	5645	5674	4922
Par	69	69	74

Advised golfing ability — 0 12 24 36
Niveau de jeu recommandé
Hcp required Handicap exigé — certificate

CLUB HOUSE & AMENITIES / CLUB HOUSE ET ANNEXES — 7/10

Pro shop	Pro-shop	
Driving range	Practice	
Sheltered	couvert	no
On grass	sur herbe	yes
Putting-green	putting-green	yes
Pitching-green	pitching green	yes

HOTEL FACILITIES / ENVIRONNEMENT HOTELIER — 7/10

HOTELS HÔTELS

Thorpeness GC Hotel — Thorpeness on site
30 rooms, £ 85 pp (Green fee included)
Tel (44) 01728 - 452 176, Fax (44) 01728 - 453 868

Wentworth Hotel — Aldeburgh 4 km
38 rooms, D £ 70
Tel (44) 01728 - 452 312, Fax (44) 01728 - 454 343

Brudenell — Aldeburgh 4 km
47 rooms, D £ 90
Tel (44) 01728 - 452 071, Fax (44) 01728 - 454 082

RESTAURANTS RESTAURANTS

Thorpeness GC Hotel — Thorpeness on site
Tel (44) 01728 - 452176

New Regatta — Aldeburgh 4 km
Tel (44) 01728 - 452011

670

THURLESTONE

This is a magnificent spot where you savour every moment along a rugged coastline with rocky cliffs and pounding waves. This course is beside the sea, but most of the holes are pretty high up. Only the dunes are missing to make this a text-book links course, although the sandy soil is just right and the layout well worthy of the label. After much hesitation, the original short 9 hole course was happily extended and altered by Harry Colt; the back 9 are 1,000 yards longer than the front 9 and have added a good deal of zip to the course. The first seven holes are short, rather treacherous and very technical in style, while the remainder are longer and more open but still to be played with care and caution when the wind blows. In windy weather, punchers of the ball will have fun while the others can always divide their score by two or else admire the landscape and visit the region.

C'est un magnifique endroit à savourer chaque instant le long d'une côte tourmentée, avec d'impressionnantes falaises où la mer livre ses assauts. Ce parcours est situé en bordure de mer, mais la plupart des trous sont bien en hauteur. Il ne manque que les dunes pour en faire un links comme dans les livres, mais le sol sablonneux a la qualité requise, et le dessin est à la hauteur. Après bien des hésitations, le petit 9 trous initial fut heureusement modifié et agrandi par Harry Colt : le retour est près de 1000 mètres plus long que l'aller et a donné de la vigueur au tracé. Les sept premiers trous sont courts, assez traîtres et très techniques, les suivants plus longs et ouverts, à négocier avec attention et prudence quand le vent souffle. Les «puncheurs» de balles pourront alors s'y régaler, les autres diviseront leur score par deux, à moins de se contenter d'admirer le paysage ou de visiter la région.

Thurlestone Golf Club — 1897

Thurlestone
ENG - KINGSBRIDGE, S. Devon TQ7 3NZ

Office	Secrétariat	(44) 01548 - 560 405
Pro shop	Pro-shop	(44) 01548 - 560 715
Fax	Fax	(44) 01548 - 560 405
Situation	Situation	

6 km W of Kingsbridge (pop. 5 081) - 8 km W of Salcombe

Annual closure	Fermeture annuelle	no
Weekly closure	Fermeture hebdomadaire	no

Fees main season	Tarifs haute saison	18 holes
	Week days	We/Bank holidays
	Semaine	We/Férié
Individual Individuel	£ 26	£ 26
Couple Couple	£ 52	£ 52
£ 13 under 17 years		

Caddy	Caddy	no
Electric Trolley	Chariot électrique	£ 10/day
Buggy	Voiturette	no
Clubs	Clubs	£ 10/day

Credit cards Cartes de crédit
Visa - Mastercard (Pro shop goods only)

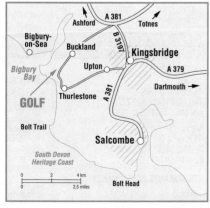

Access Accès : M5, then A38, A382 to Newton Abbott, then A381 through Totnes and Kingsbridge. In Sutton, → South Milton and Thurlestone. Follow signs.
Map 6 on page 498 Carte 6 Page 498

GOLF COURSE / PARCOURS — 16/20

Site	Site	
Maintenance	Entretien	
Architect	Architecte	Harry S. Colt
Type	Type	seaside course, open country
Relief	Relief	
Water in play	Eau en jeu	
Exp. to wind	Exposé au vent	
Trees in play	Arbres en jeu	

Scorecard / Carte de score	Chp. / Chp.	Mens / Mess.	Ladies / Da.
Length Long.	5770	5626	5086
Par	71	71	73

Advised golfing ability	0	12	24	36
Niveau de jeu recommandé				
Hcp required	Handicap exigé	28 Men, 36 Ladies		

CLUB HOUSE & AMENITIES / CLUB HOUSE ET ANNEXES — 6/10

Pro shop	Pro-shop	
Driving range	Practice	
Sheltered	couvert	no
On grass	sur herbe	yes
Putting-green	putting-green	yes
Pitching-green	pitching green	yes

HOTEL FACILITIES / ENVIRONNEMENT HOTELIER — 4/10

HOTELS HÔTELS
Thurlestone Hotel — Thurlestone
68 rooms, D £ 90 — cn site
Tel (44) 01548 - 560 382
Fax (44) 01548 - 561 069

Henley — Bigbury-on-Sea
7 rooms, D £ 80 (dinner inc.)
Tel (44) 01548 - 810 240
Fax (44) 01548 - 810 020

RESTAURANTS RESTAURANT
Church House — Churchstow
Tel (44) 01548 - 852 237 — 6 km

671

With tighter fairways and rough as wild as the tops of the dunes, Trevose would be much more difficult. But this is first and foremost a holiday location, where regular golfers return each year with their children. The kids eventually get to play the «big» 18-hole course after cutting their teeth on the two 9-holers. Spectacular, charming and technical, Trevose is a course for golfers of all levels where the best players will never grow tired. This Harry Colt layout is highly strategic and very honest, even though not all the hazards are visible, but there are seldom any really unpleasant surprises. They say that a friendly atmosphere adds to the pleasure of playing golf, and that is certainly true here, even with the wind. And that King Arthur met Merlin the Wizard nearby. It might even have been over a meal in the clubhouse, because the food is excellent.

Avec des fairways plus étroits, un rough aussi sauvage que les sommets des dunes, Trevose serait bien plus difficile encore. Mais c'est d'abord un lieu de vacances, où les habitués reviennent chaque année, avec les enfants qui finissent un jour par passer au «grand» 18 trous après avoir débuté et pris de l'expérience sur les deux 9 trous. Spectaculaire, plein de charme, technique, Trevose est un parcours pour tous les niveaux, où les meilleurs ne s'ennuient jamais. Le dessin de Harry Colt est très stratégique et très franc, même si les obstacles ne sont pas tous bien visibles, mais on a rarement de mauvaises surprises. On dit qu'une atmosphère amicale contribue au plaisir du jeu, c'est bien le cas ici, même avec le vent. Le Roi Arthur aurait rencontré l'Enchanteur Merlin dans les environs, c'était peut-être ici au Clubhouse, car les repas sont excellents.

Trevose Golf & Country Club — 1925

Constantine Bay
ENG - PADSTOW, Cornwall PL28 8J13

Office	Secrétariat	(44) 01841 - 520 208
Pro shop	Pro-shop	(44) 01841 - 520 261
Fax	Fax	(44) 01841 - 521 057
Situation	Situation	

6 km from Padstow (pop. 4 250)

Annual closure	Fermeture annuelle	no
Weekly closure	Fermeture hebdomadaire	no
Fees main season	Tarifs haute saison	18 holes

	Week days Semaine	We/Bank holidays We/Férié
Individual Individuel	£ 33	£ 33
Couple Couple	£ 66	£ 66

low season, £ 22 / mid-season, £ 28

Caddy	Caddy	no
Electric Trolley	Chariot électrique	£ 5/18 holes
Buggy	Voiturette	£ 17/18 holes
Clubs	Clubs	no

Credit cards Cartes de crédit
VISA - MasterCard (except bar)

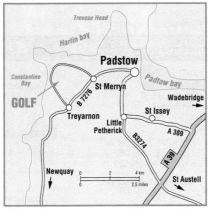

Access Accès : M5 Exit 31, then A30 (→ Exeter) through Bodwin, then B3274 on right after Victoria → Padstow. → St Merryn. Follow signs to golf.
Map 6 on page 498 Carte 6 Page 498

GOLF COURSE PARCOURS — 17/20

Site	Site	
Maintenance	Entretien	
Architect	Architecte	Harry S. Colt
Type	Type	seaside course, links
Relief	Relief	
Water in play	Eau en jeu	
Exp. to wind	Exposé au vent	
Trees in play	Arbres en jeu	

Scorecard Carte de score	Chp. Chp.	Mens Mess.	Ladies Da.
Length Long.	5947	5792	5142
Par	71	71	73

Advised golfing ability Niveau de jeu recommandé	0	12	24	36

Hcp required Handicap exigé — 28 Men, 36 Ladies

CLUB HOUSE & AMENITIES CLUB HOUSE ET ANNEXES — 7/10

Pro shop	Pro-shop	
Driving range	Practice	
Sheltered	couvert	no
On grass	sur herbe	yes
Putting-green	putting-green	yes
Pitching-green	pitching green	yes

HOTEL FACILITIES ENVIRONNEMENT HOTELIER — 7/10

HOTELS HÔTELS

Treglos — Constantine Bay
41 rooms, D £ 65 — 1 km
Tel (44) 01841 - 520 727
Fax (44) 01841 - 521 163

Metropole — Padstow
44 rooms, D £ 100 — 5 km
Tel (44) 01841 - 532 486
Fax (44) 01841 - 532 867

RESTAURANTS RESTAURANTS

Seafood — Padstow
Tel (44) 01841 - 532 485 — 5 km

St Petroc's Bistro — Padstow
Tel (44) 01841 - 532 700 — 5 km

672

What with coastal erosion having washed away three of the original holes and the problems of ownership which caused some bad blood and the need to borrow less favourable terrain, the course has evolved considerably since its creation. Today, everything seems to have settled down. Laid out on more hilly landscape than its (near) neighbour Hoylake, Wallasey requires a lot of serious thought as to where to place your drive in order to attack the greens from the best position and keep well away from the dunes, bushes and fairway bunkers (few in number but the penalty is always high). With that said, the pleasure you get from hitting good recovery shots on this sort of course is such that you might almost stray off the straight and narrow deliberately in order to add to your fond memories. So try match-play, or even the stableford points system, whose homonymous inventor came from Wallasey and certainly knew a thing or two about the problems of counting a score once you reach a certain number.

L'érosion de la côte ayant supprimé trois des trous originaux, des problèmes de propriété ayant empoisonné le club, le parcours a évolué depuis sa création, devant emprunter des terrains moins favorables, mais tout cela semble résolu. Dans un paysage plus mouvementé que celui de son (presque) voisin Royal Liverpool, Wallasey demande quelque réflexion sur le placement des drives afin d'attaquer les greens en bonne position, et ne pas se retrouver dans les dunes, les buissons, les bunkers de fairway - peu nombreux mais pénalisants. Cela dit, le plaisir de réussir les recoveries sur ce genre de parcours est tel que l'on pourrait presque faire exprès de s'égarer pour se fabriquer des souvenirs ! Alors, jouez en match-play, ou en stableford, l'inventeur de la formule qui porte son nom venait d'ici, il savait donc à quoi s'en tenir sur la difficulté de compter à partir d'un certain chiffre.

Wallasey Golf Club — 1891
Bayswater Road
ENG - WALLASEY, Cheshire L45 8LA

Office	Secrétariat	(44) 0151 - 691 1024
Pro shop	Pro-shop	(44) 0151 - 638 3888
Fax	Fax	(44) 0151 - 691 1024
Situation	Situation	

5 km from Liverpool (pop. 452 450)

Annual closure	Fermeture annuelle	no
Weekly closure	Fermeture hebdomadaire	no

Fees main season Tarifs haute saison — 18 holes

	Week days Semaine	We/Bank holidays We/Férié
Individual Individuel	£ 27	£ 32
Couple Couple	£ 54	£ 64

Full weekdays: £ 32/full weekend days: £ 37

Caddy	Caddy	on request/£ 25
Electric Trolley	Chariot électrique	no
Buggy	Voiturette	no
Clubs	Clubs	no

Credit cards Cartes de crédit
VISA - Eurocard - MasterCard - AMEX - DC
(Pro shop goods only)

GOLF COURSE / PARCOURS — 17/20

Site	Site	▮▮▮▮▮▮▯
Maintenance	Entretien	▮▮▮▮▮▮▮
Architect	Architecte	Tom Morris/J. Braid Taylor/Hawtree...
Type	Type	seaside course, links
Relief	Relief	▮▮▮▯▯▯▯
Water in play	Eau en jeu	▮▯▯▯▯▯▯
Exp. to wind	Exposé au vent	▮▮▮▮▮▯▯
Trees in play	Arbres en play	▮▯▯▯▯▯▯

Scorecard / Carte de score	Chp. / Chp.	Mens / Mess.	Ladies / Da.
Length Long.	5946	5710	5241
Par	72	72	74

Advised golfing ability — 0 12 24 36
Niveau de jeu recommandé — ▮▮▮▮▮▮▯
Hcp required — Handicap exigé — certificate

CLUB HOUSE & AMENITIES / CLUB HOUSE ET ANNEXES — 7/10

Pro shop	Pro-shop	▮▮▮▮▮▮▯
Driving range	Practice	▮▮▯▯▯▯▯
Sheltered	couvert	no
On grass	sur herbe	no
Putting-green	putting-green	yes
Pitching-green	pitching green	yes

673

HOTEL FACILITIES / ENVIRONNEMENT HOTELIER — 7/10

HOTELS HÔTELS
Grove Hotel - 14 rooms, D £ 50 — Wallasey 2 km
Tel (44) 0151 - 630 4558, Fax (44) 0151 - 639 0028

Leasowe Castle Hotel — Moreton
22 rooms, D £ 66 — 2 km
Tel (44) 0151 - 606 9191, Fax (44) 0151 - 678 5551

Bowler Hat — Birkenhead
32 rooms, D £ 85 — 3 km
Tel (44) 0151 - 652 4931, Fax (44) 0151 - 653 8127

Twelfth Man Lodge — Greasby
30 rooms, D £ 39 — 4 km
Tel (44) 0151 - 677 5445, Fax (44) 0151 - 678 5085

RESTAURANTS RESTAURANTS
Grove Hotel - Tel (44) 0151 - 630 4558 — Wallasey 2 km
Lee Ho - Tel (44) 0151 - 677 6440 — Moreton 2 km

Access Accès : Liverpool, Wallasey tunnel to Jct 1.
Follow signs to New Brighton. Golf on A 551.
Map 5 on page 497 Carte 5 Page 497

The history of Walton Heath is closely tied to politics, with many members being Ministers (including Winston Churchill in his younger days) or Peers. The Prince of Wales was club captain in 1935, but apparently that was not enough for the club to receive the royal seal. Soil and space are both ideal here, despite being so close to London, but sand and heather land were of no use to farmers in those days. The wind can be an important factor here, as the course is high up. There are trees, but they don't detract from a great feeling of open space, or relieve the anxiety as you eye the ubiquitous heather and wonder how on earth anyone could ever get out of there. It is especially dangerous on the 12th hole, where you need a long drive to have any hope of reaching a very well-protected green. Although this «New» course is not easy, the members will tell you that it is two shots easier than its «Old» neighbour. We suggest you check that out for yourself.

L' histoire de Walton Heath est étroitement liée à la politique, avec quantité de membres ministres, dont Winston Churchill, ou appartenant à la Chambre des Lords. Le Prince de Galles en a été capitaine en 1935, sans que le club en soit annobli pour autant. Les parcours ont eu un sol idéal, et de l'espace, même à proximité de Londres car les terres de sable et de bruyère étaient inutilisées pour l'agriculture. Le vent y est un facteur important, car nous sommes ici en hauteur. Malgré la présence des arbres, on éprouve une grande sensation d'espace, avec un soupçon d'inquiétude devant l'omniprésence de la bruyère, dont aucun traité ne vous enseigne comment en sortir. Elle est spécialement dangereuse au 12, où il faut un long drive pour espérer toucher le green très défendu. Bien que ce «New» ne soit pas facile, les membres vous diront qu'il est de deux coups plus facile que le «Old.» A vérifier par vous-même !

Walton Heath Golf Club — 1904
Deans Lane, Walton-on-the-Hill
ENG - TADWORTH, Surrey, KT20 7TP

Office	Secrétariat	(44) 01737 - 812 380
Pro shop	Pro-shop	(44) 01737 - 812 152
Fax	Fax	(44) 01737 - 814 225
Situation	Situation	

7 km from Reigate (pop. 52 010) - 5 km from Epsom

Annual closure	Fermeture annuelle	no
Weekly closure	Fermeture hebdomadaire	no
Fees main season	Tarifs haute saison	18 holes

	Week days Semaine	We/Bank holidays We/Férié
Individual Individuel	£ 67	—
Couple Couple	£ 134	—

Weekends: visitors only with a member

Caddy	Caddy	on request/£ 20+tip
Electric Trolley	Chariot électrique	no
Buggy	Voiturette	no
Clubs	Clubs	£ 7.50/18 holes

Credit cards Cartes de crédit
VISA - Eurocard - MasterCard - AMEX - JCB

Access Accès : M25 Jct 8. A217 → Sutton. After 3 km (2 m.) B270 into Mill Lane, then left along B2032. Deans Lane on the right after 1.5 km (1 m.).
Map 8 on page 503 Carte 8 Page 503

674

GOLF COURSE / PARCOURS — 16/20

Site	Site	
Maintenance	Entretien	
Architect	Architecte	
Type	Type	inland, heathland
Relief	Relief	
Water in play	Eau en jeu	
Exp. to wind	Exposé au vent	
Trees in play	Arbres en jeu	

Scorecard Carte de score	Chp. Chp.	Mens Mess.	Ladies Da.
Length Long.	5948	5643	5328
Par	72	72	74

Advised golfing ability	0	12	24	36
Niveau de jeu recommandé				

Hcp required Handicap exigé — certificate

CLUB HOUSE & AMENITIES / CLUB HOUSE ET ANNEXES — 7/10

Pro shop	Pro-shop	
Driving range	Practice	
Sheltered	couvert	2 indoor nets
On grass	sur herbe	yes
Putting-green	putting-green	yes
Pitching-green	pitching green	yes

HOTEL FACILITIES / ENVIRONNEMENT HOTELIER — 6/10

HOTELS HÔTELS

Nutfield Priory — Redhill
52 rooms, D £ 120 — 7 km
Tel (44) 01737 - 822 066, Fax (44) 01737 - 823 321

Bridge House — Reigate
37 rooms, D £ 75 — 4 km
Tel (44) 01737 - 246 801, Fax (44) 01737 - 223 756

Cranleigh — Reigate
9 rooms, D £ 75 — 7 km
Tel (44) 01737 - 223 417, Fax (44) 01737 - 223 734

RESTAURANTS RESTAURANTS

Gemini - Tel (44) 01737 - 812179 — Tadworth 2 km

The Dining Room — Reigate
Tel (44) 01737 - 226 650 — 7 km

La Barbe — Reigate
Tel (44) 01737 - 241 966 — 7 km

Herbert Fowler designed the courses for this club where James Braid was the first professional. He was here for 50 years and although his name does not figure anywhere, it would be hard to imagine him never having retouched the original layout here and there, or never having given others the benefit of his invaluable advice. With the soft turf, the layout and even the sensation of space, you might think yourself on a links course, if it weren't for the pine, birch and oak trees, and the heather. And when the wind blows (this is the highest spot in Surrey), the illusion is complete. The wide, deep bunkers are a feature you'll remember for many a month, as they outline the holes to perfection and attract any ball sailing slightly off course. The greens are well grassed, fast, fair and particularly well defended. A difficult course with its very own character, but every golfer will improve his game here as long as he remembers the one basic rule of golf... humility.

Herbert Fowler a dessiné les parcours de ce club dont James Braid a été le premier professionnel. Il y est resté pendant plus de 50 ans, et si son nom n'apparaît pas, on imagine mal qu'il n'ait jamais eu à retoucher çà et là le dessin original, ou à donner quelques précieux conseils. Par la qualité du gazon comme par le dessin ou même la sensation d'espace, on pourait se croire sur un links, n'était la présence de pins, de bouleaux, de chênes et de bruyère. Et quand le vent souffle (c'est le plus haut point du Surrey), l'illusion est complète. Les bunkers larges et profonds sont un élément dont on se souvient, tant ils dessinent les trous à la perfection, en attirant les balles un peu trop écartées. Les greens sont bien fournis, rapides et francs, et surtout très défendus. C'est un parcours difficile, au caractère bien marqué, mais tous les joueurs y feront des progrès s'ils l'abordent avec modestie.

Walton Heath Golf Club — 1903

Deans Lane, Walton-on-the-Hill
ENG - TADWORTH, Surrey, KT20 7TP

Office	Secrétariat	(44) 01737 - 812 380
Pro shop	Pro-shop	(44) 01737 - 812 152
Fax	Fax	(44) 01737 - 814 225
Situation	Situation	

7 km from Reigate (pop. 52 010) - 5 km from Epsom

Annual closure	Fermeture annuelle	no
Weekly closure	Fermeture hebdomadaire	no
Fees main season	Tarifs haute saison	18 holes

	Week days Semaine	We/Bank holidays We/Férié
Individual Individuel	£ 67	—
Couple Couple	£ 134	—
Weekends: only with a member		

Caddy	Caddy	on request/£ 20+tip
Electric Trolley	Chariot électrique	no
Buggy	Voiturette	no
Clubs	Clubs	£ 7.50/18 holes

Credit cards Cartes de crédit
VISA - Eurocard - MasterCard - AMEX - JCB

Access Accès : M25 Jct 8. A217 → Sutton. After 3 km (2 m.) B270 into Mill Lane, then left along B2032. Deans Lane on the right after 1.5 km (1 m.).
Map 8 on page 503 Carte 8 Page 503

GOLF COURSE / PARCOURS — 18/20

Site	Site	
Maintenance	Entretien	
Architect	Architecte	Herbert Fowler
Type	Type	inland, heathland
Relief	Relief	
Water in play	Eau en jeu	
Exp. to wind	Exposé au vent	
Trees in play	Arbres en jeu	

Scorecard Carte de score	Chp. Chp.	Mens Mess.	Ladies Da.
Length Long.	6121	5705	5346
Par	72	71	74

Advised golfing ability Niveau de jeu recommandé	0	12	24	36
Hcp required Handicap exigé	certificate			

CLUB HOUSE & AMENITIES / CLUB HOUSE ET ANNEXES — 7/10

Pro shop	Pro-shop	
Driving range	Practice	
Sheltered	couvert	2 indoor nets
On grass	sur herbe	yes
Putting-green	putting-green	yes
Pitching-green	pitching green	yes

HOTEL FACILITIES / ENVIRONNEMENT HOTELIER — 7/10

HOTELS HÔTELS

Nutfield Priory — Redhill
52 rooms, D £ 120 — 7 km
Tel (44) 01737 - 822 066, Fax (44) 01737 - 823 321

Bridge House — Reigate
37 rooms, D £ 75 — 4 km
Tel (44) 01737 - 246 801, Fax (44) 01737 - 223 756

Cranleigh — Reigate
9 rooms, D £ 75 — 7 km
Tel (44) 01737 - 223 417, Fax (44) 01737 - 223 734

RESTAURANTS RESTAURANTS

Gemini — Tadworth
Tel (44) 01737 - 812179 — 2 km

The Dining Room — Reigate
Tel (44) 01737 - 226 650 — 7 km

La Barbe — Reigate
Tel (44) 01737 - 241 966 — 7 km

675

WARWICKSHIRE (THE)

This is a complex of four inter-combinable nine-hole courses. The East and North courses are rather hilly, the South and West courses are simply sloping. Karl Litten's design is unashamedly American with a lot of dangerous water hazards (except on the North where there are more trees). Carefully placing your shots is important, and if you are an attacking player you should follow your instinct, as any hesitation can cost you dearly. The greens must be attacked with high shots, but when we visited they were very firm and so will surely cause problems for average-players. The length of each hole is such that we would suggest the forward tees for all except the very good player, and would recommend beginners to head for the pitch 'n putt course. With a very flexible combination of courses, spectacular golf and very modern facilities, this is a very well designed resort but not quite as hospitable as it could be. Our advice: rent a buggy and shoot 36 holes.

C'est un ensemble de quatre fois neuf trous combinables, l'Est et le Nord étant assez accidentés, le Sud et l'Ouest simplement ondulés. L'architecture de Karl Litten est américaine sans honte, avec beaucoup d'obstacles d'eau dangereux (sauf le Nord, plus arboré). Il est partout nécessaire de bien placer la balle, mais aussi d'attaquer sans réserves si on a ce caractère, car les hésitations ne pardonnent pas. Les greens doivent être attaqués comme des cibles, mais ils étaient très fermes lors de notre visite, ce qui ne facilitait pas la tâche des joueurs moyens. La longueur de chacun des neuf trous incite à ne recommander les départs arrière qu'aux très bons amateurs, et à conseiller aux presque débutants d'aller sur le parcours de par 3. Flexible dans ses combinaisons, spectaculaire, avec des équipements très modernes, c'est un ensemble très bien conçu, mais pas vraiment chaleureux. Notre conseil : 36 trous en voiturette.

The Warwickshire — 1993

Leek Wootton
ENG - WARWICK, Warwickshire CV35 7QT

Office	Secrétariat	(44) 01926 - 409 409
Pro shop	Pro-shop	(44) 01926 - 409 409
Fax	Fax	(44) 01926 - 408 409
Situation	Situation	

5 km N of Warwick (pop. 22 709)
13 km S of Coventry (pop. 294 387)

Annual closure	Fermeture annuelle	no
Weekly closure	Fermeture hebdomadaire	no

Fees main season	Tarifs haute saison	18 holes
	Week days Semaine	**We/Bank holidays** We/Férié
Individual Individuel	£ 40	£ 40
Couple Couple	£ 80	£ 80

Many golf packages for 36 holes, different fees in winter and summer

Caddy	Caddy	on request/£ 30
Electric Trolley	Chariot électrique	no
Buggy	Voiturette	£ 20/18 holes
Clubs	Clubs	£ 12.50/18 holes

Credit cards Cartes de crédit
VISA - Eurocard - MasterCard - AMEX

Access Accès : M40 Jct 15, then A46 → Coventry.
Follow signs to Leek Wootton (B4115).
Map 7 on page 500 Carte 7 Page 500

GOLF COURSE / PARCOURS — 15/20

Site	Site	
Maintenance	Entretien	
Architect	Architecte	Karl Litten
Type	Type	parkland
Relief	Relief	
Water in play	Eau en jeu	
Exp. to wind	Exposé au vent	
Trees in play	Arbres en jeu	

Scorecard / Carte de score	Chp. / Chp.	Mens / Mess.	Ladies / Da.
Length Long.	6500	6000	5000
Par	72	72	72

Advised golfing ability Niveau de jeu recommandé	0	12	24	36
Hcp required Handicap exigé	certificate			

CLUB HOUSE & AMENITIES / CLUB HOUSE ET ANNEXES — 7/10

Pro shop	Pro-shop	
Driving range	Practice	
Sheltered	couvert	10 bays
On grass	sur herbe	no
Putting-green	putting-green	yes
Pitching-green	pitching green	yes

HOTEL FACILITIES / ENVIRONNEMENT HOTELIER — 8/10

HOTELS HÔTELS
Chesford Grange - 150 rooms, D £ 90 Kenilworth 3 km
Tel (44) 01926 - 859 331, Fax (44) 01926 - 859 075

De Montfort - 96 rooms, D £ 95 Kenilworth 4 km
Tel (44) 01926 - 855 944, Fax (44) 01926 - 857 830

Mallory Court Royal Leamington Spa
10 rooms, D £ 200+ 4 km
Tel (44) 01926 - 330 214, Fax (44) 01926 - 451 714

Manor House (Forte) Royal Leamington Spa
53 rooms, D £ 80 4 km
Tel (44) 01926 - 423 251, Fax (44) 01926 - 425 933

RESTAURANTS RESTAURANTS
Simpson's - Tel (44) 01926 - 864 567 Kenilworth 4 km
Bosquet - Tel (44) 01926 - 852 463 Kenilworth 4 km
Les Plantagenets Royal Leamington Spa
Tel (44) 01926 - 453 171 4 km

If you don't get lost in the very comfortable and totally gigantic clubhouse at Wentworth (a little over the top, maybe?), try to forget the West course and go for the East. This was the first course laid out at Wentworth by Harry Colt and many prefer it to its illustrious neighbour. It simply has not had the benefit of the same rejuvenation programmes nor maybe the same standard of green-keeping, but the soil is more pleasant (sand) and drier, and the heather adds a touch of colour. It is difficult to explain other than that we felt this a more «cheerful» layout, without the same severity that you find on the West course. Very fair and with some very amusing greens, this course has been under-estimated for too long. The full Wentworth complex has been supplemented with a third course, «Edinburgh», which despite everything it has to offer is not necessarily worth a green-fee of some £85!

Si vous ne vous êtes pas perdu dans le Clubhouse très confortable et totalement gigantesque (un peu «too much?») de Wentworth, tournez un jour le dos au «West» et dirigez-vous vers «l'East.» Ce fut le premier des parcours dessinés par Harry Colt à Wentworth, et beaucoup le préfèrent à son illustre voisin. Il n'a simplement pas bénéficié des mêmes programmes de rajeunissement, ni peut-être du même entretien, mais le sol y est plus agréable (c'est du sable), plus sec, et la bruyère ajoute une touche de couleur. Il est difficile d'expliquer autrement qu'en disant qu'il est plus «souriant,» dénué de cette sévérité que l'on peut trouver au parcours West. Franc, avec des greens souvent amusants, ce parcours a été trop longtemps sous-estimé. Cet ensemble de Wentworth a été complété par un troisième parcours, «Edinburgh» qui, en dépit de ses qualités, ne vaut certainement pas un green-fee de 85 Livres...

Wentworth Golf Club — 1924

Wentworth Drive
ENG - VIRGINIA WATER, Surrey GU25 4 LS

Office	Secrétariat	(44) 01344 - 842 201
Pro shop	Pro-shop	(44) 01344 - 843 353
Fax	Fax	(44) 01344 - 842 804
Situation	Situation	

7 km from Ascot (pop. 150 244)
10 km from Staines (pop. 51 167)

Annual closure	Fermeture annuelle	no
Weekly closure	Fermeture hebdomadaire	no
Fees main season	Tarifs haute saison	18 holes

	Week days Semaine	We/Bank holidays We/Férié
Individual Individuel	£ 85	—
Couple Couple	£ 170	—

No visitors at weekends

Caddy	Caddy	on request/£ 25+tip
Electric Trolley	Chariot électrique	no
Buggy	Voiturette	£ 35/18 holes
Clubs	Clubs	£ 25/18 holes

Credit cards Cartes de crédit
VISA - Eurocard - MasterCard - AMEX - DC

Access Accès : London, A30. Left road opposite A329 turning to Ascot.
Map 8 on page 502 Carte 8 Page 502

GOLF COURSE / PARCOURS — 16/20

Site	Site	
Maintenance	Entretien	
Architect	Architecte	Harry S. Colt
Type	Type	inland, forest
Relief	Relief	
Water in play	Eau en jeu	
Exp. to wind	Exposé au vent	
Trees in play	Arbres en jeu	

Scorecard Carte de score	Chp. Chp.	Mens Mess.	Ladies Da.
Length Long.	5558	5354	4855
Par	68	68	72

Advised golfing ability		0 12 24 36
Niveau de jeu recommandé		
Hcp required	Handicap exigé	28 Men, 36 Ladies

CLUB HOUSE & AMENITIES / CLUB HOUSE ET ANNEXES — 8/10

Pro shop	Pro-shop	
Driving range	Practice	
Sheltered	couvert	10 mats
On grass	sur herbe	yes
Putting-green	putting-green	yes
Pitching-green	pitching green	yes

HOTEL FACILITIES / ENVIRONNEMENT HOTELIER — 7/10

HOTELS HÔTELS

Royal Berkshire - 60 rooms, D £ 140   Sunninghill 3 km
Tel (44) 01344 - 23 322, Fax (44) 01344 - 27 100

Berystede - 90 rooms, D £ 120   Sunninghill 5 km
Tel (44) 01344 - 23 311, Fax (44) 01344 - 872 301

Great Fosters   Egham
42 rooms, D £ 140   5 km
Tel (44) 01784 - 433 822, Fax (44) 01784 - 472 455

Thames Lodge   Staines
44 rooms, D £ 95   10 km
Tel (44) 01784 - 464 433, Fax (44) 01784 - 454 858

RESTAURANTS RESTAURANTS

Stateroom (Royal Berkshire)   Sunninghill
Tel (44) 01344 - 23 322   3 km

Royal Forresters   Ascot
Tel (44) 01344 - 884 747   5 km

677

This is one of those courses that has become familiar to many through the staging here every year of the PGA and the World Match-Play Championships. The price of the green-fee is such that you'd better get here in good shape if you really want to enjoy your day. Another solution is to take advantage of the special rates and play between October and March, although the landscape is not always very pretty at that time of year. You just get a clearer view of some of the superb houses on this very exclusive site. The «West» course is a great test of golf, where the yardage book will prove most handy to get a clearer idea of the position of difficulties, particularly some not very visible ditches. The positioning of hazards here is subtlety itself and nothing is left to chance. Your game must be absolutely tip-top, with a lot of inspiration to boot in the tricky run from the 13th to the 15th holes. Our judgment is a little more reserved for the two par 5s at the end of a course which is unquestionably one of the best inland layouts in England.

Ce parcours est de ceux que la télévision a rendus familiers, grâce au PGA Championship et au World Match-Play qui s'y disputent tous les ans. Et le prix du green-fee est tel qu'il faut y arriver en forme pour vraiment savourer sa journée, ou alors profiter de tarifs spéciaux d'octobre à mars, mais le paysage n'est pas très gai à cette période, sauf que les vues sont plus dégagées sur les superbes maisons de ce domaine très exclusif. Le parcours «Ouest» est un grand test de golf, où le carnet de parcours sera fort utile pour identifier les difficultés, notamment des fossés pas très visibles. Le placement des obstacles est d'une subtilité exceptionnelle, et rien de bon ici n'est dû au hasard. Il faut un jeu absolument complet, et beaucoup d'inspiration dans le très délicat passage du 13 au 15. On sera plus réservé sur les deux par 5 clôturant ce parcours, qui reste incontestablement l'un des meilleurs «inland» du pays.

Wentworth Golf Club — 1926

Wentworth Drive
ENG - VIRGINIA WATER, Surrey GU25 4 LS

Office	Secrétariat	(44) 01344 - 842 201
Pro shop	Pro-shop	(44) 01344 - 843 353
Fax	Fax	(44) 01344 - 842 804
Situation	Situation	

7 km from Ascot (pop. 150 244)
10 km from Staines (pop. 51 167)

Annual closure	Fermeture annuelle	no
Weekly closure	Fermeture hebdomadaire	no

Fees main season	Tarifs haute saison	18 holes
	Week days Semaine	We/Bank holidays We/Férié
Individual Individuel	£ 140	—
Couple Couple	£ 280	—

No visitors at weekends -
Reduced greenfees from October to March

Caddy	Caddy	on request/£ 25+tip
Electric Trolley	Chariot électrique	no
Buggy	Voiturette	£ 35/18 holes
Clubs	Clubs	£ 25/18 holes

Credit cards Cartes de crédit
VISA - Eurocard - MasterCard - AMEX - DC

678

Access Accès : London, A30. Left road opposite A329 turning to Ascot. **Map 8 on page 502** Carte 8 Page 502

GOLF COURSE PARCOURS — 18/20

Site	Site	
Maintenance	Entretien	
Architect	Architecte	Harry S. Colt
Type	Type	inland, forest
Relief	Relief	
Water in play	Eau en jeu	
Exp. to wind	Exposé au vent	
Trees in play	Arbres en jeu	

Scorecard Carte de score	Chp. Chp.	Mens Mess.	Ladies Da.
Length Long.	6261	6008	5440
Par	73	73	75

Advised golfing ability Niveau de jeu recommandé	0	12	24	36

Hcp required Handicap exigé — 24 Men, 32 Ladies

CLUB HOUSE & AMENITIES CLUB HOUSE ET ANNEXES — 8/10

Pro shop	Pro-shop	
Driving range	Practice	
Sheltered	couvert	10 mats
On grass	sur herbe	yes
Putting-green	putting-green	yes
Pitching-green	pitching green	yes

HOTEL FACILITIES ENVIRONNEMENT HOTELIER — 7/10

HOTELS HÔTELS
Royal Berkshire - 60 rooms, D £ 140   Sunninghill 3 km
Tel (44) 01344 - 23 322, Fax (44) 01344 - 27 100

Berystede - 90 rooms, D £ 120   Sunninghill 5 km
Tel (44) 01344 - 23 311, Fax (44) 01344 - 872 301

Great Fosters - 42 rooms, D £ 140   Egham 5 km
Tel (44) 01784 - 433 822, Fax (44) 01784 - 472 455

Thames Lodge   Staines
44 rooms, D £ 95   10 km
Tel (44) 01784 - 464 433, Fax (44) 01784 - 454 858

RESTAURANTS RESTAURANTS

Stateroom (Royal Berkshire)   Sunninghill
Tel (44) 01344 - 23 322   3 km

Royal Forresters   Ascot
Tel (44) 01344 - 884 747   5 km

Without wishing to appear «reactionary», there are a number of trends in modern course design which don't always go down very well. Take the length of the par 5s here, for example, and particularly hole N°5, which is a full 635 yards. Admittedly professional golfers hit the ball further than they used to, but this can be a windy course, the ground can often be wet and while the normal tee-boxes bring everything down to more human proportions, there must be a happy medium somewhere for good golfers who don't have to be huge-hitters. It is a pity that such an ambitious facility, with some magnificent views, seems to have forgotten somewhat that playing golf is about enjoyment, that the aim of the game is not for a golfer to end up on his knees with his swing in tatters. Even though the course is flat, you will appreciate this very interesting and often captivating layout much more in a buggy, competing with friends more than with the course.

Sans être un vieux réactionnaire, on peut ne pas apprécier certaines tendances des architectes modernes. Ici, tous les par 5 le sont vraiment, le trou n°5 atteignant 570 mètres (635 yards). Il est vrai que les pros tapent plus fort qu'avant, mais le vent n'est pas rare ici, le sol peut être humide (non ?), et si les départs «normaux» ramènent les trous à des proportions normales, il y a sans doute un juste milieu pour les golfeurs d'un bon niveau sans carrure d'athlètes. Il est dommage qu'un équipement aussi ambitieux, offrant des vues magnifiques, ait un peu oublié la dimension de plaisir du joueur, ou, en tout cas, qu'il ne doit pas finir à genoux et le swing en compote. Même si le terrain est très plat, on appréciera beaucoup plus en voiturette ce tracé intéressant et souvent captivant, en dehors de tout esprit de compétition, sauf bien sûr avec les amis.

West Berkshire Golf Club		1978
Chaddleworth		
ENG - NEWBURY, Berks RG16 0HS		

Office	Secrétariat	(44) 01488 - 638 574
Pro shop	Pro-shop	(44) 01488 - 638 851
Fax	Fax	(44) 01488 - 638 781
Situation	Situation	

8 km NW from Newbury (pop. 136 700)
7 km NE of Hungerford (pop. 6 174)

Annual closure	Fermeture annuelle	no
Weekly closure	Fermeture hebdomadaire	no

Fees main season	Tarifs haute saison	18 holes
	Week days Semaine	**We/Bank holidays** We/Férié
Individual Individuel	£ 18	£ 22
Couple Couple	£ 36	£ 44

Full weekday: £ 26 - Visitors after 12.30 pm at weekends

Caddy	Caddy	no
Electric Trolley	Chariot électrique	no
Buggy	Voiturette	£ 10/18 holes
Clubs	Clubs	£ 10/18 holes

Credit cards Cartes de crédit VISA - MasterCard

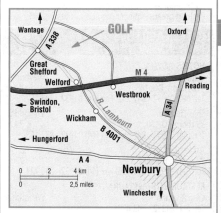

Access Accès : London M4. Jct 14 A338, → RAF Welford, Club house on right.
Map 7 on page 500 Carte 7 Page 500

GOLF COURSE
PARCOURS

15/20

Site	Site	
Maintenance	Entretien	
Architect	Architecte	John Stagg
Type	Type	open country
Relief	Relief	
Water in play	Eau en jeu	
Exp. to wind	Exposé au vent	
Trees in play	Arbres en jeu	

Scorecard Carte de score	**Chp.** Chp.	**Mens** Mess.	**Ladies** Da.
Length Long.	6353	5618	5200
Par	73	73	74

Advised golfing ability Niveau de jeu recommandé	0	12	24	36

Hcp required	Handicap exigé	no

CLUB HOUSE & AMENITIES
CLUB HOUSE ET ANNEXES

7/10

Pro shop	Pro-shop	
Driving range	Practice	
Sheltered	couvert	no
On grass	sur herbe	yes
Putting-green	putting-green	yes
Pitching-green	pitching green	yes

HOTEL FACILITIES
ENVIRONNEMENT HOTELIER

7/10

679

HOTELS HÔTELS

Bear at Hungerford		Hungerford
41 rooms, D £ 85		7 km
Tel (44) 01488 - 682 512		
Fax (44) 01488 - 684 357		

Three Swans		Hungerford
15 rooms, D £ 70		7 km
Tel (44) 01488 - 682 721		
Fax (44) 01488 - 681 708		

Stakis Newbury		Newbury
109 rooms, D £ 90		8 km
Tel (44) 01635 - 247 010, Fax (44) 01635 - 247 077		

RESTAURANTS RESTAURANTS

Just William's		Hungerford
Tel (44) 01488 - 681 199		7 km
Blue Boar Inn		Newbury
Tel (44) 01635 - 248 236		4 km

Although the club-house is situated close to the road, you still get the impression of being in the heart of Surrey's tree-covered countryside and find it hard to imagine that in such green surroundings a drought virtually killed the fairways here some years back. This is a rather flat course where the difficulties are clearly visible, but no-one ever said that seeing was avoiding. It is made even narrower than the trees suggest by the position of fairway bunkers, especially on the 16th, where the fairway slopes towards the sand hazards. This long hole is part of an excellent finishing stretch with the 15th, ending in a very undulating green, the 17th, a very well-guarded par 3, and the 18th, where you can risk it and go for the green in two. These last four holes are in fact what make West Byfleet a good course rather than just a pretty one, although it is still not quite in the very top class. The course being open on week-ends is in pleasant contrast with the other top courses in the region, but book a tee-time all the same.

Bien que le Club house soit situé près de la route, on garde l'impression d'être effectivement dans les belles parties boisées de la campagne du Surrey. C'est un parcours assez plat où les difficultés sont bien visibles mais il ne suffit pas de les voir pour les éviter : il est rendu plus étroit encore que les arbres ne l'indiquent par le placement des bunkers de fairway, en particulier au 16 où les pentes du fairway inclinent vers ces obstacles. Ce long trou fait partie d'un finale de très bonne qualité, avec le 15 et son green très modelé du 15, le 17 (par 3) avec ses solides défenses, le 18, où l'on peut être tenté d'attaquer le green en 2, mais avec des risques. ce sont en fait ces quatre trous qui font passer West Byfleet du statut de joli parcours à celui de bon parcours. Et le fait qu'il soit ouvert en week-end tranche singulièrement avec les autres grands parcours de la région, mais il est prudent de réserver un départ.

West Byfleet Golf Club — 1906

Sheerwater Road
ENG - WEST BYFLEET, Surrey KT14 6AA

Office	Secrétariat	(44) 01932 - 345 230
Pro shop	Pro-shop	(44) 01932 - 346 584
Fax	Fax	(44) 01932 - 346 584
Situation	Situation	

40 km from London (pop. 6 679 699)
2 km from Weybridge (pop. 7 919)

Annual closure	Fermeture annuelle	no
Weekly closure	Fermeture hebdomadaire	no

Fees main season
Tarifs haute saison full day

	Week days Semaine	We/Bank holidays We/Férié
Individual Individuel	£ 38.50	£ 38.50
Couple Couple	£ 77	£ 77

Caddy	Caddy	£ 25
Electric Trolley	Chariot électrique	£ 5
Buggy	Voiturette	£ 20
Clubs	Clubs	£ 11

Credit cards Cartes de crédit
VISA- Eurocard - MasterCard - AMEX - DC - JCB

680

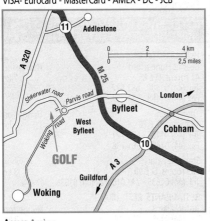

Addlestone
Byfleet
London
West Byfleet
Cobham
GOLF
Guildford
Woking

0 — 2 — 4 km
0 — 2,5 miles

A 320 / M 25 / A 3

11 / 10

Sheerwater road / Parvis road / Woking road

Access Accès :
Map 8 on page 503 Carte 8 Page 503

GOLF COURSE / PARCOURS — 14/20

Site	Site	
Maintenance	Entretien	
Architect	Architecte	Mr Buchanan
Type	Type	inland, parkland
Relief	Relief	
Water in play	Eau en jeu	
Exp. to wind	Exposé au vent	
Trees in play	Arbres en jeu	

Scorecard Carte de score	Chp. Chp.	Mens Mess.	Ladies Da.
Length Long.	5590	5307	5087
Par	70	70	72

Advised golfing ability Niveau de jeu recommandé	0	12	24	36
Hcp required Handicap exigé	24			

CLUB HOUSE & AMENITIES / CLUB HOUSE ET ANNEXES — 6/10

Pro shop	Pro-shop	
Driving range	Practice	
Sheltered	couvert	under construction
On grass	sur herbe	yes
Putting-green	putting-green	yes
Pitching-green	pitching green	yes

HOTEL FACILITIES / ENVIRONNEMENT HOTELIER — 8/10

HOTELS HÔTELS

Oatlands Park — Weybridge
112 rooms, D £ 145 — 4 km
Tel (44) 01932 - 847 242, Fax (44) 01932 - 842 252

Ship Thistle — Weybridge
39 rooms, D 120 — 3 km
Tel (44) 01932 - 848 364, Fax (44) 01932 - 857 153

Ashley Park — Walton-on-Thames
29 rooms, D £ 80 — 7 km
Tel (44) 01932 - 220 196, Fax (44) 01932 - 248 721

RESTAURANTS RESTAURANTS

Casa Romana — Weybridge
Tel (44) 01932 - 843 470 — 3 km

Edwinns — Sheperton
Tel (44) 01932 - 223 543 — 8 km

On the first hole at West Cornwall, you understand the religious and sporting nature of the game of golf, as you line up your drive on the steeple of the village church, the birthplace of Jim Barnes, one of the few British golfers to have won both the British and the US Opens. The course has not changed much since his time. It is rather short and a little devious in that the sloping terrain can easily draw your ball off the fairway. At the same time the railway line exerts a strange attraction on slicers over four holes. Once you are out of «Calamity Corner», where two par 3s and a short par 4 (holes 5 to 7) have ruined many a card, you will need a cool head for the remaining 11 holes in the dunes, up until the 18th, where you are in for a gentle landing downhill. A very natural and imaginative course, West Cornwall is excellent golfing before visiting the pretty fishing village and the artists of Saint Ives.

Le premier trou de West Cornwall permet de comprendre la nature religieuse et sportive du golf, il faut s'aligner sur le clocher de l'église du village où est né Jim Barnes, l'un des rares Britanniques à avoir remporté le British et l'US Open. Et le parcours n'a pas dû changer beaucoup. Assez court, il n'est pas d'une parfaite franchise, car les pentes peuvent sortir la balle du fairway, et la voie ferrée attire étrangement les sliceurs sur quatre trous. Une fois sorti indemne de «Calamity Corner,» où deux par 3 et un minuscule par 4 (du 5 au 7) ont détruit bien des cartes, il faut garder son sang-froid pour les onze trous restant, toujours dans les dunes, et jusqu'au 18, un atterrissage en douceur et en descente. Très naturel et imaginatif, West Cornwall est un parcours à connaître, avant d'aller flâner à St Ives, joli village de pêcheurs et d'artistes.

West Cornwall Golf Club — 1889

Church Lane, Lelant
ENG - ST IVES, Cornwall TR26 3D2

Office	Secrétariat	(44) 01736 - 753 401
Pro shop	Pro-shop	(44) 01736 - 753 177
Fax	Fax	
Situation	Situation	

3 km SE of St Ives (pop. 7 254)
16 km NE of Penzance (pop. 20 284)

Annual closure	Fermeture annuelle	no
Weekly closure	Fermeture hebdomadaire	no

Fees main season
Tarifs haute saison full day

	Week days Semaine	We/Bank holidays We/Férié
Individual Individuel	£ 20	£ 25
Couple Couple	£ 40	£ 50

half price when playing with a member

Caddy	Caddy	no
Electric Trolley	Chariot électrique	no
Buggy	Voiturette	no
Clubs	Clubs	£ 10/day

Credit cards Cartes de crédit
Visa - Eurocard - Mastercard (Pro shop goods only)

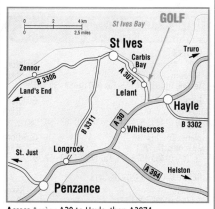

GOLF

St Ives Bay
St Ives
Carbis Bay
Truro
Zennor
B 3306
Land's End
Lelant
Hayle
B 3311
Whitecross
B 3302
St. Just
Longrock
A 394
Helston
Penzance

Access Accès : A30 to Hayle, then A3074
(Golf signposted)
Map 6 on page 498 Carte 6 Page 498

GOLF COURSE / PARCOURS — 16/20

Site	Site	
Maintenance	Entretien	
Architect	Architecte	Reverend Tyack, vicar of Lelant...
Type	Type	seaside course, links
Relief	Relief	
Water in play	Eau en jeu	
Exp. to wind	Exposé au vent	
Trees in play	Arbres en jeu	

Scorecard Carte de score	Chp. Chp.	Mens Mess.	Ladies Da.
Length Long.	5354	5180	4890
Par	69	69	73

Advised golfing ability Niveau de jeu recommandé	0	12	24	36
Hcp required	Handicap exigé		28 Men, 36 Ladies	

CLUB HOUSE & AMENITIES / CLUB HOUSE ET ANNEXES — 7/10

Pro shop	Pro-shop	
Driving range	Practice	
Sheltered	couvert	no
On grass	sur herbe	yes
Putting-green	putting-green	yes
Pitching-green	pitching green	yes

HOTEL FACILITIES / ENVIRONNEMENT HOTELIER — 6/10

HOTELS HÔTELS

Boskerris		Carbis Bay
19 rooms, D £ 60		2 km
Tel (44) 01736 - 795 295		
Fax (44) 01736 - 798 632		
Porthminster		St Ives
46 rooms, D £ 90		4 km
Tel (44) 01736 - 795 221		
Fax (44) 01736 - 797 043		
Ped'n Olva		St Ives
35 rooms, D £ 50		4 km
Tel (44) 01736 - 796 222		
Fax (44) 01736 - 797 710		

RESTAURANTS RESTAURANT
Pig'n'Fish - Tel (44) 01736 - 794 204 — St Ives 4 km

681

This is the third of a compact threesome of courses, the other two being virtual neighbours Woking and Worplesdon. In fact these are three courses belonging to the same club, and each has its own personality. We suppose you are bound to prefer one of the three, but each to his own, as they say. West Hill is very short and only moderately contoured over land strewn with pines, birch and conifers. The heather narrows the fairways and even cuts them in two on the 5th and 17th holes, two par 5s where that age-old decision arises once again: do I carry the hazard or lay up short? In fact the whole course calls for constant thought on the best way of driving, hitting the second shot and approaching the greens. This is why it is always such fun to play. A natural and well-landscaped course whose sandy soil drains easily, West Hill has inimitable charm, matched only perhaps by the other two «Ws»...

C'est le troisième d'un trio compact, avec Woking et Worplesdon, pratiquement voisins. Comme s'il s'agissait de trois parcours d'un même club, alors que chacun a préservé sa personnalité. Que l'on préfère l'un à l'autre est in-évitable, mais «chacun a son goût.» West Hill est très court, avec un relief très modéré, et un espace arboré de pins, de bouleaux et de sapins. La bruyère rétrécit les fairways, et vient parfois même les interrompre comme au 5 et au 17, deux par 5 où il faut prendre la décision de risquer de passer ou de rester court. L'ensemble du par-cours demande une réflexion constante sur la meilleure façon de driver, de jouer le second coup, d'approcher, c'est pourquoi il reste aussi amusant. Naturel et bien paysagé, bien draînant avec son sol sablonneux, West Hill a un charme inimitable, sauf par les deux autres «W,» peut-être...

West Hill Golf Club — 1909
Bagshot Road
ENG - BROOKWOOD, Surrey GU24 0BH

Office	Secrétariat	(44) 01483 - 474 365
Pro shop	Pro-shop	(44) 01483 - 473 172
Fax	Fax	(44) 01483 - 474 252
Situation	Situation	

8 km from Guildford (pop. 122 378) - 6 km from Woking

Annual closure	Fermeture annuelle	no
Weekly closure	Fermeture hebdomadaire	no

Fees main season — Tarifs haute saison — full day

	Week days Semaine	We/Bank holidays We/Férié
Individual Individuel	£ 45	—
Couple Couple	£ 90	—

Weekends: only with a member

Caddy	Caddy	on request/£ 20+tip
Electric Trolley	Chariot électrique	no
Buggy	Voiturette	no
Clubs	Clubs	£ 30/18 holes

Credit cards Cartes de crédit
VISA - Eurocard - AMEX (not for greenfees)

682

Access Accès : London A3 → Guildford. At Cobham, A245 on right. Through Woking. At Brookwood, turn left on A322 → Guildford. Entrance on left next to railway bridge. Map 8 on page 502 Carte 8 Page 502

GOLF COURSE PARCOURS — 15/20

Site	Site	
Maintenance	Entretien	
Architect	Architecte	Willie Park Jack White
Type	Type	inland, heathland
Relief	Relief	
Water in play	Eau en jeu	
Exp. to wind	Exposé au vent	
Trees in play	Arbres en jeu	

Scorecard Carte de score	Chp. Chp.	Mens Mess.	Ladies Da.
Length Long.	5731	5731	0
Par	69	69	0

Advised golfing ability Niveau de jeu recommandé	0	12	24	36

Hcp required — Handicap exigé — certificate

CLUB HOUSE & AMENITIES
CLUB HOUSE ET ANNEXES — 6/10

Pro shop	Pro-shop	
Driving range	Practice	
Sheltered	couvert	2 mats
On grass	sur herbe	yes
Putting-green	putting-green	yes
Pitching-green	pitching green	no

HOTEL FACILITIES
ENVIRONNEMENT HOTELIER — 6/10

HOTELS HÔTELS
Angel Posting House — Guildford
18 rooms, D £ 105 — 8 km
Tel (44) 01483 - 64 555, Fax (44) 01483 - 33 770

Forte Crest — Guildford
109 rooms, D £ 109 — 8 km
Tel (44) 01483 - 574 444, Fax (44) 01483 - 302 960

Blanes Court Hotel — Guildford
29 rooms, D £ 70 — 8 km
Tel (44) 01483 - 573 171, Fax (44) 01483 - 32 780

RESTAURANTS RESTAURANTS
Michel's — Ripley
Tel (44) 01483 - 224 777 — 10 km

Café de Paris — Guildford
Tel (44) 01483 - 34 896 — 8 km

The string of great courses running from Liverpool to Southport is unmatched anywhere in the world. And although West Lancashire is undoubtedly one of them, it has seldom staged top tournaments. The views over the Mersey estuary and the Welsh mountains are superb from the clubhouse, yet are less visible from the actual course, which lies sheltered behind a line of dunes. This is not a very hilly course, a fact that tends to give it an air of austerity but also its very own personality. What's more, this impression of infinity makes it very difficult to judge distances. It is already a tough task choosing the right club for the wind, avoiding bunkers, many of which just swallow up your ball, and getting to grips with firm, subtle and very slick greens. But despite everything, game strategy is pretty obvious, even though a few hazards are hard to spot from the tee-boxes.

Nulle part au monde on ne trouve une telle succession de grands parcours que de Liverpool à Southport. West Lancashire y figure sans conteste, alors qu'il a rarement reçu de grandes épreuves. Du Clubhouse, les vues sont superbes sur l'estuaire de la Mersey et les montagnes du Pays de Galles, mais on les voit peu du parcours, à l'abri derrière un cordon de dunes. Le relief n'est pas ici très prononcé, ce qui lui donne un caractère d'austérité, mais aussi sa personnalité. De plus, cette impression d'infinité rend très difficile le jugement des distances : il est déjà délicat de choisir les bons clubs en fonction du vent, d'éviter les bunkers, dont beaucoup sont d'une grande voracité, de négocier des greens fermes, subtils et très rapides. La stratégie est malgré tout assez évidente, alors que certains obstacles sont peu visibles des départs.

West Lancashire Golf Club — 1873

Hall Road West, Blundellsands
ENG - LIVERPOOL, Lancs L23 8SZ

Office	Secrétariat	(44) 0151 - 924 1076
Pro shop	Pro-shop	(44) 0151 - 924 5662
Fax	Fax	
Situation	Situation	

1.5 km from Crosby (pop. 22 000)
14 km from Liverpool (pop. 452 450)

Annual closure	Fermeture annuelle	no
Weekly closure	Fermeture hebdomadaire	no
Fees main season	Tarifs haute saison	18 holes

	Week days Semaine	We/Bank holidays We/Férié
Individual Individuel	£ 28	£ 50
Couple Couple	£ 56	£ 100
Full weekdays: £ 40		

Caddy	Caddy	on request
Electric Trolley	Chariot électrique	no
Buggy	Voiturette	no
Clubs	Clubs	£ 5/18 holes

Credit cards Cartes de crédit
VISA - Eurocard - MasterCard - AMEX - DC - JCB
(Pro shop goods only)

Access Accès : Liverpool, A565 to Crosby.
+Follow signs to club by Hall Road Rail Station
Map 5 on page 497 Carte 5 Page 497

GOLF COURSE / PARCOURS — 17/20

Site	Site	▬▬▬▬▭
Maintenance	Entretien	▬▬▬▬▭
Architect	Architecte	Unknown C.K. Cotton (1960)
Type	Type	links
Relief	Relief	
Water in play	Eau en jeu	▬▬▭▭▭
Exp. to wind	Exposé au vent	▬▬▬▬▭
Trees in play	Arbres en jeu	▬▬▭▭▭

Scorecard Carte de score	Chp. Chp.	Mens Mess.	Ladies Da.
Length Long.	6086	5594	5135
Par	72	70	73

Advised golfing ability Niveau de jeu recommandé	0	12	24	36
Hcp required Handicap exigé	28 Men, 36 Ladies			

CLUB HOUSE & AMENITIES / CLUB HOUSE ET ANNEXES — 7/10

Pro shop	Pro-shop	▬▬▬▬▭
Driving range	Practice	▬▬▭▭▭
Sheltered	couvert	no
On grass	sur herbe	yes
Putting-green	putting-green	yes
Pitching-green	pitching green	yes

683

HOTEL FACILITIES / ENVIRONNEMENT HOTELIER — 7/10

HOTELS HÔTELS

Blundellsands - 41 rooms, D £ 70 — Crosby 3 km
Tel (44) 0151 - 924 6515, Fax (44) 0151 - 931 5364

Atlantic Tower Thistle — Liverpool
223 rooms, D £ 90 — 15 km
Tel (44) 0151 - 227 4444, Fax (44) 0151 - 236 3973

Liverpool Moat House — Liverpool
244 rooms, D £ 98 — 15 km
Tel (44) 0151 - 471 9988, Fax (44) 0151 - 709 2706

Park - 62 rooms, D £ 34 — Netherton 3 km
Tel (44) 0151 - 525 7555, Fax (44) 0151 - 525 2481

RESTAURANTS RESTAURANTS

Ristorante del Secolo — Liverpool
Tel (44) 0151 - 236 4004 — 15 km

Blundellsands — Crosby
Tel (44) 0151 - 924 6515 — 3 km

West Surrey is one of those courses where you soon start feeling excited about your game as all the hazards and the tactics you need to overcome them are crystal clear. This is important, because placing the drive is of prime importance if you want a relatively simple approach shot. So players who are playing to form should card their handicap and perhaps even better if they excel on the greens. In Summer the course gets a little harder because the fairways are not watered and the ball will roll on easily into the long thick rough from where only a wedge can be of any use. With this said, there are not many other hazards to contend with. With a longer outward 9 and tight back 9, there is something for every kind of player, and the long-hitters who keep out of the trees will enjoy a number of birdie opportunities on the par 5s.

West Surrey est de ces parcours où l'on éprouve vite de bonnes sensations, parce que l'on voit aussi clairement les obstacles que la tactique à mettre en oeuvre. C'est important car le placement du drive est essentiel pour garantir un second coup assez facile. Ainsi, les joueurs qui sont à leur bon niveau joueront normalement leur handicap, et mieux même s'ils sont inspirés sur les greens. En été, le parcours est plus difficile car les fairways ne sont pas arrosés, et l'on roule assez facilement dans des roughs longs et épais, d'où on ne peut souvent sortir qu'avec un wedge. Cela dit, il n'y a pas beaucoup d'autres obstacles. Avec un aller plus long, mais un retour plus étroit, tous les types de joueurs sont bien servis, et les longs frappeurs sachant éviter les arbres trouveront de belles occasions de birdies sur les par 5.

West Surrey Golf Club — 1910

Enton Green
ENG - GODALMING, Surrey GU8 5AF

Office	Secrétariat	(44) 01483 - 421 275
Pro shop	Pro-shop	(44) 01483 - 417 278
Fax	Fax	(44) 01483 - 415 419
Situation	Situation	

6 km from Guildford (pop. 122 378) - next to Godalming

Annual closure	Fermeture annuelle	no
Weekly closure	Fermeture hebdomadaire	no
		Tuesday 08 → 12

Fees main season Tarifs haute saison — 18 holes

	Week days Semaine	We/Bank holidays We/Férié
Individual Individuel	£ 38.50	£ 50*
Couple Couple	£ 77	£ 100*
Restrictions at weekends (please call)		

Caddy	Caddy	no
Electric Trolley	Chariot électrique	£ 6/18 holes
Buggy	Voiturette	no
Clubs	Clubs	£ 10/18 holes

Credit cards Cartes de crédit
VISA - Eurocard - MasterCard - AMEX - DC - JCB
(not for green fees)

Access Accès : A3 (→ Portsmouth) through Guildford. Turn left to Milford. At traffic lights turn left onto A 3100 (→Portsmouth). Right onto Station Lane. Golf 3 km down (2 m.) on right side.
Map 7 on page 500 Carte 7 Page 500

684

GOLF COURSE / PARCOURS — 15/20

Site	Site	
Maintenance	Entretien	
Architect	Architecte	Herbert Fowler
Type	Type	parkland
Relief	Relief	
Water in play	Eau en jeu	
Exp. to wind	Exposé au vent	
Trees in play	Arbres en jeu	

Scorecard Carte de score	Chp. Chp.	Mens Mess.	Ladies Da.
Length Long.	5633	5842	4970
Par	71	71	72

Advised golfing ability Niveau de jeu recommandé	0	12	24	36
Hcp required Handicap exigé	certificate			

CLUB HOUSE & AMENITIES / CLUB HOUSE ET ANNEXES — 7/10

Pro shop	Pro-shop	
Driving range	Practice	
Sheltered	couvert	no
On grass	sur herbe	yes (summer)
Putting-green	putting-green	yes
Pitching-green	pitching green	yes

HOTEL FACILITIES / ENVIRONNEMENT HOTELIER — 7/10

HOTELS HÔTELS
Inn on the Lake - 17 rooms, D £ 80 — Godalming 3 km
Tel (44) 01483 - 415 575, Fax (44) 01483 - 860 445

Kings Arms and Royal — Godalming 3 km
16 rooms, D £ 60
Tel (44) 01483 - 421 545, Fax (44) 01483 - 415 403

Angel Posting House and Livery — Guildford 7 km
18 rooms, D £ 105
Tel (44) 01483 - 64 555, Fax (44) 01483 - 33 770

Bramley Grange - 45 rooms, D £ 90 — Bramley 3 km
Tel (44) 01483 - 893 434, Fax (44) 01483 - 893 835

RESTAURANTS RESTAURANTS
White Horse - Tel (44) 01483 - 208 258 — Hascombe 3 km
Café de Paris - Tel (44) 01483 - 34 896 — Guildford 7 km
Squirrel at Hurtmore — Hurtmore
Tel (44) 01483 - 860 223 — 5 km

WEST SUSSEX

18	7	6

The good news for most amateurs is that West Sussex is not a long course. The bad news is that there is only one par 5, hole N°1, where your swing might not quite be in the right groove to hit the green in two. There are also a number of holes where you will hope to get by unscathed, for example the 6th and 15th, two tough par 3s where you need to carry water, and the 16th, a beautiful par 4 whose green looks depressingly tiny beyond a wide ravine. Here, you have every opportunity to shoot a good round as long as your game is in tip-top condition, and although the greens are very well protected, there is often an easy way in. You need to play every shot there is, one at a time, firstly in your mind, then with your club. This absolute gem of a course does not have the recognition it deserves, but the people here seem to have opted for the sweet life, preferring to leave the limelight for others.

La bonne nouvelle pour la plupart des amateurs, c'est que West Sussex n'est pas bien long ! La mauvaise, c'est qu'il y a un seul par 5, et c'est le 1, où l'on n'est généralement pas assez assoupli pour vraiment attaquer le green en deux. Il y a aussi quelques trous dont il faut sortir indemne, comme le 6 et le 15, deux solides par 3 où il faut passer l'eau, ou le 16, très beau par 4 dont le green paraît minuscule au delà d'un large ravin. Autrement, il est ici beaucoup d'occasions de réussir si l'on a amené son meilleur jeu, d'autant que les greens sont bien protégés, mais qu'ils laissent très souvent une ouverture. Il faut ici savoir jouer tous les coups, et un seul à la fois, d'abord avec sa tête puis avec son club. Ce merveilleux petit bijou n'a pas la notoriété qu'il mérite, mais, ici, on a choisi de vivre heureux, sans souci des projecteurs trop violents.

West Sussex Golf Club — 1931
ENG - PULBOROUGH, West Sussex RH20 2EN

Office	Secrétariat	(44) 01798 - 875 563
Pro shop	Pro-shop	(44) 01798 - 872 426
Fax	Fax	(44) 01798 - 875 563

Situation Situation
2.5 km from Pulborough (pop. 4 309)
25 km from Brighton (pop. 228 946)

Annual closure	Fermeture annuelle	no
Weekly closure	Fermeture hebdomadaire	no

Fees main season
Tarifs haute saison 18 holes

	Week days Semaine	We/Bank holidays We/Férié
Individual Individuel	£ 35	£ 40
Couple Couple	£ 70	£ 80

Full weekdays: £ 45 - No visitors on Friday

Caddy	Caddy	no
Electric Trolley	Chariot électrique	£ 5/18 holes
Buggy	Voiturette	no
Clubs	Clubs	£ 7.50/18 holes

Credit cards Cartes de crédit
VISA - MasterCard (Pro shop goods only)

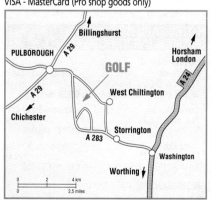

Access Accès : M25 Jct 9, A24 → Worthing. At Washington, A283 on the right through Storrington → Pulborough. Golf course on the right.
Map 7 on page 500 Carte 7 Page 500

GOLF COURSE PARCOURS — 18/20

Site	Site	
Maintenance	Entretien	
Architect	Architecte	Sir Guy Campbell C.K. Hutchinson
Type	Type	inland, heathland
Relief	Relief	
Water in play	Eau en jeu	
Exp. to wind	Exposé au vent	
Trees in play	Arbres en jeu	

Scorecard Carte de score	Chp. Chp.	Mens Mess.	Ladies Da.
Length Long.	5600	5320	5020
Par	68	68	73

Advised golfing ability Niveau de jeu recommandé	0	12	24	36
Hcp required Handicap exigé	certificate			

CLUB HOUSE & AMENITIES
CLUB HOUSE ET ANNEXES — 7/10

Pro shop	Pro-shop	
Driving range	Practice	
Sheltered	couvert	1 mat
On grass	sur herbe	yes
Putting-green	putting-green	yes
Pitching-green	pitching green	yes

HOTEL FACILITIES
ENVIRONNEMENT HOTELIER — 6/10

HOTELS HÔTELS
Chequers — Pulborough 3 km
11 rooms, D £ 75
Tel (44) 01798 - 872 486
Fax (44) 01798 - 872 715

Little Thakeham — Storrington 4 km
7 rooms, D £ 130
Tel (44) 01903 - 744 416
Fax (44) 01903 - 745 022

Mill House — Ashington 10 km
12 rooms, D £ 80
Tel (44) 01670 - 892 426, Fax (44) 01670 - 892 855

RESTAURANTS RESTAURANTS
Stane Street Hollow — Pulborough 5 km
Tel (44) 01798 - 872819

Manley's — Storrington 4 km
Tel (44) 01903 - 742331

685

The beginning of the course is not so simple, between the sand-dunes and out-of-bounds. If the wind is blowing, don't go for the pin, you will be asking for trouble. The 15th is also surprising, because you have to cut the ball over an out-of-bounds area. Try and get a round with some local players so they can tell you about the traps that are not always clearly in view. For example, the rough is never the same from one season to the next and even disappears altogether in the Winter (hardly the best time to come here anyway). Facing the Welsh coast, Weston-Super-Mare provides some spectacular views over the Bristol Channel and the general flatness of the course means you can easily play 36 holes in a day when on holiday. Similar to Saunton in style but without offering quite the same challenge, this is a course in the grand links tradition.

Le début du parcours n'est pas si simple, entre les dunes et le hors-limites. S'il y a du vent, ne jouez pas directement les drapeaux, vous risquez des problèmes. Le 15 est aussi surprenant, où il faut couper au-dessus du hors-limites. Essayez donc de faire une partie avec des joueurs locaux, ils vous en apprendront les pièges pas toujours bien visibles, notamment que le rough n'est jamais le même suivant la saison, et qu'il est absent en hiver. Mais il est vari que l'on vient rarement ici en cette période de l'année. En face du Pays de Galles, Weston-super-Mare offre des vues spectaculaires sur le Bristol Channel. Son absence de relief en fait un parcours idéal pour jouer 36 trous en vacances. Assez proche par son style de Saunton, sans prétendre à son exigence, c'est un parcours de grande tradition de links.

Weston-Super-Mare Golf Club — 1892

Uphill Road North
ENG - WESTON-SUPER-MARE, Bristol BS23 4NQ

Office	Secrétariat	(44) 01934 - 626 968
Pro shop	Pro-shop	(44) 01934 - 633 360
Fax	Fax	(44) 01934 - 626 968
Situation	Situation	

2 km S of Weston-Super-Mare (pop. 64 935)
23 km SW of Bristol (pop. 376 146)

Annual closure	Fermeture annuelle	no
Weekly closure	Fermeture hebdomadaire	no

Fees main season
Tarifs haute saison full day

	Week days Semaine	We/Bank holidays We/Férié
Individual Individuel	£ 24	£ 35
Couple Couple	£ 48	£ 70

Caddy	Caddy	no
Electric Trolley	Chariot électrique	no (but batteries)
Buggy	Voiturette	no
Clubs	Clubs	yes (ask pro)

Credit cards Cartes de crédit
Visa - Mastercard (Pro shop goods only)

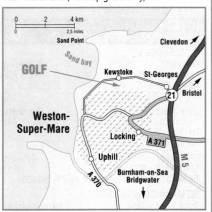

GOLF
Sand Point
Sand bay
Clevedon
Kewstoke
St-Georges
21 Bristol
Weston-Super-Mare
Locking A 371
Uphill
M 5
A 370
Burnham-on-Sea
Bridgwater

Access Accès : • M5 Jct 21, then A370 to Weston-Super-Mare. Follow signs. • From Bristol centre, A370.
Map 6 on page 499 Carte 6 Page 499

GOLF COURSE / PARCOURS — 16/20

Site	Site	▬▬▬▬
Maintenance	Entretien	▬▬▬▬
Architect	Architecte	Tom Dunn
Type	Type	seaside course, links
Relief	Relief	▬▬
Water in play	Eau en jeu	▬▬
Exp. to wind	Exposé au vent	▬▬▬
Trees in play	Arbres en jeu	▬

Scorecard Carte de score	Chp. Chp.	Mens Mess.	Ladies Da.
Length Long.	5651	5540	5006
Par	70	70	72

Advised golfing ability	0	12	24	36
Niveau de jeu recommandé				

Hcp required	Handicap exigé	certificate

CLUB HOUSE & AMENITIES / CLUB HOUSE ET ANNEXES — 6/10

Pro shop	Pro-shop	▬▬▬
Driving range	Practice	▬▬
Sheltered	couvert	no
On grass	sur herbe	yes
Putting-green	putting-green	yes
Pitching-green	pitching green	yes

HOTEL FACILITIES / ENVIRONNEMENT HOTELIER — 7/10

HOTELS HÔTELS

Beachlands — Weston-Super-Mare
17 rooms, D £ 80 — on site
Tel (44) 01934 - 621 401, Fax (44) 01934 -621 966

Grand Atlantic — Weston-Super-Mare
76 rooms, D £ 75 — 2 km
Tel (44) 01934 - 626 543, Fax (44) 01934 - 415 048

Commodore — Weston-Super-Mare
18 rooms, D £ 70 — 2 km
Tel (44) 01934 - 415 778, Fax (44) 01934 - 636 483

RESTAURANTS RESTAURANTS

Duets — Weston-Super-Mare
Tel (44) 01934 - 413 428 — 3 km

Claremont Vaults — Weston-Super-Mare 2 km

686

WHEATLEY

This course is on the edge of the city of Doncaster, one of England's more famous horse-racing venues. And although there are many houses all around, you forget all about them once out on the course. The club-house, recently refurbished, is simple with no superfluous frills or outstanding architecture, yet the restaurant serves good food, something you don't always find in British club-houses. The peat and sandy soil provide good drainage and top quality grass, especially since the fairways are protected in winter: players hit their shots off a little mat. This tree-lined course is easily walkable despite a few slopes on the back nine, where you find most of the difficulties; trouble is evenly spread over alternating tricky and easier holes to ensure a pleasant rhythm to your round. This is a good course to play with all the family, although the best players looking for a testing challenge might end up a little frustrated.

Ce parcours est en limites de la ville de Doncaster, assez connue par les amateurs de chevaux de course. Bien qu'il y ait de nombreuses maisons alentour, on les oublie totalement une fois sur le parcours. Le Club house a été récemment rénové, mais reste simple, sans luxe excessif ni architecture très remarquable. Cependant, le restaurant est de bonne qualité, ce qui n'est pas toujours le cas dans les golfs britanniques, il faut bien le dire. Le sol de sable et de tourbe assure un bon drainage, et un gazon de bonne qualité, d'autant que les fairways sont protégés en hiver : les joueurs tapent leurs coups à partir de petits tapis ! Le parcours bien boisé est facile à jouer à pied, malgré quelques petits reliefs au retour. C'est là que l'on trouve d'ailleurs les trous les plus problématiques, alors que les difficultés sont bien réparties, l'alternance de trous faciles et de trous délicats assurant un rythme de jeu agréable. C'est un bon parcours à jouer pour la détente, les meilleurs joueurs seront un peu frustrés dans leurs attentes de grands défis.

Wheatley Golf Club — 1923

Armthorpe Road
ENG - DONCASTER, S. Yorkshire DN2 5QB

Office	Secrétariat	(44) 01302 - 831 655
Pro shop	Pro-shop	(44) 01302 - 834 085
Fax	Fax	
Situation	Situation	

2 km from Doncaster (pop. 288 854)

Annual closure	Fermeture annuelle	no
Weekly closure	Fermeture hebdomadaire	no

Fees main season
Tarifs haute saison 18 holes

	Week days Semaine	We/Bank holidays We/Férié
Individual Individuel	£ 25	£ 35
Couple Couple	£ 50	£ 70

Full day: £ 30/£ 40

Caddy	Caddy	no
Electric Trolley	Chariot électrique	no
Buggy	Voiturette	no
Clubs	Clubs	no

Credit cards Cartes de crédit
VISA - Eurocard - MasterCard - AMEX - JCB - Switch

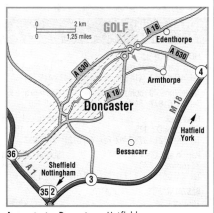

Access Accès : Doncaster → Hatfield,
then Armthorpe Road on right hand side.
Map 4 on page 495 Carte 4 Page 495

GOLF COURSE / PARCOURS — 14/20

Site	Site	
Maintenance	Entretien	
Architect	Architecte	Unknown
Type	Type	parkland
Relief	Relief	
Water in play	Eau en jeu	
Exp. to wind	Exposé au vent	
Trees in play	Arbres en jeu	

Scorecard Carte de score	Chp. Chp.	Mens Mess.	Ladies Da.
Length Long.	5765	5598	5237
Par	71	71	73

Advised golfing ability		0 12 24 36
Niveau de jeu recommandé		
Hcp required	Handicap exigé	certificate

CLUB HOUSE & AMENITIES / CLUB HOUSE ET ANNEXES — 6/10

Pro shop	Pro-shop	
Driving range	Practice	
Sheltered	couvert	
On grass	sur herbe	yes
Putting-green	putting-green	yes
Pitching-green	pitching green	yes

HOTEL FACILITIES / ENVIRONNEMENT HOTELIER — 6/10

HOTELS HÔTELS

Grand St. Leger — Doncaster
20 rooms, D £ 90 — 3 km
Tel (44) 01302 - 364 111, Fax (44) 01302 - 329 865

Mount Pleasant — Doncaster
34 rooms, D £ 70 — 8 km
Tel (44) 01302 - 868 696, Fax (44) 01302 - 865 130

The Regent Hotel — Doncaster
50 rooms, D £ 80 — 5 km
Tel (44) 01302 - 364 180, Fax (44) 01302 - 322 331

RESTAURANTS RESTAURANTS

Mount Pleasant — Doncaster
Tel (44) 01302 - 868 696 — 8 km

The Bistro — Doncaster,3 km
Hamilton's — Doncaster
Tel (44) 01302 - 760 770 — 3 km

687

This is the kind of course you would like to keep to yourself. Very much underrated and often completely unknown, it is a sort of delectable gem that long-hitters will look down upon until they reach the 14th tee. In a none too impressive site of heathland and on the springy turf that comes with peat, the layout was designed by Harry Colt, who knew a thing or two about teasing dog-legs. Missing the open side of the fairway calls for some acrobatics through or over the trees, or some sheepish save-shots back into play. If you score well it's because you thought it out well. The greens are well defended, distinctly well contoured, pretty huge and a pleasure to putt on. What lingers here is an impression of happiness, of having discovered something personal, but which you have to share with others...

C'est le genre de parcours que l'on aimerait garder pour soi. Très sous-estimé, souvent complètement ignoré, c'est une sorte de délicieux petit bijou que les longs frappeurs regarderont de haut jusqu'au moment où ils parviendront au départ du 14. Dans un site de terre de bruyère pas spécialement impressionnant, sur ce gazon élastique que donne un sol de tourbe, le tracé est signé Harry Colt, qui savait notamment faire des doglegs provoquants, où manquer l'ouverture oblige à des coups d'acrobate, ou encore à des retours penauds en sécurité sur le fairway. Et si l'on a bien scoré, c'est que l'on a bien pensé. Bien défendus, très travaillés, et plutôt vastes, les greens sont un plaisir à négocier. C'est cette impression de bonheur qui reste ici, d'avoir découvert quelque chose, même si on est loin d'être le seul...

Whittington Heath Golf Club — 1886

Tamworth Road
ENG - LICHFIELD, Staffs WS14 9PW

Office	Secrétariat	(44) 01543 - 432 317
Pro shop	Pro-shop	(44) 01543 - 432 261
Fax	Fax	(44) 01543 - 432 317
Situation	Situation	

6 km from Lichfield (pop. 28 666)
20 km from Birmingham (pop. 961 041)

Annual closure	Fermeture annuelle	no
Weekly closure	Fermeture hebdomadaire	no

Fees main season
Tarifs haute saison 18 holes

	Week days Semaine	We/Bank holidays We/Férié
Individual Individuel	£ 24	—
Couple Couple	£ 48	—

Full weekdays: £ 32 - No visitors at w/ends

Caddy	Caddy	no
Electric Trolley	Chariot électrique	no
Buggy	Voiturette	no
Clubs	Clubs	no

Credit cards Cartes de crédit
Visa - Mastercard (Pro shop & green fees)

688

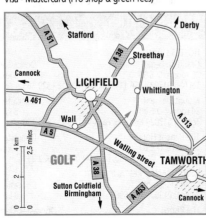

Access Accès : On A51, 4 km from Lichfield Station
Map 7 on page 500 Carte 7 Page 500

GOLF COURSE
PARCOURS — 17/20

Site	Site	
Maintenance	Entretien	
Architect	Architecte	Harry S. Colt
Type	Type	inland, heathland
Relief	Relief	
Water in play	Eau en jeu	
Exp. to wind	Exposé au vent	
Trees in play	Arbres en jeu	

Scorecard Carte de score	Chp. Chp.	Mens Mess.	Ladies Da.
Length Long.	5841	5542	5117
Par	70	70	72

Advised golfing ability Niveau de jeu recommandé		0 12 24 36
Hcp required	Handicap exigé	65, C.J. Poxon

CLUB HOUSE & AMENITIES
CLUB HOUSE ET ANNEXES — 6/10

Pro shop	Pro-shop	
Driving range	Practice	
Sheltered	couvert	no
On grass	sur herbe	no
Putting-green	putting-green	yes
Pitching-green	pitching green	yes

HOTEL FACILITIES
ENVIRONNEMENT HOTELIER — 7/10

HOTELS HÔTELS
Little Barrow - 24 rooms, D £ 60 — Lichfield 6 km
Tel (44) 01543 - 414 500, Fax (44) 01543 - 415 734

Travel Inn - 40 rooms, D £ 35 — Tamworth 5 km
Tel (44) 01827 - 54 414, Fax (44) 01827 - 310 420

New Hall — Sutton Coldfield
62 rooms, D £ 125 — 15 km
Tel (44) 0121 - 378 2442, Fax (44) 0121 - 378 4637

Parson and Clerk — Sutton Coldfield
36 rooms, D £ 40 — 13 km
Tel (44) 0121 - 353 1747, Fax (44) 0121 - 352 1340

RESTAURANTS RESTAURANTS
Thrales — Lichfield
Tel (44) 01543 - 255 091 — 6 km

La Truffe — Sutton Coldfield
Tel (44) 0121 - 355 5836 — 13 km

WILMSLOW

16	7	6

In a typical landscape of rural Cheshire, golf at Wilmslow is a civilized affair with distinct disdain for the ostentatious. Although there is a pleasantly old-fashioned feel to the course, maintenance is definitely modern and probably the best in the region. It is generally prepared in such a way as to not intimidate the less experienced players while providing a respectable challenge for low-handicappers. They can start by attempting to drive the green on hole N°1, cutting the corner of this par 4 by hitting it over the trees. The most surprising thing here is the unity of style, even though a dozen or so architects have altered the layout in their own way, from James Braid to Tom Simpson to Fred Hawtree to Dave Thomas. At least no-one thought of removing the many cross-bunkers that modern-day architects hardly know how to use any more. A course with all the components of a good test of golf, a stiff challenge for the better player, a "human" course that neither flatters the hacker nor demands too much of single-figure handicappers.

Dans un paysage typique du Cheshire rural, le golf à Wilmslow est chose civilisée, dédaignant toute ostentation. Bien que l'on ait ici une sensation agréablement «old fashion», rien de tel dans l'entretien du parcours, l'un des meilleurs de la région sur ce plan. Il est généralement préparé de manière à ne pas intimider le joueur peu aguerri, tout en offrant des défis respectables aux meilleurs. Le plus surprenant ici est l'unité de style, bien qu'une bonne dizaine d'architectes se soient penchés sur ce dessin, de James Braid à Tom Simpson, de Fred Hawtree à Dave Thomas. Au moins personne n'aura songé à en effacer les nombreux «cross-bunkers» que les architectes modernes ne savent plus guère mettre en oeuvre. Un parcours avec tous les éléments d'un bon test, résistant bien aux meilleurs, un parcours à l'échelle humaine, ni pour faire briller les mauvais joueurs à bon compte, ni pour demander l'impossible aux bons.

Wilmslow Golf Club — 1903

Great Warford, Mobberley
ENG - KNUTSFORD, Cheshire WA16 7AY

Office	Secrétariat	(44) 01565 - 872 148
Pro shop	Pro-shop	(44) 01565 - 873 620
Fax	Fax	(44) 01565 - 872 172
Situation	Situation	

20 km S of Manchester (pop. 404 861)
3 km from Wilmslow (pop. 28 827)

Annual closure	Fermeture annuelle	no
Weekly closure	Fermeture hebdomadaire	no

Fees main season	Tarifs haute saison	18 holes
	Week days Semaine	**We/Bank holidays** We/Férié
Individual Individuel	£ 40	£ 50
Couple Couple	£ 80	£ 100
Full day: £ 50/£ 60		
Caddy	Caddy	no
Electric Trolley	Chariot électrique	£ 7
Buggy	Voiturette	no
Clubs	Clubs	£ 10

Credit cards Cartes de crédit
VISA - MasterCard (Pro shop goods only)

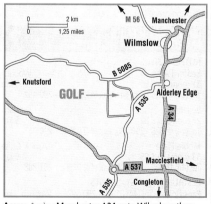

Access Accès : Manchester A34 onto Wilmslow, then B5085 → Mobberley, Knutsford, turn left → David Lewis Centre for Epilepsy, Golf course on left hand side. **Map 4 on page 494** Carte 4 Page 494

GOLF COURSE / PARCOURS — 16/20

Site	Site	
Maintenance	Entretien	
Architect	Architecte	S. Herd, J. Braid T. Simpson, G.Duncan
Type	Type	inland, open country
Relief	Relief	
Water in play	Eau en jeu	
Exp. to wind	Exposé au vent	
Trees in play	Arbres en jeu	

Scorecard Carte de score	Chp. Chp.	Mens Mess.	Ladies Da.
Length Long.	6044	6044	5293
Par	72	72	74

Advised golfing ability		0	12	24	36
Niveau de jeu recommandé					
Hcp required	Handicap exigé	certificate			

CLUB HOUSE & AMENITIES / CLUB HOUSE ET ANNEXES — 7/10

Pro shop	Pro-shop	
Driving range	Practice	
Sheltered	couvert	practice area
On grass	sur herbe	yes
Putting-green	Putting-green	yes
Pitching green	Pitching-green	yes

HOTEL FACILITIES / ENVIRONNEMENT HOTELIER — 6/10

HOTELS HÔTELS

Stanneylands — Wilmslow
31 rooms, D £ 89 — 5 km
Tel (44) 01625 - 525 225, Fax (44) 01625 - 537 282

Mottram Hall Hotel — Wilmslow/Prestbury
132 rooms, D £ 165 — 8 km
Tel (44) 01625 - 828 135, Fax (44) 01625 - 828 950

Alderley Edge Hotel — Alderley Edge
46 rooms, D £ 115 — 2 km
Tel (44) 01625 - 583 033, Fax (44) 01625 - 586 343

RESTAURANTS RESTAURANTS

Belle Epoque — Knutsford
Tel (44) 01565 - 633 060 — 3 km

Alderley Edge — Alderley Edge
Tel (44) 01625 - 583 033 — 2 km

Plough & Flail - Tel (44) 01565 - 873 537 — Mobberley 1 km

689

In a very elegant setting with an equally comfortable clubhouse, both the courses at Woburn are pleasantly sited well away from the noise of the outside world. The Duchess course is above average but not in the same league as the Duke, made famous by the British Masters and the Women's British Open. Except for the first few holes, this is a rather flat layout which winds its way through a beautiful old forest of pine and chestnut trees, sufficiently in play for the rough not to be too difficult. The sandy soil makes for pleasant golfing all the year round, enhanced by the excellence of the greens, which are never easy to read. The holes all have a distinct individual character but without detracting from a pleasant unity of style. The back-tees are for very good players only, especially from the 13th onward, where some of the par-4s are quite formidable. In such a serious layout, the only regret might be a slight lack of fantasy (maybe a touch of British humour might help).

D'une grande élégance générale, l'ensemble des deux parcours de Woburn bénéficie d'une situation bien à l'écart du monde. Le parcours «Duchess» est honorable, mais ne saurait lutter avec le «Dukes,» rendu célèbre par le British Masters et le Women's British Open. Assez plat, sauf dans ses premiers trous, il est insinué dans une belle et ancienne forêt, où dominent les pins et les châtaigniers, assez présents dans le jeu pour que les roughs ne soient pas trop difficiles. Le sol sablonneux le rend très agréable à jouer toute l'année, et la qualité des greens, pas faciles à lire, augmente encore ce plaisir. Les trous sont bien individualisés, tout en offrant une bonne unité de style. On ne conseillera les départs arrière qu'aux très bons joueurs, surtout à partir du 13, où quelques par 4 sont redoutables. Sur un tracé aussi sérieux, on regrettera peut-être un léger manque de fantaisie (d'humour anglais?)

Woburn Golf & Country Club — 1976

Bow Brickhill
ENG - MILTON KEYNES, Bucks MK17 9 LJ

Office	Secrétariat	(44) 01908 - 370 756
Pro shop	Pro-shop	(44) 01908 - 647 987
Fax	Fax	(44) 01908 - 370 756
Situation	Situation	

10 km from Milton Keynes (pop. 176 330)
35 km from Bedford (pop. 73 917)

Annual closure	Fermeture annuelle	no
Weekly closure	Fermeture hebdomadaire	no

Christmas Day only

Fees main season	Tarifs haute saison	18 holes
	Week days Semaine	We/Bank holidays We/Férié
Individual Individuel	*	*
Couple Couple	*	*

On request: depends on number, time of the year, availability. Visitors must

Caddy	Caddy	no
Electric Trolley	Chariot électrique	no
Buggy	Voiturette	£ 40/18 holes
Clubs	Clubs	£ 20/18 holes

Credit cards Cartes de crédit VISA - MasterCard - AMEX

690

Access Accès : London M1 North. Jct 13 into Woburn Sands. Left to Woburn. After 0.75 km (1/2 m), right at sign. **Map 7 on page 500** Carte 7 Page 500

GOLF COURSE / PARCOURS — 18/20

Site	Site	
Maintenance	Entretien	
Architect	Architecte	Charles Lawrie
Type	Type	inland, forest
Relief	Relief	
Water in play	Eau en jeu	
Exp. to wind	Exposé au vent	
Trees in play	Arbres en jeu	

Scorecard Carte de score	Chp. Chp.	Mens Mess.	Ladies Da.
Length Long.	6264	5898	5454
Par	72	72	75

Advised golfing ability Niveau de jeu recommandé	0	12	24	36
Hcp required Handicap exigé	28 Men, 36 Ladies			

CLUB HOUSE & AMENITIES / CLUB HOUSE ET ANNEXES — 7/10

Pro shop	Pro-shop	
Driving range	Practice	
Sheltered	couvert	no
On grass	sur herbe	no
Putting-green	putting-green	yes
Pitching-green	pitching green	yes

HOTEL FACILITIES / ENVIRONNEMENT HOTELIER — 7/10

HOTELS HÔTELS

Bedford Arms — Woburn
51 rooms, D £ 80 — 5 km
Tel (44) 01525 - 290 441, Fax (44) 01525 - 290 432

Bell Inn — Woburn
27 rooms, D £ 82 — 5 km
Tel (44) 01525 - 290 280, Fax (44) 01525 - 290 017

Moore Place — Aspley Guise
53 rooms, D £ 85 — 6 km
Tel (44) 01908 - 282 000, Fax (44) 01908 - 281 888

RESTAURANTS RESTAURANTS

Paris House - Tel (44) 01525 - 290 692 — Woburn 5 km

Shenley Church Inn — Milton Keynes
Tel (44) 01908 - 505 467 — 12 km

Bell Inn — Woburn
Tel (44) 01525 - 290 280 — 5 km

The second of the threesome of «Ws», we could almost write the same report for each one, although each does have its own personality. Here it all starts with the clubhouse, as British as a cricket pavilion where you drink tea after your round. Otherwise the landscape is the same as on the other two courses, with heather just about everywhere you look. Isn't it about time someone invented a special «heather wedge» to help get balls back onto the fairway? And heather it is that puts the most pressure on your tee-shot here, where apprehension will always be your worst enemy. Add to this first class bunkering and very subtle, medium-sized greens that need time and patience to figure out and you realise that although a very fair proposition, Woking is a difficult course for carding a good score. A charming site, but watch out for its bite...

Avec West Hill et Worplesdon, ce sont de faux triplés. On pourrait d'ailleurs imaginer le même texte, avec trois copies. Chacun a son caractère. Celui-ci commence par son Clubhouse, à ce point British que l'on imagine un pavillon de cricket, où l'on boit le thé à la fin de la partie. Sinon, le paysage est analogue, avec une omniprésente bruyère dont il faudra bien que quelqu'un dessine un jour un «heather wedge» pour en sortir. C'est d'ailleurs cette possibilité qui met tant de pression sur les coups de départ : en golf aussi, la peur est mauvaise conseillère. Et si l'on ajoute un bunkering de premier ordre, ainsi que des greens de taille moyenne, mais d'une telle subtilité qu'il faut du temps et de la patience pour les comprendre, on se doute que, en dépit de sa franchise, Woking n'est pas un parcours évident à scorer. Derrière le charme du lieu, il y a de solides mâchoires.

Woking Golf Club — 1893
Pond Road, Hook Heath
ENG - WOKING, Surrey GU22 0JZ

Office	Secrétariat	(44) 01483 - 760 053
Pro shop	Pro-shop	(44) 01483 - 769 582
Fax	Fax	(44) 01483 - 772 441
Situation	Situation	

6 km from Guildford (pop. 122 378)
48 km from Central London (pop. 6 679 700)

Annual closure	Fermeture annuelle	no
Weekly closure	Fermeture hebdomadaire	no
Fees main season	Tarifs haute saison	full day

	Week days Semaine	We/Bank holidays We/Férié
Individual Individuel	£ 45	—
Couple Couple	£ 90	—

Weekends: only with a member

Caddy	Caddy	on request
Electric Trolley	Chariot électrique	£ 10/18 holes
Buggy	Voiturette	no
Clubs	Clubs	£ 10/18 holes
Credit cards Cartes de crédit		no

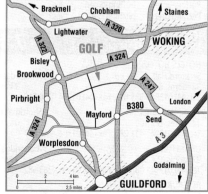

Access Accès : London A3 → Guildford.
At Cobham, A245 on right. Through Woking.
→ St Johns Village. Hollibank Road, turn right into
Golf Club Road. Entrance on right at end.
Map 8 on page 502 Carte 8 Page 502

GOLF COURSE / PARCOURS — 16/20

Site	Site	
Maintenance	Entretien	
Architect	Architecte	Tom Dunn
Type	Type	inland, heathland
Relief	Relief	
Water in play	Eau en jeu	
Exp. to wind	Exposé au vent	
Trees in play	Arbres en jeu	

Scorecard Carte de score	Chp. Chp.	Mens Mess.	Ladies Da.
Length Long.	5706	5361	5055
Par	70	70	73

Advised golfing ability Niveau de jeu recommandé	0	12	24	36

Hcp required — Handicap exigé — certificate

CLUB HOUSE & AMENITIES / CLUB HOUSE ET ANNEXES — 6/10

Pro shop	Pro-shop	
Driving range	Practice	
Sheltered	couvert	no
On grass	sur herbe	yes
Putting-green	putting-green	yes
Pitching-green	pitching green	yes

HOTEL FACILITIES / ENVIRONNEMENT HOTELIER — 6/10

HOTELS HÔTELS

Angel Posting House — Guildford
18 rooms, D £ 105 — 6 km
Tel (44) 01483 - 64 555, Fax (44) 01483 - 33 770

Forte Crest — Guildford
109 rooms, D £ 109 — 6 km
Tel (44) 01483 - 574 444, Fax (44) 01483 - 302 960

Blanes Court Hotel — Guildford
29 rooms, D £ 70 — 6 km
Tel (44) 01483 - 573 171, Fax (44) 01483 - 32 780

RESTAURANTS RESTAURANTS

Michel's — Ripley
Tel (44) 01483 - 224 777 — 6 km

Café de Paris — Guildford
Tel (44) 01483 - 34 896 — 6 km

691

WOODBRIDGE

| 14 | 7 | 7 |

Since 1893, Woodbridge has moved with the times and got equipped with a modern clubhouse in the early 1970s. Once much wider, the course has become much tighter as the trees have grown, a factor rarely given full consideration but one which can and will significantly change the designer's original intentions. A lot of courses should be studying the question right now. As it happens, the trees at Woodbridge hardly make it the ideal course for wayward hitters or beginners, unless they can master a 1 iron off the tee, which for the latter at least is hardly likely. This is a pity because here you have a very good test of golf where many holes widen out after the driving area and things get a little easier if you stay out of the heather. Those of you who can flight the ball either way will enjoy Woodbridge, a fine course and an excellent test, but never an ordeal. Very pleasant to play with the family, for fun.

Depuis 1893, Woodbridge a évolué avec le temps, et s'est doté d'un Clubhouse moderne vers 1970. Autrefois large, le parcours est devenu beaucoup plus étroit avec la croissance des arbres : c'est un élément rarement pris en compte, alors qu'il peut beaucoup modifier les intentions des architectes. Cette question doit en tout cas se poser pour beaucoup de parcours. En l'occurrence, ce détail empêche de conseiller Woodbridge aux frappeurs pas trop précis et aux débutants, à moins qu'ils ne soient des maîtres du fer 1, ce qui serait étonnant, du moins chez les débutants. C'est dommage car c'est un très bon test de golf, beaucoup de trous s'élargissent après la zone de drive, et les choses vont mieux si l'on a évité la bruyère. Les travailleurs de balle s'amuseront beaucoup sur ce beau parcours, un bon test sans être une bataille, et très agréable à jouer en famille, pour le plaisir.

Woodbridge Golf Club — 1893

Bromeswell Heath
ENG - WOODBRIDGE, Suffolk IP12 2PF

Office	Secrétariat	(44) 01394 - 382 038
Pro shop	Pro-shop	(44) 01394 - 383 213
Fax	Fax	(44) 01394 - 382 392
Situation	Situation	

13 km from Ipswich (pop. 2 654)
15 km from Aldeburgh (pop. 130 157)

Annual closure	Fermeture annuelle	no
Weekly closure	Fermeture hebdomadaire	no
Fees main season	Tarifs haute saison	18 holes

	Week days Semaine	We/Bank holidays We/Férié
Individual Individuel	£ 30	—
Couple Couple	£ 60	—

Full day: £ 35/70 - No visitors on main course at weekends

Caddy	Caddy	no
Electric Trolley	Chariot électrique	no
Buggy	Voiturette	no
Clubs	Clubs	no

Credit cards Cartes de crédit
Visa - Mastercard (Pro shop goods only)

692

GOLF COURSE PARCOURS 14/20

Site	Site	
Maintenance	Entretien	
Architect	Architecte	F.W. Hawtree
Type	Type	inland, heathland
Relief	Relief	
Water in play	Eau en jeu	
Exp. to wind	Exposé au vent	
Trees in play	Arbres en jeu	

Scorecard Carte de score	Chp. Chp.	Mens Mess.	Ladies Da.
Length Long.	5670	5456	5137
Par	70	70	73

Advised golfing ability Niveau de jeu recommandé	0	12	24	36
Hcp required Handicap exigé	certificate			

CLUB HOUSE & AMENITIES CLUB HOUSE ET ANNEXES 7/10

Pro shop	Pro-shop	
Driving range	Practice	
Sheltered	couvert	no
On grass	sur herbe	yes
Putting-green	putting-green	yes
Pitching-green	pitching green	yes

HOTEL FACILITIES ENVIRONNEMENT HOTELIER 7/10

HOTELS HÔTELS
Seckford Hall — Woodbridge
32 rooms, D £ 90 — 3 km
Tel (44) 01394 - 385 678, Fax (44) 01394 - 380 610

Wood Hall Hotel — Shottisham
14 rooms, D £ 100 — 6 km
Tel (44) 01394 - 411 283, Fax (44) 01394 - 410 007

Ufford Park — Woodbridge
37 rooms, D £ 80 — 3 km
Tel (44) 01394 - 383 555, Fax (44) 01394 - 383 582

RESTAURANTS RESTAURANTS
Seckford Hall — Woodbridge 3 km
Tel (44) 01394 - 385678

Ufford Park - Tel (44) 01394 -383555 Woodbridge 3 km

Woodhall Hotel — Shottisham
Tel (44) 01394 - 411283 — 6 km

Access Accès : Ipswich A12. At Woodbridge, B1084 through Melton. Over bridge. Left at roundabout. Golf course 200 m on the right.
Map 7 on page 501 Carte 7 Page 501

WOODBURY PARK THE OAKS

15	9	6

As this course belongs to Nigel Mansell, it is only logical to drive around it rather than walk. It is actually pretty hilly but it won't wear you out, at least not physically. Mentally, chronic hookers might find their ball in deep trouble on at least one half of the holes. Opened in 1992, this 18-hole course is still maturing, although the well-wooded countryside has retained its typical Devonshire landscape. Holes through the woods alternate with holes over open space where water hazards beckon (on 7 holes). Add to this some pretty huge and deep bunkers with high lips and you can feel a very distinct American influence where target golf is the order of the day. There is no way you can roll your ball onto the greens. This is a very interesting test where you should play from the tee-boxes designed for your level of ability. Beginners will certainly feel more comfortable on the neighbouring 9-holer, unless they prefer a little fishing, the swimming pool, tennis courts or aerobics available in this very well equipped resort.

Comme ce golf appartient à Nigel Mansell, il est assez logique de le jouer en voiture ! Il est effectivement assez accidenté mais pas épuisant, sauf mentalement pour les spécialistes du hook, qui risquent la sortie de route sur une bonne moitié des trous. Ouvert en 1992, le 18 trous n'a pas encore atteint sa maturité, même si le paysage bien boisé a gardé son style de campagne typique du Devon. Il alterne les trous très boisés et les espaces plus ouverts, où les obstacles d'eau sont dangereux (sur sept trous). Si l'on ajoute les bunkers plutôt vastes, profonds avec des faces très relevées, on a ici une sensation très nette d'influence américaine, et il n'est pas question de faire rouler la balle. C'est un test très intéressant, si l'on joue les départs à son niveau. Les débutants seront plus à l'aise sur le 9 trous voisin, à moins de se livrer aux plaisirs de la pêche, de la piscine, du tennis ou de l'aréobic que propose ce club très bien équipé.

Woodbury Park
Golf & Country Club
1992

Woodbury Castle, Woodbury
ENG - EXETER EX5 1JJ

Office	Secrétariat	(44) 01395 - 233 382
Pro shop	Pro-shop	(44) 01395 - 233 382
Fax	Fax	(44) 01395 - 233 384
Situation	Situation	

9 km SE of Exeter (pop. 98 125)

Annual closure	Fermeture annuelle	no
Weekly closure	Fermeture hebdomadaire	no
Fees main season	Tarifs haute saison	full day

	Week days Semaine	We/Bank holidays We/Férié
Individual Individuel	£ 35	£ 45
Couple Couple	£ 70	£ 90

Caddy	Caddy	no
Electric Trolley	Chariot électrique	no
Buggy	Voiturette	£ 20/18 holes
Clubs	Clubs	£ 12.50/18 holes

Credit cards Cartes de crédit
VISA - MasterCard

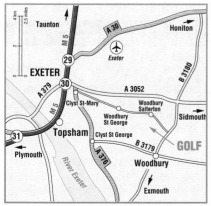

Access Accès : M5 Jct 30. A376 to Sidmouth/Exmouth. Take A3052 to Sidmouth. Turn right at Half Way House Inn. **Map 6 on page 499** Carte 6 Page 499

GOLF COURSE
PARCOURS
15/20

Site	Site	
Maintenance	Entretien	
Architect	Architecte	J. Hamilton Stutt
Type	Type	inland, parkland
Relief	Relief	
Water in play	Eau en jeu	
Exp. to wind	Exposé au vent	
Trees in play	Arbres en jeu	

Scorecard	Chp.	Mens	Ladies
Carte de score	Chp.	Mess.	Da.
Length Long.	6252	6030	5201
Par	72	72	73

Advised golfing ability	0	12	24	36
Niveau de jeu recommandé				
Hcp required	Handicap exigé	certificate		

CLUB HOUSE & AMENITIES
CLUB HOUSE ET ANNEXES
9/10

Pro shop	Pro-shop	
Driving range	Practice	
Sheltered	couvert	18 bays
On grass	sur herbe	yes
Putting-green	putting-green	yes (3)
Pitching-green	pitching green	yes

693

HOTEL FACILITIES
ENVIRONNEMENT HOTELIER
6/10

HOTELS HÔTELS

Rougemont Thistle — Exeter 9 km
88 rooms, D £ 75
Tel (44) 01392 - 54 982, Fax (44) 01392 - 420 928

Exeter Arms Toby — Exeter 9 km
37 rooms, D £ 60
Tel (44) 01392 - 435 353, Fax (44) 01392 - 420 826

RESTAURANTS RESTAURANTS

Golsworthy's — Exeter 9 km
Tel (44) 01392 - 217 736

Lamb's — Exeter 9 km
Tel (44) 01392 - 54 269

Woodhall Spa is still a very important leisure and holiday centre, like a sort of wood-strewn oasis in the middle of the Lincolnshire countryside. It is similar to Pinehurst in the United States but with only one course (a second is opening shortly). And what a course this is, regularly ranked amongst the best in Britain. Originally laid out by Vardon and Colt amidst pines, birch-trees and heather on ideal sandy soil, it was re-designed by the owner, Hotchkin. The number one requirement is to keep your drive in play and the ball alive in order to square up to some of the toughest second (and third) shots you could imagine. You then avoid the bunkers: you can spend quite some time there, especially on the par 3s. Might we add that to avoid putting beginners off the game altogether, here they will be better off watching or carrying someone's bag. Hiring a caddie is also money well spent.

Ancienne ville d'eau, Woodhall Spa est resté un centre de loisirs et de vacances important, comme une sorte d'oasis boisée au milieu de la campagne du Lincolnshire, à l'instar de Pinehurst aux USA, mais avec un seul parcours (un second ouvre bientôt). Quel parcours aussi, régulièrement classé parmi les meilleurs de Grande-Bretagne. Tracé par Vardon et Colt dans les pins, les bouleaux et la bruyère, sur un sol sablonneux idéal, il a été redessiné par le propriétaire, Hotchkin. Il exige d'abord de garder la balle en jeu du départ, afin d'être encore vivant pour affronter quelques-uns des deuxièmes coups les plus difficiles qui soient (comme les troisièmes !), où il importe d'éviter des bunkers où l'on peut rester longtemps, notamment sur les par 3. On ajoutera seulement que les débutants doivent porter le sac des autres joueurs s'ils ne veulent pas se décourager, et que prendre un caddie est un bon investissement.

Woodhall Spa Golf Club — 1905

The Broadway
ENG - WOODHALL SPA, Lincolnshire LN10 6PU

Office	Secrétariat	(44) 01526 - 352 511
Pro shop	Pro-shop	(44) 01526 - 352 511
Fax	Fax	(44) 01526 - 352 778
Situation	Situation	

21 km E of Lincoln (pop. 80 218)
10 km SW of Horncastle (pop. 4 994)

Annual closure	Fermeture annuelle	no
Weekly closure	Fermeture hebdomadaire	no

Fees main season
Tarifs haute saison 18 holes

	Week days Semaine	We/Bank holidays We/Férié
Individual Individuel	£ 40	£ 40
Couple Couple	£ 80	£ 80

Full day £ 65 - Prior arrangement with the Secretary

Caddy	Caddy	on request/£ 20
Electric Trolley	Chariot électrique	no
Buggy	Voiturette	no
Clubs	Clubs	no

Credit cards Cartes de crédit
VISA - MasterCard - AMEX - Switch

694

Access Accès : On B1191 10 km SW of Horncastle
Map 4 on page 495 Carte 4 Page 495

GOLF COURSE / PARCOURS — 18/20

Site	Site	
Maintenance	Entretien	
Architect	Architecte	Col. S.V. Hotchkin
Type	Type	inland, heathland
Relief	Relief	
Water in play	Eau en jeu	
Exp. to wind	Exposé au vent	
Trees in play	Arbres en jeu	

Scorecard Carte de score	Chp. Chp.	Mens Mess.	Ladies Da.
Length Long.	6250	5897	5203
Par	73	71	73

Advised golfing ability		0	12	24	36
Niveau de jeu recommandé					
Hcp required	Handicap exigé	20 Men, 30 Ladies			

CLUB HOUSE & AMENITIES / CLUB HOUSE ET ANNEXES — 7/10

Pro shop	Pro-shop	
Driving range	Practice	
Sheltered	couvert	20 bays (floodlit)
On grass	sur herbe	no
Putting-green	putting-green	yes
Pitching-green	pitching green	yes

HOTEL FACILITIES / ENVIRONNEMENT HOTELIER — 8/10

HOTELS HÔTELS

Golf Hotel — Woodhall Spa
50 rooms, D £ 65 — 2 km
Tel (44) 01526 - 353 535, Fax (44) 01526 - 353 096

Petwood House Hotel — Woodhall Spa
47 rooms, D £ 90 — 2 km
Tel (44) 01526 - 352 411, Fax (44) 01526 - 353 473

Dower House — Woodhall Spa
7 rooms, D £ 60 — 1 km
Tel (44) 01526 - 352 588, Fax (44) 01526 - 354 045

Forte Posthouse - 70 rooms, D £ 60 — Lincoln 25 km
Tel (44) 01522 - 520 341, Fax (44) 01522 - 510 780

RESTAURANTS RESTAURANTS

Hornblowers - Tel (44) 01526 - 342 124 — Coningsby 4 km
Jew's House - Tel (44) 01522 - 524 851 — Lincoln 25 km

WORPLESDON

This is the third of the three «Ws» around Woking, designed by John Abercromby, who worked with, amongst others, the inimitable Tom Simpson. On arriving you notice the winding first hole and the beautiful houses around the course. You never grow tired of that sensation of privilege you get from playing golf over wide open spaces. A watering system has further enhanced green-keeping, and the greens are very quick, so you'd better stay on the right side of the slopes and the right tier of the multi-tiered greens. If you are looking for a brilliant score, the pin placements here will dictate game strategy. While West Hill and Woking are, in a way, courses where the tee-shot is all-important, Worplesdon calls for excellence on your second shot. Choosing between the three would be like having to refuse the starter, main course or dessert in a good restaurant.

C'est le troisième de la trinité de Woking, cette fois dessiné par John Abercromby, qui a travaillé notamment avec l'inimitable Tom Simpson. En arrivant, on remarque d'une part les méandres du premier trou, et la beauté des maisons environnantes. On ne saurait être insensible à cette sensation de privilège que donne le golf dans de beaux espaces. Et l'arrosage a fait encore progresser l'entretien. Les greens sont souvent très rapides, ce qui implique d'être du bon côté des pentes, et sur le bon plateau quand il y en a plusieurs. Le placement des drapeaux va en fait dicter toute la stratégie si l'on veut faire un score brillant. Si West Hill et Woking sont, un peu, des parcours de mise en jeu, Worplesdon est un parcours de seconds coups. On ne saurait choisir, pas plus qu'on ne refuse l'entrée, le plat ou le dessert dans un bon restaurant...

Worplesdon Golf Club — 1908

Heath House Road
ENG - WOKING, Surrey GU22 0RA

Office	Secrétariat	(44) 01483 - 472 277
Pro shop	Pro-shop	(44) 01483 - 473 287
Fax	Fax	(44) 01483 - 473 303
Situation	Situation	

6 km from Guildford (pop. 122 378)
49 km from Central London (pop. 6 679 700)

Annual closure	Fermeture annuelle	no
Weekly closure	Fermeture hebdomadaire	no
Fees main season	Tarifs haute saison	full day

	Week days Semaine	We/Bank holidays We/Férié
Individual Individuel	£ 55	—
Couple Couple	£ 110	—

Weekends: only with a member

Caddy	Caddy	on request/£ 25
Electric Trolley	Chariot électrique	no
Buggy	Voiturette	no
Clubs	Clubs	£ 10/18 holes

Credit cards Cartes de crédit
VISA - Eurocard - AMEX - DC (not for green fees)

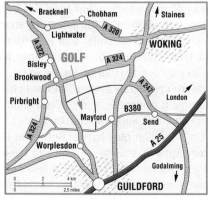

Access Accès : London A3 → Guildford. At Cobham, A245 on right. At Woking, A320 → Guildford, After railway bridge, turn left into Heath House. Golf entrance on right. **Map 8 on page 502** Carte 8 Page 502

GOLF COURSE / PARCOURS — 16/20

Site	Site	
Maintenance	Entretien	
Architect	Architecte	John Abercromby
Type	Type	inland, heathland
Relief	Relief	
Water in play	Eau en jeu	
Exp. to wind	Exposé au vent	
Trees in play	Arbres en jeu	

Scorecard Carte de score	Chp. Chp.	Mens Mess.	Ladies Da.
Length Long.	5760	5760	5040
Par	71	71	73

Advised golfing ability
Niveau de jeu recommandé   0   12   24   36

Hcp required   Handicap exigé   20 Men, 30 Ladies

CLUB HOUSE & AMENITIES / CLUB HOUSE ET ANNEXES — 7/10

Pro shop	Pro-shop	
Driving range	Practice	
Sheltered	couvert	no
On grass	sur herbe	yes
Putting-green	putting-green	yes
Pitching-green	pitching green	no

HOTEL FACILITIES / ENVIRONNEMENT HOTELIER — 6/10

695

HOTELS HÔTELS

Angel Posting House — Guildford
18 rooms, D £ 105 — 6 km
Tel (44) 01483 - 64 555, Fax (44) 01483 - 33 770

Forte Crest — Guildford
109 rooms, D £ 109 — 6 km
Tel (44) 01483 - 574 444, Fax (44) 01483 - 302 960

Blanes Court Hotel — Guildford
29 rooms, D £ 70 — 6 km
Tel (44) 01483 - 573 171, Fax (44) 01483 - 32 780

RESTAURANTS RESTAURANTS

Michel's — Ripley
Tel (44) 01483 - 224 777 — 10 km

Café de Paris — Guildford
Tel (44) 01483 - 34 896 — 6 km

As a country, Scotland is a small in terms of land surface but quite exceptional when it comes to golf, with courses sometimes laid out one after the other in an uninterrupted sequence on either side of the country. There are huge clusters of links course on both the east coast and the west coast of Ayrshire. Here we have included the great links courses but also some lesser known gems around Glasgow and Edinburgh, or between Aberdeen and Inverness. But besides the links courses - the glory of Scotland - we have also elected to present a number of inland clubs, some of which have been laid out over areas of immense beauty, for example in the Highlands. Of course some might consider their yardage to be bordering on the "ridiculous" by today's standards, but they are certainly more than a match for your average long-hitter.

As here we are at the very heart of golf, we could quite easily have included "North Inch" in Perth, a course that was played by King James VI in 1603, or again Askernish on the isle of South Uist, but rather than opt for history or unusual surroundings, we preferred Shiskine in Blackwaterfoot which, although only having twelve holes, remains an amazing reference in course design and for the game of golf. This is particularly relevant at a time when the temptation from America or influence from south of the border has pushed green-fees upward, and when golf in Scotland has always been and fortunately always will be a game for everyone. With money to spare you can build courses like the now highly reputed Loch Lomond or Skibo, which would have deserved inclusion, but no visitors are allowed. With money to spare you can shift mountains, dig lakes, model and sometimes even massacre natural landscape, but you won't change the sun's path across the sky or the rhythm of the seasons. In Scotland, golf courses were created by Mother Nature helped by the genius of a few brilliant designers, and golf is a shining light for all. Some courses are snow-bound in Winter, it sometimes rains and the wind can play havoc. But while the best time to play is from April to September, you can tee-off virtually all year... just don't forget to pack a few thick sweaters. You don't come to Scotland the way you would fly to the Caribbean. You come here to play, breathe and live golf.

Ecosse

L 'Ecosse est un petit pays en superficie mais un exceptionnel pays de golf, où les parcours peuvent se succéder de manière pratiquement ininterrompue sur les grandes concentrations de links des côtes Est comme de la côte de l'Ayrshire à l'Ouest. Nous avons inclus ici les plus grands links, mais aussi de petites merveilles moins connues, rassemblés autour de Glasgow et d'Edimbourg, mais aussi d'Aberdeen à Inverness. En dehors des links qui ont fait la gloire de l'Ecosse, nous avons aussi choisi de vous présenter des parcours «inland», dont la plupart ont été comme posés sur des espaces d'une intense beauté, comme dans les Highlands. Bien sûr, on pourra estimer leur longueur parfois «ridicule,» mais en ramener un bon score n'est pas à la portée du premier cogneur venu.

Sans aucun doute, comme nous sommes au cœur du golf, nous aurions presque pu inclure le *"North Inch"* de Perth, sur un terrain où a joué le roi James VI en 1603, ou encore Askernish dans l'île de South Uist, mais, quitte à être historique ou dépaysant, nous avons préféré Shiskine à Blackwaterfoot, qui compte peut-être douze trous, mais constitue une étonnante référence d'architecture et de jeu. Il n'est pas inutile de rappeler les fondamentaux du dessin de parcours, ou tout au moins les garnds témoignages du passé, à l'heure où la tentation américaine ou l'exemple des grands clubs modernes anglais ont poussé les green-fees vers le haut, alors même que le golf en Ecosse a toujours été un jeu pour tous, et le reste fort heureusement.

Avec beaucoup d'argent, on peut créer des parcours comme Loch Lomond ou Skibo, de fameuse réputation, qui auraient évidemment mérite de figurer ici, mais ils n'acceptent aucun visiteur. Avec beaucoup d'argent, on peut déplacer des montagnes, creuser des lacs, modeler la nature, la torturer parfois, mais on ne changera pas la course du soleil ni le rythme des saisons. En Ecosse, les golfs ont été fait par la nature et quelques architectes de génie, le soleil du golf brille pour tous, certains parcours sont enneigés en hiver, la pluie tombe parfois, le vent souffle aussi, et si la meilleure saison va d'avril à septembre, on peut jouer pratiquement toute l'année... avec de gros pulls dans la valise. On ne vient pas en Ecosse comme dans les Caraïbes. On vient ici pour jouer au golf, pour respirer le golf, vivre le golf.

697

The Millennium Guide

There is no shortage of golf courses in the region of Deeside, each one having its own character often shaped by the setting. Aboyne is a real park and is by and large flat, except on the edge of the course where the holes run around a small hill and the slopes from the 11th to the 14th holes take us into more rocky countryside. Reassuringly, particularly for your game strategy, the course is free of hidden hazards as no-one likes to fall into that sort of trap the first time they play a new course. There are though just a few elevated or tiered greens that might cause you trouble. Generally speaking, Aboyne is a little similar to Ballater, only with a little more variety in hole layout.

Cette région du Deeside ne manque pas de parcours de golf, chacun avec son propre caractère, souvent fonction de l'environnement. Aboyne est un véritable parc, généralement plat. Sauf à l'extrémité du parcours où les trous tournent autour d'une petite colline et ces quelques reliefs du 11 au 14 qui nous amènent dans un paysage de lande rocailleuse. Quand on joue un parcours pour la première fois, il n'est pas toujours agréable d'être piégé par des obstacles cachés, mais ici, ce n'est pas le cas, ce qui peut rassurer sur la stratégie à mettre en oeuvre. Seuls quelques greens surélevés, ou à plateau peuvent causer quelques surprises. En règle général, Aboyne est un peu similaire de caractère avec Ballater, mais avec un peu plus de variété de dessin des trous.

Aboyne Golf Club — 1883

Formaston Park
SCO - ABOYNE, Aberdeenshire AB34 5 HE

Office	Secrétariat	(44) 013398 -870 78
Pro shop	Pro-shop	(44) 013398 -863 28
Fax	Fax	(44) 013398 -875 92
Situation	Situation	

48 km W of Aberdeen (pop. 204 885)
19 km W of Banchory (pop. 6 230)

Annual closure	Fermeture annuelle	no
Weekly closure	Fermeture hebdomadaire	no

Fees main season
Tarifs haute saison 18 holes

	Week days Semaine	We/Bank holidays We/Férié
Individual Individuel	£ 18	£ 24
Couple Couple	£ 36	£ 48

Full days: £ 22 - £ 28 (Weekends)

Caddy	Caddy	on request
Electric Trolley	Chariot électrique	no
Buggy	Voiturette	no
Clubs	Clubs	yes

Credit cards Cartes de crédit Eurocard - MasterCard

Access Accès : Aberdeen, A93. In Aboyne, turn off to right at club entrance.
Map 1 on page 489 Carte 1 Page 489

698

GOLF COURSE / PARCOURS — 14/20

Site	Site	
Maintenance	Entretien	
Architect	Architecte	Archie Simpson
Type	Type	parkland
Relief	Relief	
Water in play	Eau en jeu	
Exp. to wind	Exposé au vent	
Trees in play	Arbres en jeu	

Scorecard Carte de score	Chp. Chp.	Mens Mess.	Ladies Da.
Length Long.	5447	5112	4906
Par	68	67	72

Advised golfing ability Niveau de jeu recommandé	0	12	24	36
Hcp required Handicap exigé	no			

CLUB HOUSE & AMENITIES / CLUB HOUSE ET ANNEXES — 6/10

Pro shop	Pro-shop	
Driving range	Practice	
Sheltered	couvert	no
On grass	sur herbe	no
Putting-green	putting-green	yes
Pitching-green	pitching green	yes

HOTEL FACILITIES / ENVIRONNEMENT HOTELIER — 6/10

HOTELS HÔTELS
Birse Lodge — Aboyne, close
12 rooms, D £ 70
Tel (44) 01339 - 886 253

Tullich Lodge — Ballater, 14 km
10 rooms, D £ 200 (with dinner)
Tel (44) 013397 - 55 406
Fax (44) 013397 - 55 397

RESTAURANTS RESTAURANTS
The Boat Inn (Pub) — Aboyne, close
Tel (44) 01339 - 886 137

Alloa is one of a bunch of very good inland courses in Scotland, in a region little known by golfing tourists. You shouldn't pass through here without stopping off and playing this fine course, once again restyled by James Braid. Where hasn't the man left his mark in Scotland? If you are a «collector» of James Braid courses, you will recognise his strategic placing of bunkers denoting an astute knowledge of both the game at the highest level and of average players' abilities, a rare feature from a former champion such as he. While there are courses for driving and courses for approach shots, this one demands both to reach greens which are sometimes elevated and even blind and call for special care. This is a hilly course so physical fitness will help.

Alloa fait partie du petit peloton des très bons parcours «inland» d'Ecosse, dans une région assez peu connue des touristes golfiques. Il ne faudrait pas passer par là sans connaître cette belle réalisation, une fois de plus remaniée par James Braid, mais où n'est-il pas intervenu ? Si vous «collectionnez» ses réalisations, vous retrouverez ici un placement stratégique des obstacles, dénotant une connaissance aiguë du jeu au plus haut niveau mais aussi des joueurs moyens, ce qui est plus rare de la part d'un ancien champion comme lui. S'il est des parcours de drivers et des parcours de «seconds coups,» celui-ci exige autant des départs aux greens, avec une attention particulière pour ces derniers, parfois surélevés, voire aveugles. Le relief est ici bien marqué, attention à venir en bonne forme physique.

Alloa Golf Club — 1891

Schawpark
SCO - SAUCHIE, Clackmannanshire FK10 3AX

Office	Secrétariat	(44) 01259 - 722 745
Pro shop	Pro-shop	(44) 01259 - 724 476
Fax	Fax	
Situation	Situation	

24 km W of Dunfermline (pop. 29 436)

Annual closure	Fermeture annuelle	no
Weekly closure	Fermeture hebdomadaire	no

Fees main season
Tarifs haute saison 18 holes

	Week days Semaine	We/Bank holidays We/Férié
Individual Individuel	£ 20	£ 25
Couple Couple	£ 40	£ 50

Full days: £ 25 - £ 30 (weekends)

Caddy	Caddy	no
Electric Trolley	Chariot électrique	yes
Buggy	Voiturette	no
Clubs	Clubs	yes

Credit cards Cartes de crédit
VISA - Eurocard - MasterCard - AMEX - DC

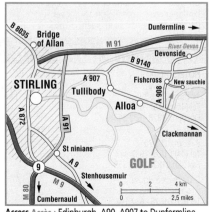

Access Accès : Edinburgh, A90, A907 to Dunfermline and Alloa. Turn right onto A908.
course on the right in the village of Sauchie.
Map 2 on page 491 Carte 2 Page 491

GOLF COURSE / PARCOURS — 15/20

Site	Site	
Maintenance	Entretien	
Architect	Architecte	James Braid
Type	Type	parkland
Relief	Relief	
Water in play	Eau en jeu	
Exp. to wind	Exposé au vent	
Trees in play	Arbres en jeu	

Scorecard Carte de score	Chp. Chp.	Mens Mess.	Ladies Da.
Length Long.	5570	5460	4895
Par	70	69	73

Advised golfing ability Niveau de jeu recommandé	0	12	24	36
Hcp required Handicap exigé	no			

CLUB HOUSE & AMENITIES / CLUB HOUSE ET ANNEXES — 7/10

Pro shop	Pro-shop	
Driving range	Practice	
Sheltered	couvert	no
On grass	sur herbe	yes
Putting-green	putting-green	yes
Pitching-green	pitching green	yes

HOTEL FACILITIES / ENVIRONNEMENT HOTELIER — 6/10

HOTELS HÔTELS
Gean House — Alloa
7 rooms, D £ 140 — 5 km
Tel (44) 01259 - 219 275
Fax (44) 01259 - 213 827

Stirling Highland — Stirling
70 rooms, D £ 90 — 14 km
Tel (44) 01786 - 475 444
Fax (44) 01786 - 462 929

RESTAURANTS RESTAURANTS
Farriers — Alva
Tel (44) 01259 - 762 702 — 5 km

Unicorn Inn — Kincardine
Tel (44) 01259 - 730 704 — 6 km

699

Within the immediate vicinity of Blairgowrie, Dundee and Perth, the Alyth course does not have the fame it deserves, partly because fame today comes through hosting top tournaments. This course now is too short for that but is way above average in terms of appeal. With good, well protected greens, endless trees and heather edging the fairways and dangerous bunkers, Alyth requires great accuracy and is ideal for getting your ironwork into good shape. A few very good holes and some superb views over the Perthshire countryside add extra appeal to a guaranteed good day's golfing. The region of Angus also offers a variety facilities for leisure and excursions.

A proximité immédiate de Blairgowrie, Dundee et Perth, le parcours d'Alyth n'a pas connu la notoriété qu'il mérite, en partie parce qu'elle se fait aujourd'hui en recevant de grands tournois. Ce parcours est aujourd'hui trop court pour cela, mais son intérêt est nettement au-dessus de la moyenne. Avec de bons greens correctement défendus contre les assauts, des arbres nombreux et la bruyère bordant les fairways, des bunkers dangereux, il demande une grande précision, et c'est idéal pour travailler son jeu de fers. Quelques très bons trous et des vues superbes sur la campagne du Perthshire ajoutent un intérêt supplémentaire à une bonne journée de golf garanti sans souffrances. Et cette région de l'Angus offre de multiples opportunités de loisirs et d'excursions.

Alyth Golf Club — 1894

Pitcrocknie
SCO - ALYTH, Perthshire PH10 7AB

Office	Secrétariat	(44) 01828 - 632 268
Pro shop	Pro-shop	(44) 01828 - 633 411
Fax	Fax	(44) 01828 - 633 491
Situation	Situation	

8 km E of Blairgowrie (pop. 5 208)
24 km NW of Dundee (pop. 165 873)

Annual closure	Fermeture annuelle	no
Weekly closure	Fermeture hebdomadaire	no

Fees main season	Tarifs haute saison	18 holes
	Week days Semaine	We/Bank holidays We/Férié
Individual Individuel	£ 20	£ 25
Couple Couple	£ 40	£ 50

Full day: £ 30 - £ 40 (weekends)

Caddy	Caddy	on request
Electric Trolley	Chariot électrique	£ 4/18 holes
Buggy	Voiturette	no
Clubs	Clubs	no
Credit cards Cartes de crédit		no

700

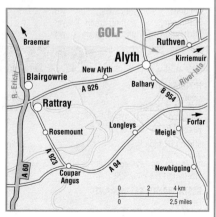

Access Accès : Edinburgh M90, Exit 11 → Perth, then A94 through Coupar to Meigle. Turn right on B954. Golf 1.5 km (1 m.) before Alyth.
Map 1 on page 489 Carte 1 Page 489

GOLF COURSE / PARCOURS — 14/20

Site	Site	
Maintenance	Entretien	
Architect	Architecte	Tom Morris James Braid
Type	Type	heathland
Relief	Relief	
Water in play	Eau en jeu	
Exp. to wind	Exposé au vent	
Trees in play	Arbres en jeu	

Scorecard Carte de score	Chp. Chp.	Mens Mess.	Ladies Da.
Length Long.	5646	5409	4770
Par	70	70	71

Advised golfing ability Niveau de jeu recommandé	0	12	24	36
Hcp required	Handicap exigé	certificate		

CLUB HOUSE & AMENITIES / CLUB HOUSE ET ANNEXES — 6/10

Pro shop	Pro-shop	
Driving range	Practice	
Sheltered	couvert	not yet
On grass	sur herbe	yes
Putting-green	putting-green	yes
Pitching-green	pitching green	no

HOTEL FACILITIES / ENVIRONNEMENT HOTELIER — 6/10

HOTELS HÔTELS

Lands of Loyal 14 rooms, D £ 79 Tel (44) 01828 - 633 151 Fax (44) 01828 - 633 313	Alyth 1 km
Alyth Hotel 8 rooms, D £ 70 Tel (44) 01828 - 632 447 Fax (44) 01828 - 632 355	Alyth 1 km
Drumnacree House 6 rooms, D £ 80 Tel (44) 01828 - 632 194	Alyth 1 km

RESTAURANTS RESTAURANTS

Lands of Loyal Tel (44) 01828 - 633 151	Alyth 1 km

AYR (BELLEISLE)

16 **5** **7**

Most of the visitors to this region head for Prestwick, Royal Troon and Turnberry and might easily neglect a number of little gems of which this is a typical example. Designed by James Braid (who else?) in 1927 to meet the huge demand for new courses, Belleisle was laid out in a public park close to the sea but without the features of a links. This is nevertheless a challenging course with a lot of character where there is something almost odd about the views over the sea in the setting of trees. With no hidden dangers, golfing can be enjoyed without fear as long as you choose the right clubs and the right way of playing them. The weather will decide whether you aim high or low. An ideal course for week-end golfing when the «big» courses are crowded.

La plupart des visiteurs de la région se concentrent sur Prestwick, Royal Troon et Turnberry, et risquent de négliger quelques petits joyaux. En voici un exemple typique. Dessiné par James Braid en 1927 pour satisfaire une demande galopante de nouveaux parcours, Belleisle a été créé dans un parc public proche de la mer, mais sans les caractéristiques des links. Il n'empêche qu'il s'agit d'un parcours exigeant, avec beaucoup de caractère, où certains points de vue sur l'eau ont quelque chose d'étrange dans cet environnement d'arbres. Sans aucun danger caché, ce parcours peut être immédiatement dégusté sans crainte, du moment que l'on y choisit les bons clubs et la bonne manière de s'en servir. Suivant le temps, on pourra y jouer balles roulées ou balles levées. Idéal pour jouer en week-end quand les «grands» sont très difficiles d'accès.

Belleisle Golf Course — 1927

Belleisle Park, Doonfoot Road
SCO - AYR, Ayrshire KA7 4DU

Office	Secrétariat	(44) 01292 - 441 258
Pro shop	Pro-shop	(44) 01292 - 441 314
Fax	Fax	(44) 01292 - 442 632
Situation	Situation	

1 km from Ayr (pop. 47 872)

Annual closure	Fermeture annuelle	no
Weekly closure	Fermeture hebdomadaire	no

Fees main season
Tarifs haute saison 18 holes

	Week days Semaine	We/Bank holidays We/Férié
Individual Individuel	£ 18.50	£ 20
Couple Couple	£ 37	£ 40

Full days: £ 26 - £ 30 (weekends)

Caddy	Caddy	on request
Electric Trolley	Chariot électrique	no
Buggy	Voiturette	no
Clubs	Clubs	£ 10/18 holes

Credit cards Cartes de crédit
VISA - Eurocard - MasterCard

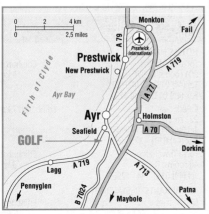

Access Accès : 1 km S of Ayr in Belleisle Park
Map 3 on page 492 Carte 3 Page 492

GOLF COURSE
PARCOURS — **16**/20

Site	Site	
Maintenance	Entretien	
Architect	Architecte	James Braid
Type	Type	parkland
Relief	Relief	
Water in play	Eau en jeu	
Exp. to wind	Exposé au vent	
Trees in play	Arbres en jeu	

Scorecard Carte de score	Chp. Chp.	Mens Mess.	Ladies Da.
Length Long.	5855	5509	5150
Par	71	71	74

Advised golfing ability Niveau de jeu recommandé	0	12	24	36
Hcp required Handicap exigé	no			

CLUB HOUSE & AMENITIES
CLUB HOUSE ET ANNEXES — **5**/10

Pro shop	Pro-shop	
Driving range	Practice	
Sheltered	couvert	no
On grass	sur herbe	yes
Putting-green	putting-green	yes
Pitching-green	pitching green	no

HOTEL FACILITIES
ENVIRONNEMENT HOTELIER — **7**/10

HOTELS HÔTELS
Fairfield House — Ayr
33 rooms, D £ 120 — 3 km
Tel (44) 01292 - 267 461, Fax (44) 01292 - 261 456

Kylestrome — Ayr
12 rooms, D £ 80 — 3 km
Tel (44) 01292 - 262 474, Fax (44) 01292 - 260 863

Pickwick — Ayr 2 km
15 rooms, D £ 70
Tel (44) 01292 - 260 111, Fax (44) 01292 - 285 348

Northpark House — Alloway
5 rooms, D £ 85 — 2 km
Tel (44) 01292 - 442 336, Fax (44) 01292 - 445 572

RESTAURANTS RESTAURANTS
Fouters — Ayr
Tel (44) 01292 - 261 391 — 3 km

701

While the family is visiting Edinburgh or doing some shopping, you'll have the time to play 18 holes at Baberton to the south-west of the city. Created in 1893 and designed by the great Wille Park Jnr, this is no longer a tournament course but some of the par 4s and par 3s are anything but easy. Without being really dangerous, the trees, bunkers and ditches are in play just enough to bother average players, who make up the major share of green-fees here during the week. The trees are particularly beautiful especially in their Autumn colours, when we visited. Don't be surprised if you're late getting back, as the Clubhouse reserves a warm welcome to all. The best idea would be for the family to come and meet you there.

Pendant que la famille visite Edinburgh ou fait du shopping, vous avez le temps de faire 18 trous à Baberton, au sud-ouest de la ville. Fondé en 1893 et dessiné par le grand Willie Park Jr, ce n'est plus aujourd'hui un parcours de championnat, bien que certains de ses par 4 et ses cinq par 3 ne soient pas des plus faciles. Sans être vraiment dangereux, les arbres, les bunkers et les fossés sont assez en jeu pour inquiéter le joueur moyen, qui fournit l'essentiel de la clientèle extérieure en semaine. Les arbres sont ici particulièrement beaux, spécialement dans leurs teintes d'automne. Et si vous êtes en retard pour rejoindre les vôtres, rien d'étonnant, le Clubhouse est accueillant. La bonne idée, c'est qu'ils vous rejoignent ici.

Baberton Golf Club — 1893

50 Baberton Avenue, Juniper Green
SCO - EDINBURGH EH14 5DU

Office	Secrétariat	(44) 0131 - 453 4911
Pro shop	Pro-shop	(44) 0131 - 453 3555
Fax	Fax	
Situation	Situation	

9 km SW of Edinburgh centre (pop. 418 914)

Annual closure	Fermeture annuelle	no
Weekly closure	Fermeture hebdomadaire	no

Fees main season
Tarifs haute saison 18 holes

	Week days Semaine	We/Bank holidays We/Férié
Individual Individuel	£ 18.50	—
Couple Couple	£ 37	—

Full weekday: £ 28.50 - Weekends: members only

Caddy	Caddy	no
Electric Trolley	Chariot électrique	no
Buggy	Voiturette	no
Clubs	Clubs	yes

Credit cards Cartes de crédit — no

702

Access Accès : Edinburgh A70 Slateford Road and Lanark Road until by-pass (A720), Juniper Green and Baberton Junction.
Map 3 on page 493 Carte 3 Page 493

GOLF COURSE / PARCOURS — 14/20

Site	Site	
Maintenance	Entretien	
Architect	Architecte	Willie Park
Type	Type	parkland
Relief	Relief	
Water in play	Eau en jeu	
Exp. to wind	Exposé au vent	
Trees in play	Arbres en jeu	

Scorecard Carte de score	Chp. Chp.	Mens Mess.	Ladies Da.
Length Long.	5601	5601	4985
Par	69	69	72

Advised golfing ability Niveau de jeu recommandé	0	12	24	36

Hcp required Handicap exigé — no

CLUB HOUSE & AMENITIES / CLUB HOUSE ET ANNEXES — 6/10

Pro shop	Pro-shop	
Driving range	Practice	
Sheltered	couvert	no
On grass	sur herbe	no
Putting-green	putting-green	yes
Pitching-green	pitching green	no

HOTEL FACILITIES / ENVIRONNEMENT HOTELIER — 8/10

HOTELS HÔTELS

Forte Posthouse 204 rooms, D £ 70 Tel (44) 0131 - 334 0390 Fax (44) 0131 - 334 9237		Edinburgh 5 km
Caledonian 223 rooms, D £ 200 Tel (44) 0131 - 459 9988 Fax (44) 0131 - 225 6632		Edinburgh 7 km
Forte Travelodge 40 rooms, D £ 35 Tel (44) 0131 - 441 4296		Edinburgh 3 km

RESTAURANTS RESTAURANTS

Mackenzies Tel (44) 0131 - 441 2587		Edinburgh 2 km
Indian Cavalry Club Tel (44) 0131 - 228 3282		Edinburgh 5 km

Here we are just a few miles from Balmoral Castle, the Royal Family's summer residence, in a beautiful region of the Highlands along the banks of the river Dee, which borders the course. The area is more popular for tourism than golf, or even for fishing or hunting from Spring to late Autumn only (at 2,000 ft. above sea level, the winter weather always has the final say). The course, rather hilly although never too exhausting to walk on a soft carpet of grass, winds its way through heather, broom and trees. James Braid and Harry Vardon added their personal touch to a very pleasant layout, where the land has been used very intelligently. This may not be the world's most difficult course but playing here certainly is time well spent.

Nous ne sommes qu'à quelques kilomètres du château de Balmoral, résidence d'été de la famille royale, dans une très belle région des Highlands, en bordure de la rivière Dee servant de limite au parcours. On vient plus ici pour le tourisme que pour le golf, ou encore pour la pêche et la chasse, du printemps à la fin de l'automne, car nous sommes à 600 mètres d'altitude. Les reliefs du parcours sont assez prononcés, bien que l'ensemble ne soit pas épuisant, grâce à un gazon très fourni, insinué dans la bruyère, les genêts et les arbres. James Braid et Harry Vardon ont apporté leur touche personnelle à un dessin très agréable, où le terrain a été utilisé avec beaucoup d'à-propos. Ce n'est peut-être pas le parcours le plus difficile du monde, mais on n'y perdra jamais son temps.

Ballater Golf Club — 1892

Victoria Road
SCO - BALLATER, Aberdeenshire AB35 5QX

Office	Secrétariat	(44) 013397 - 55 567
Pro shop	Pro-shop	(44) 013397 - 55 658
Fax	Fax	(44) 013397 - 55 057
Situation	Situation	

67 km W of Aberdeen (pop. 204 885)

Annual closure	Fermeture annuelle	no
Weekly closure	Fermeture hebdomadaire	no

Chances of snow in winter months

Fees main season
Tarifs haute saison 18 holes

	Week days Semaine	We/Bank holidays We/Férié
Individual Individuel	£ 18	£ 21
Couple Couple	£ 36	£ 42

Full day: £ 26 - £ 30 (weekends)

Caddy	Caddy	on request
Electric Trolley	Chariot électrique	yes
Buggy	Voiturette	yes
Clubs	Clubs	yes

Credit cards Cartes de crédit
VISA - MasterCard - Switch

Access Accès : Aberdeen, A93 West → Ballater, Balmoral Castle
Map 1 on page 489 Carte 1 Page 489

GOLF COURSE / PARCOURS — 15/20

Site	Site	
Maintenance	Entretien	
Architect	Architecte	James Braid
Type	Type	parkland
Relief	Relief	
Water in play	Eau en jeu	
Exp. to wind	Exposé au vent	
Trees in play	Arbres en jeu	

Scorecard / Carte de score	Chp. / Chp.	Mens / Mess.	Ladies / Da.
Length Long.	5545	5638	5278
Par	70	67	71

Advised golfing ability Niveau de jeu recommandé		0 12 24 36
Hcp required Handicap exigé	no	

CLUB HOUSE & AMENITIES / CLUB HOUSE ET ANNEXES — 6/10

Pro shop	Pro-shop	
Driving range	Practice	
Sheltered	couvert	no
On grass	sur herbe	no
Putting-green	putting-green	no
Pitching-green	pitching green	no

HOTEL FACILITIES / ENVIRONNEMENT HOTELIER — 7/10

HOTELS HÔTELS

Craigendarroch - 38 rooms, D £ 140 — Ballater
Tel (44) 013397 - 55 858 - Fax (44) 013397 - 55 447

Tullich Lodge — Ballater
10 rooms, D £ 200 (with dinner)
Tel (44) 013397 - 55 406 - Fax (44) 013397 - 55 397

Darroch Leargh - 18 rooms, D £ 90 — Ballater
Tel (44) 013397 - 55 443 - Fax (44) 013397 - 55 252

Glen Lui - 19 rooms, D £ 65 — Ballater
Tel (44) 013397 - 55 402 - Fax (44) 013397 - 55 545

RESTAURANTS RESTAURANTS

Oaks — Ballater
Tel (44) 01339 - 55 858

Highlander — Ballater

703

Starting out from Aberdeen, the A93 runs up the Grampian mountains alongside the river Dee. You won't be alone in making this climb, the salmon have been doing it for centuries, as you will probably see from the Brigg O'Feugh, an 18th century bridge in the middle of the village of Banchory. The splendours of Royal Deeside include this golf course, which lies right alongside the river. Recently restyled by some keen local golfers, this is a combination of wide open space and tree-lined fairways. Big-hitting is not always an essential virtue on this ideal holiday course, but the par 3s are long (except the 16th) and tricky. The best is certainly hole N°11 (180 yards/162 metres) with OB to the left and a burn in front of the green. There are also half a dozen or so short par 4s that are fun to play. Non-golfers have lots to do in this region and can even take an indiscreet look at Balmoral Castle, the Queen's summer residence.

En partant d'Aberdeen, la A93 s'enfonce dans les Grampians, en longeant la rivière Dee. Vous ne serez pas seul à remonter, les saumons le font aussi depuis des siècles, comme on peut les apercevoir du Brigg o'Feugh, un pont du XVIIIè siècle au milieu du village de Banchory. Parmi les splendeurs du Royal Deeside, ce parcours qui longe la rivière, récemment remanié par des enthousiastes golfeurs locaux associe les espaces ouverts avec des fairways bordés d'arbres. La force de frappe n'est pas une qualité obligatoire sur ce parcours idéal pour des vacances, mais les par 3 sont longs (sauf le 16) et délicats. Le meilleur d'entre eux est sans doute le 11, de 162 mètres (180 yards), avec hors-limites à gauche et un «burn» devant le green. On remarquera aussi une demi-douzaine de courts par 4 très amusants. Quant aux non golfeurs, ils ne manqueront pas de sources d'intérêt dans cette région, et jetteront un coup d'oeil indiscret sur le Château de Balmoral, résidence d'été de la Reine.

Banchory Golf Club — 1906

Kinnesky Road
SCO - BANCHORY AB31 5TA

Office	Secrétariat	(44) 01330 - 822 365
Pro shop	Pro-shop	(44) 01330 - 822 447
Fax	Fax	(44) 01330 - 822 491
Situation	Situation	

29 km W of Aberdeen (pop. 204 885)

Annual closure	Fermeture annuelle	no
Weekly closure	Fermeture hebdomadaire	no

Fees main season
Tarifs haute saison 18 holes

	Week days Semaine	We/Bank holidays We/Férié
Individual Individuel	£ 17	£ 21
Couple Couple	£ 34	£ 42

Full day: £ 23 - £ 26 (weekends)

Caddy	Caddy	no
Electric Trolley	Chariot électrique	yes
Buggy	Voiturette	yes
Clubs	Clubs	yes

Credit cards Cartes de crédit	no

704

Map

Lumphanan, Garlogie, A 980, B 977, Brathens, Aboyne, Aberdeen, Banchory, Bridge of Canny, A 93, River Dee, GOLF, Bridge of Feugh, A 957, Strachan, B 974, Montrose, Water of Dye, Stonehaven

Access Accès : Aberdeen, A93, Golf in village centre.
Map 1 on page 489 Carte 1 Page 489

GOLF COURSE PARCOURS — 14/20

Site	Site	■■■■■□□
Maintenance	Entretien	■■■■■□□
Architect	Architecte	Local enthusiasts

Type	Type	parkland
Relief	Relief	■■□□□□□
Water in play	Eau en jeu	■■□□□□□
Exp. to wind	Exposé au vent	■■■■■□□
Trees in play	Arbres en jeu	■■■■■□□

Scorecard Carte de score	Chp. Chp.	Mens Mess.	Ladies Da.
Length Long.	5255	4990	4732
Par	69	68	71

Advised golfing ability	0	12	24	36
Niveau de jeu recommandé				
Hcp required	Handicap exigé	no		

CLUB HOUSE & AMENITIES
CLUB HOUSE ET ANNEXES — 7/10

Pro shop	Pro-shop	■■■■□□□
Driving range	Practice	■■■□□□□
Sheltered	couvert	no
On grass	sur herbe	no
Putting-green	putting-green	yes
Pitching-green	pitching green	yes

HOTEL FACILITIES
ENVIRONNEMENT HOTELIER — 7/10

HOTELS HÔTELS

Tor-Na-Coille — Banchory
24 rooms, from D £ 76 — 0.5 km
Tel (44) 01330 - 822 242, Fax (44) 01330 - 824 012

Raemoir House — Banchory
20 rooms, from D £ 85 — 5 km
Tel (44) 01330 - 824 884, Fax (44) 01330 - 822 171

Burnett Arms — Banchory
16 rooms, D £ 62 — 0.5 km
Tel (44) 01330 - 824 944, Fax (44) 01330 - 825 553

RESTAURANTS RESTAURANTS

Milton — Crathes
Tel (44) 01330 - 844 566 — 6 km

Parker's — Banchory
Tel (44) 01330 - 824 789 — 0.5 km

In a magnificent resort located in some of Scotland's finest countryside, this course designed by Thomas and Alliss in 1974 brought a welcome alternative to the famous Rosemount course. There is of course a definite American influence in this layout over a thickly treed landscape (pine-trees especially). The fairways are narrow and then the heather makes things a little more complicated, but the designers have often left a few open corridors to the greens to make things easier for Scottish golfers who are not always experts at lofting the ball. We would have liked a little more breathing space for the tee-shot, as players who are neither too long nor too straight will have a tough time if they choose to play from the back tees. The course has aged well even though some might find this still just a touch artificial.

Dans ce magnifique ensemble situé dans un des très beaux paysages d'Ecosse, ce parcours de Thomas et Alliss a apporté en 1974 une alternative bienvenue au fameux Rosemount Course. Bien sûr, on trouve une certaine influence américaine dans leur dessin tracé dans un paysage très boisé (surtout de pins). Les fairways sont étroits, la bruyère complique ensuite les choses, mais les architectes ont souvent laissé quelques passages en ouverture des greens pour faciliter le travail des joueurs écossais pas toujours virtuoses des balles levées. On aimerait parfois une plus grande sensation d'espace au moment de driver, car les joueurs ni très longs, ni très droits souffriront s'ils choisissent les départs reculés. Le parcours a bien vieilli, bien qu'on puisse toujours le trouver un rien artificiel.

Blairgowrie Golf Club — 1974

Rosemount
SCO - BLAIRGOWRIE, Perthshire PH10 6LG

Office	Secrétariat	(44) 01250 - 872 622
Pro shop	Pro-shop	(44) 01250 - 872 594
Fax	Fax	(44) 01250 - 875 451
Situation	Situation	

35 km from Perth (pop. 123 495)

Annual closure	Fermeture annuelle	no
Weekly closure	Fermeture hebdomadaire	no

Fees main season	Tarifs haute saison	18 holes
	Week days	We/Bank holidays
	Semaine	We/Férié
Individual Individuel	£ 40	£ 45
Couple Couple	£ 80	£ 90

Day ticket for a round on both courses: £ 60- £ 75 (Weekends)

Caddy	Caddy	on request
Electric Trolley	Chariot électrique	
Buggy	Voiturette	£ 17/18 holes
Clubs	Clubs	£ 5-20/18 holes

Credit cards Cartes de crédit
VISA - Eurocard - MasterCard - AMEX - DC - JCB

Access Accès : Edinburgh M90 to Perth, then A93 → Blairgowrie (golf 2 km South of Blairgowrie)
Map 1 on page 489 Carte 1 Page 489

GOLF COURSE / PARCOURS — 15/20

Site	Site	
Maintenance	Entretien	
Architect	Architecte	Dave Thomas
		Peter Alliss
Type	Type	heathland, inland
Relief	Relief	
Water in play	Eau en jeu	
Exp. to wind	Exposé au vent	
Trees in play	Arbres en jeu	

Scorecard	Chp.	Mens	Ladies
Carte de score	Chp.	Mess.	Da.
Length Long.	6290	5805	5420
Par	72	71	73

Advised golfing ability		0 12 24 36
Niveau de jeu recommandé		
Hcp required	Handicap exigé	certificate

CLUB HOUSE & AMENITIES / CLUB HOUSE ET ANNEXES — 8/10

Pro shop	Pro-shop	
Driving range	Practice	
Sheltered	couvert	no
On grass	sur herbe	yes
Putting-green	putting-green	yes
Pitching-green	pitching green	no

705

HOTEL FACILITIES / ENVIRONNEMENT HOTELIER — 6/10

HOTELS HÔTELS

Rosemount	Golf	
12 rooms, D £ 55	on site	
Tel (44) 01250 - 872 604		
Fax (44) 01250 - 874 496		

Kinloch House	Blairgowrie	
21 rooms, D £ 165 (w. dinner)	3 km	
Tel (44) 01250 - 884 237		
Fax (44) 01250 - 884 333		

Altamount House	Blairgowrie	
7 rooms, D £ 75	2 km	
Tel (44) 01250 - 873 512		
Fax (44) 01250 - 876 200		

RESTAURANTS RESTAURANTS

Rosemount	Golf	
Tel (44) 01250 - 872 604	on site	

For many golfers this is one of the best British inland courses. It's a pity they had to sacrifice two or three holes to cater to the building of the Lansdowne course but James Braid had already altered the original layout by Alister MacKenzie. Despite this, Rosemount has lost nothing of its charm and of the marvellous feeling of tranquillity you get when playing here, as each hole is clearly separated from the others by a thick row of trees. The wildlife and flora add to the beauty of the spot, particularly in Autumn, and to this excellent course where you need to play in every direction. Beneath its kindly exterior, Rosemount cleverly conceals perhaps not the hazards but at least its difficulties. And as it is never tiring to play, it is worth more than the one visit.

C'est pour beaucoup l'un des meilleurs parcours intérieurs de Grande-Bretagne. On regrette un peu le sacrifice de deux ou trois trous au moment de la construction du Lansdowne Course, mais James Braid avait déjà retouché le travail original d'Alister MacKenzie. Rosemount n'a rien perdu pour autant de son charme, et de la merveilleuse sensation de paix qu'on y éprouve, chaque trou étant nettement séparé des autres par d'épais rideaux d'arbres. La vie sauvage et le flore ajoutent encore à la beauté du lieu, notamment en automne. En plus, c'est un excellent parcours où il faut savoir jouer dans tous les sens, et qui cache bien, sinon ses obstacles, du moins ses difficultés sous des dehors souriants. Comme il n'est pas non plus fatigant à jouer, il mérite mieux qu'une simple visite.

Blairgowrie Golf Club

1889

Rosemount
SCO - BLAIRGOWRIE, Perthshire PH10 6LG

Office	Secrétariat	(44) 01250 - 872 622
Pro shop	Pro-shop	(44) 01250 - 872 594
Fax	Fax	(44) 01250 - 875 451
Situation	Situation	

35 km from Perth (pop. 123 495)

Annual closure	Fermeture annuelle	no
Weekly closure	Fermeture hebdomadaire	no

Fees main season Tarifs haute saison · 18 holes

	Week days Semaine	We/Bank holidays We/Férié
Individual Individuel	£ 50	£ 55
Couple Couple	£ 100	£ 110

Day ticket for a round on both courses: £ 60- £ 75 (Weekends)

Caddy	Caddy	on request
Electric Trolley	Chariot électrique	
Buggy	Voiturette	£ 17/18 holes
Clubs	Clubs	£ 5-20/18 holes

Credit cards Cartes de crédit
VISA - Eurocard - MasterCard - AMEX - DC - JCB

706

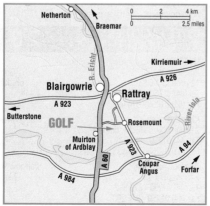

Netherton
Braemar

0 2 4 km
0 2,5 miles

Kirriemuir →

A 926

Blairgowrie · ● **Rattray**

A 923

← Butterstone

GOLF

Rosemount

Muirton of Ardblay

A 923 · A 94

A 60

Coupar Angus · Forfar

A 984

R. Ericht · River Isla

Access Accès : Edinburgh M90 to Perth, then A93 →
Blairgowrie (golf 2 km South of Blairgowrie)
Map 1 on page 489 Carte 1 Page 489

GOLF COURSE / PARCOURS

18/20

Site	Site	
Maintenance	Entretien	
Architect	Architecte	Alister MacKenzie James Braid
Type	Type	heathland, inland
Relief	Relief	
Water in play	Eau en jeu	
Exp. to wind	Exposé au vent	
Trees in play	Arbres en jeu	

Scorecard Carte de score	Chp. Chp.	Mens Mess.	Ladies Da.
Length Long.	6014	5693	5445
Par	72	70	74

Advised golfing ability · 0 12 24 36
Niveau de jeu recommandé
Hcp required · Handicap exigé · certificate

CLUB HOUSE & AMENITIES / CLUB HOUSE ET ANNEXES

8/10

Pro shop	Pro-shop	
Driving range	Practice	
Sheltered	couvert	no
On grass	sur herbe	yes
Putting-green	putting-green	yes
Pitching-green	pitching green	no

HOTEL FACILITIES / ENVIRONNEMENT HOTELIER

6/10

HOTELS HÔTELS

Rosemount · Golf · on site
12 rooms, D £ 55
Tel (44) 01250 - 872 604
Fax (44) 01250 - 874 496

Kinloch House · Blairgowrie · 3 km
21 rooms, D £ 165 (w. dinner)
Tel (44) 01250 - 884 237
Fax (44) 01250 - 884 333

Altamount House · Blairgowrie 2 km
7 rooms, D £ 75
Tel (44) 01250 - 873 512
Fax (44) 01250 - 876 200

RESTAURANTS RESTAURANTS

Rosemount · Golf · on site
Tel (44) 01250 - 872 604

Boat of Garten is the gateway to the Cairngorms, with some of the highest peaks in the UK, and lies within the immediate vicinity of a natural reserve created to protect wildlife, a few miles from the mountain resort of Aviemore to which it is linked by a charming steam train. The flora and fauna (deers and ospreys are often seen on the course) are worth the visit in this region as much as the distilleries. And there is also a golf course, a little but not too hilly over the first few holes, whose general excellence makes this more than just an added distraction or a site for spectacular panoramas. The rolling fairways often present hanging lies more often associated with seaside golf courses. James Braid's layout is top notch and features one of the best holes in Scotland (the 6th) which is saying something. A holiday course, but what a holiday !

A proximité immédiate d'une réserve naturelle créée pour protéger les orfraies, à quelques kilomètres de la station de montagne d'Aviemore, reliée par un charmant train à vapeur, Boat of Garten marque l'entrée dans les Cairngorns, parmi les plus hautes montagnes de Grande-Bretagne. La flore et la faune de cette région valent le déplacement autant que les distilleries. Il y a aussi un parcours de golf, un peu accidenté dans les premiers trous, mais sans excès, et dont la qualité générale en fait plus qu'une distraction annexe ou le site de panoramas spectaculaires. Les fairways présentent souvent des ondulations dignes des golfs de bord de mer. Le dessin de James Braid est de première qualité, notamment au 6, l'un des meilleurs trous de toute l'Ecosse. Un parcours de vacances, mais de bonnes vacances.

Boat of Garten Golf Club — 1932

SCO - BOAT OF GARTEN, Inverness-shire PH24 3BQ

Office	Secrétariat	(44) 01479 - 831 282
Pro shop	Pro-shop	(44) 01479 - 831 282
Fax	Fax	(44) 01479 - 831 523
Situation	Situation	

8 km from Aviemore (pop. 2 214)
48 km SE of Inverness (pop. 62 186)

Annual closure	Fermeture annuelle	yes 1/11 → 1/4
Weekly closure	Fermeture hebdomadaire	no

Fees main season
Tarifs haute saison 18 holes

	Week days Semaine	We/Bank holidays We/Férié
Individual Individuel	£ 21	£ 26
Couple Couple	£ 42	£ 52

Full day: £ 26 - £ 31 (weekends)

Caddy	Caddy	on request/£ 20
Electric Trolley	Chariot électrique	£ 5/18 holes
Buggy	Voiturette	no
Clubs	Clubs	£ 5/18 holes

Credit cards Cartes de crédit
VISA - MasterCard - Delta - Switch - Solo - JCB

Access Accès : Inverness, A9 and A95.
2 km North of Aviemore. Follow signs to village.
Map 1 on page 489 Carte 1 Page 489

GOLF COURSE / PARCOURS — 14/20

Site	Site	
Maintenance	Entretien	
Architect	Architecte	James Braid
Type	Type	heathland
Relief	Relief	
Water in play	Eau en jeu	
Exp. to wind	Exposé au vent	
Trees in play	Arbres en jeu	

Scorecard Carte de score	Chp. Chp.	Mens Mess.	Ladies Da.
Length Long.	5340	5340	4640
Par	69	69	71

Advised golfing ability Niveau de jeu recommandé	0	12	24	36

Hcp required Handicap exigé certificate

CLUB HOUSE & AMENITIES / CLUB HOUSE ET ANNEXES — 6/10

Pro shop	Pro-shop	
Driving range	Practice	
Sheltered	couvert	no
On grass	sur herbe	no
Putting-green	putting-green	yes
Pitching-green	pitching green	yes

HOTEL FACILITIES / ENVIRONNEMENT HOTELIER — 7/10

HOTELS HÔTELS

The Boat Hotel — Boat of Garten
35 rooms, D £ 50 — 1 km
Tel (44) 01479 - 831 258, Fax (44) 01479 - 831 414

The Craigard Hotel — Boat of Garten
18 rooms, D £ 70 — 1 km
Tel (44) 01479 - 831 206, Fax (44) 01479 - 831 423

Heathbank House — Boat of Garten
7 rooms, D £ 70 — 1 km
Tel (44) 01479 - 831 234

RESTAURANTS RESTAURANTS

Heathbank House — Boat of Garten
Tel (44) 01479 - 831 234 — 1 km

Craggan Mill — Grantown on Spey
Tel (44) 01479 - 872 288 — 5 km

707

	15	7	7

This course is found no further than the end of the world, a little after Dornoch and Golspie, where the length of the days in summer could almost let you play all three in the same day. Brora is one of the great traditional links, fine-tuned in 1924 after a design by James Braid. Electric fences protect all the greens from the sheep employed to keep the grass cropped. The tee-boxes and greens are often elevated, built between dunes of between 5 and 12 metres high, and the texture of the turf is particularly pleasant, especially for putting. Although rather short, Brora is not an easy course, even though sometimes you might prefer slightly more penalising rough (especially for the guys you're playing with). This is a club of perfect hospitality, where the 19th hole is both reward and consolation. More should be said about this side of Brora to people who are not curious enough to come and discover the course.

Ce n'est pas plus loin que le bout du monde, un peu après Dornoch et Golspie, là où la longueur des journées de début d'été vous permettraient presque de jouer les trois le même jour. Brora est un des grands links traditionnels, peaufiné en 1924 d'après un dessin de James Braid. Des clôtures électriques préservent chaque green des moutons chargés de tondre. Les départs et greens sont souvent surélevés, construits entre des dunes de 5 à 12 mètres de haut, la texture du gazon particulièrement agréable, notamment au putting. Bien qu'assez court, Brora n'est pas un parcours facile, même si l'on souhaiterait parfois (pour ses adversaires !) un rough plus pénalisant. Un club à la parfaite hospitalité, où le 19ème trou est à la fois récompense et consolation, dont on aimera parler à ceux qui ne sont pas assez curieux pour le connaître.

Brora Golf Club — 1891

Golf Road
SCO - BRORA, Highland KW9 6QS

Office	Secrétariat	(44) 01408 - 621 417
Pro shop	Pro-shop	(44) 01408 - 621 473
Fax	Fax	(44) 01408 - 622 157
Situation	Situation	

85 km N of Inverness (pop. 62 186)

Annual closure	Fermeture annuelle	no
Weekly closure	Fermeture hebdomadaire	no

Fees main season
Tarifs haute saison 18 holes

	Week days Semaine	We/Bank holidays We/Férié
Individual Individuel	£ 20	£ 25
Couple Couple	£ 40	£ 50

Second round on the same day: £ 10

Caddy	Caddy	on request/£ 20
Electric Trolley	Chariot électrique	yes
Buggy	Voiturette	no
Clubs	Clubs	£ 7/18 holes

Credit cards Cartes de crédit VISA - Access - Delta

Access Accès : Inverness, A9 to the North
Map 1 on page 489 Carte 1 Page 489

GOLF COURSE PARCOURS — 15/20

Site	Site	
Maintenance	Entretien	
Architect	Architecte	James Braid
Type	Type	links
Relief	Relief	
Water in play	Eau en jeu	
Exp. to wind	Exposé au vent	
Trees in play	Arbres en jeu	

Scorecard Carte de score	Chp. Chp.	Mens Mess.	Ladies Da.
Length Long.	5560	5328	4800
Par	69	69	70

Advised golfing ability	0	12	24	36
Niveau de jeu recommandé				
Hcp required	Handicap exigé	no		

CLUB HOUSE & AMENITIES
CLUB HOUSE ET ANNEXES — 7/10

Pro shop	Pro-shop	
Driving range	Practice	
Sheltered	couvert	no
On grass	sur herbe	yes
Putting-green	putting-green	yes
Pitching-green	pitching green	yes

HOTEL FACILITIES
ENVIRONNEMENT HOTELIER — 7/10

HOTELS HÔTELS
Royal Marine Hotel — Brora / on site
22 rooms, D £ 90
Tel (44) 01408 - 621 252
Fax (44) 01408 - 621 181

Links Hotel — Brora / on site
24 rooms, D £ 90
Tel (44) 01408 - 621 225
Fax (44) 01408 - 621 383

RESTAURANTS RESTAURANTS
Garden Room — Brora / 1 km
Tel (44) 01408 - 621 252

Brora Golf Club — Brora / on site
Tel (44) 01408 - 621 417

BRUNTSFIELD

For many continental Europeans, playing golf virtually in town is a unique experience. This club used to be right in the middle of Edinburg but has since moved to the outskirts where space is a little less cramped. Willie Park and the great Alistair Mackenzie are responsible for a very pleasant layout at the edge of some hills but where steep slopes have been avoided. This park-style course is generally in excellent condition with immaculate fairways and not over-sized greens. In addition to traditional bunkers, trees are often a dangerous hazard if you play without thinking. This course is a good test for everyone before they square up to more formidable tests on either side of the Forth. Enjoy the excellent restaurant.

Pour bien des continentaux, jouer au golf quasiment en ville est une expérience unique. Ce club était autrefois en plein milieu d'Edinburgh, mais il a émigré à la périphérie, moins à l'étroit. Willie Park et le grand Alister Mackenzie sont responsables d'un tracé très plaisant, en bordure de collines, mais où les fortes pentes ont été évitées. Ce véritable parc est généralement en excellente condition, avec des fairways impeccables et des greens pas très vastes. En plus des bunkers traditionnels, les arbres constituent souvent des obstacles dangereux, si l'on ne réfléchit pas assez. C'est un bon test pour tous, avant d'affronter des adversaires plus redoutables, d'un côté ou de l'autre du Forth. A signaler enfin, l'excellent restaurant.

Bruntsfield Links Golfing Society — 1898

32 Barnton Avenue
SCO - EDINBURGH EH4 6JH

Office	Secrétariat	(44) 0131 - 336 1479
Pro shop	Pro-shop	(44) 0131 - 336 4050
Fax	Fax	(44) 0131 - 336 5538
Situation	Situation	

5 km of Edinburgh City Centre

Annual closure	Fermeture annuelle	no
Weekly closure	Fermeture hebdomadaire	no

Fees main season	Tarifs haute saison	18 holes
	Week days Semaine	**We/Bank holidays** We/Férié
Individual Individuel	£ 36	£ 42
Couple Couple	£ 72	£ 84
Full day: £ 50 - £ 55 (weekends)		

Caddy	Caddy	no
Electric Trolley	Chariot électrique	no
Buggy	Voiturette	£ 10/18 holes
Clubs	Clubs	no

Credit cards Cartes de crédit
VISA - MasterCard (Pro Shop only)

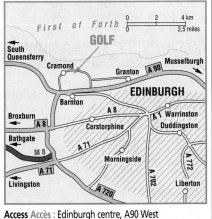

Access Accès : Edinburgh centre, A90 West
(Queenferry Road) Right into Quality St
and Crammond Road, then left into Barnton Avenue.
Map 3 on page 493 Carte 3 Page 493

GOLF COURSE / PARCOURS — 15/20

Site	Site	
Maintenance	Entretien	
Architect	Architecte	Willie Park Alister MacKenzie
Type	Type	parkland
Relief	Relief	
Water in play	Eau en jeu	
Exp. to wind	Exposé au vent	
Trees in play	Arbres en jeu	

Scorecard Carte de score	Chp. Chp.	Mens Mess.	Ladies Da.
Length Long.	5830	5560	5007
Par	71	70	70

Advised golfing ability Niveau de jeu recommandé	0	12	24	36
Hcp required Handicap exigé	36			

CLUB HOUSE & AMENITIES / CLUB HOUSE ET ANNEXES — 8/10

Pro shop	Pro-shop	
Driving range	Practice	
Sheltered	couvert	members only
On grass	sur herbe	members only
Putting-green	putting-green	yes
Pitching-green	pitching green	yes

HOTEL FACILITIES / ENVIRONNEMENT HOTELIER — 9/10

HOTELS HÔTELS

Edinburgh Capital — Edinburgh
111 rooms, D £ 100 — 3 km
Tel (44) 0131 - 535 9988, Fax (44) 0131 - 334 9712

Forte Posthouse — Edinburgh
204 rooms, D £ 70 — 3 km
Tel (44) 0131 - 334 0390, Fax (44) 0131 - 334 9237

Lodge — Edinburgh
12 rooms, D £ 80 — 5 km
Tel (44) 0131 - 337 3682, Fax (44) 0131 - 313 1700

RESTAURANTS RESTAURANTS

Pompadour — Edinburgh
Tel (44) 0131 - 459 9988 — 6 km

Martins — Edinburgh
Tel (44) 0131 - 225 3106 — 6 km

709

While Donald Ross or Tom Simpson might define their designer art as the straight hole, James Braid prefers the dog-leg. Here on the former training grounds for the horses of the Dukes of Montrose, Braid designed a good dozen holes, which were shortened somewhat to cater to members who found the layout a little too difficult. The site is almost flat and so easy on the legs, but keep away from the thick rough which can be really sticky in wet weather. The river Endrick, although theoretically out of reach for normal shots, seems to attract balls like a magnet and it is true that your average hacker is pretty good at going where he never wanted to. Since this course is close to Loch Lomond, Scotland's most private course, come and dream here. You will be made most welcome.

Si l'aboutissement de l'art de Donald Ross ou de Tom Simpson en tant qu'architectes, c'est le trou rectiligne, celui de James Braid, c'est le dog-leg. Ici, sur les anciennes pistes d'entraînement des chevaux des Ducs de Montrose, il en a dessiné une bonne dizaine. Un peu raccourcis depuis, car on estimait que son tracé était trop difficile pour les membres. Le terrain est pratiquement plat, ce qui le rend facile à marcher, mais il vaut mieux échapper aux roughs, très épais quand le temps est à la pluie. Mais rien n'oblige à y aller ! La rivière Endrick est théoriquement hors de portée des coups normaux, mais elle semble avoir un effet magnétique, tant il est vrai que les golfeurs moyens réussissent surtout à aller là où ils ne veulent pas aller. Comme ce parcours est proche de Loch Lomond, le club le plus fermé d'Ecosse, venez rêver ici, vous serez les bienvenus.

Buchanan Castle Golf Club — 1936
SCO - DRYMEN, Glasgow G63 0HY

Office	Secrétariat	(44) 01360 - 660 369
Pro shop	Pro-shop	(44) 01360 - 660 330
Fax	Fax	
Situation	Situation	

29 km N of Glasgow (pop. 662 853)

Annual closure	Fermeture annuelle	no
Weekly closure	Fermeture hebdomadaire	no
Fees main season	Tarifs haute saison	18 holes

	Week days Semaine	We/Bank holidays We/Férié
Individual Individuel	£ 30	—
Couple Couple	£ 60	—

No visitors on Saturdays - Some visitors allowed on Sundays (ask)

Caddy	Caddy	no
Electric Trolley	Chariot électrique	on request
Buggy	Voiturette	no
Clubs	Clubs	yes

Credit cards Cartes de crédit   no

710

GOLF COURSE / PARCOURS — 14/20

Site	Site	
Maintenance	Entretien	
Architect	Architecte	James Braid

Type	Type	parkland
Relief	Relief	
Water in play	Eau en jeu	
Exp. to wind	Exposé au vent	
Trees in play	Arbres en jeu	

Scorecard Carte de score	Chp. Chp.	Mens Mess.	Ladies Da.
Length Long.	5538	5180	4795
Par	70	68	71

Advised golfing ability Niveau de jeu recommandé	0 12 24 36
Hcp required Handicap exigé	26 Men, 36 Ladies

CLUB HOUSE & AMENITIES / CLUB HOUSE ET ANNEXES — 6/10

Pro shop	Pro-shop	
Driving range	Practice	
Sheltered	couvert	no
On grass	sur herbe	yes
Putting-green	putting-green	yes
Pitching-green	pitching green	yes

HOTEL FACILITIES / ENVIRONNEMENT HOTELIER — 6/10

HOTELS HÔTELS

Buchanan Arms	Drymen
52 rooms, D £ 115	1 km
Tel (44) 01360 - 660 588	
Fax (44) 01360 - 660 943	

Cameron House (De Vere)	Balloch
68 rooms, D £ 130	5 km
Tel (44) 01389 - 755 565	
Fax (44) 01389 - 759 522	

RESTAURANTS RESTAURANTS

Georgian Room (Cameron House)	Balloch
Tel (44) 01389 - 755 565	5 km

Queen Elizabeth Forest Park / Aberfoyle / Stirling / **GOLF** / Milton of Buchanan / Loch Lomond / **Drymen** / Endrick water / Balfron / Gartness / A 81 / Croftamie / Killearn / Alexandria / A 809 / A 875 / Milngavie

Access Accès : Glasgow, A81 to Milngavie, then A809, A811, off the A811 → Drymen, Golf just South of Drymen.
Map 2 on page 490 Carte 2 Page 490

BURNTISLAND

14 6 6

The club was founded in 1797 but the course dates back to the end of the 19th century. Laid out by Willie Park Jr., it was restyled by the inevitable James Braid. At the time, this was one of the few courses to open on a Sunday. Built on a little hill overlooking the Firth of Forth, it is still very walkable but a number of elevated greens call for very careful club selection. Likewise, the natural topology has been used with great skill, as you might expect from the afore-mentioned architects. Alongside the many links courses along the coast leading up to Saint Andrews, Burntisland provides the alternative of a parkland style which is highly satisfactory to look at and to play. A candidly open course when the wind stays away, it can turn nasty when the weather gets rough, as all the holes seem to be laid out in different directions. So on a windy day this is a good test for technique and for your nerves. The club-house is modern, functional and unpretentious with a warm welcome.

Le Club a été fondé en 1797 mais le parcours date de la fin du XIXème siècle. Tracé par Willie Park Jr, il a été remanié par l'inévitable James Braid. A l'époque, c'était l'un des seul parcours du pays ouvert le dimanche. Il est construit sur une petite colline dominant le Firth of Forth, mais reste tout à fait jouable à pied. Cependant, quelques greens en élévation exigent un choix de club très exact. De même, les contours du terrain ont été utilisés avec beaucoup de savoir-faire, comme on peut l'attendre de tels architectes. A côté des nombreux links de la côte menant jusqu'à St Andrews, Burntisland offre l'alternative d'une esthétique «parkland» très satisfaisante visuellement et golfiquement. Assez franc quand il n'y pas de vent, ce parcours peut devenir plus méchant s'il souffle, car les trous changent sans cesse d'orientation. C'est alors un bon test pour la technique et les nerfs. Le Clubhouse est moderne, fonctionnel et sans prétention.

Burntisland Golf House		**1898**
Dodhead		
SCO - BURNTISLAND, Fife KY3 9HS		

Office	Secrétariat	(44) 01592 - 874 093
Pro shop	Pro-shop	(44) 01592 - 872 116
Fax	Fax	(44) 01592 - 874 093
Situation	Situation	

30 km NE of Edinburgh (pop. 418 914)

Annual closure	Fermeture annuelle	no
Weekly closure	Fermeture hebdomadaire	no

Fees main season
Tarifs haute saison 18 holes

	Week days Semaine	We/Bank holidays We/Férié
Individual Individuel	£ 15	£ 25
Couple Couple	£ 30	£ 50

Full days: £ 25 - £ 35 (weekends)

Caddy	Caddy	on request
Electric Trolley	Chariot électrique	no
Buggy	Voiturette	no
Clubs	Clubs	yes

Credit cards Cartes de crédit VISA - MasterCard - JCB

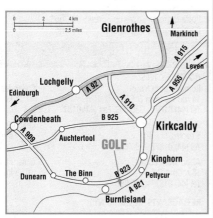

Access Accès : Edinburgh, M90 Jct 1, A921 → Kirkcaldy, Golf on B923, 1.5 km (1 m.) East of Burntisland.
Map 3 on page 493 Carte 3 Page 493

GOLF COURSE
PARCOURS

14/20

Site	Site	
Maintenance	Entretien	
Architect	Architecte	Willie Park
Type	Type	parkland
Relief	Relief	
Water in play	Eau en jeu	
Exp. to wind	Exposé au vent	
Trees in play	Arbres en jeu	

Scorecard Carte de score	Chp. Chp.	Mens Mess.	Ladies Da.
Length Long.	5430	5020	4635
Par	70	69	70

Advised golfing ability	0	12	24	36
Niveau de jeu recommandé				

Hcp required Handicap exigé certificate

CLUB HOUSE & AMENITIES
CLUB HOUSE ET ANNEXES

6/10

Pro shop	Pro-shop	
Driving range	Practice	
Sheltered	couvert	no
On grass	sur herbe	no
Putting-green	putting-green	yes
Pitching-green	pitching green	yes

HOTEL FACILITIES
ENVIRONNEMENT HOTELIER

6/10

HOTELS HÔTELS

Kingswood 9 rooms, D £ 70 Tel (44) 01592 - 872 329 Fax (44) 01592 - 873 123	Burntisland 1.5 km
Balbirnie House 28 rooms, D £ 150 Tel (44) 01592 - 610 066 Fax (44) 01592 - 610 529	Glenrothes 15 km
Rescobie - 10 rooms, D £ 70 Tel (44) 01592 - 742 143 Fax (44) 01592 - 620 231	Leslie 15 km
King Malcolm Thistle 48 rooms, D £ 85 Tel (44) 01383 - 722 611 Fax (44) 01383 - 730 865	Dunfermline 15 km

711

This is the region of Trossachs, dotted with hills and lochs and a lot of wild-life, including deer which come down from the Perthshire hills in spring. It is also the region which inspired Walter Scott and Daniel Defoe and helped create the character of Rob Roy. In fact, the museum celebrating this popular hero is situated in Callender. The golf-course of the same name is laid out over an idyllic site which is ideal for spending a few days holiday without feeling too bad about your game. Old Tom Morris help build this course, and as on most courses that stretch back almost to the origins of golf, length is not a vital factor. Having said that, the par 3s take some reaching and there are seven of them to contend with here. There is also only one par 5, so the tempo is a little different from usual. The dangers include several ditches and other hazards, which call for some careful shot-making. Open and uncomplicated, this is hardly your unforgettable course but we would defy anyone not to have fun playing it.

C'est la région des Trossachs, parsemée de collines et de lochs, avec une faune importante : au printemps, les cerfs descendent des collines du Perthshire. Cette région qui a inspiré Walter Scott, et Daniel Defoe avec le personnage de Rob Roy. Le Musée célébrant ce héros populaire se trouve d'ailleurs à Callender. Le parcours du même nom est dans un site idyllique, idéal pour passer quelques jours de vacances sans trop faire honte à ses clubs. Comme sur les parcours encore proches des origines, la longueur n'est pas l'élément essentiel, bien que les par 3 soient souvent très respectables de ce point de vue. Il y en a sept ici, et un seul par 5, ce qui créée un rythme de jeu assez inhabituel. Plusieurs fossés et autres obstacles d'eau demandent un travail de balle très réfléchi et attentif. Franc et sans complication, ce n'est certes pas un parcours inoubliable, mais on défie quiconque de ne pas y prendre plaisir.

Callander Golf Club — 1890

Aveland Road
SCO - CALLANDER, Perthshire FK7 8EN

Office	Secrétariat	(44) 01877 - 330 090
Pro shop	Pro-shop	(44) 01877 - 330 975
Fax	Fax	(44) 01877 - 330 062
Situation	Situation	

19 km of Stirling (pop. 30 515)

Annual closure	Fermeture annuelle	no
Weekly closure	Fermeture hebdomadaire	no

Fees main season
Tarifs haute saison 18 holes

	Week days Semaine	We/Bank holidays We/Férié
Individual Individuel	£ 20	£ 26
Couple Couple	£ 40	£ 52

Full day: £ 26 - £ 31 (weekends)

Caddy	Caddy	on request
Electric Trolley	Chariot électrique	no
Buggy	Voiturette	no
Clubs	Clubs	no
Credit cards Cartes de crédit		no

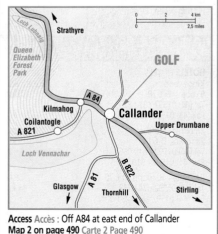

GOLF

Strathyre

Queen Elizabeth Forest Park

Loch Lubnaig

A 84

Kilmahog

Coilantogle
A 821

Callander

Upper Drumbane

Loch Vennachar

Glasgow   Thornhill   Stirling

Access Accès : Off A84 at east end of Callander
Map 2 on page 490 Carte 2 Page 490

GOLF COURSE / PARCOURS — 13/20

Site	Site	
Maintenance	Entretien	
Architect	Architecte	Tom Morris
Type	Type	parkland
Relief	Relief	
Water in play	Eau en jeu	
Exp. to wind	Exposé au vent	
Trees in play	Arbres en jeu	

Scorecard Carte de score	Chp. Chp.	Mens Mess.	Ladies Da.
Length Long.	4687	4047	4181
Par	66	63	68

Advised golfing ability	0	12	24	36
Niveau de jeu recommandé				
Hcp required	Handicap exigé	certificate		

CLUB HOUSE & AMENITIES / CLUB HOUSE ET ANNEXES — 6/10

Pro shop	Pro-shop	
Driving range	Practice	
Sheltered	couvert	no
On grass	sur herbe	no
Putting-green	putting-green	no
Pitching-green	pitching green	no

HOTEL FACILITIES / ENVIRONNEMENT HOTELIER — 7/10

HOTELS HÔTELS

Roman Camp Hotel — Callander
14 rooms, from D £ 91 — 1 km
Tel (44) 01877 - 330 003, Fax (44) 01877 - 331 533

Riverview House — Callander
5 rooms, D £ 40 — 1 km
Tel (44) 01877 - 330 635

Abbotsford Lodge — Callander
18 rooms, D £ 46 — 0.75 km
Tel (44) 01877 - 330 066

RESTAURANTS RESTAURANTS

The Byre Inn — Brig O'Turk
Tel (44) 01877 - 376 292 — 10 km

Braeval Old Mill — Aberfoyle
Tel (44) 01877 - 382 711 — 12 km

CARDROSS

14	6	5

This course provides some pretty views over the Firth of Clyde and the countryside around Dumbarton. Laid out in moderately hilly parkland landscape, it is a good test of golf for players of all abilities, even though the course is hardly the latest thing in modern golf design. The main difficulty lies with the classic and very numerous bunkers. The heavy clay soil can get sticky in winter and the very thick turf stops the ball from rolling very far in spring and summer. Under these conditions, every yard of fairway really counts. The course was laid out in 1904 by Willie Fernie from Troon, and the changes made since then have not changed the spirit of this old and respectable golf club. Other clubs in the region certainly enjoy a better reputation and probably have more spectacular courses than this (and higher green-fees, too), but the frankness of this layout, the pleasure of playing here and the way the course is adapted to players of all abilities, make this a pretty useful round of golf when you are in the region (except on week-ends).

Au sud du Loch Lomond, ce parcours offre de jolis panoramas sur le Firth of Clyde et la campagne de Dumbarton. Tracé dans un paysage de parc modérément accidenté, c'est un bon test de golf pour tous niveaux, même s'il n'est pas du tout dernier modernisme. Ce sont d'ailleurs de classiques et nombreux bunkers qui sont la principale difficulté. Le terrain argileux est assez lourd en hiver, et son gazon très fourni empêche les balles de rouler beaucoup à la belle saison : dans ces conditions, chaque mètre du parcours compte. Le dessin en a été fait en 1904 par Willie Fernie, de Troon, et les changements apportés depuis n'en ont pas modifié l'esprit. Certes, d'autres Clubs de la région ont des réputations mieux établies, et sans doute des parcours plus spectaculaires (et aussi des green-fees plus élevés), mais la franchise de celui-ci, l'agrément du lieu, l'adaptation à tous les types de joueurs en font un golf utile dans cette région.

Cardross Golf Club — 1904

Main Road
SCO - CARDROSS, Dumbarton G82 5LB

Office	Secrétariat	(44) 01389 - 841 754
Pro shop	Pro-shop	(44) 01389 - 841 350
Fax	Fax	(44) 01389 - 841 754
Situation	Situation	

8 km W of Dumbarton (pop. 77 173)
30 km NW of Glasgow (pop. 662 853)

Annual closure	Fermeture annuelle	no
Weekly closure	Fermeture hebdomadaire	no

Fees main season	Tarifs haute saison	18 holes	
	Week days Semaine	**We/Bank holidays** We/Férié	
Individual Individuel	£ 22	—	
Couple Couple	£ 44	—	

Full weekday: £ 32 - No visitors at weekends

Caddy	Caddy	on request
Electric Trolley	Chariot électrique	no
Buggy	Voiturette	no
Clubs	Clubs	£ 10/18 holes

Credit cards Cartes de crédit VISA (Pro Shop only)

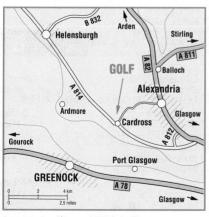

Access Accès : Glasgow, M8 Exit Jct 30, then A814 to Cardross
Map 3 on page 492 Carte 3 Page 492

GOLF COURSE / PARCOURS — 14/20

Site	Site	
Maintenance	Entretien	
Architect	Architecte	Willie Fernie James Braid
Type	Type	parkland
Relief	Relief	
Water in play	Eau en jeu	
Exp. to wind	Exposé au vent	
Trees in play	Arbres en jeu	

Scorecard Carte de score	Chp. Chp.	Mens Mess.	Ladies Da.
Length Long.	5887	5607	5238
Par	71	71	76

Advised golfing ability Niveau de jeu recommandé	0	12	24	36
Hcp required Handicap exigé	no			

CLUB HOUSE & AMENITIES / CLUB HOUSE ET ANNEXES — 6/10

Pro shop	Pro-shop	
Driving range	Practice	
Sheltered	couvert	no
On grass	sur herbe	yes
Putting-green	putting-green	yes
Pitching-green	pitching green	yes

HOTEL FACILITIES / ENVIRONNEMENT HOTELIER — 5/10

HOTELS HÔTELS
Cameron House Hotel — Loch Lomond
96 rooms, D £ 93 — 11 km
Tel (44) 01389 - 755 565
Fax (44) 01389 - 759 522

RESTAURANTS RESTAURANTS
Cameron House — Loch Lomond
Tel (44) 01389 - 755 565 — 11 km

713

Of course you don't come here only to play this «Burnside Course», but if you consider this simply as a warm-up round before playing the Championship course, then watch out: this is not a layout for beginners. It is certainly much shorter than its prestigious older companion but does have enough difficulties for it to hold its head high. It is laid out in a similar setting, the only blemish being that it runs alongside the railway track. Bunkers form the main line of defence, but there is also a number of trees which accentuate the countryside appearance found here and there on the Championship course. On a site that could contain in all almost a dozen courses, this layout more than does itself justice. And the appeal of the environment benefits from the hotel opened for the British Open in 1999.

Certes, on ne vient pas ici uniquement pour jouer ce «Burnside Course», mais s'il s'agit simplement de s'échauffer avant de jouer le «Championship», méfiance car ce n'est pas un parcours pour débutants. Il est certes beaucoup plus court que son prestigieux aîné, mais présente assez de difficultés pour garder la tête haute. Il est d'ailleurs situé dans un environnement similaire, son seul défaut étant de longer davantage la voie ferrée. Les bunkers constituent la défense essentielle, avec aussi pas mal d'arbres, ce qui accentue un aspect campagne que l'on retrouve çà et là sur le «Championship.» Dans un site qui pourrait au total contenir une bonne dizaine de parcours, celui-ci est plus qu'honorable. Et la séduction autrefois incertaine de l'environnement a bénéficié de l'uinauguration d'un hotelpour le mémorable British Open 1999.

Carnoustie Golf Links — 1914

Links Parade
SCO- CARNOUSTIE, Angus, DD7 7JE

Office	Secrétariat	(44) 01241 - 853 789
Pro shop	Pro-shop	
Fax	Fax	(44) 01241 - 852 720
Situation	Situation	

17 km NE of Dundee (pop. 165 873)
9 km SW of Abroath

Annual closure	Fermeture annuelle	no
Weekly closure	Fermeture hebdomadaire	no

Fees main season Tarifs haute saison — 18 holes

	Week days Semaine	We/Bank holidays We/Férié
Individual Individuel	£ 20	£ 20
Couple Couple	£ 40	£ 40

Burnside + Championship (same day): £ 70

Caddy	Caddy	£ 26
Electric Trolley	Chariot électrique	no
Buggy	Voiturette	no
Clubs	Clubs	nearby Pro shop

Credit cards Cartes de crédit
VISA - Eurocard - MasterCard - AMEX

714

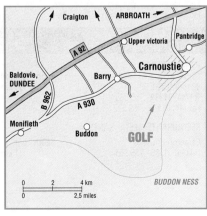

Access Accès : Dundee, A92 and A930
Map 2 on page 491 Carte 2 Page 491

GOLF COURSE / PARCOURS — 14/20

Site	Site	
Maintenance	Entretien	
Architect	Architecte	Unknown
Type	Type	links
Relief	Relief	
Water in play	Eau en jeu	
Exp. to wind	Exposé au vent	
Trees in play	Arbres en jeu	

Scorecard Carte de score	Chp. Chp.	Mens Mess.	Ladies Da.
Length Long.	5478	5478	5478
Par	68	68	72

Advised golfing ability — 0   12   24   36
Niveau de jeu recommandé
Hcp required Handicap exigé — no

CLUB HOUSE & AMENITIES / CLUB HOUSE ET ANNEXES — 5/10

Pro shop	Pro-shop	
Driving range	Practice	
Sheltered	couvert	no
On grass	sur herbe	no
Putting-green	putting-green	no
Pitching-green	pitching green	no

HOTEL FACILITIES / ENVIRONNEMENT HOTELIER — 6/10

HOTELS HÔTELS

Carnoustie Golf Hotel		Carnoustie
85 rooms, D £ 149		on site
Tel (49) 01241 - 411 999, Fax (49) 01241 - 411 998		
Stakis Dundee		Dundee
104 rooms, D £ 90		18 km
Tel (44) 01382 - 22 9271, Fax (44) 01382 - 200 072		
Kingsley		Arbroath
16 rooms, D £ 35		9 km
Tel (44) 01241 - 879 933		
Tayview		Broughty Ferry
11 rooms, D £ 65		12 km
Tel (44) 01382 - 779 438		

RESTAURANTS RESTAURANTS

11 Park Avenue		Carnoustie
Tel (44) 01241 - 853 336		3 km

The return of the British Open to Carnoustie saw the 18th hole disaster and barefoot antics of Jean van de Velde and a surprise win for Paul Lawrie, a little unusual in a history marked by wins from such greats as Armour, Cotton, Ben Hogan, Player and Watson. It was a pity that the more attacking players were cut down by the preparation of a course that even in its natural state and without wind, is already a formidable adversary. Contrary to many links courses, this one is very difficult without the wind. When the wind does blow, it can be a real brute. There are no large dunes, just a sort of space where the sea has apparently withdrawn to leave room for a few streams, bushes, a little scrub and long grass. Designers have successively added a few very nasty bunkers, very tricky greens and optical illusions that make club choice very difficult. If you survive the first 15 holes, the last 3 can easily finish you off. For this inhuman greatness, some prefer Carnoustie to the Old Course at St Andrews. There is little to choose...

Le retour du British Open aura vu le désastre loufoque de van de Velde et la victoire surprise de Paul Lawrie, insolites dans une histoire marquée par les victoires de Armour, Cotton, Ben Hogan, Player et Watson. On regrettera que les attaquants aient eu le souffle coupé par la préparation d'un parcours déjà bien assez terrible au naturel, même s'il n'y a pas de vent. Au contraire d'autres links, celui-ci est très difficile même quand il ne souffle pas. Et s'il souffle, c'est carrément une brute. Pas de grandes dunes ici, mais une sorte d'espace d'où la mer se serait retirée doucement pour laisser place à quelques ruisseaux, aux buissons, à de rares arbustes, aux longues herbes. Les architectes y ont successivement ajouté quelques bunkers très méchants, des greens d'une grande subtilité, et des illusions d'optique qui rendent très difficile le choix de clubs. Et si l'on a survécu à quinze trous, les trois derniers peuvent vous achever. Pour cette grandeur inhumaine, certains préfèrent Carnoustie au «Old Course» de St Andrews... Il n'est pas inférieur.

Carnoustie Golf Links — 1842

Links Parade
SCO- CARNOUSTIE, Angus, DD7 7JE

Office	Secrétariat	(44) 01241 - 853 789
Pro shop	Pro-shop	
Fax	Fax	(44) 01241 - 852 720
Situation	Situation	

17 km NE of Dundee (pop. 165 873)
9 km SW of Abroath

Annual closure	Fermeture annuelle	no
Weekly closure	Fermeture hebdomadaire	no

Fees main season Tarifs haute saison		18 holes
	Week days Semaine	We/Bank holidays We/Férié
Individual Individuel	£ 60	£ 60
Couple Couple	£ 120	£ 120

Championship + Burnside (same day): £ 70

Caddy	Caddy	£ 26
Electric Trolley	Chariot électrique	no
Buggy	Voiturette	no
Clubs	Clubs	nearby Pro shop

Credit cards Cartes de crédit
VISA - Eurocard - MasterCard - AMEX

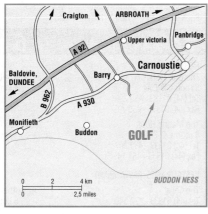

Access Accès : Dundee, A92 and A930
Map 2 on page 491 Carte 2 Page 491

GOLF COURSE / PARCOURS — 19/20

Site	Site	▬▬▬▬▬▬
Maintenance	Entretien	▬▬▬▬▬▬
Architect	Architecte	Tom Morris James Braid
Type	Type	links, seaside course
Relief	Relief	
Water in play	Eau en jeu	▬▬▬
Exp. to wind	Exposé au vent	▬▬▬▬
Trees in play	Arbres en jeu	▬▬

Scorecard Carte de score	Chp. Chp.	Mens Mess.	Ladies Da.
Length Long.	6643	6246	6127
Par	72	72	73

Advised golfing ability Niveau de jeu recommandé	0 12 24 36
Hcp required Handicap exigé	28 Men, 36 Ladies

CLUB HOUSE & AMENITIES / CLUB HOUSE ET ANNEXES — 5/10

Pro shop	Pro-shop	▭▭
Driving range	Practice	▭▭
Sheltered	couvert	no
On grass	sur herbe	no
Putting-green	putting-green	no
Pitching-green	pitching green	no

715

HOTEL FACILITIES / ENVIRONNEMENT HOTELIER — 6/10

HOTELS HÔTELS

Carnoustie Golf Hotel — Carnoustie
85 rooms, D £ 149 — on site
Tel (49) 01241 - 411 999, Fax (49) 01241 - 411 998

Stakis Dundee — Dundee
104 rooms, D £ 90 — 18 km
Tel (44) 01382 - 22 9271, Fax (44) 01382 - 200 072

Kingsley — Arbroath
16 rooms, D £ 35 — 9 km
Tel (44) 01241 - 879 933

Tayview - 11 rooms, D £ 65 — Broughty Ferry
Tel (44) 01382 - 779 438 — 12 km

RESTAURANTS RESTAURANTS

11 Park Avenue — Carnoustie
Tel (44) 01241 - 853 336 — 3 km

Don't expect impressive dunes here. In fact, the east coast of Scotland is less undulating than the west side, which feels the full brunt of Atlantic storms. Crail is the 7th oldest club in the history of golf and its course goes by the name of Balcomie Links. This is reputed to be one of the most hospitable clubs in the whole country and its closeness to St Andrews has in no way gone to its head. The best golf here is to be found with the opening and closing holes, where the sea is very much in play (more than anywhere else in this region), but the rest of the course, more inland in style, is still exposed to the wind and interesting enough for players to keep «focused» right to the end. Less manicured and more natural than other layouts, Crail is a club with ambition, as witnessed by the future opening of Craighead, a second 18-hole course.

Que l'on n'attende pas ici de dunes impressionnantes. Le relief de la côte Est de l'Ecosse est d'ailleurs moins mouvementé que celui de la côte Ouest, soumise à toutes les tempêtes. Crail est le 7ème plus ancien club de l'histoire du golf, et son parcours porte le nom de Balcomie Links. C'est un des clubs les plus accueillants de tout le pays, selon sa réputation, et sa proximité de St Andrews ne l'a pas rendu plus prétentieux. Le meilleur est ici contenu dans les premiers et derniers trous, ceux qui mettent la mer en jeu (plus que partout ailleurs dans cette région), mais le reste du parcours, plus «inland,» n'est pas moins exposé au vent, et assez intéressant pour que l'on reste concentré jusqu'à la fin. Moins manucuré que d'autres, plus naturel aussi, Crail a de l'ambition, dont témoigne la prochaine ouverture d'un second 18 trous, Craighead.

Crail Golfing Society — 1895

Balcomie Clubhouse, Fifeness
SCO - CRAIL, Fife KY10 3XN

Office	Secrétariat	(44) 01333 - 450 686
Pro shop	Pro-shop	(44) 01333 - 450 960
Fax	Fax	(44) 01333 - 450 416
Situation	Situation	

14 km S of St Andrews (pop. 11 136)

Annual closure	Fermeture annuelle	no
Weekly closure	Fermeture hebdomadaire	no
Fees main season	Tarifs haute saison	18 holes

	Week days Semaine	We/Bank holidays We/Férié
Individual Individuel	£ 25	£ 30
Couple Couple	£ 50	£ 60

Caddy	Caddy	on request
Electric Trolley	Chariot électrique	no
Buggy	Voiturette	no
Clubs	Clubs	£ 10/18 holes

Credit cards Cartes de crédit
VISA - Eurocard - MasterCard - JCB

716

Access Accès : Edinburgh A92 to Kirkcaldy, then A915 through Leven, B942 and A 917 through Crail until Golf Hotel, turn right → Golf.
Map 3 on page 493 Carte 3 Page 493

GOLF COURSE / PARCOURS — 15/20

Site	Site	
Maintenance	Entretien	
Architect	Architecte	Tom Morris
Type	Type	links
Relief	Relief	
Water in play	Eau en jeu	
Exp. to wind	Exposé au vent	
Trees in play	Arbres en jeu	

Scorecard / Carte de score	Chp. / Chp.	Mens / Mess.	Ladies / Da.
Length Long.	5390	4945	4760
Par	69	67	70

Advised golfing ability		0	12	24	36
Niveau de jeu recommandé					
Hcp required	Handicap exigé	no			

CLUB HOUSE & AMENITIES / CLUB HOUSE ET ANNEXES — 6/10

Pro shop	Pro-shop	
Driving range	Practice	
Sheltered	couvert	no
On grass	sur herbe	no
Putting-green	putting-green	yes
Pitching-green	pitching green	no

HOTEL FACILITIES / ENVIRONNEMENT HOTELIER — 6/10

HOTELS HÔTELS

The Golf Hotel — Crail
5 rooms, D £ 44 — 1 km
Tel (44) 01333 - 450 206
Fax (44) 01333 - 450 795

The Marine Hotel — Crail
8 rooms, D £ 60 — 1 km
Tel (44) 01333 - 450 207
Fax (44) 01333 - 451 145

RESTAURANTS RESTAURANT

The Cellar — Ansruther
Tel (44) 01333 - 477 540 — 6 km

For a start, we would not recommend Crieff to any one without sturdy legs, as the course is largely laid out on the side of a hill. Most golfers though get used to the climbing but not always to shaping their shots or choosing the right strategy with due consideration given to the slopes. This Ferntower course follows a part of the layout created by Archie Simpson then re-designed by James Braid (the remaining section is on the Dornock course), but the final work, completed in 1980, was made in a way to avoid any excessive disparity in style. Of course you need to play here several times to understand the full layout, but it's fun every time because the enjoyment of playing here is more than enhanced by the warm reception and hospitality. The people from Crieff really do make you feel at home.

Déjà, on ne saurait conseiller Crieff à ceux dont les jambes sont faibles, car il a été construit largement à flanc de colline, mais la plupart des golfeurs s'en accommoderont. Les pentes doivent d'ailleurs souvent être prises en considération pour établir une stratégie efficace, comme pour choisir les meilleures trajectoires. Ce Ferntower Course a repris une partie du tracé créé par Archie Simpson puis remanié par James Braid (les autres sont sur le Dornock Course), mais les travaux définitifs achevés en 1980 ont été assez bien menés pour que l'on n'ait pas trop de disparités de style. Certes, il est utile de jouer plusieurs fois pour bien comprendre ce tracé, mais on le fera avec plaisir quand on ajoute au plaisir du jeu celui de la réception et de l'accueil : on se sent ici en famille.

Crieff Golf Club — 1891

Perth Road
SCO - CRIEFF, Perthshire PH7 3LR

Office	Secrétariat	(44) 01764 - 652 397
Pro shop	Pro-shop	(44) 01764 - 652 909
Fax	Fax	(44) 01764 - 655 096
Situation	Situation	

27 km W of Perth (pop. 123 495)

Annual closure	Fermeture annuelle	no
Weekly closure	Fermeture hebdomadaire	no
Fees main season	Tarifs haute saison	18 holes

	Week days Semaine	We/Bank holidays We/Férié
Individual Individuel	£ 21	£ 29
Couple Couple	£ 42	£ 58
Full days: £ 36		

Caddy	Caddy	on request
Electric Trolley	Chariot électrique	no
Buggy	Voiturette	no
Clubs	Clubs	yes

Credit cards Cartes de crédit
VISA - Mastercard - Access (only in Pro shop)

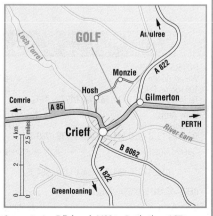

Access Accès : Edinburgh M90 to Perth, then A85 →
Crieff. Golf on right at the edge of town.
Map 2 on page 491 Carte 2 Page 491

GOLF COURSE
PARCOURS — 15/20

Site	Site	
Maintenance	Entretien	
Architect	Architecte	Bob Simpson James Braid
Type	Type	parkland
Relief	Relief	
Water in play	Eau en jeu	
Exp. to wind	Exposé au vent	
Trees in play	Arbres en jeu	

Scorecard Carte de score	Chp. Chp.	Mens Mess.	Ladies Da.
Length Long.	5830	5830	5830
Par	71	71	76

Advised golfing ability Niveau de jeu recommandé		0 12 24 36
Hcp required	Handicap exigé	certificate

CLUB HOUSE & AMENITIES
CLUB HOUSE ET ANNEXES — 7/10

Pro shop	Pro-shop	
Driving range	Practice	
Sheltered	couvert	no
On grass	sur herbe	yes
Putting-green	putting-green	yes
Pitching-green	pitching green	yes

717

HOTEL FACILITIES
ENVIRONNEMENT HOTELIER — 7/10

HOTELS HÔTELS
Crieff Hydro — Golf adjacent
225 rooms, D £ 120
Tel (44) 01764 - 655 555
Fax (44) 01764 - 653 087

Murraypark Hotel — Crieff close
19 rooms, D £ 70
Tel (44) 01764 - 653 731
Fax (44) 01764 - 655 311

RESTAURANTS RESTAURANT
Murraypark — Crieff close
Tel (44) 01764 - 653 731

This is one of the very few Tom Simpson courses in Scotland, a masterpiece on a par with County Louth, another hidden gem but this time in Ireland. They say that Slain Castle in the background inspired Bram Stoker for his Dracula. Well you'll find drama enough here and maybe blood on your card too when the wind starts to blow and the designer, as if in a game of chess, takes your pieces one by one as the course unwinds. You will find every challenge to test your game: subtle, well-protected greens, strategic fairway bunkers, deep green-side bunkers, burns, blind shots, majestic long holes or teasing shorter ones. There was once a grand hotel on the site but it was demolished, a fact that might explain the relative anonymity from which Cruden Bay deserves to emerge... but don't tell anybody.

C'est un des seuls parcours de Tom Simpson en Ecosse, un chef-d'oeuvre à mettre à côté de County Louth, lui aussi un des joyaux cachés, mais d'Irlande cette fois. On dit que Slain Castle, en arrière plan du lieu, a inspiré Bram Stoker pour son «Dracula.» Nul doute qu'il y aura aussi des drames et du sang sur les cartes de score quand le vent souffle un peu, et que la patiente partie d'échec de l'architecte avec les joueurs tourne à la déconfiture des seconds. Greens subtils et bien défendus, bunkers de fairway stratégiques, profonds bunkers de green, petits «burns» piégeux, coups aveugles, longs trous majestueux ou petits trous provocants : on a ici tous les défis pour mettre son jeu à l'épreuve. Il y avait autrefois un grand hôtel sur place, il a été détruit, ce qui explique le relatif anonymat dont Cruden Bay mérite de sortir. Mais ne le dites à personne...

Cruden Bay Golf Club		1899
Aulton Road, Cruden Bay		
SCO - PETERHEAD, Aberdeenshire AB42 0NN		

Office	Secrétariat	(44) 01779 - 812 285
Pro shop	Pro-shop	(44) 01779 - 812 414
Fax	Fax	(44) 01779 - 812 945
Situation	Situation	

40 km N of Aberdeen (pop. 204 885)
12 km S of Peterhead (pop. 20 789)

Annual closure	Fermeture annuelle	no
Weekly closure	Fermeture hebdomadaire	no

Fees main season	Tarifs haute saison	18 holes
	Week days Semaine	We/Bank holidays We/Férié
Individual Individuel	£ 40	£ 50
Couple Couple	£ 80	£ 100

Some weekend restrictions: ask before

Caddy	Caddy	on request/£ 20+tip
Electric Trolley	Chariot électrique	no
Buggy	Voiturette	no
Clubs	Clubs	£ 7.50/18 holes

Credit cards Cartes de crédit VISA - MasterCard

GOLF COURSE / PARCOURS — 18/20

Site	Site	▬▬▬▬▬
Maintenance	Entretien	▬▬▬▬
Architect	Architecte	Tom Simpson
Type	Type	links
Relief	Relief	▬
Water in play	Eau en jeu	▬▬
Exp. to wind	Exposé au vent	▬▬▬▬
Trees in play	Arbres en jeu	▬▬

Scorecard Carte de score	Chp. Chp.	Mens Mess.	Ladies Da.
Length Long.	5820	5480	5243
Par	70	70	74

Advised golfing ability		0	12	24	36
Niveau de jeu recommandé					
Hcp required	Handicap exigé	certificate			

CLUB HOUSE & AMENITIES / CLUB HOUSE ET ANNEXES — 7/10

Pro shop	Pro-shop	▬▬▬▬
Driving range	Practice	▬▬▬▬
Sheltered	couvert	10 mats
On grass	sur herbe	yes
Putting-green	putting-green	yes
Pitching-green	pitching green	yes

HOTEL FACILITIES / ENVIRONNEMENT HOTELIER — 6/10

HOTELS HÔTELS

Waterside Inn — Peterhead
109 rooms, D £ 95 — 13 km
Tel (44) 01779 - 471 121, Fax (44) 01779 - 470 670

Udny Arms — Newburgh
24 rooms, D £ 60 — 10 km
Tel (44) 01358 - 789 444, Fax (44) 01779 - 789 012

Queens Hotel — Aberdeeen
26 rooms, D £ 90 — 35 km
Tel (44) 01224 - 206 999, Fax (44) 01224 - 584 352

RESTAURANTS RESTAURANTS

Udny Arms — Newburgh
Tel (44) 01358 - 789 444 — 10 km

Waterside Inn — Peterhead
Tel (44) 01779 - 471 121 — 13 km

718

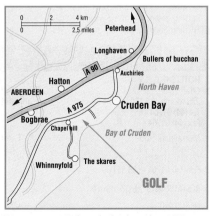

Access Accès : A92 through Aberdeen, then A975 →
Peterhead to Cruden Bay.
Map 1 on page 489 Carte 1 Page 489

With two 18-hole courses, one of which is in the international league, this golfing complex controlled by Marriott is a very high class resort with a full-facility hotel, particularly for non-golfers (tennis, swimming pool, fitness, etc.). The East Course, designed by James Braid, has played host to some major tournaments, including the Solheim Cup in 1992. Although some aspects of the course are reminiscent of a links, here we are in a beautiful park where trees are important not so much as dangerous hazards but for outlining the holes. Water comes into play but only on two holes. So really if you drive straight you're half-way there, but only half-way. You need some accurate ironwork to hit the well-protected greens, so a few rudiments of target golf will more than come in handy. A good test of golf.

Avec deux parcours de 18 trous, dont un de classe internationale, cet ensemble contrôlé par Marriott est devenu un complexe de tout premier ordre avec un hôtel très bien équipé, notamment pour les non-golfeurs (tennis, piscine, mise en forme, etc). Dessiné par James Braid, l'East Course a accueilli de grandes épreuves, dont la Solheim Cup en 1992. Bien que certains aspects puissent rappeler les links, nous sommes ici dans un parc de toute beauté, où les arbres jouent un certain rôle, mais ils définissent plus les trous qu'ils ne constituent des obstacles dangereux. L'eau n'est en jeu que sur deux trous. De fait, si l'on drive bien, on aura fait une bonne partie du chemin, mais c'est loin d'être suffisant : il faut être d'autant plus précis que les greens sont bien défendus, ce qui exige parfois de connaître les secrets du «target golf.» Un bon test de golf.

Marriott Dalmahoy Golf & Country Club — 1927

Kirknewton
SCO - EDINBURGH EH27 8EB

Office	Secrétariat	(44) 0131 - 333 1845
Pro shop	Pro-shop	(44) 0131 - 333 1845
Fax	Fax	(44) 0131 - 333 1433
Situation	Situation	

12 km SW of Edinburgh (pop. 418 914)

Annual closure	Fermeture annuelle	no
Weekly closure	Fermeture hebdomadaire	no

Fees main season	Tarifs haute saison	18 holes
	Week days Semaine	We/Bank holidays We/Férié
Individual Individuel	£ 55*	£ 75*
Couple Couple	£ 110	£ 150

* Non residents

Caddy	Caddy	on request/£ 25
Electric Trolley	Chariot électrique	no
Buggy	Voiturette	£ 24/18 holes
Clubs	Clubs	£ 19/18 holes

Credit cards Cartes de crédit
VISA - Eurocard - MasterCard - AMEX - DC

Access Accès : From Edinburgh, on A 71 → Livingston
Map 3 on page 493 Carte 3 Page 493

GOLF COURSE PARCOURS — 17/20

Site	Site	
Maintenance	Entretien	
Architect	Architecte	James Braid
Type	Type	parkland
Relief	Relief	
Water in play	Eau en jeu	
Exp. to wind	Exposé au vent	
Trees in play	Arbres en jeu	

Scorecard Carte de score	Chp. Chp.	Mens Mess.	Ladies Da.
Length Long.	6030	5836	5356
Par	72	71	75

Advised golfing ability Niveau de jeu recommandé	0	12	24	36
Hcp required Handicap exigé	certificate			

CLUB HOUSE & AMENITIES CLUB HOUSE ET ANNEXES — 8/10

Pro shop	Pro-shop	
Driving range	Practice	
Sheltered	couvert	12 bays (floodlit)
On grass	sur herbe	no
Putting-green	putting-green	yes
Pitching-green	pitching green	yes

HOTEL FACILITIES ENVIRONNEMENT HOTELIER — 8/10

HOTELS HÔTELS

Marriott Dalmahoy — Golf, on site
214 rooms, D from £ 158 (w.GF)
Tel (44) 0131 - 333 1845, Fax (44) 0131 - 333 1433

Malmaison — Edinburgh, 12 km
25 rooms, D £ 85
Tel (44) 0131 - 555 6868, Fax (44) 0131 - 555 6989

RESTAURANTS RESTAURANTS

L'Auberge — Edinburgh, 12 km
Tel (44) 0131 - 556 5888

Aye (Japanese) — Edinburgh, 12 km
Tel (44) 0131 - 320 1238

719

DOWNFIELD

Located in the north-west confines of Dundee, Downfield is without a doubt one of the very great British inland courses, even though it is still little known outside of Scotland and even less so to players from continental Europe. If you are in the region it would be a great pity to miss it. C.K. Cotton has designed an un-compromising challenge in an already very heavily wooded area. The course's park style means that the ball doesn't roll much so each yard of the course really counts on your card. Only good drivers can hope to get a good score, as long they keep on the straight and narrow. But short-game experts will feel very welcome here, as well. At an equal distance from St Andrews and Carnoustie, this is an excellent stop-over and a serious test of golf, more sheltered from the wind.

Situé aux limites nord-ouest de Dundee, Downfield est sans conteste un des très bons parcours «inland» de Grande-Bretagne, bien qu'il reste peu connu en dehors des limites de l'Ecosse, et ne parlons même pas des joueurs du continent. Il serait fort dommage de le négliger si l'on passe dans les environs. C.K. Cotton a créé un défi sans compromis dans un espace déjà très boisé. La nature de parc implique que la balle roule peu sur les fairways, et chaque mètre de ce parcours compte sur la carte. Seuls les bons drivers peuvent espérer un score honorable, du moment qu'ils ne s'égarent pas trop. Mais les maîtres du petit jeu y sont aussi les bienve-nus. A égale distance des golfs de Carnoustie et de St Andrews, voici une halte de qualité, et un sérieux test... plus à l'abri du vent.

Downfield Golf Club — 1932

Turnberry Avenue
SCO - DUNDEE DD2 3QP

Office	Secrétariat	(44) 01382 - 825 595
Pro shop	Pro-shop	(44) 01382 - 889 246
Fax	Fax	(44) 01382 - 813 111
Situation	Situation	

3 km from Dundee (pop. 165 873)

Annual closure	Fermeture annuelle	no
Weekly closure	Fermeture hebdomadaire	no

Fees main season	Tarifs haute saison		18 holes
		Week days Semaine	We/Bank holidays We/Férié
Individual Individuel		£ 33	£ 38
Couple Couple		£ 66	£ 76

Caddy	Caddy	£ 20
Electric Trolley	Chariot électrique	£ 8/18 holes
Buggy	Voiturette	£ 18/18 holes
Clubs	Clubs	£ 6/18 holes

Credit cards Cartes de crédit — yes

720

GOLF COURSE / PARCOURS — 17/20

Site	Site	
Maintenance	Entretien	
Architect	Architecte	C.K. Cotton
Type	Type	parkland
Relief	Relief	
Water in play	Eau en jeu	
Exp. to wind	Exposé au vent	
Trees in play	Arbres en jeu	

Scorecard	Chp.	Mens	Ladies
Carte de score	Chp.	Mess.	Da.
Length Long.	6208	5702	5330
Par	73	70	74

Advised golfing ability	0	12	24	36
Niveau de jeu recommandé				
Hcp required	Handicap exigé	no		

CLUB HOUSE & AMENITIES / CLUB HOUSE ET ANNEXES — 6/10

Pro shop	Pro-shop	
Driving range	Practice	
Sheltered	couvert	no
On grass	sur herbe	yes
Putting-green	putting-green	yes
Pitching-green	pitching green	yes

HOTEL FACILITIES / ENVIRONNEMENT HOTELIER — 7/10

HOTELS HÔTELS

Swallow Hotel — Dundee
107 rooms, D £ 100 — 3 km
Tel (44) 01382 - 641 122, Fax (44) 01382 - 568 340

Stakis Dundee — Dundee
104 rooms, D £ 90 — 5 km
Tel (44) 01382 - 22 9271, Fax (44) 01382 - 200 072

Travel Inn — Dundee
40 rooms, D £ 40 — 5 km
Tel (44) 01382 - 20 3240, Fax (44) 01382 - 568 431

RESTAURANTS RESTAURANTS

Birkhill Inn — Dundee
Tel (44) 01382 - 581 297 — 2 km

Beefeater — Dundee
Tel (44) 01382 - 561 115 — 5 km

Raffles — Dundee
Tel (44) 01382 - 226 344 — 4 km

Access Accès : In Dundee, A90 Kingsway (Ring Road). A923 Coupar Angus Road. 50 m, right Faraday St, 1st left on Harrison Rd. 200 m, T junction, left onto Dalamhoy Dr. 400 m, left.
Map 1 on page 489 Carte 1 Page 489

DUDDINGSTON

15	7	9

One of the good Edinburgh courses, of which there are several dozen. The club has a good sporting reputation with an encouraging policy for young golfers that is none too common in the often crowded big city clubs. Located immediately behind Arthur's Seat to the east of the castle, this is a park course with the meanders of Braid's burn to make life a misery for golfers who like a round without hazards. The trees are also dangerously in play when there are no fairway bunkers. This moderately hilly course is well worth playing, especially since the designers always kept the cohorts of average players very much in mind. In the olden days it was often thus. A very pleasant course and a hospitable club, but only on weekdays.

L'un des bons parcours d'Edinburgh, qui en compte plusieurs dizaines. Celui-ci s'est fait une bonne réputation sportive, avec une politique de jeunes pas toujours si fréquente dans les grands clubs citadins, souvent très fréquentés. Situé immédiatement derrière Arthur's Seat, à l'est du château, c'est un golf de parc, avec les méandres du Braid's burn pour empoisonner la vie de ceux qui aiment la vie sans obstacles. Et les arbres viennent aussi dangereusement en jeu quand les bunkers de fairway manquent à l'appel. D'un relief modéré, c'est un parcours à connaître, d'autant que les architectes n'ont jamais perdu de vue les armées de joueurs moyens. Mais il est vrai que l'on y pensait davantage autrefois. Un parcours très plaisant, et un club accueillant, mais seulement en semaine.

Duddingston Golf Club — 1895

Duddingston Road West
SCO - EDINBURGH EH15 3QD

Office	Secrétariat	(44) 0131 - 661 7688
Pro shop	Pro-shop	(44) 0131 - 661 4301
Fax	Fax	(44) 0131 - 661 4301
Situation	Situation	

3 km E of Edinburgh centre (pop. 418 914)

Annual closure	Fermeture annuelle	no
Weekly closure	Fermeture hebdomadaire	no
Fees main season	Tarifs haute saison	18 holes

	Week days Semaine	We/Bank holidays We/Férié
Individual Individuel	£ 28	—
Couple Couple	£ 56	—

Caddy	Caddy	no
Electric Trolley	Chariot électrique	no
Buggy	Voiturette	yes
Clubs	Clubs	yes
Credit cards Cartes de crédit		no

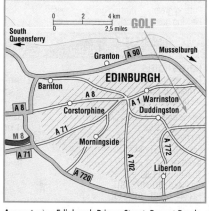

Access Accès : Edinburgh Princes Street, Regent Road, London Road, turn off right to Willowbrae Road, right to Duddingston Road West (near Duddingston Loch).
Map 3 on page 493 Carte 3 Page 493

GOLF COURSE PARCOURS — 15/20

Site	Site	
Maintenance	Entretien	
Architect	Architecte	Willie Park
Type	Type	parkland
Relief	Relief	
Water in play	Eau en jeu	
Exp. to wind	Exposé au vent	
Trees in play	Arbres en jeu	

Scorecard Carte de score	Chp. Chp.	Mens Mess.	Ladies Da.
Length Long.	5845	5556	5091
Par	71	71	69

Advised golfing ability Niveau de jeu recommandé	0	12	24	36
Hcp required Handicap exigé	no			

CLUB HOUSE & AMENITIES CLUB HOUSE ET ANNEXES — 7/10

Pro shop	Pro-shop	
Driving range	Practice	
Sheltered	couvert	no
On grass	sur herbe	no
Putting-green	putting-green	yes
Pitching-green	pitching green	yes

HOTEL FACILITIES ENVIRONNEMENT HOTELIER — 9/10

HOTELS HÔTELS

King James Thistle — Edinburgh
147 rooms, D £ 110 — 3 km
Tel (44) 0131 - 556 0111, Fax (44) 0131 - 557 5333

17 Abercromby Place — Edinburgh
6 rooms, D £ 70 — 5 km
Tel (44) 0131 - 557 8036, Fax (44) 0131 - 558 3453

Balmoral Forte — Edinburgh
189 rooms, D £ 130 — 5 km
Tel (44) 0131 - 556 2414, Fax (44) 0131 - 557 8740

RESTAURANTS RESTAURANTS

Merchants — Edinburgh
Tel (44) 0131 - 225 4009 — 3 km

Ciro's — Edinburgh
Tel (44) 0131 - 668 4207 — 3 km

721

DUFF HOUSE ROYAL

| 15 | 6 | 6 |

There are courses you play in tournaments and courses you prefer for a bright stroll. This is one of the latter, where enjoyment comes first. Although designer Alister MacKenzie also laid out Augusta and Cypress Point, here he was looking above all else to satisfy golfers of all levels. The difficulties are there, certainly (clever bunkering, trees or the estuary of the river Deveron) but they are never insurmountable or unavoidable. So you can hope to reach the green without too much to-do, keeping to your handicap on rather flat terrain, but be careful not to waste those precious handicap strokes: the greens are often two-tiered with tricky slopes and are well protected.

Il y a des parcours pour s'affronter en compétition et d'autres pour faire une intelligente balade. Celui-ci fait évidemment partie de la seconde catégorie, celle du plaisir avant tout. Certes, l'architecte Alister MacKenzie a aussi créé Augusta et Cypress Point, mais il a surtout cherché ici à satisfaire tous les niveaux. Les difficultés sont présentes (bunkering intelligent, arbres, ou l'embouchure de la rivière Deveron) mais jamais insurmontables ou impossibles à éviter. On peut ainsi espérer arriver paisiblement sur le green en utilisant sagement ses points de handicap sur le terrain assez plat, mais il faut rester attentif à ne pas les gâcher : les greens sont souvent ici à double plateau, avec des pentes subtiles. Ils sont aussi bien protégés.

Duff House Royal — 1909
The Barnyards
SCO - BANFF, AB45 3SX

Office	Secrétariat	(44) 01261 - 812 062
Pro shop	Pro-shop	(44) 01261 - 812 075
Fax	Fax	(44) 01261 - 812 224
Situation	Situation	

1 km from Banff (pop. 4 402)

Annual closure	Fermeture annuelle	no
Weekly closure	Fermeture hebdomadaire	no
Fees main season	Tarifs haute saison	18 holes

	Week days Semaine	We/Bank holidays We/Férié
Individual Individuel	£ 18	£ 25
Couple Couple	£ 36	£ 50

Full days: £ 25 - £ 30 (weekends)

Caddy	Caddy	yes
Electric Trolley	Chariot électrique	yes
Buggy	Voiturette	no
Clubs	Clubs	yes
Credit cards Cartes de crédit		yes

722

Access Accès : Aberdeen, A947 → Banff and Macduff.
In Macduff, cross the river Deveron, course next to the bridge, up the rise towards Banff.
Map 1 on page 489 Carte 1 Page 489

GOLF COURSE PARCOURS — 15/20

Site	Site	▬▬▬▬
Maintenance	Entretien	▬▬▬▬
Architect	Architecte	Alister MacKenzie
Type	Type	parkland
Relief	Relief	▬
Water in play	Eau en jeu	▬▬
Exp. to wind	Exposé au vent	▬▬
Trees in play	Arbres en jeu	▬▬

Scorecard Carte de score	Chp. Chp.	Mens Mess.	Ladies Da.
Length Long.	5665	5665	5665
Par	69	69	69

Advised golfing ability		0 12 24 36
Niveau de jeu recommandé		▬▬▬
Hcp required	Handicap exigé	no

CLUB HOUSE & AMENITIES CLUB HOUSE ET ANNEXES — 6/10

Pro shop	Pro-shop	▬▬
Driving range	Practice	▬▬
Sheltered	couvert	no
On grass	sur herbe	no
Putting-green	putting-green	yes
Pitching-green	pitching green	no

HOTEL FACILITIES ENVIRONNEMENT HOTELIER — 6/10

HOTELS HÔTELS
Eden House — Banff
5 rooms, D £ 68 — 8 km
Tel (44) 01261 - 821 282

Fife Lodge — Banff
7 rooms, D £ 50 — 1 km
Tel (44) 01261 - 812 436
Fax (44) 01261 - 812 636

Banff Springs Hotel — Banff
30 rooms, D £ 80 — 1.5 km
Tel (44) 01261 - 812 881
Fax (44) 01261 - 815 546

RESTAURANTS RESTAURANTS
Banff Springs Hotel — Banff
Tel (44) 01261 - 812 881 — 1.5 km

DUKE'S COURSE ST ANDREWS

16	7	8

Five times British Open winner Peter Thompson designed this course at the request of the Old Course Hotel. It was intended for hotel patrons owing to the problem of getting firm guaranteed tee-off times on the adjacent Old Course. Contrary to its illustrious neighbour, the Duke's Course is 3 miles inland and very different in character. It is situated on high land offering magnificent views over the old town of St Andrews and the mountains to the north beyond the bay of St Andrews. Owing to the steep slopes and distances between green and next tee, we would advise a buggy, something that would certainly be seen as sacrilege on the «real» St Andrews. Difficult, intelligent and well landscaped, the Duke's is a solid test of golf, best played from the front tees.

Cinq fois vainqueur du British Open, Peter Thomson a dessiné ce parcours à la demande du Old Course Hotel et à l'intention de ses clients, en raison de la difficulté d'obtenir des départs garantis sur le «Old Course» jouxtant cet hôtel. Contrairement à son illustre voisin, le «Duke's» est un parcours intérieur à 5 km de la mer, et d'un caractère très différent. Il se situe sur un terrain élevé, propose des vues magnifiques sur la vieille ville de St Andrews, et sur les montagnes au nord au delà de la baie de St Andrews. A cause du relief et des distances entre greens et départs, on conseillera l'usage de la voiturette, qui serait une hérésie sur le «vrai» St Andrews. Difficile, intelligent, bien paysagé, le «Duke's» propose un solide test de golf, où l'on conseillera les départs avancés.

The Duke's Golf Club — 1995

Craigton
SCO - ST ANDREWS, Fife KY16 8NS

Office	Secrétariat	(44) 01334 - 474 371
Pro shop	Pro-shop	(44) 01334 - 474 371
Fax	Fax	(44) 01334 - 477 668
Situation	Situation	

5 km SE of St Andrews (pop. 11 136)

Annual closure	Fermeture annuelle	no
Weekly closure	Fermeture hebdomadaire	no
Fees main season	Tarifs haute saison	18 holes

	Week days Semaine	We/Bank holidays We/Férié
Individual Individuel	£ 50	£ 55
Couple Couple	£ 100	£ 110
Caddy Caddy		no
Electric Trolley Chariot électrique		no
Buggy Voiturette		£ 30/18 holes
Clubs Clubs		£ 25/18 holes

Credit cards Cartes de crédit
VISA - Eurocard - MasterCard - AMEX - DC - JCB

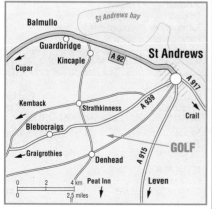

Access Accès : A91 → St Andrews through Guardbridge, then right to Strathkinness, go through towards Craigtoun (on left). Follow signs to Craigtoun Country Park).
Map 3 on page 493 Carte 3 Page 493

GOLF COURSE PARCOURS — 16/20

Site	Site	▬▬▬▬▬▭
Maintenance	Entretien	▬▬▬▬▭▭
Architect	Architecte	Peter Thomson
Type	Type	parkland
Relief	Relief	
Water in play	Eau en jeu	▬▭▭▭▭▭
Exp. to wind	Exposé au vent	▬▬▭▭▭▭
Trees in play	Arbres en jeu	▬▬▬▭▭▭

Scorecard Carte de score	Chp. Chp.	Mens Mess.	Ladies Da.
Length Long.	6616	6145	5528
Par	72	72	72

		0	12	24	36
Advised golfing ability Niveau de jeu recommandé			▬▬▬▬▭		
Hcp required	Handicap exigé	36			

CLUB HOUSE & AMENITIES CLUB HOUSE ET ANNEXES — 7/10

Pro shop	Pro-shop	▬▬▬▭▭
Driving range	Practice	▬▬▬▭▭
Sheltered	couvert	no
On grass	sur herbe	yes (05 → 09)
Putting-green	putting-green	yes
Pitching-green	pitching green	yes

HOTEL FACILITIES ENVIRONNEMENT HOTELIER — 8/10

HOTELS HÔTELS

Old Course Hotel — St Andrews
125 rooms, D £ 315 — 5 km
Tel (44) 01334 - 474 371, Fax (44) 01334 - 477 668

Russell Hotel — St Andrews
10 rooms, from D £ 65 — 5 km
Tel (44) 01334 - 473 447, Fax (44) 01334 - 478 279

St Andrews Golf Hotel — St Andrews
22 rooms, D £ 130 — 5 km
Tel (44) 01334 - 472 611, Fax (44) 01334 - 472 188

RESTAURANTS RESTAURANTS

The Cellar — Ansruther
Tel (44) 01333 - 477 540 — 12 km

The Peat Inn — Peat Inn
Tel (44) 01334 - 840 206 — 8 km

723

This is one of the best courses in south-west Scotland, a region too often neglected by foreign tourists. Off the beaten track, Dumfries & County is generally in excellent condition and very pleasant on the eye with the river Nith alongside the course. This adds a pastoral note to a very tree-bound landscape. Designed by Willie Fernie, this is one of those collection of courses which will probably never mark the history of golf design but which you are glad to have played. An unpretentious layout, it is happy to be just a rather difficult course to test the average player, kind enough not to put off the rather less experienced golfer and clever enough to tease the experts. The one hole no-one will forget is the tiny 14th, a par-3.

C'est un des meilleurs parcours du sud-ouest de l'Ecosse, une région trop souvent négligée par les touristes étrangers. Hors des sentiers battus, Dumfries & County est généralement en excellente condition, et très plaisant visuellement, avec la rivière Nith le long du terrain, qui ajoute une note pastorale à un paysage très arboré. Dessiné par Willie Fernie, il fait partie de cet ensemble de golfs qui ne marqueront sans doute pas l'histoire de l'architecture de golf, mais que l'on est heureux de connaître. Sans prétention aucune, il se contente d'être un parcours assez difficile pour tester les joueurs moyens, assez aimable pour ne pas rebuter les joueurs peu expérimentés, assez astucieux pour provoquer les experts. Ils garderont au moins le souvenir du minuscule 14, un par 3.

Dumfries & County Golf Club — 1912

Nunfields, Edinburgh Road
SCO - DUMFRIES DG1 1JX

Office	Secrétariat	(44) 01387 - 253 585
Pro shop	Pro-shop	(44) 01387 - 268 918
Fax	Fax	
Situation	Situation	

1.5 km N of Dumfries (pop. 21 164)

Annual closure	Fermeture annuelle	no
Weekly closure	Fermeture hebdomadaire	no
Fees main season	Tarifs haute saison	18 holes

	Week days Semaine	We/Bank holidays We/Férié
Individual Individuel	£ 25	£ 25
Couple Couple	£ 50	£ 50

Restrictions at weekends during summer months

Caddy	Caddy	no
Electric Trolley	Chariot électrique	yes
Buggy	Voiturette	no
Clubs	Clubs	yes

Credit cards Cartes de crédit no (Pro Shop only)

GOLF COURSE / PARCOURS — 15/20

Site	Site	
Maintenance	Entretien	
Architect	Architecte	Willie Fernie
Type	Type	parkland
Relief	Relief	
Water in play	Eau en jeu	
Exp. to wind	Exposé au vent	
Trees in play	Arbres en jeu	

Scorecard Carte de score	Chp. Chp.	Mens Mess.	Ladies Da.
Length Long.	5418	5418	4954
Par	68	68	72

Advised golfing ability Niveau de jeu recommandé		0 12 24 36
Hcp required	Handicap exigé	no

CLUB HOUSE & AMENITIES / CLUB HOUSE ET ANNEXES — 7/10

Pro shop	Pro-shop	
Driving range	Practice	
Sheltered	couvert	no
On grass	sur herbe	yes
Putting-green	putting-green	yes
Pitching-green	pitching green	no

HOTEL FACILITIES / ENVIRONNEMENT HOTELIER — 5/10

HOTELS HÔTELS

Cairndale		Dumfries
76 rooms, D £ 105		2 km
Tel (44) 01387 - 254 111, Fax (44) 01387 - 250 155		
Station		Dumfries
32 rooms, D £ 80		1.5 km
Tel (44) 01387 - 254 316, Fax (44) 01387 - 250 388		

RESTAURANTS RESTAURANTS

Golf restaurant		Dumfries
Tel (44) 01387 - 253 585		on site
Cairndale		Dumfries
Tel (44) 01387 - 254 111		2 km

724

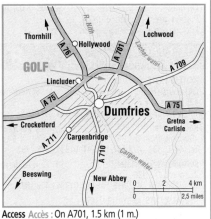

Access Accès : On A701, 1.5 km (1 m.)
North of Dumfries
Map 2 on page 491 Carte 2 Page 491

One of the classic courses of East Lothian, nestling on a narrow strip of land along a rocky seashore hardly big enough for two fairways. This means that you have not only the sea but also a wall and out-of-bounds to contend with, so when the wind blows you just might feel you haven't a friend on earth. In this case do what all amateurs used to do and go around in match-play, a very exciting format on this type of course. The most memorable part of the course is from the 7th to the 16th holes, as the holes close to the clubhouse are rather squeezed together. This is where the Firth of Forth becomes the North Sea and the view of this mass of water adds to the pleasure of playing golf in the bracing sea-air.

C'est un des classiques de l'East Lothian, blotti sur une étroite bande le long d'un rivage rocheux, avec à peine assez de place pour deux fairways. Ce qui implique que non seulement la mer est en jeu, mais aussi un mur et des hors-limites. Autrement dit, les jours de vent, les joueurs peuvent avoir l'impression de n'avoir que des adversaires. Alors, qu'ils se réfugient dans la formule de tous les amateurs d'autrefois, le match-play, toujours très excitant sur des parcours de ce style. Ici, on retiendra particulièrement le passage du 7 au 16, les trous proches du Clubhouse étant plus resserrés. C'est ici que le Firth of Forth devient vraiment la Mer du Nord, et la vue de cette immensité ajoute encore au plaisir du jeu de golf dans un air vivifiant.

Dunbar Golf Club — 1856

East Links
SCO - DUNBAR, East Lothian, EH42 1LT

Office	Secrétariat	(44) 01368 - 862 317
Pro shop	Pro-shop	(44) 01368 - 862 086
Fax	Fax	(44) 01368 - 865 202
Situation	Situation	

48 km E of Edinburgh (pop. 418 914)

Annual closure	Fermeture annuelle	no
Weekly closure	Fermeture hebdomadaire	no

Fees main season	Tarifs haute saison	18 holes
	Week days Semaine	We/Bank holidays We/Bank holidays
Individual Individuel	£ 25	£ 35
Couple Couple	£ 35	£ 70

Caddy	Caddy	£ 20 + tip
Electric Trolley	Chariot électrique	£ 6/18 holes
Buggy	Voiturette	no
Clubs	Clubs	£ 10/18 holes

Credit cards Cartes de crédit VISA - MasterCard

GOLF COURSE / PARCOURS — 16/20

Site	Site	▬▬▬▬▬
Maintenance	Entretien	▬▬▬▬▬
Architect	Architecte	Tom Morris
Type	Type	seaside course
Relief	Relief	▬▬
Water in play	Eau en jeu	▬
Exp. to wind	Exposé au vent	▬▬▬
Trees in play	Arbres en jeu	▬

Scorecard Carte de score	**Chp.** Chp.	**Mens** Mess.	**Ladies** Da.
Length Long.	5848	5848	5848
Par	71	71	74

Advised golfing ability Niveau de jeu recommandé	0	12	24	36

Hcp required Handicap exigé — certificate

CLUB HOUSE & AMENITIES / CLUB HOUSE ET ANNEXES — 5/10

Pro shop	Pro-shop	▬▬▬▬
Driving range	Practice	▭
Sheltered	couvert	no
On grass	sur herbe	no
Putting-green	putting-green	no
Pitching-green	pitching green	no

HOTEL FACILITIES / ENVIRONNEMENT HOTELIER — 6/10

HOTELS HÔTELS

Marine — Dunbar
9 rooms, D £ 32 — close
Tel (44) 01368 - 863 315

Marine Hotel — North Berwick
74 rooms, D £ 80 — 15 km
Tel (44) 01620 - 892 406
Fax (44) 01620 - 894 480

Courtyard — Dunbar
6 rooms, D £ 50 — close
Tel (44) 01368 - 864 169

RESTAURANTS RESTAURANTS

Courtyard — Dunbar
Tel (44) 01368 - 864 169 — close

Access Accès : 1 km E of Dunbar on A1 and A1087
Map 2 on page 491 Carte 2 Page 491

725

This city was the capital of Scotland up until 1603 and still carries the vestiges of its prestigious past. Now while the kingdom of Fife is famous for its links, shaped by nature over several hundred years, this particular course is an inland layout which has much to be said for it but without quite the same nobility. Tradition here goes back more than 110 years, and although the course was simply modernised at the beginning of the 1950s, no great change was made to the 600 year-old clubhouse. Trees and bunkers form the traditional hazards of a well-balanced course which is moderately hilly and fun for all. In short, this is your standard middle-of-the-road course that will sometimes have you raring to go. The watchword here is always fun.

La ville fut la capitale de l'Ecosse jusqu'en 1603, et porte les vestiges d'un prestigieux passé. Mais si le royaume de Fife est célèbre par ses links patinés depuis des siècles par la nature, le présent parcours «inland» ne manque pas de qualités, sans prétendre à tant de noblesse. Sa tradition remonte à plus de 110 ans, il a simplement été modernisé au début des années 50, sans que l'on touche beaucoup au Clubhouse, datant de plus de six siècles. Les arbres et les bunkers forment les obstacles traditionnels d'un parcours bien équilibré dans ses difficultés, modérément mouvementé, amusant pour tous les niveaux. Bref, un modèle de golf «middle-of-the-road,» que l'on pourrait parfois avoir envie de violenter un peu, mais le maître mot est ici le plaisir...

Dunfermline Golf Club — 1953

Pitfirrane, Crossford
SCO - DUNFERMLINE, Fife KY12 7QW

Office	Secrétariat	(44) 01383 - 723 534
Pro shop	Pro-shop	(44) 01383 - 729 061
Fax	Fax	
Situation	Situation	

3 km W of Dunfermline (pop.29 436)
27 km NW of Edinburgh (pop. 418 914)

Annual closure	Fermeture annuelle	no
Weekly closure	Fermeture hebdomadaire	no
Fees main season	Tarifs haute saison	18 holes

	Week days Semaine	We/Bank holidays We/Férié
Individual Individuel	£ 20	£ 25*
Couple Couple	£ 40	£ 50

* Sunday only - Full day: £ 30 - £ 35 (Sunday)

Caddy	Caddy	no
Electric Trolley	Chariot électrique	no
Buggy	Voiturette	no
Clubs	Clubs	no
Credit cards Cartes de crédit		no

Access Accès : On A994, West of Dunfermline
Map 2 on page 491 Carte 2 Page 491

GOLF COURSE PARCOURS — 15/20

Site	Site	
Maintenance	Entretien	
Architect	Architecte	Stutt & Co
Type	Type	parkland
Relief	Relief	
Water in play	Eau en jeu	
Exp. to wind	Exposé au vent	
Trees in play	Arbres en jeu	

Scorecard Carte de score	Chp. Chp.	Mens Mess.	Ladies Da.
Length Long.	5575	5263	4917
Par	72	70	72

Advised golfing ability		0	12	24	36
Niveau de jeu recommandé					
Hcp required	Handicap exigé	certificate			

CLUB HOUSE & AMENITIES CLUB HOUSE ET ANNEXES — 7/10

Pro shop	Pro-shop	
Driving range	Practice	
Sheltered	couvert	no
On grass	sur herbe	yes
Putting-green	putting-green	yes
Pitching-green	pitching green	yes

HOTEL FACILITIES ENVIRONNEMENT HOTELIER — 7/10

HOTELS HÔTELS
Keavil House Hotel — Crossford
33 rooms, D £ 75 — 0,5 km
Tel (44) 01383 - 736 258, Fax (44) 01383 - 621 600

The Pitfirrane Arms Hotel — Crossford
41 rooms, D from £ 52 — 0,5 km
Tel (44) 01383 - 736 132, Fax (44) 01383 - 621 760

King Malcolm Thistle Hotel — Dunfermline
48 rooms, from D £ 64 — 4 km
Tel (44) 01383 - 722 611, Fax (44) 01383 - 730 865

RESTAURANTS RESTAURANTS

Noble Cuisine — Dunfermline
Tel (44) 01383 - 620 555 — 4 km

King Malcolm — Dunfermline
Tel (44) 01383 - 722 611 — 4 km

Although close to Glasgow, this course is located away from any residential area. We are out in the country on Scottish moorland with its typical covering of whin (gorse) and heather, very many trees and a stream that crosses the course, running down the side of the fairways and sometimes cutting across them at strategic distances. This was only to be expected from James Braid. It is very easy to see your ball end up there if you don't give enough thought to flight and roll. Mid-handicappers, though, can always choose a line of flight without too many risks, although the experts will be keen to flex their muscles. In a word, a good score here is not as easy as all that. The clubhouse is spacious but the course crowded enough for us to advise you to book your tee-off time in advance.

Bien qu'il soit proche de Glasgow, ce parcours est situé en dehors de toute zone résidentielle. Nous sommes à la campagne, dans la lande écossaise, avec sa végétation typique d'ajoncs et de bruyère, de nombreux arbres, mais aussi un ruisseau qui parcourt l'espace, longeant les fairways ou venant les interrompre, de manière stratégique, ce qu'il fallait attendre de James Braid. Il est très facile d'y voir les balles y terminer leur course si l'on n'a pas réfléchi un peu sur leur portée et leur roulement. Cependant, les handicaps moyens peuvent toujours choisir des lignes de jeu sans grands risques, alors que les experts voudront montrer leurs muscles. Bref, il n'est pas si facile de scorer ici. Le Clubhouse est spacieux, mais le parcours assez fréquenté pour que l'on conseille de réserver les départs à l'avance.

East Renfrewshire Golf Course — 1923

Pilmuir, Newton Mearns
SCO - GLASGOW G77 6RT

Office	Secrétariat	(44) 01355 - 500 256
Pro shop	Pro-shop	(44) 01355 - 500 206
Fax	Fax	
Situation	Situation	

15 km S of centre of Glasgow (pop. 622 853)

Annual closure	Fermeture annuelle	no
Weekly closure	Fermeture hebdomadaire	no

Fees main season Tarifs haute saison — 18 holes

	Week days Semaine	We/Bank holidays We/Férié
Individual Individuel	£ 30	£ 30
Couple Couple	£ 60	£ 60

Full day: £ 40

Caddy	Caddy	no
Electric Trolley	Chariot électrique	no
Buggy	Voiturette	no
Clubs	Clubs	yes

Credit cards Cartes de crédit
VISA - Eurocard - MasterCard - AMEX - DC

Access Accès : Glasgow M8 and M77/A77 → Kilmarnock. Club on the right shortly after Newton Mearns.
Map 3 on page 492 Carte 3 Page 492

GOLF COURSE PARCOURS — 15/20

Site	Site	
Maintenance	Entretien	
Architect	Architecte	James Braid
Type	Type	inland, moorland
Relief	Relief	
Water in play	Eau en jeu	
Exp. to wind	Exposé au vent	
Trees in play	Arbres en jeu	

Scorecard Carte de score	Chp. Chp.	Mens Mess.	Ladies Da.
Length Long.	5577	5577	4668
Par	70	70	71

Advised golfing ability
Niveau de jeu recommandé   0 12 24 36

Hcp required Handicap exigé   certificate

CLUB HOUSE & AMENITIES
CLUB HOUSE ET ANNEXES — 6/10

Pro shop	Pro-shop	
Driving range	Practice	
Sheltered	couvert	no
On grass	sur herbe	yes
Putting-green	putting-green	yes
Pitching-green	pitching green	yes

HOTEL FACILITIES
ENVIRONNEMENT HOTELIER — 8/10

HOTELS HÔTELS
Glasgow Hilton — Glasgow
315 rooms, D £ 120 — 15 km
Tel (44) 0141 - 204 5555, Fax (44) 0141 - 204 5004

One Devonshire Gardens — Glasgow
25 rooms, D £ 135 — 15 km
Tel (44) 0141 - 339 2001, Fax (44) 0141 - 337 1663

Carrick — Glasgow
121 rooms, D £ 65 — 15 km
Tel (44) 0141 - 248 2355, Fax (44) 0141 - 221 1014

RESTAURANTS RESTAURANTS
One Devonshire Gardens — Glasgow
Tel (44) 0141 - 339 2001 — 15 km

Buttery — Glasgow
Tel (44) 0141 - 221 8188 — 15 km

727

This course is located virtually in town, or should we say village, as Edzell has often been voted «the best preserved village in Scotland». It was certainly one of the most stylishly frequented for many a year, as princes and maharajahs would come here for the fishing and hunting at the edge of the Highlands, and certainly to play this course designed in 1895 by Bob Simpson of Carnoustie. Laid out over gorse-land, this is a gem of a course, with a wide variety of holes, small, well-kept greens, soft fairways and hazards of all shapes and sizes, including bunkers, a steep-banked river and trees. This is one of the places in Scotland where you can still feel «out of time», as you are so far away from the main roads. Don't expect a Japanese-style clubhouse on this kind of course; what really matters here is hospitality, and here you will find that aplenty.

Ce parcours est pratiquement en ville. Ou en village, car Edzell a été souvent élu comme «le village le mieux préservé d'Ecosse.» Il fut longtemps aussi le «mieux» fréquenté, car princes et maharadjahs venaient ici pêcher, chasser en bordure des Highlands, et sans doute aussi jouer sur ce parcours créé en 1895 par Bob Simpson de Carnoustie. Tracé en terre de bruyère, c'est un petit bijou, avec des trous très variés, de petits greens bien entretenus, des fairways souples et des obstacles en tous genres, depuis les bunkers jusqu'à la rivière et ses rives abruptes en passant par les bois. C'est un des endroits d'Ecosse où l'on peut le plus se croire hors du temps, parce qu'on se trouve aussi à l'écart des grandes routes. Dans ce genre de golf, que l'on n'attende pas un Clubhouse à la japonaise : l'essentiel est dans la chaleur de l'accueil.

The Edzell Golf Club — 1895

High Street
SCO - EDZELL, by Brechin, Tayside DD9 7TF

Office	Secrétariat	(44) 01356 - 647 283
Pro shop	Pro-shop	(44) 01356 - 648 462
Fax	Fax	(44) 01356 - 648 094
Situation	Situation	

8 km N of Brechin
20 km NW of Montrose (pop. 8 473)

Annual closure	Fermeture annuelle	no
Weekly closure	Fermeture hebdomadaire	no

Fees main season	Tarifs haute saison	18 holes
	Week days Semaine	We/Bank holidays We/Férié
Individual Individuel	£ 21	£ 27
Couple Couple	£ 42	£ 41
Full weekdays: £ 31		

Caddy	Caddy	no
Electric Trolley	Chariot électrique	no
Buggy	Voiturette	£ 12/18 holes
Clubs	Clubs	yes

Credit cards Cartes de crédit — no

GOLF COURSE / PARCOURS — 14/20

Site	Site	▰▰▰▰▰▱
Maintenance	Entretien	▰▰▰▰▰▱
Architect	Architecte	Bob Simpson
Type	Type	heathland, parkland
Relief	Relief	▰▱▱▱▱
Water in play	Eau en jeu	▰▱▱▱▱
Exp. to wind	Exposé au vent	▰▰▱▱▱
Trees in play	Arbres en jeu	▰▰▰▱▱

Scorecard Carte de score	Chp. Chp.	Mens Mess.	Ladies Da.
Length Long.	5776	5498	5040
Par	71	71	74

Advised golfing ability Niveau de jeu recommandé		0	12	24	36

Hcp required — Handicap exigé — no

CLUB HOUSE & AMENITIES / CLUB HOUSE ET ANNEXES — 6/10

Pro shop	Pro-shop	▰▰▰▰▱
Driving range	Practice	▰▰▰▰▱
Sheltered	couvert	9 mats
On grass	sur herbe	yes
Putting-green	putting-green	yes
Pitching-green	pitching green	yes

HOTEL FACILITIES / ENVIRONNEMENT HOTELIER — 3/10

HOTELS HÔTELS
Glenesk Hotel — Edzell
25 rooms, D £ 82 — adjacent
Tel (44) 01356 - 648 319
Fax (44) 01356 - 647 333

728

Access Accès : Dundee A90. After Brechin,
B966 to Edzell. Golf alongside main entrance to village.
Map 1 on page 489 Carte 1 Page 489

This course has the enviable reputation of being one of the best inland courses in northern Scotland. At all events it is a very good test of golf, and although its length may seem a little outdated, there is only the one par 5 and this can often dash any hope of carding a good score. Precision is at a premium here, but hazards are in good view and so can help you recover an efficient game strategy. Eight of the par-4s are longer than 390 yards, so you can understand Elgin's reputation for being a serious examination of every green-feer's talent. For want of beating any records, you can always enjoy the view over the old city of Elgin to the north (well worth a visit) and to the south the superb Cairngorm Mountains (well worth exploring).

Ce parcours a la réputation enviable d'être l'un des meilleurs parcours «intérieurs» du nord de l'Ecosse. C'est en tout cas un très bon test de golf, et si sa longueur peut le faire paraître désuet, il y a un seul par 5, ce qui complique bien souvent l'espérance d'un bon score. La précision est ici très précis, mais les obstacles sont assez en vue pour établir rapidement une stratégie efficace. Huit des par 4 mesurant plus de 360 mètres, on comprend que la réputation de Elgin soit aussi d'être un sérieux examen du talent des visiteurs. A défaut de battre tous les records, ceux-ci pourront se livrer à la contemplation du panorama sur la vieille cité d'Elgin au nord (à visiter) et, au sud, sur les superbes Cairngorm Mountains (à explorer).

Elgin Golf Club — 1926

Birnie Road
SCO - ELGIN, Moray IV30 3SX

Office	Secrétariat	(44) 01343 - 542 338
Pro shop	Pro-shop	(44) 01343 - 542 884
Fax	Fax	(44) 01343 - 542 341
Situation	Situation	

1 km from Elgin (pop. 11 855)
62 km E of Inverness (pop. 62 186)

Annual closure	Fermeture annuelle	no
Weekly closure	Fermeture hebdomadaire	no

Fees main season	Tarifs haute saison	18 holes
	Week days Semaine	We/Bank holidays We/Férié
Individual Individuel	£ 22	£ 28
Couple Couple	£ 44	£ 56

Caddy	Caddy	£10
Electric Trolley	Chariot électrique	no
Buggy	Voiturette	no
Clubs	Clubs	£ 10/18 holes

Credit cards Cartes de crédit — no

Access Accès : Aberdeen or Inverness A96 to Elgin.
Golf on A941 just South of town limits
Map 1 on page 489 Carte 1 Page 489

GOLF COURSE / PARCOURS — 15/20

Site	Site	
Maintenance	Entretien	
Architect	Architecte	John MacPherson
Type	Type	parkland
Relief	Relief	
Water in play	Eau en jeu	
Exp. to wind	Exposé au vent	
Trees in play	Arbres en jeu	

Scorecard	Chp.	Mens	Ladies
Carte de score	Chp.	Mess.	Da.
Length Long.	5834	5608	5290
Par	69	69	74

Advised golfing ability	0	12	24	36
Niveau de jeu recommandé				
Hcp required	Handicap exigé	no		

CLUB HOUSE & AMENITIES / CLUB HOUSE ET ANNEXES — 7/10

Pro shop	Pro-shop	
Driving range	Practice	
Sheltered	couvert	16 mats
On grass	sur herbe	no
Putting-green	putting-green	yes
Pitching-green	pitching green	no

HOTEL FACILITIES / ENVIRONNEMENT HOTELIER — 6/10

HOTELS HÔTELS

Mansion House — Elgin
23 rooms, D £ 120 — 1 km
Tel (44) 01343 - 548 811
Fax (44) 01343 - 547 916

Mansfield House — Elgin
16 rooms, D £ 80 — 1 km
Tel (44) 01343 - 540 883
Fax (44) 01343 - 552 491

RESTAURANTS RESTAURANTS

Mansion House — Elgin
Tel (44) 01343 - 548 811 — 1 km

729

15	6	6

This is where James Braid learnt his golf, and you can understand why he became such a great champion and such a good course designer. Elie is a delightful course, as picturesque as they come with a number of rural features that will stay for ever, notably its location virtually in the middle of the village. But if you get the impression you are in for a pleasure cruise, watch out. The traps here are as frequent as the number of shots that, although not completely blind, do raise a few questions and eyebrows. Exposure to the wind is so fierce that there is no point in worrying about the theoretical par for each hole. It changes from one day to the next. Likewise you'll learn how to bump and run the ball by asking the locals who are always willing to give advice. One of the region's most amusing courses.

C'est ici que James Braid a appris le golf, l'on comprend qu'il soit devenu un si grand champion, et un si bon architecte. Elie est un délicieux parcours, aussi pittoresque que possible, avec certains aspects rustiques à préserver, notamment sa situation quasiment au milieu du village. Mais si l'on a l'impression de s'y livrer à une partie de plaisir, il faut méfiance garder. Les pièges sont ici aussi nombreux que les coups sinon aveugles, du moins bien soulignés de points d'interrogation. L'exposition au vent est si importante qu'il ne faut pas se soucier du par théorique de chaque trou, il change d'un jour à l'autre. De même on y apprendra à faire rouler la balle, en demandant aux joueurs locaux, qui n'hésitent jamais à livrer leurs bons conseils... avec l'accent. L'un des plus amusants parcours de la région.

Golf House Club Elie — 1875
SCO - ELIE, LEVEN, Fife, KY9 1AS

Office	Secrétariat	(44) 01333 - 330 336
Pro shop	Pro-shop	(44) 01333 - 320 955
Fax	Fax	(44) 01333 - 330 895
Situation	Situation	

19 km S of St Andrews (pop. 11 136)
65 km E of Edinburgh (pop. 418 914)

Annual closure	Fermeture annuelle	no
Weekly closure	Fermeture hebdomadaire	no

Fees main season	Tarifs haute saison	18 holes
	Week days Semaine	We/Bank holidays We/Férié
Individual Individuel	£ 32	£ 40
Couple Couple	£ 64	£ 80

Full days: £ 45 - £ 55 (weekends)

Caddy	Caddy	£ 15
Electric Trolley	Chariot électrique	yes
Buggy	Voiturette	no
Clubs	Clubs	yes
Credit cards Cartes de crédit		no

730

GOLF COURSE PARCOURS — 15/20

Site	Site	■■■■□
Maintenance	Entretien	■■■■□
Architect	Architecte	Unknown
Type	Type	links
Relief	Relief	■■□□□
Water in play	Eau en jeu	■□□□□
Exp. to wind	Exposé au vent	■■■■□
Trees in play	Arbres en jeu	■□□□□

Scorecard	Chp.	Mens	Ladies
Carte de score	Chp.	Mess.	Da.
Length Long.	5697	5697	5697
Par	70	70	75

Advised golfing ability	0	12	24	36
Niveau de jeu recommandé			■■■	
Hcp required	Handicap exigé	no		

CLUB HOUSE & AMENITIES CLUB HOUSE ET ANNEXES — 6/10

Pro shop	Pro-shop	■■■□□
Driving range	Practice	■■■□□
Sheltered	couvert	no
On grass	sur herbe	no
Putting-green	putting-green	yes
Pitching-green	pitching green	no

HOTEL FACILITIES ENVIRONNEMENT HOTELIER — 6/10

HOTELS HÔTELS
Old Manor — Leven
20 rooms, D £ 100 — 5 km
Tel (44) 01333 - 320 368
Fax (44) 01333 - 320 911

Balbirnie House — Glenrothes
28 rooms, D £ 150 — 8 km
Tel (44) 01592 - 610 066
Fax (44) 01592 - 610 529

RESTAURANTS RESTAURANTS

Bouquet Garni — Elie
Tel (44) 01333 - 330 374 — close

Cellar — Ansruther
Tel (44) 01333 - 310 378 — 4 km

Access Accès : Edinburgh M90, A92 to Kirkcaldy, then A917. Golf 8 km in the centre of village.
Map 3 on page 492 Carte 3 Page 492

13	6	6

This is not the most engaging site for golf. With a cricket pitch right in the middle, here you have the two most mysterious games ever invented by man sitting side by side. The course was built over several stages on flat terrain in the village of Larbert. The first three holes form a sort of loop. From N° 4 to N° 10 (plus the 18th), you have another set of holes, then a third running from hole number 11 to 17. On this course, where the rhythm of the layout is strange to say the least, the par 3s are called «short holes», even though two of them are in the region of 200 yards and the three others never shorter than 165 yards. By contrast, two of the three par 5s provide a reasonable opportunity for a birdie. When it comes to counting your score, you will see that playing to your handicap is anything but easy, an annoying state of affairs when considering how flat and short the course is overall. Lovers of spectacular courses probably would not play here every day, but a round from time to time is always time well spent.

Ce n'est pas le site le plus engageant. Avec un terrain de cricket au milieu de ce golf, voici côte-à-côte les deux jeux les plus mystérieux que l'homme ait inventé. Le parcours a été créé en plusieurs temps sur cet espace plat dans le village de Larbert. Les trois premiers trous forment une boucle. Du 4 au 10 (avec le 18), nous avons encore un autre ensemble, le troisième allant du 11 au 17. Dans cette réalisation au rythme un peu étrange, les par 3 sont peut-être appelés «short holes» en anglais, ils n'ont rien de court, deux d'entre eux dépassant les 180 mètres, les trois autres ne sont jamais inférieurs à 150 mètres. Deux des trois par 5 fournissent de raisonnables occasions de birdie. A l'heure des comptes, il n'est guère facile de jouer son handicap. Certes, les amateurs de parcours spectaculaires ne joueront pas ici tous les jours, mais une visite de temps en temps n'est jamais du temps perdu.

Falkirk Tryst Golf Club — 1885
86 Burn,head Road
SCO - LARBERT, Stirlingshire FK5 4BD

Office	Secrétariat	(44) 01324 - 562 415
Pro shop	Pro-shop	(44) 01324 - 562 091
Fax	Fax	
Situation	Situation	

40 km W of Edinburgh (pop. 418 914)

Annual closure	Fermeture annuelle	no
Weekly closure	Fermeture hebdomadaire	

Fees main season
Tarifs haute saison full day

	Week days Semaine	We/Bank holidays We/Férié
Individual Individuel	£ 25	—
Couple Couple	£ 50	—

No visitors at weekends

Caddy	Caddy	no
Electric Trolley	Chariot électrique	yes
Buggy	Voiturette	no
Clubs	Clubs	yes

Credit cards Cartes de crédit — no

Access Accès : On A88. Access from M876 (from W), A9 from N and S, M9 and A905 from East.
Map 2 on page 491 Carte 2 Page 491

GOLF COURSE / PARCOURS — 13/20

Site	Site	
Maintenance	Entretien	
Architect	Architecte	Unknown
Type	Type	inland, links
Relief	Relief	
Water in play	Eau en jeu	
Exp. to wind	Exposé au vent	
Trees in play	Arbres en jeu	

Scorecard Carte de score	Chp. Chp.	Mens Mess.	Ladies Da.
Length Long.	5532	5112	4993
Par	70	67	71

Advised golfing ability
Niveau de jeu recommandé | 0 12 24 36
Hcp required Handicap exigé no

CLUB HOUSE & AMENITIES / CLUB HOUSE ET ANNEXES — 6/10

Pro shop	Pro-shop	
Driving range	Practice	
Sheltered	couvert	no
On grass	sur herbe	no
Putting-green	putting-green	yes
Pitching-green	pitching green	yes

HOTEL FACILITIES / ENVIRONNEMENT HOTELIER — 6/10

HOTELS HÔTELS
Stakis Park — Falkirk
55 rooms, D £ 85 — 5 km
Tel (44) 01324 - 628 331, Fax (44) 01324 - 611 593

Airth Castle — Airth
75 rooms, D £ 140 — 5 km
Tel (44) 01324 - 831 411, Fax (44) 01324 - 831 419

Grange Manor — Falkirk
7 rooms, D £ 80 — 3 km
Tel (44) 01324 - 474 836, Fax (44) 01324 - 665 861

Topps Farm - 8 rooms, D £ 45 — Denny 5 km
Tel (44) 01324 - 822 471, Fax (44) 01324 - 823 099

RESTAURANTS RESTAURANTS
Regent — Stirling
Tel (44) 01786 - 472 513 — 15 km

731

Old Tom Morris came from Forfar to lay out the first nine holes of this course in beautiful landscape dotted with heather. In 1925, the Club asked James Braid to come and complete the course, which he did for the princely sum of £10. At that rate you can understand why the man travelled Scotland far and wide, designing hundreds of courses and managing to earn his living as a golf-course designer. Today, the course has been enhanced by some tall pine-trees, but you can still feel Tom Morris' beloved springy turf underfoot. Not a long course - although it is only a par 69 with just the one par 5 - it is still exciting to play, especially the par 3s and a number of blind shots for a few extra thrills. If you are in the region, Forfar is well worth a visit.

Old Tom Morris vint de Saint Andrews pour tracer les neuf premiers trous de ce parcours dans un beau paysage parsemé de bruyère. En 1925, le Club demanda à James Braid de le compléter, ce qu'il fit pour la somme de 10 Livres. A ce tarif, on comprend qu'il ait sillonné l'Ecosse pour dessiner une multitude de parcours et parvenir à gagner sa vie d'architecte de golf ! Aujourd'hui, de grands pins viennent agrémenter le tracé, mais on y trouve toujours ce sol élastique que Tom Morris aimait tant. De longueur assez modeste - mais c'est un par 69 avec un seul par 5 - il n'en est pas moins passionnant à jouer, en particulier avec ses très beaux par 3, et quelques coups aveugles pour donner un peu d'émotions. Si vous êtes dans la région, Forfar mérite une halte.

Forfar Golf Club

1871

Cunning Hill, Arbroath Road
SCO - FORFAR, Angus DD8 2RL

Office	Secrétariat	(44) 01307 - 463 773
Pro shop	Pro-shop	(44) 01307 - 465 683
Fax	Fax	(44) 01307 - 468 495
Situation	Situation	

2.5 km E of Forfar (pop. 14 159)
27 km N of Dundee (pop. 165 873)

Annual closure	Fermeture annuelle	no
Weekly closure	Fermeture hebdomadaire	

Fees main season
Tarifs haute saison 18 holes

	Week days Semaine	We/Bank holidays We/Férié
Individual Individuel	£ 17	£ 22
Couple Couple	£ 34	£ 44

Full day: £ 24 - £ 32 (weekends)

Caddy	Caddy	no
Electric Trolley	Chariot électrique	£ 5/18 holes
Buggy	Voiturette	no
Clubs	Clubs	no

Credit cards Cartes de crédit no

732

Access Accès : Dundee A929 to Forfar, then A932 East
Map 1 on page 489 Carte 1 Page 489

GOLF COURSE
PARCOURS

14/20

Site	Site	
Maintenance	Entretien	
Architect	Architecte	Tom Morris James Braid
Type	Type	heathland
Relief	Relief	
Water in play	Eau en jeu	
Exp. to wind	Exposé au vent	
Trees in play	Arbres en jeu	

Scorecard	Chp.	Mens	Ladies
Carte de score	Chp.	Mess.	Da.
Length Long.	5507	5236	4945
Par	69	69	72

Advised golfing ability	0	12	24	36
Niveau de jeu recommandé				
Hcp required	Handicap exigé	certificate		

CLUB HOUSE & AMENITIES
CLUB HOUSE ET ANNEXES

6/10

Pro shop	Pro-shop	
Driving range	Practice	
Sheltered	couvert	no
On grass	sur herbe	no
Putting-green	putting-green	yes
Pitching-green	pitching green	no

HOTEL FACILITIES
ENVIRONNEMENT HOTELIER

6/10

HOTELS HÔTELS

Chapelbank House		Forfar
4 rooms, D £ 70		2 km
Tel (44) 01307 - 463 151		
Fax (44) 01307 - 461 922		
Royal Hotel		Forfar
19 rooms, D £ 70		2 km
Tel (44) 01307 - 462 691		

RESTAURANTS RESTAURANTS

Chapelbank House		Forfar
Tel (44) 01307 - 463 151		2 km
August Moon		Forfar
Tel (44) 01307 - 468 688		2 km

FORTROSE & ROSEMARKIE

16 6 5

This delightful course is sited on a promontory on Black Isle and gives a magnificent view over Cromarty Firth. It's shortish length might make you feel that only accuracy is of any importance here, and that's true if the wind keeps low, which is rare. Twice restyled by James Braid, it uses the land in remarkable fashion and is extremely dangerous in the way the sea comes into play. You will need a broad pair of shoulders to keep your score down on an off-day, but you don't have to keep score. Doubtless a little kinder than its neighbours Royal Dornoch and Nairn, this gently rolling course is magic for everyone, and remarkable value for money. On the 17th, watch out for the stone marking the tomb of the «last» Scottish witch. Was she really the last?

Ce délicieux parcours est situé sur un promontoire sur la Black Isle et offre un spectacle magnifique sur le Cromarty Firth. Sa longueur très modérée pourrait faire croire que seule va compter la précision. C'est vrai si le vent ne souffle pas, ce qui est bien rare. Révisé à deux reprises par James Braid, il utilise le terrain de manière remarquable, et met en jeu la mer de manière fort dangereuse. Il faut certes avoir les épaules larges pour serrer le score quand le jeu n'est pas au rendez-vous... mais on n'est pas obligé de compter les coups. Moins brutal sans doute que ses voisins Royal Dornoch et Nairn, ce parcours gentiment ondulé est un régal pour tous, avec un rapport qualité/prix remarquable. A remarquer au 17, la pierre marquant la tombe de la «dernière» sorcière d'Ecosse. La dernière, vraiment ?

Fortrose & Rosemarkie — 1888

Ness Road East, Fortrose
SCO - BLACK ISLE, Ross-shire IV10 8SE

Office	Secrétariat	(44) 01381 - 620 529
Pro shop	Pro-shop	(44) 01381 - 620 733
Fax	Fax	
Situation	Situation	

21 km NE of Inverness (pop. 62 186)

Annual closure	Fermeture annuelle	no
Weekly closure	Fermeture hebdomadaire	

Fees main season
Tarifs haute saison 18 holes

	Week days Semaine	We/Bank holidays We/Férié
Individual Individuel	£ 18	£ 25
Couple Couple	£ 36	£ 50

Caddy	Caddy	no
Electric Trolley	Chariot électrique	no
Buggy	Voiturette	no
Clubs	Clubs	on request

Credit cards Cartes de crédit VISA - MasterCard

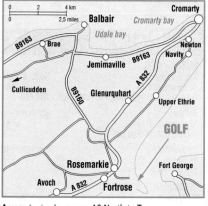

0 2 4 km	Cromarty
0 2,5 miles **Balbair**	Cromarty bay
Udale bay	
B9163 **Brae**	**Newton**
Jemimaville B9163	**Navity**
A 832	
Cullicudden B9160 **Glenurquhart**	**Upper Ethrie**
	GOLF
Rosemarkie	**Fort George**
Avoch A 832 **Fortrose**	

Access Accès : Inverness, A9 North to Tore.
At roundabout, A382 to Fortrose
Map 1 on page 488 Carte 1 Page 488

GOLF COURSE / PARCOURS

16/20

Site	Site	
Maintenance	Entretien	
Architect	Architecte	James Braid
Type	Type	links
Relief	Relief	
Water in play	Eau en jeu	
Exp. to wind	Exposé au vent	
Trees in play	Arbres en jeu	

Scorecard Carte de score	Chp. Chp.	Mens Mess.	Ladies Da.
Length Long.	5331	5095	4876
Par	71	71	71

Advised golfing ability		0 12 24 36
Niveau de jeu recommandé		
Hcp required	Handicap exigé	28 Men, 36 Ladies

CLUB HOUSE & AMENITIES / CLUB HOUSE ET ANNEXES

6/10

Pro shop	Pro-shop	
Driving range	Practice	
Sheltered	couvert	no
On grass	sur herbe	no
Putting-green	putting-green	yes
Pitching-green	pitching green	no

HOTEL FACILITIES / ENVIRONNEMENT HOTELIER

5/10

HOTELS HÔTELS

Royal — Cromarty
10 rooms, D £ 55 — 15 km
Tel (44) 01381 - 600 217

Ballyfeary House — Inverness
8 rooms, D £ 68 — 25 km
Tel (44) 01463 - 235 572, Fax (44) 01463 - 717 583

Craigmonie Hotel — Inverness
35 rooms, D £ 90 — 25 km
Tel (44) 01463 - 231 649, Fax (44) 01463 - 233 720

RESTAURANTS RESTAURANTS

Dunain Park — Inverness
Tel (44) 01463 - 230 512 — 25 km

Culloden House — Inverness
Tel (44) 01463 - 790 461 — 25 km

733

This is the «East Links» of North Berwick, less well known than its neighbour doubtless because it is less of a complete links and has several inland holes. It is laid out over two levels but is still easy on the legs. Designed at the turn of the century and tastefully restyled by MacKenzie Ross with a considerate thought for all players, it offers some splendid views over the Firth of Forth and over the famous bird reserve of Bass Rock in the open sea. It is not over-long (compared as always with today's standards) but is still a stiff test of golf, especially with the wind which although not too blustery is never far away. Green-fees will at least remember the drive from the 18th tee, from a severely elevated tee, and the excitement of a number of blind shots.

C'est le «East Links» de North Berwick, moins connu que son voisin, sans doute parce qu'il a un caractère moins totalement «links», avec plusieurs trous nettement «inland.» Construit sur deux niveaux, il n'est pas fatigant à jouer. Créé au début du siècle, remanié par Mackenzie Ross avec beaucoup de goût et de souci d'adaptation à tous les joueurs, il propose de superbes vues sur le Firth of Forth et sur la fameuse réserve d'oiseaux du Bass Rock, au large. Bien qu'il ne soit pas très long (toujours en regard des célèbres critères modernes), c'est néanmoins un solide test de jeu, spécialement avec le vent, pas toujours violent, mais toujours présent. Les visiteurs garderont d'ici au moins le souvenir du drive du 18, depuis un départ très en hauteur, et celui de quelques émotions sur certains coups aveugles.

Glen Golf Club — 1906

Tantallon Terrace
SCO - NORTH BERWICK, East Lothian EH39 4LE

Office	Secrétariat	(44) 01620 - 895 288
Pro shop	Pro-shop	(44) 01620 - 894 596
Fax	Fax	(44) 01620 - 895 447
Situation	Situation	

25 km E of Edinburgh (pop. 418 914)

Annual closure	Fermeture annuelle	no
Weekly closure	Fermeture hebdomadaire	no

Fees main season
Tarifs haute saison 18 holes

	Week days Semaine	We/Bank holidays We/Férié
Individual Individuel	£ 18	£ 23
Couple Couple	£ 36	£ 46

Caddy	Caddy	on request
Electric Trolley	Chariot électrique	£ 5/18 holes
Buggy	Voiturette	no
Clubs	Clubs	£ 10/18 holes

Credit cards Cartes de crédit — no

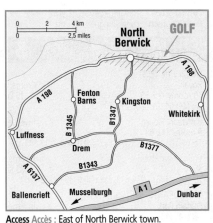

Access Accès : East of North Berwick town.
Follow seafront road from harbour. Course signposted.
Map 3 on page 493 Carte 3 Page 493

GOLF COURSE PARCOURS — 14/20

Site	Site	
Maintenance	Entretien	
Architect	Architecte	Mackenzie Ross
Type	Type	seaside course
Relief	Relief	
Water in play	Eau en jeu	
Exp. to wind	Exposé au vent	
Trees in play	Arbres en jeu	

Scorecard Carte de score	Chp. Chp.	Mens Mess.	Ladies Da.
Length Long.	5523	5293	5116
Par	69	69	72

Advised golfing ability — 0 12 24 36
Niveau de jeu recommandé
Hcp required — Handicap exigé — no

CLUB HOUSE & AMENITIES CLUB HOUSE ET ANNEXES — 7/10

Pro shop	Pro-shop	
Driving range	Practice	
Sheltered	couvert	no
On grass	sur herbe	yes
Putting-green	putting-green	yes
Pitching-green	pitching green	yes

HOTEL FACILITIES ENVIRONNEMENT HOTELIER — 7/10

HOTELS HÔTELS

Marine Hotel — North Berwick
74 rooms, D £ 80 — 3 km
Tel (44) 01620 - 892 406, Fax (44) 01620 - 894 480

Belhaven — North Berwick
12 rooms, D £ 45 — 2 km
Tel (44) 01620 - 893 009

Nether Abbey — North Berwick
16 rooms, D £ 55 — 3 km
Tel (44) 01620 - 892 802

RESTAURANTS RESTAURANTS

Tantallon Inn — North Berwick
Tel (44) 01620 - 892 238 — 0.5 km

The Grange — North Berwick
Tel (44) 01620 - 895 894 — 1 km

734

GLENEAGLES KING'S ☀ ⌇ 18 9 7

You come here as a true golfing fanatic, and to hell with the cost. The Gleneagles hotel, an absolute must, is a genuine palace hotel in an idyllic region of the Highlands. At the end of the first world war, James Braid designed the first two 18-hole courses - the King's and Queen's - while the third, the Monarch, was laid out by Jack Nicklaus. The King's Course is without a doubt the finest of the three, magnificently crafted from the surrounding landscape, winding its way through trees, bushes and hills and teeming with wildlife. The course has one essential quality, namely the variety of holes and a sort of indefinable logic in its balance. The artistry in the shapes of greens and bunkers only adds to the visual and technical pleasure of playing this challenging, very technical and remarkably well-groomed course. Exposure to the wind may vary considerably, depending on how protected the fairways are.

On vient ici en passionné du golf, en décidant de ne pas compter ses sous. Le Gleneagles Hotel, point de passage obligatoire, est un véritable palace, dans une région idyllique des Highlands. A la fin de la première Guerre Mondiale, James Braid dessina les deux premiers 18 trous, le King's et le Queen's, le troisième le Monarch's, ayant été créé par Jack Nicklaus. Le premier nommé reste sans doute le plus savoureux des trois. Magnifiquement sculpté dans la campagne environnante, insinué au milieu des arbres, des buissons, des collines, parcourus d'une vie animale intense, il a une qualité essentielle, la variété des trous et une sorte de logique indéfinissable de rythme. Et la sensualité des formes des greens ou des bunkers ne fait qu'ajouter au plaisir visuel et technique de ce parcours exigeant, très technique, remarquablement entretenu. L'exposition au vent peut varier considérablement, suivant la protection ou non des fairways.

Gleneagles Hotel & Golf Courses — 1919

Gleneagles Hotel
SCO - AUCHTERARDER, Perthshire PH3 1NF

Office	Secrétariat	(44) 01764 - 694 469
Pro shop	Pro-shop	(44) 01764 - 694 362
Fax	Fax	(44) 01764 - 694 383
Situation	Situation	

30 km SW of Perth (pop. 123 495)
85 km NW of Edinburgh (pop. 418 914)

Annual closure	Fermeture annuelle	no
Weekly closure	Fermeture hebdomadaire	no
Fees main season	Tarifs haute saison	full day

	Week days Semaine	We/Bank holidays We/Férié
Individual Individuel	£ 110*	£ 110*
Couple Couple	£ 220	£ 220
Residents greenfees: £ 90		
Caddy	Caddy	£ 30
Electric Trolley	Chariot électrique	no
Buggy	Voiturette	£ 30 (Monarch only)
Clubs	Clubs	£ 30/18 holes

Credit cards Cartes de crédit
VISA - Eurocard - MasterCard - AMEX - DC - JCB

Access Accès : • Glasgow A80, M9, A9. Turn left at junction with A823 signed Crieff & Gleneagles • Edinburgh M90. Jct 2, then A823 through Dunfermline, → Crieff. **Map 2 on page 490** Carte 2 Page 490

GOLF COURSE PARCOURS — 18/20

Site	Site	
Maintenance	Entretien	
Architect	Architecte	James Braid
Type	Type	moorland
Relief	Relief	
Water in play	Eau en jeu	
Exp. to wind	Exposé au vent	
Trees in play	Arbres en jeu	

Scorecard Carte de score	Chp. Chp.	Mens Mess.	Ladies Da.
Length Long.	5888	5574	5345
Par	70	68	75

Advised golfing ability — 0 12 24 36
Niveau de jeu recommandé
Hcp required Handicap exigé — no

CLUB HOUSE & AMENITIES CLUB HOUSE ET ANNEXES — 9/10

Pro shop	Pro-shop	
Driving range	Practice	
Sheltered	couvert	10 mats
On grass	sur herbe	yes (04 → 10)
Putting-green	putting-green	yes
Pitching-green	pitching green	yes

HOTEL FACILITIES ENVIRONNEMENT HOTELIER — 7/10

HOTELS HÔTELS
Gleneagles Hotel — Golf
234 rooms, from D £ 130 (ask) — on site
Tel (44) 01764 - 662 231
Fax (44) 01764 - 662 134

RESTAURANTS RESTAURANTS
Strathearn — Gleneagles Hotel
Tel (44) 01764 - 662 231 — on site

Dormy Grill — Gleneagles Hotel
Tel (44) 01764 - 662 231 — on site

735

We could talk for ever about the suitability of Jack Nicklaus' design for the Monarch's course at Gleneagles, but so much earth was shifted that not all the scars have healed and mother nature has yet to regain the upper hand. Despite certain reverences to the artistry of James Braid, the design can look distinctly American and often artificial in this landscape. With this said, the course is of an excellent strategic standard, as might be expected, even though Nicklaus was visibly thinking more of the proficient golfer than the less experienced hacker. The superb setting will silence even those people who feel that the difference in style with the other two courses is over the top. No-one, though, can fault the imagination employed here.

On pourrait éternellement discuter de l'adéquation du dessin de Jack Nicklaus pour le «Monarch's» à Gleneagles, mais tant de terre a été remuée que toutes les cicatrices ne sont pas encore refermées, que la nature n'a pas encore repris tous ses droits. En dépit de certaines révérences aux modelages de James Braid, le dessin peut apparaître nettement américain, souvent artificiel dans le paysage. Cela dit, le parcours est d'une excellente qualité stratégique, comme on pouvait s'y attendre, même si Nicklaus a visiblement plus pensé aux bons joueurs qu'aux joueurs peu expérimentés. L'environnement superbe fera taire même ceux qui estiment que la différence esthétique excessive par rapport aux deux autres parcours. Tous devront s'incliner au moins devant l'imagination déployée ici.

Gleneagles Hotel & Golf Courses　1993

Gleneagles Hotel
SCO - AUCHTERARDER, Perthshire PH3 1NF

Office	Secrétariat	(44) 01764 - 694 469
Pro shop	Pro-shop	(44) 01764 - 694 362
Fax	Fax	(44) 01764 - 694 383
Situation	Situation	

30 km SW of Perth (pop. 123 495)
85 km NW of Edinburgh (pop. 418 914)

Annual closure	Fermeture annuelle	no
Weekly closure	Fermeture hebdomadaire	no
Fees main season	Tarifs haute saison	full day

	Week days Semaine	We/Bank holidays We/Férié
Individual Individuel	£ 110	£ 110
Couple Couple	£ 220	£ 220
Residents greenfees: £ 90		

Caddy	Caddy	£ 30
Electric Trolley	Chariot électrique	no
Buggy	Voiturette	£ 30 (Monarch only)
Clubs	Clubs	£ 30/18 holes

Credit cards　Cartes de crédit
VISA - Eurocard - MasterCard - AMEX - DC - JCB

736

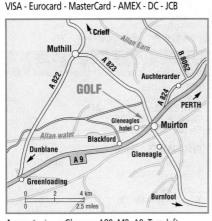

Access Accès : • Glasgow A80, M9, A9. Turn left at junction with A823 signed Crieff & Gleneagles • Edinburgh M90. Jct 2, then A823 through Dunfermline, → Crieff. **Map 2 on page 490** Carte 2 Page 490

GOLF COURSE PARCOURS　17/20

Site	Site	▰▰▰▰▱
Maintenance	Entretien	▰▰▰▱▱
Architect	Architecte	Jack Nicklaus
Type	Type	moorland
Relief	Relief	▰▰▱▱▱
Water in play	Eau en jeu	▰▰▰▱▱
Exp. to wind	Exposé au vent	▰▰▰▱▱
Trees in play	Arbres en jeu	▰▰▰▱▱

Scorecard Carte de score	Chp. Chp.	Mens Mess.	Ladies Da.
Length Long.	6444	5581	4610
Par	72	72	72

Advised golfing ability Niveau de jeu recommandé		0　12　24　36
Hcp required	Handicap exigé	no

CLUB HOUSE & AMENITIES CLUB HOUSE ET ANNEXES　9/10

Pro shop	Pro-shop	▰▰▰▰▱
Driving range	Practice	▰▰▰▰▱
Sheltered	couvert	10 mats
On grass	sur herbe	yes (04 → 10)
Putting-green	putting-green	yes
Pitching-green	pitching green	yes

HOTEL FACILITIES ENVIRONNEMENT HOTELIER　7/10

HOTELS HÔTELS

Gleneagles Hotel — Golf
234 rooms, from D £ 130 (ask) — on site
Tel (44) 01764 - 662 231
Fax (44) 01764 - 662 134

RESTAURANTS RESTAURANTS

Strathearn — Gleneagles Hotel
Tel (44) 01764 - 662 231 — on site

Dormy Grill — Gleneagles Hotel
Tel (44) 01764 - 662 231 — on site

In a series of courses like these, there is often an ugly duckling that is reserved for the lesser players or which you play to take a break from the others. Queen's is certainly not as long, as difficult or as exposed as its fellow courses, but it is not really much more than a foil for the other two. Elsewhere it would be a very good course. Kinder, gentler and might we say more feminine and enhanced with pretty stretches of water, this is in fact a more ornamental course. And while it is more reassuring because it offers less resistance to good golfers, it is still essential playing when you are here. From Spring to late Autumn, Gleneagles is one of the finest places in the world to stay and play golf, even though there are perhaps more thrilling masterpieces elsewhere.

Dans un tel ensemble de parcours, il y a souvent un «vilain petit canard,» un parcours que l'on réserve aux moins bons joueurs, ou qui figure là comme un repos pour le guerrier. Certes, le «Queen's» n'est pas aussi long, aussi difficile, aussi exposé que ses deux compagnons, mais ce n'en est pas moins bien mieux qu'un faire-valoir. Ailleurs, ce serait un très bon parcours. Plus aimable, plus doux (faut-il dire plus féminin ?), orné de jolies pièces d'eau, il est finalement plus ornementé. Et s'il doit rassurer par une moindre résistance, il n'en est pas moins inévitable quand on se trouve ici. Du printemps à la fin de l'automne, Gleneagles est un des plus beaux endroits au monde pour séjourner, et aussi pour jouer au golf, même si l'on trouve ailleurs des chef-d'oeuvres plus émouvants.

Gleneagles Hotel & Golf Courses — 1917

Gleneagles Hotel
SCO - AUCHTERARDER, Perthshire PH3 1NF

Office	Secrétariat	(44) 01764 - 694 469
Pro shop	Pro-shop	(44) 01764 - 694 362
Fax	Fax	(44) 01764 - 694 383
Situation	Situation	

30 km SW of Perth (pop. 123 495)
85 km NW of Edinburgh (pop. 418 914)

Annual closure	Fermeture annuelle	no
Weekly closure	Fermeture hebdomadaire	no
Fees main season	Tarifs haute saison	full day

	Week days Semaine	We/Bank holidays We/Férié
Individual Individuel	£ 110	£ 110
Couple Couple	£ 220	£ 220

Residents greenfees: £ 90

Caddy	Caddy	£ 30
Electric Trolley	Chariot électrique	no
Buggy	Voiturette	£ 30 (Monarch only)
Clubs	Clubs	£ 30/18 holes

Credit cards Cartes de crédit
VISA - Eurocard - MasterCard - AMEX - DC - JCB

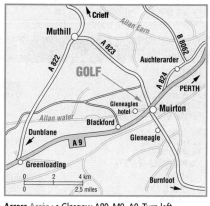

Access Accès : • Glasgow A80, M9, A9. Turn left at junction with A823 signed Crieff & Gleneagles • Edinburgh M90. Jct 2, then A823 through Dunfermline, → Crieff. **Map 2 on page 490** Carte 2 Page 490

GOLF COURSE / PARCOURS — 15/20

Site	Site	▭
Maintenance	Entretien	▭
Architect	Architecte	James Braid
Type	Type	moorland
Relief	Relief	▭
Water in play	Eau en jeu	▭
Exp. to wind	Exposé au vent	▭
Trees in play	Arbres en jeu	▭

Scorecard Carte de score	Chp. Chp.	Mens Mess.	Ladies Da.
Length Long.	5428	5150	5001
Par	68	68	74

Advised golfing ability		0 12 24 36
Niveau de jeu recommandé		
Hcp required	Handicap exigé	no

CLUB HOUSE & AMENITIES / CLUB HOUSE ET ANNEXES — 9/10

Pro shop	Pro-shop	▭
Driving range	Practice	▭
Sheltered	couvert	10 mats
On grass	sur herbe	yes (04 → 10)
Putting-green	putting-green	yes
Pitching-green	pitching green	yes

737

HOTEL FACILITIES / ENVIRONNEMENT HOTELIER — 7/10

HOTELS HÔTELS
Gleneagles Hotel — Golf on site
234 rooms, from D £ 130 (ask)
Tel (44) 01764 - 662 231
Fax (44) 01764 - 662 134

RESTAURANTS RESTAURANTS
Strathearn — Gleneagles Hotel on site
Tel (44) 01764 - 662 231

Dormy Grill — Gleneagles Hotel on site
Tel (44) 01764 - 662 231

GOLSPIE

Golspie is particularly interesting for the shape and layout of the course. Over limited space, you start off virtually in a park before moving on to pure links holes (not necessarily the best), then into woods and heather before returning to park landscape. There is no shortage of interesting holes of all shapes and sizes, with some very long and very short par 4s, five par 3s and just the one par 5. A very pleasant course to play on holiday, far from the crowds who flock to more fashionable and less remote venues, Golspie also offers some beautiful views over the coast, north and south. A word should go the excellent green-keeping despite only very few staff working on the course. Play here in Summer, when the wind keeps away, before playing Brora and Dornoch.

Golspie est particulièrement intéressant en raison de sa conformation. Sur un espace restreint, on part quasiment d'un parc pour passer ensuite par des trous de pur links (ce ne sont pas forcément les meilleurs), puis dans les bois, la bruyère et enfin revenir au parc. Les trous intéressants ne manquent pas ici, de tous genres car on trouve des longs par 4 mais aussi de très courts, cinq par 3 et un seul par 5. Très agréable à jouer en vacances, loin de la foule qui choisit des endroits plus à la mode, ou moins lointains, Golspie offre en outre des vues très belles sur la côte, au nord comme au sud. On signalera enfin l'excellente qualité de l'entretien, malgré un personnel très restreint. A jouer en été, quand le vent est amical, et avant de jouer Brora et Dornoch.

Golspie Golf Club — 1889

Ferry Road
SCO - GOLSPIE, Sutherland KW10 6ST

Office	Secrétariat	(44) 01408 - 633 266
Pro shop	Pro-shop	(44) 01408 - 633 266
Fax	Fax	(44) 01408 - 633 393
Situation	Situation	

18 km N of Dornoch (pop. 2 042)
80 km N of Inverness (pop. 62 186)

Annual closure	Fermeture annuelle	no
Weekly closure	Fermeture hebdomadaire	no
Fees main season	Tarifs haute saison	18 holes

	Week days Semaine	We/Bank holidays We/Férié
Individual Individuel	£ 18	£ 18
Couple Couple	£ 36	£ 36

Full days: £ 20 - £ 25 (weekends)

Caddy	Caddy	on request
Electric Trolley	Chariot électrique	yes
Buggy	Voiturette	no
Clubs	Clubs	yes

Credit cards Cartes de crédit VISA - MasterCard

Access Accès : Off the main A9.
Turn right after railway crossing. Golf on the sea side.
Map 1 on page 489 Carte 1 Page 489

GOLF COURSE PARCOURS — 14/20

Site	Site	
Maintenance	Entretien	
Architect	Architecte	James Braid (1926)
Type	Type	links, parkland
Relief	Relief	
Water in play	Eau en jeu	
Exp. to wind	Exposé au vent	
Trees in play	Arbres en jeu	

Scorecard Carte de score	Chp. Chp.	Mens Mess.	Ladies Da.
Length Long.	5360	5167	4766
Par	68	68	71

Advised golfing ability	0	12	24	36
Niveau de jeu recommandé				
Hcp required	Handicap exigé	no		

CLUB HOUSE & AMENITIES CLUB HOUSE ET ANNEXES — 5/10

Pro shop	Pro-shop	
Driving range	Practice	
Sheltered	couvert	n,o
On grass	sur herbe	yes
Putting-green	putting-green	yes
Pitching-green	pitching green	no

HOTEL FACILITIES ENVIRONNEMENT HOTELIER — 4/10

HOTELS HÔTELS
Royal Marine — Brora
24 rooms, D £ 90 — 10 km
Tel (44) 01408 - 621 252
Fax (44) 01408 - 621 181

Morangie House — Tain
26 rooms, D £ 80 — 24 km
Tel (44) 01862 - 892 281
Fax (44) 01862 - 892 872

Golf Links — Golspie
9 rooms, D £ 40 — close
Tel (44) 01408 - 633 408

RESTAURANTS RESTAURANTS
Morangie House — Tain
Tel (44) 01862 - 892 281 — 24 km

738

This is the kind of course you want to show those golfers who know only the links courses in Scotland. But why go and play mountain courses, you may ask? Firstly because they are located in superb, untamed regions and then because they are flat enough not to tire the legs of people who spend the rest of the year behind a desk. And perhaps you'll find more things to do outside golf (for non-golfers) in the Highlands than beside the sea. Close to Boat of Garten and Aviemore, this course was designed by Willie Park and James Braid. It has no needless complications, is very short (even for a par 68), is quick to play and is playable by golfers of all levels. The best players might find it a little on the easy side, but there is nothing to stop them from trying to beat the course record (60)

Le genre de parcours à mettre sous les yeux de ceux qui ne connaissent de l'Ecosse que le pays des links. Pourquoi aller jouer ses parcours de montagne ? D'abord parce qu'ils se trouvent dans des régions superbes et sauvages, ensuite parce qu'ils sont souvent assez plats pour ne pas effrayer ceux qui passent leur vie dans un bureau. Parce que l'on trouve peut-être plus d'activités annexes (pour ceux qui ne jouent pas) dans les Highlands qu'en bord de mer. A proximité de Boat of Garten et d'Aviemore, des réserves des Cairngorns, ce parcours de Willie Park et Braid est sans complications inutiles, très court (même pour un par 68), rapide à jouer et bien adapté à tous les niveaux. Les meilleurs le trouveront un peu limité pour eux, mais rien ne les empêche de battre le record (60) !

Grantown on Spey Golf Club — 1890

Golf Course Road
SCO - GRANTOWN ON SPEY, Morayshire PH26 3HY

Office	Secrétariat	(44) 01479 - 872 079
Pro shop	Pro-shop	(44) 01479 - 872 079
Fax	Fax	(44) 01479 - 873 725
Situation	Situation	

56 km SE of Inverness (pop. 62 186)

| Annual closure | Fermeture annuelle | no |
| Weekly closure | Fermeture hebdomadaire | no |

Cubhouse closed 11 → 03 inclusive

Fees main season Tarifs haute saison — full day

	Week days / Semaine	We/Bank holidays / We/Férié
Individual Individuel	£ 18	£ 23
Couple Couple	£ 36	£ 46

Caddy	Caddy	no
Electric Trolley	Chariot électrique	no
Buggy	Voiturette	yes
Clubs	Clubs	£ 7/18 holes

Credit cards Cartes de crédit
VISA - Eurocard - MasterCard

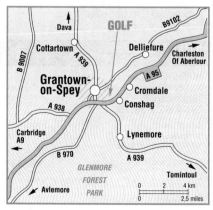

Access Accès : Inverness, A9, A938 & A95 to Grantown.
Course lies off the road to Nairn and Forres, on NE side of Grantown Map 1 on page 489 Carte 1 Page 489

GOLF COURSE / PARCOURS — 14/20

Site	Site	
Maintenance	Entretien	
Architect	Architecte	A.C. Brown/W. Park James Braid
Type	Type	parkland
Relief	Relief	
Water in play	Eau en jeu	
Exp. to wind	Exposé au vent	
Trees in play	Arbres en jeu	

Scorecard / Carte de score	Chp. / Chp.	Mens / Mess.	Ladies / Da.
Length Long.	5198	4930	4801
Par	70	69	72

Advised golfing ability
Niveau de jeu recommandé — 0 12 24 36

Hcp required Handicap exigé — no

CLUB HOUSE & AMENITIES / CLUB HOUSE ET ANNEXES — 6/10

Pro shop	Pro-shop	
Driving range	Practice	
Sheltered	couvert	no
On grass	sur herbe	no
Putting-green	putting-green	yes
Pitching-green	pitching green	no

HOTEL FACILITIES / ENVIRONNEMENT HOTELIER — 7/10

HOTELS HÔTELS
Muckrach Lodge — Dulnain Bridge
9 rooms, from D£ 90 — 5 km
Tel (44) 01479 - 851 257, Fax (44) 01479 - 851 325

Culdearn House — Grantown
9 rooms, D £ 100 (w. dinner) — 0.5 km
Tel (44) 01479 - 872 106, Fax (44) 01479 - 873 641

Ravenscourt House — Grantown
6 rooms, D £ 55 — 0.5 km
Tel (44) 01479 - 872 286, Fax (44) 01479 - 873 260

RESTAURANTS RESTAURANTS
Craggan Mill — Grantown
Tel (44) 01479 - 872 288 — 0.5 km

La Taverna — Aviemore
Tel (44) 01479 - 810 636 — 22 km

739

Of the three courses at Gullane, the N° 1 is unquestionably the most spectacular and the most challenging in golfing terms, although its two neighbours are a pleasant alternative on holiday or for less experienced golfers in the family. The slow climb along an impressive hill takes you gradually up above the Firth of Forth until you can make out the famous Muirfield links not far away. But Gullane is much more than an observatory. Wide open spaces, where only the tall rough can break the feeling of immensity, accommodate a high class course where the work of anonymous designers consisted primarily in laying out the greens, digging the bunkers (often deep) and leaving time do the rest. If you want to enjoy rather than endure this often austere course, give it everything you've got.

Des trois parcours de Gullane, le 1 est sans conteste le plus spectaculaire et le plus exigeant au plan golfique, bien que ses deux voisins apportent une alternative heureuse en vacances, ou pour les membres moins expérimentés de la famille. La lente montée le long d'une imposante colline permet de s'élever peu à peu au-dessus du Firth of Forth, jusqu'à distinguer non loin les fameux links de Muirfield. Mais Gullane est bien plus qu'un observatoire. Les vastes espaces, où seul le haut rough peut rompre le sentiment d'immensité, accueillent un parcours de haute volée, où le travail anonyme des architectes a surtout consisté à aménager les greens, creuser les bunkers (souvent profonds) et laisser faire le temps. Ici, sur ce tracé souvent austère, on exprime tout son golf, ou on le subit...

Gullane Golf Club   1844

West Links Road
SCO - GULLANE, East Lothian EH31 2BB

Office	Secrétariat	(44) 01620 - 842 255
Pro shop	Pro-shop	(44) 01620 - 842 255
Fax	Fax	(44) 01620 - 842 327
Situation	Situation	

29 km E of Edinburgh (pop. 418 914)

Annual closure	Fermeture annuelle	no
Weekly closure	Fermeture hebdomadaire	no

Fees main season
Tarifs haute saison 18 holes

	Week days Semaine	We/Bank holidays We/Férié
Individual Individuel	£ 56	£ 70
Couple Couple	£ 112	£ 140
Full Weekdays: £ 80		

Caddy	Caddy	£ 20
Electric Trolley	Chariot électrique	£ 5/18 holes
Buggy	Voiturette	£ 20/18 holes
Clubs	Clubs	£ 15/18 holes

Credit cards Cartes de crédit
VISA - Eurocard - MasterCard - AMEX

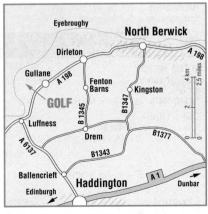

Eyebroughy
North Berwick
Dirleton
A 198
Gullane
A 198
Fenton Barns
Kingston
GOLF
B1347
B 1345
Luffness
Drem
B1377
A 6137
B1343
Ballencrieff
A 1
Haddington
Dunbar
Edinburgh
4 km
2.5 miles

Access Accès : Edinburgh A198 to Gullane
Map 3 on page 493 Carte 3 Page 493

GOLF COURSE
PARCOURS   17/20

Site	Site	
Maintenance	Entretien	
Architect	Architecte	Unknown
Type	Type	seaside course, links
Relief	Relief	
Water in play	Eau en jeu	
Exp. to wind	Exposé au vent	
Trees in play	Arbres en jeu	

Scorecard Carte de score	Chp. Chp.	Mens Mess.	Ladies Da.
Length Long.	5884	5530	5530
Par	71	71	75

Advised golfing ability Niveau de jeu recommandé	0 12 24 36
Hcp required Handicap exigé	24 Men, 30 Ladies

CLUB HOUSE & AMENITIES
CLUB HOUSE ET ANNEXES   8/10

Pro shop	Pro-shop	
Driving range	Practice	
Sheltered	couvert	no
On grass	sur herbe	yes
Putting-green	putting-green	yes
Pitching-green	pitching green	yes

HOTEL FACILITIES
ENVIRONNEMENT HOTELIER   7/10

HOTELS HÔTELS
Mallard Hotel   Gullane
18 rooms, D £ 76   2 km
Tel (44) 01620 - 843 288

Brown's Hotel   Haddington
5 rooms, D £ 78   3 km
Tel (44) 01620 - 822 254

Maitlandfield House   Haddington
22 rooms, D £ 90   3 km
Tel (44) 01620 - 826 513, Fax (44) 01620 - 826 713

RESTAURANTS RESTAURANTS
Brown's   Haddington
Tel (44) 01620 - 822 254   3 km

La Potinière   Gullane
Tel (44) 01620 - 843 214   2 km

The fine layout of this well-known Glaswegian club unwinds between rows of fully grown trees a few miles to the south-west of the city centre. It is one of the easiest-to-reach courses around Glasgow, useful to know in that although a private club, it willingly welcomes visitors during the week. Of course it doesn't offer the array of technical challenges found on the great championship courses but it has often been used for some very high level tournaments which testify to its status. The Scottish Open was one such before it moved on to Gleneagles and then Carnoustie. Good drivers will feel easy here, the others will need all their expertise to reach the well-protected greens which pitch well. There are very few bump 'n run shots to be played here, rather more in the American target golf style, despite the very British nature of the course overall.

Le beau tracé de ce club bien connu de Glasgow s'étire entre des rangées d'arbres bien adultes, à quelques kilo-mètres au sud-ouest du centre ville. C'est un des golfs de Glasgow les plus faciles d'accès. Et d'autant plus que, bien qu'il soit privé, il accueille volontiers les visteurs en semaine. Certes, le parcours ne présente pas la variété des défis techniques des plus grands parcours de championnat, mais il a souvent été utilisé pour de très bonnes épreuves, ce qui témoigne de son rang : nous ne citerons que le Scottish Open, qui émigra ensuite à Gleneagles puis Carnoustie. Les bons drivers y seront ici à l'aise. Les autres devront témoigner de virtuosité pour rejoindre des greens bien protégés, mais qui tiennent bien la balle. Ici, peu de «bump'n run,» mais plutôt un jeu de cible à l'américaine, malgré le caractère général très britannique de l'ensemble.

Haggs Castle Golf Club — 1910
70 Dumbreck Road
SCO - GLASGOW G41 4SN

Office	Secrétariat	(44) 0141 - 427 0480
Pro shop	Pro-shop	(44) 0141 - 427 3355
Fax	Fax	(44) 0141 - 427 1157
Situation	Situation	

5 km SW of Glasgow centre (pop. 662 853)

Annual closure	Fermeture annuelle	no
Weekly closure	Fermeture hebdomadaire	

Fees main season
Tarifs haute saison 18 holes

	Week days Semaine	We/Bank holidays We/Férié
Individual Individuel	£ 27	—
Couple Couple	£ 54	—

No visitors at weekends

Caddy	Caddy	on request
Electric Trolley	Chariot électrique	no
Buggy	Voiturette	no
Clubs	Clubs	on request
Credit cards Cartes de crédit		no

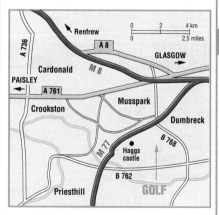

Access Accès : A7 end of Jct 1 off M77.
SW of Glasgow city centre.
Map 3 on page 492 Carte 3 Page 492

GOLF COURSE / PARCOURS — 15/20

Site	Site	
Maintenance	Entretien	
Architect	Architecte	Unknown
Type	Type	parkland
Relief	Relief	
Water in play	Eau en jeu	
Exp. to wind	Exposé au vent	
Trees in play	Arbres en jeu	

Scorecard Carte de score	Chp. Chp.	Mens Mess.	Ladies Da.
Length Long.	5908	5441	5070
Par	72	69	73

Advised golfing ability	0	12	24	36
Niveau de jeu recommandé				
Hcp required Handicap exigé	certificate			

CLUB HOUSE & AMENITIES / CLUB HOUSE ET ANNEXES — 7/10

Pro shop	Pro-shop	
Driving range	Practice	
Sheltered	couvert	no
On grass	sur herbe	no
Putting-green	putting-green	yes
Pitching-green	pitching green	no

HOTEL FACILITIES / ENVIRONNEMENT HOTELIER — 9/10

HOTELS HÔTELS

Swallow Glasgow — Glasgow
117 rooms, D £ 130 — 3 km
Tel (44) 0141 - 427 3146, Fax (44) 0141 - 427 4059

Glasgow Hilton — Glasgow
315 rooms, D £ 120 — 5 km
Tel (44) 0141 - 204 5555, Fax (44) 0141 - 204 5004

Forte Crest - 248 rooms, D £ 100 — Glasgow 5 km
Tel (44) 0141 - 248 2656, Fax (44) 0141 - 221 8986

RESTAURANTS RESTAURANTS

Camerons (Hilton) — Glasgow
Tel (44) 0141 - 204 5511 — 5 km

One Devonshire Gardens — Glasgow
Tel (44) 0141 - 339 2001 — 7 km

Rogano — Glasgow
Tel (44) 0141 - 248 4055 — 5 km

741

This may not be the masterpiece of the century when it comes to course design, and as a course off the beaten track, you wouldn't expect it to be. But if you want to know what everyday golf is like in Scotland, come along to Huntly. You'll easily find a playing partner and learn things about the country that you will never find in any book. Flattish and running alongside the river Deveron (in play on a few holes), this is an excellent course for playing with the family or on holiday, and one where you can card a flattering score without deceiving yourself. But be careful, the trees and often very thick rough can humble anyone who takes this course too lightly. You might not want to travel 500 km just to play a round of golf here, but if you did you would spend a great day, somewhere between Aberdeen and Nairn.

D'accord, ce n'est pas le chef-d'oeuvre du siècle en matière d'architecture de golf, mais on ne saurait en rechercher autant à l'écart des chemins très fréquentés du golf. Mais pour quelqu'un qui veut connaître le golf des Ecossais au quotidien, Huntly est un des parcours à connaître, où il trouvera facilement des partenaires de jeu, et apprendra à connaître le pays en dehors des livres. Peu accidenté, le long de la rivière Deveron qui joue son rôle sur quelques-uns des trous, c'est un excellent parcours pour jouer en famille et en vacances, où il est possible de faire un score flatteur sans se faire d'illusions sur sa propre valeur. Mais il faut faire attention, les arbres et un rough souvent épais peuvent étrangler celui qui prendrait ce parcours à la légère. Certes, on ne fait pas 500 kilomètres pour venir ici, mais il n'empêche que vous passerez une bonne journée ici, disons entre Aberdeen et Nairn.

Huntly Golf Club — 1892

Cooper Park
SCO - HUNTLY, Aberdeenshire AB54 4SH

Office	Secrétariat	(44) 01466 - 792 643
Pro shop	Pro-shop	(44) 01466 - 794 181
Fax	Fax	
Situation	Situation	

62 km NW of Aberdeen (pop. 204 885)

Annual closure	Fermeture annuelle	no
Weekly closure	Fermeture hebdomadaire	no

Fees main season
Tarifs haute saison 18 holes

	Week days Semaine	We/Bank holidays We/Férié
Individual Individuel	£ 18	£ 24
Couple Couple	£ 36	£ 48

Caddy	Caddy	no
Electric Trolley	Chariot électrique	no
Buggy	Voiturette	yes
Clubs	Clubs	yes
Credit cards Cartes de crédit		yes

GOLF COURSE / PARCOURS — 14/20

Site	Site	
Maintenance	Entretien	
Architect	Architecte	Unknown
Type	Type	parkland
Relief	Relief	
Water in play	Eau en jeu	
Exp. to wind	Exposé au vent	
Trees in play	Arbres en jeu	

Scorecard Carte de score	Chp. Chp.	Mens Mess.	Ladies Da.
Length Long.	4913	7764	4187
Par	66	64	67

Advised golfing ability
Niveau de jeu recommandé   0   12   24   36

Hcp required   Handicap exigé   no

CLUB HOUSE & AMENITIES / CLUB HOUSE ET ANNEXES — 6/10

Pro shop	Pro-shop	
Driving range	Practice	
Sheltered	couvert	no
On grass	sur herbe	yes
Putting-green	putting-green	yes
Pitching-green	pitching green	no

HOTEL FACILITIES / ENVIRONNEMENT HOTELIER — 6/10

HOTELS HÔTELS

Castle Hotel — Huntly 1 km
20 rooms, D £ 60
Tel (44) 01466 - 792 696
Fax (44) 01466 - 792 641

Huntly Hotel — Huntly 1 km
9 rooms, D £ 50
Tel (44) 01466 - 792 703

RESTAURANTS RESTAURANTS

Tandoorie — Huntly 1 km
Tel (44) 01466 - 792 667

742

Access Accès : Aberdeen A96 to Huntly. Golf approx. 1 km from town centre, adjacent to the Gordon School and Huntly Castle. **Map 1 on page 489** Carte 1 Page 489

16	7	8

The completion of a new, first-rate club-house provides an additional argument for this often underrated course in the capital of the Scottish highlands. The site is excellent with views over the hills on either side of Loch Ness, and the occasional glimpse over Moray Firth. The course is lined by any number of trees (not always as tall as you might imagine), the fairways are generously wide and it takes a pretty wild mis-hit to reach the tall rough. On this moderately hilly terrain, there is only one really blind shot, from the 16th tee. Otherwise the layout is very frank and hides nothing. Pleasant to play in normal weather, it can turn nasty under championship conditions, when a tough round can turn distinctly nightmarish on the 14th, one of the toughest par 4s in the north of Scotland. Inverness certainly does not have the layout or setting to claim parity with Nairn or Dornoch, but in its own style it can and does hold its head high.

L'achèvement d'un nouveau Clubhouse de premier ordre apporte un argument de plus à ce parcours souvent sous-estimé, celui de la capitale des Highlands. Le site est de grande qualité, avec les vues sur les collines de part et d'autre du Loch Ness, et des aperçus de temps à autre sur le Firth. De nombreux arbres longent le parcours, pas toujours immenses d'ailleurs, les fairways sont de largeur généreuse, et il faut faire des efforts pour s'égarer dans le haut rough. Sur ce terrain modérément accidenté, on ne trouve qu'un seul coup vraiment aveugle, au drive du 16. Sinon, le dessin est d'une grande franchise. Agréable en temps normal, il peut montrer les dents en conditions de championnat, culminant au 14, l'un des par 4 les plus difficiles du nord de l'Ecosse. Certes, Inverness ne prétend ni par son dessin, ni par son cadre à être l'égal de Nairn ou de Dornoch, mais dans son propre style, il peut lever la tête.

Inverness Golf Club — 1908

Culcabock
SCO - INVERNESS IV2 3XQ

Office	Secrétariat	(44) 01463 - 239 882
Pro shop	Pro-shop	(44) 01463 - 231 989
Fax	Fax	(44) 01463 - 239 882
Situation	Situation	

1,5 km S of Inverness (pop. 62 186)

Annual closure	Fermeture annuelle	no
Weekly closure	Fermeture hebdomadaire	no

Fees main season
Tarifs haute saison full day

	Week days Semaine	We/Bank holidays We/Férié
Individual Individuel	£ 32	£ 35
Couple Couple	£ 64	£ 70

Caddy	Caddy	on request
Electric Trolley	Chariot électrique	no
Buggy	Voiturette	yes
Clubs	Clubs	yes

Credit cards Cartes de crédit — no

Access Accès : A9 North. First turn off → Inverness. Roundabout, turn right (5th exit). Next roundabout, Club on left. **Map 1 on page 488** Carte 1 Page 488

GOLF COURSE / PARCOURS — 16/20

Site	Site	
Maintenance	Entretien	
Architect	Architecte	Unknown
Type	Type	park
Relief	Relief	
Water in play	Eau en jeu	
Exp. to wind	Exposé au vent	
Trees in play	Arbres en jeu	

Scorecard Carte de score	Chp. Chp.	Mens Mess.	Ladies Da.
Length Long.	5700	5204	5068
Par	69	67	72

Advised golfing ability Niveau de jeu recommandé	0	12	24	36

Hcp required Handicap exigé — 35

CLUB HOUSE & AMENITIES / CLUB HOUSE ET ANNEXES — 7/10

Pro shop	Pro-shop	
Driving range	Practice	
Sheltered	couvert	no
On grass	sur herbe	no
Putting-green	putting-green	yes
Pitching-green	pitching green	yes

743

HOTEL FACILITIES / ENVIRONNEMENT HOTELIER — 8/10

HOTELS HÔTELS

Craigmonie Hotel — Inverness
35 rooms, D £ 90 — 1 km
Tel (44) 01463 - 231 649, Fax (44) 01463 - 233 720

Kingsmills Hotel — Inverness
82 rooms, D £ 155 — 100 m
Tel (44) 01463 - 237 166, Fax (44) 01463 - 225 208

Culloden House — Culloden
28 rooms, D £ 190 — 6 km
Tel (44) 01463 - 790 461, Fax (44) 01463 - 792 181

RESTAURANTS RESTAURANTS

Inverness Golf Club — Inverness
Tel (44) 01463 - 233 259 — on site

Culloden House — Culloden
Tel (44) 01463 - 790 461 — 6 km

Much closer to the holiday resort of Troon than to Kilmarnock, Barassie is also much more than a friendly leisure course. Although near the sea it often feels like an inland course, but don't let that fool you. This is an impressive challenge even for the best players and each visit is the opportunity to discover new surprises and enjoy it again and again. A few blind shots add a little spice to the fun and the difficulties are evenly spread around the course. You'll need the full range of shots here to see you home, but then again you do on virtually every course of this type. Testimony to the excellence of this layout is the fact that this is one of the courses for the final qualification rounds when the British Open is played at Troon. It has also hosted some of the greatest amateur tournaments. Essential visiting when in this region that is spoilt for great courses.

Bien plus près de la station de vacances de Troon que de Kilmarnock, Barassie est beaucoup plus qu'un aimable parcours de loisirs. Bien qu'il soit proche de la mer, il offre parfois la sensation d'être un parcours «inland,» mais il ne faut pas se laisser piéger : il présente un imposant défi, même aux meilleurs, et chaque visite est l'occasion de surprises, et d'un plaisir renouvelé. Quelques coups aveugles ajoutent un peu de piment, les difficultés sont très bien équilibrées, et il faudra toute la panoplie de coups du sac pour en sortir, mais c'est pratiquement le cas sur tous les parcours de ce type. Témoin de sa qualité, c'est l'un des parcours des ultimes qualifications quand le British Open se joue à Royal Troon, il a aussi été le site de grandes compétitions amateur. A ne pas manquer dans cette région richissime en grands golfs.

Kilmarnock (Barassie) Golf Club — 1894

29, Hillhouse Road, Barassie
SCO - TROON, Ayrshire KA10 6SY

Office	Secrétariat	(44) 01292 - 313 920
Pro shop	Pro-shop	(44) 01292 - 311 322
Fax	Fax	(44) 01292 - 313 920
Situation	Situation	

3 km N of Troon (pop. 15 116)
45 km SW of Glasgow (pop. 662 853)

Annual closure	Fermeture annuelle	no
Weekly closure	Fermeture hebdomadaire	no
Fees main season	Tarifs haute saison	full day

	Week days Semaine	We/Bank holidays We/Férié
Individual Individuel	£ 38	—
Couple Couple	£ 76	—

Full weekday: £ 58 - No visitors:
wednesday & weekends

Caddy	Caddy	on request
Electric Trolley	Chariot électrique	no
Buggy	Voiturette	no
Clubs	Clubs	£ 15/18 holes

Credit cards Cartes de crédit — no

GOLF COURSE / PARCOURS — 17/20

Site	Site	
Maintenance	Entretien	
Architect	Architecte	Theodore Moon
Type	Type	links
Relief	Relief	
Water in play	Eau en jeu	
Exp. to wind	Exposé au vent	
Trees in play	Arbres en jeu	

Scorecard Carte de score	Chp. Chp.	Mens Mess.	Ladies Da.
Length Long.	6203	5902	5511
Par	72	72	74

Advised golfing ability	0	12	24	36
Niveau de jeu recommandé				

Hcp required Handicap exigé — no

CLUB HOUSE & AMENITIES / CLUB HOUSE ET ANNEXES — 6/10

Pro shop	Pro-shop	
Driving range	Practice	
Sheltered	couvert	no
On grass	sur herbe	yes
Putting-green	putting-green	yes
Pitching-green	pitching green	yes

HOTEL FACILITIES / ENVIRONNEMENT HOTELIER — 8/10

HOTELS HÔTELS

Piersland House 19 rooms, D £ 95 Tel (44) 01292 - 314 747, Fax (44) 01292 - 315 613		Troon 3 km
South Beach Hotel 29 rooms, D £ 90 Tel (44) 01292 - 312 033, Fax (44) 01292 - 318 438		Troon 3 km
Marine Highland 66 rooms, D £ 120 Tel (44) 01292 - 314 444, Fax (44) 01292 - 316 922		Troon 3 km

RESTAURANTS RESTAURANTS

Piersland House Tel (44) 01292 - 314 747		Troon 3 km
Hospitality Inn Tel (44) 01294 - 274 272		Irvine 3 km

744

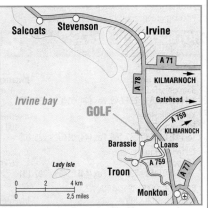

Access Accès : On A78 3 km N of Troon, opposite Barassie railway station
Map 3 on page 492 Carte 3 Page 492

KINGUSSIE

This highlands course, located at 1,000 ft. above sea level, provides some breath-taking views over Speyside and the Cairngorms. The river Gynack crosses the course and comes into play on several occasions. Kingussie was originally designed on farmland, and Harry Vardon has made so much out of it that you'd willingly believe he had shifted tons of earth. He was unable to avoid a few blind shots over rather hilly terrain, but they are few and far between. The course is not really too tiring, either; the designer was a great champion and knew what can be asked of an amateur golfer. On this terrain of peat and moor-land, the ball never rolls much so the course plays every yard of its length. With a charming setting and warm welcome, Kingussie is a good holiday course.

Situé à environ 300 mètres d'altitude, ce parcours des Highlands offre de vastes panoramas sur le Speyside et les montagnes des Cairngorms. La rivière Gynack parcourt le site, venant en jeu sur quelques trous. A l'origine, ce parcours a été dessiné sur un terrain d'élevage, et Harry Vardon en a tiré un tel parti que l'on croirait qu'il a déplacé des tonnes de terre. Avec cet espace assez accidenté, il n'a pu éviter quelques coups aveugles, mais ils sont bien rares. De plus, on ne peut pas dire que ce parcours soit épuisant : l'architecte était un grand champion, il savait ce qu'on peut demander à un amateur. Sur ce terrain de tourbe et de lande, la balle ne roule jamais beaucoup, ce qui rend à peine plus long ce parcours. Le charme de l'environnement, comme l'accueil font de Kingussie un bon golf de vacances.

Kingussie Golf Club — 1891
Gynack Road
SCO - KINGUSSIE, Inverness-shire PH21 1LR

Office	Secrétariat	(44) 01540 - 661 600
Pro shop	Pro-shop	(44) 01540 - 661 600
Fax	Fax	(44) 01540 - 662 066
Situation	Situation	

20 km from Aviemore (pop. 2 214)

Annual closure	Fermeture annuelle	no
Weekly closure	Fermeture hebdomadaire	

Chances of snow during winter months

Fees main season
Tarifs haute saison full day

	Week days Semaine	We/Bank holidays We/Férié
Individual Individuel	£ 20	£ 25
Couple Couple	£ 40	£ 50

Caddy	Caddy	no
Electric Trolley	Chariot électrique	no
Buggy	Voiturette	yes
Clubs	Clubs	£ 5/18 holes

Credit cards Cartes de crédit — no

Access Accès : Just off main A9
Map 1 on page 488 Carte 1 Page 488

GOLF COURSE / PARCOURS — 15/20

Site	Site	
Maintenance	Entretien	
Architect	Architecte	Harry Vardon
Type	Type	mountain
Relief	Relief	
Water in play	Eau en jeu	
Exp. to wind	Exposé au vent	
Trees in play	Arbres en jeu	

Scorecard Carte de score	Chp. Chp.	Mens Mess.	Ladies Da.
Length Long.	5813	4813	4575
Par	66	66	73

Advised golfing ability Niveau de jeu recommandé	0	12	24	36

Hcp required Handicap exigé — no

CLUB HOUSE & AMENITIES / CLUB HOUSE ET ANNEXES — 4/10

Pro shop	Pro-shop	
Driving range	Practice	
Sheltered	couvert	no
On grass	sur herbe	yes
Putting-green	putting-green	yes
Pitching-green	pitching green	yes

745

HOTEL FACILITIES / ENVIRONNEMENT HOTELIER — 5/10

HOTELS HÔTELS
Scot House — Kingussie close
9 rooms, D £ 95 (dinner included)
Tel (44) 01540 - 661 351
Fax (44) 01540 - 661 111

Columba House — Kingussie close
7 rooms, D £ 45
Tel (44) 01540 - 661 402

RESTAURANTS RESTAURANTS
The Cross — Kingussie close
Tel (44) 01540 - 661 166

LADYBANK

Although not a links, Ladybank is used as a qualifying course for the British Open when held at St Andrews. In other words it is held in high esteem by the game's governing bodies, and deserves to be. Amidst pine-trees, heather and gorse, this is a technical challenge of the highest order where accuracy is at a premium. You are best advised to keep well away from the formidable rough here where you can lose balls, clubs and perhaps even players too! But while good players may suffer, the humbler hacker can get by with a minimum of careful thought. With superb use of the land, pleasantly contoured fairways and well-defended greens where there is always one safe way in, Ladybank really is worth the trip.

Bien qu'il ne s'agisse pas d'un links, Ladybank est utilisé comme parcours de qualification pour le British Open quand il a lieu à St Andrews. C'est dire qu'il est tenu en haute estime par les pouvoirs sportifs. Il le mérite. Au milieu des pins, de la bruyère et des ajoncs, c'est un défi technique de première grandeur, où la précision est d'abord essentielle, car il vaut mieux ne pas s'égarer dans les roughs redoutables où l'on perd les balles, les clubs et sans doute aussi les joueurs ! Mais si les bons joueurs peuvent souffrir, les joueurs plus humbles et modestes tireront leur épingle du jeu avec un minimum de réflexion. Par sa superbe utilisation du terrain, son relief agréable, ses greens bien défendus mais qui laissent toujours une porte ouverte, Ladybank mérite vraiment le détour.

Ladybank Golf Club — 1879
Annsmuir
SCO - LADYBANK, Fife KY7 7RA

Office	Secrétariat	(44) 01337 - 830 814
Pro shop	Pro-shop	(44) 01337 - 830 725
Fax	Fax	(44) 01337 - 831 505
Situation	Situation	

9 km from Cupar (pop. 8 174)

Annual closure	Fermeture annuelle	no
Weekly closure	Fermeture hebdomadaire	no

Fees main season
Tarifs haute saison 18 holes

	Week days Semaine	We/Bank holidays We/Férié
Individual Individuel	£ 28	£ 39
Couple Couple	£ 56	£ 78

Full day: £ 40

Caddy	Caddy	no
Electric Trolley	Chariot électrique	no
Buggy	Voiturette	yes (2)
Clubs	Clubs	on request

Credit cards Cartes de crédit VISA - MasterCard

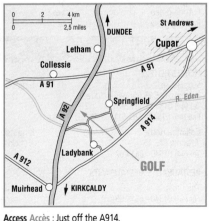

Access Accès : Just off the A914,
between Glenrothes and Dundee
Map 3 on page 493 Carte 3 Page 493

GOLF COURSE PARCOURS — 17/20

Site	Site	
Maintenance	Entretien	
Architect	Architecte	Tom Morris
Type	Type	heathland
Relief	Relief	
Water in play	Eau en jeu	
Exp. to wind	Exposé au vent	
Trees in play	Arbres en jeu	

Scorecard Carte de score	Chp. Chp.	Mens Mess.	Ladies Da.
Length Long.	6043	5707	5707
Par	71	71	73

Advised golfing ability Niveau de jeu recommandé	0 12 24 36
Hcp required	Handicap exigé	certificate

CLUB HOUSE & AMENITIES CLUB HOUSE ET ANNEXES — 7/10

Pro shop	Pro-shop	
Driving range	Practice	
Sheltered	couvert	no
On grass	sur herbe	yes
Putting-green	putting-green	yes
Pitching-green	pitching green	yes

HOTEL FACILITIES ENVIRONNEMENT HOTELIER — 5/10

HOTELS HÔTELS
Crusoe Hotel — Lower Largo
13 rooms, D £ 92 — 15 km
Tel (44) 01333 - 320 759, Fax (44) 01333 - 320 865

Laurel Bank — Markinch, Leven
11 rooms, D £ 55 — 10 km
Tel (44) 01592 - 611 205

Old Manor — Leven
20 rooms, D £ 100 — 15 km
Tel (44) 01333 - 320 368, Fax (44) 01333 - 320 911

RESTAURANTS RESTAURANTS
Ostler's Close — Cupar
Tel (44) 01334 - 655 574 — 9 km

Crusoe Hotel — Lower Largo
Tel (44) 01333 - 320 759 — 15 km

LANARK

They say that the total length of courses designed by James Braid exceeds the combined length and width of Great Britain. That's probably true inasmuch as he basically retouched a lot of existing courses. This layout was designed by Old Tom Morris, another prolific designer, but at the time «designing» was primarily a question of laying out the route of the course and the position of bunkers and greens. The course was then completed by the work of nature. Lanark is one of those courses where golf seems always to have been a part of the scene on land of heather and moorland which make such excellent playing surfaces. Not overly long, moderately hilly and with only one or two blind shots, this is a no-nonsense course and a serious test for all levels. A genuinely hidden treasure of Scottish golf.

On dit que la longueur totale des parcours dessinés par James Braid totalise plus de la longueur et de la largeur de la Grande-Bretagne. C'est sans doute vrai, dans la mesure où il a essentiellement retouché beaucoup de parcours existants. Celui-ci avait été dessiné par Old Tom Morris, lui aussi architecte très prolifique : mais, à l'époque, il s'agissait avant tout de définir l'itinéraire du parcours, l'emplacement des greens et bunkers. Un parcours devait s'arranger de la nature. Lanark est l'un de ces sites où le golf paraît avoir toujours été présent, en terre de bruyère et de lande qui fait de bons tapis de jeu. Pas trop long, avec un relief modéré, et seulement un ou deux coups aveugles, c'est un parcours sans autres histoires que celles que l'on y fait, un test sérieux pour tous niveaux. Un petit bijou bien caché du golf écossais.

Lanark Golf Club — 1851

The Moor, Whiteless Road
SCO - LANARK, ML11 7RX

Office	Secrétariat	(44) 01555 - 663 219
Pro shop	Pro-shop	(44) 01555 - 661 456
Fax	Fax	
Situation	Situation	

1 km from Lanark town centre

Annual closure	Fermeture annuelle	no
Weekly closure	Fermeture hebdomadaire	no

Fees main season
Tarifs haute saison 18 holes

	Week days Semaine	We/Bank holidays We/Férié
Individual Individuel	£ 25	—
Couple Couple	£ 50	—

Full Weekdays: £ 38 - No visitors at weekends

Caddy	Caddy	no
Electric Trolley	Chariot électrique	no
Buggy	Voiturette	£ 14/18 holes
Clubs	Clubs	no
Credit cards Cartes de crédit		no

Access Accès : • Edinburgh, A71, then A706 to Lanark
• Glasgow, M74 and A72 to Lanark
Map 2 on page 491 Carte 2 Page 491

GOLF COURSE / PARCOURS — 16/20

Site	Site	
Maintenance	Entretien	
Architect	Architecte	Tom Morris James Braid
Type	Type	moorland
Relief	Relief	
Water in play	Eau en jeu	
Exp. to wind	Exposé au vent	
Trees in play	Arbres en jeu	

Scorecard Carte de score	Chp. Chp.	Mens Mess.	Ladies Da.
Length Long.	5845	5570	5330
Par	70	70	74

Advised golfing ability Niveau de jeu recommandé	0 12 24 36
Hcp required Handicap exigé	certificate

CLUB HOUSE & AMENITIES / CLUB HOUSE ET ANNEXES — 6/10

Pro shop	Pro-shop	
Driving range	Practice	
Sheltered	couvert	no
On grass	sur herbe	no
Putting-green	putting-green	yes
Pitching-green	pitching green	no

HOTEL FACILITIES / ENVIRONNEMENT HOTELIER — 5/10

HOTELS HÔTELS

Abington Hotel — Abington, by Biggar
28 rooms, D £ 74 — 15 km
Tel (44) 01864 - 502 467
Fax (44) 01864 - 502 223

Cartland Bridge — Lanark
17 rooms, D £ 58-68 — 2 km
Tel (44) 01555 - 664 426

RESTAURANTS RESTAURANTS

La Vigna — Lanark
Tel (44) 01555 - 664 320 — 2 km

Crown Tavern — Lanark
Tel (44) 01555 - 662 465 — 2 km

747

LETHAM GRANGE OLD COURSE

15	7	5

This course was opened in 1987 at the foot of the splendid Letham Grange Hotel and was designed by gentleman farmer Ken Smith who drew his inspiration from the Augusta National course, hoping that one day this might become known as the Scottish Augusta. In actual fact there are very few similarities but this is nonetheless a pretty and rather challenging layout with tree-lined fairways and a few rather dangerous water hazards. The course is rather hilly in places, which means a few blind shots. Target golf is virtually an obligation here, and this is why you don't always get the impression of playing in Scotland. But despite everything, it is fun playing here with friends of all levels, of whom the least experienced will probably enjoy more the second, shorter course.

Ce parcours a été créé en 1987 au pied du splendide Letham Grange Hotel, et dessiné par Ken Smith, un gentleman farmer qui s'inspira d'Augusta National en espérant que ce parcours pourrait un jour être appelé le «Augusta d'Ecosse.» En fait, on trouve peu de ressemblances, mais c'est malgré tout un joli tracé, assez exigeant, aux fairways bordés d'arbres, avec quelques obstacles d'eau assez dangereux. Le relief est parfois assez prononcé, ce qui implique quelques coups aveugles. Ici, le target golf est quasiment une obligation, c'est pourquoi on n'a pas forcément l'impression de se trouver en Ecosse. Malgré tout, on aura plaisir à évoluer ici avec des amis de tous niveaux, dont les moins expérimentés aimeront jouer le second parcours, plus court.

Letham Grange Golf Club — 1985

Letham Grange Hotel
SCO - COLLISTON, by Arbroath, Angus DD11 4 RL

Office	Secrétariat	(44) 01241 - 890 373
Pro shop	Pro-shop	(44) 01241 - 890 377
Fax	Fax	(44) 01241 - 890 725
Situation	Situation	

8 km N of Arbroath (pop. 24 002)
32 km E of Dundee (pop. 165 873)

Annual closure	Fermeture annuelle	yes
		1/1 → 31/1
Weekly closure	Fermeture hebdomadaire	no

Fees main season Tarifs haute saison 18 holes

	Week days Semaine	We/Bank holidays We/Férié
Individual Individuel	£ 27.50	£ 35
Couple Couple	£ 55	£ 70

Caddy	Caddy	on request
Electric Trolley	Chariot électrique	no
Buggy	Voiturette	yes
Clubs	Clubs	yes

Credit cards Cartes de crédit
VISA - Eurocard - MasterCard - AMEX - DC - JCB

748

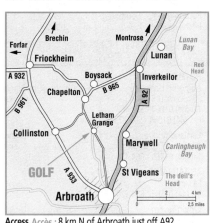

Access Accès : 8 km N of Arbroath just off A92.
Well signposted.
Map 1 on page 489 Carte 1 Page 489

GOLF COURSE PARCOURS — 15/20

Site	Site	
Maintenance	Entretien	
Architect	Architecte	D. Steel/GK. Smith
Type	Type	parkland
Relief	Relief	
Water in play	Eau en jeu	
Exp. to wind	Exposé au vent	
Trees in play	Arbres en jeu	

Scorecard Carte de score	Chp. Chp.	Mens Mess.	Ladies Da.
Length Long.	6341	5777	5254
Par	73	73	75

Advised golfing ability   0   12   24   36
Niveau de jeu recommandé
Hcp required   Handicap exigé   no

CLUB HOUSE & AMENITIES CLUB HOUSE ET ANNEXES — 7/10

Pro shop	Pro-shop	
Driving range	Practice	
Sheltered	couvert	no
On grass	sur herbe	yes
Putting-green	putting-green	yes
Pitching-green	pitching green	yes

HOTEL FACILITIES ENVIRONNEMENT HOTELIER — 5/10

HOTELS HÔTELS
Letham Grange Hotel — Golf
42 rooms, from D £ 60 — on site
Tel (44) 01241 - 890 373
Fax (44) 01241 - 890 414

RESTAURANTS RESTAURANTS

But'n'Ben — Arbroath
Tel (44) 01241 - 877 233 — 5 km

The original course was shared with the Lundin Golf Club. But when the railways arrived in the region, the course was split nine holes on one side and nine on the other, with each club creating an extra nine holes. So instead of one good course, here we have two, as adjacent now as they were in the past. Most of the holes at Leven are pure links style, but two or three are close to the heather-bound inland courses that are so common in both Scotland and England. Here again the wind has a say in things, because Leven is distinctly vulnerable when played by long-hitters and skilled technicians in fine weather. In this case even the least experienced players will have fun, although the last few holes can easily upset their card. The least they should do is avoid the deep fairway bunkers and the traps around the green.

Le parcours original a été partagé avec le Lundin Golf Club, à l'arrivée du chemin de fer dans la région. Chacun étant reparti de son côté avec neuf trous a créé neuf autres trous. Au lieu d'un seul bon parcours, en voilà deux, toujours mitoyens. La plupart de trous de Leven ont un caractère de pur link, mais deux ou trois sont assez proches des parcours inland de bruyère, que l'on trouve souvent en Ecosse comme en Angleterre. Là encore, le vent fait la différence, car Leven s'avère assez fragile face aux solides frappeurs et aux bons techniciens quand le temps est beau. Alors, même les moins expérimentés y trouveront leur plaisir, mais les derniers trous peuvent leur créer des problèmes. Qu'ils évitent en tous cas les profonds bunkers de fairway comme de défense de green.

Leven Golfing Society — 1846

P.O. Box 14609, Links Road
SCO - LEVEN, Fife KY9 1LG

Office	Secrétariat	(44) 01333 - 424 229
Pro shop	Pro-shop	(44) 01333 - 421 390
Fax	Fax	(44) 01333 - 424 229
Situation	Situation	

20 km SW of St Andrews (pop. 11 136)

Annual closure	Fermeture annuelle	no
Weekly closure	Fermeture hebdomadaire	no

Fees main season Tarifs haute saison		18 holes
	Week days Semaine	We/Bank holidays We/Férié
Individual Individuel	£ 25	£ 30
Couple Couple	£ 50	£ 60

Caddy	Caddy	no
Electric Trolley	Chariot électrique	no
Buggy	Voiturette	no
Clubs	Clubs	no
Credit cards Cartes de crédit		no

Access Accès : Edinburgh, M90 then A92 (Jct3), A955.
Golf East of Leven, on Promenade.
Map 3 on page 493 Carte 3 Page 493

GOLF COURSE / PARCOURS — 16/20

Site	Site	
Maintenance	Entretien	
Architect	Architecte	Unknown
Type	Type	links, seaside course
Relief	Relief	
Water in play	Eau en jeu	
Exp. to wind	Exposé au vent	
Trees in play	Arbres en jeu	

Scorecard Carte de score	Chp. Chp.	Mens Mess.	Ladies Da.
Length Long.	5882	5475	5217
Par	71	69	73

Advised golfing ability Niveau de jeu recommandé	0	12	24	36
Hcp required Handicap exigé	no			

CLUB HOUSE & AMENITIES / CLUB HOUSE ET ANNEXES — 6/10

Pro shop	Pro-shop	
Driving range	Practice	
Sheltered	couvert	no
On grass	sur herbe	no
Putting-green	putting-green	no
Pitching-green	pitching green	no

HOTEL FACILITIES / ENVIRONNEMENT HOTELIER — 6/10

HOTELS HÔTELS
Old Manor Hotel — Lundin Links
24 rooms, D £ 115 — 3 km
Tel (44) 01333 - 320 368, Fax (44) 01333 - 320 911

Lundin Links Hotel — Lundin Links
21 rooms, D £ 122 — 3 km
Tel (44) 01333 - 320 201, Fax (44) 01333 - 320 930

Crusoe Hotel — Lundin Links
16 rooms, D £ 95 — 3 km
Tel (44) 01333 - 320 759, Fax (44) 01333 - 320 865

RESTAURANTS RESTAURANTS
Old Manor Hotel — Lundin Links
Tel (44) 01333 - 320 368 — 3 km

Lundin Links Hotel — Lundin Links
Tel (44) 01333 - 320 207 — 3 km

749

LONGNIDDRY

14	7	6

According to legend, Mary Queen of Scots played golf somewhere around here in 1567, but it was only 350 years later that Harry Colt designed the present course, subsequently restyled by James Braid and MacKenzie Ross. Despite a breath-taking view over the Firth of Forth, this is not a links course, rather a parkland affair with friendly yardage. The sandstone club-house is simple but offers a warm welcome, while the actual course gives an impression of tranquillity, beauty and elegance. There is nothing treacherous about it, you just have to keep well away from the trees (usually pines) and not think too much about making par as written on your card. In theory there are no par 5s here, but some of the long par 4s could be considered as such, balanced by two or three others which are definite birdie holes. The greens are good and receptive to well-hit approach shots, whether pitched or rolled. Regretfully, some of the original two-tiered greens have disappeared.

Mary Reine d'Ecosse aurait joué au golf dans les environs en 1567, mais il fallut 350 ans de plus pour que Harry Colt désigne le présent parcours, retouché ensuite par James Braid et Mackenzie Ross. Malgré une vue imprenable sur le Firth of Forth, il n'a rien d'un links, mais plutôt une allure de parc, de longueur assez bénigne. Le Clubhouse en grès est sans prétention, mais très accueillant. Quant au parcours, il dégage une impression de calme, de beauté et d'élégance. Rien de traître ici, il convient seulement de se tenir à l'écart des arbres (souvent des pins), et de ne pas trop tenir compte du par de la carte. Ici, il n'y a en théorie pas de par 5, mais certains longs par 4 en tiennent lieu, et deux ou trois par 4 sont des trous à birdie. Les greens sont de bonne qualité, réceptifs à des approches bien jouées, éventuellement roulées, on peut seulement regretter que certains greens à double plateau des origines aient disparu.

Longniddry Golf Club — 1921
SCO - LONGNIDDRY, East Lothian EH32 0NL

Office	Secrétariat	(44) 01875 - 852 241
Pro shop	Pro-shop	(44) 01875 - 852 228
Fax	Fax	(44) 01875 - 853 371
Situation	Situation	

19 km E of Edinburgh (pop. 418 914)

Annual closure	Fermeture annuelle	no
Weekly closure	Fermeture hebdomadaire	no

Fees main season
Tarifs haute saison 18 holes

	Week days Semaine	We/Bank holidays We/Férié
Individual Individuel	£ 27	£ 35
Couple Couple	£ 54	£ 70
Full weekdays: £ 38		

Caddy	Caddy	on request/£ 15
Electric Trolley	Chariot électrique	no
Buggy	Voiturette	no
Clubs	Clubs	on request

Credit cards Cartes de crédit VISA - MasterCard

Access Accès : Edinburgh, A1, A198.
Course reached via Links Road at North of the village.
Map 3 on page 493 Carte 3 Page 493

GOLF COURSE
PARCOURS

14/20

Site	Site	
Maintenance	Entretien	
Architect	Architecte	Harry S. Colt Ross / Braid
Type	Type	parkland
Relief	Relief	
Water in play	Eau en jeu	
Exp. to wind	Exposé au vent	
Trees in play	Arbres en jeu	

Scorecard Carte de score	Chp. Chp.	Mens Mess.	Ladies Da.
Length Long.	5660	5660	5246
Par	68	68	73

Advised golfing ability	0	12	24	36
Niveau de jeu recommandé				
Hcp required Handicap exigé	28 Men, 36 Ladies			

CLUB HOUSE & AMENITIES
CLUB HOUSE ET ANNEXES

7/10

Pro shop	Pro-shop	
Driving range	Practice	
Sheltered	couvert	no
On grass	sur herbe	yes
Putting-green	putting-green	yes
Pitching-green	pitching green	yes

HOTEL FACILITIES
ENVIRONNEMENT HOTELIER

6/10

HOTELS HÔTELS

Mallard Hotel		Gullane
18 rooms, D £ 76		10 km
Tel (44) 01620 - 843 288		
Brown's Hotel		Haddington
5 rooms, D £ 78		12 km
Tel (44) 01620 - 822 254		
Maitlandfield House Hotel		Haddington
22 rooms, D £ 50-90		12 km
Tel (44) 01620 - 826 513, Fax (44) 01620 - 826 713		

RESTAURANTS RESTAURANTS

Greywalls Hotel		Gullane
Tel (44) 01620 - 842 144		10 km
La Potinière		Gullane
Tel (44) 01620 - 843 214		10 km

750

14	6	8

Lying to the south of Edinburgh at the boundary with the Pentland Hills, this course has undergone many a change since its inception in 1893. Four such major alterations were made by James Braid and the last change in 1993 seems to have given the course its final complexion (but who knows?). The terrain is full of slopes, some of which are really steep (especially out in the middle section), so we would recommend this to fit players only. The reward is the beauty of vistas over the Firth of Forth from atop the hill. The course has a number of excellent holes, whose contours seem to follow those of the natural terrain. The downside is that you need to play here several times to establish any sort of game strategy. As on any unknown course, give matchplay a shot first time around.

Au sud d'Edinburgh et à la limite des Pentland Hills, ce parcours créé en 1893 a connu bien des modifications, dont au moins quatre majeures sous la direction de James Braid, et une dernière en 1993 qui semble lui avoir donné son caractère définitif (mais sait-on jamais ?). Le terrain est très vallonné, parfois de façon assez brutale (surtout dans la partie centrale) et l'on ne conseillera qu'aux joueurs en forme de s'y mesurer. La récompense, c'est la beauté des points de vue sur le Firth of Forth, au sommet de la colline. On trouve ici bon nombre d'excellents trous de golf, dont le tracé a suivi les contours des reliefs. Mais le revers de la médaille, c'est qu'il faut avoir joué plusieurs fois pour bien établir une stratégie. Comme sur tous les parcours inconnus, jouez au début en match-play...

Lothianburn Golf Club — 1893

106A Biggar Road
SCO - EDINBURGH EH10 7DU

Office	Secrétariat	(44) 0131 - 445 5067
Pro shop	Pro-shop	(44) 0131 - 445 2288
Fax	Fax	
Situation	Situation	

limits of Edinburgh city (pop. 418 914)

Annual closure	Fermeture annuelle	no
Weekly closure	Fermeture hebdomadaire	

Fees main season
Tarifs haute saison 18 holes

	Week days Semaine	We/Bank holidays We/Férié
Individual Individuel	£ 16	£ 22
Couple Couple	£ 32	£ 44

Full days: £ 22 - £ 27 (Weekends)

Caddy	Caddy	no
Electric Trolley	Chariot électrique	no
Buggy	Voiturette	yes
Clubs	Clubs	yes

Credit cards Cartes de crédit — no

Access Accès : City by-pass. Lothianburn exit.
Map 3 on page 493 Carte 3 Page 493

GOLF COURSE / PARCOURS — 14/20

Site	Site	
Maintenance	Entretien	
Architect	Architecte	James Braid
Type	Type	hilly
Relief	Relief	
Water in play	Eau en jeu	
Exp. to wind	Exposé au vent	
Trees in play	Arbres en play	

Scorecard Carte de score	Chp. Chp.	Mens Mess.	Ladies Da.
Length Long.	5090	5090	4438
Par	71	71	70

Advised golfing ability Niveau de jeu recommandé	0	12	24	36
Hcp required Handicap exigé	28 Men/Ladies			

CLUB HOUSE & AMENITIES / CLUB HOUSE ET ANNEXES — 6/10

Pro shop	Pro-shop	
Driving range	Practice	
Sheltered	couvert	no
On grass	sur herbe	no
Putting-green	putting-green	yes
Pitching-green	pitching green	no

751

HOTEL FACILITIES / ENVIRONNEMENT HOTELIER — 8/10

HOTELS HÔTELS

Forte Posthouse — Edinburgh
204 rooms, D £ 70 — 6 km
Tel (44) 0131 - 334 0390, Fax (44) 0131 - 334 9237

Caledonian — Edinburgh
223 rooms, D £ 200 — 8 km
Tel (44) 0131 - 459 9988, Fax (44) 0131 - 225 6632

Forte Travelodge — Edinburgh
40 rooms, D £ 35 — 1 km
Tel (44) 0131 - 441 4296

RESTAURANTS RESTAURANTS

Mackenzies — Edinburgh
Tel (44) 0131 - 441 2587 — 2 km

Indian Cavalry Club — Edinburgh
Tel (44) 0131 - 228 3282 — 5 km

Arriving here, you seem to be carrying on from Gullane in a whole cluster of courses the equivalent of which is to be found only at St Andrews or Pinehurst. Although Luffness New is not as well known as its neighbours or even nearby Muirfield, it is a course of great character which is always in perfect condition (the greens are famous for this). It rewards the good shots and punishes the bad ones, the way it should be not always is. The wind is an important factor but the direction changes at almost every hole. With a network of bunkers and formidable, omnipresent rough, carding a good score here is the sign of a talented player. Even if you are short of talent, you'll still have fun.

En arrivant ici, on se retrouve dans la continuité des parcours de Gullane, et dans une véritable galaxie dont on ne retrouve l'équivalent qu'à St Andrews ou, plus encore, Pinehurst. Bien que Luffness New n'ait pas la notoriété de ses voisins ou, plus encore, de Muirfield tout proche, c'est un parcours de caractère fort, toujours en bon état (ses greens sont célèbres), qui récompense les bons coups et punit les mauvais, ce qui devrait toujours être le cas, mais n'est pas si fréquent. Le vent y est un facteur important, mais l'orientation change pratiquement à chaque trou. Avec le réseau de bunkers et un rough aussi redoutable qu'omniprésent, signer un bon score ici est une preuve de talent. Si l'on en manque, on s'y amusera aussi beaucoup.

Luffness New Golf Club — 1894
SCO - ABERLADY EH32 0QA

Office	Secrétariat	(44) 01620 - 843 336
Pro shop	Pro-shop	(44) 01620 - 843 114
Fax	Fax	(44) 01620 - 842 933
Situation	Situation	

27 km E of Edinburgh (pop. 418 914)

Annual closure	Fermeture annuelle	no
Weekly closure	Fermeture hebdomadaire	no

Fees main season — Tarifs haute saison — 18 holes

	Week days Semaine	We/Bank holidays We/Férié
Individual Individuel	£ 35	—
Couple Couple	£ 70	—

Full weekday: £ 50 - No visitors at weekends - Restrictions for Ladies (ask)

Caddy	Caddy	no
Electric Trolley	Chariot électrique	no
Buggy	Voiturette	no
Clubs	Clubs	no

Credit cards Cartes de crédit — no

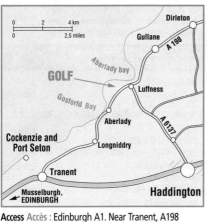

752

Access Accès : Edinburgh A1. Near Tranent, A198 through Longniddry and Aberlady.
Turn off right to Luffness Clubhouse.
Map 3 on page 493 Carte 3 Page 493

GOLF COURSE / PARCOURS — 16/20

Site	Site	■■■■□
Maintenance	Entretien	■■■■□
Architect	Architecte	Tom Morris
Type	Type	links
Relief	Relief	■■□□□
Water in play	Eau en jeu	■□□□□
Exp. to wind	Exposé au vent	■■■□□
Trees in play	Arbres en jeu	■□□□□

Scorecard Carte de score	Chp. Chp.	Mens Mess.	Ladies Da.
Length Long.	5576	5576	5576
Par	69	69	73

Advised golfing ability
Niveau de jeu recommandé

0	12	24	36

Hcp required — Handicap exigé — certificate

CLUB HOUSE & AMENITIES / CLUB HOUSE ET ANNEXES — 5/10

Pro shop	Pro-shop	■■■□□
Driving range	Practice	■■□□□
Sheltered	couvert	no
On grass	sur herbe	no
Putting-green	putting-green	yes
Pitching-green	pitching green	no

HOTEL FACILITIES / ENVIRONNEMENT HOTELIER — 6/10

HOTELS HÔTELS

Mallard Hotel — Gullane
18 rooms, D £ 76 — 4 km
Tel (44) 01620 - 843 288

Brown's Hotel — Haddington
5 rooms, D £ 78 — 5 km
Tel (44) 01620 - 822 254

Maitlandfield House — Haddington
22 rooms, D £ 90 — 5 km
Tel (44) 01620 - 826 513, Fax (44) 01620 - 826 713

RESTAURANTS RESTAURANTS

Brown's — Haddington
Tel (44) 01620 - 822 254 — 5 km

La Potinière — Gullane
Tel (44) 01620 - 843 214 — 4 km

The twin brother to Leven Links, Lundin was born from a split in 1868, where each course took 9 holes and went their own way up to 18. Don't wait for the annual tournament that bring both courses together, just try and play this course which originated beside the sea. Restyled like so many other courses by James Braid, this is a good old links - there is even an old railway track running through the middle - used for the qualifying rounds when the British Open is held at Saint Andrews. You'll find some holes in heathland, particularly the 12th and 13th holes, where the view over the Forth is impressive, from the confines of Edinburgh to Muirfield, just opposite. On the course the major hazard is the wind, and let's hope that the watering system is not over-used. Soft terrain kills a little of the subtlety of playing a links course and requires less creativity from the golfer.

Frère jumeau de Leven Links, Lundin est né d'une scission en 1868, chacun gardant neuf trous et complétant son parcours. N'attendez pas la compétition annuelle qui les réunit, essayez aussi de jouer ce parcours des origines le long de la mer. Remodelé comme bien d'autres par James Braid, c'est un vrai bon links (avec même une ancienne voie ferrée au milieu) utilisé pour les qualifications du British Open quand il est à Saint Andrews. Mais on y trouve aussi des trous en terrain de bruyère, en particulier au 12 et au 13, d'où la vue est impressionnante sur le Forth, des confins d'Edimbourg à Muirfield, en face. Sur le parcours, le vent est le principal obstacle, mais on peut souhaiter que l'arrosage ne soit pas trop utilisé, un terrain mou retire un peu de leur subtilité aux links, et exige moins de créativité.

Lundin Golf Club		1868
Golf Road		
SCO - LUNDIN LINKS, Fife KY8 6BA		

Office	Secrétariat	(44) 01333 - 320 202
Pro shop	Pro-shop	(44) 01333 - 320 051
Fax	Fax	(44) 01333 - 329 743
Situation	Situation	

20 km SW of St Andrews (pop. 11 136)
17 km E of Kirkcaldy

Annual closure	Fermeture annuelle	no
Weekly closure	Fermeture hebdomadaire	no

Fees main season	Tarifs haute saison	18 holes
	Week days	We/Bank holidays
	Semaine	We/Férié
Individual Individuel	£ 29	£ 37 *
Couple Couple	£ 58	£ 74 *

Full weekdays: £ 37
* Saturday: after 2.30 pm - Not on Sundays.

Caddy	Caddy	on request
Electric Trolley	Chariot électrique	no
Buggy	Voiturette	no
Clubs	Clubs	no
Credit cards Cartes de crédit		yes

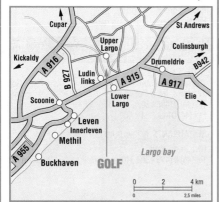

Access Accès : Edinburgh A92 and A915. In the village of Lundin Links on the sea front, turn right at the Royal Bank of Scotland, thereafter first right and second left.
Map 3 on page 493 Carte 3 Page 493

GOLF COURSE
PARCOURS

16/20

Site	Site	
Maintenance	Entretien	
Architect	Architecte	James Braid
Type	Type	links
Relief	Relief	
Water in play	Eau en jeu	
Exp. to wind	Exposé au vent	
Trees in play	Arbres en jeu	

Scorecard	Chp.	Mens	Ladies
Carte de score	Chp.	Mess.	Da.
Length Long.	5846	5846	5846
Par	71	71	75

Advised golfing ability	0	12	24	36
Niveau de jeu recommandé				
Hcp required	Handicap exigé	certificate		

CLUB HOUSE & AMENITIES
CLUB HOUSE ET ANNEXES

6/10

Pro shop	Pro-shop	
Driving range	Practice	
Sheltered	couvert	no
On grass	sur herbe	yes
Putting-green	putting-green	yes
Pitching-green	pitching green	no

753

HOTEL FACILITIES
ENVIRONNEMENT HOTELIER

7/10

HOTELS HÔTELS
Old Manor Hotel — Lundin Links
24 rooms, D £ 115 — 0.4 km
Tel (44) 01333 - 320 368, Fax (44) 01333 - 320 911

Lundin Links Hotel — Lundin Links
21 rooms, D £ 122 — 0.3 km
Tel (44) 01333 - 320 201, Fax (44) 01333 - 320 930

Crusoe Hotel — Lundin Links
16 rooms, D £ 95 — 0.4 km
Tel (44) 01333 - 320 759, Fax (44) 01333 - 320 865

RESTAURANTS RESTAURANTS
Old Manor Hotel — Lundin Links
Tel (44) 01333 - 320 368 — 0.4 km

Lundin Links Hotel — Lundin Links
Tel (44) 01333 - 320 207 — 0.3 km

So far away from the «civilised» world, this course, where designer Willie Campbell worked wonders, could but adapt to existing terrain. With a 100-year-old hotel or small cottages, there is no shortage of accommodation or pleasure facilities, aided by some exceptional pure malt whiskies smoked over a peat fire, even tastier when drunk after some wholesome sporting activities. The beaches are superb and the views equally magnificent and romantic. The fairways lie like a carpet and form nothing less than a good, pure and authentic golf course. There are few places in the world that feel so different to what you know already as Machrie. You can get here by boat, but it's a long haul, or by plane in a quick hop from Glasgow.

Autant à l'écart du monde «civilisé», ce parcours ne pouvait que s'adapter au terrain existant, et l'architecte Willie Campbell en a tiré des merveilles. Avec un hôtel plus que centenaire ou de petits cottages, le lieu ne manque pas de possibilités d'accueil, ni de plaisirs : on y distille alentour d'exceptionnels whiskies pur malt fumé à la tourbe, on s'y livre à de saines activités sportives avant de les déguster. Les plages sont superbes, les vues magnifiques, romantiques. Le parcours est posé comme un tapis sur le sol, c'est un pur, vrai et bon parcours de golf. Il est peu d'endroits au monde qui soient si «différents» de tout ce que l'on connaît. On peut y aller en bateau, mais c'est long, ou en avion : c'est un saut de puce depuis Glasgow.

Machrie Hotel & Golf Links — 1891

Western Cottage, Port Ellen
SCO - ISLE OF ISLAY, PA42 7AT

Office	Secrétariat	(44) 01496 - 302 310
Pro shop	Pro-shop	(44) 01496 - 302 310
Fax	Fax	(44) 01496 - 302 404
Situation	Situation	

5 km from Port Ellen (Isle of Islay)

Annual closure	Fermeture annuelle	no
Weekly closure	Fermeture hebdomadaire	no

Fees main season Tarifs haute saison — 18 holes

	Week days Semaine	We/Bank holidays We/Férié
Individual Individuel	£ 17.50	£ 17.50
Couple Couple	£ 35	£ 35

Caddy	Caddy	on request
Electric Trolley	Chariot électrique	no
Buggy	Voiturette	no
Clubs	Clubs	yes

Credit cards Cartes de crédit
VISA - Eurocard - MasterCard

754

ISLAY

Bowmore
Laggan bay
Glenegedale
GOLF
Islay port Ellen
A 846
Ardbeg
Risabus
Port Ellen
Kilnaughton bay
Lower Killeyan

0 — 2 — 4 km
0 — 2,5 miles

Access Accès : • By Plane, 25 mn from Glasgow (twice daily flights)
• Road & Ferry, 5 hrs from Glasgow
Map 2 on page 490 Carte 2 Page 490

GOLF COURSE / PARCOURS — 17/20

Site	Site	▬▬▬▬▬
Maintenance	Entretien	▬▬▬▬▬
Architect	Architecte	Willie Campbell Donald Steel
Type	Type	links
Relief	Relief	▬▬▬
Water in play	Eau en jeu	▬▬
Exp. to wind	Exposé au vent	▬▬▬
Trees in play	Arbres en jeu	▬

Scorecard Carte de score	Chp. Chp.	Mens Mess.	Ladies Da.
Length Long.	5665	5331	4741
Par	71	71	69

Advised golfing ability — 0 12 24 36
Niveau de jeu recommandé
Hcp required Handicap exigé — no

CLUB HOUSE & AMENITIES / CLUB HOUSE ET ANNEXES — 7/10

Pro shop	Pro-shop	▬▬▬
Driving range	Practice	▬▬▬
Sheltered	couvert	no
On grass	sur herbe	yes
Putting-green	putting-green	yes
Pitching-green	pitching green	yes

HOTEL FACILITIES / ENVIRONNEMENT HOTELIER — 5/10

HOTELS HÔTELS
The Machrie Hotel — Golf
27 rooms, from £ 65 — on site
Tel (44) 01496 - 302 310
Fax (44) 01496 - 302 404

RESTAURANTS RESTAURANTS
Byre Restaurant — Golf
Tel (44) 01496 - 302 310 — on site

MACHRIHANISH

18	6	4

The road you take to reach here is as long as it is picturesque, the only problem being that you can't stay for ever. The course is superb, as are the distilleries and the hospitality of the inhabitants of Kintyre here at the ends of the world. So step into this wide open space «created by the Almighty to play golf», as Old Tom Morris would say, who knew a good sales pitch when he saw one and could design a course or two. He obviously lent our Good Lord a hand here to make this marvellous test of golf between the dunes and the foot of the hills. With a simply beautiful first hole, a par 4 over the sea, where the men will envy the ladies. For the fairer sex this is a par 5, for many male players too. You won't regret a single second of your visit here.

La route pour arriver ici est aussi longue que splendide. Le seul problème est qu'il faut ensuite repartir. S'arracher à Machrihanish est d'autant plus dur que si le parcours est superbe, les distilleries ne le sont pas moins, et l'accueil des habitants du Kintyre d'autant plus agréable que l'on est au bout de l'ancien monde, et du monde tout court. Alors, immergez-vous dans un espace «créé par le Tout-Puissant pour jouer au golf» comme disait Old Tom Morris qui avait le sens du commerce, et du dessin de golf aussi. Car il est évidemment venu en aide au Seigneur pour en faire un merveilleux test de golf entre les dunes et le pied des collines. Avec un premier trou de toute beauté, un par 4 à jouer au-dessus de la mer où les hommes jalouseront les dames : c'est pour elles un par 5... pour beaucoup d'hommes aussi ! Vous ne regretterez rien du voyage.

Machrihanish Golf Club	1876
Machrihanish	
SCO - CAMPBELTOWN, Argyll PA28 6PT	

Office	Secrétariat	(44) 01586 - 810 213
Pro shop	Pro-shop	(44) 01586 - 810 277
Fax	Fax	(44) 01586 - 810 221
Situation	Situation	
8 km S of Campbeltown		

Annual closure	Fermeture annuelle	no
Weekly closure	Fermeture hebdomadaire	no

Fees main season	Tarifs haute saison		full day
		Week days Semaine	We/Bank holidays We/Férié
Individual Individuel		£ 40*	£ 50*
Couple Couple		£ 80*	£ 100*

* Weekdays: Sunday to Friday -
18 holes, weekdays only: £ 25

Caddy	Caddy	on request
Electric Trolley	Chariot électrique	no
Buggy	Voiturette	no
Clubs	Clubs	yes

Credit cards Cartes de crédit VISA - MasterCard

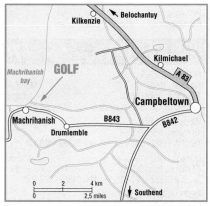

Access Accès : • By air: from Glasgow, 15 mn flight to Machrihanish Airport. • By car: 3 hrs drive by A82, A83, via Tarbet, Inverraray... or Ferry to Isle of Arran, and to Claonaig. **Map 2 on page 490** Carte 2 Page 490

GOLF COURSE
PARCOURS

18/20

Site	Site	
Maintenance	Entretien	
Architect	Architecte	Tom Morris
Type	Type	links
Relief	Relief	
Water in play	Eau en jeu	
Exp. to wind	Exposé au vent	
Trees in play	Arbres en jeu	

Scorecard	Chp.	Mens	Ladies
Carte de score	Chp.	Mess.	Da.
Length Long.	5670	5425	5025
Par	70	70	72

Advised golfing ability	0	12	24	36
Niveau de jeu recommandé				
Hcp required	Handicap exigé	no		

CLUB HOUSE & AMENITIES
CLUB HOUSE ET ANNEXES

6/10

Pro shop	Pro-shop	
Driving range	Practice	
Sheltered	couvert	no
On grass	sur herbe	yes
Putting-green	putting-green	yes
Pitching-green	pitching green	yes

HOTEL FACILITIES
ENVIRONNEMENT HOTELIER

4/10

HOTELS HÔTELS

Balegreggan Country House	Campbeltown
4 rooms, from D £ 70	8 km
Tel (44) 01586 - 552 062	

Westbank	Campbeltown
8 rooms, D £ 34	8 km
Tel (44) 01586 - 553 660	

755

We know that golf was played here in the first half of the 17th century but the first signs of a real course really date from 1850. Like nearby Carnoustie, the course is shared by five different clubs, as is the Ashludie Course, a little more modest and restful but nonetheless interesting. The wide open spaces of the «great» course naturally leaves it exposed to the wind, but anything else would come as a great surprise. Classic and discreet in design with no hidden traps, Monifieth is respectable in length and deserves to be better known outside Scotland. This is one of the best surprises that any visitor could hope to find on the east coast. A course for connoisseurs but pleasant for players of all levels.

On sait que le golf a été pratiqué ici dès la première moitié du XVIIème siècle, mais les premiers signes d'un véritable parcours datent vraiment de 1850. Comme le tout proche Carnoustie, le parcours est partagé par cinq clubs différents, de même que le «Ashludie Course», plus modeste et reposant, mais néanmoins intéressant. Les vastes espaces où s'épanouit le «grand» parcours l'exposent bien sûr au vent, mais c'est le contraire qui serait étonnant. D'une architecture classique et sobre, sans pièges dissimulés, et d'une longueur très respectable, Monifieth devrait connaître une meilleure notoriété hors des frontières, et c'est l'une des meilleures surprises que les visiteurs pourront trouver de ce côté de l'Ecosse. Un parcours pour connaisseurs, mais agréable à tous niveaux de jeu.

Monifieth Golf Club — 1850

Medal Starter's Box, Princes Street
SCO - MONIFIETH, Dundee DD5 4AW

Office	Secrétariat	(44) 01382 - 535 553
Pro shop	Pro-shop	(44) 01382 - 532 945
Fax	Fax	(44) 01382 - 535 553
Situation	Situation	

8 km E of Dundee (pop. 165 873

Annual closure	Fermeture annuelle	no
Weekly closure	Fermeture hebdomadaire	np

Fees main season
Tarifs haute saison 18 holes

	Week days Semaine	We/Bank holidays We/Férié
Individual Individuel	£ 26	£ 30
Couple Couple	£ 52	£ 60

Full day: £ 34 - £ 40 (weekends)

Caddy	Caddy	on request/£ 25
Electric Trolley	Chariot électrique	no
Buggy	Voiturette	no
Clubs	Clubs	yes

Credit cards Cartes de crédit — no

756

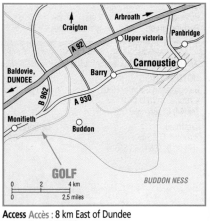

Access Accès : 8 km East of Dundee
on coast road (A930)
Map 2 on page 491 Carte 2 Page 491

GOLF COURSE / PARCOURS — 17/20

Site	Site	
Maintenance	Entretien	
Architect	Architecte	Unknown
Type	Type	links
Relief	Relief	
Water in play	Eau en jeu	
Exp. to wind	Exposé au vent	
Trees in play	Arbres en jeu	

Scorecard Carte de score	Chp. Chp.	Mens Mess.	Ladies Da.
Length Long.	6056	5877	5361
Par	71	71	73

Advised golfing ability		0	12	24	36
Niveau de jeu recommandé					
Hcp required	Handicap exigé	certificate			

CLUB HOUSE & AMENITIES / CLUB HOUSE ET ANNEXES — 7/10

Pro shop	Pro-shop	
Driving range	Practice	
Sheltered	couvert	no
On grass	sur herbe	yes
Putting-green	putting-green	yes
Pitching-green	pitching green	yes

HOTEL FACILITIES / ENVIRONNEMENT HOTELIER — 7/10

HOTELS HÔTELS
Panmure Hotel — Monifieth
13 rooms, from D £ 64 — adjacent
Tel (44) 01382 - 532 911, Fax (44) 01382 - 535 859

Woodlands Hotel — Broughty Ferry
18 rooms, from D £ 64 — 2.5 km
Tel (44) 01382 - 480 033, Fax (44) 01382 - 480 126

Queen's Hotel — Dundee
47 rooms, from D £ 52 — 8 km
Tel (44) 01382 - 322 515, Fax (44) 01382 - 202 668

RESTAURANTS RESTAURANTS
Panmure Hotel — Monifieth
Tel (44) 01382 - 532 911 — adjacent

L'Auberge — Broughty Ferry
Tel (44) 01382 - 730 890 — 5 km

A great classic shared by three golf clubs, as is Carnoustie a few miles down the coast. If the history books are right, then this is the 5th oldest club in the world and golf has been played on the grounds of the Earl of Montrose since the 16th century. It is true that there is tradition in the air here, with a tinge of austerity as well. Here you'll find all the finest components that go to make up a great links course: deep bunkers, wonderfully soft soil, bushes and towering dunes covered by wild grass that shape the winding fairways and greens. Very reasonable in length, although this can change in a matter of minutes when the wind blows, this excellent course (complemented by the little Broomfield Course) has been a little neglected for the benefit of more powerful neighbours, but the course is so steeped in history that it should be a part of your own experience.

Un grand classique partagé par trois clubs de golf, comme Carnoustie, quelques kilomètres plus bas sur la côte. L'histoire voudrait que ce soit le 5ème club du monde, et que l'on ait joué sur ces terres du Marquis de Montrose depuis le XVIè siècle. Il est vrai que l'on respire ici la tradition, non sans une certaine austérité. On trouve ici à l'état pur ce qui fait la grandeur des links, de profonds bunkers, un sol merveilleusement souple, des buissons, de hautes dunes envahies d'herbes folles entre lesquelles s'insinuent les fairways et les greens. De longueur très raisonnable, mais que le vent peut bien sûr métamorphoser d'un instant à l'autre, cet excellent parcours (complété par le petit Broomfield Course) a été un peu négligé au profit de puissants voisins, mais il témoigne de toute une histoire, et doit faire partie de la vôtre.

Montrose Links Trust   1562

Traill Drive
SCO - MONTROSE, Angus DD10 8SW

Office	Secrétariat	(44) 01674 - 672 932
Pro shop	Pro-shop	(44) 01674 - 672 634
Fax	Fax	(44) 01674 - 671 800
Situation	Situation	

in Montrose (pop. 8 473)
35 km E of Dundee (pop. 165 873)

Annual closure	Fermeture annuelle	no
Weekly closure	Fermeture hebdomadaire	no

Fees main season	Tarifs haute saison	18 holes
	Week days Semaine	We/Bank holidays We/Férié
Individual Individuel	£ 25	£ 30*
Couple Couple	£ 50	£ 60

Saturdays: visitors between 2.35 and 3.38 pm only.

Caddy	Caddy	no
Electric Trolley	Chariot électrique	£ 5/18 holes
Buggy	Voiturette	no
Clubs	Clubs	£ 8/18 holes

Credit cards Cartes de crédit
VISA - MasterCard - JCB

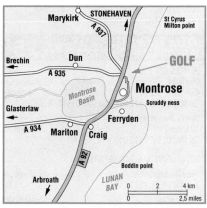

Access Accès : A90, turn off at Brechin and follow A935 to Montrose. Golf 0.8 km (1/2 m) from town centre.
Map 1 on page 489 Carte 1 Page 489

GOLF COURSE
PARCOURS   17 /20

Site	Site	
Maintenance	Entretien	
Architect	Architecte	Willie Park Jr
Type	Type	links
Relief	Relief	
Water in play	Eau en jeu	
Exp. to wind	Exposé au vent	
Trees in play	Arbres en jeu	

Scorecard	Chp.	Mens	Ladies
Carte de score	Chp.	Mess.	Da.
Length Long.	5887	5670	5134
Par	71	71	73

Advised golfing ability	0	12	24	36
Niveau de jeu recommandé				
Hcp required Handicap exigé	certificate			

CLUB HOUSE & AMENITIES
CLUB HOUSE ET ANNEXES   5 /10

Pro shop	Pro-shop	
Driving range	Practice	
Sheltered	couvert	no
On grass	sur herbe	no
Putting-green	putting-green	yes
Pitching-green	pitching green	yes

757

HOTEL FACILITIES
ENVIRONNEMENT HOTELIER   6 /10

HOTELS HÔTELS
Park Hotel   Montrose
59 rooms, D £ 90   1 km
Tel (44) 01674 - 673 415
Fax (44) 01674 - 677 091

Links Hotel   Montrose
22 rooms, D £ 74   1 km
Tel (44) 01674 - 671 000
Fax (44) 01674 - 672 698

RESTAURANTS RESTAURANTS
Park Hotel   Montrose
Tel (44) 01674 - 673 415   1 km

This is not the best known links in Scotland but it is a good one. Firstly for its antiquated charm, because like the Old Course at St Andrews, it starts and ends in town, in Lossiemouth, the name by which the course is also sometimes known. A large part of this «old» course was designed by Old Tom Morris, although patient changes have given the layout its present-day look, custom-made for the requirements of modern golf. Players of all levels will enjoy this course, and the less experienced golfers can get acquainted with the subtle side of links golf without too much to worry about. Moray is also home to the «New Course» designed by Henry Cotton, a very pleasant layout but without the cachet of its «old» stable-mate. We would also emphasise the mildness of the climate here and the superb views over the Moray Firth. Highly recommended.

Ce n'est pas le plus connu des links d'Ecosse, mais ce n'est pas le moindre. Par son charme désuet d'abord : comme le Old Course de St Andrews, il commence et s'achève en ville, à Lossiemouth, qui lui a donné parfois son nom. Ce «Old» a en grande partie été conçu par Old Tom Morris, mais de patientes modifications lui ont donné son visage actuel, parfaitement adapté aux exigences du golf moderne. Cependant, les joueurs de tous niveaux y prendront plaisir, et les moins expérimentés pourront s'y familiariser avec les subtilités du golf de links sans être trop intimidés. De plus, on trouve également à Moray le «New Course» dessiné par Henry Cotton, très agréable mais moins empreint de la grandeur du «Old.» On soulignera enfin la douceur du climat local, et les vues superbes sur le Moray Firth. Visite conseillée !

Moray Golf Club — 1889

Stotfield Road
SCO - LOSSIEMOUTH, Moray JV31 6QS

Office	Secrétariat	(44) 01343 - 812 018
Pro shop	Pro-shop	(44) 01343 - 813 330
Fax	Fax	(44) 01343 - 815 102
Situation	Situation	

9 km N of Elgin (pop. 11 855)

Annual closure	Fermeture annuelle	no
Weekly closure	Fermeture hebdomadaire	no

Fees main season
Tarifs haute saison 18 holes

	Week days Semaine	We/Bank holidays We/Férié
Individual Individuel	£ 30	£ 40
Couple Couple	£ 60	£ 80

Full days: £ 40 - £ 50 (weekends)

Caddy	Caddy	on request
Electric Trolley	Chariot électrique	no
Buggy	Voiturette	no
Clubs	Clubs	yes

Credit cards Cartes de crédit only Pro-shop

758

GOLF

Lossiemouth

B 9040
Burnside
spey bay
Duffus
A 941
B 9103
B 9012
Elgin
Bishopmill
Linkwood

0 — 2 — 4 km
0 — 2,5 miles

Access Accès : Inverness, A96 to Elgin, then A941 North.
Map 1 on page 489 Carte 1 Page 489

GOLF COURSE PARCOURS — 17/20

Site	Site	
Maintenance	Entretien	
Architect	Architecte	Tom Morris
Type	Type	links
Relief	Relief	
Water in play	Eau en jeu	
Exp. to wind	Exposé au vent	
Trees in play	Arbres en jeu	

Scorecard Carte de score	Chp. Chp.	Mens Mess.	Ladies Da.
Length Long.	6066	5735	5580
Par	71	70	75

Advised golfing ability		0 12 24 36
Niveau de jeu recommandé		
Hcp required	Handicap exigé	24

CLUB HOUSE & AMENITIES CLUB HOUSE ET ANNEXES — 5/10

Pro shop	Pro-shop	
Driving range	Practice	
Sheltered	couvert	no
On grass	sur herbe	no
Putting-green	putting-green	yes
Pitching-green	pitching green	yes

HOTEL FACILITIES ENVIRONNEMENT HOTELIER — 5/10

HOTELS HÔTELS
Stotfield — Lossiemouth
45 rooms, D £ 70 — adjacent
Tel (44) 01343 - 812 011, Fax (44) 01343 - 814 820

Skerry Brae Hotel — Lossiemouth
10 rooms, — adjacent
Tel (44) 01343 - 812 040

RESTAURANTS RESTAURANTS
1629 Restaurant — Lossiemouth
Tel (44) 01343 - 813 743 — 1 km

Skerry Brae — lossiemouth
Tel (44) 01343 - 812 040 — adjacent

The course of the Honourable Company of Edinburg Golfers, who drew up the first collection of the rules of golf, is first and foremost one of the great courses used for the British Open. Winners here include Nicklaus, Trevino and Faldo, three players of very different talent, suggesting that great courses adapt to all styles of play. While there are no spectacular dunes and no sea in the immediate vicinity for this to be labelled a reference links course, the thick and very tall rough, deep bunkering that reflects a shrewd golfing mind, narrow (but welcoming) fairways and tricky greens where you need magic fingers, make it a reference course, full stop. The course asks a lot of players when it comes to shaping the right shot. A good shot is rewarded but any flaw is a shortcut to disaster. This is a great test of golf. The clubhouse is superb, historically very instructive and a great place to eat.

Le parcours de l'Honourable Company of Edinburgh Golfers, qui a établi le premier recueil de règles de golf est surtout l'un des grands parcours du British Open, où ont triomphé notamment Nicklaus, Trevino et Faldo, trois hommes aux talents dissemblables, comme quoi les grands golfs s'adaptent à tous les types de jeu. S'il manque de dunes spectaculaires et de proximité immédiate de la mer pour être un links de référence, les roughs épais et très hauts, de profonds bunkers placés avec une très grande connaissance du jeu, des fairways étroits (mais accueillants), des greens subtils où il faut avoir des doigts de fée en font une référence. Ici, on exige beaucoup du joueur afin qu'il fasse le coup qui convient. Un bon coup est récompensé, mais toute défaillance amène un désastre. Un grand test de golf. Le Club house est superbe, historiquement très instructif, et la table excellente.

Honourable Company of Edinburgh Golfers — 1891

Muirfield
SCO - GULLANE, E. Lothian, EH31 2EG

Office	Secrétariat	(44) 01620 - 842 123
Pro shop	Pro-shop	no Pro shop
Fax	Fax	(44) 01620 - 842 977
Situation	Situation	

30 km E of Edinburgh (pop. 418 914)

Annual closure	Fermeture annuelle	no
Weekly closure	Fermeture hebdomadaire	no
Fees main season	Tarifs haute saison	18 holes

	Week days Semaine	We/Bank holidays We/Férié
Individual Individuel	£ 95	—
Couple Couple	£ 190	—

Ask for availability - No visitors at weekends

Caddy	Caddy	on request
Electric Trolley	Chariot électrique	no
Buggy	Voiturette	limited use
Clubs	Clubs	no
Credit cards Cartes de crédit		no

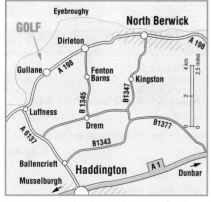

GOLF
Eyebroughy
North Berwick
Dirleton
A 198
Gullane — A 198
Fenton Barns
Kingston
Luffness
B 1345
B 1347
Drem
B 1377
A 6137
B 1343
Ballencrieff
Haddington
A 1
Dunbar
Musselburgh
4 km / 2.5 miles

Access Accès : Edinburgh A198 along Firth of Forth. Turn left at the end of Gullane, follow signs to Greywalls Hotel.
Map 3 on page 493 Carte 3 Page 493

GOLF COURSE / PARCOURS — 19/20

Site	Site	
Maintenance	Entretien	
Architect	Architecte	Tom Morris Harry S. Colt
Type	Type	links
Relief	Relief	
Water in play	Eau en jeu	
Exp. to wind	Exposé au vent	
Trees in play	Arbres en jeu	

Scorecard Carte de score	Chp. Chp.	Mens Mess.	Ladies Da.
Length Long.	6336	6007	0
Par	73	73	0

Advised golfing ability Niveau de jeu recommandé		0 12 24 36
Hcp required	Handicap exigé	certificate

CLUB HOUSE & AMENITIES / CLUB HOUSE ET ANNEXES — 7/10

Pro shop	Pro-shop	
Driving range	Practice	
Sheltered	couvert	practice area only
On grass	sur herbe	yes
Putting-green	putting-green	yes
Pitching-green	pitching green	yes

759

HOTEL FACILITIES / ENVIRONNEMENT HOTELIER — 6/10

HOTELS HÔTELS

Greywalls — Gullane / on site
22 rooms, D £ 95
Tel (44) 01620 - 842 144
Fax (44) 01620 - 842 241

Green Craigs — Aberlady / 3 km
6 rooms, D £ 90
Tel (44) 01875 - 870 301
Fax (44) 01875 - 870 440

RESTAURANTS RESTAURANTS

La Potinière — Gullane / 0.5 km
Tel (44) 01620 - 843 214

Greywalls — Gullane / next to golf
Tel (44) 01620 - 842 144

Murcar lies alongside Royal Aberdeen but has never been awarded the royal seal. But if they say that mongrels are a tougher species than pedigrees, then Murcar is definitely a course not to be missed. Only just a little shorter than its neighbour, the course is a permanent challenge which should never be taken lightly even when there's no wind. And that's about as rare as the layout of holes here, where there are three par 3s, three par 5s and twelve par 4s. The latter include those devilishly tricky short par 4s that you think you can drive in one, only to end up on your knees praying for a bogey. Naturally you won't find the tremendous challenges that await you on the monster courses in Scotland, but Murcar deserves much more than just a quick look. We had seen it in better condition than when we visited this time, but this is certainly only a temporary fault.

Il jouxte le parcours de Royal Aberdeen et n'a pas eu droit à l'annoblissement. Mais si on dit que les bâtards sont les plus vigoureux, Murcar est effectivement un parcours à ne pas manquer. A peine plus court que son voisin, il présente un défi permanent, à ne jamais prendre à la légère, même quand le vent ne souffle pas, ce qui est tout aussi rare que la distribution avec trois par 3, trois par 5 et douze par 4, dont ces démoniaques petits trous techniques que l'on croit pouvoir driver et qui vous mettent à genoux. Certes, l'on n'attendra pas ici d'aussi formidables défis que dans le groupe des grands monstres d'Ecosse, mais Murcar mérite beaucoup mieux qu'un simple regard. Certes, nous l'avons vu en meilleure condition qu'au moment de notre visite, mais c'était sans doute provisoire...

Murcar Golf Club — 1909
Bridge of Don
SCO - ABERDEEN, Aberdeenshire AB23 8BD

Office	Secrétariat	(44) 01224 - 704 345
Pro shop	Pro-shop	(44) 01224 - 704 370
Fax	Fax	(44) 01224 - 704 354
Situation	Situation	

8 km N of Aberdeen (pop. 204 885)

Annual closure	Fermeture annuelle	no
Weekly closure	Fermeture hebdomadaire	no

Fees main season
Tarifs haute saison 18 holes

	Week days Semaine	We/Bank holidays We/Férié
Individual Individuel	£ 28	£ 43
Couple Couple	£ 56	£ 86

Full Weekdays: £ 38

Caddy	Caddy	on request
Electric Trolley	Chariot électrique	no
Buggy	Voiturette	no
Clubs	Clubs	yes
Credit cards Cartes de crédit		no

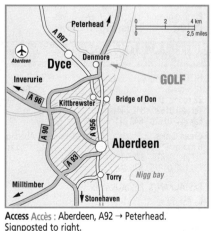

Access Accès : Aberdeen, A92 → Peterhead.
Signposted to right.
Map 1 on page 489 Carte 1 Page 489

GOLF COURSE / PARCOURS — 15/20

Site	Site	
Maintenance	Entretien	
Architect	Architecte	Archie Simpson James Braid
Type	Type	links
Relief	Relief	
Water in play	Eau en jeu	
Exp. to wind	Exposé au vent	
Trees in play	Arbres en jeu	

Scorecard Carte de score	Chp. Chp.	Mens Mess.	Ladies Da.
Length Long.	5679	5287	5036
Par	70	68	73

Advised golfing ability		0 12 24 36
Niveau de jeu recommandé		
Hcp required	Handicap exigé	certificate

CLUB HOUSE & AMENITIES / CLUB HOUSE ET ANNEXES — 6/10

Pro shop	Pro-shop	
Driving range	Practice	
Sheltered	couvert	no
On grass	sur herbe	yes
Putting-green	putting-green	yes
Pitching-green	pitching green	no

HOTEL FACILITIES / ENVIRONNEMENT HOTELIER — 6/10

HOTELS HÔTELS
Marcliffe at Piffodels — Aberdeen
42 rooms, D £ 150 — 9 km
Tel (44) 01224 - 861 000, Fax (44) 01224 - 868 860

Quality — Bridge of Don
123 rooms, D £ 120 — 4 km
Tel (44) 01224 - 706 707, Fax (44) 01224 - 823 923

Corner House — Aberdeen
17 rooms, D £ 58 — 8 km
Tel (44) 01224 - 313 063

RESTAURANTS RESTAURANTS
Courtyard on the Lane — Aberdeen
Tel (44) 01224 - 213 795 — 8 km

Silver Darling — Aberdeen
Tel (44) 01224 - 576 229 — 8 km

760

Located in a well-forested setting not far from Perth, this country course was opened in 1981 and has quickly built up an excellent reputation among local players for its pleasant site, the hazards and the challenge of playing here. This is by no means an easy course but is one of those layouts which quickly help you forget a bad score. If your card is bad, there's no blaming the course. Game strategy is obvious from the first time out, difficulties are evenly spread around the course with just the right balance of stress and relaxation, and the greens are well designed and protected. This is one of the best-equipped golf clubs you can find, with a real driving range and a very comfortable hotel.

Situé dans un environnement bien boisé non loin de Perth, ce parcours campagnard né en 1981 s'est vite bâti une excellente réputation parmi les joueurs de la région, en raison de l'agrément du site, mais aussi des difficultés présentées et du «challenge» offert. Ce n'est certes pas un parcours facile, mais il fait partie de ceux qui vous font vite oublier un mauvais score. En tout cas, on ne pourra pas en accuser le parcours. La stratégie de jeu y est assez évidente dès la première visite, les difficultés sont bien réparties, avec ce qu'il faut de tension et de détente, les greens bien dessinés et bien défendus. Le Club est l'un des mieux équipés que l'on puisse trouver, notamment avec un vrai pratice et un hôtel très confortable.

Murrayshall Golf Club — 1981

Murrayshall Country House Hotel
SCO - SCONE, Perthshire PH2 7PH

Office	Secrétariat	(44) 01738 - 551 171
Pro shop	Pro-shop	(44) 01738 - 552 784
Fax	Fax	(44) 01738 - 552 595
Situation	Situation	

8 km NE of Perth (pop. 123 495)

Annual closure	Fermeture annuelle	no
Weekly closure	Fermeture hebdomadaire	no

Fees main season
Tarifs haute saison 18 holes

	Week days Semaine	We/Bank holidays We/Férié
Individual Individuel	£ 22	£ 27
Couple Couple	£ 44	£ 54

Full days: £ 30 - £ 45 (weekends)

Caddy	Caddy	on request/£ 15
Electric Trolley	Chariot électrique	£ 7.50/18 holes
Buggy	Voiturette	£ 20/18 holes
Clubs	Clubs	£ 15/18 holes

Credit cards Cartes de crédit
VISA - Eurocard - MasterCard - AMEX

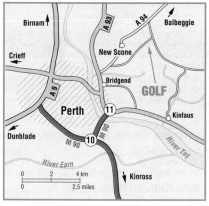

Access Accès : Edinburgh M90 to Perth,
then A94 → Coupar Angus, Golf at Scone.
Map 2 on page 491 Carte 2 Page 491

GOLF COURSE / PARCOURS — 14/20

Site	Site	▮▮▮▮▯
Maintenance	Entretien	▮▮▮▮▯
Architect	Architecte	Hamilton Stutt
Type	Type	parkland
Relief	Relief	▮▮▯▯▯
Water in play	Eau en jeu	▮▮▯▯▯
Exp. to wind	Exposé au vent	▮▮▮▯▯
Trees in play	Arbres en jeu	▮▮▮▯▯

Scorecard Carte de score	Chp. Chp.	Mens Mess.	Ladies Da.
Length Long.	5862	5502	4842
Par	73	72	74

Advised golfing ability Niveau de jeu recommandé	0 12 24 36	
Hcp required	Handicap exigé	no

CLUB HOUSE & AMENITIES / CLUB HOUSE ET ANNEXES — 7/10

Pro shop	Pro-shop	▮▮▮▯▯
Driving range	Practice	▮▮▮▯▯
Sheltered	couvert	11 mats
On grass	sur herbe	no
Putting-green	putting-green	yes
Pitching-green	pitching green	yes

761

HOTEL FACILITIES / ENVIRONNEMENT HOTELIER — 8/10

HOTELS HÔTELS

Murrayshall Country House — Golf
30 rooms, D £ 100 — on site
Tel (44) 01738 - 551 171, Fax (44) 01738 - 552 595

Queens Hotel — Perth
51 rooms, D £ 100 — 8 km
Tel (44) 01738 - 442 222

Salutation Hotel — Perth
84 rooms, D £ 80 — 8 km
Tel (44) 01738 - 630 066, Fax (44) 01738 - 633 598

RESTAURANTS RESTAURANTS

Old Masters (Murrayshall) — Golf
Tel (44) 01738 - 551 171 — on site

Patrick's — Perth
Tel (44) 01738 - 624 114 — 8 km

This is one of the great Scottish links and for many a year was one of the country's best guarded secrets. The heather, broom and gorse complete a fine collection of hazards preying on your ball once you have avoided the traps along the Moray Firth. But on the whole Nairn is a remarkable challenge, notably with greens that are often firm and very quick. If you add James Braid's high class bunkering, you'll understand that you don't drive past without stopping off a day or three to test your game on the long golfing road that leads the visitor from Aberdeen to Inverness then to Dornoch and beyond. The landscape is maybe plainer than on other courses in the region, but it is also a little more sheltered, if that is the right word.

C'est l'un des grands links d'Ecosse et ce fut longtemps l'un de ses secrets les mieux gardés. La bruyère, les genêts et les ajoncs complètent une belle collection d'entraves à la liberté des balles, une fois que l'on a déjoué les pièges le long du Moray Firth. Mais Nairn est dans l'ensemble un défi remarquable, avec notamment des greens souvent fermes et très rapides. Si l'on ajoute la contribution majeure de James Braid, un «bunkering» de haute volée, on aura compris que l'on ne saurait passer devant la porte sans s'arrêter un bon moment pour tester sa forme, sur la longue route golfique menant d'Aberdeen à Inverness puis Dornoch et au-delà. Le paysage est moins mouvementé que sur d'autres parcours de la région, mais il est aussi un peu plus abrité... si l'on peut dire.

Nairn Golf Club — 1887

Seabank Road
SCO - NAIRN, IV12 4HB

Office	Secrétariat	(44) 01667 - 453 208
Pro shop	Pro-shop	(44) 01667 - 452 787
Fax	Fax	(44) 01667 - 456 328
Situation	Situation	

24 km E of Inverness (pop. 62 186)

Annual closure	Fermeture annuelle	no
Weekly closure	Fermeture hebdomadaire	no

Full catering: only 04 → 10 inclusive

Fees main season
Tarifs haute saison 18 holes

	Week days Semaine	We/Bank holidays We/Férié
Individual Individuel	£ 60	£ 55
Couple Couple	£ 120	£ 110

Caddy	Caddy	on request/£ 22
Electric Trolley	Chariot électrique	£ 6/18 holes
Buggy	Voiturette	no
Clubs	Clubs	£ 12/18 holes

Credit cards Cartes de crédit VISA - MasterCard

762

GOLF COURSE
PARCOURS

19/20

Site	Site	
Maintenance	Entretien	
Architect	Architecte	Tom Morris James Braid
Type	Type	links
Relief	Relief	
Water in play	Eau en jeu	
Exp. to wind	Exposé au vent	
Trees in play	Arbres en jeu	

Scorecard Carte de score	Chp. Chp.	Mens Mess.	Ladies Da.
Length Long.	6138	5890	5562
Par	72	71	75

Advised golfing ability Niveau de jeu recommandé		0 12 24 36
Hcp required	Handicap exigé	certificate

CLUB HOUSE & AMENITIES
CLUB HOUSE ET ANNEXES

7/10

Pro shop	Pro-shop	
Driving range	Practice	
Sheltered	couvert	no
On grass	sur herbe	yes
Putting-green	putting-green	yes
Pitching-green	pitching green	no

HOTEL FACILITIES
ENVIRONNEMENT HOTELIER

8/10

HOTELS HÔTELS

Golf View — Nairn close
48 rooms, D £ 90
Tel (44) 01667 - 452 301, Fax (44) 01667 - 455 267

Lochloy House — Nairn 4 km
8 rooms, D £ 130
Tel (44) 01667 - 455 355, Fax (44) 01667 - 454 809

Windsor Hotel — Nairn close
40 rooms, D £ 75
Tel (44) 01667 - 453 108, Fax (44) 01667 - 456 108

RESTAURANTS RESTAURANTS

Longhouse — Nairn close
Tel (44) 01667 - 455 532

Golf View Hotel — Nairn close
Tel (44) 01667 - 452 301

Access Accès : Off A96 Inverness to Nairn road.
Golf to the West of town centre.
Map 1 on page 489 Carte 1 Page 489

NAIRN DUNBAR

15 | 6 | 7

This course is located to the east of the town, as opposed to its famous cousin. It was originally created for the Craftsmen's Guild, as is often the case in Great Britain. Remodelled and changed on many different occasions, it now seems to have found its final form. Close to the sea and the estuary, it has been intelligently tailored to the site with a lot of inventive flair which gives the course variety. There aren't many bunkers, but the bushes, gorse and a few trees are all there to get in the way and give this a rather unusual appearance for a course so close to the sea, although the soil is very much that of a links. Even though this is not really in the top drawer of Scottish courses, it is very pleasant (the 10th hole if excellent) and the atmosphere very friendly.

Ce parcours est situé à l'est de la ville, à l'opposé de son célèbre cousin. Il fut originellement créé pour le club des artisans, comme on en trouvait beaucoup en Grande-Bretagne. Remodelé et modifié à de multiples reprises, il semble avoir trouvé sa forme définitive. Près de la mer et de l'embouchure de la rivière, il a été intelligemment adapté au site, avec beaucoup d'esprit d'invention, qui lui donne une grande variété. Les bunkers sont peu nombreux, mais buissons, ajoncs et quelques arbres viennent contrarier les joueurs, et donnent un aspect un peu inhabituel à un parcours si proche de la mer, mais avec un sol de links pour nous le rappeler. Même s'il n'appartient pas absolument à l'élite, c'est un golf très plaisant (le 10 est de premier ordre), et l'atmosphère y est très amicale.

Nairn Dunbar Golf Club — 1899

Lochloy Road
SCO - NAIRN, IV12 5AE

Office	Secrétariat	(44) 01667 - 452 741
Pro shop	Pro-shop	(44) 01667 - 453 964
Fax	Fax	(44) 01667 - 456 897
Situation	Situation	

25 km E of Inverness (pop. 62 186)

Annual closure	Fermeture annuelle	no
Weekly closure	Fermeture hebdomadaire	no

Fees main season
Tarifs haute saison full day

	Week days Semaine	We/Bank holidays We/Férié
Individual Individuel	£ 30	£ 35
Couple Couple	£ 60	£ 70

Caddy	Caddy	on request
Electric Trolley	Chariot électrique	yes
Buggy	Voiturette	£ 15/18 holes
Clubs	Clubs	£ 10/18 holes

Credit cards Cartes de crédit VISA - Access

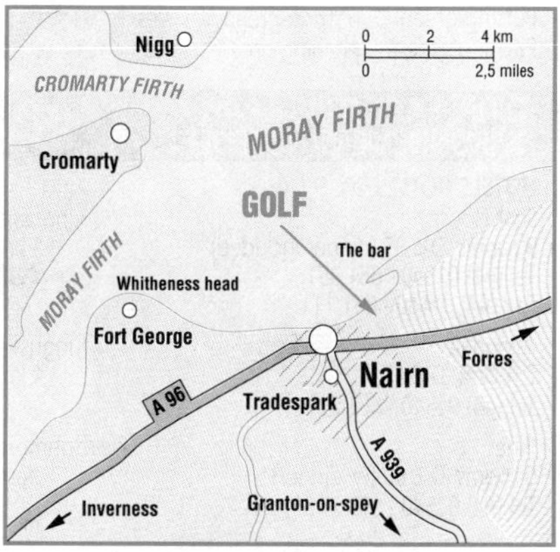

Access Accès : Inverness A96 through Nairn. Golf at the end of town.
Map 1 on page 489 Carte 1 Page 489

GOLF COURSE / PARCOURS — 15/20

Site	Site	
Maintenance	Entretien	
Architect	Architecte	Unknown
Type	Type	links
Relief	Relief	
Water in play	Eau en jeu	
Exp. to wind	Exposé au vent	
Trees in play	Arbres en jeu	

Scorecard Carte de score	Chp. Chp.	Mens Mess.	Ladies Da.
Length Long.	6108	5726	5196
Par	72	72	75

Advised golfing ability 0 12 24 36
Niveau de jeu recommandé
Hcp required Handicap exigé no

CLUB HOUSE & AMENITIES / CLUB HOUSE ET ANNEXES — 6/10

Pro shop	Pro-shop	
Driving range	Practice	
Sheltered	couvert	no
On grass	sur herbe	no
Putting-green	putting-green	yes
Pitching-green	pitching green	no

HOTEL FACILITIES / ENVIRONNEMENT HOTELIER — 7/10

HOTELS HÔTELS

Golf View — Nairn
48 rooms, D £ 90 — close
Tel (44) 01667 - 452 301, Fax (44) 01667 - 455 267

Lochloy House — Lochloy
8 rooms, D £ 120 — 4 km
Tel (44) 01667 - 455 355, Fax (44) 01667 - 454 809

Claymore House — Nairn
16 rooms, D £ 75 — close
Tel (44) 01667 - 453 731, Fax (44) 01667 - 455 290

RESTAURANTS RESTAURANTS

Longhouse — Nairn
Tel (44) 01667 - 455 532 — close

Golf View — Nairn
Tel (44) 01667 - 452 301 — close

NEWTONMORE

The neighbour to Kingussie and a good complementary course to play when spending a few days in the beautiful region of the Cairngorms. A large part of the course is laid out in the plain of the river Spey, which runs alongside several holes. The first and last two holes are on higher land with heather that is fortunately cut back, while the others run through heavier and flatter terrain generously lined with copses of conifers. Over the years, James Braid's original layout has been lengthened but this is by no means a monster. The different holes are well designed with a certain emphasis on variety, but there is nothing to get too excited about. The bottom-line is that this is a very pleasant course for holidays and the family in a magnificent setting. The club-house is not over-large but Scottish hospitality means everything here.

C'est le voisin de Kingussie, et un bon complément quand on passe quelques jours dans cette belle région des Cairngorms. Le parcours est situé en grande partie dans la plaine de la rivière Spey, qui longe plusieurs trous. Les deux premiers et deux derniers trous se trouvent plus en hauteur, en terre de bruyère assez dégagée, alors que les autres trous, en terrain plus lourd et plus plat, sont généreusement boisés de bosquets de conifères. Au fil des ans, le parcours originale de James Braid a été allongé, sans être pour autant un monstre, loin de là. Les différents trous sont bien dessinés, avec un certain souci de variété, mais les émotions restent assez limitées. En fait, il s'agit d'un très agréable parcours à faire en vacances et en famille, dans un cadre magnifique. Le Clubhouse n'est pas grand, mais l'hospitalité écossaise n'y est pas un vain mot.

Newtonmore Golf Club — 1893

Golf Course Road
SCO - NEWTONMORE, Highland PH20 1AT

Office	Secrétariat	(44) 01540 - 673 328
Pro shop	Pro-shop	(44) 01540 - 673 878
Fax	Fax	(44) 01540 - 673 878
Situation	Situation	

68 km S of Inverness (pop. 62 186)
4 km S of Kingussie (pop. 1 298)

Annual closure	Fermeture annuelle	no
Weekly closure	Fermeture hebdomadaire	no

Fees main season
Tarifs haute saison 18 holes

	Week days Semaine	We/Bank holidays We/Férié
Individual Individuel	£ 13	£ 15
Couple Couple	£ 26	£ 30

Caddy	Caddy	on request
Electric Trolley	Chariot électrique	no
Buggy	Voiturette	£ 12/18 holes
Clubs	Clubs	yes
Credit cards Cartes de crédit		no

GOLF COURSE
PARCOURS — 14/20

Site	Site	
Maintenance	Entretien	
Architect	Architecte	James Braid

Type	Type	inland
Relief	Relief	
Water in play	Eau en jeu	
Exp. to wind	Exposé au vent	
Trees in play	Arbres en jeu	

Scorecard Carte de score	Chp. Chp.	Mens Mess.	Ladies Da.
Length Long.	5487	4950	4813
Par	70	67	73

Advised golfing ability		0 12 24 36
Niveau de jeu recommandé		
Hcp required	Handicap exigé	no

CLUB HOUSE & AMENITIES
CLUB HOUSE ET ANNEXES — 5/10

Pro shop	Pro-shop	
Driving range	Practice	
Sheltered	couvert	no
On grass	sur herbe	no
Putting-green	putting-green	yes
Pitching-green	pitching green	no

HOTEL FACILITIES
ENVIRONNEMENT HOTELIER — 5/10

HOTELS HÔTELS
Scot House — Kingussie
9 rooms, D £ 95 (dinner included) — 4 km
Tel (44) 01540 - 661 351
Fax (44) 01540 - 661 111

Avondale — Kingussie
7 rooms, D £ 43 — 4 km
Tel (44) 01540 - 661 731

Pines — Newtonmore
6 rooms, D £ 68 (w. dinner) — close
Tel (44) 01540 - 673 271

RESTAURANTS RESTAURANTS
The Cross — Kingussie
Tel (44) 01540 - 661 166 — 4 km

764

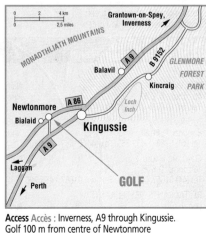

Access Accès : Inverness, A9 through Kingussie.
Golf 100 m from centre of Newtonmore
Map 1 on page 488 Carte 1 Page 488

This is probably one of the courses that is closest to the origins of the game, where you start off along the beach trying to avoid passers-by who watch without a smile. It's then onto a wide strip of land with a few, reasonably high dunes, and a wall you'll have to get over one day to reach the green. Although this is flattish terrain, there are a few blind holes. North Berwick was modelled by mother nature and the sands of time, although they did need an architect (unknown) to build «Perfection (a par 4) and the famous «Redan», a diabolical and often imitated par 3. At once archaic and very modern, seemingly friendly but ferocious when the wind blows (any high ball can be disastrous), North Berwick slowly unveils its secrets which you can only discover with a good measure of patience and humility.

C'est probablement l'un des parcours les plus proches des origines, où l'on commence le long de la plage en essayant d'éviter les promeneurs qui vous regardent sans rire, on se promène ensuite dans une large bande de terrain avec quelques dunes pas trop hautes. Il y a un mur au-dessus duquel il faudra passer un jour pour atteindre le green. Il y a quelques coups aveugles bien que le terrain soit assez plat. C'est la nature et les siècles qui ont modelé North Berwick, mais il a bien fallu un architecte (inconnu) pour faire le «Perfection» (par 4) et le célèbre «Redan», par 3 diabolique souvent copié. A la fois archaïque et très moderne, apparemment aimable et sauvage quand le vent le balaie (toute balle haute provoque un désastre), North Berwick révèle lentement ses secrets. Il faut savoir les découvrir avec patience et humilité.

North Berwick Golf Club   1832
New Club House, Beach Road
SCO - NORTH BERWICK, East Lothian, EH39 4BB

Office	Secrétariat	(44) 01620 - 892 135
Pro shop	Pro-shop	(44) 01620 - 893 233
Fax	Fax	(44) 01620 - 893 274
Situation	Situation	

37 km E of Edinburgh (pop. 418 914)

Annual closure	Fermeture annuelle	no
Weekly closure	Fermeture hebdomadaire	no

Fees main season
Tarifs haute saison 18 holes

	Week days Semaine	We/Bank holidays We/Férié
Individual Individuel	£ 36	£ 54
Couple Couple	£ 72	£ 108

Full days: £ 54 - £ 72 (weekends)

Caddy	Caddy	on request/£ 18.50
Electric Trolley	Chariot électrique	no
Buggy	Voiturette	no
Clubs	Clubs	£ 10/18 holes

Credit cards Cartes de crédit VISA - MasterCard

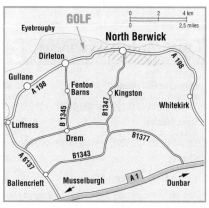

Access Accès : Edinburgh, by-pass and A1 → Berwick upon Tweed. Exit for A198, follow to North Berwick.
Map 3 on page 493 Carte 3 Page 493

GOLF COURSE
PARCOURS   18/20

Site	Site	
Maintenance	Entretien	
Architect	Architecte	Unknown
Type	Type	links
Relief	Relief	
Water in play	Eau en jeu	
Exp. to wind	Exposé au vent	
Trees in play	Arbres en jeu	

Scorecard	Chp.	Mens	Ladies
Carte de score	Chp.	Mess.	Da.
Length Long.	5842	5490	5233
Par	71	70	74

Advised golfing ability	0	12	24	36
Niveau de jeu recommandé				
Hcp required	Handicap exigé	25 Men, 35 Ladies		

CLUB HOUSE & AMENITIES
CLUB HOUSE ET ANNEXES   7/10

Pro shop	Pro-shop	
Driving range	Practice	
Sheltered	couvert	no
On grass	sur herbe	yes
Putting-green	putting-green	yes
Pitching-green	pitching green	no

HOTEL FACILITIES
ENVIRONNEMENT HOTELIER   8/10

HOTELS HÔTELS
Marine Hotel — North Berwick adjacent
74 rooms, D £ 80
Tel (44) 01620 - 892 406
Fax (44) 01620 - 894 480

Blenheim House Hotel — North Berwick close
11 rooms, D £ 68
Tel (44) 01620 - 892 385
Fax (44) 01620 - 894 010

RESTAURANTS RESTAURANTS
Marine Hotel — North Berwick adjacent
Tel (44) 01620 - 892 406

The Grange — North Berwick close
Tel (44) 01620 - 895 894

765

PANMURE

Although this course has paled somewhat in the shadow of neighbouring Carnoustie, Panmure (like the other neighbour Monifieth) does not fall far short from featuring in the same class. Anywhere else it would be very highly rated, so take advantage of your stay in the region to play it. In a rather hilly landscape, sometimes even dotted with oddly-shaped dunes, you'll have to be pretty hot with your bump and run shots, regardless of wind direction, in order to control the flight of your shots even though from first reading the card you might think that the course has nothing over-difficult to offer. The greens are extremely well protected and the putting surface is always tricky but never impossible. A classic and very forthright links to which access is restricted on weekends but where a warm welcome awaits the visitor on weekdays.

Bien qu'il ait un peu pâli du puissant voisinage de Carnoustie, il manque peu de chose à Panmure (tout comme à Monifieth, son autre voisin) pour figurer dans sa même classe. Partout ailleurs, il serait hautement considéré : profitez d'être dans la région pour le découvrir. Dans un paysage assez mouvementé, parfois même orné de petites dunes de formes curieuses, il vous faudra savoir jouer les balles roulées, que le vent soit dans n'importe quel sens, pour bien contrôler vos trajectoires de balles, même si la lecture de la carte peut faire penser que les difficultés ne sont pas immenses. Les greens sont très bien défendus, leurs surfaces subtiles mais sans exagérations. Un links classique d'une grande franchise, où l'accès est limité en week-end, mais l'accueil chaleureux en semaine.

Panmure Golf Club 1899

Barry
SCO- CARNOUSTIE, Angus DD7 7RT

Office	Secrétariat	(44) 01241 - 855 120
Pro shop	Pro-shop	(44) 01241 - 852 460
Fax	Fax	(44) 01241 - 859 737
Situation	Situation	

16 km E of Dundee (pop. 165 873)

Annual closure	Fermeture annuelle	no
Weekly closure	Fermeture hebdomadaire	no

Fees main season
Tarifs haute saison 18 holes

	Week days Semaine	We/Bank holidays We/Férié
Individual Individuel	£ 32	£ 32*
Couple Couple	£ 64	£ 64*

* Not Saturdays - Full Weekday: £ 48

Caddy	Caddy	on request
Electric Trolley	Chariot électrique	no
Buggy	Voiturette	£ 20/18 holes
Clubs	Clubs	yes

Credit cards Cartes de crédit
VISA - Eurocard - MasterCard - JCB

766

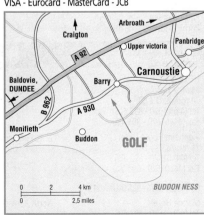

Access Accès : Dundee A930 to Barry Village. Golf 1 km
Map 2 on page 491 Carte 2 Page 491

GOLF COURSE
PARCOURS

17 /20

Site	Site	
Maintenance	Entretien	
Architect	Architecte	Unknown
Type	Type	links
Relief	Relief	
Water in play	Eau en jeu	
Exp. to wind	Exposé au vent	
Trees in play	Arbres en jeu	

Scorecard Carte de score	Chp. Chp.	Mens Mess.	Ladies Da.
Length Long.	5925	5538	5215
Par	70	70	73

Advised golfing ability		0 12 24 36
Niveau de jeu recommandé		
Hcp required	Handicap exigé	no

CLUB HOUSE & AMENITIES
CLUB HOUSE ET ANNEXES

6 /10

Pro shop	Pro-shop	
Driving range	Practice	
Sheltered	couvert	1 mat
On grass	sur herbe	yes (own balls)
Putting-green	putting-green	yes
Pitching-green	pitching green	yes

HOTEL FACILITIES
ENVIRONNEMENT HOTELIER

5 /10

HOTELS HÔTELS
Carnoustie Golf Hotel — Carnoustie
85 rooms, D £ 149 — 16 km
Tél (49) 01241 - 411 999, Fax (49) 01241 - 411 998

Stakis Dundee — Dundee
104 rooms, D £ 90 — 6 km
Tél (44) 01382 - 22 9271, Fax (44) 01382 - 200 072

Kingsley — Arbroath
16 rooms, D £ 35 — 10 km
Tél (44) 01241 - 879 933

Tayview - 11 rooms, D £ 65 — Broughty Ferry
Tél (44) 01382 - 779 438

RESTAURANTS RESTAURANTS
11 Park Avenue — Carnoustie 3 km
Tél (44) 01241 - 853 336

After the more famous Cruden Bay, you are strongly recommended to drive on a few more miles. The curiosity here is firstly that you have to cross a car-park bridge up to the rather Spartan clubhouse, where there is no locker-room for visitors. This very interesting course often looks like a links but is more like a park course when it ventures inland. It doesn't appear to have been altered a great deal since the various retouching operations firstly by Willie Park then by Braid and Auchterlonie. Bushes, rough, bunkers and ditches are the basic hazards on this layout where very little sand has ever been moved. But the terrain was made for an interesting course and there was enough space to lay-out another excellent 9-hole course, where the lesser golfer can get to grips with the game.

Après le plus célèbre Cruden Bay, il est fortement conseillé de pousser quelques kilomètres plus loin. La curiosité, c'est d'abord de devoir traverser un pont, du parking jusqu'au Clubhouse assez spartiate, où les visiteurs n'ont pas de vestiaire. Ce très intéressant parcours aux allures de links le plus souvent, parfois de parc dans les parties les plus intérieures, ne paraît pas avoir été beaucoup modifié depuis les différentes interventions de Willie Park d'abord, Braid et Auchterlonie ensuite. Buissons, roughs, bunkers et fossés constituent l'essentiel des obstacles sur ce dessin où peu de sable a été bougé. Mais le terrain se prêtait à un parcours intéressant, et l'espace était assez vaste pour que l'on trouve également ici un 9 trous de bonne facture où les moins compétents pourront s'aguerrir.

Peterhead Golf Club 1891

Craigewan Links, Riverside Drive
SCO - PETERHEAD, Aberdeenshire AB42 1LT

Office	Secrétariat	(44) 01779 - 472 149
Pro shop	Pro-shop	no Pro shop
Fax	Fax	(44) 01779 - 480 725
Situation	Situation	

56 km N of Aberdeen (pop. 204 885)

Annual closure	Fermeture annuelle	no
Weekly closure	Fermeture hebdomadaire	no

Fees main season
Tarifs haute saison full day

	Week days Semaine	We/Bank holidays We/Férié
Individual Individuel	£ 20	£ 27
Couple Couple	£ 40	£ 54

Caddy	Caddy	no
Electric Trolley	Chariot électrique	no
Buggy	Voiturette	no
Clubs	Clubs	no

Credit cards Cartes de crédit · no

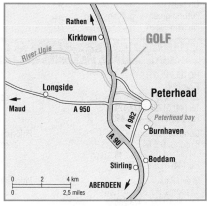

Access Accès : Aberdeen, A92 North, turn right on A952 → Peterhead. Go for north edge of town. Park on south of river Ugie. Walk across bridge to Clubhouse. **Map 1 on page 489** Carte 1 Page 489

GOLF COURSE
PARCOURS **15**/20

Site	Site	
Maintenance	Entretien	
Architect	Architecte	Willie Park James Braid
Type	Type	seaside course, links
Relief	Relief	
Water in play	Eau en jeu	
Exp. to wind	Exposé au vent	
Trees in play	Arbres en jeu	

Scorecard Carte de score	Chp. Chp.	Mens Mess.	Ladies Da.
Length Long.	5642	5263	4930
Par	70	69	72

Advised golfing ability	0 12 24 36
Niveau de jeu recommandé	
Hcp required Handicap exigé	certificate

CLUB HOUSE & AMENITIES
CLUB HOUSE ET ANNEXES **5**/10

Pro shop	Pro-shop	
Driving range	Practice	
Sheltered	couvert	practice area
On grass	sur herbe	no
Putting-green	putting-green	yes
Pitching-green	pitching green	yes

HOTEL FACILITIES
ENVIRONNEMENT HOTELIER **4**/10

HOTELS HÔTELS
Waterside Inn — Peterhead
109 rooms, D £ 95 — 1 km
Tél (44) 01779 - 471 121, Fax (44) 01779 - 470 670

Red House Hotel — Peterhead
12 rooms, D £ 98 — 1 km
Tél (49) 01779 - 812 215, Fax (49) 01779 - 812 320

Meldrum House — Oldmeldrum
9 rooms, D £ 120 — 28 km
Tél (44) 01651 - 872 294, Fax (44) 01651 - 872 464

Udry Arms - 24 rooms, D £ 60 — Newburgh 30 km
Tél (44) 01358 - 789 444, Fax (44) 01779 - 789 012

RESTAURANTS RESTAURANTS
Udny Arms — Newburgh
Tél (44) 01358 - 789 444 — 30 km

767

A visit here in Winter would probably come as something as a surprise, as even at a moderate altitude, snow is not rare. This little town, one of Queen Victoria's favourite destinations, is surrounded by hills edged with pine-trees and looks it best in Summer, when nature and the course are in full bloom and the salmon are on their way up to Loch Faskally. Accommodation here is both extensive and good standard and there is even a theatre. The actual course lies on a hill above Pitlochry, and although the first few holes are something of a climb, the layout soon levels out and the view from the top of the course really is worth the effort. Slopes have been used so intelligently that you don't always notice them, and while tee-boxes and greens are frequently at the same level, you'll find a few surprises in store as you progress from one to the other. Interestingly, the bunkers here contain quartz sand.

Venir par ici en hiver pourrait bien vous surprendre. Même à une altitude modérée, il n'est pas rare d'y voir de la neige. Les collines bordées de pins entourent la petite ville, que la reine Victoria adorait. Il faut venir ici en été, quand la végétation est à sa plénitude, et que les saumons remontent le Loch Faskally. L'hébergement est ici aussi abondant que de qualité, on trouve même un théâtre. Le parcours est situé sur une colline au-dessus de Pitlochry, le début est physiquement assez difficile, mais les choses s'arrangent rapidement, et la vue du haut du parcours valait cet effort. On ne remarque pas toujours les pentes, car elles sont intelligemment utilisées, les départs et les greens sont fréquemment au même niveau, mais on peut avoir entre les deux quelques surprises. A remarquer, le sable de quartz dans les bunkers.

Pitlochry Golf Club   1909

Golf Course Road
SCO - PITLOCHRY, TH16 5QY

Office	Secrétariat	(44) 01796 - 472 314
Pro shop	Pro-shop	(44) 01796 - 472 792
Fax	Fax	(44) 01796 - 473 599
Situation	Situation	

45 km N of Perth (pop. 123 495)
close to Pitlochry (Pop. 3 126)

Annual closure	Fermeture annuelle	no
Weekly closure	Fermeture hebdomadaire	no

Chances of snow during winter months

Fees main season	Tarifs haute saison	18 holes

	Week days Semaine	We/Bank holidays We/Férié
Individual Individuel	£ 14.50	£ 19
Couple Couple	£ 29	£ 38

Caddy	Caddy	on request
Electric Trolley	Chariot électrique	yes
Buggy	Voiturette	no
Clubs	Clubs	yes
Credit cards Cartes de crédit		yes

0 ——— 2 ——— 4 km
0 ——— 2,5 miles

Glen Garry · Glen Briat
Kingussie
GOLF
A 9
Glen Breraran
Killiecrankie
Rattray
B 8019
B 8019
Aberfeldy
Pitlochry
TAY FOREST PARK
Balliemuigh
Milton · A 827
PERTH

Access Accès : Edinburgh M90 then A9 to Pitlochry.
Turn uphill at sign in middle of town.
Map 1 on page 489 Carte 1 Page 489

GOLF COURSE
PARCOURS   14/20

Site	Site	▰▰▰▱▱
Maintenance	Entretien	▰▰▰▱▱
Architect	Architecte	W. Fernie
Type	Type	mountain
Relief	Relief	▰▰▱▱▱
Water in play	Eau en jeu	▰▱▱▱▱
Exp. to wind	Exposé au vent	▰▰▰▰▱
Trees in play	Arbres en jeu	▰▰▰▱▱

Scorecard	Chp.	Mens	Ladies
Carte de score	Chp.	Mess.	Da.
Length Long.	5290	5290	5290
Par	69	69	72

Advised golfing ability		0	12	24	36
Niveau de jeu recommandé					
Hcp required	Handicap exigé	certificate			

CLUB HOUSE & AMENITIES
CLUB HOUSE ET ANNEXES   6/10

Pro shop	Pro-shop	▰▰▰▱▱
Driving range	Practice	▰▰▱▱▱
Sheltered	couvert	no
On grass	sur herbe	yes
Putting-green	putting-green	yes
Pitching-green	pitching green	no

HOTEL FACILITIES
ENVIRONNEMENT HOTELIER   7/10

HOTELS HÔTELS

Pine Trees 20 rooms, D £ 95 Tel (44) 01796 - 472 121 Fax (44) 01796 - 472 460	Pitlochry close
Dunfallandy House 8 rooms, D £ 64 Tel (44) 01796 - 472 648 Fax (44) 01796 - 472 017	Pitlochry close
Green Park 37 rooms, D £ 95 Tel (44) 01796 - 473 248 Fax (44) 01796 - 473 520	Pitlochry close

RESTAURANTS RESTAURANTS

East Haugh House Tel (44) 01796 - 473 121	Pitlochry 4 km

768

This course dominates the little village of Portpatrick from atop the cliffs overlooking the Irish sea, with views stretching to the distant Isle of Man, the Irish coast and the Mull of Kintyre. Although close to the ocean, this is not a dunes links, although the scrub and bushes are just as dangerous. Because of its location it is very exposed to the prevailing south-westerlies, and of course overcoming, or at least accepting, this element is essential, particularly when it comes to club selection. Make full allowance for side-winds or head-winds or any possible combination of the two. This is a pretty spot to spend a holiday, especially as the little 9-holer is ideal for beginners to cut their teeth or even for non-golfers in the family to hit a ball or two. It is also the opportunity to discover a little known region of Scotland.

Ce parcours domine le petit village de Portpatrick du haut des falaises dominant la mer d'Irlande, avec des vues dans le lointain sur l'Ile de Man, la côte irlandaise et le Mull of Kintyre. Il est proche de l'océan, mais ce n'est pas un links de dunes, bien que les bosquets et arbustes y jouent un rôle identique. A cause de sa situation, il est très exposé aux vents dominants de sud-ouest. Bien sûr, savoir maîtriser - ou au moins accepter - cet élément est ici une nécessité, notamment au moment du choix des clubs : prévoir large par vent contre ou latéral, ou toutes combinaisons imaginables des deux. C'est un joli endroit où passer pendant les vacances, d'autant que le petit 9-trous est idéal pour aguerrir les débutants, voire initier les non-golfeurs de la famille. C'est aussi l'occasion de découvrir une région peu connue d'Ecosse...

Portpatrick Golf Club — 1903

Golf Course Road,
SCO - PORTPATRICK, STRANRAER, Wigtownshire DG9 8TB

Office	Secrétariat	(44) 01776 - 810 273
Pro shop	Pro-shop	(44) 01776 - 810 273
Fax	Fax	(44) 01776 - 810 811
Situation	Situation	

8 km from Stranraer (pop. 11 348)

Annual closure	Fermeture annuelle	no
Weekly closure	Fermeture hebdomadaire	no

Fees main season
Tarifs haute saison 18 holes

	Week days Semaine	We/Bank holidays We/Férié
Individual Individuel	£ 19	£ 28
Couple Couple	£ 38	£ 56

Full days: £ 28 - £ 33 (weekends)

Caddy	Caddy	on request
Electric Trolley	Chariot électrique	on request
Buggy	Voiturette	on request
Clubs	Clubs	£ 6/18 holes

Credit cards Cartes de crédit
VISA - Eurocard - MasterCard - AMEX - DC

Access Accès : Glasgow, A77 through Ayr, Turnberry, to Stranraer, then A716 and A77 to Portpatrick.
Map 2 on page 490 Carte 2 Page 490

GOLF COURSE / PARCOURS — 15/20

Site	Site	
Maintenance	Entretien	
Architect	Architecte	C.W. Hunter
Type	Type	seaside course, parkland
Relief	Relief	
Water in play	Eau en jeu	
Exp. to wind	Exposé au vent	
Trees in play	Arbres en jeu	

Scorecard Carte de score	Chp. Chp.	Mens Mess.	Ladies Da.
Length Long.	5401	5061	4707
Par	70	70	70

Advised golfing ability		0 12 24 36
Niveau de jeu recommandé		
Hcp required	Handicap exigé	24 Men, 36 Ladies

CLUB HOUSE & AMENITIES / CLUB HOUSE ET ANNEXES — 6/10

Pro shop	Pro-shop	
Driving range	Practice	
Sheltered	couvert	no
On grass	sur herbe	yes
Putting-green	putting-green	yes
Pitching-green	pitching green	yes

HOTEL FACILITIES / ENVIRONNEMENT HOTELIER — 7/10

HOTELS HÔTELS

Knockinaam Lodge — Portpatrick
10 rooms, D £ 150 — 4 km
Tel (44) 01776 - 810 471
Fax (44) 01776 - 810 435

Fernhill — Portpatrick
20 rooms, D £ 100 — 0,5 km
Tel (44) 01776 - 810 220
Fax (44) 01776 - 810 596

North West Castle — Stranraer
67 rooms, D £ 70 — 8 km
Tel (44) 01776 - 704 413
Fax (44) 01776 - 702 646

RESTAURANTS RESTAURANTS

Knockinaam Lodge — Portpatrick
Tel (44) 01776 - 810 471 — 4 km

769

POWFOOT

It has often been said that the finest turf in the world is to be found close to Solway Firth. Whatever, the grass at Powfoot does nothing to undermine that claim. And although the course is not specifically a links, the type of soil here means you play it as if it were. There is a lot of gorse to worry wayward hitters, although the fairways are wide enough for players to open their shoulders, as long as the wind behaves itself. Mid- and high-handicappers can rest assured: this is a friendly layout and they shouldn't be over-awed by the one or two blind shots. The surprises in store from off-target shots are more often pleasant than unpleasant. The better players will need to think harder to keep the ball straight and avoid the very many bunkers, which were laid out by James Braid. Need we say more? Excellent golfing.

On a souvent dit que l'on trouvait les meilleurs gazons du monde près du Solway Firth. Celui de Powfoot prouve en tout cas que ce n'est pas faux. Et bien que le parcours ne soit pas spécifiquement un links, la nature du sol fait qu'on le joue comme tel. Les ajoncs sont ici abondants pour inquiéter les joueurs imprécis, mais les fairways sont assez larges pour qu'ils oublient leurs craintes, tant que le vent ne souffle pas trop... Que les joueurs de handicap moyen ou élevé se rassurent, c'est un tracé des plus amicaux, et les quelques coups aveugles ne devraient pas trop les préoccuper : ils auront plus de bonnes surprises que de mauvaises avec leurs écarts imprévus ! Les meilleurs joueurs devront réfléchir davantage à garder la balle assez droite, à éviter les nombreux bunkers : James Braid les a disposés, il n'est pas nécessaire d'en dire plus. Une halte de qualité.

Powfoot Golf Club		1903
Cummertrees		
SCO - ANNAN, Dumfriesshire DG12 5QE		
Office	Secrétariat	(44) 01461 - 700 276
Pro shop	Pro-shop	(44) 01461 - 700 327
Fax	Fax	(44) 01461 - 700 276
Situation	Situation	
19 km SE of Dumfries (pop. 21 164)		
Annual closure	Fermeture annuelle	no
Weekly closure	Fermeture hebdomadaire	no
Fees main season	Tarifs haute saison	18 holes

	Week days Semaine	We/Bank holidays We/Férié
Individual Individuel	£ 23	£ 23
Couple Couple	£ 46	£ 46
Full day: £ 30		
Caddy	Caddy	no
Electric Trolley	Chariot électrique	no
Buggy	Voiturette	no
Clubs	Clubs	no

Credit cards Cartes de crédit VISA - JCB - Switch

GOLF COURSE
PARCOURS

16/20

Site	Site	
Maintenance	Entretien	
Architect	Architecte	James Braid
Type	Type	links
Relief	Relief	
Water in play	Eau en jeu	
Exp. to wind	Exposé au vent	
Trees in play	Arbres en jeu	

Scorecard Carte de score	Chp. Chp.	Mens Mess.	Ladies Da.
Length Long.	5710	5475	5010
Par	70	70	74

Advised golfing ability		0	12	24	36
Niveau de jeu recommandé					
Hcp required	Handicap exigé	no			

CLUB HOUSE & AMENITIES
CLUB HOUSE ET ANNEXES

6/10

Pro shop	Pro-shop	
Driving range	Practice	
Sheltered	couvert	
On grass	sur herbe	yes
Putting-green	putting-green	yes
Pitching-green	pitching green	yes

HOTEL FACILITIES
ENVIRONNEMENT HOTELIER

4/10

HOTELS HÔTELS

Cairndale — Dumfries
76 rooms, D £ 105 — 15 km
Tel (44) 01387 - 254 111
Fax (44) 01387 - 250 155

Station — Dumfries
32 rooms, D £ 80 — 15 km
Tel (44) 01387 - 254 316
Fax (44) 01387 - 250 388

RESTAURANTS RESTAURANTS

Cairndale — Dumfries
Tel (44) 01387 - 254 111 — 15 km

770

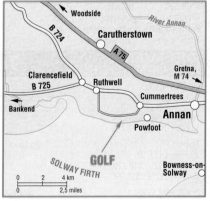

Access Accès : Glasgow, M74 and A74. Exit 18 after Lockerbie, B723 → Annan. B724 → Cummertrees. After 5 km (3 m.), pass under railway bridge, turn sharp left → Golf.
Map 2 on page 4491 Carte 2 Page 4491

PRESTWICK

18	6	7

This was the first course used for the British Open but was withdrawn from the course rotation in 1925 for being too short and perhaps, too, for a number of eccentric features such as the blind par-3 fifth hole or the second shot on the 17th, where the green is nowhere to be seen. But no lover of authentic golf will miss playing this delightful and one-of-a-kind links course which is kept in excellent condition. Like many courses in Scotland, it unwinds between a railway track and the sea. It has been lengthened since the days when there were only twelve holes but this has added to the course's variety if not its unity. The bunkers here are particularly tough, especially the famous Cardinal, which cuts hole N°3 in two. Prestwick thrives on hospitality (on week-days) and memories of the past that you can't and won't miss in the clubhouse.

Ce fut le premier parcours du British Open, mais il fut retiré de la rotation des parcours en 1925, pour sa longueur insuffisante, mais peut-être aussi quelques aspects excentriques comme le 5, un par 3 aveugle, ou le second coup du 17, où le green n'est pas plus visible. Mais aucun amoureux de golfeur uthentique ne manquera de jouer ce links savoureux et unique en son genre, où l'entretien est d'excellente qualité. Comme beaucoup de parcours en Ecosse, il se déroule entre la voie ferrée et la mer. Il a été allongé depuis l'époque où il ne comptait que 12 trous, mais cela a contribué à ajouter à sa variété, sinon à son unité. Les bunkers ici sont particulièrement féroces, notamment le fameux Cardinal, qui coupe le 3 en deux parties. Prestwick cultive l'hospitalité (en semaine) et les souvenirs des temps passés, que vous ne manquerez pas au Club house.

Prestwick Golf Club — 1851

2 Links Road
SCO - PRESTWICK, Ayrshire KA9 1QG

Office	Secrétariat	(44) 01292 - 477 404
Pro shop	Pro-shop	(44) 01292 - 479 483
Fax	Fax	(44) 01292 - 477 255
Situation	Situation	

4 km N of Ayr (pop. 47 872)
50 km SW of Glasgow (pop. 662 853)

Annual closure	Fermeture annuelle	no
Weekly closure	Fermeture hebdomadaire	no

Fees main season	Tarifs haute saison	18 holes
	Week days / Semaine	We/Bank holidays / We/Férié
Individual Individuel	—	—
Couple Couple	—	—

Restrictions for visitors (weekdays only):
ask for details

Caddy	Caddy	on request
Electric Trolley	Chariot électrique	yes
Buggy	Voiturette	no
Clubs	Clubs	yes

Credit cards Cartes de crédit
VISA - MasterCard - AMEX (Pro shop)

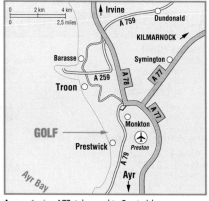

Access Accès : A77, take road to Prestwick,
Golf adjacent to railway station
Map 3 on page 492 Carte 3 Page 492

GOLF COURSE / PARCOURS — 18/20

Site	Site	
Maintenance	Entretien	
Architect	Architecte	Unknown
Type	Type	links
Relief	Relief	
Water in play	Eau en jeu	
Exp. to wind	Exposé au vent	
Trees in play	Arbres en jeu	

Scorecard / Carte de score	Chp. / Chp.	Mens / Mess.	Ladies / Da.
Length Long.	6068	6068	0
Par	72	72	0

Advised golfing ability		0	12	24	36
Niveau de jeu recommandé					
Hcp required	Handicap exigé	certificate			

CLUB HOUSE & AMENITIES / CLUB HOUSE ET ANNEXES — 6/10

Pro shop	Pro-shop	
Driving range	Practice	
Sheltered	couvert	no
On grass	sur herbe	yes
Putting-green	putting-green	yes
Pitching-green	pitching green	yes

HOTEL FACILITIES / ENVIRONNEMENT HOTELIER — 7/10

HOTELS HÔTELS

Carlton Toby — Prestwick close
37 rooms, D £ 80
Tel (44) 01292 - 476 811
Fax (44) 01292 - 474 845

Fairfield House — Ayr 4 km
33 rooms, D £ 120
Tel (44) 01292 - 267 461
Fax (44) 01292 - 261 456

Pickwick — Ayr 3 km
15 rooms, D £ 70
Tel (44) 01292 - 260 111
Fax (44) 01292 - 285 348

RESTAURANTS RESTAURANTS

Fouters — Ayr 4 km
Tel (44) 01292 - 261 391

771

The reputation of the other Prestwick course has doubtless helped keep this course out of the limelight. That might be so with non-Scots, but the local players know that this is not just another course that should be included when making an intelligent and exhaustive survey of good courses in Ayrshire. This is a genuine typical Scottish links laid out between the sea and a railway line, both of which come into play depending on where the wind is blowing from. While some of the natural bunkers can keep you out of the wind, you'll have to get out of them sooner or later to affront the tricky slopes of the huge greens, which are often firm and slick. With difficulties spread evenly over the 18 holes, don't put too much faith in the lengths written on the card. You can certainly play to your handicap here, but it's no walk-over either.

La réputation de l'autre Prestwick a sans doute maintenu celui-ci dans une certaine obscurité, au moins auprès des étrangers car les joueurs de la région savent qu'il ne s'agit pas là d'un parcours indifférent, à inclure dans une exploration intelligente et exhaustive des bons parcours de l'Ayrshire. Il s'agit là d'un vrai et typique «Scottish links,» situé entre la mer et le chemin de fer, qui viennent tous deux en jeu selon que le vent souffle d'un côté ou de l'autre. Et si certains bunkers naturels vous fourniront un abri, il faudra pourtant bien en sortir un jour pour affronter les subtils reliefs de greens vastes, souvent fermes et bien roulants. Avec des difficultés bien réparties tout au long des 18 trous, il ne faut pas se fier aux longueurs inscrites sur la carte. Certes, on peut jouer ici son handicap, mais ce n'est pas donné d'avance.

Prestwick St Nicholas Golf Club — 1892

Grangemuir Road
SCO - PRESTWICK, Ayrshire KA9 1SN

Office	Secrétariat	(44) 01292 - 477 608
Pro shop	Pro-shop	(44) 01292 - 473 904
Fax	Fax	(44) 01292 - 473 900
Situation	Situation	

3 km N of Ayr (pop. 47 872)
51 km SW of Glasgow (pop. 662 853)

Annual closure	Fermeture annuelle	no
Weekly closure	Fermeture hebdomadaire	no
Fees main season	Tarifs haute saison	18 holes

	Week days Semaine	We/Bank holidays We/Férié
Individual Individuel	£ 30	£ 35
Couple Couple	£ 60	£ 70

Full weekdays: £ 50 - Visitors at weekends: Sunday p.m. only

Caddy	Caddy	on request
Electric Trolley	Chariot électrique	no
Buggy	Voiturette	no
Clubs	Clubs	yes
Credit cards Cartes de crédit		yes

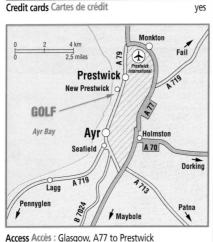

Access Accès : Glasgow, A77 to Prestwick
Map 3 on page 492 Carte 3 Page 492

GOLF COURSE PARCOURS — 16/20

Site	Site	
Maintenance	Entretien	
Architect	Architecte	Charles Hunter James Allan
Type	Type	links
Relief	Relief	
Water in play	Eau en jeu	
Exp. to wind	Exposé au vent	
Trees in play	Arbres en jeu	

Scorecard Carte de score	Chp. Chp.	Mens Mess.	Ladies Da.
Length Long.	5416	5416	4836
Par	69	69	70

Advised golfing ability		0 12 24 36
Niveau de jeu recommandé		
Hcp required	Handicap exigé	no

CLUB HOUSE & AMENITIES CLUB HOUSE ET ANNEXES — 6/10

Pro shop	Pro-shop	
Driving range	Practice	
Sheltered	couvert	no driving range
On grass	sur herbe	no
Putting-green	putting-green	yes
Pitching-green	pitching green	yes

HOTEL FACILITIES ENVIRONNEMENT HOTELIER — 7/10

HOTELS HÔTELS
Carlton Toby — Prestwick / close
37 rooms, D £ 80
Tel (44) 01292 - 476 811
Fax (44) 01292 - 474 845

Fairfield House — Ayr / 4 km
33 rooms, D £ 120
Tel (44) 01292 - 267 461
Fax (44) 01292 - 261 456

Pickwick — Ayr / 4 km
15 rooms, D £ 70
Tel (44) 01292 - 260 111
Fax (44) 01292 - 285 348

RESTAURANTS RESTAURANTS
Fouters — Ayr / 4 km
Tel (44) 01292 - 261 391

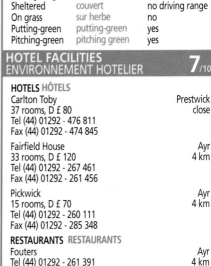

ROXBURGHE (THE)

15 7 7

The Duke and Duchess of Roxburghe were personally involved in the decoration and style of the Roxburghe Hotel and everyone should visit their «home sweet home», i.e. the hundreds of rooms in the Floors Castle. Fishing, clay pigeon-shooting, riding and tennis are some of the activities on offer on this estate located very close to the English border, plus an 18-hole course designed by Dave Thomas alongside a river, following the natural relief of the estate and alternating stretches in the forest and the attractive park (the course is not always easy to walk). Modern in style with many different hazards, it demands target golf more than your usual bump and run shots. A high-class location for a sporting holiday in very pretty countryside. Excellent practice for your game.

Le Duc et la Duchesse de Roxburghe ont mis eux-même la main à la décoration et au style de l'hôtel Roxburghe, et l'on ne manquera pas de visiter leur «sweet home», c'est-à-dire les centaines de pièces du Floors Castle. Pêche, tir au pigeon d'argile, équitation et tennis sont quelques-unes des activités proposées dans ce domaine tout proche de la frontière avec l'Angleterre, auxquelles s'ajoute un 18 trous dessiné par Dave Thomas en bordure de rivière. Il suit les reliefs naturels du domaine et alterne passages en forêt et esthétique de parc (le parcours n'est pas toujours facile à marcher). De style moderne, avec de multiples obstacles, exigeant un jeu de cible plus que des coups roulés, c'est un lieu de vacances sportives de très bonne facture, dans un très joli paysage. Très beau practice !

The Roxburghe Golf Course — 1997

The Roxburghe Hotel
SCO - KELSO, Roxburghshire TD5 8JZ

Office	Secrétariat	(44) 01573 - 450 331
Pro shop	Pro-shop	(44) 01573 - 450 333
Fax	Fax	(44) 01573 - 450 611
Situation	Situation	

5 km SW of Kelso (pop. 6 167)

Annual closure	Fermeture annuelle	no
Weekly closure	Fermeture hebdomadaire	no

Fees main season	Tarifs haute saison		18 holes
		Week days Semaine	We/Bank holidays We/Férié
Individual Individuel		£ 35	£ 40
Couple Couple		£ 70	£ 80

Caddy	Caddy	on request/£ 20
Electric Trolley	Chariot électrique	no
Buggy	Voiturette	£ 20/18 holes
Clubs	Clubs	£ 20/18 holes

Credit cards Cartes de crédit
VISA - MasterCard - AMEX - DC

Access Accès : Edinburgh A68. After St Boswells and before Jedburgh, turn left on A698, Golf approx.10 km (6 m.).
Map 2 on page 491 Carte 2 Page 491

GOLF COURSE / PARCOURS — **15**/20

Site	Site	
Maintenance	Entretien	
Architect	Architecte	Dave Thomas
Type	Type	parkland
Relief	Relief	
Water in play	Eau en jeu	
Exp. to wind	Exposé au vent	
Trees in play	Arbres en jeu	

Scorecard Carte de score	Chp. Chp.	Mens Mess.	Ladies Da.
Length Long.	6471	5943	5167
Par	72	72	72

Advised golfing ability — 0 12 24 36
Niveau de jeu recommandé
Hcp required Handicap exigé — 24

CLUB HOUSE & AMENITIES / CLUB HOUSE ET ANNEXES — **7**/10

Pro shop	Pro-shop	
Driving range	Practice	
Sheltered	couvert	no
On grass	sur herbe	yes
Putting-green	putting-green	yes
Pitching-green	pitching green	yes

HOTEL FACILITIES / ENVIRONNEMENT HOTELIER — **7**/10

HOTELS HÔTELS

The Roxburghe Hotel 22 rooms, D £ 145 Tel (44) 01573 - 450 331 Fax (44) 01573 - 450 611	Golf on site
Ednam House 32 rooms, D £ 93 Tel (44) 01573 - 224 168 Fax (44) 01573 - 226 319	Kelso 5 km
Dryburgh Abbey 24 rooms, D £ 110 Tel (44) 01835 - 822 261 Fax (44) 01835 - 823 945	St Boswells 10 km

RESTAURANTS RESTAURANTS

The Roxburghe Tel (44) 01573 - 450 331	Golf on site

773

A page of golf was written here, less than 2 miles from the «city of granite». Royal Aberdeen originated in 1780, was the world's sixth golf club and the first to adopt the 5-minute rule when looking for your ball. You probably won't lose yours as long as you play «Balgownie» (its more familiar name) carefully, avoid the bushes and tall grass and, in a word, stay in the fairway. You'll probably have a tougher time distinguishing the fairways amongst the dunes, keeping a solid swing when the wind blows a little too hard, or remembering to turn around at the 9th, as the holes that continue belong to Murcar. A little off the beaten golf-trotter track, this is one of the great classics for every links-collector, fun to play every time.

A seulement 3 km de la «ville de granit» s'est tournée une page du golf : le Royal Aberdeen trouve ses origines en 1780, c'est le sixième club du monde et le premier à avoir adopté la règle de cinq minutes pour chercher une balle. Mais on ne risque pas trop d'en perdre si l'on joue sagement «Balgownie» (comme on le connaît mieux), en évitant les buissons et les hautes herbes. Bref si l'on ne quitte pas le fairway. On perdra davantage la tête à repérer certains fairways parmi les dunes, à garder un swing solide quand le vent souffle un peu trop fort, ou si l'on oublie de revenir en arrière au 9 : les trous qui suivent appartiennent à Murcar. Un peu en dehors des sentiers touristiques du golf, c'est un des grands classiques quand on fait collection de links. Et c'est toujours un plaisir d'y revenir.

Royal Aberdeen Golf Club — 1888

Balgownie, Links Road, Bridge of Don
SCO- ABERDEEN AB23 8AT

Office	Secrétariat	(44) 01224 - 702 571
Pro shop	Pro-shop	(44) 01224 - 702 221
Fax	Fax	(44) 01224 - 826 591
Situation	Situation	

3 km from Aberdeen (pop. 204 885)

Annual closure	Fermeture annuelle	no
Weekly closure	Fermeture hebdomadaire	no

Fees main season	Tarifs haute saison	18 holes
	Week days Semaine	**We/Bank holidays** We/Férié
Individual Individuel	£ 55	£ 65
Couple Couple	£ 110	£ 130
Weekdays: full day £ 75		

Caddy	Caddy	on request
Electric Trolley	Chariot électrique	£ 6/18 holes
Buggy	Voiturette	no
Clubs	Clubs	£ 10/18 holes

Credit cards Cartes de crédit
VISA - Eurocard - MasterCard - JCB

774

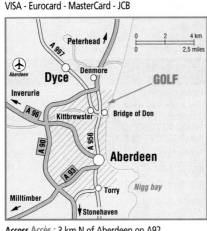

Access Accès : 3 km N of Aberdeen on A92.
Cross River Don, on right at first traffic lights,
on Links Road to golf course.
Map 1 on page 489 Carte 1 Page 489

GOLF COURSE / PARCOURS — 18/20

Site	Site	
Maintenance	Entretien	
Architect	Architecte	Bob Simpson James Braid
Type	Type	links
Relief	Relief	
Water in play	Eau en jeu	
Exp. to wind	Exposé au vent	
Trees in play	Arbres en jeu	

Scorecard Carte de score	Chp. Chp.	Mens Mess.	Ladies Da.
Length Long.	5915	5915	0
Par	70	70	0

Advised golfing ability Niveau de jeu recommandé	0	12	24	36
Hcp required Handicap exigé	24			

CLUB HOUSE & AMENITIES / CLUB HOUSE ET ANNEXES — 7/10

Pro shop	Pro-shop	
Driving range	Practice	
Sheltered	couvert	no
On grass	sur herbe	no
Putting-green	putting-green	yes
Pitching-green	pitching green	yes

HOTEL FACILITIES / ENVIRONNEMENT HOTELIER — 8/10

HOTELS HÔTELS

Marcliffe at Piffodels — Aberdeen
42 rooms, D £ 150 — 6 km
Tel (44) 01224 - 861 000, Fax (44) 01224 - 868 860

Quality — Bridge of Don
123 rooms, D £ 120 — 2 km
Tel (44) 01224 - 706 707, Fax (44) 01224 - 823 923

Corner House — Aberdeen
17 rooms, D £ 58 — 5 km
Tel (44) 01224 - 313 063

RESTAURANTS RESTAURANTS

Courtyard on the Lane — Aberdeen
Tel (44) 01224 - 213 795 — 5 km

Silver Darling — Aberdeen
Tel (44) 01224 - 576 229 — 5 km

This club was apparently formed in 1735 and played the Brunstfield Links behind Edinburgh Castle. Today it lies adjoined to the Brunstfield Club (whose history runs parallel to this club) in the north-west of the city in magnificently laid out park landscape. The work of Old Tom Morris and then James Braid, this course has its own very personal character with alternating old trees and young saplings standing alone or in clumps. Accuracy is recommended, needless to say, as for many golfers this is a «second-shot» course where you have to be so efficient to hit the greens or save your score when you miss them. The putting surfaces are such a pleasure to play that sometimes you would like to putt a little more often. Well worth knowing, but not easy to reach.

Ce club aurait été formé en 1735, et aurait eu comme parcours les Bruntsfield Links derrière le Château d'Edinburgh. Toujours est-il qu'il est aujourd'hui mitoyen au Club de Bruntsfield (dont l'histoire est parallèle), au nord-ouest de la ville, et dans un paysage de parc magnifiquement sculpté. Dû aux crayons bien connus de Old Tom Morris, puis de James Braid, ce parcours possède un caractère très personnel, avec son alternance d'arbres anciens et de jeunes pousses, solitaires ou en bosquets. Inutile de dire que la précision est recommandée, car c'est pour beaucoup un parcours «de seconds coups,» tant il faut être efficace pour rejoindre les greens, et pour sauver le score quand on les a manqués. Les surfaces de putting sont d'ailleurs un tel régal que l'on aimerait devoir faire plein de putts ! A connaître, mais l'accès n'y est pas facile.

Royal Burgess Golfing Society of Edinburgh — 1894

181 Whitehouse Road, Barnton
SCO - EDINBURGH EH4 6BY

Office	Secrétariat	(44) 0131 - 339 2075
Pro shop	Pro-shop	(44) 0131 - 339 6474
Fax	Fax	(44) 0131 - 339 3712
Situation	Situation	

5 km NW of Edinburgh centre (pop. 418 914)

Annual closure	Fermeture annuelle	no
Weekly closure	Fermeture hebdomadaire	no
Fees main season	Tarifs haute saison	18 holes

	Week days Semaine	We/Bank holidays We/Férié
Individual Individuel	£ 40	—
Couple Couple	£ 80	—

Weekends: members only
Restrictions for Ladies (ask before)

Caddy	Caddy	on request
Electric Trolley	Chariot électrique	yes
Buggy	Voiturette	no
Clubs	Clubs	yes
Credit cards Cartes de crédit		no

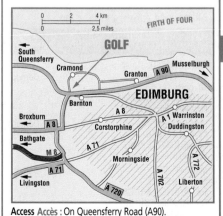

Access Accès : On Queensferry Road (A90).
Turn right at Barnton roundabout
on Whitehouse Road.
Map 3 on page 493 Carte 3 Page 493

GOLF COURSE PARCOURS — 16/20

Site	Site	
Maintenance	Entretien	
Architect	Architecte	Tom Morris James Braid
Type	Type	parkland
Relief	Relief	
Water in play	Eau en jeu	
Exp. to wind	Exposé au vent	
Trees in play	Arbres en jeu	

Scorecard Carte de score	Chp. Chp.	Mens Mess.	Ladies Da.
Length Long.	5910	5910	0
Par	71	71	0

Advised golfing ability
Niveau de jeu recommandé   0   12   24   36

Hcp required   Handicap exigé   24

CLUB HOUSE & AMENITIES CLUB HOUSE ET ANNEXES — 7/10

Pro shop	Pro-shop	
Driving range	Practice	
Sheltered	couvert	no
On grass	sur herbe	yes
Putting-green	putting-green	yes
Pitching-green	pitching green	no

HOTEL FACILITIES ENVIRONNEMENT HOTELIER — 9/10

HOTELS HÔTELS

Edinburgh Capital — Edinburgh
111 rooms, D £ 100
Tel (44) 0131 - 535 9988, Fax (44) 0131 - 334 9712

Forte Posthouse — Edinburgh
204 rooms, D £ 70
Tel (44) 0131 - 334 0390, Fax (44) 0131 - 334 9237

Lodge — Edinburgh
12 rooms, D £ 80
Tel (44) 0131 - 337 3682, Fax (44) 0131 - 313 1700

RESTAURANTS RESTAURANTS

Pompadour — Edinburgh
Tel (44) 0131 - 459 9988

Martins — Edinburgh
Tel (44) 0131 - 225 3106

775

Golf has been played here since about 1616, but it was Old Tom Morris and particularly the admirable Donald Ross who had the honour of really designing the course before John Sutherland added the final gloss. For untamed natural beauty and the challenge it offers any player, Royal Dornoch is one of the world's greatest courses. Located away from any large towns, this is a haven of peace and tranquillity in a unique atmosphere where you can chew long and hard over your technical flaws and the philosophy of golf. In fact it is only this isolation that has kept this gem of a course from being on the British Open rotation. In July you might often see some of the top champions who come here to re-acclimatise themselves to links golfing, the beginning and the end for every true golfer. Two of the greatest fans of Dornoch and none other than Tom Watson and Ben Crenshaw.

Le golf a été pratiqué sur le site depuis 1616 environ, mais ce fut à Old Tom Morris et surtout à l'admirable Donald Ross que revinrent l'honneur de dessiner vraiment le parcours, plus tard peaufiné par John Sutherland. Pour sa beauté sauvage et naturelle, pour les défis qu'il présente aux joueurs, Royal Dornoch est un des plus grands parcours au monde. Situé à l'écart des grandes villes, c'est un havre de paix à l'atmosphère unique où l'on peut méditer sur ses faiblesses techniques et la philosophie du jeu, et seul cet isolement a pu empêcher cette merveille d'être l'un des parcours du British Open. En juillet, il n'est pas rare d'y croiser de grands champions, venus se réacclimater au jeu sur les links, l'alpha et l'oméga du vrai golfeur. Tom Watson et Ben Crenshaw notamment n'ont pas été les moins élogieux sur «Dornoch.»

Royal Dornoch Golf Club — 1877

Golf Road
SCO - DORNOCH, Sutherland IV25 3LW

Office	Secrétariat	(44) 01862 - 810 219
Pro shop	Pro-shop	(44) 01862 - 810 902
Fax	Fax	(44) 01862 - 810 792
Situation	Situation	

72 km N of Inverness (pop. 62 186)

Annual closure	Fermeture annuelle	no
Weekly closure	Fermeture hebdomadaire	no

Fees main season
Tarifs haute saison 18 holes

	Week days Semaine	We/Bank holidays We/Férié
Individual Individuel	£ 55	£ 65
Couple Couple	£ 110	£ 130

GF £ 60 for Championship + Struie courses

Caddy	Caddy	on request/£ 25
Electric Trolley	Chariot électrique	£ 5/18 holes
Buggy	Voiturette	£ 20/18 holes
Clubs	Clubs	£ 10/18 holes

Credit cards Cartes de crédit VISA - MasterCard

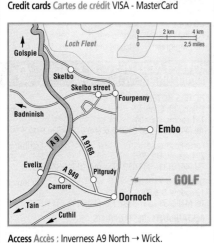

Access Accès : Inverness A9 North → Wick.
Golf on A949 to the east of the town.
Map 1 on page 488 Carte 1 Page 488

GOLF COURSE / PARCOURS — 19/20

Site	Site	
Maintenance	Entretien	
Architect	Architecte	Tom Morris Donald Ross
Type	Type	links
Relief	Relief	
Water in play	Eau en jeu	
Exp. to wind	Exposé au vent	
Trees in play	Arbres en jeu	

Scorecard Carte de score	Chp. Chp.	Mens Mess.	Ladies Da.
Length Long.	5927	5630	5420
Par	70	70	76

Advised golfing ability Niveau de jeu recommandé		0 12 24 36
Hcp required	Handicap exigé	24 Men, 35 Ladies

CLUB HOUSE & AMENITIES / CLUB HOUSE ET ANNEXES — 7/10

Pro shop	Pro-shop	
Driving range	Practice	
Sheltered	couvert	no
On grass	sur herbe	yes
Putting-green	putting-green	yes
Pitching-green	pitching green	yes

HOTEL FACILITIES / ENVIRONNEMENT HOTELIER — 7/10

HOTELS HÔTELS

Burghfield House — Dornoch
30 rooms, D £ 62
Tel (44) 01862 - 810 212
Fax (44) 01862 - 810 404

Dornoch Castle — Dornoch
17 rooms, D £ 66
Tel (44) 01862 - 810 216
Fax (44) 01862 - 810 981

Mallin House — Dornoch
10 rooms, D £ 52
Tel (44) 01862 - 810 335
Fax (44) 01862 - 810 810

RESTAURANTS RESTAURANTS

Morangie House Hotel — Tain
Tel (44) 01862 - 892 281 — 10 km

776

ROYAL MUSSELBURGH

<table>
<tr><td>16</td><td>8</td><td>7</td></tr>
</table>

The club was founded in 1774 but we imagine that golf was played at the Old Musselburgh long before that. That course still exists but its original tenants left on one side to form the Muirfield club and on the other to open this course in 1925. This is not a links but a park course laid out around a majestic barony used as the clubhouse. James Braid designed the first layout, but in 1939 the Club asked Mungo park to give it a thorough overhaul. The very many trees form impressive lines of defence completed by some very effective bunkering to swallow any wayward shot. This is not a long course but there is only one par 5, something that generally speaking bothers the long-hitters on the look-out for «easy» birdies. This well-balanced course is a pleasant alternative when you have had enough of wind howling over the dunes.

Le Club a été fondé en 1774, mais on présume que le «Old Musselburgh» avait vu jouer au golf bien avant. Il existe toujours mais ses premiers locataires sont partis d'un côté créer Muirfield, et de l'autre celui-ci, en 1925. Il ne s'agit pas d'un links, mais d'un golf de parc, autour d'une majestueuse baronnie utilisée comme Club-house. James Braid créa le premier tracé, mais le Club demanda en 1939 à Mungo Park de le réviser sérieusement. Les nombreux arbres forment des défenses imposantes, complétées par un bunkering très efficace pour recueillir les coups un peu égarés. Ce n'est pas un parcours bien long, mais il n'a qu'un seul par 5, ce qui gêne en général beaucoup les frappeurs en quête de birdies faciles. Bien équilibré, c'est une bonne alternative quand on est un peu saoûlé par le vent dans les dunes.

Royal Musselburgh Golf Club		1926
Prestongrange House		
SCO - PRESTONPANS, East Lothian EH32 9RP		
Office	Secrétariat	(44) 01875 - 810 276
Pro shop	Pro-shop	(44) 01875 - 810 139
Fax	Fax	(44) 01875 - 810 276
Situation	Situation	
13 km E of Edinburgh (pop. 418 914)		
Annual closure	Fermeture annuelle	no
Weekly closure	Fermeture hebdomadaire	no

Fees main season
Tarifs haute saison 18 holes

	Week days Semaine	We/Bank holidays We/Férié
Individual Individuel	£ 20	£ 20
Couple Couple	£ 40	£ 40

Full days: £ 35 (any)

Caddy	Caddy	on request/£ 25
Electric Trolley	Chariot électrique	£ 4/18 holes
Buggy	Voiturette	no
Clubs	Clubs	£ 6/18 holes
Credit cards Cartes de crédit		no

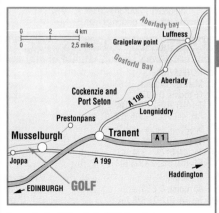

Access Accès : 13 km East of Edinburgh
on B361 → North Berwick.
Map 3 on page 493 Carte 3 Page 493

GOLF COURSE
PARCOURS
16/20

Site	Site	
Maintenance	Entretien	
Architect	Architecte	James Braid Mungo Park
Type	Type	parkland
Relief	Relief	
Water in play	Eau en jeu	
Exp. to wind	Exposé au vent	
Trees in play	Arbres en jeu	

Scorecard Carte de score	Chp. Chp.	Mens Mess.	Ladies Da.
Length Long.	5701	5346	5048
Par	70	70	72

Advised golfing ability		0 12 24 36
Niveau de jeu recommandé		
Hcp required	Handicap exigé	certificate

CLUB HOUSE & AMENITIES
CLUB HOUSE ET ANNEXES
8/10

Pro shop	Pro-shop	
Driving range	Practice	
Sheltered	couvert	no
On grass	sur herbe	no
Putting-green	putting-green	yes
Pitching-green	pitching green	no

777

HOTEL FACILITIES
ENVIRONNEMENT HOTELIER
7/10

HOTELS HÔTELS
Woodside Hotel   Musselburgh
11 rooms, D £ 74   2 km
Tel (44) 0131 - 665 0404

Granada Lodge   Musselburgh
44 rooms, D £ 45   5 km
Tel (44) 0131 - 653 6070
Fax (44) 0131 - 653 6106

RESTAURANTS RESTAURANTS
Woodside Hotel   Musselburgh
Tel (44) 0131 - 665 0404   2 km

Caprice   Musselburgh
Tel (44) 0131 - 665 2991   2 km

The «Championship» course is the most remarkable of the five courses around Troon and has staged many a British Open. It also offers magnificent views of the Firth of Clyde towards the Isle of Arran and the Mull of Kintyre, lulling you into a false sense of tranquillity. On this tremendous links course, the outward 9 may seem comparatively easy, but the back 9 is one of the most horrendous in the world of golf. It is the wind that makes all the difference, especially as here it is often a side wind adding even more spice to the course. At the famous «postage-stamp» hole, the green can seem more like a pin-head when the wind is playing tricks. All those golfers who love Castles in Spain, huge trees bathed in sunlight and flattering scores can be on their way. Sure there's the Gulf Stream nearby, and sure you'll see more impressive dunes elsewhere, but this is no place for the mild or meek-hearted.

Le «Championship» est le plus remarquable des cinq parcours autour de Troon, et a été le théâtre de nombreux British Open. Il offre des vues magnifiques au-delà du Firth of Clyde vers l'Ile d'Arran et le Mull of Kintyre, dans une trompeuse tranquillité. Sur ce formidable links, l'aller peut paraître assez facile et le retour un des plus féroces au monde. Mais le vent fera la différence, d'autant qu'il est souvent en travers, et ajoute encore à l'intérêt du parcours : au fameux «Postage Stamp», le green est encore plus petit qu'un timbre-poste quand il souffle. Que ceux qui aiment les châteaux en Espagne, les grands arbres baignés de soleil et les scores flatteurs passent leur chemin. Certes, le Gulf Stream passe par ici, certes, les dunes peuvent être encore plus impressionnantes ailleurs, mais on n'est pas ici au royaume de la douceur.

Royal Troon Golf Club	1878
SCO - TROON, Ayrshire KA10 6EP	

Office	Secrétariat	(44) 01292 - 311 555
Pro shop	Pro-shop	(44) 01292 - 313 281
Fax	Fax	(44) 01292 - 318 204
Situation	Situation	

8 km N of Prestwick (pop. 13 705)
20 km N of Ayr (pop. 47 872)

Annual closure	Fermeture annuelle	no
Weekly closure	Fermeture hebdomadaire	no

Fees main season
Tarifs haute saison full day

	Week days Semaine	We/Bank holidays We/Férié
Individual Individuel	£ 115	—
Couple Couple	£ 230	—

Visitors: Monday, Tuesday, Thursday only.
Ladies on other course only.

Caddy	Caddy	on request/£ 25
Electric Trolley	Chariot électrique	yes
Buggy	Voiturette	no
Clubs	Clubs	£ 25/18 holes

Credit cards Cartes de crédit
VISA - Mastercard (Greenfees & Proshop only)

778

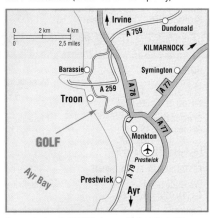

Access Accès : On B749 between Prestwick and Troon
Map 3 on page 492 Carte 3 Page 492

GOLF COURSE PARCOURS   19/20

Site	Site	▬▬▬▬▬▬▬
Maintenance	Entretien	▬▬▬▬▬▬▬
Architect	Architecte	Willie Fernie
Type	Type	links
Relief	Relief	▬▬▬
Water in play	Eau en jeu	▬▬
Exp. to wind	Exposé au vent	▬▬▬
Trees in play	Arbres en jeu	▬▬

Scorecard Carte de score	Chp. Chp.	Mens Mess.	Ladies Da.
Length Long.	6458	6042	0
Par	71	71	74

Advised golfing ability	0 12 24 36
Niveau de jeu recommandé	▬▬▬▬▬
Hcp required	Handicap exigé 20

CLUB HOUSE & AMENITIES CLUB HOUSE ET ANNEXES   7/10

Pro shop	Pro-shop	▬▬▬▬▬
Driving range	Practice	▬▬▬
Sheltered	couvert	practice area
On grass	sur herbe	yes
Putting-green	putting-green	yes
Pitching-green	pitching green	yes

HOTEL FACILITIES ENVIRONNEMENT HOTELIER   7/10

HOTELS HÔTELS

Marine Highland	Troon
66 rooms, D £ 120	close
Tel (44) 01292 - 314 444	
Fax (44) 01292 - 316 922	

Piersland House	Troon
19 rooms, D £ 95	close
Tel (44) 01292 - 314 747	
Fax (44) 01292 - 315 613	

Travel Inn	Prestwick
40 rooms, D £ 35	4 km
Tel (44) 01292 - 678 262	

RESTAURANTS RESTAURANTS

Highgrove House	Troon
Tel (44) 01292 - 312 511	3 km

SCOTSCRAIG

16 6 6

This is one of Scotland's oldest courses, whose reputation has not really benefited from the closeness of St Andrews, at least not with outsiders. The road that gets you here is nothing special, but when you reach the course, all that changes. A little links and a little inland with heather, this is a course that is none too tiring to play but one which requires a lot of concentration to play well. The wind plays a vital role, it must be said, but so do the deep bunkers and the well-contoured greens which, like the course as a whole, are in good condition. Scotscraig has been used as a qualifying course for the British Open, which speaks volumes for its quality as a test of golf, but this doesn't stop less experienced players from having a go themselves.

C'est un des plus anciens golfs d'Ecosse, dont la réputation n'a pas vraiment bénéficié de la proximité de St Andrews, en tout cas auprès des étrangers à la région. La route d'arrivée n'est pas merveilleuse, mais tout change dès que l'on arrive. Un peu links, un peu inland avec de la bruyère, c'est un parcours peu fatigant à jouer mais qui demande beaucoup d'attention pour être maîtrisé. Le vent y joue un rôle essentiel, faut-il le dire, mais aussi les profonds bunkers, les greens bien modelés et généralement en bon état, comme le parcours. Scotscraig a été utilisé comme parcours qualificatif pour le British Open, c'est le signe de sa qualité de test, mais que cela n'empêche pas les joueurs moins expérimentés de l'affronter.

Scotscraig Golf Club		1817
Golf Road		
SCO - TAYPORT, Fife DD6 9DZ		
Office	Secrétariat	(44) 01382 - 552 515
Pro shop	Pro-shop	(44) 01382 - 552 855
Fax	Fax	(44) 01382 - 553 130
Situation	Situation	
16 km N of St Andrews (pop. 11 136)		
Annual closure	Fermeture annuelle	no
Weekly closure	Fermeture hebdomadaire	no
Fees main season	Tarifs haute saison	18 holes

	Week days Semaine	We/Bank holidays We/Férié
Individual Individuel	£ 28	£ 33
Couple Couple	£ 56	£ 66
Full weekday: £ 40		

Caddy	Caddy	on request
Electric Trolley	Chariot électrique	no
Buggy	Voiturette	no
Clubs	Clubs	yes
Credit cards Cartes de crédit		no

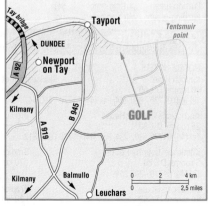

Access Accès : Edinburgh, M90 Jct 3, then A92 and A914 → Dundee. Before Tay Bridge, turn right to Tayport on B945. Golf signposted to left in Tayport.
Map 2 on page 491 Carte 2 Page 491

GOLF COURSE
PARCOURS

16/20

Site	Site	
Maintenance	Entretien	
Architect	Architecte	James Braid (1920s)
Type	Type	links, heathland
Relief	Relief	
Water in play	Eau en jeu	
Exp. to wind	Exposé au vent	
Trees in play	Arbres en jeu	

Scorecard Carte de score	Chp. Chp.	Mens Mess.	Ladies Da.
Length Long.	5960	5960	5960
Par	69	69	74

Advised golfing ability		0 12 24 36
Niveau de jeu recommandé		
Hcp required	Handicap exigé	certificate

CLUB HOUSE & AMENITIES
CLUB HOUSE ET ANNEXES

6/10

Pro shop	Pro-shop	
Driving range	Practice	
Sheltered	couvert	no
On grass	sur herbe	yes
Putting-green	putting-green	yes
Pitching-green	pitching green	no

HOTEL FACILITIES
ENVIRONNEMENT HOTELIER

6/10

HOTELS HÔTELS

Stakis Dundee	Dundee
104 rooms, D £ 90	7 km
Tel (44) 01382 - 22 9271	
Fax (44) 01382 - 200 072	

Shaftesbury	Dundee
12 rooms, D £ 70	7 km
Tel (44) 01382 - 669 216	
Fax (44) 01382 - 641 598	

Travel Inn	Dundee
40 rooms, D £ 40	7 km
Tel (44) 01382 - 20 3240	
Fax (44) 01382 - 568 431	

RESTAURANTS RESTAURANTS

Stakis Dundee	Dundee
Tel (44) 01382 - 229 271	7 km

779

This is the one exception to our rule of featuring only 18-hole courses. Shiskine has only twelve but it is one of the most frequently visited courses by the world's golf designers. There is one blind shot on virtually each hole and signals in every direction telling players when it is safe to play. This is golf in its original pure style and enjoyment (but also with its own idiosyncrasies). The sheep are there to crop the sprinkler-free fairways, which haven't changed at all since the course first opened. That was when Willie Fernie brought the very best out of a space of land without even the most primitive excavator to call on. The greens are amazingly good, when you finally reach them. You need to play here a hundred times in order to fully understand the ins and outs of the course, but who's objecting.

La seule exception à notre règle de ne signaler que des parcours de 18 trous. Le Shiskine n'a que douze trous, mais c'est un des parcours les plus visités par les architectes du monde entier. On trouve un coup aveugle sur pratiquement chaque trou, et des signaux dans tous les sens pour préciser aux joueurs quand ils peuvent jouer en toute sécurité. C'est ici le golf dans sa pureté et son plaisir originels (mais aussi ses excès baroques), avec des moutons pour tondre des fairways sans arrosage, qui n'ont pas bougé depuis la création. Alors, Willie Fernie avait tiré la quintessence d'un espace où il ne disposait pas du moindre engin de terrassement. Les greens y sont d'une surprenante qualité... quand on y parvient enfin. Il faut jouer ici cent fois pour comprendre toutes les astuces, mais on ne demande que çà.

Shiskine Golf & Tennis Club — 1896

Shiskine
SCO - BLACKWATERFOOT, Isle of Arran KA27 8 HA

Office	Secrétariat	(44) 01770 - 860 226
Pro shop	Pro-shop	(44) 01770 - 860 226
Fax	Fax	(44) 01770 - 860 205
Situation	Situation	

Isle of Arran (pop. 4 474)

Annual closure	Fermeture annuelle	no
Weekly closure	Fermeture hebdomadaire	no

Fees main season
Tarifs haute saison 12 holes round

	Week days Semaine	We/Bank holidays We/Férié
Individual Individuel	£ 13	£ 18
Couple Couple	£ 26	£ 36

Caddy	Caddy	no
Electric Trolley	Chariot électrique	no
Buggy	Voiturette	yes
Clubs	Clubs	yes

Credit cards Cartes de crédit — no

Access Accès : Ferry from Ardrossan to Brodick.
Cross island via String Road (20 km)
to village of Blackwaterfoot.
Map 2 on page 490 Carte 2 Page 490

GOLF COURSE / PARCOURS — 17/20

Site	Site	▰▰▰▰▱
Maintenance	Entretien	
Architect	Architecte	Willie Fernie
Type	Type	links
Relief	Relief	▰▰▰▱▱
Water in play	Eau en jeu	▰▱▱▱▱
Exp. to wind	Exposé au vent	▰▰▰▰▱
Trees in play	Arbres en jeu	▰▱▱▱▱

Scorecard Carte de score	Chp. Chp.	Mens Mess.	Ladies Da.
Length Long.	2745	2745	2561
Par	42	42	44

Advised golfing ability		0 12 24 36
Niveau de jeu recommandé		▰▰▰▰
Hcp required	Handicap exigé	no

CLUB HOUSE & AMENITIES / CLUB HOUSE ET ANNEXES — 5/10

Pro shop	Pro-shop	▰▰▰▱▱
Driving range	Practice	▰▰▱▱▱
Sheltered	couvert	no
On grass	sur herbe	no
Putting-green	putting-green	yes
Pitching-green	pitching green	no

HOTEL FACILITIES / ENVIRONNEMENT HOTELIER — 5/10

HOTELS HÔTELS

Kinloch Hotel — Blackwaterfoot
40 rooms, D £ 60 — 1 km
Tel (44) 01770 - 860 444, Fax (44) 01770 - 860 447

Auchrannie Country House — Brodick
26 rooms, D £ 80 — 20 km
Tel (44) 01770 - 302 234, Fax (44) 01770 - 302 812

Kilmichael Country House — Brodick
5 rooms, D £ 80 — 20 km
Tel (44) 01770 - 302 219

Dunvegan House — Brodick
10 rooms, D £ 52 — 20 km
Tel (44) 01770 - 302 811

RESTAURANTS RESTAURANTS

Carraigh Mhor — Lamlash
Tel (44) 01770 - 600 453 — 22 km

780

SOUTHERNESS

18 **6** **5**

A course for connoisseurs off the traditional golfing trail but your journey will be more than rewarded by a superb day out. This is one of the most recent links to date in Scotland, designed by Mackenzie Ross while he was working on Turnberry. The excellence of the design, very elaborate despite the course's natural look, quickly caught the attention of the better players, who appreciate the distinctive layout and the variety of challenge, with a special mention for the 12th, one of the finest par 4s in Scotland. Golfing here can be very enjoyable when the weather is fine, but that doesn't happen all that often. What's more, the holes are always running in different directions, thus calling for constant improvisation. Generally flat with only a few welcome slopes and difficulties that are always visible, this course is well worth the trip.

Un golf de connaisseurs, à l'écart des sentiers traditionnels, mais le déplacement sera récompensé par une superbe journée. C'est l'un des derniers en date des links d'Ecosse, dessiné par Mackenzie Ross alors qu'il ressuscitait Turnberry. La qualité du dessin, très travaillé malgré son apparence naturelle, a vite attiré l'attention des bons joueurs. Ils apprécient la distinction du tracé, la diversité des défis proposés, avec une mention particulière pour le 12, un des plus beaux par 4 d'Ecosse. Le golf peut ici être très plaisant quand le temps est calme, mais ce n'est pas si fréquent. De plus, les trous vont dans des directions toujours différentes, ce qui oblige à un sens constant de l'improvisation. Généralement plat, avec quelques ondulations bienvenues, mais des difficultés toujours visibles, ce parcours vaut le voyage.

Southerness Golf Club	1947
Clubhouse	
SCO - SOUTHERNESS, Dumfries, DG2 8AZ	

Office	Secrétariat	(44) 01387 - 880 677
Pro shop	Pro-shop	(44) 01387 - 880 677
Fax	Fax	(44) 01387 - 880 644
Situation	Situation	
24 km S of Dumfries (pop. 21 164)		
Annual closure	Fermeture annuelle	no
Weekly closure	Fermeture hebdomadaire	no
Fees main season	Tarifs haute saison	full day

	Week days Semaine	We/Bank holidays We/Férié
Individual Individuel	£ 30	£ 40
Couple Couple	£ 60	£ 80

Caddy	Caddy	on request
Electric Trolley	Chariot électrique	no
Buggy	Voiturette	no
Clubs	Clubs	no

Credit cards Cartes de crédit
VISA - Eurocard - MasterCard

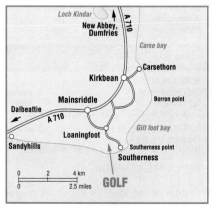

Access Accès : Glasgow M74 to Abbington.
Edinburgh A702 to Abington. Then A74 to Beattock and A701 to Dumfries. Then A710. After Kirkbean, left to Southerness. **Map 2 on page 491** Carte 2 Page 491

GOLF COURSE
PARCOURS
18/20

Site	Site	
Maintenance	Entretien	
Architect	Architecte	Mackenzie Ross
Type	Type	links
Relief	Relief	
Water in play	Eau en jeu	
Exp. to wind	Exposé au vent	
Trees in play	Arbres en jeu	

Scorecard Carte de score	Chp. Chp.	Mens Mess.	Ladies Da.
Length Long.	5975	5556	5116
Par	69	69	73

Advised golfing ability	0	12	24	36
Niveau de jeu recommandé				
Hcp required Handicap exigé	28			

CLUB HOUSE & AMENITIES
CLUB HOUSE ET ANNEXES
6/10

Pro shop	Pro-shop	
Driving range	Practice	
Sheltered	couvert	no
On grass	sur herbe	yes
Putting-green	putting-green	yes
Pitching-green	pitching green	no

HOTEL FACILITIES
ENVIRONNEMENT HOTELIER
5/10

HOTELS HÔTELS
Cairngill House — Sandyhills
7 rooms, D £ 50 — 5 km
Tel (44) 01387 - 780 681

Cairndale Hotel — Dumfries
76 rooms, D £ 80 — 24 km
Tel (44) 01387 - 254 111
Fax (44) 01387 - 250 555

Cavens House — Kirkbean
6 rooms, D £ 56 — 2 km
Tel (44) 01387 - 880 234

781

Notably shorter than its three most prestigious neighbours, the Eden Course is a very respectful course and probably, if not the most forthright then at least the least difficult of the three to figure out first time around, even though the wind will always be there to make things a little harder. This is a more conventional course, laid out in two loops of 9 holes, but the hazards are intelligently placed with a good number of bunkers from which average players will find escaping a little easier than on the other courses around here. Don't underestimate the Eden course, it can be fun playing here when everyone is swarming over the other courses of the golf factory that St Andrews has now become.

Notablement plus court que ses trois voisins les plus prestigieux, l'Eden Course est cependant un parcours plus qu'honorable, et probablement sinon le plus franc des trois, du moins le moins difficile à déchiffrer au premier abord, même si le vent vient tout autant y compliquer les choses. De fait, c'est un parcours plus conventionnel, au point même d'avoir deux boucles de 9 trous, mais les obstacles sont intelligemment placés, les bunkers sont assez nombreux, mais les joueurs moyens pourront en sortir un jour (ce n'est pas toujours facile sur les autres parcours du site !). Il ne faut pas le sous-estimer, et le plaisir de jouer ici n'est pas négligeable quand tout le monde s'agite dans les autres ateliers de cette véritable usine à golf que St Andrews est devenu.

St Andrews Links — 1914

Pilmour Cottage
SCO - ST ANDREWS, Fife, KY16 9SF

Office	Secrétariat	(44) 01334 - 466 666
Pro shop	Pro-shop	
Fax	Fax	(44) 01334 - 477 036
Situation	Situation	

St Andrews (pop. 11 136)
30 km SE of Dundee (pop. 165 873)

Annual closure	Fermeture annuelle	no
Weekly closure	Fermeture hebdomadaire	no

Fees main season	Tarifs haute saison	18 holes
	Week days Semaine	We/Bank holidays We/Férié
Individual Individuel	£ 23	£ 23
Couple Couple	£ 46	£ 46

Caddy	Caddy	£ 28
Electric Trolley	Chariot électrique	no
Buggy	Voiturette	no
Clubs	Clubs	£ 20/18 holes

Credit cards Cartes de crédit
VISA - Eurocard - MasterCard

782

Balmullo
St Andrews bay
GOLF
Guardbridge
Kincaple
A 92
St Andrews
Cupar
A 917
Kemback
Strathkinness
Crail
Blebocraigs
A 939
Graigrothies
Denhead
Peat Inn
0   2   4 km
0   2,5 miles

Access Accès : Edinburgh, M90, Jct 8,
then A91 to St Andrews.
Map 3 on page 493 Carte 3 Page 493

GOLF COURSE PARCOURS — 14/20

Site	Site	
Maintenance	Entretien	
Architect	Architecte	Unknown
Type	Type	links
Relief	Relief	
Water in play	Eau en jeu	
Exp. to wind	Exposé au vent	
Trees in play	Arbres en jeu	

Scorecard Carte de score	Chp. Chp.	Mens Mess.	Ladies Da.
Length Long.	5588	5588	4987
Par	70	70	73

Advised golfing ability		0 12 24 36
Niveau de jeu recommandé		
Hcp required	Handicap exigé	no

CLUB HOUSE & AMENITIES CLUB HOUSE ET ANNEXES — 8/10

Pro shop	Pro-shop	
Driving range	Practice	
Sheltered	couvert	14 mats
On grass	sur herbe	yes
Putting-green	putting-green	yes
Pitching-green	pitching green	yes

HOTEL FACILITIES ENVIRONNEMENT HOTELIER — 8/10

HOTELS HÔTELS
Old Course Hotel — St Andrews
125 rooms, D £ 315 — adjacent
Tel (44) 01334 - 474 371, Fax (44) 01334 - 477 668

Rufflets Country House — St Andrews
25 rooms, D £ 138 — 2 km
Tel (44) 01334 - 472 594, Fax (44) 01334 - 478 703

RESTAURANTS RESTAURANTS

The Peat Inn — Peat Inn
Tel (44) 01334 - 840 206 — 8 km

Grange Inn — St Andrews
Tel (44) 01334 - 472 670 — 2 km

Cellar — Ansruther
Tel (44) 01333 - 310 378 — 17 km

Having celebrated its centenary in 1997, the Jubilee Course has been given a recent face-lift and is now the longest course at St Andrews. Although laid out in a single stretch with no return to the Club House at the 9th, there are no double fairways. The course is a little more hilly and gives some pretty viewpoints in a region which is rather flat. There is little in the way of vegetation on the holes close to the sea if you except tall grass, but this layout requires accurate driving and a lot of concentration. Like the others, the course is run by St Andrews Links Management and the Links Trust which built a very well equipped clubhouse open to all. Needless to say any trip should be organised in advance, especially between April and September.

Centenaire en 1997, le «Jubilee» a bénéficié d'une récente cure de rajeunissement qui en a fait le plus long de St Andrews. On ne trouve pas ici les fameux double fairways, bien que le parcours se déroule aussi d'un seul trait, sans retour au Club-house au 9. On trouve aussi davantage de relief, et donc quelques jolis points de vue dans une région somme toute peu accidentée. Les trous proches de la mer ont une végétation assez limitée, les hautes herbes mises à part, mais l'ensemble demande des drives précis, et généralement beaucoup d'attention. Comme les autres, ce parcours est géré par le St Andrews Links Management, et le Links Trust, qui a construit un Club-house de très bien équipé, et ouvert à tous. Inutile de dire qu'il est nécessaire d'organiser son voyage à l'avance, surtout d'avril à septembre.

St Andrews Links — 1897

Pilmour Cottage
SCO - ST ANDREWS, Fife, KY16 9SF

Office	Secrétariat	(44) 01334 - 466 666
Pro shop	Pro-shop	
Fax	Fax	(44) 01334 - 477 036
Situation	Situation	

St Andrews (pop. 11 136)
30 km SE of Dundee (pop. 165 873)

Annual closure	Fermeture annuelle	no
Weekly closure	Fermeture hebdomadaire	no
Fees main season	Tarifs haute saison	18 holes

	Week days Semaine	We/Bank holidays We/Férié
Individual Individuel	£ 35	£ 35
Couple Couple	£ 70	£ 70

Caddy	Caddy	£ 28
Electric Trolley	Chariot électrique	no
Buggy	Voiturette	no
Clubs	Clubs	£ 20/18 holes

Credit cards Cartes de crédit
VISA - Eurocard - MasterCard

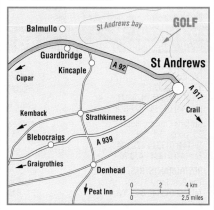

Access Accès : Edinburgh, M90, Jct 8, then A91 to St Andrews.
Map 3 on page 493 Carte 3 Page 493

GOLF COURSE / PARCOURS — 16/20

Site	Site	▮▮▮▮▮▯
Maintenance	Entretien	▮▮▮▮▮▯
Architect	Architecte	Unknown Donald Steel
Type	Type	links
Relief	Relief	▮▮▯▯▯▯
Water in play	Eau en jeu	▮▯▯▯▯▯
Exp. to wind	Exposé au vent	▮▮▮▯▯▯
Trees in play	Arbres en jeu	▮▮▮▯▯▯

Scorecard Carte de score	Chp. Chp.	Mens Mess.	Ladies Da.
Length Long.	6218	5150	5525
Par	72	69	75

Advised golfing ability		0 12 24 36
Niveau de jeu recommandé		▮▮▮▮▮▯
Hcp required	Handicap exigé	no

CLUB HOUSE & AMENITIES / CLUB HOUSE ET ANNEXES — 8/10

Pro shop	Pro-shop	▮▮▮▮▮▯
Driving range	Practice	▮▮▮▮▮▮
Sheltered	couvert	14 mats
On grass	sur herbe	yes
Putting-green	putting-green	yes
Pitching-green	pitching green	yes

783

HOTEL FACILITIES / ENVIRONNEMENT HOTELIER — 8/10

HOTELS HÔTELS

Old Course Hotel — St Andrews
125 rooms, D £ 315 — adjacent
Tel (44) 01334 - 474 371
Fax (44) 01334 - 477 668

Rufflets Country House — St Andrews
25 rooms, D £ 138 — 2 km
Tel (44) 01334 - 472 594
Fax (44) 01334 - 478 703

RESTAURANTS RESTAURANTS

The Peat Inn — Peat Inn
Tel (44) 01334 - 840 206 — 8 km

Grange Inn — St Andrews
Tel (44) 01334 - 472 670 — 2 km

Cellar — Ansruther
Tel (44) 01333 - 310 378 — 17 km

Fortunately, there are several other excellent golf courses at St Andrews when it is impossible to play the Old Course. The New Course is one of them and does not settle for playing second fiddle to its illustrious neighbour. Some local players even consider this their favourite course. At all events it is a very demanding layout, rather similar to the Old Course in its general physiognomy and the way it demands technical skill and powers of invention. Here you don't play the club you need for such and such a distance, rather the club that will roll the ball up to the pin. Hazard-wise there are no trees, naturally, only threatening thick gorse and bunkers like those on the Old Course which collect any ball coming their way. The greens are huge and undulating and the turf a pleasure to walk and play on.

Heureusement, quand il est impossible de jouer le «Old Course», il reste plusieurs excellents autres parcours à St Andrews. Le «New» est de ceux-là, et bien plus que le second violon de son voisin géographique immédiat. On trouve même des joueurs locaux pour en faire leur favori ! C'est en tout cas un parcours très exigeant, assez proche de son aîné pour sa physionomie générale et pour ce qu'il réclame de qualités techniques et de capacités d'invention. Ici, on ne joue pas le club qu'il faut pour telle distance, mais celui qui fera arriver la balle en roulant jusqu'au drapeau. Côté obstacles, pas d'arbres bien sûr, mais des ajoncs menaçants et denses, et aussi des bunkers comme ceux du «Old», qui recueillent toutes les balles qui passent aux alentours. Les greens sont très vastes et ondulés, et le gazon un plaisir à fouler et à jouer.

St Andrews Links — 1895

Pilmour Cottage
SCO - ST ANDREWS, Fife, KY16 9SF

Office	Secrétariat	(44) 01334 - 466 666
Pro shop	Pro-shop	
Fax	Fax	(44) 01334 - 477 036
Situation	Situation	

St Andrews (pop. 11 136)
30 km SE of Dundee (pop. 165 873)

Annual closure	Fermeture annuelle	no
Weekly closure	Fermeture hebdomadaire	no

Fees main season	Tarifs haute saison	18 holes
	Week days Semaine	We/Bank holidays We/Férié
Individual Individuel	£ 35	£ 35
Couple Couple	£ 70	£ 70

Caddy	Caddy	£ 28
Electric Trolley	Chariot électrique	no
Buggy	Voiturette	no
Clubs	Clubs	£ 20/18 holes

Credit cards Cartes de crédit
VISA - Eurocard - MasterCard

784

Access Accès : Edinburgh, M90, Jct 8, then A91 to St Andrews.
Map 3 on page 493 Carte 3 Page 493

GOLF COURSE / PARCOURS — 17/20

Site	Site	
Maintenance	Entretien	
Architect	Architecte	Unknown
Type	Type	links
Relief	Relief	
Water in play	Eau en jeu	
Exp. to wind	Exposé au vent	
Trees in play	Arbres en jeu	

Scorecard Carte de score	Chp. Chp.	Mens Mess.	Ladies Da.
Length Long.	6038	6038	5479
Par	71	71	76

Advised golfing ability
Niveau de jeu recommandé
0   12   24   36

Hcp required   Handicap exigé   24 Men, 36 Ladies

CLUB HOUSE & AMENITIES / CLUB HOUSE ET ANNEXES — 8/10

Pro shop	Pro-shop	
Driving range	Practice	
Sheltered	couvert	14 mats
On grass	sur herbe	yes
Putting-green	putting-green	yes
Pitching-green	pitching green	yes

HOTEL FACILITIES / ENVIRONNEMENT HOTELIER — 8/10

HOTELS HÔTELS
Old Course Hotel — St Andrews
125 rooms, D £ 315 — adjacent
Tel (44) 01334 - 474 371
Fax (44) 01334 - 477 668

Rufflets Country House — St Andrews
25 rooms, D £ 138 — 2 km
Tel (44) 01334 - 472 594
Fax (44) 01334 - 478 703

RESTAURANTS RESTAURANTS
The Peat Inn — Peat Inn
Tel (44) 01334 - 840 206 — 8 km

Grange Inn — St Andrews
Tel (44) 01334 - 472 670 — 2 km

Cellar — Ansruther
Tel (44) 01333 - 310 378 — 17 km

Is there anything left to write about the Old Course? The world's most famous venue is a public course even though you do need to be patient if you want to play here. It is well thought of to say that this is the greatest course in the British Isles, so often in the public eye that when you come here for the first time you get the impression you have already played it. Be wise and take a caddy, as the devilish subtleties, traps, double fairways and double greens make every decision a tough one. The work of no real designer, the Old Course has been shaped by the passing centuries, the wind, champions and green-keepers. The atmosphere alone is enough to intimidate or even terrorise amateurs stepping onto the first tee. But if you disregard the «religiousness» of this hallowed site there are, dare we say it, many more challenging links courses when the weather is calm (may the gods of golf forgive us). You cannot not play the Old Course.

Est-il encore possible d'écrire sur l'Old Course ? Le plus célèbre parcours du monde, est un golf public, même s'il faut de la patience pour pouvoir le jouer. Il est bien vu de dire que c'est le plus grand parcours des Iles Britanniques, tellement montré qu'on a l'impression de déjà l'avoir joué quand on vient pour la première fois. Mais il reste prudent de prendre un caddie car ses diaboliques subtilités, ses pièges, ses double fairways et double greens rendent difficiles toutes les décisions. Sans véritable architecte, le «Old» a été admirablement façonné par les siècles, le vent, les champions, les green-keepers, et rien que son atmosphère rend les amateurs sinon terrorisés, du moins intimidés au départ du 1. Si l'on fait abstraction de la «religiosité du lieu», il est des links bien plus exigeants, quand le temps est calme. Mais a t-on le droit de le dire sans aller en enfer ? L'Old Course est inévitable.

St Andrews Links — XVth Century

Pilmour Cottage
SCO - ST ANDREWS, Fife, KY16 9SF

Office	Secrétariat	(44) 01334 - 466 666
Pro shop	Pro-shop	
Fax	Fax	(44) 01334 - 477 036
Situation	Situation	

St Andrews (pop. 11 136)
30 km SE of Dundee (pop. 165 873)

Annual closure	Fermeture annuelle	no
Weekly closure	Fermeture hebdomadaire	no
Fees main season	Tarifs haute saison	18 holes

	Week days Semaine	We/Bank holidays We/Férié
Individual Individuel	£ 75	£ 75
Couple Couple	£ 150	£ 150

Caddy	Caddy	£ 28
Electric Trolley	Chariot électrique	no
Buggy	Voiturette	no
Clubs	Clubs	£ 20/18 holes

Credit cards Cartes de crédit
VISA - Eurocard - MasterCard

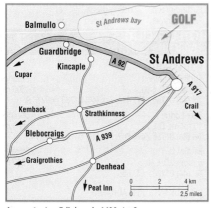

GOLF

Balmullo
St Andrews bay
Guardbridge
Kincaple — A 92 — **St Andrews**
Cupar
A 917
Kemback
Strathkinness
Crail
Blebocraigs — A 939
Graigrothies
Denhead
Peat Inn

0 — 2 — 4 km
0 — 2,5 miles

Access Accès : Edinburgh, M90, Jct 8, then A91 to St Andrews.
Map 3 on page 493 Carte 3 Page 493

GOLF COURSE / PARCOURS — 18/20

Site	Site	
Maintenance	Entretien	
Architect	Architecte	Unknown
Type	Type	links
Relief	Relief	
Water in play	Eau en jeu	
Exp. to wind	Exposé au vent	
Trees in play	Arbres en jeu	

Scorecard Carte de score	Chp. Chp.	Mens Mess.	Ladies Da.
Length Long.	6300	6004	5512
Par	72	72	76

Advised golfing ability
Niveau de jeu recommandé   0   12   24   36

Hcp required   Handicap exigé   24 Men, 36 Ladies

CLUB HOUSE & AMENITIES / CLUB HOUSE ET ANNEXES — 8/10

Pro shop	Pro-shop	
Driving range	Practice	
Sheltered	couvert	14 mats
On grass	sur herbe	yes
Putting-green	putting-green	yes
Pitching-green	pitching green	yes

785

HOTEL FACILITIES / ENVIRONNEMENT HOTELIER — 8/10

HOTELS HÔTELS
Old Course Hotel — St Andrews adjacent
125 rooms, D £ 315
Tel (44) 01334 - 474 371
Fax (44) 01334 - 477 668

Rufflets Country House — St Andrews 2 km
25 rooms, D £ 138
Tel (44) 01334 - 472 594
Fax (44) 01334 - 478 703

RESTAURANTS RESTAURANTS
The Peat Inn — Peat Inn 8 km
Tel (44) 01334 - 840 206

Grange Inn — St Andrews 2 km
Tel (44) 01334 - 472 670

Cellar — Ansruther 17 km
Tel (44) 01333 - 310 378

In the shadow of Stirling castle, this is the gateway to the Highlands, a strategic position of key importance in the never-ending battles between the English and Scots. The city is also a sort of strategic point for setting out to play golf in all directions. This privileged position also works wonders for the charm of the golf course, despite being one of the lesser known in the region. It is still very interesting to play, even more so when you set out to play well. Designed and developed by James Braid and Henry Cotton, this is one of a whole host of courses in the UK where yardage is a little limited and which sometimes could do with a little updating to give a new lease of life (with all due respect, naturally). Having said that, the space available here was limited and the architects made intelligent use of what they had. As for the club-house, let's say that you are perhaps better off admiring the countryside rather than the architecture (very functional).

A l'ombre du château de Stirling, c'est la porte des Highlands, une position stratégique capitale dans les incessantes batailles entre l'Angleterre et l'Ecosse. La ville est aussi une sorte de point stratégique pour aller jouer vers tous les points cardinaux. Cette situation privilégiée fait beaucoup pour le charme du parcours, bien qu'il ne soit pas l'un des plus connus de la région. Il est pourtant très intéressant à jouer, et plus encore à tenter de bien y jouer. Dessiné et développé par James Braid et Henry Cotton, il fait partie de cette cohorte de parcours de Grande Bretagne à la longueur un peu limitée, et qui auraient parfois besoin d'un (respectueux) coup de jeunesse pour prendre un nouvel élan. Cela dit, l'espace disponible n'était pas immense, et les architectes en ont tiré un parti intelligent. Pour finir, il vaut mieux regarder le paysage que l'architecture (fonctionnelle) du Club house...

Stirling Golf Club — 1869

Queen's Road
SCO - STIRLING, FK8 3AA

Office	Secrétariat	(44) 01786 - 464 098
Pro shop	Pro-shop	(44) 01786 - 471 490
Fax	Fax	(44) 01786 - 450 748
Situation	Situation	

1 km from Stirling (pop. 30 515)

Annual closure	Fermeture annuelle	no
Weekly closure	Fermeture hebdomadaire	no
Fees main season	Tarifs haute saison	18 holes

	Week days Semaine	We/Bank holidays We/Férié
Individual Individuel	£ 20	£ 20
Couple Couple	£ 40	£ 40
Full day: £ 30		

Caddy	Caddy	no
Electric Trolley	Chariot électrique	no
Buggy	Voiturette	no
Clubs	Clubs	£ 12/18 holes

Credit cards Cartes de crédit
VISA - Eurocard - MasterCard - AMEX

786

Access Accès : Edinburgh, M9 Jct 10 → Stirling.
First road on the right, follow signs to Golf Course
Map 2 on page 490 Carte 2 Page 490

GOLF COURSE / PARCOURS — 13/20

Site	Site	
Maintenance	Entretien	
Architect	Architecte	James Braid C.K. Cotton
Type	Type	parkland
Relief	Relief	
Water in play	Eau en jeu	
Exp. to wind	Exposé au vent	
Trees in play	Arbres en jeu	

Scorecard Carte de score	Chp. Chp.	Mens Mess.	Ladies Da.
Length Long.	5858	5858	5858
Par	72	72	74

Advised golfing ability
Niveau de jeu recommandé   0   12   24   36

Hcp required   Handicap exigé   no

CLUB HOUSE & AMENITIES / CLUB HOUSE ET ANNEXES — 6/10

Pro shop	Pro-shop	
Driving range	Practice	
Sheltered	couvert	no
On grass	sur herbe	yes
Putting-green	putting-green	yes
Pitching-green	pitching green	yes

HOTEL FACILITIES / ENVIRONNEMENT HOTELIER — 7/10

HOTELS HÔTELS

Stirling Highland — Stirling
70 rooms, D £ 90 — 500 m
Tel (44) 01786 - 475 444, Fax (44) 01786 - 462 929

Park Lodge — Stirling
10 rooms, D £ 75 — 500 m
Tel (44) 01786 - 474 862, Fax (44) 01786 - 449 748

Fairfield — Stirling
6 rooms, D £ 40 — 800 m
Tel (44) 01786 - 472 685

RESTAURANTS RESTAURANTS

Regent (Chinese) — Stirling
Tel (44) 01786 - 472 513 — 600 m

Park Lodge — Stirling
Tel (44) 01786 - 474 862 — 500 m

13	5	5

The clubhouse is not as comfortable and facilities not as comprehensive as continental golfers prefer, but this course is so far off the beaten track that you don't really mind. It lies on a sort of platform atop some often wind-swept cliffs. When it is stormy, just settle for the view. By contrast when the sun shines, you'll see that the difficulties are more psychological than real and there are enough of them for the designer not to have added any more. This is evidently not a course for beginners, who would be best advised to take the day off, pull someone's cart or take a lesson or two. Basically, this has to be one of the courses where playing to your handicap is the toughest, even though the course is not long. There are seven par 3s, each one a real handful.

Le Clubhouse n'est pas aussi confortable et les services pas aussi complets que les golfeurs continentaux le souhaitent, mais ce parcours semble tellement à l'écart du monde qu'on ne se pose pas ces questions. Il est situé sur une sorte de plate-forme au sommet des falaises, souvent très ventée : les jours de tempête, il faut se contenter de regarder. En revanche, par beau temps, on peut apprécier que les difficultés sont encore plus psychologiques que réelles. D'ailleurs, elles sont assez nombreuses au naturel pour que l'architecte n'en ait pas rajouté. Evidemment, ce n'est pas un parcours pour débutants : ce jour-là, ils tireront le chariot et prendront une leçon. En fin de compte, c'est sans doute un des parcours où il est le plus difficile de jouer son handicap, bien qu'il ne soit pas long... Il y a sept par 3, pas faciles.

Stonehaven Golf Club — 1888

Cowie
SCO - STONEHAVEN, Aberdeenshire AB39 3RH

Office	Secrétariat	(44) 01569 - 762 124
Pro shop	Pro-shop	
Fax	Fax	(44) 01569 - 765 973
Situation	Situation	

25 km S of Aberdeen (pop. 204 885)

Annual closure	Fermeture annuelle	no
Weekly closure	Fermeture hebdomadaire	no

Fees main season	Tarifs haute saison	18 holes
	Week days Semaine	We/Bank holidays We/Férié
Individual Individuel	£ 15	£ 20
Couple Couple	£ 30	£ 40

£ 10 after 4.00 pm - No visitors on Saturdays

Caddy	Caddy	no
Electric Trolley	Chariot électrique	no
Buggy	Voiturette	no
Clubs	Clubs	yes

Credit cards Cartes de crédit VISA - Mastercard

Access Accès : A92 S of Aberdeen,
Golf 1.5 km (1 m.) before Stonehaven.
Map 1 on page 489 Carte 1 Page 489

GOLF COURSE
PARCOURS — 13/20

Site	Site	
Maintenance	Entretien	
Architect	Architecte	George Duncan
Type	Type	seaside course
Relief	Relief	
Water in play	Eau en jeu	
Exp. to wind	Exposé au vent	
Trees in play	Arbres en jeu	

Scorecard Carte de score	Chp. Chp.	Mens Mess.	Ladies Da.
Length Long.	4664	4390	4103
Par	66	64	68

Advised golfing ability Niveau de jeu recommandé	0	12	24	36

Hcp required Handicap exigé certificate

CLUB HOUSE & AMENITIES
CLUB HOUSE ET ANNEXES — 5/10

Pro shop	Pro-shop	
Driving range	Practice	
Sheltered	couvert	no
On grass	sur herbe	no
Putting-green	putting-green	yes
Pitching-green	pitching green	yes

787

HOTEL FACILITIES
ENVIRONNEMENT HOTELIER — 5/10

HOTELS HÔTELS

Muchalls Castle 8 rooms, D £ 120 Tel (44) 01569 - 731 170 Fax (44) 01569 - 731 480	Stonehaven 5 km
Raemoir House 20 rooms, from D £ 85 Tel (44) 01330 - 824 884 Fax (44) 01330 - 822 171	Banchory 15 km
Tor-Na-Coille 24 rooms, from D £ 76 Tel (44) 01330 - 822 242 Fax (44) 01330 - 824 012	Banchory 15 km

RESTAURANTS RESTAURANTS

Lairhillock Tel (44) 01569 - 730 001	Netherley 10 km

STRATHAVEN

15	7	6

Located some 22 miles from Glasgow, this is one of those gems tucked away in the west of Scotland. It is an inland course with more than a touch of heathland in a layout which winds its way between fir trees and long established woodland. The layout was extended to 18 holes in 1965 in a style that is very much in keeping with the original course. Bunkers are strategically located and the rough very penalising, both of which call for careful game strategy. For many, this is a course for accurate drivers, sometimes a little treacherous, which needs to be played several times over before getting to grips with the traps and appreciating its many qualities. Even when you reach the very tricky greens, you are still not through because you need a magic putter here to pick up strokes. Many high-level tournaments have been played here, a token of the course's overall excellence.

A quelques 45 km de Glasgow, c'est un des petits bijoux cachés à l'ouest de l'Ecosse, et un parcours «inland» dont le dessin s'insinue entre les sapins et un paysage boisé. Le tracé a été porté à 18 trous en 1965, dans un style qui reste très cohérent avec l'original. Les bunkers sont stratégiquement placés et le rough très pénalisant, ce qui oblige à bien réfléchir sur la tactique à mettre en oeuvre. C'est pour beaucoup un parcours de drivers précis, parfois un peu traître, et il faut jouer plusieurs fois pour en comprendre à la fois les pièges et en savourer toutes les qualités. Et une fois arrivé sur des greens très subtils, le travail n'est pas fini, il faut un toucher d'orfèvre pour y gagner des points. De nombreux bons tournois ont été disputés ici, c'est une marque de qualité.

Strathaven Golf Club — 1908

Overton Avenue, Glasgow Road
SCO - STRATHAVEN, Strathclyde, ML10 6NL

Office	Secrétariat	(44) 01357 - 520 421
Pro shop	Pro-shop	(44) 01357 - 521 812
Fax	Fax	(44) 01357 - 570 539
Situation	Situation	

12 km SE of East Kilbride (pop. 73 378)

Annual closure	Fermeture annuelle	no
Weekly closure	Fermeture hebdomadaire	no

Fees main season
Tarifs haute saison full day

	Week days Semaine	We/Bank holidays We/Férié
Individual Individuel	£ 35	—
Couple Couple	£ 70	—

Weekends: members only

Caddy	Caddy	no
Electric Trolley	Chariot électrique	no
Buggy	Voiturette	no
Clubs	Clubs	no
Credit cards Cartes de crédit		no

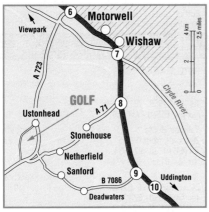

Access Accès : Glasgow, A726.
Golf in the outskirts of Strathaven city.
Map 3 on page 492 Carte 3 Page 492

788

GOLF COURSE PARCOURS — 15/20

Site	Site	
Maintenance	Entretien	
Architect	Architecte	Willie Fernie J.R. Stutt
Type	Type	parkland
Relief	Relief	
Water in play	Eau en jeu	
Exp. to wind	Exposé au vent	
Trees in play	Arbres en jeu	

Scorecard Carte de score	Chp. Chp.	Mens Mess.	Ladies Da.
Length Long.	5665	5665	5066
Par	71	71	73

Advised golfing ability
Niveau de jeu recommandé

0 12 24 36

Hcp required Handicap exigé 28 Men, 36 Ladies

CLUB HOUSE & AMENITIES
CLUB HOUSE ET ANNEXES — 7/10

Pro shop	Pro-shop	
Driving range	Practice	
Sheltered	couvert	no
On grass	sur herbe	no
Putting-green	putting-green	yes
Pitching-green	pitching green	no

HOTEL FACILITIES
ENVIRONNEMENT HOTELIER — 6/10

HOTELS HÔTELS

Strathaven Hotel — Strathaven
22 rooms, D £ 75 — 2 km
Tel (44) 01357 - 521 778

Stakis East Kilbride — East Kilbride
73 rooms, D £ 90 — 5 km
Tel (44) 01357 - 36 300, Fax (44) 01357 - 33 552

Stuart — East Kilbride
38 rooms, D £ 75 — 2 km
Tel (44) 01357 - 21 161, Fax (44) 01357 - 64 410

RESTAURANTS RESTAURANTS

Simpsons (Stakis) — East Kilbride
Tel (44) 01357 - 36 300 — 5 km

Waterside Inn — Strathaven

Although it doesn't have the aura of Dornoch, Tain is worth much more than just a casual visit. All the more so in that green-keeping here is on a par with that found at «posher» courses. The site is superb and very quiet and the alternating heather and seaside holes produce a variety of landscapes, but playing here always requires a shrewd brain. Nothing is given away and players constantly have to adapt to new problems. The greens are never very large and the tricky breaks can be disastrous if you're not really careful. Ongoing work in the clubhouse should enhance still further the enjoyment of playing here, especially considering the value for money and warm welcome.

Sans avoir l'aura de Dornoch, Tain mérite néanmoins bien plus qu'un regard distrait. Et d'autant plus que l'entretien rivalise généralement avec celui de parcours plus huppés. Le site en est superbe et très tranquille, l'alternance de trous de links et de trous dans la bruyère apporte une variété de paysages, mais le jeu doit constamment être réfléchi. Rien n'est donné, et le joueur doit sans cesse s'adapter à de nouveaux problèmes. Les greens ne sont jamais très grands, et leurs subtiles ondulations peuvent provoquer des désastres si l'on n'y prête pas attention. Les travaux en cours au Club house devraient augmenter encore le plaisir que l'on éprouve ici, d'autant que le rapport qualité-prix-accueil est très favorable !

Tain Golf Club — 1890

Chapel Road
SCO - TAIN, Ross-shire, IV19 1PA

Office	Secrétariat	(44) 01862 - 892 314
Pro shop	Pro-shop	(44) 01862 - 893 313
Fax	Fax	
Situation	Situation	

56 km N of Inverness (pop. 62 186)
1 km of Tain (pop. 4 540)

Annual closure	Fermeture annuelle	no
Weekly closure	Fermeture hebdomadaire	no
Fees main season	Tarifs haute saison	18 holes

	Week days Semaine	We/Bank holidays We/Férié
Individual Individuel	£ 24	£ 30
Couple Couple	£ 48	£ 60

Full day: £ 30/£ 36 pp

Caddy	Caddy	on request
Electric Trolley	Chariot électrique	yes
Buggy	Voiturette	£ 20/18 holes
Clubs	Clubs	yes

Credit cards Cartes de crédit VISA - MasterCard

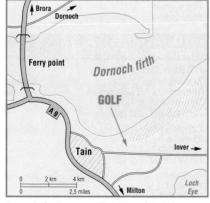

Access Accès : Inverness, A9 → Dornoch to Tain.
From Tain town centre,
down Castle Brae over railway, past cemetery
Map 1 on page 488 Carte 1 Page 488

GOLF COURSE PARCOURS — 17/20

Site	Site	
Maintenance	Entretien	
Architect	Architecte	Tom Morris
Type	Type	links, heathland
Relief	Relief	
Water in play	Eau en jeu	
Exp. to wind	Exposé au vent	
Trees in play	Arbres en jeu	

Scorecard Carte de score	Chp. Chp.	Mens Mess.	Ladies Da.
Length Long.	5855	5586	5170
Par	71	70	73

Advised golfing ability		0 12 24 36
Niveau de jeu recommandé		
Hcp required	Handicap exigé	no

CLUB HOUSE & AMENITIES CLUB HOUSE ET ANNEXES — 6/10

Pro shop	Pro-shop	
Driving range	Practice	
Sheltered	couvert	no
On grass	sur herbe	no
Putting-green	putting-green	yes
Pitching-green	pitching green	yes

HOTEL FACILITIES ENVIRONNEMENT HOTELIER — 6/10

HOTELS HÔTELS

Morangie House — Tain
26 rooms, D £ 80 — 0.5 km
Tel (44) 01862 - 892 281, Fax (44) 01862 - 892 872

Mansfield House — Tain
17 rooms, D £ 80 — 0.5 km
Tel (44) 01862 - 892 052, Fax (44) 01862 - 892 260

Golf View House — Tain
5 rooms, D £ 40 — 0.5 km
Tel (44) 01862 - 892 856

RESTAURANTS RESTAURANTS

Morangie Hotel — Tain
Tel (44) 01862 - 892 281 — 0.5 km

Mansfield House — Tain
Tel (44) 01862 - 892 052 — 0.5 km

789

TAYMOUTH CASTLE

13	4	6

James Braid made the best possible use of limited space and restricted potential for contouring generally flat terrain. But even he was hard put to avoid a number of up and down holes and a hint of monotony. Whenever the course moves on to higher ground, the standard of the holes follows suit. In such an attractive region as this, the landscape is an added value of prime importance with the surrounding woods and hills. As the winter months are pretty wet here, even by Scottish standards, the best time to play is in summer or early autumn, for the colours. Most of the very many trees line and define the fairways, but some interfere to the point where they may be considered as hazards. Hit the ball in the right direction off the tee to keep out of trouble. This is not a great course, but there are few others in the immediate neighbourhood and, when all is said and done, this is a good layout despite the overall sobriety.

James Braid a tiré le meilleur parti possible d'un espace assez limité et de possibilités restreintes de modelage d'un terrain généralement plat. Mais il lui était difficile d'éviter un certain nombre d'allers et retours et une légère monotonie. Dès que le parcours s'élève un peu, la qualité des trous fait de même. Dans une région aussi attrayante, le paysage est une valeur ajoutée de premier ordre, avec les bois et les collines environnants. Les mois d'hiver étant assez humides - même pour un Ecossais - on viendra ici en été ou en début d'automne, pour les couleurs. La plupart des nombreux arbres longent et définissent les fairways, mais certains empiètent assez pour prendre le statut d'obstacles : il est alors sage de bien étudier la trajectoire des coups de départ. En définitive, ce n'est pas un «grand» parcours, mais il y en a peu dans les environs immédiats, et celui-ci est de qualité, dans sa sobriété.

Taymouth Castle Golf Course 1923

Kenmore
SCO - ABERFELDY, Perthshire PH15 2NT

Office	Secrétariat	(44) 01887 - 830 228
Pro shop	Pro-shop	(44) 01887 - 830 228
Fax	Fax	(44) 01887 - 830 765
Situation	Situation	

60 km NW of Perth (pop. 123 495)
9 km W of Aberfeldy (pop. 4 083)

Annual closure	Fermeture annuelle	no
Weekly closure	Fermeture hebdomadaire	no

Clubhouse closed 11 → 03

Fees main season	Tarifs haute saison	18 holes

	Week days Semaine	We/Bank holidays We/Férié
Individual Individuel	£ 17	£ 21
Couple Couple	£ 34	£ 42

Caddy	Caddy	no
Electric Trolley	Chariot électrique	no
Buggy	Voiturette	£ 15/18 holes
Clubs	Clubs	£ 10/18 holes
Credit cards Cartes de crédit		no

790

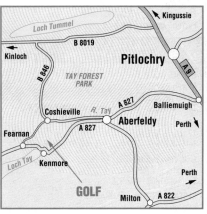

Access Accès : Perth, A9 North to Ballinluig, then A827 through Aberfeldy. Kenmore is approx. 9 km farther on the same road. **Map 1 on page 489** Carte 1 Page 489

GOLF COURSE PARCOURS 13/20

Site	Site	▬▬▬▬▬
Maintenance	Entretien	▬▬▬▬
Architect	Architecte	James Braid
Type	Type	parkland
Relief	Relief	▬▬
Water in play	Eau en jeu	▬
Exp. to wind	Exposé au vent	▬▬▬
Trees in play	Arbres en jeu	▬▬▬▬

Scorecard Carte de score	Chp. Chp.	Mens Mess.	Ladies Da.
Length Long.	5520	5220	4598
Par	69	69	72

Advised golfing ability Niveau de jeu recommandé	0	12	24	36
Hcp required	Handicap exigé	no		

CLUB HOUSE & AMENITIES CLUB HOUSE ET ANNEXES 4/10

Pro shop	Pro-shop	▬▬▬▬
Driving range	Practice	▬▬
Sheltered	couvert	no
On grass	sur herbe	no
Putting-green	putting-green	yes
Pitching-green	pitching green	no

HOTEL FACILITIES ENVIRONNEMENT HOTELIER 6/10

HOTELS HÔTELS

Kenmore Hotel — Kenmore, close
39 rooms, D £ 125 (with dinner)
Tel (44) 01887 - 830 205
Fax (44) 01887 - 830 262

Farleyer House — Aberfeldy, 5 km
15 rooms, D £ 150
Tel (44) 01887 - 820 332
Fax (44) 01887 - 829 430

The Weem — Aberfeldy, 7 km
8 rooms, D £ 50
Tel (44) 01887 - 820 381
Fax (44) 01887 - 820 187

RESTAURANTS RESTAURANTS

Farleyer House — Aberfeldy, 5 km
Tel (44) 01887 - 820 332

After the city, seaside and sometimes upland courses, here we are out in the country with some pretty views over the surrounding hills. Created by Willie Fernie and then restyled in 1979, this is a very short but rather technical layout designed more for families or friendly rounds but also completed with remarkable concern for quality. You need to be accurate because the greens are small and often treacherous and multi-tiered. Although rather hilly, it is still very much a rural park and its difficulties shouldn't be taken lightly. Judging by the success of the club's prodigal son Andrew Coltart, this is a good course to learn on. The clubhouse of this «village course» is unpretentious but warm. Close by, art enthusiasts will visit Drumlanrig Castle which houses a fine collection of paintings and mementoes of Bonnie Prince Charlie.

Après les golfs des villes, du bord de mer, des montagnes parfois aussi, nous voici à la campagne, avec de jolies vues sur les collines alentour. Créé par Willie Fernie, remanié en 1979, c'est un tracé très court, assez technique, très orienté vers le jeu en famille ou entre amis, mais avec un souci de qualité à remarquer. Il faut être précis, car les greens sont petits, souvent assez traîtres, parfois à plateaux. Assez accidenté, il conserve néanmoins un caractère de parc rural, et il ne faut pas prendre à la légère ses difficultés. Si l'on en juge par la réussite de l'enfant du club, Andrew Coltart, c'est un parcours formateur. Le Clubhouse de ce «golf de village» est modeste, mais chaleureux. A proximité, les amateurs d'art visiteront le Drumlanrig Castle, avec une riche collection de peinture et des souvenirs du Bonnie Prince Charlie.

Thornhill Golf Club — 1893

Blacknest
SCO - THORNHILL, Dumfries-shire DG3 5DW

Office	Secrétariat	(44) 01848 - 330 546
Pro shop	Pro-shop	
Fax	Fax	
Situation	Situation	

22 km NW of Dumfries (pop. 21 164)

Annual closure	Fermeture annuelle	no
Weekly closure	Fermeture hebdomadaire	no

Fees main season
Tarifs haute saison full day

	Week days Semaine	We/Bank holidays We/Férié
Individual Individuel	£ 22	£ 28
Couple Couple	£ 44	£ 56

Caddy	Caddy	no
Electric Trolley	Chariot électrique	no
Buggy	Voiturette	no
Clubs	Clubs	on request

Credit cards Cartes de crédit — no

GOLF

Sanquhar — A 702 — Dalveen — River Nith

Thornhill — Mitchellslacks

Burnhead — A 702 — Gatelawbridge — Loch Ettrick

Moniaive — A 76 — Campie

Closeburnmill

Closeburn — Park — Chanterelle Burn

0 — 2 — 4 km
0 — 2,5 miles — Dumfries

Access Accès : Glasgow, M74 - Edinburgh A702. In Abington, A74, then A702 to Thornhill. Golf on A76 (turn East in middle of village).
Map 2 on page 491 Carte 2 Page 491

GOLF COURSE / PARCOURS — 15/20

Site	Site	
Maintenance	Entretien	
Architect	Architecte	Willie Fernie
Type	Type	heathland, parkland
Relief	Relief	
Water in play	Eau en jeu	
Exp. to wind	Exposé au vent	
Trees in play	Arbres en jeu	

Scorecard Carte de score	Chp. Chp.	Mens Mess.	Ladies Da.
Length Long.	5562	5562	4925
Par	71	71	74

Advised golfing ability
Niveau de jeu recommandé — 0 12 24 36

Hcp required Handicap exigé — 28 Men, 36 Ladies

CLUB HOUSE & AMENITIES / CLUB HOUSE ET ANNEXES — 6/10

Pro shop	Pro-shop	
Driving range	Practice	
Sheltered	couvert	no
On grass	sur herbe	yes
Putting-green	putting-green	yes
Pitching-green	pitching green	no

791

HOTEL FACILITIES / ENVIRONNEMENT HOTELIER — 5/10

HOTELS HÔTELS

Blackaddie House — Sanquhar
10 rooms, D £ 60 — 19 km
Tel (44) 01659 - 50 270
Fax (44) 01659 - 50 270

Cairndale — Dumfries
76 rooms, D £ 105 — 22 km
Tel (44) 01387 - 254 111
Fax (44) 01387 - 250 155

Station — Dumfries
32 rooms, D £ 80 — 22 km
Tel (44) 01387 - 254 316
Fax (44) 01387 - 250 388

Regularly playing host to the British Open has forged this course's reputation as one of the world's greatest championship venues. The course is located at the southernmost end of a majestic series of links in Ayrshire and offers a splendid view over the Isle of Arran, the dark and mysterious Mull of Kintyre and the rock of Ailsa. Try and play here in fine weather (it happens more often than you might imagine) as the wind can make this a hellish course to handle. After an almost innocent first few holes, you soon find the sea down the left for the 8 most spectacular holes with the famous lighthouse, but the finish is no less gripping. Brought back to life after the war thanks to the work of MacKenzie Ross, the Ailsa course is challenging, untamed and beguiling. It simply has to be experienced at least once in a lifetime, at any price (and here it is not just any price). A course to savour from end to end, without worrying too much about your card.

La venue régulière du British Open a fait sa réputation parmi les plus grands parcours de championnat au monde. Situé dans la partie la plus au sud d'une série majestueuse de links de l'Ayrshire, il offre un spectacle splendide sur l'île d'Arran, le sombre et mystérieux Mull of Kintyre et le rocher d'Ailsa. A savourer par beau temps (plus fréquent qu'on ne le croit !), car le vent peut transformer le parcours en enfer du jeu. Après un départ presque innocent, on trouve vite la mer à main gauche, pour les huit trous les plus spectaculaires, avec le célèbre phare, mais la conclusion n'est pas moins prenante. Ressuscité après la guerre grâce au travail de MacKenzie Ross, l'Ailsa est exigeant, sauvage, enchanteur, il constitue une expérience à connaître au moins une fois dans sa vie, à n'importe quel prix (c'est effectivement le cas...). Un parcours à savourer de bout en bout, sans trop penser au score.

Turnberry Hotel Golf Courses 1903
SCO - TURNBERRY, Ayrshire, KA26 9LT

Office	Secrétariat	(44) 01655 - 331 000
Pro shop	Pro-shop	(44) 01655 - 334 048
Fax	Fax	(44) 01655 - 331 069
Situation	Situation	

24 km S of Ayr (pop. 47 872)

Annual closure	Fermeture annuelle	no
Weekly closure	Fermeture hebdomadaire	no
Fees main season	Tarifs haute saison	18 holes

	Week days Semaine	We/Bank holidays We/Férié
Individual Individuel	£ 120*	£ 150*
Couple Couple	£ 240	£ 300

* Hotel residents: £ 90 pp

Caddy	Caddy	£ 25
Electric Trolley	Chariot électrique	no
Buggy	Voiturette	no
Clubs	Clubs	£ 40/day

Credit cards Cartes de crédit
VISA - Eurocard - MasterCard - AMEX - DC

792

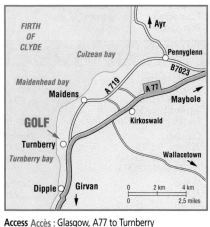

FIRTH OF CLYDE
Ayr
Culzean bay
Pennyglenn
B7023
Maidenhead bay
Maidens
A 719
A 77
Maybole
GOLF
Kirkoswald
Turnberry
Turnberry bay
Wallacetown
Dipple
Girvan
0   2 km   4 km
0   2,5 miles

Access Accès : Glasgow, A77 to Turnberry
Map 3 on page 492 Carte 3 Page 492

GOLF COURSE PARCOURS 19/20

Site	Site	
Maintenance	Entretien	
Architect	Architecte	Mackenzie Ross, remod. in 1945
Type	Type	links
Relief	Relief	
Water in play	Eau en jeu	
Exp. to wind	Exposé au vent	
Trees in play	Arbres en jeu	

Scorecard Carte de score	Chp. Chp.	Mens Mess.	Ladies Da.
Length Long.	6348	5860	5239
Par	70	69	75

Advised golfing ability   0   12   24   36
Niveau de jeu recommandé
Hcp required   Handicap exigé   no

CLUB HOUSE & AMENITIES CLUB HOUSE ET ANNEXES 9/10

Pro shop	Pro-shop	
Driving range	Practice	
Sheltered	couvert	no
On grass	sur herbe	yes
Putting-green	putting-green	yes
Pitching-green	pitching green	yes

HOTEL FACILITIES ENVIRONNEMENT HOTELIER 8/10

HOTELS HÔTELS
Turnberry Hotel
132 rooms, from D £ 200   on site
Tel (44) 01655 - 331 000
Fax (44) 01655 - 331 706

RESTAURANTS RESTAURANTS
3 restaurants   at the Hotel
Tel (44) 01655 - 331 000

If it were located anywhere else than beside one of the world's greatest courses, Arran would be considered to be a course of very considerable merit. Shorter than Ailsa and better protected from the sea but not the wind, there is no shortage of charm or technical challenge. Golfers who take it only as a warm-up round before playing the Ailsa course are in for a shock, as this is a worthy adversary for any player. And an ideal companion to Ailsa for a bit of a breather before turning into one of the world's most delightful grand hotels with white walls and red tiled roof. Okay, so you have to dig into your savings to play and stay here, but if there are places in this world where pecuniary considerations come last, this has to be one of them.

S'il était situé ailleurs qu'à côté d'un des plus grands parcours du monde, l'Arran serait considéré comme un parcours de très grand mérite. Plus court que l'Ailsa Course, plus protégé de la mer, mais pas vraiment du vent, il ne manque ni de charme, ni surtout de propositions techniques à résoudre. Ceux qui croient y trouver seulement une occasion de s'échauffer avant de jouer l'Ailsa risquent les désillusions : c'est un adversaire de valeur pour n'importe quel joueur. Et un complément idéal pour reprendre son souffle, avant de rejoindre l'un des grands hôtels les plus attachants au monde, avec ses murs blanchis et ses toits de tuiles rousses. Certes, il faut casser sa tirelire pour séjourner et jouer ici, mais s'il y a des endroits sans prix, celui-ci en fait partie.

Turnberry Hotel Golf Courses
SCO - TURNBERRY, Ayrshire, KA26 9LT

Office	Secrétariat	(44) 01655 - 331 000
Pro shop	Pro-shop	(44) 01655 - 334 048
Fax	Fax	(44) 01655 - 331 069
Situation	Situation	

24 km S of Ayr (pop. 47 872)

Annual closure	Fermeture annuelle	no
Weekly closure	Fermeture hebdomadaire	no

Fees main season	Tarifs haute saison	18 holes
	Week days	We/Bank holidays
	Semaine	We/Férié
Individual Individuel	£ 55*	£ 55*
Couple Couple	£ 110	£ 110

Hotel residents: £ 40 pp

Caddy	Caddy	£ 25
Electric Trolley	Chariot électrique	no
Buggy	Voiturette	no
Clubs	Clubs	£ 40/day

Credit cards Cartes de crédit
VISA - Eurocard - MasterCard - AMEX - DC

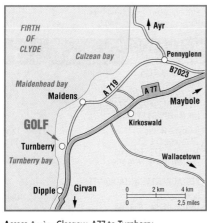

FIRTH OF CLYDE

Ayr

Culzean bay

Pennyglenn

B7023

Maidenhead bay

Maidens

A 719

A 77

Maybole

GOLF

Kirkoswald

Turnberry

Turnberry bay

Wallacetown

Dipple

Girvan

0 — 2 km — 4 km
0 — 2,5 miles

Access Accès : Glasgow, A77 to Turnberry
Map 3 on page 492 Carte 3 Page 492

GOLF COURSE
PARCOURS
16/20

Site	Site	
Maintenance	Entretien	
Architect	Architecte	Mackenzie Ross, remod. in 1945
Type	Type	links
Relief	Relief	
Water in play	Eau en jeu	
Exp. to wind	Exposé au vent	
Trees in play	Arbres en jeu	

Scorecard	Chp.	Mens	Ladies
Carte de score	Chp.	Mess.	Da.
Length Long.	5475	5475	5020
Par	68	68	72

Advised golfing ability	0	12	24	36
Niveau de jeu recommandé				
Hcp required	Handicap exigé	no		

CLUB HOUSE & AMENITIES
CLUB HOUSE ET ANNEXES
9/10

Pro shop	Pro-shop	
Driving range	Practice	
Sheltered	couvert	no
On grass	sur herbe	yes
Putting-green	putting-green	yes
Pitching-green	pitching green	yes

HOTEL FACILITIES
ENVIRONNEMENT HOTELIER
8/10

HOTELS HÔTELS
Turnberry Hotel
132 rooms, from D £ 200 — on site
Tel (44) 01655 - 331 000
Fax (44) 01655 - 331 706

RESTAURANTS RESTAURANTS
3 restaurants — at the Hotel
Tel (44) 01655 - 331 000

793

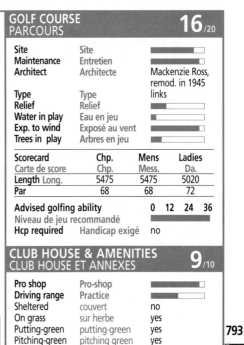

A very pretty course on the Ayrshire coast, without the claim to fame of its prestigious neighbours but always very welcoming on weekdays. The site is as magnificent as it is peaceful, with superb views over the Isle of Arran, Ailsa Craig and the north-west hills. But this 18-hole course is worth much more than its scenery. A very reasonable length makes this interesting prey for good golfers and the best players will find more than one opportunity to shine. The spread of difficulties makes for a well-balanced round of golf with only a single burn to interrupt the links landscape: bunkers that look to have been here since time began, thick bushes and the few trees that the wind has left standing. And of course the sea, whose incursions often tend to complicate the job of club officials.

Un très joli parcours de la côte de l'Ayrshire, sans prétendre aux grands titres de gloire de ses prestigieux voisins, mais toujours accueillant en semaine. Le site est aussi magnifique et très tranquille, avec des vues superbes sur l'Île d'Arran, Ailsa Craig et les collines du nord-ouest. Mais ce 18 trous vaut mieux que son panorama. Sa longueur très raisonnable en fait une proie intéressante pour les golfeurs de niveau honorable, et les meilleurs y trouveront plus d'une occasion de s'y casser les dents. La répartition des difficultés offre un bon rythme de jeu, un «burn» venant seul rompre leur nature propre aux links : des bunkers qui paraissent là depuis l'éternité, des buissons bien épais, quelques arbres ayant résisté au vent. Et à la mer, dont l'action vient parfois compliquer la tâche des responsables du Club.

The West Kilbride Golf Club   1893

33-35 Fullerton Drive, Seamill
SCO - WEST KILBRIDE, Ayrshire KA23 9HT

Office	Secrétariat	(44) 01294 - 823 911
Pro shop	Pro-shop	(44) 01294 - 823 042
Fax	Fax	(44) 01294 - 823 911
Situation	Situation	

56 km SW of Glasgow (pop. 662 853)

Annual closure	Fermeture annuelle	no
Weekly closure	Fermeture hebdomadaire	no

Fees main season	Tarifs haute saison	18 holes
	Week days Semaine	We/Bank holidays We/Férié
Individual Individuel	£ 25	—
Couple Couple	£ 50	—

Full weekday: £ 38 - No visitors at weekends

Caddy	Caddy	no
Electric Trolley	Chariot électrique	yes
Buggy	Voiturette	no
Clubs	Clubs	£ 5/18 holes

Credit cards Cartes de crédit
VISA - Eurocard - MasterCard - AMEX - DC - JCB

794

Access Accès : Glasgow, A80 → Airport. At Jct 29, A737 through Paisley, Beith. After Dalry turn right on B781. In West Kilbride, turn right towards the sea.
Map 3 on page 492 Carte 3 Page 492

GOLF COURSE
PARCOURS   16/20

Site	Site	■■■■■■□
Maintenance	Entretien	■■■■■■□
Architect	Architecte	Tom Morris James Braid
Type	Type	links
Relief	Relief	■■□□□
Water in play	Eau en jeu	■■□□□
Exp. to wind	Exposé au vent	■■■■□
Trees in play	Arbres en jeu	■□□□□

Scorecard Carte de score	Chp. Chp.	Mens Mess.	Ladies Da.
Length Long.	5898	5898	5292
Par	71	71	72

Advised golfing ability		0 12 24 36
Niveau de jeu recommandé		■■■■■□
Hcp required	Handicap exigé	certificate

CLUB HOUSE & AMENITIES
CLUB HOUSE ET ANNEXES   7/10

Pro shop	Pro-shop	■■■■□
Driving range	Practice	■■□□□
Sheltered	couvert	no
On grass	sur herbe	no
Putting-green	putting-green	yes
Pitching-green	pitching green	yes

HOTEL FACILITIES
ENVIRONNEMENT HOTELIER   5/10

HOTELS HÔTELS

Hospitality Inn		Irvine
126 rooms, D £ 100		6 km
Tel (44) 01294 - 274 272		
Fax (44) 01294 - 277 287		
Brisbane House		Largs
23 rooms, D £ 80		5 km
Tel (44) 01475 - 687 200		
Fax (44) 01475 - 676 295		

RESTAURANTS RESTAURANTS

Braidwoods		Dalry
Tel (44) 01294 - 833 544		6 km

WESTERN GAILES

Between the seaside dunes and the railway lines, Western Gailes is one of the best links down the whole coast of Scotland. Totally exposed to the prevailing south-west wind, it subtly changes its nature even if the wind varies just a few degrees. There are only three par 3s, every one more difficult than it looks. Rather strangely for a course that is hardly much wider than two fairways, the clubhouse is almost in the middle. This means you play one half of the front 9 and one half of the back 9 with the wind behind you, and holes 5 to 13 with the wind in your face. This calls for some careful thinking over the line of play and attack. This private club welcomes visitors, even of the female variety, although there are no ladies tees. We'll just say that for them, this is an excellent par 74.

Entre les dunes de bord de mer et la voie ferrée, Western Gailes est un des meilleurs links de toute cette côte de l'Ecosse. Totalement exposé aux vents dominants de sud-ouest, il change subtilement de caractère selon que l'orientation se modifie de quelques degrés seulement. Il n'y a que trois par 3 ici, mais tous plus difficiles qu'ils ne paraissent. Assez curieusement pour un parcours guère plus large que deux fairways, le Club-house est presqu'au milieu : on joue ainsi la moitié de l'aller et la moitié du retour vent avec, et toute la partie du 5 au 13 vent contre, ce qui exige pas mal de réflexion sur la ligne de jeu... et la façon de négocier. Ce club privé est accueillant aux visiteurs, même féminins, bien qu'elles n'aient pas ici de départs spécifiques : disons que c'est pour elles un excellent par 74.

Western Gailes Golf Club — 1898

Gailes
SCO - IRVINE, Ayrshire KA11 5AE

Office	Secrétariat	(44) 01294 - 311 649
Pro shop	Pro-shop	(44) 01294 - 311 649
Fax	Fax	(44) 01294 - 312 312
Situation	Situation	

5 km N of Troon (pop. 15 116)

Annual closure	Fermeture annuelle	no
Weekly closure	Fermeture hebdomadaire	no

Restaurant closed 10 → 04 inclusive

Fees main season Tarifs haute saison — 18 holes

	Week days Semaine	We/Bank holidays We/Férié
Individual Individuel	£ 60	£ 70
Couple Couple	£ 120	£ 140

Visitors: only Monday, Tuesday (except Ladies), Wednesday and Friday.

Caddy	Caddy	on request/£ 25
Electric Trolley	Chariot électrique	no
Buggy	Voiturette	no
Clubs	Clubs	no

Credit cards Cartes de crédit VISA - Mastercard

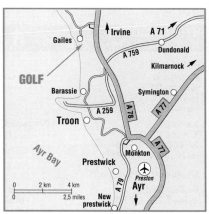

Access Accès : On A78, 3 km S of junction with A 71.
Map 3 on page 492 Carte 3 Page 492

GOLF COURSE / PARCOURS — 17/20

Site	Site	
Maintenance	Entretien	
Architect	Architecte	Original greenkeeper links
Type	Type	
Relief	Relief	
Water in play	Eau en jeu	
Exp. to wind	Exposé au vent	
Trees in play	Arbres en jeu	

Scorecard Carte de score	Chp. Chp.	Mens Mess.	Ladies Da.
Length Long.	6110	6040	5622
Par	71	71	75

Advised golfing ability	0	12	24	36
Niveau de jeu recommandé				
Hcp required	Handicap exigé	24		

CLUB HOUSE & AMENITIES / CLUB HOUSE ET ANNEXES — 5/10

Pro shop	Pro-shop	
Driving range	Practice	
Sheltered	couvert	small practice area
On grass	sur herbe	no
Putting-green	putting-green	yes
Pitching-green	pitching green	yes

795

HOTEL FACILITIES / ENVIRONNEMENT HOTELIER — 7/10

HOTELS HÔTELS
Hospitality Inn — Irvine — 2 km
126 rooms, D £ 100
Tel (44) 01294 - 274 272
Fax (44) 01294 - 277 287

Marine Highland — Troon — 5 km
66 rooms, D £ 120
Tel (44) 01292 - 314 444
Fax (44) 01292 - 316 922

RESTAURANTS RESTAURANTS
Highgrove House — Troon — 5 km
Tel (44) 01292 - 312 511

WESTERWOOD

This is one of the very ambitious projects of recent years, designed by Dave Thomas and Seve Ballesteros in search of commercial success. The site is beautiful with an excellent hotel atop a hill, guaranteeing a scenic view and exposure to the wind. The course unwinds around the hotel but is never very hilly. The only real regret is that the course gets very wet when it rains and stays very dry for the rest of the time, which doesn't make playing very easy either way. You have to play long and straight, the greens are very well protected and the wind can make life complicated even in the middle of the trees. An often interesting and sometimes even spectacular course which is well worth playing in fine weather. Still in its infancy, Westerwood can only get better.

C'est l'un des projets très ambitieux de ces dernières années, avec les signatures de Dave Thomas et Seve Ballesteros pour rechercher le succès commercial. Le site est très beau, avec un excellent hôtel au sommet d'une colline, ce qui garantit le panorama, mais aussi l'exposition au vent. Le parcours se déroule à son pied, mais les reliefs ne sont pas très importants. Le seul vrai regret que l'on puisse avoir est qu'il soit très humide quand il a plu, et très sec par ailleurs, ce qui ne facilite pas le jeu dans un cas comme dans l'autre. Car il faut être long, précis, les greens sont très bien défendus et le vent peut compliquer les choses, même au milieu des arbres. Un parcours souvent intéressant, parfois même spectaculaire et qui vaut la peine d'être découvert par beau temps. Mais il est encore jeune et ne peut que progresser.

The Westerwood
Hotel, Golf & Country Club

1989

St Andrews Drive
SCO - WESTERWOOD, Cumbernauld G68 0EW

Office	Secrétariat	(44) 01236 - 452 772
Pro shop	Pro-shop	(44) 01236 - 725 181
Fax	Fax	(44) 01236 - 738 478
Situation	Situation	

23 km NE of Glasgow (pop. 662 853)

Annual closure	Fermeture annuelle	no
Weekly closure	Fermeture hebdomadaire	no
Fees main season	Tarifs haute saison	18 holes

	Week days Semaine	We/Bank holidays We/Férié
Individual Individuel	£ 22.50	£ 27.50
Couple Couple	£ 45	£ 55
Caddy	Caddy	on request/£ 15
Electric Trolley	Chariot électrique	no
Buggy	Voiturette	yes
Clubs	Clubs	yes

Credit cards Cartes de crédit
VISA - Eurocard - MasterCard - AMEX - DC - JCB

Access Accès : Glasgow, A80. turn off at Cumbernauld on the road labelled to Dullatur. At first roundabout, look for Westerwood sign (not obvious!).
Map 2 on page 490 Carte 2 Page 490

GOLF COURSE
PARCOURS

14/20

Site	Site	
Maintenance	Entretien	
Architect	Architecte	Seve Ballesteros Dave Thomas
Type	Type	parkland
Relief	Relief	
Water in play	Eau en jeu	
Exp. to wind	Exposé au vent	
Trees in play	Arbres en jeu	

Scorecard Carte de score	Chp. Chp.	Mens Mess.	Ladies Da.
Length Long.	6030	5560	4965
Par	72	72	75

Advised golfing ability Niveau de jeu recommandé		0 12 24 36
Hcp required	Handicap exigé	no

CLUB HOUSE & AMENITIES
CLUB HOUSE ET ANNEXES

8/10

Pro shop	Pro-shop	
Driving range	Practice	
Sheltered	couvert	no
On grass	sur herbe	yes
Putting-green	putting-green	yes
Pitching-green	pitching green	yes

HOTEL FACILITIES
ENVIRONNEMENT HOTELIER

6/10

HOTELS HÔTELS
Westerwood — Golf
49 rooms, D £ 85 — on site
Tel (44) 01236 - 457 171
Fax (44) 01236 - 738 478

Travel Inn — Cumbernauld
37 rooms, D £ 35 — 3 km
Tel (44) 01236 - 725 339
Fax (44) 01236 - 736 380

RESTAURANTS RESTAURANTS

The Tipsy Laird — Golf
Tel (44) 01236 - 457 171 — on site

796

In a region where there are many high quality courses, the Whitekirk promoters scored a significant victory over those who thought there wouldn't be enough space for another one. This course is a fine example of what can still be done with a restricted budget but with the determination to offer visitors excellent value for money. Practice facilities are of a standard seldom found in the UK, the greens are excellent, the layout very varied and the views (free of charge) over the Firth of Forth are magnificent. Naturally this layout cannot really match the genuine links courses found in the vicinity here, but it is a very serious design and strategy is immediately obvious without any hidden traps. This is essential for a «pay-as-you-play» course.

Dans une région présentant des parcours d'une telle qualité, les promoteurs de Whitekirk ont remporté une belle victoire sur ceux qui estimaient qu'il n'y avait plus de place disponible. Ce parcours est un bon exemple de ce que l'on peut encore faire avec un budget limité, mais avec la détermination d'offrir un bon rapport qualité-prix aux visiteurs de passage. Ils y trouveront des installations d'entraînement d'une rare qualité en Grande-Bretagne, des greens excellents, un tracé très varié et (gratuitement) de très belles vues sur le Firth of Forth. Certes, ce parcours ne peut tout à fait lutter avec les véritables links que l'on peut trouver alentour, mais son dessin a été sérieusement réalisé, la stratégie est immédiatement évidente, sans pièges dissimulés, ce qui est essentiel pour un parcours «pay-as-you-play.»

Whitekirk Golf Course — 1995

Whitekirk
SCO - Nr NORTH BERWICK, E. Lothian EH39 5PR

Office	Secrétariat	(44) 01620 - 870 300
Pro shop	Pro-shop	(44) 01620 - 870 300
Fax	Fax	(44) 01620 - 870 330
Situation	Situation	

5 km SE of North Berwick (pop. 5 871)

Annual closure	Fermeture annuelle	no
Weekly closure	Fermeture hebdomadaire	no
Fees main season	Tarifs haute saison	18 holes

	Week days Semaine	We/Bank holidays We/Férié
Individual Individuel	£ 18	£ 25
Couple Couple	£ 36	£ 50

Full days: £ 30 - £ 35 (weekends)

Caddy	Caddy	on request
Electric Trolley	Chariot électrique	yes
Buggy	Voiturette	£ 12/18 holes
Clubs	Clubs	£ 8/18 holes

Credit cards Cartes de crédit
VISA - Eurocard - MasterCard

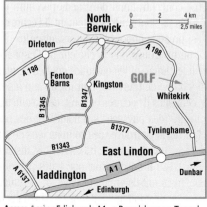

Access Accès : Edinburgh A1 → Berwick-upon-Tweed.
After East Linton, A198 on the left.
Golf on left side after Whitekirk village.
Map 3 on page 493 Carte 3 Page 493

GOLF COURSE / PARCOURS — 15/20

Site	Site	▦▦▦▦▯
Maintenance	Entretien	▦▦▦▦▯
Architect	Architecte	Cameron Sinclair
Type	Type	open country
Relief	Relief	▦▦▯▯▯
Water in play	Eau en jeu	▦▦▦▯▯
Exp. to wind	Exposé au vent	▦▦▦▯▯
Trees in play	Arbres en jeu	▦▯▯▯▯

Scorecard Carte de score	Chp. Chp.	Mens Mess.	Ladies Da.
Length Long.	5842	5645	4835
Par	72	72	72

Advised golfing ability Niveau de jeu recommandé		0 12 24 36 ▦▦▦▦
Hcp required Handicap exigé	no	

CLUB HOUSE & AMENITIES / CLUB HOUSE ET ANNEXES — 7/10

Pro shop	Pro-shop	▦▦▦▦▯
Driving range	Practice	▦▦▦▦▯
Sheltered	couvert	no
On grass	sur herbe	yes
Putting-green	putting-green	yes
Pitching-green	pitching green	yes

HOTEL FACILITIES / ENVIRONNEMENT HOTELIER — 7/10

HOTELS HÔTELS
Marine Hotel — North Berwick
74 rooms, D £ 80 — 5 km
Tel (44) 01620 - 892 406
Fax (44) 01620 - 894 480

Courtyard — Dunbar
6 rooms, D £ 50 — 12 km
Tel (44) 01368 - 864 169

RESTAURANTS RESTAURANTS

Marine — North Berwick
Tel (44) 01620 - 892 406 — 5 km

797

Pays de Galles

The Millennium Guide

In the British Isles, Wales is not the best known country for golf, at least to players on the continent, who are often only familiar with those courses seen on the television during the British Open or other top tournaments. Yet Wales has one of the highest concentrations of great courses seen anywhere in the world. The problem is that they are sometimes so far away from any major city that it is virtually impossible for them to organise any of the world's top tournaments. You won't find the sunny climes of Spain here, but the Gulf Stream does bring a lot of mild weather and a few spots of rain are always good for the skin. So there are very few tourists, which can only be good news for golf-trotters, who often have hundreds of acres of forest, miles of rugged coastline or sandy beaches, and splendid landscapes all to themselves. And these are courses where you will have more than one opportunity to find playing partners and to discover the Welsh people, who are the very picture of their country: sometimes a little rough on the edges, discreet, always proud and deeply hospitable. All they need do now is tell the rest of the world that their golf courses are first-rate, but do they really want to get involved in big publicity and promotion campaigns? If a happy life means a hidden life out-of-the-way, then real happiness is right here.

Dans les Iles Britanniques, le Pays de Galles n'est pas le pays le plus connu pour le golf, en tout cas par les continentaux, qui ne connaissent souvent que les parcours vus à la télévision au moment de championnats comme le British Open. Pourtant, le Pays de Galles réunit l'une des plus fortes concentrations de grands parcours par rapport au nombre total, mais ils sont parfois tellement à l'écart des grandes métropoles qu'il est presque impossible d'y organiser les plus grandes compétitions. Ici, on ne trouve pas la chaleur de l'Espagne, mais le Gulf Stream adoucit le climat, et les quelques gouttes de pluie attendrissent la peau. S'il y a peu de touristes, tant mieux : on a souvent pour soi tout seul des centaines d'hectares de forêt, des kilomètres de côtes sauvages ou de plages, des paysages splendides, et des parcours de golf où l'on aura l'occasion de trouver des compagnons de jeu, de découvrir des Gallois à l'image de leur pays, rudes parfois, discrets , chaleureux et fiers. Il leur reste à faire savoir que leurs parcours sont de première grandeur, mais ont-ils vraiment envie de se lancer dans de grandes campagnes de promotion ? S'il faut être bien caché pour vivre heureux, le bonheur est ici.

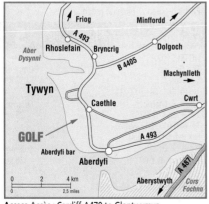

ABERDOVEY

17 7 7

You can get here by train, bringing your clubs with you, a throw-back to the times when courses were always close to railway tracks. The line here does indeed run alongside the course but not enough to make a nuisance of itself. And that's probably good news, because this layout, which has benefited from the flair of designers Fowler, Colt and Braid, is one of the best in Wales. Located in the Dovey estuary at the foot of some hills, this is a flat course lying alongside the pretty resort of Aberdovey, hence the rather crowded fairways in Summer. As the Old Course at St. Andrews, the holes are in a straight line out and in, thus making play a little easier in the wind. Yet the shifting landscape and dunes bring variety and sometimes even surprises like at the 3rd, a par 3 where the green is totally out of view. Aberdovey is Ian Woosnam's retreat between tournaments. So if it suits him, it'll probably suit you, too.

On peut venir en train avec ses clubs, ce qui rappelle le temps où les golfs étaient près du chemin de fer. Certes, il longe tout le parcours, mais pas assez souvent pour être une nuisance. Heureusement, car ce tracé, où des gloires comme Fowler, Colt et Braid ont laissé leur «patte» est un des meilleurs du pays. Dans l'embouchure de la Dovey, au pied des collines, c'est un parcours plat, à côté de la jolie station balnéaire d'Aberdovey, d'où une forte fréquentation en été. A l'instar du Old Course de St Andrews, les trous sont pratiquement alignés en aller et retour, ce qui facilite le jeu quand il y a du vent, mais les mouvements du terrain et les dunes apportent de la variété, parfois même de la surprise comme au 3, un par 3 où le green est totalement dissimulé. Pour Ian Woosnam, Aberdovey est une retraite entre les tournois. Si c'est bien pour lui...

Aberdovey Golf Club		1892
WAL - ABERDOVEY, Gwynedd LL35 0RT		

Office	Secrétariat	(44) 01654 - 767 493
Pro shop	Pro-shop	(44) 01654 - 767 602
Fax	Fax	(44) 01654 - 767 027
Situation	Situation	

5 km NW of Aberdovey (Aberdyfi)
140 km from Cardiff (pop. 279 055)

Annual closure	Fermeture annuelle	no
Weekly closure	Fermeture hebdomadaire	no
Fees main season	Tarifs haute saison	18 holes

	Week days Semaine	We/Bank holidays We/Férié
Individual Individuel	£ 29*	£ 35*
Couple Couple	£ 58	£ 70
* Full day: £ 42/£ 50		

Caddy	Caddy	no
Electric Trolley	Chariot électrique	yes
Buggy	Voiturette	yes
Clubs	Clubs	no

Credit cards Cartes de crédit   VISA - MasterCard
(Green fees & goods, only at Pro shop)

Access Accès : Cardiff A470 to Glantwymyn,
then A489 to Machynlleth, A493 through
Aberdyfi. Golf course NW near Railway Station.
Map 5 on page 496 Carte 5 Page 496

GOLF COURSE
PARCOURS
17 /20

Site	Site	
Maintenance	Entretien	
Architect	Architecte	Braid, Fowler, Colt
Type	Type	seaside course, links
Relief	Relief	
Water in play	Eau en jeu	
Exp. to wind	Exposé au vent	
Trees in play	Arbres en jeu	

Scorecard	Chp.	Mens	Ladies
Carte de score	Chp.	Mess.	Da.
Length Long.	5865	5551	5314
Par	71	71	74

Advised golfing ability	0 12 24 36
Niveau de jeu recommandé	
Hcp required Handicap exigé	certificate

CLUB HOUSE & AMENITIES
CLUB HOUSE ET ANNEXES
7 /10

Pro shop	Pro-shop	
Driving range	Practice	
Sheltered	couvert	no
On grass	sur herbe	yes
Putting-green	putting-green	yes
Pitching-green	pitching green	yes

HOTEL FACILITIES
ENVIRONNEMENT HOTELIER
7 /10

HOTELS HÔTELS
Plas Penhelig Country House   Aberdovey
11 rooms, D £ 80   6 km
Tél (44) 01654 - 767 676
Fax (44) 01654 - 767 783

Trefeddian   Aberdovey
46 rooms, D £ 80   3 km
Tél (44) 01654 - 767 213
Fax (44) 01654 - 767 777

Penhelig Arms   Aberdovey
10 rooms, D £ 75   5 km
Tél (44) 01654 - 767 215
Fax (44) 01654 - 767 690

RESTAURANTS RESTAURANTS
Plas Penhelig Country House   Aberdovey
Tél (44) 01654 - 767 676   6 km

799

Located to the west of Llanelli and not so far from Swansea, this is one of the oldest courses in Wales, overlooking Camarthen Bay. The fairways are very busy in Summer, so be warned. The first and last two holes have a rather marked inland character, but for the rest of the course you have the prevailing south-westerlies to contend with. Holes 3 to 8 run parallel to the sea with a head-wind, holes 9 to 15 are played with the wind behind you. With tight fairways, dangerous rough and other unwelcome but easily identifiable hazards, you play here with your clubs and your brains. The greens are on the large side and equally difficult to read, which would explain why the course record here is only 70. Even though players of all levels can measure up to this test, the least experienced should not hold out too much hope when the wind roars (except perhaps for learning how to play with it).

Situé à l'ouest de Llanelli, et pas si loin de Swansea, ce parcours très fréquenté en été, et l'un des plus anciens du Pays de Galles, domine la baie de Carmarthen. Les deux premiers et deux derniers trous ont un caractère inland assez marqué. Ensuite, il faut jouer avec le vent dominant, car les trous du 3 ou 8 sont joués parallèlement à la mer et vent contre, les trous 9 à 15 se jouent vent avec... Avec les fairways étroits, un rough et des obstacles bien dangereux, mais aussi bien identifiables, il faut jouer avec ses clubs, mais aussi sa tête. Les greens sont assez grands, mais aussi très difficiles à lire, ce qui explique que le record ne soit ici que de 70. Et même si les joueurs de tous niveaux trouveront le test à leur mesure, les moins expérimentés ne doivent pas trop espérer quand le vent souffle (sinon apprendre à jouer...)

Ashburnham Golf Club — 1894

Cliff Terrace
WAL - BURRY PORT, Dyfed SA16 0HN

Office	Secrétariat	(44) 01554 - 832 269
Pro shop	Pro-shop	(44) 01554 - 833 846
Fax	Fax	(44) 01554 - 832 269
Situation	Situation	

8 km W of Llanelli - 25 km W of Swansea (pop. 181 906)

Annual closure	Fermeture annuelle	no
Weekly closure	Fermeture hebdomadaire	no
Fees main season	Tarifs haute saison	18 holes

	Week days Semaine	We/Bank holidays We/Férié
Individual Individuel	£ 27.50*	£ 32.50*
Couple Couple	£ 55	£ 65

* Full day: £ 32.50/£ 42.50 - Restrictions at weekends: ask before coming

Caddy	Caddy	no
Electric Trolley	Chariot électrique	yes
Buggy	Voiturette	no
Clubs	Clubs	yes

Credit cards Cartes de crédit
VISA - MasterCard (for Green fees & goods, only at Pro shop)

800

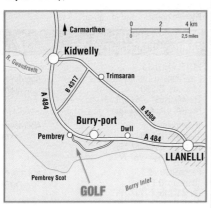

↑ Carmarthen

Kidwelly
R. Gwendraeth
Trimsaran
B 4317
A 484
B 4308
Burry-port
Dwll
A 484
Pembrey
LLANELLI
Pembrey Scot
GOLF
Burry Inlet

0 — 2 — 4 km
0 — 2,5 miles

Access Accès : Cardiff M4. Jct 48, A4138 to Llanelli, then A484 to Burry Port.
Map 6 on page 498 Carte 6 Page 498

GOLF COURSE PARCOURS — 17/20

Site	Site	
Maintenance	Entretien	
Architect	Architecte	Unknown
Type	Type	links
Relief	Relief	
Water in play	Eau en jeu	
Exp. to wind	Exposé au vent	
Trees in play	Arbres en jeu	

Scorecard Carte de score	Chp. Chp.	Mens Mess.	Ladies Da.
Length Long.	6312	5652	5007
Par	72	72	75

Advised golfing ability		0 12 24 36
Niveau de jeu recommandé		
Hcp required	Handicap exigé	certificate

CLUB HOUSE & AMENITIES CLUB HOUSE ET ANNEXES — 6/10

Pro shop	Pro-shop	
Driving range	Practice	
Sheltered	couvert	no
On grass	sur herbe	yes
Putting-green	putting-green	yes
Pitching-green	pitching green	yes

HOTEL FACILITIES ENVIRONNEMENT HOTELIER — 5/10

HOTELS HÔTELS

The George | Burry Port
5 rooms, D £ 45 | 2 km
Tél (44) 01554 - 832 211

Swansea Marriott | Swansea
117 rooms, D £ 76 | 25 km
Tél (44) 01792 - 642 020
Fax (44) 01792 - 650 345

Forte Crest | Swansea
99 rooms, D £ 69 | 25 km
Tél (44) 01792 - 651 074, Fax (44) 01792 - 456 044

RESTAURANTS RESTAURANTS

Four Seasons | Carmarthen
Tél (44) 01267 - 290 238 | 20 km

Annie's | Swansea
Tél (44) 01792 - 655 603 | 25 km

CARDIFF

This course is virtually in the middle of town, one but not the only reason why it is impossible to play here without being accompanied by a member. Quite simply, this is an excellent course, even considered by some to be one of the three best inland courses in Wales, despite the relatively short yardage. This very well maintained course is a classic example of parkland golfing, where the growing trees have gradually become a crucial factor. A few water hazards and particularly the very cleverly arranged green-side bunkers make the golfer's job a whole lot more difficult. What's more, the greens are medium-sized only, thus calling for even greater accuracy. In this respect it is interesting to note that modern courses seldom require any more virtuosity than their elders, just a little more power. From the back tees here, there are some short and some long par 4s, but virtually nothing in between. A great and appealing challenge.

Ce parcours est pratiquement situé en pleine ville : il est impossible d'y jouer en week-end autrement qu'avec un membre, mais c'est surtout un excellent parcours, considéré par certains comme l'un des trois meilleurs parcours «inland» du Pays de Galles, bien qu'il soit plutôt côté «court» que côté «long». Très bien entretenu, c'est un exemple classique de «parkland», dans lequel la croissance des arbres en a fait progressivement un facteur de jeu crucial. Quelques obstacles d'eau et surtout des bunkers de green disposés de manière très intelligente rendent la tâche plus complexe. Les greens sont de taille plutôt moyenne, ce qui oblige plus encore à être précis. Il est d'ailleurs intéressant de constater que les parcours modernes ne réclament guère plus de virtuosité que les anciens, juste un peu plus de puissance. On remarquera que, des départs arrière, il y a ici des par 4 courts et longs mais presqu'aucun de longueur moyenne.

Cardiff Golf Club — 1921

Sherborne Avenue
WAL - CYNCOED, CARDIFF CF2 6SJ

Office	Secrétariat	(44) 01222 - 753 067
Pro shop	Pro-shop	(44) 01222 - 754 772
Fax	Fax	(44) 01222 - 752 134
Situation	Situation	

3 km N. of Cardiff (pop. 279 055)

Annual closure	Fermeture annuelle	no
Weekly closure	Fermeture hebdomadaire	no

Monday, Restaurant only

Fees main season	Tarifs haute saison	full day
	Week days Semaine	We/Bank holidays We/Férié
Individual Individuel	£ 35	£ 35*
Couple Couple	£ 70	£ 70*

* Only with a member at week ends

Caddy	Caddy	no
Electric Trolley	Chariot électrique	no
Buggy	Voiturette	no
Clubs	Clubs	yes
Credit cards Cartes de crédit		no

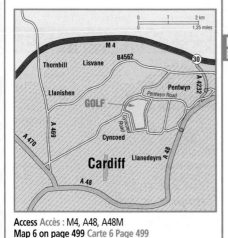

Access Accès : M4, A48, A48M
Map 6 on page 499 Carte 6 Page 499

GOLF COURSE / PARCOURS — 14/20

Site	Site	
Maintenance	Entretien	
Architect	Architecte	Robert Walker
Type	Type	parkland
Relief	Relief	
Water in play	Eau en jeu	
Exp. to wind	Exposé au vent	
Trees in play	Arbres en jeu	

Scorecard Carte de score	Chp. Chp.	Mens Mess.	Ladies Da.
Length Long.	5412	5180	4750
Par	70	70	73

Advised golfing ability Niveau de jeu recommandé	0 12 24 36
Hcp required Handicap exigé	certificate

CLUB HOUSE & AMENITIES / CLUB HOUSE ET ANNEXES — 6/10

Pro shop	Pro-shop	
Driving range	Practice	
Sheltered	couvert	practice area
On grass	sur herbe	yes
Putting-green	putting-green	yes
Pitching-green	pitching green	yes

801

HOTEL FACILITIES / ENVIRONNEMENT HOTELIER — 8/10

HOTELS HÔTELS

Park - 115 rooms, D £ 100 — Cardiff 4 km
Tél (44) 01222 - 383 471, Fax (44) 01222 - 399 309

Cardiff Bay - 65 rooms, D £ 110 — Cardiff 5 km
Tél (44) 01222 - 465 888, Fax (44) 01222 - 481 491

Townhouse — Cardiff
8 rooms, D £ 50 — 4 km
Tél (44) 01222 - 239 399, Fax (44) 01222 - 223 214

RESTAURANTS RESTAURANTS

De Courcey's — Pentyrch
Tél (44) 01222 - 892 23 — 4 km

Blas-ar-Gymru — Cardiff
Tél (44) 01222 - 892 232 — 4 km

Le Cassoulet — Cardiff
Tél (44) 01222 - 221 905 — 5 km

CARDIGAN

This is not the best known Welsh course, but it does bear comparison with Tenby or Glamorganshire. The club-house buildings, although not the smartest in the world, are at least functional, while the view over the sea, particularly from the 16th, costs nothing even for the «never-break-a-hundred» hacker. The club dates back to 1895, but the course has been restyled several times, the last effort being conducted by Hawtree and Sons without altering the feel of the original. Yardage is in line with modern-day requirements, while the gorse and fern form the most obvious hazards for mis-hits; your ball somehow always seem to end up there whenever the wind blows it off course. In fact, this is a subtle blend of a links course, cliffs and pasture-land on a rather hilly setting, but the greens can generally be reached with low shots, at least if you work your way between the bunkers. A high standard course, with a special mention going to the visual and technical excellence of the last three holes.

Ce n'est pas le plus connu des parcours gallois, mais il peut soutenir la comparaison avec des parcours tels que Tenby ou Glamorganshire. Certes, les bâtiments du Clubhouse ne sont pas les plus stylés du monde, mais il sont au moins fonctionnels. Quant à la vue sur l'Océan, en particulier au départ du 16, elle est offerte, même aux mauvais joueurs. Le club date de 1895, mais le parcours a été plusieurs fois remanié, la dernière fois par le cabinet Hawtree & Sons sans en modifier l'esprit. Sa longueur répond à présent aux critères modernes. Les ajoncs et les fougères constituent l'une des menaces les plus flagrantes pour les balles, et si le vent les détourne, c'est toujours vers les obstacles. En fait, c'est un mélange assez subtil de links, de parcours de falaise, de pâturages, le tout assez accidenté, mais les greens acceptent en général les approches roulées, du moins si les bunkers les laissent passer.

Cardigan Golf Club — 1928

Gwbert on Sea
WAL - CARDIGAN SA43 1PR

Office	Secrétariat	(44) 01239 - 621 775
Pro shop	Pro-shop	(44) 01239 - 615 359
Fax	Fax	(44) 01239 - 621 775
Situation	Situation	

3 km from Cardigan (pop. 4 409)

Annual closure	Fermeture annuelle	no
Weekly closure	Fermeture hebdomadaire	

Fees main season
Tarifs haute saison 18 holes

	Week days Semaine	We/Bank holidays We/Férié
Individual Individuel	£ 20	£ 25
Couple Couple	£ 40	£ 50

Caddy	Caddy	no
Electric Trolley	Chariot électrique	no
Buggy	Voiturette	£ 15
Clubs	Clubs	yes

Credit cards Cartes de crédit
VISA - Eurocard - MasterCard

Access Accès : A 487 Cardigan to Aberystwyth Road.
Fork left at War Memorial, 2 km.
Map 6 on page 498 Carte 6 Page 498

GOLF COURSE / PARCOURS — 15/20

Site	Site	
Maintenance	Entretien	
Architect	Architecte	I.E. Grant Hawtree & Son
Type	Type	links, meadowland
Relief	Relief	
Water in play	Eau en jeu	
Exp. to wind	Exposé au vent	
Trees in play	Arbres en jeu	

Scorecard Carte de score	Chp. Chp.	Mens Mess.	Ladies Da.
Length Long.	6019	5784	5022
Par	72	72	74

Advised golfing ability Niveau de jeu recommandé	0 12 24 36	
Hcp required	Handicap exigé	certificate

CLUB HOUSE & AMENITIES / CLUB HOUSE ET ANNEXES — 6/10

Pro shop	Pro-shop	
Driving range	Practice	
Sheltered	couvert	practice area
On grass	sur herbe	yes
Putting-green	putting-green	yes
Pitching-green	pitching green	no

HOTEL FACILITIES / ENVIRONNEMENT HOTELIER — 5/10

HOTELS HÔTELS
Gwbert Hotel — Gwbert-on-Sea
20 rooms, D £ 70 — 1 km
Tél (44) 01239 - 612 638
Fax (44) 01239 - 621 474

Penrallt — Aberporth
17 rooms, D £ 95 — 10 km
Tél (44) 01239 - 810 227
Fax (44) 01239 - 811 375

Manor House — Fishguard
6 rooms, D £ 50 — 30 km
Tél (44) 01348 - 873 260

RESTAURANTS RESTAURANTS
Three Main Street — Fishguard
Tél (44) 01348 - 874 275 — 30 km

Gwbert Hotel — Gwbert-on-Sea
Tél (44) 01239 - 612 638 — 1 km

802

If you have the time, have a drink or (even better) take lunch after your round facing one of the most splendid sights to be seen on the Welsh coast. This should offer some consolation for shooting over your handicap on a course that J.H. Taylor obviously had great fun building. Don't be fooled by the yardage, relatively short except for the first hole, an intimidating long and tough par 4. And watch out for the 17th, where the two-tiered green is treacherous enough to ruin any card. With this said, if you can move the ball both ways, have a certain instinct for the game and a fair degree of humility, approach this course with serious but modest pretentions. There are no gimmicks here, no needless trimmings and no huge back-fills of earth: it is quite simply a great test of golf, pleasant to walk despite the rolling terrain and a peaceful site out in the countryside. It gets pretty wet here in winter so try to make it in spring or summer.

Si vous en avez le temps, prenez un verre ou (encore mieux) déjeunez après votre parcours devant l'un des plus beaux panoramas que l'on puisse trouver sur la campagne galloise. Cela vous consolera de ne pas avoir cassé le par sur un parcours que J.H. Taylor a dû prendre beaucoup de plaisir à dessiner. Sa longueur modérée ne doit pas faire illusion. D'ailleurs, le parcours commence par un long et difficile par 4 pour vous intimider, et le 17 se termine par un green à double plateau, assez traître pour vous casser la carte. Mais si vous avez quelque talent du maniement de balle, l'instinct du jeu, et une certaine humilité, prenez ce parcours avec sérieux et modestie. pas de «gimmicks» ici, pas de décoration inutile, pas de grands mouvements de terrain, c'est tout simplement un très bon test de golf, agréable à marcher en dépit de ses ondulations, un lieu de calme aussi en pleine campagne. Il peut être humide en hiver, venez plutôt aux beaux jours.

Carmarthen Golf Club — 1928

Rhydymarchog, Blaen-y-Coed Road
WAL - CARMARTHEN SA33 6EH

Office	Secrétariat	(44) 01267 - 281 588
Pro shop	Pro-shop	(44) 01267 - 281 493
Fax	Fax	(44) 01267 - 281 214
Situation	Situation	

6 km NW of Carmarthen

Annual closure	Fermeture annuelle	no
Weekly closure	Fermeture hebdomadaire	no

Wednesday, Restaurant only

Fees main season
Tarifs haute saison 18 holes

	Week days Semaine	We/Bank holidays We/Férié
Individual Individuel	£ 18	£ 25
Couple Couple	£ 36	£ 50

Half price when playing with a member

Caddy	Caddy	no
Electric Trolley	Chariot électrique	
Buggy	Voiturette	
Clubs	Clubs	yes

Credit cards Cartes de crédit VISA - MasterCard

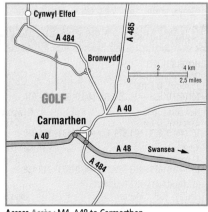

Access Accès : M4, A48 to Carmarthen,
A40 → Abergwilli, then A484 North,
left on Blaen-y-Coed road.
Map 6 on page 498 Carte 6 Page 498

GOLF COURSE / PARCOURS — 15/20

Site	Site	
Maintenance	Entretien	
Architect	Architecte	J.H. Taylor
Type	Type	parkland
Relief	Relief	
Water in play	Eau en jeu	
Exp. to wind	Exposé au vent	
Trees in play	Arbres en jeu	

Scorecard Carte de score	Chp. Chp.	Mens Mess.	Ladies Da.
Length Long.	5621	5433	4815
Par	71	71	72

Advised golfing ability Niveau de jeu recommandé		0 12 24 36
Hcp required	Handicap exigé	certificate

CLUB HOUSE & AMENITIES / CLUB HOUSE ET ANNEXES — 7/10

Pro shop	Pro-shop	
Driving range	Practice	
Sheltered area	couvert	large practice
On grass	sur herbe	yes
Putting-green	putting-green	yes
Pitching-green	pitching green	yes

803

HOTEL FACILITIES / ENVIRONNEMENT HOTELIER — 4/10

HOTELS HÔTELS

Cwmtwrch Hotel		Nantgaredig
6 rooms, D £ 60		12 km

Tél (44) 01267 - 290 238, Fax (44) 01267 - 290 808

Farm Retreats		Capel Dewi
3 rooms, D £ 50		13 km

Tél (44) 01267 - 290 799, Fax (44) 01267 - 290 003

Pantgwyn		Carmarthen
3 rooms, D £ 55		15 km

Tél (44) 01267 - 290 247, Fax (44) 01267 - 290 880

RESTAURANTS RESTAURANTS

Ty Mawr Country House		Brechfa
Tél (44) 01267 - 202 332		15 km

Four Seasons (Cwmtwrch Hotel)		Carmarthen
Tél (44) 01267 - 290 238		7 km

Alongside a remarkable hotel, you find here a real driving range, two-stories high, and a very well-appointed clubhouse. This ambitious golfing resort is organised around two courses (a third is presently under construction) designed by Robert Trent Jones, who thus returned to the land of his ancestors. You'll find the remains of a Roman Way here, and also of a Roman gladiator school, although the battles waged here nowadays are of a more pacific nature, fought over a little white ball. In this hilly landscape (a buggy is a good idea for the less athletic players), the designer has laid out a very American style course calling for accurate play to get the ball onto huge, well-contoured greens. On the way you'll be negotiating lakes, ravines, woods, other stretches of water and huge sand-traps. No effort was spared to make Celtic Manor a highly impressive and successful venture.

A côté d'un hôtel remarquable, on trouve ici un vrai driving-range à deux étages et un Clubhouse remarquablement équipé. Cet ambitieux complexe a été organisé autour de deux parcours dûs au crayon de Robert Trent Jones (un troisième est en travaux), revenu ainsi sur la terre de ses ancêtres. On trouve ici les restes d'une voie romaine, et même d'une école de gladiateurs, mais on aura ici à batailler de manière plus pacifique. Dans ce paysage vallonné (voiturette conseillée pour les moins en forme), l'architecte a placé un parcours très américain de style, avec la nécessité, en passant au large des lacs, des ravins, des bois, des cours d'eau, des immenses bunkers, de poser sa balle sur de vastes greens très travaillés. Rien n'a été épargné pour faire de Celtic Manor une impressionnante réussite.

Celtic Manor — 1995
Coldra Woods
WAL - NEWPORT NP6 2YA

Office	Secrétariat	(44) 01633 - 413 000
Pro shop	Pro-shop	(44) 01633 - 410 268
Fax	Fax	(44) 01633 - 412 910
Situation	Situation	

25 km E of Cardiff (pop. 279 055)
5 km NE of Newport (pop. 133 318)

Annual closure	Fermeture annuelle	no
Weekly closure	Fermeture hebdomadaire	no
Fees main season	Tarifs haute saison	18 holes

	Week days Semaine	We/Bank holidays We/Férié
Individual Individuel	£ 30	£ 35
Couple Couple	£ 60	£ 70

Caddy	Caddy	on request
Electric Trolley	Chariot électrique	yes
Buggy	Voiturette	yes
Clubs	Clubs	yes

Credit cards Cartes de crédit
VISA - MasterCard - AMEX - Switch

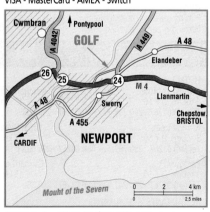

Cwmbran — Pontypool
GOLF — A 48
Elandeber
26 — 25 — 24 — M 4 — Llanmartin
A 48 — Swerry — Chepstow BRISTOL
A 455 — **NEWPORT**
CARDIF
Mouth of the Severn
0 — 2 — 4 km
0 — 2,5 miles

Access Accès : M4 Jct 24, then A48 → Newport.
First right at Royal Oak Public House.
Turn right at top of the hill. Golf on right hand side.
Map 6 on page 499 Carte 6 Page 499

GOLF COURSE / PARCOURS — 18/20

Site	Site	
Maintenance	Entretien	
Architect	Architecte	R. Trent Jones Sr
Type	Type	parkland
Relief	Relief	
Water in play	Eau en jeu	
Exp. to wind	Exposé au vent	
Trees in play	Arbres en jeu	

Scorecard Carte de score	Chp. Chp.	Mens Mess.	Ladies Da.
Length Long.	6371	5998	4430
Par	70	70	70

Advised golfing ability — 0   12   24   36
Niveau de jeu recommandé
Hcp required   Handicap exigé   certificate

CLUB HOUSE & AMENITIES / CLUB HOUSE ET ANNEXES — 9/10

Pro shop	Pro-shop	
Driving range	Practice	
Sheltered	couvert	28 floodlit bays
On grass	sur herbe	yes
Putting-green	putting-green	yes
Pitching-green	pitching green	yes

HOTEL FACILITIES / ENVIRONNEMENT HOTELIER — 7/10

HOTELS HÔTELS
Celtic Manor Hotel — Golf
75 rooms, D £ 100 — on site
Tél (44) 01633 - 413 000, Fax (44) 01633 - 412 910

Newport Lodge — Newport
27 rooms, D £ 67 — 5 km
Tél (44) 01633 - 821 818, Fax (44) 01633 - 856 360

Knoll — Newport
11 rooms, D £ 40 — 5 km
Tél (44) 01633 - 263 557, Fax (44) 01633 - 212 168

RESTAURANTS RESTAURANTS
Hedley's (Celtic Manor) — on site
Tél (44) 01633 - 413 000

804

Sections of the artificial port for the 1944 Normandy landings were built behind the green on the 2nd hole. This is only one page of history amongst many others, as the city has even held onto its medieval ramparts. The course is much flatter than its counterparts on the western and southern coasts, but there is never any question of tedium thanks to subtle shifts in landscape and the ubiquitous gorse. Naturally, you can add to this the course's own specific headaches, including length from the back tees. Playing further forward can put it within easier reach. In every case this is a perfectly honest layout, where the penalty to pay matches the gravity of your mis-hit. Very natural and with obvious personality, Conwy deserves a prolonged and respectful visit.

Derrière le green du 2 ont été construites en 1943 des portions du port artificiel du débarquement de 1944. Ce n'est qu'une page d'histoire parmi d'autres, car la ville a conservé jusqu'à ses remparts médiévaux. Le parcours est beaucoup plus plat que ceux des côtes ouest et sud, mais il échappe à la monotonie grâce à de subtils mouvements de terrain, et aussi à l'omniprésence de buissons d'ajoncs. Il faut encore y ajouter les difficultés propres du parcours, très long des départs les plus reculés, mais plus accessible des départs avancés. En tous les cas, il est d'une parfaite franchise, les punitions étant à la hauteur de la gravité des fautes commises. Très naturel, avec son évidente personnalité, Conwy mérite une visite aussi prolongée que respectueuse.

Conwy (Caernarvonshire) Golf Club 1890

Morfa
WAL - CONWY, Gwynedd LL32 8 ER

Office	Secrétariat	(44) 01492 - 592 423
Pro shop	Pro-shop	(44) 01492 - 593 225
Fax	Fax	(44) 01492 - 593 363
Situation	Situation	

8 km W of Colwyn Bay (pop. 9 471)
4 km S of Llandudno (pop. 18 647)

Annual closure	Fermeture annuelle	no
Weekly closure	Fermeture hebdomadaire	no

Fees main season
Tarifs haute saison 18 holes

	Week days Semaine	We/Bank holidays We/Férié
Individual Individuel	£ 25	£ 30
Couple Couple	£ 50	£ 60

Caddy	Caddy	no
Electric Trolley	Chariot électrique	yes
Buggy	Voiturette	yes
Clubs	Clubs	yes

Credit cards Cartes de crédit   no

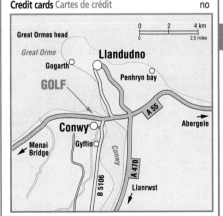

Great Ormes head
Great Orme
Gogarth
Llandudno
Penrhyn bay
GOLF
A 55
Conwy
Abergele
Menai Bridge
Gyffin
A 470
B 5106
Llanrwst

Access Accès : A55 to Conwy and follow signs to Conwy Marina.
Map 5 on page 496 Carte 5 Page 496

GOLF COURSE
PARCOURS   **17**/20

Site	Site	
Maintenance	Entretien	
Architect	Architecte	Unknown
Type	Type	links
Relief	Relief	
Water in play	Eau en jeu	
Exp. to wind	Exposé au vent	
Trees in play	Arbres en jeu	

Scorecard Carte de score	Chp. Chp.	Mens Mess.	Ladies Da.
Length Long.	6049	5819	5299
Par	72	72	74

Advised golfing ability		0 12 24 36
Niveau de jeu recommandé		
Hcp required	Handicap exigé	certificate

CLUB HOUSE & AMENITIES
CLUB HOUSE ET ANNEXES   **7**/10

Pro shop	Pro-shop	
Driving range	Practice	
Sheltered	couvert	28 floodlit bays
On grass	sur herbe	yes
Putting-green	putting-green	yes
Pitching-green	pitching green	yes

HOTEL FACILITIES
ENVIRONNEMENT HOTELIER   **8**/10

HOTELS HÔTELS

Bodysgallen Hall   Llandudno
34 rooms, D £ 120   6 km
Tél (44) 01492 - 584 466, Fax (44) 01492 - 582 519

Berthlwyd Hall   Conwy
9 rooms, D £ 65   3 km
Tél (44) 01492 - 592 409, Fax (44) 01492 - 572 290

Old Rectory   Llansanffraid Glan Conwy
6 rooms, D £ 100   6 km
Tél (44) 01492 - 580 611, Fax (44) 01492 - 584 555

RESTAURANTS RESTAURANTS

Martin's   Llandudno
Tél (44) 01492 - 870 070   6 km

Old Rectory   Llansanffraid Glan Conwy
Tél (44) 01492 - 580 611   6 km

Paysanne - Tél (44) 01492 - 582 079   Deganwy 5 km

805

This is the fourth oldest club in Wales. Perched above the Bristol Channel, it provides some splendid views over Glamorgan and Monmouthshire, and over the English counties on the other side as well. The architect is unknown, but he sure knew his job. Aside from links courses, this is how our ancestors enjoyed their golfing; forget the acres of white sand, the shining blue lakes and manicured grass. Tee it up, hit the approach from whatever position you happen to be in and try and stop your ball on firm, slick greens. With this said, the general condition of the course is excellent but here they prefer the course to be good and play well rather than just look beautiful. This is a totally forthright course where you can't lie about your game or hide any chinks in the armour: it is tradition in its finest and most vivid form, with some golfing history to boot. This is where Dr. Frank Stableford invented the scoring system that bears his name.

Du haut de son perchoir au dessus du Bristol Channel, ce parcours offre des vues sur le Glamorgan et le Monmouthshire, mais aussi sur trois Comtés anglais. On ne connaît pas son architecte mais il connaissait son métier. Mis à part les links, c'est ainsi que nos ancêtres vivaient le golf : oubliez les hectares de sable blanc, les lacs aux hauts bleues, les brins de gazon au garde-à-vous. Tapez la balle sur le tee, puis jouez votre approche comme sa position vous l'impose, et tâchez d'arrêter votre balle sur un green ferme et roulant. Cela dit, l'état général du parcours est excellent, mais rien n'est fait pour faire «beau» au détriment de «bien». La franchise du parcours est absolue, et vous ne pourrez pas mentir avec lui, maquiller vos défauts, c'est la tradition dans ce qu'elle a de mieux, et de plus vivant. En plus, vous avez l'histoire : c'est ici que le Dr Frank Stableford inventa la formule de jeu qui porte son nom.

The Glamorganshire Golf Club — 1890

Lavernock Road
ENG - PENARTH CF64 5UP

Office	Secrétariat	(44) 01222 - 701 185
Pro shop	Pro-shop	(44) 01222 - 707 401
Fax	Fax	(44) 01222 - 701 185
Situation	Situation	

16 km from Cardiff (pop. 279 055)

Annual closure	Fermeture annuelle	no
Weekly closure	Fermeture hebdomadaire	no

Fees main season
Tarifs haute saison 18 holes

	Week days Semaine	We/Bank holidays We/Férié
Individual Individuel	£ 30	£ 35
Couple Couple	£ 60	£ 70

Caddy	Caddy	no
Electric Trolley	Chariot électrique	no
Buggy	Voiturette	£ 20
Clubs	Clubs	yes

Credit cards Cartes de crédit VISA - MasterCard

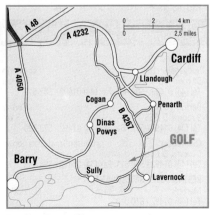

Access Accès : Cardiff South → Pennarth.
B 4267 → Golf
Map 6 on page 499 Carte 6 Page 499

GOLF COURSE PARCOURS — 14/20

Site	Site	
Maintenance	Entretien	
Architect	Architecte	Unknown
Type	Type	parkland
Relief	Relief	
Water in play	Eau en jeu	
Exp. to wind	Exposé au vent	
Trees in play	Arbres en jeu	

Scorecard Carte de score	Chp. Chp.	Mens Mess.	Ladies Da.
Length Long.	5451	5281	4916
Par	70	70	72

Advised golfing ability		0 12 24 36
Niveau de jeu recommandé		
Hcp required	Handicap exigé	certificate

CLUB HOUSE & AMENITIES CLUB HOUSE ET ANNEXES — 7/10

Pro shop	Pro-shop	
Driving range	Practice	
Sheltered	couvert	practice area
On grass	sur herbe	yes
Putting-green	putting-green	yes
Pitching-green	pitching green	yes

HOTEL FACILITIES ENVIRONNEMENT HOTELIER — 8/10

HOTELS HÔTELS

Mount Sorrel — Barry
43 rooms, D £ 90 — 7 km
Tél (44) 01446 - 740 069, Fax (44) 01446 - 746 600

Cardiff Bay Hotel — Cardiff
65 rooms, D £ 100 — 16 km
Tél (44) 01222 - 465 888, Fax (44) 01222 - 481 491

Ferrier's Hotel — Cardiff
26 rooms, D £ 50 — 16 km
Tél (44) 01222 - 383 413, Fax (44) 01222 - 383 413

Clare Court Hotel — Cardiff
8 rooms, D £ 40 — 16 km
Tél (44) 01222 - 344 839, Fax (44) 01222 - 665 856

RESTAURANTS RESTAURANTS

Quayle's - Tél (44) 01222 - 341 264 — Cardiff 16 km
Armless Dragon - Tél (44) 01222 - 382 357 Cardiff 16 km

806

A bridge has made Anglesey a peninsula and Trearddur Bay (as Holyhead is properly known) a better known course. Local players will tell you some horrible stories about lost golfers and terrifying scores, but Wales is also known as a land of tall stories. This course is difficult in the wind, but that is true for all links courses. It is short enough not to have staged very many prestigious tournaments, and rather hilly with tight, neatly contoured fairways. The natural rough is often dotted with thick heather, broom, gorse and even ferns, so it is an honest test for players of all levels (it was designed by James Braid, which says it all) with some of the best greens in the country. Exciting to play, intelligent and imaginative, Holyhead is well worth going out of your way for and in Summer is quite superb.

Le pont a fait d'Anglesey une presqu'île, et de «Trearddur Bay» (comme on appelle Holyhead) une oeuvre mieux connue. Les joueurs locaux vous raconteront quelques horribles histoires sur des golfeurs perdus et des scores terrifiants, mais le Pays de Galles est aussi celui des contes de fées. Ce parcours est difficile par grand vent, mais c'est le cas de tous les links. Assez court, ce qui explique qu'il n'ait pas reçu beaucoup de championnats très prestigieux, pas trop accidenté, il a des fairways étroits, bien modelés, des roughs naturels souvent parsemés d'une dense végétation de bruyère, de genêts, d'ajoncs et même de fougères. C'est un test d'une grande franchise pour tous les niveaux (il est signé James Braid, une référence), avec des greens parmi les meilleurs du pays. Superbe au printemps, excitant à jouer, intelligent et imaginatif, Holyhead mérite le détour.

Holyhead (Caergybi) Golf Club — 1912

Lon Carreg Fawr, Trearddur Bay
WAL - HOLYHEAD, Gwynedd LL65 2YG

Office	Secrétariat	(44) 01407 - 763 279
Pro shop	Pro-shop	(44) 01407 - 762 022
Fax	Fax	(44) 01407 - 763 279
Situation	Situation	

3 km S of Holyhead (pop. 11 796)

Annual closure	Fermeture annuelle	no
Weekly closure	Fermeture hebdomadaire	no

Fees main season	Tarifs haute saison	18 holes
	Week days Semaine	We/Bank holidays We/Férié
Individual Individuel	£ 19*	£ 25*
Couple Couple	£ 38	£ 50

Full day: £ 25/£29

Caddy	Caddy	no
Electric Trolley	Chariot électrique	no
Buggy	Voiturette	no
Clubs	Clubs	yes

Credit cards Cartes de crédit
VISA - Mastercard (Pro shop only)

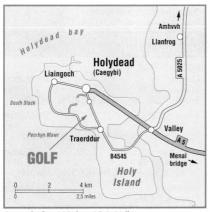

Access Accès : A55 then A5. In Valley,
turn left on B4545.
Map 5 on page 496 Carte 5 Page 496

GOLF COURSE / PARCOURS — 16/20

Site	Site	▇▇▇▇▇▇▫
Maintenance	Entretien	▇▇▇▇▇▫▫
Architect	Architecte	James Braid
Type	Type	heathland
Relief	Relief	▇▇▫▫▫▫
Water in play	Eau en jeu	▇▫▫▫▫▫▫
Exp. to wind	Exposé au vent	▇▇▇▇▫▫▫
Trees in play	Arbres en jeu	▇▇▫▫▫▫

Scorecard Carte de score	Chp. Chp.	Mens Mess.	Ladies Da.
Length Long.	5922	5180	4825
Par	71	68	72

Advised golfing ability Niveau de jeu recommandé	0	12	24	36

Hcp required — Handicap exigé — certificate

CLUB HOUSE & AMENITIES / CLUB HOUSE ET ANNEXES — 7/10

Pro shop	Pro-shop	▇▇▇▇▇▫
Driving range	Practice	▇▇▫▫▫▫
Sheltered	couvert	no
On grass	sur herbe	no
Putting-green	putting-green	yes
Pitching-green	pitching green	yes

HOTEL FACILITIES / ENVIRONNEMENT HOTELIER — 5/10

HOTELS HÔTELS

Trearddur Bay Hotel 32 rooms, D £ 60 Tél (44) 01407 - 860 301 Fax (44) 01407 - 861 181	Holyhead 3 km
Moranedd 6 rooms, D £ 49 Tél (44) 01407 - 860 324	Trearddur Bay 3 km

RESTAURANTS RESTAURANTS

Trearddur Bay Hotel Tél (44) 01407 - 860 301	Holyhead 3 km

807

This course is located in the Mumbles, a water sports centre at the entrance to the Gower peninsula, a listed site. Although rather hilly in places, Langland Bay is perfectly walkable, offering a splendid enough view to fire any imagination. However the small greens, a bunch of bunkers and threatening rough quickly bring you back to golfing reality. The hazards were clearly forged with the course and are dangerous without being downright treacherous. Everything is on an open table in front of you, so it is up to you to cross swords with the hazards in the great tradition of openness and challenge that remains the James Braid hallmark. Imaginative but totally natural, the course has unique charm, and although yardage is short to today's standards, par (gross or net) is never a walk-over. A number of international players are members here, so they too must find this course to their liking and to their standard.

Ce parcours est situé dans les Mumbles, centre de sports nautiques, et à l'entrée de la péninsule de Gower, qui est un site classé. Le site est assez accidenté à certains endroits mais il est assez facile de jouer à pied. La vue splendide va vite vous occuper, mais de petits greens, une quantité de bunkers et un rough menaçant vous ramènent vite aux réalités du parcours. Les obstacles ont été bien fondus dans le parcours, ils sont dangereux sans être traîtres. Tout est exposé devant vous, à vous de combattre les périls, dans la grande tradition de franchise et d'exigence mesurée de James Braid. Imaginatif tout en restant naturel, c'est un parcours au charme unique, et bien qu'il manque de longueur selon nos critères du jour, il n'est guère facile d'attaquer le par (en brut ou en net) avec toutes les chances de succès. Le club compte nombre de joueurs internationaux parmi ses membres, ils doivent sans doute trouver ce parcours à leur goût et à leur niveau.

Langland Bay Golf Club — 1901

The Mumbles
WAL - SWANSEA SA3 4QR

Office	Secrétariat	(44) 01792 - 361 721
Pro shop	Pro-shop	(44) 01792 - 366 186
Fax	Fax	(44) 01792 - 361 082
Situation	Situation	

10 km S. of Swansea (pop. 181 906)

Annual closure	Fermeture annuelle	no
Weekly closure	Fermeture hebdomadaire	no

Fees main season
Tarifs haute saison 18 holes

	Week days Semaine	We/Bank holidays We/Férié
Individual Individuel	£ 28	£ 30
Couple Couple	£ 56	£ 60

Caddy	Caddy	no
Electric Trolley	Chariot électrique	no
Buggy	Voiturette	no
Clubs	Clubs	no

Credit cards Cartes de crédit — no

Access Accès : M4 exit 47 A4216 unto Swansea,
then A4216 and to the end of A4067.
Then → The Mumbles.
Map 6 on page 498 Carte 6 Page 498

GOLF COURSE / PARCOURS — 15/20

Site	Site	▰▰▰▰▱
Maintenance	Entretien	▰▰▰▰▱
Architect	Architecte	James Braid
Type	Type	seaside course, parkland
Relief	Relief	▰▰▰▱▱
Water in play	Eau en jeu	▰▰▰▱▱
Exp. to wind	Exposé au vent	▰▰▰▱▱
Trees in play	Arbres en jeu	▰▰▱▱▱

Scorecard Carte de score	Chp. Chp.	Mens Mess.	Ladies Da.
Length Long.	5272	5146	4804
Par	70	70	73

Advised golfing ability Niveau de jeu recommandé	0	12	24	36
Hcp required	Handicap exigé	certificate		

CLUB HOUSE & AMENITIES / CLUB HOUSE ET ANNEXES — 7/10

Pro shop	Pro-shop	▰▰▰▰▱
Driving range	Practice	▰▰▰▱▱
Sheltered	couvert	practice area
On grass	sur herbe	yes
Putting-green	putting-green	yes
Pitching-green	pitching green	yes

HOTEL FACILITIES / ENVIRONNEMENT HOTELIER — 7/10

HOTELS HÔTELS

Osborne — The Mumbles
32 rooms, D £ 95 — 1 km
Tél (44) 01792 - 366 274, Fax (44) 01792 - 363 100

Norton House — The Mumbles
15 rooms, D £ 80 — 1 km
Tél (44) 01792 - 404 891, Fax (44) 01792 - 403 210

Forte Crest — Swansea
99 rooms, D £ 69 — 10 km
Tél (44) 01792 - 651 074, Fax (44) 01792 - 456 044

Wittemberg — The Mumbles
11 rooms, D £ 52 — 1 km
Tél (44) 01792 - 369 696, Fax (44) 01792 - 366 995

RESTAURANTS RESTAURANTS

Annie's — Swansea
Tél (44) 01792 - 655 603 — 10 km

808

This seaside resort owes it existence and reputation to the railways. It has preserved a very Victorian feel and physiognomy, still resisting the flash modern age of cars and planes. Yet there is nothing stuffy about this corner of the world, the air along the huge pier and sheltered promenades is far too keen for that. The course was created in the early part of the 20th century, designed by a one Tom Jones (whatever happened to him?) in a superb setting and beautiful parkland style with a few links features to add a little extra spice. This is another example of traditional architecture given few resources to shift earth but a great deal of imagination in using existing terrain. Trees, bunkers and a few well-placed ponds provide the main ingredients of a pleasant challenge, where holiday-makers can have fun and good amateur golfers let rip. A particularly high mark should go to the excellence of maintenance, especially the greens.

Cette station balnéaire a dû à la fois sa construction et sa notoriété au chemin de fer. Elle en a gardé un esprit et une physionomie très victoriens, résistant au modernisme et au clinquant, à l'heure de l'automobile, de la moto et de l'avion. Rien pourtant ici ne sent la poussière, l'air est trop vif le long de l'immense jetée et des promenades abritées. Ce parcours est né au début du XXème siècle, sous le crayon d'un Tom Jones qui n'a guère laissé de traces indélébiles. Celui-ci bénéficie d'un environnement superbe, d'une esthétique de golf «parkland» avec quelques traits de links pour épicer le plat. C'est encore un bon exemple de l'architecture traditionnelle, disposant de peu de moyens pour remuer la terre, mais de pas mal d'imagination pour utiliser le terrain existant. Des arbres, des bunkers, et quelques mares bien placées fournissent les éléments d'un challenge agréable, où les vacanciers pourront s'amuser, et les bons amateurs se déchaîner. La qualité de l'entretien et en particulier des greens est à noter.

Llandudno (Maesdu) Golf Club   1915

Hospital Road
WAL - LLANDUDNO LL30 1HU

Office	Secrétariat	(44) 01492 - 876 450
Pro shop	Pro-shop	5 195450
Fax	Fax	(44) 01492 - 871 570
Situation	Situation	

1,5 km S of Llandudno (pop. 18 647)

Annual closure	Fermeture annuelle	no
Weekly closure	Fermeture hebdomadaire	no

Fees main season
Tarifs haute saison 18 holes

	Week days Semaine	We/Bank holidays We/Férié
Individual Individuel	£ 25	£ 30
Couple Couple	£ 50	£ 60

Caddy	Caddy	no
Electric Trolley	Chariot électrique	no
Buggy	Voiturette	£ 16
Clubs	Clubs	yes

Credit cards Cartes de crédit   no

GOLF COURSE
PARCOURS   15/20

Site	Site	
Maintenance	Entretien	
Architect	Architecte	Tom Jones
Type	Type	parkland
Relief	Relief	
Water in play	Eau en jeu	
Exp. to wind	Exposé au vent	
Trees in play	Arbres en jeu	

Scorecard Carte de score	Chp. Chp.	Mens Mess.	Ladies Da.
Length Long.	5891	5630	5095
Par	72	72	75

Advised golfing ability Niveau de jeu recommandé	0 12 24 36	
Hcp required	Handicap exigé	certificate

CLUB HOUSE & AMENITIES
CLUB HOUSE ET ANNEXES   5/10

Pro shop	Pro-shop	
Driving range	Practice	
Sheltered	couvert	practice area
On grass	sur herbe	yes
Putting-green	putting-green	yes
Pitching-green	pitching green	yes

809

HOTEL FACILITIES
ENVIRONNEMENT HOTELIER   8/10

HOTELS HÔTELS
Bodysgallen Hall   Llandudno 4 km
34 rooms, D £ 120
Tél (44) 01492 - 584 466, Fax (44) 01492 - 582 519

St. Tudno - 21 rooms, D £ 120   Llandudno 1 km
Tél (44) 01492 - 874 411, Fax (44) 01492 - 860 407

Empire - 43 rooms, D £ 95   Llandudno 1 km
Tél (44) 01492 - 584 466, Fax (44) 01492 - 583 519

Bedford   Llandudno
27 rooms, D £ 46   1 km
Tél (44) 01492 - 876 647, Fax (44) 01492 - 860 185

RESTAURANTS RESTAURANTS
Martin's   Llandudno
Tél (44) 01492 - 870 070   1 km

Richard's Bistro   Llandudno
Tél (44) 01492 - 877 924   1 km

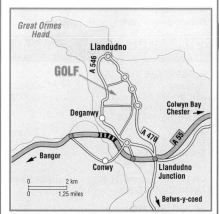

Access Accès : Manchester & Liverpool, A55,
then A470 to Llandudno. Golf near the Hospital.
Map 5 on page 496 Carte 5 Page 496

This course is important for several reasons. Firstly, its name is nigh on impossible to pronounce, secondly this is the site where the former Great Britain was defeated by the Romans after some heroic resistance, thirdly a small part of the course is in England and a larger part in Wales, and lastly this is where the young Woosnam learned the game. On top of that it also happens to be a good golf course, where the natural topology has been utilized with excellent insight into the game of golf and a marked degree of wisdom. As a result, a number of greens are elevated and a few ditches look safely far away but are in fact much closer and are just waiting for your ball to come their way. The perspectives here can be deceiving, therefore, even though the hilly terrain is easily walkable. Varied and pleasing to the eye, there is no let-up here if you want to card a good score, but you can also have fun with friends or the family. In short, a real good course becoming increasingly popular and busy.

Ce golf est important pour plusieurs raisons. D'abord, son nom est impossible. Puis, c'est ici que le roi de l'ancienne Grande Bretagne fut défait par les Romains après une héroïque résistance. Ensuite, le parcours est minoritairement en Angleterre, majoritairement au Pays de Galles. Enfin, c'est ici que le jeune Ian Woosnam a exercé ses premiers talents. Tout cela dit, c'est aussi un bon parcours de golf, où les accidents variés du terrain ont été utilisés avec un bon sens du jeu, mais aussi une certaine sagesse. Quelques greens sont ainsi surélevés, quelques fossés vous paraissent bien lointains, mais ils sont très proches pour les balles. Les perspectives offertes par les dénivelées sont parfois trompeuses, même si les reliefs ne sont pas un obstacle au jeu à pied. Varié, plaisant visuellement, il ne permet guère de répit si l'on veut bien scorer. mais on peut aussi s'y amuser entre amis ou en famille.

Llanymynech Golf Club 1933
Pant
ENG - OSWESTRY SY10 8LB

Office	Secrétariat	(44) 01691 - 830 983
Pro shop	Pro-shop	(44) 01691 - 830 879
Fax	Fax	
Situation	Situation	

10 km S of Oswestry (pop. 33 508)

Annual closure	Fermeture annuelle	no
Weekly closure	Fermeture hebdomadaire	no

Fees main season
Tarifs haute saison 18 holes

	Week days Semaine	We/Bank holidays We/Férié
Individual Individuel	£ 16	£ 20
Couple Couple	£ 32	£ 40

Full day: £ 25. Reductions for Juniors.

Caddy	Caddy	no
Electric Trolley	Chariot électrique	no
Buggy	Voiturette	no
Clubs	Clubs	yes

Credit cards Cartes de crédit   no

810

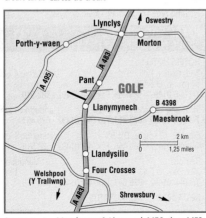

Access Accès : Manchester & Liverpool: M56, then M53, A55, A483 unto Ruabon, A5 unto Oswestry, then A483 again → Welshpool. Golf on right hand side (Pant).
Map 5 on page 496 Carte 5 Page 496

GOLF COURSE
PARCOURS   14/20

Site	Site	
Maintenance	Entretien	
Architect	Architecte	Unknown
Type	Type	open country, upland
Relief	Relief	
Water in play	Eau en jeu	
Exp. to wind	Exposé au vent	
Trees in play	Arbres en jeu	

Scorecard Carte de score	Chp. Chp.	Mens Mess.	Ladies Da.
Length Long.	5503	5310	4695
Par	70	70	71

Advised golfing ability		0 12 24 36
Niveau de jeu recommandé		
Hcp required	Handicap exigé	no

CLUB HOUSE & AMENITIES
CLUB HOUSE ET ANNEXES   6/10

Pro shop	Pro-shop	
Driving range	Practice	
Sheltered	couvert	practice area
On grass	sur herbe	yes
Putting-green	putting-green	yes
Pitching-green	pitching green	yes

HOTEL FACILITIES
ENVIRONNEMENT HOTELIER   4/10

HOTELS HÔTELS
Wynnstay   Oswestry
26 rooms, D £ 80   10 km
Tél (44) 01691 - 655 621
Fax (44) 01691 - 670 606

Ashfield   Trefonen
10 rooms, D £ 40   7 km
Tél (44) 01691 - 655 200
Fax (44) 01691 - 657 367

Old Mill Inn - 5 rooms, D £ 40   Llanforda 8 km
Tél (44) 01691 - 657 058

RESTAURANTS RESTAURANTS
Sebastian   Oswestry 10 km
Tél (44) 01691 - 655 444

Old Mill Inn - Tél (44) 01691 - 657 058   Llanforda 8 km

Purchasing this course allowed the Marriott group to rejuvenate and put the whole site centre-stage, with notably the arrival of the Solheim Cup in 1996. With a hotel now set up in the little 14th century manor here, the venue has become a leading resort which comprises two courses, the best known and most demanding of which is the «Old Course», named thus because it dates from only 1961. Designed by Ken Cotton, this has all the style of a typical park-land course where the finishing holes bring a lot of water into play. It is certainly not the world's most subtle course, but this honesty has the advantage of letting the golfer feel immediately at home and of carding the score he or she really deserves. We would advise green-feers not to go for the back-tees, especially on the 18th, a huge par 3.

L'achat de ce golf par le groupe Marriott a permis un rajeunissement notable, mais lui a aussi donné un coup de projecteur accentué par la venue de la Solheim Cup 1996. Avec son hôtel installé dans un petit manoir du XIVème siècle, c'est devenu un «resort» important, qui comprend deux parcours dont le plus connu et le plus exigeant est le le «Old Course,» dénommé ainsi bien qu'il ne date que de 1961. Dessiné par Ken Cotton, c'est un parcours typique de l'esthétique des parcs, avec un finale où l'eau est très en jeu. Ce n'est sans doute pas le parcours le plus subtil du monde, mais cette franchise a l'avantage de permettre immédiatement de s'y sentir à l'aise, et de faire le score que l'on mérite vraiment. On conseillera aux visiteurs de ne pas choisir les départs arrière, surtout au 18, énorme par 3.

Marriott St Pierre
Hotel & Country Club
1961

St Pierre Park
WAL - CHEPSTOW, Gwent NP6 6YA

Office	Secrétariat	(44) 01291 - 625 261
Pro shop	Pro-shop	(44) 01291 - 621 400
Fax	Fax	(44) 01291 - 629 975
Situation	Situation	

20 km E of Newport (pop. 133 318)

Annual closure	Fermeture annuelle	no
Weekly closure	Fermeture hebdomadaire	no
Fees main season	Tarifs haute saison	full day

	Week days Semaine	We/Bank holidays We/Férié
Individual Individuel	£ 55	—
Couple Couple	£ 110	—

Weekends: members and hotel guests only

Caddy	Caddy	on request
Electric Trolley	Chariot électrique	yes
Buggy	Voiturette	yes
Clubs	Clubs	yes

Credit cards Cartes de crédit
VISA - Eurocard - AMEX - DC

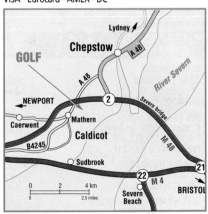

Access Accès : Newport A48 → Chepstow.
Golf 3 km (2 m. before Chepstow).
Map 6 on page 499 Carte 6 Page 499

GOLF COURSE
PARCOURS
16/20

Site	Site	
Maintenance	Entretien	
Architect	Architecte	C.K. Cotton
Type	Type	parkland
Relief	Relief	
Water in play	Eau en jeu	
Exp. to wind	Exposé au vent	
Trees in play	Arbres en jeu	

Scorecard Carte de score	Chp. Chp.	Mens Mess.	Ladies Da.
Length Long.	6280	5920	5337
Par	71	71	75

Advised golfing ability	0	12	24	36
Niveau de jeu recommandé				
Hcp required Handicap exigé	certificate			

CLUB HOUSE & AMENITIES
CLUB HOUSE ET ANNEXES
8/10

Pro shop	Pro-shop	
Driving range	Practice	
Sheltered	couvert	10 bays
On grass	sur herbe	yes
Putting-green	putting-green	yes
Pitching-green	pitching green	yes

811

HOTEL FACILITIES
ENVIRONNEMENT HOTELIER
7/10

HOTELS HÔTELS
Marriott Hotel — Golf
148 rooms, D £ 110 — on site
Tél (44) 01291 - 625 261, Fax (44) 01291 - 629 975

George — Chepstow
14 rooms, D £ 95 — 3 km
Tél (44) 01291 - 625 363, Fax (44) 01291 - 627 418

Beaufort — Chepstow
18 rooms, D £ 50 — 3 km
Tél (44) 01291 - 622 497, Fax (44) 01291 - 627 389

RESTAURANTS RESTAURANTS
Marriott Hotel — Golf
Tél (44) 01291 - 625 261 — on site

Parva Farmhouse — Tintern
Tél (44) 01291 - 689 411 — 8 km

This course is hardly close to the major tourist routes, but the site at least deserves a visit. Perched atop cliffs, it is very similar to a links course although some holes prefer heather to dunes. The course was founded in 1907, re-styled by J.H. Taylor and James Braid and completed in 1993. The site also houses a 9-holer between two sea inlets. The 18 hole course is no walk-over but never too tough or unfair. You also have to play every shot in the book, compounded by the fact that you often have a choice between playing safe or «going for it». The latter option can turn out to be foolhardy indeed on certain blind-shots. Never mind, you can stop off at the pub close to the 12th hole to boost your sagging spirits before squaring up to a wonderful finish, of which for us the 15th is the crowning moment. Maintenance is excellent and the clubhouse extends a warm welcome.

Ce n'est pas exactement sur les autoroutes de touristes, mais le site au moins mérite une visite. Perché sur les falaises, il est apparenté à un links, bien que certains trous soient assez proches des terrains de bruyère. Ce golf a été fondé en 1907, remanié par J.H. Taylor et James Braid, et achevé en 1993. On y trouve aussi un petit 9 trous entre deux bras de mer. Le 18 trous n'est pas facile, mais n'est jamais trop sévère ni injuste. On doit d'autant plus y jouer toute la gamme des coups de golf que l'on a souvent le choix entre la sécurité et l'héroïsme, qui peut s'avérer folie sur certains coups aveugles. Mais on peut faire une halte pour reprendre ses esprits au pub non loin du green du 12, afin d'affronter un très beau finish, dont le 15 est pour nous le sommet. L'entretien est de très bonne qualité, et le Clubhouse très chaleureux.

Nefyn & District Golf Club   1907

Morfa Nefyn
WAL - PWLLHELI, Gwynedd LL53 6DA

Office	Secrétariat	(44) 01758 - 720 966
Pro shop	Pro-shop	(44) 01758 - 720 102
Fax	Fax	(44) 01758 - 720 476
Situation	Situation	

3 km W of Nefyn (pop. 2 548)
32 km W of Caernarfon (pop. 9 695)

Annual closure	Fermeture annuelle	no
Weekly closure	Fermeture hebdomadaire	no

Fees main season
Tarifs haute saison 18 holes

	Week days Semaine	We/Bank holidays We/Férié
Individual Individuel	£ 25*	£ 30*
Couple Couple	£ 50	£ 60

*Full day: £ 30/£ 35

Caddy	Caddy	on request
Electric Trolley	Chariot électrique	yes
Buggy	Voiturette	£ 15/18 holes
Clubs	Clubs	yes

Credit cards Cartes de crédit
VISA - MasterCard (Pro shop only)

812

GOLF COURSE / PARCOURS   16/20

Site	Site	
Maintenance	Entretien	
Architect	Architecte	James Braid J.H. Taylor
Type	Type	seaside course, links
Relief	Relief	
Water in play	Eau en jeu	
Exp. to wind	Exposé au vent	
Trees in play	Arbres en jeu	

Scorecard Carte de score	Chp. Chp.	Mens Mess.	Ladies Da.
Length Long.	5958	5750	5420
Par	71	71	75

Advised golfing ability	0	12	24	36

Niveau de jeu recommandé

Hcp required Handicap exigé   certificate

CLUB HOUSE & AMENITIES / CLUB HOUSE ET ANNEXES   7/10

Pro shop	Pro-shop	
Driving range	Practice	
Sheltered	couvert	no
On grass	sur herbe	yes
Putting-green	putting-green	yes
Pitching-green	pitching green	yes

HOTEL FACILITIES / ENVIRONNEMENT HOTELIER   5/10

HOTELS HÔTELS

Caeau Capel Hotel   Nefyn
18 rooms, D £ 37   2 km
Tél (44) 01758 - 720 240

Plas Bodegroes   Pwllheli
8 rooms, D £ 100 (w/dinner)   12 km
Tél (44) 01758 - 612 363
Fax (44) 01758 - 701 247

Abersoch Harbour   Abersoch
14 rooms, D £ 60   25 km
Tél (44) 01758 - 712 406

RESTAURANTS RESTAURANTS

Plas Bodegroes   Pwllheli
Tél (44) 01758 - 612 363   12 km

Caeau Capel   Nefyn
Tél (44) 01758 - 720 240   2 km

GOLF

Porth-Dinilaen
Llithraen
Nefyn
Morfa Nefyn
Groesflordd
Edern
B 4354
B 4417
Criccieth
A 497
Bodluan
Tudweiliog
B 4415
Pwllhei
Aberdaron
A 499
B 4413
Abersoch
Y Gamlas
0   2   4 km
0   2,5 miles

Access Accès : North coast Lleyn Peninsula, on B4417
Map 5 on page 496 Carte 5 Page 496

A week's golfing in the Cardiff and Swansea region can be a week of playing a different course every day and of getting to know some superb and visually very contrasting layouts. Between St. Pierre and Porthcawl, close to Celtic Manor, the Newport course is one of the best examples of a park-land golf course you could ever hope to find. What's more, green-keeping is excellent and the welcome from both the clubhouse and members is warm and friendly. They are rightly extremely proud of a varied layout with very reasonable yardage, spread over rolling landscape which is very pleasant to walk. You won't find any breath-taking designer ploys or excesses, just a sort of sobriety in a pretty country landscape. A quality course, quite simply.

Une semaine de golf dans la région de Cardiff et Swansea peut permettre de ne jamais jouer deux fois le même parcours, et d'en jouer de superbes, d'esthétiques très différentes, voire opposées. Entre St Pierre et Porthcawl, près de Celtic Manor, le parcours de Newport est l'un des meilleurs exemples de golfs de parcs que l'on puisse trouver. Ce qui ne gâte rien, l'entretien y est toujours très soigné, et l'accueil, du club comme des membres, très amical et chaleureux. Ils sont fiers à juste raison d'un tracé très varié, et de longueur très raisonnable sur un terrain vallonné, mais où il est agréable de jouer à pied. On ne trouvera pas ici de trouvailles architecturales à couper le souffle, ni d'excès, mais une sorte de sobriété dans un joli paysage de campagne. La qualité, tout simplement.

Newport Golf Club — 1903

Great Oak, Rogerstone
WAL - NEWPORT, Gwent NP1 9FX

Office	Secrétariat	(44) 01633 - 892 643
Pro shop	Pro-shop	(44) 01633 - 893 271
Fax	Fax	(44) 01633 - 896 676
Situation	Situation	

6 km W of Newport (pop.133 318)

Annual closure	Fermeture annuelle	no
Weekly closure	Fermeture hebdomadaire	no

Fees main season
Tarifs haute saison 18 holes

	Week days Semaine	We/Bank holidays We/Férié
Individual Individuel	£ 30	£ 40
Couple Couple	£ 60	£ 80

Weekends: members only

Caddy	Caddy	no
Electric Trolley	Chariot électrique	yes
Buggy	Voiturette	no
Clubs	Clubs	yes
Credit cards Cartes de crédit		no

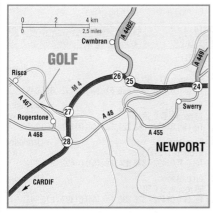

GOLF
Risca
Cwmbran
Rogerstone
Swerry
NEWPORT
CARDIF

0 — 2 — 4 km
0 — 2,5 miles

Access Accès : M4 Jct 27, then B4591.
Golf 1 km (1/2 m) W of exit.
Map 6 on page 499 Carte 6 Page 499

GOLF COURSE / PARCOURS — 15/20

Site	Site	
Maintenance	Entretien	
Architect	Architecte	Unknown
Type	Type	parkland
Relief	Relief	
Water in play	Eau en jeu	
Exp. to wind	Exposé au vent	
Trees in play	Arbres en jeu	

Scorecard Carte de score	Chp. Chp.	Mens. Mess.	Ladies Da.
Length Long.	5852	5632	5195
Par	72	72	74

Advised golfing ability Niveau de jeu recommandé	0	12	24	36

Hcp required   Handicap exigé   certificate

CLUB HOUSE & AMENITIES / CLUB HOUSE ET ANNEXES — 6/10

Pro shop	Pro-shop	
Driving range	Practice	
Sheltered	couvert	no
On grass	sur herbe	yes
Putting-green	putting-green	yes
Pitching-green	pitching green	yes

HOTEL FACILITIES / ENVIRONNEMENT HOTELIER — 7/10

HOTELS HÔTELS

Westgate — Newport
69 rooms, D £ 75 — 3 km
Tél (44) 01633 - 244 444, Fax (44) 01633 - 246 616

Newport Lodge — Newport
27 rooms, D £ 67 — 3 km
Tél (44) 01633 - 821 818, Fax (44) 01633 - 856 360

Parkway — Cwmbran
70 rooms, D £ 82.50 — 6 km
Tél (44) 01633 - 871 199, Fax (44) 01633 - 869 160

Celtic Manor Hotel — Newport
73 rooms, D £ 99 — 5 km
Tél (44) 01633 - 413 000, Fax (44) 01633 - 412 910

RESTAURANTS RESTAURANTS

Hedley's (Celtic Manor) — Newport
Tél (44) 01633 - 413 000 — 5 km

813

Llandudno is the seaside resort where a one Charles Dodgson, alias Lewis Carroll, treated his friends' children to readings of the stories that were to become Alice in Wonderland. It is also a resort where you can also ride on one of the few cable-car tramways in the world - there is another in San Francisco - to get to Great Orme's Head and see the Bronze Age copper mines. You will also find this rather little known links course, described by none other than Henry Cotton as a «gem». After a hesitant start, you are plunged into a landscape of dunes through which the course somehow winds it way. The front nine stretch alongside a railway line, the back nine return along the coastline, but the holes never run one behind the other; the direction they head in can cause a few surprises on your card. From one day to the next, a capricious wind can make life extremely complicated. There are good and bad things you will remember about this course, things like blind shots or weird ball positions and stances.

Llandudno, c'est la station balnéaire où Charles Dodgson, alias Lewis Carroll, racontait aux enfants de ses amis les futures histoires d'Alice au Pays des Merveilles. C'est aussi là que l'on peut prendre l'un des seuls tramways à câble du monde, avec celui de San Francisco, pour monter au Great Orme's Head, avec ses mines de cuivre de l'Age du Bronze. C'est enfin le site de ce links assez méconnu, décrit par Henry Cotton comme un «joyau». Après un départ hésitant, on plonge dans un paysage de dunes où se coule le parcours. Les neuf premiers trous longent une voie ferrée, les neuf derniers reviennent le long de la mer, mais l'orientation des trousl peut créer des surprises sur la carte. D'un jour à l'autre, les caprices du vent peuvent encore compliquer les choses. On se souviendra ici du bon et du mauvais caractère du parcours, qui peuvent vous réserver aussi bien des coups aveugles que des positions de balle (et de stance) bizarres.

North Wales Golf Club — 1894

72 Brynian Road
WAL - WEST SHORE, LLANDUDNO LL30 2 DZ

Office	Secrétariat	(44) 01492 - 875 325
Pro shop	Pro-shop	(44) 01492 - 876 878
Fax	Fax	(44) 01492 - 875 325
Situation	Situation	

1 km from Llandudno (pop. 18 647)

Annual closure	Fermeture annuelle	no
Weekly closure	Fermeture hebdomadaire	no

Fees main season
Tarifs haute saison 18 holes

	Week days Semaine	We/Bank holidays We/Férié
Individual Individuel	£ 23*	£ 30*
Couple Couple	£ 46	£ 60

£ 16 and £ 20 from November to March

Caddy	Caddy	no
Electric Trolley	Chariot électrique	no
Buggy	Voiturette	£ 25
Clubs	Clubs	yes

Credit cards Cartes de crédit	no

814

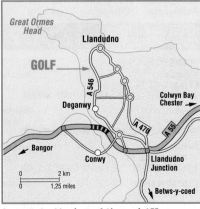

Access Accès : Manchester & Liverpool, A55, then A470 to Llandudno.
Golf 1 km West of Llandudno on West Shore
Map 5 on page 496 Carte 5 Page 496

GOLF COURSE PARCOURS — 17/20

Site	Site	
Maintenance	Entretien	
Architect	Architecte	Unknown
Type	Type	links
Relief	Relief	
Water in play	Eau en jeu	
Exp. to wind	Exposé au vent	
Trees in play	Arbres en jeu	

Scorecard Carte de score	Chp. Chp.	Mens Mess.	Ladies Da.
Length Long.	5623	5331	5072
Par	71	71	73

Advised golfing ability Niveau de jeu recommandé	0	12	24	36
Hcp required Handicap exigé	certificate			

CLUB HOUSE & AMENITIES CLUB HOUSE ET ANNEXES — 6/10

Pro shop	Pro-shop	
Driving range	Practice	
Sheltered	couvert	practice area
On grass	sur herbe	yes
Putting-green	putting-green	yes
Pitching-green	pitching green	yes

HOTEL FACILITIES ENVIRONNEMENT HOTELIER — 8/10

HOTELS HÔTELS

Imperial — Llandudno
97 rooms, D £ 90 — 1 km
Tél (44) 01492 - 877 466, Fax (44) 01492 - 878 043

Tan Lan — Llandudno
18 rooms, D £ 50 — 1 km
Tél (44) 01492 - 860 221, Fax (44) 01492 - 860 221

Bryn Derwen — Llandudno
9 rooms, D £ 80 — 1 km
Tél (44) 01492 - 876 804, Fax (44) 01492 - 876 804

Ambassador — Llandudno
65 rooms, D £ 60 — 1,5 km
Tél (44) 01492 - 876 886, Fax (44) 01492 - 876 347

RESTAURANTS RESTAURANTS

Number 1's Bistro — Llandudno 1 km
Tél (44) 01492 - 877 924

Café Niçoise - Tél (44) 01492 - 531 555 Colwyn Bay 8 km

NORTHOP COUNTRY PARK

16	9	6

As the Tour Operators say, this is a good «product». The club-house is opulent and spacious, the adjacent hotel is luxurious, the park is a beauty and maintenance virtually faultless. The course is recent but has already hosted many high-level tournaments like the British Girls. It was designed by John Jacobs, one of the legendary names in modern golf instruction. Here, he was at his best, even though a little more extravagance in the graphics of the layout might sometimes have been welcome over what is a spectacular complex. Nevertheless, the whole course has been carefully designed in a rather classic British style and it is becoming better and better as each passing year adds to its maturity. One decisive advantage here is that nothing is concealed from view and both reward and sanction are equal to the risk taken or mistake made. You can almost feel the teacher behind the architect. Amongst other excellent holes, the 8th is most memorable, a downhill par 5, together with the 16th, a slight dog-leg with trees and water .

Un beau produit. Le Clubhouse est riche et grand, l'Hôtel adjacent est luxueux, le parc est beau, l'entretien presque sans fautes. Le parcours est récent, mais il a déjà reçu de nombreuses bonnes épreuves, comme la British Girls. Son auteur est John Jacobs, l'une des légendes de l'enseignement moderne de golf. Ici, il est à son meilleur, même si on pourrait souhaiter parfois un peu plus de «folie» graphique dans un ensemble par ailleurs spectaculaire. Il reste que l'ensemble est très soigné, assez classiquement britannique, et que chaque année ajoutant de la maturité, il se bonifie en vieillissant. Avantage décisif : rien n'est caché ici, et la récompense comme la punition sont à la hauteur du risque pris ou de la faute commise. On sent bien là l'enseignant derrière l'architecte ! Entre autres trous de qualité, on se souviendra du 8, un par 5 en descente, comme du 16, en léger dog-leg avec des arbres et pas mal d'eau.

Northop Country Park		**1993**
WAL - NORTHOP, Nr Chester, CH7 6WA		

Office	Secrétariat	(44) 01352 - 840 440
Pro shop	Pro-shop	(44) 01352 - 840 440
Fax	Fax	(44) 01352 - 840 445
Situation	Situation	
20 km SW of Chester (pop. 115 971)		
Annual closure	Fermeture annuelle	no
Weekly closure	Fermeture hebdomadaire	no

Fees main season
Tarifs haute saison 18 holes

	Week days Semaine	We/Bank holidays We/Férié
Individual Individuel	£ 30	£ 35
Couple Couple	£ 60	£ 70

Caddy	Caddy	no
Electric Trolley	Chariot électrique	no
Buggy	Voiturette	£ 15
Clubs	Clubs	£ 10

Credit cards Cartes de crédit VISA - MasterCard

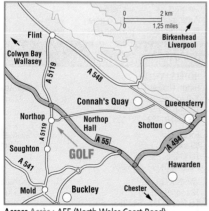

Access Accès : A55 (North Wales Coast Road).
Exit at Northop Connah's Quay.
Northop Country Park is on left side of exit road.
Map 5 on page 496 Carte 5 Page 496

GOLF COURSE
PARCOURS

16/20

Site	Site	
Maintenance	Entretien	
Architect	Architecte	John Jacobs
Type	Type	parkland
Relief	Relief	
Water in play	Eau en jeu	
Exp. to wind	Exposé au vent	
Trees in play	Arbres en jeu	

Scorecard Carte de score	Chp. Chp.	Mens Mess.	Ladies Da.
Length Long.	6128	5765	4945
Par	72	72	72

Advised golfing ability		0	12	24	36
Niveau de jeu recommandé					
Hcp required	Handicap exigé	yes			

CLUB HOUSE & AMENITIES
CLUB HOUSE ET ANNEXES

9/10

Pro shop	Pro-shop	
Driving range	Practice	
Sheltered	couvert	6 bays
On grass	sur herbe	yes
Putting-green	putting-green	yes
Pitching-green	pitching green	yes

815

HOTEL FACILITIES
ENVIRONNEMENT HOTELIER

6/10

HOTELS HÔTELS
St David's Park Hotel — close
145 rooms, D £ 85
Tél (44) 01244 - 520 800, Fax (44) 01244 - 520 930

Kinsale Hall — Holywell
27 rooms, D £ 90 — 10 km
Tél (44) 01745 - 560 001, Fax (44) 01745 - 561 298

Holiday Inn Garden Court — Chester
55 rooms, D £ 90 — 15 km
Tél (44) 01244 - 550 011, Fax (44) 01244 - 550 763

RESTAURANTS RESTAURANTS
Crabwall Manor — Chester
Tél (44) 01244 - 851 666 — 15 km

Craxton Wood — Puddington
Tél (44) 0151 - 339 4717 — 15 km

Firstly there are the superb views over a rugged coastline, the sea, smugglers' beaches and dunes, then the countryside with remains of castles. In a highly romantic setting, don't ever let this course catch you napping. At first sight it can be intimidating with steep hills that make club selection a delicate business (there are a few blind shots to contend with) but the difficulties are not insurmountable even for a mid-handicapper, unless the wind begins to blow a little too hard. In calm weather, Pennard certainly could not claim to be a major championship course, but it is incredibly enjoyable both visually and technically. And when you do finally get to grips with it, you feel that you could be a good player. Green-keeping is of a very high standard, and the greens are slick and firm all year round (Winters are very mild here). Discovery recommended.

D'abord il y a des vues superbes sur les côtes découpées, la mer, des plages de contrebandiers, les dunes, la campagne, des châteaux en ruines. Dans un site hautement romantique, il ne faut pas rêver pour jouer ce parcours. Il peut intimider au premier abord avec ses reliefs qui compliquent notamment la sélection des clubs (quelques coups aveugles), mais ses difficultés ne sont pas insurmontables, même pour un joucur moyen, sauf si le vent se met à souffler un peu fort. Certes, par temps calme, Pennard ne saurait prétendre être un parcours de grands championnats, mais il procure un plaisir fou, visuellement et techniquement. Et quand vous parvenez à l'apprivoiser, vous avez l'impression d'être un grand joueur. L'entretien est ici très soigné, les greens rapides et fermes toute l'année (les hivers sont assez doux). A découvrir !

Pennard Golf Club — 1896
2, Southgate Road, Southgate
WAL - SWANSEA SA3 2BT

Office	Secrétariat	(44) 01792 - 233 131
Pro shop	Pro-shop	(44) 01792 - 233 451
Fax	Fax	(44) 01792 - 234 797
Situation	Situation	

12 km W of Swansea (pop. 181 906)

Annual closure	Fermeture annuelle	no
Weekly closure	Fermeture hebdomadaire	no

Fees main season
Tarifs haute saison full day

	Week days Semaine	We/Bank holidays We/Férié
Individual Individuel	£ 24	£ 30
Couple Couple	£ 48	£ 60

Caddy	Caddy	no
Electric Trolley	Chariot électrique	no
Buggy	Voiturette	no
Clubs	Clubs	yes
Credit cards Cartes de crédit		no

GOLF COURSE / PARCOURS — 18/20

Site	Site	
Maintenance	Entretien	
Architect	Architecte	James Braid C.K. Cotton links
Type	Type	
Relief	Relief	
Water in play	Eau en jeu	
Exp. to wind.	Exposé au vent	
Trees in play	Arbres en jeu	

Scorecard Carte de score	Chp. Chp.	Mens Mess.	Ladies Da.
Length Long.	5701	5508	4880
Par	71	71	73

Advised golfing ability		0 12 24 36
Niveau de jeu recommandé		
Hcp required	Handicap exigé	no

CLUB HOUSE & AMENITIES / CLUB HOUSE ET ANNEXES — 6/10

Pro shop	Pro-shop	
Driving range	Practice	
Sheltered	couvert	no
On grass	sur herbe	yes
Putting-green	putting-green	yes
Pitching-green	pitching green	yes

HOTEL FACILITIES / ENVIRONNEMENT HOTELIER — 6/10

HOTELS HÔTELS

Hilton National — Swansea 12 km
120 rooms, D £ 75
Tél (44) 01792 - 310 330
Fax (44) 01792 - 797 535

Forte Crest — Swansea 15 km
99 rooms, D £ 69
Tél (44) 01792 - 651 074
Fax (44) 01792 - 456 044

Windsor Lodge — Swansea 15 km
18 rooms, D £ 60
Tél (44) 01792 - 642 158
Fax (44) 01792 - 648 996

RESTAURANTS RESTAURANT

Annie's — Swansea 15 km
Tél (44) 01792 - 655 603

816

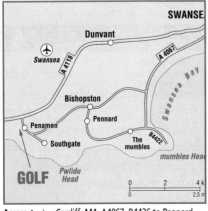

SWANSE
Dunvant
Swansea
A4118
A4067
Swansea Bay
Bishopston
Penamen
Pennard
Southgate
The mumbles
B4422
mumbles Hea
GOLF
Pwlidu Head
0   2   4 k
0   2,5 m

Access Accès : Cardiff, M4, A4067, B4436 to Pennard Church, → Golf
Map 6 on page 498 Carte 6 Page 498

There is not much missing at Pyle & Kenfig for this to rank amongst the very great courses. For once, a course of this type returns to the clubhouse at the 9th and in doing so emphasises the difference between the front and back nines, separated by a road. Although the outward half is not to be sniffed at, it doesn't have the dune landscape of the epic back nine, which has a single par 5 but some beefy par 3s and huge par 4s (from hole 16 to 18 with a head-wind to boot). The greatest difficulties are the rough, the positions you can get yourself into when straying off the fairway and the cleverly placed pot bunkers. The greens are on the flat side and generally reachable with bump and run shots, luckily for the players, because they are of course often very exposed to the wind. Not an easy course, but very forthright.

Il ne manque pas grand-chose à Pyle & Kenfig pour être dans la cour des très grands parcours. Pour une fois, un parcours de ce type revient au Clubhouse au 9, cela ne fait que souligner la différence entre l'aller et le re-tour, séparés par une route. Bien que l'aller ne soit pas négligeable, il lui manque le caractère dunaire d'un re-tour héroïque, où l'on trouve un seul par 5, mais des par 3 très musclés et d'énormes par 4 (du 16 au 18, contre les vents dominants). Les plus grandes difficultés sont les roughs, les positions où l'on se trouve par rapport à la balle quand on s'égare hors des fairways, et de profonds bunkers (trop) bien placés. Les greens sont assez plats, leur accès généralement possible en roulant, ce qui est fort heureux car l'exposition au vent est bien sûr importante. Un parcours pas facile, mais franc.

Pyle & Kenfig Golf Club — 1922

Waun-y-Mer
WAL - KENFIG, Mid Glamorgan CF33 4PU

Office	Secrétariat	(44) 01656 - 783 093
Pro shop	Pro-shop	(44) 01656 - 772 446
Fax	Fax	(44) 01656 - 772 822
Situation	Situation	

40 km W of Cardiff (pop. 279 055)
10 km E of Port Talbot (pop. 51 023)

Annual closure	Fermeture annuelle	no
Weekly closure	Fermeture hebdomadaire	no
Fees main season	Tarifs haute saison	18 holes

	Week days Semaine	We/Bank holidays We/Férié
Individual Individuel	£ 30	*
Couple Couple	£ 60	*

* Weekends: with members only (£ 17.50)

Caddy	Caddy	no
Electric Trolley	Chariot électrique	yes
Buggy	Voiturette	no
Clubs	Clubs	yes

Credit cards Cartes de crédit
VISA -Mastercard - AMEX

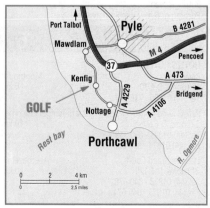

Access Accès : M4, Jct 37, → Porthcawl,
at 3rd roundabout, 1st right
Map 6 on page 499 Carte 6 Page 499

GOLF COURSE / PARCOURS — 17/20

Site	Site	
Maintenance	Entretien	
Architect	Architecte	Harry S. Colt
Type	Type	links, open country
Relief	Relief	
Water in play	Eau en jeu	
Exp. to wind	Exposé au vent	
Trees in play	Arbres en jeu	

Scorecard Carte de score	Chp. Chp.	Mens Mess.	Ladies Da.
Length Long.	6086	5571	4941
Par	71	71	74

Advised golfing ability Niveau de jeu recommandé	0 12 24 36
Hcp required Handicap exigé	certificate

CLUB HOUSE & AMENITIES / CLUB HOUSE ET ANNEXES — 7/10

Pro shop	Pro-shop	
Driving range	Practice	
Sheltered	couvert	no
On grass	sur herbe	yes
Putting-green	putting-green	yes
Pitching-green	pitching green	yes

817

HOTEL FACILITIES / ENVIRONNEMENT HOTELIER — 5/10

HOTELS HÔTELS
Fairways Hotel — Porthcawl
25 rooms, D £ 65 — 2 km
Tél (44) 01656 - 782 085, Fax (44) 01656 - 785 351

The Porthcawl Hotel — Porthcawl
28 rooms, D £ 44 — 2 km
Tél (44) 01656 - 782 257

Heritage Hotel — Porthcawl
8 rooms, D £ 50 — 2 km
Tél (44) 01656 - 771 881

Dormy House — Royal Porthcawl
9 rooms, D £ 40 — 2 km
Tél (44) 01656 - 782 251, Fax (44) 01656 - 771 687

RESTAURANTS RESTAURANT
Heritage Hotel — Porthcawl
Tél (44) 01656 - 771 881 — 2 km

You sometimes wonder why some good courses never reach the sort of stardom they might deserve. Here, despite the excellent road from Birmingham to Cardiff running close by, the reason might be the absence of any top tournament. From another angle, this tranquillity is a blessing for players who love to feel alone in the world. Although laid out over «rolling» landscape, the course's name comes from the Rolls family (as in Royce), whose estate overlooks the course. It is sited around a forest-covered hill in a park-land landscape lined with some superb trees. Walking can be a little hard on the legs but there are buggies to give you the time to admire the landscape and wild-life or to drive on and reconnoitre some of the blind shots that await you. As far as the course's very own personality is concerned, you'll remember best of all the magnificent par 3s.

On se demande pourquoi de bons parcours restent à l'écart de la célébrité. Dans le cas présent, l'excellente route de Birmingham à Cardiff passant pourtant à côté, il manque peut-être un grand tournoi. D'un autre côté, cette tranquillité est une bénédiction pour les joueurs, qui adorent être seuls au monde, c'est bien connu. Certes le terrain est «rolling,» mais le nom vient de la famille Rolls (comme Royce) dont la propriété domine le parcours, dessiné autour d'une grande colline boisée, dans un paysage de parc et de bois superbes. Marcher peut-être ici fatigant, mais il y a des voiturettes pour se donner le temps d'admirer le paysage et la vie sauvage, ou d'aller repérer les lieux sur les quelques coups aveugles. Pour ce qui est de la personnalité du parcours, on se souviendra notamment des très beaux par 3.

The Rolls of Monmouth — 1982

The Hendre
WAL - MONMOUTH, Gwent NP5 4HG

Office	Secrétariat	(44) 01600 - 715 353
Pro shop	Pro-shop	(44) 01600 - 715 353
Fax	Fax	(44) 01600 - 713 115
Situation	Situation	

7 km W of Monmouth (pop. 8 204)
58 km NE of Cardiff (pop. 279 055)

Annual closure	Fermeture annuelle	no
Weekly closure	Fermeture hebdomadaire	no

Fees main season	Tarifs haute saison	18 holes
	Week days Semaine	We/Bank holidays We/Férié
Individual Individuel	£ 32	£ 37
Couple Couple	£ 64	£ 74
Monday offer: £ 26		

Caddy	Caddy	no
Electric Trolley	Chariot électrique	yes
Buggy	Voiturette	£ 25/18 holes
Clubs	Clubs	no

Credit cards Cartes de crédit VISA - AMEX - DC

Access Accès : Cardiff, M4 East, Jct 24, then A449 to Monmouth. Golf on B4233 (Abergavenny Road), 5 km W of Monmouth.
Map 6 on page 499 Carte 6 Page 499

GOLF COURSE PARCOURS — 15/20

Site	Site	
Maintenance	Entretien	
Architect	Architecte	Urbis Planning
Type	Type	parkland, hilly
Relief	Relief	
Water in play	Eau en jeu	
Exp. to wind	Exposé au vent	
Trees in play	Arbres en jeu	

Scorecard Carte de score	Chp. Chp.	Mens Mess.	Ladies Da.
Length Long.	6127	5718	5215
Par	72	72	75

Advised golfing ability		0	12	24	36
Niveau de jeu recommandé					
Hcp required	Handicap exigé	no			

CLUB HOUSE & AMENITIES CLUB HOUSE ET ANNEXES — 6/10

Pro shop	Pro-shop	
Driving range	Practice	
Sheltered	couvert	no
On grass	sur herbe	yes
Putting-green	putting-green	yes
Pitching-green	pitching green	yes

HOTEL FACILITIES ENVIRONNEMENT HOTELIER — 6/10

HOTELS HÔTELS
Riverside — Monmouth
17 rooms, D £ 70 — 6 km
Tél (44) 01600 - 715 577

Penyclawdd Court — Llanfihangel Crucorney
3 rooms, D £ 60 — 10 km
Tél (44) 01873 - 890 719
Fax (44) 01873 - 890 848

Llansantffraed Court — Abergavenny
21 rooms, D £ 120 — 10 km
Tél (44) 01873 - 840 678
Fax (44) 01873 - 840 674

RESTAURANTS RESTAURANT
Clytha Arms — Raglan
Tél (44) 01873 - 840 206 — 8 km

818

The is the most famous course in Wales and does full honour to its reputation. Royal Porthcawl is an absolute must for great course «trophy-hunters». It is, of course, a links, although half a dozen very distinctive holes are more heather-land in style and are played on a sort of high plateau overlooking the Bristol Channel. Contrary to many links, where holes are often laid out in line, the holes here shoot out in all directions and make club selection a real headache, depending on the wind. This is a part of what goes to make up the greatness and test value of this layout, where the slightest technical shortcoming will cost you dearly, and where the uninterrupted view over the sea might make you wish you had gone to the beach instead. A true masterpiece, beautifully maintained, which has staged some memorable Curtis Cup and Walker Cup matches and five British Amateur Championships.

C'est le plus fameux parcours du Pays de Galles, il honore dignement sa réputation, et doit figurer dans le «tableau» des chasseurs de grands golfs. C'est évidemment un links, bien qu'une demi-douzaine de trous de caractère un peu plus «terre de bruyère» trouvent place sur une sorte de haut plateau dominant le Canal de Bristol. Au contraire de nombreux links, dont les trous sont souvent alignés, ceux-ci tournent dans toutes les directions, à vous donner le vertige quant au choix de clubs suivant le vent. C'est une part de ce qui fait la grandeur et la valeur de test de ce parcours, où la moindre faiblesse technique se paie cher, où la vue constante de la mer peut vous faire regretter de ne pas avoir choisi d'aller à la plage. Un vrai chef-d'oeuvre merveilleusement entretenu, où se sont déroulées de mémorables Curtis Cup et Walker Cup, ainsi que cinq British Amateur.

Royal Porthcawl Golf Club — 1891
WAL - PORTHCAWL, Mid Glamorgan CF36 3VW

Office	Secrétariat	(44) 01656 - 782 251
Pro shop	Pro-shop	(44) 01656 - 773 702
Fax	Fax	(44) 01656 - 771 687
Situation	Situation	

40 km W of Cardiff (pop. 279 055)
10 km E of Port Talbot (pop. 51 023)

Annual closure	Fermeture annuelle	no
Weekly closure	Fermeture hebdomadaire	no
Fees main season	Tarifs haute saison	18 holes

	Week days Semaine	We/Bank holidays We/Férié
Individual Individuel	£ 40*	£ 50*
Couple Couple	£ 80	£ 100

*Full day: £ 50/£ 60 - Weekends & Wednesdays: with members only & guests of

Caddy	Caddy	on request
Electric Trolley	Chariot électrique	yes
Buggy	Voiturette	no
Clubs	Clubs	yes

Credit cards Cartes de crédit VISA - MasterCard

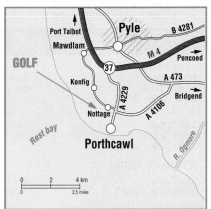

GOLF
Port Talbot
Mawdlam
Pyle
B 4281
M 4
Pencoed
Kenfig
37
A 473
A 4229
A 4106
Bridgend
Nottage
Rest bay
Porthcawl
R. Ogmore

0   2   4 km
0   2,5 miles

Access Accès : M4 Jct 37. At Porthcawl seafront, right → Locks Common, then left.
Map 6 on page 499 Carte 6 Page 499

GOLF COURSE / PARCOURS — 19/20

Site	Site	▰▰▰▰▱
Maintenance	Entretien	▰▰▰▰▱
Architect	Architecte	Charles Gibson

Type	Type	links
Relief	Relief	▰▰▰▱▱
Water in play	Eau en jeu	▰▱▱▱▱
Exp. to wind	Exposé au vent	▰▰▰▰▱
Trees in play	Arbres en jeu	▰▱▱▱▱

Scorecard Carte de score	Chp. Chp.	Mens Mess.	Ladies Da.
Length Long.	6083	5608	5231
Par	72	72	75

Advised golfing ability		0 12 24 36
Niveau de jeu recommandé		▰▰▰▱
Hcp required	Handicap exigé	certificate

CLUB HOUSE & AMENITIES / CLUB HOUSE ET ANNEXES — 7/10

Pro shop	Pro-shop	▰▰▰▰▱
Driving range	Practice	▰▰▰▱▱
Sheltered	couvert	2 bays
On grass	sur herbe	yes
Putting-green	putting-green	yes
Pitching-green	pitching green	yes

HOTEL FACILITIES / ENVIRONNEMENT HOTELIER — 6/10

HOTELS HÔTELS

Fairways Hotel — Porthcawl
25 rooms, D £ 65 — 1 km
Tél (44) 01656 - 782 085, Fax (44) 01656 - 785 351

The Porthcawl Hotel — Porthcawl
28 rooms, D £ 44 — 3 km
Tél (44) 01656 - 782 257

Heritage Hotel — Porthcawl
8 rooms, D £ 50 — 2 km
Tél (44) 01656 - 771 881

Dormy House — Royal Porthcawl
9 rooms, D £ 40 — on site
Tél (44) 01656 - 782 251, Fax (44) 01656 - 771 687

RESTAURANTS RESTAURANT

Heritage Hotel — Porthcawl
Tél (44) 01656 - 771 881 — 2 km

819

Overlooked by the extraordinary medieval Harlech castle with a fortified stairway running down to the sea, this course (named after the patron saint of Wales) is more majestic than ever. The pros say this is the toughest par 69 in the world, but one thing is sure: for the ordinary mortal, playing 3 strokes over your handicap is already a right «royal» exploit. The constant changes in hole direction are a further disruptive factor for golfers who already have to contend with the optical illusions created by the dune environment and the sensation of space. The shot you need to master here is of course the low ball and you need a good measure of flair to place your bump 'n run shots close to the pin. High shots will more often than not end up in spots where your recovery can be «most amusing». A great course.

Dominé par l'extraordinaire château médiéval d'Harlech, avec son escalier fortifié allant jusqu'à la mer, ce parcours (portant le nom du patron du Pays de Galles) acquiert une majesté supplémentaire. Les profession- nels disent qu'il s'agit du par 69 le plus difficile du monde. Une chose est sûre, pour le commun des mortels, jouer trois au-dessus de son handicap est déjà «royal». Les changements constants d'orientation des trous perturbent les joueurs, déjà aux prises avec les illusions de distance que donne l'environnement de dunes, mais aussi la sensation d'espace. Le coup à maîtriser est bien sûr la balle basse, et il faut beaucoup de flair pour placer les obligatoires «bump'n run» à proximité du trou. Quant aux balles hautes, elles terminent leur course dans des endroits d'où il est amusant de s'extraire. Un grand parcours.

Royal St David's Golf Club — 1894
WAL - HARLECH, Gwynedd LL46 2UB

Office	Secrétariat	(44) 01766 - 780 361
Pro shop	Pro-shop	(44) 01766 - 780 851
Fax	Fax	(44) 01766 - 781 110
Situation	Situation	

3 km from Harlech (pop. 1 880)

| Annual closure | Fermeture annuelle | no |
| Weekly closure | Fermeture hebdomadaire | no |

Fees main season	Tarifs haute saison	18 holes
	Week days Semaine	We/Bank holidays We/Férié
Individual Individuel	£ 30	£ 38
Couple Couple	£ 60	£ 76

Booking essential at weekends

Caddy	Caddy	no
Electric Trolley	Chariot électrique	yes
Buggy	Voiturette	yes
Clubs	Clubs	yes

Credit cards Cartes de crédit VISA - Mastercard

820

Access Accès : Manchester M56, A55 to Bangor, then A487 South to Porthmadog, A470 and A496 → Harlech. Golf on right side before Harlech.
Map 5 on page 496 Carte 5 Page 496

GOLF COURSE / PARCOURS — 18/20

Site	Site	■■■■■■□
Maintenance	Entretien	■■■■■■□
Architect	Architecte	Unknown
Type	Type	links
Relief	Relief	■■■■□
Water in play	Eau en jeu	■■■□□
Exp. to wind	Exposé au vent	■■■■□
Trees in play	Arbres en jeu	■□□□□

Scorecard Carte de score	Chp. Chp.	Mens Mess.	Ladies Da.
Length Long.	5848	5713	5266
Par	69	69	74

Advised golfing ability		0 12 24 36
Niveau de jeu recommandé		■■■■■
Hcp required	Handicap exigé	certificate

CLUB HOUSE & AMENITIES / CLUB HOUSE ET ANNEXES — 6/10

Pro shop	Pro-shop	■■■■□
Driving range	Practice	■■■□□
Sheltered	couvert	no
On grass	sur herbe	yes
Putting-green	putting-green	yes
Pitching-green	pitching green	yes

HOTEL FACILITIES / ENVIRONNEMENT HOTELIER — 5/10

HOTELS HÔTELS
St David's Hotel — Harlech adjacent
60 rooms, D £ 40
Tél (44) 01766 - 780 366
Fax (44) 01766 - 780 820

Castle Cottage — Harlech 3 km
6 rooms, D £ 52
Tél (44) 01766 - 780 479

RESTAURANTS RESTAURANT
Castle Cottage — Harlech close
Tél (44) 01766 - 780 479

A good number of specialists lent a hand in laying out this course, including Fernie, Vardon, Braid, Fowler, Willie Park, H.S. Colt and, more recently Donald Steel. Perched high up overlooking Porthcawl, Southerndown has resisted any attempts at serious human interference and stayed very natural in style. And it is true that the land was ideal for the building of a golf course. The fairways are cropped by sheep, who never go on strike and work most methodically. Very British in its sloping and hilly design but never over-tiring on the legs, this is not a links because the terrain is clay (well drained) but there are more bushes than trees in play. Still, you are playing links-style golf here, hitting searing low shots. A tough test from the back tees, a little easier from the front and all in all, well worth getting to know.

Bien des spécialistes se sont penchés sur ce parcours : Fernie, Vardon, Braid, Fowler, Willie Park, H.S. Colt et dernièrement Donald Steel. Perché haut et dominant Porthcawl, Southerndown a pourtant réussi à se préserver des atteintes et rester très naturel: il est vrai que le terrain se prêtait idéalement à la construction d'un golf. Les fairways sont d'ailleurs tondus par les moutons, qui ne font jamais grève et travaillent avec méthode ! Très britannique dans son dessin typique des terrains en pente, mais sans fatigue excessive, ce n'est pas un links, parce que le terrain est argileux (bien drainé) et bien que l'on y trouve plus de buissons que d'arbres en jeu, mais il faut utiliser le même type de jeu, avec des balles pénétrantes et basses. Difficile des départs arrière, il s'adoucit quand on avance un peu. A connaître.

Southerndown Golf Club — 1905

Ewenny
WAL - BRIDGEND, Mid. Glam. CF32 0QP

Office	Secrétariat	(44) 01656 - 880 476
Pro shop	Pro-shop	(44) 01656 - 880 326
Fax	Fax	(44) 01656 - 880 371
Situation	Situation	

5 km SW of Bridgend (pop. 14 311)

Annual closure	Fermeture annuelle	no
Weekly closure	Fermeture hebdomadaire	no

Fees main season	Tarifs haute saison	18 holes
	Week days Semaine	We/Bank holidays We/Férié
Individual Individuel	£ 25	£ 35
Couple Couple	£ 50	£ 70

Weekends: only with a member

Caddy	Caddy	no
Electric Trolley	Chariot électrique	no
Buggy	Voiturette	no
Clubs	Clubs	yes
Credit cards Cartes de crédit		no

Access Accès : On the coast road Bridgend to Ogmore-by-Sea.
Turn off at Pelican Inn (opp. Ogmore Castle)
Map 6 on page 499 Carte 6 Page 499

GOLF COURSE / PARCOURS — 16/20

Site	Site	
Maintenance	Entretien	
Architect	Architecte	Willie Fernie
Type	Type	downland
Relief	Relief	
Water in play	Eau en jeu	
Exp. to wind	Exposé au vent	
Trees in play	Arbres en jeu	

Scorecard	Chp.	Mens	Ladies
Carte de score	Chp.	Mess.	Da.
Length Long.	5840	5395	5049
Par	70	69	74

Advised golfing ability		0	12	24	36
Niveau de jeu recommandé					
Hcp required	Handicap exigé	certificate			

CLUB HOUSE & AMENITIES / CLUB HOUSE ET ANNEXES — 7/10

Pro shop	Pro-shop	
Driving range	Practice	
Sheltered	couvert	no
On grass	sur herbe	yes
Putting-green	putting-green	yes
Pitching-green	pitching green	yes

HOTEL FACILITIES / ENVIRONNEMENT HOTELIER — 7/10

HOTELS HÔTELS

Heronston — Bridgend
76 rooms, D £ 80 — 3 km
Tél (44) 01656 - 668 811
Fax (44) 01656 - 667 391

Coed-y-Mwstwr — Coychurch
22 rooms, D £ 100 — 6 km
Tél (44) 01656 - 860 261
Fax (44) 01656 - 863 122

RESTAURANTS RESTAURANTS

Frolics — Southerndown
Tél (44) 01656 - 880 127 — 3 km

Great House — Laleston
Tél (44) 01656 - 657 644 — 7 km

821

Firstly there is a landscape of pot-holed dunes, looking as if they have been stirred by the wind for years on end. And then comes the course, fashioned by men and nature for centuries with the sporadic help of James Braid, as witnessed by the contours of some of the greens and the location of the many bunkers. There are very few continental golfers who have heard much about Welsh courses. This one is a must as you travel around the magnificent coastline of this very likeable country. Depending on the weather, the course can turn into a major championship test or a superb walk in the bracing sea-air. This is the time to test your creativity and invent special shots, because you will often end up in situations that are completely new to you. Tenby is a surprising, honest and charming course to play.

D'abord, il y a un paysage de dunes agitées comme par des années de bombardements, un parcours façonné par les hommes et la nature pendant plus d'un siècle, avec l'aide sporadique de James Braid, visible par les contours de certains greens, et le placement de nombreux bunkers. Rares sont les golfeurs du continent qui ont entendu parler des parcours du Pays de Galles. Celui-ci est incontournable dans un circuit des côtes magnifiques de ce pays attachant. Suivant le temps, il prendra des allures de grand test de championnat, ou de superbe promenade dans un air vivifiant. C'est alors le moment de tester votre créativité, d'inventer des coups de golf, parce que vous serez souvent dans des situations inconnues. Surprenant et franc, Tenby est aussi un parcours de charme.

Tenby Golf Club — 1888

The Burrows
WAL - TENBY, Dyfed SA70 7NP

Office	Secrétariat	(44) 01834 - 842 978
Pro shop	Pro-shop	(44) 01834 - 844 447
Fax	Fax	(44) 01834 - 842 978
Situation	Situation	

W of Tenby (pop. 4 809)

Annual closure	Fermeture annuelle	no
Weekly closure	Fermeture hebdomadaire	no

Fees main season
Tarifs haute saison 18 holes

	Week days Semaine	We/Bank holidays We/Férié
Individual Individuel	£ 25	£ 30
Couple Couple	£ 50	£ 60

Caddy	Caddy	no
Electric Trolley	Chariot électrique	no
Buggy	Voiturette	no
Clubs	Clubs	yes

Credit cards Cartes de crédit — no

Access Accès : Cardiff, M4 West, A48, A477, A478 to Tenby. Golf near railway station.
Map 6 on page 498 Carte 6 Page 498

GOLF COURSE
PARCOURS — 18/20

Site	Site	▰▰▰▱▱
Maintenance	Entretien	▰▰▰▰▱
Architect	Architecte	James Braid
Type	Type	links
Relief	Relief	▰▰▱▱▱
Water in play	Eau en jeu	▱▱▱▱▱
Exp. to wind	Exposé au vent	▰▰▰▰▱
Trees in play	Arbres en jeu	▱▱▱▱▱

Scorecard Carte de score	Chp. Chp.	Mens Mess.	Ladies Da.
Length Long.	5767	5120	4943
Par	69	68	73

Advised golfing ability
Niveau de jeu recommandé — 0 12 24 36

Hcp required — Handicap exigé — certificate

CLUB HOUSE & AMENITIES
CLUB HOUSE ET ANNEXES — 7/10

Pro shop	Pro-shop	▰▰▰▰▱
Driving range	Practice	▰▰▰▱▱
Sheltered	couvert	no
On grass	sur herbe	yes
Putting-green	putting-green	yes
Pitching-green	pitching green	yes

HOTEL FACILITIES
ENVIRONNEMENT HOTELIER — 6/10

HOTELS HÔTELS

Waterwynch House — Tenby
14 rooms, D £ 65 — 3 km
Tél (44) 01834 - 842 464
Fax (44) 01834 - 845 076

Penally Abbey — Penally
12 rooms, D £ 100 — 2 km
Tél (44) 01834 - 843 033
Fax (44) 01834 - 844 714

Heywood Mount Hotel — Tenby
21 rooms, D £ 52 — 1.5 km
Tél (44) 01834 - 842 087

St Brides Hotel — Saundersfoot
43 rooms, D £ 62.50 — 6 km
Tél (44) 01834 - 812 304
Fax (44) 01834 - 813 303

822

This resort features hotel, fitness and beauty centre, indoor squash and tennis courts, gymnasiums and swimming pools. Add to this a high-tech training facility and suddenly you are light-years away from a traditional golf-club where you bring your own balls to hit across a field before making for the first tee. Here the aim is to host big events, even though the course is a little of the short side. Ten holes feature water in play, thus giving a slight American flavour to what is otherwise a very British country setting, and calling for target golf on virtually every hole. Luckily, the architect also remembered that a course needs players all year, which is why even though the yardage is reasonable overall, the front tees provide an intriguing challenge which remains within the bounds of human possibility. The character of the location and excellence of the Lake Course mean this is recommended golfing every time. Another 9-hole layout (the Hensol Course) is perfect for beginners to build up their confidence.

Ce complexe comprend hôtel, centre de mise en forme et de beauté, squash et tennis indoor, gymnases et autres piscine. Avec un centre d'entraînement high tech, nous voilà loin du club traditionnel où l'on amène ses propres balles pour taper dans un champ. Ici, on veut accueillir de grandes épreuves, bien que l'ensemble soit un peu court. Dix trous ont de l'eau en jeu, ce qui donne un caractère un peu américain à un paysage autrement très britannique, et impose un jeu de cible pratiquement sur tous les trous. Heureusement, l'architecte a aussi pensé qu'il faut des joueurs toute l'année, c'est pourquoi, même si la longueur générale est raisonnable, les départs avancés procurent un challenge intéressant, mais sans rien d'inhumain. Le caractère du lieu et la qualité de ce «Lake Course» incitent à le recommander. Un autre 9 trous (Hensol Course) permet aux joueurs golfiquement timides de prendre de l'assurance.

Vale of Glamorgan
Golf & Country Club　　1994

Hensol Park
WAL - HENSOL, near BRIDGEND CF7 8JY

Office	Secrétariat	(44) 01443 - 222 221
Pro shop	Pro-shop	(44) 01443 - 222 221
Fax	Fax	(44) 01443 - 222 221
Situation	Situation	

32 km from Cardiff (pop. 279 055)

Annual closure	Fermeture annuelle	no
Weekly closure	Fermeture hebdomadaire	no
Fees main season	Tarifs haute saison	18 holes

	Week days Semaine	We/Bank holidays We/Férié
Individual Individuel	£ 30	£ 30
Couple Couple	£ 60	£ 60

Soft spikes mandatory

Caddy	Caddy	no
Electric Trolley	Chariot électrique	no
Buggy	Voiturette	yes
Clubs	Clubs	yes

Credit cards Cartes de crédit
VISA - Eurocard - MasterCard - AMEX - DC

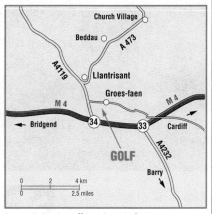

Access Accès : Just off Junction 34 of M4
Map 6 on page 499 Carte 6 Page 499

GOLF COURSE
PARCOURS　　16/20

Site	Site	■■■■■■□
Maintenance	Entretien	■■■■■■□
Architect	Architecte	Peter Johnson
Type	Type	parkland
Relief	Relief	■■■□□
Water in play	Eau en jeu	■■■■□
Exp. to wind	Exposé au vent	■■■□□
Trees in play	Arbres en jeu	■■■□□

Scorecard Carte de score	Chp. Chp.	Mens Mess.	Ladies Da.
Length Long.	5761	5455	5172
Par	72	72	74

Advised golfing ability Niveau de jeu recommandé	0　12　24　36 ■■■■■
Hcp required	Handicap exigé	certificate

CLUB HOUSE & AMENITIES
CLUB HOUSE ET ANNEXES　　8/10

Pro shop	Pro-shop	■■■■□
Driving range	Practice	■■■■□
Sheltered	couvert	20 bays
On grass	sur herbe	no
Putting-green	putting-green	yes
Pitching-green	pitching green	yes

HOTEL FACILITIES
ENVIRONNEMENT HOTELIER　　7/10

HOTELS HÔTELS

Vale of Glamorgan Hotel - 150 rooms,　　Hensol
Tél (44) 01443 - 222 221　　on site
Fax (44) 01443 - 222 221

Greyhound Inn　　Llantrisant
10 rooms, D £ 58　　6 km
Tél (44) 01291 - 672 505
Fax (44) 01291 - 673 255

Coed-y-Mwstwr　　Coychurch
22 rooms, D £ 100　　12 km
Tél (44) 01656 - 860 261
Fax (44) 01656 - 863 122

Forte Travelodge　　Pencoed
40 rooms, D £ 35　　8 km
Tél (44) 01656 - 864 404
Fax (44) 01656 - 850 950

823

IRELAND'S LONG DISTANCE DRIVERS DRIVE PEUGEOT

THE DRIVE OF YOUR LIFE

PEUGEOT

Orlande
Orlande du Nord

H ere, we have included in succession courses from the Republic of Ireland and Northern Ireland. When trimming the list down to 100, we deliberately focused on the most representative courses, especially the links courses, which continental golfers seldom have the chance to play locally. With nearly 250 eighteen-hole and 113 nine-hole courses or 200,000 registered players, there is no shortage of space for visitors, and Ireland is a golfing destination renowned the world over. You will always be made most welcome, but don't expect to find any magnificent driving ranges (you often find just rough practice areas where you can hit your own balls), or sumptuous club-houses. Here, modern facilities and luxury come second to the excellence of the course and warm hospitality. A letter of introduction from your own club is never a bad idea, and also remember to book your tee-off times.

V ous trouverez ici, successivement, les parcours de la République d'Irlande et d'Irlande du Nord. Pour choisir les 100 meilleurs d'entre eux, nous avons volontairement mis l'accent sur les plus représentatifs, en particulier les links, que les golfeurs continentaux ont rarement l'habitude de trouver chez eux. Avec près de 250 parcours de 18 trous et 113 de 9 trous pour 200.000 joueurs licenciés, la place ne manque pas pour les visiteurs, et le territoire de l'Irlande est une destination touristique connue du monde entier. Vous y serez toujours le bienvenu, mais ne vous attendez pas à trouver des practices magnifiques (on trouve souvent de simples zones où l'on tape ses propres balles), ni toujours des Club-house somptueux). Ici, le modernisme et le luxe passent après la qualité du parcours et la chaleur de l'accueil. Une lettre d'introduction de votre club n'est jamais inutile. Pensez aussi à réserver vos départs.

827

MICHELIN

d'après cartes n°923 - 2ème édition - 1999 et n° 986 -
19ème édition - 2000. Autorisation n° 9904173.

Map No 2
Carte n°2

km
0   10   20

828

MICHELIN

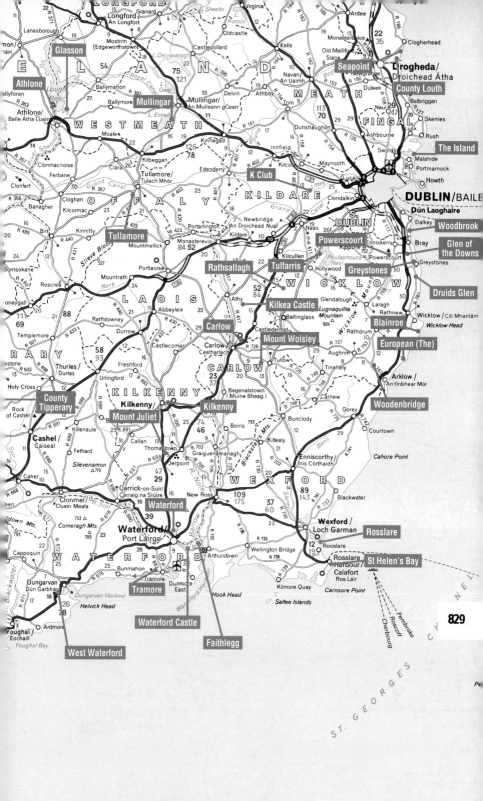

829

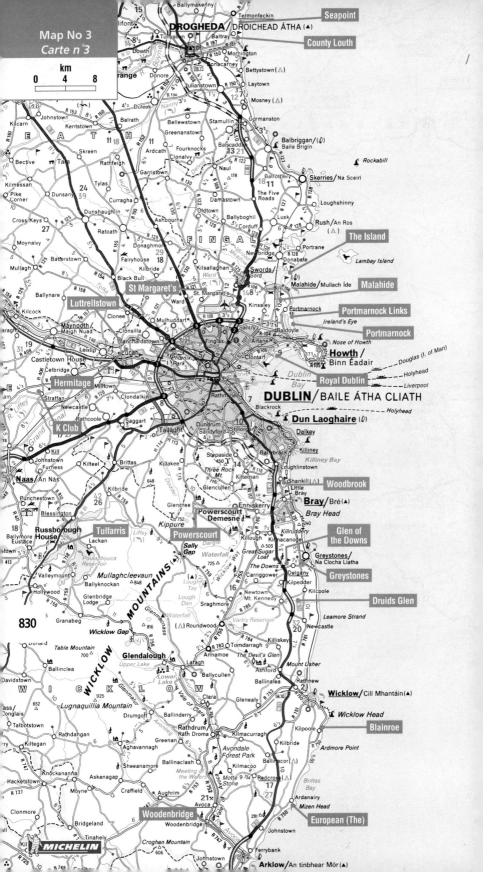

CLASSIFICATION OF IRISH COURSES
CLASSEMENT DES PARCOURS IRLANDAIS

This classification gives priority consideration
to the score awarded to the actual course.

Ce classement donne priorité à la note attribuée au parcours.

I: Republic of Ireland   U: Northern Ireland (Ulster)

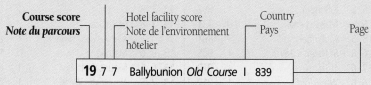

Club-house and facilities
Note du Club-house et annexes

Course score
Note du parcours

Hotel facility score
Note de l'environnement
hôtelier

Country
Pays

Page

19 7 7   Ballybunion *Old Course*   I   839

Score			Course	Country	Page	Note			Golfplatz		Seite
19	7	7	Ballybunion *Old Course*	I	839	**16**	7	6	Woodenbridge	I	918
19	7	8	Portmarnock	I	894	**15**	6	7	Adare	I	836
19	6	7	Royal County Down	U	934	**15**	6	5	Ballyliffin *Old Course*	I	842
19	7	7	Royal Portrush			**15**	5	6	Belvoir Park	U	922
			Dunluce Links	U	935	**15**	6	6	Clandeboye		
18	5	6	County Louth	I	855				*Dufferin Course*	U	926
18	5	6	European (The)	I	867	**15**	3	5	Cork GC	I	854
18	6	6	Lahinch	I	883	**15**	7	5	County Tipperary	I	857
18	9	8	Mount Juliet	I	889	**15**	5	5	Dooks	I	861
18	7	6	Tralee	I	908	**15**	6	6	Dundalk	I	864
17	6	5	Ballyliffin *Glashedy Links*	I	841	**15**	7	6	Fota Island	I	869
17	4	3	County Sligo	I	856	**15**	6	7	Hermitage	I	876
17	8	8	K Club	I	877	**15**	7	8	Killarney *Mahony's Point*	I	881
17	7	8	Portmarnock Links	I	895	**15**	6	5	Kirkistown Castle	U	927
17	6	7	Waterville	I	914	**15**	7	6	Knock	U	928
16	7	7	Ballybunion			**15**	7	6	Limerick County	I	885
			Cashen (New Course)	I	838	**15**	7	6	Lisburn	U	929
16	6	6	Carlow	I	847	**15**	7	7	Luttrellstown	I	886
16	5	3	Carn	I	848	**15**	6	7	Monkstown	I	888
16	6	6	Castlerock	U	925	**15**	7	7	Old Head	I	893
16	6	4	Dingle (Ceann Sibeal)	I	859	**15**	7	7	Powerscourt	I	897
16	5	6	Donegal (Murvagh)	I	860	**15**	7	6	Rathsallagh	I	898
16	9	7	Druids Glen	I	863	**15**	7	7	Royal Belfast	U	933
16	7	6	Enniscrone	I	866	**15**	6	6	Seapoint	I	902
16	7	7	Glasson	I	872	**15**	8	6	Slieve Russell	I	904
16	5	8	Grange	I	874	**15**	7	7	The Island	I	907
16	7	8	Killarney *Killeen Course*	I	880	**15**	6	5	Tullamore	I	911
16	5	5	Portsalon	I	896	**15**	7	7	Westport	I	916
16	7	7	Portstewart			**15**	7	6	Woodbrook	I	917
			Strand Course	U	932	**14**	6	4	Ardglass	U	920
16	7	6	Rosapenna	I	899	**14**	7	6	Ballykisteen	I	840
16	8	7	Royal Dublin	I	901	**14**	6	6	Bangor	U	921
16	7	7	St Margaret's	I	906	**14**	6	7	Beaufort	I	843

831

CLASSIFICATION OF IRISH COURSES

Score	Course	Country	Page	Score	Course	Country	Page
14 7 7	Bhearna	I	844	13 7 6	Castle Hume	U	924
14 6 6	Castletroy	I	850	13 4 6	Charleville	I	851
14 6 6	Connemara	I	853	13 6 7	Citywest	I	852
14 5 5	Courtown	I	858	13 7 8	Elm Park	I	865
14 7 7	Dromoland Castle	I	862	13 7 6	Faithlegg	I	868
14 7 6	Galway Bay	I	870	13 6 6	Galway GC	I	871
14 6 5	Greenore	I	875	13 4 7	Glen of the Downs	I	873
14 6 6	Kilkea Castle	I	878	13 7 6	Kilkenny	I	879
14 6 5	Killorglin	I	882	13 7 6	Lee Valley	I	884
14 5 6	Massereene	U	931	13 7 8	Malahide		
14 5 5	Mullingar	I	891		Red + Blue + Yellow	I	887
14 6 6	St Helen's Bay	I	905	13 6 6	Malone	U	930
14 7 6	Tulfarris	I	910	13 6 5	Mount Wolsley	I	890
14 6 6	Waterford	I	912	13 7 5	Newcastle West	I	892
14 5 6	Waterford Castle	I	913	13 5 6	Rosslare	I	900
13 6 6	Athlone	I	837	13 7 7	Royal Portrush Valley	U	936
13 6 6	Blainroe	I	845	13 6 6	Shannon	I	903
13 6 7	Bundoran	I	846	13 7 6	Tramore	I	909
13 6 5	Cairndhu	U	923	13 6 5	Warrenpoint	U	937
13 6 8	Castle	I	849	12 7 6	West Waterford	I	915

CLASSIFICATION OF HOTELS FACILITIES
CLASSEMENT DE L'ENVIRONNEMENT HOTELIER

This classification gives priority consideration
to the score awarded to the hotel facilities.

Ce classement donne priorité à la note attribuée à l'environnement hôtelier

I: Republic of Ireland   U: Northern Ireland (Ulster)

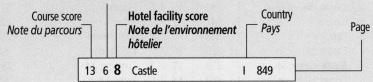

Club-house and facilities
Note du Club-house et annexes

Course score
Note du parcours

Hotel facility score
Note de l'environnement hôtelier

Country
Pays

Page

13 6 **8**   Castle   I   849

Score	Course	Country	Page	Score	Course	Country	Page
13 6 8	Castle	I	849	19 7 8	Portmarnock	I	894
13 7 8	Elm Park	I	865	17 7 8	Portmarnock Links	I	895
16 5 8	Grange	I	874	15 6 7	Adare	I	836
17 8 8	K Club	I	877	16 7 7	Ballybunion		
16 7 8	Killarney Killeen Course	I	880		Cashen (New Course)	I	838
15 7 8	Killarney Mahony's Point	I	881	19 7 7	Ballybunion Old Course	I	839
13 7 8	Malahide			14 6 7	Beaufort	I	843
	Red + Blue + Yellow	I	887	14 7 7	Bhearna	I	844
18 9 8	Mount Juliet	I	889	13 6 7	Bundoran	I	846

Ireland

Score	Course	Country	Page
13 6 **7**	Citywest	I	852
14 7 **7**	Dromoland Castle	I	862
16 9 **7**	Druids Glen	I	863
16 7 **7**	Glasson	I	872
13 4 **7**	Glen of the Downs	I	873
15 6 **7**	Hermitage	I	876
15 7 **7**	Luttrellstown	I	886
15 6 **7**	Monkstown	I	888
15 7 **7**	Old Head	I	893
16 7 **7**	Portstewart		
	Strand Course	U	932
15 7 **7**	Powerscourt	I	897
15 7 **7**	Royal Belfast	U	933
19 6 **7**	Royal County Down	U	934
16 8 **7**	Royal Dublin	I	901
19 7 **7**	Royal Portrush		
	Dunluce Links	U	935
13 7 **7**	Royal Portrush *Valley*	U	936
16 7 **7**	St Margaret's	I	906
15 7 **7**	The Island	I	907
17 6 **7**	Waterville	I	914
15 7 **7**	Westport	I	916
13 6 **6**	Athlone	I	837
14 7 **6**	Ballykisteen	I	840
14 6 **6**	Bangor	U	921
15 5 **6**	Belvoir Park	U	922
13 6 **6**	Blainroe	I	845
16 6 **6**	Carlow	I	847
13 7 **6**	Castle Hume	U	924
16 6 **6**	Castlerock	U	925
14 6 **6**	Castletroy	I	850
13 4 **6**	Charleville	I	851
15 6 **6**	Clandeboye		
	Dufferin Course	U	926
14 6 **6**	Connemara	I	853
18 5 **6**	County Louth	I	855
16 5 **6**	Donegal (Murvagh)	I	860
15 6 **6**	Dundalk	I	864
16 7 **6**	Enniscrone	I	866
18 5 **6**	European (The)	I	867
13 7 **6**	Faithlegg	I	868
15 7 **6**	Fota Island	I	869
14 7 **6**	Galway Bay	I	870
13 6 **6**	Galway GC	I	871
14 6 **6**	Kilkea Castle	I	878
13 7 **6**	Kilkenny	I	879
15 7 **6**	Knock	U	928
18 6 **6**	Lahinch	I	883
13 7 **6**	Lee Valley	I	884
15 7 **6**	Limerick County	I	885
15 7 **6**	Lisburn	U	929
13 6 **6**	Malone	U	930
14 5 **6**	Massereene	U	931
15 7 **6**	Rathsallagh	I	898
16 7 **6**	Rosapenna	I	899
13 5 **6**	Rosslare	I	900
15 6 **6**	Seapoint	I	902
13 6 **6**	Shannon	I	903
15 8 **6**	Slieve Russell	I	904
14 6 **6**	St Helen's Bay	I	905
18 7 **6**	Tralee	I	908
13 7 **6**	Tramore	I	909
14 7 **6**	Tulfarris	I	910
14 6 **6**	Waterford	I	912
14 5 **6**	Waterford Castle	I	913
12 7 **6**	West Waterford	I	915
15 7 **6**	Woodbrook	I	917
16 7 **6**	Woodenbridge	I	918
17 6 **5**	Ballyliffin *Glashedy Links*	I	841
15 6 **5**	Ballyliffin *Old Course*	I	842
13 6 **5**	Cairndhu	U	923
15 3 **5**	Cork GC	I	854
15 7 **5**	County Tipperary	I	857
14 5 **5**	Courtown	I	858
15 5 **5**	Dooks	I	861
14 6 **5**	Greenore	I	875
14 6 **5**	Killorglin	I	882
15 6 **5**	Kirkistown Castle	U	927
13 6 **5**	Mount Wolsley	I	890
14 5 **5**	Mullingar	I	891
13 7 **5**	Newcastle West	I	892
16 5 **5**	Portsalon	I	896
15 6 **5**	Tullamore	I	911
13 6 **5**	Warrenpoint	U	937
14 6 **4**	Ardglass	U	920
16 6 **4**	Dingle (Ceann Sibéal)	I	859
16 5 **3**	Carn	I	848
17 4 **3**	County Sligo	I	856

833

Ireland

RECOMMENDED GOLFING STAY
SEJÓUR DE GOLF RECOMMANDÉ

Exciting courses where a stay of a few days is to be recommended.
Les parcours dont les qualités permettent de conseiller un séjour de plusieurs jours.

Score	Course		Country Page		Score	Course		Country Page	
	Ballybunion *Old Course*	I	19 7 7	839		Mount Juliet	I	18 9 8	889
	Ballyliffin *Glashedy Links*	I	17 6 5	841		Portmarnock	I	19 7 8	894
	Ballyliffin *Old Course*	I	15 6 5	842		Portmarnock Links	I	17 7 8	895
	County Louth	I	18 5 6	855		Portstewart *Strand Course*	U	16 7 7	932
	County Sligo	I	17 4 3	856		Royal County Down	U	19 6 7	934
	Druids Glen	I	16 9 7	863		Royal Dublin	I	16 8 7	901
	European (The)	I	18 5 6	867		Royal Portrush				
	K Club	I	17 8 8	877		*Dunluce Links*	U	19 7 7	935
	Killarney *Killeen Course*	I	16 7 8	880		Royal Portrush *Valley*	U	13 7 7	936
	Killarney *Mahony's Point*	I	15 7 8	881		Tralee	I	18 7 6	908
	Lahinch	I	18 6 6	883		Waterville	I	17 6 7	914

FÜR EINEN FERIENAUFENTHALT EMPFOHLEN
RECOMMENDED GOLFING HOLIDAYS

Charleville	I	13 4 6	851

834

TYPE OF COURSE
TYPE DE PARCOURS

Type of course / Golf course		Page	Type of course / Golf course		Page	Type of course / Golf course		Page
forest			Glen of the Downs	I	873	**links**		
Woodenbridge	I	918	K Club	I	877	Ballybunion *Cashen*		
			Malone	U	930	*(New Course)*	I	838
inland			Massereene	U	931	Ballybunion		
Adare	I	836	Powerscourt	I	897	*Old Course*	I	839
Bangor	U	921	Rathsallagh	I	898	Ballyliffin *Glashedy*		
Charleville	I	851	St Margaret's	I	906	*Links*	I	841
Clandeboye			Woodbrook	I	917	Ballyliffin *Old Course*	I	842
Dufferin Course	U	926				Bundoran	I	846
Dundalk	I	864				Carn	I	848

PEUGEOT GOLF GUIDE 2000/2001

Ireland

Type of course / Golf course		Page	Type of course / Golf course		Page	Type of course / Golf course		Page
Castlerock	U	925	Bundoran	I	846	Newcastle West	I	892
Connemara	I	853	Cairndhu	U	923	Powerscourt	I	897
County Louth	I	855	Carlow	I	847	Rathsallagh	I	898
County Sligo	I	856	Castle	I	849	Royal Belfast	U	933
Dingle (Ceann Sibeal)	I	859	Castle Hume	U	924	Shannon	I	903
Donegal (Murvagh)	I	860	Castletroy	I	850	Slieve Russell	I	904
Dooks	I		Charleville	I	851	St Helen's Bay	I	905
Enniscrone	I	866	Citywest	I	852	St Margaret's	I	906
European (The)	I	867	Cork GC	I	854	Tramore	I	909
Kirkistown Castle	U	927	County Tipperary	I	857	Tulfarris	I	910
Lahinch	I	883	Courtown	I	858	Tullamore	I	911
Lee Valley	I	884	Dromoland Castle	I	862	Warrenpoint	U	937
Portmarnock	I	894	Druids Glen	I	863	Waterford	I	912
Portmarnock Links	I	895	Dundalk	I	864	Waterford Castle	I	913
Portsalon	I	896	Elm Park	I	865	West Waterford	I	915
Portstewart			Faithlegg	I	868	Westport	I	916
Strand Course	U	932	Fota Island	I	869	Woodenbridge	I	918
Rosapenna	I	899	Galway GC	I	871			
Rosslare	I	900	Glasson	I	872	**seaside course**		
Royal County Down	U	934	Grange	I	874	Ardglass	U	920
Royal Dublin	I	901	Hermitage	I	876	Ballyliffin		
Royal Portrush			K Club	I	877	*Glashedy Links*	I	841
Dunluce Links	U	935	Kilkea Castle	I	878	Blainroe	I	845
Royal Portrush			Kilkenny	I	879	Cairndhu	U	923
Valley	U	936	Killarney			Castlerock	U	925
Seapoint	I	902	*Killeen Course*	I	880	Dingle (Ceann Sibeal)	I	859
St Helen's Bay	I	905	Killarney			Dooks	I	861
The Island	I	907	*Mahony's Point*	I	881	Enniscrone	I	866
Tralee	I	908	Kirkistown Castle	U	927	Galway Bay	I	870
Warrenpoint	U	937	Killorglin	I	882	Galway GC	I	871
Waterville	I	914	Knock	U	928	Greenore	I	875
			Lee Valley	I	884	Old Head	I	893
open country			Limerick County	I	885	Rosslare	I	900
Bhearna	I	844	Lisburn	U	929	Tramore	I	909
Newcastle West	I	892	Luttrellstown	I	886	Westport	I	916
			Malahide *Red +*					
parkland			*Blue + Yellow*	I	887	**copse**		
Adare	I	836	Malone	U	930	Clandeboye		
Athlone	I	837	Massereene	U	931	*Dufferin Course*	U	926
Ballykisteen	I	840	Monkstown	I	888			
Beaufort	I	843	Mount Juliet	I	889			
Belvoir Park	U	922	Mount Wolsley	I	890			
Blainroe	I	845	Mullingar	I	891			

835

From time to time, being iconoclastic can make a pleasant change. There could be no doubting that Adare was designed by Robert Trent Jones, because this could just as easily be a course on the Costa del Sol. In other words, there is no real "feeling" with the Irish landscape, probably on account of the over-extensive earthworks and grading used to shape the course, the give-away bunker designs and the huge water hazard on the front 9, which cost a fortune to build. But this is still a great course once you forget its artificial side, which anyway is less apparent on the way in. Here, golfers have to cope with the river Maigue and indigenous trees such as oak, beech, pine and cedar. There is no hidden trap, which only emphasises the psychological fear factor. Long and challenging, the course is almost certainly too tough for high-handicappers on account of the very many hazards. Even the better players will find it hard going.

De temps à autre, il n'est pas désagréable d'être iconoclaste : Adare a certes été dessiné par Robert Trent Jones, mais pourrait tout aussi bien se trouver sur la Costa del Sol. Autrement dit, on ne trouvera pas ici de véritable «sympathie» avec le paysage irlandais, en raison sans doute de mouvements de terrain trop importants, de dessin de bunkers trop révélateurs de leur auteur, de l'immense obstacle d'eau de l'aller, dont l'aménagement a coûté une fortune. Mais il reste un grand parcours de golf, dont on oubliera le côté parfois artificiel, d'ailleurs moins sensible au retour : il met essentiellement en jeu la rivière Maigue, et les arbres natifs du lieu : chênes, hêtres, pins ou cèdres. Aucun piège n'est caché, ce qui accentue le facteur psychologique de crainte. Long et exigeant, ce parcours est sans doute très difficile pour les handicaps élevés, en raison de la multiplicité des obstacles, les autres n'y connaîtront guère de repos...

Adare Golf Club — 1995

Adare Manor
IRL - ADARE, Co Limerick

Office	Secrétariat	(353) 061 - 395 044
Pro shop	Pro-shop	(353) 061 - 395 044
Fax	Fax	(353) 061 - 396 987
Situation	Situation	

10 km S. of Limerick (pop. 52 083)

Annual closure	Fermeture annuelle	no
Weekly closure	Fermeture hebdomadaire	no

Fees main season	Tarifs haute saison	18 holes
	Week days Semaine	We/Bank holidays We/Férié
Individual Individuel	IR£ 45	IR£ 45
Couple Couple	IR£ 90	IR£ 90

Special fees for early tee-times

Caddy	Caddy	IR£ 16/18 holes
Electric Trolley	Chariot électrique	no
Buggy	Voiturette	IR£ 30/18 holes
Clubs	Clubs	IR£ 12/18 holes

Credit cards Cartes de crédit
VISA - Eurocard - MasterCard - AMEX

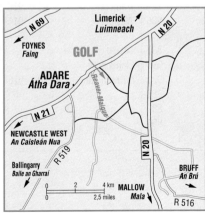

Access Accès : Limerick, N7 → Adare.
Patrick's Well, straight through the fork in road,
first left in village at gates, right to proshop
Map 2 on page 828 Carte 2 Page 828

GOLF COURSE / PARCOURS — 15/20

Site	Site	
Maintenance	Entretien	
Architect	Architecte	R. Trent Jones Sr
Type	Type	inland, parkland
Relief	Relief	
Water in play	Eau en jeu	
Exp. to wind	Exposé au vent	
Trees in play	Arbres en jeu	

Scorecard Carte de score	Chp. Chp.	Mens Mess.	Ladies Da.
Length Long.	6489	5993	4925
Par	72	72	72

Advised golfing ability		0 12 24 36
Niveau de jeu recommandé		
Hcp required	Handicap exigé	28 Men, 36 Ladies

CLUB HOUSE & AMENITIES / CLUB HOUSE ET ANNEXES — 6/10

Pro shop	Pro-shop	
Driving range	Practice	
Sheltered	couvert	no
On grass	sur herbe	yes
Putting-green	putting-green	yes
Pitching-green	pitching green	yes

HOTEL FACILITIES / ENVIRONNEMENT HOTELIER — 7/10

HOTELS HÔTELS

Adare Manor Hotel	on site
64 rooms, D IR£ 192	
Tel (353) 061 - 396 566, Fax (353) 061 - 396 124	

Woodlands Hotel	Adare
57 rooms, D IR£ 70	2 km
Tel (353) 061 - 396 118, Fax (353) 061 - 396 073	

Dunraven Arms Hotel	Adare
66 rooms, D IR£ 104	0.5 km
Tel (353) 061 - 396 633, Fax (353) 061 - 396 541	

RESTAURANTS RESTAURANTS

Wild Geese	Adare
Tel (353) 061 - 396 451	1 km

Dunraven Arms	Adare
Tél(353) 061 - 396 633	0.5 km

836

The gently rolling course of Athlone is magnificently sited on a peninsula overlooking Lough Ree. An old course that was remodelled in the late 1930s, the lack of yardage might lead to the better players under-estimating its difficulty and will invite them to play from the back-tees. It demands a wide variety of shots, especially when the wind blows from the lake, and skills in flighting the ball will help. The woods are on the outskirts of the course, as are most of the water hazards, although some isolated trees can come into play. Otherwise, you just avoid the bunkers, whose only criticism is the bland uniformity in design and shape. The greens are generally in good condition and moderately contoured, but they do tend to be soft in winter. Long-hitters will have fun on the three rather short par 5s, but accuracy is always important. Watch out for some tight fairways.

Doucement vallonné, le parcours d'Athlone dispose d'une situation magnifique sur une péninsule dominant le Lough Ree. Déjà ancien, bien que révisé à la fin des années 30, son manque de longueur ne doit pas le faire sous estimer par les joueurs de bon niveau, à qui on conseillera bien sûr les départs arrière. Il demande une grande variété de coups, surtout quand le vent vient du lac, il faut alors savoir travailler la balle. Les bois sont à la périphérie du parcours, de même que la plupart des obstacles d'eau, mais certains arbres isolés peuvent venir en jeu. Autrement, il suffit d'éviter les bunkers, auxquels on peut simplement reprocher une certaine uniformité de dessin et de forme. Les greens sont généralement en bonne condition et de relief modéré, mais ils peuvent être assez mous en hiver. Les longs frappeurs s'amuseront sur trois par 5 assez courts, mais ne devront pas oublier la précision, les fairways peuvent être étroits.

Athlone Golf Club — 1892

Hodson Bay
IRL - ATHLONE, Co. Westmeath

Office	Secrétariat	(353) 0902 - 92 073
Pro shop	Pro-shop	(353) 0902 - 94 285
Fax	Fax	(353) 0902 - 94 080
Situation	Situation	

5 km from Athlone (pop. 8 170)
120 km from Dublin (pop. 859 976)

Annual closure	Fermeture annuelle	no
Weekly closure	Fermeture hebdomadaire	no
Fees main season	Tarifs haute saison	18 holes

	Week days Semaine	We/Bank holidays We/Férié
Individual Individuel	IR£ 15	IR£ 18
Couple Couple	IR£ 30	IR£ 36

Caddy	Caddy	on request/IR£ 10
Electric Trolley	Chariot électrique	no
Buggy	Voiturette	IR£ 15
Clubs	Clubs	IR£ 10

Credit cards Cartes de crédit VISA - MasterCard

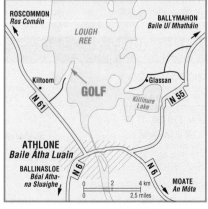

ROSCOMMON
Ros Comáin
LOUGH REE
BALLYMAHON
Baile Uí Mhatháin
Kiltoom
Glassan
GOLF
Killinure Lake
N 61
N 55
ATHLONE
Baile Átha Luain
BALLINASLOE
Béal Atha-na Sluaighe
N 6
N 6
MOATE
An Móta
0 2 4 km
0 2,5 miles

Access Accès : Athlone, N61 → Roscommon.
Golf beside Hodson Bay Hotel
Map 2 on page 829 Carte 2 Page 829

GOLF COURSE / PARCOURS — 13/20

Site	Site	
Maintenance	Entretien	
Architect	Architecte	J. McAllister Fred Hawtree
Type	Type	parkland
Relief	Relief	
Water in play	Eau en jeu	
Exp. to wind	Exposé au vent	
Trees in play	Arbres en jeu	

Scorecard Carte de score	Chp. Chp.	Mens Mess.	Ladies Da.
Length Long.	5922	5773	5104
Par	71	71	75

Advised golfing ability		0 12 24 36
Niveau de jeu recommandé		
Hcp required	Handicap exigé	no

CLUB HOUSE & AMENITIES / CLUB HOUSE ET ANNEXES — 6/10

Pro shop	Pro-shop	
Driving range	Practice	
Sheltered	couvert	no
On grass	sur herbe	yes
Putting-green	putting-green	yes
Pitching-green	pitching green	yes

HOTEL FACILITIES / ENVIRONNEMENT HOTELIER — 6/10

HOTELS HÔTELS

Hodson Bay Hotel — Athlone
100 rooms, D IR£ 100 — beside golf
Tel (353) 0902 - 92 404, Fax (353) 0902 - 92 688

Prince of Wales Hotel — Athlone
73 rooms, D IR£ 60 — 6 km
Tel (353) 0902 - 72 626, Fax (353) 0902 - 75 658

Shamrock Lodge — Athlone
25 rooms, D IR£ 60 — 5 km
Tel (353) 0902 - 92 601

RESTAURANTS RESTAURANTS

Cornloft — on road 362
Tel (353) 0902 - 94 753 — 6 km

Le Chateau — Athlone
Tel (353) 0902 - 94 517 — 5 km

837

Designing a new course in a mythical site such as this can be fatal to any course architect. But Robert Trent Jones has already designed enough great courses of his own to shrug off any mention of comparison, and his personality told him not to ape the old course, even though the dune-peppered landscape is similar (and sometimes even more impressive). The result here is a course that is slightly harder to decipher, where there is less room for intuition and more for knowledge of distance when choosing your clubs. A little American touch, even though approach shots can still be played "British" style. However, he has made maximum use of the terrain's natural contours and limited earthworks, while giving each hole its own individual character. The course's forceful personality (it is not everyone's cup of tea) would make this a must anywhere else, but here it lives in the shadow of the "Old Course".

Pour un architecte, signer un nouveau parcours dans un site aussi mythique peut être meurtrier. Robert Trent Jones avait déjà créé assez de grands parcours pour ne pas craindre la comparaison, et sa personnalité ne l'incitait pas à essayer de singer le «Old», bien que le paysage dunaire soit similaire (parfois plus impressionnant encore). De fait, il a créé un parcours plus complexe à déchiffrer, où la place de l'intuition est moins importante que la connaissance des distances pour choisir les clubs. Une petite touche américaine... même si les petites approches peuvent être souvent jouées «à la britannique». Cependant, il a su utiliser au maximum les contours naturels du terrain et limiter les terrassements, tout en donnant la touche de caractère individuel à chaque trou. La forte personnalité de ce parcours (qui ne fait pas toujours l'unanimité) en ferait n'importe où ailleurs un «must», mais le «Old» lui fait forcément ombrage.

Ballybunion Golf Club — 1971
Sandhill Road
IRL - BALLYBUNION, Co Kerry

Office	Secrétariat	(353) 068 - 27 146
Pro shop	Pro-shop	(353) 068 - 27 146
Fax	Fax	(353) 068 - 27 387
Situation	Situation	

1 km from Ballybunion Town (pop. 1 346)

Annual closure	Fermeture annuelle	no
Weekly closure	Fermeture hebdomadaire	no

Fees main season	Tarifs haute saison	18 holes
	Week days Semaine	**We/Bank holidays** We/Férié
Individual Individuel	IR£ 30	IR£ 30
Couple Couple	IR£ 60	IR£ 60

IR£ 72 for both courses (same day)

Caddy	Caddy	IR£ 15/18 holes
Electric Trolley	Chariot électrique	no
Buggy	Voiturette	no
Clubs	Clubs	IR£ 20/18 holes

Credit cards Cartes de crédit VISA - MasterCard

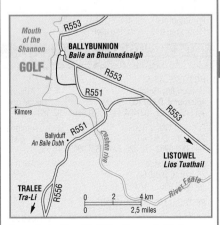

Access Accès : Limerick, N21 → Newcastle West,
→ Listowel, → Ballybunion
Map 2 on page 828 Carte 2 Page 828

GOLF COURSE PARCOURS — 16/20

Site	Site	
Maintenance	Entretien	
Architect	Architecte	R. Trent Jones Sr
Type	Type	links
Relief	Relief	
Water in play	Eau en jeu	
Exp. to wind	Exposé au vent	
Trees in play	Arbres en jeu	

Scorecard Carte de score	Chp. Chp.	Mens Mess.	Ladies Da.
Length Long.	5830	5350	5160
Par	72	72	72

Advised golfing ability Niveau de jeu recommandé	0	12	24	36

Hcp required Handicap exigé — 24 Men, 36 Ladies

CLUB HOUSE & AMENITIES CLUB HOUSE ET ANNEXES — 7/10

Pro shop	Pro-shop	
Driving range	Practice	
Sheltered	couvert	
On grass	sur herbe	yes
Putting-green	putting-green	yes
Pitching-green	pitching green	no

HOTEL FACILITIES ENVIRONNEMENT HOTELIER — 7/10

HOTELS HÔTELS
Golf Hotel — Ballybunion
96 rooms, D IR£ 60 — 2 km
Tel (353) 068 - 27 111
Fax (353) 068 - 27 166

Cliff House Hotel — Ballybunion
51 rooms, D IR£ 70 — 2 km
Tel (353) 068 - 27 398
Fax (353) 068 - 27 783

RESTAURANTS RESTAURANTS
Three Mermaids — Listowel
Tel (353) 068 - 21 184 — 15 km

Harty-Costello — Ballybunion
Tel (353) 068 - 27 129 — 1 km

838

There are some courses you could write a book about, where anything less you know will fail to do them justice. The old course at Ballybunion is one such course. On a windless day (a rare occurrence), it's not easy playing here. In a strong wind, it can be hell. But losing out to a living masterpiece such as this is sheer bliss. The numbers on your card lose all their significance: there are no such things as par 3s, par 4s or par 5s, all that matters is survival. After a few almost ordinary holes (relatively speaking), the pulse starts to quicken on the 6th. The rest is one long epic adventure where you need ball control in every direction, skills with every club in the bag and technique for high and low shots alike. At the same time you'll admire the layout. Lost between huge sand dunes, the fairway looks so narrow, the greens tiny and the bunkers absolutely ruthless. Tom Watson considers this ultimate test of technique and inspiration to be the greatest course in the world. Suffice it to say, every golfer will have to check it out for himself or herself, one day or another.

Faute de pouvoir écrire un livre sur certains parcours, il faudrait ne rien en dire. Le «Old Course» de Ballybunion est de ceux-là. Sans vent (c'est rare), il n'est pas facile. Il devient infernal par vent fort, mais quel bonheur d'être battu par un chef-d'oeuvre aussi vivant : alors, les chiffres inscrits sur la carte ne signifient plus rien. Plus de par 3, 4 ou 5, il s'agit de survivre. Après quelques trous presque anodins (c'est relatif !), le pouls s'accélère à partir du 6, la suite n'est plus qu'une longue épopée, où il faut travailler la balle dans tous les sens, jouer tous les clubs et tous les coups, maîtriser les balles hautes comme les balles au ras du sol. Et admirer le génie du dessin. Perdus dans d'immenses dunes, le fairway paraît bien étroit, les greens minuscules, les bunkers sans pitié. Tom Watson considère cet examen suprême de la technique et de l'inspiration comme le plus grand parcours du monde, tout golfeur doit le vérifier un jour.

Ballybunion Golf Club 1893
Sandhill Road
IRL - BALLYBUNION, Co Kerry

Office	Secrétariat	(353) 068 - 27 146
Pro shop	Pro-shop	(353) 068 - 27 146
Fax	Fax	(353) 068 - 27 387
Situation	Situation	

1 km from Ballybunion Town (pop. 1 346)

Annual closure	Fermeture annuelle	no
Weekly closure	Fermeture hebdomadaire	no

Fees main season	Tarifs haute saison	18 holes

	Week days Semaine	We/Bank holidays We/Férié
Individual Individuel	IR£ 55	IR£ 55
Couple Couple	IR£ 110	IR£ 110

IR£ 72 for both courses (same day)

Caddy	Caddy	IR£ 15/18 holes
Electric Trolley	Chariot électrique	no
Buggy	Voiturette	no
Clubs	Clubs	IR£ 20/18 holes

Credit cards Cartes de crédit VISA - MasterCard

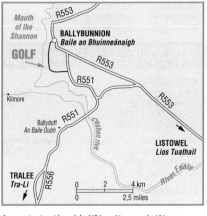

Mouth of the Shannon
GOLF
BALLYBUNNION
Baile an Bhuinneánaigh
R553
R551
Kilmore
Ballyduff
An Baile Dubh
R551
LISTOWEL
Lios Tuathail
TRALEE
Tra-Li
R556
0 2 4 km
0 2,5 miles
River Féale
Cashen river

Access Accès : Limerick, N21 → Newcastle West,
→ Listowel, → Ballybunion
Map 2 on page 828 Carte 2 Page 828

GOLF COURSE PARCOURS 19/20

Site	Site	
Maintenance	Entretien	
Architect	Architecte	L. Hewson T. Simpson
Type	Type	links
Relief	Relief	
Water in play	Eau en jeu	
Exp. to wind	Exposé au vent	
Trees in play	Arbres en jeu	

Scorecard Carte de score	Chp. Chp.	Mens Mess.	Ladies Da.
Length Long.	6241	6201	5004
Par	71	71	74

Advised golfing ability		0 12 24 36
Niveau de jeu recommandé		
Hcp required	Handicap exigé	28 Men, 36 Ladies

CLUB HOUSE & AMENITIES
CLUB HOUSE ET ANNEXES 7/10

Pro shop	Pro-shop	
Driving range	Practice	
Sheltered	couvert	
On grass	sur herbe	yes
Putting-green	putting-green	yes
Pitching-green	pitching green	no

HOTEL FACILITIES
ENVIRONNEMENT HOTELIER 7/10

HOTELS HÔTELS
Golf Hotel
96 rooms, D IR£ 60
Tel (353) 068 - 27 111
Fax (353) 068 - 27 166
Ballybunion
2 km

Cliff House Hotel
51 rooms, D IR£ 70
Tel (353) 068 - 27 398
Fax (353) 068 - 27 783
Ballybunion
2 km

RESTAURANTS RESTAURANTS
Three Mermaids
Tel (353) 068 - 21 184
Listowel
15 km

Harty-Costello
Tel (353) 068 - 27 129
Ballybunion
1 km

839

Laid out over a former horse farm and riding stables, Ballykisteen looks like a large park where trees and water form the main hazards. But the designers (Des Smyth and Declan Branigan) spared a thought for everyone. The further back you tee off, the narrower the fairways become, and the great number of tees means you can adapt each round to your ability. The course calls for every shot in the book: here a fade, there a draw. The greens are guarded to allow either the good old bump and run shots, or the new-style target shot approaches. Water is in play on ten holes, but with varying degrees of difficulty. It is at its worst on the 15th (with out-of-bounds to the left), one of Ireland's most demanding par 3s - the bogey should be gratefully accepted. Forthright and well-balanced, Ballykisteen perhaps lacks in yardage, but who's complaining?

Réalisé dans un ancien élevage de chevaux, Ballykisteen présente un caractère de grand parc, où les arbres et l'eau constituent les dangers. Mais les architectes (le champion irlandais Des Smyth et Declan Branigan) ont pensé à tout le monde. Plus on recule de départ, plus le parcours est étroit, et la multiplicité des départs permet de se faire un parcours «à sa main». Le dessin exige tous les coups de golf : certains trous demandent une balle en fade, un nombre égal réclame le draw. Les greens sont protégés soit des balles roulées (bump and run), soit des balles levées (target golf). L'eau vient en jeu sur dix trous, mais avec différents niveaux de difficulté. Elle est au maximum sur le 15 (avec hors-limites à gauche), un des plus exigeants par 3 d'Irlande : le bogey y est très acceptable ! Honnête et bien équilibré, Ballykisteen manque peut-être un peu de longueur, mais qui s'en plaindra ?

Ballykisteen Golf Club — 1995
IRL - MONARD, Co Tipperary

Office	Secrétariat	(353) 062 - 33 333
Pro shop	Pro-shop	(353) 062 - 33 333
Fax	Fax	(353) 062 - 33 668
Situation	Situation	

5 km from Tipperary
32 km from Limerick (pop. 52 083)

Annual closure	Fermeture annuelle	no
Weekly closure	Fermeture hebdomadaire	no

Fees main season	Tarifs haute saison	18 holes
	Week days Semaine	We/Bank holidays We/Férié
Individual Individuel	IR£ 22	IR£ 22
Couple Couple	IR£ 44	IR£ 44

Caddy	Caddy	on request/IR£ 15
Electric Trolley	Chariot électrique	no
Buggy	Voiturette	IR£ 20/18 holes
Clubs	Clubs	IR£ 8/18 holes

Credit cards Cartes de crédit VISA - MasterCard - DC

GOLF COURSE / PARCOURS — 14/20

Site	Site	
Maintenance	Entretien	
Architect	Architecte	Des Smyth D. Branigan
Type	Type	parkland
Relief	Relief	
Water in play	Eau en jeu	
Exp. to wind	Exposé au vent	
Trees in play	Arbres en jeu	

Scorecard Carte de score	Chp. Chp.	Mens Mess.	Ladies Da.
Length Long.	6150	5713	5110
Par	72	72	74

Advised golfing ability		0	12	24	36
Niveau de jeu recommandé					
Hcp required	Handicap exigé	28 Men, 36 Ladies			

CLUB HOUSE & AMENITIES / CLUB HOUSE ET ANNEXES — 7/10

Pro shop	Pro-shop	
Driving range	Practice	
Sheltered	couvert	no
On grass	sur herbe	yes
Putting-green	putting-green	yes
Pitching-green	pitching green	yes

HOTEL FACILITIES / ENVIRONNEMENT HOTELIER — 6/10

HOTELS HÔTELS

Royal Hotel — Tipperary
16 rooms, D IR£ 50 — 4 km
Tel (353) 062 - 33 244
Fax (353) 062 - 33 596

Aherlow House — Glen of Aherlow
30 rooms, D IR£ 70 — 10 km
Tel (353) 062 - 56 153
Fax (353) 062 - 56 212

RESTAURANTS RESTAURANTS

Cranleys — Tipperary
Tel (353) 062 - 33 917 — 5 km

The Brown Trout — Tipperary
Tel (353) 062 - 51 912 — 5 km

840

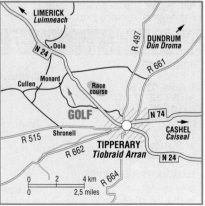

Access Accès : Tipperary N24 → Limerick.
Golf 5 km, opposite Tipperary Racecourse
Map 2 on page 828 Carte 2 Page 828

This recent course outstrips its neighbour in terms of technical play. The landscape is even more moon-like, with massive dunes, but a little grading work has resulted in levelling out a number of drive landing areas and in creating a collection of fairway and green-side bunkers that you are sure to encounter every now and then. This course grabs you by the throat from the word go and doesn't let you go. You need to hit low shots into the wind and with the wind, otherwise your ball will float upwards like a feather. You need to know how to fade and draw the ball to get around the dog-legs, you need brains and nerves to approach the greens, to stay on the putting surface and make the putt. You need a cool head to go fetch your ball instead of admiring the landscape (especially Glashedy Rock, off the coast). You need to play here and spend some time on the course to measure what you are capable of.

Ce récent parcours dépasse son voisin en matière de technicité. Le paysage est encore plus lunaire, avec des dunes massives, où quelques terrassements ont permis d'adoucir certaines zones d'arrivée de drive, mais aussi de creuser une collection de bunkers de fairway et de green que l'on ne manquera pas d'expérimenter. Ce parcours vous prend à la gorge dès les premiers trous, et ne vous lâchera plus. Il faudra faire des balles basses, contre le vent, mais aussi avec, pour ne pas les voir voler comme des plumes. Il faudra maîtriser les effets de fade et de draw pour négocier les dog-legs, il faudra de la science et des nerfs pour attaquer les greens, pour y rester, et pour putter. Il faudra du sang-froid pour revenir à sa balle au lieu d'admirer le paysage (notamment sur le Glashedy Rock, au large). Il faudra jouer ici, y faire une retraite de golf pour mesurer vos capacités. Et attendre encore un peu pour situer ce parcours à sa vraie place dans la hiérarchie des parcours.

Ballyliffin Golf Club — 1995
IRL - BALLYLIFFIN, Co Donegal

Office	Secrétariat	(353) 077 - 76 119
Pro shop	Pro-shop	(353) 077 - 76 119
Fax	Fax	(353) 077 - 76 672
Situation	Situation	

40 km from Derry (72 334)
160 km from Belfast (279 237)

Annual closure	Fermeture annuelle	no
Weekly closure	Fermeture hebdomadaire	no

Fees main season	Tarifs haute saison	18 holes
	Week days Semaine	We/Bank holidays We/Férié
Individual Individuel	IR£ 20	IR£ 30
Couple Couple	IR£ 40	IR£ 60

Caddy	Caddy	on request/IR£ 10
Electric Trolley	Chariot électrique	no
Buggy	Voiturette	IR£ 20/18 holes
Clubs	Clubs	IR£ 10

Credit cards Cartes de crédit
VISA - Eurocard - MasterCard - Access

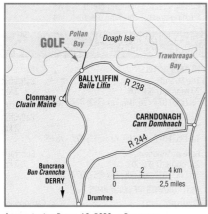

Access Accès : Derry, A2, R238 → Buncrana, Dumfree, Ballyliffin
Map 1 on page 827 Carte 1 Page 827

GOLF COURSE PARCOURS — 17/20

Site	Site	
Maintenance	Entretien	
Architect	Architecte	Pat Ruddy Tom Craddock
Type	Type	links, seaside
Relief	Relief	
Water in play	Eau en jeu	
Exp. to wind	Exposé au vent	
Trees in play	Arbres en jeu	

Scorecard Carte de score	Chp. Chp.	Mens Mess.	Ladies Da.
Length Long.	6456	6154	5328
Par	72	73	72

Advised golfing ability		0 12 24 36
Niveau de jeu recommandé		
Hcp required	Handicap exigé	28 Men, 36 Ladies

CLUB HOUSE & AMENITIES CLUB HOUSE ET ANNEXES — 6/10

Pro shop	Pro-shop	
Driving range	Practice	
Sheltered	couvert	no
On grass	sur herbe	yes
Putting-green	putting-green	yes
Pitching-green	pitching green	yes

841

HOTEL FACILITIES ENVIRONNEMENT HOTELIER — 5/10

HOTELS HÔTELS
The Strand — Ballyliffin
20 rooms, D IR£ 108 — 2 km
Tel (353) 077 - 76 107, Fax (353) 077 - 76 486

Ballyliffin Hotel — Ballyliffin
13 rooms, D IR£ 90 — 2 km
Tel (353) 077 - 76 106, Fax (353) 077 - 76 658

Lake of Shadows — Buncrana
23 rooms, D IR£ 50 — 17 km
Tel (353) 077 - 61 005, Fax (353) 077 - 62 131

RESTAURANTS RESTAURANTS
Corncrake — Carndonagh
Tel (353) 077 - 74 534 — 12 km

Ubiquitous Chip — Burcrana
Tel (353) 077 - 62 530 — 16 km

The trip to the northern tip of Ireland is not the easiest in the world, but the recent addition of another 18 holes has made this one of the country's finest golfing destinations. Summer days are very long here, enough to give anyone more than their fill of golf, no matter how tempting a proposition these courses may be. Nick Faldo called the Old Links here "the most natural course ever" when making a surprise visit that did much for the site's recognition. Here, you play the ball where it lies, on rolling fairways between the rough, sometimes with no visible limits, and rarely on the flat. The landscape has an amazing austere beauty to it, between the ocean, hills and endless stretches of dunes, tall grass and bushes, dotted with the odd white house in the distance. In this huge sanctuary of tranquillity, every player cuts his own path, as if he were the first to play here. A bit short, did you say? That's just the way it is, and no more.

Le voyage à l'extrême nord de l'Irlande n'est pas des plus faciles, mais la récente addition d'un autre 18 trous à celui-ci en fait une des plus belles destinations du pays. Les journées d'été y sont très longues, assez pour se donner une... indigestion de golf, alors que ces parcours sont bien digestes ! Le «Old Links» a été qualifié par Nick Faldo de «Golf le plus naturel qui soit» lors d'une visite surprise qui a beaucoup fait pour la notoriété du lieu. Ici, on joue la balle où elle est, sur des fairways ondulant entre les roughs, parfois sans limite visible, où l'on joue rarement la balle à plat. Le paysage est stupéfiant d'austère beauté, entre les flots de l'océan, les collines et des étendues infinies de dunes, de buissons, d'herbes hautes, ponctuées par de rares maisons blanches dans le lointain. Dans cet espace immense de paix, chacun trace son chemin, comme s'il était le premier à jouer ici. Le parcours est un peu court ? Il est ce qu'il est, c'est tout.

Ballyliffin Golf Club — 1947
IRL - BALLYLIFFIN, Co Donegal

Office	Secrétariat	(353) 077 - 76 119
Pro shop	Pro-shop	(353) 077 - 76 119
Fax	Fax	(353) 077 - 76 672
Situation	Situation	

40 km from Derry (72 334)
160 km from Belfast (279 237)

Annual closure	Fermeture annuelle	no
Weekly closure	Fermeture hebdomadaire	no
Fees main season	Tarifs haute saison	18 holes

	Week days Semaine	We/Bank holidays We/Férié
Individual Individuel	IR£ 15	IR£ 20
Couple Couple	IR£ 30	IR£ 40

Caddy	Caddy	on request/IR£ 10
Electric Trolley	Chariot électrique	no
Buggy	Voiturette	IR£ 20/18 holes
Clubs	Clubs	IR£ 10

Credit cards Cartes de crédit
VISA - Eurocard - MasterCard - Access

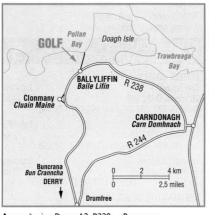

GOLF Pollan Bay — Doagh Isle — Trawbreaga Bay
BALLYLIFFIN Baile Lifín R 238
Clonmany Cluain Maine
CARNDONAGH Carn Domhnach
R 244
Buncrana Bun Cranncha
DERRY
Drumfree

0 2 4 km
0 2,5 miles

Access Accès : Derry, A2, R238 → Buncrana, Dumfree, Ballyliffin
Map 1 on page 827 Carte 1 Page 827

GOLF COURSE PARCOURS — 15/20

Site	Site	
Maintenance	Entretien	
Architect	Architecte	unknown
Type	Type	links
Relief	Relief	
Water in play	Eau en jeu	
Exp. to wind	Exposé au vent	
Trees in play	Arbres en jeu	

Scorecard Carte de score	Chp. Chp.	Mens Mess.	Ladies Da.
Length Long.	5750	0	0
Par	72	0	0

Advised golfing ability — 0 12 24 36
Niveau de jeu recommandé
Hcp required Handicap exigé — Men 28, Ladies 36

CLUB HOUSE & AMENITIES CLUB HOUSE ET ANNEXES — 6/10

Pro shop	Pro-shop	
Driving range	Practice	
Sheltered	couvert	no
On grass	sur herbe	yes
Putting-green	putting-green	yes
Pitching-green	pitching green	yes

HOTEL FACILITIES ENVIRONNEMENT HOTELIER — 5/10

HOTELS HÔTELS
The Strand — Ballyliffin
20 rooms, D IR£ 108 — 2 km
Tel (353) 077 - 76 107, Fax (353) 077 - 76 486

Ballyliffin Hotel — Ballyliffin
13 rooms, D IR£ 90 — 2 km
Tel (353) 077 - 76 106, Fax (353) 077 - 76 658

Lake of Shadows — Buncrana
23 rooms, D IR£ 50 — 17 km
Tel (353) 077 - 61 005, Fax (353) 077 - 62 131

RESTAURANTS RESTAURANTS
Corncrake — Carndonagh
Tel (353) 077 - 74 534 — 12 km

Ubiquitous Chip — Burcrana
Tel (353) 077 - 62 530 — 16 km

842

It was not so easy to create a new course within the immediate vicinity of Killarney, but with such a superb setting (the Mcgillicuddy Reeks form an impressive backdrop) and even the ruins of castle Gore to add a touch of history to the back nine, the appeal of the site could only enhance the actual course. Designed by Arthur Springs over pleasantly rolling and woody terrain, this recent course needs time to mellow, although it is already in very good condition. Of special note are the excellence of the par 3s (especially the 8th), the care taken over the placement of hazards, especially the bunkers, the use of trees and the variety of greens, sometimes elevated or multi-tiered and requiring some accurate ironwork. You can seldom roll the ball here. A few blind shots call for a careful choice of line, but things are generally rather obvious. A pleasant course for all.

Il n'était pas si facile de créer un nouveau golf à proximité immédiate de celui de Killarney, mais la séduction du lieu ne pouvait que profiter au parcours lui-même avec une situation aussi favorable (les Mcgillicuddy Reeks sont en toile de fond), et même les ruines du Castle Core pour donner une touche d'histoire aux neuf derniers trous. Dessiné par Arthur Springs sur un terrain agréablement vallonné et boisé, ce récent parcours a besoin de gagner en maturité, mais sa condition est déjà très bonne. On y remarquera en particulier la qualité des pars 3 (notamment le 8), le soin apporté au placement des obstacles, des bunkers en particulier, la mise en jeu des arbres et la diversité des greens, parfois surélevés ou à plateaux, obligeant à un jeu de fers précis : il est rarement possible de faire rouler la balle. Certains coups aveugles obligent à bien choisir la ligne de jeu, mais elle reste assez évidente. Un parcours agréable pour tous.

Beaufort Golf Club — 1994
IRL - BEAUFORT, Co. Kerry

Office	Secrétariat	(353) 064 - 44 440
Pro shop	Pro-shop	(353) 064 - 44 440
Fax	Fax	(353) 064 - 44 752
Situation	Situation	

11 km W of Killarney (pop. 7 275)
10 km E of Killorglin (pop. 1 229)

Annual closure	Fermeture annuelle	no
Weekly closure	Fermeture hebdomadaire	no

Fees main season	Tarifs haute saison	18 holes
	Week days Semaine	We/Bank holidays We/Férié
Individual Individuel	IR£ 25	IR£ 28
Couple Couple	IR£ 50	IR£ 56

Caddy	Caddy	on request/IR£ 10
Electric Trolley	Chariot électrique	no
Buggy	Voiturette	no
Clubs	Clubs	IR£ 10

Credit cards Cartes de crédit VISA

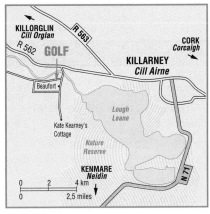

Access Accès : Killarney, R562 to Beaufort.
Golf signposted
Map 2 on page 828 Carte 2 Page 828

GOLF COURSE
PARCOURS
14/20

Site	Site	
Maintenance	Entretien	
Architect	Architecte	Arthur Spring
Type	Type	parkland
Relief	Relief	
Water in play	Eau en jeu	
Exp. to wind	Exposé au vent	
Trees in play	Arbres en jeu	

Scorecard	Chp.	Mens	Ladies
Carte de score	Chp.	Mess.	Da.
Length Long.	6005	5535	4803
Par	71	71	71

Advised golfing ability		0	12	24	36
Niveau de jeu recommandé					
Hcp required	Handicap exigé	no			

CLUB HOUSE & AMENITIES
CLUB HOUSE ET ANNEXES
6/10

Pro shop	Pro-shop	
Driving range	Practice	
Sheltered	couvert	no
On grass	sur herbe	no
Putting-green	putting-green	yes
Pitching-green	pitching green	no

HOTEL FACILITIES
ENVIRONNEMENT HOTELIER
7/10

HOTELS HÔTELS

Dunloe Castle		Beaufort
120 rooms, D IR£ 100		2 km
Tel (353) 064 - 44 111, Fax (353) 064 - 44 583		
Hotel Europe		Killarney
205 rooms, D IR£ 120		6 km
Tel (353) 064 - 31 900, Fax (353) 064 - 32 118		
Aghadoe Heights		Killarney
60 rooms, D IR£ 165		7 km
Tel (353) 064 - 31 766, Fax (353) 064 - 31 345		

RESTAURANTS RESTAURANTS

Fredrick's at the Heights		Killarney
Tel (353) 064 - 31 766		7 km
Gaby's		Killarney
Tel (353) 064 - 32 519		11 km

843

This course was laid out over a marsh with granite subsoil, but intensive draining was carried out, and the condition is already excellent. The undulating site is magnificent, between the Bay of Galway and the hills of County Clare in the distance, countryside which was one of the major areas affected by the great hunger of the 19th century. Begun in 1996, the layout have been patiently completed. Although in the middle of the countryside with many water hazards to contend with, the style of the course has a strong links flavour, meaning that golfers who prefer seaside courses will feel the most comfortable over these 18 holes, where the difficulties gradually pile up as you progress. This is perhaps not the best course in the world but the peaceful setting, the keen air, the wild beauty of the nature all around and the sheer pleasure of playing here make it a rather unique layout, a good round of golf next to the Galway courses before moving on up to Connemara.

Ce parcours a été construit sur un marécage avec sous-sol de granit (il affleure çà et là), mais avec un drainage intensif, il est déjà en très bonne condition. Le site vallonné est magnifique, entre la baie de Galway et les collines du County Clare au loin, dans un des haut-lieux (si l'on peut dire) de la grande famine au XIXème siècle. Commencée en 1996, la construction du parcours, et du Club house ont été patiemment poursuivis. Bien qu'il y ait de nombreux obstacles d'eau, le style du parcours dégage un parfum de links. Et les amoureux des parcours en bord de mer se sentiront à l'aise dans la montée en puissance de ces 18 trous, où les difficultés augmentent à mesure que l'on progresse. Ce n'est peut être pas le meilleur parcours du monde, mais la tranquillité du lieu, l'air vif, la sauvage beauté de la nature, le plaisir de jouer ici rendent ce parcours assez unique, à côté de ceux de Galway, et avant de jouer le Connemara.

Bhearna Golf Club — 1996

Corboley
IRL - BARNA, Co. Galway

Office	Secrétariat	(353) 091 - 592 677
Pro shop	Pro-shop	(353) 091 - 592 677
Fax	Fax	(353) 091 - 592 674
Situation	Situation	

Galway (pop. 50 855), 11 km

Annual closure	Fermeture annuelle	no
Weekly closure	Fermeture hebdomadaire	no

Fees main season	Tarifs haute saison	18 holes
	Week days Semaine	We/Bank holidays We/Férié
Individual Individuel	IR£ 20	IR£ 22
Couple Couple	IR£ 40	IR£ 44

Caddy	Caddy	on request, IR£ 15
Electric Trolley	Chariot électrique	no
Buggy	Voiturette	IR£ 20/18 holes
Clubs	Clubs	IR£ 10/18 holes

Credit cards Cartes de crédit
VISA - Eurocard - MasterCard - AMEX - DC

GOLF COURSE PARCOURS — 14/20

Site	Site	
Maintenance	Entretien	
Architect	Architecte	R.J. Browne
Type	Type	open country
Relief	Relief	
Water in play	Eau en jeu	
Exp. to wind	Exposé au vent	
Trees in play	Arbres en jeu	

Scorecard Carte de score	Chp. Chp.	Mens Mess.	Ladies Da.
Length Long.	6174	5746	4684
Par	72	72	70

Advised golfing ability		0	12	24	36
Niveau de jeu recommandé					
Hcp required	Handicap exigé	no			

CLUB HOUSE & AMENITIES
CLUB HOUSE ET ANNEXES — 7/10

Pro shop	Pro-shop	
Driving range	Practice	
Sheltered	couvert	12 bays under construction
On grass	sur herbe	yes
Putting-green	putting-green	yes
Pitching-green	pitching green	yes

HOTEL FACILITIES
ENVIRONNEMENT HOTELIER — 7/10

HOTELS HÔTELS

Connemara Coast Hotel — Galway
112 rooms, D IR£ 130 — 10 km
Tel (353) 091 - 592 108, Fax (353) 091 - 592 065

Brennans Yard — Galway
24 rooms, D IR£ 100 — 10 km
Tel (353) 091 - 568 186, Fax (353) 091 - 568 262

Ardilaun Hotel — Galway
89 rooms, D IR£ 120 — 10 km
Tel (353) 091 - 521 433, Fax (353) 091 - 521 546

RESTAURANTS RESTAURANTS

Donnellys — Barna 3 km

White Gables — Moycullen 1 km

844

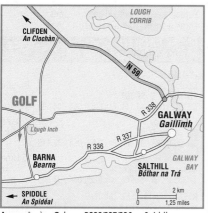

Access Accès : Galway, R338/337/336 → Spiddle.
At the end of Barna (Bearna), turn right → Golf
Map 1 on page 826 Carte 1 Page 826

A seaside course but not a links, with pronounced hilly relief between the 2nd and 8th holes before becoming a little easier. The architects have made good use of difficult terrain for golf but were unable to prevent the 6th, 7th and 14th from being rather tricky little numbers. The 4 closing holes more than make up for this minor shortcoming. In a region where there is no shortage of very good courses, Blainroe compares well. Water is in play on two holes only, news that will delight those players who have been playing with the same ball all season, and the basic difficulties, excluding the wind, are the 58 bunkers, all more strategic than really penalising. When the ground is dry, the greens are open enough to allow rolled shots. Players of all abilities can enjoy their golf here, but single-figure handicappers might prefer to wait for the wind to make this a tougher challenge.

Un parcours de bord de mer, mais sans être un links, avec des reliefs prononcés entre le 2 et le 8, mais ensuite nettement assagis. Les architectes ont fait bon usage d'un terrain difficile à adapter au golf, et n'ont pu éviter de rendre le 6, le 7 et le 14 assez «tricky», mais les quatre derniers trous rachètent ces faiblesses ponctuelles. Dans une région où les très bons parcours ne manquent pas, Blainroe s'est taillé une place très honorable. L'eau n'y vient en jeu que sur deux trous, ce qui ne manquera pas de plaire à ceux qui jouent avec la même balle depuis des années, et les difficultés essentielles (en dehors du vent) sont les 58 bunkers, tous plus stratégiques que vraiment pénalisants. Quand le terrain est sec, les greens sont assez ouverts pour permettre de faire rouler la balle. Tous les niveaux de jeu peuvent s'exprimer ici, mais les meilleurs attendront le vent pour trouver un challenge encore plus décisif.

Blainroe Golf Club — 1978
IRL - BLAINROE, Co. Wicklow

Office	Secrétariat	(353) 0404 - 68 168
Pro shop	Pro-shop	(353) 0404 - 68 168
Fax	Fax	(353) 0404 - 69 369
Situation	Situation	

6 km S of Wicklow (pop. 5 847)
51 km from Dublin (pop. 859 976)

Annual closure	Fermeture annuelle	no
Weekly closure	Fermeture hebdomadaire	no
Fees main season	Tarifs haute saison	18 holes

	Week days Semaine	We/Bank holidays We/Férié
Individual Individuel	IR£ 25	IR£ 35
Couple Couple	IR£ 50	IR£ 70

Caddy	Caddy	IR£ 10/18 holes
Electric Trolley	Chariot électrique	no
Buggy	Voiturette	no
Clubs	Clubs	IR£ 10

Credit cards Cartes de crédit
VISA - MasterCard - AMEX

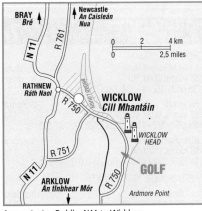

Access Accès : Dublin, N11 to Wicklow.
R750 (Coast Road) to Golf.
Map 3 on page 830 Carte 3 Page 830

GOLF COURSE / PARCOURS — 13/20

Site	Site	
Maintenance	Entretien	
Architect	Architecte	Hawtree & Sons
Type	Type	seaside course, parkland
Relief	Relief	
Water in play	Eau en jeu	
Exp. to wind	Exposé au vent	
Trees in play	Arbres en jeu	

Scorecard Carte de score	Chp. Chp.	Mens Mess.	Ladies Da.
Length Long.	6175	6070	5365
Par	72	72	74

Advised golfing ability Niveau de jeu recommandé	0	12	24	36
Hcp required	Handicap exigé	no		

CLUB HOUSE & AMENITIES / CLUB HOUSE ET ANNEXES — 6/10

Pro shop	Pro-shop	
Driving range	Practice	
Sheltered	couvert	no
On grass	sur herbe	yes
Putting-green	putting-green	yes
Pitching-green	pitching green	yes

845

HOTEL FACILITIES / ENVIRONNEMENT HOTELIER — 6/10

HOTELS HÔTELS
Tinakilly House Hotel — Rathnew
29 rooms, D IR£ 130 — 10 km
Tel (353) 0404 - 69 274, Fax (353) 0404 - 67 806

Blainroe Golf Hotel — adjacent
10 rooms, D IR£ 70
Tel (353) 0404 - 67 500, Fax (353) 0404 - 69 737

Grand Hotel — Wicklow
32 rooms, D IR£ 70 — 6 km
Tel (353) 0404 - 67 337, Fax (353) 0404 - 69 607

RESTAURANTS RESTAURANTS
The Old Rectory — Wicklow
Tel (353) 0404 - 67 048 — 6 km

The Bakery — Wicklow
Tel (353) 0404 - 66 770 — 6 km

The shortest courses are not always the easiest, often lacking par 5s to make those coveted birdies. Bundoran is one such number, and is also a part of history, being over 100 years old. Between the wars, the course was reshaped and toughened up by the grand champion Harry Vardon (the designer of Little Aston and the first designer of Woodhall Spa in England). Alternating park-land country with links holes, this is a good quality test that is ideal for a few rounds with friends or the family. Of course, with the wind, which can blow very hard indeed, things may get tough. Visitors enjoy a picturesque setting with several holes running alongside the ocean (you can even see people surfing) and some superb beaches. When exploring for golf in the north-west of Ireland - which is making itself a nice little international reputation - Bundoran is a highly recommendable stop-off.

Les parcours les plus courts ne sont pas toujours les plus faciles : il y a peu de pars 5 pour faire des birdies ! Bundoran en fait partie. Comme il fait partie de l'histoire, car il a plus d'un siècle d'existence. Entre les deux guerres, il a été remodelé et durci par le grand champion Harry Vardon (l'auteur de Little Aston et le premier architecte de Woodhall Spa, en Angleterre). Alternant les paysages de parc et les vrais trous de links, c'est un test de bonne qualité, idéal pour quelques bonnes parties de golf entre amis ou en famille, mais qui (bien sûr) prend de la puissance avec le vent, parfois très fort ici. Il fait profiter ses visiteurs d'une situation pittoresque, avec plusieurs trous le long de l'océan (on y voit souvent des surfeurs) et de superbes plages. Dans une exploration golfique du Nord-Ouest de l'Irlande, qui commence à acquérir une réputation internationale, Bundoran est une halte très recommandable.

Bundoran Golf Club — 1894
IRL - BUNDORAN, Co Donegal

Office	Secrétariat	(353) 072 - 41 302
Pro shop	Pro-shop	(353) 072 - 41 302
Fax	Fax	(353) 072 - 42 014
Situation	Situation	

1 km from Bundoran
40 km from Sligo (pop. 17 302)

Annual closure	Fermeture annuelle	no
Weekly closure	Fermeture hebdomadaire	no

Fees main season
Tarifs haute saison 18 holes

	Week days Semaine	We/Bank holidays We/Férié
Individual Individuel	IR£ 16	IR£ 18
Couple Couple	IR£ 28	IR£ 32

Caddy	Caddy	on request/IR£ 10
Electric Trolley	Chariot électrique	no
Buggy	Voiturette	IR£ 20/18 holes
Clubs	Clubs	IR£ 10

Credit cards Cartes de crédit — no

GOLF COURSE / PARCOURS — 13/20

Site	Site	▬▬▬
Maintenance	Entretien	▬▬▬
Architect	Architecte	Harry Vardon
Type	Type	links, parkland
Relief	Relief	▬▬
Water in play	Eau en jeu	▬▬
Exp. to wind	Exposé au vent	▬▬
Trees in play	Arbres en jeu	▬

Scorecard Carte de score	Chp. Chp.	Mens Mess.	Ladies Da.
Length Long.	5599	5234	5178
Par	69	69	75

Advised golfing ability Niveau de jeu recommandé	0	12	24	36

Hcp required Handicap exigé — no

CLUB HOUSE & AMENITIES / CLUB HOUSE ET ANNEXES — 6/10

Pro shop	Pro-shop	▬▬
Driving range	Practice	▬▬
Sheltered	couvert	no
On grass	sur herbe	yes
Putting-green	putting-green	yes
Pitching-green	pitching green	yes

HOTEL FACILITIES / ENVIRONNEMENT HOTELIER — 7/10

HOTELS HÔTELS

Great Northern Hotel — Bundoran, on site
98 rooms, D IR£ 90
Tel (353) 072 - 41 204, Fax (353) 072 - 41 114

Holyrood — Bundoran, 1 km
85 rooms, D IR£ 60
Tel (353) 072 - 41 232, Fax (353) 072 - 41 100

Allingham Arms — Bundoran, 1 km
88 rooms, D IR£ 50
Tel (353) 072 - 41 075, Fax (353) 072 - 41 171

RESTAURANTS RESTAURANTS

Le Chateaubrianne — Bundoran, 2 km
Tel (353) 072 - 42 160

Fitzgerald's Bistro — Bundoran, 2 km
Tel (353) 072 - 41 336

846

Access Accès : On N15 Sligo to Donegal
Map 1 on page 826 Carte 1 Page 826

There are some designers that always arouse our curiosity. Alongside Braid, Colt or Mackenzie, one such is Tom Simpson, whose philosophy has been taken up by numerous modern course architects, but not always so successfully. For Simpson, a course must be demanding for champions, less and less difficult the further forward the tee, and the most dangerous hazards should be designed to worry the very best players. This spirit abounds at Carlow, where virtually nothing has changed since the earliest days. It could be lengthened, that's for sure, but this par 70 stands up well to every assault. All the difficulties are visible, but the strategic and aesthetic subtleties appear only gradually: the bunkering, the shaping of the fairways and the use of a little elevated land and rare water hazards reveal an in-depth knowledge of the game of golf. A engaging course, off the beaten track.

Il est des signatures qui éveillent la curiosité. A côté de Braid, Colt ou Mackenzie, Tom Simpson est de celles-là. Sa philosophie a été reprise par de nombreux architectes modernes, pas toujours avec un tel succès : un parcours doit être exigeant pour les champions, de moins en moins difficile à mesure que l'on avance de départ, et les obstacles les plus dangereux doivent inquiéter avant tout les premiers nommés. On retrouve cet esprit à Carlow, où pratiquement rien n'a changé depuis les origines. Certes, on pourrait l'allonger un peu, mais ce par 70 résiste aux assauts. Toutes les difficultés sont visibles, mais les subtilités stratégiques et esthétiques n'apparaissent que progressivement : le placement des bunkers, le travail de modelage des fairways, l'utilisation des quelques élévations de terrain et des rares obstacles d'eau révèlent une connaissance profonde du jeu. Un parcours attachant, hors des sentiers battus.

Carlow Golf Club   1937
Deerpark, Dublin Road
IRL - CARLOW, Co Carlow

Office	Secrétariat	(353) 0503 - 31 695
Pro shop	Pro-shop	(353) 0503 - 41 745
Fax	Fax	(353) 0503 - 40 065
Situation	Situation	

5 km from Carlow

Annual closure	Fermeture annuelle	no
Weekly closure	Fermeture hebdomadaire	no

Fees main season
Tarifs haute saison 18 holes

	Week days Semaine	We/Bank holidays We/Férié
Individual Individuel	IR£ 20	IR£ 25
Couple Couple	IR£ 40	IR£ 50

Caddy	Caddy	on request
Electric Trolley	Chariot électrique	no
Buggy	Voiturette	IR£ 20/18 holes
Clubs	Clubs	IR£ 10

Credit cards Cartes de crédit VISA - MasterCard

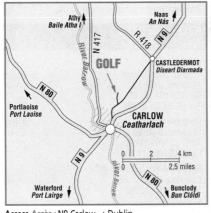

Athy Baile Atha I
Naas An Nás
River Barrow
N 417
R 418
N 9
GOLF
CASTLEDERMOT Diseart Diarmada
N 80
Portlaoise Port Laoise
N 9
CARLOW Ceatharlach
River Barrow
N 80
Waterford Port Lairge
Bunclody Bun Clóidi

| 0 | 2 | 4 km |
| 0 | 2,5 miles | |

Access Accès : N9 Carlow → Dublin
Map 2 on page 829 Carte 2 Page 829

GOLF COURSE
PARCOURS   16/20

Site	Site	▰▰▰▰▱
Maintenance	Entretien	▰▰▰▰▱
Architect	Architecte	Tom Simpson
Type	Type	parkland
Relief	Relief	▰▰▱▱▱
Water in play	Eau en jeu	▰▰▱▱▱
Exp. to wind	Exposé au vent	▰▰▰▱▱
Trees in play	Arbres en jeu	▰▰▰▱▱

Scorecard Carte de score	Chp. Chp.	Mens Mess.	Ladies Da.
Length Long.	5844	5731	5218
Par	70	70	75

Advised golfing ability		0	12	24	36
Niveau de jeu recommandé	▰▰▰▰▱				
Hcp required	Handicap exigé	no			

CLUB HOUSE & AMENITIES
CLUB HOUSE ET ANNEXES   6/10

Pro shop	Pro-shop	▰▰▰▱▱
Driving range	Practice	▰▰▰▱▱
Sheltered	couvert	no
On grass	sur herbe	yes
Putting-green	putting-green	yes
Pitching-green	pitching green	no

HOTEL FACILITIES
ENVIRONNEMENT HOTELIER   6/10

HOTELS HÔTELS

Royal Hotel   Carlow
34 rooms, D IR£ 48   5 km
Tel (353) 0503 - 31 621, Fax (353) 0503 - 31 621

Seven Oaks Hotel   Carlow
32 rooms, D IR£ 70   5 km
Tel (353) 0503 - 31 308, Fax (353) 0503 - 32 155

Kilkea Castle   Castledermot
38 rooms, D IR£ 120   8 km
Tel (353) 0503 - 45 156, Fax (353) 0503 - 45 187

RESTAURANTS RESTAURANTS

Kilkea Castle   Castledermot
Tel (353) 0503 - 45 156   8 km

Tonlegee House   Athy
Tel (353) 0507 - 31 473   15 km

847

Also known by the name of Belmullet, this is yet another world's end course, with impressive views over the rocky coast to the north of Mayo and Blacksod Bay. It is also one of the most recent designs by Eddie Hackett (over 80 years old). The course is very hilly, so we would advise a buggy for all seniors if they want to keep a cool head. Everyone else would be well advised to study the course closely (without counting their score first time out), because a lot of shots and greens turn blind if you are too far off the fairway, and the eight dog-legs are difficult to cope with if you don't get the right distance and angle for the green. Carn is an exciting prospect in match-play, because miracles are as frequent as disasters. However, this course is not to everyone's liking, especially to players who like parks with a pretty castle in the middle, but it is an essential experience in a site very exposed to the wind. But then, which links is not?

Egalement connu sous le nom de Belmullet, avec d'impressionnants panoramas sur la côte sauvage au nord du Mayo et Blacksod Bay, c'est encore un parcours au bout du monde, et l'un des plus récents de Eddie Hackett (à plus de 80 ans). Comme il est très accidenté, on conseillera aux seniors de prendre une voiturette, s'ils veulent garder la tête froide. Et à tout le monde de bien l'étudier (sans compter leur score la première fois) car beaucoup de coups et de greens seront aveugles s'ils s'écartent trop du fairway, et les huit doglegs seront difficiles à négocier si l'on évalue mal les distances pour avoir l'ouverture. En match-play, Carn est passionnant, car les miracles sont aussi fréquents que les désastres. Ce parcours excitant ne plaira pas à tout le monde, notamment à ceux qui aiment les parcs avec joli château, mais c'est une expérience à vivre, dans un site très exposé au vent, mais que serait un links sans lui ?

Carn Golf Links — 1993

IRL - BELMULLET, Co Mayo

Office	Secrétariat	(353) 097 - 82 292
Pro shop	Pro-shop	(353) 097 - 82 292
Fax	Fax	(353) 097 - 81477
Situation	Situation	

1 km from Belmullet
60 km from Ballina (pop. 6 563)

Annual closure	Fermeture annuelle	no
Weekly closure	Fermeture hebdomadaire	no
Fees main season	Tarifs haute saison	18 holes

	Week days Semaine	We/Bank holidays We/Férié
Individual Individuel	IR£ 17	IR£ 17
Couple Couple	IR£ 27	IR£ 27

Caddy	Caddy	IR£ 10/18 holes
Electric Trolley	Chariot électrique	no
Buggy	Voiturette	IR£ 20/18 holes
Clubs	Clubs	IR£ 8

Credit cards Cartes de crédit
VISA - Eurocard - MasterCard

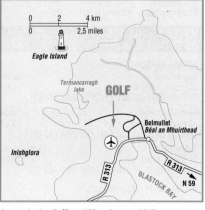

0	2	4 km
0	2,5 miles

Eagle Island

Termancarragh lake

GOLF

Belmullet
Béal an Mhuirthead

Inishglora

R 313

R 313

BLASTOCK BAY

N 59

Access Accès : Ballina, N59 to Bangor. R313 to Belmullet. → Airport. Golf on the right
Map 1 on page 826 Carte 1 Page 826

GOLF COURSE
PARCOURS — 16/20

Site	Site	
Maintenance	Entretien	
Architect	Architecte	Eddie Hackett
Type	Type	links
Relief	Relief	
Water in play	Eau en jeu	
Exp. to wind	Exposé au vent	
Trees in play	Arbres en jeu	

Scorecard Carte de score	Chp. Chp.	Mens Mess.	Ladies Da.
Length Long.	6090	5804	4704
Par	72	72	73

Advised golfing ability		0 12 24 36
Niveau de jeu recommandé		
Hcp required	Handicap exigé	no

CLUB HOUSE & AMENITIES
CLUB HOUSE ET ANNEXES — 5/10

Pro shop	Pro-shop	
Driving range	Practice	
Sheltered	couvert	no
On grass	sur herbe	yes
Putting-green	putting-green	yes
Pitching-green	pitching green	no

HOTEL FACILITIES
ENVIRONNEMENT HOTELIER — 3/10

HOTELS HÔTELS

Western Strand Hotel — Belmullet
15 rooms, D IR£ 25 — 1 km
Tel (353) 097 - 81 096
Fax (353) 097 - 81 096

Downhill Hotel — Ballina
50 rooms, D IR£ 93 — 60 km
Tel (353) 096 - 21 033
Fax (353) 096 - 21 338

RESTAURANTS RESTAURANTS

Club House Restaurant — on site
Tel (353) 097 - 82 292

The River Boat Inn — Ballina
Tel (353) 096 - 22 183 — 60 km

848

Here we are virtually in town, enough to turn green with envy many a continental city-dweller who has to drive miles and miles to find a course. Here, though, you still feel a distinct change of surroundings after a very pleasant drive up to a pretty club-house. The course, designed by Harry Colt, is already old and weathered by the years; the trees and grass have a sort of polished sheen look to them, rather like on old furniture. The rather flat layout is like a pleasant walk in a large park, with trees placed (or used) strategically so that they don't actually form a wood. Visually, they look even more dangerous. Equally well «placed» are the fairway and green-side bunkers, but it is fair to say that here you seldom have a truly long shot to play, which makes it even more annoying to miss the greens. A good old top class course, well-maintained and very pleasant for a round with the family... or to show off your skills with lesser players than yourself.

On est pratiquement en pleine ville, mais on a une certaine impression de dépaysement, après une arrivée très agréable sur le site et la vision d'un joli Club house. Dû au crayon expert de Harry Colt, ce parcours déjà ancien est poli par les années, les arbres et le gazon ont cette sorte de «patine» que l'on associe aux meubles anciens. Assez plat, le tracé constitue une sorte de promenade dans un grand parc, les arbres étant davantage placés (ou utilisés) stratégiquement qu'ils ne constituent des bois à proprement parler. Ils n'en paraissent que plus dangereux visuellement. Tout aussi «bien» placés, les bunkers de fairway et bunkers de greens, mais il faut dire que l'on a rarement de longs coups à jouer ici : il n'en est que plus vexant de manquer les greens. Un bon vieux parcours de bonne classe, bien entretenu, très agréable à jouer en famille... ou pour briller avec des amis moins expérimentés.

Castle Golf Club — 1913

Woodside Drive
IRL - RATHFARNHAM - DUBLIN 14

Office	Secrétariat	(353) 01 - 490 4207
Pro shop	Pro-shop	(353) 01 - 490 4207
Fax	Fax	(353) 01 - 490 0264
Situation	Situation	

Dublin (pop. 859 976), 6 km from city centre

Annual closure	Fermeture annuelle	no
Weekly closure	Fermeture hebdomadaire	no
Fees main season	Tarifs haute saison	18 holes

	Week days Semaine	We/Bank holidays We/Férié
Individual Individuel	IR£ 35	IR£ 35
Couple Couple	IR£ 70	IR£ 70

Caddy	Caddy	IR£ 20
Electric Trolley	Chariot électrique	no
Buggy	Voiturette	no
Clubs	Clubs	no

Credit cards Cartes de crédit
VISA - Eurocard - MasterCard - AMEX - DC

Access Accès : In Dublin, → Castle, Harold's Cross Road, Lower Dodder Park Road, Woodside Drive (Golf at Rathfarnham).
Map 3 on page 830 Carte 3 Page 830

GOLF COURSE / PARCOURS — 13/20

Site	Site	
Maintenance	Entretien	
Architect	Architecte	Harry S. Colt
Type	Type	parkland
Relief	Relief	
Water in play	Eau en jeu	
Exp. to wind	Exposé au vent	
Trees in play	Arbres en jeu	

Scorecard Carte de score	Chp. Chp.	Mens Mess.	Ladies Da.
Length Long.	5733	5508	5104
Par	70	70	72

Advised golfing ability Niveau de jeu recommandé	0	12	24	36
Hcp required	Handicap exigé	no		

CLUB HOUSE & AMENITIES / CLUB HOUSE ET ANNEXES — 6/10

Pro shop	Pro-shop	
Driving range	Practice	
Sheltered	couvert	no
On grass	sur herbe	yes (practice area)
Putting-green	putting-green	yes
Pitching-green	pitching green	no

HOTEL FACILITIES / ENVIRONNEMENT HOTELIER — 8/10

HOTELS HÔTELS
Rathmines Plaza Hotel — Rathmines
54 rooms, D IR£ 80 — 6 km
Tel (353) 01 - 496 6966, Fax (353) 01 - 491 0603

Orwell Lodge Hotel - 10 rooms, D IR£ 80 — Rathgae
Tel (353) 01 - 497 7258, Fax (353) 01 - 497 9913 — 3 km

Red Cow Morans Hotel — Clondalkin
1233 rooms, D IR£ 140 — 14 km
Tel (353) 01 - 459 3650, Fax (353) 01 - 459 1588

RESTAURANTS RESTAURANTS
Johnnie Foxes — Glencullen 17 km
Tel (353) 01 - 295 5647

Killakee Restaurant — Rathfarnham 5 km
Tél (353) 01 - 493 2645

Yellow House — Rathfarnham 5 km
Tél (353) 01 - 493 2994

849

Here is a good example of a course where maintenance can change everything. After a few years of comparative neglect, Castletroy can once again boast the manicured label with clearly cut fairways, making it a whole different course. Three new greens have been re-laid on sand, leading to a slight difference from the rest in terms of roll and pitch, but nothing to shout about. It is always pleasant to feel this impression of a huge park. In fact the trees outline the holes more than form a real wood, but they still swallow up any mis-hit drive with great relish. Accuracy is the watchword here, with OB on holes 1 & 2 calling for tidy shot-making from the outset, whatever the club. This is particularly true on hole N°12, an excellent dog-leg with an elevated and highly contoured green, or the 13th, a pretty par 3 with a small green way down below. And as the more you play here the more you enjoy the course, Castletroy is back on the itinerary of demanding golfers.

Un bon exemple de parcours où l'entretien peut tout changer. Après quelques années d'errance, Castletroy est redevenu bien «manucuré», ses fairways nettement dessinés, et tout change. Trois nouveaux greens ont été refaits sur du sable, ce qui provoque un peu de différence de roulement et de tenue avec les autres, mais cela ne choque pas trop. On retrouve avec plaisir cette impression de grand parc. Mais les arbres définissent plus les trous qu'ils ne sont de véritables bois, mais ils accueillent avec un plaisir évident les drives un peu écartés! La précision est d'ailleurs le maître mot, avec les hors-limites aux 1 et 2 qui vous imposent d'entrée la rigueur. En particulier pour négocier des trous délicats comme le 12, excellent dog-leg avec green en hauteur et très travaillé, ou le 13, joli par 3 avec un petit green en contrebas. Castletroy fait son retour sur les itinéraires des golfeurs exigeants.

Castletroy Golf Club — 1937
IRL - CASTLETROY, Co. Limerick

Office	Secrétariat	(353) 01 - 458 8566
Pro shop	Pro-shop	
Fax	Fax	
Situation	Situation	
Limerick (pop. 52 083), 3.5 km		
Annual closure	Fermeture annuelle	no
Weekly closure	Fermeture hebdomadaire	no

Fees main season
Tarifs haute saison 18 holes

	Week days Semaine	We/Bank holidays We/Férié
Individual Individuel	IR£ 22	IR£ 25
Couple Couple	IR£ 44	IR£ 50

Caddy	Caddy	IR£ 20
Electric Trolley	Chariot électrique	no
Buggy	Voiturette	IR£ 30
Clubs	Clubs	IR£ 10

Credit cards Cartes de crédit
VISA - MasterCard - AMEX - DC

850

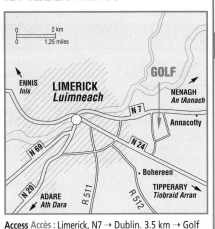

Access Accès : Limerick, N7 → Dublin. 3.5 km → Golf
Map 2 on page 828 Carte 2 Page 828

GOLF COURSE
PARCOURS — **14**/20

Site	Site	
Maintenance	Entretien	
Architect	Architecte	Eddie Hackett
Type	Type	parkland
Relief	Relief	
Water in play	Eau en jeu	
Exp. to wind	Exposé au vent	
Trees in play	Arbres en jeu	

Scorecard Carte de score	Chp. Chp.	Mens Mess.	Ladies Da.
Length Long.	5793	5617	5256
Par	71	71	75

Advised golfing ability		0	12	24	36
Niveau de jeu recommandé					
Hcp required	Handicap exigé	no			

CLUB HOUSE & AMENITIES
CLUB HOUSE ET ANNEXES — **6**/10

Pro shop	Pro-shop	
Driving range	Practice	
Sheltered	couvert	3 mats
On grass	sur herbe	yes
Putting-green	putting-green	yes
Pitching-green	pitching green	yes

HOTEL FACILITIES
ENVIRONNEMENT HOTELIER — **6**/10

HOTELS HÔTELS

Castletroy Park Hotel — Castletroy
107 rooms, D IR£ 100 — 1 km
Tel (353) 061 - 335 566, Fax (353) 061 - 331 117

Jury's Hotel — Limerick
95 rooms, D IR£ 120 — 4 km
Tel (353) 061 - 327 777, Fax (353) 061 - 326 400

Royal George Hotel — Limerick
54 rooms, D IR£ 55 — 8 km
Tel (353) 061 - 414 566, Fax (353) 061 - 317 171

RESTAURANTS RESTAURANTS

Moll Darby's — Limerick
Tel (353) 061 - 411 511 — 4 km

Freddy's Bistro — Limerick
Tel (353) 061 - 418 749 — 4 km

One of the best courses to the north of Cork has just been supplemented by an extra 9 holes, to make it even more pleasant to play. At the heart of the Golden Vale at the foot of the Ballyhoura Mountains, this is one of Ireland's best known farming regions and a good opportunity to note that the Irish are not just a people of sailors and fishermen. On this subject, the nearby Blackwater river is one of the finest sites in Ireland for tickling trout. This very busy course is in excellent condition (greens and fairways) but the bunkers are average only and rainy days are not ideal for playing here. The very many trees are often dangerous and clearly suggest a 3-wood rather than the driver. As the course is relatively short, this is not too much of a problem. It was designed more for club members than for over-demanding green-feers, but if you are in the region, you won't be disappointed.

L'un des meilleurs parcours au nord de Cork vient d'être complété par un 9 trous supplémentaire, qui en augmente encore l'agrément. Au coeur de la «Golden Vale», au pied des Ballyhoura Mountains, c'est l'une des régions agricoles les plus connues d'Irlande, une bonne occasion de vérifier que les Irlandais ne sont pas seulement un peuple de marins et de pêcheurs. A ce propos, la proche rivière Blackwater est l'un des meilleurs sites d'Irlande pour taquiner le poisson. Ce parcours très fréquenté est en excellente condition (greens et fairways), mais les bunkers sont simplement moyens, et les périodes pluvieuses ne sont pas idéales. Les arbres abondants sont souvent dangereux, ils incitent à laisser le driver dans le sac : comme le parcours n'est pas long, ce n'est pas un problème. Il a été conçu davantage pour les membres d'un club que pour des visiteurs trop exigeants. Si vous passez dans la région, vous ne serez pas déçu.

Charleville Golf Club — 1941

Smiths Road
IRL - CHARLEVILLE (RATH LUIRC), Co Cork

Office	Secrétariat	(353) 063 - 81 257
Pro shop	Pro-shop	(353) 063 - 81 274
Fax	Fax	(353) 063 - 81 274
Situation	Situation	

45 km from Limerick (pop. 52 083)
58 km from Cork (pop. 174 400)

Annual closure	Fermeture annuelle	no
Weekly closure	Fermeture hebdomadaire	no

Fees main season
Tarifs haute saison 18 holes

	Week days Semaine	We/Bank holidays We/Férié
Individual Individuel	IR£ 13.50	IR£ 15
Couple Couple	IR£ 27	IR£ 30
Students, IR£ 7		

Caddy	Caddy	IR£ 10/18 holes
Electric Trolley	Chariot électrique	no
Buggy	Voiturette	no
Clubs	Clubs	no

Credit cards Cartes de crédit
VISA - MasterCard - AMEX

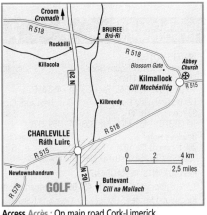

Access Accès : On main road Cork-Limerick
Map 2 on page 828 Carte 2 Page 828

GOLF COURSE PARCOURS — 13/20

Site	Site	
Maintenance	Entretien	
Architect	Architecte	E. Connaughton
Type	Type	inland, parkland
Relief	Relief	
Water in play	Eau en jeu	
Exp. to wind	Exposé au vent	
Trees in play	Arbres en jeu	

Scorecard Carte de score	Chp. Chp.	Mens Mess.	Ladies Da.
Length Long.	5845	5647	4585
Par	71	71	72

Advised golfing ability	0	12	24	36
Niveau de jeu recommandé				
Hcp required	Handicap exigé	28 Men, 36 Ladies		

CLUB HOUSE & AMENITIES CLUB HOUSE ET ANNEXES — 4/10

Pro shop	Pro-shop	
Driving range	Practice	
Sheltered	couvert	4 mats
On grass	sur herbe	yes
Putting-green	putting-green	yes
Pitching-green	pitching green	yes

HOTEL FACILITIES ENVIRONNEMENT HOTELIER — 6/10

HOTELS HÔTELS

Deerpark — Charleville
20 rooms, D IR£ 45 — 1.5 km
Tel (353) 063 - 81 581, Fax (353) 063 - 81 581

Hibernian Hotel — Mallow
49 rooms, D IR£ 70 — 40 km
Tel (353) 022 - 21 588, Fax (353) 022 - 22 632

Duhallow Hotel — 6 km Kenturk
22 rooms, D IR£ 50 — 40 km
Tel (353) 029 - 56 042, Fax (353) 029 - 56 152

RESTAURANTS RESTAURANTS

Longueville — Mallow
Tel (353) 027 - 47 156 — 24 km

The Coffee Pot — Charleville
Tel (353) 063 - 81 203 — adjacent

851

This is a green-fee course easily playable on week-ends and boasting good practice facilities (20 mats on the driving range are lit-up). It is a whole different picture from the recent, very fashionable private clubs in the region of Dublin. Christy O'Connor Jr. has cleverly made the most of limited space, where imposing trees provided a good working base and pleasant setting. Intelligent but not unduly stressful deployment of water, the use of some natural topography to lay a number of greens and careful bunkering have resulted in a varied, interesting and instructive course: here you have to play every shot in the book, but everyone can try their luck once in a while. Visually, some holes like the 8th and 9th definitely look a little artificial in this landscape, but time will change all that. A very useful addition at a time when fashion seems to be swinging a little too much in favour of upmarket courses.

C'est un parcours au green-fee, facilement accessible en week-end et pourvu de bonnes installations d'entraînement (20 postes du driving range sont éclairés). Rien à voir avec les récents grands clubs privés très «fashionable» de la région de Dublin. Mais Christy O'Connor Jr a astucieusement tiré parti d'un espace limité, où l'implantation d'arbres déjà imposants a fourni à la fois une base de travail et un environnement plaisant. Une mise en place intelligente mais pas trop stressante d'obstacles d'eau, l'utilisation de quelques reliefs naturels pour implanter certains greens, un bunkering soigné ont contribué à en faire un parcours varié, intéressant et formateur : ici, on doit jouer tous les coups de golf, mais tous les golfeurs pourront tenter leur chance. Visuellement, certains trous comme le 8 et le 9 paraissent certes un peu artificiels dans le paysage, mais le temps effacera cela. Une réalisation fort utile, en un temps où l'on a un peu trop tendance à privilégier le «haut de gamme».

Citywest Golf Club — 1994
IRL - SAGGART, Co Dublin

Office	Secrétariat	(353) 01 - 458 8566
Pro shop	Pro-shop	(353) 01 - 401 0900
Fax	Fax	(353) 01 - 458 8565
Situation	Situation	

16 km W. of Dublin (pop. 859 976)

Annual closure	Fermeture annuelle	no
Weekly closure	Fermeture hebdomadaire	no

Fees main season
Tarifs haute saison 18 holes

	Week days Semaine	We/Bank holidays We/Férié
Individual Individuel	IR£ 25	IR£ 30
Couple Couple	IR£ 50	IR£ 60

Hotel guests: IR£ 20

Caddy	Caddy	on request/IR£ 30
Electric Trolley	Chariot électrique	no
Buggy	Voiturette	IR£ 20/18 holes
Clubs	Clubs	IR£ 12/18 holes

Credit cards Cartes de crédit
VISA - Eurocard - MasterCard - AMEX

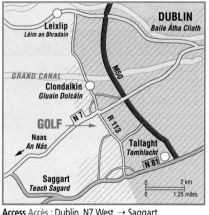

Access Accès : Dublin, N7 West. → Saggart.
Golf 2 km
Map 3 on page 830 Carte 3 Page 830

GOLF COURSE
PARCOURS — 13/20

Site	Site	
Maintenance	Entretien	
Architect	Architecte	Christy O'Connor Jr
Type	Type	parkland
Relief	Relief	
Water in play	Eau en jeu	
Exp. to wind	Exposé au vent	
Trees in play	Arbres en jeu	

Scorecard Carte de score	Chp. Chp.	Mens Mess.	Ladies Da.
Length Long.	6022	5683	4910
Par	70	70	71

Advised golfing ability Niveau de jeu recommandé	0	12	24	36
Hcp required Handicap exigé	no			

CLUB HOUSE & AMENITIES
CLUB HOUSE ET ANNEXES — 6/10

Pro shop	Pro-shop	
Driving range	Practice	
Sheltered	couvert	20 mats
On grass	sur herbe	yes
Putting-green	putting-green	yes
Pitching-green	pitching green	yes

HOTEL FACILITIES
ENVIRONNEMENT HOTELIER — 7/10

HOTELS HÔTELS
Citywest Country House Hotel — on site
39 rooms, D IR£ 118/178
Tel (353) 01 - 458 8566, Fax (353) 01 - 458 8565

Doyles Green Isle Hotel — Newlands Cross
90 rooms, D IR£ 80 — 5 km
Tel (353) 01 - 459 3406, Fax (353) 01 - 459 2178

Bowley's Hotel — Newlands Cross
200 rooms, D IR£ 100 — 5 km
Tel (353) 01 - 464 0140, Fax (353) 01 - 464 0900

RESTAURANTS RESTAURANT
Terrace Room - Tel (353) 01 - 458 8566 — Saggart on site
Kingswood House — Naas Road
Tel (353) 01 - 459 2428 — 2 km
The Common's - Tél(353) 01 - 475 2597 — Dublin15 km

852

When setting eyes on a site as exceptional, as romantic and as captivating as this, set between the ocean and national park mountains, one imagines nothing less than boundless enthusiasm. Here, you are transported hundreds of years back in history, and the actual course looks as if it has always been a part of the picture. But as with Waterville, the total absence of any relief over the first few holes is disappointing, and the serious business only starts at the 8th. Then come a number of gems (the 8th, 9th and 13th) and all the closing holes from the 15th onward. If you started out playing some slack golf, the course will soon very roughly remind you of the real state of your game, and inexperienced players can easily suffer. The fairway bunkers are more or less dangerous, depending on the wind, and the same goes for the rough and some formidable thickets (often around the greens). The original budget was restricted, but we'd be willing to pay a little more to finance a few improvements to the front 9.

On aimerait bien être complètement enthousiaste quand on voit un site aussi exceptionnel, romantique et attachant, entre l'Océan et les montagnes du Parc National. On est transporté des milliers d'années en arrière, et le golf lui-même donne l'impression d'avoir toujours été là. Un peu comme à Waterville, on peut regretter le manque total de relief des premiers trous, les choses sérieuses ne commençant vraiment qu'à partir du 8. Alors, on trouve quelques joyaux (8, 9, 13) et toute la fin, à partir du 15. Si vous avez commencé avec un jeu négligent, le parcours vous rappelle brutalement à la réalité de votre golf, et les joueurs peu expérimentés risquent de souffrir. Selon le vent, les bunkers de fairway peuvent être dangereux ou non, de même que le rough et quelques redoutables buissons (souvent autour des greens). Le budget initial était limité, on serait prêt à payer plus cher pour financer quelques travaux sur l'aller.

Connemara Golf Club

Ballyconneely
IRL - CLIFDEN, Co Galway

Office	Secrétariat	(353) 095 - 23 602
Pro shop	Pro-shop	(353) 095 - 23 502
Fax	Fax	(353) 095 - 23 662
Situation	Situation	

16 km from Clifden (pop. 808)

Annual closure	Fermeture annuelle	no
Weekly closure	Fermeture hebdomadaire	no

Fees main season
Tarifs haute saison 18 holes

	Week days Semaine	We/Bank holidays We/Férié
Individual Individuel	IR£ 25	IR£ 25
Couple Couple	IR£ 50	IR£ 50

Caddy	Caddy	on request/IR£ 15
Electric Trolley	Chariot électrique	no
Buggy	Voiturette	IR£ 20/18 holes
Clubs	Clubs	IR£ 12/18 holes

Credit cards Cartes de crédit
VISA - Eurocard - MasterCard

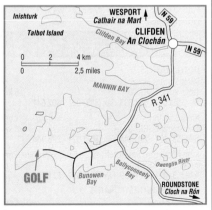

Access Accès : Galway N59 › Clifden. 16 km S of Clifden, golf in seaside village of Ballyconneely
Map 1 on page 826 Carte 1 Page 826

GOLF COURSE
PARCOURS

14/20

Site	Site	
Maintenance	Entretien	
Architect	Architecte	Eddie Hackett
Type	Type	links
Relief	Relief	
Water in play	Eau en jeu	
Exp. to wind	Exposé au vent	
Trees in play	Arbres en jeu	

Scorecard Carte de score	Chp. Chp.	Mens Mess.	Ladies Da.
Length Long.	6611	6263	5055
Par	72	72	72

Advised golfing ability Niveau de jeu recommandé	0	12	24	36

Hcp required   Handicap exigé   28 Men, 36 Ladies

CLUB HOUSE & AMENITIES
CLUB HOUSE ET ANNEXES

6/10

Pro shop	Pro-shop	
Driving range	Practice	
Sheltered	couvert	no
On grass	sur herbe	yes
Putting-green	putting-green	yes
Pitching-green	pitching green	no

HOTEL FACILITIES
ENVIRONNEMENT HOTELIER

6/10

HOTELS HÔTELS

Abbey Glen   Clifden
32 rooms, D IR£ 69   16 km
Tel (353) 095 - 21 201, Fax (353) 095 - 21 797

Rock Glen   Clifden
29 rooms, D IR£ 90   16 km
Tel (353) 095 - 21 035, Fax (353) 095 - 21 737

Erriseask Hotel   Ballyconneely
13 rooms, D IR£ 80   5 km
Tel (353) 095 - 23 553, Fax (353) 095 - 23 639

RESTAURANTS RESTAURANT

O'Grady's Seafood   Clifden
Tel (353) 095 - 21 450   16 km

High Moors   Clifden
Tel (353) 095 - 21 342   16 km

853

This course, which is more than 100 years old, was remodelled by Alistair Mackenzie, one of the great names from the classical era (he was the joint designer of Augusta, no less). Although well off the beaten golfer's track, Cork G.C. is well worth the visit. Located in a park on an island opposite the port of Cork, this is a marvellously technical course and you are constantly amazed at how easy it can be to drop so many strokes on such an honest and apparently benign course. But here, placing the drive is crucial, hazards are magnificently well placed and the putting surfaces are not easy to read. Water comes into play on only a few holes (ditches), but the rough can be as formidable as a huge lake. This very prettily landscaped and very well kept course has victoriously weathered the passing of time. Discover or return to Cork G.C. before setting out to explore the very many sights to see in this pretty region.

Ce parcours plus que centenaire a été remodelé par Alistair Mackenzie, l'un des grands architectes de l'ère classique (c'est le co-auteur d'Augusta). Bien qu'il figure à l'écart des grands circuits golfiques, il mérite largement la visite. Dans un paysage de parc et situé dans une petite île face au port de Cork, c'est une petite merveille de technicité, et l'on s'étonne constamment de perdre autant de points sur un tracé aussi franc et apparemment aimable. Mais le placement des drives y est crucial, les obstacles sont magnifiquement placés, les surfaces de green sont peu faciles à lire. L'eau ne vient en jeu que sur quelques trous (fossés), mais le rough peut être tout aussi redoutable que l'immense lac. Ce parcours très joliment paysagé et très bien entretenu a victorieusement subi les atteintes du temps. A découvrir, ou redécouvrir, avant d'explorer les richesses touristiques de cette jolie région.

Cork Golf Club · 1888
IRL - LITTLE ISLAND, Co Cork

Office	Secrétariat	(353) 021 - 353 451
Pro shop	Pro-shop	(353) 021 - 353 451
Fax	Fax	(353) 021 - 353 410
Situation	Situation	

8 km from Cork (pop. 174 400)
30 km from Cobh (pop. 6 227)

Annual closure	Fermeture annuelle	no
Weekly closure	Fermeture hebdomadaire	no

Fees main season
Tarifs haute saison 18 holes

	Week days Semaine	We/Bank holidays We/Férié
Individual Individuel	IR£ 35	IR£ 40
Couple Couple	IR£ 70	IR£ 80

Caddy	Caddy	IR£ 15/18 holes
Electric Trolley	Chariot électrique	no
Buggy	Voiturette	no
Clubs	Clubs	IR£ 12/18 holes

Credit cards Cartes de crédit
VISA - MasterCard - AMEX

854

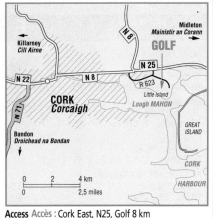

Access Accès : Cork East, N25, Golf 8 km
Map 2 on page 828 Carte 2 Page 828

GOLF COURSE
PARCOURS · 15/20

Site	Site	▆▆▆▆
Maintenance	Entretien	▆▆▆▆
Architect	Architecte	Alistair Mackenzie
Type	Type	parkland
Relief	Relief	▆▆
Water in play	Eau en jeu	▆
Exp. to wind	Exposé au vent	▆▆▆
Trees in play	Arbres en jeu	▆▆

Scorecard Carte de score	Chp. Chp.	Mens Mess.	Ladies Da.
Length Long.	6115	5910	5262
Par	72	72	74

Advised golfing ability		0 12 24 36
Niveau de jeu recommandé		▆▆▆
Hcp required	Handicap exigé	no

CLUB HOUSE & AMENITIES
CLUB HOUSE ET ANNEXES · 3/10

Pro shop	Pro-shop	▆▆▆
Driving range	Practice	▆▆
Sheltered	couvert	no
On grass	sur herbe	yes
Putting-green	putting-green	yes
Pitching-green	pitching green	yes

HOTEL FACILITIES
ENVIRONNEMENT HOTELIER · 5/10

HOTELS HÔTELS

Silver Springs Hotel — Cork
109 rooms, D IR£ 90 — 6 km
Tel (353) 021 - 507 533, Fax (353) 021 - 507 641

Jurys Cork Inn — Cork
133 rooms, D IR£ 50 — 8 km
Tel (353) 021 - 276 444, Fax (353) 021 - 276 144

John Barleycorn Inn Hotel — Glanmire, Cork
0 rooms, D IR£ 50 — 4 km
Tel (353) 021 - 821 499, Fax (353) 021 - 821 221

RESTAURANTS RESTAURANTS

Oyster Tavern — Cork
Tel (353) 021 - 272 716 — 8 km

Flemings — Cork
Tel (353) 021 - 821 621 — 8 km

How do you explain the fame of a golf course? County Louth (or Baltray) has never hosted major international tournaments, is not one of the star courses in the south-west of Ireland and is an hour's drive from Dublin, where there is no shortage of top courses. But recognition comes from being known by the connoisseurs. While some courses may be controversial, this one is acclaimed by all. The dunes may not be as Dantesque as elsewhere and all the difficulties are there to be seen, but this course needs a humble and clear-headed approach and close observation of each detail to appreciate the aristocratic grandeur of the whole layout. Designer Tom Simpson was perhaps the greatest strategist of all for the placing and design of bunkers, and here you recognise his cachet from hole 1 to 18. Whichever direction the wind blows, it is always in play. The fairways are comparatively wide but the rough and thickets are deadly. This sheer gem deserves both respect and glory.

A quoi tient la célébrité d'un parcours ? County Louth (ou Baltray) n'a pas reçu de grandes compétitions internationales, ne fait pas partie des vedettes du Sud-Ouest, est à une heure de Dublin, où les grands parcours ne manquent pas. Mais on reconnaît un connaisseur s'il le connaît. S'il est des parcours controversés, celui-ci fait l'unanimité. Certes, les dunes n'y sont pas aussi dantesques qu'ailleurs, on distingue toutes les difficultés, mais il faut l'aborder avec humilité et lucidité, en observer chaque détail pour apprécier la grandeur aristocratique de l'ensemble. L'architecte Tom Simpson était peut-être le plus grand stratège du placement et du dessin même des bunkers : on reconnaît sa signature du premier au dernier trou. Quelle que soit la direction du vent, il s'en trouve toujours en jeu. Les fairways sont relativement larges, mais les roughs et les buissons sont redoutables. Ce pur joyau mérite le respect, et la gloire.

County Louth Golf Club — 1892

Baltray
IRL - DROGHEDA, Co Louth

Office	Secrétariat	(353) 041 - 22 329
Pro shop	Pro-shop	(353) 041 - 22 444
Fax	Fax	(353) 041 - 22 969
Situation	Situation	

5 km from Drogheda (pop. 23 848)

Annual closure	Fermeture annuelle	no
Weekly closure	Fermeture hebdomadaire	no

Fees main season
Tarifs haute saison 18 holes

	Week days Semaine	We/Bank holidays We/Férié
Individual Individuel	IR£ 40	IR£ 50
Couple Couple	IR£ 80	IR£ 100

Caddy	Caddy	IR£ 20/18 holes
Electric Trolley	Chariot électrique	no
Buggy	Voiturette	IR£ 20/18 holes
Clubs	Clubs	IR£ 12/18 holes

Credit cards Cartes de crédit VISA - MasterCard

Access Accès : Dublin, M1 North → Drogheda.
7 km NE of Drogheda on R167
Map 3 on page 830 Carte 3 Page 830

GOLF COURSE PARCOURS — 18/20

Site	Site	
Maintenance	Entretien	
Architect	Architecte	Tom Simpson (1937)
Type	Type	links
Relief	Relief	
Water in play	Eau en jeu	
Exp. to wind	Exposé au vent	
Trees in play	Arbres en jeu	

Scorecard Carte de score	Chp. Chp.	Mens Mess.	Ladies Da.
Length Long.	6113	5952	5740
Par	73	73	75

Advised golfing ability		0 12 24 36
Niveau de jeu recommandé		
Hcp required	Handicap exigé	no

CLUB HOUSE & AMENITIES CLUB HOUSE ET ANNEXES — 5/10

Pro shop	Pro-shop	
Driving range	Practice	
Sheltered	couvert	no
On grass	sur herbe	yes
Putting-green	putting-green	yes
Pitching-green	pitching green	yes

855

HOTEL FACILITIES ENVIRONNEMENT HOTELIER — 6/10

HOTELS HÔTELS
Boyne Valley Hotel — Drogheda
35 rooms, D IR£ 60 — 5 km
Tel (353) 041 - 37 737, Fax (353) 041 - 39 188

Neptune — Bettystown
25 rooms, D IR£ 45 — 10 km
Tel (353) 041 - 27 107, Fax (353) 041 - 27 243

Westcourt — Drogheda
20 rooms, D IR£ 60 — 5 km
Tel (353) 041 - 30 965, Fax (353) 041 - 30 970

RESTAURANTS RESTAURANTS
Buttergate — Drogheda
Tel (353) 041 - 34 759 — 6 km

Triple House — Termonfeckin
Tel (353) 041 - 22 616 — 3 km

From the fairways, magnificent views over the Atlantic, the bay of Drumcliff and Ben Bulben warrant a trip to County Sligo. But this is also home to one of Ireland's greatest golf courses. As windless days are few and far between, the elements are an overriding factor: the fairways are wide enough, but balls too far left or right are snapped up by the bunkers and rough, both equally penalising. With this said, and if we exclude two or three blind shots, all the hazards are clearly visible and the player knows perfectly well what needs to be done to avoid them. It is simply a question of doing it! Golfers with little experience or even less nerve can choose their own tees, they are all well placed to vary the shape of the course. With 9 holes overlooking the site and the other half in a valley, you can look forward to a few climbs (nothing too exhausting) and elevated greens, but none are blind. A great links to savour, yard by yard.

Depuis le parcours, les vues magnifiques sur l'Atlantique, la baie de Drumcliff et le mont Ben Bulben justifieraient le voyage à County Sligo. Mais c'est aussi l'un des plus grands parcours d'Irlande. Comme les jours sans vent sont rares, c'est un facteur dominant : les fairways sont larges, mais un petit écart amène vite la balle dans les roughs et les bunkers, tout aussi pénalisants. Cela dit, à l'exception de deux ou trois coups aveugles, tous les obstacles sont visibles, et l'on sait parfaitement ce qu'il faut éviter, à défaut de le faire ! Les golfeurs peu expérimentés ou pas trop courageux pourront choisir leurs tees de départ, ils sont tous très bien placés pour varier le parcours. Avec une moitié des trous dominant le site et l'autre moitié dans une vallée, on peut s'attendre à quelques montées (elles ne sont pas épuisantes), et à quelques greens surélevés, mais aucun n'est aveugle. Un grand links à savourer mètre par mètre.

County Sligo Golf Club   1894
IRL - ROSSES POINT, Co Sligo

Office	Secrétariat	(353) 071 - 77 134
Pro shop	Pro-shop	(353) 071 - 77 171
Fax	Fax	(353) 071 - 77 460
Situation	Situation	

8 km from Sligo (pop. 17 332)

Annual closure	Fermeture annuelle	no
Weekly closure	Fermeture hebdomadaire	no

Fees main season
Tarifs haute saison 18 holes

	Week days Semaine	We/Bank holidays We/Férié
Individual Individuel	IR£ 27	IR£ 35
Couple Couple	IR£ 54	IR£ 60

Caddy	Caddy	IR£ 15-20/18 holes
Electric Trolley	Chariot électrique	no
Buggy	Voiturette	IR£ 20/18 holes
Clubs	Clubs	IR£ 10/18 holes

Credit cards Cartes de crédit   no

GOLF COURSE PARCOURS   17 /20

Site	Site	
Maintenance	Entretien	
Architect	Architecte	Harry S. Colt Alison
Type	Type	links
Relief	Relief	
Water in play	Eau en jeu	
Exp. to wind	Exposé au vent	
Trees in play	Arbres en jeu	

Scorecard Carte de score	Chp. Chp.	Mens Mess.	Ladies Da.
Length Long.	6043	5840	5280
Par	71	71	75

Advised golfing ability   0 12 24 36
Niveau de jeu recommandé

Hcp required   Handicap exigé   28 Men, 36 Ladies

CLUB HOUSE & AMENITIES CLUB HOUSE ET ANNEXES   4 /10

Pro shop	Pro-shop	
Driving range	Practice	
Sheltered	couvert	no
On grass	sur herbe	yes
Putting-green	putting-green	yes
Pitching-green	pitching green	no

HOTEL FACILITIES ENVIRONNEMENT HOTELIER   3 /10

HOTELS HÔTELS
Yeats Country Hotel   Rosses Point
79 rooms, D IR£ 70   on site
Tel (353) 071 - 77 221, Fax (353) 071 - 77 203

Ballincar House Hotel   Rosses Point
30 rooms, D IR£ 110   4 km
Tel (353) 071 - 45 361, Fax (353) 071 - 44 198

Sligo Park Hotel   Sligo
89 rooms, D IR£ 80   8 km
Tel (353) 071 - 60 291, Fax (353) 071 - 69 556

RESTAURANTS RESTAURANTS
The Moorings   Rosses Point
Tel (353) 071 - 77 112   1 km

Austies   Rosses Point
Tel (353) 071 - 77 111   2 km

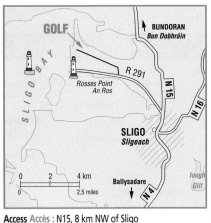

Access Accès : N15, 8 km NW of Sligo
Map 1 on page 826 Carte 1 Page 826

856

A long way to Tipperary? Not from Shannon, Cork or Dublin at any rate, although this course is rather off the traditional golfing track and it's a pity, because professional golfer Philip Walton has also shown himself to be a good course architect. He has used the natural contours well, along with the lakes and the river that cross the course rather dangerously on the 4th, and there are visible signs of the so-called American influence, particularly around the greens. These have been carefully designed and call more for lofted approaches rather than the traditional British style run shots. Designed for all levels of play, this rather, but never excessively, long course (even from the back) was designed on rolling terrain (easily walkable) around an 18th century manor, now converted into a hotel.. As a result, this is now a very agreeable week-end destination in the peaceful Irish countryside.

De Shannon, de Cork ou de Dublin, ce n'est pas une longue route pour aller à Tipperary... Pourtant, ce parcours reste en dehors des circuits golfiques traditionnels, et c'est dommage, car l'excellent professionnel Philip Walton s'y révèle également bon architecte. Il a ainsi très bien utilisé les contours naturels, les lacs et la rivière qui traverse de manière dangereuse le 4, avec une influence de l'architecture dite américaine que l'on retrouve dans le dessin des greens, très travaillés, et qui appellent davantage un jeu de balles levées que des «bump 'n run» à la britannique. Conçu pour tous les niveaux de jeu, ce parcours assez long, mais sans excès (même du fond) a été construit sur un terrain assez ondulé (facile à marcher) autour d'un manoir du XVIIIème siècle transformé en hôtel, ce qui en fait une destination de week-end tout à fait acceptable.

County Tipperary Golf & Country Club — 1993

Dundrum House Hotel
IRL - DUNDRUM, Co Tipperary

Office	Secrétariat	(353) 062 - 71 116
Pro shop	Pro-shop	(353) 062 - 71 116
Fax	Fax	(353) 062 - 71 366
Situation	Situation	

8 km N of Tipperary - 9 km W of Cashel (pop. 2 473)

Annual closure	Fermeture annuelle	no
Weekly closure	Fermeture hebdomadaire	no
Fees main season	Tarifs haute saison	18 holes

	Week days Semaine	We/Bank holidays We/Férié
Individual Individuel	IR£ 20	IR£ 24
Couple Couple	IR£ 40	IR£ 48

Caddy	Caddy	no
Electric Trolley	Chariot électrique	IR£ 5
Buggy	Voiturette	IR£ 20/18 holes
Clubs	Clubs	IR£ 8/18 holes

Credit cards Cartes de crédit VISA - MasterCard - AMEX

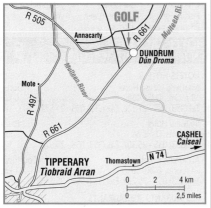

Access Accès : • Dublin N7 to Portlaoise. N8 to Cashel. R505 to Dundrum
• Cork N8 to Cashel. R505 to Dundrum
Map 2 on page 829 Carte 2 Page 829

GOLF COURSE / PARCOURS — 15/20

Site	Site	
Maintenance	Entretien	
Architect	Architecte	Philip Walton
Type	Type	parkland
Relief	Relief	
Water in play	Eau en jeu	
Exp. to wind	Exposé au vent	
Trees in play	Arbres en jeu	

Scorecard Carte de score	Chp. Chp.	Mens Mess.	Ladies Da.
Length Long.	6150	5700	5100
Par	72	72	72

Advised golfing ability		0 12 24 36
Niveau de jeu recommandé		
Hcp required	Handicap exigé	no

CLUB HOUSE & AMENITIES / CLUB HOUSE ET ANNEXES — 7/10

Pro shop	Pro-shop	
Driving range	Practice	
Sheltered	couvert	no
On grass	sur herbe	no
Putting-green	putting-green	yes
Pitching-green	pitching green	no

HOTEL FACILITIES / ENVIRONNEMENT HOTELIER — 5/10

HOTELS HÔTELS

Dundrum House Hotel — Dundrum
60 rooms, D IR£ 90 — on site
Tel (353) 062 - 71 116, Fax (353) 062 - 71 366

Royal Hotel — Tipperary
16 rooms, D IR£ 50 — 8 km
Tel (353) 062 - 33 244, Fax (353) 062 - 33 596

Rectory House Hotel — Dundrum
10 rooms, D IR£ 55 — 2 km
Tel (353) 062 - 71 266, Fax (353) 062 - 71 115

RESTAURANTS RESTAURANTS

Rosemore — Dundrum House Hotel
Tel (353) 062 - 71 116 — on site

Cashel Palace — Cashel
Tel (353) 062 - 61 411 — 5 km

857

Alongside the monster-length courses in this region like the European and Druid's Glen, albeit in different styles, the parkland landscape and unpretentiousness of the Courtown course is like a breath of fresh air. Although the course lies close to the sea, trees form a natural shelter from the frequent wind, even though in return off-target big-hitters might find them a little too big for comfort. Add to this country scene the rolling contours of small hills and you get a course that is pleasant and varied: no two holes are the same. With medium-sized greens that are thickly grassed and true, plus a nice balance between holes presumed to be easy and others that are more demanding, Courtown is one of those good but somewhat old-fashioned courses - compared to today's modern designs - that everyone enjoys playing, even if you would never drive 200 miles out of your way to do so.

A côté des monstres de longueur que peuvent être, dans cette région et dans des styles différents, the European et Druids Glen, la longueur réduite, le paysage de parc et l'absence de prétention d'un Courtown constituent une sorte de respiration. Bien que le parcours soit très près de la mer, les arbres constituent un abri naturel contre un vent souvent présent, même si, en contrepartie, les frappeurs auront affaire à des adversaires de (grande) taille. Et quand on ajoute à ce tableau champêtre les ondulations mesurées de petites collines, on obtient un ensemble agréable et varié : il n'y a pas deux trous identiques. Avec des greens de taille moyenne mais bien garnis et francs, un bon équilibre entre les trous présumés faciles et d'autres plus exigeants, Courtown fait partie de ces bons parcours un peu surannés par rapport à une certaine modernité de la conception que chacun a plaisir à jouer même si l'on ne fait pas 500 km de route rien que pour le visiter.

Courtown Golf Club — 1936
IRL - COURTOWN, GOREY, Co. Wexford

Office	Secrétariat	(353) 055 - 25 166
Pro shop	Pro-shop	(353) 055 - 25 166
Fax	Fax	(353) 055 - 25 553
Situation	Situation	

Gorey (pop. 2 198), 6 km
Dublin (pop. 859 976), 95 km

Annual closure	Fermeture annuelle	no
Weekly closure	Fermeture hebdomadaire	no

Fees main season
Tarifs haute saison 18 holes

	Week days Semaine	We/Bank holidays We/Férié
Individual Individuel	IR£ 18	IR£ 23
Couple Couple	IR£ 36	IR£ 46

Caddy	Caddy	no
Electric Trolley	Chariot électrique	no
Buggy	Voiturette	IR£ 15
Clubs	Clubs	no
Credit cards Cartes de crédit		no

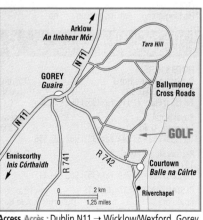

Access Accès : Dublin N11 → Wicklow/Wexford. Gorey, R742 → Courtown, Golf on the left.
Map 2 on page 829 Carte 2 Page 829

858

GOLF COURSE / PARCOURS — 14/20

Site	Site	
Maintenance	Entretien	
Architect	Architecte	Harris & Associates
Type	Type	parkland
Relief	Relief	
Water in play	Eau en jeu	
Exp. to wind	Exposé au vent	
Trees in play	Arbres en jeu	

Scorecard Carte de score	Chp. Chp.	Mens Mess.	Ladies Da.
Length Long.	5898	5725	4981
Par	71	71	73

Advised golfing ability Niveau de jeu recommandé	0	12	24	36
Hcp required Handicap exigé	no			

CLUB HOUSE & AMENITIES / CLUB HOUSE ET ANNEXES — 5/10

Pro shop	Pro-shop	
Driving range	Practice	
Sheltered	couvert	no
On grass	sur herbe	yes (practice area)
Putting-green	putting-green	yes
Pitching-green	pitching green	no

HOTEL FACILITIES / ENVIRONNEMENT HOTELIER — 5/10

HOTELS HÔTELS

Marlfield House Hotel — Gorey
19 rooms, D IR£ 150 — 6 km
Tel (353) 055 - 21 124, Fax (353) 055 - 21 572

Bayview Hotel — Courtown
13 rooms, D IR£ 66 — 1 km
Tel (353) 055 - 25 307, Fax (353) 055 - 25 576

Ardamine Hotel — Courtown
24 rooms, D IR£ 36 — 1 km
Tel (353) 055 - 25 264, Fax (353) 055 - 25 548

RESTAURANTS RESTAURANTS

Marlfield House — Gorey
Tel (353) 055 - 21 124 — 6 km

The Old Rectory — Wicklow
Tel (353) 0404 - 67 048 — 40 km

DINGLE (CEANN SIBEAL)

16 6 4

The first thing here is the magic of an outstanding site, overlooking Dingle Bay, the Blasket Islands and Mount Brandon, on a peninsula where you can find the vestiges of the stone age or the beginnings of Christianity. The many panels in Gaelic only add to the impression of a journey back in time. Designed by Eddie Hackett and Christy O'Connor Jnr., this course looks as if it has always been here, and is a real pleasure to play on long summer days, even if the wind blows or if it rains a little (this may sometimes occur in Ireland). Without pretending to be in the same league as Ballybunion or Waterville, this is an interesting course for everyone, where emphasis should be laid on trying to play low shots. The main difficulty is making clean contact with the ball on sandy soil, escaping from bunkers and avoiding a meandering stream which comes into play on about ten holes. A delightful experience.

D'abord, il y a la magie d'une situation exceptionnelle sur la baie de Dingle, les Blasket Islands et le Mount Brandon, dans une péninsule où l'on trouve des vestiges de l'Age de pierre ou des débuts du christianisme. La présence de nombreux panneaux en gaélique accentue encore cette impression de voyage en remontant le temps. Créé par Eddie Hackett et Christy O'Connor Jr, ce parcours paraît avoir toujours été là, et c'est un plaisir d'y jouer pendant les longues journées d'été, même si le vent souffle, ou s'il pleut un peu (ce qui arrive parfois en Irlande). Sans prétendre appartenir à la même division que Ballybunion ou Waterville, c'est un parcours intéressant pour tous, où l'on jouera de préférence des balles basses, où la principale difficulté consiste à bien contacter la balle sur le sol sablonneux, à s'échapper des bunkers, et à éviter les méandres d'un cours d'eau, en jeu sur une dizaine de trous. Avec le charme en plus.

Golf Chumann Cean Sibeal — 1972

Ballyoughteragh
IRL - BALLYFERRITER, Co Kerry

Office	Secrétariat	(353) 066 - 56 408
Pro shop	Pro-shop	(353) 066 - 56 255
Fax	Fax	(353) 066 - 56 409
Situation	Situation	

2 km from Ballyferriter
16 km from Dingle

Annual closure	Fermeture annuelle	no
Weekly closure	Fermeture hebdomadaire	no
Fees main season	Tarifs haute saison	18 holes

	Week days Semaine	We/Bank holidays We/Férié
Individual Individuel	IR£ 22	IR£ 22
Couple Couple	IR£ 44	IR£ 44

Caddy	Caddy	on request/IR£ 10
Electric Trolley	Chariot électrique	no
Buggy	Voiturette	no
Clubs	Clubs	IR£ 10

Credit cards Cartes de crédit VISA - MasterCard

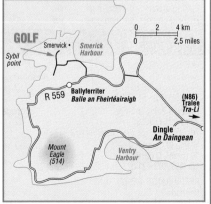

GOLF
Sybil point
Smerwick • Smerick Harbour
R 559 Ballyferriter Balle an Fheirtéairaigh
(N86) Tralee Tra-Li
Dingle An Daingean
Mount Eagle (514)
Ventry Harbour

0 — 2 — 4 km
0 — 2,5 miles

Access Accès : Tralee N86 → Derrymore, Camp, Anascaul, Dingle. R559 → Ballynana, Ballyferriter (Dingle Peninsula)
Map 2 on page 828 Carte 2 Page 828

GOLF COURSE PARCOURS — **16**/20

Site	Site	▓▓▓▓▓▓░░
Maintenance	Entretien	▓▓▓▓▓▓░░
Architect	Architecte	Eddie Hackett Christy O'Connor Jr
Type	Type	seaside course, links
Relief	Relief	
Water in play	Eau en jeu	▓▓▓▓▓░░░
Exp. to wind	Exposé au vent	▓▓▓▓▓▓░░
Trees in play	Arbres en jeu	▓▓▓░░░░░

Scorecard Carte de score	Chp. Chp.	Mens Mess.	Ladies Da.
Length Long.	6030	5870	4700
Par	72	72	73

Advised golfing ability Niveau de jeu recommandé	0	12	24	36

Hcp required Handicap exigé no

CLUB HOUSE & AMENITIES CLUB HOUSE ET ANNEXES — **6**/10

Pro shop	Pro-shop	▓▓▓▓▓░░░
Driving range	Practice	▓▓▓▓░░░░
Sheltered	couvert	no
On grass	sur herbe	yes
Putting-green	putting-green	yes
Pitching-green	pitching green	no

HOTEL FACILITIES ENVIRONNEMENT HOTELIER — **4**/10

HOTELS HÔTELS

Dingle Skellig — Dingle
100 rooms, D IR£ 90 — 16 km
Tél (353) 066 - 51 144, Fax (353) 066 - 51 501

Benners Hotel — Dingle
24 rooms, D IR£ 60 — 16 km
Tél (353) 066 - 51 638, Fax (353) 066 - 51 412

Dun an Oir Golf Hotel — on site
20 rooms, D IR£ 50
Tél (353) 066 - 56 133, Fax (353) 066 - 56 153

RESTAURANTS RESTAURANTS

Doyle's Seafood Bar — Dingle
Tél (353) 066 - 51 174 — 16 km

Beginish — Dingle
Tél (353) 066 - 51 588 — 16 km

859

DONEGAL (MURVAGH)

Be warned, this is not a course for the faint-hearted. A word of advice: if your driving is not in tip-top condition, and unless you couldn't give the proverbial two hoots about playing 10 strokes over your handicap, avoid the back tees. The tiger tees are definitely no-go, except if you have the wind behind you all the way (and St Patrick to watch over you). You guessed it, this is the longest course in all of Ireland. Some of the par 4s are real monsters, not to mention the 16th, a par 3, that is inaccessible to the common run of people. From the front tees, however, it is a little easier, and the effort of walking over hilly terrain will be rewarded by a great day's golfing. The greens are often open to bump and runs, and the short game experts can have a whale of a time. The surrounding dunes and general layout make this a very good, spectacular and exciting links course, but emphasis is more on the roughness of the course than on the finesse you find with the really great courses of this type.

Ce n'est pas un parcours de gamins. Un bon conseil : à moins d'avoir réglé votre driving à la perfection, de vous moquer éperdument de jouer dix coups au-dessus de votre handicap, évitez les départs arrière. A moins d'avoir vent avec sur tous les trous (il faut St Patrick pour veiller sur vous), évitez les départs de championnat, c'est le plus long parcours d'Irlande. Quelques par 4 sont de véritables monstres, sans même parler du 16, un par 3 inaccessible au commun des mortels. Cela dit, il s'adoucit un peu des départs avancés, et les efforts de la marche sur ce terrain accidenté seront récompensés par une belle journée de golf. Les greens sont souvent accessibles en roulant, et les virtuoses du petit jeu pourront s'y régaler. L'environnement de dunes, et le tracé général en font un très bon links, spectaculaire et excitant, mais l'accent a été mis davantage sur la rudesse que sur la finesse des plus grands parcours du genre.

Donegal Golf Club — 1960
IRL - LAGHY, Co Donegal

Office	Secrétariat	(353) 073 - 34 054
Pro shop	Pro-shop	(353) 073 - 34 054
Fax	Fax	(353) 073 - 34 377
Situation	Situation	

7 km from Donegal Town (pop. 2 193)

Annual closure	Fermeture annuelle	no
Weekly closure	Fermeture hebdomadaire	no
Fees main season	Tarifs haute saison	18 holes

	Week days Semaine	We/Bank holidays We/Férié
Individual Individuel	IR£ 18	IR£ 25
Couple Couple	IR£ 36	IR£ 50

Caddy	Caddy	on request/IR£ 12
Electric Trolley	Chariot électrique	no
Buggy	Voiturette	IR£ 20/18 holes
Clubs	Clubs	no
Credit cards Cartes de crédit		no

Access Accès : • Sligo, N15 → Donegal. 3 km before Donegal, turn left to Mullinasole/Murvagh peninsula • Donegal N15 South →Ballyshannon. Laghy, turn right to Mullinasole/Murvagh peninsula
Map 1 on page 826 Carte 1 Page 826

GOLF COURSE / PARCOURS — 16/20

Site	Site	
Maintenance	Entretien	
Architect	Architecte	Eddie Hackett
Type	Type	links
Relief	Relief	
Water in play	Eau en jeu	
Exp. to wind	Exposé au vent	
Trees in play	Arbres en jeu	

Scorecard Carte de score	Chp. Chp.	Mens Mess.	Ladies Da.
Length Long.	6574	6249	5253
Par	73	73	75

Advised golfing ability	0 12 24 36
Niveau de jeu recommandé	
Hcp required Handicap exigé	28 Men, 36 Ladies

CLUB HOUSE & AMENITIES / CLUB HOUSE ET ANNEXES — 5/10

Pro shop	Pro-shop	
Driving range	Practice	
Sheltered	couvert	no
On grass	sur herbe	yes
Putting-green	putting-green	yes
Pitching-green	pitching green	yes

HOTEL FACILITIES / ENVIRONNEMENT HOTELIER — 6/10

HOTELS HÔTELS
Sand House — Rossnowlagh
40 rooms, D IR£ 100 — 7 km
Tél (353) 072 - 51 777, Fax (353) 072 - 52 100

Harvey's Point Country — Donegal
20 rooms, D IR£ 90 — 12 km
Tél (353) 073 - 22 208, Fax (353) 073 - 22 352

Highland Central — Donegal 7 km
90 rooms, D IR£ 93
Tél (353) 073 - 21 027, Fax (353) 073 - 22 295

RESTAURANTS RESTAURANTS
Belshade — Donegal
Tél (353) 073 - 22 660 — 7 km

The Castle Bar — Donegal
Tél(353) 073 - 21 062 — 7 km

Harvey's Point Country — Donegal
Tél (353) 073 - 22 208 — 12 km

860

DOOKS

15 5 5

A very good links course, whose international fame has been eclipsed somewhat by its prestigious neighbours. While this course alone may not warrant a long journey, it would be a shame not to include Dooks in any golfing itinerary to south-west Ireland. It is an excellent practice outing before getting to grips with some even more difficult courses nearby. Opened in the 19th century, it was completed in 1973 by Eddie Hackett, with praiseworthy concern for preserving unity of style. There are no gigantic dunes here, just endless mounds and dales which add to the course's character and complicate the round just enough to keep everyone happy. Not very long but often narrow, Dooks gets tougher with the wind. The greens are not huge but are well-guarded, so accuracy and a sharp short game are the order of the day, with excellent scope for bump and run approach shots. The one or two blind shots merely add to the excitement.

Un très bon parcours de links, dont la notoriété internationale a été éclipsée par de prestigieux voisins. S'il ne justifie pas à lui seul un long voyage, il serait fort dommage de ne pas l'intégrer à un séjour golfique dans le Sud-Ouest de l'Irlande. C'est même un très bon galop d'entraînement avant d'affronter des adversaires encore plus difficiles. Créé au siècle dernier, il a été complété en 1973 par Eddie Hackett, avec un louable souci de lui conserver son unité. On ne trouve pas ici de dunes gigantesques, mais les nombreuses buttes et dépressions ajoutent à son caractère, et compliquent assez le jeu pour plaire à tous. Pas très long, mais souvent étroit, il prend de la force avec le vent. Les greens ne sont pas immenses, et bien protégés, il convient alors d'être très exact, ou de sortir son meilleur petit jeu, en favorisant ces approches roulées qui sont un des plaisirs des links, avec quelques coups aveugles pour donner des émotions.

Dooks Golf Club — 1889
IRL - GLENBEIGH, Co Kerry

Office	Secrétariat	(353) 066 - 68 205
Pro shop	Pro-shop	(353) 066 - 68 205
Fax	Fax	(353) 066 - 68 476
Situation	Situation	

24 km from Killarney (pop. 7 275)
8 km from Killorglin (pop. 1 229)

Annual closure	Fermeture annuelle	no
Weekly closure	Fermeture hebdomadaire	no
Fees main season	Tarifs haute saison	18 holes

	Week days Semaine	We/Bank holidays We/Férié
Individual Individuel	IR£ 20	IR£ 20
Couple Couple	IR£ 40	IR£ 40
Caddy	Caddy	on request/IR£ 15
Electric Trolley	Chariot électrique	IR£ 8/18 holes
Buggy	Voiturette	no
Clubs	Clubs	no

Credit cards Cartes de crédit
VISA - Eurocard - MasterCard - AMEX

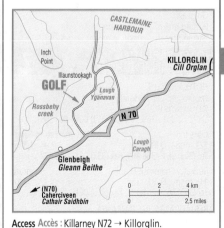

Access Accès : Killarney N72 → Killorglin.
N70 → Glenbeigh (Ring of Kerry).
Golf 3 km from Glenbeigh
Map 2 on page 828 Carte 2 Page 828

GOLF COURSE / PARCOURS — 15/20

Site	Site	▬▬▬▬▬▬▭
Maintenance	Entretien	▬▬▬▬▬▬▭
Architect	Architecte	Eddie Hackett
Type	Type	links, seaside course
Relief	Relief	▬▬▭▭▭▭
Water in play	Eau en jeu	▬▭▭▭▭▭
Exp. to wind	Exposé au vent	▬▬▬▭▭▭
Trees in play	Arbres en jeu	▬▬▭▭▭▭

Scorecard Carte de score	Chp. Chp.	Mens Mess.	Ladies Da.
Length Long.	6010	5702	4848
Par	70	70	70

Advised golfing ability		0 12 24 36
Niveau de jeu recommandé		▬▬▬▬▬▭
Hcp required	Handicap exigé	24 Men, 36 Ladies

CLUB HOUSE & AMENITIES / CLUB HOUSE ET ANNEXES — 5/10

Pro shop	Pro-shop	▬▬▬▬▭
Driving range	Practice	▬▬▭▭▭
Sheltered	couvert	no
On grass	sur herbe	no
Putting-green	putting-green	yes
Pitching-green	pitching green	no

HOTEL FACILITIES / ENVIRONNEMENT HOTELIER — 5/10

HOTELS HÔTELS

Ard Na Sidhe — Caragh Lake, Killorglin
20 rooms, D IR£ 158 — 5 km
Tel (353) 066 - 69 105, Fax (353) 066 - 69 282

Glenbeigh Hotel — Glenbeigh
16 rooms, D IR£ 50 — 3 km
Tel (353) 066 - 68 333, Fax (353) 066 - 68 404

Falcon Inn Hotel — Glenbeigh
13 rooms, D IR£ 36 — 3 km
Tel (353) 066 - 68 215, Fax (353) 066 - 68 411

RESTAURANTS RESTAURANTS

Nicks — Killorglin
Tel (353) 066 - 61 219 — 7 km

Red Fox Inn — Glenbeigh
Tel (353) 066 - 69 184 — 2 km

861

Give Robert Trent Jones Snr. a big lake (in play on many of the holes) and a reasonably sized parkland estate, and he will produce a course that is well above average. He probably lacked a bit of space here to create the length he usually gives his courses, so he laid more emphasis on the technical side. Being able to flight the ball is a decisive advantage here. Although only very slightly hilly, certain rolling fairways have resulted in blind tee shots, but the greens and traps along the way are clearly visible for the second shot (or at least they should be). People who are used to Trent Jones courses will recognise his strategic style for locating bunkers and the work made on and around the greens, which are always fascinating to putt on. Dromoland Castle has earned itself a very handy reputation, particularly thanks to the work made on the course in recent years.

Donnez un grand lac (en jeu sur de nombreux trous) et un parc de taille raisonnable à Robert Trent Jones Sr, il saura vous faire un parcours nettement au dessus de la moyenne. Il a sans doute manqué un peu d'espace pour lui donner la longueur habituelle de ses parcours, il a donc mis davantage l'accent sur la technicité. Ainsi, savoir travailler la balle est un avantage décisif. Bien que le relief soit limité, certaines ondulations du terrain ont imposé des départs aveugles, mais les greens et leurs défenses sont bien visibles au second coup. Les habitués des golfs de Trent Jones reconnaîtront son style stratégique de placement de bunkers, ainsi que le travail effectué sur les greens, toujours intéressants à putter. Dromoland Castle a acquis une très bonne réputation, en particulier grâce au travail effectué sur le parcours depuis quelques années.

Dromoland Castle Golf Club — 1985
IRL - NEWMARKET-ON-FERGUS, Co Clare

Office	Secrétariat	(353) 061 - 368 444
Pro shop	Pro-shop	(353) 061 - 368 444
Fax	Fax	(353) 061 - 363 355
Situation	Situation	

28 km from Limerick (pop. 52 083)
11 km from Ennis (pop. 13 730)

Annual closure	Fermeture annuelle	no
Weekly closure	Fermeture hebdomadaire	no

Fees main season
Tarifs haute saison 18 holes

	Week days Semaine	We/Bank holidays We/Férié
Individual Individuel	IR£ 22	IR£ 27
Couple Couple	IR£ 44	IR£ 54
Caddy	Caddy	IR£ 15/18 holes
Electric Trolley	Chariot électrique	no
Buggy	Voiturette	IR£ 30/18 holes
Clubs	Clubs	IR£ 10

Credit cards Cartes de crédit
VISA - Eurocard - MasterCard - AMEX - DC

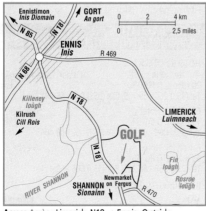

Access Accès : Limerick, N18 → Ennis. Outside Newmarket-on-Fergus, right → Dromoland Castle
Map 2 on page 828 Carte 2 Page 828

GOLF COURSE
PARCOURS — **14**/20

Site	Site	
Maintenance	Entretien	
Architect	Architecte	R. Trent Jones Sr
Type	Type	parkland
Relief	Relief	
Water in play	Eau en jeu	
Exp. to wind	Exposé au vent	
Trees in play	Arbres en jeu	

Scorecard Carte de score	Chp. Chp.	Mens Mess.	Ladies Da.
Length Long.	5719	5646	5542
Par	71	71	71

Advised golfing ability		0 12 24 36
Niveau de jeu recommandé		
Hcp required	Handicap exigé	no

CLUB HOUSE & AMENITIES
CLUB HOUSE ET ANNEXES — **7**/10

Pro shop	Pro-shop	
Driving range	Practice	
Sheltered	couvert	no
On grass	sur herbe	yes
Putting-green	putting-green	yes
Pitching-green	pitching green	yes

HOTEL FACILITIES
ENVIRONNEMENT HOTELIER — **7**/10

HOTELS HÔTELS

Dromoland Castle Hotel — on site
73 rooms, D IR£ 202
Tel (353) 061 - 368 144, Fax (353) 061 - 363 355

Clare Inn — Newmarket-on-Fergus
121 rooms, D IR£ 70 — 1,5 km
Tel (353) 061 - 368 161, Fax (353) 061 - 368 622

Bunratty Shamrock Hotel — Bunratty
115 rooms, D IR£ 115 — 12 km
Tel (353) 061 - 361 177, Fax (353) 061 - 471 252

RESTAURANTS RESTAURANTS

Earl of Thomond — on site
Tel (353) 061 - 368 144

Weavers Inn — Newmarket-on-Fergus
Tel (353) 061 - 368 482 — 1,5 km

862

You might easily imagine the club-house here in a chic suburb of London. It is certainly impressive for comfort, but it lacks Irish warmth. Likewise, you might find this course just about anywhere in the United States, and the very American style is compounded by the necessity to be practised in the art of target golf. These remarks come to mind only because of the course's stated cultural identity, as the problem for any foreign visitor is to decipher the signposts showing the way here - they are all written in Gaelic. With this said, we are talking about an excellent and often intimidating course, notably the 12th, 13th and 14th (another Amen corner), the only holes that are really hilly and often less challenging than they look, at least if you avoid playing the "tiger-tees" and stick more or less to the fairway. Very spectacular and extremely well kept, this luxury course is well worth a close inspection.

On imaginerait bien le Club-house dans la banlieue chic de Londres. Il est certes impressionnant de confort, mais il manque la chaleur irlandaise. De même, on pourrait trouver le parcours n'importe où aux USA, son style très américain étant accentué par la nécessité de jouer un «target golf». Ces remarques ne viennent à l'esprit qu'en raison de l'identité culturelle affichée : le problème pour un étranger est de déchiffrer les panneaux pour y parvenir, ceux-ci étant exclusivement rédigés en gaélique. Cela dit, il reste un excellent parcours, souvent très intimidant, notamment aux 12, 13 et 14 (l'Amen Corner), seuls trous au relief vraiment accidenté, mais souvent moins exigeant qu'il n'y paraît, si l'on évite du moins les départs de championnat, et si l'on ne s'écarte pas trop de la piste. Très spectaculaire, remarquablement entretenu, ce parcours de grand luxe mérite une visite attentive.

Druids Glen Golf Club — 1995
IRL - NEWTOWN MOUNT KENNEDY, Co Wicklow

Office	Secrétariat	(353) 01 - 287 3600
Pro shop	Pro-shop	(353) 01 - 287 3600
Fax	Fax	(353) 01 - 287 3699
Situation	Situation	

2 km from Kilcoole
35 km from Dublin (pop. 859 976)

Annual closure	Fermeture annuelle	no
Weekly closure	Fermeture hebdomadaire	no

Fees main season
Tarifs haute saison 18 holes

	Week days Semaine	We/Bank holidays We/Férié
Individual Individuel	IR£ 75	IR£ 75
Couple Couple	IR£ 150	IR£ 150
Caddy Caddy		on request/IR£ 20
Electric Trolley Chariot électrique		no
Buggy Voiturette		no
Clubs Clubs		IR£ 15/18 holes

Credit cards Cartes de crédit
VISA - Eurocard - AMEX - DC

DUBLIN
Greystones *Na Clocha Litha*
Kilcoole *Cill Chomhghaill*
Newtown MtKennedy *Baile an Chinnéidigh*
GOLF
R 761
N 11
R 761
ARKLOW
0 — 2 — 4 km
0 — 2,5 miles

Access Accès : Dublin, N11 South.
Turn left at Newtown Mt Kennedy (signpost). Golf 2 km
Map 3 on page 830 Carte 3 Page 830

GOLF COURSE PARCOURS — 16/20

Site	Site	
Maintenance	Entretien	
Architect	Architecte	Pat Ruddy M. Craddock
Type	Type	parkland
Relief	Relief	
Water in play	Eau en jeu	
Exp. to wind	Exposé au vent	
Trees in play	Arbres en jeu	

Scorecard Carte de score	Chp. Chp.	Mens Mess.	Ladies Da.
Length Long.	6416	5997	4773
Par	72	72	72

Advised golfing ability Niveau de jeu recommandé	0	12	24	36
Hcp required Handicap exigé	no			

CLUB HOUSE & AMENITIES CLUB HOUSE ET ANNEXES — 9/10

Pro shop	Pro-shop	
Driving range	Practice	
Sheltered	couvert	no
On grass	sur herbe	yes
Putting-green	putting-green	yes
Pitching-green	pitching green	yes

HOTEL FACILITIES ENVIRONNEMENT HOTELIER — 7/10

HOTELS HÔTELS
Glenview Hotel — Glen of the Downs
40 rooms, D IR£ 130 — 8 km
Tel (353) 01 - 287 3399, Fax (353) 01 - 287 7511

Tinakilly House Hotel — Rathnew
29 rooms, D IR£ 130 — 15 km
Tel (353) 0404 - 69 274, Fax (353) 0404 - 67 806

Hunter's Hotel — Rathnew
16 rooms, D IR£ 65 — 15 km
Tel (353) 0404 - 40 106, Fax (353) 0404 - 40 338

RESTAURANTS RESTAURANTS
Wicklow Arms — Delgany
Tel (353) 01 - 287 46 11 — 6 km
Cooper's - Tel (353) 01 - 287 3914 — Greystones 6 km
Hungry Monk Tel (353) 01 - 287 5759 — Greystones 6 km

863

On a road linking some of the very greatest Irish courses, Dundalk is located between County Louth and Royal County Down. You certainly won't be wasting your time stopping off here, in the shadow of the Cooley Mountains and with the Mountains of Mourne in the background. Rejuvenated by Alliss and Thomas, this is one of the country's most under-rated inland courses. Firstly, it is a course to test your driver, with a few long and very tough par 4s and strategically located fairway bunkers. The architects have also tightened the entrances to many of the greens, thus attaching greater importance to spot-on second shots, which are, nonetheless, made easier by the elimination of blind approaches. A generally very open course, you need to get into your stride right away, as many of the difficulties are concentrated over the first seven holes. With little difference between the white and yellow tees, there's every chance that inexperienced golfers will find this tough going score-wise.

Sur une route des très grands parcours d'Irlande, Dundalk se situe entre County Louth et Royal County Down, mais l'on ne perdra pas son temps en marquant une halte ici, à l'ombre des Cooley Mountains, avec au loin les Mountains of Mourne. Rajeuni par Alliss et Thomas, c'est l'un des «inland « les plus sous-estimés du pays. C'est d'abord un parcours pour tester les drivers, avec quelques longs par 4 très difficiles, et des bunkers de fairway très stratégiques. Les architectes ont aussi rétréci les entrées de beaucoup de greens, ce qui accentue la nécessité de seconds coups précis, mais facilités par l'élimination des coups aveugles. Généralement très ouvert, il oblige à prendre vite le rythme, avec une forte concentration des difficultés sur les sept premiers trous. Il y a peu de différences entre les départs arrière et les départs hommes normaux : les golfeurs peu expérimentés auront du mal à y scorer...

Dundalk Golf Club
Blackrock
IRL - DUNDALK, Co Louth

1904

Office	Secrétariat	(353) 042 - 21 731
Pro shop	Pro-shop	(353) 042 - 22 022
Fax	Fax	(353) 042 - 22 022
Situation	Situation	

5 km S. of Dundalk (pop. 25 843)

Annual closure	Fermeture annuelle	no
Weekly closure	Fermeture hebdomadaire	no

Fees main season
Tarifs haute saison full day

	Week days Semaine	We/Bank holidays We/Férié
Individual Individuel	IR£ 20	IR£ 25
Couple Couple	IR£ 40	IR£ 50

Caddy	Caddy	IR£ 10/18 holes
Electric Trolley	Chariot électrique	IR£ 2/18 holes
Buggy	Voiturette	no
Clubs	Clubs	no

Credit cards Cartes de crédit
VISA - Eurocard - MasterCard

864

CASTLEBLAYNEY
Baile na Lorgan
Newry
N 53
Dundalk Harbour
DUNDALK
Dún Dealgan
R 211
R 172
GOLF
N 52
N 1
BLACKROCK
Na Creagacha Dubha
0   2   4 km
0   2,5 miles
ARDEE
Baile Átha-
Fhirdhia
CASTLEBELLINGHAM
Baile an
Ghearlánaigh
DUNDALK BAY

Access Accès : Dublin → Belfast,
1 km N. of Blackrock Village
Map 1 on page 827 Carte 1 Page 827

GOLF COURSE
PARCOURS

15/20

Site	Site	
Maintenance	Entretien	
Architect	Architecte	T. Shannon Alliss & Thomas
Type	Type	inland, parkland
Relief	Relief	
Water in play	Eau en jeu	
Exp. to wind	Exposé au vent	
Trees in play	Arbres en jeu	

Scorecard Carte de score	Chp. Chp.	Mens Mess.	Ladies Da.
Length Long.	6160	6028	5134
Par	72	72	73

Advised golfing ability
Niveau de jeu recommandé

0	12	24	36

Hcp required   Handicap exigé   28 Men, 36 Ladies

CLUB HOUSE & AMENITIES
CLUB HOUSE ET ANNEXES

6/10

Pro shop	Pro-shop	
Driving range	Practice	
Sheltered	couvert	no
On grass	sur herbe	yes
Putting-green	putting-green	yes
Pitching-green	pitching green	yes

HOTEL FACILITIES
ENVIRONNEMENT HOTELIER

6/10

HOTELS HÔTELS

Fairways Hotel 48 rooms, D IR£ 75 Tel (353) 042 - 21 500 Fax (353) 042 - 21 511		Dundalk 1 km
Derryhill Hotel 23 rooms, D IR£ 60 Tel (353) 042 - 35 471 Fax (353) 042 - 35 471		Dundalk 8 km

RESTAURANTS RESTAURANTS

Mashie + Spoon Tel (353) 042 - 22 255		on site
Jade Garden Tel (353) 042 - 30 378		Dundalk 5 km

After an impressive drive up to the club-house past twenty or so tennis courts, you feel very much in a club here, where silence is almost guaranteed by the vicinity of St. Vincent's Hospital and the keen air of Dublin Bay. Strangely enough, the course begins with a par 3 that is not to be under-estimated, as two trees threaten the tee shot. In fact they give you some idea of the landscape ahead, compounded by a meandering stream which is in play on almost half the holes and devours any mis-hit shot. The city park atmosphere is confirmed by the virtual absence of rough, so it's fair to say that a good score is a distinct possibility. Yet the impression of this being an easy course is soon dented by some well-located bunkers and greens in any number of shapes and contours that call for cool-thinking when planning your approach shot. Variety is also to the fore in the layout of each hole, with things coming to a head over the finishing holes where a whole string of difficulties can easily ruin your card or swing the match.

Après une arrivée impressionnante et la vue d'une vingtaine de courts de tennis, on se sent bien dans un club où le silence est garanti par la proximité de St. Vincent's Hospital, et l'air vif par Dublin Bay. Assez curieusement, le parcours débute par un par 3 à ne pas sous-estimer, deux arbres menaçant le tee-shot. Ils donnent d'ailleurs une idée de l'environnement à venir, auquel s'ajoutent vite les méandres d'un petit cours d'eau, en jeu sur près de la moitié des trous, et fort gourmand en balles. L'atmosphère de grand parc citadin est confirmée par l'absence quasi totale de rough dans le jeu, favorisant la qualité des scores, il faut bien le dire. Cependant, l'impression de facilité est vite contrée par des bunkers bien placés, et par la variété de formes et d'ondulations des greens, obligeant à réfléchir sur le choix du type d'approche. L'enchaînement des difficultés dans les derniers trous peut facilement faire basculer un score ou un match.

Elm Park Golf Club — 1925

Nutley House, Nutley Lane
IRL - DONNYBROOK, DUBLIN 4

Office	Secrétariat	(353) 01 - 269 3438
Pro shop	Pro-shop	(353) 01 - 269 2650
Fax	Fax	(353) 01 - 269 4505
Situation	Situation	

Dublin (pop. 859 976), 7 km

Annual closure	Fermeture annuelle	no
Weekly closure	Fermeture hebdomadaire	no

Fees main season	Tarifs haute saison		18 holes
		Week days	We/Bank holidays
		Semaine	We/Férié
Individual Individuel		IR£ 35	IR£ 45
Couple Couple		IR£ 70	IR£ 90

Caddy	Caddy	IR£ 20
Electric Trolley	Chariot électrique	no
Buggy	Voiturette	on request
Clubs	Clubs	IR£ 12

Credit cards Cartes de crédit
VISA - Eurocard - MasterCard

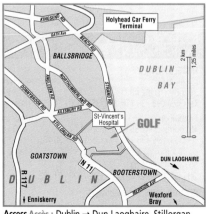

Access Accès : Dublin → Dun Laoghaire. Stillorgan Road (dual carriage way), turn off onto Nutley Lane. Golf course besides St. Vincent's Hospital.
Map 3 on page 830 Carte 3 Page 830

GOLF COURSE / PARCOURS — 13/20

Site	Site	
Maintenance	Entretien	
Architect	Architecte	Unknown
Type	Type	parkland
Relief	Relief	
Water in play	Eau en jeu	
Exp. to wind	Exposé au vent	
Trees in play	Arbres en jeu	

Scorecard	Chp.	Mens	Ladies
Carte de score	Chp.	Mess.	Da.
Length Long.	5355	5150	4974
Par	69	69	72

Advised golfing ability	0	12	24	36
Niveau de jeu recommandé				
Hcp required	Handicap exigé	no		

CLUB HOUSE & AMENITIES / CLUB HOUSE ET ANNEXES — 7/10

Pro shop	Pro-shop	
Driving range	Practice	
Sheltered	couvert	6 mats
On grass	sur herbe	yes
Putting-green	putting-green	yes
Pitching-green	pitching green	yes

HOTEL FACILITIES / ENVIRONNEMENT HOTELIER — 8/10

HOTELS HÔTELS

Doyne Montrose Hotel — Dublin
179 rooms, D IR£ 60 — 2 km
Tel (353) 01 - 269 3311, Fax (353) 01 - 269 1164

Jurys Hotel - 394 rooms, D IR£ 180 — Dublin 5 km
Tel (353) 01 - 660 5000, Fax (353) 01 - 660 5540

Burlington Hotel — Dublin
451 rooms, D IR£ 160 — 6 km
Tel (353) 01 - 660 5222, Fax (353) 01 - 660 3172

RESTAURANTS RESTAURANTS

Da Vincenzo — Dublin
Tel (353) 01 - 660 9906 — 3 km

Beaufield News — Skillorgan
Tel (353) 01 - 288 0375 — 3 km

Roly's Bistro - Tél(353) 01 - 668 2611 — Dublin 5 km

865

For many a year, Enniscrone was the most underrated links in Ireland, or at least one of the least known. The rediscovery of this region has pulled it out of the shadows, and although lacking the subtle features associated with the greatest links courses, it is well worth the trip. Weaker souls would be well advised to hire a buggy or, even better, take a caddie, so they don't have to carry their bag. The front 9 never really venture into the coastal dunes and emphasis is primarily on length off the tee, with difficulties caused by a number of ditches. From the 9th hole onward, excursions into moon landscape are much more frequent, with a number of holes calling for some pretty accurate ironwork. You only see the sea from the 17th tee, but you can feel it close by. The frequent wind can easily make Enniscrone doubly challenging and only the better player can hope to make any impression on the course.

Enniscrone a longtemps été l'un des links les plus sous-estimés d'Irlande, ou du moins les plus méconnus. La redécouverte de cette région l'a tiré de l'ombre. Bien qu'il manque des subtilités associées aux plus grands parcours de links, il mérite largement le détour, mais on conseillera aux constitutions fragiles de le jouer en voiturette ou (mieux) de prendre un caddie, pour ne pas avoir de sac à porter. L'aller ne pénètre pas vraiment dans les dunes côtières, et l'accent est porté essentiellement sur la longueur au drive, avec des difficultés dûes à la présence de fossés. A partir du 9, les voyages dans un paysage lunaire sont bien plus effectifs, avec quelques trous où les coups de fer devront être exacts. On n'aperçoit l'océan qu'au départ du 17, mais on la sent toujours très proche. Le vent fréquent peut facilement doubler l'exigence d'Enniscrone, et seuls les joueurs de niveau honorable pourront espérer se tirer vraiment d'affaire...

Enniscrone Golf Club — 1925
IRL - ENNISCRONE, Co Sligo

Office	Secrétariat	(353) 096 - 36 297
Pro shop	Pro-shop	(353) 096 - 36 297
Fax	Fax	(353) 096 - 36 657
Situation	Situation	

13 km N of Ballina (pop. 6 563)

Annual closure	Fermeture annuelle	no
Weekly closure	Fermeture hebdomadaire	no

Fees main season
Tarifs haute saison 18 holes

	Week days Semaine	We/Bank holidays We/Férié
Individual Individuel	IR£ 18	IR£ 24
Couple Couple	IR£ 25	IR£ 32

Caddy	Caddy	IR£ 10/18 holes
Electric Trolley	Chariot électrique	no
Buggy	Voiturette	IR£ 20/18 holes
Clubs	Clubs	IR£ 12

Credit cards Cartes de crédit
VISA - Eurocard - Mastercard

866

Access Accès : Killala Bay, 12 km North of Ballina
Map 1 on page 826 Carte 1 Page 826

GOLF COURSE
PARCOURS — 16/20

Site	Site	
Maintenance	Entretien	
Architect	Architecte	Eddie Hackett
Type	Type	seaside course, links
Relief	Relief	
Water in play	Eau en jeu	
Exp. to wind	Exposé au vent	
Trees in play	Arbres en jeu	

Scorecard Carte de score	Chp. Chp.	Mens Mess.	Ladies Da.
Length Long.	6044	5958	5076
Par	72	72	73

Advised golfing ability Niveau de jeu recommandé	0	12	24	36

Hcp required Handicap exigé — 28 Men, 36 Ladies

CLUB HOUSE & AMENITIES
CLUB HOUSE ET ANNEXES — 7/10

Pro shop	Pro-shop	
Driving range	Practice	
Sheltered	couvert	6 mats
On grass	sur herbe	yes
Putting-green	putting-green	yes
Pitching-green	pitching green	no

HOTEL FACILITIES
ENVIRONNEMENT HOTELIER — 6/10

HOTELS HÔTELS

Castle Arms — Enniscrone
24 rooms, D IR£ 40 — 1 km
Tel (353) 096 - 36 156, Fax (353) 096 - 36 156

Benbulben — Enniscrone
16 rooms, D IR£ 55 (with dinner) — 3 km
Tel (353) 096 - 36 185, Fax (353) 096 - 36 185

Downhill Hotel — Ballina
50 rooms, D IR£ 93 — 13 km
Tel (353) 096 - 21 033, Fax (353) 096 - 21 338

RESTAURANTS RESTAURANTS

Clark's — Enniscrone
Tel (353) 096 - 36 405 — adjacent

Alpine Hotel — Enniscrone
Tel (353) 096 - 36 252 — adjacent

EUROPEAN (THE)

How a site like this remained unknown until the late 1980s will always be a mystery. The creation of "The European" was the work of Pat Ruddy, a professional, enthusiast, journalist and course designer. This is his masterpiece, and looks almost hand-made. Between the dunes, the beach, the fairways, the greens and the bunkers bolstered by railway line sleepers (the sand-wedge is the only way out), there was just enough room for a little marsh and a water hazard that is as worrying as it is unexpected. This course is a great trip to the land of golf where each round is so varied, so demanding and so exciting that no-one would care to mention the layout's one or two weaknesses. It takes time to appreciate the course's finer points, but the only thing on your mind when leaving is knowing when you can come back. The atmosphere of freshness and golfing purism that reigns here is the icing on the cake, as opposed to clubs where personal wealth seems to be the only criterion for playing.

Comment un site comme celui-ci est resté ignoré jusqu'à la fin des années 1980 restera un éternel mystère. La création de «The European» est dûe à Pat Ruddy, enthousiaste professionnel, journaliste et architecte. C'est son chef-d'oeuvre, donnant l'impression d'avoir été fait à la main. Entre les dunes, la plage, les fairways, les greens et des bunkers renforcés de traverses de chemin de fer (sandwedge obligatoire), il restait à peine place pour un petit marais, et pour un obstacle d'eau aussi préoccupant qu'inattendu. Ce parcours est un grand voyage au pays du golf, où l'on n'a pas le courage de relever des faiblesses de dessin tant le jeu y est varié, exigeant, excitant. Il faut du temps pour en apprécier toutes les nuances, mais on a une seule idée en le quittant, c'est d'y revenir. L'atmosphère de fraîcheur et de purisme golfique qui règne ici est la cerise sur un gâteau, à l'opposé de clubs où la fortune paraît le seul critère pour jouer.

The European Club — 1989
IRL - BRITTAS BAY, Co Wicklow

Office	Secrétariat	(353) 0404 - 47 415
Pro shop	Pro-shop	(353) 0404 - 47 415
Fax	Fax	(353) 0404 - 47 449
Situation	Situation	

12 km from Wicklow (pop. 5 847)
10 km from Arklow

Annual closure	Fermeture annuelle	no
Weekly closure	Fermeture hebdomadaire	no

Fees main season
Tarifs haute saison 18 holes

	Week days Semaine	We/Bank holidays We/Férié
Individual Individuel	IR£ 35	IR£ 35
Couple Couple	IR£ 70	IR£ 70
Caddy	Caddy	IR£ 15-20/18 holes
Electric Trolley	Chariot électrique	no
Buggy	Voiturette	IR£ 25/18 holes
Clubs	Clubs	IR£ 20/18 holes

Credit cards Cartes de crédit
VISA - Eurocard - MasterCard

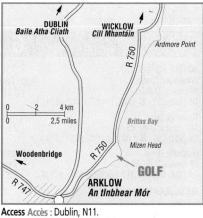

DUBLIN
Baile Atha Cliath

WICKLOW
Cill Mhantáin

Ardmore Point
R 750

0   2   4 km
0   2,5 miles

Brittas Bay

Mizen Head

Woodenbridge
R 750

GOLF

R 747

ARKLOW
An tInbhear Mór

Access Accès : Dublin, N11.
56 km turn left at Jack White's Inn.
Turn right at T Junction → Brittas Bay. 2 km
Map 3 on page 830 Carte 3 Page 830

GOLF COURSE / PARCOURS — 18/20

Site	Site	
Maintenance	Entretien	
Architect	Architecte	Pat Ruddy
Type	Type	links
Relief	Relief	
Water in play	Eau en jeu	
Exp. to wind	Exposé au vent	
Trees in play	Arbres en jeu	

Scorecard Carte de score	Chp. Chp.	Mens Mess.	Ladies Da.
Length Long.	6187	5922	5153
Par	71	71	71

Advised golfing ability		0 12 24 36
Niveau de jeu recommandé		
Hcp required	Handicap exigé	no

CLUB HOUSE & AMENITIES / CLUB HOUSE ET ANNEXES — 5/10

Pro shop	Pro-shop	
Driving range	Practice	
Sheltered	couvert	under construction
On grass	sur herbe	yes
Putting-green	putting-green	yes
Pitching-green	pitching green	yes

HOTEL FACILITIES / ENVIRONNEMENT HOTELIER — 6/10

HOTELS HÔTELS

Grand Hotel — Wicklow
32 rooms, D IR£ 70 — 11 km
Tel (353) 0404 - 67 337, Fax (353) 0404 - 69 607

Tinakilly House Hotel — Rathnew
29 rooms, D IR£ 130 — 14 km
Tel (353) 0404 - 69 274, Fax (353) 0404 - 67 806

Hunter's Hotel — Rathnew
16 rooms, D IR£ 65 — 14 km
Tel (353) 0404 - 40 106, Fax (353) 0404 - 40 338

RESTAURANTS RESTAURANTS

Old Rectory — Wicklow
Tel (353) 0404 - 67 048 — 12 km

Tinakilly House — Rathnew
Tel (353) 0404 - 69 274 — 14 km

867

The south-eastern coast is not the most popular with golftrotters, and that's a good reason for discovering the region once you have visited the rest. A recent course, Faithlegg was laid out over a former estate, as you can see with the old trees, which outline the fairways, the enclosure wall and the gardens. They add extra style and difficulties to the course as a whole. The architect has designed a very varied layout with no excessively steep hills, although some hazards are hardly visible and so complicate matters slightly in terms of strategy. With this said, they only await the really wayward shot. This is an averagely difficult and very competent course, the one criticism being the very ordinary bunkers with sand a little on the coarse side. However, you can get round the course quickly, as the rough is lenient and the undergrowth kept neatly trimmed.

La côte Sud-Est n'est pas la plus fréquentée par les touristes golfiques, c'est une bonne raison de l'explorer quand vous aurez parcouru les régions plus classiques. Ouvert depuis peu, Faithlegg a été construit dans une ancienne propriété, comme on le remarque avec les arbres très adultes qui définissent les trous, le mur d'enceinte et les jardins : ils apportent une beauté supplémentaire et quelques difficultés au parcours. L'architecte a conçu un tracé très varié, sans reliefs excessifs, certains obstacles d'eau par exemple ne sont guère visibles, ce qui complique légèrement la stratégie, mais ils ne recueillent que les balles très écartées du bon chemin. De difficulté moyenne, c'est une réalisation sérieuse. On peut cependant estimer que la forme des bunkers ne sort pas de l'ordinaire, et que le sable pourrait être plus fin. En revanche, la vitesse de jeu est garantie par la clémence des roughs et le bon entretien des sous-bois.

Faithlegg Golf Club — 1992
IRL - FAITHLEGG, Co. Waterford

Office	Secrétariat	(353) 051 - 382 241
Pro shop	Pro-shop	(353) 051 - 382 241
Fax	Fax	(353) 051 - 382 664
Situation	Situation	

7 km from Waterford (pop. 40 328)

Annual closure	Fermeture annuelle	no
Weekly closure	Fermeture hebdomadaire	no

Fees main season
Tarifs haute saison 18 holes

	Week days Semaine	We/Bank holidays We/Férié
Individual Individuel	IR£ 22	IR£ 25
Couple Couple	IR£ 44	IR£ 50

Caddy	Caddy	on request/IR£ 10/15
Electric Trolley	Chariot électrique	no
Buggy	Voiturette	IR£ 20/18 holes
Clubs	Clubs	IR£ 10

Credit cards Cartes de crédit VISA - MasterCard

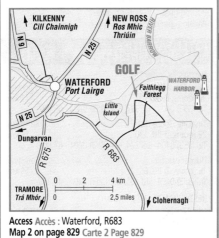

KILKENNY Cill Chainnigh
NEW ROSS Ros Mhic Thriúin
RIVER BARROW
N 9
N 25
GOLF
WATERFORD Port Lairge
Faithlegg Forest
WATERFORD HARBOR
Little Island
N 25
Dungarvan
R 675
R 683
TRAMORE Trá Mhór
0   2   4 km
0   2,5 miles
Clohernagh

Access Accès : Waterford, R683
Map 2 on page 829 Carte 2 Page 829

GOLF COURSE / PARCOURS — 13/20

Site	Site	■■■■
Maintenance	Entretien	■■■■
Architect	Architecte	Patrick Merrigan
Type	Type	parkland
Relief	Relief	■■
Water in play	Eau en jeu	■■■
Exp. to wind	Exposé au vent	■■
Trees in play	Arbres en jeu	■■■■

Scorecard Carte de score	Chp. Chp.	Mens Mess.	Ladies Da.
Length Long.	6057	5712	5160
Par	72	72	73

Advised golfing ability
Niveau de jeu recommandé   0   12   24   36

Hcp required   Handicap exigé   no

CLUB HOUSE & AMENITIES / CLUB HOUSE ET ANNEXES — 7/10

Pro shop	Pro-shop	■■■
Driving range	Practice	■■■
Sheltered	couvert	no
On grass	sur herbe	yes
Putting-green	putting-green	yes
Pitching-green	pitching green	no

HOTEL FACILITIES / ENVIRONNEMENT HOTELIER — 6/10

HOTELS HÔTELS

Waterford Castle — Waterford
19 rooms, D IR£ 170 — 3.5 km
Tel (353) 051 - 878 203, Fax (353) 051 - 879 316

Tower Hotel — Waterford
141 rooms, D IR£ 85 — 7 km
Tel (353) 051 - 875 801, Fax (353) 051 - 870 129

Granville Hotel — Waterford
74 rooms, D IR£ 72 — 7 km
Tel (353) 051 - 55 111, Fax (353) 051 - 870 307

RESTAURANTS RESTAURANTS

Dwyer's — Waterford
Tel (353) 051 - 77 478 — 7 km

Prendiville's — Waterford
Tel (353) 051 - 78 851 — 7 km

868

This is the brainchild of Kevin Mulcahy, the son of the founder of Waterville. It is not a links, but it makes no difference, and the designers McEvoy and O'Connor Jnr. have made a point of including some seaside features like pot bunkers and a double green, amongst the many other difficulties. These start with the greens, moderately contoured, but only the short putts are more or less straight. You often see water (as far as the port of Cork) but it only comes into play on half a dozen holes, dangerously so on the 12th, 14th and 18th. The other hazards are primarily trees, green-side bunkers and a few stone walls here and there. This course is suitable for all players, who often have the choice between lofted and ground shots. Here, you hone your short game and play with your brains. You will also see a few ostriches, monkeys or llamas roaming in the adjacent natural park.

C'est l'enfant de Kevin Mulcahy, fils du fondateur de Waterville. Que ce ne soit pas un links n'enlève rien à ses qualités, et les architectes McEvoy et O'Connor Jr n'ont pas manqué d'en citer quelques traits, comme quelques pot-bunkers et un double-green, parmi bien d'autres difficultés. A commencer par les greens, de relief modéré, mais où seuls les petits putts seront quasiment droits. On voit souvent l'eau (jusqu'au port de Cork), elle ne vient réellement en jeu que sur une demi-douzaine de trous, et de manière dangereuse au 12, au 14 et au 18. Les autres obstacles sont principalement de grands arbres, les bunkers de green et un petit mur çà et là. Ce parcours convient à tous les joueurs, qui auront souvent le choix entre les balles portées (target golf) et les approches roulées. Ici, on travaille son petit jeu, on joue avec sa tête et on peut apercevoir quelques autruches, singes ou lamas en balade hors du parc naturel adjacent.

Fota Island Golf Club — 1993
IRL - CARRIGTWOHILL, Co Cork

Office	Secrétariat	(353) 021 - 883 700
Pro shop	Pro-shop	(353) 021 - 883 710
Fax	Fax	(353) 021 - 883 713
Situation	Situation	

14 km from Cork (pop. 174 400)
10 km from Cobh (pop. 6 227)

Annual closure	Fermeture annuelle	no
Weekly closure	Fermeture hebdomadaire	no

Fees main season
Tarifs haute saison 18 holes

	Week days Semaine	We/Bank holidays We/Férié
Individual Individuel	IR£ 27	IR£ 30
Couple Couple	IR£ 54	IR£ 60

Caddy	Caddy	on request/IR£ 12
Electric Trolley	Chariot électrique	no
Buggy	Voiturette	IR£ 25/18 holes
Clubs	Clubs	IR£ 12/18 holes

Credit cards Cartes de crédit VISA - MasterCard - AMEX

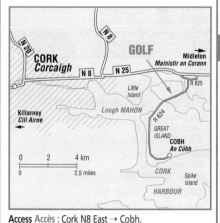

Access Accès : Cork N8 East → Cobh.
R624 → Fota Island
Map 2 on page 828 Carte 2 Page 828

GOLF COURSE / PARCOURS — 15/20

Site	Site	
Maintenance	Entretien	
Architect	Architecte	Christy O'Connor Jr Peter McEvoy
Type	Type	parkland
Relief	Relief	
Water in play	Eau en jeu	
Exp. to wind	Exposé au vent	
Trees in play	Arbres en jeu	

Scorecard Carte de score	Chp. Chp.	Mens Mess.	Ladies Da.
Length Long.	6197	5788	4967
Par	72	72	72

Advised golfing ability Niveau de jeu recommandé	0 12 24 36
Hcp required Handicap exigé	24 Men, 36 Ladies

CLUB HOUSE & AMENITIES / CLUB HOUSE ET ANNEXES — 7/10

Pro shop	Pro-shop	
Driving range	Practice	
Sheltered	couvert	no
On grass	sur herbe	yes
Putting-green	putting-green	yes
Pitching-green	pitching green	no

869

HOTEL FACILITIES / ENVIRONNEMENT HOTELIER — 6/10

HOTELS HÔTELS

Midleton Park	Cork
40 rooms, D IR£	7 km
Tel (353) 021 - 631 767, Fax (353) 021 - 631 605	
Rochestown Hotel	Cork
63 rooms, D IR£ 85	12 km
Tel (353) 021 - 892 233, Fax (353) 021 - 892 178	
Silver Springs Hotel	Cork
109 rooms, D IR£ 90	12 km
Tel (353) 021 - 507 533, Fax (353) 021 - 507 641	

RESTAURANTS RESTAURANTS

Ballymaloe House	Midleton
Tel (353) 021 - 352 531	33 km
Crawford Gallery	Cork
Tel (353) 021 - 274 415	15 km

Overlooking the Atlantic and the town of Galway, this recent course provides some outstanding viewpoints, but don't let them blur your judgment. The terrain given to Christy O'Connor Jnr. was naturally nothing more than ordinary, but he has made a great job of it and designed in a lot of appeal at the expense of some highly appropriate earthworks. As usual, the bunkers are very well placed and ready to collect any ball that doesn't quite manage to short-cut the dog-legs. There are also three lakes, but there are in play on three holes only. The many tee-off areas spread the range of difficulties, but only the back tees make this a severe test. The general difficulties are clearly visible and game strategy is obvious; this is important because the wind can turn nasty and make it even more essential to know how to play with it and against it. Welcome to a course designed with considerable talent, lacking only that intangible touch of greatness that separates the excellent from the exceptional.

Dominant l'océan et la ville de Galway, ce récent parcours offre des points de vue exceptionnels. Mais ils ne doivent pas influencer le jugement ! Le terrain mis à la disposition de Christy O'Connor Jr était naturellement assez ordinaire, il en a tiré un très bon parti, et l'a même rendu séduisant, au prix de travaux de terrassement très adéquats. Ses bunkers sont comme d'habitude très bien placés, et prêts à accueillir ceux qui ne parviennent pas à couper les dog-legs. De même, trois lacs sont mis en jeu, mais sur trois trous seulement. Les nombreux départs proposent un éventail de difficultés, seuls les départs arrière rendent ce parcours sévère. Les difficultés générales sont bien visibles, et la stratégie de jeu évidente : c'est important car le vent peut devenir méchant, et renforcer encore la nécessité de savoir jouer avec et contre lui. Un parcours réalisé avec talent, auquel ne manque que l'indéfinissable grandeur qui fait les exceptions.

Galway Bay Golf & Country Club — 1993

Renville
IRL - ORANMORE, Co Galway

Office	Secrétariat	(353) 091 - 790 500
Pro shop	Pro-shop	(353) 091 - 790 503
Fax	Fax	(353) 091 - 790 510
Situation	Situation	

5 km from Oranmore Village
13 km from Galway (pop. 50 855)

Annual closure	Fermeture annuelle	no
Weekly closure	Fermeture hebdomadaire	no

Fees main season	Tarifs haute saison	18 holes	
		Week days Semaine	**We/Bank holidays** We/Férié
Individual Individuel		IR£ 30	IR£ 35
Couple Couple		IR£ 60	IR£ 70

Weekdays: IR£ 45 for 2 rounds
Week-ends: IR£ 53 for 2 rounds

Caddy	Caddy	on request/IR£ 20
Electric Trolley	Chariot électrique	no
Buggy	Voiturette	IR£ 20/18 holes
Clubs	Clubs	IR£ 10

Credit cards Cartes de crédit
VISA - Eurocard - MasterCard

(map)

TUAM Tualm · N 339 · N 84 · N 17 · R 339 · N 64 · N 6 · GALWAY Gaillimh · Castle ⊕ · ORANMORE Orán Mór · GALWAY BAY · GOLF · N 18 · Dunbulcaun Bay · 0 — 2 — 4 km · 0 — 2,5 miles · GORT An Gort

Access Accès : Galway N6 → Oranmore, → Renville
Map 1 on page 826 Carte 1 Page 826

GOLF COURSE / PARCOURS — 14/20

Site	Site	▬▬▬▬
Maintenance	Entretien	▬▬▬▬
Architect	Architecte	Christy O'Connor Jr
Type	Type	seaside course
Relief	Relief	▬▬
Water in play	Eau en jeu	▬▬
Exp. to wind	Exposé au vent	▬▬▬
Trees in play	Arbres en jeu	▬▬

Scorecard Carte de score	Chp. Chp.	Mens Mess.	Ladies Da.
Length Long.	6533	6091	5205
Par	72	72	74

Advised golfing ability		0	12	24	36
Niveau de jeu recommandé					
Hcp required	Handicap exigé	28 Men, 36 Ladies			

CLUB HOUSE & AMENITIES / CLUB HOUSE ET ANNEXES — 7/10

Pro shop	Pro-shop	▬▬▬
Driving range	Practice	▬▬▬
Sheltered	couvert	no
On grass	sur herbe	yes
Putting-green	putting-green	yes
Pitching-green	pitching green	yes

HOTEL FACILITIES / ENVIRONNEMENT HOTELIER — 6/10

HOTELS HÔTELS

Corrib Great Southern — Galway
179 rooms, D IR£ 117 — 8 km
Tel (353) 091 - 755 281, Fax (353) 091 - 751 390

Galway Ryan — Galway
96 rooms, D IR£ 120 — 9 km
Tel (353) 091 - 753 181, Fax (353) 091 - 753 187

Oranmore Lodge Hotel — Oranmore
40 rooms, D IR£ 80 — 5 km
Tel (353) 091 - 794 400, Fax (353) 091 - 790 227

RESTAURANTS RESTAURANTS

Paddy Burkes — Clarinbridge
Tel (353) 091 - 796 226 — 7 km

Galway Bay Golf Club — on site
Tel (353) 091 - 790 500

GALWAY GC

We expect a lot from a great designer such as Alistair Mackenzie, but there's no denying the fact that Galway GC is now in need of a little careful remodelling from a modern designer who can preserve the course's style and spirit. The trees have obviously grown considerably since 1923, compounding the course's general tightness, the only real difficulty for the modern player. Precision play and flighting the ball take precedence over length, to the extent that long-hitters can leave the driver firmly in the bag and card a better score in return. On the other hand, average players will doubtless find the course long enough as it is. The space available was used to good effect and there are a lot of bunkers which are never excessively penalising. If we add to all this the superb views over Galway Bay, Burren and the Aran islands, plus the very busy city of Galway, then there is a welcome for you here.

On attend beaucoup de la signature d'un très grand architecte tel que Alister Mackenzie, mais il faut bien reconnaître que ce parcours mériterait un «lifting» attentif de la part d'un architecte moderne soucieux de lui conserver son esthétique et son esprit. Les arbres ont dû beaucoup pousser depuis 1923, accentuant l'étroitesse du parcours, seule véritable difficulté pour un joueur d'aujourd'hui. La précision et le travail de balle prennent nettement le pas sur la longueur, au point que les longs joueurs pourront laisser le driver dans le sac, avec une incidence favorable sur leur score. En revanche, les joueurs moyens trouveront sans doute la longueur du parcours suffisante ! L'espace disponible a été bien utilisé, le bunkering est important, mais rarement de manière trop pénalisante. Si l'on ajoute les points de vue superbes sur la baie de Galway, le Burren et les Iles d'Arran, et la proximité de la ville très animée de Galway... bienvenue ici.

Galway Golf Club		1893
Blackrock		
IRL - SALTHILL, GALWAY, Co Galway		
Office	Secrétariat	(353) 091 - 522 033
Pro shop	Pro-shop	(353) 091 - 523 038
Fax	Fax	(353) 091 - 522 033
Situation	Situation	
2 km from Galway (pop. 50 855)		
Annual closure	Fermeture annuelle	no
Weekly closure	Fermeture hebdomadaire	no

Fees main season
Tarifs haute saison 18 holes

	Week days Semaine	We/Bank holidays We/Férié
Individual Individuel	IR£ 18	IR£ 23
Couple Couple	IR£ 36	IR£ 46

Caddy	Caddy	on request/IR£ 15
Electric Trolley	Chariot électrique	IR£ 5/18 holes
Buggy	Voiturette	IR£ 25/18 holes
Clubs	Clubs	IR£ 8/18 holes

Credit cards Cartes de crédit VISA - MasterCard

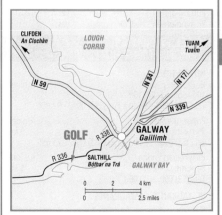

Access Accès : Galway R336 West.
Golf at the end of the Promenade at Salthill.
Map 1 on page 826 Carte 1 Page 826

GOLF COURSE
PARCOURS
13/20

Site	Site	
Maintenance	Entretien	
Architect	Architecte	Alistair Mackenzie
Type	Type	seaside course, parkland
Relief	Relief	
Water in play	Eau en jeu	
Exp. to wind	Exposé au vent	
Trees in play	Arbres en jeu	

Scorecard Carte de score	Chp. Chp.	Mens Mess.	Ladies Da.
Length Long.	5832	5598	4752
Par	70	71	73

Advised golfing ability	0	12	24	36
Niveau de jeu recommandé				
Hcp required	Handicap exigé	28 Men, 36 Ladies		

CLUB HOUSE & AMENITIES
CLUB HOUSE ET ANNEXES
6/10

Pro shop	Pro-shop	
Driving range	Practice	
Sheltered	couvert	no
On grass	sur herbe	yes
Putting-green	putting-green	yes
Pitching-green	pitching green	no

HOTEL FACILITIES
ENVIRONNEMENT HOTELIER
6/10

HOTELS HÔTELS

Corrib Great Southern	Galway
179 rooms, D IR£ 117	1 km
Tel (353) 091 - 755 281, Fax (353) 091 - 751 390	

Spinnaker Hotel	Galway
20 rooms, D IR£ 60	adjacent
Tel (353) 091 - 526 788, Fax (353) 091 - 526 650	

Glenlo Abbey	Galway
45 rooms, D IR£ 150	2 km
Tel (353) 091 - 526 666, Fax (353) 091 - 527 800	

RESTAURANTS RESTAURANTS

Moran's Oyster Cottage	Kilcolgan
Tel (353) 091 - 796 113	10 km

Cavey's Westwood	Galway
Tel (353) 091 - 21 442	3 km

871

Very positively adapting a course to players of all abilities is something you would expect from a fine connoisseur of amateur and professional golf such as Christy O'Connor Jnr. Given a remarkable site, long a favourite haunt of hikers and cyclists, he visibly rose to the occasion, and the views over Lough Ree are as magnificent as his deployment of the course on several holes. Other lakes add to both the course's scenic beauty and difficulty. And if we add to this a lot of very careful design on and around the greens, intelligently placed bunkers and the general balance of the layout, you will understand that this is one of the finest recent additions to the collection of Irish courses and one that will leave nobody indifferent. A little hilly but not excessively so, Glasson calls for a very precise game strategy and a cool head at all times. One further detail: you can reach the 18th tee by boat from Athlone.

On peut attendre d'un fin connaisseur du golf amateur et professionnel comme Christy O'Connor Jr une adaptation très sûre à tous les niveaux de jeu. Disposant d'un site remarquable, depuis longtemps connu des amateurs de randonnées cyclistes et pédestres, il en a visiblement été exalté, les vues sur le Lough Ree sont aussi magnifiques que sa mise en jeu sur quelques trous. D'autres lacs contribuent aussi bien à la beauté scénique du parcours qu'à sa difficulté. Et si l'on ajoute le travail très soigné des greens, le placement intelligent des bunkers et l'équilibre général du tracé, on aura compris qu'il s'agit d'une des meilleures additions récentes à la collection des golfs irlandais, et qui ne peut laisser indifférent. Un peu accidenté, mais sans excès, Glasson demande une stratégie de jeu très précise et de garder la tête froide. Pour l'anecdote, on peut parvenir en bateau au départ du 18, depuis Athlone.

Glasson Golf Club — 1993

Glasson
IRL - ATHLONE, Co West Meath

Office	Secrétariat	(353) 0902 - 85 120
Pro shop	Pro-shop	(353) 0902 - 85 120
Fax	Fax	(353) 0902 - 85 444
Situation	Situation	

9 km from Athlone (pop. 8 170)

Annual closure	Fermeture annuelle	no
Weekly closure	Fermeture hebdomadaire	no

Fees main season
Tarifs haute saison 18 holes

	Week days Semaine	We/Bank holidays We/Férié
Individual Individuel	IR£ 25	IR£ 30
Couple Couple	IR£ 50	IR£ 60

Caddy	Caddy	on request/IR£ 15
Electric Trolley	Chariot électrique	no
Buggy	Voiturette	IR£ 20/18 holes
Clubs	Clubs	IR£ 12/18 holes

Credit cards Cartes de crédit VISA - MasterCard

GOLF COURSE PARCOURS — 16/20

Site	Site	
Maintenance	Entretien	
Architect	Architecte	Christy O'Connor Jr
Type	Type	parkland
Relief	Relief	
Water in play	Eau en jeu	
Exp. to wind	Exposé au vent	
Trees in play	Arbres en jeu	

Scorecard Carte de score	Chp. Chp.	Mens Mess.	Ladies Da.
Length Long.	6510	6083	5100
Par	72	72	73

Advised golfing ability Niveau de jeu recommandé	0	12	24	36

Hcp required Handicap exigé 24 Men, 36 Ladies

CLUB HOUSE & AMENITIES CLUB HOUSE ET ANNEXES — 7/10

Pro shop	Pro-shop	
Driving range	Practice	
Sheltered	couvert	no
On grass	sur herbe	yes
Putting-green	putting-green	yes
Pitching-green	pitching green	yes

HOTEL FACILITIES ENVIRONNEMENT HOTELIER — 7/10

HOTELS HÔTELS

Hodson Bay Hotel — Athlone
100 rooms, D IR£ 100 — 12 km
Tel (353) 0902 - 92 404, Fax (353) 0902 - 92 688

Prince of Wales — Athlone
75 rooms, D IR£ 70 — 9 km
Tel (353) 0902 - 72 626, Fax (353) 0902 - 75 658

Ballykeeran Lodge — Athlone
8 rooms, D IR£ 32 — 5 km
Tel (353) 0902 - 85 063

RESTAURANTS RESTAURANTS

Grogans — Glasson Village
Tel (353) 0902 - 85 158 — 2 km

Glasson Village — Glasson/Athlone
Tel (353) 0902 - 85 001 — 2 km

Access Accès : 10 km N.E. of Athlone on N55.
Cavan road
Map 2 on page 829 Carte 2 Page 829

This is a recent addition to a very large number of courses in County Wicklow, but its condition already makes it look much older. Laid out about 200 ft above sea level, it provides some splendid views over the Irish Sea and surrounding hills. The slopes are a feature of the course, which nonetheless is still definitely walkable. Architect Peter McEvoy, a remarkable golfer himself, has very carefully used the natural topology and the trees and ponds to produce a pretty layout. Likewise, the greens are sometimes elevated; if not, they are well guarded by bunkers. Straightforwardness is a valuable asset here on a course where golfing psychology is important: the hazards are often less dangerous than they seem. Although we could not rank Glen of the Downs in the top pack of courses in Ireland, it is still very pleasant and will be even more so when a real club-house opens, planned for October 2000.

Dans le Co. Wicklow, c'est une récente addition à un ensemble de parcours déjà fort important, mais son état est déjà celui d'un parcours bien plus ancien. Situé à une soixantaine de mètres au-dessus du niveau de la mer, il offre des vues splendides à la fois sur la Mer d'Irlande et sur les collines de la région. Ces reliefs sont d'ailleurs une marque du parcours, bien qu'il soit très jouable à pied. L'architecte (et très grand joueur) Peter McEvoy a très habilement utilisé ces accidents naturels, ainsi que les arbres et les petites mares pour poser joliment son tracé. De même, les greens sont parfois surélevés et bien défendus par des bunkers quand ils ne le sont pas. La franchise est de mise dans ce parcours, avec un aspect psychologique important : les obstacles sont souvent moins dangereux qu'on ne le croit. Bien qu'on ne puisse classer Glen of the Downs dans le peloton de tête des parcours d'Irlande, il n'en reste pas moins très agréable, et le sera en plus avec un véritable Club house, prévu pour octobre 2000.

Glen of the Downs Golf Club — 1997
IRL - DELGANY, Co Wicklow

Office	Secrétariat	(353) 01 - 287 0065
Pro shop	Pro-shop	(353) 01 - 287 6240
Fax	Fax	(353) 01 - 287 0063
Situation	Situation	

Dublin (pop. 859 976), 30 km

Annual closure	Fermeture annuelle	no
Weekly closure	Fermeture hebdomadaire	no

Fees main season
Tarifs haute saison 18 holes

	Week days Semaine	We/Bank holidays We/Férié
Individual Individuel	IR£ 40	IR£ 50
Couple Couple	IR£ 80	IR£ 100

Caddy	Caddy	no
Electric Trolley	Chariot électrique	IR£ 10
Buggy	Voiturette	IR£ 20
Clubs	Clubs	IR£ 15

Credit cards Cartes de crédit
VISA - MasterCard - AMEX - DC

BRAY Bré
0 — 2 km
0 — 1,25 miles
DUBLIN Baile Átha Cliath
N 11
R 768
R 761
GREYSTONES Na Clocha Liatha
R 755
Kindlestown Forest
N 11
R 762
GOLF →
Roundwood An Tóchar
Wicklow Cill Mhantáin

Access Accès : Dublin, N11 → Wicklow/Wexford.
Kilmacanogue → Greystones. → Glen of the Downs.
Map 3 on page 830 Carte 3 Page 830

GOLF COURSE / PARCOURS — 13/20

Site	Site	
Maintenance	Entretien	
Architect	Architecte	Peter McEvoy
Type	Type	inland
Relief	Relief	
Water in play	Eau en jeu	
Exp. to wind	Exposé au vent	
Trees in play	Arbres en jeu	

Scorecard Carte de score	Chp. Chp.	Mens Mess.	Ladies Da.
Length Long.	5830	5410	4780
Par	71	71	71

Advised golfing ability
Niveau de jeu recommandé — 0 12 24 36
Hcp required — Handicap exigé — no

CLUB HOUSE & AMENITIES / CLUB HOUSE ET ANNEXES — 4/10

Pro shop	Pro-shop	
Driving range	Practice	
Sheltered	couvert	no
On grass	sur herbe	no
Putting-green	putting-green	yes
Pitching-green	pitching green	yes

HOTEL FACILITIES / ENVIRONNEMENT HOTELIER — 7/10

HOTELS HÔTELS
Glenview Hotel — Glen of the Downs
40 rooms, D IR£ 130 — 3 km
Tel (353) 01 - 287 3399, Fax (353) 01 - 287 7511

Summerhill Hotel — Enniskerry
30 rooms, D IR£ 50 — 8 km
Tel (353) 01 - 286 7928, Fax (353) 01 - 286 79 29

Powerscourt Arms Hotel — Enniskerry
12 rooms, D IR£ 50 — 8 km
Tel (353) 01 - 282 89 03, Fax (353) 01 - 286 49 09

RESTAURANTS RESTAURANTS
Enniscree Lodge — Enniskerry
Tel (353) 01 - 286 3542 — 8 km

Tinakilly House — Rathnew
Tel (353) 0404 - 69 274 — 15 km

Cooper's - Tel (353) 01 - 287 3914 — Greystones 5 km

873

The great James Braid created fewer courses in Ireland than in Scotland, but alongside Tullamore or Mullingar, Grange is one of his more excellent designs. No wonder then that the club has a large number of members to make week-end green-fees a difficult proposition. Here in the city they preserve tradition, at least for having retained the wooden club-house built in the 1940s and kept the design of the course as close as possible to the original. You will appreciate the very subtle bunkering and the strategic use of water on the 18th. By and large, the course looks to be tight and tough all the way, in fact only the first 6 holes really fit this category. But the impression of narrowness never leaves you: James Braid knew a thing a two about the psychology of your average golfer. But there again, the trees have doubtless grown a lot over the past one hundred years or so. Some of the greens are elevated (depending on terrain topology), all are well guarded and only a handful can really be reached by rolling the ball in.

James Braid n'a pas créé autant de parcours en Irlande qu'en Ecosse mais, à côté de Tullamore ou Mullingar, Grange figure parmi ses excellentes créations : les membres sont nombreux et il est très difficile d'y jouer en week-ends. Ici, on cultive la tradition, au moins pour avoir conservé le Club house en bois des années 40, et le dessin du parcours aussi original que possible. En règle générale, le parcours paraît étroit et difficile, bien que seuls les six premiers trous le soient vraiment, mais l'impression demeure : James Braid connaissait très bien la psychologie de l'amateur. D'un autre côté, les arbres ont sans doute aussi beaucoup poussé en près de cent ans... Côté greens, quelques uns sont en élévation (suivant les accidents du terrain), tous sont bien défendus, seule une poignée d'entre eux étant vraiment accessibles en roulant.

Grange Golf Club — 1910
IRL - RATHFARNHAM, DUBLIN 16

Office	Secrétariat	(353) 01 - 493 2889
Pro shop	Pro-shop	(353) 01 - 493 2299
Fax	Fax	(353) 01 - 493 2832
Situation	Situation	

Dublin (pop. 859 976), 10 km

Annual closure	Fermeture annuelle	no
Weekly closure	Fermeture hebdomadaire	no

Fees main season	Tarifs haute saison	18 holes	
		Week days Semaine	We/Bank holidays We/Férié
Individual Individuel		IR£ 35	IR£ 40
Couple Couple		IR£ 70	IR£ 80

No green-fees on Saturdays

Caddy	Caddy	IR£ 15
Electric Trolley	Chariot électrique	no
Buggy	Voiturette	no
Clubs	Clubs	IR£ 10

Credit cards Cartes de crédit
VISA - MasterCard - AMEX - DC

Access Accès : • Dublin, New Street, at Harold Cross, take left on Harold Cross Road. Left on Grange Road.
• Or Western Parkway to the end, straight on Knocklyon, Scholars, Taylor Lane, Grange Road.
Map 3 on page 830 Carte 3 Page 830

GOLF COURSE / PARCOURS — 16/20

Site	Site	
Maintenance	Entretien	
Architect	Architecte	James Braid
Type	Type	parkland
Relief	Relief	
Water in play	Eau en jeu	
Exp. to wind	Exposé au vent	
Trees in play	Arbres en jeu	

Scorecard Carte de score	Chp. Chp.	Mens Mess.	Ladies Da.
Length Long.	5517	5420	5154
Par	68	68	73

Advised golfing ability		0 12 24 36
Niveau de jeu recommandé		
Hcp required	Handicap exigé	

CLUB HOUSE & AMENITIES / CLUB HOUSE ET ANNEXES — 5/10

Pro shop	Pro-shop	
Driving range	Practice	
Sheltered	couvert	no
On grass	sur herbe	yes (practice area)
Putting-green	putting-green	yes
Pitching-green	pitching green	yes

HOTEL FACILITIES / ENVIRONNEMENT HOTELIER — 8/10

HOTELS HÔTELS
Rathmines Plaza Hotel — Rathmines
54 rooms, D IR£ 80 — 5 km
Tel (353) 01 - 496 6966, Fax (353) 01 - 491 0603

Orwell Lodge Hotel — Rathgae
10 rooms, D IR£ 80 — 12 km
Tel (353) 01 - 497 7258, Fax (353) 01 - 497 9913

Red Cow Morans Hotel — Clondalkin
1233 rooms, D IR£ 140 — 7 km
Tel (353) 01 - 459 3650, Fax (353) 01 - 459 1588

RESTAURANTS RESTAURANTS
Johnnie Foxes — Glencullen
Tel (353) 01 - 295 5647 — 15 km

Killakee Restaurant — Rathfarnham
Tél(353) 01 - 493 2645 — 8 km

Yellow House — Rathfarnham
Tel (353) 01 - 493 2994 — 3 km

This age-old course, completed and overhauled by Eddie Hackett, is a mixture of wooded inland course and links, resulting in a lot of variety and an original appearance. There are even surprises in store, with the presence of the old disused railway line, whose infrastructure offers protection from the Irish sea and serves as a platform (no pun intended) for four elevated tees. If you like surprises, this course harbours a number of traps and is no walk-over first time out. Six greens are blind, there is a double green (2 and 10), a few hazards are invisible on several holes, a ditch makes its presence felt on four holes and there are ponds for a watery grave on three others. Fortunately, if you miss the fairway, the rough is perfectly playable. Laid out along Carlingford Lough, close to the pretty fishing village of Carlingford (an oyster centre), this is a very amusing, far from easy and rather uncommon course.

Ce parcours centenaire complété et révisé par Eddie Hackett est un mélange de parcours inland boisé et de links, ce qui lui donne beaucoup de variété, mais aussi un visage assez original. Il est même surprenant à cause de la présence d'une ancienne ligne de chemin de fer, aujourd'hui désaffectée, dont l'infrastructure protège de la mer d'Irlande, et sert de base pour quatre départs surélevés. Si vous aimez les surprises, ce parcours recèle pas mal de pièges, et n'est pas évident à première vue : six greens sont aveugles, on trouve un double green (2 et 10), quelques obstacles sont invisibles sur plusieurs trous, un fossé vient en jeu sur quatre trous, et des mares sur trois trous. Heureusement, si l'on manque les fairways, le rough reste tout à fait jouable. Le long du Carlingford Lough, près du joli village de pêcheurs de Carlingford (la capitale des huîtres), c'est un parcours très amusant, pas facile et dépaysant.

Grenore Golf Club 1896
IRL - GRENORE, Co Louth

Office	Secrétariat	(353) 042 - 73 678
Pro shop	Pro-shop	(353) 042 - 73 678
Fax	Fax	(353) 042 - 73 678
Situation	Situation	

12 km from Dundalk (pop. 25 843)
16 km from Newry

Annual closure	Fermeture annuelle	no
Weekly closure	Fermeture hebdomadaire	no

Fees main season
Tarifs haute saison 18 holes

	Week days Semaine	We/Bank holidays We/Férié
Individual Individuel	IR£ 14	IR£ 20
Couple Couple	IR£ 28	IR£ 40

Caddy	Caddy	no
Electric Trolley	Chariot électrique	no
Buggy	Voiturette	no
Clubs	Clubs	no

Credit cards Cartes de crédit no

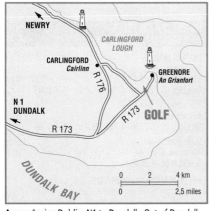

NEWRY
CARLINGFORD LOUGH
CARLINGFORD Cairlinn
R 176
GREENORE An Grianfort
N 1 DUNDALK
R 173 GOLF
R 173
DUNDALK BAY

| 0 | 2 | 4 km |
| 0 | | 2,5 miles |

Access Accès : Dublin, N1 to Dundalk. Out of Dundalk, turn right on R173 to Grenore. Golf 12 km
Map 1 on page 827 Carte 1 Page 827

GOLF COURSE PARCOURS 14/20

Site	Site	
Maintenance	Entretien	
Architect	Architecte	Eddie Hackett
Type	Type	seaside course
Relief	Relief	
Water in play	Eau en jeu	
Exp. to wind	Exposé au vent	
Trees in play	Arbres en jeu	

Scorecard Carte de score	Chp. Chp.	Mens Mess.	Ladies Da.
Length Long.	5954	5700	5198
Par	71	71	74

Advised golfing ability		0	12	24	36
Niveau de jeu recommandé					
Hcp required	Handicap exigé	24 Men, 36 Ladies			

CLUB HOUSE & AMENITIES CLUB HOUSE ET ANNEXES 6/10

Pro shop	Pro-shop	
Driving range	Practice	
Sheltered	couvert	no
On grass	sur herbe	yes
Putting-green	putting-green	yes
Pitching-green	pitching green	no

HOTEL FACILITIES ENVIRONNEMENT HOTELIER 5/10

HOTELS HÔTELS
Ballymascanlon Hotel — Dundalk
36 rooms, D IR£ — 12 km
Tel (353) 042 - 71 124

Village Hotel — Carlingford
13 rooms, D IR£ 45 — 2 km
Tel (353) 042 - 73 116

RESTAURANTS RESTAURANTS
Jordans Townhouse — Carlingford
Tel (353) 042 - 73 223 — 3 km

McKevitts Village — Carlingford
Tel (353) 042 - 73 116 — 3 km

875

HERMITAGE

<table>
<tr><td>15</td><td>6</td><td>7</td></tr>
</table>

This course has led a quiet existence since the turn of the century and continues to figure regularly amongst the better Irish golf courses. There is nothing of the links about it, sure, but its park-landscape configuration (the trees are superb) on the banks of the Liffey, the moderately hilly relief (two or three steep climbs) and the closeness to Dublin make this a very interesting stop-off. It is not very long (especially from the normal tees) but it does require a lot of precision play and probably every club in your bag. A few blind shots and greens add a little uncertainty to it all, and the 10th (a par 3 along the Liffey river) is an exciting prospect with the green way down below you. You shouldn't under-estimate Hermitage, it is capable of baring its teeth to anyone who is not permanently on his or her toes. This is a very fine example of an inland course and has hosted a number of top tournaments. It may not always stand up to the best player, but it has lost none of its charm.

Ce golf vit paisiblement depuis le début du siècle, et continuer à figurer régulièrement parmi les bons parcours d'Irlande. Certes, il n'a rien d'un links, mais sa configuration de grand parc (les arbres sont superbes) en bordure de la Liffey, son relief modéré (deux ou trois fortes montées) et sa proximité de Dublin en font une étape fort intéressante. Il n'est pas très long (surtout des départs normaux), mais il demande pas mal de précision, et l'utilisation probable de tous les clubs du sac. Quelques coups et un green aveugles ajoutent un peu d'incertitude, et le 10 (un par 3 le long de la Liffey) amène quelque émotion, avec son green très en contrebas du départ. On ne doit pas sous-estimer Hermitage, il est capable de montrer les dents à ceux qui négligeraient de conserver en permanence leur concentration. Ce très bel exemple de parcours «inland» a reçu de grandes compétitions, il conserve tout son charme.

Hermitage Golf Club — 1902
Ballydowd
IRL - LUCAN, Co Dublin

Office	Secrétariat	(353) 01 - 626 4781
Pro shop	Pro-shop	(353) 01 - 626 8072
Fax	Fax	(353) 01 - 626 4781
Situation	Situation	

12 km from Dublin (pop. 859 976)
4 km from Maynooth (pop. 6 027)

Annual closure	Fermeture annuelle	no
Weekly closure	Fermeture hebdomadaire	no

Fees main season
Tarifs haute saison 18 holes

	Week days Semaine	We/Bank holidays We/Férié
Individual Individuel	IR£ 32	IR£ 45
Couple Couple	IR£ 64	IR£ 90

Weekdays: IR£ 21 before 9.00 am

Caddy	Caddy	on request/IR£ 15
Electric Trolley	Chariot électrique	IR£ 5
Buggy	Voiturette	no
Clubs	Clubs	IR£ 10/18 holes

Credit cards Cartes de crédit VISA - MasterCard

876

Access Accès : Dublin, N4 West
Map 3 on page 830 Carte 3 Page 830

GOLF COURSE PARCOURS — 15/20

Site	Site	
Maintenance	Entretien	
Architect	Architecte	M. McKenna
Type	Type	parkland
Relief	Relief	
Water in play	Eau en jeu	
Exp. to wind	Exposé au vent	
Trees in play	Arbres en jeu	

Scorecard Carte de score	Chp. Chp.	Mens Mess.	Ladies Da.
Length Long.	6051	5833	5215
Par	71	71	75

Advised golfing ability
Niveau de jeu recommandé — 0 12 24 36
Hcp required — Handicap exigé — 24 Men, 36 Ladies

CLUB HOUSE & AMENITIES
CLUB HOUSE ET ANNEXES — 6/10

Pro shop	Pro-shop	
Driving range	Practice	
Sheltered	couvert	no
On grass	sur herbe	yes
Putting-green	putting-green	yes
Pitching-green	pitching green	yes

HOTEL FACILITIES
ENVIRONNEMENT HOTELIER — 7/10

HOTELS HÔTELS
Spa Hotel — Lucan
53 rooms, D IR£ 64 — 4 km
Tel (353) 01 - 628 0494, Fax (353) 01 - 628 0841

Finnstown House Hotel — Lucan
45 rooms, D IR£ 70 — 6 km
Tel (353) 01 - 628 0644, Fax (353) 01 - 628 1088

Springfield Hotel — Leixlip
40 rooms, D IR£ 44 — 2 km
Tel (353) 01 - 624 4925

RESTAURANTS RESTAURANTS
Finnstown — Lucan
Tel (353) 01 - 628 0644 — 6 km

Ryans — Dublin
Tel (353) 01 - 820 8210 — 6 km

This is one of the most ambitious projects ever carried out in Ireland, ands will be the site of the 2005 Ryder Cup. Straffan House has been converted into a top luxury hotel and a course built without counting the cost, the whole piece co-ordinated by the Jefferson Smurfit group, one of the country's most dynamic entrepreneurs. Arnold Palmer pitched and won the official tender to design the course and has come up with one of his most exacting layouts. In length and tactical difficulty, it is reminiscent of Bay Hill in Florida. Only the most accomplished golfers can hope to cope without feeling too disillusioned about their game. Even from the front tees, this is an uncompromising challenge, so don't waste time counting your strokes, or even your balls if you start flirting too boldly with the water, especially over the closing holes. What with the closeness of the river Liffey, we would suggest you play here in summer.

C'est le site de la Ryder Cup 2005, et l'une des plus ambitieuses réalisations jamais effectuées en Irlande, avec la transformation de la Straffan House en hôtel de grand luxe, et la construction d'un parcours où l'argent n'a pas été compté, sous la houlette du Jefferson Smurfit Group, l'une des entreprises les plus dynamiques du pays. Arnold Palmer est sorti vainqueur du concours d'architectes, il a livré l'un de ses parcours les plus exigeants : par sa longueur et ses difficultés tactiques, il n'est pas sans rappeler Bay Hill en Floride. Et seul les golfeurs accomplis pourront prétendre le négocier sans trop perdre d'illusions sur leur golf. Même des départs avancés, il reste un challenge sans concessions, on évitera donc de compter ses coups, et parfois même ses balles, si l'on flirte trop audacieusement avec l'eau, notamment dans les derniers trous. En dépit d'importants drainages, la proximité de la rivière Liffey incite à le recommander en été.

The K Club — 1991
IRL - STRAFFAN, Co Kildare

Office	Secrétariat	(353) 01 - 601 7300
Pro shop	Pro-shop	(353) 01 - 601 7321
Fax	Fax	(353) 01 - 601 7399
Situation	Situation	

34 km W of Dublin (pop. 859 976)

Annual closure	Fermeture annuelle	no
Weekly closure	Fermeture hebdomadaire	no

Fees main season
Tarifs haute saison 18 holes

	Week days Semaine	We/Bank holidays We/Férié
Individual Individuel	IR£ 120	IR£ 120
Couple Couple	IR£ 240	IR£ 240

Caddy	Caddy	on request/IR£ 25
Electric Trolley	Chariot électrique	IR£ 10
Buggy	Voiturette	IR£ 30/18 holes
Clubs	Clubs	IR£ 30/18 holes

Credit cards Cartes de crédit
VISA - Eurocard - MasterCard - AMEX - DC

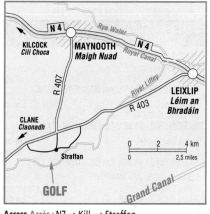

Access Accès : N7 → Kill, → Straffan
Map 3 on page 830 Carte 3 Page 830

GOLF COURSE / PARCOURS — 17/20

Site	Site	■■■■■□
Maintenance	Entretien	■■■■■□
Architect	Architecte	Arnold Palmer
Type	Type	inland, parkland
Relief	Relief	■■□□□□
Water in play	Eau en jeu	■■■■□□
Exp. to wind	Exposé au vent	■■□□□□
Trees in play	Arbres en jeu	■■■■□□

Scorecard Carte de score	Chp. Chp.	Mens Mess.	Ladies Da.
Length Long.	6519	6063	4990
Par	72	72	73

Advised golfing ability Niveau de jeu recommandé	0	12	24	36
			■■■	

Hcp required Handicap exigé — 28 Men, 36 Ladies

CLUB HOUSE & AMENITIES / CLUB HOUSE ET ANNEXES — 8/10

Pro shop	Pro-shop	■■■■□□
Driving range	Practice	■■■■□□
Sheltered	couvert	no
On grass	sur herbe	yes
Putting-green	putting-green	yes
Pitching-green	pitching green	yes

HOTEL FACILITIES / ENVIRONNEMENT HOTELIER — 8/10

HOTELS HÔTELS
Kildare Hotel and Country Club — on site
45 rooms, D IR£ 260
Tel (353) 01 - 627 3333, Fax (353) 01 - 627 3312

Leixlip House Hotel — Leixlip 10 km
16 rooms, D IR£ 100
Tel (353) 01 - 624 2268, Fax (353) 01 - 624 4177

Moyglare Manor — Maynooth 10 km
16 rooms, D IR£ 130
Tel (353) 01 - 628 63 51, Fax (353) 01 - 628 5405

RESTAURANTS RESTAURANTS
The Legends — K Club on site
Tel (353) 01 - 627 3111

The Burly Turk — K Club on site
Tel (353) 01 - 627 3111

877

At first sight, this is an impressive complex. Kilkea Castle is the oldest inhabited castle in Ireland and provides a splendid setting for this golf and hotel resort, where you can also try your hand at archery, clay-pigeon shooting and horse-riding, one of Ireland's national sports. Seen in comparison with the hotel's facilities, the green-fee is by no means prohibitive and in any case is in line with the very respectful quality of the course. The architects have used the natural terrain, streams and ponds for purposes of effect and also for game strategy. Existing trees are reasonably in play and new plantations should enhance the scenery and nature of hazards still further. They also tried to please everyone, so less experienced players always have the chance to stay away from trouble while others will face up to the challenge without too much trepidation.

Au premier regard, l'ensemble est impressionnant. Kilkea Castle est le plus ancien château habité d'Irlande, il constitue un cadre splendide à cet ensemble golf et hôtel, où l'on peut également pratiquer le tir à l'arc, le tir au pigeon d'argile et l'équitation, un des sports nationaux de l'Irlande. En comparaison des équipements de l'hôtel, le green-fee n'est pas ici prohibitif, en tout cas par rapport à la très honorable qualité du parcours. Les architectes ont utilisé le terrain naturel, les cours d'eau et les mares avec beaucoup de sens de l'effet, mais aussi de la stratégie du jeu. Les arbres existants du domaine sont raisonnablement en jeu, et de nouvelles plantations devraient encore faire évoluer le décor et la nature des obstacles. On a aussi cherché ici à contenter tout le monde, tous les niveaux de jeu. Ainsi, les joueurs les moins aguerris ont toujours des possibilités de rester à l'écart des problèmes, les autres affronteront sans trop de peur les défis du lieu.

Kilkea Castle Golf Club 1994
IRL - CASTLEDERMOT, Co. Kildare

Office	Secrétariat	(353) 0503 - 45 555
Pro shop	Pro-shop	(353) 0503 - 45 555
Fax	Fax	(353) 0503 - 45 505
Situation	Situation	

Dublin (pop. 859 976), 65 km

Annual closure	Fermeture annuelle	no
Weekly closure	Fermeture hebdomadaire	no

Fees main season
Tarifs haute saison 18 holes

	Week days Semaine	We/Bank holidays We/Férié
Individual Individuel	IR£ 25	IR£ 25
Couple Couple	IR£ 50	IR£ 50

Caddy	Caddy	no
Electric Trolley	Chariot électrique	no
Buggy	Voiturette	no
Clubs	Clubs	IR£ 15

Credit cards Cartes de crédit
VISA - Eurocard - MasterCard - AMEX

878

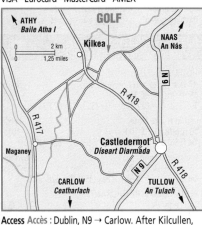

Access Accès : Dublin, N9 → Carlow. After Kilcullen, Ballymount, turn off at High Cross → Kilkea Castle.
Map 2 on page 828 Carte 2 Page 828

GOLF COURSE
PARCOURS   **14**/20

Site	Site	
Maintenance	Entretien	
Architect	Architecte	Andrew Gilbert
		Jim Cassidy
Type	Type	parkland
Relief	Relief	
Water in play	Eau en jeu	
Exp. to wind	Exposé au vent	
Trees in play	Arbres en jeu	

Scorecard Carte de score	Chp. Chp.	Mens Mess.	Ladies Da.
Length Long.	6097	5891	5076
Par	70	70	72

Advised golfing ability Niveau de jeu recommandé	0	12	24	36
Hcp required Handicap exigé	no			

CLUB HOUSE & AMENITIES
CLUB HOUSE ET ANNEXES   **6**/10

Pro shop	Pro-shop	
Driving range	Practice	
Sheltered	couvert	no
On grass	sur herbe	yes (practice area)
Putting-green	putting-green	yes
Pitching-green	pitching green	yes

HOTEL FACILITIES
ENVIRONNEMENT HOTELIER   **6**/10

HOTELS HÔTELS
Kilkea Castle Hotel   Castledermot
36 rooms, D IR£ 190   on site
Tel (353) 0503 - 45 156, Fax (353) 0503 - 45 187

Royal Hotel   Carlow
34 rooms, D IR£ 48   12 km
Tel (353) 0503 - 31 621, Fax (353) 0503 - 31 621

Seven Oaks Hotel   Carlow
32 rooms, D IR£ 70   12 km
Tel (353) 0503 - 31 308, Fax (353) 0503 - 32 155

RESTAURANTS RESTAURANTS
Kilkea Castle   Castledermot
Tel (353) 0503 - 45 156   on site

Tonlegee House - Tel (353) 0507 - 31 473   Athy19 km

Rathsallagh House   Dunlavin
Tel (353) 045 - 403 112   36 km

13	7	6

The thousands of trees planted in the 1960s and 1970s have grown and compounded the difficulty of this course. But being on the short side, it is within the grasp of most golfers, although the best will see this more as a good practice course rather than a top-level test of skill. Here, then, is the opportunity to look after the rest of the family or the lesser players in the group. They will, though, need to be careful on the par 3s, on the 11th, a long par 4, and on the closing holes, which can spoil a good card. The main hazards are generally speaking the trees, which neatly outline the holes, the fairway bunkers (they can be punishing at times) and the sand around the greens. The greens themselves are forthright, medium-sized and not bumpy enough to be really difficult to read. This is a pleasant day's golfing over terrain where holes alternate over flat and rolling landscape.

La croissance des milliers d'arbres plantés dans les années 60 et 70 a accru la difficulté de ce parcours. Cependant, sa faible longueur le place à la portée de tous les niveaux de jeu, mais les meilleurs doivent le considérer comme un bon parcours d'entraînement, et non comme un test de première grandeur : ce sera l'occasion pour eux de s'occuper des autres joueurs de la famille ou du groupe ! Mais ils devront être vigilants sur les pars 3, sur le 11(un long par 4) et sur les derniers trous, qui peuvent endommager un bon score. Les principaux obstacles sont en général les arbres, qui définissent bien les trous, les bunkers de fairway (ils pourraient être plus punitifs), et les bunkers défendant les greens. Ces derniers sont francs, de taille moyenne, ne sont pas assez accidentés pour être vraiment difficiles à lire. Et comme le relief du terrain alterne les trous plats et les trous plus vallonnés, c'est une agréable promenade.

Kilkenny Golf Club — 1896
IRL - GLENDINE, Co Kilkenny

Office	Secrétariat	(353) 056 - 22 125
Pro shop	Pro-shop	(353) 056 - 61 730
Fax	Fax	(353) 056 - 22 125
Situation	Situation	

1.5 km from Kilkenny (pop. 8 515)

Annual closure	Fermeture annuelle	no
Weekly closure	Fermeture hebdomadaire	no

Fees main season
Tarifs haute saison 18 holes

	Week days Semaine	We/Bank holidays We/Férié
Individual Individuel	IR£ 20	IR£ 22
Couple Couple	IR£ 40	IR£ 44

Caddy	Caddy	IR£ 10/15
Electric Trolley	Chariot électrique	no
Buggy	Voiturette	IR£ 20/18 holes
Clubs	Clubs	IR£ 6

Credit cards Cartes de crédit VISA - MasterCard

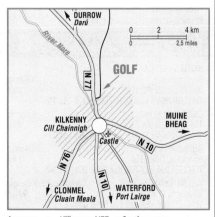

Access Accès : Kilkenny, N77 → Castlecomer.
Golf 1.5 km
Map 2 on page 829 Carte 2 Page 829

GOLF COURSE PARCOURS — 13/20

Site	Site	
Maintenance	Entretien	
Architect	Architecte	
Type	Type	parkland
Relief	Relief	
Water in play	Eau en jeu	
Exp. to wind	Exposé au vent	
Trees in play	Arbres en jeu	

Scorecard Carte de score	Chp. Chp.	Mens Mess.	Ladies Da.
Length Long.	5857	5600	5112
Par	71	71	73

Advised golfing ability
Niveau de jeu recommandé   0   12   24   36
Hcp required   Handicap exigé   no

CLUB HOUSE & AMENITIES CLUB HOUSE ET ANNEXES — 7/10

Pro shop	Pro-shop	
Driving range	Practice	
Sheltered	couvert	no
On grass	sur herbe	yes
Putting-green	putting-green	yes
Pitching-green	pitching green	no

HOTEL FACILITIES ENVIRONNEMENT HOTELIER — 6/10

HOTELS HÔTELS
Mount Juliet House — Thomastown
32 rooms, D from IR£ 120 — 16 km
Tel (353) 056 - 24 455, Fax (353) 056 - 24 522

Hotel Kilkenny — Kilkenny
60 rooms, D IR£ 100 — 3 km
Tel (353) 056 - 62 000, Fax (353) 056 - 65 984

Newpark Hotel — Kilkenny
84 rooms, D IR£ 100 — 3 km
Tel (353) 056 - 22 122, Fax (353) 056 - 61 111

RESTAURANTS RESTAURANTS
Lacken House — Kilkenny
Tel (353) 056 - 61 085 — 3 km

Kytlers Inn — Kilkenny
Tel (353) 056 - 21 064 — 3 km

879

Although the closing holes here are not quite as spectacular as those on its illustrious neighbour, Killeen is generally considered to be the most challenging course of this remarkable complex. It staged the Irish Open in 1991 and 1992, when Nick Faldo triumphed. Some of the original holes designed by Sir Guy Campbell are included here, but the basic layout is the work of Eddie Hackett and Billy O'Sullivan. The landscape is that of a huge park with every imaginable hazard. Let's start with the trees: from the back tees, the fairways look and are narrow, and demand very accurate driving. As you move forward, they obligingly become a little wider. The path to the green is dotted with strategically placed bunkers, and water hazards also play a significant role. While it is difficult to prefer one or the other of the Killarney courses (everyone to his own), the purists say that Killeen just has the edge.

Bien qu'il ne produise pas un finish aussi spectaculaire que son voisin, Killeen est généralement considéré comme le plus exigeant de ce remarquable complexe. C'est d'ailleurs celui qui a reçu l'Irish Open, notamment en 1991 et 1992 quand Nick Faldo s'y imposa. Quelques-uns des trous du tracé original de Sir Guy Campbell ont été repris ici, mais l'essentiel en est dû à Eddie Hackett et Billy O'Sullivan. Le paysage est celui d'un vaste parc, avec tous les obstacles imaginables. A commencer par les arbres : des départs arrière, les fairways paraissent étroits et imposent un driving très précis, mais ils s'élargissent amicalement pour les départs plus avancés. Le chemin des greens est alors très fourni en bunkers stratégiques, et les obstacles d'eau jouent également un rôle important. S'il est difficile de préférer l'un ou l'autre parcours de Killarney (chacun son goût), celui-ci est un soupçon supérieur selon les puristes.

Killarney Golf Club — 1971

O'Mahoney's Point
IRL - KILLARNEY, Co Kerry

Office	Secrétariat	(353) 064 - 31 034
Pro shop	Pro-shop	(353) 064 - 31 165
Fax	Fax	(353) 064 - 33 065
Situation	Situation	

3 km from Killarney (pop. 7 275)

Annual closure	Fermeture annuelle	no
Weekly closure	Fermeture hebdomadaire	no

Fees main season
Tarifs haute saison 18 holes

	Week days Semaine	We/Bank holidays We/Férié
Individual Individuel	IR£ 38	IR£ 38
Couple Couple	IR£ 76	IR£ 76

Caddy	Caddy	IR£ 15/18 holes
Electric Trolley	Chariot électrique	no
Buggy	Voiturette	no
Clubs	Clubs	IR£ 11/18 holes

Credit cards Cartes de crédit
VISA - Eurocard - MasterCard - AMEX - DC

880

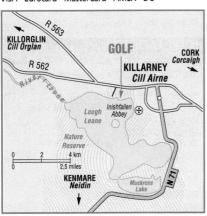

Access Accès : Killarney W, 3 km on R562 → Killorglin
Map 2 on page 828 Carte 2 Page 828

GOLF COURSE PARCOURS — 16/20

Site	Site	▰▰▰▰▱
Maintenance	Entretien	▰▰▰▰▱
Architect	Architecte	Eddie Hackett Billy O'Sullivan
Type	Type	parkland
Relief	Relief	▰▰▱▱▱
Water in play	Eau en jeu	▰▰▱▱▱
Exp. to wind	Exposé au vent	▰▰▱▱▱
Trees in play	Arbres en jeu	▰▰▰▱▱

Scorecard Carte de score	Chp. Chp.	Mens Mess.	Ladies Da.
Length Long.	6474	5993	4928
Par	72	72	74

Advised golfing ability Niveau de jeu recommandé		0 12 24 36
Hcp required	Handicap exigé	28 Men, 36 Ladies

CLUB HOUSE & AMENITIES CLUB HOUSE ET ANNEXES — 7/10

Pro shop	Pro-shop	▰▰▰▰▱
Driving range	Practice	▰▰▰▱▱
Sheltered	couvert	no
On grass	sur herbe	yes
Putting-green	putting-green	yes
Pitching-green	pitching green	no

HOTEL FACILITIES ENVIRONNEMENT HOTELIER — 8/10

HOTELS HÔTELS

Europe Hotel — Killarney
205 rooms, D IR£ 132 — 1 km
Tel (353) 064 - 31 900, Fax (353) 064 - 32 118

Castlerosse Hotel — Killarney
114 rooms, D IR£ 110 — 1 km
Tel (353) 064 - 31 144, Fax (353) 064 - 31 031

Aghadoe Heights — Killarney
60 rooms, D IR£ 165 — 1 km
Tel (353) 064 - 31 766, Fax (353) 064 - 31 345

Ard Na Sidhe — Caragh Lake, Killorglin
20 rooms, D IR£ 158 — 22 km
Tel (353) 066 - 69 105, Fax (353) 066 - 69 282

RESTAURANTS RESTAURANTS

Dingle's - Tel (353) 064 - 31 079 — Killarney 4 km
Failte Restaurant - Tél(353) 064 - 33 404 — Killarney 4 km

A lively place to be at night, this charming little town is a major tourist centre and an ideal holiday stop-off to explore the lakes in the National Park, the Kerry mountains... and the prestigious golf courses of south-west Ireland. The two 18-hole courses at Killarney are a part of these, and golfers often tend to show a slight sentimental preference for this one, especially the 3 closing holes, which include the 18th, a tough par 3 magnificently set alongside Lough Leane. Try and arrange to play here in the early evening to watch the sun set, when the surrounding forests blossom in the colours of autumn (play Killeen in the morning). A rather short course, it is less of a handful than it looks at first sight, but it does require a careful short game around very well-guarded greens. The beauty of the environment, the trees and the layout add to the pleasure of your day spent here, and the best players in your group will enjoy a good round without having to dig too deeply into their reserves.

Très animée le soir, cette charmante petite ville est un grand centre touristique, un lieu de séjour idéal pour explorer les lacs du National Park, les monts du Kerry... et pour aller jouer les prestigieux parcours du Sud-Ouest. Les deux 18 trous de Killarney en font partie, et les joueurs ont souvent une petite préférence sentimentale pour celui-ci, notamment pour les trois derniers trous, dont le magnifique 18, un par 3 difficile et magnifiquement situé le long du Lough Leane : il faut s'arranger pour le jouer au coucher du soleil, quand les forêts environnantes prennent leurs couleurs d'automne (jouer Killeen le matin). Assez court, ce parcours est moins difficile à négocier qu'il n'y paraît à première vue, mais il réclame un petit jeu attentif, car les greens sont bien défendus. La beauté de l'environnement, des arbres et du dessin ajoute au plaisir de la journée, et les meilleurs joueurs du groupe auront plaisir à briller sans trop puiser dans leurs réserves.

Killarney Golf Club — 1891
O'Mahoney's Point
IRL - KILLARNEY, Co Kerry

Office	Secrétariat	(353) 064 - 31 034
Pro shop	Pro-shop	(353) 064 - 31 165
Fax	Fax	(353) 064 - 33 065
Situation	Situation	

3 km from Killarney (pop. 7 275)

Annual closure	Fermeture annuelle	no
Weekly closure	Fermeture hebdomadaire	no

Fees main season
Tarifs haute saison 18 holes

	Week days Semaine	We/Bank holidays We/Férié
Individual Individuel	IR£ 38	IR£ 38
Couple Couple	IR£ 76	IR£ 76

Caddy	Caddy	IR£ 15/18 holes
Electric Trolley	Chariot électrique	no
Buggy	Voiturette	no
Clubs	Clubs	IR£ 11/18 holes

Credit cards Cartes de crédit
VISA - Eurocard - MasterCard - AMEX - DC

KILLORGLIN
Cill Orglan
R 563
R 562
River Laune
GOLF
KILLARNEY
Cill Airne
CORK
Corcaigh
Inishfallen
Abbey
Lough
Leane
Nature
Reserve
0   2   4 km
0   2,5 miles
KENMARE
Neidin
Muckross
Lake
N 71

Access Accès : Killarney W, 3 km on R562 → Killorglin
Map 2 on page 828 Carte 2 Page 828

GOLF COURSE / PARCOURS — 15/20

Site	Site	▬▬▬▬▬▬□
Maintenance	Entretien	▬▬▬▬▬▬□
Architect	Architecte	Sir Guy Campbell
Type	Type	parkland
Relief	Relief	▬□□□□□
Water in play	Eau en jeu	▬▬▬□□□
Exp. to wind	Exposé au vent	▬▬▬▬□□
Trees in play	Arbres en jeu	▬▬▬▬□□

Scorecard Carte de score	Chp. Chp.	Mens Mess.	Ladies Da.
Length Long.	6164	5826	4932
Par	72	72	74

Advised golfing ability		0 12 24 36
Niveau de jeu recommandé		▬▬▬▬▬▬
Hcp required	Handicap exigé	28 Men, 36 Ladies

CLUB HOUSE & AMENITIES / CLUB HOUSE ET ANNEXES — 7/10

Pro shop	Pro-shop	▬▬▬▬▬□
Driving range	Practice	▬▬▬▬□□
Sheltered	couvert	no
On grass	sur herbe	yes
Putting-green	putting-green	yes
Pitching-green	pitching green	no

881

HOTEL FACILITIES / ENVIRONNEMENT HOTELIER — 8/10

HOTELS HÔTELS
Europe Hotel — Killarney
205 rooms, D IR£ 132 — 1 km
Tel (353) 064 - 31 900, Fax (353) 064 - 32 118

Castlerosse Hotel — Killarney
114 rooms, D IR£ 110 — 1 km
Tel (353) 064 - 31 144, Fax (353) 064 - 31 031

Aghadoe Heights — Killarney
60 rooms, D IR£ 165 — 1 km
Tel (353) 064 - 31 766, Fax (353) 064 - 31 345

Ard Na Sidhe — Caragh Lake, Killorglin
20 rooms, D IR£ 158 — 22 km
Tel (353) 066 - 69 105, Fax (353) 066 - 69 282

RESTAURANTS RESTAURANTS
Dingle's - Tel (353) 064 - 31 079 — Killarney 4 km
Failte Restaurant - Tel (353) 064 - 33 404 — Killarney 4 km

As the courses in this region are very busy, catering to not only tourists but also the locals, this recent course was more than welcome. It was designed by the busiest of all Irish designers, Eddie Hackett. Running on the side of hill, the terrain overlooks Dingle Bay (the weaker souls will find the course tiring to walk) and gives golfers some pretty viewpoints over the estuary, the Slieve Mish Mountains opposite and Macgillicuddy's Reeks to the west. Although not outstanding, Killorglin is well worth a visit, especially for a round with friends or the family, without undue suffering (except, of course, when the wind gets up). The difficulties are easily seen but are more psychological than real. You can even play to your handicap first time round, providing you don't misjudge your approach shots - some greens are elevated, others multi-tiered.

Les parcours de la région étant très fréquentés, non seulement par les touristes, mais aussi par la clientèle locale, ce récent parcours était plus que bienvenu. C'est le plus occupé des architectes irlandais, Eddie Hackett, qui en est l'auteur. À flanc de colline, le terrain domine la baie de Dingle (les plus fatigués souffriront à pied), ce qui offre aux joueurs quelques jolis points de vue sur cet estuaire, comme sur les Slieve Mish Mountains en face et, à l'ouest, sur les Macgilliguddy Reeks. Sans être exceptionnel, le parcours de Killorglin mérite la visite, notamment pour y faire une partie amicale ou en famille, sans trop souffrir, sauf quand le vent souffle fort, bien sûr. Les difficultés sont aisément identifiables, mais sont plus psychologiques que réelles. Dès la première fois, on peut y jouer son handicap, à condition de bien juger ses approches : certains greens sont surélevés et quelques-uns à plateaux.

Killorglin Golf Club — 1992

Stealroe
IRL - KILLORGLIN, Co. Kerry

Office	Secrétariat	(353) 066 - 61 979
Pro shop	Pro-shop	(353) 066 - 61 979
Fax	Fax	(353) 066 - 61 437
Situation	Situation	

21 km from Killarney (pop. 7 275)
24 km from Tralee (pop. 17 225)

Annual closure	Fermeture annuelle	no
Weekly closure	Fermeture hebdomadaire	no
Fees main season	Tarifs haute saison	18 holes

	Week days Semaine	We/Bank holidays We/Férié
Individual Individuel	IR£ 14	IR£ 16
Couple Couple	IR£ 28	IR£ 32

Caddy	Caddy	on request/IR£ 10
Electric Trolley	Chariot électrique	no
Buggy	Voiturette	no
Clubs	Clubs	IR£ 10

Credit cards Cartes de crédit
VISA - Eurocard - MasterCard - AMEX

Access Accès : Killarney, N72 W to Killorglin. Killorglin bridge, turn right on N70. Golf, 1.6 km.
Map 2 on page 828 Carte 2 Page 828

GOLF COURSE
PARCOURS — 14/20

Site	Site	
Maintenance	Entretien	
Architect	Architecte	Eddie Hackett
Type	Type	parkland
Relief	Relief	
Water in play	Eau en jeu	
Exp. to wind	Exposé au vent	
Trees in play	Arbres en jeu	

Scorecard Carte de score	Chp. Chp.	Mens Mess.	Ladies Da.
Length Long.	5821	5358	4678
Par	72	72	74

Advised golfing ability		0 12 24 36
Niveau de jeu recommandé		
Hcp required	Handicap exigé	no

CLUB HOUSE & AMENITIES
CLUB HOUSE ET ANNEXES — 6/10

Pro shop	Pro-shop	
Driving range	Practice	
Sheltered	couvert	no
On grass	sur herbe	no
Putting-green	putting-green	no
Pitching-green	pitching green	yes

HOTEL FACILITIES
ENVIRONNEMENT HOTELIER — 5/10

HOTELS HÔTELS

Bianconi — Killorglin
15 rooms, D IR£ 50 — 1.6 km
Tel (353) 066 - 61 146, Fax (353) 066 - 61 950

Dunloe Castle — Killarney
120 rooms, D IR£ 120 — 14 km
Tel (353) 064 - 44 111, Fax (353) 064 - 44 583

Europe — Killarney
205 rooms, D IR£ 125 — 17 km
Tel (353) 064 - 31 900, Fax (353) 064 - 32 118

RESTAURANTS RESTAURANTS

Bianconi — Killorglin
Tel (353) 066 - 61 146 — 1.6 km

The Fishery — Killorglin
Tel (353) 066 - 61 670 — 1.6 km

882

LAHINCH

Lahinch has long held pride of place in the collection of great courses in south-west Ireland. The surrounding dunes invite visual comparison with Ballybunion, although it is not quite as challenging. For example, if you can keep on the straight and narrow here, approach shots to the greens are altogether an easier matter, with bump and run shots a distinct possibility. But you need to know the course to cope, to appreciate the effects of the wind, to identify where hazards are placed and to come to terms with the sand-dunes, where balls can end up in some unusual positions. Care is rewarded on this spectacular layout, where high variety is the watchword and where flighters of the ball will have fun (beginners probably much less so). Look out for the extraordinary 5th and 6th holes, the first a par 5, where the second shot has to fly over a huge dune, the latter a par 3 with a blind green.

Dans la collection des grands parcours du sud-ouest de l'Irlande, Lahinch tient depuis longtemps une belle place. Son environnement de grandes dunes le rapproche visuellement de Ballybunion, bien qu'il ne soit pas aussi exigeant. Par exemple, si l'on parvient à rester droit, les approches des greens y sont moins complexes, ceux-ci étant généralement accessibles avec des coups roulés. Mais il faut bien connaître ce parcours pour le négocier, apprécier les effets du vent, identifier la place des obstacles, composer avec les dunes, où la balle peut se trouver dans des situations «intéressantes». La prudence sera récompensée sur ce tracé spectaculaire et d'une très grande variété, où les virtuoses des effets de balle s'amuseront beaucoup (les débutants beaucoup moins). A signaler, les extraordinaires trous 5 et 6, un par 5 où le second coup doit survoler une énorme dune, et un par 3 avec un green aveugle.

Lahinch Golf Club — 1892
IRL - LAHINCH, Co Clare

Office	Secrétariat	(353) 065 - 81 003
Pro shop	Pro-shop	(353) 065 - 81 408
Fax	Fax	(353) 065 - 81 592
Situation	Situation	

0.5 km from Lahinch (pop. 550)
32 km from Ennis (pop. 13 730)

Annual closure	Fermeture annuelle	no
Weekly closure	Fermeture hebdomadaire	no
Fees main season	Tarifs haute saison	18 holes

	Week days Semaine	We/Bank holidays We/Férié
Individual Individuel	IR£ 45	IR£ 45
Couple Couple	IR£ 90	IR£ 90
Green-fees on Castle Course: IR£ 25		
Caddy	Caddy	IR£ 15/18 holes
Electric Trolley	Chariot électrique	IR£ 7,50
Buggy	Voiturette	no
Clubs	Clubs	IR£ 12/18 holes

Credit cards Cartes de crédit
VISA - Eurocard - MasterCard

Access Accès : N18 Limerick → Ennis,
N85 Ennis → Ennistymon, → Lahinch, 3 km
Map 2 on page 828 Carte 2 Page 828

GOLF COURSE / PARCOURS — 17/20

Site	Site	
Maintenance	Entretien	
Architect	Architecte	Old Tom Morris
		Alistair MacKenzie
Type	Type	links
Relief	Relief	
Water in play	Eau en jeu	
Exp. to wind	Exposé au vent	
Trees in play	Arbres en jeu	

Scorecard Carte de score	Chp. Chp.	Mens Mess.	Ladies Da.
Length Long.	6123	5890	4997
Par	72	72	74

Advised golfing ability Niveau de jeu recommandé	0 12 24 36
Hcp required Handicap exigé	28 Men, 36 Ladies

CLUB HOUSE & AMENITIES / CLUB HOUSE ET ANNEXES — 6/10

Pro shop	Pro-shop	
Driving range	Practice	
Sheltered	couvert	no
On grass	sur herbe	yes
Putting-green	putting-green	yes
Pitching-green	pitching green	no

HOTEL FACILITIES / ENVIRONNEMENT HOTELIER — 6/10

HOTELS HÔTELS

Aberdeen Arms — Lahinch
55 rooms, D IR£ — 5
Tel (353) 065 - 81 100, Fax (353) 065 - 81 228

Atlantic Hotel — Lahinch
14 rooms, D IR£ 50 — 5
Tel (353) 065 - 81 049, Fax (353) 065 - 81 029

Falls Hotel — Ennistymon
100 rooms, D IR£ 50 — 3 km
Tel (353) 065 - 71 004, Fax (353) 065 - 71 367

RESTAURANTS RESTAURANTS

Mr Eamons — Lahinch
Tel (353) 065 - 81 050 — 2

Aberdeen Arms — Lahinch
Tel (353) 065 - 81 100 — 5

883

LEE VALLEY

13	7	6

A rather hilly site for players out of condition or those who have taken a little too kindly to delicious Irish food and drink. Over this pleasantly landscaped and country style terrain, Christy O'Connor Jnr has produced a perfectly honest layout, where good shots are rewarded. It still needs getting to know to cope with some tricky holes, like the 10th or the tough 18th, to keep away from the numerous water hazards (on the 8th and 15th especially), and to read the greens, which are sometimes a real handful. There are many different tee-off areas, so the course adjusts easily to players of all abilities and to how you might be feeling on any one particular day. Lee Valley will present its final face once the trees have grown, but it is already one of the busiest courses in the region, which goes to prove that players like to come back here.

Un site parfois bien accidenté pour les joueurs en forme physique moyenne... ou qui auront un peu trop goûté les spécialités irlandaises. Sur ce terrain au paysage très agréable et campagnard, mais pas idéal pour un golf, Christy O'Connor Jr a produit un dessin d'une parfaite honnêteté, où les bons coups de golf sont récompensés, même si une bonne connaissance du terrain permet de mieux négocier quelques trous, comme le 10 ou le difficile 18, d'échapper aux nombreux obstacles d'eau, au 8 et au 15 notamment, et enfin de bien interpréter les greens, parfois d'une grande subtilité. La multiplicité des départs permet d'adapter facilement le parcours à tous les niveaux de jeu, ou à l'inspiration du jour. Lee Valley prendra son véritable visage quand tous les arbres auront poussé, mais c'est déjà l'un des parcours les plus fréquentés de la région, ce qui prouve que les joueurs aiment y revenir.

Lee Valley Golf & Country Club — 1993

Clashanure
IRL - OVENS, Co Cork

Office	Secrétariat	(353) 021 - 331 721
Pro shop	Pro-shop	(353) 021 - 331 758
Fax	Fax	(353) 021 - 331 695
Situation	Situation	

14 km from Cork (pop. 174 400)
10 km from Blarney (pop. 2 043)

Annual closure	Fermeture annuelle	no
Weekly closure	Fermeture hebdomadaire	no

Fees main season	Tarifs haute saison	18 holes
	Week days Semaine	We/Bank holidays We/Férié
Individual Individuel	IR£ 25	IR£ 27
Couple Couple	IR£ 50	IR£ 54

IR£ 15 before 10.30 am

Caddy	Caddy	on request/IR£ 12
Electric Trolley	Chariot électrique	IR£ 6
Buggy	Voiturette	IR£ 25/18 holes
Clubs	Clubs	IR£ 10/18 holes

Credit cards Cartes de crédit
VISA - MasterCard - AMEX

884

```
                0    2    4 km
                |----|----|
                0     2,5 miles

   GOLF
        ⊕                    CORK
       St Senan's Abbey     Corcaigh
                          CORK HARBOUR
   N 22   Ovens        BALLINCOLLIG
                       Baile an Chollaig
   ← Killarney
     Cill Airne                    N 71
                       Bandon
                       Droichead na Bandan
```

Access Accès : Cork, N22 → Killarney.
At Ballincolig, → Ovens
Map 2 on page 828 Carte 2 Page 828

GOLF COURSE / PARCOURS — 13/20

Site	Site	
Maintenance	Entretien	
Architect	Architecte	Christy O'Connor Jr
Type	Type	parkland, hilly
Relief	Relief	
Water in play	Eau en jeu	
Exp. to wind	Exposé au vent	
Trees in play	Arbres en jeu	

Scorecard Carte de score	Chp. Chp.	Mens Mess.	Ladies Da.
Length Long.	6050	5795	4900
Par	72	72	72

Advised golfing ability		0	12	24	36
Niveau de jeu recommandé					
Hcp required	Handicap exigé	24 Men, 36 Ladies			

CLUB HOUSE & AMENITIES / CLUB HOUSE ET ANNEXES — 7/10

Pro shop	Pro-shop	
Driving range	Practice	
Sheltered	couvert	15 mats
On grass	sur herbe	yes
Putting-green	putting-green	yes
Pitching-green	pitching green	yes

HOTEL FACILITIES / ENVIRONNEMENT HOTELIER — 6/10

HOTELS HÔTELS

Blarney Park Hotel — Blarney
65 rooms, D IR£ 60 — 10 km
Tel (353) 021 - 385 281
Fax (353) 021 - 381 506

Oriel House Hotel — Ballincollig
10 rooms, D IR£ 40 — 6 km
Tel (353) 021 - 870 888
Fax (353) 021 - 397 760

RESTAURANTS RESTAURANTS

Clashanure — Lee Valley GC
Tel (353) 021 - 331 721 — on site

Christys — Blarney
Tel (353) 021 - 385 011 — 12 km

15 7 6

The cottages on site are an excellent base camp for exploring the courses in this region, especially this one. Des Smyth has used the terrain to good effect, but we will have to wait until the trees grow to see how it will look in the end. For the moment, the saplings are obviously not a problem, but the same cannot be said for the collection of bunkers and obligatory water hazards found on modern courses. Very difficult from the back tees, it is a little kinder further forward, from where we recommend you play unless you are a long driver. A few tees and greens are played blind, which requires good knowledge of the course to fix any definite strategy, especially on the back 9, which happens to be much flatter than the first half of the course. The greens are hospitable but certain pin positions can make them a tricky proposition. This very competent layout is already rated amongst the country's top twenty or thirty inland courses.

Les cottages sur place en font une bonne base pour explorer les golfs de la région, et notamment celui-ci. Des Smyth a bien utilisé le terrain, mais il faudra attendre qu'il prenne son visage définitif, le temps que grandissent les nombreux arbres plantés. Pour l'instant, ils ne sont pas un facteur de difficulté, au contraire de la collection de bunkers et d'obstacles d'eau incontournables dans les parcours modernes. Très difficile des départs arrière, il est plus amical des autres, on les conseillera, à moins d'avoir affaire à de bons frappeurs. Quelques départs et greens sont aveugles, imposant une bonne connaissance du parcours pour avoir une stratégie précise, notamment au retour, qui est en revanche plus plat que l'aller. Les greens sont accueillants, mais certaines positions de drapeau peuvent les rendre très délicats. Cette très solide réalisation figure déjà parmi les vingt ou trente meilleurs parcours inland du pays.

Limerick County
Golf & Country Club
1994

IRL - BALLYNEETY, Co Limerick

Office	Secrétariat	(353) 061 - 351 881
Pro shop	Pro-shop	(353) 061 - 351 881
Fax	Fax	(353) 061 - 351 384
Situation	Situation	

11 km from Limerick (pop. 52 083)

Annual closure	Fermeture annuelle	no
Weekly closure	Fermeture hebdomadaire	no

Fees main season
Tarifs haute saison 18 holes

	Week days Semaine	We/Bank holidays We/Férié
Individual Individuel	IR£ 20	IR£ 25
Couple Couple	IR£ 40	IR£ 50

Weekdays: IR£ 12.50 before 9.30 am

Caddy	Caddy	on request/IR£ 12
Electric Trolley	Chariot électrique	no
Buggy	Voiturette	IR£ 20/18 holes
Clubs	Clubs	IR£ 10/18 holes
Credit cards Cartes de crédit		VISA - MasterCard

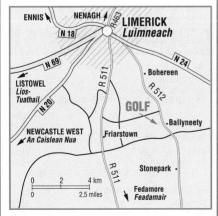

Access Accès : Limerick, R512
Map 2 on page 828 Carte 2 Page 828

GOLF COURSE
PARCOURS
15/20

Site	Site	
Maintenance	Entretien	
Architect	Architecte	Des Smyth
Type	Type	parkland
Relief	Relief	
Water in play	Eau en jeu	
Exp. to wind	Exposé au vent	
Trees in play	Arbres en jeu	

Scorecard	Chp.	Mens	Ladies
Carte de score	Chp.	Mess.	Da.
Length Long.	6194	5784	5050
Par	72	72	73

Advised golfing ability	0	12	24	36
Niveau de jeu recommandé				
Hcp required	Handicap exigé		28 Men, 36 Ladies	

CLUB HOUSE & AMENITIES
CLUB HOUSE ET ANNEXES
7/10

Pro shop	Pro-shop	
Driving range	Practice	
Sheltered	couvert	20 mats
On grass	sur herbe	yes
Putting-green	putting-green	yes
Pitching-green	pitching green	yes

885

HOTEL FACILITIES
ENVIRONNEMENT HOTELIER
6/10

HOTELS HÔTELS

Castletroy Park Hotel — Limerick
107 rooms, D IR£ 120 — 8 km
Tel (353) 061 - 335 566, Fax (353) 061 - 335 117

Jurys Hotel — Limerick
95 rooms, D IR£ 90 — 11 km
Tel (353) 061 - 327 77, Fax (353) 061 - 326 400

Limerick Ryan Hotel — Limerick
180 rooms, D IR£ 70 — 11 km
Tel (353) 061 - 453 922, Fax (353) 061 - 326 333

RESTAURANTS RESTAURANTS

Moll Darby's — Limerick
Tel (353) 061 - 411 511 — 11 km

Freddy's Bistro — Limerick
Tel (353) 061 - 418 749 — 11 km

In the grounds of a famous castle hotel, whose illustrious guests have included Queen Victoria, Fred Astaire, Ronald Reagan and Rainiers of Monaco, this recent course was designed by Nicholas Bielenberg. It is laid out in a huge park, where age-old trees add beauty and majesty to a matchless atmosphere of tranquility. The few straight up and down holes are rather a pity, although the fairways are clearly separated by trees and water. These two elements are the main hazards here, especially the many lakes and ponds, which call for long, lofted shots (on about half a dozen holes). This might not be too much to the liking of high-handicappers, but target golf buffs will have fun. The geographical relief is only very slight and enough to give each hole clear definition. Very long from the tiger-tees, this is a stiff challenge for any golfer, although much more approachable from the front tees.

Dans le domaine d'un célèbre Château-hôtel, qui a reçu des gloires telles que la Reine Victoria, Fred Astaire, Ronald Reagan ou Rainier de Monaco, ce récent parcours a été dessiné par Nicholas Bielenberg, dans un immense parc avec des arbres centenaires, qui ajoutent leur beauté et leur majesté à une atmosphère incomparable de tranquillité. On peut regretter certains allers et retours du tracé, malgré que les fairways soient bien séparés par les bois et l'eau. Ces deux éléments constituent des difficultés évidentes, notamment les nombreux lacs et mares, qui obligent souvent à porter la balle (sur une demi-douzaine de trous environ). Si cela ne plaira guère aux handicaps élevés, les habitués du «target golf» auront de quoi s'amuser. Le relief est très modéré, et suffisant pour assurer une bonne définition des trous. Très long des départs de championnat, ce parcours reste un «challenge», mais plus abordable, des départs avancés.

Luttrellstown Golf & Country Club — 1993
IRL - CLONSILLA, Co Dublin

Office	Secrétariat	(353) 01 - 808 9988
Pro shop	Pro-shop	(353) 01 - 808 9988
Fax	Fax	(353) 01 - 820 5218
Situation	Situation	

10 km from Dublin (pop. 859 976)

Annual closure	Fermeture annuelle	no
Weekly closure	Fermeture hebdomadaire	no

Fees main season
Tarifs haute saison 18 holes

	Week days Semaine	We/Bank holidays We/Férié
Individual Individuel	IR£ 40	IR£ 45
Couple Couple	IR£ 80	IR£ 90

Caddy	Caddy	on request/IR£ 20
Electric Trolley	Chariot électrique	no
Buggy	Voiturette	IR£ 25/18 holes
Clubs	Clubs	IR£ 10/18 holes

Credit cards Cartes de crédit
VISA - MasterCard - AMEX - DC

886

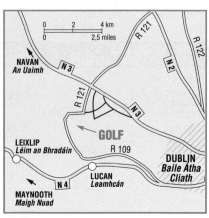

Access Accès : 10 km NW from Dublin
on N3 → Clonsilla
Map 3 on page 830 Carte 3 Page 830

GOLF COURSE / PARCOURS — 15/20

Site	Site	
Maintenance	Entretien	
Architect	Architecte	Nicholas Bielenberg
Type	Type	parkland
Relief	Relief	
Water in play	Eau en jeu	
Exp. to wind	Exposé au vent	
Trees in play	Arbres en jeu	

Scorecard Carte de score	Chp. Chp.	Mens Mess.	Ladies Da.
Length Long.	6384	6032	5246
Par	72	72	72

Advised golfing ability Niveau de jeu recommandé	0	12	24	36

Hcp required Handicap exigé — 24 Men, 36 Ladies

CLUB HOUSE & AMENITIES / CLUB HOUSE ET ANNEXES — 7/10

Pro shop	Pro-shop	
Driving range	Practice	
Sheltered	couvert	no
On grass	sur herbe	yes
Putting-green	putting-green	yes
Pitching-green	pitching green	no

HOTEL FACILITIES / ENVIRONNEMENT HOTELIER — 7/10

HOTELS HÔTELS

Burlington Hotel — Dublin
451 rooms, D IR£ 160 — 10 km
Tel (353) 01 - 660 5222, Fax (353) 01 - 660 3172

Jurys Christchurch Inn — Dublin
182 rooms, D IR£ 64 — 10 km
Tel (353) 01 - 475 0111, Fax (353) 01 - 475 0488

West County Hotel — Lucan
50 rooms, D IR£ 74 — 5 km
Tel (353) 01 - 626 4011, Fax (353) 01 - 623 1378

RESTAURANTS RESTAURANTS

Annadale — Lucan
Tel (353) 01 - 628 0622 — 4 km

Scott's — Castleknock
Tel (353) 01 - 821 3482 — 3 km

If you want to play every Eddie Hackett course in Ireland, you sure have a lot of golfing to do. With the experience of age, he was very kind here with the average week-enders, who return the compliment and come to play here in droves on 27 holes combinable in every different way. In addition to the actual layout, the wind and wetness of the terrain can seriously dent any hopes of a good card. First time around, a number of blinds shots should require some reconnaissance work, but the course is by no means hilly. Bunkering is high quality, as is the use of water hazards, especially on the par 3s. Another side to the course's resistance is the elevation of certain greens, calling for some accurate ironwork. Once on the green, the surfaces are easy to read (perhaps too easy ?). A recent course, Malahide needs time to mature but is already good fun in amongst the region's great links courses.

Si vous voulez jouer tous les parcours d'Eddie Hackett en Irlande, vous n'avez pas fini... Avec l'expérience de l'âge, il a été ici très amical avec les golfeurs moyens : ils se lui rendent bien et viennent nombreux sur les 27 trous, combinables à volonté. En dehors du tracé lui-même, le vent et l'humidité du terrain peuvent perturber les prétentions à bien scorer. La première fois, certains coups aveugles nécessitent une certaine reconnaissance, mais le parcours est facilement jouable à pied. Le «bunkering» est de grande qualité, de même que l'utilisation des obstacles d'eau, notamment sur les pars 3. Autre facteur de résistance du parcours, l'élévation de certains greens, qui oblige à des coups de fer très exacts, mais les surfaces de putting ne sont guère complexes à lire (pas assez ?). De construction récente, Malahide a besoin de prendre de la maturité, c'est déjà une bonne récréation entre les grands links de la région.

Malahide Golf Club — 1991
Beechwood, The Grange
IRL - MALAHIDE, Co Dublin

Office	Secrétariat	(353) 01 - 846 1611
Pro shop	Pro-shop	(353) 01 - 846 0002
Fax	Fax	(353) 01 - 846 1270
Situation	Situation	

18 km from Dublin (pop 859 976)

Annual closure	Fermeture annnuelle	no
Weekly closure	Fermeture hebdomadaire	no

Fees main season
Tarifs haute saison 18 holes

	Week days Semaine	We/Bank holidays We/Férié
Individual Individuel	IR£ 30	IR£ 40
Couple Couple	IR£ 55	IR£ 75

Caddy	Caddy	on request/IR£ 25
Electric Trolley	Chariot électrique	no
Buggy	Voiturette	no
Clubs	Clubs	IR£ 15

Credit cards Cartes de crédit
VISA - Eurocard - MasterCard - AMEX

Access Accès : Dublin to Portmarnock Village. Left turn at traffic lights beside Church. Golf 3 km from there.
Map 3 on page 830 Carte 3 Page 830

GOLF COURSE PARCOURS — 13/20

Site	Site	
Maintenance	Entretien	
Architect	Architecte	Eddie Hackett
Type	Type	parkland
Relief	Relief	
Water in play	Eau en jeu	
Exp. to wind	Exposé au vent	
Trees in play	Arbres en jeu	

Scorecard Carte de score	Chp. Chp.	Mens Mess.	Ladies Da.
Length Long.	6066	5742	5146
Par	71	70	74

Advised golfing ability Niveau de jeu recommandé	0	12	24	36
Hcp required	Handicap exigé	Men 28, Ladies 36		

CLUB HOUSE & AMENITIES CLUB HOUSE ET ANNEXES — 7/10

Pro shop	Pro-shop	
Driving range	Practice	
Sheltered	couvert	no
On grass	sur herbe	yes
Putting-green	putting-green	yes
Pitching-green	pitching green	no

887

HOTEL FACILITIES ENVIRONNEMENT HOTELIER — 8/10

HOTELS HÔTELS
Grand Hotel — Malahide
100 rooms, D IR£ 95 — 1 km
Tel (353) 01 - 845 0000, Fax (353) 01 - 845 0987

Portmarnock Links Hotel — Portmarnock
110 rooms, D IR£ 190 — 4 km
Tel (353) 01 - 846 0611, Fax (353) 01 - 846 2442

Sands Hotel — Portmarnock
10 rooms, D IR£ 70 — 2 km
Tel (353) 01 - 846 0003, Fax (353) 01 - 846 0420

RESTAURANTS RESTAURANTS
Bon Appetit — Malahide
Tel (353) 01 - 845 0314 — 1 km

Colonnade — Malahide
Tel (353) 01 - 845 0000 — 1 km

MONKSTOWN

15 6 7

This course was built in the early 20th century then restyled in 1971, but it remains on the short side, probably much to the pleasure of the majority of golfers, no matter how modern their equipment. The two parts of the course are distinctly different, with the outward 9 overlooking Cork harbour. Indeed, variety is one of the course's strong points, giving numerous opportunities to try different shots. The majority of hazards are clearly visible from the tee, but the architects could not or would not avoid a number of blind shots, imposed by the sloping terrain. The overall topology and the position of trees call for some long, hard thinking, as do the 80 bunkers, all of which are very much in play. Add to this the setting provided by an old 17th century castle and the excellence of the greens - long considered to be the best in the country - and you will understand why Monkstown deserves to find out just how good a golfer you are.

Créé au début du XXème siècle, ce parcours a été remanié en 1971, mais est resté assez court, ce qui n'est pas pour déplaire à la majorité des joueurs, quel que soit leur armement golfique moderne. Les deux parties de ce parcours sont sensiblement différentes, avec les 9 premiers trous dominant le port de Cork. La variété est d'ailleurs l'un des points forts de ce tracé, ce qui offre parallèlement une très grande variété d'occasions de coups différents. La plus grande partie des obstacles sont bien visibles du départ, mais les architectes n'ont pas pu ou voulu éviter certains coups aveugles, que la configuration du terrain pouvait imposer. Les contours du terrain comme la position des arbres imposent une certaine réflexion, de même que la présence de 80 bunkers dont aucun n'est en dehors du jeu. Si l'on ajoute le décor formé par un vieux château du XVIIè siècle et la qualité des greens, longtemps considérés comme les meilleurs du pays, on aura compris que Monkstown mérite de connaître la qualité de votre golf.

Monkstown Golf Club — 1908

Parkgarry
IRL - MONKSTOWN, Co. Cork

Office	Secrétariat	(353) 021 - 841 376
Pro shop	Pro-shop	(353) 021 - 841 686
Fax	Fax	(353) 021 - 841 376
Situation	Situation	

Cork (pop. 174 400), 12 km

Annual closure	Fermeture annuelle	no
Weekly closure	Fermeture hebdomadaire	no

Fees main season	Tarifs haute saison	18 holes
	Week days	We/Bank holidays
	Semaine	We/Férié
Individual Individuel	IR£ 23	IR£ 26
Couple Couple	IR£ 46	IR£ 52

Caddy	Caddy	IR£ 20
Electric Trolley	Chariot électrique	no
Buggy	Voiturette	IR£ 20
Clubs	Clubs	IR£ 12

Credit cards Cartes de crédit
VISA - MasterCard - AMEX - DC

Access Accès : Cork, South East along
R610 → Glenbrook/Monkstown
Map 2 on page 828 Carte 2 Page 828

GOLF COURSE / PARCOURS — 15/20

Site	Site	
Maintenance	Entretien	
Architect	Architecte	Peter O'Hare
		T. Carey, B. Murphy
Type	Type	parkland
Relief	Relief	
Water in play	Eau en jeu	
Exp. to wind	Exposé au vent	
Trees in play	Arbres en jeu	

Scorecard	Chp.	Mens	Ladies
Carte de score	Chp.	Mess.	Da.
Length Long.	5669	5441	4862
Par	70	70	73

Advised golfing ability — 0 12 24 36
Niveau de jeu recommandé
Hcp required — Handicap exigé — no

CLUB HOUSE & AMENITIES / CLUB HOUSE ET ANNEXES — 6/10

Pro shop	Pro-shop	
Driving range	Practice	
Sheltered	couvert	no
On grass	sur herbe	yes (practice area)
Putting-green	putting-green	yes
Pitching-green	pitching green	yes

HOTEL FACILITIES / ENVIRONNEMENT HOTELIER — 7/10

HOTELS HÔTELS
Rochestown Park — Cork
115 rooms, D IR£ 80 — 6 km
Tel (353) 021 - 892 233, Fax (353) 021 - 892 178

Metropole Hotel — Cork
113 rooms, D IR£ 70 — 10 km
Tel (353) 021 - 508 122, Fax (353) 021 - 506 450

Maryborough House Hotel — Cork
57 rooms, D IR£ 100 — 6 km
Tel (353) 021 - 365 555, Fax (353) 021 - 365 662

Redclyffe Guest House — Cork
13 rooms, D IR£ 40 — 15 km
Tel (353) 021 - 273 220, Fax (353) 021 - 811 373

RESTAURANTS RESTAURANTs
The Bosun — Monkstown 3 km
Gregory's — Carrigaline 12 km

888

There is hardly a country in the world where Jack Nicklaus has not left his mark as a course designer, with, it should be said, mixed success. If he claims to be the greatest course designer, our reply is that there are probably many better than he around the world. It all depends on what a designer can squeeze out of a given space. At Mount Juliet, Nicklaus was presented with a magnificent estate, profusely covered with oak, lime and beech trees. A lot of use has been found for water (there is even a waterfall) and very US-style bunkers, or sand-traps, as they say. The greens, vast and well-designed, only add to the difficulties of a course which demands a complete game from start to finish and, in particular an aptitude for target golf. The many different tee-off areas cater to players of differing abilities, but given the overall length the back-tees should most definitely be reserved for single-figure handicappers. Spectacular and remarkable intelligent, this is an excellent Nicklaus vintage.

Il n'est guère de pays au monde où Jack Nicklaus n'ait laissé sa trace en tant qu'architecte, avec - il faut bien le dire - des bonheurs divers. Et s'il annonce vouloir être le plus grand architecte, on répondra qu'il y a beaucoup de meilleurs architectes du monde ! Tout dépend du parti qu'ils tirent d'un espace. A Mount Juliet, il a trouvé une magnifique propriété, généreusement occupée par les chênes, les tilleuls, les hêtres. Un généreux usage a été fait de l'eau (il y a même une cascade), et de bunkers au profil très américain. Et les greens eux-mêmes, vastes et bien travaillés, ajoutent aux difficultés : ce parcours exige un jeu complet, du départ au dernier trou, et singulièrement un jeu de «target golf». La diversité des départs permet de l'adapter aux possibilités des joueurs, mais sa longueur réserve les départs arrière aux handicaps à un chiffre. Spectaculaire et remarquablement intelligent, c'est un excellent Nicklaus...

Mount Juliet Golf Club — 1991
IRL - THOMASTOWN, Co Kilkenny

Office	Secrétariat	(353) 056 - 24 455
Pro shop	Pro-shop	(353) 056 - 24 455
Fax	Fax	(353) 056 - 24 522
Situation	Situation	

16 km from Kilkenny (pop. 8 515)

Annual closure	Fermeture annuelle	no
Weekly closure	Fermeture hebdomadaire	no

Fees main season	Tarifs haute saison	18 holes
	Week days Semaine	We/Bank holidays We/Férié
Individual Individuel	IR£ 70	IR£ 75
Couple Couple	IR£ 140	IR£ 150

Early or late tee-times (off peak hours): IR£ 40

Caddy	Caddy	on request/IR£ 16
Electric Trolley	Chariot électrique	no
Buggy	Voiturette	no
Clubs	Clubs	IR£ 15/18 holes

Credit cards Cartes de crédit
VISA - MasterCard - AMEX - DC

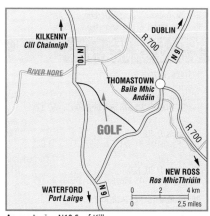

KILKENNY
Cill Chainnigh
N 10
RIVER NORE
DUBLIN
R 700
N 9
THOMASTOWN
Baile Mhic
Andáin
GOLF
R 700
NEW ROSS
Ros MhicThriúin
WATERFORD
Port Lairge
N 9
0   2   4 km
0   2,5 miles

Access Accès : N10 S. of Kilkenny
N9 S. of Carlow
Map 2 on page 829 Carte 2 Page 829

GOLF COURSE PARCOURS — 18/20

Site	Site	▬▬▬▬□
Maintenance	Entretien	▬▬▬▬□
Architect	Architecte	Jack Nicklaus
Type	Type	parkland
Relief	Relief	▬▬▬□□
Water in play	Eau en jeu	▬▬▬▬□
Exp. to wind	Exposé au vent	▬▬▬□□
Trees in play	Arbres en jeu	▬▬▬▬□

Scorecard Carte de score	Chp. Chp.	Mens Mess.	Ladies Da.
Length Long.	7111	6705	5554
Par	72	72	73

Advised golfing ability Niveau de jeu recommandé	0	12	24	36
Hcp required Handicap exigé	28 Men, 36 Ladies			

CLUB HOUSE & AMENITIES CLUB HOUSE ET ANNEXES — 9/10

Pro shop	Pro-shop	▬▬▬▬□
Driving range	Practice	▬▬▬▬□
Sheltered	couvert	5 bays
On grass	sur herbe	yes
Putting-green	putting-green	yes
Pitching-green	pitching green	yes

HOTEL FACILITIES ENVIRONNEMENT HOTELIER — 8/10

HOTELS HÔTELS

Mount Juliet House		Thomastown
32 rooms, D from IR£ 120		on site
Tel (353) 056 - 24 455, Fax (353) 056 - 24 522		

Hunters Yard		Thomastown
13 rooms, D IR£ 120		on site
Tel (353) 056 - 24 455, Fax (353) 056 - 24 522		

Newpark Hotel		Kilkenny
84 rooms, D IR£ 100		17 km
Tel (353) 056 - 22 122, Fax (353) 056 - 61 111		

RESTAURANTS RESTAURANTS

Parliament House		Kilkenny
Tel (353) 056 - 63 666		16 km

Langtons		Kilkenny
Tel (353) 056 - 65 133		16 km

889

MOUNT WOLSLEY

13	6	5

This new course is quite typical of the style of Christy O'Connor Jr., with water hazards (especially on the outward nine) and fairway bunkers which some might feel often unfairly penalise good shots. High-level lady players will also feel frustrated as their tee-boxes are often too far forward (a frequent feature these days). However this very likeable course is most welcome in a lovely region and the overall honesty of the layout is conducive to attacking golf without the fear of too many unpleasant surprises. We noted the variety of design and protection for the greens, thus allowing all sorts of approach shots. The course is already in very respectable condition.

Ce nouveau parcours est tout à fait typique du style architectural de Christy O'Connor Jr, avec ses obstacles d'eau (surtout à l'aller) et ses bunkers de fairway, mais on peut trouver que ces derniers pénalisent souvent les bons coups. Les femmes de bon niveau seront aussi frustrées, car leurs départs sont souvent trop avancés (c'est aujourd'hui fréquent). Cependant, cette sympathique réalisation est bienvenue dans une région très agréable, et la franchise générale du tracé permet de l'attaquer sans trop de crainte des mauvaises surprises. Il faut enfin remarquer la variété de dessin et de défense des greens, ce qui permet toutes sortes d'approches. L'état du parcours est déjà très honorable.

Mount Wolsley Golf Club — 1996
IRL - TULLOW, Co. Carlow

Office	Secrétariat	(353) 0503 - 51 674
Pro shop	Pro-shop	(353) 0503 - 51 674
Fax	Fax	(353) 0503 - 52 123
Situation	Situation	

80 km S of Dublin, 14 km E of Carlow on N. 81

Annual closure	Fermeture annuelle	no
Weekly closure	Fermeture hebdomadaire	no

Fees main season
Tarifs haute saison 18 holes

	Week days Semaine	We/Bank holidays We/Férié
Individual Individuel	IR£ 25	IR£ 30
Couple Couple	IR£ 50	IR£ 60

Caddy	Caddy	no
Electric Trolley	Chariot électrique	no
Buggy	Voiturette	IR£ 20/18 holes
Clubs	Clubs	IR£ 10/18 holes

Credit cards Cartes de crédit
VISA - MasterCard - AMEX - DC

890

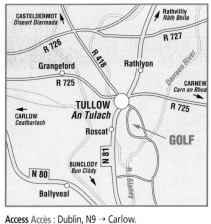

Access Accès : Dublin, N9 → Carlow.
In Castledermot, R418 to Tullow
Map 2 on page 829 Carte 2 Page 829

GOLF COURSE PARCOURS — 13/20

Site	Site	
Maintenance	Entretien	
Architect	Architecte	Christy O'Connor Jr
Type	Type	parkland
Relief	Relief	
Water in play	Eau en jeu	
Exp. to wind	Exposé au vent	
Trees in play	Arbres en jeu	

Scorecard Carte de score	Chp. Chp.	Mens Mess.	Ladies Da.
Length Long.	6497	6140	4963
Par	72	72	74

Advised golfing ability Niveau de jeu recommandé	0	12	24	36
Hcp required	Handicap exigé	no		

CLUB HOUSE & AMENITIES CLUB HOUSE ET ANNEXES — 6/10

Pro shop	Pro-shop	
Driving range	Practice	
Sheltered	couvert	
On grass	sur herbe	yes
Putting-green	putting-green	yes
Pitching-green	pitching green	yes

HOTEL FACILITIES ENVIRONNEMENT HOTELIER — 5/10

HOTELS HÔTELS
Mount Wolsley Hotel — Tullow, on site
20 rooms, D IR£ 80
Tel (353) 0503 - 51 674, Fax (353) 0503 - 52 123

Royal Hotel — Carlow, 14 km
34 rooms, D IR£ 48
Tel (353) 0503 - 31 621, Fax (353) 0503 - 31 621

Kilkea Castle — Castledermot, 8 km
38 rooms, D IR£ 120
Tel (353) 0503 - 45 156, Fax (353) 0503 - 45 187

RESTAURANTS RESTAURANTS
Mount Wolsley Hotel — Tullow, on site
Tel (353) 0503 - 51 674

Kilkea Castle — Castledermot, 8 km
Tel (353) 0503 - 45 156

MULLINGAR

14 5 5

James Braid, who reshaped this course in 1937, considered Mullingar to be one of his best designs. A little on the short side today (there was little space available at the time), this is still a very popular course with Irish players, although it has still to gain an international reputation. It shouldn't leave foreigners feeling too lost, as you can find similar courses in the UK and on the continent, which only show how typical an inland design this is. The one slight difference would be the need to go for target golf, as the greens are very well guarded up front. The hazards are dangerous and call for precision play (the par 3s are excellent). Skills in working the ball both ways, although not decisive, do give an advantage here. A pleasant course for all levels (the ladies tees are nicely well forward) and one you won't be sorry to discover.

James Braid, qui remodela ce parcours en 1937, le considérait comme un de ses meilleurs dessins. Aujourd'hui un peu court (l'espace disponible était réduit), c'est malgré tout un golf très populaire auprès des joueurs irlandais, mais sa réputation internationale reste à établir. Il ne devrait pas trop dépayser les étrangers, car on pourrait trouver aussi bien en Grande-Bretagne que sur le continent des parcours similaires, tant il est typique de l'esthétique et de l'architecture des «inland». Une seule nuance dans cette appréciation : il vaut mieux jouer des balles de «target golf», car les greens sont bien défendus frontalement. Les obstacles sont dangereux, obligeant à un jeu précis (les pars 3 sont excellents), et si l'on sait travailler la balle, l'avantage sera sinon décisif, du moins important. Un parcours plaisant, pour tous niveaux (les départs dames sont gentiment avancés) et que l'on ne sera pas déçu de découvrir.

Mullingar Golf Club — 1894

Mullingar
IRL - BELVEDERE, Co West Meath

Office	Secrétariat	(353) 044 - 48 366
Pro shop	Pro-shop	(353) 044 - 40 088
Fax	Fax	(353) 044 - 41 499
Situation	Situation	

5 km from Mullingar (pop. 8 003)

Annual closure	Fermeture annuelle	no
Weekly closure	Fermeture hebdomadaire	no

Fees main season
Tarifs haute saison 18 holes

	Week days Semaine	We/Bank holidays We/Férié
Individual Individuel	IR£ 20	IR£ 25
Couple Couple	IR£ 40	IR£ 50

Caddy	Caddy	no
Electric Trolley	Chariot électrique	no
Buggy	Voiturette	IR£ 20/18 holes
Clubs	Clubs	IR£ 7/18 holes
Credit cards Cartes de crédit		no

GOLF COURSE / PARCOURS — 14/20

Site	Site	
Maintenance	Entretien	
Architect	Architecte	James Braid
Type	Type	parkland
Relief	Relief	
Water in play	Eau en jeu	
Exp. to wind	Exposé au vent	
Trees in play	Arbres en jeu	

Scorecard Carte de score	Chp. Chp.	Mens Mess.	Ladies Da.
Length Long.	5913	5721	4991
Par	72	72	74

Advised golfing ability
Niveau de jeu recommandé — 0 12 24 36
Hcp required — Handicap exigé — 28 Men, 36 Ladies

CLUB HOUSE & AMENITIES / CLUB HOUSE ET ANNEXES — 5/10

Pro shop	Pro-shop	
Driving range	Practice	
Sheltered	couvert	no
On grass	sur herbe	yes
Putting-green	putting-green	yes
Pitching-green	pitching green	no

HOTEL FACILITIES / ENVIRONNEMENT HOTELIER — 5/10

HOTELS HÔTELS

Bloomfield House — Mullingar — 500 m
33 rooms, D IR£ 74
Tel (353) 044 - 40 894
Fax (353) 044 - 43 767

Greville Arms — Mullingar — 5 km
40 rooms, D IR£ 70
Tel (353) 044 - 48 563
Fax (353) 044 - 48 052

RESTAURANTS RESTAURANTS

Hacketts — Mullingar — 5 km
Tel (353) 044 - 49 755

Oscars — Mullingar — 5 km
Tel (353) 044 - 44 909

891

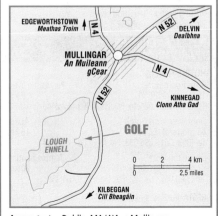

Access Accès : Dublin, M4 / N4 → Mullingar.
In Mullingar, R52 to Belvedere
Map 2 on page 829 Carte 2 Page 829

This is a rather hilly course out in the country, running alongside the village of Ardagh with its pretty stone houses. The averagely fit player, though, shouldn't have too much trouble walking the course. Plant-lovers will admire the fine varieties of fully-grown trees, which have been designed into the layout to clearly define the fairways and make life a little more sticky for players. However, water is the main difficulty, with dangerous lakes and streams, but they are clearly visible and there is nothing to force you into them... if you choose the right clubs. The greens are very generously designed and are easier to reach with lofted shots than with bump and rolls. They are all visible on the second shot, even when the tee shot is blind. Despite being a young course, this layout is already showing signs of healthy maturity and should develop well over the coming years.

Tout à côté du village d'Ardagh, avec ses jolis maisons de pierre, ce parcours en pleine campagne est assez accidenté, mais les joueurs en bonne santé ne devraient pas avoir trop de mal à marcher à pied. Les amateurs de plantes y admireront quelques belles espèces d'arbres en pleine maturité, incorporés au tracé de manière à bien définir les trous, mais aussi à compliquer le travail des joueurs. L'eau constitue cependant la difficulté essentielle, avec des lacs et cours d'eau dangereux. Mais ils sont bien visibles, et rien n'oblige à y envoyer ses balles... si l'on choisit les bons clubs. Les greens ont été généreusement dessinés, ils sont plus facilement accessibles en portant la balle qu'en la faisant rouler. Ils sont tous visibles au second coup, même quand les drives sont aveugles. Malgré sa jeunesse, ce parcours montre beaucoup de maturité, et devrait favorablement évoluer avec le temps.

Newcastle West Golf Club — 1938
IRL - ARDAGH, Co. Limerick

Office	Secrétariat	(353) 069 - 76 500
Pro shop	Pro-shop	(353) 069 - 76 500
Fax	Fax	(353) 069 - 76 511
Situation	Situation	

40 km from Limerick (pop. 52 083)
10 km from Newcastle West

Annual closure	Fermeture annuelle	no
Weekly closure	Fermeture hebdomadaire	no

Fees main season
Tarifs haute saison full day

	Week days Semaine	We/Bank holidays We/Férié
Individual Individuel	IR£ 18	IR£ 18
Couple Couple	IR£ 36	IR£ 36

Caddy	Caddy	on request
Electric Trolley	Chariot électrique	no
Buggy	Voiturette	IR£ 20/18 holes
Clubs	Clubs	IR£ 7

Credit cards Cartes de crédit
VISA - Eurocard - MasterCard

GOLF COURSE
PARCOURS — 13/20

Site	Site	
Maintenance	Entretien	
Architect	Architecte	Arthur Spring
Type	Type	parkland, open country
Relief	Relief	
Water in play	Eau en jeu	
Exp. to wind	Exposé au vent	
Trees in play	Arbres en jeu	

Scorecard Carte de score	Chp. Chp.	Mens Mess.	Ladies Da.
Length Long.	5773	5381	4834
Par	71	71	72

Advised golfing ability		0	12	24	36
Niveau de jeu recommandé					
Hcp required	Handicap exigé	no			

CLUB HOUSE & AMENITIES
CLUB HOUSE ET ANNEXES — 7/10

Pro shop	Pro-shop	
Driving range	Practice	
Sheltered	couvert	no
On grass	sur herbe	yes
Putting-green	putting-green	yes
Pitching-green	pitching green	yes

HOTEL FACILITIES
ENVIRONNEMENT HOTELIER — 5/10

HOTELS HÔTELS

River Room Hotel — Newcastle West
15 rooms, D IR£ 39 — 9 km
Tel (353) 069 - 62 244, Fax (353) 069 - 62 244

Dunraven Arms Hotel — Adare
66 rooms, D IR£ 104 — 16 km
Tel (353) 061 - 396 633, Fax (353) 061 - 396 541

Devon Inn Hotel — Templeglantine
37 rooms, D IR£ 50 — 20 km
Tel (353) 069 - 84 122, Fax (353) 069 - 84 255

RESTAURANTS RESTAURANTS

Mustard Seed — Ballingarry
Tel (353) 069 - 68 508 — 8 km

The Arches — Adare
Tel (353) 061 - 396 246 — 14 km

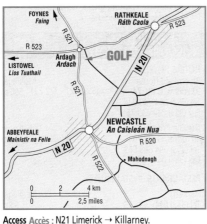

Access Accès : N21 Limerick → Killarney.
Golf near Armagh. Follow signposts
Map 2 on page 828 Carte 2 Page 828

892

OLD HEAD

Like a boat leaving its harbour, this new course is exposed to all winds. So there was really little point in adding an array of difficulties to those already inherent in an excellent and virtually sea-bound setting. Perched atop cliffs but not really a links course in the strict sense of the term, this is still one of the most exciting courses to play at the present time. The number of tee-boxes helps adapt the course to its strengths and the forces of nature, but you are best advised to opt for match-play rather than aim to score to your handicap. The pretty town of Kinsale deserved a class course, and here it is, laid out by a host of designers (Kirby, Carr, Merrigan, Hackett and Higgins). Not surprisingly, the purist may point of a little lack of unity in style.

Comme un navire sortant du port, ce nouveau parcours est exposé à tous les vents. Il n'était alors pas utile d'ajouter une profusion de difficultés à celles imposées par un site exceptionnel, pratiquement encerclé par la mer. Situé au sommet des falaises, sans être un links à proprement parler, il n'en est pas moins l'un des plus excitants à jouer actuellement. Le nombre de tees permet d'adapter le parcours à ses forces et celles de la nature, mais il vaudra mieux y jouer en match-play que de faire la course derrière son handicap. La jolie ville de Kinsale méritait un parcours de grande classe. Dessiné par une armée d'architectes (Kirby, Carr, Merrigan, Hackett et Higgins), il manquera cependant un peu d'unité de style aux yeux des puristes...

Old Head Golf Links 1997
IRL - KINSALE, Co. Cork

Office	Secrétariat	(353) 021 - 778 444
Pro shop	Pro-shop	(353) 021 - 778 444
Fax	Fax	(353) 021 - 778 022
Situation	Situation	

10 km S of Kinsale (pop. 1800)
48 km from Cork (pop. 174 400)

Annual closure	Fermeture annuelle	yes
		1/12→28/2
Weekly closure	Fermeture hebdomadaire	

Fees main season
Tarifs haute saison 18 holes

	Week days Semaine	We/Bank holidays We/Férié
Individual Individuel	IR£ 50	IR£ 60
Couple Couple	IR£ 100	IR£ 120
Caddy Caddy		IR£ 15
Electric Trolley Chariot électrique		no
Buggy Voiturette		IR£ 30/18 holes
Clubs Clubs		IR£ 20/18 holes

Credit cards Cartes de crédit
VISA - MasterCard - AMEX - DC

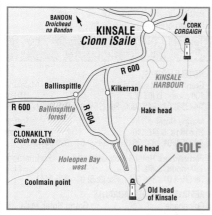

Access Accès : Cork → Kinsale, R 600 → Ballinspittle
Map 2 on page 828 Carte 2 Page 828

GOLF COURSE
PARCOURS 15/20

Site	Site	
Maintenance	Entretien	
Architect	Architecte	Ron Kirby, Joe Carr
		P. Merrigan...
Type	Type	seaside course
Relief	Relief	
Water in play	Eau en jeu	
Exp. to wind	Exposé au vent	
Trees in play	Arbres en jeu	

Scorecard Carte de score	Chp. Chp.	Mens Mess.	Ladies Da.
Length Long.	6080	5657	4827
Par	72	72	72

Advised golfing ability Niveau de jeu recommandé	0	12	24	36
Hcp required	Handicap exigé	no		

CLUB HOUSE & AMENITIES
CLUB HOUSE ET ANNEXES 7/10

Pro shop	Pro-shop	
Driving range	Practice	
Sheltered	couvert	no
On grass	sur herbe	yes (03#10)
Putting-green	putting-green	yes
Pitching-green	pitching green	no

HOTEL FACILITIES
ENVIRONNEMENT HOTELIER 7/10

HOTELS HÔTELS
Actons Hotel - 56 rooms, D IR£ 70 Kinsale 10 km
Tel (353) 021 - 772 135, Fax (353) 021 - 772 231

Trident Hotel Kinsale
58 rooms, D IR£ 70 10 km
Tel (353) 021 - 772 301, Fax (353) 021 - 774 173

Innishannon House Hotel Innishannon
14 rooms, D IR£ 90 20 km
Tel (353) 021 - 775 121, Fax (353) 021 - 775 609

RESTAURANTS RESTAURANTS
The Vintage - Tel (353) 021 - 772 502 Kinsale 10 km

Blue Haven Hotel Kinsale
Tel (353) 021 - 774 075 10 km

The White House - Tel (353) 021 - 772 125 Kinsale10 km

893

A masterpiece. Straight to the point, honest, blunt and diabolical when the wind blows. While Ballybunion can sometimes appear a little baroque, Portmarnock posts an almost austere classicism. There is not one hazard too many, and not one too few to collect wayward shots, not to mention the rough, which is knee-high in places. The greens are huge, subtly contoured and formidably well-guarded. Every shot has to be perfect, from tee to final putt, otherwise stick your tail between your legs and accept that what you get is no more than what you give, with no chance of blaming a single hidden difficulty. If there is one course in this world to be admired for its power, visual amazement, intelligence and variety within unity of style, then it has to be Portmarnock. It is also a great lesson in sobriety for all the world's golf-course designers. You haven't lived if you haven't played Portmarnock at least once. There again, you could also spend your whole life playing here.

Un chef-d'oeuvre. Direct, franc, brutal, et diabolique quand le vent souffle. Si Ballybunion peut paraître parfois baroque, Portmarnock est d'un classicisme presque austère. Il n'y a pas un obstacle superflu, mais il n'en manque pas un pour recevoir les coups égarés, sans même parler d'un rough qui peut monter jusqu'aux genoux. Les greens sont vastes, leurs contours subtils, leurs défenses redoutables. Tous les coups doivent être parfaits, du départ au dernier putt, sinon, il faut faire preuve d'humilité, accepter de ne recevoir que ce que vous donnez, sans pouvoir accuser une seule difficulté cachée. S'il est un parcours admirable par sa puissance, sa grandeur visuelle, son intelligence, sa diversité à l'intérieur même d'une unité de style, c'est Portmarnock. C'est aussi une grande leçon de sobriété pour tous les architectes du monde. On ne saurait vivre sans avoir joué ici une fois, on pourrait aussi y passer sa vie.

Portmarnock Golf Club — 1894
IRL - PORTMARNOCK, Co. Dublin

Office	Secrétariat	(353) 01 - 846 2968
Pro shop	Pro-shop	(353) 01 - 846 2634
Fax	Fax	(353) 01 - 846 2601
Situation	Situation	

16 km NE of Dublin (pop. 859 976)

Annual closure	Fermeture annuelle	no
Weekly closure	Fermeture hebdomadaire	Wednesday

Restaurant open all days

Fees main season	Tarifs haute saison	18 holes

	Week days Semaine	We/Bank holidays We/Férié
Individual Individuel	IR£ 60	IR£ 75
Couple Couple	IR£ 120	IR£ 150

No women at weekend or public holidays!!!

Caddy	Caddy	on request/IR£ 20
Electric Trolley	Chariot électrique	no
Buggy	Voiturette	no
Clubs	Clubs	IR£ 15.50/full day

Credit cards Cartes de crédit
VISA - Eurocard - MasterCard - AMEX - DC

894

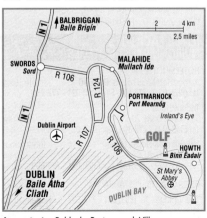

Access Accès : Baldoyle, Portmarnock Village.
Golf Links bar, turn right. Golf 1,5 km
Map 3 on page 830 Carte 3 Page 830

GOLF COURSE PARCOURS — 19/20

Site	Site	■■■■■■
Maintenance	Entretien	■■■■■■
Architect	Architecte	WG Pikeman George Ross
Type	Type	links
Relief	Relief	
Water in play	Eau en jeu	■■
Exp. to wind	Exposé au vent	■■■■
Trees in play	Arbres en jeu	■

Scorecard Carte de score	Chp. Chp.	Mens Mess.	Ladies Da.
Length Long.	6497	6251	5304
Par	72	72	72

Advised golfing ability Niveau de jeu recommandé	0 12 24 36
Hcp required Handicap exigé	28 Men, 36 Ladies

CLUB HOUSE & AMENITIES CLUB HOUSE ET ANNEXES — 7/10

Pro shop	Pro-shop	■■■■
Driving range	Practice	■■■■
Sheltered	couvert	no
On grass	sur herbe	yes
Putting-green	putting-green	yes
Pitching-green	pitching green	yes

HOTEL FACILITIES ENVIRONNEMENT HOTELIER — 8/10

HOTELS HÔTELS
Grand Hotel Malahide — Malahide
100 rooms, D IR£ 90 — 5 km
Tel (353) 01 - 845 0000, Fax (353) 01 - 845 0987

Marine Hotel — Sutton
26 rooms, D IR£ 110 — 5 km
Tel (353) 01 - 832 2613, Fax (353) 01 - 839 04 42

Portmarnock Hotel & Golf Links — Portmarnock
110 rooms, D IR£ 115 — 1 km
Tel (353) 01 - 846 0611, Fax (353) 01 - 846 2442

RESTAURANTS RESTAURANTS
Colonnade — Grand Hotel, Malahide
Tel (353) 01 - 845 0000 — 5 km

Meridian Restaurant — Marine Hotel, Sutton
Tel (353) 01 - 839 0000 — 5 km

PORTMARNOCK LINKS ⅃ 17 7 8

Assuming such a prestigious name was a stiff task, but Bernhard Langer and Stan Eby accepted the challenge and came up with a great course. Only history will tell how great, but their initial achievement was to approach the site with a degree of modesty, and to learn from others - including its illustrious neighbour and other gems such as Carnoustie and Muirfield - without copying a single thing. There is nothing visually excessive and no signature hole, just a natural layout in unforgiving, changing landscape. While the first holes are visually unimpressive, their technical challenge is something else. From the 8th hole onward, the terrain becomes a little more lively and the choice of club a little tougher in a spectacular landscape of dunes. There is no water (to speak of) and no trees, either, nothing but bushes, dangerous rough, magnificently designed and located bunkers and greens that are really exciting to play. The result is more than anyone could ever have hoped for.

Il était difficile de porter un nom aussi prestigieux. Bernhard Langer et Stan Eby ont relevé le défi, et réussi un grand parcours. L'histoire dira sa place exacte, mais la réussite première est d'avoir abordé modestement ce site, de n'avoir rien copié tout en retenant les leçons de l'illustre voisin, mais aussi de merveilles telles que Carnoustie ou Muirfield. Rien ici d'excessif visuellement, pas de trou-signature, rien que le déroulement naturel dans un paysage rude et changeant. Si les premiers trous ne sont pas visuellement impressionnants, quels challenges techniques ils présentent ! A partir du 8, le terrain devient plus animé, le choix de club plus difficile dans un paysage spectaculaire de dunes. Ici, pas d'eau (ou presque), pas d'arbres, rien que des buissons, un rough dangereux, des bunkers magnifiquement dessinés et placés, des greens passionnants à jouer. Le résultat dépasse les espérances.

Portmarnock Hotel & Golf Links	1995		
IRL - PORTMARNOCK, Co Dublin			

Office	Secrétariat	(353) 01 - 846 1800
Pro shop	Pro-shop	(353) 01 - 846 1800
Fax	Fax	(353) 01 - 846 1077
Situation	Situation	

8 km from Dublin (pop. 859 976)

Annual closure	Fermeture annuelle	no
Weekly closure	Fermeture hebdomadaire	no

Fees main season
Tarifs haute saison 18 holes

	Week days Semaine	We/Bank holidays We/Férié
Individual Individuel	IR£ 50	IR£ 50
Couple Couple	IR£ 100	IR£ 100
Hotel guests: IR£ 30		

Caddy	Caddy	on request/IR£ 20
Electric Trolley	Chariot électrique	no
Buggy	Voiturette	no
Clubs	Clubs	IR£ 15/18 holes

Credit cards Cartes de crédit
VISA - MasterCard - AMEX

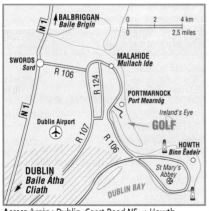

Access Accès : Dublin, Coast Road NE → Howth.
Map 3 on page 830 Carte 3 Page 830

GOLF COURSE / PARCOURS — 17/20

Site	Site	
Maintenance	Entretien	
Architect	Architecte	Bernhard Langer
Type	Type	links
Relief	Relief	
Water in play	Eau en jeu	
Exp. to wind	Exposé au vent	
Trees in play	Arbres en jeu	

Scorecard Carte de score	Chp. Chp.	Mens Mess.	Ladies Da.
Length Long.	6195	5909	4987
Par	71	71	71

Advised golfing ability Niveau de jeu recommandé	0 12 24 36
Hcp required Handicap exigé	24 Men, 36 Ladies

CLUB HOUSE & AMENITIES / CLUB HOUSE ET ANNEXES — 7/10

Pro shop	Pro-shop	
Driving range	Practice	
Sheltered	couvert	yes
On grass	sur herbe	yes
Putting-green	putting-green	yes
Pitching-green	pitching green	yes

HOTEL FACILITIES / ENVIRONNEMENT HOTELIER — 8/10

HOTELS HÔTELS
Portmarnock Links Hotel — Portmarnock on site
110 rooms, D IR£ 190
Tel (353) 01 - 846 0611, Fax (353) 01 - 846 2442

Grand Hotel — Malahide 4 km
100 rooms, D IR£ 95
Tel (353) 01 - 845 0000, Fax (353) 01 - 845 0987

Sands Hotel — Portmarnock 1 km
10 rooms, D IR£ 70
Tel (353) 01 - 846 0003, Fax (353) 01 - 846 0420

RESTAURANTS RESTAURANTS
Bon Appetit - Tel (353) 01 - 845 0314 — Malahide 4 km

Old Street Wine Bar — Malahide 4 km
Tél(353) 01 - 845 1882

Ostborne (at Hotel) - Tél(353) 01 846 0611 — on site

895

PORTSALON

Portsalon is an outstanding site, between the beach of Ballymostocker bay, one of the world's finest, and the Knockalla mountains. This age-old course is today run by local Irishmen, which means a friendly welcome guaranteed every time. The course is a shortish links with no real geographical relief, and so is ideal for a romantic stroll, even for the non-golfers in the family. The terrain has stayed very natural, with unpredictable kicks that are all part of the fun of golf, when they bounce and rebound in the right direction. The rough is not too severe and the bunkers are nicely, but not excessively, in play. Golfers who are new to the game will enjoy the opportunity here to learn about the architecture of a links course, without undue suffering, especially continental Europeans, who have little contact with this style of golf. The water on the 3rd and 15th shouldn't bother them too much, either. The wind is, of course, an element to be reckoned with, but it puts colour into your cheeks and gives you a hearty appetite for after the round.

Portsalon bénéficie d'une situation exceptionnelle, entre la plage de Ballymostocker Bay, l'une des plus belles du monde, et les Knockalla Mountains. Ce golf centenaire est aujourd'hui géré par des Irlandais locaux, c'est une garantie d'accueil amical. Le parcours est un links de longueur réduite, sans relief trop prononcé, ce qui permet une promenade romantique, même pour les non-golfeurs de la famille. Le terrain est resté très naturel, avec les rebonds imprévisibles qui font le plaisir du jeu... quand ils sont favorables. Le rough n'est pas trop sévère, les bunkers bien en jeu, mais sans excès. Les golfeurs peu expérimentés auront ici une belle occasion d'apprendre à aimer sans douleur l'architecture de links, notamment les Européens du continent, peu familiarisés avec elle. Et la présence de l'eau, au 3 et au 15, ne devrait pas trop les gêner. Bien sûr, le vent est un élément important, mais il donne bonne mine et ouvre l'appétit.

Portsalon Golf Club — 1881

Portsalon
IRL - FANAD, Co Donegal

Office	Secrétariat	(353) 074 - 59 459
Pro shop	Pro-shop	(353) 074 - 59 459
Fax	Fax	(353) 074 - 59 459
Situation	Situation	

50 km from Derry (pop. 72 334)
32 km from Letterkenny (pop. 7 166)

Annual closure	Fermeture annuelle	no
Weekly closure	Fermeture hebdomadaire	no

Fees main season	Tarifs haute saison	18 holes
	Week days Semaine	We/Bank holidays We/Férié
Individual Individuel	IR£ 10	IR£ 12
Couple Couple	IR£ 20	IR£ 24

Caddy	Caddy	IR£ 10/18 holes
Electric Trolley	Chariot électrique	no
Buggy	Voiturette	no
Clubs	Clubs	no

Credit cards Cartes de crédit — no

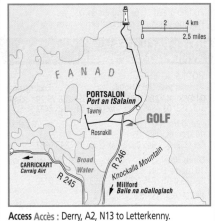

Access Accès : Derry, A2, N13 to Letterkenny.
R245 to Rathmelton, Milford.
R246 to Portsalon (Fanad Peninsula)
Map 1 on page 827 Carte 1 Page 827

GOLF COURSE / PARCOURS — 16/20

Site	Site	
Maintenance	Entretien	
Architect	Architecte	Mr Thompson
Type	Type	links
Relief	Relief	
Water in play	Eau en jeu	
Exp. to wind	Exposé au vent	
Trees in play	Arbres en jeu	

Scorecard	Chp.	Mens	Ladies
Carte de score	Chp.	Mess.	Da.
Length Long.	5354	5354	4499
Par	69	69	70

Advised golfing ability	0	12	24	36
Niveau de jeu recommandé				
Hcp required	Handicap exigé	no		

CLUB HOUSE & AMENITIES / CLUB HOUSE ET ANNEXES — 5/10

Pro shop	Pro-shop	
Driving range	Practice	
Sheltered	couvert	no
On grass	sur herbe	no
Putting-green	putting-green	yes
Pitching-green	pitching green	no

HOTEL FACILITIES / ENVIRONNEMENT HOTELIER — 5/10

HOTELS HÔTELS

Rathmullan House — Rathmullan
21 rooms, D IR£ 100 — 10 km
Tel (353) 074 - 59 115, Fax (353) 074 - 58 200

Pier Hotel, D IR£ 60 — Rathmullan 10 km
Tel (353) 074 - 59 115

Castle Grove Hotel — Letterkenny
8 rooms, D IR£ 65 — 30 km
Tel (353) 074 - 51 118, Fax (353) 074 - 51 384

RESTAURANTS RESTAURANTS

Portsalon Store — Portsalon
Tel (353) 074 - 59 107 — 1 km

Rosapenna Hotel — Downings
Tel (353) 074 - 55 301

896

POWERSCOURT

This is a magnificent site alongside the little town of Enniskerry, the gateway to the "Military Road" that crosses the wild landscape of the Wicklow Mountains in the immediate vicinity of Powerscourt Castle (hence the name of the course). The course winds it way around a majestic estate over some sharp slopes that might make a buggy advisable for senior players. Amateur champion Peter McEvoy has produced a championship course that is as honest as it is technically demanding, where water comes into play on only two holes (including the superb 16th hole, a par 3 and obvious tribute to the 12th at Augusta). The main hazards are the large trees and very strategically placed bunkers. Powerscourt is still a very young course but the sand-based greens are already in excellent condition ; for the moment, the fairways still need to gain a little firmness and the back-tees are best left alone...

C'est un site magnifique, à côté de la petite ville d'Enniskerry, porte d'entrée de la «Military Road» traversant les paysages sauvages des Wicklow Mountains, à proximité immédiate du Château de Powerscourt, dont le golf a emprunté le nom. Le parcours a été insinué dans cet espace majestueux, au prix de quelques reliefs incitant à conseiller une voiturette aux seniors. Le grand champion amateur Peter McEvoy en a fait un parcours de championnat aussi franc qu'exigeant techniquement, où l'eau n'est en jeu que sur deux trous (dont le superbe 16, un par 3 en référence évidente au 12 d'Augusta). Les grands arbres constituent les principaux obstacles, avec des bunkers très stratégiques. Powerscourt est très jeune encore, mais les greens en sable sont déjà en excellente condition, alors que les fairways ont besoin d'acquérir un peu de fermeté : il vaut mieux ne pas jouer des départs arrière pour l'instant...

Powerscourt Golf Club — 1996

Powerscourt Estate
IRL - ENNISKERRY, Co Wicklow

Office	Secrétariat	(353) 01 - 204 6033
Pro shop	Pro-shop	(353) 01 - 204 6033
Fax	Fax	(353) 01 - 286 3561
Situation	Situation	

19 km S of Dublin (pop. 859 976)
1 km from Enniskerry

Annual closure	Fermeture annuelle	no
Weekly closure	Fermeture hebdomadaire	no

Fees main season
Tarifs haute saison 18 holes

	Week days Semaine	We/Bank holidays We/Férié
Individual Individuel	IR£ 50	IR£ 60
Couple Couple	IR£ 100	IR£ 120

Caddy	Caddy	on request
Electric Trolley	Chariot électrique	no
Buggy	Voiturette	IR£ 30/18 holes
Clubs	Clubs	IR£ 15/18 holes

Credit cards Cartes de crédit
VISA - MasterCard - AMEX - Laser

Access Accès : N11, South of Bray
Map 3 on page 830 Carte 3 Page 830

GOLF COURSE PARCOURS — 15/20

Site	Site	
Maintenance	Entretien	
Architect	Architecte	Peter McEvoy
Type	Type	inland, parkland
Relief	Relief	
Water in play	Eau en jeu	
Exp. to wind	Exposé au vent	
Trees in play	Arbres en jeu	

Scorecard Carte de score	Chp. Chp.	Mens Mess.	Ladies Da.
Length Long.	6410	5858	5322
Par	72	72	75

Advised golfing ability		0 12 24 36
Niveau de jeu recommandé		
Hcp required	Handicap exigé	no

CLUB HOUSE & AMENITIES
CLUB HOUSE ET ANNEXES — 7/10

Pro shop	Pro-shop	
Driving range	Practice	
Sheltered	couvert	no
On grass	sur herbe	yes
Putting-green	putting-green	yes
Pitching-green	pitching green	yes

HOTEL FACILITIES
ENVIRONNEMENT HOTELIER — 7/10

HOTELS HÔTELS

Summerhill Hotel - 30 rooms, D IR£ 50 — Enniskerry
Tel (353) 01 - 286 7928, Fax (353) 01 - 286 79 29 — close

Glenview Hotel — Delgany
43 rooms, D IR£ 125 — 13 km
Tel (353) 01 - 287 3399, Fax (353) 01 - 287 7511

Charlesland Golf & Country C. — Greystones
12 rooms, D IR£ 66 — 16 km
Tel (353) 01 - 287 6764, Fax (353) 01 - 287 3882

RESTAURANTS RESTAURANTS

Roly's Bistro — Dublin
Tel (353) 01 - 668 2611 — 15 km

Cooper's - Tel (353) 01 - 287 3914 — Greystones 13 km

Hungry Monk — Greystones
Tel (353) 01 - 287 5759 — 13 km

897

Welcome to a huge park, where the age-old trees provide a sumptuous splash of colour come Autumn. Away from the madding crowd, the trees here are in fact a real factor to complicate the course and your game. The slopes are sometimes steep and might hinder some senior players, but they also add to the problem of club selection. This is compounded by well-guarded and cleverly designed greens, where you can rarely get home without lofting the ball. A noticeable feature is the variety of the holes, with more than a few slight dog-legs that ideally call for some flighted shots (when the ground is damp the course plays very long). There is water on seven holes, and it is often dangerous. Although generally honest and open, the course nonetheless harbours a few traps, including the 6th, a par 5 peppered with bunkers, ponds and ditches and a tricky hole to master. Other features are the difficulty of the closing holes and the very family atmosphere that reigns throughout the club.

Un immense parc avec des arbres centenaires, dont les couleurs automnales sont somptueuses. A l'écart des bruits du monde, leur présence est un facteur de difficulté effective dans le jeu. Les dénivellées sont parfois importantes, et peuvent poser des problèmes aux seniors, mais aussi pour bien choisir son club, et d'autant plus que les greens sont très défendus, très travaillés : on peut rarement y entrer en faisant rouler la balle. On remarquera aussi la variété des trous, avec pas mal de légers dog-legs obligeant à travailler ses effets (le parcours est très long quand le sol est humide). L'eau est présente sur sept trous, souvent de manière dangereuse. Généralement assez franc, ce parcours recèle néanmoins quelques pièges, dont le 6, un par 5 truffé de bunkers, de mares et de fossés, et bien délicat à décrypter. A signaler aussi, la difficulté des derniers trous, et l'atmosphère très familiale qui règne ici.

Rathsallagh Golf Club   1995
IRL - DUNLAVIN, Co Wicklow

Office	Secrétariat	(353) 045 - 403 316
Pro shop	Pro-shop	(353) 045 - 403 316
Fax	Fax	(353) 045 - 403 295
Situation	Situation	

4 km from Dunlavin (pop. 720)

Annual closure	Fermeture annuelle	no
Weekly closure	Fermeture hebdomadaire	no

Fees main season
Tarifs haute saison 18 holes

	Week days Semaine	We/Bank holidays We/Férié
Individual Individuel	IR£ 30	IR£ 40
Couple Couple	IR£ 60	IR£ 80

Weekdays: IR£ 20 before 9.30 am

Caddy	Caddy	on request
Electric Trolley	Chariot électrique	IR£ 8
Buggy	Voiturette	IR£ 25/18 holes
Clubs	Clubs	IR£ 25/18 holes

Credit cards Cartes de crédit VISA - MasterCard

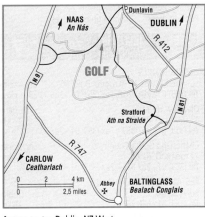

Access Accès : Dublin, N7 West.
N9 → Waterford. → Dunlavin
Map 2 on page 829 Carte 2 Page 829

GOLF COURSE PARCOURS   15 /20

Site	Site	■■■■■□□
Maintenance	Entretien	■■■■■□
Architect	Architecte	Peter McEvoy Ch. O'Connor Jr
Type	Type	inland, parkland
Relief	Relief	■■■■□□
Water in play	Eau en jeu	■■■□□□
Exp. to wind	Exposé au vent	■■□□□□
Trees in play	Arbres en jeu	■■■■■□

Scorecard Carte de score	Chp. Chp.	Mens Mess.	Ladies Da.
Length Long.	6321	5940	5033
Par	72	72	73

Advised golfing ability	0	12	24	36
Niveau de jeu recommandé				
Hcp required	Handicap exigé	28 Men, 36 Ladies		

CLUB HOUSE & AMENITIES CLUB HOUSE ET ANNEXES   7 /10

Pro shop	Pro-shop	■■■■□□
Driving range	Practice	■■■□□
Sheltered	couvert	2 mats
On grass	sur herbe	yes
Putting-green	putting-green	yes
Pitching-green	pitching green	no

HOTEL FACILITIES ENVIRONNEMENT HOTELIER   6 /10

HOTELS HÔTELS
Rathsallagh House   on site
17 rooms, D IR£ 160
Tel (353) 045 - 403 112
Fax (353) 045 - 403 343

Kilkee Castle   Castledermot
36 rooms, D IR£ 120   20 km
Tel (353) 0503 - 45 156
Fax (353) 0503 - 45 187

RESTAURANTS RESTAURANTS
Rathsallagh House   on site
Tel (353) 045 - 403 112

Priory Inn   Carlow-Kilkenny Road
Tel (353) 045 - 403 355   4 km

898

ROSAPENNA

Originally designed by Old Tom Morris in 1893, Rosapenna was reshaped by James Braid and Harry Vardon in 1906 before Eddie Hackett added the final touches in 1993. With names like these, the course should, on the face of it, be quite something, and it is. This is one of the obligatory stop-offs in the long trek of exploring golfing treasures in the north-west of Ireland, often unknown to foreign tourists but not so to the Irish themselves. Playing on a links is like going back to the origins of the game, when intuition and inspiration held the upper hand over pure technique, when the size of your score was merely relative because match-play was the formula that reigned supreme with amateur golfers. Exposure to the wind makes Rosapenna a tricky number to play, and even if the traps are seldom hidden, playing here several times makes it easier to choose tactics. Lack of experience could be a serious setback for high-handicappers.

D'abord dessiné par Old Tom Morris en 1893, Rosapenna a bénéficié des aménagements de James Braid et Harry Vardon en 1906, avant que Eddie Hackett lui donne la dernière touche en 1993. Avec de tels signataires, ce parcours ne peut laisser indifférent, à priori ! Il constitue effectivement l'un des étapes obligées dans une longue exploration des trésors golfiques du Nord-Ouest, souvent ignorés par les touristes étrangers, alors que les Irlandais en ont pris souvent le chemin. Jouer sur un links, c'est retrouver les origines du jeu, où l'intuition et l'inspiration prenaient le pas sur la technique pure, où l'importance du score était toute relative quand le match-play était la formule reine des amateurs. L'exposition au vent rend forcément Rosapenna délicat à jouer, et même si les pièges sont rarement dissimulés, jouer plusieurs fois améliore les choix tactiques. Le manque d'expérience peut gêner les golfeurs très moyens.

Rosapenna Hotel & Golf Links		1893
IRL - DOWNINGS, Co Donegal		

Office	Secrétariat	(353) 074 - 55 301
Pro shop	Pro-shop	(353) 074 - 55 301
Fax	Fax	(353) 074 - 55 128
Situation	Situation	
40 km from Letterkenny (pop. 7 166)		
Annual closure	Fermeture annuelle	no
Weekly closure	Fermeture hebdomadaire	no

Fees main season
Tarifs haute saison 18 holes

	Week days Semaine	We/Bank holidays We/Férié
Individual Individuel	IR£ 20	IR£ 25
Couple Couple	IR£ 40	IR£ 50

Caddy	Caddy	on request
Electric Trolley	Chariot électrique	no
Buggy	Voiturette	IR£ 20/18 holes
Clubs	Clubs	IR£ 10

Credit cards Cartes de crédit
VISA - Eurocard - MasterCard - DC

Rosguill
Sheep Haven
Mulray Bay
R 248
FANAD
GOLF
CARRICKART
Carraig Airt
R 245
Millford
Baile na nGalloglach
R 245
N 56
LETTERKENNY
Leitir Ceanainn
0   2   4 km
0   2,5 miles

Access Accès : Letterkenny: R245 to Rathmelton, Millford, Cranford, Carrigart. Golf 2 km → Rosapenna
Map 1 on page 827 Carte 1 Page 827

GOLF COURSE
PARCOURS
16/20

Site	Site	■■■■□
Maintenance	Entretien	■■■■□
Architect	Architecte	Old Tom Morris Braid, Vardon
Type	Type	links
Relief	Relief	■■□□□
Water in play	Eau en jeu	■□□□□
Exp. to wind	Exposé au vent	■■■■□
Trees in play	Arbres en jeu	■□□□□

Scorecard Carte de score	Chp. Chp.	Mens Mess.	Ladies Da.
Length Long.	5950	5644	4555
Par	71	70	74

Advised golfing ability Niveau de jeu recommandé	0 12 24 36 ■■■■
Hcp required Handicap exigé	Men 24, Ladies 36

CLUB HOUSE & AMENITIES
CLUB HOUSE ET ANNEXES
7/10

Pro shop	Pro-shop	■■■□□
Driving range	Practice	■■■□□
Sheltered	couvert	6 mats
On grass	sur herbe	yes
Putting-green	putting-green	yes
Pitching-green	pitching green	yes

HOTEL FACILITIES
ENVIRONNEMENT HOTELIER
6/10

HOTELS HÔTELS
Rosapenna Hotel   on site
46 rooms, D IR£ 95
Tél (353) 074 - 55 301, Fax (353) 074 - 55 128

Shandon Hotel   Marble Hill
55 rooms, D IR£ 80   13 km
Tél (353) 074 - 36 137, Fax (353) 074 - 36 430

Arnold's Hotel   Dunfaghy
34 rooms, D IR£ 60   25 km
Tél (353) 074 - 36 208, Fax (353) 074 - 36 352

RESTAURANTS RESTAURANTS
Rosapenna Hotel   on site
Tél (353) 074 - 55 301

The Cove   Dunfaghy
Tél (353) 074 - 36 300   25 km

899

This course is located on a peninsula, and what with there being no trees to protect it, is clearly exposed to the wind. This element makes any links course an exciting proposition and adds to the pleasure when you can keep control. It can, though, easily upset the more inexperienced player. This is the main difficulty at Rosslare, which otherwise can appear a little dated to top level players. The bunkers are more strategic than really penalising and the well-watered greens will still hold slightly miscued shots, but before reaching them you need an accurate tee-shot to avoid the unforgiving rough. One particular feature here is the excellence of the par 3s and the closing holes along the sea, which are superb in matchplay. Today better suited to holiday golf than tournaments, Rosslare is a good course on which to become acclimatised with links golf.

La situation de ce parcours sur une péninsule et l'absence d'arbres protecteurs impliquent une forte exposition au vent. Cet élément rend très excitants les parcours de links, et renforce le plaisir quand on réussit à en maîtriser les effets. Mais il tourne la tête des joueurs peu expérimentés ! C'est la principale difficulté de Rosslare, autrement un peu désuet au regard des joueurs du meilleur niveau. Les bunkers sont plus stratégiques que vraiment pénalisants, l'arrosage des greens a facilité la réception des coups imparfaits, mais il faut encore de la précision au drive pour pouvoir les attaquer, car le rough peut être méchant. On distinguera particulièrement ici la qualité des pars 3, et celle des derniers trous le long de la mer, qui offrent un espace superbe en matchplay. Aujourd'hui mieux adapté à un golf de vacances que de championnat, Rosslare est un bon parcours pour se familiariser avec l'architecture de links.

Rosslare Golf Club — 1905
IRL - ROSSLARE STRAND, Co Wicklow

Office	Secrétariat	(353) 053 - 32 113
Pro shop	Pro-shop	(353) 053 - 32 238
Fax	Fax	(353) 053 - 32 203
Situation	Situation	

18 km from Wexford (pop. 15 393)

Annual closure	Fermeture annuelle	no
Weekly closure	Fermeture hebdomadaire	no

Fees main season
Tarifs haute saison 18 holes

	Week days Semaine	We/Bank holidays We/Férié
Individual Individuel	IR£ 20	IR£ 25
Couple Couple	IR£ 40	IR£ 50

Caddy	Caddy	no
Electric Trolley	Chariot électrique	no
Buggy	Voiturette	IR£ 20/18 holes
Clubs	Clubs	IR£ 6

Credit cards Cartes de crédit — no

900

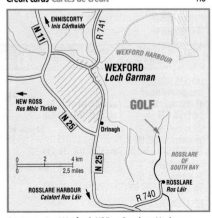

Access Accès : Wexford, N25 → Rosslare Harbour.
1 km after Killinick, left on R740 to Rosslare.
Golf → Rosslare Point/Burrow
Map 2 on page 829 Carte 2 Page 829

GOLF COURSE
PARCOURS — **13**/20

Site	Site	
Maintenance	Entretien	
Architect	Architecte	
Type	Type	seaside course, links
Relief	Relief	
Water in play	Eau en jeu	
Exp. to wind	Exposé au vent	
Trees in play	Arbres en jeu	

Scorecard Carte de score	Chp. Chp.	Mens Mess.	Ladies Da.
Length Long.	5920	5650	5075
Par	72	72	73

Advised golfing ability — 0   12   24   36
Niveau de jeu recommandé
Hcp required — Handicap exigé — no

CLUB HOUSE & AMENITIES
CLUB HOUSE ET ANNEXES — **5**/10

Pro shop	Pro-shop	
Driving range	Practice	
Sheltered	couvert	no
On grass	sur herbe	yes
Putting-green	putting-green	yes
Pitching-green	pitching green	yes

HOTEL FACILITIES
ENVIRONNEMENT HOTELIER — **6**/10

HOTELS HÔTELS
Kelly's Resort — Rosslare Strand
99 rooms, D IR£ 85 — 1 km
Tél (353) 053 - 32 114, Fax (353) 053 - 32 222

Cedars Hotel — Rosslare Strand
34 rooms, D IR£ 58 — 1 km
Tél (353) 053 - 32 124, Fax (353) 053 - 32 243

Great Southern — Rosslare Harbour
100 rooms, D IR£ 70 — 4 km
Tél (353) 053 - 33 233, Fax (353) 053 - 33 543

RESTAURANTS RESTAURANTS
Ocean Bed Seafood Restaurant — Wexford
Tél (353) 053 - 23 935 — 20 km

Kelly's Resort — Rosslare Strand
Tél (353) 053 - 32 114 — 1 km

ROYAL DUBLIN

16 8 7

Although not inside the very closed club of exceptional golf courses, Royal Dublin is an excellent example of a classic links, peppered with deep fairway and green-side bunkers (sometimes very penalising indeed) and a number of bushes, but these are often more decorative or useful for gauging distance than really dangerous. Although the terrain is none too hilly, there are a couple of blind drives but nothing blind when approaching the greens. You could almost call this a kind course if the prevailing wind wasn't blowing in your face on the way in. This makes the back 9 an even trickier proposition, which demands certain skills in drawing the ball, a feat that many will find harder than others. A very natural looking course and very busy, being so close to Dublin, this layout has started to show its age and probably needs a little restyling (especially in terms of yardage) if it is to recover its championship course status.

Bien qu'il n'appartienne pas au club très fermé des parcours exceptionnels, Royal Dublin est un excellent exemple de links classique, avec ses profonds bunkers de fairway et de greens (parfois très pénalisants), des buissons, mais souvent plus décoratifs ou utiles comme points de repère que vraiment dangereux. Bien que le terrain soit peu accidenté, on trouve ici quelques drives aveugles, mais aucun green de la sorte. On pourrait presque le qualifier d'aimable si le vent dominant n'était contraire au retour, ce qui rend cette partie du parcours encore plus délicate, exigeant notamment une bonne maîtrise des effets de draw, ce qui n'est pas donné à tout le monde ! Très naturel d'aspect, très fréquenté aussi en raison de sa proximité de Dublin, ce parcours porte un peu son âge, mais aurait sans doute besoin d'un petit lifting (notamment au niveau de la longueur), s'il souhaite du moins retrouver un statut de parcours de championnat.

Royal Dublin Golf Club		1885
Bull Island		
IRL - DUBLIN 3		

Office	Secrétariat	(353) 01 - 833 6346
Pro shop	Pro-shop	(353) 01 - 833 6477
Fax	Fax	(353) 01 - 833 6504
Situation	Situation	
7 km E of Dublin (pop. 859 976)		
Annual closure	Fermeture annuelle	no
Weekly closure	Fermeture hebdomadaire	no
Fees main season	Tarifs haute saison	18 holes

	Week days Semaine	We/Bank holidays We/Férié
Individual Individuel	IR£ 45	IR£ 55
Couple Couple	IR£ 90	IR£ 110

No Ladies on Week-ends and Public Holidays!!!

Caddy	Caddy	IR£ 15 (+ Tip)
Electric Trolley	Chariot électrique	no
Buggy	Voiturette	no
Clubs	Clubs	IR£ 15

Credit cards Cartes de crédit
VISA - MasterCard - AMEX - DC

Access Accès : Dublin City, Coast road → Howth.
Bull Island Bridge, turn right
Map 3 on page 830 Carte 3 Page 830

GOLF COURSE
PARCOURS
16/20

Site	Site	
Maintenance	Entretien	
Architect	Architecte	H.S. Colt
Type	Type	links
Relief	Relief	
Water in play	Eau en jeu	
Exp. to wind	Exposé au vent	
Trees in play	Arbres en jeu	

Scorecard Carte de score	Chp. Chp.	Mens Mess.	Ladies Da.
Length Long.	6281	6030	5439
Par	72	72	74

Advised golfing ability Niveau de jeu recommandé	0	12	24	36
Hcp required Handicap exigé	28 Men, 36 Ladies			

CLUB HOUSE & AMENITIES
CLUB HOUSE ET ANNEXES
8/10

Pro shop	Pro-shop	
Driving range	Practice	
Sheltered	couvert	no
On grass	sur herbe	yes
Putting-green	putting-green	yes
Pitching-green	pitching green	yes

901

HOTEL FACILITIES
ENVIRONNEMENT HOTELIER
7/10

HOTELS HÔTELS
Marine Hotel - 26 rooms, D IR£ 110   Sutton 7 km
Tél (353) 01 - 832 2613, Fax (353) 01 - 839 04 42

Grand Hotel Malahide   Malahide
100 rooms, D IR£ 90   10 km
Tél (353) 01 - 845 0000, Fax (353) 01 - 845 0987

Portmarnock Hotel & Golf Links   Portmarnock
110 rooms, D IR£ 115   7 km
Tél (353) 01 - 846 0611, Fax (353) 01 - 846 2442

RESTAURANTS RESTAURANTS
Colonnade   Grand Hotel, Malahide
Tél (353) 01 - 845 0000   10 km

King Sitric Fish   East Pier, Howth
Tél (353) 01 - 832 5235   8 km

Roly's Bistro - Tél (353) 01 - 668 2611   Dublin 13 km

SEAPOINT

15	6	6

From the 14th at County Louth, you can see practically all the neighbouring course of Seapoint, opened only recently. Here, it is a return to similar moonscape scenery, but with a large section of the course winding through heather and a more rural landscape. This is rather an attractive contrast, and gives the impression of a course gradually building up speed through to the closing holes, all very spectacular and exciting when using the match-play format. The wind often has a word or two to say, and good ball control is required, especially with the tee shot, in order to avoid the fairway bunkers and get a good view of the greens to keep out of the often dangerous green-side traps. These greens are large and distinguished more by general slopes than by individual contouring. By and large, the difficulties are clearly visible (water comes into play on the 4th and 9th holes), so at least you can start out here with a degree of confidence. Well worth knowing.

Depuis le 14 de County Louth, on aperçoit pratiquement tout le parcours voisin de Seapoint, ouvert récemment. On y retrouve au retour un paysage dunaire analogue, alors qu'une grande partie se déroule dans la bruyère et un paysage plus rural. Ce contraste est d'ailleurs assez séduisant, et donne une impression de montée en puissance progressive, jusqu'aux derniers trous, très spectaculaires et excitants en match-play. Le vent joue souvent un rôle et il faut un bon contrôle de balle, en particulier depuis les départs, pour éviter les bunkers de fairway et avoir une ouverture suffisante sur les greens pour échapper à leurs bunkers, souvent dangereux. Ces greens sont largement dimensionnés, et caractérisés davantage par des pentes générales que par des ondulations ponctuelles. En règle générale, les difficultés sont bien visibles (eau en jeu au 4 et au 9), ce qui permet d'aborder Seapoint avec un minimum de confiance.

Seapoint Golf Club — 1993
IRL - TERMONFECKIN, Co Louth

Office	Secrétariat	(353) 041 - 22 333
Pro shop	Pro-shop	(353) 041 - 22 333
Fax	Fax	(353) 041 - 22 331
Situation	Situation	

8 km from Drogheda (pop. 23 848)

Annual closure	Fermeture annuelle	no
Weekly closure	Fermeture hebdomadaire	no

Fees main season
Tarifs haute saison 18 holes

	Week days Semaine	We/Bank holidays We/Férié
Individual Individuel	IR£ 25	IR£ 30
Couple Couple	IR£ 45	IR£ 54

Caddy	Caddy	on request/IR£ 15
Electric Trolley	Chariot électrique	no
Buggy	Voiturette	no
Clubs	Clubs	no

Credit cards Cartes de crédit VISA - MasterCard

902

Access Accès : Drogheda, Termonfeckin Road
Map 3 on page 830 Carte 3 Page 830

GOLF COURSE
PARCOURS — 15/20

Site	Site	▰▰▰▰▱
Maintenance	Entretien	▰▰▰▰▱
Architect	Architecte	Des Smyth Declan Branigan
Type	Type	links
Relief	Relief	
Water in play	Eau en jeu	▰▰▰▱▱
Exp. to wind	Exposé au vent	▰▰▰▰▱
Trees in play	Arbres en jeu	▰▰▱▱▱

Scorecard Carte de score	Chp. Chp.	Mens Mess.	Ladies Da.
Length Long.	6339	5904	4999
Par	72	72	73

Advised golfing ability	0	12	24	36
Niveau de jeu recommandé			▰▰▰	
Hcp required	Handicap exigé	28 Men, 36 Ladies		

CLUB HOUSE & AMENITIES
CLUB HOUSE ET ANNEXES — 6/10

Pro shop	Pro-shop	▰▰▰▰▱
Driving range	Practice	▰▰▰▱▱
Sheltered	couvert	no
On grass	sur herbe	yes
Putting-green	putting-green	yes
Pitching-green	pitching green	no

HOTEL FACILITIES
ENVIRONNEMENT HOTELIER — 6/10

HOTELS HÔTELS

Boyne Valley — Drogheda
37 rooms, D IR£ 82 — 8 km
Tél (353) 041 - 37 737, Fax (353) 041 - 39188

West Court House — Drogheda
27 rooms, D IR£ 75 — 15 km
Tél (353) 041 - 30 965, Fax (353) 041 - 30 970

Ross Naree — Drogheda
19 rooms, D IR£ 46 — 9 km
Tél (353) 041 - 37 673, Fax (353) 041 - 33 116

RESTAURANTS RESTAURANTS

Triple House — Termonfeckin
Tél (353) 041 - 22 616 — 1 km

Donegans — Monasterboice
Tél (353) 041 - 37 383 — 5 km

Located close to Shannon airport, this is a good starting point for a golfing holiday in the region, with enough difficulties to get you into your stride. High handicappers, though, might not feel so confident about it. In a park landscape, the trees are always in play, but there are not enough of them to trouble even the most claustrophobic player, despite the tightness of some fairways. The essential difficulties are the bunkers and many water hazards, which call for some straight driving and good club selection for the second shot. Most holes give you the choice of lofted approaches or rolled shots. But just following the layout is not enough here, you need to take the initiative. With well-spread hazards and a pleasant variety of holes, this complete course requires some powerful hitting when playing from the back-tees. A very competent course in its style.

Situé près de l'aéroport de Shannon, c'est un bon point de départ pour un séjour golfique dans la région, avec assez de difficultés pour prendre le bon rythme, mais les handicaps élevés auront du mal à se mettre en confiance. Dans un paysage de parc, les arbres entrent en jeu, et si certains trous sont étroits, ils ne sont pas assez nombreux pour gêner les claustrophobes. Les difficultés essentielles sont les bunkers et les nombreux obstacles d'eau, qui imposent pas mal de précision au drive, et un choix de club précis aux seconds coups. Sur la plupart des trous, on peut avoir les options de porter la balle ou de jouer des balles roulées. Il ne suffit pas ici de se laisser porter par le tracé, encore faut-il prendre des initiatives. Avec ses obstacles bien répartis et une bonne variété des trous, ce parcours complet demande aussi quelque puissance si l'on choisit les départs arrière. Une solide réalisation dans son genre.

Shannon Golf Club
IRL - SHANNON, Co. Clare
1966

Office	Secrétariat	(353) 061 - 471 849
Pro shop	Pro-shop	(353) 061 - 471 551
Fax	Fax	(353) 061 - 471 507
Situation	Situation	

2 km from Shannon (pop. 7 920)
23 km from Limerick (pop. 52 083)

Annual closure	Fermeture annuelle	no
Weekly closure	Fermeture hebdomadaire	no

Fees main season
Tarifs haute saison 18 holes

	Week days Semaine	We/Bank holidays We/Férié
Individual Individuel	IR£ 22	IR£ 27
Couple Couple	IR£ 44	IR£ 54

Caddy	Caddy	on request/IR£ 25
Electric Trolley	Chariot électrique	IR£ 15
Buggy	Voiturette	IR£ 25/18 holes
Clubs	Clubs	IR£ 15

Credit cards Cartes de crédit VISA - MasterCard

Access Accès : Limerick, N18 → Ennis.
N19 to Shannon. Golf 800 m from Shannon Airport.
Map 2 on page 828 Carte 2 Page 828

GOLF COURSE
PARCOURS
13/20

Site	Site	▮▮▮▮▯
Maintenance	Entretien	▮▮▮▮▯
Architect	Architecte	John D. Harris
Type	Type	parkland
Relief	Relief	▮▯▯▯▯
Water in play	Eau en jeu	▮▮▮▮▯
Exp. to wind	Exposé au vent	▮▮▯▯▯
Trees in play	Arbres en jeu	▮▮▮▯▯

Scorecard Carte de score	Chp. Chp.	Mens Mess.	Ladies Da.
Length Long.	6186	5863	5209
Par	72	72	74

Advised golfing ability		0	12	**24**	36
Niveau de jeu recommandé				▮▮▮▮	
Hcp required	Handicap exigé		Men 24, Ladies 36		

CLUB HOUSE & AMENITIES
CLUB HOUSE ET ANNEXES
6/10

Pro shop	Pro-shop	▮▮▮▯▯
Driving range	Practice	▮▮▮▯▯
Sheltered	couvert	no
On grass	sur herbe	yes
Putting-green	putting-green	yes
Pitching-green	pitching green	yes

903

HOTEL FACILITIES
ENVIRONNEMENT HOTELIER
6/10

HOTELS HÔTELS

Great Southern Hotel — Shannon Airport
115 rooms, D IR£ 90 — 1 km
Tel (353) 061 - 471 122, Fax (353) 061 - 471 982

Fitzpatrick Shamrock Hotel — Bunratty
115 rooms, D IR£ 100 — 9 km
Tel (353) 061 - 361 177, Fax (353) 061 - 471 252

West County Inn — Ennis
110 rooms, D IR£ 66 — 20 km
Tel (353) 065 - 28 421, Fax (353) 065 - 28 801

RESTAURANTS RESTAURANTS

MacCloskey's — Bunratty
Tel (353) 061 - 364 082 — 9 km

Mr Pickwick's — Shannon
Tel (353) 061 - 364 290 — 2 km

The early 1990s saw the advent of a fine group of excellent new courses in Ireland, often tied in with hotels. Slieve Russell is one such project in a region that hitherto had earned a reputation as being a paradise for anglers, and whose isolation should appeal to golfers who want to get away from the world for a few days spent in the heart of nature. The landscape is park-land in style, but certain geographical features are reminiscent of a links course. Two large lakes come into play, joined by a stretch of water which lurks just as threateningly, and complete a full barrage of difficulties: sometimes very thick rough, thickets, fairway and green-side bunkers and greens with sometimes very pronounced contours. Of the more memorable holes, we noted the excellence of the par 3s (especially the 16th), the 2nd, where the water is already upon you, and the 13th, a magnificent par 5 alongside Lough Rud. This course has very quickly forged itself a pretty fine reputation, and understandably so.

Le début des années 90 a vu naître en Irlande un bon groupe d'excellents nouveaux parcours, souvent associés à des hôtels. Slieve Russell est de ceux-ci, dans une région jusqu'ici réputée comme un paradis des pêcheurs, et dont l'isolement devrait séduire les golfeurs qui veulent se retirer du monde, du moins en pleine nature et au moins quelques jours. Il se trouve dans un paysage de parc, mais certains reliefs font parfois penser aux links. Deux grands lacs viennent en jeu, réunis par un cours d'eau tout aussi menaçant. Ils complètent un arsenal de difficultés : rough parfois épais, buissons, bunkers de fairway et de greens, ceux-ci protégeant des greens au relief parfois prononcé. Parmi quelques trous mémorables, on soulignera la qualité des par 3 (notamment le 16), du 2, où l'eau est déjà présente, et du 13, un magnifique par 5 le long du Lough Rud. Ce parcours s'est fait une jolie réputation, on comprend pourquoi.

Slieve Russell Golf Club — 1992
IRL - BALLYCONNELL, Co Cavan

Office	Secrétariat	(353) 049 - 26 458
Pro shop	Pro-shop	(353) 049 - 26 444
Fax	Fax	(353) 049 - 26 474
Situation	Situation	

11 km from Belturbet
25 km from Cavan (pop. 3 332)

Annual closure	Fermeture annuelle	no
Weekly closure	Fermeture hebdomadaire	no
Fees main season	Tarifs haute saison	18 holes

	Week days Semaine	We/Bank holidays We/Férié
Individual Individuel	IR£ 28	IR£ 36
Couple Couple	IR£ 56	IR£ 72

Hotel residents : IR£ 19 (W/D) and IR£ 26 (W/E)

Caddy	Caddy	on request/IR£ 20
Electric Trolley	Chariot électrique	no
Buggy	Voiturette	IR£ 25/18 holes
Clubs	Clubs	IR£ 10/18 holes

Credit cards Cartes de crédit
VISA - Eurocard - MasterCard - AMEX

904

ENNISKILLEN

GOLF

A 509

R 200   BALLYCONNEL
Béal Atha Connaill

R 205   N 3

BELTURBET   R 197
Béal Tarbirt

Ballinamore   R 200
Béal an Atha Móir

| 0 | 2 | 4 km |
| 0 | | 2,5 miles |

Access Accès : Dublin, N3 → Cavan.
Belturbet, R200 → Ballyconnell
Map 1 on page 827 Carte 1 Page 827

GOLF COURSE
PARCOURS — 15/20

Site	Site	▬▬▬▬▬▬▬
Maintenance	Entretien	▬▬▬▬▬▬▬
Architect	Architecte	Paddy Merrigan
Type	Type	parkland
Relief	Relief	▬▬▬▬
Water in play	Eau en jeu	▬▬▬▬▬
Exp. to wind	Exposé au vent	▬▬▬
Trees in play	Arbres en jeu	▬▬▬▬

Scorecard	Chp.	Mens	Ladies
Carte de score	Chp.	Mess.	Da.
Length Long.	6449	6018	4849
Par	72	72	72

Advised golfing ability		0 12 24 36
Niveau de jeu recommandé		▬▬▬▬▬
Hcp required	Handicap exigé	no

CLUB HOUSE & AMENITIES
CLUB HOUSE ET ANNEXES — 8/10

Pro shop	Pro-shop	▬▬▬▬▬
Driving range	Practice	▬▬▬▬
Sheltered	couvert	no
On grass	sur herbe	yes
Putting-green	putting-green	yes
Pitching-green	pitching green	yes

HOTEL FACILITIES
ENVIRONNEMENT HOTELIER — 6/10

HOTELS HÔTELS
Slieve Russell Hotel — Ballyconnell
150 rooms, D IR£ 150 — on site
Tel (353) 049 - 26 442, Fax (353) 049 - 26 474

GUEST ROOMS CHAMBRES D'HÔTE
An Crannog — Ballyconnell
5 rooms, D IR£ 32 — 1 km
Tel (353) 049 - 26 545

Greenmount — Ballyconnell
5 rooms, D IR£ 32 — 2 km
Tel (353) 049 - 26 628

RESTAURANTS RESTAURANTS
Summit — Golf Club
Tel (353) 049 - 26 444 — on site

Erin Bistro — Belturbet, 11 km

14	6	6

Some 6,000 trees have been planted at St Helen's Bay, and they will of course underline the park landscape of a part of this course. Philip Walton, who made his golf-designer debut here, visibly had the amateur golfer in mind. Sure, there is water on six holes, but it is more psychologically scaring than terribly dangerous, the fairway bunkers are on the lenient side and the greens (moderately sized) are well defended but leave a way open for rolled approach shots, if preferred to lofted pitches. From the 14th hole onward, you are in links country, and the going gets tougher as you progress. The coup de grâce awaits you at the 17th and 18th holes, where your card can end in tatters... or maybe not, since you have had 16 holes to hone your swing. One of the major assets of this course is its versatility, and it gives a lot of pleasure to players of all levels. We should mention, in closing, that the "wall of famine", dating from 1846, comes into play on three holes.

6.000 arbres ont été plantés à St Helen's Bay, qui vont accentuer le paysage de parc d'une partie du parcours. Philip Walton, dont c'est le premier dessin, a visiblement pensé aux amateurs. Certes, l'eau vient en jeu sur six trous, mais de manière plus psychologique que terriblement dangereuse, les bunkers de fairway ne sont pas trop pénalisants, les greens (de dimension confortable) sont bien défendus, mais on peut en aborder la plupart en faisant rouler la balle, ou en la portant, au choix. A partir du 14, nous voici dans un paysage de links, dont la difficulté va croissant, pour culminer au 17 et au 18, deux trous pour détruire sa carte, ou pour la soigner : vous avez 16 trous pour vous y préparer ! La versatilité du parcours est l'un de ses arguments majeurs, il donne beaucoup de plaisir aux joueurs de tous niveaux. Pour l'anecdote, soulignons la mise en jeu sur trois trous du «mur de la famine», qui remonte à 1846.

St Helen's Bay Golf & Country Club 1993

Kilrane
IRL - ROSSLARE HARBOUR, Co. Wexford

Office	Secrétariat	(353) 053 - 33 234
Pro shop	Pro-shop	(353) 053 - 33 669
Fax	Fax	(353) 053 - 33 803
Situation	Situation	

13 km from Wexford (pop. 15 393)
2 km from Rosslare Harbour

Annual closure	Fermeture annuelle	no
Weekly closure	Fermeture hebdomadaire	no

Fees main season	Tarifs haute saison	18 holes
	Week days Semaine	**We/Bank holidays** We/Férié
Individual Individuel	IR£ 20	IR£ 20
Couple Couple	IR£ 40	IR£ 40

Caddy	Caddy	IR£ 10/18 holes
Electric Trolley	Chariot électrique	IR£ 6
Buggy	Voiturette	IR£ 20/18 holes
Clubs	Clubs	IR£ 8

Credit cards Cartes de crédit
VISA - Eurocard - MasterCard - AMEX

Access Accès : Dublin, N11 to Wexford.
N25 to Rosslare Harbour
Map 2 on page 829 Carte 2 Page 829

GOLF COURSE
PARCOURS
14/20

Site	Site	
Maintenance	Entretien	
Architect	Architecte	Philip Walton
Type	Type	links, parkland
Relief	Relief	
Water in play	Eau en jeu	
Exp. to wind	Exposé au vent	
Trees in play	Arbres en jeu	

Scorecard Carte de score	Chp. Chp.	Mens Mess.	Ladies Da.
Length Long.	6091	5813	4967
Par	72	72	72

Advised golfing ability		0	12	24	36
Niveau de jeu recommandé					
Hcp required	Handicap exigé	no			

CLUB HOUSE & AMENITIES
CLUB HOUSE ET ANNEXES
6/10

Pro shop	Pro-shop	
Driving range	Practice	
Sheltered	couvert	no
On grass	sur herbe	yes
Putting-green	putting-green	yes
Pitching-green	pitching green	no

HOTEL FACILITIES
ENVIRONNEMENT HOTELIER
6/10

HOTELS HÔTELS

Kelly's Resort — Rosslare Strand
99 rooms, D IR£ 85 — 5 km
Tel (353) 053 - 32 114, Fax (353) 053 - 32 222

Great Southern — Rosslare Harbour
100 rooms, D IR£ 70 — 4 km
Tel (353) 053 - 33 233, Fax (353) 053 - 33 543

Cedars Hotel — Rosslare Strand
34 rooms, D IR£ 58 — 5 km
Tel (353) 053 - 32 124, Fax (353) 053 - 32 243

RESTAURANTS RESTAURANTS

Coopers — Killinick
Tel (353) 053 - 58 942 — 6 km

Lobster Pot — Carne
Tel (353) 053 - 31 110 — 3 km

905

Before designing Druid's Glen, Pat Ruddy and Tom Craddock gave Dublin one of its best inland courses, at the expense of significant earthwork, as the former farming land was singularly lacking in geographical relief. They evidently had champion golfers in mind, but didn't forget the average amateur player either. Yet despite the many different tee-off areas, they haven't really managed to make it easy. Many of the greens are very well-guarded, and the style of golf is more American than British, meaning a lot of lofted iron shots, long and short. There are a few memorable holes, like the 8th or 12th, two real par 5s reachable only in three, and the 7th and 18th, two grand par 4s. These are all holes where water lurks dangerously. Elsewhere, the bunkers are comparatively flat and so don't set too many problems, even for players who have an aversion to sand. A course well worth getting to know.

Avant de produire Druids Glen, Pat Ruddy et Tom Craddock ont donné à Dublin l'un de ses meilleurs parcours intérieurs, au prix de terrassements importants, car ces anciens terrains agricoles manquaient singulièrement de relief. S'ils ont pensé aux champions, ils n'ont pas oublié les amateurs moyens, mais ils n'ont pas vraiment réussi, malgré le nombre de départs, à le rendre facile. Il faut dire que de nombreux greens sont très défendus, et que l'on joue plus un golf à l'américaine qu'à la «britannique», avec l'obligation de porter haut les coups de fer, y compris les petites approches. Quelques trous sont mémorables, comme le 8 et le 12, deux véritables par 5 à trois coups, le 7 et surtout le 18, deux par 4 de grand style. Ce sont tous des trous où l'eau est dangereuse. Ailleurs, les bunkers sont relativement plats, ce qui ne pose pas trop de problèmes, même à ceux qui n'adorent pas le sable. Un parcours à connaître.

St Margaret's Golf & Country Club — 1992
IRL - ST MARGARET'S, Co Dublin

Office	Secrétariat	(353) 01 - 864 0400
Pro shop	Pro-shop	(353) 01 - 864 0400
Fax	Fax	(353) 01 - 864 0289
Situation	Situation	

20 km from Dublin (pop. 859 976)
10 km from Malahide (pop. 12 088)

Annual closure	Fermeture annuelle	no
Weekly closure	Fermeture hebdomadaire	no

Fees main season
Tarifs haute saison 18 holes

	Week days Semaine	We/Bank holidays We/Férié
Individual Individuel	IR£ 40	IR£ 40
Couple Couple	IR£ 80	IR£ 80

Caddy	Caddy	IR£ 25/18 holes
Electric Trolley	Chariot électrique	no
Buggy	Voiturette	IR£ 25/18 holes
Clubs	Clubs	IR£ 15/18 holes

Credit cards Cartes de crédit VISA - MasterCard - AMEX

906

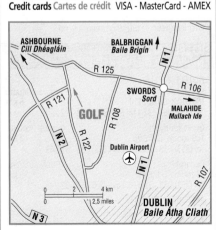

ASHBOURNE Cill Dhéagláin
BALBRIGGAN Baile Brigín
R 125
SWORDS Sord
R 106
R 121
GOLF
R 108
MALAHIDE Mullach Ide
N 2
R 122
Dublin Airport
DUBLIN Baile Átha Cliath
N 3
0 — 2 — 4 km
0 — 2,5 miles

Access Accès : 6 km W. of Dublin Airport
Map 3 on page 830 Carte 3 Page 830

GOLF COURSE
PARCOURS
16/20

Site	Site	
Maintenance	Entretien	
Architect	Architecte	Pat Ruddy Tom Craddock
Type	Type	parkland, inland
Relief	Relief	
Water in play	Eau en jeu	
Exp. to wind	Exposé au vent	
Trees in play	Arbres en jeu	

Scorecard Carte de score	Chp. Chp.	Mens Mess.	Ladies Da.
Length Long.	6226	5967	5195
Par	73	73	75

Advised golfing ability Niveau de jeu recommandé	0	12	24	36
Hcp required Handicap exigé	24 Men, 36 Ladies			

CLUB HOUSE & AMENITIES
CLUB HOUSE ET ANNEXES
7/10

Pro shop	Pro-shop	
Driving range	Practice	
Sheltered	couvert	no
On grass	sur herbe	yes
Putting-green	putting-green	yes
Pitching-green	pitching green	no

HOTEL FACILITIES
ENVIRONNEMENT HOTELIER
7/10

HOTELS HÔTELS
Forte Travelodge — Swords
40 rooms, D IR£ 32 — 6 km
Tel (353) 01 - 840 9233, Fax (353) 01 - 832 4476

Grand Hotel — Malahide
100 rooms, D IR£ 95 — 10 km
Tel (353) 01 - 845 0000, Fax (353) 01 - 845 0987

Forte Crest — Dublin Airport
188 rooms, D IR£ 110 — 6 km
Tel (353) 01 - 844 4211, Fax (353) 01 - 842 5874

RESTAURANTS RESTAURANTS
Red Bank — Skerries
Tel (353) 01 - 849 1005 — 15 km

Old School House — Swords
Tel (353) 01 - 840 2846 — 8 km

A hundred years after it was first created, the original design here was drastically remodelled by Fred Hawtree and Eddie Hackett. In the past, you could only reach the course by boat. Now, they have made it meaner but removed some of its beauty in the process. In contrast, there are no more blind greens, even though the terrain is hilly (but not too punishing). A kind course when there is little or no wind, The Island can turn nasty when the wind blows, especially on the holes close to the sea. This is when you need the deliberate low shot and, if that were not enough, the ability to stop the ball on the greens at the same time. Here you learn how to fashion every shot in the book, so much so that this club has schooled an impressive list of top men and lady players, which goes to show that power play on its own is not enough. It's one of the best venues for the region's golfing technicians.

Cent ans après sa naissance, Fred Hawtree et Eddie Hackett ont révisé de manière drastique le dessin original d'un parcours auquel on ne pouvait autrefois accéder qu'en barque. Ils lui ont donné de la rudesse, mais retiré un peu de la beauté. En revanche, il n'y a plus de greens aveugles, même si le terrain est un peu accidenté (pas de manière punitive). Assez aimable par vent faible ou nul, The Island peut devenir très méchant par vent fort, en particulier sur les trous proches de la mer, il faut alors maîtriser les balles basses, mais ce n'est pas suffisant, il faut en même temps arrêter la balle sur les greens. Ici, on apprend à fabriquer tous les coups de golf. Tellement bien que ce club a formé une liste impressionnante de joueurs et surtout de bonnes joueuses, comme quoi la puissance ne suffit pas. C'est un des garnds lieux de rendez-vous des techniciens de la région,

The Island Golf Club
1890
IRL - DONABATE, Co Dublin

Office	Secrétariat	(353) 01 - 843 6205
Pro shop	Pro-shop	(353) 01 - 843 5002
Fax	Fax	(353) 01 - 843 6860
Situation	Situation	

20 km from Dublin (pop. 859 976)

Annual closure	Fermeture annuelle	no
Weekly closure	Fermeture hebdomadaire	no

Fees main season
Tarifs haute saison 18 holes

	Week days Semaine	We/Bank holidays We/Férié
Individual Individuel	IR£ 35	IR£ 45
Couple Couple	IR£ 70	IR£ 90

Caddy	Caddy	on request/IR£ 25
Electric Trolley	Chariot électrique	no
Buggy	Voiturette	no
Clubs	Clubs	IR£ 25/18 holes

Credit cards Cartes de crédit VISA - MasterCard

Access Accès : Dublin, N1 → Belfast. Turn right to Donabate. Side road to The Island signposted.
Map 3 on page 830 Carte 3 Page 830

GOLF COURSE
PARCOURS
15/20

Site	Site	
Maintenance	Entretien	
Architect	Architecte	Fred Hawtree Eddie Hackett
Type	Type	links
Relief	Relief	
Water in play	Eau en jeu	
Exp. to wind	Exposé au vent	
Trees in play	Arbres en jeu	

Scorecard Carte de score	Chp. Chp.	Mens Mess.	Ladies Da.
Length Long.	6078	5791	5447
Par	71	71	70

Advised golfing ability
Niveau de jeu recommandé   0 12 24 36

Hcp required Handicap exigé   28 Men, 36 Ladies

CLUB HOUSE & AMENITIES
CLUB HOUSE ET ANNEXES
7/10

Pro shop	Pro-shop	
Driving range	Practice	
Sheltered	couvert	no
On grass	sur herbe	yes
Putting-green	putting-green	yes
Pitching-green	pitching green	yes

HOTEL FACILITIES
ENVIRONNEMENT HOTELIER
7/10

HOTELS HÔTELS

Forte Crest — Dublin Airport
188 rooms, D IR£ 110 — 8 km
Tel (353) 01 - 844 4211, Fax (353) 01 - 842 5874

Dunes Hotel — Donabate
16 rooms, D IR£ 50 — 5 km
Tel (353) 01 - 843 6153, Fax (353) 01 - 843 6111

Pier Hotel — Skerries
10 rooms, D IR£ 35 — 10 km
Tel (353) 01 - 849 1708, Fax (353) 01 - 849 1708

RESTAURANTS RESTAURANTS

The Food Fare — Dublin Airport
Tel (353) 01 - 844 4085 — 8 km

Giovanni's — Malahide
Tel (353) 01 - 845 1733 — 8 km

907

Give a golfer terrain like this and he will give you a course to match his designer skills, imagination and audacity. Arnold Palmer had no shortage of the latter and he learnt the former; Tralee (with the complicity of mother nature) is one of his greatest courses. The front 9 unwind partly atop a cliff overhanging the ocean, which comes dangerously into play if direction and accuracy are wayward. The back 9 are even more impressive, amidst huge dunes in their natural state. Here, you often need to carry the ball a long way and you will be best advised to play from the front tees if your drive and long ironwork are not quite up to scratch. A heroic course, not always as refined in diabolical details as say Ballybunion, Portrush or County Down, but essential visiting for every true golfing enthusiast.

Donnez un terrain comme celui-ci à un golfeur, il vous fera un parcours à la hauteur de ses connaissances d'architecte, de son imagination et de son audace. Le champion Arnold Palmer ne manquait pas de ces dernières qualités, il a appris les premières et Tralee (avec la complicité de la nature) est l'une de ses plus grandes réussites. L'aller se déroule partiellement au sommet d'une falaise longeant l'océan, qui vient dangereusement en jeu si l'on manque de direction et de précision. Le retour est plus impressionnant encore, au milieu d'énormes dunes à l'état sauvage. Là, il faut souvent porter loin la balle, et l'on aura intérêt à choisir les départs avancés si la qualité du drive et des longs fers n'est pas à la hauteur des défis. Un parcours héroïque, pas toujours aussi raffiné dans les détails diaboliques que Ballybunion, Portrush ou County Down, mais incontournable pour tout véritable amoureux du golf.

Tralee Golf Club — 1895

West Barron
IRL - ARDFERT, Co Kerry

Office	Secrétariat	(353) 066 - 36 379
Pro shop	Pro-shop	(353) 066 - 36 379
Fax	Fax	(353) 066 - 36 008
Situation	Situation	

12 km from Tralee (pop. 17 225)

Annual closure	Fermeture annuelle	no
Weekly closure	Fermeture hebdomadaire	no

Fees main season
Tarifs haute saison 18 holes

	Week days Semaine	We/Bank holidays We/Férié
Individual Individuel	IR£ 45	IR£ 45
Couple Couple	IR£ 90	IR£ 90

No green-fees on Sunday
Early tee times: IR£ 35 (→ 9.30 am)

Caddy	Caddy	on request/IR£ 15
Electric Trolley	Chariot électrique	no
Buggy	Voiturette	no
Clubs	Clubs	no

Credit cards Cartes de crédit VISA - Mastercard

GOLF COURSE / PARCOURS — 18/20

Site	Site	
Maintenance	Entretien	
Architect	Architecte	Arnold Palmer
Type	Type	links
Relief	Relief	
Water in play	Eau en jeu	
Exp. to wind	Exposé au vent	
Trees in play	Arbres en jeu	

Scorecard Carte de score	Chp. Chp.	Mens Mess.	Ladies Da.
Length Long.	6252	5961	4792
Par	71	71	72

Advised golfing ability Niveau de jeu recommandé	0 12 24 36
Hcp required Handicap exigé	24 Men, 36 Ladies

CLUB HOUSE & AMENITIES / CLUB HOUSE ET ANNEXES — 7/10

Pro shop	Pro-shop	
Driving range	Practice	
Sheltered	couvert	no
On grass	sur herbe	yes
Putting-green	putting-green	yes
Pitching-green	pitching green	yes

HOTEL FACILITIES / ENVIRONNEMENT HOTELIER — 6/10

HOTELS HÔTELS

Brandon Hotel — Tralee 12 km
160 rooms, D IR£ 70
Tel (353) 066 - 23 333, Fax (353) 066 - 25 019

Grand Hotel — Tralee 12 km
44 rooms, D IR£ 70
Tel (353) 066 - 21 499, Fax (353) 066 - 22 877

Imperial — Tralee 12 km
29 rooms, D IR£ 44
Tel (353) 066 - 27 755, Fax (353) 066 - 27 800

RESTAURANTS RESTAURANTS

Tankard — Tralee 2 km
Tel (353) 066 - 36 349

Oyster Tavern — Tralee 3 km
Tel (353) 066 - 36 102

908

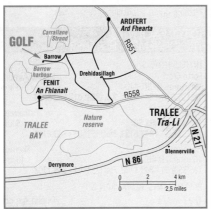

Access Accès : Fenit Road, 12 km NW of Tralee
Map 2 on page 828 Carte 2 Page 828

TRAMORE

Tramore is first and foremost an impressive site by the sea, which in the past caused more than a few problems in stormy weather. The present course has no links holes and is much better protected. The clay soil and heathery terrain drain the course well owing to its elevated position, and the sloping terrain makes an easy walk. This is a driver's course, where long-hitters have an obvious advantage. However, while they can open their shoulders on the first few holes, they will need to keep on the straight and narrow coming home, where the course gets much narrower. Generally speaking, the hazards (especially trees) are placed to catch wayward shots, and players lacking power should avoid the back-tees. Tramore is suitable for players of all levels, but there is just a touch of extra difficulty on the last four holes, especially on the 16th, where a little stream comes into play rather dangerously.

Tramore, c'est d'abord une situation impressionnante en bord de mer, qui a posé autrefois bien des problèmes lors de grandes tempêtes. Le parcours actuel n'a pas de trous de links, il est beaucoup mieux protégé. Le sol d'argile et de terre de bruyère est bien drainant en raison de sa situation surélévée, et les pentes du terrain sont assez favorables à la marche. C'est un parcours de driver où les joueurs longs seront évidemment avantagés, mais s'ils pourront se déchaîner dans les premiers trous, ils devront aussi être droits vers la fin, bien plus étroite. En règle générale, les obstacles (surtout les arbres) sont placés pour recevoir les coups écartés, les joueurs pas trop puissants auront intérêt à ne pas jouer des départs arrière. Tramore convient à tous les niveaux de jeu, avec une nuance de difficulté supplémentaire sur les quatre derniers trous, particulièrement au 16, où un ruisseau vient en jeu de manière dangereuse.

Tramore Golf Club — 1894

Newtown Hill
IRL - TRAMORE, Co Waterford

Office	Secrétariat	(353) 051 - 386 170
Pro shop	Pro-shop	(353) 051 - 381 706
Fax	Fax	(353) 051 - 390 961
Situation	Situation	

10 km from Waterford City (pop. 40 328)

Annual closure	Fermeture annuelle	no
Weekly closure	Fermeture hebdomadaire	no

Fees main season
Tarifs haute saison 18 holes

	Week days Semaine	We/Bank holidays We/Férié
Individual Individuel	IR£ 25	IR£ 30
Couple Couple	IR£ 50	IR£ 60

Caddy	Caddy	IR£ 10/18 holes
Electric Trolley	Chariot électrique	no
Buggy	Voiturette	IR£ 20/18 holes
Clubs	Clubs	IR£ 8/18 holes

Credit cards Cartes de crédit VISA - MasterCard

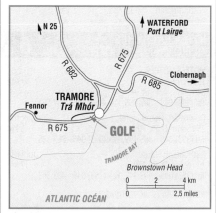

Access Accès : Cork → Tramore. Left junction, outcoast road to top of the hill
Map 2 on page 829 Carte 2 Page 829

GOLF COURSE
PARCOURS — 13/20

Site	Site	
Maintenance	Entretien	
Architect	Architecte	Capt. Tippett
Type	Type	seaside course, parkland
Relief	Relief	
Water in play	Eau en jeu	
Exp. to wind	Exposé au vent	
Trees in play	Arbres en jeu	

Scorecard Carte de score	Chp. Chp.	Mens Mess.	Ladies Da.
Length Long.	6055	5871	5146
Par	72	72	75

Advised golfing ability		0	12	24	36
Niveau de jeu recommandé					
Hcp required	Handicap exigé	no			

CLUB HOUSE & AMENITIES
CLUB HOUSE ET ANNEXES — 7/10

Pro shop	Pro-shop	
Driving range	Practice	
Sheltered	couvert	no
On grass	sur herbe	yes
Putting-green	putting-green	yes
Pitching-green	pitching green	no

HOTEL FACILITIES
ENVIRONNEMENT HOTELIER — 6/10

HOTELS HÔTELS

O'Sheds Hotel — Tramore
14 rooms, D IR£ 55 — 1.5 km
Tel (353) 051 - 381 246, Fax (353) 051 - 390 144

Grand Hotel — Tramore
80 rooms, D IR£ 68 — 1.5 km
Tel (353) 051 - 381 414, Fax (353) 051 - 386 428

The Majestic Hotel — Tramore
57 rooms, D IR£ 33 — 1.5 km
Tel (353) 051 - 381 761, Fax (353) 051 - 381 766

RESTAURANTS RESTAURANTS

Pine Rooms — Tramore
Tel (353) 051 - 381 683 — 2 km

Esquire — Tramore
Tel (353) 051 - 386 237 — 2 km

909

Although the buildings, particularly the hotel, were still not finished when this Guide went to press, the course promises a great deal. It is very attractively located on the shores of lake Blessington and the layout, restyled and completed by P.J. Merrigan, is well suited to all levels of golfing ability. The fairways are wide, with bold routes to beckon the long-hitters and safer ways forward for the lesser players, and the use of trees, sand and water as hazards is cleverly balanced. In this respect, the fairway and green-side bunkers are particularly well located. The design successfully manages to retain a certain local colour despite the "foreign" architectural influences, because the natural landscape has been left unspoilt. High-handicappers will certainly find it something of a stiff challenge, but they will be glad to have had a go. This still very young course has a brilliant future ahead of it, and we would not be at all surprised if it were to become one of Ireland's very best inland courses.

Bien que les bâtiments, et notamment l'hôtel, ne soient encore achevés à parution de ce Guide, ce golf est des plus prometteurs. Sa situation en bordure du lac de Blessington est séduisante, le tracé remodelé et complété par P.J. Merrigan est bien adapté à tous les niveaux de jeu, avec des fairways larges, des chemins audacieux pour les frappeurs, et d'autres plus sûrs pour les prudents, une utilisation très équilibrée des arbres, de l'eau et du sable comme obstacles : les bunkers de fairways et de greens sont judicieusement placés. Le paysage naturel ayant été préservé, le dessin réussit à conserver une certaine couleur "locale" en dépit d'influences architecturales "étrangères". Certes, les joueurs peu expérimentés trouveront le challenge un peu difficile, mais ils seront heureux de l'avoir affronté. Encore très jeune, c'est un parcours d'avenir : on ne serait pas étonné qu'il devienne l'un des meilleurs "inland" du pays.

Tulfarris Golf Club — 1987
Blessington Lakes
Blessington, Co Wicklow

Office	Secrétariat	(353) 045 - 867 555
Pro shop	Pro-shop	(353) 045 - 867 555
Fax	Fax	(353) 045 - 867 561
Situation	Situation	

Dublin (pop. 859 976), 40 km

Annual closure	Fermeture annuelle	no
Weekly closure	Fermeture hebdomadaire	no

Fees main season
Tarifs haute saison 18 holes

	Week days Semaine	We/Bank holidays We/Férié
Individual Individuel	IR£ 45	IR£ 50
Couple Couple	IR£ 90	IR£ 100

Caddy	Caddy	on request/IR£ 15
Electric Trolley	Chariot électrique	no
Buggy	Voiturette	IR£ 25/18 holes
Clubs	Clubs	yes

Credit cards Cartes de crédit
VISA - Eurocard - MasterCard - AMEX - DC

910

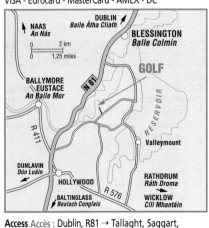

Access Accès : Dublin, R81 → Tallaght, Saggart, Tullow. Just after Blessington, turn left → Reservoir
Map 3 on page 830 Carte 3 Page 830

GOLF COURSE PARCOURS — 14/20

Site	Site	
Maintenance	Entretien	
Architect	Architecte	Paddy Merrigan
Type	Type	parkland
Relief	Relief	
Water in play	Eau en jeu	
Exp. to wind	Exposé au vent	
Trees in play	Arbres en jeu	

Scorecard Carte de score	Chp. Chp.	Mens Mess.	Ladies Da.
Length Long.	6410	6064	5325
Par	72	72	72

Advised golfing ability   0 12 24 36
Niveau de jeu recommandé
Hcp required   Handicap exigé   no

CLUB HOUSE & AMENITIES CLUB HOUSE ET ANNEXES — 7/10

Pro shop	Pro-shop	
Driving range	Practice	
Sheltered	couvert	no
On grass	sur herbe	yes
Putting-green	putting-green	yes
Pitching-green	pitching green	yes

HOTEL FACILITIES ENVIRONNEMENT HOTELIER — 6/10

HOTELS HÔTELS
Tulfarris House — on site
64 rooms, not yet set, ask Spring of 2000
Tel (353) 045 - 867 555, Fax (353) 045 - 867 561

Downshire House Hotel — Blessington
25 rooms, D IR£ 70 — 5 km
Tel (353) 045 - 865 199, Fax (353) 045 - 865 335

Rathsallagh House — Dunlavin
17 rooms, D IR£ 170 — 17 km
Tel (353) 045 - 403 112, Fax (353) 045 - 403 343

RESTAURANTS RESTAURANTS
Rathsallagh House — Dunlavin
Tel (353) 045 - 403 112 — 17 km

TULLAMORE

15 6 5

This has long been one of Ireland's very good inland courses (it is over 100 years old). Reviewed by James Braid in 1926, it has been rejuvenated by Paddy Merrigan and given a planting programme involving 5,000 trees to add to the surrounding forest (oak and beech trees). So trees should become an even more significant factor here, alongside the classic bunkers and a meandering stream. The shape of the fairways brings the rough into play in a very honest way, only really penalising the truly wayward shot. The clearly visible hazards clearly show the best way forward, a friendly gesture which is repeated right around this very open and forthright course. And even though yardage is low, this is still a course where scoring can be difficult; you need to be very accurate to get to a good position on averagely sized greens, which pitch and bite nicely. This is a flat course, and an interesting day's golf.

C'est depuis longtemps (il est centenaire) l'un des très bons parcours inland. Revu par James Braid en 1926, il fait l'objet d'un rajeunissement par Paddy Merrigan, et d'un programme de plantations de 5.000 arbres, à côté des bunkers classiques et des méandres d'un ruisseau. Les arbres devraient donc devenir un facteur encore plus important, à côté des bunkers classiques et des méandres d'un ruisseau. Le dessin des fairways met en jeu le rough, mais de façon très honnête, ne pénalisant vraiment que les coups très écartés. Les obstacles bien visibles indiquent clairement la ligne de jeu, cet aspect amical se confirme sur ce parcours d'une grande franchise. Il reste cependant difficile d'y réaliser un très bon score, même si la longueur est réduite : il faut beaucoup de précision pour être en bonne position sur des greens de taille moyenne, mais assez réceptifs. Si l'on ajoute que ce parcours est plat, le détour est intéressant.

Tullamore Golf Club		**1896**
Brookfield		
IRL - TULLAMORE, Co Offaly		
Office	Secrétariat	(353) 0506 - 21 439
Pro shop	Pro-shop	(353) 0506 - 51 757
Fax	Fax	(353) 0506 - 51 757
Situation	Situation	
90 km from Dublin (pop. 859 976)		
2 km from Tullamore(pop. 8 622)		
Annual closure	Fermeture annuelle	no
Weekly closure	Fermeture hebdomadaire	no

Fees main season
Tarifs haute saison 18 holes

	Week days Semaine	We/Bank holidays We/Férié
Individual Individuel	IR£ 11	IR£ 13
Couple Couple	IR£ 22	IR£ 26

Caddy	Caddy	on request/IR£ 15
Electric Trolley	Chariot électrique	no
Buggy	Voiturette	no
Clubs	Clubs	IR£ 10/18 holes
Credit cards Cartes de crédit		no

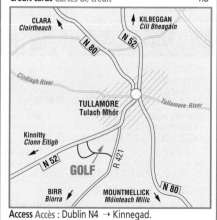

Access Accès : Dublin N4 → Kinnegad.
N6 → Kilbeggan. N52 → Tullamore.
R421 → Kinnitty, 2 km from Tullamore
Map 2 on page 829 Carte 2 Page 829

GOLF COURSE
PARCOURS
15/20

Site	Site	▇▇▇▇▇▇▇▇
Maintenance	Entretien	▇▇▇▇▇▇▇
Architect	Architecte	James Braid
		Paddy Merrigan
		parkland
Type	Type	
Relief	Relief	▇▇▇▇
Water in play	Eau en jeu	▇▇
Exp. to wind	Exposé au vent	▇▇▇
Trees in play	Arbres en jeu	▇▇▇▇

Scorecard	Chp.	Mens	Ladies
Carte de score	Chp.	Mess.	Da.
Length Long.	5779	5555	5070
Par	71	71	74

Advised golfing ability	0	12	24	36
Niveau de jeu recommandé		▇▇▇▇		
Hcp required Handicap exigé	no			

CLUB HOUSE & AMENITIES
CLUB HOUSE ET ANNEXES
6/10

Pro shop	Pro-shop	▇▇▇▇▇
Driving range	Practice	
Sheltered	couvert	no
On grass	sur herbe	yes
Putting-green	putting-green	yes
Pitching-green	pitching green	yes

HOTEL FACILITIES
ENVIRONNEMENT HOTELIER
5/10

HOTELS HÔTELS
Moorhill House Hotel — Tullamore
12 rooms, D IR£ 50 — 3 km
Tel (353) 0506 - 21 395
Fax (353) 0506 - 52 424

RESTAURANTS RESTAURANTS
Moorhill House — Tullamore
Tel (353) 0506 - 21 395 — 2 km
Sli Dala — Kinnitty
Tel (353) 0509 - 37 318 — 20 km

911

The first nine holes, designed by the great Willie Park Jnr., were completed by the no less great James Braid. From these two we would have expected a course to resist the skilled player and show a kinder face to the less experienced golfer. This is indeed the case, but today its yardage might seem a little on the short side. Likewise, although the fairway bunkers are strategically well placed, their design has faded over the years. This is perfect on a day when you want golf to be fun. In contrast, the green-side bunkers are well-placed to gather the wayward shot, and you will need to play some sharp short and medium irons. The greens are medium-sized, slightly contoured and are virtually all elevated above ground level, thus emphasising the need for accuracy. This pleasant course leaves a pleasant memory thanks to the 18th hole, a downhill par 4 with a splendid scenic view from the tee.

Les neuf premiers trous conçus par le grand Willie Park Jr ont été complétés par le non moins grand James Braid. On pouvait attendre d'eux un parcours résistant aux efforts des joueurs de haut niveau, et plus amical pour les moins expérimentés. C'est effectivement le cas, mais on peut trouver aujourd'hui sa longueur insuffisante, de même que, si le placement des bunkers de fairway est très stratégique, leur dessin s'est affadi au cours des années. Le jour où l'on a envie que le golf soit amusant, c'est parfait ! En revanche, les bunkers de green sont bien placés pour accueillir les coups insuffisants de précision, et l'on devra bien toucher ses petits et moyens fers. Les greens sont de surface moyenne, faiblement ondulés, mais ils sont pratiquement tous au-dessus du niveau du sol, ce qui accentue la nécessité d'être précis. De ce plaisant parcours, on retiendra le 18, un par 4 en descente avec une vue panoramique splendide depuis le départ.

Waterford Golf Club — 1934
IRL - NEWRATH, Co Waterford

Office	Secrétariat	(353) 051 - 876 748
Pro shop	Pro-shop	(353) 051 - 854 256
Fax	Fax	(353) 051 - 853 405
Situation	Situation	

3 km from Waterford (pop. 40 328)

Annual closure	Fermeture annuelle	no
Weekly closure	Fermeture hebdomadaire	no

Fees main season
Tarifs haute saison 18 holes

	Week days Semaine	We/Bank holidays We/Férié
Individual Individuel	IR£ 22	IR£ 25
Couple Couple	IR£ 44	IR£ 50

Caddy	Caddy	on request/IR£ 10
Electric Trolley	Chariot électrique	IR£ 7
Buggy	Voiturette	IR£ 20/18 holes
Clubs	Clubs	IR£ 10

Credit cards Cartes de crédit — no

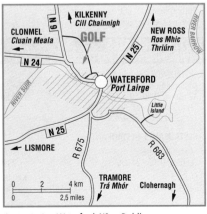

912

Access Accès : Waterford, N9 → Dublin.
Golf 3 km
Map 2 on page 829 Carte 2 Page 829

GOLF COURSE
PARCOURS — 14/20

Site	Site	
Maintenance	Entretien	
Architect	Architecte	Willie Park Jr
		James Braid
Type	Type	parkland
Relief	Relief	
Water in play	Eau en jeu	
Exp. to wind	Exposé au vent	
Trees in play	Arbres en jeu	

Scorecard Carte de score	Chp. Chp.	Mens Mess.	Ladies Da.
Length Long.	5722	5491	5168
Par	71	71	74

Advised golfing ability — 0   12   24   36
Niveau de jeu recommandé
Hcp required   Handicap exigé — no

CLUB HOUSE & AMENITIES
CLUB HOUSE ET ANNEXES — 6/10

Pro shop	Pro-shop	
Driving range	Practice	
Sheltered	couvert	no
On grass	sur herbe	yes
Putting-green	putting-green	yes
Pitching-green	pitching green	no

HOTEL FACILITIES
ENVIRONNEMENT HOTELIER — 6/10

HOTELS HÔTELS

Tower Hotel — Waterford
141 rooms, D IR£ 85 — 5 km
Tel (353) 051 - 875 801, Fax (353) 051 - 870 129

Granville Hotel — Waterford
74 rooms, D IR£ 72 — 5 km
Tel (353) 051 - 55 111, Fax (353) 051 - 870 307

Jurys Hotel — Waterford
98 rooms, D IR£ 90 — 4 km
Tel (353) 051 - 832 111, Fax (353) 051 - 832 863

RESTAURANTS RESTAURANTS

Granville Hotel — Waterford
Tel (353) 051 - 855 111 — 5 km

Prendiville's — Waterford
Tel (353) 051 - 78 851 — 7 km

WATERFORD CASTLE

14 5 6

A few minutes on a ferry to cross the Suir river, and there you are in a sanctuary of peace and quiet where, if you break into your piggy bank, you can enjoy a dream stay at the on-site hotel and admire some of the walls, which date back to the middle ages. This is perhaps not the course where you would spend the rest of your golfing days, but despite its young age it is in excellent condition and shouldn't be overlooked when in the region. The architects have worked wonders with the physical relief (none too hilly) and the trees which neatly demarcate the holes. This is not really a championship course, but the hazards have been placed to worry the very good players more than the average week-end golfer, who will, or should, have fun here. The large greens make it essential to choose the right club to get close to the pin. A number of water hazards add to the course's appeal.

Quelques minutes de ferry pour traverser la rivière Suir, et vous voilà dans une enclave de tranquillité où vous pourrez faire un séjour de rêve à l'hôtel sur place (certains des murs remontent au Moyen-Âge) si vous cassez un peu la tirelire... Le parcours n'est peut-être pas celui que l'on choisirait pour passer le reste de sa vie, mais il est en très bon état malgré sa jeunesse, et ne saurait être ignoré quand on visite la région. Les architectes ont tiré un excellent parti des reliefs (peu importants) du terrain, et des nombreux arbres pour définir les trous dans l'espace. Il ne s'agit pas vraiment d'un parcours de championnat, mais les obstacles ont été placés pour perturber plutôt les très bons joueurs que les joueurs moyens, qui s'y amuseront beaucoup. Les greens, de grande dimension, obligent à faire les bons choix de clubs pour se trouver près des drapeaux. Les obstacles d'eau ajoutent à l'intérêt de ce parcours.

Waterford Castle Golf Club		1992
The Island		
IRL - BALLYNAKILL, Co Waterford		
Office	Secrétariat	(353) 051 - 871 633
Pro shop	Pro-shop	(353) 051 - 841 569
Fax	Fax	(353) 051 - 871 634
Situation	Situation	
1,5 km from Waterford (pop. 40 328)		
Annual closure	Fermeture annuelle	no
Weekly closure	Fermeture hebdomadaire	no

Fees main season	Tarifs haute saison	18 holes
	Week days Semaine	**We/Bank holidays** We/Férié
Individual Individuel	IR£ 24	IR£ 27
Couple Couple	IR£ 48	IRL 54
IR£ 16.50 before 10 a.m.		

Caddy	Caddy	on request/IR£ 15
Electric Trolley	Chariot électrique	no
Buggy	Voiturette	IR£ 20
Clubs	Clubs	IR£ 10

Credit cards Cartes de crédit
VISA - MasterCard - AMEX

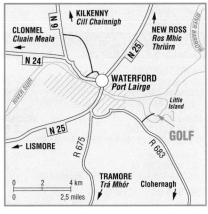

Access Accès : Waterford, R683. 4 km Ballinakill Road, private ferry to the Island
Map 2 on page 829 Carte 2 Page 829

GOLF COURSE / PARCOURS

14/20

Site	Site	
Maintenance	Entretien	
Architect	Architecte	Des Smyth Declan Brannigan
Type	Type	parkland
Relief	Relief	
Water in play	Eau en jeu	
Exp. to wind	Exposé au vent	
Trees in play	Arbres en jeu	

Scorecard Carte de score	Chp. Chp.	Mens Mess.	Ladies Da.
Length Long.	6209	5810	5073
Par	72	72	72

Advised golfing ability Niveau de jeu recommandé	0	12	24	36
Hcp required Handicap exigé	no			

CLUB HOUSE & AMENITIES / CLUB HOUSE ET ANNEXES

5/10

Pro shop	Pro-shop	
Driving range	Practice	
Sheltered	couvert	no
On grass	sur herbe	yes
Putting-green	putting-green	yes
Pitching-green	pitching green	yes

913

HOTEL FACILITIES / ENVIRONNEMENT HOTELIER

6/10

HOTELS HÔTELS
Waterford Castle Hotel — on site
19 rooms, D IR£ 200
Tel (353) 051 - 878 203, Fax (353) 051 - 879 316

Tower Hotel — Waterford
141 rooms, D IR£ 85 — 4 km
Tel (353) 051 - 875 801, Fax (353) 051 - 870 129

Granville Hotel — Waterford
74 rooms, D IR£ 72 — 4 km
Tel (353) 051 - 55 111, Fax (353) 051 - 870 307

RESTAURANTS RESTAURANTS
Dwyer's — Waterford
Tel (353) 051 - 77 478 — 4 km

Waterford Castle — on site
Tel (353) 051 - 878 203

WATERVILLE

⅃ 17 6 7

The pleasure of playing Waterville starts on the road, the "Ring of Kerry", which you first take from the south, from Killarney. The first nine holes unwind over very flat countryside, but the remainder, snaking their way through sand dunes, are impressive to say the least. The design work, no matter how natural it might look today, was considerable: there are no blind holes, virtually flat fairways and almost no dog-legs (except the 16th). But with sometimes blustery side-winds, you need to know how to flight the ball to keep it in play. If we add to this the fact that the putting surfaces are a little less enigmatic than those at Ballybunion, for example, the overall problem here stems from its length (a "man's course", as they say), plus the technical side to the second shot once the drive has avoided the rough and a number of fairway bunkers. A great course, to be played off the front tees.

Le plaisir de jouer Waterville commence sur la route, le «Ring of Kerry» qu'il faut prendre d'abord par le sud, depuis Killarney. Les neuf premiers trous se déroulent dans un paysage de campagne très plat, mais la suite, insinuée dans les dunes, est impressionnante. Le travail architectural, pour naturel qu'il paraisse aujourd'hui, a été important : pas de trous aveugles, des fairways quasiment plats, quasiment aucun dog-leg (sauf le 16). Mais il faudra savoir travailler la balle pour la garder en jeu, avec des vents latéraux souvent violents. Si l'on ajoute que les surfaces de greens ne sont pas aussi énigmatiques qu'elles peuvent l'être à Ballybunion par exemple, la difficulté générale de Waterville tient certes beaucoup à sa longueur, comme on l'a dit («un parcours d'hommes» !), on peut aussi parler de la technicité des seconds coups, une fois que le drive a évité les roughs et certains bunkers de fairway. Un grand parcours, à jouer des départs avancés.

Waterville	1889
IRL - WATERVILLE, Co Kerry	

Office	Secrétariat	(353) 066 - 74 102
Pro shop	Pro-shop	(353) 066 - 74 102
Fax	Fax	(353) 066 - 74 482
Situation	Situation	

4 km from Waterville (pop. 463)

Annual closure	Fermeture annuelle	no
Weekly closure	Fermeture hebdomadaire	no

Fees main season
Tarifs haute saison 18 holes

	Week days Semaine	We/Bank holidays We/Férié
Individual Individuel	IR£ 40	IR£ 40
Couple Couple	IR£ 80	IR£ 80

Caddy	Caddy	IR£ 15/18 holes
Electric Trolley	Chariot électrique	no
Buggy	Voiturette	IR£ 35/18 holes
Clubs	Clubs	IR£ 10/18 holes

Credit cards Cartes de crédit
VISA - Eurocard - MasterCard - AMEX - DC

914

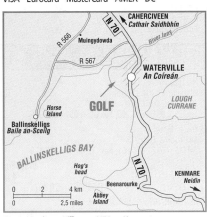

Access Accès : • Killarney N71 → Kenmate.
N70 → Parknasilla, Waterville • Killarney → Killorglin.
N70 → Glenbeigh, Cahirciveen, Waterville
Map 2 on page 828 Carte 2 Page 828

GOLF COURSE PARCOURS — **17**/20

Site	Site	
Maintenance	Entretien	
Architect	Architecte	Eddie Hackett John A. Mulcahy
Type	Type	links
Relief	Relief	
Water in play	Eau en jeu	
Exp. to wind	Exposé au vent	
Trees in play	Arbres en jeu	

Scorecard Carte de score	Chp. Chp.	Mens Mess.	Ladies Da.
Length Long.	6430	5954	4789
Par	72	73	73

Advised golfing ability Niveau de jeu recommandé	0	12	24	36
Hcp required Handicap exigé	28 Men, 36 Ladies			

CLUB HOUSE & AMENITIES CLUB HOUSE ET ANNEXES — **6**/10

Pro shop	Pro-shop	
Driving range	Practice	
Sheltered	couvert	
On grass	sur herbe	yes
Putting-green	putting-green	yes
Pitching-green	pitching green	yes

HOTEL FACILITIES ENVIRONNEMENT HOTELIER — **7**/10

HOTELS HÔTELS
Club Med — Waterville
88 rooms, D IR£ 110 — 3 km
Tel (353) 066 - 74 133, Fax (353) 066 - 74 483

Butler Arms — Waterville
35 rooms, D IR£ 110 — 2 km
Tel (353) 066 - 74 144, Fax (353) 066 - 74 520

Bayview Hotel — Waterville
10 rooms, D IR£ 48 — 2 km
Tel (353) 066 - 74 122, Fax (353) 066 - 74 680

RESTAURANTS RESTAURANTS
Sheilin Seafood — Waterville
Tel (353) 066 - 74 231 — nearby

Villa Maria — Waterville
Tel (353) 066 - 74 635 — nearby

The Pratt family, all fanatical golfers, made their dream come true by building this course, which they continue to run today. This sort of initiative would bring a smile to anyone's face, and the choice of Eddie Hackett as architect has led to a course nicely tailored to the pleasantly rolling landscape without any extravagant earthworks, and a thought spared for golfers of all levels. The setting is calm indeed, on the banks of the Brickey River, which sometimes comes into play rather dangerously. But it really is difficult to design a course for all golfers, and while mid-handicappers will love this, the 24+ hacker will probably suffer (they shouldn't bother counting their score). To score, you need to cope well with holes 12 to 16 where water, trees and bushes play a crucial part. The splendid environment of small mountains also plays a significant role in the charm of this site.

Fanatique de golf, la famille Pratt a transformé son rêve en réalité en construisant ce parcours qu'elle continue à diriger. On regarde avec sympathie ce genre d'initiative, et le choix d'Eddie Hackett comme architecte signifiait qu'il allait s'adapter à un terrain agréablement vallonné sans y faire de gigantesques terrassements, et qu'il penserait à tous les niveaux. La situation du golf est très tranquille, sur les rives de la Brickey River, qui vient parfois en jeu de manière menaçante. Il est très difficile de faire un parcours pour tous les joueurs et si les golfeurs moyens trouveront leur bonheur, les handicaps les plus élevés souffriront un peu (qu'ils ne comptent pas leur score). Pour y faire une bonne carte, il faudra en particulier bien négocier les trous 12 à 16, où l'eau, les arbres et les buissons jouent un rôle crucial. L'environnement splendide de petites montagnes joue un rôle important dans la séduction du lieu.

West Waterford Golf Club — 1992

Coolcormack
IRL - DUNGARVAN, Co. Waterford

Office	Secrétariat	(353) 058 - 43 216
Pro shop	Pro-shop	(353) 058 - 43 216
Fax	Fax	(353) 058 - 44 343
Situation	Situation	

5 km of Dungarvan (pop. 6920)

Annual closure	Fermeture annuelle	no
Weekly closure	Fermeture hebdomadaire	no

Fees main season
Tarifs haute saison 18 holes

	Week days Semaine	We/Bank holidays We/Férié
Individual Individuel	IR£ 18	IR£ 22
Couple Couple	IR£ 36	IR£ 40

Caddy	Caddy	IR£ 10/18 holes
Electric Trolley	Chariot électrique	IR£ 5
Buggy	Voiturette	IR£ 20/18 holes
Clubs	Clubs	IR£ 8
Credit cards Cartes de crédit		no

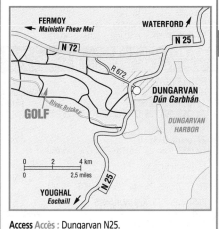

FERMOY
Mainistir Fhear Maí
WATERFORD
N 72
N 25
R 672
DUNGARVAN
Dún Garbhán
River Brickey
DUNGARVAN HARBOR
GOLF
0   2   4 km
0   2,5 miles
N 25
YOUGHAL
Eochaill

Access Accès : Dungarvan N25.
By-pass on Aglish Road.
Map 2 on page 829 Carte 2 Page 829

GOLF COURSE / PARCOURS — 12/20

Site	Site	■■■■■□
Maintenance	Entretien	■■■■□□
Architect	Architecte	Eddie Hackett
Type	Type	parkland
Relief	Relief	■■■□□□
Water in play	Eau en jeu	■■■■□□
Exp. to wind	Exposé au vent	■■□□□□
Trees in play	Arbres en jeu	■■■■□□

Scorecard Carte de score	Chp. Chp.	Mens Mess.	Ladies Da.
Length Long.	6162	5902	4773
Par	72	72	72

Advised golfing ability Niveau de jeu recommandé		0 12 24 36
Hcp required	Handicap exigé	28 Men, 36 Ladies

CLUB HOUSE & AMENITIES / CLUB HOUSE ET ANNEXES — 7/10

Pro shop	Pro-shop	■■■■□□
Driving range	Practice	■■■■□□
Sheltered	couvert	no
On grass	sur herbe	yes
Putting-green	putting-green	yes
Pitching-green	pitching green	yes

HOTEL FACILITIES / ENVIRONNEMENT HOTELIER — 6/10

HOTELS HÔTELS

Park Hotel Dungarvan — Dungarvan
40 rooms, D IR£ 80 — 5 km
Tel (353) 058 - 42 899, Fax (353) 058 - 42 899

Lawlors — Dungarvan
89 rooms, D IR£ 60 — 5 km
Tel (353) 058 - 41 122, Fax (353) 058 - 41 000

Gold Coast Golf Hotel — Ballynacourty-Dungarvan
37 rooms, D IR£ 80 — 7 km
Tel (353) 058 - 42 249, Fax (353) 058 - 43 378

RESTAURANTS RESTAURANTS

Mary's Restaurant — Dungarvan
Tel (353) 058 - 41 974 — 5 km

Richmond House — Cappoquin
Tel (353) 058 - 54 278 — 9 km

915

Although located on the edge of Clew Bay, this is essentially a parkland course. For many players, it will be the opportunity to catch their breath between Connemara and Carn or Enniscrone, and to find a little shelter when the wind is playing havoc elsewhere. The views here are just magnificent, between the bay and the blessed mountain of Croagh Patrick, where Ireland's patron saint spent 40 days of fasting and prayer. We wouldn't ask golfers to do the same, as they'll need all their strength to cope with this top-class course. The only slight short-coming is the relative blandness of the first few holes, but the challenge grows stronger on the way in, with a special mention going to the very pretty 14th, a par 3, and especially the 15th, a splendid and very long par 5 along the bay. The hazards are visibly in play and clear enough to make strategy pretty obvious on your first visit.

Bien qu'il soit situé en bordure de la Clew Bay, ce parcours présente un caractère de parc. Ce sera pour beaucoup de joueurs l'occasion de reprendre leur souffle entre Connemara et Carn ou Enniscrone, et de trouver quelque abri, quand le vent joue un rôle important. Les vues sont ici magnifiques, entre la baie et la «montagne sacrée», le Croagh Patrick, où le saint patron de l'Irlande aurait passé 40 jours de jeûne et de prières. On n'en demandera pas autant aux golfeurs, qui ont besoin de toutes leurs forces sur ce parcours de qualité. La seule nuance dans ce jugement, c'est la relative faiblesse des premiers trous, mais le challenge devient plus exigeant au retour, avec une mention particulière pour le 14, très joli par 3, et surtout le 15, un splendide par 5 très long en bordure de la baie. Les obstacles sont honnêtement en jeu, et assez visibles pour que la stratégie soit évidente dès la première visite.

Westport Golf Club
1908

Carrowholly
IRL - WESTPORT, Co Mayo

Office	Secrétariat	(353) 098 - 28 262
Pro shop	Pro-shop	(353) 098 - 27 481
Fax	Fax	(353) 098 - 27 217
Situation	Situation	

16 km from Castlebar
32 km from Ballinrobe

Annual closure	Fermeture annuelle	no
Weekly closure	Fermeture hebdomadaire	no

Fees main season
Tarifs haute saison 18 holes

	Week days Semaine	We/Bank holidays We/Férié
Individual Individuel	IR£ 18	IR£ 22.50
Couple Couple	IR£ 36	IR£ 45

Caddy	Caddy	on request / IR£ 12
Electric Trolley	Chariot électrique	IR£ 7/18 holes
Buggy	Voiturette	IR£ 20/18 holes
Clubs	Clubs	IR£ 12/18 holes

Credit cards Cartes de crédit	no

GOLF COURSE
PARCOURS
15/20

Site	Site	
Maintenance	Entretien	
Architect	Architecte	Fred Hawtree
Type	Type	seaside course, parkland
Relief	Relief	
Water in play	Eau en jeu	
Exp. to wind	Exposé au vent	
Trees in play	Arbres en jeu	

Scorecard	Chp.	Mens	Ladies
Carte de score	Chp.	Mess.	Da.
Length Long.	6355	6095	5233
Par	73	73	74

Advised golfing ability	0	12	24	36
Niveau de jeu recommandé				
Hcp required	Handicap exigé	no		

CLUB HOUSE & AMENITIES
CLUB HOUSE ET ANNEXES
7/10

Pro shop	Pro-shop	
Driving range	Practice	
Sheltered	couvert	no
On grass	sur herbe	yes
Putting-green	putting-green	yes
Pitching-green	pitching green	no

HOTEL FACILITIES
ENVIRONNEMENT HOTELIER
7/10

HOTELS HÔTELS

Hotel Westport — Westport
49 rooms, D IR£ 60 — 4 km
Tel (353) 098 - 25 122, Fax (353) 098 - 26 739

Railway Hotel — Westport
27 rooms, D IR£ 60 — 4 km
Tel (353) 098 - 25 166, Fax (353) 098 - 25 090

Castlecourt Hotel — Westport
0 rooms, D IR£ 55 — 4 km
Tel (353) 098 - 25 444, Fax (353) 098 - 25 444

RESTAURANTS RESTAURANTS

Ardmore House — Westport
Tel (353) 098 - 25 994 — 4 km

The Moorings — Westport
Tel (353) 098 - 25 874 — 4 km

916

Access Accès : 4 km from Westport on Newport Road
Map 1 on page 828 Carte 1 Page 828

This course was for many a year a star attraction to the south of Dublin, often hosting the Carroll's Irish Open in the 1960s and the Irish Senior Open in 1998. Complete re-laying of the tees and greens some years ago, under the supervision of Peter McEvoy, has helped to restore the course's prestige and raise the challenge that awaits you. Clearly, the alternating inland and seaside holes provide a close examination of the talent of skilled players and the lesser player too, because the layout is reasonably playable by golfers of all abilities. This rather flat course overlooks the Irish sea from atop cliffs, even though only holes 10 to 12 actually run along the coast. Although there are no huge difficulties, the wind can make life tricky, especially since the trees do little to break it. The only flaw is the Dublin to Wexford railway line, but this type of interference was commonplace in the past and together with the old-style club-house helps to create a site full of the charm of yesteryear.

Ce golf a souvent reçu le Carroll's Irish Open dans les années 60, et l'Irish Senior Open en 1998. Une réfection complète des départs et des greens il y a quelques années, sous l'autorité de Peter McEvoy, a contribué à lui rendre son prestige et à augmenter la qualité du défi. Il faut dire que l'alternance des trous inland et des trous de bord de mer permet un examen complet du talent des bons joueurs. Et des moins bons, car Woodbrook est raisonnablement jouable à tous les niveaux. Assez plat, il domine du haut des falaises la mer d'Irlande, bien que seuls les trous du 10 au 12 longent effectivement la côte. Les difficultés ne sont pas immenses, mais le vent peut compliquer les choses, et les arbres présents ne sont pas vraiment des remparts. Seul défaut, le passage de la voie ferrée, mais ce genre d'interférence était autrefois fréquent, et contribue comme le Club house à donner au lieu un certain charme d'antan.

Woodbrook Golf Club — 1926

Dublin Road
IRL - BRAY, Co. Wicklow

Office	Secrétariat	(353) 01 - 282 4799
Pro shop	Pro-shop	(353) 01 - 282 4799
Fax	Fax	(353) 01 - 282 4799
Situation	Situation	

Dublin (pop. 859 976), 20 km

Annual closure	Fermeture annuelle	no
Weekly closure	Fermeture hebdomadaire	no

Fees main season
Tarifs haute saison 18 holes

	Week days Semaine	We/Bank holidays We/Férié
Individual Individuel	IR£ 50	IR£ 55
Couple Couple	IR£ 100	IR£ 110

Caddy	Caddy	IR£ 20
Electric Trolley	Chariot électrique	no
Buggy	Voiturette	no
Clubs	Clubs	IR£ 15

Credit cards Cartes de crédit
VISA - MasterCard - AMEX - DC

★ Town center
DUBLIN
Baile Átha Cliath
Dalkey Deilginis
Killiney Cill Inion Léinín
N 11
2 km
1,25 miles
R 117 Carrickgollagan Forest
R 119
GOLF
BRAY Bré

Access Accès : Dublin, N11. R761 → Bray.
1.5 km before Bray → Woodbrook Golf Club
Map 3 on page 830 Carte 3 Page 830

GOLF COURSE PARCOURS — 15/20

Site	Site	■■■■□□
Maintenance	Entretien	■■■■■□
Architect	Architecte	Peter McEvoy (remod)
Type	Type	inland
Relief	Relief	■■□□□□
Water in play	Eau en jeu	■□□□□□
Exp. to wind	Exposé au vent	■■■■□□
Trees in play	Arbres en jeu	■■■■□□

Scorecard Carte de score	Chp. Chp.	Mens Mess.	Ladies Da.
Length Long.	6362	6276	5609
Par	72	72	74

Advised golfing ability Niveau de jeu recommandé	0	12	24	36
Hcp required Handicap exigé	no			

CLUB HOUSE & AMENITIES CLUB HOUSE ET ANNEXES — 7/10

Pro shop	Pro-shop	■■■■□□
Driving range	Practice	■■■■□□
Sheltered	couvert	no
On grass	sur herbe	yes (practice area)
Putting-green	putting-green	yes
Pitching-green	pitching green	yes

HOTEL FACILITIES ENVIRONNEMENT HOTELIER — 6/10

HOTELS HÔTELS
Royal Hotel - 91 rooms, D IR£ 70 — Bray
Tel (353) 01 - 286 2935, Fax (353) 01 - 286 7373 — 3 km

Powerscourt Arms Hotel — Enniskerry
12 rooms, D IR£ 50 — 10 km
Tel (353) 01 - 282 89 03, Fax (353) 01 - 286 49 09

Glenview Hotel — Glen of the Downs
40 rooms, D IR£ 130 — 12 km
Tel (353) 01 - 287 3399, Fax (353) 01 - 287 7511

RESTAURANTS RESTAURANTS
Morels Bistro — Dun Laoghaire
Tel (353) 01 - 230 0210 — 15 km

Enniscree Lodge — Enniskerry
Tel (353) 01 - 286 3542 — 15 km

Tinakilly Country House — Rathnew
Tel (353) 0404 - 69 274 — 30 km

917

Woodenbrige is located in the very pretty Vale of Avoca, famous for its tweeds, and essential visiting in the spring when the cherry trees are in full blossom. You will be following in the footsteps of the poet Thomas Moore. Created 100 years ago, this fine course became very popular when Paddy Merrigan upgraded it to 18 holes in 1993. The only vegetation are the few trees, here and there (woods outline the course's boundaries), which come very much into play from time to time, but the main hazards are the bunkers (none too penalising) and water, notably the river Avoca, which naturally abounds in this region. There are no unpleasant surprises for visitors, as the difficulties are clearly visible from each tee and add to the course's overall honesty. There is no great need to flight your shots, and only the variety of approach shots (lofted or run) call for real talent.

Woodenbridge est situé dans la très jolie Vallée d'Avoca, célèbre pour ses tweeds, et qu'il faut voir au printemps, quand les cerisiers sont en fleurs : vous y suivrez les traces du poète Thomas Moore. Créé il y a cent ans, ce bon parcours est devenu très populaire quand Paddy Merrigan l'a porté à 18 trous en 1993. La seule végétation est ici constituée par des arbres çà et là (les bois marquant les limites du golf), ils sont parfois très en jeu, mais les obstacles principaux sont les bunkers (pas trop pénalisants quand on s'y retrouve) et des obstacles d'eau - notamment la rivière Avoca - naturellement abondants dans cette région. Les visiteurs ne risquent pas de mauvaises surprises, les difficultés sont bien visibles de chaque départ, ajoutant à la franchise générale du tracé. Il n'est pas utile de beaucoup travailler la balle, seule la variété des approches (balles levées ou balles roulées) exigeant un certain talent.

Woodenbridge Golf Club — 1897

Woodenbridge
IRL - ARKLOW, Co Wicklow

Office	Secrétariat	(353) 0402 - 35 202
Pro shop	Pro-shop	(353) 0402 - 35 202
Fax	Fax	(353) 0402 - 31 402
Situation	Situation	

74 km from Dublin (pop. 859 976)
7 km from Arklow

Annual closure	Fermeture annuelle	no
Weekly closure	Fermeture hebdomadaire	no
Fees main season	Tarifs haute saison	18 holes

	Week days Semaine	We/Bank holidays We/Férié
Individual Individuel	IR£ 25	IR£ 30
Couple Couple	IR£ 50	IR£ 60

Caddy	Caddy	on request/IR£ 20
Electric Trolley	Chariot électrique	no
Buggy	Voiturette	no
Clubs	Clubs	no
Credit cards Cartes de crédit		no

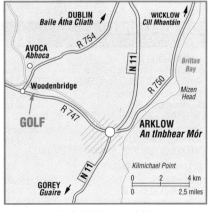

Access Accès : Dublin N11 South → Arklow.
7 km NW of Arklow on R747
Map 3 on page 830 Carte 3 Page 830

GOLF COURSE / PARCOURS — 16/20

Site	Site	
Maintenance	Entretien	
Architect	Architecte	Paddy Merrigan, 1993
Type	Type	forest, parkland
Relief	Relief	
Water in play	Eau en jeu	
Exp. to wind	Exposé au vent	
Trees in play	Arbres en jeu	

Scorecard Carte de score	Chp. Chp.	Mens Mess.	Ladies Da.
Length Long.	6350	6074	5490
Par	71	71	72

Advised golfing ability Niveau de jeu recommandé	0 12 24 36
Hcp required Handicap exigé	24 Men, 36 Ladies

CLUB HOUSE & AMENITIES / CLUB HOUSE ET ANNEXES — 7/10

Pro shop	Pro-shop	
Driving range	Practice	
Sheltered	couvert	no
On grass	sur herbe	yes
Putting-green	putting-green	yes
Pitching-green	pitching green	no

HOTEL FACILITIES / ENVIRONNEMENT HOTELIER — 6/10

HOTELS HÔTELS
Woodenbridge Hotel — Arklow
12 rooms, D IR£ 60 — 1 km
Tel (353) 0402 - 35 146, Fax (353) 0402 - 35 573

Valley Hotel — Woodenbridge
10 rooms, D IR£ 40 — 1 km
Tel (353) 0402 - 35 200, Fax (353) 0402 - 35 542

Arklow Bay Hotel — Arklow
38 rooms, D IR£ 50 — 7 km
Tel (353) 0402 - 32 309, Fax (353) 0402 - 32 300

RESTAURANTS RESTAURANTS
Sheepwalk House — Avoca
Tel (353) 0402 - 35 189 — 8 km

Mitchell's — Laragh, Glendalough
Tel (353) 0404 - 45 302 — 28 km

If you have a whole day to spare, stop off on the Lahinch road for a great round of golf in a huge and moderately hilly park, full of country charm. This course is a typical product of modern architecture, with a few water hazards, including a big lake that is fully in play on the 7th, present on the 6th and 7th holes and extending onward to the 12th. There are only a few fairway bunkers, but their role of dissuasion is assumed more often by the trees here. The shape of the dog-legs calls ideally for flighted shots in both directions so as to be in a better position for the second shot and reach the well-designed greens without too much trouble. Here, you need a complete and consistent game, and are helped by the clearly staggered tee-boxes which allow everyone to play a round according to the shape of his or game. There is nothing exceptionally difficult on this pleasant and welcoming course, which is a good address.

Si vous disposez d'une grande journée, arrêtez vous sur la route de Lahinch pour une bonne partie de golf, dans un vaste parc au relief modéré, au charme très campagnard. Ce parcours est typique des architectures modernes, avec quelques obstacles d'eau, dont un grand lac venant fortement en jeu au 7, mais aussi au 6 et au 8, avant d'en retrouver la prolongation au 12. On trouve assez peu de bunkers de fairway, mais leur rôle de dissuasion est bien occupé par les arbres. La forme des dog-legs amène à travailler la balle dans les deux sens pour mieux négocier les coups suivants, et parvenir sans encombre sur des greens bien dessinés et bien construits. Il faut ici un jeu complet et cohérent, avec l'avantage de départs très bien étagés, permettant à chacun de se faire un parcours selon ses capacités du moment. Sans difficultés exceptionnelles, cette réalisation plaisante et très accueillante est une bonne adresse.

Woodstock Golf & Country Club — 1993

Shanaway Road
IRL - ENNIS, Co Clare

Office	Secrétariat	(353) 065 - 42 406
Pro shop	Pro-shop	(353) 065 - 42 463
Fax	Fax	(353) 065 - 20 304
Situation	Situation	

4 km from Ennis (pop. 13 730)

Annual closure	Fermeture annuelle	no
Weekly closure	Fermeture hebdomadaire	no

Fees main season
Tarifs haute saison 18 holes

	Week days Semaine	We/Bank holidays We/Férié
Individual Individuel	IR£ 20	IR£ 20
Couple Couple	IR£ 40	IR£ 40

Caddy	Caddy	IR£ 12/18 holes
Electric Trolley	Chariot électrique	no
Buggy	Voiturette	IR£ 20/18 holes
Clubs	Clubs	IR£ 10/18 holes

Credit cards Cartes de crédit VISA - MasterCard

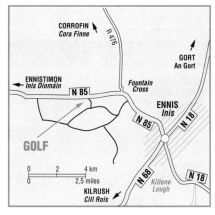

CORROFIN
Cora Finne
R 476

GORT
An Gort

ENNISTIMON
Inis Diomáin
N 85

Fountain
Cross

ENNIS
Inis
N 85
N 18

GOLF

0   2   4 km
0   2,5 miles

N 68
N 18

Killene
Lough

KILRUSH
Cill Rois

Access Accès : Ennis → Lahinch. 2.5 km, signposted left at pub.
Map 2 on page 828 Carte 2 Page 828

GOLF COURSE / PARCOURS — 13/20

Site	Site	
Maintenance	Entretien	
Architect	Architecte	Arthur Spring
Type	Type	inland, parkland
Relief	Relief	
Water in play	Eau en jeu	
Exp. to wind	Exposé au vent	
Trees in play	Arbres en jeu	

Scorecard Carte de score	Chp. Chp.	Mens Mess.	Ladies Da.
Length Long.	5879	5513	5062
Par	71	71	73

Advised golfing ability Niveau de jeu recommandé	0	12	24	36

Hcp required   Handicap exigé   no

CLUB HOUSE & AMENITIES / CLUB HOUSE ET ANNEXES — 5/10

Pro shop	Pro-shop	
Driving range	Practice	
Sheltered	couvert	no
On grass	sur herbe	yes
Putting-green	putting-green	yes
Pitching-green	pitching green	no

919

HOTEL FACILITIES / ENVIRONNEMENT HOTELIER — 6/10

HOTELS HÔTELS

Templegate Hotel — Ennis — 2 km
34 rooms, D IR£ 65
Tel (353) 065 - 23 300, Fax (353) 065 - 23 322

Auburn Lodge — Ennis — 2 km
100 rooms, D IR£ 76
Tel (353) 065 - 21 247, Fax (353) 065 - 21 202

Old Grand Hotel — Ennis — 2 km
58 rooms, D IR£ 100
Tel (353) 065 - 28 127, Fax (353) 065 - 28 112

RESTAURANTS RESTAURANTS

The Four Seasons — Ennis — on site
Tel (353) 065 - 42 406

Branigans — Ennis — 2 km
Tel (353) 065 - 20 211

In this region, occupied by the Vikings, pirates and smugglers, you will also find the vestiges of a castle built by the Normans alongside the club-house. Other good news for non-golfers is the nearby Strangford Lough, a real sanctuary for birds. But back to golf. As the course runs impressively atop coastal cliffs, this is one of the country's finest sites, with a view as far as the Isle of Man (on a clear day). Worth seeing, and worth playing, too. An age-old course from an unknown architect, this is a good layout and links course with no steep relief and none of those enormous dunes that can have such an effect on easily influenced players. You need to play several rounds to grasp the subtleties of the course, because there are quite a few blind drives and so a high risk of ending up in the rough or bushes, that do your card no good at all. And that's no to mention the exposure to the wind, which hardly helps matters. The bunkers are rather small, as are the greens. First time out, have fun with a match-play round.

Dans ce pays occupé par les Vikings, les pirates et les contrebandiers, on trouve aussi, à côté du Club-house, les vestiges d'un château bâti par les Normands. A proximité, le Strangford Lough est un véritable sanctuaire d'oiseaux. Et comme la situation du parcours sur de hautes falaises est impressionnante, c'est un des grands sites du pays, avec une vue jusqu'à l'Ile de Man (quand il fait beau). A voir mais aussi à jouer. Centenaire, et d'architecte inconnu, c'est un bon tracé, un links au relief très modéré, mais sans les dunes énormes qui peuvent ailleurs effrayer les joueurs influençables. Il faut plusieurs visites pour en comprendre les subtilités, on trouve pas mal de départs aveugles, avec le risque de se retrouver dans un rough ou des buissons dangereux pour le score. Et l'exposition au vent n'arrange rien en ce domaine. Les bunkers sont assez petits, mais les greens aussi... La première fois, amusez-vous en match-play.

Ardglass Golf Club   1896

Castle Place
NIRL - ARDGLASS, Co Down BT30 7 TP

Office	Secrétariat	(44) 01396- 841 219
Pro shop	Pro-shop	(44) 01396- 841 022
Fax	Fax	(44) 01396- 841 841
Situation	Situation	

11 km from Downpatrick
48 km from Belfast (pop. 279 237)

Annual closure	Fermeture annuelle	no
Weekly closure	Fermeture hebdomadaire	no

Monday Restaurant

Fees main season Tarifs haute saison   18 holes

	Week days Semaine	We/Bank holidays We/Férié
Individual Individuel	£ 15	£ 21
Couple Couple	£ 30	£ 42

Caddy	Caddy	on request/£ 15
Electric Trolley	Chariot électrique	no
Buggy	Voiturette	no
Clubs	Clubs	£ 5

Credit cards Cartes de crédit   VISA - Mastercard
(Pro-shop only)

920

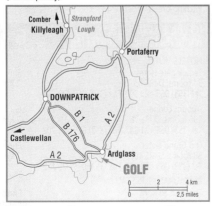

Access Accès : Belfast, A24, A7 to Downpatrick.
B1 to Ardglass. → Golf
Map 1 on page 827 Carte 1 Page 827

GOLF COURSE
PARCOURS   14/20

Site	Site	
Maintenance	Entretien	
Architect	Architecte	
Type	Type	seaside course
Relief	Relief	
Water in play	Eau en jeu	
Exp. to wind	Exposé au vent	
Trees in play	Arbres en jeu	

Scorecard Carte de score	Chp. Chp.	Mens Mess.	Ladies Da.
Length Long.	5500	5500	4765
Par	70	70	70

Advised golfing ability Niveau de jeu recommandé	0	12	24	36
Hcp required Handicap exigé		Men 24, Ladies 36		

CLUB HOUSE & AMENITIES
CLUB HOUSE ET ANNEXES   6/10

Pro shop	Pro-shop	
Driving range	Practice	
Sheltered	couvert	no
On grass	sur herbe	yes
Putting-green	putting-green	yes
Pitching-green	pitching green	no

HOTEL FACILITIES
ENVIRONNEMENT HOTELIER   4/10

HOTELS HÔTELS

Abbey Lodge	Downpatrick
22 rooms, D £ 45	11 km
Tel (44) 01396 - 614 511	
Brook Cottage	Newcastle
12 rooms, D £ 46	30 km
Tel (44) 013967 - 22 204, Fax (44) 013967 - 22 193	
Burrendale Hotel	Newcastle
50 rooms, D £ 80	30 km
Tel (44) 013967 - 22 599, Fax (44) 013967 - 22 328	

RESTAURANTS RESTAURANTS

Aldo's	Ardglass
Tel (44) 01396 - 841 315	1 km
Seaford Inn	Seaford
Tel (44) 01396 - 812 232	22 km

BANGOR

The course is located virtually in the city of Bangor, David Feherty's home town, where, so they say, you'll see the finest landscapes in the whole of Northern Ireland. Bird-watching enthusiasts are just a few minutes away from the boat that takes them to the Copeland Islands, inhabited only by birds, and you are not far from the pretty town of Newtownards. Inveterate golfers, on the other hand, will enjoy playing on this course, rather off the beaten track, a little dated in terms of yardage but great fun to play all the same. James Braid laid out a few elevated greens, others being multi-tiered, plus a few fairway bunkers that are both strategic and punishing. Some of the doglegs (the 5th, 13th, 14th and 15th holes) call for very accurate driving. In all, a course where you would probably not spend the rest of your life playing, but a good addition to the region's other courses.

Le golf est situé pratiquement dans la ville de Bangor, ville natale du champion David Feherty, où l'on trouve paraît-il les plus beaux paysages d'Irlande du Nord. Les amateurs d'ornithologie n'auront que quelques minutes à faire pour embarquer à destination des Copeland Islands, où ne vivent plus que des oiseaux, ou pour découvrir la jolie ville de Newtownards. Quant aux golfeurs invétérés, ils pourront s'exprimer sur ce parcours hors des sentiers battus, un peu daté en ce qui concerne la longueur, mais très amusant au demeurant. James Braid y a disposé quelques greens surélevés, d'autres à double plateau, et quelques bunkers de fairway à la fois stratégiques et punitifs. Certains dog-legs (5, 13, 14 et 15) demandent un driving très précis pour être maîtrisés. Au total, un parcours sur lequel on ne jouerait peut-être pas toute sa vie, mais un bon complément aux autres parcours de la région.

Bangor Golf Club — 1903

Broadway
NIR - BANGOR, Co. Down BT20 4RH

Office	Secrétariat	(44) 01247- 270 922
Pro shop	Pro-shop	(44) 01247- 462 164
Fax	Fax	(44) 01247- 453 394
Situation	Situation	

10 km from Newtownards
20 km from Belfast (pop. 279 237)

Annual closure	Fermeture annuelle	no
Weekly closure	Fermeture hebdomadaire	no

Fees main season
Tarifs haute saison 18 holes

	Week days Semaine	We/Bank holidays We/Férié
Individual Individuel	£ 20	£ 28
Couple Couple	£ 40	£ 56

Saturday: members only

Caddy	Caddy	no
Electric Trolley	Chariot électrique	no
Buggy	Voiturette	no
Clubs	Clubs	£ 5

Credit cards Cartes de crédit VISA - Access - Mastercard

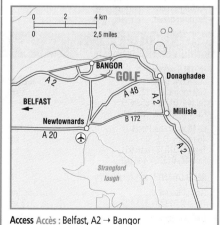

Access Accès : Belfast, A2 → Bangor
Map 1 on page 827 Carte 1 Page 827

GOLF COURSE / PARCOURS — 14/20

Site	Site	
Maintenance	Entretien	
Architect	Architecte	James Braid
Type	Type	inland
Relief	Relief	
Water in play	Eau en jeu	
Exp. to wind	Exposé au vent	
Trees in play	Arbres en jeu	

Scorecard Carte de score	Chp. Chp.	Mens Mess.	Ladies Da.
Length Long.	5781	5577	5113
Par	71	71	72

Advised golfing ability Niveau de jeu recommandé	0	12	24	36

Hcp required Handicap exigé no

CLUB HOUSE & AMENITIES / CLUB HOUSE ET ANNEXES — 6/10

Pro shop	Pro-shop	
Driving range	Practice	
Sheltered	couvert	no
On grass	sur herbe	yes
Putting-green	putting-green	yes
Pitching-green	pitching green	yes

HOTEL FACILITIES / ENVIRONNEMENT HOTELIER — 6/10

HOTELS HÔTELS

Royal Hotel — Bangor
50 rooms, D £ 72 — 1.5 km
Tel (44) 01247 - 271 866, Fax (44) 01247 - 467 810

Crawfordsburn Inn — Crawfordsburn
33 rooms, D £ 90 — 5 km
Tel (44) 01247 - 853 255, Fax (44) 01247 - 852 775

Sands Hotel — Bangor
12 rooms, D £ 75 — 1.5 km
Tel (44) 01247 - 270 696, Fax (44) 01247 - 271 678

RESTAURANTS RESTAURANTS

Shanks — Bangor
Tel (44) 01247 - 853 313 — 8 km

Jenny Watts — Bangor
Tel (44) 01247 - 270 401 — 2.5 km

921

BELVOIR PARK

15 5 6

The energetic rejuvenation of this course has turned it into one of the region's hidden gems in the region of Belfast, without ever affecting the intelligence of Harry Colt's original layout. Very reasonable in length, it is a real pleasure to play in this lush green park, well protected from the city noise by woods and thick curtains of trees, which also separate the fairways and call for unfailing accuracy. Despite everything, the fairways are of a fair width, and while there are fairway bunkers, their design rarely makes them dangerous. Ditches on the 10th and 12th are the only water hazards, but they play a key role. The course is generally not too hilly, except on the 3rd and 17th, the latter being a part of a very difficult finish, where many a card can fall apart. Fun to play and very prettily landscaped, Belvoir Park is rated amongst the country's finest inland courses.

Le rajeunissement énergique de ce parcours en a fait l'un des petits bijoux cachés de la région de Belfast, sans pour autant altérer l'intelligence du tracé original de Harry Colt, d'une longueur très raisonnable. C'est un plaisir d'évoluer dans ce grand parc en pleine verdure, bien protégé des bruits de la ville par de petits bois et d'épais rideaux d'arbres, séparant bien les fairways, tout en impliquant une certaine précision. Malgré tout, les fairways restent d'une largeur très acceptable, et si les bunkers y sont présents, leur dessin les rend rarement très dangereux. Les fossés au 10 et au 12 sont les seuls obstacles d'eau, mais ils y jouent un rôle fondamental. Le parcours est généralement de relief très modéré, sauf au 3 et au 17, ce dernier trou faisant partie d'un «finish» très difficile, où bien des cartes vont s'alourdir. Amusant à jouer, très joliment paysagé, Belvoir Park figure parmi les très bons parcours «inland» du pays.

Belvoir Park Golf Club — 1927
Church Road, Newtownbreda
NIR - BELFAST BT8 4AN

Office	Secrétariat	(44) 01232- 491 693
Pro shop	Pro-shop	(44) 01232- 646 714
Fax	Fax	(44) 01232- 646 113
Situation	Situation	

5 km S from Belfast (pop. 279 237)

Annual closure	Fermeture annuelle	no
Weekly closure	Fermeture hebdomadaire	no

Fees main season
Tarifs haute saison full day

	Week days Semaine	We/Bank holidays We/Férié
Individual Individuel	£ 33	£ 38
Couple Couple	£ 66	£ 76

Caddy	Caddy	no
Electric Trolley	Chariot électrique	no
Buggy	Voiturette	£ 20/18 holes
Clubs	Clubs	£ 10/18 holes
Credit cards Cartes de crédit		no

922

GOLF COURSE
PARCOURS
15/20

Site	Site	
Maintenance	Entretien	
Architect	Architecte	Harry S. Colt
Type	Type	parkland
Relief	Relief	
Water in play	Eau en jeu	
Exp. to wind	Exposé au vent	
Trees in play	Arbres en jeu	

Scorecard Carte de score	Chp. Chp.	Mens Mess.	Ladies Da.
Length Long.	5958	5739	5152
Par	71	70	73

Advised golfing ability
Niveau de jeu recommandé   0   12   24   36
Hcp required   Handicap exigé   24 Men, 36 Ladies

CLUB HOUSE & AMENITIES
CLUB HOUSE ET ANNEXES
5/10

Pro shop	Pro-shop	
Driving range	Practice	
Sheltered	couvert	no
On grass	sur herbe	yes
Putting-green	putting-green	yes
Pitching-green	pitching green	no

HOTEL FACILITIES
ENVIRONNEMENT HOTELIER
6/10

HOTELS HÔTELS
Stormont Hotel — Belfast
109 rooms, D £ 115 — 5 km
Tel (44) 01232 - 658 621
Fax (44) 01232 - 480 240

La Mon House Hotel — Belfast
46 rooms, D £ 20 — 5 km
Tel (44) 01232 - 448 631
Fax (44) 01232 - 448 026

RESTAURANTS RESTAURANTS
Antica Roma — Belfast
Tel (44) 01232 - 311 121 — 2 km

La Belle Epoque — Belfast
Tel (44) 01232 - 323 244 — 3 km

BELFAST

Ballynafeigh

GOLF

Balmoral

Downpatrick
Newcastle

Belvoir

Access Accès : Belfast A24 → Saintfield.
Turn off Ormeau Road (Newtownbreda)
Map 1 on page 827 Carte 1 Page 827

CAIRNDHU

There are trees here, but if you hit your ball into the woods, you are almost certainly out of bounds. Cairndhu is a seaside course (not really a links) along the Antrim coast road. This is the beginner's road leading from Belfast to the great links courses in the north, and the views are often quite spectacular. Excellence of setting and environment are, though, virtually a constant factor throughout Ireland. Don't be too put out when setting eyes on the contours and relief of the first few holes, things calm down a little after the 4th hole and the terrain gently rolls, nothing more. The course demands some straight driving and accurate approach shots, especially when homing in on a number of small greens, although "average" hitters will basically be playing mid to short irons. Don't place too much faith in your own instinct for gauging distances, because here they can be misleading. The architect has made the most of the terrain and it would be a pity not to get to known a course like this.

Il y a des arbres, mais si vous envoyez votre balle dans les bois, elle est sans doute hors limites. Cairndhu est un parcours de bord de mer (pas vraiment un links), le long de l'Antrim Coast Road. C'est le chemin des écoliers pour aller de Belfast aux grands links du nord, et les vues y sont parfois spectaculaires, mais cette qualité d'environnement est quasiment une constante dans toute l'Irlande. A moins d'être cardiaque, ne vous affolez pas trop à la vue du relief des premiers trous, il s'adoucit après le 4 pour laisser place à de sobres ondulations. Ce parcours réclame de la précision au drive et aux approches, particulièrement pour attaquer certains greens de petite taille, mais les frappeurs «normaux» auront alors essentiellement à jouer des moyens et petits fers. Ne vous fiez pas trop à votre instinct pour les distances, il peut vous tromper. L'architecte a tiré un bon parti du terrain, il serait dommage de ne pas le connaître.

Cairndhu Golf Club — 1928

192 Coast Road, Ballygally
NIRL - LARNE, Co Antrim

Office	Secrétariat	(44) 01574- 583 324
Pro shop	Pro-shop	(44) 01574- 583 324
Fax	Fax	(44) 01574- 583 477
Situation	Situation	

6 km from Larne (pop. 17 575)

Annual closure	Fermeture annuelle	no
Weekly closure	Fermeture hebdomadaire	no

Fees main season	Tarifs haute saison	18 holes
	Week days Semaine	We/Bank holidays We/Férié
Individual Individuel	£ 15	£ 24
Couple Couple	£ 30	£ 48

Caddy	Caddy	on request
Electric Trolley	Chariot électrique	no
Buggy	Voiturette	no
Clubs	Clubs	£ 10/18 holes

Credit cards Cartes de crédit
VISA - MasterCard (Green-fees only)

CARNLOUGH
BALLYGALLEY
GOLF
Carncastle
A2
LARNE
Ballymena
A8
Larne
Lough
ISLAND
MAGEE
BALLYCLARE
A2
WHITEHEAD

0   2   4 km
0   2,5 miles

Access Accès : Belfast, M2 → Antrim. Exit 4. A8 to Larne. A2 to Ballygally
Map 1 on page 827 Carte 1 Page 827

GOLF COURSE / PARCOURS — 13/20

Site	Site	
Maintenance	Entretien	
Architect	Architecte	T. Morrison
Type	Type	seaside course, parkland
Relief	Relief	
Water in play	Eau en jeu	
Exp. to wind	Exposé au vent	
Trees in play	Arbres en jeu	

Scorecard Carte de score	Chp. Chp.	Mens Mess.	Ladies Da.
Length Long.	5500	5436	4861
Par	70	70	73

Advised golfing ability Niveau de jeu recommandé	0	12	24	36
Hcp required	Handicap exigé	no		

CLUB HOUSE & AMENITIES / CLUB HOUSE ET ANNEXES — 6/10

Pro shop	Pro-shop	
Driving range	Practice	
Sheltered	couvert	no
On grass	sur herbe	yes
Putting-green	putting-green	yes
Pitching-green	pitching green	no

HOTEL FACILITIES / ENVIRONNEMENT HOTELIER — 5/10

HOTELS HÔTELS

Ballygally Castle Hotel — Ballygally
30 rooms, D £ 69 — 3 km
Tel (44) 01574 - 583 212
Fax (44) 01574 - 583 681

Magheramorne House — Larne
22 rooms, D £ 80 — 6 km
Tel (44) 01574 - 279 444
Fax (44) 01574 - 260 138

Londonderry Arms Hotel — Carnlough
21 rooms, D £ 65 — 18 km
Tel (44) 01574 - 885 255
Fax (44) 01574 - 885 263

RESTAURANTS RESTAURANT

Lynden Heights — Ballygally
Tel (44) 01574 - 583 560 — 3 km

923

Golf in Northern Ireland has developed more particularly in County Down, around Belfast and along the northern coast. There are, of course, pleasant courses in other areas, but they could hardly be rated as unforgettable playing experiences and anyway, tourists don't have time enough to play them all. Located on the banks of Lower Lough Erne, a paradise for anglers, nature and history-lovers, Castle Hume is an exception to the above. A recent course, it will need a few years for the several thousand saplings to grow to see how the course will eventually look, and the club-house is still on the drawing board. But the course itself is worth the visit. The architect has visibly been influenced by the American style, and accurate target golf is called for to cope with a course where water hazards have enhanced what is already a stiff challenge. Castle Hume is already an address to be recommended.

Le golf en Irlande du Nord a surtout été développé dans le County Down, autour de Belfast et sur la côte Nord. Bien sûr, on trouve aussi des parcours sympathiques dans les autres régions, mais ils ne sauraient vraiment prendre place parmi les réalisations mémorables, et les touristes ne disposent pas d'assez de temps pour les visiter tous. Situé en bordure du Lower Lough Erne, un paradis des pêcheurs et des amateurs de nature comme d'histoire, Castle Hume fait exception. Récemment construit, il faudra attendre que les milliers d'arbres plantés aient poussé pour qu'il prenne son allure définitive, et le Club-house reste à l'état de projet, mais le parcours vaut la visite. L'architecte a visiblement été influencé par le style américain, et il faudra jouer des approches levées précises pour bien le négocier, d'autant que les obstacles d'eau relèvent le niveau du défi, mais Castle Hume est déjà une adresse recommandable.

Castle Hume Golf Club 1991

Belleek Road
NIR - ENNISKILLEN, Co. Fermanagh BT93 7ED

Office	Secrétariat	(44) 01365- 327 077
Pro shop	Pro-shop	(44) 01365- 327 075
Fax	Fax	(44) 01365- 327 076
Situation	Situation	

6 km from Enniskillen (pop. 11 436)

Annual closure	Fermeture annuelle	no
Weekly closure	Fermeture hebdomadaire	no

Fees main season
Tarifs haute saison 18 holes

	Week days Semaine	We/Bank holidays We/Férié
Individual Individuel	£ 15	£ 20
Couple Couple	£ 30	£ 40

Caddy	Caddy	no
Electric Trolley	Chariot électrique	no
Buggy	Voiturette	£ 15/18 holes
Clubs	Clubs	£ 5

Credit cards Cartes de crédit VISA - MasterCard - Access

Access Accès : Belfast M1 exit 15 (Dungannon).
A4 to Enniskillen, A46 → Belleek.
Map 1 on page 827 Carte 1 Page 827

GOLF COURSE PARCOURS 13/20

Site	Site	
Maintenance	Entretien	
Architect	Architecte	Tony Carroll
Type	Type	parkland
Relief	Relief	
Water in play	Eau en jeu	
Exp. to wind	Exposé au vent	
Trees in play	Arbres en jeu	

Scorecard	Chp.	Mens	Ladies
Carte de score	Chp.	Mess.	Da.
Length Long.	5941	5685	4980
Par	72	72	72

Advised golfing ability		0	12	24	36
Niveau de jeu recommandé					
Hcp required	Handicap exigé	no			

CLUB HOUSE & AMENITIES
CLUB HOUSE ET ANNEXES 7/10

Pro shop	Pro-shop	
Driving range	Practice	
Sheltered	couvert	no
On grass	sur herbe	yes
Putting-green	putting-green	yes
Pitching-green	pitching green	yes

HOTEL FACILITIES
ENVIRONNEMENT HOTELIER 6/10

HOTELS HÔTELS
Killyhevlin Hotel — Enniskillen
45 rooms, D £ 80 — 6 km
Tel (44) 01365 - 323 481, Fax (44) 01365 - 324 726

Fort Lodge — Enniskillen
35 rooms, D £ 70 — 6 km
Tel (44) 01365 - 323 275, Fax (44) 01365 - 323 275

Manor House — Killadeas, Enniskillen
46 rooms, D £ 80 — 15 km
Tel (44) 01365 6- 21 561, Fax (44) 01365 6- 21 545

RESTAURANTS RESTAURANTS
Franco's — Enniskillen
Tel (44) 01365 - 324 424 — 6 km

Mulligan's — Enniskillen
Tel (44) 01365 - 322 059 — 6 km

924

CASTLEROCK

16 6 6

Already at a venerable age, Castlerock is certainly not one of the best known links courses, but it would be shame to overlook it. It certainly won't disappoint the better players, and it is also more within the reach of mid- to high-handicappers than its prestigious neighbours. This is a great introduction for people who have never played links golf ; it has a very natural look to it, is in a beautifully wild setting and has the traditional difficulties found on this type of course. The bunkers, though, are appreciably less severe than elsewhere. To maintain the suspense, you will find a few blind drives, but the hazards everywhere are visible enough for you to forget, temporarily at least, that golf is a sport where there's no justice. Smallish greens call for great precision, and if you miss them you will have the opportunity to put your newly-honed short game to the test. Another important factor here is the warm welcome in the clubhouse.

Ayant déjà atteint un âge vénérable, Castlerock ne figure sans doute pas parmi les links les plus connus, mais il serait bien regrettable de le négliger. Il ne décevra en rien les meilleurs joueurs, mais il est aussi davantage à la portée du golfeur de handicap moyen ou élevé que ses voisins prestigieux. Pour ceux qui n'ont jamais joué un links, c'est une bonne initiation, par son aspect très naturel, la beauté sauvage de son environnement de dunes, et les difficultés traditionnelles de ce type de parcours : les bunkers sont notamment moins sévères qu'ailleurs. Pour maintenir le suspense, on trouve quelques drives aveugles, mais les obstacles sont partout assez visibles pour ne pas trop s'apercevoir que le golf est un sport sans justice. Des greens de surface assez réduite obligent à une certaine précision. Si on les manque, ce sera l'occasion de mettre en valeur sa virtuosité au petit jeu. La qualité de l'accueil est aussi à souligner.

Castlerock Golf Club		1901
Circular Road		
NIR - CASTLEROCK, Co Derry		

Office	Secrétariat	(44) 01265- 848 314
Pro shop	Pro-shop	(44) 01265- 848 314
Fax	Fax	(44) 01265- 848 714
Situation	Situation	

90 km from Belfast (pop. 279 237)
9 km from Coleraine (pop. 20 721)

Annual closure	Fermeture annuelle	no
Weekly closure	Fermeture hebdomadaire	no

Fees main season	Tarifs haute saison	18 holes
	Week days Semaine	We/Bank holidays We/Férié
Individual Individuel	£ 30	£ 40
Couple Couple	£ 60	£ 80

Caddy	Caddy	on request/£ 20
Electric Trolley	Chariot électrique	no
Buggy	Voiturette	no
Clubs	Clubs	on request/£ 10

Credit cards Cartes de crédit VISA - Mastercard - AMEX

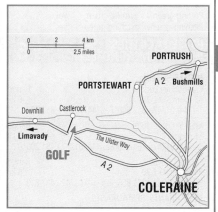

Access Accès : Belfast M2 North → Antrim.
Turn right to A26 → Ballymena/Coleraine.
Coleraine A2 → Castlerock
Map 1 on page 827 Carte 1 Page 827

GOLF COURSE
PARCOURS

16/20

Site	Site	
Maintenance	Entretien	
Architect	Architecte	Ben Sayers
Type	Type	links, seaside course
Relief	Relief	
Water in play	Eau en jeu	
Exp. to wind	Exposé au vent	
Trees in play	Arbres en jeu	

Scorecard Carte de score	Chp. Chp.	Mens Mess.	Ladies Da.
Length Long.	6115	5850	5299
Par	73	73	75

Advised golfing ability		0 12 24 36
Niveau de jeu recommandé		
Hcp required	Handicap exigé	28 Men, 36 Ladies

CLUB HOUSE & AMENITIES
CLUB HOUSE ET ANNEXES

6/10

Pro shop	Pro-shop	
Driving range	Practice	
Sheltered	couvert	no
On grass	sur herbe	yes
Putting-green	putting-green	yes
Pitching-green	pitching green	no

HOTEL FACILITIES
ENVIRONNEMENT HOTELIER

6/10

HOTELS HÔTELS
Golf Hotel — Castlerock — 1 km
16 rooms, D £ 50
Tel (44) 01265 - 848 204, Fax (44) 01265 - 848 295

Lodge — Coleraine — 8 km
20 rooms, D £ 70
Tel (44) 01265 - 44 848

Marine Hotel — Castlerock — 2 km
9 rooms, D £ 40
Tel (44) 01265 - 848 456

RESTAURANTS RESTAURANTS
Bushtown House — Coleraine — 8 km
Tel (44) 01265 - 58 367

The Lodge — Coleraine — 8 km
Tel (44) 01265 - 44 848

925

Standing alongside the short and amusing "Ava Course", Clandeboye is a layout of greater calibre in its variety and technical demands on players. Yardage is definitely no difficulty, especially for the long-hitters (they will enjoy the wide fairways), but players who are too short might have problems in carrying the ball. What's more, the uneven soil can also create some interesting lies. Game strategy is pretty obvious, as the difficulties are easily identifiable from the tee, albeit in a sometimes intimidating way. There is just the one blind green here, and the few elevated greens call for accurately and cleanly hit approach shots, especially since the putting surfaces are rather firm. Add to this the water, stream and ditches and you will realise that playing to your handicap here requires careful thought and attention.

A côté du «Ava Course», court et assez amusant, Clandeboye propose ici un parcours de plus grand calibre, par sa diversité et ses exigences techniques. Sa longueur n'est certes pas un facteur de difficulté particulière, en particulier pour les longs frappeurs (ils pourront se déchaîner sur des fairways larges), mais certains joueurs courts risquent d'avoir des problèmes quand il faut porter la balle. Par ailleurs, le sol irrégulier provoque quelques positions de balle intéressantes. La stratégie est assez évidente, les difficultés étant facilement identifiables de chaque départ, mais elles peuvent intimider. On trouve ici un seul green aveugle, quelques greens surélevés, les approches devront y être d'autant plus précises et les coups bien touchés que les surfaces de putting sont souvent assez fermes. Ajoutons la présence de cours d'eau et de fossés, et vous aurez compris que jouer son handicap demande de la réflexion et de l'attention.

Clandeboye Golf Club   1933

Tower Road, Conlig
NIRL - NEWTOWNWARDS, Co Down BT23 3PN

Office	Secrétariat	(44) 01247- 271 767
Pro shop	Pro-shop	(44) 01247- 271 750
Fax	Fax	(44) 01247- 473 711
Situation	Situation	

4 km from Newtownwards and Bangor
15 km from Belfast (pop. 279 237)

Annual closure	Fermeture annuelle	no
Weekly closure	Fermeture hebdomadaire	no
Fees main season	Tarifs haute saison	18 holes

	Week days Semaine	We/Bank holidays We/Férié
Individual Individuel	£ 25	£ 30
Couple Couple	£ 50	£ 60
Ava Course: £ 20 / £ 25		
Caddy	Caddy	no
Electric Trolley	Chariot électrique	no
Buggy	Voiturette	£ 20/18 holes
Clubs	Clubs	£ 5

Credit cards Cartes de crédit
VISA - MasterCard - Access

926

Access Accès : Belfast, A20 to Newtownwards.
A21 → Bangor.
Map 1 on page 827 Carte 1 Page 827

GOLF COURSE PARCOURS   `15`/20

Site	Site	
Maintenance	Entretien	
Architect	Architecte	W.R. Robinson
Type	Type	inland, copse
Relief	Relief	
Water in play	Eau en jeu	
Exp. to wind	Exposé au vent	
Trees in play	Arbres en jeu	

Scorecard Carte de score	Chp. Chp.	Mens Mess.	Ladies Da.
Length Long.	5916	5700	5180
Par	71	71	73

Advised golfing ability   0   12   24   36
Niveau de jeu recommandé
Hcp required   Handicap exigé   no

CLUB HOUSE & AMENITIES CLUB HOUSE ET ANNEXES   `6`/10

Pro shop	Pro-shop	
Driving range	Practice	
Sheltered	couvert	no
On grass	sur herbe	yes
Putting-green	putting-green	yes
Pitching-green	pitching green	yes

HOTEL FACILITIES ENVIRONNEMENT HOTELIER   `6`/10

HOTELS HÔTELS
Clandeboye Lodge   Bangor
43 rooms, D £ 75   6 km
Tel (44) 01247 - 852 500, Fax (44) 01247 - 852 772

Marine Court Hotel   Bangor
51 rooms, D £ 80   6 km
Tel (44) 01247 - 451 100, Fax (44) 01247 - 451 200

O'Hara's Royal   Bangor
34 rooms, D £ 70   6 km
Tel (44) 01247 - 271 866, Fax (44) 01247 - 467 810

RESTAURANTS RESTAURANTS
Shanks   Bangor
Tel (44) 01247 - 853 313   6 km

Poachers Arms (Clandeboye L.)   Bangor
Tel (44) 01247 - 853 311   6 km

KIRKISTOWN CASTLE 15 6 5

With breath-taking views over the Irish Sea, gently contoured landscape and a sandy soil, you can understand why James Braid exclaimed "if only this spot were within 50 miles of London !" Not far from the sea but closer to a lush park-land style than anything else, it does nonetheless have something of the links about it, not to mention the wind, which blows wherever it wants to and magnifies every error and difficulty. The course's bunkering is particularly remarkable, but the green-side bunkers generally leave a way open for bump and run shots, which are just the job for firm greens like these. This pretty course is a high-class design, which is only to be expected from its architect, and offers a refreshing and quaintly old-fashioned alternative to modern layouts splattered with water hazards. Even with a par 69 and low yardage, this friendly course is well worth a visit.

Avec ses vues admirables et imprenables sur la mer d'Irlande, son relief très modéré et un sol sablonneux, on comprend que James Braid en ait dit : «Si seulement ce terrain se trouvait à moins de 50 miles de Londres !» Non loin de la mer, mais plus proche d'un parc que d'un véritable links, il en présente malgré tout certains aspects, sans parler du vent, qui souffle où il veut, mais qui amplifie toutes les erreurs et les difficultés. Le bunkering de ce parcours est particulièrement remarquable, mais les bunkers de greens laissent généralement une ouverture, ce qui permet de jouer les «bump 'n run» bien adaptés à des greens fermes. Ce joli parcours bénéficie d'un dessin de haut niveau, que l'on pouvait attendre de son architecte, et offre une alternative rafraîchissante et un peu surannée aux tracés modernes envahis d'obstacles d'eau. Même avec un par 69 et sa longueur réduite, ce parcours amical mérite une visite.

Kirkistown Castle 1902
142, Main Road, Cloughey
NIR - NEWTOWNARDS, Co Down BT22 1JA

Office	Secrétariat	(44) 01247 - 771 233
Pro shop	Pro-shop	(44) 01247 - 771 004
Fax	Fax	(44) 01247 - 771 699
Situation	Situation	

38 km SE of Bangor
30 km SE of Newtownards

Annual closure	Fermeture annuelle	no
Weekly closure	Fermeture hebdomadaire	no

Fees main season	Tarifs haute saison	18 holes
	Week days	We/Bank holidays
	Semaine	We/Férié
Individual Individuel	£ 15	£ 20
Couple Couple	£ 30	£ 40

Restrictions on Week ends

Caddy	Caddy	£ 10/18 holes
Electric Trolley	Chariot électrique	no
Buggy	Voiturette	no
Clubs	Clubs	£ 10

Credit cards Cartes de crédit
VISA - MasterCard - Access (Green fees & Pro Shop only)

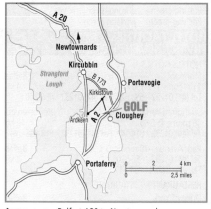

Newtownards
Kircubbin
Strangford Lough
B 173 Portavogie
Kirkistown
A 20
GOLF Cloughey
Ardkeen
Portaferry
0   2   4 km
0   2,5 miles

Access Accès : Belfast A20 to Newtownards.
A20 to Kircubbin. B173 to Cloughey
Map 1 on page 827 Carte 1 Page 827

GOLF COURSE
PARCOURS 15/20

Site	Site	
Maintenance	Entretien	
Architect	Architecte	James Braid
Type	Type	links, parkland
Relief	Relief	
Water in play	Eau en jeu	
Exp. to wind	Exposé au vent	
Trees in play	Arbres en jeu	

Scorecard	Chp.	Mens	Ladies
Carte de score	Chp.	Mess.	Da.
Length Long.	5550	5335	5120
Par	70	69	73

Advised golfing ability	0	12	24	36
Niveau de jeu recommandé				
Hcp required	Handicap exigé	no		

CLUB HOUSE & AMENITIES
CLUB HOUSE ET ANNEXES 6/10

Pro shop	Pro-shop	
Driving range	Practice	
Sheltered	couvert	no
On grass	sur herbe	yes
Putting-green	putting-green	yes
Pitching-green	pitching green	yes

927

HOTEL FACILITIES
ENVIRONNEMENT HOTELIER 5/10

HOTELS HÔTELS
Coastal Lodge Hotel Cloughey
9 rooms, D £ 25 500 m
Tel (44) 012477 - 72 100

Portaferry Hotel Portaferry
14 rooms, D £ 89 7 km
Tel (44) 012477 - 28 231, Fax (44) 012477 - 28 999

Strangford Arms Newtownards
40 rooms, D £ 80 20 km
Tel (44) 01232 - 814 141, Fax (44) 01232 - 818 846

RESTAURANTS RESTAURANTS
Portaferry Hotel Portaferry
Tel (44) 012477 - 28 231 7 km

Copeland's Donaghady
Tel (44) 01247 - 888 189 25 km

This is a generally flat course with a hill in the middle, which you climb twice, although climb is hardly the word. As with all courses close to Belfast, Knock is very busy on week-ends and the week-days are quieter for green-feers. They will have a lot of fun here, unless their swing is off-colour or they start spraying their drives. If you go into the woods, a little recovery shot back to the fairway is all you can hope for. Most of the holes are lined with trees, which make for a peaceful setting, but wayward hitters will suffer the consequences. The hazards are clearly visible and you feel confident from the very first visit ; all you need do is avoid the meanders of two streams which come and go over the course. Although not one of the country's most spectacular and original courses, Knock is at the very least extremely pleasant to play, perhaps more so for mid-handicappers than for the more proficient golfers.

C'est un parcours généralement plat, avec une colline en son centre, que l'on grimpe deux fois, mais il ne s'agit certes pas d'une escalade ! Comme tous les golfs à proximité de Belfast, il est très fréquenté en week-end, mais la semaine est plus calme pour les visiteurs. Il s'y amuseront beaucoup, sauf si leur swing est malade ce jour là et qu'ils «arrosent» au drive : il leur faudra bien souvent se contenter de se recentrer s'ils se sont un peu enfoncés dans les bois. La plupart des trous sont bordés d'arbres, ce qui garantit une tranquillité certaine, mais il faut en subir les conséquences. Les obstacles sont ici bien visibles, on se sent en confiance dès la première visite, il suffira d'éviter les méandres de deux cours d'eau qui vont et viennent sur le parcours. S'il ne figure pas parmi les golfs les plus spectaculaires et originaux du pays, Knock est du moins très agréable à jouer, peut-être davantage pour les joueurs moyens que pour les meilleurs.

Knock Golf Club — 1895

Summerfield, Dundonald
NIRL - BELFAST BT16 OQX

Office	Secrétariat	(44) 01232- 483 251
Pro shop	Pro-shop	(44) 01232- 483 825
Fax	Fax	
Situation	Situation	

7 km from Belfast (pop. 279 237)
9 km from Newtownards

Annual closure	Fermeture annuelle	no
Weekly closure	Fermeture hebdomadaire	no

Fees main season
Tarifs haute saison 18 holes

	Week days Semaine	We/Bank holidays We/Férié
Individual Individuel	£ 20	£ 25
Couple Couple	£ 40	£ 50

Caddy	Caddy	no
Electric Trolley	Chariot électrique	no
Buggy	Voiturette	no
Clubs	Clubs	£ 10/18 holes

Credit cards Cartes de crédit — no

Access Accès : Belfast, A20 → Newtownards
Map 1 on page 827 Carte 1 Page 827

GOLF COURSE / PARCOURS — 15/20

Site	Site	
Maintenance	Entretien	
Architect	Architecte	Harry Colt, McKenzie Allison
Type	Type	parkland
Relief	Relief	
Water in play	Eau en jeu	
Exp. to wind	Exposé au vent	
Trees in play	Arbres en jeu	

Scorecard Carte de score	Chp. Chp.	Mens Mess.	Ladies Da.
Length Long.	5800	5615	5205
Par	70	70	73

Advised golfing ability Niveau de jeu recommandé	0	12	24	36

Hcp required Handicap exigé — no

CLUB HOUSE & AMENITIES / CLUB HOUSE ET ANNEXES — 7/10

Pro shop	Pro-shop	
Driving range	Practice	
Sheltered	couvert	no
On grass	sur herbe	yes
Putting-green	putting-green	yes
Pitching-green	pitching green	yes

HOTEL FACILITIES / ENVIRONNEMENT HOTELIER — 6/10

HOTELS HÔTELS

Stormont — Belfast
110 rooms, D £ 130 — 4 km
Tel (44) 01232 - 658 621, Fax (44) 01232 - 480 240

Strangford Arms — Newtownards
40 rooms, D £ 80 — 10 km
Tel (44) 01232 - 814 141, Fax (44) 01232 - 818 846

Park Avenue - 70 rooms, D £ 90 — Belfast
Tel (44) 01232 - 656 520, — 8 km
Fax (44) 01232 - 471 417

RESTAURANTS RESTAURANTS

Duke of York — Belfast
Tel (44) 01232 - 241 062 — 9 km

Strand — Belfast
Tel (44) 01232 - 682 266 — 9 km

LISBURN

A beautiful tree-lined drive leads to the Lisburn Golf Club, and sets the mood. Here, you are in the wide open space of park-land and meadows, with the feeling of tranquillity that prevails throughout the Irish countryside. But don't let such bucolic thoughts go to your head, as this course is far-from-easy, especially from the back tees. With that said, the men's yellow and ladies tees are well forward, so most golfers can breathe easily. Created in 1905, Lisburn was overhauled by Fred Hawtree, whose strategic positioning of fairway and green-side bunkers is clear to see, although the latter seldom block the front of the greens. The terrain is rather flat and only one hole could really be called blind, the 17th, a tricky hole before finishing on a spectacular downhill par 3, itself something of a rarity. This very pretty layout is well worth visiting if you are up Belfast way.

Une belle allée bordée d'arbres conduit au Golf de Lisburn, et donne l'ambiance. Nous allons nous trouver dans un espace de grand parc et de prairies, avec le sentiment de tranquillité associé à la campagne irlandaise. Mais il ne faudra pas se laisser endormir par des pensées bucoliques, ce parcours n'est pas des plus faciles, notamment du fond, mais les départs hommes et dames sont assez avancés pour que la majorité des golfeurs s'y trouve à l'aise. Créé en 1905, il a été révisé par Fred Hawtree, dont on peut remarquer le positionnement stratégique des bunkers de fairway et de greens, mais ces derniers masquent rarement l'entrée des greens. Le terrain est assez plat, et un seul green peut être considéré comme aveugle, au 17, un trou délicat, avant de finir par un par 3 spectaculaire en descente : une disposition très rare sur un parcours. Cette très jolie réalisation mérite le détour si vous passez à Belfast.

Lisburn Golf Club — 1905

68 Eglantine Road
NIR - LISBURN, Co Antrim

Office	Secrétariat	(44) 01846- 677 216
Pro shop	Pro-shop	(44) 01846- 677 217
Fax	Fax	(44) 01846- 603 608

Situation Situation
14 km from Belfast (pop. 279 237)
4 km from Lisburg

Annual closure	Fermeture annuelle	no
Weekly closure	Fermeture hebdomadaire	no
Fees main season	Tarifs haute saison	18 holes

	Week days Semaine	We/Bank holidays We/Férié
Individual Individuel	£ 25	*
Couple Couple	£ 50	*

* only with a member at week ends

Caddy	Caddy	no
Electric Trolley	Chariot électrique	no
Buggy	Voiturette	no
Clubs	Clubs	£ 15/18 holes

Credit cards Cartes de crédit
VISA - MasterCard (Pro shop goods only)

BELFAST
M1
A1
LISBURN
Craigavon Mazetown
M1 **GOLF**
R. Lagan Ravernet
Dromore

Access Accès : Belfast M1 → Lisburn.
Turn left to A1 → Hillsborough.
Golf 4 km S of Lisburn
Map 1 on page 827 Carte 1 Page 827

GOLF COURSE / PARCOURS — 15/20

Site	Site	▰▰▰▰▱
Maintenance	Entretien	▰▰▰▰▱
Architect	Architecte	Fred Hawtree
Type	Type	parkland
Relief	Relief	▰▰▱▱▱
Water in play	Eau en jeu	▰▰▱▱▱
Exp. to wind	Exposé au vent	▰▰▰▱▱
Trees in play	Arbres en jeu	▰▰▰▰▱

Scorecard Carte de score	Chp. Chp.	Mens Mess.	Ladies Da.
Length Long.	6075	5754	5049
Par	72	72	72

Advised golfing ability
Niveau de jeu recommandé

0	12	24	36

Hcp required Handicap exigé 24 Men, 36 Ladies

CLUB HOUSE & AMENITIES / CLUB HOUSE ET ANNEXES — 7/10

Pro shop	Pro-shop	▰▰▰▰▱
Driving range	Practice	▰▰▰▱▱
Sheltered	couvert	no
On grass	sur herbe	yes
Putting-green	putting-green	yes
Pitching-green	pitching green	yes

HOTEL FACILITIES / ENVIRONNEMENT HOTELIER — 6/10

HOTELS HÔTELS

Whites Gables - 31 rooms, D £ 75 — Lisburn 4 km
Tel (44) 01846 - 682 755
Fax (44) 01846 - 689 532

Aldergrove International — Belfast
108 rooms, D £ 80 — 12 km
Tel (44) 01849 - 422 033

Forte Posthouse — Belfast
82 rooms, D £ 70 — 4 km
Tel (44) 01232 - 612 101

RESTAURANTS RESTAURANTS

Tidy Doffer — Hillsborough
Tel (44) 01846 - 689 188 — 2 km

Ashoka — Belfast
Tel (44) 01232 - 660 362 — 12 km

929

MALONE

13 6 6

A course with forty bunkers, both necessary and sufficient, as water hazards also play a significant role on certain holes : the 7th, 15th and 16th, a pretty and short par 3 where the tee-box and green bite into a large lake, and again on the 18th, a superb par 4 where slicers might spend a few nervous moments. Created in 1895, the Malone Golf Club moved to this pleasantly rolling terrain in the early 1960s. It is a typical Fred Hawtree design with well-guarded greens of all different sizes, but with the front door left open for crisply hit rolled shots. The existing natural setting was hardly touched, the course being a frank and finely landscaped layout designed around the trees. Of course, visitors used to the British inland style will hardly notice any particular local character, but if you are in the region, you will find this a challenge of high standard.

On trouve une quarantaine de bunkers ici, à la fois nécessaires et suffisants, car les obstacles d'eau jouent un grand rôle, au 7, au 15, au 16, joli par 3 court où le départ et le green empiètent sur un lac de neuf hectares, et encore au 18, superbe par 4 où les slicers risquent d'éprouver des émotions fortes. Créé en 1895, le club de Malone a émigré sur ce terrain agréablement vallonné au début des années 60, avec un dessin assez typique de Fred Hawtree, avec des greens de dimensions variées, bien défendus, mais laissant souvent la porte ouverte aux approches roulées bien touchées. Il n'a guère modifié la nature existante, mais y a inscrit un tracé bien paysagé en fonction des arbres, et d'une parfaite franchise. Certes, les visiteurs habitués au style britannique «inland» ne trouveront pas ici de caractère local très fort, mais si vous vous trouvez dans la région, vous trouverez ici un challenge de très bonne qualité.

Malone Golf Club		1895
240, Upper Malone Road		
NIRL - DUNMURRY, Co Belfast BT17 9LB		
Office	Secrétariat	(44) 01232- 612 758
Pro shop	Pro-shop	(44) 01232- 614 917
Fax	Fax	(44) 01232- 431 394
Situation	Situation	
8 km S of Belfast (pop. 279 237)		
Annual closure	Fermeture annuelle	no
Weekly closure	Fermeture hebdomadaire	no

Fees main season
Tarifs haute saison 18 holes

	Week days Semaine	We/Bank holidays We/Férié
Individual Individuel	£ 33	£ 38
Couple Couple	£ 66	£ 76

Caddy	Caddy	on request/£ 15
Electric Trolley	Chariot électrique	£ 5/18 holes
Buggy	Voiturette	£ 20/18 holes
Clubs	Clubs	£ 10

Credit cards Cartes de crédit VISA - Eurocard
MasterCard - AMEX (Green-fees & Pro-shop goods only)

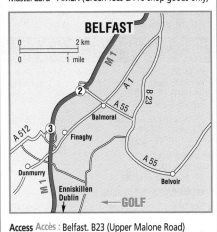

Access Accès : Belfast. B23 (Upper Malone Road)
Map 1 on page 827 Carte 1 Page 827

GOLF COURSE PARCOURS **13**/20

Site	Site	
Maintenance	Entretien	
Architect	Architecte	Fred Hawtree
Type	Type	inland, parkland
Relief	Relief	
Water in play	Eau en jeu	
Exp. to wind	Exposé au vent	
Trees in play	Arbres en jeu	

Scorecard Carte de score	Chp. Chp.	Mens Mess.	Ladies Da.
Length Long.	6084	5680	5213
Par	71	71	72

Advised golfing ability   0   12   24   36
Niveau de jeu recommandé
Hcp required   Handicap exigé   no

CLUB HOUSE & AMENITIES CLUB HOUSE ET ANNEXES **6**/10

Pro shop	Pro-shop	
Driving range	Practice	
Sheltered	couvert	no
On grass	sur herbe	yes
Putting-green	putting-green	yes
Pitching-green	pitching green	yes

HOTEL FACILITIES ENVIRONNEMENT HOTELIER **6**/10

HOTELS HÔTELS
Forte Posthouse   Dunmurry
82 rooms, D £ 85   2 km
Tel (44) 01232 - 612 101, Fax (44) 01232 - 626 546

Wellington Park   Belfast
50 rooms, D £ 60   7 km
Tel (44) 01232 - 381 111, Fax (44) 01232 - 665 410

Lansdowne Court   Belfast
25 rooms, D £ 70   7 km
Tel (44) 01232 - 773 317, Fax (44) 01232 - 370 125

RESTAURANTS RESTAURANTS

Roscoff   Belfast
Tel (44) 01232 - 331 532   6 km

Nicks Warehouse   Belfast
Tel (44) 01232 - 439 690   7 km

930

MASSEREENE

14	**5**	**6**

The course's location on the banks of Lough Neagh, the largest lake in the British Isles, is a convincing argument in its favour. There are others. Created in 1895, the course was tampered with on several occasions before Fred Hawtree came along in 1961 and brought some order and consistency to the layout. There are any number of trees here, many of which have been planted and are already of an age to come clearly into play (especially on the 17th). The front 9, on clay, can be heavy going in winter, but the back 9 are laid out over sandy soil which drains easily when it rains. There are a lot of hazards, basically bunkers (and water on the 16th), not always very deep but always well-placed and clearly visible. The variety in the size and shape of greens adds to the diversity of holes, and while beginners will unquestionably suffer, good players can test their driving accuracy. A course worth discovering.

Sa situation en bordure du Lough Neagh, le plus grand lac des Iles Britanniques, est un argument de taille (si l'on peut dire). Ce n'est pas le seul. Fondé en 1895, il a été modifié à de multiples reprises, avant que Fred Hawtree vienne mettre un peu d'ordre et de cohérence dans le tracé, en 1961. On trouve de nombreux arbres, dont beaucoup ont été plantés, mais ils ont assez atteint leur maturité pour venir nettement en jeu (spécialement au 17). L'aller, sur un sol argileux, peut être assez mou en hiver, mais le retour bénéficie d'un sol sablonneux, et bien drainant en cas de pluie. Les obstacles sont nombreux, essentiellement les bunkers (de l'eau au 16), mais pas très profonds, toujours bien placés et bien visibles. La variété de dimension et de forme des greens contribue à la diversité des trous, et si les débutants souffriront sans doute, les bons joueurs pourront y tester la précision de leurs drives. Un parcours à découvrir.

Massereene Golf Club — 1895

51 Lough Road
NIRL - ANTRIM BT41 4OQ

Office	Secrétariat	(44) 01849 - 428 096
Pro shop	Pro-shop	(44) 01849 - 464 074
Fax	Fax	(44) 01849 - 487 661
Situation	Situation	

1.5 km from Antrim
35 km from Belfast (pop. 279 237)

Annual closure	Fermeture annuelle	no
Weekly closure	Fermeture hebdomadaire	no
Fees main season	Tarifs haute saison	18 holes

	Week days Semaine	We/Bank holidays We/Férié
Individual Individuel	£ 20	£ 25
Couple Couple	£ 40	£ 50

Caddy	Caddy	on request
Electric Trolley	Chariot électrique	no
Buggy	Voiturette	no
Clubs	Clubs	yes

Credit cards Cartes de crédit — VISA - Mastercard
(Green-fees & Pro-shop only)

Access Accès : A26 S of Antrim. 1 km, right turn at leisure center. Golf 1.5 km along this road
Map 1 on page 827 Carte 1 Page 827

GOLF COURSE / PARCOURS — 14/20

Site	Site	
Maintenance	Entretien	
Architect	Architecte	Fred Hawtree
Type	Type	inland, parkland
Relief	Relief	
Water in play	Eau en jeu	
Exp. to wind	Exposé au vent	
Trees in play	Arbres en jeu	

Scorecard Carte de score	Chp. Chp.	Mens Mess.	Ladies Da.
Length Long.	5980	5760	0
Par	72	72	0

Advised golfing ability Niveau de jeu recommandé	0	12	24	36
Hcp required Handicap exigé	no			

CLUB HOUSE & AMENITIES / CLUB HOUSE ET ANNEXES — 5/10

Pro shop	Pro-shop	
Driving range	Practice	
Sheltered	couvert	no
On grass	sur herbe	no
Putting-green	putting-green	yes
Pitching-green	pitching green	yes

HOTEL FACILITIES / ENVIRONNEMENT HOTELIER — 6/10

HOTELS HÔTELS

Dunadry Hotel & Country Club — Dunadry
67 rooms, D £ 110 — 6 km
Tel (44) 01849 - 432 474, Fax (44) 01849 - 433 389

Deerpark Hotel — Antrim
19 rooms, D £ 70 — 1.5 km
Tel (44) 01849 - 462 480, Fax (44) 01849 - 467 126

Galgorm Manor — Ballymena
23 rooms, D £ 90 — 15 km
Tel (44) 01266 - 881 001, Fax (44) 01266 - 880 080

RESTAURANTS RESTAURANTS

Roscoff — Belfast
Tel (44) 01232 - 331 532 — 30 km

Dunadry Hotel — Dunadry
Tel (44) 01849 - 432 474 — 6 km

931

The seaside resorts of Portrush and Portstewart are very busy, but foreign tourists come here for the golf. Kept in the shadows of its illustrious neighbour for many a year, the Portstewart (Championship) course has been recently restyled and toughened up, and is now a very respectable test of golf which unquestionably deserves a good visit. Seven new holes have been built over an area of what were virgin dunes, and the old holes were used as a base for a 9 holer, which has completed a second 18 hole course (the "Old" course). From the back tees Portstewart is a very competent course with a dangerous collection of bunkers, but you can still play to your handicap... when the wind is just a breeze and the fairways roll well. The most intimidating hole is the first, a par 4, where you probably will have to make do with the bogey. The next holes are spectacular but not quite as fearsome as they look. Make a point of playing here.

Les stations balnéaires de Portrush et Portstewart sont très fréquentées, mais les touristes étrangers viennent pour jouer au golf ! Longtemps à l'ombre de son illustre voisin, le parcours de Portstewart (Championship) a été récemment rajeuni et durci, c'est maintenant devenu un test fort respectable, qui mérite sans discussion le détour. Sept nouveaux trous ont été construits dans un espace de dunes autrefois vierge, et les anciens trous ont servi de base pour un 9 trous, complétant un autre 18 trous (le "Old»). Des départs arrière, c'est devenu un très solide parcours, avec notamment une collection dangereuse de bunkers, mais il reste possible d'y jouer son handicap... quand le vent s'appelle brise, et quand les fairways roulent bien. Le trou le plus intimidant est le 1, un par 4 où il faut savoir se contenter d'un bogey. Les trous sont ensuite très spectaculaires, mais un peu moins terribles qu'ils ne paraissent.

Portstewart Golf Club — 1894

117, Strand Road
NIR - PORTSTEWART BT55 7PG

Office	Secrétariat	(44) 01265- 832 015
Pro shop	Pro-shop	(44) 01265- 832 601
Fax	Fax	(44) 01265- 834 077
Situation	Situation	

75 km from Belfast (pop. 279 237)
8 km from Coleraine (pop. 20 721)

Annual closure	Fermeture annuelle	no
Weekly closure	Fermeture hebdomadaire	no

Fees main season
Tarifs haute saison 18 holes

	Week days Semaine	We/Bank holidays We/Férié
Individual Individuel	£ 45	£ 65
Couple Couple	£ 90	£ 130

Caddy	Caddy	on request/£20
Electric Trolley	Chariot électrique	£ 6.50/18 holes
Buggy	Voiturette	no
Clubs	Clubs	£ 7.50/18 holes
Credit cards Cartes de crédit		VISA - Mastercard

932

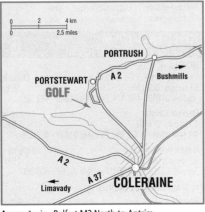

PORTRUSH
A 2 **Bushmills**
PORTSTEWART GOLF
A 2
A 37 **COLERAINE**
Limavady

Access Accès : Belfast M2 North to Antrim.
Turn right on A26 to Ballymena and Coleraine.
Coleraine A2 → Portstewart
Map 1 on page 827 Carte 1 Page 827

GOLF COURSE / PARCOURS — 16/20

Site	Site	
Maintenance	Entretien	
Architect	Architecte	Willie Park Jr Des Giffin
Type	Type	links
Relief	Relief	
Water in play	Eau en jeu	
Exp. to wind	Exposé au vent	
Trees in play	Arbres en jeu	

Scorecard Carte de score	Chp. Chp.	Mens Mess.	Ladies Da.
Length Long.	6167	5979	5301
Par	72	72	74

Advised golfing ability Niveau de jeu recommandé	0	12	24	36

Hcp required	Handicap exigé	28 Men, 36 Ladies

CLUB HOUSE & AMENITIES / CLUB HOUSE ET ANNEXES — 7/10

Pro shop	Pro-shop	
Driving range	Practice	
Sheltered	couvert	no
On grass	sur herbe	yes
Putting-green	putting-green	yes
Pitching-green	pitching green	no

HOTEL FACILITIES / ENVIRONNEMENT HOTELIER — 7/10

HOTELS HÔTELS
Edgewater — Portstewart
31 rooms, D £ 70 — adjacent
Tel (44) 01265 - 832 224, Fax (44) 01265 - 832 224

O'Neills Causeway Coast Hotel — Portrush
101 rooms, D £ 75 — 5 km
Tel (44) 01265 - 822 435, Fax (44) 01265 - 824 495

Royal Court Hotel — Portrush
18 rooms, D £ 85 — 8 km
Tel (44) 01265 - 822 236, Fax (44) 01265 - 823 176

RESTAURANTS RESTAURANTS
Cromore Halt — Portstewart
Tel (44) 01265 - 836 888 — 2 km

Some Place Else — Portrush
Tel (44) 01265 - 824 945 — 4 km

ROYAL BELFAST

15 7 7

As you might expect from a course with a regal title in a capital city, Royal Belfast is a rather exclusive club, but it is certainly not impossible to play here (especially during the week) if you book a tee-off time. Although you shouldn't expect the warm atmosphere of a vacation club in Florida, it would be a shame not to play the oldest established club in Ireland, not only for historical reasons but also because of the good course, modified slightly in the 1920s by Harry Colt. Although clearly visible, the hazards are genuinely dangerous (there is a total of 61 bunkers) and need extreme precision if they are to be avoided. So this is hardly what you would call a course for beginners. In addition, the greens are well-guarded and should be approached from exactly the right angle to keep your score down. Course upkeep is excellent.

Comme on peut l'attendre d'un golf avec un titre de noblesse et situé dans une capitale, Royal Belfast est un club assez exclusif, mais il n'est certes pas impossible d'y jouer (surtout en semaine) en réservant à l'avance. Bien sûr, il ne faut pas y attendre l'ambiance chaleureuse d'un club de vacances en Floride ! Il serait malgré tout dommage de ne pas visiter le plus ancien club établi en Irlande, non seulement pour raisons historiques, mais aussi parce qu'il dispose d'un bon parcours, auquel Harry Colt a apporté quelques modifications dans les années 20. Bien que les obstacles soient visibles, ils sont effectivement dangereux (il y a 61 bunkers au total), et demandent une grande précision pour être évités. De fait, ce n'est pas exactement un parcours pour débutants ! De plus, les greens sont bien protégés, et il faut les aborder avec un angle d'attaque correct pour préserver un bon score. L'entretien est excellent.

Royal Belfast Golf Club — 1891

Station Road, Craigavad
NIRL - HOLYWOOD, Co Down BT18 OBP

Office	Secrétariat	(44) 01232- 428 165
Pro shop	Pro-shop	(44) 01232- 428 586
Fax	Fax	(44) 01232- 421 404

Situation Situation
13 km from Belfast (pop. 279 237)
9 km from Bangor

Annual closure	Fermeture annuelle	no
Weekly closure	Fermeture hebdomadaire	no

Fees main season	Tarifs haute saison		18 holes
		Week days	We/Bank holidays
		Semaine	We/Férié
Individual Individuel		£ 30	£ 40
Couple Couple		£ 60	£ 80

Caddy	Caddy	no
Electric Trolley	Chariot électrique	no
Buggy	Voiturette	no
Clubs	Clubs	yes

Credit cards Cartes de crédit   VISA - Mastercard
(Green fees & Pro shop goods only)

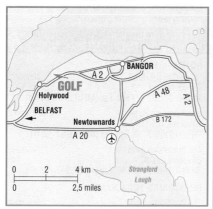

Access Accès : Belfast, A2 → Bangor.
Map 1 on page 827 Carte 1 Page 827

GOLF COURSE / PARCOURS — **15**/20

Site	Site	▬▬▬
Maintenance	Entretien	▬▬▬
Architect	Architecte	Harry S. Colt
Type	Type	parkland
Relief	Relief	
Water in play	Eau en jeu	
Exp. to wind	Exposé au vent	
Trees in play	Arbres en jeu	

Scorecard	Chp.	Mens	Ladies
Carte de score	Chp.	Mess.	Da.
Length Long.	5676	5575	5000
Par	71	70	72

Advised golfing ability		0	12	24	36
Niveau de jeu recommandé					
Hcp required	Handicap exigé	24 Men, 36 Ladies			

CLUB HOUSE & AMENITIES / CLUB HOUSE ET ANNEXES — **7**/10

Pro shop	Pro-shop	▬▬▬
Driving range	Practice	▬▬
Sheltered	couvert	
On grass	sur herbe	yes
Putting-green	putting-green	yes
Pitching-green	pitching green	no

933

HOTEL FACILITIES / ENVIRONNEMENT HOTELIER — **7**/10

HOTELS HÔTELS
Culloden Hotel — Holywood
89 rooms, D £ 140 — 1.5 km
Tel (44) 01232 - 425 223, Fax (44) 01232 - 426 777

Old Inn-Crawfords Burn — Bangor
33 rooms, D £ 90 — 6 km
Tel (44) 01247 - 853 255, Fax (44) 01247 - 852 175

Clandeboye Lodge — Bangor
43 rooms, D £ 75 — 9 km
Tel (44) 01247 - 852 500, Fax (44) 01247 - 852 772

RESTAURANTS RESTAURANTS

Sullivans — Holywood
Tel (44) 01232 - 421 000 — 6 km

Shanks — Bangor
Tel (44) 01247 - 853 313 — 9 km

Choosing between Ballybunnion, Royal Portrush, Portmarnock and Royal County Down is like trying to give an order of preference to four children. This is a masterly links, with enough blind shots and tricky greens to make a caddie well worthwhile on your first visit. Designed by Old Tom Morris, the course has been modernised with no loss of character or majesty, and without the hazards losing their strategic role : the rough, bushes, bunkers and huge dunes collect poor or over-ambitious shots. For a decent score, your game has to be up to the standard demanded by the course, and a degree of humility will also help you to come to terms with the hazards, without which the game of golf would be boring. If you can, tee off from the 10th ; despite their excellence, the last 9 holes are a little less impressive than the front 9, which wind their way through sand dunes. This is, perhaps, the only hint of a blemish on an otherwise perfect masterpiece.

Choisir entre Ballybunion, Royal Portrush, Portmarnock et Royal County Down, c'est comme classer ses enfants par ordre de préférence. Celui-ci est un links magistral, avec assez de coups aveugles et des greens assez délicats à lire pour inciter à prendre un caddie la première fois. Conçu par Old Tom Morris, ce parcours a été modernisé sans perdre son caractère et sa grandeur, sans que les obstacles perdent leur rôle stratégique : les roughs, les buissons, les bunkers, les immenses dunes accueillent tous les coups médiocres ou trop audacieux. Il faut un jeu à la hauteur du parcours pour y scorer, mais aussi beaucoup d'humilité pour accepter les hasards sans lesquels le golf serait bien ennuyeux. Si l'on peut, on commencera par le retour : en dépit de leur qualité golfique, les derniers trous ne sont pas aussi impressionnnants que les autres, insinués dans les dunes. C'est la seule petite ombre à un tableau de maître.

Royal County Down — 1889
NIR - NEWCASTLE, Co Down

Office	Secrétariat	(44) 013967 - 23 314
Pro shop	Pro-shop	(44) 013967 - 22 419
Fax	Fax	(44) 013967 - 26 281
Situation	Situation	

48 km S of Belfast (pop. 279 237)
1 km from Newcastle (pop. 7 214)

Annual closure	Fermeture annuelle	no
Weekly closure	Fermeture hebdomadaire	no

Fees main season Tarifs haute saison 18 holes

	Week days Semaine	We/Bank holidays We/Férié
Individual Individuel	£ 60	£ 80
Couple Couple	£ 120	£ 160

No GF on Saturdays

Caddy	Caddy	£ 20/18 holes
Electric Trolley	Chariot électrique	£ 5/18 holes
Buggy	Voiturette	no
Clubs	Clubs	£ 15/18 holes

Credit cards Cartes de crédit VISA - MasterCard - AMEX

Ballynahinch BELFAST
Downpatrick
Clough
CASTLEWELLAN
DUNDRUM BAY
GOLF NEWCASTLE
Annalong

0 2 4 km / 0 2,5 miles

Access Accès : Belfast A24, 50 km through Newcastle on A2
Map 1 on page 827 Carte 1 Page 827

934

GOLF COURSE PARCOURS — 19/20

Site	Site	
Maintenance	Entretien	
Architect	Architecte	Old Tom Morris
Type	Type	links
Relief	Relief	
Water in play	Eau en jeu	
Exp. to wind	Exposé au vent	
Trees in play	Arbres en jeu	

Scorecard Carte de score	Chp. Chp.	Mens Mess.	Ladies Da.
Length Long.	6335	6084	5672
Par	71	71	76

Advised golfing ability — 0 12 24 36
Niveau de jeu recommandé
Hcp required Handicap exigé — 28 Men, 36 Ladies

CLUB HOUSE & AMENITIES CLUB HOUSE ET ANNEXES — 6/10

Pro shop	Pro-shop	
Driving range	Practice	
Sheltered	couvert	
On grass	sur herbe	yes
Putting-green	putting-green	yes
Pitching-green	pitching green	no

HOTEL FACILITIES ENVIRONNEMENT HOTELIER — 7/10

HOTELS HÔTELS

Slieve Donard Hotel — Newcastle
130 rooms, D £ 110 — 500 m
Tel (44) 013967 - 23 681, Fax (44) 013967 - 24 830

Glasdrumman Hotel — Glasdrumman
10 rooms, D £ 115 — 11 km
Tel (44) 013967 - 68 585, Fax (44) 013967 - 67 041

The Burrendale Hotel — Newcastle
68 rooms, D £ 80 — 1 km
Tel (44) 013967 - 22 599, Fax (44) 013967 - 22 328

RESTAURANTS RESTAURANTS

The Pavillion — Newcastle
Tel (44) 013967 - 26 239 — adjacent

Mario's — Newcastle
Tel (44) 013967 - 23 912 — 1 km

ROYAL PORTRUSH DUNLUCE LINKS 19 7 7

Being so close to the Giant's Causeway effectively brings to mind how a course can dwarf your golf. The Dunluce course is rated as one of Ireland's greatest courses, a fact you can easily check for yourself. Over an area covered with enormous dunes, the course comes and goes in a perfectly nothing-to-hide manner. In fact, it never leaves you alone and not a single hole fails to impress, so woe betide the golfer who drops his guard. You need not only extreme skill with club and ball, but also nerves of steel so as not to shrink from the difficulties you are sure to encounter sooner or later. Even the greens, with some tantalising slopes, demand unfailing concentration. You need a certain level of golfing ability to appreciate the subtler sides to this devilish course, which really snarls when the wind gets up. Harry Colt considered this to be his masterpiece. It is, quite simply, a masterpiece.

La proximité de la «Chaussée des Géants» fait penser que l'on est un nain, golfiquement parlant du moins. Le «Dunluce» de Royal Portrush passe pour être l'un des plus grands parcours d'Irlande, vous le vérifierez aisément. Dans un espace occupé par d'énormes dunes, le parcours va et vient avec une franchise parfaite. Il n'est pas un trou pour vous laisser tranquille ou indifférent, pour vous permettre de baisser la garde. Il faut non seulement une grande maîtrise de ses clubs et du maniement de la balle, mais aussi des nerfs d'acier pour ne pas fléchir devant les difficultés, à un moment ou à un autre. Même les greens exigent une concentration sans faille, avec leurs pentes déconcertantes. Il faut un certain niveau de jeu pour apprécier les subtilités de ce parcours démoniaque, dont les dents sont encore plus acérées avec le vent. Harry Colt le considérait comme «son» chef-d'oeuvre. C'est un chef d'oeuvre, tout simplement.

Royal Portrush Golf Club 1888
Bushmills Road
NIR - PORTRUSH, Co Antrim

Office	Secrétariat	(44) 01265- 822 311
Pro shop	Pro-shop	(44) 01265- 823 335
Fax	Fax	(44) 01265- 823 139
Situation	Situation	

90 km from Belfast (pop. 279 237)
8 km N of Coleraine (pop. 20 721)

Annual closure	Fermeture annuelle	no
Weekly closure	Fermeture hebdomadaire	no

Fees main season
Tarifs haute saison 18 holes

	Week days Semaine	We/Bank holidays We/Férié
Individual Individuel	£ 70	£ 80
Couple Couple	£ 140	£ 160

Caddy	Caddy	on request/£ 20
Electric Trolley	Chariot électrique	£ 7.50/18 holes
Buggy	Voiturette	no
Clubs	Clubs	£ 10/18 holes
Credit cards Cartes de crédit		VISA - MasterCard

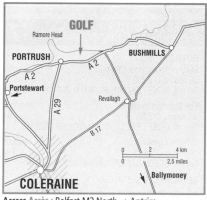

GOLF
Ramore Head
PORTRUSH
A 2
Portstewart
A 29
BUSHMILLS
A 2
Revallagh
B 17
0   2   4 km
0   2,5 miles
Ballymoney
COLERAINE

Access Accès : Belfast M2 North → Antrim.
Turn right to A26 → Ballymena/Coleraine.
Coleraine → Portrush
Map 1 on page 827 Carte 1 Page 827

GOLF COURSE / PARCOURS 19/20

Site	Site	▰▰▰▰▱
Maintenance	Entretien	▰▰▰▰▰
Architect	Architecte	Harry S. Colt
Type	Type	links
Relief	Relief	▰▰▱▱▱
Water in play	Eau en jeu	▰▱▱▱▱
Exp. to wind	Exposé au vent	▰▰▰▱▱
Trees in play	Arbres en jeu	▱▱▱▱▱

Scorecard Carte de score	Chp. Chp.	Mens Mess.	Ladies Da.
Length Long.	6137	6000	5601
Par	72	72	75

Advised golfing ability Niveau de jeu recommandé		0 12 24 36
Hcp required Handicap exigé		24 Men, 36 Ladies

CLUB HOUSE & AMENITIES / CLUB HOUSE ET ANNEXES 7/10

Pro shop	Pro-shop	▰▰▰▰▱
Driving range	Practice	▰▰▰▱▱
Sheltered	couvert	no
On grass	sur herbe	yes
Putting-green	putting-green	yes
Pitching-green	pitching green	yes

935

HOTEL FACILITIES / ENVIRONNEMENT HOTELIER 7/10

HOTELS HÔTELS

Magherabuoy House Hotel — Portrush
38 rooms, D £ 100 — 2 km
Tel (44) 01265 - 823 907, Fax (44) 01265 - 824 687

The Eglinton Hotel — Portrush
30 rooms, D £ 60 — 1 km
Tel (44) 01265 - 822 371, Fax (44) 01265 - 823 155

O'Neills Causeway Coast Hotel — Portrush
101 rooms, D £ 75 — 1 km
Tel (44) 01265 - 822 435, Fax (44) 01265 - 824 495

RESTAURANTS RESTAURANTS

Ramore — Portrush
Tel (44) 01265 - 824 313 — 2 km

Some Place Else — Portrush
Tel (44) 01265 - 824 945 — 2 km

How can we assess the "second course" at Portrush ? Would we rate it a very good course if it went by any other name ? The answer is seemingly yes, even though it is some way from the greatness and majesty of Dunluce Links. Located, as its name suggests, in a valley between dunes, there are, strangely enough, no more than twenty bunkers, and the par 3s are particularly devoid of sand. Otherwise, the rolling terrain, rough, bushes and wind are trouble enough to upset most players, especially when the end-targets are as small as they generally are here. The nature of the terrain will also pose a few problems for players who are used to the immaculately prepared fairways of inland courses. As with all links courses, this is a test of ball-play and feeling, and the natural setting only adds to the appeal. Golfers who end up discovering this course by chance are generally surprised at the overall excellence of the layout. A very good practice course.

Comment juger le «second parcours» de Royal Portrush ? S'il portait un autre nom, serait-il considérée comme un très bon parcours ? A l'évidence oui, même s'il est loin de la grandeur et de la majesté du «Dunluce Links». Situé comme son nom l'indique dans une vallée entre les dunes, il ne compte curieusement qu'une vingtaine de bunkers, particulièrement sur les par 3. Autrement, les ondulations du terrain, les roughs, les buissons et le vent suffisent amplement à troubler les joueurs, surtout quand les cibles finales sont petites, ce qui est généralement le cas. Et la nature du terrain posera forcément des problèmes aux joueurs habitués aux fairways impeccablement garnis des parcours intérieurs. Comme tous les links, celui-ci est un test de toucher de balle, et son aspect naturel ajoute à la séduction. Ceux qui sont amenés à le découvrir par hasard sont généralement surpris de sa qualité générale.

Royal Portrush Golf Club   1889
Bushmills Road
NIR - PORTRUSH, Co Antrim

Office	Secrétariat	(44) 01265- 822 311
Pro shop	Pro-shop	(44) 01265- 823 335
Fax	Fax	(44) 01265- 823 139
Situation	Situation	

90 km from Belfast (pop. 279 237)
8 km N of Coleraine (pop. 20 721)

Annual closure	Fermeture annuelle	no
Weekly closure	Fermeture hebdomadaire	no

Fees main season
Tarifs haute saison 18 holes

	Week days Semaine	We/Bank holidays We/Férié
Individual Individuel	£ 24	£ 32
Couple Couple	£ 48	£ 64

Caddy	Caddy	on request/£ 20
Electric Trolley	Chariot électrique	£ 7.50/18 holes
Buggy	Voiturette	no
Clubs	Clubs	£ 10/18 holes
Credit cards Cartes de crédit		VISA - MasterCard

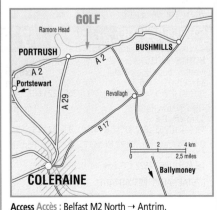

GOLF
Ramore Head
PORTRUSH
A 2
Portstewart
A 29
Revallagh
B 17
BUSHMILLS
A 2
0   2   4 km
0   2,5 miles
Ballymoney
COLERAINE

Access Accès : Belfast M2 North → Antrim.
Turn right to A26 → Ballymena/Coleraine.
Coleraine → Portrush
Map 1 on page 827 Carte 1 Page 827

GOLF COURSE PARCOURS   13/20

Site	Site	
Maintenance	Entretien	
Architect	Architecte	Unknown
Type	Type	links
Relief	Relief	
Water in play	Eau en jeu	
Exp. to wind	Exposé au vent	
Trees in play	Arbres en jeu	

Scorecard Carte de score	Chp. Chp.	Mens Mess.	Ladies Da.
Length Long.	5700	5450	4995
Par	70	68	72

Advised golfing ability	0 12 24 36
Niveau de jeu recommandé	
Hcp required	Handicap exigé	no

CLUB HOUSE & AMENITIES CLUB HOUSE ET ANNEXES   7/10

Pro shop	Pro-shop	
Driving range	Practice	
Sheltered	couvert	no
On grass	sur herbe	yes
Putting-green	putting-green	yes
Pitching-green	pitching green	yes

HOTEL FACILITIES ENVIRONNEMENT HOTELIER   7/10

HOTELS HÔTELS
Magherabuoy House Hotel   Portrush
38 rooms, D £ 100   2 km
Tel (44) 01265 - 823 907, Fax (44) 01265 - 824 687

The Eglinton Hotel   Portrush
30 rooms, D £ 60   1 km
Tel (44) 01265 - 822 371, Fax (44) 01265 - 823 155

O'Neills Causeway Coast Hotel   Portrush
101 rooms, D £ 75   1 km
Tel (44) 01265 - 822 435, Fax (44) 01265 - 824 495

RESTAURANTS RESTAURANTS
Ramore   Portrush
Tel (44) 01265 - 824 313   2 km

Some Place Else   Portrush
Tel (44) 01265 - 824 945   2 km

936

WARRENPOINT

The setting for the Warrenpoint course, between mountains and Carringford bay, provides some breath-taking scenery and gives a marvellous sensation of space. To appreciate it fully, though, you will need to disregard the noise of the adjacent road, which is a shame. This is otherwise a very pleasant course, maybe more for mid- to high-handicappers than for the more skilled exponents, who might feel a little frustrated if expecting an adversary measuring up to their ability. But we need courses for every taste and anyway, there is no shortage of tough courses in Ireland. This layout requires no great length off the tee (which is a reserved privilege, anyway) but it does call for a sharp and subtle short game, as some approaches and bunkers around the greens are tricky. But these difficulties are generally on either side of the greens, so you can lay up short and stay out of trouble. A pleasant stop-off on "hard-working" holidays.

La situation du golf de Warrenpoint, entre les montagnes et la baie de Carringford permet des points de vue majestueux, donnant une sensation merveilleuse d'espace, mais il faut, pour en profiter, faire abstraction du bruit de la route adjacente... C'est dommage, car ce parcours est autrement très agréable, peut-être davantage encore pour les handicaps moyens et élevés, alors que les meilleurs joueurs seront un peu frustrés s'ils attendent un adversaire à la mesure de leur talent. Mais il faut des golfs pour tous les goûts, alors on ne manque pas de parcours difficiles. Celui-ci ne requiert pas une grande longueur (elle n'est pas donnée à tout le monde), mais plutôt de la finesse de petit jeu, car certains abords de greens sont délicats, de même que les bunkers. Mais ces difficultés sont plutôt de part et d'autre des greens, ce qui autorise à jouer court pour ne pas en souffrir. Une halte sympathique pour des vacances studieuses.

Warrenpoint Golf Club		1893
Lower Dromore Road		
NIRL - WARRENPOINT, Co Down BT34 3LN		
Office	Secrétariat	(44) 016937- 53 695
Pro shop	Pro-shop	(44) 016937- 52 371
Fax	Fax	(44) 016937- 52 918
Situation	Situation	
50 km from Belfast (pop. 279 237)		
8 km from Newry		
Annual closure	Fermeture annuelle	no
Weekly closure	Fermeture hebdomadaire	no

Fees main season
Tarifs haute saison 18 holes

	Week days Semaine	We/Bank holidays We/Férié
Individual Individuel	£ 20	£ 30
Couple Couple	£ 40	£ 60

Caddy	Caddy	no
Electric Trolley	Chariot électrique	£ 10/18 holes
Buggy	Voiturette	no
Clubs	Clubs	£ 10

Credit cards Cartes de crédit   no

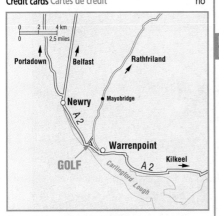

Access Accès : Belfast, A1 to Newry.
A2 → Warrenpoint.
Map 1 on page 827 Carte 1 Page 827

GOLF COURSE
PARCOURS
13/20

Site	Site	
Maintenance	Entretien	
Architect	Architecte	Unknown
Type	Type	parkland, hilly
Relief	Relief	
Water in play	Eau en jeu	
Exp. to wind	Exposé au vent	
Trees in play	Arbres en jeu	

Scorecard Carte de score	Chp. Chp.	Mens Mess.	Ladies Da.
Length Long.	6161	5778	5377
Par	71	71	72

Advised golfing ability Niveau de jeu recommandé	0 12 24 36
Hcp required Handicap exigé	no

CLUB HOUSE & AMENITIES
CLUB HOUSE ET ANNEXES
6/10

Pro shop	Pro-shop	
Driving range	Practice	
Sheltered	couvert	no
On grass	sur herbe	yes
Putting-green	putting-green	yes
Pitching-green	pitching green	no

937

HOTEL FACILITIES
ENVIRONNEMENT HOTELIER
5/10

HOTELS HÔTELS
Kilmorey Arms Hotel — Kilkeel
50 rooms, D £ 40 — 20 km
Tel (44) 016937 - 62 220
Fax (44) 016937 - 65 399

Carlingford Bay Hotel — Warrenpoint
24 rooms, D £ 50 — 1 km
Tel (44) 016937 - 73 521
Fax (44) 016937 - 74 202

RESTAURANTS RESTAURANTS
The Brass Monkey — Newry
Tel (44) 01693 - 63 176 — 8 km

Aylesfort House — Warrenpoint
Tel (44) 016937 -72 255 — 100 m

406

PEUGEOT

AUTO GRATIFICAZIONE

pininfarina

PEUGEOT 406 COUPÉ

E'difficile immaginare un paese più piacevole e con il clima migliore dell'Italia, nel quale la storie si trova ovunque intorno a te ma si integra perfettamente con la vita moderna super-attiva. Anche se l'inverno può essere abbastanza freddo al nord, a parte nella regione dei laghi, il golf è uno sport che si pratica tutto l'anno. Per il momento ci sono solo poco più di 100 campi e neanche 60.000 giocatori. Mentre la Spagna e il Portogallo hanno riempito le loro coste di campi e turisti-golfisti, l'Italia ha trascurato questo aspetto ed ha costruito percorsi principalmente per la popolazione locale, in particolar modo intorno alle città più importanti e sopratutto nel nord del paese. E' veramente un piacere giocare a golf qui, oltretutto, di solito si trovano club-houses molto eleganti e ben attrezzate che sono il punto d'incontro della buona società e dove si mangia molto bene. Si dice che il golf sia un'arte di vivere: in Italia lo è certamente.

It is hard to imagine a more agreeable country and favourable climate than Italy, where history is all around you and closely integrated with very active modern-day life. Even though the winters can be rather cold in the north, excepting the lakes region, golf is an all-year sport. Yet, there are only about a hundred courses and not even 60,000 players. While Spain and Portugal have covered their coastlines with courses and touring golfers, Italy has neglected this side of the equation and has built courses mainly for local populations and particularly around major cities, mainly in the North of the country. It is such a pleasure playing golf here, though, with generally very elegant and well-equipped club-houses which make a point of cultivating social life and great food. They say that golf is an art of living; in Italy it certainly is.

939

The Millennium Guide

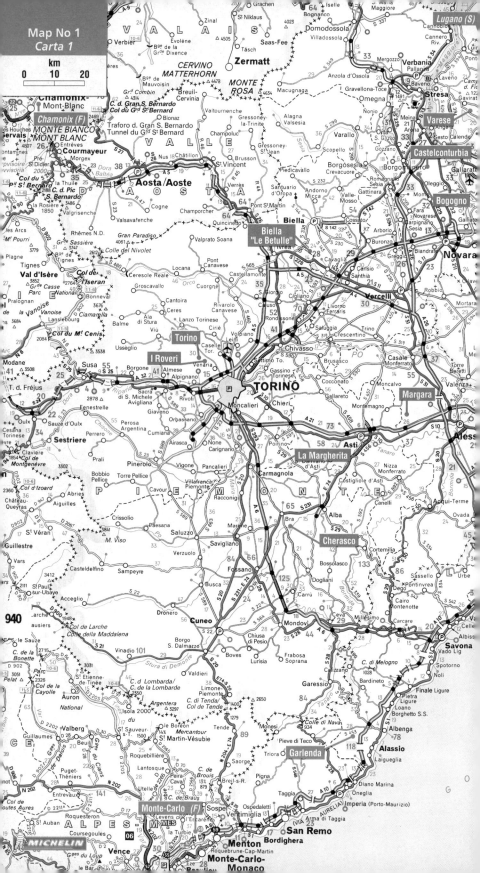

MICHELIN

d'après carte n°988 - 23ème édition - 2000.
Autorisation n°9904173.

943

CRES

MICHELIN

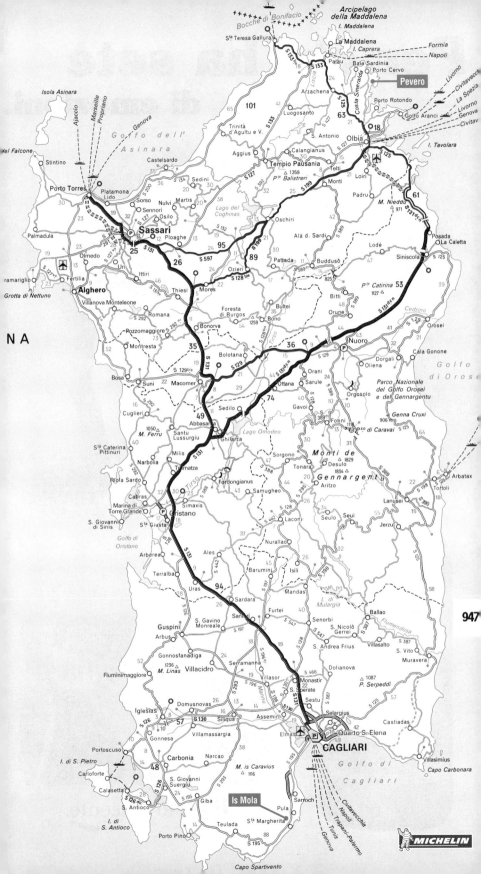

Per chi ha sete
di emozioni.

Il gusto vincente.

CLASSIFICA DEI PERCORSI
CLASSIFICATION OF COURSES

This classification gives priority consideration
to the score awarded to the actual course.

Questa classifica è ordinata secondo il punteggio assegnato al percorso.

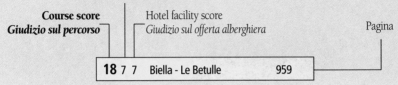

Club-house and facilities
Giudizio sul Club-house

Course score
Giudizio sul percorso

Hotel facility score
Giudizio sul offerta alberghiera

Pagina

18 7 7   Biella - Le Betulle   959

Nota	Percorso	Pagina	Nota	Percorso	Pagina
18 7 7	Biella - Le Betulle	959	**14** 6 7	Cosmopolitan	968
18 8 7	Castelconturbia		**14** 8 9	Firenze - Ugolino	969
	Giallo + Azzurro	963	**14** 7 8	Gardagolf	972
17 8 7	Bogogno	960	**14** 7 8	Garlenda	973
17 7 8	I Roveri	974	**14** 8 8	Le Pavoniere	979
17 8 7	Le Querce	980	**14** 7 7	Lignano	982
16 7 8	Is Molas	975	**14** 7 8	Modena	986
16 9 7	Le Robinie	981	**14** 8 7	Monticello	989
16 8 8	Marco Simone	983	**14** 7 7	Padova	991
16 8 9	Milano	985	**14** 7 8	Punta Ala	996
16 7 6	Olgiata	990	**14** 8 7	Varese	1002
16 8 8	Pevero	994	**13** 7 7	Asolo	956
16 7 7	Poggio dei Medici	995	**13** 7 7	Bologna	961
16 8 9	Roma - Acquasanta	999	**13** 6 8	Ca' della Nave	962
16 8 8	Torino - La Mandria		**13** 6 9	Cervia	966
	Percorso Blu	1001	**13** 7 7	Cherasco	967
16 7 9	Venezia	1003	**13** 7 7	La Margherita	976
16 8 9	Villa D'Este	1005	**13** 7 7	La Pinetina	977
15 8 8	Barlassina	957	**13** 6 8	La Rocca	978
15 7 8	Bergamo - L'Albenza		**13** 7 7	Margara	984
	Blu + Giallo	958	**13** 9 8	Molinetto	987
15 7 7	Castelgandolfo	964	**13** 8 7	Montecchia	988
15 8 8	Castello di Tolcinasco	965	**13** 7 9	Parco de' Medici	993
15 7 8	Franciacorta	971	**13** 7 8	Rapallo	997
15 8 8	Palazzo Arzaga	992	**13** 7 6	Riva dei Tessali	998
14 8 7	Albarella	954	**13** 7 8	Verona	1004
14 7 7	Ambrosiano	955			

949

Segafredo ZANETTI

Espresso

CON PASSIONE ED ESPERIENZA ABBIAMO PORTATO LA CULTURA

DEL VERO ESPRESSO ITALIANO NEL MONDO, SEGUENDO

CON CURA IL NOSTRO CAFFÈ IN OGNI FASE, DALLE PIANTAGIONI

FINO A CASA VOSTRA. PER QUESTO OGGI LE NOSTRE

MISCELE SONO TRA LE PIÙ APPREZZATE NEL MONDO

CLASSIFICA DEI SERVIZI ALBERGHIERI
CLASSIFICATION OF HOTELS FACILITIES

This classification gives priority consideration
to the score awarded to the hotel facilities.

Questa classifica è ordinata secondo il punteggio assegnato ai servizi alberghieri.

Club-house and facilities
Giudizio sul Club-house

Course score
Giudizio sul percorso

Hotel facility score
Giudizio sul offerta alberghiera

Pagina

| 13 | 6 | **9** | Cervia | 966 |

Nota			Percorso	Pagina	Nota			Percorso	Pagina
13	6	9	Cervia	966	13	7	8	Verona	1004
14	8	9	Firenze - Ugolino	969	14	8	7	Albarella	954
16	8	9	Milano	985	14	7	7	Ambrosiano	955
13	7	9	Parco de' Medici	993	13	7	7	Asolo	956
16	8	9	Roma - Acquasanta	999	18	7	7	Biella - Le Betulle	959
16	7	9	Venezia	1003	17	8	7	Bogogno	960
16	8	9	Villa D'Este	1005	13	7	7	Bologna	961
15	8	8	Barlassina	957	18	8	7	Castelconturbia	
15	7	8	Bergamo - L'Albenza					*Giallo + Azzurro*	963
			Blu + Giallo	958	15	7	7	Castelgandolfo	964
13	6	8	Ca' della Nave	962	13	7	7	Cherasco	967
15	8	8	Castello di Tolcinasco	965	14	6	7	Cosmopolitan	968
15	7	8	Franciacorta	971	13	7	7	La Margherita	976
14	7	8	Gardagolf	972	13	7	7	La Pinetina	977
14	7	8	Garlenda	973	17	8	7	Le Querce	980
17	7	8	I Roveri	974	16	9	7	Le Robinie	981
16	7	8	Is Molas	975	14	7	7	Lignano	982
13	6	8	La Rocca	978	13	7	7	Margara	984
14	8	8	Le Pavoniere	979	13	8	7	Montecchia	988
16	8	8	Marco Simone	983	14	8	7	Monticello	989
14	7	8	Modena	986	14	7	7	Padova	991
13	9	8	Molinetto	987	16	7	7	Poggio dei Medici	995
15	8	8	Palazzo Arzaga	992	14	8	7	Varese	1002
16	8	8	Pevero	994	16	7	6	Olgiata	990
14	7	8	Punta Ala	996	13	7	6	Riva dei Tessali	998
13	7	8	Rapallo	997					
16	8	8	Torino - La Mandria						
			Percorso Blu	1001					

951

Italia

SOGGIORNO GOLFISTICO CONSIGLIATI
RECOMMENDED GOLFING STAY

Percorso	Nota	Pagina	Percorso	Nota	Pagina
Bogogno	17 8 7	960	I Roveri	17 7 8	974
Castelconturbia			Torino - La Mandria		
Giallo + Azzurro	18 8 7	963	*Percorso Blu*	16 8 8	1001

LUOGO DI VACANZA CONSIGLIATI
RECOMMENDED GOLFING HOLIDAYS

Percorso	Nota	Pagina	Percorso	Nota	Pagina
Albarella	14 8 7	954	Palazzo Arzaga	15 8 8	992
Cervia	13 6 9	966	Pevero	16 8 8	994
Cosmopolitan	14 6 7	968	Punta Ala	14 7 8	996
Gardagolf	14 7 8	972	Rapallo	13 7 8	997
Garlenda	14 7 8	973	Riva dei Tessali	13 7 6	998
Is Molas	16 7 8	975	Venezia	16 7 9	1003
Lignano	14 7 7	982	Villa D'Este	16 8 9	1005

MESI CONSIGLIATI
RECOMMENDED SEASONS

952

Percorso	Nota	Pagina	Percorso	Nota	Pagina
`1 2 3 4 5 6 7 8 9 10 11 12`			`1 2 3 4 5 6 7 8 9 10 11 12`		
Cosmopolitan	14 6 7	968	Castelgandolfo	15 7 7	964
Garlenda	14 7 8	973	Marco Simone	16 8 8	983
Is Molas	16 7 8	975	Parco de' Medici	13 7 9	993
Pevero	16 8 8	994			
Punta Ala	14 7 8	996	`1 2 3 4 5 6 7 8 9 10 11 12`		
Rapallo	13 7 8	997	Olgiata	16 7 6	990
Riva dei Tessali	13 7 6	998			
Roma - Acquasanta	16 8 9	999	`1 2 3 4 5 6 7 8 9 10 11 12`		
			Asolo	13 7 7	956
`1 2 3 4 5 6 7 8 9 10 11 12`			Bergamo - L'Albenza		
Albarella	14 8 7	954	*Blu + Giallo*	15 7 8	958
Franciacorta	15 7 8	971	Ca' della Nave	13 6 8	962
Gardagòlf	14 7 8	972	Castello di Tolcinasco	15 8 8	965
Le Querce	17 8 7	980	Cervia	13 6 9	966
Lignano	14 7 7	982	Firenze - Ugolino	14 8 9	969
Palazzo Arzaga	15 8 8	992	La Margherita	13 7 7	976
Venezia	16 7 9	1003	La Pinetina	13 7 7	977

Percorso	Nota	Pagina		Percorso	Nota	Pagina
1 2 3 4 5 6 7 8 9 10 11 12				1 2 3 4 5 6 7 8 9 10 11 12		
La Rocca	13 6 8	978		Cherasco	13 7 7	967
Le Pavoniere	14 8 8	979		1 2 3 4 5 6 7 8 9 10 11 12		
Le Robinie	16 9 7	981		Ambrosiano	14 7 7	955
Milano	16 8 9	985		Bogogno	17 8 7	960
Modena	14 7 8	986		Bologna	13 7 7	961
Molinetto	13 9 8	987		I Roveri	17 7 8	974
Montecchia	13 8 7	988		Margara	13 7 7	984
Monticello	14 8 7	989		Padova	14 7 7	991
Poggio dei Medici	16 7 7	995		Torino - La Mandria		
Varese	14 8 7	1002		*Percorso Blu*	16 8 8	1001
Verona	13 7 8	1004		1 2 3 4 5 6 7 8 9 10 11 12		
Villa D'Este	16 8 9	1005		Biella - Le Betulle	18 7 7	959
1 2 3 4 5 6 7 8 9 10 11 12				Castelconturbia *Giallo + Azzurro*	18 8 7	963
Barlassina	15 8 8	957				

TIPO DI PERCORSO
TYPE OF COURSE

Tipo	Pagina	Tipo	Pagina	Tipo	Pagina
copse		Bogogno	960	Le Robinie	981
Riva dei Tessali	998	I Roveri	974	Margara	984
		La Pinetina	977	Modena	986
country		Punta Ala	996	Montecchia	988
Ambrosiano	955	Torino - La Mandria		Roma - Acquasanta	999
Asolo	956	*Percorso Blu*	1001		
Bogogno	960	Villa D'Este	1005	**parkland**	
Bologna	961	Castelconturbia		Barlassina	957
Ca' della Nave	962	*Giallo + Azzurro*	963	Cervia	966
Castello di Tolcinasco	965			La Margherita	976
Cherasco	967	**hilly**		Le Pavoniere	979
Franciacorta	971	Bologna	961	Milano	985
Gardagolf	972	Firenze - Ugolino	969	Olgiata	990
Garlenda	973	La Pinetina	977	Varese	1002
Is Molas	975	Le Querce	980		
La Rocca	978	Marco Simone	983	**residential**	
Marco Simone	983	Rapallo	997	Albarella	954
Molinetto	987	Varese	1002	Castelgandolfo	964
Monticello	989			Castello di Tolcinasco	965
Padova	991	**links**		I Roveri	974
Palazzo Arzaga	992	Albarella	954	Molinetto	987
Poggio dei Medici	995	Castelconturbia		Olgiata	990
Rapallo	997	*Giallo + Azzurro*	963	Parco de' Medici	993
Verona	1004	Cosmopolitan	968		
		Lignano	982	**seaside course**	
forest				Cervia	966
Bergamo - L'Albenza		**open country**		Pevero	994
Blu + Giallo	958	Le Querce	980	Roma - Acquasanta	999
Biella - Le Betulle	959	Le Pavoniere	979	Venezia	1003

953

Situato in una piccola isola nel delta del Po, vicino a Venezia e a Padova è un golf molto conosciuto in Italia, in particolare perchè ha ospitato numerosi tornei internazionali. E' stato costruito su un terreno molto aperto dove la vegetazione è poco significativa, molto vicino al mare ed alla spiaggia. Circondato da piccole dune di sabbia, il percorso può far pensare ad un links. Certo il gioco può cambiare radicalmente quando soffia forte il vento, il che non accade raramente ma è solitamente misurato e non di tipo britannico: l'Adriatico non è il mare del Nord o l'Atlantico! Infatti è un piacevolissimo percorso di vacanza, ben tenuto e dove può giocare tutta la famiglia. Le difficoltà sono solitamente ben visibili e i rilievi praticamente inesistenti: se mai si può dire che manca un po' di movimento. John Harris e Marco Croze hanno evidentemente pensato prima ai dilettanti, ma anche se il record è 63, i migliori giocatori dovranno fare molta attenzione per fare uno score basso.

Albarella, located on a small peninsula in the estuary of the river Po near Venice and Padova, is one of Italy's best known courses, having hosted a many international tournaments. It was laid out on open terrain with little in the way of vegetation, close to the sea and beaches. Surrounded by small sand-dunes, certain aspects of this course are reminiscent of a typical links course. The way it plays can certainly change drastically when the wind blows, a frequent occurrence here, but this British side to the course has its limits, as this is, after all, the Adriatic not the North Sea or the Atlantic. In actual fact this is a very good holiday course, well kept and easy to play with all the family. Hazards are clearly visible and there is no relief to speak of. The more critically-minded might feel that the course could have been given more shape, but John Harris and Marco Croze obviously had amateur golfers in mind when designing the layout. The course record is 63, but the better players will have to be on top of their game if they want to card low scores.

Circolo Golf Albarella — 1972

Isola di Albarella
I - 45010 ROSOLINA (RO)

Office	Segreteria	(39) 0426 330 124
Pro shop	Pro shop	(39) 0426 330 896
Fax	Fax	(39) 0426 330 830
Situation	Localita'	

Chioggia (pop. 52.471) 24 km - Venezia (pop. 293.731), 45 km

Annual closure	Chiusura annuale	no
Weekly closure	Chiusura settimanale	tuesday

Fees main season
Tariffe alta stagione 18 holes

	Week days Settimana	We/Bank holidays Feriale/Festivo
Individual Individuale	L. 80.000	L. 100.000
Couple Coppia	L. 160.000	L. 200.000

Caddy	Caddy	no
Electric Trolley	Carello elettrico	no
Buggy	Car	L 60.000
Clubs	Bastoni	L 50.000

Credit cards Carte di credito
VISA- Eurocard - MasterCard

Access Itinerario : A4 Milano-Venezia. Exit (Uscita) Padova Est. SS16 → Chioggia. In Chioggia, Strada Romea → Ravenna. After Rosolina, turn left to Isola Albarella. → Golf
Map 2 on page 942 Carta 2 Pagina 942

GOLF COURSE / PERCORSO — 14/20

Site	Paesaggio	
Maintenance	Manutenzione	
Architect	Architetto	John Harris Marco Croze
Type	Tipologia	links, residential
Relief	Relievo terreno	
Water in play	Acqua in gioco	
Exp. to wind	Esposto al vento	
Trees in play	Alberi in gioco	

Scorecard Carta-score	Chp. Camp.	Mens Uomini	Ladies Donne
Length Lunghezza	5370	6100	6100
Par	72	72	72

Advised golfing ability Livello di gioco consigliato	0	12	24	36

Hcp required Handicap richiesto 34

CLUB HOUSE & AMENITIES / CLUB HOUSE E SERVIZI — 8/10

Pro shop	Pro shop	
Driving range	Campo pratica	
Sheltered	coperto	4 mats
On grass	in erba	yes
Putting-green	Putting-green	yes
Pitching-green	Green-pratica	yes

HOTEL FACILITIES / ALBERGHI — 7/10

HOTELS ALBERGHI
Hotel Capo Nord — Albarella
41 rooms, D L. 158.000 — 3 km
Tel (39) 0426 330 139

Golf Hotel — Albarella
22 rooms, D L. 180.000 — on site
Tel (39) 0426 367 811, Fax (39) 0426 330 628

RESTAURANTS RISTORANTE
Sottovento — Norge Polesine
Tel (39) 0426 340 138 — 12,5 km

Due Leoni — Ariano nel Polesine
Tel (39) 0426 372 129 — 25 km

Franco — Chioggia
Tel (39) 041 4950 301 — 24 km

Questo percorso recente è molto vicino a Milano ma anche a Pavia, dove la sua università ha ospitato nientemeno che il Petrarca e Leonardo da Vinci. La città è stata anche una roccaforte dei Visconti che stabilirono il loro mausoleo a nord della città, alla Certosa di Pavia, una straordinaria chiesa lombarda tra il gotico e il rinascimentale. La Certosa non è che a qualche chilometro dall'Ambrosiano e coloro che non amamo più di tanto la storia e l'antichità potranno fare questo percorso anche due volte al giorno. Siccome è particolarmente piatto è difficile capire subito la strategia di gioco e visualizzare i suoi tranelli. La disposizione intelligente dei numerosi ostacoli ne fa un percorso divertente e di qualità anche se il paesaggio non è eccezionale. Si può rivelare più delicato dalle partenze di campionato.

Sure, this recent course is close to Milan, but it is also not far from Pavia, at whose university Petrarch and Leonardo da Vinci studied in days gone by. This was also one of the strongholds of the Visconti, who built their mausoleum to the north of the city at Certosa di Pavia (Charterhouse of Pavia), an extraordinary Lombardy-style church somewhere between the Gothic and Renaissance styles. It is also just a few miles from Ambrosiano. Golfers who have no time for history or old buildings can play this course twice in a day. Being virtually shorn of trees, it is hard to immediately appreciate game strategy and visualize the traps. The clever layout of the very many hazards makes this a very amusing and high quality course, even though the landscape is nothing to write home about. It is, however, a much trickier proposition when played from the tiger tees.

Golf Club Ambrosiano — 1994

Cascina Bertacca
I - 20080 BUBBIANO (MI)

Office	Segreteria	(39) 02 9084 0820
Pro shop	Pro shop	(39) 02 9084 0820
Fax	Fax	(39) 02 9084 9365
Situation	Localita'	

Milano (pop. 1 032 808), 29 km -
Pavia (pop. 74 065), 30 km

Annual closure	Chiusura annuale	no
Weekly closure	Chiusura settimanale	tuesday

Fees main season
Tariffe alta stagione full day

	Week days Settimana	We/Bank holidays Feriale/Festivo
Individual Individuale	L. 60.000	L. 90.000
Couple Coppia	L. 120.000	L. 180.000
Caddy	Caddy	no
Electric Trolley	Carello elettrico	no
Buggy	Car	L. 60.000
Clubs	Bastoni	L. 30.000

Credit cards Carte di credito
VISA - Eurocard - MasterCard - Cartasi

Access Itinerario : A7 Milano-Genova, Exit (Uscita)
Binasco, right → Motta Visconti. 7 km, → Bubbiano.
→ Golf. **Map 1 on page 941** Carta 1 Pagina 941

GOLF COURSE
PERCORSO

14/20

Site	Paesaggio	
Maintenance	Manutenzione	
Architect	Architetto	Cornish & Silva
Type	Tipologia	country
Relief	Relievo terreno	
Water in play	Acqua in gioco	
Exp. to wind	Esposto al vento	
Trees in play	Alberi in gioco	

Scorecard Carta-score	Chp. Camp.	Mens Uomini	Ladies Donne
Length Lunghezza	6281	6047	5316
Par	72	72	72

Advised golfing ability		0	12	24	36
Livello di gioco consigliato					

Hcp required	Handicap richiesto	no

CLUB HOUSE & AMENITIES
CLUB HOUSE E SERVIZI

7/10

Pro shop	Pro shop	
Driving range	Campo pratica	
Sheltered	coperto	5 mats
On grass	in erba	yes
Putting-green	Putting-green	yes
Pitching-green	Green-pratica	yes

HOTEL FACILITIES
ALBERGHI

7/10

HOTELS ALBERGHI

Corona — Binasco
50 rooms, D. L. 120.000 — 8 km
Tel (39) 02 905 2280, Fax (39) 02 905 434

Europa — Rosate
40 rooms, D. L. 110.000 — 3 km
Tel (39) 02 908 7612

Comtur - 49 rooms, D. L. 235.000 — Binasco
Tel (39) 02 900 2020 — 7 km

RESTAURANTS RISTORANTE

Al Cassinino — Pavia (Str. 35)
Tel (39) 0382 422 097

I Castagni - Tel(39) 0381 42 860 — Vigevano 16 km

Re Artù - Tel(39) 02 908 5123 — Gaggiano 15 km

Antica Trattoria del Gallo — Gaggiano
Tel (39) 02 908 52 76 — 15 km

955

Con la sua ubicazione vicino a Vicenza, Treviso, Padova, Venezia ed anche alla Svizzera, Asolo è uno dei percorsi da conoscere quando si visita questa superba regione del Veneto. Da aggiungere a questa lista le famose cittadine di Asolo con i suoi castelli e i suoi palazzi e Bassano del Grappa, conosciuta per le sue piccole case dipinte, le ceramiche e... la grappa! Questo percorso è immerso in un posto molto bello ed ampio e comprenderà in breve tempo tre percorsi di 9 buche combinabili tra loro in diversi percorsi di 18 buche. Stan Eby, della European Golf Design, ha concepito questo tracciato dove le difficoltà sono ben equilibrate ed è quindi accessibile ai giocatori di ogni livello anche se non sempre è particolarmente stimolante. Tutto qui è stato fatto con grande serietà e con una buona conoscenza dei vari livelli di gioco, ma gli amanti dei percorsi di carattere avrebbero amato un po' più di audacia nell'estetica. Asolo resta comunque un percorso da visitare quando si è nella regione.

Being close to Vicenza, Treviso, Padova, Venice and even Switzerland, Asolo is a course to play when exploring this superb region. We can add Asolo to this list of famous cities, with fortress and palaces, and Bassano del Grappa, famous for its little painted houses, porcelain and... Grappa liqueur! The golf course is spread over a very beautiful and uncluttered site and will shortly comprise three combinable 9 hole courses to form several different 18-hole layouts. Stan Eby from European Golf Design designed this course, which is well-balanced in the difficulties it presents, playable by golfers of all abilities but not always necessarily very exciting. Everything has been done very thoroughly here, with good insight into different levels of golfing skill, although golfers who like more personalized courses might have preferred a little more daring here and there. Nonetheless, Asolo is a course that deserves a visit when in the region.

Asolo Golf Club — 1997

Via Ronche
I - 31034 CAVASO DEL TOMBA (TV)

Office	Segreteria	(39) 0423 942 000
Pro shop	Pro shop	(39) 0423 942 217
Fax	Fax	(39) 0423 543 226
Situation	Localita'	

Treviso (pop. 81.328), 35 km
Bassano del Grappa (pop. 39.625)

Annual closure	Chiusura annuale	no
Weekly closure	Chiusura settimanale	tuesday

Fees main season
Tariffe alta stagione full day

	Week days Settimana	We/Bank holidays Feriale/Festivo
Individual Individuale	L. 80.000	L. 120.000
Couple Coppia	L. 160.000	L. 240.000
Caddy Caddy		L. 40.000
Electric Trolley Carello elettrico	no	
Buggy Car		L. 60.000
Clubs Bastoni		L. 30.000

Credit cards Carte di credito
VISA - Eurocard - MasterCard - AMEX - DC - Cartasi

956

Access Itinerario : Treviso, S348, → Possagno and Cavaso del Tomba. Golf 2 km after Cavaso.
Map 2 on page 942 Carta 2 Pagina 942

GOLF COURSE / PERCORSO — 13/20

Site	Paesaggio	
Maintenance	Manutenzione	
Architect	Architetto	European Golf Design
Type	Tipologia	country
Relief	Relievo terreno	
Water in play	Acqua in gioco	
Exp. to wind	Esposto al vento	
Trees in play	Alberi in gioco	

Scorecard Carta-score	Chp. Camp.	Mens Uomini	Ladies Donne
Length Lunghezza	6242	5873	5161
Par	72	72	72

Advised golfing ability		0 12 24 36
Livello di gioco consigliato		
Hcp required	Handicap richiesto	34

CLUB HOUSE & AMENITIES / CLUB HOUSE E SERVIZI — 7/10

Pro shop	Pro shop	
Driving range	Campo pratica	
Sheltered	coperto	10 mats
On grass	in erba	yes
Putting-green	Putting-green	yes
Pitching-green	Green-pratica	yes

HOTEL FACILITIES / ALBERGHI — 7/10

HOTELS ALBERGHI

Villa Cipriani — Asolo
31 rooms, D. L. 705.000 — 8 km
Tel (39) 0423 523 411, Fax (39) 0423 529 411

Al Sole — Asolo
23 rooms, D. L. 350.000 — 8 km
Tel (39) 0423 528 111, Fax (39) 0423 528 399

Victoria — Bassano del Grappa
23 rooms, D. L. 140.000 — 15 km
Tel (39) 0424 503 620, Fax (39) 0424 503 130

RESTAURANTS RISTORANTE

Belvedere — Bassano del Grappa 15 km
Tel (39) 0424 524 988

Ai Due Archi - Tel (39) 0423 952 201 — Asolo 8 km

Tavernetta - Tel (39) 0423 952 273 — Asolo 8 km

BARLASSINA

| 15 | 8 | 8 |

Aperto nel 1956, il disegno dell'architetto inglese John Morrison è stato modificato nel 1988, per quel che riguarda il tracciato di alcune buche e di molti greens. E' situato in una regione abbastanza ondulata ad un ventina di chilometri a nord di Milano, poco distante dalle strade che portano al lago di Como. La natura è particolarmente piacevole e le buche sono ritagliate in mezzo al bosco anche se abbastanza larghe: gli alberi sono in gioco senza essere veramente pericolosi, e apportano un elemento di decoro importante per il piacere degli occhi. In questo grande parco, la passeggiata è tanto piacevole che non è necessario essere un gran campione per divertirsi e non si è impegnati in colpi particolarmente difficili. Però se si parte dai tees di campionato non ci si può permettere di fare troppi errori. Tra i numerosi percorsi intorno a Milano, Barlassina merita una visita, ma non durante il week-end dove il gioco è riservato ai soci.

Opened in 1956, this layout from British architect John Morrison was altered in 1988 with changes made to a number of holes and to the configuration of several greens. It is located over rolling countryside some twenty or so kilometres to the north of Milan, just off the road leading to Lake Como. The surroundings are pleasant indeed and the course full of trees, but still with rather wide fairways. Although in play, the trees are not all that dangerous and serve more as decoration and an addition to the course's visual appeal. In this large park, the walk is all the more enjoyable in that you don't have to be a top champion to tame the course, or know how to hit the so-called technical shots. With that said, if you play from the tips, you have little room for error if you want to score well. Of the many courses around Milan, Barlassina is well worth a visit, except on week-ends when the course is reserved for members only.

Barlassina Country Club — 1956

Via Privata Golf 42
I - 20030 BIRAGO DI CAMNAGO (MI)

Office	Segreteria	(39) 0362 560 621
Pro shop	Pro shop	(39) 0362 560 621
Fax	Fax	(39) 0362 560 834
Situation	Localita'	

Milano (pop. 1.302.808), 26 km - Como, 25 km

Annual closure	Chiusura annuale	no
Weekly closure	Chiusura settimanale	monday

Fees main season
Tariffe alta stagione 18 holes

	Week days Settimana	We/Bank holidays Feriale/Festivo
Individual Individuale	L. 110.000	L. 155.000
Couple Coppia	L. 220.000	L. 310.000

Green-fees on week days only (Ospiti solo durante i giorni feriali)

Caddy	Caddy	L. 35.000
Electric Trolley	Carello elettrico	no
Buggy	Car	no
Clubs	Bastoni	L. 20.000

Credit cards Carte di credito		no

Access Itinerario : Milano North, take the S35 → Como. Exit (Uscita Seveso/Barlassina.
Map 1 on page 941 Carta 1 Pagina 941

GOLF COURSE / PERCORSO — 15/20

Site	Paesaggio	
Maintenance	Manutenzione	
Architect	Architetto	J. Morrison
Type	Tipologia	parkland
Relief	Relievo terreno	
Water in play	Acqua in gioco	
Exp. to wind	Esposto al vento	
Trees in play	Alberi in gioco	

Scorecard Carta-score	Chp. Camp.	Mens Uomini	Ladies Donne
Length Lunghezza	6197	6197	5418
Par	72	72	72

Advised golfing ability		0 12 24 36
Livello di gioco consigliato		
Hcp required	Handicap richiesto 34	

CLUB HOUSE & AMENITIES / CLUB HOUSE E SERVIZI — 8/10

Pro shop	Pro shop	
Driving range	Campo pratica	
Sheltered	coperto	8 mats
On grass	in erba	yes
Putting-green	Putting-green	yes
Pitching-green	Green-pratica	yes

HOTEL FACILITIES / ALBERGHI — 8/10

HOTELS ALBERGHI

Albergo della Rotonda — Saronno
92 rooms, D L. 400.000 — 12 km
Tel (39) 02 967 032 32, Fax (39) 02 967 027 70

Principe di Savoia — Milano
252 rooms, D. L. 1.000.000 — 19 km
Tel (39) 02 62 301, Fax (39) 02 659 5838

Umberto Primo — Seregno
52 rooms, D. L. 200.000 — 7 km
Tel (39) 0362 223 377, Fax (39) 0362 221 931

RESTAURANTS RISTORANTE

Osteria del Pomiroeu — Seregno
Tel (39) 0362 237 973 — 7 km

Le Querce - Tel (39) 031 731 336 — Cantù 15 km

La Rimessa — Mariano Comense
Tel (39) 031 749 668 — 6 km

957

Se le 9 buche «blu» e le 9 buche «gialle» sono considerate il percorso di campionato, le 9 buche «rosse» costituiscono un'alternativa di qualità all'uno o all'altro e aggiungono ancora del pepe ad un disegno che non ne avrebbe bisogno grazie ai suoi par 4 ed ai par 5 difficili da raggiungere in due colpi. E' sicuramente la varietà la carta migliore dell'Albenza con i suoi passaggi tra i boschi e i suoi spazi aperti, la sua alternanza di buche lunghe e corte, la necessità di giocare un golf di precisione o meglio all'inglese. Bisogna «lavorare» spesso la palla per avere dei colpi al green più facili e riflettere bene sulla scelta dei bastoni. Un percorso di grande «formazione» se lo si giudica dalla carriera e dal gioco molto completo di Costantino Rocca, che ha cominciato qui come caddie prima di diventare un grandissimo campione. Questo personaggio, pieno di personalità avrebbe potuto figurare nella commedia dell'arte nata proprio a Bergamo.

If we consider the «blue» and «yellow» 9-hole courses to be the 18 hole championship course, the «red» course is an excellent alternative to both and adds a little spice to a layout that is pretty hot as it is, in particular on account of the par 4s and the par 5s that are tough to reach in two. Talking of spice, variety is certainly one of the key assets of «L'Albenza», which winds its way now through the woods, now over open space, alternating short and long holes, or target golf and the more British bump and run approach. You often have to work the ball one way or the other for an easier shot at the greens, and club choice requires careful thinking. This is a very «educational» course, judging by very complete game of Costantino Rocca, who started off here as a caddie before becoming one of the world's best golfers. A colourful figure, Rocca could easily have figured in the «Commedia dell'Arte» which, as it happens, was founded in Bergamo.

Golf Club Bergamo - L'Albenza 1961
Via Longoni 12
I - 24030 ALMENNO SAN BARTOLOMEO (BG)

Office	Segreteria	(39) 035 640 028
Pro shop	Pro shop	(39) 035 643 288
Fax	Fax	(39) 035 643 066
Situation	Localita'	

Bergamo (pop. 117.619), 15 km Brescia (pop. 190.518), 50 km
Annual closure Chiusura annuale no

Weekly closure Chiusura settimanale monday

Fees main season
Tariffe alta stagione 18 holes

	Week days Settimana	We/Bank holidays Feriale/Festivo
Individual Individuale	L. 80.000	L. 120.000
Couple Coppia	L. 160.000	L. 240.000
Caddy Caddy		L. 40.000
Electric Trolley Carello elettrico		L. 15.000
Buggy Car		no
Clubs Bastoni		L. 10.000

Credit cards Carte di credito
VISA - Eurocard - MasterCard - AMEX - DC

958

Access Itinerario : A4 Milano-Venezia, Exit (Uscita)
Capriate. Turn right → Ponte San Pietro. At old house,
turn left → Lecco. 2 km right → Almenno San
Bartolomeo. Golf on left hand side.
Map 1 on page 941 Carta 1 Pagina 941

GOLF COURSE PERCORSO 15/20

Site	Paesaggio	▭▭▭▭
Maintenance	Manutenzione	▭▭▭▭
Architect	Architetto	Cotton & Sutton
Type	Tipologia	forest
Relief	Relievo terreno	▭▭▭
Water in play	Acqua in gioco	▭▭
Exp. to wind	Esposto al vento	▭▭
Trees in play	Alberi in gioco	▭▭▭▭

Scorecard Carta-score	Chp. Camp.	Mens Uomini	Ladies Donne
Length Lunghezza	6220	6100	5368
Par	72	72	72

Advised golfing ability 0 12 24 36
Livello di gioco consigliato ▭▭▭
Hcp required Handicap richiesto 34

CLUB HOUSE & AMENITIES CLUB HOUSE E SERVIZI 7/10

Pro shop	Pro shop	▭▭▭▭
Driving range	Campo pratica	▭▭▭
Sheltered	coperto	12 mats
On grass	in erba	yes
Putting-green	Putting-green	yes
Pitching-green	Green-pratica	yes

HOTEL FACILITIES ALBERGHI 8/10

HOTELS ALBERGHI
Castello di Clanezzo — Clanezzo
12 rooms, D.L. 120.000 — 3 km
Tel (39) 035 641 567, Fax (39) 035 641 567

Starhotel Cristallo Palace — Bergamo
90 rooms, D. L. 365.000 — 15 km
Tel (39) 035 311 211, Fax (39) 035 312 031

Radisson SAS Hotel — Bergamo
86 rooms, D. L. 300.000 — 15 km
Tel (39) 035 308 111, Fax (39) 035 308 308

RESTAURANTS RISTORANTE
Ponte di Briolo — Valbrembo
Tel (39) 035 611 197 — 5 km

Trattoria del Tone — Curno
Tel (39) 035 613 166 — 8 km

Caprese - Tel (39) 035 611 148 — Mozzo 6 km

Biella è la sede di uno dei più sobri e migliori golf della penisola, dove il disegno dell'architetto si è nascosto dietro alla bellezza di un paesaggio e di un terreno che sembrano fatti apposta per il golf. Se a questo si aggiunge il talento di un architetto come John Morrison abbiamo veramente il massimo. Il percorso è stato allungato nel corso degli anni per rispondere alle esigenze del gioco moderno, ma vi consigliamo di giocare dai tees normali per non soffrire troppo a meno di non avere una tecnica di prim'ordine. Di spirito assolutamente britannico, il percorso mette in gioco dei bunkers piazzati strategicamente, dei fossi diabolici e alberi in abbondanza, querce, castagni e betulle. Il tutto con una varietà notevole: sobrietà, infatti, non vuol dire monotonia. Un grande test di golf in un ambiente superbo, può essere un po' difficile per i giocatori poco esperti. Da conoscere, ancor meglio con un soggiorno nella «Dormy House» del circolo.

Biella has made a name for Italian design. It is also the site of one of the more discreet but also one of the greatest golf courses in the whole of Italy, a course where architectural design plays second fiddle to the beauty of the landscape and terrain that were just made for golf. Yet it still took the designer skills of John Morrison to perfect the chemistry. The course has since been lengthened to meet the demands of the modern game, but unless you have the technique of a budding champion, we would recommend the normal tees to avoid needless suffering. There is a very British feel to this course, which brings strategically located bunkers into play, along with diabolic ditches and no end of oak, chestnut and birch trees. Add to all this a remarkable touch of variety and you'll realize that here, sobriety does not necessarily mean monotony. All in all, a great test of golf in superb surroundings, but maybe a little too tough for inexperienced players. For an even more enjoyable experience, try and stay in the course's «Dormy House» hotel.

Golf Club Biella - Le Betulle 1958

Località Valcarrozza
I - 13887 MAGNANO (BI)

Office	Segreteria	(39) 015 679 151
Pro shop	Pro shop	(39) 015 679 151
Fax	Fax	(39) 015 679 276
Situation	Localita'	

Biella (pop. 47.713), 18 km - Torino (pop. 914.818), 75 km

Annual closure	Chiusura annuale	no
Weekly closure	Chiusura settimanale	monday

Fees main season
Tariffe alta stagione 18 holes

	Week days Settimana	We/Bank holidays Feriale/Festivo
Individual Individuale	L. 90.000	L. 120.000
Couple Coppia	L. 180.000	L. 240.000

Caddy	Caddy	yes
Electric Trolley	Carello elettrico	no
Buggy	Car	L. 60.000
Clubs	Bastoni	L. 30.000

Credit cards Carte di credito
VISA - Eurocard - MasterCard - AMEX

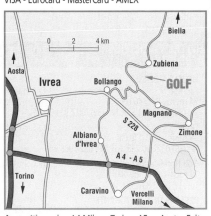

↑ Biella

0   2   4 km

↑ Aosta

Ivrea   Bollango   Zubiena   **GOLF**

S 228   Magnano

Albiano d'Ivrea   Zimone

A 4 - A 5

↓ Torino   Caravino   Vercelli Milano

Access Itinerario : A4 Milano-Torino, A5 → Aosta. Exit (Uscita) Albiano, → Biella. Cross the S228 and take S338 → Biella. Golf 2 km
Map 1 on page 940 Carta 1 Pagina 940

GOLF COURSE
PERCORSO

18/20

Site	Paesaggio	
Maintenance	Manutenzione	
Architect	Architetto	John Morrison
Type	Tipologia	forest
Relief	Relievo terreno	
Water in play	Acqua in gioco	
Exp. to wind	Esposto al vento	
Trees in play	Alberi in gioco	

Scorecard Carta-score	Chp. Camp.	Mens Uomini	Ladies Donne
Length Lunghezza	6497	6125	5390
Par	73	73	73

Advised golfing ability		0	12	24	36
Livello di gioco consigliato					
Hcp required	Handicap richiesto 34				

CLUB HOUSE & AMENITIES
CLUB HOUSE E SERVIZI

7/10

Pro shop	Pro shop	
Driving range	Campo pratica	
Sheltered	coperto	10 mats
On grass	in erba	yes
Putting-green	Putting-green	yes
Pitching-green	Green-pratica	yes

959

HOTEL FACILITIES
ALBERGHI

7/10

HOTELS ALBERGHI
Dormy House   Magnano
20 rooms, D. L. 150.000   on site
Tel (39) 015 679 151, Fax (39) 015 679 276

Astoria - 50 rooms, D. L. 190.000   Biella
Tel (39) 015 402 750, Fax (39) 015 351 047   18 km

Michelangelo   Biella
21 rooms, D. L. 190.000   18 km
Tel (39) 015 8492 362, Fax (39) 015 8492 649

Augustus - 38 rooms, D. L. 190.000   Biella 18 km
Tel (39) 015 24 554, Fax (39) 015 29 257

RESTAURANTS RISTORANTE
La Bessa Tel (39) 015 679 186   Magnano 4 km

Prinz Grill da Beppe e Teresio   Biella
Tel (39) 015 23 876   18 km

San Paolo - Tel (39) 015 8493 236   Biella18 km

Aperto nel 1996, Bogogno si è subito imposto come uno dei campi più spettacolari d'Italia d'altronde c'era da attenderselo da un architetto come Robert Von Hagge che raramente disegna campi «minimalisti». Ma bisogna dire che i suoi movimenti del terreno non sono mai inutili, sono fatti per variare prospettiva, creare difficoltà, dividere le buche una dall'altra, quando il terreno è piatto. L'aspetto visivo è comunque molto importante e assume a volte un aspetto quasi scozzese... Ma siamo in Italia, culla del teatro: la scenografia delle Alpi e del Monte Rosa è valorizzata al massimo dalla bellezza grafica del percorso. Gli attori avranno grandi spazi per fare le loro evoluzioni, che saranno però difficili da interpretare. Bisogna avere nervi saldi e mestiere per arrivare alla fine con un buono score in tasca perchè gli ostacoli sono in agguato ovunque. Un altro percorso di 18 buche si integrerà a questo creando uno dei più bei complessi golfistici del paese.

In 1996, Bogogno immediately became established as one of Italy's most spectacular courses, as one might expect from architect Robert von Hagge, who seldom has much time for «minimalism». It should be said though that the way he contours the terrain is never gratuitous and is designed to vary the viewpoints, to add difficulty and isolate holes when the terrain is flat. The visual aspect is very important and if you look closely enough there is almost a touch of Scotland here and there. However, this is Italy and the land of drama, and the backdrop of the Alps and Monte Rosa is enhanced by the graphic beauty of the course. Players will find the wide open space they need to perform but can easily fluff their lines. To keep your score down, you need nerves of steel and a good measure of skill, as there is no shortage of hazards in all shapes and sizes. A second 18 hole course will be completing what is one of the country's finest golfs.

Circolo Golf Bogogno — 1996

Via S. Isidoro 1
I - 28010 BOGOGNO (NO)

Office	Segreteria	(39) 0322 863 794
Pro shop	Pro shop	(39) 0322 863 339
Fax	Fax	(39) 0322 863 798
Situation	Localita'	

Novara (pop. 102.404), 30 km
Milano (pop. 1.302.808), 66 km

Annual closure	Chiusura annuale	no
Weekly closure	Chiusura settimanale	monday

Fees main season
Tariffe alta stagione 18 holes

	Week days Settimana	We/Bank holidays Feriale/Festivo
Individual Individuale	L. 100.000	L. 130.000
Couple Coppia	L. 200.000	L. 260.000
Caddy	Caddy	L. 40.000
Electric Trolley	Carello elettrico	L. 20.000
Buggy	Car	L. 50.000
Clubs	Bastoni	L. 35.000

Credit cards Carte di credito VISA- Eurocard - MasterCard

960

Access Itinerario : A4 Milano-Torino, Exit (Uscita) Novara. Then S229 → Borgomanero. About 29 km, turn right → Cressa. 800 m turn left to Bogogno.
Map 1 on page 940 Carta 1 Pagina 940

GOLF COURSE / PERCORSO — 17/20

Site	Paesaggio	
Maintenance	Manutenzione	
Architect	Architetto	Robert von Hagge
Type	Tipologia	country, forest
Relief	Relievo terreno	
Water in play	Acqua in gioco	
Exp. to wind	Esposto al vento	
Trees in play	Alberi in gioco	

Scorecard Carta-score	Chp. Camp.	Mens Uomini	Ladies Donne
Length Lunghezza	6485	5755	4947
Par	72	72	72

Advised golfing ability
Livello di gioco consigliato — 0 12 24 36

Hcp required Handicap richiesto 34

CLUB HOUSE & AMENITIES / CLUB HOUSE E SERVIZI — 8/10

Pro shop	Pro shop	
Driving range	Campo pratica	
Sheltered	coperto	8 mats
On grass	in erba	yes
Putting-green	Putting-green	yes
Pitching-green	Green-pratica	yes

HOTEL FACILITIES / ALBERGHI — 7/10

HOTELS ALBERGHI

San Rocco — Orta San Giulio
74 rooms, D. L. 460.000 — 20 km
Tel (39) 0322 911 977, Fax (39) 0322 911 964

Orta — Orta San Giulio
35 rooms, D. L. 170.000 — 20 km
Tel (39) 0322 90 253, Fax (39) 0322 905 646

Golf Hotel Castelconturbia — Agrate Conturbia
19 rooms, D. L. 180.000 — 3 km
Tel (39) 0322 832 337

RESTAURANTS RISTORANTE

Pinocchio — Borgomanero
Tel (39) 0322 82 273 — 3 km

Il Bersagliere — Borgomanero
Tel (39) 0322 82 277 — 6 km

BOLOGNA

Bologna è da molti secoli una città che potremmo definire come una studentessa maggiorenne. Senza essere una delle città più turistiche d'Italia, non manca nè di monumenti che di musei importanti. E' anche uno dei centri più significativi per la gastronomia del paese. Se si aggiunge la sua attività industriale e quella della vicina Modena c'è da chiedersi come mai questa regione non sia più ricca di percorsi di golf. Aperto da più di 40 anni, questo percorso è stato disegnato da Henry Cotton e John Harris su di un terreno ondulato ai piedi degli Appennini. Il suo aspetto generale ricorda i percorsi britannici dell'interno con i greens ben difesi dai bunkers, ma senza un disegno particolarmente originale. Non si verrà qui per trovare delle grandi emozioni di gioco, nè per vedere panorami eclatanti, ma il giusto grado di difficoltà rende il percorso piacevole per la grande maggioranza dei giocatori anche se ai migliori mancherà il sapore della grande sfida.

For centuries, Bologna has been one of the top cities for students, and although not one of Italy's leading tourist destinations, there is no shortage of significant landmarks and museums. It is also one of the country's top areas for food and drink. If we add to this the region's industrial activity and that of the neighbouring city of Modena, then the scarcity of golf courses might come as something of a surprise. Opened some forty years ago, this course was laid out by Henry Cotton and John Harris over rolling terrain at the foot of the Apennines. Its overall shape is reminiscent of British inland courses, with greens well protected by bunkers and nothing particularly original about the layout as a whole. You certainly wouldn't come here just for thrills or striking visual beauty, but the moderation in the layout of hazards makes this a pleasant course for almost every player. Only the very best might rue the absence of a tougher challenge.

Golf Club Bologna — 1959

Via Sabbatini 69
I - 40050 MONTE SAN PIETRO (BO)

Office	Segreteria	(39) 051 969 100
Pro shop	Pro shop	(39) 051 969 505
Fax	Fax	(39) 051 6720 017
Situation	Localita'	

Bologna (pop. 383.761), 15 km
Modena (pop. 175.013), 25 km

Annual closure	Chiusura annuale	no
Weekly closure	Chiusura settimanale	tuesday

Fees main season
Tariffe alta stagione 18 holes

	Week days Settimana	We/Bank holidays Feriale/Festivo
Individual Individuale	L. 80.000	L. 100.000
Couple Coppia	L. 160.000	L. 200.000
Caddy	Caddy	L. 50.000
Electric Trolley	Carello elettrico	L. 30.000
Buggy	Car	L. 50.000
Clubs	Bastoni	L. 30.000

Credit cards Carte di credito — no

Access Itinerario : A1 (Autostrada del Sole) Exit (Uscita) Casalecchio, S569 (Vigolese e di Bazzano) → Maranello, Vignola. After Ponte Ronca, turn left → Golf
Map 2 on page 942 Carta 2 Pagina 942

GOLF COURSE
PERCORSO — 13/20

Site	Paesaggio	
Maintenance	Manutenzione	
Architect	Architetto	Cotton & Harris
Type	Tipologia	country, hilly
Relief	Relievo terreno	
Water in play	Acqua in gioco	
Exp. to wind	Esposto al vento	
Trees in play	Alberi in gioco	

Scorecard Carta-score	Chp. Camp.	Mens Uomini	Ladies Donne
Length Lunghezza	6098	5949	5226
Par	72	72	72

Advised golfing ability	0	12	24	36
Livello di gioco consigliato				

Hcp required Handicap richiesto 34

CLUB HOUSE & AMENITIES
CLUB HOUSE E SERVIZI — 7/10

Pro shop	Pro shop	
Driving range	Campo pratica	
Sheltered	coperto	5 mats
On grass	in erba	yes
Putting-green	Putting-green	yes
Pitching-green	Green-pratica	yes

HOTEL FACILITIES
ALBERGHI — 7/10

HOTELS ALBERGHI

Alla Rocca — Bazzano
50 rooms, D. L. 240.000 — 5 km
Tel (39) 051 831 217, Fax (39) 051 830 690

Garden — Anzola Emilia
56 rooms, D. L. 340.000 — 4 km
Tel (39) 051 735 200, Fax (39) 051 735 673

Grand Hotel Baglioni — Bologna
125 rooms, D. L. 600.000 — 15 km
Tel (39) 051 225 445, Fax (39) 051 234 840

RESTAURANTS RISTORANTE

Il Ristorante da Dino — Anzola Emilia
Tel (39) 051 732 364 — 4 km

Trattoria al Parco — Bazzano
Tel (39) 051 830 800 — 5 km

Battibecco — Bologna
Tel (39) 051 223 298 — 15 km

961

Il golf è situato nella campagna veneziana, un po' a lato dalla rotta per Treviso, in una delle proprietà di campagna dove si rifugiavano i ricchi veneziani durante l'estate. Restano ancora una parte dei favolosi giardini e la villa Grimani Morosini, datata XVI secolo e ora restaurata ma non adibita a club-house. Questo percorso di Arnold Palmer riprende alcuni tratti tipici dell'Italia: ad esempio l'acqua, onnipresente come a Venezia, sotto forma di canali e di piccoli laghi, soprattutto alla 14, dove sia il fairway che il green sono praticamente ognuno su un'isola. Palmer ha fatto parecchi movimenti di terra per creare questo percorso molto intelligente, divertente da giocare con gli amici, dove le difficoltà sono più apparenti che reali, salvo qualche grandissimo bunker che i dilettanti mediocri non amano proprio. Il disegno dei greens è di buona qualità, sono ben difesi ma qualche volta facilmente accessibili facendo rotolare la palla. Questo tracciato molto buono meriterebbe una manutenzione impeccabile... da sorvegliare!

This course is located in the Venetian countryside a little way off the Treviso road on one of those country estates where the wealthier Venetians used to spend their summer. Still here are some superb gardens and the 16th century Villa Grimani Morosini, now restored but not used as a club-house. This Arnold Palmer layout is the only course to utilize the typical features of Italy, obviously meaning omnipresent water - we are close to Venice after all - in the shape of canals and little lakes. This is very much the case on the 14th hole, where the fairway and green are virtually islands on their own. Palmer excavated a lot of earth to build this very intelligent course, which is fun to play with friends and where the difficulties are more apparent than real, except for a number of very large sand-traps that your average hacker dislikes intensely. This very good layout deserves immaculate green-keeping... so watch this space.

Ca' della Nave Golf Club — 1987

Piazza della Vittoria 14
I - 30030 MARTELLAGO (VE)

Office	Segreteria	(39) 041 540 1555
Pro shop	Pro shop	(39) 041 540 1555
Fax	Fax	(39) 041 540 1555
Situation	Localita'	

Mestre, 8 km - Venezia (pop. 293 731), 19 km

Annual closure	Chiusura annuale	no
Weekly closure	Chiusura settimanale	tuesday

Fees main season
Tariffe alta stagione full day

	Week days Settimana	We/Bank holidays Feriale/Festivo
Individual Individuale	L. 80.000	L. 100.000
Couple Coppia	L. 160.000	L. 200.000
Caddy	Caddy	no
Electric Trolley	Carello elettrico	no
Buggy	Car	L. 50.000
Clubs	Bastoni	L. 30.000

Credit cards Carte di credito
VISA - Eurocard - MasterCard - AMEX - DC - Cartasi

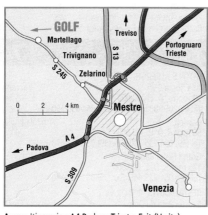

Access Itinerario : A4 Padova-Trieste. Exit (Uscita) Castelfranco Veneto. In Mestre S245 → Zelarino e Trivignano. Go to Martellago. Golf on the right, at the end of town.
Map 2 on page 942 Carta 2 Pagina 942

GOLF COURSE / PERCORSO — 13/20

Site	Paesaggio	
Maintenance	Manutenzione	
Architect	Architetto	Arnold Palmer
Type	Tipologia	country
Relief	Relievo terreno	
Water in play	Acqua in gioco	
Exp. to wind	Esposto al vento	
Trees in play	Alberi in gioco	

Scorecard Carta-score	Chp. Camp.	Mens Uomini	Ladies Donne
Length Lunghezza	6041	5800	4825
Par	72	72	72

Advised golfing ability Livello di gioco consigliato: 0 12 24 36

Hcp required Handicap richiesto 34

CLUB HOUSE & AMENITIES / CLUB HOUSE E SERVIZI — 6/10

Pro shop	Pro shop	
Driving range	Campo pratica	
Sheltered	coperto	5 mats
On grass	in erba	yes
Putting-green	Putting-green	yes
Pitching-green	Green-pratica	yes

HOTEL FACILITIES / ALBERGHI — 8/10

HOTELS ALBERGHI

Michelangelo — Mestre 9 km
51 rooms, D. L. 440.000
Tel (39) 041 986 600, Fax (39) 041 986 052

Park Hotel Villa Giustinian — Mirano 5 km
38 rooms, D. L. 180.000
Tel (39) 041 570 0200, Fax (39) 041 570 0355

Villa Soranzo Conestabile — Scorzè 5 km
22 rooms, D. L. 220.000
Tel (39) 041 445 027, Fax (39) 041 584 0088

Cipriani - 59 rooms, D. L. 1.650.000 — Venezia 18 km
Tel (39) 041 520 7744, Fax (39) 041 520 3930

RESTAURANTS RISTORANTE

Marco Polo - Tel (39) 041 989 855 — Mestre 8 km

Autoespresso — Marghera 10 km
Tel (39) 041 930 214

962

Anche se i tre percorsi di 9 buche sono intercambiabili tra loro per fare percorsi differenti, è il tracciato «blu e giallo» quello che è stato scelto per l'Open d'Italia nel 1998. Ovunque si riconosce la firma di Robert Trent Jones e non solo per i bunkers frastagliati, l'aspetto strategico qui è particolarmente importante. Bisogna diffidare della larghezza ingannevole dei fairways, anche se c'è sempre una parte ideale da dove attaccare meglio i greens che sono molto grandi con pendenze spesso diaboliche. Il gioco consiste allora sia nell'evitare gli errori giocando in difesa che nell' attaccare con decisione. Castelconturbia richiede riflessione e il saper eseguire i colpi che si vogliono fare: dominarlo non è certo possibile per un giocatore inesperto! I pendii non sono molto rilevanti ma alcuni greens sopraelevati richiedono un'attenzione speciale. Un complesso superbo impossibile da ignorare.

Although the three 9 hole courses can be combined to produce different layouts, the blue and yellow courses were the two chosen for the Italian Open in 1998. The hallmark of Robert Trent Jones is omnipresent, and not only in the jagged sand traps. The strategic aspect is particularly important, and watch out for the deceiving width of fairways. Remember, too, that there is always the right side from which to attack greens in the best position, especially since the greens in question are pretty huge with diabolical slopes and breaks. Golf here consists in cutting out mistakes and in stopping short of all-out attack. Castelconturbia requires a lot of thought and the ability to turn thought into deed, so inexperienced players will find it hard going. The course is on the flat side, although some of the raised greens require special care. A superb resort, not to be missed.

Golf Club Castelconturbia — 1987

Via Suno 10
I - 28010 AGRATE CONTURBIA (NO)

Office	Segreteria	(39) 0322 832 093
Pro shop	Pro shop	(39) 0322 832 596
Fax	Fax	(39) 0322 832 428
Situation	Localita'	

Novara (pop. 102.404), 33 km - Milano, 63 km)

Annual closure	Chiusura annuale	no
Weekly closure	Chiusura settimanale	tuesday

Fees main season
Tariffe alta stagione full day

	Week days Settimana	We/Bank holidays Feriale/Festivo
Individual Individuale	95.000	150.000
Couple Coppia	190.000	300.000

Green-fees on week days only
(Ospiti solo durante i giorni feriali)

Caddy	Caddy	L. 30.000
Electric Trolley	Carello elettrico	no
Buggy	Car	L. 80.000
Clubs	Bastoni	si

Credit cards Carte di credito
VISA - Eurocard - MasterCard - AMEX - DC

Access Itinerario : A4 Milano-Torino, Exit (Uscita) Novara. Then S229 → Borgomanero. About 29 km, turn right → Cressa and Agrate Conturbia.
Map 1 on page 940 Carta 1 Pagina 940

GOLF COURSE / PERCORSO — 18/20

Site	Paesaggio	
Maintenance	Manutenzione	
Architect	Architetto	R. Trent Jones Sr
Type	Tipologia	forest, links
Relief	Relievo terreno	
Water in play	Acqua in gioco	
Exp. to wind	Esposto al vento	
Trees in play	Alberi in gioco	

Scorecard Carta-score	Chp. Camp.	Mens Uomini	Ladies Donne
Length Lunghezza	6230	5888	5145
Par	72	72	72

Advised golfing ability Livello di gioco consigliato	0	12	24	36

Hcp required Handicap richiesto 34

CLUB HOUSE & AMENITIES / CLUB HOUSE E SERVIZI — 8/10

Pro shop	Pro shop	
Driving range	Campo pratica	
Sheltered	coperto	10 mats
On grass	in erba	yes
Putting-green	Putting-green	yes
Pitching-green	Green-pratica	yes

HOTEL FACILITIES / ALBERGHI — 7/10

HOTELS ALBERGHI

Golf Hotel — Agrate Conturbia
19 rooms, D. L. 180.000 — on site
Tel (39) 0322 832 337, Fax (39) 0322 832 428

Concorde — Arona
82 rooms, D. L. 240.000 — 20 km
Tel (39) 0322 249 321, Fax (39) 0322 249 372

Giardino — Arona
56 rooms, D. L. 145.000 — 20 km
Tel (39) 0322 45 994, Fax (39) 0322 249 401

Atlantic - 79 rooms, D. L. 210.000 — Arona
Tel (39) 0322 46 521 — 20 km

RESTAURANTS RISTORANTE

Pinocchio — Borgomanero
Tel (39) 0322 82 273 — 6 km

Taverna Pittore - Tel (39) 0322 293 366 — Arona 20 km

963

Questo piccolo paese è conosciuto per essere la residenza estiva del Papa, in un'antica zona vulcanica dove il clima è molto mite. E' soprattutto la zona di Alba Longa che la leggenda narra sia stata fondata da Enea e che si sia poi opposta a Roma nella guerra tra Orazi e Curiazi. Questo percorso è l'ideale per ur match-play perchè le insidie ripartite da Robert Trent Jones non mancano, come ad esempio un lago che entra ir gioco pericolosamente in diverse buche. In più in questo paesaggio di pini marittimi e olivi che addolciscono il rigore del gioco e quello del sole, si ritroveranno i soliti bunkers e i greens a volte difficilissimi da decifrare dell'architetto americano. Per rilassarsi la club-house è veramente molto piacevole. Questa antica villa del XVII secolo ben restaurata, domina su tutto il percorso.

This little town is known for being the Pope's summer residence in a formerly volcanic region with a warm, balmy climate. It is importantly the site of Alba Longa which, according to legend was founded by Aeneas and then opposed Rome in the fighting with the Horatii and the Curiatii. So this layout is ideal for head-to-head match-play, as there is no shortage of traps spread around the course by Robert Trent Jones, especially a lake which comes into play most dangerously on several holes. Otherwise, you find the usual bunkers and often hard-to-read greens favoured by the American architect in a landscape of maritime pines and olive trees, which temper the course and the sunshine too. For relaxation after your round, the club-house is a real treat, a well-restored former 17th century patrician villa which overlooks the whole course.

Country Club Castelgandolfo — 1988

Via di Santo Spirito 13
I - 00040 CASTELGANDOLFO (RM)

Office	Segreteria	(39) 06 931 2301
Pro shop	Pro shop	(39) 06 931 1065
Fax	Fax	(39) 06 931 2244
Situation	Localita'	

Roma (pop. 2 653 245), 26 km

Annual closure	Chiusura annuale	no
Weekly closure	Chiusura settimanale	monday

Fees main season
Tariffe alta stagione full day

	Week days Settimana	We/Bank holidays Feriale/Festivo
Individual Individuale	L. 70.000	L. 90.000
Couple Coppia	L. 140.000	L. 180.000

Caddy	Caddy	L. 50.000
Electric Trolley	Carello elettrico	no
Buggy	Car	L. 60.000
Clubs	Bastoni	L. 25.000

Credit cards Carte di credito
VISA - Eurocard - MasterCard - AMEX - DC

964

R O M A Ciampino
G.R.A
VIA APPIA
S 7
Frattochie
Castel Gandolfo
GOLF →
Albano
Laziale
Pavona
0   2   4 km

Access Itinerario : Roma, Via Appia Nuova. At Ciampino, go right to Via Nettunense. 2 km → Golf.
Map 3 on page 945 Carta 3 Pagina 945

GOLF COURSE / PERCORSO — 15/20

Site	Paesaggio	
Maintenance	Manutenzione	
Architect	Architetto	R. Trent Jones Sr
Type	Tipologia	residential
Relief	Relievo terreno	
Water in play	Acqua in gioco	
Exp. to wind	Esposto al vento	
Trees in play	Alberi in gioco	

Scorecard Carta-score	Chp. Camp.	Mens Uomini	Ladies Donne
Length Lunghezza	6205	5855	5143
Par	72	72	72

Advised golfing ability		0	12	24	36
Livello di gioco consigliato					

Hcp required Handicap richiesto 34

CLUB HOUSE & AMENITIES / CLUB HOUSE E SERVIZI — 7/10

Pro shop	Pro shop	
Driving range	Campo pratica	
Sheltered	coperto	9 mats
On grass	in erba	yes
Putting-green	Putting-green	yes
Pitching-green	Green-pratica	yes

HOTEL FACILITIES / ALBERGHI — 7/10

HOTELS ALBERGHI

Castelvecchio — Castel Gandolfo
50 rooms, D. L. 200.000 — 3 km
Tel (39) 06 936 0308, Fax (39) 06 936 0579

Grand Hotel Helio Cabala — Marino
50 rooms, D. L. 270.000 — 3 km
Tel (39) 06 9366 1391, Fax (39) 06 9366 1125

Park Hotel Villa Grazioli — Grottaferrata
58 rooms, D. L. 450.000 — 6 km
Tel (39) 06 945 400, Fax (39) 06 941 3506

RESTAURANTS RISTORANTE

Antico Ristorante Pagnanelli — Castel Gandolfo
Tel (39) 06 936 0004 — 3 km

Hostaria al Vecchio Fico — Grottaferrata
Tel (39) 06 945 9261 — 6 km

Da Mario - La Cavola d'Oro — Grottaferrata
Tel (39) 06 9431 5755 — 8 km

Per i grandi giocatori che si sono tolti lo sfizio di disegnare campi da golf, il punto di forza della buona riuscita è sempre stata la qualità dei loro ingegneri ed architetti. Gary Player ha fatto l'esperienza , ma l'ha fatta anche Jack Nicklaus che pur ha firmato soltanto opere molto ben riuscite. Arnold Palmer ha avuto dei periodi di qualità variabile e il Castello di Tolcinasco fa parte di quelle di buona qualità pur non essendo eccezionale. Questo terreno molto aperto a sud di Milano si prestava per un tracciato all'americana, dove grossi bunkers e ostacoli d'acqua costituiscono la maggior parte delle difficoltà, obbligando a giocare un golf molto preciso. Difficile dai tees di campionato, questo percorso (un po' artificiale) diventa nettamente più facile dalle partenze avanti, cosicché può essere adatto a tutti i livelli di gioco pur essendo un buon percorso di gara. I dilettanti medi si divertiranno comunque molto qui anche marcando il loro score.

For the game's top players who have moved into course design, the key to success has always been the excellence of their engineers and architects. Gary Player learnt from experience, and so has Jack Nicklaus, whose courses have not always been top rate. Arnold Palmer has had a few patchy periods as well, but Castello di Tolcinasco is a layout of high, not to say outstanding quality. This rather open terrain to the south of Milan was just perfect for an American-style layout, where the majority of hazards are huge sand traps and water, which call for accurate target golf. Tough from the back tees, this course (a little artificial, it might be said) becomes a little more human the further forward you move, which just goes to show that you can take account of all levels of playing ability yet still design a good tournament course. Whatever, average mid-handicappers will have a lot of fun here, even if they count their score.

Castello di Tolcinasco G & CC — 1993

Loc. Tolcinasco
I - 20090 PIEVE EMANUELE (MI)

Office	Segreteria	(39) 02 904 672 01
Pro shop	Pro shop	(39) 02 904 672 10
Fax	Fax	(39) 02 904 672 26
Situation	Localita'	

Milano (pop. 1.302.808), 8 km

Annual closure	Chiusura annuale	no
Weekly closure	Chiusura settimanale	monday

Fees main season
Tariffe alta stagione 18 holes

	Week days Settimana	We/Bank holidays Feriale/Festivo
Individual Individuale	L. 80.000	L. 100.000
Couple Coppia	L. 160.000	L. 200.000

Caddy	Caddy	L. 50.000
Electric Trolley	Carello elettrico	no
Buggy	Car	L. 60.000
Clubs	Bastoni	no

Credit cards Carte di credito
VISA - Eurocard - MasterCard - AMEX - DC

Access Itinerario : Milano Duomo, Via Torino, C° di Porto Ticinese, C° San Gottardo, straight in Via dei Missaglia. At traffic lights go left. 3 km, Castello di Tolcinasco. **Map 1 on page 941** Carta 1 Pagina 941

GOLF COURSE PERCORSO 15/20

Site	Paesaggio	
Maintenance	Manutenzione	
Architect	Architetto	Arnold Palmer
Type	Tipologia	country, residential
Relief	Relievo terreno	
Water in play	Acqua in gioco	
Exp. to wind	Esposto al vento	
Trees in play	Alberi in gioco	

Scorecard Carta-score	Chp. Camp.	Mens Uomini	Ladies Donne
Length Lunghezza	6322	5788	4999
Par	72	72	72

Advised golfing ability		0 12 24 36
Livello di gioco consigliato		
Hcp required	Handicap richiesto	no

CLUB HOUSE & AMENITIES CLUB HOUSE E SERVIZI 8/10

Pro shop	Pro shop	
Driving range	Campo pratica	
Sheltered	coperto	15 mats
On grass	in erba	yes
Putting-green	Putting-green	yes
Pitching-green	Green-pratica	yes

HOTEL FACILITIES ALBERGHI 8/10

HOTELS ALBERGHI
Residence Club Milano 3 — Basiglio
62 rooms, D. L. 220.000 — 3 km

Royal Garden Hotel — Assago
111 rooms, D. L. 350.000 — 11 km
Tel (39) 02 457 811, Fax (39) 02 457 029 01

Four Seasons — Milano
82 rooms, D. L. 965.000 — 12 km
Tel (39) 02 770 88, Fax (39) 02 770 850 00

RESTAURANTS RISTORANTE
Sadler — Milano
Tel (39) 02 581 044 51 — 13 km

Aimo e Nadia — Milano
Tel (39) 02 416 886 — 12 km

La Scaletta — Milano
Tel (39) 02 581 0029 — 10 km

965

La reputazione di Cesenatico, Riccione e sopratutto di Milano Marittima ha varcato le frontiere e questo percorso doveva essere logicamente un incentivo maggiore per coloro che amano le vacanze sportive. Non bisogna poi dimenticare la vicinanza con Ravenna con i suoi monumenti e i mosaici che figurano tra i tesori mondiali. Tracciato su un terreno piatto, un po' tra i pini o sulle dune sabbiose, il percorso disegnato da Marco Croze riprendre alcuni tratti tipici dei «links» ed altri dei percorsi americani. Ma l'architetto ha cercato di riportare qui una certa «italianità», una sorta di eleganza nel disegno, a volte persino un po' eccessiva. Solo il vento può allora inasprire la sfida offerta ai giocatori. Detto questo, Cervia resta un percorso molto piacevole sul quale giocare, perchè anche se gli ostacoli sono sempre in gioco non sono mai scoraggianti nè insormontabili. E' stato richiesto all'architetto un percorso divertente per tutti i golfisti e lui ha ben svolto il suo compito.

This section of the Adriatic coast is one of the most popular and entertaining (great fun to be had). The reputation of Cesenatico, Riccione and Milano Marittima has spread abroad and this course should logically be an extra attraction for people who prefer the more sporting style of holiday. Let's not forget nearby Ravenna, whose monuments and mosaics feature amongst the world's treasures. Spread over flat terrain amidst both pine trees and sandy dunes, this Marco Croze layout has some of the features of a real links course but also a slight American flavour, but you won't find the raw brutality of a Scottish links. The architect has apparently looked to add a little «Italian touch», a sort of elegance of design which sometimes goes a little over the top. In this case, only the wind can stiffen the challenge. With this said, Cervia is a very pleasant an fun course to play, especially since all the hazards are in play but never insurmountable.

Adriatic Golf Club Cervia — 1985

Via Jelenia Gora 6
I - 48016 MILANO MARITTIMA (RA)

Office	Segreteria	(39) 0544 992 786
Pro shop	Pro shop	(39) 0544 993 788
Fax	Fax	(39) 0544 993 410
Situation	Localita'	

Ravenna (pop. 137 721), 22 km
Forli (pop. 107 461), 28 km

Annual closure	Chiusura annuale	no
Weekly closure	Chiusura settimanale	monday

Fees main season
Tariffe alta stagione 18 holes

	Week days Settimana	We/Bank holidays Feriale/Festivo
Individual Individuale	L. 85 000	L. 100 000
Couple Coppia	L. 170 000	L. 200 000

Caddy	Caddy	on request, L.40 000
Electric Trolley	Carello elettrico	no
Buggy	Car	L. 55.000
Clubs	Bastoni	L. 25.000

Credit cards Carte di credito
VISA - Eurocard - MasterCard - AMEX - DC

966

GOLF COURSE / PERCORSO — 13/20

Site	Paesaggio	
Maintenance	Manutenzione	
Architect	Architetto	Marco Croze
Type	Tipologia	seaside course, parkland
Relief	Relievo terreno	
Water in play	Acqua in gioco	
Exp. to wind	Esposto al vento	
Trees in play	Alberi in gioco	

Scorecard Carta-score	Chp. Camp.	Mens Uomini	Ladies Donne
Length Lunghezza	6296	6029	5185
Par	72	72	72

Advised golfing ability	0	12	24	36
Livello di gioco consigliato				

Hcp required Handicap richiesto 34

CLUB HOUSE & AMENITIES / CLUB HOUSE E SERVIZI — 6/10

Pro shop	Pro shop	
Driving range	Campo pratica	
Sheltered	coperto	5 mats
On grass	in erba	yes
Putting-green	Putting-green	yes
Pitching-green	Green-pratica	yes

HOTEL FACILITIES / ALBERGHI — 9/10

HOTELS ALBERGHI

Mare e Pineta — Milano Marittima
170 rooms, D L. 300 000 — 500 m
Tel (39) 0544 992 262, Fax (39) 0544 992 739

Deanna Golf Hotel — Milano Marittima
68 rooms, D L. 260 000 — 300 m
Tel (39) 0544 991 365, Fax (39) 0544 994 251

Grand Hotel Cervia — Cervia
56 rooms, D 290 000 — 1 km
Tel (39) 0544 970 500, Fax (39) 0544 972 086

RESTAURANTS RISTORANTE

Al Caminetto — Milano Marittima
Tel (39) 0544 994 479 — 500 m

Dal Marinio — Milano Marittima
Tel (39) 0544 975 479 — 500 m

Al Teatro - Tel (39) 0544 716 39 — Cervia 1 km

Access Itinerario : A14 Bologna-Rimini. Exit (Uscita) Cesena. → Cervia, → Pineta and Milano Marittima. → Golf **Map 2 on page 942** Carta 2 Pagina 942

E' la regione di Alba, quella dei vini di nomea internazionale come il Barbera e il Barolo e dei tartufi bianchi. Un po' più in alto c'è Asti. Effettivamente siamo a metà strada tra Torino e il mare, questo golf di Cherasco può far parte di due rotte diverse. Creato nel 1982 si snoda su un terreno relativamente ondulato, ma si può giocare a piedi senza difficoltà. Il percorso non è lungo ma bisogna essere abbastanza dritti per prendere il fairway nella posizione migliore, altrimenti non è raro essere obbligati a far girare la palla. Gli ostacoli d'acqua entrano in gioco senza essere di grande pericolo. In realtà tutto qui è fatto con misura senza voler intimidire troppo i giocatori mediocri: un percorso di qualità, come sa disegnarli Marco Croze, ma senza una personalità spiccata.

This is the region of Alba, of internationally reputed wines such as Barbera and Barolos, and of «tartufi bianchi» (white truffles). A little higher up and you are in Asti, although in fact here you are mid-way between Turin and the Mediterranean, meaning that the Cherasco course can be fitted in when heading for two potential destinations. Created in 1982, it stretches over rolling but definitely walkable terrain. This is not a long course, but you need to hit it straight to reach the fairways in the right position; being able to bend the ball will come in handy. More, some water hazards come into play but present no real danger. All in all, everything here is very measured in a bid not to cause too much trouble for mid-handicappers. A class course designed as Marco Croze knows how, but with no real personality.

Golf Club Cherasco — 1982

Loc. Fraschetta
I - 12062 CHERASCO (CN)

Office	Segreteria	(39) 0172 489 772
Pro shop	Pro shop	(39) 0172 489 772
Fax	Fax	(39) 0172 488 304
Situation	Localita'	

Cuneo (pop. 54 743), 47 km - Alba (pop. 29 876), 21 km

Annual closure	Chiusura annuale	no
Weekly closure	Chiusura settimanale	tuesday

Fees main season
Tariffe alta stagione 18 holes

	Week days Settimana	We/Bank holidays Feriale/Festivo
Individual Individuale	L. 60.000	L. 80.000
Couple Coppia	L. 120.000	L. 160.000

Caddy	Caddy	L. 30.000
Electric Trolley	Carello elettrico	L. 15.000
Buggy	Car	L. 50.000
Clubs	Bastoni	L. 15.000

Credit cards Carte di credito
VISA - Eurocard - MasterCard - AMEX - DC - Cartasi

Access Itinerario : Alba → Bra (S231), left → Santa Vittoria d'Alba, → Pollenzo. Left at traffic lights, 1 km, then left again.
Map 1 on page 940 Carta 1 Pagina 940

GOLF COURSE
PERCORSO — 13/20

Site	Paesaggio	▮▮▮▮▮▮▯
Maintenance	Manutenzione	▮▮▮▮▮▮▯
Architect	Architetto	Marco Croze
Type	Tipologia	country
Relief	Relievo terreno	▮▮▮▯▯
Water in play	Acqua in gioco	▮▮▯▯▯
Exp. to wind	Esposto al vento	▮▮▯▯▯
Trees in play	Alberi in gioco	▮▮▮▯▯

Scorecard Carta-score	Chp. Camp.	Mens Uomini	Ladies Donne
Length Lunghezza	5947	5600	5140
Par	72	72	72

Advised golfing ability		0	12	24	36
Livello di gioco consigliato					

Hcp required Handicap richiesto 34

CLUB HOUSE & AMENITIES
CLUB HOUSE E SERVIZI — 7/10

Pro shop	Pro shop	▮▮▮▮▯
Driving range	Campo pratica	▮▮▮▮▯
Sheltered	coperto	5 mats
On grass	in erba	yes
Putting-green	Putting-green	yes
Pitching-green	Green-pratica	yes

HOTEL FACILITIES
ALBERGHI — 7/10

HOTELS ALBERGHI

La Tour		Cervere
13 rooms, D. L. 130.000		5 km
Tel (39) 0172 474 691, Fax (39) 0172 474 693		
I Castelli		Alba
84 rooms, D. L. 180.000		20 km
Tel (39) 0173 361 978, Fax (39) 0172 361 974		
Elisabeth - 27 rooms, D. L. 140.000		Bra
Tel (39) 0172 422 486, Fax (39) 0172 412 214		5 km

RESTAURANTS RISTORANTE

La Corte Albertina		Pollenzo
Tel (39) 0172 458 159		3 km
Il Vicoletto		Alba
Tel(39) 0173 363 196		20 km
Antica Corona Reale da Renzo		Cervere
Tel(39) 0172 474 132		3 km
La Lumaca - Tel (39) 0172 489 421		Cherasco 2 km

967

Un viaggio intelligente alla scoperta dell'Italia passa obbligatoriamente da Pisa. Qui si visiterà sicuramente il famoso campanile di marmo bianco ma anche il magnifico insieme degli altri edifici della piazza del Duomo, con il Battistero, il Camposanto e ovviamente il Duomo, il tutto in stile principalmente romanico. Scendendo verso Livorno, città portuale molto viva, si può fare una sosta al Cosmopolitan, un percorso aperto di recente. E' stato disegnato da David Mezzacane su un terreno piatto e senza alberi. Lo stile links era il migliore per animare questo posto dove soltanto il posizionamento degli ostacoli d'acqua ha un leggero sapore americano. Malgrado tutto, l'insieme conserva un aspetto naturale del tutto inaspettato. Qui è difficile giocare il proprio handicap soprattutto quando tira vento e ancor più dalle partenze arretrate. Ma la larghezza dei fairways e la buona dimensione dei greens perdono gli errori dei giocatori inesperti.

A smart trip to discover Italy has to include a visit to Pisa to see the famous white marble bell-tower and the other wonderful buildings on the Piazza del Duomo, with the Battistero, Camposanto (closed cemetery), and of course the Duomo, all built primarily in pure Roman style. Driving down towards Livorno, a very lively harbour town, you can stop off at the recently opened Cosmopolitan course designed over flat and tree-less terrain. A links style was essential here to create some sort of lively addition to the open space, and only the introduction of a few water hazards gives this a slight American flavour. Despite everything, the whole course has retained an unexpected very natural appearance. Playing to your handicap here is a tall order, especially when the wind blows and even more so when playing from the back-tees. Yet the wide fairways and nicely-sized greens help forgive the shortcomings of inexperienced players.

Cosmopolitan Golf & Country Club 1993

Via Pisorno 60
56018 TIRRENIA (PI)

Office	Segreteria	(39) 050 33 633
Pro shop	Pro shop	(39) 050 384 002
Fax	Fax	(39) 050 384 707
Situation	Localita'	

Pisa (pop. 93 133), 18 km - Livorno (pop. 163 073), 11 km

Annual closure	Chiusura annuale	no
Weekly closure	Chiusura settimanale	monday

Fees main season
Tariffe alta stagione full day

	Week days Settimana	We/Bank holidays Feriale/Festivo
Individual Individuale	L. 70.000	L. 80.000
Couple Coppia	L. 140.000	L. 160.000

Caddy	Caddy	no
Electric Trolley	Carello elettrico	no
Buggy	Car	L. 50.000
Clubs	Bastoni	L. 25.000

Credit cards Carte di credito
VISA - Eurocard - MasterCard - DC - Cartasi

968

Access Itinerario : Pisa → Marina di Pisa.
→ Tirrenia and Livorno
Map 3 on page 944 Carta 3 Pagina 944

GOLF COURSE
PERCORSO   14/20

Site	Paesaggio	
Maintenance	Manutenzione	
Architect	Architetto	David Mezzacane

Type	Tipologia	links
Relief	Relievo terreno	
Water in play	Acqua in gioco	
Exp. to wind	Esposto al vento	
Trees in play	Alberi in gioco	

Scorecard	Chp.	Mens	Ladies
Carta-score	Camp.	Uomini	Donne
Length Lunghezza	6291	5830	5125
Par	72	72	72

Advised golfing ability		0 12 24 36
Livello di gioco consigliato		
Hcp required	Handicap richiesto 34	

CLUB HOUSE & AMENITIES
CLUB HOUSE E SERVIZI   6/10

Pro shop	Pro shop	
Driving range	Campo pratica	
Sheltered	coperto	no
On grass	in erba	yes
Putting-green	Putting-green	yes
Pitching-green	Green-pratica	yes

HOTEL FACILITIES
ALBERGHI   7/10

HOTELS ALBERGHI

Grand Hotel Golf		Tirrenia
77 rooms, D. L. 290.000		700 m
Tel (39) 050 37 545, Fax (39) 050 32 111		
San Francesco		Tirrenia
25 rooms, D. L. 250.000		1 km
Tel (39) 050 33 572, Fax (39) 050 33 630		
Europa Park Hotel		Pisa
13 rooms, D. L. 140.000		18 km
Tel (39) 050 500 732, Fax (39) 050 554 930		

RESTAURANTS RISTORANTE

Dante e Ivana		Tirrenia
Tel (39) 050 32 549		1 km
Al Ristoro dei Vecchi Macelli		Pisa
Tel (39) 050 20 424		18 km
A Casa Mia - Tel (39) 050 879 265		Pisa 12 km

Il Circolo Golf Firenze è il più vecchio d'Italia ma si è insediato in questo luogo soltanto nel 1933. Disegnato dalla studio Blandford & Gannon è stato modificato in seguito da Piero Mancinelli. Il posto è molto piacevole ed è dunque garantito di trascorrere una bella giornata. Si consiglia il golf cart ai giocatori non in forma fisica perfetta, perchè il terreno è molto mosso. Manca un poco di lunghezza per i professionisti di oggi, ma resta un buon percorso di gara per i dilettanti tra i quali la precisione conta ben più che la forza bruta. Ci sono dei par 3 abbastanza lunghi ma anche una collezione impressionante di corti par 4 dove si cerca costantemente il birdie, senza peraltro farne molti perchè i greens sono generalmente piccoli, abbastanza ben disegnati e difesi. L'Ugolino non è certamente un esempio di modernità, ma merita certamente una visita anche se un viaggio a Firenze lascia poco tempo libero...

The Circolo Golf Firenze (Florence Golf Club) is the oldest in Italy but opened here only in 1933. Designed by Blandford & Gannon, it was subsequently altered by Piero Mancinelli. This is a very pleasant site with a great day's golfing assured. We would simply advise a buggy for players whose physical condition is not what it was, as the course is rather hilly. For today's professionals, Ugolino is doubtless a little short, but this is still an excellent course for amateur tournaments, where accuracy counts for much more than brute strength. The par 3s are rather long, but there is also an impressive group of short par 4s, where you might be tempted to think about birdies. Whether or not you make them remains in some doubt, as the greens are generally small, well contoured and well protected. Ugolino is by no means an example of modernity but it certainly deserves a visit, even if a trip to Florence, one of the world's finest cities, leaves little time for sport. Certainly worth a try... together, of course, with a glass of local Chianti wine.

Circolo Golf Ugolino — 1933

Via Chiantigiana 3
I - 50015 GRASSINA (FI)

Office	Segreteria	(39) 055 2301 009
Pro shop	Pro shop	(39) 055 2301 278
Fax	Fax	(39) 055 2301 141
Situation	Localita'	

Firenze (pop. 379.687), 12 km

Annual closure	Chiusura annuale	no
Weekly closure	Chiusura settimanale	monday

Fees main season
Tariffe alta stagione full day

	Week days Settimana	We/Bank holidays Feriale/Festivo
Individual Individuale	L. 95.000	L. 110.000
Couple Coppia	L. 190.000	L. 220.000

Caddy	Caddy	no
Electric Trolley	Carello elettrico	no
Buggy	Car	L. 70.000
Clubs	Bastoni	L. 30.000

Credit cards Carte di credito
VISA - Eurocard - MasterCard - AMEX - Cartasi

Access Itinerario : A1 Exit (Uscita) Firenze South (Sud). Turn right to Grassina then S222 (Chiantigiana). Golf 4 km on the left.
Map 3 on page 944 Carta 3 Pagina 944

GOLF COURSE PERCORSO — 14/20

Site	Paesaggio	
Maintenance	Manutenzione	
Architect	Architetto	Blandford & Gannon
Type	Tipologia	hilly
Relief	Relievo terreno	
Water in play	Acqua in gioco	
Exp. to wind	Esposto al vento	
Trees in play	Alberi in gioco	

Scorecard Carta-score	Chp. Camp.	Mens Uomini	Ladies Donne
Length Lunghezza	5800	5676	4994
Par	72	72	72

Advised golfing ability Livello di gioco consigliato	0	12	24	36

Hcp required Handicap richiesto 34

CLUB HOUSE & AMENITIES CLUB HOUSE E SERVIZI — 8/10

Pro shop	Pro shop	
Driving range	Campo pratica	
Sheltered	coperto	12 mats
On grass	in erba	yes
Putting-green	Putting-green	yes
Pitching-green	Green-pratica	yes

HOTEL FACILITIES ALBERGHI — 9/10

HOTELS ALBERGHI

Excelsior 152 rooms, D. L. 950.000 Tel (39) 055 264 201, Fax (39) 055 210 278	Firenze	12 km
Brunelleschi 88 rooms, D. L. 480.000 Tel (39) 055 290 311, Fax (39) 055 219 653	Firenze	12 km
Sheraton Firenze 319 rooms, D. L. 400.000 Tel (39) 055 64 901, Fax (39) 055 680 747	Firenze	5 km

RESTAURANTS RISTORANTE

Enoteca Pinchiorri Tel (39) 055 242 777	Firenze	12 km
Bottega del Moro Tel (39) 055 853 753	Greve in Chianti	5 km
Sabatini - Tel (39) 055 211 559	Firenze 12 km	

969

In campagna
l'ospitalità discreta

Una villa locanda in collina, tra le Alpi e il Lago d'Iseo, dove nascono grandi vini, il golf è di casa, il paesaggio segreto e il clima dolce.

Qui, proprio qui, Gualtiero Marchesi ha rinnovato l'amore per la cucina.

Cultura, cantine, carattere, cortesia, cuore... molto e tutto in Franciacorta.

A villa, transformed into a hotel, placed in the hills, between the Alps and Lake Iseo, a region where great wines are produced, where golf is a widespread sport, where the landscape is secret and the climate mild.

It is here that Gualtiero Marchesi has rediscovered his love for cuisine.

Culture, wines, character, courtesy, warmth... all of which can be found in Franciacorta.

Convenzione green fee con:
Green fee special price for:

**Franciacorta Golf • Garda Golf • La Rossera • L'Albenza
Palazzo Arzaga • Sommacampagna**

L'ALBERETA
LOCANDA IN FRANCIACORTA

Via Vittorio Emanuele 11, 25030 Erbusco (Bs) Italy
Hotel tel. 030.7760550 fax 030.7760573 **Restaurant** tel. 030.7760562
e-mail: albereta@terramoretti.it http://www.terramoretti.it
40 minuti da Milano - *40 minutes from Milan*
Airport: Milano, Linate e Malpensa - Bergamo, Orio al Serio - Verona, Villafranca

Il golf di Franciacorta si trova vicino al lago d'Iseo. Anche se non è il più celebre dei grandi laghi italiani, merita di essere conosciuto per il suo aspetto selvaggio, così come per il Monte Isola che si trova in mezzo al lago e dal quale si gode un panorama superbo sulle Alpi bergamasche. Con il «Domaine Imperial» in Svizzera, questo percorso è l'unico esempio in Europa dello stile, spesso controverso, di Pete Dye, che qui ha collaborato con Marco Croze uno dei più prolifici architetti italiani. E' stato tracciato su un terreno mosso ma non troppo faticoso. Lo stile è decisamente americano con ostacoli d'acqua su circa la metà delle buche e con due greens in un'isola: non si può certo arrivare a rotolo! Malgrado ciò i giocatori medi avranno da divertirsi perchè le difficoltà sono ben visibili e la strategia di gioco evidente.

The Golf de Franciacorta is situated close to Lake Iseo. This is not the most famous of the Italian «Great Lakes», but the wild scenery here is well worth seeing, as is the Monte Isola, located in the middle of the lake and offering superb views over the Alps. Along with the Domaine Impérial in Switzerland, this course is one of the rare examples in Europe of the often controversial style (but always true to the spirit of golf) of American designer Pete Dye, who here worked together with Marco Croze, one of the more prolific Italian course architects. The course is laid out on slightly hilly but never tiring terrain. The style is blatantly American, with water on almost half the holes and two island greens, so you can forget the bump and run shots. Despite this, average players can have a lot of fun, as all the difficulties are clear to see and game strategy is obvious.

Golf di Franciacorta — 1986

Loc. Castagnola
I - 25040 CORTE FRANCA (BS)

Office	Segreteria	(39) 030 984 167
Pro shop	Pro shop	(39) 030 9828 330
Fax	Fax	(39) 030 984 343
Situation	Localita'	

Brescia (pop. 190 518), 28 km
Bergamo (pop. 117 619), 32 km

Annual closure	Chiusura annuale	no
Weekly closure	Chiusura settimanale	tuesday

Fees main season
Tariffe alta stagione 18 holes

	Week days Settimana	We/Bank holidays Feriale/Festivo
Individual Individuale	L. 70.000	L. 100.000
Couple Coppia	L. 140.000	L. 200.000

Caddy	Caddy	no
Electric Trolley	Carello elettrico	no
Buggy	Car	L. 60.000
Clubs	Bastoni	L. 40.000

Credit cards Carte di credito — no

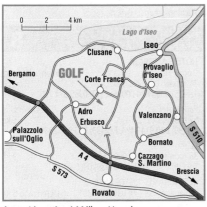

Access Itinerario : A4 Milano-Venezia.
Exit (Uscita) Rovato, turn left then right → Iseo.
6 km → golf on left hand side
Map 1 on page 941 Carta 1 Pagina 941

GOLF COURSE / PERCORSO — 15/20

Site	Paesaggio	▇▇▇▇▇▇▭
Maintenance	Manutenzione	▇▇▇▇▇▭▭
Architect	Architetto	Pete Dye Marco Croze
Type	Tipologia	country
Relief	Relievo terreno	▇▇▇▇▭▭▭
Water in play	Acqua in gioco	▇▇▇▇▇▭▭
Exp. to wind	Esposto al vento	▇▇▭▭▭▭▭
Trees in play	Alberi in gioco	▇▇▇▇▭▭▭

Scorecard Carta-score	Chp. Camp.	Mens Uomini	Ladies Donne
Length Lunghezza	5924	5762	5095
Par	72	72	72

Advised golfing ability	0	12	24	36
Livello di gioco consigliato				

Hcp required Handicap richiesto 34

CLUB HOUSE & AMENITIES / CLUB HOUSE E SERVIZI — 7/10

Pro shop	Pro shop	▇▇▇▇▇▭▭
Driving range	Campo pratica	▇▇▇▇▇▇▭
Sheltered	coperto	4 mats
On grass	in erba	yes
Putting-green	Putting-green	yes
Pitching-green	Green-pratica	yes

HOTEL FACILITIES / ALBERGHI — 8/10

HOTELS ALBERGHI

L'Albereta — Erbusco
32 rooms, D. L. 750.000 — 9 km
Tel (39) 030 7760 562, Fax (39) 030 7760 573

Relaisfranciacorta — Corte Franca
44 rooms, D. L. 210.000 — 3 km
Tel (39) 030 988 4234, Fax (39) 030 988 4224

Franciacorta Golf Hotel — Corte Franca
40 rooms, D. L. 210.000 — 12 km
Tel (39) 035 913 333, Fax (39) 035 913 600

RESTAURANTS RISTORANTE

Gualtiero Marchesi (Albereta) — Erbusco
Tel (39) 030 7760 562 — 9 km

Santa Giulia - Tel (39) 030 9828 348 — Timoline 2 km

La Mongolfiera dei Sodi — Erbusco
Tel (39) 030 7268 303 — 9 km

971

Grazie alla protezione delle Dolomiti che mitigano il vento, il lago di Garda vanta un clima formidabile, particolarmente dolce d'inverno. Per la sua ubicazione appena sopra al lago, la sua vista spettacolare e la sua vicinanza a Brescia, Bergamo e Milano, Gardagolf ha fatto in fretta ad ottenere un grande successo, tanto che può essere difficile riuscire a giocare nel week-end. Ma questa regione è abbastanza seducente per trascorrerci più giorni se non addirittura settimane. Disegnato dallo Studio Cotton, Penninck & Steel, con 9 buche piatte e 9 buche in collina è considerato difficile dai tees di campionato (uomini e donne), ma niente vi obbliga a sceglierli. L'acqua entra in gioco su circa un terzo delle buche e i bunkers sia del fairway che dei greens sono stati giudiziosamente piazzati. Qui non bisogna fare colpi particolari, i giocatori dritti ne trarranno beneficio, tanto più che i greens non richiedono studi particolari essendo generalmente piatti. Un buon percorso in una bellissima regione.

Protected by the Dolomites, which cut out the wind, Lake Garda enjoys a wonderful climate which is surprisingly mild in winter. Located above the lake, spectacular in more ways than one and located close to Brescia, Bergamo and Milan, Gardagolf has rapidely become a popular venue and week-end green-fees can be hard to come by. Nonetheless, this region has appeal enough to spend several days or even weeks looking around. Designed by architects Cotton, Penninck & Steel, with nine flat holes and nine hilly numbers, the course is considered to be hard from the back tees (men and ladies) but there is no obligation to play from the tips. Water is in play on half a dozen holes and the green-side and fairway bunkers are cleverly located. There is no great need to work the ball in any direction, and straight-hitters should do well, especially as the greens have no hidden perils and are generally rather flat. A good course in a superb region.

Gardagolf Country Club   1986
Via A. Omodeo 2
I - 25080 SOIANO DEL LAGO (BS)

Office	Segreteria	(39) 0365 674 707
Pro shop	Pro shop	(39) 0365 674 173
Fax	Fax	(39) 0365 674 788
Situation	Localita'	

Brescia (pop. 190 518), 46 km - Bergamo, 77 km

Annual closure	Chiusura annuale	no
Weekly closure	Chiusura settimanale	monday
		(01/11 → 31/03)

Fees main season
Tariffe alta stagione 18 holes

	Week days Settimana	We/Bank holidays Feriale/Festivo
Individual Individuale	L. 85.000	L. 115.000
Couple Coppia	L. 170.000	L. 230.000

Caddy	Caddy	L. 30.000
Electric Trolley	Carello elettrico	L 20.000
Buggy	Car	L. 60.000
Clubs	Bastoni	L. 20.000

Credit cards Carte di credito   no

GOLF COURSE
PERCORSO   14/20

Site	Paesaggio	
Maintenance	Manutenzione	
Architect	Architetto	Cotton, Pennink Steel & Partners
Type	Tipologia	country
Relief	Relievo terreno	
Water in play	Acqua in gioco	
Exp. to wind	Esposto al vento	
Trees in play	Alberi in gioco	

Scorecard Carta-score	Chp. Camp.	Mens Uomini	Ladies Donne
Length Lunghezza	6505	6040	5353
Par	72	72	72

Advised golfing ability	0	12	24	36
Livello di gioco consigliato				

Hcp required   Handicap richiesto 34

CLUB HOUSE & AMENITIES
CLUB HOUSE E SERVIZI   7/10

Pro shop	Pro shop	
Driving range	Campo pratica	
Sheltered	coperto	8 mats
On grass	in erba	yes
Putting-green	Putting-green	yes
Pitching-green	Green-pratica	yes

HOTEL FACILITIES
ALBERGHI   8/10

HOTELS ALBERGHI
Dormy House   Soiano del Garda
11 rooms, D. L. 200.000   on site
Tel (39) 0365 674 000, Fax (39) 0365 674 788

Park Hotel   Desenzano
57 rooms, D. L. 210.000   5 km
Tel (39) 030 914 3494, Fax (39) 030 914 2280

Laurin   Salò
36 rooms, D. L. 450.000   9 km
Tel (39) 0365 22 022, Fax (39) 0365 22 382

RESTAURANTS RISTORANTE
Esplanade - Tel (39) 030 914 3361   Desenzano 5 km

Vecchia Lugana   Sirmione-Lugana
Tel (39) 030 919 6023   16 km

Al Porto   Moniga del Garda
Tel (39) 0365 502 069   5 km

972

Access Itinerario : A4 Milano-Venezia.
Exit (Uscita) Desenzano. → Salò. 5 km after Moniga cross, turn left at traffic lights. Golf 2 km
Map 1 on page 941 Carta 1 Pagina 941

Questo percorso è nato dalla volontà di fare della Riviera italiana una sorta di Costa del Sol o anche della Riviera francese così piena di campi di golf. Ma questo progetto molto intelligente non è andato avanti. Garlenda è stato costruito sulle colline che dominano le stazioni balneari di Alassio e Albenga ed è un percorso abbastanza corto che invita al divertimento. John Harris lo ha disegnato con gusto rispettando il paesaggio, da una parte all'altra del fiume Lerrone che attraversa la 13 a lungo par 3. Gli alberi sono di ostacolo in numerose buche, obbligando a volte a colpi particolari per avvicinarsi il più possibile ai greens, spesso di piccole dimensioni ma disegnati senza troppe difficoltà. Divertente per giocare con la famiglia e con gli amici anche di livello diverso, Garlenda non pretende di essere un grande percorso da campionato, ma offre una buona occasione per trascorrere una bella vacanza grazie alla presenza all'interno del campo dell'Hotel «La Meridiana» (Relais-Châteaux) e delle camere sopra la club-house.

This course was born from the desire to make the Italian Riviera a match for the Costa Del Sol or even the French Riviera, where golf courses abound. Unfortunately, this clever project never quite made it. This course was built in the hills overlooking the resorts of Albenga and Alassio, and is short enough to avoid scaring off the average golfer. John Harris designed the lay-out with taste and good landscaping sense on either side of the river Lerrone, which crosses the 13th hole, a long par 3. Trees are a threat on many holes and invite the player to work the ball both ways in order to get as close as possible to the greens, which are often small but designed without too many difficulties. Fun to play with the family and friends, even of very different abilities, Garlenda does not claim to be a great championship course but offers a fine opportunity to stay here, courtesy of the «La Meridiana» (Relais-Châteaux) and rooms belonging to the club.

Golf Club Garlenda — 1965

Piazzetta Galleani - Via del Golf 7
I - 17033 GARLENDA (SV)

Office	Segreteria	(39) 0182 580 012
Pro shop	Pro shop	(39) 0182 580 012
Fax	Fax	(39) 0182 580 561
Situation	Localita'	

Albenga (pop. 22.642), 8 km - Genova (pop. 659.754), 75 km

Annual closure	Chiusura annuale	no
Weekly closure	Chiusura settimanale	wednesday (01/09 → 30/06)

Fees main season
Tariffe alta stagione 18 holes

	Week days Settimana	We/Bank holidays Feriale/Festivo
Individual Individuale	L. 80.000	L. 130.000
Couple Coppia	L. 160.000	L. 260.000

Caddy	Caddy	L. 30.000
Electric Trolley	Carello elettrico	L. 10.000
Buggy	Car	L. 60.000
Clubs	Bastoni	L. 20.000

Credit cards Carte di credito
VISA - Eurocard - MasterCard - DC

GOLF COURSE / PERCORSO — 14/20

Site	Paesaggio	
Maintenance	Manutenzione	
Architect	Architetto	John Harris
Type	Tipologia	country
Relief	Relievo terreno	
Water in play	Acqua in gioco	
Exp. to wind	Esposto al vento	
Trees in play	Alberi in gioco	

Scorecard Carta-score	Chp. Camp.	Mens Uomini	Ladies Donne
Length Lunghezza	6095	5960	5240
Par	72	72	72

Advised golfing ability — 0 12 24 36
Livello di gioco consigliato
Hcp required Handicap richiesto 34

CLUB HOUSE & AMENITIES / CLUB HOUSE E SERVIZI — 7/10

Pro shop	Pro shop	
Driving range	Campo pratica	
Sheltered	coperto	8 mats
On grass	in erba	yes (1/5 → 30.9)
Putting-green	Putting-green	yes
Pitching-green	Green-pratica	yes

973

HOTEL FACILITIES / ALBERGHI — 8/10

HOTELS ALBERGHI
La Meridiana — Garlenda
14 rooms, D. L. 390.000 — 500 m
Tel (39) 0182 580 271, Fax (39) 0182 580 150

Hermitage — Garlenda
11 rooms, D. L. 220.000 — 500 m
Tel (39) 0182 582 976, Fax (39) 0182 582 975

Club House — Garlenda
7 rooms, D. L. 110.000 — on site
Tel (39) 0182 580 012, Fax (39) 0182 580 561

RESTAURANTS RISTORANTE
Palma - Tel (39) 0182 640 314 — Alassio 10 km

Pernambucco — Albenga
Tel (39) 0182 53 458 — 8 km

Lanterna Blu-da Tonino — Porto Maurizio (Imperia)
Tel(39) 0183 63 859 — 25 km

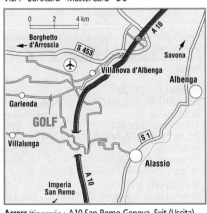

Access Itinerario : A10 San-Remo-Genova. Exit (Uscita) Albenga. Turn right → Albenga then right at turnabout under the motorway to Villanova d'Albenga and Garlenda. **Map 1 on page 940** Carta 1 Pagina 940

Questa antica riserva di caccia era il luogo ideale per la costruzione di un ambizioso complesso golfistico alle porte di Torino dove gli alberi secolari avrebbero sia isolato le buche una dall'altra , che creato una barriera naturale alle ambizioni dei giocatori poco precisi. Qui ci sono 27 buche ma il terzo percorso è decisamente sottotono rispetto alle vere 18 buche disegnate da Trent Jones e così i principianti potranno abituarsi progressivamente. Nel percorso di campionato, a parte la lunghezza , si noterà l'utilizzo molto strategico degli ostacoli d'acqua, nonchè la posizione e il disegno molto elaborato dei bunkers. Qui bisogna saper giocare tutti i colpi ma soprattutto fare traiettorie alte, «all'americana», perchè è molto raro poter attaccare i greens, che sono oltretutto molto protetti, facendo rotolare la palla. Le superfici dei greens sono ben disegnate e possono dare problemi di putting. I Roveri è proprio uno dei più bei percorsi d'Italia.

This former hunting estate was the ideal setting for building an ambitious golfing resort close to Turin. The age-old trees both demarcate and isolate the holes and form a natural barrier to the ambitions of wayward hitters. There are 27 holes here, although the par-3 course is a notch below the other two 9-hole layouts, probably to help the club's members who are just starting out. On the «championship» 18 hole course (designed by Trent Jones), yardage aside, you will notice the very strategic deployment of water and the very carefully plotted position and design of bunkers. You have to know how to hit it every way here, especially those US-style target golf shots, since you don't get much chance to roll the ball onto very well defended greens. Once there, the putting surfaces are nicely contoured and can pose a number of problems. I Roveri is definitely one of the very best courses in Italy.

I Roveri Golf Club — 1971

Rotta Cerbiatta 24
I - 10070 FIANO TORINESE (TO)

Office	Segreteria	(39) 011 923 5719
Pro shop	Pro shop	(39) 011 923 5223
Fax	Fax	(39) 011 923 5669
Situation	Localita'	

Torino (pop. 914.818), 16 km

Annual closure	Chiusura annuale	no
Weekly closure	Chiusura settimanale	monday

Fees main season
Tariffe alta stagione 18 holes

	Week days Settimana	We/Bank holidays Feriale/Festivo
Individual Individuale	L. 95.000	L. 120.000
Couple Coppia	L. 190.000	L. 240.000

Caddy	Caddy	yes
Electric Trolley	Carello elettrico	no
Buggy	Car	L. 50.000
Clubs	Bastoni	no
Credit cards Carte di credito		no

Access Itinerario : Milano to Torino, A4 - A45
Exit (Uscita) Venaria. → Lanzo. Golf to the left.
Map 1 on page 940 Carta 1 Pagina 940

974

GOLF COURSE PERCORSO — 17/20

Site	Paesaggio	
Maintenance	Manutenzione	
Architect	Architetto	R. Trent Jones Sr
Type	Tipologia	forest, residential
Relief	Relievo terreno	
Water in play	Acqua in gioco	
Exp. to wind	Esposto al vento	
Trees in play	Alberi in gioco	

Scorecard Carta-score	Chp. Camp.	Mens Uomini	Ladies Donne
Length Lunghezza	6566	6218	5471
Par	72	72	72

Advised golfing ability	0	12	24	36
Livello di gioco consigliato				

Hcp required Handicap richiesto 34

CLUB HOUSE & AMENITIES CLUB HOUSE E SERVIZI — 7/10

Pro shop	Pro shop	
Driving range	Campo pratica	
Sheltered	coperto	6 mats
On grass	in erba	yes
Putting-green	Putting-green	yes
Pitching-green	Green-pratica	yes

HOTEL FACILITIES ALBERGHI — 8/10

HOTELS ALBERGHI

Jet Hotel — Caselle Torinese
79 rooms, D. L. 270.000 — 8 km
Tel (39) 011 991 3733, Fax (39) 011 996 1544

Hotel Atlantic — Borgaro Torinese
110 rooms, D. L. 295.000 — 13 km
Tel (39) 011 450 0055, Fax (39) 011 470 1783

Hotel Pacific — Borgaro Torinese
54 rooms, D. L. 270.000 — 13 km
Tel (39) 011 470 4666, Fax (39) 011 470 3293

RESTAURANTS RISTORANTE

Dolce Stil Novo - Tel (39) 011 921 1110 — Cirié 7 km
Mario - Tel(39) 011 920 3490 — Cirié 8 km
Antica Zecca — Caselle Torinese
Tel (39) 011 996 1403 — 8 km
Balbo - Tel(39) 011 839 5775 — Torino16 km

E' uno dei due (eccellenti) percorsi di 18 buche in Sardegna, vicino al capoluogo dell'isola, Cagliari. Anche se non si trova esattamente in riva al mare ne subisce nettamente l'influenza: oltre alle difficoltà del tracciato e agli ostacoli, il vento è un fattore essenziale del gioco. Così come lo è la lunghezza, di tutto rispetto, anche se il percorso di solito è abbastanza duro, il che rende però più pericolosi gli ostacoli d'acqua. Disegnato dai britannici Cotton e Pennink, il percorso è stato costruito sotto la direzione di Piero Mancinelli uno dei più grandi architetti italiani del nostro tempo. Ben equilibrato nel tracciato, Is Molas ha saputo fondersi bene con le forme originali del terreno e conservare un aspetto naturale, tra il mare e le colline boschive. Spettacolare e originale, è un percorso piacevole e appassionante per giocarci. E per chi non gioca a golf la bellezza del mare è incomparabile.

This is one of the two excellent 18-hole courses in Sardinia, close to Cagliari, the island's «capital». Although not exactly beside the sea, the course clearly comes under its influence, and the wind is a key factor when playing here, just as much as the difficulties of the layout and the hazards. The course's very respectable length also has to be considered, even though the fairways often roll a lot and make the water hazards more dangerous in the process. Designed by British designers Cotton and Pennink, the course was actually built under the supervision of Piero Mancinelli, one of the great Italian course architects of our day and age. A well-balanced layout, Is Molas has successfully hugged the contours of the terrain and retained its very natural appearance between the sea and tree-covered hills. Spectacular and original, the course is at once pleasant to look at and exciting to play. For non-golfers, there is all the fun of the seaside just next door.

Circolo Golf Is Molas 1975
Loc. Is Molas
I - SANTA MARGHERITA DI PULA (CA)

Office	Segreteria	(39) 070 924 1013
Pro shop	Pro shop	(39) 070 924 1070
Fax	Fax	(39) 070 924 1015
Situation	Localita'	

Cagliari (pop. 170.786), 35 km

Annual closure	Chiusura annuale	no
Weekly closure	Chiusura settimanale	no

Fees main season
Tariffe alta stagione full day

	Week days Settimana	We/Bank holidays Feriale/Festivo
Individual Individuale	L. 100.000	L. 100.000
Couple Coppia	L. 200.000	L. 200.000

Caddy	Caddy	L. 30.000
Electric Trolley	Carello elettrico	no
Buggy	Car	L. 60.000
Clubs	Bastoni	L. 30.000

Credit cards Carte di credito
VISA - Eurocard - MasterCard - AMEX - DC

Access Itinerario : Cagliari, S195 south to Pula. 3 km after Pula, turn right → Golf
Map 4 on page 949 Carta 4 Pagina 949

GOLF COURSE
PERCORSO 16 /20

Site	Paesaggio	
Maintenance	Manutenzione	
Architect	Architetto	Cotton, Pennink Piero Mancinelli
Type	Tipologia	country
Relief	Relievo terreno	
Water in play	Acqua in gioco	
Exp. to wind	Esposto al vento	
Trees in play	Alberi in gioco	

Scorecard Carta-score	Chp. Camp.	Mens Uomini	Ladies Donne
Length Lunghezza	6383	6197	5395
Par	72	72	72

Advised golfing ability 0 12 24 36
Livello di gioco consigliato
Hcp required Handicap richiesto 34

CLUB HOUSE & AMENITIES
CLUB HOUSE E SERVIZI 7 /10

Pro shop	Pro shop	
Driving range	Campo pratica	
Sheltered	coperto	5 mats
On grass	in erba	yes
Putting-green	Putting-green	yes
Pitching-green	Green-pratica	yes

HOTEL FACILITIES
ALBERGHI 8 /10

HOTELS ALBERGHI
Is Molas Golf Hotel Is Molas
84 rooms, D. L. 370.000 on site
Tel (39) 070 924 1006, Fax (39) 070 924 1002

Costa del Fiori Santa Margherita
62 rooms, D. L. 590.000 5 km
Tel (39) 070 924 5333, Fax (39) 070 924 5335

Nora Club Hotel Pula
25 rooms, D. L. 220.000 4 km
Tel (39) 070 924 5450, Fax (39) 070 920 9129

New Barcaleva Santa Margherita
27 rooms, D. L. 280.000 5 km
Tel (39) 070 929 0476, Fax (39) 070 929 0480

RESTAURANTS RISTORANTE
Dal Corsaro - Tel (39) 070 664 318 Cagliari 35 km
Il Molo - Tel (39) 070 308 959 Cagliari 35 km

975

LA MARGHERITA

13	7	7

Anche se non gode nei turisti stranieri del prestigio della vicina Milano, di Firenze, Roma, Venezia o Napoli, la città di Torino non manca né di argomenti né di seduzione. Il centro monumentale della città con Via Roma e i palazzi avrebbe dovuto fare tanto per la sua gloria quanto la squadra di calcio della Juventus. Tra i golf intorno a Torino, La Margherita è uno dei più recenti. E' stato tracciato da Marco Croze e Giorgio Ferraris in uno spazio moderatamente mosso, ai bordi di una pineta, ma praticamente senza alberi sul percorso. Solo i movimenti del terreno, gli ostacoli d'acqua e i bunkers potevano renderlo particolare e interessante. Gli architetti hanno lavorato con intelligenza e il risultato è stimolante per ogni livello di gioco, salvo che per i giocatori veramente inesperti.

Although in the eyes of tourists Turin lacks the prestige of Milan, Florence, Rome, Venice or Naples, this attractive northern city has a lot going for it. The monument-strewn city centre, with the Via Roma and Palazzi, should have done as much for its name as the Juventus football team has. Of the courses around Turin, La Margherita is one of the most recent. It was laid out by Marco Croze and Giorgio Ferraris in an area somewhat lacking in excitement, on the edge of a pine forest but virtually without any trees on the actual course. Excavated terrain, water hazards and bunkers were the only way to add variety and appeal. The architects did their job cleverly, whence an interesting course for players of all abilities except, no doubt, the real beginner.

Golf Club La Margherita — 1989

Strada Pralormo 29
I - 10022 CARMAGNOLA (TO)

Office	Segreteria	(39) 011 979 5113
Pro shop	Pro shop	(39) 011 979 5113
Fax	Fax	(39) 011 979 5204
Situation	Localita'	

Torino (pop. 914 818), 36 km

Annual closure	Chiusura annuale	no
Weekly closure	Chiusura settimanale	tuesday

Fees main season
Tariffe alta stagione full day

	Week days Settimana	We/Bank holidays Feriale/Festivo
Individual Individuale	L. 60.000	L. 90.000
Couple Coppia	L. 120.000	L. 180.000

Caddy	Caddy	no
Electric Trolley	Carello elettrico	yes
Buggy	Car	L. 60.000
Clubs	Bastoni	yes
Credit cards Carte di credito		no

976

Asti →

A 21 — Torino — Santena — S 29 — 0 2 4 km
S 393 — Villastellone — Poirino
A 6 — Casanova — GOLF — Pralormo
Carmagnola — Torino Carmagnola — Ternavasso

Access Itinerario : Torino A6 → Savona. Exit (Uscita) Carmagnola. Turn left → Pralormo. 8 km, turn left → Golf
Map 1 on page 940 Carta 1 Pagina 940

GOLF COURSE PERCORSO — 13/20

Site	Paesaggio	▮▮▮▮▯
Maintenance	Manutenzione	▮▮▮▮▯
Architect	Architetto	Marco Croze Giorgio Ferraris
Type	Tipologia	parkland
Relief	Relievo terreno	▮▮▯▯▯
Water in play	Acqua in gioco	▮▮▮▯▯
Exp. to wind	Esposto al vento	▮▮▮▯▯
Trees in play	Alberi in gioco	▮▮▮▮▯

Scorecard Carta-score	Chp. Camp.	Mens Uomini	Ladies Donne
Length Lunghezza	6379	6062	5412
Par	72	72	72

Advised golfing ability Livello di gioco consigliato	0	12	24	36

Hcp required   Handicap richiesto 34

CLUB HOUSE & AMENITIES CLUB HOUSE E SERVIZI — 7/10

Pro shop	Pro shop	▮▮▮▮▯
Driving range	Campo pratica	▮▮▮▯▯
Sheltered	coperto	5 mats
On grass	in erba	yes (04 → 10)
Putting-green	Putting-green	yes
Pitching-green	Green-pratica	yes

HOTEL FACILITIES ALBERGHI — 7/10

HOTELS ALBERGHI

Lo Scoiattolo — Pralormo
52 rooms, D. L. 120.000 — 2 km
Tel (39) 011 948 1148, Fax (39) 011 948 1481

Italia — Carmagnola
20 rooms, D. L. 100.000 — 6 km
Tel (39) 011 972 0496

Le Meridien Lingotto — Torino
229 rooms, D. L. 450.000 — 12 km
Tel (39) 011 664 2000, Fax (39) 011 664 2001

RESTAURANTS RISTORANTE

La Carmagnola — Carmagnola
Tel (39) 011 971 2673 — 6 km

San Marco - Tel (39) 011 972 0485   Carmagnola 6 km

La Prima Smarrita - Tel (39) 011 317 9657 Torino 15 km

Se avete scelto di alloggiare nelle camere del golf, Como è lontano solo una quindicina di chilometri: gli amanti di storia e di architettura apprezzeranno la ricchezza del Duomo costruito nel XIV secolo e anche la sobrietà romanica della Basilica di Sant'Abbondio e di San Fedele. Dopo si potrà ritrovare la quiete alla Pinetina. Il percorso è stato disegnato da John Harris e Gianni Albertini e costruito in due tempi in un terreno molto scosceso che lo rende abbastanza impegnativo fisicamente (è consigliato il golf cart). Questa ubicazione offre degli scorci magnifici sulle montagne. Come dice il suo nome, numerosi pini bordano i fairways obbligando sovente a far girare la palla per recuperare colpi sbagliati; qualche ostacolo d'acqua complica ancor più la vita. Quando si ha giocato un po' di volte, si interpreta meglio questo tracciato un po' «tricky» e si può pensare di fare un buono score, trascorrendo una piacevole giornata.

Although we decided to stay in the course's own guestrooms, lake Como is a mere fifteen kilometres down the road. Lovers of history and architecture will appreciate the wealth of Duomo, built during 14th century, and the Romanesque sobriety of the Basilica di Sant'Abbondio and San Fedele. Then it is on to the peace and quiet of La Pinetina, a course designed by John Harris and Gianni Albertini over two stages and hilly terrain which results in this being a tiring course to walk (buggy recommended). The good thing, naturally, is the magnificent view over the mountains. As its name would suggest, the fairways here are lined with pine-trees and wayward balls will need bending back to the short stuff. Then a few water hazards make life a little difficult, as well. After several rounds here, you have a clearer insight into this rather tricky layout and you can even think about carding a good score and having a great day's golfing in the process.

La Pinetina Golf Club — 1971

Via al Golf 4
I - 22070 APPIANO GENTILE (CO)

Office	Segreteria	(39) 031 933 202
Pro shop	Pro shop	(39) 031 890 857
Fax	Fax	(39) 031 890 342
Situation	Localita'	

Como (pop. 83 637), 15 km - Milano (pop. 1 302 808), 35 km

Annual closure	Chiusura annuale	no
Weekly closure	Chiusura settimanale	tuesday

Fees main season
Tariffe alta stagione 18 holes

	Week days Settimana	We/Bank holidays Feriale/Festivo
Individual Individuale	L. 84.000	L. 132.000
Couple Coppia	L. 168.000	L. 264.000

Caddy	Caddy	L. 40.000
Electric Trolley	Carello elettrico	no
Buggy	Car	L. 72.000
Clubs	Bastoni	L. 42.000

Credit cards Carte di credito
VISA - Eurocard - MasterCard - AMEX

Access Itinerario : Milano A8, A9 → Como, Exit (Uscita) Lomazzo, turn right → Guanzate and Appiano Gentile. **Map 1 on page 941** Carta 1 Pagina 941

GOLF COURSE / PERCORSO — 13/20

Site	Paesaggio	
Maintenance	Manutenzione	
Architect	Architetto	John Harris G. Albertini
Type	Tipologia	forest, hilly
Relief	Relievo terreno	
Water in play	Acqua in gioco	
Exp. to wind	Esposto al vento	
Trees in play	Alberi in gioco	

Scorecard Carta-score	Chp. Camp.	Mens Uomini	Ladies Donne
Length Lunghezza	5233	5922	5684
Par	71	71	71

Advised golfing ability Livello di gioco consigliato	0	12	24	36

Hcp required Handicap richiesto 34

CLUB HOUSE & AMENITIES / CLUB HOUSE E SERVIZI — 7/10

Pro shop	Pro shop	
Driving range	Campo pratica	
Sheltered	coperto	6 mats
On grass	in erba	yes
Putting-green	Putting-green	yes
Pitching-green	Green-pratica	yes

HOTEL FACILITIES / ALBERGHI — 7/10

HOTELS ALBERGHI

Canturio 30 rooms, D. L. 170.000 Tel (39) 031 716 035, Fax (39) 031 720 211		Cantù 5 km
Terminus 37 rooms, D. L. 220.000 Tel (39) 031 329 111, Fax (39) 031 302 550		Como 15 km
Villa Flori 44 rooms, D. L. 320.000 Tel (39) 031 573 105, Fax (39) 031 570 379		Como 15 km

RESTAURANTS RISTORANTE

Tradate - Tel (39) 0331 841 401	Tradate 4 km
Tarantola Tel (39) 031 930 990	Appiano Gentile 2 km
Al Ponte - Tel (39) 031 712 561	Cantù 5 km

977

La Rocca è stato costruito a sud dell'affascinante città di Parma, all'inizio delle colline addossate alle diramazioni degli Appennini. Un poì più lontano, visitando la fortezza di Torrechiara, ci si può calare nei panni di un valoroso guerriero. All'inizio 9 buche, La Rocca è passato a 18 buche nel 1986 con un disegno tra i migliori dell'architetto italiano, Marco Croze. Al primo impatto lo si può giudicare un po' troppo americano, ma come potrebbe essere altrimenti con gli ostacoli d'acqua che entrano in gioco in modo così strategico su molte buche? Bisogna anche tenere conto dei numerosi boschetti di querce e di acacie che delimitano bene le buche e che possono obbligarvi a fare qualche colpo particolare. Siccome il percorso è onesto non è necessario giocarci più volte per conoscere le sottigliezze e scegliere la strategia migliore. Piacevole d'aspetto e disegnato con gusto è una buona realizzazione.

La Rocca was built to the south of the charming city of Parma on the first slopes of the foothills to the Apennines. A little further on, you can look for a little fighting spirit and inspiration by visiting the fortress of Torrechiara. Originally a 9-hole course, La Rocca was extended to 18 in 1986 with a layout by the most prolific of Italian golf course architects, Marco Croze. There is an obvious American influence here, it could hardly be otherwise with water hazards placed so strategically on several holes. Watch out, too, for the many groups of trees - oak and acacia - which clearly outline the holes and force you to try and bend the ball one way or another. This is an open course which shows its hand, so you don't need to play several rounds to understand the finer points and choose the right strategy. A good course, visually pleasing and tastefully laid out.

Golf Club La Rocca — 1986

Via Campi 8
I - 43038 SALA BAGANZA (PR)

Office	Segreteria	(39) 0521 834 037
Pro shop	Pro shop	(39) 0521 833 969
Fax	Fax	(39) 0521 834 575
Situation	Localita'	

Parma (pop. 167 165), 15 km

Annual closure	Chiusura annuale	no
Weekly closure	Chiusura settimanale	monday

Fees main season
Tariffe alta stagione 18 holes

	Week days Settimana	We/Bank holidays Feriale/Festivo
Individual Individuale	L. 60.000	L. 80.000
Couple Coppia	L. 120.000	L. 160.000

Caddy	Caddy	no
Electric Trolley	Carello elettrico	no
Buggy	Car	L. 60.000
Clubs	Bastoni	L. 25.000

Credit cards Carte di credito	no

Access Itinerario : A1 Exit (Uscita) Parma-Ovest.
Parma → La Spezia and Collecchio.
Before going into Collecchio, → Sala Baganza → Golf.
Map 1 on page 941 Carta 1 Pagina 941

GOLF COURSE PERCORSO — 13/20

Site	Paesaggio	
Maintenance	Manutenzione	
Architect	Architetto	Marco Croze
Type	Tipologia	country
Relief	Relievo terreno	
Water in play	Acqua in gioco	
Exp. to wind	Esposto al vento	
Trees in play	Alberi in gioco	

Scorecard Carta-score	Chp. Camp.	Mens Uomini	Ladies Donne
Length Lunghezza	6052	5688	5089
Par	71	71	71

Advised golfing ability   0   12   24   36
Livello di gioco consigliato
Hcp required   Handicap richiesto 34

CLUB HOUSE & AMENITIES CLUB HOUSE E SERVIZI — 6/10

Pro shop	Pro shop	
Driving range	Campo pratica	
Sheltered	coperto	4 mats
On grass	in erba	yes
Putting-green	Putting-green	yes
Pitching-green	Green-pratica	yes

HOTEL FACILITIES ALBERGHI — 8/10

HOTELS ALBERGHI

Grand Hotel Baglioni — Parma
169 rooms, D. L. 450.000 — 9 km
Tel (39) 0521 292 929, Fax (39) 0521 292 828

Palace Hotel Maria Luigia — Parma
94 rooms, D. L. 410.000 — 9 km
Tel (39) 0521 281 032, Fax (39) 0521 231 126

Villa Ducale — Parma
28 rooms, D. L. 240.000 — 9 km
Tel (39) 0521 272 727, Fax (39) 0521 780 756

RESTAURANTS RISTORANTE

Parizzi — Parma
Tel (39) 0521 285 952 — 9 km

Villa Maria Luigia di Ceci — Collecchio
Tel (39) 0521 805 489 — 4 km

La Greppia - Tel (39) 0521 233 686 — Parma 9 km

978

LE PAVONIERE

14	8	8

Dopo aver visitato in lungo e in largo Firenze è ora di girare verso ovest. Scoprire Montecatini Terme, una piacevole stazione termale per rimettersi in forma dopo gli eccessi di bistecca alla fiorentina o di Chianti e sopratutto Prato, per tanto tempo all'ombra di Firenze, ma alla quale non mancano le qualità. Si vedrà in particolare il Duomo, il Palazzo Pretorio o la sorprendente fortezza del Castello dell' Imperatore. O ancora, ad una decina di chilometri, Le Pavoniere, aperto nel 1996 e disegnato da Arnold Palmer come il Castello di Tolcinasco in Lombardia. Si ritrova l'ispirazione sempre molto strategica del campione americano, dove gli ostacoli sono messi in gioco con grande intelligenza e con una buona conoscenza delle possibilità dei giocatori di tutti i livelli, anche se i più inesperti rischiano di soffrire un po'. Abbastanza piatto, questo percorso nasconde qualche sottigliezza che permette di non annoiarsi e i greens sono abbastanza grandi per offrire tante posizioni di bandiere diverse.

After a good look at Florence, it is time to head west of the city and discover Montecatini Terme, a pretty spa resort for treating people suffering from too much Bistecca alla Fiorentina or Chianti, and particularly Prato, for many a year overshadowed by Florence but nonetheless a town of many attractions. Visit Duomo, the Palazzo Pretorio or the amazing fortress of Castello dell'Imperatore. Or again, a few miles further on, play Le Pavoniere, opened in 1986 and designed by Arnold Palmer, as was Castello di Tolcinasco in Lombardy. You can feel Arnie's highly strategic inspiration, where hazards are very cleverly brought into play, and his excellent knowledge of players of differing abilities. All the same, the less experienced players might suffer a little here anyway. Although rather flat, the course is subtle enough to be played and enjoyed often, and the greens big enough to offer very many different pin positions.

Golf Club Le Pavoniere — 1986

Via della Fattoria 6/29, Loc. Tavola
I - 50040 PRATO

Office	Segreteria	(39) 0574 620 855
Pro shop	Pro shop	(39) 0574 620 855
Fax	Fax	(39) 0574 624 558
Situation	Localita'	

Prato (pop. 169 927), 10 km - Firenze, 20 km

Annual closure	Chiusura annuale	no
Weekly closure	Chiusura settimanale	monday
		01/10 →31/03

Fees main season
Tariffe alta stagione 18 holes

	Week days Settimana	We/Bank holidays Feriale/Festivo
Individual Individuale	L. 70.000	L. 90.000
Couple Coppia	L. 140.000	L. 180.000
Caddy	Caddy	L. 50.000
Electric Trolley	Carello elettrico	no
Buggy	Car	L. 50.000
Clubs	Bastoni	L. 25.000

Credit cards Carte di credito
VISA - Eurocard - MasterCard - AMEX

Access Itinerario : A11 Exit (Uscita) Prato Ovest. Take right → Poggio a Caiano. Right → Tavola. After four traffic lights, don't turn left, take the dead end way (senza uscita) **Map 3 on page 944** Carta 3 Pagina 944

GOLF COURSE PERCORSO — 14/20

Site	Paesaggio	
Maintenance	Manutenzione	
Architect	Architetto	Arnold Palmer
Type	Tipologia	parkland, open country
Relief	Relievo terreno	
Water in play	Acqua in gioco	
Exp. to wind	Esposto al vento	
Trees in play	Alberi in gioco	

Scorecard Carta-score	Chp. Camp.	Mens Uomini	Ladies Donne
Length Lunghezza	6465	6137	5323
Par	72	72	72

Advised golfing ability Livello di gioco consigliato	0	12	24	36

Hcp required Handicap richiesto 34

CLUB HOUSE & AMENITIES CLUB HOUSE E SERVIZI — 8/10

Pro shop	Pro shop	
Driving range	Campo pratica	
Sheltered	coperto	12 mats
On grass	in erba	yes
Putting-green	Putting-green	yes
Pitching-green	Green-pratica	yes

HOTEL FACILITIES ALBERGHI — 8/10

HOTELS ALBERGHI

Hermitage — Poggio a Caiano
58 rooms, D. L. 130.000 — 5 km
Tel (39) 055 877 040, Fax (39) 055 879 7057

Art Hotel Museo — Prato
108 rooms, D. L. 250.000 — 10 km
Tel (39) 0574 5787, Fax (39) 0574 578 880

San Marco - 41 rooms, D. L. 150.000 — Prato 10 km
Tel (39) 0574 21 321, Fax (39) 0574 22 378

RESTAURANTS RISTORANTE

Il Piraña — Prato
Tel (39) 0574 25 746 — 10 km

Da Delfina — Artimino
Tel (39) 055 871 8119 — 15 km

Osvaldo Baroncelli — Prato
Tel (39) 0574 23 810 — 10 km

979

Le Querce annuncia il programma: ci saranno delle querce sul percorso. Inaugurato nel 1990 è composto dal Centro Tecnico Nazionale della Federazione Italiana Golf ma anche da un club privato. Le sue qualità sono state messe in evidenza nell'edizione 1991 della World Cup, ma anche i giocatori meno esperti si potranno accomodare a meno che non partano dalle partenze arretrate! Perchè altrimenti è obbligatorio avere una potenza e una precisione assolute. Comunque è un campo molto onesto e la strategia di gioco in rapporto ai pericoli e agli ostacoli è molto evidente. Gli avvallamenti obbligano anche a pensare bene prima di scegliere un bastone, perchè i greens sono molto grandi, ben difesi e con parecchie pendenze: il putting non è mai facile se si è lontani dalla buca. Vi segnaliamo infine delle sequenze che possono decidere o meno la buona riuscita, dalla 4 alla 6 e dalla 13 alla 15. Due «Amen Corner» sono abbastanza scontati così vicino alla Città Santa!

Le Querce is a course lined with oak-trees, which was opened in 1990 as a national golf centre for the Italian Golf Federation but also as a private club. The hosting of the World Cup here in 1991 highlighted the course's many qualities, but the not-so-good players can handle this okay as long they keep well away from the back tees. Playing from the tips is a very demanding experience for both power and precision. This is a very open course, though, and game strategy with respect to the dangers and hazards is clear enough. The sloping terrain calls for thoughtful club selection, because while the greens are on the large side, they are well guarded and steeply contoured; putting here is never easy if you are too far from the hole. To finish, make a note of two stretches which can make or break your card: 4 through 6 and 13 through 15... two «Amen Corners» and a natural state of affairs being so close to the Holy City.

Golf Club Le Querce — 1990

Via Cassia Km 44,500
I - 01015 SUTRI (VT)

Office	Segreteria	(39) 0761 600 789
Pro shop	Pro shop	(39) 0761 600 789
Fax	Fax	(39) 0761 600 142
Situation	Localita'	

Viterbo (pop. 60 319), 31 km - Roma (pop. 2 653 245), 51 km

Annual closure	Chiusura annuale	no
Weekly closure	Chiusura settimanale	no

Fees main season
Tariffe alta stagione full day

	Week days Settimana	We/Bank holidays Feriale/Festivo
Individual Individuale	L. 80.000	L. 100.000
Couple Coppia	L. 160.000	L. 200.000

Caddy	Caddy	no
Electric Trolley	Carello elettrico	L. 15.000
Buggy	Car	L. 50.000
Clubs	Bastoni	L. 10.000

Credit cards Carte di credito
VISA - Eurocard - MasterCard - AMEX - DC

980

Sutri
Viterbo
Nepi
GOLF →
Monterosi
0   1,5   3 km
Roma
Trevignano
Romano
Sette Vene
Lago di
Bracciano

Access Itinerario : Roma, Via Cassia. Before Monterosi, at the end of a long and straight road, take left → Golf.
Map 3 on page 945 Carta 3 Pagina 945

GOLF COURSE / PERCORSO — 17/20

Site	Paesaggio	■■■■■□
Maintenance	Manutenzione	■■■■■□
Architect	Architetto	Jim Fazio

Type	Tipologia	open country, hilly
Relief	Relievo terreno	■■■■□□
Water in play	Acqua in gioco	■■□□□□
Exp. to wind	Esposto al vento	■■■□□□
Trees in play	Alberi in gioco	■■■■□□

Scorecard Carta-score	Chp. Camp.	Mens Uomini	Ladies Donne
Length Lunghezza	6462	6052	5305
Par	72	72	72

Advised golfing ability
Livello di gioco consigliato   0   12   24   36
Hcp required   Handicap richiesto 34

CLUB HOUSE & AMENITIES / CLUB HOUSE E SERVIZI — 8/10

Pro shop	Pro shop	■■■■■□
Driving range	Campo pratica	■■■■■□
Sheltered	coperto	10 mats
On grass	in erba	yes
Putting-green	Putting-green	yes
Pitching-green	Green-pratica	yes

HOTEL FACILITIES / ALBERGHI — 7/10

HOTELS ALBERGHI

Il Borgo di Sutri — Sutri, 2 km
16 rooms, D. L. 220.000
Tel (39) 0761 607 690, Fax (39) 0761 608 308

Hotel Sallus e delle Terme — Viterbo, 31 km
100 rooms, D. L. 240.000
Tel (39) 0761 3581, Fax (39) 0761 354 262

Balletti Palace Hotel — Viterbo, 31 km
105 rooms, D. L. 160.000
Tel (39) 0761 344 777, Fax (39) 0761 344 777

RESTAURANTS RISTORANTE

L'Altra Bottiglia — Civita Castellana, 15 km
Tel (39) 0761 517 403

Il Vescovado Tel (39) 0761 608 811 — Sutri 8 km

La Zaffera - Tel (39) 0761 344 265 — Viterbo 31 km

A metà strada tra Milano, Varese e il Lago Maggiore, Le Robinie è uno dei più recenti golf italiani e anche uno dei più prestigiosi grazie alla firma di Jack Nicklaus. Esistono architetti meno di moda o ancora più creativi ma questo nome continua ad essere una garanzia di grande qualità anche se si può obiettare che tutti i suoi percorsi seguono un po' lo stesso modello secondo l'ingegnere che ha realmente seguito i lavori. Su un terreno così piatto, l'esperienza americana è stata di grande utilità e i lavori di movimentazione sono stati veramente di prim'ordine con numerosi ostacoli d'acqua creati per recuperare terra e riportarla in modo da ottenere tanti anfiteatri che dominano le buche. Di estremo rilievo anche l'accuratezza con la quale sono stati disegnati i bunkers e i greens che donano un aspetto grafico veramente perfetto. Dalle partenze di campionato questo percorso è consigliato solo ai giocatori esperti, per gli altri, i tees normali sono l'ideale per trascorrere una bella giornata di golf.

Mid-way between Milan, Varese and the unavoidable Lake Maggiore, Le Robinie is one of Italy's more recent courses and one of the most prestigious too, courtesy of its designer Jack Nicklaus. There are other, less fashionable and perhaps more creative architects, but the Golden Bear label is a quality guarantee even if all his courses do tend to follow more or less the same model, depending on the engineer. On terrain as flat as this, American experience is useful indeed and the excavation work made to contour the course was quite remarkable, including many water hazards in order to recover the earth which has been arranged to form amphitheatres around the holes. A lot of thought also went into the shapes of bunkers and greens, giving a very graphic look to the whole layout. From the back tees, this very open and forthright course is for experienced players only. Further forward and you are in for a great day's golfing.

Golf Club Le Robinie — 1992

Via per Busto Arsizio 9
I - 21058 SOLBIATE OLONA (VA)

Office	Segreteria	(39) 0331 329 260
Pro shop	Pro shop	(39) 0331 329 272
Fax	Fax	(39) 0331 329 266
Situation	Localita'	

Varese (pop. 84.187), 27 km
Milano (pop. 1.302.808), 35 km

Annual closure	Chiusura annuale	no
Weekly closure	Chiusura settimanale	tuesday

Fees main season
Tariffe alta stagione 18 holes

	Week days Settimana	We/Bank holidays Feriale/Festivo
Individual Individuale	L. 80.000	L. 120.000
Couple Coppia	L. 160.000	L. 240.000

Caddy	Caddy	L. 35.000
Electric Trolley	Carello elettrico	no
Buggy	Car	L. 50.000
Clubs	Bastoni	L. 30.000

Credit cards Carte di credito
VISA - Eurocard - MasterCard - AMEX - DC

Access Itinerario : A8 (Autostrada dei Laghi). Exit (Uscita) Busto Arsizio. Right then left, golf 2 km
Map 1 on page 941 Carta 1 Pagina 941

GOLF COURSE / PERCORSO — 16/20

Site	Paesaggio	
Maintenance	Manutenzione	
Architect	Architetto	Jack Nicklaus
Type	Tipologia	open country
Relief	Relievo terreno	
Water in play	Acqua in gioco	
Exp. to wind	Esposto al vento	
Trees in play	Alberi in gioco	

Scorecard Carta-score	Chp. Camp.	Mens Uomini	Ladies Donne
Length Lunghezza	6520	6168	5378
Par	72	72	72

Advised golfing ability	0	12	24	36
Livello di gioco consigliato				

Hcp required   Handicap richiesto 34

CLUB HOUSE & AMENITIES / CLUB HOUSE E SERVIZI — 9/10

Pro shop	Pro shop	
Driving range	Campo pratica	
Sheltered	coperto	19 mats
On grass	in erba	yes
Putting-green	Putting-green	yes
Pitching-green	Green-pratica	yes

HOTEL FACILITIES / ALBERGHI — 7/10

HOTELS ALBERGHI

Pineta — Busto Arsizio
52 rooms, D. L. 300.000 — 4 km
Tel (39) 0331 381 220, Fax (39) 0331 381 220

Jet Hotel — Gallarate
40 rooms, D. L. 280.000 — 9 km
Tel (39) 0331 772 100, Fax (39) 0331 772 686

Astoria — Busto Arsizio
48 rooms, D. L. 170.000 — 4 km
Tel (39) 0331 636 422

RESTAURANTS RISTORANTE

Ma.Ri.Na — Olgiate Olona
Tel (39) 0331 640 463 — 2 km

Casa Radice - Tel (39) 0331 620 454 Busto Arsizio 4 km

Cinque Campanili — Busto Arsizio
Tel (39) 0331 630 493 — 4 km

981

Lignano è una stazione balneare di primaria importanza in Friuli, sulle rive dell'Adriatico e più o meno a metà strada tra Venezia e Trieste. La spiaggia lunga otto chilometri, consente di trascorrere soggiorni molto piacevoli con la famiglia in una delle villette di Lignano Sabbiadoro o di Lignano Pineta. Il golfista potrà quindi dedicarsi al suo gioco preferito senza rimorsi quando i bambini sono al mare. Il percorso, disegnato da Marco Croze è particolarmente piatto, con pochi alberi. Si ritrova un po' lo stile «links» con un disegno intelligente dei fairways e dei grandi bunkers, e un po' lo stile «Florida» quando gli ostacoli entrano in gioco. Abbastanza difficile dalle partenze arretrate quando soffia vento, è più facile giocare il proprio handicap quando si è più modesti e non troppo ambiziosi. Bisogna giocare due o tre volte per apprezzare le sottigliezze del percorso, ma non ci si annoierà restando qualche giorno.

Lignano is one of the topmost seaside resorts in Friuli on the shores of the Adriatic, about half-way between Venice and Trieste. The 5-mile long beach is perfect for very pleasant family holidays in the small towns of Lignano Sabbiadoro or Lignano Pineta. You guessed it, golfers can go about their favourite pastime with a clear conscience when the children are on the beach. This course, designed by Marco Croze, is virtually flat with few trees. It combines a sort of links style, where terrain has been cleverly contoured and given some large bunkers, with some very Floridian features when the water hazards come into play. A rather tough proposition from the back tees when the wind blows, it is easier to play to your handicap when swallowing your pride and not being too ambitious (i.e. opt for the front tees). You need two or three rounds to appreciate the finer points of this layout, but you won't get bored playing here if you are around for several days.

Golf Club Lignano — 1991
Via della Bonifica
I - 33054 LIGNANO SABBIADORO (UD)

Office	Segreteria	(39) 0431 428 025
Pro shop	Pro shop	(39) 0431 423 274
Fax	Fax	(39) 0431 423 230
Situation	Localita'	

Portegruaro (pop. 24 461), 32 km

Annual closure	Chiusura annuale	no
Weekly closure	Chiusura settimanale	no

Fees main season
Tariffe alta stagione 18 holes

	Week days Settimana	We/Bank holidays Feriale/Festivo
Individual Individuale	L. 90.000	L. 110.000
Couple Coppia	L. 180.000	L. 220.000

Caddy	Caddy	no
Electric Trolley	Carello elettrico	no
Buggy	Car	L. 60.000
Clubs	Bastoni	L. 15.000

Credit cards Carte di credito
VISA - Eurocard - MasterCard - AMEX - DC -Cartasi

GOLF COURSE / PERCORSO — 14/20

Site	Paesaggio	
Maintenance	Manutenzione	
Architect	Architetto	Marco Croze
Type	Tipologia	links
Relief	Relievo terreno	
Water in play	Acqua in gioco	
Exp. to wind	Esposto al vento	
Trees in play	Alberi in gioco	

Scorecard Carta-score	Chp. Camp.	Mens Uomini	Ladies Donne
Length Lunghezza	6369	6069	5328
Par	72	72	72

Advised golfing ability — 0 12 24 36
Livello di gioco consigliato
Hcp required — Handicap richiesto 34

CLUB HOUSE & AMENITIES / CLUB HOUSE E SERVIZI — 7/10

Pro shop	Pro shop	
Driving range	Campo pratica	
Sheltered	coperto	15 mats
On grass	in erba	yes
Putting-green	Putting-green	yes
Pitching-green	Green-pratica	yes

HOTEL FACILITIES / ALBERGHI — 7/10

HOTELS ALBERGHI

Greif — Lignano Pineta
74 rooms, D. L. 450.000 — 2 km
Tel (39) 0431 422 261, Fax (39) 0431 422 261

Marina Uno — Lignano Riviera
87 rooms, D. L. 360.000 — 2 km
Tel (39) 0431 427 171, Fax (39) 0431 427 171

Golf Inn — Lignano
24 rooms, D. L. 140.000 — on site
Tel (39) 0431 428 025, Fax (39) 0431 423 230

Park Hotel — Lignano Pineta
49 rooms, D. L. 240.000 — 2 km
Tel (39) 0431 422 380, Fax (39) 0431 428 079

RESTAURANTS RISTORANTE

Newport - Tel (39) 0431 427 171 — Lignano Riviera 2 km
Bidin - Tel (39) 0431 71 988 — Lignano 2 km

Access Itinerario : A4 Venezia-Trieste, Exit (Uscita) Latisana, → Lignano. 24 km, take right → Golf.
Map 2 on page 944 Carta 2 Pagina 944

Si può scommettere che ben pochi turisti stranieri che vengono a visitare Roma hanno mai sentito parlare di Tivoli. Invece è uno dei posti più magici che si possano immaginare, soprattutto per i giardini e le fontane di Villa d'Este o per la ricchezza archeologica di Villa Adriana, antica dimora dell'imperatore Adriano. Le 27 buche del golf Marco Simone si trovano a meno di 10 chilometri in una campagna molto ondulata (è consigliato il golf cart). A ridosso di un antico castello di proprietà della stilista Laura Biagiotti, la club-house è immensa e i servizi lussuosi con tennis, piscina e centro bellezza che sono però riservati ai soci. Il percorso disegnato con molta fantasia da Jim Fazio ha il merito di essere difficile dalle partenze di campionato ma, con perfetta logica, diventa più facile man mano che si accorciano le partenze. Gli ostacoli d'acqua così come le forme dei greens e dei bunkers gli confluiscono uno stile americano, mitigato dal paesaggio della campagna romana. Un gran bel percorso già vicino alla maturità.

You can bet that very few foreign tourists coming to visit Rome have heard of Tivoli. Yet it is one of the most magic spots imaginable, particularly with the gardens and fountains of la Villa d'Este or the archaeological wealth of the Villa Adriana, the former mansion of Emperor Hadrian. The 27 holes that grace the Marco Simone golf club are less than 10 kilometres away, laid out over steeply rolling countryside (buggy recommended). Leaning against a former castle belonging to designer Laura Biagiotti, the club-house is huge and facilities luxurious, including tennis courts, swimming pool and health centre, but reserved for members only. The course, designed with much imagination has the merit of being tough from the back tees but easier the further forward you go. Water hazards and the shaping of greens and bunkers create anAmerican feel, tempered only by the landscape of the Roman countryside. A very good course, already mature.

Golf Marco Simone — 1991
Via di Marco Simone 84/88
I - 00012 GUIDONIA MONTECELLO (RM)

Office	Segreteria	(39) 0774 366 469
Pro shop	Pro shop	(39) 0774 367 060
Fax	Fax	(39) 0774 366 476
Situation	Localita'	

Tivoli (pop. 52 735), 9 km
Roma (pop. 2 653 245), 37 km

Annual closure	Chiusura annuale	no
Weekly closure	Chiusura settimanale	tuesday

Fees main season
Tariffe alta stagione 18 holes

	Week days Settimana	We/Bank holidays Feriale/Festivo
Individual Individuale	L. 80.000	L. 120.000
Couple Coppia	L. 160.000	L. 240.000

Caddy	Caddy	yes
Electric Trolley	Carello elettrico	no
Buggy	Car	L. 70.000
Clubs	Bastoni	L. 30.000

Credit cards Carte di credito
VISA - Eurocard - MasterCard - AMEX - DC - Cartasi

Access Itinerario : Roma, «Grande Raccordo Anulare» (Ring road), Exit (Uscita) 11, → Mentana. → Guidonia.
Map 3 on page 945 Carta 3 Pagina 945

GOLF COURSE
PERCORSO **16**/20

Site	Paesaggio	
Maintenance	Manutenzione	
Architect	Architetto	Jim Fazio
Type	Tipologia	country, hilly
Relief	Relievo terreno	
Water in play	Acqua in gioco	
Exp. to wind	Esposto al vento	
Trees in play	Alberi in gioco	

Scorecard Carta-score	Chp. Camp.	Mens Uomini	Ladies Donne
Length Lunghezza		6343	0 0
Par	72	72	72

Advised golfing ability			0	12 24 36	
Livello di gioco consigliato					
Hcp required	Handicap richiesto	34			

CLUB HOUSE & AMENITIES
CLUB HOUSE E SERVIZI **8**/10

Pro shop	Pro shop	
Driving range	Campo pratica	
Sheltered	coperto	10 mats
On grass	in erba	yes
Putting-green	Putting-green	yes
Pitching-green	Green-pratica	yes

983

HOTEL FACILITIES
ALBERGHI **8**/10

HOTELS ALBERGHI
Grand Hotel Duca d'Este — Bagni di Tivoli
176 rooms, D. L. 250.000 — 5 km
Tel (39) 0774 3883, Fax (39) 0774 388 101

Torre Sant'Angelo — Tivoli
31 rooms, D. L. 250.000 — 9 km
Tel (39) 0774 332 533, Fax (39) 0774 332 533

Sirene - 40 rooms, D. L. 230.000 — Villa Adriana
Tel (39) 0774 330 605, Fax (39) 0774 330 608 — 7 km

Golf Club Marco Simone — Guidonia
27 rooms, appartamenti — on site
Tel (39) 0774 366 469, Fax (39) 0774 366 476

RESTAURANTS RISTORANTE
Adriano - Tel (39) 0774 382 235 — Villa Adriana 7 km

Antiqua Host. dei Carrettieri — Tivoli
Tel (39) 0774 330 159 — 9 km

Questo golf è situato in una regione industriale e non particolarmente turistica, fatta eccezione per il periodo del Palio o della festa del vino ad Asti (in settembre). Si può arrivarci da Torino attraversando il Monferrato fermandosi nei suoi castelli per degustare i famosi vini piemontesi tra i quali il Barolo ed il Barbera. In questa occasione o durante un viaggio d'affari, una visita a Margara non è certo tempo perso. Si può anche soggiornare nell'immensa costruzione che ospita la club-house e dalla quale si gode la vista di tutto il percorso. Tre percorsi di 9 buche sono combinabili tra loro e sono stati disegnati dal professionista Agostino Reale e da Glauco Lolli Ghetti, figlio del proprietario di questa vecchia tenuta agricola. Il percorso è abbastanza mosso e questo obbliga ad un' attenta selezione dei bastoni da scegliere. Gli ostacoli sono quelli classici con bunkers privi di grande fantasia e una curiosità alla 11, dove il green é interamente circondato da un fosso.

This course is located in an industrial part of the country, off the tourist trail, except during the period of Palio or the Wine Festival in Asti (September). Starting out from Turin, you can also take the Monferrato road with its castles and taste all the wines of Piedmont, including the famous Barolo and Barbera. On such an occasion, or during a business trip, a visit to Margara is time well spent. You can even stay here in the impressive club-house buildings, which overlook almost all the course. There are three combinable 9-hole courses, designed by the professional player Agostino Reale and Glauco Lolli Ghetti, son of the proprietor of this former farming estate. The course is a little hilly and so calls for careful club selection. Hazards are standard affairs with some slightly unimaginative bunkering and one curiosity at the 11th hole, where the green is completely surrounded by a ditch.

Golf Club Margara — 1975

Via Tenuta Margara 25
I - 15043 FUBINE (AL)

Office	Segreteria	(39) 0131 778 555
Pro shop	Pro shop	(39) 0131 778 555
Fax	Fax	(39) 0131 778 772
Situation	Localita'	

Alessandria (pop. 90.852), 17 km
Asti (pop. 73.281), 29 km

Annual closure	Chiusura annuale	no
Weekly closure	Chiusura settimanale	monday

Fees main season
Tariffe alta stagione 18 holes

	Week days Settimana	We/Bank holidays Feriale/Festivo
Individual Individuale	L. 60.000	L. 90.000
Couple Coppia	L. 120.000	L. 180.000

Caddy	Caddy	no
Electric Trolley	Carello elettrico	yes
Buggy	Car	L. 50.000
Clubs	Bastoni	si

Credit cards Carte di credito
VISA - Eurocard - MasterCard

984

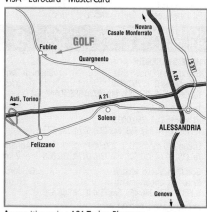

Access Itinerario : A21 Torino-Piacenza.
Exit (Uscita) Felizzano. Turn left on S10.
In Felizzano take left → Fubine. 3 km → golf
Map 1 on page 940 Carta 1 Pagina 940

GOLF COURSE / PERCORSO — 13/20

Site	Paesaggio	▰▰▰▱
Maintenance	Manutenzione	▰▰▰▱
Architect	Architetto	
Type	Tipologia	open country
Relief	Relievo terreno	▰▰▰▱
Water in play	Acqua in gioco	▰▱▱▱
Exp. to wind	Esposto al vento	▰▱▱▱
Trees in play	Alberi in gioco	▰▰▰▱

Scorecard Carta-score	Chp. Camp.	Mens Uomini	Ladies Donne
Length Lunghezza	6198	6045	5319
Par	72	72	72

Advised golfing ability			0	12	24 36
Livello di gioco consigliato					
Hcp required	Handicap richiesto	34			

CLUB HOUSE & AMENITIES / CLUB HOUSE E SERVIZI — 7/10

Pro shop	Pro shop	▰▰▰▱
Driving range	Campo pratica	▰▰▰▱
Sheltered	coperto	10 mats
On grass	in erba	yes
Putting-green	Putting-green	yes
Pitching-green	Green-pratica	yes

HOTEL FACILITIES / ALBERGHI — 7/10

HOTELS ALBERGHI

Alli Due Buoi Rossi — Alessandria
50 rooms, D. L. 340.000 — 17 km
Tel (39) 0131 445 252, Fax (39) 0131 445 255

Dormy House — Fubine
10 rooms, D. L. 100.000 — on site
Tel (39) 0131 778 555, Fax (39) 0131 778 772

Lux — Alessandria
52 rooms, D. L. 190.000 — 17 km
Tel (39) 0131 251 661, Fax (39) 0131 441 091

RESTAURANTS RISTORANTE

La Braja — Montemagno
Tel (39) 0141 653 925 — 10 km

La Fermata — Alessandria
Tel (39) 0131 251 350 — 17 km

Castello di Lajone — Piepasso (Quattordio)
Tel (39) 0131 773 692 — 10 km

Situato in prossimità del capoluogo lombardo dentro al Parco di Monza, è sicuramente uno dei circoli italiani più prestigiosi che ama portare avanti le tradizioni e lo conferma l'incontro annuale dei suoi soci con quelli del Royal & Ancient Golf Club of St. Andrews. Glannon e Blanford lo hanno disegnato su di un terreno piatto, dove gli alberi maestosi sono sia il mezzo per isolarsi completamente, che un'impenetrabile barriera dai principianti maldestri. I numerosi bunkers difendono molto bene i greens di medie dimensioni, leggermente ondulati e ben tenuti. Giocando qui si ha la sensazione di muoversi in un parco immenso dove il silenzio è interrotto soltanto nei giorni in cui si disputano le corse sul circuito di Monza. Con i suoi percorsi, per un totale di 27 buche, che ben si adattano a tutti i livelli di gioco e con la sua grande club-house funzionale e lussuosa che ha sostituito il vecchio casino di caccia, il Golf Club Milano ha ancora davanti a sè un florido avvenire.

Located close to the capital of Lombardy in the Parco di Monza, this is obviously one of the most prestigious Italian clubs cultivating real golfing tradition, as testified by the annual encounter with the members of the Royal & Ancient at St Andrews. Gannon and Blanford laid the course out over flat terrain, where majestic trees create both a feeling of isolation and pleasant exclusivity, and a formidable line of defence for hitters who slug rather than think. The very many bunkers ably defend the average-sized greens that are slightly contoured and very well maintained. Here you get the feeling of playing in a huge park, where the silence is disturbed only on those days when the Monza race-track is in action. With good courses (27 holes in all) well suited to all standards of play, plus a huge, functional and luxurious club-house, which has replaced the former hunting lodge, the Golf Club Milano has a great future in store.

Golf Club Milano — 1928

Viale Mulini San Giorgio 7
I - 20052 PARCO DI MONZA (MI)

Office	Segreteria	(39) 039 303 081
Pro shop	Pro shop	(39) 039 304 561
Fax	Fax	(39) 039 304 427
Situation	Localita'	

Milano (pop. 1.302.808), 25 km
Bergamo (pop. 117.619), 29 km

Annual closure	Chiusura annuale	no
Weekly closure	Chiusura settimanale	monday

Fees main season
Tariffe alta stagione 18 holes

	Week days Settimana	We/Bank holidays Feriale/Festivo
Individual Individuale	L. 100.000	L. 150.000
Couple Coppia	L. 200.000	L. 300.000
Caddy Caddy		L. 30.000
Electric Trolley Carello elettrico		no
Buggy Car		L. 60.000
Clubs Bastoni		L. 30.000

Credit cards Carte di credito
VISA - Eurocard - MasterCard

Access Itinerario : Milano A4, Tangenziale Est.
Exit (Uscita) Vimercate. Take left → Villasanta.
Cross road to Lecco, → Villasanta. First traffic lights,
turn right → San Giorgio. → Parco di Monza, Golf
Map 1 on page 941 Carta 1 Pagina 941

GOLF COURSE / PERCORSO — 16/20

Site	Paesaggio	
Maintenance	Manutenzione	
Architect	Architetto	Blandford & Gannon
Type	Tipologia	parkland
Relief	Relievo terreno	
Water in play	Acqua in gioco	
Exp. to wind	Esposto al vento	
Trees in play	Alberi in gioco	

Scorecard Carta-score	Chp. Camp.	Mens Uomini	Ladies Donne
Length Lunghezza	6403	6239	5509
Par	72	72	72

Advised golfing ability   0   12   24   36
Livello di gioco consigliato
Hcp required   Handicap richiesto 34

CLUB HOUSE & AMENITIES / CLUB HOUSE E SERVIZI — 8/10

Pro shop	Pro shop	
Driving range	Campo pratica	
Sheltered	coperto	8 mats
On grass	in erba	yes
Putting-green	Putting-green	yes
Pitching-green	Green-pratica	yes

HOTEL FACILITIES / ALBERGHI — 9/10

HOTELS ALBERGHI

De La Ville — Monza — 2 km
55 rooms, D. L. 370.000
Tel (39) 039 382 581, Fax (39) 039 367 647

Della Regione — Monza — 2 km
90 rooms, D. L. 250.000
Tel (39) 039 387 205, Fax (39) 039 380 254

Sant' Eustorgio — Arcore — 4 km
35 rooms, D. L. 200.000
Tel (39) 039 601 3718, Fax (39) 039 617 531

RESTAURANTS RISTORANTE

Giannino — Milano — 25 km
Tel (39) 02 551 955 82

Pierino Penati — Viganò — 17 km
Tel (39) 039 956 020

Derby Grill — Monza — 5 km
Tel (39) 039 382 581

985

Le scarpe, i treni e soprattutto le automobili (Ferrari a Maranello) hanno creato la reputazione di Modena... così come il suo Duomo e la bella collezione di dipinti della Galleria Estense. Aperto nel 1987, il percorso del Modena Golf & Country Club è stato disegnato da Bernhard Langer, senza dubbio all'epoca della sua collaborazione con Buckley. Più tardi il campione tedesco si è molto evoluto perfezionandosi nel suo mestiere di architetto. Il suo disegno segue fedelmente gli aspetti del terreno poco movimentato dove gli alberi non sono un pericolo. La strategia di gioco è ben evidente. Gli ostacoli sono costituiti maggiormente dai bunkers e dall'acqua presente spesso e in particolare su due par 3 e alla 18 dove l'audacia può essere ricompensata o distruggere un buono score. E' un perfetto percorso per un circolo con soci di diverso livello. I giocatori migliori non saranno appagati e i cultori dei campi naturali lo troveranno un po' troppo artificiale ma è destinato a migliorare nel tempo.

Footwear, rolling stock and particularly cars (Ferrari in Maranello) have forged the reputation of Modena... together with the Duomo and the fine collection of paintings at the Galleria Estense. Created in 1987, the Modena Golf & Country Club course was designed by Bernhard Langer, certainly during the period when he was working with Buckley. Since then, the German champion has covered a lot of ground and acquired maturity in his work as a course architect. Here, the design faithfully hugs the contours of rather flat terrain, where trees are not a danger. Playing strategy is obvious as soon as you are on the course. Hazards are basically the bunkers and very present water hazards, especially on two of the par 3s and at the end, on the 18th, where daring may be rewarded or simply ruin your card. This is a real members' course where playing levels are necessarily very different, and where the more skilled player might feel a little frustrated. Lovers of natural courses will find this layout a little artificial, but one which with age should mature well.

Modena Golf & Country Club — 1987

Via Castelnuovo Rangone 4
I - 41050 COLOMBARO DI FORMIGINE (MO)

Office	Segreteria	(39) 0359 553 482
Pro shop	Pro shop	(39) 0359 553 696
Fax	Fax	(39) 0359 553 696
Situation	Localita'	

Modena (pop. 175.013), 20 km
Bologna (pop. 383.761), 40 km

Annual closure	Chiusura annuale	no
Weekly closure	Chiusura settimanale	tuesday

Fees main season
Tariffe alta stagione 18 holes

	Week days Settimana	We/Bank holidays Feriale/Festivo
Individual Individuale	L. 60.000	L. 90.000
Couple Coppia	L. 120.000	L. 180.000

Caddy	Caddy	no
Electric Trolley	Carello elettrico	no
Buggy	Car	L. 60.000
Clubs	Bastoni	L. 20.000

Credit cards Carte di credito
VISA - Eurocard - MasterCard - AMEX - DC

Access Itinerario : A1 (Autostrada del Sole), Exit (Uscita) Modena Sud. Go right → Modena for 5 km. A12 to the left. 12 km, Golf on the left hand side.
Map 2 on page 942 Carta 2 Pagina 942

GOLF COURSE / PERCORSO — 14/20

Site	Paesaggio	
Maintenance	Manutenzione	
Architect	Architetto	Bernhard Langer
Type	Tipologia	open country
Relief	Relievo terreno	
Water in play	Acqua in gioco	
Exp. to wind	Esposto al vento	
Trees in play	Alberi in gioco	

Scorecard Carta-score	Chp. Camp.	Mens Uomini	Ladies Donne
Length Lunghezza	6423	6097	5350
Par	72	72	72

Advised golfing ability	0	12	24	36
Livello di gioco consigliato				

Hcp required Handicap richiesto 34

CLUB HOUSE & AMENITIES / CLUB HOUSE E SERVIZI — 7/10

Pro shop	Pro shop	
Driving range	Campo pratica	
Sheltered	coperto	10 mats
On grass	in erba	yes
Putting-green	Putting-green	yes
Pitching-green	Green-pratica	yes

HOTEL FACILITIES / ALBERGHI — 8/10

HOTELS ALBERGHI

Executive — Fiorano Modenese
51 rooms, D. L. 270.000 — 3 km
Tel (39) 0536 832 010, Fax (39) 0536 830 229

La Fenice — Formigine
48 rooms, D. L. 145.000 — 3 km
Tel (39) 059 573 344, Fax (39) 059 573 455

Real Fini — Modena
91 rooms, D. L 360.000 — 20 km
Tel (39) 059 238 091, Fax (39) 059 364 804

RESTAURANTS RISTORANTE
Fini - Tel (39) 059 223 314 — Modena 15 km
Arnaldo-Clinica Gastronomica — Rubiera
Tel (39) 059 626 124 — 10 km
Borso d'Este - Tel (39) 059 214 114 — Modena 20 km

986

MOLINETTO

E' uno dei numerosi e più recenti golf intorno a Milano, sulla strada di Gorgonzola... Aperto nel 1983, il percorso ha ospitato dopo soli due anni l'Open d'Italia e da allora ha continuato a migliorarsi con movimenti del terreno. E' stato tracciato su un terreno assolutamente piatto con numerosi piccoli laghi molto spesso in gioco. I fairways sono logicamente stretti data la scarsa lunghezza del percorso e i greens di medie dimensioni sono abbastanza ben disegnati e ben difesi. Al Molinetto i promotori hanno cercato di raggiungere un bacino d'utenza molto vasto e non necessariamente composto da golfisti provetti per formare un grande circolo plurisportivo. Lo confermano la presenza di un campo pratica di grandi dimensioni, di una piscina e anche di numerosissimi campi da tennis.

This is one of the many and most recent golf courses of Milan on the road to Gorgonzola... Since is was opened in 1983, Molinetto has acquired an excellent reputation and even hosted the Italian Open after just two years. Since then, it has undergone a number of significant improvements, especially in terms of contouring. It is laid out over a plain with a whole number of little lakes that are frequently in play. The fairways are rather narrow, which may seem logical given the course's short yardage; likewise, the greens are not enormous but rather well designed and protected. Here again, the promoters set their sights on a wide customer base, without necessarily much experience of golf, in order to create a multi-sports club; whence the huge driving range, swimming pool and any number of tennis courts.

Molinetto Country Club — 1982

SS. Padana Superiore 11
I - 20063 CERNUSCO SUL NAVIGLIO (MI)

Office	Segreteria	(39) 02 921 051 28
Pro shop	Pro shop	(39) 02 921 499 54
Fax	Fax	(39) 02 921 066 35
Situation	Localita'	

Milano (pop. 1.302.808), 6 km

Annual closure	Chiusura annuale	no
Weekly closure	Chiusura settimanale	monday

Fees main season
Tariffe alta stagione 18 holes

	Week days Settimana	We/Bank holidays Feriale/Festivo
Individual Individuale	L. 80.000	L. 100.000
Couple Coppia	L. 160.000	L. 200.000

Caddy	Caddy	no
Electric Trolley	Carello elettrico	L. 10.000
Buggy	Car	no
Clubs	Bastoni	yes

Credit cards Carte di credito
VISA - Eurocard - MasterCard - AMEX - DC

Access Itinerario : Milano, Via Palmanova →
Vimodrome. S11 → Cernusco and Gorgonzola. Golf
on the left hand side
Map 1 on page 941 Carta 1 Pagina 941

GOLF COURSE / PERCORSO — 13/20

Site	Paesaggio	
Maintenance	Manutenzione	
Architect	Architetto	S. Carrera L. Rota Caremoli
Type	Tipologia	country, residential
Relief	Relievo terreno	
Water in play	Acqua in gioco	
Exp. to wind	Esposto al vento	
Trees in play	Alberi in gioco	

Scorecard Carta-score	Chp. Camp.	Mens Uomini	Ladies Donne
Length Lunghezza	5901	5901	5193
Par	71	71	71

Advised golfing ability Livello di gioco consigliato	0	12	24	36

Hcp required   Handicap richiesto 34

CLUB HOUSE & AMENITIES / CLUB HOUSE E SERVIZI — 9/10

Pro shop	Pro shop	
Driving range	Campo pratica	
Sheltered	coperto	4 mats
On grass	in erba	yes
Putting-green	Putting-green	yes
Pitching-green	Green-pratica	yes

HOTEL FACILITIES / ALBERGHI — 8/10

HOTELS ALBERGHI
Concorde — Cernusco sul Naviglio
37 rooms, D. L. 150.000 — 1 km
Tel (39) 02 921 005 49

Jolly Hotel Milano 2 — Segrate (Milano)
149 rooms, D. L. 300.000 — 10 km
Tel (39) 02 2175, Fax (39) 02 264 101 15

Country Hotel Borromeo — Peschiera Borromeo
75 rooms, D. L. 365.000 — 10 km
Tel (39) 02 547 5121, Fax (39) 02 553 007 08

RESTAURANTS RISTORANTE
Vecchia Filanda — Cernusco sul Naviglio 1 km
Tel (39) 02 924 9200

San Martino - Tel (39) 0363 490 75 — Treviglio 18 km
Osteria dei Fauni - Tel (39) 02 269 214 11 — Segrate 7 km
Aimo e Nadia - Tel (39) 02 416 886 — Milano 12 km

987

Questo percorso è stato aperto nel 1992 vicino alle stazioni termali di Abano Terme e Montegrotto e soprattutto a due passi dalla bella città di Padova, che per tanto tempo ha vissuto all'ombra della vicina Venezia. Ci si emozionerà davanti agli affreschi di Mantegna e Giotto e se avete già pregato S. Antonio da Padova per salvare qualcuno potrete farlo ancora a Montecchia per evitare gli ostacoli d'acqua disseminati in questo tracciato di Tom Macauley! Non ha avuto un compito facile su un terreno così piatto dove ha creato movimenti scavando e aggiungendo terra altrove. Le qualità tecniche del percorso, accessibile a giocatori di ogni livello, non impediscono la continuità nel gioco, ma ci si ricorda poco del tracciato a meno di averci giocato varie volte. Un altro percorso di 9 buche aggiunge maggior interesse a questo circolo molto piacevole.

This course was opened in 1992 close to the spa resorts of Abano Terme and Montegrotto Terme, and particularly within the vicinity of the fine city of Padua, which spent many a year in the shadows of neighbouring Venice. The frescoes of Mantegna and Giotto are exciting visiting. While in earlier times they used to pray to Saint Antonio de Padua for shipwrecked mariners, prayers can still be heard in Montecchia to avoid the water hazards that are very much in play on this Tom Macauley layout. Designing the course was no easy job on such flat land, but he succeeded in contouring the fairways by digging here to add over there. However, the technical qualities of the course, playable by golfers of all abilities, cannot conceal a slight problem of uniformity. This is not a layout that sticks in the mind, unless of course you play it several times. A 9-hole layout has added to the appeal of what is a very pleasant course.

Golf della Montecchia — 1992

Via Montecchia 16
I - 35030 SELVAZZANO DENTRO (PD)

Office	Segreteria	(39) 049 805 5550
Pro shop	Pro shop	(39) 049 805 5965
Fax	Fax	(39) 049 805 5737
Situation	Localita'	

Padova (pop. 211 985), 7 km
Venezia (pop. 293 731), 42 km

Annual closure	Chiusura annuale	no
Weekly closure	Chiusura settimanale	monday

Fees main season
Tariffe alta stagione 18 holes

	Week days Settimana	We/Bank holidays Feriale/Festivo
Individual Individuale	L. 90.000	L. 110.000
Couple Coppia	L. 180.000	L. 220.000

Caddy	Caddy	no
Electric Trolley	Carello elettrico	no
Buggy	Car	L. 65.000
Clubs	Bastoni	L. 30.000

Credit cards Carte di credito
VISA - Eurocard - MasterCard - AMEX - DC

988

Access Itinerario : A4 Verona-Venezia. Exit (Uscita) Padova-Ovest. Take the Corso Australia, right to Tencarola, right again → Selvazzano Dentro. → Golf
Map 2 on page 942 Carta 2 Pagina 942

GOLF COURSE PERCORSO — 13/20

Site	Paesaggio	
Maintenance	Manutenzione	
Architect	Architetto	Tom Macauley
Type	Tipologia	open country
Relief	Relievo terreno	
Water in play	Acqua in gioco	
Exp. to wind	Esposto al vento	
Trees in play	Alberi in gioco	

Scorecard Carta-score	Chp. Camp.	Mens Uomini	Ladies Donne
Length Lunghezza	6318	6078	5326
Par	72	72	72

Advised golfing ability	0	12	24	36
Livello di gioco consigliato				

Hcp required — Handicap richiesto 34

CLUB HOUSE & AMENITIES CLUB HOUSE E SERVIZI — 8/10

Pro shop	Pro shop	
Driving range	Campo pratica	
Sheltered	coperto	12 mats
On grass	in erba	yes
Putting-green	Putting-green	yes
Pitching-green	Green-pratica	yes

HOTEL FACILITIES ALBERGHI — 7/10

HOTELS ALBERGHI
La Piroga — Selvazzano Dentro
62 rooms, D. L. 150.000 — 3 km
Tel (39) 049 637 966, Fax (39) 049 637 966

Bristol Buja — Abano Terme
116 rooms, D. L. 230.000 — 6 km
Tel (39) 049 866 9390, Fax (39) 049 667 910

Donatello — Padova
49 rooms, D. L. 255.000 — 7 km
Tel (39) 049 875 0634, Fax (39) 049 875 0829

RESTAURANTS RISTORANTE
Le Calendre - Tel (39) 049 630 303 — Rubano 6 km
Relais — Selvazzano Dentro
Tel (39) 049 805 5323 — 2 km
Trattoria Casa Vecia — Monterosso
Tel (39) 049 860 0138 — 8 km

E' uno dei grandi classici italiani, reso celebre sia dai numerosi Open d'Italia che qui sono stati organizzati, che per la manutenzione molto accurata dei suoi due percorsi. A pochi chilometri, il delizioso lago di Como rende il posto perfetto per trascorrere lunghi fine settimana o piacevoli vacanze. Il percorso «rosso» è stato costruito in una pianura ornata da varie specie di alberi con le Alpi in sullo sfondo. Le difficoltà qui sono ben visibili e distribuite con saggezza per non infastidire troppo i giocatori medi e testare l'intelligenza e la tattica dei migliori che saranno i soli a poter pretendere di partire dalle partenze di campionato in particolare nei due lunghi par 3, dei quali la 7 con il green circondato dall'acqua. Comunque, i fairways sono abbastanza larghi, i rough non pericolosi e gli ostacoli più frequenti sono costituiti dai bunkers e dagli alberi. Questo bel percorso avrebbe senz'altro meritato un po' più di fantasia nel disegno.

This is one of the great classic courses in Italy, made famous by the Italian Open championships held here and by the very meticulous maintenance and green-keeping on both 18-hole courses. The wonderful lake Como, a few miles down the road, makes this a great spot for a week-end or longer holiday. The «Rosso» course is laid out in a plain lined with little copses and with the Alps as a backdrop. The difficulties are clearly in view and judiciously spread in order to avoid overwhelming the average player. Instead, they test the intelligence and tactical sense of the better golfers. What's more, only the better player will feel easy playing from the back-tees, particularly on the two very long par 3s, one green of which is surrounded by water (hole N° 7). Elsewhere, the fairways are rather wide, the rough can be dangerous and the most frequently encountered hazards are bunkers and trees. A good course but one which might have deserved a little more imagination from a graphical viewpoint.

Golf Club Monticello — 1974

Via Volta 4
I - 22070 CASSINA RIZZARDI (CO)

Office	Segreteria	(39) 031 928 055
Pro shop	Pro shop	(39) 031 928 003
Fax	Fax	(39) 031 880 207
Situation	Localita'	

Como (pop. 83.637), 11 km - Milano (pop. 1.302.808), 45 km

Annual closure	Chiusura annuale	no
Weekly closure	Chiusura settimanale	no

Fees main season
Tariffe alta stagione 18 holes

	Week days Settimana	We/Bank holidays Feriale/Festivo
Individual Individuale	L. 80.000	L. 120.000
Couple Coppia	L. 160.000	L. 240.000

No green-fees on week ends
(Ospiti solo durante i giorni feriali)

Caddy	Caddy	L. 40.000
Electric Trolley	Carello elettrico	no
Buggy	Car	L. 70.000
Clubs	Bastoni	L. 30.000

Credit cards Carte di credito — no

← Varese
S 342 — Olgiate Comasco
Binago — Lucino
GOLF
Como
A 9
Fino Mornasco
Appiano Gentile
0 — 2 — 4 km
Tradate — Guanzate
Lurago Marinone — Milano

Access Itinerario : Milano, A8 and A9 → Como. Exit (Uscita) Fino Mornasco. Turn left. Golf to the right.
Map 1 on page 941 Carta 1 Pagina 941

GOLF COURSE / PERCORSO — 14/20

Site	Paesaggio	
Maintenance	Manutenzione	
Architect	Architetto	Biratti, Cavalsani Fazio, Dassù
Type	Tipologia	country
Relief	Relievo terreno	
Water in play	Acqua in gioco	
Exp. to wind	Esposto al vento	
Trees in play	Alberi in gioco	

Scorecard Carta-score	Chp. Camp.	Mens Uomini	Ladies Donne
Length Lunghezza	6270	6047	5321
Par	72	72	72

Advised golfing ability — 0 12 24 36
Livello di gioco consigliato
Hcp required — Handicap richiesto 34

CLUB HOUSE & AMENITIES / CLUB HOUSE E SERVIZI — 8/10

Pro shop	Pro shop	
Driving range	Campo pratica	
Sheltered	coperto	8 mats
On grass	in erba	yes
Putting-green	Putting-green	yes
Pitching-green	Green-pratica	yes

HOTEL FACILITIES / ALBERGHI — 7/10

HOTELS ALBERGHI

Canturio		Cantù
30 rooms, D. L. 170.000		7 km
Tel (39) 031 716 035, Fax (39) 031 720 211		
Terminus		Como
37 rooms, D. L. 220.000		11 km
Tel (39) 031 329 111, Fax (39) 031 302 550		
Villa Flori		Como
44 rooms, D. L. 320.000		11 km
Tel (39) 031 573 105, Fax (39) 031 570 379		

RESTAURANTS RISTORANTE

Tradate		Tradate
Tel (39) 0331 841 401		10 km
Tarantola		Appiano Gentile
Tel (39) 031 930 990		3 km
Al Ponte - Tel (39) 031 712 561		Cantù 7 km

989

Costruito nella proprietà della scuderia che ha dato cavalli come Nearco e Ribot, questo grande circolo romano comprende 27 buche disegnate da Charles Kenneth Cotton e realizzate da Piero Mancinelli. Il percorso principale di 18 buche ha ricevuto tutti gli elogi in occasione delle due edizioni della World Cup nel 1968 e nel 1984. E' un percorso classico, dove l'acqua interviene soltanto su due buche perchè i maggiori ostacoli sono i numerosi alberi e i bunkers. Nei fairways questi ultimi sono penalizzanti sopratutto per i giocatori migliori e questo rassicurerà molto i visitatori. Abbastanza piatto ha tuttavia qualche buca con il drive cieco, ma senza eccessi: generalmente questo percorso non nasconde le sue difficoltà. Ogni buca ha il suo carattere e questo ne facilita la memorizzazione. Inoltre c'è sempre una piacevole sensazione di spazio e di isolamento tra un fairway e l'altro. Uno dei grandi percorsi italiani.

Built over a former horse-rearing estate which produced such horses as Nearco and Ribot, this great Roman club boasts 27 holes designed by Charles Kenneth Cotton and laid out by Piero Mancinelli. The main 18-hole course was much acclaimed during the 1968 and 1984 World Cups held here. This is a classic course, where water comes into play only on two holes and where the main hazards are the very many trees and bunkers. In the fairways, bunkers are most penalizing for the better players, which might reassure visitors. Rather flat, there are nonetheless a few holes where you are driving blind, but within reason: generally speaking, this course reveals what it has in store. Interestingly, each hole has its own character, so you remember them well. Each hole, too, gives a great sensation of space and isolation from one fairway to another. One of the great Italian courses.

Olgiata Golf Club — 1961

Largo Olgiata 15
I - 00123 ROMA

Office	Segreteria	(39) 06 3088 9141
Pro shop	Pro shop	(39) 06 3088 4344
Fax	Fax	(39) 06 3088 9968
Situation	Localita'	

Roma (pop. 2 653 245), 19 km

Annual closure	Chiusura annuale	no
Weekly closure	Chiusura settimanale	monday

Fees main season
Tariffe alta stagione full day

	Week days Settimana	We/Bank holidays Feriale/Festivo
Individual Individuale	L. 70.000	L. 120.000
Couple Coppia	L. 140.000	L. 240.000

Caddy	Caddy	no
Electric Trolley	Carello elettrico	no
Buggy	Car	L. 60.000
Clubs	Bastoni	L. 20.000

Credit cards Carte di credito
VISA - Eurocard - MasterCard - AMEX - DC - Cartasi

990

Access Itinerario : Roma, «Grande Raccordo Anulare» (Ring road), Exit (Uscita) Via Cassia.
S493 to the left → Bracciano, → Golf on the right.
Map 3 on page 945 Carta 3 Pagina 945

GOLF COURSE / PERCORSO — 16/20

Site	Paesaggio	
Maintenance	Manutenzione	
Architect	Architetto	Henry Cotton Piero Mancinelli
Type	Tipologia	parkland, residential
Relief	Relievo terreno	
Water in play	Acqua in gioco	
Exp. to wind	Esposto al vento	
Trees in play	Alberi in gioco	

Scorecard Carta-score	Chp. Camp.	Mens Uomini	Ladies Donne
Length Lunghezza	6347	6054	5306
Par	72	72	72

Advised golfing ability — 0 12 24 36
Livello di gioco consigliato
Hcp required — Handicap richiesto 34

CLUB HOUSE & AMENITIES / CLUB HOUSE E SERVIZI — 7/10

Pro shop	Pro shop	
Driving range	Campo pratica	
Sheltered	coperto	8 mats
On grass	in erba	yes
Putting-green	Putting-green	yes
Pitching-green	Green-pratica	yes

HOTEL FACILITIES / ALBERGHI — 6/10

HOTELS ALBERGHI
Relais I Due Laghi   Le Cerque(Anguillaria Sabazia)
28 rooms, D. L. 250.000   12 km
Tel (39) 06 9960 7059, Fax (39) 06 9960 7068

Villa San Dominique   Roma (Via Cassia)
62 rooms, D. L. 210.000   8 km

Tel (39) 06 3036 0147Colony Flaminio   Roma
28 rooms, D. L. 230.000   12 km
Tel (39) 06 3630 1843, Fax (39) 06 3630 9495

RESTAURANTS RISTORANTE
Chalet del Lago   Anguilleria Sabazia
Tel (39) 06 9960 7053   10 km

Il Grottino da Norina   Anguilleria Sabazia
Tel (39) 06 996 8181   10 km

L'Ortica - Tel (39) 06 3338 709   Roma 12 km

E' il campo più vicino a Montecchia, realizzato su un terreno praticamente piatto ai piedi dei Colli Euganei, colline di origine vulcanica colme di frutteti e di vigne da dove sgorgano le sorgenti termali, conosciute fin dall'epoca dei Romani che hanno dato origine alle stazioni di Abano Terme ed altre vicine. Il percorso disegnato da John Harris è di buona qualità e si adatta alla maggioranza dei giocatori. Qualche ostacolo d'acqua è stato scavato in modo da poter recuperare terra per effettuare qualche movimento in superficie. Le buche più pericolose vanno dalla 5 alla 8. Agli alberi esistenti, sono stati aggiunti molti altri arbusti che crescono velocemente. Il tracciato non esige virtuosismi particolari e i migliori giocatori qui potranno brillare con una certa facilità. Un percorso abbastanza corto, di solito molto frequentato nei week-end (la club-house è enorme ed ha 15 camere a disposizione) e piacevole per giocare con tutta la famiglia.

This is the neighbouring course to Montecchia, on flat terrain at the foot of the Colli Euganei, volcanic hills dotted with orchards and vineyards and the source of hot springs already appreciated by the ancient Romans. They spawned a number of spa resorts, including Abano Terme and others in the same region. This course, designed by John Harris, is quality golfing and ideal for most players. A few water hazards have been dug out to collect some welcome earth with which to contour the course elsewhere, and are particularly dangerous from hole 5 to hole 8. The existing vegetation has been supplemented by many others trees and bushes, which are growing slowly but surely. The layout does not require any special skills and the best players might card a good score without being unduly tested. A rather short course, often busy on week-ends (the club-house is huge with 15 guestrooms) and pleasant to play with all the family.

Golf Club Padova — 1964

Via Noiera 57
I - 35030 VALSANZIBIO DI GALZIGNANO TERME (PA)

Office	Segreteria	(39) 049 913 0078
Pro shop	Pro shop	(39) 049 913 1140
Fax	Fax	(39) 049 913 1193
Situation	Localita'	

Padova (pop. 211.985), 17 km
Venezia (pop. 293.731), 40 km

Annual closure	Chiusura annuale	no
Weekly closure	Chiusura settimanale	monday

Fees main season
Tariffe alta stagione 18 holes

	Week days Settimana	We/Bank holidays Feriale/Festivo
Individual Individuale	L. 90.000	L. 110.000
Couple Coppia	L. 180.000	L. 220.000
Caddy Caddy		no
Electric Trolley Carello elettrico		yes
Buggy Car		L. 50.000
Clubs Bastoni		no

Credit cards Carte di credito
VISA - Eurocard - MasterCard

PADOVA Abano Terme
Montegrotto Terme
GOLF
Galzignano Terme
Cataio
Valsanzibio
Arquà Petrarca
Monselice
Rovigo
A 13
S 16
0 2 4 km

Access Itinerario : A13 Padova-Bologna. Exit (Uscita) Terme Euganee. In Battaglia Terme, turn right. 6 km, Galzignano. Turn left → Valsanzibio. Golf on the left
Map 2 on page 942 Carta 2 Pagina 942

GOLF COURSE / PERCORSO — 14/20

Site	Paesaggio	▓▓▓▓▓░░
Maintenance	Manutenzione	▓▓▓▓▓░░
Architect	Architetto	John Harris
Type	Tipologia	country
Relief	Relievo terreno	▓▓░░░░░
Water in play	Acqua in gioco	▓▓▓░░░░
Exp. to wind	Esposto al vento	▓▓▓░░░░
Trees in play	Alberi in gioco	▓▓▓▓░░░

Scorecard Carta-score	Chp. Camp.	Mens Uomini	Ladies Donne
Length Lunghezza	6053	5920	5328
Par	72	72	72

Advised golfing ability
Livello di gioco consigliato — 0 12 24 36
Hcp required Handicap richiesto 34

CLUB HOUSE & AMENITIES / CLUB HOUSE E SERVIZI — 7/10

Pro shop	Pro shop	▓▓▓▓░░░
Driving range	Campo pratica	▓▓▓▓▓░░
Sheltered	coperto	10 mats
On grass	in erba	yes
Putting-green	Putting-green	yes
Pitching-green	Green-pratica	yes

HOTEL FACILITIES / ALBERGHI — 7/10

HOTELS ALBERGHI

Majestic Hotel Terme — Galzignano Terme
94 rooms, D. L. 225.000 — 1 km
Tel (39) 049 919 4000, Fax (39) 049 919 4250

Sporting Hotel Terme — Galzignano Terme
92 rooms, D. L. 230.000 — 1 km
Tel (39) 049 919 5000, Fax (39) 049 919 5250

Green Park Hotel Terme — Galzignano Terme
86 rooms, D. L. 215.000 — 1 km
Tel (39) 049 919 7000, Fax (39) 049 919 7250

RESTAURANTS RISTORANTE

Antico Brolo - Tel (39) 049 664 555 — Padova 17 km

Belle Parti-Toulá — Padova
Tel (39) 049 875 1822 — 17 km

La Montanella — Arquà Petrarca
Tel (39) 0429 718 200 — 3 km

991

PALAZZO ARZAGA ❋ 15 | 8 | 8

Con un tale numero di percorsi di assoluta qualità nella regione dei laghi in Lombardia, stiamo vedendo nascere una vera destinazione golfistica in paesaggi da sogno e a due passi da grandi città turistiche , commerciali e artistiche come Milano o ancora Brescia e Verona. Il nuovo golf di Palazzo Arzaga si trova tra queste due ultime città, appena sopra al lago di Garda. Aperto nel 1998, è un complesso ambizioso, con un hotel sontuoso in una antica villa, tennis, spa di Saturnia e la piscina (riservata ai soci). In questo bel posto che comprenderà 36 buche con un altro tracciato disegnato da Gary Player, il figlio di Jack Nicklaus ha disegnato un percorso di stile assolutamente americano, con pochi alberi in gioco, ma con molti ostacoli d'acqua e bunkers. I greens sono grandi, a volte a due livelli o sopraelevati e il loro pendenze contribuiscono a rendere difficile la riuscita di un buono score. Questo percorso è comunque adatto a tutti i livelli di gioco ma deve un po' maturare prima di passare dallo stadio dei «buoni» percorsi a quello dei «grandi».

With so many top class courses in the region of the Lombardy lakes, we could be witnessing the birth of a real golfing destination, set in dream landscapes within the.immediate vicinity of major tourist, business and cultural cities such as Milan or even Brescia and Verona. The new Palazzo Arzaga course lies between these two cities just above lake Garda. This is an ambitious resort opened in 1998 with a sumptuous hotel in a patrician villa, tennis courts, a spa as at Saturnia and swimming pool (reserved for members). In this very fine site, which will eventually comprise 36 holes of golf (Gary Player is designing a second course), Jack Nicklaus Junior has designed a bltantly American-styled layout with few trees coming into play but a lot of water and sand. The greens are huge, sometimes tiered and elevated and contoured enough to compound the task of carding a good score here. Still, the course is playable by everyone but needs a little maturing before moving up from the rating of «good» course to «great» course.

Palazzo Arzaga — 1998

Loc. Carzago
I - 25080 CAVALGESE DELLA RIVIERA

Office	Segreteria	(39) 030 680 600
Pro shop	Pro shop	(39) 030 680 6171
Fax	Fax	(39) 030 680 178
Situation	Localita'	

Brescia (pop. 190 518), 28 km - Verona (pop. 254 748), 45 km

Annual closure	Chiusura annuale	no
Weekly closure	Chiusura settimanale	no

Fees main season
Tariffe alta stagione 18 holes

	Week days Settimana	We/Bank holidays Feriale/Festivo
Individual Individuale	L. 95.000	L. 125.000
Couple Coppia	L. 190.000	L. 250.000

Caddy	Caddy	no
Electric Trolley	Carello elettrico	L. 15.000
Buggy	Car	L. 60.000
Clubs	Bastoni	L. 40.000

Credit cards Carte di credito
VISA - Eurocard - MasterCard - AMEX - DC

992

Access Itinerario : A4 Milano-Venezia. Exit (Uscita) Desenzano. Turn left, then left again → Brescia. → Sedena. 2 km turn right. 300 m to the left.
Map 1 on page 941 Carta 1 Pagina 941

GOLF COURSE / PERCORSO — 15/20

Site	Paesaggio	
Maintenance	Manutenzione	
Architect	Architetto	Jack Nicklaus Jr
Type	Tipologia	country
Relief	Relievo terreno	
Water in play	Acqua in gioco	
Exp. to wind	Esposto al vento	
Trees in play	Alberi in gioco	

Scorecard Carta-score	Chp. Camp.	Mens Uomini	Ladies Donne
Length Lunghezza	6062	5885	5220
Par	72	72	72

Advised golfing ability Livello di gioco consigliato	0	12	24	36

Hcp required Handicap richiesto 34

CLUB HOUSE & AMENITIES / CLUB HOUSE E SERVIZI — 8/10

Pro shop	Pro shop	
Driving range	Campo pratica	
Sheltered	coperto	10 mats
On grass	in erba	yes
Putting-green	Putting-green	yes
Pitching-green	Green-pratica	yes

HOTEL FACILITIES / ALBERGHI — 8/10

HOTELS ALBERGHI
Palazzo Arzaga Golf e Spa — Cavalgese
80 rooms, D. L. 630.000 — on site
Tel (39) 030 680 600, Fax (39) 030 680 178

Park Hotel — Desenzano del Garda
57 rooms, D. L. 210.000 — 7,5 km
Tel (39) 030 914 3494, Fax (39) 030 914 2280

Grand Hotel Fasano — Fasano
75 rooms, D. L. 450.000 — 15 km
Tel (39) 0365 290 220, Fax (39) 0365 290 221

RESTAURANTS RISTORANTE
Esplanade — Desenzano del Garda
Tel (39) 030 914 3361 — 7,5 km

Villa Fiordaliso — Gardone Riviera
Tel (39) 0365 20 158 — 10 km

Locanda Santa Giulia — Padenghe sul Garda
Tel (39) 030 99 950 — 5 km

PARCO DE' MEDICI

Il percorso di 18 buche è stato completato da altre 9 buche (par 34). E' stato parzialmente costruito su di una tenuta di caccia usata da Papa Leone X nel XV secolo. Si trova molto vicino al centro di Roma e all'aeroporto e questo ne facilita l'accesso. Il terreno è molto piatto e la sua monotonia è rotta da qualche movimento del terreno e dai numerosi laghi nei quali si possono vedere numerosi uccelli... Ma anche la propria palla tuffarsi se non si è precisi. Abbastanza lungo dalle partenze arretrate è molto più facile quando si ha la modestia di partire dalle partenze avanti anche se non stimola particolarmente la fantasia. Disegnato da David Mezzacane e Peter Fazio, Parco dei Medici rappresenta bene l'architettura moderna molto strategica, con grandi greens ben protetti dove bisogna giocare preferibilmente un «target golf». Una grande club-house, un albergo, una piscina e due tennis in erba completano questa struttura di buon livello.

The 18-hole course has been supplemented by a 9-holer (par 34) and was partly laid out over a former hunting estate belonging to Pope Leon X in the 15th century. For easy access, the course is within the immediate vicinity of downtown Rome and the airport. The terrain is very flat but the monotony is broken by contouring and the very many stretches of water that are home to a good many birds and a resting place for even more balls if you don't hit it straight. Rather long from the back-tees and very exposed to the wind, the layout is much easier when you are humble enough to move further forward, but somehow it doesn't leave a lasting impression. Designed by David Mezzacane and Peter Fazio, Parco de' Medici clearly portrays the highly strategic modern style of course architecture with large, well-guarded greens and a preference for target golf. A huge club-house, grand hotel, a pool and two grass tennis courts complete the very high standard facilities here.

Golf Club Parco de' Medici — 1990

Viale Parco de' Medici 165/167
I - 00148 ROMA

Office	Segreteria	(39) 06 655 3477
Pro shop	Pro shop	(39) 06 655 3477
Fax	Fax	(39) 06 655 3344
Situation	Localita'	

close to Roma (pop. 2 653 245)

Annual closure	Chiusura annuale	no
Weekly closure	Chiusura settimanale	tuesday

Fees main season
Tariffe alta stagione 18 holes

	Week days Settimana	We/Bank holidays Feriale/Festivo
Individual Individuale	L. 90.000	L. 100.000
Couple Coppia	L. 180.000	L. 200.000

Caddy	Caddy	L. 50.000
Electric Trolley	Carello elettrico	no
Buggy	Car	L. 50.000
Clubs	Bastoni	L. 25.000

Credit cards Carte di credito
VISA - Eurocard - MasterCard - AMEX - DC - Cartasi

Access Itinerario : Roma, → Fiumicino,
Exit (Uscita) Magliana Vecchia. → Golf
Map 3 on page 945 Carta 3 Pagina 945

GOLF COURSE / PERCORSO — 13/20

Site	Paesaggio	
Maintenance	Manutenzione	
Architect	Architetto	David Mezzacane
Type	Tipologia	residential
Relief	Relievo terreno	
Water in play	Acqua in gioco	
Exp. to wind	Esposto al vento	
Trees in play	Alberi in gioco	

Scorecard Carta-score	Chp. Camp.	Mens Uomini	Ladies Donne
Length Lunghezza	6303	5908	5200
Par	71	71	71

Advised golfing ability 0 12 24 36
Livello di gioco consigliato
Hcp required Handicap richiesto 34

CLUB HOUSE & AMENITIES / CLUB HOUSE E SERVIZI — 7/10

Pro shop	Pro shop	
Driving range	Campo pratica	
Sheltered	coperto	9 mats
On grass	in erba	yes
Putting-green	Putting-green	yes
Pitching-green	Green-pratica	yes

HOTEL FACILITIES / ALBERGHI — 9/10

HOTELS ALBERGHI

Sheraton Golf Parco de' Medici — Roma — 300 m
285 rooms, D. L. 335.000
Tel (39) 06 658 588, Fax (39) 06 658 587 42

Holiday Inn Parco de' Medici — Roma — 500 m
317 rooms, D. L. 450.000
Tel (39) 06 65 581, Fax (39) 06 657 7005

Dei Congressi — Roma — 10 km
105 rooms, D. L. 260.000
Tel (39) 06 592 6021, Fax (39) 06 591 1903

RESTAURANTS RISTORANTE

Checchino del 1887 — Roma — 12 km
Tel (39) 06 574 6318

Il Convivio — Roma — 12 km
Tel (39) 06 686 9432

Quinzi Gabrieli - Tel (39) 06 687 9389 — Roma 12 km

993

Questa regione chiamata Costa Smeralda è stata scoperta turisticamente nel 1961, sotto la spinta di un gruppo di investitori guidati da Karim Aga Khan. E' diventata una delle regioni preferite dal «jet-set» con ville da sogno, porti turistici, tennis-club e con il Golf del Pevero, fiore all'occhiello del luogo, quasi di fronte al non meno famoso (e più recente) Golf di Sperone in Corsica. I due campi sono stati disegnati da Robert Trent Jones. Il Pevero è sontuoso, scavato in mezzo alle rocce coperte di macchia mediterranea, interrotte da scorci stupendi e da un mare dai mille colori. Il disegno impone strategia e la lunghezza è relativa, ma ci vuole molta tecnica per fare un buono score. E' un percorso fantastico per un match-play soprattutto quando il vento soffia forte da un momento all'altro: diventa allora veramente difficile contare i propri (numerosi) colpi. Un luogo di vacanza da sogno...

This region, known as the Costa Smeralda, began to be exploited as tourist material in 1961, spurred on by Karim Aga Khan and a consortium of investors. It has become one of the jet-set's favourite playgrounds with its palace hotels, marinas, tennis clubs and the site's crowning glory, the Pevero golf course, lying almost directly opposite the no less famous (and more recent) Golf de Sperone in Corsica. Both were designed by Robert Trent Jones. The Pevero site is simply sumptuous, between tree-covered hills, a rocky coastline broken only by some splendid coves and a sea of ever changing colour. This layout is highly strategic, yardage is a matter of relative importance and a good score calls for the virtuosity of a fine technician. This is a marvellous course for match-play golf, especially when the wind blows, as it does on occasions. In this case counting your strokes (certainly more than you bargained for) is meaningless. A dream holiday location.

Pevero Golf Club — 1971
Loc. Cala di Volpe
I - 07020 PORTO CERVO (SS)

Office	Segreteria	(39) 0789 96 210
Pro shop	Pro shop	(39) 0789 96 210
Fax	Fax	(39) 0789 96 572
Situation	Localita'	

Olbia (pop. 44.600), 30 km

Annual closure	Chiusura annuale	no
Weekly closure	Chiusura settimanale	tuesday

Fees main season
Tariffe alta stagione full day

	Week days Settimana	We/Bank holidays Feriale/Festivo
Individual Individuale	L. 120.000	L. 225.000
Couple Coppia	L. 240.000	L. 450.000

GF with mandatory golf car (con obbligo del cart compreso nel prezzo)

Caddy	Caddy	no
Electric Trolley	Carello elettrico	no
Buggy	Car	yes
Clubs	Bastoni	L. 75.000

Credit cards Carte di credito
VISA - Eurocard - MasterCard - AMEX - DC

994

GOLF COURSE
PERCORSO — 16/20

Site	Paesaggio	▆▆▆▆▆▃
Maintenance	Manutenzione	▆▆▆▆▆▆
Architect	Architetto	R. Trent Jones Sr
Type	Tipologia	seaside course
Relief	Relievo terreno	▆▆▆▆▆▃
Water in play	Acqua in gioco	▆▆▃
Exp. to wind	Esposto al vento	▆▆▆▆▆▃
Trees in play	Alberi in gioco	▆▆▆▃

Scorecard Carta-score	Chp. Camp.	Mens Uomini	Ladies Donne
Length Lunghezza	6150	5858	5135
Par	72	72	72

Advised golfing ability Livello di gioco consigliato	0	12	24	36

Hcp required   Handicap richiesto 34

CLUB HOUSE & AMENITIES
CLUB HOUSE E SERVIZI — 8/10

Pro shop	Pro shop	▆▆▆▆▆▆
Driving range	Campo pratica	▆▆▆▆▆▃
Sheltered	coperto	5 mats
On grass	in erba	yes
Putting-green	Putting-green	yes
Pitching-green	Green-pratica	yes

HOTEL FACILITIES
ALBERGHI — 8/10

HOTELS ALBERGHI

Cala di Volpe — Cala di Volpe
123 rooms, D. L. 925.000 — 1 km
Tel (39) 0789 976 111, Fax (39) 0789 976 617

Cervo & Conference Center — Porto Cervo
108 rooms, D.L. 1.100.000 — 5 km
Tel (39) 0789 931 111, Fax (39) 0789 931 613

Nibaru — Cala di Volpe
45 rooms, D. L. 320.000 — 2 km
Tel (39) 0789 96 038, Fax (39) 0789 96 474

RESTAURANTS RISTORANTE

Gianni Pedrinelli — Porto Cervo
Tel (39) 0789 92 436 — 3 km

Casablanca — Baia Sardinia
Tel (39) 0789 99 006 — 10 km

La Conchiglia - Tel (39) 0789 99 864 Baia Sardinia 6 km

Access Itinerario : Olbia → Porto Cervo (Costa Smeralda). Golf on the right hand side.
Map 4 on page 947 Carta 4 Pagina 947

A Firenze non c'è solo Firenze. C'è anche una campagna meravigliosa, dolce, affascinante e naturalmente equilibrata. In mezzo a colline coperte di vigne, olivi, pini e cipressi, con una cucina raffinata e vini stupendi, si può pensare che il tempo si sia fermato. Il nome di questo golf (la collina dei Medici) riassume la storia e il paesaggio di Firenze. Bisognerà attendere che gli alberi crescano per vedere l'aspetto definitivo di questo percorso aperto nel 1992 in uno spazio molto vasto. Il lavoro effettuato dal campione italiano Baldovino Dassù e dall' architetto Alvise Rossi Fioravanti è stato pieno di fantasia, per come è stato utilizzato il terreno, come sono stati disegnati fairways e greens e per come sono stati fatti entrare in gioco gli ostacoli: rough, bunkers e acqua. Molto ondulato, esige una buona forma fisica. Su questo percorso difficile, si consiglia di giocare dalle partenze normali, a meno di essere veramente di livello superiore. Se giocherete qui una volta sola, il match-play è la formula migliore per divertirsi.

Florence is a little more than just the city of Florence; there is also some wonderfully sweet and charming countryside where everything is visual and natural harmony. In the middle of hills covered with vines, olive, pine and cypress trees, and in a land of sophisticated food and admirable wines, you could be forgiven for thinking that time has stood still. The name of this course («The Hill of the Medici») sums up both the history and landscape of Florence. However, the trees here will need to grow a little before the course fully matures. It was opened in 1992 over very wide open space and designed by the Italian champion Baldovino Dassù and course architect Alvise Rossi Fioravanti. They have showed a great deal of imagination in the way they used the terrain, contoured the fairways and greens and brought hazards into play, namely rough, sand and water. A very hilly course which is better played by the fitter golfer, and a difficult one, too, where the front tees are to be advised unless you can boast a single-figure handicap.

Poggio dei Medici Golf Club		**1992**
Via San Gavino 27		
I - 50038 SCARPERIA (FI)		
Office	Segreteria	(39) 055 843 0436
Pro shop	Pro shop	(39) 055 843 0436
Fax	Fax	(39) 055 843 0439
Situation	Localita'	
Firenze (pop. 379 687), 25 km		
Annual closure	Chiusura annuale	no
Weekly closure	Chiusura settimanale	tuesday

Fees main season
Tariffe alta stagione 18 holes

	Week days Settimana	We/Bank holidays Feriale/Festivo
Individual Individuale	L. 78.000	L. 96.000
Couple Coppia	L. 156.000	L. 192.000

Caddy	Caddy	L. 50.000
Electric Trolley	Carello elettrico	no
Buggy	Car	L. 50.000
Clubs	Bastoni	L. 35.000

Credit cards Carte di credito
VISA - Eurocard - MasterCard - AMEX - DC - Cartasi

Access Itinerario : Firenze, S65 → Bologna,
→ San Pietro a Sieve, → Gabbiano.
Map 3 on page 944 Carta 3 Pagina 944

GOLF COURSE
PERCORSO

16/20

Site	Paesaggio	
Maintenance	Manutenzione	
Architect	Architetto	Baldovino Dassù A. Rossi Fioravanti
Type	Tipologia	country
Relief	Relievo terreno	
Water in play	Acqua in gioco	
Exp. to wind	Esposto al vento	
Trees in play	Alberi in gioco	

Scorecard Carta-score	Chp. Camp.	Mens Uomini	Ladies Donne
Length Lunghezza	6338	6082	5352
Par	73	73	73

Advised golfing ability
Livello di gioco consigliato

0   12   24   36

Hcp required Handicap richiesto 34

CLUB HOUSE & AMENITIES
CLUB HOUSE E SERVIZI

7/10

Pro shop	Pro shop	
Driving range	Campo pratica	
Sheltered	coperto	5 mats
On grass	in erba	yes
Putting-green	Putting-green	yes
Pitching-green	Green-pratica	yes

995

HOTEL FACILITIES
ALBERGHI

7/10

HOTELS ALBERGHI
Park Hotel Ripaverde   Borgo San Lorenzo
57 rooms, D. L. 300.000   8 km
Tel (39) 055 849 6003, Fax (39) 055 845 9379

Villa Campestri   Campestri (Vicchio)
15 rooms, D. L. 270.000   15 km
Tel (39) 055 849 0107, Fax (39) 055 849 0108

Villa San Michele   Fiesole
26 rooms, D. L. 1.580.000   20 km
Tel (39) 055 59 451, Fax (39) 055 598 734

RESTAURANTS RISTORANTE
Fattoria Il Palagio   Scarperia
Tel (39) 055 846 376   2 km

La Panacea del Bartolini   Olmo
Tel (39) 055 548 972   20 km

Il Feriolo   Borgo San Lorenzo
Tel (39) 055 840 9928   5 km

Non lontano dalla città storica di Siena (che merita parecchi giorni di visita), in faccia alla Corsica, vicino a importanti stazioni balneari, Punta Ala è un luogo di vacanze di primo ordine per tutta la famiglia e la qualità del golf permette ai giocatori di passare dei momenti sia divertenti che di buon agonismo. Disegnato da Giulio Cavalsani all'inizio degli anni 60 si snoda su di un terreno molto accidentato (il golf-cart è consigliato) che obbliga a riflettere in continuazione. La presenza costante di alberi, complica ancora di più la situazione per coloro che cercano di fare un buono score: diventa allora indispensabile saper «lavorare» bene la palla in tutte le direzioni per uscire dalla pineta quando ci si è finiti dentro. Abbastanza lungo dalle partenze arretrate, è più piacevole dalle partenze normali. In un posto molto tranquillo, un campo ben riuscito.

Not far from the historical city of Sienna (worth a visit of several days), opposite Corsica and next to some top seaside resorts, Punta Ala is a first-rate holiday destination for all the family. The excellence of the golf course also means that golfers can both have fun and get down to some serious golfing. Designed by Giulio Cavalsani in the early 1960s, it is laid out over some very hilly terrain (buggy recommended) which calls for unwavering concentration. In addition, the unending presence of trees complicates matters still further if you are looking, say, to break 90. You simply have to be able to work the ball in all directions to get that mis-hit ball safely out of the pine trees. Rather a long course from the back tees, Punta Ala is much kinder when you tee off further forward. A pretty course in a very calm setting.

Golf Club Punta Ala — 1964

Via del Golf 1
I - 58040 PUNTA ALA (GR)

Office	Segreteria	(39) 0564 922 121
Pro shop	Pro shop	(39) 0564 922 420
Fax	Fax	(39) 0564 920 182
Situation	Localita'	

Grosseto (pop. 72.453), 35 km

Annual closure	Chiusura annuale	no
Weekly closure	Chiusura settimanale	no

Fees main season
Tariffe alta stagione 18 holes

	Week days Settimana	We/Bank holidays Feriale/Festivo
Individual Individuale	L. 100.000	L. 100.000
Couple Coppia	L. 200.000	L. 200.000

Caddy	Caddy	no
Electric Trolley	Carello elettrico	no
Buggy	Car	L. 60.000
Clubs	Bastoni	L. 30.000

Credit cards Carte di credito
VISA - Eurocard - MasterCard - DC - Cartasi

996

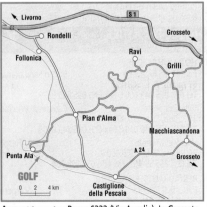

Access Itinerario : Roma S322 (Via Aurelia). In Grosseto, → Castiglione della Pescaia and Punta Ala
Map 3 on page 944 Carta 3 Pagina 944

GOLF COURSE / PERCORSO — 14/20

Site	Paesaggio	
Maintenance	Manutenzione	
Architect	Architetto	Giulio Cavalsani
Type	Tipologia	forest
Relief	Relievo terreno	
Water in play	Acqua in gioco	
Exp. to wind	Esposto al vento	
Trees in play	Alberi in gioco	

Scorecard Carta-score	Chp. Camp.	Mens Uomini	Ladies Donne
Length Lunghezza	6213	6036	5311
Par	72	72	72

Advised golfing ability	0	12	24	36
Livello di gioco consigliato				

Hcp required Handicap richiesto 34

CLUB HOUSE & AMENITIES / CLUB HOUSE E SERVIZI — 7/10

Pro shop	Pro shop	
Driving range	Campo pratica	
Sheltered	coperto	6 mats
On grass	in erba	yes
Putting-green	Putting-green	yes
Pitching-green	Green-pratica	yes

HOTEL FACILITIES / ALBERGHI — 8/10

HOTELS ALBERGHI

Golf Hotel Porto Laconia — Punta Ala
106 rooms, D. L. 250.000 — 500 m
Tel (39) 0564 922 026

Gallia Palace Hotel — Punta Ala
78 rooms, D. L. 620.000 — 2 km
Tel (39) 0564 922 022, Fax (39) 0564 920 229

Hotel Alleluja — Punta Ala
38 rooms, D. L. 850.000 — 1,5 km
Tel (39) 0564 922 050, Fax (39) 0564 920 734

RESTAURANTS RISTORANTE

Corallo — Castiglione della Pescaia
Tel (39) 0564 933 668 — 12 km

Pierbacco — Castiglione della Pescaia
Tel (39) 0564 933 522 — 12 km

Lo Scalino - Tel (39) 0564 922 168 — Punta Ala 1 km

Come molti golf europei Rapallo è nato vicino ad un luogo di villeggiatura situato nella parte orientale della Riviera, più mossa e selvaggia della parte occidentale, da Genova a Ventimiglia. Rapallo è una delle più eleganti stazioni balneari italiane e il percorso si snoda sulle colline che la circondano. Di lunghezza ridotta, ma rispettabile al momento della costruzione negli anni 30, il percorso non ha che due par 5 (la 2 e la 7) quattro par 3 e dodici par 4 tra i 255 e i 385 metri. L'architetto ha seguito armoniosamente i movimenti del terreno per fare il tracciato facendo entrare in gioco alberi e corsi d'acqua come ostacoli naturali. I greens di taglia piccola obbligano a molta precisione con gli approcci dato che sono oltretutto molto ben difesi. Un golf piacevole da giocare tra amici, relativamente facile dalle partenze normali, che permette di emergere senza troppi sforzi.

Like many continental golf courses, Rapallo was designed near a holiday centre on the eastern side of the Riviera, a steeper and wilder section of coastline than further west, running from Genoa to Ventimiglia. Rapallo is one of Italy's most elegant seaside resorts and the golf course is laid out over the hills that overlook the town below. Today considered a short course (although this sort of yardage was quite respectable in the 1930s when it was first laid out), Rapallo has only two par 5s (the 2nd and 7th holes), four par 3s and twelve par 4s of between 255 and 385 metres. The architect used the terrain's natural contours to build a smoothly flowing layout, playing with trees and water as natural hazards. The small greens calls for accurate approach shots, especially since they are well guarded. A pleasant course for a round with friends and relatively easy from the front tees. A good opportunity to shine without too much effort.

Circolo Golf e Tennis Rapallo — 1930
Via Mameli 377
I - 16035 RAPALLO (GE)

Office	Segreteria	(39) 0185 261 777
Pro shop	Pro shop	(39) 0185 261 777
Fax	Fax	(39) 0185 261 779
Situation	Localita'	

Rapallo (pop. 28 176), 2 km
Genova (pop. 659 754), 50 km

Annual closure	Chiusura annuale	no
Weekly closure	Chiusura settimanale	tuesday

Fees main season
Tariffe alta stagione full day

	Week days Settimana	We/Bank holidays Feriale/Festivo
Individual Individuale	L. 80.000	L. 120.000
Couple Coppia	L. 160.000	L. 240.000

Caddy	Caddy	L. 35.000
Electric Trolley	Carello elettrico	no
Buggy	Car	L. 55.000
Clubs	Bastoni	L. 15.000

Credit cards Carte di credito
VISA - Eurocard - MasterCard - AMEX - DC

Access Itinerario : A12 Genova-Livorno. Exit (Uscita)
Rapallo → Centro Cittadino. Golf 200 m on the right.
Map 1 on page 941 Carta 1 Pagina 941

GOLF COURSE / PERCORSO — 13/20

Site	Paesaggio	
Maintenance	Manutenzione	
Architect	Architetto	
Type	Tipologia	country, hilly
Relief	Relievo terreno	
Water in play	Acqua in gioco	
Exp. to wind	Esposto al vento	
Trees in play	Alberi in gioco	

Scorecard Carta-score	Chp. Camp.	Mens Uomini	Ladies Donne
Length Lunghezza	5625	5625	4955
Par	70	70	70

Advised golfing ability — 0 12 24 36
Livello di gioco consigliato
Hcp required — Handicap richiesto 34

CLUB HOUSE & AMENITIES / CLUB HOUSE E SERVIZI — 7/10

Pro shop	Pro shop	
Driving range	Campo pratica	
Sheltered	coperto	15 mats
On grass	in erba	no
Putting-green	Putting-green	yes
Pitching-green	Green-pratica	yes

HOTEL FACILITIES / ALBERGHI — 8/10

HOTELS ALBERGHI

Excelsior Palace Hotel — Rapallo
131 rooms, D. L. 580.000 — 2 km
Tel (39) 0185 230 666, Fax (39) 0185 230 214

Rosabianca — Rapallo
16 rooms, D. L. 300.000 — 1,5 km
Tel (39) 0185 50 390, Fax (39) 0185 65 035

Astoria — Rapallo
19 rooms, D. L. 280.000 — 1,5 km
Tel (39) 0185 273 533, Fax (39) 0185 62 793

RESTAURANTS RISTORANTE

Hostaria Vecchia Rapallo — Rapallo
Tel (39) 0185 50 053 — 2 km

Luca - Tel (39) 0185 60 323 — Rapallo 2,5 km

Eden - Tel (39) 0185 50 553 — Rapallo 2 km

997

Questa parte della Puglia non è la più conosciuta dai turisti stranieri, ma si dovrebbe assistere alla processione della settimana Santa a Taranto per entrare nella dimensione religiosa del profondo sud, o ancora andare a visitare più a nord la stupefacente città di Matera con le sue case rudimentali. A Taranto c'è anche il Museo Archeologico Nazionale che fa rivivere in modo particolare la presenza greca nell'antichità. Infine la costa, disseminata di spiagge immense, come il lido di Metaponto, è un posto di vacanza di tutto rispetto. Il percorso di Riva dei Tessali è uno dei rari nel sud Italia. I numerosi alberi assicurano l'ombra, molto spesso gradita e nello stesso tempo sono una delle principali difficoltà del percorso insieme agli ostacoli d'acqua. Disegnato da Marco Croze, non è molto lungo ma i greens di medie dimensioni sono ben difesi. Potrebbe essere più spettacolare, ma almeno è un percorso alla portata di tutti.

The region of Apulia is hardly the part of Italy best known to foreign tourists, yet the Holy Week processions in Taranto (they give great insight into the depth of religious feeling in southern Italy) and a trip to the amazing town of Metera with its troglodyte dwellings further north are essential visiting. Taranto also boasts a Museo Archeologico Nazionale, which recalls the presence of the ancient Greeks in this part of Europe. Last but not least, the beach-lined seaboard, for example the Lido di Metaponto, makes this a remarkable holiday destination. Riva dei Tessali is one of the rare golf courses to be found in the south of Italy, where the very many trees offer welcome shade and provide one of the course's main difficulties, together with water. Designed by Marco Croze, the course is on the short side and has average-sized greens that are well defended. Not the most spectacular layout in the world but at least playable by everyone.

Golf Club Riva dei Tessali — 1968
I - 74011 CASTELLANETA (TA)

Office	Segreteria	(39) 099 843 9251
Pro shop	Pro shop	(39) 099 843 9251
Fax	Fax	(39) 099 843 1844
Situation	Localita'	

Taranto (pop. 210.536), 34 km

Annual closure	Chiusura annuale	no
Weekly closure	Chiusura settimanale	tuesday

Fees main season
Tariffe alta stagione 18 holes

	Week days Settimana	We/Bank holidays Feriale/Festivo
Individual Individuale	L. 70.000	L. 70.000
Couple Coppia	L. 140.000	L. 140.000

Caddy	Caddy	yes
Electric Trolley	Carello elettrico	no
Buggy	Car	L. 40.000
Clubs	Bastoni	L. 25.000

Credit cards Carte di credito
VISA - Eurocard - MasterCard - AMEX - DC

998

Castellaneta Bari — Palagiano
0 2 4 km
Ginosa Matera
S 580
S 106
Taranto
Castellaneta Marina
GOLF
Riva dei Tessali
Ginosa Marina

Access Itinerario : Bari A14 → Taranto. At the end of motorway, go to Palagiano. S106dir, turn right on S106. 18 km, → Riva dei Tessali
Map 4 on page 946 Carta 4 Pagina 946

GOLF COURSE PERCORSO — 13/20

Site	Paesaggio	
Maintenance	Manutenzione	
Architect	Architetto	Marco Croze
Type	Tipologia	copse
Relief	Relievo terreno	
Water in play	Acqua in gioco	
Exp. to wind	Esposto al vento	
Trees in play	Alberi in gioco	

Scorecard Carta-score	Chp. Camp.	Mens Uomini	Ladies Donne
Length Lunghezza	5947	5709	5095
Par	72	72	72

Advised golfing ability Livello di gioco consigliato	0 12 24 36
Hcp required Handicap richiesto	34

CLUB HOUSE & AMENITIES CLUB HOUSE E SERVIZI — 7/10

Pro shop	Pro shop	
Driving range	Campo pratica	
Sheltered	coperto	no
On grass	in erba	yes
Putting-green	Putting-green	yes
Pitching-green	Green-pratica	yes

HOTEL FACILITIES ALBERGHI — 6/10

HOTELS ALBERGHI
Riva dei Tessali Golf Hotel — Castellaneta Marina
70 rooms, D. L. 250.000 — 2,5 km
Tel (39) 099 843 9251, Fax (39) 099 843 1844

Grand Hotel Delfino — Taranto
198 rooms, D. L. 260.000 — 34 km
Tel (39) 099 732 3232, Fax (39) 099 730 4654

Europa — Taranto
40 rooms, D. L. 220.000 — 34 km
Tel (39) 099 454 4111, Fax (39) 099 454 4115

RESTAURANTS RISTORANTE
La Ruota — Massafra
Tel (39) 099 880 7710 — 25 km

Il Caffè — Taranto
Tel (39) 099 452 5097 — 34 km

In un paesaggio calmo e serafico, non si potrebbe mai immaginare di essere a un passo dal centro di Roma e a poche centinaia di metri da Cinecittà. Invece siamo sulla via Appia «nuova» a fianco di quella «antica» e la vista dell'Acquedotto che portava l'acqua potabile alla capitale dell'Impero ci ricorda costantemente la grandiosità della sua storia. Il percorso dell'Acquasanta ne fa parte, perchè è il più vecchio golf d'Italia, dove sono passate tutte le teste coronate e gli attori del cinema. E' un grande percorso all'antica inserito in una vegetazione superba ma non soffocante. Dolcemente ondulato è attraversato da piccoli corsi d'acqua piazzati davanti ai greens. E' molto vario nel disegno e proprio per questo non annoia mai. Spettacolare e nello stesso tempo naturale il percorso si integra delicatamente nel paesaggio della campagna romana. Quando il golf è Dolce Vita...

In countryside as lazy and as peaceful as this, it is hard to believe you are so close to the centre of Rome and a few hundred metres from Cinecitta. Maybe we are on the «new» Via Appia, alongside the old one. The view from the aqueduct that carried spring water to the capital of the Roman empire is a constant reminder of the history that surrounds this part of Italy. The Acquasanta course is all part of it, being the oldest club in Italy and one that has entertained kings, princes and movie stars. Above all, it is a great old-style course in a superb setting of plants and trees, although the latter are never too present. This is a pleasantly sloping course crossed by streams, often just in front of the greens. And thanks to the variety of the layout, you never tire of playing here. Both spectacular and natural, the course blends delicately into the landscape of typical Roman countryside. Golf very much «dolce vita» style.

Circolo del Golf di Roma — 1903

Via Appia Nuova 716/A - Loc. Acquasanta
I - 00178 ROMA

Office	Segreteria	(39) 06 780 3407
Pro shop	Pro shop	(39) 06 783 951 68
Fax	Fax	(39) 06 783 462 19
Situation	Localita'	

Roma (pop. 2 653 245), 7 km

Annual closure	Chiusura annuale	no
Weekly closure	Chiusura settimanale	monday

Fees main season
Tariffe alta stagione 18 holes

	Week days Settimana	We/Bank holidays Feriale/Festivo
Individual Individuale	L. 80.000	L. 110.000
Couple Coppia	L. 160.000	L. 220.000

Week-end: with members only (ospiti accettati con soci)

Caddy	Caddy	yes
Electric Trolley	Carello elettrico	no
Buggy	Car	no
Clubs	Bastoni	L. 30.000
Credit cards Carte di credito		no

R O M A

GOLF

Cinecittà

0 2 4 km

Cecchignola

Castel Gandolfo

Access Itinerario : Roma, Via Appia Nuova. At N° 716/A, small road with a stone → Golf
Map 3 on page 945 Carta 3 Pagina 945

GOLF COURSE / PERCORSO — 16/20

Site	Paesaggio	
Maintenance	Manutenzione	
Architect	Architetto	
Type	Tipologia	open country, residential
Relief	Relievo terreno	
Water in play	Acqua in gioco	
Exp. to wind	Esposto al vento	
Trees in play	Alberi in gioco	

Scorecard Carta-score	Chp. Camp.	Mens Uomini	Ladies Donne
Length Lunghezza	6000	5854	5101
Par	71	71	71

Advised golfing ability Livello di gioco consigliato	0	12	24	36

Hcp required Handicap richiesto 34

CLUB HOUSE & AMENITIES / CLUB HOUSE E SERVIZI — 8/10

Pro shop	Pro shop	
Driving range	Campo pratica	
Sheltered	coperto	7 mats
On grass	in erba	yes
Putting-green	Putting-green	yes
Pitching-green	Green-pratica	yes

HOTEL FACILITIES / ALBERGHI — 9/10

HOTELS ALBERGHI

Forum — Roma
73 rooms, D. L. 490.000 — 7 km
Tel (39) 06 679 2446, Fax (39) 06 678 6479

Quirinale — Roma
210 rooms, D.L. 470.000 — 5 km
Tel (39) 06 4707, Fax (39) 06 482 0099

Appia Park Hotel — Roma
17 rooms, D. L. 240.000 — 1 km
Tel (39) 06 718 0180

RESTAURANTS RISTORANTE

Il Convivio - Tel (39) 06 686 9432 — Roma 5 km
Sans Souci - Tel (39) 06 482 1814 — Roma 8 km
Agata e Romeo - Tel (39) 06 446 5842 — Roma 4 km
Alberto Ciaria - Tel (39) 06 581 8668 — Roma 5 km

999

Everything's changed.
Except the way we think about cars.

A passion for design.

Since 1930, cars that have marked an era, made history, set a style. Years of constant, independent research into shapes, aerodynamics, new materials, safety, environmental impact. Pininfarina: a practical contribution to the ongoing technical and aesthetical progress of the car.

The manufacturing rationale.

A full cycle, full service capability: from styling prototype to product and process engineering and on to the production of 50,000 cars a year. Pininfarina: a longstanding culture of quality and constantly updated expertise applied to the creation of unique cars, designed and built using cutting edge technologies, skilfully finished by man.

Factory of ideas. Factory of automobiles.

E' il fratello maggiore e il vicino di casa de I Roveri, un complesso di 36 buche dove il percorso migliore è quello «Blu». Di lunghezza assolutamente rispettabile è stato disegnato da John Morrison prima di subire qualche modifica recente da Graham Cooke. Gli alberi centenari sono sempre presenti, ma la larghezza dei fairways è sufficiente per non sentirsi soffocati. I bunkers difendono bene i greens di questo percorso dal carattere britannico. Alcuni ostacoli d'acqua naturali sono stati messi in gioco con intelligenza, ma comunque è sempre possibile recuperare i propri errori. Nell'insieme è un percorso dove si cammina facilmente, è molto piacevole con un bel paesaggio e impegna abbastanza i giocatori con handicap basso senza essere troppo difficile per i giocatori mediocri. Il percorso «giallo» è immerso nella stessa natura ma ha più acqua in gioco.

This is the elderly neighbour to «I Roveri», a 36 hole resort the most challenging section of which is the «Percorso Blu». With very respectable yardage, it was designed by John Morrison and underwent a number of more recent changes under the supervision of Graham Cooke. Age-old trees are almost everywhere but the fairways are wide enough to avoid any risk of claustrophobia. The greens are well defended by bunkers on a course that has classic British character. A few stretches of water have been cleverly brought into play, but here again it is always possible to make up for your mistakes. In all, this gives an easily walkable, very pleasant and well-landscaped course that is demanding enough for low-handicap golfers and not too tough for high-handicappers. The other course, the «Percorso giallo» is more or less the same sort of layout only with more water in play.

Circolo Golf Torino — 1924

Via Grange 137
I - 10070 FIANO TORINESE

Office	Segreteria	(39) 011 923 5440
Pro shop	Pro shop	(39) 011 923 6028
Fax	Fax	(39) 011 923 5886
Situation	Localita'	

Torino (pop. 914.818), 16 km

Annual closure	Chiusura annuale	no
Weekly closure	Chiusura settimanale	monday

Fees main season
Tariffe alta stagione 18 holes

	Week days Settimana	We/Bank holidays Feriale/Festivo
Individual Individuale	L. 110.000	L. 155.000
Couple Coppia	L. 220.000	L. 310.000
Caddy	Caddy	L. 50.000
Electric Trolley	Carello elettrico	L. 10.000
Buggy	Car	L. 50.000
Clubs	Bastoni	L. 15.000

Credit cards Carte di credito — no

Fiano — Cirié — Lanzo Torinese — Robassomero — GOLF — Caselle Torinese — PARCO REGIONALE LA MANDRIA — Venaria — TORINO

0   2   4 km

Access Itinerario : Milano to Torino, A4 - A45 Exit (Uscita) Venaria. → Lanzo. Golf to the left.
Map 1 on page 940 Carta 1 Pagina 940

GOLF COURSE / PERCORSO 16/20

Site	Paesaggio	
Maintenance	Manutenzione	
Architect	Architetto	John Morrison Cooke/Harris/Croze
Type	Tipologia	forest
Relief	Relievo terreno	
Water in play	Acqua in gioco	
Exp. to wind	Esposto al vento	
Trees in play	Alberi in gioco	

Scorecard Carta-score	Chp. Camp.	Mens Uomini	Ladies Donne
Length Lunghezza	6216	5943	5212
Par	72	72	72

Advised golfing ability	0	12	24	36
Livello di gioco consigliato				

Hcp required Handicap richiesto 34

CLUB HOUSE & AMENITIES / CLUB HOUSE E SERVIZI 8/10

Pro shop	Pro shop	
Driving range	Campo pratica	
Sheltered	coperto	8 mats
On grass	in erba	yes
Putting-green	Putting-green	yes
Pitching-green	Green-pratica	yes

HOTEL FACILITIES / ALBERGHI 8/10

HOTELS ALBERGHI
Jet Hotel — Caselle Torinese
79 rooms, D. L. 270.000 — 8 km
Tel (39) 011 991 3733, Fax (39) 011 996 1544

Turin Palace Hotel — Torino
120 rooms, D. L. 410.000 — 16 km
Tel (39) 011 562 5511, Fax (39) 011 562 2187

Relais Villa Sassi — Torino
17 rooms, D. L. 440.000 — 16 km
Tel (39) 011 898 0556, Fax (39) 011 898 0095

RESTAURANTS RISTORANTE
Del Cambio - Tel (39) 011 543 760 — Torino 16 km

La Prima Smarrita — Torino
Tel (39) 011 317 9657 — 20 km

Rendez Vous — Torino
Tel (39) 011 887 666 — 18 km

1001

Varese è una città dallo sviluppo abbastanza recente, situata tra il lago di Lugano e Milano. Il campo da golf è stato costruito appena sopra al lago di Varese, che è uno dei più piccoli laghi lombardi dove il clima è particolarmente dolce e soleggiato. I golfisti più religiosi non potranno fare a meno di una visita al Sacro Monte dove viene fatto un continuo pellegrinaggio alla Vergine e da dove si può godere un fantastico panorama sui laghi e le montagne. Questa regione non è solamente turistica e questo percorso merita una visita per la sua particolarità. Non è molto lungo, ma il terreno piuttosto mosso esige una buona forma fisica e una buona padronanza nelle situazioni delicate e nei pendii. La scelta del bastone non è mai facile perchè alcuni greens sono sopraelevati e molti con due livelli esigono una buona precisione. Ci si consola facilmente da eventuali delusioni con la superba club-house (un antico monastero) e ammirando la bellezza del paesaggio.

Varese is a city that has developed only recently, located between Lake Lugano and Milan. This course was built above Lake Varese, one of the smallest lakes in Lombardy, where the climate is particularly mild and sunny. The more religious-minded golfer won't want to miss visiting the Sacro Monte, the site of a great pilgrimage to the Virgin Mary plus the added bonus of wonderful views over lakes and mountains. This region is not only a tourist destination, it also worth visiting for the originality of this course. It might not be very long but the hilly terrain requires a certain level of fitness and control when hitting the ball from tricky situations and sloping lies. Club selection is seldom straightforward, especially since a number of greens are elevated and many are two-tiered, making accuracy a must. If your round didn't go so well, the superb club-house (a former monastery) offers solace and consolation from where you can admire the beautiful landscape.

Golf Club Varese — 1934

Via Vitorio Veneto 32
I - 21020 LUVINATE (VA)

Office	Segreteria	(39) 0332 229 302
Pro shop	Pro shop	(39) 0332 821 043
Fax	Fax	(39) 0332 222 107
Situation	Localita'	

Varese (pop. 84.187), 5 km
Milano (pop. 1.302.808), 55 km

Annual closure	Chiusura annuale	no
Weekly closure	Chiusura settimanale	monday

Fees main season
Tariffe alta stagione 18 holes

	Week days Settimana	We/Bank holidays Feriale/Festivo
Individual Individuale	L. 80.000	L. 120.000
Couple Coppia	L. 160.000	L. 240.000

Caddy	Caddy	L. 40.000
Electric Trolley	Carello elettrico	no
Buggy	Car	L. 60.000
Clubs	Bastoni	L. 20.000

Credit cards Carte di credito — no

GOLF COURSE / PERCORSO — 14/20

Site	Paesaggio	
Maintenance	Manutenzione	
Architect	Architetto	Cecil R. Blandford Peter Gannon
Type	Tipologia	parkland, hilly
Relief	Relievo terreno	
Water in play	Acqua in gioco	
Exp. to wind	Esposto al vento	
Trees in play	Alberi in gioco	

Scorecard Carta-score	Chp. Camp.	Mens Uomini	Ladies Donne
Length Lunghezza	6105	5942	5238
Par	72	72	72

Advised golfing ability Livello di gioco consigliato		0 12 24 36
Hcp required	Handicap richiesto 34	

CLUB HOUSE & AMENITIES / CLUB HOUSE E SERVIZI — 8/10

Pro shop	Pro shop	
Driving range	Campo pratica	
Sheltered	coperto	15 mats
On grass	in erba	no
Putting-green	Putting-green	yes
Pitching-green	Green-pratica	no

HOTEL FACILITIES / ALBERGHI — 7/10

HOTELS ALBERGHI

Palace Hotel — Varese — 4 km
112 rooms, D. L. 400.000
Tel (39) 0332 327 100, Fax (39) 0332 312 870

City Hotel — Varese — 4 km
47 rooms, D. L. 235.000
Tel (39) 0332 281 304, Fax (39) 0332 232 882

Bel Sit — Comerio — 7 km
30 rooms, D. L. 115.000
Tel (39) 0332 737 705

RESTAURANTS RISTORANTE

Lago Maggiore — Varese 5 km
Tel (39) 0332 231 183

Da Annetta - Tel (39) 0332 490 230 — Capolago 5 km

Colonne — Santa Maria Del Monte
Tel (39) 0332 224 633 — 5 km

1002

Access Itinerario : Varese, Via Manzoni, Via Sacco, Via S. Sanvito → Gavirate/Laveno. 5 km → Golf
Map 1 on page 940 Carta 1 Pagina 940

Si dice che Venezia sia magica all'alba e a notte fonda, quindi rimane tutta la giornata per giocare a golf su questo percorso nell'estremità ovest del Lido, di fronte alla città dei Dogi, in una stazione balneare molto elegante dove c'è anche uno dei pochissimi casinò italiani. Ma questo percorso è molto più che un campo per quell'altro gioco d'azzardo che è il golf. Disegnato da Cruikshank e rivisto da C.K. Cotton e Marco Croze, si sviluppa su terreno di dune sabbiose in mezzo a pioppi, pini ed olivi. La sua architettura tipicamente britannica si è perfettamente armonizzata negli anni e non costringe a porsi troppi problemi tattici quando non si è in forma. Bisogna comunque fare attenzione: in un ambiente così piacevole, gli errori arrivano in fretta e possono costare cari sullo score o in match-play. Qualche ostacolo d'acqua e spesso il vento aggiungono ancora un po' di pepe a questo eccellente «piatto» golfistico.

As Venice is sheer magic at dawn and nightfall, you have the whole day in between to play this course at the far western tip of the Lido, opposite the city of Doges, a very chic seaside resort which is also home to one of the rare casinos to be found in Italy. This course, however, is much more than just space in which you can try your luck at golf. Designed by Cruikshank and restyled by C.K. Cotton and Marco Croze, it stretches over dune land amidst poplar, pine and olive trees. The obvious British architecture here has aged well and you find yourself rather happy not to have to ask too many tactical questions when your game is off-colour. Caution is required nonetheless, as mistakes can occur so easily in such a pleasant setting and prove costly for your card or match-play score. A few water hazards and frequent wind add a little spice to this excellent feast of golf.

Circolo Golf Venezia — 1928

Via del Forte
I - 30011 ALBERONI (VE)

Office	Segreteria	(39) 041 731 333
Pro shop	Pro shop	(39) 041 276 0361
Fax	Fax	(39) 041 731 339
Situation	Localita'	

Venezia (pop. 293.731), 11 km

Annual closure	Chiusura annuale	no
Weekly closure	Chiusura settimanale	monday

Fees main season
Tariffe alta stagione full day

	Week days Settimana	We/Bank holidays Feriale/Festivo
Individual Individuale	L. 90.000	L. 100.000
Couple Coppia	L. 180.000	L. 200.000

Week-end : 2 days L. 140.000 (indiv.) / L. 240.000 (couple)

Caddy	Caddy	L. 60.000
Electric Trolley	Carello elettrico	no
Buggy	Car	no
Clubs	Bastoni	L. 25.000

Credit cards Carte di credito
VISA - MasterCard - AMEX - DC

Mestre — VENEZIA — Punta Sabbioni — Lido di Venezia — Alberoni — GOLF

Access Itinerario : Venezia to Lido with vaporetto
Map 2 on page 942 Carta 2 Pagina 942

GOLF COURSE / PERCORSO — 16/20

Site	Paesaggio	
Maintenance	Manutenzione	
Architect	Architetto	CK Cotton/
	Cruikshank	Marco Croze
Type	Tipologia	seaside course
Relief	Relievo terreno	
Water in play	Acqua in gioco	
Exp. to wind	Esposto al vento	
Trees in play	Alberi in gioco	

Scorecard Carta-score	Chp. Camp.	Mens Uomini	Ladies Donne
Length Lunghezza	6199	6039	5353
Par	72	72	72

Advised golfing ability Livello di gioco consigliato	0	12	24	36
Hcp required	Handicap richiesto 34			

CLUB HOUSE & AMENITIES / CLUB HOUSE E SERVIZI — 7/10

Pro shop	Pro shop	
Driving range	Campo pratica	
Sheltered	coperto	5 mats
On grass	in erba	yes
Putting-green	Putting-green	yes
Pitching-green	Green-pratica	yes

HOTEL FACILITIES / ALBERGHI — 9/10

HOTELS ALBERGHI

Danieli — Venezia
221 rooms, D. L. 1.045.000 — 11 km
Tel (39) 041 522 6480, Fax (39) 041 520 0208

Excelsior — Venezia Lido
196 rooms, D. L. 850.000 — 3 km
Tel (39) 041 526 0201, Fax (39) 041 526 7276

Villa Mabapa - 60 rooms, D. L. 420.000 — Venezia Lido
Tel (39) 041 526 0590, Fax (39) 041 526 9441 — 3 km

RESTAURANTS RISTORANTE

Trattoria Favorita — Venezia Lido
Tel (39) 041 526 1626 — 3 km

Harry's Bar - Tel (39) 041 528 5777 — Venezia 11 km

Osteria da Fiore - Tel (39) 041 721 308 — Venezia 11 km

Al Vecio Cantier — Venezia Lido
Tel (39) 041 526 8130 — 3 km

1003

Se si amano le belle storie, Verona è il posto giusto per versare qualche lacrima sul tragico amore di Romeo e Giulietta. Autentiche o create per gli animi sensibili, la casa (Via Cappello) e la tomba di Giulietta meritano un giro dopo un'opera all'Arena o un caffè in Piazza delle Erbe. Verona è in ogni modo una città bellissima e la vicinanza con il lago di Garda le dà ancora un argomento in più. Il golf club Verona è stato fondato nel 1963 e il percorso è stato realizzato in due tempi da John Harris in uno stile assolutamente britannico conforme a quello dell'architetto. Molto mosso, obbliga i giocatori meno in forma ad usare il golf cart e a stare molto attenti ad attaccare i greens sopraelevati (e un green cieco). Le prime nove buche sono abbastanza strette e «tricky» con qualche pericoloso fuori limite, le buche di ritorno sono più larghe con qualche ostacolo d'acqua ma permettono di non compromettere un buon score ottenuto sulle prime.

When you love tear-jerking tales of love and grief, you can hardly wish for a better setting than Verona, home to the tragic story of Romeo and Juliette. The house (Via Cappello) and tomb of Juliette are worth going out your way for, after an opera at the Arenas or a coffee on the Piazza delle Erbe. Whichever way you look at it, Verona is a superb city made even more attractive by the closeness of Lake Garda. The Verona Golf Club was founded in 1963 and the course laid out in two stages by John Harris, in a British parkland style consistent with the architect's own style. Very hilly, this course warrants a buggy for the more unfit golfer and a lot of concentration to hit some elevated greens (and one blind green as well). The first holes are rather narrow and tricky to negotiate - some dangerous out-of-bounds await the mis-hit shot - while the back 9 are wider with a few water hazards and shouldn't do too much damage to your card if you have scored well over the front nine.

Golf Club Verona — 1963

Loc. Ca' del Sale 15
I - 37066 SOMMACAMPAGNA (VR)

Office	Segreteria	(39) 045 510 060
Pro shop	Pro shop	(39) 045 510 317
Fax	Fax	(39) 045 510 242
Situation	Localita'	

Verona (pop. 254 748), 13 km

Annual closure	Chiusura annuale	no
Weekly closure	Chiusura settimanale	tuesday

Fees main season
Tariffe alta stagione full day

	Week days Settimana	We/Bank holidays Feriale/Festivo
Individual Individuale	L. 96.000	L. 120.000
Couple Coppia	L. 192.000	L. 240.000

Caddy	Caddy	L. 40.000
Electric Trolley	Carello elettrico	no
Buggy	Car	L. 60.000
Clubs	Bastoni	yes

Credit cards Carte di credito	no

Access Itinerario : A4 Milano-Venezia, Exit (Uscita) Sommacampagna. 1 km, take right then left → Golf.
Map 2 on page 942 Carta 2 Pagina 942

GOLF COURSE / PERCORSO — 13/20

Site	Paesaggio	
Maintenance	Manutenzione	
Architect	Architetto	John Harris
Type	Tipologia	country
Relief	Relievo terreno	
Water in play	Acqua in gioco	
Exp. to wind	Esposto al vento	
Trees in play	Alberi in gioco	

Scorecard Carta-score	Chp. Camp.	Mens Uomini	Ladies Donne
Length Lunghezza	6037	6037	5241
Par	72	72	72

Advised golfing ability Livello di gioco consigliato	0	12	24	36
Hcp required Handicap richiesto	34			

CLUB HOUSE & AMENITIES / CLUB HOUSE E SERVIZI — 7/10

Pro shop	Pro shop	
Driving range	Campo pratica	
Sheltered	coperto	12 mats
On grass	in erba	yes
Putting-green	Putting-green	yes
Pitching-green	Green-pratica	yes

HOTEL FACILITIES / ALBERGHI — 8/10

HOTELS ALBERGHI

Quadrante Europe — Caselle di Sommacampagna
117 rooms, D. L. 250.000 — 5 km
Tel (39) 045 858 1400, Fax (39) 045 858 1402

Gabbia d'Oro — Verona
27 rooms, D. L. 540.000 — 13 km
Tel (39) 045 800 3060, Fax (39) 045 590 293

Bologna — Verona
32 rooms, D. L. 250.000 — 13 km
Tel (39) 045 800 6830, Fax (39) 045 801 0602

RESTAURANTS RISTORANTE

Il Desco — Verona
Tel (39) 045 595 358 — 13 km

Merica - Tel (39) 045 515 160 — Sommacampagna 2 km

Tre Marchetti - Tel (39) 045 803 0463 — Verona 13 km

1004

Disegnato nel 1926 da Peter Gannon, Villa d'Este è diventato rapidamente uno dei gioielli golfistici italiani. Merito è anche della sua posizione vicino al magnifico lago di Como, che si snoda in lunghezza e dove i piccoli porticcioli si succedono ai giardini esotici delle sue ville da sogno. La più bella è stata trasformata a Cernobbio in uno dei più affascinanti hotel, luogo di soggiorno ideale... Se non si devono fare i conti con il prezzo. Ai bordi del piccolo lago di Montorfano, Villa d'Este è un percorso abbastanza mosso in mezzo a pini, castani e querce ma si può facilmente giocare anche a piedi. Non è lungo, ma per fare un buono score bisogna mettere a punto una tecnica eccellente e saper fare colpi elaborati. Ci sono sei par 3 e solo due par 5 offrono buone possibilità per un birdie. Una club-house superba dà il tocco finale a questo posto tranquillo ed elegante.

Designed in 1926 by Peter Gannon, Villa d'Este has rapidly become one of the gems of Italian golf courses, much of which is due to a location close to the long Lake Como, where small harbours give way to exotic gardens around superb villas. The finest of these villas in Cernobbio has been transformed into one of the most charming hotels you could wish to find, the ideal site for a holiday... if not on too tight a budget. Villa d'Este, alongside the small lake of Montorfano, is a rather hilly course set amidst pine, chestnut and birch trees but is easily walkable all the same. Yardage is not too demanding but you need to develop good technique to play well here, bending the ball both ways especially on the six par 3s. There are only two par 5s but both offer a real chance of a birdie. A superb club-house adds the final touch to this tranquil and elegant site.

Circolo Golf Villa d'Este — 1926

Via Cantù 13
I - 22030 MONTORFANO (CO)

Office	Segreteria	(39) 031 200 200
Pro shop	Pro shop	(39) 031 553 050
Fax	Fax	(39) 031 200 786
Situation	Localita'	

Como (pop. 83.637), 9 km - Varese (pop. 84.187), 30 km

Annual closure	Chiusura annuale	no
Weekly closure	Chiusura settimanale	tuesday

Fees main season
Tariffe alta stagione full day

	Week days Settimana	We/Bank holidays Feriale/Festivo
Individual Individuale	L. 110.000	L. 155.000
Couple Coppia	L. 220.000	L. 310.000

Week-end: with members only (ospiti accettati con soci)

Caddy	Caddy	yes
Electric Trolley	Carello elettrico	no
Buggy	Car	no
Clubs	Bastoni	L. 20.000

Credit cards Carte di credito
VISA - Eurocard - MasterCard - AMEX

Access Itinerario : A9 → Como.
Exit (Uscita) Como-Sud. Turn right → Cantù.
5 km → Montorfano. Golf on left hand side.
Map 1 on page 941 Carta 1 Pagina 941

GOLF COURSE / PERCORSO — 16/20

Site	Paesaggio	
Maintenance	Manutenzione	
Architect	Architetto	Peter Gannon
Type	Tipologia	forest
Relief	Relievo terreno	
Water in play	Acqua in gioco	
Exp. to wind	Esposto al vento	
Trees in play	Alberi in gioco	

Scorecard Carta-score	Chp. Camp.	Mens Uomini	Ladies Donne
Length Lunghezza	5727	5544	4869
Par	69	69	69

Advised golfing ability
Livello di gioco consigliato — 0 12 24 36

Hcp required Handicap richiesto 34

CLUB HOUSE & AMENITIES / CLUB HOUSE E SERVIZI — 8/10

Pro shop	Pro shop	
Driving range	Campo pratica	
Sheltered	coperto	12 mats
On grass	in erba	no
Putting-green	Putting-green	yes
Pitching-green	Green-pratica	yes

HOTEL FACILITIES / ALBERGHI — 9/10

HOTELS ALBERGHI
Grand Hotel Villa d'Este — Cernobbio
166 rooms, D. L. 980.000 — 13 km
Tel (39) 031 3481, Fax (39) 031 348 844

Villa Fiori — Como
44 rooms, D. L. 320.000 — 9 km
Tel (39) 031 573 105, Fax (39) 031 570 379

Santandrea Golf Hotel — Montorfano
12 rooms, D. L. 120.000 — 3 km
Tel (39) 031 200 220, Fax (39) 031 200 220

RESTAURANTS RISTORANTE
Imbarcadero — Como
Tel (39) 031 270 166 — 9 km

Il Cantuccio - Tel (39) 031 628 736 — Albavilla 8 km

Crotto del Lupo — Como
Tel (39) 031 570 881 — 9 km

1005

406 Coupé

PEUGEOT

JE VOELT JE LEKKERDER IN EEN PEUGEOT.

ⓝederland

The Millennium Guide

Met meer dan 125.000 spelers behoort Nederland tot de landen van Europa met een sterke groei. Er zijn meer dan 70 18-holes-banen, die logischerwijze vooral rond de grote steden liggen. Wat betekent dat het er vooral in de weekends druk kan zijn. Maar de afstanden van ene naar de andere kant van dit land zijn nooit erg groot en het wegennet is vrij dich, waardoor je een groot gebied rond de verblijfplaats kunt bereiken. Naast de 'grote' banen aan de kust heeft het land golftechnisch nog meer in zijn mars, met banen die vaak goed in het lanschap zijn opgenomen. Het is een weinig bekende bestemming, die vooral en de zomer ontdekt moet worden.

The Netherlands, with 125,000 golfers, is one of the countries in Europe where golf is developing fast. There are about 70 eighteen-hole courses, naturally spread around large cities, thus implying busy week-ends. But here, distances from one end of the country to the other are never too great, and the very dense road system makes for easy travelling round and about your holiday location. Alongside the great seaside courses, the country has a number of solid arguments to attract golftrotters, with courses that, more often than not, blend in very tastefully with the natural landscape. This is still a little known destination, and one well worth discovering during the warmer months.

1007

RANGSCHIKKING VAN DE TERREINEN
CLASSIFICATION OF COURSES

Deze rangschikking houdt eerst en vooral rekening met het cijfer,
dat aan het terrein werd toegekend.

This classification gives priority consideration
to the score awarded to the actual course.

Cijfer van het Club-House & dependances
Club-house and facilities

Cijfer van het terrein
Course score ⌐

Cijfer van hotelaccomodatie in de omgeving
Hotel facility score

18 8 6		Eindhoven		1019	Blz *Page*

Cijfer			Baan	Blz	Cijfer			Baan	Blz
18	8	6	Eindhoven	1019	**15**	6	7	Hoge Kleij	1028
18	7	8	Haagsche	1025	**15**	5	3	Nunspeet *North/East*	1033
18	8	8	Kennemer	1030	**15**	7	7	Oosterhout	1034
18	7	8	Noordwijk	1032	**15**	7	7	Rosendael	1037
16	8	5	Cromstrijen	1016	**15**	7	5	Sint Nicolaasga	1038
16	8	7	De Pan	1017	**15**	6	6	Sybrook	1039
16	8	5	Efteling	1018	**15**	7	6	Twente	1041
16	7	6	Herkenbosch	1026	**15**	7	6	Wouwse Plantage	1042
16	7	7	Hilversum	1027	**14**	7	6	Anderstein	1013
16	8	8	Houtrak	1029	**14**	4	5	Gelpenberg	1020
16	7	7	Purmerend	1035	**14**	7	4	Grevelinghout	1024
15	7	7	Amsterdam	1012	**14**	6	7	Lauswolt	1031
15	7	3	Batouwe	1014	**14**	6	5	Rijk van Nijmegen	
15	7	6	Broekpolder	1015				*Nijmeegse Baan*	1036
15	7	7	Gendersteyn	1021	**14**	7	6	Toxandria	1040
15	7	6	Goes	1022	**14**	7	7	Zuid Limburgse	1043
15	7	6	Graafschap	1023					

RANGSCHIKKING VAN DE HOTELACCOMODATIE
CLASSIFICATION OF HOTELS FACILITIES

Cijfer van het Club-House & dependances
Club-house and facilities

Cijfer van het terrein
Course score ⌐

Cijfer van hotelaccomodatie in de omgeving
Hotel facility score

18 7 **8**		Haagsche		1025	Blz *Page*

Cijfer			Baan	Blz	Cijfer			Baan	Blz
18	7	**8**	Haagsche	1025	16	8	**7**	De Pan	1017
16	8	**8**	Houtrak	1029	15	7	**7**	Gendersteyn	1021
18	8	**8**	Kennemer	1030	16	7	**7**	Hilversum	1027
18	7	**8**	Noordwijk	1032	15	6	**7**	Hoge Kleij	1028
15	7	**7**	Amsterdam	1012	14	6	**7**	Lauswolt	1031

Netherlands

Cijfer			Baan	Blz	Cijfer			Baan	Blz
15	7	7	Oosterhout	1034	15	7	6	Twente	1041
16	7	7	Purmerend	1035	15	7	6	Wouwse Plantage	1042
15	7	7	Rosendael	1037	16	8	5	Cromstrijen	1016
14	7	7	Zuid Limburgse	1043	16	8	5	Efteling	1018
14	7	6	Anderstein	1013	14	4	5	Gelpenberg	1020
15	7	6	Broekpolder	1015	14	6	5	Rijk van Nijmegen	
18	8	6	Eindhoven	1019				Nijmeegse Baan	1036
15	7	6	Goes	1022	15	7	5	Sint Nicolaasga	1038
15	7	6	Graafschap	1023	14	7	5	Grevelingenhout	1024
16	7	6	Herkenbosch	1026	15	7	3	Batouwe	1014
15	6	6	Sybrook	1039	15	5	3	Nunspeet North/East	1033
14	7	6	Toxandria	1040					

AAN TE RADEN VAKANTIEVERBLIJF
RECOMMENDED GOLFING STAY

Baan	Cijfer			Blz	Baan	Cijfer			Blz
De Pan	16	8	7	1017	Hilversum	16	7	7	1027
Eindhoven	18	8	6	1019	Kennemer	18	8	8	1030
Haagsche	18	7	8	1025	Noordwijk	18	7	8	1032

TYPE BAAN
TYPE OF COURSE

Baan	Blz	Baan	Blz	Baan	Blz
forest		**open country**		Purmerend	1035
De Pan	1017	Amsterdam	1012	Sint Nicolaasga	1038
Eindhoven	1019	Batouwe	1014	Twente	1041
Gelpenberg	1020	Broekpolder	1015	Wouwse Plantage	1042
Graafschap	1023	Cromstrijen	1016		
Herkenbosch	1026	Efteling	1018	**polder**	
Hilversum	1027	Goes	1022	Amsterdam	1012
Hoge Kleij	1028	Houtrak	1029	Batouwe	1014
Lauswolt	1031	Oosterhout	1034	Broekpolder	1015
Nunspeet North/East	1033	Purmerend	1035	Goes	1022
Rosendael	1037	Sint Nicolaasga	1038	Houtrak	1029
Sybrook	1039	Wouwse Plantage	1042	Purmerend	1035
Toxandria	1040			Sint Nicolaasga	1038
Twente	1041	**parkland**			
Zuid Limburgse	1043	Anderstein	1013		
		Gendersteyn	1021		
links		Grevelingenhout	1024		
Haagsche	1025	Rijk van Nijmegen			
Kennemer	1030	Nijmeegse Baan	1036		
Noordwijk	1032	Oosterhout	1034		

1011

Toen de oude Amsterdamse de helft van zijn holes aan de Spoorwegen verloor, vertrok de club naar een nieuw, open terrein aan de westkant van de stad (soms een beetje rumoerig door de overvliegende vliegtuigen). Aanvankelijk waren er problemen waardoor alle greens moesten worden gerenoveerd. Die ingreep en het verder groeien van de jonge aanplant, zullen de baan sterk verbeteren. De eerste zeven holes zijn niet om over naar huis te schrijven, met alleen de fairway bunkers en de wind als moeilijkheidsfactor. Dan wordt het spannender met twee par-4 holes en water. Water speelt ook een belangrijke rol op de tweede negen, vooral op de 14e (een par-5 dogleg met twee vijvers) en de 18e waar de green wordt afgeschermd door water. Een prachtige slothole. De baan is niet te druk.

When the old Amsterdam Golf Club lost half of its holes to the railways, the club moved out into a very open area to the west of the city (sometimes a little noisy because of the airport). Owing to a number of serious problems, the greens have all been re-laid and their maturity should do much to improve the terrain still further; the same goes for the newly planted trees and bushes. The seven first holes are not much to write home about, the only difficulties being the bunker fairways and wind. Then, it gets a little more exciting with two par 4s and water hazards. Water, in fact, is very much to the fore on the way in, especially on the 14th (a par 5 dog-leg with two ponds and two ditches) and the 18th, where the green is again guarded by water to make an excellent final hole. The course is not too crowded.

Amsterdamse Golfclub — 1990

Bauduinlaan 35
NL - 1047 HK AMSTERDAM

Office	Secretariaat	(31) 020 - 497 7866
Pro shop	Pro shop	(31) 020 - 497 4906
Fax	Fax	(31) 020 - 497 5966
Situation	Locatie	

Amsterdam (pop. 724 096), 10 km

| Annual closure | Jaarlijkse sluiting | no |
| Weekly closure | Wekelijkse sluitingsdag | no |

Fees main season
Hoogseizoen tarieven 18 holes

	Week days Weekdagen	We/Bank holidays We/Feestdagen
Individual Individueel	Fl 125,-	Fl 125,-
Couple Paar	Fl 250,-	Fl 250,-

Caddy	Caddy	no
Electric Trolley	Electrische trolley	Fl 7.50,-
Buggy	Buggy	Fl 25,-/18 holes
Clubs	Clubs	Fl 25,-

Credit cards Creditkaarten — no

1012

Access Toegang : Amsterdam N5/A5 → Haarlem.
Exit Spaarnwoude. 1 km → Ruigoord/Houtrak
Map 1 on page 1008 Auto kaart 1 Blz 1008

GOLF COURSE
BAAN — 15/20

Site	Terrein	
Maintenance	Onderhoud	
Architect	Architect	Paul Rolin Gerard Jol (1993)
Type	Type baan	polder, open country
Relief	Reliëf	
Water in play	Waterhazards	
Exp. to wind	Windgevoelig	
Trees in play	Bomen	

Scorecard Scorekaart	Chp. Back tees	Mens Heren	Ladies Damen
Length Lengte	6103	5948	5084
Par	72	72	72

Advised golfing ability — 0 12 24 36
Aanbevolen golfvaardigheid
Hcp required — Vereiste hcp — yes, certificate

CLUB HOUSE & AMENITIES
CLUB HOUSE EN ANNEXEN — 7/10

Pro shop	Pro shop	
Driving range	Oefenbaan	
Sheltered	overdekt	5 mats
On grass	op gras	no, 15 mats open air
Putting-green	putting-green	yes
Pitching-green	pitching-green	yes

HOTEL FACILITIES
HOTELS IN OMGEVING — 7/10

HOTELS HOTELS

Radisson SAS — Amsterdam
246 rooms, D Fl. 375,- — 15 km
Tel (31) 020 - 623 1231
Fax (31) 020 - 520 8200

Canal House — Amsterdam
26 rooms, D Fl. 225,- — 15 km
Tel (31) 020 - 622 5182
Fax (31) 020 - 624 1317

RESTAURANTS RESTAURANTS

La Rive — Amsterdam
Tel (31) 020 - 622 6060 — 10 km

De Bokkedorns — Overveen/Haarlem
Tel (31) 023 - 526 3600 — 15 km

ANDERSTEIN

14	7	6

De spoorweg en de A12 op de achtergrond van een aantal holes zouden niet teveel de aandacht van de vele kwaliteiten van deze baan moeten afleiden. Het vroegere familiedomein is omgetoverd in een 18-holes baan, met het clubhuis in de gerestaureerde en onlangs nog eens gerenoveerde boerenstal. Bij de uitbreiding zijn acht van de oorspronkelijke holes intact gebleven. Die zijn vrij smal omdat er in eerste aanleg niet veel ruimte was. Van de tien nieuwe holes liggen er vijf in open land. Het zijn doglegs met brede fairways, twee grote vijvers en strategisch geplaatste fairway bunkers. De overige vijf liggen meer tussen de bomen, zoals de oorspronkelijke holes. Alles bij elkaar is het een aantrekkelijke baan geworden, met allerlei moeilijkheden. Allereerst al de noodzaak om aan de grote variatie in holes te wennen. Je moet er eigenlijk meerdere keren spelen om de baan te gaan begrijpen. Doe dit vooral door de week, want in de weekenden zijn er veel leden op de been/baan.

The railway line and road that form a backdrop to some holes here should not conceal the many virtues of this course. The erstwhile family property was extended and built into a private 18 hole course, and the old farmhouse, now the clubhouse, has recently been restored. Eight of the first nine holes have been preserved and are very narrow - they were built over a restricted amount of space. Of the ten new holes, five run through wide open land in the form of doglegs with broad fairways, two major water hazards and strategically located fairway bunkers. The other five are in woodland, like the original holes. In all, this has become a very attractive course, offering all sorts of difficulty, the first of which is to get accustomed to the very different nature of each hole. You definitely need to play here several times to understand the course. If you do, make it a week-day, as there are a lot of members at week-ends.

Golfclub Anderstein — 1987

Woudenbergseweg 13 A
NL 3953 ME MAARSBERGEN

Office	Secretariaat	(31) 0343 - 431 330
Pro shop	Pro shop	(31) 0343 - 431 560
Fax	Fax	(31) 0343 - 432 062
Situation	Locatie	

Utrecht (pop. 234 106), 20 km

Annual closure	Jaarlijkse sluiting	no
Weekly closure	Wekelijkse sluitingsdag	no

Fees main season
Hoogseizoen tarieven 18 holes

	Week days Weekdagen	We/Bank holidays We/Feestdagen
Individual Individueel	Fl 100,-	*
Couple Paar	Fl 200,-	*

* Week-end: members only

Caddy	Caddy	no
Electric Trolley	Electrische trolley	Fl 7,50,-
Buggy	Buggy	no
Clubs	Clubs	no

Credit cards Creditkaarten — no

Access Toegang : A 12 Utrecht-Arnhem.
Exit 22 → Maarsbergen, N226. 500 m turn left
Map 1 on page 1008 Auto kaart 1 Blz 1008

GOLF COURSE
BAAN — 14/20

Site	Terrein	
Maintenance	Onderhoud	
Architect	Architect	J. Dudok van Heel Gerard Jol (1989)
Type	Type baan	parkland
Relief	Reliëf	
Water in play	Waterhazards	
Exp. to wind	Windgevoelig	
Trees in play	Bomen	

Scorecard Scorekaart	Chp. Back tees	Mens Heren	Ladies Damen
Length Lengte	6015	5719	4910
Par	72	72	72

Advised golfing ability Aanbevolen golfvaardigheid	0 12 24 36	
Hcp required Vereiste hcp	no	

CLUB HOUSE & AMENITIES
CLUB HOUSE EN ANNEXEN — 7/10

Pro shop	Pro shop	
Driving range	Oefenbaan	
Sheltered	overdekt	6 mats
On grass	op gras	no, 20 mats open air
Putting-green	putting-green	yes
Pitching-green	pitching-green	yes

HOTEL FACILITIES
HOTELS IN OMGEVING — 6/10

HOTELS HOTELS

Motel Maarsbergen — Maarsbergen
38 rooms, D Fl. 95,- — 500 m
Tel (31) 0343 - 431 341
Fax (31) 0343 - 431 379

De Hoefslag — Bosch en Duin
34 rooms, D FL 220,- — 15 km
Tel (31) 030 - 225 1051
Fax (31) 030 - 228 5821

RESTAURANTS RESTAURANTS

De Hoefslag — Bosch en Duin
Tel (31) 030 - 225 1051 — 15 km

1013

Deze nieuwe baan ligt in open terrein, midden tussen de grote rivieren. Bij de aanleg stonden er al een handjevol bomen en die zijn goed in het ontwerp ingepast. Ze staan langs de fairways of beschermen enkele greens, waardoor spelers twee keer moeten denken voordat ze een driver uit de tas halen. Er komen heel wat waterhazards in het spel, zoals op de 15e, een par-3 met een eilandgreen, of de 18e waar water de green beschermd tegen mislukte approaches. De negen andere holes hebben gewoon veel bunkers vooral op de fairways, zeker op twee holes. Honderden jonge bomen zijn aangeplant, maar die zijn nog niet groot genoeg om veel bescherming tegen de wind te bieden. Hoewel de baan vrij kort is, zijn het vooral de elementen, zoals wind en water, die dwingen tot een nauwkeurige clubkeuze. De beste tijd om Batouwe te spelen is in het voorjaar, als de fruitbomen in de Betuwe in bloei staan.

This recent course has been laid out over wide open space between the main rivers in the centre of Holland. There were a handful of trees, and these have been intelligently used by the designer. They line certain fairways and protect a number of greens, forcing players to think twice before taking the driver out of the bag. A lot of water hazards come into play, like on the par 3 15th, with an island green, or the 18th, where water protects the green from mis-hit approach shots. Most of the other holes just have lots of bunkers, especially of the fairway variety, numerous on two holes in particular. Hundreds of other trees have been planted but are no size as yet, so there is precious little protection from the wind - even though the course itself is on the short side, the elements are a key factor here for choosing the right club. The best time to play Batouwe is in the Spring, when the region's fruit trees are in full blossom.

Betuws Golfcentrum de Batouwe — 1993

Ost Kanaalweg 1
NL - 4011 LA ZOELEN

Office	Secretariaat	(31) 0344 - 624 370
Pro shop	Pro shop	(31) 0344 - 624 370
Fax	Fax	(31) 0344 - 613 096
Situation	Locatie	

Tiel (pop. 33 571), 3 km

Annual closure	Jaarlijkse sluiting	no
Weekly closure	Wekelijkse sluitingsdag	no

Fees main season
Hoogseizoen tarieven 18 holes

	Week days Weekdagen	We/Bank holidays We/Feestdagen
Individual Individueel	Fl 80,-	Fl 95,-
Couple Paar	Fl 160,-	Fl 190,-

Caddy	Caddy	Fl 10,-
Electric Trolley	Electrische trolley	no
Buggy	Buggy	Fl 10,-
Clubs	Clubs	Fl 5,-

Credit cards Creditkaarten VISA - Eurocard - MasterCard

1014

Access Toegang : A15 Rotterdam-Arnhem/Nijmegen.
Exit 33 → Maurik. 3.5 km → Echtfeld. Golf 1 km
Map 1 on page 1008 Auto kaart 1 Blz 1008

GOLF COURSE / BAAN — 15/20

Site	Terrein	
Maintenance	Onderhoud	
Architect	Architect	Alan Rijks
Type	Type baan	polder, open country
Relief	Reliëf	
Water in play	Waterhazards	
Exp. to wind	Windgevoelig	
Trees in play	Bomen	

Scorecard Scorekaart	Chp. Back tees	Mens Heren	Ladies Damen
Length Lengte	5775	5775	4839
Par	72	72	72

Advised golfing ability
Aanbevolen golfvaardigheid — 0 12 24 36
Hcp required — Vereiste hcp — no

CLUB HOUSE & AMENITIES / CLUB HOUSE EN ANNEXEN — 7/10

Pro shop	Pro shop	
Driving range	Oefenbaan	
Sheltered	overdekt	6 mats
On grass	op gras	no, 10 mats open air
Putting-green	putting-green	yes
Pitching-green	pitching-green	yes

HOTEL FACILITIES / HOTELS IN OMGEVING — 3/10

HOTELS HOTELS

't Paviljoen — Rhenen
32 rooms, D Fl 165,- — 20 km
Tel (31) 0317 - 619 003
Fax (31) 0317 - 617 213

RESTAURANTS RESTAURANTS

Gravin van Buren — Buren
Tel (31) 0344 - 571 663 — 7 km

't Kalkoentje — Rhenen
Tel (31) 0317 - 612 344 — 20 km

BROEKPOLDER

Hier vindt u een voorbeeld van een nog vrij nieuwe baan, waar de oorspronkelijk nogal kale ruimte geleidelijk aan voller en rijker wordt. Na de aanleg in 1983 zijn bomen en struiken nu bijna volgroeid hetgeen zowel bescherming tegen de wind biedt als een visuele verbetering is. De ontwikkeling van de baan wordt versterkt door recente ingrepen die wat oorspronkelijke zwaktes hebben opgeheven. Waterhazards komen op vijf holes in het spel en vormen met de sloten de belangrijkste hindernissen. Ook bunkers spelen een rol in de verdediging van de grote greens. Sommige holes zijn behoorlijk aan de lange kant, maar toch is de baan geschikt voor spelers van alle niveaus. Broekpolder ligt maar een paar meter boven het zeeniveau, maar dat is voldoende om een paar mooie vergezichten over de omliggende polders op te leveren, met de haveninstallatie van Rotterdam op de achtergrond.

Here is an example of a recently built course, where the original barren space is gradually becoming richer, visibly developing and maturing year in year out. Since 1983, the trees and bushes are already almost full grown, bringing greater protection from the wind and visual improvement. The course's evolution has also been marked by recent changes, which have put right some of the flaws exposed by the course's immaturity. The water hazards come into play on four holes, and, with a number of ditches, form the main difficulties. The bunkers, too, provide a firm line of defence for the large greens. We might add that some of the holes are on the long side, but overall the course can be played by golfers of all levels. Broekpolder is only a few metres above sea level, but that's enough to provide some pretty views over the surrounding lakes and fields, with the port of Rotterdam in the background.

Golfclub Broekpolder — 1983

Watersportweg 100
NL - 3138 HD VLAARDINGEN

Office	Secretariaat	(31) 010 - 249 5555
Pro shop	Pro shop	(31) 010 - 474 7610
Fax	Fax	(31) 010 - 474 4094
Situation	Locatie	

Rotterdam (pop. 598 521), 12 km

Annual closure	Jaarlijkse sluiting	no
Weekly closure	Wekelijkse sluitingsdag	no

Fees main season
Hoogseizoen tarieven 18 holes

	Week days Weekdagen	We/Bank holidays We/Feestdagen
Individual Individueel	Fl 100,-	Fl 125,-
Couple Paar	Fl 200,-	Fl 250,-

Caddy	Caddy	no
Electric Trolley	Electrische trolley	no
Buggy	Buggy	no
Clubs	Clubs	no

Credit cards Creditkaarten Eurocard - MasterCard

Access Toegang : A20 Rotterdam → Vlaardingen.
Exit 8 → Broekpolderweg, Golf 3 km
Map 1 on page 1008 Auto kaart 1 Blz 1008

GOLF COURSE / BAAN — **15**/20

Site	Terrein	
Maintenance	Onderhoud	
Architect	Architect	Frank Pennink Gerard Jol (1991)
Type	Type baan	polder, open country
Relief	Reliëf	
Water in play	Waterhazards	
Exp. to wind	Windgevoelig	
Trees in play	Bomen	

Scorecard Scorekaart	Chp. Back tees	Mens Heren	Ladies Damen
Length Lengte	6429	6048	5313
Par	72	72	72

Advised golfing ability Aanbevolen golfvaardigheid	0	12	24	36
Hcp required Vereiste hcp	30			

CLUB HOUSE & AMENITIES / CLUB HOUSE EN ANNEXEN — **7**/10

Pro shop	Pro shop	
Driving range	Oefenbaan	
Sheltered	overdekt	20 mats
On grass	op gras	no, 20 mats open air
Putting-green	putting-green	yes
Pitching-green	pitching-green	yes

HOTEL FACILITIES / HOTELS IN OMGEVING — **6**/10

HOTELS HOTELS

Delta - 78 rooms, D Fl 140,- Vlaardingen 5 km
Tel (31) 010 - 434 5477, Fax (31) 010 - 434 9525

New York Rotterdam
73 rooms, D Fl 135,- 20 km
Tel (31) 010 - 439 0500, Fax (31) 010 - 484 2701

Parkhotel Rotterdam
187 rooms, D Fl 335,- 15 km
Tel (31) 010 - 436 3611, Fax (31) 010 - 436 4212

RESTAURANTS RESTAURANTS

Parkheuvel Rotterdam
Tel (31) 010 - 475 0011 15 km

La Duchesse Schiedam
Tel (31) 010 - 426 4626 10 km

1015

CROMSTRIJEN

Deze nog vrij nieuwe baan, niet ver van Rotterdam, ligt in een wijd open gebied. Weliswaar dichtbij een autoweg, maar ook met fraaie vergezichten over de omliggende weidegebieden. De plaatselijke autoriteiten keurden de aanleg van een golfbaan goed op voorwaarde dat die open zou staan voor iedereen. Het resultaat daarvan is een openbare 9-holes baan naast een besloten 18-holes baan. Het meest opvallende natuurlijke element wordt gevormd door vier rijen met hoge bomen. De stukken water daartussen zijn uitgebouwd tot een klein meertje, dat meerdere keren in het spel komt. Een andere moeilijkheidsfactor bestaat uit de 75 strategisch geplaatste bunkers en, natuurlijk, uit de wind. Er is veel jonge aanplant, bedoeld om deze vlakke baan een beetje vorm te geven. De greens zijn groot, goed gevormd, goed ontworpen en sterk bewaakt. De baan is door Tom McAuley ontworpen voor alle type golfers en wordt zeer goed onderhouden baan. Naarmate de baan rijpt, zal het een van de meeste interessante banen van het land worden. Het clubhuis straalt al de allure uit die bij die status past.

This recent course, situated not far from Rotterdam, is laid out in wide open space, close to a motorway but with scenic views over farmland. The local authorities agreed to building the course as long as it was open to everyone. The result is a public 9-holer next to a private 18-hole course. The most striking natural elements are the four rows of trees. The patches of water have been extended to form a real lake, which comes into play several times. The other hazards are the 75 strategically placed bunkers and, of course, the wind. A great many shrubs have been planted as well, to give this flat course a little relief. The greens are huge, well-contoured, well-designed and very safely- guarded. As it matures, this Tom McAuley course, designed for all golfers and very well upkept, should become one of the most interesting in Holland. The clubhouse already has the majestic allure worthy of such a status.

Golfclub Cromstrijen — 1991
Veerweg 26
NL - 3281 LX NUMANSDORP

Office	Secretariaat	(31) 0186 - 654 455
Pro shop	Pro shop	(31) 0186 - 654 336
Fax	Fax	(31) 0186 - 654 681
Situation	Locatie	

Rotterdam (pop. 598 521), 20 km
Dordrecht (pop. 113 394), 15 km

Annual closure	Jaarlijkse sluiting	no
Weekly closure	Wekelijkse sluitingsdag	no

Fees main season
Hoogseizoen tarieven full day

	Week days Weekdagen	We/Bank holidays We/Feestdagen
Individual Individueel	Fl 80,-	Fl 95,-
Couple Paar	Fl 160,-	Fl 190,-

Caddy	Caddy	no
Electric Trolley	Electrische trolley Fl 7,50 /18 holes	
Buggy	Buggy	no
Clubs	Clubs	Fl 25,-
Credit cards Creditkaarten		no

Access Toegang : Rotterdam A29. Exit 22 → Havens Numansdorp, → Veenhaven
Map 1 on page 1008 Auto kaart 1 Blz 1008

GOLF COURSE / BAAN — 16/20

Site	Terrein	
Maintenance	Onderhoud	
Architect	Architect	Tom MacAuley
Type	Type baan	open country
Relief	Reliëf	
Water in play	Waterhazards	
Exp. to wind	Windgevoelig	
Trees in play	Bomen	

Scorecard Scorekaart	Chp. Back tees	Mens Heren	Ladies Damen
Length Lengte	6128	5934	5039
Par	72	72	72

Advised golfing ability
Aanbevolen golfvaardigheid — 0 12 24 36
Hcp required — Vereiste hcp — no

CLUB HOUSE & AMENITIES / CLUB HOUSE EN ANNEXEN — 8/10

Pro shop	Pro shop	
Driving range	Oefenbaan	
Sheltered	overdekt	12 mats
On grass	op gras	no, 6 mats open air
Putting-green	putting-green	yes
Pitching-green	pitching-green	yes

HOTEL FACILITIES / HOTELS IN OMGEVING — 5/10

HOTELS HOTELS
Het Wapen van Willemstad — Willemstad
6 rooms, D Fl. 150,- — 8 km
Tel (31) 0168 - 473 450
Fax (31) 0168 - 473 705

Zuiderparkhotel — Rotterdam
117 rooms, D Fl. 175,- — 20 km
Tel (31) 010 - 485 0055
Fax (31) 010 - 485 6304

RESTAURANTS RESTAURANTS
Wapen van Willemstad — Willemstad
Tel (31) 0168 - 473 450 — 8 km

Hosman Frères — Schiedam
Tel (31) 010 - 426 4096 — 25 km

DE PAN

Harry Colt heeft zijn stempel op meerdere banen in Nederland gezet en zijn ontwerpen zijn altijd een plezierige ervaring. Een korte bootreis was voor hem voldoende om hier naartoe te komen vanuit zijn geboorteland Engeland, waar hij ook een aantal meesterwerken afleverde (Sunningdale, Wentworth en Ganton, bijvoorbeeld). Hij was onder andere een van de eerste grote ontwerpers van banen in het binnenland. De Pan is een van die uitstekende voorbeelden van zijn vermogen net het juiste aantal hazards op te nemen om wat pikants aan het spel toe te voegen. Op heel natuurlijke wijze werkend met de omgeving en altijd een paar strategische verrassingen toevoegend, zoals een aantal fascinerende doglegs en veeleisende par-3 holes. De baan heeft meer glooiing dan je zou verwachten zo midden in Holland. De belangrijkste obstakels om te ontwijken zijn de bomen en een paar goed geplaatste bunkers. De fraai vorm gegeven greens worden goed bewaakt, maar sommigen zijn van elke verdediging ontbloot. Weggestopt in de bossen, ver van alle lawaai, is deze aantrekkelijke baan er een die u echt aan uw collectie moet toevoegen.

You often find the mark of Harry Colt in the Netherlands, and it's always a pleasure. Coming here was a short boat trip from his native England, where he also produced a number of masterpieces (Sunningdale, Wentworth and Ganton, for example). Among other things, he was one of the first great designers of inland courses. This is one excellent example of his skill in placing just the right number of hazards needed to add a little spice to the game, working very naturally with the surroundings and always adding a few strategic surprises, such as a number of compelling dog-legs and tough par 3s. The course undulates a little more than you might expect in this part of Holland, and the major hazards to be avoided are the trees and a few well-located bunkers. The nicely contoured greens are well-guarded, but some have no defence at all. Tucked away in the woods far from any noise, this fine course is most definitely one to add to your collection.

Utrechse Golf Club De Pan		1929
Amersfoortseweg 1		
NL - 3735 LJ BOSCH EN DUIN		
Office	Secretariaat	(31) 030 - 695 5223
Pro shop	Pro shop	(31) 030 - 695 6427
Fax	Fax	(31) 030 - 696 3769
Situation	Locatie	
Utrecht (pop. 234 106), 10 km		
Annual closure	Jaarlijkse sluiting	no
Weekly closure	Wekelijkse sluitingsdag	no

Fees main season
Hoogseizoen tarieven 18 holes

	Week days Weekdagen	We/Bank holidays We/Feestdagen
Individual Individueel	Fl 125,-	*
Couple Paar	Fl 250,-	*

* We: members only

Caddy	Caddy	no
Electric Trolley	Electrische trolley	no
Buggy	Buggy	no
Clubs	Clubs	no
Credit cards Creditkaarten		no

Access Toegang : Utrecht A28 → Amersfoort,
Exit 3 → Den Dolder. 500 m left. 1.7 km parallel road
Map 1 on page 1008 Auto kaart 1 Blz 1008

GOLF COURSE
BAAN
16/20

Site	Terrein	
Maintenance	Onderhoud	
Architect	Architect	Harry S. Colt
Type	Type baan	forest
Relief	Reliëf	
Water in play	Waterhazards	
Exp. to wind	Windgevoelig	
Trees in play	Bomen	

Scorecard Scorekaart	Chp. Back tees	Mens Heren	Ladies Damen
Length Lengte	6088	5707	4951
Par	72	72	72

Advised golfing ability		0	12	24	36
Aanbevolen golfvaardigheid					
Hcp required	Vereiste hcp	28			

CLUB HOUSE & AMENITIES
CLUB HOUSE EN ANNEXEN
8/10

Pro shop	Pro shop	
Driving range	Oefenbaan	
Sheltered	overdekt	6 mats
On grass	op gras	no, 4 mats open air
Putting-green	putting-green	yes
Pitching-green	pitching-green	yes

HOTEL FACILITIES
HOTELS IN OMGEVING
7/10

HOTELS HOTELS
De Hoefslag — Bosch en Duin
34 rooms, D FL 220,- — 1 km
Tel (31) 030 - 225 1051
Fax (31) 030 - 228 5821

Kerkebosch — Zeist
30 rooms, D Fl 195,- — 5 km
Tel (31) 030 - 691 4734
Fax (31) 030 - 691 3114

RESTAURANTS RESTAURANTS
De Hoefslag — Bosch en Duin
Tel (31) 030 - 225 1051 — 1 km

Wilhelmina Park — Utrecht
Tel (31) 030 - 251 0693 — 10 km

1017

Deze nieuwe baan is onderdeel van het bekende, gelijknamige attractiepark (ideaal voor de niet-golfers in de familie), waarvan sommige onderdelen vanaf de fairways te zien zijn. De baan ligt in een landelijke omgeving met aan weerszijden een natuurgebied. Veel open ruimtes waardoor de richting en kracht van de wind een grote rol spelen, omdat maar vier holes beschermd liggen. Bij gebrek aan bomen is water de belangrijkste hindernis, in de vorm van grote vijvers langs de baan of voor de green. Op de derde hole kronkelt een kreekje door de fairway, waardoor spelers voor de keuze worden gesteld rechts of links te spelen. De greens zijn groot, goed gevormd en beschermd door handig geplaatste bunkers omgeven door heuveltjes en andere vormen van aarden wallen. Met smaak ontworpen door Donald Steel. Een prettige en boeiende baan geschikt voor spelers van alle nivo's. Goed aangelegd en goed onderhouden.

This very recent course is part of the celebrated "De Efteling" theme park (ideal for non-golfers in the family), which you can actually see from the fairways. The whole piece is located in a rural spot surrounded by two nature reserves. There is a lot of very open space here, which gives great importance to the direction and strength of the wind, as only four holes are protected. For want of trees, water is the main hazard to cope with, in the shape of large ponds lining the fairways or in front of the greens. At the 3rd, a stretch of water winds its way down the fairway, forcing players to choose from which side of the fairway they want to play the hole. The greens are huge, well-contoured and protected by cleverly placed bunkers surrounded by mounds and other forms of earthwork. Tastefully designed by Donald Steel, this is a very pleasant and entertaining course for golfers of all abilities. Well built and well upkept.

Golfpark de Efteling — 1995
Veldstraat 6
NL - 5176 NB KAATSHEUVEL

Office	Secretariaat	(31) 0416 - 288 399
Pro shop	Pro shop	(31) 0416 - 288 399
Fax	Fax	(31) 0416 - 281 095
Situation	Locatie	

Tilburg (pop. 163 383), 10 km

Annual closure	Jaarlijkse sluiting	no
Weekly closure	Wekelijkse sluitingsdag	no

Fees main season
Hoogseizoen tarieven 18 holes

	Week days Weekdagen	We/Bank holidays We/Feestdagen
Individual Individueel	Fl 75,-	Fl 85,-
Couple Paar	Fl 150,-	Fl 170,-

Caddy	Caddy	no
Electric Trolley	Electrische trolley	no
Buggy	Buggy	Fl 40,-
Clubs	Clubs	Fl 20,-

Credit cards Creditkaarten
VISA - Eurocard - MasterCard - AMEX - DC

1018

Access Toegang : A59, Exit 37 → Efteling → Golfpark
Map 1 on page 1008 Auto kaart 1 Blz 1008

GOLF COURSE
BAAN — 16/20

Site	Terrein	
Maintenance	Onderhoud	
Architect	Architect	Donald Steel
Type	Type baan	open country
Relief	Reliëf	
Water in play	Waterhazards	
Exp. to wind	Windgevoelig	
Trees in play	Bomen	

Scorecard Scorekaart	Chp. Back tees	Mens Heren	Ladies Damen
Length Lengte	6258	5960	5072
Par	72	72	72

Advised golfing ability
Aanbevolen golfvaardigheid — 0 12 24 36
Hcp required Vereiste hcp — no

CLUB HOUSE & AMENITIES
CLUB HOUSE EN ANNEXEN — 8/10

Pro shop	Pro shop	
Driving range	Oefenbaan	
Sheltered	overdekt	6 mats
On grass	op gras	yes
Putting-green	putting-green	yes
Pitching-green	pitching-green	yes

HOTEL FACILITIES
HOTELS IN OMGEVING — 5/10

HOTELS HOTELS
De Efteling — Kaatsheuvel
121 rooms, D Fl 200,- — 1 km
Tel (31) 0416 - 282 000
Fax (31) 0416 - 281 515

De Postelse Hoeve — Tilburg
35 rooms, D Fl 200,- — 10 km
Tel (31) 013 - 463 6335
Fax (31) 013 - 463 9390

RESTAURANTS RESTAURANTS
De Pepermolen — Waalwijk
Tel (31) 0416 - 339 308 — 8 km

Valentijn — Tilburg
Tel (31) 013 - 543 3386 — 10 km

Een van de beste banen in het binnenland met een nivo van onderhoud dat overeenkomt met de hoge kwaliteit van de geboden faciliteiten. De baan ligt midden in een prachtig bos met beekjes en vennetjes. Twee lussen van negen holes omcirkelen grote stukken bos, waardoor spelers een gevoel van afzonde-ring en rust krijgen dat zeer bevorderlijk voor de concentratie is. Hoewel de fairways breed zijn - goed nieuws voor krachtpatsers - is het oppassen geblazen voor de doglegs, die vragen om met effect geslagen ballen, zowel naar links als naar rechts. Dit is een baan voor technisch ervaren spelers, met goed ontworpen greens, bewaakt door grote bunkers. Kenmerkend voor Harry Colt, duidelijk een van de grootste golf-architecten uit de eerste helft van deze eeuw. Zijn ontwerpen zijn veeleisend voor de goede, maar toch ook mild voor de stomme slagen van de gemiddelde speler. Een aardig element is het grote ven voor het clubhuis dat in de zomer als openlucht zwembad fungeert.

One of Holland's best inland courses with a standard upkeep to match the general quality of facilities. The course is laid out in a magnificent forest with streams and ponds. The trees are right in the middle of the two parts of the course, out and in, and this gives players an impression of isolation and tranquillity that can be very useful for concentration. Although the fairways are wide - good news for big-hitters - still watch out for the dog-legs winding left and right and calling for a number of flighted shots in both directions. This is a course for skilled technicians, with well designed putting surfaces and greens well-guarded by large bunkers, another distinctive feature of Harry Colt, definitely one of the greatest course designers from the first half of the century. His layouts demand a great deal from good players but are somehow more lenient on duff shots from the average hacker.

Eindhovensche Golf — 1930

Eindhovenseweg 300
NL - 5553 VB VALKENSWAARD

Office	Secretariaat	(31) 040 - 201 4816
Pro shop	Pro shop	(31) 040 - 204 4546
Fax	Fax	(31) 040 - 204 4038
Situation	Locatie	

Eindhoven (pop. 196 130), 10 km

| Annual closure | Jaarlijkse sluiting | no |
| Weekly closure | Wekelijkse sluitingsdag | no |

Fees main season
Hoogseizoen tarieven full day

	Week days Weekdagen	We/Bank holidays We/Feestdagen
Individual Individueel	Fl 100,-	Fl 100,-
Couple Paar	Fl 200,-	Fl 200,-

NGF members Fl 25,- reduction

Caddy	Caddy	no
Electric Trolley	Electrische trolley	no
Buggy	Buggy	no
Clubs	Clubs	no
Credit cards Creditkaarten		no

Access Toegang : Eindhoven A2 → Weert.
Exit 33. N69 → Valkenswaard. Golf 4 km
Map 1 on page 1008 Auto kaart 1 Blz 1008

GOLF COURSE / BAAN — 18/20

Site	Terrein	
Maintenance	Onderhoud	
Architect	Architect	Harry S. Colt

Type	Type baan	forest
Relief	Reliëf	
Water in play	Waterhazards	
Exp. to wind	Windgevoelig	
Trees in play	Bomen	

Scorecard Scorekaart	Chp. Back tees	Mens Heren	Ladies Damen
Length Lengte	6176	5918	5048
Par	72	72	72

Advised golfing ability
Aanbevolen golfvaardigheid
0   12   24   36

Hcp required Vereiste hcp   36, We 24

CLUB HOUSE & AMENITIES / CLUB HOUSE EN ANNEXEN — 8/10

Pro shop	Pro shop	
Driving range	Oefenbaan	
Sheltered	overdekt	5 mats
On grass	op gras	yes
Putting-green	putting-green	yes
Pitching-green	pitching-green	yes

1019

HOTEL FACILITIES / HOTELS IN OMGEVING — 6/10

HOTELS HOTELS

Dorint Hotel — Eindhoven
191 rooms, D Fl 190,- — 8 km
Tel (31) 040 - 232 6111
Fax (31) 040 - 244 0148

Holiday Inn Hotel — Eindhoven
201 rooms, D Fl 190,- — 8 km
Tel (31) 040 - 243 3222
Fax (31) 040 - 244 9235

RESTAURANTS RESTAURANTS

De Waterkers — Eindhoven
Tel (31) 040 - 212 4999 — 7 km

Karpendonkse Hoeve — Eindhoven
Tel (31) 040 - 281 3663 — 7 km

GELPENBERG

14	4	5

Zoals veel banen in Nederland is de Gelpenberg in twee fasen tot stand gekomen. En zoals vaker liggen negen holes in een bosgebied en de andere in vroeger agrarisch, meer open terrein. Hier zijn de eerste negen holes betrekkelijk smal, met bomen als voornaamste hindernis. Middenin het bos liggen flinke stukken hei, die op vier holes in het spel komen en voldoende problemen geven om het praktisch ontbreken van fairway-bunkers te verklaren. Omdat er zes doglegs bij zijn, is een goede strategie en effectvolle slagen (in de goede richting) een 'must'. De tweede negen zijn veel breder, maar ook meer beïnvloed door de wind. Een klein meertje komt op drie holes in het spel, net als een paar grote fairway bunkers, zoals op de 18e. De bunker die op de slothole de fairway doorkruist moet een van de grootste van Europa zijn. Een baan die het waard is gespeeld te worden, door spelers van elk nivo.

Like several courses in the Netherlands, Gelpenberg was designed in two stages. Like the others, you find nine holes amidst an old forest and the others on former farming land, which is much more open. Here, the front 9 are tight, with trees as the main hazards, so take care to avoid them. In the middle of the forest, there is a huge area of heather, which comes into play on four holes and causes enough difficulty to explain the virtual absence of fairway bunkers. And as there are 6 dog-legs to cope with, choosing the right strategy and flighting the ball (in the right direction) are important. The back 9 are much wider, but also much exposed to the wind. A small lake comes into play on three holes, as do some large fairway bunkers, notably on the 18th. The bunker splitting the fairway on this final hole must be one of the largest in Europe. A course well worth getting to know, for players of all levels.

Drentse Golfclub De Gelpenberg — 1972

Aelderholt 4
NL - 7874 TZ AALDEN

Office	Secretariaat	(31) 0591 - 372 343
Pro shop	Pro shop	(31) 0591 - 372 174
Fax	Fax	(31) 0591 - 371 800
Situation	Locatie	

Emmen (pop. 93 476), 15 km

Annual closure	Jaarlijkse sluiting	no
Weekly closure	Wekelijkse sluitingsdag	no

Fees main season
Hoogseizoen tarieven 18 holes

	Week days Weekdagen	We/Bank holidays We/Feestdagen
Individual Individueel	Fl 60,-	Fl 70,-
Couple Paar	Fl 120,-	Fl 140,-

Caddy	Caddy	no
Electric Trolley	Electrische trolley	no
Buggy	Buggy	no
Clubs	Clubs	no

Credit cards Creditkaarten — no

1020

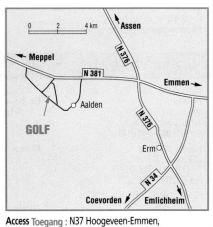

Access Toegang : N37 Hoogeveen-Emmen,
Exit Oosterhesselen → Zweeloo → Golf
Map 1 on page 1009 Auto kaart 1 Blz 1009

GOLF COURSE / BAAN — 14/20

Site	Terrein	▇▇▇▇
Maintenance	Onderhoud	▇▇▇▇
Architect	Architect	Frank Pennink Donald Steel
Type	Type baan	forest
Relief	Reliëf	▇▇
Water in play	Waterhazards	▇▇
Exp. to wind	Windgevoelig	▇▇▇
Trees in play	Bomen	▇▇▇▇

Scorecard Scorekaart	Chp. Back tees	Mens Heren	Ladies Damen
Length Lengte	6031	6031	5093
Par	71	71	71

Advised golfing ability
Aanbevolen golfvaardigheid — 0   12   24   36

Hcp required	Vereiste hcp	nee

CLUB HOUSE & AMENITIES / CLUB HOUSE EN ANNEXEN — 4/10

Pro shop	Pro shop	▇▇▇▇
Driving range	Oefenbaan	▇▇▇
Sheltered	overdekt	5 mats
On grass	op gras	no, 15 mats open air
Putting-green	putting-green	yes
Pitching-green	pitching-green	yes

HOTEL FACILITIES / HOTELS IN OMGEVING — 5/10

HOTELS HOTELS

Ten Cate — Emmen
33 rooms, D Fl 125,- — 15 km
Tel (31) 0591 - 617 600
Fax (31) 0591 - 618 432

Boorland — Emmen
14 rooms, D 135,- — 15 km
Tel (31 591) 613 746
Fax (31 591) 616 525

RESTAURANTS RESTAURANTS

Idylle — Zweeloo
Tel (31) 0591 - 371 857 — 2 km

Zuudbarge — Emmen
Tel (31) 0591 - 630 813 — 16 km

Deze baan is aangelegd in een landelijk gebied, tussen een autoweg en wat industrie. Alhoewel ook een aantal holes verborgen ligt in de bossen, waardoor een vredige atmosfeer is geschapen. Hoewel de baan nog jong is, ogen de bomen zeer volwassen. De fairways mogen wat korter gemaaid (er is nauwelijks een semi-rough). Twee vijvers en een paar kleine vennetjes komen op verschillende manieren in het spel, zoals op de 6e, een par-3 waarvan de tee (niet de green) op een eiland ligt. De tweede negen strekken zich uit over een tot 20 meter verhoogd stuk land, zodat spelers worden geconfronteerd met blinde slagen en sterk hellende fairways. Het hoogste punt levert een fraai uitzicht over de omgeving op. Het vormt een welkome onderbreking van het vlakke deel van de baan. De greens kunnen lastig zijn, afhankelijk van de pin-positie en een aantal afslagen zijn veeleisend, maar er is altijd ruimte om een veilige weg te vinden. Geschikt voor alle type golfers.

This course is laid out in a rural zone between a motorway and industrial estate, although several holes are tucked away in a woodland area and help give the site something of a peaceful atmosphere. Although still very young, the trees create an air of maturity, even though the grass is not yet mown short enough (there is no semi-rough). Two lakes and several little ponds come into play in different ways, like on the 6th, a par 3 where the tee is an island (but not the green). The back 9 are built over a plot of fallow land some 20 metres high, where players are confronted with a few blind shots and many sloping lies. This altitude offers some pretty views over the region and breaks up the rather flat nature of the course. The greens can be difficult, depending on the pin positions, and a number of drives can be tricky, but there is always room to play safe. For golfers of all levels.

Golfbaan Gendersteyn — 1995
Postbus 453
NL - 5500 AL VELDHOVEN

Office	Secretariaat	(31) 040 - 253 4444
Pro shop	Pro shop	(31) 040 - 254 7101
Fax	Fax	(31) 040 - 254 9747
Situation	Locatie	

Eindhoven (pop. 196 130), 8 km

Annual closure	Jaarlijkse sluiting	no
Weekly closure	Wekelijkse sluitingsdag	no

Fees main season
Hoogseizoen tarieven 18 holes

	Week days / Weekdagen	We/Bank holidays / We/Feestdagen
Individual Individueel	Fl 65,-	Fl 85,-
Couple Paar	Fl 130,-	Fl 170,-

Caddy	Caddy	no
Electric Trolley	Electrische trolley	Fl 7,50
Buggy	Buggy	Fl 50,-
Clubs	Clubs	Fl 5,-

Credit cards Creditkaarten — no

Access Toegang : A2 Eindhoven → Antwerpen.
Exit 32 → Veldhoven → Eersel. Golf 2 km
Map 1 on page 1008 Auto kaart 1 Blz 1008

GOLF COURSE / BAAN — 15/20

Site	Terrein	
Maintenance	Onderhoud	
Architect	Architect	Alan Rijks
Type	Type baan	parkland
Relief	Reliëf	
Water in play	Waterhazards	
Exp. to wind	Windgevoelig	
Trees in play	Bomen	

Scorecard / Scorekaart	Chp. / Back tees	Mens / Heren	Ladies / Damen
Length Lengte	5965	5770	4869
Par	72	72	72

Advised golfing ability
Aanbevolen golfvaardigheid — 0 12 24 36

Hcp required Vereiste hcp — no

CLUB HOUSE & AMENITIES / CLUB HOUSE EN ANNEXEN — 7/10

Pro shop	Pro shop	
Driving range	Oefenbaan	
Sheltered	overdekt	10 mats
On grass	op gras	no, 6 mats open air
Putting-green	putting-green	yes
Pitching-green	pitching-green	yes

HOTEL FACILITIES / HOTELS IN OMGEVING — 7/10

HOTELS HOTELS

Dorint Hotel — Eindhoven
191 rooms, D Fl 190,- — 8 km
Tel (31) 040 - 232 6111, Fax (31) 040 - 244 0148

Holiday Inn Hotel — Eindhoven
201 rooms, D Fl 190,- — 8 km
Tel (31) 040 - 243 3222, Fax (31) 040 - 244 9235

Motel Eindhoven — Eindhoven
175 rooms, D FL 100,- — 8 km
Tel (31) 040 - 212 3435, Fax (31) 040 - 212 0774

RESTAURANTS RESTAURANTS

De Waterkers — Eindhoven
Tel (31) 040 - 212 4999 — 7 km

Karpendonkse Hoeve — Eindhoven 7 km
Tel (31) 040 - 281 3663

1021

GOES

Van een afstand lijkt deze baan misschien op een van de vele nieuwe 'polderbanen'. Maar als je op de fairways loopt vallen direct de glooiingen en heuveltjes op, die elke slag een beetje moeilijker dan normaal kunnen maken. Deze heuveltjes zijn gemaakt met de grond die vrijkwam bij het graven van de waterpartijen die op dertien holes in het spel komen. Soms alleen langs de kant van de fairway, maar in veel gevallen vlak voor de green. Water is niet de enige hindernis om rekening mee te houden. Er ligt een flink aantal bunkers op strategische plaatsen. De greens zijn alle wat glooiend, maar zonder de overdreven contouren die je op veel nieuwe banen tegenkomt. Als afsluiting van het hele project is een ruim nieuw clubhuis gebouwd, dat een fraai uitzicht over de baan biedt.

From a distance, Goes may look like one of the many new courses in the flat Dutch «polderland». But once walking its fairways you will notice the subtle undulations and hills that frequently make your next shot a little more awkward. These slopes result from the clever use of soil dug out to create the many water hazards that come into play, sometimes edging the fairway but on several occasions in front of the greens. And water is not the only hazard to cope with, as a fair number of bunkers are strategically located on the fairways. The greens are rather distinctly contoured but don't have the excessive bumps often seen on today's new courses. Now that the new clubhouse has opened its doors, the facilities are complete and up-to-standard.

Goese Golf — 1995
Krukweg 52
NL - 4465 BH GOES

Office	Secretariaat	(31) 0113 - 229 557
Pro shop	Pro shop	(31) 0113 - 229 557
Fax	Fax	(31) 0113 - 229 554
Situation	Locatie	

Goes (pop. 33 300), 1 km

Annual closure	Jaarlijkse sluiting	no
Weekly closure	Wekelijkse sluitingsdag	no

Fees main season
Hoogseizoen tarieven per dag

	Week days Weekdagen	We/Bank holidays We/Feestdagen
Individual Individueel	Fl 75,-	Fl 85,-
Couple Paar	Fl 150,-	Fl 170,-

Caddy	Caddy	no
Electric Trolley	Electrische trolley	Fl 20,-/18 holes
Buggy	Buggy	Fl 40,-/18 holes
Clubs	Clubs	Fl 25,-/18 holes

Credit cards Creditkaarten
VISA - Eurocard - MasterCard - AMEX

1022

Zizrikzee

0 2 4 km

THOLEN

N 255 N 256

Middelsburg
Veerse mer
Whilheminadorp

GOLF

Oost-Souburg
GOES Kattendijke
N 289
Bergen op Zoom

De Poel M 58

Ooster schelde

Access Toegang : A58 → N256 → Goes Centrum
→ Goese Meer
Map 1 on page 1008 Auto kaart 1 Blz 1008

GOLF COURSE / BAAN — 15/20

Site	Terrein	
Maintenance	Onderhoud	
Architect	Architect	Donald Steel H. Hertzberger
Type	Type baan	polder, open country
Relief	Reliëf	
Water in play	Waterhazards	
Exp. to wind	Windgevoelig	
Trees in play	Bomen	

Scorecard Scorekaart	Chp. Back tees	Mens Heren	Ladies Damen
Length Lengte	6269	6110	5145
Par	72	72	72

Advised golfing ability Aanbevolen golfvaardigheid	0	12	24	36
Hcp required Vereiste hcp	no			

CLUB HOUSE & AMENITIES / CLUB HOUSE EN ANNEXEN — 7/10

Pro shop	Pro shop	
Driving range	Oefenbaan	
Sheltered	overdekt	9 mats
On grass	op gras	no, 9 mats open air
Putting-green	putting-green	yes
Pitching-green	pitching-green	yes

HOTEL FACILITIES / HOTELS IN OMGEVING — 6/10

HOTELS HOTELS
Bolsjoi — Goes, 3 km
12 rooms, D Fl 145,-
Tel (31) 0113 - 232 323
Fax (31) 0113 - 251 755

Le Manoir — Kruiningen, 15 km
8 rooms, D Fl 300,-
Tel (31) 0113 - 381 753
Fax (31) 0113 - 381 763

RESTAURANTS RESTAURANTS
Inter Scaldes — Kruiningen, 15 km
Tel (31) 0113 - 381 753

Nolet-Reymerswale — Yerseke, 14 km
Tel (31) 0113 - 517 642

Het specifieke karakter van deze goed ontworpen baan is de afwisseling tussen open en bebost terrein, een typische eigenschap van het hele gebied. Het uit zich hier in het feit dat bijna de helft van de holes begint in een open stuk en eindigt temidden van bomen. Of andersom. In tegenstelling tot veel nieuwe banen is hier weinig grond verzet, zelfs niet voor de waterhazards die klein en heel natuurlijk zijn. De meeste fairways zijn breed en mild voor afgedwaalde ballen, maar enkele losse bomen kunnen voor flinke problemen zorgen. In combinatie met de wind (in de open gedeelten) kunnen zij elke hoop op een goede score de nek omdraaien. Ondanks het ontbreken van reliëf valt er van prachtige vergezichten te genieten, vooral in de herfst. De greens zijn middelgroot, niet moeilijk te lezen en over het algemeen niet spectaculair. Wel afdoende bewaakt door bunkers.

The full character of this competently designed course lies with its alternating forest and open landscape, a frequent feature throughout the region. It is plain to see on almost half the holes, which start under the open sky and end up in the trees, or inversely. As opposed to many recent courses, there has been little artificial moving of earth, even for the water hazards that are small and very natural. Most of the fairways are wide and forgiving for wayward shots, but several isolated trees can spell serious trouble. Combined with the wind (in the more exposed sections), they can dash any hope of playing to your handicap, a feat that otherwise is more than possible. Despite the lack of relief, there are some beautiful views to be had here, especially in the Autumn. The greens are mid-sized, pretty easy to read and generally, but none too imaginatively, well-guarded by a brace of bunkers.

Golf & Country Club De Graafschap   0
Sluitdijk 4
NL - 7241 RR LOCHEM

Office	Secretariaat	(31) 0573 - 254 323
Pro shop	Pro shop	(31) 0573 - 258 179
Fax	Fax	(31) 0573 - 258 450
Situation	Locatie	
Deventer (pop. 69 079), 22 km		
Annual closure	Jaarlijkse sluiting	no
Weekly closure	Wekelijkse sluitingsdag	no

Fees main season
Hoogseizoen tarieven full day

	Week days	We/Bank holidays
	Weekdagen	We/Feestdagen
Individual Individueel	Fl 90,-	Fl 100,-
Couple Paar	Fl 180,-	Fl 200,-

Caddy	Caddy	no
Electric Trolley	Electrische trolley	no
Buggy	Buggy	no
Clubs	Clubs	Fl 25,-

Credit cards Creditkaarten   no

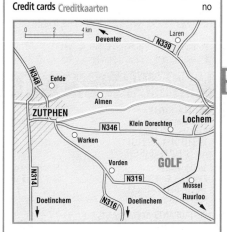

Access Toegang : A1 Amsterdam -Enschede. Exit 23.
N348 → Zutphen. N346 → Lochem. Golf km 11.5
Map 1 on page 1009 Auto kaart 1 Blz 1009

GOLF COURSE
BAAN   15/20

Site	Terrein	▦
Maintenance	Onderhoud	▦
Architect	Architect	Eschauzier & Thate
Type	Type baan	forest
Relief	Reliëf	▪
Water in play	Waterhazards	▦
Exp. to wind	Windgevoelig	▦
Trees in play	Bomen	▦

Scorecard	Chp.	Mens	Ladies
Scorekaart	Back tees	Heren	Damen
Length Lengte	6306	6059	5277
Par	72	72	72

Advised golfing ability   0   12   24   36
Aanbevolen golfvaardigheid
Hcp required   Vereiste hcp   no

CLUB HOUSE & AMENITIES
CLUB HOUSE EN ANNEXEN   7/10

Pro shop	Pro shop	▦
Driving range	Oefenbaan	▦
Sheltered	overdekt	9 mats
On grass	op gras	no, 9 mats open air
Putting-green	putting-green	yes
Pitching-green	pitching-green	yes

HOTEL FACILITIES
HOTELS IN OMGEVING   6/10

HOTELS HOTELS
De Scheperskamp   Lochem
46 rooms, D Fl. 185,-   3 km
Tel (31) 0573 - 254 051
Fax (31) 0573 - 257 150

't Hof van Gelre   Lochem
49 rooms, D Fl. 150,-   3 km
Tel (31) 0573 - 253 351
Fax (31) 0573 - 254 245

RESTAURANTS RESTAURANTS
Mondani   Lochem
Tel (31) 0573 - 257 595   3 km

Galantijn   Zutphen
Tel (31) 0575 - 525 555   8 km

1023

Wat kunt u anders verwachten in de provincie Zeeland dan een straffe wind? Grevelingenhout is ontworpen in een mooi gebied langs de rivierendelta, waar zeilen de traditionele sport is. Het is de eerste golfbaan in Nederland waar ook gewoond kan worden, al zijn de huizen op de vrij kleine stukken grond niet altijd wonderen van architectuur. Zij zijn gescheiden van de baan door vijvertjes en sloten, die op bijna alle holes in het spel komen. We hopen maar dat de aangeplante bomen en struiken de bewoners, en de spelers, geleidelijk wat meer privacy zullen bieden. Dit is een goede golfbaan om spelers aan water te laten wennen. Dat komt op fraaie wijze in het spel op de 12e (een par-3) over een vijver en de 9e en de 18e, die een dubbelgreen delen, bewaakt door water. Het zal niet verbazen dat al die nattigheid het grootste obstakel vormt, samen met de wind. Het zou spelers ertoe kunnen aanzetten juist hier matchplay te spelen.

What else would you expect in the province of Zeeland than persistent wind? Grevelingenhout was designed in a pretty region along the delta, where sailing is the traditional sport. This is Holland's first residential course, although the houses built on small plots of land are hardly wonders of architecture. They are separated from the fairways by ponds and other stretches of water, which come into play on most holes. We can only hope that the newly planted trees and bushes will offer the inhabitants, and players, a little more privacy. This is a good course for accustoming all golfers to the problems posed by water, which is excellently brought into play on the 12th (a par 3 over water) and the 9th and 18th holes, which share a very well-guarded double green. Water is, not surprisingly, the key difficulty here, together with the wind we talked about, and this should incite most golfers to opt for the match-play format.

Golfclub Grevelingenhout — 1989

Oudendijk 3
NL - 4311 NA BRUINISSE

Office	Secretariaat	(31) 0111 - 482 650
Pro shop	Pro shop	(31) 0111 - 482 650
Fax	Fax	(31) 0111 - 481 566

Situation Locatie
Goes (pop. 33 281), 30 km
Rotterdam (pop. 598 521), 50 km

Annual closure	Jaarlijkse sluiting	no
Weekly closure	Wekelijkse sluitingsdag	no

Fees main season
Hoogseizoen tarieven full day

	Week days Weekdagen	We/Bank holidays We/Feestdagen
Individual Individueel	Fl 75,-	Fl 95,-
Couple Paar	Fl 150,-	Fl 190,-

Caddy	Caddy	no
Electric Trolley	Electrische trolley	Fl 40,-
Buggy	Buggy	no
Clubs	Clubs	no

Credit cards Creditkaarten   no

1024

Access Toegang : Rotterdam A29, Exit Middelharnis,
N59 → Zierikzee. Exit Aquadelta
Map 1 on page 1008 Auto kaart 1 Blz 1008

GOLF COURSE / BAAN — 14/20

Site	Terrein	
Maintenance	Onderhoud	
Architect	Architect	Donald Harradine
Type	Type baan	parkland
Relief	Reliëf	
Water in play	Waterhazards	
Exp. to wind	Windgevoelig	
Trees in play	Bomen	

Scorecard Scorekaart	Chp. Back tees	Mens Heren	Ladies Damen
Length Lengte	6193	5951	5144
Par	72	72	72

Advised golfing ability Aanbevolen golfvaardigheid	0	12	24	36
Hcp required Vereiste hcp	no			

CLUB HOUSE & AMENITIES / CLUB HOUSE EN ANNEXEN — 7/10

Pro shop	Pro shop	
Driving range	Oefenbaan	
Sheltered	overdekt	6 mats
On grass	op gras	no, 6 mats open air
Putting-green	putting-green	yes
Pitching-green	pitching-green	yes

HOTEL FACILITIES / HOTELS IN OMGEVING — 4/10

HOTELS HOTELS
Mondragon   Zierikzee
8 rooms, D Fl 195,-   10 km
Tel (31) 0111 - 413 051
Fax (31) 0111 - 415 997

Schuddebeurs   Schuddebeurs
21 rooms, D Fl 205,-   15 km
Tel (31) 0111 - 415 651
Fax (31) 0111 - 413 103

RESTAURANTS RESTAURANTS
De drie Morianen   Zierikzee
Tel (31) 0111 - 412 931   10 km

Mondragon   Zierikzee
Tel (31) 0111 - 412 670   10 km

De Hollandse kust leent zich uitstekend voor de aanleg van prachtige banen en deze is daar een goed voorbeeld van. Naar het ontwerp van de architecten Colt en Alison die borg stonden voor een uitdagend ontwerp. Het is maar goed dat de lengte niet overdreven is, want het komt vaak voor dat je slagen verliest in dichte struiken of in diepe bunkers. Maar als u door de wind met rust gelaten wordt en alle aandacht aan uw swing kunt besteden, dan hebt u een goede kans een mooi resultaat te scoren. Zoals je in de duinen kan verwachten zijn er maar weinig echt vlakke stukken op de fairways. Veel uphill of downhill slagen dus, plus interessante situaties rond de greens. De Haagsche heeft talloze internationale wedstrijden (waaronder het Dutch Open) mogen ontvangen. Het is de moeite waard hier een dag voor uit te trekken. Zowaar een linksbaan zonder het Kanaal te hoeven oversteken.

The Dutch coast is a marvellous site for building great courses, and this is one of the finest. The cachet of designers Colt and Alison speaks volumes for the challenging style of this layout. Although not excessively long, there are more than enough opportunities to drop shots, in the thickets lining the fairways or in the pot bunkers. If the wind leaves you alone, with just your problems of swing to cope with, you will have every chance of returning a good score. As you might expect among sand dunes, there are few really flat lies on the fairways, a lot of shots uphill and down, and some tantalising situations around the greens. Haagsche has hosted a number of international events (including the Dutch Open) and, with its counterparts along the coast, deserves a special golfing holiday. Here is a great links to play without having to ferry across the Channel.

Koninklijke Haagsche Golf & Countryclub   **1938**

Groot Haesenbroekseweg 22
NL - 2243 EC WASSENAAR

Office	Secretariaat	(31) 070 - 517 9607
Pro shop	Pro shop	(31) 070 - 517 9822
Fax	Fax	(31) 070 - 514 0171
Situation	Locatie	

Den Haag (pop. 445 279), 4 km

Annual closure	Jaarlijkse sluiting	no
Weekly closure	Wekelijkse sluitingsdag	no

Fees main season
Hoogseizoen tarieven full day

	Week days Weekdagen	We/Bank holidays We/Feestdagen
Individual Individueel	Fl. 160,-	*
Couple Paar	Fl. 320,-	*

* Week-end: members only

Caddy	Caddy	no
Electric Trolley	Electrische trolley	Fl. 20,-
Buggy	Buggy	no
Clubs	Clubs	Fl. 50,-

Credit cards Creditkaarten   no

Access Toegang : A44 → Wassenaar
Map 1 on page 1008 Auto kaart 1 Blz 1008

GOLF COURSE BAAN   **18**/20

Site	Terrein	▬▬▬▬▬□□
Maintenance	Onderhoud	▬▬▬▬▬▬□
Architect	Architect	Harry S. Colt Allison
Type	Type baan	links
Relief	Reliëf	
Water in play	Waterhazards	▬▬▬▬□□□
Exp. to wind	Windgevoelig	▬▬□□□□□
Trees in play	Bomen	▬▬▬▬▬□□

Scorecard Scorekaart	Chp. Back tees	Mens Heren	Ladies Damen
Length Lengte	6142	5674	5006
Par	72	72	72

Advised golfing ability	0	12	24	36
Aanbevolen golfvaardigheid		▬▬▬□		
Hcp required Vereiste hcp	26			

CLUB HOUSE & AMENITIES CLUB HOUSE EN ANNEXEN   **7**/10

Pro shop	Pro shop	▬▬▬▬▬□□
Driving range	Oefenbaan	▬▬▬▬□□□
Sheltered	overdekt	12 mats
On grass	op gras	yes
Putting-green	putting-green	yes
Pitching-green	pitching-green	yes

HOTEL FACILITIES HOTELS IN OMGEVING   **8**/10

HOTELS HOTELS

Des Indes   Den Haag
70 rooms, D Fl. 505,-   5 km
Tel (31) 070 - 363 2932, Fax (31) 070 - 356 2863

Kurhaus - 233 rooms, D Fl. 400,-   Scheveningen
Tel (31) 070 - 416 2636, Fax (31) 070 - 416 2646   5 km

Green Park 92 rooms, D Fl. 290,-   Leidschendam
Tel (31) 070 - 320 9280, Fax (31) 070 - 327 4907   7 km

Auberge de Kievit   Wassenaar
23 rooms, D Fl. 350,-   1 km
Tel (31) 070 - 511 9232, Fax (31) 070 - 511 0969

RESTAURANTS RESTAURANTS

Auberge de Kievit   Wassenaar
Tel (31) 070 - 511 9232   1 km

't Ganzenest   Den Haag
Tel (31) 070 - 389 6709   5 km

1025

Dit is waarschijnlijk een van de laatste keren dat de aanleg van een baan in zulke bebost terrein werd toegestaan. In dit geval was het verkrijgen van een kapvergunning iets makkelijker, omdat het om mijnhout ging. Er is nog steeds veel daarvan blijven staan, en die bomen zijn de belangrijkste hindernis, vooral op de smallere holes en de vele doglegs. De begroeiing onder de bomen kan heel dicht zijn, hetgeen een extra afstraffing van onnauwkeurige slagen oplevert (neem wat extra ballen mee als u niet zo zuiver slaat). Dit is het enige zwakke punt in wat verder een knappe baan is, waarvan een deel over een heuvel is gedrapeerd, hetgeen resulteert in moeilijke uphill en downhill slagen. Er ligt daarentegen niet zoveel water. Al komt wat er ligt wel duidelijk in het spel, zoals op de fraaie 11e hole. De greens zijn tamelijk groot, goed ontworpen en goed bewaakt.

This is probably one of the last courses that the authorities will allow to be built in such a wooded area. Permission to fell trees was granted because they were lean pines planted for the mining industry. There are a lot of them left and they form the main hazard, especially on a number of tight holes and numerous dog-legs. The undergrowth is thick to say the least and adds an extra and perhaps unwarranted difficulty, given that mis-hit shots are already punished enough (bring a stock of balls if you are wayward off the tee). This is the only real flaw in what is an intelligent course, a part of which hugs a steepish hill, thus giving some tricky holes uphill and down. In contrast, there is little water to bother you, although what there is well in play, as on the very fine 11th hole. The greens are rather large, well-contoured and well-guarded.

Burggolf Herkenbosch   **1992**
Stationsweg 100
NL - 6075 CD HERKENBOSCH

Office	Secretariaat	(31) 0475 - 531 458
Pro shop	Pro shop	(31) 0475 - 535 804
Fax	Fax	(31) 0475 - 533 580
Situation	Locatie	

Roermond (pop. 43 110), 5 km

Annual closure	Jaarlijkse sluiting	no
Weekly closure	Wekelijkse sluitingsdag	no
Fees main season	Hoogseizoen tarieven	18 holes

	Week days Weekdagen	We/Bank holidays We/Feestdagen
Individual Individueel	Fl 75,-	Fl 100,-
Couple Paar	Fl 150,-	Fl 200,-

Caddy	Caddy	no
Electric Trolley	Electrische trolley	Fl 15,-
Buggy	Buggy	no
Clubs	Clubs	Fl 7,50

Credit cards Creditkaarten
VISA - Eurocard - MasterCard

1026

Access Toegang :A2 Maastricht-Weert-Eindhoven.
Exit 40. N68, A68 → Roermond. N68,
N281 → Herkenbosch → Golf
Map 1 on page 1009 Auto kaart 1 Blz 1009

GOLF COURSE / BAAN   16/20

Site	Terrein	■■■■■□
Maintenance	Onderhoud	■■■■□□
Architect	Architect	Joan Dudok van Heel B. Steensels
Type	Type baan	forest
Relief	Reliëf	■■■■□□
Water in play	Waterhazards	■■□□□□
Exp. to wind	Windgevoelig	■■□□□□
Trees in play	Bomen	■■■■■□

Scorecard Scorekaart	Chp. Back tees	Mens Heren	Ladies Damen
Length Lengte	5682	5682	4924
Par	71	71	71

Advised golfing ability		0 12 24 36
Aanbevolen golfvaardigheid		■■■■■■□
Hcp required	Vereiste hcp	We: 36

CLUB HOUSE & AMENITIES / CLUB HOUSE EN ANNEXEN   7/10

Pro shop	Pro shop	■■■■□
Driving range	Oefenbaan	■■■■□
Sheltered	overdekt	6 mats
On grass	op gras	no, 10 mats open
air		
Putting-green	putting-green	yes
Pitching-green	pitching-green	yes

HOTEL FACILITIES / HOTELS IN OMGEVING   6/10

HOTELS HOTELS

Kasteeltje Hattem   Roermond
11 rooms, D Fl. 250,-   5 km
Tel (31) 0475 - 319 222, Fax (31) 0475 - 319 292

Landhotel Cox - 54 rooms, D Fl. 175,-   Roermond
Tel (31) 0475 - 329 966, Fax (31) 0475 - 325 142   5 km

Boshotel - 60 rooms, D Fl. 150,-   Vlodrop
Tel (31) 0475 - 534 959, Fax (31) 0475 - 534 580   3 km

RESTAURANTS RESTAURANTS

Kasteel Daelenbroek   Herkenbosch
Tel (31) 0475 - 532 465   2 km

La Cascade   Roermond
Tel (31) 0475 - 319 274   5 km

Sinds deze baan aan het begin van de eeuw is aangelegd, heeft hij een aantal ingrijpende wijzigingen ondergaan. Hoewel sommige van die aanpassingen twijfelachtig zijn, blijft Hilversum wat het altijd is geweest: een verbluffend voorbeeld van een goed ontwerp voor een baan in het binnenland. Door de vele oude bomen zijn de meeste fairways behoorlijk smal, waardoor ze precisie en effectvolle slagen vereisen. De zanderige heuvels, die vaak tot slagen van glooiende hellingen dwingen, verhogen het technisch aspect van het spel. De spaarzame fairway-bunkers zijn goed geplaatst en moeilijk, de middelgrote greens worden goed bewaakt en de heidevelden voegen extra moeilijkheden aan de baan toe. De baan is heel rustig (de enige verstoring kan komen van fietsers of ruiters) en heeft het onderhoudsnivo de laatste tijd sterk verbeterd. Dat zou te maken kunnen hebben met het Dutch Open dat hier vanaf 1994 wordt gespeeld.

Since it was created at the turn of the century, this course has undergone a number of significant changes. Although some of these are questionable, the course is still the strikingly good example of excellent inland design it always has been. Owing to the very many old trees, some fairways are very tight and require precision and flighted shots. The sandy slopes, which often call for shots played from sloping lies, augment the technical aspect of golf here. The few fairway bunkers you come across are still well-placed and tough, the mid-sized greens are well-guarded and the heather adds an extra difficulty to the course. Very quiet (the only disturbance here might come from cyclists or horse-riders), Hilversum has significantly improved its standard of course upkeep: to prove it, the Dutch Open has been played here since 1994.

Hilversumsche Golf Club — 1910

Soestdijkerstraatsweg 172
NL - 1213 XJ HILVERSUM

Office	Secretariaat	(31) 035 - 685 7060
Pro shop	Pro shop	(31) 035 - 685 7140
Fax	Fax	(31) 035 - 685 3813
Situation	Locatie	

Hilversum (pop. 84 213), 2 km

Annual closure	Jaarlijkse sluiting	no
Weekly closure	Wekelijkse sluitingsdag	no

Fees main season
Hoogseizoen tarieven 18 holes

	Week days Weekdagen	We/Bank holidays We/Feestdagen
Individual Individueel	Fl 75,-	Fl 100,-
Couple Paar	Fl 150,-	Fl 200,-

Caddy	Caddy	no
Electric Trolley	Electrische trolley	Fl 7,50,-
Buggy	Buggy	no
Clubs	Clubs	Fl 50,-
Credit cards Creditkaarten		no

Access Toegang : Amsterdam A1 → Hilversum.
A27 → Utrecht. Exit 33 → Hilversum. → Golf
Map 1 on page 1008 Auto kaart 1 Blz 1008

GOLF COURSE / BAAN — 16/20

Site	Terrein	
Maintenance	Onderhoud	
Architect	Architect	Burrows Del C. van Krimpen
Type	Type baan	forest
Relief	Reliëf	
Water in play	Waterhazards	
Exp. to wind	Windgevoelig	
Trees in play	Bomen	

Scorecard Scorekaart	Chp. Back tees	Mens Heren	Ladies Damen
Length Lengte	6098	5859	5102
Par	72	72	72

Advised golfing ability
Aanbevolen golfvaardigheid   0   12   24   36

Hcp required Vereiste hcp   26

CLUB HOUSE & AMENITIES / CLUB HOUSE EN ANNEXEN — 7/10

Pro shop	Pro shop	
Driving range	Oefenbaan	
Sheltered	overdekt	6 mats
On grass	op gras	no, 6 mats open air
Putting-green	putting-green	yes
Pitching-green	pitching-green	yes

1027

HOTEL FACILITIES / HOTELS IN OMGEVING — 7/10

HOTELS HOTELS
Lapershoek — Hilversum
63 rooms, D Fl. 225,- — 2 km
Tel (31) 035 - 623 1341
Fax (31) 035 - 628 4360

De Hooge Vuursche — Baarn
20 rooms, D Fl. 300,- — 2 km
Tel (31) 035 - 541 2541
Fax (31) 035 - 542 3288

RESTAURANTS RESTAURANTS
Joffers — Hilversum
Tel (31) 035 - 621 4556 — 2 km

De Kastanjehof — Lage Vuursche
Tel (31) 035 - 666 8248 — 3 km

Deze opvallende baan, in het midden van het land, was een van de eerste van een serie nieuwe privé banen die begin jaren '80 werden aangelegd. Een groot deel van de baan ligt temidden van bestaande bossen, de rest in meer open terrein. Door dat laatste biedt de Hoge Klej een groter gevoel van ruimte dan de 'oudere' buren Hilversum en De Pan. Op enkele holes is goed gebruik gemaakt van de hoogteverschillen, terwijl de overige holes vrij vlak zijn. Dat maakt de baan toegankelijk voor elk nivo speler. Het mag dan geen spectaculaire baan zijn, er zitten een paar mooie holes tussen, met een grote variatie in vormen, maten en moeilijkheden. Maar dat kun je verwachten van ontwerpers en kenners als Steel en Pennink, die zich nooit druk maken om al te subtiele details. De oefenfaciliteiten houden gelijke tred met de kwaliteit van de baan en hetzelfde kan worden gezegd van het clubhuis (met een goed restaurant).

This remarkable course, in the centre of Holland, was one of the first of a series of new private courses built in the first half of the 1980s. A large section was laid out in trees, the rest in wide open spaces, and this gives «Hoge Kleij» a much more definite impression of space than its elder neighbours at Hilversum and De Pan. The differences in level on several holes have been cleverly used, while the rest of the course is flat, making it easier for players of all levels and ages. This is hardly a spectacular course, but there are some competent holes here and a wide variety of shapes, sizes and difficulties. Again, this is only to be expected from designers and fine connoisseurs of golf such as Steel and Pennink, who never care unduly about excessively sophisticated details. Practice facilities are consistent with the standard of the course design, and the same can be said for the clubhouse (with a good restaurant).

Bolfclub De Hoge Kleij — 1986

Appelweg 4
NL - 3832 RK LEUSDEN

Office	Secretariaat	(31) 033 - 461 6944
Pro shop	Pro shop	(31) 033 - 463 8221
Fax	Fax	(31) 033 - 465 2921
Situation	Locatie	

Amersfoort (pop. 110 117), 2 km
Utrecht (pop. 234 106), 15 km

| Annual closure | Jaarlijkse sluiting | no |
| Weekly closure | Wekelijkse sluitingsdag | no |

Fees main season
Hoogseizoen tarieven 18 holes

	Week days Weekdagen	We/Bank holidays We/Feestdagen
Individual Individueel	Fl. 65,-	Fl. 95,-
Couple Paar	Fl. 130,-	Fl. 190,-

Caddy	Caddy	no
Electric Trolley	Electrische trolley	no
Buggy	Buggy	no
Clubs	Clubs	Fl. 40,-
Credit cards Creditkaarten		no

GOLF COURSE / BAAN — 15/20

Site	Terrein	
Maintenance	Onderhoud	
Architect	Architect	Donald Steel Frank Pennink
Type	Type baan	forest
Relief	Reliëf	
Water in play	Waterhazards	
Exp. to wind	Windgevoelig	
Trees in play	Bomen	

Scorecard Scorekaart	Chp. Back tees	Mens Heren	Ladies Damen
Length Lengte	6244	6046	5243
Par	72	72	72

Advised golfing ability
Aanbevolen golfvaardigheid   0   12   24   36

Hcp required   Vereiste hcp   We: 29

CLUB HOUSE & AMENITIES / CLUB HOUSE EN ANNEXEN — 6/10

Pro shop	Pro shop	
Driving range	Oefenbaan	
Sheltered	overdekt	6 mats
On grass	op gras	no, 12 mats open air
Putting-green	putting-green	yes
Pitching-green	pitching-green	yes

HOTEL FACILITIES / HOTELS IN OMGEVING — 7/10

HOTELS HOTELS

De Klepperman   Hoevelaken
79 rooms, D Fl. 285,-   5 km
Tel (31) 033 - 253 4120, Fax (31) 033 - 253 7434

Den Treek   Leusden
18 rooms, D Fl. 125,-   2 km
Tel (31) 033 - 286 1425, Fax (31) 033 - 286 3007

Berghotel   Amersfoort
92 rooms, D Fl. 210,-   3 km
Tel (31) 033 - 462 0444, Fax (31) 033 - 465 0505

RESTAURANTS RESTAURANTS

Mariënhof - Tel (31) 033 - 463 2979   Amersfoort 2 km
Tollius - Tel (31) 033 - 465 1793   Amersfoort 2 km

1028

Access Toegang : A28 Utrecht-Amersfoort, Exit 5
Map 1 on page 1008 Auto kaart 1 Blz 1008

Deze aantrekkelijke baan is aangelegd in de eerste drooglegging van het IJ (net als de naastgelegen baan van de Amsterdamse Golfclub) en zal, zolang de aangebrachte beplanting nog bescheiden is, het karakter van een polderbaan hebben. Maar geleidelijk zal dat veel gevarieerder worden. Ook al omdat bij de aanleg optimaal gebruik is gemaakt van de oude bomen die nog net op een puntje van het terrein staan, waar nu een volledige par-3 in verscholen ligt. En er zijn twaalfhonderd vrachtwagens met verse grond aangevoerd, waarmee licht glooiende contouren zijn geschapen. Verder zijn er heel wat waterpartijen, die vooral aan de buitenkant van het terrein zorgen voor een natuurlijke overgang naar de weilanden. Vanuit het iets hoger gelegen clubhuis is er een prachtig zicht op zes holes die van of naar dit centrale punt lopen.

This attractive course was built in the first land-recovery of the IJ-estuary (just like the adjacent course of the Amsterdamse Golfclub). So as long as the newly planted trees and bushes are still small, it will be ranked as a «polderbaan». But the nature of the course will gradually change, if only because of the clever use that has been made of some remaining trees in a corner of the terrain, now hiding a full par-3 hole. In addition, more than 1200 truckloads of new soil were brought in and used to create slight undulations, and there are various ponds serving as water hazards. On the outskirts of the course, they provide a natural transition to the surrounding meadowlands. From the somewhat elevated clubhouse you enjoy a magnificent view over six holes running in or out.

Golfclub Houtrak — 1997

Machineweg 1b
NL - 1165 NB HALFWEG

Office	Secretariaat	(31) 023 - 513 2933
Pro shop	Pro shop	(31) 023 - 513 2933
Fax	Fax	(31) 023 - 513 2935
Situation	Locatie	

Amsterdam (pop. 724 096), 10 km

Annual closure	Jaarlijkse sluiting	no
Weekly closure	Wekelijkse sluitingsdag	no

Fees main season
Hoogseizoen tarieven 18 holes

	Week days Weekdagen	We/Bank holidays We/Feestdagen
Individual Individueel	Fl 100,-	Fl 100,-
Couple Paar	Fl 200,-	Fl 200,-

Caddy	Caddy	no
Electric Trolley	Electrische trolley	no
Buggy	Buggy	yes
Clubs	Clubs	yes

Credit cards Creditkaarten — no

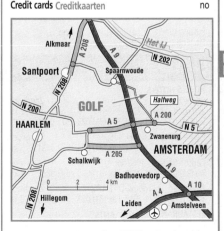

Access Toegang : Amsterdam, N5/A5 → Haarlem.
Exit Spaarnwoude. 200 m turn left.
Map 1 on page 1008 Auto kaart 1 Blz 1008

GOLF COURSE / BAAN — 16/20

Site	Terrein	
Maintenance	Onderhoud	
Architect	Architect	Gerard Jol
Type	Type baan	polder, open country
Relief	Reliëf	
Water in play	Waterhazards	
Exp. to wind	Windgevoelig	
Trees in play	Bomen	

Scorecard Scorekaart	Chp. Back tees	Mens Heren	Ladies Damen
Length Lengte	6392	6163	5194
Par	72	72	72

Advised golfing ability	0	12	24	36
Aanbevolen golfvaardigheid				

Hcp required Vereiste hcp — certificate

CLUB HOUSE & AMENITIES / CLUB HOUSE EN ANNEXEN — 8/10

Pro shop	Pro shop	
Driving range	Oefenbaan	
Sheltered	overdekt	10 mats
On grass	op gras	no
Putting-green	putting-green	yes
Pitching-green	pitching-green	yes

HOTEL FACILITIES / HOTELS IN OMGEVING — 8/10

HOTELS HOTELS
Radisson SAS — Amsterdam
246 rooms, D Fl. 375,- — 10 km
Tel (31) 020 - 623 1231, Fax (31) 020 - 520 8200

Canal House — Amsterdam
26 rooms, D Fl. 225,- — 10 km
Tel (31) 020 - 622 5182, Fax (31) 020 - 624 1317

Ambassade - 46 rooms, D Fl. 325,- — Amsterdam
Tel (31) 020 - 626 2333, Fax (31) 020 - 624 5321 — 10 km

RESTAURANTS RESTAURANTS
La Rive - tel. (31) 020 - 622 6060 — Amsterdam 10 km

De Bokkedoorns — Overveen1
Tel (31) 023 - 526 3600 — 5 km

Tout Court — Amsterdam
Tel (31) 020 - 625 8637 — 10 km

1029

Als Holland een vlak land is, dan liggen hier haar bergen. Duintoppen, wind en sobere vegetatie zijn de kenmerken van een echte linksbaan. De Kennemer is een van de mooiste voorbeeld daarvan in Europa. Je kunt de zee dan wel niet zien van hieruit, het stijlvolle, zeer traditionele clubhuis zal u zeker bekoren. De baan, ontworpen door Harry Colt in 1920, is in 1985 met negen holes uitgebreid, maar het gedeelte waar dit gebeurde had minder natuurlijke aanleg daarvoor. De hoogte-verschillen zijn beperkt (met wat blinde slagen), al zal menige bal uiteindelijk na wat stuiteren en rollen op een interessante plaats tot rust komen. Laat de afwezigheid van water en de schaarste aan bomen (enkele vliegdennen) u niet overmoedig maken. De bunkers zijn talrijk en goed geplaatst, de struiken ontbreken niet. Als u ze weet te ontlopen, kunt u een goede score neerzetten. Op voorwaarde dat de wind niet te hard waait, maar dit spreekt vanzelf op dit type baan.

If Holland is a flat country, then here are her mountains. High dunes, wind and scant vegetation are the unmistakable features of a links course, of which Kennemer is one of the finest examples in Europe. You don't really see the sea, but you will appreciate the stylish and very traditional clubhouse. Designed by Harry Colt in 1920, the original course was supplemented with an additional 9 holes in 1985, but the natural terrain has not quite worked as well for the newer layout. The course is moderately hilly (with a few blind shots), enough for slightly wayward shots to kick, roll and end up in some pretty interesting positions. Don't feel too confident about the absence of water and the scarcity of trees; there are loads of bunkers, all well placed, and there is no shortage of prickly gorse, either. Keep out of them and you might hope to sign for a good score, providing the wind doesn't blow too hard. On this type of course, that goes without saying. An absolute must.

Kennemer Golf & Country Club   1927
Kennemerweg 78
NL - 2042 XT ZANDVOORT

Office	Secretariaat	(31) 023 - 571 8456
Pro shop	Pro shop	(31) 023 - 571 4974
Fax	Fax	(31) 023 - 571 9520
Situation	Locatie	

Haarlem (pop. 150 213), 8 km

Annual closure	Jaarlijkse sluiting	no
Weekly closure	Wekelijkse sluitingsdag	no

Fees main season
Hoogseizoen tarieven 18 holes

	Week days Weekdagen	We/Bank holidays We/Feestdagen
Individual Individueel	Fl. 125,-	Fl. 125,-
Couple Paar	Fl. 250,-	Fl. 250,-

Caddy	Caddy	no
Electric Trolley	Electrische trolley	no
Buggy	Buggy	no
Clubs	Clubs	Fl. 25,-

Credit cards Creditkaarten   no

Access Toegang : Haarlem, Aerdenhout → Zandvoort
Map 1 on page 1008 Auto kaart 1 Blz 1008

GOLF COURSE / BAAN   **18**/20

Site	Terrein	
Maintenance	Onderhoud	
Architect	Architect	Harry S. Colt
Type	Type baan	links
Relief	Reliëf	
Water in play	Waterhazards	
Exp. to wind	Windgevoelig	
Trees in play	Bomen	

Scorecard	Chp.	Mens	Ladies
Scorekaart	Back tees	Heren	Damen
Length Lengte	6045	5738	5006
Par	72	72	72

Advised golfing ability		0	12	24	36
Aanbevolen golfvaardigheid					
Hcp required	Vereiste hcp	28			

CLUB HOUSE & AMENITIES / CLUB HOUSE EN ANNEXEN   **8**/10

Pro shop	Pro shop	
Driving range	Oefenbaan	
Sheltered	overdekt	3 mats
On grass	op gras	no, 10 mats open air
Putting-green	putting-green	yes
Pitching-green	pitching-green	yes

HOTEL FACILITIES / HOTELS IN OMGEVING   **8**/10

HOTELS HOTELS

Elysée Beach   Zandvoort
200 rooms, D Fl. 225,-   3 km
Tel (31) 023 - 571 3234, Fax (31) 023 - 571 9094

Palace -53 rooms, D Fl. 175,-   Zandvoort
Tel (31) 023 - 571 2911, Fax (31) 023 - 572 0131   3 km

Carlton Square - 106 rooms, D Fl. 275,-   Haarlem
Tel (31) 023 - 531 9091, Fax (31) 023 - 532 9853   8 km

Zuiderbad - 27 rooms, D Fl. 180,-   Zandvoort
Tel (31) 023 - 571 2613, Fax (31) 023 - 571 3190   3 km

RESTAURANTS RESTAURANTS

De Bokkedoorns   Overveen
Tel (31) 023 - 526 3600   12 km

Landgoed Groenendaal   Heemstede
Tel (31) 023 - 528 1555   3 km

Opnieuw een golfbaan die in twee fasen tot stand is gekomen, maar waar de samenwerking Pennink-Steel, twee ontwerpers met eenzelfde achtergrond, een vrij consistent en gelijkmatig resultaat heeft opgeleverd. Vooral omdat de meeste holes in een bosgebied liggen, met nadruk op eenheid van stijl. Zoals altijd kunnen de bomen het leven zuur maken voor zwierige spelers. Je moet echt recht slaan en je niet teveel om de lengte bekommeren (zeker niet van de medaltees), wat de meeste spelers als muziek in de oren zal klinken. Er zijn maar weinig fairway-bunkers en die er zijn leveren niet al te veel problemen op. Ook bij de greens liggen niet veel bunkers, zodat de meeste greens met een stuiterend schot gehaald kunnen worden. De greens zelf zijn middelgroot, redelijk gevormd en makkelijk te lezen. Zoals je in dit waterrijke gebied mag verwachten komt water regelmatig in het spel, soms onverwachts, zelfs een beetje stiekem. Het gelijknamige hotel voegt extra allure aan de baan toe.

Yet another course built in two parts, but the partnership between Pennink and Steel, two designers of the same culture, has produced a rather consistent and even result, especially since the majority of holes are laid out in a forest to accentuate unity of style. But as always, trees also make life complicated for wayward players. You have to play straight here and not necessarily look for length all the time (not from the front tees, anyway), which is probably good news for most players. There are few fairway bunkers, and the ones there are don't add much to the overall difficulty. Green-side bunkers are scarce, too, meaning that most greens can be approached with bump and run shots. The greens themselves are mid-sized, moderately contoured and easy to read. As you might expect in a province with so many lakes, water comes into play, sometimes surprisingly and even sneakily. The hotel on site simply adds to the course's overall appeal.

Golf en Country Club Lauswolt — 1966
Van Harinxmaweg 8a
NL - 9244 CJ BEESTERZWAAG

Office	Secretariaat	(31) 0512 - 382 594
Pro shop	Pro shop	(31) 0512 - 383 869
Fax	Fax	(31) 0512 - 383 739
Situation	Locatie	

Drachten (pop. 50 440), 5 km
Groningen (pop. 170 535), 40 km

Annual closure	Jaarlijkse sluiting	no
Weekly closure	Wekelijkse sluitingsdag	no
Fees main season	Hoogseizoen tarieven	full day

	Week days Weekdagen	We/Bank holidays We/Feestdagen
Individual Individueel	Fl 110,-	Fl 150,-
Couple Paar	Fl 220,-	Fl 300,-

Caddy	Caddy	no
Electric Trolley	Electrische trolley	Fl 7,50
Buggy	Buggy	no
Clubs	Clubs	Fl 20,-

Credit cards Creditkaarten
VISA - Eurocard - MasterCard - AMEX - DC

Access Toegang : A7 Groningen-Drachten,
Exit 28 → Beetsterzwaag
Map 1 on page 1008 Auto kaart 1 Blz 1008

GOLF COURSE BAAN — 14/20

Site	Terrein	
Maintenance	Onderhoud	
Architect	Architect	Frank Pennink Donald Steel
Type	Type baan	forest
Relief	Reliëf	
Water in play	Waterhazards	
Exp. to wind	Windgevoelig	
Trees in play	Bomen	

Scorecard Scorekaart	Chp. Back tees	Mens Heren	Ladies Damen
Length Lengte	6152	5916	5353
Par	72	72	72

Advised golfing ability Aanbevolen golfvaardigheid	0	12	24	36
Hcp required Vereiste hcp	36			

CLUB HOUSE & AMENITIES CLUB HOUSE EN ANNEXEN — 6/10

Pro shop	Pro shop	
Driving range	Oefenbaan	
Sheltered	overdekt	4 mats
On grass	op gras	no, 10 mats open air
Putting-green	putting-green	yes
Pitching-green	pitching-green	yes

1031

HOTEL FACILITIES HOTELS IN OMGEVING — 7/10

HOTELS HOTELS
Landgoed Lauswolt — Golf
58 rooms, D Fl. 250,- — on site
Tel (31) 0512 - 381 245, Fax (31) 0512 - 381 496

Het Witte Huis — Beetsterzwaag
8 rooms, D Fl. 130,- — 1 km
Tel (31) 0512 - 382 222, Fax (31) 0512 - 382 307

Hotel Drachten - 48 rooms, D Fl. 155,- — Drachten
Tel (31) 0512 - 520 705, Fax (31) 0512 - 523 232 — 5 km

RESTAURANTS RESTAURANTS
Landgoed Lauswolt — Golf
Tel (31) 0512 - 381 245 — on site

De Wilgenhoeve — Drachten
Tel (31) 0512 - 512 510 — 5 km

De derde parel in de trilogie van Nederlandse linksbanen. Met magnifiek uitzicht over de duinen en de bollenvelden in het binnenland. Een klassieke lay-out, waarbij alleen natuurlijke elementen in het spel komen. Met alle moeilijkheden van het golfspel in de duinen, zoals potbunkers, blinde slagen en de wind. Slechts vijf holes liggen in bebost terrein. Ook hier kennen de fairways maar weinig vlakke stukken, dus is een goede techniek nodig voor elke slag. En om de bal laag te houden als het waait. De meeste greens worden omringd door rough of heuveltjes, zonder al te veel bunkers, maar denk niet dat scoren gemakkelijk is. Andere interessante elementen zijn de dichte struiken in de rough, een enkel poeltje en de renovatie van het clubhuis. Een uitdagende baan, die tot de beste van Europa gerekend kan worden (bij voorkeur spelen op een werkdag).

The third absolute gem in the magnificent trilogy of Dutch links, one that offers some magnificent views over the dunes and inland, covered with fields of flowers in the Spring. The layout is a classic, bringing into play only natural elements and the difficulties of golfing amidst sand dunes, including pot bunkers, blind shots and exposure to the wind. Only five holes are laid out over woody terrain. Again, there are few flat lies, so good technique is needed to shape the shot and to hit low balls when the wind blows. As most of the greens are surrounded by rough or rolling mounds, there aren't too many bunkers, but don't ever think scoring is easy. Other interesting features are the thick bushes in the middle of the rough, a single water hazard and the welcome renovation of the clubhouse. A challenging layout that has to be rated amongst the front-running courses in Europe (choose a week-day to play here).

Noordwijkse Golfclub
Randweg 25
NL - 2204 AL NOORDWIJK

Office	Secretariaat	(31) 0252 - 373 763
Pro shop	Pro shop	(31) 0252 - 373 763
Fax	Fax	(31) 0252 - 370 044
Situation	Locatie	

Leiden (pop. 114 892), 15 km

Annual closure	Jaarlijkse sluiting	no
Weekly closure	Wekelijkse sluitingsdag	no

Fees main season
Hoogseizoen tarieven 18 holes

	Week days Weekdagen	We/Bank holidays We/Feestdagen
Individual Individueel	Fl 125,-	*
Couple Paar	Fl 250,-	*

* Week-end: members only

Caddy	Caddy	no
Electric Trolley	Electrische trolley	no
Buggy	Buggy	no
Clubs	Clubs	yes

Credit cards Creditkaarten
VISA - Eurocard - MasterCard

1032

Access Toegang : Amsterdam, A4, A44 → Leiden.
Exit 3 → Noordwijk aan Zee.
6 km → Nordwijkerhout. 1 km → Zee
Map 1 on page 1008 Auto kaart 1 Blz 1008

GOLF COURSE
BAAN 18/20

Site	Terrein	■■■■■□
Maintenance	Onderhoud	■■■■■□
Architect	Architect	Frank Pennink
Type	Type baan	links
Relief	Reliëf	■■■■□□
Water in play	Waterhazards	■□□□□
Exp. to wind	Windgevoelig	■■■■□
Trees in play	Bomen	■■□□□

Scorecard Scorekaart	Chp. Back tees	Mens Heren	Ladies Damen
Length Lengte	6242	5875	5029
Par	72	72	72

Advised golfing ability Aanbevolen golfvaardigheid	0	12	24	36
	■	■	■	

Hcp required Vereiste hcp 28

CLUB HOUSE & AMENITIES
CLUB HOUSE EN ANNEXEN 7/10

Pro shop	Pro shop	■■■■□
Driving range	Oefenbaan	■■■■□
Sheltered	overdekt	5 mats
On grass	op gras	no, 3 mats open air
Putting-green	putting-green	yes
Pitching-green	pitching-green	yes

HOTEL FACILITIES
HOTELS IN OMGEVING 8/10

HOTELS HOTELS
Huis ter Duin   Noordwijk
238 rooms, D Fl. 400,-   6 km
Tel (31) 071 - 361 9220, Fax (31) 071 - 361 9401

Noordwijk   Noordwijk
62 rooms, D Fl. 200,-   6 km
Tel (31) 071 - 361 8900, Fax (31) 071 - 361 7882

De Witte Raaf - 35 rooms, D Fl. 170,-   Noordwijk
Tel (31) 0252 - 375 984, Fax (31) 0252 - 377 578   1 km

RESTAURANTS RESTAURANTS
Cleyburg   Noordwijk-Binnen
Tel (31) 071 - 364 8448   8 km

De Palmentuin   Noordwijk
Tel (31) 071 - 361 9340   6 km

15 **5** **3**

Temidden van oude bospercelen zijn drie lussen van elk negen holes aangelegd. Het levert een aantrekkelijke, maar ook vrij smalle golfbaan op. Misschien is het terrein net iets te klein voor 27 holes en zou een 18-holesbaan meer op zijn plaats zijn geweest. Hoewel, als je geen probleem hebt met holes die soms wat kunstmatig aandoen, blijft er een 'spannende' baan over. Vooral de 'North'-baan, waar op de zesde hole een zandverstuiving voor een soort superbunker zorgt. De 'North' en 'East' baan eindigen beide op een grote dubbelgreen. Het clubhuis en de oefenfaciliteiten zijn groot genoeg om meerdere groepen te hulsvesten. Wel vreemd: in de kleedkamers zijn golfschoenen uit den boze. Dus altijd schone sokken meenemen !

Three loops of 9 holes have each been cut out of the existing woodland, making a pretty but somewhat narrow layout. Maybe the total area was just too small for 27 holes and a full-size 18-holer with an additional par-3 course would have been more appropriate. Yet if you accept that some holes are a little artificial, what is left is still an attractive layout, especially the North course, where the 6th hole features a huge natural sandtrap in the form of a drifting dune. Both the North and East courses finish on a large twin green. The clubhouse and practice facilities are good enough to handle groups easily, the only strange phenomenon here being the fact that golf shoes are not allowed in the locker-rooms.

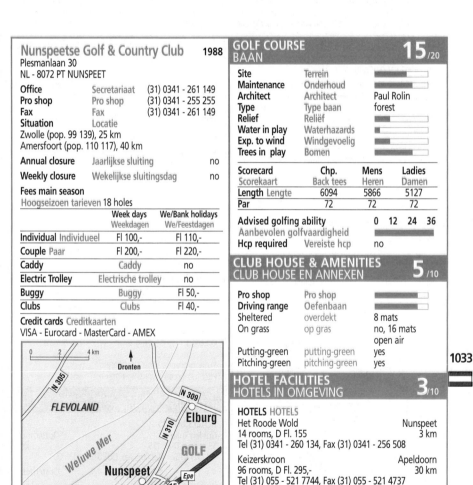

Nunspeetse Golf & Country Club — 1988

Plesmanlaan 30
NL - 8072 PT NUNSPEET

Office	Secretariaat	(31) 0341 - 261 149
Pro shop	Pro shop	(31) 0341 - 255 255
Fax	Fax	(31) 0341 - 261 149
Situation	Locatie	

Zwolle (pop. 99 139), 25 km
Amersfoort (pop. 110 117), 40 km

Annual closure	Jaarlijkse sluiting	no
Weekly closure	Wekelijkse sluitingsdag	no

Fees main season
Hoogseizoen tarieven 18 holes

	Week days Weekdagen	We/Bank holidays We/Feestdagen
Individual Individueel	Fl 100,-	Fl 110,-
Couple Paar	Fl 200,-	Fl 220,-
Caddy	Caddy	no
Electric Trolley	Electrische trolley	no
Buggy	Buggy	Fl 50,-
Clubs	Clubs	Fl 40,-

Credit cards Creditkaarten
VISA - Eurocard - MasterCard - AMEX

Access Toegang : A28 Exit 14 (Zwolle-Amersfoort)
→ Nunspeet. Take right
Map 1 on page 1009 Auto kaart 1 Blz 1009

GOLF COURSE BAAN — 15/20

Site	Terrein	
Maintenance	Onderhoud	
Architect	Architect	Paul Rolin
Type	Type baan	forest
Relief	Reliëf	
Water in play	Waterhazards	
Exp. to wind	Windgevoelig	
Trees in play	Bomen	

Scorecard Scorekaart	Chp. Back tees	Mens Heren	Ladies Damen
Length Lengte	6094	5866	5127
Par	72	72	72

Advised golfing ability Aanbevolen golfvaardigheid	0	12	24	36
Hcp required Vereiste hcp	no			

CLUB HOUSE & AMENITIES CLUB HOUSE EN ANNEXEN — 5/10

Pro shop	Pro shop	
Driving range	Oefenbaan	
Sheltered	overdekt	8 mats
On grass	op gras	no, 16 mats open air
Putting-green	putting-green	yes
Pitching-green	pitching-green	yes

1033

HOTEL FACILITIES HOTELS IN OMGEVING — 3/10

HOTELS HOTELS
Het Roode Wold — Nunspeet
14 rooms, D Fl. 155 — 3 km
Tel (31) 0341 - 260 134, Fax (31) 0341 - 256 508

Keizerskroon — Apeldoorn
96 rooms, D Fl. 295,- — 30 km
Tel (31) 055 - 521 7744, Fax (31) 055 - 521 4737

Dennenheuvel - 28 rooms, D Fl. 170,- — Epe
Tel (31) 0578 - 612 326, Fax (31) 0578 - 621 857 — 10 km

RESTAURANTS RESTAURANTS
't Soerel - Tel (31) 0578 - 688 276 — Epe 10 km

De Echoput — Apeldoorn
Tel (31) 055 - 519 1248 — 30 km

Het Jachthuis — Apeldoorn
Tel (31) 055 - 519 1397 — 30 km

Helaas is een deel van het aangrenzende industrieterrein zichtbaar en is de autoweg continu hoorbaar. Voor het overige waant u zich hier temidden van het buitenleven (weilanden, graanvelden, koeien) op een baan die veel aandacht voor ecologie heeft. Zo wordt de rough lang gehouden om de knaagdieren te huisvesten, die op hun beurt roofvogels aantrekken. Ondanks de relatief jonge leeftijd oogt de baan vrij volwassen. Een paar losse bomen en struiken zijn in het ontwerp opgenomen en vormen zo hindernissen, net als waterpartijen, talloze bunkers en de wind, die altijd aanwezig lijkt. Vier vijvertjes komen in het spel op acht holes, waarbij ze op de 5e en 15e recht voor de green liggen. Twee fraaie par-3 holes, die vooral onervaren spelers ontzag zullen inboezemen. Behalve een paar blinde bunkers heeft de baan een eerlijk karakter. Uitgezonderd misschien de 16e hole, een controversiële dogleg.

Unfortunately, a number of buildings from the nearby industrial estate can still be seen and the noise from the road is never-ending. Otherwise, you are in the country here (meadows, fields of wheat and cows) and the club pays very special attention to the environment. Hence a rough that is left to grow rather tall, attracting rodents, falcons and eagles. Despite its tender age, this course is remarkably mature. A few isolated trees or copses are fully integrated into the course and form one of the difficulties, along with the water hazards, numerous bunkers and the wind, which is always a frequent feature. Four small lakes come into play on eight holes, forming frontal hazards on the 5th and 15th holes, two fine par 3s which could be a real handful for inexperienced players. Despite a few hidden hazards, the course is forthright in style, except the 16th, a very controversial dog-leg.

Oosterhoutse Golf Club — 1989

Dukaatstraat 21
NL - 4903 RN OOSTERHOUT

Office	Secretariaat	(31) 0162 - 421 210
Pro shop	Pro shop	(31) 0162 - 436 397
Fax	Fax	(31) 0162 - 433 285
Situation	Locatie	

Breda (pop. 129 125), 5 km

Annual closure	Jaarlijkse sluiting	no
Weekly closure	Wekelijkse sluitingsdag	no

Fees main season
Hoogseizoen tarieven 18 holes

	Week days Weekdagen	We/Bank holidays We/Feestdagen
Individual Individueel	Fl 70,-	Fl 75,-
Couple Paar	Fl 140,-	Fl 150,-

Caddy	Caddy	no
Electric Trolley	Electrische trolley	Fl 10,-
Buggy	Buggy	no
Clubs	Clubs	no
Credit cards Creditkaarten		no

Access Toegang : A27, Exit 17 → Rijen.
200 m, turn right. → Golf
Map 1 on page 1008 Auto kaart 1 Blz 1008

GOLF COURSE BAAN — 15/20

Site	Terrein	
Maintenance	Onderhoud	
Architect	Architect	Joan Dudok van Heel
Type	Type baan	open country, parkland
Relief	Reliëf	
Water in play	Waterhazards	
Exp. to wind	Windgevoelig	
Trees in play	Bomen	

Scorecard Scorekaart	Chp. Back tees	Mens Heren	Ladies Damen
Length Lengte	6182	5907	5110
Par	71	72	72

Advised golfing ability Aanbevolen golfvaardigheid		0 12 24 36
Hcp required Vereiste hcp		no

CLUB HOUSE & AMENITIES CLUB HOUSE EN ANNEXEN — 7/10

Pro shop	Pro shop	
Driving range	Oefenbaan	
Sheltered	overdekt	9 mats
On grass	op gras	no, 8 mats open air
Putting-green	putting-green	yes
Pitching-green	pitching-green	yes

HOTEL FACILITIES HOTELS IN OMGEVING — 7/10

HOTELS HOTELS
Golden Tulip — Oosterhout
53 rooms, D Fl. 175,- — 3 km
Tel (31) 0162 - 452 003, Fax (31) 0162 - 435 003

A.C. Hotel — Oosterhout
63 rooms, D Fl. 100,- — 3 km
Tel (31) 0162 - 453 643, Fax (31) 0162 - 434 662

Korenbeurs — Made
54 rooms, D Fl. 165,- — 5 km
Tel (31) 0162 - 682 150, Fax (31) 0162 - 684 647

RESTAURANTS RESTAURANTS
Le Bouc — Oosterhout
Tel (31) 0162 - 450 888 — 3 km

De Arent - Tel (31) 076 - 514 4601 — Breda 5 km

PURMEREND

16 7 7

Purmerend is een goed voorbeeld van een golfbaan-ontwerp in een polder, het vlakke boerenland in de loop der eeuwen aan de zee onttrokken. De bodem is rijk en vruchtbaar, maar elke vorm van fysiek reliëf moet kunstmatig worden aangebracht. Zoals op de meeste nieuwe banen zijn er vijvers en sloten gegraven en is de aarde gebruikt om hoogtes en heuveltjes te creëren. Of dat lukt hangt af van het talent van de ontwerper. In dit geval komen we dicht bij het sublieme, en dat zal nog duidelijker worden als de vele nieuw geplante bomen en bosjes tot wasdom zijn gekomen. Voorlopig bepalen de kracht en richting van de wind of de baan moeilijk of makkelijk is. De speler moet vooral het water en de vele bunkers zien te ontlopen. Met zijn redelijke lengte is dit een baan voor alle categoriën spelers. Naast de hier beschreven 18 holes (geel-blauw) is er een iets kortere 9-holes baan (rood).

Purmerend is a good example of golf-course architecture in a polder landscape, i.e. the flat farming land that has been won back from the sea over the centuries. The soil is rich and fertile, but each physical feature has had to be created artificially. As with most modern courses, they have dug ponds and ditches, and shifted earth to design mounds and other hillocks. Success depends on the talent of the designer. In this case, we are close to excellence, and this should become more apparent as the many newly-planted trees and bushes begin to mature. For the time being, the strength and direction of the wind make the course more difficult or easier to play. The player's job is to avoid the water hazards and plentiful bunkers. Very walkable and reasonable in length, this is a layout playable by golfers of all abilities, and also features a smaller 9 hole course.

Burg Golf Purmerend — 1990

Westerweg 60
NL - 1445 AD PURMEREND

Office	Secretariaat	(31) 0299 - 481 650
Pro shop	Pro shop	(31) 0299 - 481 650
Fax	Fax	(31) 0299 - 447 081
Situation	Locatie	

Amsterdam (pop. 724 096), 15 km

Annual closure	Jaarlijkse sluiting	no
Weekly closure	Wekelijkse sluitingsdag	no
Fees main season	Hoogseizoen tarieven	18 holes

	Week days Weekdagen	We/Bank holidays We/Feestdagen
Individual Individueel	Fl. 75,-	Fl. 100,-
Couple Paar	Fl. 150,-	Fl. 200,-

Caddy	Caddy	no
Electric Trolley	Electrische trolley	Fl. 50,-
Buggy	Buggy	no
Clubs	Clubs	Fl. 40,-

Credit cards Creditkaarten
VISA - Eurocard - MasterCard - AMEX - DC

Access Toegang : Amsterdam A7 Exit 6 → Purmerend-Noord. Take right → Volendam
Map 1 on page 1008 Auto kaart 1 Blz 1008

GOLF COURSE BAAN — 16/20

Site	Terrein	
Maintenance	Onderhoud	
Architect	Architect	Tom MacAuley
Type	Type baan	polder, open country
Relief	Reliëf	
Water in play	Waterhazards	
Exp. to wind	Windgevoelig	
Trees in play	Bomen	

Scorecard Scorekaart	Chp. Back tees	Mens Heren	Ladies Damen
Length Lengte	5781	5781	5148
Par	72	72	72

Advised golfing ability Aanbevolen golfvaardigheid	0	12	24	36
Hcp required Vereiste hcp	no			

CLUB HOUSE & AMENITIES CLUB HOUSE EN ANNEXEN — 7/10

Pro shop	Pro shop	
Driving range	Oefenbaan	
Sheltered	overdekt	no
On grass	op gras	no, mats open air
Putting-green	putting-green	yes
Pitching-green	pitching-green	yes

HOTEL FACILITIES HOTELS IN OMGEVING — 7/10

HOTELS HOTELS

Purmerend — Purmerend
85 rooms, D Fl. 180,- — 3 km
Tel (31) 0299 - 481 666, Fax (31) 0299 - 644 691

Damhotel — Edam
10 rooms, D Fl. 120,- — 3 km
Tel (31) 0299 - 371 766, Fax (31) 0299 - 373 031

De Fortuna — Edam
26 rooms, D Fl. 152,- — 3 km
Tel (31) 0299 - 371 671, Fax (31) 0299 - 371 469

RESTAURANTS RESTAURANTS

La Ciboulette — Zuidoostbeemster
Tel (31) 0299 - 683 585 — 4 km

Manno — Neck
Tel (31) 0299 - 423 949 — 5 km

1035

Deze baan was een van der eerste commerciële projecten in Nederland en als zodanig zeer succesvol. Oorspronkelijk lagen er twee kortere 9-holesbanen en een 18-holes wedstrijdbaan. De 9-holesbanen zijn samengevoegd en uitgebreid tot een volwaardige 18-holesbaan, de Groesbeekse Baan. Nog steeds wat korter, maar ook veel heuvelachtiger dan de andere, de Nijmeegse Baan. Hoewel de vele bosjes die tussen de holes zijn geplant wat bescherming bieden, is de wind een factor om terdege rekening mee te houden. Net als met de vele, soms van de tee niet-zichtbare bunkers. Er zijn meerder holes met blinde slagen naar de green. Alles bij elkaar een prettige baan in een golvend landschap, dat in Nederland niet veel voorkomt.

This course was one of the early commercial golf projects in the Netherlands and a rather successful one, too. It originally consisted of one 18-hole course and two short 9-holers, but the latter have been merged into a second 18-hole course (Groesbeekse Baan). It is a little shorter but also much more hilly than its senior companion, the Nijmeegse Baan. Although the many bushes planted between the holes seem to offer some protection from the wind, it is still a factor to consider. As are the many bunkers, some of which are not easily visible from the tees. There are also several holes with blind shots to the greens. Altogether, this is a pleasant course in rolling countryside not often seen in the Netherlands, with excellent clubhouse and practice facilities.

Golfbaan Rijk van Nijmegen — 1987
Postweg 17
NL - 6561 KJ GROESBEEK

Office	Secretariaat	(31) 024 - 397 6644
Pro shop	Pro shop	(31) 024 - 397 6644
Fax	Fax	(31) 024 - 397 6942
Situation	Locatie	

Nijmegen (pop. 147 000), 5 km

Annual closure	Jaarlijkse sluiting	no
Weekly closure	Wekelijkse sluitingsdag	no

Fees main season
Hoogseizoen tarieven 18 holes

	Week days Weekdagen	We/Bank holidays We/Feestdagen
Individual Individueel	Fl 70,-	Fl 85,-
Couple Paar	Fl 140,-	Fl 170,-

Caddy	Caddy	no
Electric Trolley	Electrische trolley	no
Buggy	Buggy	Fl 40,-
Clubs	Clubs	Fl 10,-

Credit cards Creditkaarten
VISA - Eurocard - MasterCard - AMEX - DC

1036

Access Toegang : Nijmegen: A73,
Exit 3 → Groesbeek → Nijmegen
Map 1 on page 1009 Auto kaart 1 Blz 1009

GOLF COURSE BAAN — 14/20

Site	Terrein	
Maintenance	Onderhoud	
Architect	Architect	Paul Rolin
Type	Type baan	parkland
Relief	Reliëf	
Water in play	Waterhazards	
Exp. to wind	Windgevoelig	
Trees in play	Bomen	

Scorecard Scorekaart	Chp. Back tees	Mens Heren	Ladies Damen
Length Lengte	6076	6010	5307
Par	72	72	72

Advised golfing ability
Aanbevolen golfvaardigheid   0 12 24 36
Hcp required Vereiste hcp   no

CLUB HOUSE & AMENITIES CLUB HOUSE EN ANNEXEN — 6/10

Pro shop	Pro shop	
Driving range	Oefenbaan	
Sheltered	overdekt	24 mats
On grass	op gras	no, 9 mats open air
Putting-green	putting-green	yes
Pitching-green	pitching-green	yes

HOTEL FACILITIES HOTELS IN OMGEVING — 5/10

HOTELS HOTELS
Hotel Erica - 59 rooms, D Fl. 200,-   Berg en Dal 2 km
Tel (31) 024 - 684 3514, Fax (31) 024 - 684 3613

Hotel Val Monte   Berg en Dal
103 rooms, D Fl. 175,-   2 km
Tel (31) 024 - 684 2000, Fax (31) 024 - 684 3353

Jachtslot Mookerheide   Molenhoek
20 rooms, D Fl. 250,-   6 km
Tel (31) 024 - 358 3035, Fax (31) 024 - 358 4355

RESTAURANTS RESTAURANTS
Jachslot Mookerheide   Molenhoek
Tel (31) 024 - 358 3035   6 km

Chalet Brakenstein   Nijmegen
Tel (31) 024 - 355 3949   5 km

Claudius - Tel (31) 024 - 322 1456   Nijmegen 5 km

De enige zwakke schakel hier is de rumoerige nabijheid van twee autowegen, hoewel die niet bestonden aan het eind van de vorige eeuw toen deze baan tussen bos, heide en doornenstruiken werd aangelegd. Dit zijn de oudste holes in Nederland en de eerste negen volgen nog het originele ontwerp. In de loop der tijden zijn ingrijpende veranderingen aangebracht, hoewel het oorspronkelijke plan van Del Court van Krimpen onaangetast is gebleven. We vermoeden dat Harry Colt iets met de latere wijzigingen te maken heeft gehad. Het zou niet verbazen, gegeven de positionering van de hazards en het natuurlijk karakter van de baan, die in licht heuvelachtig terrein ligt. De tweede negen holes zijn in 1977 gereedgekomen in een stijl die aansluit op de eerste negen. Let ook eens op de grappige holes, zoals de 13e, een korte dogleg met een hoger liggende tee en green. En alle par-3 holes, echte juweeltjes. Rosendaal is zonder twijfel een van Neerlands beste banen.

The only weak link here is the noisy proximity of two motorways, although they didn't exist at the turn of the century when this course was created through forest, heather and gorse. This was Holland's very first course, and the front nine are the original layout. Significant changes have been made, although the original design of Del Court van Krimpen remains unspoiled. We suspect that Harry Colt had something to do with these changes, it wouldn't be surprising given the layout of hazards and the natural character of the course over slightly hilly terrain. The back nine were completed in 1977 in a style consistent with the front nine. Make a note of some amusing holes here, like the 13th, a short dog-leg with elevated tee and green, and all the par 3, pure gems. Rosendael is unquestionably one of Holland's best inland courses.

Rosendelsche Golfclub
1906

Apeldoornseweg 450
NL - 6816 SN ARNHEM

Office	Secretariaat	(31) 026 - 442 1438
Pro shop	Pro shop	(31) 026 - 443 7283
Fax	Fax	(31) 026 - 351 1196
Situation	Locatie	

Arnhem (pop. 133 670), 2 km

Annual closure	Jaarlijkse sluiting	no
Weekly closure	Wekelijkse sluitingsdag	no

Fees main season
Hoogseizoen tarieven full day

	Week days Weekdagen	We/Bank holidays We/Feestdagen
Individual Individueel	Fl. 100,-	*
Couple Paar	Fl. 200,-	*

* Week-end: members only

Caddy	Caddy	no
Electric Trolley	Electrische trolley	no
Buggy	Buggy	no
Clubs	Clubs	yes

Credit cards Creditkaarten no

Access Toegang : Arnhem A12. Exit 26,
take left, then right
Map 1 on page 1009 Auto kaart 1 Blz 1009

GOLF COURSE
BAAN
15/20

Site	Terrein	
Maintenance	Onderhoud	
Architect	Architect	D.C. van Krimpen F. Pennink
Type	Type baan	forest
Relief	Reliëf	
Water in play	Waterhazards	
Exp. to wind	Windgevoelig	
Trees in play	Bomen	

Scorecard Scorekaart	Chp. Back tees	Mens Heren	Ladies Damen
Length Lengte	6324	6057	5159
Par	72	72	72

Advised golfing ability Aanbevolen golfvaardigheid	0	12	24	36
Hcp required Vereiste hcp	36			

CLUB HOUSE & AMENITIES
CLUB HOUSE EN ANNEXEN
7/10

Pro shop	Pro shop	
Driving range	Oefenbaan	
Sheltered	overdekt	2 mats
On grass	op gras	no, 10 mats open air
Putting-green	putting-green	yes
Pitching-green	pitching-green	yes

HOTEL FACILITIES
HOTELS IN OMGEVING
7/10

HOTELS HOTELS

Rijnhotel — Arnhem
56 rooms, D Fl 205,- — 4 km
Tel (31) 026 - 443 4642, Fax (31) 026 - 445 4847

Groot Warnsborn — Arnhem
29 rooms, D Fl. 250,- — 5 km
Tel (31) 026 - 445 5751, Fax (31) 026 - 443 1010

Postiljon - 84 rooms, D Fl. 180,- — Arnhem
Tel (31) 026 - 357 3333, Fax (31) 026 - 357 3361 — 1 km

RESTAURANTS RESTAURANTS

De Steenen Tafel — Arnhem
Tel (31) 026 - 443 5313 — 1 km

Chez Arie — Arnhem
Tel (31) 026 - 445 6191 — 5 km

1037

	15	7	5

Er is maar weinig reliëf in Friesland, de provincie van de wijde horizon en telkens wisselende luchten. In dit land van meren en weilanden vormen koeien en paarden een deel van het landschap. Er liggen maar weinig golfbanen, maar dit is een van de beste, heel fraai opgenomen in de omgeving. Een vlakke baan, niet erg lang, met brede fairways en weinig bomen, maar des te meer struiken om u dwars te zitten. Long-hitters kunnen zich laten gaan, maar moeten wel rekening houden met de wind, die het leven aardig zuur kan maken. Hetzelfde geldt voor de waterhazards (vijvertjes en sloten) die op zo'n twaalf holes in het spel komen. Deze nog vrij nieuwe baan is snel gerijpt en biedt veel variatie, zowel visueel (er is een hoop grond verplaatst) als golftechnisch. Een minpunt zijn de lange afstanden tussen de holes. Heel bijzonder is de klokkenstoel op het kerkhofje, aan drie zijden door de baan ingesloten.

There is little relief to speak of in the Frise, a region of endless horizons and changing skies. In this land of lakes, pastureland and crops, cows and horses are all part of the landscape. Golf courses are few and far between here, but this is one of the best, blending in very nicely with the surrounding countryside. Very flat, not very long but with wide fairways, it has few trees to bother you but quite a few bushes. Long-hitters will let rip, but will still have to watch out for the wind, which can make life very difficult. The same goes for the water hazards (ponds and ditches), in play on about a dozen holes. This recent course has quickly matured and has considerable variety to it, both visually (a lot of earth was moved) and technically. The one minor flaw are the long walks between holes, and the one peculiarity the little cemetery in front of the clubhouse, overlooked by a bell-tower and surrounded on three sides by the course.

Burggolf Sint Nicolaasga		1990
Legemeersterweg 18		
NL - 8527 DS LEGEMEER		
Office	Secretariaat	(31) 0513 - 499 466
Pro shop	Pro shop	(31) 0513 - 499 466
Fax	Fax	(31) 0513 - 499 091
Situation	Locatie	
Heerenveen (pop. 38 936), 15 km		
Annual closure	Jaarlijkse sluiting	no
Weekly closure	Wekelijkse sluitingsdag	no
Fees main season	Hoogseizoen tarieven	18 holes

	Week days Weekdagen	We/Bank holidays We/Feestdagen
Individual Individueel	Fl 75,-	Fl 85,-
Couple Paar	Fl 150,-	Fl 170,-

Caddy	Caddy	no
Electric Trolley	Electrische trolley	no
Buggy	Buggy	Fl 40,-
Clubs	Clubs	Fl 20,-

Credit cards Creditkaarten
VISA - Eurocard - MasterCard - AMEX - DC - Pinpas

1038

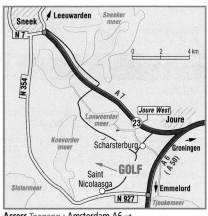

Access Toegang : Amsterdam A6 →
Groningen/Leeuwarden.
Exit 19 → Woudsend. 3.5 km → Golf
Map 1 on page 1008 Auto kaart 1 Blz 1008

GOLF COURSE
BAAN
15/20

Site	Terrein	
Maintenance	Onderhoud	
Architect	Architect	Paul Rolin
		Alan Rijks
Type	Type baan	polder,
		open country
Relief	Reliëf	
Water in play	Waterhazards	
Exp. to wind	Windgevoelig	
Trees in play	Bomen	

Scorecard	Chp.	Mens	Ladies
Scorekaart	Back tees	Heren	Damen
Length Lengte	6038	5765	4993
Par	72	72	72

Advised golfing ability	0	12	24	36
Aanbevolen golfvaardigheid				
Hcp required Vereiste hcp	no			

CLUB HOUSE & AMENITIES
CLUB HOUSE EN ANNEXEN
7/10

Pro shop	Pro shop	
Driving range	Oefenbaan	
Sheltered	overdekt	10 mats
On grass	op gras	no, 15 mats
		open air
Putting-green	putting-green	yes
Pitching-green	pitching-green	yes

HOTEL FACILITIES
HOTELS IN OMGEVING
5/10

HOTELS HOTELS
Hotel Legemeer   Legemeer
14 rooms, D FL 170,-
Tel (31) 0513 - 432 999, Fax (31) 0513 - 432 876

Lauswolt   Beetsterzwaag
58 rooms, Fl 195,-   35 km
Tel (31) 0527 - 291 833, Fax (31) 0527 - 291 836

Postiljon 55 rooms, D Fl 145,-   Heerenveen
Tel (31) 0513 - 618 618, Fax (31) 0513 - 629 100   15 km

RESTAURANTS RESTAURANTS
Kaatje bij de Sluis   Blokzijl
Tel (31) 0527 - 291 833   20 km

Sir Sebastian   Heerenveen
Tel (31) 0513 - 650 408   15 km

Deze baan ligt buiten de traditionele toeristische routes, in het groene land van Twente, dichtbij Duitsland. Veel water, weilanden, dichte bossen en grote boerderijen, waarvan de architectuur kennelijk de inspiratie vormde toen het clubhuis met binnenplaats werd ontworpen. Sybrook is een van de weinige nieuwe banen die in bosgebied mochten worden aangelegd. Bossen waarin nog volop wild voorkomt. Die ziet u dan ook regelmatig in de vroege ochtend of avond. Er zijn wat waterhazards, maar niet overdreven veel. De aantrekkingskracht van deze baan zit in een aantal doorkijkjes en de bloeiende rhododendrons. Het is geen ideale baan voor onstuimige spelers, want er wordt om voorzichtigheid en precisie gevraagd. Ondanks de jonge leeftijd, maakt de baan een volwassen indruk. Het is een lange baan, dus voor de meeste spelers zijn de backtees taboe.

This is a course off the traditional tourist track in the very green region of Twente, close to Germany. Water abounds, as do pasture-land, thick forest and large farms, whose architecture obviously inspired that of the Clubhouse, built with an inner courtyard. Sybrook is one of the few new courses laid out in a forest, which is still home to all sorts of wild animals. You will see a lot of furry creatures at dawn or in the early evening. Several small water hazards come into play, but never excessively so. The appeal of this course is all the greater for a number of views over the countryside and the flowering rhododendrons. Sybrook is not the ideal course for the reckless player, as it demands care, a little thought and considerable accuracy. Despite its infancy, there is a clear impression of maturity. This is a long course, so we would advise the front tees for most players.

Golf & Countryclub 't Sybrook — 1994

Veendijk 100
NL - 7525 PZ ENSCHEDE

Office	Secretariaat	(31) 0541 - 530 331
Pro shop	Pro shop	(31) 0541 - 530 331
Fax	Fax	(31) 0541 - 531 690
Situation	Locatie	

Enschede (pop. 147 624), 5 km
Hengelo (pop. 75 000), 10 km

Annual closure	Jaarlijkse sluiting	no
Weekly closure	Wekelijkse sluitingsdag	no

Fees main season
Hoogseizoen tarieven 18 holes

	Week days Weekdagen	We/Bank holidays We/Feestdagen
Individual Individueel	Fl. 80,-	Fl. 80,-
Couple Paar	Fl. 160,-	Fl. 160,-
Caddy Caddy		no
Electric Trolley Electrische trolley		no
Buggy Buggy		no
Clubs Clubs		yes

Credit cards Creditkaarten
VISA - Eurocard - MasterCard - AMEX

HENGELO

ENSCHEDE

Access Toegang : Hengelo A1 Exit 33 → Enschede. 2,5 km, take left
Map 1 on page 1009 Auto kaart 1 Blz 1009

GOLF COURSE / BAAN — 15/20

Site	Terrein	
Maintenance	Onderhoud	
Architect	Architect	Alan Rijks Paul Rolin
Type	Type baan	forest
Relief	Reliëf	
Water in play	Waterhazards	
Exp. to wind	Windgevoelig	
Trees in play	Bomen	

Scorecard Scorekaart	Chp. Back tees	Mens Heren	Ladies Damen
Length Lengte	6242	5951	5093
Par	72	72	72

Advised golfing ability
Aanbevolen golfvaardigheid — 0 12 24 36

Hcp required	Vereiste hcp	no

CLUB HOUSE & AMENITIES / CLUB HOUSE EN ANNEXEN — 6/10

Pro shop	Pro shop	
Driving range	Oefenbaan	
Sheltered	overdekt	yes
On grass	op gras	no, mats open air
Putting-green	putting-green	yes
Pitching-green	pitching-green	yes

HOTEL FACILITIES / HOTELS IN OMGEVING — 6/10

HOTELS HOTELS
De Broeierd — Enschede
30 rooms, D Fl. 200,- — 5 km
Tel (31) 053 - 435 9882, Fax (31) 053 - 434 0502

Dish — Enschede
80 rooms, D Fl. 135,- — 5 km
Tel (31) 053 - 486 6666, Fax (31) 053 - 435 3104

't Lansink — Hengelo
18 rooms, D Fl. 125,- — 10 km
Tel (31) 074 - 291 0066, Fax (31) 074 - 243 5891

RESTAURANTS RESTAURANTS
't Koesthuis - Tel (31) 053 - 432 866 — Enschede 5 km

Mondriaan — Hengelo
Tel (31) 074 - 291 5321 — 10 km

1039

Een ontwerp van John S.F. Morrison, die werd geholpen door Harry Colt en Sir Guy Campbell. De baan is in de loop der tijd aangepast en recent met twee holes uitgebreid. Zo midden in een bos laat de baan een indruk van rust achter, als je het lawaai van de weg en de nabij gelegen vliegbasis even wegdenkt. In grote lijnen is het een echte Britse baan, zonder veel verrassingen, met natuurlijk de bomen als belangrijkste hindernis (er zijn veel doglegs). Vooral vanaf de backtees kan de baan soms erg nauw ogen. De ruwweg twintig natuurlijk aandoende fairway-bunkers spelen een belangrijke rol door hun strategische ligging. De greens zijn middelgroot, goed ontworpen, goed bewaakt en over het algemeen open genoeg om allerlei soorten approaches toe te staan. Aardigheidje: de 150-meter markers bestaan uit nestkastjes in de bomen.

Designed by John S.F. Morrison, who worked with Harry Colt and Sir Guy Campbell, this course has been altered and recently lengthened with two new holes. Laid out in a forest, it exudes an impression of tranquillity, if you can forget the slight traffic noise and the planes from a nearby air base. The general style is rather British and offers no great surprises, while the main difficulties are, naturally, the trees (there are a lot of dog-legs), especially from the back-tees from where the fairways at times look despairingly narrow. The twenty or so very natural-looking fairway bunkers also play an important role through their strategic positioning. The greens are mid-size, slightly contoured, neatly designed, well-guarded and, by and large, open enough to allow all types of approach shots. Interestingly, the 150 yard-to-green markers are nests placed in the trees.

Noord-Brabantsche Golfclub Toxandria — 1928

Veenstraat 89
NL - 5124 NC MOLENSCHOT

Office	Secretariaat	(31) 0161 - 411 200
Pro shop	Pro shop	(31) 0161 - 411 200
Fax	Fax	(31) 0161 - 411 715
Situation	Locatie	

Breda (pop. 129 125), 5 km

Annual closure	Jaarlijkse sluiting	no
Weekly closure	Wekelijkse sluitingsdag	no
Fees main season	Hoogseizoen tarieven	18 holes

	Week days Weekdagen	We/Bank holidays We/Feestdagen
Individual Individueel	Fl. 85,-	Fl. 110,-
Couple Paar	Fl. 170,-	Fl. 220,-

Caddy	Caddy	no
Electric Trolley	Electrische trolley	no
Buggy	Buggy	no
Clubs	Clubs	no
Credit cards Creditkaarten		no

1040

Access Toegang : A27 Utrecht-Breda Exit 16.
N263 → Rijen. 4 km → Molenschot
Map 1 on page 1008 Auto kaart 1 Blz 1008

GOLF COURSE / BAAN — 14/20

Site	Terrein	
Maintenance	Onderhoud	
Architect	Architect	J. Morrison
Type	Type baan	forest
Relief	Reliëf	
Water in play	Waterhazards	
Exp. to wind	Windgevoelig	
Trees in play	Bomen	

Scorecard Scorekaart	Chp. Back tees	Mens Heren	Ladies Damen
Length Lengte	6140	5974	5188
Par	72	72	72

Advised golfing ability Aanbevolen golfvaardigheid	0	12	24 36
Hcp required Vereiste hcp	no		

CLUB HOUSE & AMENITIES / CLUB HOUSE EN ANNEXEN — 7/10

Pro shop	Pro shop	
Driving range	Oefenbaan	
Sheltered	overdekt	8 mats
On grass	op gras	no, mats open air
Putting-green	putting-green	yes
Pitching-green	pitching-green	yes

HOTEL FACILITIES / HOTELS IN OMGEVING — 6/10

HOTELS HOTELS

De Herbergh — Rijen
44 rooms, D Fl. 130,- — 2 km
Tel (31) 0161 - 224 318, Fax (31) 0161 - 222 327

Motel Gilze-Rijen — Rijen
134 rooms, D Fl. 100,- — 2 km
Tel (31) 0161 - 454 951, Fax (31) 0161 - 452 171

Mercure Hotel — Breda
40 rooms, D Fl. 225,- — 5 km
Tel (31) 0161 - 522 0200, Fax (31) 0161 - 521 4967

RESTAURANTS RESTAURANTS

La Grille d'Or — Breda
Tel (31) 0161 - 520 4333 — 5 km

Mirabelle — Breda
Tel (31) 0161 - 565 6650 — 5 km

Tientallen jaren bracht de Twentsche Golfclub door op een kleine, maar fijne 9-holesbaan, ingeklemd tussen de Hengelo en Enschede. Die baan ligt er nog steeds, maar de club is verhuisd naar een ruimere «outfit» in de bossen ten westen van de dubbelstad. Het decor van de baan wordt gevormd door oude bossen, met daartussen opvallend veel open ruimtes (van nature) en opvallend veel water (aangelegd) in de vorm van vijf vijvers. Soms hebben die alleen een decoratieve functie, maar op negen holes komt het water ook echt in het spel. Naast de bomen en het water is de lengte een factor om rekening mee te houden. Vooral op de tweede negen, met drie par-4 holes rond de 400 meter. Het nieuwe clubhuis heeft door het hoge rode pannendak het karakter van een Twentsche boerderij.

For dozens of years the Twentsche Golfclub was based at a short but pretty 9-hole course, stuck in between Hengelo and Enschede. That original course is still open, but the club moved to a larger outfit in the woods west of the Twin-cities. The stage there is set by old forests, with a remarkable amount of open space (natural) and an equally remarkable amount of water (artificial) in the form of five ponds. Often the water only serves as decoration but on nine holes it actually comes into play. Apart from the water and the trees, length is a factor to reckon with, especially on the back-nine, with three par-4 holes around 440 yards. The newly-built clubhouse resembles a traditional local farmhouse thanks to its bright red tiled roof.

Twentsche Golf Club — 1997

Almelosestraat 17
NL - 7495 TG AMBT-DELDEN

Office	Secretariaat	(31) 074 - 384 1167
Pro shop	Pro shop	(31) 074 - 384 1054
Fax	Fax	(31) 074 - 384 1067
Situation	Locatie	

Hengelo (pop. 75 000), 10 km

Annual closure	Jaarlijkse sluiting	no
Weekly closure	Wekelijkse sluitingsdag	no

Fees main season
Hoogseizoen tarieven 18 holes

	Week days Weekdagen	We/Bank holidays We/Feestdagen
Individual Individueel	Fl 80,-	Fl 90,-
Couple Paar	Fl 160,-	Fl 180,-

Caddy	Caddy	no
Electric Trolley	Electrische trolley	no
Buggy	Buggy	no
Clubs	Clubs	yes
Credit cards Creditkaarten		no

Wierden **Almelo**
0   2   4 km
N 743
Bornerbroek   **Borne**
Deventer Apeldoorn A 1   A 35
Borne West
GOLF
Deldenerbroek   Delden   **Hengelo**
Goor N 346   **Delden**
Enschede ↓
Twente kanaal

Access Toegang : Amsterdam, A1 → Hengelo, Exit 28, N347, then N346 → Delden, then → Bornebroek.
Map 1 on page 1009 Auto kaart 1 Blz 1009

GOLF COURSE / BAAN — 15/20

Site	Terrein	▰▰▰▰▱▱
Maintenance	Onderhoud	▰▰▰▰▱▱
Architect	Architect	Tom MacAuley
Type	Type baan	forest, parkland
Relief	Reliëf	▰▰▱▱▱▱
Water in play	Waterhazards	▰▰▰▱▱▱
Exp. to wind	Windgevoelig	▰▰▱▱▱▱
Trees in play	Bomen	▰▰▰▰▱▱

Scorecard Scorekaart	Chp. Back tees	Mens Heren	Ladies Damen
Length Lengte	6296	6178	5241
Par	72	72	72

Advised golfing ability
Aanbevolen golfvaardigheid   0   12   24   36

Hcp required Vereiste hcp   certificate

CLUB HOUSE & AMENITIES / CLUB HOUSE EN ANNEXEN — 7/10

Pro shop	Pro shop	▰▰▰▰▱▱
Driving range	Oefenbaan	▰▰▰▱▱▱
Sheltered	overdekt	7 mats
On grass	op gras	no
Putting-green	putting-green	yes
Pitching-green	pitching-green	yes

HOTEL FACILITIES / HOTELS IN OMGEVING — 6/10

HOTELS HOTELS

Carelshaven — Delden
20 rooms, D Fl. 165,- — 4 km
Tel (31) 074 - 376 1305
Fax (31) 074 - 376 1291

't Lansing — Hengelo
6 rooms, D Fl. 120,- — 10 km
Tel (31) 074 - 291 0066
Fax (31) 074 - 243 5891

RESTAURANTS RESTAURANTS

In de Kop'ren Smorre — Markelo
Tel (31) 0547 - 361 344 — 10 km

In den Drost van Twenthe — Delden
Tel (31) 074 - 376 4055 — 3 km

1041

15 7 6

De oorspronkelijk aangelegde holes liggen in bebost terrein, waar bomen natuurlijk de belangrijkste hindernis vormen. Zeker op de vier dog-legs en de lange smalle 6e, nu 15e hole. Zo ook op de daaropvolgende schitterende par-3, waar de bomen voor de green weinig ruimte voor fouten laten. Later werden negen nieuwe holes aangelegd, op vroegere landbouwgrond, met vier kleine vijvertjes en een paar sloten, maar ook met bredere fairways. Oude en nieuwe holes zijn door elkaar gemengd, wat variatie in het spel, maar ook behoorlijke afstanden tussen de holes heeft opgeleverd. Een nadeel is dat je tegen de tijd dat je aan de 'oude' greens gewend bent, overstapt naar de nieuwe en omgekeerd. Dat maakt het spel niet eenvoudiger, maar misschien hebben alleen de wat betere spelers hier last van.

The front nine were laid out in woody terrain and trees naturally form the main difficulty, especially on the four dog-legs and the long, narrow 15th. Likewise, on the 16th, a beautiful par 3, the trees in front of the green leave little room for error. They then created nine new holes, over much more open farming land, with four small water hazards and a few ditches, but with much wider fairways. The old and new holes have been intermingled, thus varying the pleasure but sometimes leaving considerable distances between green and next tee. Another obvious drawback is that by the time you get accustomed to the grass and greens on the old holes, you are back to the new ones, and vice versa. This does not make scoring easy, and it just might be that better players are more affected by this subtle difference than their less experienced counterparts.

Wouwse Plantage   1982
Zoomvlietweg 66
NL - 4624 RP BERGEN OP ZOOM

Office	Secretariaat	(31) 0165 - 379 593
Pro shop	Pro shop	(31) 0165 - 379 547
Fax	Fax	(31) 0165 - 379 888
Situation	Locatie	

Roosendaal (pop. 62 784), 10 km
Bergen op Zoom (pop. 47 483), 15 km

Annual closure	Jaarlijkse sluiting	no
Weekly closure	Wekelijkse sluitingsdag	no
Fees main season	Hoogseizoen tarieven	18 holes

	Week days Weekdagen	We/Bank holidays We/Feestdagen
Individual Individueel	Fl 70,-	Fl 80,-
Couple Paar	Fl 140,-	Fl 160,-

Caddy	Caddy	no
Electric Trolley	Electrische trolley	Fl 7,50,-
Buggy	Buggy	no
Clubs	Clubs	Fl 35,-
Credit cards	Creditkaarten	no

1042

Access Toegang : A58 Breda → Bergen op Zoom.
Exit 26 → Wouwse Plantage. 100 m,
turn right then left (Zoomvlietweg). Golf 3.5 km.
Map 1 on page 1008 Auto kaart 1 Blz 1008

GOLF COURSE
BAAN   **15**/20

Site	Terrein	
Maintenance	Onderhoud	
Architect	Architect	Donald Steel Paul Rolin
Type	Type baan	open country, parkland
Relief	Reliëf	
Water in play	Waterhazards	
Exp. to wind	Windgevoelig	
Trees in play	Bomen	

Scorecard Scorekaart	Chp. Back tees	Mens Heren	Ladies Damen
Length Lengte	5909	5909	5111
Par	72	72	72

Advised golfing ability		0 12 24 36
Aanbevolen golfvaardigheid		
Hcp required Vereiste hcp	36	

CLUB HOUSE & AMENITIES
CLUB HOUSE EN ANNEXEN   **7**/10

Pro shop	Pro shop	
Driving range	Oefenbaan	
Sheltered	overdekt	5 mats
On grass	op gras	no, 5 mats open air
Putting-green	putting-green	yes
Pitching-green	pitching-green	yes

HOTEL FACILITIES
HOTELS IN OMGEVING   **6**/10

HOTELS HOTELS
De Draak   Bergen op Zoom
48 rooms, D Fl. 250,-   8 km
Tel (31) 0164 - 235 000, Fax (31) 0164 - 236 001

De Gouden Leeuw   Bergen op Zoom
28 rooms, D Fl. 200,-   8 km
Tel (31) 0164 - 235 000, Fax (31) 0164 - 236 001

De Draak   Roosendaal
49 rooms, D Fl. 195,-   10 km
Tel (31) 0165 - 555 400, Fax (31) 0165 - 560 660

RESTAURANTS RESTAURANT
Mijn Keuken - Tel (31) 0165 - 530 2208   Wouw 5 km

Moerstede   Bergen op Zoom
Tel (31) 0164 - 258 800   8 km

gewonnen zou wel eens meer toeristen naar dit heerlijke gebied kunnen trekken. We zitten hier dicht bij Aken, een van de belangrijkste Duitse steden, waarvan de historische waarde, sinds de grootse plannen van Karel de Grote, nooit in twijfel is getrokken. Dit gebied is ook het hoogste van Nederland... iets onder de 300 meter (elk land heeft zijn bergen, Moeder Natuur bepaalt hoe hoog ze zijn!). De baan werd aangelegd als een 9-holes baan en werd uitgebreid tot 18 holes in 1990. De 'oude' holes lopen door een bos, terwijl acht van de 'nieuwe' holes in een open landschap liggen met sterke hoogteverschillen en prachtige vergezichten. Al met al is de baan goed te bespelen, voor iedereen. Om je handicap te spelen moet je wel de bomen op de eerste negen tee te ontlopen en op de twee negen vooral nauwkeurige teeshots afleveren. Afgedwaalde ballen komen snel op onplezierige plaatsen terecht, op sterk glooiende hellingen.

Maastricht's newly acquired fame, or notoriety, in Europe should attract the tourists to this lovely region. Here, we are very close to Aachen, one of the great German cities whose historical importance, since the great European designs of Charlemagne, has never been questioned. The region is also one of the highest in the Netherlands...a little below 300 metres (each country has its natural mountains, mother nature decides how high!). The course here began as a 9-holer and was extended to 18 holes in 1980. The first holes wind their way through a forest, while 8 of the last 9 are in open countryside with sharp differences in level and some beautiful views. All in all, the course is easily walkable, for everyone. Playing to your handicap demands avoidance of the trees on the way out and carefully placed drives on the way in. Wayward shots can leave your ball in some very tricky positions, with steeply sloping lies.

Zuid Limburgse Golf & Countryclub   1956
Dalbissenweg 22
NL - 6281 NC MECHELEN

Office	Secretariaat	(31) 043 - 455 1254
Pro shop	Pro shop	(31) 043 - 455 1254
Fax	Fax	(31) 043 - 455 1576
Situation	Locatie	

Maastricht (pop. 118 102), 18 km
Aachen (Deutschland), 15 km

Annual closure	Jaarlijkse sluiting	no
Weekly closure	Wekelijkse sluitingsdag	no

Fees main season
Hoogseizoen tarieven full day

	Week days Weekdagen	We/Bank holidays We/Feestdagen
Individual Individueel	Fl. 60,-	Fl. 90,-
Couple Paar	Fl. 120,-	Fl. 180,-

Caddy	Caddy	no
Electric Trolley	Electrische trolley	no
Buggy	Buggy	no
Clubs	Clubs	yes

Credit cards Creditkaarten   no

Access Toegang : N278 Maastricht → Aachen.
Gulpen → Landsrade.
Map 1 on page 1009 Auto kaart 1 Blz 1009

GOLF COURSE
BAAN   14/20

Site	Terrein	
Maintenance	Onderhoud	
Architect	Architect	FW Hawtree Rolin / Snelders
Type	Type baan	forest
Relief	Reliëf	
Water in play	Waterhazards	
Exp. to wind	Windgevoelig	
Trees in play	Bomen	

Scorecard Scorekaart	Chp. Back tees	Mens Heren	Ladies Damen
Length Lengte	5924	5924	5071
Par	71	71	71

Advised golfing ability Aanbevolen golfvaardigheid	0	12	24	36
Hcp required Vereiste hcp	We: 30			

CLUB HOUSE & AMENITIES
CLUB HOUSE EN ANNEXEN   7/10

Pro shop	Pro shop	
Driving range	Oefenbaan	
Sheltered	overdekt	2 mats
On grass	op gras	no, 8 mats open air
Putting-green	putting-green	yes
Pitching-green	pitching-green	yes

HOTEL FACILITIES
HOTELS IN OMGEVING   7/10

HOTELS HOTELS

Kasteel Wittem   Wittem
12 rooms, D Fl. 210,-   12 km
Tel (31) 043 - 450 1208, Fax (31) 043 - 450 1260

Landgoed Schoutenhof   Epen
10 rooms, D Fl. 170,-   8 km
Tel (31) 043 - 455 2002, Fax (31) 043 - 455 2605

Brull - 32 rooms, D Fl. 140,-   Mechelen
Tel (31) 043 - 455 1263, Fax (31) 043 - 455 2300   4 km

RESTAURANTS RESTAURANTS

De Leuf   Ubachsberg
Tel (31) 045 - 575 0226   4 km

De Bloasbalg   Wahlwiller
Tel (31) 043 - 451 1364   5 km

1043

Norge

The Millennium Guide

D et hevdes at skigåing er like viktig for nordmenn som sykling er det for danskene. En logisk antagelse med tanke på at landet er dekket med snø en stor del av året. Til tross for dette kan det være overraskende mildt på vestkysten – takket være Golfstrømmens innflytelse. Fra Oslo til Bergen kan du spille golf i perioden april til oktober, og for 70.000 nordmenn er golfkøllene en slags sommerutgave av skistavene. Som i alle de nordiske landene er golf en sportsaktivitet på lik linje med de fleste andre idretter. Golf er heller ikke så snobbete som den kan oppleves i andre europeiske land. Naturligvis er ikke alle de 74 banene (24 av dem er 18 hulls) i så god stand og velstelt som Augusta, men så fort vinteren har tatt farvel fremstår banene i bra stand. Sesongåpning på den enkelte bane avhenger mye av våren og hvor raskt snø og frost slipper taket.

T hey say that skiing is as important to the Norwegians as cycling is to the Danes, a logical assumption when snow covers the whole country for a good part of the year. Despite this, the west coast can be surprisingly mild thanks to the warming influence of the Gulf Stream. You can play golf between April and October from Bergen to Oslo, and for 55,000 Norwegians, golf clubs are the summer version of ski poles. As in all northern countries, golf here is a sporting activity like any other and golfing snobbery is never as blatant in Norway as it can be in other countries of Europe. Naturally, the 74 courses (24 eighteen-holers) are not all as well manicured as Augusta, but they are very quickly groomed into good condition once winter is over. Opening dates depend entirely on the thawing frost and snow.

1044

RANGERING AV BANENE
CLASSIFICATION OF COURSES

Denne rangeringen er basert på poeng som er gitt den aktuelle banen.

This classification gives priority consideration
to the score awarded to the actual course.

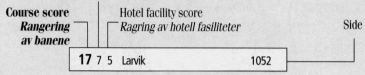

Club-house and facilities
Rangering av Klubhus

Course score
Rangering
av banene

Hotel facility score
Ragring av hotell fasiliteter

Side

17 7 5   Larvik   1052

Rangering	Golfbanene	Side	Rangering	Golfbanene	Side
17 7 5	Larvik	1052	**14** 6 6	Grenland	1050
16 6 5	Borre	1049	**14** 6 4	Nes	1053
16 6 7	Stavanger	1056	**14** 6 6	Tyrifjord	1057
15 7 5	Arendal	1048	**13** 7 6	Hauger	1051
15 7 9	Oslo	1054	**13** 6 4	Sorknes	1055

RANGERING AV HOTELL FASILITETER
CLASSIFICATION OF HOTELS FACILITIES

Rangering	Golfbanene	Side	Rangering	Golfbanene	Side
15 7 **9**	Oslo	1054	15 7 **5**	Arendal	1048
16 6 **7**	Stavanger	1056	16 6 **5**	Borre	1049
14 6 **6**	Grenland	1050	17 7 **5**	Larvik	1052
13 7 **6**	Hauger	1051	14 6 **4**	Nes	1053
14 6 **6**	Tyrifjord	1057	13 6 **4**	Sorknes	1055

BANETYPE TYPE OF COURSES

Rangering	Golfbanene		Side	Rangering	Golfbanene		Side
forest				**open country**			
Grenland	14 6 6		1050	Borre	16 6 5		1049
Sorknes	13 6 4		1055	Hauger	13 7 6		1051
hilly				Nes	14 6 4		1053
Tyrifjord	14 6 6		1057	Oslo	15 7 9		1054
inland				Stavanger	16 6 7		1056
Arendal	15 7 5		1048	Larvik	17 7 5		1052
links				**parkland**			
Larvik	17 7 5		1052	Grenland	14 6 6		1050
				Tyrifjord	14 6 6		1057

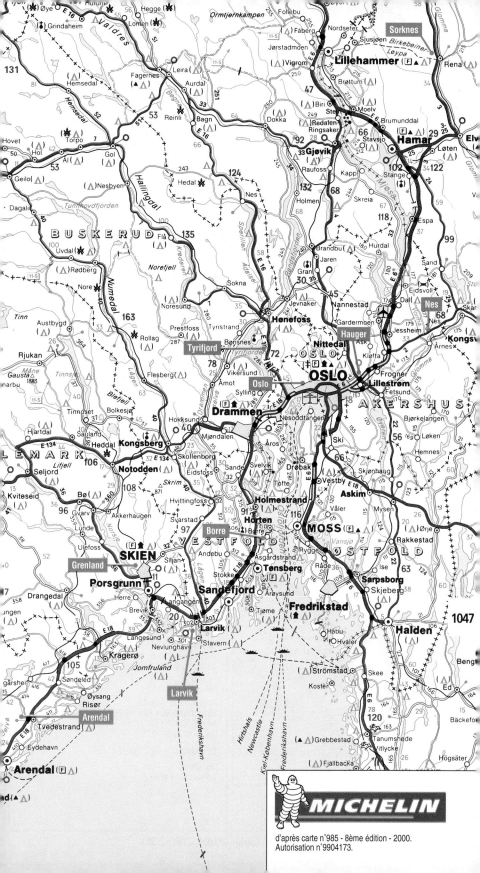

Arendal blir ofte kalt Nordens Venezia på grunn av de mange kanalene som rant gjennom byen. Denne golfbanen er ytterligere et argument som tjener byens livskraft, bygd i 1991 uten hjelp fra noen golfbanearkitekter. For en gang skyld har denne form for vågestykke blitt en suksess. Den er mye bakker (du bør være i god fysisk form) og enkelte vanskeligheter ser man ikke før de dukker opp. Får man imidlertid kontroll på vanskelighetene viser banen seg å være en meget god utfordring. Det er ikke en lang bane, men den er utmerket balansert og greenene er vel designet på måte som kan gjøre det vanskelig å spille til sitt handicap. Mens de første ni hullene er heller åpne, så medfører trær og vannhinder at det må utvises forsiktighet på hjemturens ni siste hull. Det er en stor fordel å ha spilt banen tidligere, og det gjelder å merke seg at klubbhuset er åpent rundt på skisesongen.

Arendal used to be called the Venice of the North on account of the very many canals that ran through the town. Most of these have disappeared today, but a good number of wooden buildings and houses still testify to the former importance of Arendal. This golf course is further argument in favour of the town's vitality, built in 1991 without the services of a golf architect. For once, this sort of venture has been successful. It is rather hilly (you need to be in good shape physically) and some of the difficulties are hidden from view, but once under control, it proves to be a very good challenge. This is not a long course but it is nicely balanced and the greens are designed well enough to make playing to your handicap a sometimes awkward proposition. In addition, while the front 9 are rather open, the trees and water hazards on the way home call for extreme caution. Well worth getting to know, and note that the club-house stays open all year for the skiing season.

Arendal og Omegn Golfklubb 1991
Nes Verk
N - 4900 TVEDESTRAND

Office	Kontor	(47) 371 603 60
Pro shop	Pro shop	(47) 371 603 60
Fax	Fax	(47) 371 602 11
Situation	Beliggenhet	

Arendal, 20 km

Annual closure	Årlig stenging	1/11 → 30/4
Weekly closure	Ukentlig stenging	no

Fees main season
Tariffer i høysesongen 18 holes

	Week days Ukedager	We/Bank holidays Week-end/Frydag
Individual Individuell	NOK 230,-	NOK 280,-
Couple Par	NOK 460,-	NOK 560,-

Juniors: – 50 %

Caddy	Caddy	no
Electric Trolley	Elektrisk vogn	no
Buggy	Golfbil	yes
Clubs	Køller	yes

Credit cards Kredittkort
VISA - Eurocard - MasterCard - AMEX - DC - JCB

1048

Access Adkomst : Arendal, E18 → Tvedestrand
Exit «Fjanesvingen». Golf 2 km from E18 on 112
Map 1 on page 1047 Kort 1 på side: 1047

GOLF COURSE
GOLFBANEN 15/20

Site	Område	
Maintenance	Vedlikehold	
Architect	Arkitekt	Unknown
Type	Type	inland
Relief	Relief	
Water in play	Vann-hinder	
Exp. to wind	Utsatt for vind	
Trees in play	Tre-hinder	

Scorecard	Chp.	Mens	Ladies
Scorecard	Champ.-tee	Herre-tees	Dame-tees
Length Lengde	5785	5528	4683
Par	72	72	72

Advised golfing ability	0	12	24	36
Anbefalt golfnivå				

Hcp required Obligatorisk Hcp 35

CLUB HOUSE & AMENITIES
KLUBHUS OG OMGIVELSER 7/10

Pro shop	Pro shop	
Driving range	Treningsbane	
Sheltered	ly	yes
On grass	på gress	yes (Summer)
Putting-green	putting-green	yes
Pitching-green	pitching-green	yes

HOTEL FACILITIES
HOTELFASILITETER 5/10

HOTELS HOTEL-FASILITETER
Tvedestrand Fjordhotel   Tvedestrand
18 rooms, D NOK 990,-   10 km
Tel (47) 371 626 55
Fax (47) 371 626 18

Scandic Hotel Arendal   Arendal
80 rooms, D NOK 845,-/1295,-   20 km
Tel (47) 370 251 60
Fax (47) 370 267 07

RESTAURANTS RESTAURANT

Vertshuset   Tvedestrand
Tel (47) 371 612 61   10 km

Folk som assosierer Norge med fjorder vil bli overrasket over de mange små buktene med fiskelandsbyer som ligger sørvest for Oslo. Før du tar dem i nærmere øyesyn er det verdt å gjøre et stopp ved Borre, like ved Horten. Banen ble anlagt rundt den noble herregården Semb. Deler av banen ligger på et tidligere jordbruksområde mens de øvrige hullene snor seg igjennom et skoglandskap. Tommy Nordström har gjort denne banen til en av de beste i landet. En bane som gir utfordringer for de gode spillerne, men som samtidig tar vare på de med høyt handicap. Den er vakkert bygd, men man likevel klart å gi den et naturlig utseende. Den avslører mange slags vanskeligheter og utfordringer, og du vil snarlig beklage din manglende evne til å slå ballene kontrollert i de forskjellige retningene. Banen er ikke spesielt preget av bakker og den er lett å gå rundt. Banen preges av ypperlige greener og med et meget hyggelig miljø. På Borre opplever man en golfrunde som helst ikke vil ta slutt. Så derfor, hvorfor ikke komme tilbake ved en senere anledning?

People who associate Norway with fjords will be surprised by the little coves and fishing villages lying to the southwest of Oslo. Before you see them for yourselves, stop off and play a round at Borre, close to Horten. The course was laid out around the noble mansion of Semb, partly over an old farm and partly over more woodland landscape. Tommy Nordstrom has made this into one of the country's best courses, one that is both challenging for the better golfer and well suited to higher-handicappers. Well landscaped but still with a crisp natural look, it clearly reveals difficulties of every kind and soon has you regretting your inability to bend the ball deliberately in either direction. The course is not too hilly and easily walkable, and with well-guarded, excellent greens and a very pleasant environment, this is one round of golf you will be sorry to finish. But there again, who is to stop you from coming back for more?

Barre Golfklubb — 1991
Semb Hovedgård
N - 3186 HORTEN

Office	Kontor	(47) 330 730 79
Pro shop	Pro shop	(47) 330 739 70
Fax	Fax	(47) 330 732 41
Situation	Beliggenhet	
Horten, 2,5 km		
Annual closure	Årlig stenging	1/11→31/3
Weekly closure	Ukentlig stenging	no

Fees main season
Tariffer i høysesongen full day

	Week days Ukedager	We/Bank holidays Week-end/Frydag
Individual Individuell	NOK 250,-	NOK 300,-
Couple Par	NOK 500,-	NOK 600,-

Juniors: – 50%

Caddy	Caddy	no
Electric Trolley	Elektrisk vogn	no
Buggy	Golfbil	yes
Clubs	Køller	yes

Credit cards Kredittkort
VISA - Eurocard - MasterCard - AMEX - DC - JCB

Access Adkomst : 2,5 km S of Horten city centre
Map 1 on page 1047 Kort 1 på side: 1047

GOLF COURSE / GOLFBANEN — 16/20

Site	Område	
Maintenance	Vedlikehold	
Architect	Arkitekt	Tommy Nordström
Type	Type	open country
Relief	Relief	
Water in play	Vann-hinder	
Exp. to wind	Utsatt for vind	
Trees in play	Tre-hinder	

Scorecard Scorecard	Chp. Champ.-tee	Mens Herre-tees	Ladies Dame-tees
Length Lengde	5788	5788	4964
Par	72	72	72

Advised golfing ability Anbefalt golfnivå	0	12	24	36

Hcp required Obligatorisk Hcp 35

CLUB HOUSE & AMENITIES / KLUBHUS OG OMGIVELSER — 6/10

Pro shop	Pro shop	
Driving range	Treningsbane	
Sheltered	ly	no
On grass	på gress	yes
Putting-green	putting-green	yes
Pitching-green	pitching-green	yes

1049

HOTEL FACILITIES / HOTELFASILITETER — 5/10

HOTELS HOTEL-FASILITETER
Hotel Horten Brygge — Horten
23 rooms, D NOK 650,- — 2,5 km
Tel (47) 330 204 20
Fax (47) 330 204 21

RESTAURANTS RESTAURANT
Fishland — Horten
Tel (47) 330 488 10 — 2,5 km

Dette er banen i Skien, den største byen i Telemark fylke. Telemark er skisportens mekka. Skidisiplinen med samme navn og ordet slalåm har sin opprinnelse fra dette området. Golfbanen er imidlertid overraskende lite preget av bakker. Her slår vi ut fra tee og finner et åpent område mellom parklandskap og skog. Samtidig er fairwayene godt adskilt, men gir like fullt en følelse av intimitet. Banen byr ikke på noen fremtredende vanskeligheter og den er aldri kjedelig å spille. Jan Sederholm har fremskaffet en meget god layout på banen som passer golfere på alle nivåer, selv om de beste kanskje synes den er i korteste laget. Sant nok, men den morsom å spille og har mange nok utfordringer til å gi deg stor glede og tilfredsstillelse av å slå gode slag. En bra bane, varm atmosfære og et vakkert landskap.

This is the Skien golf course, the biggest town in the province of Telemark, a sort of Mecca for skiers. The skiing style of the same name and the word slalom were born right here. The golf course, however, is surprisingly unhilly. Here we are teeing off over open space between park and forest, where the fairways are generously separated for a little golfing intimacy. With no outstanding difficulties on a course that is never bland or boring to play, this is a very good layout by Jan Sederholm for all types of golfer, although the best might find it a little short. That may well be, but it is still great fun, with considerable difficulties and a stiff enough challenge not only for enjoyment but also for the opportunity and satisfaction of hitting some good shots, i.e. the 10% shots that go with the remaining 90%. A good course, warm atmosphere and beautiful landscapes.

Grenland Golfklubb — 1994

Luksefjellvn. 578
N - 3721 SKIEN

Office	Kontor	(47) 355 907 03
Pro shop	Pro shop	(47) 355 903 00
Fax	Fax	(47) 355 906 10
Situation	Beliggenhet	

Skien, 6 km

| Annual closure | Årlig stenging | 1/11 → 31/3 |
| Weekly closure | Ukentlig stenging | no |

Fees main season
Tariffer i høysesongen full day

	Week days Ukedager	We/Bank holidays Week-end/Frydag
Individual Individuell	NOK 250,-	NOK 250,-
Couple Par	NOK 500,-	NOK 500,-

Caddy	Caddy	no
Electric Trolley	Elektrisk vogn	no
Buggy	Golfbil	yes
Clubs	Køller	yes

Credit cards Kredittkort
VISA - Eurocard - MasterCard - AMEX - DC - JCB

1050

Access Adkomst : Skien, Rv.32 North → Siljan, turn on road Luksfjellveien
Map 1 on page 1047 Kort 1 på side: 1047

GOLF COURSE
GOLFBANEN — 14/20

Site	Område	▰▰▰▱
Maintenance	Vedlikehold	▰▰▰▱
Architect	Arkitekt	Jan Sederholm
Type	Type	forest, parkland
Relief	Relief	▰▰▱▱
Water in play	Vann-hinder	▰▱▱▱
Exp. to wind	Utsatt for vind	▰▰▱▱
Trees in play	Tre-hinder	▰▰▱▱

Scorecard Scorecard	Chp. Champ.-tee	Mens Herre-tees	Ladies Dame-tees
Length Lengde	5777	5777	4960
Par	72	72	72

Advised golfing ability Anbefalt golfnivå	0	12	24	36

Hcp required   Obligatorisk Hcp 35

CLUB HOUSE & AMENITIES
KLUBHUS OG OMGIVELSER — 6/10

Pro shop	Pro shop	▰▰▰▱
Driving range	Treningsbane	▱▱▱▱
Sheltered	ly	no
On grass	på gress	yes
Putting-green	putting-green	yes
Pitching-green	pitching-green	yes

HOTEL FACILITIES
HOTELFASILITETER — 6/10

HOTELS HOTEL-FASILITETER
Rica Ibsen Hotel — Skien
119 rooms, D NOK 840,-/1210,- — 8 km
Tel (47) 355 249 90
Fax (47) 355 261 86

RESTAURANTS RESTAURANT
Jegermesteren — Skien
Tel (47) 355 241 73 — 8 km

Spørsmålet er om Hauger en god mesterskapsbane? Det er utvilsomt en fysisk test å spille 18 hull. Seniorer og mindre veltrente golfere kanskje har mer igjen av å tilbringe noen timer i det fantastiske klubbhuset som tidligere var en forpakterbolig og betrakte det bakre landskapet som omgir banen. Etter å ha spilt banen vil man for alltid huske greenene. De er meget raske og ondulerte. Under disse forholdene vil du kanskje spille til ditt handicap, men det skal godt gjøres å senke det. Enkelte av hullene pærer preg av en linksbane med en meget lang og tøff rough. Andre hull minner mer om en park- og innlandsbane. Sagt med andre ord: Du trenger å mestre de fleste type slag og det er viktig å slå rett. Om du ikke tenker for mye på scoren er Hauger en utrolig bra bane hvis man ønsker å lære seg å spille på alle typer baner. For å være ærlig vil vi dessverre ikke anbefale banen for spillere med høyere enn handicap 15, eller kanskje 18. Med litt mer «normale» greener ville Hauger utvilsomt vært en mesterskapsbane.

The question is: is this course a good championship test? It is certainly a demanding physical test, where seniors and the less athletic golfer might do better to wait in the superb farmhouse used as a club-house and admire the beautiful scenery. This is also a memorable course for the greens, all very slick and sometimes with contours that some might consider a little over the top. Under these conditions, you might just about play to your handicap but you will be hard pushed to lower it. Some of the holes have a distinctive links flavour with very tough, tall rough, others are more like inland or parkland holes. In other words, you will need the full panoply of shots and have to hit it straight. If you don't pay too much attention to your score, Hauger is an excellent course for learning and sustaining an all-round game. We wouldn't honestly recommend this to players with a handicap higher than 15 or maybe 18, which is a pity. With more reasonable greens, it really would have been a good championship test.

Hanger Golfklubb — 1996

Ramstadvn. 18
N - 1480 SLATTUM

Office	Kontor	(47) 670 784 00
Pro shop	Pro shop	(47) 670 790 30
Fax	Fax	(47) 670 799 09
Situation	Beliggenhet	

Lillestrøm, 10 km - Oslo (pop. 458 500), 20 km

Annual closure	Årlig stenging	1/11 → 30/4
Weekly closure	Ukentlig stenging	no

Fees main season
Tariffer i høysesongen 18 holes

	Week days Ukedager	We/Bank holidays Week-end/Frydag
Individual Individuell	NOK 350,-	NOK 400,-
Couple Par	NOK 700,-	NOK 800,-
Juniors: – 50 %		

Caddy	Caddy	no
Electric Trolley	Elektrisk vogn	no
Buggy	Golfbil	no
Clubs	Køller	yes

Credit cards Kredittkort
VISA - Eurocard - MasterCard - AMEX - DC - JCB

Access Adkomst : Oslo, E6 North.
Left on Rv.122 by Olavsgaard Hotel. 1 km → Golf
Map 1 on page 1047 Kort 1 på side: 1047

GOLF COURSE / GOLFBANEN — 13/20

Site	Område	
Maintenance	Vedlikehold	
Architect	Arkitekt	Jeremy Turner
Type	Type	open country
Relief	Relief	
Water in play	Vann-hinder	
Exp. to wind	Utsatt for vind	
Trees in play	Tre-hinder	

Scorecard Scorecard	Chp. Champ.-tee	Mens Herre-tees	Ladies Dame-tees
Length Lengde	5974	5974	4987
Par	72	72	72

Advised golfing ability — 0 12 24 36
Anbefalt golfnivå
Hcp required Obligatorisk Hcp 28 Men/32 Ladies

CLUB HOUSE & AMENITIES / KLUBHUS OG OMGIVELSER — 7/10

Pro shop	Pro shop	
Driving range	Treningsbane	
Sheltered	ly	yes
On grass	på gress	yes (Summer)
Putting-green	putting-green	yes
Pitching-green	pitching-green	yes

HOTEL FACILITIES / HOTELFASILITETER — 6/10

HOTELS HOTEL-FASILITETER

Quality Olavsgaard Hotel — Skjetten, 2,5 km
162 rooms, D NOK 890,-/1395,-
Tel (47) 638 477 00
Fax (47) 638 476 00

Grand Hotel — Oslo, 20 km
281 rooms, D NOK 300,-
Tel (47) 224 293 90
Fax (47) 224 212 25

RESTAURANTS RESTAURANT

Quality Olavsgaard — Skjetten, 2,5 km
Tel (47) 638 477 00

Bagatelle — Oslo, 20 km
Tel (47) 224 463 97

Spiesestedet Feinschmecker — Oslo, 20 km
Tel (47) 224 417 77

1051

Du vil for alltid huske denne banen som en stor vakker park med til dels en fantastisk utsikt over sjøen. Banen ligger like ved Fritzøe Gård med noen minneverdige arkitektoniske innslag som erindrer deg om å være på en linksbane. Her gjelder det å holde seg unna roughen. Den er både lang og saftig, og kan gi deg traumatiske opplevelser i forsøk på å komme ut på fairway igjen - hvis du i det hele tatt finner ballen. Dette til tross, både fairwayene og den korte roughen er brede nok for de fleste spillerne. Problemet er kanskje størst for de som virkelig vil slå langt og kan komme ut av kurs. Det er visselig ikke arkitekt Jan Sederholms stil å straffe for hardt de som hører hjemme blant middels- og høyhandicapere. Det eneste skjønnhetsfeilen ved banen er at den er for flat og hullene for i de fleste tilfeller den samme utforming. Heldigvis har vanskelighetene på banen en forskjellig og særegen karakter. Larvik er udiskutabelt en av de beste banene i Norge, og det vil være synd om man ikke får spilt banen hvis man en sjelden gang er i landet.

You may well remember this as a big, beautiful park with some great views over the sea, and as a course close to Fritzsøe Gård with some memorable architectural features reminiscent of a links course. So first off, be careful to avoid the tall rough, from where escape can be traumatic, if ever you find your ball. However, the fairways and short rough are still wide enough for most players, except the really big hitters who might stray a little too much off-course. It is certainly not the usual style of architect Jan Sederholm to punish too severely the slightly wayward shots from mid- to high-handicappers. The only slight blemish is the overall flatness of the course, creating a certain sameness on most holes. Fortunately the difficulties are more distinctive. Larvik is unquestionably one of the country's finest courses and it would be a pity not to play it if you come to Norway only on rare occasions.

Larvik Golfklubb — 1994

Fritzsøe Gård
N - 3267 LARVIK

Office	Kontor	(47) 331 401 40
Pro shop	Pro shop	(47) 331 406 80
Fax	Fax	(47) 331 401 49
Situation	Beliggenhet	
Larvik, 3 km		
Annual closure	Årlig stenging	1/12→31/3
Weekly closure	Ukentlig stenging	no

Fees main season
Tariffer i høysesongen 18 holes

	Week days Ukedager	We/Bank holidays Week-end/Frydag
Individual Individuell	NOK 200,-	NOK 300,-
Couple Par	NOK 500,-	NOK 600,-

Juniors: – 50 %

Caddy	Caddy	no
Electric Trolley	Elektrisk vogn	no
Buggy	Golfbil	yes
Clubs	Køller	yes

Credit cards Kredittkort
VISA - Eurocard - MasterCard - AMEX - DC - JCB

1052

Access Adkomst : Oslo, E18 → Skien/Kristiansand.
Rv.301 to Stavern. 3km, right → Fritzsøe Gård.
Map 1 on page 1047 Kort 1 på side: 1047

GOLF COURSE / GOLFBANEN — 17/20

Site	Område	
Maintenance	Vedlikehold	
Architect	Arkitekt	Jan Sederholm
Type	Type	links, open country
Relief	Relief	
Water in play	Vann-hinder	
Exp. to wind	Utsatt for vind	
Trees in play	Tre-hinder	

Scorecard Scorecard	Chp. Champ.-tee	Mens Herre-tees	Ladies Dame-tees
Length Lengde	5828	5828	5093
Par	72	72	72

Advised golfing ability Anbefalt golfnivå	0	12	24	36

Hcp required Obligatorisk Hcp 35

CLUB HOUSE & AMENITIES / KLUBHUS OG OMGIVELSER — 7/10

Pro shop	Pro shop	
Driving range	Treningsbane	
Sheltered	ly	yes
On grass	på gress	yes
Putting-green	putting-green	yes
Pitching-green	pitching-green	yes

HOTEL FACILITIES / HOTELFASILITETER — 5/10

HOTELS HOTEL-FASILITETER
Quality Grand Hotel Farris — Larvik
88 rooms, D NOK 950,-/1220,- — 3 km
Tel (47) 331 878 00
Fax (47) 331 870 45

RESTAURANTS RESTAURANT
Skipperstua — Stavern
Tel (47) 331 992 15 — 3 km

Her i utkanten av Oslo ligger banen omkranset av jordbruksområder. Det er også en region med mange innsjøer som gjør området meget populært for ekskursjoner, spesielt videre nordover i retning Trollparken. En praktfullt distrikt som sprer seg videre utover mot fjellområdene hvor de berømte trollene har sitt tilholdssted. Heldigvis kommer ikk trollene så langt sør i og med at golfere er hyggelige fyrer. Banen er av meget høy standard og er utviklet av klubbens egne medlemmer. Her må man slå rett og det gjelder å besinne seg når man slår ut fra tee-stedene. De som har designet banen har unngått å skape noe trolsk over det hele. I stedet later det til at man har latt seg inspirere av linksbaner. En av de virkelige vanskelighetene er lengdene ut fra tee når du spiller helst bakerst. Selv om du slår ut litt lenger fremme krever det et anstendig utslag om du vil spille deg rundt på handicap. En bane full av gode hensikter.

Here, we are in the outer suburbs of Oslo in crop-growing country which surrounds the whole course. It is also a region of lakes, very popular for excursions, especially northwards to the Trollpark, a magnificent, sprawling region of mountains inhabited by those long-nosed dwarfs which scare Norwegian children stiff. Fortunately, the trolls do not come this far south, as golfers are decent chaps. This high-standard course, created by club members, calls for some straight shot-making and cool management of some pretty perilous tee-shots. It might well lack subtlety and greatness, but at least the designers avoided creating anything too weird; in places, they even seem to have used links courses as a model of inspiration. One of the main difficulties is length off the tee when playing from the tips, and even a little further forward you will need a decent tee-shot if you want play anything like your handicap. A course full of good intentions.

Nes Golfklubb — 1992

Postbox 86
N - 2160 VORMSUND

Office	Kontor	(47) 639 029 29
Pro shop	Pro shop	(47) 639 021 60
Fax	Fax	(47) 639 026 80
Situation	Beliggenhet	

Oslo (pop. 458 500), 50 km

Annual closure	Årlig stenging	yes
		1/11 → 30/4
Weekly closure	Ukentlig stenging	no

Fees main season
Tariffer i høysesongen full day

	Week days Ukedager	We/Bank holidays Week-end/Frydag
Individual Individuell	NOK 250,-	NOK 280,-
Couple Par	NOK 500,-	NOK 360,-

Caddy	Caddy	no
Electric Trolley	Elektrisk vogn	no
Buggy	Golfbil	yes
Clubs	Køller	yes

Credit cards Kredittkort
VISA - Eurocard - MasterCard - AMEX - DC - JCB

GOLF COURSE / GOLFBANEN — 14/20

Site	Område	
Maintenance	Vedlikehold	
Architect	Arkitekt	Unknown
Type	Type	open country
Relief	Relief	
Water in play	Vann-hinder	
Exp. to wind	Utsatt for vind	
Trees in play	Tre-hinder	

Scorecard Scorecard	Chp. Champ.-tee	Mens Herre-tees	Ladies Dame-tees
Length Lengde	6382	6001	5203
Par	72	72	72

Advised golfing ability
Anbefalt golfnivå — 0 12 24 36

Hcp required Obligatorisk Hcp 35

CLUB HOUSE & AMENITIES / KLUBHUS OG OMGIVELSER — 6/10

Pro shop	Pro shop	
Driving range	Treningsbane	
Sheltered	ly	yes
On grass	på gress	no
Putting-green	putting-green	yes
Pitching-green	pitching-green	yes

HOTEL FACILITIES / HOTELFASILITETER — 4/10

HOTELS HOTEL-FASILITETER
Vormsund Golfhotell — Vormsund
20 rooms, D NOK 1100,- (w. GF) — 1 km
Tel (47) 639 008 99
Fax (47) 639 020 08

RESTAURANTS RESTAURANT
Vormsund Golfhotell — Vosmsund
Tel (47) 639 008 99 — 1 km

1053

Access Adkomst : Oslo, E6 North.
Kløfta, turn right on Rv.2. → Vormsund
Map 1 on page 1047 Kort 1 på side: 1047

I denne meget hyggelige by gjelder det å ta turen om Ibsen museet, Nasjonalgalleriet og Edvard Munch museet for deretter å besøke Bygdøy og Viking museet. Ditt neste stopp blir 18 hulls banen på Bogstad, bare fire kilometer fra sentrum av landets hovedstad. Banen ble anlagt i 1925 og har opp gjennom årene gjennom en stadig utvikling. Den er lokalisert ved Bogstadvannet som ligger i et typisk norsk skoglandskap med fin utsikt til Holmenkollen og den berømte hoppbakken. Banen er omgitt av mye trær, men de er der mest som dekorasjon og utgjør sjelden noe fare for selve spillet unntatt for å skape noen få dog-leg hull. Vannet er ute av spill med unntak av hull 16, et meget vakkert par 3 hull over Bogstadvannet. Ellers er problemene godt spredt rundt om på banen og hullene kan oppfattes som meget forskjellige, alt fra de mest stressede til de mest avslappende. Greenene er store og til dels ondulerte. Derfor vil majoriteten av de som spiller her komme trygt rundt de 18 hullene uten altfor store problemer.

In this very pleasant city, make it along to the Ibsen Museum, the National Gallery (Najonalgalleriet) and the Edvard Münch museum, then visit the Bigdøy peninsula to see the Viking boat museum. Your next stop will be the 18-hole Oslo golf course, recently restyled. It is located on the edge of Lake Bogstad in a typically Norwegian forest setting with some fine views over the hills of Holmenkollen. There are a lot of trees on the course, but more for decoration than to provide any real danger, or to create a few dog-leg holes. Water keeps nicely out of the way except on the 16th, a pretty par 3 over a lake. Otherwise, the trouble is well spread around the course with some very different holes alternating stress and relaxation. The greens are on the large side and sometimes elevated and well-guarded, but the majority of players shouldn't have too much trouble getting home safely. You are best advised to play here during weekdays.

Oslo Golfklubb — 1925
Bogstad, Ankerveien 127
N - 0757 OSLO

Office	Kontor	(47) 225 105 65
Pro shop	Pro shop	(47) 225 054 92
Fax	Fax	(47) 225 105 61
Situation	Beliggenhet	

8 km of Oslo city centre

Annual closure	Årlig stenging	1/11 → 30/4
Weekly closure	Ukentlig stenging	no

Fees main season
Tariffer i høysesongen 18 holes

	Week days Ukedager	We/Bank holidays Week-end/Frydag
Individual Individuell	NOK 350,-	NOK 400,-
Couple Par	NOK 700,-	NOK 800,-

Juniors: – 50%

Caddy	Caddy	no
Electric Trolley	Elektrisk vogn	no
Buggy	Golfbil	no
Clubs	Køller	yes

Credit cards Kredittkort
VISA - Eurocard - MasterCard - AMEX - DC - JCB

1054

GOLF Maridalsvannet
Sørkedalen
258
168 Røa 102
160
Eiksmarka E6
Haslum
160 Bryn
E 18
Sandvika E 18
Drammen
Oslofjorden
0 2 4 km

Access Adkomst : Follow signs → Bogstad Camping.
10 mn drive from centre of town
Map 1 on page 1047 Kort 1 på side: 1047

GOLF COURSE / GOLFBANEN — 15/20

Site	Område	
Maintenance	Vedlikehold	
Architect	Arkitekt	Unknown
Type	Type	parkland
Relief	Relief	
Water in play	Vann-hinder	
Exp. to wind	Utsatt for vind	
Trees in play	Tre-hinder	

Scorecard Scorecard	Chp. Champ.-tee	Mens Herre-tees	Ladies Dame-tees
Length Lengde	5769	5769	5004
Par	72	72	72

Advised golfing ability Anbefalt golfnivå	0	12	24	36

Hcp required Obligatorisk Hcp 20 Men/28 Ladies

CLUB HOUSE & AMENITIES / KLUBHUS OG OMGIVELSER — 7/10

Pro shop	Pro shop	
Driving range	Treningsbane	
Sheltered	ly	yes
On grass	på gress	no
Putting-green	putting-green	yes
Pitching-green	pitching-green	yes

HOTEL FACILITIES / HOTELFASILITETER — 9/10

HOTELS HOTEL-FASILITETER
Holmenkollen Park Hotel — Oslo
221 rooms, D NOK 1645,-/1645,- — 3 km
Tel (47) 229 220 00, Fax (47) 221 461 92

Clarion Royal Christiania — Oslo
378 rooms, D NOK 1495,- — 7 km
Tel (47) 231 080 00, Fax (47) 231 080 80

Gyldenløve — Oslo
168 rooms, D NOK 810,- — 6 km
Tel (47) 226 010 90, Fax (47) 226 033 90

RESTAURANTS RESTAURANT
Frogneseteren — Oslo
Tel (47) 221 408 90 — 5 km

Le Canard — Oslo
Tel (47) 225 434 00 — 7 km

Storstedet Rena blir delt av Norges lengste elv Glomma. En av sideelvene heter Skynna som renner tvers gjennom golfbanen og utgjør en av de store hindringene. Den andre store hindringen er furuskogen. Banen ble lagt ut av J. Søgaard tidlig på 1990-tallet. På slutten av runden vil du huske greenen på hull 18 som er formet som et hjerte. Imidlertid handler banen om mer enn bare den fancy trimmingen av nevnte green. For det første, til tross for plasseringen utenfor allfarvei i bunn på en avsidesliggende dal så er det totalt sett en bra bane. For det andre, vedlikeholdet er bra og det er i seg selv en prestasjon når man tar klimaet i betraktning. Og til slutt, den generelle balansen i layout er fantastisk med en blanding av vanskelige og lette hull. Du vil huske banen for de mange forskjellige slagene som trengs for å komme rundt og det gjelder spesielt tre tøffe hull, inkludert det 17 (par 3 med vann). Vel verdt å vite, selv om det ikke er noen enkel sak å komme hit.

Rena is crossed by the longest river in Norway, the Glomma, into which flows the Skynna, which also crosses this course and forms one of the major hazards. The other is the pine forest through which the course was laid out by J. Søgaard in the early 1990s. Over the closing stages you will remember the 18th green, a heart-shaped affair, but Sorknes has more to be said for it than that sort of fancy trimming. Firstly, despite its out-of-the-way location at the bottom of a remote valley, it is a good course overall. Secondly, maintenance is good, no mean feat in a climate that is anything but tropical, and finally the general balance of the layout is excellent, with easier and tougher holes evenly arranged. The variety of shots you will need to play makes this a course to remember with three tough holes, including the 17th, a par 3 with water. Well worth knowing, even if getting here is no easy matter.

Sorknes Golfklubb 1992

Sorknes Gård, P.b. 70
N - 2450 RENA

Office	Kontor	(47) 624 408 70
Pro shop	Pro shop	(47) 624 408 70
Fax	Fax	(47) 624 400 27
Situation	Beliggenhet	
Rena, 3 km		
Annual closure	Årlig stenging	1/11 → 30/4
Weekly closure	Ukentlig stenging	no

Fees main season
Tariffer i høysesongen full day

	Week days Ukedager	We/Bank holidays Week-end/Frydag
Individual Individuell	NOK 220,-	NOK 300,-
Couple Par	NOK 440,-	NOK 600,-

Caddy	Caddy	no
Electric Trolley	Elektrisk vogn	no
Buggy	Golfbil	no
Clubs	Køller	yes

Credit cards Kredittkort
VISA - Eurocard - MasterCard - AMEX - DC

GOLF
Koppang
Sorknes
602
601
Skramstad
Hole
Elverum
Hamar
Nybergsund
Nordby
215
Rena
Mørstad
Bolstad

0   2   4 km

Access Adkomst : Oslo, E6, Rv.3 → Rena.
Golf 3 km from Rena city centre.
Map 1 on page 1047 Kort 1 på side: 1047

GOLF COURSE / GOLFBANEN 13/20

Site	Område	
Maintenance	Vedlikehold	
Architect	Arkitekt	Junl Søgaard
Type	Type	forest
Relief	Relief	
Water in play	Vann-hinder	
Exp. to wind	Utsatt for vind	
Trees in play	Tre-hinder	

Scorecard Scorecard	Chp. Champ.-tee	Mens Herre-tees	Ladies Dame-tees
Length Lengde	5695	5695	4930
Par	72	72	72

Advised golfing ability Anbefalt golfnivå	0	12	24	36

Hcp required Obligatorisk Hcp 35

CLUB HOUSE & AMENITIES / KLUBHUS OG OMGIVELSER 6/10

Pro shop	Pro shop	
Driving range	Treningsbane	
Sheltered	ly	yes
On grass	på gress	no
Putting-green	putting-green	yes
Pitching-green	pitching-green	yes

HOTEL FACILITIES / HOTELFASILITETER 4/10

HOTELS HOTEL-FASILITETER
Nordlandia Østerdalen Hotel — Elverum — 30 km
82 rooms, D NOK 690,-
Tel (47) 624 401 00
Fax (47) 624 409 99

RESTAURANTS RESTAURANT
Fairway to Heaven — Elverum — 30 km
Tel (47) 624 401 00

1055

Den tidligere havnen for sardinfiske er nå senter for oljeproduksjonen i Nordsjøen, men byen er fremdeles like sjarmerende som tidligere år. Stavanger er også byen hvor man kan innlede reisen langs den vakre Vestlandskysten. Norge slik du ser det på postkortene. Golfbanen, som ligger ved bredden Stokkavannet, ble anlagt midt i blant et kupert, men ikke urimelig bakkete landskap med fjell, trær, busker og myrer. Baneskaperne har klart å skape en naturskjønn og attraktivt ramme på og rundt banen som inneholder vanskeligheter av alle slag. Den har fått et meget godt rykte på seg fra de beste norske golfspillerne til tross for at lengden er forholdsvis kort. Banen er først og fremst for gode tekniske spillere. Du være nøyaktig og du må hele tiden skifte taktikk avhengig av tidligere slag. Derfor det gjelder det hele tide å gjøre riktig køllevalg. Hvis du vil ha en god score, prøv å utforske banen liten på forhånd. Hull 1, for eksempel, har et blind utslag med driven og et blindt innspill på greenen. Sagt på en annen måte, hvis du bruker 95 slag oftere enn du vanligvis gjør så må du begynne å spille taktisk for å komme rundt banen og ha glede av det.

This former sardine fishing port is now the North Sea oil production centre but is still as charming as ever. It is also the starting point for visiting the wonderful Fjord coast, the Norway you see on postcards. The present course, on the shores of Lake Stokka, was laid out amidst rolling but not unduly hilly countryside of rocks, trees, bushes and marshes, creating a picturesque and attractive setting, and difficulties of all sorts. It has acquired an excellent reputation with top Norwegian players, despite relatively short yardage, as this is a course for the golfing technician. You have to be accurate, be able to change tactics depending on the previous shot and be spot-on when choosing the right club to play. If you are set on carding a good score, try a little reconnoitring beforehand. Hole number one, for example, has a blind drive and a blind green to boot. With this said, if you break 95 more often than not, enjoy it.

Stavanger Golfklubb — 1956

Longebakke 45
N - 4042 HAFRSFJORD

Office	Kontor	(47) 515 570 25
Pro shop	Pro shop	(47) 515 554 31
Fax	Fax	(47) 515 573 11
Situation	Beliggenhet	

Stavanger, 5 km

Annual closure	Årlig stenging	1/12 → 31/3
Weekly closure	Ukentlig stenging	no

Fees main season
Tariffer i høysesongen full day

	Week days Ukedager	We/Bank holidays Week-end/Frydag
Individual Individuell	NOK 250,-	NOK 250,-
Couple Par	NOK 500,-	NOK 500,-

Caddy	Caddy	no
Electric Trolley	Elektrisk vogn	no
Buggy	Golfbil	no
Clubs	Køller	yes

Credit cards Kredittkort
VISA - Eurocard - MasterCard - AMEX - DC - JCB

GOLF COURSE / GOLFBANEN — 16/20

Site	Område	
Maintenance	Vedlikehold	
Architect	Arkitekt	Fred Smith
Type	Type	parkland
Relief	Relief	
Water in play	Vann-hinder	
Exp. to wind	Utsatt for vind	
Trees in play	Tre-hinder	

Scorecard Scorecard	Chp. Champ.-tee	Mens Herre-tees	Ladies Dame-tees
Length Lengde	5494	5494	4863
Par	71	71	71

Advised golfing ability
Anbefalt golfnivå — 0   12   24   36

Hcp required — Obligatorisk Hcp 35

CLUB HOUSE & AMENITIES / KLUBHUS OG OMGIVELSER — 6/10

Pro shop	Pro shop	
Driving range	Treningsbane	
Sheltered	ly	no
On grass	på gress	no
Putting-green	putting-green	yes
Pitching-green	pitching-green	yes

HOTEL FACILITIES / HOTELFASILITETER — 7/10

HOTELS HOTEL-FASILITETER

Radisson SAS Atlantic Hotel — Stavanger
352 rooms, D NOK 750,-/1495,- — 5 km
Tel (47) 517 600 05
Fax (47) 517 600 01

Rica Park Hotel — Stavanger
59 rooms, D NOK 895,-/1325,- — 5 km
Tel (47) 517 005 00
Fax (47) 517 004 00

RESTAURANTS RESTAURANT

Bevaremegvel — Stavanger
Tel (47) 518 438 60 — 5 km

1056

Access Adkomst : Stavanger Rv 510 to Madla.
300 m Rv 509
Map 1 on page 1046 Kort 1 på side: 1046

	14	**6**	**6**

35 kilometer utenfor Oslo finner du en bane som for alltid vil gi deg gode minner selv om scoren ble ødelagt etter å ha spilt en runde. Fredfullt plassert på en øy med god utsikt over Tyrifjorden. Her oppleves en storartet panoramautsikt som du bare får lyst til å nyte resten av dagen, særlig hvis legger og føtter verker etter ansluttet spill. God fysisk form er så absolutt en fordel her. Du bør også være i golfmessig god form for å få en god score på denne banen som er designet av Jan Sederholm og Tor Eia. Hvert hull har sin egen personlighet. Et stort antall blinde slag og greener gjør at man har noe å kappes med og det er så absolutt en fordel å spille med et medlem på den første runden. Han eller hun vil kunne fortelle deg hvor noen av de usynlige fellene og hindringene gjemmer seg. Riktignok påvirker farene deg mer psykisk enn det de i virkelighet er. Det er to hull som må tåle mye kritikk og det gjelder hullene 14 og 18. Her bør noe gjøres. Det er så absolutt en fordel å være kjentmann på banen. Og det er godt å kjenne til banen.

Located peacefully on an island overlooking the Tyrifjorden, this course provides a magnificent panorama that you could spend the whole day admiring, especially if your legs are not up to the walk and climb. Fitness is a distinct advantage here. Your game has to be in pretty good shape, too, to play this course designed by Jan Sederholm and Tor Eia with good landscaping sense. Each hole has its own personality, but with a number of blind shots and greens to cope with, we would suggest playing with a club member the first time out. He or she will tell you where the sometimes invisible traps and hazards lie, even though the danger is more psychological than real. The only real criticism would concern holes 14 and 18, which leave a lot to be desired. Otherwise, if you can forget about the landscape, which will necessarily affect your judgment, this course is worth getting to know. You won't find many others in the region!

Tyrifjord Golfklubb   1996
Postbox 91
N - 3529 RØYSE

Office	Kontor	(47) 321 613 60
Pro shop	Pro shop	(47) 321 613 62
Fax	Fax	(47) 321 613 40
Situation	Beliggenhet	

Oslo (pop. 458 500), 35 km

Annual closure	Årlig stenging	1/11 → 30/4
Weekly closure	Ukentlig stenging	no

Fees main season
Tariffer i høysesongen full day

	Week days Ukedager	We/Bank holidays Week-end/Frydag
Individual Individuell	NOK 250,-	NOK 300,-
Couple Par	NOK 500,-	NOK 600,-

Juniors: – 50%

Caddy	Caddy	no
Electric Trolley	Elektrisk vogn	no
Buggy	Golfbil	no
Clubs	Køller	no

Credit cards Kredittkort
VISA - Eurocard - MasterCard - AMEX - DC - JCB

Hønefoss
Helgelandsmoen
Stein
Steinsfjorden
Gomnes
Vik
Sundøya
Sundvollen
Bönsnes
GOLF Storøya
0   2   4 km
Gulsrud   Tyrifjorden
Tandberg   Oslo
Drammen   Pilterud

Access Adkomst : Oslo, E18 to Sandvika,
E16 → Hønefoss. Golf on Storøya
Map 1 on page 1047 Kort 1 på side: 1047

GOLF COURSE
GOLFBANEN   **14**/20

Site	Område	
Maintenance	Vedlikehold	
Architect	Arkitekt	Jan Sederholm Tor Eia
Type	Type	hilly, parkland
Relief	Relief	
Water in play	Vann-hinder	
Exp. to wind	Utsatt for vind	
Trees in play	Tre-hinder	

Scorecard Scorecard	Chp. Champ.-tee	Mens Herre-tees	Ladies Dame-tees
Length Lengde	5747	5747	4960
Par	72	72	72

Advised golfing ability Anbefalt golfnivå	0 12 24 36
Hcp required Obligatorisk Hcp	36

CLUB HOUSE & AMENITIES
KLUBHUS OG OMGIVELSER   **6**/10

Pro shop	Pro shop	
Driving range	Treningsbane	
Sheltered	ly	yes
On grass	på gress	no
Putting-green	putting-green	yes
Pitching-green	pitching-green	yes

HOTEL FACILITIES
HOTELFASILITETER   **6**/10

HOTELS HOTEL-FASILITETER
Klokken Hotel   Hønefoss
130 rooms, D NOK 990,-   5 km
Tel (47) 321 322 00
Fax (47) 321 327 93

RESTAURANTS RESTAURANT
Sundvolden Hotel   Tyrifjord
Tel (47) 321 621 00   5 km

1057

**A DIFERENÇA ENTRE ESTILO E MODA
É QUE O ESTILO NÃO SE MUDA. APERFEIÇOA-SE.**

NOVO PEUGEOT 406. Na mesma linha, mais próximo da perfeição.

O HOMEM EVOLUI. A TECNOLOGIA ACOMPANHA. *406*

PEUGEOT

Portugal

The Millennium Guide

Com um clima privilegiado, Portugal é desde há muito tempo um refúgio de inverno para os turistas do Norte da Europa e em particular golfistas. O País conta com cerca de 6 500 golfistas e 40 percursos de 18 buracos. Todos estão abertos ao público, mas aos fins de semana congestionam-se um pouco com os sócios dos Clubes, sobretudo na região de Lisboa. Assim, é sempre melhor reservar, os tempos de saída, nomeadamente na região do Algarve, ao sul de Portugal, onde os visitantes são em grande número, do Outono à Primavera. O Verão é contudo uma época agradável, onde uma suave brisa maritimal, atenua o calor.

With a privileged climate, Portugal has long been a winter refuge for tourists from northern Europe, and especially for golfers. The country has only 6,500 players and around 40 eighteen-hole courses. All are open to the public, but they do tend to get crowded on weekends with club members, especially in the Lisbon area. It is, therefore, always preferable to book a tee-off time, especially in the Algarve in the south of the country, where visitors abound from Autumn to Spring. Summer is also a pleasant time to play, with a cooling sea breeze to ease the heat.

1059

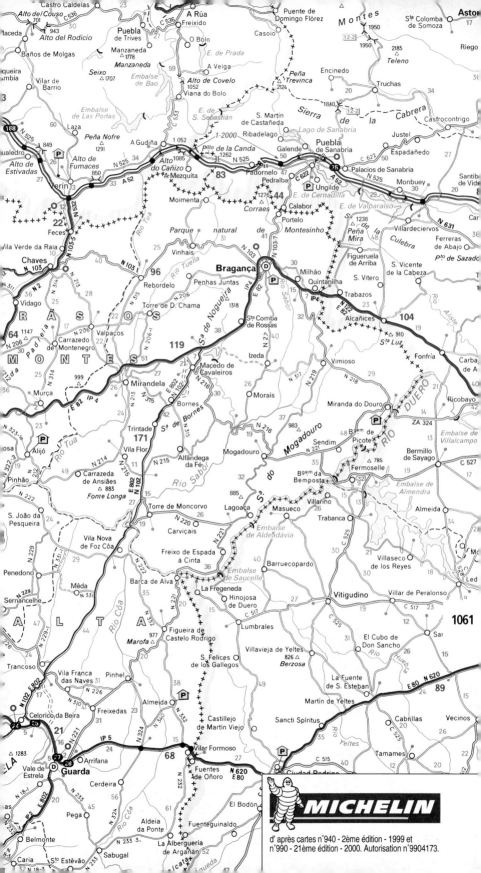

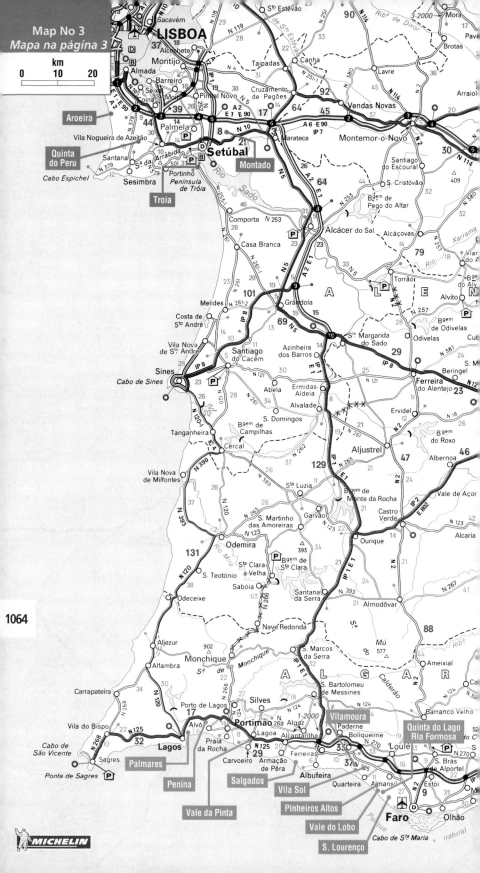

Beyond the 18th hole.

*If you're looking for golf that drives you beyond the 18th hole,
look no further than Portugal, where you find, in charming surroundings, so many
courses designed by world famous architects. Hook or slice and the ball will take
you to a wonderful beach or an old manor house in the countryside.
Or if you middle the fairway and fancy your chances, have your partner buy you
an unforgettable seafood dinner, and you'll find no finer 19th hole.
For challenging golf, all year round, it has to be Portugal.*

Portugal. The choice.

Portugal

AIR PORTUGAL

ICEP Icep Office du Commerce et du Tourisme du Portugal • Paris
Tel: (01) 56 88 30 80 • Minitel: 3615 Portugal (2.23 Franc la minute)
http://www.portugalinsite.pt

CLASSIFICAÇÃO DOS PERCURSOS
CLASSIFICATION OF COURSES

Nota do Club-House e anexos
Club house and facilities score

Nota do percurso
(Course score)

Nota do envolvimento hoteleiro
Hotel facility score

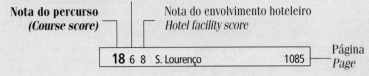

18 6 8   S. Lourenço   1085

Página
Page

Nota			Percurso		Página	Nota			Percurso		Página
18	6	8	S. Lourenço	※ ♪	1085	14	7	7	Pinheiros Altos	※	1078
17	6	8	Penha Longa	※ ♪	1076	14	8	7	Quinta da Beloura		1080
17	6	5	Praia d'El Rey	※ ♪	1079	14	7	6	Salgados	※	1086
16	7	7	Vilamoura *Vilamoura I*			14	6	6	Vale da Pinta	※	1088
			(Old Course)	※ ♪	1091	14	7	7	Vila Sol	※	1090
15	6	6	Aroeira		1068	14	7	7	Vilamoura		
15	4	4	Golden Eagle		1071				*Vilamoura III (Laguna)*	※ ♪	1093
15	7	8	Quinta do Lago *B/C*	※ ♪	1082	13	7	6	Belas	※	1069
15	7	8	Quinta do Lago			13	7	7	Estoril	※	1070
			Ria Formosa	※ ♪	1083	13	7	6	Montado		1073
15	6	5	Quinta do Peru	※	1084	13	6	7	Palheiro	※	1074
15	6	5	Troia	♪	1087	13	7	5	Palmares	※	1075
15	6	7	Vale do Lobo	※		13	7	7	Quinta da Marinha	※	1081
			Royal Golf Course		1089	13	7	7	Vilamoura		
14	6	5	Madeira	※ ♪	1072				*Vilamoura II (Pinhal)*	※ ♪	1092
14	7	7	Penina	※	1077						

CLASSIFICAÇÃO DO ENVOLVIMENTO HOTELEIRO
CLASSIFICATION OF HOTELS FACILITIES

Nota			Percurso	Página	Nota			Percurso	Página
17	6	**8**	Penha Longa	1076	13	7	**7**	Vilamoura	
15	7	**8**	Quinta do Lago *B/C*	1082				*Vilamoura II (Pinhal)*	1092
15	7	**8**	Quinta do Lago *Ria Formosa*	1083	14	7	**7**	Vilamoura	
18	6	**8**	S. Lourenço	1085				*VilamouraIII (Laguna)*	1093
13	7	**7**	Estoril	1070	15	6	**6**	Aroeira	1068
13	6	**7**	Palheiro	1074	13	7	**6**	Belas	1069
14	7	**7**	Penina	1077	13	7	**6**	Montado	1073
14	7	**7**	Pinheiros Altos	1078	14	7	**6**	Salgados	1086
14	8	**7**	Quinta da Beloura	1080	14	6	**6**	Vale da Pinta	1088
13	7	**7**	Quinta da Marinha	1081	14	6	**5**	Madeira	1072
15	6	**7**	Vale do Lobo		13	7	**5**	Palmares	1075
			Royal Golf Course	1089	17	6	**5**	Praia d'El Rey	1079
14	7	**7**	Vila Sol	1090	15	6	**5**	Quinta do Peru	1084
16	7	**7**	Vilamoura		15	6	**5**	Troia	1087
			Vilamoura I (Old Course)	1091	15	4	**4**	Golden Eagle	1071

1067

AROEIRA

A primeira impressão é a de um ambiente muito agradável entre pinheiros e flores silvestres, habitat natural de diversos tipos de aves. Sem interferir com esse quadro o arquitecto Frank Pennink realizou um percurso de uma grande franqueza, e com um traçado muito simples, onde os obstáculos (a excepção das árvores) raramente sao perigosos. Os jogadores médios e os prin-cipiantes sentem-se logo à vontade neste percurso amigável, onde se caminha facilmente e onde os "rough" não são muito penalizantes. Os melhores jogadores, no entanto, podem achá-lo um pouco monotono para jogar muitas vezes, uma vez que lhe faltam verdadeiros desafios, com a excepção do 11, redesenhado por Robert Trent Jones. Em contrapartida a Aroeira é um local ideal para se jogar uma partida em família ou para uma partida entre amigos.

The first impression is one of a very pleasant setting of pine-trees and wild flowers, and the natural habitat for numerous birds. Without spoiling the scenery, architect Frank Penninck has laid out a clear and candid course of rather simple design, where the hazards are seldom too dangerous (except the trees). High-handicappers and beginners will feel immediately at home on this friendly and easily-walkable course, where the rough and undergrowth could never be called penalising. The better players might possibly find it boring to play regularly, given the absence of real challenge. Only the 11th hole, redesigned by Robert Trent Jones, stands out from a pretty colourless picture. By contrast, Aroeira is the ideal spot for a round with all the family and for giving less experienced players welcome practice.

C.G. Aroeira — 1971

Herdade da Aroeira - Fonte da Jelha
P - 2825 MONTE DE CAPARICA

Office	Secretariado	(351) 021 - 297 1314
Pro shop	Pro-shop	(351) 021 - 296 1802
Fax	Fax	(351) 021 - 297 1238
Situation	Localização	

Lisboa, (pop. 662 782), 11 km
Setubal (pop. 89 106), 48 km

Annual closure	Fecho anual	no
Weekly closure	Fecho semanal	no

Fees main season
Tarifas de época alta 18 holes

	Week days Semana	We/Bank holidays Fim de sem./Feriad
Individual Individual	9 000 Esc	12 000 Esc
Couple Casal	18 000 Esc	24 000 Esc

Caddy	Caddy	no
Electric Trolley	Trolley eléctrico	2 000 Esc.
Buggy	Buggy	7 000 Esc.
Clubs	Tacos	3 500 Esc.

Credit cards Cartão de crédito VISA - AMEX - DC

1068

Access Acesso : A2 Lisboa → Setubal,
N377 → Caparica, Golf
Map 2 on page 1063 Mapa 2 Página 1063

GOLF COURSE
PERCURSO — 15/20

Site	Sitio	■■■■
Maintenance	Conversa	■■■■
Architect	Arquitecto	Frank Pennink
Type	Tipo	forest
Relief	Relevo	■■
Water in play	Lago	■
Exp. to wind	Exposto ao vento	■■■
Trees in play	Arvores	■■■■

Scorecard Cartão de resultados	Chp. Camp.	Mens Homens	Ladies Senhoras
Length Compriment	6040	5700	5241
Par	72	72	72

Advised golfing ability
Nivel de jogo recomendado   0   12   24   36

Hcp required   Handicap exigido   28 Men, 36 Ladies

CLUB HOUSE & AMENITIES
CLUB HOUSE E ANEXOS — 6/10

Pro shop	Pro-shop	■■■
Driving range	Campo de prática	■■■
Sheltered	coberto	4 places
On grass	om relva	yes
Putting-green	putting-green	yes
Pitching-green	pitching-green	no

HOTEL FACILITIES
INFRAESTRUCTURAS HOTELEIRAS — 6/10

HOTELS HOTELS

Costa da Caparica   Caparica
340 rooms, D 19 500 Esc.   3 km
Tel (351) 01 - 291 03 10
Fax (351) 01 - 291 06 87

Praia do Sol   Caparica
53 rooms, D 8 500 Esc.   3 km
Tel (351) 01 - 290 00 12
Fax (351) 01 - 290 25 41

RESTAURANTS RESTAURANTES

Centyonze   São João da Caparica
Tel (351) 01 - 290 39 68   4 km

Maniés   Caparica
Tel (351) 01 - 290 33 98   3 km

BELAS ❁ 13 | 7 | 6

Situada numa das grandes regiões golfísticas de Portugal, Belas está próxima de Lisboa, mas tanbêm do Palácio de Queluz, uma espêcie de pequeno Versailles, com laivos de «rococo», alternando os quartos íntimos com as salas de aparato, tudo rodeado de magníficos jardins... Não se encontrará em Belas um gosto tão ostentivo na decoração. A essência de um percurso de golf não reside verdadeiramente no luxo nem na simetria dos jardins â francesa. O Arquitecto moldou o seu traçado num terreno bastante aberto e muito acidentado onde temos o direito de preferir jogar com um «buggy» (pode dizer que é por causa do Sol). Devido a certos aspectos vísuais e técnicos, pelo tipo de jogo que é necessário desenvolver, Belas pode lembrar Pevero ou Is Molas. Em todo o caso é pêlos seus desafios que representa um bom futuro percurso de campeonato, ao ponto que os «handicaps» mais elevados terão sem duvida alguma dificuldade em retirar um enorme prazer em jogá-lo.

Located in one of Portugal's top golfing regions, Belas is close to Lisbon and also to the Castle of Queluz, a sort of smaller form of Versailles with a touch of rococo and alternating small chambers and huge state rooms, all surrounded by superb gardens. You won't find such an ostentatious taste for decoration at Belas, as the essence of a golf course is neither sheer luxury nor the symmetry of French style gardens. The architect has laid out this course over rather open, rolling terrain where you have every right to prefer playing with a buggy (say it is because of the sun). Through certain visual and technical aspects and through the type of game you need to produce, Belas is reminiscent of Pevero or Is Molas. In any case, given the challenges here, this is a future excellent championship course, even to the extent of it not always being too much fun for high-handicappers. The course unwinds smoothly with a neat balance of all forms of hazard.

Belas Club de Campo — 1997
Casal de Carregueira
P - 2745 BELAS

Office	Secretariado	(351) 021 - 962 6130
Pro shop	Pro-shop	(351) 021 - 962 6130
Fax	Fax	(351) 021 - 962 6131
Situation	Localização	

Lisboa (pop. 662 782), 18 km

Annual closure	Fecho anual	no
Weekly closure	Fecho semanal	no

Fees main season
Tarifas de época alta 18 holes

	Week days Semana	We/Bank holidays Fim de sem./Feriad
Individual Individual	12 000 Esc.	14 000 Esc.
Couple Casal	24 000 Esc.	28 000 Esc.

Members of Portuguese Clubs: – 50 %

Caddy	Caddy	no
Electric Trolley	Trolley eléctrico	no
Buggy	Buggy	6 000 Esc.
Clubs	Tacos	4 500 Esc.

Credit cards Cartão de crédito
VISA - Eurocard - AMEX - DC

Access Acesso : Lisboa, N 117 → Sintra/Queluz and Belas. Follow signs to Golf.
Map 2 on page 1062 Mapa 2 Página 1062

GOLF COURSE / PERCURSO — 13/20

Site	Sitio	
Maintenance	Conversa	
Architect	Arquitecto	Rocky Roquemore
Type	Tipo	open country
Relief	Relevo	
Water in play	Lago	
Exp. to wind	Exposto ao vento	
Trees in play	Arvores	

Scorecard Cartão de resultados	Chp. Camp.	Mens Homens	Ladies Senhoras
Length Compriment	6380	6065	4995
Par	72	72	72

Advised golfing ability	0	12	24	36
Nivel de jogo recomendado				

Hcp required Handicap exigido 28 Men/36 Ladies

CLUB HOUSE & AMENITIES / CLUB HOUSE E ANEXOS — 7/10

Pro shop	Pro-shop	
Driving range	Campo de prática	
Sheltered	coberto	no
On grass	om relva	yes
Putting-green	putting-green	yes
Pitching-green	pitching-green	yes

HOTEL FACILITIES / INFRAESTRUCTURAS HOTELEIRAS — 6/10

HOTELS HOTELS

Pousada D. Maria I. — Queluz
24 rooms, D 28 000 Esc. — 6 km
Tel (351) 01 - 435 61 58
Fax (351) 01 - 435 61 89

Palacio de Seteais — Sintra
29 rooms, D 40 000 Esc. — 12 km
Tel (351) 01 - 923 32 00
Fax (351) 01 - 923 42 77

RESTAURANTS RESTAURANTES

Cozinha Velha — Queluz
Tel (351) 01 - 435 61 58 — 6 km

Tacho Real — Sintra
Tel (351) 01 - 923 52 77 — 12 km

Solar de Sáo Pedro — Sintra
Tel (351) 01 - 923 18 60 — 12 km

1069

ESTORIL ✺ | 13 | 7 | 7

Inaugurado em 1945, é um dos campos mais conhecidos de Portugal. Inserido numa paisagem típica da região, bastante acidentado mas não muito cansativo. Mackenzie Ross desenhou um percurso de estilo britânico de uma grande sobriedade estética. O enquadramento de pinheiros e eucaliptos não só é muito agradável como desenha bem os buracos, os quais não são especialmente perigosos se se evitar utilizar o "drive". Tem de ser direito mas a dimensão curta do percurso permite realizar resultados gratificantes. É porem necessário dominar o jogo curto uma vez que é muito fácil falhar os greenes bastante pequenos. Pode tambem, para facilitar, recorrer aos "caddies" locais, muito experientes e muito uteis para evitar as diversas armadilhas de um percurso do género "tricky". Divertido a atraente, o campo do Estoril merecia uma melhor manutençao da que observámos quando para merecer uma nota melhor.

Opened in 1945, this is one of Portugal's better known courses. In countryside that is typical of this region, i.e. rolling landscape but nothing too steep, MacKenzie Ross has designed a beautifully discreet, British style course. There was hardly any need to enhance this setting of eucalyptus and pine trees, which are not only agreeable to the eye but also neatly outline each hole. And they are none too dangerous if you leave the driver in the bag. You have to play straight here, and the lack of yardage can give some flattering scores, as long as your short game is in good shape. The small greens are easy to miss. The first time out, you can hire an experienced local caddy, who will certainly prove most useful in avoiding the many traps on what is a tricky course. Estoril is fun and appealing, but for a better score it deserves better upkeep than what we saw during our visits.

Estoril Golf Club — 1945
Avenida da Republica
P - 2765 ESTORIL

Office	Secretariado	(351) 01 - 468 0176
Pro shop	Pro-shop	(351) 01 - 468 0176
Fax	Fax	(351) 01 - 468 2796
Situation	Localização	

Lisboa, (pop. 662 782), 23 km
Sintra (pop. 20 574), 5 km

Annual closure	Fecho anual	no
Weekly closure	Fecho semanal	no

Fees main season
Tarifas de época alta 18 holes

	Week days Semana	We/Bank holidays Fim de sem./Feriad
Individual Individual	8 250 Esc	11 000 Esc
Couple Casal	16 500 Esc	22 000 Esc

Caddy	Caddy	4 000 Esc.
Electric Trolley	Trolley eléctrico	no
Buggy	Buggy	5 500 Esc.
Clubs	Tacos	2 500 Esc.

Credit cards Cartão de crédito VISA - AMEX

1070

Access Acesso : A5 Lisboa → Cascais,
N9 → Estoril, Sintra
Map 2 on page 1062 Mapa 2 Página 1062

GOLF COURSE / PERCURSO — 13/20

Site	Sítio	
Maintenance	Conversa	
Architect	Arquitecto	Mackenzie Ross
Type	Tipo	forest
Relief	Relevo	
Water in play	Lago	
Exp. to wind	Exposto ao vento	
Trees in play	Arvores	

Scorecard Cartão de resultados	Chp. Camp.	Mens Homens	Ladies Senhoras
Length Compriment	5238	5238	4569
Par	69	69	69

Advised golfing ability		0 12 24 36
Nivel de jogo recomendado		
Hcp required	Handicap exigido	no

CLUB HOUSE & AMENITIES / CLUB HOUSE E ANEXOS — 7/10

Pro shop	Pro-shop	
Driving range	Campo de prática	
Sheltered	coberto	6 places
On grass	om relva	yes
Putting-green	putting-green	yes
Pitching-green	pitching-green	no

HOTEL FACILITIES / INFRAESTRUCTURAS HOTELEIRAS — 7/10

HOTELS HOTELS

Palacio — Estoril
162 rooms, D 28 000 Esc — 4 km
Tel (351) 01 - 468 04 00, Fax (351) 01 - 468 48 67

Lennox Country Club — Estoril
30 rooms, D 17 600 Esc. — 4 km
Tel (351) 01 - 468 04 24, Fax (351) 01 - 467 08 59

Atlantis — Alcabideche
129 rooms, D 12 000 Esc — 3 km
Tel (351) 01 - 469 07 21, Fax (351) 01 - 469 07 40

RESTAURANTS RESTAURANTES

English Bar — Estoril
Tel (351) 01 - 468 04 13 — 4 km

A Choupana — S. Joân do Estoril
Tel (351) 01 - 468 30 99 — 6 km

GOLDEN EAGLE

15	4	4

Este percurso recente, oferece uma boa ocasião para ir ver Obidos, uma linda cidade tanto medieval como renascentista, dominada pôr um castelo onde está instalada a Pousada. Não é mesmo ao lado do golf, mas julgamos que um jogador não tem dificuldade de fazer meia hora de automóvel pois não? Com o dever cultural cumprido e com a consciência tranquila ela poderá consagrar-se ao percurso. De passagem lamentar-se-à que não se tenha dado ao campo um nome português, mesmo sendo os britânicos uma boa parte do contingente de turistas de golf em Portugal. Numa bonita paisagem campestre com uma ondulação agradável, Rocky Roquemore apresentou um bom «test» de golf, muito franco, com alguns greens muito bem protegidos, mas com as dificuldades sempre visíveis e sem golpes cegos apesar do relevo. O seu comprimento é muito respeitável mas as saídas da frente encurtam-no em 450 metros, o que encantará aqueles que regressam sempre enfadados com a sua procura de distância.

This course is a good opportunity to go and see Obidos, a very pretty medieval and renaissance town overlooked by a castle which houses the Pousada, a hotel and restaurant comparable to the Spanish Paradors. This is not quite alongside the golf course, but a half-hour ride for a golfer is nothing, surely. With a clear conscience after your shot of culture, it's time to think about golfing. Firstly, what a pity they chose an English rather than Portuguese name for the course, even though the Brits form a big proportion of the golf-trotting tourists coming to Portugal. In a pretty country landscape with pleasant rolling valleys, Rocky Roquemore has produced a good and very candid test of golf with some very well defended greens, visible difficulties and no blind shots, despite the topology. Yardage is very respectable, but the front tees shorten the course by 450 metres, a joy and relief for golfers who strive for distance but actually get very little.

Golf Course / Percurso

Golden Eagle Golf Club — 1994
Quinta do Brinçal - Arroquelas
P - 2040 RIO MAIOR

Office	Secretariado	(351) 0243 - 908 148
Pro shop	Pro-shop	(351) 0243 - 908 148
Fax	Fax	(351) 0243 - 908 149
Situation	Localização	

Lisboa (pop. 662 782), 59 km

Annual closure	Fecho anual	no
Weekly closure	Fecho semanal	no

Fees main season
Tarifas de época alta 18 holes

	Week days Semana	We/Bank holidays Fim de sem./Feriad
Individual Individual	6 000 Esc.	8 000 Esc.
Couple Casal	12 000 Esc.	16 000 Esc.

Caddy	Caddy	2 500 Esc.
Electric Trolley	Trolley eléctrico	no
Buggy	Buggy	6 000 Esc.
Clubs	Tacos	no

Credit cards Cartão de crédito
VISA - Eurocard - AMEX - DC

Rio Maior

0   2   4 km

Obidos
Caldas da Rainha

114   Fátima

GOLF

Santarém

Cartaxo

Aveiras
de Cima

Aveiras
de Baixo

Lisboa

Access Acesso : Lisboa, A1. Km 46 in Avéiras,
→ Rio Maior. Quebradas, → Golf.
Map 2 on page 1062 Mapa 2 Página 1062

GOLF COURSE / PERCURSO — 15/20

Site	Sitio	
Maintenance	Conversa	
Architect	Arquitecto	Rocky Roquemore
Type	Tipo	inland
Relief	Relevo	
Water in play	Lago	
Exp. to wind	Exposto ao vento	
Trees in play	Arvores	

Scorecard Cartão de resultados	Chp. Camp.	Mens Homens	Ladies Senhoras
Length Comprimento	6203	5744	5018
Par	72	72	72

Advised golfing ability — 0 12 24 36
Nível de jogo recomendado
Hcp required Handicap exigido — 28 Men/36 Ladies

CLUB HOUSE & AMENITIES / CLUB HOUSE E ANEXOS — 4/10

Pro shop	Pro-shop	
Driving range	Campo de prática	
Sheltered	coberto	no
On grass	om relva	yes
Putting-green	putting-green	yes
Pitching-green	pitching-green	yes

1071

HOTEL FACILITIES / INFRAESTRUCTURAS HOTELEIRAS — 4/10

HOTELS HOTELS
Quinta da Ferraria — Ribeira de São João
13 rooms, D 13 000 Esc. — 1 km
Tel (351) 043 - 950 01, Fax (351) 043 - 956 96

Estal. do Convento — Obidos
31 rooms, D 13 000 Esc — 30 km
Tel (351) 062 - 95 92 16, Fax (351) 062 - 95 91 59

Pousada do Castelo — Obidos
9 rooms, D 30 000 Esc. — 30 km
Tel (351) 062 - 959 105, Fax (351) 062 - 959 148

RESTAURANTS RESTAURANTES

Pousada do Castelo — Obidos
Tel (351) 062 - 959 105 — 30 km

A Ilustre Casa de Ramiro — Obidos
Tel (351) 043 - 959 194 — 30 km

MADEIRA ✽ ♪ | 14 | 6 | 5

A várias centenas de metros de altitude, este percurso oferece panorámicas de uma beleza fántastica, sobre a Ilha da Madeira e o Oceano Atlântico. É um dos percursos mais extraordinários da Europa. O inconveniente da sua situação, em média montanha, é a de que se torna bastante cansativo par jogar a pé, mas a beleza do espectáculo, nomeadamente nos buracos 12 e 13, valem alguns esforços. O Arquitecto Robert Trent Jones jogou com delícia e imaginação sobre um terreno extraordinário e propõe aos jogadores de todos os níveis desafios apaixonantes. Estes terão que estudar bem a estratégia a seguir em cada buraco sem se distraírem demasiado com a paisagem. As dificuldades são múltiplas mas sempre bem visíveis, com uma vegetação muito rica, "roughs" bastante densos, "bunkers" muito em jogo, "greens" bem trabalhados mas tendo um único obstáculo de água. Em contrapardida o seu comprimento mantém-se razoável... se não houver vento. Aconselha-se jogar em "match-play", é um percurso muito divertido.

At several hundred metres above sea-level, this course primarily offers a fantastically beautiful panorama over the island of Madeira and the Atlantic ocean. The drawback of being half-way up a mountain is the toll it takes on your feet and legs. But the beauty of the site, especially on the 12th and 13th holes is well worth the effort. Designer Robert Trent Jones used a lot of fun and imagination over this remarkable terrain and offers some exciting challenges to players of all abilities, who will need to consider carefully their strategy on each hole, without being distracted by the scenery. The difficulties are many and varied, but always there to be seen: lush vegetation, pretty thick rough, omnipresent bunkers, well-designed greens but just the one water hazard. In contrast, yardage is reasonable... as long as the wind doesn't blow. Try it in match-play, it's great fun. A new 9 hole-course has just been opened on the west side of this course.

Golfe da Madeira — 1991

Casais Proximos - S° Ant° da Serra
P - 9200 MACHICO / MADEIRA

Office	Secretariado	(351) 0291 - 552 321
Pro shop	Pro-shop	(351) 0291 - 552 321
Fax	Fax	(351) 0291 - 552 367
Situation	Localização	

Machico (pop. 2 142), 6 km
Funchal (pop. 99 244), 26 km

Annual closure	Fecho anual	no
Weekly closure	Fecho semanal	no

Fees main season
Tarifas de época alta 18 holes

	Week days Semana	We/Bank holidays Fim de sem./Feriad
Individual Individual	8 000 Esc	8 000 Esc
Couple Casal	16 000 Esc	16 000 Esc

Caddy	Caddy	3 000 Esc.
Electric Trolley	Trolley eléctrico	2 000 Esc.
Buggy	Buggy	6 000 Esc.
Clubs	Tacos	2 800 Esc.

Credit cards Cartão de crédito VISA - AMEX - DC

1072

Access Acesso : E 101 Funchal → Machico.
N 675 → Sto da Serra
Map 0 on page 0 Mapa 0 Página 0

GOLF COURSE / PERCURSO — 14/20

Site	Sitio	
Maintenance	Conversa	
Architect	Arquitecto	Robert Trent Jones
Type	Tipo	mountain
Relief	Relevo	
Water in play	Lago	
Exp. to wind	Exposto ao vento	
Trees in play	Arvores	

Scorecard Cartão de resultados	Chp. Camp.	Mens Homens	Ladies Senhoras
Length Comprimento	6039	5496	4511
Par	72	72	72

Advised golfing ability		0 12 24 36
Nivel de jogo recomendado		
Hcp required	Handicap exigido	no

CLUB HOUSE & AMENITIES / CLUB HOUSE E ANEXOS — 6/10

Pro shop	Pro-shop	
Driving range	Campo de prática	
Sheltered	coberto	no
On grass	om relva	yes
Putting-green	putting-green	yes
Pitching-green	pitching-green	no

HOTEL FACILITIES / INFRAESTRUCTURAS HOTELEIRAS — 5/10

HOTELS HOTELS

Reids — Funchal
148 rooms, D 54 000 Esc — 21 km
Tel (351) 091 - 700 71 7, Fax (351) 091 - 700 71 7

Cliff Bay Resort — Funchal
97 rooms, D 45 000 Esc — 21 km
Tel (351) 091 - 76 18 18, Fax (351) 091 - 76 25 25

Madeira Carlton — Funchal
374 rooms, D 37 000 Esc. — 21 km
Tel (351) 091 - 23 10 31, Fax (351) 091 - 22 33 77

RESTAURANTS RESTAURANTES

Casa Velha — Funchal
Tel (351) 091 - 22 57 49 — 21 km

Trattoria — Funchal
Tel (351) 091 - 76 69 99 — 21 km

MONTADO

Em contrapartida com alguns campos prestigiados mas muitas vezes muito difíceis de jogar para os jogadores médios, o percurso do Montado oferece um desenho muito agradável da autoria de Duarte Sottomayor e que nos dará prazer em jogar muitas vezes sem anfado. Situado num local campestre muito agradável, as suas dificuldades são bem equilibradas, mas poderíamos desejar greens por vezes melhor protegidos, uma vez que temos frequentemente de jogar ferros curtos depois de um bom drive. Poucos jogadores, no entanto, se queixarão. Se vieram aqui de férias poderão jogar confortavelmente os seus handicaps. Trata-se de um percurso sem complicações com obstáculos de água que estão pouco em jogo, situado numa região que tinha necessidade de percursos deste género.

Alongside the prestigious courses in this part of the world, which are often very tough to play for average players, Montado is a very pleasant course designed by Duarte Sottomayor and fun to play several times over. This is a pleasant country setting where difficulties are neatly balanced, but we might have preferred more tightly protected greens, as after a good drive the second shot is often a short iron. Few players will really complain about that if they are here on holiday and they should play to their handicap quite comfortably. An uncomplicated course where water hazards are not too much in the way, and located in a region that was badly in need of this type of layout.

Club de Golf de Montado

Apartado 40 Algeruz
P - 2950 PALMELA

Office	Secretariado	(351) 065 - 706 648
Pro shop	Pro-shop	(351) 065 - 706 648
Fax	Fax	(351) 065 - 706 775
Situation	Localização	

Setubal (pop. 89 106), 7 km
Lisboa (pop. 662 782), 45 km

Annual closure	Fecho anual	no
Weekly closure	Fecho semanal	no

Fees main season
Tarifas de época alta 18 holes

	Week days Semana	We/Bank holidays Fim de sem./Feriad
Individual Individual	3 500 Esc	5 000 Esc
Couple Casal	7 000 Esc	10 000 Esc

Caddy	Caddy	no
Electric Trolley	Trolley eléctrico	yes
Buggy	Buggy	yes
Clubs	Tacos	yes

Credit cards Cartão de crédito
VISA - AMEX

Access Acesso : Lisboa, A2 → Palmela, Poceirão, Algeruz.
Map 3 on page 1064 Mapa 3 Página 1064

GOLF COURSE
PERCURSO — 13/20

Site	Sitio	
Maintenance	Conversa	
Architect	Arquitecto	Duarte Sottomayor
Type	Tipo	parkland
Relief	Relevo	
Water in play	Lago	
Exp. to wind	Exposto ao vento	
Trees in play	Arvores	

Scorecard Cartão de resultados	Chp. Camp.	Mens Homens	Ladies Senhoras
Length Compriment	6003	5702	4849
Par	72	72	72

Advised golfing ability	0 12 24 36
Nivel de jogo recomendado	
Hcp required Handicap exigido 24	

CLUB HOUSE & AMENITIES
CLUB HOUSE E ANEXOS — 7/10

Pro shop	Pro-shop	
Driving range	Campo de prática	
Sheltered	coberto	4 places
On grass	om relva	yes
Putting-green	putting-green	yes
Pitching-green	pitching-green	yes

1073

HOTEL FACILITIES
INFRAESTRUCTURAS HOTELEIRAS — 6/10

HOTELS

Novotel — Setubal
105 , D 9 000 Esc — 8 km
Tel (351) 065 - 52 28 09
Tel (351) 065 - 52 29 12

Pousada de S. Felipe — Setubal
16 , D 18 000 Esc — 15 km
Tel (351) 065 - 52 38 44
(351) 065 - 53 25 38

Mar e Sol — Setubal
71 , D 8 000 Esc — 7 km
Tel (351) 065 - 53 46 03, (351) 065 - 53 20 36

RESTAURANTS RESTAURANTES

A Roda - Tel (351) 065 - 292 64 — Setubal 7 km

O Beco — Setubal
Tel (351) 065 - 52 46 17 — 7 km

Este percurso está localizado muito perto da Quinta do Palheiro Ferreiro, vasta mansão rodeada de um parque à inglesa com milhares de flores raras e de árvores exóticas. Do golf tem-se magníficas vistas sobre o Funchal e a costa sul da Madeira, 800 metros mais abaixo. Esta situação de um golf de montanha, tem a vantagem de ser dominante e exótica, tem o inconveniente de apresentar desníveis difíceis de aguentar a pé durante 18 buracos. A tarefa do arquitecto Cabell Robinson não era das mais fáceis. Não foi capaz de evitar por isso algumas pancadas cegas. Para alem disso encontram-se aqui alguns buracos sem grande interesse, sem duvida devido a falta de espaço, mas também alguns buracos esplendidos. São tanto «tricky» como espectaculares, acessivel a todos os niveis, este percurso não deixará ninguém indiferente e criará lembranças tanto gloriosas como visuais... sobretudo quando os carrinhos evitam o cansaço fisico.

This course is located close to «la Quinta do Palheiro Ferreiro», a huge house surrounded by English-style gardens with thousands of rare flowers and exotic trees. From the course you get some superb vistas over Funchal and the southern coast of Madeira, 800 metres further down. This sort of mountainous golf course location has the advantage of being dominant; the downside is the steep sloping terrain which for 18 holes of golf is tough going on foot. The job of Cabell Robinson was anything but easy, and not surprisingly he was unable to avoid a few blind shots. In fact, there are a few holes here that offer no real appeal, probably because of the lack of space. There are, however, some splendid holes to make up for it. Tricky and spectacular and playable by all, this course won't leave you indifferent, but will give some great memories both visually and for the golf you played, especially when taking a buggy to avoid what is a very tiring walk.

Palheiro Golfe — 1994

Palheiro Ferreiro, São Gonçalo
P - 9000 FUNCHAL - MADEIRA

Office	Secretariado	(351) 0291 - 792 116
Pro shop	Pro-shop	(351) 0291 - 792 116
Fax	Fax	(351) 0291 - 792 456
Situation	Localização	

Funchal (pop. 99 244), 8 km

Annual closure	Fecho anual	no
Weekly closure	Fecho semanal	no

Fees main season
Tarifas de época alta 18 holes

	Week days Semana	We/Bank holidays Fim de sem./Feriad
Individual Individual	11 000 Esc.	11 000 Esc.
Couple Casal	22 000 Esc.	22 000 Esc.

Caddy	Caddy	on request
Electric Trolley	Trolley eléctrico	no
Buggy	Buggy	6 000 Esc.
Clubs	Tacos	4 000 Esc.

Credit cards Cartão de crédito
VISA - Eurocard - MasterCard - AMEX - DC

1074

Access Acesso : Funchal, → Airport.
Leave at Camacha, follow the signs.
Map 0 on page 0 Mapa 0 Página 0

GOLF COURSE / PERCURSO — 13/20

Site	Sítio	
Maintenance	Conversa	
Architect	Arquitecto	Cabell Robinson
Type	Tipo	mountain
Relief	Relevo	
Water in play	Lago	
Exp. to wind	Exposto ao vento	
Trees in play	Arvores	

Scorecard Cartão de resultados	Chp. Camp.	Mens Homens	Ladies Senhoras
Length Comprimento	6022	5847	4921
Par	71	71	71

Advised golfing ability		0 12 24 36
Nivel de jogo recomendado		
Hcp required	Handicap exigido	36

CLUB HOUSE & AMENITIES / CLUB HOUSE E ANEXOS — 6/10

Pro shop	Pro-shop	
Driving range	Campo de prática	
Sheltered	coberto	no
On grass	om relva	no (6 mats)
Putting-green	putting-green	yes
Pitching-green	pitching-green	yes

HOTEL FACILITIES / INFRAESTRUCTURAS HOTELEIRAS — 7/10

HOTELS HOTELS

Reids — Funchal
148 rooms, D 54 000 Esc — 8 km
Tel (351) 091 - 700 71 7, Fax (351) 091 - 700 71 7

Cliff Bay Resort — Funchal
97 rooms, D 45 000 Esc — 8 km
Tel (351) 091 - 76 18 18, Fax (351) 091 - 76 25 25

Madeira Carlton — Funchal
374 rooms, D 37 000 Esc. — 8 km
Tel (351) 091 - 23 10 31, Fax (351) 091 - 22 33 77

RESTAURANTS RESTAURANTES

Casa Velha — Funchal
Tel (351) 091 - 22 57 49 — 8 km

Trattoria — Funchal
Tel (351) 091 - 76 69 99 — 8 km

PALMARES ✹ 13 | 7 | 5

Como muitos dos percursos portugueses foi desenhado por Frank Pennink a partir de dois espaços diferentes: cinco buracos são à beira mar, com uma arquitectura que faz lembrar um "links", os outros desenvolvem-se entre pinheiros, muito mais acidentados e com magníficas vistas sobre o Atlântico. Os buracos de borda de água constituem o encanto e o interesse principal deste percurso que para alem disso tem um desenho muito simples. Alguns "drives" podem causar problemas mas os golfistas de todos os níveis não encontrarão muitas dificuldades para alêm das criadas pelo seu proprio jogo. Os "greens" são muito simples, bastante pequenos e pouco defendidos. Nesta bela paisagem seria de mau gosto estragar o prazer! Se este percurso não dá para maravilhar, não deixa de ser muito agradável para se passar uma tarde em família ou com um grupo de amigos aínda que de níveis diferentes.

Like many courses in Portugal, Palmares was designed by Frank Pennink using two different sorts of space: five holes run along the seashore in true links style, the others are laid out amidst a much hillier pine forest with some magnificent views over the Atlantic. The seaboard holes give the course its basic charm and appeal, as otherwise the design is fairly simple. Some tee-shots can cause problems, but apart from those arising from your own game, there are no real difficulties here, whatever your playing ability. The greens are very simple, smallish and wide open. In such pretty countryside, it would have been in very poor taste to make life too difficult. This course might not be over-exciting, but it is great fun to play with the family or friends, whatever their ability.

Palmares Golf	1976
Apartado 74	
P - 8600 LAGOS	

Office	Secretariado	(351) 0282 - 340 900
Pro shop	Pro-shop	(351) 0282 - 340 900
Fax	Fax	(351) 0282 - 762 534
Situation	Localização	
Lagos (pop.11 746), 6 km		
Portimão (pop. 21 196), 15 km		
Annual closure	Fecho anual	no
Weekly closure	Fecho semanal	no

Fees main season
Tarifas de época alta 18 holes

	Week days Semana	We/Bank holidays Fim de sem./Feriad
Individual Individual	9 500 Esc	9 500 Esc
Couple Casal	17 000 Esc	17 000 Esc

Caddy	Caddy	no
Electric Trolley	Trolley eléctrico	no
Buggy	Buggy	6 000 Esc.
Clubs	Tacos	4 000 Esc.

Credit cards Cartão de crédito VISA - AMEX

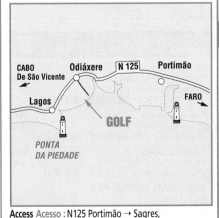

CABO De São Vicente — Odiáxere — N 125 — Portimão
Lagos — FARO
GOLF
PONTA DA PIEDADE

Access Acesso : N125 Portimão → Sagres, → Meia Praia
Map 3 on page 1064 Mapa 3 Página 1064

GOLF COURSE / PERCURSO — 13/20

Site	Sitio	
Maintenance	Conversa	
Architect	Arquitecto	Frank Pennink
Type	Tipo	seaside course, inland
Relief	Relevo	
Water in play	Lago	
Exp. to wind	Exposto ao vento	
Trees in play	Arvores	

Scorecard Cartão de resultados	Chp. Camp.	Mens Homens	Ladies Senhoras
Length Compriment	5961	5614	5020
Par	71	71	71

Advised golfing ability		0 12 24 36
Nivel de jogo recomendado		
Hcp required	Handicap exigido	28 Men, 36 Ladies

CLUB HOUSE & AMENITIES / CLUB HOUSE E ANEXOS — 7/10

Pro shop	Pro-shop	
Driving range	Campo de prática	
Sheltered	coberto	no
On grass	om relva	yes
Putting-green	putting-green	yes
Pitching-green	pitching-green	no

1075

HOTEL FACILITIES / INFRAESTRUCTURAS HOTELEIRAS — 5/10

HOTELS HOTELS
De Lagos — Lagos
317 rooms, D 14 300 Esc. — 12 km
Tel (351) 082 - 76 99 67, Fax (351) 082 - 76 99 20

Meia Praia — Meia Praia
65 rooms, D 7 500 Esc. — 4 km
Tel (351) 082 - 76 99 80, Fax (351) 082 - 76 99 80

Golfinho — Praia Dona
262 rooms, D 27 000 Esc. — 16 km
Tel (351) 082 - 76 99 00, Fax (351) 082 - 76 99 99

RESTAURANTS RESTAURANTES
O Castelo — Lagos
Tel (351) 082 - 76 09 57 — 6 km

O Galeão — Lagos
Tel (351) 082 - 76 39 09 — 6 km

PENHA LONGA ✹) 17 6 8

Localizado num belo local histórico, semeado de vestigios do passado, é um dos bons exitos dos ultimos anos. O desenho de Robert Trent Jones Junior é muito imaginativo e seduzirá primeiramente os bons jogadores que deverão saber ultrapassar com habilidade os numerosos obstáculos que se lhes deparam, para alem do terreno acidentado que oferece, porem, belas vistas do mar e da serra. O comprimento do percurso e a sua variedade exigem um jogo muito complete desde as saídas até aos "greens" de boa dimensao e bem modelados. Os jogadores menos habilitados podera escolher as saidas mais avançadas para retirar ao jogo um máximo de prazer. É certo que as dificuldades subsistem, mas se não derem demasiada importância ao "score" terão muitas ocasiões de exercer a sua destrêsa, ou mesmo de progredir sobre um percurso exigente depois de terem feito a mão nalgum percurso, mais facil, da região. A manutenção é geralmente muito bom.

In a beautiful historical site, dotted with vestiges from the past, this is one of the best courses in recent years. The very imaginative design of Robert Trent Jones Jnr. will firstly appeal to very good players, who will need all their skills to negotiate the numerous hazards and the steep hills, which offer some beautiful views over the sea and mountain. The length and variety of the course demand a good, all-round game from tee to green, most of the latter being large and well contoured. Lesser players will play from the front tees to really enjoy themselves. The difficulties are still there, of course, but if they don't pay too much attention to dropped strokes, average golfers will have many opportunities to exercise their skills and even make progress on a demanding course. This is a good test after getting warmed up on some of the easier courses in the region. Upkeep is generally good.

Penha Longa Golf Club 1994
Quinta da Penha Longa - Linho
P - 2710 SINTRA

Office	Secretariado	(351) 021 - 924 9011
Pro shop	Pro-shop	(351) 021 - 924 9011
Fax	Fax	(351) 021 - 924 9024
Situation	Localização	

Lisboa (pop. 662 782), 25 km
Sintra (pop. 33 664), 2 km

Annual closure	Fecho anual	no
Weekly closure	Fecho semanal	no

Fees main season
Tarifas de época alta 18 holes

	Week days Semana	We/Bank holidays Fim de sem./Feriad
Individual Individual	17 000 Esc.	17 000 Esc.
Couple Casal	34 000 Esc.	34 000 Esc.

Special fees for Hotel guests

Caddy	Caddy	4 000 Esc.
Electric Trolley	Trolley eléctrico	2 000 Esc.
Buggy	Buggy	6 300 Esc.
Clubs	Tacos	3 700 Esc.

Credit cards Cartão de crédito VISA - AMEX

Access Acesso : N9 Estoril → Sintra,
→ Lagon Azul
Map 2 on page 1062 Mapa 2 Página 1062

GOLF COURSE
PERCURSO 17 /20

Site	Sitio	
Maintenance	Conversa	
Architect	Arquitecto	R. Trent Jones Jr
Type	Tipo	mountain, residential
Relief	Relevo	
Water in play	Lago	
Exp. to wind	Exposto ao vento	
Trees in play	Arvores	

Scorecard Cartão de resultados	Chp. Camp.	Mens Homens	Ladies Senhoras
Length Compriment	6290	5942	5100
Par	72	72	72

Advised golfing ability		0	12	24	36
Nivel de jogo recomendado					

Hcp required	Handicap exigido	no

CLUB HOUSE & AMENITIES
CLUB HOUSE E ANEXOS 6 /10

Pro shop	Pro-shop	
Driving range	Campo de prática	
Sheltered	coberto	4 places
On grass	om relva	yes
Putting-green	putting-green	yes
Pitching-green	pitching-green	yes

HOTEL FACILITIES
INFRAESTRUCTURAS HOTELEIRAS 8 /10

HOTELS HOTELS

Caesar Park Penha Longa	Sintra
160 rooms, D 41 000 Esc.	100 m
(351) 01 - 924 90 11, Fax (351) 01 - 924 90 07	
Palacio de Seteais	Sintra
29 rooms, D 40 000 Esc.	3 km
(351) 01 - 923 32 00, Fax (351) 01 - 923 42 77	
Quinta da Capela	Sintra
5 rooms, D 24 000 Esc.	3 km
(351) 01 - 929 01 70, Fax (351) 01 - 929 34 25	

RESTAURANTS RESTAURANTES

Penha Longa	Sintra
(351) 01 - 924 90 11	100 m
Tacho Real	Sintra
(351) 01 - 923 52 77	3 km

1076

Tendo estado fechado para obras durante alguns meses, o primeiro Campo de Golfe do Algarve em termos de antiguade, sofreu alguns melhoramentos mas sem grandes moficações. Continua um percurso longo e difícil dos «Tees» de campeonato, tornando-se mais acessivel dos «Tees» normais. Bastante plano e tendo algumas árvores a dificultar as pancadas não chegam no entanto a ser perigosas. O seu traçado salienta-se por um bom número de «bunkers» com bom desenho mas sem nada de especial a assinalar. A sua colocação sugere um estilo británico que se torna evidente se nos lembrarmos que foi desenhado por Henry Cotton. A Penina pode por vezes lembrar «Carnoustie» sem no entanto se poder considerar um verdadeiro «links» o que aumentaria ainda a sua dificuldade. Se conseguirmos bater longe e direito, a bola estará sempre em boa posição. Os greens, bastante grandes e razoavelmente planos não causam problemas - embora haja necessidade de os atingir... De salientar os 4 par 5 da 2a volta. A sua situação e o equipamento hoteleiro da Penina fazem dele um destino de sucesso.

The Algarve's very first course has in recent years been given a fresh look, but with no notable changes. It is still long and tough from the back tees, but mellows the further forward you go. Very flat and covered with a variety of trees which, although in play, are none too dangerous, this layout is marked by the huge number of bunkers, correctly designed but with no real personality. Their positioning testifies to an obvious British style, knowing that the course was in fact designed by Henry Cotton. Besides, Penina is a little reminiscent of Carnoustie in some ways, but without the links features, which would only increase the difficulty here. If you can drive long and straight, you will always find your ball in a good position. The greens, which are pretty large and generally flat, pose no real problem, the trouble is reaching them. A noticeable feature are the four par 5s on the back nine. An excellent destination.

Penina Golf & Resort Hotel		1966
ALVOR		
P - PORTIMÃO - Algarve		
Office	Secretariado	(351) 0282 - 415 415
Pro shop	Pro-shop	(351) 0282 - 415 415
Fax	Fax	(351) 0282 - 220 59
Situation	Localização	
Portimão (pop. 21 196), 4 km		
Annual closure	Fecho anual	no
Weekly closure	Fecho semanal	no

Fees main season		
Tarifas de época alta 18 holes		
	Week days Semana	We/Bank holidays Fim de sem./Feriad
Individual Individual	13 500 Esc.	13 500 Esc.
Couple Casal	27 000 Esc.	27 000 Esc.

Special fees for Penina Hotel guests

Caddy	Caddy	no
Electric Trolley	Trolley eléctrico	2 000 Esc.
Buggy	Buggy	7 500 Esc.
Clubs	Tacos	4 000 Esc.

Credit cards Cartão de crédito
VISA - Eurocard - MasterCard - AMEX - DC

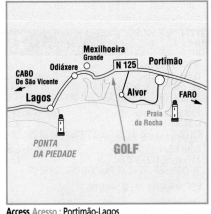

Access Acesso : Portimão-Lagos
Map 3 on page 1064 Mapa 3 Página 1064

GOLF COURSE PERCURSO — 14/20

Site	Sitio	
Maintenance	Conversa	
Architect	Arquitecto	Henry Cotton
Type	Tipo	open country
Relief	Relevo	
Water in play	Lago	
Exp. to wind	Exposto ao vento	
Trees in play	Arvores	

Scorecard Cartão de resultados	Chp. Camp.	Mens Homens	Ladies Senhoras
Length Compriment	6439	6054	5322
Par	73	73	73

Advised golfing ability	0	12	24	36
Nivel de jogo recomendado				
Hcp required	Handicap exigido	no		

CLUB HOUSE & AMENITIES CLUB HOUSE E ANEXOS — 7/10

Pro shop	Pro-shop	
Driving range	Campo de prática	
Sheltered	coberto	4 places
On grass	om relva	yes
Putting-green	putting-green	yes
Pitching-green	pitching-green	yes

1077

HOTEL FACILITIES INFRAESTRUCTURAS HOTELEIRAS — 7/10

HOTELS HOTELS
Penina Hotel — Golf on site
192 rooms, D 30 000 Esc.
Tel (351) 082 - 415 415
Fax (351) 082 - 415 000

Alvor Praia — Praia dos Três Irmãos 8 km
217 rooms, D 45 000 Esc.
Tel (351) 082 - 45 89 00, Fax (351) 082 - 45 89 99

Algarve — Praia da Rocha 7 km
220 rooms, D 35 000 Esc.
Tel (351) 082 - 41 50 01, Fax (351) 082 - 41 59 99

RESTAURANTS RESTAURANTES
Titanic — Praia da Rocha
Tel (351) 082 - 22 371 — 7 km

Falésia — Praia da Rocha
Tel (351) 082 - 23 524 — 7 km

Os dois 9 buracos são muito diferentes. Os primeiros, muito acidentados e cansativos, desenvolvem-se entre pinheiros, sempre em jogo. Os segundos são planos, com àgua, practicamente em todos os buracos. Esta falta de unidade pode explicar-se pela intervenção de McEvoy a Howard Swan sobre o desenho original de Ronald Fream. O ritmo de jogo pode ser prejudicado para os jogadores que se deixem perturbar pelo ambiente circundante. A qualidade e o desenho dos "greens", alguns difíceis de lêr, é um dos pontos positivos, para mais por estarem bem defendidos, o que torna os "aproches" muito interessantes. Não o é um percurso para se jogar todos os dias, mas merece algumas vistas muito atentas, desde que se jogue das saídas de trás e se esteja em boa forma física. Muito próximo do parque natural da Ria Formosa este golf dispõe de muito boas instalações de treino, nomeadamente para o jogo curto.

The two 9-hole courses are very different. The front nine, hilly and tiring, are laid out in a pine forest, where trees come very much into play. The back nine are flatter, with water on virtually every hole. This lack of unity might be explained by the work made by McEvoy and Howard Swan on Ronald Fream's original design, and it might upset players who are over-attentive to surroundings. Otherwise, the excellence and design of the greens, some of which are tricky to read, are very positive points, all the more so in that their defence makes for some very interesting approach shots. This is not a course you would play every day, but it does deserve some careful visiting, providing you and your game are fit enough for the back-tees. Close to the Ria Formosa Nature Park, the course boasts excellent practice facilities, particularly for the short game.

Pinheiros Campo de Golf — 1989

Quinta do Lago
P - 8135 ALMANSIL

Office	Secretariado	(351) 0289 - 394 340
Pro shop	Pro-shop	(351) 0289 - 394 340
Fax	Fax	(351) 0289 - 394 392
Situation	Localização	
Faro (pop. 33 664), 15 km		
Annual closure	Fecho anual	no
Weekly closure	Fecho semanal	no

Fees main season
Tarifas de época alta 18 holes

	Week days Semana	We/Bank holidays Fim de sem./Feriad
Individual Individual	15 000 Esc	15 000 Esc
Couple Casal	30 000 Esc	30 000 Esc

Special fees for members of Algarve golf clubs.

Caddy	Caddy	no
Electric Trolley	Trolley eléctrico	2 000 Esc.
Buggy	Buggy	7 500 Esc.
Clubs	Tacos	5 000 Esc.

Credit cards Cartão de crédito
VISA - MasterCard - AMEX - DC

1078

Loulé

E 1 - IP 1

Portimão ←

Quarteira
Vale do Lobo
Almancil N 125 São Lourenço
Quinta
do Lago FARO
GOLF

Vila real
Huelva →

Access Acesso : N 125 Faro → Portimão.
Almansil → Vale do Lobo
Map 3 on page 1064 Mapa 3 Página 1064

GOLF COURSE / PERCURSO — 14/20

Site	Sitio	▬▬▬▬▬▭
Maintenance	Conversa	▬▬▬▬▭▭
Architect	Arquitecto	Ronald Fream
Type	Tipo	forest, open country
Relief	Relevo	▬▬▬▬▬▭
Water in play	Lago	▬▬▬▬▭▭
Exp. to wind	Exposto ao vento	▬▬▬▭▭▭
Trees in play	Arvores	▬▬▬▬▬▭

Scorecard Cartão de resultados	Chp. Camp.	Mens Homens	Ladies Senhoras
Length Compriment	6057	5614	4762
Par	71	71	71

Advised golfing ability   0 12 24 36
Nivel de jogo recomendado
Hcp required   Handicap exigido   28 Men, 36 Ladies

CLUB HOUSE & AMENITIES / CLUB HOUSE E ANEXOS — 7/10

Pro shop	Pro-shop	▬▬▬▬▬▭
Driving range	Campo de prática	▬▬▬▬▭▭
Sheltered	coberto	no
On grass	om relva	yes
Putting-green	putting-green	yes
Pitching-green	pitching-green	yes

HOTEL FACILITIES / INFRAESTRUCTURAS HOTELEIRAS — 7/10

HOTELS HOTELS
Quinta do Lago   Quinta do Lago
132 rooms, D 17 000 Esc.   3 km
Tel (351) 089 - 39 66 66, Fax (351) 089 - 39 63 93

Four Seasons Fairways   Quinta do Lago
D 12 000 Esc   2 km
Tel (351) 089 - 39 80 20, Fax (351) 089 - 39 80 29

Dona Filipa   Vale do Lobo
147 rooms, D 31 500 Esc.   8 km
Tel (351) 089 - 39 41 41, Fax (351) 089 - 39 42 88

RESTAURANTS RESTAURANTES
Casa Velha   2 km
Tel (351) 089 - 39 49 83

Bobby Jones Club   Vilar do Golf 1 km

Durante muito tempo braço direito de Robert Trent Jones, Cabell Robinson impos-se como um arquitecto imaginativo e muito conhecedor a todos os niveis do golf. Praia D'El Rey é disso a demonstração. Com uma bela localização à beira mar rodeado de pinheiros, por vezes espectaculares, este percurso tem muitos aspectos em que se assemelha a um Links tradicional, obrigando a bem trabalhar a bola. Quando o vento sopra, porem raramente tão violentamente como na Escócia ou Irlanda, isto acrescenta um condimento especial a u prato de grande qualidade. A despeito da sua juventude, Praia d'El Rey promete vir a ser um dos grandes percursos da península Ibérica. Tem ainda a vantagem de permitir tanto partidas de golf de alto nível como jornadas agradáveis em família.

For many years Robert Trent Jones' right-hand man, Cabell Robinson has become established as an imaginative designer and excellent connoisseur of golf played at all levels. Praia d'El Rey is further demonstration of his expertise. Set on a very beautiful and often spectacular sea-side site enhanced with pine-trees on some holes, the course has many facets of a traditional links with the need to work the ball all ways. And while the wind is kinder than in Scotland or Ireland, it can often add a little spice to what is already a savoury dish. Although still in infancy, Praia d'El Rey promises to emerge as one of the great courses on the Iberian peninsula, with the extra pleasure of allowing rounds of golf for highly skilled players and enjoyable days with the family.

Praia d'El Rey   1997
Vale de Janelas, Apartado 2
P - 2510 OBIDOS

Office	Secretariado	(351) 062 - 909 626
Pro shop	Pro-shop	(351) 062 - 909 626
Fax	Fax	(351) 062 - 909 629
Situation	Localização	

Peniche (pop. 15 304), 5 km

Annual closure	Fecho anual	no
Weekly closure	Fecho semanal	no

Fees main season
Tarifas de época alta 18 holes

	Week days Semana	We/Bank holidays Fim de sem./Feriad
Individual Individual	5 000 Esc	7 000 Esc
Couple Casal	10 000 Esc	14 000 Esc

Caddy	no
Electric Trolley	no
Buggy	5 500 Esc.
Clubs	yes

Credit cards Cartão de crédito VISA - AMEX

GOLF

Lagoa de Odidos

Peniche   Baleal   Caldas da Rainha   Obidos

N 114

Atouguia da Baleia   Serra d'El-Rei

N 8

0   3   6 km   Lisboa

Access : Lisboa, A8-IC1 → Obidos, N114 → Peniche.
Map 2 on page 1062 Mapa 2 Página 1062

GOLF COURSE
PERCURSO   17/20

Site	Sitio	
Maintenance	Conversa	
Architect	Arquitecto	Cabell Robinson
Type	Tipo	seaside course, links
Relief		
Water in play		
Exp. to wind		
Trees in play		

Scorecard Cartão de resultados	Chp. Camp.	Mens Homens	Ladies Senhoras
Length Compriment	6467	5586	5216
Par	72	72	72

Advised golfing ability   0   12   24   36
Nivel de jogo recomendado
Hcp required   Handicap exigido 28

CLUB HOUSE & AMENITIES
CLUB HOUSE E ANEXOS   6/10

Pro shop	Pro-shop	
Driving range	Campo de prática	
Sheltered	coberto	6 places
On grass	om relva	yes
Putting-green	putting-green	yes
Pitching-green	pitching-green	yes

HOTEL FACILITIES
INFRAESTRUCTURAS HOTELEIRAS   5/10

HOTELS HOTELS
Caldas Internacional   Caldas da Rainha
83 rooms, D 8 500 Esc   15 km
Tel (351) 062 - 83 23 07, (351) 062 - 84 44 82

Estal. do Convento   Obidos
31 rooms, D 13 000 Esc   12 km
Tel (351) 062 - 95 92 16, (351) 062 - 95 91 59

Dona Leonor   Caldas da Rainha
30 rooms, D 6 500 Esc   15 km
Tel (351) 062 - 84 21 71, (351) 062 - 84 21 72

RESTAURANTS RESTAURANTES
Pousada do Castelho   Obidos
Tel (351) 062 - 95 91 05   12 km

A Ilustre Casa de Ramiro   Obido
Tel (351) 062 - 95 91 94   12 km

1079

QUINTA DA BELOURA

Desenhado por Duarte Sotto Mayor, secundo a concepção de Rocky Roquemore é o mais recente percurso desta região. O envolvimento imobiliário deverá vir a ser gradualmente escondido pela plantação de pinheiros, carvalhos, palmeiras etc, o que permitirá de melhor defenir os "fairways". Os obstáculos de agua e os "bunkers" estão pouco em jogo, à excepção de alguns lagos perigosos, principalmente nos últimos buracos. Porem, todas as dificuldades estão bem à vista, nada é aqui uma fonte de surpresas, nem mesmo os "greens" bem desenhados e fáceis de lêr. Percebe-se que não hoyuve aqui à intenção de fazer um percurso de campeonato nem para os jogadores muito compridos nem para os mestres do jogo curto que não vão encontrar motivos para saciar as suas emoções. Tem de jogar-se bastante direito mas os jogadores de nível médio ou mesmo os principiantes conseguirão fazer.

This is the region's newest course, designed by Duarte Sottomayor and Rocky Roquemore. The surrounding property development should gradually be blotted out by a plantation programme of new pine, oak and/or palm trees, also designed to outline the fairways. The sand and water hazards are seldom in play, with the exception of a few dangerous lakes, especially over the last holes. But all the difficulties here are clear to see with no surprises, not even on the greens, which are rather well designed and easy to read. Visibly, no-one was aiming to build a course for tournaments, big-hitters or short-game wizards, who will probably find this lay-out a little low on excitement. The key is to play straight, and then high-handicappers and even beginners can card an honourable score.

Quinta da Beloura Golf Club — 1994

Estrada de Albarraque
P - 2710 SINTRA

Office	Secretariado	(351) 01 - 924 0021
Pro shop	Pro-shop	(351) 01 - 924 0021
Fax	Fax	(351) 01 - 924 0061
Situation	Localização	

Sintra, (pop. 20 574), 3 km
Estoril (pop. 25 230), 4 km

Annual closure	Fecho anual	no
Weekly closure	Fecho semanal	no

Fees main season
Tarifas de época alta 18 holes

	Week days Semana	We/Bank holidays Fim de sem./Feriad
Individual Individual	6 000 Esc	8 500 Esc
Couple Casal	12 000 Esc	17 000 Esc

Caddy	Caddy	no
Electric Trolley	Trolley eléctrico	no
Buggy	Buggy	5 500 Esc.
Clubs	Tacos	2 000 Esc.

Credit cards Cartão de crédito VISA - AMEX

Access Acesso : N9 Estoril-Sintra, → Alcabideche
Map 2 on page 1062 Mapa 2 Página 1062

1080

GOLF COURSE / PERCURSO — 14/20

Site	Sitio	
Maintenance	Conversa	
Architect	Arquitecto	Duarte Sotto Mayor residential
Type	Tipo	
Relief	Relevo	
Water in play	Lago	
Exp. to wind	Exposto ao vento	
Trees in play	Arvores	

Scorecard Cartão de resultados	Chp. Camp.	Mens Homens	Ladies Senhoras
Length Compriment	5917	5474	5092
Par	72	72	73

Advised golfing ability Nível de jogo recomendado		0 12 24 36
Hcp required Handicap exigido		28 Men, 36 Ladies

CLUB HOUSE & AMENITIES / CLUB HOUSE E ANEXOS — 8/10

Pro shop	Pro-shop	
Driving range	Campo de prática	
Sheltered	coberto	no
On grass	om relva	yes
Putting-green	putting-green	yes
Pitching-green	pitching-green	yes

HOTEL FACILITIES / INFRAESTRUCTURAS HOTELEIRAS — 7/10

HOTELS HOTELS

Atlantis — Estoril 3 km
129 rooms, D 12 000 Esc
Tel (351) 01 - 469 07 21, Fax (351) 01 - 469 07 40

Palacio — Estoril 15 km
162 rooms, D 28 000 Esc
Tel (351) 01 - 468 04 00, Fax (351) 01 - 468 48 67

Estoril Eden — Estoril 18 km
162 rooms, D 15 000 Esc.
Tel (351) 01 - 467 05 73, Fax (351) 01 - 467 08 48

RESTAURANTS RESTAURANTES

A. Choupana — S. Joán do Estoril 8 km

Solar de São Pedro — Sintra 3 km
Tel (351) 01 - 923 18 60

Embora situado numa imensa zona de pinhal, este percurso merecia que lhe tivessem concecido um pouco mais de espaço para permitor a Robert Trent Jones de dar averdadeira medida do seu talento. O seu desenho é de muito boa qualidade, mas para conseguir um par 71, teve de criar 5 pares 5 para contrabalançar os 6 pares 3 (entre os quais os belos 5 e 14) o que provoca um ritmo de jogo pouco habitual. Aqueles que conhecem o estilo do arquitecto não ficam surprendidos mas terão a impressão que já jogaram aqueles buracos noutro lugar qualquer. Isto não retira muito ao prazer do jogo e do local, donde se pode apreciar algumas lindas vistas do mar, nomeadamente n° 13, o buraco modêlo do percurso. As dificuldades são numerosas, equilibradas e bem visíveis, permitindo jogar o percurso desde a primeira vez sem temer armadilhas escondidas. Em contrapartida náo fica muito por descobrir se o percurso fôr jogado frequentemente. Por pouco, tinha-se obtido um exito total.

Although sited in a huge pine estate, this course would have deserved a little more space to enable Trent Jones to fully express his many talents. This is certainly an excellent layout, but to achieve a par 71, he had to create five par 5s to offset the six par 3s (including the pretty 5th and 14th holes). Hence a rather unusually balanced course. Those of you who know the designer's style will not be surprised, but you will get the impression of having already played some of these holes before. But don't let that detract from the pleasure of golfing on a site that offers some beautiful views over the sea, notably from the 13th, the course's signature hole. Difficulties are manifold but visible, so new-comers need have no fear of hidden hazards. In contrast, you will soon get to the bottom of everything the course has to offer if you play here often. This looks very much like a missed opportunity to create a great golf course.

Club-Golf da Quinta da Marinha
Quinta da Marinha
P - 2750 CASCAIS

Office	Secretariado	(351) 01 - 486 9881
Pro shop	Pro-shop	(351) 01 - 486 9881
Fax	Fax	(351) 01 - 486 9032
Situation	Localização	

Cascais (pop. 29 882), 6 km
Lisboa (pop. 662 782), 26 km

Annual closure	Fecho anual	no
Weekly closure	Fecho semanal	no

Fees main season
Tarifas de época alta 18 holes

	Week days Semana	We/Bank holidays Fim de sem./Feriad
Individual Individual	8 500 Esc	10 500 Esc
Couple Casal	17 000 Esc	21 000 Esc

– 30% for Portuguese clubs members

Caddy	Caddy	no
Electric Trolley	Trolley eléctrico	no
Buggy	Buggy	6 000 Esc.
Clubs	Tacos	4 500 Esc.

Credit cards Cartão de crédito VISA - AMEX

Access Acesso : Lisboa A5, → Cascais,
N 247 → Praia do Guincho
Map 2 on page 1062 Mapa 2 Página 1062

GOLF COURSE
PERCURSO   13 /20

Site	Sítio	▰▰▰▱▱
Maintenance	Conversa	▰▰▰▰▱
Architect	Arquitecto	Robert Trent Jones
Type	Tipo	forest, residential
Relief	Relevo	▰▰▱▱▱
Water in play	Lago	▰▱▱▱▱
Exp. to wind	Exposto ao vento	▰▰▰▱▱
Trees in play	Arvores	▰▰▰▰▱

Scorecard Cartão de resultados	Chp. Camp.	Mens Homens	Ladies Senhoras
Length Compriment	6014	5606	5081
Par	71	71	71

Advised golfing ability Nivel de jogo recomendado	0	12	24	36

Hcp required   Handicap exigido   no

CLUB HOUSE & AMENITIES
CLUB HOUSE E ANEXOS   7 /10

Pro shop	Pro-shop	▰▰▰▰▱
Driving range	Campo de prática	▰▰▰▰▱
Sheltered	coberto	no
On grass	om relva	yes
Putting-green	putting-green	yes
Pitching-green	pitching-green	no

HOTEL FACILITIES
INFRAESTRUCTURAS HOTELEIRAS   7 /10

HOTELS HOTELS
Estoril Sol - 298 rooms, D 27 000 Esc.   Cascais 3 km
Tel (351) 01 - 483 28 31, Fax (351) 01 - 483 22 80

Atlantic Gardens   Cascais
150 rooms, D 22 000 Esc.   8 km
Tel (351) 01 - 483 37 37, Fax (351) 01 - 483 52 26

Cidadela   Cascais
106 rooms, D 35 000 Esc.   9 km
Tel (351) 01 - 483 29 21, Fax (351) 01 - 486 72 26

Estalagem Senhora da Guia   Cascais
39 rooms, D 24 000 Esc.   3 km
Tel (351) 01 - 487 92 39, Fax (351) 01 - 486 92 27

RESTAURANTS RESTAURANTES
Fortaleza do Guincho   Cascais
Tel (351) 01 - 487 04 91   3 km

Porto de Santa Maria   Praia do Guincho
Tel (351) 01 - 487 02 40   3 km

1081

A despeito da qualidade dos outros grupos de 9 buracos, a combinaçao dos percursos B e C é a mais satis-fatória e a que foi mais utilizada nas grandes competições. O seu comprimento não deve assustar. E razoável a partir das saídas normais. A largura dos "fairways" e o equilibrio do comprimento dos buracos, torna o percurso acessível a todos os jogadores com alguma experiência. Para mais, anatureza arenosa do terreno permite não so an-dar com prazer, mas tambem fazer roalr muito a bola. Os obstáculos de àgua entram em jogo em alguns buracos mas a principal dificuldade são os pinheiros que sobresaiem de outros tipos de vegetação. Pelo seu equilibrio, este percurso permite um jogo confortável sem criar problemas inuteis aos golfistas em férias. A Quinta do Lago conquis-tou uma bela reputação, seria merecida se a manutenção fosse sempre impecável.

Despite the excellence of the two other 9-hole courses, the B & C combination is the most satisfying and the most widely used for top tournaments. The yardage is nothing to be afraid of and is reasonable from the normal tees. And the width of the fairways and nicely balanced length of holes make this a course playable by any golfer with some experience. What's more, the sandy sub-soil makes it a pleasure to walk and gives balls a lot of extra roll. Water hazards are in play only on a few holes, and the main difficulties are the pine-trees looming over the hea-ther, and the broom. A nicely balanced course for a relaxed round of golf, and one that doesn't create needless pro-blems for golfers on holiday. Quinta do Lago has acquired a great reputation, which would be deserved if upkeep were immaculate all the time.

Quinta do Lago Golf Club — 1974
P - 8135 ALMANCIL (Algarve)

Office	Secretariado	(351) 0289 - 390 700
Pro shop	Pro-shop	(351) 0289 - 390 700
Fax	Fax	(351) 0289 - 394 013
Situation	Localização	

Faro (pop. 33 664), 12 km

Annual closure	Fecho anual	no
Weekly closure	Fecho semanal	no

Fees main season
Tarifas de época alta 18 holes

	Week days Semana	We/Bank holidays Fim de sem./Feriad
Individual Individual	15 000 Esc	15 000 Esc
Couple Casal	30 000 Esc	30 000 Esc

Special fees for members of Portuguese golf clubs

Caddy	Caddy	no
Electric Trolley	Trolley eléctrico	no
Buggy	Buggy	7 500 Esc.
Clubs	Tacos	4 250 Esc.

Credit cards Cartão de crédito VISA - AMEX

1082

Access Acesso : N 125 Faro → Portimão,
Almancil → Quinta do Lago
Map 3 on page 1064 Mapa 3 Página 1064

GOLF COURSE / PERCURSO — 15/20

Site	Sitio	■■■■□
Maintenance	Conversa	■■■□□
Architect	Arquitecto	William Mitchell
Type	Tipo	forest, residential
Relief	Relevo	■□□□□
Water in play	Lago	■■□□□
Exp. to wind	Exposto ao vento	■■■□□
Trees in play	Arvores	■■■■□

Scorecard Cartão de resultados	Chp. Camp.	Mens Homens	Ladies Senhoras
Length Comprimento	6488	5870	5192
Par	72	72	72

Advised golfing ability	0	12	24	36
Nivel de jogo recomendado		■■■■		

Hcp required Handicap exigido 28 Men, 36 Ladies

CLUB HOUSE & AMENITIES / CLUB HOUSE E ANEXOS — 7/10

Pro shop	Pro-shop	■■■■□
Driving range	Campo de prática	■■■□□
Sheltered	coberto	no
On grass	om relva	no (25 mats)
Putting-green	putting-green	yes
Pitching-green	pitching-green	yes

HOTEL FACILITIES / INFRAESTRUCTURAS HOTELEIRAS — 8/10

HOTELS HOTELS
Quinta do Lago — Quinta do Lago
132 rooms, D 17 000 Esc. — 3 km
Tel (351) 089 - 39 66 66
Fax (351) 089 - 39 63 93

Dona Filipa — Vale do Lobo
147 rooms, D 31 500 Esc. — 6 km
Tel (351) 089 - 39 41 41
Fax (351) 089 - 39 42 88

RESTAURANTS RESTAURANTES
Casa Velha — Quinta do Lago
Tel (351) 089 - 39 49 83 — 3 km

São Gabriel — Almancil
Tel (351) 089 - 39 45 21 — 5 km

Sob o nome de Ria Formosa reuniram-se os percursos A e D da Quinta do Lago, desenhados por dois arquitectos diferentes, William Mitchell e Rocky Roquemore. Resulta num certo desequilibrio visual e golfístico, uma vez que as personalidades dos dois signatários é forçosamente diferente. Este "defeito" contribui, porem, para da muita variedade aos 18 buracos que são, pelo menos, identicos no ponto de vista da vegetação. A estrategia é bastante simples, os "greens" são desenhados com gosto, o desenho geral é bastante imaginativo com uma estética principalmente americana, principalmente pela integração de vários lagos, sobretudo aos primeiros 9 buracos. Em relação ao outro percurso do complexo é aínda mais adequado a todos os níveis de jogo, quer se trate de jogar para o seu próprio resultado ou numa competiçao. Se juntarmos a este vasto complexo o belo e mítico percurso do São Lourenço confirma-se a necessidade de uma visita.

The A & D courses of Quinta do Lago, collectively called Ria Formosa, were designed by two different architects, William Mitchell and Joseph Lee. The result is a slight feeling of visual and golfing imbalance created by two necessarily different personalities and styles. In fact, this "flaw" actually adds a lot of variety to the 18-hole layout, where the vegetation at least is the same. Game strategy is simple to see, the greens have been tastefully designed and the general layout is rather imaginative and mainly American in style with the presence of several lakes, especially on the front nine. Compared to the other course on the same site, the A & D combination is even better suited to all levels, whichever way you play. Add to this huge golf resort the fabulous neighbouring course of San Lorenzo, then a long visit is called for.

Quinta do Lago Golf Club — 1977
P - 8135 ALMANCIL (Algarve)

Office	Secretariado	(351) 0289 - 390 700
Pro shop	Pro-shop	(351) 0289 - 390 700
Fax	Fax	(351) 0289 - 394 013
Situation	Localização	

Faro (pop. 33 664), 12 km

Annual closure	Fecho anual	no
Weekly closure	Fecho semanal	no

Fees main season
Tarifas de época alta 18 holes

	Week days Semana	We/Bank holidays Fim de sem./Feriad
Individual Individual	15 000 Esc	15 000 Esc
Couple Casal	30 000 Esc	30 000 Esc

Special fees for members of Portuguese golf clubs

Caddy	Caddy	no
Electric Trolley	Trolley eléctrico	no
Buggy	Buggy	7 500 Esc.
Clubs	Tacos	4 250 Esc.

Credit cards Cartão de crédito VISA - AMEX

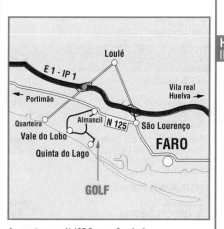

Loulé
E 1 - IP 1
Vila real
Huelva →
← Portimão
Quarteira Almancil N 125 São Lourenço
Vale do Lobo
Quinta do Lago **FARO**
GOLF

Access Acesso : N 125 Faro → Portimão,
Almancil → Quinta do Lago
Map 3 on page 1064 Mapa 3 Página 1064

GOLF COURSE PERCURSO — 15/20

Site	Sitio	
Maintenance	Conversa	
Architect	Arquitecto	William Mitchell Rocky Roquemore
Type	Tipo	forest, residential
Relief	Relevo	
Water in play	Lago	
Exp. to wind	Exposto ao vento	
Trees in play	Arvores	

Scorecard Cartão de resultados	Chp. Camp.	Mens Homens	Ladies Senhoras
Length Compriment	6205	5804	5031
Par	72	72	72

Advised golfing ability		0 12 24 36
Nivel de jogo recomendado		
Hcp required	Handicap exigido	28 Men, 36 Ladies

CLUB HOUSE & AMENITIES CLUB HOUSE E ANEXOS — 7/10

Pro shop	Pro-shop	
Driving range	Campo de prática	
Sheltered	coberto	no
On grass	om relva	no (25 mats)
Putting-green	putting-green	yes
Pitching-green	pitching-green	yes

HOTEL FACILITIES INFRAESTRUCTURAS HOTELEIRAS — 8/10

HOTELS HOTELS

Quinta do Lago
132 rooms, D 17 000 Esc.
Tel (351) 089 - 39 66 66
Fax (351) 089 - 39 63 93
Quinta do Lago
3 km

Dona Filipa
147 rooms, D 31 500 Esc.
Tel (351) 089 - 39 41 41
Fax (351) 089 - 39 42 88
Vale do Lobo
6 km

RESTAURANTS RESTAURANTES

Casa Velha
Tel (351) 089 - 39 49 83
Quinta do Lago
3 km

São Gabriel
Tel (351) 089 - 39 45 21
Almancil
5 km

1083

A visão de algumas realizações imobiliarias é largamente compensada pelos belas paisagens. Esta agradável impressão é confirmada pela qualidade do percurso, muito recente mas já em boa condição. Com aos excepções de 2 pares 3, compridos e bem protegidos por lagos, este desenho de Rocky Roquemore adapta-se muito bem a todo o tipo de jogadores se não escolherem as saídas mais longas. O sentimento dominante é o de um percurso bem equilibrado e de uma grande franquesa com os obstáculos bem visiveis. As dificuldades são bastante numerosas para evitar o aborrecimento sem no entanto se tornar opressivo, tendo "greens" bem desenhados. Construido no meio de um agradável pinhal, com um relêvo moderado está evidentemente destinado a dar prazer e os melhores jogadores tirarão dele o melhor partido a partir das saídas de trás. A qualidade das instalações de treino permitem que se passe uma agradável jornada.

The sight of several property development projects is compensated by some beautiful landscapes, and this pleasant impression is confirmed by the excellence of the course, a very recent layout but one that is already in good condition. With the exception of two par 3s, both long and tightly defended by water, this Rocky Roquemore design is well suited to players of all abilities if they avoid the back-tees. The overall feeling is one of a nicely balanced and candid course, where hazards are clearly there to be seen. Although evenly spaced to give golfers room to breathe, there are enough difficulties to keep you on your toes, and the greens are interesting. Laid out in a flattish and pleasant pine forest, this course is obviously designed for fun, and the better players will be better off playing from the back. The standard of practice facilities makes this a good day's golfing.

Club Quinta do Peru — 1994
Vila Nogueira de Azeirão
P - 2950 AZEIRÃO

Office	Secretariado	(351) 021 - 213 4320
Pro shop	Pro-shop	(351) 021 - 213 4320
Fax	Fax	(351) 021 - 210 6960
Situation	Localização	

Lisboa (pop. 662 782), 46 km
Setubal (pop. 89 106), 12 km

Annual closure	Fecho anual	no
Weekly closure	Fecho semanal	no

Fees main season
Tarifas de época alta 18 holes

	Week days Semana	We/Bank holidays Fim de sem./Feriad
Individual Individual	10 000 Esc	15 000 Esc
Couple Casal	20 000 Esc	30 000 Esc

Caddy	Caddy	no
Electric Trolley	Trolley eléctrico	2 000 Esc.
Buggy	Buggy	5 000 Esc.
Clubs	Tacos	3 000 Esc.

Credit cards Cartão de crédito VISA - AMEX

1084

Access Acesso : A2 Lisboa → Setubal,
N10 → Azeitão, Golf
Map 2 on page 1062 Mapa 2 Página 1062

GOLF COURSE
PERCURSO   **15**/20

Site	Sitio	
Maintenance	Conversa	
Architect	Arquitecto	Rocky Roquemore
Type	Tipo	forest, residential
Relief	Relevo	
Water in play	Lago	
Exp. to wind	Exposto ao vento	
Trees in play	Arvores	

Scorecard Cartão de resultados	Chp. Camp.	Mens Homens	Ladies Senhoras
Length Compriment	6074	5617	4486
Par	72	72	72

Advised golfing ability   0   12   24   36
Nivel de jogo recomendado
Hcp required   Handicap exigido   28 Men, 36 Ladies

CLUB HOUSE & AMENITIES
CLUB HOUSE E ANEXOS   **6**/10

Pro shop	Pro-shop	
Driving range	Campo de prática	
Sheltered	coberto	4 places
On grass	om relva	yes
Putting-green	putting-green	yes
Pitching-green	pitching-green	no

HOTEL FACILITIES
INFRAESTRUCTURAS HOTELEIRAS   **5**/10

HOTELS HOTELS

Bonfim	Setubal
100 rooms, D 13 500 Esc.	12 km
Tel (351) 01 - 53 41 11	
Fax (351) 01 - 53 48 58	
Estalagem Quinta das Torres	Azeitão
12 rooms, D 10 000 Esc.	9 km
Tel (351) 01 - 208 00 01	
Fax (351) 01 - 219 06 07	

RESTAURANTS RESTAURANTES

Quinta das Torres	Azeitão
Tel (351) 01 - 218 00 01	9 km
A Roda	Setubal
Tel (351) 065 - 292 64	12 km

E incontestávelmente o N° 1 de Portugal, pelo seu traçado pelo seu ambiente e pela sua manutenção. Num belo local rodeado de casas de grande qualidade, Joseph Lee demonstrou uma grande imaginação e uma preocupação de espectaculo visual e golfístico. Aqui é necessário não só utilizar todos os ferros do saco, mas tambem utilizá-los de forma diferente tão importante se torna a colocação das pancadas para se conseguir um bom resultado. Há um encontro de todas as dificuldades: arevores, "bunkers", lagos e largos braços da Ria Formosa. A tranquilidade e a beleza da paisagem incitam a dar o melhor de si próprio e a responder aos desafios técnicos postos pelo arquitecto. E certo que os jogadores inexperientes terão dificuldades, mas para aqueles que tem um handicap razoável será o culminar de uma viagem golfistica. Quanto aos jogadores de bom nível, terão aqui um máximo de prazer ao tentarem enfrentar este percurso.

This is unquestionably Portugal's top course for its design, setting and upkeep. Given a very beautiful site, dotted by some equally attractive villas, Joseph Lee employed heaps of imagination and considerable concern for golf as a visual spectacle. Here, you not only use every club in your bag, you also use clubs in different ways. That's how important positioning the ball can be for a good score. The course has every difficulty in the book: trees, fairway bunkers, lakes and a large arm of the Ria Formosa. The tranquillity and beauty of the landscape prompt the golfer to play above himself and meet the technical challenges laid down by the designer. Inexperienced players will have problems, sure, but with a decent handicap, a day spent here can be the perfect climax to a golfing holiday. The better players will have fun trying to tame a course such as this.

S. Lourenço Golf Club — 1988

Quinta do Lago
P - 8135 ALMANCIL

Office	Secretariado	(351) 0289 - 396 522
Pro shop	Pro-shop	(351) 0289 - 396 522
Fax	Fax	(351) 0289 - 396 908
Situation	Localização	

Faro (pop.33 664), 15 km

Annual closure	Fecho anual	no
Weekly closure	Fecho semanal	no

Fees main season
Tarifas de época alta 18 holes

	Week days Semana	We/Bank holidays Fim de sem./Feriad
Individual Individual	24 500 Esc	24 500 Esc
Couple Casal	49 000 Esc	49 000 Esc

Caddy	Caddy	no
Electric Trolley	Trolley eléctrico	yes
Buggy	Buggy	9 000 Esc.
Clubs	Tacos	5 000 Esc.

Credit cards Cartão de crédito VISA - AMEX

GOLF COURSE / PERCURSO — 18/20

Site	Sitio	
Maintenance	Conversa	
Architect	Arquitecto	Joseph Lee
Type	Tipo	seaside course, forest
Relief	Relevo	
Water in play	Lago	
Exp. to wind	Exposto ao vento	
Trees in play	Arvores	

Scorecard Cartão de resultados	Chp. Camp.	Mens Homens	Ladies Senhoras
Length Compriment	6238	5837	5171
Par	72	72	72

Advised golfing ability 0 12 24 36
Nivel de jogo recomendado
Hcp required Handicap exigido 28 Men, 36 Ladies

CLUB HOUSE & AMENITIES / CLUB HOUSE E ANEXOS — 6/10

Pro shop	Pro-shop	
Driving range	Campo de prática	
Sheltered	coberto	no
On grass	om relva	yes
Putting-green	putting-green	yes
Pitching-green	pitching-green	no

HOTEL FACILITIES / INFRAESTRUCTURAS HOTELEIRAS — 8/10

HOTELS HOTELS

Quinta do Lago — Quinta do Lago
132 rooms, D 17 000 Esc. — 2 km
Tel (351) 089 - 39 66 66
Fax (351) 089 - 39 63 93

Dona Filipa — Vale do Lobo
147 rooms, D 31 500 Esc. — 3 km
Tel (351) 089 - 39 41 41
Fax (351) 089 - 39 42 88

RESTAURANTS RESTAURANTES

Casa Velha — Quinta do Lago
Tel (351) 089 - 39 49 83 — 3 km

São Gabriel — Almancil
Tel (351) 089 - 39 45 21 — 5 km

Access Acesso : N125 Faro → Portimão,
Almancil → Quinta do Lago
Map 3 on page 1064 Mapa 3 Página 1064

1085

Aqueles que não gostam de àgua, arriscam-se a passar aqui um mau bocado, uma vez que está presente em jogo em todos os buracos mas é o prêço a pagar para ter uma paisagem marinha muito agradável e desnuda. O comprimento do percurso não é deshumano (tem de se utilizar muitas vezes ferros curtos) e os jogadores direitos estarão à vontade bem como aqueles que controlam bem a bola: a colocação das pancadas de saída é muito importante para se estar bem posicionado para atacar os "greens" bem defendidos. São bastante planos sem terem um desenho escepcional, sendo para alem disso fáceis de lêr. Como a maior parte dos percursos de Portugal este traçado de Pedro de Vasconcellos (revisto por Robert Muir Graves) é acessivel a todos os jogadores. Não podem esperar cumprir fácilmente os seus handicaps mas encontrarão multiplas ocasiões para se habituarem à presença da àgua, muitas vezes intimidatórias para os amadores.

Golfers who are allergic to water might have a tough time here, as just about every hole has its water hazard. This is the price you pay for a very pleasant and bare marine landscape. The course is very reasonable in length (the second shot is often a short iron) and straight-hitters and flighters of the ball will feel at home. Placing the tee-shot is more important than usual to get a better angle at the very well defended greens, which are rather flat, easy to read and pleasantly designed. Like the majority of courses in Portugal, this Pedro de Vasconcelos layout (restyled by Robert Muir Graves) is playable for golfers of all abilities. They won't find it easy to play to their handicap, but they will find numerous opportunities to get used to the sort of water hazard that often intimidates the average golfer.

Salgados Golf Club — 1995
Apartado 2266 - Vale do Rabelho
P - 8200 ALBUFEIRA

Office	Secretariado	(351) 089 - 591 111
Pro shop	Pro-shop	(351) 089 - 591 111
Fax	Fax	(351) 089 - 591 112
Situation	Localização	

Armação de Pêra (pop. 2 894), 8 km
Albufeira (pop. 4 324), 9 km

| Annual closure | Fecho anual | no |
| Weekly closure | Fecho semanal | no |

Fees main season
Tarifas de época alta 18 holes

	Week days Semana	We/Bank holidays Fim de sem./Feriad
Individual Individual	8 500 Esc	8 500 Esc
Couple Casal	17 000 Esc	17 000 Esc

Caddy	Caddy	no
Electric Trolley	Trolley eléctrico	2 000 Esc.
Buggy	Buggy	6 000 Esc.
Clubs	Tacos	3 000 Esc.

Credit cards Cartão de crédito VISA - AMEX

1086

Access Acesso : N125 Faro-Portimão, → Vale de Parra
Map 3 on page 1064 Mapa 3 Página 1064

GOLF COURSE
PERCURSO — 14 /20

Site	Sitio	
Maintenance	Conversa	
Architect	Arquitecto	Pedro Vasconcelos

Type	Tipo	seaside course
Relief	Relevo	
Water in play	Lago	
Exp. to wind	Exposto ao vento	
Trees in play	Arvores	

Scorecard Cartão de resultados	Chp. Camp.	Mens Homens	Ladies Senhoras
Length Compriment	6080	5640	5157
Par	72	72	72

Advised golfing ability Nivel de jogo recomendado	0	12	24	36
Hcp required	Handicap exigido 35			

CLUB HOUSE & AMENITIES
CLUB HOUSE E ANEXOS — 7 /10

Pro shop	Pro-shop	
Driving range	Campo de prática	
Sheltered	coberto	no
On grass	om relva	yes
Putting-green	putting-green	yes
Pitching-green	pitching-green	no

HOTEL FACILITIES
INFRAESTRUCTURAS HOTELEIRAS — 6 /10

HOTELS HOTELS
Almansor - 290 rooms, D 28 000 Esc.   Carvoeira 14 km
Tel (351) 082 - 35 80 26, Fax (351) 082 - 35 87 70

Alisios - 100 rooms, D 20 000 Esc.   Albufeira 18 km
Tel (351) 082 - 58 92 84, Fax (351) 082 - 58 92 88

Vila Galé Praia   Albufeira
40 rooms, D 24 000 Esc.   11 km
(351) 082 - 59 10 50, Fax (351) 082 - 59 14 36

Aparthotel Cristal   Carvoeira 14 km
117 rooms, D 24 000 Esc.
(351) 082 - 35 86 01, Fax (351) 082 - 35 86 48

RESTAURANTS RESTAURANTES
Centianes - Tel (351) 082 - 35 87 24   Carvoeira 19 km
Vila Joya - Tel (351) 082 - 59 17 95   Albufeira 3 km

Foi durante muito tempo o melhor percurso de Portugal. Mas uma manutenção muito irregular e mediocre, reduziram bastante o seu prestígio. É pena porque a inteligência estratégica de Robert Trent Jones foi magistral. Localizado numa peninsula à beira mar, êle interpretou a tradição dos "links" com a presença constante da areia bem como um envolvimento de pinheiros e plantas silvestres especificas da região. O percurso parece por vezes mais estreito do que é na realidade mas os obstáculos são bem visiveis e estão bem colocados, come por exemplo alguns "bunkers" profundos: defendem vigorosamente "greens" geralmente bastante pequenos e bem modelados. Troia é um grande desafio para os bons jogadores mas tambem é umteste apaixonante para os outros: é sempre muito instrutivo jogar num grande percurso de golf, num quadro atraente e natural.

For many year this was the best course in Portugal, but inadequate and inconsistent upkeep has considerably dulled its prestige. This is a pity, because the strategic intelligence deployed by designer Robert Trent Jones is brilliant. Over a seaboard peninsula, he has given his own interpretation of the links tradition with ubiquitous sand and a setting of maritime pines and wild plants, both typical of this region. The course often looks tighter than it actually is, but the hazards are clear to see and well located, particularly several deep bunkers. They provide stern defence for greens that are generally rather small and well-contoured. Troia is a great challenge for the better player and an exciting test for the rest. There is always something to learn from playing a great golf course in a natural and attractive setting.

Troia Golf — 1981
Complexo Turistico de Troia
P - 2900 SETUBAL

Office	Secretariado	(351) 065 - 494 112
Pro shop	Pro-shop	(351) 065 - 494 112
Fax	Fax	(351) 065 - 494 315
Situation	Localização	

Setubal (pop. 89 106 h), 2 km
Lisboa (pop. 662 782), 42 km

Annual closure	Fecho anual	no
Weekly closure	Fecho semanal	no

Fees main season
Tarifas de época alta full day

	Week days Semana	We/Bank holidays Fim de sem./Feriad
Individual Individual	6 000 Esc	12 000 Esc
Couple Casal	12 000 Esc	24 000 Esc

– 20 % for members of Portuguese golf clubs.

Caddy	Caddy	no
Electric Trolley	Trolley eléctrico	no
Buggy	Buggy	7 000 Esc.
Clubs	Tacos	3 500 Esc.

Credit cards Cartão de crédito
VISA - Eurocard - MasterCard - AMEX - DC

← LISBOA A 2
N 10 Setúbal
Azeitão
Tróia
RESERVA NATURAL DO ESTUARIO DO SADO
GOLF
BAIA DE SETÚBAL
Costa da Galé
0 2 4 km

Access Acesso : Lisboa → Setubal. Ferry-boat.
N 253-1 → Melides
Map 2 on page 1062 Mapa 2 Página 1062

GOLF COURSE / PERCURSO — 15/20

Site	Sitio	
Maintenance	Conversa	
Architect	Arquitecto	Robert Trent Jones
Type	Tipo	seaside course, links
Relief	Relevo	
Water in play	Lago	
Exp. to wind	Exposto ao vento	
Trees in play	Arvores	

Scorecard Cartão de resultados	Chp. Camp.	Mens Homens	Ladies Senhoras
Length Compriment	6337	5861	5426
Par	72	72	72

Advised golfing ability Nivel de jogo recomendado		0 12 24 36
Hcp required	Handicap exigido	no

CLUB HOUSE & AMENITIES / CLUB HOUSE E ANEXOS — 6/10

Pro shop	Pro-shop	
Driving range	Campo de prática	
Sheltered	coberto	no
On grass	om relva	yes
Putting-green	putting-green	yes
Pitching-green	pitching-green	yes

HOTEL FACILITIES / INFRAESTRUCTURAS HOTELEIRAS — 5/10

HOTELS HOTELS

Magnolia Mar		Troia
132 rooms, D 16 000 Esc.		2 km
(351) 065 - 4 42 21		
Fax (351) 065 - 4 41 62		

RESTAURANTS RESTAURANTES

Soltroia Beach Club	Troia 2 km
Mira Ponte	Troia 2 km

1087

VALE DA PINTA ✴ 14 | 6 | 6

Muito ondulado, mas não deixa de ser fácil para jogar a pé.. Este percurso foi desenhado pelo Americano Ronald Fream. Os que conhecem o seu estilo poderão julgar que ele aqui não foi tão exigente para os golfistas como em outros locais. Visivelmente manteve o espirito de que são sobretudo turistas de nível de jogo médio que visitam a região. Para mais, quis preservar a natureza do terreno e portanto não abusou dos obstáculos de água. Os "greens" são bastante profundos e requerem uma boa precisão nos "approaches" mas estão razoavelmente defendidos, o que acentua a impressão "amigável" do percurso. As saídas múltiplas permitem adaptá-lo a todos os níveis de jogo e a distrairse sem ter a sensação de ser um percurso fácil de mais. Os melhores jogadores ficam "aguados". Durante o passeio, poder-se-ão admirar belas oliveiras, algumas com mais de 700 anos; existe um exemplar que se calcula que tenha 1200 anos: se ele pudesse contar-nos a sua vida!

A little hilly but nonetheless easily walkable, this course was designed by Ronald Fream. Those of you who know his style might consider that he has been less demanding here than elsewhere, and visibly he bore in mind the fact that the region is visited primarily by mid-to-high handicappers on holiday. He also set out to preserve the natural look of the terrain and did not overdo the water hazards. The greens are rather deep and call for accurate approach shots, but they are reasonably defended, a fact that underlines the friendly feeling you get with this course. The many different tee-areas adapt the course easily to all players, who can enjoy themselves without feeling that the course is too easy, but the best might want more than this. In passing, a word of admiration for the beautiful olive-trees, some of which are over 700 years old. One is even 1200 years old: its life-story would make interesting reading!.

Vale da Pinta		1992
Quinta de Gramacho		
P - 8400 Lagoa		

Office	Secretariado	(351) 082 - 34 21 68
Pro shop	Pro-shop	(351) 082 - 34 21 68
Fax	Fax	(351) 082 - 34 21 89
Situation	Localização	

Carvoeiro, 13 km
Faro (pop. 33 664), 42 km

Annual closure	Fecho anual	no
Weekly closure	Fecho semanal	no

Fees main season
Tarifas de época alta 18 holes

	Week days Semana	We/Bank holidays Fim de sem./Feriad
Individual Individual	9 000 Esc.	9 000 Esc.
Couple Casal	18 000 Esc.	18 000 Esc.

Caddy	Caddy	no
Electric Trolley	Trolley eléctrico	2 500 Esc.
Buggy	Buggy	5 500 Esc.
Clubs	Tacos	2 500 Esc.

Credit cards Cartão de crédito VISA - AMEX - DC

1088

GOLF COURSE / PERCURSO — 14/20

Site	Sitio	
Maintenance	Conversa	
Architect	Arquitecto	Ronald Fream
Type	Tipo	inland, residential
Relief	Relevo	
Water in play	Lago	
Exp. to wind	Exposto ao vento	
Trees in play	Arvores	

Scorecard Cartão de resultados	Chp. Camp.	Mens Homens	Ladies Senhoras
Length Compriment	5861	5382	4528
Par	71	71	71

Advised golfing ability Nivel de jogo recomendado	0 12 24 36
Hcp required Handicap exigido	28 Men, 36 Ladies

CLUB HOUSE & AMENITIES / CLUB HOUSE E ANEXOS — 6/10

Pro shop	Pro-shop	
Driving range	Campo de prática	
Sheltered	coberto	6 places
On grass	om relva	yes
Putting-green	putting-green	yes
Pitching-green	pitching-green	yes

HOTEL FACILITIES / INFRAESTRUCTURAS HOTELEIRAS — 6/10

HOTELS HOTELS
Almansor - 290 rooms, D 28 000 Esc.   Carvoeira 3 km
Tel (351) 082 - 35 80 26, Fax (351) 082 - 35 87 70

Alisios - 100 rooms, D 20 000 Esc.   Albufeira 13 km
Tel (351) 082 - 58 92 84, Fax (351) 082 - 58 92 88

Vila Galé Praia   Albufeira
40 rooms, D 24 000 Esc.   13 km
Tel (351) 082 - 59 10 50, Fax (351) 082 - 59 14 36

Aparthotel Cristal   Carvoeira
117 rooms, D 24 000 Esc.   3 km
Tel (351) 082 - 35 86 01, Fax (351) 082 - 35 86 48

RESTAURANTS RESTAURANTES
Centianes - Tel (351) 082 - 35 87 24   Carvoeria 3 km
Vila Joya - Tel (351) 082 - 59 17 95   Albufeira 13 km

Access Acesso : N125 Lagos-Faro. Lagoa → Carvoeiro
Map 3 on page 1064 Mapa 3 Página 1064

Era um dos mais famosos percursos de Portugal, sobretudo devido a um dos seus buracos (agora é o 16) que se jogar por cima de uma serie de três falésias. Os restantes 26 buracos não estavam à mesma altura. Acrescentando-lhe 9 buracos novos e alguns melhoramentos, eis que surge o percurso «Royal», fruto do trabalho realizado com um intervalo de 30 anos entre Henry Cotton e Rocky Roquemore. Os restantes 18 buracos passaram a chamar-se «Ocean Course». No «Royal» nota-se que os estilos dos dois arquitectos se fundem harmoniosamente, numa espécie de cásamento entre a estética e os estilos de jogo americano e britânico. Há que felicitar Roquemore por ter evitado com inteligência as rupturas visuais brutais, embora cada buraco tenha a personalidade suficiente para ser memorizado. Vale do Lobo propõe-se agora um excelente teste de golf, acrescido do facto de ser um lindo percurso, arborizado por milhares de pinheiros, oliveiras, figueiras, larangeiras que invadem frequentemente a linha de jogo.

This used to be one of Portugal's most famous courses, especially for one of the holes here (now the 16th) played over three rows of cliffs. The other 26 holes unfortunately were not always up to standard. Today, with nine new holes and a little rejuvenation, here is the «Royal» course, the work of Henry Cotton and Rocky Roquemore with a 30 year interval in between. The other 18 holes are now the «Ocean» course. On the Royal, the styles of the two architects blend together perfectly, sort of dovetailing the visual appeal and styles of American and British courses. Roquemore must be congratulated for having cleverly avoided any clashes in overall visual harmony, even though each hole has enough personality to stick in the memory. Vale do Lobo now offers an excellent test of golf in addition to being a very pretty course covered with thousands of pine, olive, fig and orange trees which come into play. A must.

Vale do Lobo Golf Club — 1968
P - 8135 ALMANCIL

Office	Secretariado	(351) 089 - 393 939
Pro shop	Pro-shop	(351) 089 - 393 939
Fax	Fax	(351) 089 - 394 713
Situation	Localização	

Faro (pop. 33 664), 21 km

Annual closure	Fecho anual	no
Weekly closure	Fecho semanal	no

Fees main season
Tarifas de época alta 18 holes

	Week days Semana	We/Bank holidays Fim de sem./Feriad
Individual Individual	18 000 Esc.	18 000 Esc.
Couple Casal	36 000 Esc.	36 000 Esc.

Caddy	Caddy	no
Electric Trolley	Trolley eléctrico	no
Buggy	Buggy	7 000 Esc.
Clubs	Tacos	6 000 Esc.

Credit cards Cartão de crédito
VISA - Eurocard - AMEX - DC

Access Acesso : Faro, Road 125 → Albufeira.
Turn in Amancil and follow signs to Vale do Lobo.
Map 3 on page 1064 Mapa 3 Página 1064

GOLF COURSE / PERCURSO — 15/20

Site	Sitio	
Maintenance	Conversa	
Architect	Arquitecto	Henry Cotton Rocky Roquemore
Type	Tipo	seaside course, forest
Relief	Relevo	
Water in play	Lago	
Exp. to wind	Exposto ao vento	
Trees in play	Arvores	

Scorecard Cartão de resultados	Chp. Camp.	Mens Homens	Ladies Senhoras
Length Compriment	6050	5650	4925
Par	72	72	72

Advised golfing ability — 0 12 24 36
Nivel de jogo recomendado
Hcp required — Handicap exigido — 28 Men/36 Ladies

CLUB HOUSE & AMENITIES / CLUB HOUSE E ANEXOS — 6/10

Pro shop	Pro-shop	
Driving range	Campo de prática	
Sheltered	coberto	6 mats
On grass	om relva	yes
Putting-green	putting-green	yes
Pitching-green	pitching-green	yes

HOTEL FACILITIES / INFRAESTRUCTURAS HOTELEIRAS — 7/10

HOTELS HOTELS
Dona Filipa — Vale do Lobo
147 rooms, D 31 500 Esc. — 100 m
Tel (351) 089 - 39 41 41
Fax (351) 089 - 39 42 88

Quinta do Lago — Quinta do Lago
132 rooms, D 17 000 Esc. — 3 km
Tel (351) 089 - 39 66 66
Fax (351) 089 - 39 63 93

RESTAURANTS RESTAURANTES
Ermitage — Almancil
Tel (351) 089 - 394 329 — 4 km

O Tradicional — Almancil
Tel (351) 089 - 399 093 — 6 km

1089

Criado em 1991 numa zona de pinhal com alguns sobreiros bem como algumas figueiras a amendoeiras. Vila Sol foi desenhada po Donald Steel que não procurou em renegar o seu espírito britânico. Renunciou a quaisquer movimentos de terra espectaculares, conservando o lado natural do terreno. Pode lastimar-se que não tenha um traçado mais original, mas não dixa de ser um percurso bem adaptado a uma grande variedade de jogadores embora os primeiros buracos sejam um pouco difíceis para amadores. Podem tranquilizar-se, o seguimento é mas tranquilo. Bastante estreito, o percurso pode causar problemas aos jogadores imprecisos. Deverão jogar com cuidado para evitar as árvores e salvar o seu par. Com excepção do "green" do 11, os outros são bastante visíveis pouco defendidos, planos a de dimensão média. Com muito boa manutenção este percurso não é uma obra prima, mas merece o desvio.

Created in 1991 over an estate of pine, cork-oak, fig and almond trees, Vila Sol was laid out by Donald Steel, who worked in a distinctly British style. Preferring to keep the terrain's natural look, there was no spectacular earth-moving. This is an arguable point, as we would have liked a more personal layout. As it is, the course is very honest and playable by all golfers, even though the first holes are a tough test for the average hacker. They can relax, though, because the course tends to ease off later on. This is a rather tight course which can cause problems to wayward hitters. Getting out of the trees to save par requires some well-flighted recovery shots. With the exception of the 11th hole, all the greens are visible, relatively undefended, rather flat and medium-sized. A well upkept course, hardly a masterpiece but well worth the trip.

Golf de Vila Sol		1991
Alto do Semino. Est. Nacional 396, km 24,8		
P - 8125 QUARTEIRA		
Office	Secretariado	(351) 0289 - 300 505
Pro shop	Pro-shop	(351) 0289 - 300 505
Fax	Fax	(351) 0289 - 300 592
Situation	Localização	
Quarteira (pop.8 905), 3 km		
Faro (pop. 33 664), 18 km		
Annual closure	Fecho anual	no
Weekly closure	Fecho semanal	no

Fees main season
Tarifas de época alta 18 holes

	Week days Semana	We/Bank holidays Fim de sem./Feriad
Individual Individual	14 250 Esc.	14 250 Esc.
Couple Casal	28 500 Esc.	28 500 Esc.
– 50 % for members of Portuguese golf clubs		
Caddy	Caddy	no
Electric Trolley	Trolley eléctrico	2 000 Esc.
Buggy	Buggy	8 000 Esc.
Clubs	Tacos	4 000 Esc.

Credit cards Cartão de crédito VISA - AMEX

1090

Access Acesso : N1, N125 → Faro, N 396 → Quarteira
Map 3 on page 1064 Mapa 3 Página 1064

GOLF COURSE / PERCURSO — 14/20

Site	Sitio	▰▰▰
Maintenance	Conversa	▰▰▰
Architect	Arquitecto	Donald Steel
Type	Tipo	forest, residential
Relief	Relevo	▰▰
Water in play	Lago	▰
Exp. to wind	Exposto ao vento	▰▰▰
Trees in play	Arvores	▰▰▰▰

Scorecard Cartão de resultados	Chp. Camp.	Mens Homens	Ladies Senhoras
Length Compriment	6189	5880	5338
Par	72	72	72

Advised golfing ability	0	12	24	36
Nível de jogo recomendado	▰▰▰▰▰			
Hcp required	Handicap exigido	28 Men, 36 Ladies		

CLUB HOUSE & AMENITIES / CLUB HOUSE E ANEXOS — 7/10

Pro shop	Pro-shop	▰▰▰
Driving range	Campo de prática	▰▰▰
Sheltered	coberto	no
On grass	om relva	yes
Putting-green	putting-green	yes
Pitching-green	pitching-green	yes

HOTEL FACILITIES / INFRAESTRUCTURAS HOTELEIRAS — 7/10

HOTELS HOTELS
Marinotel — Vilamoura
364 rooms, D 50 000 Esc. — 3 km
Tel (351) 89 - 38 99 88, Fax (351) 89 - 38 98 69

Atlantis — Vilamoura
302 rooms, D 40 000 Esc. — 4 km
Tel (351) 089 - 38 99 77, Fax (351) 089 - 38 99 62

Ampalius — Vilamoura
357 rooms, D 33 500 Esc. — 4 km
Tel (351) 089 - 38 09 10, Fax (351) 089 - 38 09 11

RESTAURANTS RESTAURANTES
Al Garb (Atlantis) — Vilamoura
Tel (351) 089 - 38 99 77 — 4 km

Gril Sirius — Vilamoura
Tel (351) 089 - 38 99 88 — 3 km

VILAMOURA I (OLD COURSE) ✳ ♪ | 16 | 7 | 7 |

Construídos entre 1973 e 1990, o complexo de três percursos de Vilamoura foi-se pouco a pouco modernizando. O primeiro, Vilamoura I, continua a ser o mais interessante e a sua renovação, em particular, dos greens, acrescenta ao prazer da sua reabertura. O arquitecto Frank Pennink soube preservar a naturalidade de uma paisagem magnífica, servida de uma bela vegetação. O seu percurso lembra muitas vezes a arquitectura dos golfes britânicos de interior, com a vantagem do clima. Embora tenha um par 73, é suficientemente longo para perturbar os jogadores imprecisos, pois as arvores estão muito em jogo. Os pares 3 também não são fáceis. E um persurso para técnicistas, expertos na arte de trabalhar a bola, mas os cinco pares 5 podem salvar os resultados de outro modo ameaçados. Um excelente test bem rejuvenescido.

Built between 1973 and 1990, the three-course complex at Vilamoura has gradually been modernised. The oldest, Vilamoura 1, is still the most interesting and its restyling, especially the greens, has made its re-opening all the more enjoyable. Designer Frank Pennink has successfully preserved the natural look of magnificent landscape and vegetation. The layout is often reminiscent of some of the great British parkland courses, with the climate as an added benefit. Although a par 73, it is long enough to upset wayward hitters as the trees are very much in play. The par 3s are no walk-over, either, making this a course for the technically-minded golfer who excels in working the ball. But rest assured, the par 5s can save a card that the other holes might have condemned to the litter-bin. An excellent test of golf, now looking wonderfully younger.

VILAMOURA GOLF CLUB — 1969
P - 8125 VILAMOURA

Office	Secretariado	(351) 0289 - 310 166
Pro shop	Pro-shop	(351) 0289 - 301 166
Fax	Fax	(351) 0289 - 380 726
Situation	Localização	

Quarteira (pop. 8 905), 3 km
Faro, (pop. 33 664), 20 km

Annual closure	Fecho anual	no
Weekly closure	Fecho semanal	no

Fees main season
Tarifas de época alta 18 holes

	Week days Semana	We/Bank holidays Fim de sem./Feriad
Individual Individual	18 000 Esc.	18 000 Esc.
Couple Casal	36 000 Esc.	36 000 Esc.

Caddy	Caddy	no
Electric Trolley	Trolley eléctrico	2 000 Esc.
Buggy	Buggy	6 000 Esc.
Clubs	Tacos	4 000 Esc.

Credit cards Cartão de crédito VISA - AMEX

← Portimão

Loulé

E 1 - IP 1

Villamoura

FARO

N 396   N 125

GOLF   Quarteira

Quinta do Lago

0   2   4 km

Access Acesso : N125 Lagos-Faro. → Vilamoura
Map 3 on page 1064 Mapa 3 Página 1064

GOLF COURSE — PERCURSO — 16/20

Site	Sitio	▰▰▰▰▱
Maintenance	Conversa	▰▰▰▰▱
Architect	Arquitecto	Frank Pennink
Type	Tipo	forest
Relief	Relevo	▰▱▱▱▱
Water in play	Lago	▰▱▱▱▱
Exp. to wind	Exposto ao vento	▰▰▱▱▱
Trees in play	Arvores	▰▰▰▰▱

Scorecard Cartão de resultados	Chp. Camp.	Mens Homens	Ladies Senhoras
Length Compriment	6254	5988	5789
Par	73	73	73

Advised golfing ability		0 12 24 36
Nivel de jogo recomendado		▰▰▰▱
Hcp required	Handicap exigido	28 Men, 36 Ladies

CLUB HOUSE & AMENITIES — CLUB HOUSE E ANEXOS — 7/10

Pro shop	Pro-shop	▰▰▰▰▱
Driving range	Campo de prática	▰▰▰▰▱
Sheltered	coberto	3 bays
On grass	om relva	yes
Putting-green	putting-green	yes
Pitching-green	pitching-green	yes

HOTEL FACILITIES — INFRAESTRUCTURAS HOTELEIRAS — 7/10

HOTELS HOTELS

Marinotel — Vilamoura
364 rooms, D 50 000 Esc. — 3 km
Tel (351) 89 - 38 99 88, Fax (351) 89 - 38 98 69

Atlantis — Vilamoura
302 rooms, D 40 000 Esc. — 4 km
Tel (351) 089 - 38 99 77, Fax (351) 089 - 38 99 62

Ampalius — Vilamoura
357 rooms, D 33 500 Esc. — 4 km
Tel (351) 089 - 38 09 10, Fax (351) 089 - 38 09 11

RESTAURANTS RESTAURANTES

Al Garb (Atlantis) — Vilamoura
Tel (351) 089 - 38 99 77 — 4 km

Gril Sirius — Vilamoura
Tel (351) 089 - 38 99 88 — 3 km

1091

VILAMOURA II (PINHAL) ✹ ⟩ | 13 | 7 | 7

O complexo de Vilamoura, apresenta percursos de interesse diferente, mas é um local muito aprazível para uma estadia, numa região onde a religião dos numeroses visitantes é o culto di Golf. Vilamoura II foi desenhada num vasto pinhal, o que impõe uma grande precisão aos jogadores, para mais sendo os "greens" bastante pequenos e sem grande modulação. Desenhado de inicio por Frank Pennink, foi parcialmente modificado por Robert Trent Jones, o que lhe da um certo toque "Americano", no estilo tradicional do arquitecto, nomeadamente quanto aos obstáculos de água do 5 e do 8. Para os que têm distância, o 17 oferece uma boa oportunidade de correr um risco, cortando o "dog-leg" para tentar chegar ao green em 2 pancadas. Agradável para percorrer, com algumas vistas sobre o Atlántico. Oferece algumas boas sombras, mas as arvores são essencialmente obstáculos, uma vez que os bunkers estão raramente em jogo.

The Vilamoura resort offers courses with differing appeal, but is without a doubt a very pleasant holiday venue in a region where many visitors religiously come along to worship the gods of golf. Vilamoura II was laid out in a huge pine forest, which calls for some precision play compounded by some smallish and uncontoured greens. Getting there is the main problem. Originally designed by Franck Pennink, it has been partly restyled by Robert Trent Jones, who gave the course some American touches along the way in his traditional manner. These include the only water hazards on the 5th and 8th holes. The 17th offers big-hitters an interesting opportunity to risk cutting corners around a dog-leg to hit the green in two. This is a pleasant course to play, with a few viewpoints over the Atlantic, and some welcome shade in summer. But once again, the trees are the main hazard, with bunkers seldom coming into play.

VILAMOURA GOLF CLUB — 1976
P - 8125 VILAMOURA

Office	Secretariado	(351) 0289 - 310 166
Pro shop	Pro-shop	(351) 0289 - 301 166
Fax	Fax	(351) 0289 - 380 726
Situation	Localização	

Quarteira (pop. 8 905), 3 km
Faro, (pop. 33 664), 20 km

Annual closure	Fecho anual	no
Weekly closure	Fecho semanal	no

Fees main season
Tarifas de época alta 18 holes

	Week days Semana	We/Bank holidays Fim de sem./Feriad
Individual Individual	11 500 Esc.	11 500 Esc.
Couple Casal	23 000 Esc.	23 000 Esc.

Caddy	Caddy	no
Electric Trolley	Trolley eléctrico	2 000 Esc.
Buggy	Buggy	6 000 Esc.
Clubs	Tacos	4 000 Esc.

Credit cards Cartão de crédito VISA - AMEX

◄— Portimão
Loulé
E 1 - IP 1
Villamoura
FARO
N 396
N 125
GOLF Quarteira
Quinta do Lago
0   2   4 km

Access Acesso : N125 Lagos-Faro. → Vilamoura
Map 3 on page 1064 Mapa 3 Página 1064

GOLF COURSE / PERCURSO — 13/20

Site	Sitio	▰▰▰▱▱
Maintenance	Conversa	▰▰▰▰▱
Architect	Arquitecto	Frank Pennink
Type	Tipo	forest
Relief	Relevo	▰▱▱▱▱
Water in play	Lago	▰▰▱▱▱
Exp. to wind	Exposto ao vento	▰▰▱▱▱
Trees in play	Arvores	▰▰▰▰▱

Scorecard Cartão de resultados	Chp. Camp.	Mens Homens	Ladies Senhoras
Length Compriment	6300	5880	5212
Par	72	72	72

Advised golfing ability	0	12	24	36
Nivel de jogo recomendado	▰▰▰▰▰			

Hcp required   Handicap exigido 28 Men, 36 Ladies

CLUB HOUSE & AMENITIES / CLUB HOUSE E ANEXOS — 7/10

Pro shop	Pro-shop	▰▰▰▱▱
Driving range	Campo de prática	▰▰▱▱▱
Sheltered	coberto	3 bays
On grass	om relva	yes
Putting-green	putting-green	yes
Pitching-green	pitching-green	yes

HOTEL FACILITIES / INFRAESTRUCTURAS HOTELEIRAS — 7/10

HOTELS HOTELS

Marinotel — Vilamoura 3 km
364 rooms, D 50 000 Esc.
Tel (351) 89 - 38 99 88, Fax (351) 89 - 38 98 69

Atlantis — Vilamoura 4 km
302 rooms, D 40 000 Esc.
Tel (351) 089 - 38 99 77, Fax (351) 089 - 38 99 62

Ampalius — Vilamoura 4 km
357 rooms, D 33 500 Esc.
Tel (351) 089 - 38 09 10, Fax (351) 089 - 38 09 11

RESTAURANTS RESTAURANTES

Al Garb (Atlantis) — Vilamoura 4 km
Tel (351) 089 - 38 99 77

Gril Sirius — Vilamoura 3 km
Tel (351) 089 - 38 99 88

VILAMOURA III (LAGUNA) ✴ ♩ | 14 | 7 | 7

Em comparação com Vilamoura II, este percurso tem uma estética e uma paisagem muito diferente. De facto, é constituido por 3 grupos de 9 buracos que se combinam (Pinhal, Lago, Marina) próximo do mar. O desenho é do arquitecto Joseph Lee (e Rocky Roquemore) um dos grandes representantes da "Escola da Florida", come se nota sobretudo nos percursos Lago e Marina que são, alias, os mais interessantes. Como o seu nome indica a água está muito presente: em cerca de metade dos buracos. Mas o aspecto natural do terreno foi mantido. Os jogadores com distância podem exprimir-se ai melhor do que nos outros percursos do complexo, visto terem "fairways" mais largos e o arvoredo ser menos ameaçador, mesmo que visualmente seja mais intimidador do que o é na realidade. Vilamoura III é, apesar de tudo, mais difícil para fazer resultado: é o mais divertido para "match-play". Os greens têm um desenho interessante mas há que cuidar da manutenção, aliás como no resto do complexo que é uma verdadeira fábrica de golfe.

In a different style and landscape as the two others, this course consists in fact of three combinable 9-holers (Pinhal, Lago and Marina), close to the Atlantic. It was designed by Joseph Lee (and Rocky Roquemore), one of the great representatives of the Florida school, as is clear to see on the "Lago" and "Marina" course, the most interesting of the three, as it happens. As their name suggests, water is in great supply on about half the holes, but the terrain's natural look has been preserved. Big-hitters can hit more freely than on the other courses in this resort, as the fairways are wider and the trees less threatening. Even though it looks more intimidating than it plays, making a good score can be hard going, so match-play is often more fun. The greens are interestingly designed, but upkeep needs watching here and throughout the resort, where golf is non-stop production-business.

VILAMOURA GOLF CLUB — 1990
P - 8125 VILAMOURA

Office	Secretariado	(351) 0289 - 310 166
Pro shop	Pro-shop	(351) 0289 - 301 166
Fax	Fax	(351) 0289 - 380 726
Situation	Localização	

Quarteira (pop. 8 905), 3 km
Faro, (pop. 33 664), 20 km

Annual closure	Fecho anual	no
Weekly closure	Fecho semanal	no

Fees main season
Tarifas de época alta 18 holes

	Week days Semana	We/Bank holidays Fim de sem./Feriad
Individual Individual	10 000 Esc.	10 000 Esc.
Couple Casal	20 000 Esc.	20 000 Esc.

Caddy	Caddy	no
Electric Trolley	Trolley eléctrico	2 000 Esc.
Buggy	Buggy	6 000 Esc.
Clubs	Tacos	4 000 Esc.

Credit cards Cartão de crédito VISA - AMEX

← Portimão
Loulé
E 1 - IP 1
Villamoura
FARO
N 396
N 125
GOLF
Quarteira
Quinta do Lago
0   2   4 km

Access Acesso : N125 Lagos-Faro. → Vilamoura
Map 3 on page 1064 Mapa 3 Página 1064

GOLF COURSE / PERCURSO — 14/20

Site	Sitio	
Maintenance	Conversa	
Architect	Arquitecto	Joseph Lee
		Rocky Roquemore
Type	Tipo	open country
Relief	Relevo	
Water in play	Lago	
Exp. to wind	Exposto ao vento	
Trees in play	Arvores	

Scorecard Cartão de resultados	Chp. Camp.	Mens Homens	Ladies Senhoras
Length Compriment	6130	5760	4900
Par	72	72	72

Advised golfing ability 0   12   24   36
Nivel de jogo recomendado
Hcp required Handicap exigido 28 Men, 36 Ladies

CLUB HOUSE & AMENITIES / CLUB HOUSE E ANEXOS — 7/10

Pro shop	Pro-shop	
Driving range	Campo de prática	
Sheltered	coberto	3 bays
On grass	om relva	yes
Putting-green	putting-green	yes
Pitching-green	pitching-green	yes

HOTEL FACILITIES / INFRAESTRUCTURAS HOTELEIRAS — 7/10

HOTELS HOTELS
Marinotel — Vilamoura
364 rooms, D 50 000 Esc. — 3 km
Tel (351) 89 - 38 99 88, Fax (351) 89 - 38 98 69

Atlantis — Vilamoura
302 rooms, D 40 000 Esc. — 4 km
Tel (351) 089 - 38 99 77, Fax (351) 089 - 38 99 62

Ampalius — Vilamoura
357 rooms, D 33 500 Esc. — 4 km
Tel (351) 089 - 38 09 10, Fax (351) 089 - 38 09 11

RESTAURANTS RESTAURANTES

Al Garb (Atlantis) — Vilamoura
Tel (351) 089 - 38 99 77 — 4 km

Gril Sirius — Vilamoura
Tel (351) 089 - 38 99 88 — 3 km

1093

Mi vecino dice que no le gusta

¿Conoces la fábula del zorro y las uvas?

Cuando le solté la frase, con una media sonrisa, me miró en silencio. Después empezó un discurso sobre el materialismo, la superficialidad, el rodearse de cosas innecesarias... Realmente, estuvo a punto de convencerme. Volví a casa sintiéndome un poco culpable. Más tarde, a eso de las 9 me asomé a la terraza. En la calle todo estaba tranquilo. Miré el coche y recordé las palabras de mi vecino. Una pequeña nube ensombreció mi orgullo de flamante propietario.

Entonces, lo vi. Estaba en la terraza. Como Apoyado en la barandilla. Como yo. Contemplar mi coche. Como yo. La nube desapareció.

Peugeot. Para disfrutar del automóv

406 Coupé

PEUG

Espana

The Millennium Guide

España cuenta con unos 130.000 golfistas aproximadamente, 130 recorridos de 18 hoyos y más de 60 de 9 hoyos. Sin embargo el golf, a pesar de los numerosos campeones nacionales, no es un deporte muy popular en el país. La situación geográfica y su clima han favorecido las inversiones en el turismo desde hace mucho tiempo con un éxito evidente, sobre todo en los meses de invierno. Y el golf es un elemento de primera categoría en el desarrollo turístico : en los campos de golf de las costas orientales y meridionales se oye hablar en todos los idiomas del norte de Europa. El clima es un factor primordial de este éxito, y no hay que pensar que los meses más fríos sean los únicos aconsejables para hacer turismo o jugar al golf cómodamente.

Por regla general los socios de los clubs gozan de prioridad y el precio de los green-fees son a veces disuasivos por su alto precio. Excepto en los recorridos verdaderamente comerciales, es aconsejable presentarse con una carta de recomendación de su proprio club y un certificado con el handicap.

There are around 130,000 registered golfers in Spain playing more than 130 eighteen-hole courses and over 60 nine-hole layouts. Yet despite the prestige that comes from having a number of international stars, golf is still not a particularly popular sport in Spain. By contrast, the country's geographic location and climate have led to already long-standing investment in tourism with patent success, particularly during the winter months. Golf today represents a blue-chip argument in favour of this development. On the fairways lining the eastern and southern coasts of Spain, you can hear just about every language from Northern Europe. The country's climate has, of course, played a key role in this success, but don't for a minute think that the cooler months are the only time for an agreeable visit to Spain or even for a golfing holiday.

As a general rule, club members have full priority and green fees are high enough to be prohibitive. Excepting the truly commercial courses, it is preferable to carry a letter of introduction from your own club and proof of handicap.

1095

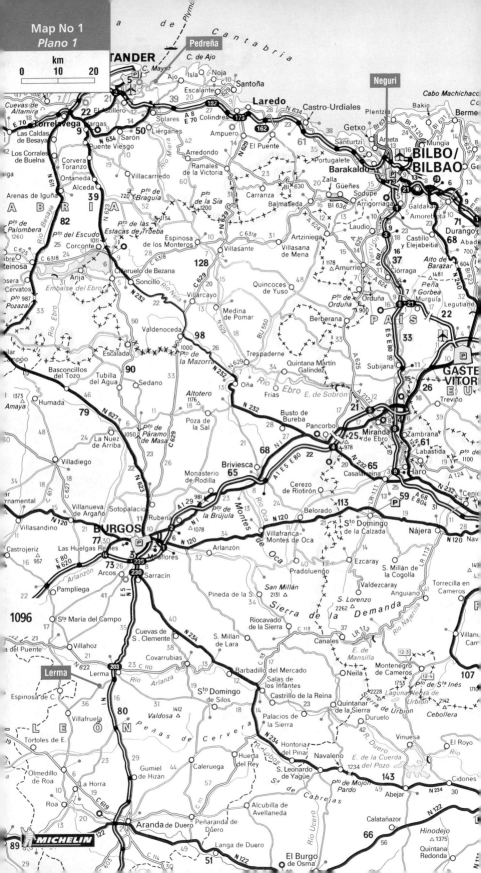

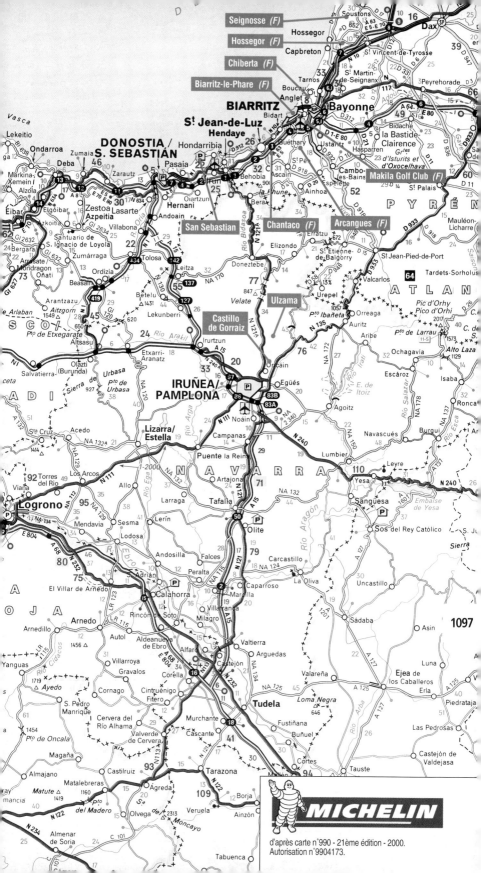

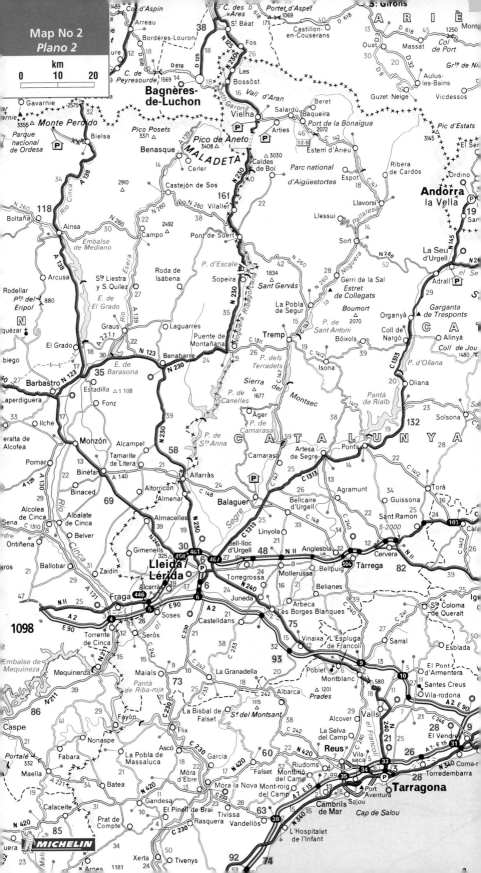

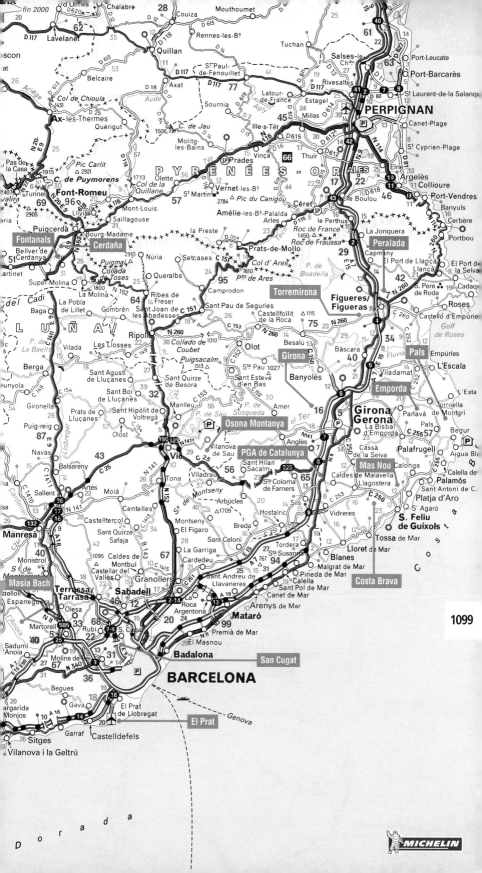

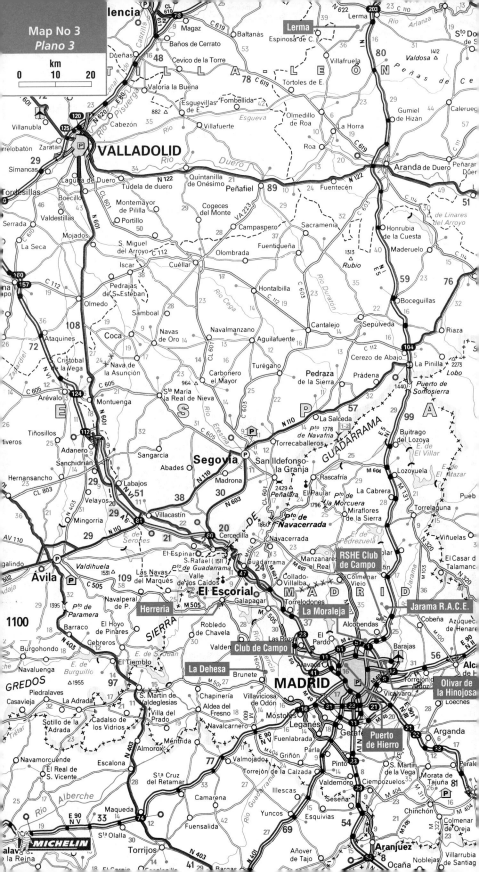

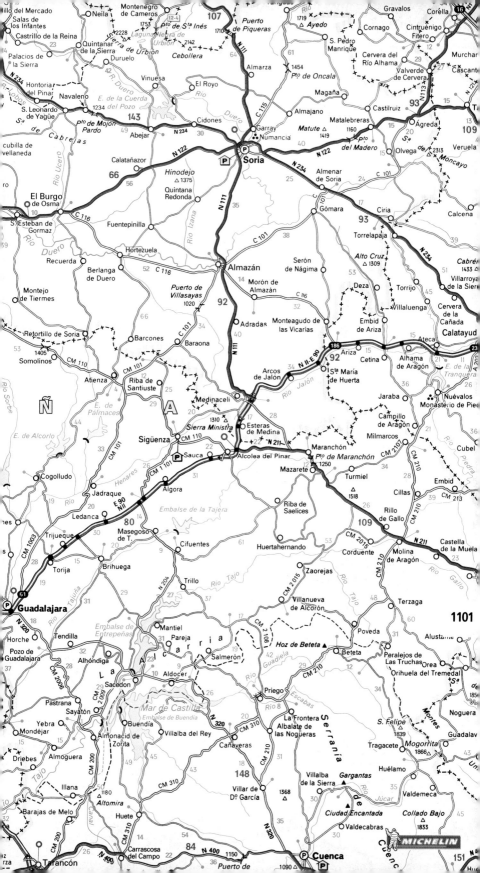

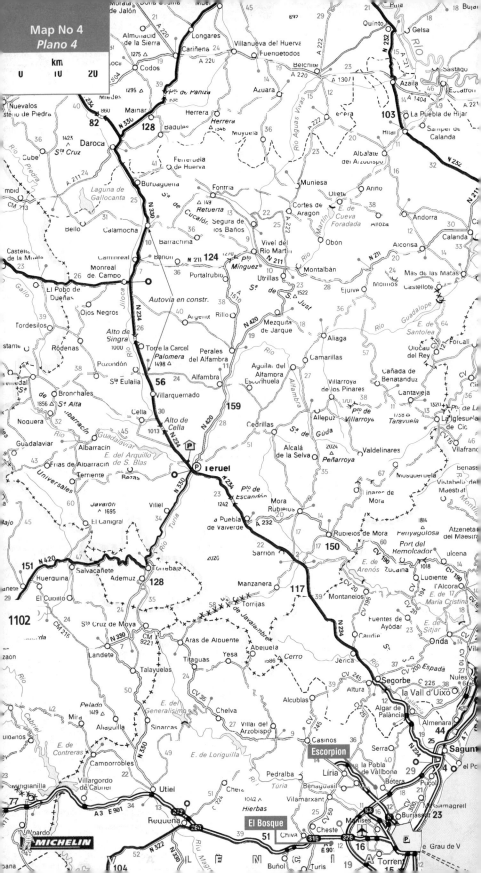

1103

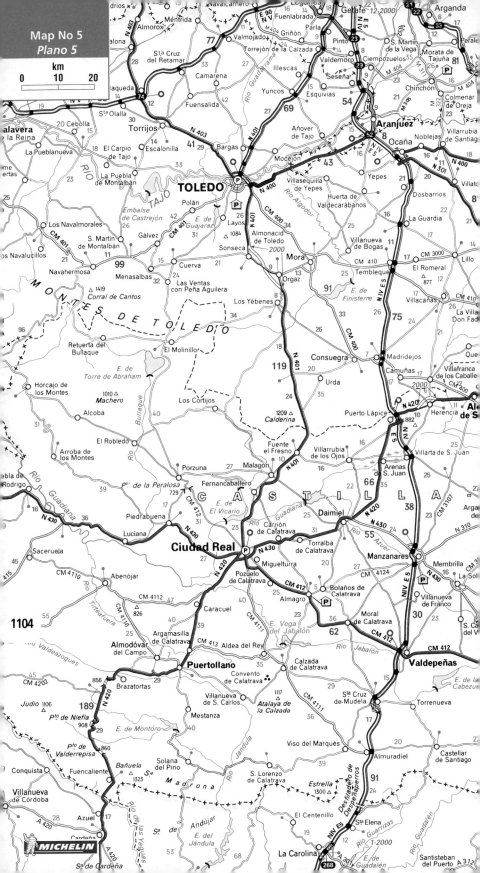

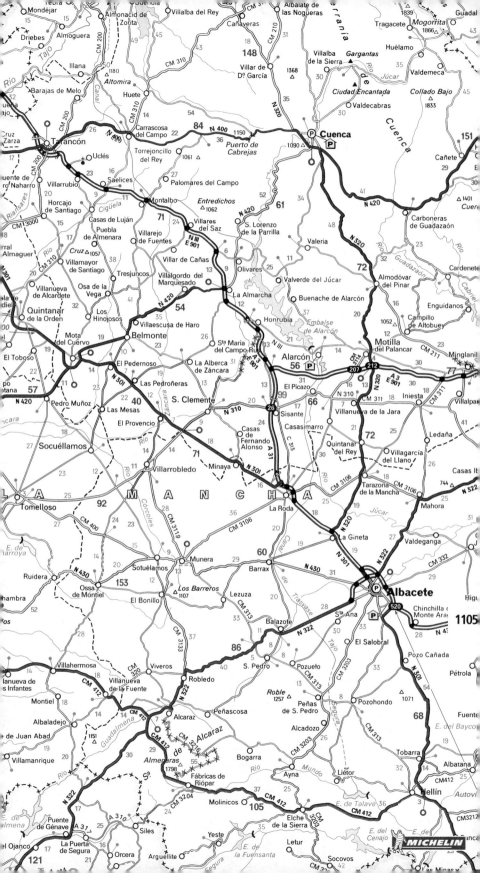

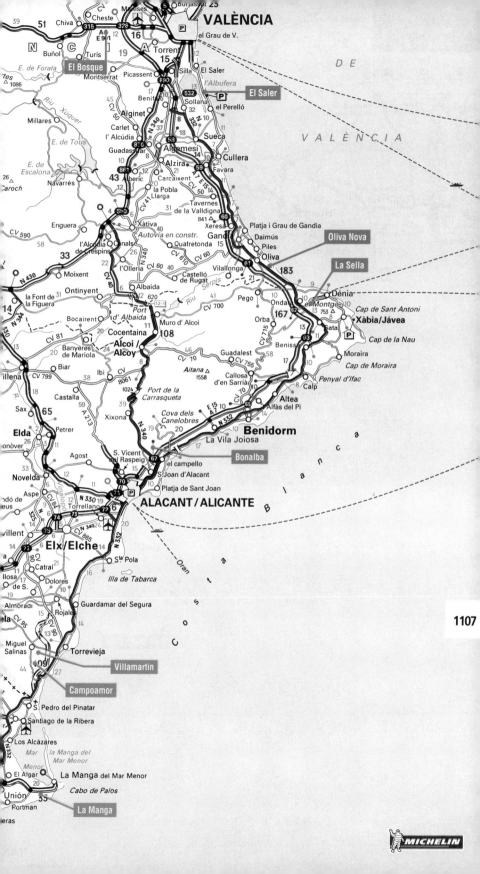

km
0   10   20

106

1108

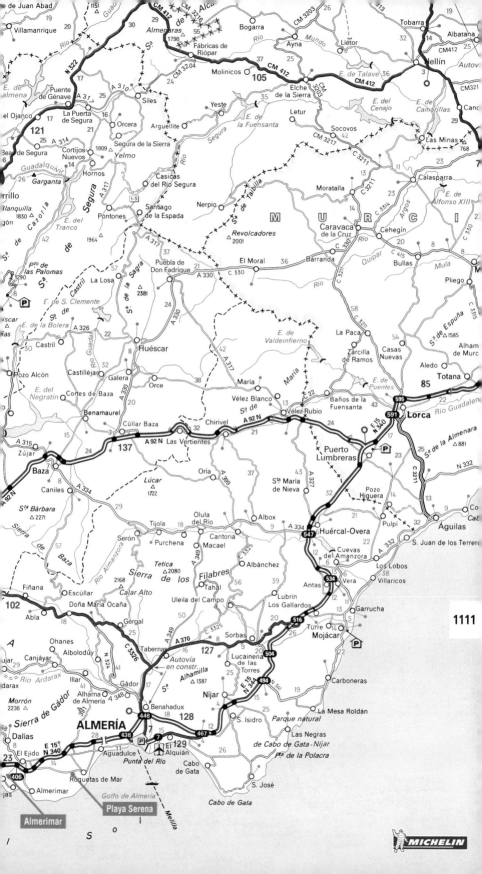

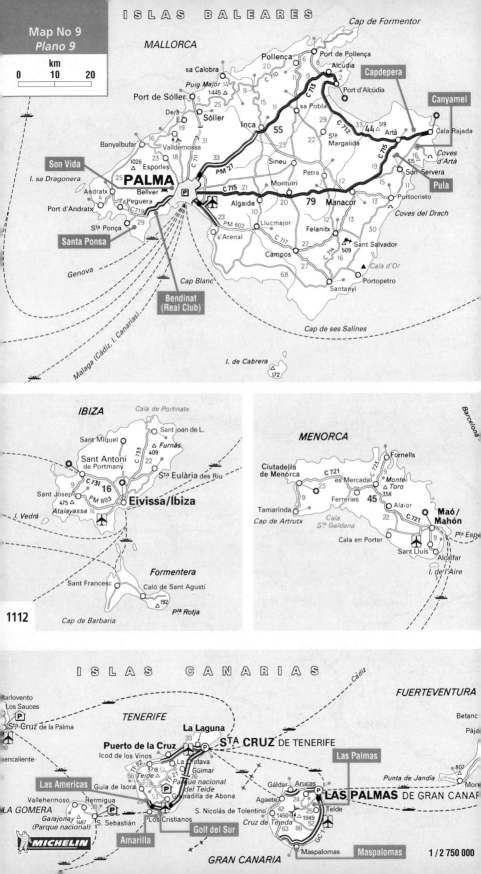

CLASIFICACION DE LOS RECORRIDOS
CLASSIFICATION OF COURSES

Esta clasificación da prioridad a la nota atribuida al recorrido.
This classification gives priority consideration
to the score awarded to the actual course.

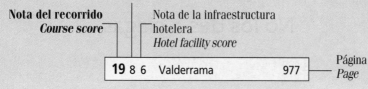

Nota del club-house y anejos
Club-house and facilities

Nota del recorrido
Course score

Nota de la infraestructura
hotelera
Hotel facility score

| **19** 8 6 | Valderrama | 977 |

Página
Page

Nota	Recorrido	Página		Nota	Recorrido	Página
19 8 6	Valderrama	1213		**16** 7 6	Pals	1192
18 7 6	El Saler	1144		**16** 6 5	Peralada	1195
18 6 5	Fontanals	1148		**16** 8 9	Puerta de Hierro	
18 7 7	Las Brisas	1171			*Puerta de Hierro 1*	1199
18 7 7	PGA de Catalunya	1196		**16** 6 6	Ulzama	1212
18 8 9	Puerta de Hierro			**16** 7 6	Villamartin	1214
	Puerta de Hierro 2	1200		**16** 7 6	Zaudin	1215
18 7 6	Real Sociedad			**15** 7 7	Amarilla	1128
	Club de Campo	1202		**15** 6 6	Canyamel	1134
18 7 6	Sotogrande	1209		**15** 7 6	Capdepera	1135
17 7 7	Aloha	1127		**15** 7 6	El Prat *Amarillo*	1142
17 7 7	Castillo de Gorraiz	1136		**15** 7 7	Golf d'Aro	1150
17 7 6	El Prat *Verde*	1143		**15** 6 6	Herreria	1155
17 7 6	Emporda	1145		**15** 7 7	La Manga *Norte*	1162
17 8 6	La Cala *Norte*	1158		**15** 7 8	La Moraleja *La Moraleja 1*	1165
17 7 4	Lerma	1174		**15** 8 7	La Quinta	1167
17 8 7	Montecastillo	1185		**15** 6 5	La Sella	1168
17 7 7	Neguri	1187		**15** 7 8	Marbella	1178
17 8 6	San Roque	1203		**15** 7 6	Masia Bach	1179
17 7 8	Sevilla	1207		**15** 7 7	Montenmedio	1186
16 7 6	Bonmont	1132		**15** 7 9	Pineda	1197
16 8 8	Club de Campo	1138		**14** 6 5	Alcaidesa	1123
16 7 4	El Bosque	1141		**14** 7 5	Alhaurin	1124
16 7 8	Golf del Sur	1151		**14** 6 6	Almerimar	1126
16 8 8	Islantilla	1156		**14** 6 6	Bonalba	1131
16 8 6	La Cala *Sur*	1159		**14** 6 6	Campoamor	1133
16 7 8	La Moraleja *La Moraleja 2*	1166		**14** 7 7	Cerdaña	1137
16 7 7	La Zagaleta	1169		**14** 7 6	Estepona	1147
16 7 8	Las Americas	1170		**14** 6 5	Granada	1152
16 7 7	Los Naranjos	1176		**14** 7 6	Guadalhorce	1153
16 7 8	Maspalomas	1180		**14** 7 7	Guadalmina *Sur*	1154
16 7 6	Mediterraneo	1181		**14** 7 4	La Dehesa	1160
16 6 7	Mijas *Los Lagos*	1182		**14** 7 7	La Manga *Oeste*	1163
16 7 7	Novo Sancti Petri	1188		**14** 7 7	La Manga *Sur*	1164

1113

PEUGEOT GOLF GUIDE 2000/2001

Si se trata de dar golpes de palo

No los des a ciegas

PORTADA DEL Nº44 MARZO 1999

EL GOLPE MÁS PROFESIONAL

Alesport, S.A. Gran Via 8-10, 7ª planta 08908 L´Hospitalet de Llobregat (Barcelona). Tel. 93 431 55 33. Fax 93 422 06 93
Pº de la Castellana, 268. 7º D, 28046 Madrid. Tel. 91 733 33 11 Fax:91 733 37 63
Dirección de Web: http://www.alesport.com, Correo electrónico (e-m ail): sologolf@alesport.com

Nota			Recorrido	Página	Nota			Recorrido	Página
14	8	8	Las Palmas	1172	13	8	4	Escorpion	1146
14	6	7	Los Arqueros	1175	13	7	5	Girona	1149
14	6	7	Oliva Nova	1189	13	7	6	Jarama R.A.C.E.	1157
14	7	4	Osona Montanya	1191	13	7	6	La Duquesa	1161
14	6	4	Panoramica	1193	13	7	5	Lauro	1173
14	6	5	Pedreña	1194	13	4	6	Málaga	1177
14	6	6	San Sebastián	1204	13	6	7	Mijas Los Olivos	1183
14	6	7	Son Vida	1208	13	5	5	Monte Mayor	1184
14	7	7	Torrequebrada	1211	13	7	8	Olivar de la Hinojosa	1190
13	8	8	Almenara	1125	13	6	4	Playa Serena	1198
13	6	7	Atalaya Old Course	1129	13	6	5	Pula	1201
13	6	7	Bendinat	1130	13	6	5	Sant Cugat	1205
13	7	7	Costa Brava	1139	13	6	7	Santa Ponsa	1206
13	6	6	Costa Dorada	1140	13	7	7	Torremirona	1210

CLASIFICACION DE LA INFRAESTRUCTURA HOTELERA
CLASSIFICATION OF HOTELS FACILITIES

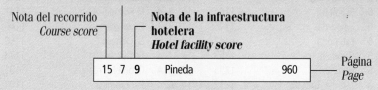

Nota del club-house y anejos
Club-house and facilities

Nota del recorrido
Course score

Nota de la infraestructura hotelera
Hotel facility score

| 15 | 7 | 9 | Pineda | 960 |

Página
Page

Nota			Recorrido	Página	Nota			Recorrido	Página
15	7	9	Pineda	1197	16	7	8	Maspalomas	1180
16	8	9	Puerta de Hierro		13	7	8	Olivar de la Hinojosa	1190
			Puerta de Hierro 1	1199	17	7	8	Sevilla	1207
18	8	9	Puerta de Hierro		17	7	7	Aloha	1127
			Puerta de Hierro 2	1200	15	7	7	Amarilla	1128
13	8	8	Almenara	1125	13	6	7	Atalaya Old Course	1129
16	8	8	Club de Campo	1138	13	6	7	Bendinat	1130
16	7	8	Golf del Sur	1151	17	7	7	Castillo de Gorraiz	1136
16	8	8	Islantilla	1156	14	7	7	Cerdaña	1137
15	7	8	La Moraleja La Moraleja 1	1165	13	7	7	Costa Brava	1139
16	7	8	La Moraleja La Moraleja 2	1166	15	7	7	Golf d'Aro	1150
16	7	8	Las Americas	1170	14	7	7	Guadalmina Sur	1154
14	8	8	Las Palmas	1172	15	7	7	La Manga Norte	1162
15	7	8	Marbella	1178	14	7	7	La Manga Oeste	1163

1115

CLASIFICACION DE LA INFRAESTRUCTURA HOTELERA

Nota	Recorrido	Página	Nota	Recorrido	Página
14 7 7	La Manga *Sur*	1164	16 8 6	La Cala *Sur*	1159
15 8 7	La Quinta	1167	13 7 6	La Duquesa	1161
16 7 7	La Zagaleta	1169	13 4 6	Málaga	1177
18 7 7	Las Brisas	1171	15 7 6	Masia Bach	1179
14 6 7	Los Arqueros	1175	16 7 6	Mediterraneo	1181
16 7 7	Los Naranjos	1176	16 7 6	Pals	1192
16 6 7	Mijas *Los Lagos*	1182	18 7 6	Real Sociedad	
13 6 7	Mijas *Los Olivos*	1183		Club de Campo	1202
17 8 7	Montecastillo	1185	17 8 6	San Roque	1203
15 7 7	Montenmedio	1186	14 6 6	San Sebastián	1204
17 7 7	Neguri	1187	18 7 6	Sotogrande	1209
16 7 7	Novo Sancti Petri	1188	16 6 6	Ulzama	1212
14 6 7	Oliva Nova	1189	19 8 6	Valderrama	1213
18 7 7	PGA de Catalunya	1196	16 7 6	Villamartin	1214
13 6 7	Santa Ponsa	1206	16 7 6	Zaudin	1215
14 6 7	Son Vida	1208	14 6 5	Alcaidesa	1123
13 7 7	Torremirona	1210	14 7 5	Alhaurin	1124
14 7 7	Torrequebrada	1211	18 6 5	Fontanals	1148
14 6 6	Almerimar	1126	13 7 5	Girona	1149
14 6 6	Bonalba	1131	14 6 5	Granada	1152
16 7 6	Bonmont	1132	15 6 5	La Sella	1168
14 6 6	Campoamor	1133	13 7 5	Lauro	1173
15 6 6	Canyamel	1134	13 5 5	Monte Mayor	1184
15 7 6	Capdepera	1135	14 6 5	Pedreña	1194
13 6 6	Costa Dorada	1140	16 6 5	Peralada	1195
15 7 6	El Prat *Amarillo*	1142	13 6 5	Pula	1201
17 7 6	El Prat *Verde*	1143	13 6 5	Sant Cugat	1205
18 7 6	El Saler	1144	16 7 4	El Bosque	1141
17 7 6	Emporda	1145	13 8 4	Escorpion	1146
14 7 6	Estepona	1147	14 7 4	La Dehesa	1160
14 7 6	Guadalhorce	1153	17 7 4	Lerma	1174
15 6 6	Herreria	1155	14 7 4	Osona Montanya	1191
13 7 6	Jarama R.A.C.E.	1157	14 6 4	Panoramica	1193
17 8 6	La Cala *Norte*	1158	13 6 4	Playa Serena	1198

1116

PEUGEOT

ESTANCIA DE GOLF RECOMENDADA
RECOMMENDED GOLFING STAY

Golfplatz	Note			Seite	Golfplatz	Note			Seite
Almerimar	14	6	6	1126	La Manga *Sur*	14	7	7	1164
Aloha	17	7	7	1127	La Moraleja *La Moraleja 1*	15	7	8	1165
Canyamel	15	6	6	1134	La Moraleja *La Moraleja 2*	16	7	8	1166
Castillo de Gorraiz	17	7	7	1136	La Quinta	15	8	7	1167
Club de Campo	16	8	8	1138	Las Brisas	18	7	7	1171
El Prat *Amarillo*	15	7	6	1142	Los Naranjos	16	7	7	1176
El Prat *Verde*	17	7	6	1143	Mediterraneo	16	7	6	1181
El Saler	18	7	6	1144	Mijas *Los Lagos*	16	6	7	1182
Emporda	17	7	6	1145	Mijas *Los Olivos*	13	6	7	1183
Fontanals	18	6	5	1148	Montecastillo	17	8	7	1185
Guadalmina *Sur*	14	7	7	1154	Neguri	17	7	7	1187
Islantilla	16	8	8	1156	Pals	16	7	6	1192
La Cala *Norte*	17	8	6	1158	San Roque	17	8	6	1203
La Cala *Sur*	16	8	6	1159	San Sebastián	14	6	6	1204
La Dehesa	14	7	4	1160	Sotogrande	18	7	6	1209
La Manga *Norte*	15	7	7	1162	Valderrama	19	8	6	1213
La Manga *Oeste*	14	7	7	1163	Villamartin	16	7	6	1214

VACACIONES RECOMENDADAS
RECOMMENDED GOLFING HOLIDAYS

Golfplatz	Note			Seite	Golfplatz	Note			Seite
Aloha	17	7	7	1127	La Manga *Sur*	14	7	7	1164
Bonmont	16	7	6	1132	La Sella	15	6	5	1168
Capdepera	15	7	6	1135	Marbella	15	7	8	1178
Costa Dorada	13	6	6	1140	Maspalomas	16	7	8	1180
El Bosque	16	7	4	1141	Mediterraneo	16	7	6	1181
El Saler	18	7	6	1144	Mijas *Los Lagos*	16	6	7	1182
Emporda	17	7	6	1145	Mijas *Los Olivos*	13	6	7	1183
Islantilla	16	8	8	1156	Novo Sancti Petri	16	7	7	1188
La Cala *Norte*	17	8	6	1158	Pals	16	7	6	1192
La Cala *Sur*	16	8	6	1159	Playa Serena	13	6	4	1198
La Manga *Norte*	15	7	7	1162	Pula	13	6	5	1201
La Manga *Oeste*	14	7	7	1163	Torrequebrada	14	7	7	1211

1117

TIPO DE RECORRIDOS
TYPE OF COURSE

1118

Tipo/ Recorrido	Nota	Página	Tipo/ Recorrido	Nota	Página
open country			**residential**		
Atalaya *Old Course*	13 6 7	1129	Aloha	17 7 7	1127
Bonmont	16 7 6	1132	Atalaya *Old Course*	13 6 7	1129
El Prat *Amarillo*	15 7 6	1142	Bendinat	13 6 7	1130
Emporda	17 7 6	1145	Bonmont	16 7 6	1132
Fontanals	18 6 5	1148	Campoamor	14 6 6	1133
Granada	14 6 5	1152	Castillo de Gorraiz	17 7 7	1136
Guadalhorce	14 7 6	1153	Costa Brava	13 7 7	1139
La Duquesa	13 7 6	1161	La Manga *Norte*	15 7 7	1162
Olivar de la Hinojosa	13 7 8	1190	La Manga *Sur*	14 7 7	1164
Peralada	16 6 5	1195	La Quinta	15 8 7	1167
Santa Ponsa	13 6 7	1206	Las Brisas	18 7 7	1171
			La Zagaleta	16 7 7	1169
parkland			Los Naranjos	16 7 7	1176
Aloha	17 7 7	1127	Panoramica	14 6 4	1193
Amarilla	15 7 7	1128	Sant Cugat	13 6 5	1205
Castillo de Gorraiz	17 7 7	1136	Son Vida	14 6 7	1208
Golf d'Aro	15 7 7	1150	Santa Ponsa	13 6 7	1206
Golf del Sur	16 7 8	1151	Zaudin	16 7 6	1215
Guadalmina *Sur*	14 7 7	1154			
Las Americas	16 7 8	1170	**seaside course**		
Las Brisas	18 7 7	1171	Alcaidesa	14 6 5	1123
Las Palmas	14 8 8	1172	Almerimar	14 6 6	1126
Los Naranjos	16 7 7	1176	El Prat *Verde*	17 7 6	1143
Montenmedio	15 7 7	1186	Guadalmina *Sur*	14 7 7	1154
Oliva Nova	14 6 7	1189	Islantilla	16 8 8	1156
PGA de Catalunya	18 7 7	1196	Málaga	13 4 6	1177
Pineda	15 7 9	1197	Novo Sancti Petri	16 7 7	1188
Puerta de Hierro			Pedreña	14 6 5	1194
Puerta de Hierro 1	16 8 9	1199	Playa Serena	13 6 4	1198
Puerta de Hierro			Sotogrande	18 7 6	1209
Puerta de Hierro 2	18 8 9	1200			
San Roque	17 8 6	1203	**hilly, residential**		
Son Vida	14 6 7	1208	El Bosque	16 7 4	1141
Sotogrande	18 7 6	1209			
Torremirona	13 7 7	1210			
Valderrama	19 8 6	1213			

Spain

1119

RELIEVE DE LOS RECORRIDOS
GEOGRAPHICAL RELIEF

Con poco relieve / Rather flat

Medianamente accidentado / Averagely hilly

Muy accidentado / Very hilly

1120

Course				
Almerimar	14	6	6	1126
Playa Serena	13	6	4	1198
El Prat *Amarillo*	15	7	6	1142
El Prat *Verde*	17	7	6	1143
Escorpion	13	8	4	1146
Guadalmina *Sur*	14	7	7	1154
Málaga	13	4	6	1177
Oliva Nova	14	6	7	1189
Olivar de la Hinojosa	13	7	8	1190
Pineda	15	7	9	1197
Santa Ponsa	13	6	7	1206
Sevilla	17	7	8	1207
Atalaya *Old Course*	13	6	7	1129
El Saler	18	7	6	1144
Emporda	17	7	6	1145
Fontanals	18	6	5	1148
Granada	14	6	5	1152
Lerma	17	7	4	1174
Los Naranjos	16	7	7	1176
Maspalomas	16	7	8	1180
Mediterraneo	16	7	6	1181
Novo Sancti Petri	16	7	7	1188
Panoramica	14	6	4	1193
Sotogrande	18	7	6	1209
Torremirona	13	7	7	1210
La Moraleja *La Moraleja 1*	15	7	8	1165
La Moraleja *La Moraleja 2*	16	7	8	1166
Las Brisas	18	7	7	1171
Mijas *Los Lagos*	16	6	7	1182
Pals	16	7	6	1192
Peralada	16	6	5	1195
Amarilla	15	7	7	1128
Bonmont	16	7	6	1132
Capdepera	15	7	6	1135
Club de Campo	16	8	8	1138

Course				
Costa Dorada	13	6	6	1140
Guadalhorce	14	7	6	1153
Lauro	13	7	5	1173
Marbella	15	7	8	1178
Mijas *Los Olivos*	13	6	7	1183
Montenmedio	15	7	7	1186
Pula	13	6	5	1201
Son Vida	14	6	7	1208
Valderrama	19	8	6	1213
Zaudin	16	7	6	1215
Aloha	17	7	7	1127
Bonalba	14	6	6	1131
Costa Brava	13	7	7	1139
Golf d'Aro	15	7	7	1150
Islantilla	16	8	8	1156
Jarama R.A.C.E.	13	7	6	1157
La Dehesa	14	7	4	1160
La Duquesa	13	7	6	1161
La Manga *Norte*	15	7	7	1162
La Manga *Oeste*	14	7	7	1163
La Manga *Sur*	14	7	7	1164
Las Americas	16	7	8	1170
Neguri	17	7	7	1187
Puerta de Hierro				
Puerta de Hierro 1	16	8	9	1199
Puerta de Hierro				
Puerta de Hierro 2	18	8	9	1200
San Roque	17	8	6	1203
Villamartin	16	7	6	1214
Alcaidesa	14	6	5	1123
Bendinat	13	6	7	1130
Campoamor	14	6	6	1133
Canyamel	15	6	6	1134
Castillo de Gorraiz	17	7	7	1136
Cerdaña	14	7	7	1137
Golf del Sur	16	7	8	1151
Herreria	15	6	6	1155
La Quinta	15	8	7	1167
La Sella	15	6	5	1168

Spain

Ano/ Recorrido	Nota			Página
Masia Bach	15	7	6	1179
Montecastillo	17	8	7	1185
Pedreña	14	6	5	1194
Real Sociedad Club de Campo	18	7	6	1202
San Sebastián	14	6	6	1204
Torrequebrada	14	7	7	1211
Alhaurin	14	7	5	1124
Almenara	13	8	8	1125
El Bosque	16	7	4	1141
Estepona	14	7	6	1147
Girona	13	7	5	1149
La Cala *Norte*	17	8	6	1158

Ano/ Recorrido	Nota			Página
Osona Montanya	14	7	4	1191
PGA de Catalunya	18	7	7	1196
Sant Cugat	13	6	5	1205
Ulzama	16	6	6	1212
La Cala *Sur*	16	8	6	1159
La Zagaleta	16	7	7	1169
Las Palmas	14	8	8	1172
Los Arqueros	14	6	7	1175
Monte Mayor	13	5	5	1184

EPOCA DEL AÑO ACONSEJADA
RECOMMENDED SEASONS

Ano/ Recorrido	Nota			Página
[1 2 3 4 5 6 7 8 9 10 11 12]				
Amarilla	15	7	7	1128
Bendinat	13	6	7	1130
Bonalba	14	6	6	1131
Campoamor	14	6	6	1133
Canyamel	15	6	6	1134
Capdepera	15	7	6	1135
Costa Dorada	13	6	6	1140
El Bosque	16	7	4	1141
El Saler	18	7	6	1144
Escorpion	13	8	4	1146
Golf d'Aro	15	7	7	1150
Golf del Sur	16	7	8	1151
La Manga *Norte*	15	7	7	1162
La Manga *Oeste*	14	7	7	1163
La Manga *Sur*	14	7	7	1164
La Sella	15	6	5	1168
Las Americas	16	7	8	1170
Las Palmas	14	8	8	1172
Maspalomas	16	7	8	1180
Mediterraneo	16	7	6	1181
Montenmedio	15	7	7	1186
Oliva Nova	14	6	7	1189
Pals	16	7	6	1192
Peralada	16	6	5	1195
PGA de Catalunya	18	7	7	1196

Ano/ Recorrido	Nota			Página
Pineda	15	7	9	1197
Pula	13	6	5	1201
San Roque	17	8	6	1203
Santa Ponsa	13	6	7	1206
Son Vida	14	6	7	1208
Sotogrande	18	7	6	1209
Torremirona	13	7	7	1210
Valderrama	19	8	6	1213
Villamartin	16	7	6	1214
[1 2 3 4 5 6 7 8 9 10 11 12]				
Costa Brava	13	7	7	1139
El Prat *Amarillo*	15	7	6	1142
El Prat *Verde*	17	7	6	1143
Girona	13	7	5	1149
Novo Sancti Petri	16	7	7	1188
Sant Cugat	13	6	5	1205
[1 2 3 4 5 6 7 8 9 10 11 12]				
Bonmont	16	7	6	1132
Club de Campo	16	8	8	1138
Emporda	17	7	6	1145
Masia Bach	15	7	6	1179
San Sebastián	14	6	6	1204

1121

EPOCA DEL AÑO ACONSEJADA

Ano/ Recorrido		Nota		Página
1 2 3 4 5 6 7 8 9 10 11 12				
Castillo de Gorraiz	17	7	7	1136
Jarama R.A.C.E.	13	7	6	1157
La Dehesa	14	7	4	1160
La Moraleja *La Moraleja 1*	15	7	8	1165
La Moraleja *La Moraleja 2*	16	7	8	1166
Neguri	17	7	7	1187
Olivar de la Hinojosa	13	7	8	1190
Osona Montanya	14	7	4	1191
Pedreña	14	6	5	1194
Puerta de Hierro				
Puerta de Hierro 1	16	8	9	1199
Puerta de Hierro				
Puerta de Hierro 2	18	8	9	1200
1 2 3 4 5 6 7 8 9 10 11 12				
Fontanals	18	6	5	1148
Herreria	15	6	6	1155
Lerma	17	7	4	1174
Ulzama	16	6	6	1212
1 2 3 4 5 6 7 8 9 10 11 12				
Granada	14	6	5	1152
1 2 3 4 5 6 7 8 9 10 11 12				
Real Sociedad				
Club de Campo	18	7	6	1202
1 2 3 4 5 6 7 8 9 10 11 12				
Cerdaña	14	7	7	1137
1 2 3 4 5 6 7 8 9 10 11 12				
Alcaidesa	14	6	5	1123

Ano/ Recorrido		Nota		Página
1 2 3 4 5 6 7 8 9 10 11 12				
Guadalhorce	14	7	6	1153
Islantilla	16	8	8	1156
La Duquesa	13	7	6	1161
La Quinta	15	8	7	1167
La Zagaleta	16	7	7	1169
Las Brisas	18	7	7	1171
Lauro	13	7	5	1173
Los Arqueros	14	6	7	1175
Los Naranjos	16	7	7	1176
Monte Mayor	13	5	5	1184
Montecastillo	17	8	7	1185
Panoramica	14	6	4	1193
Playa Serena	13	6	4	1198
Sevilla	17	7	8	1207
Torrequebrada	14	7	7	1211
Zaudin	16	7	6	1215
1 2 3 4 5 6 7 8 9 10 11 12				
Alhaurin	14	7	5	1124
Almenara	13	8	8	1125
Almerimar	14	6	6	1126
Aloha	17	7	7	1127
Atalaya *Old Course*	13	6	7	1129
Estepona	14	7	6	1147
Guadalmina *Sur*	14	7	7	1154
La Cala *Norte*	17	8	6	1158
La Cala *Sur*	16	8	6	1159
Málaga	13	4	6	1177
Marbella	15	7	8	1178
Mijas *Los Lagos*	16	6	7	1182
Mijas *Los Olivos*	13	6	7	1183

ALTITUD DE LOS RECORRIDOS > 500 m
COURSES ALTITUDE

Altitud/ Recorrido		Nota		Página
500 Castillo de Gorraiz	17	7	7	1136
500 Ulzama	16	6	6	1212
600 Puerta de Hierro				
Puerta de Hierro 2	18	8	9	1200
600 La Moraleja *La Moraleja 2*	16	7	8	1166
600 Purta de Hierro				
Puerta de Hierro 1	16	8	9	1199
600 La Moraleja *La Moraleja 1*	15	7	8	1165
600 La Dehesa	14	7	4	1160
600 Jarama R.A.C.E.	13	7	6	1157

Altitud/ Recorrido		Nota		Página
600 Olivar de la Hinojosa	13	7	8	1190
650 Club de Campo	16	8	8	1138
680 Granada	14	6	5	1152
740 Real Sociedad				
Club de Campo	18	7	6	1202
830 Osona Montanya	14	7	4	1191
840 Lerma	17	7	4	1174
950 Herreria	15	6	6	1155
1100 Fontanals	18	6	5	1148
1100 Cerdaña	14	7	7	1137

Las obras realizadas en los últimos meses han mejorado sensiblemente la calidad del campo y el estado del terreno. La obra más evidente puede concretarse en la prolongación del 15, colocando el green tras un arroyo y convirtiendo el hoyo en par 5 para que el campo sea 72. Ahora el campo responde a la espectacularidad de sus vistas sobre el Mediterráneo y la enorme Roca de Gibraltar que domina gran parte del recorrido. El campo se ha bautizado como links porque está junto al mar y hay que saber jugar con viento, pero la naturaleza del suelo, el diseño y la preparación de las zonas de caída de la bola son beignos y cómodos para que jugadores de cualquier edad y handicap puedan disfrutar de un buen día de golf, sin prescindir del reto de saber dirigir la bola. Los greenes no son inmensos ni excesivamente complicados pero para hacer una buena tarjeta o ganar un partido hay que afinar en el juego corto y pegar recto.

The work carried out in early 1999 has significantly improved the quality and maintenance of this course. The most obvious improvements consisted in lengthening the 15th hole, with the green now placed beyond a stretch of water to make this a par 5 and the course a par 72. Right now, the course is even more in keeping with the spectacular vista over the Mediterranean sea and the massive rock of Gibraltar, which dominates a large part of the course. Alcaidesa has been called a links because it is situated along the coastline and because you need to know how to handle the wind. However, the type of soil, layout and breadth of the landing areas are well suited to players of all ages and abilities who are looking for a good day's golfing without having to bend the ball one way or the other. The greens are neither oversized nor too complicated, but to card a good score or win your bet, you will need to hit it straight and have a sharp short game.

Alcaidesa Links Golf Course   1991
Apdo de Correos 125
E - 11360 SAN ROQUE (CADIZ)

Office	Secretaria	(34) 956 - 791 040
Pro shop	Pro-shop	(34) 956 - 791 040
Fax	Fax	(34) 956 - 791 041
Situation	Situación	

Algeciras (pop. 101 556), 15 km
Gibraltar (pop. 28 350) 10 km

Annual closure	Cierre anual	no
Weekly closure	Cierre semanal	no

Fees main season
Precios tempor. alta 18 holes

	Week days Semana	We/Bank holidays Fin de sem./fiestas
Individual Individual	8 500 Pts	8 500 Pts
Couple Pareja	17 000 Pts	17 000 Pts
Caddy Caddy	no	
Electric Trolley Carro eléctrico	no	
Buggy Coche	5 000 Pts/18 holes	
Clubs Palos	2 500 Pts/18 holes	

Credit cards Tarjetas de crédito
VISA - MasterCard - AMEX - DC

Access Acceso : Marbella → Estepona,
Sotogrande → Cadiz, Golf on the left (km 124,6)
Map 7 on page 1109 Plano 7 Página 1109

GOLF COURSE
RECORRIDO   **14**/20

Site	Emplazamiento	
Maintenance	Mantenimiento	
Architect	Arquitecto	P. Alliss
		Clive Clark
Type	Tipo	seaside course
Relief	Relieve	
Water in play	Agua	
Exp. to wind	Exp. al viento	
Trees in play	Arboles	

Scorecard Tarjeta	Chp. Campeonato	Mens Caballeros	Ladies Damas
Length Longitud	6158	5459	4586
Par	72	72	72

Advised golfing ability   0 12 24 36
Nivel de juego aconsejado
Hcp required   Handicap exigido 28 Men., 36 Ladies

CLUB HOUSE & AMENITIES
CLUB HOUSE Y DEPENDENCIAS   **6**/10

Pro shop	Pro-shop	
Driving range	Campo de prácticas	
Sheltered	cubierto	no
On grass	sobre hierba	yes
Putting-green	putting-green	yes
Pitching-green	pitching-green	yes

HOTEL FACILITIES
HOTELES CERCANOS   **5**/10

HOTELS HOTELES
Soto Grande   Sotogrande
46 rooms, D 19 950 Pts   8 km
Tel (34) 956 - 794 386, Fax (34) 956 - 794 333

San Roque   San Roque
50 rooms, D 20 000 Pts   2 km
Tel (34) 956 - 613 030, Fax (34) 956 - 613 012

La Solana   San Roque
19 rooms, D 9 500 Pts   5 km
Tel (34) 956 - 780 236, Fax (34) 956 - 780 236

RESTAURANTS RESTAURANTES
Los Remos   San Roque
Tel (34) 956 - 698 412   5 km

Pedro   San Roque
Tel (34) 956 - 698 453   5 km

1123

Al lado de Mijas, este ambicioso proyecto, aún no acabado, es prometedor, sobre todo teniendo en cuenta que la firma de Ballesteros es una excelente publicidad. En un magnífico entorno, con vistas espectaculares hacia la montaña, ha diseñado un recorrido bastante accidentado (a veces demasiado), que exige un juego preciso, aunque sólo sea para evitar algunos barrancos,e incluso el rough, a menudo en la línea de juego y muy ösalvaje. Favorece a aquellos que juegan en «fade», por lo que los jugadores con tendencia al «slice» no se sentirán muy perjudicados. Un buen número de tees de salida permite adaptar el recorrido a todos los niveles de juego, pero los jugadores con poca experiencia tendrán problemas. Los obstáculos de agua dan a veces un aspecto americano a este diseño que a pesar de todo está en armonía con el paisaje. Hay que tener muy en cuenta el recorrido anejo de 18 hoyos reservado a los «junior» , ... y a los padres si los niños les invitan!

Next door to Mijas, this ambitious and still incomplete resort promises a great deal, all the more so in that the label of Ballesteros is a commercial argument of the highest order. In a magnificent setting with spectacular views over mountains, Seve has designed a very, and sometimes too, hilly course, which demands precision golf, if only to avoid a number of precipices or even the rough, a frequent hazard and growing wild. It is a course for players who fade the ball, allowing the amateur slice more leeway than they might usually find. The many different tees make this a course for all levels, but inexperienced players will have problems. Water hazards sometimes give the layout a very American style, although the general character blends harmoniously with the setting. Worthy of note is the adjoining 18-hole course reserved for juniors, and their parents if invited by the kids!

Alhaurin Golf — 1992

Alhaurin El Grande
E - 29650 CTRA DE MIJAS KM 6 (MALAGA)

Office	Secretaria	(34) 952 - 595 970
Pro shop	Pro-shop	(34) 952 - 596 049
Fax	Fax	(34) 952 - 594 586
Situation	Situación	

Fuengirola (pop. 43 048), 15 km
Alhaurin, 3 km

| Annual closure | Cierre anual | no |
| Weekly closure | Cierre semanal | no |

Fees main season
Precios tempor. alta 18 holes

	Week days Semana	We/Bank holidays Fin de sem./fiestas
Individual Individual	6 200 Pts	6 200 Pts
Couple Pareja	12 400 Pts	12 400 Pts

Caddy	Caddy	no
Electric Trolley	Carro eléctrico	1 900 Pts/18 holes
Buggy	Coche	3 500 Pts/18 holes
Clubs	Palos no	1 900 Pts/18 holes

Credit cards Tarjetas de crédito VISA - AMEX

Alhaurín el Grande

GOLF · Mijas · E 15 N340 · MALAGA

FUENGIROLA

Mijas Costa

MARBELLA

Access Acceso : Malaga → Marbella. Exit (Salida) «Churiana», → Mijas → Alhaurín El Grande
Map 7 on page 1109 Plano 7 Página 1109

1124

GOLF COURSE / RECORRIDO — 14/20

Site	Emplazamiento	
Maintenance	Mantenimiento	
Architect	Arquitecto	Seve Ballesteros
Type	Tipo	mountain
Relief	Relieve	
Water in play	Agua	
Exp. to wind	Exp. al viento	
Trees in play	Arboles	

Scorecard Tarjeta	Chp. Campeonato	Mens Caballeros	Ladies Damas
Length Longitud	6221	5857	4941
Par	72	72	72

| Advised golfing ability Nivel de juego aconsejado | 0 | 12 | 24 | 36 |
| Hcp required Hcp exigido | no | | | |

CLUB HOUSE & AMENITIES / CLUB HOUSE Y DEPENDENCIAS — 7/10

Pro shop	Pro-shop	
Driving range	Campo de prácticas	
Sheltered	cubierto	
On grass	sobre hierba	yes
Putting-green	putting-green	yes
Pitching-green	pitching-green	no

HOTEL FACILITIES / HOTELES CERCANOS — 5/10

HOTELS HOTELES

Hotel Alhaurin Golf — Alhaurin
38 rooms, D 15 500 Pts.
Tel (34) 952 - 595 800, Fax (34) 952 - 594 195

Byblos — Fuengirola / 12 km
144 rooms, D 39 500 Pts
Tel (34) 952 - 473 050, Fax (34) 952 - 476 783

Mijas — Mijas / 6 km
97 rooms, D 14 700 Pts
Tel (34) 952 - 485 800, Fax (34) 952 - 485 825

RESTAURANTS RESTAURANTES

La Ventilla — Alhaurin
Tel (34) 952 - 595 800

Valparaiso — Cta de Fuengirola / 8 km
Tel (34) 952 - 485 996

La Inmobiliaria Sotogrande, que hace varios años vendió el campo «de abajo» (el primero de la zona) a los socios, ha decidido ahora desarrollar el negocio del turismo de golf. Almenara es la primera realidad de un complejo en el que están previstos dos campos de golf y dos hoteles, que se halla sobre el campo de Valderrama y linda con el de San Roque. Este campo, abierto en la primavera de 1999, está construido en un terreno de fuerte desnivel y el diseño de Dave Thomas le añade dificultad, con calles estrechas y sus típicos bunkers de calle de altos taludes que castigan todas las bolas que no estén perfectamente dirigidas. No es un campo largo y por causa de los peligros que flanquean y cruzan las calles es recomendable dejar el driver en la bolsa en muchos hoyos del recorrido. La construcción es buena, el mantenimiento está muy cuidado y los greens, no especialmente grandes pero con interesantes movimientos, son excelentes. No es obligatorio jugar en coche, pero pocas piernas resistirán hacerlo a pie.

The Sotogrande Real Estate Company, which firstly sold the «lower» terrain (the first) to members of the Sotogrande golf club, has decided to extend its activities to golf tourism. Almenara is the first complex which has provided for golf courses and hotels, located between the Valderrama and San Roque courses. The Almenara course, opened in the Spring of 1999, has been built over very hilly terrain and the Dave Thomas layout adds even more difficulties with narrow fairways and typical, high-lipped fairway bunkers, which catch anything hit off-target. This is not a wide course and what with the danger lurking alongside or across the fairways you are often better off leaving the driver in the bag. A well built course where maintenance is good and the greens - never very large but interestingly contoured - are excellent. You don't have to play with a buggy, but if you don't you sure will need sturdy legs.

Almenara Golf Hotel — 1999

Avenida Almenara s/n.
E - 11310 SOTOGRANDE

Office	Secretaria	(34) 956 - 790 300
Pro shop	Pro-shop	(34) 956 - 790 300
Fax	Fax	(34) 956 - 790 046
Situation	Situación	

Algeciras (pop. 101 556), 30 km
Estepona (pop. 36 307), 30 km

Annual closure	Cierre anual	no
Weekly closure	Cierre semanal	no

Fees main season
Precios tempor. alta 18 holes

	Week days Semana	We/Bank holidays Fin de sem./fiestas
Individual Individual	9 000 Pts	9 000 Pts
Couple Pareja	18 000 Pts	18 000 Pts
Caddy Caddy		no
Electric Trolley Carro eléctrico		500 Pts/18 holes
Buggy Coche		5 000 Pts/18 holes
Clubs Palos		3 000 Pts/18 holes

Credit cards Tarjetas de crédito
VISA - Eurocard - MasterCard - AMEX

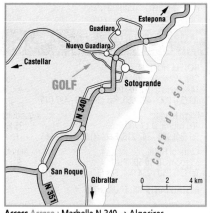

Access Acceso : Marbella N-340 → Algeciras.
Exit (salida 127). → Valderrama, Sotogrande Alto.
Map 7 on page 1109 Plano 7 Página 1109

GOLF COURSE / RECORRIDO — 13/20

Site	Emplazamiento	
Maintenance	Mantenimiento	
Architect	Arquitecto	Dave Thomas
Type	Tipo	inland, forest
Relief	Relieve	
Water in play	Agua	
Exp. to wind	Exp. al viento	
Trees in play	Arboles	

Scorecard Tarjeta	Chp. Campeonato	Mens Caballeros	Ladies Damas
Length Longitud	6168	5726	4783
Par	72	72	72

Advised golfing ability — 0 12 24 36
Nivel de juego aconsejado

Hcp required Handicap exigido 28 Men, 36 Ladies

CLUB HOUSE & AMENITIES / CLUB HOUSE Y DEPENDENCIAS — 8/10

Pro shop	Pro-shop	
Driving range	Campo de prácticas	
Sheltered	cubierto	no
On grass	sobre hierba	yes
Putting-green	putting-green	yes
Pitching-green	pitching-green	yes

HOTEL FACILITIES / HOTELES CERCANOS — 8/10

HOTELS HOTELES

Almenara Hotel y Golf — Sotogrande
150 rooms, D 35 000 Pts — on site
Tel (34) 956 790 306, Fax (34) 956 790 046

Hotel Sotogrande — Sotogrande
46 rooms, D 19 000 Pts — 5 km
Tel (34) 956 794 386, Fax (34) 956 794 333

Hotel Club Marítimo — Sotogrande
39 rooms, D 22 000 Pts — 5 km
Tel (34) 956 790 200, Fax (34) 956 794 333

RESTAURANTS RESTAURANTES

Los Remos - Tel (34) 956 - 698 412 — San Roque 10 km

Vicente - Tel (34) 956 790 212 — Sotogrande 5 km

Clau en el Don Benito — San Roque
Tel (34) 956 782 342 — 10 km

1125

Situado en un zona urbanizada con toda clase de distracciones, colaboraron en su diseño Ron Kirby y Gary Player. Tiene una vegetación rica que, en contraste con el fondo de montañas áridas, da la impresión de un oasis. Ha sido comprado por una sociedad japonesa con la intención de transformar este complejo en uno de los grandes centros turísticos del sur de Europa. Sus calles anchas, sus bunkers grandes y sus amplios obstáculos de agua en la línea de juego en una media docena de hoyos, dan a este recorrido un incontestable estilo de inspiración americana. Su longitud puede parecer importante desde cualquiera de los tees de salida, pero las bolas por lo general ruedan bastante. El punto álgido del recorrido se encuentra en el hoyo 12, un par 3, más bien largo, con el green en medio de una isla y que intimidará a muchos jugadores !.

Located in a built-up area where there are all sorts of leisure facilities, this course was designed at a period when Ron Kirby and Gary Player were working together. Lush vegetation affords a pleasant, oasis-style contrast with the arid mountains in the background. The course has been taken over by a Japanese group, which is keen to transform the complex into one of the biggest tourist resorts in southern Europe. With wide fairways, large bunkers and huge water hazards in play on half a dozen holes, the course is unquestionably American in style. It may seem a little long, whichever tee you use, but the ball generally rolls a long way here. The highlight of the course is the 12th hole, a rather long par 3 with an island green. A daunting prospect for many a player.

Golf Almerimar S.L.   1976
Urb. Almerimar
E - 04700 EL EJIDO - ALMERIA

Office	Secretaria	(34) 950 - 497 454
Pro shop	Pro-shop	(34) 950 - 497 454
Fax	Fax	(34) 950 - 497 233
Situation	Situación	

El Ejido (pop. 41 700), 10 km
Almería (pop. 159 587), 32 km

Annual closure	Cierre anual	no
Weekly closure	Cierre semanal	no

Fees main season
Precios tempor. alta full day

	Week days Semana	We/Bank holidays Fin de sem./fiestas
Individual Individual	6 400 Pts	6 400 Pts
Couple Pareja	12 800 Pts	12 800 Pts

Caddy	Caddy	on request
Electric Trolley	Carro eléctrico	no
Buggy	Coche	4 100 Pts/18 holes
Clubs	Palos	2 000 Pts/18 holes

Credit cards Tarjetas de crédito
VISA - MasterCard - AMEX

1126

Access Acceso : Almería N340 → El Ejido, Almerimar
Map 8 on page 1111 Plano 8 Página 1111

GOLF COURSE
RECORRIDO   **14**/20

Site	Emplazamiento	
Maintenance	Mantenimiento	
Architect	Arquitecto	Gary Player Ron Kirby
Type	Tipo	seaside course
Relief	Relieve	
Water in play	Agua	
Exp. to wind	Exp. al viento	
Trees in play	Arboles	

Scorecard Tarjeta	Chp. Campeonato	Mens Caballeros	Ladies Damas
Length Longitud	5981	5892	5101
Par	72	72	72

Advised golfing ability		0	12	24	36
Nivel de juego aconsejado					
Hcp required	Handicap exigido	28 Men, 36 Ladies			

CLUB HOUSE & AMENITIES
CLUB HOUSE Y DEPENDENCIAS   **6**/10

Pro shop	Pro-shop	
Driving range	Campo de prácticas	
Sheltered	cubierto	no
On grass	sobre hierba	yes
Putting-green	putting-green	yes
Pitching-green	pitching-green	no

HOTEL FACILITIES
HOTELES CERCANOS   **6**/10

HOTELS HOTELES
Golf Hotel Almerimar   Golf
147 rooms, D 11 100 Pts   400 m
Tel (34) 950 - 497 050, Fax (34) 950 - 497 019

Porto Magno   Aguadulce
400 rooms, D 17 700 Pts.   35 km
Tel (34) 950 - 342 216, Fax (34) 950 - 342 965

Costasol Hotel   Almería
55 rooms, D 10 500 Pts.   30 km
Tel (34) 950 - 234 011, Fax (34) 950 - 234 011

RESTAURANTS RESTAURANTES

El Segoviano   Almerimar
Tel (34) 950 - 480 084   10 km

El Bello Rincón   Ctra de Almería
Tel (34) 950 - 238 427   25 km

Ya desde su apertura sedujo este recorrido diseñado por Javier Arana y las recientes obras efectuadas lo han mejorado aún más. Aquí es primordial la precisión de los golpes, sobre todo los de salida: Aloha no es un recorrido muy largo, pero sí a veces estrecho y accidentado. Los árboles son a menudo peligrosos, ciertos greens son ciegos, otros en alto, pero que ruedan siempre bien. Por tanto hay que permanecer constantemente atento, sobre todo para pegar a la bola con efecto en cualquier dirección. Con su original diseño, este recorrido deja una impresión de gran armonía e inteligente utilización golfística del terreno, sobre todo en tres hoyos de gran calidad: el 1, el 12 y el 18. Algunas inclinaciones naturales del campo pueden ser peligrosas, al igual que muchos obstáculos de agua, sobre todo a la vuelta. Agradable y bien decorado, Aloha es una excelente test de golf y un lugar donde no se cansa uno de jugar.

This course, designed by Javier Arana, was an attractive proposition from the first day it opened, and recent work has helped to improve the overall layout. It is important here to place your shots carefully, especially off the tee. Aloha is not a very long course, but it is sometimes tight and hilly; the trees are often dangerous and a number of greens are blind, multi-tiered and very fast. You have to keep your wits about you all the time, especially when trying to work the ball in all directions. Although an original layout, Aloha leaves an impression of harmony and intelligent use of terrain from a golfing point of view, especially on holes 1, 12 and 18, all three excellent. A number of natural banks can cause problems, as can several water hazards, particularly on the back nine. Pleasant to play and well laid out, Aloha is an excellent test of golf which is always a pleasure to play.

Club de Golf Aloha — 1975
Nueva Andalucia
E - 29660 MARBELLA (MALAGA)

Office	Secretaria	(34) 952 - 813 750
Pro shop	Pro-shop	(34) 952 - 814 755
Fax	Fax	(34) 952 - 812 389
Situation	Situación	

San Pedro de Alcantara, 3 km
Marbella (pop. 84 410), 7 km

Annual closure	Cierre anual	no
Weekly closure	Cierre semanal	no

Fees main season
Precios tempor. alta 18 holes

	Week days Semana	We/Bank holidays Fin de sem./fiestas
Individual Individual	18 000 Pts	18 000 Pts
Couple Pareja	36 000 Pts	36 000 Pts

Caddy	Caddy	4 000 Pts
Electric Trolley	Carro eléctrico	1 500 Pts/18 holes
Buggy	Coche	5 000 Pts/18 holes
Clubs	Palos	2 000 Pts/18 holes

Credit cards Tarjetas de crédito
VISA - Eurocard - MasterCard - AMEX - JCB

Access Acceso : Marbella → Cadiz.
Nueva Andalucia km 180, turn right → Golf
Map 7 on page 1109 Plano 7 Página 1109

GOLF COURSE / RECORRIDO — 17/20

Site	Emplazamiento	▬▬▬▬▭
Maintenance	Mantenimiento	▬▬▬▬▭
Architect	Arquitecto	Javier Araña
Type	Tipo	residential, parkland
Relief	Relieve	▬▬▬▭▭
Water in play	Agua	▬▬▭▭▭
Exp. to wind	Exp. al viento	▬▬▭▭▭
Trees in play	Arboles	▬▬▬▭▭

Scorecard Tarjeta	Chp. Campeonato	Mens Caballeros	Ladies Damas
Length Longitud	6242	5936	5167
Par	72	72	72

Advised golfing ability
Nivel de juego aconsejado — 0 12 24 36 ▬▬▬▬

Hcp required Handicap exigido 28 Men, 36 Ladies

CLUB HOUSE & AMENITIES / CLUB HOUSE Y DEPENDENCIAS — 7/10

Pro shop	Pro-shop	▬▬▬▭
Driving range	Campo de prácticas	▬▬▬▭
Sheltered	cubierto	no
On grass	sobre hierba	yes
Putting-green	putting-green	yes
Pitching-green	pitching-green	no

HOTEL FACILITIES / HOTELES CERCANOS — 7/10

HOTELS HOTELES
Andalucia Plaza — Nueva Andalucia
415 rooms, D 30 500 Pts — 4 km
Tel (34) 952 - 812 000, Fax (34) 952 - 814 792

Puente Romano — Marbella, Cta de Cádiz
217 rooms, D 52 000 Pts. — 2 km
Tel (34) 952 - 820 900, Fax (34) 952 - 775 766

Pyr Hotel — Puerto Banus
319 rooms, D 15 700 Pts — 2 km
Tel (34) 952 - 817 353, Fax (34) 952 - 817 907

RESTAURANTS RESTAURANTES
Cypriano — Puerto Banús
Tel (34) 952 - 811 077 — 5 km

Taberna del Alabardero — Puerto Banús
Tel (34) 952 - 812 794 — 5 km

1127

Este es un buen campo de vacaciones. Está en un plano descendente hacia el mar por lo cual algunos hoyos disfrutan de unas vistas espléndidas dominando el Atlántico y otros hoyos lo sortean audazmente. El 5 es un par 3 de 115 metros que se conoce como Pebble Beach porque hay que tirar sobre un acantilado. El 6, en cambio, es un par 4 de 331 metros, en subida, de espaldas al mar, que domina el Teide, el volcán dormido y nevado en invierno que preside el panorama desde le centro de la isla. No es un campo difícil ni especialmente largo, suele soplar una brisa marina que refresca y motiva al buen jugador a desplegar los recursos de su juego con viento. Unas recientes obras de mantenimiento han mejorado sensiblemente el estado general del campo. El pitch & putt es recomendable por su esmerado ciudado y decoración.

Here is an excellent holiday course. It is located on a slope stretching down to the sea and offers some holes with splendid views over the Atlantic and others a little less spectacular but just as interesting and daring. Hole N°5 for example is a par 3 of 115 metres, reminiscent of Pebble Beach because you have to hit the tee-shot over a cliff. By contrast, the 6th is an uphill 331-metre par 4, turning away from the sea, overlooked by the Teide, a dormant volcano whose winter snows enhance the panorama in the middle of the island. Amarilla is not an impossible course, nor is it particularly long, and there is often a stiff sea breeze which refreshes and encourages golfers who know how to cope with wind. Recent maintenance work has significantly improved the condition of the course, and the pitch 'n putt layout is highly recommended for its manicured appearance and decoration.

Amarilla Golf & Country Club   1989
E - 38639 SAN MIGUEL DE ABONA - TENERIFE

Office	Secretaria	(34) 922 - 730 319
Pro shop	Pro-shop	(34) 922 - 730 319
Fax	Fax	(34) 922 - 730 085
Situation	Situación	

Santa Cruz de Tenerife (pop. 203 000), 60 km
Playa de Las Americas, 15 km

Annual closure	Cierre anual	no
Weekly closure	Cierre semanal	no

Fees main season
Precios tempor. alta 18 holes

	Week days Semana	We/Bank holidays Fin de sem./fiestas
Individual Individual	9 000 Pts	9 000 Pts
Couple Pareja	18 000 Pts	18 000 Pts
Caddy	Caddy	no
Electric Trolley	Carro eléctrico	no
Buggy	Coche	4 500 Pts/18 holes
Clubs	Palos	800 Pts/18 holes

Credit cards Tarjetas de crédito
VISA - Eurocard - MasterCard - AMEX

1128

Access Acceso : Motorway TF1 / Autovia del Sur - Tenerife Sur. Exit (Salida) San Miguel de Abona-Los Abrigos. Go towards the sea, → Las Galletas
Map 9 on page 1112 Plano 9 Página 1112

GOLF COURSE
RECORRIDO   **15**/20

Site	Emplazamiento	
Maintenance	Mantenimiento	
Architect	Arquitecto	Donald Steel
Type	Tipo	parkland
Relief	Relieve	
Water in play	Agua	
Exp. to wind	Exp. al viento	
Trees in play	Arboles	

Scorecard Tarjeta	Chp. Campeonato	Mens Caballeros	Ladies Damas
Length Longitud	6077	5782	4967
Par	72	72	72

Advised golfing ability		0	12	24	36
Nivel de juego aconsejado					
Hcp required	Handicap exigido	28 Men, 36 Ladies			

CLUB HOUSE & AMENITIES
CLUB HOUSE Y DEPENDENCIAS   **7**/10

Pro shop	Pro-shop	
Driving range	Campo de prácticas	
Sheltered	cubierto	no
On grass	sobre hierba	yes, 15 places
Putting-green	putting-green	yes
Pitching-green	pitching-green	yes

HOTEL FACILITIES
HOTELES CERCANOS   **7**/10

HOTELS HOTELES

Arona GH		Los Cristianos
399 rooms, D 27 000 Pts		10 km
Tel (34) 922 - 750 678		
Fax (34) 922 - 750 243		
Paradise Park		Los Cristianos
480 rooms, D 19 000 Pts		10 km
Tel (34) 922 - 794 762		
Fax (34) 922 - 750 193		

RESTAURANTS RESTAURANTES

El Rincón del Arroz		Los Cristianos
Tel (34) 922 - 797 370		10 km
Avencio		El Médano
Tel (34) 922 - 176 079		2 km
El Rable		San Isidro
Tel (34) 922 - 390 698		10 km

El más que aceptable 18 hoyos «Rosner» es sin duda más difícil que éste, pero es demasiado acidentado y todo el mundo no tiene el presupuesto - o el deseo - para añadir al green-fee el precio de un coche eléctrico casi obligatorio si no se quiere terminar a cuatro pates. Este campo es mucho más plano, y pese a no estar entre las mejores realizaciones de la región, posee suficientes cualidades como para justificar una visita. Tal vez los buenos jugadores encuentren que sus dificultades son escasas, pero el golfista medio, sobre todo si está de vacaciones, pensará que son más que suficientes. Las calles son anchas, los greenes rápidos y bastante ondulados lo que exige mucho a la hora de patear. Como los obstáculos son muy visibles, la estrategia es clara y eso puede conducir a conseguir un buen resultado en la primera visita. Si preferimos divertir nos antes que concentrarnos, el match play es muy agradable. Siendo el terreno muy arcilloso es preferible evitar las épocas de lluvias.

The very fortright «New» 18 hole course is unquestionably tougher than this one, but it is very hilly and not everyone has the budget (or inclination) to supplement their green-fee with the virtually compulsory buggy (if you don't want to end up crawling home on all fours, that is). This layout is much flatter, and without attaining the standard of some other courses in the region, it has enough going for it to warrant a visit. While the experts might find the challenge a little limited, the average hacker will certainly find it quite enough to handle... if they are in the holiday mood. The fairways are wide and the greens rather sharply contoured and quick, so putting requires careful consideration. Since the hazards are clearly visible, game strategy is clear and you might even attempt to card a good score first time out. If you prefer having fun to concentrating, match-play is an enjoyable solution. The terrain contains a lot of clay, so avoid rainy days.

Atalaya Golf & Country Club — 1968
Ctra de Benahavis km. 0.7 - San Pedro
E - 29680 ESTEPONA (MALAGA)

Office	Secretaria	(34) 952 - 882 812
Pro shop	Pro-shop	(34) 952 - 888 142
Fax	Fax	(34) 952 - 887 897
Situation	Situación	

Estepona (pop. 36 307), 12 km
San Pedro de Alcantara, 3 km

Annual closure	Cierre anual	no
Weekly closure	Cierre semanal	no

Fees main season
Precios tempor. alta 18 holes

	Week days Semana	We/Bank holidays Fin de sem./fiestas
Individual Individual	8 500 Pts	8 500 Pts
Couple Pareja	17 000 Pts	17 000 Pts

Caddy	Caddy	no
Electric Trolley	Carro eléctrico	no
Buggy	Coche	5 000 Pts/18 holes
Clubs	Palos	4 000 Pts/18 holes

Credit cards Tarjetas de crédito VISA -AMEX

Access Acceso : Marbella → Estepona
Map 7 on page 1109 Plano 7 Página 1109

GOLF COURSE
RECORRIDO — **13**/20

Site	Emplazamiento	
Maintenance	Mantenimiento	
Architect	Arquitecto	B. Von Limburger
Type	Tipo	open country, residential
Relief	Relieve	
Water in play	Agua	
Exp. to wind	Exp. al viento	
Trees in play	Arboles	

Scorecard Tarjeta	Chp. Campeonato	Mens Caballeros	Ladies Damas
Length Longitud	6142	5856	5188
Par	72	72	72

Advised golfing ability Nivel de juego aconsejado	0	12	24	36

Hcp required   Handicap exigido   28 Men, 36 Ladies

CLUB HOUSE & AMENITIES
CLUB HOUSE Y DEPENDENCIAS — **6**/10

Pro shop	Pro-shop	
Driving range	Campo de prácticas	
Sheltered	cubierto	no
On grass	sobre hierba	yes
Putting-green	putting-green	yes
Pitching-green	pitching-green	yes

HOTEL FACILITIES
HOTELES CERCANOS — **7**/10

HOTELS HOTELES

Atalaya Park   Estepona
448 rooms, D 25 200 Pts   1,5 km
Tel (34) 952 - 884 801, Fax (34) 952 - 885 735

El Paraiso   Estepona
182 rooms, D 27 000 Pts   3 km
Tel (34) 952 - 883 000, Fax (34) 952 - 882 019

Guadalmina   San Pedro
80 rooms, D 27 200 Pts   4 km
Tel (34) 952 - 882 211, Fax (34) 952 - 882 291

RESTAURANTS RESTAURANTES

El Gamonal   San Pedro de Alcantara
Tel (34) 952 - 789 921   4 km

Los Nieto   San Pedro de Alcantara
Tel (34) 952 - 883 491   3 km

1129

Agrandado en 1995, Bendinat sigue siendo un recorrido muy corto en el que los desniveles impiden apreciar bien las distancias, especialmente a la hora de atacar unos green a menudo en alto y bien diseñados por el arquitecto Martin Hawtree. Sin embargo el diseño de los bunkers y calles no son muy originales. Conviene ser prudente cuando se juega por primera vez ya que es difícil encontrar las bolas que se salen de calle. En el primer hoyo ya uno se da cuenta que no será fácil obtener un buen resultado. No obstante resulta muy divertido jugar en match-play incluso entre jugadores de diferentes niveles. El relieve del campo aconseja alquilar un coche, sobre todo si hace calor. Bien es verdad que la proximidad del mar refresca un poco, pero el viento puede ser molesto. No es un golf inolvidable, pero merece la pena conocerlo.

Enlarged in 1995, Bendinat is still a very short course, although the steep slopes do tend to confuse appreciation of distance, an important factor here to hit a number of elevated greens, well designed by designer Martin Hawtree. Unfortunately, the bunkers and fairways are not quite in the same class. Your first round will require a cautious approach, as balls that leave the fairway are never easy to find. From the very first hole, you can tell that a good score here is quite some achievement. It is, though, fun to play in match-play, even with players of different abilities. This hilly course calls for a buggy, especially in hot weather, although the sea close-by brings a welcome cooling breeze, and wind that can cause a few upsets on the course. Bendinat is hardly unforgettable, but is worth a visit.

Real Club de Bendinat — 1986

Campoamor S/N
E - 07181 CALVIA - MALLORCA

Office	Secretaria	(34) 971- 405 200
Pro shop	Pro-shop	(34) 971- 405 450
Fax	Fax	(34) 971- 700 786
Situation	Situación	

Palma (pop. 308 616), 7 km

Annual closure	Cierre anual	no
Weekly closure	Cierre semanal	no

Fees main season
Precios tempor. alta 18 holes

	Week days Semana	We/Bank holidays Fin de sem./fiestas
Individual Individual	9 000 Pts	9 000 Pts
Couple Pareja	18 000 Pts	18 000 Pts

Caddy	Caddy	no
Electric Trolley	Carro eléctrico	no
Buggy	Coche	6 000 Pts/18 holes
Clubs	Palos	2 500 Pts/18 holes

Credit cards Tarjetas de crédito
VISA - Eurocard - MasterCard

1130

```
              Palma
              de Mallorca
0   1 km       →

        GOLF
                         ○
   C719
                San Agustin
                 Illetas
   Portals Nous
Palma Nova

      Bahia de Palma
```

Access Acceso : Palma → Bendinat,
Golf between Illetas and Portals Nous
Map 9 on page 1112 Plano 9 Página 1112

GOLF COURSE / RECORRIDO — 13/20

Site	Emplazamiento	▆▆▆▆▆▆▁
Maintenance	Mantenimiento	▆▆▆▆▆▆▁
Architect	Arquitecto	Fred Hawtree
Type	Tipo	residential, hilly
Relief	Relieve	▆▆▆▆▆▆▆
Water in play	Agua	▆▆▁▁▁▁▁
Exp. to wind	Exp. al viento	▆▆▆▆▆▁▁
Trees in play	Arboles	▆▆▆▁▁▁▁

Scorecard Tarjeta	Chp. Campeonato	Mens Caballeros	Ladies Damas
Length Longitud	5650	5650	4990
Par	70	70	70

Advised golfing ability	0	12	24	36
Nivel de juego aconsejado	▆▆▆▆▆▆▁			

Hcp required Handicap exigido 27 Men, 35 Ladies

CLUB HOUSE & AMENITIES / CLUB HOUSE Y DEPENDENCIAS — 6/10

Pro shop	Pro-shop	▆▆▆▆▆▁▁
Driving range	Campo de prácticas	▆▆▆▆▁▁▁
Sheltered	cubierto	no
On grass	sobre hierba	yes
Putting-green	putting-green	yes
Pitching-green	pitching-green	yes

HOTEL FACILITIES / HOTELES CERCANOS — 7/10

HOTELS HOTELES

Bendinat — Bendinat
32 rooms, D 31 500 Pts. — 2 km
Tel (34) 971 - 675 725
Fax (34) 971 - 677 276

Punta Negra — Palmanova
69 rooms, D 25 200 Pts. — 3 km
Tel (34) 971 - 680 762
Fax (34) 971 - 683 919

Son Caliu — Palmanova
235 rooms, D 23 100 Pts — 3 km
Tel (34) 971 - 682 200
Fax (34) 971 - 683 720

RESTAURANTS RESTAURANTES

Binnacle — Portals Nous
Tel (34) 971 - 676 977 — 5 km

BONALBA

Confirma la clase de Ramón Espinosa. Bonalba a pesar de su corta existencia es un recorrido que hay que conocer. La diversidad de los hoyos y la variedad de golpes que hay que jugar constituye un desafío para los más técnicos que tendrán que evitar numerosos laguitos, en línea de juego en una buena mitad del recorrido, que aparecen después de los primeros hoyos que sirven de precalentamiento. Pero no hay que dejarse impresionar por esas dificultades: con tees de salida adelantados, resultará divertido para cualquier jugador. Sólo los buenos pegadores escogerán las salidas de atrás, donde la longitud y colocación de los obstáculos dan al recorrido su verdadera fisionomía. No obstante, para emitir un juicio más definitivo hay que esperar que la vegetación se desarrolle: se han plantado 3.000 árboles, especialmente palmeras. Pero ya desde ahora es un recorrido que merece la pena conocer.

This is definitely a Ramon Espinosa layout which, despite its tender years, is a course worth knowing. The variety between holes and shots makes this a good challenge for technicans, who like the rest have to negotiate a number of small lakes, in play on half the holes, especially at the beginning. Thereafter the going gets a little easier. But don't be put off by the water; if they play from the front tees, players of all abilities can get along together here. Only the big-hitters will prefer the back-tees, where the length of the layout and position of hazards give the course its true physionomy. To really judge, though, we'll wait until the plants and trees start to grow. Some 3,000 were planted, especially palm trees, but this is already a course well worth knowing about.

Club de Golf Bonalba		1995
Partida de Bonalba S/N		
E - 03110 MUCHAMIEL-ALICANTE		
Office	Secretaria	(34) 965 - 955 337
Pro shop	Pro-shop	(34) 965 - 955 337
Fax	Fax	(34) 965 - 955 337
Situation	Situación	
Alicante (pop. 275 111), 15 km		
Annual closure	Cierre anual	no
Weekly closure	Cierre semanal	no

Fees main season		
Precios tempor. alta 18 holes		
	Week days Semana	We/Bank holidays Fin de sem./fiestas
Individual Individual	5 000 Pts	6 000 Pts
Couple Pareja	10 000 Pts	12 000 Pts

Caddy	Caddy	no
Electric Trolley	Carro eléctrico	1 200 Pts/18 holes
Buggy	Coche	3 000 Pts/18 holes
Clubs	Palos	1 500 Pts/18 holes

Credit cards Tarjetas de crédito
VISA - MasterCard - AMEX

Access Acceso : A7 → Alicante,
Exit (Salida) 67 → Alcoy → Busot → Golf
Map 6 on page 1107 Plano 6 Página 1107

GOLF COURSE
RECORRIDO   14/20

Site	Emplazamiento	
Maintenance	Mantenimiento	
Architect	Arquitecto	Ramón Espinosa
Type	Tipo	country, hilly
Relief	Relieve	
Water in play	Agua	
Exp. to wind	Exp. al viento	
Trees in play	Arboles	

Scorecard	Chp.	Mens	Ladies
Tarjeta	Campeonato	Caballeros	Damas
Length Longitud	6367	6096	5483
Par	72	72	72

Advised golfing ability	0	12	24	36
Nivel de juego aconsejado				
Hcp required	Handicap exigido	28 Men, 36 Ladies		

CLUB HOUSE & AMENITIES
CLUB HOUSE Y DEPENDENCIAS   6/10

Pro shop	Pro-shop	
Driving range	Campo de prácticas	
Sheltered	cubierto	no
On grass	sobre hierba	no (24 mats)
Putting-green	putting-green	yes
Pitching-green	pitching-green	yes

HOTEL FACILITIES
HOTELES CERCANOS   6/10

HOTELS HOTELES
Meliá Alicante   Alicante
540 rooms, D 21 500 Pts.   15 km
Tel (34) 965 - 205 000, Fax (34) 965 - 204 756

San Juan   Campello
29 rooms, D 7 900 Pts.   2 km
Tel (34) 965 - 652 308, Fax (34) 965 - 652 642

Villa San Juan   San Juan de Alicante
40 rooms, D 7 900 Pts.   3 km
Tel (34) 965 - 652 308, Fax (34) 965 - 652 642

RESTAURANTS RESTAURANTES
El Patio de San Juan   San Juan de Alicante
Tel (34) 965 - 656 800   3 km

La Maestra   San Juan de Alicante
Tel (34) 965.- 658 560   3 km

1131

Las dificultades económicas han frenado la expansión de este golf residencial y si el recorrido estuviese mejor cuidado se le podría atribuir una mejor nota. Robert Trent Jones Jr, siguiendo la tradición de su padre, ha creado un diseño muy estratégico en el que constantemente hay que calcular los riesgos antes de jugar. Lo ha construido con un refinamiento estético muy personal, removiendo grandes cantidades de tierra, tarea indispensable para poder jugar en un terreno tan rocoso. Construido alrededor del «Barranco», una especie de riachuelo omnipresente y protegido por numerosos bunkers, el recorrido presenta dificultades bien diseminadas y permite un buen ritmo de juego, especialmente a los jugadores con experiencia, ya que a los demás les costará bastante jugar su handicap. Los greens son amplios y bien diseñados, algunos tienen múltiples escalones, pero ninguno es ciego. Sin caer en la exageración y teniendo en cuenta las cuestas, se aconseja alquilar un coche.

Financial problems have jeopardised the expansion of this residential course and better green-keeping would certainly have meant a higher score. In the family tradition, Robert Trent Jones Jnr. has designed a highly strategic layout, where risks constantly need calculating before each shot. He has modeled space in his very own tasteful and stylish way, but also with impressive contouring of the land. And this was necessary for this rocky terrain to be at all playable. Revolving around the "Barocco", a sort of omnipresent wadi, and defended by numerous bunkers, the course has an even spread of hazards to provide good golf at a good pace. At least for experienced players, as the less proficient golfer will have a problem playing to his handicap. The greens are huge and very well designed; some have several tiers, but none is blind. Without being too steep, the course is hilly enough to advise taking a buggy.

Bonmont - Terres Noves — 1990
E - 43300 MONT-ROIG DEL CAMP (TARRAGONA)

Office	Secretaria	(34) 977 - 818 140
Pro shop	Pro-shop	(34) 977 - 818 140
Fax	Fax	(34) 977 - 818 146
Situation	Situación	

Hospitalet del Infante (pop. 2 690), 6 km
Cambrils (pop. 14 903), 15 km

Annual closure	Cierre anual	no
Weekly closure	Cierre semanal	no

Fees main season
Precios tempor. alta full day

	Week days Semana	We/Bank holidays Fin de sem./fiestas
Individual Individual	5 500 Pts	8 000 Pts
Couple Pareja	11 000 Pts	16 000 Pts
Caddy	Caddy	no
Electric Trolley	Carro eléctrico	no
Buggy	Coche	5 000 Pts/18 holes
Clubs	Palos	3 000 Pts/18 holes

Credit cards Tarjetas de crédito
VISA - Eurocard - MasterCard - AMEX - DC

1132

Access Acceso : A7 Barcelona → Valencia, Exit (salida) 38. Hospitalet del Infante → Mora, 2 km → Mont Roig, Golf 4 km
Map 4 on page 1103 Plano 4 Página 1103

GOLF COURSE / RECORRIDO — 16/20

Site	Emplazamiento	
Maintenance	Mantenimiento	
Architect	Arquitecto	R. Trent Jones Jr
Type	Tipo	residential, open country
Relief	Relieve	
Water in play	Agua	
Exp. to wind	Exp. al viento	
Trees in play	Arboles	

Scorecard Tarjeta	Chp. Campeonato	Mens Caballeros	Ladies Damas
Length Longitud	6371	6050	5501
Par	72	72	72

Advised golfing ability Nivel de juego aconsejado	0	12	24	36

Hcp required — Handicap exigido — 27 Men, 36 Ladies

CLUB HOUSE & AMENITIES / CLUB HOUSE Y DEPENDENCIAS — 7/10

Pro shop	Pro-shop	
Driving range	Campo de prácticas	
Sheltered	cubierto	no
On grass	sobre hierba	yes
Putting-green	putting-green	yes
Pitching-green	pitching-green	yes

HOTEL FACILITIES / HOTELES CERCANOS — 6/10

HOTELS HOTELES

Pino Alto — Hospitalet del Infante
137 rooms, D 17 300 Pts. — 6 km
Tel (34) 977 - 811 000, Fax (34) 977 - 810 907

Bonmont — Golf
19 rooms, D 17 000 Pts. — 500 m
Tel (34) 977 - 818 140, Fax (34) 977 - 818 146

Termes Montbrio — Montbrio
133 rooms, D 18 800 Pts. — 8 km
Tel (34) 977 - 814 000, Fax (34) 977 - 826 251

RESTAURANTS RESTAURANTES

Can Bosch — Cambrils
Tel (34) 977 - 360 019 — 15 km

Casa Gatell — Cambrils
Tel (34) 977 - 360 057 — 15 km

La belleza del lugar anuncia una agradable jornada en medio de un paisaje con poco arbolado en el que predomina la vegetación de monte. Es un recorrido no muy accidentado con una longitud que gustará a los pegadores que podrán intentar llegar a green en dos pares 4 muy cortos (el 11 y el 13) y ganar puntos en los pares 5. El diseño de Sanz y García no denota una gran imaginación ya que lo que han intentado ante todo es agradar a todos los jugadores, logrando un recorrido muy funcional. Con greens correctos y poco protegidos se pueden obtener buenos resultados que agradarán a los jugadores. Bien es verdad que se pueden encontrar en la región recorridos más difíciles, pero Campoamor es un buen test para afinar su juego sin demasiadas dificultades. Un verdadero recorrido para las vacaciones.

A very pretty site heralds a pleasant day's golfing in rather open countryside, where the garrigue shrub is the main and most attractive form of vegetation. The course is not hilly, and the length will appeal to big-hitters, who can try and reach two very short par 4s (the 11th and 13th) from the tee and pick up points on the par 5s. The Sanz and Garcia layout has nothing exceptionally imaginative about it, but their aim was to appeal to players, so the course's functional side is a positive point. The greens are good but have few bunkers, and the opportunities are there to card a good score, always a welcome treat for the wounded ego. You can certainly find more challenging courses than this in the region, but Campoamor is a great place to sharpen up your game without too many mishaps. A real holiday course.

Real Club de Golf Campoamor   1989

Ctra de Torrevieja a Cartagena, km 9
E - 03192 DEHESA DE CAMPOAMOR -
ORIHUELA (ALICANTE)

Office	Secretaria	(34) 965 - 321 366
Pro shop	Pro-shop	(34) 965 - 320 104
Fax	Fax	(34) 965 - 322 454
Situation	Situación	

Alicante (pop. 275 111), 57 km
Torrevieja (pop. 25 891), 8 km

Annual closure	Cierre anual	no
Weekly closure	Cierre semanal	no

Fees main season
Precios tempor. alta 18 holes

	Week days Semana	We/Bank holidays Fin de sem./fiestas
Individual Individual	5 000 Pts	5 000 Pts
Couple Pareja	10 000 Pts	10 000 Pts

Damas GF 3500 Pts

Caddy	Caddy	no
Electric Trolley	Carro eléctrico	1 200 Pts/18 holes
Buggy	Coche	4 000 Pts/full day
Clubs	Palos	1 500 Pts/full day

Credit cards Tarjetas de crédito   no

Orihuela
Laguno Salada de Torrevieja
Alicante
San Miguel de Salinas A 351
TORREVIEJA
Villamartin N 332
La Veleta
La Zenia
GOLF
0   2   4 km
Dehesa de Campoamor

Access Acceso : N332 Torrevieja → Dehesa de Campoamor, Cabo Roig, Km 48 → Golf
Map 6 on page 1107 Plano 6 Página 1107

GOLF COURSE
RECORRIDO   14/20

Site	Emplazamiento	
Maintenance	Mantenimiento	
Architect	Arquitecto	Gregorio Sanz Carmelo Garcia
Type	Tipo	hilly, residential
Relief	Relieve	
Water in play	Agua	
Exp. to wind	Exp. al viento	
Trees in play	Arboles	

Scorecard Tarjeta	Chp. Campeonato	Mens Caballeros	Ladies Damas
Length Longitud	6203	6056	5094
Par	72	72	72

Advised golfing ability Nivel de juego aconsejado	0	12	24	36

Hcp required   Handicap exigido   28 Men, 36 Ladies

CLUB HOUSE & AMENITIES
CLUB HOUSE Y DEPENDENCIAS   6/10

Pro shop	Pro-shop	
Driving range	Campo de prácticas	
Sheltered	cubierto	no
On grass	sobre hierba	yes
Putting-green	putting-green	yes
Pitching-green	pitching-green	yes

HOTEL FACILITIES
HOTELES CERCANOS   6/10

HOTELS HOTELES

Torrejoven   Torrevieja
105 rooms, D 8 800 Pts.   4 km
Tel (34) 965 - 714 052, Fax (34) 965 - 715 315

Orihuela Costa   La Zenia
15 rooms, D 14 700 Pts   8 km
Tel (34) 966 - 760 800, Fax (34) 966 - 761 326

Meridional   Guardamar del Segura
52 rooms, D 12 900 Pts   20 km
Tel (34) 965 - 728 340, Fax (34) 965 - 728 306

RESTAURANTS RESTAURANTES

Cabo Roig   Torrevieja
Tel (34) 966 - 760 290   8 km

Morales   Los Montesinos
Tel (34) 966 - 721 293

1133

CANYAMEL

Emplazado dentro de un paisaje típico de la montaña mallorquina, es un éxito de José Gancedo el haber conseguido realizar algunos hoyos espectaculares en la parte más accidentada (los nueve hoyos de la ida). Se ha preservado la naturaleza, así como algunas tapias e incluso una antigua granja que delimita el ángulo del dog-leg del hoyo 9. Al igual que en otros golfs de la isla hay que reflexionar antes de atacar, logrando muchas veces mejores resultados si se juega la seguridad y se sabe evitar las dificultades. Mejor es preservar sus fuerzas para atacar unos greens a menudo en alto, con escalones y bien protegidos. Su longitud es razonable y hay que juagarlo varias veces para mejor apreciar la progresión de los resultados. No se aburre uno.

In a typical setting of Majorcan countryside and mountains, Canyamel is a pretty little number designed by José Gancedo. The hillier part of the course (the front 9) includes some quite spectacular holes. The land's natural beauty has been preserved, together with some low walls and even an old farmhouse marking the corner of the dog-leg on hole N° 9. As with many other courses on the island, this is not a layout to attack without thinking first. Playing safe often gives better results. If you keep out of trouble, the going is easier and you can save your strength (important here) to negotiate some tricky approach shots to elevated, multi-tiered and well-defended greens. Very human in length, Canyamel is a course you want to play several times, not to understand it (it has little to hide) but to enjoy getting your score down. Good fun all the way.

Canyamel Golf — 1987

Carretera de las Cuevas s/n
E - 07589 CAPDEPERA MALLORCA

Office	Secretaria	(34) 971 - 841 313
Pro shop	Pro-shop	(34) 971 - 841 313
Fax	Fax	(34) 971 - 841 384
Situation	Situación	

Palma (pop. 308 616), 76 km

Annual closure	Cierre anual	no
Weekly closure	Cierre semanal	no

Fees main season
Precios tempor. alta 18 holes

	Week days Semana	We/Bank holidays Fin de sem./fiestas
Individual Individual	9 200 Pts	9 200 Pts
Couple Pareja	18 400 Pts	18 400 Pts

Caddy	Caddy	no
Electric Trolley	Carro eléctrico	no
Buggy	Coche	6 000 Pts/18 holes
Clubs	Palos	2 500 Pts/18 holes

Credit cards Tarjetas de crédito
VISA - MasterCard

1134

Access Acceso : C715 Palma → Manacor
→ Artá → Canyamel
Map 9 on page 1112 Plano 9 Página 1112

GOLF COURSE / RECORRIDO — 15/20

Site	Emplazamiento	
Maintenance	Mantenimiento	
Architect	Arquitecto	J. Gancedo
Type	Tipo	country, mountain
Relief	Relieve	
Water in play	Agua	
Exp. to wind	Exp. al viento	
Trees in play	Arboles	

Scorecard Tarjeta	Chp. Campeonato	Mens Caballeros	Ladies Damas
Length Longitud	6017	5841	5393
Par	73	73	73

Advised golfing ability 0 12 24 36
Nivel de juego aconsejado
Hcp required Handicap exigido 27 Men, 35 Ladies

CLUB HOUSE & AMENITIES / CLUB HOUSE Y DEPENDENCIAS — 6/10

Pro shop	Pro-shop	
Driving range	Campo de prácticas	
Sheltered	cubierto	no
On grass	sobre hierba	yes
Putting-green	putting-green	yes
Pitching-green	pitching-green	yes

HOTEL FACILITIES / HOTELES CERCANOS — 6/10

HOTELS HOTELES

Aguait — Cala Rajada
188 rooms, D 15 400 Pts. — 15 km
Tel (34) 971 - 563 408, Fax (34) 971 - 565 106

Canyamel Park — Capdepera
133 rooms, D 14 700 Pts. — 1 km
Tel (34) 971 - 565 511, Fax (34) 971 - 565 614

S'Entrador Playa — Cala Guya
207 rooms, D 12 600 Pts — 8 km
Tel (34) 971 - 564 312, Fax (34) 971 - 564 517

RESTAURANTS RESTAURANTES

Ses Rotjes — Cala Rajada
Tel (34) 971 - 563 108 — 15 km

Los Pablos — Capdepera
Tel (34) 971 - 565 543 — 5 km

Es una obra de Dan Maples que ha trabajado mucho en Carolina del Norte y en Florida. De hecho los seis lagos le dan un aire de estilo americano sin desfigurar el paisaje natural. Desde las salidas de atrás es un excelente recorrido de competición que se puede «dulcificar» escogiendo tees de salida más avanzados, logrando así que las calles parezcan menos estrechas. Tiene muchos bunkers y bosques de los que es difícil salir. Hay que saber manejar bien todos los palos, sin olvidar el pat en unos greens bastante grandes y con ondulaciones nada fáciles de apreciar. Si a la belleza de algunas vistas hacia la montaña añadimos la calidad de los cuidados de mantenimiento, comprenderemos mejor por qué Capdepera se sitúa entre los mejores recorridos de Mallorca.

This is one of the few courses in Europe designed by Dan Maples, who has worked extensively in North Carolina and Florida. The American style is evident with the six artificial lakes, which in no way upset the natural look of the landscape and terrain. This is an excellent tournament course from the back-tees and one which gradually mellows as you move further forward. From the front, the course doesn't look as tight, and the many bunkers and tough undergrowth seem less harrowing. You will need every club in the bag, not forgetting the putter on greens which are on the large side, well-shaped and not always easy to read. Add to this some pretty viewpoints over the mountains and good general upkeep and you will understand why we consider this to be a class golf course, one of the very best in Majorca.

Capdepera Golf - Roca Viva — 1991
Ctra Arta - Capdepera - Apdo 202
E - 07570 ARTA (MALLORCA)

Office	Secretaria	(34) 971 - 818 500
Pro shop	Pro-shop	(34) 971 - 818 500
Fax	Fax	(34) 971 - 818 193
Situation	Situación	

Palma (pop. 308 616), 70 km

Annual closure	Cierre anual	no
Weekly closure	Cierre semanal	no

Fees main season
Precios tempor. alta 18 holes

	Week days Semana	We/Bank holidays Fin de sem./fiestas
Individual Individual	9 200 Pts	9 200 Pts
Couple Pareja	18 400 Pts	18 400 Pts

Caddy	Caddy	no
Electric Trolley	Carro eléctrico	900 Pts/18 holes
Buggy	Coche	6 000 Pts/18 holes
Clubs	Palos	3 000 Pts/18 holes

Credit cards Tarjetas de crédito
VISA - Eurocard - MasterCard - AMEX

Access Acceso : C715 Palma → Artá,
→ Capdepera Km 3,5
Map 9 on page 1112 Plano 9 Página 1112

GOLF COURSE
RECORRIDO — 15/20

Site	Emplazamiento	
Maintenance	Mantenimiento	
Architect	Arquitecto	Dan Maples
Type	Tipo	country, hilly
Relief	Relieve	
Water in play	Agua	
Exp. to wind	Exp. al viento	
Trees in play	Arboles	

Scorecard Tarjeta	Chp. Campeonato	Mens Caballeros	Ladies Damas
Length Longitud	6284	5919	4800
Par	72	72	72

Advised golfing ability — 0 12 24 36
Nivel de juego aconsejado
Hcp required   Handicap exigido   27 Men, 36 Ladies

CLUB HOUSE & AMENITIES
CLUB HOUSE Y DEPENDENCIAS — 7/10

Pro shop	Pro-shop	
Driving range	Campo de prácticas	
Sheltered	cubierto	no
On grass	sobre hierba	yes
Putting-green	putting-green	yes
Pitching-green	pitching-green	yes

HOTEL FACILITIES
HOTELES CERCANOS — 6/10

HOTELS HOTELES

Aguait — Cala Rajada
188 rooms, D 15 400 Pts. — 3 km
Tel (34) 971 - 563 408, Fax (34) 971 - 565 106

Serrano Palace — Cala Rajada
150 rooms, D 30 000 Pts. — 3 km
Tel (34) 971 - 563 350, Fax (34) 971 - 563 630

Canyamel Park — Capdepera
133 rooms, D 14 700 Pts. — 4 km
Tel (34) 971 - 565 511, Fax (34) 971 - 565 614

RESTAURANTS RESTAURANTES

Ses Rotjes — Cala Rajada
Tel (34) 971 - 563 108 — 15 km

Los Pablos — Capdepera
Tel (34) 971 - 565 543 — 5 km

1135

CASTILLO DE GORRAIZ

) **17** **7** **7**

No había muchos golfs en la región de Pamplona y teniendo en cuenta que el de Ulzama ha sido ampliado a 18 hoyos muy recientemente, la creación de Castillo de Gorraiz ha sido muy bien acogida. Las instalaciones son muy completas con un amplísimo campo de prácticas, tenis y piscina. Su creador es Cabell Robinson, autor también de La Cala en la Costa del Sol y de soberbios recorridos en Marruecos. Ha sabido aprovechar el terreno reservando una parte a residencias entre las que serpentean las calles anchas y muy abiertas. Los tees de salida son elevados dominando los hoyos. No siempre es necesario utilizar el drive ya que al peligro de roughs densos recomienda la prudencia si no se tiene mucha precisión. Tres grandes obstáculos de agua se encuentran en la línea de juego, lo que obliga a bien calcular tanto la distancia como la precisión de los golpes. Un golf bien logrado.

Given that the region of Pamplona is not too well off for golf courses and that Ulzama has only recently been upgraded to a full 18-holer, the advent of Castillo de Gorraiz was most welcome. Facilities are excellent, with a huge driving range, tennis courts and a pool. The course is the work of Cabell Robinson, who designed La Cala on the Costa del Sol and some superb courses in Morocco (including the King's Course in Agadir and the astonishing Amelkis in Marrakesh). Here he has worked wonders with the terrain, a part of which is reserved for villas through which the wide and very open fairways wind their way around the course. The tee-boxes are elevated so you are looking down on the holes, and you don't always have to use the driver; danger from the thick rough calls for care if accuracy is not your forte. At the other end of the fairway, the huge, roundly-contoured greens give you the opportunity to show your putting skills. Three large water hazards are also in play, so length as well as accuracy is at a premium. A very fine course.

Club de Golf Castillo de Gorraiz		**1995**
Urbanizacion Gorraiz		
E - 31620 VALLE DE EGUES (Navarra)		

Office	Secretaria	(34) 948 - 337 073
Pro shop	Pro-shop	(34) 948 - 337 073
Fax	Fax	(34) 948 - 337 315
Situation	Situación	
Pamplona (pop. 191 197), 5 km		
Annual closure	Cierre anual	no
Weekly closure	Cierre semanal	no

Fees main season
Precios tempor. alta 18 holes

	Week days Semana	We/Bank holidays Fin de sem./fiestas
Individual Individual	5 000 Pts	6 000 Pts
Couple Pareja	10 000 Pts	12 000 Pts

Caddy	Caddy	no
Electric Trolley	Carro eléctrico	700 Pts/18 holes
Buggy	Coche	3 000 Pts/18 holes
Clubs	Palos	1 000 Pts/18 holes

Credit cards Tarjetas de crédito VISA

1136

Access Acceso : A-15 Exit (Salida) Pamplona
→ Francia. Turn at Olaz-Huarte
Map 1 on page 867 Plano 1 Página 867

GOLF COURSE
RECORRIDO

17 /20

Site	Emplazamiento	
Maintenance	Mantenimiento	
Architect	Arquitecto	Cabell Robinson
Type	Tipo	parkland, residential
Relief	Relieve	
Water in play	Agua	
Exp. to wind	Exp. al viento	
Trees in play	Arboles	

Scorecard Tarjeta	Chp. Campeonato	Mens Caballeros	Ladies Damas
Length Longitud	6321	6036	5131
Par	72	72	72

Advised golfing ability		0	12	24	36
Nivel de juego aconsejado					
Hcp required	Handicap exigido	no			

CLUB HOUSE & AMENITIES
CLUB HOUSE Y DEPENDENCIAS

7 /10

Pro shop	Pro-shop	
Driving range	Campo de prácticas	
Sheltered	cubierto	12 mats
On grass	sobre hierba	no, 21 mats open air
Putting-green	putting-green	yes
Pitching-green	pitching-green	yes

HOTEL FACILITIES
HOTELES CERCANOS

7 /10

HOTELS HOTELES
Iruña Park — Pamplona
225 rooms, D 20 400 Pts — 7 km
Tel (34) 948 - 173 200, Fax (34) 948 - 172 387

Tres Reyes — Pamplona
160 rooms, D 21 000 Pts — 7 km
Tel (34) 948 - 226 600, Fax (34) 948 - 222 930

Aguirre 12 rooms, D 5 300 Pts — Pamplona
Tel (34) 948 - 330 375 — 5 km

RESTAURANTS RESTAURANTES
Hartza — Pamplona 5 km
Tel (34) 948 - 224 568

Egües - Tel (34) 948 - 330 081 — Egües 5 km

Josetxo - Tel (34) 948 - 222 097 — Pamplona 5 km

Situado en plena naturaleza, este recorrido es algo más que un simple paseo. Era de esperar dada la fama de Javier Arana, cuyos diseños dejan siempre de lado lo que es trivial y son testimonio de un gran conocimiento del golf. Ha sabido adaptarse a un terreno en el que las desnivelaciones ya eran suficientes para no añadir más dificultades. Las calles son claras, sin trampas, lo esencial del juego se desarrolla en las llegadas a green, donde es necesario evitar árboles y algunos bunkers peligrosos. No muy largo, a veces estrecho, este recorrido exige precisión, favorece el placer del golf entre jugadores de diferente nivel o en familia. Robusto y natural, no es un recorrido de campeonato, pero todos los amateurs se sentirán agusto sin que por eso se pueda decir que es un golf fácil. Unicos defectos: aguanta mal la lluvia y los greens normales están cerrados en invierno.

Located out in the country, this course is more than just a pleasant walk. And this is only to be expected from Javier Arana, whose layouts are always out of the ordinary and reveal considerable golfing intelligence. He has played a lot with the terrain and the marked differences in relief in order not to add too many hazards. With the fairways free of traps, the key to playing the course is around the greens, avoiding the trees and the few dangerous bunkers. Not particularly long and sometimes tight, this course places emphasis on accuracy and provides shared golfing pleasure among players of different levels or with the family. Rugged and natural, Cerdaña is definitely not a championship course, but all week-end golfers will feel at home here, without ever finding the course too easy. The only faults are a terrain that doesn't take too well to heavy rain, and the greens that are closed in winter.

Real Club de Golf de Cerdaña — 1929

Apartat de correus 63
E - 17520 PUIGCERDA (Girona)

Office	Secretaria	(34) 972 - 141 408
Pro shop	Pro-shop	(34) 972 - 141 040
Fax	Fax	(34) 972 - 881 338
Situation	Situación	

Puigcerdà (pop. 6 414), 1 km
Barcelona (pop. 1 681 132), 150 km

Annual closure	Cierre anual	no
Weekly closure	Cierre semanal	no

Fees main season
Precios tempor. alta 18 holes

	Week days Semana	We/Bank holidays Fin de sem./fiestas
Individual Individual	10 000 Pts	10 000 Pts
Couple Pareja	20 000 Pts	20 000 Pts
Caddy	Caddy	no
Electric Trolley	Carro eléctrico	1 000 Pts/18 holes
Buggy	Coche	5 000 Pts/18 holes
Clubs	Palos	1 000 Pts/18 holes

Credit cards Tarjetas de crédito
VISA - Eurocard - MasterCard - AMEX

0   2   4 km

FONT-ROMEU (FRANCE)
Puigcerdà
Bolvir
Ger
GOLF
N 260
Prats de Cerdanya
Alp
Bellver de Cerdanya
La Molina
BERGA   Túnel del Cadí

Access Acceso : Barcelona A18 → Manresa
→ «Tunel del Cadi y Puigcerda»
Map 2 on page 869 Plano 2 Página 869

GOLF COURSE / RECORRIDO — 14/20

Site	Emplazamiento	
Maintenance	Mantenimiento	
Architect	Arquitecto	Javier Araña
Type	Tipo	hilly
Relief	Relieve	
Water in play	Agua	
Exp. to wind	Exp. al viento	
Trees in play	Arboles	

Scorecard Tarjeta	Chp. Campeonato	Mens Caballeros	Ladies Damas
Length Longitud	5886	5726	5015
Par	71	71	71

Advised golfing ability Nivel de juego aconsejado	0	12	24	36

Hcp required   Handicap exigido   27 Men, 36 Ladies

CLUB HOUSE & AMENITIES / CLUB HOUSE Y DEPENDENCIAS — 7/10

Pro shop	Pro-shop	
Driving range	Campo de prácticas	
Sheltered	cubierto	7 mats
On grass	sobre hierba	yes
Putting-green	putting-green	yes
Pitching-green	pitching-green	yes

HOTEL FACILITIES / HOTELES CERCANOS — 7/10

HOTELS HOTELES

Torre del Remei — Bolvir de Cerdaña
11 rooms, D 39 900 Pts — l km
Tel (34) 972 - 140 182, Fax (34) 972 - 140 449

Chalet del Golf — Puigcerda
11 rooms, D 18 900 Pts — 500 m
Tel (34) 972 - 880 950, Fax (34) 972 - 880 966

Puigcerda — Puigcerda
39 rooms, D 9 500 Pts. — 1 km
Tel (34) 972 - 882 181, Fax (34) 972 - 881 256

RESTAURANTS RESTAURANTES

Torre del Remei — Bolvir de Cerdaña
Tel (34) 972 - 140 182 — 1 km

La Tieta — Puigcerda
Tel (34) 972 - 880 156 — 2 km

1137

Una vez más, Javier Arana demuestra aquí estar entre los mejores arquitéctos del siglo. Es una pena que no haya expresado su talento fuera de las fronteras españolas. A la vez exigente por su longitud así como por la precisión que requiere, éste campo nos proporciona un placer siempre renovado. De mediano relieve, no se deja descubrir tan facilmente y hacen falta muchas veces para llegar a entender todas sus sutilezas. Los árboles y los bunkers de recorrido constituyen sus principales dificultades, y le damos las gracias a Arana de no haber creado demasiados problemas en los accesos a los greenes. Tan sólo el estado de estos nos incita a revisar nuestra opinión, aunque se está llevando a cabo la reconstrucción de todos y cada uno de los greenes lo que servirá a que vuelva a ser uno de los grandes campos en el futuro. Hay que decir que el índice de ocupación del campo es altísimo ya que el Club de Campo es uno de los más grandes de España. Aconsejamos por tanto a los vistantes de evitar los fines de semana.

Here again, Javier Arana gives a further demonstration of why he will go down as one of the century's greatest architects. What a shame his great talent is not on show outside his home country. Demanding both in length and accuracy, this course, located just outside Madrid, is a real joy to play everytime. Averagely hilly (but easy to walk), the course is not easy to discover and needs several rounds to grasp the subtler points. The trees and fairway bunkers are the main difficulties, and we should be grateful to Arana for not having created too many difficulties when approaching the greens. The state of the putting surfaces is the only slight blemish on our appreciation, but whole-scale replanting should lead to an improvement in the future. It should also be said that the course is very busy in what is certainly Spain's biggest golf club. So follow our advice and avoid week-ends.

Club de Campo Villa de Madrid — 1932
Carretera de Castilla km 2
E - 28040 MADRID

Office	Secretaria	(34) 915 - 502 010
Pro shop	Pro-shop	(34) 915 - 502 010
Fax	Fax	(34) 915 - 502 023
Situation	Situación	

Madrid (pop. 3 084 373), 1 km

Annual closure	Cierre anual	no
Weekly closure	Cierre semanal	no

Fees main season
Precios tempor. alta 18 holes

	Week days Semana	We/Bank holidays Fin de sem./fiestas
Individual Individual	6 750 Pts	12 775 Pts
Couple Pareja	13 500 Pts	25 550 Pts

Access to the club (Acceso al Club): 1 850 Pts (weekdays), 3 725 Pts (We)

Caddy	Caddy	no
Electric Trolley	Carro eléctrico	1 250 Pts/18 holes
Buggy	Coche	4 300 Pts/18 holes
Clubs	Palos	2 800 Pts/18 holes

Credit cards Tarjetas de crédito — no

1138

Access Acceso : Madrid, Carretera de Castilla
→ Segovia
Map 3 on page 870 Plano 3 Página 870

GOLF COURSE
RECORRIDO — 16/20

Site	Emplazamiento	
Maintenance	Mantenimiento	
Architect	Arquitecto	Javier Arana
Type	Tipo	forest
Relief	Relieve	
Water in play	Agua	
Exp. to wind	Exp. al viento	
Trees in play	Arboles	

Scorecard Tarjeta	Chp. Campeonato	Mens Caballeros	Ladies Damas
Length Longitud	6335	6094	5169
Par	72	72	72

Advised golfing ability		0 12 24 36
Nivel de juego aconsejado		
Hcp required	Handicap exigido	28 Men, 36 Ladies

CLUB HOUSE & AMENITIES
CLUB HOUSE Y DEPENDENCIAS — 8/10

Pro shop	Pro-shop	
Driving range	Campo de prácticas	
Sheltered	cubierto	112 mats
On grass	sobre hierba	yes
Putting-green	putting-green	yes
Pitching-green	pitching-green	yes

HOTEL FACILITIES
HOTELES CERCANOS — 8/10

HOTELS HOTELES
Princesa — Madrid — 3 km
275 rooms, D 34 900 Pts
Tel (34) 915 - 422 100, Fax (34) 915 - 427 328

Melia Madrid — Madrid — 3 km
276 rooms, D 27 800 Pts
Tel (34) 915 - 418 200, Fax (34) 915 - 411 988

Moncloa Garden — Madrid — 4 km
121 rooms, D 17 300 Pts
Tel (34) 915 - 424 582, Fax (34) 915 - 427 169

RESTAURANTS RESTAURANTES
El Amparo - Tel (34) 914 - 316 456 — Madrid 6 km

Taberna de Alabardero — Madrid — 5 km
Tel (34) 915 - 472 577

La Trainera - Tel (34) 915 - 760 575 — Madrid 5 km

El gabinete del arquitecto Hamilton Stutt no es de los más conocidos, pero aquí ha construido un recorrido simpático, sin dificultades infranqueables permitiendo que jugadores de todos los niveles y edades pasen un día agradable. El relieve es mesurado, las pendientes suaves, alternando hoyos anchos y estrechos rodeados de pinos a menudo en la línea de juego y alcornoques, lo que obliga a pegar con efecto a la bola para contornearlos, pasar por arriba... o por debajo.Los greens están bien protegidos, correctamente diseñados y la mayor parte de las veces se puede aprochar haciendo rodar la bola. Sólo hay un hoyo ciego, reflejando así la filosofía del recorrido: el golf es para todo el mundo y si hay recorridos exigentes también tiene que haber otros para los golfistas de nivel medio. Este forma parte de esa categoría, pero los buenos jugadores tampoco se aburrirán.

Hamilton Stutt is not the most famous name in golf course design, but here they have produced a pleasant course without insuperable difficulties on which players of all levels and all ages can spend an enjoyable day. The ground relief is moderate, with a few gentle slopes and alternating wide and tight fairways edged by pine and oak trees that are often very much in play. The player will often have to work the ball to get around them, put the ball over the top... or keep low below the branches. The greens are well defended and correctly designed, but most of them can be approached with chip shots. Only one green is blind, which reflects the thinking behind the whole course, namely golf is for everyone, and while there are demanding courses, there should also be courses for average players. This is one such course, but even the best players will have fun.

Club de Golf Costa Brava 1968

Urbanitzacio Golf Costa Brava
E - 17246 SANTA CRISTINA D'ARO (GIRONA)

Office	Secretaria	(34) 972 - 837 150
Pro shop	Pro-shop	(34) 972 - 837 055
Fax	Fax	(34) 972 - 837 272
Situation	Situación	

San Feliu de Guixols (pop. 16 088), 7 km
Girona (pop. 70 409), 30 km

Annual closure	Cierre anual	no
Weekly closure	Cierre semanal	no

Fees main season
Precios tempor. alta 18 holes

	Week days Semana	We/Bank holidays Fin de sem./fiestas
Individual Individual	8 000 Pts	8 000 Pts
Couple Pareja	16 000 Pts	16 000 Pts

Caddy	Caddy	no
Electric Trolley	Carro eléctrico	no
Buggy	Coche	5 000 Pts/18 holes
Clubs	Palos	1 500 Pts/18 holes

Credit cards Tarjetas de crédito
VISA - Eurocard - MasterCard - AMEX

Access Acceso : C250 Sant Feliu → Girona,
Santa Cristina d'Aro → Golf
Map 2 on page 869 Plano 2 Página 869

GOLF COURSE
RECORRIDO 13/20

Site	Emplazamiento	
Maintenance	Mantenimiento	
Architect	Arquitecto	Hamilton Stutt & Co
Type	Tipo	residential, hilly
Relief	Relieve	
Water in play	Agua	
Exp. to wind	Exp. al viento	
Trees in play	Arboles	

Scorecard Tarjeta	Chp. Campeonato	Mens Caballeros	Ladies Damas
Length Longitud	5573	5445	4670
Par	70	70	70

Advised golfing ability	0	12	24	36
Nivel de juego aconsejado				

Hcp required   Handicap exigido 27 Men, 36 Ladies

CLUB HOUSE & AMENITIES
CLUB HOUSE Y DEPENDENCIAS 7/10

Pro shop	Pro-shop	
Driving range	Campo de prácticas	
Sheltered	cubierto	4 mats
On grass	sobre hierba	yes
Putting-green	putting-green	yes
Pitching-green	pitching-green	yes

HOTEL FACILITIES
HOTELES CERCANOS 7/10

HOTELS HOTELES

Golf Costa Brava		Santa Cristina
91 rooms, D 15 700 Pts.		50 m
Tel (34) 972 - 835 151, Fax (34) 972 - 837 588		

Hostal de la Gavina		S'Agaró
74 rooms, D 36 750 Pts		7 km
Tel (34) 972 - 321 100, Fax (34) 972 - 321 573		

Park Hotel San Jorge		Calonge
104 rooms, D 26 250 Pts		12 km
Tel (34) 972 - 652 311, Fax (34) 972 - 652 576		

RESTAURANTS RESTAURANTES

Els Tinars		Llagostera
Tel (34) 972 - 830 626		6 km

Les Panolles		Santa Cristina
Tel (34) 972 - 837 011		1 km

1139

El lugar es agradable y descansado. A pesar de que el recorrido se sitúa muy a menudo en la falda de la ladera y es muy ondulado, no se necesita alquilar un coche. Las calles con hierba bien tupida sostienen bien la bola, los greens la aguantan bien, sólo algunos olivos aislados o agrupados pueden perturbar la trayectoria de juego: no es un recorrido de gran dificultad y gustará a la mayoría de los jugadores. El recorrido no ofrece emociones fuertes, aunque la vuelta, a partir del 12, es más técnica que la ida, especialmente en los dos pares 5 (el 13 y el 16). Sin embargo, los arquitectos podrían haber tenido un poco más de imaginación colocando dificultades en lugares más amenazadores. En la familia de golfs gratos y agradables para todos los niveles de juego, Costa Dorada ocupa un buen lugar.

The site is pleasant and relaxing after reaching the course set in a little palm grove. Although much of Costa Dorada is laid out on the side of a hill with rolling fairways, it is easily walkable. The lushly-grassed fairways carry the ball well and the greens pitch well, too. Only a few isolated or bunches of olive trees can get in the way of your ball, so this is not too complicated a course to get around. Most players will like its honest style, but they shouldn't expect too much in the way of excitement, even though from the 12th hole onwards the course becomes more technical, especially the two par 5s (especially holes 13 and 16). We might have expected a little more imagination from the architects, with hazards perhaps located in a more threatening manner. But in the family of pleasant and encouraging courses for all levels of play, Costa Dorada is a front-runner.

Club de Golf Costa Dorada Tarragona — 1982

Apdo 600
E - 43080 TARRAGONA

Office	Secretaria	(34) 977 - 653 361
Pro shop	Pro-shop	(34) 977 - 653 361
Fax	Fax	(34) 977 - 653 028
Situation	Situación	

Tarragona (pop. 112 802), 5 km

Annual closure	Cierre anual	no
Weekly closure	Cierre semanal	no

Fees main season
Precios tempor. alta 18 holes

	Week days Semana	We/Bank holidays Fin de sem./fiestas
Individual Individual	6 000 Pts	10 000 Pts
Couple Pareja	12 000 Pts	20 000 Pts
Caddy Caddy		on request
Electric Trolley Carro eléctrico		no
Buggy Coche		4 000 Pts/18 holes
Clubs Palos		2 500 Pts/full day

Credit cards Tarjetas de crédito
VISA - MasterCard

1140

Access Acceso : A7 Barcelona → Valencia, Exit (Salida) 32, RN340 → Tarragona, Ctra El Catllar, Golf 2,7 km.
Map 4 on page 873 Plano 4 Página 873

GOLF COURSE RECORRIDO — 13/20

Site	Emplazamiento	▰▰▰▰▱▱
Maintenance	Mantenimiento	▰▰▰▰▱▱
Architect	Arquitecto	José Gancedo V. Sardá Saenger
Type	Tipo	hilly
Relief	Relieve	▰▰▰▱▱▱
Water in play	Agua	▰▰▱▱▱▱
Exp. to wind	Exp. al viento	▰▰▱▱▱▱
Trees in play	Arboles	▰▰▰▰▱▱

Scorecard Tarjeta	Chp. Campeonato	Mens Caballeros	Ladies Damas
Length Longitud	6223	5978	5136
Par	72	72	72

Advised golfing ability Nivel de juego aconsejado	0	12	24	36

Hcp required Handicap exigido no

CLUB HOUSE & AMENITIES CLUB HOUSE Y DEPENDENCIAS — 6/10

Pro shop	Pro-shop	▰▰▰▰▱▱
Driving range	Campo de prácticas	▰▰▰▱▱▱
Sheltered	cubierto	6 mats
On grass	sobre hierba	yes
Putting-green	putting-green	yes
Pitching-green	pitching-green	no

HOTEL FACILITIES HOTELES CERCANOS — 6/10

HOTELS HOTELES

Imperial Tarraco — Tarragona 6 km
155 rooms, D 18 700 Pts
Tel (34) 977 - 233 040
Fax (34) 977 - 216 566

Lauria — Tarragona 6 km
72 rooms, D 10 500 Pts
Tel (34) 977 - 236 712
Fax (34) 977 - 236 700

RESTAURANTS RESTAURANTES

Sol Ric — Tarragona 6 km
Tel (34) 977 - 232 032

Can Sala (Les Fonts) — N 240, 2 km, Tarragona 4 km
Tel (34) 977 - 228 575

La buena calidad del conjunto inmobiliario no sólo no molesta a los jugadores sino que se adapta muy bien al estilo americano del recorrido. Si añadimos que más vale alquilar un coche, uno podría creerse en Estados Unidos. El Bosque figura entre los buenos éxitos de Robert Trent Jones en España. El relieve es importante, se juega a menudo en pendiente y felizmente la estrategia de juego es clara ya que si los obstáculos son bien visibles, no dejan de ser peligrosos. La primera vez uno se siente acosado (para obtener un buen resultado) por una serie de greens ciegos que requieren trayectorias altas. No hay que dudar tirar a bandera puesto que los greens aguantan bien la bola. Los hoyos están bien integrados en el paisaje cuyo diseño y dificultades son variados, sobre todo cuatro excelentes dog-legs. Hay que hacer mención especial de los pares 3.

The surrounding real estate is a stylish programme and won't bother the players, especially since the properties fit in very well with what is a very American-style course. Add to that the definite advantage of playing with a buggy and you might think you actually were on American soil. El Bosque is one of the great success-stories of Robert Trent Jones in Spain. It is hilly, you are often faced with a sloping lie, but the game strategy is pretty clear. And that's lucky, because although the hazards are visible, they are very dangerous. First time out, players looking for a good score will have trouble only with a series of blind greens which demand high approach shots. Go for the pin, too, because these greens pitch well. The holes blend in well with the landscape, and the design and difficulties vary considerably. In particular there are four beautiful dog-legs. A special mention should go to the quality of the par 3s.

El Bosque Golf & Country Club 1975

Carretera de Godelleta, km 4,1
E - 46370 CHIVA (VALENCIA)

Office	Secretaria	(34) 961 - 808 000
Pro shop	Pro-shop	(34) 961 - 808 000
Fax	Fax	(34) 961 - 808 001
Situation	Situación	

Valencia (pop. 751 734), 20 km
Chiva (pop. 7 562), 5 km

Annual closure	Cierre anual	no
Weekly closure	Cierre semanal	no

Fees main season
Precios tempor. alta 18 holes

	Week days Semana	We/Bank holidays Fin de sem./fiestas
Individual Individual	8 000 Pts	8 000 Pts
Couple Pareja	16 000 Pts	16 000 Pts

Caddy	Caddy	no
Electric Trolley	Carro eléctrico	no
Buggy	Coche	4 500 Pts/18 holes
Clubs	Palos	2 500 Pts/18 holes

Credit cards Tarjetas de crédito VISA - AMEX

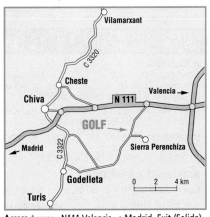

Access Acceso : N111 Valencia → Madrid, Exit (Salida) Godelleta. Km. 324, → Godelleta, Golf km. 4,1
Map 4 on page 873 Plano 4 Página 873

GOLF COURSE RECORRIDO 16/20

Site	Emplazamiento	
Maintenance	Mantenimiento	
Architect	Arquitecto	Robert Trent Jones
Type	Tipo	country, hilly, residential
Relief	Relieve	
Water in play	Agua	
Exp. to wind	Exp. al viento	
Trees in play	Arboles	

Scorecard Tarjeta	Chp. Campeonato	Mens Caballeros	Ladies Damas
Length Longitud	6367	5995	5178
Par	72	72	72

Advised golfing ability
Nivel de juego aconsejado   0   12   24   36

Hcp required   Handicap exigido   28 Men, 36 Ladies

CLUB HOUSE & AMENITIES CLUB HOUSE Y DEPENDENCIAS 7/10

Pro shop	Pro-shop	
Driving range	Campo de prácticas	
Sheltered	cubierto	25 mats
On grass	sobre hierba	yes
Putting-green	putting-green	yes
Pitching-green	pitching-green	yes

HOTEL FACILITIES HOTELES CERCANOS 4/10

HOTELS HOTELES
Sidi Saler — El Saler
276 rooms, D 23 600 Pts — 24 km
Tel (34) 961 - 610 411, Fax (34) 961 - 610 838

Melia Valencia Palace — Valencia
199 rooms, D 27 900 Pts — 30 km
Tel (34) 963 - 375 037, Fax (34) 963 - 375 532

Sol Azafata — Manises
126 rooms, D 15 600 Pts — 10 km
Tel (34) 961 - 546 100, Fax (34) 961 - 532 019

RESTAURANTS RESTAURANTES
Azafata — Manises
Tel (34) 961 - 546 100 — 10 km

Albacar — Valencia
Tel (34) 963 - 951 005 — 30 km

1141

Abierto en 1987, ha quedado un poco eclipsado por la cercanía del recorrido «Verde». Es hora de reha-bilitarlo incluso si la proximidad del aeropuerto es más molesta e incluso a veces insoportable. Es una pena , ya que este recorrido enriquecido de pinos, palmeras y numerosos obstáculos de agua, tiene su propia personalidad con inspiración americana de los golfs de Florida o del Sur de California. El arquitecto Dave Thomas ha construido un recorrido franco, sin trampas camufladas: se le puede atacar de entrada y lograr jugar su handi-cap..., si no hay mucho viento. Adeñás de los obstáculos de agua, los bunkers son numerosos y peligrosos, espe-cialmente los de calle, inteligentemente colocados, bien cuidados y rodeados de montículos. Grandes y bien di-señados, los greens no son ni fáciles ni desconcertantes.

The nearby "Green" course has somewhat eclipsed its "Yellow" neighbour, opened in 1987. So it's time this course was restored to favour, even though the closeness of the airport is much more irksome and sometimes even unbearable. It's a pity, because lined with pines, palm trees and numerous water hazards, it has its own per-sonality, largely inspired by the American style of courses such as those found in Florida or southern California. Architect Dave Thomas has produced an honest course without concealing the traps, so you can get to grips with your game and hope to play to your handicap... if there's not too much wind. Away from the water, there are many dangerous bunkers, especially on the fairways, all of which are cleverly placed, well-designed and edged with mounds. The greens, all large and very well-designed, are not easy but never really disconcerting.

Real Club de Golf «El Prat» 1987

Ap. de Correus 10
E - 08820 EL PRAT DE LLOBREGAT (BARCELONA)

Office	Secretaria	(34) 933 - 790 278
Pro shop	Pro-shop	(34) 933 - 790 278
Fax	Fax	(34) 933 - 705 102
Situation	Situación	

Barcelona (pop. 1 681 132), 10 km
El Prat, 1 km

Annual closure	Cierre anual	no
Weekly closure	Cierre semanal	no

Fees main season
Precios tempor. alta full day

	Week days Semana	We/Bank holidays Fin de sem./fiestas
Individual Individual	12 380 Pts	24 840 Pts
Couple Pareja	24 760 Pts	49 680 Pts

Caddy	Caddy	on request
Electric Trolley	Carro eléctrico	580 Pts/18 holes
Buggy	Coche	4 035 Pts/18 holes
Clubs	Palos	3 000 Pts/full day

Credit cards Tarjetas de crédito
VISA - MasterCard

1142

Barcelona map area — Sant Bol, L'Hospitalet de Llobregat, El Prat de Llobregat, Castelldefels, GOLF
A2, A16, C 246
0 2 4 km

Access Acceso : C246 → Sitges
→ El Prat de Llobregat, El Prat, Golf 1 km
Map 2 on page 869 Plano 2 Página 869

GOLF COURSE
RECORRIDO **15**/20

Site	Emplazamiento	▰▰▰▱▱
Maintenance	Mantenimiento	▰▰▰▰▱
Architect	Arquitecto	David Thomas
Type	Tipo	open country
Relief	Relieve	▰▰▱▱▱
Water in play	Agua	▰▰▰▱▱
Exp. to wind	Exp. al viento	▰▰▰▰▱
Trees in play	Arboles	▰▰▰▱▱

Scorecard Tarjeta	Chp. Campeonato	Mens Caballeros	Ladies Damas
Length Longitud	6172	5873	5079
Par	72	72	72

Advised golfing ability		0	12	24	36
Nivel de juego aconsejado			▰		
Hcp required	Handicap exigido	28 Men, 36 Ladies			

CLUB HOUSE & AMENITIES
CLUB HOUSE Y DEPENDENCIAS **7**/10

Pro shop	Pro-shop	▰▰▰▰▱
Driving range	Campo de prácticas	▰▰▰▰▱
Sheltered	cubierto	8 mats
On grass	sobre hierba	yes
Putting-green	putting-green	yes
Pitching-green	pitching-green	yes

HOTEL FACILITIES
HOTELES CERCANOS **6**/10

HOTELS HOTELES

Alfa Aeropuerto	Mercabarna
99 rooms, D 23 000 Pts.	5 km
Tel (34) 933 - 362 564, Fax (34) 933 - 355 592	
Rallye - 107 rooms, D 22 000 Pts	Barcelona
Tel (34) 933 - 399 050, Fax (34) 934 - 110 790	10 km
Barcelona Plaza Hotel	Barcelona
357 rooms, D 26 300 Pts	10 km
Tel (34) 934 - 262 600, Fax (34) 934 - 262 351	

RESTAURANTS RESTAURANTES

Casa Alcaide - Tel (34) 933 - 791 012	El Prat 1 km
Gran Mercat (Hotel Alfa) Tel(34) 933 - 362 564	Mercabarna 5 km
Via Veneto - Tel (34) 932 - 007 244	Barcelona 10 km
Neichel - Tel (34) 932 - 038 408	Barcelona 10 km

Con toda razón, uno de los recorridos más famosos de España. Llano y al borde del mar, despliega algunos de sus hoyos entre pinos, aunque la mayor parte, por haberse secado, han desaparecido del resto del recorrido. En cambio algunas palmeras pueden complicar la vida y trayectoria de los jugadores. Sin que su arquitectura sea la de los tradicionales links, sin embargo presenta un aspecto típicamente briánico, tal vez una forma de homenaje por parte del arquitecto Javier Arana. Si los bunkers son numerosos tanto en calle como alrededor de los greens, en general no están en la línea de juego, lo que permite escoger entre aprochar por alto o hacer rodar la bola y cambiar de juego en función del viento. Los roughs, difíciles a causa de la hierba bermuda, sí que están en la línea de juego. Muy equilibrado, sin artificios, este grande de España pertenece a la mejor nobleza.

One of Spain's most famous courses, and quite rightly so. Flat and by the sea, the first holes wind their way through the pines, but on the rest of the course most of the trees have disappeared because of disease. In contrast, certain palm trees can make life difficult for off-line shots. Without having the typical architecture of a links course, it offers traditional British character, perhaps as a form of tribute from the architect Javier Arana. While bunkers are plentiful on the fairways and around the greens, they are not generally in the line of fire, thus allowing players to choose between pitching and chipping onto the greens, and to vary their play depending on the wind. The rough, however, is very much to the fore, and the Bermuda grass can be a tough proposition. Well-balanced and totally honest, this great little Spanish number is of the very best vintage.

Real Club de Golf «El Prat» 1954

Ap. de Correus 10
E - 08820 EL PRAT DE LLOBREGAT (BARCELONA)

Office	Secretaria	(34) 933 - 790 278
Pro shop	Pro-shop	(34) 933 - 790 278
Fax	Fax	(34) 933 - 705 102
Situation	Situación	

Barcelona (pop. 1 681 132), 10 km
El Prat, 1 km

Annual closure	Cierre anual	no
Weekly closure	Cierre semanal	no

Fees main season
Precios tempor. alta full day

	Week days Semana	We/Bank holidays Fin de sem./fiestas
Individual Individual	12 380 Pts	24 840 Pts
Couple Pareja	24 760 Pts	49 680 Pts

Caddy	Caddy	on request
Electric Trolley	Carro eléctrico	580 Pts/18 holes
Buggy	Coche	4 035 Pts/18 holes
Clubs	Palos	3 000 Pts/full day

Credit cards Tarjetas de crédito VISA - MasterCard

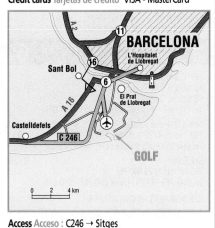

Access Acceso : C246 → Sitges
→ El Prat de Llobregat, El Prat, Golf 1 km
Map 2 on page 869 Plano 2 Página 869

GOLF COURSE RECORRIDO 17 /20

Site	Emplazamiento	▰▰▰
Maintenance	Mantenimiento	▰▰▰
Architect	Arquitecto	Javier Araña
Type	Tipo	seaside course
Relief	Relieve	▰
Water in play	Agua	▰▰
Exp. to wind	Exp. al viento	▰▰
Trees in play	Arboles	▰▰▰

Scorecard Tarjeta	Chp. Campeonato	Mens Caballeros	Ladies Damas
Length Longitud	6224	5947	5124
Par	73	73	73

Advised golfing ability	0 12 24 36
Nivel de juego aconsejado	▰▰▰
Hcp required	Handicap exigido 28 Men, 36 Ladies

CLUB HOUSE & AMENITIES CLUB HOUSE Y DEPENDENCIAS 7 /10

Pro shop	Pro-shop	▰▰▰
Driving range	Campo de prácticas	▰▰▰
Sheltered	cubierto	8 mats
On grass	sobre hierba	yes
Putting-green	putting-green	yes
Pitching-green	pitching-green	yes

HOTEL FACILITIES HOTELES CERCANOS 6 /10

HOTELS HOTELES
Alfa Aeropuerto - 99 rooms, D 23 000 Pts. Mercabarna
Tel (34) 933 - 362 564, Fax (34) 933 - 355 592   5 km

Rallye - 107 rooms, D 22 000 Pts   Barcelona
Tel (34) 933 - 399 050, Fax (34) 934 - 110 790   10 km

Barcelona Plaza Hotel   Barcelona
357 rooms, D 26 300 Pts   10 km
Tel (34) 934 - 262 600, Fax (34) 934 - 262 351

RESTAURANTS RESTAURANTES
Casa Alcaide - Tel (34) 933 - 791 012   El Prat 1 km

Gran Mercat (Hotel Alfa)   Mercabarna
Tel (34) 933 - 362 564   5 km

Via Veneto - Tel (34) 932 - 007 244   Barcelona 10 km

Neichel - Tel (34) 932 - 038 408   Barcelona 10 km

1143

El placer de saborear uno de los mejores recorridos de Europa sólo puede verse alterado por un cuidado mediano. Los hoyos de links (del 5 al 9 y del 16 al 18) pueden compararse a los mejores recorridos del Reino Unido a los que el gran arquitecto Javier Arana ha rendido homenaje. Los demás hoyos presentan la misma estética y sólo el bosque les da un aspecto diferente. Hay muchos greens y obstáculos ciegos, lo que es característico en este tipo de recorridos que se amoldan a las dunas. Los greens son inmensos con caídas y ondulaciones difíciles. Por supuesto, jugar aquí su handicap es problemático, hay que dominar todos los golpes de golf, sobre todo con viento, y es casi una alegría perder ante tal recorrido. Incluso en neto será muy difícil igualar la proeza de Bernhard Langer, que logró aquí un 62 el último día del Open de España en 1984...

Only rather average standards of upkeep might spoil the joys of savouring one of Europe's best courses. The links holes (5 to 9 and 16 to 18) bear comparison with the best courses in the UK, to which architect Javier Arana has paid tribute here. The other holes are equally attractive, but run through a forest. There are a lot of blind greens and hazards here, and this is typical of this kind of course which hugs the dunes. The greens are often huge and the slopes hard to read. Naturally, playing to your handicap on a course of this standard can pose problems, as it takes every shot in the book, especially when the wind is up. But losing to a course like this is almost a pleasure. Even with a net score, you will be hard put to equal the achievement of Bernhard Langer, who carded a 62 here in the last round of the 1984 Spanish Open...

Campo de Golf El Saler — 1968

Parador Nacional «Luis Vivès»
E - 46012 EL SALER (VALENCIA)

Office	Secretaria	(34) 961 - 610 384
Pro shop	Pro-shop	(34) 961 - 610 384
Fax	Fax	(34) 961 - 627 016
Situation	Situación	

Valencia, (pop. 777 427), 8 km

Annual closure	Cierre anual	no
Weekly closure	Cierre semanal	no

Fees main season
Precios tempor. alta 18 holes

	Week days Semana	We/Bank holidays Fin de sem./fiestas
Individual Individual	8 000 Pts	8 000 Pts
Couple Pareja	16 000 Pts	16 000 Pts

Caddy	Caddy	no
Electric Trolley	Carro eléctrico	2 000 Pts/18 holes
Buggy	Coche	4 500 Pts/18 holes
Clubs	Palos	1 500 Pts/18 holes

Credit cards Tarjetas de crédito
VISA - Eurocard - AMEX

1144

VALENCIA

0   2   4 km

Pinedo
Catarroja
Pista de Silla
V15
Silla
El Saler
GOLF
A 7
N 332
L'Albufera
Hipòdromo
N 340
Gandía
Sueca

Access Acceso : V15 Valencia → El Saler, Golf 8 km
Map 6 on page 877 Plano 6 Página 877

GOLF COURSE / RECORRIDO — 18/20

Site	Emplazamiento	
Maintenance	Mantenimiento	
Architect	Arquitecto	Javier Araña
Type	Tipo	links
Relief	Relieve	
Water in play	Agua	
Exp. to wind	Exp. al viento	
Trees in play	Arboles	

Scorecard Tarjeta	Chp. Campeonato	Mens Caballeros	Ladies Damas
Length Longitud	6355	6044	5182
Par	72	72	72

Advised golfing ability Nivel de juego aconsejàdo	0	12	24	36
Hcp required Handicap exigido	no			

CLUB HOUSE & AMENITIES / CLUB HOUSE Y DEPENDENCIAS — 7/10

Pro shop	Pro-shop	
Driving range	Campo de prácticas	
Sheltered	cubierto	no
On grass	sobre hierba	yes
Putting-green	putting-green	yes
Pitching-green	pitching-green	yes

HOTEL FACILITIES / HOTELES CERCANOS — 6/10

HOTELS HOTELES

Parador « Luis Vivés » — El Saler
58 rooms, D 19 400 Pts.
Tel (34) 961 - 611 186, Fax (34) 961 - 627 016

Melia Valencia Palace — Valencia
199 rooms, D 27 900 Pts 10 km
Tel (34) 963 - 375 037, Fax (34) 963 - 375 532

Sidi Saler — El Saler
276 rooms, D 23 600 Pts 4 km
Tel (34) 961 - 610 411, Fax (34) 961 - 610 838

RESTAURANTS RESTAURANTES

Oscar Torrijos - Tel (34) 963 - 732 949 Valencia 10 km
Sidi Saler - Tel (34) 961 - 610 411 El Saler 5 km
Rias Gallegas - Tel (34) 963 - 572 007 Valencia 10 km

Empordá tendrá en el futuro 36 hoyos. Por el momento y antes de que se haya acabado de construir el club-house, previsto para finales de esta primavera, 18 hoyos ya han alcanzado su madurez (se han abierto otros 9). Los admiradores de von Hagge no se sorprenderán del diseño característico de montículos que separan las calles, sobre todo en los hoyos sin árboles. Fuera de calle, los roughs están cortados a diferentes alturas hasta convertirse en hierbas altas en los montículos. Esta preparación refinada se confirma con unos greens de excelente calidad, bien diseñados y a menudo muy largos, lo que complica la elección del palo en función de la colocación de las banderas. Si se tiene en cuenta los numerosos tees de salida, la longitud del recorrido puede variar al infinito. Espectacular y muy bien concebido, jugar aquí es apasionante y se ha convertido en uno de los grandes recorridos de Cataluña

Eventually, Emporda will feature 36 holes. For the time being, even before the completion of the club-house, scheduled for this spring, 18 holes have reached maturity (and 9 others are now open). Admirers of von Hagge will not be surprised by this layout, with mounds separating fairways, particularly on the holes without trees. Off the fairway there are two levels of rough before the high grass on the mounds. The same refined preparation is to be found on the excellent greens, which are well designed and often very long, another factor to complicate club selection according to pin positions. When looking at the very many tees, the length of this course can vary enormously. A spectacular, very well "crafted" and exciting course to play, whatever your level, this is already one of the great courses in Catalonia.

Emporda Golf Club		1991
Ctra de Palafrugell a Torroella		
E - 17257 GUALTA (GIRONA)		
Office	Secretaria	(34) 972 - 760 450
Pro shop	Pro-shop	(34) 972 - 760 450
Fax	Fax	(34) 972 - 757 100
Situation	Situación	
Palafrugell (pop. 17 343), 17 km		
Girona (pop. 70 409), 40 km		
Annual closure	Cierre anual	no
Weekly closure	Cierre semanal	no

Fees main season
Precios tempor. alta full day

	Week days Semana	We/Bank holidays Fin de sem./fiestas
Individual Individual	9 000 Pts	9 000 Pts
Couple Pareja	18 000 Pts	18 000 Pts

Caddy	Caddy	no
Electric Trolley	Carro eléctrico	1 600 Pts/18 holes
Buggy	Coche	5 000 Pts/18 holes
Clubs	Palos	2 000 Pts/full day

Credit cards Tarjetas de crédito
VISA - Eurocard - MasterCard - AMEX

Access Acceso : A7 Exit (Salida) 6 → Girona, GE643 →
Parlavà, Torroella, GE650 → Pals / Palafrugell
Map 2 on page 869 Plano 2 Página 869

GOLF COURSE
RECORRIDO **17**/20

Site	Emplazamiento	
Maintenance	Mantenimiento	
Architect	Arquitecto	Robert von Hagge
Type	Tipo	forest, open country
Relief	Relieve	
Water in play	Agua	
Exp. to wind	Exp. al viento	
Trees in play	Arboles	

Scorecard Tarjeta	Chp. Campeonato	Mens Caballeros	Ladies Damas
Length Longitud	6160	5855	4969
Par	71	71	71

Advised golfing ability		0 12 24 36
Nivel de juego aconsejado		
Hcp required	Handicap exigido	28 Men, 36 Ladies

CLUB HOUSE & AMENITIES
CLUB HOUSE Y DEPENDENCIAS **7**/10

Pro shop	Pro-shop	
Driving range	Campo de prácticas	
Sheltered	cubierto	no
On grass	sobre hierba	yes
Putting-green	putting-green	yes
Pitching-green	pitching-green .	yes

HOTEL FACILITIES
HOTELES CERCANOS **6**/10

HOTELS HOTELES
La Costa   Platja de Pals
120 rooms, D 25 200 Pts   10 km
Tel (34) 972 - 667 740, Fax (34) 972 - 667 736

Mas de Torrent   Torrent
30 rooms, D 30 500 Pts   13 km
Tel (34) 972 - 303 292, Fax (34) 972 - 303 293

Hotel Aiguablava   Fornells
90 rooms, D 15 700 Pts   15 km
Tel (34) 972 - 622 058, Fax (34) 972 - 622 112

RESTAURANTS RESTAURANTES
Can Bech   Fontanilles
Tel (34) 972 - 759 317   5 km

Sa Punta - Tel (34) 972 - 667 376   Pals 17 km

Mas Pou - Tel (34) 972 - 634 125   Palau-Sator 6 km

1145

ESCORPION

13	8	4

Construido en un antiguo naranjal, Escorpión ofrece una vegetación compuesta de naranjos y también de palmeras y algarrobos. Se puede jugar fácilmente sin coche. Sus excelentes cuidados realzan el interés de un diseño sencillo y no excepcional. Si bien hay que deplorar la semejanza repetitiva de los pares 4 (en dog-leg), debe resaltarse al menos la calidad técnica de los pares 5 y de los pares 3. No obstante, no se puede decir que este recorrido sea muy difícil por lo que se puede jugar fácilmente en familia o entre amigos de diferentes niveles de juego. Los greens son buenos, bien diseñados y los ante-green poco protegidos: se pueden atacar haciendo rodar la bola. Hay agua en la línea de juego de ocho hoyos, sin que ésto pueda asustar al jugador con cierta precisión. Finalmente, hay que resaltar la calidad y belleza del conjunto que alberga el club-house, muy bien restaurado.

Built in a former orange orchard, Escorpion naturally has a lot of orange trees, together with palm trees and carobs. It is easily walkable and the excellent maintenance work enhances the appeal of what is an honest, but never exceptional, layout. The repetitive style of the par 4s (all dog-legs) is a pity, but the par 3s and 5s are high standard, technical holes. With that said, no-one would consider this to be a tough course, and it is fun to play with the family or friends. The greens are grassy and well-designed, and the few frontal and green-side hazards mean you can often roll the ball onto the putting surface. Water is in play on eight of the holes, but should not unduly scare the more accurate players. One last item is the club house, whose splendid buildings have been beautifully renovated.

Club de Golf Escorpion — 1975

Apartado de Correos No 1
E - 46117 - BETERA (VALENCIA)

Office	Secretaria	(34) 961 - 601 211
Pro shop	Pro-shop	(34) 961 - 601 211
Fax	Fax	(34) 961 - 690 187
Situation	Situación	

Valencia (pop. 777 427), 20 km

Annual closure	Cierre anual	no
Weekly closure	Cierre semanal	no

Fees main season
Precios tempor. alta 18 holes

	Week days Semana	We/Bank holidays Fin de sem./fiestas
Individual Individual	8 000 Pts	*
Couple Pareja	16 000 Pts	*

* Members only (solo socios)

Caddy	Caddy	no
Electric Trolley	Carro eléctrico	1 500 Pts/18 holes
Buggy	Coche	4 500 Pts/18 holes
Clubs	Palos	1 500 Pts/18 holes

Credit cards Tarjetas de crédito — no

1146

Access Acceso : A7 → Ademús, Exit (Salida) 11,
→ Betera (3,5 km)
Map 4 on page 1103 Plano 4 Página 1103

GOLF COURSE / RECORRIDO — 13/20

Site	Emplazamiento	
Maintenance	Mantenimiento	
Architect	Arquitecto	Ron Kirby
Type	Tipo	country
Relief	Relieve	
Water in play	Agua	
Exp. to wind	Exp. al viento	
Trees in play	Arboles	

Scorecard Tarjeta	Chp. Campeonato	Mens Caballeros	Ladies Damas
Length Longitud	6319	6091	5293
Par	72	72	72

Advised golfing ability
Nivel de juego aconsejado — 0 12 24 36

Hcp required — Handicap exigido — 28 Men, 36 Ladies

CLUB HOUSE & AMENITIES / CLUB HOUSE Y DEPENDENCIAS — 8/10

Pro shop	Pro-shop	
Driving range	Campo de prácticas	
Sheltered	cubierto	5 mats
On grass	sobre hierba	yes
Putting-green	putting-green	yes
Pitching-green	pitching-green	yes

HOTEL FACILITIES / HOTELES CERCANOS — 4/10

HOTELS HOTELES

Sidi Saler — El Saler
276 rooms, D 23 600 Pts — 25 km
Tel (34) 961 - 610 411, Fax (34) 961 - 610 838

Melia Valencia Palace — Valencia
199 rooms, D 27 900 Pts — 20 km
Tel (34) 963 - 375 037, Fax (34) 963 - 375 532

Feria — Valencia
140 rooms, D 11 100 Pts — 10 km
Tel (34) 963 - 644 411, Fax (34) 963 - 645 483

RESTAURANTS RESTAURANTES

Azafata — Manises
Tel (34) 961 - 546 100 — 15 km

Albacar — Valencia
Tel (34) 963 - 951 005 — 20 km

Es de esperar que este paisaje de montaña no quede alterado por los proyectos de construcción inmobiliaria, que el recorrido conserve un aspecto natural, en contraste con los grandes recorridos ajardinados, y que la flora y fauna salvajes conserven sus hábitos y su medio ambiente. En una buena mitad del recorrido hay muchas subidas y bajadas por lo que se aconseja alquilar un coche. El arquitecto José Luis López, con inteligencia y buen sentido de golf, ha sabido transformar este terreno difícil. Los greens está¿n bien diseñados,son de buena calidad e interesantes de jugar. Por lo que respecta a las dificultades, hay que evaluar con mucha precisión las ondulaciones del terreno para escoger el buen palo, evitar los roughs poco acogedores. No hay que dejarse impresionar por el hoyo 3, ni por el muy largo par cinco llamado «la pista de esquí», ni tampoco por los lagos del hoyo 10. Si se quiere cambiar del ambiente «chic» de los recorridos de la costa, Estepona es un buen destino.

Hopefully, this mountain landscape will not be spoilt by real estate projects, the course will retain its natural appearance, in contrast with larger, more manicured courses, and the wild flora and fauna will carry on living and growing the way they are. A good half of the course is very hilly, so a buggy is more than recommended. Architect José-Luis Lopez has shaped this difficult terrain intelligently and with a good golfing mind. The well-designed and good quality greens are interesting to play. The course's difficulties involve more often than not assessing the changes in relief to choose the right clubs, avoiding the most unwelcome rough, and not being overwhelmed by the third hole, a very long par 5 called the «ski trail», or by the lakes around the tenth. Estepona is a handy address to make a change from the posher world of the coastal courses.

Estepona Golf

Apdo Correos 532
E - 29680 ESTEPONA (MALAGA)

Office	Secretaria	(34) 952 - 113 081
Pro shop	Pro-shop	(34) 952 - 113 081
Fax	Fax	(34) 952 - 113 080
Situation	Situación	

Gibraltar (pop. 28 339), 40 km
Estepona (pop. 36 307), 10 km

Annual closure	Cierre anual	no
Weekly closure	Cierre semanal	no

Fees main season
Precios tempor. alta 18 holes

	Week days Semana	We/Bank holidays Fin de sem./fiestas
Individual Individual	6 000 Pts	6 000 Pts
Couple Pareja	12 000 Pts	12 000 Pts

Caddy	Caddy	no
Electric Trolley	Carro eléctrico	no
Buggy	Coche	4 500 Pts/18 holes
Clubs	Palos	1 200 Pts/18 holes

Credit cards Tarjetas de crédito VISA

Access Acceso : CN 340 Marbella → Cadiz, Estepona km 150
Map 7 on page 1109 Plano 7 Página 1109

GOLF COURSE
RECORRIDO
14/20

Site	Emplazamiento	
Maintenance	Mantenimiento	
Architect	Arquitecto	José Luis Lopez
Type	Tipo	mountain
Relief	Relieve	
Water in play	Agua	
Exp. to wind	Exp. al viento	
Trees in play	Arboles	

Scorecard Tarjeta	Chp. Campeonato	Mens Caballeros	Ladies Damas
Length Longitud	6001	5610	5137
Par	72	72	72

Advised golfing ability		0	12	24	36
Nivel de juego aconsejado				
Hcp required	Handicap exigido	no		

CLUB HOUSE & AMENITIES
CLUB HOUSE Y DEPENDENCIAS
7/10

Pro shop	Pro-shop	
Driving range	Campo de prácticas	
Sheltered	cubierto	no
On grass	sobre hierba	yes
Putting-green	putting-green	yes
Pitching-green	pitching-green	no

HOTEL FACILITIES
HOTELES CERCANOS
6/10

HOTELS HOTELES

El Paraiso — Estepona
182 rooms, D 27 000 Pts — 8 km
Tel (34) 952 - 883 000, Fax (34) 952 - 882 019

Atalaya Park — Estepona
448 rooms, D 25 200 Pts — 8 km
Tel (34) 952 - 884 801, Fax (34) 952 - 885 735

Andalucia Plaza — Nueva Andalucia
415 rooms, D 30 500 Pts — 18 km
Tel (34) 952 - 812 000, Fax (34) 952 - 814 792

RESTAURANTS RESTAURANTES

De Medici - Tel (34) 952 - 884 687 — Estepona 8 km
El Rocio - Tel (34) 952 - 800 046 — Estepona 8 km
Casa de mi Azuela — Estepona
Tel (34) 952 - 791 967 — 8 km

1147

Fontanals se sitúa en primera línea entre los golfs de la Costa Brava. Rodeado de montañas, aunque llano, con algunas ondulaciones, es un test de primer orden con multitud de obstáculos, encontrándose los más peligrosos en los hoyos más cortos. Numerosos bunkers de calle y de green, con contornos muy elaborados (un poco al estilo de Trent Jones), ponen a prueba el sentido táctico y la virtuosidad del jugador, sin que la suerte intervenga para nada en un buen resultado. Se ha cuidado mucho la estética con muretes o guijarros delimitando los obstáculos de agua. Por momentos impresionante y siempre espectacular, este recorrido de Ramón Espinosa es largo , propicio a los buenos pegadores y en general a los jugadores con experiencia y con un buen juego corto. Difícilmente se le encontrarán defectos a esta obra maestra en la que sólo el club-house está sin acabar.

The Fontanals course is already at the forefront of courses along the Costa Brava. Surrounded by mountains but flat with only a few rolling fairways, this is a test of golf of the highest order with a multitude of hazards, the most dangerous of which are reserved for the short holes. Countless fairway and green-side bunkers, all carefully shaped (a little in the style of Trent Jones), are a great test for the tactical mind and virtuosity of any player, and luck plays no role in a good score. Very special care has been given to the visual side, with the water hazards neatly lined with low walls or pebbles. Often impressive and sometimes quite spectacular, this course by Ramon Espinosa is long and can be recommended to long-hitters and in general to experienced players with a sharp short game. They will be hard pushed to find any faults in this superb achievement, were only the club house remains to be completed.

Golf Fontanals de Cerdanya — 1994

E - 17538 SORIGUEROLA,
FONTANALS DE CERDANYA (GIRONA)

Office	Secretaria	(34) 972 - 144 374
Pro shop	Pro-shop	(34) 972 - 144 374
Fax	Fax	(34) 972 - 890 856
Situation	Situación	

Puigcerdà (pop. 6 414), 12 km

Annual closure	Cierre anual	no
Weekly closure	Cierre semanal	

no restaurant closed on tuesdays

Fees main season
Precios tempor. alta 18 holes

	Week days Semana	We/Bank holidays Fin de sem./fiestas
Individual Individual	5 500 Pts	14 000 Pts
Couple Pareja	11 000 Pts	28 000 Pts
Caddy Caddy		no
Electric Trolley Carro eléctrico		no
Buggy Coche		5 000 Pts/18 holes
Clubs Palos		1 000 Pts/full day

Credit cards Tarjetas de crédito
VISA - Eurocard - MasterCard

1148

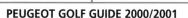

Access Acceso : Barcelona A18 → Manresa /
Puigcerdà. Manresa E9 → Puigcerdà,
Alp → Golf on left hand side
Map 2 on page 1099 Plano 2 Página 1099

GOLF COURSE
RECORRIDO — 18/20

Site	Emplazamiento	
Maintenance	Mantenimiento	
Architect	Arquitecto	Ramón Espinosa
Type	Tipo	open country
Relief	Relieve	
Water in play	Agua	
Exp. to wind	Exp. al viento	
Trees in play	Arboles	

Scorecard Tarjeta	Chp. Campeonato	Mens Caballeros	Ladies Damas
Length Longitud	6454	6159	5256
Par	72	72	72

Advised golfing ability — 0 12 24 36
Nivel de juego aconsejado
Hcp required — Handicap exigido — 28 Men, 36 Ladies

CLUB HOUSE & AMENITIES
CLUB HOUSE Y DEPENDENCIAS — 6/10

Pro shop	Pro-shop	
Driving range	Campo de prácticas	
Sheltered	cubierto	14 mats
On grass	sobre hierba	yes
Putting-green	putting-green	yes
Pitching-green	pitching-green	yes

HOTEL FACILITIES
HOTELES CERCANOS — 5/10

HOTELS HOTELES
Torre del Remei — Bolvir de Cerdanya
11 rooms, D 39 900 Pts — 10 km
Tel (34) 972 - 140 182
Fax (34) 972 - 140 449

Chalet del Golf — Puigcerda
11 rooms, D 18 900 Pts — 9 km
Tel (34) 972 - 880 950
Fax (34) 972 - 880 966

RESTAURANTS RESTAURANTES
Torre del Remei — Bolvir de Cerdanya
Tel (34) 972 - 140 182 — 10 km

La Vila — Puigcerdà
Tel (34) 972 - 140 804 — 8 km

Un recorrido con bastantes cuestas que requiere estar en buena forma física. Mejor alquilar un coche para concentrarse exclusivamente en el juego. El diseño, aunque no es excepcional, tiene el mérito de valorizar el emplaziamento del recorrido. Casi todos los hoyos tienen una buena panorámica ya que los tees de salida están generalmente en alto y los obstáculos de agua bien visibles, contrariamente a lo que sucede con algunos bunkers. No es un recorrido que se pueda recomendar a jugadores sin experiencia ya que requiere buena técnica y saber pegar con efecto a la bola: es indispensable jugar estratégicamente pues los obstáculos son peligrosos. Los greens no son muy grandes pero sí bastante ondulados. Bastante largo desde las salidas de atrás, aconsejamos que se juegue desde salidas más adelantadas.

This hilly course calls for fitness and stamina, but in a buggy you will be able to focus more on your game. And you need to, because Girona is full of trees and as a result rather, but nor excessively, tight. There is nothing exceptional about the design, but the layout is good and adds value to the site. The general vision of holes is good, because tees are usually elevated, meaning that hazards are also clearly in view, except for a few bunkers. We wouldn't recommend this course too much to inexperienced players, because it demands sound technique and sometimes the ability to flight the ball both ways. Strategy is important because the hazards are dangerous. The greens are medium-sized with a lot of slopes. A rather long course from the back tees, so play further forward.

Club de Golf Girona — 1992
E - 17481 SANT JULIÀ DE RAMIS (GIRONA)

Office	Secretaria	(34) 972 - 171 641
Pro shop	Pro-shop	(34) 972 - 170 011
Fax	Fax	(34) 972 - 171 682
Situation	Situación	

Girona (pop. 70 500), 4 km

Annual closure	Cierre anual	no
Weekly closure	Cierre semanal	no

Fees main season
Precios tempor. alta 18 holes

	Week days Semana	We/Bank holidays Fin de sem./fiestas
Individual Individual	4 800 Pts	7 000 Pts
Couple Pareja	9 600 Pts	14 000 Pts

Caddy	Caddy	on request
Electric Trolley	Carro eléctrico	2 000 Pts/18 holes
Buggy	Coche	5 500 Pts/18 holes
Clubs	Palos	1 800 Pts/18 holes

Credit cards Tarjetas de crédito VISA - MasterCard

Access Acceso : A7 Exit (salida) 6, C150 → Banyoles,
Golf on left hand side → La Mota
Map 2 on page 1099 Plano 2 Página 1099

GOLF COURSE
RECORRIDO — 13/20

Site	Emplazamiento	
Maintenance	Mantenimiento	
Architect	Arquitecto	Hawtree & Sons
Type	Tipo	mountain
Relief	Relieve	
Water in play	Agua	
Exp. to wind	Exp. al viento	
Trees in play	Arboles	

Scorecard Tarjeta	Chp. Campeonato	Mens Caballeros	Ladies Damas
Length Longitud	6100	6058	5190
Par	72	72	71

Advised golfing ability	0 12 24 36
Nivel de juego aconsejado	
Hcp required Handicap exigido	28 Men, 36 Ladies

CLUB HOUSE & AMENITIES
CLUB HOUSE Y DEPENDENCIAS — 7/10

Pro shop	Pro-shop	
Driving range	Campo de prácticas	
Sheltered	cubierto	6 mats
On grass	sobre hierba	yes
Putting-green	putting-green	yes
Pitching-green	pitching-green	no

HOTEL FACILITIES
HOTELES CERCANOS — 5/10

HOTELS HOTELES

Carlemany	Girona
87 rooms, D 14 500 Pts.	10 km
Tel (34) 972 - 211 212	
Fax (34) 972 - 214 994	

RESTAURANTS RESTAURANTES

Albereda	Girona
Tel (34) 972 - 226 002	10 km
Quatre Estacions	Banyoles
Tel (34) 972 - 573 300	3 km

1149

GOLF D'ARO

Encaramado en la cima de una pequeña montaña, como un mirador dominando la geografía espectacular de la Costa Brava -mar y pinos-, es un campo impresionante en la mayoría de sus hoyos. Ramón Espinosa pensó más en los buenos jugadores que los altos de handicap, los cuales tienen que asustarse ante los profundos barrancos que flanquean una docena de hoyos y están llenos de matorrales. Más vale no relajar la concentración y es mejor la precisión que la distancia. Antes de pensar en el resultado más vale reconocer el terreno una o dos veces, aunque sólo sea para identificar los sitios peligros os, calcular las distancias y... cuántas bolas conviene llevar en la bolsa. Nada fácil, pero interesante en un escenario realmente espectacular. Diferentes problemas y cambios de propiedad había relegado el mantenimiento del campo hasta límites muy preocupantes. Ello ha dejado el campo en condiciones de juego aceptables aunque todavía hay que trabajar para devolverlo al esplendor con que se abrió a finales de los años ochenta.

Perched on the summit of a little mountain, like a watchtower overlooking the spectacular scenery of the Costa Brava - all sea and pines -, this is an impressively spacious course, at least for most of the holes. Ramon Espinosa obviously had the good golfer in mind more than the high-handicapper, who might not be too impressed by some fearsomely deep ravines filled with dense bushes lining about a dozen holes. Focus is the key word here, with accuracy taking priority over distance. You would be wise to reconnoitre the course a few times before thinking about a good score, locating the danger spots and taking account of distance and the number of balls you might need. Nothing is easy but everything is interesting in this truly spectacular setting. Various problems to do with changes of ownership have sometimes caused concern over the state of maintenance here; all it needed was a return to acceptable playing conditions.

Club Golf d'Aro — 1990

Apdo Correos 429
E - 17250 PLATJA D'ARO (GIRONA)

Office	Secretaria	(34) 972 - 826 900
Pro shop	Pro-shop	(34) 972 - 816 727
Fax	Fax	(34) 972 - 826 906
Situation	Situación	

Platja d'Aro (pop. 4 785), 4 km
Sant Feliu de Guixols (pop.16 088 h), 10 km

Annual closure	Cierre anual	no
Weekly closure	Cierre semanal	no

Fees main season
Precios tempor. alta 18 holes

	Week days Semana	We/Bank holidays Fin de sem./fiestas
Individual Individual	8 500 Pts	9 100 Pts
Couple Pareja	17 000 Pts	18 200 Pts
Caddy Caddy	no	
Electric Trolley Carro eléctrico	2 000 Pts/18 holes	
Buggy Coche	5 000 Pts/18 holes	
Clubs Palos	2 000 Pts/18 holes	

Credit cards Tarjetas de crédito
VISA - Eurocard - MasterCard - AMEX

1150

Access Acceso : Barcelona, A2. Exit (Salida) 9.
Platja d'Aro, turn right → Urban. Mas Nou
Map 2 on page 1099 Plano 2 Página 1099

GOLF COURSE
RECORRIDO — 15/20

Site	Emplazamiento	
Maintenance	Mantenimiento	
Architect	Arquitecto	Ramón Espinosa
Type	Tipo	mountain, parkland
Relief	Relieve	
Water in play	Agua	
Exp. to wind	Exp. al viento	
Trees in play	Arboles	

Scorecard Tarjeta	Chp. Campeonato	Mens Caballeros	Ladies Damas
Length Longitud	6218	6004	5031
Par	72	72	72

Advised golfing ability Nivel de juego aconsejado	0 12 24 36
Hcp required Handicap exigido	28 Men, 36 Ladiess

CLUB HOUSE & AMENITIES
CLUB HOUSE Y DEPENDENCIAS — 7/10

Pro shop	Pro-shop	
Driving range	Campo de prácticas	
Sheltered	cubierto	10 mats
On grass	sobre hierba	yes
Putting-green	putting-green	yes
Pitching-green	pitching-green	yes

HOTEL FACILITIES
HOTELES CERCANOS — 7/10

HOTELS HOTELES

Park Hotel San Jorge — Calonge
104 rooms, D 26 250 Pts — 4 km
Tel (34) 972 - 652 311, Fax (34) 972 - 652 576

La Gavina — S'Agaró
74 rooms, D 27 500 Pts — 10 km
Tel (34) 972 - 32 11 00, Fax (34) 972 - 32 15 73

Platjapark — Platja d'Aro
200 rooms, D 14 200 Pts — 4 km
Tel (34) 972 - 81 68 05, Fax (34) 972 - 81 68 03

RESTAURANTS RESTAURANTES

Las Panolles - Tel (34) 972 - 837 011 — Platja d'Aro 8 km

Carles Camos-Big Rock — Platja d'Aro 3 km
Tel (34) 972 - 818 012

Arabi - Tel (34) 972 - 816 376 — Platja d'Aro 5 km

Este es un campo con tres recorridos de 9 hoyos que se pueden combinar entre sí. El recorrido principal consiste en jugar los campos Sur y Norte. Recientes obras de acondicionamiento han mejorado mucho el estado del campo. Sus hoyos más famosos son el 2 del Sur, un par 3 de 193 metros cuyo green es una isla verde rodeada de bunker de arena negra propia de la zona, y el hoyo 4 del recorrido Norte, un par 4 de 289 metros impresionante porque sube de espaldas al mar junto a un formidable barranco. Es un recorrido muy variado en el que Pepe Gancedo hace sus peculiares guiños al jugador, bien poniéndole ante un golpe original, bien reclamándole un approach de buen tacto. Las referencias y la decoración del campo se fundamentan en la flora autóctona que, además de alegrar los ojos, enmarca al jugador en el hoyo.

This course comprises 3 combinable nine-holers, but the reference course is certainly the South and North played together. Recent development work has done much to improve the general condition of the course, where perhaps the most remarkable hole is N°2 on the South layout, a par 3 of 193 metres, where the green is a sort of green island amidst bunkers full of the region's black sand. Almost as impressive is hole N°4 on the North course, a great par 4 of just 289 metres, where the terraced steps up the fairway towards the sea present a tremendous barrier. This is a very varied layout where Pepe Gancedo had players very much in mind, asking them to carefully place their shots before thinking about doing anything too original, and calling for a sharp short game. The decoration is the island's natural flora which not only is a sight to behold but also comes into play.

Golf del Sur — 1989
E - 38660 SAN MIGUEL DE ABONA - TENERIFE

Office	Secretaria	(34) 922 - 738 170
Pro shop	Pro-shop	(34) 922 - 738 170
Fax	Fax	(34) 922 - 738 272
Situation	Situación	

Santa Cruz de Tenerife (pop. 203 000), 75 km
Playa de Las Americas, 15 km

Annual closure	Cierre anual	no
Weekly closure	Cierre semanal	no

Fees main season
Precios tempor. alta 18 holes

	Week days Semana	We/Bank holidays Fin de sem./fiestas
Individual Individual	9 400 Pts	9400 Pts
Couple Pareja	18 800 Pts	18 800 Pts
Caddy Caddy	no	
Electric Trolley Carro eléctrico	no	
Buggy Coche	4 500 Pts/18 holes	
Clubs Palos	2 500 Pts/18 holes	

Credit cards Tarjetas de crédito
VISA - MasterCard - AMEX

Access Acceso : Motorway TF1 / Autovia del Sur,
Exit (Salida) 24 (Km 62.5), → Los Abrigos.
First right to Urbanización Golf del Sur
Map 9 on page 1112 Plano 9 Página 1112

GOLF COURSE
RECORRIDO — 16/20

Site	Emplazamiento	
Maintenance	Mantenimiento	
Architect	Arquitecto	José Gancedo
Type	Tipo	parkland
Relief	Relieve	
Water in play	Agua	
Exp. to wind	Exp. al viento	
Trees in play	Arboles	

Scorecard Tarjeta	Chp. Campeonato	Mens Caballeros	Ladies Damas
Length Longitud	5870	5578	4829
Par	72	72	72

Advised golfing ability		0	12	24	36
Nivel de juego aconsejado					
Hcp required	Handicap exigido	28 Men, 36 Ladies			

CLUB HOUSE & AMENITIES
CLUB HOUSE Y DEPENDENCIAS — 7/10

Pro shop	Pro-shop	
Driving range	Campo de prácticas	
Sheltered	cubierto	no
On grass	sobre hierba	yes, 20 places
Putting-green	putting-green	yes
Pitching-green	pitching-green	yes

HOTEL FACILITIES
HOTELES CERCANOS — 8/10

HOTELS HOTELES

Jardin Tropical — Costa Adeje
421 rooms, D 22 000 Pts — 15 km
Tel (34) 913 - 458 284, Fax (34) 922 - 746 060

Arona GH — Los Cristianos
399 rooms, D 27 000 Pts — 7 km
Tel (34) 922 - 750 678, Fax (34) 922 - 750 243

Paradise Park — Los Cristianos
480 rooms, D 19 000 Pts — 7 km
Tel (34) 922 - 794 762, Fax (34) 922 - 750 193

RESTAURANTS RESTAURANTES

El Rincón del Arroz — Los Cristianos 7 km
Tel (34) 922 - 797 370

El Jable - Tel (34) 922 - 390 698 — San Isidro 7 km

Avencio - Tel (34) 922 - 176 079 — El Médano 2 km

1151

14	6	5

A noventa minutos de la costa, este recorrido no sólo ofrece una buena oportunidad de jugar al golf cuando se va a visitar la soberbia ciudad de Granada, sino que merece la pena por sí mismo. Está situado en altura frente a Sierra Nevada, pero sin demasiadas cuestas, su longitud es razonable, salvo en los pares 3 y en los demás hoyos (sobre todo a la vuelta) si se sale de atrás. Las dificultades están colocadas de manera estratégica y peligrosa si no se tiene mucha precisión, especialmente los temibles obsáculos de agua entre los hoyos 15 y 17. Los greens están bien diseñados, son bastante grandes, bien protegidos, con sutiles ondulaciones. En este tipo de recorrido con dificultades bien repartidas, no hay que dudar en atacar en cuanto la ocasión se presente. Se aconsejará jugar con golfistas de mismo nivel para apreciar mejor los desafíos tácticos, pero es un recorrido muy agradable para todo tipo de jugadores.

This course, 90 minutes inland, not only provides a great opportunity to play golf when visiting the superb city of Granada, it is also well worth playing. At altitude, it stands opposite the Sierra Nevada, although the layout is rather flat and the length reasonable, except the par 3s and if you choose to play from the back tees (especially on the back nine). Hazards are strategically placed and often dangerous for wayward shots, especially the formidable water hazards between the 15th and 17th holes. The greens are well-designed, rather large and well defended with tricky slopes. This is a type of course where the difficulties are evenly spread, inviting players to attack whenever the opportunity arises. We recommend playing here with golfers of your own level in order to better appreciate the tactical challenges, but the course is a pleasant day's golfing for everyone.

Granada Club de Golf — 1986

Av. Delos Cosarios, 1
E - 18110 LAS GABIAS (GRANADA)

Office	Secretaria	(34) 958 - 584 436
Pro shop	Pro-shop	(34) 958 - 584 436
Fax	Fax	(34) 958 - 584 060
Situation	Situación	

Granada (pop. 287 864), 8 km

Annual closure	Cierre anual	no
Weekly closure	Cierre semanal	no

Fees main season
Precios tempor. alta 18 holes

	Week days Semana	We/Bank holidays Fin de sem./fiestas
Individual Individual	5 000 Pts	5 000 Pts
Couple Pareja	10 000 Pts	10 000 Pts

Caddy	Caddy	no
Electric Trolley	Carro eléctrico	no
Buggy	Coche	4 500 Pts/18 holes
Clubs	Palos	800 Pts/18 holes

Credit cards Tarjetas de crédito
VISA - Eurocard - Mastercard - AMEX

1152

Access Acceso : Granada N323 → Mortril,
Armilla → C340 → Gabia La Grande
Map 8 on page 1110 Plano 8 Página 1110

GOLF COURSE / RECORRIDO — 14/20

Site	Emplazamiento	▮▮▮▮
Maintenance	Mantenimiento	▮▮▮▮
Architect	Arquitecto	Ibergolf
Type	Tipo	open country
Relief	Relieve	▮▮
Water in play	Agua	▮▮▮
Exp. to wind	Exp. al viento	▮▮▮
Trees in play	Arboles	▮▮▮

Scorecard Tarjeta	Chp. Campeonato	Mens Caballeros	Ladies Damas
Length Longitud	6037	5623	5135
Par	71	71	71

Advised golfing ability	0	12	24	36

Nivel de juego aconsejado
Hcp required Handicap exigido no

CLUB HOUSE & AMENITIES / CLUB HOUSE Y DEPENDENCIAS — 6/10

Pro shop	Pro-shop	▮▮▮
Driving range	Campo de prácticas	▮▮▮▮
Sheltered	cubierto	no
On grass	sobre hierba	yes
Putting-green	putting-green	yes
Pitching-green	pitching-green	yes

HOTEL FACILITIES / HOTELES CERCANOS — 5/10

HOTELS HOTELES

Melia Granada — Granada — 8 km
191 rooms, D 18 800 Pts
Tel (34) 958 - 227 400, Fax (34) 958 - 227 403

Carmen — Granada — 8 km
283 rooms, D 18 900 Pts
Tel (34) 958 - 258 300, Fax (34) 958 - 256 462

Princesa Ana — Granada — 8 km
59 rooms, D 16 800 Pts
Tel (34) 958 - 287 447, Fax (34) 958 - 273 954

RESTAURANTS RESTAURANTES

Bogavante — Granada — 8 km
Tel (34) 958 - 259 112

Tavares — Granada — 8 km
Tel (34) 958 - 226 769

En la campiña al oeste de Málaga, este recorrido diseñado por el finlandés Kosti Kuronen presenta dos caras: los nueve primeros hoyos son bastante clásicos, los nueve últimos más imaginativos con greens en alto, calles y lagos bien cuidados. Los greens son de excelente calidad, a veces dobles (6 y 8, 12 y 16), rápidos y bien protegidos, y aguantan bien la bola. El conjunto no es que sea excepcional, pero es muy agradable y divertido el jugar todas las fórmulas de golf, tanto con jugadores de mismo nivel como de niveles muy diferentes. Sobre todo reserva sus dificultades a los mejores, respondiendo exactamente a la definición de un buen campo de golf, y el hecho de que no sea necesario alquilar un coche hace que sea muy placentero el jugar en familia. Algunas trampas estratégicas le dan un cierto encanto e incitan a jugarlo varias veces.

In the countryside to the west of Malaga, this course, designed by Finnish architect Kosti Kuronen, offers two different faces. The front nine are classical holes, while the back nine are more imaginative with elevated greens, lakes and well laid out fairways. The greens are excellent, sometimes double (6 and 8, 12 and 16), fast and well-defended, but they pitch well. This is probably not an exceptional course, but it is very pleasant and fun to play with players of your own standard or with anyone, for that matter. In fact, the difficulties of Guadalhorce, as with any good course, are reserved for the better players, and being easily playable on foot it is great fun to play with all the family. A few strategic traps add a little spice to the round and make you want to come back and play it again, and again.

Guadalhorce Club de Golf — 1990

Apartado de Correos 48
E - 29590 CAMPANILLAS-MALAGA

Office	Secretaria	(34) 952 - 179 378
Pro shop	Pro-shop	(34) 952 - 179 440
Fax	Fax	(34) 952 - 179 372
Situation	Situación	

Málaga (pop. 534 683), 6 km
Fuengirola (pop. 43 048), 15 km

Annual closure	Cierre anual	no
Weekly closure	Cierre semanal	no

Fees main season
Precios tempor. alta 18 holes

	Week days	We/Bank holidays
	Semana	Fin de sem./fiestas
Individual Individual	6 000 Pts	6 000 Pts
Couple Pareja	12 000 Pts	12 000 Pts
Caddy	Caddy	no
Electric Trolley	Carro eléctrico	no
Buggy	Coche	3 500 Pts/18 holes
Clubs	Palos	1 500 Pts/18 holes

Credit cards Tarjetas de crédito
VISA - Mastercard - AMEX

Access Acceso : Málaga → Parque Tecnologico,
Exit (Salida) «Campanillas», 2 km, Golf
Map 7 on page 1109 Plano 7 Página 1109

GOLF COURSE
RECORRIDO — **14**/20

Site	Emplazamiento	
Maintenance	Mantenimiento	
Architect	Arquitecto	Kosti Kuronen
Type	Tipo	open country, hilly
Relief	Relieve	
Water in play	Agua	
Exp. to wind	Exp. al viento	
Trees in play	Arboles	

Scorecard	Chp.	Mens	Ladies
Tarjeta	Campeonato	Caballeros	Damas
Length Longitud	6194	5860	4992
Par	72	72	72

Advised golfing ability	0	12	24	36
Nivel de juego aconsejado				

Hcp required — Handicap exigido 28 Men, 36 Ladies

CLUB HOUSE & AMENITIES
CLUB HOUSE Y DEPENDENCIAS — **7**/10

Pro shop	Pro-shop	
Driving range	Campo de prácticas	
Sheltered	cubierto	4 mats
On grass	sobre hierba	yes
Putting-green	putting-green	yes
Pitching-green	pitching-green	yes

HOTEL FACILITIES
HOTELES CERCANOS — **6**/10

HOTELS HOTELES

Malaga Palacio — Malaga — 12 km
221 rooms, D 19 500 Pts
Tel (34) 952 - 215 185, Fax (34) 952 - 215 185

Guadalmar — Malaga — 5 km
200 rooms, D 17 200 Pts
Tel (34) 952 - 231 703, Fax (34) 952 - 240 385

Larios — Malaga — 12 km
40 rooms, D 20 000 Pts
Tel (34) 952 - 222 200, Fax (34) 952 - 222 407

RESTAURANTS RESTAURANTES

Adolfo — Malaga
Tel (34) 952 - 601 914

Cueva del Camborio — Malaga
Tel (34) 952 - 347 816

1153

Es el segundo recorrido creado en la Costa del Sol, diseñado por el legendario Javier Arana. Mucho más llano que el «Norte», sin embargo sus calles son más anchas, con árboles a menudo en la línea de juego. Al tener pocas carreteras que lo atraviesen, se juega más tranquilamente, al menos en los hoyos que dan al mar. Más difícil de lo que parece, sobre todo con viento, no se siúa entre los más exigentes de la costa, máxime teniendo en cuenta que sus dificultades son perfectamente visibles y la estrategia de juego evidente. Un riachuelo está en la línea de juego en varios hoyos, pero no es demasiado peligroso. La ida tiene algunos hoyos bastante largos, mientras que a la vuelta hay algunos bastante cortos, especialmente pares 4 cortitos en los que los bienvenidos birdies pueden aliviar la tarjeta , pares 3 de buena calidad (sobre todo el 11) y dos pares 5 de los que en uno al menos (el 17) se puede llegar en dos golpes. Hay que conocerlo.

This is the second course opened on the Costa del Sol designed by the legendary Javier Arana. Much flatter than the «Norte», it also has wider fairways and more trees, which often get in the way. There are fewer roads around, so it is a quieter course, at least for the holes facing the sea. Harder than it looks, especially when the wind is up, it is not the most challenging course on this coast, especially since the hazards are perfectly visible and playing strategy rather obvious. A small river comes into play on several holes but is rarely too dangerous. The front nine include some rather long holes, while the inward half has a number of shortish holes, notably the short part 4s, where a few welcome birdies can do your score-card a world of good, enjoyable par 3s (especially the 11th) and two par 5s, of which at least one (the 17th) is reachable in two. Worth knowing.

Guadalmina Club de Golf — 1959

Urb. Guadalmina Alta
E - 29678 SAN PEDRO DE ALCANTARA (MALAGA)

Office	Secretaria	(34) 952 - 886 522
Pro shop	Pro-shop	(34) 952 - 882 023
Fax	Fax	(34) 952 - 883 483
Situation	Situación	

San Pedro de Alcantara, 1 km
Estepona (pop. 36 307), 14 km

Annual closure	Cierre anual	no
Weekly closure	Cierre semanal	no

Fees main season
Precios tempor. alta 18 holes

	Week days Semana	We/Bank holidays Fin de sem./fiestas
Individual Individual	8 000 Pts	8 000 Pts
Couple Pareja	16 000 Pts	16 000 Pts

Caddy	Caddy	no
Electric Trolley	Carro eléctrico	1 500 Pts/18 holes
Buggy	Coche	5 200 Pts/18 holes
Clubs	Palos	2 200 Pts/18 holes

Credit cards Tarjetas de crédito VISA - AMEX

Access Acceso : N340 Marbella
→ San Pedro de Alcantara
Map 7 on page 1109 Plano 7 Página 1109

GOLF COURSE
RECORRIDO — 14/20

Site	Emplazamiento	
Maintenance	Mantenimiento	
Architect	Arquitecto	Javier Araña
Type	Tipo	seaside course, parkland
Relief	Relieve	
Water in play	Agua	
Exp. to wind	Exp. al viento	
Trees in play	Arboles	

Scorecard Tarjeta	Chp. Campeonato	Mens Caballeros	Ladies Damas
Length Longitud	6025	5874	5130
Par	72	72	72

Advised golfing ability		0	12	24	36
Nivel de juego aconsejado					

Hcp required Handicap exigido 28 Men, 36 Ladies

CLUB HOUSE & AMENITIES
CLUB HOUSE Y DEPENDENCIAS — 7/10

Pro shop	Pro-shop	
Driving range	Campo de prácticas	
Sheltered	cubierto	no
On grass	sobre hierba	yes
Putting-green	putting-green	yes
Pitching-green	pitching-green	no

HOTEL FACILITIES
HOTELES CERCANOS — 7/10

HOTELS HOTELES

Guadalmina — San Pedro
80 rooms, D 27 200 Pts — 1 km
Tel (34) 952 - 882 211, Fax (34) 952 - 882 291

El Paraiso — Estepona
182 rooms, D 27 000 Pts — 3 km
Tel (34) 952 - 883 000, Fax (34) 952 - 882 019

Atalaya Park — Estepona 2 km
448 rooms, D 25 200 Pts
Tel (34) 952 - 884 801, Fax (34) 952 - 885 735

RESTAURANTS RESTAURANTES

Meridiana - Tel (34) 952 - 776 190 — Marbella
Bistrot Cristian - Tel (34) 952 - 811 006 — Puerto Banús
Los Nietos — San Pedro de Alcantara
Tel (34) 952 - 883 491 — 1 km

1154

15 6 6

Es muy raro poder jugar a proximidad de monumentos históricos como el Monasterio de San Lorenzo del Escorial que domina el recorrido. La Herreria es tan espectacular como las vistas que proporciona. En el diseño de Antonio Lucena Gómez los peligros vienen de los árboles y los bunkers, que defienden al mismo las caídas de drive como los greenes, bastante lisos pero a la vez bien moldeados. Estas dificultades no son nunca infranqueables sea cual sea el nivel del jugador ya que son muy visibles para permitir adoptar una estrategia que nos permita eludir las malas sorpresas. Si el 2 es un par 5 muy complicado, las vistas panorámicas de los hoyos 12, 13 y 14 permiten reposar el espíritu antes de abordar el hoyo 18, uno de los mejores pares 4 de España...

It is rare indeed to be able to swing a club so close to historical landmarks such as the Monasterio de San Lorenzo de El Escorial, which overlooks this course. La Herreria is also one of the truly public courses in the Madrid area, even though private courses are beginning to open up to visitors. The site is as spectacular as the vistas from the course, designed by Antonio Lucena Gomez. The main hazards are the trees and bunkers, guarding both the drive landing zone and the greens, the latter being flat but well shaped. These difficulties are never impossible to negotiate, whatever your level of proficiency, and are visible enough to adopt a strategy to avoid unpleasant surprises. While the second hole is a rather complicated par 5, the scenic views from the 12th, 13th and 14 th holes are enough to calm frayed nerves before attacking the 18th, one of the best par 4s in Spain.

La Herreria Club de Golf — 1968

Ctra de Robledo S/N
E - 28200 SAN LORENZO DE EL ESCORIAL (MADRID)

Office	Secretaria	(34) 918 - 905 111
Pro shop	Pro-shop	(34) 918 - 905 617
Fax	Fax	(34) 918 - 907 154
Situation	Situación	

San Lorenzo de El Escorial (pop. 8 704), 2 km
Madrid (pop. 3 084 673), 57 km

Annual closure	Cierre anual	no
Weekly closure	Cierre semanal	no

Fees main season
Precios tempor. alta 18 holes

	Week days Semana	We/Bank holidays Fin de sem./fiestas
Individual Individual	6 500 Pts	9 500 Pts
Couple Pareja	13 000 Pts	19 000 Pts

Caddy	Caddy	no
Electric Trolley	Carro eléctrico	1 000 Pts/18 holes
Buggy	Coche	4 500 Pts/18 holes
Clubs	Palos	no
Credit cards Tarjetas de crédito		no

Segovia
Arévalo
1902
Tablada
Guadarrama
N VI
47
Madrid
Vallée de los Caidos
M 600
1754
E. de la Aceña
San Lorenzo de EL Escorial
GOLF
El Escorial
M 505
0 2 4 km

Access Acceso : Madrid A6 → Segovia. Exit (Salida)
El Escorial, M600 → San Lorenzo de El Escorial.
→ Robledo de Chavela, Golf on the left
Map 3 on page 1100 Plano 3 Página 1100

GOLF COURSE
RECORRIDO — **15**/20

Site	Emplazamiento	
Maintenance	Mantenimiento	
Architect	Arquitecto	Antonio Lucena Gomez
Type	Tipo	forest, hilly
Relief	Relieve	
Water in play	Agua	
Exp. to wind	Exp. al viento	
Trees in play	Arboles	

Scorecard Tarjeta	Chp. Campeonato	Mens Caballeros	Ladies Damas
Length Longitud	6050	6050	5121
Par	72	72	72

Advised golfing ability		0 12 24 36
Nivel de juego aconsejado		
Hcp required	Handicap exigido	28 Men, 36 Ladies

CLUB HOUSE & AMENITIES
CLUB HOUSE Y DEPENDENCIAS — **6**/10

Pro shop	Pro-shop	
Driving range	Campo de prácticas	
Sheltered	cubierto	no
On grass	sobre hierba	yes
Putting-green	putting-green	yes
Pitching-green	pitching-green	no

1155

HOTEL FACILITIES
HOTELES CERCANOS — **6**/10

HOTELS HOTELES
Victoria Palace — San Lorenzo
90 rooms, D 18 400 Pts — 2 km
Tel (34) 918 - 901 511, Fax (34) 918 - 901 248

Cristina — San Lorenzo
16 rooms, D 6 300 Pts — 2 km
Tel (34) 918 - 901 961, Fax (34) 918 - 901 204

Miranda Suizo — San Lorenzo
52 rooms, D 11 600 Pts — 2 km
Tel (34) 918 - 904 711, Fax (34) 918 - 904 352

RESTAURANTS RESTAURANTES
Charolés — San Lorenzo
Tel (34) 918 - 905 975 — 2 km

Parilla Principe — San Lorenzo
Tel (34) 918 - 901 611 — 2 km

Con 27 hoyos y un bonito club-house de estilo andaluz, el conjunto de este ambicioso proyecto domina el Atlántico. Los magníficos árboles de este inmenso parque han sido preservados y constituyen una de las dificultades con bosquecitos que penalizan. Adeñás de los numerosos bunkers bien diseñados y de un cierto número de obstáculos de agua, greens ondulados y a menudo en alto hacen muy técnico un recorrido generalmente utilizado como el principal 18 hoyos. Raramente existen trampas escondidas y se puede afrontar sin miedo. La anchura de las calles pueden dar la impresión de que es un recorrido fácil, pero es una impresión ilusoria, sobre todo desde las salidas de atrás. Si al gusto de jugar se añade el placer de la vista (especialmente el Océano en el 12), Islantilla es una de las buenas sorpresas de estos últimos años y merece la pena conocerlo.

The 27 holes and attractive Andalusian style clubhouse of this ambitious complex overlook the Atlantic Ocean. The fine trees in this huge park have been spared and form some of the difficulties along with penalising undergrowth. In addition to the well-designed bunkers and a number of water hazards, the well-contoured and often elevated greens (some are blind) help make the 18 holes generally used as the main course a rather technical layout. But since the traps are rarely concealed, there is not a great deal to be afraid of. The wide fairways perhaps give the impression of a course that is easy to score on, but this is only an impression, especially when playing from the back tees. If you combine the pleasure of playing and the surrounding view (notably over the ocean on hole N° 12), Islantilla is one of the nicest surprises in recent years and well worth the trip.

Islantilla		1991
Ctra La Antilla - Isla Cristina		
E - 21410 HUELVA		
Office	Secretaria	(34) 959 - 486 039
Pro shop	Pro-shop	(34) 959 - 486 039
Fax	Fax	(34) 959 - 486 104
Situation	Situación	
Sevilla (pop. 704 857), 147 km		
Huelva (pop. 144 579), 40 km		
Annual closure	Cierre anual	no
Weekly closure	Cierre semanal	no

Fees main season		
Precios tempor. alta 18 holes		
	Week days Semana	We/Bank holidays Fin de sem./fiestas
Individual Individual	7 000 Pts	7 000 Pts
Couple Pareja	14 000 Pts	14 000 Pts
Caddy Caddy		on request
Electric Trolley Carro eléctrico		1 750 Pts/18 holes
Buggy Coche		5 000 Pts/18 holes
Clubs Palos		2 250 Pts/18 holes

Credit cards Tarjetas de crédito
VISA - AMEX - DC

1156

0   2,5   5 km
Huelva
LEPE
El Empalme
Pozo del Camino
La Rendondela
Isla Cristina
La Antilla
GOLF

Access Acceso : Huelva, N431 → Ayamonte,
Lepe → La Antilla, Golf 3 km
Map 7 on page 1108 Plano 7 Página 1108

GOLF COURSE
RECORRIDO   16/20

Site	Emplazamiento	
Maintenance	Mantenimiento	
Architect	Arquitecto	Enrique Canales Luis Recasens
Type	Tipo	seaside course, forest
Relief	Relieve	
Water in play	Agua	
Exp. to wind	Exp. al viento	
Trees in play	Arboles	

Scorecard Tarjeta	Chp. Campeonato	Mens Caballeros	Ladies Damas
Length Longitud	5926	5389	4686
Par	72	72	72

Advised golfing ability	0	12	24	36
Nivel de juego aconsejado				
Hcp required Handicap exigido	28 Men, 36 Ladies			

CLUB HOUSE & AMENITIES
CLUB HOUSE Y DEPENDENCIAS   8/10

Pro shop	Pro-shop	
Driving range	Campo de prácticas	
Sheltered	cubierto	no
On grass	sobre hierba	yes
Putting-green	putting-green	yes
Pitching-green	pitching-green	yes

HOTEL FACILITIES
HOTELES CERCANOS   8/10

HOTELS HOTELES
Confortel Islantilla — Islantilla
344 rooms, D 19 000 Pts — 1 km
Tel (34) 959 - 486 017, Fax (34) 959 - 486 070

Paraiso Playa — Isla Cristina
35 rooms, D 9 000 Pts — 3 km
Tel (34) 959 - 331 873, Fax (34) 959 - 343 745

Sol y Mar — Isla Cristina
16 rooms, D 8 400 Pts — 3 km
Tel (34) 959 - 332 050, Fax (34) 959 - 332 050

RESTAURANTS RESTAURANTES
El Coral — La Antilla
Tel (34) 959 - 481 406 — 2 km

Meson La Isla — Isla Cristina
Tel (34) 959 - 343 018 — 5 km

JARAMA R.A.C.E.

13 7 6

El interesante diseño de Arana se ve desgraciadamente alterado por el paso de los años y por una tierra demasiado vieja que provoca problemas de drenaje en tiempo humedo, problemas que sin embargo el Real Automovil Club de España están tratando remediar. Bien situado, con magníficas vistas, sería un sitio muy tranquilo para jugar si la proximidad del circuito automovilístico no trajese a veces problemas sonoros. Sería una pena sin embargo no aceptar una visita al campo ya que si requiere una cierta longitud (¡sobre todo desde atrás!), es lo suficientemente amplio para permitir cualquier error de dirección muy frecuentes con el driver. Cierto es que los árboles y los bunkers de recorrido constituyen sus principales defensas, pero serán sobre todo los tiros a green que proporcionarán a los jugadores imprecisos los principales problemas. Será más por la precisión que por la longitud que podremos aspirar a jugar nuestro handicap.

Javier Arana's interesting design has unfortunately been badly affected by aging terrain and a few drainage problems in wet weather. We are told that the Royal Automobile Club of Spain (the course's owner) envisage remedying this very shortly. Well located with some wonderful views, this would be a very quiet place to play if it weren't for the racing track close-by (going by the same name of Jarama), which can be noisy at times. It would, though, be a shame to turn down a visit here, because while the course demands length off the tee (especially from the back), it is wide enough to forgive the all too frequent sliced or hooked drive. Although the trees and fairway bunkers form a solid wall of defence, the biggest problems here for wayward hitters are approach shots to greens. Accuracy more than length is called for if you want to hope to play to your handicap.

Club Jarama R.A.C.E.   1967
Carretera de Madrid Burgos km 28,100
E - 28700 S.S. DE LOS REYES-MADRID

Office	Secretaria	(34) 916 - 570 011
Pro shop	Pro-shop	(34) 916 - 570 011
Fax	Fax	(34) 916 - 570 462
Situation	Situación	

Madrid (pop. 3 084 673), 28 km

Annual closure	Cierre anual	no
Weekly closure	Cierre semanal	no

Fees main season
Precios tempor. alta 18 holes

	Week days Semana	We/Bank holidays Fin de sem./fiestas
Individual Individual	8 000 Pts	15 000 Pts
Couple Pareja	16 000 Pts	30 000 Pts

Caddy	Caddy	no
Electric Trolley	Carro eléctrico	800 Pts/18 holes
Buggy	Coche	4 000 Pts/18 holes
Clubs	Palos	3 000 Pts/18 holes
Credit cards Tarjetas de crédito		no

Ciudalcampo
GOLF
Ciudad Sto Domingo
Colmenar Viejo
Fuente del Fresno
Km 25
Tres Cantos
M 607
N I
S. Sebastián de los Reyes
Burgos
M 616
17
16
MADRID
M 40

Access Acceso : Carretera Madrid → Burgos, Km 28,100
Map 3 on page 1100 Plano 3 Página 1100

GOLF COURSE
RECORRIDO   **13** /20

Site	Emplazamiento	
Maintenance	Mantenimiento	
Architect	Arquitecto	Javier Arana
Type	Tipo	country
Relief	Relieve	
Water in play	Agua	
Exp. to wind	Exp. al viento	
Trees in play	Arboles	

Scorecard Tarjeta	Chp. Campeonato	Mens Caballeros	Ladies Damas
Length Longitud	6497	6070	5109
Par	72	72	72

Advised golfing ability		0 12 24 36
Nivel de juego aconsejado		
Hcp required	Handicap exigido	28 Men, 36 Ladies

CLUB HOUSE & AMENITIES
CLUB HOUSE Y DEPENDENCIAS   **7** /10

Pro shop	Pro-shop	
Driving range	Campo de prácticas	
Sheltered	cubierto	60 mats
On grass	sobre hierba	yes
Putting-green	putting-green	yes
Pitching-green	pitching-green	yes

HOTEL FACILITIES
HOTELES CERCANOS   **6** /10

HOTELS HOTELES
Chamartin   Madrid
360 rooms, D 20 000 Pts   20 km
Tel (34) 913 - 344 900, Fax (34) 917 - 330 214

Melia Castilla   Madrid
900 rooms, D 34 000 Pts   20 km
Tel (34) 915 - 675 000, Fax (34) 915 - 675 051

La Moraleja   Alcobendas
37 rooms, D 20 200 Pts   15 km
Tel (34) 916 - 618 055, Fax (34) 916 - 612 188

RESTAURANTS RESTAURANTES
Mesón Tejas Verde   S.S. de Los Reyes
Tel (34) 916 - 527 307   10 km

Vicente - Tel (34) 916 - 513 171 S.S. de Los Reyes 10 km

Izamar - Tel (34) 916 - 543 893 S.S. de Los Reyes 10 km

1157

Es un verdadero éxito el haber podido alojar dos recorridos en una región tan montañosa..., ¡ se necesita estar en excelente condición física para prescindir de un coche! . El «Norte» ofrece buenas ocasiones de utilizar el drive, pero en general es tan importante colocar la bola y los roughs tan peligrosos (matorrales), que la madera 3 es más que suficiente. Las ondulaciones del recorrido y las impresiones ópticas exigen reflexión tanto en cada golpe como en la elección del palo, por lo que se aconseja ñás bien a jugadores ya experimentados. Sólo después de haberlo jugado una o dos veces se puede intentar obtener un buen resultado, pero es un recorrido para jugar sobre todo en match-play, apasionante por el diseño de las caídas de los greens, generalmente protegidos por grandes y profundos bunkers. Pequeño consuelo en caso de decepción: sólo hay agua en dos hoyos y la vista panorámica sobre esta región salvaje es magnífica.

Accommodating two courses into such a moutainous region is something of an exploit, but you need to be pretty fit to refuse a buggy. The «Norte» offers some fine opportunities to take the driver out of the bag, but as a general rule, positioning the ball is so important and the rough so dangerous (scrub) that the 3-wood (or long-iron) will suffice. The general relief of this course and the optical illusions call for careful consideration when choosing the club before every shot, which is why we recommend it for experienced players. After one or two reconnaissance rounds they might think about scoring, but this is a course made for match-play, an exciting format on these contoured greens which are generally well-defended by large, deep bunkers. A minor compensation in the event of wayward shot-making is the thought that water only comes into play on two holes and the vista over this wild region is magnificent.

La Cala Resort

1990

La Cala de Mijas
E - 29647 MIJAS COSTA (MALAGA)

Office	Secretaria	(34) 952 - 669 033
Pro shop	Pro-shop	(34) 952 - 669 000
Fax	Fax	(34) 952 - 669 039
Situation	Situación	

Marbella (pop. 84 410), 20 km
Mijas (pop. 32 835), 10 km

Annual closure	Cierre anual	no
Weekly closure	Cierre semanal	no

Fees main season
Precios tempor. alta 18 holes

	Week days Semana	We/Bank holidays Fin de sem./fiestas
Individual Individual	8 000 Pts	8 000 Pts
Couple Pareja	16 000 Pts	16 000 Pts

Caddy	Caddy	no
Electric Trolley	Carro eléctrico	no
Buggy	Coche	5 000 Pts/18 holes
Clubs	Palos	3 000 Pts/18 holes

Credit cards Tarjetas de crédito
VISA - MasterCard - AMEX

1158

Access Acceso : Málaga, N340 → Fuengirola,
Cala de Mijas → Golf
Map 7 on page 1109 Plano 7 Página 1109

GOLF COURSE
RECORRIDO
17/20

Site	Emplazamiento	
Maintenance	Mantenimiento	
Architect	Arquitecto	Cabell Robinson
Type	Tipo	mountain
Relief	Relieve	
Water in play	Agua	
Exp. to wind	Exp. al viento	
Trees in play	Arboles	

Scorecard Tarjeta	Chp. Campeonato	Mens Caballeros	Ladies Damas
Length Longitud	6187	5782	4759
Par	72	73	73

Advised golfing ability Nivel de juego aconsejado	0	12	24	36
Hcp required Handicap exigido	28 Men, 36 Ladies			

CLUB HOUSE & AMENITIES
CLUB HOUSE Y DEPENDENCIAS
8/10

Pro shop	Pro-shop	
Driving range	Campo de prácticas	
Sheltered	cubierto	no
On grass	sobre hierba	yes
Putting-green	putting-green	yes
Pitching-green	pitching-green	yes

HOTEL FACILITIES
HOTELES CERCANOS
6/10

HOTELS HOTELES

La Cala Resort — Golf
83 rooms, D 31 500 Pts
Tel (34) 952 - 669 000, Fax (34) 952 - 669 039

Byblos — Fuengirola 6 km
144 rooms, D 39 500 Pts
Tel (34) 952 - 473 050, Fax (34) 952 - 476 783

Mijas — Mijas 20 km
97 rooms, D 14 700 Pts
Tel (34) 952 - 485 800, Fax (34) 952 - 485 825

RESTAURANTS RESTAURANTES

El Olivar — Mijas 20 km
Tel (34) 952 - 486 196

El Tomate — Fuengirola 6 km
Tel (34) 952 - 473 599

Preferir uno u otro de los dos recorridos de La Cala es una cuestión de gusto. El «Sur» da la impresión de ser un poco más corto, o en todo caso que perdona más lo errores. También aquí los desniveles son engañosos y no hay que fiarse de la longitud teórica de los hoyos. Los drive aterrizan a menudo en zonas en alto y una vegetación densa forma una buena parte de los roughs. Algunas pendientes pronunciadas alrededor de los greens exigen un buen juego corto y mucha intuición. Al igual que en el «Norte», poco importa el resultado cuando se juega por primera vez y para mantener intacto el placer de jugar hay que aceptar las cosas como vienen y con un cierto sentido del humor. Si es mejor que los principiantes se abstengan y prefieran las excelentes instalaciones del campo de prácticas, los jugadores más aguerridos alquilarán un coche para saborear una jornada apasionante.

Preference for one or the other of La Cala courses is a matter of taste. The «Sur» gives the impression of being a little less long, or in any case of being more forgiving for mis-hit shots. Here, too, the terrain's physical contours are misleading and not too much faith should be put in the theoretical lengths of holes. The drive often lands on plateaus which players should not stray too far from, as a large part of rough here is dense vegetation. A number of steep slopes around the greens call for a sharp short game and loads of intuition. As with the «Norte», the score is of little consequence when playing the course for the first time. To really enjoy yourself, take things as they come and never lose your sense of humour. While beginners should refrain from playing the course and stick to the excellent practice facilities, the more proficient players can hop in a buggy and soak up an exciting day's golf.

La Cala Resort — 1990

La Cala de Mijas
E - 29647 MIJAS COSTA (MALAGA)

Office	Secretaria	(34) 952 - 669 033
Pro shop	Pro-shop	(34) 952 - 669 000
Fax	Fax	(34) 952 - 669 039
Situation	Situación	

Marbella (pop. 84 410), 20 km
Mijas (pop. 32 835), 10 km

Annual closure	Cierre anual	no
Weekly closure	Cierre semanal	no

Fees main season
Precios tempor. alta 18 holes

	Week days Semana	We/Bank holidays Fin de sem./fiestas
Individual Individual	8 000 Pts	8 000 Pts
Couple Pareja	16 000 Pts	16 000 Pts

Caddy	Caddy	no
Electric Trolley	Carro eléctrico	no
Buggy	Coche	5 000 Pts/18 holes
Clubs	Palos	3 000 Pts/18 holes

Credit cards Tarjetas de crédito
VISA - MasterCard - AMEX

Mijas
N 340
Malaga
FUENGIROLA
GOLF
Mijas Costa
Marbella
COSTA DEL SOL
0   2   4 km

Access Acceso : Málaga, N340 → Fuengirola,
Cala de Mijas → Golf
Map 7 on page 1109 Plano 7 Página 1109

GOLF COURSE / RECORRIDO — 16/20

Site	Emplazamiento	
Maintenance	Mantenimiento	
Architect	Arquitecto	Cabell Robinson
Type	Tipo	mountain
Relief	Relieve	
Water in play	Agua	
Exp. to wind	Exp. al viento	
Trees in play	Arboles	

Scorecard Tarjeta	Chp. Campeonato	Mens Caballeros	Ladies Damas
Length Longitud	5960	5440	4530
Par	71	71	71

Advised golfing ability		0 12 24 36
Nivel de juego aconsejado		
Hcp required	Handicap exigido	28 Men, 36 Ladies

CLUB HOUSE & AMENITIES / CLUB HOUSE Y DEPENDENCIAS — 8/10

Pro shop	Pro-shop	
Driving range	Campo de prácticas	
Sheltered	cubierto	no
On grass	sobre hierba	yes
Putting-green	putting-green	yes
Pitching-green	pitching-green	yes

1159

HOTEL FACILITIES / HOTELES CERCANOS — 6/10

HOTELS HOTELES
La Cala Resort — Golf
83 rooms, D 31 500 Pts
Tel (34) 952 - 669 000, Fax (34) 952 - 669 039

Byblos — Fuengirola
144 rooms, D 39 500 Pts — 6 km
Tel (34) 952 - 473 050, Fax (34) 952 - 476 783

Mijas — Mijas
97 rooms, D 14 700 Pts — 20 km
Tel (34) 952 - 485 800, Fax (34) 952 - 485 825

RESTAURANTS RESTAURANTES
El Olivar — Mijas
Tel (34) 952 - 486 196 — 20 km

El Tomate — Fuengirola
Tel (34) 952 - 473 599 — 6 km

El recorrido de La Dehesa forma parte de un gran complejo concebido para el ocio familiar, siendo igual de agradable para el golfista como para el no golfista, éste último se ve reducido demasiadas veces a ser un mero acompañante durante las vacaciones de golf. Las instalaciones de entrenamiento les permitirá incluso iniciarse en la práctica del golf. A la hora de diseñar el campo, Manuel Piñero pensó en todos los jugadores: es un campo competitivo, pero existen siempre soluciones para salirse de los peligros que encierra. Estos son numerosos durante los 18 hoyos, pero están los suficientemente a la vista para poder decidir rápidamente atacar a ser prudente. Los greenes son suficientemente amplios, bien defendidos, pero agradables de atacar y de jugar. Los espacios muy abiertos, el respeto del entorno existente y las magníficas vistas de la Sierra Madrileña dan al lugar una gran belleza.

The La Dehesa course is part of a large resort designed for family recreation, an equally pleasant spot for golfers and non-golfers alike. On a golfing day, the latter are often left having to accompany their playing partners, but not so here. What's more, the practice facilities might even entice them into having a swing themselves. In designing this course, Manuel Pinero spared a thought for everyone: it is a competitive layout, but there are always solutions for getting around the main difficulties. There is indeed a lot of danger, well spread over the 18 holes, but hazards are visible enough for anyone to decide quickly whether to «go for it» or «lay up». Wide open space, the respect for existing natural beauty and some magnificent views over the Madrid Sierra make this a wonderful spot for golf.

Golf La Dehesa — 1992
Avenida de la Universidad S/N
E - 28691 VILLANUEVA DE LA CAÑADA (MADRID)

Office	Secretaria	(34) 918 - 157 022
Pro shop	Pro-shop	(34) 918 - 157 022
Fax	Fax	(34) 918 - 155 468
Situation	Situación	

Madrid (pop. 3 084 673), 28 km
Brunete (pop. 2 505), 5 km

Annual closure	Cierre anual	no
Weekly closure	Cierre semanal	no

Fees main season
Precios tempor. alta 18 holes

	Week days Semana	We/Bank holidays Fin de sem./fiestas
Individual Individual	6 000 Pts	16 000 Pts
Couple Pareja	12 000 Pts	32 000 Pts

Caddy	Caddy	no
Electric Trolley	Carro eléctrico	1 000 Pts/18 holes
Buggy	Coche	4 000 Pts/18 holes
Clubs	Palos	2 500 Pts/18 holes

Credit cards Tarjetas de crédito — no

1160

Villanueva de la Cañada — GOLF — MADRID
El Escorial
M 600 — km 10 — M 40
Brunete — M 511
M 600 — Villaviciosa de Odón
Navalcarnero
Talavera de la Reina — N V
0   4   8 km

Access Acceso : Madrid M4O,
Exit (Salida) 41 → Boadilla. Exit (Salida) 8 →
Villanueva de la Cañada → Universidad → Brunete
Map 3 on page 1100 Plano 3 Página 1100

GOLF COURSE / RECORRIDO — 14/20

Site	Emplazamiento	
Maintenance	Mantenimiento	
Architect	Arquitecto	Manuel Piñero
Type	Tipo	country
Relief	Relieve	
Water in play	Agua	
Exp. to wind	Exp. al viento	
Trees in play	Arboles	

Scorecard Tarjeta	Chp. Campeonato	Mens Caballeros	Ladies Damas
Length Longitud	6444	6037	5146
Par	72	72	72

Advised golfing ability		0 12 24 36
Nivel de juego aconsejado		
Hcp required	Handicap exigido	28 Men, 36 Ladies

CLUB HOUSE & AMENITIES / CLUB HOUSE Y DEPENDENCIAS — 7/10

Pro shop	Pro-shop	
Driving range	Campo de prácticas	
Sheltered	cubierto	20 mats
On grass	sobre hierba	yes
Putting-green	putting-green	yes
Pitching-green	pitching-green	yes

HOTEL FACILITIES / HOTELES CERCANOS — 4/10

HOTELS HOTELES
Husa Princesa — Madrid
275 rooms, D 34 900 Pts. — 30 km
Tel (34) 915 - 422 100, Fax (34) 915 - 423 501

Majadahonda — Majadahonda
41 rooms, D 19 400 Pts — 15 km
Tel (34) 916 - 382 122, Fax (34) 916 - 382 157

Victoria Palace — El Escorial
90 rooms, D 18 400 Pts — 1 km
Tel (34) 918 - 901 511, Fax (34) 918 - 901 248

RESTAURANTS RESTAURANTES
Zalacain — Madrid
Tel (34) 915 - 614 840 — 28 km

El Vivero — Brunete
Tel (34) 918 - 159 222 — 5 km

LA DUQUESA

13 7 6

Rodeando la colina de El Hacho, verdadero balcón sobre el mar con una magnífica vista sobre Gibraltar, La Duquesa es uno de los múltiples recorridos de Robert Trent Jones en el sur de España. Pero no es el más difícil: los greens están a menudo en alto y algunas veces son ciegos, no con excesivas caídas, hay numerosos bunkers de los que no es difícil salir, las calles a menudo inclinadas pero no con excesivo peligro. Los roughs son tupidos, aunque bien alejados de la calle, los obstáculos de agua poco numerosos (dos lagos), este recorrido permite jugar con toda la familia sin que ningún jugador se sienta «desplazado». A pesar de las numerosas cuestas no es necesario un coche. Gozarán de una cierta ventaja los jugadores con precisión, pero también los buenos pegadores tendrán ocasión de expresarse. El recorrido de La Duquesa forma parte de un club con múltiples instalaciones (especialmente un puerto de recreo).

Running right around the El Hacho hill, which provides a balcony over the Mediterranean and a fine view of Gibraltar, La Duquesa is one of a number of courses designed by Robert Trent Jones in the south of Spain. But it is not the most difficult: the greens are often elevated and sometimes blind, but only gently contoured. There are loads of bunkers but they are not too difficult to escape from, the fairways sometimes have a sideways slope, but this is nothing too dangerous. With thick but generally distant rough and only a few water hazards (two lakes), this is a course for all the family without any one player feeling left behind. Despite the slopes, the course is easily playable on foot. Precision play is rewarded but the long-hitters also have good opportunity to swing the driver. The La Duquesa course is located within a resort which includes a number of other facilities (in particular a marina).

Golf & Country Club La Duquesa — 1987

Urb. El Hacho - km. 143,5
E - 29691 MANILVA (MALAGA)

Office	Secretaria	(34) 952 - 890 425
Pro shop	Pro-shop	(34) 952 - 890 725
Fax	Fax	(34) 952 - 890 425
Situation	Situación	

Estepona (pop. 36 307), 15 km
Gibraltar (pop. 28 339), 30 km

Annual closure	Cierre anual	no
Weekly closure	Cierre semanal	no

Fees main season
Precios tempor. alta 18 holes

	Week days Semana	We/Bank holidays Fin de sem./fiestas
Individual Individual	6 000 Pts	6 000 Pts
Couple Pareja	12 000 Pts	12 000 Pts

Caddy	Caddy	no
Electric Trolley	Carro eléctrico	no
Buggy	Coche	5 000 Pts/18 holes
Clubs	Palos	2 000 Pts/18 holes

Credit cards Tarjetas de crédito
VISA - Eurocard - MasterCard - AMEX

ESTEPONA
N 340
Playa de Estepona
0   2   4 km
Manilva
San Luis de Sabinillas
La Duquesa
GOLF
Algeciras
COSTA DEL SOL

Access Acceso : Estepona N340 → Cadiz, Manilva, Golf
Map 7 on page 1109 Plano 7 Página 1109

GOLF COURSE / RECORRIDO — 13/20

Site	Emplazamiento	
Maintenance	Mantenimiento	
Architect	Arquitecto	Robert Trent Jones
Type	Tipo	open country, hilly
Relief	Relieve	
Water in play	Agua	
Exp. to wind	Exp. al viento	
Trees in play	Arboles	

Scorecard Tarjeta	Chp. Campeonato	Mens Caballeros	Ladies Damas
Length Longitud	6142	5672	4772
Par	72	72	72

Advised golfing ability
Nivel de juego aconsejado   0   12   24   36
Hcp required   Handicap exigido 28 Men, 36 Ladies

CLUB HOUSE & AMENITIES / CLUB HOUSE Y DEPENDENCIAS — 7/10

Pro shop	Pro-shop	
Driving range	Campo de prácticas	
Sheltered	cubierto	3 mats
On grass	sobre hierba	yes
Putting-green	putting-green	yes
Pitching-green	pitching-green	yes

HOTEL FACILITIES / HOTELES CERCANOS — 6/10

HOTELS HOTELES

La Duquesa — Golf
93 rooms, D 16 800 Pts — 500 m
Tel (34) 952 - 891 211, Fax (34) 952 - 891 630

Sotogrande — Sotogrande
46 rooms, D 19 950 Pts — 10 km
Tel (34) 956 - 794 386, Fax (34) 956 - 794 333

San Roque — San Roque
50 rooms, D 20 000 Pts — 10 km
Tel (34) 956 - 613 030, Fax (34) 956 - 613 012

RESTAURANTS RESTAURANTES

Meson del Castillo — Manilva
Tel (34) 952 - 890 766 — 2 km

Macues — Manilva
Tel (34) 952 - 890 339 — 2 km

1161

Mucha gente lo prefiere a pesar de ser más corto que el «Sur». No se trata de una oposición sino de subrayar la diversidad de los dos recorridos y permitir pasar de uno a otro según se esté más o menos en forma. El «Norte», aunque mucho más corto, no se le puede considerar como un recorrido fácil ya que exige mucha precisión. Tan bien cuidado como su vecino, la longitud de los hoyos es muy variada y con un poco de intuición no es muy difícil evitar las trampas. Los greens no son muy grandes y están poco protegidos, lo que evita la presión a los los jugadores con poca experiencia. El paisaje es agradable, pero mejor evitarlo en los días de mucho calor en pleno verano. La Manga es una «fábrica» de golf, y aunque hay muchas distracciones deportivas, sin embargo los amantes de cultura y turismo pueden quedar un poco defraudados.

Although much shorter than its "South" sister, the "North" does have its supporters. We won't set out to compare the two, only to emphasise the variety they offer, allowing players to switch from one to the other depending on their game. Although much less long, the "North" can still be a handful because of the emphasis on precision. Generally as well upkept as its neighbour, the course offers considerable variety in the length of holes, but with a little intuition, you can get around the traps. The greens are not huge and not well defended, so they take some of the pressure off inexperienced players. The landscape is pleasant, but the course could hardly be recommended at the height of summer. La Manga is a golfing mega-centre, and while there are many other sports and leisure activities in the area, non-golfing lovers of culture and sightseeing might soon wish they were somewhere else.

Hyatt La Manga Club de Golf — 1970

Los Belones
E - 30385 CARTAGENA - MURCIA

Office	Secretaria	(34) 968 - 331 234
Pro shop	Pro-shop	(34) 968 - 331 234
Fax	Fax	(34) 968 - 331 235
Situation	Situación	

Cartagena (pop. 173 061), 30 km
Murcia (pop. 338 250), 75 km

Annual closure	Cierre anual	no
Weekly closure	Cierre semanal	no

Fees main season
Precios tempor. alta full day

	Week days Semana	We/Bank holidays Fin de sem./fiestas
Individual Individual	20 000 Pts	20 000 Pts
Couple Pareja	40 000 Pts	40 000 Pts

Caddy	Caddy	on request
Electric Trolley	Carro eléctrico	2 000 Pts/18 holes
Buggy	Coche	6 000 Pts/18 holes
Clubs	Palos	5 500 Pts/18 holes

Credit cards Tarjetas de crédito
VISA - MasterCard - AMEX - DC

1162

Access Acceso : Murcia → Cartagena, → La Manga
Map 6 on page 1107 Plano 6 Página 1107

GOLF COURSE / RECORRIDO — 15/20

Site	Emplazamiento	
Maintenance	Mantenimiento	
Architect	Arquitecto	Thomas/Puttman Arnold Palmer
Type	Tipo	residential, hilly
Relief	Relieve	
Water in play	Agua	
Exp. to wind	Exp. al viento	
Trees in play	Arboles	

Scorecard Tarjeta	Chp. Campeonato	Mens Caballeros	Ladies Damas
Length Longitud	5780	5518	5139
Par	71	71	71

Advised golfing ability	0	12	24	36
Nivel de juego aconsejado				
Hcp required Handicap exigido	no			

CLUB HOUSE & AMENITIES / CLUB HOUSE Y DEPENDENCIAS — 7/10

Pro shop	Pro-shop	
Driving range	Campo de prácticas	
Sheltered	cubierto	no
On grass	sobre hierba	yes
Putting-green	putting-green	yes
Pitching-green	pitching-green	yes

HOTEL FACILITIES / HOTELES CERCANOS — 7/10

HOTELS HOTELES

Hyatt Principe Felipe — Golf
192 rooms, D 45 200 Pts.
Tel (34) 968 - 137 234
Fax (34) 968 - 137 272

Villa La Manga — La Manga
60 rooms, D 16 400 Pts. — 10 km
Tel (34) 968 - 145 222
Fax (34) 968 - 145 353

RESTAURANTS RESTAURANTES

Amapola Restaurant — La Manga
Tel (34) 968 - 137 234 — 10 km

Borsalino — La Manga
Tel (34) 968 - 563 130 — 10 km

En el complejo golfístico de la Manga, la apertura de un tercer recorrido de 18 hoyos era esperada desde hacía ya mucho tiempo. De hecho se trata de los 9 hoyos existentes desde 1970, rejuvenecidos y completados por Dave Thomas. Los que conocen su trabajo en San Roque encontrarán aquí muchos de los aspectos visuales - sobre todo en la forma de los bunkers - del campo gaditano aunque el conjunto no pretenda igualar ese éxito. La limitacíon del espacio ha influido en ello, lo que ha motivado que el arquitécto haya preferido hacer un campo más corto pero a la voz más técnico. Los nueve últimos hoyos son muy acidentados, más que los primeros, pero caminar por ellos no es complicado. Arboles y arbustos han sido habilmente colocados así como tres lagos. Los pares 3 son bastante largos, y si los pegadores pueden aspirar a tocar los pares 5 de dos, también pueden aspirar al birdie en algunos pares 4 muy cortos. Un tanto difícil para los jugadores poco experimentados, este recorrido es muy divertido para los buenos jugadores.

The opening of a third 18-hole course at La Manga golf resort had been awaited for some time. It is in fact an extension of an existing 9-holer built in 1970, rejuvenated and completed by Dave Thomas. If you know his course at San Roque, you will recognise several of the same visual aspects here, notably in the shape of the bunkers, but the course as a whole is not quite in the same class. There was less space to play with, so the architect preferred to create a rather short, but nonetheless very technical layout. The back 9 are a little hillier than the rest of the course, although walking is never an ordeal. Trees and thickets have been cleverly brought into play, as have three lakes. The par 3s are on the long side, and while long-hitters will attempt to reach the par 5s in two, they can also hope for the elusive birdie on some very short par 4s. A course that is a little difficult for learners, but great fun for the better players.

Hyatt La Manga Club de Golf   1970
Los Belones
E - 30385 CARTAGENA - MURCIA

Office	Secretaria	(34) 968 - 331 234
Pro shop	Pro-shop	(34) 968 - 331 234
Fax	Fax	(34) 968 - 331 235
Situation	Situación	

Cartagena (pop. 173 061), 30 km
Murcia (pop. 338 250), 75 km

Annual closure	Cierre anual	no
Weekly closure	Cierre semanal	no

Fees main season
Precios tempor. alta full day

	Week days Semana	We/Bank holidays Fin de sem./fiestas
Individual Individual	20 000 Pts	20 000 Pts
Couple Pareja	40 000 Pts	40 000 Pts

Caddy	Caddy	on request
Electric Trolley	Carro eléctrico	2 000 Pts/18 holes
Buggy	Coche	6 000 Pts/18 holes
Clubs	Palos	5 500 Pts/18 holes

Credit cards Tarjetas de crédito
VISA - MasterCard - AMEX - DC

Access Acceso : Murcia → Cartagena, → La Manga
Map 6 on page 1107 Plano 6 Página 1107

GOLF COURSE
RECORRIDO   14/20

Site	Emplazamiento	
Maintenance	Mantenimiento	
Architect	Arquitecto	Dave Thomas
Type	Tipo	country
Relief	Relieve	
Water in play	Agua	
Exp. to wind	Exp. al viento	
Trees in play	Arboles	

Scorecard Tarjeta	Chp. Campeonato	Mens Caballeros	Ladies Damas
Length Longitud	5971	5680	4922
Par	73	73	73

Advised golfing ability	0	12	24	36
Nivel de juego aconsejado				

Hcp required   Handicap exigido   no

CLUB HOUSE & AMENITIES
CLUB HOUSE Y DEPENDENCIAS   7/10

Pro shop	Pro-shop	
Driving range	Campo de prácticas	
Sheltered	cubierto	no
On grass	sobre hierba	yes
Putting-green	putting-green	yes
Pitching-green	pitching-green	yes

1163

HOTEL FACILITIES
HOTELES CERCANOS   7/10

HOTELS HOTELES
Hyatt Principe Felipe   Golf
192 rooms, D 45 200 Pts.
Tel (34) 968 - 137 234, Fax (34) 968 - 137 272

Villa La Manga   La Manga
60 rooms, D 16 400 Pts.   10 km
Tel (34) 968 - 145 222, Fax (34) 968 - 145 353

RESTAURANTS RESTAURANTES

Amapola Restaurant   La Manga
Tel (34) 968 - 137 234   10 km

Borsalino   La Manga
Tel (34) 968 - 563 130   10 km

El complejo de La Manga es desde hace mucho tiempo uno de los más famosos de España con construcciones immobiliarias que no todos apreciarán. El recorrido «Sur» es el más largo y sin duda el más franco, aunque sea necesario juagarlo varias veces para impregnarse de sus sutilezas. Arnold Palmer ha modificado, con gran acierto, el diseño original mejorando su aspecto visual y acentuando una estética de carácter americano, aunque bien es verdad que hubiera podido diseñar mejor tanto los bunkers como los greens. Hay muchos obstáculos de agua pequeños, especialmente en el 17 y el 18. La longitud de este recorrido es un excelente test: si logra jugar su handicap querrá decir que posee un juego muy completo. Sin que sea una obra maestra y teniendo en cuenta el lugar, es un recorrido que no se debe ignorar.

La Manga has long been one of Spain's most famous resorts and a site for real estate property development that is not to everyone's taste. The "South" course is the longest and certainly the most open, even though you need several rounds to understand the more subtle sides to it. Arnold Palmer made a few welcome visual changes to the original layout, emphasising the American style design, but the great man's restyling was unable to hide the fact that the bunkers and greens could have been redesigned better. The course is dotted with little water hazards, especially on the 17th and 18th holes. The length of the course makes it a good test, and if you play to your handicap, you will have shown good all-round skills and versatility. This is not your actual masterpiece, but the facilities on site make this a course not to be missed.

Hyatt La Manga Club de Golf — 1970

Los Belones
E - 30385 CARTAGENA - MURCIA

Office	Secretaria	(34) 968 - 331 234
Pro shop	Pro-shop	(34) 968 - 331 234
Fax	Fax	(34) 968 - 331 235
Situation	Situación	

Cartagena (pop. 173 061), 30 km
Murcia (pop. 338 250), 75 km

Annual closure	Cierre anual	no
Weekly closure	Cierre semanal	no

Fees main season
Precios tempor. alta full day

	Week days Semana	We/Bank holidays Fin de sem./fiestas
Individual Individual	20 000 Pts	20 000 Pts
Couple Pareja	40 000 Pts	40 000 Pts

Caddy	Caddy	on request
Electric Trolley	Carro eléctrico	2 000 Pts/18 holes
Buggy	Coche	6 000 Pts/18 holes
Clubs	Palos	5 500 Pts/18 holes

Credit cards Tarjetas de crédito
VISA - MasterCard - AMEX - DC

1164

Access Acceso : Murcia → Cartagena, → La Manga
Map 6 on page 1107 Plano 6 Página 1107

GOLF COURSE / RECORRIDO — 14/20

Site	Emplazamiento	
Maintenance	Mantenimiento	
Architect	Arquitecto	Thomas/Puttman Arnold Palmer
Type	Tipo	residential, country
Relief	Relieve	
Water in play	Agua	
Exp. to wind	Exp. al viento	
Trees in play	Arboles	

Scorecard Tarjeta	Chp. Campeonato	Mens Caballeros	Ladies Damas
Length Longitud	6361	6065	5490
Par	72	72	72

Advised golfing ability		0 12 24 36
Nivel de juego aconsejado		
Hcp required	Handicap exigido	28 Men, 36 Ladies

CLUB HOUSE & AMENITIES / CLUB HOUSE Y DEPENDENCIAS — 7/10

Pro shop	Pro-shop	
Driving range	Campo de prácticas	
Sheltered	cubierto	no
On grass	sobre hierba	yes
Putting-green	putting-green	yes
Pitching-green	pitching-green	yes

HOTEL FACILITIES / HOTELES CERCANOS — 7/10

HOTELS HOTELES

Hyatt Principe Felipe — Golf
192 rooms, D 45 200 Pts.
Tel (34) 968 - 137 234
Fax (34) 968 - 137 272

Villa La Manga — La Manga 10 km
60 rooms, D 16 400 Pts.
Tel (34) 968 - 145 222
Fax (34) 968 - 145 353

RESTAURANTS RESTAURANTES

Amapola Restaurant — La Manga 10 km
Tel (34) 968 - 137 234

Borsalino — La Manga 10 km
Tel (34) 968 - 563 130

En la época de la construcción de éste campo (como de Muirfield Village en los Estados Unidos), Jack Nicklaus trabajada con Desmond Muirhead, uno de los arquitéctos más originales de éste siglo, y uno de los menos orientados sobre la longitud a cualquier precio. Si La Moraleja 1 es bastante corto, exige la máxima precisión si se quiere conseguir un buen resultado, sobre todo porque los greenes son bastante pequeños, muy ondulados, rápidos y muy bien defendidos. Si se les quiere atacar en buena posición, es importante colocar correctamente el drive, lo que no siempre es fácil, y mucha lucidez a la hora de seleccionar el palo: sobre los 4 pares 4 cortos será recomendable jugar un hierro de salida. Los pegadores impenitentes podrán intentar los más posible de los greenes, o atacar de dos los pares 5, sobre todo en match-play ya que los peligros son constantes. Un campo muy divertido sin ser por ello una obra maestra inolvidable.

When building this course (the same goes for Muirfield Village in the United States)), Jack Nicklaus was working with Desmond Muirhead, one of the most original course designers of our day, and one who doesn't go for length at any price. While La Moraleja 1 is on the short side, it demands extreme accuracy for a good card, especially since the greens are only average in size, steeply contoured, quick and very well guarded. To be in the right position to make your approach, the drive has to be exactly in the right place, a feat that is not always so easy and one that demands clear-headed club selection. On the four very short par 4s, for example, you are best advised to use a long iron. Incorrigible big-hitters can attempt to get as close as possible to the green and also reach the par 5s in two, at least in match-play, the ideal formula given the profusion of dangerous hazards. A very amusing course, but hardly an unforgettable master-piece.

Golf La Moraleja — 1976

Paseo Marquesa Viuda de Aldana, 50
E - 28109 LA MORALEJA-MADRID

Office	Secretaria	(34) 916 - 500 700
Pro shop	Pro-shop	(34) 916 - 500 700
Fax	Fax	(34) 916 - 504 331
Situation	Situación	

Madrid (pop. 3 084 673), 12 km

Annual closure	Cierre anual	no
Weekly closure	Cierre semanal	no

Fees main season
Precios tempor. alta 18 holes

	Week days Semana	We/Bank holidays Fin de sem./fiestas
Individual Individual	8 000 Pts	20 000 Pts
Couple Pareja	16 000 Pts	40 000 Pts

members' guests only (solo invitados de socios)

Caddy	Caddy	no
Electric Trolley	Carro eléctrico	1 000 Pts/18 holes
Buggy	Coche	4 200 Pts/18 holes
Clubs	Palos	2 000 Pts/18 holes

Credit cards Tarjetas de crédito — no

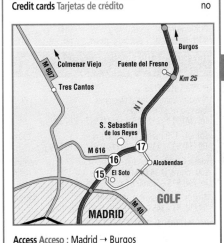

Access Acceso : Madrid → Burgos
Map 3 on page 1100 Plano 3 Página 1100

GOLF COURSE RECORRIDO — 15/20

Site	Emplazamiento	
Maintenance	Mantenimiento	
Architect	Arquitecto	Jack Nicklaus Desmond Muirhead
Type	Tipo	country
Relief	Relieve	
Water in play	Agua	
Exp. to wind	Exp. al viento	
Trees in play	Arboles	

Scorecard Tarjeta	Chp. Campeonato	Mens Caballeros	Ladies Damas
Length Longitud	5992	5706	4937
Par	72	72	72

Advised golfing ability Nivel de juego aconsejado	0	12	24	36

Hcp required Handicap exigido members' guests

CLUB HOUSE & AMENITIES CLUB HOUSE Y DEPENDENCIAS — 7/10

Pro shop	Pro-shop	
Driving range	Campo de prácticas	
Sheltered	cubierto	no
On grass	sobre hierba	no (30 mats)
Putting-green	putting-green	yes
Pitching-green	pitching-green	no

HOTEL FACILITIES HOTELES CERCANOS — 8/10

HOTELS HOTELES

Novotel-Campo de las Naciones — 600 m
246 rooms, D 19 300 Pts
Tel (34) 917 - 211 818, Fax (34) 917 - 211 122

Sofitel - 179 rooms, D 39 000 Pts — 100 m
Tel (34) 917 - 210 070, Fax (34) 917 - 210 515

Melia Castilla - 900 rooms, D 34 000 Pts — Madrid
Tel (34) 915 - 675 000, Fax (34) 915 - 675 051 — 10 km

Aristos - 24 rooms, D 19 000 Pts — Madrid
Tel (34) 91 - 345 04 50, Fax (34) 91 - 345 10 23

RESTAURANTS RESTAURANTES

Zalacain - Tel (34) 915 - 614 840 — Madrid 10 km

Principe de Viana — Madrid
Tel (34) 914 - 571 549 — 10 km

El Olivo - Tel (34) 913 - 591 535 — Madrid 10 km

1165

Este segundo recorrido del gran club de La Moraleja ha sido diseñado por los arquitéctos asociados a Jack Nicklaus. Este no lo ha firmado, pero su influencia sobre sus colaboradores se deja sentir. Los greenes son de grand tamaño, y los tres putts no son raros, sobre todo si se está alejado de la bandera. Es entonces cuando las numerosas caídas y la rapidez de la superficie exigen una gran concentración en la lectura del green y mucho toque. Están bien protegidos por el agua, por árboles, por unos bunkers muy dibujados, sobre todo en el 9 y 18, cuando protegen éste doble green. La primera mitad es tal vez menos impresionante pero ello no significa ni mucho menos que se deba bajar la guardia. Hay que estar alerta los 18 hoyos puesto que las dificultades surgen cuando uno menos se lo espera. La estrategia de juego en función de la forma del momento juega pues un papel determinante. Tiene que conocerse aunque se deben evitar los fines de semana.

This second golf course on the Club La Moraleja was designed by architects associated with Jack Nicklaus, and although not carrying his signature, the great man evidently had some influence on his partners. The greens are huge and three-putts not an uncommon occurrence, especially if you are nowhere near the pin, as the numerous slopes and speed of the putting surfaces call for careful reading and a delicate touch. They are often well-guarded by water, sometimes by trees and by well-designed bunkers, especially on the 9th and 18th holes, which share a double green. The first half of the course is less intimidating, but that doesn't mean you can take things easy. Stay on your toes the whole time, because the difficulties here crop up when you least expect them. As a result, game strategy, depending on the shape of your game, plays a significant role. Well worth knowing, but avoid week-ends.

Golf La Moraleja

Paseo Marquesa Viuda de Aldana, 50
E - 28109 LA MORALEJA-MADRID

Office	Secretaria	(34) 916 - 500 700
Pro shop	Pro-shop	(34) 916 - 500 700
Fax	Fax	(34) 916 - 504 331
Situation	Situación	

Madrid (pop. 3 084 673), 12 km

Annual closure	Cierre anual	no
Weekly closure	Cierre semanal	no

Fees main season
Precios tempor. alta 18 holes

	Week days Semana	We/Bank holidays Fin de sem./fiestas
Individual Individual	8 000 Pts	20 000 Pts
Couple Pareja	16 000 Pts	40 000 Pts

members' guests only (solo invitados de socios)

Caddy	Caddy	no
Electric Trolley	Carro eléctrico	1 000 Pts/18 holes
Buggy	Coche	4 200 Pts/18 holes
Clubs	Palos	2 000 Pts/18 holes

Credit cards Tarjetas de crédito — no

1166

Access Acceso : Madrid → Burgos
Map 3 on page 1100 Plano 3 Página 1100

GOLF COURSE
RECORRIDO   16/20

Site	Emplazamiento	
Maintenance	Mantenimiento	
Architect	Arquitecto	Golden Bear Design Associates
Type	Tipo	country
Relief	Relieve	
Water in play	Agua	
Exp. to wind	Exp. al viento	
Trees in play	Arboles	

Scorecard Tarjeta	Chp. Campeonato	Mens Caballeros	Ladies Damas
Length Longitud	6451	5888	5014
Par	72	72	72

Advised golfing ability	0	12	24	36
Nivel de juego aconsejado				

Hcp required Handicap exigido members'guests

CLUB HOUSE & AMENITIES
CLUB HOUSE Y DEPENDENCIAS   7/10

Pro shop	Pro-shop	
Driving range	Campo de prácticas	
Sheltered	cubierto	no
On grass	sobre hierba	no (30 mats)
Putting-green	putting-green	yes
Pitching-green	pitching-green	no

HOTEL FACILITIES
HOTELES CERCANOS   8/10

HOTELS HOTELES

Novotel-Campo de las Naciones 246 rooms, D 19 300 Pts Tel (34) 917 - 211 818, Fax (34) 917 - 211 122	600 m
Sofitel - 179 rooms, D 39 000 Pts Tel (34) 917 - 210 070, Fax (34) 917 - 210 515	100 m
Melia Castilla 900 rooms, D 34 000 Pts Tel (34) 915 - 675 000, Fax (34) 915 - 675 051	Madrid 10 km
Aristos - 24 rooms, D 19 000 Pts Tel (34) 91 - 345 04 50, Fax (34) 91 - 345 10 23	Madrid

RESTAURANTS RESTAURANTES

Zalacain - Tel (34) 915 - 614 840	Madrid 10 km
Principe de Viana - Tel (34) 914 - 571 549	Madrid 10 km
El Olivo - Tel (34) 913 - 591 535	Madrid 10 km

Dos grandes campeones, Antonio Garrido y Manuel Piñeiro, han diseñado uno de los recorridos más técnicos de la región , con un total de 27 hoyos, siendo la combinación de «San Pedro» y de «Guadaiza» la más larga. Como las distancias no son excesivas, los jugadores precisos se encontrarán más agusto que los pegadores a pesar de que las zonas de caída del drive sean anchas y los tees de salida a menudo en alto. Hay dificultades de todas clases : árboles, bunkers de green, ríos y lagos no siempre a la vista. El relieve es bastante accidentado, sin que sea exagerado, lo que complica la apreciación de los aproches: conviene tirar a bandera para evitar los putts largos ya que las caídas de green son difíciles de apreciar. No todo el mundo apreciará el entorno inmobiliario (cosa inevitable en la región) escondido parcialmente por la vegetación de este gran jardín.

Two top champions, Antonio Garrido and Manuel Pinero, designed this, one of the region's most technical golf courses comprising 27 holes. The «San Pedro» and «Guadaiza» together form the longest 18-hole combination. Not being over-long, accurate players will probably feel more at home than the big hitters, even though the landing areas for drives are pretty wide and the tees often elevated. There are all kinds of hazards here, from trees to green-side bunkers to rivers and lakes, and they are not always very visible. This is pretty hilly terrain, a factor which complicates the approach shot. It is also important to go for the pin to avoid over-long putts, as the greens are tricky to read. The property development surroundings are not to everyone's liking but are unavoidable in this part of the world and are partly concealed by the trees.

La Quinta Golf & Country Club   1989

Nueva Andalucia
E - 29660 MARBELLA (MALAGA)

Office	Secretaria	(34) 952 - 762 390
Pro shop	Pro-shop	(34) 952 - 762 390
Fax	Fax	(34) 952 - 783 466
Situation	Situación	

San Pedro de Alcantara, 3 km
Marbella (pop. 84 410), 16 km

Annual closure	Cierre anual	no
Weekly closure	Cierre semanal	no

Fees main season
Precios tempor. alta 18 holes

	Week days Semana	We/Bank holidays Fin de sem./fiestas
Individual Individual	9 000 Pts	9 000 Pts
Couple Pareja	18 000 Pts	18 000 Pts

Caddy	Caddy	on request
Electric Trolley	Carro eléctrico	1 500 Pts/18 holes
Buggy	Coche	5 000 Pts/18 holes
Clubs	Palos	3 000 Pts/18 holes

Credit cards Tarjetas de crédito
VISA - MasterCard - AMEX

Access Acceso : Marbella N340 → San Pedro de Alcantara, → Ronda, Golf 3 km
Map 7 on page 1109 Plano 7 Página 1109

GOLF COURSE / RECORRIDO   15/20

Site	Emplazamiento	
Maintenance	Mantenimiento	
Architect	Arquitecto	Manuel Piñero Antonio Garrido
Type	Tipo	residential, hilly
Relief	Relieve	
Water in play	Agua	
Exp. to wind	Exp. al viento	
Trees in play	Arboles	

Scorecard Tarjeta	Chp. Campeonato	Mens Caballeros	Ladies Damas
Length Longitud	5597	5517	4810
Par	72	72	72

Advised golfing ability Nivel de juego aconsejado	0 12 24 36
Hcp required Handicap exigido	28 Men, 36 Ladies

CLUB HOUSE & AMENITIES / CLUB HOUSE Y DEPENDENCIAS   8/10

Pro shop	Pro-shop	
Driving range	Campo de prácticas	
Sheltered	cubierto	10 mats
On grass	sobre hierba	yes
Putting-green	putting-green	yes
Pitching-green	pitching-green	yes

HOTEL FACILITIES / HOTELES CERCANOS   7/10

HOTELS HOTELES

Puente Romano   Marbella, Cta de Cádiz
217 rooms, D 52 000 Pts.   3 km
Tel (34) 952 - 820 900, Fax (34) 952 - 775 766

Pyr Hotel   Puerto Banus
319 rooms, D 15 700 Pts   2 km
Tel (34) 952 - 817 353, Fax (34) 952 - 817 907

RESTAURANTS RESTAURANTES

Albatros   Golf
Tel (34) 952 - 762 333

Cipriano   Puerto Banús
Tel (34) 952 - 811 077   5 km

1167

Situado en la falda de una montaña no es un recorrido excesivamente cansado, pero en pleno verano es mejor alquilar un coche. De longitud moderada, si se domina con maestría todos los palos se puede lograr un buen resultado. Pinos, naranjos, olivos y almendros le dan un cierto colorido y suponen muchos problemas para jugadores sin precisión. Con una arquitectura bastante personal, La Sella demuestra que sus creadores conocían muy bien toda la gama de jugadores, adaptando las dificulta"des a los diferentes tees de salida. Efectivamente, Juan de la Cuadra lo diseñó con la experta ayuda de José María Olazabal. Si se falla la llegada a green, habrá que emplear toda la virtuosidad del campeón español para salvar el par.... La Sella es uno de los buenos golfs de la región.

Although laid out on the side of a mountain, the course can be walked, although a buggy is advisable in mid-summer to get a bit of air. La Sella is not too long, but if all your clubs are in good working order, a good score should not be beyond you. The pine, orange, olive and almond trees bring a touch of colour and relief, and sometimes a number of problems for wayward hitters. A very personal design, La Sella shows how much the architects knew about players of all ability, as difficulties are geared to the different tees. Not surprisingly, the course was laid out by Juan de la Cuadra, expertly assisted by José-Maria Olazabal. If you miss the greens, you will need some of the Spanish champion's virtuosity to save par. La Sella is a good address in the region.

Club de Golf La Sella — 1991

Ctra La Jara - Jesus Pobre
E - 03749 JESUS POBRE - DENIA (ALICANTE)

Office	Secretaria	(34) 966 - 454 252
Pro shop	Pro-shop	(34) 966 - 454 163
Fax	Fax	(34) 966 - 454 201
Situation	Situación	

Denia (pop. 25 157), 8 km
Jávea (pop. 16 603), 8 km

Annual closure	Cierre anual	no
Weekly closure	Cierre semanal	no

Fees main season
Precios tempor. alta 18 holes

	Week days Semana	We/Bank holidays Fin de sem./fiestas
Individual Individual	6 500 Pts	6 500 Pts
Couple Pareja	13 000 Pts	13 000 Pts

Caddy	Caddy	no
Electric Trolley	Carro eléctrico	no
Buggy	Coche	4 000 Pts/18 holes
Clubs	Palos	2 000 Pts/18 holes

Credit cards Tarjetas de crédito
VISA - MasterCard - AMEX

1168

Access Acceso : A7 Valencia - Alicante,
Exit (Salida) 62 → Denia → Jara → Golf
Map 6 on page 1107 Plano 6 Página 1107

GOLF COURSE RECORRIDO 15/20

Site	Emplazamiento	
Maintenance	Mantenimiento	
Architect	Arquitecto	Juan de la Cuadra J.M. Olazabal
Type	Tipo	country, hilly
Relief	Relieve	
Water in play	Agua	
Exp. to wind	Exp. al viento	
Trees in play	Arboles	

Scorecard Tarjeta	Chp. Campeonato	Mens Caballeros	Ladies Damas
Length Longitud	6072	5919	5118
Par	72	72	72

Advised golfing ability — 0 12 24 36
Nivel de juego aconsejado
Hcp required Handicap exigido 28 Men, 36 Ladies

CLUB HOUSE & AMENITIES CLUB HOUSE Y DEPENDENCIAS 6/10

Pro shop	Pro-shop	
Driving range	Campo de prácticas	
Sheltered	cubierto	2 mats
On grass	sobre hierba	yes
Putting-green	putting-green	yes
Pitching-green	pitching-green	yes

HOTEL FACILITIES HOTELES CERCANOS 5/10

HOTELS HOTELES

Romano — Denia — 6 km
6 rooms, D 18 900 Pts
Tel (34) 966 - 421 789, Fax (34) 966 - 422 958

Parador de Jávea — Jávea — 10 km
65 rooms, D 13 700 Pts.
Tel (34) 965 - 790 200, Fax (34) 965 - 790 308

El Rodat — Jávea — 8 km
25 rooms, D 15 800 Pts
Tel (34) 966 - 470 710, Fax (34) 966 - 471 550

RESTAURANTS RESTAURANTES

Romano — Denia — 6 km
Tel (34) 966 - 421 789

El Pegoli - Tel (34) 965 - 780 135 — Denia 6 km

La Casa del Arroz - Tel (34) 965 - 781 047 — Denia 6 km

Es un recorrido muy privado, merece la pena esforzarse en conocer algún socio para que le inviten a jugar. Es aconsejable coger un coche ya que los desnivelaciones son grandes: es casi un recorrido de montaña, situado a menos de diez kilómetros de la Costa del Sol. Hay que jugar sin miedo a perder bolas, evitar los barrancos y sobrevolar bastantes obstáculos de agua. No obstante, cualquier jugador (no los principiantes!) puede adaptarse al recorrido utilizando uno de los muchos tees de salida construidos por el arquitecto. La estética es bastante americana, un poco similar a ciertos recorridos de California del Sur. Las calles son bastante anchas, los greens muy amplios, con caídas y rápidos. El mantenimiento es de muy buena calidad, cosa no muy difícil de obtener dado el limitado número de jugadores.

A very private course but one which is worth the effort involved in getting to know members well enough to be invited. They will certainly recommend a buggy because there is some steep climbing to do on what is almost a mountain style course, less than 7 miles from the Costa del Sol. Here you should not be too afraid of losing balls, just make sure you avoid the ravines and lift the ball over the many water hazards. Despite these obvious pitfalls, players of all levels (but not beginners) can play here because there are so many different tee-boxes. The style is definitely American and rather similar to some of the courses in southern California. The fairways are wide and the greens large, often multi-tiered, slick and fast. An emphatic word, too, for the excellence of green-keeping, perhaps a task made easier when there are so few players out on the course.

Club de Golf La Zagaleta — 1994

Carretera de Ronda 38
E - 29679 BENHAVIS (Malaga)

Office	Secretaria	(34) 952 - 855 453
Pro shop	Pro-shop	(34) 952 - 855 453
Fax	Fax	(34) 952 - 855 419
Situation	Situación	

San Pedro de Alcantara, 12 km

Annual closure	Cierre anual	no
Weekly closure	Cierre semanal	no

Fees main season
Precios tempor. alta 18 holes

	Week days Semana	We/Bank holidays Fin de sem./fiestas
Individual Individual	25 000 Pts	25 000 Pts
Couple Pareja	50 000 Pts	50 000 Pts

Caddy	Caddy	no
Electric Trolley	Carro eléctrico	yes
Buggy	Coche	5 000 Pts/18 holes
Clubs	Palos	yes

Credit cards Tarjetas de crédito
VISA - Eurocard - MasterCard - AMEX

Access Acceso : San Pedro → Ronda
Map 7 on page 1109 Plano 7 Página 1109

GOLF COURSE RECORRIDO — 16/20

Site	Emplazamiento	
Maintenance	Mantenimiento	
Architect	Arquitecto	Bradford Benz
Type	Tipo	hilly, residential
Relief	Relieve	
Water in play	Agua	
Exp. to wind	Exp. al viento	
Trees in play	Arboles	

Scorecard Tarjeta	Chp. Campeonato	Mens Caballeros	Ladies Damas
Length Longitud	6039	5709	5279
Par	72	72	72

Advised golfing ability 0 12 24 36
Nivel de juego aconsejado
Hcp required Handicap exigido 28 Men, 36 Ladies

CLUB HOUSE & AMENITIES CLUB HOUSE Y DEPENDENCIAS — 7/10

Pro shop	Pro-shop	
Driving range	Campo de prácticas	
Sheltered	cubierto	no
On grass	sobre hierba	yes
Putting-green	putting-green	yes
Pitching-green	pitching-green	yes

HOTEL FACILITIES HOTELES CERCANOS — 7/10

HOTELS HOTELES

Atalaya Park — Estepona
448 rooms, D 25 200 Pts — 8 km
Tel (34) 952 - 884 801, Fax (34) 952 - 885 735

El Paraiso — Estepona
182 rooms, D 27 000 Pts — 10 km
Tel (34) 952 - 883 000, Fax (34) 952 - 882 019

Guadalmina — San Pedro
80 rooms, D 27 200 Pts — 12 km
Tel (34) 952 - 882 211, Fax (34) 952 - 882 291

RESTAURANTS RESTAURANTES

El Gamonal — San Pedro
Tel (34) 952 - 883 375 — 12 km

Los Nieto — San Pedro
Tel (34) 952 - 883 491 — 12 km

1169

Es el más «urbano» de los campos del sur de Tenerife, en un oasis verde del formidable complejo hotelero y residencial Playa de Las Américas-Costa Adeje. Pero el ladrillo -y las últimas grúas- de los alrededores guarda prudente distancia y a ello colabora un diseño abierto con múltiples referencias -palmeras y agua, sobre todo- que ocupan la atención del jugador. No es un campo largo -en el 4 y en el 14 los pegadores tirarán a green- pero hay que tener cuidado con los fuera límites, el agua, los bunkers bien colocados y los greenes, muy francos, que son grandes, rápidos y movidos y, por lo tanto, hay que jugarlos con respeto. Habitualmente sopla una brisa que refresca la temperatura y altera un poco el vuelo de la bola. El mantenimiento del campo merece un aplauso especial.

This is the most residential of all the courses on the south coast of Tenerife, lying in the lush oasis of the huge hotel and residential resort of la Playa de las Americas Costa Adeje. Turn your eyes away from the bricks and last few cranes that surround the course and take a close look at a layout that has much to be said for it, especially the palm trees and water hazards that should keep you busy for some time. This is not a very long course (the longer-hitters can try and drive the green on holes 4 and 14), but watch out for OB, the water and some well-placed bunkers close to the greens. The putting surfaces are true, large and slick, so treat them with respect. To cool the summer heat, there is often a refreshing little breeze blowing here, and it can easily have an influence on where your ball ends up, so again, care is called for. A special mention should go to the excellent standard of maintenance and green-keeping.

Golf Las Americas   1998
Playa de Las Americas
E - 38650 ARONA - TENERIFE

Office	Secretaria	(34) 922 - 752 005
Pro shop	Pro-shop	(34) 922 - 752 005
Fax	Fax	(34) 922 - 795 250
Situation	Situación	

Santa Cruz de Tenerife (pop. 203 000), 75 km

Annual closure	Cierre anual	no
Weekly closure	Cierre semanal	no

Fees main season
Precios tempor. alta 18 holes

	Week days Semana	We/Bank holidays Fin de sem./fiestas
Individual Individual	10 500 Pts	10 500 Pts
Couple Pareja	21 000 Pts	21 000 Pts

Caddy	Caddy	no
Electric Trolley	Carro eléctrico	no
Buggy	Coche	4 500 Pts/full day
Clubs	Palos	2 500 Pts/full day

Credit cards Tarjetas de crédito
VISA - Eurocard - MasterCard - AMEX

Access Acceso : Motorway TF1/ Autovia del Sur,
km 72 Exit (Salida) 28
Map 9 on page 1112 Plano 9 Página 1112

GOLF COURSE
RECORRIDO   16/20

Site	Emplazamiento	
Maintenance	Mantenimiento	
Architect	Arquitecto	Rubens Henriquez
Type	Tipo	parkland
Relief	Relieve	
Water in play	Agua	
Exp. to wind	Exp. al viento	
Trees in play	Arboles	

Scorecard Tarjeta	Chp. Campeonato	Mens Caballeros	Ladies Damas
Length Longitud	6039	5860	5026
Par	72	72	72

Advised golfing ability   0   12   24   36
Nivel de juego aconsejado
Hcp required   Handicap exigido 28 Men, 36 Ladies

CLUB HOUSE & AMENITIES
CLUB HOUSE Y DEPENDENCIAS   7/10

Pro shop	Pro-shop	
Driving range	Campo de prácticas	
Sheltered	cubierto	no
On grass	sobre hierba	yes, 20 places
Putting-green	putting-green	yes
Pitching-green	pitching-green	yes

HOTEL FACILITIES
HOTELES CERCANOS   8/10

HOTELS HOTELES

Noelia Sur	Playa Las Americas
416 rooms, D 22 000 Pts	100 m
Tel (34) 922 - 793 511, Fax (34) 922 - 793 609	

Jardin Tropical	Costa Adeje
421 rooms, D 22 000 Pts	5 km
Tel (34) 913 - 458 284, Fax (34) 922 - 746 060	

Arona GH	Los Cristianos
399 rooms, D 27 000 Pts	5 km
Tel (34) 922 - 750 678, Fax (34) 922 - 750 243	

RESTAURANTS RESTAURANTES

El Patio - Tel (34) 922 - 750 678	Costa Adeje 5 km
El Jable - Tel (34) 922 - 390 698	San Isidro5 km
La Cava - Tel (34) 922 - 790 493	Los Cristianos 5 km

1170

LAS BRISAS

Uno de los grandes recorridos de la Costa del Sol, aunque conservando una dimensión humana por el gran número de tees de salida que permiten que los jugadores de nivel medio puedan evolucionar sin miedo. Rodeado de bonitos chalés, el terreno es poco accidentado, y numerosos greens en alto complican los aproches. Numerosos bunkers y obsáculos de agua (en la línea de juego en 12 hoyos) protegen los greens. Aquí es necesario poseer un juego preciso y muy completo (hoyos estrechos alternan con otros más anchos), se debe tirar a bandera y saber dar toda clase de golpes para obtener un buen resultado. Ya en el green queda todavía mucho por hacer ya que no es fácil calcular las caídas. Es apasionante jugar en este golf tanto en stroke-play como en match-play, es el más divertido de todos los «monumentos» de la región, aunque sólo sea por su seducción visual añadida a la calidad del desafío.

One of the really great courses on the Costa del Sol but one that has kept a very human dimension through the number of tees, allowing players of average standard to play the course without feeling terrorised. Surrounded by beautiful villas, the terrain is pretty even but the many elevated greens make approach shots a tricky business. The greens are well protected by the many bunkers and water hazards (affecting 12 holes in all). Las Brisas calls for accurate, comprehensive golf (tight holes alternate with wider fairways) and the ability to play most shots in order to card a good score. The emphasis here is on American-style target golf. Although once on the greens, you are still far from home and dry, because none of them are easy to read. An exciting course for stroke-play and match-play, this is the most amusing of the region's golfing landmarks, if only for the view which adds to the amazing challenge of golf.

Real Club de Golf Las Brisas — 1968

Apartado 147 - Nueva Andalucia
E - 29660 MARBELLA (MALAGA)

Office	Secretaria	(34) 952 - 810 875
Pro shop	Pro-shop	(34) 952 - 811 257
Fax	Fax	(34) 952 - 815 518

Situation — Situación
Marbella (pop. 84 410), 15 km
San Pedro de Alcantara, 6 km

Annual closure	Cierre anual	no
Weekly closure	Cierre semanal	no

Fees main season
Precios tempor. alta 18 holes

	Week days Semana	We/Bank holidays Fin de sem./fiestas
Individual Individual	15 000 Pts	15 000 Pts
Couple Pareja	30 000 Pts	30 000 Pts

Caddy	Caddy	3 500 Pts/18 holes
Electric Trolley	Carro eléctrico	2 000 Pts/18 holes
Buggy	Coche	5 000 Pts/18 holes
Clubs	Palos	2 000 Pts/18 holes

Credit cards Tarjetas de crédito VISA - MasterCard

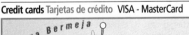

MARBELLA N 340

Sierra Bermeja
C.339
El Ángel
Nueva Andalucia
San Pedro de Alcantara
Estepona
N 340
Playas de Marbella
GOLF
COSTA DEL SOL

0 2 4 km

Access Acceso : Marbella N340 → San Pedro de Alcantara, Nueva Andalucia (km 174), turn right → Golf
Map 7 on page 1109 Plano 7 Página 1109

GOLF COURSE
RECORRIDO — 18/20

Site	Emplazamiento	▰▰▰▰▱
Maintenance	Mantenimiento	▰▰▰▰▱
Architect	Arquitecto	Robert Trent Jones
Type	Tipo	residential, parkland
Relief	Relieve	▰▰▱▱▱
Water in play	Agua	▰▰▰▱▱
Exp. to wind	Exp. al viento	▰▰▱▱▱
Trees in play	Arboles	▰▰▰▱▱

Scorecard Tarjeta	Chp. Campeonato	Mens Caballeros	Ladies Damas
Length Longitud	6163	5893	5096
Par	72	72	72

Advised golfing ability — 0 12 24 36
Nivel de juego aconsejado ▰▰▰▱
Hcp required Handicap exigido 28 Men, 36 Ladies

CLUB HOUSE & AMENITIES
CLUB HOUSE Y DEPENDENCIAS — 7/10

Pro shop	Pro-shop	▰▰▰▰▱
Driving range	Campo de prácticas	▰▰▰▱▱
Sheltered	cubierto	4 mats
On grass	sobre hierba	yes
Putting-green	putting-green	yes
Pitching-green	pitching-green	yes

HOTEL FACILITIES
HOTELES CERCANOS — 7/10

HOTELS HOTELES

Puente Romano — Marbella
217 rooms, D 52 000 Pts — 4 km
Tel (34) 952 - 820 900, Fax (34) 952 - 775 766

Melia Don Pepe — Marbella
200 rooms, D 41 400 Pts — 8 km
Tel (34) 952 - 770 300, Fax (34) 952 - 779 954

Pyr Hotel — Puerto Banus
319 rooms, D 15 700 Pts — 13 km
Tel (34) 952 - 817 353, Fax (34) 952 - 817 907

RESTAURANTS RESTAURANTES

Cipriano — Puerto Banús
Tel (34) 952 - 811 077 — 4 km

Bistrot Cristian — Puerto Banús
Tel (34) 952 - 811 006 — 4 km

1171

Es el club más antiguo de España, fundado en 1891 en las afueras de Las Palmas. La expansión de la ciudad obligó a trasladarlo en 1956 y se asienta ahora en un paraje natural, llamado los Llanos de Bandama, a 14 kilómetros de la ciudad. El ambiente del club y su diseño natural mantienen la tradición inglesa de sus fundadores. El terreno es muy escarpado y la casa-club de estilo clásico, domina todo el recorrido y ofrece unas espléndidas vistas sobre las rocas volcánicas y barrancos que lo rodean. El campo no es de medidas largas, pero hay varios hoyos en subida que hay que tratar con el máximo respeto. Es preciso dominar el vuelo de la bola para mantener la bola en juego en un recorrido, que sin ser estrecho, incita al jugador a pensar cuál es el mejor sitio para colocar cada salida.

This is Spain's oldest golf club, whose course was originally laid out in the suburbs of Las Palmas de Gran Canaria. In 1956, as the city expanded, the club moved out into the country close to Llanos de Bandama, some 14 km from the city. The atmosphere in this club, just like the actual course, faithfully upholds the British tradition laid down by the club's founding members. The course is very hilly (but only a limited number of buggies are available) and the very classically styled club-house overlooks the whole course providing a magnificent scenic view of the surrounding volcanic rocks and ravines. The 18 holes (designed by MacKenzie Ross but restyled since) are not particularly wide and there are quite a few uphill holes that need to be negotiated very carefully. Accuracy is of the essence to keep the ball in play on a course where the tight fairways force the golfer to think long and hard about careful placing of the ball before each shot.

RCG de Las Palmas — 1891

Carreterra de Bandana S/N
E - 35380 SANTA BRIGIDA (Gran Canaria)

Office	Secretaria	(34) 928 - 350 104
Pro shop	Pro-shop	(34) 928 - 350 104
Fax	Fax	(34) 928 - 350 110
Situation	Situación	

Las Palmas (pop. 360 483), 14 km

Annual closure	Cierre anual	no
Weekly closure	Cierre semanal	no

Fees main season
Precios tempor. alta 18 holes

	Week days Semana	We/Bank holidays Fin de sem./fiestas
Individual Individual	9 000 Pts	*
Couple Pareja	18 000 Pts	*

* Members only (sólo socios)

Caddy	Caddy	3 000 Pts/18 holes
Electric Trolley	Carro eléctrico	500 Pts/18 holes
Buggy	Coche	restricted
Clubs	Palos	2 000 Pts/18 holes

Credit cards Tarjetas de crédito
VISA - Eurocard - MasterCard - AMEX

1172

Access Acceso : Las Palmas C811 → Santa Brigida.
On the left, → Golf
Map 9 on page 1112 Plano 9 Página 1112

GOLF COURSE
RECORRIDO — 14/20

Site	Emplazamiento	
Maintenance	Mantenimiento	
Architect	Arquitecto	Mackenzie Ross Juan Dominguez
Type	Tipo	parkland
Relief	Relieve	
Water in play	Agua	
Exp. to wind	Exp. al viento	
Trees in play	Arboles	

Scorecard Tarjeta	Chp. Campeonato	Mens Caballeros	Ladies Damas
Length Longitud	5915	5666	5190
Par	71	71	71

Advised golfing ability Nivel de juego aconsejado	0	12	24	36

Hcp required   Handicap exigido   28 Men, 36 Ladies

CLUB HOUSE & AMENITIES
CLUB HOUSE Y DEPENDENCIAS — 8/10

Pro shop	Pro-shop	
Driving range	Campo de prácticas	
Sheltered	cubierto	15 mats
On grass	sobre hierba	yes
Putting-green	putting-green	yes
Pitching-green	pitching-green	yes

HOTEL FACILITIES
HOTELES CERCANOS — 8/10

HOTELS HOTELES
Golf Bandama — Santa Brigida
38 rooms, D 20 000 Pts — on site
Tel (34) 928 - 353 354, Fax (34) 928 - 351 290

Santa Catalina — Las Palmas
187 rooms, D 20 000 Pts — 14 km
Tel (34) 928 - 243 040, Fax (34) 928 - 242 764

Santa Brigida - 41 rooms, D 14 000 Pts — Santa Brigida
Tel (34) 928 - 355 511, Fax (34) 928 - 355 701 — 3 km

RESTAURANTS RESTAURANTES

Amaiur - Tel (34) 928 - 370 717 — Las Palmas 14 km

Las Grutas de Artiles — Santa Brigida 7 km
Tel (34) 928 - 640 575

El Novillo Precoz — Las Palmas
Tel (34) 928 - 221 659 — 14 km

LAURO

13 **7** **5**

Al final de una carretera de montaña, está situado en un lugar muy tranquilo. Cada hoyo lleva el nombre de un célebre torero, pero no por eso se trata de un recorrido agresivo que exija dotes de combate. Al contrario, la belleza de los paisajes inspira calma y el recorrido en sí mismo es más bien acogedor, incluso para los jugadores con poca experiencia. Cantidad de olivos bordean la mayor parte de las calles y algunos obstáculos de agua están situados en plena línea de juego (hoyos 9,14,17 y 18) sin ser temibles. De razonable dificultad, prácticamente sin trampas escondidas (los obstáculos son perfectamente visibles), Lauro Golf es un recorrido muy noble y el sitio ideal para evaluar el nivel de su juego actual y sus propias posibilidades frente a jugadores de nivel equivalente. Los mejores pueden obtener resulta"dos halagadores para su propio «ego».

This course is a quiet little place at the end of a mountain road. Each hole bears the name of a famous torero but the course itself is far from being aggressive and does not call for any real fighting virtues. On the contrary, the beautiful landscape inspires peace and quiet and the layout is a friendly one, even for inexperienced players. Numerous olive trees line most of the fairways and certain water hazards are very much to the fore (on the 9th, 14th, 17th and 18th holes) but never fearsome. Never too demanding with virtually no hidden traps (all hazards are clearly visible) and benign greens, Lauro Golf is a very honest layout and the ideal spot to assess your current game and potential and to measure up with players of similar ability. The better players can card flattering scores and do their ego a world of good.

Lauro Golf   1992
Los Caracolillos
E - 29130 ALHAURIN DE LA TORRE (MALAGA)

Office	Secretaria	(34) 952 - 412 767
Pro shop	Pro-shop	(34) 952 - 412 767
Fax	Fax	(34) 952 - 414 757
Situation	Situación	

Alhaurin de la Torre, 5 km
Málaga (pop. 534 683), 15 km

Annual closure	Cierre anual	no
Weekly closure	Cierre semanal	no

Fees main season
Precios tempor. alta 18 holes

	Week days Semana	We/Bank holidays Fin de sem./fiestas
Individual Individual	6 000 Pts	6 000 Pts
Couple Pareja	11 000 Pts	11 000 Pts

Caddy	Caddy	no
Electric Trolley	Carro eléctrico	no
Buggy	Coche	4 000 Pts/18 holes
Clubs	Palos	2 000 Pts/18 holes

Credit cards Tarjetas de crédito
VISA - Eurocard - Mastercard - AMEX

MALAGA

GOLF

C 344

Alhaurìn el Grande

Torremolinos

N 340

COSTA DEL SOL

Marbella

Access Acceso : Málaga, N340 → Torremolinos,
Exit (salida) «Churiana», C344, turn right to Alhaurín
Map 7 on page 1109 Plano 7 Página 1109

GOLF COURSE
RECORRIDO   13/20

Site	Emplazamiento	
Maintenance	Mantenimiento	
Architect	Arquitecto	Falco Nardi
Type	Tipo	country
Relief	Relieve	
Water in play	Agua	
Exp. to wind	Exp. al viento	
Trees in play	Arboles	

Scorecard Tarjeta	Chp. Campeonato	Mens Caballeros	Ladies Damas
Length Longitud	5971	5679	4864
Par	72	72	72

Advised golfing ability	0	12	24	36
Nivel de juego aconsejado				

Hcp required   Handicap exigido   28 Men, 36 Ladies

CLUB HOUSE & AMENITIES
CLUB HOUSE Y DEPENDENCIAS   7/10

Pro shop	Pro-shop	
Driving range	Campo de prácticas	
Sheltered	cubierto	no
On grass	sobre hierba	yes
Putting-green	putting-green	yes
Pitching-green	pitching-green	no

HOTEL FACILITIES
HOTELES CERCANOS   5/10

HOTELS HOTELES
Larios   Malaga
40 rooms, D 20 000 Pts   18 km
Tel (34) 952 - 222 200, Fax (34) 952 - 222 407

Tryp Costa Golf   Chiclana
195 rooms, 20 900 Pts   10 km
Tel (34) 956 - 494 535, Fax (34) 956 - 494 626

Byblos   Fuengirola
144 rooms, D 39 500 Pts   12 km
Tel (34) 952 - 473 050, Fax (34) 952 - 476 783

RESTAURANTS RESTAURANTES
El Olivar   Mijas 5 km
Tel (34) 952 - 486 196

Valparaiso   Mijas → Fuengirola
Tel (34) 952 - 485 996   7 km

1173

Uno de los arquitéctos más originales de su época, José Gancedo, ha diseñado en un magnífico paraje un campo a la vez espectacular y lleno de encanto. Si se le puede considerar como difícil para los buenos jugadores, sobre todo desde las barras de atrás, se adapta sin embargo perfectamente a los jugadores todos los niveles. Tendrán aún más placer ya que no es imposible cumplir su handicap, siempre y cuando sean conscientes de sua limitaciones. El trazado exige una excelente estrategia y un buen dominio de la bola. Suele recompensar más al jugador técnico que coloca la bola que al pegador que puede encontrar dificultades con los árboles o los obstáculos de agua. Sin embargo en el 18 los pegadores tendrán la oportunidad de jugar a green por encima del lago, sobre todo si juegan en match-play, la fórmula ideal para descubrir el campo. Bien equilibrado en su desarrollo, con un buen diseño, Lerma pertenece sin duda a la categoría de campos «inteligentes».

José Gancedo, one of today's most original architects, has designed a spectacular and truly charming layout over a beautiful site. While considered tough for the better players, especially from the back-tees, it is nonetheless largely suitable for players of all abilities. They will find it all the more pleasing in that playing to their handicap is not impossible, as long as they know their limits. The course demands tight strategy and excellent ball control, and generally will reward the accurate technician more than the long-hitters, who may have problems with the trees and water. But on the 18th, they can try and hit the green over the lake, especially in match-play, the ideal format when discovering this course. Well-balanced and nicely-landscaped, Lerma is undoubtedly one of the more «intelligent» courses.

Club de Golf de Lerma — 1992

Autovía Madrid-Burgos Km 195,5
E - 09340 LERMA (BURGOS)

Office	Secretaria	(34) 947 - 171 214
Pro shop	Pro-shop	(34) 947 - 171 214
Fax	Fax	(34) 947 - 171 216
Situation	Situación	

Burgos (pop. 169 111), 45 km
Lerma (pop. 2 417), 8 km

Annual closure	Cierre anual	no
Weekly closure	Cierre semanal	monday

Fees main season
Precios tempor. alta 18 holes

	Week days Semana	We/Bank holidays Fin de sem./fiestas
Individual Individual	5 500 Pts	7 500 Pts
Couple Pareja	11 000 Pts	15 000 Pts

Caddy	Caddy	no
Electric Trolley	Carro eléctrico	1 500 Pts/18 holes
Buggy	Coche	5 000 Pts/18 holes
Clubs	Palos	2 000 Pts/18 holes

Credit cards Tarjetas de crédito VISA - MasterCard

1174

Access Acceso : Madrid → Burgos, Km 195
Map 3 on page 1100 Plano 3 Página 1100

GOLF COURSE / RECORRIDO — 17/20

Site	Emplazamiento	▰▰▰▰▱
Maintenance	Mantenimiento	▰▰▰▰▱
Architect	Arquitecto	José Gancedo
Type	Tipo	country, forest
Relief	Relieve	▰▰▱▱▱
Water in play	Agua	▰▰▱▱▱
Exp. to wind	Exp. al viento	▰▰▰▱▱
Trees in play	Arboles	▰▰▰▰▱

Scorecard Tarjeta	Chp. Campeonato	Mens Caballeros	Ladies Damas
Length Longitud	6263	5905	5064
Par	72	72	72

Advised golfing ability Nivel de juego aconsejado	0	12	24	36

Hcp required Handicap exigido 28 Men, 36 Ladies

CLUB HOUSE & AMENITIES / CLUB HOUSE Y DEPENDENCIAS — 7/10

Pro shop	Pro-shop	▰▰▰▱▱
Driving range	Campo de prácticas	▰▰▰▰▱
Sheltered	cubierto	8 mats
On grass	sobre hierba	yes
Putting-green	putting-green	yes
Pitching-green	pitching-green	yes

HOTEL FACILITIES / HOTELES CERCANOS — 4/10

HOTELS HOTELES
Alisa — Lerma, 8 km
36 rooms, D 8 400 Pts
Tel (34) 947 - 170 250, Fax (34) 947 - 171 160

Docar - 15 rooms, D 6 000 Pts — Lerma, 8 km
Tel (34) 947 - 171 073

Landa Palace — Burgos, 42 km
42 rooms, D 24 200 Pts
Tel (34) 947 - 206 343, Fax (34) 947 - 264 676

Maria Luisa — Burgos, 45 km
44 rooms, D 11 000 Pts
Tel (34) 947 - 22 80 00, Fax (34) 947 - 22 80 80

RESTAURANTS RESTAURANTES
Lis 2 - Tel (34) 947 - 170 126 — Lerma 8 km
Casa Ojeda - Tel (34) 947 - 209 052 — Burgos 45 km

Desde los paisajes áridos de la carretera que sube a Ronda, da la impresión de ser un golf «extremado». En realidad no lo es, pero sus pronunciadas cuestas aconsejan utilizar un coche para jugar más fácilmente en este recorrido cuya construcción exigió enormes obras para nivelar el terreno. No es muy largo, estrecho en algunos sitios, los obstáculos son peligrosos y situados en la línea de juego, lo que incita a jugar con cierta prudencia. Teniendo en cuenta que el arquitecto es Seve Ballesteros, atraerá más bien a los jugadores de ataque que serán recompensados por sus golpes audaces, sobre todo los que juegan en «fade» o los especialistas de bolas altas cuyo objetivo son unos greens no inmensos, sin grandes trampas, que aguantan bien la bola y su trayectoria a la hora de patear. De gran imaginación y espectacular, se recomienda conocerlo antes de seguir camino hacia la bella ciudad de Ronda.

From the road and arid landscape leading to Ronda,, the impression is one of an extremely hilly golf course. This is not quite the case, but the steep slopes call for the use of a buggy to play a little more easily on a course whose construction demanded very considerable grading work. It is not very long, but sometimes tight, and the hazards are always in play and dangerously placed. The result can sometimes be an over-cautious approach when playing the course. Designed by Seve Ballesteros, Los Arqueros should appeal to attacking players and will reward bold strokes. This is particularly true for players who fade the ball or who are specialists of high shots aimed at the smallish greens, which have little in the way of traps, pitch well and putt true. Imaginative and sometimes quite spectacular, this course is to be recommended before getting back on the road and heading for the beautiful town of Ronda.

Los Arqueros Golf — 1990

Ctra Ronda, km. 166,5
E - 29679 BENAHAVIS (MALAGA)

Office	Secretaria	(34) 952 - 784 712
Pro shop	Pro-shop	(34) 952 - 784 600
Fax	Fax	(34) 952 - 786 707
Situation	Situación	

San Pedro de Alcantara
Marbella (pop. 84 410), 10 km

Annual closure	Cierre anual	no
Weekly closure	Cierre semanal	no

Fees main season
Precios tempor. alta 18 holes

	Week days Semana	We/Bank holidays Fin de sem./fiestas
Individual Individual	7 500 Pts	7 500 Pts
Couple Pareja	15 000 Pts	15 000 Pts

Caddy	Caddy	no
Electric Trolley	Carro eléctrico	no
Buggy	Coche	4 000 Pts/18 holes
Clubs	Palos	2 000 Pts/18 holes

Credit cards Tarjetas de crédito
VISA - Eurocard - MasterCard - AMEX - DC - JCB

Access Acceso : Marbella N340 → Cadiz, San Pedro de Alcantara, C339 → Ronda, Golf 4 km on the left
Map 7 on page 1109 Plano 7 Página 1109

GOLF COURSE / RECORRIDO — 14/20

Site	Emplazamiento	
Maintenance	Mantenimiento	
Architect	Arquitecto	Seve Ballesteros
Type	Tipo	mountain, hilly
Relief	Relieve	
Water in play	Agua	
Exp. to wind	Exp. al viento	
Trees in play	Arboles	

Scorecard Tarjeta	Chp. Campeonato	Mens Caballeros	Ladies Damas
Length Longitud	5843	5460	4970
Par	72	72	72

Advised golfing ability
Nivel de juego aconsejado

0   12   24   36

Hcp required   Handicap exigido   28 Men, 36 Ladies

CLUB HOUSE & AMENITIES / CLUB HOUSE Y DEPENDENCIAS — 6/10

Pro shop	Pro-shop	
Driving range	Campo de prácticas	
Sheltered	cubierto	no
On grass	sobre hierba	yes
Putting-green	putting-green	yes
Pitching-green	pitching-green	yes

HOTEL FACILITIES / HOTELES CERCANOS — 7/10

HOTELS HOTELES

Andalucia Plaza   Nueva Andalucia
415 rooms, D 30 500 Pts   6 km
Tel (34) 952 - 812 000, Fax (34) 952 - 814 792

Coral Beach   Nueva Andalucia
150 rooms, D 34 700 Pts   8 km
Tel (34) 952 - 824 500, Fax (34) 952 - 826 257

Pyr Hotel   Puerto Banus
319 rooms, D 15 700 Pts   10 km
Tel (34) 952 - 817 353, Fax (34) 952 - 817 907

RESTAURANTS RESTAURANTES

El Rodeito   Nueva Andalucia
Tel (34) 952 - 815 699   6 km

Cipriano   Puerto Banús
Tel (34) 952 - 811 077   10 km

1175

En el corazón del «Valle del golf» en Nueva Andalucía, Los Naranjos, sin ser un monstruo, es uno de los más famosos diseños de Robert Trent Jones. Las mejoras en el mantenimiento del recorrido y la construcción de un nuevo club-house han contribuido a restaurar su gloria. Los nueve primeros hoyos, ligeramente accidentados, obligan a reflexionar tanto sobre la elección del palo como sobre la trayectoria de la bola. La vuelta es prácticamente llana, insinuándose entre naranjos, y más favorable a los pegadores que no dudarán en salir de atrás. Los jugadores más razonables encontrarán que este recorrido es ya bastante largo desde los tees de salida «normales». ¿Por qué sufrir si se puede evitar? En cada partido hallarán toda clase de situaciones diferentes de las que podrán gozar. Los greens están bien protegidos, son muy grandes y se ven bien las caídas.

At the heart of "Golf Valley" in Nueva Andalucia, "Los Naranjos" (meaning Orange Trees) is one of Robert Trent Jones' more famous designs but it is no monster. Considerably improved upkeep and the building of a new club house have helped restore its former glory. The front nine, on slightly broken terrain, require careful thought as much for the choice of club as for the trajectory of the ball. The back nine are virtually flat holes winding their way between the orange trees. They will appeal to long hitters who in every case won't think twice about playing the course from the back tees. More reasonable players will find the course long enough from the "normal" tees; after all, why suffer when you don't have to? All sorts of different situations arise every time you play here, so the course is sure-fire enjoyment every time. The greens are well-defended, often huge but never too difficult to read.

Los Naranjos Golf Club — 1977
APDO 64
E - 29660 MARBELLA (MALAGA)

Office	Secretaria	(34) 952 - 812 428
Pro shop	Pro-shop	(34) 952 - 815 206
Fax	Fax	(34) 952 - 811 428
Situation	Situación	

Marbella (pop. 84 410), 15 km
San Pedro de Alcantara, 6 km

Annual closure	Cierre anual	no
Weekly closure	Cierre semanal	no

Fees main season
Precios tempor. alta 18 holes

	Week days Semana	We/Bank holidays Fin de sem./fiestas
Individual Individual	11 000 Pts	11 000 Pts
Couple Pareja	22 000 Pts	22 000 Pts

Caddy	Caddy	yes
Electric Trolley	Carro eléctrico	1 500 Pts/18 holes
Buggy	Coche	5 000 Pts/18 holes
Clubs	Palos	2 500 Pts/full day

Credit cards Tarjetas de crédito
VISA - Eurocard - MasterCard - AMEX

1176

Access Acceso : Marbella N340 → Cadiz,
Nueva Andalucia (km 180), turn right → Golf
Map 7 on page 1109 Plano 7 Página 1109

GOLF COURSE / RECORRIDO — 16/20

Site	Emplazamiento	
Maintenance	Mantenimiento	
Architect	Arquitecto	Robert Trent Jones
Type	Tipo	parkland, residential
Relief	Relieve	
Water in play	Agua	
Exp. to wind	Exp. al viento	
Trees in play	Arboles	

Scorecard Tarjeta	Chp. Campeonato	Mens Caballeros	Ladies Damas
Length Longitud	6457	6038	5143
Par	72	72	72

Advised golfing ability	0	12	24	36

Nivel de juego aconsejado
Hcp required Handicap exigido 28 Men, 36 Ladies

CLUB HOUSE & AMENITIES / CLUB HOUSE Y DEPENDENCIAS — 7/10

Pro shop	Pro-shop	
Driving range	Campo de prácticas	
Sheltered	cubierto	no
On grass	sobre hierba	yes
Putting-green	putting-green	yes
Pitching-green	pitching-green	yes

HOTEL FACILITIES / HOTELES CERCANOS — 7/10

HOTELS HOTELES
Puente Romano — Marbella
217 rooms, D 52 000 Pts — 5 km
Tel (34) 952 - 820 900, Fax (34) 952 - 775 766

Andalucia Plaza — Nueva Andalucia
415 rooms, D 30 500 Pts — 1,5 km
Tel (34) 952 - 812 000, Fax (34) 952 - 814 792

Pyr Hotel — Puerto Banus
319 rooms, D 15 700 Pts — 4 km
Tel (34) 952 - 817 353, Fax (34) 952 - 817 907

RESTAURANTS RESTAURANTES
Meson El Coto — San Pedro → Ronda
Tel (34) 952 - 785 123 — 7 km

El Rodeito — Nueva Andalucia
Tel (34) 952 - 815 699 — 6 km

No solamente es el primer recorrido de golf abierto en la famosa Costa del Sol, sino también el primer campo propiedad y dirigido por la empresa estatal Paradores, rama hostelera del Turismo oficial. Paradores ha puesto interés en tener el campo en buenas condiciones y prolongar hasta las puertas de Málaga el turismo de golf que tiene su epicentro alrededor de Marbella. El campo es un monumento histórico construído por H.S. Colt y supervisado por Tom Simpson, que alterna el diseño de parque natural, entre árboles frondosos, con los hoyos al borde de la playa a los que solamente faltan las dunas para que sea un auténtico links. El lugar tiene un gran encanto natural y los primeros nueve hoyos son especialmente interesantes, con bunkers muy bien situados y una distribución de espacios que anima a emplear todos los recursos del buen juego corto.

This was not only the very first course on the Costa del Sol, it is now also the first course to be controlled and managed by the state enterprise Paradores, the hotel branch of Spanish Tourism. Paradores set out to keep the course in sufficiently good condition in order to prolong Marbella-based golf tourism down as far as Malaga. The course is a sort of historical monument designed by H.S. Colt under the supervision of Tom Simpson. The result is an alternating string of natural parkland holes, very thick trees and seaside holes where only the dunes are lacking for this to look like a real links course. The natural site has a lot of charm about it, especially the particularly interesting front nine. Bunkers are well located and space has been cleverly used to add spice to the back nine, where a tight short game comes in very handy.

Real Club de Campo de Málaga — 1925

Apdo 324
E - 29080 MALAGA

Office	Secretaria	(34) 952 - 376 677
Pro shop	Pro-shop	(34) 952 - 372 072
Fax	Fax	(34) 952 - 376 612
Situation	Situación	

Torremolinos (pop. 35 309), 4 km
Málaga (pop. 534 683), 10 km

Annual closure	Cierre anual	no
Weekly closure	Cierre semanal	no

Fees main season
Precios tempor. alta 18 holes

	Week days Semana	We/Bank holidays Fin de sem./fiestas
Individual Individual	6 800 Pts	6 800 Pts
Couple Pareja	13 600 Pts	13 600 Pts

Caddy	Caddy	no
Electric Trolley	Carro eléctrico	no
Buggy	Coche	5 000 Pts/18 holes
Clubs	Palos	1 700 Pts/18 holes

Credit cards Tarjetas de crédito
VISA - Eurocard - MasterCard - AMEX

Access Acceso : Málaga → Torremolinos,
on the left → Parador del Golf
Map 7 on page 1109 Plano 7 Página 1109

GOLF COURSE / RECORRIDO — 13/20

Site	Emplazamiento	
Maintenance	Mantenimiento	
Architect	Arquitecto	H.S. Colt Tom Simpson
Type	Tipo	seaside course
Relief	Relieve	
Water in play	Agua	
Exp. to wind	Exp. al viento	
Trees in play	Arboles	

Scorecard Tarjeta	Chp. Campeonato	Mens Caballeros	Ladies Damas
Length Longitud	6204	6040	5134
Par	72	72	72

Advised golfing ability		0 12 24 36
Nivel de juego aconsejado		
Hcp required	Handicap exigido	28 Men, 36 Ladies

CLUB HOUSE & AMENITIES / CLUB HOUSE Y DEPENDENCIAS — 4/10

Pro shop	Pro-shop	
Driving range	Campo de prácticas	
Sheltered	cubierto	21 mats
On grass	sobre hierba	yes
Putting-green	putting-green	yes
Pitching-green	pitching-green	yes

HOTEL FACILITIES / HOTELES CERCANOS — 6/10

HOTELS HOTELES

Parador Málaga 60 rooms, D 18 400 Pts Tel (34) 952 - 381 255 Fax (34) 952 - 388 963	Golf 100 m
Guadalmar 200 rooms, D 17 200 Pts Tel (34) 952 - 231 703 Fax (34) 952 - 240 385	Malaga 3 km

RESTAURANTS RESTAURANTES

Casa Pedro Tel (34) 952 - 290 013	Málaga 3 km
Calycanto Tel (34) 952 - 212 222	Málaga 3 km

1177

La nueva dirección del club ha vuelto a dar vida a este recorrido con cierta imaginación, aunque por momentos tortuoso, de Robert Trent Jones. Muy en cuesta, es mejor alquilar un coche y a pesar de las dificultades que ello implica habría que actualizarlo. La gran diversidad de hoyos y de golpes que hay que jugar es asombrosa, encontrando los famosos bunkers del arquitecto y algunos obstáculos de agua peligrosos que requieren un serio análisis de su buena forma de juego, antes de tomar una decisión entre el ataque o la prudencia. Teniendo en cuenta que los greenes tienen muchas caídas: hay que atacar resueltamente a bandera. No se trata ni mucho menos de un recorrido imposible, pero los jugadores sin handicap sufrirán más que los otros. Algunas hondonadas y sinuosidades del terreno son una seria amenaza para los drives en algunos hoyos. Bien es verdad que por momentos el maravilloso panorama sobre el mar puede servir de consuelo a ciertos desastres.

A change of management has breathed new life into this imaginative but sometimes tortuous course, designed by Robert Trent Jones. This is rather broken terrain, making walking a little difficult, but the demanding layout is very much back in the modern trend. The variety of holes and the shots they require is remarkable. There are, of course, the architect's hallmark bunkers and a number of dangerous water hazards, which call for serious analysis of current playing form before deciding whether to attack or lay up. All the more so in that the greens are well designed and definitely favour players who go for the pin. It is not an impossible course, far from it, but high-handicappers will suffer, especially with the few ravines and hollows that pose a serious threat to a number of tee-shots. The scenic views over the sea will more than compensate should disaster strike.

Golf Club Marbella — 1988
Ctra Cadiz, Km. 188
E - 29002 MARBELLA (MALAGA)

Office	Secretaria	(34) 952 - 830 500
Pro shop	Pro-shop	(34) 952 - 830 500
Fax	Fax	(34) 952 - 834 353
Situation	Situación	

Marbella (pop. 24 410), 5 km
Fuengirola (pop. 43 048), 20 km

Annual closure	Cierre anual	no
Weekly closure	Cierre semanal	no

Fees main season
Precios tempor. alta 18 holes

	Week days Semana	We/Bank holidays Fin de sem./fiestas
Individual Individual	9 000 Pts	9 000 Pts
Couple Pareja	18 000 Pts	18 000 Pts

Caddy	Caddy	no
Electric Trolley	Carro eléctrico	no
Buggy	Coche	5 000 Pts/18 holes
Clubs	Palos	4 000 Pts/18 holes

Credit cards Tarjetas de crédito
VISA - MasterCard - AMEX

1178

Access Acceso : Marbella N340 → Fuengirola, Golf km 188
Map 7 on page 1109 Plano 7 Página 1109

GOLF COURSE / RECORRIDO 15/20

Site	Emplazamiento	
Maintenance	Mantenimiento	
Architect	Arquitecto	Robert Trent Jones
Type	Tipo	hilly
Relief	Relieve	
Water in play	Agua	
Exp. to wind	Exp. al viento	
Trees in play	Arboles	

Scorecard Tarjeta	Chp. Campeonato	Mens Caballeros	Ladies Damas
Length Longitud	5933	5558	4661
Par	71	71	71

Advised golfing ability
Nivel de juego aconsejado 0 12 24 36
Hcp required Handicap exigido 28 Men, 36 Ladies

CLUB HOUSE & AMENITIES / CLUB HOUSE Y DEPENDENCIAS 7/10

Pro shop	Pro-shop	
Driving range	Campo de prácticas	
Sheltered	cubierto	no
On grass	sobre hierba	yes
Putting-green	putting-green	yes
Pitching-green	pitching-green	yes

HOTEL FACILITIES / HOTELES CERCANOS 8/10

HOTELS HOTELES
Los Monteros — Marbella 1 km
168 rooms, D 37 000 Pts
Tel (34) 952 - 771 700
Fax (34) 952 - 825 846

Artola — Artola 7 km
32 rooms, D 12 600 Pts
Tel (34) 952 - 831 390
Fax (34) 952 - 830 450

RESTAURANTS RESTAURANTES
La Fonda — Marbella 3 km
Tel (34) 952 - 772 512

Santiago — Marbella 3 km
Tel (34) 952 - 774 339

Es mejor utilizar un coche sobre todo en los tramos accidentados de un hoyo a otro, a pesar de que el relieve del recorrido en sí mismo sea moderado. José María Olazábal ha sabido sacar provecho de un terreno a primera vista más bien quebrado y peligroso. El relieve impide muy a menudo ver los greens desde los tees de salida de los pares 4 y 5, pero los bunkers de calle indican la línea de juego y acogen las bolas imprecisas. Los pares 3, generalmente con hondanadas en medio, parecen peligrosos pero de longitud razonable. Los greens tienen muchas caídas, son o muy largos o muy anchos y aguantan bien la bola. Incluso cuando la posición de las banderas puede dificultar seriamente el juego ,sobre todo si se ha salido de atrás, Masia Bach es un recorrido menos peligroso de lo que generalmente piensan los jugadores si logran conservar su aplomo y una cierta precisión.

A buggy can come in handy here to cross the broken terrain between holes, but much of the course here is not too hilly. José Maria Olazabal has brought the best out of what, at first sight, looks to be much more rugged and dangerous terrain. Indeed, the relief often obscures any view of the greens from the tees on the par 4s and 5s, but the fairway bunkers show the line of play and often stop mishit balls in their tracks. Generally laid out with large hollows between tee and green, the par 3s look dangerous but their lengths are very reasonable. The greens are very undulating, sometimes very long or very wide, and pitch well. Even though the pin positions can sometimes seriously complicate play when driving from the back-tees, Masia Bach is a friendlier course for players of all levels than people might think. As long as they keep a cool head, and play straight.

Club de Golf Masia Bach — 1990

Ctra de Martorell-Capellades - Km 19,5
E - 08635 SANT ESTEVE SESROVIRES (BARCELONA)

Office	Secretaria	(34) 937 - 726 310
Pro shop	Pro-shop	(34) 937 - 726 310
Fax	Fax	(34) 937 - 726 356
Situation	Situación	

Martorell (pop. 16 793), 7 km
Barcelona, (pop. 1 754 900), 25 km

Annual closure	Cierre anual	no
Weekly closure	Cierre semanal	monday

Fees main season
Precios tempor. alta 18 holes

	Week days Semana	We/Bank holidays Fin de sem./fiestas
Individual Individual	8 000 Pts	20 000 Pts
Couple Pareja	16 000 Pts	40 000 Pts
Caddy Caddy		no
Electric Trolley Carro eléctrico		750 Pts/18 holes
Buggy Coche		4 000 Pts/18 holes
Clubs Palos		4 000 Pts/18 holes

Credit cards Tarjetas de crédito
VISA - Eurocard - MasterCard - AMEX

Access Acceso : Barcelona A2/A7 → Tarragona,
Exit (Salida) 25 → Martorell, B224 → Capellades,
Golf on right hand side
Map 2 on page 1099 Plano 2 Página 1099

GOLF COURSE / RECORRIDO — 15/20

Site	Emplazamiento	
Maintenance	Mantenimiento	
Architect	Arquitecto	José Maria Olazábal
Type	Tipo	mountain
Relief	Relieve	
Water in play	Agua	
Exp. to wind	Exp. al viento	
Trees in play	Arboles	

Scorecard Tarjeta	Chp. Campeonato	Mens Caballeros	Ladies Damas
Length Longitud	6271	6039	5161
Par	72	72	72

Advised golfing ability Nivel de juego aconsejado	0	12	24	36

Hcp required Handicap exigido 28 Men, 36 Ladies

CLUB HOUSE & AMENITIES / CLUB HOUSE Y DEPENDENCIAS — 7/10

Pro shop	Pro-shop	
Driving range	Campo de prácticas	
Sheltered	cubierto	7 mats
On grass	sobre hierba	yes
Putting-green	putting-green	yes
Pitching-green	pitching-green	yes

HOTEL FACILITIES / HOTELES CERCANOS — 6/10

HOTELS HOTELES

Las Torres	Sant Esteve
22 rooms, D 6 800 Pts	5 km
Tel (34) 937 - 714 181	
Fax (34) 937 - 713 462	
Manel	Martorell
29 rooms, D 7 000 Pts	4 km
Tel (34) 937 - 752 387	
Fax (34) 937 - 752 387	

RESTAURANTS RESTAURANTES

Las Torres	Sant Esteve
Tel (34) 937 - 714 181	5 km

1179

Prácticamente en el borde del mar y cerca de la ciudad, Maspalomas fue construido en un terreno muy llano cerca de las dunas, lo que le da un aspecto de links que uno no se espera encontrar en la Isla de Gran Canaria. La paternidad de Mackenzie Ross (autor de la reconstrucción de Turnberry) ofrece la garantía de autenticidad de estilo. Aunque es un recorrido de competición muy exigente, sin embargo es un buen golf para ir de vacaciones. Es un par 73 de longitud razonable, pero con dificuldades enormes, que invita a los jugadores a proceder sin complejos y según sus posibilidades. No hay que dormirse ni extraviarse en las dunas, donde el rough es muy peligroso. Grandes bunkers con una arena de agradable color amarillo esperan las bolas poco precisas. La flora subtropical compuesta de palmeras, pinos canarios y marítimos, ibiscos, buganvillas, etc., confiere un color muy particular a este diseño bastante britanico...

Virtually by the sea and in town, Maspalomas was built on a very flat land. Its layout, close to sand-dunes, gives it a links style which you wouldn't expect to find on Grand Canary island, and the patronage of Mackenzie Ross (who re-designed Turnberry) provides a sure-fire guarantee of authenticity in terms of style. Although this is a rather challenging tournament course, it still makes for very good holiday golfing and so is very «functional» golfing facility in this part of the world. This is a par 73 of reasonable with no insurmountable difficulties, inviting players to «go for it» to the best of their ability. But they'll need to keep on their toes and not stray into the dunes where the rough can make a big dent in your card. Large bunkers filled with pretty yellow sand also wait the mis-hit ball (and others too). The sub-tropical vegetation of palm-trees, Canary pines, hibiscus-trees and bougainvillaea add special colour to this very British-style layout.

Club de Golf Maspalomas — 1968

Auda de Neckerman S/N
E - 35100 MASPALOMAS (Gran Canaria)

Office	Secretaria	(34) 928 - 762 581
Pro shop	Pro-shop	(34) 928 - 768 751
Fax	Fax	(34) 928 - 768 245
Situation	Situación	

Las Palmas (pop. 360 483), 30 km

Annual closure	Cierre anual	no
Weekly closure	Cierre semanal	no

Fees main season
Precios tempor. alta 18 holes

	Week days Semana	We/Bank holidays Fin de sem./fiestas
Individual Individual	9 500 Pts	89 500 Pts
Couple Pareja	19 000 Pts	19 000 Pts

Caddy	Caddy	no
Electric Trolley	Carro eléctrico	no
Buggy	Coche	5 000 Pts/18 holes
Clubs	Palos	1 700 Pts/18 holes

Credit cards Tarjetas de crédito
VISA - Eurocard - MasterCard

1180

Access Acceso : Autopista Sur, → Maspalomas
Map 9 on page 1112 Plano 9 Página 1112

GOLF COURSE / RECORRIDO — 16/20

Site	Emplazamiento	
Maintenance	Mantenimiento	
Architect	Arquitecto	Mackenzie Ross
Type	Tipo	forest
Relief	Relieve	
Water in play	Agua	
Exp. to wind	Exp. al viento	
Trees in play	Arboles	

Scorecard Tarjeta	Chp. Campeonato	Mens Caballeros	Ladies Damas
Length Longitud	6189	6037	5210
Par	73	73	73

Advised golfing ability 0 12 24 36
Nivel de juego aconsejado
Hcp required Handicap exigido 30

CLUB HOUSE & AMENITIES / CLUB HOUSE Y DEPENDENCIAS — 7/10

Pro shop	Pro-shop	
Driving range	Campo de prácticas	
Sheltered	cubierto	12 mats
On grass	sobre hierba	yes
Putting-green	putting-green	yes
Pitching-green	pitching-green	yes

HOTEL FACILITIES / HOTELES CERCANOS — 8/10

HOTELS HOTELES
Ifa-Faro - 183 rooms, D 41 800 Pts — Maspalomas
Tel (34) 928 - 142 214, Fax (34) 928 - 141 940 — 3 km

Palm Beach — Maspalomas
347 rooms, D 69 400 Pts — 3 km
Tel (34) 928 - 140 806, Fax (34) 928 - 141 808

Oasis — Maspalomas
319 rooms, D 48 300 Pts — 3 km
Tel (34) 928 - 141 448, Fax (34) 928 - 141 192

RESTAURANTS RESTAURANTES
La Aquarela — Maspalomas
Tel (34) 928 - 140 178 — 1 km

Amaiur - Tel (34) 928 - 761 414 — Maspalomas 1 km

Orangerie - Tel (34) 928 - 140 806 — Maspalomas 3 km

Este recorrido ha contribuido a la fama creciente de su arquitecto Ramón Espinosa. Es una joya depositada en un amplio valle, sus sutiles dificultades lo hacen más delicado de lo que a primera vista parece, sin por ello desalentar a los jugadores de nivel medio. Los bunkers de calle y de green están inteligentemente situados y bien visibles e indican la táctica de juego que hay que adoptar. Algunos árboles aislados obligan a pegar la bola con efecto y algunos lagos pequeñitos están en línea de juego en siete hoyos, completando una panoplia de dificultades muy variadas. Los greens, tan tupidos como las calles, son falsamente planos y desconcertantes si no se les examina con mucha atención. Inteligente y franco, es un recorrido para todo el mundo y se puede aconsejar tanto por su armonía como por su cuidadoso mantenimiento: se pasa una óptima jornada.

This course has done much to enhance the growing reputation of architect Ramon Espinosa. This is a gem of a course located in a wide valley, and the subtly placed hazards make it tougher than you might think at first sight, but not to the point of scaring off the lesser players. The fairway and green-side bunkers are cleverly located and visible enough to help your game tactics. A few isolated trees call for elaborate shots, moving the ball both ways, and small ponds are in play on seven holes, thus completing a highly varied panoply of hazards. The greens, as grassy as the fairways, are deceptively flat and disconcerting if not read carefully. An intelligent and honest course, this is a golfing arena for everyone. Being well-balanced and well-cared for, it is a course well worth recommending for spending a great day out.

Club de Campo Mediterraneo   1978

Urbanización «La Coma» S/N
E - 12190 BORRIOL (CASTELLON DE LA PLANA)

Office	Secretaria	(34) 964 - 321 227
Pro shop	Pro-shop	(34) 964 - 322 080
Fax	Fax	(34) 964 - 321 357
Situation	Situación	

Castellón de la Plana (pop. 138 489), 5 km

Annual closure	Cierre anual	no
Weekly closure	Cierre semanal	no

Fees main season
Precios tempor. alta 18 holes

	Week days Semana	We/Bank holidays Fin de sem./fiestas
Individual Individual	6 000 Pts	6 000 Pts
Couple Pareja	12 000 Pts	12 000 Pts

Caddy	Caddy	no
Electric Trolley	Carro eléctrico	1 500 Pts/18 holes
Buggy	Coche	3 500 Pts/18 holes
Clubs	Palos	1 500 Pts/18 holes
Credit cards Tarjetas de crédito		no

GOLF →

La Coma

Tarragona →

Benicássim

46

47 A 7

Castellón de la Plana

Villarreal

N 340

Valencia

0   4   8 km

Access Acceso : A7 Barcelona-Valencia,
Exit (Salida) 46 → Castellón Norte.
700 m on the right → «Club de Campo». Golf 2,5 km
Map 4 on page 1103 Plano 4 Página 1103

GOLF COURSE
RECORRIDO   16/20

Site	Emplazamiento	
Maintenance	Mantenimiento	
Architect	Arquitecto	Ramón Espinosa
Type	Tipo	country
Relief	Relieve	
Water in play	Agua	
Exp. to wind	Exp. al viento	
Trees in play	Arboles	

Scorecard Tarjeta	Chp. Campeonato	Mens Caballeros	Ladies Damas
Length Longitud	6239	6038	5266
Par	72	72	72

Advised golfing ability		0 12 24 36
Nivel de juego aconsejado		
Hcp required	Handicap exigido	28 Men, 36 Ladies

CLUB HOUSE & AMENITIES
CLUB HOUSE Y DEPENDENCIAS   7/10

Pro shop	Pro-shop	
Driving range	Campo de prácticas	
Sheltered	cubierto	no
On grass	sobre hierba	yes
Putting-green	putting-green	yes
Pitching-green	pitching-green	yes

HOTEL FACILITIES
HOTELES CERCANOS   6/10

HOTELS HOTELES

Intur Castellón	Castellón
123 rooms, D 17 900 Pts	5 km
Tel (34) 964 - 225 000, Fax (34) 964 - 232 606	
Turcosa	El Grao/Castellón
70 rooms, D 12 200 Pts	7 km
Tel (34) 964 - 283 600, Fax (34) 964 - 284 737	
Mindoro	Castellón
103 rooms, D 15 500 Pts	5 km
Tel (34) 964 - 222 300, Fax (34) 964 - 233 154	

RESTAURANTS RESTAURANTES

Mare Nostrum	El Grao/Castellón
Tel (34) 964 - 282 929	7 km
Tasca del Puerto	El Grao/Castellón
Tel (34) 964 - 284 481	7 km

1181

De los dos recorridos de Mijas, éste es para los «pegadores» y el que da mayor sensación de espacio. Bien es verdad que hay ocho lagos en la línea de juego en una decena de hoyos, pero las calles son anchas. Y menos mal, porque Los Lagos es muy largo, sin muchas cuestas, lo que permite jugarlo sin recurrir a un coche. Algo característico de Trent Jones es la disposición de los bunkers, no sólo para defender los greens, sino para dificultar la tarea de quienes intentan cortar en los dog-legs. Además, presenta una cierta variedad visual en hoyos que son muy semejantes entre sí. Los greens son extensos, con bastantes caídas, en muy buen estado, y su rapidez no impide que aguanten bien la bola: cosa muy importante ya que a menudo hay que aprochar con hierros largos. Que los jugadores medianos no se desanimen, pueden acortar el recorrido escogiendo tees de salida más adelantados.

Of the two courses at Mijas, this is the one for the big-hitters and for the greatest impression of open space. Sure, the eight lakes are very much to the fore on ten holes, but the fairways are wide. And so they should be, because "Los Lagos" is very long. But it is a pleasant course to play walking, as the terrain is relatively flat. Typical of Trent Jones, the bunkers are there not only to defend the greens but also to trap players who try and cut corners on the dog-legs. They also add a little variety to holes that are often very similar in style. The greens are huge, undulating and in good condition, and although fast they pitch well. This is important because approach shots often call for a long iron. Average players should not lose heart though, as they can shorten the course considerably by playing off the front-tees.

Mijas Golf International — 1976

Apdo de Coreos 145
E - 29640 FUENGIROLA (MALAGA)

Office	Secretaria	(34) 952 - 476 843
Pro shop	Pro-shop	(34) 952 - 468 038
Fax	Fax	(34) 952 - 467 943
Situation	Situación	

Málaga (pop. 534 683), 25 km

Annual closure	Cierre anual	no
Weekly closure	Cierre semanal	no

Fees main season
Precios tempor. alta 18 holes

	Week days Semana	We/Bank holidays Fin de sem./fiestas
Individual Individual	8 000 Pts	8 000 Pts
Couple Pareja	16 000 Pts	16 000 Pts

Caddy	Caddy	no
Electric Trolley	Carro eléctrico	2 000 Pts/18 holes
Buggy	Coche	5 500 Pts/18 holes
Clubs	Palos	3 500 Pts/18 holes

Credit cards Tarjetas de crédito
VISA - MasterCard - 4B

GOLF COURSE RECORRIDO — 16/20

Site	Emplazamiento	
Maintenance	Mantenimiento	
Architect	Arquitecto	Robert Trent Jones
Type	Tipo	country
Relief	Relieve	
Water in play	Agua	
Exp. to wind	Exp. al viento	
Trees in play	Arboles	

Scorecard Tarjeta	Chp. Campeonato	Mens Caballeros	Ladies Damas
Length Longitud	6367	6007	5148
Par	71	71	71

Advised golfing ability — 0 12 24 36
Nivel de juego aconsejado
Hcp required Handicap exigido 28 Men, 36 Ladies

CLUB HOUSE & AMENITIES CLUB HOUSE Y DEPENDENCIAS — 6/10

Pro shop	Pro-shop	
Driving range	Campo de prácticas	
Sheltered	cubierto	no
On grass	sobre hierba	yes
Putting-green	putting-green	yes
Pitching-green	pitching-green	no

HOTEL FACILITIES HOTELES CERCANOS — 7/10

HOTELS HOTELES

Byblos — Mijas
144 rooms, D 39 500 Pts — 200 m
Tel (34) 952 - 473 050, Fax (34)·952 - 476 783

Florida — Fuengirola
116 rooms, D 11 600 Pts — 3 km
Tel (34) 952 - 476 100, Fax (34) 952 - 581 529

Mijas — Mijas
97 rooms, D 14 700 Pts — 5 km
Tel (34) 952 - 485 800, Fax (34) 952 - 485 825

RESTAURANTS RESTAURANTES

El Olivar - Tel (34) 952 - 486 196 — Mijas 5 km

El Tomate — Fuengirola 3 km
Tel (34) 952 - 473 599

El Mirlo Blanco - Tel (34) 952 - 460 250 — Mijas 5 km

1182

Access Acceso : Málaga N340 → Cadiz. Exit (Salida) «Cambio de Sentido», Fuengirola → Mijas, Golf 3 km
Map 7 on page 1109 Plano 7 Página 1109

De los dos recorridos de Mijas, Los Olivos conviene más a los jugadores de nivel medio. Por supuesto es estrecho, rodeado de numerosos olivos, algunos lagos pueden perturbar a los jugadores con poca técnica, su relieve es ligeramente más accidentado que el de «Los Lagos», pero encontrarán un trazado más a su medida y al alcance de sus posibilidades. Los greens son más pequeños, algunos ciegos, pero aguantan correctamente la bola y la progresión general del recorrido lo hace más divertido para jugar en familia cuando el resultado es menos importante que el placer. No es un recorrido para atacar y ciertamente no fue diseñado para ello. Da la impresión que Trent Jones quiso poner de relieve en Mijas dos facetas muy diferentes de su buen hacer. En todo caso, este conjunto permite que todos puedan escoger según su forma actual.

When choosing between the two courses at Mijas, average players are perhaps better off playing Los Olivos. The course is certainly tight and bordered by numerous olive trees, there are a few lakes to scare players with limited technique and the relief is in part much more broken than its sister course, Los Lagos. But the layout is probably much more within their scope and ability. The greens are smaller and some are blind, but they pitch pretty well and the general layout makes this course fun for playing with the family when scores are less important than having a good time. It is not a course for attacking players and visibly was not designed to be so. You get the impression that Trent Jones wanted to demonstrate two very different facets of his architectural know-how at Mijas. In any case, this golfing resort allows everyone to choose according to the shape of his or her game.

Mijas Golf International

1976

Apdo de Coreos 145
E - 29640 FUENGIROLA (MALAGA)

Office	Secretaria	(34) 952 - 476 843
Pro shop	Pro-shop	(34) 952 - 468 038
Fax	Fax	(34) 952 - 467 943
Situation	Situación	

Málaga (pop. 534 683), 25 km

Annual closure	Cierre anual	no
Weekly closure	Cierre semanal	no

Fees main season
Precios tempor. alta 18 holes

	Week days Semana	We/Bank holidays Fin de sem./fiestas
Individual Individual	8 000 Pts	8 000 Pts
Couple Pareja	16 000 Pts	16 000 Pts

Caddy	Caddy	no
Electric Trolley	Carro eléctrico	2 000 Pts/18 holes
Buggy	Coche	5 500 Pts/18 holes
Clubs	Palos	3 500 Pts/18 holes

Credit cards Tarjetas de crédito VISA - MasterCard - 4B

Alhaurin el Grande

Malaga
MA 485
Mijas
GOLF
N 340
MA 426
FUENGIROLA
COSTA DEL SOL
0 4 8 km
Mijas Costa
Marbella

Access Acceso : Málaga N340 → Cadiz. Exit (Salida) «Cambio de Sentido», Fuengirola → Mijas, Golf 3 km
Map 7 on page 1109 Plano 7 Página 1109

GOLF COURSE / RECORRIDO

13/20

Site	Emplazamiento	
Maintenance	Mantenimiento	
Architect	Arquitecto	Robert Trent Jones
Type	Tipo	country, hilly
Relief	Relieve	
Water in play	Agua	
Exp. to wind	Exp. al viento	
Trees in play	Arboles	

Scorecard Tarjeta	Chp. Campeonato	Mens Caballeros	Ladies Damas
Length Longitud	6009	5866	4969
Par	72	72	72

Advised golfing ability Nivel de juego aconsejado	0	12	24	36
Hcp required Handicap exigido	28 Men, 36 Ladies			

CLUB HOUSE & AMENITIES / CLUB HOUSE Y DEPENDENCIAS

6/10

Pro shop	Pro-shop	
Driving range	Campo de prácticas	
Sheltered	cubierto	no
On grass	sobre hierba	yes
Putting-green	putting-green	yes
Pitching-green	pitching-green	no

HOTEL FACILITIES / HOTELES CERCANOS

7/10

HOTELS HOTELES

Byblos — Mijas
144 rooms, D 39 500 Pts — 200 m
Tel (34) 952 - 473 050, Fax (34) 952 - 476 783

Florida — Fuengirola
116 rooms, D 11 600 Pts — 3 km
Tel (34) 952 - 476 100, Fax (34) 952 - 581 529

Mijas — Mijas
97 rooms, D 14 700 Pts — 5 km
Tel (34) 952 - 485 800, Fax (34) 952 - 485 825

RESTAURANTS RESTAURANTES

El Olivar - Tel (34) 952 - 486 196 — Mijas 5 km

El Tomate — Fuengirola
Tel(34) 952 - 473 599 — 3 km

El Mirlo Blanco - Tel (34) 952 - 460 250 — Mijas 5 km

1183

El golf más extravagante de toda la región y sin duda de España. Diseñado por Pepe Gancedo, este recorrido o gusta o se detesta. En plena montaña y muy expuesto al viento, reserva toda clase de sorpresas, hasta tal punto que algunos hoyos «normales» parecen insulsos. Sinuoso entre rocas, franqueando quebradas, bajando colinas, en medio de una vegetación salvaje y tupida, hay que conservar el dominio de sí mismo. Si se sale de calle, ¡o desgracia!. Pero las reglas locales son indulgentes: toda bola perdida se considera que reposa en un obstáculo de agua lateral. Uno se encuentra solo ante su propio juego como si estuviese al otro lado del mundo. Que el emblema del recorrido sea un toro no es mera casualidad: hay que luchar contra él, aguantar sus embistes, esquivar sus ataques. Se acaba agotado pero encantado de los magníficos paisajes. Un recorrido barroco, de gran inteligencia e imposible de ignorar.

The most extravagant course in the whole region and certainly in the whole of Spain. Designed by Pepe Gancedo, you either love it or hate it, with no middle ground. Right in the mountains and very exposed to the wind, it reserves every sort of surprise to the extent where certain "normal" holes look positively insipid. Winding its way through rocks, crossing gorges and running down hills amidst wild thick vegetation, the course calls for a cool head. Too bad if you miss the fairways. But the local rules are pretty lenient, as any lost ball is considered to be in a side water hazard. Here you are at the world's end, alone with your game of golf. It is no accident to see that the course's emblem is a bull; you have to fight it, stave off its charges and sidestep its attacks. You leave the 18th green exhausted but delighted with the magnificent landscapes. A baroque course of great intelligence, and one that is impossible to overlook.

Monte Mayor Golf Club

Urbanizacion Los Naranjos - Nueva Andalucia
E - 29660 MARBELLA (MALAGA)

Office	Secretaria	(34) 952 - 113 088
Pro shop	Pro-shop	(34) 952 - 113 088
Fax	Fax	(34) 952 - 113 087
Situation	Situación	

Estepona (pop. 36 307), 14 km
Marbella (pop. 84 410), 22 km

Annual closure	Cierre anual	no
Weekly closure	Cierre semanal	no

Fees main season
Precios tempor. alta 18 holes

	Week days Semana	We/Bank holidays Fin de sem./fiestas
Individual Individual	8 500 Pts	8 500 Pts
Couple Pareja	17 000 PtS	17 000 PTS

Green fees include golf cars

Caddy	Caddy	no
Electric Trolley	Carro eléctrico	no
Buggy	Coche	4 000 Pts/18 holes
Clubs	Palos	2 500 Pts/18 holes

Credit cards Tarjetas de crédito
VISA - Mastercard - AMEX

1184

Access Acceso : Marbella N340 → Estepona. Exit (Salida) «La Cancelada». Km 163,6 on the right → Golf
Map 7 on page 1109 Plano 7 Página 1109

GOLF COURSE
RECORRIDO

13 /20

Site	Emplazamiento	
Maintenance	Mantenimiento	
Architect	Arquitecto	P. Gancedo
Type	Tipo	mountain
Relief	Relieve	
Water in play	Agua	
Exp. to wind	Exp. al viento	
Trees in play	Arboles	

Scorecard Tarjeta	Chp. Campeonato	Mens Caballeros	Ladies Damas
Length Longitud	5652	5354	4800
Par	71	71	71

Advised golfing ability	0	12	24	36
Nivel de juego aconsejado				
Hcp required	Handicap exigido		28 Men, 36 Ladies	

CLUB HOUSE & AMENITIES
CLUB HOUSE Y DEPENDENCIAS

5 /10

Pro shop	Pro-shop	
Driving range	Campo de prácticas	
Sheltered	cubierto	no
On grass	sobre hierba	no
Putting-green	putting-green	yes
Pitching-green	pitching-green	no

HOTEL FACILITIES
HOTELES CERCANOS

5 /10

HOTELS HOTELES

Atalaya Park 448 rooms, D 25 200 Pts Tel (34) 952 - 884 801 Fax (34) 952 - 885 735	Estepona 14 km
Pyr Hotel 319 rooms, D 15 700 Pts Tel (34) 952 - 817 353 Fax (34) 952 - 817 907	Puerto Banus 25 km

RESTAURANTS RESTAURANTES

El Carnicero Tel (34) 952 - 886 307	La Cancelada 6 km
El Rocio Tel (34) 952 - 800 046	Estepona 14 km

Era de esperar encontrarse un día con la firma de Jack Nicklaus en el sur de España. Ha sacado buen partido de un terreno moderadamente accidentado, y si los greens están frecuentemente en alto, no hay hoyos ciegos ni hoyos en subida, lo que confirma su filosofía de que: «hay que ver lo que hay que hacer». Prueba de ello el 18 con el tee de salida allá en alto. En realidad es un recorrido franco y difícil de lidiar, pero su dificultad general no impide el jugarlo en familia (salvo los principiantes), siempre y cuando cada uno se mantenga tranquilo y no se obsesione por el resultado. Todas las dificultades se concentran en la línea de juego (sobre todo los obstáculos de agua), y hay muchos fuera de límites. La variedad de situaciones incita a jugarlo varias veces para comprender mejor sus sutilezas. Espectacular y original (por la región), este recorrido no reniega el espíritu americano de su autor. Los que conocen sus otras realizaciones no quedarán sorprendidos.

It was only to be expected that one day Jack Nicklaus would leave his mark in southern Spain. He has extracted the best out of a moderately hilly terrain, and while the greens are frequently elevated, there are no blind or uphill holes, thus illustrating the great man's philosophy of: "you have to see what you have to do". Witness hole N° 18 with a very elevated tee. As a result, this is a very open but very tricky course to get around, but the general difficulty does not prevent this from being a course for all the family (but not beginners) as long as you keep cool and don't get obsessed with your score. All the hazards are very much in play, especially the water and even more so the out-of-bounds. The variety of situations will make you want to play Montecastillo several times to fully understand the more subtle sides to the course. Spectacular and original (for the region, that is), the course does not break with the American spirit of its designer.

Montecastillo Hotel & Golf Resort   1992

Carretera de Arcos, km. 9,6
E - 11406 JEREZ DE LA FRONTERA (Cádiz)

Office	Secretaria	(34) 956 - 151 200
Pro shop	Pro-shop	(34) 956 - 151 200
Fax	Fax	(34) 956 - 151 209
Situation	Situación	

Jerez (pop. 184 364), 8 km
Sevilla (pop. 704 857), 70 km

Annual closure	Cierre anual	no
Weekly closure	Cierre semanal	no

Fees main season
Precios tempor. alta 18 holes

	Week days Semana	We/Bank holidays Fin de sem./fiestas
Individual Individual	9 000 Pts	9 000 Pts
Couple Pareja	18 000 Pts	18 000 Pts

Caddy	Caddy	no
Electric Trolley	Carro eléctrico	no
Buggy	Coche	5 000 Pts/18 holes
Clubs	Palos	2 000 Pts/18 holes

Credit cards Tarjetas de crédito
VISA - Eurocard - MasterCard - AMEX - DC

Access Acceso : Jerez, N342 → Arcos de la Frontera,
9,8 km turn right, Golf 1,5 km
Map 7 on page 1108 Plano 7 Página 1108

GOLF COURSE
RECORRIDO   17/20

Site	Emplazamiento	
Maintenance	Mantenimiento	
Architect	Arquitecto	Jack Nicklaus
Type	Tipo	country
Relief	Relieve	
Water in play	Agua	
Exp. to wind	Exp. al viento	
Trees in play	Arboles	

Scorecard Tarjeta	Chp. Campeonato	Mens Caballeros	Ladies Damas
Length Longitud	6424	6043	5230
Par	72	72	72

Advised golfing ability   0   12   24   36
Nivel de juego aconsejado
Hcp required   Handicap exigido 28 Men, 36 Ladies

CLUB HOUSE & AMENITIES
CLUB HOUSE Y DEPENDENCIAS   8/10

Pro shop	Pro-shop	
Driving range	Campo de prácticas	
Sheltered	cubierto	18 mats
On grass	sobre hierba	yes
Putting-green	putting-green	yes
Pitching-green	pitching-green	yes

HOTEL FACILITIES
HOTELES CERCANOS   7/10

HOTELS HOTELES
Montecastillo   Montecastillo
120 rooms, D 24 700 Pts   100 m
Tel (34) 956 - 151 200, Fax (34) 956 - 151 209

La Cueva Park   Jerez de la Frontera
58 rooms, D 12 600 Pts.
Tel (34) 956 - 189 120, Fax (34) 956 - 189 121

Royal Sherry   Jerez de la Frontera
173 rooms, D 18 700 Pts   7 km
Tel (34) 956 - 303 011, Fax (34) 956 - 311 300

RESTAURANTS RESTAURANTES
Tendido 6   Jerez de la Frontera
Tel (34) 956 - 344 835   10 km

Mesón La Cueva   Montecastillo
Tel (34) 956 - 189 020   1 km

1185

MONTENMEDIO

15	7	7

La Dehesa de Montenmedio es un recorrido reciente de buena calidad en general, salido del pincel de Alejandro Maldonado y que creemos es, hasta ahora, su realización más prestigiosa. La región está cada día mejor equipada de golfs, y es cada vez más difícil encontrar terrenos entre Málaga, Marbella y Gibraltar. Las novedades van hacia el oeste. En este recorrido, por el momento no se aceptan más de 60 jugadores al día, distribuidos en partidas a veinte minutos de intervalo, lo que garantiza una gran comodidad de juego. Las calles y greens son anchos favoreciendo a los jugadores de tipo medio que son la mayor parte de los visitantes de la región. La mayor parte de las veces en los segundos golpes hacia los greens se pueden utilizar hierros medianos. Los pares 3 exigen mucha precisión. No obstante hay que permanecer vigilitantes y no atacar de cualquier manera, ya que la configuración natural del terreno ha sido preservada al igual que la vegetación, mientras que el agua es un elemento más bien decorativo que no dificulta el juego.

La Dehesa de Montenmedio is a brand new course of generally excellent standard thanks to the design skills of Alejandro Maldonado, from whom this is the most prestigious achievement to date as far as we know. This region is being given more and more courses as land becomes increasingly scarce between Malaga, Marbella and Gibraltar. The west is where it is all happening. For the time being this course admits only 60 players a day teeing off at 20 minutes intervals, so you are in for a relaxed round. The fairways and greens are wide, which is good news for the average players who form the core of green-feers visiting the region. Most of their approach shots will be medium-irons, and the par 3s call for an accurate tee-shot. However, they will need to be careful and not go for the greens in any old way, because the designer has kept the terrain's natural contours and vegetation. There is water but it is more decorative than really in play.

Dehesa Montenmedio
Golf & Country Club — 1996
CN. 340 - Km 42,500
E - 11150 VEJER DE LA FRONTERA-BARBATE (CADIZ)

Office	Secretaria	(34) 956 - 451 216
Pro shop	Pro-shop	(34) 956 - 455 004
Fax	Fax	(34) 956 - 451 295
Situation	Situación	

Cadiz (pop.157 355), 42 km

Annual closure	Cierre anual	no
Weekly closure	Cierre semanal	no

Fees main season
Precios tempor. alta 18 holes

	Week days Semana	We/Bank holidays Fin de sem./fiestas
Individual Individual	12 000 Pts	12 000 Pts
Couple Pareja	24 000 Pts	24 000 Pts

Only 60 playesr each day (solo 60 jugadores al dia)

Caddy	Caddy	no
Electric Trolley	Carro eléctrico	500 Pts/18 holes
Buggy	Coche	5 000 Pts/18 holes
Clubs	Palos	2 000 Pts/18 holes

Credit cards Tarjetas de crédito
VISA - MasterCard - AMEX - DC

Access Acceso : N340 Cadiz → Algeciras.
Map 7 on page 1109 Plano 7 Página 1109

GOLF COURSE
RECORRIDO — 15/20

Site	Emplazamiento	▰▰▰▰▰▱
Maintenance	Mantenimiento	▰▰▰▰▰▱
Architect	Arquitecto	Alejandro Maldonado
Type	Tipo	parkland
Relief	Relieve	▰▰▰▰▱▱
Water in play	Agua	▰▰▰▱▱▱
Exp. to wind	Exp. al viento	▰▰▰▱▱▱
Trees in play	Arboles	▰▰▰▰▱▱

Scorecard Tarjeta	Chp. Campeonato	Mens Caballeros	Ladies Damas
Length Longitud	5897	5751	5563
Par	71	71	71

Advised golfing ability	0	12	24	36
Nivel de juego aconsejado				

Hcp required Handicap exigido 28 Men, 36 Ladies

CLUB HOUSE & AMENITIES
CLUB HOUSE Y DEPENDENCIAS — 7/10

Pro shop	Pro-shop	▰▰▰▰▱▱
Driving range	Campo de prácticas	▰▰▰▰▰▱
Sheltered	cubierto	no
On grass	sobre hierba	yes
Putting-green	putting-green	yes
Pitching-green	pitching-green	yes

HOTEL FACILITIES
HOTELES CERCANOS — 7/10

HOTELS HOTELES

Convento de San Francisco — Vejer
25 rooms, D 9 700 Pts
Tel (34) 956 - 451 001
Fax (34) 956 - 451 004

Royal Andalus Golf — Chiclana de la Frontera
263 rooms, D 17 900 Pts
Tel (34) 956 - 494 109
Fax (34) 956 - 494 490

Flamenco — Conil
114 rooms, D 10 500 Pts
Tel (34) 956 - 440 711
Fax (34) 956 - 440 542

RESTAURANTS RESTAURANTES

Torres — Barbate
Tel (34) 956 - 430 985 — 5 km

1186

Junto a El Saler, El Prat o el Club de Campo, Neguri es uno de los grandes ejemplos del estilo de Javier Arana, a la vez humilde (en su respeto a la tradición), y muy personal (en su interpretación). Considerado como un club privado, abre sus puertas entre semana a los jugadores de fuera nunca muy numerosos ya que Bilbao no es un destino prioritario para el turismo. Campo para los entendidos, Neguri está en perfectos condiciones aunque la tierra éste demasiado cansada. A su trazado clásico y de una rara elegancia, pocos cambios han sido incorporados desde sus orígines aunque numerosos pinos hayan sido plantados para sustituir las especies desaparecidas en primera línea de calle. Ha sido una saludable iniciatitiva ya que reconstruirán, con el conjunto de bunkers, las principales dificultades de juego. Muy difícil desde las barras de atrás, Neguri es un poco más asequible desde las otras salidas, pero sus sutilezas exigen un cierto nivel de juego para poder ser apreciadas plenamente.

Neguri is one of the great examples of the Javier Arana style, at once humble (in his respect of tradition) and very personal (in his interpretation). Neguri half-opens its doors to green-feers during the week, although visitors can hardly be accused of invading the course given that Bilbao is not yet a major tourist destination. A course for connoisseurs, Neguri is in good condition, although the soil seems to be growing a little weary. Few changes have been made to the original layout, a classic design of uncommon elegance, but a large number of pine-trees have been planted to replace the trees that have disappeared from the front-line of the fairway limits. This is a welcome initiative, because with the bunkers the trees form the course's main difficulties. Very tough from the back-tees, Neguri mellows slightly when playing further forward, but the course's subtleties require a certain standard of skill to be fully appreciated.

Real Sociedad de Golf de Neguri — 1911
Campo «La Galea», Aptdo de Correos 9
E - 48990 ALGORTA (Vizcaya)

Office	Secretaria	(34) 944 - 910 200
Pro shop	Pro-shop	(34) 944 - 910 200
Fax	Fax	(34) 944 - 605 611
Situation	Situación	

Algorta (pop. 79 517), 2 km
Bilbao (pop. 372 054), 13 km

Annual closure	Cierre anual	no
Weekly closure	Cierre semanal	no

Fees main season
Precios tempor. alta 18 holes

	Week days Semana	We/Bank holidays Fin de sem./fiestas
Individual Individual	12 000 Pts	15 000 Pts
Couple Pareja	24 000 Pts	30 000 Pts

Caddy	Caddy	5 000 Pts/18 holes
Electric Trolley	Carro eléctrico	750 Pts/18 holes
Buggy	Coche	4 000 Pts/18 holes
Clubs	Palos	no

Credit cards Tarjetas de crédito VISA

Mar Cantábrico
Santa Maria de Getxo
GOLF
C 6320
Algorta
Mungia
Ciérvana
San Mamès
San Vicente de Baracaldo
A 8
A 8
BILBAO
0 3 6 km
Burgos
A 68

Access Acceso : Bilbao → Getxo, → Algorta
Map 1 on page 1096 Plano 1 Página 1096

GOLF COURSE / RECORRIDO — 17/20

Site	Emplazamiento	
Maintenance	Mantenimiento	
Architect	Arquitecto	Javier Arana
Type	Tipo	forest
Relief	Relieve	
Water in play	Agua	
Exp. to wind	Exp. al viento	
Trees in play	Arboles	

Scorecard Tarjeta	Chp. Campeonato	Mens Caballeros	Ladies Damas
Length Longitud	6280	6054	5112
Par	72	72	72

Advised golfing ability Nivel de juego aconsejado	0 12 24 36
Hcp required Handicap exigido	28 Men, 36 Ladies

CLUB HOUSE & AMENITIES / CLUB HOUSE Y DEPENDENCIAS — 7/10

Pro shop	Pro-shop	
Driving range	Campo de prácticas	
Sheltered	cubierto	20 mats
On grass	sobre hierba	yes
Putting-green	putting-green	yes
Pitching-green	pitching-green	yes

HOTEL FACILITIES / HOTELES CERCANOS — 7/10

HOTELS HOTELES

Los Tamarises — Algorta 4 km
42 rooms, D 17 900 Pts
Tel (34) 944 - 910 005, Fax (34) 944 - 911 310

Igeretxe Agustín — Algorta 2 km
21 rooms, D 13 400 Pts
Tel (34) 944 - 910 009, Fax (34) 944 - 608 599

Lopez de Aro — Bilbao 13 km
53 rooms, D 28 600 Pts
Tel (34) 944 - 235 500, Fax (34) 944 - 234 500

RESTAURANTS RESTAURANTES

Jolastoki - Tel (34) 949 - 912 031 — Neguri
Cubita - Tel (34) 944 - 911 700 — Algorta 2 km
Zortziko - Tel (34) 944 - 239 743 — Bilbao 13 km

1187

NOVO SANCTI PETRI ✳ 16 | 7 | 7

Todas las combinaciones de estos tres 9 hoyos dan una longitud mas o menos equivalente, no se puede distinguir un 18 y un 9 hoyos. El rigor del diseño y el reparto de dificultades se añaden a la homogeneidad del lugar. De relieve moderado, este conjunto está desprovisto de trampas, pero no de dificultades. Ballesteros ha diseñado 27 hoyos de estilo mas bien americano, con obstáculos de agua (excepto en el recorrido «Azul»), numerosos bunkers bien hechos, poco profundos, y árboles (muchos recién plantados). Las calles generalmente estrechas requieren una gran precisión para no irse al rough bien tupido o a los bunkers de calle. Favorece a los jugadores con tendencia al «hook», y los aproches hacia los amplios greens han de hacerse por alto ya que están bien protegidos. El club propone muchas otras actividades deportivas.

As every combination of these three 9-hole courses gives an 18 hole course of more or less the same length, you can't say that this is an 18 hole and 9 hole complex. The very thorough layout and the distribution of hazards add further to the site's uniformity. Only moderately hilly, the course is free of traps but not of hazards. Ballesteros designed this complex in a rather American style with water hazards (except on the "Azul" course), numerous well-designed but shallow bunkers, and trees (there are a lot of young plantations). The generally tight fairways call for great accuracy to avoid the very dense rough and the fairway bunkers. It is a course for hook-shots, and the approach shots to the well-defended huge greens often require a high ball. The club features a number of other recreational activities.

Golf Novo Sancti Petri S.A. 1991
Urb. Novo Sancti Petri - Playa de la Barrosa
E - 11139 CHICLANA DE LA FRONTERA - CADIZ

Office	Secretaria	(34) 956 - 494 005
Pro shop	Pro-shop	(34) 956 - 494 005
Fax	Fax	(34) 956 - 494 350
Situation	Situación	

Jerez (pop. 184 364), 50 km
Chiclana de la Frontera (pop. 46 610), 11 km

Annual closure	Cierre anual	no
Weekly closure	Cierre semanal	no

Fees main season
Precios tempor. alta 18 holes

	Week days Semana	We/Bank holidays Fin de sem./fiestas
Individual Individual	7 500 Pts	7 500 Pts
Couple Pareja	15 000 Pts	15 000 Pts
Caddy	Caddy	5 000 Pts/18 holes
Electric Trolley	Carro eléctrico	no
Buggy	Coche	4 500 Pts/18 holes
Clubs	Palos	2 000 Pts/18 holes

Credit cards Tarjetas de crédito
VISA - Eurocard - MasterCard - AMEX - DC

1188

CADIZ
A 4
Puerto Real
San Fernando
Chiclana de la Frontera
0 2,5 5 km
Los Gallos
Novo Sancti Petri
GOLF
La Barrosa

Access Acceso : N340 Chiclana de la Frontera
→ Sancti Petri
Map 7 on page 1108 Plano 7 Página 1108

GOLF COURSE RECORRIDO 16/20

Site	Emplazamiento	■■■■■□
Maintenance	Mantenimiento	■■■■■□
Architect	Arquitecto	Seve Ballesteros
Type	Tipo	seaside course
Relief	Relieve	■■□□□□
Water in play	Agua	■■■□□□
Exp. to wind	Exp. al viento	■■■□□□
Trees in play	Arboles	■■■■□□

Scorecard Tarjeta	Chp. Campeonato	Mens Caballeros	Ladies Damas
Length Longitud	6510	6169	5337
Par	72	72	72

Advised golfing ability		0	12	24	36
Nivel de juego aconsejado					
Hcp required	Handicap exigido	28 Men, 36 Ladies			

CLUB HOUSE & AMENITIES CLUB HOUSE Y DEPENDENCIAS 7/10

Pro shop	Pro-shop	■■■■□□
Driving range	Campo de prácticas	■■■■□□
Sheltered	cubierto	no
On grass	sobre hierba	yes
Putting-green	putting-green	yes
Pitching-green	pitching-green	yes

HOTEL FACILITIES HOTELES CERCANOS 7/10

HOTELS HOTELES
Royal Andalus Golf — Playa de la Barrosa
263 rooms, D 23 100 Pts — 100 m
Tel (34) 956 - 494 109, Fax (34) 956 - 494 490

Tryp Costa Golf — La Barrosa
195 rooms, D 20 900 Pts. — 10 km
Tel (34) 956 - 494 535, Fax (34) 956 - 494 626

Playa La Barrosa — Playa de la Barrosa
264 rooms, D 23 600 Pts. — 500 m
Tel (34) 956 - 494 824, Fax (34) 956 - 494 860

RESTAURANTS RESTAURANTES
Novo Golf Gachito — Chiclana dela Frontera
Tel (34) 956 - 495 249 — 100 m

El Faro — Cádiz
Tel (34) 956 - 211 068 — 25 km

Esta es una de las más recientes realizaciones de Severiano Ballesteros. En el extremo sur de la Costa Valenciana, lindando con la superturística y residencial costa de Alicante donde los campos de golf se multiplican para atender la demanda y preferencias de alemanes y centroeuropeos en general, Oliva Nova ofrece un campo completo por su cuidado mantenimiento y los diversos elementos del trazado que permiten jugar golpes muy variados. El agua es un elemento de riesgo que aparece constantemente, tanto señalando la referencia de dirección de los golpes de salida como enmarcando muchos greenes. Los greenes son delicados de atacar y de jugar, por sus caídas acusadas y porque varios de ellos están construídos en pendiente, en subida por la parte delantera y en bajada por el fondo. En un terreno llano próximo al mar, que disfruta por la tanto de la refrescante brisa marina, el recorrido necesita un tiempo para que la vegetación plantada adquiera envergadura.

This is one of the more recent designs by Severiano Ballesteros to the extreme south of the Costa Valenciana, where golf courses are mushrooming to attract customers from Northern Europe and especially Germany. Oliva Nova is a very complete and well-groomed course, where the layout calls for a whole variety of shots. Water is a risk element that is constantly around to attract shots hit slightly off the fairway or to guard any number of greens. The latter are difficult both to approach and to play, being sharply contoured and in many cases built on slopes, where the front part of the green slopes sideways and the rear section runs away. Close to the sea (the cooling sea-breeze is often much appreciated), this course calls for a little patience until the newly planted plants and trees start to really grow.

Oliva Nova Golf — 1997
E - 46780 OLIVA

Office	Secretaria	(34) 962 - 855 975
Pro shop	Pro-shop	(34) 962 - 855 975
Fax	Fax	(34) 962 - 855 975
Situation	Situación	

Valencia (pop. 777 427), 76 km
Gandía (pop. 52 000), 8 km

Annual closure	Cierre anual	no
Weekly closure	Cierre semanal	no

Fees main season
Precios tempor. alta 18 holes

	Week days Semana	We/Bank holidays Fin de sem./fiestas
Individual Individual	6 500 Pts	6 500 Pts
Couple Pareja	13 000 Pts	13 000 Pts

Caddy	Caddy	no
Electric Trolley	Carro eléctrico	1 000 Pts/18 holes
Buggy	Coche	4 000 Pts/18 holes
Clubs	Palos	2 000 Pts/18 holes

Credit cards Tarjetas de crédito
VISA - Eurocard - MasterCard - AMEX

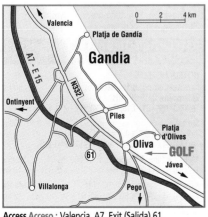

Access Acceso : Valencia, A7. Exit (Salida) 61.
Go through Oliva → Gandía.
Km 209 on N-332, turn left → Golf.
Map 6 on page 1107 Plano 6 Página 1107

GOLF COURSE / RECORRIDO — 14/20

Site	Emplazamiento	
Maintenance	Mantenimiento	
Architect	Arquitecto	Seve Ballesteros
Type	Tipo	parkland, inland
Relief	Relieve	
Water in play	Agua	
Exp. to wind	Exp. al viento	
Trees in play	Arboles	

Scorecard Tarjeta	Chp. Campeonato	Mens Caballeros	Ladies Damas
Length Longitud	6270	6037	5157
Par	72	72	72

Advised golfing ability		0	12	24	36
Nivel de juego aconsejado					

Hcp required Handicap exigido 28 Men, 36 Ladies

CLUB HOUSE & AMENITIES / CLUB HOUSE Y DEPENDENCIAS — 6/10

Pro shop	Pro-shop	
Driving range	Campo de prácticas	
Sheltered	cubierto	no
On grass	sobre hierba	yes
Putting-green	putting-green	yes
Pitching-green	pitching-green	yes

HOTEL FACILITIES / HOTELES CERCANOS — 7/10

HOTELS HOTELES
Oliva Nova Beach & Golf Hotel — Oliva 1 km
90 rooms, D 21 000 Pts
Tel (34) 96 - 285 33 00, Fax (34) 96 - 285 51 08

Bayren I — Gandía 14 km
161 rooms, D 18 000 Pts
Tel (34) 96 - 284 03 00, Fax (34) 96 - 284 06 53

Don Ximo Club Hotel — Gandía 14 km
68 rooms, D 15 000 Pts
Tel (34) 96 - 284 53 93, Fax (34) 96 - 284 12 69

RESTAURANTS RESTAURANTES
Kiko Port - Tel (34) 962 - 856 152 — Oliva 6 km
Soqueta - Tel (34) 962 - 851 452 — Oliva 6 km
Gamba — Gandía 14 km
Tel (34) 962 - 841 310

1189

En España al igual que en numerosos páises, los jugadores profesionales sucumben a la tentación del diseño de campos, con suertes diversas. José Rivero no sólo se ha preocupado de sus colegas de alto nivel, ha pensado igualmente en todos los niveles, y éste recorrido (próximo al Campo de las Naciones y al aeropuerto) les convendrá perfectamente. Si un exceso de longitud y suficientemente amplio ofrece al debutante y al jugador experto la posibilidad de pasar una jornada agradable en un sitio esplendido. Sin embargo para conseguir un buen resultado, se necesitará saber jugar todo tipo de golpes, tener una estrategia de juego eficaz, y sacar a relucir sus dotes de buen pateador ya que si las ondulaciones son moderadas, algunas posiciones de banderas pueden ser peligrosas cuando nuestro tiro a green no ha sido muy preciso. Un mejor mantenimiento del rough y de las zonas de salida redundaría en beneficio del placer que procurá el campo.

In Spain as in many other countries, professional golfers fall for the lure of course design, with mixed results. José Rivero not only set out to satisfy his professional colleagues, he also spared many a thought for players of all abilities. This course (close to Campo de Las Naciones and the airport) will suit them just fine. Very wide without being agressively long, it allows beginners and experts alike to spend a great day on a pleasant site. To score well, though, you will need to play the full panoply of shots, decide upon and stick to an effective game strategy and putt your best, because while the greens are reasonably contoured, certain pin positions can be dangerous when the approach shot strays off target. Slightly tidier green-keeping, especially for the rough and around the tee-boxes, could only enhance the pleasure of playing here.

Golf Olivar de la Hinojosa — 1996

Avenida de Dublin, Campo de Las Naciones
E - 28042 MADRID

Office	Secretaria	(34) 917 - 211 889
Pro shop	Pro-shop	(34) 917 - 211 889
Fax	Fax	(34) 917 - 210 661
Situation	Situación	

Madrid (pop. 3 084 673), 12 km

Annual closure	Cierre anual	no
Weekly closure	Cierre semanal	no

Fees main season
Precios tempor. alta 18 holes

	Week days Semana	We/Bank holidays Fin de sem./fiestas
Individual Individual	5 800 Pts	5 800 Pts
Couple Pareja	11 600 Pts	11 600 Pts

Caddy	Caddy	no
Electric Trolley	Carro eléctrico	800 Pts/18 holes
Buggy	Coche	4 000 Pts/18 holes
Clubs	Palos	1 200 Pts/18 holes

Credit cards Tarjetas de crédito VISA - AMEX - DC - 4 B

Access Acceso : Madrid → Aeropuerto → Ifema
Map 3 on page 1100 Plano 3 Página 1100

GOLF COURSE
RECORRIDO

13/20

Site	Emplazamiento	
Maintenance	Mantenimiento	
Architect	Arquitecto	José Rivero
Type	Tipo	open country
Relief	Relieve	
Water in play	Agua	
Exp. to wind	Exp. al viento	
Trees in play	Arboles	

Scorecard Tarjeta	Chp. Campeonato	Mens Caballeros	Ladies Damas
Length Longitud	6163	6053	5183
Par	72	72	72

Advised golfing ability	0	12	24	36
Nivel de juego aconsejado				

Hcp required Handicap exigido 28 Men, 36 Ladies

CLUB HOUSE & AMENITIES
CLUB HOUSE Y DEPENDENCIAS

7/10

Pro shop	Pro-shop	
Driving range	Campo de prácticas	
Sheltered	cubierto	21 mats
On grass	sobre hierba	yes
Putting-green	putting-green	yes
Pitching-green	pitching-green	yes

HOTEL FACILITIES
HOTELES CERCANOS

8/10

HOTELS HOTELES

Novotel-Campo de las Naciones — 600 m
246 rooms, D 19 300 Pts
Tel (34) 917 - 211 818, Fax (34) 917 - 211 122

Sofitel — 100 m
179 rooms, D 39 000 Pts
Tel (34) 917 - 210 070, Fax (34) 917 - 210 515

Melia Castilla - 900 rooms, D 34 000 Pts — Madrid
Tel (34) 915 - 675 000, Fax (34) 915 - 675 051 — 12 km

Aristos - 24 rooms, D 19 000 Pts — Madrid
Tel (34) 91 - 345 04 50, Fax (34) 91 - 345 10 23 — 12 km

RESTAURANTS RESTAURANTES

Zalacain - Tel (34) 915 - 614 840 — Madrid

Principe de Viana - Tel (34) 914 - 571 549 — Madrid

El Olivo - Tel (34) 913 - 591 535 — Madrid

1190

Dave Thomas no ha querido añadir demasiadas dificultades técnicas a un recorrido bastante físico por sus cuestas. Naturalmente, hay árboles en la línea de juego, también algunos obstáculos de agua y aunque los bunkers de green están alejados son poco visibles (están como hundidos) al igual que los bunkers de calle. Los greens tienen en general un declive bastante importante y pueden ser peligrosos cuando son rápidos. Todo ello hace que la estrategia de juego sea delicada cuando no se conoce el recorrido. Una vez conocido se pueden cortar los dog-legs con un buen drive, ya sea voleando los árboles o imprimiendo efecto a la bola. Agradable y variado merece la pena jugarlo varias veces, pero dada su situación en altura y en el interior, no se aconseja ir en invierno a no ser que se quiera contemplar el panorama de los Pirineos nevados desde la terraza del precioso club-house.

Dave Thomas did not want to add too many technical difficulties to an already hilly and physically quite demanding course. The trees are there, of course, together with a little water, but while the green-side bunkers are not too close to the greens, they are hard to see (they are sunk into dips). The same goes for the fairway bunkers. There is quite a lot of slope on the greens, which can be difficult when playing fast. All this makes for a tricky choice of game strategy when playing the course for the first time. When you know the course, long drivers can cut corners on the dog-legs either by hitting over the trees or by flighting the ball. Pleasant and varied, this pretty course is well worth a few visits, but the high-altitude location inland is not to be recommended in winter, except perhaps to gaze over the panorama of the snow-covered Pyrenees from the terrace of the very elegant club-house.

Club de Golf Osona Montanya 1989

Masia el Estanyol
E - 08553 EL BRULL (BARCELONA)

Office	Secretaria	(34) 938 - 840 170
Pro shop	Pro-shop	(34) 938 - 840 170
Fax	Fax	(34) 938 - 840 407
Situation	Situación	

Barcelona (pop. 1 754 900), 60 km
Vic / Vich (pop. 30 060), 17 km

Annual closure	Cierre anual	no
Weekly closure	Cierre semanal	no

Fees main season
Precios tempor. alta full day

	Week days Semana	We/Bank holidays Fin de sem./fiestas
Individual Individual	6 000 Pts	12 500 Pts
Couple Pareja	12 000 Pts	25 000 Pts

Caddy	Caddy	on request
Electric Trolley	Carro eléctrico	1 300 Pts/18 holes
Buggy	Coche	5 000 Pts/18 holes
Clubs	Palos	3 000 Pts/18 holes

Credit cards Tarjetas de crédito VISA - MasterCard

Access Acceso : Barcelona, N152 → Vic (Vich).
Tona → Seva, El Brull
Map 2 on page 1099 Plano 2 Página 1099

GOLF COURSE
RECORRIDO
14/20

Site	Emplazamiento	
Maintenance	Mantenimiento	
Architect	Arquitecto	David Thomas
Type	Tipo	forest, hilly
Relief	Relieve	
Water in play	Agua	
Exp. to wind	Exp. al viento	
Trees in play	Arboles	

Scorecard Tarjeta	Chp. Campeonato	Mens Caballeros	Ladies Damas
Length Longitud	6036	5810	5032
Par	72	72	72

Advised golfing ability	0	12	24	36
Nivel de juego aconsejado				

Hcp required   Handicap exigido 28 Men, 36 Ladies

CLUB HOUSE & AMENITIES
CLUB HOUSE Y DEPENDENCIAS
7/10

Pro shop	Pro-shop	
Driving range	Campo de prácticas	
Sheltered	cubierto	25 mats
On grass	sobre hierba	yes
Putting-green	putting-green	yes
Pitching-green	pitching-green	no

HOTEL FACILITIES
HOTELES CERCANOS
4/10

HOTELS HOTELES

El Montanya   Montanya
120 rooms, D 11 600 Pts   4 km
Tel (34) 938 - 840 606
Fax (34) 938 - 840 558

Ciutat de Vic   Vic
36 rooms, D 10 500 Pts   20 km
Tel (34) 938 - 892 551
Fax (34) 938 - 891 447

RESTAURANTS RESTAURANTES

Estanyol   Golf
Tel (34) 938 - 840 354

El Montanya   Montanya
Tel (34) 938 - 840 004

1191

PALS

Pals no ha usurpado su reputación. Su situación entre pinos, su tranquilidad, su moderado relieve (algunos greens en alto), la flexibilidad entre diferentes tees de salida, lo convierten en un recorrido atractivo para todos los niveles. Su terreno arenoso aguanta bien la lluvia y ofrece una confortable alfombra a los jugadores. Su diseño clásico (FW Hawtree) pone esencialmente en línea de juego árboles y bunkers que protegen los greens. El bosque no sólo es denso, lo que obliga a pegar un buen drive para evitarlo y buenos golpes para salir de él, sino que además la envergadura de los pinos, en forma de sombrilla, estrecha las calles y alguna que otra vez la bola queda encaramada en las ramas. El arquitecto ha revalorizado este terreno ideal para construir un golf conservando su aspecto natural. Los greens son fáciles de apreciar pero no muy grandes.

The reputation of Pals is rightfully deserved. This is firstly a very appealing course for all levels, laid out in the quiet of pinetrees, with mainly smooth unbroken terrain (only a few elevated greens) and the flexibility afforded by several different tees. The sandy terrain also soaks up any rain very quickly and provides a very comfortable carpet for players to play on. The classic design (F.W. Hawtree) basically brings bunkers into play to defend the greens, and uses trees. The forest is not only pretty thick - requiring good drives to keep out, and very good recovery shots to get out, of the woods - but the span of these parasol pines tends to make the fairways narrower, and the branches sometimes even keep the balls! The architect has successfully developed this ideal terrain for building a golf course while preserving its natural character. The greens are comparatively easy to read and not very large.

Club Golf de Pals — 1966

Carretera de Pals
E - 17256 PALS (GIRONA)

Office	Secretaria	(34) 972 - 636 006
Pro shop	Pro-shop	(34) 972 - 667 964
Fax	Fax	(34) 972 - 637 009
Situation	Situación	

Palafrugell (pop. 17 343), 12 km
Pals (pop. 1 675), 4 km

Annual closure	Cierre anual	no
Weekly closure	Cierre semanal	no

Fees main season
Precios tempor. alta 18 holes

	Week days Semana	We/Bank holidays Fin de sem./fiestas
Individual Individual	6 000 Pts	10 000 Pts
Couple Pareja	12 000 Pts	20 000 Pts

Caddy	Caddy	no
Electric Trolley	Carro eléctrico	no
Buggy	Coche	5 000 Pts/18 holes
Clubs	Palos	1 900 Pts/18 holes

Credit cards Tarjetas de crédito
VISA - Eurocard - MasterCard - AMEX

1192

Access Acceso : A7 Exit (Salida) 6 → Girona,
C255 → Palafrugell, GE650 → Pals.
Map 2 on page 1099 Plano 2 Página 1099

GOLF COURSE / RECORRIDO — 16/20

Site	Emplazamiento	
Maintenance	Mantenimiento	
Architect	Arquitecto	Frederic Hawtree
Type	Tipo	forest
Relief	Relieve	
Water in play	Agua	
Exp. to wind	Exp. al viento	
Trees in play	Arboles	

Scorecard Tarjeta	Chp. Campeonato	Mens Caballeros	Ladies Damas
Length Longitud	6222	5940	5081
Par	73	73	73

Advised golfing ability
Nivel de juego aconsejado   0 12 24 36

Hcp required   Handicap exigido 28 Men, 36 Ladies

CLUB HOUSE & AMENITIES / CLUB HOUSE Y DEPENDENCIAS — 7/10

Pro shop	Pro-shop	
Driving range	Campo de prácticas	
Sheltered	cubierto	12 mats
On grass	sobre hierba	yes
Putting-green	putting-green	yes
Pitching-green	pitching-green	yes

HOTEL FACILITIES / HOTELES CERCANOS — 6/10

HOTELS HOTELES

Mas de Torrent — Torrent
30 rooms, D 30 500 Pts — 6 km
Tel (34) 972 - 303 292, Fax (34) 972 - 303 293

Parador d'Aiguablava — Begur
87 rooms, D 20 500 Pts — 10 km
Tel (34) 972 - 622 162, Fax (34) 972 - 622 166

La Costa — Platja de Pals
120 rooms, D 25 200 Pts — 200 m
Tel (34) 972 - 667 740, Fax (34) 972 - 667 736

RESTAURANTS RESTAURANTES

Alfred — Pals
Tel (34) 972 - 636 274 — 5 km

La Xicra — Palafrugell
Tel (34) 972 - 305 630 — 12 km

Panorámica es un campo joven, situado en un espacio relativamente llano, cómodo y agradable para el amateur medio. La primera vuelta tienes tres pares 3 y tres pares 5, sin demasiadas complicaciones, capaces de animar a muchos jugadores a realizar una buena vuelta. Hay varios tees de salida en alto que invitan a pegar drives fáciles y, desde las marcas medias, el campo no es excesivamente largo. También hay varios greens en alto, sin visión para precisar el approach. El rough suele estar corado muy bajo y el estado general del mantenimiento del campo es excelente. Ello hace suponer que a este campo le favorecerá el paso del tiempo, por ejemplo, cuando crezcan los árboles que se han plantado y se asiente el entorno. En una zona de rica gastronomía mediterránea, pero sin tradición golfística, el campo todavía tiene una ocupación reducida. Con una casa-club confortable, sus servicios e instalaciones son típicos del campo de vacaciones.

Panoramica is still a young course over a relatively flat setting, enjoyable and playable by the average golfer. The outward nine include three par 3s and three par 5s without too many difficulties, and might prompt many of you to card a good score. All the tee-boxes are elevated, which will tempt a lot of players to use the driver, and from the forward tees the course is not too long. Likewise, the greens are more or less elevated so you don't always get a clear view of the approach you should be playing. The rough is not too long and overall green-keeping is of an excellent standard. This course will obviously improve with time, for example when the many young trees have grown to full maturity. In a region rich in Mediterranean gastronomy but not so well off for golf courses, Panoramica is not too busy just yet, although the comfortable clubhouse, facilities and services make this a typical vacation course.

Panoramica Golf & Country Club — 1995

Urbanización Panoramica
E - 12320 SAN JORGE (CASTELLON)

Office	Secretaria	(34) 964 - 493 072
Pro shop	Pro-shop	(34) 964 - 493 064
Fax	Fax	(34) 964 - 493 063
Situation	Situación	

Vinaròs (pop. 19 202), 15 km
Peñíscola (pop. 3 077), 25 km

Annual closure	Cierre anual	no

Weekly closure	Cierre semanal

no restaurant closed on mondays

Fees main season
Precios tempor. alta 18 holes

	Week days Semana	We/Bank holidays Fin de sem./fiestas
Individual Individual	5 500 Pts	8 000 Pts
Couple Pareja	11 000 Pts	16 000 Pts
Caddy Caddy	no	
Electric Trolley Carro eléctrico	1 200 Pts/18 holes	
Buggy Coche	4 000 Pts/18 holes	
Clubs Palos	1 500 Pts/18 holes	

Credit cards Tarjetas de crédito
VISA - Eurocard - MasterCard

Access Acceso : A7 Barcelona-Valencia,
Exit (Salida) 42 → Vinaròs. 1 km. → Sant Raphaël
on the right. 6 km on the left, → Golf
Map 4 on page 1103 Plano 4 Página 1103

GOLF COURSE RECORRIDO — 14/20

Site	Emplazamiento	
Maintenance	Mantenimiento	
Architect	Arquitecto	Bernhard Langer
Type	Tipo	country, forest, residential
Relief	Relieve	
Water in play	Agua	
Exp. to wind	Exp. al viento	
Trees in play	Arboles	

Scorecard Tarjeta	Chp. Campeonato	Mens Caballeros	Ladies Damas
Length Longitud	6429	6037	5001
Par	72	72	72

Advised golfing ability Nivel de juego aconsejado	0	12	24	36

Hcp required	Handicap exigido	28 Men, 36 Ladies

CLUB HOUSE & AMENITIES CLUB HOUSE Y DEPENDENCIAS — 6/10

Pro shop	Pro-shop	
Driving range	Campo de prácticas	
Sheltered	cubierto	no
On grass	sobre hierba	yes
Putting-green	putting-green	yes
Pitching-green	pitching-green	yes

HOTEL FACILITIES HOTELES CERCANOS — 4/10

HOTELS HOTELES
Parador — Benicarló
108 rooms, D 15 200 Pts — 20 km
Tel (34) 964 - 470 100
Fax (34) 964 - 470 934

Hosteria del Mar — Peñíscola
85 rooms, D 16 200 Pts. — 29 km
Tel (34) 964 - 480 600
Fax (34) 964 - 481 363

RESTAURANTS RESTAURANTES
El Langostino de Oro — Vinaròs
Tel (34) 964 - 451 204 — 15 km

El Faro — Vinaròs
Tel (34) 964 - 456 362 — 15 km

1193

En éste marco incomparable, con unas vistas magníficas, Severiano Ballesteros hizo su aprendizaje. Y cuando recorremos éste trazado muy británico (con todas las astucias estratégicas de su diseñador Harry Colt), cuando debemos negociar con los árboles, y muchas veces salirnos de ellos, entendemos que el campeón español haya acumulado todos los recursos para salirse de las situaciones más difíciles. Aquí hace falta pegar recto (lo que no es precisamente su fuerte). Bastante accidentado, con roughs a menudo muy densos, el campo tiene algunos greenes ciegos lo que complica todavía más sus aspectos técnicos que compensan ampliamente su falta de longitud. Sin embargo el jugador medio que sepa jugar recto se las arreglará muy bien, sobre todo en match-play, ya que es un campo perfecto para asumir riesgos. En cuanto a los mejores, deberán aplacar sus ansias y adaptar su técnica a la situación.

This impressive site, with some magnificent views, is where Severiano Ballesteros learnt his trade. When you play this classical layout (with all the strategic tricks of architect Harry Colt) and as you cope with all the trees and sometimes struggle to find your way out of them, you realise that the Spanish champion learnt his amazing art of recovery in very tough conditions indeed. Here, you have to drive straight (that was never Seve's forte). Rather hilly, with some often thick rough, this highly-reputed course includes a few blind greens, which complicate a still further the technical aspects of playing here and easily make up for the lack of yardage. With this said, average and straight players should get by just fine, especially in match-play, because this is the ideal terrain for taking risks. As for the wunderkinds, they'll just have to keep a check on their adrenaline flow and adjust their technique to matters at hand.

Real Golf de Pedreña

Apartado, 233
E - 39 080 SANTANDER

Office	Secretaria	(34) 942 - 500 001
Pro shop	Pro-shop	(34) 942 - 500 001
Fax	Fax	(34) 942 - 500 421
Situation	Situación	

Santander (pop. 196 218), 24 km

Annual closure	Cierre anual	no
Weekly closure	Cierre semanal	no

Fees main season
Precios tempor. alta 18 holes

	Week days Semana	We/Bank holidays Fin de sem./fiestas
Individual Individual	10 000 Pts	*
Couple Pareja	20 000 Pts	*

* Week ends: member's guests only (solo invitados de socios)

Caddy	Caddy	3 500 Pts/18 holes
Electric Trolley	Carro eléctrico	1 000 Pts/18 holes
Buggy	Coche	5 000 Pts/18 holes
Clubs	Palos	1 500 Pts/18 holes

Credit cards Tarjetas de crédito — no

1194

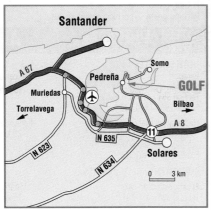

Santander

A 67
Pedreña
Muriedas
Torrelavega
Somo
GOLF
Bilbao
A 8
N 635
N 623
N 634
Solares
11

0   3 km

Access Acceso : Bilbao, N 634, N 635 → Santander.
Map 1 on page 1096 Plano 1 Página 1096

GOLF COURSE
RECORRIDO

14/20

Site	Emplazamiento	
Maintenance	Mantenimiento	
Architect	Arquitecto	Harry S. Colt
Type	Tipo	seaside course, forest
Relief	Relieve	
Water in play	Agua	
Exp. to wind	Exp. al viento	
Trees in play	Arboles	

Scorecard Tarjeta	Chp. Campeonato	Mens Caballeros	Ladies Damas
Length Longitud	5764	5511	4764
Par	70	70	70

Advised golfing ability	0	12	24	36
Nivel de juego aconsejado				

Hcp required Handicap exigido 28 Men, 36 Ladies

CLUB HOUSE & AMENITIES
CLUB HOUSE Y DEPENDENCIAS

6/10

Pro shop	Pro-shop	
Driving range	Campo de prácticas	
Sheltered	cubierto	5 mats
On grass	sobre hierba	yes
Putting-green	putting-green	yes
Pitching-green	pitching-green	no

HOTEL FACILITIES
HOTELES CERCANOS

5/10

HOTELS HOTELES

Real - 123 rooms, D 22 800 Pts Tel (34) 942 - 272 550, Fax (34) 942 - 274 573		Santander 24 km
NH Ciudad de Santander 60 rooms, D 19 400 Pts Tel (34) 942 - 227 965, Fax (34) 942 - 217 303		Santander 24 km
Sardinero 108 rooms, D 18 400 Pts Tel (34) 942 - 271 100, Fax (34) 942 - 271 698		Santander 24 km

RESTAURANTS RESTAURANTES

La Sardina Tel (34) 942 - 271 035		Santander 24 km
Mesón Segoviano Tel (34) 942 - 311 010		Santander 24 km
Rhin - Tel (34) 942 - 273 034		Santander 24 km

Un recorrido táctico. En primer lugar hay que sobrepasar los bunkers, saber evitarlos o quedarse corto: en cada par 4, un bunker de calle acoge las caídas de drive entre 190 y 240 metros desde las salidas de atrás. Después y en cinco hoyos hay que decidir si se puede sobrepasar un río situado a unos treinta metros antes del green. Pero estas dificultades no menguan la franqueza de un recorrido en el que algunos dog-legs y varios fuera de límites ayudan a mantener la concentración. Poniendo empeño se puede jugar su handicap. En todo caso, es un recorrido agradable para jugar en familia dejando que cada uno escoja el tee de salida que más le convenga. Al igual que las calles y los greens (hay 8 con doble escalón), los roughs son densos, sembrados de olivos y es de desear que el proyecto de construcción de casas se lleve a cabo en los espacios vacíos entre algunos hoyos.

This is a tactical course. First of all you have to avoid the sand by either carrying the bunkers or laying up short. Because on each par 4, a fairway bunker lurks close to the drive landing zone, from 190 to 240 metres from the back-tees. Then, on five holes you have to decide whether to carry a widish river located about thirty metres in front of the greens. But these difficulties take absolutely nothing away from the course's openness, where a few gentle dog-legs and out-of-bounds help keep players focused. With a little concentration, you might even play to your handicap at Peralada. But at all events, this is a pleasant course for all the family where everyone can choose the tees that suit them best. Like the fairways and the greens (8 of which have two tiers), the thick rough is dotted with olive trees. Hopefully, the villas under development in the open spaces between certain holes will soon be finished.

Peralada Golf Club — 1993

Paraje la Garriga
E - 17491 PERALADA (GIRONA)

Office	Secretaria	(34) 972 - 538 287
Pro shop	Pro-shop	(34) 972 - 538 287
Fax	Fax	(34) 972 - 538 236
Situation	Situación	

Figueras (pop. 35 301), 6 km

Annual closure	Cierre anual	no
Weekly closure	Cierre semanal	no

Fees main season	Precios tempor. alta		18 holes
		Week days Semana	**We/Bank holidays** Fin de sem./fiestas
Individual Individual		6 000 Pts	8 000 Pts
Couple Pareja		12 000 Pts	16 000 Pts

Caddy	Caddy	no
Electric Trolley	Carro eléctrico	no
Buggy	Coche	5 000 Pts/18 holes
Clubs	Palos	2 500 Pts/18 holes

Credit cards Tarjetas de crédito
VISA - Eurocard - MasterCard - AMEX

Access Acceso : A7 Perpignan-Barcelona,
Exit (Salida) 4, N260 → Llança y Portbou,
Golf on the left → Peralada
Map 2 on page 1099 Plano 2 Página 1099

GOLF COURSE
RECORRIDO — 16/20

Site	Emplazamiento	
Maintenance	Mantenimiento	
Architect	Arquitecto	Jorge Soler
Type	Tipo	open country
Relief	Relieve	
Water in play	Agua	
Exp. to wind	Exp. al viento	
Trees in play	Arboles	

Scorecard Tarjeta	Chp. Campeonato	Mens Caballeros	Ladies Damas
Length Longitud	6128	5886	4947
Par	72	72	72

Advised golfing ability Nivel de juego aconsejado	0	12	24	36

Hcp required Handicap exigido 28 Men, 36 Ladies

CLUB HOUSE & AMENITIES
CLUB HOUSE Y DEPENDENCIAS — 6/10

Pro shop	Pro-shop	
Driving range	Campo de prácticas	
Sheltered	cubierto	no
On grass	sobre hierba	yes
Putting-green	putting-green	yes
Pitching-green	pitching-green	yes

HOTEL FACILITIES
HOTELES CERCANOS — 5/10

HOTELS HOTELES

Terraza	Roses
98 rooms, D 19 400 Pts	15 km
Tel (34) 972 - 256 154, Fax (34) 972 - 256 866	

Bon Retorn	Figueras
50 rooms, D 10 400 Pts	6 km
Tel (34) 972 - 504 623, Fax (34) 972 - 673 979	

Vista Bella	Roses
35 rooms, D 26 300 Pts	18 km
Tel (34) 972 - 256 200, Fax (34) 942 - 253 213	

RESTAURANTS RESTAURANTES

Mas Pau	Figueras
Tel (34) 972 - 546 154	6 km

La Llar	Roses
Tel (34) 972 - 255 368	15 km

1195

La apertura en junio de 1999 del golf de Caldes de Malavella, pocos kilómetros al sur de Girona y dentro de la zona de influencia turística de la Costa Brava, enriquece sobremanera la oferta de buen golf en el noreste de España. El recorrido es bello, bueno y exigente, con excelentes vistas que llegan hasta los Pirineos. Las calles son anchas y onduladas, abiertas en un frondoso bosque de pinos y alcornoques, pero el raf es implacable, y los dos grandes lagos, entre el 3 y el 5 y entre el 11 y el 13, añaden dimensión y vistas escénicas al campo. Los greenes, muy defendidos tanto por la distancia como por bunkers, agua y accidentes del terreno, tienen unas dimensiones espléndidas y gran movimiento para el disfrute del buen pateador. Los desniveles y las distancias de green a tee demandan una buena preparación física del jugador que, sin duda, verá gratamente compensado su esfuerzo ante la inteligencia del diseño que premia el buen golpe, la buena calidad de la construcción y el estado de este soberbio recorrido.

The opening of this course close to Girona at the heart of the Costa Brava has enhanced the bunch of great courses in this part of Spain. This one is at once good, beautiful and demanding, with some wonderful views over the Pyrenees. The fairways are wide and rolling, laid out in a forest with pine and cork-oak trees, but the rough is uncompromising and the two large lakes placed between the 3rd and 5th and the 11th and 13th holes add a scenic dimension to the whole layout. The greens, difficult to reach through sheer length and tightly guarded by sand-traps, water and sloping terrain, provide added interest for good putters. The hilly terrain and distance between green and tee-box are best suited to the physically fit golfer who, in return, will be rewarded for his or her effort by the intelligence of a layout which helps the best shots, and by the excellence that has gone into the building and maintaining of this very fine course.

PGA Golf de Catalunya — 1999

Carretera II, Km 701
E - 17455 CALDES DE MALAVELLA

Office	Secretaria	(34) 972 - 472 577
Pro shop	Pro-shop	(34) 972 - 472 577
Fax	Fax	(34) 972 - 470 493
Situation	Situación	

Girona (pop. 71 000), 13 km N

Annual closure	Cierre anual	no
Weekly closure	Cierre semanal	no

Fees main season
Precios tempor. alta 18 holes

	Week days Semana	We/Bank holidays Fin de sem./fiestas
Individual Individual	6 500 Pts	9 000 Pts
Couple Pareja	13 000 Pts	18 000 Pts

Caddy	Caddy	no
Electric Trolley	Carro eléctrico	1 200 Pts/18 holes
Buggy	Coche	5 000 Pts/18 holes
Clubs	Palos	2 000 Pts/18 holes

Credit cards Tarjetas de crédito
VISA - Eurocard - MasterCard - AMEX

Access Acceso : Barcelona, A2 Exit (salida) 9.
N2 → Girona. Golf after Km 701 point.
Map 2 on page 1099 Plano 2 Página 1099

1196

GOLF COURSE
RECORRIDO — 18/20

Site	Emplazamiento	
Maintenance	Mantenimiento	
Architect	Arquitecto	Neil Coles
		Angel Gallardo
Type	Tipo	parkland, forest
Relief	Relieve	
Water in play	Agua	
Exp. to wind	Exp. al viento	
Trees in play	Arboles	

Scorecard Tarjeta	Chp. Campeonato	Mens Caballeros	Ladies Damas
Length Longitud	6588	6226	5310
Par	72	72	72

Advised golfing ability		0	12	24	36
Nivel de juego aconsejado					

Hcp required — Handicap exigido — 28 Men, 36 Ladies

CLUB HOUSE & AMENITIES
CLUB HOUSE Y DEPENDENCIAS — 7/10

Pro shop	Pro-shop	
Driving range	Campo de prácticas	
Sheltered	cubierto	no
On grass	sobre hierba	yes (100 places)
Putting-green	putting-green	yes
Pitching-green	pitching-green	yes

HOTEL FACILITIES
HOTELES CERCANOS — 7/10

HOTELS HOTELES

Balneario Vichy Catalan — Caldes de Malavella
82 rooms, D 17 000 Pts — 5 km
Tel (34) 972 - 47 00 00, Fax (34) 972 - 47 22 99

Carlemany — Girona
87 rooms, D 14 500 Pts. — 13 km
Tel (34) 972 - 211 212, Fax (34) 972 - 214 994

La Gavina - 74 rooms, D 27 500 Pts — S'Agaró
Tel (34) 972 - 32 11 00, Fax (34) 972 - 32 15 73 — 28 km

RESTAURANTS RESTAURANTES

Can Geli — Caldes de Malavella 1 km
Tel (34) 972 - 470 275

Hostal de la Granota — Vidreras 6 km
Tel(34) 972 - 853 044

Cal Ros - Tel (34) 972 - 217 379 — Girona 14 km

Se trata de un recorrido con todas las características de un Country Club, con actividades sociales y deportivas variadas (tenis, piscina, paddle) al lado de Sevilla, lo que le asegura una fuerte frecuentación. Esencialmente son los invitados de los socios quienes pueden jugar. Creado en 1939, el recorrido sólo tenía 9 hoyos, y ha habido que esperar hasta 1992 para verlo convertido en un 18 hoyos con una longitud respetable. Su estética es la de un verdadero parque con abundante vegetación, cosa bella y apreciable sobre todo en los veranos calurosos. Los hoyos están bien estructurados y el ritmo de juego es excelente. Hay que ser muy precisos en los segundos golpes ya que los greens no son muy grandes. En realidad es un recorridos muy formador que ha facilitado excelentes jugadores a los equipos nacionales españoles.

Pineda is part of a real country-club concept with a wide variety of social and sporting activities (tennis, swimming-pool, paddle-tennis) at the gates of Seville. This makes it a busy course and explains why the majority of visitors are member guests. Created in 1939, Pineda originally had only 9 holes and was extended to 18 holes and a very respectable yardage only in 1992. This is a park-style course with lush vegetation which most will find pretty welcome, particularly on hot summer afternoons. The holes are neatly proportioned and the layout well-balanced, but your approach shots must be accurate to hit the smallish greens. This is in fact a very instructive course, as it has provided many excellent players who have go on to play in the Spanish national teams.

Real Golf Club Pineda de Sevilla — 1939

Apartado 1049
E - 41080 SEVILLA

Office	Secretaria	(34) 954 - 611 400
Pro shop	Pro-shop	(34) 954 - 611 400
Fax	Fax	(34) 954 - 617 704
Situation	Situación	

Sevilla (pop. 70 4857), 3 km

Annual closure	Cierre anual	no
Weekly closure	Cierre semanal	no

Fees main season
Precios tempor. alta 18 holes

	Week days Semana	We/Bank holidays Fin de sem./fiestas
Individual Individual	8 500 Pts	8 500 Pts
Couple Pareja	17 000 Pts	17 000 Pts

Only with members (solo con socios)

Caddy	Caddy	no
Electric Trolley	Carro eléctrico	1 500 Pts/18 holes
Buggy	Coche	no
Clubs	Palos	2 500 Pts/18 holes

Credit cards Tarjetas de crédito — no

SEVILLA

GOLF

Av. de la Paz
Av. de Jerez
Hipódromo
SE 401
Utrera
SE 30
Cádiz
0 — 1 km

Access Acceso : CN IV Sevilla → Cadiz, in El Cortijo de Pineda
Map 7 on page 1109 Plano 7 Página 1109

GOLF COURSE / RECORRIDO — 15/20

Site	Emplazamiento	
Maintenance	Mantenimiento	
Architect	Arquitecto	R.& F. M. Benjumea Luis Recasens
Type	Tipo	parkland
Relief	Relieve	
Water in play	Agua	
Exp. to wind	Exp. al viento	
Trees in play	Arboles	

Scorecard Tarjeta	Chp. Campeonato	Mens Caballeros	Ladies Damas
Length Longitud	6147	6037	5077
Par	72	72	72

Advised golfing ability
Nivel de juego aconsejado — 0   12   24   36

Hcp required Handicap exigido — 28 Men, 36 Ladies

CLUB HOUSE & AMENITIES / CLUB HOUSE Y DEPENDENCIAS — 7/10

Pro shop	Pro-shop	
Driving range	Campo de prácticas	
Sheltered	cubierto	10 mats
On grass	sobre hierba	yes
Putting-green	putting-green	yes
Pitching-green	pitching-green	yes

HOTEL FACILITIES / HOTELES CERCANOS — 9/10

HOTELS HOTELES

Principe de Asturias — Sevilla 4 km
288 rooms, D 33 600 Pts
Tel (34) 954 - 462 222, Fax (34) 954 - 460 428

Alfonso XIII — Sevilla 3 km
124 rooms, D 52 500 Pts
Tel (34) 954 - 222 850, Fax (34) 954 - 216 033

Al-Andalus Palace — Sevilla 3 km
327 rooms, D 17 300 Pts
Tel (34) 954 - 230 600, Fax (34) 954 - 230 200

RESTAURANTS RESTAURANTES

La Dorada — Sevilla 4 km
Tel (34) 954 - 921 066

La Albahaca - Tel (34) 954 - 220 714 — Sevilla 4 km

El Espigon - Tel (34) 954 - 626 851 — Sevilla 4 km

1197

Con obstáculos de agua en la línea de juego en 12 hoyos, es un recorrido que no se aborda con tranquilidad, al menos por los golfistas poco acostumbrados a esta caraterística esencial de los golfs «modernos». Con el mar al lado, manifiestan en cierto modo la importancia que tiene el agua en el sur de Europa. La vegetación de pinos, acacias y palmeras adornan un paisaje bastante llano en el que se puede jugar sin necesidad de alquilar un coche. Sin embargo es necesario ser largo y preciso ya que los pares 4 de esta recorrido, diseñado por Gallardo y Aliss, son bastante difíciles desde los tees de salida de atrás (más aún con viento). Con los tees más adelantados se convierte en más humano y divertido para jugar en match-play. Si bien es verdad que los greens son pequeños, en pendiente y bien protegidos, en realidad no es un recorrido tan difícil como parece.

With water hazards on 12 holes, this is not one of the most reassuring layouts in the world, at least for golfers who are unused to this key component of "modern" courses. In their own way, they and the neighbouring sea seem to emphasise the importance of water in southern European society. Pine, acacia and palm trees add an element of landscaping to a course where there is virtually no relief and which is easy to walk. It does nonetheless demand length and precision play, as a number of long par 4s make this Gallardo and Alliss layout a tough proposition from the back tees (especially when the wind blows). Teeing off further foward makes the course more playable and more fun, and even though the smallish and often sloping greens are well-defended, it is easier to play than it looks.

Club de Golf Playa Serena 1979

Urbanización Playa Serena S/N
E - 04740 ROQUETAS DE MAR (ALMERIA)

Office	Secretaria	(34) 950 - 333 055
Pro shop	Pro-shop	(34) 950 - 333 055
Fax	Fax	(34) 950 - 333 055
Situation	Situación	

Roquetas de Mar (pop. 32 361), 1 km
Almería (pop. 159 587), 18 km

Annual closure	Cierre anual	no
Weekly closure	Cierre semanal	no

Fees main season
Precios tempor. alta 18 holes

	Week days Semana	We/Bank holidays Fin de sem./fiestas
Individual Individual	8 000 Pts	8 000 Pts
Couple Pareja	16 000 Pts	16 000 Pts

Caddy	Caddy	no
Electric Trolley	Carro eléctrico	1 500 Pts/18 holes
Buggy	Coche	3 500 Pts/18 holes
Clubs	Palos	1 500 Pts/18 holes

Credit cards Tarjetas de crédito
VISA - Eurocard - MasterCard

1198

← El Ejido
N 340
Almería →
Roquetas de Mar
Playa Serena
GOLF
← Almerimar
Salinas
Playa de Cerrillos
0   2   4 km

Access Acceso : Almería N340, → Roquetas de Mar
Map 8 on page 1111 Plano 8 Página 1111

GOLF COURSE
RECORRIDO 13/20

Site	Emplazamiento	
Maintenance	Mantenimiento	
Architect	Arquitecto	A. Gallardo, Alliss
Type	Tipo	seaside course
Relief	Relieve	
Water in play	Agua	
Exp. to wind	Exp. al viento	
Trees in play	Arboles	

Scorecard Tarjeta	Chp. Campeonato	Mens Caballeros	Ladies Damas
Length Longitud	6301	6070	5174
Par	72	72	72

Advised golfing ability | | 0 | 12 | 24 | 36
Nivel de juego aconsejado

Hcp required	Handicap exigido	no

CLUB HOUSE & AMENITIES
CLUB HOUSE Y DEPENDENCIAS 6/10

Pro shop	Pro-shop	
Driving range	Campo de prácticas	
Sheltered	cubierto	no
On grass	sobre hierba	yes
Putting-green	putting-green	yes
Pitching-green	pitching-green	yes

HOTEL FACILITIES
HOTELES CERCANOS 4/10

HOTELS HOTELES
Playa Capricho   Roquetas
330 rooms, D 21 000 Pts   1 km
Tel (34) 950 - 333 100, Fax (34) 950 - 333 806

Playa Linda   Roquetas
129 rooms, D 18 900 Pts   1 km
Tel (34) 950 - 334 500, Fax (34) 950 - 334 110

Playa Azul - 211 rooms, D 11 600 Pts   Roquetas
Tel (34) 950 - 333 311, Fax (34) 950 - 333 311   1 km

Costa Sol - 55 rooms, D 10 000 Pts.   Almería
Tel (34) 950 - 23 40 11, Fax (34) 950 - 23 40 11   20 km

RESTAURANTS RESTAURANTES
Al-Baida - Tel (34) 950 - 333 821   Roquetas de Mar
La Colmena - Tel (34) 950 - 333 565   Roquetas de Mar
Il Teatro - Tel (34) 950 - 333 710   Playa Serena 2 km

Este recorrido, diseñado por Tom Simpson en 1904, ha sido remodelado en los años 70. Ofrece un aspecto de colinas y bosque con constantes desniveles en harmonía con la naturaleza del terreno. Los greens tienen una superficie de tipo medio, son de muy buena calidad y particularmente rápidos. Es un recorrido de competición muy bueno, no excesivamente ancho, lo que requiere una gran precisión de juego para obtener un buen resultado por parte de los jugadores scratch. Sin embargo, los de handicap de tipo medio tienen siempre la posibilidad de jugar la seguridad en casi todos los hoyos. No hay obstáculos de agua ni otras dificultades que requieran golpes particularmente delicados para hacer el par o el bogey. Este club prestigioso - en el que se entra sólo con invitacion - tiene un segundo recorridos de 18 hoyos, basado en un diseño muy americano de Robert Trent Jones, con numerosos obstáculos de agua.

Designed in 1904 by Tom Simpson, this course was remodelled in the 1970s. The skyline is one of hills and woods with constantly sloping landscape embracing the natural terrain. The greens are generally average in size, of excellent standard, fast and slick. A very good tournament course which is not over-wide, Puerta de Hierro calls for extreme accuracy if you want to card a good score. But even mid-handicappers will not find this too troublesome because you can always play safe on every hole. There are no water hazards, either, or other difficulties that force you to shape those delicate shots to make par or scrape a bogey. This prestigious club - you'll need to be invited to play here - also boasts a second 18-hole course rebuilt over a very American layout by Robert Trent Jones with an array of water hazards, re-opened in 1998.

Real Club de la Puerta de Hierro — 1904

Avda de Miraflores S/N
E - 28035 MADRID

Office	Secretaria	(34) 913 - 161 745
Pro shop	Pro-shop	(34) 913 - 161 745
Fax	Fax	(34) 913 - 738 111
Situation	Situación	

Madrid (pop. 3 084 673), 4 km

Annual closure	Cierre anual	no
Weekly closure	Cierre semanal	no

Fees main season
Precios tempor. alta recorrido

	Week days Semana	We/Bank holidays Fin de sem./fiestas
Individual Individual	*	*
Couple Pareja	*	*

With members only (solo con socios)

Caddy	Caddy	yes
Electric Trolley	Carro eléctrico	yes
Buggy	Coche	yes
Clubs	Palos	yes

Credit cards Tarjetas de crédito — no

El Escorial Hipódromo
N VI
Sinesio Delgado
N 500
Av P. de Hierro
Carretera de Castilla
GOLF
0 1 2 km
MADRID
Casa de Campo
Museo del Prado
Plaza Mayor
Parquê Badajoz
Zoológico
N V

Access Acceso : Next to the Ciudad Universitaria, besides the Urbanización Puerta de Hierro
Map 3 on page 1100 Plano 3 Página 1100

GOLF COURSE / RECORRIDO — 16/20

Site	Emplazamiento	
Maintenance	Mantenimiento	
Architect	Arquitecto	Tom Simpson John Harris
Type	Tipo	parkland
Relief	Relieve	
Water in play	Agua	
Exp. to wind	Exp. al viento	
Trees in play	Arboles	

Scorecard Tarjeta	Chp. Campeonato	Mens Caballeros	Ladies Damas
Length Longitud	6347	5914	4962
Par	72	72	72

Advised golfing ability — 0 12 24 36
Nivel de juego aconsejado
Hcp required Handicap exigido 28 Men, 36 Ladies

CLUB HOUSE & AMENITIES / CLUB HOUSE Y DEPENDENCIAS — 8/10

Pro shop	Pro-shop	
Driving range	Campo de prácticas	
Sheltered	cubierto	25 mats
On grass	sobre hierba	yes
Putting-green	putting-green	yes
Pitching-green	pitching-green	yes

HOTEL FACILITIES / HOTELES CERCANOS — 9/10

HOTELS HOTELES

Santo Mauro — Madrid
33 rooms, D 35 000 Pts — 4 km
Tel (34) 91 - 319 69 00, Fax (34) 91 - 308 54 77

Melia Castilla — Madrid
900 rooms, D 34 000 Pts — 4 km
Tel (34) 915 - 675 000, Fax (34) 915 - 675 051

NH La Habana — Madrid
157 rooms, D 18 000 Pts — 4 km
Tel (34) 91 - 345 82 84, Fax (34) 91 - 457 75 79

RESTAURANTS RESTAURANTES

Teatro Real - Tel (34) 915 - 160 670 — Madrid 4 km
La Trainera - Tel (34) 915 - 760 575 — Madrid 4 km
Zalacain - Tel (34) 915 - 614 840 — Madrid 4 km

1199

Las nuevas vías rápidas de la periferia de Madrid afectaron al viejo campo «de debajo» de Puerta de Hierro que nunca había conseguido hacerse famoso. Robert Trent Jones hijo recibió el encargo de recomponer estos otros 18 hoyos que el club necesita para sus dos mil jugadores activos y el resultado es un recorrido de considerable dificultad e innegable belleza. Encinas, pinos y monte bajo componen el marco de unas calles anchas que suben y bajan siguiendo el relieve del terreno. En la mayoría de los hoyos es preciso pegar largo y colocar el golpe de salida en el lugar preciso para poder atacar unos greenes amplísimos, bien defendidos por enormes bunkers, con acentuados movimientos y plataformas que obligan a medir muy bien los pats. Por todo ello hay que considerarlo un magnífico test para la más alta competición e incluso un campo muy interesante para jugarlo desde los tees alternativos.

The new expressways around the city of Madrid have had their effect on the old «lower» course of Puerta de Hierro, which has lost quite a bit of its fame and appeal. Robert Trent Jones Jnr. was assigned with redesigning the 18 holes of the second course that the club needed for its 2,000 active members. The result is this extremely difficult but very beautiful course, where oak-trees, pines and little mounds line fairways, which hug the natural contours of the terrain. On most of the holes you need to be long and place your shot with considerable precision in order to attack the huge greens. These are well guarded by vast sand-traps, are sharply contoured and sometimes multi-tiered to make putting a trickier business than usual. Nonetheless, Puerta de Hierro 2 is a magnificent test for the highest level tournaments and also a very interesting course for the lesser player hitting it from the front tees.

Real Club de la Puerta de Hierro   1998
Avda de Miraflores S/N
E - 28035 MADRID

Office	Secretaria	(34) 913 - 161 745
Pro shop	Pro-shop	(34) 913 - 161 745
Fax	Fax	(34) 913 - 738 111
Situation	Situación	

Madrid (pop. 3 084 673), 4 km

Annual closure	Cierre anual	no
Weekly closure	Cierre semanal	no

Fees main season
Precios tempor. alta 18 holes

	Week days Semana	We/Bank holidays Fin de sem./fiestas
Individual Individual	*	*
Couple Pareja	*	*

* With members only (solo con socios)

Caddy	Caddy	yes
Electric Trolley	Carro eléctrico	yes
Buggy	Coche	yes
Clubs	Palos	yes

Credit cards Tarjetas de crédito · no

1200

Access Acceso : Next to the Ciudad Universitaria, besides the Urbanización Puerta de Hierro
Map 3 on page 1100 Plano 3 Página 1100

GOLF COURSE
RECORRIDO   **18**/20

Site	Emplazamiento	
Maintenance	Mantenimiento	
Architect	Arquitecto	R. Trent Jones Jr
Type	Tipo	parkland
Relief	Relieve	
Water in play	Agua	
Exp. to wind	Exp. al viento	
Trees in play	Arboles	

Scorecard Tarjeta	Chp. Campeonato	Mens Caballeros	Ladies Damas
Length Longitud	0	0	0
Par	0	0	0

Advised golfing ability	0	12	24	36
Nivel de juego aconsejado				

Hcp required · Handicap exigido · 28 Men, 36 Ladies

CLUB HOUSE & AMENITIES
CLUB HOUSE Y DEPENDENCIAS   **8**/10

Pro shop	Pro-shop	
Driving range	Campo de prácticas	
Sheltered	cubierto	25 mats
On grass	sobre hierba	yes
Putting-green	putting-green	yes
Pitching-green	pitching-green	yes

HOTEL FACILITIES
HOTELES CERCANOS   **9**/10

HOTELS HOTELES
Santo Mauro   Madrid
33 rooms, D 35 000 Pts   4 km
Tel (34) 91 - 319 69 00, Fax (34) 91 - 308 54 77

Melia Castilla   Madrid
900 rooms, D 34 000 Pts   4 km
Tel (34) 915 - 675 000, Fax (34) 915 - 675 051

NH La Habana   Madrid
157 rooms, D 18 000 Pts   4 km
Tel (34) 91 - 345 82 84, Fax (34) 91 - 457 75 79

RESTAURANTS RESTAURANTES
Teatro Real - Tel (34) 915 - 160 670   Madrid 4 km
La Trainera   Madrid
Tel (34) 915 - 760 575   4 km
Zalacain - Tel (34) 915 - 614 840   Madrid 4 km

Inaugurado en 1.995, es un recorrido prometedor, con espacios ya bien tupidos a pesar de su corta existencia. Dado su relieve no es necesario alquilar un coche. Los greens, bastante en alto, hay que atacarlos elevando bien la bola. La anchura de las calles da sensación de espacio, cosa que agradará a los pegadores, pero no hay que fiarse ya que algunos obstáculos no son muy visibles. El arquitecto Francisco López Segales no ha pretendido realizar cosas espectaculares sino que ha mantenido la tradición británica con inteligencia y buen gusto. Y en todo caso ha logrado un recorrido que hay que seguir de cerca con interés, bien adaptado a los diferentes niveles de juego y bien integrado en un paisaje que ofrece magníficas vistas panorámicas sobre el mar y la montaña.

Opened in 1995, Pula is a promising course with an already well-grassed and pleasant playing surface, despite its early age. Only slightly hilly, the course is easy to walk, but elevated greens call for controlled high approach shots. The width of the fairways gives a pleasant sensation of open space, and will appeal to big-hitters, although they should watch out for a number of hazards that are not always clearly visible. Designer Francisco Lopes Segales has not attempted any sort of exploit in style and has followed a British tradition with intelligence and good taste. At all events, he has succeeded in creating a course whose development deserves to be watched closely. It is well suited to players of all abilities, fits in beautifully with the landscape and offers fine panoramas over the sea and mountains.

Pula Golf   1995
Ctra Son Servera - Capdepera km. 3
E - 07550 SON SERVERA (MALLORCA)

Office	Secretaria	(34) 971 - 567 481
Pro shop	Pro-shop	(34) 971 - 567 481
Fax	Fax	(34) 971 - 817 035
Situation	Situación	

Palma (pop. 308 616), 70 km

Annual closure	Cierre anual	no
Weekly closure	Cierre semanal	no

Fees main season
Precios tempor. alta 18 holes

	Week days Semana	We/Bank holidays Fin de sem./fiestas
Individual Individual	10 000 Pts	10 000 Pts
Couple Pareja	20 000 Pts	20 000 Pts

Caddy	Caddy	no
Electric Trolley	Carro eléctrico	no
Buggy	Coche	6 000 Pts/18 holes
Clubs	Palos	2 000 Pts/18 holes

Credit cards Tarjetas de crédito
VISA - Eurocard - MasterCard - AMEX - DC

Access Acceso : Palma C715 → Manacor, → Son
Servera, Pula Golf on left hand side → Capdepera
Map 9 on page 1112 Plano 9 Página 1112

GOLF COURSE
RECORRIDO   13/20

Site	Emplazamiento	▬▬▬▬▭
Maintenance	Mantenimiento	▬▬▬▬▬▭
Architect	Arquitecto	F.L. Segales
Type	Tipo	country
Relief	Relieve	▬▬▬▭▭
Water in play	Agua	▬▬▭▭▭
Exp. to wind	Exp. al viento	▬▬▬▭▭
Trees in play	Arboles	▬▬▬▭▭

Scorecard	Chp.	Mens	Ladies
Tarjeta	Campeonato	Caballeros	Damas
Length Longitud	6003	6003	5077
Par	71	71	71

Advised golfing ability		0 12 24 36
Nivel de juego aconsejado		▬▬▬▬▬
Hcp required	Handicap exigido	28 Men, 36 Ladies

CLUB HOUSE & AMENITIES
CLUB HOUSE Y DEPENDENCIAS   6/10

Pro shop	Pro-shop	▬▬▬▬▭
Driving range	Campo de prácticas	▬▬▬▭▭
Sheltered	cubierto	10 mats
On grass	sobre hierba	yes
Putting-green	putting-green	yes
Pitching-green	pitching-green	yes

HOTEL FACILITIES
HOTELES CERCANOS   5/10

HOTELS HOTELES
Eurotel Golf Punta Rotja   Son Servera
202 rooms, D 25 900 Pts.   4 km
Tel (34) 971 - 840 000, Fax (34) 971 - 840 115

Aguait   Cala Rajada
188 rooms, D 15 400 Pts.   10 km
Tel (34) 971 - 563 408, Fax (34) 971 - 565 106

Petit Hotel Cases de Pula   Golf
10 rooms, D 33 600 Pts
Tel (34) 971 - 567 492, Fax (34) 971 - 567 271

RESTAURANTS RESTAURANTES

S'Era de Pula   Son Servera
Tel (34) 971 - 567 940   7 km

Son Floriana   Son Servera
Tel (34) 971 - 586 075   10 km

1201

Construido en una pequeña colina, en un terreno muy típico de los alrededores de Madrid, este nuevo recorrido de la Real Sociedad Hípica Española de Club de Campo ofrece una gran variedad de distancias y tipo de hoyos gracias a sus múltiples tees de salida. Nos encontramos con el afán de variedad de Robert von Hagge y su diseño bien característico: roughs espesos, calles muy cuidadas en superficie, greens amplios con múltiples desniveles, constituyendo un recorrido destinado más bien a los buenos jugadores. Pero también los jugadores inteligentes y sagaces técnicos sabrán salvar un buen resultado si son diestros en el juego corto. La ambición del club es clara: organizar grandes competiciones internacionales. Cercano al circuito del Jarama, el golf añade un nuevo elemento a una región bien servida en golfs de calidad (Jarama R.A.C.E., La Moraleja).

Built on a little hill, typical of the type of terrain found around Madrid, the new course belonging to the Real Sociedad Hípica Española de Club de Campo offers an amazing combination of distances and types of hole thanks to the many different tee-boxes. This reflects the emphasis on variety which is the trademark of Robert von Hagge (who also designed Emporda). Other distinctive features are the thick rough, highly contoured fairways and huge, multi-tiered greens which generally tend to make this a course for good players. It is also intended for smart players and fine craftsmen who can save their card if their short game is on song. The club's ambition is clearly to host major international competitions. Close to the Jarama circuit, this layout is a new addition to a region already spoilt for excellent courses (Jarama R.A.C.E., La Moraleja).

Real Sociedad Hipica Española Club de Campo — 1997

Ctra de Burgos - Km 26,400
E - 28709 SAN SEBASTIAN DE LOS REYES

Office	Secretaria	(34) 916 - 571 018
Pro shop	Pro-shop	(34) 916 - 571 018
Fax	Fax	(34) 916 - 571 022
Situation	Situación	

Madrid (pop. 3 084 673), 26 km

Annual closure	Cierre anual	no
Weekly closure	Cierre semanal	no

Fees main season
Precios tempor. alta 18 holes

	Week days Semana	We/Bank holidays Fin de sem./fiestas
Individual Individual	20 000 Pts	20 000 Pts
Couple Pareja	40 000 Pts	40 000 Pts

With members only (solo con socios)

Caddy	Caddy	no
Electric Trolley	Carro eléctrico	600 Pts/18 holes
Buggy	Coche	3 500 Pts/18 holes
Clubs	Palos	3 000 Pts/18 holes

Credit cards Tarjetas de crédito — no

1202

Access Acceso : CN I - Km 26,400
Map 3 on page 1100 Plano 3 Página 1100

GOLF COURSE / RECORRIDO — 18/20

Site	Emplazamiento	
Maintenance	Mantenimiento	
Architect	Arquitecto	Robert von Hagge
Type	Tipo	forest, hilly
Relief	Relieve	
Water in play	Agua	
Exp. to wind	Exp. al viento	
Trees in play	Arboles	

Scorecard Tarjeta	Chp. Campeonato	Mens Caballeros	Ladies Damas
Length Longitud	6464	6071	5104
Par	72	72	72

Advised golfing ability — 0 12 24 36
Nivel de juego aconsejado

Hcp required — Handicap exigido — no

CLUB HOUSE & AMENITIES / CLUB HOUSE Y DEPENDENCIAS — 7/10

Pro shop	Pro-shop	
Driving range	Campo de prácticas	
Sheltered	cubierto	no
On grass	sobre hierba	yes
Putting-green	putting-green	yes
Pitching-green	pitching-green	yes

HOTEL FACILITIES / HOTELES CERCANOS — 6/10

HOTELS HOTELES

Princesa — Madrid 20 km
275 rooms, D 34 900 Pts
Tel (34) 915 - 422 100, Fax (34) 915 - 427 328

Melia Madrid — Madrid 20 km
276 rooms, D 27 800 Pts
Tel (34) 915 - 418 200, Fax (34) 915 - 411 988

Moncloa Garden — Madrid 20 km
121 rooms, D 17 300 Pts
Tel (34) 915 - 424 582, Fax (34) 915 - 427 169

RESTAURANTS RESTAURANTES

El Amparo - Tel (34) 914 - 316 456 — Madrid 10 km

Taberna de Alabardero — Madrid 10 km
Tel (34) 915 - 472 577

La Trainera - Tel (34) 915 - 760 575 — Madrid 10 km

SAN ROQUE

17	8	6

San Roque gustará incluso a los que no les gustan los golfs inmobiliarios. En primer lugar porque las casas y residencias que lo rodean son magníficas, y en segundo lugar porque están apartadas del recorrido. No es necesario alquilar un coche y está bien protegido por los árboles, excepto un tramo expuesto al viento, entre el 13 y el 15, que bordea la colina. Muy largo saliendo desde atrás y con una ida muy estrecha, es más «humano» con los tees de salida adelantados para los jugadores con un handicap superior a 10. Exige ser un jugador completo, con mucho «feeling» para negociar los aproches a greens con muchas caídas y que están perfectamente protegidos, así como una gran finura en el juego corto. Si a ésto añadimos la calidad de las instalaciones y de su mantenimiento, comprenderemos que Tony Jacklin y Dave Thomas han diseñado uno de los grandes recorridos de la Costa. Unico reproche: su dificultad para los jugadores con poca experiencia (difícil para jugar en familia).

Golfers who don't like property development courses will love San Roque. Firstly because the villas and residences are magnificent, secondly because the course is some distance from them. The terrain is easy for walking and well protected by trees, except the 13th and 15th holes, laid out on the side of a hill and exposed to the wind. Very long off the back-tees, compounded by tight fairways on the front nine, the course is more "human" when played from the front-tees for players with handicaps in double figures. It demands an all-round game and a lot of feeling to negotiate the approach shots to greens that are very undulating and perfectly well-defended. A well-honed short game is also in order. Add to these compliments the quality of upkeep and of the facilities and you will understand how Tony Jacklin and Dave Thomas have designed one of the coast's great courses... not really easy for inexperienced players!

San Roque — 1990

CN. 340 - Km 126,5
E - 11360 SAN ROQUE (CADIZ)

Office	Secretaria	(34) 956 - 613 030
Pro shop	Pro-shop	(34) 956 - 613 030
Fax	Fax	(34) 956 - 613 013
Situation	Situación	

Algeciras (pop. 101 556), 20 km
San Roque (pop. 23 092), 6 km

Annual closure	Cierre anual	no
Weekly closure	Cierre semanal	no

Fees main season
Precios tempor. alta 18 holes

	Week days Semana	We/Bank holidays Fin de sem./fiestas
Individual Individual	10 000 Pts	10 000 Pts
Couple Pareja	20 000 Pts	20 000 Pts

Caddy	Caddy	no
Electric Trolley	Carro eléctrico	no
Buggy	Coche	5 500 Pts/18 holes
Clubs	Palos	2 500 Pts/18 holes

Credit cards Tarjetas de crédito
VISA - MasterCard - AMEX - DC

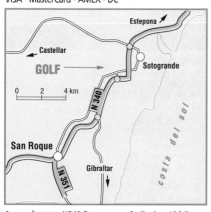

Access Acceso : N340 Estepona → Cadiz, km 126,5
turn right → Golf
Map 7 on page 1109 Plano 7 Página 1109

GOLF COURSE / RECORRIDO — 17/20

Site	Emplazamiento	
Maintenance	Mantenimiento	
Architect	Arquitecto	Dave Thomas Tony Jacklin
Type	Tipo	parkland, hilly
Relief	Relieve	
Water in play	Agua	
Exp. to wind	Exp. al viento	
Trees in play	Arboles	

Scorecard Tarjeta	Chp. Campeonato	Mens Caballeros	Ladies Damas
Length Longitud	6440	6048	5479
Par	72	72	72

Advised golfing ability Nivel de juego aconsejado	0	12	24	36

Hcp required Handicap exigido — 28 Men, 36 Ladies

CLUB HOUSE & AMENITIES / CLUB HOUSE Y DEPENDENCIAS — 8/10

Pro shop	Pro-shop	
Driving range	Campo de prácticas	
Sheltered	cubierto	no
On grass	sobre hierba	yes
Putting-green	putting-green	yes
Pitching-green	pitching-green	yes

1203

HOTEL FACILITIES / HOTELES CERCANOS — 6/10

HOTELS HOTELES

San Roque — San Roque
50 rooms, D 20 000 Pts — 100 m
Tel (34) 956 - 613 030, Fax (34) 956 - 613 012

La Solana — San Roque
19 rooms, D 9 500 Pts — 7 km
Tel (34) 956 - 780 236, Fax (34) 956 - 780 236

Sotogrande — Sotogrande
46 rooms, D 19 950 Pts — 7 km
Tel (34) 956 - 794 386, Fax (34) 956 - 794 333

RESTAURANTS RESTAURANTES

Los Remos — San Roque
Tel (34) 956 - 698 412 — 7 km

Pedro — San Roque
Tel (34) 956 - 698 453 — 7 km

Es la cuna y feudo del gran campeón español José Maria Olazábal, a quien se puede ver muy amenudo en el campo de práticas?. El recorrido fue diseñado por el profesional francés Pierre Hirigoyen en un terreno con muchas cuestas y con una media docena de hoyos en una planicie bastante húmeda con algunos obstáculos de agua. La dificuldad esencial, a parte de dejar la pelota en calle, radica en no ponerse nervioso ni desmoralizarse ante los muchos desniveles del terreno. Sin embargo, los obstáculos son visibles y se puede decir que es un recorrido claro con algunos greens en alto dando lugar a situaciones muy variadas alrededor de los mismos, lo que explica la virtuosidad adquirida por Olazábal. Es muy difícil jugar su handicap desde las salidas de atrás, a pesare de que no sea excesivamente largo, por lo que es mejor escoger salidas más avanzadas. No es un recorrido que guste a todos, pero posee un personalidad incontestable. Las montañas son realmente muy bonitas...

It is the home course and fief of the top Spanish champion Olazábal, who can often be seen on the driving range. The course was designed by the French pro Pierre Hirigoyen over very hilly terrain, although half a dozen holes are flattish, dampish and protected by a few hazards. The essential difficulty here, apart from keeping your ball in the fairway, is keeping cool head and not letting the steep slopes get the better of you. Luckily, the hazards are clearly in view and the course hides nothing, apart from a number of elevated greens. There is a variety of interesting situations around the greens, which might explain the virtuosity of Olazábal in this area, developed out on the course. A good score is a tough proposition from the back tees, but a distinct possibility when playing further forward. Not everyone loves this course, but it does have definite personality. And the mountains look beautiful.

Real Golf Club de San Sebastián — 1968

Chalet Borda Gain Apartado 6
E - 20280 HONDARRIBIA - GUIPUZCOA

Office	Secretaria	(34) 943 - 616 845
Pro shop	Pro-shop	(34) 943 - 616 845
Fax	Fax	(34) 943 - 611 491
Situation	Situación	

Irún (pop. 53 861), 3 km - San Sebastián (pop. 176 019), 18 km

Annual closure	Cierre anual	no
Weekly closure	Cierre semanal	no

Fees main season
Precios tempor. alta 18 holes

	Week days Semana	We/Bank holidays Fin de sem./fiestas
Individual Individual	9 000 Pts	*
Couple Pareja	18 000 Pts	*

* Week ends: members & guests only (solo socios)

Caddy	Caddy	on request
Electric Trolley	Carro eléctrico	1 000 Pts/18 holes
Buggy	Coche	no
Clubs	Palos	500 Pts/18 holes

Credit cards Tarjetas de crédito
VISA - Eurocard - MasterCard - AMEX - DC

1204

Access Acceso : San Sebastián A8 → Irún, Biarritz.
Exit (Salida) 4 → Aeropuerto, Golf 3 km
St Jean de Luz → Irún, Golf 3 km → San Sebastián
Map 1 on page 1096 Plano 1 Página 1096

GOLF COURSE / RECORRIDO — 14/20

Site	Emplazamiento	▰▰▰▰▱
Maintenance	Mantenimiento	▰▰▰▱▱
Architect	Arquitecto	Pierre Hirigoyen
Type	Tipo	forest, hilly
Relief	Relieve	▰▰▰▰▰
Water in play	Agua	▰▰▱▱▱
Exp. to wind	Exp. al viento	▰▰▱▱▱
Trees in play	Arboles	▰▰▰▱▱

Scorecard Tarjeta	Chp. Campeonato	Mens Caballeros	Ladies Damas
Length Longitud	5962	5790	4883
Par	71	71	71

Advised golfing ability		0 12 24 36
Nivel de juego aconsejado		▰▰▰▰▱
Hcp required	Handicap exigido	28 Men, 36 Ladies

CLUB HOUSE & AMENITIES / CLUB HOUSE Y DEPENDENCIAS — 6/10

Pro shop	Pro-shop	▰▰▰▱▱
Driving range	Campo de prácticas	▰▰▰▱▱
Sheltered	cubierto	20 mats
On grass	sobre hierba	yes
Putting-green	putting-green	yes
Pitching-green	pitching-green	yes

HOTEL FACILITIES / HOTELES CERCANOS — 6/10

HOTELS HOTELES

Parador de Hondarribia	Hondarribia (Fuenterrabia)	
36 rooms, D 20 000 Pts.		5 km
Tel (34) 943 - 645 500, Fax (34) 943 - 642 153		
Obispo	Hondarribia (Fuenterrabia)	
17 rooms, D 16 000 Pts.		5 km
Tel (34) 943 - 645 400, Fax (34) 943 - 642 386		
Tryp Urdanibia	Irún	
115 rooms, D 15 000 Pts.		1 km
Tel (34) 943 - 630 440, Fax (34) 943 - 630 410		

RESTAURANTS RESTAURANTES

Ramón Roteta		Irún
Tel (34) 943 - 641 693		5 km
Ibaiondo		Irún
Tel (34) 943 - 632 888		1 km

A pesar de ser un terreno accidentado, es tan fácil jugar caminando en Sant Cugat que sólo tiene un coche para alquilar. No es difícil lograr un buen resultado: las dificultades están a la vista, rara vez en la línea de juego, hasta tal punto que se puede aprochar a green haciendo rodar la bola (evitando sobrepasarlos). Algunos obstáculos de agua, algunos bunkers de green, árboles y bosque, son las mayores dificultades de este recorrido. Su escasa longitud permite no sólo jugar fácilmente su handicap sino que lo hace muy agradable para jugar en match-play: pueden caer muchos birdies. Los buenos jugadores se explayarán agusto y no dudarán en intentar llegar a green con el drive en ciertos pares 4. Los principiantes conseguirán sus primeros pares. Un golf para todos y de buena calidad.

Despite the broken terrain, San Cugat is easy to walk around, which is just as well as there is only one buggy. And it is not too difficult to shoot a good score, either. The hazards are clearly in view and seldom affect your game, to the extent that many greens can be approached with chip shots (but beware overshooting the green!). A few water hazards, certain green-side bunkers, trees and woods form the basic part of the course's difficulties. Being a short course, most players should play to their handicap without too much problem, and it is also fun for match-play, with birdies more common than usual. Very good players will have lots of fun and won't think twice about driving the green on a number of short par 4s, while beginners should easily find their feet. A good quality golf-course, for everyone to enjoy.

Club de Golf Sant Cugat — 1914

C/Villa, S/N
E - 08190 SANT CUGAT DEL VALLES (BARCELONA)

Office	Secretaria	(34) 936 - 743 908
Pro shop	Pro-shop	(34) 936 - 743 958
Fax	Fax	(34) 936 - 755 152
Situation	Situación	

Barcelona (pop. 1 681 132), 20 km

Annual closure	Cierre anual	no
Weekly closure	Cierre semanal	monday

Fees main season
Precios tempor. alta 18 holes

	Week days Semana	We/Bank holidays Fin de sem./fiestas
Individual Individual	9 000 Pts	20 000 Pts
Couple Pareja	18 000 Pts	40 000 Pts

Caddy	Caddy	on request
Electric Trolley	Carro eléctrico	1 500 Pts/18 holes
Buggy	Coche	4 000 Pts/18 holes
Clubs	Palos	2 500 Pts/full day
Credit cards Tarjetas de crédito		no

Access Acceso : Barcelona E9 → Sant Cugat del Vallès
Map 2 on page 1099 Plano 2 Página 1099

GOLF COURSE / RECORRIDO — 13/20

Site	Emplazamiento	▪▪▪▪▪▪▫▫
Maintenance	Mantenimiento	▪▪▪▪▪▪▫▫
Architect	Arquitecto	
Type	Tipo	hilly, residential
Relief	Relieve	▪▪▪▪▪▪▫▫
Water in play	Agua	▪▪▫▫▫▫▫▫
Exp. to wind	Exp. al viento	▪▪▪▪▫▫▫▫
Trees in play	Arboles	▪▪▪▪▪▪▫▫

Scorecard Tarjeta	Chp. Campeonato	Mens Caballeros	Ladies Damas
Length Longitud	5214	5214	4578
Par	70	70	70

Advised golfing ability	0	12	24	36
Nivel de juego aconsejado		▪▪▪▪▪▪		
Hcp required	Handicap exigido	28 Men, 36 Ladies		

CLUB HOUSE & AMENITIES / CLUB HOUSE Y DEPENDENCIAS — 6/10

Pro shop	Pro-shop	▪▪▪▪▪▪▫▫
Driving range	Campo de prácticas	▪▪▪▪▪▫▫▫
Sheltered	cubierto	15 mats
On grass	sobre hierba	yes
Putting-green	putting-green	yes
Pitching-green	pitching-green	yes

HOTEL FACILITIES / HOTELES CERCANOS — 5/10

HOTELS HOTELES

Novotel — Sant Cugat
150 rooms, D 16 500 Pts — 2 km
Tel (34) 935 - 894 141
Fax (34) 935 - 893 031

RESTAURANTS RESTAURANTES

La Fonda — Sant Cugat
Tel (34) 936 - 755 426

1205

Con dos recorridos (de lo cuales uno es privado) y tres otros en proyecto, Santa Ponsa se está convirtiendo en un conjunto residencial imponente y difícil de ignorar cuando se está jugando: los jugadores no encontrarán ninguna intimidad. El diseño de Folco Nardi es sobrio, aunque convencional, sin inspiración excepcional y curiosamente más difícil con los tees de salida adelantados. La longitud puede intimidar a los jugadores de tipo medio y a las señoras: la primera vez es mucho más divertido jugar en match-play que intentar cumplir su handicap. Los greens, de una superficie normal, son más bien planos y protegidos sólo por los costados, lo que permite llegar haciendo rodar la bola...La mayor dificultad son los obstáculos de agua. Los cuidados de mantenimiento son correctos.

With two courses (one of which is private) and three others on the drawing board, Santa Ponça is an impressive residential resort, a fact that can be hard to forget even when you are on the course. There is very little privacy. Folco Nardi's layout is discreet and rather conventional with nothing exceptional in terms of inspiration. Strangely, the course is harder to play from the front tees than from the back. Owing to the very little difference between tee-positions, the length of the course can be intimidating for high-handicappers and ladies. First time out, match-play will be much more fun than trying to play your handicap. The medium-sized greens are generally flat and are defended on the sides only, so you can roll (or top!) the ball onto the green. The main hazard is the water. Upkeep is good.

Golf Santa Ponsa I — 1977

Urb. Nova Santa Ponsa
E - 07180 CALVIA (MALLORCA)

Office	Secretaria	(34) 971 - 690 211
Pro shop	Pro-shop	(34) 971 - 694 925
Fax	Fax	(34) 971 - 693 364
Situation	Situación	

Palma (pop. 308 616), 16 km

Annual closure	Cierre anual	no
Weekly closure	Cierre semanal	no

Fees main season
Precios tempor. alta 18 holes

	Week days Semana	We/Bank holidays Fin de sem./fiestas
Individual Individual	8 700 Pts	8 700 Pts
Couple Pareja	17 400 Pts	17 400 Pts

Caddy	Caddy	no
Electric Trolley	Carro eléctrico	no
Buggy	Coche	6 000 Pts/18 holes
Clubs	Palos	2 500 Pts/18 holes

Credit cards Tarjetas de crédito VISA - MasterCard

1206

Access Acceso : Palma PM1 → Andraix, Viejo Molino, turn left → Santa Ponsa, → Golf
Map 9 on page 1112 Plano 9 Página 1112

GOLF COURSE / RECORRIDO — 13/20

Site	Emplazamiento	▰▰▰
Maintenance	Mantenimiento	▰▰▰
Architect	Arquitecto	Falco Nardi
Type	Tipo	residential, open country
Relief	Relieve	▰▰
Water in play	Agua	▰▰▰
Exp. to wind	Exp. al viento	▰▰▰
Trees in play	Arboles	▰▰▰

Scorecard Tarjeta	Chp. Campeonato	Mens Caballeros	Ladies Damas
Length Longitud	6543	6106	5241
Par	72	72	72

Advised golfing ability		0 12 24 36
Nivel de juego aconsejado		▰▰▰
Hcp required	Handicap exigido	28 Men, 36 Ladies

CLUB HOUSE & AMENITIES / CLUB HOUSE Y DEPENDENCIAS — 6/10

Pro shop	Pro-shop	▰▰▰
Driving range	Campo de prácticas	▰▰▰
Sheltered	cubierto	10 mats
On grass	sobre hierba	yes
Putting-green	putting-green	yes
Pitching-green	pitching-green	yes

HOTEL FACILITIES / HOTELES CERCANOS — 7/10

HOTELS HOTELES

Golf Santa Ponsa — Santa Ponsa
13 rooms, D 32 600 Pts — 1 km
Tel (34) 971 - 690 211, Fax (34) 971 - 694 853

Bahia del Sol — Santa Ponsa
161 rooms, D 12 600 Pts — 3 km
Tel (34) 971 - 691 150, Fax (34) 971 - 690 650

Casablanca — Santa Ponsa
87 rooms, D 7 400 Pts — 3 km
Tel (34) 971 - 690 361, Fax (34) 971 - 690 551

RESTAURANTS RESTAURANTES

Miguel — Santa Ponsa
Tel (34) 971 - 690 913 — 3 km

La Rotonda — Santa Ponsa
Tel (34) 971 - 690 219 — 3 km

Con una gran preocupación por los detalles y la estrategia, José María Olazábal ha «firmado» este recorrido. Al limitar la talla de los greens, ha querido favorecer el juego corto, uno de sus puntos fuertes. Al ser un malabarista con la bola, ha creado un recorrido que necesita dominar perfectamente todos los efectos y trayectorias (altas y bajas). Hay un gran número de bunkers y obstáculos de agua en la línea de juego, completados por 12.000 árboles y matorrales plantados para lograr un recorrido más complejo... y no sólo para protegerse del sol en verano. Equilibrado en su conjunto se adapta bien a los diferentes niveles de juego y se complica a medida que se retroceden los tees de salida. Franco y fácil de jugar sin coche, el Real Golf de Sevilla es una síntesis del estilo americano y de los links. Todo este conjunto de cualidades explican su éxito.

A course carrying the José-Maria Olazabal "label" where a lot of attention has gone into the finest detail and strategy. By restricting ther size of the greens, he has highlighted the short game, one of his own fortes. And because Olazabal is a worker of the ball, the course demands skills for every trajectory (high and low) and for fashioning the ball both ways. The course has a large number of bunkers and water hazards, all very much in play, and these will be completed by the 12,000 trees and bushes that have been planted to make the course a little trickier... and not only to provide shade from the sun in summer. This is a finely balanced layout that adapts easily to different levels of skill and becomes more complex from the back-tees. Open and easy to walk, the Real Golf de Seville is a sort of synthesis combining American and links style golf. Might this explain the course's success?

Real Club de Golf de Sevilla — 1991

Apdo 29
E - 41089 MONTEQUINTO - SEVILLA

Office	Secretaria	(34) 954 - 124 301
Pro shop	Pro-shop	(34) 954 - 124 301
Fax	Fax	(34) 954 - 124 229
Situation	Situación	

Sevilla (pop. 704 857), 10 km

Annual closure	Cierre anual	no
Weekly closure	Cierre semanal	no

Fees main season
Precios tempor. alta 18 holes

	Week days Semana	We/Bank holidays Fin de sem./fiestas
Individual Individual	8 000 Pts	15 000 Pts
Couple Pareja	16 000 Pts	30 000 Pts

Caddy	Caddy	no
Electric Trolley	Carro eléctrico	1 150 Pts/18 holes
Buggy	Coche	4 500 Pts/18 holes
Clubs	Palos	2 200 Pts/18 holes

Credit cards Tarjetas de crédito
VISA - Eurocard - MasterCard - AMEX

SEVILLA

Access Acceso : Sevilla SE401 → Utrera
Map 7 on page 1109 Plano 7 Página 1109

GOLF COURSE / RECORRIDO — 17/20

Site	Emplazamiento	
Maintenance	Mantenimiento	
Architect	Arquitecto	José Maria Olazábal
Type	Tipo	country
Relief	Relieve	
Water in play	Agua	
Exp. to wind	Exp. al viento	
Trees in play	Arboles	

Scorecard Tarjeta	Chp. Campeonato	Mens Caballeros	Ladies Damas
Length Longitud	6319	6067	5128
Par	72	72	72

Advised golfing ability
Nivel de juego aconsejado 0 12 24 36
Hcp required Handicap exigido 28 Men, 36 Ladies

CLUB HOUSE & AMENITIES / CLUB HOUSE Y DEPENDENCIAS — 7/10

Pro shop	Pro-shop	
Driving range	Campo de prácticas	
Sheltered	cubierto	10 mats
On grass	sobre hierba	yes
Putting-green	putting-green	yes
Pitching-green	pitching-green	yes

HOTEL FACILITIES / HOTELES CERCANOS — 8/10

HOTELS HOTELES

Hotel Ciudad de Sevilla — Sevilla 3 km
95 rooms, D 13 700 Pts
Tel (34) 954 - 230 505, Fax (34) 954 - 238 539

Principe de Asturias — Sevilla 10 km
288 rooms, D 33 600 Pts
Tel (34) 954 - 462 222, Fax (34) 954 - 460 428

Melia Sevilla - 361 rooms, D 20 600 Pts — Sevilla 10 km
Tel (34) 954 - 421 511, Fax (34) 954 - 422 977

Puerta de Triana - 65 rooms, D 10 000 Pts — Sevilla 8 km
Tel (34) 954 - 215 404, Fax (34) 954 - 215 401

RESTAURANTS RESTAURANTES

Taberna Alabardero — Sevilla 10 km
Tel (34) 954 - 560 637

La Albahaca - Tel (34) 954 - 220 714 — Sevilla 10 km

1207

Sus numerosos dog-legs ofrecen la oportunidad de arriesgar para acortar aún más este recorrido cuyas principales dificultades son los bunkers (colocados a uno y otro lado de los greens), algún que otro obstáculo de agua (en el 16 y 18) y losárboles: pinos, palmeras, almendros.... Desde las salidas da la impresión de ser un recorrido estrecho y con sorpresas, pero las calles se ensanchan a la caída de los drives. FW Hawtree ha sabido sacar buen partido de un terreno ondulado sin querer mostrar excesivas pretensiones arquitectónicas. Los greens son redondos, sin fantasías, planos, no muy grandes y ligeramente en alto. A pesar del carácter residencial, Son Vida conserva un aspecto muy natural. La calidad de su mantenimiento y su equilibrio nos incitan a aconsejarlo a todos los jugadores, cualquiera que sea su handicap.

The very many dog-legs provide the opportunity to take risks and shorten this course still further. The main hazards are the bunkers (on either side of the green), a few rare water hazards (on the 16th and 18th holes) and the pine, palm and almond trees. The course often looks very tight from the tee, and this can cause surprise, but the fairways open out to reach a fair width at driving length. F.W. Hawtree has made good use of averagely hilly terrain but was obviously not attempting any real architectural exploit. In particular, the greens are round, fancy-free, flat, not very large and slightly elevated. Despite the residential side, Son Vida still has a very natural appearance to it, upkeep is good and the balanced layout makes this a course we would recommend to players of all abilities.

Son Vida Golf S.A. 1964

Urb./Son Vida S/N
E - 07013 PALMA DE MALLORCA

Office	Secretaría	(34) 971 - 791 210
Pro shop	Pro-shop	(34) 971 - 791 210
Fax	Fax	(34) 971 - 791 127
Situation	Situación	

Palma (pop. 308 616), 3 km

Annual closure	Cierre anual	no
Weekly closure	Cierre semanal	no

Fees main season
Precios tempor. alta 18 holes

	Week days Semana	We/Bank holidays Fin de sem./fiestas
Individual Individual	8 800 Pts	8 800 Pts
Couple Pareja	17 600 Pts	17 600 Pts

Caddy	Caddy	no
Electric Trolley	Carro eléctrico	no
Buggy	Coche	5 900 Pts/18 holes
Clubs	Palos	2 200 Pts/18 holes

Credit cards Tarjetas de crédito VISA - MasterCard

GOLF
Son Vida
La Villeta
C 711
Palma de Mallorca
PM 20
Illetas
PM 1
Bahia de Palma

Access Acceso : Palma, Salida Son Rapinya
→ Urbanizacion Son Vida
Map 9 on page 1112 Plano 9 Página 1112

1208

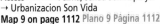

GOLF COURSE
RECORRIDO 14/20

Site	Emplazamiento	
Maintenance	Mantenimiento	
Architect	Arquitecto	F.W. Hawtree
Type	Tipo	parkland, residential
Relief	Relieve	
Water in play	Agua	
Exp. to wind	Exp. al viento	
Trees in play	Arboles	

Scorecard Tarjeta	Chp. Campeonato	Mens Caballeros	Ladies Damas
Length Longitud	5740	5740	4910
Par	72	72	72

Advised golfing ability Nivel de juego aconsejado	0	12	24	36
Hcp required Handicap exigido	28 Men, 36 Ladies			

CLUB HOUSE & AMENITIES
CLUB HOUSE Y DEPENDENCIAS 6/10

Pro shop	Pro-shop	
Driving range	Campo de prácticas	
Sheltered	cubierto	10 mats
On grass	sobre hierba	yes
Putting-green	putting-green	yes
Pitching-green	pitching-green	yes

HOTEL FACILITIES
HOTELES CERCANOS 7/10

HOTELS HOTELES

Son Vida
171 rooms, D 39 500 Pts
Tel (34) 971 - 790 000, Fax (34) 971 - 790 017
Son Vida
1 km

Arabella Golf
92 rooms, D 37 900 Pts
Tel (34) 971 - 799 999, Fax (34) 971 - 799 997
Son Vida
1 km

Saratoga
187 rooms, D 17 600 Pts
Tel (34) 971 - 727 240, Fax (34) 971 - 727 312
Palma
6 km

RESTAURANTS RESTAURANTES

El Pato
Tel (34) 971 - 791 500
Golf

Diplomatic
Tel (34) 971 - 726 482
Palma
6 km

Abierto en 1964, es uno de los clubs con más solera de la Costa y uno de los mejores recorridos. La prioridad la tienen los socios, aunque se admiten visitantes (reservar de antemano). En un sitio muy tranquilo, rodeado de casas espléndidas, con variedad de árboles (pinos, olivos, alcornoques, eucaliptus y palmeras), es más duro de lo que uno quisiera y menos de lo que parece. Gracias en parte a la ausencia casi total de rough, lo que permite que los «pegadores» puedan expresarse con todas sus fuerzas sin más preocupación que la de evitar los numerosos obstáculos de agua concentrados sobre todo en los últimos hoyos. Los golfistas de diferentes niveles se deleitarán con esta armoniosa preparación del recorrido, a pesar de que los greens sean extensos, con muchas caídas y a menudo asesinen el resultado. Bien acompasado, con dificultades bien repartidas, Sotogrande es uno de los grandes ejemplos de la arquitectura de Trent Jones.

Opened in 1964, this is one of the coast's poshest golf clubs and one of the best courses. Members have priority but it is open to visitors (book in advance). On a very quiet site, encircled by majestic houses and enhanced with numerous trees (pine, olive, oak, eucalyptus and palm trees), it is at once harder than you would like and easier than it looks. This is partly because of the virtual absence of rough, enabling long-hitters to open their shoulders with no worries other than avoiding the numerous water hazards, concentrated particularly over the last holes. But players of all levels will have fun with this friendly preparation, even though the greens are huge, very undulating and often murderous for the score card. Very well paced with difficulties evenly spread around the course, Sotogrande is one of the great examples of architecture à la Trent Jones.

Real Club de Golf Sotogrande — 1964
Paseo del Parque S/N
E - 11310 SOTOGRANDE - CADIZ

Office	Secretaria	(34) 956 - 795 050
Pro shop	Pro-shop	(34) 956 - 795 722
Fax	Fax	(34) 956 - 795 029
Situation	Situación	

Algeciras (pop. 101 556), 30 km
Estepona (pop. 36 307), 30 km

Annual closure	Cierre anual	no
Weekly closure	Cierre semanal	no

Fees main season
Precios tempor. alta 18 holes

	Week days Semana	We/Bank holidays Fin de sem./fiestas
Individual Individual	18 000 Pts	18 000 Pts
Couple Pareja	36 000 Pts	36 000 Pts
Caddy	Caddy	on request
Electric Trolley	Carro eléctrico	1 200 Pts/18 holes
Buggy	Coche	5 000 Pts/18 holes
Clubs	Palos	2 500 Pts/full day

Credit cards Tarjetas de crédito
VISA - MasterCard - AMEX

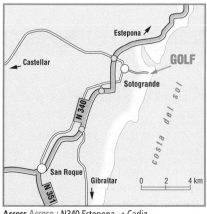

Access Acceso : N340 Estepona → Cadiz.
Sotogrande, Golf on the left
Map 7 on page 1109 Plano 7 Página 1109

GOLF COURSE
RECORRIDO — 18/20

Site	Emplazamiento	
Maintenance	Mantenimiento	
Architect	Arquitecto	Robert Trent Jones
Type	Tipo	seaside course, parkland
Relief	Relieve	
Water in play	Agua	
Exp. to wind	Exp. al viento	
Trees in play	Arboles	

Scorecard Tarjeta	Chp. Campeonato	Mens Caballeros	Ladies Damas
Length Longitud	6224	5853	5077
Par	72	72	72

Advised golfing ability		0 12 24 36
Nivel de juego aconsejado		
Hcp required	Handicap exigido	28 Men, 36 Ladies

CLUB HOUSE & AMENITIES
CLUB HOUSE Y DEPENDENCIAS — 7/10

Pro shop	Pro-shop	
Driving range	Campo de prácticas	
Sheltered	cubierto	no
On grass	sobre hierba	yes
Putting-green	putting-green	yes
Pitching-green	pitching-green	yes

1209

HOTEL FACILITIES
HOTELES CERCANOS — 6/10

HOTELS HOTELES

Sotogrande — Sotogrande
46 rooms, D 19 950 Pts — 3 km
Tel (34) 956 - 794 386, Fax (34) 956 - 794 333

Club Maritimo — Sotogrande
39 rooms, D 20 000 Pts — 3 km
Tel (34) 956 - 790 200, Fax (34) 956 - 790 377

San Roque — San Roque
50 rooms, D 20 000 Pts — 10 km
Tel (34) 956 - 613 030, Fax (34) 956 - 613 012

RESTAURANTS RESTAURANTES

Los Remos — San Roque
Tel (34) 956 - 698 412 — 15 km

Pedro — San Roque
Tel (34) 956 - 698 453 — 15 km

Este campo se halla en el centro de una planicie con unas vistas espléndidas sobre las estribaciones de los Pirineos que han recogido en sus cuadros famosos pintores locales. Le faltan unos cuantos años para que la vegetación plantada con él crezca y se asiente pero uno de los tesoros del emplazamiento es su luz y el colorido de la naturaleza que lo rodea. Es un campo cómodo de jugar, prácticamente llano. No es largo, aunque los pegadores podrán disfrutar en dos pares 4 exigentes, y permite jugar con cierta tranquilidad, aunque el recorrido sorprende gratamente de vez en cuando con tiros que merecen una gran concentración, como la salida del 10, un par 3 con agua a la izquierda, o la del 15, un par 3 con el green en alto. El campo, pues, es versátil porque los jugadores expertos pueden hallar en él ocasiones de plantearse el reto de dar el golpe precisamente indicado, y los jugadores de mayor handicap tienen muchas opciones para cubrir su recorrido sin excesivos riesgos.

This course lies at the centre of a plain giving some splendid views over the foothills of the Pyrenees, as illustrated by four famous local artists. Of course it will take years for the young plantation to grow and mature but the location of this layout already provides magnificent light and colours from the natural setting all around. This is a virtually flat and easy course to play. It is not wide, though, but big-hitters will enjoy two demanding par 4s in particular. It also has a few surprises in store when shots call for extra concentration, like at the 10th hole, a par 3 with water to the left, or the 15th, another par 3 with an elevated green. This is a versatile course in that skilled players have the chance to attack the pin if they play straight, while the higher-handicap golfer has a number of options open to him or her to get around the course without any excessive risk-taking.

Torremirona Golf Club — 1993

Ctra. N-260, Km 46
E - 17744 NAVATA

Office	Secretaria	(34) 972 - 553 737
Pro shop	Pro-shop	(34) 972 - 553 737
Fax	Fax	(34) 972 - 553 716
Situation	Situación	

Figueras (pop. 35 301), 10 km

Annual closure	Cierre anual	no
Weekly closure	Cierre semanal	no

Fees main season
Precios tempor. alta 18 holes

	Week days Semana	We/Bank holidays Fin de sem./fiestas
Individual Individual	6 500 Pts	7 750 Pts
Couple Pareja	11 000 Pts	13 500 Pts

Caddy	Caddy	no
Electric Trolley	Carro eléctrico	2 000 Pts/18 holes
Buggy	Coche	6 000 Pts/18 holes
Clubs	Palos	3 000 Pts/18 holes

Credit cards Tarjetas de crédito
VISA - Eurocard - MasterCard - AMEX

1210

Access Acceso : Figueras, N260 → Olot, Km 46, turn right.
Map 2 on page 1099 Plano 2 Página 1099

GOLF COURSE / RECORRIDO — 13/20

Site	Emplazamiento	
Maintenance	Mantenimiento	
Architect	Arquitecto	Tecnoa Eugenio Aguado
Type	Tipo	parkland, inland
Relief	Relieve	
Water in play	Agua	
Exp. to wind	Exp. al viento	
Trees in play	Arboles	

Scorecard Tarjeta	Chp. Campeonato	Mens Caballeros	Ladies Damas
Length Longitud	6192	5949	5124
Par	72	72	72

Advised golfing ability	0	12	24	36
Nivel de juego aconsejado				

Hcp required   Handicap exigido   28 Men, 36 Ladies

CLUB HOUSE & AMENITIES / CLUB HOUSE Y DEPENDENCIAS — 7/10

Pro shop	Pro-shop	
Driving range	Campo de prácticas	
Sheltered	cubierto	no
On grass	sobre hierba	yes (25 places)
Putting-green	putting-green	yes
Pitching-green	pitching-green	yes

HOTEL FACILITIES / HOTELES CERCANOS — 7/10

HOTELS HOTELES

Torremirona — Navata, on site
49 rooms, D 27 000 Pts
Tel (34) 972 - 56 67 00, Fax (34) 972 - 56 67 67

Durán — Figueras, 10 km
65 rooms, D 10 000 Pts
Tel (34) 972 - 50 12 50, Fax (34) 972 - 50 26 09

Empordá — Figueras, 11 km
42 rooms, D 13 000 Pts
Tel (34) 972 - 50 05 65, Fax (34) 972 - 50 93 58

RESTAURANTS RESTAURANTES

Empordá - Tel (34) 972 - 500 562 — Figueras 11 km
Mas Pau - Tel (34) 972 - 546 154 — Avinyonet 5 km
Durán - Tel (34) 972 - 501 250 — Figueras 10 km

Fiel a su filosofía, Pepe Gancedo ha adaptado el recorrido a un terreno cuyo relieve hace que sea muy complejo y difícil el jugar sin coche. La calidad de los golpes de salida es de importancia capital: se puede perder todo de entrada con golpes demasiado desperdigados. No hay que dejarse engañar por su reducida distancia, ya que las múltiples dificultades hacen que hasta los golpes del juego corto sean delicados: árboles, bosque, rough, bunkers y obstáculos de agua se encuentran en la línea de juego. La belleza del panorama es de poco consuelo si se pierde el control de la bola. Al menos las primeras veces hay que jugar en match-play: de esta manera el recorrido es divertido (incluso en los hoyos ciegos) excepto para los jugadores con poca experiencia en quienes aumentará la presión cuando les vayan quedando pocas bolas...

True to his philosophy, Pepe Gancedo has adapted the course to the terrain, whose relief makes it difficult not only to walk but also to play. Here, the tee-shot is of prime importance. A wild drive and all may be lost. And don't be fooled by the short yardage because the numerous hazards make even the shortest irons a tricky business. Trees, woods, rough, bunkers and water are all very much to the fore, and the beauty of the scenery is scant consolation should you lose your grip and your game. For the first couple of rounds, you are better off in match-play, in which case the course can be great fun (even on the few blind holes) except for the less experienced players, who will feel the pressure even more when they start running out of balls...

Golf Torrequebrada — 1977

Apdo de Correos 120
E - 29630 BENALMADENA COSTA (MALAGA)

Office	Secretaria	(34) 952 - 561 102
Pro shop	Pro-shop	(34) 952 - 561 544
Fax	Fax	(34) 952 - 561 129
Situation	Situación	

Torremolinos (pop. 35 309), 8 km
Fuengirola (pop. 43 048), 5 km

Annual closure	Cierre anual	no
Weekly closure	Cierre semanal	no

Fees main season
Precios tempor. alta 18 holes

	Week days Semana	We/Bank holidays Fin de sem./fiestas
Individual Individual	9 000 Pts	9 000 Pts
Couple Pareja	18 000 Pts	18 000 Pts

Caddy	Caddy	no
Electric Trolley	Carro eléctrico	no
Buggy	Coche	5 000 Pts/18 holes
Clubs	Palos	3 000 Pts/18 holes

Credit cards Tarjetas de crédito
VISA - Eurocard - Mastercard - AMEX - DC

Access Acceso : Málaga → Marbella.
Torremolinos → Benalmadena Costa.
Map 7 on page 1109 Plano 7 Página 1109

GOLF COURSE
RECORRIDO — 14/20

Site	Emplazamiento	
Maintenance	Mantenimiento	
Architect	Arquitecto	J. Gancedo
Type	Tipo	hilly
Relief	Relieve	
Water in play	Agua	
Exp. to wind	Exp. al viento	
Trees in play	Arboles	

Scorecard Tarjeta	Chp. Campeonato	Mens Caballeros	Ladies Damas
Length Longitud	5806	5513	4680
Par	72	72	72

Advised golfing ability		0 12 24 36
Nivel de juego aconsejado		
Hcp required	Handicap exigido	28 Men, 36 Ladies

CLUB HOUSE & AMENITIES
CLUB HOUSE Y DEPENDENCIAS — 7/10

Pro shop	Pro-shop	
Driving range	Campo de prácticas	
Sheltered	cubierto	no
On grass	sobre hierba	yes
Putting-green	putting-green	yes
Pitching-green	pitching-green	yes

HOTEL FACILITIES
HOTELES CERCANOS — 7/10

HOTELS HOTELES

Torrequebrada — Benalmadena
350 rooms, D 30 500 Pts — 2 km
Tel (34) 952 - 446 000, Fax (34) 952 - 445 702

Triton — Benalmadena
186 rooms, D 22 000 Pts — 2 km
Tel (34) 952 - 443 240, Fax (34) 952 - 442 649

Sol La Roca — Benalmadena
156 rooms, D 16 300 Pts — 2 km
Tel (34) 952 - 441 740, Fax (34) 952 - 443 255

RESTAURANTS RESTAURANTES

Mar de Alboran — Benalmadena
Tel (34) 952 - 446 427 — 2 km

Chef Alonso — Benalmadena
Tel (34) 952 - 443 435 — 2 km

1211

ULZAMA

Creado en 1965, Ulzama se ha convertido en 18 hoyos en 1990. Situado a 500 metros de altura, discurre en un terreno bastante accidentado en el que los jugadores poco en forma acabarán agotados. La adaptación del recorrido al terreno es extraordinaria: se trata de una de las últimas obras del gran arquitecto Javier Arana. Toda la panorámica transcurre en medio de un inmenso bosque. Aunque las calles no son muy estrechas, el jugador que no logre mantener la bola bien recta será «recompensado» a la altura de sus errores. Es un recorrido natural, con un paisaje análogo al de un parque con unos greens de superficie media y bastante llanos. Felizmente no hay muchos bunkers ya que muchos golpes son ciegos. Hay que conocerlo antes para lograr un buen resultado. Para el jugador de tipo medio es un reccorido de longitud asequible en el que los pares 3 son bastante largos exceptuando el hoyo n° 2.

Opened in 1965, Ulzama was extended to 18 holes only in 1990. At over 1500 ft. above sea-level, it unfolds over hilly terrain where the less fit player will probably feel the strain. But the way the course has been adapted to the lie of the land is quite remarkable, hardly a surprise when you learn that this is one of the latest courses by the great designer Javier Arana. The major visual feature is basically its layout in a majestic oak forest. With this said, the fairways are never too tight, which doesn't mean to say that players who make a mess of their tee-shot and don't hit it straight won't be penalised accordingly. This course is a very natural-looking layout in landscape reminiscent of park-land with average-sized, rather flat greens. Bunkers are limited in number, which is probably a good thing given the number of blind shots, and you need to know the course well before any hope of shooting a good score. For the average player, this is a course of reachable length but the par 3s are on the long side (except hole N° 2)

Club de Golf Ulzama — 1965

Valle Ulzama
E - 31799 GUERENDIAIN-ULZAMA (NAVARRA)

Office	Secretaria	(34) 948 - 305 162
Pro shop	Pro-shop	(34) 948 - 305 162
Fax	Fax	(34) 948 - 305 162
Situation	Situación	

Pamplona (pop. 191 197), 22 km

Annual closure	Cierre anual	no
Weekly closure	Cierre semanal	no

Fees main season
Precios tempor. alta 18 holes

	Week days Semana	We/Bank holidays Fin de sem./fiestas
Individual Individual	6 000 Pts	7 000 Pts
Couple Pareja	12 000 Pts	14 000 Pts

Caddy	Caddy	no
Electric Trolley	Carro eléctrico	1 000 Pts/18 holes
Buggy	Coche	4 000 Pts/18 holes
Clubs	Palos	no

Credit cards Tarjetas de crédito VISA

1212

Access Acceso : Pamplona, N-121 → Irun.
Turn in Ostiz (km 15) → Lizaso (Valle Ulzama) after 6 km.
Map 1 on page 1097 Plano 1 Página 1097

GOLF COURSE / RECORRIDO — 16/20

Site	Emplazamiento	
Maintenance	Mantenimiento	
Architect	Arquitecto	Javier Arana F. Redon/J. Guiber
Type	Tipo	forest
Relief	Relieve	
Water in play	Agua	
Exp. to wind	Exp. al viento	
Trees in play	Arboles	

Scorecard Tarjeta	Chp. Campeonato	Mens Caballeros	Ladies Damas
Length Longitud	6232	6065	5154
Par	73	72	72

Advised golfing ability	0	12	24	36
Nivel de juego aconsejado				

Hcp required Handicap exigido 28 Men, 36 Ladies

CLUB HOUSE & AMENITIES / CLUB HOUSE Y DEPENDENCIAS — 6/10

Pro shop	Pro-shop	
Driving range	Campo de prácticas	
Sheltered	cubierto	no
On grass	sobre hierba	yes
Putting-green	putting-green	yes
Pitching-green	pitching-green	yes

HOTEL FACILITIES / HOTELES CERCANOS — 6/10

HOTELS HOTELES

Ventas Ulzama — Puerto Belate
15 rooms, D 5 500 Pts — 8 km
Tel (34) 948 - 305 138, Fax (34) 948 - 305 138

Lorentxo — Olabe
9 rooms, D 5 300 Pts — 10 km
Tel (34) 948 - 332 486, Fax (34) 948 - 332 679

Aguirre — Oricain
12 rooms, D 5 300 Pts — 14 km
Tel (34) 948 - 330 375

RESTAURANTS RESTAURANTES

Josetxo - Tel (34) 948 - 222 097 — Pamplona 21 km

La Chistera - Tel (34) 948 - 210 512 — Pamplona 21 km

Castillo de Javier — Pamplona
Tel (34) 948 - 221 894 — 21 km

VALDERRAMA

	19	8	6

Valderrama ha adquirido notoriedad internacional bajo la impulsión de su propietario Jaime Ortiz-Patiño, quien impuso no sólo modificaciones del recorrido original (sobre todo el 17) sino que ha exigido un mantenimiento del campo de excepcional calidad (hasta uno teme sacar chuletas). La dificultad estratégica del trazado, la omnipresencia de árboles, la dimensión de los bunkers y algunos obstáculos de agua, le obligan a uno a estudiar muy bien cada golpe. Las caídas de los greens aumentan aún más la presión. Es inútil esperar jugar su handicap, incluso a los grandes campeones les cuesta muchísimo jugar el par. Es un golf privado donde se admiten visitantes previa reserva. No hay que perdérselo.

Valderrama has gained international fame through the energy of proprietor Jaime Ortiz-Patiño, who not only insisted on making changes to the original layout (notably to the 17th hole) but also demanded exceptional standards of course upkeep (you hardly dare take a divot!). The strategic difficulty, omnipresent trees, the size of the bunkers and a few water hazards keep the player constantly on his wits for every stroke. And the pressure is made worse when it comes to reading the greens. Don't bother about playing to your handicap, as even the top champions find making par a tough enough task. But the quality of this challenge is enough to make anyone want to walk in footsteps of the professionals after the 1997 "summit" at Valderrama, when the Ryder Cup was staged here. This is a private course but is open to green-feers who book in advance. Not to be missed.

Club de Golf Valderrama — 1975

Avda de Los Cortijos S/N
E - 11310 SOTOGRANDE - SAN ROQUE - CADIZ

Office	Secretaria	(34) 956 - 791 200
Pro shop	Pro-shop	(34) 956 - 795 775
Fax	Fax	(34) 956 - 796 292
Situation	Situación	

Algeciras (pop. 101 556), 30 km
Estepona (pop. 36 307), 30 km

Annual closure	Cierre anual	yes
		1/6→30/6
Weekly closure	Cierre semanal	no

Fees main season
Precios tempor. alta 18 holes

	Week days Semana	We/Bank holidays Fin de sem./fiestas
Individual Individual	30 000 Pts	30 000 Pts
Couple Pareja	60 000 Pts	60 000 Pts

Mostly members & guests: book in advance

Caddy	Caddy	5 000 Pts/18 holes
Electric Trolley	Carro eléctrico	no
Buggy	Coche	5 000 Pts/18 holes
Clubs	Palos	2 500 Pts/18 holes

Credit cards Tarjetas de crédito VISA - AMEX

Access Acceso : N340 Estepona → Cadiz. Sotogrande, Golf on the right
Map 7 on page 1109 Plano 7 Página 1109

GOLF COURSE
RECORRIDO — 19/20

Site	Emplazamiento	
Maintenance	Mantenimiento	
Architect	Arquitecto	Robert Trent Jones
Type	Tipo	parkland
Relief	Relieve	
Water in play	Agua	
Exp. to wind	Exp. al viento	
Trees in play	Arboles	

Scorecard Tarjeta	Chp. Campeonato	Mens Caballeros	Ladies Damas
Length Longitud	6311	5983	5091
Par	71	71	71

Advised golfing ability		0 12 24 36
Nivel de juego aconsejado		
Hcp required	Handicap exigido	28 Men, 36 Ladies

CLUB HOUSE & AMENITIES
CLUB HOUSE Y DEPENDENCIAS — 8/10

Pro shop	Pro-shop	
Driving range	Campo de prácticas	
Sheltered	cubierto	no
On grass	sobre hierba	yes
Putting-green	putting-green	yes
Pitching-green	pitching-green	yes

HOTEL FACILITIES
HOTELES CERCANOS — 6/10

HOTELS HOTELES

Sotogrande — Sotogrande
46 rooms, D 19 950 Pts — 3 km
Tel (34) 956 - 794 386, Fax (34) 956 - 794 333

San Roque — San Roque
50 rooms, D 20 000 Pts — 10 km
Tel (34) 956 - 613 030, Fax (34) 956 - 613 012

La Solana — San Roque
19 rooms, D 9 500 Pts — 15 km
Tel (34) 956 - 780 236, Fax (34) 956 - 780 236

RESTAURANTS RESTAURANTES

Los Remos — San Roque
Tel (34) 956 - 698 412 — 15 km

Pedro — San Roque
Tel (34) 956 - 698 453 — 15 km

1213

Aunque todavía no goza de fama internacional, merece la pena ir a Villamartín. Sin que sea un recorrido excesivamente largo, Paul Putman, con mucha imaginación, ha sabido adaptar su diseño al terreno, dándole gran personalidad: se aconseja que sólo los mejores elijan los tees de salida de atrás. Varios pares 4 más bien cortos permiten disfrutar un poquito. El agua, que tan poco gusta a los jugadores de tipo medio, se halla verdaderamente en línea de juego en tres hoyos (sobre todo en el 9), y preferirán admirar los árboles, raramente en línea de juego pero muy presentes. Los greens son de buen tamaño, con ligeras ondulaciones y aguantan bien la bola aún cuando el golpe no sea perfecto. Es un recorrido adaptable fácilmente para jugar en familia y con jugadores de niveles diferentes, y en general muy bien cuidado.

Although yet to forge a great international reputation, Villamartin is well worth going out of your way for. While not a terribly long course, the layout has personality and has been cleverly adopted to the terrain thanks to Paul Putman's keen imagination. In our opinion, the back-tees are for the best players only. A number of short par 4s are fun to play, and water is only really in play on three holes (especially the 9th). High-handicappers, who tend not to like water, can preferably admire the trees, which although rarely in play, are very much a part of the course. The greens are large, rolling and pitch well, even from slightly mishit shots. This is a most versatile and generally well-prepared course, easy to play with the family or with players of all different levels.

Campo de Golf Villamartin — 1972
Apdo 29
E - 03189 ORIHUELA COSTA (ALICANTE)

Office	Secretaria	(34) 966 - 765 127
Pro shop	Pro-shop	(34) 966 - 765 127
Fax	Fax	(34) 966 - 765 170
Situation	Situación	

Torrevieja (pop. 25 891), 7 km
Alicante (pop. 275 111), 50 km

Annual closure	Cierre anual	no
Weekly closure	Cierre semanal	no

Fees main season
Precios tempor. alta 18 holes

	Week days Semana	We/Bank holidays Fin de sem./fiestas
Individual Individual	7 000 Pts	7 000 Pts
Couple Pareja	14 000 Pts	14 000 Pts

Caddy	Caddy	no
Electric Trolley	Carro eléctrico	1 000 Pts/18 holes
Buggy	Coche	4 000 Pts/18 holes
Clubs	Palos	1 500 Pts/full day

Credit cards Tarjetas de crédito — no

1214

Access Acceso : N332 → Cartagena,
55 km S. de Alicante. Torrevieja → Golf
Map 6 on page 1107 Plano 6 Página 1107

GOLF COURSE
RECORRIDO — 16/20

Site	Emplazamiento	
Maintenance	Mantenimiento	
Architect	Arquitecto	P. Puttman
Type	Tipo	country, hilly
Relief	Relieve	
Water in play	Agua	
Exp. to wind	Exp. al viento	
Trees in play	Arboles	

Scorecard Tarjeta	Chp. Campeonato	Mens Caballeros	Ladies Damas
Length Longitud	6132	6037	5259
Par	72	72	72

Advised golfing ability — 0 12 24 36
Nivel de juego aconsejado
Hcp required — Handicap exigido — 28 Men, 36 Ladies

CLUB HOUSE & AMENITIES
CLUB HOUSE Y DEPENDENCIAS — 7/10

Pro shop	Pro-shop	
Driving range	Campo de prácticas	
Sheltered	cubierto	no
On grass	sobre hierba	yes
Putting-green	putting-green	yes
Pitching-green	pitching-green	yes

HOTEL FACILITIES
HOTELES CERCANOS — 6/10

HOTELS HOTELES
Torrejoven — Torrevieja
105 rooms, D 8 800 Pts. — 3 km
Tel (34) 965 - 714 052, Fax (34) 965 - 715 315

Meridional — Guadamar
52 rooms, D 12 900 Pts — 20 km
Tel (34) 965 - 728 340, Fax (34) 965 - 728 306

Orihuela Costa — La Zenia
15 rooms, D 14 700 Pts — 1 km
Tel (34) 966 - 760 800, Fax (34) 966 - 761 326

RESTAURANTS RESTAURANTES
Cabo Roig — Torrevieja
Tel (34) 966 - 760 290 — 4 km

Morales — Torrevieja
Tel (34) 966 - 721 293 — 4 km

En veinte años, el arquitecto Gary Player ha evolucionado. Sus recorridos son más detallistas y las dificultades más variadas. Aparte de unos cuantos hoyos dispuestos en ida y vuelta y la distancia a veces larga de un hoyo a otro, Zaudín figura entre las buenas realizaciones del Sur de España. Palmeras, naranjos y grandes lagos hacen pensar en Florida, pero los olivos están tan presentes como en el panorama de Sevilla. Aquí, el drive de salida en los pares 4 y 5 no plantea grandes problemas pero los aproches son delicados (especialmente en 17 y 18). Una vez en el green, no hay malas sorpresas, no son inmensos ni tortuosos. La distancia razonable del recorrido y la calidad de las instalaciones hacen que sea una realización prometedora.

The architecture of Gary Player has evolved in 20 years: his courses are now much more intricate in the smaller details and offer a greater variety of difficulty. If we exclude the large number of holes running parallel up and down and the sometimes long walk between holes, Zaudin is one of the great golfing achievements in southern Spain. The palm trees, orange trees and large lakes are reminiscent of Florida, but olive groves are as present as the views over Seville. The tee-shots on the par 4s and par 5s pose no real danger but the approach shots are often tricky affairs (especially on the 17th and 18th holes). Once on the greens, there are no unpleasant surprises in store. They are not huge, but they are not too tortuous, either. The reasonable length of this course and the standard of facilities make this a most inviting location.

Zaudin Golf — 1993

Ctra Mairena-Tomares Km 1,5
E - 41940 TOMARES (SEVILLA)

Office	Secretaria	(34) 954 - 154 159
Pro shop	Pro-shop	(34) 954 - 154 159
Fax	Fax	(34) 954 - 154 159
Situation	Situación	

Sevilla (pop. 704 857), 10 km

Annual closure	Cierre anual	no
Weekly closure	Cierre semanal	no

Fees main season
Precios tempor. alta full day

	Week days Semana	We/Bank holidays Fin de sem./fiestas
Individual Individual	5 000 Pts	7 000 Pts
Couple Pareja	10 000 Pts	14 000 Pts

Caddy	Caddy	no
Electric Trolley	Carro eléctrico	1 000 Pts/18 holes
Buggy	Coche	3 500 Pts/18 holes
Clubs	Palos	2 000 Pts/18 holes

Credit cards Tarjetas de crédito
VISA - Eurocard - MasterCard - AMEX

Access Acceso : SE 30 Mairena → Tomares, Km 1,5
Map 7 on page 1108 Plano 7 Página 1108

GOLF COURSE / RECORRIDO — 16/20

Site	Emplazamiento	
Maintenance	Mantenimiento	
Architect	Arquitecto	Gary Player
Type	Tipo	country, residential
Relief	Relieve	
Water in play	Agua	
Exp. to wind	Exp. al viento	
Trees in play	Arboles	

Scorecard Tarjeta	Chp. Campeonato	Mens Caballeros	Ladies Damas
Length Longitud	6192	5869	4967
Par	71	71	71

Advised golfing ability		0	12	24	36
Nivel de juego aconsejado					
Hcp required	Handicap exigido	28 Men, 36 Ladies			

CLUB HOUSE & AMENITIES / CLUB HOUSE Y DEPENDENCIAS — 7/10

Pro shop	Pro-shop	
Driving range	Campo de prácticas	
Sheltered	cubierto	10 mats
On grass	sobre hierba	yes
Putting-green	putting-green	yes
Pitching-green	pitching-green	no

HOTEL FACILITIES / HOTELES CERCANOS — 6/10

HOTELS HOTELES

Alcora — S. Juan de Aznalfarache
401 rooms, D 21 000 Pts — 500 m
Tel (34) 954 - 769 400, Fax (34) 954 - 170 128

Melia Sevilla — Sevilla
361 rooms, D 20 600 Pts — 15 km
Tel (34) 954 - 421 511, Fax (34) 954 - 422 977

Sol Macarena - 317 rooms, D 16 700 Pts — Sevilla
Tel (34) 954 - 375 700, Fax (34) 954 - 381 803 — 10 km

Cervantes - 46 rooms, D 10 000 Pts — Sevilla 10 km
Tel (34) 954 - 900 280, Fax (34) 954 - 900 536

RESTAURANTS RESTAURANTES

Taberna Alabardero — Sevilla 15 km
Tel (34) 954 - 560 637

Egaña Oriza - Tel (34) 954 - 227 211 — Sevilla15 km

1215

Golf Digest

NUMMER 7 1999 PRIS 49:50
(FINLAND 40 FIM, NORGE 55 NOK)
Sveriges bäst säljande
golfmagasin!

DE OFFRAR ALLT FÖR GOLFEN

NU SLÅR HAN TILL
CHRISTOPHER HANELL – VÅR NÄSTA VÄRLDSSTJÄRNA

OUT OF BOUNDS
REGLERNA VI HATAR

BAKOM KULISSERNA
RYDER CUP – SLAGET I BOSTON

VINN KLUBBOR OCH BAG
Värde: 12 000 kronor!

Äventyr i Skottland

Plus: Golfarna som slår alla rekord! • Så får du bollen att lyfta!
Portugal: Gröna viner & snabba greener • Bollkriget – så gick det • Möllö by the sea
Varm och torr i regn och blåst • Potbunkern – farligt vacker • En hjältes sista ord
Varför går det så långsamt? • Callaways nya järn

Lev lite grönare

**Elegant och djärv. Golf Digest är tidningen
som alltid går ett steg längre.
Det är i Golf Digest du hittar de bästa restipsen,
smartaste instruktionerna och roligaste
historierna. Läs och överraskas!**

Sverige

The Millennium Guide

Från maj till september är dagarna långa och fyllda av dagsljus. Ofta är det möjligt att hinna med två rundor om dagen. Med mer än 400 000 golfare fördelade på över 400 banor är Sverige en av de ledande golfnationerna i Europa.. Utvecklingen beror naturligtvis mycket på det stöd som spelet åtnjuter och att golf betraktas som vilken sport som helst, i jämnhöjd med fotboll, tennis och skidåkning. Detta har inneburit att Sverige har fått fram en rad stora golfspelare: Jesper Parnevik, Per-Ulrik Johansson och Jarmo Sandelin är bara tre av många exempel. Och eftersom Sverige är ett jämlikt land, såväl inom idrottens värld som inom övriga områden, är antalet kvinnliga stjärnor lika imponerande! Tänk bara på Liselotte Neumann, Helen Alfredsson och den fenomenala Annika Sörenstam.

From May to September, southern Europeans can easily play golf in Sweden over long periods of daylight which often allow at least two rounds a day. With more than 400,000 players for almost 400 eighteen-hole courses, Sweden is one of the leading golf countries on the continent of Europe. Thanks to golf being considered above all else as a sport like soccer, tennis or skiing, and thanks finally to intelligent organization and media exposure, Sweden has produced an amazing number of champion golfers. Amongst the men, Jesper Parnevik, Per-Ulrik Johansson and Jarmo Sandelin are just three out of a whole bunch of good players. And as Sweden cultivates equality in sport and elsewhere, the output of top women players is equally impressive, with star players such as Liselotte Neumann, Helen Alfredsson or the phenomenal Annika Sorenstam.

1217

d'après carte n°985 - 8ème édition - 2000.
Autorisation n°9904173.

VI RANKAR BANORNA
CLASSIFICATION OF COURSES

Rankingen syftar endast på golfbanan.
This classification gives priority consideration
to the score awarded to the actual course.

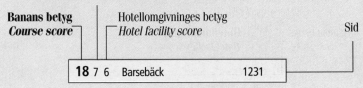

Klubhus och omgivning betyg
Club-house and facilities

Banans betyg
Course score

Hotellomgivninges betyg
Hotel facility score

Sid

18 7 6	Barsebäck	1231	

Betyg	Bana	Sid	Betyg	Bana	Sid
18 7 6	Barsebäck	1231	**15** 6 3	Fjällbacka	1243
18 7 5	Falsterbo	1242	**15** 6 7	Göteborg	1249
18 8 7	Halmstad	1252	**15** 7 5	Gränna	1250
18 7 5	Örebro	1266	**15** 5 8	Kalmar	1255
17 7 6	Bro-Bålsta	1235	**15** 6 6	Karlstad	1257
17 7 7	Kristianstad	1258	**15** 6 6	Kungsbacka	1259
17 6 7	Ljunghusen	1261	**15** 7 5	Mölle	1264
17 5 7	Skövde	1270	**15** 7 8	Rya	1268
17 7 8	Stenungsund	1272	**15** 7 5	Söderhåsen	1271
17 8 6	Ullna	1278	**15** 7 5	Värnamo	1280
16 6 5	Åtvidaberg	1230	**15** 6 7	Växjö	1282
16 7 7	Båstad *Old Course*	1232	**14** 7 6	A 6	1229
16 6 7	Bokskogen	1233	**14** 9 6	Drottningholm	1236
16 7 7	Bråviken	1234	**14** 7 7	Ekerum	1237
16 7 7	Flommen	1244	**14** 7 5	Eslöv	1238
16 7 4	Forsbacka	1245	**14** 7 7	Falkenberg	1241
16 7 5	Frösåker	1247	**14** 6 7	Forsgården	1246
16 8 6	Haninge	1253	**14** 6 6	Gävle	1248
16 7 7	Jönköping	1254	**14** 6 6	Karlshamn	1256
16 7 5	Lunds Akademiska	1262	**14** 8 6	Lindö Park	1260
16 6 6	Österåker	1267	**14** 6 5	Skellefteå	1269
16 8 9	Stockholm	1273	**14** 7 7	Torekov	1276
16 7 7	Täby	1275	**14** 6 7	Tranås	1277
16 7 7	Vasatorp	1281	**13** 7 6	Gullbringa	1251
16 6 5	Visby	1283	**13** 7 6	Lyckorna	1263
15 7 6	European Tour Club		**13** 7 5	Öijared *Gamla banan*	1265
	(Kungsängen)	1239	**13** 6 6	Sundsvall	1274
15 9 5	Fågelbro	1240	**13** 6 6	Upsala	1279

1223

Sweden

VI RANKAR HOTELLEN
CLASSIFICATION OF HOTELS FACILITIES

Rankingen syftar endast på Hotellen
This classification gives priority consideration
to the score awarded to the hotel facilities.

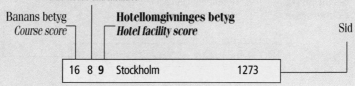

Klubhus och omgivninges betyg
Club-house and facilities

Banans betyg
Course score

Hotellomgivninges betyg
Hotel facility score

Sid

16 8 **9**	Stockholm		1273	

Betyg	Bana	Sid	Betyg	Bana	Sid
16 8 **9**	Stockholm	1273	14 6 **6**	Gävle	1248
15 5 **8**	Kalmar	1255	13 7 **6**	Gullbringa	1251
15 7 **8**	Rya	1268	16 8 **6**	Haninge	1253
17 7 **8**	Stenungsund	1272	14 6 **6**	Karlshamn	1256
16 7 **7**	Båstad	1232	15 6 **6**	Karlstad	1257
16 6 **7**	Bokskogen	1233	15 6 **6**	Kungsbacka	1259
16 7 **7**	Bråviken	1234	14 8 **6**	Lindö Park	1260
14 7 **7**	Ekerum	1237	13 7 **6**	Lyckorna	1263
14 7 **7**	Falkenberg	1241	16 6 **6**	Österåker	1267
16 7 **7**	Flommen	1244	13 6 **6**	Sundsvall	1274
14 6 **7**	Forsgården	1246	17 8 **6**	Ullna	1278
15 6 **7**	Göteborg	1249	13 6 **6**	Upsala	1279
18 8 **7**	Halmstad	1252	16 6 **5**	Åtvidaberg	1230
16 7 **7**	Jönköping	1254	14 7 **5**	Eslöv	1238
17 7 **7**	Kristianstad	1258	15 9 **5**	Fågelbro	1240
17 6 **7**	Ljunghusen	1261	18 7 **5**	Falsterbo	1242
17 5 **7**	Skövde	1270	16 7 **5**	Frösåker	1247
16 7 **7**	Täby	1275	15 7 **5**	Gränna	1250
14 7 **7**	Torekov	1276	16 7 **5**	Lunds Akademiska	1262
14 6 **7**	Tranås	1277	15 7 **5**	Mölle	1264
16 7 **7**	Vasatorp	1281	13 7 **5**	Öijared	1265
15 6 **7**	Växjö	1282	18 7 **5**	Örebro	1266
14 7 **6**	A 6	1229	14 6 **5**	Skellefteå	1269
18 7 **6**	Barsebäck	1231	15 7 **5**	Söderhåsen	1271
17 7 **6**	Bro-Bålsta	1235	15 7 **5**	Värnamo	1280
14 9 **6**	Drottningholm	1236	16 6 **5**	Visby	1284
15 7 **6**	European Tour Club		16 7 **4**	Forsbacka	1245
	(Kungsängen)	1239	15 6 **3**	Fjällbacka	1243

1224

REKOMMENDERAD GOLFVISTELSE
RECOMMENDED GOLFING STAY

Bana	Betyg			Sid	Bana	Betyg			Sid
Barsebäck	18	7	6	1231	Ljunghusen	17	6	7	1261
Falsterbo	18	7	5	1242	Örebro	18	7	5	1266
Halmstad	18	8	7	1252	Skövde	17	5	7	1270
Kalmar	15	5	8	1255					

REKOMMENDERAD SEMESTERORT
RECOMMENDED HOLIDAYS

Bana	Betyg			Sid	Bana	Betyg			Sid
Båstad	16	7	7	1232	Kungsbacka	15	6	6	1259
Ekerum	14	7	7	1237	Ljunghusen	17	6	7	1261
Falsterbo	18	7	5	1242	Mölle	15	7	5	1264
Fjällbacka	15	6	3	1243	Rya	15	7	8	1268
Flommen	16	7	7	1244	Torekov	14	7	7	1276
Forsgården	14	6	7	1246					

REKOMMENDERADE MÅNADER
RECOMMENDED SEASONS

1225

Bana	Betyg			Sid	Bana	Betyg			Sid
`1 2 3 4 5 6 7 8 9 10 11 12`					`1 2 3 4 5 6 7 8 9 10 11 12`				
Barsebäck	18	7	6	1231	Falsterbo	18	7	5	1242
Båstad	16	7	7	1232	Göteborg	15	6	7	1249
Ekerum	14	7	7	1237	Lyckorna	13	7	6	1263
Eslöv	14	7	5	1238	Rya	15	7	8	1268
Flommen	16	7	7	1244					
Kristianstad	17	7	7	1258	`1 2 3 4 5 6 7 8 9 10 11 12`				
Ljunghusen	17	6	7	1261	Forsbacka	16	7	4	1245
Mölle	15	7	5	1264	Kalmar	15	5	8	1255
Söderhåsen	15	7	5	1271	Skövde	17	5	7	1270
Torekov	14	7	7	1276	Täby	16	7	7	1275
Vasatorp	16	7	7	1281	Växjö	15	6	7	1282
Visby	16	6	5	1283					

REKOMMENDERADE MÅNADER

Bana	Betyg		Sid	Bana	Betyg		Sid
				Örebro	18	7 5	1266
1 2 3 4 **5 6 7 8 9** 10 11 12				Österåker	16	6 6	1267
A 6	14	7 6	1229	Stenungsund	17	7 8	1272
Åtvidaberg	16	6 5	1230	Stockholm	16	8 9	1273
Bokskogen	16	6 7	1233	Tranås	14	6 7	1277
Bråviken	16	7 7	1234	Ullna	17	8 6	1278
Bro-Bålsta	17	7 6	1235	Värnamo	15	7 5	1280
Drottningholm	14	9 6	1236				
European Tour Club				1 2 3 4 **5 6 7 8 9 10** 11 12			
(Kungsängen)	15	7 6	1239	Falkenberg	14	7 7	1241
Fågelbro	15	9 5	1240	Öijared	13	7 5	1265
Fjällbacka	15	6 3	1243	Upsala	13	6 6	1279
Forsgården	14	6 7	1246				
Frösåker	16	7 5	1247	1 2 3 4 5 **6 7 8** 9 10 11 12			
Gränna	15	7 5	1250	Karlstad	15	6 6	1257
Gullbringa	13	7 6	1251				
Halmstad	18	8 7	1252	1 2 3 4 5 **6 7 8 9** 10 11 12			
Haninge	16	8 6	1253	Gävle	14	6 6	1248
Jönköping	16	7 7	1254	Skellefteå	14	6 5	1269
Karlshamn	14	6 6	1256	Sundsvall	13	6 6	1274
Kungsbacka	15	6 6	1259				
Lindö Park	14	8 6	1260				
Lunds Akademiska	16	7 5	1262				

NIVÅSKILLNADER I LANDSKAPET
GEOGRAPHICAL RELIEF

Bana	Betyg		Sid	Bana	Betyg		Sid
				Haninge	16	8 6	1253
Barsebäck	18	7 6	1231	Kristianstad	17	7 7	1258
Fjällbacka	15	6 3	1243	Kungsbacka	15	6 6	1259
Flommen	16	7 7	1244	Örebro	18	7 5	1266
Kalmar	15	5 8	1255	Österåker	16	6 6	1267
Ljunghusen	17	6 7	1261	Skellefteå	14	6 5	1269
Visby	16	6 5	1283	Stenungsund	17	7 8	1272
				Ullna	17	8 6	1278
				Upsala	13	6 6	1279
Åtvidaberg	16	6 5	1230	Värnamo	15	7 5	1280
Bokskogen	16	6 7	1233	Vasatorp	16	7 7	1281
Bro-Bålsta	17	7 6	1235				
Ekerum	14	7 7	1237				
Fågelbro	15	9 5	1240	Bråviken	16	7 7	1234
Falsterbo	18	7 5	1242	Drottningholm	14	9 6	1236
Frösåker	16	7 5	1247	Forsgården	14	6 7	1246
Gävle	14	6 6	1248	Göteborg	15	6 7	1249
Gränna	15	7 5	1250	Gullbringa	13	7 6	1251
Halmstad	18	8 7	1252	Karlshamn	14	6 6	1256

1226

Sweden

Bana	Betyg	Sid	Bana	Betyg	Sid
Karlstad	15 6 6	1257	European Tour Club		
Lindö Park	14 8 6	1260	(Kungsängen)	15 7 6	1239
Lunds Akademiska	16 7 5	1262	Forsbacka	16 7 4	1245
Sundsvall	13 6 6	1274	Öijared	13 7 5	1265
Torekov	14 7 7	1276	Skövde	17 5 7	1270
Tranås	14 6 7	1277	Stockholm	16 8 9	1273
Växjö	15 6 7	1282	Täby	16 7 7	1275

Bana	Betyg	Sid	Bana	Betyg	Sid
Båstad	16 7 7	1232	Lyckorna	13 7 6	1263
Falkenberg	14 7 7	1241			
Jönköping	16 7 7	1254			
Rya	15 7 8	1268	Mölle	15 7 5	1264
Söderhåsen	15 7 5	1271			

Bana	Betyg	Sid
A 6	14 7 6	1229
Eslöv	14 7 5	1238

BANTYP
TYPE OF COURSE

Bana	Betyg	Sid	Bana	Betyg	Sid
forest			Växjö	15 6 7	1282
A 6	14 7 6	1229			
Åtvidaberg	16 6 5	1230	**hilly**		
Bråviken	16 7 7	1234	A 6	14 7 6	1229
European Tour Club			European Tour Club		
(Kungsängen)	15 7 6	1239	(Kungsängen)	15 7 6	1239
Fågelbro	15 9 5	1240	Mölle	15 7 5	1264
Falkenberg	14 7 7	1241	Flommen	16 7 7	1244
Forsbacka	16 7 4	1245			
Gävle	14 6 6	1248	**links**		
Gullbringa	13 7 6	1251	Falsterbo	18 7 5	1242
Halmstad	18 8 7	1252			
Haninge	16 8 6	1253	**open country**		
Karlshamn	14 6 6	1256	Bro-Bålsta	17 7 6	1235
Karlstad	15 6 6	1257	Fjällbacka	15 6 3	1243
Öijared Gamla banan	13 7 5	1265	Forsgården	14 6 7	1246
Örebro	18 7 5	1266	Gränna	15 7 5	1250
Skellefteå	14 6 5	1269	Kristianstad	17 7 7	1258
Söderhåsen	15 7 5	1271	Lindö Park	14 8 6	1260
Sundsvall	13 6 6	1274	Stenungsund	17 7 8	1272
Tranås	14 6 7	1277	Torekov	14 7 7	1276
Upsala	13 6 6	1279			
Värnamo	15 7 5	1280			
Vasatorp	16 7 7	1281			

1227

Bana	Betyg			Sid
parkland				
Barsebäck	18	7	6	1231
Båstad *Old Course*	16	7	7	1232
Bokskogen	16	6	7	1233
Bråviken	16	7	7	1234
Bro-Bålsta	17	7	6	1235
Drottningholm	14	9	6	1236
Ekerum	14	7	7	1237
Eslöv	14	7	5	1238
Falkenberg	14	7	7	1241
Fjällbacka	15	6	3	1243
Forsbacka	16	7	4	1245
Frösåker	16	7	5	1247
Gävle	14	6	6	1248
Göteborg	15	6	7	1249
Gränna	15	7	5	1250
Gullbringa	13	7	6	1251
Halmstad	18	8	7	1252
Haninge	16	8	6	1253
Jönköping	16	7	7	1254
Kalmar	15	5	8	1255
Karlshamn	14	6	6	1256
Karlstad	15	6	6	1257
Kristianstad	17	7	7	1258
Kungsbacka	15	6	6	1259
Lindö Park	14	8	6	1260
Lunds Akademiska	16	7	5	1262
Lyckorna	13	7	6	1263
Mölle	15	7	5	1264
Öijared *Gamla banan*	13	7	5	1265

Bana	Betyg			Sid
Örebro	18	7	5	1266
Österåker	16	6	6	1267
Rya	15	7	8	1268
Skövde	17	5	7	1270
Söderhåsen	15	7	5	1271
Stenungsund	17	7	8	1272
Stockholm	16	8	9	1273
Sundsvall	13	6	6	1274
Täby	16	7	7	1275
Tranås	14	6	7	1277
Ullna	17	8	6	1278
Upsala	13	6	6	1279
Värnamo	15	7	5	1280
Vasatorp	16	7	7	1281
Växjö	15	6	7	1282
Visby	16	6	5	1283
seaside course				
Barsebäck	18	7	6	1231
Falsterbo	18	7	5	1242
Flommen	16	7	7	1244
Frösåker	16	7	5	1247
Kungsbacka	15	6	6	1259
Ljunghusen	17	6	7	1261
Lyckorna	13	7	6	1263
Rya	15	7	8	1268
Täby	16	7	7	1275
Torekov	14	7	7	1276
Visby	16	6	5	1283

1228

PEUGEOT

Om du är på väg norrut på E4 i det svindlande vackra landskapet rekommenderas ett besök på denna till namnet märkliga bana. Den är designad av Peter Nordwall, som här har ritat greener som ligger väl skyddade och som i varje fall för honom är förvånansvärt små. De är med andra ord inte alldeles lätta att träffa. Banan är relativt kuperad och bjuder på några ställen på en härlig utsikt. Detta innebär också att du under rundan kommer ställas inför några blinda slag, och dessutom skär en ravin in i spelet på flera hål och hotar att ställa till det för dig. Som på alla banor av den här typen krävs det några rundor innan du känner dig hemma. Försök att hålla huvudet kallt eller ännu bättre – lira en runda med en medlem som känner till alla problemen. Eller så struntar du helt enkelt i att föra scorekort! Vad du än väljer – på A 6 kommer du finna det svårt att gå på din handicap. Så därför gör det inte så mycket om du spelar med sämre spelare än du själv. Gå ut med hela familjen eller med vänner med högre handicap.

Before heading northward across the superb landscapes to be seen on the A4 motorway (speed limits vary between 90 and 100 km), this course going by the strange name A6 is well worth a round or two. It was designed by Peter Nordwall, who produced some well-guarded greens that are smaller than usual (for him) and so a little trickier to approach. The course is on the steep side, which gives a wild natural setting but also a number of blind shots and a dangerous ravine in play on several holes. As with every course like this, it is difficult to get a clear idea of game strategy first time out. To tackle it with as cool a head as possible, try to play a round with a member, do your own reconnoitring or simply forget about keeping score. Whatever, it will never be easy to play to your handicap here, so make the most of it and play with the family or friends who are not as good as you.

A 6 Golfklubb   1989

Centralvägen
S - 553 05 JÖNKÖPING

Office	Sekretariat	(46) 036 - 30 81 30
Pro shop	Pro shop	(46) 036 - 71 91 05
Fax	Fax	(46) 036 - 30 81 40
Situation	Läge	

Jönköping, 3 km

Annual closure	Årlig stängning	no
Weekly closure	Daglig stängning	no

Fees main season
Tariff hög säsong full day

	Week days Veckodag	We/Bank holidays Lör/Söndag/Helgdag
Individual Individuellt	SKr 220:-	SKr 240:-
Couple Par	SKr 440:-	SKr 480:-

Juniors: – 50% / 2 Seniors, 2 Juniors
(Familijegreenfee): SKr 500:-

Caddy	Caddie	no
Electric Trolley	El vagn	no
Buggy	Golfbil	no
Clubs	Klubbor	SKr 100:-

Credit cards Kredit kort VISA - AMEX

Access Tillfart : E4 Jönköping → Husqvarna.
→ «Nya A 6».
Map 1 on page 1218 Karta 1 se sid: 1218

GOLF COURSE BANA   14/20

Site	Läge	▰▰▰▰▱
Maintenance	Underhåll	▰▰▰▰▱
Architect	Arkitekt	Peter Nordwall
Type	Typ	forest, hilly
Relief	Relief	▰▰▰▰▱
Water in play	Vatten på spelfältet	▰▰▱▱▱
Exp. to wind	Vindutsatt	▰▰▰▱▱
Trees in play	Träd på spelfältet	▰▰▰▰▱

Scorecard Scorekort	Chp. Back tees	Mens Herrtee	Ladies Damtee
Length Längd	6268	5668	4881
Par	72	72	72

Advised golfing ability Rekommenderad spelnivå	0	12	24	36
Hcp required Hcp erfordrad	36			

CLUB HOUSE & AMENITIES CLUB HOUSE ET ANNEXES   7/10

Pro shop	Pro shop	▰▰▰▱▱
Driving range	Träningsbana	▰▰▰▱▱
Sheltered	täkt	no
On grass	på gräs	yes
Putting-green	putting-green	yes
Pitching-green	pitching-green	yes

HOTEL FACILITIES HOTELL OMGIVNING   6/10

HOTELS

Jönköpings Hotell & Konferens   Jönköping
60 rooms, D SKr 710/1030:-   on site
Tel (46) 036 - 17 18 00
Fax (46) 036 - 17 18 35

Comfort Home Hotel Victoria   Jönköping
90 rooms, D SKr 695/1245:-   5 km
Tel (46) 036 - 71 28 00
Fax (46) 036 - 71 50 50

RESTAURANTS RESTAURANG

Restaurang Borgmästaren   Jönköping
Tel (46) 036 - 16 14 40   3 km

Restaurang Dragon   Jönköping
Tel (46) 036 - 17 28 00   3 km

Krogen Svarta Börsen   Jönköping
Tel (46) 036 - 71 22 22   3 km

1229

ÅTVIDABERG

| 16 | 6 | 5 |

Banan i Åtvidaberg smälter in i landskapet mellan skogar och sjöar. I ett land med mängder av vattendrag hittar du naturligtvis också vattenhinder på banan. Det finns dock inget konstgjort amerikanskt över dessa, utan de är naturliga och typiska för sin omgivning. Initialt kanske du tycker att detta är en lätt bana, men skenet bedrar och om du inte passar dig hamnar du lätt i problem. Här finns massor med skog och även enskilda träd kommer i spel. Flera skarpa doglegs kräver att du är duktig på att manövrera bollen. Akta dig också för bunkrarna. Greenerna är mellanstora och ett par stycken är upphöjda. Allt som allt gör det att du behöver spela banan några gånger för att komma underfull med den. Hur som helst, en weekend på hotellet som ligger på banan är ett frestande förslag. Låt oss avsluta med att berömma det 11e hålet, en fantastisk par 5 som går utmed en sjö. Åtvidaberg är en charmerande upplevelse, och dessutom är man snart klara med ombyggnaden av banan som kommer att göra den ännu bättre.

Typical of the surrounding countryside, the Åtvidaberg course is set amidst lakes and forests. In a land dotted with countless stretches of water, the water hazards here are very much Swedish style. At first sight you might think this an easy course, but although playable by golfers of all abilities, it can also be dangerous. With the woods, a few isolated trees here and there (hole N° 10 for example), several dog-legs where skills in bending the ball will come in handy, a number of traps around the course, and average-sized and sometimes elevated greens, you will need to play several times to get to grips with this challenging layout. Anyway, a week-end's stay in the on-course hotel (with restaurant) will always be a tempting proposition. In a few words, special praise in order for the excellent 11th hole, a beautiful par 5 alongside a lake, the charm of the whole site and the soon-to-be completed work designed to improve this course still further.

Åtvidabergs Golfklubb — 1956

Box 180
S - 597 41 ÅTVIDABERG

Office	Sekretariat	(46) 0120 - 354 25
Pro shop	Pro shop	(46) 0120 - 126 95
Fax	Fax	(46) 0120 - 135 02
Situation	Läge	
Åtvidaberg, 1 km		
Annual closure	Årlig stängning	no
Weekly closure	Daglig stängning	no

Fees main season
Tariff hög säsong 18 holes

	Week days Veckodag	We/Bank holidays Lör/Söndag/Helgdag
Individual Individuellt	SKr 200:-	SKr 220:-
Couple Par	SKr 400:-	SKr 440:-
Juniors : – 50 %		

Caddy	Caddie	no
Electric Trolley	El vagn	no
Buggy	Golfbil	SKr 150:-
Clubs	Klubbor	SKr 100:-

Credit cards Kredit kort
VISA - Eurocard - MasterCard - DC

1230

Access Tillfart : Linköping, R35 → Åtvidaberg, → Golf.
Map 1 on page 1219 Karta 1 se sid: 1219

GOLF COURSE / BANA — 16/20

Site	Läge	
Maintenance	Underhäll	
Architect	Arkitekt	Douglas Brasier Peter Nordwall
Type	Typ	forest
Relief	Relief	
Water in play	Vatten på spelfältet	
Exp. to wind	Vindutsatt	
Trees in play	Träd på spelfältet	

Scorecard Scorekort	Chp. Back tees	Mens Herrtee	Ladies Damtee
Length Längd	5857	5747	4930
Par	72	72	72

Advised golfing ability Rekommenderad spelnivå	0	12	24	36

Hcp required	Hcp erforrad	36

CLUB HOUSE & AMENITIES / KLUBBHUS OCH OMGIVNING — 6/10

Pro shop	Pro shop	
Driving range	Träningsbana	
Sheltered	täkt	3 mats
On grass	på gräs	no, 20 mats open air
Putting-green	putting-green	yes
Pitching-green	pitching-green	yes

HOTEL FACILITIES / HOTELL OMGIVNING — 5/10

HOTELS

Trädgårdshotellet 15 rooms, D SKr 1180:- Tel (46) 0120 150 70 Fax (46) 0120 150 70	Åtvidaberg on site
Stallet 67 rooms, D SKr 1345:- Tel (46) 0120 855 00 Fax (46) 0120 142 19	Åtvidaberg 1 km

RESTAURANTS RESTAURANG

Trädgårdshotellet Tel (46) 0120 150 70	Åtvidaberg on site
Bysjö Krog Tel (46) 0120 145 40	Åtvidaberg 1 km

Från klubbhuset har du en fantastisk vy över Öresund som skiljer Sverige och Danmark åt. Träningsmöjligheterna är utomordentliga, och eftersom banan rankas som en av de bästa i Sverige är en runda här ett måste. Vid sidan av the "Old Course" finns här ytterligare en bana ritad av Donald Steele. De första hålen vindlar genom tät skog, vilket kräver raka utslag samt en förmåga att manövrera bollen och att du är duktig på att rädda dig ur svåra lägen. Därefter når banan fram till vattnet och i stället för precisionsgolf blir det nu viktigt att kunna slå låga slag för att undgå vinden (en måttlig bris är dock vanligare än en kuling). För spelare som hoppas på ett lågt resultat är Barsebäck alltid en utmaning. Om inte annat får du glädja dig åt den omväxlande rundan som layouten bjuder. Den här banan kan du spela gång på gång utan att tröttna på den.

The Club house here gives a splendid view over the Öresund, a large stretch of the North Sea which separates Sweden and Denmark. Practice facilities are also first rate, and as the course rates as one of the best in Sweden, a round or two here is a must. This is the «Old Course», subsequently supplemented by another Donald Steel 18-hole layout, some holes of which were successfully used to form a composite course for the Scandinavian Masters one year. The first holes wind their way through thick but well-cleared woods, which require straight driving, an ability to bend the ball and skilled recovery shots. Then the course reaches the seaboard, where target golf has to give way to the ability to hit low, bump and run shots and take account of the always windy conditions (often a breeze rather than a gale). Although challenging for golfers looking for low scores, Barsebäck is still playable by the less skilled player, if only for experience in learning different styles of play. A superb course you can play over and over again and still get excited about.

Barsebäck Golf & Country Club		1969
S - 246 55 LÖDDEKÖPINGE		

Office	Sekretariat	(46) 046 - 77 62 30
Pro shop	Pro shop	(46) 046 - 77 51 27
Fax	Fax	(46) 046 - 77 26 30
Situation	Läge	
Lund, 20 km		
Annual closure	Årlig stängning	no
Weekly closure	Daglig stängning	no

Fees main season
Tariff hög säsong 18 holes

	Week days Veckodag	We/Bank holidays Lör/Söndag/Helgdag
Individual Individuellt	SKr 340:-	SKr 340:-
Couple Par	SKr 680:-	SKr 680:-
Juniors : - 50 %		

Caddy	Caddie	no
Electric Trolley	El vagn	SKr 150:-
Buggy	Golfbil	SKr 200:-
Clubs	Klubbor	SKr 150:-

Credit cards Kredit kort
VISA - Eurocard - MasterCard - AMEX - DC

Access Tillfart : E6 Malmö-Helsingborg:
Exit Löddeköpinge. → Golfbana.
Map 1 on page 1218 Karta 1 se sid: 1218

GOLF COURSE BANA 18/20

Site	Läge	
Maintenance	Underhåll	
Architect	Arkitekt	Ture Bruce
Type	Typ	seaside course, parkland
Relief	Relief	
Water in play	Vatten på spelfältet	
Exp. to wind	Vindutsatt	
Trees in play	Tråd på spelfältet	

Scorecard Scorekort	Chp. Back tees	Mens Herrtee	Ladies Damtee
Length Längd	6250	5905	4950
Par	72	72	72

Advised golfing ability Rekommenderad spelnivå	0	12	24	36
Hcp required Hcp erfodrad	36			

CLUB HOUSE & AMENITIES CLUB HOUSE ET ANNEXES 7/10

Pro shop	Pro shop	
Driving range	Träningsbana	
Sheltered	tåkt	7 mats
On grass	på gräs	yes
Putting-green	putting-green	yes
Pitching-green	pitching-green	yes

HOTEL FACILITIES HOTELL OMGIVNING 6/10

HOTELS

Grand Hotell — Lund
84 rooms, D SKr 1695:- — 20 km
Tel (46) 046 - 280 61 00, Fax (46) 046 - 280 61 50

Lundia — Lund
97 rooms, D SKr 1550:- — 20 km
Tel (46) 046 - 280 65 00, Fax (46) 046 - 280 65 10

Järavallen — Barsebäck
40 rooms, D SKr 1500:- — on site
Tel (46) 046 - 77 70 50, Fax (46) 046 - 77 58 98

RESTAURANTS RESTAURANG

Grand Hotell — Lund
Tel (46) 046 - 280 61 00 — 20 km

Bantorget 9 — Lund
Tel (46) 046 - 32 02 00 — 20 km

1231

BÅSTAD OLD COURSE ✺ | 16 | 7 | 7

Banan designades på 30-talet av Hawtree och Taylor, och smälter på ett fint sätt in i landskapet. Den rankas regelbundet bland de 20 bästa i Sverige. Initialt finansierades den av Ludvig Nobel (Alfreds brorson) för att attrahera engelska affärsmän. Banan är belägen på en halvö och har ett gammalt och mycket charmigt klubbhus. Den är ordentligt kuperad, vilket ger dig många intressanta lägen under din vandring. Detta gör bara layouten ännu bättre. Medelhandicaparen kommer att lära sig mycket under rundans gång, han behöver dock inte oroa sig över att bli av med särskilt många bollar. Största svårigheten är de ofta starkt ondulerade greenerna som tenderar att vara mycket snabba. Är du inte vän med din putter kan det stå dig riktigt dyrt. Flera av greenerna är också upphöjda, vilket kräver höga slag in mot dem. Varje hål är minnesvärt skiljer sig från det föregående utan att harmonin störs.

The town of Båstad is one of Sweden's most famous seaside resorts. Designed in 1930 by Hawtree and Taylor, the natural-looking but well-landscaped «Old Course» is regularly ranked in the country's top 20 golf courses. It was financed by Ludvig Nobel (the nephew of Alfred) with the purpose of attracting British golfers. Located on a peninsula with a very old-style club-house, all 18 holes involve a lot of climbing and provide all sorts of situations from where that little white ball has to be hit. This makes the layout all the more interesting... and instructive for mid-handicappers, who shouldn't have too much trouble with lost balls. One of the main difficulties lies with the greens, which are steeply contoured and often very slick. An off-day with the putter can be an expensive business stroke-wise. More, as some of the putting surfaces are elevated, high approach shots are the order of the day. Each hole is different and memorable, but this does nothing to deter from the overall impression of harmony and the measured layout of difficulties.

Båstad Golfklubb — 1930

Boarp, Box 1037
S - 269 21 BÅSTAD

Office	Sekretariat	(46) 0431 - 731 36
Pro shop	Pro shop	(46) 0431 - 732 81
Fax	Fax	(46) 0431 - 733 31
Situation	Läge	
Båstad, 4 km		
Annual closure	Årlig stängning	no
Weekly closure	Daglig stängning	no

Fees main season
Tariff hög säsong full day

	Week days Veckodag	We/Bank holidays Lör/Söndag/Helgdag
Individual Individuellt	SKr 300:-	SKr 300:-
Couple Par	SKr 600:-	SKr 600:-
Juniors: – 50 %		

Caddy	Caddie	no
Electric Trolley	El vagn	no
Buggy	Golfbil	SKr 150:-
Clubs	Klubbor	SKr 50:-

Credit cards Kredit kort
VISA - Eurocard - MasterCard - AMEX - DC

1232

Naturreservat
Kattvik **GOLF**
Halmstad ↑
Skummeslövsstrand
Torekov ←
115
Hov
Båstad
V. Karup
O. Karup
Grevie
105
E6 / E20
Ängelholm
Malmö ↓
0   2   4 km
Förslöv

Access Tillfart : E6. Båstad → Torekov. → Golf.
Map 1 on page 1218 Karta 1 se sid: 1218

GOLF COURSE / BANA — 16/20

Site	Läge	▬▬▬▬▬□
Maintenance	Underhåll	▬▬▬▬▬□
Architect	Arkitekt	Hawtree & Taylor
Type	Typ	parkland
Relief	Relief	▬▬▬▬▬□
Water in play	Vatten på spelfältet	▬▬□□□
Exp. to wind	Vindutsatt	▬▬□□□
Trees in play	Träd på spelfältet	▬▬▬▬□

Scorecard Scorekort	Chp. Back tees	Mens Herrtee	Ladies Damtee
Length Längd	5632	5520	4787
Par	71	71	71

Advised golfing ability		0 12 24 36
Rekommenderad spelnivå		
Hcp required	Hcp erfordrad	36

CLUB HOUSE & AMENITIES / KLUBBHUS OCH OMGIVNING — 7/10

Pro shop	Pro shop	▬▬▬▬□
Driving range	Träningsbana	▬▬▬▬□
Sheltered	tåkt	4 mats
On grass	på gräs	no, 20 mats open air
Putting-green	putting-green	yes
Pitching-green	pitching-green	yes

HOTEL FACILITIES / HOTELL OMGIVNING — 7/10

HOTELS
Kattegatt	Torekov
11 rooms, D SKr 1640:-	12 km
Tel (46) 0431 - 36 30 02	
Fax (46) 0431 - 36 30 03	
Hemmeslöv	Båstad
90 rooms, D SKr 800:-	4 km
Tel (46) 0431 - 742 65	
Fax (46) 0431 - 748 88	

RESTAURANTS RESTAURANG
Kattegatt	Båstad
Tel (46) 0431 - 36 30 02	8 km
Margretetorp	Båstad
Tel (46) 0431 - 45 44 50	11 km
Enehall	Båstad
Tel (46) 0431 - 750 15	10 km

Den här banan arrangerade PLM Open under många år. Och inte undra på det! Banan är ett bra test, framför allt om du väljer att spela från backtee eller om du inte är så lång med drivern. Under sommaren är ruffarna tjocka och besvärliga, och fångar effektivt upp varje felriktat slag. Trots detta är vandringen mellan de höga bokarna så njutningsfylld att inte ens en liten vit boll kan förstöra din dag. Du behöver inte spela särskilt många rundor för att snabbt förstå att de flesta hinder ser du redan från tee. Banan är bredare än vad den verkar att vara. De största svårigheterna ligger i längden och några minst sagt knepiga greener. Allt detta gör Bokskogen till en bra värdemätare för hur du slår bollen. Även medelhandicapare kommer att ha stort utbyte av rundan om de inte förväntar sig underverk på scorekortet. Bokskogen ligger 20 kilometer från Malmö, och här finns förutom den nyss nämnda banan ytterligare en 18-hålare. Den senare är något kortare och mer lättspelad.

This course hosted the PLM Open for many a year and remains a very well maintained layout with no shortage of trouble if you play from the back tees or have a problem of length. In addition, the rough grows tall and thick in the summer and presents a serious threat to wayward shots. Despite this, the walk through a large forest of birch trees is so pleasant that even a little white ball can't really spoil your enjoyment. You don't need many rounds here to understand the layout, as all hazards are clearly visible, the course is wider than it looks and the main difficulty lies with reaching and successfully negotiating some pretty lively greens, which are often multi-tiered and elevated. All this makes Bokskogens a good yardstick for how well you are striking the ball, and a course playable by mid-handicappers if they don't go out looking for miracle scores. Some twenty kilometres from Malmö, this is a fine golfing complex with a second and somewhat shorter 18 hole course for your added enjoyment.

Bokskogens Golfklubb   1964
Torrups Nygård
S - 230 40 BARA

Office	Sekretariat	(46) 046 - 48 11 21
Pro shop	Pro shop	(46) 046 - 48 11 53
Fax	Fax	(46) 046 - 48 10 81
Situation	Läge	
Malmö, 20 km		
Annual closure	Årlig stängning	no
Weekly closure	Daglig stängning	no

Fees main season
Tariff hög säsong 18 holes

	Week days Veckodag	We/Bank holidays Lör/Söndag/Helgdag
Individual Individuellt	SKr 250:-	SKr 300:-
Couple Par	SKr 500:-	SKr 600:-
Juniors: 100:-		

Caddy	Caddie	no
Electric Trolley	El vagn	no
Buggy	Golfbil	SKr 100:-
Clubs	Klubbor	SKr 150:-

Credit cards Kredit kort
VISA - Eurocard - MasterCard - AMEX - DC

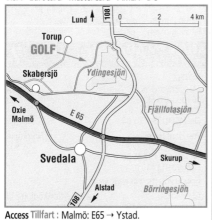

Access Tillfart : Malmö: E65 → Ystad.
Exit Oxie, → Skabersjö,
turn right at church, left at Torup, → Golf.
Map 1 on page 1218 Karta 1 se sid: 1218

GOLF COURSE
BANA   16/20

Site	Läge	▬▬▬
Maintenance	Underhåll	▬▬▬
Architect	Arkitekt	Anders Amilon Jan Sederholm
Type	Typ	parkland
Relief	Relief	▬
Water in play	Vatten på spelfältet	▬
Exp. to wind	Vindutsatt	▬
Trees in play	Tråd på spelfältet	▬▬▬

Scorecard Scorekort	Chp. Back tees	Mens Herrtee	Ladies Damtee
Length Längd	6306	6006	5238
Par	72	72	72

Advised golfing ability	0	12	24	36
Rekommenderad spelnivå			▬▬	
Hcp required Hcp erfordrad	36			

CLUB HOUSE & AMENITIES
CLUB HOUSE ET ANNEXES   6/10

Pro shop	Pro shop	▬▬▬
Driving range	Träningsbana	▬▬▬
Sheltered	täkt	3 mats
On grass	på gräs	yes
Putting-green	putting-green	yes
Pitching-green	pitching-green	no

HOTEL FACILITIES
HOTELL OMGIVNING   7/10

HOTELS

Mäster Johan	Malmö
69 rooms, D SKr 1695:-	20 km
(46) 040 - 664 64 00, Fax (46) 040 - 664 64 01	
Scandic Hotel Triangeln	Malmö
210 rooms, D SKr 1689:-	20 km
(46) 040 - 693 47 00, Fax (46) 040 - 693 47 11	
Savoy Hotel	Malmö
109 rooms, D SKr 1450:-	20 km
(46) 040 - 702 30, Fax (46) 040 - 664 48 50	

RESTAURANTS RESTAURANG

Johan P Saluhallen	Malmö
Tel (46) 040 - 97 18 18	20 km
Årstiderna - Tel (46) 040 - 23 09 10	Malmö 20 km
Nyströms Gastronomi	Malmö
Tel (46) 040 - 30 53 03	20 km

1233

Det är ett nöje att bara köra upp till klubbhuset och restaurangen som ryms i familjen Mannheims gamla herrgård. Banan ligger utlagd på mark som har skapat en högst varierande upplevelse: öppna landskap, park-landskap och skog borgar för variation hela vägen. Trots topografin har arkitekten Björn Magnusson lyckats bygga en bana med väl synliga hinder från tee, vilket gör det enklare för golfaren att hitta den bästa strategin. Bråviken kan vid första anblicken verka vara ganska vänlig, men du måste hela tiden vara på din vakt: misstag bestraf-fas snabbt och hårt. Framför allt måste du vara försiktig med alla de taggiga buskar som växer runt greenerna. Om din boll hamnar där är den ospelbar, och i värsta fall förlorad. Detta om detta, förutom banan vill vi även påpeka att at-mosfären är vänlig och avslappnad, vilket bör få alla golfare att känna sig som hemma. Bråviken är väl värd att besöka.

The pleasure starts with the drive up to the club-house and restaurant, both located in the former manor of Mannheim. The estate over which the course has been laid out results in very different styles of hole: wide open space, parkland or forest mean variety all the way. Despite the topology, architect Björn Magnusson succeeded in never concealing the hazards from every tee-box, thus making it easier to draw up the most effective game stra-tegy possible. Bråviken might appear very friendly at first sight, but watch out all the same: mistakes are quickly and severely punished. Be especially careful with the bramble bushes around the greens, where your ball will end up at best unplayable, at worst lost. What we can say is that the sanction is at least proportional to the mistake you make. Add to this the relaxed and friendly atmosphere here, and every golfer will feel confident about playing the course. Well worth getting to know.

Bråvikens Golfklubb — 1992

Manheims Säten
S - 605 91 NORRKÖPING

Office	Sekretariat	(46) 034 - 34 00 41
Pro shop	Pro shop	(46) 034 - 34 00 91
Fax	Fax	(46) 034 - 34 00 45
Situation	Läge	

Norrköping, 8 km

Annual closure	Årlig stängning	no
Weekly closure	Daglig stängning	no

Fees main season
Tariff hög säsong 18 holes

	Week days Veckodag	We/Bank holidays Lör/Söndag/Helgdag
Individual Individuellt	SKr 220:-	SKr 280:-
Couple Par	SKr 440:-	SKr 560:-

Juniors: 160:-/220:-

Caddy	Caddie	no
Electric Trolley	El vagn	no
Buggy	Golfbil	no
Clubs	Klubbor	SKr 100:-

Credit cards Kredit kort
VISA - Eurocard - MasterCard - AMEX - JCB

1234

Access Tillfart : Norrköping, 209 → Airport (Flygplats).
881 → Djurön, → Golf
Map 1 on page 1219 Karta 1 se sid: 1219

GOLF COURSE BANA — 16/20

Site	Läge	
Maintenance	Underhåll	
Architect	Arkitekt	Brian Magnusson
Type	Typ	forest, parkland
Relief	Relief	
Water in play	Vatten på spelfältet	
Exp. to wind	Vindutsatt	
Trees in play	Träd på spelfältet	

Scorecard Scorekort	Chp. Back tees	Mens Herrtee	Ladies Damtee
Length Längd	6040	5635	5000
Par	72	72	72

Advised golfing ability Rekommenderad spelnivå	0	12	24	36
Hcp required	Hcp erfordrad	no		

CLUB HOUSE & AMENITIES KLUBBHUS OCH OMGIVNING — 7/10

Pro shop	Pro shop	
Driving range	Träningsbana	
Sheltered	täkt	5 mats
On grass	på gräs	no, 15 mats open air
Putting-green	putting-green	yes
Pitching-green	pitching-green	yes

HOTEL FACILITIES HOTELL OMGIVNING — 7/10

HOTELS

Mauritzbergs Slott — Vikbolandet
16 rooms, D SKr 2100:- — 22 km
Tel (46) 0125 - 501 00
Fax (46) 0125 - 501 04

President Hotel — Norrköping
78 rooms, D SKr 1295:- — 9 km
Tel (46) 011 - 12 95 20
Fax (46) 011 - 10 07 10

RESTAURANTS RESTAURANG

Guskelov — Norrköping 8 km
Tel (46) 011 - 13 44 00

Bacchus — Norrköping 8 km
Tel (46) 011 - 10 07 40

O'Leary's - Tel (46) 011 - 10 51 07 — Norrköping 8 km

Här är banan där Annika och Charlotta Sörenstam växte upp och lärde sig att spela, och med det i bakhuvudet förstår man varför bägge har blivit så duktiga med puttern. Om du kan putta här så kan du nämligen putta överallt! Peter Nordwall har designat greener med så skarpa konturer att en del är på gränsen till att vara orättvisa. De är också väldigt stora, så stora att bunkrar och vattenhinder knappast kommer i spel när du slår in mot dem. Från tee är det dock en helt annan historia, speciellt för de långtslående som kan råka i alla möjliga sorters svårigheter om utslaget blir snett. Med detta sagt kan vi konstatera att det är en mycket intelligent layout med väl synliga hinder från tee. Medelgolfaren, som inte slår så långt, kan sprida bollarna rätt rejält och ändå komma undan med det. Om vi dessutom tillägger att banan ligger i ett fantastiskt och böljande landskap så förstår du varför det utan vidare är värt att tillbringa en hel dag här.

This is where Anika and Charlotta Sorenstam learned their trade and it is no wonder that both are such good putters. If you can putt well here, you can putt well anywhere. These greens are very sharply contoured even to the extent of sometimes appearing almost unfair. They are also very large, even too large in relation to the type of shot you need to play. They are so big in fact that the bunkers and water hazards don't even come into play, although they definitely do for the tee-shot, particularly for the longer-hitters. With this said, the layout is plainly intelligent, hazards are clearly visible from the tee-box and strategy obvious enough. Moreover, the «average» player has all the room in the world to hit a bad shot and not really suffer the consequences. If we complete the picture by saying that the site is one of pleasantly rolling terrain and set in a beautiful natural setting, you will understand that this course is well worth a full day's golfing.

Bro-Bålsta Golfklubb — 1982
Nygårdsvägen
S - 197 91 BRO

Office	Sekretariat	(46) 08 - 582 413 00
Pro shop	Pro shop	(46) 08 - 582 413 05
Fax	Fax	(46) 08 - 582 400 06
Situation	Läge	
Stockholm, 40 km		
Annual closure	Årlig stängning	no
Weekly closure	Daglig stängning	no

Fees main season
Tariff hög säsong full day

	Week days Veckodag	We/Bank holidays Lör/Söndag/Helgdag
Individual Individuellt	SKr 300:-	SKr 350:-
Couple Par	SKr 600:-	SKr 700:-
Juniors: – 50%		

Caddy	Caddie	no
Electric Trolley	El vagn	no
Buggy	Golfbil	no
Clubs	Klubbor	SKr 150:-

Credit cards Kredit kort
VISA - Eurocard - MasterCard

Access Tillfart : Stockholm E18 → Enköping.
Exit Bålsta. 1 km → Golf
Map 2 on page 1220 Karta 2 se sid: 1220

GOLF COURSE — BANA — 17/20

Site	Läge	
Maintenance	Underhåll	
Architect	Arkitekt	Peter Nordwall
Type	Typ	parkland, open country
Relief	Relief	
Water in play	Vatten på spelfältet	
Exp. to wind	Vindutsatt	
Trees in play	Tråd på spelfältet	

Scorecard Scorekort	Chp. Back tees	Mens Herrtee	Ladies Damtee
Length Längd	6505	5890	5160
Par	73	73	73

Advised golfing ability Rekommenderad spelnivå	0	12	24	36
Hcp required	Hcp erfordrad	36		

CLUB HOUSE & AMENITIES — CLUB HOUSE ET ANNEXES — 7/10

Pro shop	Pro shop	
Driving range	Träningsbana	
Sheltered	täkt	3 mats
On grass	på gräs	yes
Putting-green	putting-green	yes
Pitching-green	pitching-green	yes

HOTEL FACILITIES — HOTELL OMGIVNING — 6/10

HOTELS
Tamsvik — Bålsta
120 rooms, D SKr 995:- — 5 km
Tel (46) 08 - 582 421 00, Fax (46) 08 - 582 425 29

Grand Hotel — Stockholm
307 rooms, D SKr 2700:- — 40 km
Tel (46) 08 - 679 3500, Fax (46) 08 - 611 8606

Diplomat Hotel — Stockholm
128 rooms, D SKr 2295:- — 40 km
Tel (46) 08 - 459 6800, Fax (46) 08 - 459 6820

RESTAURANTS RESTAURANG
Fredsgatan 12 - Tel (46) 08 - 248 052 Stockholm 40 km

Franska Matsalen — Stockholm
Tel (46) 08 - 679 3584 — 40 km

Cliff Barnes - Tel (46) 08 - 318 070 — Stockholm 40 km

1235

Drottningholms slott är arkitektoniskt en korsning mellan barock och neoklassisk stil, ett Versailles i miniatyr. På sommaren är teatern här en fantastisk plats för operauppsättningar. Kinaslottet och trädgårdarna är också värda ett besök. Det senare gäller även för banan, även om den knappast bjuder på några större överraskningar väl du har spelat några rundor här. Banan är en blandning av parkbanekaraktär och öppna landskap. Den är byggd av Sköld och Sundblom, och är en trevlig bekantskap för medelgolfaren och låghandicaparen. För den som hoppas på en riktigt bra score är Drottningholm en bra utmaning. Inte minst för att en missad fairway oftast innebär ett besök i den tjocka ruffen eller i skogen. Vattenhinder kommer egentligen bara i spel på två av hålen, det femte och det 18e. Däremot är det viktigt att kunna skruva bollen från tee, framför allt på dogleg-hålen, om du inte vill ställas inför ett "blint" inspel.

Between the Baroque and the neo-classical, the castle of Drottningholm is a sort of unpretentious Château de Versailles for a monarchy that thrives on simplicity. In summer, the theatre here is a marvellous setting for operas, while the Chinese pavilion (Kina Slott) and the gardens are both well worth the visit. The same goes for the course here, even though after a few rounds you will find nothing to really surprise you. The site is a blend of parkland and wide open space, as Swedish as the layout of Sköld and Sundblom. This course is pleasant to play for mid- and low-handicappers and a real challenge for golfers looking to card a low score, as a missed fairway can be very costly, especially on account of the trees and tall rough (particularly in summer). The water hazards only really come into play on the 5 and 18th holes, while a number of tee-shots call for some bending of the ball, especially on the dog-leg holes (five of the par 4s), if you don't want to be left with a «blind» shot.

Drottningholms Golfklubb — 1959
PL 183
S - 178 93 DROTTNINGHOLM

Office	Sekretariat	(46) 08 - 759 0085
Pro shop	Pro shop	(46) 08 - 759 0314
Fax	Fax	(46) 08 - 759 0851
Situation	Läge	

Stockholm, 25 km

Annual closure	Årlig stängning	no
Weekly closure	Daglig stängning	no

Fees main season
Tariff hög säsong full day

	Week days Veckodag	We/Bank holidays Lör/Söndag/Helgdag
Individual Individuellt	SKr 300:-	SKr 300:-
Couple Par	SKr 600:-	SKr 600:-

Juniors: – 50 %

Caddy	Caddie	no
Electric Trolley	El vagn	no
Buggy	Golfbil	no
Clubs	Klubbor	SKr 300:-

Credit cards Kredit kort VISA - Eurocard - MasterCard

1236

Access Tillfart : Stockholm, Drottningholmsvägen.
→ Slottet. Exit Lovö Kyrka. 300 m → Golf
Map 2 on page 1220 Karta 2 se sid: 1220

GOLF COURSE
BANA — 14/20

Site	Läge	
Maintenance	Underhåll	
Architect	Arkitekt	Rafael Sundblom
		Nils Sköld
Type	Typ	parkland
Relief	Relief	
Water in play	Vatten på spelfältet	
Exp. to wind	Vindutsatt	
Trees in play	Tråd på spelfältet	

Scorecard Scorekort	Chp. Back tees	Mens Herrtee	Ladies Damtee
Length Längd	6125	5745	5040
Par	71	71	71

Advised golfing ability		0	12	24	36
Rekommenderad spelnivå					
Hcp required	Hcp erfordrad	30 Men, 35 Ladies			

CLUB HOUSE & AMENITIES
KLUBBHUS OCH OMGIVNING — 9/10

Pro shop	Pro shop	
Driving range	Träningsbana	
Sheltered	täkt	2 mats
On grass	på gräs	no, 25 mats open air
Putting-green	putting-green	yes
Pitching-green	pitching-green	yes

HOTEL FACILITIES
HOTELL OMGIVNING — 6/10

HOTELS

Grand Hotel — Stockholm
307 rooms, D SKr 2700:- — 25 km
(46) 08 - 679 3500, Fax (46) 08 - 611 8606

First Hotel Reisen — Stockholm
144 rooms, D 1895 SKr:- — 25 km
(46) 08 - 223 260, Fax (46) 08 - 201 559

Diplomat Hotel — Stockholm
128 rooms, D SKr 2295:- — 25 km
(46) 08 - 459 6800, Fax (46) 08 - 459 6820

RESTAURANTS RESTAURANG

Fredsgatan 12 - Tel (46) 08 - 248 052 — Stockholm 25 km

Franska Matsalen — Stockholm
(46) 08 - 679 3584 — 25 km

Cliff Barnes - Tel (46) 08 - 318 070 — Stockholm 25 km

Till Öland kommer man via den sex kilometer långa Ölandsbron. Här finns fyra golfbanor. Den bästa är Ekerum, en 27-hålsanläggning. Totalt är ön 12 mil lång, och består huvudsakligen av hedar där många intressanta växter och fårglar går att finna. En vandring eller en cykeltur över Stora Alvaret (på den södra delen av ön) är en ljuvlig upplevelse. Hotellet på golfbanan är en bra utgångspunkt, framför allt för barnfamiljer. Att spela den här banan är också en upplevelse utöver det vanliga. Den sluttar ned mot havet, är lättpromenerad och inte alltför svår om du kan hålla dig borta från ruffen. Faktum är att varje gång du går ut här känns det som om du har en bra score på gång. Men att träffa greenerna på rätt antal slag är inte hela hemligheten. Greenerna är enorma, många av dem har platåer och är starkt ondulerade. Att hålla treputten borta är inte så lätt. Banans omgivningar höjer upplevelsen, för om vi ska vara ärlig är inte detta ett mästerverk, men du slösar definitivt inte bort din tid om du spelar här.

With 27 holes, this is the largest of the four courses on the Island of Öland, linked by a 4 mile bridge to the south-eastern coast of mainland Sweden. The island, some 80 miles long, partly consists of vast moor-land which is home to some very interesting plants and birds. A walk or bicycle ride over Stora Alvaret (the southern part of the island) is a wonderful experience and the golf course hotel is an excellent base-camp for family expeditions. Playing this course is something of an experience as well. It slopes down towards a stretch of sea, is easy to play walking and not too tough if you can keep out of some very thick rough. In fact, every time you play you feel you can card a very good score, but hitting the greens in regulation is simply not enough. The putting surfaces are huge, often multi-tiered and highly-contoured and very conducive to three-putting. Of course the quality of the landscape «enhances» what is probably not an outstanding course, but you aren't wasting your time playing here.

Ekerum Golfklubb & Resort		1990
S - 387 92 BORGHOLM		

Office	Sekretariat	(46) 0485 - 800 20
Pro shop	Pro shop	(46) 0485 - 808 77
Fax	Fax	(46) 0485 - 800 10
Situation	Läge	

Borgholm, 15 km - Kalmar, 27 km

Annual closure	Årlig stängning	no
Weekly closure	Daglig stängning	no

Fees main season
Tariff hög säsong full day

	Week days Veckodag	We/Bank holidays Lör/Söndag/Helgdag
Individual Individuellt	SKr 190:-	SKr 190:-
Couple Par	SKr 380:-	SKr 380:-
Juniors: – 50%		

Caddy	Caddie	no
Electric Trolley	El vagn	no
Buggy	Golfbil	SKr 200:-
Clubs	Klubbor	SKr 100:-

Credit cards Kredit kort
VISA - Eurocard - MasterCard - AMEX - DC

GOLF

Mönsterås
Ryssby
Skäggenäs
Borgholm
Revsudden
Stora Rör   Rälla
Kalmarsund
Lindsdal   Glömminge
Nybro   Öland
Ölandsbron   Algutsrum
✈
Kalmar
Karlskrona
Färjestaden

Access Tillfart : Kalmar → Ölandsbron. → Bergholm.
Turn left → Ekerum Golf & Resort.
Map 1 on page 1219 Karta 1 se sid: 1219

GOLF COURSE
BANA   **14**/20

Site	Läge	
Maintenance	Underhäll	
Architect	Arkitekt	Peter Nordwall
Type	Typ	parkland
Relief	Relief	
Water in play	Vatten på spelfältet	
Exp. to wind	Vindutsatt	
Trees in play	Träd på spelfältet	

Scorecard Scorekort	Chp. Back tees	Mens Herrtee	Ladies Damtee
Length Längd	6518	6055	4997
Par	72	72	72

Advised golfing ability Rekommenderad spelnivå	0	12	24	36
Hcp required Hcp erfordrad	36			

CLUB HOUSE & AMENITIES
CLUB HOUSE ET ANNEXES   **7**/10

Pro shop	Pro shop	
Driving range	Träningsbana	
Sheltered	tåkt	no
On grass	på gräs	yes
Putting-green	putting-green	yes
Pitching-green	pitching-green	yes

HOTEL FACILITIES
HOTELL OMGIVNING   **7**/10

HOTELS
Ekerum	Borgholm
70 rooms, D SKr 1195:-	on site
Tel (46) 0485 - 808 00, Fax (46) 0485 - 800 10	

Halltorps Gästgiveri	Borgholm
36 rooms, D SKr 990:-	1 km
Tel (46) 0485 - 850 00, Fax (46) 0485 - 850 01	

Strand Hotel	Borgholm
134 rooms, D SKr 1090:-	15 km
Tel (46) 0485 - 888 88, Fax (46) 0485 - 888 99	

RESTAURANTS RESTAURANG
Halltorps Gästgiveri	Borgholm
Tel (46) 0485 - 850 00	1 km

Hotell Borgholm	Borgholm
Tel (46) 0485 - 770 60	15 km

1237

Klubbhuset ligger mitt på ett öppet fält, men på sommaren är det betydligt charmigare när färgstarka jord-bruksfält svarar för inramningen. Flera av hålen är ganska kuperade, vilket kan tyckas vara aningen ovanligt i Skåne. Banan byggdes i två etapper, de senare byggda hålen har något större greener och är inte fullt så förrä-diska. Även om vi befinner oss långt från havet brukar vinden kunna blåsa rätt rejält, vilket torkar upp greenerna och gör dem hårda och snabba. Första nio är vidöppna och där får vinden fritt spelrum, medan andra nio bjuder på mer lä. De fyra sista hålen kan lätt förstöra ett scorekort, om det nu inte redan är förstört av bågra sneda slag. Den största faran är den tjocka ruffen. Sagt det kan vi konstatera att höghandicaparen kan ha riktigt kul här. Det finns nämligen inte alltför många vattenhinder att förlora bollen i, även om det kan vara nog så besvärligt att slå ur ruffen. En bana som ligger en bit från allfarsvägen men som definitivt är värd en runda eller två.

The club-house is set out over wide open space but the colourful fields in summer add considerable charm. In addition, some of the holes are hilly, and a little reminiscent of the downs of Sussex or Kent. The 18-hole layout was built in two stages; the later holes have larger and slightly less treacherous greens than the others, but all the putting surfaces tend to get dry and quick when the wind blows, even though we are relatively far from the seaboard. The wind actually blows all it likes over the wide open front nine, then swirls through the trees on the back nine. The last four holes can easily ruin any card that has not already been punished by inaccurate shot-making. The one thing your card won't survive, though, is the tall rough. With this said, high-handicap golfers will have fun, there is little water and so few opportunities to lose balls, even if playing them can sometimes be difficult. A good course off the beaten track.

Eslövs Golfklubb — 1968

Box 150
S - 241 22 ESLÖV

Office	Sekretariat	(46) 0413 - 186 10
Pro shop	Pro shop	(46) 0413 - 162 13
Fax	Fax	(46) 0413 - 186 13
Situation	Läge	

Eslöv, 13 km

Annual closure	Årlig stängning	no
Weekly closure	Daglig stängning	no

Fees main season
Tariff hög säsong full day

	Week days Veckodag	We/Bank holidays Lör/Söndag/Helgdag
Individual Individuellt	SKr 200:-	SKr 250:-
Couple Par	SKr 400:-	SKr 500:-

Juniors: 100:-/130:-

Caddy	Caddie	no
Electric Trolley	El vagn	no
Buggy	Golfbil	no
Clubs	Klubbor	SKr 50:-

Credit cards Kredit kort VISA - Eurocard - MasterCard

GOLF COURSE / BANA — 14/20

Site	Läge	▮▮▮▮▮▯
Maintenance	Underhåll	▮▮▮▮▮▯
Architect	Arkitekt	Ture Bruce
Type	Typ	parkland
Relief	Relief	▮▮▮▮▮▯
Water in play	Vatten på spelfältet	▮▮▯▯▯▯
Exp. to wind	Vindutsatt	▮▮▮▯▯▯
Trees in play	Tråd på spelfältet	▮▮▮▯▯▯

Scorecard Scorekort	Chp. Back tees	Mens Herrtee	Ladies Damtee
Length Längd	5825	5630	4845
Par	70	70	70

Advised golfing ability	0	12	24	36
Rekommenderad spelnivå	▮▮▮▮▮▮▮▯			
Hcp required	Hcp erfordrad	36		

CLUB HOUSE & AMENITIES / KLUBBHUS OCH OMGIVNING — 7/10

Pro shop	Pro shop	▮▮▮▮▮▯
Driving range	Träningsbana	▮▮▮▮▯▯
Sheltered	täkt	6 mats
On grass	på gräs	yes
Putting-green	putting-green	yes
Pitching-green	pitching-green	yes

HOTEL FACILITIES / HOTELL OMGIVNING — 5/10

HOTELS

Hotell Stensson	Eslöv
80 rooms, D SKr 1095:-	5 km
Tel (46) 0413 - 160 10	
Fax (46) 0413 - 102 16	
Hotell Villasjöhusen	Eslöv
6 rooms, D SKr 560:-	3 km
Tel (46) 0413 - 120 18	
Fax (46) 0413 - 120 18	

RESTAURANTS RESTAURANG

Medborgarhuset	Eslöv
Tel (46) 0413 - 106 64	5 km
Cupido	Eslöv
Tel (46) 0413 - 102 42	5 km

1238

Access Tillfart : Malmö, E22 → Lund, Kristianstad.
E113 → Eslöv. → «Ellinge».
Map 1 on page 1218 Karta 1 se sid: 1218

Den här anläggningen, som också kallas för Kungsängen, består av 36 hål – den kortare slingan heter Queen's Course och den längre slingan heter King's Course, som vi avhandlar här. King's Course designades av Anders Forsbrand och målsättningarna var två: Dels skulle det bli en mästerskapsbana, dels skulle den vara spelbar för oss amatörer som i slutändan betalar kalaset. Detta är en mycket lång bana, kuperad och väldigt tekniskt krävande. King's är knappast en bana för den med ett högt handicap eller som bara spelar golf för att få gå ut och gå i naturen. Å andra sidan, golfare som letar efter en utmaning som testar deras tålamod och förmåga att scora väl ska definitivt åka hit. Några av hålen är rent layout-mässigt mindre lyckade, andra är helt magnifika (exempelvis 18e). Ännu återstår det dock lite tid innan banan har mognat och kan börja leva upp till alla högt ställda förväntningar.

Also known as Kungsängen, this course comprises two 18-hole layouts, of which the Queen's Course is on the short side, and the King's the one we are reviewing here. It was designed by Anders Forsbrand with a view to becoming a championship course, but it shouldn't be forgotten that week in, week out, it is we amateurs who play and pay. This is a very long layout that is technically extremely demanding and very hilly: as there are neither carts nor caddies, it takes a fit golfer to enjoy playing here. Kings is definitely not a course to be recommended to people who think of golf as a purely leisure activity or to high-handicappers. On the other hand, golfers who look to test their patience and their ability to score well, work on their strategy or develop their technique must come and play this course. While they may dispute the golfing spirit of some holes, others are simply excellent (especially the 18th). It will take a while for this course to reach full maturity and see whether it lives up to its promises.

European Tour Club 1992

Box 133
S - 196 21 KUNGSÄNGEN

Office	Sekretariat	(46) 08 - 584 507 30
Pro shop	Pro shop	(46) 08 - 584 507 31
Fax	Fax	(46) 08 - 584 710 02
Situation	Läge	

Stockholm, 25 km

Annual closure	Årlig stängning	no
Weekly closure	Daglig stängning	no

Fees main season
Tariff hög säsong full day

	Week days Veckodag	We/Bank holidays Lör/Söndag/Helgdag
Individual Individuellt	SKr 450:-	SKr 450:-
Couple Par	SKr 900:-	SKr 900:-

Juniors: – 50 %

Caddy	Caddie	no
Electric Trolley	El vagn	no
Buggy	Golfbil	no
Clubs	Klubbor	SKr 250:-

Credit cards Kredit kort
VISA - Eurocard - MasterCard - AMEX - DC

Access Tillfart : Stockholm, E18 → Enköping.
Exit Tibble/Brunna. → Golf
Map 2 on page 1220 Karta 2 se sid: 1220

GOLF COURSE BANA — 15/20

Site	Läge	▬▬▬▬▬□
Maintenance	Underhåll	▬▬▬▬□□
Architect	Arkitekt	Anders Forsbrand
Type	Typ	forest, hilly
Relief	Relief	▬▬▬▬▬□
Water in play	Vatten på spelfältet	▬▬▬▬□□
Exp. to wind	Vindutsatt	▬▬▬□□□
Trees in play	Träd på spelfältet	▬▬▬▬▬□

Scorecard Scorekort	Chp. Back tees	Mens Herrtee	Ladies Damtee
Length Längd	6248	5784	4827
Par	72	72	72

Advised golfing ability Rekommenderad spelnivå		0 12 24 36
Hcp required	Hcp erfordrad	36

CLUB HOUSE & AMENITIES CLUB HOUSE ET ANNEXES — 7/10

Pro shop	Pro shop	▬▬▬▬□□
Driving range	Träningsbana	▬▬▬▬□□
Sheltered	täkt	no
On grass	på gräs	no, 35 mats open air
Putting-green	putting-green	yes
Pitching-green	pitching-green	yes

HOTEL FACILITIES HOTELL OMGIVNING — 6/10

HOTELS

Tamsvik -	Bålsta 15 km
Tel (46) 08 - 582 421 00, Fax (46) 08 - 582 425 29	
Grand Hotel	Stockholm
307 rooms, D SKr 2700:-	25 km
Tel (46) 08 - 679 3500, Fax (46) 08 - 611 8606	
First Hotel Reisen	Stockholm
144 rooms, D 1895 SKr:-	25 km
Tel (46) 08 - 223 260, Fax (46) 08 - 201 559	

RESTAURANTS RESTAURANG

Svenska Pizzaköket	Stockholm
Tel (46) 08 - 150 061	25 km
Ocean	Stockholm
Tel (46) 08 - 652 4090	25 km
Franska Matsalen	Stockholm
Tel (46) 08 - 679 3584	25 km

1239

Många stockholmare har sommarhus i närheten, och under högsäsong är därför trycket hårt på Fågelbro. Paradoxalt nog ser du aldrig havet från banan, vilket dock inte förtar intrycket av att detta är en härlig naturupplevelse. Designen är mycket amerikansk, vilket märks sista nio där vatten kommer i spel på hela sex av hålen. Första nio är helt annorlunda och har mycket mer av parkbanekaraktär. Fågelbro är inte lång men har du problem med dina utslag kommer du snart att hamna i svårigheter. Lyckligtvis behöver du inte använda drivern så ofta – följ ett gott råd och låt den stanna i bagen. Här finns knappast ett enda hål där du kan slappna av, vilket höghandicapare inte kommer att uppskatta. Å andra sidan kommer belöningen efter rundan i klubbhuset som är ett av Sveriges charmigaste. Baren är härligt hemtrevlig och restaurangen är kort och gott – magnifik.

To get here from Stockholm, you have to drive between land and water along the edge of the Skärgården, an incredible archipelago of more than 20,000 islands and reefs stretching some 140 km into the Baltic Sea. This is the summer or week-end residence of many of the capital city's inhabitants and Fågelbro is one of the busiest courses. Paradoxically this is a wonderful natural setting where you never see the sea. The design is pure American, meaning that water is in play on six of the last nine holes, while the front nine are spread over what looks like a huge park. Fågelbro is not long but will pose problems on days when your driving is not up to scratch. Fortunately, the driver is seldom indispensable so keep it in your bag on this narrow course where the borderline between a good and bad score is slim indeed. There is not a single hole where you can relax, and high handicappers won't like that. There is however the reward of the club-house, one of the most charming of its kind in the whole of Sweden. The bar is very cosy and the restaurant simply excellent.

Fågelbro Golf & Country Club — 1991

Fågelbro Säteri
S - 139 60 VÄRMDÖ

Office	Sekretariat	(46) 08 - 571 418 00
Pro shop	Pro shop	(46) 08 - 571 418 00
Fax	Fax	(46) 08 - 571 406 71
Situation	Läge	

Stockholm, 35 km

Annual closure	Årlig stängning	no
Weekly closure	Daglig stängning	no

Fees main season
Tariff hög säsong full day

	Week days Veckodag	We/Bank holidays Lör/Söndag/Helgdag
Individual Individuellt	SKr 360:-	SKr 400:-
Couple Par	SKr 720:-	SKr 800:-

Juniors: 200:-/250:-

Caddy	Caddie	no
Electric Trolley	El vagn	no
Buggy	Golfbil	SKr 250:-
Clubs	Klubbor	SKr 250:-

Credit cards Kredit kort
VISA - Eurocard - MasterCard - AMEX - DC

GOLF COURSE / BANA — 15/20

Site	Läge	
Maintenance	Underhäll	
Architect	Arkitekt	Björn Eriksson
Type	Typ	forest
Relief	Relief	
Water in play	Vatten på spelfältet	
Exp. to wind	Vindutsatt	
Trees in play	Träd på spelfältet	

Scorecard Scorekort	Chp. Back tees	Mens Herrtee	Ladies Damtee
Length Längd	5974	5445	4535
Par	71	71	71

Advised golfing ability
Rekommenderad spelnivå — 0 12 24 36

Hcp required — Hcp erfordrad — 24 Men, 30 Ladies

CLUB HOUSE & AMENITIES / KLUBBHUS OCH OMGIVNING — 9/10

Pro shop	Pro shop	
Driving range	Träningsbana	
Sheltered	täkt	2 mats
On grass	på gräs	no, 16 mats open air
Putting-green	putting-green	yes
Pitching-green	pitching-green	no

HOTEL FACILITIES / HOTELL OMGIVNING — 5/10

HOTELS

Fågelbrohus — Golfklubb
72 rooms, D SKr 1245:- — 100 m
Tel (46) 08 - 571 401 00, Fax (46) 08 - 571 401 71

Grand Hotel — Stockholm
307 rooms, D SKr 2700:- — 35 km
Tel (46) 08 - 679 3500, Fax (46) 08 - 611 8606

First Hotel Reisen — Stockholm
144 rooms, D 1895 SKr:- — 35 km
Tel (46) 08 - 223 260, Fax (46) 08 - 201 559

RESTAURANTS RESTAURANG

Fågelbro - Tel (46) 08 - 759 0750 — Stockholm 35 km

Fredsgatan 12 - Tel (46) 08 - 248 052 — Stockholm 35 km

Franska Matsalen — Stockholm 35 km
Tel (46) 08 - 679 3584

1240

Access Tillfart : Stockholm, Väg 222 → Stavanäs/Djurö
Map 2 on page 1221 Karta 2 se sid: 1221

I Falkenberg finner man många företag med keramik- och krukproduktion. Det är också en av de bästa städerna om man vill fånga en lax, vilket till och med går att göra i Ätran som rinner rakt igenom staden. Konstälskare får också sitt lystmäte tillfredsställt genom ett besök i kyrkan. Golfbanan ligger nära havet mitt i ett skogsparti, inte helt ovanligt i ett land där skogen är en nationell resurs. Banan smälter mjukt in i ett mjukt böljande landskap, där träden är mer dekorativa än riktigt farliga. Det samma gäller för bunkrarna, åarna och dammarna – de är i spel, men utgör inte någon överdriven hotbild. Därmed får man också en klar idé över filosofin bakom den här banan: Det är viktigt att bygga mästerskapsanläggningar för de bästa spelarna, men det är lika viktigt att konstruera banor för medelgolfaren. Detta är en bana som du som medlem kan spela gång på gång utan att tröttna. Som greenfee-spelare är det också möjligt att ta sig runt Falkenberg utan att behöva vara ett taktiskt snille.

Falkenberg is a production centre for ceramics and pottery and also one of the leading sites for salmon-fishing, even in the river Ätran which crosses the city. Art lovers will also enjoy the paintings in the church of Skt Laurentil. The golf course is laid out close to the sea in the middle of a forest, a contrast often found in a country where timber and its derivative are a major national resource. Yet this is not an oppressive course and some of the terrain is rather more like rolling landscape, where the trees are more decorative than truly dangerous. Likewise, the bunkers, rivers and ponds are in play but never excessively so, giving a general idea of the measured side to this course: it is important to create layouts that can easily be played by the average golfer. This is the type of course where you can play as a member and never grow tired of it, or where you can come and play once or twice without having to do too much tactical thinking.

Falkenbergs Golfklubb — 1962

Golfvägen
S - 311 72 FALKENBERG

Office	Sekretariat	(46) 0346 - 502 87
Pro shop	Pro shop	(46) 0346 - 505 60
Fax	Fax	(46) 0346 - 509 97
Situation	Läge	

Falkenberg, 5 km

Annual closure	Årlig stängning	no
Weekly closure	Daglig stängning	no

Fees main season
Tariff hög säsong full day

	Week days Veckodag	We/Bank holidays Lör/Söndag/Helgdag
Individual Individuellt	SKr 250:-	SKr 250:-
Couple Par	SKr 500:-	SKr 500:-

Juniors: – 50%

Caddy	Caddie	no
Electric Trolley	El vagn	yes
Buggy	Golfbil	no
Clubs	Klubbor	yes

Credit cards Kredit kort
VISA - Eurocard - MasterCard - AMEX - DC - JCB

Access Tillfart : E6. Avfart (exit) 50. 500 m, → Golf
Map 1 on page 1218 Karta 1 se sid: 1218

GOLF COURSE / BANA — 14/20

Site	Läge	
Maintenance	Underhäll	
Architect	Arkitekt	Unknown
Type	Typ	forest, parkland
Relief	Relief	
Water in play	Vatten på spelfältet	
Exp. to wind	Vindutsatt	
Trees in play	Träd på spelfältet	

Scorecard Scorekort	Chp. Back tees	Mens Herrtee	Ladies Damtee
Length Längd	6125	5785	5084
Par	72	72	72

Advised golfing ability Rekommenderad spelnivå	0	12	24	36

Hcp required	Hcp erfordrad	35

CLUB HOUSE & AMENITIES / CLUB HOUSE ET ANNEXES — 7/10

Pro shop	Pro shop	
Driving range	Träningsbana	
Sheltered	täkt	10 mats
On grass	på gräs	yes
Putting-green	putting-green	yes
Pitching-green	pitching-green	yes

HOTEL FACILITIES / HOTELL OMGIVNING — 7/10

HOTELS

Grand Hotel Falkenberg	Falkenberg
71 rooms, D SKr 1210:-	5 km

Tel (46) 0346 - 144 50
Fax (46) 0346 - 829 25

Hotel Strandbaden	Falkenberg
135 rooms, D SKr 1035:-	5 km

Tel (46) 0346 - 71 49 00
Fax (46) 0346 - 161 11

RESTAURANTS RESTAURANG

Restaurant Hertigen	Falkenberg
Tel (46) 0346 - 100 18	5 km

Laxbutiken	Falkenberg
Tel (46) 0346 - 511 10	5 km

Harry's Restaurant och Pub	Falkenberg
Tel (46) 0346 - 100 77	5 km

1241

Detta är en av få linksbanor utanför Storbritannien där det känns som om du befinner dig på Skottlands östkust. Banan är omgärdad av vatten på tre sidor, och framför allt på första nio hålen finns också ett antal dammar. Övriga problem är den tjocka ruffen och bunkrar som lurar antingen på sidorna eller mitt i fairway. Greenerna kan man ofta närma sig med låga rullslag. Blåser det inte är banan i det närmaste ofarlig. Men de dagar när det friskar i, och det gör det nästan alltid, måste du ha god bollkontroll och kreativa lösningar. Spelare med bra känsla blir belönade, framför allt när det kommer till att rädda par runt greenerna. Några få rader av träd i banans ytterområde avskärmar Falsterbo från resten av omgivningen, och en gammal fyr mitt i området är ett pittoreskt inslag i en miljö som annars saknar starka färger. Längre söderut än så här kommer du inte i Sverige, och på våren är det här platsen att se de första gässen och änderna. Några väljer till och med att stanna och bygga bo i detta golfparadis. Vi förstår varför!

One of the pure links courses outside the British Isles. Surrounded by water on three sides, there is also a number of ponds, particularly on the front nine. The other problems are basically the tall rough and bunkers, which lurk on either side and across the fairways, and beside greens which can often be reached with bump and run shots. Without wind, this course is almost tame. When the wind blows, which is mostly does, you need good ball control and constant creativity. Players with good hands and touch are rewarded, particularly when it comes to saving par around the greens. A few rows of trees on the outskirts isolate the course from its surroundings and an old lighthouse adds a touch of colour to a rather bleak landscape. This is the southernmost part of Sweden where you first see the ducks and geese flying back to herald the first days of spring. Some even stop to nest alongside this little golfer's paradise, and understandably so.

Falsterbo Golfklubb   1911
Fyrvägen
S - 239 40 FALSTERBO

Office	Sekretariat	(46) 040 - 47 00 78
Pro shop	Pro shop	(46) 040 - 47 52 52
Fax	Fax	(46) 040 - 47 27 22
Situation	Läge	

Malmö, 30 km

Annual closure	Årlig stängning	no
Weekly closure	Daglig stängning	no

Fees main season
Tariff hög säsong full day

	Week days Veckodag	We/Bank holidays Lör/Söndag/Helgdag
Individual Individuellt	SKr 220:-	SKr 280:-
Couple Par	SKr 440:-	SKr 560:-

19/6 → 20/8: GF SKr 350:- / Juniors: – 50%

Caddy	Caddie	no
Electric Trolley	El vagn	no
Buggy	Golfbil	no
Clubs	Klubbor	SKr 150:-

Credit cards Kredit kort
VISA - Eurocard - MasterCard - AMEX - DC

1242
🇩🇰

Access Tillfart : Malmö, E6 South (Syd).
→ Skanör/Falsterbo.
Map 1 on page 1218   Karta 1 se sid: 1218

GOLF COURSE BANA   18/20

Site	Läge	
Maintenance	Underhåll	
Architect	Arkitekt	Gunnar Bauer
Type	Typ	links, seaside course
Relief	Relief	
Water in play	Vatten på spelfältet	
Exp. to wind	Vindutsatt	
Trees in play	Tråd på spelfältet	

Scorecard Scorekort	Chp. Back tees	Mens Herrtee	Ladies Damtee
Length Längd	6065	5785	5040
Par	71	71	71

Advised golfing ability Rekommenderad spelnivå		0 12 24 36
Hcp required Hcp erfordrad	32	

CLUB HOUSE & AMENITIES KLUBBHUS OCH OMGIVNING   7/10

Pro shop	Pro shop	
Driving range	Träningsbana	
Sheltered	tåkt	no
On grass	på gräs	yes
Putting-green	putting-green	yes
Pitching-green	pitching-green	yes

HOTEL FACILITIES HOTELL OMGIVNING   5/10

HOTELS

Hotell Gässlingen 13 rooms, D SKr 1300:- Tel (46) 040 - 45 91 00 Fax (46) 040 - 35 91 13	Skanör 5 km
Hotell Spelabäcken 18 rooms, D SKr 850:- Tel (46) 040 - 47 53 00 Fax (46) 040 - 47 32 42	Skanör 1 km

RESTAURANTS RESTAURANG

Skänors Gästgiveri Tel (46) 040 - 47 56 90	Skanör 4 km
Kaptensgården Tel (46) 040 - 47 07 50	Falsterbo 1 km
Vellinge Gästgiveri Tel (46) 040 - 42 48 65	Vellinge 7 km

FJÄLLBACKA

15 **6** **3**

För inte så länge sedan tycktes det att Fjällbacka låg alldeles för långt bort från allfarsvägarna. Men platsen har sin berömmelse inte endast tack vare att Ingrid Bergman brukade åka hit på semestern: Detta är hummerns, krabbans och musslans huvudstad. Banan, som ritades av Erik Röös, öppnade 1967 och är resultatet av det arbete som visionären Harry Järund la ner. I dag är det en mycket välkänd bana belägen i ett ganska fantastiskt landskap, smala strängar av platt mark kantade av bergig terräng. Fairways vaktas på sina ställen av klippor, ungefär som på banorna i Arizona, enda skillnaden är att "öknen" här är grön och att en å rinner genom området och på flera ställen korsar banan. Fjällbacka är inte lång, men spelaren som kan manövrera bollen och då och då slå ett punchslag under vinden blir belönad därefter. Trots att detta är en inlandsbana är känslan av seasidegolf stark, framför allt när man måste spela klassiska rullslag in mot greenerna.

Fjällbacka, long considered too far out of the way, owes its reputation not only to the fact that Ingrid Bergman used to come here in summer, but also to its status as one of the northern capitals of lobster, crab and oysters. This course was opened in 1967, promoted by a visionary named Harry Järund and designed by Erik Röös. Today, it has become a very well known course over a quite amazing site, a rocky region with patches of soil. The fairways are sort of guarded by the rocks, rather like on some of the courses in Arizona, the only difference being that the «desert» here is all green and crossed by a river that often comes into play. The course is not long, but players who can bend the ball, play knock-down shots or punch the ball will get their reward. Despite this being an inland course, there is still a seaside atmosphere, particularly when it comes to playing some good old bump and run shots to well-contoured greens.

Fjällbacka Golfklubb		1967
PL 2005		
S - 450 71 FJÄLLBACKA		
Office	Sekretariat	(46) 0525 - 311 50
Pro shop	Pro shop	(46) 0525 - 315 60
Fax	Fax	(46) 0525 - 321 22
Situation	Läge	
Fjällbacka, 2 km - Göteborg, 120 km		
Annual closure	Årlig stängning	no
Weekly closure	Daglig stängning	no

Fees main season
Tariff hög säsong 18 holes

	Week days Veckodag	We/Bank holidays Lör/Söndag/Helgdag
Individual Individuellt	SKr 180:-	SKr 220:-
Couple Par	SKr 360:-	SKr 440:-
Juniors: – 50%		

Caddy	Caddie	no
Electric Trolley	El vagn	no
Buggy	Golfbil	SKr 150:-
Clubs	Klubbor	SKr 100:-

Credit cards Kredit kort VISA - Eurocard - MasterCard

Access Tillfart : Göteborg E6. Dingle,
R163 → Fjällbacka. Golf 2 km north of Fjällbacka.
Map 1 on page 1218 Karta 1 se sid: 1218

GOLF COURSE
BANA
15/20

Site	Läge	
Maintenance	Underhåll	
Architect	Arkitekt	Erik Röös
Type	Typ	parkland, open country
Relief	Relief	
Water in play	Vatten på spelfältet	
Exp. to wind	Vindutsatt	
Trees in play	Träd på spelfältet	

Scorecard Scorekort	Chp. Back tees	Mens Herrtee	Ladies Damtee
Length Längd	5935	5655	4985
Par	72	72	72

Advised golfing ability Rekommenderad spelnivå	0	12	24	36
Hcp required Hcp erfordrad	36			

CLUB HOUSE & AMENITIES
CLUB HOUSE ET ANNEXES
6/10

Pro shop	Pro shop	
Driving range	Träningsbana	
Sheltered	täkt	6 mats
On grass	på gräs	yes
Putting-green	putting-green	yes
Pitching-green	pitching-green	yes

HOTEL FACILITIES
HOTELL OMGIVNING
3/10

HOTELS
Stara Hottelet — Fjällbacka
22 rooms, D SKr 1160:- — 2 km
Tel (46) 0525 - 310 03
Fax (46) 0525 - 310 93

RESTAURANTS RESTAURANG
Restaurant Klassen — Fjällbacka
Tel (46) 0525 - 310 03 — 2 km

1243

Tillsammans med Falsterbo och Ljunghusen utgör Flommen en berömd trio, där Falsterbo, förstås, är den mest omtalade banan utanför Sverige. Vad gäller närheten till vatten så är det ett faktum som inte bara gör sig påmint för att Flommen ligger på en halvö – nix, här kommer vatten i spel på varje hål. Här finns inga träd, bara den eviga vinden, året om. För friluftsmänniskan är detta en mycket upphetsande bana, måhända lite mindre för golfaren som inte är i form eller som älskar att ströva i skogen. Hindrena syns tydligt från tee och är mycket farliga oavsett om vi talar om ruffen, bunkrarna eller vattnet (översvämningar kan vara ett problem). Några av greenerna är upphöjda, en del är svårlästa och kenpigaatt träffa. För matchspel är detta en idealisk bana eftersom ingenting kan tas för givet. Den modige har en fördel över den överdrivet försiktige. Om dina bollar tar slut får du ägna dig åt att tillsammans med alla fågelskådare studera det fantastiska naturlivet.

With Falsterbo and Ljunghusens, Flommens makes up a famous threesome of courses, the best known of which outside Sweden is Falsterbo. This sort of peninsula gives you all the more the impression of being surrounded by water in that the stuff comes into play on virtually every hole. There are no trees here, just wind all year, so an exciting course for sports lovers, a little less so for golfers who prefer a stroll through the forest or who are not on top of their game. The hazards are visible enough and effectively dangerous, whether rough, bunkers or, of course, water. And the greens are sometimes elevated (the terrain is subject to flooding on occasions), not always flat and difficult to approach. This is your ideal course for match-play, as here nothing is ever over: daring is sometimes more rewarding than extreme caution. If you run out of balls, take time off to explore a region where the wild-life is quite exceptional and attracts a good number of bird-watchers.

Flommens Golfklubb — 1935

Fädriften
S - 239 40 FALSTERBO

Office	Sekretariat	(46) 040 - 47 50 17
Pro shop	Pro shop	(46) 040 - 47 50 16
Fax	Fax	(46) 040 - 47 31 57
Situation	Läge	

Malmö, 30 km – Höllviken, 8 km

Annual closure	Årlig stängning	no
Weekly closure	Daglig stängning	no

Fees main season
Tariff hög säsong full day

	Week days Veckodag	We/Bank holidays Lör/Söndag/Helgdag
Individual Individuellt	SKr 260:-	SKr 260:-
Couple Par	SKr 520:-	SKr 520:-
Juniors: – 50 %		

Caddy	Caddie	no
Electric Trolley	El vagn	no
Buggy	Golfbil	no
Clubs	Klubbor	

Credit cards Kredit kort
VISA - Eurocard - MasterCard - AMEX

1244

Access Tillfart : Malmö, E6 → Vellinge, → Skanör-Falsterbo, → Falsterbo. → Flommens Golfklubb.
Map 1 on page 1218 Karta 1 se sid: 1218

GOLF COURSE / BANA — 16/20

Site	Läge	
Maintenance	Underhåll	
Architect	Arkitekt	Stig Bergendorff Stig Kristersson
Type	Typ	seaside course, links
Relief	Relief	
Water in play	Vatten på spelfältet	
Exp. to wind	Vindutsatt	
Trees in play	Tråd på spelfältet	

Scorecard Scorekort	Chp. Back tees	Mens Herrtee	Ladies Damtee
Length Längd	6035	5745	4955
Par	72	72	72

Advised golfing ability Rekommenderad spelnivå	0	12	24	36
Hcp required	Hcp erfordrad	36		

CLUB HOUSE & AMENITIES / KLUBBHUS OCH OMGIVNING — 7/10

Pro shop	Pro shop	
Driving range	Träningsbana	
Sheltered	tåkt	no
On grass	på gräs	yes
Putting-green	putting-green	yes
Pitching-green	pitching-green	yes

HOTEL FACILITIES / HOTELL OMGIVNING — 7/10

HOTELS

Hotel Gässlingen — Skanör
13 rooms, D SKr 1300:- — 4 km
Tel (46) 040 - 45 91 00
Fax (46) 040 - 35 91 13

Hotell Spelabäcken — Skanör
18 rooms, D SKr 850:- — 1 km
Tel (46) 040 - 47 53 00
Fax (46) 040 - 47 32 42

RESTAURANTS RESTAURANG

Skänors Gästgiveri — Skanör
Tel (46) 040 - 47 56 90 — 10 km

Vellinge Gästgiveri — Vellinge
Tel (46) 040 - 42 48 65 — 15 km

Kaptensgården — Falsterbo
Tel (46) 040 - 47 07 50 — 1 km

Många svenska banor är vackert infogade i naturen. Forsbacka är inget undantag. Banan ligger nära Åmål, en liten stad på Vätterns strand. Den är belägen i ett underbart landskap mellan sjöar och skog, ungefär som man föreställer sig ett svenskt vykort. Men eftersom den är ganska kuperad och här inte finns några golfbilar rekommenderar vi den endast till den som är i bra fysisk form och som inte är rädd för vatten, träd eller höga kullar. Som på de flesta kuperade banor vill man gärna veta vilka hinder som finns framför en, här finns dock inga gömda elakheter så länge du håller dig på fairway. De mest minnesvärda hålen är sjuan och nian, som bägge kräver långa slag och stor precision. Många golfare tycker att Forsbacka är en av Sveriges vackraste banor, andra kanske tycker att den är i väl förrädiska laget. Hur som helst, du måste spela här för att bilda dig en egen uppfattning.

Many Swedish courses are beautifully immersed in nature, and this is one of them. Forsbacka is close to Åmål, a small town on the shores of the Vänern, the largest lake in western Europe. The course offers a wonderful landscape of lakes and forests, rather like a postcard of Sweden, but being rather hilly and given the absence of carts we would recommend it only for golfers who are in good shape physically and for whom water, trees and slopes hold no fears. As with all hilly courses, we would like to see the hazards ahead, but here there are not really any hidden traps or unpleasant surprises in store. On this exciting course, perhaps the most memorable holes are from 7 to 9, where that hardest of combinations - length and accuracy - is a total and absolute necessity. For many golfers, Forsbacka is one of Sweden's most beautiful parkland courses, others might find it a little treacherous. Whatever, you will need to play it yourself to form your own opinion, which certainly won't be one of indifference.

Forsbacka Golfklubb — 1971

Box 136
S - 662 23 ÅMÅL

Office	Sekretariat	(46) 0532 - 430 73
Pro shop	Pro shop	(46) 0532 - 431 19
Fax	Fax	(46) 0532 - 431 16
Situation	Läge	

Åmål, 7 km - Karlstad, 75 km

Annual closure	Årlig stängning	no
Weekly closure	Daglig stängning	no

Fees main season
Tariff hög säsong full day

	Week days Veckodag	We/Bank holidays Lör/Söndag/Helgdag
Individual Individuellt	SKr 200:-	SKr 250:-
Couple Par	SKr 400:-	SKr 500:-

Juniors: 100:-/150:-

Caddy	Caddie	no
Electric Trolley	El vagn	no
Buggy	Golfbil	SKr 100:-
Clubs	Klubbor	SKr 90:-

Credit cards Kredit kort VISA - Eurocard - MasterCard

Access Tillfart : R45 Vänersborg-Karlstad.
Exit R164 → Bengtsfors. → Golf
Map 2 on page 1224 Karta 2 se sid: 1224

GOLF COURSE / BANA — 16/20

Site	Läge	▓▓▓▓▓▓░
Maintenance	Underhåll	▓▓▓▓▓▓░
Architect	Arkitekt	Nils Sköld
Type	Typ	forest, parkland
Relief	Relief	▓▓▓▓▓░░
Water in play	Vatten på spelfältet	▓▓▓▓░░░
Exp. to wind	Vindutsatt	▓▓▓░░░░
Trees in play	Träd på spelfältet	▓▓▓▓▓░░

Scorecard Scorekort	Chp. Back tees	Mens Herrtee	Ladies Damtee
Length Längd	6040	5755	5050
Par	72	72	72

Advised golfing ability Rekommenderad spelnivå		0	12	24	36
Hcp required	Hcp erfordrad	36			

CLUB HOUSE & AMENITIES / CLUB HOUSE ET ANNEXES — 7/10

Pro shop	Pro shop	▓▓▓▓▓▓░
Driving range	Träningsbana	▓▓▓▓▓░░
Sheltered	täkt	1 mat
On grass	på gräs	no, 12 mats open air
Putting-green	putting-green	yes

HOTEL FACILITIES / HOTELL OMGIVNING — 4/10

HOTELS
Dalhall — Åmål
20 rooms, D SKr 790:- — 10 km
Tel (46) 0532 - 166 90
Fax (46) 0532 - 129 67

RESTAURANTS RESTAURANG

Stadshotellet — Åmål
Tel (46) 0532 - 120 20 — 7 km

Barhörnan — Åmål
Tel (46) 0532 - 146 00 — 7 km

1245

Forsgården har 27 hål, varav en riktig 18-hålare. Omgärdad av hus och vägar är kanske inte detta den vanligaste eller mest upphetsande plats för en bana. Men väl ute på banan ser du tack vare naturens terräng ingenting av detta. Forsgården är en mästerskapsbana där hindrena ofta är mer i spel för låghandicaparen än för höghandicaparen. Landningsområdena för driven är smala, och det är lätt att hamna i såväl sand som vatten. Att attackera greenerna är inte heller särskilt lätt. De är väl skyddade av kullar, sluttningar och bunkrar. Att ha ett taktiskt sinne på Forsgården är ett stort plus, allt eftersom dina beslut kan betyda skillnaden mellan katastrof och succé. Bästa exemplet på detta är trean, en kort par 4, men nog så knepigt om du spelar det fel. Forsgården är ett bra test på din golf, även om den måhända kunde ha varit aningen charmigare.

The lovely little hamlet of Kungsbacka with its pastel-coloured houses is an essential stop-off when touring this region to the south of Göteborg, which is flat and lined with huge and very busy beaches during the summer. The Forsgården Golfklub consists of 27 holes, including a real 18-hole course. Surrounded by houses and roads, this open space is hardly the most attractive or typical course around, but once out on the course you are isolated from the outside world by the terrain's natural relief. This is a championship course where the hazards affect more the play of low-handicappers than that of the 18-plus hacker, a logical state of affairs. So certain landing areas for the drive are threatened by sand or hazards, with water very definitely in play. Attacking the greens is never easy, either, as they are well guarded by mounds, slopes and other bunkers. Having a game strategy is essential here, as the decisions you take can result in a disastrous or successful round of golf. The best example is hole number 3, a short par 4, with all the usual risks involved.

Forsgårdens Golfklubb — 1989

Gamla Forsvågen 1
S - 434 47 KUNGSBACKA

Office	Sekretariat	(46) 0300 - 719 97
Pro shop	Pro shop	(46) 0300 - 183 27
Fax	Fax	(46) 0300 - 719 87
Situation	Läge	

Göteborg, 27 km

Annual closure	Årlig stängning	no
Weekly closure	Daglig stängning	no

Fees main season
Tariff hög säsong 18 holes

	Week days Veckodag	We/Bank holidays Lör/Söndag/Helgdag
Individual Individuellt	SKr 240:-	SKr 280:-
Couple Par	SKr 480:-	SKr 560:-
Juniors: – 50%		

Caddy	Caddie	no
Electric Trolley	El vagn	no
Buggy	Golfbil	SKr 200:-
Clubs	Klubbor	SKr 180:-

Credit cards Kredit kort
VISA - Eurocard - MasterCard - AMEX - DC

1246

Access Tillfart : Göteborg E6 → Kungsbacka. → Fjäras
Map 1 on page 1218 Karta 1 se sid: 1218

GOLF COURSE / BANA — 14/20

Site	Läge	
Maintenance	Underhåll	
Architect	Arkitekt	Sune Linde
Type	Typ	open country
Relief	Relief	
Water in play	Vatten på spelfältet	
Exp. to wind	Vindutsatt	
Trees in play	Träd på spelfältet	

Scorecard Scorekort	Chp. Back tees	Mens Herrtee	Ladies Damtee
Length Längd	6310	5755	4840
Par	72	72	72

Advised golfing ability — 0 12 24 36
Rekommenderad spelnivå
Hcp required Hcp erfordrad — 36

CLUB HOUSE & AMENITIES / KLUBBHUS OCH OMGIVNING — 6/10

Pro shop	Pro shop	
Driving range	Träningsbana	
Sheltered	täkt	4 mats
On grass	på gräs	yes
Putting-green	putting-green	yes
Pitching-green	pitching-green	yes

HOTEL FACILITIES / HOTELL OMGIVNING — 7/10

HOTELS
Hotell Halland — Kungsbacka
30 rooms, D SKr 1050:- — 3 km
Tel (46) 0300 - 775 30, Fax (46) 0300 - 162 25

Hotell Nattmössan — Kungsbacka
20 rooms, D SKr 850:- — 5 km
Tel (46) 0300 - 775 30, Fax (46) 0300 - 162 25

Säröhus — Särö
83 rooms, D SKr 1095:- — 12 km
Tel (46) 031 - 93 60 90, Fax (46) 031 - 93 61 85

RESTAURANTS RESTAURANG
Pio Pepe — Kungsbacka
Tel (46) 0300 - 199 04 — 3 km

Hotell Halland — Kungsbacka
Tel (46) 0300 - 775 30 — 3 km

FRÖSÅKER

16 | 7 | 5

Även om detta är en relatiivt ny bana har den snabbt fått ett utomordentligt rykte. Inledningen är måhända lite tam, men sedan tar saker och ting fart och när du slutligen når 18e står du inför ett av Sveriges allra bästa hål. Hindrena på Frösåker kommer i alla former och harmonierar väl med landskapet i övrigt. Sista nio är betydligt mer utmanande än de första, och det är lätt att frestas att ta risker. Om du slår någorlunda rakt, förmår att hålla dig kall och har en hyglig teknik så har du alla möjligheter att komma in på ett bra resultat. För den som slår snett kan ruffen vålla stora problem, särskilt med tanke på att höga inspel med gott om bakskruv är ett måste på flera av hålen. En aning för svår för den inte fullt så erfarne golfaren, en njutning för alla andra.

An hour away from Stockholm, Frösåker is also very close to Västerås, where amongst other things you will find a very beautiful cathedral and an old district full of timber houses. Although very new, this course has quickly built up an excellent reputation. Before reaching the magnificent 18th, one of the finest holes in the whole country, you start off with a few rather indifferent holes. Then things start to get more exciting in a much more attractive park landscape, where hazards of all shapes and sizes are brought into play, clearly and with a sense of harmony. The back 9 are even more demanding than the outward half and you will be tempted to take risks. If you are a reasonably straight hitter, can keep a cool head and have the proper technique to work the ball, you will come through with flying colours. For the more wayward hitters, the rough can be more than a handful, especially since approach shots to the greens are not easy and call for high shots with a little spin if possible. A wee difficult for inexperienced players, a real pleasure for the better golfers.

Frösåker Golfklubb — 1989

Box 17015
S - 720 17 VÄSTERÅS

Office	Sekretariat	(46) 021 - 254 01
Pro shop	Pro shop	(46) 021 - 250 24
Fax	Fax	(46) 021 - 254 85
Situation	Läge	
Västerås, 20 km		
Annual closure	Årlig stängning	no
Weekly closure	Daglig stängning	no

Fees main season
Tariff hög säsong 18 holes

	Week days Veckodag	We/Bank holidays Lör/Söndag/Helgdag
Individual Individuellt	SKr 240:-	SKr 300:-
Couple Par	SKr 400:-	SKr 500:-
Juniors: 120:-/180:-		

Caddy	Caddie	no
Electric Trolley	El vagn	no
Buggy	Golfbil	SKr 150:-
Clubs	Klubbor	yes

Credit cards Kredit kort
VISA - Eurocard - MasterCard - AMEX - DC

Access Tillfart : Stockholm E18
→ Enköping/Västerås. → Kärrbo.
Map 2 on page 1221 Karta 2 se sid: 1221

GOLF COURSE
BANA

16/20

Site	Läge	▐▐▐▐▐▯▯
Maintenance	Underhäll	▐▐▐▐▐▯▯
Architect	Arkitekt	Sune Linde
Type	Typ	seaside course, parkland
Relief	Relief	▐▐▯▯▯▯
Water in play	Vatten på spelfältet	▐▐▐▐▯▯
Exp. to wind	Vindutsatt	▐▐▐▐▯▯
Trees in play	Träd på spelfältet	▐▐▐▐▯▯

Scorecard Scorekort	Chp. Back tees	Mens Herrtee	Ladies Damtee
Length Längd	6400	5820	4950
Par	72	72	72

Advised golfing ability Rekommenderad spelnivå	0	12	24	36
Hcp required	Hcp erfordrad	36		

CLUB HOUSE & AMENITIES
CLUB HOUSE ET ANNEXES

7/10

Pro shop	Pro shop	▐▐▐▐▐▯▯
Driving range	Träningsbana	▐▐▐▐▯▯
Sheltered	tåkt	2 mats
On grass	på gräs	yes
Putting-green	putting-green	yes
Pitching-green	pitching-green	yes

HOTEL FACILITIES
HOTELL OMGIVNING

5/10

HOTELS
Radisson — Västerås
203 rooms, D SKr 1325:- — 6 km
Tel (46) 021 - 10 10 10
Fax (46) 021 - 10 10 91

Stadshotellet — Västerås
137 rooms, D SKr 1245:- — 6 km
Tel (46) 021 - 18 04 20
Fax (46) 021 - 10 28 10

RESTAURANTS RESTAURANG
Da Vincis — Västerås
Tel (46) 021 - 18 82 20 — 10 km

Lemone — Västerås
Tel (46) 021 - 410 60 75 — 10 km

1247

Här ligger två banor utlagda i en ganska flack terräng i ett skogs- och parklandskap. Arkitekterna Nils Sköld, Jan Sederholm och Björn Eriksson är välkända namn i Sverige. Framför allt är vattenhindren en ständig källa till oro, och ibland är de direkt farliga. Om du endast spelar Gävle en gång kanske du inte ser de mer subtila poängerna med layouten, och då är det väl tveksamt om det är värt att åka 20 mil för att spela här. Men banan är definitivt en av de bättre norr om Stockholm, och den förtjänar absolut mer än en snabbvisit. Så har du tagit dig över Dalälven, stanna till ett tag. Även om det bara är 10 mil till Stockholm så märker du på atmosfären att du har kommit en bit norrut i landet. Ett utflyktsmål vi absolut vill tipsa om är Storsjön, nära Sandviken och bara tio minuter bort med bil – en av de mest pittoreska vyer man kan hitta i den här regionen.

Two courses are laid out over a rather flat terrain in a combination of forest and parkland styles. Architects Nils Sköld, Jan Sederholm and Björn Eriksson are well known names in Sweden and with their new Avan layout, they designed a course where the risk factor is even greater than here on Gävle course. The water hazards in particular are a constant threat and sometimes downright dangerous. If you play this course once only, you will be hard pushed to understand the more subtle points of the layout. You probably would not travel 200 miles just to play here, but it really is one of the better courses to the north of Stockholm. It deserves more than a fleeting visit when you are in this region, crossed by the Dalälven, one of the twisting rivers running down from the mountains that separate Sweden from Norway. There is indeed a very Nordic flavour to this part of the world, which lies about 100 kilometres from the Swedish capital. If you make it this far north, go and visit lake Storsjön, about a ten minute drive next to Sandviken, one of the most picturesque sights in this part of the country.

Gävle Golfklubb — 1949
Bönavägen 23
S - 805 95 GÄVLE

Office	Sekretariat	(46) 026 - 12 03 33
Pro shop	Pro shop	(46) 026 - 12 14 10
Fax	Fax	(46) 026 - 51 64 68
Situation	Läge	

Gävle, 3 km

Annual closure	Årlig stängning	no
Weekly closure	Daglig stängning	no

Fees main season
Tariff hög säsong full day

	Week days Veckodag	We/Bank holidays Lör/Söndag/Helgdag
Individual Individuellt	SKr 200:-	SKr 250:-
Couple Par	SKr 400:-	SKr 500:-

Juniors: – 50%

Caddy	Caddie	no
Electric Trolley	El vagn	no
Buggy	Golfbil	SKr 200:-
Clubs	Klubbor	SKr 100:-

Credit cards Kredit kort VISA - Eurocard - MasterCard

1248

Access Tillfart : Stockholm, E4 → Gävle. 83
→ Trödje. → FredrikSkans.
Map 2 on page 1221 Karta 2 se sid: 1221

GOLF COURSE
BANA — 14/20

Site	Läge	
Maintenance	Underhåll	
Architect	Arkitekt	Sköld, Sederholm Eriksson
Type	Typ	forest, parkland
Relief	Relief	
Water in play	Vatten på spelfältet	
Exp. to wind	Vindutsatt	
Trees in play	Träd på spelfältet	

Scorecard Scorekort	Chp. Back tees	Mens Herrtee	Ladies Damtee
Length Längd	5915	5720	4875
Par	72	72	72

Advised golfing ability Rekommenderad spelnivå	0	12	24	36

Hcp required   Hcp erfordrad   no

CLUB HOUSE & AMENITIES
KLUBBHUS OCH OMGIVNING — 6/10

Pro shop	Pro shop	
Driving range	Träningsbana	
Sheltered	täkt	no
On grass	på gräs	yes
Putting-green	putting-green	yes
Pitching-green	pitching-green	yes

HOTEL FACILITIES
HOTELL OMGIVNING — 6/10

HOTELS

Scandic Hotel		Gävle
200 rooms, D SKr 660:-		5 km
Tel (46) 026 - 18 80 60		
Fax (46) 026 - 14 18 60		
Hotell Winn		Gävle
200 rooms, D 770/1260 SEK		7 km
Tel (46) 026 - 17 70 00		
Fax (46) 026 - 64 70 09		

RESTAURANTS RESTAURANG

Johanssons Köle		Gävle
Tel (46) 026 - 10 07 34		3 km
Church Street Saloon		Gävle
Tel (46) 026 - 12 62 11		3 km
Bali Garden		Gävle
Tel (46) 026 - 12 43 22		3 km

Detta är Sveriges äldsta bana, och få en starttid här på en helg är snudd på omöjligt. Den byggdes 1904, och träden som då planterades har nu hunnit växa sig stora och mäktiga vilket gör en del hål synnerligen knixiga. Här är du inte mycket hjälpt av råstyrka, betydligt bättre är att fokusera på precisionen. Men det ska du nog lyckas med eftersom banan är ganska kort och ligger i ett böljande landskap som inte är alltför fysiskt krävande. Dessutom är konditionen på banan nästan alltid i högklass, vilket gör att man gärna åker hit för att spela en vänskaplig match. Göteborg, eller i folkmun Hovås, kräver inte en gudabenådad talang, däremot ett hyggligt spel med fairwayträna och mellanjärnen samt de korta järnen. Det här är en perfekt bana att spela och ladda upp på inför tuffare uppgifter, eller som avslutning på en trevlig dag i staden, där vi rekommenderar ett besök i hamnen, centrum, Konstmuseumet eller Röhsska Museumet.

This is the oldest course in Sweden where playing on week-ends is nigh on impossible. It was designed in 1904, and some of the oldest holes are all the narrower and trickier today in that the trees have grown upwards and outwards since they were first planted. It is on these holes in particular that brute force is best left in the locker room and replaced by emphasis on accuracy. This should not be too much of a handicap, though, as the course is short and set out over rolling terrain, which you can walk quite easily. Indeed, the condition of the greens and fairways makes the course even more pleasant to play and it can be great fun playing friendly matches here. Göteborg does not require any particular heaven-sent talent, just all-round skills for fairway woods and your medium and short irons. It is a good course to hone your game before squaring up to more demanding challenges or after a pleasant visit to a city where there is much to see, particularly the harbour, the city centre, the Konstmuseum and the Röhsska Museet (decorative arts).

Göteborgs Golfklubb — 1904

Box 2056
S - 436 02 HOVÅS

Office	Sekretariat	(46) 031 - 28 24 44
Pro shop	Pro shop	(46) 031 - 28 61 59
Fax	Fax	(46) 031 - 68 53 33
Situation	Läge	

Göteborg, 15 km

Annual closure	Årlig stängning	no
Weekly closure	Daglig stängning	no

Fees main season
Tariff hög säsong 18 holes

	Week days Veckodag	We/Bank holidays Lör/Söndag/Helgdag
Individual Individuellt	SKr 250:-	SKr 300:-
Couple Par	SKr 500:-	SKr 600:-

Juniors: – 50%

Caddy	Caddie	no
Electric Trolley	El vagn	no
Buggy	Golfbil	no
Clubs	Klubbor	no

Credit cards Kredit kort VISA - Mastercard - AMEX

Access Tillfart : Göteborg, V 158 → Särö.
Map 1 on page 1218 Karta 1 se sid: 1218

GOLF COURSE
BANA — 15/20

Site	Läge	▰▰▰▰
Maintenance	Underhäll	▰▰▰▰
Architect	Arkitekt	Anders Person
Type	Typ	parkland
Relief	Relief	▰▰▱
Water in play	Vatten på spelfältet	▰▰▱
Exp. to wind	Vindutsatt	▰▰▰
Trees in play	Träd på spelfältet	▰▰▰▰

Scorecard Scorekort	Chp. Back tees	Mens Herrtee	Ladies Damtee
Length Längd	5575	5250	4630
Par	70	70	70

Advised golfing ability Rekommenderad spelnivå	0	12	24	36

Hcp required   Hcp erfordrad   30

CLUB HOUSE & AMENITIES
CLUB HOUSE ET ANNEXES — 6/10

Pro shop	Pro shop	▰▰▰
Driving range	Träningsbana	▰▰▰
Sheltered	täkt	2 mats
On grass	på gräs	no (mats open air)
Putting-green	putting-green	yes
Pitching-green	pitching-green	no

1249

HOTEL FACILITIES
HOTELL OMGIVNING — 7/10

HOTELS

Quality Hotel 11 — Göteborg
133 rooms, D SKr 1350:- — 15 km
Tel (46) 031 - 779 11 11, Fax (46) 031 - 779 11 10

Sheraton Göteborgs Hotel — Göteborg
333 rooms, D SKr 2180:- — 15 km
Tel (46) 031 - 80 60 00, Fax (46) 031 - 15 98 88

Victors - 35 rooms, D SKr 1250:- — Göteborg
Tel (46) 031 - 17 41 80, Fax (46) 031 - 13 96 10 — 15 km

RESTAURANTS RESTAURANG

Westra Piren — Göteborg
Tel (46) 031 - 51 95 55 — 15 km

Le Village — Göteborg
Tel (46) 031 - 24 20 03 — 15 km

Fiskekrogen — Göteborg
Tel (46) 031 - 10 10 05 — 15 km

GRÄNNA

15 7 5

Oavsett om du kommer norr eller söderifrån hamnar du på E 4 utmed Vätterns strand. Detta är tveklöst Sveriges vackraste väg. Inte heller lär du bli besviken på Gränna. Damer, äldre spelare och juniorer kan njuta fullt ut – här finns nämligen inga omöjliga hinder som inte går att slå över med utslaget. Vad gäller medelhandicapare så kommer de också att trivas eftersom de sällan når hindrena som är så strategiskt placerade att de endast bekymrar de bättre spelarna. Från utslagsplatserna är det generella intrycket att fairways är mycket smala. Men detta är faktiskt en synvilla och mer ett psykologiskt problem än ett reellt, vilket kanske kan förklara att den som spelar här för första gången ofta är överdrivet försiktig. På Gränna kan man tydligt se banarkitekten Peter Nordwalls signum: Stora greener! Normalt innebär detta att de även blir aningen försvarslösa, men eftersom de på Gränna är starkt kuperade kommer du att inse att den viktigaste klubban i bagen är din putter.

You will love the trip down the E4 road alongside the Vättern, and Gränna will certainly not disappoint you either. Average players will be happy, as the hazards out on the course are seldom in play for them, and the better players will be in their element, as the main hazards are reserved just for them. From the tee-boxes (generally elevated) you get the impression of the fairways here being very narrow. This is in fact an optical illusion and psychological trap, which explains why golfers playing here for the first time tend to be over-cautious. The course clearly carries the hallmarks of architect Peter Nordwall, i.e. very large greens, a feature that tends to blunt their defences, but as the contours are very pronounced, the putter once again will be the most important club in your bag. Excepting three or four very ordinary holes, Gränna really is worth a visit, as is the village of the same name to see the coloured houses and taste the local barley sugar called polkagrisar.

Gränna Golfklubb — 1989

Västanå Slott
S - 563 92 GRÄNNA

Office	Sekretariat	(46) 0390 - 100 02
Pro shop	Pro shop	(46) 0500 - 106 29
Fax	Fax	(46) 0500 - 100 34
Situation	Läge	

Jönköping, 32 km

Annual closure	Årlig stängning	no
Weekly closure	Daglig stängning	no

Fees main season
Tariff hög säsong full day

	Week days Veckodag	We/Bank holidays Lör/Söndag/Helgdag
Individual Individuellt	SKr 200:-	SKr 250:-
Couple Par	SKr 400:-	SKr 500:-
Juniors: 100:-		

Caddy	Caddie	no
Electric Trolley	El vagn	no
Buggy	Golfbil	SKr 150:-
Clubs	Klubbor	SKr 200:-

Credit cards Kredit kort
VISA - Eurocard - MasterCard - AMEX - DC

1250

Access Tillfart : Gränna E4.
5 km Exit Gyllene Uttern. → Västanå Slott.
Map 1 on page 1218 Karta 1 se sid: 1218

GOLF COURSE / BANA — **15**/20

Site	Läge	
Maintenance	Underhåll	
Architect	Arkitekt	Peter Nordwall
Type	Typ	parkland, open country
Relief	Relief	
Water in play	Vatten på spelfältet	
Exp. to wind	Vindutsatt	
Trees in play	Träd på spelfältet	

Scorecard Scorekort	Chp. Back tees	Mens Herrtee	Ladies Damtee
Length Längd	5967	5515	4741
Par	72	72	72

Advised golfing ability Rekommenderad spelnivå	0	12	24	36

Hcp required   Hcp erfordrad   36

CLUB HOUSE & AMENITIES / KLUBBHUS OCH OMGIVNING — **7**/10

Pro shop	Pro shop	
Driving range	Träningsbana	
Sheltered	täkt	2 mats
On grass	på gräs	no, 16 mats open air
Putting-green	putting-green	yes
Pitching-green	pitching-green	yes

HOTEL FACILITIES / HOTELL OMGIVNING — **5**/10

HOTELS
Västanå Slott - 20 rooms, D SKr 850:-   Gränna
Tel (46) 0390 - 500 00, Fax (46) 0390 - 41 18 75   on site

Stora Hotellet   Jönköping
114 rooms, D SKr 1295:-   32 km
Tel (46) 036 - 10 00 00, Fax (46) 036 - 71 93 20

John Bauer   Jönköping
100 rooms, D SKr 1200:-   32 km
Tel (46) 036 - 34 90 00, Fax (46) 036 - 71 93 20

RESTAURANTS RESTAURANG
Västanå Slott - Tel (46) 0390 - 107 00   Gränna on site

Esters Restaurang   Jönköping
Tel (46) 036 - 34 90 00   32 km

Trottoaren   Jönköping
Tel (46) 036 - 10 00 00   32 km

GULLBRINGA

Den här banan är verkligen strategiskt placerad, nära Göteborg och mittemellan semesterparadiset Marstrand och lilla Kungälv, där du finner massor med småhus som omgärdar en kyrka byggd i trä. De 27 hålen är är utlagda i ett härligt parklandskap med björkskog och små kullar och dalar. Banans placering är alltså idealisk, och layouten signerad Douglas Brasier, är med beröm godkänd. På många hål kommer träd i spel, liksom dammar, diken och förrädiska out-of-bounds-gränser. Du kommer snart att inse att här krävs det en sund taktik, precision och tålamod för att leverera en score på eller under din handicap. Gullbringa är inte 1900-talets största arkitektoniska mästerverk, men den ligger i en härlig miljö och är oftast i väldigt bra kondition. Har du en gång varit här kommer du att vilja åka tillbaka.

Not only is this course close to Göteborg, it is also about mid-way between the seaside resort and port of Marstrand (reachable only by ferry) and the little town of Kungälv, which is full of little houses and a church built out of painted wood. The 27 holes of this course are nicely placed in a magnificent landscape of park-land, a birch forest, little hills and vales. In fact an ideal setting for a very decent layout indeed by Douglas Brasier. Trees are a threat on many holes, as are ponds, ditches and the dreaded out-of-bounds. You will have realized that good strategy, accuracy and thoroughness are required to card a good score and even to play to your handicap. Gullbringa is hardly the masterwork of the century in architectural terms, as it lacks a little punch. But with good green-keeping and a marvellous location, you are always happy to come back for more of the same.

Gullbringa Golfklubb — 1968
S - 442 95 KUNGÄLV

Office	Sekretariat	(46) 0303 - 22 71 61
Pro shop	Pro shop	(46) 0303 - 22 70 27
Fax	Fax	(46) 0303 - 22 77 78
Situation	Läge	

Göteborg, 30 km - Kungälv, 14 km

Annual closure	Årlig stängning	no
Weekly closure	Daglig stängning	no

Fees main season
Tariff hög säsong full day

	Week days Veckodag	We/Bank holidays Lör/Söndag/Helgdag
Individual Individuellt	SKr 220:-	SKr 220:-
Couple Par	SKr 440:-	SKr 440:-

Juniors: – 50%

Caddy	Caddie	no
Electric Trolley	El vagn	no
Buggy	Golfbil	no
Clubs	Klubbor	

Credit cards Kredit kort
VISA - Eurocard - MasterCard - JCB

Access Tillfart : Göteborg, E6. Kungälv,
V 168 → Marstrand. 14 km, → Golf
Map 1 on page 1218 Karta 1 se sid: 1218

GOLF COURSE / BANA — 13/20

Site	Läge	
Maintenance	Underhåll	
Architect	Arkitekt	Douglas Brasier
Type	Typ	forest, parkland
Relief	Relief	
Water in play	Vatten på spelfältet	
Exp. to wind	Vindutsatt	
Trees in play	Träd på spelfältet	

Scorecard Scorekort	Chp. Back tees	Mens Herrtee	Ladies Damtee
Length Längd	5585	5585	4819
Par	71	71	71

Advised golfing ability Rekommenderad spelnivå	0	12	24	36
Hcp required	Hcp erfordrad	no		

CLUB HOUSE & AMENITIES / CLUB HOUSE ET ANNEXES — 7/10

Pro shop	Pro shop	
Driving range	Träningsbana	
Sheltered	täkt	2 mats
On grass	på gräs	no, 18 mats open air
Putting-green	putting-green	yes
Pitching-green	pitching-green	yes

HOTEL FACILITIES / HOTELL OMGIVNING — 6/10

HOTELS

Grand Hotell Marstrand	Marstrand	
22 rooms, D SKr 1495:-	12 km	
Tel (46) 0303 - 603 22		
Fax (46) 0303 - 600 53		

RESTAURANTS RESTAURANG

Tre Kockar	Kungälv
Tel (46) 0303 - 101 23	14 km
Lasse-Majas Krog	Marstrand
Tel (46) 0303 - 611 22	12 km
Lökeberg Konferens Hotell	Kungälv
Tel (46) 0303 - 22 71 91	14 km

1251

HALMSTAD 〉 | 18 | 8 | 7 |

Banan ligger vid Tylösand, vilket är den populäraste stranden i staden. I övrigt rekommenderar vi att du besöker Stortorget och Miniland. Efter detta ska du absolut ta dig tid för en runda golf på en av Sveriges allra bästa banor – utlagd i en tät tallskog och även om du inte kan se havet kan du på många ställen höra och känna det. Varje hål är kantat av träd, och därför finns det heller inget behov för ruff. Träden ger dig känslan av att hålen är längre och smalare än vad de verkligen är, och resultatet blir ofta att du spelar alltför försiktigt. Ett antal fairwaybunkers är extra luriga (framför allt på tvåan), för att inte tala om ån som rinner genom banan, och som lätt ställer till med problem på 12e och 16e hålen. I matchspel kan vad som helst hända där! Lyckligtvis är många av hindrena utom räckhåll för höghandicaparen – därför är också Halmstad relativt sett tuffare för den bättre spelaren. Är du inspirerad blir du dock belönad!

This course is at Tylösand, where essential visiting includes the «Miniland» attraction, a sort of miniature Sweden with 73 reduced-scale models of the finest landmarks and characters from tales and legends in this part of the world. Then move on and play one of the greatest courses in Sweden, laid out in a pine forest where you can always hear the sea without actually seeing it. Each hole is lined with trees, which are so dominant that there is no need for rough. They also give the impression of long, narrow fairways and often result in the golfer playing too cautiously. A few fairway bunkers also lurk dangerously (especially on the second hole), as do a number of streams and ditches, like on the 12th and 16th holes. These can make all the difference in a match-play round. On the other hand, many of the hazards are out of reach for high-handicappers, meaning that Halmstad is a tougher proposition for the better players, but one that rewards inspired play. Completed by another shorter and less challenging 18-hole course, Halmstad is a must.

Halmstad Golfklubb		1938
Tylösand		
S - 302 73 HALMSTAD		

Office	Sekretariat	(46) 035 - 302 80
Pro shop	Pro shop	(46) 035 - 309 76
Fax	Fax	(46) 035 - 323 08
Situation	Läge	
Halmstad, 9 km		
Annual closure	Årlig stängning	no
Weekly closure	Daglig stängning	no

Fees main season
Tariff hög säsong 18 holes

	Week days Veckodag	We/Bank holidays Lör/Söndag/Helgdag
Individual Individuellt	SKr 400:-	SKr 400:-
Couple Par	SKr 800:-	SKr 800:-
Juniors: 240:-		

Caddy	Caddie	no
Electric Trolley	El vagn	SKr 85:-
Buggy	Golfbil	no
Clubs	Klubbor	SKr 100:-

Credit cards Kredit kort
VISA - Eurocard - MasterCard - AMEX

1252

Access Tillfart : Halmstad, → Tylösand.
Map 1 on page 1218 Karta 1 se sid: 1218

GOLF COURSE
BANA 18/20

Site	Läge	
Maintenance	Underhåll	
Architect	Arkitekt	Rafael Sundblom
Type	Typ	forest, parkland
Relief	Relief	
Water in play	Vatten på spelfältet	
Exp. to wind	Vindutsatt	
Trees in play	Tråd på spelfältet	

Scorecard Scorekort	Chp. Back tees	Mens Herrtee	Ladies Damtee
Length Längd	6317	5955	5116
Par	72	72	72

Advised golfing ability	0 12 24 36
Rekommenderad spelnivå	
Hcp required	Hcp erfordrad	28 Men, 36 Ladies

CLUB HOUSE & AMENITIES
KLUBBHUS OCH OMGIVNING 8/10

Pro shop	Pro shop	
Driving range	Träningsbana	
Sheltered	tåkt	3 mats
On grass	på gräs	yes
Putting-green	putting-green	yes
Pitching-green	pitching-green	yes

HOTEL FACILITIES
HOTELL OMGIVNING 7/10

HOTELS
Hotell Mårtensson — Halmstad
103 rooms, D SKr 1385:- — 9 km
Tel (46) 035 - 177 575, Fax (46) 035 - 125 875

Scandic Hotell — Halmstad
129 rooms, D SKr 1387:- — 9 km
Tel (46) 035 - 218 800, Fax (46) 035 - 148 956

Hotell Continental — Halmstad
46 rooms, D SKr 1165:- — 9 km
Tel (46) 035 - 176 300, Fax (46) 035 - 128 604

RESTAURANTS RESTAURANG
Pio & Company — Halmstad
Tel (46) 035 - 210 669 — 9 km

Mårtensson — Halmstad
Tel (46) 035 - 177 575 — 9 km

Klosterköket — Halmstad
Tel (46) 035 - 124 050 — 9 km

Strax söder om Stockholm ligger denna utomordentliga bana och med ett rykte om sig att vara en riktig mästerskapsanläggning. Detta ska dock inte avskräcka medelhandicaparen som kommer att ha en härlig runda framför sig, låt vara att han kanske inte blir alltför stolt över scoren. För det första: Klubbhuset är någonting alldeles extra, ett slott från 1400-talet. För det andra: Banan är en mix mellan öppna hål och parkbane-karaktär. Och eftersom vatten kommer i spel på sju av hålen så kan man verkligen säga att detta är en komplett bana. Långtslående kan sträcka ut ordentligt då fyra av par 5-hålen är möjliga att nå på två slag. Det kan behövas eftersom det är lätt att scoren drar iväg på par 4-hålen och par 3-hålen. Greenerna är mycket bra designade, ganska stora och kuperade och med riktigt besvärliga lutningar på några ställen. De är dessutom väl skyddade bakom bunkrar och kullar som gör det eftersträvansvärt med höga inspel. Arkitekten har lyckats bygga en behaglig bana som kräver all din skicklighet.

This excellent course, lying to the south of Stockholm, has the reputation of being a fine championship test. This shouldn't deter mid-handicappers, who will have a lot of fun playing here, even though they might not be too proud of their card. Firstly, the club-house is a real picture, in an old 15th century castle. Then, the course itself mixes open holes with park-land and forest. And as water comes into play on seven holes, you could call this a complete course. Long-hitters can give it a real whack, probably reaching four of the par 5s in two and putting a few strokes in the bank in the process. They will need them on the par 3s and par 4s. The greens are well-designed, rather large and well contoured; some even have a number of very steep slopes. They are also well-guarded by bunkers and a series of mounds which call for high approach shots. The architect has succeeded in designing an enjoyable course, for which you will need all your skill and technique.

Haninge Golfklubb		1986
Årsta Slott		
S - 136 91 HANINGE		

Office	Sekretariat	(46) 08 - 500 322 70
Pro shop	Pro shop	(46) 08 - 500 322 35
Fax	Fax	(46) 08 - 500 323 40
Situation	Läge	

Stockholm, 30 km

Annual closure	Årlig stängning	no
Weekly closure	Daglig stängning	no

Fees main season
Tariff hög säsong full day

	Week days Veckodag	We/Bank holidays Lör/Söndag/Helgdag
Individual Individuellt	SKr 300:-	SKr 300:-
Couple Par	SKr 600:-	SKr 600:-

Juniors: – 50%

Caddy	Caddie	no
Electric Trolley	El vagn	no
Buggy	Golfbil	no
Clubs	Klubbor	SKr 125:-

Credit cards Kredit kort VISA - Eurocard - MasterCard

Access Tillfart : Stockholm, 73 → Nynäshamn.
→ Dalarö. → «Årsta Havsbad»
Map 2 on page 1221 Karta 2 se sid: 1221

GOLF COURSE
BANA
16/20

Site	Läge	
Maintenance	Underhåll	
Architect	Arkitekt	Jan Sederholm
Type	Typ	forest, parkland
Relief	Relief	
Water in play	Vatten på spelfältet	
Exp. to wind	Vindutsatt	
Trees in play	Träd på spelfältet	

Scorecard Scorekort	Chp. Back tees	Mens Herrtee	Ladies Damtee
Length Längd	6242	5874	5094
Par	73	73	73

Advised golfing ability Rekommenderad spelnivå	0	12	24	36
Hcp required Hcp erfordrad	36			

CLUB HOUSE & AMENITIES
CLUB HOUSE ET ANNEXES
8/10

Pro shop	Pro shop	
Driving range	Träningsbana	
Sheltered	täkt	2 mats
On grass	på gräs	yes
Putting-green	putting-green	yes
Pitching-green	pitching-green	yes

1253

HOTEL FACILITIES
HOTELL OMGIVNING
6/10

HOTELS

Grand Hotel	Stockholm
307 rooms, D SKr 2700:-	20 km
Tel (46) 08 - 679 3500, Fax (46) 08 - 611 8606	

First Hotel Reisen	Stockholm
144 rooms, D 1895 SKr:-	20 km
Tel (46) 08 - 223 260, Fax (46) 08 - 201 559	

City Hotel Slöjdgatan	Stockholm
292 rooms, D SKr 1680:-	20 km
Tel (46) 08 723 72 00, Fax (46) 08 723 72 09	

RESTAURANTS RESTAURANG

Paul and Norbert	Stockholm
Tel (46) 08 661 72 36	20 km

Franska Matsalen	Stockholm
Tel (46) 08 - 679 3584	20 km

Clas På Hörnet	Stockholm
Tel (46) 08 16 51 30	20 km

Staden är en bra start för en resa runt Vättern, Sveriges näst största sjö, berömd för sitt kalla, klara och för all del stormiga vatten när vinden ligger på. Bara några minuter söder om staden ligger banan i en kuperad terräng med ett charmerande klubbhus i centrum. Den öppnades 1938 och är med dagens mått mätt ganska kort, och här kan faktiskt även vardagshackaren hoppas på att träffa parfyrorna på två slag. Problemet är att man sällan får ett rakt läge utan ständigt står i sluttningar. På så vis är Jönköping ingen lätt nöt att knäcka, framför allt som de flesta hinder finns runt de väldesignade och snabba greenerna. De spelare med bra teknik och ett smart huvud på axlarna har en stor fördel. Trevligt är också att alla spelare, oavsett skicklighet, kan spela med varandra och ha stort utbyte av rundan – vilket inte är så vanligt som man kanske tror. Jönköping är ett bra exempel på att längd faktiskt inte är allt.

This little town is the starting point for trips around the Vättern, Sweden's second largest lake known for its clear, cold and rough water when the wind blows. Just a few minutes to the south of the town, this 18-hole course is laid out over hilly terrain around a charming club house. Opened in 1938, today it might be considered very short, where even the average hacker can hope (repeat, hope) to hit the longest par 4s in two. But like everyone else, they won't often find flat lies from where to hit the next shot. In fact, Jönköpings is all the more dangerous because of its shortness; most of the difficulties lie on and around the greens, which are excellent and well-designed putting surfaces given unfailing protection by sand and other hazards. The wily technicians and players with brawn and brain in good working order will probably score better than the rest. Players of all abilities can happily play together, a fun factor that is less frequent than one might think. Jönköping is a fine example of a good course not necessarily having to be a long course.

Jönköpings Golfklubb		1938
Kettilstorp		
S - 556 27 JÖNKÖPING		

Office	Sekretariat	(46) 036 - 765 67
Pro shop	Pro shop	(46) 036 - 763 90
Fax	Fax	(46) 036 - 765 11
Situation	Läge	
Jönköping, 3 km		
Annual closure	Årlig stängning	no
Weekly closure	Daglig stängning	no

Fees main season
Tariff hög säsong full day

	Week days Veckodag	We/Bank holidays Lör/Söndag/Helgdag
Individual Individuellt	SKr 250:-	SKr 300:-
Couple Par	SKr 500:-	SKr 600:-
Juniors: – 50%		

Caddy	Caddie	no
Electric Trolley	El vagn	no
Buggy	Golfbil	no
Clubs	Klubbor	SKr 100:-

Credit cards Kredit kort VISA - Eurocard - MasterCard

1254

Access Tillfart : Jönköping R40 → Göteborg.
Exit Kettilstorp.
Map 1 on page 1218 Karta 1 se sid: 1218

GOLF COURSE
BANA   16/20

Site	Läge	▰▰▰▰▱
Maintenance	Underhåll	▰▰▰▰▱
Architect	Arkitekt	F. Deyer
Type	Typ	parkland
Relief	Relief	▰▰▱▱▱
Water in play	Vatten på spelfältet	▰▰▱▱▱
Exp. to wind	Vindutsatt	▰▱▱▱▱
Trees in play	Träd på spelfältet	▰▰▰▱▱

Scorecard Scorekort	Chp. Back tees	Mens Herrtee	Ladies Damtee
Length Längd	5564	5313	4717
Par	70	70	70

Advised golfing ability Rekommenderad spelnivå	0	12	24	36
Hcp required	Hcp erfordrad	33 Men, 36 Ladies		

CLUB HOUSE & AMENITIES
KLUBBHUS OCH OMGIVNING   7/10

Pro shop	Pro shop	▰▰▰▰▱
Driving range	Träningsbana	▰▰▰▱▱
Sheltered	täkt	15 mats
On grass	på gräs	no, 15 mats
open air		
Putting-green	putting-green	yes
Pitching-green	pitching-green	yes

HOTEL FACILITIES
HOTELL OMGIVNING   7/10

HOTELS
Stora Hotellet	Jönköping
114 rooms, D SKr 1295:-	3 km
Tel (46) 036 - 10 00 00	
Fax (46) 036 - 71 93 20	

John Bauer	Jönköping
100 rooms, D SKr 1200:-	3 km
Tel (46) 036 - 34 90 00	
Fax (46) 036 - 71 93 20	

RESTAURANTS RESTAURANG
Trottoaren	Jönköping
Tel (46) 036 - 10 00 00	3 km

Esters Restaurang	Jönköping
Tel (46) 036 - 34 90 00	3 km

Bron mellan Öland och Kalmar betyder numera att du kan spela Ekerum och Kalmar på samma dag, eller varför inte trycka in två rundor i Kalmar? Här finns nämligen två utmärkta banor. Mästerskapsbanan är resultatet av elva hål från den gamla banan, byggd 1947, och sju hål från den nya banan som öppnade 1992. Låt vara att många tyckte det var ett helgerån att blanda nytt och gammalt när så gjordes, men bortsett från några av de nya greenerna har det blivit en lyckad mix. Från klubbbhuset tittar du ut över Östersjön, och på första hålet spelar du till och med över vattnet. Efter ettan får du vara beredd på att alla klubbor kommer i spel om du vill undvika hindrena, dit ett antal strategiskt placerade träd får räknas. På Kalmar gäller det att hålla sig borta från skogen. Av största betydelse är att tänka innan du slår och att använda dig av de resurser du har för dagen, en bra teknik skadar inte heller. Eftersom de flesta hinder syns tydligt från tee får du leta efter en annan ursäkt för en misslyckad score!

The bridge between Öland and Kalmar now means you can play Ekerum and Kalmar in one summer's day, and maybe even squeeze in 36 holes in Kalmar. This championship course is in fact a mix of 11 holes from the old course, created in 1947, with seven holes from the new course opened in 1992. Some saw this as plain sacrilege, but you have to admit that the two go together well (except perhaps the new greens). The whole complex magnificently overlooks the Baltic and the first hole is in fact played over water. The rest of the programme calls for every club in your bag, if only to avoid the hazards, which include some very dangerous trees. Here more than usual, if you keep long and straight you will be literally out of the woods. Course management is vital using whatever resources you have on that particular day, and good golfing technique. As all the difficulties are clearly in view, you will have to find another excuse for a bad score.

Kalmar Golfklubb — 1947

Box 278
S - 391 23 KALMAR

Office	Sekretariat	(46) 0480 - 47 21 11
Pro shop	Pro shop	(46) 0480 - 47 20 49
Fax	Fax	(46) 0480 - 47 23 14
Situation	Läge	

Kalmar, 8 km

Annual closure	Årlig stängning	no
Weekly closure	Daglig stängning	no

Fees main season
Tariff hög säsong full day

	Week days Veckodag	We/Bank holidays Lör/Söndag/Helgdag
Individual Individuellt	SKr 250:-	SKr 250:-
Couple Par	SKr 500:-	SKr 500:-

Juniors: 100:- / 2 adults + 2 children: SKr 400:-

Caddy	Caddie	no
Electric Trolley	El vagn	no
Buggy	Golfbil	SKr 150:-
Clubs	Klubbor	SKr 125:-

Credit cards Kredit kort
VISA - Eurocard - MasterCard - DC

Access Tillfart : Kalmar E22 Exit Kalmar N/Lindsdal.
Map 1 on page 1219 Karta 1 se sid: 1219

GOLF COURSE / BANA — 15/20

Site	Läge	
Maintenance	Underhäll	
Architect	Arkitekt	Sundblom/Gierdsjö Sköld/Sune Linde
Type	Typ	parkland
Relief	Relief	
Water in play	Vatten på spelfältet	
Exp. to wind	Vindutsatt	
Trees in play	Träd på spelfältet	

Scorecard Scorekort	Chp. Back tees	Mens Herrtee	Ladies Damtee
Length Längd	6028	5685	4864
Par	72	72	72

Advised golfing ability Rekommenderad spelnivå	0	12	24	36

Hcp required Hcp erfordrad 36

CLUB HOUSE & AMENITIES / CLUB HOUSE ET ANNEXES — 5/10

Pro shop	Pro shop	
Driving range	Träningsbana	
Sheltered	täkt	12 mats
On grass	på gräs	no, 7 mats open air
Putting-green	putting-green	yes
Pitching-green	pitching-green	yes

HOTEL FACILITIES / HOTELL OMGIVNING — 8/10

HOTELS

Packhuset — Kalmar 8 km
68 rooms, D SKr 1350:-
Tel (46) 0480 - 570 00, Fax (46) 0480 - 866 42

Slottshotellet — Kalmar 8 km
44 rooms, D SKr 1450:-
Tel (46) 0480 - 882 60, Fax (46) 0480 - 882 66

Kalmarsund Hotell — Kalmar 8 km
85 rooms, D SKr 1310:-
Tel (46) 0480 - 181 00, Fax (46) 0480 - 41 13 37

RESTAURANTS RESTAURANG

Kalmar Hamnkrog — Kalmar 8 km
Tel (46) 0480 - 41 10 20

Matïsse - Tel (46) 0480 - 272 86 — Kalmar 8 km

Källaren Kronan - Tel (46) 0480 - 41 14 00 — Kalmar 8 km

1255

Detta är en historisk region, som har sett allt från en rysk ubåt stranda på klipporna till en 26 kilo tung lax fångas i Mörrum. Banan är utlagd genom tät skog där det inte finns några som helst flyktvägar att hoppas på. Hemligheten är att ignorera träden, för faktum är att fairways är bredare än vad de verkar. Hur som helst, det har sin charm att rädda sig ur skogen, och det är även möjligt då ett stort arbete har lagts ned på att rensa undervegetationen. Nåväl, för den mer klaustrofobiske och snedslående golfaren är kanske inte "charm" det rätta ordet. Han kommer att få det svårt att slappna av och njuta av spelet. Men det är heller ingen idé att vara överdrivet försiktig från tee eftersom detta bara leder till långa andraslag in mot greener som på sina ställen vaktas av djupa och rymningssäkra bunkrar. Greenerna har också sin historia: Många är upphöjda eller ligger precis intill sluttningar vilket kräver ett taktiskt sinne då det inte alltid går att rulla in bollen. Det sägs att efter en runda här så drömmer du i veckor om stora, vackra träd.

An historical region, where a Russian submarine once came to grief on the rocks just off the coast and where a 55 lb. salmon was caught, close to Mörrum, one of the great fishery centres that are so important to Swedish gastronomy. The golf course was laid out through a forest, from which there is no escaping on virtually every hole. The secret is to try to ignore it, as the fairways are wider than they look. And anyway, it's such fun hitting little recovery shots from out of the trees because the undergrowth has been thoroughly cleared. Fun might not be the word for the more claustrophobic golfer or way at the bottom of a hill; this calls for careful thinking and often rules out the bump and run shot. They say that after playing here you spend the next few weeks dreaming about big beautiful trees.

Karlshamns Golfklubb — 1966

Box 188
S - 374 23 KARLSHAMN

Office	Sekretariat	(46) 0454 - 500 85
Pro shop	Pro shop	(46) 0454 - 541 41
Fax	Fax	(46) 0454 - 501 60
Situation	Läge	

Karlshamn, 7 km

Annual closure	Årlig stängning	no
Weekly closure	Daglig stängning	no

Fees main season
Tariff hög säsong 18 holes

	Week days Veckodag	We/Bank holidays Lör/Söndag/Helgdag
Individual Individuellt	SKr 200:-	SKr 250:-
Couple Par	SKr 400:-	SKr 500:-

Juniors: – 50% / 2 Seniors + 2 Juniors: SKr 500:-

Caddy	Caddie	no
Electric Trolley	El vagn	no
Buggy	Golfbil	no
Clubs	Klubbor	SKr 150:-

Credit cards Kredit kort VISA - Eurocard - MasterCard

1256.

Access Tillfart : Karlshamn E22 → Kristianstad.
Mörrum, R29. Golf north of Mörrum.
Map 1 on page 1219 Karta 1 se sid: 1219

GOLF COURSE BANA — 14/20

Site	Läge	
Maintenance	Underhåll	
Architect	Arkitekt	Douglas Brasier R. Victorsson
Type	Typ	forest, parkland
Relief	Relief	
Water in play	Vatten på spelfältet	
Exp. to wind	Vindutsatt	
Trees in play	Träd på spelfältet	

Scorecard Scorekort	Chp. Back tees	Mens Herrtee	Ladies Damtee
Length Längd	6039	5750	5002
Par	72	72	72

Advised golfing ability Rekommenderad spelnivå	0 12 24 36
Hcp required Hcp erfordrad	36

CLUB HOUSE & AMENITIES KLUBBHUS OCH OMGIVNING — 6/10

Pro shop	Pro shop	
Driving range	Träningsbana	
Sheltered	täkt	2 mats
On grass	på gräs	yes
Putting-green	putting-green	yes
Pitching-green	pitching-green	no

HOTEL FACILITIES HOTELL OMGIVNING — 6/10

HOTELS

First Hotel Karlshamn — Karlshamn
132 rooms, D SKr 1285:- — 7 km
Tel (46) 0454 - 890 00
Fax (46) 0454 - 891 50

Scandic Hotel — Karlshamn
9 rooms, D SKr 1322:- — 10 km
Tel (46) 0454 -166 60
Fax (46) 0454 - 186 66

RESTAURANTS RESTAURANG

Lord Nelson — Karlshamn
Tel (46) 0454 - 845 35 — 7 km

Loch Ness — Karlshamn
Tel (46) 0454 - 126 00 — 7 km

Gourmet Grön — Karlshamn
Tel (46) 0454 - 164 40 — 7 km

Detta är i hjärtat av Värmland – ett landskap av skogar, forsar, sjöar, små bondgårdar och härliga måltider. Det var också hemvist för Selma Lagerlöf, författaren till Nils Holgerssons underbara resor, som är en underbar hyllning till Sverige. Lagerlöfs hus ligger mindre än en timmes resa från banan, som vindlar genom lummig skog och är en njutning för den som gillar vildmarksliv, något som kan skänka tröst åt den som olyckligtvis inte har någon av sina bästa dagar, vilket är lätt hänt här om man inte driver bollen bra från tee. Banan är mycket lång, och på vår och höst är den ofta blöt och tung. Då är många av par 4-hålen svåra att nå även för den bättre spelaren. Men Karlstad är inte bara skog, det finns också relativt öppna partier, vilket vi är tacksamma för. Flertalet av greenerna är dock väldigt svårlästa, och troligen är banan relativt sett svårare för låghandicaparen än för höghandicaparen som inte behöver träffa varje green på rätt antal slag.

This is the capital of Värmland, a landscape of forests, streams, lakes, small farms and rich food (sausage, roast pork with oat mash). It is also the region of Selma Lagerlöf, the author of The Travels of Nils Holgersson, which is nothing less than an ode to Sweden. His house is less than an hour away from the course. Karlstad runs through a forest and is a real treat for lovers of wildlife, a sort of communion with nature, which can offer some solace and compensation for the disappointing score they might have to settle for here, unless they are hitting their driver really well. The course is very long, wet outside summer, and some of the par 4s are hard to reach, even for the better player. Yet its openness works in its favour, despite a number of greens that are difficult to read. In actual fact, the lower handicap golfer is more likely to suffer here than the lesser golfers, who can easily put up with not hitting greens in regulation.

Karlstad Golfklubb — 1958

Höja 510
S - 655 92 KARLSTAD

Office	Sekretariat	(46) 054 - 86 63 53
Pro shop	Pro shop	(46) 054 - 86 62 70
Fax	Fax	(46) 054 - 86 64 78
Situation	Läge	
Karlstad, 8 km		
Annual closure	Årlig stängning	no
Weekly closure	Daglig stängning	no

Fees main season
Tariff hög säsong full day

	Week days Veckodag	We/Bank holidays Lör/Söndag/Helgdag
Individual Individuellt	SKr 250:-	SKr 250:-
Couple Par	SKr 500:-	SKr 500:-
Juniors: – 50%		

Caddy	Caddie	no
Electric Trolley	El vagn	no
Buggy	Golfbil	SKr 150:-
Clubs	Klubbor	SKr 150:-

Credit cards Kredit kort
VISA - Eurocard - MasterCard - DC

Access Tillfart : Karlstad E18. Exit R63 → Filipstad.
4 km → Golf
Map 2 on page 1220 Karta 2 se sid: 1220

GOLF COURSE / BANA — **15**/20

Site	Läge	
Maintenance	Underhåll	
Architect	Arkitekt	Nils Sköld
		Sune Linde
Type	Typ	forest, parkland
Relief	Relief	
Water in play	Vatten på spelfältet	
Exp. to wind	Vindutsatt	
Trees in play	Träd på spelfältet	

Scorecard Scorekort	Chp. Back tees	Mens Herrtee	Ladies Damtee
Length Längd	6215	5985	5060
Par	72	72	72

Advised golfing ability 0 12 24 36
Rekommenderad spelnivå
Hcp required Hcp erfordrad — 36

CLUB HOUSE & AMENITIES / CLUB HOUSE ET ANNEXES — **6**/10

Pro shop	Pro shop	
Driving range	Träningsbana	
Sheltered	täkt	8 mats
On grass	på gräs	yes
Putting-green	putting-green	yes
Pitching-green	pitching-green	yes

HOTEL FACILITIES / HOTELL OMGIVNING — **6**/10

HOTELS
Plaza Hotel — Karlstad
121 rooms, D SKr 1385:- — 5 km
Tel (46) 054 - 10 02 00
Fax (46) 054 - 10 02 24

Stadshotellet — Karlstad
139 rooms, D SKr 1250:- — 6 km
Tel (46) 054 - 29 30 00
Fax (46) 054 - 29 30 31

RESTAURANTS RESTAURANG
Tiffany — Karlstad
Tel (46) 054 - 15 33 88 — 7 km

Vivaldi — Karlstad
Tel (46) 054 - 10 02 00 — 5 km

1257

I Skåne känner du omedelbart impulserna från Danmark, vilket är rätt logiskt med tanke på hur länge landskapet tillhörde danskarna. Det var ju inte förrän i början av 1800-talet som Skåne en gång för alla blev svenskt och Sverige fick sin naturliga kustlinje. Detta är jordbruksland i ett långsamt böljande landskap, och den topografin återspeglar sig också i banan. Kristianstad ligger inte långt från havet – sandjorden och layouten påminner också om en linksbana, fast i själva verket befinner vi oss i ett parklandskap. Många greener närmar man sig bäst med låga rullslag, framför allt de dagar när vinden ligger på. Banan ändrar gång på gång karaktär, såväl visuellt som rent strategiskt. Ibland är den vänlig, ibland direkt fientlig. Nyckelhålen är 14-16 – massor med vatten kommer i spel och en otålig själ riskerar att bestraffas hårt. De här hindrena ska dock inte hindra höghandicaparen från att spela här. Banan har nyligen byggts om, och blivit ännu bättre.

Scania (Skåne) is the Swedish south, where there is a definite Danish influence, a logical enough state of affairs when you realize that Denmark only granted Sweden its natural maritime frontier in the early 18th century. Here, we are in farming country in a landscape of gently rolling valleys, and this course reflects the same topology. Located not far from the sea, the sandy soil and layout are reminiscent of a links course, although in reality the setting is one large park. The grass is wonderful and many of the greens can be reached with low running shots, a considerable advantage given how windy it can be here. The key holes are 14 through 16, spectacular numbers with a lot of water where impatience can cost you dearly. These difficulties, however, should not prevent the higher-handicap golfers from playing here and rubbing shoulders with the better players. The course has been recently restyled, for the better.

Kristianstads Golfklubb 1924
Box 41
S - 296 21 ÅHUS

Office	Sekretariat	(46) 044 - 24 76 56
Pro shop	Pro shop	(46) 044 - 24 74 29
Fax	Fax	(46) 044 - 24 76 35
Situation	Läge	

Kristianstad, 18 km

Annual closure	Årlig stängning	no
Weekly closure	Daglig stängning	no

Fees main season
Tariff hög säsong full day

	Week days Veckodag	We/Bank holidays Lör/Söndag/Helgdag
Individual Individuellt	SKr 240:-	SKr 240:-
Couple Par	SKr 400:-	SKr 400:-

Juniors: 130:-

Caddy	Caddie	no
Electric Trolley	El vagn	no
Buggy	Golfbil	SKr 100:-
Clubs	Klubbor	SKr 95:-

Credit cards Kredit kort
VISA - Eurocard - MasterCard - AMEX - DC

1258

Access Tillfart : Malmö, E22 → Kristianstad.
118 → Åhus. Rondell i Åhus → Golf
Map 1 on page 1218 Karta 1 se sid: 1218

GOLF COURSE
BANA 17 /20

Site	Läge	■■■■■□
Maintenance	Underhåll	■■■■■□
Architect	Arkitekt	Douglas Brasier Tommy Nordström
Type	Typ	parkland, open country
Relief	Relief	■■□□□□
Water in play	Vatten på spelfältet	■■■■□□
Exp. to wind	Vindutsatt	■■■■■□
Trees in play	Träd på spelfältet	■■■■□□

Scorecard Scorekort	Chp. Back tees	Mens Herrtee	Ladies Damtee
Length Längd	6046	5675	4940
Par	71	71	71

Advised golfing ability	0	12	24	36
Rekommenderad spelnivå		■■■■■		
Hcp required Hcp erfordrad	36			

CLUB HOUSE & AMENITIES
KLUBBHUS OCH OMGIVNING 7 /10

Pro shop	Pro shop	■■■■□
Driving range	Träningsbana	■■■■□
Sheltered	täkt	2 mats
On grass	på gräs	yes
Putting-green	putting-green	yes
Pitching-green	pitching-green	yes

HOTEL FACILITIES
HOTELL OMGIVNING 7 /10

HOTELS
Åhustrand — Åhus
57 rooms, D SKr 650:- — 3 km
Tel (46) 044 - 28 93 00, Fax (46) 044 - 24 94 80

Kastanjelund — Åhus
24 rooms, D SKr 720:- — 6 km
Tel (46) 044 - 23 25 33, Fax (46) 044 - 23 21 77

Kristian IV — Kristianstad
86 rooms, D SKr 1385:- — 14 km
Tel (46) 044 - 12 63 00, Fax (46) 044 - 12 41 40

RESTAURANTS RESTAURANG
Kippers Källare — Kristianstad
Tel (46) 044 - 10 62 00 — 14 km

Kung Kristian — Kristianstad
Tel (46) 044 - 21 00 34 — 14 km

Banan öppnade 1974, arkitekten heter Frank Pennink, och det finns ingen som helst anledning varför du skulle spela dåligt här, inte med tanke på att här finns ett magnifikt övningsfält, tre puttinggreener och fyra pitchinggreener... Men, men – banan är en sällsynt tuff nöt att knäcka, Först och främst måste du lära dig att växla mellan olika typer av golf. Till en början spelar vi i ett parklandskap, sedan övergår det till golf med seasidekänsla och därefter golf i tät, ogenomtränglig skog. Den trånga avslutningen där vinden torkar upp greenerna och gör dem hårda är en alldeles egen historia, inte minst med tanke på hur svårt det är att få bollen att stanna kvar på det finklippta. Svårigheten ligger alltså i att ställa om från att ha försökt lura vinden med låga slag till att spela klassisk målgolf med höga slag. Detta är ett riktigt nervtest! För höghandicaparen kan det bli lite väl mycket av det goda, om han nu inte förmår att ta det med jämnmod och inse att han ännu har mycket att lära. Har han den distansen kan han mycket väl spela Kungsbacka.

There is no reason why you should play badly here, after all there is a huge driving range, three putting greens and four pitching greens to practice on. No reason that is, except for the course itself. Firstly you have to adjust to some abrupt changes of surroundings, from parkland to seaboard to forest. You start off over wide open space and end up down a narrow strait where the wind can twist and turn, dry the greens and make those approach shots even tougher. From the roll-on shots by the sea you then have to change modes to target golf. For the nerves, nothing is simple here, especially since the last section of the course is the most demanding. This is a tough proposition for high-handicappers, who will be hard pushed to keep up with the better players. Yet if they can take it like a man and realize willingly that they still have much to learn, then there's no reason why they should not play a round or two here.

Kungsbacka Golfklubb — 1974
Hamra Gård 515
S - 429 44 SÄRÖ

Office	Sekretariat	(46) 031 - 93 61 71
Pro shop	Pro shop	(46) 031 - 93 62 79
Fax	Fax	(46) 031 - 93 50 85
Situation	Läge	

Göteborg, 25 km

Annual closure	Årlig stängning	no
Weekly closure	Daglig stängning	no

Fees main season
Tariff hög säsong 18 holes

	Week days Veckodag	We/Bank holidays Lör/Söndag/Helgdag
Individual Individuellt	SKr 220:-	SKr 260:-
Couple Par	SKr 440:-	SKr 520:-

Juniors: – 50%

Caddy	Caddie	no
Electric Trolley	El vagn	no
Buggy	Golfbil	SKr 200:-
Clubs	Klubbor	SKr 150:-

Credit cards Kredit kort VISA - Eurocard - MasterCard

Access Tillfart : Göteborg, E6 → Kungsbacka.
Exit 60 → Särö. 7 km → Golf
Map 1 on page 1218 Karta 1 se sid: 1218

GOLF COURSE BANA — 15/20

Site	Läge	■■■■■
Maintenance	Underhäll	■■■■
Architect	Arkitekt	Frank Pennink
Type	Typ	seaside course, parkland
Relief	Relief	■■
Water in play	Vatten på spelfältet	■■■
Exp. to wind	Vindutsatt	■■■
Trees in play	Träd på spelfältet	■■■■

Scorecard Scorekort	Chp. Back tees	Mens Herrtee	Ladies Damtee
Length Längd	6096	5831	5030
Par	72	72	72

Advised golfing ability		0	12	24	36
Rekommenderad spelnivå				■■	
Hcp required	Hcp erfordrad	36			

CLUB HOUSE & AMENITIES CLUB HOUSE ET ANNEXES — 6/10

Pro shop	Pro shop	■■■■
Driving range	Träningsbana	■■■
Sheltered	täkt	8 mats
On grass	på gräs	no, 22 mats open air
Putting-green	putting-green	ja
Pitching-green	pitching-green	ja

HOTEL FACILITIES HOTELL OMGIVNING — 6/10

HOTELS

Säröhus - 83 rooms, D SKr 1095:- — Särö
Tel (46) 031 - 93 60 90, Fax (46) 031 - 93 61 85 — 4 km

Hotell Holland — Kungsbacka
30 rooms, D SKr 1050:- — 12 km
Tel (46) 0300 - 775 30, Fax (46) 0300 - 162 25

Hotell Nattmösan — Kungsbacka
20 rooms, D SKr 850:- — 10 km
Tel (46) 0300 - 775 30, Fax (46) 0300 - 162 25

RESTAURANTS RESTAURANG

Hotell Holland — Kungsbacka
Tel (46) 0300 - 775 30 — 12 km

Pio Pepe - Tel (46) 0300 - 199 04 — Kungsbacka 11 km

Kliv in Kök & Bar — Kungsbacka
(46) 0300 - 199 04 — 11 km

1259

Anläggningen i sin helhet är suverän, den andra banan på området är en mycket trevlig bekantskap och klubbhuset har allt man kan önska sig. Huvudbanan är ett mycket intressant test, även om man önskar att den konditionsmässigt vore aningen jämnare i kvaliteten. Vatten kommer i spel på nära häften av hålen men om du undviker att chansa ska det inte behöva ställa till med något problem. Därmed sagt – är du villig att ta risker så kommer du att bli belönad om du lyckas. Tre av par 5-hålen är exempelvis möjliga att nå på två slag, om du kan hantera pressen, vill säga. Landskapet är relativt platt, och vid en jämförelse med andra svenska banor möjligen aningen tråkigt. Å andra sidan har det det goda med sig att du inte blir distraherad av fantastiska scenerier. Men åtskilliga av hålen kommer att bjuda på all underhållning du kan önska dig. Det finns många banor som är mer imponerande och upphetsande än Lindö, men likväl är banan definitivt värd ett besök.

All the facilities here are excellent, the second course is a nice little layout and the club-house is well equipped. The main course, despite inconsistent green-keeping, makes for very interesting golf. Water comes into play on nearly half the holes but should be easily avoided if you are as afraid of water as you are of taking risks. With this said, the more daring golfers will find their reward, for example on three of the par 5s, which are definitely reachable in two if you can handle the pressure. The landscape is rather flat and perhaps a little monotonous, at least when compared with the panoramas around which most Swedish courses are built, but when you come to play here you won't be distracted by the scenery, which is a help. Some holes, moreover, are spectacular enough to leave their mark. There are certainly more impressive and, objectively speaking, more decisive courses than this, but Lindö Park is well worth a visit.

Stockholm Lindö Park GK 1984
S - 186 92 VALLENTUNA

Office	Sekretariat	(46) 08 - 511 750 00
Pro shop	Pro shop	(46) 08 - 511 754 52
Fax	Fax	(46) 08 - 511 706 13
Situation	Läge	

Stockholm, 30 km

Annual closure	Årlig stängning	no
Weekly closure	Daglig stängning	no

Fees main season
Tariff hög säsong full day

	Week days Veckodag	We/Bank holidays Lör/Söndag/Helgdag
Individual Individuellt	SKr 300:-	SKr 400:-
Couple Par	SKr 600:-	SKr 800:-

Juniors: – 50%

Caddy	Caddie	no
Electric Trolley	El vagn	no
Buggy	Golfbil	no
Clubs	Klubbor	SKr 200:-

Credit cards Kredit kort
VISA - Eurocard - MasterCard

1260

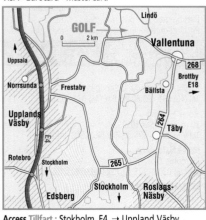

Access Tillfart : Stokholm, E4. → Uppland Väsby.
268 → Vallentuna. 9 km → «Stockholm Lindö Park».
Map 2 on page 1220 Karta 2 se sid: 1220

GOLF COURSE
BANA **14**/20

Site	Läge	
Maintenance	Underhäll	
Architect	Arkitekt	Ture Bruce Åke Persson
Type	Typ	parkland, open country
Relief	Relief	
Water in play	Vatten på spelfältet	
Exp. to wind	Vindutsatt	
Trees in play	Tråd på spelfältet	

Scorecard Scorekort	Chp. Back tees	Mens Herrtee	Ladies Damtee
Length Längd	6050	5795	5025
Par	72	72	72

Advised golfing ability Rekommenderad spelnivå	0	12	24	36
Hcp required	Hcp erfordrad	36		

CLUB HOUSE & AMENITIES
KLUBBHUS OCH OMGIVNING **8**/10

Pro shop	Pro shop	
Driving range	Träningsbana	
Sheltered	tåkt	22 mats
On grass	på gräs	yes
Putting-green	putting-green	yes
Pitching-green	pitching-green	yes

HOTEL FACILITIES
HOTELL OMGIVNING **6**/10

HOTELS

Radisson SAS Royal Park	Stockholm
184 rooms, D SKr 1900:-	25 km
Tel (46) 08 - 624 55 00, Fax (46) 08 - 85 85 66	
Silja Hotel Ariadne	Stockholm
283 rooms, D SKr 1960:-	30 km
Tel (46) 08 - 665 78 00, Fax (46) 08 - 662 76 70	
First Hotel Reisen	Stockholm
144 rooms, D 1895 SKr:-	30 km
Tel (46) 08 - 223 260, Fax (46) 08 - 201 559	

RESTAURANTS RESTAURANG

Edsbacka Krog	Sollentuna
Tel (46) 08 - 85 08 15	15 km
Stallmästaregården	Stockholm
Tel (46) 08 - 610 13 00	30 km

Några tips innan du slår ut: När du begraver bollen i tjock ljung (vilket du kommer att göra), så försök att ta dig därifrån så fort som möjligt, även om detta innebär att du bara hackar bollen några meter till höger eller vänster. En annan sak: När du har en nedförsputt i medvind så behöver du...äsch, glöm det! För att scora väl på den här banan måste du ha stor fantasi och hela tiden befinna dig på rätt sida om flaggan. På den här typen av seaside-bana räcker det alltså inte med att ha tränat som en galning på övningsfältet. Här krävs andra kunskaper! Du måste kunna manövrera bollen åt bägge hållen. På sätt och vis är detta klassisk linksgolf, även om du inte kommer se några gigantiska sandklitter som du kan göra på Irland. Vad som däremot finns här är ljung – tjock och ogenomtränglig på sommaren. Därför verkar också fairways från utslagsplatserna vara löjligt smala. Men detta är faktiskt inte riktigt sant, och spelare av alla skicklighetsgrader verkligen ha ett fint utbyte av en runda här. I varje fall så länge som du är villig att eftertänksamt ta dig an varje slag, ett i taget.

To score well, you must show a certain amount of creativity from tee to green. On this kind of seaside course, the standard shots you learn at practice are not enough. You have to know how to bend that ball in every direction. You won't find the spectacular sights of huge Irish-style dunes here, but you will be confronted with each and every feature of links play. With the addition of heather - thick and ubiquitous in the summer months - you get the impression from the tee-box that the fairways are ridiculously narrow. This in fact is not really true, as Ljunghusens is a distinctly playable course for golfers of all abilities, as long as you are willing to review your strategy at each shot. Your reward will be to contemplate with a positive eye this huge stretch of purple, yellow and green, which really comes to life in the summer twilight.

Ljunghusens Golfklubb — 1932
Kinellsväg
S - 236 42 HÖLLVIKEN

Office	Sekretariat	(46) 040 - 45 03 84
Pro shop	Pro shop	(46) 040 - 45 25 61
Fax	Fax	(46) 040 - 45 42 65
Situation	Läge	

Malmö, 30 km - Falsterbo, 1 km

Annual closure	Årlig stängning	no
Weekly closure	Daglig stängning	no

Fees main season
Tariff hög säsong full day

	Week days Veckodag	We/Bank holidays Lör/Söndag/Helgdag
Individual Individuellt	SKr 250:-	SKr 300:-
Couple Par	SKr 500:-	SKr 600:-

We 05 → 09 & every day in 07: limitation of Green fees (Begr antal tider for gäs

Caddy	Caddie	no
Electric Trolley	El vagn	no
Buggy	Golfbil	SKr 100:-
Clubs	Klubbor	SKr 100:-

Credit cards Kredit kort
VISA - Eurocard - MasterCard - AMEX - DC

Access Tillfart : Malmö: E6 → Falsterbo.
Map 1 on page 1218 Karta 1 se sid: 1218

GOLF COURSE / BANA — 17/20

Site	Läge	■■■■□
Maintenance	Underhåll	■■■■□
Architect	Arkitekt	Douglas Brasier
Type	Typ	seaside course
Relief	Relief	■■□□□
Water in play	Vatten på spelfältet	■■■□□
Exp. to wind	Vindutsatt	■■■■□
Trees in play	Tråd på spelfältet	■■□□□

Scorecard Scorekort	Chp. Back tees	Mens Herrtee	Ladies Damtee
Length Längd	6115	5895	5120
Par	72	72	72

Advised golfing ability Rekommenderad spelnivå	0	12	24	36

Hcp required — Hcp erfordrad — 36

CLUB HOUSE & AMENITIES / CLUB HOUSE ET ANNEXES — 6/10

Pro shop	Pro shop	■■■■□
Driving range	Träningsbana	■■■□□
Sheltered	tåkt	2 mats
On grass	på gräs	yes
Putting-green	putting-green	yes
Pitching-green	pitching-green	yes

HOTEL FACILITIES / HOTELL OMGIVNING — 7/10

1261

HOTELS

Hotell Gässlingen — Skanör
13 rooms, D SKr 1300:- — 8 km
Tel (46) 040 - 45 91 00
Fax (46) 040 - 35 91 13

Hotell Spelabäcken — Skanör
18 rooms, D SKr 850:- — 6 km
Tel (46) 040 - 47 53 00
Fax (46) 040 - 47 32 42

RESTAURANTS RESTAURANG

Skänors Gästgiveri — Skanör
Tel (46) 040 - 47 56 90 — 10 km

Vellinge Gästgiveri — Vellinge
Tel (46) 040 - 42 48 65 — 15 km

Kaptensgården — Falsterbo
Tel (46) 040 - 47 07 50 — 1 km

Lund är en härlig plats att besöka, bubblande av liv, vilket kanske inte är så konstigt med tanke på att det är Sveriges näst största universitetsstad. Ett av många utflyktsmål vi rekommenderar att besöka är den stora domkyrkan. Några kilometer österut från själva staden ligger i en nationalpark en bana ritad 1936 av Morrison, vars namn är förknippat med många av Europas bästa banor. Under sommaren växer ruffen tjock och vild, och straffar sneda drives obarmhärtigt. Första nio är som en vandring genom en lummig park. Andra nio ligger öppnare och är svårare. Helt logiskt kommer banans klimax i avslutningen. På hålen 16-18 förenar sig ruffen, vattnet och skogen i ett gemensamt försök att förstöra din score. Om du klarar detta så kan du spela var som helst! Alla älskar den här charmerande platsen, men det är troligen en utmaning som uppskattas mer av den bättre spelaren.

Lund is a very pleasant, bustling place and Sweden second's largest university city. Art-lovers should make a point of visiting the Romanesque cathedral and the astronomical clock with automatons. Several miles to the east lies a national park and a golf course designed in 1936 by Morrison, whose name is linked with many of the top courses in Europe. Here in summer, the rough grows high and thick and punishes wild driving unrelentlessly. The outward nine are like a walk through a huge tree-strewn park, the back nine are laid out over more open space, but are tougher to play. Quite logically the climax comes over the finishing holes, 16 through 18, where water, rough and trees join forces to ruin your card. If you can resist this treatment, you can play just about everywhere. Everyone loves this spot, it's so charming, but it is a challenge that is probably better appreciated and accepted by the more proficient players.

Lunds Akademiska Golfklubb — 1936
Kungsmarken
S - 225 92 LUND

Office	Sekretariat	(46) 046 - 990 04
Pro shop	Pro shop	(46) 046 - 990 96
Fax	Fax	(46) 046 - 991 46
Situation	Läge	

Lund, 10 km

Annual closure	Årlig stängning	no
Weekly closure	Daglig stängning	no

Fees main season
Tariff hög säsong full day

	Week days Veckodag	We/Bank holidays Lör/Söndag/Helgdag
Individual Individuellt	SKr 160:-	SKr 200:-
Couple Par	SKr 280:-	SKr 360:-

Juniors: – 50%

Caddy	Caddie	no
Electric Trolley	El vagn	no
Buggy	Golfbil	SKr 100:-
Clubs	Klubbor	SKr 100:-

Credit cards Kredit kort
VISA - Eurocard - MasterCard - AMEX - DC

1262

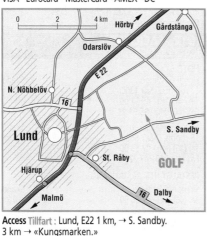

Access Tillfart : Lund, E22 1 km, → S. Sandby.
3 km → «Kungsmarken.»
Map 1 on page 1218 Karta 1 se sid: 1218

GOLF COURSE / BANA — 16/20

Site	Läge	
Maintenance	Underhäll	
Architect	Arkitekt	J. Morrison S. Böstrom
Type	Typ	parkland
Relief	Relief	
Water in play	Vatten på spelfältet	
Exp. to wind	Vindutsatt	
Trees in play	Tråd på spelfältet	

Scorecard Scorekort	Chp. Back tees	Mens Herrtee	Ladies Damtee
Length Längd	6040	5705	5030
Par	72	72	72

Advised golfing ability Rekommenderad spelnivå	0	12	24	36
Hcp required Hcp erfordrad	36			

CLUB HOUSE & AMENITIES / KLUBBHUS OCH OMGIVNING — 7/10

Pro shop	Pro shop	
Driving range	Träningsbana	
Sheltered	täkt	2 mats
On grass	på gräs	no, 17 mats open air
Putting-green	putting-green	yes
Pitching-green	pitching-green	yes

HOTEL FACILITIES / HOTELL OMGIVNING — 5/10

HOTELS

Grand Hotell — Lund
84 rooms, D SKr 1695:- — 10 km
Tel (46) 046 - 280 61 00
Fax (46) 046 - 280 61 50

Lundia — Lund
97 rooms, D SKr 1550:- — 10 km
Tel (46) 046 - 280 65 00
Fax (46) 046 - 280 65 10

RESTAURANTS RESTAURANG

Bantorget 9 — Lund
Tel (46) 046 - 32 02 00 — 10 km

Grand Hotell — Lund
Tel (46) 046 - 280 61 00 — 10 km

Ljungskile ligger mitt emot Orust, som är den största ön i den bohusländska skärgården, separerad från fastlandet av Hakefjorden, där man under många år byggde fantastiska träbåtar. Vyn från banan är alldeles fantastisk, och ibland undrar du nog om det är naturupplevelserna eller de branta backarna som får dig att tappa andan. Lyckligtvis är detta ingen lång bana, men är du inte i en bra fysisk form blir nog helhetsupplevelsen lidande. De flesta golfare kommer snart att inse fördelarna med att hålla huvudet kallt och inte överarbeta saker och ting. Detta är ingen bana där du kan sträcka ut på varje hål, tvärtom, det är en fördel att försiktigt knuffa fram bollen i banan. Det skadar inte heller om du kan manövrera bollen åt bägge hållen (fade och draw), framför allt med tanke på alla träden som hotar att förstöra scoren. Layouten är synnerligen fantasifull, och det är som med en del människor man möter – ju bättre man lär känna dem desto mer uppskattar man dem.

The village of Ljungskile is situated just opposite Orust, the largest island of an archipelago separated from the mainland by the Hakefjorden, where the building of wooden ships was the major activity for many a year, along with farming. The view from the course is absolutely magnificent, enough to make you wonder sometimes whether it is the steep climbs or the landscape that has taken your breath away. Fortunately this is not a very long course, although lack of fitness might spoil some of the fun. Most golfers though will think first and foremost about keeping a cool head and not trying to overdo things. There is no question here of «letting rip»; you have to carefully negotiate each shot and even bend the ball both ways to have any chance of scoring, as there are trees everywhere. This very fetching course was designed with no shortage of imagination, but the relief, in particular, means that you might get the impression of a slightly deceitful layout. Like some people, the better you get to know it, the more you like it.

Lyckorna Golfklubb — 1968

Box 66
S - 459 22 LJUNGSKILE

Office	Sekretariat	(46) 0522 - 201 76
Pro shop	Pro shop	(46) 0522 - 290 29
Fax	Fax	(46) 0522 - 223 04
Situation	Läge	

Göteborg, 45 km - Ljungskile, 7 km

Annual closure	Årlig stängning	no
Weekly closure	Daglig stängning	no

Fees main season
Tariff hög säsong full day

	Week days Veckodag	We/Bank holidays Lör/Söndag/Helgdag
Individual Individuellt	SKr 200:-	SKr 200:-
Couple Par	SKr 400:-	SKr 400:-

Juniors: – 50%

Caddy	Caddie	no
Electric Trolley	El vagn	no
Buggy	Golfbil	no
Clubs	Klubbor	SKr 200:-

Credit cards Kredit kort
VISA - Eurocard - MasterCard - JCB

Access Tillfart : Göteborg, E6 → Uddevalla.
Lyckornamotet, → Golf
Map 1 on page 1218 Karta 1 se sid: 1218

GOLF COURSE / BANA — 13/20

Site	Läge	
Maintenance	Underhåll	
Architect	Arkitekt	Anders Amilon
Type	Typ	seaside course, parkland
Relief	Relief	
Water in play	Vatten på spelfältet	
Exp. to wind	Vindutsatt	
Trees in play	Träd på spelfältet	

Scorecard Scorekort	Chp. Back tees	Mens Herrtee	Ladies Damtee
Length Längd	6090	5470	5015
Par	72	72	72

Advised golfing ability Rekommenderad spelnivå		0 12 24 36
Hcp required Hcp erfordrad		34

CLUB HOUSE & AMENITIES / CLUB HOUSE ET ANNEXES — 7/10

Pro shop	Pro shop	
Driving range	Träningsbana	
Sheltered	täkt	2 mats
On grass	på gräs	yes
Putting-green	putting-green	yes
Pitching-green	pitching-green	yes

HOTEL FACILITIES / HOTELL OMGIVNING — 6/10

HOTELS

Ljungskile Turisthotell 12 rooms, D SKr 495:- Tel (46) 0522 - 200 39	Ljungskile 4 kms
Villa Sjötorp 9 rooms, D SKr 840:- Tel (46) 0522 - 201 74 Fax (46) 0522 - 201 74	Lyckorna

RESTAURANTS RESTAURANG

Lyckorna Restaurang Tel (46) 0522 - 222 55	Ljungskile 7 km
Särla Restaurang Tel (46) 0522 - 244 44	Ljungskile 7 km
Restaurang Bellamare Tel (46) 0522 - 295 45	Ljungskile 7 km

1263

Vägen upp till Kullaberg förbi Höganäs är med alla sina fiskeläger vacker som ett vykort. Detta är Sveriges keramik-centrum, och väl framme i Mölle kan du begrunda det faktum att du nu är på platsen där män och kvinnor för första gången fick sola och bada tillsammans. Golfbanan ligger högre upp i en nationalpark, och att den är belägen där förklarar också varför antalet bunkrar är begränsat på banan (endast elva stycken). Nåväl, de flesta greener är små, uppbyggda på platåer och ligger väl skyddade. Du behöver kunna slå höga inspel här, men många hål kräver också att du behärskar låga rullslag. Banan är kraftigt kuperad, vilket kan vara slitsamt (det finns inga golfbilar). Om du ska kunna klara dig runt här och träffa greenerna måste du ha ett brett register av olika typer av slag, framför allt med mellanjärnen och de korta järnen. Eftersom banan inte är särskilt lång kan du gott lämna drivern hemma. Layouten bör passa de flesta spelarkategorier, men vi varnar för vinden, den kan vara riktigt besvärlig.

The road along the Kullen peninsula is as pretty as a picture with fishing villages and the town of Höganäs, the centre of the Swedish ceramics and sandstone pottery industry on the way to Mölle, the first seaside resort in Sweden where men and women were able to bathe together. The golf course is higher up in a national park, a fact that limited the number of bunkers (11 green-side traps). No matter, many of the greens are small, elevated and well-guarded, but only one is really blind. You need to hit the ball high here, of course, but approach shots hit along the ground (deliberately) are often a better solution. Hilly enough to deter tired legs (there are no carts), Mölle requires all sorts of shots, especially with medium and short irons, to hit the greens. This is not really a long course and the driver can easily stay in the bag all day. Over a layout that is well suited to all playing abilities, the wind can be the most bothersome element to distract from the pleasure of playing here.

Mölle Golfklubb — 1944
Box 44
S - 260 42 MÖLLE

Office	Sekretariat	(46) 042 - 34 75 20
Pro shop	Pro shop	(46) 042 - 34 70 12
Fax	Fax	(46) 042 - 34 75 23
Situation	Läge	

Mölle, 3 km - Helsingborg, 30 km

Annual closure	Årlig stängning	no
Weekly closure	Daglig stängning	no

Fees main season
Tariff hög säsong full day

	Week days Veckodag	We/Bank holidays Lör/Söndag/Helgdag
Individual Individuellt	SKr 260:-	SKr 260:-
Couple Par	SKr 520:-	SKr 520:-

Juniors: – 50 %

Caddy	Caddie	no
Electric Trolley	El vagn	no
Buggy	Golfbil	SKr 100:-
Clubs	Klubbor	SKr 150:-

Credit cards Kredit kort VISA - Eurocard - MasterCard

1264

Map
Kullagården
0   2   4 km
Mölle
Arild
GOLF
Jonstorp
Brunnby
Nyhamnsläge
R111
Höganäs
Helsingborg   Väsby   Ängelholm
112

Access Tillfart : Helsingborg, R111 → Höganäs/Mölle.
Mölle, → Kullens Fyr.
Map 1 on page 1218 Karta 10 se sid: 1218

GOLF COURSE / BANA — 15/20

Site	Läge	▬▬▬▬▬▭
Maintenance	Underhåll	▬▬▬▬▭▭
Architect	Arkitekt	Ture Bruce
Type	Typ	parkland, hilly
Relief	Relief	
Water in play	Vatten på spelfältet	▬▬▭▭▭▭
Exp. to wind	Vindutsatt	▬▬▬▬▭▭
Trees in play	Tråd på spelfältet	▬▬▬▬▬▭

Scorecard Scorekort	Chp. Back tees	Mens Herrtee	Ladies Damtee
Length Längd	5467	5312	4627
Par	70	70	70

Advised golfing ability	0	12	24	36
Rekommenderad spelnivå				
Hcp required Hcp erfordrad		32 Men, 36 Ladies		

CLUB HOUSE & AMENITIES / KLUBBHUS OCH OMGIVNING — 7/10

Pro shop	Pro shop	▬▬▬▬▭▭
Driving range	Träningsbana	▬▬▬▭▭▭
Sheltered	täkt	no
On grass	på gräs	yes
Putting-green	putting-green	yes
Pitching-green	pitching-green	yes

HOTEL FACILITIES / HOTELL OMGIVNING — 5/10

HOTELS
Kullabergs Värdshus — Mölle
89 rooms, D SKr 1295:- — on site
Tel (46) 042 - 18 53 90, Fax (46) 042 - 14 96 16

Hotel Nouveau — Helsingborg
15 rooms, D SKr 945:- — 30 km
Tel (46) 042 - 34 74 20, Fax (46) 042 - 34 74 31

Marina Plaza — Helsingborg
190 rooms, D SKr 1295:- — 30 km
Tel (46) 042 - 19 21 00, Fax (46) 042 - 14 96 16

RESTAURANTS RESTAURANG
Le Petit — Helsingborg
Tel (46) 042 - 21 97 27 — 30 km

Oskar Trapp — Helsingborg
Tel (46) 042 - 14 60 44 — 30 km

Gastro — Helsingborg
Tel (46) 042 - 24 34 70 — 30 km

Mindre än fyra mil från Göteborg ligger denna 36-hålsanläggning med sitt majestätiska klubbhus. Bägge banorna är relativt korta. Vi väljer här att skriva om Gamla Banan, par 71 och som öppnade 1965. Den har ritats av Brasier, Röss och Amilon. En del av banan vindlar genom ett parkliknande landskap medan den andra delen är byggd i kuperad terräng. Träd kommer hela tiden i spel och utgör precis som bunkrarna och vattenhindren ett hot mot scoren. Det här är en bana som du måste lära känna innan du kan hoppas på en bra score. Det viktigaste är att slå rakt från tee, även om detta innebär att du måste offra lite längd och välja en kortare klubba. Du tjänar också på att spela strategiskt och kunna ändra taktik där det behövs. Här kan den något sämre spelaren lära sig mycket av den som är lite bättre i hur man ska tänka på banan. Detta är en fantasifull och intelligent bana som är väl värd att lära känna, även om de kuperade partierna kommer slita en del på orken.

Located less than 40 kilometres from Göteborg, this is a 36-hole complex with a majestic club-house at the end of a pretty little road. Both courses are on the short side, but this one, the Gamla Banan (old course) is a par 71 laid out in 1965 by Douglas Brasier, Röss and Amilon. One part of the course winds its way through a sort of park, the other is laid out over hilly terrain. Trees come into play throughout and are often dangerous, and as bunkers and water hazards are also very present, you need to reconnoitre the course before hoping to card a good score. Not only do you need to drive it straight, even if that means sacrificing length off the tee, you also need to establish good game strategy for each hole and be able to change tactics according to the situation at hand. In this respect, good players with a group or with their family can give lesser players a few useful lessons in course management. An imaginative and intelligent course which is well worth getting to know, even if it does call for a little physical effort over the more hilly stretches.

Öijared Golfklubb   1965

Pl 1082
S - 448 92 FLODA

Office	Sekretariat	(46) 0302 - 306 04
Pro shop	Pro shop	(46) 0302 - 311 45
Fax	Fax	(46) 0302 - 353 70
Situation	Läge	
Floda, 10 km		
Annual closure	Årlig stängning	no
Weekly closure	Daglig stängning	no

Fees main season
Tariff hög säsong full day

	Week days Veckodag	We/Bank holidays Lör/Söndag/Helgdag
Individual Individuellt	SKr 200:-	SKr 240:-
Couple Par	SKr 400:-	SKr 480:-
Juniors: – 50 %		

Caddy	Caddie	no
Electric Trolley	El vagn	no
Buggy	Golfbil	no
Clubs	Klubbor	SKr 100:-

Credit cards Kredit kort
VISA - Eurocard - MasterCard - AMEX - DC

Access Tillfart : Göteborg, E20 → Alingsås/Stockholm.
30 km → Nääs. 5 km → Golf
Map 1 on page 1218 Karta 1 se sid: 1218

GOLF COURSE / BANA   **13**/20

Site	Läge	
Maintenance	Underhåll	
Architect	Arkitekt	Douglas Brasier Röhss, Amilon
Type	Typ	forest, parkland
Relief	Relief	
Water in play	Vatten på spelfältet	
Exp. to wind	Vindutsatt	
Trees in play	Träd på spelfältet	

Scorecard Scorekort	Chp. Back tees	Mens Herrtee	Ladies Damtee
Length Längd	5561	5561	4855
Par	71	71	71

Advised golfing ability Rekommenderad spelnivå	0	12	24	36

Hcp required Hcp erfordrad   36

CLUB HOUSE & AMENITIES / CLUB HOUSE ET ANNEXES   **7**/10

Pro shop	Pro shop	
Driving range	Träningsbana	
Sheltered	täkt	12 mats
On grass	på gräs	no, 12 mats open air
Putting-green	putting-green	yes
Pitching-green	pitching-green	yes

HOTEL FACILITIES / HOTELL OMGIVNING   **5**/10

HOTELS
Nääs Slott   Floda
10 rooms, D SKr 990:-   4 km
Tel (46) 0302 - 318 39, Fax (46) 0302 - 304 44

Good Morning Hotel   Lerum
68 rooms, D SKr 495/545:-   10 km
Tel (46) 0302 - 170 00, Fax (46) 0302 - 713 65

RESTAURANTS RESTAURANG

Nääs Värdshus Spiltan   Floda
Tel (46) 0302 - 312 42   4 km

Farmors Hörna   Lerum
Tel (46) 0302 - 153 33   10 km

Ming House   Lerum
Tel (46) 0302 - 124 66   10 km

1265

Trots att den inte är monsterlång räknas Örebro som en av de bästa banorna i Sverige. Det är en trrevlig plats att besöka med ett charmigt klubbhus och ett övningsfält som är bland det bästa vi kan erbjuda här i landet. Pitch- och puttbanan är också en höjdare! När du väl har värmt upp kan du börja fundera över att attackera banrekordet som innehas av Joakim Haeggman och Pierre Fulke på 63 slag. Båda spelarna är kända för sin skicklighet med drivern, och det kommer du också behöva. Detta gäller framför allt för första nio där träden är mer i spel än på sista nio. Dessutom skadar det inte att vara utrustad med en stor portion tålamod och ta chanserna när de dyker upp. Du måste också vara smart när du attackerar greenerna, av vilka fler ligger på platåer. Örebro är en härlig utmaning där en sund teknik är att föredra framför muskler.

Despite its «reasonable» length, Örebro is generally considered to be one of the very best courses in Sweden. It is a pleasant spot, the club-house very agreeable, the driving range is one of the best in the country (but not sheltered) and there is a pitch and putt course that is great fun. When nicely warmed up, you can start to think about getting out there and trying to beat the course record of 63 set by Joakim Haeggman and Pierre Fulke. Both players are straight drivers and you will need the same accuracy, at least on the front nine, where the forest poses more of a threat than on the inward nine. You need to be patient here and grasp the right opportunities provided by your own talent or any luck that comes your way. You also need to be smart to appreciate some of the approach shots to greens that are sometimes elevated but never oversized. Örebro is a mighty challenge but places emphasis more on technique than power, an asset for golfers who always look to their swing (or change of club) to hit the ball 20 yards further.

Örebro Golfklubb — 1962

Lanna
S - 719 93 VINTROSA

Office	Sekretariat	(46) 019 - 29 10 65
Pro shop	Pro shop	(46) 019 - 29 10 45
Fax	Fax	(46) 019 - 29 10 55
Situation	Läge	

Örebro, 20 km

Annual closure	Årlig stängning	no
Weekly closure	Daglig stängning	no

Fees main season
Tariff hög säsong full day

	Week days Veckodag	We/Bank holidays Lör/Söndag/Helgdag
Individual Individuellt	SKr 260:-	SKr 300:-
Couple Par	SKr 420:-	SKr 500:-

Juniors: 130:-

Caddy	Caddie	no
Electric Trolley	El vagn	no
Buggy	Golfbil	SKr 200:-
Clubs	Klubbor	SKr 100:-

Credit cards Kredit kort
VISA - Eurocard - MasterCard - AMEX - DC

1266

Tysslingen
Arboga Hjälmaren
GOLF
Karlskoga
Örebro
Vintrosa
E 18
E 20
Hidinge
Fjugesta
0   2   4 km   Hallsberg

Access Tillfart : Örebro, E18 → Oslo.
20 km, → «Lanna»
Map 2 on page 1220 Karta 2 se sid: 1220

GOLF COURSE / BANA — 18/20

Site	Läge	
Maintenance	Underhäll	
Architect	Arkitekt	Flera

Type	Typ	forest, parkland
Relief	Relief	
Water in play	Vatten på spelfältet	
Exp. to wind	Vindutsatt	
Trees in play	Träd på spelfältet	

Scorecard Scorekort	Chp. Back tees	Mens Herrtee	Ladies Damtee
Length Längd	6160	5860	5065
Par	71	71	71

Advised golfing ability Rekommenderad spelnivå	0 12 24 36
Hcp required Hcp erfordrad	36

CLUB HOUSE & AMENITIES / KLUBBHUS OCH OMGIVNING — 7/10

Pro shop	Pro shop	
Driving range	Träningsbana	
Sheltered	täkt	no
On grass	på gräs	yes
Putting-green	putting-green	yes
Pitching-green	pitching-green	yes

HOTEL FACILITIES / HOTELL OMGIVNING — 5/10

HOTELS

Golf Hotellet — Örebro — on site
12 rooms, D SKr 600:-
Tel (46) 019 - 29 10 65, Fax (46) 019 - 29 10 55

Stora Hotellet — Örebro — 20 km
132 rooms, D SKr 1295:-
Tel (46) 019 - 15 69 00, Fax (46) 019 - 15 69 50

Scandic Grand Hotel — Örebro — 20 km
220 rooms, D SKr 1398:-
Tel (46) 019 - 15 02 00, Fax (46) 019 - 18 58 14

RESTAURANTS RESTAURANG

Slottohällaren — Örebro — 20 km
Tel (46) 019 - 15 69 00

Babar - Tel (46) 019 - 10 19 00 — Örebro 20 km

Tulins - Tel (46) 019 - 13 25 30 — Örebro 20 km

Det amerikanska sättet att bygga banor har haft ett stort inflytande i Europa. Allt fler banor byggs som är väldigt straffande i sin natur. Österåker är inget undantag från den här trenden som har sitt upphov i dagens nya teknologi som har gett oss järnklubbor som går allt högre och wedgar som får mer och mer loft. Många av greenerna vaktas av ett stort antal hinder, de är dessutom relativt hårda vilket gör att du måste slå höga pitch-slag mot dem för att få bollen att stanna. Om du har en lobbwedge – stoppa den i bagen! Du behöver dessutom långa, raka utslag – framför allt under sommaren då ruffen växer hög. En tuff utmaning, framför allt de första nio som är betydligt trixigare än andra nio som är längre men inte fullt så krävande. Om du har en dålig svingdag får du förlita dig på ditt närspel, men eftersom detta är något förunnat låghandicappare så kan spelare med högre handicap få det besvärligt. För att göra saken än mer problematisk så är vatten i spel på åtta av hålen.

This course is no exception to the trend that today's equipment tends to favour, namely irons designed to hit higher balls, including very wide-angle wedges. A lot of the greens here are guarded at the front by a number of hazards, and as they are also pretty firm you have to hit high pitches and be able to stop the ball on the putting surface. If you have a lob-wedge, put it in your bag. Otherwise, what with the tall rough in summer, you need some straight driving as well, a tough proposition early in the day because the front nine are a good deal trickier than the back nine, which are longer but less demanding. If your swing is off-colour, your short game should help you out, but as this part of golf is not always the forte of high-handicappers, they could be in trouble. To top it all, some fearsome water is in play on eight holes. The holes to remember on this course are the spectacular par 3s.

Österåkers Golfklubb — 1990

Hagby 1:1
S - 184 92 ÅKERSBERGA

Office	Sekretariat	(46) 08 - 540 851 90
Pro shop	Pro shop	(46) 08 - 540 684 49
Fax	Fax	(46) 08 - 540 668 32
Situation	Läge	

Stockholm, 20 km

Annual closure	Årlig stängning	no
Weekly closure	Daglig stängning	no

Fees main season
Tariff hög säsong full day

	Week days Veckodag	We/Bank holidays Lör/Söndag/Helgdag
Individual Individuellt	SKr 300:-	SKr 350:-
Couple Par	SKr 600:-	SKr 700:-

Juniors: – 50%

Caddy	Caddie	no
Electric Trolley	El vagn	no
Buggy	Golfbil	no
Clubs	Klubbor	SKr 175:-

Credit cards Kredit kort
VISA - Eurocard - MasterCard - AMEX - DC

Access Tillfart : Stockholm, E18 → Norrtälje.
→ Åkersberga, → Waxholm
Map 2 on page 1220 Karta 2 se sid: 1220

GOLF COURSE / BANA — 16/20

Site	Läge	
Maintenance	Underhåll	
Architect	Arkitekt	Sven Tumba Jan Sederholm
Type	Typ	parkland
Relief	Relief	
Water in play	Vatten på spelfältet	
Exp. to wind	Vindutsatt	
Trees in play	Tråd på spelfältet	

Scorecard Scorekort	Chp. Back tees	Mens Herrtee	Ladies Damtee
Length Längd	6145	5790	5010
Par	72	72	72

Advised golfing ability Rekommenderad spelnivå	0	12	24	36

Hcp required Hcp erfordrad 29 Men, 34 Ladies

CLUB HOUSE & AMENITIES / CLUB HOUSE ET ANNEXES — 6/10

Pro shop	Pro shop	
Driving range	Träningsbana	
Sheltered	tåkt	6 mats
On grass	på gräs	no, 30 mats open air
Putting-green	putting-green	yes
Pitching-green	pitching-green	yes

HOTEL FACILITIES / HOTELL OMGIVNING — 6/10

HOTELS

Silja Hotel Ariadne — Stockholm Värtahamnen
283 rooms, D SKr 1960:- — 17 km
Tel (46) 08 - 665 78 00, Fax (46) 08 - 662 76 70

Lord Nelson — Stockholm
31 rooms, D SKr 1890:- — 20 km
Tel (46) 08 - 23 23 90, Fax (46) 08 - 10 10 89

Victory - Tel 45 rooms, D SKr 2390:- — Stockholm
Tel (46) 08 - 14 30 90, Fax (46) 08 - 20 21 77 — 20 km

RESTAURANTS RESTAURANG

Eriks - Tel (46) 08 - 23 85 00 — Stockholm 20 km

Stallmästeregården — Stockholm
Tel (46) 08 - 610 13 00 — 17 km

Den Gyldene Freden — Stockholm
Tel (46) 08 - 24 97 60 — 20 km

1267

Även när bron mellan Malmö och Köpenhamn har byggts kommer man fortfarande kunna tura mellan Helsingborg och Helsingør, den kortaste vägen mellan Sverige och Danmark. Från Rya, strax söder om Helsingborg, ser man inte bara Öresund utan även Danmark på andra sidan sundet. Bortsett från fem ganska kuperade hål är resten av banan platt och varierar i stil mellan links och parkbanekaraktär. På några hål kommer träd i spel, annars är det vattenhinder som är de största hoten, framför allt på det fjärde och det åttonde, som kan vara svåra för höghandicaparen. Nåja, det åttonde hålet ställer till med problem för alla – ett vattenhinder skär igenom fairway precis framför greenen på detta par 5-hål som måste räknas vara ett av de bästa i hela landet. 16e är också minnesvärt – en par 3 med sundet och Danmark i bakgrunden.

Even when the motorway-train link from Malmö to København is open, there will still be the ferry link between Helsingborg and Helsingør, the shortest way of getting from one country to the other. From the Rya course, to the south of Helsingborg, you can see not only the Öresund strait but also Denmark on the other side. Aside from five rather hilly holes, the rest of the course is flat with a style varying from links to parkland. Trees are in play only on a few holes, otherwise the hazards that are present are very dangerous, particularly on holes 4 and 8, where water will cause trouble for the high-handicap golfers. In fact, hole N° 8 will cause problems for everyone, with water crossing the fairway next to the green of this superb par 5, which has to rate as one of the finest holes in the whole country. The 16th, too, is a great hole, a short par 3 with the sea and Denmark in the background. At the end of your round, you can take the children to the beach (less than 60 yards away) and even go for a swim.

Rya Golfklubb		1935
PL 5500		
S - 255 92 HELSINGBORG		
Office	Sekretariat	(46) 042 - 22 01 82
Pro shop	Pro shop	(46) 042 - 22 16 88
Fax	Fax	(46) 042 - 22 03 94
Situation	Läge	
Helsingborg, 10 km		
Annual closure	Årlig stängning	no
Weekly closure	Daglig stängning	no

Fees main season			
Tariff hög säsong full day			
		Week days Veckodag	We/Bank holidays Lör/Söndag/Helgdag
Individual Individuellt		SKr 260:-	SKr 260:-
Couple Par		SKr 520:-	SKr 520:-
Junios: 150:-			

Caddy	Caddie	no
Electric Trolley	El vagn	no
Buggy	Golfbil	no
Clubs	Klubbor	SKr 100:-

Credit cards Kredit kort VISA - Eurocard - MasterCard

Access Tillfart : Malmö E6 → Helsingborg.
→ Rydebäck. → Golf
Map 1 on page 1218 Karta 1 se sid: 1218

GOLF COURSE
BANA   15/20

Site	Läge	▬▬▬▬▬▭
Maintenance	Underhåll	▬▬▬▬▬▭
Architect	Arkitekt	Rafael Sundblom
Type	Typ	seaside course, parkland
Relief	Relief	▬▬▬▬▭▭
Water in play	Vatten på spelfältet	▬▬▬▭▭▭
Exp. to wind	Vindutsatt	▬▬▬▬▬▭
Trees in play	Träd på spelfältet	▬▬▭▭▭▭

Scorecard	Chp.	Mens	Ladies
Scorekort	Back tees	Herrtee	Damtee
Length Längd	5857	5558	4846
Par	71	71	71

Advised golfing ability		0	12	24	36
Rekommenderad spelnivå		▬▬▬▬▬▬			
Hcp required	Hcp erfordrad	32			

CLUB HOUSE & AMENITIES
KLUBBHUS OCH OMGIVNING   7/10

Pro shop	Pro shop	▬▬▬▬▬▭
Driving range	Träningsbana	▬▬▬▬▭▭
Sheltered	täkt	2 mats
On grass	på gräs	yes
Putting-green	putting-green	yes
Pitching-green	pitching-green	yes

HOTEL FACILITIES
HOTELL OMGIVNING   8/10

HOTELS

Marina Plaza	Helsingborg
190 rooms, D SKr 1295:-	7 km
Tel (46) 042 - 19 21 00, Fax (46) 042 - 14 96 16	

Hotell Nouveau	Helsingborg
89 rooms, D SKr 1145:-	7 km
Tel (46) 042 - 18 53 90, Fax (46) 042 - 14 08 85	

Grand Hotell	Helsingborg
116 rooms, D SKr 1490:-	7 km
Tel (46) 042 - 12 01 70, Fax (46) 042 - 21 88 33	

RESTAURANTS RESTAURANG

Le Petit	Helsingborg
Tel (46) 042 - 21 97 27	7 km

Oskar Trapp	Helsingborg
Tel (46) 042 - 14 60 44	7 km

Gastro	Helsingborg
Tel (46) 042 - 24 34 70	7 km

Skellefteå ligger i ett ingenmansland mellan norr och söder i Sverige. Ändå finns polcirkeln på ett relativt nära avstånd, och här kan sommardagarna kännas oändliga. Om du är tillräckligt vältränad kan du spela flera banor om dagen och ändå hinna njuta av var och en av dem. Banan är ganska flack och från utslagsplatserna kan du se de flesta av hindren. Fairway kantas av träd, och dessa undviker du bäst genom en smula klokskap förenat med skicklighet: Spela försiktigt när du behöver det, slå en kontrollerad fade, och så vidare. Till sist besegrar sunt förnuft ren råstyrka. Fyra talangfulla arkitekter har byggt denna bana i omgångar mellan 1970-1995, vilket kan få en att tro att detta skulle ge en splittrad helhetsbild, men så är det inte. Skellefteå är utan vidare den bästa banan i den här regionen. För lite extra inspiration inför nästa runda rekommenderas ett besök i gamla stan.

This is not yet the great North, but it is not the south either; the Polar Circle is not so far away and summer days can seem endless. If you are fit enough, you will have the time to play several courses in a day and fully appreciate the difficulties of each one. From the tees on this relatively flat and tree-strewn terrain, you can see most of the hazards, which are most effectively avoided with a little skill and thought, i.e. playing short here, fading the ball there, and so forth. At the final count, using your head is more important than physical strength. Four talented architects helped to design this course between 1970 and 1995, which has still nonetheless retained a certain unity. All in all, this is a good and the most impressive course to be found in this part of Sweden. Spare a little time to see the old Parish village of Bonnstan, you might find a little extra inspiration for your next round.

Skellefteå Golfklubb — 1970
Roönnbäcken
S - 931 92 SKELLEFTEÅ

Office	Sekretariat	(46) 0910 - 128 10
Pro shop	Pro shop	(46) 0303 - 779 866
Fax	Fax	(46) 0303 - 779 777
Situation	Läge	
Skellefteå, 5 km		
Annual closure	Årlig stängning	no
Weekly closure	Daglig stängning	no

Fees main season
Tariff hög säsong full day

	Week days Veckodag	We/Bank holidays Lör/Söndag/Helgdag
Individual Individuellt	SKr 200:-	SKr 200:-
Couple Par	SKr 400:-	SKr 400:-
Juniors: – 50 %		

Caddy	Caddie	no
Electric Trolley	El vagn	no
Buggy	Golfbil	no
Clubs	Klubbor	SKr 150:-

Credit cards Kredit kort
VISA - Eurocard - MasterCard - AMEX - DC - JCB

Access Tillfart : E4 → Skellefteå.
V 364 → Burträsk. 5 km → Golf, Rönnbäcken.
Map 3 on page 1222 Karta 3 se sid: 1222

GOLF COURSE BANA — 14/20

Site	Läge	
Maintenance	Underhåll	
Architect	Arkitekt	Sköld, Karlsson Nordwall, Larsson
Type	Typ	forest
Relief	Relief	
Water in play	Vatten på spelfältet	
Exp. to wind	Vindutsatt	
Trees in play	Tråd på spelfältet	

Scorecard Scorekort	Chp. Back tees	Mens Herrtee	Ladies Damtee
Length Längd	6187	5801	4971
Par	72	72	72

Advised golfing ability Rekommenderad spelnivå	0	12	24	36
Hcp required Hcp erfordrad	no			

CLUB HOUSE & AMENITIES CLUB HOUSE ET ANNEXES — 6/10

Pro shop	Pro shop	
Driving range	Träningsbana	
Sheltered	tåkt	no
On grass	på gräs	yes
Putting-green	putting-green	yes
Pitching-green	pitching-green	yes

HOTEL FACILITIES HOTELL OMGIVNING — 5/10

HOTELS

First Hotel Statt 131 rooms, D SKr 690/1235:- Tel (46) 0910 - 141 40 Fax (46) 0910 - 126 28	Skellefteå 3 km
Scandic Hotel 131 rooms, D SKr 660/1385:- Tel (46) 0910 - 383 00 Fax (46) 0910 - 77 84 11	Skellefteå 5 km

RESTAURANTS RESTAURANG

Restaurang Vitberget Tel (46) 0910 - 77 58 00	Skellefteå 12 km
Nordanågårdens Värdshus Tel (46) 0910 - 533 50	Skellefteå 5 km
Carl Victor Tel (46) 0910 - 100 29	Skellefteå 5 km

1269

Det här är en bra bas om man ska utforska områdena kring Sveriges två största sjöar, Vänern och Vättern. Besöka exempelvis Mariestad, där kan du ta en sväng runt den magnifika kyrkan eller bara strosa runt bland de vackra trähusen. Precis utanför Skövde hittar man golfbanan med det lilla, men charmiga klubbhuset byggt högst upp på en kulle, och för att ta sig dit krävs nästan lika mycket energi som att spela banan (alla med dålig kondition är härmed varnade). Genom att studera greenernas storlek förstår man snabbt vem som har designat banan: Peter Nordwall, förstås. Han har lagt ut en lång och svår bana, där bra bollträff är ett måste. På Skövde är allting stort, från utslagsplatserna till amerikansk-inspirerade fairways. För faktum är att de är bredare än vad de verkar vara vid första anblicken. Tur är det, för första gången ser du bara hinder – skog och tjock ruff. En av banans stora förtjänster är att den är så omväxlande, vilket verkligen kräver att du kan använda alla klubbor i bagen.

This town is more than anything a base-camp to explore the two great Swedish lakes of Vättern and Vänern, on the shores of which you will find the little town of Mariestad and certainly visit the cathedral and old wooden houses. Just outside the town, a charming but small club-house (another one is planned) stands atop a hill which requires about as much stamina to reach as the course does to play (veterans be warned). The size of the greens are a good clue to who designed this course, none other than Peter Nordwall, who has laid out a long and difficult course, where the ball needs to be hit crisp and clean. Everything is big here, from the tee-boxes to the rather American style fairways. In fact, the holes are wider than you think and all you see are the hazards of trees and tall rough. One of the qualities of this course is the variety of holes and of the shots you need to play.

Skövde Golfklubb — 1991

Box 269
S - 541 26 SKÖVDE

Office	Sekretariat	(46) 0500 - 41 15 35
Pro shop	Pro shop	(46) 0500 - 41 25 37
Fax	Fax	(46) 0500 - 41 01 16
Situation	Läge	

Skövde, 5 km

Annual closure	Årlig stängning	no
Weekly closure	Daglig stängning	no

Fees main season
Tariff hög säsong full day

	Week days Veckodag	We/Bank holidays Lör/Söndag/Helgdag
Individual Individuellt	SKr 220:-	SKr 220:-
Couple Par	SKr 380:-	SKr 380:-

Juniors: 140:- / Family of 4 (Familjegreenfee): SKr 500:-

Caddy	Caddie	no
Electric Trolley	El vagn	no
Buggy	Golfbil	no
Clubs	Klubbor	

Credit cards Kredit kort
VISA - Eurocard - MasterCard - AMEX - DC

1270

Access Tillfart : Jönköping R47/48 → Skövde. R49 → Skara. Cementa/Rockwool, → Simsjön. Golf 2 km
Map 1 on page 1218 Karta 1 se sid: 1218

GOLF COURSE
BANA — 17/20

Site	Läge	
Maintenance	Underhåll	
Architect	Arkitekt	Peter Nordwall
Type	Typ	parkland
Relief	Relief	
Water in play	Vatten på spelfältet	
Exp. to wind	Vindutsatt	
Trees in play	Träd på spelfältet	

Scorecard Scorekort	Chp. Back tees	Mens Herrtee	Ladies Damtee
Length Längd	6215	5740	4885
Par	72	72	72

Advised golfing ability 0 12 24 36
Rekommenderad spelnivå
Hcp required Hcp erfordrad 36

CLUB HOUSE & AMENITIES
KLUBBHUS OCH OMGIVNING — 5/10

Pro shop	Pro shop	
Driving range	Träningsbana	
Sheltered	täkt	5 mats
On grass	på gräs	yes
Putting-green	putting-green	yes
Pitching-green	pitching-green	yes

HOTEL FACILITIES
HOTELL OMGIVNING — 7/10

HOTELS
Billingehus — Skövde 3 km
240 rooms, D SKr 1350:-
Tel (46) 0500 - 44 57 00, Fax (46) 0500 - 48 38 80

Billingen — Skövde 4 km
106 rooms, D SKr 1195:-
Tel (46) 0500 - 41 07 90, Fax (46) 0500 - 41 73 10

Knista Hotel — Skövde 10 km
79 rooms, D SKr 1140:-
Tel (46) 0500 - 46 31 70, Fax (46) 0500 - 46 30 75

RESTAURANTS RESTAURANG
Skafferiet — Skövde 5 km
Tel (46) 0500 - 41 11 77

Parnassen — Skövde 5 km
Tel (46) 0500 - 41 19 12

Orient Palace - Tel (46) 0500 - 48 98 83 — Skövde 5 km

Sista biten upp mot klubbhuset är magnifik med träd på bägge sidor. Detta är ett typiskt skånskt landskap, och tankarna går till dignande smörgåsbord med lax, sill, ål och mycket mer. Banan kan dock lätt trycka ned din positivism med all skog, tjock ruff och strategiskt utplacerade diken. Var kylig: Det viktigaste är att ha ett bra huvud och förmåga att anpassa sig när saker inte riktigt går som det är tänkt. Sedan skadar det förstås inte heller med en smula ödmjukhet! Om du tycker om att spela banor som utvecklar dig som golfare kommer du älska att spela här. Även höghandicapare klarar sig runt om de inte överskattar sin egen kapacitet, vill säga. Greenerna är relativt små, och ofta väldigt snabba. Många är upphöjda och kräver ett delikat närspel – särskilt många greenträffar på rätt antal slag kan du nämligen inte räkna med. Detta gäller framför allt på par 4-hålen som är tuffa att nå på två slag.

The drive to this course set amidst an ocean of trees is simply splendid, the same goes for the typical countryside of Skåne, the country's southernmost province, famous for its smörgåsbord, a sort of huge brunch based on fish (salmon, herring and eels in season) and meat (particularly duck and goose). A forest, tall rough and a few very well located ditches can easily wear down the optimism of any golfer here. The basic requirements are good game strategy, the ability to adapt when things don't go quite the way you planned (this does happen) and a certain degree of humility (as always). You will love playing here if you appreciate courses which help make you become a better golfer. High-handicappers, as long as they don't overestimate their playing ability, will get by without too much damage. The greens are rather small, frequently fast and slick, often elevated and always requiring a lot of touch to stop the ball when your approach has missed its target. Many holes stick in the mind, particularly the 2nd, a par 4 which is tough to reach in two shots and a good yardstick for gauging the shape of your game on any one particular day.

Söderhåsens Golfklubb		1972
Box 41		
S - 260 50 BILLESHOLM		
Office	Sekretariat	(46) 042 - 733 37
Pro shop	Pro shop	(46) 042 - 724 45
Fax	Fax	(46) 042 - 739 63
Situation	Läge	
Helsingborg, 20 km		
Annual closure	Årlig stängning	no
Weekly closure	Daglig stängning	no

Fees main season		
Tariff hög säsong full day		
	Week days Veckodag	We/Bank holidays Lör/Söndag/Helgdag
Individual Individuellt	SKr 250:-	SKr 250:-
Couple Par	SKr 500:-	SKr 500:-
Juniors: – 50 %		

Caddy	Caddie	no
Electric Trolley	El vagn	no
Buggy	Golfbil	SKr 200:-
Clubs	Klubbor	SKr 100:-

Credit cards Kredit kort
VISA - Eurocard - MasterCard - AMEX - DC

Helsingborg
Astorp
Bjuv
Mörarp
Risekatslösa
Billesholm
Kågeröd
GOLF→
110
Hässlunda
Landskrona
Ekeby
Landskrona / Malmö

Access Tillfart : Malmö, E6. R110. → Golf
Map 1 on page 1218 Karta 1 se sid: 1218

GOLF COURSE BANA   **15**/20

Site	Läge	▰▰▰▰▱
Maintenance	Underhåll	▰▰▰▰▱
Architect	Arkitekt	Ture Bruce
Type	Typ	forest, parkland
Relief	Relief	▰▰▱▱▱
Water in play	Vatten på spelfältet	▰▰▱▱▱
Exp. to wind	Vindutsatt	▰▰▱▱▱
Trees in play	Träd på spelfältet	▰▰▰▰▱

Scorecard Scorekort	Chp. Back tees	Mens Herrtee	Ladies Damtee
Length Längd	6050	5657	4879
Par	71	71	71

Advised golfing ability Rekommenderad spelnivå	0	12	24	36
Hcp required Hcp erfordrad	36			

CLUB HOUSE & AMENITIES CLUB HOUSE ET ANNEXES   **7**/10

Pro shop	Pro shop	▰▰▰▰▱
Driving range	Träningsbana	▰▰▰▰▱
Sheltered	täkt	2 mats
On grass	på gräs	yes
Putting-green	putting-green	yes
Pitching-green	pitching-green	yes

1271

HOTEL FACILITIES HOTELL OMGIVNING   **5**/10

HOTELS
Marina Plaza — Helsingborg
190 rooms, D SKr 1295:- — 20 km
Tel (46) 042 - 19 21 00, Fax (46) 042 - 14 96 16

Hotell Nouveau — Helsingborg
89 rooms, D SKr 1145:- — 20 km
Tel (46) 042 - 18 53 90, Fax (46) 042 - 14 08 85

Grand Hotell — Helsingborg
116 rooms, D SKr 1490:- — 20 km
Tel (46) 042 - 12 01 70, Fax (46) 042 - 21 88 33

RESTAURANTS RESTAURANG
Gastro Tel (46) 042 - 24 34 70 — Helsingborg 20 km

Le Petit — Helsingborg
Tel (46) 042 - 21 97 27 — 20 km

Oskar Trapp — Helsingborg
Tel (46) 042 - 14 60 44 — 20 km

Från Stenungsund styr du vidare över Almöbron mot Tjörn. Utsikten med alla fjordar och öar går inte av för hackor. Från banan kan du skymta havet, men i grunden är detta en inlandsbana. Peter Nordwall har ritat på sitt speciella sätt, med andra ord: allting är stort. Anråseå, som skär genom banan, har han dock inte lyckats förvandla till en ocean. Hur som helst, atmosfären är en skotsk seaside-känsla, och layouten fordrar att du kan slå flera typer av slag med hygglig bollträff. Banan är mycket ung, dock ska sägas att den verkar vara betydligt äldre. Skötseln är tipp-topp! Detta är en riktig mästerskapsbana, vilket innebär att alla hinder finns åtminstone 200 meter från tee – höghandicapare kan därmed lugnt andas ut. Fast på greenerna kommer de att mötas av samma problem som de bättre spelarna – här är det känsla och fantasi som gäller.

From the Stenungsund course, you can make out the sea in the distance, although this is very much an inland course. Here again, Peter Nordwall has done everything in his own, oversized style, and while he has brought the Anräseå river into play, at least he was unable to transform it into an ocean. All the same, you still find a sort of Scottish seaside course atmosphere here, a layout which requires the full range of shots and some solid striking of the ball. Still very young, the course looks much older, especially thanks to maintenance and green-keeping. A real championship course indeed, but as all the hazards are at least 220 yards (200 metres) from the tee, mid- and high-handicappers can breathe easily. They will however be on an equal footing with the better players when tackling the huge greens, where touch and feel count for much more than long game technique.

Stenungsund Golfklubb — 1993
Lundby 7480
S - 444 93 SPEKERÖD

Office	Sekretariat	(46) 0303 - 77 84 70
Pro shop	Pro shop	(46) 0303 - 77 81 88
Fax	Fax	(46) 0303 - 77 83 50
Situation	Läge	

Göteborg, 45 km

Annual closure	Årlig stängning	no
Weekly closure	Daglig stängning	no

Fees main season
Tariff hög säsong full day

	Week days Veckodag	We/Bank holidays Lör/Söndag/Helgdag
Individual Individuellt	SKr 220:-	SKr 220:-
Couple Par	SKr 390:-	SKr 390:-

Juniors: – 50 %

Caddy	Caddie	no
Electric Trolley	El vagn	no
Buggy	Golfbil	SKr 150:-
Clubs	Klubbor	SKr 100:-

Credit cards Kredit kort — no

GOLF COURSE BANA — 17/20

Site	Läge	▬▬▬▬▭
Maintenance	Underhåll	▬▬▬▬▬
Architect	Arkitekt	Peter Nordwall
Type	Typ	parkland, open country
Relief	Relief	
Water in play	Vatten på spelfältet	▬▬▬▭▭
Exp. to wind	Vindutsatt	▬▬▬▬▭
Trees in play	Träd på spelfältet	▬▬▭▭▭

Scorecard Scorekort	Chp. Back tees	Mens Herrtee	Ladies Damtee
Length Längd	6238	5825	4936
Par	72	72	72

Advised golfing ability Rekommenderad spelnivå	0	12	24	36
Hcp required	Hcp erfordrad	36		

CLUB HOUSE & AMENITIES KLUBBHUS OCH OMGIVNING — 7/10

Pro shop	Pro shop	▬▬▬▬▭
Driving range	Träningsbana	▬▬▬▬▭
Sheltered	tåkt	no
On grass	på gräs	yes
Putting-green	putting-green	yes
Pitching-green	pitching-green	yes

HOTEL FACILITIES HOTELL OMGIVNING — 8/10

HOTELS
Stenungsbaden Yacht Club — Stenungsund
200 rooms, D SKr 1190:- — 5 km
Tel (46) 0303 - 831 00, Fax (46) 0303 - 844 43

Solliden — Stenungsund
13 rooms, D SKr 945:- — 5 km
Tel (46) 0303 - 698 70, Fax (46) 0303 - 870 00

Hotel Reis — Stenungsund
17 rooms, D SKr 595:- — 5 km
Tel (46) 0303 - 77 00 11, Fax (46) 0303 - 824 72

RESTAURANTS RESTAURANG
Bara Kök och Bar — Stenungsund
Tel (46) 0303 - 654 50 — 5 km

Sjökanten Tel (46) 0303 - 77 00 40 — Stenungsund 5 km

Stenungsbaden — Stenungsund
Tel (46) 0303 - 831 00 — 5 km

1272

Access Tillfart : Göteborg, E6 → «Stora Höga-motet».
→ Ucklum. 1,5 km Golf
Map 1 on page 1218 Karta 1 se sid: 1218

Layouten har en skotsk känsla, framför allt i hur bunkrarna har lagts ut. Detta är inget att förvånas över då såväl Morrison som Nicholson har varit inblandade i banbygget. Greenerna ligger väl skyddade bakom hinder, de är svåra att läsa, många har branta sluttningar och i en del fall ställs man dessutom inför ett blint inspel. De blinda slagen är dock ett mindre problem för de långtslående. Naturen är relativt kuperad, och med tanke på hur nära banan ligger staden är det förvånansvärt tyst och stilla. Träden ser inte bara till att dämpa oväsendet runt omkring de är dessutom en ständig oroskälla för oss golfare, inte minst på banans sex dogleg-hål. Om du ska göra en bra score här måste du ha ordning på spelet. Par år 69, och eftersom det finns få par 5-hål är birdiemöjligheterna begränsade. Banan är sällsynt charmig och oftast i excellent kondition. Se bara till att vara ute i god tid om du vill boka en starttid.

The layout has a certain Scottish flavour to it, particularly in the way the bunkers are laid out. This is hardly surprising, as Morrison had a lot to do with the design, along with Nicholson; greens that are already tough to read, sharply contoured and sometimes blind are also very well guarded. The blind shots are perhaps less of a problem for long hitters, as the layout is rather hilly and strangely quiet for a city course. The trees dampen the surrounding noise but are also a major hazard, especially on the six dog-legs. To score here, you simply have to play very well, especially since being a par 69, there are few par 5s to bring that welcome birdie or two. A charming course in superb condition, situated in a splendid city, the Stockholms Golfklub is not easy to play, but if you have enough patience to secure a tee-off time, you will be well rewarded.

Stockholms Kolfklubb — 1932

Kevingestrand 20
S - 182 57 DANDERYD

Office	Sekretariat	(46) 08 - 544 907 15
Pro shop	Pro shop	(46) 08 - 544 907 11
Fax	Fax	(46) 08 - 544 907 12
Situation	Läge	

Stockholm, 7 km

| Annual closure | Årlig stängning | no |
| Weekly closure | Daglig stängning | no |

Fees main season
Tariff hög säsong full day

	Week days Veckodag	We/Bank holidays Lör/Söndag/Helgdag
Individual Individuellt	SKr 300:-	SKr 400:-
Couple Par	SKr 600:-	SKr 800:-

Juniors: – 50%

Caddy	Caddie	no
Electric Trolley	El vagn	no
Buggy	Golfbil	no
Clubs	Klubbor	SKr 200:-

Credit cards Kredit kort VISA - Eurocard - MasterCard

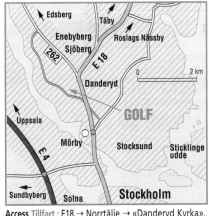

Access Tillfart : E18 → Norrtälje → «Danderyd Kyrka», 262 → Sollentuna, → Golf
Map 2 on page 1220 Karta 2 se sid: 1220

GOLF COURSE / BANA — 16/20

Site	Läge	
Maintenance	Underhåll	
Architect	Arkitekt	John Morrison M. Nicholson
Type	Typ	parkland
Relief	Relief	
Water in play	Vatten på spelfältet	
Exp. to wind	Vindutsatt	
Trees in play	Träd på spelfältet	

Scorecard Scorekort	Chp. Back tees	Mens Herrtee	Ladies Damtee
Length Längd	5437	5164	4552
Par	69	69	69

Advised golfing ability		0 12 24 36
Rekommenderad spelnivå		
Hcp required	Hcp erfordrad	30 Men, 36 Ladies

CLUB HOUSE & AMENITIES / CLUB HOUSE ET ANNEXES — 8/10

Pro shop	Pro shop	
Driving range	Träningsbana	
Sheltered	tåkt	no
On grass	på gräs	no, 14 mats open air
Putting-green	putting-green	yes
Pitching-green	pitching-green	yes

HOTEL FACILITIES / HOTELL OMGIVNING — 9/10

HOTELS

Stockholm Plaza — Stockholm
147 rooms, D SKr 1850:- — 6 km
Tel (46) 08 - 14 51 20, Fax (46) 08 - 10 34 92

Scandic Hotel Park — Stockholm
195 rooms, D SKr 2185:- — 6 km
Tel (46) 08 - 22 96 20, Fax (46) 08 - 21 62 68

Mornington — Stockholm
141 rooms, D SKr 1595:- — 6 km
Tel (46) 08 - 663 12 40, Fax (46) 08 - 662 21 79

RESTAURANTS RESTAURANG

Videgård - Tel (46) 08 - 411 61 53 — Stockholm 6 km

Operakällaren — Stockholm
Tel (46) 08 - 676 58 00 — 7 km

Wedholms Fisk - Tel (46) 08 - 611 78 74 Stockholm 7 km

1273

Även om du inte ska förvänta dig greener av Augusta Nationals kvalitet, eller ens jämförbara med de du finner i Malmö, så har klubben, genom ett fantastiskt greenkeeper-arbete, handskats framgångsrikt med de bistra förutsättningar som naturen bjuder. Låt vara att våren när vi besökte Skellefteå så hade greenkeepern ingen som helst hjälp av vädret. Naturens skönhet var dock ett minne värt att bevara. Detta är en region som lever på skogen och här är öppna ytor nästan något exotiskt. Träden ställer sålunda till en hel del besvär för golfaren. På många av par 4-hålen är det därför ett smartare val att slå ut med ett långt järn än med en driver. Landskapet är böljande, men backarna blir aldrig riktigt branta, ett par av greenerna är dock upphöjda och kräver väl avvägda inspel. Vattenhindrena är lättråknade och ruffen är ganska snäll. Vad golfaren måste komma underfull med på Skellefteå är träden, men till och med höghandicaparen bör finna en väg mellan dem.

Although you shouldn't expect grass the quality of Augusta's or even the turf you find around Malmö, the club has successfully coped with the challenging natural conditions through top-rate green-keeping. Even though the spring we were there was hardly a help weather-wise, the beauty of the scenery and trees are a sight to behold. In a region of forestry activity, the open spaces are almost exotic for this part of the world and some of the trees sufficiently in play to make a nuisance of themselves, so much so that a long iron off the tee is a better bet than the driver on most of the par 4s. Although none too steep, this rolling landscape gives two or three blind or raised greens, which call for caution on the approach shot. Water hazards are rare and the rough not too unkind. The golfer is left to come to terms with the trees, but even high-handicappers should find a way through.

Sundsvalls Golfklubb — 1953

Golfvägen 5
S - 862 34 KVISSLEBY

Office	Sekretariat	(46) 060 - 56 14 90
Pro shop	Pro shop	(46) 060 - 56 10 30
Fax	Fax	(46) 060 - 56 19 09
Situation	Läge	

Sundsvall, 17 km

Annual closure	Årlig stängning	no
Weekly closure	Daglig stängning	no

Fees main season
Tariff hög säsong full day

	Week days Veckodag	We/Bank holidays Lör/Söndag/Helgdag
Individual Individuellt	SKr 200:-	SKr 220:-
Couple Par	SKr 400:-	SKr 440:-

Juniors: – 50%

Caddy	Caddie	no
Electric Trolley	El vagn	no
Buggy	Golfbil	no
Clubs	Klubbor	SKr 100:-

Credit cards Kredit kort
VISA - Eurocard - MasterCard - AMEX - DC - JCB

1274

Access Tillfart : Sundsvall, E4 → Kvissleby. → Essvik.
Map 3 on page 1222 Karta 3 se sid: 1222

GOLF COURSE / BANA — 13/20

Site	Läge	
Maintenance	Underhåll	
Architect	Arkitekt	Rafel Sundblom Nils Skild
Type	Typ	forest, parkland
Relief	Relief	
Water in play	Vatten på spelfältet	
Exp. to wind	Vindutsatt	
Trees in play	Tråd på spelfältet	

Scorecard Scorekort	Chp. Back tees	Mens Herrtee	Ladies Damtee
Length Längd	5850	5850	4930
Par	71	71	71

Advised golfing ability Rekommenderad spelnivå	0	12	24	36
Hcp required Hcp erfordrad	36			

CLUB HOUSE & AMENITIES / KLUBBHUS OCH OMGIVNING — 6/10

Pro shop	Pro shop	
Driving range	Träningsbana	
Sheltered	täkt	no
On grass	på gräs	yes
Putting-green	putting-green	yes
Pitching-green	pitching-green	yes

HOTEL FACILITIES / HOTELL OMGIVNING — 6/10

HOTELS
First Hotel Strand — Sundsvall 17 km
203 rooms, D SKr 750/1385:-
Tel (46) 060 - 12 18 00
Fax (46) 060 - 61 92 02

Hotell Ankaret — Svartvik 2 km
17 rooms, D SKr 450:-
Tel (46) 060 - 56 16 10
Fax (46) 060 - 56 16 75

RESTAURANTS RESTAURANG
Matkrogen i Sundsvall — Sundsvall 17 km
Tel (46) 060 - 17 36 00

Restaurang Oscar — Sundsvall 17 km
Tel (46) 060 - 12 98 11

Svartviles Herrgård — Kvissleby 5 km
Tel (46) 060 - 36 12 51

När du tänker tillbaka på din runda kan du reflektera en stund över att det var här som Jesper Parnevik lärde sig spela golf. Då förstår man varför han blev den mästare som han är på att manövrera och kontrollera bollen. På Täby kommer nämligen alla klubbor i bagen till användning. Du kommer definitivt råka ut för några rejäla överraskningar. Banan ligger i ett kuperat skogsområde, och det är sällan som du får ett platt läge (vilket kan vara knepigt för höghandicaparen). På 14e kliver du plötsligt ut ur skogen och de fyra följande hålen ändrar banan karaktär. Nu är det seaside-golf som gäller! Fast havet heter här Vallentunasjön. På Täby, som på så många andra banor, är det viktigt att kunna skruva bollen från tee för att få ett så bra inspelsläge som möjligt (om du nu inte behärskar att slå bollen spikrakt, vilket är det svåraste slaget i golf). Om du bara har en dag över för golfspel så spela Ullna på förmiddagen och Täby på eftermiddagen.

At the end of the day on a veranda overlooking the 18th green, when looking back over your round, you might well remember that Jesper Parnevik learned his trade here. No wonder he became such a good worker of the ball. At Täby, you need every club in your bag and every shot in the book. Expect a few surprises too, as the holes are laid out in the middle of a forest over hilly terrain, meaning that you are hardly ever playing the ball from a flat lie (not easy for high-handicappers). Suddenly, when playing holes 14 through 17, you are in a whole change of scenery, similar to a seaside course except that here the course unwinds alongside lake Vallentunasjön. At Täby as elsewhere, astute placing of the drive is essential off the tee, fading and drawing the ball (unless you hit it perfectly straight, perhaps the hardest thing to do in golf). If you only have one day for golfing, play Ullna in the morning and Täby in the afternoon.

Täby Golfklubb — 1968
Skålhamra Gård
S - 187 70 TÄBY

Office	Sekretariat	(46) 08 - 510 234 22
Pro shop	Pro shop	(46) 08 - 510 233 36
Fax	Fax	(46) 08 - 510 234 41
Situation	Läge	

Stockholm, 25 km

Annual closure	Årlig stängning	no
Weekly closure	Daglig stängning	no

Fees main season
Tariff hög säsong full day

	Week days / Veckodag	We/Bank holidays / Lör/Söndag/Helgdag
Individual Individuellt	SKr 350:-	SKr 400:-
Couple Par	SKr 700:-	SKr 800:-

Juniors: – 50%

Caddy	Caddie	no
Electric Trolley	El vagn	no
Buggy	Golfbil	SKr 250:-
Clubs	Klubbor	SKr 200:-

Credit cards Kredit kort VISA - Eurocard - MasterCard

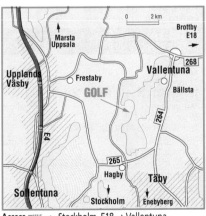

Access Tillfart : Stockholm, E18 → Vallentuna, «Danderyds Kyrka». 3 km → «Skålhamra 7»
Map 2 on page 1220 Karta 2 se sid: 1220

GOLF COURSE / BANA — 16/20

Site	Läge	
Maintenance	Underhåll	
Architect	Arkitekt	Nils Sköld
Type	Typ	seaside course, parkland
Relief	Relief	
Water in play	Vatten på spelfältet	
Exp. to wind	Vindutsatt	
Trees in play	Träd på spelfältet	

Scorecard / Scorekort	Chp. / Back tees	Mens / Herrtee	Ladies / Damtee
Length Längd	6105	5812	5036
Par	72	72	72

Advised golfing ability		0	12	24	36
Rekommenderad spelnivå					
Hcp required Hcp erfordrad	36				

CLUB HOUSE & AMENITIES / CLUB HOUSE ET ANNEXES — 7/10

Pro shop	Pro shop	
Driving range	Träningsbana	
Sheltered	täkt	3 mats
On grass	på gräs	no, 24 mats open air
Putting-green	putting-green	yes
Pitching-green	pitching-green	yes

HOTEL FACILITIES / HOTELL OMGIVNING — 7/10

HOTELS

Radisson SAS Royal Park — Stockholm
184 rooms, D SKr 1900:- — 20 km
Tel (46) 08 - 624 55 00, Fax (46) 08 - 85 85 66

Silja Hotel Ariadne — Stockholm
283 rooms, D SKr 1960:- — 25 km
Tel (46) 08 - 665 78 00, Fax (46) 08 - 662 76 70

First Hotel Reisen — Stockholm
144 rooms, D 1895 SKr:- — 25 km
Tel (46) 08 - 223 260, Fax (46) 08 - 201 559

RESTAURANTS RESTAURANG

Edsbacka Krog — Sollentuna
Tel (46) 08 - 85 08 15 — 15 km

Stallmästaregården — Stockholm
Tel (46) 08 - 610 13 00 — 25 km

1275

Torekov ligger längst ute på Bjärehalvön, en halvö norr om Helsingborg. Banan öppnade redan 1925 men byggdes om i början av 90-talet av Nils Sköld. Vi kan tillägga att han lyckades väl. Klimatet och sandjorden gör det i princip möjligt att spela året om här. Banan är kort, men kräver bra drives eller långa järnslag från tee för att ge dig möjlighet att spela in mot greenerna med ett mellanjärn eller ett kort järn. Det är i varje fall vad du kan hoppas på de dagar det är vindstilla, vilket händer ungefär två gånger om året. De andra 363 dagarna får du plocka fram ditt skotska spel och studsa och rulla bollen upp på greener som ofta är hårda och snabba. Det finns definitivt bättre golfbanor än denna, men få har en större charm och ett sådant lugnt behagligt tempo. Några monsterhål finns inte så detta är en perfekt bana för hela familjen att åka till. Dessutom, har du bra bollträff finns möjligheten till en låg runda.

Torekov is situated at the tip of Bjärehalvön, a peninsula to the north of Malmö and Helsingborg. The course was opened in 1925, but it was significantly altered in the early 1990s by Nils Sköld, for the better we might add. The climate and largely sandy soil make this course playable virtually all year (a rare occurrence in Sweden). A very short layout, it calls for excellent driving or long irons off the tee to end up with a short or medium iron going into the green, at least if the wind is quiet. This is the case about two days a year. For the other days, you will have to call on all your Scottish flair when selecting the right club to play and master the bump and run shot to hit greens that are often firm and slick. There are better courses than this, but few have greater charm and such an easy pace and tempo. There are few high-risk holes, so this is an ideal course for family holidays, where the pleasure of playing together counts for more than carding a reasonable score. At the same time, if you want to shoot a low score, you are of course very free to do so.

Torekovs Golfklubb — 1925
Box 81
S - 260 93 TOREKOV

Office	Sekretariat	(46) 0431 - 36 35 72
Pro shop	Pro shop	(46) 0431 - 36 41 21
Fax	Fax	(46) 0431 - 36 49 16
Situation	Läge	
Båstad, 15 km		
Annual closure	Årlig stängning	no
Weekly closure	Daglig stängning	no

Fees main season
Tariff hög säsong full day

	Week days Veckodag	We/Bank holidays Lör/Söndag/Helgdag
Individual Individuellt	SKr 260:-	SKr 260:-
Couple Par	SKr 520:-	SKr 520:-
Juniors: – 50%		

Caddy	Caddie	no
Electric Trolley	El vagn	SKr 100:-
Buggy	Golfbil	SKr 150:-
Clubs	Klubbor	SKr 100:-

Credit cards Kredit kort
VISA - Eurocard - MasterCard - AMEX

1276

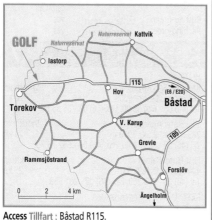

Access Tillfart : Båstad R115.
Map 1 on page 1218 Karta 1 se sid: 1218

GOLF COURSE BANA — 14/20

Site	Läge	▰▰▰
Maintenance	Underhåll	▰▰▰
Architect	Arkitekt	Nils Sköld
Type	Typ	seaside course, open country
Relief	Relief	▰▰▰
Water in play	Vatten på spelfältet	▰▰▰▰
Exp. to wind	Vindutsatt	▰▰▰▰
Trees in play	Tråd på spelfältet	▰▰

Scorecard Scorekort	Chp. Back tees	Mens Herrtee	Ladies Damtee
Length Längd	5707	5707	5027
Par	72	72	72

Advised golfing ability	0	12	24	36
Rekommenderad spelnivå				
Hcp required Hcp erfordrad	36			

CLUB HOUSE & AMENITIES
KLUBBHUS OCH OMGIVNING — 7/10

Pro shop	Pro shop	
Driving range	Träningsbana	
Sheltered	täkt	1 mat
On grass	på gräs	no, 14 mats open air
Putting-green	putting-green	ja
Pitching-green	pitching-green	ja

HOTEL FACILITIES
HOTELL OMGIVNING — 7/10

HOTELS

Kattegatt — Torekov
11 rooms, D SKr 1640:- — 5 km
Tel (46) 0431 - 36 30 02, Fax (46) 0431 - 36 30 03

Margretetorp — Ängelholm
60 rooms, D SKr 1585:- — 20 km
Tel (46) 0431 - 45 44 50, Fax (46) 0431 - 45 48 77

Hemmestör — Båstad
90 rooms, D SKr 800:- — 20 km
Tel (46) 0431 - 742 65, Fax (46) 0431 - 748 88

RESTAURANTS RESTAURANG

Kattegatt — Torekov
Tel (46) 0431 - 36 30 02 — 5 km

Enehall — Båstad
Tel (46) 0431 - 750 15 — 10 km

Margretetorp — Båstad
Tel (46) 0431 - 45 44 50 — v

Staden ligger mitt i djupaste Småland, omgiven av skogar och mörkblåa sjöar – ett paradis för fotvandrare och sportfiskare. Banan står att finna österut nära sjön Sommen. Den är smal och slingrar sig fram mellan träden, men någon större längd från tee behövs inte utan en trätrea räcker ofta långt. Detta är ett smart sätt att undvika strategiskt utlagda fairwaybunkers som annars är som en magnet för bollen. Många doglegs gör också att den som verkligen kan manövrera bollen har julafton här. Redan på första hålet kan långtslående försöka nå greenen med utslaget, men frågan är om de känner sig bekväma på en smal bana som denna? Har de en bra dag med drivern kommer de dock ha att hamna väldigt nära greenen på några par 4-hål. Greenerna är för övrigt typiska för hur man byggde på 50-talet. De är små, mycket ondulerade och är svåra att stanna en boll på. Därför krävs mycket känsla i närspelet. Åk hit, om det så bara är för att uppleva charmen med den här platsen

The town is situated in the middle of Småland, a region of forests and blue-steel lakes, a sort of paradise for hikers and anglers. The course lies to the east, very close to lake Sommen. It is a narrow layout amongst trees, but no great length is required off the tee and a 3-wood will often do very nicely. This is also a very reassuring club to hit in that the fairway bunkers seem to have a magnetic effect on mis-hit drives. More, the very many dog-legs ideally call for skill in bending the ball both ways, making this a home from home course for technicians and tacticians. Long-hitters can certainly go for the green as from hole number one, but generally speaking they won't feel quite as comfortable on this sort of course. With a good tee-shot, though, they will probably end up with a short iron into the greens, which are typically 1950s style: on the small side, very contoured and hard to stop the ball on. Worth knowing, if only for the charm of the site.

Tranås Golfklubb — 1952

Box 430
S - 573 25 TRANÅS

Office	Sekretariat	(46) 0140 - 31 16 61
Pro shop	Pro shop	(46) 0140 - 169 20
Fax	Fax	(46) 0140 - 161 61
Situation	Läge	

Jönköping, 78 km

Annual closure	Årlig stängning	no
Weekly closure	Daglig stängning	no

Fees main season
Tariff hög säsong full day

	Week days Veckodag	We/Bank holidays Lör/Söndag/Helgdag
Individual Individuellt	SKr 180:-	SKr 200:-
Couple Par	SKr 360:-	SKr 400:-

Juniors: 80:-

Caddy	Caddie	no
Electric Trolley	El vagn	no
Buggy	Golfbil	SKr 100:-
Clubs	Klubbor	SKr 100:-

Credit cards Kredit kort VISA - Eurocard - MasterCard

Access Tillfart : Jönköping E4 → Linköping. Gränna
Exit R133 → Tranås, R32 → Tranås. 2 km N, → Golf
Map 1 on page 1229 Karta 1 se sid: 1229

GOLF COURSE
BANA — 14/20

Site	Läge	
Maintenance	Underhåll	
Architect	Arkitekt	Sundholm
Type	Typ	forest, parkland
Relief	Relief	
Water in play	Vatten på spelfältet	
Exp. to wind	Vindutsatt	
Trees in play	Träd på spelfältet	

Scorecard Scorekort	Chp. Back tees	Mens Herrtee	Ladies Damtee
Length Längd	6014	5768	5022
Par	72	72	72

Advised golfing ability Rekommenderad spelnivå	0	12	24	36

Hcp required   Hcp erfordrad   36

CLUB HOUSE & AMENITIES
KLUBBHUS OCH OMGIVNING — 6/10

Pro shop	Pro shop	
Driving range	Träningsbana	
Sheltered	tåkt	1 mat
On grass	på gräs	no, 14 mats open air
Putting-green	putting-green	yes
Pitching-green	pitching-green	yes

HOTEL FACILITIES
HOTELL OMGIVNING — 7/10

HOTELS

Statt Hotell — Tranås, 5 km
52 rooms, D SKr 970:-
Tel (46) 0140 - 566 00, Fax (46) 0140 - 561 51

Badhotellet — Tranås, 5 km
57 rooms, D SKr 725:-
Tel (46) 0140 - 462 00, Fax (46) 0140 - 461 85

Hotell Äberg — Tranås, 3 km
20 rooms, D SKr 740:-
Tel (46) 0140 - 130 80, Fax (46) 0140 - 562 02

RESTAURANTS RESTAURANG

Queens — Tranås, 3 km
Tel (46) 0140 - 539 99

Krogen — Tranås, 3 km
Tel (46) 0140 - 161 45

1277

ULLNA

17	8	6

En dag på Ullna måste börja med att du står och filosoferar i klubbhusets värme och blickar ut över Ullnasjön och ser solen reflektera i vattnet. Det här kommer definitivt få dig i rätt sinnesstämning. Tredje hålet är en kort och oförglömlig par 3a med en ögreen. Faktum är att du finner vatten så gott som överallt, på tolv av hålen kommer vatten i spel. För att leverera en bra score här är det nödvändigt att du är i absolut toppform. Ullna är en väldigt ärlig bana som inte gömmer sina hinder – de syns tydligt från tee. Den är dessutom nästan helt platt, och sammantaget är den ett av de finaste exempel på "targetgolf" som finns i Sverige. De duktiga spelarna kommer säkert göra en eller annan birdie för att kompensera för oundvikliga bogeys. Sven Tumba, banarkitekten, har dock inte gjort livet lätt för höghandicaparen, som kommer att tvingas plocka upp bollen på många hål (om han har några kvar, vill säga). Ullna är spektakulär, konstgjord och välmanikyrerad, och en högst oförglömlig upplevelse. Och då inte bara för de 4 och de 17 hålen, som är bland de bästa som man kan finna i Sverige.

Contemplating the sun reflecting on the lake in the morning will put you in the right frame of mind for your round, because water is almost everywhere, coming into play on 12 holes. You will need to be on top of your game to card a good score. This is a very forthright course which clearly shows it hand in terms of hazards; it is also virtually flat and one of the finest examples of target golf in the whole of Sweden. All the same, while the best players should come through unscathed and find a few birdies to make up for the inevitable bogeys, architect Sven Tumba did not spare too many thoughts for the higher-handicappers, who will spend a lot of time picking up their balls (if they have any left). Spectacular, artificial and finely contoured, Ullna is a memorable course, and not only for holes 4 and 17, two of the finest in the country.

Ullna Golf & Country Club — 1981
Rosenkälla
S - 184 94 Åkersberga

Office	Sekretariat	(46) 08 - 510 260 75
Pro shop	Pro shop	(46) 08 - 510 264 20
Fax	Fax	(46) 08 - 510 260 68
Situation	Läge	

Stockholm, 27 km

Annual closure	Årlig stängning	no
Weekly closure	Daglig stängning	no

Fees main season
Tariff hög säsong full day

	Week days Veckodag	We/Bank holidays Lör/Söndag/Helgdag
Individual Individuellt	SKr 425:-	SKr 425:-
Couple Par	SKr 850:-	SKr 850:-

Juniors: 160:-

Caddy	Caddie	no
Electric Trolley	El vagn	no
Buggy	Golfbil	SKr 250:-
Clubs	Klubbor	SKr 300:-

Credit cards Kredit kort
VISA - Eurocard - MasterCard - AMEX - DC

1278

Access Tillfart : Stockholm, E 18 → Norrtälje.
→ Åkersberga, → Gribbylund, → Golf
Map 2 on page 1220 Karta 2 se sid: 1220

GOLF COURSE BANA — 17/20

Site	Läge	
Maintenance	Underhåll	
Architect	Arkitekt	Sven Tumba
Type	Typ	parkland
Relief	Relief	
Water in play	Vatten på spelfältet	
Exp. to wind	Vindutsatt	
Trees in play	Tråd på spelfältet	

Scorecard Scorekort	Chp. Back tees	Mens Herrtee	Ladies Damtee
Length Längd	6210	5750	4915
Par	72	72	72

Advised golfing ability Rekommenderad spelnivå	0	12	24	36

Hcp required Hcp erfordrad   24 Men, 30 Ladies

CLUB HOUSE & AMENITIES CLUB HOUSE ET ANNEXES — 8/10

Pro shop	Pro shop	
Driving range	Träningsbana	
Sheltered	tåkt	25 mats
On grass	på gräs	no, 12 mats open air
Putting-green	putting-green	yes
Pitching-green	pitching-green	yes

HOTEL FACILITIES HOTELL OMGIVNING — 6/10

HOTELS

Silja Hotel Ariadne — Stockholm Värtahamnen
283 rooms, D SKr 1960:- 24 km
Tel (46) 08 - 665 78 00, Fax (46) 08 - 662 76 70

Lord Nelson — Stockholm
31 rooms, D SKr 1890:- 27 km
Tel (46) 08 - 23 23 90, Fax (46) 08 - 10 10 89

Victory - Tel 45 rooms, D SKr 2390:- — Stockholm
Tel (46) 08 - 14 30 90, Fax (46) 08 - 20 21 77 27 km

RESTAURANTS RESTAURANG

Eriks - Tel (46) 08 - 23 85 00 — Stockholm 27 km

Stallmästeregården — Stockholm
Tel (46) 08 - 610 13 00 24 km

Den Gyldene Freden - Tel (46) 08 - 24 97 60 — Stockholm

Staden Uppsala är berömd för sin katedral, sina museum och en historia som ofta har varit våldsam, såväl politiskt som intellektuellt. Uppsala är också hem för landets äldsta universitet. Fast något vilt studentliv kan vi knappast förknippa Upsala Golfklubb med, även om vi får allt fler yngre golfare i landet. Banan är ganska flack och växlar mellan parkbanekaraktär och skog, en typisk svensk landskapsbild med andra ord. Framför allt de långa par 4-hålen kräver väl träffade drives om du ska ha en möjlighet att nå greenerna på rätt antal slag. Hindernas variation och placering kräver att du håller huvudet kallt. Det här är en typisk inlandsbana, därmed inte sagt att det för jämnan är vindstilla. Vinden kan på den här banan spela en avgörande betydelse. Detta är en mästerskapsbana ofta använd för stora nationella tävlingar.

The city of Uppsala is famous for its Gothic cathedral, museums and tangible vestiges of an eventful and oftentimes violent past history both intellectually and politically. It is home to the country's oldest university. The Upsala Golfklubb course lies well away from the hustle and bustle of young undergraduates, even though young golfers make up a large contingent of Swedish golfers. A rather flat layout in a landscape of parkland and forest frequently found in a country so attached to nature, the course calls for long drives on all the par 4s if you want to hit the greens in regulation. The standard, variety and location of hazards call for tight strategy, and for a course which, to all intents and purposes, is an inland layout, the wind can play a major role and have a significant effect on scores. A serious course which is often used for nationwide tournaments.

Upsala Golfklubb — 1964

Håmo Gåro
S - 755 92 UPPSALA

Office	Sekretariat	(46) 018 - 46 01 20
Pro shop	Pro shop	(46) 018 - 46 12 41
Fax	Fax	(46) 018 - 46 12 05
Situation	Läge	

Uppsala, 4 km

Annual closure	Årlig stängning	no
Weekly closure	Daglig stängning	no

Fees main season
Tariff hög säsong full day

	Week days Veckodag	We/Bank holidays Lör/Söndag/Helgdag
Individual Individuellt	SKr 240:-	SKr 320:-
Couple Par	SKr 480:-	SKr 640:-

Juniors: – 50%

Caddy	Caddie	no
Electric Trolley	El vagn	no
Buggy	Golfbil	no
Clubs	Klubbor	

Credit cards Kredit kort
VISA - Eurocard - MasterCard - AMEX - JCB

Access Tillfart : Uppsala, V 55 →
Enköping/Norrköping/Sala. 4 km V 72.
Map 2 on page 1221 Karta 2 se sid: 1221

GOLF COURSE / BANA — 13/20

Site	Läge	
Maintenance	Underhåll	
Architect	Arkitekt	Greger Paulsson
Type	Typ	forest, parkland
Relief	Relief	
Water in play	Vatten på spelfältet	
Exp. to wind	Vindutsatt	
Trees in play	Träd på spelfältet	

Scorecard Scorekort	Chp. Back tees	Mens Herrtee	Ladies Damtee
Length Längd	6153	5839	4978
Par	72	72	72

Advised golfing ability Rekommenderad spelnivå	0 12 24 36	
Hcp required Hcp erfordrad	36	

CLUB HOUSE & AMENITIES / KLUBBHUS OCH OMGIVNING — 6/10

Pro shop	Pro shop	
Driving range	Träningsbana	
Sheltered	täkt	no
On grass	på gräs	yes
Putting-green	putting-green	yes
Pitching-green	pitching-green	yes

HOTEL FACILITIES / HOTELL OMGIVNING — 6/10

HOTELS

Hotel Gillet/Radisson SAS — Uppsala 10 km
160 rooms, D SKr 1300:-
Tel (46) 018 - 15 53 60
Fax (46) 018 - 15 33 80

Hotel Svava — Uppsala 10 km
120 rooms, D SKr 990:-
Tel (46) 018 - 13 00 30
Fax (46) 018 - 13 22 30

RESTAURANTS RESTAURANG

Elaka Måns — Uppsala 4 km
Tel (46) 018 - 10 66 66

Domtrappkällaren — Uppsala 4 km
Tel (46) 018 - 13 09 55

Rådhussalongen — Uppsala 4 km
Tel (46) 018 - 69 50 70

1279

Tack vare E 4 ligger banan perfekt till för dig som färdas från Malmö till Stockholm, eller tvärtom. Ändå kan Värnamo, i en positiv mening, kännas som att komma till världens ände. Att släntra upp till klubbhuset en tidig morgon och titta ut över sjön Hindsen är en magisk upplevelse. Som så många andra svenska banor är Värnamo byggd på en romantisk, nästan teatralisk plats. Klarar du av par 3-hålen är du på väg mot en bra score. Fast den riktiga utmaningen finns i de något upphöjda greenerna som dessutom inte är alldeles lätta att läsa. Missar du en green skadar det inte om du har en vass lobbwedge i bagen. På Värnamo finns inga riktiga monsterhinder som avskräcker höghandicaparen, medan det för den bättre spelaren gäller att undvika skogen om han vill briljera inför släkt och vänner och visa vad han kan göra med en golfklubba. Såväl för män som kvinnor är denna halvsvåra bana definitivt att föredra framför att spela en riktig tuffing. Här vinner charmen!

This course is close to the motorway running across the country from south-west Malmö to Stockholm further northeast. But it is still far enough for the golfer to feel as if he were playing at the ends of the earth. Arriving early morning at the club house built on a small hill overlooking lake Hindsen is a magic experience. Like many Swedish courses, this has a romantic, theatrical setting, but that is only the beginning. It might be on the short side, but start off by getting the better of the par 3s and you can think about carding a good score. Here, the real challenge lies with the slightly elevated greens, which are sharply contoured and tough to read. You will also need a lot of touch. A missed green cries out for a lob-wedge, if you have one. There are no excessive hazards to deter the high-handicapper, while the better players will have to come to terms with the trees before showing friends and family what he or she can do.

Värnamo Golfklubb — 1962

Box 146
S - 331 21 VÄRNAMO

Office	Sekretariat	(46) 0370 - 230 84
Pro shop	Pro shop	(46) 0370 - 231 23
Fax	Fax	(46) 0370 - 232 16
Situation	Läge	

Jönköping, 70 km - Värnamo, 7 km

Annual closure	Årlig stängning	no
Weekly closure	Daglig stängning	no

Fees main season
Tariff hög säsong full day

	Week days Veckodag	We/Bank holidays Lör/Söndag/Helgdag
Individual Individuellt	SKr 300:-	SKr 300:-
Couple Par	SKr 300:-	SKr 300:-

Juniors: 100:-/120:-

Caddy	Caddie	no
Electric Trolley	El vagn	no
Buggy	Golfbil	SKr 200:-
Clubs	Klubbor	SKr 100:-

Credit cards Kredit kort
VISA - Eurocard - MasterCard - DC

1280

Access Tillfart : E4 Exit Värnamo Norra. →
Vetlanda/Vrigstad. Värnamo GK 5 km.
Map 1 on page 1218 Karta 1 se sid: 1218

GOLF COURSE / BANA — 15/20

Site	Läge	
Maintenance	Underhåll	
Architect	Arkitekt	Nils Sköld
Type	Typ	forest, parkland
Relief	Relief	
Water in play	Vatten på spelfältet	
Exp. to wind	Vindutsatt	
Trees in play	Träd på spelfältet	

Scorecard Scorekort	Chp. Back tees	Mens Herrtee	Ladies Damtee
Length Längd	5943	5701	4825
Par	72	72	72

Advised golfing ability Rekommenderad spelnivå	0	12	24	36
Hcp required Hcp erfordrad	120 max. (4 players)			

CLUB HOUSE & AMENITIES / CLUB HOUSE ET ANNEXES — 7/10

Pro shop	Pro shop	
Driving range	Träningsbana	
Sheltered	täkt	2 mat
On grass	på gräs	no, 22 mats open air
Putting-green	putting-green	yes
Pitching-green	pitching-green	yes

HOTEL FACILITIES / HOTELL OMGIVNING — 5/10

HOTELS

Hotell Statt — Värnamo 7 km
125 rooms, D SKr 1195:-
Tel (46) 0370 - 30 15 30
Fax (46) 0370 - 134 69

Tre Liljor — Värnamo 7 km
39 rooms, D SKr 1275:-
Tel (46) 0370 - 473 00
Fax (46) 0370 - 168 90

RESTAURANTS RESTAURANG

Harrys — Värnamo 7 km
Tel (46) 0370 - 498 00

Napoli — Värnamo 7 km
Tel (46) 0370 - 120 60

16	7	7

Vasatorp är en av många utmärkta banor som ligger runt Helsingborg, en fantastisk stad för den historieintresserade – inte minst för att detta är skådeplatsen för många krigsbataljer mellan Sverige och Danmark genom århundradena. Knappt fem kilometer bort skymtar man Helsingør. Vasatorps golfbana gömmer inga obehagliga överraskningar: Slå rakt och håll dig på fairway, och du kommer att göra en bra score (svårare än så är inte golf). Trots den täta skogen är banan förhållandevis bred – även för Ballesteros, som när han vann SEO här spred sina drives både till höger och vänster. Om du ska ha en chans att nå på rätt antal slag och få bra inspelsvinklar måste du välja drivern från tee. Många greener är omgärdade av kullar, vilket ställer höga krav på dina inspel. Greenerna är relativt stora och kan bjuda på en stor variation vad gäller flaggplaceringarna, något som kan inverka högst påtagligt på ditt resultat. Här är det amerikansk målgolf som gäller – höga inspel är att föredra framför att rulla in bollen.

This course has no traps in store: hit it straight, keep in the fairway and you will card a good score (golf is that simple). Despite the trees, the whole complex is wide, enough so for Ballesteros to have won here even though he sprayed his drives left and right into the undergrowth. Quite simply, here you have to hit the driver if you want to reach the long holes in regulation and approach the greens from the right angle. A number of sandhills and mounds can complicate your approach shots. The greens are pretty huge, with many different pin positions that can seriously damage your card, especially since here you have to play target golf rather than bump and run shots. High-handicappers are best advised to play Vasatorps in summer, when the ground is dry and affords welcome roll for added length.

Vasatorps Golfklubb   1973
Box 13035
S - 250 13 HELSINGBORG

Office	Sekretariat	(46) 042 - 23 50 58
Pro shop	Pro shop	(46) 042 - 23 50 45
Fax	Fax	(46) 042 - 23 51 35
Situation	Läge	

Helsingborg, 7 km

Annual closure	Årlig stängning	no
Weekly closure	Daglig stängning	no

Fees main season
Tariff hög säsong full day

	Week days Veckodag	We/Bank holidays Lör/Söndag/Helgdag
Individual Individuellt	SKr 260:-	SKr 260:-
Couple Par	SKr 520:-	SKr 520:-

Juniors: – 50%

Caddy	Caddie	no
Electric Trolley	El vagn	SKr 50:-
Buggy	Golfbil	no
Clubs	Klubbor	SKr 150:-

Credit cards Kredit kort
VISA - Eurocard - MasterCard - AMEX - DC

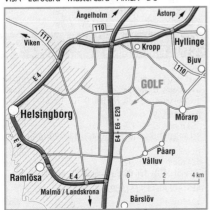

Access Tillfart : Kelsingborg, E4 West (Österut) →
«Höganäsrondellen». → Råå. Turn left at traffic
lights (Trafiklij, vä). 500 m → Kropp.
Map 1 on page 1218 Karta 1 se sid: 1218

GOLF COURSE
BANA   16/20

Site	Läge	▰▰▰▰▱
Maintenance	Underhåll	▰▰▰▰▱
Architect	Arkitekt	Ture Bruce
Type	Typ	forest, parkland
Relief	Relief	▰▰▱▱▱
Water in play	Vatten på spelfältet	▰▱▱▱▱
Exp. to wind	Vindutsatt	▰▰▱▱▱
Trees in play	Träd på spelfältet	▰▰▰▰▱

Scorecard Scorekort	Chp. Back tees	Mens Herrtee	Ladies Damtee
Length Längd	6165	5895	5510
Par	72	72	72

Advised golfing ability		0	12	24	36
Rekommenderad spelnivå		▰▰▰▰▱			
Hcp required	Hcp erfordrad	36			

CLUB HOUSE & AMENITIES
KLUBBHUS OCH OMGIVNING   7/10

Pro shop	Pro shop	▰▰▰▰▱
Driving range	Träningsbana	▰▰▰▰▱
Sheltered	täkt	7 mats
On grass	på gräs	no, 30 mats open air
Putting-green	putting-green	yes
Pitching-green	pitching-green	yes

HOTEL FACILITIES
HOTELL OMGIVNING   7/10

HOTELS
Marina Plaza   Helsingborg
190 rooms, D SKr 1295:-   7 km
Tel (46) 042 - 19 21 00, Fax (46) 042 - 14 96 16

Hotell Nouveau   Helsingborg
89 rooms, D SKr 1145:-   7 km
Tel (46) 042 - 18 53 90, Fax (46) 042 - 14 08 85

Grand Hotell   Helsingborg
116 rooms, D SKr 1490:-   7 km
Tel (46) 042 - 12 01 70, Fax (46) 042 - 21 88 33

RESTAURANTS RESTAURANG
Oskar Trapp   Helsingborg
Tel (46) 042 - 14 60 44   7 km

Gastro   Helsingborg
Tel (46) 042 - 24 34 70   7 km

1281

VÄXJÖ

Växjö golfbana designades 1961 av Douglas Brasier, en arkitekt som ligger bakom många kvalitetsbanor. Här finns massor med träd, på våren kan banan var ganska blöt och landar du i den tjocka ruffen kan du få många besvärliga lägen. Spelare med bra drives har en klar fördel här, förutsatt naturligtvis att de kan följa upp med precisa inspel mot de väl skyddade greenerna. Fast höghandicaparen kommer att uppskatta att det inte finns några riktigt besvärliga hinder precis framför utslagsplatserna. Men det ska också sägas – den här banan är inte lätt, inte för någon. Banans svårigheter är jämt fördelade över de 18 hålen, även om sluthålet bjuder på något alldeles extra. Här krävs en perfekt drive om du ska avsluta rundan på ett bra sätt. Växjö är betydligt bättre än genomsnittsbanan, layouten är av gammalt klassiskt snitt, men ändå med många fantasifulla inslag, exempelvis sjätte hålet, en par 5, där du har många alternativa spelmöjligheter att välja mellan.

This is the centre of a region specializing in glasswork, particularly the crystal of Orrefors and Åfors, or the famous Kosta Boda. In fact you will find everything to treat yourself to a fine trophy to reward your performance on this layout. Designed in 1961 by Douglas Brasier, Växjö is full of trees, often wet in the spring and autumn, and has a very thick first layer of rough from where extracting your ball can be a difficult proposition. Good drivers have a clear advantage here, providing of course that they successfully pursue their route to medium-sized, well-guarded greens. The absence of hazards immediately in front of the tee-boxes will reassure the less experienced players, even though this course is easy for no-one. The difficulties are evenly spread around the course and come to a head on the 18th hole, where the drive has to be perfect to finish your round with some satisfaction. A course above average, rather classical in style.

Växjö Golfklubb — 1961
Araby Herrgård Box 227
S - 351 05 VÄXJÖ

Office	Sekretariat	(46) 0470 - 215 15
Pro shop	Pro shop	no Proshop
Fax	Fax	(46) 042 - 215 57
Situation	Läge	

Växjö, 10 km

Annual closure	Årlig stängning	no
Weekly closure	Daglig stängning	no

Fees main season
Tariff hög säsong full day

	Week days Veckodag	We/Bank holidays Lör/Söndag/Helgdag
Individual Individuellt	SKr 200:-	SKr 220:-
Couple Par	SKr 400:-	SKr 440:-

Juniors: –50%

Caddy	Caddie	no
Electric Trolley	El vagn	no
Buggy	Golfbil	SKr 200:-
Clubs	Klubbor	

Credit cards Kredit kort VISA - Eurocard - MasterCard

GOLF COURSE / BANA — 15/20

Site	Läge	
Maintenance	Underhåll	
Architect	Arkitekt	Douglas Brasier
Type	Typ	forest, parkland
Relief	Relief	
Water in play	Vatten på spelfältet	
Exp. to wind	Vindutsatt	
Trees in play	Tråd på spelfältet	

Scorecard Scorekort	Chp. Back tees	Mens Herrtee	Ladies Damtee
Length Längd	6046	5799	5059
Par	72	72	72

Advised golfing ability — 0 12 24 36
Rekommenderad spelnivå
Hcp required Hcp erfordrad 36

CLUB HOUSE & AMENITIES / CLUB HOUSE ET ANNEXES — 6/10

Pro shop	Pro shop	
Driving range	Träningsbana	
Sheltered	tåkt	no
On grass	på gräs	no, 20 mats open air
Putting-green	putting-green	yes
Pitching-green	pitching-green	yes

HOTEL FACILITIES / HOTELL OMGIVNING — 7/10

HOTELS

First Hotel Cardinal — Växjö, 7 km
111 rooms, D SKr 1335:-
Tel (46) 0470 - 134 30, Fax (46) 0470 - 169 64

Radisson SAS — Växjö, 7 km
158 rooms, D SKr 1295:-
Tel (46) 0470 - 70 10 00, Fax (46) 0470 - 70 10 10

Hotell Statt — Växjö, 7 km
124 rooms, D SKr 1125:-
Tel (46) 0470 - 134 00, Fax (46) 0470 - 448 37

RESTAURANTS RESTAURANG

Spisen — Växjö, 7 km
Tel (46) 0470 - 123 00

Munhen - Tel (46) 0470 - 160 60 — Växjö 7 km

Teaterparken - Tel (46) 0470 - 399 00 — Växjö 7 km

Access Tillfart : Växjö, R23, R25 & R30 → Golf
Map 1 on page 1218 Karta 1 se sid: 1218

1282

Bli inte skrämd av Gotlands geografiska läge! Klimatet är milt och på sommaren flockas turisterna här. Precis som handelsmännen gjorde under medeltiden. Faktum är att Visby har så många avtryck från den här perioden att UNESCO har satt staden på sin lista över kulturminnesmärkta platser. Kustlinjen är något alldeles extra, och nästan halva banan är också utlagd nära denna, resten av hålen vindlar fram i ett skogsparti. Det finns ingen hejd på alla hinder och det krävs att du inte släpper på koncentrationen. Även greenerna är lagom knepiga. De som byggdes 1959 är små och förrädiska, medan de som byggdes i början av 90-talet är större och mer kuperade. Som du kanske förstår är vinden här en avgörande faktor, något som du kommer att känna direkt på första hålet: Längs hela högersidan lurar vatten. För att ta dig till Gotland väntar en färjetur på 4–8 timmar (beroende på vilket bolag du åker med), så en bra idé är att stanna här i några dagar och spela banan flera gånger (samt niohålsbanan som ligger på området).

For this "Nordic" region, the climate is very mild and the area is a very popular destination. In the Middle Ages, it was also a very busy trading centre, and the town of Visby has so many vestiges of this period that it is on the UNESCO world heritage list of historical sites. This course is laid out half beside the sea, half amidst trees. There is no shortage of hazards to keep you on your toes, and the greens, too, can cause their share of problems. Those built in 1959 are small and treacherous, the others, built in the 1990s, are larger and contoured. The wind here is a decisive factor, as you will see and feel straightaway on 1st hole. Here, your brushes with water begin down the right-hand side of the fairway. Getting here involves an four to eight-hour trip (by the new catamaran or by ferry), so a good idea is to stay for several days, play the course (this and the adjacent nine-hole layout), and get in some visits to cultural landmarks.

Visby Golfklubb — 1959

Kronholmen Västergarn
S - 620 020 KLINTEHAMN

Office	Sekretariat	(46) 0498 - 24 50 56
Pro shop	Pro shop	(46) 0498 - 24 51 00
Fax	Fax	(46) 0498 - 24 52 40
Situation	Läge	

Visby (Gotlands Län), 25 km

Annual closure	Årlig stängning	no
Weekly closure	Daglig stängning	no

Fees main season
Tariff hög säsong full day

	Week days Veckodag	We/Bank holidays Lör/Söndag/Helgdag
Individual Individuellt	SKr 280:-	SKr 300:-
Couple Par	SKr 560:-	SKr 600:-

Juniors: 135:-/150:-

Caddy	Caddie	no
Electric Trolley	El vagn	no
Buggy	Golfbil	SKr 100:-
Clubs	Klubbor	SKr 150:-

Credit cards Kredit kort
VISA - Eurocard - MasterCard - AMEX

Access Tillfart : Stockholm, R79 → Nynäshamn.
Ferry → Visby. R140 → Klintehamn. 25 km, → Golf
Map 1 on page 1219 Karta 1 se sid: 1219

GOLF COURSE / BANA — 16/20

Site	Läge	▪▪▪▪▪▪▫▫
Maintenance	Underhåll	▪▪▪▪▪▪▫▫
Architect	Arkitekt	Nils Sköld Peter Nordwall
Type	Typ	seaside course, parkland
Relief	Relief	▪▪▪▪▪▫▫▫
Water in play	Vatten på spelfältet	▪▪▪▪▪▪▫▫
Exp. to wind	Vindutsatt	▪▪▪▪▪▪▪▫
Trees in play	Träd på spelfältet	▪▪▪▪▪▫▫▫

Scorecard Scorekort	Chp. Back tees	Mens Herrtee	Ladies Damtee
Length Längd	6103	5868	5094
Par	72	72	72

Advised golfing ability	0	12	24	36
Rekommenderad spelnivå				
Hcp required Hcp erfordrad	36			

CLUB HOUSE & AMENITIES / KLUBBHUS OCH OMGIVNING — 6/10

Pro shop	Pro shop	▪▪▪▪▪▪▫▫
Driving range	Träningsbana	▪▪▪▪▪▪▫▫
Sheltered	täkt	2 mats
On grass	på gräs	yes
Putting-green	putting-green	yes
Pitching-green	pitching-green	yes

HOTEL FACILITIES / HOTELL OMGIVNING — 5/10

HOTELS

Visby Hotell — Visby / 30 km
134 rooms, D SKr 1520:-
Tel (46) 0498 - 20 40 00
Fax (46) 0498 - 21 13 20

Strand Hotell — Visby / 30 km
110 rooms, D SKr 1325:-
Tel (46) 0498 - 25 88 00
Fax (46) 0498 - 25 88 11

RESTAURANTS RESTAURANG

Lindgården — Visby / 30 km
Tel (46) 0498 - 21 87 00

Visby Hotell — Visby / 30 km
Tel (46) 0498 - 20 40 00

1283

Donnez des ailes à vos rêves.

C O U P É
406
Pour que l'automobile soit toujours un plaisir. **PEUGEOT**

Schweiz Suisse Svizzera

The Millennium Guide

Comme dans les autres pays d'Europe, la majeure partie des golfs présentés ici sont privés, mais ouverts au public avec quelques restrictions ou difficultés d'accès en week-end. Il convient donc de s'informer et de réserver à l'avance, et une lettre d'introduction de votre club ne sera jamais inutile. Avec 31.000 joueurs, et une quarantaine de 18 trous, la Suisse n'est pas un très grand pays golfique, mais ses parcours sont souvent situés dans des paysages superbes.

Wie auch in anderen europäischen Ländern sind die meisten Golfplätze privat, aber der Öffentlichkeit unter gewissen Vorbehalten oder Einschränkungen an den Wochenenden zugänglich. Es ist daher empfehlenswert, sich vorgängig zu informieren oder zu reservieren, und ein Empfehlungsschreiben Ihres Clubs ist sicher immer nützlich. Mit ihren 31'000 Golfern und ungefähr 40 18-Loch-Bahnen zählt die Schweiz sicherlich nicht zu den bekannten Golfländern, aber dafür befinden sich die Golfplätze in einer landschaftlich reizvollen Umgebung.

As in other European countries, the majority of golf courses featured here are private, but open to the general public with a few restrictions or dufficulties for playing on week-ends. The best idea, therefore, is to make enquiries and book in advance, and emember that a letter of introduction from your own club is always a good idea. With 31,000 players and around 40 eighteen-hole courses, Switzerland is not a big golfing country but the courses are often set amidst some fabulous landscapes.

1285

CLASSEMENT DES PARCOURS
EINTEILUNG DER GOLFPLÄTZE
CLASSIFICATION OF COURSES

Note du Club-house et annexes
Note für das Clubhaus und die Einrichtungen
Club-house and facilities

Note du parcours
Note für den Golfplatz
Course score

Note de l'environnement hôtelier
Note für das Hotelangebot der Umgebung
Hotel facility score

P. / Seite

| 18 | 8 | 6 | Domaine Impérial | 1294 |

Note			Parcours/Golfplätze	P.	Note			Parcours/Golfplätze	P.
18	8	6	Domaine Impérial	1294	14	7	6	Gruyère (La)	1298
17	7	8	Genève	1297	14	6	6	Interlaken	1299
16	7	7	Lausanne	1300	14	6	7	Neuchâtel	1305
15	7	6	Blumisberg	1291	14	7	6	Schönenberg	1308
15	6	6	Engadin	1295	13	7	6	Bad Ragaz	1290
15	6	6	Les Bois	1301	13	7	6	Breitenloo	1292
15	7	8	Lugano	1302	13	7	6	Ennetsee-Holzhäusern	1296
15	7	7	Patriziale Ascona	1307	13	6	7	Luzern	1303
15	8	7	Sempachersee	1309	13	6	5	Montreux	1304
15	7	6	Zumikon	1311	13	7	7	Niederbüren	1306
14	7	8	Crans-sur-Sierre	1293	13	6	6	Wylihof	1310

CLASSEMENT DE L'ENVIRONNEMENT HOTELIER
EINTEILUNG DES HOTELANGEBOTS DER UMGEBUNG
CLASSIFICATION OF HOTELS FACILITIES

Note			Parcours/Golfplätze	P.	Note			Parcours/Golfplätze	P.
14	7	8	Crans-sur-Sierre	S 1293	13	7	6	Breitenloo	S 1292
17	7	8	Genève	S 1297	18	8	6	Domaine Impérial	S 1294
15	7	8	Lugano	S 1302	15	6	6	Engadin	S 1295
16	7	7	Lausanne	S 1300	13	7	6	Ennetsee-Holzhäusern	S 1296
13	6	7	Luzern	S 1303	14	7	6	Gruyère (La)	S 1298
14	6	7	Neuchâtel	S 1305	14	6	6	Interlaken	S 1299
13	7	7	Niederbüren	S 1306	15	6	6	Les Bois	S 1301
15	7	7	Patriziale Ascona	S 1307	14	7	6	Schönenberg	S 1308
15	8	7	Sempachersee	S 1309	13	6	6	Wylihof	S 1310
13	7	6	Bad Ragaz	S 1290	15	7	6	Zumikon	S 1311
15	7	6	Blumisberg	S 1291	13	6	5	Montreux	S 1304

SEJOUR DE GOLF RECOMMANDÉ
FÜR GOLFFERIEN EMPFOHLEN
RECOMMENDED GOLFING STAY

VACANCES RECOMMANDEES
FÜR EINEN FERIENAUFENTHALT EMPFOHLEN
RECOMMENDED GOLFING HOLIDAYS

Domaine Impérial	18	8	6	1294	Crans-sur-Sierre	14	7	8	1293
Genève	17	7	8	1297	Engadin	15	6	6	1295
Lausanne	16	7	7	1300	Lugano	15	7	8	1302
					Patriziale Ascona	15	7	7	1307

BAD RAGAZ

13	7	6

Wie viele andere Schweizer Plätze stammt auch dieser Parcours aus der Feder Donald Harradines, einem begnadeten Architekten, der die Natur gekonnt in seine Arbeit einbezieht. Das Bergpanorama und die bewaldete Gegend verleihen Bad Ragaz einen besonderen Charme. Gestaltung und Platzcharakter bergen keine Überraschungen, aber der Golfcourse garantiert dank seinen wenig ausgeprägten Geländeformen und seiner vernünftigen Länge für Spielfreude. Zu bedauern wäre höchstens, dass der Fluss, der durch die Anlage führt, das Spiel etwas zu wenig beeinflusst. Die eher schmalen Fairways der ersten neun Loch verlangen präzise Bälle. Longhitter spielen ihre Trümpfe auf der zweiten Platzhälfte aus. In Bad Ragaz bietet sich die Chance für schmeichelhafte Scores. Warum nicht?

Like many Swiss courses, Bad Ragaz was designed by Donald Harradine, a generally academic architect who willingly lets nature keep the upper hand. Moreover, the setting for Bad Ragaz is a very pleasant site in a forest surrounded by mountains. The course itself has very little in the way of stylish surprises or outstanding personality, but it is pleasant to play for its flattish relief and very reasonable length. It is a pity that the river crossing the course was not brought into play in a more imaginative way. The front nine are rather tight and call for precision play, while the back nine give greater scope to the long-hitters. A round of golf here is perhaps the opportunity to sign for a flattering score, but why not, after all?

Bad Ragaz Golf Club — 1957
CH - 7310 BAD RAGAZ

Office	Sekretariat	(41) 081 - 303 37 17
Pro shop	Pro shop	(41) 081 - 303 53 14
Fax	Fax	(41) 081 - 303 37 27
Situation	Lage	

Bad Ragaz (pop. 4 325)
Chur (pop. 32 868), 24 km

Annual closure	Jährliche Schliessung	8/12→18/1
Weekly closure	Wöchentliche Schliessung	no

Fees main season
Preisliste hochsaison — full day

	Week days Woche	We/Bank holidays We/Feiertag
Individual Individuell	100 CHF	100 CHF
Couple Ehepaar	200 CHF	200 CHF

Caddy	Caddy	no
Electric Trolley	Elektrokarren	18 CHF
Buggy	Elektrischer Wagen	no
Clubs	Leihschläger	15 CHF

Credit cards Kreditkarten
VISA - Eurocard - MasterCard - AMEX - DC

Access Zufahrt : Motorway (Autobahn) N 13 →
Maienfeld → Bad Ragaz → Golf
Map 2 on page 1288 Karte 2 Seite 1288

GOLF COURSE
PLATZ — 13/20

Site	Lage	
Maintenance	Instandhaltung	
Architect	Architekt	Donald Harradine
Type	Typ	forest
Relief	Begehbarkeit	
Water in play	Platz mit Wasser	
Exp. to wind	Wind ausgesetzt	
Trees in play	Platz mit Bäumen	

Scorecard Scorekarte	Chp. Chp.	Mens Herren	Ladies Damen
Length Länge	5750	5494	4860
Par	70	70	70

Advised golfing ability Empfohlene Spielstärke	0	12	24	36
Hcp required	Min. Handicap	30		

CLUB HOUSE & AMENITIES
KLUBHAUS UND NEBENGEBÄUDE — 7/10

Pro shop	Pro shop	
Driving range	Übungsplatz	
Sheltered	überdacht	12 mats
On grass	auf Rasen	no
Putting-green	Putting-grün	yes
Pitching-green	Pitching-grün	yes

HOTEL FACILITIES
HOTEL BESCHREIBUNG — 6/10

HOTELS HOTELS
Grand Hotel Hof Ragaz — Bad Ragaz
133 rooms, D 560 CHF
Tel (41) 081 - 303 30 30, Fax (41) 081 - 303 30 33

Bristol — Bad Ragaz
25 rooms, D 260 CHF
Tel (41) 081 - 302 82 61, Fax (41) 081 - 302 64 94

Parkhotel Bad Ragaz — Bad Ragaz
60 rooms, D 244 CHF
Tel (41) 081 - 302 22 44, Fax (41) 081 - 302 64 39

RESTAURANTS RESTAURANT
Paradies — Bad Ragaz
Tel (41) 081 - 302 14 41

Schloss Wartenstein — Pfäfers
Tel (41) 081 - 302 40 47 — 2 km

1290

BLUMISBERG

Blumisberg - mit Aussicht auf den Jura und die Alpen - liegt in coupiertem Gelände mit stolzem Baumbestand (vor allem auf den ersten neun Loch). Die Anlage ist aber trotzdem zu Fuss zu bewältigen. Die Mehrheit der Holes bietet gut sichtbare Hindernisse, hauptsächlich Greenbunker. Die Greens sind von mittlerer Grösse, gut verteidigt, relativ wellig und einige Etagengreens eignen sich für interessante Fahnenpositionen. Schon mittlere Handicaps finden zu einem guten Spielrhythmus und geniessen die vernünftige Länge der Holes. Gute Golfer legen ihr Ballkönnen vor allem auf gewissen, schräg abfallenden Fairways in die Waagschale. Der Platz geniesst einen sehr guten Unterhalt.

With the Jura mountains on one side and the Alps on the other, Blumisberg is hilly and woody (especially the front nine), but walkable if you settle for just the 18 holes. Although a few holes require a little explanation, the vast majority hide nothing with clearly visible hazards, basically green-side bunkers. The greens are average in size, well-defended and sloping, with a number of two-tiered surfaces which make for some interesting pin positions. By and large, players can get a good rhythm going and the length of the course is reasonable enough to suit all players of decent ability. The best will be in their element here, working the ball both ways in order to card a good score. This is important, especially to handle some of the sloping fairways. Green-keeping and general upkeep are good.

Golf & Country Club Blumisberg — 1959
CH - 3184 WÜNNEWIL

Office	Sekretariat	(41) 026 - 496 34 38
Pro shop	Pro shop	(41) 026 - 496 17 27
Fax	Fax	(41) 026 - 496 35 23
Situation	Lage	

Freiburg (pop. 36 355), 17 km. Bern (pop.136 338), 17 km

Annual closure	Jährliche Schliessung	17/11→21/3
Weekly closure	Wöchentliche Schliessung	no

Fees main season
Preisliste hochsaison — full day

	Week days Woche	We/Bank holidays We/Feiertag
Individual Individuell	80 CHF	—
Couple Ehepaar	160 CHF	—

We//Holidays: with members only (nur in Mitgliederbegleitung)

Caddy	Caddy	no
Electric Trolley	Elektrokarren	12 CHF/full day
Buggy	Elektrischer Wagen	no
Clubs	Leihschläger	yes

Credit cards Kreditkarten — no

GOLF COURSE
PLATZ — 15/20

Site	Lage	
Maintenance	Instandhaltung	
Architect	Architekt	B. von Limburger
Type	Typ	forest, mountain
Relief	Begehbarkeit	
Water in play	Platz mit Wasser	
Exp. to wind	Wind ausgesetzt	
Trees in play	Platz mit Bäumen	

Scorecard Scorekarte	Chp. Chp.	Mens Herren	Ladies Damen
Length Länge	6048	5707	5014
Par	72	72	72

Advised golfing ability — 0 12 24 36
Empfohlene Spielstärke

Hcp required Min. Handicap — 30

CLUB HOUSE & AMENITIES
KLUBHAUS UND NEBENGEBÄUDE — 7/10

Pro shop	Pro shop	
Driving range	Übungsplatz	
Sheltered	überdacht	4 mats
On grass	auf Rasen	yes
Putting-green	Putting-grün	yes
Pitching-green	Pitching-grün	yes

HOTEL FACILITIES
HOTEL BESCHREIBUNG — 6/10

HOTELS HOTELS
Central — Düdingen
16 rooms, D 160 CHF — 8 km
Tel (41) 026 - 493 13 48, Fax (41) 026 - 493 34 88

Belle Epoque — Bern
17 rooms, D 285 CHF — 17 km
Tel (41) 031 - 311 43 36, Fax (41) 031 - 311 39 36

Bellevue Palace — Bern
145 rooms, D 350 CHF — 17 km
Tel (41) 031 - 320 45 45, Fax (41) 031 - 311 47 43

RESTAURANTS RESTAURANT
Central — Düdingen
Tel (41) 026 - 493 13 48 — 8 km

Le Moléson — Düdingen
Tel (41) 026 - 741 02 40 — 8 km

1291

Access Zufahrt : Autobahn E 25 Freiburg-Bern → Flamat, 6 km → Freiburg, → Golf
Map 1 on page 1286 Karte 1 Seite 1286

NEUCHÂTEL
N 1 - E 25
BERN
Köniz
Neuenegg
Flamatt
Fribourg
Dietisberg
Flamatt
Blumisberg
Wünnewil
Üeberstorf
GOLF
Fribourg
0   2   4 km
Schwarzenburg

Ein kleiner, bewaldeter Flecken auf dem Land mit Aussichten auf die umliegende Gegend. Donald Harradine hat diesen Platz (wie viele Schweizer Golfcourses) in britischem Stil in eine hügelige Landschaft gezeichnet. Das Gelände wird auf den zweiten neun Loch etwas flacher. Mit einigen Out of bounds und kleinen Wasserhindernissen sind die Schwierigkeiten nicht allzu zahlreich, aber der Ball muss auf den Fairways gut plaziert werden, um die Greens leicht angreifen zu können. Präzision im Umgang mit dem kleinen Ball kann sich als nützlich erweisen. In jedem Fall lässt sich dieser gut gepflegte Platz unter Golfern verschiedener Niveaus mit viel Spass spielen - vor allem im Sommer, wenn der Ball gut rollt.

A little patch of remote forest in the countryside, with wide spaces opening onto the surrounding region. Another Harradine course, Breitenloo has a clearly British style to it and is laid out over a gently hilly terrain (even though the back nine are flatter). Despite a number of out-of-bounds and small water hazards, the difficulties are few and far between, are evenly spread and clearly visible. Some of the greens need a carefully placed tee-shot for an easier second shot, and fading or drawing the ball can, as always, prove helpful. At all events, this well-cared for course is easily playable by all the family or with players of varying ability. All good fun, especially in summer when the ball rolls a lot.

Golf Club Breitenloo — 1966

Untere Zaüne 9
CH - 8001 ZÜRICH

Office	Sekretariat	(41) 01 - 836 40 80
Pro shop	Pro shop	(41) 01 - 836 40 80
Fax	Fax	(41) 01 - 837 10 85
Situation	Lage	

Zürich (pop. 365 043), 22 km

Annual closure	Jährliche Schliessung	31/10→31/3
Weekly closure	Wöchentliche Schliessung	no

Fees main season
Preisliste hochsaison 18 holes

	Week days Woche	We/Bank holidays We/Feiertag
Individual Individuell	100 CHF	—
Couple Ehepaar	200 CHF	—

90 CHF with ASG card - We: with members only
(nur in Mitgliederbegleitung)

Caddy	Caddy	on request
Electric Trolley	Elektrokarren	30 CHF /18 holes
Buggy	Elektrischer Wagen	no
Clubs	Leihschläger	20 CHF

Credit cards Kreditkarten — no

1292

WINTERTHUR

Oberembrach
GOLF
Oberwill
Kloten
Nürensdorf
Bassersdorf
N 20
N 1
ZÜRICH

0   2   4 km

Access Zufahrt : Zürich-Kloten → Kloten → Bassersdorf → Birchwil-Oberwil, in Oberwil → Golf
Map 1 on page 1287 Karte 1 Seite 1287

GOLF COURSE / PLATZ — 13/20

Site	Lage	
Maintenance	Instandhaltung	
Architect	Architekt	Donald Harradine
Type	Typ	parkland
Relief	Begehbarkeit	
Water in play	Platz mit Wasser	
Exp. to wind	Wind ausgesetzt	
Trees in play	Platz mit Bäumen	

Scorecard Scorekarte	Chp. Chp.	Mens Herren	Ladies Damen
Length Länge	6125	5750	5045
Par	72	72	72

Advised golfing ability Empfohlene Spielstärke		0 12 24 36
Hcp required	Min. Handicap	30

CLUB HOUSE & AMENITIES / KLUBHAUS UND NEBENGEBÄUDE — 7/10

Pro shop	Pro shop	
Driving range	Übungsplatz	
Sheltered	überdacht	2 mats
On grass	auf Rasen	yes
Putting-green	Putting-grün	yes
Pitching-green	Pitching-grün	yes

HOTEL FACILITIES / HOTEL BESCHREIBUNG — 6/10

HOTELS HOTELS

Renaissance Hôtel — Glattbrugg
204 rooms, D 245 CHF — 14 km
Tel (41) 01 - 810 85 00
Fax (41) 01 - 810 87 55

Zum Bären — Nürensdorf
14 rooms, D 215 CHF — 4 km
Tel (41) 01 - 836 42 12
Fax (41) 01 - 836 42 17

RESTAURANTS RESTAURANT

Bruno's — Glattbrugg
Tel (41) 01 - 810 03 01 — 14 km

Tübli — Zürich
Tel (41) 01 - 251 26 26 — 22 km

C'est le plus célèbre parcours de Suisse, grâce aux efforts de son président Gaston Barras pour y accueillir depuis des années le European Masters professionnel. Il n'est jamais vraiment intimidant : ses obstacles sont bien visibles, modérément en jeu, la difficulté principale reste le choix de club en fonction des dénivellations. Assez accidenté, il est d'ailleurs fatigant à jouer à pied. La splendeur du panorama sur les Alpes (Cervin, Mont Blanc, Alpes bernoises) est parfois à couper le souffle, et console des petites désillusions golfiques. En altitude, les balles volant loin, quelques drives peuvent être flatteurs. Un bon parcours de vacances, avec un entretien souvent simplement honnête. On attendait quelques remodelages de ce tracé : Seve Ballesteros a introduit des modifications au 15 et au 17, devenus plus esthétiques et délicats. La plupart des greens ont été refaits, pas toujours pour le meilleur.

This is the most famous of Swiss courses thanks to the work put in by club chairman Gaston Barras to stage the European Masters here over the past few years. The course is never really intimidating, the hazards are clearly in view and not always directly in play. The main problem is the choice of club to offset the steep gradients. It is a hilly course which can be tiring to cover on foot. The beautiful scenery of the Alps (Cervin, Mont Blanc) is quite breath-taking and enough to make up for the mishaps that can so easily mess up your card. At altitude, the ball travels further and a number of drives will prove flattering. A good holiday course where green-keeping is often no more than decent. A little restyling work has been awaited here, and Seve Ballesteros has already made changes to the 15th and 17th holes, which are now more attractive and trickier. And most of the greens hace been remodeled, not always for the best.

Golf Club de Crans-sur-Sierre — 1907
CH - 3953 CRANS-SUR-SIERRE

Office	Secrétariat	(41) 027 - 481 21 68
Pro shop	Pro-shop	(41) 027 - 481 40 61
Fax	Fax	(41) 027 - 481 95 68
Situation	Situation	

Sierre (pop.14 551), 15 km

Annual closure	Fermeture annuelle	31/10→31/5
Weekly closure	Fermeture hebdomadaire	no

Fees main season
Tarifs haute saison18 holes

	Week days Semaine	We/Bank holidays We/Férié
Individual Individuel	80 CHF	80 CHF
Couple Couple	160 CHF	160 CHF

Caddy	Caddy	on request
Electric Trolley	Chariot électrique	25 CHF
Buggy	Voiturette	65 CHF / 18 holes
Clubs	Clubs	25-35 CHF

Credit cards Cartes de crédit
VISA - Eurocard - MasterCard - AMEX - DC

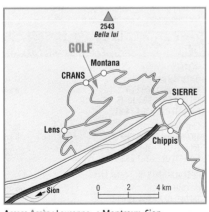

▲
2543
Bella lui
GOLF
Montana
CRANS
SIERRE
Lens
Chippis
Sión
0   2   4 km

Access Accès : Lausanne → Montreux, Sion
Sierre → Crans
Map 1 on page 1286 Carte 1 Page 1286

GOLF COURSE PARCOURS — 14/20

Site	Site	▰▰▰▰▰▰
Maintenance	Entretien	▰▰▰
Architect	Architecte	M. Nicholson Seve Ballesteros
Type	Type	parkland, mountain
Relief	Relief	
Water in play	Eau en jeu	▰
Exp. to wind	Exposé au vent	▰▰▰▰
Trees in play	Arbres en jeu	▰▰▰▰▰▰

Scorecard Carte de score	Chp. Chp.	Mens Mess.	Ladies Da.
Length Long.	6170	5785	5075
Par	72	72	72

Advised golfing ability Niveau de jeu recommandé	0 12 24 36
Hcp required Handicap exigé	36

CLUB HOUSE & AMENITIES CLUB HOUSE ET ANNEXES — 7/10

Pro shop	Pro-shop	▰▰▰▰▰
Driving range	Practice	
Sheltered	couvert	9 mats
On grass	sur herbe	yes
Putting-green	putting-green	yes
Pitching-green	pitching green	yes

HOTEL FACILITIES ENVIRONNEMENT HOTELIER — 8/10

HOTELS HÔTELS
Grand Hôtel du Golf — Crans-sur-Sierre
45 rooms, D 500 CHF
Tel (41) 027 - 41 42 42, Fax (41) 027 - 41 97 58

Alpina et Savoy — Crans-sur-Sierre
50 rooms, D 320 CHF
Tel (41) 027 - 481 21 42, Fax (41) 027 - 481 61 75

Alpha — Crans-sur-Sierre
23 rooms, D 260 CHF
Tel (41) 027 - 483 31 13, Fax (41) 027 - 483 31 19

RESTAURANTS RESTAURANT
Rôtisserie de la Reine — Crans-sur-Sierre
Tel (41) 027 - 481 18 85

Restaurant de la Poste — Montana
Tel (41) 027 - 481 27 45

1293
✚

DOMAINE IMPÉRIAL

🏌 | 18 | 8 | 6

Par son esthétique et la stratégie de jeu, ce parcours est le plus nettement américain des golfs suisses (Pete Dye !). En bordure du Lac Léman, avec de belles perspectives sur le Jura et les Alpes, il se joue sans fatigue physique, mais les fairways bien travaillés, les profonds bunkers, la diversité des obstacles (arbres , obstacles d'eau) et l'intelligence de leur placement en font un défi permanent, constamment renouvelé : on joue ici tous les clubs de son sac, et de multiples façons. On notera en particulier l'excellent rythme du parcours, la subtilité des par 3, de longueur pourtant fort raisonnable, et le modelage de greens très défendus, qu'il faut savoir «rater du bon côté». Techniquement impressionnant, il se laisse apprivoiser si l'on ajoute la réflexion à la maîtrise du jeu. L'entretien a beaucoup progressé depuis quelques années, tous les détails sont soignés, et les greens sont souvent rapides.

In style and game strategy, this is clearly the most American of all Swiss courses (designed by Pete Dye). On the banks of lake Geneva with fine views over the Jura mountains and the Alps, it is an easily walkable course, but the well-designed fairways, the deep bunkers, the variety of hazards (trees and water) and the intelligence deployed in placing them make this course a permanent challenge which will never lie down. You play every club in the bag, and in different ways. In particular, this is a good course for quick play with subtle but reasonably-lengthed par 3s and well-designed, well-defended greens which, if you are going to miss, should not be missed on the wrong side. Although technically very impressive, you can keep your head above water by playing with skill and brains. Green-keeping is much improved since a few years ; every detail is carefully tended and the greens are fast... matching the standard of the architect.

Domaine Impérial — 1987
Villa Prangins
CH - 1196 GLAND

Office	Secrétariat	(41) 022 - 999 06 00
Pro shop	Pro-shop	(41) 022 - 999 06 80
Fax	Fax	(41) 022 - 999 06 06
Situation	Situation	
Nyon (pop. 14 747), 3 km		
Annual closure	Fermeture annuelle	21/12→28/2
Weekly closure	Fermeture hebdomadaire	monday (lundi)

Fees main season Tarifs haute saison		18 holes
	Week days Semaine	We/Bank holidays We/Férié
Individual Individuel	90 CHF	*
Couple Couple	180 CHF	*

* We : Members only (membres seulement)

Caddy	Caddy	on request
Electric Trolley	Chariot électrique	20 CHF
Buggy	Voiturette	no
Clubs	Clubs	25 CHF

Credit cards Cartes de crédit
VISA - Eurocard - MasterCard - AMEX

1294

🇨🇭

Map

0 — 1 — 2 km | Gland
Gland
LAUSANNE
N 1
GOLF
Prangins
Nyon
Divonne-les-bains
NYON
Promenthoux
GENEVE
L A C   L É M A N

Access Accès : Genève-Lausanne → Gland, "Route Suisse" → Genève, 400 m on left hand side
Map 1 on page 1286 Carte 1 Page 1286

GOLF COURSE / PARCOURS — 18/20

Site	Site	
Maintenance	Entretien	
Architect	Architecte	Pete Dye
Type	Type	forest, country
Relief	Relief	
Water in play	Eau en jeu	
Exp. to wind	Exposé au vent	
Trees in play	Arbres en jeu	

Scorecard	Chp.	Mens	Ladies
Carte de score	Chp.	Mess.	Da.
Length Long.	6297	5903	4993
Par	72	72	72

Advised golfing ability	0	12	24	36
Niveau de jeu recommandé				
Hcp required	Handicap exigé	30		

CLUB HOUSE & AMENITIES / CLUB HOUSE ET ANNEXES — 8/10

Pro shop	Pro-shop	
Driving range	Practice	
Sheltered	couvert	10 mats
On grass	sur herbe	no
Putting-green	putting-green	yes
Pitching-green	pitching green	yes

HOTEL FACILITIES / ENVIRONNEMENT HOTELIER — 6/10

HOTELS HÔTELS
de la Plage — Gland
18 rooms, D 100 CHF — 4 km
Tel (41) 022 - 364 10 35
Fax (41) 022 - 364 34 81

Clos-de-Sadex — Nyon
187 rooms, D 200 CHF — 6 km
Tel (41) 022 - 361 28 31
Fax (41) 022 - 361 28 33

RESTAURANTS RESTAURANT
du Golf — on site
Tel (41) 022 - 364 45 45

Auberge du Soleil — Bursins
Tel (41) 021 - 824 13 44 — 8 km

Vor mehr als einem Jahrhundert entstanden, wurde dieser Platz mehrmals und von Mario Verdieri wesentlich verändert, hat aber dabei seinen britischen Touch nicht verloren. Der Kontrast zu den majestätischen Schneegipfeln rundum ist beeindruckend. Wasserläufe und kleine Seen sind die wesentlichen Hindernisse, aber die besten Spieler werden sich davon wenig beeindrucken lassen und richtig loslegen, da auch Bäume nicht zu stark ins Spielgeschehen eingreifen. Dieser sehr natürliche und angenehme Golfcourse würde mit der Neugestaltung gewisser Greens und einigen verteidigenden Hindernissen (man kann den Ball oft rollen lassen) anspruchsvoller werden. Doch er soll vor allem Vergnügen und gutes Scores ermöglichen und nicht Hochleistungen abverlangen.

Opened more than a century ago, this course has undergone many a facelift, essentially by Mario Verdieri, but has retained an evidently British flavour in contrast with the majestic setting of snow-capped mountains. Little lakes and rivers form the main hazards, but these should not over-concern the better players who have the chance here to open their shoulders, since the trees (a lot of very old larch trees) are never too much in play. This is a very natural and deliberately pleasing course which could be made more demanding by redesigning some of the greens and creating hazards to defend them more effectively (you can often chip and roll the ball from fairway to green). But as we said, it was designed more for fun and for producing flattering scores than for any great exploit on the part of the player.

Engadin Golf — 1893
CH - 7503 SAMEDAN

Office	Sekretariat	(41) 081 - 852 52 26
Pro shop	Pro shop	(41) 081 - 852 31 81
Fax	Fax	(41) 081 - 852 46 82
Situation	Lage	

St-Moritz (pop., 5 582), 5 km.

Annual closure	Jährliche Schliessung	1/10→30/4
Weekly closure	Wöchentliche Schliessung	no

Fees main season
Preisliste hochsaison full day

	Week days Woche	We/Bank holidays We/Feiertag
Individual Individuell	90 CHF	90 CHF
Couple Ehepaar	180 CHF	180 CHF

Caddy	Caddy	on request
Electric Trolley	Elektrokarren	no
Buggy	Elektrischer Wagen	50 CHF
Clubs	Leihschläger	30 CHF

Credit cards Kreditkarten
VISA - Eurocard - MasterCard - AMEX - DC

Access Zufahrt : Saint Moritz → Samedan, → Golf
Map 2 on page 1288 Karte 2 Seite 1288

GOLF COURSE PLATZ — 15/20

Site	Lage	▬▬▬▬▬
Maintenance	Instandhaltung	▬▬▬▬
Architect	Architekt	Mario Verdieri

Type	Typ	country
Relief	Begehbarkeit	▬▬▬
Water in play	Platz mit Wasser	▬▬▬
Exp. to wind	Wind ausgesetzt	▬▬
Trees in play	Platz mit Bäumen	▬▬▬

Scorecard Scorekarte	Chp. Chp.	Mens Herren	Ladies Damen
Length Länge	6350	6080	5320
Par	72	72	72

Advised golfing ability Empfohlene Spielstärke	0	12	24	36
Hcp required	Min. Handicap	30		

CLUB HOUSE & AMENITIES KLUBHAUS UND NEBENGEBÄUDE — 6/10

Pro shop	Pro shop	▬▬▬
Driving range	Übungsplatz	▬▬▬
Sheltered	überdacht	no
On grass	auf Rasen	no
Putting-green	Putting-grün	yes
Pitching-green	Pitching-grün	yes

HOTEL FACILITIES HOTEL BESCHREIBUNG — 6/10

HOTELS HOTELS
Alpen Golf Hotel — Samedan, 500 m
42 rooms, D 220 CHF
Tel (41) 081 - 852 52 62
Fax (41) 081 - 852 33 38

Bernina — Samedan, 1 km
59 rooms, D 280 CHF
Tel (41) 081 - 852 12 12
Fax (41) 081 - 852 36 06

RESTAURANTS RESTAURANT
Jöhri's Talvo — Champfer, 8 km
Tel (41) 081 - 852 44 55

Chesa Veglia — St. Moritz, 5 km
Tel (41) 081 - 852 35 96

1295

1995 war es soweit: der erste öffentliche Golfplatz der Schweiz wurde eröffnet. Er wurde in einer wenig schmeichelnden Industriezone erbaut, doch dieses Manko könnte mit einem soliden Bepflanzungsprogramm behoben werden. Mit dem Ziel, Golfer auszubilden und eine erschwingliche Alternative zu den Privatclubs zu bieten, wurden keine zusätzlichen golferischen Schwierigkeiten gesucht (kaum Wasserhindernisse im Spiel), was die besten Spieler enttäuschen mag. Es ist schade, dass die Greens und Bunkers nicht vielseitiger gestaltet wurden. Der sonst angenehm zu spielende Platz würde so mehr fürs Auge bieten und dem Stammspieler zu technisch vielseitigeren Herausforderungen verhelfen. Die Anlage offeriert nebst dem Golfplatz grossangelegte Trainingsmöglichkeiten.

This is at last Switzerland's first truly public golf course, opened in 1995. It has been laid out on an industrial site which is still a little unattractive but it could easily grow into something much better with a good plantation programme. The aim here is to coach golfers and offer an economical alternative to the private courses. As a result, there was no deliberate quest for difficulty (for example, there are very few water hazards in play), so the better players might feel disappointed. It is though a shame that the greens and bunkers weren't given more careful thought - they would have added a little more style and pleasure to a course which elsewhere makes for a pleasant round of golf - and that there is not more technical variety for the people who play here regularly. The whole complex also includes huge practice facilities.

Golfpark Holzhäusern 1995
CH - 6343 ROTKREUZ

Office	Sekretariat	(41) 041 - 799 70 10
Pro shop	Pro shop	(41) 041 - 799 06 19
Fax	Fax	(41) 041 - 799 70 15
Situation	Lage	

Zug (pop. 21 705), 10 km, Luzern (pop. 61 034), 20 km

Annual closure	Jährliche Schliessung	1/1→31/1
Weekly closure	Wöchentliche Schliessung	no

Fees main season
Preisliste hochsaison 18 holes

	Week days Woche	We/Bank holidays We/Feiertag
Individual Individuell	50 CHF	60 CHF
Couple Ehepaar	100 CHF	120 CHF

Caddy	Caddy	no
Electric Trolley	Elektrokarren	27 CHF
Buggy	Elektrischer Wagen	no
Clubs	Leihschläger	25 CHF

Credit cards Kreditkarten — no

GOLF COURSE
PLATZ   13/20

Site	Lage	■
Maintenance	Instandhaltung	■
Architect	Architekt	Marco Verdieri
Type	Typ	open country
Relief	Begehbarkeit	■
Water in play	Platz mit Wasser	■
Exp. to wind	Wind ausgesetzt	■
Trees in play	Platz mit Bäumen	■

Scorecard	Chp.	Mens	Ladies
Scorekarte	Chp.	Herren	Damen
Length Länge	6110	6050	5100
Par	73	73	73

Advised golfing ability		0	12	24	36
Empfohlene Spielstärke					
Hcp required	Min. Handicap	35			

CLUB HOUSE & AMENITIES
KLUBHAUS UND NEBENGEBÄUDE   7/10

Pro shop	Pro shop	■
Driving range	Übungsplatz	■
Sheltered	überdacht	40 mats
On grass	auf Rasen	yes
Putting-green	Putting-grün	yes
Pitching-green	Pitching-grün	yes

HOTEL FACILITIES
HOTEL BESCHREIBUNG   6/10

HOTELS HOTELS

Waldheim		Risch
34 rooms, D 190 CHF		2 km
Tel (41) 041 - 799 70 70		
Fax (41) 041 - 799 70 79		
Parkhotel		Zug
112 rooms, D 300 CHF		10 km
Tel (41) 041 - 711 66 11		
Fax (41) 041 - 710 66 11		

RESTAURANTS RESTAURANT

Rathauskeller		Zug
Tel (41) 041 - 711 00 58		10 km
Hecht		Zug
Tel (41) 041 - 711 01 93		10 km

Access Zufahrt : N4 oder N14 → Rotkreuz → Industrie Ost → "Golfpark"
Map 1 on page 1287 Karte 1 Seite 1287

1296

Un des parcours suisses les plus intéressants. Nul n'en sera étonné : Robert Trent Jones en est l'auteur. Dans un site magnifique surplombant le Lac Léman, il a une fois de plus signé un dessin très imaginatif et d'une grande intelligence stratégique. La multiplicité des départs et des positions de drapeaux permet de l'adapter à tous les niveaux, même si les joueurs très moyens auront du mal à y scorer. Les greens sont vastes (un double green aux 9 et 18), très dessinés, ce qui rend essentielle une bonne maîtrise du petit jeu et du putting... même si l'on réussit à bien travailler la balle au grand jeu, notamment sur les nombreux dog-legs. Une consolation pour ceux dont le swing n'est pas exceptionnel : si certains arbres peuvent poser problème, il y a peu d'obstacles d'eau (8, 16 et 17).

One of the most interesting Swiss courses, and, surprise surprise, it was designed by a one Robert Trent Jones. In a magnificent setting overlooking Lake Geneva, Jones has once again come up with a very imaginative layout calling for considerable strategic intelligence. The many different tees and pin positions make this a course for players of all ability, even though your average hacker will find scoring a tough proposition. The greens are huge (the 9th and 18th have a double green) and well designed, thus calling for good putting skills and a sharp short game, even if your long game is on tune with the ball moving both ways, particularly on the very many dog-legs. There is one consolation for high-handicappers, namely that although a few trees may cause problems, there are few water hazards (on the 8th, 16th and 17th holes only).

Golf Club de Genève		1972
70, route de la Capite		
CH - 1233 COLOGNY		
Office	Secrétariat	(41) 022 - 707 48 00
Pro shop	Pro-shop	(41) 022 - 707 48 15
Fax	Fax	(41) 022 - 707 48 20
Situation	Situation	
Genève (pop. 172 486), 5 km		
Annual closure	Fermeture annuelle	7/12→7/3
Weekly closure	Fermeture hebdomadaire	monday (lundi)

Fees main season			
Tarifs haute saison 18 holes			
		Week days Semaine	We/Bank holidays We/Férié
Individual Individuel		80 CHF	80 CHF
Couple Couple		160 CHF	160 CHF

Caddy	Caddy	on request
Electric Trolley	Chariot électrique	20 CHF
Buggy	Voiturette	no
Clubs	Clubs	20 CHF
Credit cards Cartes de crédit		no

Access Accès : Genève → Evian, → Cologny, → Golf
Map 1 on page 1286 Carte 1 Page 1286

GOLF COURSE
PARCOURS
17/20

Site	Site	▮▮▮▮▮▮▯
Maintenance	Entretien	▮▮▮▮▮▮▯
Architect	Architecte	Robert Trent Jones
Type	Type	parkland
Relief	Relief	▮▮▯▯▯
Water in play	Eau en jeu	▮▮▮▯▯
Exp. to wind	Exposé au vent	▮▮▮▯▯
Trees in play	Arbres en jeu	▮▮▮▮▯

Scorecard	Chp.	Mens	Ladies
Carte de score	Chp.	Mess.	Da.
Length Long.	6289	5626	5321
Par	72	72	72

Advised golfing ability	0 12 24 36
Niveau de jeu recommandé	▮▮▮▮▮▯
Hcp required Handicap exigé	24 Men, 26 Ladies

CLUB HOUSE & AMENITIES
CLUB HOUSE ET ANNEXES
7/10

Pro shop	Pro-shop	▮▮▮▮▮▯
Driving range	Practice	▮▮▮▮▯
Sheltered	couvert	12 mats
On grass	sur herbe	yes (04 → 10)
Putting-green	putting-green	yes
Pitching-green	pitching green	yes

HOTEL FACILITIES
ENVIRONNEMENT HOTELIER
8/10

HOTELS HÔTELS
La Cigogne		Genève
42 rooms, D 400 CHF		5 km
Tel (41) 022 - 311 42 42		
Fax (41) 022 - 311 40 65		
Century		Genève
133 rooms, D 250 CHF		5 km
Tel (41) 022 - 736 80 95		
Fax (41) 022 - 736 52 74		

RESTAURANTS RESTAURANT
Parc des Eaux-Vives		Genève
Tel (41) 022 - 735 41 40		6 km
Lion d'Or		Genève
Tel (41) 022 - 736 44 32		4 km

1297

Il n'est pas très habituel de conseiller des parcours courts, mais celui-ci, avec son par 68, est des plus amusants. Evidemment, les golfeurs du plus haut niveau n'y seront pas à l'aise, mais ils sont une minorité ! En premier lieu, Jeremy Pern a tiré un parti remarquable d'un terrain difficile à adapter au golf, et mis l'accent sur la précision, dans tous les secteurs du jeu. Qu'il s'agisse du drive, du second coup, des approches vers des greens très défendus ou du putting, cet aspect ludique est à la fois intéressant et formateur. Le parcours est assez physique, mais les fairways (étroits) sont assez plats, ce qui ne rend pas la marche trop ardue. L'imagination et l'intelligence de l'architecte en font une réussite, même s'il n'a pas eu l'espace pour s'exprimer pleinement. La qualité de l'entretien et la facilité relative pour y scorer en font une bonne adresse, relevée encore par un environnement magnifique au bord du lac de Gruyère.

It is not every day that we recommend short courses, but this one, a par 68, is most amusing. The most proficient golfers will obviously not feel too excited about it, but they are a minority anyway. Firstly, Jeremy Pern has done a remarkable job with terrain that was difficult to harness for golf and has placed emphasis on precision in every department of the game. Whether for the drive, the second shot, approaches to very well-guarded greens or putting, this fun aspect is both interesting and educational. The course is pretty hilly, although the actual fairways are rather flat (and narrow), which means easy walking. The architect's imagination and intelligence have made this a class course, even though space was restricted. The standard of green-keeping and the relative ease of scoring make this a good address, enhanced by a magnificent setting on the banks of Lake Gruyère.

Golf de la Gruyère — 1993

Le Château
CH - 1649 PONT-LA-VILLE

Office	Secrétariat	(41) 026 - 414 91 11
Pro shop	Pro-shop	(41) 026 - 414 94 00
Fax	Fax	(41) 026 - 414 92 20
Situation	Situation	

Fribourg (pop. 36 355), 12 km

Annual closure	Fermeture annuelle	2/1 → 1/3
Weekly closure	Fermeture hebdomadaire	no

Fees main season
Tarifs haute saison le parcours

	Week days Semaine	We/Bank holidays We/Férié
Individual Individuel	85 CHF	105 CHF
Couple Couple	170 CHF	210 CHF

Caddy	Caddy	on request
Electric Trolley	Chariot électrique	25 CHF
Buggy	Voiturette	50 CHF
Clubs	Clubs	35 CHF

Credit cards Cartes de crédit
VISA - MasterCard - AMEX - DC

1298

Access Accès : E25 Fribourg-Vevey
→ Rossens → Pont-la-Ville
Map 1 on page 1286 Carte 1 Page 1286

GOLF COURSE / PARCOURS — 14/20

Site	Site	▬▬▬
Maintenance	Entretien	▬▬▬
Architect	Architecte	Jeremy Pern
Type	Type	country
Relief	Relief	▬▬
Water in play	Eau en jeu	▬▬
Exp. to wind	Exposé au vent	▬▬
Trees in play	Arbres en jeu	▬▬▬

Scorecard Carte de score	Chp. Chp.	Mens Mess.	Ladies Da.
Length Long.	5058	4740	4095
Par	68	68	68

Advised golfing ability		0 12 24 36
Niveau de jeu recommandé		▬▬▬
Hcp required	Handicap exigé	36

CLUB HOUSE & AMENITIES / CLUB HOUSE ET ANNEXES — 7/10

Pro shop	Pro-shop	▬▬▬
Driving range	Practice	▬▬▬
Sheltered	couvert	3 mats
On grass	sur herbe	no
Putting-green	putting-green	yes
Pitching-green	pitching green	yes

HOTEL FACILITIES / ENVIRONNEMENT HOTELIER — 6/10

HOTELS HÔTELS

Royal Golf Hôtel — Pont-la-Ville
12 rooms, D 120 CHF — on site
Tel (41) 026 - 414 91 11, Fax (41) 026 - 414 92 20

Hôtel de la Gruyère — Gruyères
36 rooms, D 77 CHF — 8 km
Tel (41) 026 - 915 22 30, Fax (41) 026 - 915 10 28

Hôtel Cailler/Charmey — Charmey
45 rooms, D 90 CHF — 15 km
Tel (41) 026 - 927 10 13, Fax (41) 026 - 927 24 13

RESTAURANTS RESTAURANT

La Fleur de Lys — Fribourg
Tel (41) 026 - 322 79 61 — 12 km

Restaurant de la Tour — Bulle
Tel (41) 026 - 912 74 70 — 15 km

INTERLAKEN

14	6	6

Vom Thunerseeufer nur durch eine Naturschutzzone getrennt, bietet der Interlakner Golfplatz je nach Wasserstand des Sees und Regenmenge recht feuchte Bedingungen, doch er gibt ein gutes Beispiel für das Miteinander von Golf und Oekologie ab. Die recht flache Anlage steht in einem faszinierenden Kontrast zu den umliegenden Berner Alpengipfeln. Der Spielrhythmus ist ansprechend, doch die ersten fünf Loch können - bedingt durch ihre beträchtliche Länge - eine gute Scorekarte schon zu allem Anfang gefährden. Die gut und vielseitig gestalteten Greens bieten einige interessante Annäherungen. Moderate Schwierigkeiten bestimmen den Gesamteindruck dieses Golfcourses, der sich zur angenehmen Familienrunde eignet. Einige Fairways mögen vor allem aus Sicht des hintersten Abschlags schmal erscheinen. Einem Abschlag übrigens, den man bei Regen besser ignoriert.

Not far from Lake Thun, from which the course is separated by a protected natural expanse of land, this can be a very wet course when it rains but forms a good example of coexistence with ecological requirements. In contrast with the impressive mountain setting, the course is rather flat and can be played at a good pace, even though the first five holes are a tough proposition in terms of length and can spoil any hope of returning a good card. The greens are well cut out, rather varied and make for some interesting approach shots. The overriding impression is that of a course where difficulties have been kept to a reasonable minimum for a pleasant round of golf with all the family. With this said, some holes can look decidedly tight, especially from the back tees, which should be unashamedly forgotten whenever it rains.

Golf-Club Interlaken-Unterseen

Postfach 110
CH - 3800 INTERLAKEN

Office	Sekretariat	(41) 033 - 823 60 16
Pro shop	Pro shop	(41) 033 - 822 79 70
Fax	Fax	(41) 033 - 823 42 03
Situation	Lage	

Interlaken (pop. 5 176), 2 km

Annual closure	Jährliche Schliessung	15/11 → 31/3
Weekly closure	Wöchentliche Schliessung	no

Fees main season
Preisliste hochsaison 18 holes

	Week days Woche	We/Bank holidays We/Feiertag
Individual Individuell	70 CHF	80 CHF
Couple Ehepaar	140 CHF	160 CHF

Caddy	Caddy	no
Electric Trolley	Elektrokarren	25 CHF
Buggy	Elektrischer Wagen	no
Clubs	Leihschläger	30 CHF

Credit cards Kreditkarten
VISA - Eurocard - MasterCard - AMEX

INTERLAKEN
GOLF
Thun
Unterseen
Brientz
BRIENZERSEE
Interlaken
N 8
THUNERSEE
wilderswil
Unterseen
N 8
Spiez
N 8
Därligen

0   2   4 km

Access Zufahrt : N8 → Unterseen → Thunersee, Golf
Map 1 on page 1287 Karte 1 Seite 1287

GOLF COURSE
PLATZ
14/20

Site	Lage	▬▬▬▬▬
Maintenance	Instandhaltung	▬▬▬▬
Architect	Architekt	
Type	Typ	parkland, country
Relief	Begehbarkeit	▬▬▬
Water in play	Platz mit Wasser	▬▬
Exp. to wind	Wind ausgesetzt	▬▬▬
Trees in play	Platz mit Bäumen	▬▬▬

Scorecard Scorekarte	Chp. Chp.	Mens Herren	Ladies Damen
Length Länge	6274	5875	5298
Par	72	72	72

Advised golfing ability		0 12 24 36
Empfohlene Spielstärke		▬▬▬▬
Hcp required	Min. Handicap	30

CLUB HOUSE & AMENITIES
KLUBHAUS UND NEBENGEBÄUDE
6/10

Pro shop	Pro shop	▬▬▬
Driving range	Übungsplatz	▬▬▬▬
Sheltered	überdacht	4 mats
On grass	auf Rasen	yes (03 → 10)
Putting-green	Putting-grün	yes
Pitching-green	Pitching-grün	yes

HOTEL FACILITIES
HOTEL BESCHREIBUNG
6/10

HOTELS HOTELS
Landhotel Golf   Golf
26 rooms, D 184 CHF   on site
Tel (41) 033 - 823 21 31, Fax (41) 033 - 823 21 91

Victoria Jungfrau   Interlaken
227 rooms, D 550 CHF   2 km
Tel (41) 033 - 827 11 11, Fax (41) 033 - 827 37 37

Lötschberg   Interlaken
19 rooms, D 180 CHF   2 km
Tel (41) 036 - 22 25 45, Fax (41) 036 - 22 25 79

RESTAURANTS RESTAURANT
La Terrasse   Interlaken
Tel (41) 033 - 827 11 11   2 km

Hirschen   Interlaken
Tel (41) 033 - 822 15 45   2 km

1299

Un parcours séduisant et tranquille à première vue, mais dont les nombreuses difficultés se révèlent peu à peu, dans ce site très boisé. Bien rythmé dans son enchaînement, il est souvent étroit, assez vallonné, mais sans vraiment de pièges cachés. Le récent remodelage des greens par Jeremy Pern a rajeuni ce parcours classique de façon spectaculaire, et oblige plus encore à penser avant de jouer, d'autant que les bunkers de green, également retravaillés, amènent à porter souvent la balle au lieu de la faire rouler. Les joueurs moyens, qui ont souvent du mal à le faire, auront intérêt à jouer des départs avancés. Très agréable à jouer en été quand le terrain est sec, il pouvait s'avérer plus difficile dans les conditions humides, le placement de la balle au drive devenant alors encore plus crucial, mais des travaux ont nettement amélioré cet aspect des choses, tout en maintenant le cachet du parcours. Une véritable réussite où les greens, un instant menacés, ont été bien repris.

At first view, an appealing and quiet golf course, but one where the numerous difficulties gradually emerge in a very woody site. With nicely paced continuity, the fairways are often tight and rather hilly, but with no real hidden traps. Recent restyling by architect Jeremy Pern has spectacularly rejuvenated this classic course which now requires more careful thought before each shot, especially since the green-side bunkers, which have also been redesigned, often call for a high lob shot instead of the easier chip into the green. Average players, who often have problems with this kind of approach, will be better off playing from the front tees. Very pleasant to play in summer when the terrain is dry, Lausanne can prove to be a tougher proposition in wet conditions, when placing the ball off the tee becomes even more crucial. However, work has been carried out and has distinctly improved this side of things.

Golf Club de Lausanne — 1931

3, route du Golf
CH - 1000 Lausanne 25

Office	Secrétariat	(41) 021 - 784 84 84
Pro shop	Pro-shop	(41) 021 - 784 84 74
Fax	Fax	(41) 021 - 784 84 80
Situation	Situation	

Lausanne (pop. 125 395), 5 km

Annual closure	Fermeture annuelle	15/12 →21/3
Weekly closure	Fermeture hebdomadaire	no

Fees main season
Tarifs haute saison 18 holes

	Week days Semaine	We/Bank holidays We/Férié
Individual Individuel	80 CHF	100 CHF
Couple Couple	160 CHF	200 CHF

Caddy	Caddy	on request
Electric Trolley	Chariot électrique	15 CHF
Buggy	Voiturette	no
Clubs	Clubs	20 CHF

Credit cards Cartes de crédit VISA - MasterCard

1300

Access Accès : N9, Exit (Sortie) Vennes
→ Epalinges. Chalet-à-Gobet, → Le Mont, Golf
Map 1 on page 1286 Carte 1 Page 1286

GOLF COURSE / PARCOURS — 16/20

Site	Site			
Maintenance	Entretien			
Architect	Architecte	Narbel Jeremy Pern		
Type	Type	parkland		
Relief	Relief			
Water in play	Eau en jeu			
Exp. to wind	Exposé au vent			
Trees in play	Arbres en jeu			

Scorecard Carte de score	Chp. Chp.	Mens Mess.	Ladies Da.
Length Long.	6295	5900	5170
Par	72	72	72

Advised golfing ability   0 12 24 36
Niveau de jeu recommandé
Hcp required Handicap exigé 24 Men., 28 Ladies

CLUB HOUSE & AMENITIES / CLUB HOUSE ET ANNEXES — 7/10

Pro shop	Pro-shop	
Driving range	Practice	
Sheltered	couvert	4 mats
On grass	sur herbe	yes (05 → 10)
Putting-green	putting-green	yes
Pitching-green	pitching green	yes

HOTEL FACILITIES / ENVIRONNEMENT HOTELIER — 7/10

HOTELS HÔTELS

Les Chevreuils		Vers-chez-les-Blancs
30 rooms, D 215 CHF		5 km
Tel (41) 021 - 784 20 21, Fax (41) 021 - 784 15 45		
Beau Rivage Palace		Lausanne
180 rooms, D 390 CHF		6 km
Tel (41) 021 - 613 33 33, Fax (41) 021 - 613 33 34		
Mövenpick Radisson		Lausanne
265 rooms, D 240 CHF		6 km
Tel (41) 021 - 617 21 21, Fax (41) 021 - 616 15 27		

RESTAURANTS RESTAURANT

Rochat		Crissier
Tel (41) 021 - 634 05 05		10 km
La Grappe d'Or		Lausanne
Tel (41) 021 - 323 07 60		6 km

LES BOIS | 15 | 6 | 6

Le Golf Club Les Bois se trouve au milieu de la région des Franches Montagnes, typique du Jura Suisse. Un vrai décor d'opérette, superbe. Le terrain est accidenté, mais acceptable sur le plan physique. Il a été construit en deux temps, et certains greens sont encore fermes. Le parcours mélange les trous en forêt et les trous en espace plus ouvert, l'ensemble étant harmonieux et très bien équilibré. Certes, on ne voit pas tous les obstacles, et l'on ne peut concevoir une bonne stratégie de jeu avant d'avoir joué au moins trois fois, mais sachez au moins que ce parcours est aussi franc qu'on le devine, et qu'il n'est pas vraiment nécessaire de travailler la balle. En revanche, il faut savoir lire ces greens, pas évidents. Pour finir, vous garderez en particulier le souvenir des trous 14 à 16 au milieu des sapins, qui peuvent déjà figurer parmi les plus beaux trous de Suisse. Un golf de premier ordre, et jouable à tous niveaux.

The Golf Club Les Bois is located amidst the region of Franches Montagnes that is typical of the Swiss Jura mountains. A superb decor in true operetta style. The terrain is hilly but not over-demanding physically (think about an electric trolley or buggy for the less able). It was built in two phases, which is clearly evident, as some greens are still very firm. The course is a mixture of holes through a forest and holes in more open space, all harmoniously put together with clever balance. You definitely do not see all the hazards and effective game strategy is not possible before playing the course at least three times. Suffice it to say that this layout is as open and honest as you might guess and you don't really need to bend or flight the ball. What you do need to know is how to read the greens here, which are anything but straightforward. The holes you will remember are 14 through 16 in the middle of pine trees, which might rank as some of the finest holes of golf in the whole of Switzerland. A first rate course, playable by everyone.

Golf Club Les Bois — 1995
CH - 2336 LES BOIS

Office	Secrétariat	(41) 032 - 961 10 03
Pro shop	Pro-shop	(41) 032 - 961 19 44
Fax	Fax	(41) 032 - 961 10 17
Situation	Situation	

La Chaux-de-Fonds (pop. 37 500 hab.), 12 km

Annual closure	Fermeture annuelle	no
Weekly closure	Fermeture hebdomadaire	no

Fees main season
Tarifs haute saison 18 holes

	Week days Semaine	We/Bank holidays We/Férié
Individual Individuel	60 CHF	70 CHF
Couple Couple	120 CHF	140 CHF

Caddy	Caddy	no
Electric Trolley	Chariot électrique	25 CHF
Buggy	Voiturette	50 CHF
Clubs	Clubs	50 CHF

Credit cards Cartes de crédit
VISA - Eurocard - MasterCard - AMEX - DC

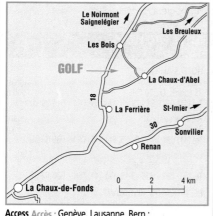

Access Accès : Genève, Lausanne, Bern :
A1 → Neuchâtel. N20 → La Chaux-de-Fonds.
Road 18 → Saignelégier.
Map 1 on page 1286 Carte 1 Page 1286

GOLF COURSE PARCOURS — 15/20

Site	Site	
Maintenance	Entretien	
Architect	Architecte	Jeremy Pern
Type	Type	forest, country
Relief	Relief	
Water in play	Eau en jeu	
Exp. to wind	Exposé au vent	
Trees in play	Arbres en jeu	

Scorecard Carte de score	Chp. Chp.	Mens Mess.	Ladies Da.
Length Long.	6027	5624	4740
Par	72	72	72

Advised golfing ability	0	12	24	36
Niveau de jeu recommandé				
Hcp required Handicap exigé	35			

CLUB HOUSE & AMENITIES
CLUB HOUSE ET ANNEXES — 6/10

Pro shop	Pro-shop	
Driving range	Practice	
Sheltered	couvert	12 mats
On grass	sur herbe	no
Putting-green	putting-green	yes
Pitching-green	pitching green	yes

HOTEL FACILITIES
ENVIRONNEMENT HOTELIER — 6/10

HOTELS HÔTELS

Le Quinquet — Les Bois
5 rooms, D 100 CHF — 2 km
Tel (41) 032 - 961 12 06, Fax (41) 032 - 961 16 51

Hôtel de la Gare — Le Noirmont
10 rooms, D 240 CHF — 10 km
Tel (41) 032 - 953 11 10, Fax (41) 032 - 953 10 59

Hôtel de la Gare et du Parc — Saignelégier
21 rooms, D 240 CHF — 20 km
Tel (41) 032 - 951 11 21, Fax (41) 032 - 951 12 32

RESTAURANTS RESTAURANT

Hôtel de la Gare — Le Noirmont
Tel (41) 032 - 953 11 10 — 10 km

Hôtel de la Gare et du Parc — Saignelégier
Tel (41) 032 - 951 11 21 — 20 km

1301

Fondata nel 1925, il percorso é stato rimodellato succesivamente da Donald Harradine e Cabell Robinson che à aggiunto qualche laghetto al corso d'acqua esistente, ma non ha potuto allungarlo per la mancanza dello spazio. I green sono ben difesi, ció che puo ostacolare il desiderio di performance. Molto franco, non ha bisogno di essere giocate dieci volte per essere capito, la vegetazione attenua molto l'impressione di va e vieni suggeriti dal disegno, e obbliga i giocatori d'un altro livello, dove possono rifarsi con la precisione, in quanto il percorso non é molto lungo. In un sito ed una piacevole regione, é un buon percorso di vacanze, la sua manutenzione deve essere migliorata per attribuirgli una nota migliore.

Opened in 1925, the course has been successively reshaped by Donald Harradine and Cabell Robinson, who added several lakes to the existing river but were unable to lengthen the course owing to lack of space. The greens are well defended, which may cut short any desire to go for the performance. You don't need to play this very honest course ten times to understand what it is about. The vegetation reduces the impression of up and down holes, suggested by the layout, and forces long-hitters to fade or draw the ball to get a good approach into the green. Good and not so good players can get along well together here, where lack of precision is offset by short yardage. In a pleasant setting and region, this is a good holiday course, but to get a better score, greenkeeping and maintenance could still do with a little improvement.

Golf Club Lugano — 1926
CH - 6983 MAGLIASO

Office	Segreteria	(41) 091 - 606 15 57
Pro shop	Pro shop	(41) 091 - 606 46 76
Fax	Fax	(41) 091 - 606 65 58
Situation	Localita'	

Lugano (pop. 25 334), 5 km

Annual closure	Chiusura annuale	no
Weekly closure	Chiusura settimanale	no

Fees main season
Tariffe alta stagione 18 holes

	Week days Settimana	We/Bank holidays Feriale/Festivo
Individual Individuale	85 CHF	110 CHF
Couple Coppia	170 CHF	220 CHF

Caddy	Caddy	no
Electric Trolley	Carello elettrico	no
Buggy	Car	110 CHF
Clubs	Bastoni	30 CHF

Credit cards Carte di credito — no

GOLF COURSE
PERCORSO — 15/20

Site	Paesaggio	
Maintenance	Manutenzione	
Architect	Architetto	Donald Harradine Cabell B. Robinson
Type	Tipologia	parkland
Relief	Relievo terreno	
Water in play	Acqua in gioco	
Exp. to wind	Esposto al vento	
Trees in play	Alberi in gioco	

Scorecard Carta-score	Chp. Camp.	Mens Uomini	Ladies Donne
Length Lunghezza	5775	5775	5040
Par	71	71	71

Advised golfing ability Livello di gioco consigliato	0	12	24	36

Hcp required Handicap richiesto 30

CLUB HOUSE & AMENITIES
CLUB HOUSE E SERVIZI — 7/10

Pro shop	Pro shop	
Driving range	Campo pratica	
Sheltered	coperto	8 mats
On grass	in erba	no
Putting-green	Putting-green	yes
Pitching-green	Green-pratica	yes

HOTEL FACILITIES
ALBERGHI — 8/10

HOTELS ALBERGHI

Villa Magliasina — Magliaso
25 rooms, D 270 CHF — 500 m
Tel (41) 091 - 611 29 29, Fax (41) 091 - 611 29 20

Principe Leopoldo — Lugano
39 rooms, D 480 CHF — 5 km
Tel (41) 091 - 985 88 55, Fax (41) 091 - 985 88 25

Locanda Esterel — Caslano
9 rooms, D 180 CHF — 1 km
Tel (41) 091 - 606 43 13, Fax (41) 091 - 606 62 02

RESTAURANTS RISTORANTE

Locanda Esterel — Caslano
Tel (41) 091 - 606 43 13 — 1 km

Al Portone — Lugano
Tel (41) 091 - 923 55 11 — 5 km

Access Itinerario : Lugano, → Ponte Tresa,
→ Magliaso, Golf
Map 1 on page 1287 Carta 1 Pagina 1287

1925 erbaut und seither mehrfach verändert, bietet dieser Golfcourse hübsche und abwechslungsreiche Aussichten auf den Vierwaldstättersee, auf Hügellandschaften und auf verschneite Berge. Bie betonten Geländeformen wurden geschickt einbezogen, denn die grossen Höhenunterschiede liegen meist zwischen den Holes. Doglegs sind wenige zu finden, aber die Bahnen sind oft schmal, verlangen gerade Schläge und den einen oder anderen Flirt mit Baümen. Bei nur einem Wasserhindernis haben gute Spieler Chancen auf tiefe Scores, obwohl Annäherungen auf oft tiefergelegene oder überhöhte Greens solide Schläge verlangen. Ein traditionelles Platzkonzept, dem aber die Schwierigkeiten eines modernen Courses nicht fehlen und die charmante Umgebung machen Luzern zum lohnenden Golfabstecher.

This course has been considerably restyled since its opening in 1925. There are a number of different pretty views over lake Lucerne, the hills and the snow-capped mountains. The terrain is steep and rather hilly but has been well utilised, as the steepest slopes are to be found primarily between holes. There are few dog-legs, as most holes are often straight and require straight shots, skirting the trees. With a single water hazard, skilled players will doubtless find this an easy course to score on, even though care is called for when attacking the greens, which are rarely on the same level as the fairway (elevated or in a hollow). We liked the charm of the site and a certain idea of old-style golf courses, without the difficulties found on many modern courses.

Luzern Golf Club — 1925

Dietschiberg
CH - 6006 LUZERN

Office	Sekretariat	(41) 041 - 420 97 87
Pro shop	Pro shop	(41) 041 - 420 97 87
Fax	Fax	(41) 041 - 420 82 48
Situation	Lage	

Luzern (pop. 61 034), 2 km

Annual closure	Jährliche Schliessung	31/10 → 1/4
Weekly closure	Wöchentliche Schliessung	no

Monday (Montag), Restaurant closed

Fees main season
Preisliste hochsaison 18 holes

	Week days Woche	We/Bank holidays We/Feiertag
Individual Individuell	80 CHF	100 CHF
Couple Ehepaar	160 CHF	200 CHF

Caddy	Caddy	no
Electric Trolley	Elektrokarren	no
Buggy	Elektrischer Wagen	no
Clubs	Leihschläger	15 CHF

Credit cards Kreditkarten
VISA - Eurocard - MasterCard - AMEX

Access Zufahrt : Luzern → Dreilinden,
→ Trachtenmuseum, Dietschibergstrasse
Map 1 on page 1287 Karte 1 Seite 1287

GOLF COURSE / PLATZ — 13/20

Site	Lage	
Maintenance	Instandhaltung	
Architect	Architekt	Ruzzo Reuss
Type	Typ	forest, mountain
Relief	Begehbarkeit	
Water in play	Platz mit Wasser	
Exp. to wind	Wind ausgesetzt	
Trees in play	Platz mit Bäumen	

Scorecard Scorekarte	Chp. Chp.	Mens Herren	Ladies Damen
Length Länge	6082	5760	4931
Par	73	72	72

Advised golfing ability Empfohlene Spielstärke	0 12 24 36
Hcp required Min. Handicap	30

CLUB HOUSE & AMENITIES / KLUBHAUS UND NEBENGEBÄUDE — 6/10

Pro shop	Pro shop	
Driving range	Übungsplatz	
Sheltered	überdacht	4 mats
On grass	auf Rasen	yes (06 → 09)
Putting-green	Putting-grün	yes
Pitching-green	Pitching-grün	yes

HOTEL FACILITIES / HOTEL BESCHREIBUNG — 7/10

HOTELS
Montana — Luzern 2 km
60 rooms, D 286 CHF
Tel (41) 041 - 410 65 65, Fax (41) 041 - 410 66 76

Grand Hôtel National — Luzern 2 km
78 rooms, D 400 CHF
Tel (41) 041 - 50 11 11, Fax (41) 041 - 51 55 39

Drei Könige — Luzern 2 km
60 rooms, D 150 CHF
Tel (41) 041 - 22 88 33, Fax (41) 041 - 22 88 52

RESTAURANTS
Zunfthaus zu Pfistern — Luzern 2 km
Tel (41) 041 - 51 36 50

Old Swiss House - Tel (41) 041 - 410 61 71 — Luzern 2 km

Le Manoir - Tel (41) 041 - 23 23 48 — Luzern 2 km

1303

MONTREUX

On pourrait souligner la beauté du panorama sur les Alpes , mais cette qualité est commune à la majorité des golfs de Suisse ! Elle contribue au moins à faire apprécier un parcours autrement sans originalité particulière, et sans obstacles d'eau. Eviter les arbres constitue le principal «challenge», car ils sont souvent en jeu, et rompent un peu la monotonie des trous, trop similaires de dessin pour frapper la mémoire. Les difficultés ne sont pas très grandes, ce qui peut réserver des parties plaisantes entre joueurs de niveau différent, mais les meilleurs resteront certainement sur leur faim. Au moment des visites, les greens étaient toujours en état moyen : ce n'est plus une question de malchance. Si vous passez dans la région...

We could point to the beautiful scenery of the Alps, but such panoramas are common to the majority of Swiss courses. But it does help the player to enjoy a course which otherwise has no particular originality and no water hazards. The main challenge is to avoid the trees, which are often in play and break the monotony of holes which are too similar to really leave an indelible impression. The difficulties are not enormous, which can lead to pleasant rounds with friends of differing ability, but the better players will feel a touch of frustration. When we visited, the greens still were in average condition, so if you are in the neighbourhood, call first to check.

Golf Club Montreux

Route d'Evian
CH - 1860 AIGLE

Office	Secrétariat	(41) 024 - 466 4616
Pro shop	Pro-shop	(41) 024 - 466 14 64
Fax	Fax	(41) 024 - 466 10 47
Situation	Situation	

Montreux (pop. 21 325), 25 km

Annual closure	Fermeture annuelle	no
Weekly closure	Fermeture hebdomadaire	no

January (janvier), restaurant closed

Fees main season
Tarifs haute saison 18 holes

	Week days Semaine	We/Bank holidays We/Férié
Individual Individuel	70 CHF	90 CHF
Couple Couple	140 CHF	180 CHF

Caddy	Caddy	no
Electric Trolley	Chariot électrique	no
Buggy	Voiturette	no
Clubs	Clubs	15 CHF
Credit cards Cartes de crédit		no

1304

Access Accès : N9 Montreux-Martigny,
Exit (sortie) Aigle, → Golf
Map 1 on page 1286 Carte 1 Page 1286

GOLF COURSE
PARCOURS   13/20

Site	Site	
Maintenance	Entretien	
Architect	Architecte	unknown
Type	Type	parkland
Relief	Relief	
Water in play	Eau en jeu	
Exp. to wind	Exposé au vent	
Trees in play	Arbres en jeu	

Scorecard Carte de score	Chp. Chp.	Mens Mess.	Ladies Da.
Length Long.	6143	5828	5092
Par	72	72	72

Advised golfing ability Niveau de jeu recommandé	0	12	24	36
Hcp required Handicap exigé	30			

CLUB HOUSE & AMENITIES
CLUB HOUSE ET ANNEXES   6/10

Pro shop	Pro-shop	
Driving range	Practice	
Sheltered	couvert	6 mats
On grass	sur herbe	yes
Putting-green	putting-green	yes
Pitching-green	pitching green	yes

HOTEL FACILITIES
ENVIRONNEMENT HOTELIER   5/10

HOTELS HÔTELS

Le Montreux Palace	Montreux
250 rooms, D 570 CHF	25 km
Tel (41) 021 - 962 12 12, Fax (41) 021 - 962 17 17	

Bonivard	Montreux/Veytaux
70 rooms, D 240 CHF	20 km
Tel (41) 021 - 963 43 41, Fax (41) 021 - 963 48 15	

Nord	Aigle
19 rooms, D 180 CHF	20 km
Tel (41) 024 - 466 10 55, Fax (41) 024 - 466 42 48	

RESTAURANTS RESTAURANT

Le Pont de Brent	Montreux-Brent
Tel (41) 021 - 964 52 30	30 km

L'Ermitage	Montreux
Tel (41) 021 - 964 44 11	25 km

Ce parcours accidenté, mais sans excès, a été dessiné dans une ancienne zone agricole au pied du Jura. L'absence d'arrosage automatique oblige à le déconseiller en temps de forte sécheresse, mais les précipitations naturelles permettent de le maintenir généralement en bon état. Les obstacles sont rarement très dangereux (quelques hors-limites), et la longueur raisonnable permet d'offrir pas mal d'occasions de birdie (ou de pars pour les joueurs moyens). Pas de pièges ici ni de complications artificielles : ce parcours a été coulé dans la nature, à l'intention évidente des familles, ou de ceux qui ne souhaitent pas trop se compliquer la vie sur un parcours (ils sont nombreux).

This is a hilly course laid out over a former farming region at the foot of the Jura mountains. There being no automatic sprinklers, it is not a course to be recommended during a drought, but natural rainfall generally tends to keep it in good condition. The hazards are rarely very dangerous (a few out-of-bounds) and the reasonable length can produce more than one opportunity to catch an elusive birdie (or the equally elusive par for lesser players). There are no traps or artificial complications here, as this course was cast in natural land, evidently intended for families or golfers who prefer not to make life any more complicated than it often can be on a golf course (and there are a lot of those).

Golf & Country Club Neuchâtel — 1975
Voëns
CH - 2072 SAINT-BLAISE

Office	Secrétariat	(41) 032 - 753 55 50
Pro shop	Pro-shop	(41) 032 - 753 70 84
Fax	Fax	(41) 032 - 753 29 40
Situation	Situation	

Neuchâtel (pop. 32 080), 5 km

Annual closure	Fermeture annuelle	15/11 → 21/3
Weekly closure	Fermeture hebdomadaire	no

Fees main season
Tarifs haute saison 18 holes

	Week days Semaine	We/Bank holidays We/Férié
Individual Individuel	70 CHF	90 CHF
Couple Couple	140 CHF	180 CHF

Caddy	Caddy	on request
Electric Trolley	Chariot électrique	no
Buggy	Voiturette	no
Clubs	Clubs	15 CHF

Credit cards Cartes de crédit — no

Lignières
Enges — BIEL
GOLF
La Chaux-de-Fonds — Cornaux
St-Blaise — Thielle — BERN
Marin
Lausanne
NEUCHÂTEL
LAC DE NEUCHÂTEL
0   2   4 km

Access Accès : Neuchâtel Exit (sortie) St Blaise,
→ Lignières or St Blaise Centre, → Chaumont
Map 1 on page 1286 Carte 1 Page 1286

GOLF COURSE / PARCOURS — 14/20

Site	Site	
Maintenance	Entretien	
Architect	Architecte	Donald Harradine
Type	Type	parkland
Relief	Relief	
Water in play	Eau en jeu	
Exp. to wind	Exposé au vent	
Trees in play	Arbres en jeu	

Scorecard Carte de score	Chp. Chp.	Mens Mess.	Ladies Da.
Length Long.	5930	5630	4870
Par	71	71	71

Advised golfing ability Niveau de jeu recommandé	0 12 24 36
Hcp required Handicap exigé	30

CLUB HOUSE & AMENITIES / CLUB HOUSE ET ANNEXES — 6/10

Pro shop	Pro-shop	
Driving range	Practice	
Sheltered	couvert	8 mats
On grass	sur herbe	no
Putting-green	putting-green	yes
Pitching-green	pitching green	yes

HOTEL FACILITIES / ENVIRONNEMENT HOTELIER — 7/10

HOTELS HÔTELS

Beaurivage — Neuchâtel
65 rooms, D 310 CHF — 9 km
Tel (41) 032 - 724 00 24, Fax (41) 032 - 724 78 94

Chaumont et Golf -88 rooms, D 200 CHF — Chaumont
Tel (41) 032 - 755 21 75, Fax (41) 032 - 753 27 22 — 2 km

Les Vieux Toits — Hauterive
10 rooms, D 175 CHF — 2 km
Tel (41) 032 - 753 42 42, Fax (41) 032 - 753 24 52

Cheval Blanc - 11 rooms, D 90 CHF — Saint-Blaise
Tel (41) 032 - 753 30 07, Fax (41) 032 - 753 30 06 — 4 km

RESTAURANTS RESTAURANT

Au Boccalino — Saint-Blaise
Tel (41) 032 - 753 36 80 — 4 km

Auberge du Grand Pin — Peseux
Tel (41) 032 - 751 77 07 — 12 km

1305

Niederbüren, entworfen von dem allseits gefragten Donald Harradine, entrollt sich wie ein schmales Band vor den Augen des Spielers, ganz so wie der Old Course von St. Andrews. Nur, dass der Platz an dem Flüsschen Thun liegt und nicht am Meer. Einzig der Entwurf entspricht britischer Tradition, der Vergleich lässt sich nicht weiter ausdehnen. Es beginnt damit, dass der Wind hier längst nicht so häufig und so gewaltig weht. Weiterhin bilden die Bunker die haupsächliche Bedrohung der Fairways, jedoch veranlassen deren Profil und Schwierigkeitsgrad zu keinerlei Besorgnis. Die Bahnen sind von Tannen gesäumt, die an ein gerades Spiel appellieren und keinerlei Fehler zulassen, wie etwa die breiten Flächen der richtigen Links. Der Platz ist insgesamt nicht zu lang und die schwierigen Passagen sind gleichmässig verteilt. Es handelt sich um ein angenehmes Areal, ideal für die ganze Familie.

Laid out by the prolific designer Donald Harradine, Niederbüren is peculiar in that it unwinds in a narrow strip, like the Old Course at St Andrews, only alongside the river Thun and not the sea. Despite the British tradition here, the comparison ends there. Firstly the wind is less frequent and more clement, then the basic hazards emerge as bunkers, although their shape and difficulty are anything but fearsome. The fairways here are lined with fir-trees, which call for accuracy and do not leave the room for error you find on real links courses. The layout is moderate in length and difficulties are evenly spread around the course. A pleasant course for all the family.

Ostschweizerischer Golf Club — 1948
CH - 9246 NIEDERBÜREN

Office	Sekretariat	(41) 071 - 422 18 56
Pro shop	Pro shop	(41) 071 - 422 18 56
Fax	Fax	(41) 071 - 422 18 25
Situation	Lage	

St-Gallen (pop. 71 917), 16 km
Winterthur (pop. 88 812), 48 km.

Annual closure	Jährliche Schliessung	1/12 → 1/3
Weekly closure	Wöchentliche Schliessung	no

Monday (Montag), restaurant closed

Fees main season
Preisliste hochsaison full day

	Week days Woche	We/Bank holidays We/Feiertag
Individual Individuell	80 CHF	100 CHF
Couple Ehepaar	160 CHF	200 CHF

Caddy	Caddy	no
Electric Trolley	Elektrokarren	25 CHF
Buggy	Elektrischer Wagen	no
Clubs	Leihschläger	20 CHF

Credit cards Kreditkarten — no

0 2 4 km
Konstanz
Wil
Winterthur
GOLF
Niederbühren
Oberbüren
Uzwil
N 1
ST-GALLEN

Access Zufahrt : Motorway 1 → St Gallen,
→ Uzwil/Oberbüren, → Niederbüren, → Golf
Map 1 on page 1287 Karte 1 Seite 1287

GOLF COURSE
PLATZ — 13/20

Site	Lage	▰▰▰▰▱
Maintenance	Instandhaltung	▰▰▰▱▱
Architect	Architekt	Donald Harradine
Type	Typ	country
Relief	Begehbarkeit	▰▰▱▱▱
Water in play	Platz mit Wasser	▰▱▱▱▱
Exp. to wind	Wind ausgesetzt	▰▰▱▱▱
Trees in play	Platz mit Bäumen	▰▰▰▰▱

Scorecard Scorekarte	Chp. Chp.	Mens Herren	Ladies Damen
Length Länge	6096	5698	5040
Par	72	72	72

Advised golfing ability	0 12 24 36
Empfohlene Spielstärke	▱▰▰▰
Hcp required Min. Handicap	30

CLUB HOUSE & AMENITIES
KLUBHAUS UND NEBENGEBÄUDE — 7/10

Pro shop	Pro shop	▰▰▰▰▱
Driving range	Übungsplatz	▰▰▰▱▱
Sheltered	überdacht	6 mats
On grass	auf Rasen	yes
Putting-green	Putting-grün	yes
Pitching-green	Pitching-grün	yes

HOTEL FACILITIES
HOTEL BESCHREIBUNG — 7/10

HOTELS HOTELS

Alte Herberge — Niederbüren
2 rooms, D 75 CHF — 1 km
Tel (41) 071 - 422 20 91

Hotel Uzwil — Uzwil
38 rooms, D 80 CHF — 10 km
Tel (41) 071 - 955 70 70, Fax (41) 071 - 955 35 55

Hotel Sonne — Gossau
8 rooms, D 140 CHF — 12 km
Tel (41) 071 - 385 16 51, Fax (41) 071 - 385 90 22

RESTAURANTS RESTAURANT

Linde — Bischofszell
Tel (41) 071 - 422 16 10 — 6 km

Alte Herberge — Niederbüren
Tel (41) 071 - 422 20 91 — 1 km

1306

Sulle rive dello splendido Lago Maggiore, una delle più belle villeggiature della Svizzera, dove il Patriziale aggiunge un'attrazione supplementare alla regione in quanto pianeggiante, e senza trappole. I molti alberi danno in estate un ombra benvenuta, senza che il sottobosco ne sia penalizzato. Lo si puo considerare come un'agreabile percorso di vacanze in famiglia, ma anche come testo di buona fattura, dove i giocatori precisi e regolari, saranno a loro agio, dovranno pero, impiegare tutte le risorse del piccolo gioco, in quanto i green non sono molto grandi ma ben difesi, e sovente in altezza. Il piacere del clima, la natura del terreno, permettono di giocare una gran parte dell'anno, ció che non é freguente in Svizzera.

Alongside the beautiful Lake Maggiore, one of the prettiest Swiss holiday sites, the "Patriziale" adds extra charm to the region, all the more so in that the course is flat with no hidden traps. The very many trees bring welcome shade in summer, and the undergrowth is never too penalising. This is what might be considered to be a very pleasant holiday course, for playing with all the family with little at stake, but also a cleverly worked out test of golf where straight and consistent players will feel at home. They will, nonetheless, need a finely tuned short game, because the greens are not enormous, are well-defended and often come with several tiers. The pleasant climate and the nature of the terrain mean being able to play here most of the year, a feature that is not all that common in Switzerland.

Golf Club Patriziale Ascona — 1928

Via al Lido 81
CH - 6612 ASCONA

Office	Segreteria	(41) 091 - 791 21 32
Pro shop	Pro shop	(41) 091 - 791 14 36
Fax	Fax	(41) 091 - 791 07 96
Situation	Localita'	

Locarno (pop. 13 796), 3 km

Annual closure	Chiusura annuale	no
Weekly closure	Chiusura settimanale	no

Fees main season
Tariffe alta stagione 18 holes

	Week days Settimana	We/Bank holidays Feriale/Festivo
Individual Individuale	80 CHF	80 CHF
Couple Coppia	160 CHF	160 CHF

Caddy	Caddy	no
Electric Trolley	Carello elettrico	20 CHF
Buggy	Car	no
Clubs	Bastoni	20 CHF

Credit cards Carte di credito   no

```
        0    2    4 km
                          Gordola
              N 13                  N 13
   GOLF
Ascona         LOCARNO          BELLINZONA →
VERBANIA                MAGGIORE
(ITALIA)         LAGO
                                    N 12
                          LUGANO
```

Access Itinerario :
Locarno → Ascona, → Via Lido, Golf
Map 1 on page 1287 Carta 1 Pagina 1287

GOLF COURSE / PERCORSO — 15/20

Site	Paesaggio	▬▬▬▬▭
Maintenance	Manutenzione	▬▬▬▬▭
Architect	Architetto	C.K. Cotton
Type	Tipologia	parkland
Relief	Relievo terreno	▬▬▭▭▭
Water in play	Acqua in gioco	▬▬▭▭▭
Exp. to wind	Esposto al vento	▬▬▭▭▭
Trees in play	Alberi in gioco	▬▬▬▬▭

Scorecard Carta-score	Chp. Camp.	Mens Uomini	Ladies Donne
Length Lunghezza	5948	5948	5268
Par	71	71	71

Advised golfing ability   0   12   24   36
Livello di gioco consigliato   ▬▬▬▬▬▭
Hcp required   Handicap richiesto 30

CLUB HOUSE & AMENITIES / CLUB HOUSE E SERVIZI — 7/10

Pro shop	Pro shop	▬▬▬▭▭
Driving range	Campo pratica	▬▬▬▬▭
Sheltered	coperto	40 matsi
On grass	in erba	yes
Putting-green	Putting-green	yes
Pitching-green	Green-pratica	yes

HOTEL FACILITIES / ALBERGHI — 7/10

HOTELS ALBERGHI

Casa Berno — Ascona
60 rooms, D 368 CHF
Tel (41) 091 - 791 32 32, Fax (41) 091 - 792 11 14

Castello del Sole — Ascona
85 rooms, D 450 CHF
Tel (41) 091 - 791 02 02, Fax (41) 091 - 791 11 18

Castello — Ascona
45 rooms, D 350 CHF
Tel (41) 091 - 791 01 61, Fax (41) 091 - 791 18 04

RESTAURANTS RISTORANTE

Ascolago — Ascona
Tel (41) 091 - 791 20 55

Osteria Giardino — Ascona
Tel (41) 091 - 791 01 01

1307

Die Lage des Platzes auf einem schmalen Terrain entlang des Flüsschens Krebs erklärt die zahlreichen aber nicht allzu spielbestimmenden Out of bounds und auch den feuchten Torfboden. Von der hintersten Abschlägen gespielt, ist der Platz recht lang. Bäume, Bunkers und zahlreiche Wasserflächen scheuen entwichene Bälle nicht und machen die Aufgaben heikel. Die Strategie ist auf jedem Hole wichtig und macht das Spiel vielfältig und interessant. Auch ohne golfarchitektonische Sonderleistungen ist Schönenberg eine ausserordentliche Anlage und dank geschützten Zonen ein gutes Beispiel für das Nebeneinander von Golf und Natur.

A lay-out on a narrow strip of terrain along the river Krebs explains both the many out-of bounds (although not too many in play) and the wetness of the soil, which is basically peat. Reasonable from the normal tees, it gets much longer from the back-tees, especially since the bunkers and many water hazards easily collect balls hit off-target. Each hole requires a definite strategy, but this and especially the variety of holes make it a pleasant course to play. Without displaying any exceptional imagination on the part of the architect, Schönenberg is a very attractive course and again shows a good example of ecology and golf living easily side by side (several areas are natural trust land). This is always a thorny problem in Switzerland.

Golf & Country Club Schönenberg 1968
CH - 8824 SCHÖNENBERG

Office	Sekretariat	(41) 01 - 788 90 40
Pro shop	Pro shop	(41) 01 - 788 90 55
Fax	Fax	(41) 01 - 788 90 45
Situation	Lage	

Zürich (pop. 365 043), 25 km

Annual closure	Jährliche Schliessung	15/11 → 20/3
Weekly closure	Wöchentliche Schliessung	no

Fees main season
Preisliste hochsaison 18 holes

	Week days Woche	We/Bank holidays We/Feiertag
Individual Individuell	90 CHF	90 CHF
Couple Ehepaar	180 CHF	180 CHF

Caddy	Caddy	no
Electric Trolley	Elektrokarren	27 CHF
Buggy	Elektrischer Wagen	no
Clubs	Leihschläger	yes

Credit cards Kreditkarten no

1308

GOLF COURSE
PLATZ 14/20

Site	Lage	▬▬▬▬
Maintenance	Instandhaltung	▬▬▬▬
Architect	Architekt	Donald Harradine
Type	Typ	country
Relief	Begehbarkeit	▬▬▬
Water in play	Platz mit Wasser	▬▬▬▬
Exp. to wind	Wind ausgesetzt	▬▬
Trees in play	Platz mit Bäumen	▬▬▬▬

Scorecard Scorekarte	Chp. Chp.	Mens Herren	Ladies Damen
Length Länge	6135	5672	4864
Par	72	72	72

Advised golfing ability		0 12 24 36
Empfohlene Spielstärke		▬▬▬▬
Hcp required	Min. Handicap	30

CLUB HOUSE & AMENITIES
KLUBHAUS UND NEBENGEBÄUDE 7/10

Pro shop	Pro shop	▬▬▬
Driving range	Übungsplatz	▬▬
Sheltered	überdacht	4 mats
On grass	auf Rasen	yes (04 -10)
Putting-green	Putting-grün	yes
Pitching-green	Pitching-grün	yes

HOTEL FACILITIES
HOTEL BESCHREIBUNG 6/10

HOTELS HOTELS

Post | Biberbrugg
13 rooms, D 120 CHF | 15 km
Tel (41) 055 - 412 27 71
Fax (41) 055 - 412 70 72

Seehotel Meierhof | Horgen
113 rooms, D 200 CHF | 5 km
Tel (41) 01 - 725 29 61
Fax (41) 01 - 725 55 23

RESTAURANTS RESTAURANT

Golf & Country Club | Schönenberg
Tel (41) 01 - 788 15 74

Eichmühle | Wädenswil
Tel (41) 01 - 780 34 44

Access Zufahrt : Zürich-Chur → Horgen
or Wädenswil, → Zug, Hirsel → Schönenberg,
Golf 1,5 km.
Map 1 on page 1287 Karte 1 Seite 1287

Die Gegend ist eher flach, bietet aber dennoch eine wunderschöne Sicht auf dem Sempachersee und liegt in der Nähe eines der bekannten Schlachtfelder des Mittelalters. Bevor Sie diesen Platz spielen, tun Sie gut daran, ihn und seine Tücken zu studieren. Er bietet einiges an Schwierigkeiten, die man entweder umgehen oder mit einigem Risiko direkt angreifen kann. Oder man kann auch etwas überraschendes versuchen... Dabei stellt man fest, dass er gar nicht so ungastlich ist. Die Fairways sind angenehm breit, denn die Bäume müssen noch wachsen, bevor der Platz seinen definitiven Charakter seigen kann. Im Moment gilt es vor allem bei den Abschlägen auf das hohe Rough zu achten, und auch die zahlreichen Wasser können sich als beachtliche Hindernisse erweisen. Die Greens sind von mittlerer Grösse aber schön gezeichnet und je nach Fahnenposition kann der Schwierigkeitsgrad recht stark variiert werden.

The site is flat but provides an outstanding view over the Sempachersee, at about 1 kilometre from a famous battlefield. Battling is perhaps the right word when it comes to contending with these 18 holes, with careful study of your opponent's strengths required before going on the offensive. The course conceals some of its difficulties but you can get around them, or take risks and «take 'em by surprise». If you succeed, it won't be such a hostile proposition after all. The area is still nicely wide open and the trees will have to grow a bit before Sempachersee shows its true colours. For the time being, watch out for the tall rough, which threatens many a tee-shot, and several water hazards that are laid out in a rather classic, albeit effective style. Greens are average in size, well-designed and provide a good number of different pin positions to make the golfer's life a little more difficult.

Golf Sempachersee		1996
CH - 6024 HILDISRIEDEN		

Office	Sekretariat	(41) 041 - 462 71 71
Pro shop	Pro shop	(41) 041 - 462 71 75
Fax	Fax	(41) 041 - 462 71 72
Situation	Lage	
Luzern (pop. 61 034), 20 km		
Annual closure	Jährliche Schliessung	no
Weekly closure	Wöchentliche Schliessung	no

Fees main season
Preisliste hochsaison 18 holes

	Week days Woche	We/Bank holidays We/Feiertag
Individual Individuell	80 CHF	*
Couple Ehepaar	160 CHF	*

* We/Holidays: with members only
(nur in Mitgliederbegleitung)

Caddy	Caddy	no
Electric Trolley	Elektrokarren	25 CHF
Buggy	Elektrischer Wagen	50 CHF
Clubs	Leihschläger	45 CHF

Credit cards Kreditkarten VISA - Eurocard - AMEX

Access Zufahrt : Luzern, N2 → Basel.
→ Sempach, Hildisrieden.
Map 1 on page 1287 Karte 1 Seite 1287

GOLF COURSE
PLATZ
15/20

Site	Lage	
Maintenance	Instandhaltung	
Architect	Architekt	Kurt Rossknecht
Type	Typ	Wald, Fachland
Relief	Begehbarkeit	
Water in play	Platz mit Wasser	
Exp. to wind	Wind ausgesetzt	
Trees in play	Platz mit Bäumen	

Scorecard Scorekarte	Chp. Chp.	Mens Herren	Ladies Damen
Length Länge	6123	5858	5153
Par	72	72	72

Advised golfing ability	0	12	24	36
Empfohlene Spielstärke				

Hcp required   Min. Handicap   30

CLUB HOUSE & AMENITIES
KLUBHAUS UND NEBENGEBÄUDE
8/10

Pro shop	Pro shop	
Driving range	Übungsplatz	
Sheltered	überdacht	10 mats
On grass	auf Rasen	yes
Putting-green	Putting-grün	yes
Pitching-green	Pitching-grün	yes

HOTEL FACILITIES
HOTEL BESCHREIBUNG
7/10

HOTELS HOTELS
Vogelsang — Eich
11 rooms, D 190 CHF — 5 km
Tel (41) 041 - 462 66 66
Fax (41) 041 - 462 66 65

Hirschen — Beromünster
12 rooms, D 120 CHF — 5 km
Tel (41) 041 - 930 33 71
Fax (41) 041 - 930 39 44

RESTAURANTS RESTAURANT
Herlisberg Wirtshaus — Herlisberg
Tel (41) 041 - 930 12 80 — 10 km

Vogelsang — Vogelsang
Tel (41) 041 - 462 66 66 — 5 km

1309

Bedingt durch seine Länge und Wasserhindernisse auf sechs Holes ist dieser Platz vor allem von den hinteren Abschlägen schwierig zu meistern. Dies um so mehr, weil Steine und schlechtes Gras in den Roughs bei unserem Besuch dem Gesamtzustand noch abträglich waren. Die Anlage ist aber jung und muss noch bearbeitet werden. Die Umgebung am Ufer der Aare ist nicht von überragender Schönheit, bietet aber einige schöne Blicke auf den Jura. Architektonisch wurde gut gearbeitet, aber die geniale Gestaltung blieb aus. Der Ball kann meist rollenderweise auf die Greens gebracht werden, was Spieler beruhigt, die sich von den Wassergefahren beeindrucken lassen. Der Platz versteckt seine golferischen Tücken kaum und kann mit gesundem Selbstvertrauen angegangen werden. Auch schon beim erstem Mal.

Judging by length and the number of water hazards (on 6 holes), this is a tough course to play from the back-tees, especially since the state of upkeep was pretty rough when we visited, notably because of the stones and weeds in the rough. But this is a young course and further work is still needed. On the banks of the Aar, the setting is hardly outstanding, despite a few pleasant views over the Jura mountains. The architecture has been given careful thought, but without any special flair for landscaping. Most of the time, players can chip the ball onto the green, which will reassure lesser players who are already under stress from the water hazards. At least the course does not have too many hidden traps, meaning that golfers can play here confidently, even the first time out.

Golf Club Wylihof — 1995
CH - 4708 LUTERBACH

Office	Sekretariat	(41) 032 - 882 28 28
Pro shop	Pro shop	(41) 032 - 882 28 28
Fax	Fax	(41) 032 - 882 28 24
Situation	Lage	

Solothurn (pop. 15 748), 8 km

Annual closure	Jährliche Schliessung	no
Weekly closure	Wöchentliche Schliessung	no

Restaurant closed during Winter

Fees main season
Preisliste hochsaison 18 holes

	Week days Woche	We/Bank holidays We/Feiertag
Individual Individuell	90 CHF	90 CHF
Couple Ehepaar	180 CHF	180 CHF

Caddy	Caddy	no
Electric Trolley	Elektrokarren	yes
Buggy	Elektrischer Wagen	80 CHF
Clubs	Leihschläger	no

Credit cards Kreditkarten
VISA - Eurocard - MasterCard

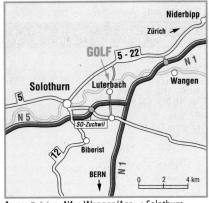

Access Zufahrt : N1→ Wangen/Aar, → Solothurn, → Koppingen, Aarbrücke, turn left → Golf
Map 1 on page 1286 Karte 1 Seite 1286

GOLF COURSE / PLATZ — 13/20

Site	Lage	
Maintenance	Instandhaltung	
Architect	Architekt	Ruzzo Reuss
Type	Typ	open country
Relief	Begehbarkeit	
Water in play	Platz mit Wasser	
Exp. to wind	Wind ausgesetzt	
Trees in play	Platz mit Bäumen	

Scorecard Scorekarte	Chp. Chp.	Mens Herren	Ladies Damen
Length Länge	6581	6105	5274
Par	73	73	73

Advised golfing ability 0 12 24 36
Empfohlene Spielstärke
Hcp required Min. Handicap 30

CLUB HOUSE & AMENITIES / KLUBHAUS UND NEBENGEBÄUDE — 6/10

Pro shop	Pro shop	
Driving range	Übungsplatz	
Sheltered	überdacht	16 mats
On grass	auf Rasen	yes
Putting-green	Putting-grün	yes
Pitching-green	Pitching-grün	yes

HOTEL FACILITIES / HOTEL BESCHREIBUNG — 6/10

HOTELS HOTELS
Krone — Solothurn
42 rooms, D 195 CHF — 10 km
Tel (41) 032 - 622 44 12
Fax (41) 032 - 622 37 24

Astoria — Solothurn
40 rooms, D 130 CHF — 10 km
Tel (41) 032 - 622 75 71
Fax (41) 032 - 623 68 57

RESTAURANTS RESTAURANT
Zunfthaus zu Wirthen — Solothurn
Tel (41) 032 - 623 33 44 — 10 km

Chutz — Langendorf
Tel (41) 032 - 622 34 71 — 8 km

1310

ZUMIKON

Die ersten neun Loch in Zumikon sind recht flach, aber sehr lang. Der Weg zurück ist mit einigen Schräglagen und Hängen wesentlich coupierter und kann Senioren Mühe bereiten. Dieser Nachteil wird aber durch kürzere Spielbahnen kompensiert. Die gut plazierten Hindernisse stören vor allem gute Golfer, beeinflussen aber das Spiel höherer Handicaps wenig. Zumikon ist ein guter Test des golferischen Könnens, lässt aber in seinem durchschnittlichen Design das gewisse Etwas an Originalität und den perfekten Unterhalt der Greens vermissen. Trotzdem langweilt sich hier niemand, und das ist für Golfer jedes Handicaps ein wichtiger Punkt.

The front nine at Zumikon are pretty flat but very long. The back nine are much hillier with a number of dangerous slopes in all directions, often a problem for senior players but one that is offset by the shorter length of holes. The hazards are generally well sited and tend to bother the better players more than the rest. Reassuring for the latter, at least. Zumikon is a very honourable test of golf, but we were sorry to see a little lack of originality and stamina in a very reasonable layout, and greens in a fair condition only, still putting this course a little way behind the best courses in Switzerland. However, there is never a dull moment here, and golfers of all levels will appreciate that.

Golf & Country Club Zurich — 1929
CH - 8126 ZUMIKON

Office	Sekretariat	(41) 01 - 918 00 50
Pro shop	Pro shop	(41) 01 - 918 00 52
Fax	Fax	(41) 01 - 918 00 39
Situation	Lage	

Zurich (pop. 365 043), 7 km

Annual closure	Jährliche Schliessung	31/10 → 1/4
Weekly closure	Wöchentliche Schliessung	no

Monday (Montag), Restaurant closed

Fees main season
Preisliste hochsaison 18 holes

	Week days Woche	We/Bank holidays We/Feiertag
Individual Individuell	100 CHF	*
Couple Ehepaar	200 CHF	*

* Week ends: members only

Caddy	Caddy	on request
Electric Trolley	Elektrokarren	20 CHF
Buggy	Elektrischer Wagen	no
Clubs	Leihschläger	20 CHF

Credit cards Kreditkarten — no

Access Zufahrt : Zürich → Forch, Zumikon → Dorfplatz → Strubenacher Strasse
Map 1 on page 1287 Karte 1 Seite 1287

GOLF COURSE
PLATZ — 15/20

Site	Lage	
Maintenance	Instandhaltung	
Architect	Architekt	Donald Harradine
Type	Typ	parkland
Relief	Begehbarkeit	
Water in play	Platz mit Wasser	
Exp. to wind	Wind ausgesetzt	
Trees in play	Platz mit Bäumen	

Scorecard Scorekarte	Chp. Chp.	Mens Herren	Ladies Damen
Length Länge	6360	5860	5155
Par	72	72	72

Advised golfing ability Empfohlene Spielstärke	0	12	24	36

Hcp required   Min. Handicap   30

CLUB HOUSE & AMENITIES
KLUBHAUS UND NEBENGEBÄUDE — 7/10

Pro shop	Pro shop	
Driving range	Übungsplatz	
Sheltered	überdacht	4 mats
On grass	auf Rasen	yes
Putting-green	Putting-grün	yes
Pitching-green	Pitching-grün	yes

HOTEL FACILITIES
HOTEL BESCHREIBUNG — 6/10

HOTELS HOTELS

Wassberg — Forch
17 rooms, D 240 CHF — 6 km
Tel (41) 01 - 980 43 00
Fax (41) 01 - 980 43 03

Ermitage am See — Küsnacht
26 rooms, D 244 CHF — 5 km
Tel (41) 01 - 910 52 22
Fax (41) 01 - 910 52 44

RESTAURANTS RESTAURANT

Golf & Country Club — Zumikon
Tel (41) 01 - 918 00 51

Petersmann's Kunststuben — Küsnacht
Tel (41) 01 - 910 07 15 — 2 km

1311

Autres pays

The Millennium Guide

Golf in Europe is in the throes of becoming a universal sport. To the east, the Czech Republic has a golfing heritage rich enough to produce several excellent courses for more than 5,000 local players, and even Russia has now one superb course. Further south, golf is an important asset for tourism and courses are beginning to spring up, catering primarily to foreign golfers as there are still not enough locals to fill the fairways. Turkey is one country which has systematically been building some good courses in the seaside areas of Antalya and Belek. In the years ahead, we can expect to see a big increase in the number of golf-playing countries.

En Europe, le golf devient un sport universel. A l'est, la République Tchèque possède un passé golfique assez riche pour avoir plusieurs bons parcours et 5.000 joueurs environ. Même la Russie possède aujourd'hui un superbe parcours. Plus au sud, le golf est un important atout pour le tourisme et les parcours commencent à sortir de terre, pour l'instant davantage destinés aux joueurs étrangers avides de soleil qu'aux joueurs locaux. La Turquie est l'un de ces pays à avoir systématiquement construit de bons parcours autour des importantes stations balnéaires de Belek et Antalya. Au cours des années à venir, on peut s'attendre à voir s'étendre encore le nombre de pays golfiques, et de parcours de qualité.

1312

Karlovy Vary was one of the great spas much visited by the aristocracy for several centuries. Goethe and Beethoven were some of the more prestigious visitors who came to treat their ills and, so they would have us believe, their love stories as well. There is no denying that the superb romantic valley in which the town is set is well worth a stay. As in many spas, golf was played here from 1904, but a new layout was designed in 1932 before being altered and improved upon thanks to the endeavours of the Golf Resort Company, two of whose shareholders are the impressive Grandhotel Pupp and the extravagant Hotel Imperial. This rather hilly course (but never too much of a climb) is of a very respectable length for players of all abilities without any insurmountable hazards. As water is not often in play, trees and bunkers are the main obstacles likely to shatter your golfing ambitions. This classic layout is well maintained and boasts some unique touches of natural romanticism and Slav charm that are simply irresistible.

Karlovy Vary a été autrefois l'une des grandes stations thermales de l'aristocratie. Goethe et Beethoven en ont été parmi les plus prestigieux visiteurs, pour soigner leurs maux, et pour quelques aventures discrètes, croit-on. Il faut dire que la superbe vallée romantique qui en est le cadre mérite un séjour. Comme dans beaucoup de villes d'eau, le golf a été pratiqué très tôt, dès 1904, mais un nouveau tracé en a été fait en 1932, modifié et amélioré depuis, grâce aux efforts de la Golf Resort Company dont deux des actionnaires sont l'impressionnant Grandhotel Pupp et l'extravagant Hotel Imperial. Le parcours assez accidenté, mais sans exagération, est d'une longueur très respectable pour tous les niveaux, mais sans que personne n'ait d'obstacle insurmontable à franchir. L'eau étant assez peu en jeu (sauf au 4), ce sont essentiellement les arbres et bunkers qui peuvent contrer vos ambitions. Ce tracé classique est bien entretenu, avec ces touches uniques de romantisme naturel et de charme slave que l'on ne peut qu'aimer.

Golf Resort Karlovy Vary a.s.   1933

Prazska 125
CZ - 360 01 Karlovy Vary

Office	Secrétariat	(420) 017 333 1101
Pro shop	Pro-shop	(420) 017 333 1000
Fax	Fax	(420) 017 333 1101
Situation	Situation	

Karlovy Vary, 6 km - Praha (pop. 1 203 230), 120 km

Annual closure	Fermeture annuelle	no
Weekly closure	Fermeture hebdomadaire	no
Fees main season	Tarifs haute saison	18 holes

	Week days Semaine	We/Bank holidays We/Férié
Individual Individuel	1100 CZK	1300 CZK
Couple Couple	2200 CZK	2600 CZK

Special fees for Grandhotel Pupp guests

Caddy	Caddy	500 CZK
Electric Trolley	Chariot électrique	400 CZK
Buggy	Voiturette	200 CZK/hour
Clubs	Clubs	800 CZK

Credit cards Cartes de crédit
VISA - Eurocard - MasterCard - AMEX - DC - JCB

Access Accès : Praha, E48 → Karlovy Vary.
700 m before Olsová Vrata and airport,
turn right → Golf.
Map 4 on page 367 Carte 4 Page 367

GOLF COURSE PARCOURS   15/20

Site	Site	
Maintenance	Entretien	
Architect	Architecte	C. Noskowski
Type	Type	parkland, forest
Relief	Relief	
Water in play	Eau en jeu	
Exp. to wind	Exposé au vent	
Trees in play	Arbres en jeu	

Scorecard Carte de score	Chp. Chp.	Mens Mess.	Ladies Da.
Length Long.	6226	5799	5475
Par	72	72	72

Advised golfing ability
Niveau de jeu recommandé   0   12   24   36

Hcp required   Handicap exigé   36

CLUB HOUSE & AMENITIES CLUB HOUSE ET ANNEXES   7/10

Pro shop	Pro-shop	
Driving range	Practice	
Sheltered	couvert	8 mats
On grass	sur herbe	yes
Putting-green	putting-green	yes
Pitching-green	pitching green	yes

HOTEL FACILITIES ENVIRONNEMENT HOTELIER   6/10

HOTELS HÔTELS
Grandhotel Pupp   Karlovy Vary
110 rooms, D 5500 CZK   4 km
Tel (420) 17 310 9111
Fax (420) 17 322 4032

RESTAURANTS RESTAURANTS

Golf restaurant   Golf club
Tel (420) 17 333 1101   on site

Other restaurants   Karlovy Vary 4 km

1313

The former Marienbad was the other major spa town frequented by the aristocracy of all nationalities and all the countries of Europe up until World War I. The number of churches of different Christian denominations tell the full story. At an altitude of 600 metres, the nobility and the «grand bourgeoisie» would come here to treat any number of affections. Today, the town is enjoying a new lease of life and golfers can come and «treat» their swing in the crisp air and deep forests of Bohemia on what is the country's oldest course. There is a chance that you might find the design of this grand parkland layout a little outmoded, but it oozes inimitable charm and presents a tougher challenge than you might expect, especially from the back tees and on some of the long par 4s like holes N° 6, 11 or 18. Water hazards are infrequent but dangerous every time, while two or three complex greens will help add to your score. With this said, reasonable players will make hay before resting their weary bones in the tastefully restored Belle Epoque style club-house.

L'ancienne Marienbad est l'autre grande station thermale de l'aristocratie de tous pays d'Europe jusqu'avant la Première Guerre Mondiale, comme en témoignent les églises de tous les cultes chrétiens. A 600 mètres d'altitude, la noblesse et la grande bourgeoisie venaient y soigner leurs affections. La ville retrouve aujourd'hui une nouvelle jeunesse, et les golfeurs pourront y soigner leurs swings dans l'air vif et les forêts profondes de Bohême sur le plus ancien parcours du pays. Certes, on pourra trouver l'architecture de golf de ce grand parc un peu surannée, mais il y a ici un charme inimitable, et un challenge plus difficile qu'on pourrait s'y attendre, en tout cas des départs arrière, en particulier sur de longs par 4 comme le 6, le 11 ou le 18. Les obstacles d'eau ne sont pas nombreux, mais tous dangereux, et deux ou trois greens un peu complexes contribuent aussi à alourdir les scores. Cependant, les joueurs raisonnables tireront sans mal leur épingle du jeu, avant de se reposer dans un Club house Belle Epoque restauré avec goût.

Golf Club Mariánské Lázne — 1905

P.O. Box 267
CZ - 353 01 MARIANSKE LAZNE

Office	Secrétariat	(420) 0165 624 300
Pro shop	Pro-shop	(420) 0165 620 251
Fax	Fax	(420) 0165 625 195
Situation	Situation	

Mariánské Lázne, 2 km
Praha (pop. 1 203 230), 160 km

Annual closure	Fermeture annuelle	1/11→1/4
Weekly closure	Fermeture hebdomadaire	no

Fees main season
Tarifs haute saison full day

	Week days Semaine	We/Bank holidays We/Férié
Individual Individuel	1100 CZK	1100 CZK
Couple Couple	2200 CZK	2200 CZK
Caddy	Caddy	on request/400 CZK
Electric Trolley	Chariot électrique	no
Buggy	Voiturette	500 CZK /18 holes
Clubs	Clubs	400 CZK

Credit cards Cartes de crédit
VISA - Eurocard - MasterCard - AMEX

GOLF COURSE / PARCOURS — 14/20

Site	Site	
Maintenance	Entretien	
Architect	Architecte	Unknown
Type	Type	parkland
Relief	Relief	
Water in play	Eau en jeu	
Exp. to wind	Exposé au vent	
Trees in play	Arbres en jeu	

Scorecard Carte de score	Chp. Chp.	Mens Mess.	Ladies Da.
Length Long.	6178	5953	5279
Par	72	72	72

Advised golfing ability Niveau de jeu recommandé		0 12 24 36
Hcp required	Handicap exigé	36

CLUB HOUSE & AMENITIES / CLUB HOUSE ET ANNEXES — 7/10

Pro shop	Pro-shop	
Driving range	Practice	
Sheltered	couvert	not yet
On grass	sur herbe	yes
Putting-green	putting-green	yes
Pitching-green	pitching green	yes

HOTEL FACILITIES / ENVIRONNEMENT HOTELIER — 6/10

HOTELS HÔTELS

Cristal Palace — Mariánské Lázne 4 km
94 rooms, D 3500 CZK
Tel (420) 165 615 111
Fax (420) 165 5012

Hotel Berlin — Mariánské Lázne 6 km
30 rooms, D 2500 CZK
Tel (420) 165 620 117
Fax (420) 165 620 118

Cesky Dur — Mariánské Lázne 1 km
10 rooms, D 1200 CZK
Tel (420) 165 622 490
Fax (420) 165 622 490

1314

Access Accès : Turn off the main road to Karlovy Vary opposite Hotel Golf
Map 4 on page 367 Carte 4 Page 367

Coming from Prague, simply treat yourself to a stop-off on the Plzen road (Plzen is a beer centre and a 1 hour drive) to play this course on the edge of the superb, tree-covered valley of Berounka, at the foot of Hrad Karlstejn, the castle built by emperor Charles IV and magnificently restored in the 19th century. This very recent course has very quickly made a name for itself thanks to the Chemapol Trophy, appealing to golfers not only for the site but also for being a very intelligent layout. It is also very modern in its careful bunkering (huge fairway traps), the bringing into play of natural contours and the variety of holes. Water comes into play only a few holes, but the profile of the many dog-legs, one or two very elevated greens and the variety of shots you need to shape make this a rather tricky challenge that golfers will only start to master after several outings. The architects set out to achieve the eternal Trent Jones project of «easy bogey, tough birdie», and they succeeded. Even shooting par is no easy feat.

Depuis Prague, offrez-vous une halte sur la route de Plzen, capitale de la bière (1 heure de route), pour jouer ce parcours au bord de la superbe vallée voisée de la Berounka, à l'ombre de Hrad Karlstejn, la château construit par l'empereur Charles IV et magnifiquement restauré au XIXè siècle. Ce golf très récent s'est tout de suite fait connaître grâce au Chemapol Trophy, il a séduit non seulement par son site, mais aussi son parcours très intelligent. Il est aussi très moderne par son bunkering soigné (vastes bunkers de fairway), la mise en jeu des reliefs, la variété des trous. L'eau n'est vraiment en jeu que sur quelques trous, mais le profil des nombreux doglegs, un ou deux- greens très en hauteur, la variété des coups à jouer en font un challenge assez délicat, que l'on ne maîtrise pas en une seule fois. Les architectes ont voulu réaliser l'éternel projet de Trent Jones «bogey facile, birdie difficile». C'est réussi : même le par n'est pas simple.

Praha Karlstejn Golf Klub 1993

P.O. Box 23
CZ - 267 27 LITEN

Office	Secrétariat	(420) 0311 684 716
Pro shop	Pro-shop	(420) 0311 684 716
Fax	Fax	(420) 0311 684 717
Situation	Situation	

Praha (pop. 1 203 230), 30 km

Annual closure	Fermeture annuelle	1/12 → 31/3
Weekly closure	Fermeture hebdomadaire	no

Fees main season
Tarifs haute saison full day

	Week days Semaine	We/Bank holidays We/Férié
Individual Individuel	1000 CZK	1800 CZK
Couple Couple	2000 CZK	3600 CZK

under 18 years old: – 50%
afternoon GF: 500/900 CZK

Caddy	Caddy	no
Electric Trolley	Chariot électrique	no
Buggy	Voiturette	1 000 CZK
Clubs	Clubs	300/500 CZK

Credit cards Cartes de crédit VISA - Eurocard - MasterCard

Access Accès : Praha, D5 → Plzen. Exit → Lodenice, Buhovice, Morina, Karlstejn.

GOLF COURSE
PARCOURS
15/20

Site	Site	
Maintenance	Entretien	
Architect	Architecte	Les Furber Jim Eremko
Type	Type	forest, hilly
Relief	Relief	
Water in play	Eau en jeu	
Exp. to wind	Exposé au vent	
Trees in play	Arbres en play	

Scorecard Carte de score	Chp. Chp.	Mens Mess.	Ladies Da.
Length Long.	6361	5880	4876
Par	72	72	72

Advised golfing ability		0	12	24	36
Niveau de jeu recommandé					
Hcp required	Handicap exigé	36			

CLUB HOUSE & AMENITIES
CLUB HOUSE ET ANNEXES
6/10

Pro shop	Pro-shop	
Driving range	Practice	
Sheltered	couvert	yes
On grass	sur herbe	yes
Putting-green	putting-green	yes
Pitching-green	pitching green	yes

HOTEL FACILITIES
ENVIRONNEMENT HOTELIER
7/10

HOTELS HOTELS

Hoffmeister
38 rooms, D 8 800 CZK
Tel (420) 02 5731 0942 - Fax (420) 02 5732 0906
Praha
30 km

Grand Hotel Bohemia
78 rooms, D 13 500 CZK
Tel (420) 02 2480 4111 - Fax (420) 02 232 9545
Praha
30 km

U Krale Karla
19 rooms, D 6 400 CZK
Tel (420) 02 538 805 - Fax (420) 02 538 811
Praha
30 km

RESTAURANTS RESTAURANTS

U Modre Kachnicky
Tel (420) 02 5732 0308
Praha
30 km

Hostinec U Kalicha
Tel (420) 02 291 945
Praha
30 km

1315

Russia had to wake up to golf one day or another, and although for the time being the majority of golfers are Western businessmen or diplomats, it is surely only a matter of time before we see a Russian champion. At least they have a great course to play on. Built over a 120 hectare estate, this layout also boasts a hotel and modern houses that reminded us of the little dachas in Doctor Zhivago. This is a Trent Jones Jnr. course through and through, looking like a little corner of America. But failing a Russian style of golf architecture, the landscape of birch-trees and lakes adds considerable local colour. Actually, through its strategic intelligence, the loving care that went into every detail of the design, the layout and balance of course difficulties and for sheer golfing excellence, this course is a must. With a number of different tee-boxes, it is also playable by everyone. The standard of accommodation makes this a top-notch week-end golf-course, albeit not necessarily within the means of your average «Moujik» on the street.

La Russie devait s'éveiller un jour au golf... et même si les diplomates et businessmen occidentaux sont les plus pratiquants, il y aura sans doute un jour de grands joueurs russes. Au moins ont-ils ici un grand parcours ! Construit à l'intérieur d'un domaine de 120 hectares, il s'accompagne d'un hôtel et de maisons modernes réminiscentes des «datchas» du Docteur Jivago. Ce parcours de Trent Jones Jr est en droite ligne de toutes ses créations, comme un petit coin d'Amérique. Néanmoins, à défaut d'une style «russe» d'architecture de golf, le paysage de bouleaux et de lacs est là pour donner la couleur locale. Par son intellignece stratégique, le soin apporté au dessin des moindres détails, la disposition et l'équilibre des difficultés, ce parcours est un «must», à la portée de tous (ou presque) par l'étagement des départs. La qualité du «réceptif» en fait un lieu de week-end de grande qualité... mais pas à la portée du «moujik» moyen.

Moscow Country Club — 1993

Nakhabino, Krasnogorsky District
MOSCOW REGION 143 430 RUSSIA

Office	Secrétariat	(7) 095 - 926 5911
Pro shop	Pro-shop	(7) 095 - 926 5910
Fax	Fax	(7) 095 - 926 5921
Situation	Situation	

Moscow, 15 km

Annual closure	Fermeture annuelle	no
Weekly closure	Fermeture hebdomadaire	monday (lundi)

Fees main season Tarifs haute saison — 18 holes

	Week days Semaine	We/Bank holidays We/Férié
Individual Individuel	US$ 50	US$ 100
Couple Couple	US$ 100	US$ 200

Caddy	Caddy	on request/US$ 15
Electric Trolley	Chariot électrique	no
Buggy	Voiturette	no
Clubs	Clubs	US$ 25

Credit cards Cartes de crédit
VISA - MasterCard - JCB

1316

Access Accès : Moscow, Volokolamskoye Shosde.
Gai Station, turn right → Krasnogorsk
and Novo-Nikolskoye. Gai Station, right turn
at sign «Moscow Country Club, 2.6 km»

GOLF COURSE / PARCOURS — 17/20

Site	Site	
Maintenance	Entretien	
Architect	Architecte	R. Trent Jones Jr
Type	Type	forest
Relief	Relief	
Water in play	Eau en jeu	
Exp. to wind	Exposé au vent	
Trees in play	Arbres en jeu	

Scorecard Carte de score	Chp. Chp.	Mens Mess.	Ladies Da.
Length Long.	6390	5953	5248
Par	72	72	72

Advised golfing ability — 0 12 24 36
Niveau de jeu recommandé
Hcp required Handicap exigé — 36

CLUB HOUSE & AMENITIES / CLUB HOUSE ET ANNEXES — 7/10

Pro shop	Pro-shop	
Driving range	Practice	
Sheltered	couvert	10 mats
On grass	sur herbe	yes
Putting-green	putting-green	yes
Pitching-green	pitching green	yes

HOTEL FACILITIES / ENVIRONNEMENT HOTELIER — 6/10

HOTELS HÔTELS
Le Meridien — Nakhabino
130 rooms, D US$ 325 — on site
Tel (7) 095 - 926 5911
Fax (7) 095 - 926 5921

Golf club restaurant — Nakhabino on site

As everywhere else in this region, this course is rather flat and the very many trees bring some welcome shade when you hit your ball slightly off-target. There is little tall rough to speak of, so getting back on the «short stuff» is no real problem. Only slightly trickier are some huge fairway bunkers, which are more in play for the mid-handicapper than they are for the better player. You might even find them a little too large, serving no purpose other than visual appeal. The green-side bunkers are no big hazard either, a reassuring thought when approaching the greens with bump and run shots... hit deliberately or otherwise. We couldn't help thinking that the design of Michel Gayon might have made more of this site, but the course is still very pleasant to play during the holidays for players of all abilities. Here, visitors will find excellent practice facilities, a few practice holes, a beach hotel and beach to ensure a holiday without too much shade (see above!). One last word: the fairways have been entirely re-seeded with Bermuda grass.

Comme dans toute cette région, le parcours de Gloria est assez plat, et de nombreux arbres apportent des ombrages bienvenus... quand on s'égare un peu. Mais comme il y a peu de haut rough, on s'en dégage facilement. Sans doute plus que de quelques immenses bunkers, davantage en jeu pour les joueurs moyens que pour les bons. Ils sont peut-être beaucoup trop grands, sans nécessité autre qu'esthétique. Les bunkers de green ne sont pas très dangereux non plus, ce qui rassure quand on approche les greens en faisant rouler la balle... volontairement ou non. L'architecte Michel Gayon aurait pu tirer meilleur parti d'un tel site, mais ce parcours reste plaisant à jouer en vacances, pour tous les niveaux. De plus, on trouve ici de très bonnes installations d'entraînement, l'hôtel sur place et la plage garantissent un séjour sans ombres. On notera enfin que les fairways ont été entièrement réensemencés en bermuda.

Gloria Golf Resort 1997

Acisu Mevkii, Belek Mail Box 27 Serik
TR - BELEK ANTALYA (Türkiye)

Office	Secrétariat	(90) 242 - 715 1520
Pro shop	Pro-shop	(90) 242 - 715 1520
Fax	Fax	(90) 242 - 715 1525
Situation		

Antalya, 45 km

Annual closure	Fermeture annuelle	no
Weekly closure	Fermeture hebdomadaire	no

Fees main season
Tarifs haute saison 18 holes

	Week days Semaine	We/Bank holidays We/Férié
Individual Individuel	50 US$	50 US$
Couple Couple	100 US$	100 US$

Seasonal tariff (ask for details)

Caddy	Caddy	15 US$
Electric Trolley	Chariot électrique	no
Buggy	Voiturette	25 US$
Clubs	Clubs	15/20 US$

Credit cards Cartes de crédit
VISA - Eurocard - MasterCard - AMEX

Access Accès : Antalya → Belek → Gloria Golf Resort

GOLF COURSE / PARCOURS 13/20

Site	Site	▬▬▬▬▭
Maintenance	Entretien	▬▬▬▬▭
Architect	Architecte	Michel Gayon
Type	Type	forest, parkland
Relief	Relief	▬▬▭▭▭
Water in play	Eau en jeu	▬▬▬▭▭
Exp. to wind	Exposé au vent	▬▬▬▭▭
Trees in play	Arbres en jeu	▬▬▬▬▭

Scorecard Carte de score	Chp. Chp.	Mens Mess.	Ladies Da.
Length Long.	6288	5900	5200
Par	72	72	72

Advised golfing ability Niveau de jeu recommandé	0 12 24 36
Hcp required Handicap exigé	28 Men/36 Ladies

CLUB HOUSE & AMENITIES / CLUB HOUSE ET ANNEXES 7/10

Pro shop	Pro-shop	▬▬▬▭▭
Driving range	Practice	▬▬▬▭▭
Sheltered	couvert	24 mats
On grass	sur herbe	no
Putting-green	putting-green	yes
Pitching-green	pitching green	yes

HOTEL FACILITIES / ENVIRONNEMENT HOTELIER 7/10

HOTELS HÔTELS
Gloria Golf Resort Hotel Gloria Golf Resort
420 rooms, D 92 US$ on site
Tel (90) 242 - 715 1520
Fax (90) 242 - 715 1525

RESTAURANTS RESTAURANT
4 restaurants Gloria Golf Resort
Tel (90) 242 - 715 1520 on site

1317

The entranceway, gardens and club-house make this a very pleasant and relaxing site. The course was laid out by David Jones and David Feherty, one of the more interesting characters in today's world of professional golf. We might also have expected a little more «fantasy» from Feherty, but while the style is a clever blend of American and British features, the constraints involved in building a course that is playable for everyone might have dampened his enthusiasm in this respect. Although the course is perfectly playable and even fun for the less experienced or reasonable golfer, it is still a tricky proposition for the low handicapper, as the fairways get very narrow when winding between trees. Hazards are well located but always in view, which is probably a good thing because strategy is important here and skills in bending the ball something of a necessity to avoid a few isolated and carefully positioned trees. In a superb setting (to a backdrop of snow-capped mountains), this is a course whose development we will be watching carefully.

L'entrée, les jardins et le Clubhouse rendent cet endroit très agréable et relaxant. Le parcours a été dessiné par David Jones et David Feherty, l'un des personnages les plus intéressants du golf professionnel d'aujourd'hui. On aurait d'ailleurs pu attendre un peu plus de «folie» de sa part, et si le style est un habile mélange de britannique et d'américain, devoir faire un parcours jouable pour tous a peut être restreint leurs élans. Ce parcours est tout à fait jouable et même amusant pour les joueurs peu expérimentés ou raisonnables, mais reste délicat pour les meilleurs joueurs, car il est souvent étroit quand il s'insinue entre les arbres. Les obstacles sont bien placés, mais toujours visibles. Heureusement, car la stratégie est ici importante, et le travail de la balle n'est pas superflu, avec quelques arbres isolés très judicieusement placés. L'environnement (avec les montagnes enneigées en arrière plan) est superbe.

National Golf Club — 1994

Belek Turizm Merkezi
TR - 07500 SERIK ANTALYA (Türkiye)

Office	Secrétariat	(90) 242 - 725 5401
Pro shop	Pro-shop	(90) 242 - 725 5401
Fax	Fax	(90) 242 - 725 5399
Situation	Situation	

Antalya, 35 km

Annual closure	Fermeture annuelle	no
Weekly closure	Fermeture hebdomadaire	no

Fees main season
Tarifs haute saison 18 holes

	Week days Semaine	We/Bank holidays We/Férié
Individual Individuel	55 US$	55 US$
Couple Couple	110 US$	110 US$

US$ or Euros. Seasonal tariffs (ask for details).

Caddy	Caddy	on request
Electric Trolley	Chariot électrique	no
Buggy	Voiturette	25 US$
Clubs	Clubs	10/20 US$

Credit cards Cartes de crédit
VISA - Eurocard - MasterCard

1318

Access Accès : Antalya → Belek.
→ National Golf Club

GOLF COURSE PARCOURS — 15/20

Site	Site	
Maintenance	Entretien	
Architect	Architecte	David Feherty David Jones
Type	Type	forest
Relief	Relief	
Water in play	Eau en jeu	
Exp. to wind	Exposé au vent	
Trees in play	Arbres en jeu	

Scorecard	Chp.	Mens	Ladies
Carte de score	Chp.	Mess.	Da.
Length Long.	6172	5410	4886
Par	72	72	72

Advised golfing ability	0	12	24	36
Niveau de jeu recommandé				
Hcp required	Handicap exigé	28 Men/36 Ladies		

CLUB HOUSE & AMENITIES CLUB HOUSE ET ANNEXES — 7/10

Pro shop	Pro-shop	
Driving range	Practice	
Sheltered	couvert	6 bays
On grass	sur herbe	yes (30 grass tees)
Putting-green	putting-green	yes
Pitching-green	pitching green	yes

HOTEL FACILITIES ENVIRONNEMENT HOTELIER — 7/10

HOTELS HÔTELS
Tatbeach Golf Hotel — Belek/Antalya
260 rooms, Seasonal (ask for tariffs) — 2 km
Tel (90) 242 - 725 4076
Fax (90) 242 - 725 4099

Sirene — Belek/Antalya
Seasonal (ask for tariffs) — 1 km
Tel (90) 242 - 725 4130

Adora Hotel — Belek Antalya
Seasonal (ask for tariffs) — 1 km
Tel (90) 242 - 725 4051
Fax (90) 242 - 725 4359

RESTAURANTS RESTAURANT
In the Hotels — Belek Antalya

NOBILIS

There is every reason to consider this excellent course as the best of the better layouts in the region. When approaching the club-house, you will notice the very pleasant landscape, with holes laid out amidst a pine forest along the river Acisu. Off the tee, the course is relatively easy; the problems for birdie-hunting golfers begin with the second shot and concern the mid-handicapper a little less than the better players. The greens especially are very well defended, particularly by often deep but visible bunkers, which are well shaped in the tradition of Dave Thomas. The secret is simple: place your drive for an easier approach, and work on bending the ball, it will come in useful. You still have all the time and leisure to focus on your game though, as there is little hilly relief to speak of, and there are no blind shots. Water is not too much of a danger here and is rarely frontal (except on hole N° 10). If we also throw in the excellent driving range, it is clear that Nobilis has everything to become a great holiday destination.

La qualité de ce parcours le place en tête des bons golfs de la région. Dès l'arrivée au Club house, le paysage est très plaisant, les trous ayant été tracés au milieu d'une pinède le long de la rivière Acisu. C'est un parcours relativement facile à driver, les difficultés commencent ensuite pour les chasseurs de birdies, mais concernent moins les handicaps moyens. Les greens sont en particulier très bien gardés, notamment par des bunkers souvent profonds mais bien visibles, et bien formés, dans la tradition de l'architecte Dave Thomas. Ainsi, il convient de bien placer les coups de départ pour faciliter l'angle d'approche, et savoir travailler la balle n'est pas un luxe. Mais on a tout le loisir de se concentrer sur le jeu, car les reliefs sont limités, il n'y a pas de coups aveugles. L'eau n'est pas ici trop dangereuse et rarement frontale (sauf au 10). Si l'on ajoute un excellent practice, Nobilis a tout pour devenir une grande destination de vacances.

Nobilis Golf Club — 1998

Acisu Mevkii Belek
TR - BELEK ANTALYA (Türkiye)

Office	Secrétariat	(90) 242 - 715 1987
Pro shop	Pro-shop	(90) 242 - 715 1987
Fax	Fax	(90) 242 - 715 1985
Situation	Situation	

Antalya, 45 km

Annual closure	Fermeture annuelle	no
Weekly closure	Fermeture hebdomadaire	no

Fees main season
Tarifs haute saison 18 holes

	Week days Semaine	We/Bank holidays We/Férié
Individual Individuel	50 US$	50 US$
Couple Couple	100 US$	100 US$

under 18 years: - 50% - Daily Ticket: 75 US$ - Seasonal tariff.

Caddy	Caddy	on request
Electric Trolley	Chariot électrique	no
Buggy	Voiturette	30 US$
Clubs	Clubs	15 US$

Credit cards Cartes de crédit
VISA - Eurocard - MasterCard

Access Accès : Antalya → Belek → Nobilis Golf Club

GOLF COURSE PARCOURS — 17/20

Site	Site	
Maintenance	Entretien	
Architect	Architecte	Dave Thomas
Type	Type	forest, parkland
Relief	Relief	
Water in play	Eau en jeu	
Exp. to wind	Exposé au vent	
Trees in play	Arbres en jeu	

Scorecard Carte de score	Chp. Chp.	Mens Mess.	Ladies Da.
Length Long.	6312	5877	5103
Par	72	72	72

Advised golfing ability
Niveau de jeu recommandé

0   12   24   36

Hcp required Handicap exigé   28 Men/36 Ladies

CLUB HOUSE & AMENITIES
CLUB HOUSE ET ANNEXES — 8/10

Pro shop	Pro-shop	
Driving range	Practice	
Sheltered	couvert	no
On grass	sur herbe	yes
Putting-green	putting-green	yes
Pitching-green	pitching green	yes

1319

HOTEL FACILITIES
ENVIRONNEMENT HOTELIER — 6/10

HOTELS

Nobilis Villas 600 → 1500 US$ (week) Tel (90) 242 - 715 1987 Fax (90) 242 - 715 1985	Nobilis Golf Club on site
Gloria Golf Resort Hotel 420 rooms, D 92 US$ Tel (90) 242 - 715 1520 Fax (90) 242 - 715 1525	Gloria Golf Resort 500 m

RESTAURANTS RESTAURANT

Club house Tel (90) 242 - 715 1987	Nobilis Golf Club on site
4 restaurants Tel (90) 242 - 715 1520	Gloria Golf Resort on site

TAT GOLF BELEK

14 7 7

This 1996 course was designed by Martin Hawtree and is one of his best. It consists of three looping 9-hole layouts that are combinable any way and similar in length. The toughest have to be the Yellow and Red courses, where the water hazards lurk quite impressively. The style of course shifts to good effect between a links and parkland layout, but style is perhaps not the right word for the monumental club-house, which spoils the view over mountains and sea. The most significant hazard is the river Besgösz (and affluents thereof) which is in play on about half the holes. It should be said, though, that water looks more dangerous than it actually is, and the drive landing area are wide open targets. The relatively flat layout is landscaped with a lot of trees and some sometimes thick rough. Bunkers are few and far between but generally well located. Such a measured approach to bringing difficulties into play gives every hope of being able to play to one's handicap without too much trouble.

Ouvert en 1996, ce parcours a été dessiné par Martin Hawtree, dont c'est l'une des meilleures réalisations. Il se compose de trois boucles de 27 trous combinables et de longueurs équivalentes, dont les plus difficiles sont le Yellow et le Red, où les obstacles d'eau peuvent impressionner. De fait, l'esthétique oscille entre le links et le parc, de manière assez heureuse, davantage que le monumental Club house, qui gâche la vue sur les montagnes et la mer. Le plus important obstacle est la rivière Besgösz (et ses affluents) qui viennent en jeu sur la moitié des trous. Cela dit, l'eau est plus présente au regard que vraiment dangereuse, et les zones d'arrivée de drive offrent de larges cibles. De nombreux arbres, un rough parfois épais viennent paysager cet ensemble relativement plat. Les bunkers ne sont pas très nombreux, mais bien placés. Cette mesure dans la mise en jeu des difficultés permet d'espérer jouer son handicap sans trop de problèmes.

TAT International Golf Belek — 1996

Tat Beach Golf Hotel - Üçkum Tepesi Mevkii P.K. 71
TR - BELEK ANTALYA (Türkiye)

Office	Secrétariat	(90) 242 - 725 5303
Pro shop	Pro-shop	(90) 242 - 725 5303
Fax	Fax	(90) 242 - 725 5299
Situation	Situation	

Antalya, 38 km

Annual closure	Fermeture annuelle	no
Weekly closure	Fermeture hebdomadaire	no

Fees main season
Tarifs haute saison 18 holes

	Week days Semaine	We/Bank holidays We/Férié
Individual Individuel	55 US$	55 US$
Couple Couple	110 US$	110 US$

Seasonal tariff (ask for details)

Caddy	Caddy	no
Electric Trolley	Chariot électrique	no
Buggy	Voiturette	25 US$
Clubs	Clubs	15/20 US$

Credit cards Cartes de crédit
VISA - Eurocard - MasterCard

1320

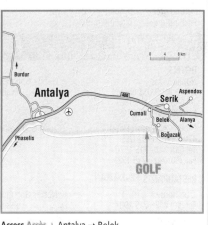

Access Accès : Antalya → Belek
→ Tatbeach Golf Hotel

GOLF COURSE PARCOURS — **14**/20

Site	Site	▪▪▪▪▪▪▢
Maintenance	Entretien	▪▪▪▪▪▪▢
Architect	Architecte	Martin Hawtree
Type	Type	seaside course, forest
Relief	Relief	▪▪▪▢▢
Water in play	Eau en jeu	▪▪▪▢▢
Exp. to wind	Exposé au vent	▪▪▢▢▢
Trees in play	Arbres en jeu	▪▪▪▪▢

Scorecard Carte de score	Chp. Chp.	Mens Mess.	Ladies Da.
Length Long.	6200	5900	5000
Par	72	72	72

Advised golfing ability			0 12 24 36
Niveau de jeu recommandé			▪▪▪▪▪▪▢
Hcp required	Handicap exigé	no	

CLUB HOUSE & AMENITIES
CLUB HOUSE ET ANNEXES — **7**/10

Pro shop	Pro-shop	▪▪▪▪▢
Driving range	Practice	▪▪▪▪▢
Sheltered	couvert	no
On grass	sur herbe	yes (20 grass tees)
Putting-green	putting-green	yes
Pitching-green	pitching green	yes

HOTEL FACILITIES
ENVIRONNEMENT HOTELIER — **7**/10

HOTELS

Tatbeach Golf Hotel — Belek/Antalya
260 rooms, Seasonal (ask for tariffs) — 800 m
Tel (90) 242 - 725 4076
Fax (90) 242 - 725 4099

Sirene — Belek/Antalya
Seasonal (ask for tariffs) — 800 m
Tel (90) 242 - 725 4130

Adora Hotel — Belek Antalya
Seasonal (ask for tariffs) — 600 m
Tel (90) 242 - 725 4051
Fax (90) 242 - 725 4359

RESTAURANTS RESTAURANT

In the Hotels — Belek Antalya

ALPHABETIC ORDER AND CLOSEST AIRPORTS
CLASSEMENT ALPHABÉTIQUE ET AÉROPORTS
CLASIFICACION ALFABETICA Y AEROPUERTOS
ALPHABETISCHE EINTEILUNG UND FLUGHAFEN
I ALFABETISK ORDNING OCH NÄRMASTE FLYGPLATSER
ORDINE ALFABETICO E AEROPORTI PIÙ VICINI

GOLF COURSE	CLASSIFICATIONS				PAGE
PARCOURS	CLASSEMENT				PAGE
RECORRIDOS	LAS CLASIFICACIONES				PÁGINA
GOLFPLATZ	EINTEILUNGEN				ZEITE
GOLFBANER	RANKINGEN				SIDE
PERCORSO	CLASSIFICA				PAGINA
A 6	S	14	7	6	Jönköping, 8 km	1229
Abenberg	D	14	7	6	Nürnberg, 30 km	382
Aberdovey	W	17	7	7	Cardiff, 140 km	799
Ableiges Les Etangs	F	15	6	4	Charles-de-Gaulle, 48 km	213
Aboyne	Sc	14	6	6	Aberdeen, 45 km	698
Adare	I	15	6	7	Shannon, 20 km	836
Ailette (L')	F	15	6	5	Charles-de-Gaulle, 109 km	214
Aisses (Les) Rouge/Blanc	F	16	5	4	Orly, 145 km	215
Aix-les-Bains	F	13	5	7	Chambéry, 13 km	216
Albarella	I	14	8	7	Venezia, 50 km	954
Albi	F	15	6	6	Albi, 4 km - Toulouse, 65 km	217
Alcaidesa	E	14	6	5	Gibraltar, 10 km	1123
Aldeburgh	Eng	13	6	7	Stansted, 140 km	522
Alhaurin	E	14	7	5	Malaga, 30 km	1124
Alloa	Sc	15	7	6	Edinburgh, 50 km	699
Almenara	E	13	8	8	Málaga, 100 km	1125
Almerimar	E	14	6	6	Almería, 48 km	1126
Aloha	E	17	7	7	Malaga, 60 km	1127
Alwoodley (The)	Eng	18	7	7	Leeds, 7 km	523
Alyth	Sc	14	6	6	Edinburgh, 96 km	700
Amarilla	E	15	7	7	Tenerife Sur, 4 km	1128
Ambrosiano	I	14	7	7	Milano, 75 km	955
Amirauté (L')	F	14	7	8	Charles-de-Gaulle, 210 km	218

1321

Amnéville	F	13	6	5	Metz-Nancy, 35 km	219
Amsterdam	N	15	7	7	Amsterdam Schiphol, 10 km	1012
Anderstein	N	14	7	6	Amsterdam-Schiphol, 60 km	1013
Anjou-Champigné	F	13	6	6	Nantes-Atlantique, 123 km	220
Annonay-Gourdan	F	13	6	5	Lyon-Satolas, 90 km	221
Antwerp	B	16	7	7	Antwerpen, 15 km	107
Apremont	F	15	8	6	Charles de Gaulle, 34 km	222
Arcachon	F	13	6	6	Bordeaux, 66 km	223
Arcangues	F	14	7	8	Biarritz-Parme, 3 km	224
Ardglass	UL	14	6	4	Belfast, 65 km	920
Arendal	Nw	15	7	5	Kristiansand, 80 km	1048
Aroeira	P	15	6	6	Lisboa, 11 km	1068
Arras	F	14	6	6	Roissy CdG, 150 km	225
Ashburnham	W	17	6	5	Cardiff, 90 km	800
Ashridge	Eng	16	7	6	Heathrow, 48 km	524
Asolo	I	13	7	7	Venezia, 66 km	956
Asserbo	Da	15	7	6	København, 70 km	133
Atalaya *Old Course*	E	13	6	7	Malaga, 75 km.	1129
Athlone	I	13	6	6	Dublin, 125 km	837
Åtvidaberg	S	16	6	5	Linköping, 35 km	1230
Augerville	F	13	5	4	Orly, 70 km	226
Augsburg	D	15	7	7	München, 90 km	383
Aura	Fi	13	5	5	Helsinki, 180 km	152
Ayr (Belleisle)	Sc	16	5	7	Glasgow, 55 km	701
Baberton	Sc	14	6	8	Edinburgh, 8 km	702
Bad Abbach-Deutenhof	D	15	7	7	München, 90 km	384
Bad Bevensen	D	15	5	7	Hamburg, 100 km	385
Bad Griesbach *Brunnwies*	D	17	9	9	München, 180 km	386
Bad Griesbach-Sagmühle	D	15	9	9	München, 180 km	387
Bad Liebenzell	D	14	7	7	Stuttgart, 40 km	388
Bad Ragaz	Ch	13	7	6	Zürich-Kloten, 100 km	1290
Bad Wörishofen	D	14	6	6	München, 120 km	389
Baden	F	15	6	5	Lorient, 45 km	227
Badgemore Park	Eng	14	7	7	Heathrow, 48 km	525
Bâle-Hagenthal	F	15	7	7	Bâle-Mulhouse, 8 km	228
Ballater	Sc	15	6	7	Dyce, 35 km	703
Ballybunion *Cashen (New Course)*	I	16	7	7	Shannon, 88 km	838
Ballybunion *Old Course*	I	19	7	7	Shannon, 88 km	839
Ballykisteen	I	14	7	6	Shannon, 50 km / Cork, 90 km	840
Ballyliffin *Glashedy Links*	I	17	6	5	Belfast, 160 km	841
Ballyliffin *Old Course*	I	15	6	5	Belfast, 160 km	842
Bamberg	D	15	7	7	Nürnberg, 40 km	390
Banchory	Sc	14	7	7	Aberdeen, 32 km	704
Bangor	UL	14	6	6	Belfast, 40 km	921
Barbaroux	F	17	7	6	Toulon-Hyères, 51 km	229
Barlassina	I	15	8	8	Milano, 35 km	957
Barsebäck	S	18	7	6	Malmö, 50 km	1231
Båstad *Old Course*	S	16	7	7	Halmstad, 30 km	1232
Bath	Eng	16	6	9	Bristol, 20 km	526
Batouwe	N	15	7	3	Amsterdam Schiphol, 80 km	1014
Baule (La) *Rouge*	F	15	7	8	Nantes, 60 km	230
Beau Desert	Eng	16	7	7	Birmingham, 30 km	527
Beaufort	I	14	6	7	Cork, 85 km	843

1322

Belas	P	13	7	6	Lisboa, 15 km	1069
Bélesbat	F	14	7	7	Orly, 40 km	231
Belle-Dune	F	16	6	5	Le Touquet, 25 km	232
Belvoir Park	UL	15	5	6	Belfast, 12 km	922
Bendinat	E	13	6	7	Palma, 15 km	1130
Bercuit	B	13	7	7	Bruxelles (Brussel), 30 km	108
Bergamo - L'Albenza *Blu + Giallo*	I	15	7	8	Bergamo, 18 km	958
Bergisch Land Wuppertal	D	16	7	7	Düsseldorf, 20 km	391
Berkhamsted	Eng	16	7	6	Heathrow, 48 km	528
Berkshire (The) *Blue Course*	Eng	17	8	7	Heathrow, 25 km	529
Berkshire (The) *Red Course*	Eng	17	8	7	Heathrow, 25 km	530
Berlin-Wannsee	D	16	8	9	Berlin, 40 km	392
Berwick-upon-Tweed	Eng	15	6	5	Newcastle, 60 km	531
Besançon	F	13	7	5	Bâle-Mulhouse, 170 km	233
Béthemont	F	14	7	5	Charles-de-Gaulle, 55 km	234
Beuerberg	D	17	7	6	München, 80 km	393
Bhearna	I	14	7	7	Galway, 20 km	844
Biarritz-le-Phare	F	14	6	8	Biarritz-Parme, 3 km	235
Biella - Le Betulle	I	18	7	7	Torino, 75 km	959
Bitburger Land	D	15	7	8	Luxembourg, 55 km	394
Bitche	F	14	6	5	Strasbourg, 80 km	236
Blackmoor	Eng	17	6	5	Heathrow, 65 km	532
Blainroe	I	13	6	6	Dublin, 65 km	845
Blairgowrie *Lansdowne*	Sc	15	8	6	Edinburgh, 90 km	705
Blairgowrie *Rosemount*	Sc	18	8	6	Edinburgh, 90 km	706
Blumisberg	Ch	15	7	6	Genève, 135 km, Zürich, 156 km	1291
Boat of Garten	Sc	14	6	7	Inverness, 45 km	707
Bodensee-Weissensberg	D	16	7	7	Zürich, 130 km / München, 180 km	395
Bogogno	I	17	8	7	Milano, 33 km	960
Bokskogen	S	16	6	7	Malmö, 7 km	1233
Bologna	I	13	7	7	Bologna, 6 km	961
Bolton Old Links	Eng	15	5	7	Manchester, 25 km	533
Bonalba	E	14	6	6	Alicante, 15 km	1131
Bondues *Blanc*	F	16	7	6	Lille-Lesquin, 20 km	237
Bondues *Jaune*	F	15	7	6	Lille-Lesquin, 20 km	238
Bonmont	E	16	7	6	Barcelona, 140 km	1132
Bordes (Les)	F	19	8	6	Orly, 130 km	239
Borre	Nw	16	6	5	Oslo, 75 km	1049
Boulie (La) *La Vallée*	F	15	7	8	Orly, 20 km	240
Bowood (Cornwall)	Eng	16	7	6	Plymouth, 65 km	534
Bowood G&CC	Eng	17	6	6	Bristol, 50 km	535
Brampton	Eng	17	7	6	Glasgow, 160 km	536
Brancepeth Castle	Eng	14	6	5	Newcastle, 20 km	537
Braunschweig	D	14	6	7	Hannover, 75 km	396
Bråviken	S	16	7	7	Norrköping, 5 km	1234
Breitenloo	Ch	13	7	6	Zürich-Kloten, 8 km	1292
Bresse (La)	F	15	6	4	Lyon, 62 km	241
Brest Iroise	F	14	7	6	Brest, 20 km	242
Bretesche (La)	F	15	7	7	Nantes, 61 km	243
Brigode	F	14	7	6	Lille, 15 km	244
Bro-Bålsta	S	17	7	6	Stockholm, 35 km	1235
Broadstone	Eng	17	7	7	Bournemouth, 17 km	538
Broekpolder	N	15	7	6	Rotterdam, 15 km	1015

1323

Brokenhurst Manor	Eng	15	6	6	Southampton, 16 km	539
Brora	Sc	15	7	7	Inverness, 92 km	708
Bruntsfield	Sc	15	8	9	Edinburgh, 10 km	709
Buchanan Castle	Sc	14	6	6	Glasgow, 33 km	710
Buckinghamshire (The)	Eng	17	8	7	Heathrow, 16 km	540
Bude & North Cornwall	Eng	15	6	5	Exeter, 70 km	541
Bundoran	I	13	6	7	Sligo, 45 km/Belfast, 176 km	846
Burnham & Berrow	Eng	18	7	6	Bristol, 38 km	542
Burntisland	Sc	14	6	6	Edinburgh, 27 km	711
Buxtehude	D	16	7	6	Hamburg, 60 km	397
Ca' della Nave	I	13	6	8	Venezia, 16 km	962
Cairndhu	UL	13	6	5	Belfast, 40 km	923
Caldy	Eng	17	7	7	Liverpool, 38 km	543
Callander	Sc	13	6	7	Glasgow, 65 km	712
Camberley Heath	Eng	16	6	6	Heathrow, 50 km	544
Came Down	Eng	15	5	6	Exeter, 53 km	545
Campoamor	E	14	6	6	Alicante, 50 km	1133
Cannes Mandelieu Old Course	F	14	7	8	Nice, 38 km	245
Cannes-Mougins	F	15	7	8	Nice, 18 km	246
Canyamel	E	15	6	6	Palma, 68 km	1134
Cap d'Agde	F	15	6	5	Béziers, 25 km	247
Capdepera	E	15	7	6	Palma, 62 km	1135
Carden Park Cheshire Course	Eng	14	8	8	Manchester, 50 km	546
Carden Park Nicklaus Course	Eng	17	8	8	Manchester, 50 km	547
Cardiff	W	14	6	8	Cardiff, 16 km	801
Cardigan	W	15	6	5	Cardiff, 140 km	802
Cardross	Sc	14	6	5	Glasgow, 25 km	713
Carlisle	Eng	17	7	7	Glasgow, 160 km	548
Carlow	I	16	6	6	Dublin, 100 km	847
Carmarthen	W	15	7	4	Cardiff, 100 km	803
Carn	I	16	5	3	Sligo, 115 km	848
Carnoustie Burnside	Sc	14	5	6	Edinburgh, 100 km	714
Carnoustie Championship	Sc	19	5	6	Edinburgh, 100 km	715
Castelconturbia Giallo + Azzurro	I	18	8	7	Milano, 30 km	963
Castelgandolfo	I	15	7	7	Roma Fiumicino, 53 km	964
Casteljaloux	F	14	6	5	Agen, 70 km	248
Castello di Tolcinasco	I	15	8	8	Milano, 50 km	965
Castillo de Gorraiz	E	17	7	7	Pamplona, 8 km	1136
Castle	I	13	6	8	Dublin, 18 km	849
Castle Hume	UL	13	7	6	Belfast, 100 km	924
Castlerock	UL	16	6	6	Belfast, 80 km	925
Castletown	Eng	18	6	8	Ronaldsway, 4 km	549
Castletroy	I	14	6	6	Shannon, 18 km	850
Celtic Manor Roman Road	W	18	9	7	Cardiff, 30 km	804
Cély	F	15	7	6	Orly, 40 km	249
Cerdaña	E	14	7	7	Barcelona, 150 km	1137
Cervia	I	13	6	9	Bologna, 96 km	966
Chailly (Château de)	F	14	8	6	Dijon-Bourgogne, 66 km	250
Chambon-sur-Lignon (Le)	F	14	5	7	Lyon, 145 km	251
Chamonix	F	15	6	7	Genève-Cointrin, 80 km	252
Champ de Bataille	F	14	6	3	Rouen, 35 km	253
Chantaco	F	14	7	7	Biarritz-Parme, 15 km	254
Chantilly Vineuil	F	18	7	6	Charles-de-Gaulle, 21 km	255

1324

Charleville	I	13	4	6	Cork, 60 km	851
Charmeil	F	16	6	6	Grenoble, 15 km	256
Chart Hills	Eng	18	8	6	Gatwick, 50 km	550
Chaumont-en-Vexin	F	14	6	4	Charles-de-Gaulle, 60 km	257
Cherasco	I	13	7	7	Torino, 85 km	967
Chesterfield	Eng	13	6	7	Manchester, 70 km	551
Cheverny	F	14	7	6	Tours-Saint-Symphorien, 70 km	258
Chiberta	F	16	6	8	Biarritz-Parme, 5 km	259
Citywest	I	13	6	7	Dublin, 20 km	852
Clandeboye *Dufferin Course*	UL	15	6	6	Belfast, 35 km	926
Clitheroe	Eng	17	7	7	Manchester, 60 km	552
Club de Campo	E	16	8	8	Madrid, 20 km	1138
Club zur Vahr (Garlstedt)	D	18	6	5	Bremen, 30 km	398
Cognac	F	13	7	5	Angoulème, 44 km	260
Collingtree Park	Eng	14	8	7	Luton, 45 km	553
Colony Club Gutenhof	A	17	8	7	Wien, 17 km	92
Connemara	I	14	6	6	Galway, 100 km	853
Conwy	W	17	7	8	Manchester, 180 km	805
Cork GC	I	15	3	5	Cork, 10 km	854
Cosmopolitan	I	14	6	7	Pisa, 15 km	968
Costa Brava	E	13	7	7	Barcelona, 100 km	1139
Costa Dorada	E	13	6	6	Barcelona, 100 km	1140
County Louth	I	18	5	6	Dublin, 36 km	855
County Sligo	I	17	4	3	Sligo, 15 km	856
County Tipperary	I	15	7	5	Cork, 90 km / Dublin, 156 km	857
Courson *Lilas/Orange*	F	15	7	3	Orly, 20 km	261
Courson *Vert/Noir*	F	16	7	3	Orly, 20 km	262
Courtown	I	14	5	5	Dublin, 105 km	858
Coxmoor	Eng	15	6	6	East Midlands, 40 km	554
Crail	Sc	15	6	6	Edinburgh, 85 km	716
Crans-sur-Sierre	Ch	14	7	8	Sion, 25 km - Genève, 200 km	1293
Crieff *Ferntower Course*	Sc	15	7	7	Edinburgh, 70 km	717
Cromstrijen	N	16	8	5	Rotterdam, 35 km	1016
Cruden Bay	Sc	18	7	6	Aberdeen, 38 km	718
Cumberwell Park	Eng	17	7	7	Bristol, 40 km	555
Dachstein Tauern / Schladming	A	15	7	5	Salzburg, 80 km	93
Dalmahoy *East Course*	Sc	17	8	8	Edinburgh, 5 km	719
Dartmouth	Eng	16	9	6	Plymouth, 60 km	556
De Pan	N	16	8	7	Amsterdam, 65 km	1017
Delamere Forest	Eng	15	6	7	Manchester, 40 km	557
Denham	Eng	15	7	7	Heathrow, 16 km	558
Dieppe-Pourville	F	14	6	5	Charles-de-Gaulle, 160 km	263
Dinard	F	13	6	7	Rennes 75 km, Dinard 6 km	264
Dingle (Ceann Sibeal)	I	16	6	4	Cork, 160 km	859
Disneyland Paris						
Never Land + Wonderland	F	16	7	8	Orly, 40 km - Roissy, 28 km	265
Divonne	F	14	6	7	Genève-Cointrin, 15 km	266
Domaine Impérial	Ch	18	8	6	Genève-Cointrin, 25 km	1294
Domont-Montmorency	F	13	7	4	Charles-de-Gaulle, 20 km	267
Domtal-Mommenheim	D	14	7	7	Frankfurt, 40 km	399
Donegal (Murvagh)	I	16	5	6	Belfast, 160 km / Sligo, 45 km	860
Donnerskirchen-Neusiedlersee	A	16	6	5	Wien, 35 km	94
Dooks	I	15	5	5	Cork, 115 km	861

1325

Europe

Downfield	Sc	17	6	7	Edinburgh, 80 km	720
Dromoland Castle	I	14	7	7	Shannon, 15 km	862
Drottningholm	S	14	9	6	Stockholm, 75 km	1236
Druids Glen	I	16	9	7	Dublin, 40 km	863
Duddingston	Sc	15	7	9	Edinburgh, 12 km	721
Duff House Royal	Sc	15	6	6	Aberdeen, 75 km	722
Duke's Course St Andrews	Sc	16	7	8	Edinburgh, 80 km	723
Dumfries & County	Sc	15	7	5	Edinburgh/Glasgow, 115 km	724
Dunbar	Sc	16	5	6	Edinburgh, 48 km	725
Dundalk	I	15	6	6	Dublin, 80 km	864
Dunfermline	Sc	15	7	7	Edinburgh, 25 km	726
Düsseldorfer	D	15	7	7	Düsseldorf, 8 km	400
East Devon	Eng	16	6	7	Exeter, 10 km	559
East Renfrewshire	Sc	15	6	8	Glasgow, 20 km	727
East Sussex National *East Course*	Eng	17	8	7	Gatwick, 35 km	560
Edzell	Sc	14	6	3	Aberdeen, 60 km	728
Efteling	N	16	8	5	Eindhoven, 40 km	1018
Eindhoven	N	18	8	6	Eindhoven, 12 km	1019
Ekerum	S	14	7	7	Kalmar, 27 km	1237
El Bosque	E	16	7	4	Valencia, 5 km	1141
El Prat *Amarillo*	E	15	7	6	Barcelona, 7 km	1142
El Prat *Verde*	E	17	7	6	Barcelona, 7 km	1143
El Saler	E	18	7	6	Valencia, 16 km	1144
Elfrather Mühle	D	14	7	7	Düsseldorf, 30 km	401
Elgin	Sc	15	7	6	Aberdeen, 100 km	729
Elie	Sc	15	6	6	Edinburgh, 80 km	730
Elm Park	I	13	7	8	Dublin, 17 km	865
Emporda	E	17	7	6	Barcelona 120 km - Perpignan, 90 km	1145
Engadin	Ch	15	6	6	Zürich, 225 km	1295
Ennetsee-Holzhäusern	Ch	13	7	6	Zürich-Kloten, 45 km	1296
Enniscrone	I	16	7	6	Sligo, 55 km	866
Esbjerg	Da	15	6	5	Billund, 70 km	134
Eschenried	D	14	7	7	München, 35 km	402
Escorpion	E	13	8	4	Valencia-Manises, 10 km	1146
Esery	F	15	7	5	Genève-Cointrin, 16 km	268
Eslöv	S	14	7	5	Malmö, 50 km	1238
Espoo	Fi	16	7	6	Helsinki, 25 km	153
Essener Oefte	D	15	8	7	Düsseldorf, 25 km	403
Estepona	E	14	7	6	Gibraltar, 40 km	1147
Estérel Latitudes	F	16	6	7	Nice, 60 km	269
Estoril	P	13	7	7	Lisboa, 25 km	1070
Etiolles *Les Cerfs*	F	15	6	5	Orly, 15 km	270
Etretat	F	14	6	5	Le Havre-Octeville, 20 km	271
Europasportregion-Zell am See Schmittenhöhe	A	16	7	6	Salzburg, 100 km	95
European (The)	I	18	5	6	Dublin, 90 km	867
European Tour Club (Kungsängen)	S	15	7	6	Stockholm, 30 km	1239
Evian	F	15	7	9	Genève-Cointrin, 52 km	272
Fågelbro	S	15	9	5	Stockholm, 75 km	1240
Fairhaven	Eng	17	7	8	Manchester, 100 km	561
Faithlegg	I	13	7	6	Cork, 135 km	868
Falkenberg	S	14	7	7	Göteborg, 115 km	1241
Falkenstein	D	18	6	7	Hamburg, 30 km	404

1326

Falkirk Tryst	Sc	13	6	6	Edinburgh, 32 km	731
Falmouth	Eng	14	6	7	Exeter, 120 km	562
Falnuee	B	14	7	4	Charleroi, 25 km	109
Falsterbo	S	18	7	5	Malmö, 45 km	1242
Fanø	Da	15	4	7	Esbjerg, 10 km	135
Feldafing	D	16	7	6	München, 80 km	405
Felixstowe Ferry Martello Course	Eng	15	6	6	Stansted, 120 km	563
Ferndown Old Course	Eng	17	7	7	Bournemouth, 7 km	564
Feucherolles	F	15	7	5	Orly, 30 km	273
Filey	Eng	13	5	5	Leeds, 110 km	565
Firenze - Ugolino	I	14	8	9	Firenze, 16 km	969
Fjällbacka	S	15	6	3	Göteborg, 130 km	1243
Flommen	S	16	7	7	Malmö, 45 km	1244
Fontainebleau	F	17	7	7	Orly, 40 km	274
Fontana	A	16	8	5	Wien, 45 km	96
Fontanals	E	18	6	5	Perpignan, 110 km	1148
Fontcaude	F	14	6	6	Montpellier- Fréjorgues, 15 km	275
Fontenailles Blanc	F	14	7	6	Orly, 55 km	276
Fontenelles (Les)	F	14	7	4	Nantes, 70 km	277
Forest of Arden Arden Course	Eng	14	8	8	Birmingham, 6 km	566
Forest Pines Forest + Pines	Eng	17	6	7	Humberside, 11 km	567
Forfar	Sc	14	6	6	Edinburgh, 120 km	732
Formby	Eng	18	7	7	Manchester, 80 km	568
Formby Hall	Eng	14	8	6	Manchester, 80 km	569
Forsbacka	S	16	7	4	Karlstad, 70 km	1245
Forsgården	S	14	6	7	Göteborg, 25 km	1246
Fortrose & Rosemarkie	Sc	16	6	5	Inverness, 40 km	733
Fota Island	I	15	7	6	Cork, 18 km	869
Franciacorta	I	15	7	8	Bergamo, 30 km	971
Frankfurter GC	D	17	7	8	Frankfurt, 5 km	406
Fränkische Schweiz	D	14	7	6	Nürnberg, 45 km	407
Frégate	F	15	7	7	Toulon Hyères, 50 km	278
Frilford Heath Red Course	Eng	14	7	7	Heathrow, 75 km	570
Frösåker	S	16	7	5	Stockholm, 80 km	1247
Fulford	Eng	17	7	8	Leeds, 35 km	571
Furesø	Da	15	7	7	København, 25 km	136
Fürstlicher GC Bad Waldsee	D	17	7	8	Stuttgart, 140 km	408
Fürstliches Hofgut Kolnhausen	D	14	7	6	Frankfurt, 60 km	409
Gainsborough-Karsten Lakes	Eng	14	8	6	Humberside, 40 km	572
Galway Bay	I	14	7	6	Galway, 6 km	870
Galway GC	I	13	6	6	Galway, 12 km	871
Ganton	Eng	19	8	5	Leeds, 60 km	573
Gardagolf	I	14	7	8	Bergamo, 73 km	972
Garlenda	I	14	7	8	Genova, 75 km	973
Garmisch-Partenkirchen	D	14	6	7	München, 110 km	410
Gävle	S	14	6	6	Stockholm, 140 km	1248
Gelpenberg	N	14	4	5	Eelde, 50 km	1020
Gendersteyn	N	15	7	7	Eindhoven, 10 km	1021
Genève	Ch	17	7	8	Genève-Cointrin, 10 km	1297
Girona	E	13	7	5	Barcelona, 120 km	1149
Glamorganshire	W	14	7	8	Cardiff, 13 km	806
Glasson	I	16	7	7	Dublin, 120 km	872
Glen	Sc	14	7	7	Edinburgh, 30 km	734

1327

Glen of the Downs	I	13	4	7	Dublin, 40 km	873
Gleneagles *King's*	Sc	18	9	7	Edinburgh, 70 km	735
Gleneagles *Monarch's*	Sc	17	9	7	Edinburgh, 70 km	736
Gleneagles *Queen's*	Sc	15	9	7	Edinburgh, 70 km	737
Gloria Golf Resort	T	13	7	7	Antalya, 42 km	1317
Goes	N	15	7	6	Rotterdam, 80 km	1022
Gog Magog *Old Course*	Eng	15	7	8	Stansted, 48 km	574
Golden Eagle	P	15	4	4	Lisboa, 55 km	1071
Golf d'Aro	E	15	7	7	Girona, 25 km	1150
Golf del Sur	E	16	7	8	Tenerife Sur, 2 km	1151
Golfresort Haugschlag-Waldviertel	A	16	7	5	Wien, 160 km	97
Golspie	Sc	14	5	4	Inverness, 90 km	738
Göteborg	S	15	6	7	Göteborg, 25 km	1249
Gouverneur (Le) *Le Breuil*	F	16	7	6	Lyon-Satolas, 40 km	279
Gouverneur (Le) *Montaplan*	F	14	7	6	Lyon-Satolas, 40 km	280
Graafschap	N	15	7	6	Amsterdam-Schiphol, 110 km	1023
Granada	E	14	6	5	Granada, 15 km	1152
Grand Ducal de Luxembourg	LU	13	6	7	Luxembourg, 1 km	127
Grande Bastide (La)	F	16	6	6	Nice, 26 km	281
Grande-Motte (La) *Les Flamants Roses*	F	16	6	4	Montpellier-Fréjorgues, 10 km	282
Grange	I	16	5	8	Dublin, 20 km	874
Gränna	S	15	7	5	Jönköping, 40 km	1250
Grantown on Spey	Sc	14	6	7	Inverness, 56 km	739
Granville *Les Dunes*	F	14	4	4	Bréville, 4 km	283
Grasse	F	13	7	6	Nice, 37 km	284
Greenore	I	14	6	5	Dublin, 104 km	875
Grenland	Nw	14	6	6	Oslo, 130 km	1050
Grenoble Bresson	F	17	7	6	Grenoble, 50 km	285
Grevelingenhout	N	14	7	4	Rotterdam, 65 km	1024
Gruyère (La)	Ch	14	7	6	Genève, 120 km	1298
Guadalhorce	E	14	7	6	Málaga, 4 km	1153
Guadalmina *Sur*	E	14	7	7	Málaga, 64 km	1154
Gujan-Mestras	F	15	7	6	Bordeaux-Mérignac, 50 km	286
Gullane *No 1*	Sc	17	8	7	Edinburgh, 50 km	740
Gullbringa	S	13	7	6	Göteborg, 45 km	1251
Gut Altentann	A	18	8	7	Salzburg, 17 km	98
Gut Kaden *Platz B + Platz C*	D	15	7	6	Hamburg, 20 km	411
Gut Lärchenhof	D	17	9	7	Köln-Bonn, 35 km	412
Gut Ludwigsberg	D	15	6	6	München, 70 km	413
Gut Thailing	D	16	7	5	München, 65 km	414
Gut Waldhof	D	15	7	5	Hamburg, 27 km	415
Gütersloh (Westfälischer GC)	D	17	7	7	Paderborn, 30 km	416
Haagsche	N	18	7	8	Amsterdam-Schiphol, 45 km	1025
Hadley Wood	Eng	16	7	7	Heathrow, 48 km	575
Haggs Castle	Sc	15	7	9	Glasgow, 9 km	741
Hainaut *Bruyere-Quesnoy-Etangs*	B	15	7	5	St-Ghislain, 10 km	110
Hallamshire	Eng	15	6	8	Leeds, 25 km	576
Halmstad	S	18	8	7	Göteborg, 160 km	1252
Hamburg-Ahrensburg	D	16	8	7	Hamburg, 20 km	417
Hamburg-Holm	D	15	6	6	Hamburg, 15 km	418
Hanau-Wilhelmsbad	D	16	6	6	Frankfurt, 25 km	419
Haninge	S	16	8	6	Stockholm, 70 km	1253
Hankley Common	Eng	16	6	6	Heathrow, 50 km	577

1328

Europe

Hannover	D	16	7	7	Hannover, 12 km	420
Hardelot *Les Pins*	F	16	6	6	Lille, 153 km	287
Harrogate	Eng	15	7	7	Leeds Bradford, 25 km	578
Hauger	Nw	13	7	6	Oslo, 20 km	1051
Haut-Poitou	F	14	6	4	Poitiers-Biart, 25 km	288
Hawkstone Park *Hawkstone*	Eng	15	8	7	Manchester, 65 km	579
Hayling	Eng	16	7	7	Southampton, 45 km	580
Hechingen-Hohenzollern	D	14	6	6	Stuttgart, 50 km	421
Helsinki	Fi	16	7	8	Helsinki, 19 km	154
Henley	Eng	14	6	7	Heathrow, 48 km	581
Herkenbosch	N	16	7	6	Maastricht, 35 km	1026
Hermitage	I	15	6	7	Dublin, 10 km	876
Herreria	E	15	6	6	Madrid, 60 km	1155
Hertfordshire (The)	Eng	15	7	7	Heathrow, 55 km	582
Hetzenhof	D	14	7	6	Stuttgart, 60 km	422
Hever	Eng	14	8	8	Gatwick, 25 km	583
High Post	Eng	15	6	7	Heathrow, 130 km	584
Hillside	Eng	18	7	7	Manchester, 80 km	585
Hilversum	N	16	7	7	Amsterdam-Schiphol, 40 km	1027
Himmerland *New Course*	Da	16	8	6	Aalborg, 50 km	137
Hindhead	Eng	16	7	6	Heathrow, 55 km	586
Hof Trages	D	15	7	5	Frankfurt, 45 km	423
Hoge Kleij	N	15	6	7	Amsterdam-Schiphol, 50 km	1028
Hohenpähl	D	15	7	6	München, 73 km	424
Holstebro	Da	16	6	5	Århus, 100 km	138
Holyhead	W	16	7	5	Manchester, 220 km	807
Hossegor	F	16	6	6	Biarritz-Parme, 28 km	289
Houtrak	N	16	8	8	Amsterdam, 20 km	1029
Hubbelrath	D	17	8	6	Düsseldorf, 18 km	425
Huddersfield (Fixby)	Eng	16	6	7	Leeds Bradford, 25 km	587
Hunstanton	Eng	17	7	6	Stansted, 150 km	588
Huntercombe	Eng	14	6	7	Heathrow, 65 km	589
Huntly	Sc	14	6	6	Aberdeen, 56 km	742
I Roveri	I	17	7	8	Torino, 7 km	974
Iffeldorf	D	16	7	6	München, 70 km	426
Ilkley	Eng	18	7	6	Leeds, 15 km	590
Im Chiemgau	D	15	7	6	München, 100 km	427
Interlaken	Ch	14	6	6	Bern, 59 km	1299
Inverness	Sc	16	7	8	Glasgow, 256 km	743
Ipswich (Purdis Heath)	Eng	16	7	7	Stansted, 84 km	591
Is Molas	I	16	7	8	Cagliari, 35 km	975
Isernhagen	D	15	7	6	Hannover, 17 km	428
Islantilla	E	16	8	8	Faro (Portugal), 69 km	1156
Isle Adam (L')	F	16	7	4	Charles-de-Gaulle, 23 km	290
Isle of Purbeck	Eng	16	7	6	Bournemouth, 16 km	592
Jakobsberg	D	15	7	6	Frankfurt, 100 km	429
Jarama R.A.C.E.	E	13	7	6	Madrid, 20 km	1157
John O'Gaunt	Eng	16	7	6	Luton 28 km/Heathrow, 65 km	593
Jönköping	S	16	7	7	Jönköping, 2 km	1254
Joyenval *Marly*	F	16	8	7	Orly, 32 km	291
Joyenval *Retz*	F	15	8	7	Orly, 32 km	292
K Club	I	17	8	8	Dublin, 44 km	877
Kalmar	S	15	5	8	Kalmar, 5 km	1255

1329

Karlovy Vary	Cz	15	7	6	Karlovy Vary, 1 km	1313
Karlshamn	S	14	6	6	Kristianstad, 60 km	1256
Karlstad	S	15	6	6	Karlstad, 6 km	1257
Keerbergen	B	14	7	6	Brussel (Bruxelles), 15 km	111
Kempferhof (Le)	F	18	8	6	Strasbourg-Entzheim, 14 km	293
Kennemer	N	18	8	8	Amsterdam-Schiphol, 20 km	1030
Kikuoka	LU	16	7	7	Luxembourg, 10 km	128
Kilkea Castle	I	14	6	6	Dublin, 70 km	878
Kilkenny	I	13	7	6	Dublin, 110 km	879
Killarney Killeen Course	I	16	7	8	Cork, 105 km	880
Killarney Mahony's Point	I	15	7	8	Cork, 105 km	881
Killorglin	I	14	6	5	Cork, 126 km	882
Kilmarnock (Barassie)	Sc	17	6	8	Glasgow, 50 km	744
Kingussie	Sc	15	4	5	Inverness, 70 km	745
Kirkistown Castle	UL	15	6	5	Belfast, 55 km	927
Knock	UL	15	7	6	Belfast, 21 km	928
Köln	D	17	6	7	Köln-Bonn, 25 km	430
Königsfeld	D	13	6	6	Stuttgart, 100 km	431
Korsør	Da	14	4	6	Odense, 40 km	139
Krefelder	D	17	7	7	Düsseldorf, 30 km	432
Kristianstad	S	17	7	7	Malmö, 90 km	1258
Kungsbacka	S	15	6	6	Göteborg, 30 km	1259
La Cala Norte	E	17	8	6	Málaga, 35 km	1158
La Cala Sur	E	16	8	6	Málaga, 35 km	1159
La Dehesa	E	14	7	4	Madrid, 35 km	1160
La Duquesa	E	13	7	6	Gibraltar, 30 km	1161
La Manga Norte	E	15	7	7	Alicante, 110 km	1162
La Manga Oeste	E	14	7	7	Alicante, 110 km	1163
La Manga Sur	E	14	7	7	Alicante, 110 km	1164
La Margherita	I	13	7	7	Torino, 61 km	976
La Moraleja La Moraleja 1	E	15	7	8	Madrid, 15 km	1165
La Moraleja La Moraleja 2	E	16	7	8	Madrid, 15 km	1166
La Moye	Eng	17	7	8	Jersey, 3 km	594
La Pinetina	I	13	7	7	Milano, 48 km	977
La Quinta	E	15	8	7	Málaga, 64 km	1167
La Rocca	I	13	6	8	Bologna, 91 km	978
La Sella	E	15	6	5	Valencia, 70 km	1168
La Zagaleta	E	16	7	7	Malaga, 65 km	1169
Lacanau	F	14	6	7	Bordeaux-Mérignac, 55 km	294
Ladybank	Sc	17	7	5	Edinburgh, 56 km	746
Lahinch	I	18	6	6	Shannon, 55 km	883
Lanark	Sc	16	6	5	Edinburgh, 48 km	747
Langland Bay	W	15	7	7	Cardiff, 65 km	808
Largue (La)	F	15	7	4	Bâle-Mulhouse, 35 km	295
Larvik	Nw	17	7	5	Oslo, 120 km	1052
Las Americas	E	16	7	8	Tenerife Sur, 15 km	1170
Las Brisas	E	18	7	7	Málaga, 60 km	1171
Las Palmas	E	14	8	8	Las Palmas, 20 km	1172
Lauro	E	13	7	5	Málaga, 10 km	1173
Lausanne	Ch	16	7	7	Genève-Cointrin, 60 km	1300
Lauswolt	N	14	6	7	Groningen-Eelde, 50 km	1031
Laval-Changé La Chabossière	F	14	7	5	Nantes, 100 km	296
Læsø Seaside	Da	15	7	5	Aalborg, 100 km	140

1330

Le Pavoniere	I	14	8	8	Firenze, 15 km	979
Le Prieuré *Ouest*	F	14	7	5	Roissy, 70 km	297
Le Querce	I	17	8	7	Roma, 95 km	980
Le Robinie	I	16	9	7	Milano, 9 km	981
Lee Valley	I	13	7	6	Cork, 14 km	884
Lerma	E	17	7	4	Madrid, 200 km	1174
Les Bois	Ch	15	6	6	Genève, 140 km	1301
Letham Grange *Old Course*	Sc	15	7	5	Edinburgh, 110 km	748
Leven	Sc	16	6	6	Edinburgh, 56 km	749
Lichtenau-Weickershof	D	15	7	6	Nürnberg, 40 km	433
Lignano	I	14	7	7	Venezia, 108 km	982
Limburg	B	16	7	4	Brussel (Bruxelles), 75 km	112
Limère	F	17	6	5	Orly, 130 km	298
Limerick County	I	15	7	6	Shannon, 40 km	885
Lindau-Bad Schachen	D	15	7	8	Zürich, 130 km/München, 180 km	434
Linden Hall	Eng	17	8	6	Newcastle, 40 km	595
Lindö Park	S	14	8	6	Stockholm, 15 km	1260
Lindrick	Eng	17	6	6	Leeds/Bradford, 40 km	596
Liphook	Eng	16	7	6	Gatwick, 48 km	597
Lisburn	UL	15	7	6	Belfast, 14 km	929
Littlestone	Eng	14	6	5	Gatwick, 110 km	598
Ljunghusen	S	17	6	7	Malmö, 45 km	1261
Llandudno (Maesdu)	W	15	5	8	Manchester, 160 km	809
Llanymynech	W	14	6	4	Manchester, 120 km	810
London Golf Club *International*	Eng	15	9	7	Gatwick, 58 km	599
Longniddry	Sc	14	7	6	Edinburgh, 30 km	750
Los Arqueros	E	14	6	7	Málaga, 65 km	1175
Los Naranjos	E	16	7	7	Málaga, 62 km	1176
Lothianburn	Sc	14	6	8	Edinburgh, 12 km	751
Lübeck-Travemünder	D	15	8	8	Hamburg, 90 km	435
Luffness New	Sc	16	5	6	Edinburgh, 30 km	752
Lugano	Ch	15	7	8	Lugano (Agno), 2 km	1302
Lundin	Sc	16	6	7	Edinburgh, 55 km	753
Lunds Akademiska	S	16	7	5	Malmö, 25 km	1262
Lüneburger Heide	D	16	7	5	Hamburg, 70 km	436
Luttrellstown	I	15	7	7	Dublin, 10 km	886
Luzern	Ch	13	6	7	Zürich, 70 km	1303
Lyckorna	S	13	7	6	Göteborg, 65 km	1263
Lytham Green Drive	Eng	15	7	8	Manchester, 100 km	600
Machrie	Sc	17	7	7	Islay Airport, 5 km	754
Machrihanish	Sc	18	6	4	Glasgow	755
Madeira	P	14	6	5	Funchal, 6 km	1072
Main-Taunus	D	14	7	6	Frankfurt, 20 km	437
Maison Blanche	F	14	7	5	Genève-Cointrin, 10 km	299
Makila Golf Club	F	14	6	8	Biarritz-Parme, 4 km	300
Málaga	E	13	4	6	Málaga, 3 km	1177
Malahide *Red + Blue + Yellow*	I	13	7	8	Dublin, 7 km	887
Malone	UL	13	6	6	Belfast, 16 km	930
Manchester	Eng	16	7	7	Manchester, 20 km	601
Mannings Heath *Waterfall Course*	Eng	14	8	6	Gatwick, 18 km	602
Manor House (Castle Combe)	Eng	15	8	7	Bristol, 45 km	603
Marbella	E	15	7	8	Málaga, 51 km	1178
Marco Simone	I	16	8	8	Roma, 73 km	983

1331

Margara	I	13	7	7	Torino, 109 km	984
Mariánské Lázne	Cz	14	7	6	Praha, 160 km	1314
Märkischer Potsdam	D	14	7	6	Berlin, 45 km	438
Marriott St Pierre Old Course	W	16	8	7	Cardiff, 45 km	811
Masia Bach	E	15	7	6	Barcelona, 40 km	1179
Maspalomas	E	16	7	8	Las Palmas, 30 km	1180
Massereene	UL	14	5	6	Belfast, 7 km	931
Master Master	Fi	15	7	7	Helsinki, 25 km	155
Mazamet-La Barouge	F	13	5	4	Toulouse-Blagnac, 90 km	301
Mediterraneo	E	16	7	6	Valencia-Manises, 70 km	1181
Médoc Les Châteaux	F	18	7	5	Bordeaux-Mérignac, 20 km	302
Médoc Les Vignes	F	15	7	5	Bordeaux-Mérignac, 20 km	303
Memmingen Gut Westerhart	D	14	6	6	München, 140	439
Mendip	Eng	15	5	7	Bristol, 30 km	604
Meon Valley Meon Course	Eng	15	8	7	Southampton, 16 km	605
Mere	Eng	15	7	7	Manchester, 8 km	606
Mijas Los Lagos	E	16	6	7	Málaga, 20 km	1182
Mijas Los Olivos	E	13	6	7	Málaga, 20 km	1183
Milano	I	16	8	9	Milano, 70 km	985
Mittelrheinischer	D	17	7	7	Frankfurt, 100 km	440
Modena	I	14	7	8	Bologna, 40 km	986
Moliets	F	17	6	5	Biarritz-Parme, 50 km	304
Molinetto	I	13	9	8	Milano, 50 km	987
Mölle	S	15	7	5	Malmö, 110 km	1264
Møn	Da	15	7	7	København, 120 km	141
Monifieth	Sc	17	7	7	Edinburgh, 96 km	756
Monkstown	I	15	6	7	Cork, 15 km	888
Mont-Garni	B	13	7	6	Bruxelles, 70 km	113
Montado	P	13	7	6	Lisboa, 50 km	1073
Monte Carlo (Mont Agel)	F	14	6	7	Nice, 20 km	305
Monte Mayor	E	13	5	5	Málaga, 65 km	1184
Montecastillo	E	17	8	7	Jerez, 7 km	1185
Montecchia	I	13	8	7	Venezia, 95 km	988
Montenmedio	E	15	7	7	Jerez, 70 km	1186
Monticello	I	14	8	7	Milano, 30 km	989
Montpellier-Massane	F	16	7	5	Montpellier-Fréjorgues, 14 km	306
Montreux	Ch	13	6	5	Genève-Cointrin, 85 km	1304
Montrose	Sc	17	5	6	Aberdeen, 72 km	757
Moor Allerton	Eng	14	6	7	Leeds Bradford, 15 km	607
Moor Park High Course	Eng	17	8	7	Heathrow, 16 km	608
Moortown	Eng	18	7	7	Leeds, 10 km	609
Moray	Sc	17	5	5	Inverness, 60 km	758
Moscow	Ru	17	7	6	Moscow, 35 km	1316
Motzener See	D	17	8	6	Berlin, 45 km	441
Mount Juliet	I	18	9	8	Dublin, 136 km	889
Mount Wolsley	I	13	6	5	Dublin, 93 km	890
Muirfield	Sc	19	7	6	Edinburgh, 40 km	759
Mülheim	D	13	6	7	Düsseldorf, 12 km	442
Mullingar	I	14	5	5	Dublin, 90 km	891
Mullion	Eng	15	5	5	Exeter, 160 km	610
München-Riedhof	D	16	7	7	München, 90 km	443
Münchner-Strasslach	D	15	6	7	München, 80 km	444
Murcar	Sc	15	6	6	Aberdeen, 12 km	760

1332

Europe

Murrayshall	Sc	14	7	8	Edinburgh, 72 km	761
Nahetal	D	14	8	6	Frankfurt, 90 km	445
Nairn	Sc	19	7	8	Inverness, 9 km	762
Nairn Dunbar	Sc	15	6	7	Inverness, 15 km	763
National L'Albatros	F	18	5	6	Orly, 32 km	307
National GC	T	15	7	7	Antalya, 32 km	1318
Neckartal	D	16	6	7	Stuttgart, 25 km	446
Nefyn & District	W	16	7	5	Manchester, 180 km	812
Neguri	E	17	7	7	Bilbao, 12 km	1187
Nes	Nw	14	6	4	Oslo, 60 km	1053
Neuchâtel	Ch	14	6	7	Genève-Cointrin, 125 km	1305
Neuhof	D	15	7	7	Frankfurt, 18 km	447
New Golf Deauville Rouge/Blanc	F	15	7	8	Charles-de-Gaulle, 220 km	308
Newbury & Crookham	Eng	15	6	7	Heathrow, 80 km	611
Newcastle West	I	13	7	5	Shannon, 55 km	892
Newport	W	15	6	7	Cardiff, 30 km	813
Newtonmore	Sc	14	5	5	Inverness, 72 km	764
Niederbüren	Ch	13	7	7	Zürich-Kloten, 80 km	1306
Nîmes-Campagne	F	16	7	6	Nîmes-Garons, 2 km	309
Nobilis	T	17	8	6	Antalya, 42 km	1319
Noordwijk	N	18	7	8	Amsterdam Schiphol, 35 km	1032
Nordcenter Benz Course	Fi	15	7	5	Helsinki,	156
North Berwick	Sc	18	7	8	Edinburgh, 50 km	765
North Foreland	Eng	13	7	7	Gatwick, 140 km	612
North Hants	Eng	17	7	6	Heathrow, 40 km	613
North Wales (Llandudno)	W	17	6	8	Manchester, 160 km	814
Northop Country Park	W	16	9	6	Manchester, 70 km	815
Notts (Hollinwell)	Eng	18	6	6	Birmingham, 69 km	614
Novo Sancti Petri	E	16	7	7	Jerez, 50 km	1188
Nunspeet North/East	N	15	5	3	Amsterdam-Schiphol, 85 km	1033
Obere Alp	D	14	7	7	Stuttgart, 135 km	448
Oberfranken	D	17	6	5	Nürnberg, 80 km	449
Oberschwaben Bad Waldsee	D	15	6	6	Stuttgart, 140 km	450
Öijared Gamla banan	S	13	7	5	Göteborg, 30 km	1265
Old Head	I	15	7	7	Cork, 20 km	893
Olgiata	I	16	7	6	Roma Fiumicino, 25 km	990
Oliva Nova	E	14	6	7	Valencia, 76 km	1189
Olivar de la Hinojosa	E	13	7	8	Madrid, 1 km	1190
Omaha Beach La Mer/Le Bocage	F	14	7	5	Caen, 40 km	310
Oostende	B	15	7	7	Brussel (Bruxelles), 115 km	114
Oosterhout	N	15	7	7	Amsterdam-Schiphol, 100 km	1034
Opio Valbonne	F	13	6	7	Nice Côte d'Azur, 29 km	311
Orchardleigh	Eng	17	7	7	Bristol, 32 km	615
Örebro	S	18	7	5	Örebro, 15 km	1266
Ormskirk	Eng	14	6	4	Manchester, 48 km	616
Öschberghof	D	15	7	7	Stuttgart, 100 km	451
Oslo	Nw	15	7	9	Oslo, 10 km	1054
Osona Montanya	E	14	7	4	Barcelona, 80 km	1191
Österåker	S	16	6	6	Stockholm, 40 km	1267
Oudenaarde	B	14	6	6	Brussel (Bruxelles), 85 km	115
Ozoir-la-Ferrière Château/Monthéty	F	13	7	5	Charles-de-Gaulle, 47 km	312
Padova	I	14	7	7	Venezia, 40 km	991
Palazzo Arzaga	I	15	8	8	Verona, 45 km	992

1333

Europe

Palheiro	P	13	6	7	Funchal, 16 km	1074
Palingbeek	B	13	6	6	Lille, 60 km	116
Palmares	P	13	7	5	Faro, 75 km	1075
Pals	E	16	7	6	Barcelona, 120 km	1192
Panmure	Sc	17	6	5	Edinburgh, 100 km	766
Pannal	Eng	15	6	7	Leeds, 20 km	617
Panoramica	E	14	6	4	Barcelona, 200 km - Valencia, 150 km	1193
Parco de' Medici	I	13	7	9	Roma Fiumicino, 15 km	993
Paris International	F	16	7	5	Charles-de-Gaulle, 15 km	313
Parkstone	Eng	16	7	8	Bournemouth, 12 km	618
Patriziale Ascona	Ch	15	7	7	Lugano, 40 km	1307
Patshull Park Hotel	Eng	13	8	8	Birmingham, 48 km	619
Pau	F	13	6	8	Pau-Pyrénées, 5 km	314
Pedreña	E	14	6	5	Santander, 7 km	1194
Penha Longa	P	17	6	8	Lisboa, 25 km	1076
Penina	P	14	7	7	Faro, 60 km	1077
Pennard	W	18	6	6	Cardiff, 50 km	816
Peralada	E	16	6	5	Perpignan (France), 60 km	1195
Perranporth	Eng	16	6	6	Plymouth, 80 km	620
Pessac	F	13	7	7	Bordeaux-Mérignac, 10 km	315
Peterhead	Sc	15	5	4	Aberdeen, 43 km	767
Pevero	I	16	8	8	Olbia, 30 km	994
PGA de Catalunya	E	18	7	7	Barcelona, 133 km	1196
Pickala *Seaside Course*	Fi	15	8	5	Helsinki, 60 km	157
Pineda	E	15	7	9	Sevilla, 15 km	1197
Pinheiros Altos	P	14	7	7	Faro, 12 km	1078
Pinnau	D	14	6	6	Hamburg, 25 km	452
Pitlochry	Sc	14	6	7	Edinburgh, 105 km	768
Playa Serena	E	13	6	4	Almería, 33 km	1198
Pleasington	Eng	16	8	6	Manchester, 45 km	621
Pléneuf-Val-André	F	17	7	5	Rennes, 90 km	316
Ploemeur Océan	F	15	7	6	Brest, 130 - Rennes, 150 km	317
Poggio dei Medici	I	16	7	7	Firenze, 28 km	995
Pont Royal	F	16	6	5	Marseille-Marignane, 50 km	318
Porcelaine (La)	F	14	6	4	Limoges-Bellegarde, 15 km	319
Pornic	F	15	6	6	Nantes-Atlantique, 41 km	320
Portal *Championship*	Eng	15	8	7	Manchester, 30 km	622
Porters Park	Eng	15	7	7	Heathrow, 30 km	623
Portmarnock	I	19	7	8	Dublin, 8 km	894
Portmarnock Links	I	17	7	8	Dublin, 8 km	895
Portpatrick (Dunskey)	Sc	15	6	7	Glasgow, 150 km	769
Portsalon	I	16	5	5	Belfast, 160 km	896
Portstewart *Strand Course*	UL	16	7	7	Belfast, 64 km	932
Powerscourt	I	15	7	7	Dublin, 20 km	897
Powfoot	Sc	16	6	4	Glasgow, 130 km	770
Praha Karlstejn	Cz	15	6	7	Praha, 50 km	1315
Praia d'El Rey	P	17	6	5	Lisboa, 75 km	1079
Prestbury	Eng	17	8	7	Manchester, 15 km	624
Prestwick	Sc	18	6	7	Glasgow, 55 km	771
Prestwick St Nicholas	Sc	16	6	7	Glasgow, 55 km	772
Prince's *Himalayas-Shore*	Eng	13	6	4	Gatwick, 145 km	625
Puerta de Hierro *Puerta de Hierro 1*	E	16	8	9	Madrid, 15 km	1199
Puerta de Hierro *Puerta de Hierro 2*	E	18	8	9	Madrid, 15 km	1200

1334

Pula	E	13	6	5	Palma, 63 km	1201
Punta Ala	I	14	7	8	Firenze, 140 km	996
Purmerend	N	16	7	7	Amsterdam-Schiphol, 25 km	1035
Pyle & Kenfig	W	17	7	5	Cardiff, 25 km	817
Quinta da Beloura	P	14	8	7	Lisboa, 26 km	1080
Quinta da Marinha	P	13	7	7	Lisboa, 28 km	1081
Quinta do Lago *B/C*	P	15	7	8	Faro, 10 km	1082
Quinta do Lago *Ria Formosa*	P	15	7	8	Faro, 10 km	1083
Quinta do Peru	P	15	6	5	Lisboa, 46 km	1084
Rapallo	I	13	7	8	Genova, 59 km	997
Raray (Château de) *La Licorne*	F	14	6	4	Roissy, 34 km	321
Rathsallagh	I	15	7	6	Dublin, 80 km	898
Ravenstein	B	17	8	7	Bruxelles, 12 km	117
Real Sociedad Club de Campo	E	18	7	6	Madrid, 20 km	1202
Rebetz	F	16	6	4	Charles-de-Gaulle, 67 km	322
Reichsstadt Bad Windsheim	D	14	6	7	Nürnberg, 50 km	453
Reichswald-Nürnberg	D	16	7	7	Nürnberg, 2 km	454
Reims-Champagne	F	13	7	6	Charles-de-Gaulle, 120 km	323
Rheinhessen	D	14	8	7	Frankfurt, 55 km	455
Rigenée	B	14	7	6	Bruxelles, 35 km	118
Rijk van Nijmegen *Nijmeegse Baan*	N	14	6	5	Eindhoven, 65 km	1036
Rinkven *Red - White*	B	14	6	5	Antwerpen, 30 km	119
Riva dei Tessali	I	13	7	6	Bari, 128 km	998
Riviéra Golf Club	F	13	7	8	Nice Côte d'Azur, 32 km	324
Rochefort-Chisan	F	14	6	4	Orly, 35 km	325
Rochester & Cobham	Eng	14	6	6	Gatwick, 65 km	626
Rolls of Monmouth (The)	W	15	6	6	Cardiff, 65 km	818
Roma - Acquasanta	I	16	8	9	Roma, 30 km	999
Roncemay	F	15	7	7	Orly, 135 km	326
Rosapenna	I	16	7	6	Sligo, 150 km / Belfast, 160 km	899
Rosendael	N	15	7	7	Amsterdam-Schiphol, 90 km	1037
Ross-on-Wye	Eng	15	5	6	Birmingham, 95 km	627
Rosslare	I	13	5	6	Dublin, 160 km	900
Roxburghe (The)	Sc	15	7	7	Edinburgh, 90 km	773
Royal Aberdeen *Balgownie Links*	Sc	18	7	8	Aberdeen, 10 km	774
Royal Ashdown Forest	Eng	14	7	6	Gatwick, 20 km	628
Royal Belfast	UL	15	7	7	Belfast, 30 km	933
Royal Birkdale (The)	Eng	19	9	7	Manchester, 80 km	629
Royal Burgess	Sc	16	7	9	Edinburgh, 4 km	775
Royal Cinque Ports	Eng	17	6	5	Gatwick, 145 km	630
Royal County Down	UL	19	6	7	Belfast, 48 km	934
Royal Cromer	Eng	15	7	6	Stansted, 120 km	631
Royal Dornoch *Championship*	Sc	19	7	7	Inverness, 82 km	776
Royal Dublin	I	16	8	7	Dublin, 13 km	901
Royal Guernsey	Eng	16	7	7	Guernsey, 8 km	632
Royal Jersey	Eng	16	7	8	Jersey, 10 km	633
Royal Latem	B	15	8	6	Brussel, 65 km	120
Royal Liverpool (Hoylake)	Eng	18	8	7	Liverpool, 35 km	634
Royal Lytham & St Anne's	Eng	19	7	8	Manchester, 100 km	635
Royal Mid-Surrey *Outer*	Eng	14	7	8	Heathrow, 17 km	636
Royal Mougins	F	17	7	8	Nice, 29 km	327
Royal Musselburgh	Sc	16	8	7	Edinburgh, 20 km	777
Royal North Devon (Westward Ho!)	Eng	18	6	6	Plymouth, 90 km	637

1335

Royal Oak	Da	15	7	5	Billund, 60 km	142
Royal Porthcawl	W	19	7	6	Cardiff, 25 km	819
Royal Portrush Dunluce Links	UL	19	7	7	Belfast, 80 km	935
Royal Portrush Valley	UL	13	7	7	Belfast, 80 km	936
Royal St David's	W	18	6	5	Manchester, 120 km	820
Royal St George's	Eng	19	7	5	Gatwick, 145 km	638
Royal Troon Old Course	Sc	19	7	7	Glasgow, 50 km	778
Royal West Norfolk (Brancaster)	Eng	17	7	6	Stansted, 150 km	639
Royal Wimbledon	Eng	16	7	8	Heathrow, 40 km	640
Royal Winchester	Eng	15	6	8	Heathrow, 90 km	641
Royal Zoute	B	18	7	7	Brussel (Bruxelles), 108 km	121
Rudding Park	Eng	15	8	8	Leeds, 20 km	642
Rungsted	Da	17	7	7	København, 40	143
Rya	S	15	7	8	Malmö, 120 km	1268
S. Lourenço	P	18	6	8	Faro, 12 km	1085
Sablé-Solesmes La Forêt/La Rivière	F	16	7	4	Orly, 250 km	328
Saint Donat	F	15	7	8	Nice, 37 km	329
Saint-Cloud Vert	F	14	7	7	Orly, 25 km	330
Saint-Endréol	F	15	7	4	Nice, 70 km	331
Saint-Germain	F	17	7	7	Orly, 30 km	332
Saint-Jean-de-Monts	F	16	6	5	Nantes, 68 km	333
Saint-Laurent	F	14	7	5	Lorient Lann-Bihoué, 40 km	334
Saint-Nom-la-Bretèche Bleu	F	15	8	8	Orly, 30 km	335
Saint-Nom-la-Bretèche Rouge	F	16	8	8	Orly, 30 km	336
Saint-Thomas	F	14	7	5	Béziers-Vias, 15 km	337
Sainte-Baume (La)	F	13	7	6	Marseille-Marignane, 73 km	338
Sainte-Maxime	F	13	7	7	Toulon, 55 km	339
Salgados	P	14	7	6	Faro, 55 km	1086
Samsø	Da	15	4	7	Århus, 50 km	144
San Roque	E	17	8	6	Gibraltar, 15 km	1203
San Sebastián	E	14	6	6	Biarritz (France), 20 km	1204
Sand Moor	Eng	14	7	7	Leeds, 10 km	643
Sandiway	Eng	17	5	7	Manchester, 35 km	644
Sant Cugat	E	13	6	5	Barcelona, 35 km	1205
Santa Ponsa	E	13	6	7	Palma, 26 km	1206
Sarfvik New Course	Fi	16	8	7	Helsinki, 25 km	158
Sart-Tilman	B	16	7	7	Liège, 20 km	122
Saunton East Course	Eng	18	7	6	Plymouth, 90 km	645
Savenay	F	14	5	4	Nantes-Atlantique, 40 km	340
Scharmützelsee Arnold Palmer	D	17	8	7	Berlin, 80 km	456
Scharmützelsee Nick Faldo	D	18	8	7	Berlin, 80 km	457
Schloss Braunfels	D	16	7	7	Frankfurt, 85 km	458
Schloss Egmating	D	15	7	7	München, 55 km	459
Schloss Klingenburg	D	15	6	6	München, 150 km	460
Schloss Langenstein	D	16	8	7	Stuttgart, 150 km	461
Schloss Liebenstein Gelb + Blau	D	16	8	7	Stuttgart, 40 km	462
Schloss Lüdersburg Old/New	D	15	7	6	Hamburg, 50 km	463
Schloss Myllendonk	D	16	7	7	Düsseldorf, 25 km	464
Schloss Nippenburg	D	17	8	6	Stuttgart, 35 km	465
Schloss Wilkendorf	D	17	7	5	Berlin, 50 km	466
Schönenberg	Ch	14	7	6	Zürich-Kloten, 30 km	1308
Scotscraig	Sc	16	6	6	Edinburgh, 95 km	779
Sct. Knuds	Da	14	5	6	Odense, 30 km	145

1336

Seacroft	Eng	17	6	4	Humberside, 80 km	646
Seapoint	I	15	6	6	Dublin, 48 km	902
Seascale	Eng	18	5	4	Manchester, 200 km	647
Seaton Carew	Eng	17	7	5	Teesside, 20 km	648
Seddiner See *Südplatz*	D	18	9	7	Berlin, 50 km	467
Seefeld-Wildmoos	A	17	8	7	Innsbruck, 20 km	99
Seignosse	F	17	7	7	Biarritz-Parme, 39 km	341
Semlin am See	D	16	8	7	Berlin, 70 km	468
Sempachersee	Ch	15	8	7	Zürich, 120 km	1309
Servanes	F	13	7	7	Marseille-Marignane, 57 km	342
Sevilla	E	17	7	8	Sevilla, 10 km	1207
Shanklin & Sandown	Eng	15	7	6	Southampton, 65 km	649
Shannon	I	13	6	6	Shannon, 1 km	903
Sherborne	Eng	15	6	7	Bristol, 45 km	650
Sheringham	Eng	15	7	6	Stansted, 120 km	651
Sherwood Forest	Eng	17	7	6	East Midlands, 40 km	652
Shiskine (Blackwaterfoot)	Sc	17	5	5	Glasgow	780
Silloth-on-Solway	Eng	18	7	4	Glasgow, 200 km	653
Simon's	Da	14	7	7	København, 40 km	146
Sint Nicolaasga	N	15	7	5	Amsterdam Schiphol, 120 km	1038
Skellefteå	S	14	6	5	Skellefteå, 10 km	1269
Skövde	S	17	5	7	Jönköping, 90 km	1270
Slaley Hall	Eng	17	8	7	Newcastle, 35 km	654
Slieve Russell	I	15	8	6	Dublin, 128 km	904
Söderhåsen	S	15	7	5	Malmö, 120 km	1271
Son Vida	E	14	6	7	Palma, 8 km	1208
Sonnenalp	D	15	7	7	München, 190 km	469
Sorknes	Nw	13	6	4	Oslo, 165 km	1055
Sotogrande	E	18	7	6	Málaga, 120 km	1209
Soufflenheim	F	16	7	4	Strasbourg, 50 km	343
Southerndown	W	16	7	7	Cardiff, 36 km	821
Southerness	Sc	18	6	5	Glasgow, 155 km	781
Southport & Ainsdale	Eng	18	7	7	Manchester, 80 km	655
Spa (Les Fagnes)	B	17	7	7	Liège, 25 km	123
Spérone	F	17	7	5	Figari, 27 km	344
Spiegelven	B	14	7	8	Maastricht, 25 km	124
St Andrews *Eden Course*	Sc	14	8	8	Edinburgh, 80 km	782
St Andrews *Jubilee Course*	Sc	16	8	8	Edinburgh, 80 km	783
St Andrews *New Course*	Sc	17	8	8	Edinburgh, 80 km	784
St Andrews *Old Course*	Sc	18	8	8	Edinburgh, 80 km	785
St Enodoc *Church Course*	Eng	18	7	4	Plymouth, 80 km	656
St George's Hill	Eng	17	7	7	Heathrow, 28 km	657
St Helen's Bay	I	14	6	6	Dublin, 160 km	905
St Laurence	Fi	14	5	4	Helsinki, 70 km	159
St Margaret's	I	16	7	7	Dublin, 6 km	906
St Mellion *Nicklaus Course*	Eng	17	9	7	Plymouth, 16 km	658
St. Dionys	D	17	7	6	Hamburg, 60 km	470
St. Eurach	D	16	7	6	München, 70 km	471
St. Leon-Rot	D	15	8	6	Frankfurt, 100 km	472
Stavanger	Nw	16	6	7	Stavanger, 10 km	1056
Steiermärkischer Murhof	A	16	7	6	Graz, 20 km	100
Stenungsund	S	17	7	8	Göteborg, 65 km	1272
Stirling	Sc	13	6	7	Edinburgh, 45 km	786

1337

Stockholm	S	16	8	9	Stockholm, 33 km	1273
Stoke Poges	Eng	17	8	8	Heathrow, 24 km	659
Stolper Heide	D	16	7	5	Berlin, 10 km	473
Stoneham	Eng	15	7	8	Southampton, 4 km	660
Stonehaven	Sc	13	5	5	Aberdeen, 25 km	787
Strasbourg Illkirch *Jaune + Rouge*	F	13	7	6	Strasbourg, 12 km	345
Strathaven	Sc	15	7	6	Glasgow, 35 km	788
Stuttgarter Solitude	D	17	5	5	Stuttgart, 25 km	474
Sundsvall	S	13	6	6	Sundsvall, 25 km	1274
Sunningdale *New Course*	Eng	18	8	8	Heathrow, 20 km	661
Sunningdale *Old Course*	Eng	18	8	8	Heathrow, 20 km	662
Swinley Forest	Eng	16	6	8	Heathrow, 20 km	663
Sybrook	N	15	6	6	Enschede Twente, 5 km	1039
Sylt	D	15	6	8	Westerland, 5 km	475
Täby	S	16	7	7	Stockholm, 30 km	1275
Tain	Sc	17	6	6	Inverness, 65 km	789
Talma	Fi	14	8	6	Helsinki,	160
Tandridge	Eng	14	7	6	Gatwick, 18 km	664
TAT Golf Belek	T	14	7	7	Antalya, 35 km	1320
Taulane	F	15	7	4	Nice, 75 km	346
Tawast	Fi	14	7	5	Helsinki	161
Taymouth Castle	Sc	13	4	6	Edinburgh, 125 km	790
Tegernseer Bad Wiessee	D	14	7	8	München, 85 km	476
Tehidy Park	Eng	13	7	6	Exeter, 200 km	665
Tenby	W	18	7	6	Cardiff, 75 km	822
The Belfry *Brabazon*	Eng	15	9	8	Birmingham, 15 km	666
The Belfry *PGA National*	Eng	15	9	8	Birmingham, 15 km	667
The Island	I	15	7	7	Dublin, 8 km	907
Thetford	Eng	14	7	5	Stansted, 90 km	668
Thorndon Park	Eng	14	7	6	Stansted, 37 km	669
Thornhill	Sc	15	6	5	Edinburgh, Glasgow, 109 km	791
Thorpeness	Eng	14	7	7	Stansted, 145 km	670
Thurlestone	Eng	16	6	4	Plymouth, 50 km	671
Torekov	S	14	7	7	Halmstad, 30 km	1276
Torino - La Mandria *Percorso Blu*	I	16	8	8	Torino, 7 km	1001
Torremirona	E	13	7	7	Barcelona, 150 km	1210
Torrequebrada	E	14	7	7	Málaga, 15 km	1211
Toulouse Palmola	F	15	7	4	Toulouse-Blagnac, 40 km	347
Toulouse-Seilh *Rouge*	F	15	7	6	Toulouse-Blagnac, 8 km	348
Touquet (Le) *La Mer*	F	17	6	7	Lille-Lesquin, 151 km	349
Touraine	F	13	7	6	Tours-Saint-Symphorien, 25 km	350
Toxandria	N	14	7	6	Eindhoven, 40 km	1040
Tralee	I	18	7	6	Cork, 120 km	908
Tramore	I	13	7	6	Cork, 120 km	909
Tranås	S	14	6	7	Jönköping, 85 km	1277
Treudelberg	D	13	8	7	Hamburg, 6 km	477
Trevose *Championship*	Eng	17	7	7	Plymouth, 80 km	672
Troia	P	15	6	5	Lisboa, 42 km	1087
Tulfarris	I	14	7	6	Dublin, 50 km	910
Tullamore	I	15	6	5	Dublin, 96 km	911
Turnberry *Ailsa Course*	Sc	19	9	8	Glasgow, 80 km	792
Turnberry *Arran Course*	Sc	16	9	8	Glasgow, 80 km	793
Tutzing	D	15	7	6	München, 80 km	478

1338

Name					Location	
Twente	N	15	7	6	Enschede Twente, 15 km	1041
Tyrifjord	Nw	14	6	6	Oslo, 45 km	1057
Ullna	S	17	8	6	Stockholm, 40 km	1278
Ulzama	E	16	6	6	Pamplona, 28 km	1212
Upsala	S	13	6	6	Stockholm, 30 km	1279
Val de Sorne	F	14	7	5	Lyon-Satolas, 134 km	351
Val Queven	F	15	6	5	Lorient Lann-Bihoué, 3 km	352
Valderrama	E	19	8	6	Málaga, 120 km	1213
Vale da Pinta	P	14	6	6	Faro, 42 km	1088
Vale do Lobo *Royal Golf Course*	P	15	6	7	Faro, 18 km	1089
Vale of Glamorgan	W	16	8	7	Cardiff, 30 km	823
Varese	I	14	8	7	Milano, 25 km	1002
Värnamo	S	15	7	5	Jönköping, 70 km	1280
Vasatorp	S	16	7	7	Malmö, 85 km	1281
Vaucouleurs (La) *Les Vallons*	F	15	7	4	Orly, 71 km	353
Växjö	S	15	6	7	Växjö, 8 km	1282
Vejle *Blue + Red Slings*	Da	15	7	7	Billund, 40 km	147
Venezia	I	16	7	9	Venezia, 13 km	1003
Verona	I	13	7	8	Verona, 5 km	1004
Vila Sol	P	14	7	7	Faro, 22 km	1090
Vilamoura *Vilamoura I (Old Course)*	P	16	7	7	Faro, 22 km	1091
Vilamoura *Vilamoura II (Pinhal)*	P	13	7	7	Faro, 22 km	1092
Vilamoura *Vilamoura III (Laguna)*	P	14	7	7	Faro, 22 km	1093
Villa D'Este	I	16	8	9	Milano, 37 km	1005
Villamartin	E	16	7	6	Alicante, 50 km	1214
Villette d'Anthon *Les Sangliers*	F	17	6	4	Lyon-Satolas, 12 km	354
Visby	S	16	6	5	Visby, 30 km	1283
Volcans (Les)	F	14	6	5	Clermont-Ferrand, 19 km	355
Walddörfer	D	16	7	6	Hamburg, 20 km	479
Wallasey	Eng	17	7	7	Liverpool, 35 km	673
Walton Heath *New Course*	Eng	16	7	6	Gatwick, 15 km	674
Walton Heath *Old Course*	Eng	18	7	7	Gatwick, 15 km	675
Wantzenau (La)	F	16	6	6	Strasbourg, 27 km	356
Warrenpoint	UL	13	6	5	Belfast, 75 km	937
Warwickshire (The)	Eng	15	7	8	Birmingham, 30 km	676
Wasserburg Anholt	D	15	7	7	Düsseldorf, 80 km	480
Waterford	I	14	6	6	Cork, 130 km / Dublin, 170 km	912
Waterford Castle	I	14	5	6	Cork, 130 km / Dublin, 170 km	913
Waterloo *La Marache*	B	16	8	7	Bruxelles, 20 km	125
Waterville	I	17	6	7	Cork, 150 km	914
Wendlohe *A-Kurs + B-Kurs*	D	16	7	6	Hamburg, 10 km	481
Wentorf-Reinbeker	D	15	7	6	Hamburg, 40 km	482
Wentworth *East Course*	Eng	16	8	7	Heathrow, 20 km	677
Wentworth *West Course*	Eng	18	8	7	Heathrow, 20 km	678
West Berkshire	Eng	15	7	7	Heathrow, 80 km	679
West Byfleet	Eng	14	6	8	Heathrow, 20 km	680
West Cornwall	Eng	16	7	6	Plymouth, 120 km	681
West Hill	Eng	15	6	6	Heathrow, 44 km	682
West Kilbride	Sc	16	7	5	Glasgow, 50 km	794
West Lancashire	Eng	17	7	7	Manchester, 80 km	683
West Surrey	Eng	15	7	7	Gatwick, 15 km	684
West Sussex	Eng	18	7	6	Gatwick, 40 km	685
West Waterford	I	12	7	6	Cork, 80 km	915

1339

Western Gailes	Sc	17	5	7	Glasgow, 50 km	795
Westerwood	Sc	14	8	6	Glasgow, 32 km	796
Weston-Super-Mare	Eng	16	6	7	Bristol, 25 km	686
Westport	I	15	7	7	Knock, 50 km	916
Wheatley	Eng	14	6	6	Leeds Bradford, 40 km	687
Whitekirk	Sc	15	7	7	Edinburgh, 50 km	797
Whittington Heath	Eng	17	6	7	Birmingham, 20 km	688
Wien-Freudenau	A	13	7	9	Wien, 12 km	101
Wilmslow	Eng	16	7	6	Manchester, 6 km	689
Wimereux	F	14	4	5	Lille-Lesquin, 143 km	357
Wittelsbacher	D	16	7	6	München, 80 km	483
Woburn *Dukes Course*	Eng	18	7	7	Heathrow, 70 km	690
Woking	Eng	16	6	6	Heathrow, 38 km	691
Woodbridge	Eng	14	7	7	Stansted, 120 km	692
Woodbrook	I	15	7	6	Dublin, 30 km	917
Woodbury Park *The Oaks*	Eng	15	9	6	Exeter, 10 km	693
Woodenbridge	I	16	7	6	Dublin, 88 km	918
Woodhall Spa	Eng	18	7	8	Humberside, 70 km	694
Worplesdon	Eng	16	7	6	Heathrow, 39 km	695
Wouwse Plantage	N	15	7	6	Eindhoven, 70 km	1042
Wylihof	Ch	13	6	6	Zurich-Kloten, 110 km	1310
Zaudin	E	16	7	6	Sevilla, 15 km	1215
Zuid Limburgse	N	14	7	7	Maastricht, 25 km	1043
Zumikon	Ch	15	7	6	Zurich-Kloten, 30 km	1311

1340

PEUGEOT

EXCHANGE CROSS RATES
TABLEAU DE CHANGE DES MONNAIES
TABELLE FÜR DIE WÄHRUNGSUMRECHNUNG

	BF	DKr	F	DM	IR£	L	Fl
Belgium (BF)	100	18.43	16.26	4.848	1.952	4800	5.483
Denmark (DKr)	54.26	10	8.824	2.631	1.059	2605	2.964
France (F)	61.50	11.33	10	2.982	1.201	2952	3.360
Germany (DM)	20.63	3.801	3.354	1	0.403	990.0	1.127
Ireland (IR£)	51.22	9.439	8.329	2.483	1	2459	2.798
Italy (L)	2.083	0.384	0.339	0.101	0.041	100	0.114
Netherlands (Fl)	18.31	3.373	2.977	0.888	0.357	878.6	1
Norway (NKr)	48.27	8.896	7.849	2.340	0.942	2317	2.637
Portugal (Esc)	20.12	3.708	3.272	0.976	0.393	965.8	1.099
Spain (Pts)	24.24	4.468	3.942	1.175	0.473	1164	1.324
Sweden (SKr)	45.82	8.445	7.451	2.222	0.895	2199	2.503
Switzerland (CHF)	25.35	4.672	4.122	1.229	0.495	1217	1.385
Un. Kingdom (£)	62.38	11.50	10.14	3.024	1.218	2994	3.408
Canada (C$)	25.06	4.619	4.076	1.215	0.489	1203	1.369
United States ($)	37.36	6.886	6.075	1.811	0.729	1793	2.041
Japan (¥)	35.37	6.518	5.751	1.715	0.690	1698	1.932
Euro (€)	40.34	7.434	6.560	1.956	0.788	1936	2.204

Danish Kroner, French Franc, Norwegian Kroner and Swedish Kroner x 10.

Belgian Franc, Yen, Escudo, Lira and Peseta x 100.

Source: Financial Times, October 20, 1999

TABELL FÖR VÄXELOMRÄKNING
CAMBIO DE DIVISAS
CAMBIO VALUTA

NKr	Esc	Pts	SKr	CHF	£	C$	$	¥	€
20.72	497.0	412.5	21.82	3.944	1.603	3.990	2.577	282.7	2.479
11.24	269.7	223.8	11.84	2.141	0.870	2.165	1.452	153.4	1.345
12.74	305.6	253.7	13.42	2.426	0.986	2.464	1.546	173.9	1.525
4.273	102.5	85.07	4.501	0.814	0.331	0.823	0.552	58.32	0.511
10.61	254.6	211.3	11.18	2.020	0.821	2.044	1.371	144.8	1.270
0.432	10.35	8.593	0.455	0.082	0.033	0.083	0.056	5.891	0.052
3.792	90.97	75.50	3.995	0.722	0.293	0.730	0.490	51.76	0.454
10	239.9	199.1	10.53	1.904	0.774	1.925	1.292	136.5	1.197
4.169	100	82.99	4.391	0.794	0.323	0.803	0.539	56.89	0.499
5.023	120.5	100	5.291	0.956	0.389	0.967	0.649	68.55	0.601
9.493	227.7	189.0	10	1.808	0.735	1.828	1.226	129.6	1.136
5.252	126.0	104.6	5.532	1	0.406	1.011	0.678	71.68	0.628
12.92	310.0	257.3	13.61	2.461	1	2.489	1.670	176.4	1.546
5.193	124.6	103.4	5.470	0.989	0.402	1	0.671	70.87	0.621
7.741	185.7	154.1	8.154	1.474	0.599	1.491	1	105.6	0.926
7.327	175.8	145.9	7.718	1.396	0.567	1.411	0.947	100	0.877
8.357	200.5	166.4	8.803	1.591	0.647	1.610	1.080	114.1	1

1343

L'ÉNERGIE DE L' INFORMATION

TECHNIQUES GRAPHIQUES

Berger-Levrault Graphique ▪ ZI de la Croix-de-Metz ▪ ROUTE DE VILLEY-SAINT-ETIENNE ▪ 54200 TOUL

Bureau commerciaux ▪ 17, RUE REMI-DUMONCEL ▪ 75014 PARIS

Téléphone ▪ 01.40.64.43.82 ▪ Fax 01.40.64.43.80